HANDBOOK OF RESEARCH ON MUSIC
TEACHING AND LEARNING

HANDBOOK

OF RESEARCH ON

MUSIC TEACHING

AND LEARNING

A Project of the Music Educators National Conference

Editor

Richard Colwell

SCHIRMER BOOKS

A Division of Macmillan, Inc.

NEW YORK

Maxwell Macmillan Canada

TORONTO

Maxwell Macmillan International

NEW YORK   OXFORD   SINGAPORE   SYDNEY

Production: Hockett Editorial Service

Schirmer Books   Maxwell Macmillan Canada, Inc.
A Division of Macmillan, Inc.   1200 Eglinton Avenue East, Suite 200
866 Third Avenue   Don Mills, Ontario M3C 3N1
New York, NY 10022

Macmillan, Inc., is part of the Maxwell
Communication Group of Companies.

Library of Congress Catalog Card Number: 91-29363

Printed in the United States of America

printing number
1   2   3   4   5   6   7   8   9   10

Library of Congress Cataloging-in-Publication Data

Handbook of research on music teaching and learning / Richard Colwell,
    editor.
        p.   cm.
    ''A project of the Music Educators National Conference.''
    Includes bibliographical references and indexes.
    ISBN 0-02-870501-7
    1. Music—instruction and study.   I. Colwell, Richard.   II. Music
Educators National Conference (U.S.)
MT1.H138   1992
780'.7—dc20   91-29363
                                                         CIP
                                                         MN

The paper used in this publication meets the minimum
requirements of American National Standard for Information
Sciences—Permanence of Paper for Printed Library Materials.
ANSI Z39.48–1984. ∞™

CONTENTS

Section
A
CONCEPTUAL FRAMEWORK   1

Section
B
RESEARCH MODES AND TECHNIQUES   73

Section
C
EVALUATION   245

Section
D
PERCEPTION AND COGNITION   331

Section

E

TEACHING AND LEARNING STRATEGIES   449

Section

F

THE TEACHING OF SPECIFIC MUSICAL SKILLS AND KNOWLEDGE IN DIFFERENT INSTRUCTIONAL SETTINGS   559

PREFACE

The format and content of this *Handbook of Research on Music Teaching and Learning* was influenced by the handbooks published by the American Educational Research Association and Macmillan and by the numerous subsequent handbooks. Especially helpful was the handbook in social studies edited by Professor James Shaver. Although this book may not serve music educators in the same way that a handbook of diseases, medications, and procedures serves the physician, its use will bear some similarities to the use of medical handbooks. The material in this handbook is pertinent, well-nigh essential, to systematic teaching and research. All oboists know of the *Vade Mecum* for oboe, the player's "constant companion"; this handbook is intended to serve a similar purpose for all teachers and students of music teaching and learning.

Acknowledgments are traditionally reserved until the end of the preface; however, in newspaper articles the most important information is presented first. I wish to acknowledge the effort of every author—each a senior member of the profession and each representing the best scholarship in the field—who undertook this task for the good of the profession. The authors received no renumeration for their work or even for their chapter-related expenses; their contributions were motivated by their belief in music education and in the importance of this project.

Administrative support for secretaries, copying, and postage from the University of Northern Colorado and from Boston University represented a major financial commitment from each institution. Graduate assistant Charlene Brown at the University of Northern Colorado cheerfully dealt with the mountains of correspondence and task-tracking required by the extensive reviews for each chapter. My associates Marcus Silvi and Robert Ambrose maintained the equilibrium at Boston University in numerous ways. Careful, extensive editing was undertaken both by section editors and by Ruth Colwell with efficiency and good humor.

The definition of music education encompasses one of the broadest of the disciplines; hence the undertaking of a handbook or research in music teaching and learning is a monumental task. Education itself is broad and complex, and the addition of music's performing, listening, and creating enlarges the challenge presented by a project such as this one. It was critical that we not knowingly exclude any area of music teaching and learning from this first handbook in the field. Therefore, chapters on teaching class piano, class voice, and music therapy stand with chapters on motivation and transfer of learning.

The aim of music instruction as a part of general education is to enhance the quality of life; the full expression of our humanness requires encounters with listening, performing, and creating music. Music is equally important in accomplishing the general goals of education such as values education, learning how to learn, knowledge of divergent cultures and viewpoints, cooperation and competition, and knowledge of how to function in a democratic society. Music is a powerful tool for those who work with students with special needs, and music is also a powerful means by which the social studies teacher can bring to life contrasting times and cultures. Indeed, given the importance of music to our own culture, it is difficult to conceive that a school board or school administrator would fail to include a strong music component in the curriculum. Music instruction can also be justified, and at an early age, for those who may wish to choose music as a career. The study of law or medicine can begin after the completion of an undergraduate degree in college, but such an approach to the education of musicians is inappropriate in the extreme. Probably in no other field is early and consistent instruction so important. The Handbook does not attempt to be complete in any one, let alone all, of the areas of music education, but it offers a starting point, an introduction, to every facet of music teaching and learning.

The profession has dictionaries: The *New Groves Dictionary of Music and Musicians,* and *New Groves Dictionary of American Music,* and other specialized dictionaries that are seminal publications. Until the "new" edition, the editors of Groves did not consider music education as a viable topic, and in the latest edition the treatment of music education is limited. This Handbook is not a dictionary; the topics are limited. However, this Handbook and Groves may come to be considered two indispensable tools for the practicing musician and teacher. Handbooks can provide unity and integrity to a discipline, giving it definition and comprehensibility. Handbooks can be economically published as there are no author royalties and no desk copies. MENC has provided advertising and visibility for the publication.

The Handbook is not designed to serve as a text for a research course; the coverage is too broad. It will, however, likely be an indispensable part of any research course. The Handbook can be described as a primary reference for music teaching and learning but it is not exhaustive. Complete reference lists are helpful but knowledge is expanding too rapidly to make such a reference list feasible. The guideline to authors was to be as sparing as possible with references; the reader can conduct computer searches to generate long and exhaustive lists.

MENC's involvement with this Handbook stemmed from David Swanzy and Ed Kvet's 1987 Loyola Symposium on publications. Maribeth Payne of Schirmer Books attended, as did I (as editor of the *Bulletin of the Council for Research in Music Education*) and somehow the chemistry of the MENC members present and the publisher catapulted us into the present project.

A two-day meeting of interested and interesting individuals, Bob Stake, Bennett Reimer, Allen Britton, Jeffrey Patchen, Eleanor Stubley, Peter Costanza, Warren George, Charles Hoffer, and myself, was held at the Indianapolis in-service meeting in 1988; to this group I proposed a Handbook of sixteen sections and eighty-three chapters. Following these discussions, President Hoffer appointed an editorial board to review what was left of the original outline, and this board convened in Chicago in May of 1988. Two days of gnawing on a second proposal resulted in the framework for the present eight-section handbook of fifty-five chapters. The eight sections include many of the major constructs to a discipline: historical-philosophical, research techniques, evaluation, cognition, research results, discipline blocks such as early childhood, general music, teacher education, and special education, and sociology and administration.

The editorial board identified potential authors but gave me the responsibility for juggling and substituting. Throughout this entire process the editorial board has provided generous moral support.

The authors and reviewers for each chapter were selected by a complicated process following the suggestions of the editorial board. Additional suggestions were solicited from many sources: publishers, department chairs, funding agencies, and research centers. Although authors also served as reviewers, every effort was made to coordinate the effort and assure that no one was asked to review more than one chapter. Every chapter received at least three reviews; some chapters received as many as six or seven. I solicited review help from psychologists, philosophers, educators, aestheticians, and the experts in the field of teaching and learning. These latter usually provided the most thorough reviews, as they themselves had written chapters for Handbook, knew the process, and knew how helpful a thorough review could be. A close alignment between chapter emphasis and reviewer was sought— for example, in the chapter by Richardson and Whitaker, reviews were obtained from the authors they cited for the basic material in the chapter. The result is a Handbook written by the authorities in the profession, an enviable accomplishment for any profession.

I am especially pleased that we were able to obtain the cooperation of authors in other English-speaking countries; the presence of Canadian, British, and Australian authors within these pages strengthens this initial definition of music education.

The authors were given freedom to present their topic under friendly circumstances. Some chapter authors list research completed and the reader is afforded a listing of selected studies. Other chapter authors interpret what is known about music teaching and learning based on experience, careful practice, tempered with some systematic research. The different approaches are reflected in the chapters on cognition and technology (Chapters 23 and 32). One chapter discusses a stable discipline, while the other discusses an area characterized by trial and error.

The authors kindly accepted the deletion of much of their valuable material. Although the number of words for each chapter was suggested in the contract, some chapters received were twice that length—and more. Excising one's own wisdom is difficult; thus the editors assumed responsibility for all omissions in the chapters that were due to the sharp pencil.

There was really no elegant way to organize the sections and chapters. This difficulty shows itself in the lack of standardization of format but also provides a dynamism to the presentation that might be lacking in a "standardized version."

The authors are due my thanks for following the timetable as closely as they did and I apologize for the nasty and satirical letters and phone calls that I from time to time injected into the process.

One effort I made to standardize the Handbook was to submit the chapter (Chapter 23) written by Professor Fiske of the University of Western Ontario to the section editors as a model. I like the format of this chapter and hope that when this book is revised sometime in the 21st century that consideration again will be given to this model.

Without first-hand knowledge of the process, some readers may wonder why it takes so long to publish a handbook. A quick review. Once the potential author is identified, there is the matter of contractual negotiation. Next the author must be informed about the project and the type of chapter that the editor has in mind for him or her to write. If the author agrees to the project, he or she submits an outline to the editor. This outline is critiqued by the general editor, section editors, and at least three reviewers. These comments are consolidated and forwarded to the author. Further negotiations on the content and format of the chapter occur at this stage in the process. Once these matters are resolved, the author submits a draft of the chapter. The draft chapter goes through the same review process, reviews that edit as well as suggest and reviews that often approach the length of the draft. Revisions are then made by the author and the chapter resubmitted. In many cases, final editing for consistency and the editor's deletions require one more version before the chapter is deemed ready for copyediting. Professional copyeditors make changes and ask numerous questions, each of which must be carefully proofed. Such a process depends upon the wisdom of editors and reviewers and considerable forbearance, patience, and frustration on the part of the authors.

As editor, I would have preferred to have the two words, teaching and learning, reversed, since learning should precede as well as follow teaching, but I was informed that teaching and learning are always thought of in that order.

Music education, like many disciplines, received its boost in research from the onset of the scientific age. The acousticians Wundt, Helmholtz, and others, and the psychologists Seashore, Kwalwasser, Mainwaring, and Lundin were among the earliest researchers in musical knowing. The findings of these individuals encouraged behaviorism, and the behaviorists assumed the leadership in research activities. As in other areas of education, the behaviorists conducted a prodigious quantity of research, much of it informative. But because they lacked a theoretical or philosophical base, their research failed to help establish the framework for a discipline and for the assignment of educational priorities. The behavioristic movement did provide a basis for the initial research in music therapy and in functional music, as well as for research into the developmental characteristics of children and some helpful work in music perception. Because we are not robots different philosophies have emerged. The first section of the Handbook attempts to address these theoretical and philosophical issues and to provide a basis for discussion and dialogue.

The content of the Handbook reflects the expansion of research knowledge. The *Journal of Research in Music Education* has been in existence for forty years, and the first AERA handbook was published nearly thirty years ago. In the past forty years we have come through a period of funded research, the accountability movement, the introduction of computers into the classroom, a surge of doctoral students, two national assessments, and several significant conferences. Presently, although the field of music education is somewhat stable, education generally is not. To the professional educator it appears that little is being spent on education research, but to the music educator educational research looks like the land of plenty. Laboratories and research development centers exist, and many school districts employ directors of research. An examination of the program for a national AERA convention suggests that the production of research on learning is an industry in itself. The training of music educators largely emphasizes musical skills and knowledge, and only after the completion of four years of undergraduate work does the newly minted teacher recognize the need for information about schools and students.

AERA handbooks on research on teaching were helpful models to us and remain of use to music educators. Unfortunately, music is viewed differently by school administrators than social studies, physics, or English, and we must survive by our own wits. We know that the certification of music teachers has resulted in a ''special'' certificate in most states,

that special status indicating that the music curriculum is unique, engendering different issues in teacher education and requiring different teacher evaluation. Music was one of the last subjects to require certification, and is presently at the forefront of using noncertified teachers to deliver instruction. The artist in residence has become a popular idea, and hundreds of private organizations provide packaged instructional sequences to schools for a fee. Artist instruction, which was intended to supplement and enrich instruction, has replaced it in many of our largest cities. This instruction requires different questions than those asked in this Handbook. The uniqueness of music education is also illustrated by the fact that NASM has as much influence as NCATE in approving programs in music teacher education, although these two organizations have differing approaches to teaching and learning. In our profession, skill training is well attended; the rest of the knowledge base is considerably thinner.

The Handbook is valuable for articulating what we don't know as much as for reporting what we do know and believe. Those areas that receive our greatest teaching emphasis are the areas with the least solid research. The belief in the profession might be that present teaching methods are fully satisfactory and that reflection and investigation will not be fruitful. For example, we have scanty evidence about the effectivness of general music and/or the various methods used to teach it. We also have little hard data on teacher education. The list could go on and on: The research on the impact of chorus is absent except for references to voice production. Band directors have been primarily interested in drop-outs from their program rather than who learns what and why.

In reflecting on the material in the Handbook and the preparation of music teachers, it is apparent that music teachers are exceptionally well prepared in their subject (at least in relationship to the subject matter preparation in other disciplines), but music teachers are less well prepared in pedagogy and general education, information that is often of current use.

Use of the Handbook will allow individuals in teaching and research to avoid pitfalls already encountered by our colleagues and to capitalize on strengths that have been attained by many successful teachers but not disseminated to the profession. Our successes have been stunning. Exemplary programs are shown on television and through frequent public performances. Thousands of students are annually encouraged to consider careers in music based on these rewarding experiences. This Handbook should document for such students the promise that exists in music teaching and learning.

The preface is the only place where I can make the point that historians use footnotes and annotated footnotes and will continue to do so despite the efforts of the American Psychological Association to influence the style of our scholarship. Stylistic diversity is not part of the lexicon of publishers, and the compromise was the use of endnotes.

As a music educator who thinks about curriculum, program, and student evaluation, I regret that there is no chapter on qualitative evaluation. Although I suggested earlier in this preface that the profession was moving away from its reliance on behaviorism, that movement is not reflected in the evaluation section. This anomaly is of interest as changes in evaluation in the 1990s are based on our work in the arts. Daniel Stufflebeam is an ex-band director and Elliot Eisner an art educator. Much of the emphasis on collecting samples of student work (like repertoire lists) stems from practices long common in music and music education. Evaluating through sampling a student's work—try-outs, contests, etc., or through a portfolio (documentation of a student having practiced, attended performances and music camps)—is not a new idea, and

yet to read the press, one would think that abandoning the bubble sheet is a new and innovative approach.

The Handbook will be used in many ways and provide assistance to teachers and students of the next decade. The Music Educators National Conference and each of us owes a debt of gratitude to this distinguished panel of authors. The names of reviewers who contributed through particularly extensive and thoughtful advice follow this preface. A complete list of reviewers begins on page xv.

Richard Colwell
Boston University

ADVISORY REVIEWERS

Jeanne Bamberger, Massachusetts Institute of Technology
Douglas Bartholomew, Montana State University
Charles Boody, Mound, Minnesota
Wayne Bowman, Brandon University
Donna Brink-Fox, Eastman School of Music
Henry Cady, University of Delaware
James Carlsen, University of Washington
Alicia Ann Clair, The University of Kansas
Lyn Corbin, Ohio State University
Gary Cziko, University of Illinois
George Duerksen, University of Kansas
Jack Easley, University of Illinois
Elliot W. Eisner, Stanford University
Robert Ennis, University of Illinois
Harold Fiske, University of Western Ontario
Mark Fonder, Ithaca College
Hildegard Froelich, University of North Texas
Mark Gall, University of Oregon
Howard Gardner, Harvard University
J. Terry Gates, State University of New York, Buffalo
Richard Graham, University of Georgia
Norman Gronlund, San Diego, California
Paul Haack, University of Minnesota
Carole Harrison, California State University, Fullerton
Samuel Hope, NASM, Reston, Virginia
Vernon A. Howard, Harvard University
Jere T. Humphreys, Arizona State University
Richard J. Jaeger, University of North Carolina, Greensboro
James Jordan, Westminster Choir College
Donald Krummel, University of Illinois
Joseph Labuta, Wayne State University
E. L. Lancaster, University of Oklahoma
Francis Larimer, Northwestern University

Paul Lehman, University of Michigan
Douglas Lemmon, Memphis State University
Barbara Lundquist, University of Washington
Martin Maehr, University of Michigan
James Major, Ohio State University
Wanda May, Michigan State University
Dorothy McDonald, The University of Iowa
Kacper Miklaszewski, Chopin Academy, Warsaw, Poland
David Myers, Georgia State University
Grant Newman, Iowa State University
Randall Pembrook, University of Missouri-Kansas City
Rosalie Pratt, Brigham Young University
James Raths, University of Vermont
Thomas Regelski, State University of New York
Carol Richardson, Northwestern University
John Richmond, University of South Florida
Jon Rieger, University of Louisville
Charles Schmidt, Indiana University
Lloyd Schmidt, Storrs, Connecticut
Ralph Smith, University of Illinois
Sandra Stauffer, Arizona State University
Eleanor V. Stubley, McGill University, Montreal
Daniel Stufflebeam, Western Michigan University
Bertil Sundin, Stockholm University
Keith Swanwick, University of London
Donald Taebel, Georgia State University
Keith Thompson, Pennsylvania State University
Darryl Walters, Temple University
Barrie Wells, Arizona State University
Ian Westbury, University of Illinois
Nancy Whitaker, University of North Carolina
David Williams, Illinois State University
Lizabeth Bradford Wing, University of Cincinnati

REVIEWERS

♦

Philip C. Abrani, Concordia University
Steven Adams, Univ. of Southern California
Clem Adelman, University of Reading
David Alexander, Southern Nazarene University
William Anderson, Kent State University
Barbara Andress, Arizona State University
Hilary Apfelstadt, University of North Carolina at Greensboro
Edward Asmus, University of Utah
Buddy Baker, University of Northern Colorado
Sam Baltzer, Shorter College
Jeanne Bamberger, Massachusetts Institute of Technology
Lee Bartel, University of Toronto
Douglas Bartholomew, Montana State University
Dale Bartlett, Michigan State University
Gretchen Beall, University of Colorado
Martin Bergee, University of Missouri
Eunice Boardman, University of Illinois
Charles Boody, Mound, Minnesota
Jackie Boswell, Arizona State University
Wayne Bowman, Brandon University
Rene Boyer-White, University of Cincinnati
David Boyle, University of Miami
Manny Brand, Southwest Texas State University
Donna Brink-Fox, Eastman School of Music
Allen P. Britton, University of Michigan
Jere Brophy, Michigan State University
Leon Burton, University of Hawaii
Joe Buttram, Ball State University
Henry Cady, University of Delaware
Max Camp, University of South Carolina
James Carlsen, University of Washington
Richard Chronister, The National Conference on Piano Pedagogy
Alicia Ann Clair, The University of Kansas
Christopher Clark, Michigan State University
Harry Clark, University of Kentucky
Annabel J. Cohen, Dalhousie University
Peter A. Cohen, Medical College of Georgia
Homer Coker, Georgia State University
Irma Collins, Murray State University
Donald Corbett, Wichita State University
Lyn Corbin, Ohio State University

Robert L. Cowden, Indiana State University
Thomas R. Curtin, Research Triangle Park, North Carolina
Robert Cutietta, Kent State University
Gary Cziko, University of Illinois
Bruce Dalby, University of New Mexico
Dennis Darling, Luther College
Alice Ann Darrow, University of Kansas
Lyle Davidson, New England Conservatory
Judith Delzell, Ohio State University
Gregory DeNardo, Bowling Green State University
Jay Dowling, University of Texas at Dallas
George Duerkson, University of Kansas
Robert Duke, University of Texas at Austin
Jack Easley, University of Illinois
Elliot W. Eisner, Stanford University
Charles Elliott, University of South Carolina
Robert Erbes, Michigan State University
Roy Ernst, Eastman School of Music
John Feierabend, Hartt School of Music
Harold Fiske, University of Western Ontario
John Flohr, Texas Woman's University
Mark Fonder, Ithaca College
Hildegard Froelich, University of North Texas
Mark Gall, University of Oregon
Howard Gardner, Harvard University
J. Terry Gates, State University of New York, Buffalo
Robert Gillespie, Ohio State University
Robert Glidden, Florida State University
Mary Goetze, Indiana University
Thomas Goolsby, University of Washington
Stewart Gordon, Los Angeles
Richard Graham, University of Georgia
John Grashel, University of Illinois
Marvin Greenberg, University of Hawaii
Norman Gronlund, San Digeo, California
Paul Haack, University of Minnesota
Lois Habteyes, Department of Education, St. Thomas
Harriet Hair, University of Georgia
Louis O. Hall, University of Maine
Donald Hamann, Kent State University
Carole Harrison, California State University, Fullerton
Jerome Hausman, Evanston, Illinois

Steven Hedden, University of Arizona
Norman Heim, University of Maryland
Jack Heller, University of South Florida
Carolyn Hildebrandt, University of California, Berkeley
Donald Hodges, University of Texas, San Antonio
Fred T. Hofstetter, University of Delaware
Samuel Hope, NASM, Reston, Virginia
Vernon A. Howard, Harvard University
Jere T. Humphreys, Arizona State University
John Hylton, University of Missouri-St. Louis
Richard J. Jaeger, University of North Carolina, Greensboro
June Jetter, University of Missouri, Kansas City
James Jordan, Westminster Choir College
Vince Kantorski, Bowling Green State
Anthony Kemp, University of Reading
John Kennedy, University of Toronto
Gerald Kneiter, California State University, Northridge
John Kratus, Case Western Reserve University
Donald Krummel, Urbana, Illinois
Edward Kvet, Central Michigan University
Joseph Labuta, Wayne State University
Morris Lai, University of Hawaii at Manoa
E. L. Lancaster, University of Oklahoma
Franics Larimer, Northwestern University
Joy E. Lawrence, Kent State University
Paul Lehman, University of Michigan
Douglas Lemmon, Memphis State University
Carol Lindeman, Greenbraie, California
Barbara Lundquist, University of Washington
James Lyke, University of Illinois
Martin Maehr, University of Michigan
James Major, Ohio State University
Victor Markovich, Witchita State University
Gary M. Martin, University of Oregon
Wanda May, Michigan State University
Victoria McArthur, Florida State University
Dorothy McDonald, The University of Iowa
Patrick McMullen, SUNY Fredonia
Margaret Merrion, Ball State University
Kacper Miklaszewski, Chopin Academy, Warsaw, Poland
Robert Miller, University of Connecticult, Storrs
Samuel Miller, University of Houston
Sally Monsour, Georgia State University
Janet Montgomery, University of Colorado, Boulder
Brian Moore, University of Nebraska
David Myers, Georgia State University
Catherine Nadon-Gabrion, University of Michigan
Grant Newman, Iowa State University
Glenn Nierman, University of Nebraska
Ivan Olson, Winona State University
David Pankratz, Alexandria, Virginia
Carol Pemberton, Eden Prairie, Minnesota
Randall Pembrook, University of Missouri, Kansas City
Raymond Perry, Max Planck Institute
Jon Piersol, Florida State University

Melvin Platt, University of Missouri
Lenore Pogonowski, Teachers College, Columbia University
Edward Rainbow, University of North Texas
Darhyl S. Ramsey, University of North Texas
James Raths, University of Vermont
Rosalie Rebollo Pratt, Brigham Young University
Thomas Regelski, State University of New York
Carol Richardson, Northwestern University
John Richmond, University of South Florida
Jon Rieger, University of Louisville
Carroll Rinehart, Tucson, Arizona
Maria Runfola, State University of New York, Buffalo
Timothy Russell, Naples, Florida
James Saker, University of Nebraska, Omaha
Ed Sandor, University of Georgia
Stanley L. Schleuter, Indiana University
Charles Schmidt, Indiana University
Lloyd Schmidt, Storrs, Connecticut
James Scholten, Ohio University
Desmond Sergeant, Southlands College
Patricia Shand, University of Toronto
Patricia Shehan Campbell, University of Washington
Donald Shetler
Rosamund Shuter-Dyson, Woking, Surrey, England
Patricia Sink, University of North Carolina, Greensboro
John Sloboda, University of Keele
Camille Smith, University of Florida
Ralph Smith, University of Illinois
Robert Soar, Fort Collins, Colorado
James Sorensen, University of Puget Sound
Sandra Stauffer, Arizona State University
Eleanor V. Stubley, McGill University, Montreal
Daniel Stufflebeam, Western Michigan University
Bertil Sundin, Stockholm University
John Swaim, University of Northern Colorado
Keith Swanwick, University of London
David Swanzy, Loyola University
Donald Taebel, Georgia State University
Keith Thompson, Pennsylvania State University
Loren Waa, University of Louisville
Robert Walker, Simon Fraser University
Patricia Wallace Hughes, University of Northern Iowa
Darryl Walters, Temple University
Cecilia Wang, University of Kentucky
Barrie Wells, Arizona State University
Betty Welsbacher, Wichita State University
Ian Westbury, University of Illinois
Nancy Whitaker, University of North Carolina
David Williams, Illinois State University
Bruce Wilson, University of Maryland
Helga Windold, Indiana University
Lizabeth Bradford Wing, University of Cincinnati
Robert Winslow, University of North Texas
Marilyn Zimmerman, University of Illinois
Jay Zorn, University of Southern California

Section

·A·

CONCEPTUAL FRAMEWORK

PHILOSOPHICAL FOUNDATIONS

Eleanor V. Stubley

MCGILL UNIVERSITY

What constitutes knowledge and how human beings come to know are complex questions which form the foundation of epistemology as a branch of philosophical discourse. Both questions are also central to the formulation of a philosophy of research in any field of educational endeavor. Education, regardless of the specific form it assumes, is commonly defined at the most basic level as the accumulation and transmission of knowledge.[1] Its formal realization requires identification of (1) a body of knowledge constituting educational content or subject matter, (2) methods through which such knowledge can be transmitted, and (3) means of assessing to what extent knowledge has been satisfactorily acquired. Educational research ultimately seeks to inform this process by identifying, verifying, and adding to the knowledge constituting educational content and by exploring how this knowledge may be transmitted most efficiently in the educational context.[2] Different conceptions of knowledge and of how human beings come to know affect the ways in which educational content are defined, which in turn affect the types of questions considered worthy of study and the ways in which research methodologies are developed and results interpreted.

Attempts to develop a philosophical basis for research in music education typically have been motivated by methodological issues and the identification of specific questions which different research methodologies can effectively address.[3] Discussion for the most part has focused on questions of objectivity, reliability, and validity, rather than the development of a comprehensive understanding of what knowledge is, how it is acquired, and the ways in which music and knowledge may be considered to be connected, if at all.[4] Music education, in other words, has often confused the concept of research as a path to knowledge with the concept of knowledge itself. We have adapted research models detailing how information about a particular discipline or phenomenon may be systematically acquired without first understanding what our discipline is, often equating information

about music and music education with the knowledge potentially accumulated and transmitted through music and music education. If research is to inform the practice of music education with respect to both the identification and verification of educational content and the development of instructional methods, the principles governing the formulation of valid research questions and the development of research methodologies need to be grounded in an understanding of music as a mode of knowing, as well as grounded in the criteria through which the reliability and validity of research results may be established.

The purpose of this chapter is to explore what developments in the field of epistemology can potentially contribute to a philosophy of research in music education. Historical conceptions of propositional knowledge provide insight into the epistemological foundations of research as a path to knowledge about music and music education. More recent developments pertaining to nonpropositional forms of knowledge help to clarify the ways in which music itself may be considered a mode of knowing. Music is explored from the perspectives of listener, performer, and composer, with critical epistemological issues surrounding each type of musical experience considered collectively as a basis for defining new goals and directions in research. The intent is not to develop a comprehensive philosophy of research, but rather to identify a starting point for the formulation of such a philosophy, by presenting an overview of the epistemological principles in which a philosophy of research in music education might be grounded.

PROPOSITIONAL KNOWLEDGE: SCHOOLS OF THOUGHT

Epistemological theories from the Greeks to the early twentieth century have tended to focus primarily on propositional knowledge, the kind of knowledge that is meant when someone is said to know such and such to be the case. This term is usually understood to denote possession of specific pieces of information having a certain truth or validity that can be linguistically conveyed to others. Some hold that this possession is a state of mind, a special form of awareness similar to but much stronger than believing, guessing, or imagining. Others link it with a capacity to perform or respond in certain ways under certain conditions, ascribing knowledge only when complex cognitive and behavioral conditions have been satisfied. As to what types of information count as propositional knowledge and how it is acquired, a wide variety of theories reflecting different conceptions of the human mind and the relationship of humans to the natural world have been proposed. Western theory has been dominated by three schools of thought: rationalism, empiricism, and pragmatism.

Rationalism, the prevalent theory up until about 400 years ago, construes the mind as a deep reservoir of a priori knowledge that is discovered and elaborated through rational analysis of ideas independent of empirical data or authoritative pronouncements. Knowledge is conceived as a fixed body of immutable, fundamental truths relevant to all times and places. Propositions express these truths, often in mathematical terms, as ideal forms that objects and phenomena in the natural world are understood to approximate. Information received directly through the senses is considered unreliable as a source of knowledge because of variations in the specific manifestations of these forms in the natural world.

As a particular school of thought, rationalism owes much to the religious doctrines that permeated thought and action in early western civilizations.[5] Humans, like the natural world in which they lived, were believed to have been created by God and placed on earth to perform a particular task understood to be part of a larger, more omnipotent vision. Casting humans in the role of dutiful servants, this belief gave meaning, purpose, and direction to life. It also accounted for formal variations among natural objects and phenomena by positing the existence of some other more ideal world to which all objects and creatures on earth aspired. In the larger scheme of things, these variations were insignificant, interpretable very simply as earthly imperfections. If humans were to fulfill God's ultimate purpose, what mattered most as knowledge was the ideal forms to which natural objects and creatures aspired.

Empiricism, like rationalism, assumes the existence of a fixed body of immutable, fundamental truths relevant to all times and places. The similarity ends here, however. Identifying information received directly through the senses as the foundation of all knowledge, empiricism dissociates knowledge from any belief structures, religious doctrines, or ideas having no perceptually verifiable reality in the natural world. The mind is conceived as a blank slate, endowed at birth with the capacity to gather, organize, and store sensory impressions. Humans learn through observation by breaking the natural world and its constituent objects into progressively smaller and smaller pieces, with the understanding that the whole is equal to the sum of its parts. Propositions express interrelationships between sensory impressions in the form of empirical generalizations or theoretical constructs abstracted from the specific contexts in which they were originally identified.

Fundamental to empiricism is the strong conviction that humans can know only those things that can be known with complete certainty. Where rationalism considers truth to be a self-evident property of propositions, empiricism defines it as a perceptually verifiable feature that must be repeatedly confirmed or established in a wide variety of situations having universal import or significance. This perspective was to a large extent a response to Nicholas Copernicus's discovery that the earth revolved around the sun.[6] Until that time, the earth had been believed to be the center of the universe, an assumption that followed logically from the belief that human beings and the natural world were God's creations. With the discovery that this was not the case, propositions previously thought to require no explanation could no longer be accepted without question. This observation led empiricists to conclude that rational analysis, insofar as it could be grounded in false propositions, was as potentially fallible as a path to knowledge as the empirical data held suspect by rationalists. If knowledge was to be known with certainty, it had to be verifiable. Human beings, consequently, could know only those invariant, objective aspects of the natural world that could be perceptually confirmed through repeated observations.

Pragmatism was an outgrowth of empiricism prompted by two late nineteenth-century scientific developments.[7] The first was the discovery of electromagnetic fields and Niels Bohr's subsequent observation that the building blocks of all matter could be construed as particles or waves, with the context established by the whole determining the behavior of its parts. Bohr's observation shattered the assumption underlying empiricism that a whole was equal to the sum of its parts, and led Albert Einstein to conclude in his monumental theory of relativity that physical concepts once thought to be perceptually verifiable were in fact creations of the human mind, no matter how unequivocally they appeared to be determined by the natural world. The second development was J. B. de Monet Lamarck's and Charles Darwin's theory of evolution and the realization that the universe and everything in it are constantly changing.

These two developments meant that knowledge could no longer be considered immutable and fixed for all times and places. Pragmatists, consequently, understand propositions to express working hypotheses rather than binding axioms. Like empiricists, pragmatists contend that humans come to know and understand the world through experience. Pragmatists, however, do not view humans as spectators looking out on the natural world, but rather as creative problem solvers in constant interaction with it. Knowledge is not the product of a fixed staring at something, but the result of an ongoing interactive process of acting and being acted upon. Humans come to know by identifying a problem or imbalance in experience, hypothesizing solutions, and exploring the desirability of the potential outcomes through direct action.[8]

Pragmatism links knowledge to the actions of a particular knower in a particular context, making knowledge and the process of knowing or acquiring knowledge virtually synonymous. It extends the empiricist concept of mind as a tool for gathering and storing information by endowing the mind with the capacity to imagine and predict outcomes, as well as to combine, analyze, and categorize sensory impressions. Pragmatism also intricately connects truth with questions of purpose, meaning, and morality, redefining the criteria through which truth is established to take into consideration context and the fact that outcomes recognized as desirable in one situation may not be equally desirable in another.

THEORIES OF PROPOSITIONAL KNOWLEDGE AS MODELS FOR THE RESEARCH ENTERPRISE

The three schools of thought have had greatest impact on research in music education as models of the research enterprise, defining the different types of information about music and music education that may be classified as knowledge and the procedures through which such knowledge may be systematically gathered and validated. The earliest research pertaining to music stemming from the Pythagorean period, with its emphasis on scales and the mathematical principles of acoustics,[9] was very much a product of the beliefs and convictions underlying rationalism. Music was a worthy subject to study because it was believed to be a means of bridging the gap between heaven and earth. What mattered as knowledge were the ideal forms that music sought to embody. Scholars attempted to define these forms by identifying scale structures governing the organization of musical materials and by formulating the acoustical principles of the celestial spheres in which such scales were believed to be grounded. Rational analysis was the path to knowledge, with the laws of logic and mathematics used as the criteria for establishing truth and validity. Although individual compositions and the sounds produced by musical instruments were often a source of inspiration, they were considered unreliable as a source of knowledge insofar as different types of music were observed to elicit different types of responses, not all of which were considered morally beneficial or desirable.[10] To assume the status of knowledge, propositions had to detail forms having universal import and value.

This type of research has played an important role in music education as a means of identifying, verifying, and adding to the knowledge constituting educational content. To begin with, the susceptibility of music to mathematical or propositional formulations gave music a place in the educational curriculum as a distinct branch of knowledge.[11] This status defined the content of music education as the study of music theory or the formal principles through which musical materials are organized and understood, principles that remain significant components of music education even in the twentieth century. Later, music theory as a scholarly discipline dedicated to the study of musical forms came into

being in an effort to extend the content of music education to accommodate and explain developments in the practice of music itself. Although the religious convictions and beliefs motivating the work of early scholars no longer have any relevancy, many of the discipline's most significant research models are rationalistic in their emphasis on the identification of formal principles having universal relevance and on analysis as a path to such knowledge. Recent forays into set theory and Shenker's analyses of compositions as exfoliations of a single, musical relationship defined by foreground, middleground, and background features that may have no perceptually verifiable reality in experience are illustrative examples.[12] The importance theorists have attached to the concept of scale in their efforts to understand the music of other cultures is another example. Indeed, the concept of scale has been so central to Western musical thought that its validity as a universal construct has only recently come to be questioned through the work of ethnomusicologists and cognitive psychologists.[13]

Empiricism as a model of the research enterprise turned attention from ideal musical forms as theoretical abstractions to music as an objective phenomenon in the natural world. Its emphasis on truth and certainty demanded that propositions be formulated on the basis of observations systematically gathered so as to ensure their relevance and generalizability beyond the immediate context. Through adaptation of the procedures used to explore other aspects of the natural world, empiricist researchers sought an understanding of music through an analysis of the perceptual properties of its constituent elements and focused study on those aspects of music that could be known through direct observation. The need to make observations as accurate and as reliable as possible necessitated the application and development of rigorous measurement and observation tools. Repeated applications of the tools with the same results across time and place served to establish the truth of the observations as knowledge.

The measurement tools borrowed from the natural sciences initially limited study to the physical properties of sound, explaining particular musical effects and phenomena in terms of the four essential elements of sound: pitch, duration, intensity, and timbre.[14] Later, these four elements became the basis for exploring auditory thresholds, the various components thought to define musical aptitude, and the different subskills believed to constitute specific performance skills.[15] This interest in the ability of human beings to hear and respond to music was made possible by the development of measurement and observational tools in the behavioral sciences that subjected humans to the same objective scrutiny as natural objects and phenomena. The interest was to a large degree prompted by the empiricist concept of the human mind as a tool for gathering, analyzing, and storing sensory impressions. If research was to inform the practice of music education, both in terms of the definition of content and the methods through which such knowledge could be most effectively transmitted, it was important to know not only what music is in the objective, physical sense, but also what different capacities facilitate the ability of humans to respond to sounds as music.[16]

The development of measurement devices and observational tools specific to musical behaviors has played an important role in the definition of music education research as a branch of research distinct from the natural and behavioral sciences. Such tools have made it possible to explore the effectiveness of different music-teaching and -learning strategies, with positive changes in musical behaviors across time used as a measure of success or effectiveness.[17] These tools have also played an important role in the definition of music education's content, with the musical behaviors they measure and the activities through which the behaviors are measured often becoming the focus of instruction.[18] Technological advances have enabled more accurate measurement and have facilitated the identification and evaluation of the various subcomponents of skills and capacities previously believed to be unsusceptible to direct observation. The elaborate measures that have been developed in recent years to evaluate choral and instrumental performance in terms of achievement across a myriad complex of subskills are notable examples.[19]

Pragmatism initially had its most significant impact on music education as an instructional approach. As a model of the research enterprise, it prompted refinements to the empiricist model in an effort to facilitate the application of research results to practice. The principles underlying pragmatism treat the process of teaching and learning as an interactive system, where the empiricist model approached it in terms of cause and effect. This, plus the association of knowledge with a particular problem, changed the focus of research from the analysis of music and musical behaviors to the study of particular problems in music teaching and learning.[20] As Clifford Geertz has described it in his explanation of "local" knowledge, there has been a movement away from the dream of finding out once and for all how teaching works, to the more modest goal of trying to figure out what is happening or did happen in a particular context.[21] Consequently, there has been a growing interest in developmental questions and in the need to explore a particular problem in a variety of different contexts and from a variety of different perspectives.[22]

This change in focus prompted two additional refinements to the empiricist model. First, it led researchers, both in the design of research studies and the interpretation of results, to distinguish between the perceptions of individual learners and those of teachers and to acknowledge that solutions to a particular problem in one context may not be equally desirable in another.[23] Second, it prompted the adaptation and development of a host of research methodologies and statistical tools designed to develop an understanding of the unique characteristics of a particular context. Various correlational designs and multidimensional factor-analysis statistical packages have, for example, enabled researchers to deepen their understanding of research results by identifying the factors and interrelationships that affect particular outcomes. The introduction of ethnographic techniques such as the case study has enabled researchers to explore the context of a particular problem or situation through direct interaction with it. Unfortunately, however, the information obtained through these tools has not been used to best advantage, with the methodologies often treated as a separate path to knowledge in the empiricist sense, rather than as a means of generating hypotheses and understanding their potential applications in particular contexts.[24]

As the previous discussion has illustrated, the current epistemological foundations of research in music education owe much to the rationalistic, empiricist, and pragmatic schools of thought. Rationalism defined the initial content of music education as a distinct branch of knowledge and led to the development of a scholarly discipline dedicated to deepening and broadening this concept of music as subject matter. The empiricist model identified a need to ascertain and evaluate the truth and certainty of propositions pertaining to music and musical behaviors as objective phenomena and provided guidelines and procedures in the form of measurement and observation tools to facilitate this process. Pragmatism has provided principles and procedures for interpreting and applying research results obtained through the empiricist model by shedding light on the particular characteristics of the context in which the propositions were originally formulated and the context in which the propositions will be applied as hypotheses for selecting specific courses of action. Empiricism and pragmatism have also affected the content of music education in that the procedures used to obtain results and formulate propositions have focused instruction on knowledge about particular aspects of music or the achievement of specific skills and capacities defined by observational tools and measures. With the exception of the religious doctrines underlying rationalistic formulations of music, however, the three schools have done little to inform an understanding of music as a distinct form of knowledge or a mode of knowing in itself.

NONPROPOSITIONAL KNOWLEDGE AND MUSIC AS A MODE OF KNOWING

Constructivism

Advances in epistemological theory in the twentieth century have revolved around the concept of constructivism, with many philosophers turning from the questions of truth and certainty that historically focused thought to questions of understanding and the representation of knowledge by the human mind. The central thesis of constructivism is that the world as we know it is a construction of the human mind. Unlike animals, humans transform their experiences of the natural world through the creation and imposition of forms and images that embody its salient features and shape it for recognition and memory. There being no experience of the natural world independent of such transformations, what humans make of the natural world is a significantly more important question than descriptions of what reality actually is in the objective sense.

Constructivism as a distinct epistemological perspective can be traced back to Immanuel Kant, who was the first to develop the idea that what exists is a product of what is thought.[25] He attributed his insight to David Hume's discovery that certain relationships among things in the natural world, such as causation, were mental constructions projected onto an "objective" world, rather than properties of the natural world itself. Ernst Cassirer extended Kant's logic to encompass nonscientific domains of experience, arguing that a broader interpretation of knowledge was needed to include the types of knowing made possible through myth, religion, and art.[26] Understanding of humans' ability to symbolically transform experience, and thereby their ability to know and understand, he argued, had been limited by an undue emphasis on the conceptual mode of thought associated with propositional knowledge and the sciences. There are also intuitional and expressional modes. The intuitional mode, Cassirer claimed, functions on the level of volitional and teleological concerns, with systematization focusing on the sensuous. The expressional mode stems from emotional or affective experience and is found in artistic and mythological cultural expressions.

Music as Expressional Mode of Knowing: Contributions of Susanne Langer

In *Philosophy in a New Key,* and later in *Feeling and Form* and *Mind,* Susanne Langer extended Cassirer's belief in an expressional mode of knowing by exploring in what senses music and the other arts could be epistemologically associated with affective and emotional experiences.[27] Her explication rests on a distinction between conventional and presentational symbols. The conventional symbols associated with language and mathematics, she argued, serve a designative function, pointing to or referring to some aspect of experience by providing general or abstract information about it. Symbols in the expressional mode of knowing, in contrast, serve a presentational function. They embody in their own structures the patterns and forms of experience that defy linguistic and propositional formulation. Presentational art symbols, she contended, "make feelings conceivable so that man can envisage and understand them without verbal helps and without the scaffolding of an occasion wherein they figure."[28] Langer found support for her position in the apparent similarity between the patterns and forms of music and the ebb and flow of tension marking ordinary experience.

The tonal structures we call "music" bear a close logical similarity to the forms of human feeling—forms of growth and of attenuation, flowing and slowing, conflict and resolution, speed, arrest, terrific excitement, calm, or subtle activation and dreamy lapses—not joy and sorrow perhaps, but the poignancy of either and both—the greatness and brevity and eternal passing of everything vitally felt. Such is the pattern, or logical form, of sentience, and the pattern of music is that same form worked out in pure measured sound and silence.[29]

Langer's description of music and the other arts as presentational symbols has had an impact on a theoretical level in

music education as a justification for music in the educational curriculum as a mode of knowing distinct from that associated with traditional academic subjects. Where mathematical, linguistic, and scientific subject areas develop the skills, competencies, and propositional knowledge base necessary to work in Kant's conceptual mode of knowing, education in music and the other arts provides a means of coming to know and to understand the realm of human feeling. Education in the arts provides a means of developing the skills, competencies, and knowledge base necessary to work in the expressional mode of knowing. Propositional knowledge about music and its organizational principles and the development of musical skills and behaviors are important as a means of developing aesthetic perception, simply defined as the capacity to respond to musical patterns and forms as expressive of human feeling.[30]

This philosophical orientation has had an impact on research in music education in three respects. First, in the area of music theory, it prompted L. B. Meyer to forge a link between aesthetic accounts of the importance of musical form and its expressive functions and psychological accounts of the nature of emotion and auditory perception. This link was a means of explaining exactly how music's patterns and forms can be considered analogous to the patterns and forms of human feeling.[31] Second, in the area of experimental research, Meyer's account of Langer's theory has led to the development of new methodologies through which musical expectation and its importance in music learning and teaching can be better understood.[32] Third, but by no means least, the concept of music education as aesthetic education has pressured the profession to examine, at least on a theoretical level, the value of quantitative and qualitative research methodologies as the only systematic paths to knowledge about music as an expressional mode of knowing. Elliot Eisner, for example, has urged us to consider the value of art criticism as a research methodology.[33] Others have explored the potential limitations of language and different behavioral observation tools as means of assessing and evaluating musical understanding and growth.[34]

Although Langer's theory has played a role in philosophical justifications of music education and thereby has had some effect on research, its impact as a comprehensive epistemological foundation has been limited. To begin with, the theory does not provide any insight into how composers, performers, and listeners make a connection between the patterns and forms of music and those of human feeling—a similarity in form [as Ludwig Wittgenstein's work in symbolic theory and the concept of resemblance has demonstrated] not necessarily guaranteeing that a connection has indeed been made.[35] Although many aestheticians and philosophers have grappled with this problem, their solutions have not been fully satisfactory. Explanations, like those of Roger Scruton and Peter Kivy, for example, do little to move understanding beyond early baroque accounts of musical expression that connect musical patterns with the patterns of human feeling through the physical gestures, body movements, and vocal inflections characterizing ordinary emotional responses.[36] Nelson Goodman's attempt to by-step the problem by demonstrating how music can be understood to refer to the properties it presents, poses another problem, namely, how to determine which of the many different qualities embodied in a work of art are actually referred to by the work of art.[37]

Langer's theory is further limited by the fact that it does not recognize that music has many different functions and values that extend beyond the expressive one traditionally associated with the body of literature defining Langer's musical heritage, functions and values that may also have epistemological significance. The problem is one that Francis Sparshott suggests is inherent in any explanation of music that approaches the concept of expressivity in symbolic terms.[38] By virtue of the traditions defining symbolic theory as a distinct branch of philosophical inquiry, such explanations must detail a symbol's designative or embodied content, evaluate the suitability of the symbolic form with respect to this content, and identify the processes through which these forms are interpreted. Because music has been experienced as expressive in so many different senses, any single theory can at best define a particular potential of music, not music itself. Langer's explication of music as a presentational symbol, for example, precludes the possibility of music functioning as a designative symbol, a function that is central to a variety of western and non-western musical traditions that systematically make use of musical representation and nonmusical references.[39] The approach, Sparshott notes further, also focuses attention on music as an object of contemplation, a perspective that does not acknowledge the value that various western and non-western traditions and cultures have attached to musical performance.[40]

Phenomenological Perspectives on Constructivism: An Alternative Basis for Exploring Music's Epistemological Value

Phenomenological interpretations of constructivism offer an alternative starting point for exploring the different senses in which music may be understood as a mode of knowing. Phenomenologists hold that knowledge is the product of a personal intentional act having social and historical dimensions. Like pragmatists, they treat it as virtually synonymous with the act of knowing or the processes through which it is acquired. Humans come to know and understand the world by actively directing their consciousness toward it and recognizing in their immediate experience elements of past experiences. The common elements function as an interpretative framework, suggesting in turn possible outcomes and appropriate courses of action. In the terms of Alfred Schutz's social phenomenology, experience is shaped through the provinces of meaning that define an individual's *lebensfeld*, or personal stock of knowledge.[41]

The intentional act has a social dimension to the extent that humans do not exist in isolation, but in a larger social context. The interactive exigencies of this social context necessitate the sharing of meanings through the development of collective frames of reference built on the common char-acteristics of personal stocks of knowledge.[42] The act has a historical dimension where ritual and a treasuring of the achievements of the past are at the roots of social interactions.[43] There is an awareness that something has been interpreted in some way in the past and that this way of shaping experience has special significance. Experience is not shaped or seen necessarily in the same way as in the past. Rather, the ritual surrounding the event enables individuals to shape their own experience within the context of shared historical frames of reference for their intrinsic value.

As a framework for understanding music as a mode of knowing, the phenomenological perspective focuses attention on the ways musical experience is shaped. The musical experience, be it that of listener, performer, or composer, is an intentional act in which individuals accept the musical event as their own, shaping what is given in relation to their own fund of past experiences and knowledge. The experience has a social dimension to the extent that musical styles define collective frames of reference through which meanings are shared in a larger social context. It has a historical dimension where tradition creates an awareness that musical sounds have been interpreted in a particular way in the past and that this way of shaping or understanding has special significance or value. A philosophy of research in music education needs to recognize that music as a mode of knowing is not defined by any particular style, historical tradition, or type of musical experience, but by the multiple ways in which musical events may be shaped or constructed at any given moment in history. This requires attention in the formulation of research questions, the development of methodologies, and the interpretation of results to (1) the question of musical style as a social and historical construction, (2) the personal fund of knowledge that individuals bring to the musical experience, and (3) the ways in which the individual, social, and historical dimensions of the musical experience interact in different contexts and situations. Insofar as the experiences of listening, performing, and composing differ, a philosophy of research must also address the critical epistemological issues associated with each type of experience as a mode of music knowing.

Listening as a Mode of Music Knowing

The constructive process defining listening as a mode of music knowing is typically identified as aesthetic perception. The term, from a phenomenological perspective, encompasses a variety of different ways of listening.[44] Michael Parsons's recent work in the visual arts suggests that these differences may be interpretable as developmental stages.[45] Parsons contends that individuals respond to art works differently because they have come to the art work with different expectations as to what art works should be like, what kinds of qualities can be found in them, and how they ought to be judged. These expectations are developed through a series of invariant stages that reflect, first, an increasing ability to construct experiences around accepted social values and norms, and later, an increasing ability to construct viewpoints and perspectives that rise beyond accepted social norms. A Stage 1 response details an essentially sensuous reaction to the art object. A Stage 2 response revolves around the concept of representation and subject matter, with attention focusing on what the art work depicts and how realistically the subject is portrayed. Stage 3 responses consider the sincerity and validity of the affective and emotional properties of a work, while Stage 4 responses focus on details of medium, form, and style in an absolute formalistic sense, with style defining how details of medium and form are viewed and valued. A Stage 5 response questions the criteria, the concepts, and the values with which a tradition constructs artistic meanings and recognizes that aesthetic values change with history.[46]

As previously noted, developmental questions have been of interest to researchers in music education since the turn of the century. To date, attempts to explore these questions from an epistemological perspective have been grounded for the most part in Jean Piaget's developmental account of conceptual thought in science and mathematics.[47] Parsons's findings offer an epistemological foundation for research which is consistent with the values underlying the inclusion of the arts in the educational curriculum. Parsons's stages provide a framework of knowing that can potentially link the development of measures for evaluating musical growth and the effectiveness of instructional strategies to the types of meanings made possible through music and the individual, social, and historical processes through which such meanings are constructed.[48] Pragmatic models of research consider this link to be essential if research is to inform the practice of music education through continued development of content and instructional method.

Application of Parsons's framework to listening as a mode of music knowing, however, requires consideration of four critical epistemological issues: (1) the role music-as-object plays in the constructive process; (2) the extent to which meanings and values associated with different stylistic traditions in the visual arts can serve as a basis for understanding music; (3) the ways in which knowledge of particular stylistic traditions can affect the musical experience at different stages of development; and (4) the types of knowing involved in the measurement of musical understanding. Parsons's framework treats the constructive process as independent of the particular features and characteristics of the art work itself. Although Parsons acknowledged that art objects are capable of many different layers of interpretation, he did not consider the fact that different stylistic traditions attach value to different types of meanings and formal relationships and that the structure of the art object can reflect these values. Music's many different functional and textual associations, for example, have often dictated the formal structure of the music itself.[49] Moreover, stylistic traditions in music, while often related to those in the visual arts, have not been limited to or defined by those of the visual arts.

The ways in which knowledge of particular stylistic traditions can affect the musical experience at different stages of development are a critical issue if a framework such as Parsons's is to serve as a baseline measure for determining the effectiveness and potential of instructional strategies. The issue is rooted in David Feldman's epistemological distinction between universal domains of human experience in which all individuals achieve a certain level of mastery and nonuniversal domains in which mastery or expertise requires indoctrination or instruction in the idiomatic traditions and characteristics of the domain itself.[50] Parsons's stages appear to encompass both universal and nonuniversal achievements in that many of the features distinguishing Stage 4 and 5 responses from the first three stages are a product of specialized knowledge of the traditions and conventions defining different styles. The features distinguishing Stage 1, 2, and 3 responses from each other, in contrast, represent different conceptions of what art with a capital "A" is capable of expressing. It is not clear how these responses would have been different, if at all, if the subjects had had some knowledge of different stylistic traditions. In order to fully understand the potential of different instructional strategies, researchers need to be able to distinguish between achievements that represent a distinct change in understanding in the Piagetian sense and those that are a product of specialized knowledge which deepens understanding without changing the fundamental character of the constructive process.

An understanding of the types of knowing involved in the measurement of musical understanding through a framework such as Parsons's can be informed by a distinction between "reflection-in-action" and "reflection-on-action," two types of knowing which have come to play an important role in research on teacher thinking. As explicated by Donald Schön, reflection-in-action describes the constructive process through which individuals come to know the unique characteristics of a particular situation as the situation unfolds.[51] Knowing is in the action taken to accommodate unanticipated events and outcomes while the action is being taken. Reflection-on-action distinguishes this type of knowing from associated thinking about action that individuals exhibit when they describe their experiences.[52] Aesthetic perception is not a passive act of reception, but a form of reflection-in-action. As the music unfolds, listeners form expectations about possible modes of musical continuation on the basis of stylistic tendencies and respond when those expectations are not realized or are delayed.[53] Verbal descriptions of this experience represent reflection-on-action, symbolic transformation of the original experience through language requiring thinking about the processes through which musical outcomes were anticipated and the knowledge accumulated through the actions constituting responses to unexpected outcomes. Although reflection-on-action can be a potentially valuable source of information about reflection-in-action, the two represent different types of knowing, and may, consequently, have different, albeit related, developmental characteristics.

Roman Ingarden's description of the literary work of art as a stratified formation offers a non-developmental approach for understanding listening as a mode of music knowing.[54] Making a clear distinction between the literary object and its experience, the literary work, Ingarden argues that the literary work consists of a variety of different meaning strata that have their own identities in terms of both their particular qualities and the role each plays with respect to the others in the structure of the work as a whole. On the most basic level, there are the strata defined by the linguistic sound formations of single words and word components. There are also strata defined by (1) the meanings of single words, sentences, and sentence complexes; (2) represented objects; (3) schematicized aspects, such as actions, events, feelings, and so forth, which defy strict representation and thereby require some experiential inference on the part of the reader; (4) the role each of these individual stratum plays in the structure of the whole; and (5) the role played by sequence.

For a variety of reasons this model has value as an epistemological foundation for research on music listening. First, the literary experience is similar to music listening in that the whole represented by the literary object or the musical score is never present to the reader or to the listener all at once as a painting or sculpture is. Second, the concept of the whole as a stratified formation accommodates the many different functions and values associated with music. Beginning with the individual notes and sounds designated in the score, there are strata defined by (1) the sensuous and acoustical properties of individual sounds and sound combinations; (2) the formal meanings articulating musical motives, gestures, phrases, sections, movements, and so forth; (3) musical gestures, themes, or tunes that function like Ingarden's represented objects; and (4) schematicized aspects such as musical style, implication, deviation, embellishment, and elaboration.[55] There are also all the different strata associated with text and other schematic nonmusical aspects, such as representational, expressive, and functional meanings that require knowledge of particular stylistic and cultural traditions on the part of the listener. Last, the importance attached to different strata by different musical traditions and listeners can be accommodated by the strata defined by the different roles individual stratum play within the whole.[56] These strata also enable a link to be established between the performer's exploration and projection of a work's formal qualities and the musical and nonmusical schematic strata that are often central to the listener's interpretation of a work.

Performing as a Mode of Music Knowing

The link between performance and knowledge was first made on the basis of the many different technical skills constituting the act of music performance—skills involved in producing vocal and instrumental sounds, reading music, counting rhythms, shaping musical phrases, adjusting intonation, and so forth. The link is rooted in Gilbert Ryle's distinction between procedural knowledge as "knowing-how" and propositional knowledge as "knowing-that."[57] Using the example of an individual who is able to perform a particular skill expertly but who is unable to explain how this skill is executed, Ryle argues that knowing-how and knowing-that designate two distinct types of knowledge that cannot be re-

duced to or derived from each other. In the words of Israel Scheffler, a skilled performance requires knowledge that can be known and demonstrated only through the performance itself, knowledge pertaining to the specific ways in which the particular steps noted in a propositional description of the skill work together to define a single, complex action.[58] Practical success serves as logical evidence justifying the validity of the knowledge.

The development of performance skills as a branch of knowledge has played an important role in music education as a path to musical understanding, a means of knowing music.[59] The underlying assumption is that understanding a work of art requires insight into the processes governing its creation. To understand a work of art, one must reconstruct it and learn to see it as the embodiment of a particular artist's creative intelligence. In order to reconstruct it, one must master certain prerequisite technical skills.

As a basis for exploring performing as a mode of music knowing, this viewpoint has certain merits. Learning to perform a work can provide students with a sense of the intelligence involved in the construction of the work. This type of understanding can also potentially enhance perception and understanding of other works. The viewpoint, however, fails to recognize that a work of art is not wholly a function of the artist's original intentions. Creation and interpretation take place in a larger social-historical context that affects the decisions made by the composer during the act of creation and the ways in which the artwork itself is later heard.[60] Even more importantly, the viewpoint fails to acknowledge the value that has been and continues to be attached to musical performance, both in western and non-western traditions. As both David Elliott and Nicholas Wolsterstoff remind us, music, in the sense of music making or performing, has a significant history that predates music as individual works of art.[61]

Elliott provides an alternative framework for exploring performing as a mode of music knowing by extending Ryle's concept of procedural knowledge from the know-how defining particular performance skills to the act of music-making itself.[62] Describing how thought and action are integrated in professional practice and making a distinction between quotation and assertion,[63] Elliott demonstrates that performing is much more than the actualization of a given work through the correct implementation of a series of particular technical performance skills.[63] First, such skills must be integrated and combined in such a way that they can be heard or interpreted as a single action, namely, a particular musical performance. Although certain principles governing this integration may be expressed in propositional format, the specific way in which they must be integrated can be known and demonstrated only through the performance itself. Second, like any intentional act, performing is "thought-full." There is an awareness that one is performing, with decisions about actions taken during the course of the performance made on the basis of an understanding of what is currently happening, musically and technically; what should or could be happening; and what strategies can be used to take what is happening closer to what should or could be happening. Third, the making of such decisions requires value judgments about what counts and what does not count in certain contexts. Performing is not simply a matter of quoting what the composer intended. It is a process through which performers develop a personal conception of a work and project it through their own actions. In the words of Alan H. Goldman: "[A] performance instantiates, exemplifies, or implicitly conveys the performer's interpretation. What it exemplifies or implicitly conveys is an explanation of the work and its elements, one that reflects the performer's view of the values inherent in the piece."[64]

It is in this last sense that Elliott finds the principal value of performing as a distinct mode of music knowing. Performing not only yields procedural knowledge of music and of musical performance, it also provides insight into the particular performance. In western traditions, where performance often begins with the composed work, this means that there are two distinct works of art, the work notated in the score and the performer's own conception of that work. Insofar as the latter is formulated in a larger social-historical context, a performance embodies a personal response to the perceived intentions of the composer, to other performances of the same work (including the performer's own), and to the audience, and as such, can yield procedural knowledge of self.

Mihalyi Csikszentmihalyi's concepts of play and constructive knowledge clarify this notion.[65] Play sustains interest and enjoyment because it orders consciousness through the creation of constructive knowledge, knowledge of one's power to control life. Play challenges. It demands the reordering of one's know-how to overcome and rise beyond obstacles and the unexpected. The kind and quality of the actions taken during the course of play, and the changes that these actions make in materials, contexts, audiences, and so on, provide constructive knowledge to the agents about their personal self and the relation of that self to others. Through musical performances, performers learn about their own capacity to control and project musical sounds that will be heard and responded to by others as authoritative assertions articulating a particular conception of how things are musically. In Elliott's words, "Musical performing provides the performer with knowledge about his or her own actions—their quality and affect—and, therefore, a sense of who he or she is."[66]

The work of Barbara and Lawrence Krader on forms of singing and self-identity extends this sense of performing to musical traditions where performance is not associated with a composed work of art.[67] Describing the folk song traditions of several Croatian communities, they note how performers in each community shaped and modified their own performance within the context of the group performance and the stylistic traditions dictated by that community. In one community, for example, voice blending was considered of central importance, with singers working during the course of a performance to equalize the volume and sharpness or timbre of all the voices singing together. It was necessary for the singers to stand close together so that they could hear and judge their own performance in relation to the rest of the group. This yielded a sense of not only self-identity, but also

group identity. Krader notes, "Identity was not constituted by the relation of self to other, but was generated thereby. Identity was not first a process of self-discovery in the sense of 'who am I?', but a process of discovery of identity, difference and connection with the other."[68]

This intricate connection between self-identity and group identity suggests that performing provides constructive knowledge not only of self, but also of culture. To the extent that one's own performance must be shaped within the broader context of a group performance that reflects a particular social-historical tradition, and to the extent that the group performance itself is affected by the actions taken by individual performers within the group, performing reorders knowledge of culture on the social dimension, as much as it reorders knowledge of self.[69]

This connection also makes differences between solo and group performance a critical epistemological issue. The issue is rooted in a distinction between separated and connected modes of knowing forming the foundation of much recent thinking in feminist theory. Carol Gilligan and Nona Lyons use the terms separate and connected to describe two different experiences of the self, one as essentially autonomous or separate from others, the other as essentially in relationship or connected to others.[70] The separate self experiences relationship in terms of "reciprocity," considering others as that self wishes to be considered. The connected self experiences relationships as "response to others in their terms." Connected knowing involves an interest in other people's ways of thinking and knowing. In the group performance, this thought is made accessible by the fact that it is manifested in the actions of the individual performers and the group as a whole. Francis Sparshott seems to allude to this distinction when he reminds us that "for some people, music is between people; for others, it is between a person and the musical piece as an organism."[71]

The concept of performing as a mode of music knowing, which yields constructive knowledge of self and culture, has several implications for research in music education. First, it reorients thought from a focus on questions about the actions involved in the performance of various technical and musical skills, to a focus on questions about what music means for the performer. It suggests the need for an understanding of what constitutes a musical decision; how musical decisions are made; the criteria used to judge artistry; and the different ways in which knowledge about (as opposed to the knowledge that is made possible through performance) music, performance, self, and culture can inform the process of learning to perform in both solo and group contexts. It also has implications for understanding listening as a mode of music knowing. Insofar as procedural knowledge of musical performance and the individual performer's conception of the work are manifested in the actual performance, both can form part of the schematicized stratum of meaning that defines the performance as object for the listener. As Thomas Carson Mark notes: "The one who knows something about the relation of the movements of the piano player to the production of the music from the piano will hear something the mere layman does not perceive."[72] Proficient performers know what to listen for in a given work, and also what to listen for in a musical performance of that work. This can contribute to the knowing of self and culture to the extent that these layers of stratified meaning are felt in relation to listeners' own constructive actions.

Composing as a Mode of Music Knowing

To date, attempts to explore composing from an epistemological perspective have been grounded in the principles underlying structuralism, as researchers have sought to develop a generative-transformational grammar of music.[73]

Although a generative-transformational grammar can provide insight into syntactic and structural principles governing the organization of particular musical patterns within certain stylistic traditions, it is limited in a number of ways as an epistemological foundation for understanding composing as a mode of knowing. First, such a grammar does not account for the many different types of meaning, significance, and value that composers attribute to their own creations.[74] Second, by focusing on an underlying "deep structure," the approach does not acknowledge the attention that composers (performers and listeners as well) give to the specific color, character, and detail of the surface features of a work. Indeed, it is often this detail that defines the unique identity of a given work of art. Third, the approach limits the number of ways in which musical patterns and formal relationships can be shaped and projected in performance, and thereby fails to recognize the ways in which different syntactic emphases can affect the meaning of the whole while retaining the essential identity of the original. The approach, in other words, like empiricist conceptions of the natural world, treats the whole as the sum of its parts. Last, the approach provides no means of accounting for the joy and satisfaction composers find while working out musical ideas and developing new modes of expression.

The concept of play underlying Elliott's explication of performance as a mode of music knowing offers an alternative starting point. Although there is a whole body of propositional knowledge pertaining to specific skills and concepts involved in or associated with composition, composing is a skilled performance that requires procedural knowledge that can be known and demonstrated only through the act of composing.[75] To borrow the words of Roger Sessions, composition is not a matter of set procedure, but a living process of growth, a searching out of possibilities.

The process of execution is first of all that of listening inwardly to the music as it shapes itself; of allowing the music to grow; of following both inspiration and conception wherever they may lead. A phrase, a motif, a rhythm, even a chord, may contain within itself in the composer's imagination, the energy which produces movement. It will lead the composer on, through the force of its own momentum and tension, to other phrases, other motifs, other chords.[76]

This searching out is "thought-full" in that critical judgments are made on the basis of knowledge of music generally, knowledge of the stylistic traditions within which the com-

poser is working, knowledge of the technique of composition, and knowledge of the particular act of composing itself in terms of an understanding of the composer's own sense of self in relation to the context in which the composer is working.[77]

The process yields constructive knowledge of self to the extent that there is a reordering of self as challenges presented by the implications of musical ideas are met and overcome. As Igor Stravinsky describes it: "We grub about in expectation of our pleasure, guided by our scent, and suddenly we stumble against an unknown obstacle. It gives us a jolt, a shock, and this shock fecundates our creative process."[78] The process can also lead to a reordering of culture when individual compositional acts are experienced as single actions constituting broader trains of musical thought that span both the musical life of the composer and the composite musical development of the culture as a whole.[79] Both types of constructive knowledge are distinct from those derived through music performing in that they are informed by knowledge of the act of composing, as opposed to the act of performing (though knowledge of the act of performing may play a role in the definition of knowledge of the act of composing). This distinction is important not only in the sense of the different techniques and concerns dominating one's musical thought while performing and composing, but also in the different ways in which self and culture are defined. Unlike performance where the number of possible modes of continuation are limited by the work of art and the different conceptions of that work held by the performers involved in the performance,[80] composition by definition has no boundaries. The composer's sense of self and culture is defined in relation to an infinite number of possibilities of musical continuation. The principles underlying particular stylistic traditions can limit the number of possibilities, but composers are not bound to work within such stylistic traditions. Indeed, the adoption of such a tradition represents a musical decision, an authoritative assertion articulating a particular conception of how things are musically for that composer. It follows logically that improvisation, by virtue of the fact that it integrates music performing and composing in a single action which is different than either performing or composing, would yield *yet* another sense of self and culture and thereby represent *yet* another mode of music knowing.[81]

This epistemological orientation to composing can also be informed by conceiving composing as a form of philosophizing. When defined as a mode of knowing, philosophy is an ongoing, critical questioning process that seeks to define the nature and value of the world. Basic beliefs about the world are intentionally explored to determine their ultimate truth, meaning, and significance. Marx Wartofsky suggests that artists are involved in the same type of critical discourse with respect to the nature and value of art as a mode of human experience when they evaluate the worth of different artistic structures and stylistic traditions.[82] Every time artists create a new art work or explore new modes of expression, they are involved in the construction of alternate "artistic" worlds, with the "truth" and merit of the beliefs underlying these constructions known as procedural knowledge manifested in the practical success of the artist's decisions.[83] In the case of music, performers and listeners can participate in this discourse to the extent that the composer's questioning process forms part of the schematicized stratum of meaning that defines one aspect of music as object.[84]

A FINAL NOTE

Epistemological questions concerning what constitutes knowledge and how human beings come to know are central to the formulation of a philosophy of research in any field of educational endeavor insofar as research seeks to inform educational practice as the transmission and accumulation of knowledge. These questions affect not only the definition of educational content as subject matter, but also the definition of research as a systematic path to knowledge. In music education, philosophical discussion of the goals and objectives of research has been rooted for the most part in the latter, with historical schools of thought concerning propositional knowledge defining the types of information about music and music education that may be classified as knowledge and the procedures through which such knowledge may be systematically gathered and validated. Rationalism, for example, has provided a research model for exploring musical forms as theoretical abstractions, with the truth and validity of propositions detailing ideal formal constructs established through the laws of logic and mathematics. Empiricism has provided guidelines and procedures for evaluating the truth and certainty of propositions pertaining to music and musical behaviors as objective phenomena. Pragmatism has provided principles and procedures for developing an understanding of the contexts in which propositions are empirically formulated in an effort to facilitate the application of research results as hypotheses for determining how teaching and learning in a particular situation may be maximized.

Although not without value, these principles and procedures are limited as a comprehensive foundation for research in music education insofar as they begin with the ways in which knowledge about music and music education may be systematically gathered, rather than with an understanding of music as a mode of knowing having distinct educational value. As a profession, we have put questions about truth, certainty, teaching, and learning before understanding what it is that is to be taught and learned. This has been due to a large degree to the fact that epistemological theories up until the early twentieth century focused for the most part on the concept of propositional knowledge as "knowing-that," a form of knowledge that does not recognize the sense of significance universally associated with music.

Advances in epistemological theory in the twentieth century focusing on knowledge as a construction of the human mind have been more helpful in this regard, turning thought from questions of truth and certainty to questions of understanding and representation. The work of symbolic theorists such as Ernst Cassirer and Susanne Langer broadened the concept of knowledge to include the nonpropositional

knowledge made possible through such nonscientific domains of human experience as art, myth, and religion. Explanations of music as symbol, however, have also proved of limited value as an epistemological foundation for research in music education in that no single explanation of music as symbol can accommodate the many different senses in which music is experienced as expressive and the value that various musical traditions have attached to musical performance.

Phenomenological interpretations of constructivism and Gilbert Ryle's distinction between propositional and procedural knowledge offer an alternative starting point. The phenomenological description of the processes through which humans come to know as a personal, intentional act having social and historical dimensions focuses attention on the ways in which musical experience is shaped. Music as a mode of knowing is not defined by any particular style, historical tradition, or type of musical experience, but by the multiple ways in which musical events may be shaped or constructed at any given moment in history. Ryle's concept of procedural knowledge defines a new orientation to epistemology in which knowing is not restricted to words and other symbols, but is also manifested in doing.

The conception of music as subject matter which emerges from these advances has several important implications for the development of a philosophy of research. First, research in music education cannot be restricted to a single definition of music's potential expressive value or to a single style or type of musical experience. Research needs to be couched in a philosophical framework that reflects the many different layers of meaning potential in music when it is experienced as object and those made possible through performing and composing. This requires attention in the formulation of research questions, the development of methodologies, and the interpretation of results to (1) the question of musical style as a social and historical construction, (2) the personal fund of knowledge that individuals bring to the musical experience, and (3) the ways in which the individual, social, and historical dimensions of the musical experience interact in different contexts and situations. The framework should recognize the ways in which the musical experiences of listener, performer, and composer are connected and the different types of constructive knowledge of self and culture that each enables. It should also accommodate change and growth, recognizing that research is itself a mode of knowing that occurs in a larger social and historical context which is constantly evolving.

Second, the recent advances broaden the focus of research from information about the acquisition of particular skills and knowledge about music to include questions of what music means for the listener, performer, and composer. If research ultimately seeks to inform the practice of music education by identifying, verifying, and adding to the knowledge constituting educational content and by exploring how this knowledge may be transmitted most efficiently in the educational context, measures for interpreting and evaluating student growth and the effectiveness of particular instructional strategies must be linked to the content and processes of music education. In the case of music listening, it is not enough to know how an individual comes to identify beat as an abstract musical concept. If music is to be taught as a mode of knowing, we need to develop methods of identifying and understanding differences in the meaning attached to different types of musical and nonmusical relationships within the context of a particular work. If these differences are to be used as measures of growth and learning for determining the effectiveness of different instructional strategies, there exists a need to understand the role the structure of music as object plays in the listening experience and the types of knowing involved in the measures used to identify growth. For the performer and composer, we need to understand what constitutes a musical decision, how musical decisions are made, and the criteria used to judge artistry. We need to understand how knowledge about music, performance, composition, self, and culture informs and affects the making of musical decisions at various stages of development and how the potential of such knowledge may be maximized as a learning tool. To do this, we will have to develop an understanding of how decisions embodied in a performer's and composer's actions can be measured and used as indicators of growth and learning.

When addressing these issues, it is essential that we remember that music teaching and learning are also distinct modes of musical experience.[85] From the phenomenological interpretation of constructivism, teaching and learning are not experiences independent of music. Music teaching and learning are different modes of knowing music as listener, performer, and composer. The epistemological foundations of research in music education must explore these two modes, not as teaching and learning, but as derivations of the more basic experiences of listening, performing, and composing in which they are grounded. It is here that epistemological theories of language, other symbolic media, and communication become important. As Vernon Howard has so eloquently illustrated in his book, *Artistry*, language and modeling are the tools of music instruction, the links between teacher and learner, with words, gestures, and sounds showing both how to go on and the standards of correct "performance" in the broad sense of that word.

In the action-oriented context of craft skills one's concern is less with what particular words mean as rendered in other words than with what it is (the phenomena) they refer to. Indeed, while the phenomenon in question—a special quality of voice, the head voice, for instance—may admit of precise discrimination, the words used to label or describe it may vary considerably. The important thing is to be able to discrimate that sound from another term. . . . By learning when and what to query in the examples, one advances en route to an understanding of what is significant about them: what to emulate, what to avoid, or ignore.[86]

As a profession, we need to develop an understanding of the potential of these links and the different ways in which this potential may be maximized for music learning and teaching in all its different forms. In closing, to modify and adapt a remark made by Maxine Greene, it seems the task of a philosophy of research in music education at this time is to awaken the profession to the full range of meaning potential in the musical experience and to encourage the reflection upon that experience for the insights and self-understanding made possible through the experiences of listening, performing, composing, and music teaching and learning through listening, performing, and composing.[87]

Notes

1. Gary D. Fenstermacher, Philosophy of research on teaching: Three aspects, in *Handbook of research on teaching,* 3rd ed., ed. M. Wittrock (New York: Macmillan, 1986) 37–39.
2. Philip W. Jackson, The functions of educational research, *Educational Researcher,* Oct. 1990, 3–9.
3. See, for example, Robert Sidnell, The dimensions of research in music education, *Bulletin of the Council for Research in Music Education,* 1972, vol. 29, 17–27. Charles Leonhard and Richard Colwell, Research in music education, *Bulletin of the Council for Research in Music Education,* 1976, vol. 49, 1–29.
4. See the exchange between Bennett Reimer, George Heller, Peter Webster, Jack Heller, and Warren Campbell in Special Issue of *Bulletin of the Council of Research in Music Education,* 1985, vol. 83, 1–40. See also Roger Rideout, Old wine in new bottles: more thoughts on Reimer, in *Bulletin of the Council for Research in Music Education,* 1987, vol. 92, 42–55.
5. Epistemology, *Encyclopedia Britannica* (Chicago: Encyclopedia Britannica Corp., 1987), particularly 474–484.
6. For further discussion of the effect of this discovery, see T. S. Kuhn, *The structure of scientific revolutions* (Chicago: Chicago University Press, 1962), 66–76.
7. Ibid., 171–173.
8. Pragmatism has been defined and interpreted in many different ways. Discussion in this paper has been based on the concept as formulated by John Dewey in *How we think* (Lexington: Heath and Company, 1933) 91–118; and Israel Scheffler in *Conditions of knowledge* (Chicago: Scott, Foresman, and Company, 1965), 4–6.
9. See Richard L. Crocker, Pythagorean mathematics and music, *The Journal of Aesthetics and Art Criticism,* 1964, vol. 22, 189–198, 325–335; Donald Ferguson, *A history of musical thought* (New York: Appleton Century, Crofts, 1959); Gottfried Wilhelm Leibniz, Principles of nature and of grace, founded on reason, in *The monadology and other philosophical writings* trans. Robert Latta (London: Oxford University Press, 1988) 405–424; D. P. Walker, *Studies in musical science in the late renaissance* (London: The Warburg Institute, 1978).
10. Plato, for example, classified music in terms of the moral effects of the different modes. Music in certain modes was not considered appropriate in sacred contexts because it tended to elicit "unseemly" behavior in secular contexts. For further explication of this classification system, see Wladyslaw Tatarkiewicz, *History of aesthetics,* vol. 2 (The Hague: Mouton, 1970) particularly 120–134.
11. Stephen Toulmin, Philosophies of the branches of knowledge, *Encyclopedia Britannica,* 663–665.

12. Relatively accessible explanations of the principles of set theory can be found in: John Rahn, *Basic atonal theory* (New York: Longman, 1980) 74–123; David Lewin: *Generalized musical intervals and transformation* (New Haven: Yale University Press, 1987), 60–156; and Robert Morris, *Composition with pitch classes: a theory of compositional design* (New Haven: Yale University Press, 1987), 1–57. A concise and balanced description of Schenker's approach can be found in Allen Forte, Heinrich Schenker, in the *New grove dictionary of music and musicians,* 1980, vol. 16, 627–628. A discussion of the importance of this type of approach in non-western musics can be found in Ernest G. McClain. *The myth of invariance* (New York: Nicholas Hays, 1976). For discussion of the different developments in this approach from the late Renaissance, see Stillman Drake, Renaissance Music and Experimental Science, *Journal of the History of Ideas,* 1970, vol. 31, 483–500.

13. See, for example, Bruno Nettl, *Twenty-nine issues in ethnomusicology* (Urbana: University of Illinois Press, 1983), particularly sections 1 and 2, and Mary Louise Serafine, *Music as cognition* (New York: Columbia University Press, 1988), 18–23, 52–60.

14. See, for example, Hermann Helmholtz, *On the sensations of tone* (New York, Dover Publications, 1954).

15. This transition is especially apparent in Carl Seashore's *Measures of musical talents,* which define musical aptitude as the sum of capacities to respond to different auditory thresholds. As James Mursell notes in the *Human values in music education* (New York: Silver Burdett, 1934), these capacities played a major role in determining students' natural ability for performing music.

16. This point is made by Carl Seashore in Measures of musical talent. *Psychology of music* (New York: McGraw-Hill, 1938), 302–308.

17. The Rubin-Rabson studies exploring different approaches to musical memory and rehearsal in piano instruction are examples of the earliest initiatives in this area.

18. One only has to trace the role different types of activities defining measures of musical aptitude and later measures of musical achievement have played in the basal textbook series of the period to see the importance of this relationship. More recently, the skills and capacities measured by Edwin Gordon's *Musical Aptitude Profile* have become central to a particular methodology, *Jump Right In,* although this relationship is slightly different from the earlier ones in that Gordon's *Profile* is part of an attempt to develop a comprehensive theory of musical learning.

19. See, for example, John Cooksey's Developing an Objective Approach to Evaluating Music Performance, in *Symposium in music education: A festschrift for Charles Leonhard,* ed. Richard Colwell (Urbana: University of Illinois Press, 1982), 197–230.

20. This change can be seen by scanning the titles recorded in the Council for Research in Music Education annual publication, *Dissertations in progress,* for the last 10 years.

21. Clifford Geertz, *Local knowledge* (New York, Basic Books, 1983), 34.

22. To name only the most obvious contributions, the centrality of developmental issues can be documented in the recent work of Howard Gardner, Lyle Davidson, and the Harvard Project Zero, Helmut Moog, David Hargreaves, and Keith Swanwick. The need to explore a particular problem in a variety of different contexts and from a variety of different perspectives is the underlying impetus for the concept of University Research Centers devoted to the study of a single issue articulated by Bennett Reimer in Toward a more scientific approach to music education research, *Bulletin of the Council for Research in Music Education,* 1985, vol. 83, 1–21.

23. These new directions, for example, are seen in Ruth I. Gustafson, The teacher-student-family triad: social systems theory applied to three case studies of problematic behaviour in music lessons, in *Bulletin of the Council for Research in Music Education,* 1987, vol. 94, 1–16.

24. This point is articulately made by Sharan Merriam and Edwin Simpson in *A guide to research educators and trainers of adults* (Malobar: Robert E. Krieger, 1984).

25. Immanuel Kant, *Critique of pure reason,* trans. J. Bernard (New York: Hafner Publishing, 1951).

26. For further elaboration of this argument, see Ernst Cassirer, *The philosophy of symbolic forms,* 3 vols. (New Haven: Yale University Press, 1953), vol. 3, 1–91 and *An essay on man: An introduction to philosophy of human culture* (New Haven: Yale University Press, 1956), 1–36.

27. Susanne Langer, *Philosophy in a new key* (Cambridge: Harvard University Press, 1942); *Feeling and form* (New York: Scribner's, 1953); *Mind: An essay on human feeling,* 3 vols. (Baltimore: John Hopkins University Press, 1967–1985).

28. Susanne Langer, *Philosophy in a new key,* 222.

29. Susanne Langer, *Feeling and form,* 27.

30. Bennett Reimer's *A philosophy of music education,* 2nd ed. (Englewood Cliffs: Prentice-Hall, 1989) is the most noteworthy statement of this position. As several important leaders in the field have noted, this position has had virtually no impact on actual classroom practice insofar as musical performance remains the central preoccupation of music education (Charles Fowler, *The crane symposium: toward an understanding of the teaching and learning of music performance,* Potsdam: Potsdam College of State University of New York, 1988, viii).

31. Leonard B. Meyer, *Emotion and meaning in music* (Chicago: University of Chicago Press, 1956), 1–82, 256–272 and *Music, the arts, and ideas: patterns and predictions in twentieth-century culture* (Chicago: University of Chicago Press, 1967), 3–41.

32. For example, the work of D. E. Berlyne at the University of Toronto in the development of "experimental aesthetics" (see *Studies in the new experimental aesthetics: Steps toward an objective psychology of aesthetic appreciation* [Toronto: John Wiley, 1974] and the work of James Carlsen and his students at the University of Washington (e.g., Developing aural perception of music in context, *Journal of Research in Music Education,* 1970–1971, 47–50); and the work of Lola Cuddy at Queen's University (e.g., Perception of structured melodic sequences, paper presented at Music Perception Conference, Paris, 1977).

33. Elliot Eisner, *The educational imagination* (New York: Macmillan, 1979).

34. See, for example, K. Durkin and R. D. Crowther, Language in music education: Research overview, *Psychology of Music,* 1982, vol. 10, 59–61; David Perkins, Talk About Art, *Journal of Aesthetic Education,* 1977, vol. 11, 87–116; F. Hare, The identification of dimensions underlying verbal and non-verbal responses to music through multidimensional scaling, unpublished doctoral dissertation, University of Toronto, 1975; Jack Heller and Warren Campbell, Models of language and intellect in music research, in *Music education for tomorrow's society: selected topics,* ed. Arthur Motycka (Jamestown: GAMT Music Press, 1976), 40–49; and Harriet Hair, Descriptive vocabulary and visual choices: Childrens' responses to conceptual changes in music, *Bulletin of the Council for Research in Music Education,* 1987, vol. 91, 59–64.

35. See Ludwig Wittgenstein, *Lectures and conversations on aesthetics, psychology, and religious belief,* ed. Cyril Barrett (Oxford: Blackwell, 1966), 1–32.

36. Roger Scruton, *The aesthetic understanding: Essays in the philosophy of art and culture* (New York: Methuen, 1983); Peter Kivy, *The corded shell: Reflections on musical expression* (Princeton: Princeton University Press, 1980). Other approaches can be found in the works of Donald Ferguson, *Music as metaphor* (New York, Greenwood Press, 1973); Wilson Coker, *Meaning and music: A theoretical introduction to musical aesthetics* (New York: The Free Press, 1970); Deryck Cook, *The language of music* (London: Oxford University Press, 1959); and Alan Tormey, *The concept of expression* (Princeton: Princeton University Press, 1971). Malcolm Budd has provided a comprehensive, critical survey of various approaches to the relationship between music and the emotions in *Music and the emotions: The philosophical theories* (Boston: Routledge and Kegan Paul, 1985). His approach in the final chapter (151–176) is noteworthy in its attempt to link cognition and feeling as a single integrated function of mind.

37. Nelson Goodman elaborates this solution in *The languages of art,* 2nd ed. (Indianapolis: Hackett, 1976) through the introduction of the concept of exemplification. Further elaboration of the problem posed by this solution can be found in Monroe Beardsley, On Understanding Music, in *On criticising music: five philosophical perspectives,* ed. Kingsley Price (Baltimore: Johns Hopkins University Press, 1981), 55–73.

38. For a comprehensive survey of this notion, see Francis Sparshott, *The theory of the arts* (Princeton: Princeton University Press, 1982), particularly 58–101, 303–345, 346–370.

39. For a comprehensive survey of the different ways in which music has been used for representational purposes and musical quotation, see Peter Kivy, *Sound and semblance,* (Princeton: Princeton University Press, 1984) and Jenefer Robinson, Music as a Representational Art, in Alperson, *What is music?,* 165–192.

40. Francis Sparshott, Aesthetics of music—limits and grounds, in Alperson, *What is music?,* 33–98. Christopher Small makes the same point in *Music, society, education* (London: John Calder, 1977), 34–58.

41. Alfred Schutz, The problem of social reality, in *Collected papers I,* ed. Maurice Hatanson (The Hague: Martinus Nijhoff, 1962), 64–90.

42. In *The Social Construction of Knowledge* (New York: Doubleday, 1966). Peter Berger and Thomas Luckmann go so far as to assert that the socially constructed world is the only one available to us, that there can be no knowing without this social dimension.

43. This interpretation of the historical dimension of knowing is presented by Richard Palmer in *Hermeneutics* (Evanston: Northwestern University Press, 1969), and Edward Carr in *What is history?* (New York: Knopf, 1967). Its application in the artistic sense has been detailed by Clifford Geertz in *The Interpretation of cultures* (New York: Basic Books, 1973) and by Timothy Rice in Toward the remodeling of ethnomusicology, *Ethnomusicology,* 1987, 469–487.

44. See, for example, Maxine Greene, *Landscapes of learning* (New York: Teachers' College Press, 1978), 159–210 and Stanley Madeja and David Perkins (ed.), *A model for aesthetic response in the arts* (St. Louis: CEMREL, 1982).

45. Michael Parsons, *How we understand art* (Cambridge: Cambridge University Press, 1987).

46. Other studies which have reported similar findings to Parson's include: James Baldwin, *Thought and things: A study of the development and meaning of thought,* 3 vols. (London: Swan Sonnenschein, 1974); Jonna Ruth Clayton, An investigation into the developmental trends in aesthetics: A study of qualitative similarities and differences in the young, unpublished doctoral dissertation, University of Utah, Salt Lake City, 1974; A. Coffey, A developmental study of aesthetic preferences for realistic and nonobjective paintings, unpublished doctoral dissertation, University of Massachusetts, Amherst, 1968; Abigail Housen, The eye of the beholder: Measuring aesthetic development, unpublished doctoral dissertation, Harvard University, Cambridge, 1983.

47. For an account of Jean Piaget's theory, see *The science of education and the psychology of the child* (New York: Orion Press, 1970); see, Mary Louise Serafine's Piagetian research in music," *Bulletin of the Council for Research in Music Education,* 1980, vol. 62, 1–21, for a discussion of early applications of Piaget's thought to music.

48. The verbal responses Parsons used to develop his framework, for example, share certain characteristics with verbal responses elicited during and after music listening. See, Otto Ortmann in Types of listeners: Genetic considerations, in *The effects of music,* ed. Max Schoen, 38–77 (London: K. Paul. Trench Trubner, 1927); or Henry Weld's An experimental study of musical enjoyment, *American Journal of Psychology,* 1912, vol. 23, 245–308. Stubley has directly explored the application of Parsons' stages to the description of musical experiences, An exploration of verbal description and reflection as a means of exploring how musical meanings are shaped and understood in light of theories of Thomas Clifton and Michael Parsons," unpublished doctoral dissertation, University of Illinois, Urbana, 1989.

49. See Joseph Kerman, *Contemplating music: Challenges to musicology,* (Cambridge: Harvard University Press, 1985).

50. David Feldman, *Beyond universals in cognitive development* (Norwood: Ablex Publishing, 1980), 1, 8–20, 27, 105–108, 117–119, 152, 160–161, 168.

51. Donald Schön, *The reflective practitioner* (New York: Basic Books, 1983), 49–69, and *Educating the reflective practitioner* (San Francisco: Jossey-Bass, 1989), 22–40.

52. Hugh Munby and Tom Russell, Educating the reflective teacher, *Journal of Curriculum Studies,* 1989, vol. 21, 71–80.

53. For further discussion of this process and the role style plays in the formulation of musical expectations, see L. B. Meyer, *Emotion and meaning in music* and *Music, the arts and ideas.* 1–69.

54. Roman Ingarden, *The literary work of art* (Evanston: Northwestern University Press, 1972), 29–33, and *Cognition of the literary work of art* (Evanston: Northwestern University Press, 1973). A third work by Ingarden, *The work of music and the problem of its identity,* (Berkeley: U of Cal Press, 1986), 34–40, begins to deal with the distinction between the work and the score. Other literary models detailing different levels of meaning, such as those by Elizabeth Rosenblatt and Jerome Bruner, might also prove of value.

55. Don Ihde's *Listening and voice: A phenomenology of sound* (Athens: Ohio University Press, 1976) and Joseph Smith, *The experiencing of musical sound: prelude to a phenomenology of music* (New York: Gordon and Breach, 1979), explore the sensuous and acoustical properties of sound. Thomas Clifton's *Music as heard* (New Haven: Yale University Press, 1983) begins work on the concept of musical gestures, themes, etc., as represented objects and schematicized aspects such as musical style, implication, and so forth. There are a wide variety of theoretical treatises that provide insight into the many different levels on which such musical relationships may be shaped.

56. A recent paper presented by Douglas Bartholomew at the Indiana (1990) Conference on Philosophy in Music Education be-

gins to explore different types of whole-part musical relationships. Roman Jakobson illustrates how different emphases on the sensuous stratum can affect the syntactic stratrum within the whole. See Musikwissenshchaft und linguistik, in his *Selected writings,* (The Hague: Mouton, 1971), 551–553. Differences in Tibby's and Mrs. Munt's responses to Beethoven's Fifth in Peter Kivy's *Music alone* (New York: Cornell University, 1990) show the potential of verbal responses to illuminate differences in the importance attached to such strata.

57. Gilbert Ryle, *The Concept of mind* (London: Hutchinson, 1963), 25–61.

58. Scheffler, *Conditions of knowledge,* 91–105

59. See, for example, Reimer, *A philosophy of music education,* and Smith, *Excellence in art education* (Reston: National Art Education Association, 1986).

60. For further explication of this point, and others pertaining to the weaknesses involved in this approach, see Israel Scheffler, Making and understanding, in *Proceedings of the forty-third annual meeting of the philosophy of education society,* (Normal: Illinois State University Press, 1988), 65–78.

61. David Elliott, Music as Knowledge, paper presented at Indiana Conference on Philosophy in Music Education, 1990, 28; Nicholas Wolterstorff, The Work of Making a Work of Music, in Alperson, *What is music?,* 115.

62. Elliott, "Music as knowledge," 28.

63. In developing these ideas, Elliott draws on the work of: Schön, *The reflective practitioner;* Saul Ross, Epistemology, intentional action and physical education, in *Philosophy of sport and physical activity,* ed. P. Galasso (Toronto: Canadian Scholars' Press, 1988), 171–189; Thomas Carson Mark, Philosophy of piano playing: Reflections on the concept of performance, *Philosophy and Phenomenological Research,* 1981, vol. 4, 299–324.

64. Alan H. Goldman, Interpreting Art and Literature, *Journal of Aesthetics and Art Criticism,* 1990, vol. 48, 203.

65. Mihayli Csikszentmihalyi and Isabella Csikszentmihalyi, *Optimal experience: Psychological studies of flow in consciousness* (Cambridge: Cambridge University Press, 1988). 3–36.

66. Elliott, Music as knowledge, 28.

67. Barbara Krader and Lawrence Krader, Slavic Folk Music: Forms of Singing and Self-Identity, *Ethnomusicology,* 1987, vol. 13, 9–17.

68. Ibid., 16.

69. This seems to be the idea underlying Clifford Geertz's description of art as culture (*The interpretation of culture)* and Peter Kivy's more recent description of music as a medium through which individuals enact the gestures and rites defining culture (paper presented at Indiana Conference on Philosophy in Music Education, 1990).

70. C. Gilligan, *In a different voice: Psychological theory and women's development* (Cambridge: Harvard University Press, 1982); N. Lyons, Two perspectives on self, relationships and morality, *Harvard Educational Review,* 1983, vol. 53, 125—145. For a more complete treatment of women's ways of knowing see Mary Belenky, Blythe Clinchy, Nancy Goldberger, and Jill Tarule, *Women's ways of knowing* (New York: Basic Books, 1986).

71. Sparshott, Aesthetics of music, 89.

72. Mark, Philosophy of Piano Playing, 321.

73. See, for example, Fred Lerdahl and Ray Jackendoff, *A generative theory of tonal music* (Cambridge: MIT, 1983).

74. See Ian Lawrence, *Composers and the nature of music education* (London: Scolar Press, 1978).

75. This is what recent studies on expert performances have sought to do: formulate these procedural integrations in propositional format. See, for example, Alf Gabrielsson, Performance of Rhythm Patterns, *Scandanavian Journal of Psychology,* 1975, vol. 15, 63–72 and S. Sternberg and R. Zukofsky, Timing by Skilled Musicians in *Psychology of music,* ed. D. Deutsch (New York: Academic Press, 1982), 182–240.

76. Roger Sessions, The Composer and His Message, in *The creative process,* ed. Brewster Ghiselin (New York: New American Library, 1985), 45.

77. This is what Igor Stravinsky alludes to when he writes that the compositional act is sustained by a chain of discoveries and shaped by a vigilant technique, the latter being interpreted as a form of control associated with music and self, both of which are subjected to higher values (*The poetics of music,* New York: Vintage Books, 1956), third lesson, pp 61–87.

78. Stravinsky, *The Poetics of Music,* 73.

79. For further explication of the different "temporal horizons" on which music may be shaped as a social and historical construction in experience, see Clifton, *Music as heard,* 50–74, 205–239.

80. Limited in the sense that interpretation must be recognizable as a performance of a particular work or else the whole process would be the creation of a new work.

81. David Sudnow's description of the stages he went through learning to improvise supports this conclusion insofar as knowledge of playing and knowledge of materials and vocabulary of jazz were not enough; the two ultimately had to be combined to create something different and new. See *Ways of the hand: Organization of improvised conduct* (London: Routledge and Kegan Paul), 1978.

82. Marx W. Wartofsky, The Liveliness of aesthetics, *Journal of Aesthetics and Art Criticism,* Special Issue on Analytical Aesthetics, 1987, 211–218.

83. Alperson rejects this possibility in Music as Philosophy, in *What is music?,* 193–206, but he deals only with philosophy as investigating the truth of propositions. The concept of success as logical evidence underlying the notion of procedural knowledge seems to allow philosophizing in nonlinguistic media.

84. The capacity to shape experience in this way is the central achievement of Parsons's fifth, and last, stage of aesthetic understanding. See Parsons, *How we understand art,* chap. 5, 121–153.

85. This point is implicit in the remarks of Christopher Small in *Music, society, education* 206–229 (See note 40) and in Patricia Shehan Campbell's observations in Orality, literacy, and music's creative potential: A comparative approach, *Bulletin of the Council for Research in Music Education,* 1989, vol. 101, 1–29.

86. Vernon Howard, *Artistry: The work of artists* (Indianapolis: Hackett Publishing, 1982), 72–73.

87. Greene, *Landscapes of learning,* 161–210. (See note 40)

References

Alperson, P. (1987). Music as philosophy. *What is music? An introduction to the philosophy of music.* New York: Haven Publications, 193–210.

Baldwin, J. (1974). *Thought and things: A study of the development and meaning of thought,* 3 vols. London: Swan Sonnenschein.

Beardsley, M. (1981). On understanding music. K. Price (ed.), *On criticising music: Five philosophical perspectives.* Baltimore: Johns Hopkins University Press, 55–73.

Belenky, M., Clinchy, B., Goldberger, N., and Tarule, J. (1986). *Women's ways of knowing.* New York: Basic Books.

Berger, P., and Luckman, T. (1966). *The Social construction of knowledge.* New York: Doubleday.

Berlyne, D. E. (1974). *Studies in the new experimental aesthetics: Steps toward an objective psychology of aesthetic appreciation.* Toronto: John Wiley.

Budd, M. (1985). *Music and the emotions: The philosophical theories.* Boston: Routledge and Kegan Paul.

Campbell, P. S. (1989). Orality, literacy, and music's creative potential: A comparative approach. *Bulletin of the Council for Research in Music Education,* vol. 101, 1–29.

Carlsen, J. (1970–1971). Developing aural perception of music in context, *Journal of Research in Music Education,* 47–50.

Carr, E. (1967). *What is history?.* New York: Alfred A Knopf.

Cassirer, E. (1953). *The philosophy of symbolic forms,* 3 vols. New Haven: Yale University Press.

Cassier, E. (1956). *An essay on man: An introduction to philosophy of human culture.* New Haven: Yale University Press.

Clayton, J. R. (1974). An investigation into the developmental trends in aesthetics: A study of qualitative similarities and differences in the young. Unpublished doctoral dissertation, University of Utah, Salt Lake City.

Clifton, T. (1983). *Music as heard.* New Haven: Yale University Press.

Coffey, A. (1968). A developmental study of aesthetic preferences for realistic and nonobjective paintings. Unpublished doctoral dissertation, University of Massachusetts, Amherst.

Coker, W. (1970). *Meaning and music: A theoretical introduction to musical aesthetics.* New York: The Free Press.

Cook, D. (1959). *The language of music.* London: Oxford University Press.

Cooksey, J. (1982). Developing an objective approach to evaluating music performance. In R. Colwell (ed.), *Symposium in music education: A festschrift for Charles Leonhard,* Urbana: University of Illinois Press.

Crocker, R. L. (1964). Pythagorean mathematics and music. *The Journal of Aesthetics and Art Criticism,* vol. 22.

Csikszentmihalyi, M., and Csikszentmihalyi, I. (1988). *Optimal experience: Psychological studies of flow in consciousness.* Cambridge: Cambridge University Press.

Cuddy, L. (1977). Perception of structured melodic sequences. Paper presented at Music Perception Conference. Paris.

Cziko, G. (1989). Unpredictability and indeterminism in human behavior: Arguments and implications for educational research. *Educational Researcher,* vol. 18, issue 3.

Dewey, J. (1933). *How we think.* Lexington: D.C. Health and Company.

Drake, S. (1970). Renaissance Music and Experimental Science. *Journal of the History of Ideas,* vol. 31, 483–500.

Durkin, K. K., and Crowther, R. D. (1982) Language in music education: Research overview. *Psychology of Music,* vol. 10, 59–61.

Eisner, E. (1979). *The educational imagination.* New York: Macmillan.

Eisner, E. (March 1984). Can educational research inform educational practice? *Phi Delta Kappan,* vol. 65, 447–452.

Elliott, D. (1990). Music as knowledge. Paper presented at Indiana Conference on Philosophy in Music Education.

Epistemology. *Encyclopedia Britannica.* Chicago: Encyclopedia Britannica Corp., 1987.

Feldman, D. (1980). *Beyond universals in cognitive development.* Norwood: Ablex Publishing Corp.

Fenstermacher, G. D. (1986). Philosophy of research on teaching: Three aspects.'' In M. Wittrock (ed.), *Handbook of research on teaching,* 3rd ed. New York: Macmillan, 37–39.

Ferguson, D. (1959). *A history of musical thought.* New York: Appleton Century, Crofts.

Ferguson, D. (1973). *Music as metaphor.* New York: Greenwood Press.

Forte, A. (1980). Heinrich Schenker. In the *New grove dictionary of music and musicians,* vol. 16, 627–628.

Fowler, C. (1988). *The Crane symposium: Toward an understanding of the teaching and learning of music performance.* Potsdam: Potsdam College of State University of New York.

Gabrielsson, A. (1975). Performance of rhythm patterns. *Scandanavian Journal of Psychology,* vol. 15, 63–72.

Geertz, C. (1973). *The interpretation of cultures.* New York: Basic Books.

Gilligan, C. (1982). *In a different voice: Psychological theory and women's development.* Cambridge: Harvard University Press.

Goldman, A. H. (1990). Interpreting art and literature. *Journal of Aesthetics and Art Criticism,* vol. 48, 203.

Goodman, N. (1976). *The languages of art,* 2nd ed. Indianapolis: Hackett.

Greene, M. (1978). *Landscapes of learning.* New York: Teachers' College Press.

Gustafson, R. I. (1987). The teacher-student-family triad: Social systems theory applied to three case studies of problematic behaviour in music lessons. *Bulletin of the Council for Research in Music Education,* vol. 94, 1–16.

Hair, H. (1987). Descriptive vocabulary and visual choices: Childrens' responses to conceptual changes in music. *Bulletin of the Council for Research in Music Education,* vol. 91, 59–64.

Hare, F. (1975). The identification of dimensions underlying verbal and non-verbal responses to music through multidimensional scaling. Unpublished doctoral dissertation, University of Toronto, Toronto.

Heller, J., and Campbell, W. (1976). Models of language and intellect in music research. In A. Motycka (ed.), *Music education for tomorrow's society: Selected topics,* edited by Jameston: GAMT Music press.

Helmholtz, H. (1954). *On the sensations of tone.* New York: Dover Publications.

Housen, A. (1983). The eye of the beholder: Measuring aesthetic development. Unpublished doctoral dissertation, Harvard University, Cambridge.

Howard, V. (1982). *Artistry: The work of artists.* Indianapolis: Hackett Publishing.

Ihde, D. (1976). *Listening and voice: A phenomenology of sound.* Athens: Ohio University Press.

Ingarden, R. (1972). *The literary work of art.* Evanston: Northwestern University Press.

Ingarden, R. (1973). *Cognition of the literary work of art.* Evanston: Northwestern University Press.

Jakobson, R. (1971). Musikwissenshchaft und linguistik. In his *Selected writings.* The Hague: Mouton, 551–553..

Jackson, P. W. (Oct. 1990). The functions of educational research. *Educational Researcher,* 19:7, 3–9.

Kant, I. (1951). *Critique of pure reason.* Translated by J. Bernard. New York: Hafner Publishing, 3–9.

Kerman, J. (1985). *Contemplating music: Challenges to musicology.* Cambridge: Harvard University Press.

Kivy, P. (1984). *Sound and semblance.* Princeton: Princeton University Press.

Kivy, P. (1980). *The corded shell: Reflections on musical expression.* Princeton: Princeton University Press.

Kivy, P. (1990). *Music alone.* New York: Cornell University.

Krader, B., and Krader, L. (1987). Slavic folk music: Forms of singing and self-identity. *Ethnomusicology,* vol. 13, 9–17.

Kuhn, T. S. (1962). *The structure of scientific revolutions*. Chicago: Chicago University Press.

Langer, S. (1942). *Philosophy in a new key*. Cambridge: Harvard University Press.

Langer, S. (1953). *Feeling and form*. New York: Scribner's.

Langer, S. (1967–1985). *Mind: An essay on human feeling*, 3 vols. Baltimore: Johns Hopkins University Press.

Lawrence, I. (1978). *Composers and the nature of music education*. London: Scolar Press.

Leibniz, G. W. (1988). Principles of nature and of grace, founded on reason. In *The monadology and other philosophical writings*, translated by Robert Latta. London: Oxford University Press, 405–424.

Leonhard, C., and Colwell, R. (1976). Research in music education. *Bulletin of the Council for Research in Music Education*, vol. 49, 1–29.

Lerdahl, F., and Jackendoff, R. (1983). *A generative theory of tonal music*. Cambridge: MIT Press.

Lewen, D. (1987). *Generalized musical intervals and transformation*. New Haven: Yale University Press.

Lyons, N. (1983). Two perspectives on self, relationships and morality. *Harvard Educational Review*, vol. 53, 125–145.

Madeja, S., and Perkins, D. ed. (1982). *A model for aesthetic response in the arts*. St. Louis: CEMREL.

Mark, T. C. (1981). Philosophy of piano playing: Reflections on the concept of performance. *Philosophy and Phenomenological Research*, vol. 4, 299–324.

McClain, E. G. (1976). *The myth of invariance*. New York: Nicholas Hays.

Merriam, S., and Simpson. E. (1984). *A guide to research for educators and trainers of adults*. Malabar: Robert E. Krieger.

Meyer, L. B. (1956). *Emotion and meaning in music*. Chicago: University of Chicago Press.

Meyer, L. B. (1967). *Music, the arts, and ideas: Patterns and predictions in twentieth-century culture*. Chicago: University of Chicago Press.

Morris, R. (1987). *Composition with pitch classes: A theory of compositional design*. New Haven: Yale University Press.

Munby, H., and Russell, T. (1989). Educating the reflective teacher. *Journal of Curriculum Studies*, vol. 21, 71–80.

Mursell, J. (1934). *Human values in music education*. New York: Silver Burdett.

Mursell, J. (1937). *Psychology of music*. New York: W. W. Norton.

Nettl, B. (1983). *Twenty-nine issues in ethnomusicology*. Urbana: University of Illinois Press.

Ortmann, O. (1927). Types of listeners: Genetic considerations.'' In Max Schoen (ed.), *The effects of music*. London: K. Paul Trench, Trubner.

Palmer, R. (1969). *Hermeneutics*. Evanston: Northwestern University Press.

Parsons, M. (1987). *How we understand art*. Cambridge: Cambridge University Press.

Perkins, D. (1977). Talk about art. *Journal of Aesthetic Education*, vol. 11, 87–116.

Piaget, J. (1970). *The science of education and the psychology of the child*. New York: Orion Press.

Rahn, J. (1980). *Basic atonal theory*. New York: Longman.

Reimer, B. (1985). Toward a more scientific approach to music education research. *Bulletin of the Council for Research in Music Education*, vol. 83, 1–21.

Reimer, B. (1989). *A philosophy of music education*, 2nd ed. Englewood Cliffs: Prentice-Hall.

Reimer, B., Heller, G., Heller, J., Campbell, W., and Webster, P. (1985). *Bulletin of the Council for Research in Music Education*, vol. 83, 1–40.

Rice, T. (1987). Toward the remodeling of ethnomusicology. *Ethnomusicology*, 31:3, 469–487.

Rideout, R. (1987). Old wine in new bottles: More thoughts on reimer. *Bulletin of the Council for Research in Music Education*, vol. 92, 42–55.

Robinson, J. (1987). Music as a representational art. In P. Alperson (ed.), *What is music? An introduction to the philosophy of music*. New York: Haven Publications.

Ross, S. (1988). Epistemology, intentional action and physical education. In P. Galasso (ed.), *Philosophy of sport and physical activity*. Toronto: Canadian Scholars' Press.

Ryle, G. (1963). *The concept of mind*. London: Hutchinson.

Scheffler, I. (1965). *Conditions of knowledge*. Chicago: Scott, Foresman, and Company.

Scheffler, I. (1988). Making and understanding. *Proceedings of the forty-third annual meeting of the philosophy of education society*. Normal: Illinois State University Press, 65–78.

Schön, D. (1983). *The reflective practitioner*. New York: Basic Books.

Schön, D. (1989). *Educating the reflective practitioner*. San Francisco: Jossey-Bass.

Schutz, A. (1962). The Problem of Social Reality. In Maurice Hatanson, (ed.), *Collected Papers I*. The Hague: Martinus Nijhoff.

Scruton, R. (1983). *The aesthetic understanding: Essays in the philosophy of art and culture*. New York: Methuen.

Seashore, C. (1938). Measures of Musical Talent. in *Psychology of music*. New York: McGraw-Hill, 302–308.

Serafine, M. L. (1988). *Music as cognition*. Columbia University Press, New York.

Serafine, M. L. (1980). Piagetian research in music. *Bulletin of the Council for Research in Music Education*, vol. 62, 1–21.

Sessions, R. (1950). *The musical experience of composer, performer, listener*. Princeton: Princeton University Press.

Sessions, R. (1985). The Composer and His Message. In B. Ghiselin (ed.), *The Creative Process*. New York: The New American Library, 45.

Sidnell, R. (1972). The dimensions of research in music education. *Bulletin of the Council for Research in Music Education*, vol. 29, 17–27.

Simpson, A. J., and Weiner E. S. C., eds. (1989). *The Oxford English dictionary*, 2nd ed. Oxford: Clarendon Press, vol. 11.

Small, C. (1977). *Music, society, education*. London: John Calder.

Smith, J. (1979). *The experiencing of musical sound; Prelude to a phenomenology of music*. New York: Gordon and Breach.

Smith, R. (1986). *Excellence in art education*. Reston: National Art Education Association.

Sparshott, F. (1987). Aesthetics of music: Limits and grounds.'' In P. Alperson (ed.), *What is Music? An Introduction to the Philosophy of Music*. New York: Haven Publications.

Sparshott, F. (1982). *The theory of the arts*. Princeton: Princeton University Press.

Sternberg, S., and Zukofsky, R. (1982). Timing by skilled musicians. In D. Deutsch (ed.), *Pyschology of Music*. New York: Academic Press.

Stravinsky, I. (1956). *The poetics of music*. New York: Vintage Books.

Stubley, E. (1989). An exploration of verbal description and reflection as a means of exploring how musical meanings are shaped and understood in light of theories of Thomas Clifton and Michael Parsons. Unpublished doctoral dissertation, University of Illinois, Urbana.

Sudnow, D. (1978). *Ways of the hand: Organization of improvised conduct*. London: Routledge and Kegan Paul.

Swanwick, K. (1988). *Music, mind, and education.* London: Routledge.

Tatarkiewicz, W. (1970). *History of aesthetics,* vol. 2. The Hague: Mouton.

Tormey, A. (1971). *The concept of expression.* Princeton: Princeton University Press.

Toulmin, S. (1987). Philosophies of the branches of knowledge. In *Encyclopedia Britannica.* Chicago: Encyclopedia Britannica Corp., 663–665.

Walker, D. P. (1978). *Studies in musical science in the late renaissance.* London: The Warburg Institute.

Wartofsky, M. W. (1987). The liveliness of aesthetics. *Journal of Aesthetics and Art Criticism, Special Issue on Analytical Aesthetics,* 211–218.

Weld, H. (1912). An experimental study of musical enjoyment. *American Journal of Psychology,* vol. 23, 245–308.

Wittgenstein, L. (1966). *Lectures and conversations on aesthetics, psychology, and religious belief.* Oxford: Blackwell.

Wolterstorff, N. (1987). The work of making a work of music. In P. Alperson (ed.), *What is music? An introduction to the philosophy of music.* New York: Haven Publications.

TOWARD A PHILOSOPHICAL FOUNDATION FOR MUSIC EDUCATION RESEARCH

Bennett Reimer

NORTHWESTERN UNIVERSITY

This chapter will explore several important issues that need to be addressed if a philosophical foundation for music education research is to be built. Implicit in this task are three presumptions, which will organize my presentation into sections: (1) that music education research is not presently and has not in the past been guided by foundational philosophical principles, (2) that it would be beneficial for the research enterprise if such principles were articulated and applied, and (3) that careful consideration of several key issues will be necessary if music education research is to be grounded in a coherent philosophical-epistemological perspective.

What will *not* be offered here is a philosophy of music education research. Whereas I will not attempt to disguise whatever preferences and proclivities I hold, I will also not aim toward a particular resolution of the philosophical issues to be raised. It is my hope that sufficient debate about these (and other such) issues will occur in the future to lead interested and capable individuals to formulate philosophical principles that would guide our research efforts.

Because I will be discussing something that does not yet exist, the consequences of its absence, and the ways our work would be likely to improve if we were to have it, I will naturally tend to focus on the shortcomings within music education research. After all, if no shortcomings existed there would be little reason to posit that we are in need of something we do not yet have. It is not particularly pleasant to set out to draw attention to weaknesses as a way of establishing that we have much room for improvement, and to indicate some of the ways we need to improve. This is especially the case in a volume of this sort, which to a large degree exists, correctly and aptly, to celebrate the achievements of music education research. That such achievements have been considerable will be amply demonstrated by much of what appears here. Music education has a very short research history

because it lies outside those disciplines in which research is the central, or at least a major, defining activity. That its research endeavor has grown so rapidly, that so many of the complexities of the activity have been mastered, that so many researchers have developed into highly competent specialists, that training programs for preparing new recruits have been established, that a large, wide-ranging literature has developed—all this and more is ample testimony to high levels of success.

Yet it can also be argued that the continuing viability of music education research will depend on significant improvements. That is the argument I will make in this chapter, in the spirit that this volume is an appropriate occasion not only to demonstrate the strengths of music education research but also to acknowledge that it can and should be stronger than it is, and to suggest how it can become so.

THE LACK OF A PHILOSOPHICAL GROUNDING FOR MUSIC EDUCATION RESEARCH

From among the ways the term "philosophy" can be construed, I will focus here on its meaning as "a system of principles for guidance in practical affairs" (*Random House Dictionary*). The term "system" implies that the principles be ordered according to a set of beliefs that achieves a convincing level of consistency and validity. Philosophical principles, to be valid and useful, cannot be simply a random collection of assumptions. A unifying core of precepts, sufficiently congruent to provide coherence, sufficiently broad to cover the scope of the enterprise, and sufficiently in consonance with what is accepted as true according to the criteria established by the community in question is necessary for a convincing and useful set of philosophical guidelines to exist.

The term "principles" refers to a particular level of mental operation. Principles provide general rules, laws, or guidelines from which specific actions or beliefs might logically spring. As generalities that capture the determining characteristics or essential qualities of a phenomenon or activity, principles provide the nexus for consistent doing and being. Without a set of principles to guide them, practical affairs can be only adventitious, lacking in the unity of purpose that is required for effectiveness.

Music education research is an enterprise employing disciplined inquiries[1] in an attempt to understand and improve the teaching and learning of music. It has been undertaken, I suggest, without a sufficient level of grounding in a coherent system of guiding principles. Few, if any, discussions exist in the music education literature about the basic questions that must be grappled with if a set of sound and useful principles is to emerge: What is valid music education research? How should music education research be organized and conducted? Who should do music education research?

In regard to the first question, we find in the infrequent discussions of music education research an unquestioning acceptance of a particular (positivist) conception of science as the basis for the activity. Few issues are raised as to what science means; how science has radically questioned its own nature during the twentieth century; the uncertain relationship of the physical and biological sciences with the so-called social sciences; the uncertain relationship of the physical, biological, and social sciences with the domain of art; the vexing dilemmas of the relation of basic research to applied research; and a host of questions about the compatibility of education as a social-political endeavor with the particular model of scientific research that music education has tended to adopt uncritically as its modus operandi.[2] This is not to say that the quantitative, positivist definition of science and of research that has dominated the history of music education research is, ipso facto, mistaken or misguided. It *is* to say that we have been mistaken and misguided not to have examined, carefully and critically and continually, how and why and when such a definition might be or might not be appropriate for our purposes. I am not questioning at this point the substantive issue of the adequacy of positivistic science as a basis for music education research (under "Several Key Issues . . ." below, I will return to this matter in some detail). I am raising the question of our need, and our failure, to think about music education research at a metacognitive level. That is the level from which principles might emerge that could help our research become more efficacious. It is important to begin to think at that level. We have not, I suggest, sufficiently engaged in professional discussions about the basic issue of what scientific truth might mean and not mean.

By contrast, we have indeed thought a great deal about the various modes or methodologies by which music education research might be carried on. Few articles or textbooks on research have neglected to discuss the differences among types of research, such as philosophical, historical, descriptive, experimental, and variations thereof. Perhaps the most inclusive treatment was provided by Robert Sidnell, who, after reviewing several classifications, proposed a three-dimensional matrix including methods of inquiry (historical, descriptive, experimental, philosophical), central variables (the teacher, the learner, the interaction of teacher and learner, content, and environment), and disciplines (education, musicology, psychology, sociology, anthropology, history).[3]

The substantial interest in types of research (there is far less discussion of central variables or disciplines) reflects the characteristic focus by music educators on issues of methodology. In every aspect of music education, from the most practical to the most theoretical, we have historically been fascinated by (if not fixated on) methodological concerns. This may stem, in part, from our need to demonstrate our capacity to be scholarly, but it is also likely to be a result of our concentration, from the early colonies to the present, on the teaching of performance, with all the attendant needs for regularity, careful sequencing, technical finesse, constant monitoring and assessing, and so forth. Such requirements, and the remarkable success the profession has achieved in meeting them, raise methodological issues to high levels of consciousness and inevitably transfer to endeavors not directly related to performance, such as research.

Therefore, discussions of the various research types or modes focus largely on the methods and techniques by which they should properly be carried out. Given the dominance of quantitative research and the great number and intricacy of technical details related to such research, whether descriptive or experimental or correlational, and the special languages, computations, and symbolic representations they require, major attention is given in the music education research literature and in research courses to their methodological particulars. Such (necessary) attention to detail fits well not only with the positivist and quantitative bent mentioned previously but also with the natural predilections of many music educators.

Little similar attention has been paid to philosophical issues related to the various research methodologies. It is generally agreed that all are necessary, but the questions of why, and in what ways, have seldom received more than cursory treatment. A step toward principles was taken by Charles Leonhard and Richard J. Colwell in their 1976 review of research and projections for the future, by their suggestion that in order to achieve better clarity about significant research topics, philosophers and scientists will have to collaborate.[4] But we have not built on this suggestion by trying to define what the characteristics of significant research topics might be, whether the four research types we generally identify are relevant to or sufficient for dealing with such topics, how each type of research might be expected to contribute toward useful knowledge, how and for what purposes each type (and others that might be identified) might collaborate or interact with the others, whether particular types might be incompatible with one of more of the others in the context of some topics, and whether combining two or more types might yield insights larger than the sum of the parts included.

Lacking examination of these issues, we cannot simply assume that so long as we have various types of research being undertaken we are doing our work responsibly. We need to attend to the principles lurking beneath the surface of our previous, largely technological discussions of the ways research can be conducted, by focusing on issues such as (1) what each type allows us to know, (2) what good such knowings are, (3) how our knowings might be enhanced by combinations and juxtapositions presently not used because of our limited understanding of which dimensions and dynamics of music education each type can be expected to clarify.

Few generalizations would seem more self-evident than that different types or modes of research yield different pictures of reality. In addition to being clearer about how that occurs so we can exercise more intelligent control over it, we also need to be clearer about what realities we are interested in exploring through research. We find few, if any, sustained discussions in the music education research literature of what it is we need to know in order to improve music education. The Leonhard and Colwell article mentioned above attempts to suggest a set of "major research questions," and other attempts have been made over the years to delineate topics that might drive the research enterprise.[5] The most frequent way such topics are suggested, however, is through the "Recommendations for Further Research" sections of doctoral dissertations and other studies, but these are generally limited to extensions of the particular topic of the dissertation or study, and no mechanism exists to gather, coordinate, and prioritize the many recommendations made. Further, such recommendations are ex post facto—they suggest follow-ups to topics that were chosen without the guidance of an overarching plan leading to that specific research effort. No such plan exists because no philosophical principles for music education research exist to provide a foundation for such planning.

One more issue should be mentioned regarding the lack of philosophical guidelines for music education research. To what degree do we expect music education research to relate to, influence, or in any way be connected with practices of teaching and learning music? We often given strong indications that we expect research to have practical consequences, as in our attempts to translate research results into language nonresearchers can understand and to explain their applications. We also exhort nonresearchers to keep up with research journals and research studies so their practices can be guided by research findings. This is all under the assumption that research frequently is or should be applicable to practice. That assumption is suspect, of course. The general literature on educational research reflects an intense examination of whether and how research relates to schooling and why it often does not, an examination carried on with particular force in our sister field of art education. We have not paid similar attention to the theoretical issues of why research in music education seems to have such little relevance for the great majority of music teachers. This has been noted outside our own field, as in the comment by Beverly Jones and June McFee in the *Handbook of Research on Teaching* (3rd ed.) that "the controversy regarding separation of research from practice which is pervasive in art education is conspicuously absent in the literature of music education."[6]

I shall return to this matter under "Several Key Issues . . . ," in my discussion of the question of who should do research. The point here is that a carefully devised set of principles for music education research would offer guidance as to whether and when we should expect practical payoffs from research, and how such payoffs might be achieved. We do not presently have such guidance available to us, accounting in large part for our disorganization as to how we approach the conduct and application of research. Such disorganization is quite atypical of music education as a whole. Why can it be argued, as I believe it validly can be, that music education research, which should be characterized by thoughtful, effective structures within which its diverse activities can be generated and carried on coherently, is largely devoid of such structures, all existing structures being ex post facto? The answer lies in the lack of a solid foundation on which a research structure can be built.

THE NEED FOR A PHILOSOPHICAL FOUNDATION FOR MUSIC EDUCATION RESEARCH

The discussion in the preceding section focused on several important factors demonstrating that we have carried out our research endeavors in the absence of guiding principles. We have not attempted to define sufficiently what we mean by science, what we can and cannot expect from science, and how we can utilize science to help us with the problems we think are important. Therefore, we cannot exercise optimum control over how we engage in science in our research endeavors. Instead we tend to "do science" in ways only vaguely related to a definition of science that is itself quite vague.

For example, a good deal of music education research has been influenced by the assumptions of behavioristic psychology, which is the paradigm case in the human sciences of positivism as it has existed in the physical-biological sciences. There is a tendency to regard such research as the very model of science, and those who have done it most and best as our most "scientific" researchers. We have not discussed whether this particular model is (1) viable within the larger fields of philosophy of science, psychology, and educational research, (2) pertinent to the needs of music education, and (3) supportive of values we hold for both music and education. If we had discussed the issue with some thoroughness and rigor, we would have discovered, I think, that (1) behavioristic assumptions were being severely questioned in both philosophy and psychology at the very time we began adopting them as the basis for much of our own research, (2) they do offer important insights and guidelines for certain aspects of music education, and (3) they do support certain values we tend to hold but are inimical to others.

What difference would it have made if we had had a reasonable level of clarity about such matters through our ongoing discussions of them? Perhaps we would have been able to use behaviorism more insightfully and powerfully, taking advantage of what it can do very well in the perspective of what it cannot do very well. Perhaps we would have been more aware that other models from psychology were and are viable for our research, and could have pursued them with the energy they deserved, achieving a balance in psychological orientations more relevant to the diverse nature of music education than we otherwise were able to achieve. We would have been able, perhaps, to recognize the importance of behavioristic research in light of its particular strengths while also being cognizant of its inherent weaknesses. In short, our philosophical-theoretical groundings could have made our research endeavors more sensible.

We are now entering a new era in psychology with a severe erosion of interest in and credibility of behaviorism and the rise of cognitive psychology along with the broader domain of cognitive science, and we are beginning to see this change reflected to some small degree in music education research. It is disconcerting to think that we might now embrace cognitive psychology as unthinkingly as we did behavioral psychology. Although the new developments in psychology clearly seem to be immensely fruitful for the music education enterprise as a whole and for research in particular, we would benefit from history if we recognized that, rather than buying uncritically into a particular psychological orientation, we would be better served to reflect on what we want and are able to get from it that might help us do what we define as being important to do. We would then not become servants of a particular psychological view, as was our tendency with behaviorism, but controllers of our scholarly destinies, using psychology as another powerful means for our benefit as we define it.

On the issue of research modes, a set of principles guiding our actions might have led us to realize that, while each must be carried on in methodologically sound ways, the more important issues have to do with the nature of each type of inquiry and with their interrelations and their limitations. Such issues are raised by the complexities of the three factors with which the field of music education deals—music, people, and education. For each factor there exists a three-part set of fundamental realities as to its nature.

In regard to music, it exists, in certain respects, as a phenomenon with a nature transcending time and place. No matter when in human history and where in human communities, music has qualities setting it apart from all other human endeavors. Yet, in certain other respects, it is a product of particular times and particular places. The universal nature of music is exemplified in specific cultural contexts, which are complex because there are usually many manifestations of music and many cross-cultural influences in particular cultures. Finally, in still other respects, music exists in singular manifestations—this specific piece or process at this specific moment for this specific occasion. Music, after all, is phenomenon underneath generality.

Human beings exhibit the very same tripartite nature. In certain respects all human beings are alike—they manifest universal qualities that set them apart from all other creatures and things. But people always exist, simultaneously, as members of particular societies at particular times, and that membership pervades all they are and can be. At this level, the complexities are enormous because differences in gender, age, and role affect the playing out of social membership. Also, people are usually members of several cultural groupings, at several levels of engagement, simultaneously, especially in the modern world where cultural isolation is rare. But further, each human being is, in certain respects, *sui generis,* with characteristics distinctive to this particular individual. People are, underneath any commonalities, unique identities.

Because music education deals with music and people in particular settings, the dimension of education also must be accounted for in the mix of factors with which research must deal. Here also we find the same tripartite division. In certain senses education is an undertaking with transhistorical, transcultural characteristics. In other senses it is embedded in history and in particular cultures, with the infinite political, social, psychological, and economic issues that fact entails. But further, every act of learning is incomparable, requiring an engagement by a unique person at a particular moment in that person's life with sets of conditions experienced only as that person can experience them. Education, after all, occurs in a single person's inner being.

Given these realities, research modes should be seen as mechanisms to throw light on one or several dimensions of music, people, and education as these dimensions interact with one another. Certain kinds of research are particularly helpful at certain levels, but are limited in providing insights at other levels. Experiments, for example, are particularly useful in probing for insights at the transpersonal level but are less useful in yielding understanding of what occurs in unique situations for particular individuals. Case studies reverse the situation. History can be organized to illuminate broad, general trends. It can also probe the nuances of specific occurrences in their manifold complexities. Every possible way to carry on research has its strengths and limitations.

Because music education deals with the interrelations of music, people, and education, each of them existing at three general levels of reality, research attempting to understand and enhance those interrelations must be both diverse and coordinated. No single approach to research can possibly cope with all levels, and no scattershot array of studies can possibly yield understanding of the organic nature of the interactions music education must influence. Until we have rationalized how and why we can employ various research modes relevantly and cohesively, we will continue to be more unscientific—that is, more unsystematic, uncoordinated, imprecise, unfocused—in our search for disciplined knowledge than we should be. To construct philosophical principles for music education research is, precisely, to provide guidance as to how we can achieve better science.

These considerations lead directly to the issue of science as being the rationalized search for solutions to human problems rather than a prescriptive technology one is obligated to follow. Our technological orientation has led us to think that "doing science" is a matter of following prescribed routines as exactly and "objectively" as possible. I will return to this notion of science under "Several Key Issues." Here, the question needing to be raised has to do with what it is that drives the research enterprise in the first place. What purposes (other than completing a dissertation, getting published, achieving tenure) do we expect research to serve? If research in music education is to be scientific in a meaningful sense, it should serve the purposes of more effective, useful, and relevant teaching and learning of music. But what would that consist of? Clearly that is a philosophical question at base: It is a question of values. Effective for what? Useful for what? Relevant for what? What *do* we want music education to achieve, so that research might help in achieving it and thereby fulfill the function of being science?

I do not intend here to answer this question, of course, having used up several hundred gallons of ink (if not blood) elsewhere in trying to answer it. I do intend to suggest that science is and must be a value-driven enterprise, and the values it is driven to help achieve are, by necessity, human values because science is a human construct and an activity pervaded with human valuing. Objective it is not—disciplined it must be. What disciplines it, I suggest, is its pursuit of meaningful values and the rigor of that pursuit. Therefore, a philosophical foundation for music education research will have to relate in several ways to a philosophy of music education, which can provide it with its significant research topics. Unless our research modes and techniques are aimed in meaningful directions, that is, employed for valid and important purposes, we will too often give the impression of being "scientoid" rather than scientific—as resembling science rather than being science.

It is not enough to argue that researchers generally pursue topics of interest—even of pressing interest—to themselves (or to their adviser or faculty in the case of dissertation topic choices). Certainly we should hope and expect that researchers will be devoted to the topics on which they will be expending the significant investments of time and energy that sizable research studies require. The issue is not the interest and devotion of particular researchers—it is the structure within which research interests and commitments are encouraged to arise and be sustained.

At present, no profession-wide structure exists to generate, coordinate, and disseminate music education research. In the absence of a planned, rationalized structure of goals to give direction to choices for individual and group efforts, research topics tend to be generated randomly. The source of topics is too often one's present interest, one's intuition as to what might be of interest to others, the availability of a technology or research process compatible with one's skills, a search for something that can be claimed as one's territory, or a hunt in the literature for loose threads that can be picked up. There are any number of ways that one might light on something reasonably persuasive and reasonably accomplishable.

Occasionally particular research settings determine the choice of topic—places where an influential historian, experimentalist, tests and measurements expert, philosopher, or the like influences (or persuades) others to do similar work, or where an individual or group of researchers interested in a particular area, such as therapy, behavioral techniques, or performance problems, similarly influences others to join in the endeavor. Such settings go a long way to fill in the vacuum that exists when no direction at all is discernible to guide the choice of research topics. For, although it would seem that maximum freedom to choose a topic exists where no prior research direction exists, such "freedom" is actually a function of vacuity—an absence of interests and commitments to which a researcher might gravitate. When any topic can be chosen, choice can occur only by chance or impulse, and the freedom to choose is an empty exercise. The existence of a goal structure within which the freedom to choose is governed by meaningful parameters with meaningful consequences allows freedom to be balanced with responsibility, and thereby gives freedom significance. As in the creation of a work of art, where choices must be made within a structure of artistic constraints, giving the choices a necessary function, research choices must be made within a structure of professionally defined constraints. These give particular choices of research a purposive function within a larger, meaningful structure.

Freedom without structure is anarchic, and music education research has suffered from an excess of disorder because its structure has been insufficient to give meaning to freedom of choice. Although those constraints in choices mentioned above have helped provide cohesion in particular instances, they are not the products of a rationalized plan to which they are consciously contributing, but rather the result of chance events that led particular people with particular interests to exert influence on those with whom they came into contact. Our profession deserves better. We deserve to build, by our conscious, directed efforts, a planned research program focusing on the significant problems and issues of music education for which research can provide assistance, in which all those engaged in research or preparing to be engaged in research can find a useful contribution to make in light of their individual intellectual strengths and personal-professional interests. Of course a structured research program can be so restrictive and prescriptive as to forestall freedom: That is the opposite end of the continuum from there being so little structure as to render freedom insignificant. Between the untenable extremes lies the possibility for balances in which an overarching plan allows our research to become directed toward the important goals we define for it, and in which individual researchers can freely find a contribution to make toward the achievement of progress also being sought by others.

The development of such plans requires the guidance of articulated principles for generating significant research topics, and then viable research contexts within which the topics can be pursued. Such contexts would provide the working conditions—optimum support of people, facilities, resources, in pursuit of defined professional goals over sufficient periods of time—for progress to be expected to occur. That is how effective science works. Science does not proceed by a random accretion of uncoordinated, unfocused studies chosen by individuals working in isolation from communities of like-minded, similarly goal-driven colleagues. If that is how science had proceeded we would, in the larger sphere of science, be faced now with what faces us in music education research—bits and pieces of insights insufficiently coordinated or integrated to add up to a larger picture.

We have done much excellent research of a variety of sorts in a variety of fields, as this volume attests. Imagine, for a moment, if all this research had been guided by well-defined goals focusing on topics mutually defined as central to the improvement of music education. Imagine, further, that this research had been carried out in contexts providing optimum coordination, so that individual (or group) studies were accomplished in ways that enchanced all possible interstudy congruences. Imagine that the studies had been carefully linked with one another to build on fruitful leads, to fill in needed gaps of knowledge, to replicate and expand successful attempts, to provide longitudinal data so lacking in our research, to probe theoretical-philosophical weaknesses, and to put ideas into practice in a variety of relevant education settings with careful monitoring and follow-ups. Surely we would have been able, under such conditions, to have approximated more closely the astonishing gains made in the traditional (and new) sciences during the past three of four decades—gains that could not possibly have been made without extraordinary degrees of coordination. Although some would argue that our subject matter is more complex than theirs, it is nevertheless reasonable to assume that we would have made far more progress than we have, and would have done so in contexts also promoting genuine communities of cooperating scholars. The human benefit of so doing is not to be lightly dismissed, in that such communities are far more likely to attract people to become professional researchers than is the "scientist as isolationist" image we have tended to portray.

There are a variety of ways to build ongoing research contexts, the research center as existing in the sciences by the hundreds if not thousands being the clearest example. This chapter is not the place to describe and discuss the details of research centers or of other ways to provide the coordination from which music education research is likely to benefit dramatically. The point is that the development of philosophical guidelines for music education research would entail, as a necessary adjunct, the building of operational research structures and policies to carry out the guidelines intelligently and cohesively. I will return to this matter in the concluding section of this chapter.

SEVERAL KEY ISSUES UNDERLYING A PHILOSOPHICAL FOUNDATION FOR MUSIC EDUCATION RESEARCH

The foundational issues for which philosophical principles are needed arise from a particular agenda. For example, a philosophy of music education is likely to grapple with issues such as the nature of music, its various social functions, what musical creation consists of, what musical experience consists of, how music "means," how education can be organized to achieve the values the philosophy claims for it, and so forth. The defining issues for music education research are likely to include the nature of scientific knowing, the modes of scientific knowing, how such knowings relate to the knowings music education is concerned with, the structures within which science can take place effectively in a field such as music education, how findings can be implemented, and so forth. The previous two sections touched on some of the kinds of issues for which philosophy might be expected to provide guidance for music education research.

Here I want to offer a few illustrative examples of foundational issues to which philosophical thinking about research is likely to have to attend, so that the nature, scope, and level of the work might become more apparent. To attempt to cover most or all such issues would be tantamount to writing a complete philosophy of research, so, obviously, only a small sample can be handled in this section. First, I will discuss in some detail the dilemma being caused by the major shifts recently occurring in the philosophy of science and the repercussions those shifts have had on the field of educational research. We, too, in music education research, will have to adapt to the new intellectual realities being thrust on us, and it is a function of philosophical guidelines to help us do so effectively.

Second, I will discuss briefly a conceptualization of the various ways one particular research mode (in this case, history) might be construed to operate, to illustrate that research, no matter of what sort, requires a basis in philosophical commitments—in value choices—in order to be carried on at all. Research, we need to understand explicitly, cannot be value free, so we must be clear about the value choices being made in any particular research methodology or endeavor, and in the subsequent educational recommendations it might yield.

Finally, I will raise an issue increasingly being raised in educational research, having to do with who should be engaged in doing such research and in what settings it can be carried on most fruitfully. This issue leads directly to the domain of research policy, much neglected if not ignored in music education, but about which philosophy might be expected to offer some clarity.

How "Scientific" Is Science?

From the beginnings of modern science some four centuries ago until the revolution in conceptions of science that occurred around the middle of this century, science was largely conceived to be the domain in which assured, inerrant knowledge (1) was assumed to be possible and (2) could be achieved through the use of appropriate methodologies. Scientific knowledge was considered to be, by its very nature, founded upon the existence of a reality beyond human subjectivity, variability, and uncertainty. That solid, unchallengeable reality could be discovered reliably either by the careful application of the human senses (bolstered by instrumentation), as empiricists like John Locke and George Berkeley believed, or by the application of reason, as rationalists like René Descartes believed. Scientific knowledge depended on the objective application of the senses or of reason—subjectivity was taboo because it intruded between the human observer and the "real" being observed. That "real"—that objectively existent actuality—could be represented accurately, once discovered, by language (construed to include symbol systems such as mathematics).

The general term for this belief system is "positivism." Although some thinkers before the middle of the twentieth century were skeptical about this view (John Dewey notably among them), most adopted it, or some form of it, as the basis for their work. And although the view was developed as applicable to the "hard" sciences, whose subject matter was the natural world, it was an easy and seemingly logical step to assume it applied equally to human affairs. The methodologies of natural science, and the quest for existent actualities, could be transferred from the traditional sciences to the human domain—the social sciences. Research in social science could be as objective and reality seeking as in the sciences exploring the natural world, and methodologies for ensuring objectivity, control of variables, statistical power, could be used to duplicate in social science what was occurring in natural science.

It was an even easier step to assume that education, as an aspect of social behavior, could be understood to be a domain in which objectively existent reality could be uncovered through the applications of scientific methodology. Education research, often teamed with the psychology most amenable to the positivist scientific model—behaviorism—adopted and implemented this model as its foundation. Music education research did likewise. Such research in education generally, and in the subdomain of music education, was predicated on the principle on which positivism was founded—that objective truth could be discovered by scientific methodologies. In education, such truth would consist of verifiable propositions applying to all learners, teachers, and disciplines in all education contexts. As Gary A. Cziko explains:

The adoption by the behavioral sciences toward the end of the nineteenth century of the research perspective and methodology used in the physical sciences is usually considered to mark the birth of "scientific" sociological, psychological, and educational research. The emphasis on quantification, objectivity, experimentation, and inferential statistical techniques still found in mainstream behavioral science clearly shows the influence of the research methods of the physical sciences on those of the behavioral sciences.[7]

Inevitably, then, the major focus for research was the first level—the universal level—of the tripartite reality in which music, people, and education exist, with some attention to the group-culture level but less attention to the individual level except as another way to reveal universals. What science is after, in the positivist view, are those underlying truths applicable in all circumstances. Such truths must be statistically verifiable: An incomparable, individual experi-

ence cannot, by its nature, be generalized to the level of a universal principle. Statistical devices must be constructed to subsume the particular within the general because scientific principles are always general principles. And the possibility of observer or experimenter bias—the particular personality, belief system, expectation system, emotional investment of the person(s) doing the research—needs to be controlled for. The more one controls for all the possible ways universality might be compromised, the better—the more "scientific"—the research.

The foundational beliefs of positivism were so severely called into question beginning in the middle of this century as to constitute what many people have called a revolution, or "paradigm shift," in the philosophy of science, leading to the period of "postpositivism" in which we are now living.[8] Every concept, from the notion of objectivity; to the idea of reliable observation; to the assumptions of verifiability, discoverable reality, control, universal principles, and constants, all were probed for inherent weaknesses. All were found to be vulnerable, not only in the human sciences, where they were obviously and painfully so, but also in the natural sciences, most notably in physics, where they had once seemed invincible. The distinguished education researcher Donald Campbell perhaps summed it up best:

Nonlaboratory social science is precariously scientific at best. But even for the strongest sciences, the theories believed to be true are radically underjustified and have, at most, the status of "better than" rather than the status of "proven." All commonsense and scientific knowledge is presumptive. In any setting in which we seem to gain new knowledge, we do so at the expense of many presumptions. . . . Single presumptions or small subsets can in turn be probed, but the total set of presumptions is not of demonstrable validity, is radically underjustified. Such are the pessimistic conclusions of the most modern developments in the philosophy of science.[9]

If it is so, as is now commonly accepted in the field of philosophy of science, that science is necessarily perspectival rather than disinterested, the perspectives and values of investigators determining what will be discovered, how it will be discovered, why it should be discovered, and what the discovery will then mean; that science is necessarily systemic rather than linear, the system in which it exists being validly described as more biological and psychological than mechanical; that science is essentially theory based, culture based, and language based, with language being a social construct itself inherently and deeply metaphoric rather than abstractly logical; that evidence can be generated only by using procedures that are themselves the products of historically embedded human value structures; that evidence gained is never sufficient to eliminate alternative theories that might explain the data equally well, so that all theories are inherently and by nature underdetermined; and that everything seemingly "objective" is itself a product of a historical value system and belief system itself subjectively determined, then several conclusions seem inevitable. The notion of truth as something reducible to single entities (the notion of "rival paradigms," in which each is a rival for the single possible truth) will have to be expanded to include the notion of truth as multiple and organic ("complementary paradigms" providing different perspectives and foci on different dimensions of a complex, multitudinous system of interactive components). The myth of science as objective, and therefore value free, needs to be recognized as itself a value position, and this position judged against others that stress not only that "value-free science" is an inherent impossibility but that the idea itself is ethically dangerous, misleading, dehumanizing, and neutralizing, preventing us from acting in responsible ways to improve the human condition according to values we can embrace openly. Such values are based on a view of reality as being not "objectively given," but instead inherently dynamic, conflictual, relative, acausal, idiosyncratic, socially constructed, and historically based. Language itself is value laden, the "appropriately scientific" language we have inherited being a historically based political mechanism to promote the subject-object dualism then valued. When values are no longer focused on promoting this dualism, language can be recognized to be a psychological-aesthetic-social phenomenon and employed openly and freely to act that way in disciplined inquiries. The conception of science as a search for objective truth can be reconceived as a search for more useful, more satisfying human meanings. Such are the assertions now current in the philosophy of science.

As one can imagine, the response to all this by the community of education research was massive, complex, and contentious. As regular readers of the publications of the American Educational Research Association, most notably the *Educational Researcher,* know, it has also been ongoing. Few issues of the journals in education research do not contain articles dealing in some way and at some level with one or another of the research implications of the shifting paradigm in science from positivism to some version of postpositivism. The arguments range across a continuum from radical critiques of and proposals to abandon past and most present educational research assumptions and practices, to attempts to adapt and retain older ideas by bending them to fit the new ideas. Entirely off the continuum in that they do not engage in the debate at all are those who are unaware that any changes have taken place, or who are unwilling or unable to acknowledge that change has occurred and simply go on doing what they have always done. This, I believe, characterizes music education research to an uncomfortable degree.

For those unaware of the philosophical change that has taken place in science, or those who choose to ignore it, the notion of education research as being devoted to the prediction and control of behavior remains extant. But some who continue to hold deterministic views argue nonetheless that it is likely to be impossible to make predictions of human behavior that are both accurate and nontrivial. As Cziko points out, it is possible to retain a belief in behavior as being "lawful" and theoretically predictable but also as too complex to expect that reliable predictions could ever be made.[10] This seems to be the position of Lee J. Cronbach and Richard Snow, who argue that individual differences interact with educational treatments over time in such massively compli-

cated, accumulative ways as to defy research discoveries. They conclude that "comprehensive and definitive experiments in the social sciences are not possible and that the most we can ever realistically hope to achieve in educational research is not prediction and control but rather only temporary understanding."[11]

But this may not go far enough, for Cronbach and Snow imply that it is only a matter of complexity that prevents prediction and therefore control. Others would argue that what influences human behavior is not the environment or other objective, external stimuli theoretically researchable, but instead, the *meanings* ascribed to life events by each individual, and that such meanings are inherently resistant to any research techniques based on positivist notions because they are a function of the totality of all previous experiences and therefore access to them is impossible. Further, even within a positivist framework, the magnitude of individual differences is so stupendous (Carl Sagan estimates that the human brain has some 10^{13} synapses permitting some 2 raised to the power 10^{13} different possible states—a number far greater than the total number of elementary particles, that is, electrons and protons, in the entire universe) that no two humans, even identical twins raised together, "can ever be really very much alike."[12] Add to this all the complicating factors of education, and one begins to appreciate the limited nature of the idea that educational research can predict and control behavior and that it should operate according to the premise that it should be devoted primarily to doing so.

But other factors add still more implications, as Cziko explains. Under the Newtonian view on which positivistic science was founded and from which positivistic education research sprang, it was assumed that all relevant variables could be measured objectively and that all events were determined by (and therefore predictable by knowledge of) preceding events. The world, and people, therefore, were thought to be causally determined. Now, although the physical sciences have discarded this view, it remains, anomalously, the dominant perspective in mainstream "scientific" educational research.

One major discovery in the physical sciences that has led to an altered view of prediction is chaos theory, in which, while each individual step in any process may be conceived to be determined causally, it is theoretically impossible to predict the outcome of any *sequence* of steps in the process even with the most precise possible knowledge of the relevant initial conditions.[13] Initially tiny differences in conditions lead to large, unpredictable differences in results because of the nonlinear effects of chaos; so that, for example, E. N. Lorenz, an important chaos theorist, was led to the conclusion that accurate, long-range forecasting of the weather is impossible no matter how much and how precise the data and how powerful the computer power to process it. Chaos theory is fast spreading in physics, mathematics, biology, astronomy, and economics, its importance being compared with that of theories of evolution, relativity, and quantum mechanics. It is likely to be an important factor in educational research because the processes occurring in education seem fruitfully conceived as following nonlinear histories in which accumulative events lead to unpredictable outcomes: This seems at least as descriptive of what tends to occur in human reality and in educational reality as deterministic explanations have been.

In addition to theories expanding on and altering deterministic views, several important nondeterministic positions have been articulated as bearing directly on what educational research can be in essence. The first is that human learning is an evolutionary process in which, as in biological evolution, chance, randomness, and "creative" (acausal) leaps play essential roles. If human cognitive learning is to any degree creative and free rather than determined and mechanical, results cannot be predicted or controlled, nor should they be. Research, under this view, is an activity intended not to deduce the predictable outcomes of particular inputs, but to describe as fully as possible the varieties of conditions under which optimal diversity of learning outcomes might occur.

Another factor leading to a sense of research different from the positivistic one has to do with consciousness, free will, and openness of choice rather than restriction of choice. Consciousness, it has been suggested, plays an interactive role in human reality, being caused by the reality in which it exists but also influencing what that reality can be. Despite many restrictions, the possibility of choosing freely from many alternatives is real in human life and learning, because consciousness, being aware of alternative possibilities, leads to unpredictable choices in that (1) choices can be freely made, and (2) alternative future possibilities cannot be predicted. Prediction (and control) of complex, creative human behavior would have to take account of the regulatory role of consciousness, but cannot do so because consciousness cannot be made known to researchers and is likely to be only dimly and partially known to individuals in that it is more like a lived process than an existent entity. The attempt to predict behavior in that most complex of all settings—education—would seem to be futile, except, perhaps, in cases so restricted to nonconscious or preconscious functions (classical operant conditioning, perhaps) as to relinquish any claim to be "education," especially when education is conceived as being a cognitive enterprise.

Finally, the advent of quantum mechanics has shown that the physical universe operates by processes far different from the Newtonian deterministic ones, in that randomness and unpredictability seem built into phenomena at the subatomic level. Observation (measurement) of particles changes the particles, entities can exist in two apparently contradictory conditions at the same time, and interconnections exist among all phenomena in ways of which we are only beginning to be aware. The implications of all this for human functioning, as in education, are complex and uncertain. (Cziko discusses a variety of factors.) But it would seem reasonable to entertain the notion that human beings may reflect in their nature some, at least, of the aspects of the indeterminacy of all matter.

If unpredictability in any or all of its guises is a factor in human learning and education, the definition of educational research as being "scientific" in a positivist sense would seem highly questionable, if not largely irrelevant. But many

educational theorists continue to argue that at certain levels and for certain purposes and under certain conditions it is still useful (or essential) to employ the kinds of research based on positivist, deterministic assumptions, because to some degree they can help us regularize what would otherwise seem chaotic, and to some degree, at some levels, they can be reasonably predictive, especially statistically, and it is helpful, if not necessary, to be able to predict, if only at the level of probabilities among groups sufficiently large to allow probabilities to appear.[14] But even advocates of probabilistic research are likely to agree that the essential (or at least operative) unpredictability of human behavior explains why traditional educational research has not advanced, or exerted the influence, or achieved what might have been expected for it from the tremendous amount of work that has been done. D. C. Phillips is a major advocate of the idea that objectivity can still serve as a regulative principle, in that research can be opened to criticism, its evidence subjected to scrutiny, and its conclusions potentially refuted by better explanations. The key to objectivity, for Phillips, is not a positivist worldview but that research be carried out in a "critical spirit."[15] Yet even Phillips is led to agree that "social scientists have not been able to discover generalizations that are reliable enough, and about which there is enough professional consensus, to form the basis for social policy. . . . While the situation may suddenly turn around . . . there seems to be no good reason for this to happen."[16]

One major response to the issues raised by the decline in the credibility of positivism was the rise of qualitative research as an alternative or addition (depending on how one stood on the question of the viability of positivism) to quantitative research. Qualitative research focuses on descriptions of an openly interpretive sort, even to the point of using language overtly for its aesthetic qualities.[17] It concentrates on individuals, as in case studies, because of the conviction that "averaging across subjects blurs our view of exactly that which we want to study,"[18] and that attempts must be made to plumb the depths of what people actually experience when they learn. Qualitative research, it is believed, opens up possibilities for understanding individuals rather than seeking transpersonal essences or pervasive laws. For these and a host of other reasons,[19] qualitative approaches to educational research have made significant inroads within the dominant culture of positivistic orientations, although this movement has caused a sociological struggle of major dimensions, the term "warfare" often being used to describe the tenor of the debate.[20] It is not just the simple matter that qualitative research provides another useful methodology, as sometimes assumed by music education researchers. It is that qualitative approaches construe human reality as being very different from the reality assumed by traditional science, raising the issue as to whether reality must continue to be conceived as unidimensional or whether it is possible for it to be multidimensional.

Where might all this ferment in educational research, brought about by the disruptions occurring in this century in our understanding of science, lead the profession? In a clever article, the eminent researcher N. L. Gage looks back at the period in which we are now living from the vantage point of the year 2009, and projects three possible scenarios for the 20 years after 1989.[21]

First, he paints the picture of what actually had occurred by 1989, a year in which the "Paradigm Wars" came to a climax. During the 1980s, he says, research in education such as had been carried on in the 1960s and 1970s took a severe beating, being characterized as "at best, inconclusive, at worst, barren," and as "inadequate to tell us anything secure and important about how teachers should proceed in the classroom." The attempt to lay a scientific basis for teaching had failed, the critics claimed, and the application of science to education had proved futile. Even if positivistic social science had succeeded, it would have been applicable only in "authoritarian, manipulative, bureaucratic systems."

Three classes of critiques were leveled in the late 1980s at the previous two or three decades of educational research. The antinaturalist critique claimed that human affairs cannot be studied with natural science techniques (hence the term "social science" is an oxymoron) because human learning is essentially intentional and purposeful and humanly meaningful. There are no causal, direct connections between teacher behavior and student learning. Human behavior is inherently not stable and uniform over time, space, and context. Teacher planning is itself subject to nonlinear events and responses, as are student learnings. Educational research, therefore, should not deal with fictions such as prediction and control, but should attempt to provide insights similar to those yielded by moral philosophers, novelists, artists, and literary critics.

The interpretivist critique focused on the immediately meaningful nature of acts of learning, in which the learner's interpretation, including human volition, human variability, humanly created meanings, and humanly constructed social realities, all are essential factors in what can be learned and how it can be learned. Positivistic research, focusing on prediction and control, should be supplanted by interpretive research, which examines the conditions of meaning created by interactions of teachers, students, subject matters, and contexts of learning.

The critical theorist's critique was aimed at the technological, rationalist, efficiency-driven, objectivist, measurement-focused nature of mainstream educational research, which neglected what is most important in education—its social, political, economic agenda. Traditional education serves traditional value systems and power systems, while properly motivated education can redress social inequities and help reconstruct society. Teaching and research of a positivist nature are essentially trivial, according to this view, aiming at the finer technical details of schooling and neglecting the social imperatives for which education exists.

All this, says Gage, had occurred by 1989, and that was the actual state of affairs at that time. Now, what did he imagine happened in the two decades following?

Scenario 1 The critics triumphed, and the kind of objectivist-quantitative "scientific" research that had been so dominant for most of the twentieth century ground to a halt. Courses in tests and measurements, statistical techniques, and research design disappeared. No one any longer used structured observations, achievement or aptitude tests, statistical treatment of data. Journals no longer published articles reporting tests of statistical significance, correlation coefficients, effect sizes, metaanalyses, or the like. Research became a matter of observing carefully and reflecting deeply, and teachers became active researchers rather than recipients of research done by others.

The results were all positive. Teachers became aware of small differences in teaching that made big differences in student learning. Student differences, both individual and cultural, finally began to be taken fully into account, so that individuals were able to optimize their learnings in settings where teachers provided optimal conditions for each child. Pupils also were sensitized to deep social issues underlying what they learned, so that far greater equality began to be achieved among previously disenfranchised groups. Education became more individually effective and more socially constructive.

Scenario 2 In this version of the future, says Gage, the focus on individual learning and on social improvement took place as in scenario 1, producing the hoped for results. But what did *not* take place was the demise of quantitative, positivistic research, because a "great awakening" occurred in the recognition that alternative modes of research were compatible and that the "incompatibilists," who had argued that quantitative and qualitative approaches could not coexist, were simply wrong. Philosophical analysis provided a basis for pragmatic solutions in which it was recognized that paradigm differences do not require paradigm conflicts. Different approaches to research were concerned with different but important aspects of education and learning, and interdisciplinary, cooperative research began to be the norm. Subject-specific issues, ethnographic issues, and meaning-generation issues were all recognized to be amenable to deeper understanding through a variety of research approaches, and the reality levels of universals and cultural characteristics and individualities were seen to be dimensions requiring a variety of research perspectives that could be mutually reinforcing.

The social sciences, it came to be recognized, need not blindly adopt assumptions about uniformity in nature as a given. But while many aspects of human reality are changeable and incomparable, some are relatively permanent and uniform, and some research should be devoted to explaining the uniformities in human life, culture, and education without adopting a strict positivist bias.

Process-product research, so strongly criticized, continued to be carried on, focusing not only on mechanical, predictable laws such as had previously been the quest but on interpretive and cognitive teacher processes, and on student products conceived as outcomes that could be reasonably investigated through essays, real-life performances, group processes, student products, and so forth, in addition to standardized testing. A great mixture of research methodologies began to occur, and a broader spectrum of educational issues and topics was investigated, reflecting psychological, anthropological, and various subject matter perspectives. Rivalries among perspectives gave way to respectful cooperation, as the hegemony of the established psychological-quantitative-positivist position opened up to include those approaches to research based on different epistemologies and discipline bases.

Thus from the jungle wars of the 1980s, educational researchers, including those concerned with teaching, emerged onto a sunlit plain—a happy and productive arena in which the strengths of all three paradigms (objective-quantitative, interpretive-qualitative, critical-theoretical) were abundantly realized, with a corresponding decrease in the harmful effects of their respective inadequacies. Educational researchers today look back with amused tolerance at the invidious recriminations that the paradigm-loyalists had hurled at other paradigms in the 1980s.[22]

Scenario 3 Finally, the possibility exists that the next 20 years will have brought no significant change. The Paradigm Wars continued to be waged and the traditional positivist view continued to hold sway with increasingly bitter attacks by those proposing "alternative paradigms." Each camp reflected differences in temperament as much as intellectual positions, the tough-minded against the tender-minded, scientific against humanistic, nomothetic against ideographic, statistical against clinical, positivist against hermeneutic, so that purely rational considerations tended to become embedded in community identification issues, and the conflicts spun on and on to the detriment of both education and educational research. "How long the war will last, and whether it will lead to the demise of social and educational research, including research on teaching, are questions that cannot be answered in the year 2009."[23]

Which scenario will prove accurate? The answer, Gage suggests, depends on how the educational research community acts. I want to suggest that the answer to what music education research becomes in the next couple of decades also depends on how the music education research community acts. We are living in a period of ideological warfare about which, to judge by what is done and what is published in the field of music education, we are largely, if not entirely, ignorant.[24] I hope we can engage ourselves in the major research issues of our day because we cannot claim full membership in the community of scholars if we remain as far outside the center of activity as we now are. But I hope we can do so in ways that avoid fruitless battles. We may not be able to emerge onto a "sunlit plain," but we should surely be able to grapple with the larger issues of research in ways that lead us toward intelligent, informed control over our destiny rather than drifting aimlessly with whatever winds we get caught in from the wars going on all around us. Philosophical reflection about music education research should help us understand the complex issues and alternatives that are now being addressed in research in the social sciences generally and education in particular, and, based on our own history, nature,

and needs, provide some useful guidelines for how we might develop to a more mature level in light of alternative possible futures. I would personally hope that we could develop as scenario 2 suggests, because of my conviction that the three levels of our reality call for research modes covering each and dealing with all the interactions among them. Philosophical guidance is needed to clarify whether and why this is the case and how we could organize our research accordingly.

Nontechnical Issues in Doing Research Responsibly

As mentioned above in the first two sections of this chapter, a good deal of interest exists in the field of music education research about the various research modes, but most of this interest is methodological and technical rather than substantive. Few discussions exist about the epistemology of research modes—what they can help us know and how their presumptions influence what they allow us to know. It is generally and offhandedly assumed that if one follows correct procedures for doing whatever type of research one is doing, the results are then assured to be valid. Unfortunately, this does not begin to address the complexities of the issue. Underneath the level of methodology is the dilemma that research choices always both reveal and conceal—reveal by focusing on a particular aspect of reality (and giving the impression that this particular aspect therefore constitutes the reality), and conceal by neglecting a great many alternative realities not being focused upon (thereby invalidating them).

All research modes are subject to this fundamental dilemma, so our consciousness needs to be raised as to how it occurs and how we can be better aware of it both in doing research and in using and assessing research. I will raise the issue here, necessarily briefly, in regard to the doing of history.

Our explanations of history as a mode of music education research are, typically, methodological. Certain procedures must be followed to do history correctly. We must choose a researchable, manageable, and, it is to be hoped, original topic. We must gather data of a variety of sorts by building a bibliography, we must ask a multitude of precise questions, and we must refine the topic and read for general context. We should use source materials carefully, including primary and secondary, easily available and less available, and newly discovered sources and oral sources; we should be careful to authenticate and verify our materials both externally and internally; we should report objectively, leaving our personal biases out; we should write up the results clearly and in a well-organized fashion, and so forth. Do all this, it is implied, and good history will have been accomplished.

Certainly much of this is valid. But when historical research is construed to consist of only these matters, as tends to be the case in the music education research literature, it distorts and misrepresents the issues that the doing of history entails. For by necessity history must infer and explain: Historical facts become "evidence" only within a framework of explanations, being incapable, in and of themselves, of meaningfulness. What are the issues raised by explanation? *That* is what we need to grapple with in our discussions of history as a mode of research.

In an essay by David B. Tyack some of these issues are addressed.[25] Tyack intends to demonstrate the influence exerted by the explanatory model chosen to present a particular history. He uses, as the basis for his demonstration, the rise of compulsory schooling in the United States over the century from the 1850s to the 1950s. By presenting several alternative explanatory models for this phenomenon, he hopes to give evidence of (and to avoid) the reductionism that results when only one particular thesis (or none at all) is the basis for a history. First, he offers a sketch of the salient events and issues relating to the compulsory school attendance movement. Although many would consider such an overview to be, in and of itself, "history," it only scratches the surface of what historical research requires. Tyack then offers five different explanatory accounts of these events and issues. Each deals with the same situation, but, because each stems from a different disciplinary or ideological framework, each defines the problems differently, chooses different units of analysis, and offers different pictures of what occurred.

Those taking the view that the advent of compulsory education is to be understood as a political phenomenon emphasize the role of the state and the use of education as a means to incorporate people into a nation-state and to legitimize the status of those who will be citizens and those who will be leaders. The ethnocultural orientation, however, sees the phenomenon of compulsory schooling quite differently, focusing on the influence of ethnic and religious groups, and their attitudes and beliefs, as playing the major roles in what could have occurred and in what therefore did occur. The organizational perspective offers a still different interpretation, probing the bureaucratic, institutional implications and downplaying the influence of religion and ethnicity. Human capital theorists, alternatively, paint a picture of the family as the decision unit in calculating what the costs and benefits of compulsory education might be, and they draw implications for how the nation as a whole was led to its decisions on the basis of a human investment paradigm. Finally, a Marxian analysis is offered, in which class struggle is the source of the dialectic mechanisms that produce societal change, and capitalist assumptions and values drive the events and decisions.[26]

What does one make of these diverse ways of construing the history of the same phenomenon? Each is valid, each is explanatory, and each directs attention to certain kinds of evidence that could be used to confirm or disprove its assertions of causation. Each is, in every sense, a "history." Can one then simply add them all up to get the sum total, that sum constituting the "real" history?

Tyack thinks not. Each of the models deals with social reality on a different level, and each is based on a different conception of what it is that underlies social change. Simple eclecticism would cause a blurring of the separate visions and a confusion of the purpose of each. So we are confronted by a principle of history—that it is not a single entity, and most assuredly not an "objective presentation" of facts, but a construction determined by values and choices, in which the assumptions and interests and preconceptions of those doing the constructing inevitably influence that which is constructed as a result.

One of my purposes in this essay has been to extend the boundaries of discussion about the history of American education. I have become convinced that much of the recent work in the field . . . has used causal models too implicitly. It has also tended to constrict the range of value judgments. . . . Entertaining explicit alternative models and probing their value assumptions may help historians to gain a more complex and accurate perception of the past and a greater awareness of the ambiguous relationship between outcome and intent—both of the actors in history and of the historians who attempt to recreate their lives.[27]

Adding to the issues raised by Tyack about what constitutes history and how it might be carried out fruitfully, is the emerging conception of education, and of educational research, as consisting of the telling of narrative stories. This view encompasses much of what is now occurring in qualitative research. It throws new light on the kinds of stories told, not told, and obscured by quantitative, "objective" research.

This perspective holds that humans are, essentially, storytelling organisms who lead storied lives as individuals and as social groups. To understand human reality requires the study of the ways humans experience their world, and human experience can be grasped most truthfully by exploring the stories that tell about the truths being lived. In a complex, detailed, and wide-ranging explanation of this way of conceiving history and the present, and its implications for understanding what educational research can be understood to be and how it might be carried out more effectively, F. Michael Connelly and D. Jean Clandinin build the case that the "real" is what humans construe to be so, and that what is most real is the life story we live.[28] Researchers are also humans living their story—not disembodied spirits endowed with extrahuman powers of objectivity. Education and research on education, including research on the history of education, require

a mutually constructed story created out of the lives of both researcher and participant. We therefore think in terms of a two-part inquiry agenda. We need to listen closely to teachers and other learners and to the stories of their lives in and out of classrooms. We also need to tell our own stories as we live our own collaborative researcher/teacher lives. Our own work then becomes one of learning to tell and live a new mutually constructed account of inquiry in teaching and learning. What emerges from this mutual relationship are new stories of teachers and learners as curriculum makers, stories that hold new possibilities for both researchers and teachers and for those who read their stories.[29]

So many changes have been and are occurring in fundamental ideas about educational research, including how we tell the story of the history of education, that to carry on our work in disregard of or ignorance about what is going on in the larger field of educational research would seem to be professionally irresponsible. Where are the ongoing, probing discussions about how the history of music education might be accomplished in ways reflecting recent scholarship about history as an endeavor?[30] Where are the counterpart discussions of every other mode of doing research, each of which is being as thoroughly reexamined as is history? Where, in short, is a philosophical grounding for research that can make our work as researchers more meaningful? Clearly we do not have one, nor do we have the lively exchange of ideas about research out of which philosophical principles might be encouraged to emerge. I am not suggesting that we must stop doing research until we have attended to our philosophical needs, or that none of the research we are doing or have done is valid because of the lack of guiding principles. But surely we are operating in less than an optimal professional situation, and it would seem important for us to begin to pay the attention it deserves to how we might improve the situation. That is, we would benefit from efforts to forge a convincing philosophical foundation for music education research that could serve as the basis for needed changes in our research policies.

Policy Issues for Music Education Research

I have pointed out elsewhere that philosophy and policy are, or should be, intimately related, in that a philosophy provides the foundation for valid policy while policy deals with issues raised by but beyond the purview of a philosophy.[31] In that efforts to philosophize about music education research have seldom been made, there has been little basis for coherent policy-making, so the research policies and practices that have emerged are generally retrospective and reactive rather than anticipatory and proactive. We have attempted to respond to perceived needs but have done little to create anticipatory policies that carry out a philosophically grounded agenda. What policy issues might emerge, then, as needing to be taken into account if a set of foundational principles underlying music education research was developed?

Just as it is likely that such philosophical thinking will raise issues relating to the nature of the scientific enterprise itself, it is also likely to raise issues about the appropriate locus for the enterprise of music education research. We have assumed, along with the field of educational research generally, that research is an activity most reasonably and appropriately carried out in university settings by university professors. An entire culture of research has arisen in both education and music education, and that culture is almost completely centered in higher education. As I am writing this, I am not aware, of course, of who all the authors are who will be contributing to this book, yet I am willing to guess with a high degree of confidence that practically all are university faculty members.

Well, what is wrong with that? A good many people in

educational research are now arguing that there is a great deal wrong with it. As pointed out by Marilyn Cochran-Smith and Susan L. Lytle, two paradigms for doing educational research have dominated over the last two decades.[32] The first, process-product research, has assumed that effective teaching can be understood by correlating particular processes such as teacher behaviors with particular products, usually defined as student achievement. This cause-effect model "emphasizes the actions of teachers rather than their professional judgments and attempts to capture the activity of teaching by identifying sets of discrete behaviors reproducible from one teacher and one classroom to the next." Under this view of the teacher as a technician, the teacher's role

is to implement the research findings of others concerning instruction, curriculum, and assessment. With this view, the primary knowledge source for the improvement of practice is research on classroom phenomena that can be observed. This research has a perspective that is 'outside-in'; in other words, it has been conducted almost exclusively by university-based researchers who are outside the day-to-day practices of schooling.[33]

How much of the research reported in the present volume follows this model? Probably most, if not all.

A second paradigm, the qualitative, deals with studies of "classroom ecology," providing detailed, descriptive accounts of classrooms and other school settings that shed light on their meanings. Here, too, although there are a small number of reports coauthored by university-based researchers and school teachers, practically all are the products of university researchers, who frame and mediate teachers' perspectives through their own perspectives as researchers.

We propose that current research on teaching within both process-product and interpretive paradigms, constrains, and at times even makes invisible, teachers' roles in the generation of knowledge about teaching and learning in classrooms. The contents of the *Handbook of Research on Teaching* (Wittrock, 1986), widely viewed as the most comprehensive synthesis of research in the field, is indicative of this exclusion. . . . The 1037-page handbook contains 35 research reviews. Although a few of these include studies carried out by university researchers in cooperation with teachers, and several focus explicitly on teachers' thinking, knowledge, and the cultures of teaching . . . none are written by school-based teachers nor . . . are published accounts of teachers' work cited. Rather, in most of the studies included, teachers are the objects of researchers' investigations and then ultimately are expected to be the consumers and implementors of their findings. Missing from the handbook are the voices of the teachers themselves, the questions that teachers ask, and the interpretive frames that teachers use to understand and improve their own classroom practices.[34]

Out of analyses such as these an important movement has been generated to reconsider whether the traditional place for educational research to be conducted—the university, with schools serving as data sources—is, in fact, the best place for achieving meaningful school change as a result of research. The term "teacher research" has arisen as indicating a need to change research from an activity presently dominated by nonschool professionals and nonschool locations to one predominantly or at least largely carried on by teachers trained also to be active researchers in the location such research is intended to influence—schools. The literature has burgeoned, and it is likely that the debate will become intense (if not heated) over the next several years.[35] We may move in the direction of a changing balance in the research culture, in which teachers themselves assume more responsibility for disciplined inquiry about the work they do, using university personnel as a source for particular needs that the teacher researchers identify. If the painful gap between research as it is presently conducted, and school use of that research, is to be bridged, it would seem that a shift in the control and conduct of research would help significantly.[36] And that raises another directly related issue—how would such teacher researchers be trained?

At present, music educators in training at the undergraduate level seldom, if ever, are introduced to, let alone trained in, research. At the master's level, students who will be taking (or returning to) school jobs are generally given one course in research, and this course typically covers the techniques and methodologies of the various research modes, with concentration on the quantitative. My sense is that most ''Introduction to Research in Music Education'' courses are intended to prepare more receptive, knowledgeable consumers of research that has been carried on by university faculty members or by doctoral students. (I would assume there are exceptions to this, in which the model of the teacher as potential researcher is followed.)

The issues here plead for policy guidance. What would, in fact, be the optimal way to structure an introductory research course, and how might a series of courses and other offerings be developed to prepare teachers to become effective school-based researchers? To what extent should the study of philosophical issues related to research be foundational for the study of research techniques and designs, given the value choices such techniques and designs necessarily entail? How do we address the issue of doctoral-level research preparation, given the complexity inherent in a situation in which many doctoral students are likely to take jobs having little to do with research? What kinds of studies would be most effective for the few choosing to specialize in research—a common program for all such students, or some common elements with subsequent specialization in a particular mode, or specialization from the start? As with the other questions I have attempted to raise in this chapter I do not intend to offer answers here, only to suggest that we should, as a profession, be seeking answers to such pressing concerns through our professional activities—journals, symposia, and so forth. Our neglect of matters of philosophy inevitably has caused a concomitant neglect of matters of policy, so that our research infrastructure is insufficiently solid to support our activities.

This situation applies as well to our research coordination and dissemination practices. Our present general research journals—*Journal of Research in Music Education;* the *Bulletin of the Council for Research in Music Education,* and the variety of state and other publications—serve to bring particular studies to attention. This is a valuable function, but it tends also to exacerbate the problem of diffuseness, in that the studies reported represent a bewildering, scattered assortment of topics and approaches demonstrating plainly the existing disordered state of our research endeavor. Even in the related, focused journals, such as *Psychology of Music,* the desired level of coordination among studies is absent because little such coordination exists. The various SRIG newsletters help to reach and define communities of shared interests, which is certainly healthy, but they also must present the research in their topic areas as such research exists in its unintegrated state.

What we do not find in any of the journals is discussions of the research enterprise qua enterprise. That, I am proposing, is precisely what we require, not only in our journals, but among all the members of the music education research community. We require it because we need guidelines for our actions, and such guidelines are not likely to emerge in the absence of a rich and ongoing professional dialogue as to what they might be. Our journals should, I think, actively seek articles on basic problems of the music education research enterprise, with occasional single-focus issues to which several people are invited to contribute. A music education research planning council, ongoing with rotating membership, might be charged with the formulation of policies to be suggested to the research community for their discussion and exploration.[37] We need to encourage young scholars to become researchers not only as practitioners, but also as theoreticians about the issues of research, and we need to demonstrate in our publications that theorizing about research is as necessary as doing particular research studies. Out of such ferment of ideas we are likely to generate unifying views—philosophical principles—that can bring sufficient order to our endeavors to help research become more valid as science and more influential in the larger sphere of music education than it has been to the present, through policies that implement the philosophical guidelines suggested. Movement in this direction would mean that ''at long last, arts education researchers would be able to orient their work to shared, explicit research priorities. This reorientation could dramatically reduce the piecemeal nature of arts education research and increase its value to arts teachers, policy makers, and administrators.''[38]

The issues raised in this chapter are, I have suggested, fundamental to the music education research enterprise, and progress in resolving them is fundamental to the improvement of that enterprise. If we actually do address such issues, every aspect of music education research will be affected, some or many of them significantly. I believe the stresses of change—even major change—are worth facing, because I believe that research should play a far more significant role in music education than it ever has played or is ever likely to play under its present aphilosophical condition. It is time, I suggest, for music education research itself to be subjected to serious and ongoing disciplined inquiry about its nature, value, and modes of functioning.

Notes

1. The term "disciplined inquiry" as the essential characteristic of research is suggested by Lee S. Shulman, Disciplines of inquiry in education: An overview, in *Complementary methods for research in education*, ed. R.M. Jaeger (Washington: American Educational Research Association, 1988), 3–17.

2. For representative examples over the years of the unquestioned acceptance of a mechanistic, positivist scientific model as a valid basis for music education research, see John W. Beattie, The Function of Research, in *Yearbook of the music educators national conference*, 1934, 89–92; Emmett M. Wilson, The teacher's use of research, in *Yearbook of the music educators national conference*, 1935, 163–166; Erwin H. Schneider and Henry L. Cady, Competency of Research, in *Evaluation and synthesis of research studies relating to music education* (Columbus: Ohio State University Research Foundation, 1965), 36–43; Robert G. Petzold, Directions for research in music education, *Bulletin of the Council for Research in Music Education* 1 (1963), 18–23; Max Kaplan, *Foundations and frontiers of music education* (New York: Holt, Rinehart and Winston, 1966), 206; Richard J. Colwell, Music education and experimental research, *Journal of Research in Music Education* 15:1 (1967), 73–84; R. Douglas Greer, Music instruction as behavior modification, in *Research in music behavior,* ed. C. K. Madsen, R. D. Greer and C. H. Madsen (New York: Teachers College Press, 1975), 3–11; Roger P. Phelps, *A guide to research in music education,* 2nd ed., (Metuchen: Scarecrow Press, 1980); Edward L. Rainbow and Hildegard C. Froehlich, *Research in music education* (New York: Schirmer, 1987).

3. Robert Sidnell, The dimensions of research in music education, *Bulletin of the Council for Research in Music Education* 29 (1972), 17–27.

4. Charles Leonhard and Richard J. Colwell, Research in music education, *Bulletin of the Council for Research in Music Education* 49 (1976), 1–29.

5. An early example of a thoughtful attempt to do so was Robert A. Choate, Research in music education, *Journal of Research in Music Education,* 13:2 (1965), 67–86.

6. Beverly J. Jones and June K. McFee, Research on teaching arts and aesthetics, in *Handbook of research on teaching,* 3rd ed., ed. M. C. Wittrock (New York: Macmillan, 1986), 912.

7. Gary A. Cziko, Unpredictability and Indeterminism in Human Behavior: Arguments and Implications for Educational Research, *Educational Researcher,* 18:3 (April, 1989), 18.

8. An extensive literature exists on the scientific revolution leading to postpositivism. A few basic sources are P. Feyerabend, *Against method* (London: Verso, 1978); R. Giere, *Explaining science: A cognitive Approach* (Chicago: University of Chicago Press, 1987); N. R. Hanson, *Patterns of discovery* (Cambridge: Cambridge University Press, 1958); Carl Hempel, *Philosophy of natural science* (Englewood Cliffs: Prentice Hall, 1966); D. Hull, *Science as a process,* (Chicago: University of Chicago Press, 1989); Thomas S. Kuhn, *The structure of scientific revolutions* (Chicago: University of Chicago Press, 1962); Graham Macdonald and Philip Pettit, *Semantics and social science* (London: Routledge and Kegan Paul, 1981); W. H. Newton-Smith, *The Rationality of science* (London: Routledge and Kegan Paul, 1981); D. C. Phillips, *Philosophy, science, and social inquiry* (Oxford: Pergamon, 1987); K. Popper, *Conjectures and refutations* (New York: Harper, 1968); Israel Scheffler, *Science and subjectivity* (New York: Bobbs-Merrill, 1967); S. Toulmin, *Foresight and understanding* (New York: Harper and Row, 1961); Walter B. Weimer, *Notes on the methodology of scientific research* (Hillsdale: Lawrence Erlbaum, 1979).

9. Donald T. Campbell, Qualitative knowing and action research, in *The social contexts of method,* ed. Michael Brenner, Peter Marsh, and Marylin Brenner (New York: St. Martin's Press, 1978), 185.

10. Cziko, Unpredictability and indeterminism, 17–19.

11. Ibid., 17.

12. Ibid., 18.

13. The most accessible (to laypeople) explanation of chaos theory is J. Glieck, *Chaos: Making a new science* (New York: Viking, 1987).

14. Ideas of this sort are presented in Richard Lehrer, Ronald C. Serlin, and Ronald Amundson, Knowledge or certainty?: A Reply to Cziko, *Educational Researcher,* 19:6 (August-September 1990), 16–19.

15. D. C. Phillips, Subjectivity and objectivity: An objective inquiry, in *Qualitative inquiry in education,* ed. Elliott W. Eisner and Alan Peshkin (New York: Teachers College Press, 1990), 35.

16. Quoted in Cziko, Unpredictability and indeterminism, 23.

17. As suggested by Elliott W. Eisner, *The educational imagination* (New York: Macmillan, 1979).

18. H. E. Gruber, From epistemic subject to unique creative person at work, *Archives de psychologie,* 53, 170 (1985), quoted in Cziko, Unpredictability and indeterminism.

19. A good overview is given in Eisner and Peshkin, eds., *Qualitative inquiry in education* (New York: Teachers College Press, 1990).

20. A fascinating glimpse of the struggle in educational research to include nonpositivistic, nonquantitative methodologies is given in the editorial by Wayne J. Urban, The social and institutional analysis section: Context and content, *American Educational Research Journal* 27:1 (Spring 1990), 1–8, in which he explains how difficult it has been to get the educational research community to allow publication of nontraditional studies. Also, for a penetrating treatment of the conflictual sociology of quantitative versus qualitative research in education, see Shulamit Reinharz, So-called training in the so-called alternative paradigm, in *The paradigm dialog,* ed. Egon Guba (Beverly Hills: Sage, 1990).

21. N. L. Gage, The paradigm wars and their aftermath: A 'historical' sketch of research on teaching since 1989, *Educational Researcher* 18:7 (October 1989), 4–10.

22. Ibid., 9.

23. Ibid.

24. It is difficult to find, in any of our research literature, discussions of issues such as are raised in my explanation here of recent events in the philosophy of science and in educational research. Notable exceptions are Jack Heller and Warren Campbell, Models of language and intellect in music research, in *Music education for tomorrow's society,* ed. Arthur Motycka (Jamestown: GAMT Music Press, 1976), 40–49; my response to this chapter, Bennett Reimer, Language or Non-language models of aesthetic stimuli, *Journal of Aesthetic Education* 11:3 (July, 1977); Warren Campbell and Jack Heller, An orientation for considering models of musical behavior, in *Handbook of music psychology,* ed. D. Hodges (Lawrence: National Association for Music Therapy, 1980); Bennett Reimer, Toward a more scientific approach to music education

research," *Bulletin of the Council for Research in Music Education* 83 (Summer 1985), 1–21.

25. David B. Tyack, Ways of seeing: An essay on the history of compulsory schooling," in *Complementary methods*, R. M. Jaeger, ed.

26. This very brief overview does little justice to the richness and complexity of the explanations Tyack offers of how each point of view determines the history it describes. Interested readers will want to study his entire chapter.

27. Tyack, Ways of seeing, 58.

28. F. Michael Connelly and D. Jean Clandinin, Stories of experience and narrative inquiry, *Educational Researcher* 19:5 (June-July 1990), 2–14.

29. Ibid., 12.

30. A hint of awareness of these issues is given by George N. Heller, Music education history and American musical scholarship: Problems and promises, *The Bulletin of Historical Research in Music Education* XI:2 (July 1990), 73, in which he recognizes that, according to several sources of the history of American music education, men play nearly all the major roles, twentieth-century achievements are neglected, racial and ethnic minorities are hardly mentioned, and music education for the handicapped is entirely absent.

31. Bennett Reimer, *A philosophy of music education*, 2nd ed. (Englewood Cliffs: Prentice Hall, 1989), 7–10.

32. Marilyn Cochran-Smith and Susan L. Lytle, Research on teaching and teacher research: The issues That divide, *Educational Researcher* 19:2 (March, 1990), 2–11.

33. Ibid., 2, 3.

34. Ibid., 3.

35. For readings on the issue of the teacher as researcher, see the references in Cochran-Smith and Lytle, Ibid., and the bibliographies in S. N. Oja and L. Smulyan, *Collaborative action research: A developmental approach* (London: Falmer Press, 1989); D. Goswami and P. P. Stillman, eds., *Reclaiming the classroom: Teacher research as an agency for change* (Upper Montclair: Boynton, 1987); D. A. Schon, *Educating the reflective practitioner* (San Francisco: Jossey-Bass, 1987); Joe L. Kincheloe, *Teachers as researchers: Qualitative inquiry as a path to empowerment* (New York: Falmer, 1990); Richard Winter, *Learning from experience: Principles and practice in action research* (New York: Falmer, 1989).

36. Other related issues pertinent to the research-practice gap are discussed by Elliot W. Eisner, Can educational research inform educational practice?," *Phi Delta Kappan* 65:7 (March 1984) 447–452.

37. For a discussion of the issues relating to the establishment of an arts policy research center, see David B. Pankratz and James Hutchens, Disciplinary and institutional bases for arts policy research centers, *Design for Arts in Education* 89:6 (July/August 1988), 28–36. Issues relating to research policy in the arts are raised in David B. Pankratz, Policies, agendas, and arts education research, *Design for Arts in Education* 90:5 (May/June 1989), 2–13.

38. David B. Pankratz, Policies, agendas, and arts education research, in *Design for Arts in Education,* 90:5, 2–13.

References

Beattie, J. W. (1934). The function of research. *Yearbook of the music educators national conference.* 89–92.

Campbell, T. C. (1978). Qualitative knowing and action research. In M. Brenner, P. Marsh, and M. Brenner (Eds.), *The social contexts of method.* New York: St. Martin's Press, 185.

Campbell, W. and Heller, J., (1980). An orientation for considering model of musical behavior. In D. Hodges (Ed.), *Handbook of music psychology.* Lawrence: National Association for Music Therapy.

Choate, R. A. (1965). Research in music education. *Journal of Research in Music Education,* 13:2, 67–86.

Cochran-Smith, M., and Lytle, S. L. (1990). Research on teaching and teacher research: The issues that divide. *Educational Researcher,* 19:2, 2–11.

Colwell, R. J. (1967). Music education and experimental research. *Journal of Research* in *Music Education,* 15:1, 73–84.

Connelly, F. M., and Clandinin, D. J. (1990). Stories of experience and narrative inquiry. *Educational Researcher,* 19:5, 2–14.

Cziko, G. A. (1989) Unpredictability and indeterminism in human behavior: Arguments and implications for educational research. *Educational Researcher,* 18:3, 18.

Eisner, E. W. (1979). *The educational imagination.* New York: Macmillan.

Eisner, E. W. (1984). Can educational research inform educational practice? *Phi Delta Kappan,* 65:7, 447–452.

Gage, N. L. (1989). The paradigm wars and their aftermath: A historical sketch of research on teaching since 1989. *Educational Researcher,* 18:7, 4–10.

Giere, R. (1984). *Explaining science: A cognitive approach.* Chicago: University of Chicago Press.

Glieck, J. (1987). *Chaos: Making a new science.* New York: Viking.

Greer, R. D. (1975). Music instruction as behavior modification. In C. K. Madsen, R. D. Greer, and C. H. Madsen (Eds.), *Research in music behavior.* New York: Teachers College Press, 3–11.

Hanson, N. R. (1958). *Patterns of discovery.* Cambridge: Cambridge University Press.

Heller, J., and Campbell, W. (1976). Models of language and intellect in music research. In A. Motycka (Ed.), *Music education for tomorrow's society.* Jamestown: GAMT Music Press, 40–49.

Heller, G. N. (1990). "Music education history and American musical scholarship: Problems and promises. *The Bulletin of Historical Research in Music Education,* 11:2, 73.

Hempel, C. (1966). *Philosophy of natural science.* Englewood Cliffs, Prentice Hall.

Hull, D. (1989). *Science as process.* Chicago. University of Chicago Press.

Jones, B. J. and McFee, J. K. (1986). Research on teaching arts and aesthetics. In M. C. Wittrock (Ed.), *Handbook of research on teaching,* 3rd ed. New York: Macmillan, 912.

Kaplan, M. (1966). *Foundations and frontiers of music education.* New York: Holt, Rinehart, and Winston, 206.

Kincheloe, J. (1990). *Teachers as researchers: Qualitative inquiry as a path to empowerment.* New York: Falmer.

Kuhn, T. S. (1962). *The structure of scientific revolutions.* Chicago: University of Chicago Press.

Lehrer, R., Serlin, R. C., and Amundson, R. (1990) Knowledge or certainty?: A reply to cziko. *Educational Researcher,* 19:6, 16–19.

Leonhard, C. and Colwell, R. J. (1976). Research in music education''. *Bulletin of the Council for Research in Music Education,* 49, 1–29.

MacDonald, G., and Pettit, P. (1981). *Semantics and social science.* London: Routledge and Kegan Paul.

Newton-Smith, W. H. (1981). *The rationality of science.* London: Routledge and Kegan Paul.

Oja, S. N., and Smulyan, L. (1989). *Collaborative action research: A developmental approach.* London: Falmer Press.

Pankratz, D. B., and Hutchens, J. (1988). Disciplinary and institutional bases for arts policy research centers. *Design for Arts in Education.* 89:6, 28–36.

Pankratz, D. B. (1989). Policies, agendas, and arts education research. *Design for Arts in Education,* 90:5, 2–13.

Petzold, R. G. (1963). Directions for research in music education. *Bulletin of the Council for Research in Music Education,* 1, 18–23.

Phelps, Roger P. (1980). *A guide to research in music education,* 2nd ed. Metuchen: Scarecrow Press.

Philips, D. C. (1990). Subjectivity and objectivity: An objective inquiry. In E. W. Eisner, and A. Peshkin (Eds.), *Qualitative inquiry in education.* New York: Teachers College Press, 35.

Popper, K. (1968). *Conjectures and refutations.* New York: Harper.

Rainbow, E. L. and Froelich H. C. (1987). *Research in music education.* New York: Schirmer.

Reimer, B. (1977). Language or non-language models of aesthetic stimuli. *Journal of Aesthetic Education,* 11:3.

Reimer, B. (1985). Toward a more scientific approach to music education research. *Bulletin for the Council for Research in Music Education,* 83, 1–21.

Reimer, B. (1989). *A philosophy of music education,* 2nd ed. Englewood Cliffs: Prentice Hall, 7–10.

Reinharz, S. (1990). So-called training in the so-called alternative paradigm. In E. Guba (Ed.) *The paradigm dialog.* Sage: Beverly Hills.

Scheffler, I. (1967). *Science and subjectivity.* New York: Bobbs-Merrill.

Schneider, E. H., and Cady, H. L. (1965). Competency of research. In *Evaluation and synthesis of research studies relating to music education.* Columbus: Ohio State University Research Foundation.

Schon, D. A. (1987). *Educating the reflective practitioner.* San Francisco: Jossey-Bass.

Shulman, L. S. (1988). Disciplines of inquiry in education: An overview. In R. M. Jaeger (Ed.), *Complementary methods for research in education.* Washington: American Education Research Association.

Sidnell, R. (1972). The dimensions of research in music education. *Bulletin of the Council for Research in Music Education,* 49, 17–27.

Stillman, P. P., and Goswami, D. (Eds.) (1987). *Reclaiming the classroom: Teacher research as an agency for change.* Upper Montclair: Boynton.

Toulmin, S. (1961). *Foresight and understanding.* New York: Harper and Row.

Tyack, D. B. (1988). Ways of seeing: An essay on the history of compulsory schooling. In R. M. Jaeger (Ed.), *Complementary methods for research in education.* Washington, DC. American Education Research Association.

Urban, W. J. (1990, Spring). The social and institutional analysis section: Context and content. *American Educational Research Journal,* 27:1, 1–8.

Weimer, W. B. (1979). *Notes on the methodology of scientific research.* Hillsdale: Lawrence Eribaum.

Wilson, E. (1935). The teacher's use of research. In *Yearbook of the music educators national conference.* 163–166.

Winter, R. (1989). *Learning from experience: Principles and practice in action research.* New York: Falmer.

·3·

MODEL BUILDING

Roger H. Edwards

ROCKWOOD PUBLIC SCHOOLS

Perhaps the least productive way for researchers to explore model building is through a trip to a public library. There one will find 90 percent of the "model" entries concerned with three things: models (airplane), models (trains), and models (fashion; see careers). And although no one can deny that these pursuits fit a legitimate, broad definition of "modeling," it is difficult to reconcile them with the production of knowledge; at best, they seem more like ways of representing knowns than like ways of exploring unknowns. However, among these disparate uses of the term, there are linkages that can serve as a starting place for exploring models and the researcher.

Many phenomena are cumbersome to be dealt with in their entirety. I may have a fascination with trains, but a number of considerations keep me from buying a locomotive and putting it in my basement. And the factors that dictate that I get a model train rather than a real one have a lot in common with the reasons researchers use models.

A sufficient justification for not having a full-size Chesapeake and Ohio 4-6-2 in my basement is that it wouldn't fit; a communality of all forms of modeling has to do with miniaturization. There is more to miniaturization than creating small replicas that will fit in basements, however. Reduction of a 185-ton locomotive to something I can pick up in one hand allows me a large measure of control. I can run my model at a scale-equivalent 100 miles per hour into a sharp turn. If the laws of physics dictate a derailment, at least no lives are lost.

Experimentation through physical reduction is not always feasible, however. Even physical things cannot always be accurately miniaturized. Does this mean that a hypothesis about the positive effects of soaking an eighteenth-century violin in lemon juice and muriatic acid must go unexplored until some naive person donates a Guarnerius for experimentation?

Not necessarily. A chemist would be able to predict how these ingredients would react with each other and with the wood and varnish of the violin. If we can further tap someone's expertise on how the chemistry and physics of a violin influence tone, we will have taken a step toward predicting the effects of this "treatment." We have informational inputs, and some knowledge of the relationships between them and of how these inputs relate to a goal. We have the beginnings of another kind of model. Now it is not the object that has been reduced but the attendant *process.* Styles of teaching, attitude formation, the administration of large music programs, and the complex scheme by which the brain facilitates the translation of musical notation into sound are common examples of the processes that concern researchers in music.

Like a 185-ton locomotive, many processes are difficult to deal with in their entirety. In the continual struggle to understand processes and to store and communicate this information, we are thus forced to find various means to put what we observe in a more comprehensible, manageable form. The resulting models are the necessary links between the real world of complex processes and a simpler world that facilitates storage, comprehension, and communication. Even more importantly for the researcher, models make manipulation possible, just as they do for the model railroader. They permit problems to be visualized, understood, and more easily solved.

Many authors have seen the centrality of modeling to the undertaking of research. London (1949), for example, says:

Fundamentally, all explanation proceeds in terms of models . . . with modular apparatus ranging from the mathematical rigor of the closely articulated symbolical, at one extreme, to the free looseness of the suggestive metaphor and simile, at the other. But no matter how constructed or arrived at, every model serves to bring order of some kind to nature or, rather, our comprehension of her. (p. 165)

Rivett (1980) is even more blunt about modeling's place in the researcher's arsenal: "All scientists are aware that the central act of the scientific method is the creation of a model" (p. 1).

SOME IMPORTANT IDEAS THAT UNDERLIE THE USE OF MODELS

Reduction and Simplification

Many of the steps employed in creating models are almost instinctive. When someone stops us on the street to ask for directions, we might appropriately respond with some kind of map. It may be a physical map showing key roads, turns, and landmarks, with arrows to indicate the directions of travel. Or more commonly, the information is communicated orally with just enough of the critical intersections and landmarks to allow the listener to construct a mental map of the proposed route. Although giving directions may not qualify us as full-fledged model builders, a map, like an N-gauge locomotive, is another form of *iconic model*. And a map and a model also have something important in common.

An effective map does not have to be complete in all respects. It concentrates on the essential points and their relationships. Similarly, an important part of model building is the ability to extract the important information from a situation and avoid the random irrelevancies that surround it. As Sisson (1975) puts it, a key skill of the model builder is that which

allows him to capture the essence, only the most important variables and relationships, so as to produce a meaningful and useful model. The creative input to the modeling process, the art of model building, is in translating a perception of the world into the essential relationships and variables, and thus into a model. (p. 7)

The Roles of Modeling

The ultimate purpose of any model is some form of utility, but it is appropriate here to stop to consider what this means. Common usage of "modeling" tends to accentuate it not as part of a process but as product oriented and tautological; that is, the purpose of modeling is to produce a model.

There are two major roles that models fill in educational research. On one side there is a representational role. We strive to construct something that captures the essence of a process. Having captured and organized its salient aspects, we better understand the process ourselves and are able to use the model as an aid in communicating this information to others. One role of a model is thus almost the same as that of a map: It is a neat, simplified means of representing, understanding, storing, and communicating information. The major

distinction is that a map represents things while a model represents actions and processes.

Representational models can play an important role in research. They can tell us how to follow a procedural regimen or show us hypothesized relationships and causal patterns. They enhance our ability to speculate about processes, consider alternatives, and develop hypotheses.

A second role of models is dynamic and generative. A model used dynamically represents not so much a destination as the vehicle for getting there. It is more like a National Weather Service forecasting model. On the basis of atmospheric conditions A, B, and C, rain is forecast for tomorrow. If tomorrow turns out to be sunny, the model must be revised to include condition D or some further interactive relationship of A and B. The model continually evolves toward greater understanding as more information becomes available. It is this more active form of model toward which the researcher aims.*

An outgrowth of this view of modeling is surprising to some: A model does not have to be correct to be useful. Researchers learn from their failed models. In Richard Snow's words, "The primary criterion for the evaluation of theory is usefulness, not truthfulness" (1973, p. 103).

The hallmark of a research model is that it grows and develops from within. The model leads to investigable hypotheses. The data that stem from testing these hypotheses lead to further refinement of the model. Some data serve to verify conjectures. Other results—like that unforecasted sunny day—lead to altering the current model or even rethinking the whole process.

Models and Theories

Tracing a process through time, we find a chain of events. They tend to be at least partially ordered and display some evidence of cause and effect. There may be a large number of subevents, and there may be complex interrelationships between them. The complete process may be so complex and interwoven as to make us question whether anyone can ever really capture its whole truth. In fact, many would argue that an attempt to explain a complex social or psychological process would be no more than a theory. In practice, this is true: A model in one sense is no more than the schematization of a theory (see Kaplan, 1964).

At one time the term "theory" had negative connotations to many people. To them, theoreticians were an elite band who contemplated only the most abstract problems, leaving others to determine what functional benefits might accrue from their solution. Not only were theorizers seen as impractical people, they were proud of it.

This view has changed. As noted by Gage (1963):

In the social sciences, theories were once expected to be overarching world views and master prescriptions like socialism and the sin-

---

*Some authors use the term "dynamic model" to refer to any model of a process. We will restrict use of this term to mean an evolving model used in an ongoing research effort.

gle tax. Now theories are developed for much more modest topics, like learning, leadership, and cooperation, and one need not don a charismatic mantle in order to attempt to theorize. (p. 94)

Views on theorizing have changed so much that Kaplan (1964) can suggest that the theorizer is really the practical person, not the speculative dreamer.

The systemization effected by a theory does have the consequence of simplifying laws and introducing order into congeries of facts. But this is a by-product of a more basic function: to make sense of what would otherwise be inscrutable or unmeaning empirical findings . . . (p. 302).

In consistency with this view, Snow (1973) defines theory as "symbolic construction designed to bring generalizable facts (or laws) into systematic connection" (p. 78). The term "symbolic construction" emphasizes the very intimate relationship between theories and models.

For a more detailed analysis of the role of theory in research, see Henry Cady's discussion in Chapter 5.

Models as Experiments

If a dynamically used model constitutes the basis of a research effort, it is instructive to consider how models relate to the design of experiments. Most experiments involve carrying out a process. We subsequently try to attribute the variation observed in one or more dependent variables to the effects of other variables. To make such attribution possible, we must control (or assume to be random and unbiased) many potential sources of such variation. Accordingly, we study experimental design and quantitative methods to learn about prototypes for setting up and analyzing such experimental situations.

An unfortunate by-product of pursuing these studies is a tendency to use these prototypes in cookbook fashion, changing or reperceiving the process so as to meet the requirements of a chosen design. This is to say that as soon as researchers select a particular experimental design or statistical methodology to analyze data, they have implicitly chosen a model of the process they are analyzing. This is not the proper sequence of events. A model must precede design and analysis, not be a result of it. Textbooks and manuals often fail to emphasize this point, and researchers, lacking a substantial knowledge of analytical methodologies, are often unaware of the choice that has been made and how important that choice is. Only after having thought through a model is one ready to decide how the research data are best gathered and analyzed. We shall illustrate this point presently.

TYPES OF MODELS

There are as many ways of delineating model types as there are authors on the subject. Using any particular system risks missing significant concepts. Nevertheless, some organized way of understanding models is necessary if we are to

become skilled in making processes tractable for thought and examination. Toward this end we will start by dividing models into two loose classes, "protomodels" and analytical "true" models.

Protomodels

Protomodels are not final model building products, but they are important in understanding the diverse kinds of thinking that lead to the development of models. Protomodels are often the seed whence a "true" model springs.

Metaphoric Models Metaphoric thinking is widespread in music and music education. Who would teach diaphragmatic breathing by simply explaining which muscles to contract? By taking advantage of prior information and proprioception, teachers use metaphor and simile to communicate the concept much more efficiently. Likewise, a performance teacher might exhort a student to "soar" on entering a romantic cantabile passage. Although we might be hard-pressed to connect a dictionary definition of "soar" to a precise statement of what the teacher wishes to hear, there is general acceptance of such methods.

The use of metaphor as an informal, heuristic basis for modeling has similar advantages. Specialists in the field of program evaluation have given us a deeper insight into how one assesses the worth of an educational program by virtue of evaluation metaphors. For many years the only major model for assessing the worth of an educational undertaking was the preordinate Tylerian model, whose metaphor was quality control: Evaluators said, "State what your final product should look like and we will tell you if it does."

Experience has shown that this approach was too narrow for many evaluative situations. A jurisprudential model (Owens and Owen, 1981) considers the task of evaluating a program as a trial in which both a prosecution and a defense gather and present evidence. Hilliard (1980) has considered educational assessment through the metaphor of medical diagnosis and healing. An investigative journalism metaphor (Guba, 1981) suggests that objectivity is not a goal of evaluation so much as fairness. This metaphor also implies that an evaluation that strives for some ultimate judgment of worth is not realistic; there are many "truths." The evaluator just pursues leads and strives for balance. The determination of "truth" is left to the various audiences for the evaluation.

Theory at the metaphoric level does not give us a verifiable model, however. It is only with a more detailed explication of the metaphor that precise representations and testable hypotheses are born. But despite the low level of metaphor as modeling product, it has great potential for expanding our thinking about process and for exploring and finding new ways to approach problems.

Snow (1973) is an eloquent backer of metaphor as a basis of theory:

"The theoretician may start with metaphors . . . producing them as a kind of image game, without much disciplined direction or general plan. . . . The metaphor captures key aspects of the phenomena of interest for the theoretician. It succinctly may schematize important insights into data and provide for apt labels for these patterns of observation. . . . One can argue that the successful theoretician simply engages more in metaphor making than other researchers, so he is more likely to turn up some useful ideas. (p. 89)

Although metaphor's potential is great, there can be pitfalls in its use. Not every metaphoric statement can be developed into a formal model. The "evaluator-as-investigative-journalist" analogy may lead to new insights into the quality of a music program. On the other hand, a "performing-artist-as-factory-robot" analogy may or may not bring anything significant to light or lead to a deeper understanding of musicians. The metaphor that last night seemed to reach to the heart of some process may seem only cutely epigrammatic the next morning.

A metaphor can also be ambiguous. Even when its intent is simply communicative, persons may not share the necessary backgrounds for successful transactions at the metaphoric level. If the student hears "sore" when you say "soar," cantabile may turn to agitato. Metaphor may be the basis for a model but does not become a model without thoughtful explication and development.

Emulative Models The term "model" has many everyday uses. Educators often refer to "model programs." In this context a model is something to be copied or emulated. Although "model" used in this way is not usually considered theory, exemplars also have potential as heuristic devices that may lead in the direction of theory.

Modeling by demonstration or exemplar is another commonly used instructional technique in music. When the metaphoric "soar" doesn't seem to be effecting the intended communication, the teacher may fall back on demonstrating an instance of soaring. Exemplifying cuts away the complexity of a situation by starting with an instance of the process rather than its generalities.

A well-known example of this perspective of modeling is Bruce Joyce and Marsha Weil's *Models of Teaching* (1972). Those familiar with the author's approach will recall that each of the many teaching models discussed is introduced with a carefully chosen instance of a theoretical approach to teaching. Each model is subsequently expanded through discussion of underlying principles and axioms. Although explaining process through exemplars is more commonly a practitioner training activity, development of exemplars into specific analytic models for the researcher is also practicable.

Descriptive Models In one sense any application of inductive or analytic thinking to a process begins the creation of a model. An orchestra manager's verbal summary of the key steps and decisions in making an annual budget thus qualifies and is a low-level, descriptive "model."

The reasons for classifying such discourse as a protomodel should be obvious, however. First, such descriptions usually lack specificity. One of the worst features of process descriptions is that they can give the illusion of specificity and completeness when they have neither.

Second, most descriptions—even when specific—lack generalizability. They may detail how some instances of budget decisioning came about, but developing a model that can cope with a related class of decisions is more complex. Most descriptions are instantiations of process, not models.

The assiduous researcher can flesh out a descriptive model into a more useful one through skilled questioning of the "expert." But in the absence of such fleshing out, it is best to consider process descriptions as having heuristic potential only.

"True" Models

Going beyond these heuristic protomodels, we now consider more formal representations of theory, those considered as "true" models.

Analytic/Symbolic Models Most characteristic of analytic models is a graphic or symbolic representation of the ingredients and flow of a process. This is usually done by some form of diagraming or flowcharting, much like what a systems analyst does before a computer program is written. The diagram makes explicit the critical inputs into the process, how subprocesses are brought together, where key decision points are, the basis on which these decisions are made, and the consequences of these decisions as they relate to other parts of the process.

Within the realm of symbolic representations exist "models" with a vast range of pertinence to research. Models can be used either representationally or as the underlying blueprint of a research effort. At their best they can be beautifully concise statements of theory with considerable potential for improved understanding and, often, dynamic usage. At their worst they can be trivial, or not a model at all.

For example, one can always jot down a few key stages of a process, draw connected boxes around them, and claim to have created a model (see Figure 3–1). But a representation such as that shown in Figure 3–1 hardly qualifies as a model of performance; it fails to portray any worthwhile theory. Note that this fails to be a model not because it is simple. Complexity is never a goal of modeling. Many elaborate constructions posing as models are like the zany inventions of Wile E. Coyote. They are largely useless except as a display of ingenuity.

Likewise, other kinds of analytic representations can be termed "model" only under the broadest of definitions. A

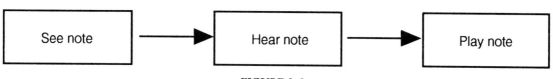

FIGURE 3–1.

Venn diagram, for instance, lacking any representation of process, also fails to qualify.

At the broadest level of "true" models, we find a particular sticky group of qualitative ones sometimes called "conceptual models." Many of these constructions are really better regarded as schematized paradigms. They are qualitative entities characterized by breadth and generality (see Gage, 1963). A paradigm is not a model of the world but, as Bailey (1978) puts it, the "mental window through which the researcher views the world" (p. 18). As an aid in thinking about process and as a basis for using subsequent observation to refine those thoughts, such mental windows have much to recommend them. They may serve an important representational need or, like protomodels, represent the germ of an idea that will later be developed into a specific model.

A central problem of conceptual models is their ambiguity. They often lead to varied interpretations of what actually happens in a process. Accordingly, attempts to verify or expand upon these models will usually lead to inconclusive results. A conceptual model may tell us, in general, on what the modeler focuses when studying the process. But few are specific enough that a second "trained" observer would see the same thing as the modeler when the two simultaneously (but independently) observed it. The lack of independent replicability severely hampers research.

In summary, conceptual models can fill a representational need. For some inherently qualitative processes, a refined conceptual model may represent a significant research product. Other conceptual models can be refined to the point where they lead to specific hypotheses and dynamic usage. Unfortunately, many never go beyond the schematized speculation stage and deserve their fate of gathering dust on library shelves.

As our need to understand the inner workings and causal links of a process grows, an increasing level of model specificity is needed. Such models typically call upon the precision of mathematics to provide the unambiguous definitions needed for all potential users to understand and apply a model in the same way.

To take a musical example of how a dynamic, symbolic model might evolve, we will explore a problem related to public support for the arts. A tax levy to support the civic symphony has been placed on the ballot twice, each time meeting with defeat. One more attempt at passage will be made next year, and someone suggests that since the previous "Support the Arts" campaign has failed, more information is needed on why the proposition has been defeated.

As an initial step we hypothesize some constructs that we feel may be relevant to voters decisions—say, musical preferences, background in musical performance, and, more specifically, public sentiment about the quality of the orchestra. On the basis of this prototype model of voter behavior, we wish to conduct a survey to gather this information from a sample of voters. How do we proceed to establish the potency of these explanatory variables and determine what steps might be taken to influence public opinion favorably and pass the increase?

One approach would be to use multiple regression to obtain parameter estimates for A (performance background), B (preferences), and C (assessment of ensemble quality). Diagrammatically, one might express this as Figure 3–2, where voting behavior is the outcome variable and A, B, and C are three independent variables, each making its own separate contribution.

But is this realistic? It seems reasonable to consider that preference is itself influenced by the performance background of the rater. Thus a better picture of the relationship might be that in Figure 3–3. Note here that A influences B and, additionally, has a direct effect (in addition to its effect through the intermediary B).

It is also possible that B influences A—people may have taken up performance avocationally as a result of sophistication obtained elsewhere. Now A and B influence each

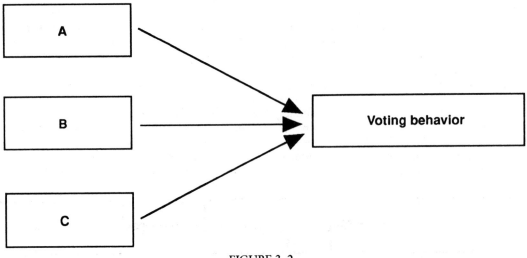

FIGURE 3–2.

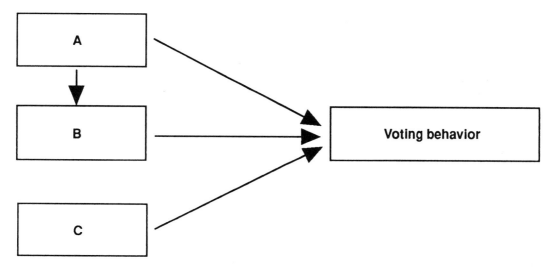

FIGURE 3–3.

other—a reciprocal relationship—and influence voting behavior (see Figure 3–4).

We will not try to complete the development of such a model here as even such a "simple" modeling situation can be very complex. In this case there would surely be other variables involved and other intervariable relationships that would suggest the need for going beyond a simple linear regression analysis of the variables and their interactions. More sophisticated methods such as path analysis or nonrecursive, multiequation regression may be needed (see Berry, 1984).

The point of this is that by looking at just a few relationship paradigms, we have done some worthwhile scientific thinking. We have the beginnings of a model. More importantly, we have avoided the common trap of letting established methodology control our thinking rather than letting

method flow from what we understand about the research situation.

The mathematics of so-called mathematical models is not usually empirical mathematics (although it can be, as in our example of voting behavior). Most mathematical models are simply another formulation of theory, primarily differing in the language used to communicate it. How mathematical a process seems to be can be surprisingly unrelated to the usefulness of mathematics in studying it.

The variables of a quantified model can represent values based on measurement or counts; they can be simple 1s and 0s, representing the existence or nonexistence of something. Relationships are expressed as procedures for calculating some variables on the basis of values of others.

Quantified models have their own set of limitations and

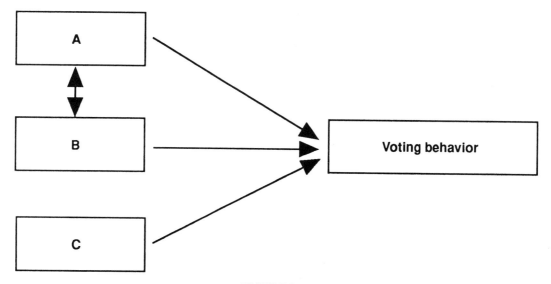

FIGURE 3–4.

pitfalls. Twenty-five years ago—before the computer explosion increased the accessibility of rapid quantification—Kaplan (1964) worried that mindless modeling could lead to "the appearance of mathematics without the reality" (p. 64).

Sisson (1975) sounds a more general warning, which applies to all forms of modeling, and, indeed, to all forms of scientific inquiry.

Model building is as much an art as a science. One of the difficulties in using a flow diagram to represent the model-building process is that the process looks more scientific than it really is. [No method] automatically produces the creative leaps required to translate a complicated real world system into a more compact and manipulable model. (p. 30)

Regarding utilization, Taffler (1981) expresses an even more ominous apprehension about quantified models. Although he is speaking to managers in industry, one can find the implied "posterior protection principle" among researchers: "Quantitative techniques sometimes have a dangerous appeal of their own; especially to managers who see in them a means of avoiding personal responsibility for decisions that might go wrong" (p. 3).

Simulation There is no specific meaning to "simulation" as the term relates to modeling, nor is a simulation a unique type of model. A small group of people can simulate the dynamics of world politics, with each person representing a country, or they can simulate the behavior of a machine, with each acting as a part or stage. In practice, simulation has come to imply a computerized model, but everyone would agree that a simulation is an *operating model,* computerized or otherwise.

There are a number of reasons for bringing a model to life through simulation. Perhaps the most important is the intellectual stimulus provided by turning the model into a set of completely nonambiguous instructions. Computers continue to sport one major defect: They do exactly what they are told to do. When the computer balks at executing some part of a model or when a completed run gives clearly impossible results, the modeler is almost inevitably wrong, at least by customary syntactic and procedural rules. The flaws in a model that works well with certain chosen situations or values may become obvious only when the modeler uses simulation under a great variety of circumstances. The process of creating a simulation and using it to watch the model in action under diverse conditions almost always aids the researcher. It reveals gaps in thinking and promotes a deeper understanding of the process being modeled.

Physical Models Physical models do not fit into any hierarchy of model sophistication. A running model train is a physical model that is little more than a moving icon. A complex set of water pipes could represent the flow of money in an economy. At the sophisticated end of the scale, the current use of computerized wind tunnels for airplane design represents the interfacing of an icon (the plane) and a replicated physical condition (the wind), with a computer controlling input variables and recording outcomes.

Sophisticated physical models are seldom used in music, but robot instrumentalists and vocalists might teach us a great deal about performance instruction—for example, what are the critical components of embouchure, and why? How well can the effect of imagery techniques used in vocal instruction be replicated by purely physiological means?

Other Terms Connected with Model Types

Some terms commonly connected with modeling have not been used in our typology. They have been omitted as separate entities so as to concentrate on the forms in which models are conceptualized and expressed. We will note some of the most common here by way of a brief glossary.

Schema Theory In recent years schema theory has been rising in favor as an aspect of modeling. But schema theory is not so much a different means of representing a model as it is an application of dynamic modeling to certain situations. Without attempting a strict differentiation, we suggest three characteristics that are usually diagnostic in differentiating between schemas and other models, as shown in Table 3–1.

Additionally, schemas are often used in a modular fashion. A group of schema modules may be assembled into a larger unit (which may also be called a schema). To illustrate, if one tries to portray the decision processes used by a band director in preparing a group for a performance, standard symbolic modeling would be the likely vehicle. Alternatively, to explain the process by which the director picks up that first mug of morning coffee (including how to tell the mug from the jar that contains clarinet reeds), schema theory is probably called for.

The increasing emphasis on schema theory for understanding musical processes is warranted. The most challenging areas of musical research are those that deal with short-term perception and action processes at the unconscious level. Those wishing to be at the forefront of the psychology of music will find an understanding of schema theory to be a twenty-first century necessity.

Stochastic (or Nondeterministic) Models These terms imply that there is one or more random variables or events in the model. This model is invaluable for mimicking selected real-life situations. Stochastic models are usually constructed by letting a computer use a random function to simulate various unpredictable conditions that are characteristic of the actual process.

Decision-Making Models This term refers to a class of models used mainly in the business world. Business has been the

Table 3–1.

	Model	Schema
Time frame of process	Longer	Shorter
Psychology	Conscious	Mostly unconscious
Processes controlled	Action	Perception and action

largest single producer of models since managers discovered that many important corporate decisions were conducive to modeling. Executives now use econometric and other models to forecast likely outcomes (fiscal and otherwise) before committing themselves to decisions involving real dollars.

EMPLOYING MODELS IN RESEARCH

Reapplication and Translation of Models

The simplest way to make use of a model is to appropriate an existing one. A model or schema generated to explain some aspect of the psychology of music can be reused. It can be put into competition with an alternative model or further developed to continue a particular investigation. A decision model for departmental budgeting may work whether the department is music or paleontology.

One of the most potentially productive means of adding to our knowledge of music is through the translation of models that have been designed for other domains. Many models and schemas have been developed to explain and investigate the processes by which reading skills are learned. Likewise, theories related to speech acquisition have many clear analogies in the development of performance skills (e.g., Cziko, 1988). By finding these analogies and translating a model into a musical setting, we may immediately develop new ways of seeing old problems. The degree to which a model or schema developed in another area can be applied to music can in itself be a worthwhile study.

A model developed in and for another field may be useless in music, regardless of how good the translation is. But, there is the corresponding possibility that a model—or part of a model—developed in another domain may also prove *more* useful when translated to a music context. We must remember that many drugs and inventions found their highest (or only) calling for purposes not intended by their originators.

Models developed in other domains may hold the key to deeper understanding of many areas in music and music education. As with metaphors, one should not dismiss interesting parallels between musical situations and nonmusical ones without giving them a chance to develop and bloom.

De Novo Generation

If a process has not been subjected to in-depth analysis before or, in the researcher's eyes, has been misanalyzed, a model may have to be built from scratch. Where does one start? First, let us note what should be obvious: Researchers should not try to model processes with which they have little familiarity. The sophistication of a complex model or an intricate simulation may be impressive, but glitz cannot make up for a lack of understanding of the process.

The major source of many inspired models is a unique, personal insight into some process, based on extensive thought, observation, or participation. The unique elements of the model may come from introspection and metacogni-

tion. How do I see (or do) this process differently than others? Why? Are there factors that most people ignore or play down that actually have a high level of potency or causality in the process? Such speculations as these suggest alternative models or may result in one's being able to analyze a process that has never received formal treatment before.

Assuming one feels knowledgeable enough to proceed, we next start some sketching of the model. This process of starting to put perceptions into some tangible form is of significance. Augmenting analytical skills with visual ones can help bring vague ideas into clear focus. The systematic effort of schematizing prompts us to ponder possible relationships among the variables that would otherwise have been ignored.

During this initial sketching stage, we should be reflecting on some fundamental questions about our model: What positive outcomes result when the process works well? How do we know when we (or the process) have failed? How can we express these outcomes as the dependent variable of a model? What factors or independent variables affect the process? This is a crucial stage in building the model, and involves detailed consideration of exactly what we want the model to do. We will consider two diverse instances of dynamic quantitative models to illustrate.

Case 1—Empirical Prediction There are empirical data on an outcome (dependent) variable and a set of input (independent) variables. The modeling task is to find values of and relationships between the variables so as to make the best prediction of the outcome. The voting behavior problem noted previously is an example of this approach.

Empirical models can also be developed for more qualitative investigations. For instance, if we wish to study characteristics of exemplary string programs in elementary schools, a modeling approach helps keep the investigation properly focused. At an early stage of the investigation, the researcher is forced to consider exactly how to define success for such a program, what the potentially important causative variables are, and so on. Even though a symbolic model may not be an important end product, a dynamic modeling approach is much superior to interviewing 50 exemplary directors and then trying to make sense of the resulting mountain of data.

Case 2—Optimization There are no empirical data on the outcome variable, but its value must be optimized (usually maximized or minimized). The modeling task is to find values and interrelationships of the independent variables that will optimize the outcome measure. The business world makes considerable use of these models to aid in corporate decision making and in studying the efficiency of processes. This form of modeling may become indistinguishable from "operations research." Fast-food chains want, for example, to keep the drive-up window traffic moving as quickly as possible to maximize revenue. Musicians may wish to maximize the efficiency of rehearsal time or minimize the time needed to teach some musical concept.

Having used this kind of thinking about output, input, and purpose, we are ready to continue with the design. Critical inputs and subprocesses are noted, lined up, and placed in boxes. The boxes are then connected by arrows showing the direction of flow in time. Conventionally the flow is left to right or top to bottom.

Some stages of the process may represent decision points. Which step or subprocess is to be done next may depend on some current value or logical condition. Such decision points or branching conditions are often put in diamond-shaped boxes. Usually there are "yes" and "no" branches emanating from the diamond, with an arrow connecting that branch to the appropriate substage toward which processing is to flow under that condition. This flow is often back toward the beginning of the model.

Even at this early stage one should keep the model representation as clear as possible. Every effort should be made to prevent crossing lines and other sources of confusion. Likewise, modelike constructions with arrows pointing to nowhere, interconnected small boxes inside bigger boxes, and other obscure representations usually serve to mystify rather than clarify.

Having made an initial sketch of the model, we next use the sketch as a guide for more detailed thought about the variables involved. Are any variables so vague as to defy verification that they even exist? If so, can we redefine them in a more meaningful way? If the model is to be of the empirical prediction variety, where will the empirical values come from?

Before going beyond this stage, one should consult with someone with modeling expertise. Discovering some fatal flaw in a model at this point is disheartening, but the heartbreak will be worse if the problem comes to light only after one has spent months trying to refine the unrefinable.

If a model is really the backbone of a research effort, the project's quality is directly related to the quality of the model employed. A good one can be the researcher's guiding light. A poor one can play the monster to the researcher's Frankenstein.

SOME EXEMPLARS FOR FURTHER STUDY

One of the best ways to learn about modeling is to read well-done studies that discuss model derivation. Among those that seem to have that heuristic quality are Newell and Simon (1972) on models of information processing, Weiner (1979) on classroom motivation, and Briars and Larkin (1984) using simulation to study problem-solving skills.

Researchers have applied modeling to music in many ways. In the area of historical research, Mark (1987) has modeled the rise of jazz in the music education curriculum. In addition to the value of his own model, Mark's discussion of model usage in historical investigations is of great value to those wishing to do research of this nature.

Howell, Cross, and West (1985) present many interesting examples of mathematical modeling in musicology. A number of the studies cited therein exemplify modeling that is representational but virtually necessary for subsequent dynamic modeling in the area of musical perception.

George Stiny and James Gips's (1978) discussion of models for aesthetic criticism, Horning's (1982) work on modeling aesthetic response to music, Markowitz's (1981) model of curricular decision making are also notable in their respective musical areas.

The important process of moving a conceptual model to a dynamic one is notable in some long-term projects of music researchers. Peter Webster's continued development of his model of creativity (see Webster, 1987) and Alfred Leblanc's work in musical taste (e.g., Leblanc, 1980) are two notable examples.

Probably the most sophisticated use of modeling in music has been Bharucha's (1987) studies in simulating aspects of musical listening. This work, based on perceptual schemas, should be of great interest to researchers in psychomusicology.

For some instructive notions of translating researchable theory to musical contexts from nonmusical ones, Cziko's exploration of music as language (1988) and Edwards's (1988) discussion of psychological transfer and performance skills may be helpful.

Summary

In music, as any other field, research has as its goal to explain observed relationships. Research in music is not a matter of relating randomly chosen musical variables, however. Typically, our choices of variables are made on the basis of a theory about one or more relationships, whether or not we ever make an explicit statement of what that theory is. Models are used to make concise, visual representation of the theory that underlies a particular research undertaking. The model not only serves as a means of concisely communicating that theory to others but also provides a framework that researchers can use to reflect on their findings and alter or refine theory on the basis of new information. In this way, research becomes more than a series of stabs in the dark; it becomes part of an evolutionary process whose goals are the increased understanding, prediction, and control of events in the musical world.

References

Bailey, K. D. (1978). *Methods of social research*. New York: Macmillan.

Berry, W. D. (1984). *Nonrecursive causal models*. Sage series on quantitative applications in the social sciences, 07–037. Beverly Hills: Sage Publications.

Bharucha, J. J. (1987). Music cognition and perceptual facilitation: A connectionist framework. *Music Perception, V*(1), 1–30.

Briars, D. J., and Larkin, J. H. (1984). An integrated model of skill in solving elementary word problems. *Cognition and Instruction, I*(3), 245–296.

Cziko, G. (1988). Implicit and explicit learning: Implications for and applications to music teaching. *The Crane Symposium: Toward an understanding of the teaching and learning of music performance*. Potsdam: Potsdam College of SUNY.

Easley, J. A. (1977). Seven modeling perspectives on teaching and learning—some interrelations and cognitive effects. *Instructional Science, 6*, 319–367.

Edwards, R. H. (1988). Transfer and performance instruction. *The Crane Symposium: Toward an understanding of the teaching and learning of music performance*. Potsdam: Potsdam College of SUNY.

Gage, N. L. (1963). Paradigms for research on teaching. In N. L. Gage, (ed.), *Handbook of research on teaching*. Chicago: Rand McNally.

Guba, E. G. (1981). Investigative reporting. In N. L. Smith (Ed.), *Metaphors for evaluation: Sources of new methods*. Beverly Hills: Sage Publications.

Guetzkow, H., Kotler, P., and Schultz, R. (1972). *Simulation in social and administrative science*. Englewood Cliffs: Prentice-Hall.

Hilliard, A. G. (1980). A medical model for educational assessment? *Journal of School Health, L*, 256–258.

Horning, T. M. (1982). The development of a model of the psychological processes which translate musical stimuli into affective experience. Unpublished doctoral dissertation, Case Western Reserve University, Cleveland.

Howell, P., Cross, I., and West, P. (1985). *Musical structure and cognition*. London: Academic Press.

Huckfeldt, R. R., Kohfeld, C. W., and Likens, T. W. (1982). *Dynamic modeling: An introduction*. Sage series on quantitative applications in the social sciences, 07–027. Beverly Hills: Sage Publications.

Joyce, B. R., and Weil, M. (1972). *Models of teaching*. Englewood Cliffs: Prentice-Hall.

Kaplan, A. (1964). *The conduct of inquiry: Methodology for behavioral science*. San Francisco: Chandler.

Leblanc, A. (1980). Outline of a proposed model of sources of variation in musical taste. *Bulletin of the Council for Research in Music Education, 61*, 29–34.

London, I. D. (1949). The role of the model in explanation. *Journal of Genetic Psychology, 74*, 165–176.

Mark, M. L. (1987). The acceptance of jazz in the music education curriculum: A model for interpreting a historical process. *Bulletin of the Council for Research in Music Education, 92*, 15–21.

Markowitz, S. P. (1981). A model for the analysis of political behavior in institutional curriculum decision-making: A case study in music education. Unpublished doctoral dissertation, Kent State University, Kent.

Newell, A., and Simon, H. A. (1972). *Human problem solving*. Englewood Cliffs: Prentice-Hall.

Owens, T. R., and Owen, T. R. Law. (1981). In N. L. Smith (Ed.), *Metaphors for evaluation: Sources of new methods*. Beverly Hills: Sage Publications.

Rivett, P. (1980). *Model building for decision analysis*. New York: John Wiley.

Sisson, R. (1975). Introduction to decision models. In S. I. Goss and R. Sisson (Eds.), *A guide to models in governmental planning and operations*. Potomac: Sauger Books.

Snow, R. E. (1973). Theory construction for research on teaching. In Travers, R. (Ed.), *Second handbook of research on teaching*. Chicago: Rand-McNally.

Stiny, G., and Gips, J. (1978). *Algorithmic aesthetics: Computer models for criticism and design in the arts*. Berkeley: University of California Press.

Stogdill, R. M. (Ed.). (1970). *The process of model-building in the behavioral sciences*. Columbus: Ohio State University Press.

Taffler, R. (1981). *Answers: Decision-making techniques for managers*. Englewood Cliffs: Prentice-Hall, 1979.

Weiner, B. (1979). A theory of motivation for some classroom experiences. *Journal of Educational Psychology, 71*, 3–25.

·4·

A HISTORY OF
MUSIC EDUCATION RESEARCH

Michael L. Mark
TOWSON STATE UNIVERSITY

Music education, like other professions, is composed of a diverse and complex grouping of subdisciplines that extend beyond the basic activity of instruction. Research is one of the subdisciplines. It is a recent phenomenon that has evolved and matured rapidly. Most of the history of music education research takes place in the twentieth century, when music in education proliferated, providing abundant topics of study for researchers. This brief history will cover early research in education; the tests and measurements movement; research in colleges and universities; the roles of the Music Educators National Conference, other organizations, the federal government, and private foundations in music education research; and the relationship between research and practice. These topics do not exhaust the subject, but they provide the best overview possible within the space limitation of a single chapter.

EARLY RESEARCH IN EDUCATION
AND MUSIC EDUCATION

Early Educational Research

Although educational surveys were done throughout much of the nineteenth century, the first widespread involvement of individual educators as researchers was during the latter part of the century, when formal means of communication were established to solve problems. For the most part, ideas were shared through papers and addresses at conferences and other meetings. Most of the information concerned practices that individual educators found to be successful in their own teaching. This *personal experience method* (Barr, Davis, and Johnson, 1953) was followed in the twentieth century by the *deliberative approach,* which consisted of discussion of problems, often by committees. The Educational Council of the Music Supervisors National Conference (discussed later) is an example of the use of the deliberative approach to solve music education problems. These were rudimentary forms of research, with little thought given to scientific method.

The first widespread movement that promoted educational research was the Child-Study Movement, which helped develop the scientific observation and study of children in the late nineteenth and early twentieth centuries. G. Stanley Hall, the recipient of the first doctorate in psychology in the United States (Harvard, 1878), was the leader in the movement to study children scientifically. This movement generated much basic research, which led to a large volume of applied research in music education in the years to follow (Humphreys, 1985; Rideout, 1982). The Child-Study Movement was succeeded by the progressive education movement, which also involved a great deal of research activity.

Edward L. Thorndike is generally considered the most prominent figure in early educational research in the United States. Thorndike was appointed instructor of genetic psychology at Teachers College of Columbia University in 1899. It was his intention to develop a science of learning. His research led him to develop methods of testing and measuring the intelligence and learning ability of children. Lewis Terman was of the same generation of educational researchers as Thorndike. Terman's classic studies of gifted children helped teachers better understand the nature of giftedness. The next generation of researchers, whose work began long before Thorndike's was completed, including Sidney Pressey, B. Frederick Skinner, and Jean Piaget, all of whom contributed significantly to educational development through their studies of behavior.

Educational theorists and psychologists attempted to emulate the techniques of American industrial planning during the first two decades of the twentieth century because manufacturing procedures were proven models for achieving goals in the most efficient manner. "Efficiency" became the key word for educators. They sought ways to make the schools operate at peak efficiency and thus educate students more effectively. To achieve efficiency it was necessary to have goals and to measure success in achieving them. Thus, another term, "standardization," found its way into educational jargon. Educators developed standards for many aspects of schooling, including standardization of the curriculum and learning objectives.

Efficiency and standardization required measurement techniques to determine whether they were successful, and so an objective measurement movement arose in the second decade of the twentieth century. It was, in part, a reaction to the findings of lack of reliability in the scoring of written examinations during the first decade of the century. Educators knew little about the abilities and achievements of their students, and realized the need to be able to measure mental characteristics accurately. Thorndike wrote in the *Seventeenth Yearbook of the National Society for the Study of Education: Part II* (1918): "Whatever exists exists in some amount" and therefore can be measured (p. 16). He led his colleagues in exploring the possibilities of quantitative methods in educational measurement.

The *Journal of Educational Research* and the American Educational Research Association (AERA) were both founded in 1920 in response to widespread interest in this type of research. Educational research broadened during the second quarter of the twentieth century, years characterized as "a period during which extraordinary stress was placed upon the processes of collecting, analyzing, and quantifying educational data" (Barr et al., Johnson, 1953 p. 4). The number of measurement instruments increased dramatically throughout the first half of the century. *The Third Mental Measurement Yearbook* (Buros, 1949) catalogs 663 tests and 549 books about measurement. AERA established the *Review of Educational Research* in 1930 to provide abstracts and digests of educational research from various sources.

Music Education Research

According to Schneider and Cady (1965, pp. 33–34), research that is relevant to music education is "related to the over-all development, analysis, and evaluation of the music education program." Such research covers the teacher, the student, the teaching-learning process, the constraining elements, and the music education program. By this definition, the earliest music education research that can be identified in western history is that of Plato, whose philosophical reflections on music in education still command the attention of music educators. It is probably not stretching a point to say that Guido d'Arezzo did research in practical music instruction in the eleventh century when he developed a system to help pupils learn to read music.

The earliest formal educational research activities in the United States were in the form of surveys, which were done throughout much of the nineteenth century by legislative bodies, government agencies, school systems, institutions of higher education, and teacher associations. The surveys were meant to determine specific facts about the status of various subjects, to learn about organizational structures, and to gain other kinds of information about the public schools. The first known attempt in the United States to collect data on music instruction by means of a survey was part of a larger project sponsored by the Connecticut General Assembly in 1837. Henry Barnard was instrumental in persuading the state legislature to collect educational data. Questionnaires were sent to all schools in the state in 1837 "(Mr. Barnard's Labors," 1856). The teachers were asked eight questions concerning music instruction:

Can you sing by note?
Can you play any instrument?
Do you teach or cause singing in school, either by rote or by note?
Do you use singing as a relieving exercise for ill humor or weariness in schools?
Do you use any instrument, or have any used, as an accompaniment to singing?
Do you teach your pupils to use the proper musical voice in singing?
Do you do so from ear, or from knowledge of the physiology of the vocal organs?
How many of your pupils prove on trial unable to understand music, or acquire even a moderate degree of proficiency in the practice?

Unfortunately, Barnard's position was eliminated shortly thereafter and Connecticut abandoned its newly established leadership in music education research. Also unfortunate is the lack of records of the results of the survey, or knowledge of whether the results affected practices in the schools of Connecticut.

Other surveys were designed to collect similar information. The U.S. Office of Education sponsored a national survey to learn the condition of music education throughout the United States in 1886 (Bergee, 1987). Two years later, the Department of Music Instruction of the National Education Association conducted another survey (Silver, 1889). Later surveys inquired into music education during the first three decades of the twentieth century. Many were sponsored by city school systems, and assumed such importance that some school systems created their own research bureaus to conduct surveys. Although they provided valuable information about the status of music education, they did not address the specific problems of teaching and learning that are the focus of much contemporary research.

Research bureaus were also established in teachers colleges and normal schools; these were instrumental in promoting educational tests and measurements. Music testing was not an interest of the bureaus, with the exception of the Bureau of Educational Measurements and Standards of the

Kansas State Normal School in Emporia. Here the *Beach Standardized Music Tests,* the first set of standardized tests of musical achievement, was published (Humphreys, 1987).

During the early part of the twentieth century, there was a strong movement toward the use of scientific principles to improve instruction. Philip C. Hayden might have been the first music educator to advocate a scientific approach to music instruction. Shortly after the turn of the century, he wrote a series of articles in which he stated that Thaddeus L. Bolton's experimental studies on musical perception proved that the ear tended to group sounds into twos, threes, and fours. Hayden demonstrated the principle at the 1905 meeting of the National Education Association, and again in 1907 at the meeting of music supervisors in Keokuk, Iowa, from which the Music Supervisors National Conference was to develop.

By the 1920s music education leaders had begun calling for research to confirm or guide practice. In 1928 Peter Dykema discussed the need for research in musical endowment, teaching methods, and "the results of teaching, practice, growth or whatever is added to endowment which produces the musical power of the individual as he grows up" (Dykema, 1928, p. 28). Kittle (1932) wrote:

Scientific research should enable us to more effectively maintain the present level, and through elimination of the unnecessary phases of our work, allow us to train our students more thoroughly in the ways that will lead to our goal of genuine and lasting appreciation of music. Science and art *can* be combined, and the proper combination will mean much to the future success of our work. (p. 39)

Jacob Kwalwasser (1935) encouraged high goals for music education research with this statement:

We must turn from the method of authority and pursue a method which promises enlightenment and greater understanding. We must search for the truth wherever it may lead. We must doubt the value of ready-made and oversimplified solutions. We must be wary of personality domination. Every teacher must be fired by the research spirit. Only by searching for the truth with care and diligence, observing the natural responses of children to various teaching situations, and studying the data so observed are we likely to convert music teaching into music pedagogy; music training into music achievement; and music learning into a joyous experience for both the child and the teacher. (p. 162)

Wilson (1936) identified a problem in 1935 that persists to the present. He said that music teachers were not interested in research or the findings of researchers, and that they must be stimulated to do research themselves.

THE TESTS AND MEASUREMENTS MOVEMENT IN MUSIC

Music education research began to mature with the basic research of Carl Seashore, Jacob Kwalwasser, Raleigh Drake, E. Thayer Gaston, Max Schoen, and others. Several laboratories were established or used for music testing in an at-

tempt to relate music education research to the discipline of psychology. Seashore's laboratory was at the State University of Iowa, where he was dean of the Graduate College (Small, 1944). Karl W. Gehrkens's laboratory was at Oberlin College (Lendrim, 1961); Charles H. Farnsworth's at Teachers College, Columbia University (Lee, 1982); and Osbourne McConathy's at Northwestern University (Platt, 1973). The tests and measurements movement influenced both music education researchers and practitioners as they came to believe that music instruction could be improved by quantitative measurement of musical characteristics. For the first time, serious attention was given to the distinction between aptitude and achievement.

Measures of Musical Aptitude

Investigators developed categories of traits by which they believed musical talent could be measured. Carl Seashore was a pioneer in the measurement of what he called "musicality." He identified capacities of musicality, including hearing, feeling, and understanding music. Seashore believed, however, that only the physical aspects of music could be quantified accurately, and so only they could be measured with any degree of accuracy. Physical measurement is possible because sound waves can be quantified, the source of sound can be controlled, and perception can be assessed. He did not attempt to measure musical feeling and understanding because they are less susceptible to accurate quantification. Seashore's theory of specifics refers to the analysis of the specific components of music (pitch, loudness, duration, rhythm, timbre, tonal memory) that he believed to be both measurable and permanent. According to Seashore, these capacities are developed early in life and do not change appreciably with training or maturity.

Seashore published his first standardized battery of musical aptitude measures, the *Seashore Measures of Musical Talents,* in 1919. It consisted of six tests for the measurement of pitch discrimination, loudness discrimination, sensitivity to differences in time intervals, recognition of differences in rhythm patterns, discrimination of degrees of consonance, and tonal memory. A revised edition, *Measures of Musical Talents,* was published by Seashore, Lewis, and Saetveit in 1939. It is the 1939 version, on long-playing disks, that is used today.

Opponents of Seashore's beliefs in the measurement of musicality were led by the psychologist James L. Mursell, who believed in musical talent as described by the Gestalt school of psychology. Viewing musicality as a whole, Mursell and others could not accept the fragmentation of musicality into separate elements. Mursell considered musicality to be more than a group of attributes dependent on sensory capacity. Seashore believed each component section of his *Measures* could be validated separately, and that a musician would be competent in most of the elements. These opposing schools have generated much controversy (and research) over the years, and the difficulty in validating musical aptitude measures has precluded a decisive solution to this day.

Other historically important measures of musical aptitude are the *Kwalwasser-Dykema Music Tests,* published in 1930, measuring several of the same aptitudes as the Seashore *Measures,* the *Tilson-Gretch Musical Aptitude Tests* (1941), the *Drake Musical Aptitude Tests* (1954, 1957), the *Kwalwasser Music Talent Test* (1953), the *Gaston Test of Musicality* (1942, 1950, 1956, 1957), the *Wing Standardized Tests of Musical Intelligence* (1939, 1948, 1957, 1960, 1961), the *Gordon Musical Aptitude Profile* (1965), and the *Measures of Musical Ability* by Bentley (1966).

Music Achievement Tests

Several tests of musical achievement were also developed and used by music educators. They included the *Beach Music Test* (1920, 1930), the *Kwalwasser-Ruch Test of Musical Accomplishment* (1925, 1927), the *Kwalwasser Test of Music Information and Appreciation* (1927), the *Knuth Achievement Tests in Music* (1936, 1966), the *Aliferis Music Achievement Test* (1947, 1949, 1950, 1954), and the *Elementary Music Achievement Tests* (1965) and *Music Achievement Tests* (1969) by Richard Colwell, among others. In addition to the above, numerous tests to measure ability, achievement, and response have been constructed, and many of them validated, by curriculum evaluators and as the subjects of dissertations and theses.

The tests and measurements movement proved to be of greater practical interest to music education practitioners than other research activities. Music educators have done much testing in practical situations, and have made many critical decisions about students on the basis of test results. Such testing is the most important example of widespread research activity affecting classroom practices.

RESEARCH IN COLLEGES AND UNIVERSITIES

Music Educators as Researchers

As the tests and measurements movement developed and matured, music educators began to take an interest in using scientific methods as the basis of their own research rather than leaving that enterprise to psychologists. Much of their work was applied research that extended the basic research of the psychologists. From the 1930s to the present, the vast majority of music education research has been done in the context of higher education. Much of it has been by the professoriat, but far more is in the form of master's degree theses and doctoral dissertations. An unfortunate aspect of graduate research is that only a small proportion of those awarded graduate degrees in music education have continued their research activities after completing their formal education.

Research topics include tests and measurements, which has remained popular to the present, and virtually every other area of interest in the music education profession.

Much of the earlier research was of a quantitative nature, being concerned with tests and measurements and surveys, but numerous historical topics were also addressed. The plethora of topics indicate healthy intellectual interest in all facets of music education, but it also has a negative side. Reimer (1985) points out that music education research has developed atheoretically, without a clear definition of its role in relation to practice or the best way for it to be undertaken to maximize knowledge. He discusses the lack of an underlying philosophy to guide research:

> Music education research, as an enterprise employing disciplined inquiries in an attempt to understand and improve the teaching and learning of music, has been . . . devoid of or certainly with an insufficient level of grounding in a coherent system of guiding principles for carrying on its affairs. (p. 18)

The growth of graduate study in music education from the 1930s has influenced music education research profoundly. Earlier, there had been little incentive for the establishment of separate doctoral programs in music education, and most doctoral study in the discipline took place within general education programs in which music was emphasized. Before the 1950s many universities required faculty to hold the master's degree. It was not until the 1950s that universities began to require the doctorate of faculty.

By midcentury the normal schools had converted to state teachers colleges, which later developed into liberal arts colleges or universities. Many offered master's degree programs in music education, and some the doctorate. These new graduate music education programs greatly increased the number of music education faculty involved in research, adding their efforts to those of faculty of the research universities.

To understand the movement toward individual research by members of the profession, it is necessary to review the history of graduate study in music education in the United States. The research traditions of both the master's and doctoral degrees are rooted in the Middle Ages. The master's degree was originally a part of the medieval guild system. The holder of the master's degree, having passed rigorous examinations and demonstrating competency in a field of study, was qualified to teach. The doctorate was an academic degree. The holder of the doctorate had great depth of knowledge in an academic field, was also licensed to teach, and was expected to be able to pursue research that would result in original contributions to knowledge. The traditional Ph.D. was always a research degree that was not intended to prepare teachers, but during the twentieth century many, if not most, holders of the Ph.D. have become teachers.

The model upon which American research universities were built is the German university. In 1876 Daniel Coit Gilman became the first president of Johns Hopkins University. He patterned the university after the University of Berlin, which was primarily devoted to the advancement of knowledge through scholarship and research. This was a radical departure for American higher education, which for the most part had prepared students for the ministry or to enter the various learned professions. Such venerable institutions as Yale and Brown Universities and the College of William and Mary were originally intended to improve the moral character of young men. The success of Johns Hopkins University as a research institution was quickly emulated by Harvard, Cornell, and Columbia Universities, the University of Michigan, and others. As in the German tradition, graduate study in the United States began as a period of extensive research training.

Yale University awarded the first American Ph.D. in 1861, but doctoral education remained relatively insignificant in terms of numbers of students until after World War I, when a new degree, the Doctor of Education, gained popularity. Harvard University was the first to award the degree (1921). It was originally intended to train school administrators and teachers, but as higher education required greater numbers of faculty with more teaching competence, the degree became very similar to the Ph.D. Except for the language requirement, there is little difference now between the Ph.D. and the Ed.D. (D.Ed. in some institutions), except that the latter is usually awarded through professional education departments. All doctoral candidates are expected to be competent researchers. They take research courses and prepare dissertations, many of which contribute significantly to knowledge.

Music faculty at all types of higher education institutions have traditionally been expected to maintain both musical and academic standards through scholarly and artistic activities to the level of other disciplines. It is the scholarly aspect of the work of the music education faculty that has led to research activities in colleges and universities. Music faculty, like other faculty, have needed advanced degrees to provide credibility for their institutions, for academic rank and tenure, for accreditation of the institution, to serve as evidence of the preparation of the faculty, and to support career advancement.

As more doctorates in music education were awarded, the research community expanded and individuals joined it for the rewards it offered. Many people who were well trained in research methodology found it to be their primary professional interest, and often a compelling personal interest as well. They continued their research activities after receiving the doctorate, writing articles for such professional journals as the *Journal of Research in Music Education* and the *Bulletin of the Council for Research in Music Education*. As research activities expanded and research outlets increased, the publication of research results came to be accepted as a major criterion for tenure and promotion. Another powerful motivation for research activity has been the recognition and prestige within the music education profession that comes with success as a published researcher.

The Expansion of Research

By the middle of the twentieth century, educational research had expanded considerably and created new opportunities for music education researchers. R. Stewart Jones (1957) reviewed the status of music education research in 1956 and found the methodological trends to include normative questionnaire studies, correlational analyses, action research, and simulated situations. Less attention was given to teaching methods and teaching materials and more to such areas as "guidance, social climate of groups, interests, aptitudes, etc." Although children were the subject of much music education research at that time, there was little research on how to teach them (Jones, 1957, p. 5). Some of the specific content areas Jones identified were group dynamics, motivational analysis, and the public and its education. He identified project interdisciplinary research in education as a new trend, which was to become firmly entrenched during the next decade with many projects supported by the federal government.

Jones also found that educational research had been slowed by three new problems: (1) educational researchers, seeking respectability, often permitted research design and quantitative procedures to take precedence over creative ideas; (2) research interests had often been diverted to those areas that could be funded; and (3) research and writing had become the primary consideration in faculty promotion at many universities, thus causing quantity of educational research to take precedence over quality.

Educational researchers have often emulated research in other disciplines throughout the twentieth century. Numerous attempts to imitate research in the physical sciences convinced many educational researchers that this task was not a productive one for the solution of educational problems. In fact, widespread agreement arose that education is more closely related to the social and behavioral sciences than to the physical sciences. Some have questioned whether music is an appropriate subject for experimental research. Bennett Reimer (1985), among others, points out that truly accurate experimental conditions cannot be created because it is not possible to control and manipulate people to the degree necessary to produce such conditions.

Bibliographies of Research Studies

Because of the vast scope of research done in American colleges and universities, a broad view of the subject is difficult to grasp. One of the ways to know the products of scholars is by means of bibliographies of research studies. Several such bibliographies have been compiled by music education scholars who have studied the research literature, and in some cases, synthesized it, thus enabling the research community to know the precedents of current research.

Humphreys (1989) compiled the "Bibliography of Theses and Dissertations Related to Music Education, 1895–1931." The study identifies 194 master's theses and 66 doctoral dissertations from 51 institutions. Only three of the works date to the nineteenth century: Thaddeus L. Bolton ("Rhythm," Clark University, 1895), John J. Dawson ("The Education Value of Vocal Music," New York University, 1895), and Charles William Johnson ("Musical Pitch and the Measurement of Intervals Among the Ancient Greeks," Johns Hopkins University, 1896). None of the nineteenth-century dissertations was written in a music department.

Major bibliographies of music education research studies have been published under the sponsorship of the Music Education Research Council. The first, "Bibliography of Research Studies in Music Education 1932–1944," was a 55-page booklet published by the State University of Iowa Press for MENC that sold for $1.00. The study was compiled by Arnold M. Small with the Committee on Research in Music Education of MENC, chaired by William S. Larson, a student of Carl Seashore. The studies included both published and unpublished research. The inclusive dates of the research reported (1932–1944) were selected arbitrarily, with the expectation that they would yield the "greatest interest and practical value." Describing the criteria for selection, Larson wrote:

Only those studies which by their titles indicated a contribution to the *teaching of music* were accepted, with due allowance being made for studies in applied Psychology of Music, notably those done at the State University of Iowa, which have contributed so much, directly or indirectly, to research in music education.

Larson compiled the *Bibliography of Research Studies in Music Education: 1932–1948* (1949). His "Bibliography of Research Studies in Music Education, 1949–1956" (1957) was published in the *Journal of Research in Music Education* in 1957. Thirty-six hundred studies completed between 1932 and 1956 were listed. Most were done to satisfy master's degree requirements, and 420 were for doctoral dissertations. Many were faculty research projects not done for degree credit. The primary criterion for inclusion in both bibliographies was the contribution of the studies to the teaching of music (Larson, 1957).

Roderick D. Gordon compiled the next major bibliography, which was published in the *Journal of Research in Music Education* in 1964. It consisted of titles of doctoral dissertations completed between 1957 and 1963. Gordon (1978) continued to compile doctoral dissertation bibliographies for publication in *JRME,* the last of which covered the period from 1972 to 1977.

THE ROLE OF THE MUSIC EDUCATORS NATIONAL CONFERENCE IN RESEARCH

Although many psychologists and music educators were actively pursuing research in various facets of music education at universities, the Music Educators National Association assumed the responsibility of serving as an umbrella organization to promote, encourage, and help develop standards for music education research. Undoubtedly research in music education would have continued without the support of a professional organization, but the MENC offered researchers benefits they would have found difficult to gain on their own. The MENC has served as a forum for the exchange of ideas and information between researchers. This has been done in many ways, some of which follow.

The Educational Council

MENC research activities began with its Educational Council, established in 1918, which later became the Music Education Research Council. The research role of the Educational Council was quite different from its current function. The Council published bulletins on various aspects of music education, including curriculum guides, information on training music supervisors, and other topics. In keeping with the trend of that time, survey data were the basis of most of the reports. Karl Gehrkens and Hollis Dann were assigned the task of making recommendations for a collegiate course of study to prepare music supervisors. The acceptance of their report on April 8, 1921, and its subsequent publication, combined with the Standard Course in Music for the Elementary Grades, was a momentous event in MENC history. The Gehrkens and Dann reports comprised *Bulletin No. 1.*

Bulletin No. 1 was followed by a series of publications on many topics that have reappeared in publications, conferences, and other forums since that time. Other early *Bulletin* titles served the membership and advanced the cause of music education through research. They include *Four-Year Course for Training Music Supervisors* (1921), *High School Credits for Applied Music Study* (1922), *Junior High School Music* (1925), *Report on Music in the One-Teacher Rural School* (1926), and *Survey on Tests and Measurements in Music Education* (1926).

In 1923 the name of the Council was changed to the National Research Council on Music Education, but its function remained the same. The name changed again in 1932, this time to the Music Education Research Council. MERC remains the research branch of the Music Educators National Conference. The Music Education Research Council was relatively inactive from 1940 until 1960. During the 1950s it began to revitalize itself by cosponsoring some publishing projects with the *Journal of Research in Music Education,* which included publication of *Bibliography of Research Studies in Music Education, 1949–1957, American Index to the Musical Quarterly* (1915–1957), and *Music Education Materials—A Selected Bibliography* (1954). Article VII of the MENC constitution identifies MERC as the governing body of the Society for Research in Music Education (SRME).

The Society for Research in Music Education

SRME was established in 1960 under the governance of MERC. The objective of SRME is "the encouragement and advancement of research in those areas pertinent to music education." It was founded for a most pragmatic reason—to facilitate compliance with postal regulations in distributing the *Journal of Research in Music Education.* Its aims are as follows:

1. Sponsor meaningful sessions of MENC national conventions devoted to reports of research studies and relevant topics.

2. Through its divisional and state units, sponsor similar sessions at the divisional and state levels.
3. Provide an effective framework for the exchange of information among persons engaged in or interested in research in music education.
4. Encourage all research in music education and in fields related to music education (Jones, 1957 p. 5).

A major responsibility was given to SMRE when *The Journal of Research in Music Education* became its official publication in 1963. MENC members who subscribe to JRME are automatically members of the Society for Research in Music Education.

Special Research Interest Groups

One of the ways in which the Music Education Research Council sought to promote and support music education research was by the establishment of several special research interest groups (SRIG), which were formed at the 1978 convention in Chicago. The SRIGs, which operate under the governance of MERC, are organizations of researchers with similar research interests. The original SRIGs were in the fields of measurement and evaluation, affective response, history, instructional strategies, perception, early childhood, and general research. New ones have been added since 1978. Most SRIGs publish newsletters and meet at MENC national conventions to discuss their particular research areas and new findings.

The MENC Historical Center

Another research activity of MENC is the MENC Historical Center, established in 1965 at the University of Maryland at College Park. The MENC and the University of Maryland College Park share the governance of the Center, the purpose of which is "to preserve the documents and materials that have reflected and influenced the history of music instruction in the United States" (*Handbook*, 1971, p. 243). The Historical Center is part of a section of the library called "Special Collections in Music," which also houses the archival collections of the International Society for Music Education; American Bandmasters Association; National Association of College Wind and Percussion Instructors; College Band Directors National Association; Mid-West International Band and Orchestra Clinic; Society for Ethnomusicology; International Clarinet Society; American String Teachers Association; Association for Recorded Sound Collectors; Music Library Association; International Association of Music Libraries, Archives, and Documentation Centers—U.S. Branch; Music OCLC Users Group; and the Irving and Margery Lowens Collection, which emphasizes American music scholarship. The International Piano Archives are also housed in the University of Maryland College Park Library, but are not part of the Special Collections in Music.

The Journal of Research in Music Education

The *JRME* is the most visible research endeavor of the MENC. It began publication in 1953 under the editorship of Allen P. Britton, who was chairman of the Editorial Committee. The original purpose of the journal was to publish "articles which report the results of research in any phase of music education." Three criteria for the acceptance of articles were listed in volume 1, number 2 (pp. 155–156) by Britton: (1) "Is the article based upon serious and extended study of some aspect of music education?" (2) "Is the author of the article a member of the music education profession?" (3) "Is the article based on an academic thesis or dissertation in music education?" The second and third criteria were not required, but were given high priority.

For several years many *JRME* articles were based largely on historical and descriptive research. By the early 1960s music educators, like educators in other fields, had begun to value experimental methods, and the contents of *JRME* reflected that trend. With the appointment of Robert G. Petzold as editor in 1972, the majority of articles had begun to reflect experimental and descriptive research techniques. James C. Carlsen became editor in 1978, George L. Duerksen (acting editor) in 1981, Jack A. Taylor in 1982, and Rudolph Radocy in 1988. The journal publishes "reports of research that clearly make a contribution to theories of music education." It includes research based on experimental, descriptive, historical, and philosophical techniques. Cornelia Yarbrough's (1984, pp. 213–220) content analysis of *JRME* from 1953 to 1983 indicated the following proportions of articles based on the various research techniques:

Historical:	16.17%
Philosophical	3.77%
Experimental	31.13%
Descriptive	41.51%
Behavioral	.63%
Other	6.29%

George Weimer (1980) provides a comparison between the emphases of *JRME* and the kinds of dissertations undertaken at universities. In a survey of 1,760 dissertations, he found 11 percent to be historical, 2 percent philosophical, 18 percent concerned with instruction in music education, 32 percent evaluation, 8 percent musical structure, and 8 percent instructional technology, in addition to 10 percent in miscellaneous categories.

OTHER ORGANIZATIONS AS OUTLETS FOR RESEARCH REPORTS

One of the effects of the growth of research during the second half of the twentieth century has been a significant increase in the number of scholarly journals through which researchers could disseminate their findings. Between 1900 and 1949, an average of 6.2 new music journals were founded each decade. Fifty-eight journals were founded during the 1950s, about 37 in the 1960s, and 41 in the 1970s. At least eight more were founded in the early 1980s (Basart, 1984). Included in these numbers are several devoted to music education research, and others that are related closely enough to be of interest to music education researchers. In 1989 alone, two new research-related journals in music education were established: *The Quarterly,* published by the University of Northern Colorado, and the *Southeastern Journal of Music Education,* published by the University of Georgia. The Florida Music Educators Association and the Canadian Music Educators Association annually devote one issue to reporting on research.

The Council for Research in Music Education

In 1963 a group of music education researchers met at the MENC convention in Minneapolis to form the Council for Research in Music Education. The Council members were researchers who had agreed to critique research studies. They assessed a few studies and disseminated the information as a pilot publication. The enthusiastic response indicated a strong need and desire in the music education research community for such a publication. CRME was initially sponsored by the University of Illinois and the Illinois Office of the Superintendent of Public Instruction, and the *Bulletin of the Council for Research in Music Education* is today published by the University of Illinois. Richard Colwell, of the University of Illinois, served as editor until 1989, when he left to become Distinguished Professor of Music at the University of Northern Colorado. Marilyn Zimmerman succeeded Colwell as editor.

Each issue of the *Bulletin* contains articles of interest to music education researchers and reviews by CMRE members of doctoral dissertations. CRME also publishes indexes of music education doctoral dissertations in progress and of recently completed dissertations available for review in the *Bulletin.*

The national journals discussed above (the *Journal of Research in Music Education* and the *Bulletin of the Council for Research in Music Education)* as well as the *Bulletin of Historical Research in Music Education* are indexed through 1984 in *Contemporary Music Education* by Michael L. Mark (1986)

The *Bulletin of Historical Research in Music Education* was founded by George Heller in 1980 as an outgrowth of the newly established History Special Research Interest Group of MENC. It is published at the University of Kansas and serves as a forum for music education historians, an outlet for publication of research findings in the history of music education, and a source of information pertinent to research in the history of the profession. It features "research of a philosophical and historical nature pertinent in any way to music education" (Heller, 1980).

UPDATE: The Applications of Research in Music Education was established in 1982 by Charles Elliott with funding from the University of South Carolina. The MENC assumed responsibility for it in 1990. Its purpose is to disseminate research findings to public school music teachers in a jargon-free manner. All articles are research based. Emphasis is on interpretation and application in the classroom rather than on research procedures and statistics.

GOVERNMENT SUPPORT FOR MUSIC EDUCATION RESEARCH

An important chapter in the history of American music education research occurred from the late 1950s to the 1970s, when the federal government became sufficiently interested in education to provide support for research in many disciplines, including music. One major effect of government involvement in educational research was the grouping of music education with the other arts education disciplines. Although government-sponsored arts education research was not always interdisciplinary, music education research was seldom identified as an entity in itself for the purpose of government funding.

The Arts and Humanities Program of the U.S. Office of Education

August Heckscher, a consultant to the U.S. Office of Education (USOE), reviewed the relationship between the government and the arts and wrote in 1963 that "at present the arts are given a low priority, or are even excluded in most educational and training programs; and basic research information in this field is scarcely pursued at all" (Murphy and Jones, 1976, p. 3). The sequence of events that led to funding for arts education research began when President Kennedy appointed Francis Keppel Commissioner of Education in 1962. Keppel in turn appointed Kathryn Bloom to be director to the Cultural Affairs Branch. Under Bloom, the Cultural Affairs Branch was renamed the Arts and Humanities Branch, which then became the Arts and Humanities Program (AHP) in 1965. The director of AHP was the Special Advisor to the Commissioner on the Arts and the Humanities, a position that strengthened the arts within the Office of Education. Unexpected support came from the President's Science Advisory Committee, which reported in 1962 that it was concerned with "the lack of balance in Federal assistance to the arts as compared to science." The committee's Panel on Educational Research and Development asked "whether curriculum reform as it has developed in science education could be applied to education in the arts" (Innovation and Experiment, 1974). An immediate result of the panel's advocacy of arts education funding was the organization of the Yale Seminar on Music Education.

In 1966 about $100 million was granted for arts education projects, mostly under the titles of the Elementary and Secondary Education Act (ESEA). The amount remained fairly constant for the next 3 years, after which it began to decline Title IV of ESEA, a relatively small program, provided funds specifically for "research and related activities in the arts and humanities." In only 2 years, 1966 and 1968, did it disburse more than $2,000,000, but it was important because "it made possible the first coherent national efforts in arts education research; it also provided an incentive for other arts education funding" (Murphy and Jones, 1976, pp. 3,4).

National and Regional Research Facilities

ESEA Title IV authorized $100 million over 5 years for national and regional research facilities, expansion of existing research and development programs, and a training program for educational researchers. Under Title IV, nine Educational Research and Development Centers were established to bring interdisciplinary talent together, to focus on crucial educational problems by means of long-range coordinated efforts, and to assist nascent educational innovations. The Educational Research and Development Centers were part of a larger group of institutions that included two Educational Policy Research Centers, two Vocational Education Research Centers, 15 Regional Educational Laboratories, and the Educational Resources Information Center (ERIC).

One of the most visible arts education projects to result from Title IV of the Cooperative Research Program was the Aesthetic Education Program of the Central Midwestern Regional Educational Laboratory (CEMREL) in St. Louis. The purpose of the project was to develop research data to support aesthetic education through arts education.

Project Zero at Harvard University received funding for aesthetic education research. It was so named because it began "with little more than a conviction of the task and some tentative notions as to where to direct our attention first." Project Zero has broadened from a research base to practical applications in schools, museums, and television. Its purpose is to investigate human symbolic functioning, with emphasis on creation and comprehension in the arts. The Project has sought participation and insights from the disciplines of philosophy, developmental and cognitive psychology, mathematics, and education, as well as the arts (Murphy and Jones, 1976, p. 21).

The Music Education Research Council received federal funds for three projects to train music education researchers (1968, 1969, 1970). The projects, known as MERC Research Institutes, were patterned after the earlier programs of the American Educational Research Association (AERA). The focus of the first workshop was research models, specifically experimental paradigms. The next year featured instructional models based on behavioral objectives. Both approaches were used at the third session (Nelson and Williams, 1977). Each session included at least 19 hours of formal instruction, additional informal tutorials, and small group discussions.

By 1970, Congressional action had reduced funding for educational research so drastically that future research training sessions could not be supported by government grants.

Other Federally Funded Research Projects

In addition to the above, ESEA Title IV funds sponsored numerous other research projects in arts education, many of which were in music education. Two of the initial grantees, Charles Spohn (1964, 1965, 1968) and Robert Petzold (1959, 1966), did a series of projects, including major longitudinal studies, that were early examples of excellence in funded research. Among the music education studies funded by Title IV were several that gained national recognition. They included the 1965 string project by Paul Rolland (1965, 1971), the Juilliard Repertory Project, parts of the Contemporary Music Project, and the Manhattanville Music Curriculum Project. In 1966 alone the USOE Arts and Humanities program supported 48 research projects in music, 46 in art, 18 in theater and dance, four in the arts in general, and 11 in the humanities. About 200 music education projects were sponsored during the 1960s, of which 30 to 40 were basic research (meaning a "search for new knowledge or better experimental confirmation of earlier findings"). About 70 were for developmental activities, and the rest were concerned with curriculum development, which USOE considered to be applied research in arts education. Of $11 million spent, about $2.1 million (20 percent) went for basic research, and $1.6 million (15 percent) for development. More than $7,000,000 (65 percent) was granted for applied research in curriculum and related matters (Murphy and Jones, 1976, p.9). Music received the most money—more than $3,000,000—and some projects were awarded amounts in the hundreds of thousands of dollars. The music and art projects differed in that the art educators were more concerned with the nature of art and aesthetics, whereas the music educators tended to concentrate more on such practical matters as teaching methods. The music grants supported 11 surveys, conferences, and curriculum studies.

The Decline of the Arts and Humanities Program

By the end of the 1960s the Arts and Humanities program was in decline; Congress had redirected its attention and resources to the social and political changes taking place in the United States. Much of its funding was redirected to the new National Endowments for the Arts and the Humanities, making it impossible for the U.S. Office of Education to continue supporting arts education research. Educational research at the federal level became the responsibility of the National Institute of Education (NIE), but it has made only limited support available for arts-related research. Some NIE projects have involved the arts, however, and as a result have been able to continue their research in arts education. The Central Midwestern Regional Education Laboratory (CEMREL) received funding, as did the Southwest Regional Education Laboratory, which was begun with Title IV funds and which took an elements approach to music education. Project Zero also received support.

In 1985 the 99th Congress recommended that the National Endowment for the Arts support arts education. One of the responses to the mandate was the establishment of the National Arts Education Research Center in 1987 at the University of Illinois and New York University, with joint funding from the United States Department of Education. The purpose of the Illinois site is "to conduct research on the status of arts education and on the processes involved in the development and implementation of arts education programs" (Leonhard, 1990). New York University's research center was continued beyond the initial 3-year period. Its purpose is to identify research projects that are school-important and to teach teachers to be researchers who can solve their own problems (Ross, 1990).

PRIVATE FOUNDATION SUPPORT OF MUSIC EDUCATION RESEARCH

Occasional instances can be found of private foundation support for music education research. Probably the most prominent example is the Contemporary Music Project, which began with a grant from the Ford Foundation in 1959 to establish the Young Composers Project. Taken over in 1963 by the Music Educators National Conference, the project was broadened to become the Contemporary Music Project for Creativity in Music Education (CMP). The Ford Foundation granted the MENC $1,380,000 to support the CMP, and later provided an additional $1,340,000. Many field research projects took place under the CMP, and one of the practical results was the development of comprehensive musicianship curricula.

Research Symposia

In the 1970s and 1980s several symposia were held to facilitate the dissemination of research information on various aspects of music education. It is noteworthy that the four symposia described here addressed widely divergent aspects of music education research—music education and psychology, music education and sociology, music education and American history, and philosophy of music education. Many of the symposia have resulted in published proceedings that have proved to be positive contributions to the literature of the particular interest groups involved.

The Ann Arbor Symposium on the Applications of Psychology to the Teaching and Learning of Music was held in 1978, 1979, and 1981 at the University of Michigan, sponsored by the university, the Theodore Presser Foundation, and the MENC. The purpose of the symposium was to explore the relationship between research in certain areas of behavioral psychology and music education. The Wesleyan Symposium on the Application of Social Anthropology to the Teaching and Learning of Music was held from August 6 to 10, 1984, under the sponsorship of Wesleyan University, MENC, and the Theodore Presser Foundation. Music in American Schools, 1838–1988, a historical research symposium, honored the 150th anniversary of the introduction of music as a curricular subject in American schools. It was held in August 1988 at the University of Maryland, at College Park. The Philosopher/Teacher in Music, a symposium on research and teaching in the philosophy of music education, was held at Indiana University in 1990.

THE RELATIONSHIP BETWEEN RESEARCH AND PRACTICE

An early example of the influence of music education research on the practice of music education is the first dissertation on a topic related to music education—Thaddeus L. Bolton's "Rhythm," which Humphreys cites as having influenced Philip C. Hayden. Hayden's 1907 demonstration of his work in teaching rhythm to children was the reason for the gathering of music supervisors at Keokuk, Iowa. That meeting led to the founding of the Music Educators National Conference. Hayden's work itself resulted from a research project that he called "Ear Training in Rhythm Forms" (Heller, 1982). Other bodies of research, such as the study of children's voices and the tests and measurements movement, have influenced music education practices.

In general, however, the relationship between research and practice in music education has not been strong. The educational psychologist Robert Glaser stated that research offers no firm scientific basis for educational practice. At best, research can assist educators in making sound decisions. He warns that research cannot substitute for creative intelligence in solving educational problems. Bennett Reimer agrees, saying the assumption that research is, or should be, applicable to practice is suspect.

Many researchers have taken the position that as the research literature grows, practitioners will find ways to use it to meet their needs. The research community, however, does not necessarily seek answers to practitioners' specific problems. Other researchers have suggested that mediators propose ways of implementing research in practice, and that teachers do their own research. The question has never been settled, however, and researchers remain a community somewhat separated from that of practitioners. In his 1986 MENC speech (unpublished), Robert Petzold discussed the relationship between research and practice. He said:

Education and music education have not yet satisfactorily solved the perennial problem of how to narrow that gap between what research has learned about ways to improve practice and what the practitioner is doing. Educational practice, based largely on tradition, common sense, experience, and common consensus is unlikely to change as a consequence of isolated studies which are seen to have little relationship to the music teaching-learning process. It is also unlikely to change until such time as practitioners themselves develop skills in evaluating and interpreting research findings that are relevant to their problems. That many practitioners lack an appreciation and understanding or research is due, in part, to the inconclusive of many of the research findings, to the kind of language used in reporting research, to the lack of communication and cooperation between researchers and practitioners, and the failure of the research community to interpret the research findings so as to produce meaningful, understandable materials targeted for use by practitioners. We already have . . . opportunities for dissemination. Until some of our research is meaningfully sensitive to the needs of practitioners and adequately conducted on significant problems, there is little reason for music teachers to be interested in our findings. Perhaps, as envisioned by the formation of SRIGs, a first step is to help music teachers work with researchers in actually *doing* some of the research.

A major reason for research having relatively little influence on practice in music education is that few researchers have carried on sustained research programs on single topic that are sufficiently evolutionary and developmental to justify the transition from theory to practice. Edwin Gordon (1980, 1984) is a rare example of a music education researcher who has pursued a single research interest over many years in order to bring his work to bear on practical teaching situations. After years of work in constructing theories, testing them in numerous studies, revising them as indicated by his findings, and retesting them, he has developed teaching materials and techniques based on his research.

As the call for educational accountability grows louder it may become necessary for practitioners to validate much of their work on the basis of research. In fact, proposed legislation in some states calls for a research base for educational practices. It would be ironic if legal requirements were to force a marriage of research and practice, when music educators have historically met with only limited success on their own. Regardless of legal issues, however, it is likely that teachers and researchers will continue to search for ways to strengthen their own endeavors by involving each other in the continued development and improvement of music education.

References

Barr, A. S., Davis, R. A., and Johnson, P. O. (1953). *Educational research and appraisal.* Chicago: J.B. Lippincott.

Basart, A. P. (1984). Editorial practice and publishing opportunities in serious English-language music journals: A survey. *Cum notis variorum, 79.* Music Library, University of California, Berkeley, 9–25.

Bergee, M. J., (1987). Ringing the changes: General John Eaton and the 1886 public school music survey. *Journal of Research in Music Education 35,* 103–116.

Buros, O. K. (1949). *The third mental measurement yearbook.* New Brunswick: Rutgers University Press.

Colwell, R. J. (undated). *A critique of research studies in music education* (Final report, USOE research project 6-10-245). Arts and Humanities Branch, U.S. Office of Education.

Dykema, P. A. (1928). A review of achievements and an outline of studies still to be made. *Journal of Proceedings for 1928* (Music Educators National Conference).

Fourth annual report (1969). (Report No. OE 6-10-061). Research and Development Center in Educational Stimulation, The University of Georgia, Athens, to the United States Office of Education.

Gordon, E. E., and Woods, G. D. (1984). *Jump right in: The music curriculum.* Chicago: G.I.A. Publications.

Gordon, E. E. (1980). *Learning sequences in music.* Chicago: G.I.A. Publications.

Gordon, R, D. (1978). Doctoral dissertations in music and music education, 1972–1977. *Journal of Research in Music Education, 26.*

Handbook of the society for research in music education. (1971). *Journal of Research in Music Education, XIX,* 243.

Heller, G. N. (1980), Call for historical research in music education. *Journal of Historical Research in Music Education* I, Vol. II., 24.

Heller, G. N. (1982). Reflections. *UPDATE: the Applications of Research in Music Education, I,* 25.

Humphreys, J. T. (1988). Applications of science: The age of standardization and efficiency in music education. *The Bulletin of Historical Research in Music Education, IX,* 4–5.

Humphreys, J. T. (1989). Bibliography of theses and dissertations related to music education, 1895–1931. *The Bulletin of Historical Research in Music Education, X,* 1–51.

Humphreys, J. T. (1985). The child-study movement and public school music education. *Journal of Research in Music Education, 33,* 79–86.

Humphreys, J. T. (1987). Music education and the school-survey movement. *The Bulletin of Historical Research in Music Education, VIII,* 33–43.

Humphreys, J. T. (1990). Thaddeus Bolton, the first dissertation in music education, and the founding of the Music Supervisors National Conference. *Journal of Research in Music Education, 38.*

Innovations and experiment in education. (1974). Progress report, Panel on Educational Research and Development, President's Science Advisory Committee. Washington: Government Printing Office.

Jones, R. S. (1957). Current trends and new directions in educational research. *Journal of Research in Music Education, 5.*

Kittle, J. L. (1932). Music education and scientific research. *Music Supervisors Journal, 18,* 39.

Kwalwasser, J. (1936). Significance of research to music education. *Music Educators National Conference Yearbook, 1935,* 162.

Larson, W. S. (1949). *Bibliography of research studies in music education: 1932–1948.* Washington: Music Educators National Conference.

Larson, W. S. (1957). Bibliography of research studies in music education, 1949–1956. *Journal of Research in Music Education, 5.*

Lee, W. R. (1982). Education through music: The life and work of Charles Hubert Farnsworth (1859–1947). Unpublished doctoral dissertation, University of Kentucky, Lexington.

Lendrim, F. T., (1961). Music for every child: The story of Karl Wilson Gehrkens. Unpublished doctoral dissertation, University of Michigan, Ann Arbor, 20–23.

Leonhard, C. (1990). The National Arts Education Research Center. *Bulletin of the Council for Research in Music Education, 105.*

Mark, M. L. (1986). *Contemporary music education.* New York: Schirmer Books.

Mr. Barnard's labors in Connecticut from 1838 to 1842 (1856). *Barnard's American Journal of Education, I* (695).

Murphy, J., and Jones, L. (1976). *Research in arts education: A federal chapter.* Washington: U.S. Department of Health, Education, and Welfare.

Nelson, C. B., and Williams, D. B. (1977). Review and survey of MENC research training institutes. *Journal of Research in Music Education, 25*: 1, 3–20.

Petzold, R. (1959). *The perception of music symbols in music reading by normal children and by children gifted musically.* U.S. Department of Health, Education, and Welfare ED 002 899.

Petzold, R. (1966). *Auditory perception of musical sounds by children in the first six grades.* U.S. Department of Health, Education, and Welfare ED 010 412.

Petzold, R., Heller, J., Colwell, R., Jason, J., and Moody, C. (1971). *Final report: Preconference educational research training pro-*

gram in music education (Project No. 0-03019, Grant No. OEG-0-70-2861[520]).

Platt, M. C. (1973). Osbourne McConathy: American music educator. *Journal of Research in Music Education, 21,* 173.

Reimer, B. (1985). Toward a more scientific approach to music education research. *Bulletin of the Council for Research in Music Education, 83,* 18.

Rideout, R. R., (1982). On early applications of psychology in music education. *Journal of Research in Music Education, 30,* 141–150.

Rolland, P. (1965). *A filmed demonstration of the teaching of Shinichi Suzuki with American preschool and grade school children and their mothers as subjects.* U.S. Department of Health, Education, and Welfare ED 003 083.

Rolland, P. (1971). *Development and trial of a two-year program of string instruction.* U.S. Department of Health, Education, and Welfare ED 054 190.

Ross, J. (1990). The National Arts Education Research Center at New York University: Challenging tradition. *The Quarterly 1, 2,* 14–21.

Schneider, E. H., and Cady, H. L. (1965). *Evaluation and synthesis of research studies relating to music education 33–35.* (Report no. E-016, U.S. Department of Health, Education and Welfare). Columbus: Ohio State University.

Silver, E. O. (1889). Special report on the condition of music instruction in the public schools of the United States. *Proceedings,* National Education Association.

Small, A. M. (Ed.). (1944). *Bibliography of research studies in music education 1931–1944.* Chicago: State University of Iowa Press for the Music Educators National Conference.

Spohn, C. L. (1964). *An evaluation of two methods using magnetic tape recording for programed instruction in the elemental materials of music.* U.S. Department of Health, Education, and Welfare ED 003 611.

Spohn, C. L. (1965). *A comparison between different stimuli combined with two methods for providing knowledge of results in music instruction.* U.S. Department of Health, Education, and Welfare ED 003 232.

Spohn, C. L. (1968). *Diagnosing and correcting individual deficiencies in learning music.* U.S. Department of Health, Education, and Welfare ED 019-292.

Thorndike, E. L. (1918). *The nature, purposes, and general methods of measurement of educational products.* Bloomington: National Society for the Study of Education, 17th Yearbook, 16.

UPDATE: The applications of research in music education (1982), *I.*

Weimer, G. (1980). *Trends in topics, methods of research and statistical techniques employed in dissertations completed for doctor's degrees in music education, 1913–1978.* Unpublished doctoral dissertation, University of Illinois, Urbana.

Wilson, M. E. (1936). Music education and scientific research. *Music Educators National Conference Yearbook, 1935,* 164.

Yarbrough, C. (1984). A content analysis of the Journal of Research in Music Education, 1953–1983. *Journal of Research in Music Education, 20,* 213–222.

·5·

SOURCES OF THEORY FOR RESEARCH IN SCHOOL MUSIC

Henry L. Cady
UNIVERSITY OF DELAWARE

Although there are philosophical and technical concepts for the role and practice of music education in schools, there is also the need for a theoretical formulation of it as a totality. Toward that end, this chapter is a discussion of theoretical thought potentially applicable to research regarding the teaching and learning of music in schools, preschool through twelfth grade.

The teaching and learning of music occur in a broad variety of situations for a variety of purposes. The consequent diversity of research interests is greater than can be included in this brief chapter. Necessarily, a selection of exemplary sources of theory in a few realms of knowledge is provided.

Key terms for the content of this chapter—"sources" and "theory"—are abstractions that require limitation for their use in formal discourse. Merton (1957) states the need for disciplined terminology: "Too often, a single term has been used to symbolize different concepts, just as the same concept has been symbolized by different terms," (p. 20). (For a discussion of the consequences of terminological confusion in sociological analyses, see Merton, 1957, pp. 20–25.)

Therefore, the following sections include (1) a discussion and an operational definition of "sources"; (2) an analysis of the term "theory," and an operational definition for it; and (3) a discussion of some theories from socially oriented fields of knowledge as examples of sources for theory construction and research in the teaching and learning of music in schools.

SOURCES DEFINED

Sources of theory for theoretical thought and theory construction in music education may be differentiated into three general kinds. Each source serves a different purpose, but in many research efforts they combine to make research processes possible by virtue of their unique combination.

The initial source for theoretical ideas is evident—it is the human mind, but a creative mind rather than one inclined to replicate and adapt. Another source is direct observation of students learning music, teachers teaching music, or the environment of music in our society both inside and outside schools, which results in analyses and interpretations. Others use these products as bases for historical searches, and to make rational analyses of music education as it is and as it ought to be. Finally, and this is the primary subject of this chapter, there are the sources in bodies of knowledge relevant to teaching and learning music, knowledge that colleagues in other disciplines have developed.

In the sense of the history of knowledge, music is now a differentiated, multidisciplinary realm. Accordingly, semantic differentiations have evolved for specializations or subsets in music research. Specifically in music education, these subsets of researchers apply knowledge from various disciplines external to music per se, such as philosophy, psychology, education, sociology, linguistics, computer technology, and history. Studies *in* music per se by scholars in music education are often directed at voids in repertoire, that is, by their composing or searching for appropriate works for pedagogical purposes.

The conversion of the concepts and the methodology of other disciplines into useful forms for research has been a major challenge for researchers in music education. The difficulty arises from the nature of music, its role in American society, and the unique behaviors required in teaching and learning music in diverse situations, as in churches, studios, and schools. Where theories exist in these subsets, they are related to, if not derived from, the theories of relevant bodies of knowledge.

"THEORY" CONSIDERED

The primary concern in and a condition for a functional inquiry is a creditable and methodologically plausible theory within which analyses of specific phenomena can be made. (Cf. Merton, 1957, pp. 3–16, for an extended discussion of this idea.) Such a theory may be in the mode of tacit knowledge or it may be explicitly detailed prior to an inquiry. Polanyi (1959) seems to make tacit knowledge the test for explicit knowledge: "We always know tacitly that we are holding our explicit knowledge to be true. . . . Tacit knowing appears to be a doing of our own, lacking the public, objective, character of explicit knowledge" (pp. 12–13).

The components of a theory are observation, well-considered assumptions, a logical structure, and a conclusion, which may be expressed in the form of interrelated propositions that are believed to be testable as hypotheses. The theory itself may be explicitly stated or tacitly known to the investigator.

Theory: A Semantic Problem

Consideration of theory and theory construction raises questions about definitions and semantic intentions. (For a discussion of definitions and concept formation in the sciences, see Hempel, 1952, pp. 2–49. Inasmuch as his exposition is based on traditional logic, his treatment has broad application.) The term "theory" is ambiguous, varying in meaning and specificity from colloquial to disciplined technical usages. Its ambiguity is found also in its use as a metaphor or figure of speech and as a synonym for "hypothesis." Furthermore, *Roget's Thesaurus* includes 19 categories under "theory," which include synonyms such as conjecture, suggestion, supposition, assumption, inference, surmise, and guesswork (Chapman, 1984).

"Theory" is used for differentiating arguments and endeavors qualitatively. One meaning is traceable to ancient Greek usage in which theory and practice were believed to be essentially different.

The object of theoretic knowledge is truth, while that of practical knowledge is action; for even when they are investigating how a thing is so, practical men study not the external principle but the relative and immediate application. (Aristotle, 1933, p. 87)

For the Greeks and Romans, art was the product of skills acquired through practice by the body; theory was the product of speculation and contemplation by the mind.

Hirst (1983) also makes a distinction between theory and practice, but of a different order:

I distinguish domains of practical theory from domains concerned simply with purely theoretical knowledge. The function of the latter is primarily explanation. The function of the former is primarily the determination of practice. The one is concerned with achieving rational understanding, the other achieving rational action. (p. 3)

Hirst's use of the term "rational" as a modifier for both understanding and action seems to be a rebuttal to the Aristote-

lian dichotomy. Also, he raises an interesting problem regarding the procedural and temporal relationship between the realities represented by "rational understanding" and "rational action," especially when applied to music as a performing art, that is, as a process-as-product phenomenon.

In contrast, Homans (1964) prefers what he considers to be the classical definition for theory: "This is the definition that identifies a theory of a phenomenon with an explanation of it by means of a deductive system" (p. 951). One can transform this definition into an expression such as "theory [explanation] of x" (adapted from Hodges, 1977, p. 19). Given the differentiated research endeavors in music education it seems advisable to modify that expression for this chapter to "sources of theory for [some subset of inquiry into school music]."

Theory as a Mode of Knowing

Theories are neither true nor false. If an explanation is comprised of truths, it is not theoretical by definition. If it is false, the assumptions or logic are false. Theories are credible because their information and logic have at least face validity. Their crucial value is their usefulness in the search for facts and the verification of understanding. They are offered as speculative designs of knowledge about a phenomenon constructed of deductive logic. (For another discussion of this point in this volume see the section "Deduction and Induction" in the chapter by Estelle Jorgensen.)

Beliefs are essentially attitudinal propositions of varying intensity. Definitions of belief include terms such as trust, faith, feeling, and confidence, which imply an interdependence of thought and emotion. (Cf. "belief" in *Webster's Dictionary*, 1948, and *The Oxford Universal Dictionary*, 1955.) The assumption here is that states of belief are inherent professional postures of scholars, and are integral in theory construction. (This use of "belief" is derived from Hodges, 1977, especially pp. 17–19.)

The genesis of theoretical exploration is found in a problem that arouses curiosity. According to Gephart (1967), such a problem is in "one of four situations: an anomaly, an unverified 'fact,' conflicting evidence, or an uncharted area" (pp. 148–153). Theories are stated in a variety of forms. The null statement is used in statistical studies to avoid the methodological difficulty of finding a truth. Theory and practice are frequently clarified by their juxtaposition, especially in the study of educational practice, as in the sequence theory-into-practice. Sometimes theories are antithetical, as in vigorous debates between technical and liberal educationists or between basic educationists and those who argue for a broad cultural interpretation of education.

What Theory Is Not

Inasmuch as a theory is a complex deductive argument, segments of it or individual statements extracted from it may be limited to specific problems; therefore they may, and often do, become formal hypotheses for investigation. The difference then between a theory and a hypothesis is that the latter is not an explanation. In Webster's third edition (1981) "hypothesis" is defined as follows: (1) "A tentative assumption made in order to draw out and test its logical or empirical consequences . . . " (2) "An assumption or concession made for the sake of argument . . . " (3) An interpretation of a practical situation or condition taken as ground for action . . . "

These may be stated in the statistical null form or in the historian's interrogatory form. For our purposes here, theories generate the hypotheses that are investigated. (Cf. "hypothesis" in *Webster's Third New International Dictionary,* 1981, and *The Oxford Universal Dictionary,* 1955.) Hypotheses derived from theory provide specific means for undertaking a search; they are methodological in kind—that is, instruments.

In music there is another peculiar problem in the use of the term "theory." Sometimes the term is misapplied as a result of the evolution of a discipline. Beginning study in so-called music theory is actually the equivalent to learning grammar, that is, learning the rules and preferred syntax in extant musical processes. These prescriptions can be defined ostensibly, that is, experiences through the senses as phenomena having well-known labels. At one time music theory statements were deduced explanations, but they are now formulas for common practice.

Another kind of confusion occurs between the concepts of theory and philosophy. They share commonalities in sources of information and fact. In a sense philosophy is explanation; but the intent of philosophy is the sharing of subjective argument with conclusions. Philosophical conclusions do not require considerations external to the experience and deductions of the individual. The proof of the conclusions is in the assumptions and logic of the argument. On the other hand, the proof of a theory is in its testing against reality external to its internal proof by deductive argument. The differences between the terms "theory" and "philosophy" is in the intent regarding generality and utility. The difference is not the value of either but rather the nature of each kind of inquiry and its products.

Theory Defined

With the preceding discussion in mind the following is offered as a definition for this chapter:

A theory is a logical deductive relationship among declarative sentences whose propositional quality yields the attitude found in statements of belief that offer an explanation of a phenomenon.

SOME SOURCES OF THEORY FOR RESEARCH FROM SOCIOLOGY, LINGUISTICS, AND HISTORY

As stated in the introduction, the purpose of this section is the identification of theories applicable to phenomena in music education. Included are three relevant disciplines—sociology of education, linguistics, and history. Numerous theoretical statements in these bodies of knowledge are spread throughout many kinds of publications.

To provide a reasonable, coherent treatment of these sources, the primary focus of suggestions for their application is music in education from preschool through secondary school, hereafter referred to as "school music."

The following is essentially a narrative synthesis of ideas common to much of the literature in each discipline, with citations of particularly significant or unusual contributions. The assumptions underlying the synthesis are founded in the nature of schools as *societal* institutions formed to transmit knowledge:

1. Their nature determines what is learned formally and systematically by children and demonstrates what knowledge is socially important by virtue of its inclusion in curricula.
2. Regardless of the nature of the knowledge being taught and learned in schools, the language(s) used in their societal environments is their primary method of communication.
3. The present evolutionary state of music education in the schools is a social history matter.

Sociology of Education

Theories of social systems can be applied to the organization of education. The concern is for school music as an enterprise within institutions that comprise social systems. The topics selected are political factors, values, social organizations, education as social organization, role theory, and knowledge.

Political Factors Social systems are products of dynamic collective sets of beliefs. Except during social upheaval, one or another set of beliefs politically dominates a social system until the desire for change exceeds the desire for stability. Beliefs about social matters are in a sense values underlying (1) preferences for modes of human behavior and (2) predictions of desired outcomes based on past experiences. These propositions regarding human living are useful in the analysis of school music. (Cf. Ostrom, 1961, p. 14; and Scott, 1964, p. 488.)

In a broad sense, education as a nationwide endeavor is a product of values pertaining to the knowledge and behavior of people as citizens, and the enrichment of societal living. In contemporary industrialized societies the primary social vehicle for realizing a system for education is the overarching political system, which acts according to its values.

The function of a political system in any society is to make choices from among the different courses of action that may be available to members of that society and to maintain the social system based upon those choices. The choices or decisions made by a political system are stated as rules, policies, or laws which prescribe a relationship among people by ordering their action and behavior with one another and with their universe. (Ostrom, 1961, p. 14)

If Ostrom's theory is correct, one may infer that tax-supported education and the role of music in it are products of this process, whether the choices are tacit or explicit.

The capabilities of a political system are dependent on the political system's prescription for education, that is, "for basic communication of knowledge which can serve as intelligence and skills" (Ostrom, 1961, p. 20). This implies that education is subsumed to the welfare of the political system, and is in part a function of the economic processes that support the political system; it provides a human investment in society's economic growth (Schultz, 1961, pp. 46–48). Accordingly, the acquisition of knowledge that does not contribute to economic growth has debatable value in terms of economic efficiency in the political system. Then, if Ostrom and Schultz are realistic, for some taxpayers in the United States, music in the education of children may have limited value or may be foregone completely. (Cf. Schultz, 1961, pp. 46–84, especially the section "Return to Education," pp. 73–82.)

Given the influence of values on choices, the organization of children's learning especially formalizes dominant collective beliefs about familiar problems: (1) who shall be taught, (2) what shall be taught, (3) who shall teach, (4) who decides what shall be taught, (5) what responsibilities shall be allocated to the custodians of learning processes, (6) what criteria shall be used in testing accountability for learning, and (7) who shall finance the learning and in what manner.

School music, if the arguments above are correct, is a product of value-laden choices made within the jurisdictions of political bodies such as school boards. The national effect is qualitative differences between educational jurisdictions regarding music education. Furthermore, the implication seems to be that education is fundamentally a political matter.

A problem then for the music education profession is the identification of the criteria by which analyses can be made of the differences among school systems. Ostrom (1961) offers criteria that seems to be useful in a variety of situations:

The basic criteria for judging the performance of a political system are: (a) the validity of its policies, (b) its standards of values or preferences, (c) its efficiency in realizing ends appropriate to these values or preferences, and (d) the responsibility of persons performing political roles in the system. (p. 17)

If these criteria are used as researchable propositions, perhaps reasonable arguments can be made that explain the nature of the support for school music across the United States.

Values Considered In the preceding discussion, the term "value" was used in the sense of beliefs or preferences for modes of behavior and predictions of desired outcomes. Because of the vulnerable role of music in tax-supported education particularly, societal values are a peculiarly intense concern of persons involved in school music. Therefore, a clear definition of the term "value" seems necessary. Several definitions are attributed to it (*Webster's Third New International Dictionary*, 1981).

In his analysis of the debate about value-neutral research among sociologists, Foss (1977) provides the following definition: "We take a broad working definition of value: beliefs about classes of objects, situations, actions, and wholes composed of them in regards to the extent that they are good, right, obligatory, or ought to be" (pp. 4, 112).

Also, he provides an addendum to his essay under the title "Values: Uses of the Term." Implicit in the term are "value judgments," which are differentiated into "judgments of obligation" (what one ought to do or is committed to) and "judgments of value" (what is preferred among choices). Within judgments of value are "moral" value judgments (good, bad, right, wrong) and "nonmoral" value judgments (without consideration for ethical attributes). Foss notes the differences among philosophical obligation, duty, and the moral element in values (Foss, 1977, pp. 113–115).

The investigator of school music may find in these differentiations discomfort among school personnel regarding the competing judgments of obligation on behalf of a significant other person and judgments of value according to one's own beliefs. As to the nature of the values toward school music in the tax-paying public, reliable and valid information is lacking.

Social Organizations Theories of organizations are applicable to all forms of bureaucratic structures offering music education. Clearly identifiable are two particular types of organizations that share the same concern for musical learning in formal education, the professional associations that support it, and the formal institutions that provide it.

A variety of associations contribute support to the teaching and learning of music in schools, such as the American String Teachers Association, the American Choral Directors Association, and the primary contributor, the Music Educators National Conference (MENC). The formal institutions that provide music education are diverse, such as private studios, tax-supported universities, and privately funded elementary schools.

Two early authors of theories about organizations were Max Weber and C. I. Barnard. Their basic ideas are summarized and integrated by Scott (1964) as follows:

Organizations are defined as collectives . . . that have been established for the pursuit of relatively specific objectives on a more or less continuous basis. . . . [Other distinctive features] include relatively fixed boundaries, a normative order, authority ranks, a communication system, and an incentive system which enables various types of participants to work together in the pursuit of common goals. (p. 488)

In a succinct synthesis of commonly accepted ideas about organizations, Merton (1957) begins with the following:

A formal, rationally organized social structure involves clearly defined patterns of activity in which, ideally, every series of actions is functionally related to the purposes of the organization. (p. 195)

He goes on to identify bureaucracy as the ideal type of such a formal organization, thereby including educational institutions.

In this theory for the analysis of such organizations, Scott (1964, p. 489) identifies three "levels" of inquiry:

1. Behavioral, or the study of the individual in the environment of the organization
2. Structural, or the explanation of the structural features and social processes in organizations
3. Ecological, or the organization as an entity interacting in a larger system of relations

Merton (1957) finds among other sociologists' works two basic categories of functions in formal organizations, which he forms into a theory:

Manifest functions and latent functions; the first referring to those objective consequences for a specified unit (person, subgroup, social or cultural system) which contribute to its adjustment or adaptation and were so intended; the second referring to unintended and unrecognized consequences of the same order. (pp. 62–63)

To summarize the preceding ideas, organizations have purposes for which persons fulfill responsibilities, communications are formed, and incentives are provided. All organizations function in a social environment with which they interact. The achievement of goals requires manifest functions; but latent functions may inhibit the success of manifest functions if they are not in agreement. These functions are found in three levels—behavioral, structural, and ecological—each of which may be analyzed in terms of stated objectives.

Education as Social Organization Clark (1964), a sociologist whose interest is in the theory of organizations, views education as a societal subsystem that is subdivided further hierarchically. For example, he limits "the definition of education to formally differentiated systems of instruction" (p. 735).

When analyzing music education in schools nationwide, those "differentiated systems" yield various kinds of subsystems having different effects on the musical learning of children—tax-supported educational institutions of all kinds varying in programs and curricula from theoretical to technical courses, church-related schools, university conservatories of music, and so forth. There are, of course, those that eschew bureaucratic relationships, such as private music schools, independent schools, individual church schools not under denominational control, and private studios.

As politicoeconomic systems with the objective of transmitting knowledge, bureaucratic subsystems have various structures. In tax-supported education, curricular choices for learning are implemented by forming school systems and subsystems within school systems, the school itself being the irreducible minimal organization.

Hallinan (1987) presents the theory that school organization is an expression of curriculum.

Viewing the curriculum as an organizational feature of the school underscores the fact that the curriculum and its organization are the primary determinants of what information students receive in school. (p. 5)

This theory recognizes the substance of the teaching-learning process as the central variable around which buildings are built, equipment is placed, and people are grouped.

Clark (1964) categorizes the sociology of education into four "sectors":

1. ". . . the connection of education to the external social structure . . ." (politics, economics, social strata, intersecting social groups—family, neighbors, peers)
2. ". . . the educational institution taken as whole, or in major segments larger than the individual agency of education . . . a web of organizations and associations . . ."
3. ". . . the internal life of the educational organization . . . (a) a formal organization, with bureaucratic and professional features; (b) a subculture, or a set of interrelated subcultures of students and faculty; and (c) a series of interactions of teachers and students centered on the formal instruction of the classroom."
4. ". . . education outside of Education, especially that which emerges as sizable organized components of other major institutions." (p. 735)

Clark's categorization, which is much like Scott's, is based on the interaction of an educational organization with other societal structures that impinge upon it and the interactive relationships within it. This categorization, for example, applies to the hierarchical structure of school music in tax-supported education.

The content of a school curriculum depends on a political body's dominant beliefs about the education and nurture of children. The evidence available from state departments of education is varied regarding the requirement of music as an essential form of knowing for children to learn (Steinel, 1985). In some states music instruction is required for all grades; in others, a requirement in only the seventh and eighth grades suggests questions about their philosophies of education. The values underlying these data are determinants of the purposes of schooling, which may or may not be functional in a broader cultural sense.

The functionality of a school system may be determined by using Ostrom's four criteria for judging the performance of a political system (see under "Political Factors" above). The success of a school system to meet school music objectives would mean that the political system's objectives for the schools are valid, the practiced standards and values are adequate, efficiency is practiced, and/or responsibilities are fulfilled. In brief, school music in such a situation is functional. If the consequences of the system are not anticipated and not desired, then school music is dysfunctional.

Roles in School Music In the preceding discussion under "Social Organizations," Scott (1964) identifies organizational variables affecting personnel: "relatively fixed boundaries, a normative order, and authority roles . . ." (p. 488). During the last quarter century, the study of these has generated an explanation of human behavior in bureaucracies known as "role theory."

With the use of this theory, a body of knowledge about human behavior has been developed that includes descriptors and methods of analysis. The following list of descriptors (key terms) is based on several authors' contributions and presents the more common terms and their definitions. (Cf.: Biddle and Thomas, 1966, pp. 28–31; Brookover and Gottlieb, 1964, pp. 321–325; Gould and Kolb, 1964, pp. 609–610; Scott, 1964, pp. 509–520; and Scileppi, 1984, pp. 60–67.)

Of primary value is the historical and comparative analysis of the definitions for role analysis terminology in Gould and Kolb (1964). A comparison between Biddle and Thomas (1966) and Biddle (1979) reveals that in a decade of conceptual and analytical changes role theory has come to include more of the subtlety and complexity in role behavior.

The key terms in role analysis are the following:

actor: the occupant of a prescribed position in an organization

role: expectations for behaviors by the occupant of a prescribed position in a social system; also those expectations applied to the individual who occupies that prescribed position

position: a prescribed location in a social group or social system; a location in a social structure

status: related to position, the expectations held for any occupant in a particular position

office: an authoritatively sanctioned and well-defined status such that the office is recognized rather than the person occupying it

convergence-divergence: the agreement and disagreement among different groups for a role, also labeled "interposition consensus"

significant others: individuals with whom the occupant of a position (actor) relates in particular ways.

reference groups: any group of people whom the occupant (actor) perceives to be significant for his or her role, that is, to the actor's professional and/or personal behavior and welfare.

The preceding list of descriptors is useful for clarifying the roles and consequent expected behaviors of personnel in schools. For example, the nature of both the economic support and the reference groups who supply it may be a distinguishing factor among music teachers in tax-supported school districts that differ in socioeconomic characteristics. (For examples of role studies see Hoffer, "Sociology and Music Education," Chapter 50 in this volume.)

Knowledge As noted above, Hallinan (1987) identifies curriculum as the central variable about which schools are organized. The brief discussion that follows is concerned with the course in music as organized knowledge for students to acquire in a social environment that determines what knowledge shall be included and how it will be taught and learned. This is a social phenomenon to be accounted for in constructing a theory of school music.

Sociologists make a distinction between a sociological theory of knowledge and a sociology of knowledge. The latter, a comparatively recent development (Teeland, 1971, p. 12), is the context for the following discussion, which includes sources of theory that connect social influences and

school curricula. Also included is a clarification of the difference between epistemology and the sociology of knowledge according to some sociologists' definitions.

Historically, curiosity about knowledge as a sociological rather than an epistemological problem began in the eighteenth century. Although epistemology is traceable to the ancient Greeks, the sociology of knowledge, as we know it today, has a classical tradition that began in the eighteenth century among French and German scholars. There was little interest in the United States until the second half of the twentieth century. As in the classical tradition, the primary concern has been theoretical thought (Hamilton, 1974, pp. 15–134, Stehr and Meja, 1984, pp. 1–18).

One finds little agreement about a definition for this field of inquiry. The following are a few examples of definitions.

What do we mean exactly by the term 'sociology of knowledge'? It is primarily the study of functional correlations which can be established between the different types, the differently emphasized forms within these types, the different systems (hierarchies of these types) of knowledge, and, on the other hand, the social frameworks, such as global societies, social classes, particular groupings and various manifestations of sociality (microsocial elements). . . . (Gurvitch, 1971, pp. 16–17)

Teeland (1971) quotes Berger and Luckman (1963, p. 11), agreeing with their view: "The sociology of knowledge is concerned with the relationship between human thought and the social context within which it arises" (p. 2). This is a derivative of Merton's (1957) assertion of an earlier date that the sociology of knowledge is "primarily concerned with the relations between knowledge and other existential factors in the society or culture" (p. 456).

Merton then provides a "Paradigm for the Sociology of Knowledge." It is based on five relationships between existence and mental productions: (1) Where are the relationships located? (2) Which are being analyzed? (3) How are they related? (4) What is the condition of their manifest and latent functions? and (5) When do the relationships occur? (pp. 460–461).

In recent years Merton's position that knowledge has an existential basis has become predominant. However, the interpretation of that belief has yielded disagreement over what circumstances produce what knowledge. A theory of school music presumably would address this disagreement. For example, a long-standing principle in music education has been educating children from what they know and from their own cultural base. But the influence of a common mass media and mass marketing of music seems to confuse the definition of cultural musical differences as a basis for selecting school music curricular content.

Sociologists find a difference between epistemology and the sociology of knowledge. The former is the study of the relation between what the perceiver receives and the object being perceived. However, when the existential condition of the perceiver is considered, as suggested above by Teeland and Merton, then social variables must be included in a theory as contributing to knowledge learned.

The epistemologist was and continues to be, though modified in interests, a philosopher (Fuller, 1988, p. xi). In the classical tradition, the sociologist is a social scientist with concern for the positivistic and empirical aspects of research into knowledge as a phenomenon. But then, Fuller insists that epistemology has always been sociologically oriented in that knowledge itself is a social phenomenon. However, for the epistemologist the question of validity is not addressed empirically but rather logically.

Another aspect of musical knowledge is its classification. Brief histories of efforts to classify knowledge in the arts and sciences by Tatarkiewicz (1973, pp. 456–462) and Speziali (1973, pp. 462–467) provide an overview of the changes in classifications from ancient Greece to this century. These changes are a result of the evolution of knowledge about each mode of thought in each body of knowledge, a difficult process. It seems that music is especially difficult to classify; it is omitted by these authors, an omission implying residual effects of the Aristotelian dichotomy.

The role of music in the school curriculum, especially tax-supported schools, may be a function of its social position as knowledge, that is, its classification according to social criteria. Apparently, the variability of that position may be attributable to the values related to the general and local public's perception of music as a mode of knowing and as functional knowledge.

Linguistics

The social study of education includes the methods of communication in the teaching-learning process. The primary method is through language, regardless of subject matter, persons, or place. Its use in musical instruction then is a problem of interest to those who seek valid teaching methods and a reasonable explanation of the nature and meaning in the subject.

The relationship of language to music is seen as a problem appropriate to this chapter because of the long and complex association between them. Yet disciplined study of that relationship is sparse.

The following discussion includes (1) some apparent reasons why the relationship is complex, (2) a brief description of linguistics, the study of language, and (3) presentations of some theoretical concepts from the four primary branches of linguistics—hermeneutics, historical-comparative method, semiotics, and structuralism—with suggestions concerning their relevance to theory construction in school music.

Underlying the following discussion are assumptions: (1) the term "music" is the label for the organized sound that musicians make; (2) musicians know what music is per se, as a body of knowledge, and especially as a mode of knowing; and (3) the score is not music but rather the "blueprint" for making it.

The Problem The relationship between music and language is essentially twofold. First, the use of the term "music" in various literary forms as analogy, simile, or metaphor has a long history. Numerous entries in Bartlett's *Familiar Quotations* illustrate this use for flights of fancy, wonders of planetary order, a wide range of emotions, nobility of human spirit, and so forth (Bartlett, 1968).

Second, musicians themselves not only have engaged in this practice but also have used common language terms as technical language, seemingly equating and even subsuming music to language. Terms such as phrase, sentence, and period have been used in musical analysis for over a century (Grove 1879–80; Apel, 1969). Some authors of books about music assume music to be a language (Spalding, 1939; Manoff, 1982). Rosen (1972) uses language as a fundamental concept in his discussion of the classical style, entitling his introductory chapter "Musical Language of the Late Eighteenth Century" (p. 19).

Implied in these usages is the existence of a satisfactory theory of music that explains music as a linguistic form or, contrarily, a satisfactory theory of language that explains music. There is also the implication that music is categorically one of many languages, that is, another means of *linguistic* expression. But then, it may be argued, the term "language" itself has evolved into a metaterm, an abstraction that includes all means of human communication. Consequently the question arises: Is it true that music is a language?

The belief in the equivalence of music and language seems to be based on their commonalities, including the use of sounded and/or written signs and symbols, such as the following:

1. Conventional elements that comprise events (sound or their signs)
2. Conventional successions of events implying meanings
3. Conventional syntax for successions of events conveying meaning
4. A grammar derived from practice of conventional syntax
5. Fulfillment of criteria for interpersonal and/or inter-group transfer of knowledge

But then this list could be applied to several nonlinguistic phenomena, possibly leading to a discussion of a unified theory of communication for all forms of human expression.

Linguistics Described The analytical, descriptive mode for the study of language is the field of linguistics; musical analysis is its equivalent in the study of music. The genesis of linguistics seems to have been in the ancient Greeks' curiosity about speech; today it includes all forms of spoken and written language.

The study of language has concentrated on three main fields: the origin of language, the relation between language and reality, and the structure of language. The first is bound up with questions of religion or cosmogeny, the second is epistemological, while the third may be called the field of pure linguistics or grammar. (Ellegard, 1973, p. 661)

Newmeyer (1986) considers linguistics a field of inquiry composed of "three orientations—humanistic, sociological, and autonomous'' (p. 8). Humanists are interested in the ''linguistic analysis of literary texts and . . . the study of figurative, aesthetic, and creative use of language in literature'' (p. 8). Sociolinguists are interested in ''the functioning of language in society'' (p. 8). Autonomous linguistics ''attempts to formulate the principles governing structural regularity in language'' (p. 8), having subareas of '' 'phonology,' the study of sound patterning; 'morphology,' the study of word formation; and 'syntax,' the study of sentence construction'' (p. 9).

Ellegard and Newmeyer speak for scholars who believe linguistics is a science, having characteristics similar to those of the social sciences, but sufficiently different to be considered autonomous. However, positivism has been rebutted by those who subscribe to a humanistic view of language.

Hermeneutics The humanistic school of philosophy has formalized a mode of linguistics under the rubric ''hermeneutics,'' a term derived from the ancient Greek word for ''interpretation.'' Its argument is that many language research findings are neither quantifiable or generalizable, that some uses of language are unique to a particular speaker. These ideas arise from a philosophy of inquiry that differentiates between human and physical phenomena:

I shall use the term 'hermeneutics' to denote all those schools of thought which make an irreducible distinction between observation and understanding, and claim that the investigation of human phenomena is, in one way or another, qualitatively different from the investigation of physical reality. (Itkonen, 1978, p. 20)

Not only is positivism rejected but also a uniform methodology is claimed to not exist.

As a purely informal characterization, it might be said that hermeneutics acquires its data through understanding meanings, intentions, values, norms, or rules, and that hermeneutic analysis consists in reflection upon what has been understood. (Itkonen, 1978, p. 20)

Thus Itkonen sustains the long-standing debate about different kinds of abstraction, and the nature of the knowledge necessary for justifying such abstractions as valid representations of reality. He also reasserts the humanist's skepticism of scientific reductionism applied to human behavior. Since children learn their culture and that culture is changing relentlessly, a subscriber to hermeneutics could assert that social scientific assumptions about data for curricular structure development and methodologies (language usage) as well are irrelevant, and that the data for curricular design are necessarily rational rather than empirical.

Historical-Comparative Method Some scholars find the beginning of modern linguistics in the close of the eighteenth century. The relationship, implying a common origin, was found then between the ancient Sanskrit language and several European languages (Newmeyer, 1986, pp. 17–18; Hoenigwald, 1973, p. 65). The procedure used in this discovery was the historical-comparative method, or diachronic method, by which comparison of linguistic elements was made between contemporary languages. Its central concern was the origin of languages (Ellegard's first field), and was the discipline for the study of languages until the beginning of this century.

Rules and procedures for this method were formalized in the first half of the nineteenth century. By the end of the nineteenth century, many linguists had accepted the idea that within languages there is structure that is independent of all other factors. The uniqueness of the rules they developed through diachronic study led scholars to believe language was an innate competence. This yielded what is now called by some ''autonomous linguistics'' (Newmeyer, 1986, p. 21–24; Hoenigwald, 1973, pp. 65–73).

In music, the historical–comparative method was used early in this century by students of folk music, who sought the origins of songs. A comparison between pre– and post–World War II elementary school music textbooks reveals the effects of that procedure. Furthermore, this early interest evolved into the disciplines of ethnomusicology and social anthropology of music, providing the cultural variety of musics available for schools today. (cf. MENC, 1985, *Becoming Human Through Music).* However, the application of this method seems to have doubtful value in analyzing the analogy or the equation between music and language.

Semiotics Ellegard's second field, semiotics, as we know it today was begun at the turn of this century by Ferdinand de Saussure (1857–1913) and C. S. Peirce (1839–1914). Saussure proposed:

A science that studies the life of signs within society is conceivable: it would be a part of social psychology and consequently of general psychology; I shall call it semiology (from the Greek *semeion,* ''sign''). Semiology would show what constitutes signs, what laws govern them. . . . Linguistics is only a part of the general science of semiology; the laws discovered in semiology will be applicable to linguistics, and the latter will circumscribe a well-defined area within the mass of anthropological facts. (Saussure, 1959, p. 16)

Peirce proposed:

Logic, in its general sense, . . . is only another name for *semeiotic* (*semeiotike*), the quasi-necessary, or formal, doctrine of signs. By describing the doctrine as ''quasi-necessary,'' or formal, I mean that we observe the characters of such signs as we know, and from such an observation, by a process which I will not object to naming Abstraction, we are led to statements, eminently fallible, and therefore in one sense by no means necessary, as to what *must be* the characters of all signs used by a ''scientific'' intelligence, that is to say, by an intelligence capable of learning by experience. (Hartshorne and Weiss, 1932, p. 134)

Guiraud (1975) interprets the two positions: ''Saussure emphasizes the social function of the sign, Peirce its logical function. But the two aspects are closely correlated and today the words semiology and semiotics refer to the same discipline'' (p. 2).

A recent author, Clarke (1987), defines ''semiotic'' as ''the discipline delimited by Peirce, with its subjects including linguistic and non-linguistic signs, and including natural events not produced for the purposes of communication'' (p. 37). This interpretation of Peirce's definition unifies all inquiry into the relationship between all signs and their reality under the term "semiotic." (Clarke uses the singular form, tracing its use to the ancient Greeks, but the use of the plural form is apparently more common.)

Students of Susanne Langer (1957, pp. 57–64) will note that her distinction between signs and symbols has become blurred inasmuch as the terms "sign" and "signification" predominate in the literature of semiotics, a dubious development. Notably, Peirce included icon, index, and symbol under sign, a distinction blurred in subsequent linguists' works (Hartshorne and Weiss, 1932, pp. 156–173). Semiotics suggests a variety of investigations in the music teaching-learning process, especially the problematic mixture of technical terms unique to music and terms in common language. The latter, vernacular terms, are dependent on linguistic, musical, and social contexts for their meaning, the context of realities but not the realities themselves.

How this semiotic problem should be analyzed is debatable. For illustrative purposes, consider Guiraud's (1975) approach:

The function of the sign is to *communicate* ideas by means of *messages*. This implies an object, a thing spoken about or *referent, signs* and therefore a *code,* a *means* of transmission and obviously an *emitter* and a *receiver.* (p. 5)

Then, citing precedents, Guiraud presents six linguistic functions (pp. 6–9):

1. Referential function—"defines the relations between the message and the object to which it refers."
2. Emotive function—"defines the relations between message and the emitter."
3. Conative or injunctive function—"defines the relation between message and the receiver"
4. Poetic or aesthetic function—"[defines] the relation between the message and itself. . . . In the arts, the referent is the message, which thus ceases to be the instrument of communication and becomes its object."
5. Phatic function—"affirms, maintains or halts communication."
6. Metalinguistic function—"defines the meaning of any signs which might not be understood by the receiver. . . . [It] refers one back to the code from which the sign takes its meaning. It plays a considerable role in the arts; 'writing' is a signal of the code." [N.B. codes are systems of social conventions.]

Much of Guiraud's approach is from information theory, semantics, and communication theory. These are also the basis of the later work of Clarke, cited above, who broadens the information base to research on animal behavior, a different categorization system, and greater specificity in examples from the visual arts. Neither of these authors refers to music; both speak of the arts as communication.

The literature explaining the application of semiotics to the arts is relatively recent, and much of it is analyses of the written word—prose, poetry, and drama. There have been efforts to apply the methods of semiotics to music, primarily vocal works, as in the early work of Bogatyrev (1936, 1976).

Di Pietro (1979) discusses the differences between spoken and musical theater. They include the semiotic function of music in support of language, scenery, actions, and "illocutionary forces which shape the actions of the stage characters" (p. 31).

Disagreement about the application of semiotic techniques to music is expressed by Orlov (1981). He finds that

musical sound meets the definition neither of sign nor of the icon. As a sign, the sound would have to have a recognizable identity and to stand for an extraneous reality, which it obviously does not. . . . As an icon, the sound would have to resemble in a way, be similar to, what it signifies (pp. 131–137)

The problem of meaning from a musician's point of view is discussed by Meyer (1967) as being of two kinds—designative and embodied (see especially Chapters 1 and 3). He distinguishes three viewpoints about signification among listeners—formal, kinetic-syntactic, and referential (pp. 42–43).

Kivy (1990) addresses the problem from a philosopher's viewpoint. He states his personal epistemological theory of music as follows: "'Music alone' as I have called it, is a quasi-syntactical structure of sound understandable solely in musical terms and having no semantic or representational content, no meaning, making reference to nothing beyond itself" (p. 202). Kivy and Meyer give music educators the poles of disagreement: Meyer believes that music has communicable intellectual content (meaning) and Kivy does not (cf. Cady, 1987). Consequently, they raise profound questions about the value of music in education, such as: Is it true that music has meaning that is communicable?

Structuralism Another field in the study of language, Ellegard's pure linguistics or structuralism, demonstrates apparent commonalities between music and language. Constructing a theory for the structure of language is methodologically similar to constructing a theory for the structure of music. Because of their rules and conventions (their grammars) both can be analyzed according to the premises of "structuralism."

According to the standard structuralist account, structures are structures *of* systems; systems function, structures in themselves do not function—but systems function because they have the structures they do. . . . structure is not merely form; form is something that can be abstracted from matter or content and considered separately, whereas structure, in the structuralist sense, is precisely the significant (as opposed to material) content of the system. (Caws, 1973, p. 322)

These are intriguing distinctions for the musician who lives with the forms of music, which are organizations of sound that result from making tonal relationships according to precedents and rules of composition within conventions of preference.

The term "structuralism" is found in the vocabulary of biology in the seventeenth century, appearing later in nineteenth-century analyses of language, literature, and philosophy. Its origin, as we know its meaning and use today, is attributed to Saussure (Caws, 1973, pp. 322–323).

The objective of structuralism is the irreducible form of language, especially spoken language. According to Salverda (1985), Saussure considered the linguistic problem to be twofold.

[First,] . . . it is the *langue,* the language system that one can distinguish behind the multitude of language phenomena, which forms the central conceptual entity that has to be studied in linguistics . . . a synchronic system of signs. (p. 11)

[Second,] . . . Saussure held it to be necessary for linguists to pay no regard to individual acts of speaking which constitute the *parole* [common speech, a diachronic variable]. (pp. 11–12)

In the 1950s a major development occurred with the introduction of generative-transformational grammar by Noam Chomsky (1957). The old rules for constructing and analyzing verbal communication were replaced with rules for two levels of structure—surface structure (*parole*) and deep structure (*langue*). The deep structure rules are intended to find the fundamental language elements that form all languages, that is, the structure of a universal language. Chomsky echoes the diachronists by asserting an innate human linguistic competence.

In music, there has been a recent substantial effort to modify Chomsky's grammar for the creation of a theory of tonal music (Lerdahl and Jackendoff, 1983). This work fulfills the definition of a theory presented earlier in this chapter.

Language in the Chomskian sense has a dual component structure—syntactic and phonological. The syntactic is useful in analyzing language that is written and spoken. The phonological is applicable to speech only. Syntactic analysis, which applies to the musical score primarily, has been the music theorist's forte. The work of Lerdahl and Jackendoff contributes to a theory of musical process as well as structure, but seems not applicable to the semantic problem.

The field of linguistics is useful in considering the nature of a theory of music per se and a theory of music education. There are apparently three integrated essential facets (aspects) of music—syntactic (logic), semantic (signification or symbolization), and affective (feeling or emotion)—as a social as well as psychological phenomenon.

Finally, there is an ethical imperative in verbal representations of music to children. Peirce addressed this imperative for his own studies by posing the following question in his "Ethics of Terminology":

What principle is there which will be perfectly determinative as to what terms and notation shall be used, and in what sense, and which at the same time possesses the requisite power to influence all right-feeling and thoughtful men? (Hartshorne and Weiss, 1932, p. 130)

History

During the last decade both the number of historians of music education and their products have increased. Evidently there is an increasing need among music educators to know the precedents and standards of the past that may be useful in our own time, especially for determining change and progress in school music.

This discussion is a brief presentation of the historian's concepts of history, historiography, and theories of history. Also, applications of those theories to school music are suggested.

Fortunately, present historiographers of school music live in a time when ideologies of history and historiography have waned, a great advantage over the past. Collingwood (1956) describes the contemporary state of historiography in this way:

Historians nowadays think that history should be (a) a science, or an answering of questions; (b) concerned with human actions in the past; (c) pursued by interpretation of evidence; and (d) for the sake of human self-knowledge. (pp. 10–11)

History and the Historian In most of their research, historians want to know what happened, where it happened, when it happened, who did it, and why was it done. The quasi-detective role of the historian is clear. Also, there is awareness of the individual historian's role in the making of history, another social peculiarity having a past of its own.

Several authors have discussed what history is, the evolution of its theories, and what a historian does (the content of this section is based on the general agreement regarding the theories of history or similar interpretive ideas found in the following sources: Bloch, 1953; Carr, 1967; Collingwood, 1956; and Nash, 1969.). One might say that the history of historiography is a description of the evolution of two contrasting assumptions about the historian's role and the historian's product. Those assumptions, discussed below, were realized to be complementary only in this century. The evolution of that relationship was a consequence of jousting through 2,500 years between the literalism of chroniclers and the romanticism of idealists.

The beginning of history, that is, the writing about events after they happened and trying to do so with information from as reliable sources as possible, either verbal or written, began in ancient Greece and was carried on by the Romans. Quasi records were kept earlier, mostly in documents related to religion, governance, business, and social history. The language used then by custom not only obscured facts about human behavior but also was mostly ceremonial in character. The historian and archeologist have had to tease out of the earliest documents the facts about human activity.

There is agreement that the beginnings of history as we know it are found in the works of Herodotus and Thucydides. They were early chroniclers of human life, less interested in the why or the threads of history than in the what, who, where, and when. They sought to record the past events in ancient Greece, an endeavor that continues today among those who seek factual information about the past. This is the present task of scholars in the history of music education, a comparatively uncharted area.

In ancient times, those who recorded events assumed that it was possible to know all of the facts; but Socrates challenged that assumption, a challenge that thrived again in eighteenth-century rationalism. Specifically, eighteenth-century rationalists believed that an interpretation of humans' life on earth was the objective of the historian, not merely the collection of data for descriptions of human behavior.

Thus two basic concepts of history were sustained by historians into this century. Establishing this dichotomy as an assumption for his essays, Carr (1967) cites the comments of two editors of *The Cambridge Modern History*. Lord Acton, in 1907, foresaw an "ultimate history" because "all information is within reach, and every problem has become capable of solution" (p. 3). In 1957, Sir George Clark disagreed with Lord Acton because historians "expect their work to be superseded again and again . . . that knowledge has come down through one or more human minds, and has been 'processed' by them" (p. 4). Not until this century has this dichotomy resolved into mutually beneficial contributions from both.

Theories of History Today, several theories of history have their supporters. The most common are discussed below as having usefulness in the study of school music.

The *"Great Man Theory"* derives from the belief that people make events and therefore history. This has been an assumption underlying collegiate music history and music appreciation texts, with few exceptions. It is also a dominant theme in Birge's history of school music (Birge, 1937).

The "Cyclical Theory" is well-known to musicians, revolving attitudes of classicism and romanticism being the framework for many music histories. The essence of this theory is in the dominant-recessive cycle of human beliefs that seems to be a product of human need for order and change; that is, order begets change begets order, and so forth. Such cycles are found in histories of education—for example, between education through an individualistic, child-centered curricular structure and through a core of basic, unchanging knowledge that all school children must learn.

There is a belief that chance, perhaps better described as serendipity, accident, or fortuitous coincidence, is the genesis of historically significant events. Carr (1967) dubs this the "Cleopatra's Nose Theory," inasmuch as her beauty was the "cause" of a succession of events (p. 128). It is a rebuttal to the Great Man Theory. So-called great men are forced into prominence by coincident events, their greatness resting on the effectiveness with which they meet events or are fortuitously directed by them, and on the consequent social legacy of their actions.

In the history of school music there is a coincidence that preceded related subsequent events. At the close of World War I military band musicians were discharged during the period that schools were increasingly interested in developing instrumental music programs. Following that coincidence there was an increase of instrumental music instruction in schools.

Causation, sometimes called "determinism," is a belief that some consecutive events have a cause-and-effect relationship. The belief is that the result of such events could not have been different. If the result had been different, the events in that succession would have been necessarily different. This belief has a long history in the human mind; however, it is contradicted by those who believe in free will.

To apply the idea of causation to events in the history of school music leads to a network of causes. It is comprised of a complex of variables of different sorts, each having a different history—teaching, curricula, school boards, community values, learning, mass communication, technological change.

Collingwood (1956) interprets causation from a different perspective. He asserts that history is about the actions of people, thoughts in the mind lead to actions, and the thoughts behind the actions are the cause of the actions. Essentially, history is the history of thought (p. 215).

Progress, for those who live in industrialized societies. is assumed to exist and to be a desirable objective. The roots or seeds of the idea are traceable to the ancient Greeks, but its contemporary meaning is comparatively recent. Ginsberg (1968) states that "the belief in progress, the idea that human history forms a movement, more or less continuous, towards a desirable future, began to take shape late in the seventeenth century" (p. 633).

Collingwood (1956) identifies two kinds of progress: "progress in nature," which he equates with evolution of natural species into more adaptable and complex forms (p. 321), and "historical progress," which he considers to be "not merely . . . new actions or thoughts or situations belonging to the same specific type, but a new specific type" (p. 324). Perhaps this could be interpreted to mean that the founding of tax-supported school music in the nineteenth-century United States was the beginning of "a new specific type" of music education.

Nisbet (1980), in a comparatively recent analysis of the concept's history and a critical discussion of its contemporary meaning, gives this definition at the beginning of his work: "Simply stated, the idea of progress holds that mankind has advanced in the past—from some aboriginal condition of primitiveness, barbarism, or even nullity—is now advancing and will continue to advance through the foreseeable future" (pp. 4–5). He then states that from the ancient Greeks to the present time there have been two propositions:

First, slow, gradual, and accumulative improvement in *knowledge,* the kind of knowledge embodied in the arts and sciences. . . .
The second . . . centers upon man's moral or spiritual condition on earth, his happiness, his freedom from torments of nature and society, and above all his serenity or tranquillity. (p. 5)

In applying the idea of progress to school music, one wonders, what phenomenon is eligible logically to be tested with the idea? Nisbet's first proposition, the improvement in knowledge, could lead to speculation about changes during this century, for example, in the content of school music textbooks and in the instructional competencies of school music teachers.

Regarding Nisbet's second proposition, it may be difficult to conceive of an application of the adjectives "moral" and "spiritual" to progress in the teaching and learning of music in schools. Both Collingwood and Nisbet, among others, argue that there are substantive problems in finding progress in the moral or spiritual aspects of human existence.

References

Apel, W. (1969). *Harvard dictionary of music* (2nd ed., rev. and enl.). Cambridge: Belknap Press of Harvard University Press.

Aristotle. (1933). *Metaphysics, book 2.* (H. Tredenick, Trans.). Loeb Classical Library. Cambridge: Harvard.

Bartlett, J. (1968). *Familiar quotations* (14th ed., rev. and enl.). (E. M. Beck, Ed.). Boston: Little, Brown.

Berger, P. L., and Luckman, T. (1963). *The social construction of reality.* New York: Penguin Books.

Biddle, B. J. (1979). *Role theory: Expectations, identities, and behaviors.* New York: Academic Press.

Biddle, B. J., and Thomas, E. J. (Eds.). (1966). *Role theory: Concepts and research.* New York: John Wiley.

Birge, E. B. (1937). *History of public school music in the United States* (New and aug. ed.). Bryn Mawr: Oliver Ditson.

Bloch, M. (1953). *The historian's craft* (P. Putnam, Trans.). New York: Vintage.

Bogatyrev, P. (1976). Folk song from a functional point of view (Y. Lockwood, Trans.). In L. Matejka and I. R. Titunik (Eds.), *Semiotics of art: Prague School contributions.* Cambridge: MIT. (Originally published in 1936)

Brookover, W. B., and Gottlieb, D. (1964). *A sociology of education* (2nd ed.). New York: American Book.

Cady, H. L. (1987). The problem of the rational in music. *Council for Research in Music Education, 90,* 30–40.

Carr, E. H. (1967). *What is history?* New York: Vintage.

Caws, P. (1973). Structuralism. In P. P. Wiener (Ed.), *Dictionary of the history of ideas* (Vol. IV, pp. 322–330). New York: Scribner.

Chapman, Robert L. (Ed.). (1984). *Roget's international thesaurus* (4th ed., rev.) New York: Harper & Row.

Chomsky, N. (1957). *Syntactic structures.* The Hague: Mouton.

Clark, B. R. (1964). Sociology of education. In R. E. L. Faris (Ed.), *Handbook of modern sociology* (pp. 734–769). Chicago: Rand McNally.

Clarke, D. S., Jr. (1987). *Principles of semiotic.* London: Routledge & Kegan Paul.

Collingwood, R. G. (1956). *The idea of history.* London: Oxford University Press.

Di Pietro, R. J. (1979). The semiotics of musical theater. Second Andrew Mellon Distinguished Lecture. Washington: Georgetown University.

Ellegard, A. (1973). Study of language. In P. P. Wiener (Ed.), *Dictionary of the history of ideas* (Vol. II, pp. 659–673). New York: Scribner.

Foss, D. C. (1977). *The value controversy in sociology: A new orientation for the profession.* San Francisco: Jossey-Bass.

Fuller, S. (1988). *Social epistemology.* Bloomington: Indiana University Press.

Gephart, W. J. (1967). Thoughts on identifying 'significant' research problems in music education. In H. L. Cady (Ed.), *A conference on research in music education* (Report No. BR-6-1388). Columbus: Ohio State University. (ERIC Document Reproduction Service No. ED 013 298).

Ginsberg, M. (1973). Progress in the modern era. In P. P. Wiener (Ed.), *Dictionary of the history of ideas* (Vol. III, pp. 633–650). New York: Scribner.

Gould, J. and Kolb, W. (Eds.). (1964). *A dictionary of the social sciences.* (Compiled under the auspices of UNESCO). New York: Free Press of Glencoe.

Grove, Sir G. (Ed. and Comp.). (1879–1889). *A dictionary of music and musicians.* London: Macmillan and Co.

Guiraud, P. (1975). *Semiology* (G. Cross, Trans.). London: Routledge & Kegan Paul.

Gurvitch, G. (1971). *The social frameworks of knowledge* (M. A. Thompson and K. A. Thompson, Trans.). Oxford: Basil Blackwell.

Hallinan, M. T. (Ed.). (1987). *The social organization of the school: New conceptualizations of the learning process.* New York: Plenum.

Hamilton, P. (1974). *Knowledge and social structure: An introduction to the classical argument in the sociology of knowledge.* London: Routledge & Kegan Paul.

Hartshorne, C., & Weiss P. (1932). *Collected papers of Charles S. Peirce: Vol II, Elements of logic.* Cambridge: Harvard University Press.

Hempel, C. G. (1952). *Fundamentals of concept formation in empirical science.* In O. Neurath, R. Carnap, and C. Morris (Eds.), *International encyclopedia of unified science: Foundations of the unity of science* (Vol. 2, No. 7). Chicago: University of Chicago.

Hirst, P. H. (1983). Educational theory. In P. H. Hirst (Ed.), *Educational theory and its foundation disciplines* (pp. 3–29). London: Routledge & Kegan Paul.

Hodges, W. (1977). *Logic.* New York: Penguin Books.

Hoenigwald, H. M. (1973). Linguistics. In P. P. Wiener (Ed.), *Dictionary of the history of ideas* (Vol. III, pp. 61–73). New York: Scribner.

Homans, G. C. (1964). Contemporary theory in sociology. In R. E. L. Faris, *Handbook of modern sociology* (pp. 951–977). Chicago: Rand McNally.

Itkonen, E. (1978). *Grammatical theory and metascience: A critical investigation into methodological and philosophical foundations of "autonomous" linguistics.* Amsterdam studies in the theory and history of linguistic science. Series IV, Current issues in linguistic theory (Vol. 5). Amsterdam: John Benjamins.

Kivy, P. (1990). *Music alone: Philosophical reflections on the purely musical experience.* Ithaca: Cornell University Press.

Langer, S. (1957). *Philosophy in a new key* (3rd. ed.). Cambridge: Harvard University Press.

Lerdahl, F., and Jackendoff, R. (1983). *A generative theory of tonal music.* Cambridge: MIT Press.

Manoff, T. (1982). *Music: A living language.* New York: W. W. Norton.

Merton, R. K. (1957). *Social theory and social structure* (Rev. and enl. ed.). New York: The Free Press.

Meyer, L. B. (1967). *Music, the arts, and ideas: Patterns and predictions in twentieth century culture.* Chicago: University of Chicago.

Music Educators National Conference. (1985). *Becoming human through music.* The Wesleyan symposium on the perspectives of social anthropology in the teaching and learning of music. Reston: Music Educators National Conference.

Nash, R. H. (Ed.). (1969). *Ideas of history: Vol I, Speculative approaches to history; Vol II, The critical philosophy of history.* New York: Dutton.

Newmeyer, F. J. (1986). *The politics of linguistics.* Chicago: University of Chicago.

Nisbet, R. (1980). *History of the idea of progress.* New York: Basic Books.

Orlov, H. (1981). Toward a semiotics of music. In W. Steiner (Ed.), *The sign in music and literature* (pp. 131–137). Austin: University of Texas.

Ostrom, V. (1961). Education and politics. In N. B. Henry (Ed.), *Social forces influencing American education. Part 2: The sixtieth yearbook of the National Association for the Study of Education* (pp. 8–45). Chicago: University of Chicago.

Polanyi, M. (1959). *The study of man.* Chicago: University of Chicago.

Rosen, C. (1972). *The classical style: Haydn, Mozart, Beethoven.* New York: W. W. Norton.

Salverda, R. (1985). *Leading conceptions in linguistics theory: Formal tendencies in structural linguistics.* Dordrecht, Holland: Foris.

Saussure, F. de. (1959). *Course in general linguistics.* (W. Baskin, Trans.). New York: Philosophical Library.

Schultz, Theodore W. (1961). Education and Economic Growth. In Nelson B. Henry (Ed.), *Social forces influencing American education: The sixtieth yearbook of the National Society for the study of education, Part II.* Chicago: University of Chicago, pp. 46–88.

Scileppi, J. A. (1984). *A systems view of education: A model for change.* Lanham: University Press of America.

Scott, W. R. (1964). Theory of organizations. In R. E. L. Faris (Ed.), *Handbook of modern sociology* (pp. 485–529). Chicago: Rand McNally.

Spalding, W. R. (1939). *Music: An art and a language* (9th ed.). Boston: Arthur P. Schmidt.

Speziali, P. (1973). Classification in the sciences. In P. P. Wiener (Ed.), *Dictionary of the history of ideas* (Vol. I, pp. 462–467). New York: Scribner.

Stehr, N., and Meja, V. (Eds.). (1984). *Society and knowledge: Contemporary perspectives in the sociology of knowledge.* New Brunswick: Transaction Books.

Steinel, D. V. (1985). *Arts in schools: State by state.* Reston: Music Educators National Conference.

Tartarkiewicz, W. (1973). Classification of the arts. In P. P. Wiener (Ed.), *Dictionary of the history of ideas* (Vol. I, pp. 456–462). New York: Scribner.

Teeland, L. A. (1971). *The relevance of the concept of reference groups to the sociology of knowledge.* Forskningsrapport Gotesborgs Universitet Sociologiska Institutionen (No. 12).

The Oxford universal dictionary on historical principles (3rd ed., rev.). (1955). Oxford: Clarendon Press.

Webster's new international dictionary of the English language (2nd ed., unabr.). (1948). Springfield: Merriam.

Webster's third new international dictionary of the English language (unabr.). (1981). Springfield: Webster-Merriam.

·B·

RESEARCH MODES AND TECHNIQUES

·6·

QUALITATIVE RESEARCH METHODOLOGY
IN MUSIC EDUCATION

Liora Bresler and Robert E. Stake
UNIVERSITY OF ILLINOIS AT URBANA-CHAMPAIGN

A freckled third grader approaches the music teacher in the corridor and hands her a stack of 3 x 5 cards. "Thirty-six," he announces proudly. Back in her office Rebecca Grant puts the cards in an envelope on which she neatly writes, "Daniel Wang, 36," and posts it on the wall near three other envelopes. This latest is Daniel's entry in the Composer's Facts competition, this week featuring Aaron Copland. Were curious eyes to pry, they would find information about Copland's birthdate, milestones, compositions, and books. Winners will get musical handbags, musical rulers, musical paraphernalia which Rebecca orders (and pays for with her own money) from a mail-order firm specializing in music items.[1]

* * *

Public Act 84-126, effective August 1, 1985, amended The School Code of Illinois to include, for the first time in state history, a requirement that the goals for learning be identified and assessed. The fine arts were one of the six primary areas designated. Broad goals for Illinois school children include understanding the sensory, formal, technical, and expressive qualities for each of the arts; demonstrating the basic skills necessary to participate in the creation and performance of the arts; and identifying significant works in the arts from major historical periods and how they reflect societies, cultures, and civilizations, past and present.

Achievement of the goals would be assessed by paper and pencil tests. Music specialists, classroom teachers, and principals expressed anger and frustration about these new mandated tests. Among the main complaints were the loss and redirection of instructional time, the lack of empathy about teaching within existing constraints, the lack of responsiveness to teacher concerns, and the lack of financial support to help the teachers learn new skills. Mark Denman, principal in East Park, reacted as follows:

"It is not fair for the state to dictate this. Unless they teach us how to teach these areas it's not realistic. You can't just legislate improvement. You can't just say we are going to raise test scores. You've got to build the groundwork. You can't impose change from the top. You've got to ignite the interest of the staff. Oftentimes people in the

State Department of Education will say: 'Do this, this, and this.' But we have no money to do it. We were not asked if we wanted to do it. We were not asked how we could do it. We work for years to improve something, then funding runs out and nothing further happens. So people are discouraged [shaking his head]. I know the intents of legislators are very good, but . . ."

* * *

It is a chilly Tuesday morning when Ms. Casieri and myself (in the role of observer, and not a very experienced one) are sitting in a half-full bus, with a group of third and fourth graders, on the way to the Civic Center to hear Humperdinck's *Hansel und Gretel*. When we are seated, a blue light is turned on, a series of Shhh's spreads in waves. The chaos subsides, an intense diminuendo, with some uncontrollable giggles as leftovers. The striking silence makes me uneasy, seems to invite a reaction. But no. The lights go down. The piano sounds.

Today's performance is a shortened version of the opera, 60 minutes rather than the 2 original hours. It is performed by a junior group of opera members, the orchestra parts transcribed to piano. An accomplished young woman plays flawlessly the difficult virtuoso part—rhythm and notes, articulations and phrasing, matching dynamics. There is much humor and jest as Hansel and Gretel tease and chase each other. Children laugh *with* the singers, an honest laugh. A good channel to release the tension of the unfamiliar—singing culture, the new form.

* * *

In this chapter we review the basic theory and method of qualitative research in music education. Qualitative approaches come with various names and descriptions: case study, field study, ethnographic research, naturalistic, phenomenological, interpretive, symbolic interactionist, or just plain descriptive. We use "qualitative research" as a general term to refer to several research strategies that share certain characteristics: (1) *noninterventionist* observation in natural settings; (2) emphasis on *interpretation* of both emic issues (those of the participants) and etic issues (those of the writer); (3) highly *contextual description* of people and events; and (4) validation of information through triangulation. These constructs will be developed later in this chapter.

Educational researchers in America have increasingly come to value what researchers elsewhere have long emphasized: the personal and political nature of education. Part of the awareness is reflected in an increased interest in the unique circumstances of school programs and performances. The study of uniqueness can be handled in a disciplined and scholarly way with qualitative inquiry. The classroom community and societal contexts become more than abstract variables.

Our chapter begins with an overview of the intellectual and methodological roots of qualitative research, its basic assumptions and goals, plus identification of kinds of research questions of central interest. In the next section, we examine qualitative research in music. First, we examine models in pedagogy, ethnomusicology, and musical biography. Then we review key studies, focusing on their unique contributions to the field, their aims and objectives, and their primary issues and findings. Of special interest is the compatibility of research methods to the training of musicians regarding teaching as art form and classroom interaction as kinetic performance. We then focus on methods and criteria of qualitative studies. We conclude by pointing to some future directions and possibilities offered by qualitative research to the field of music education.

ROOTS OF QUALITATIVE METHODOLOGY

Just as music and education can be traced back across the centuries ultimately to the crude and custom-driven habits of primitive societies, qualitative inquiry has its roots in the intuitive and survivalist behavior of early peoples. For ages we have operated on hunches and emotions, increasingly using those that brought us safety and satisfaction. Gradually we saw the wisdom of what we already were doing by observing, questioning, keeping records and interpreting, respecting the experience and rumination of elders. Gradually we formed rules for study and names for our sciences. Music educators, too, increasingly drew from philosophers and social scientists to codify research procedures.

Intellectual Roots

The intellectual roots of qualitative methodology lie in the idealist movement—in particular, William Dilthey (1900) and Max Weber (1949), who found their philosophical origins in Kantian thinking. Immanuel Kant (1969) distinguished objects and events as they appear in experience from objects and events as they are in themselves, independent of the forms imposed on them by our cognitive faculties. The for-

mer he called "phenomena"; the latter, "noumena." All we can ever know, Kant argued, are phenomena. Rather than knowing the world directly, we sense, interpret, and explain it to ourselves. All experience is mediated by mind, and all human intellect is imbued with and limited to human interpretation and representation.

Phenomenologists follow Kant in the claim that immediate experiences and sensory observations are always interpreted or classified under general concepts. Their appeal to phenomena is therefore not an appeal to simple, uninterpreted data of sensory experience. Meaning is the target of phenomenology. Phenomenologists do not assume they know what things mean to others. Emphasizing the subjective aspects, they attempt to gain entry into the conceptual world of themselves and others. Giving accounts of their reality construction, phenomenologists believe that these inward construals derive from a developing understanding of self, others, and things. The relationships between these are not "givens" but dialectical, context bound, and processual.

Qualitative researchers tend to be phenomenological in their orientation. Most maintain that knowledge is a human construction. They reason as follows: Although knowledge starts with sensory experience of external stimuli, these sensations are immediately given meaning by the recipient. Though meaning originates in outside action, only the inside interpretation is known. As far as we can tell, nothing about the stimuli is registered in awareness and memory other than our interpretations of it. This registration is not necessarily conscious or rational.

In our minds, new perceptions of stimulation mix with old, and with complexes of perception, some of which we call generalizations. Some aspects of knowledge seem generated entirely from internal deliberation, without immediate external stimulation—but no aspects are purely of the external world, devoid of human construction.

Concepts of Reality The aim of qualitative research is not to discover reality, for by phenomenological reasoning this is impossible. The aim is to construct a clearer experiential memory and to help people obtain a more sophisticated account of things. Sophistication is partly a matter of withstanding disciplined skepticism. Science strives to build universal understanding. The understanding reached by each individual will of course be to some degree unique to the beholder, but much will be held in common. Though the comprehension we seek is of our own making, it is a collective making. Each of us seeks a well-tuned comprehension, one bearing up under further human constructions: scrutiny and challenge.

The qualitative researcher chooses which realities to investigate. For researcher data or interpretation of findings, not every person's personal reality is of equal use. Society deems some interpretations better than others. People have ways of agreeing on which are the best explanations. Of course they are not always right. There is no reason to think that among people fully committed to a constructed reality all constructions are of equal value. One can believe in relativity, contextuality, and constructivism, without believing all views are of equal merit. Personal civility or political ideology may call for respecting every view, but scientific study does not.[2]

Researchers interested in the uniqueness of particular teaching or learning find value in qualitative studies because the design allows or demands extra attention to physical, temporal, historical, social, political, economic, and aesthetic contexts. Contextual epistemology requires in-depth studies, leaving less time for the refinement of theme and construct. It is true that naturalistic and phenomenological case studies are likely to be undertaken by researchers with constructivist persuasions. Why this is is not clear, but it probably would be a mistake to conclude that more than a realist logic, a constructivist logic promotes contextualist epistemology or case-specific study. It is not uncommon to find case study researchers espousing a constructivist view of reality, but the two persuasions are not one and the same.

Cultural sciences need *descriptive* as well as explanatory and predictive powers. At the beginning, middle, and end of a program of research, the researcher at times needs to concentrate on interpretive understanding (*verstehen*). The process of *verstehen* involves the ability to empathize, to recreate the experience of others within oneself.

Dilthey and Weber perceived understanding as hermeneutic, resulting from a process of interpretation. The hermeneutic experience (encounter with a work of art) is historical, linguistic, dialectical. Understanding the meaning of any particular part of a text (a word or a sentence) requires an understanding of the meaning of the whole and vice versa. Thus, achieving a meaningful interpretation requires back and forth movement between parts and whole. Understanding cannot be pursued in the absence of context and interpretive framework. The hermeneutic perspective means that human experience is context bound and that there can be no context-free or neutral scientific language with which to express what happens in the social world. At best we could have laws applying to only a limited context for a limited time.

Ethnography and Biography

The roots of qualitative research methods can be traced to ethnography and sociological fieldwork as well as literary criticism, biography, and journalism. From the end of the nineteenth century, anthropologists advocated and practiced spending extensive periods of time in the natural setting, studying cultures with the intent of learning how the culture was perceived and understood by its members (cf. Boas and Malinowski). Bronislaw Malinowski, who found himself in New Guinea and unable to return to Poland because of the outbreak of World War I, was the first social anthropologist to spend long periods in a native village to observe what was going on. He was also the first professional anthropologist to dwell on how he obtained his data and what the fieldwork experience was like. Malinowski maintained that a theory of culture had to be grounded in particular human experiences, based on observation, and inductively sought.

Case study and ethnographic methods have been part of sociology's history since the 1920s and 1930s when University of Chicago sociologists, under the influence of Robert Park, W. I. Thomas, and Herbert Blumer, were trained in the interpretive approach to human group life (Bogdan and Biklin, 1982; Denzin, 1989). Sociologists in succeeding generations turned away from the method, giving their attention to problems of measurement, validity, and reliability; survey methodologies; and laboratory experiments. Educational researchers recently have witnessed a surge of interest in interpretive approaches to the study of culture, biography, and human life. Central to this view has been the argument that societies, cultures, and the expressions of human experience can be read as social text, that is, the structures of representation that require symbolic statement (Denzin, 1989).

Literary models provide another important model for qualitative methodology. Eisner (1979, 1991) advocates the paradigmatic use of qualitative inquiry found in the arts and the world of art critics. Artists inquire in a qualitative mode both in the formulation of ends and in the use of means to achieve such ends. The art critic's task is to render the essentially ineffable qualities constituting works of art into a language that will help others perceive the world more deeply.

Thomas Barone (1987, 1990) follows Eisner in referring to works of art as relying on a continuum of scientific texts. All texts, claims Barone, are modes of fiction (borrowing the Geertz meaning of fiction—something fashioned). Each brings with it researcher/author subjectivity and personal bias, ideology, and visions, but with fictional works these are more visible, explicit. Barone reminds us that novelists do not spin their imaginary webs from within a world of pure illusion and fantasy, but that "since Henry Fielding, they also have relied upon observation of the minutae of human activity, observing social phenomena" (1987, p. 455). Often a novelist will construct a story out of the qualitative phenomena confronted in everyday experience: Sometimes they will intentionally transport themselves into the field to investigate facets of their emerging story's milieu, as did Dickens who, in preparation for *The Life Adventures of Nicholas Nickelby,* gained admittance to a notorious Yorkshire boarding school by assuming the false identity of someone seeking a school for the son of a widowed friend. The fictionalization process of the novelist, says Barone, is a rigorous and disciplined undertaking, a qualitative problem-solving process that even proceeds through several identifiable stages. A thesis, or central insight, is gradually constructed from patterned relationships between qualitative phenomena. A similar relationship between thesis and particulars exists in accomplished worlds of literary-style fiction such as autobiography, new journalism, and educational criticism. The crafting of an educational criticism closely resembles the dialectical problem-solving process of the novelist.

Rorty (1982) believes that all qualitative inquiry is continuous with literature. For Rorty, books serve the important role of advancing social and political goals of liberalism by promoting a genuine sense of human solidarity (Rorty, 1989).

Literature has been a methodological force. Biography

and autobiography have become a topic of renewed interest in literary criticism (cf. Elbaz, 1987; Cockshut, 1984), as well as in sociology (cf. Denzin, 1989) and anthropology (cf. Geertz, 1988). Feminist views have had an important influence in this discussion (cf. Jelinek, 1980; Spacks, 1976; Grumet, 1988). Jean-Paul Sartre recognized the force of literature in the preface to *The Family Idiot, Gustave Flaubert,* Vol. 1, 1821–1857 (1981):

What, at this point in time, can we know about man? It seemed to me that this question could only be answered by studying a specific case. . . . For a man is never an individual; it would be more fitting to call him a *universal singular.* Summed up and for this reason universalized by his epoch, he in turn resumes it by reproducing himself in it as singularity. Universal by the singular universality of human history, singular by the universalizing singularity of his projects, he requires simultaneous examination from both ends. (pp. ix—x)

Biography has always been an important part of musicology and music history, with oral history gaining interest. While sociology focuses on *interpretive biography*—the creation of literary, narrative accounts and representations of lived experience (Denzin, 1989)—the traditional use of biographies in music centers around life-events, especially family, patrons, and mentoring, a written account or history of an individual.

A second kind of biography (e.g., Von Gunden, 1983) is essentially a musical analysis, where biographical information of the composer and philosophy are brought in to interpret the music. Here, listening to musical works itself provides data, extending the examination of archives (e.g., documents, letters) and in-depth interviews of author and composer. Immersed in the music, the interviews, or observation data, the music education researcher attempts to find new patterns and meanings.

Qualitative vs. Quantitative Research

The quantitative research tradition, grounded in the positivist urge for a science of society, fostered adaptation of the methodology of the physical sciences to investigate social and human worlds. From the theological to the metaphysical, twentieth-century positivism saw culmination of progress and human knowledge through scientific methods. Objects of study in the social sciences are to be treated in the same way that physical scientists treat physical things. The role of the social scientist is that of recorder and theory builder for a reality existing outside human experience.

Another assumption in positivist thinking was that in regard to values, social investigation can and should be a *neutral* activity. Hence, social scientists should eliminate all bias and value-laden preconception and not be emotionally involved with their subject matter. Knowledge derived from social investigation would eventually result in the same sort of technological mastery over the social world as physical science had for the physical world. The aims of practical application would be achieved by the discovery of social laws that point at relationships among social objects, aiming, like

physical laws, at context-free social laws (Hempel, 1966; Popper, 1969).

Dilthey and Weber challenged the positivist point of view, arguing that social studies has a different ontological and epistemological status. They claimed that there we are both the subject and the object of inquiry: The subject matter concerns the product of human minds and as such is inseparably connected to our minds, bringing along all our subjectivities, cognitions, emotions, and values. Furthermore, the complexity of the social world and cultures makes it impossible to discover laws as in the physical sciences. Rather than a series of overarching causal laws, they said, emphasis must be on understanding the individual case or type.[3]

Philosophically, we are dealing here with two paradigms. The *quantitative paradigm* supports investigation of how reality exists independently of us. Ontological questions concerning what is can be kept separate from the epistemological questions about how we come to know "what is." According to that paradigm, knowledge and truth are questions of correspondence—what is true is what corresponds to reality. Done well, the activity of investigation does not affect what is being investigated.

In the *qualitative paradigm* there is a range of positions, from the idealist belief that social and human reality are created, to the milder conviction that this reality is shaped by our minds. But all the positions posit a degree of mind involvement with subject matter not acceptable to the quantitative, positivist, realist tradition. The idea that the process of investigation can be separated from what is being investigated is possible only within that realist perspective. In the realist view, an investigation is directed toward an external referent. In the idealist view, the process is external as well as internal, a part of the investigator's active participation in shaping the world (cf. Peshkin, 1988).

In actual life, no research study is purely qualitative or quantitative. In each qualitative study, enumeration and recognition of differences in amount have a place. And in each quantitative study, natural language description and interpretation are expected. The distinction as we see it is an epistemological distinction that can be identified as the distinction between inquiry for making explanations versus inquiry for promoting understanding. This distinction has best been developed by the Finnish philosopher of science Georg Hendrik von Wright (1971), who emphasized the epistemological distinction between formal explanations and experiential understanding.

Quantitative study was nourished by the scientific search for grand theory seeking generalizations that hold over diverse situations, trying to eliminate the merely situational, letting contextual effects "balance each other out." Quantitative researchers try to nullify context in order to find the most general and pervasive explanatory relationships. Research in education, including music education, has been dominated by this universalist approach, this grand search for explanation. Quantification occurs in order to permit simultaneous study of a large number of dissimilar cases, in order to put the researcher in a position to make formal generalizations about teaching and learning. Proposition-shaped knowledge obviously can be important.

It is apparent that much important knowledge about education (e.g., the calendar, the practice facilities) is situational. Qualitative researchers have a great interest in the uniqueness of the individual case, the variety of perceptions of that case, and the different intentionalities of the actors who populate that case. These interests force the researcher to find easy-access situations for repeated observations, to limit attention to small numbers of teachers and students, to rely little on objective measurement, and to probe in unexpected directions. Fixed designs are less necessary and can be less productive for providing understanding of particular cases. Still, in a discipline governed strongly by an existing composition or score, the musician may find the structures of quantitativism attractive and the open-field behavior of the qualitative researcher too improvisational.

Qualitative researchers are not devoid of interest in generalization but it does not dominate their thinking. Often the qualitative researchers' commitments to multiple interpretations become manifest in a desire to assist practitioners to interpret the situations for themselves. The intent of research then may become the provision of vicarious experience for report readers who will draw their own generalizations, combining previous experience with new. It often is research specially designed to assist practice. The choice of epistemological role for research and the immediacy of its assistance to practice should be part of our distinction between quantitative and qualitative inquiries.

Qualitative researchers too have interest in frequency, typicality, and generalizability (cf. Stake, Bresler, and Mabry, in press). Still, their craft is distinguished by a too-holistic viewing of phenomena. They examine multiple situations but each at close quarters, not forcing them into comparisons, not fixated on common variables. It is not uncommon for a qualitative researcher to ask in midstudy: "Of all things, what is it that is most important to be learned from this case?" In music education, we have need for formal generalizations and need for experiential understandings of particular situations. We need high-quality research, both quantitative and qualitative.

CHARACTERISTICS OF QUALITATIVE RESEARCH

1. It is holistic. Its contexts are well studied. It is case oriented (a case may be a student, a teacher, a classroom, a curriculum, any "bounded system"). It is relatively noncomparative, seeking more to understand its case than to understand how it differs from others.
2. It is empirical. It is field oriented, the field being the natural settings of the case. Its emphasis is on observables, including observations by informants. It strives to be naturalistic, noninterventionistic. There is a preference for natural language description. The researcher is the key instrument. For qualitative research, researchers typically spend considerable time in schools, homes, neighborhoods, and other locales learning about educational concerns. Data are collected on the premises. Qualitative researchers go to the particular settings because they are concerned with context. Action can be better understood when it is observed in the natural setting.
3. It is descriptive. Data take the form of words and graphics more than numbers. The written results of the research contain quotations to illustrate and substantiate the presentation.
4. It is interpretive. Its researchers rely on intuition with many important criteria not specified. Its on-site observers strive to keep attention free to recognize problem-relevant events. It is attuned to the fact that research is a researcher-subject interaction. Qualitative research is concerned with the different meanings that actions and events carry for different members.
5. It is empathic. It attends to the presumed intentions of those being observed. It seeks actor frames of reference, value commitments. Though planned, its design is emergent, responsive. Its issues are emic issues, progressively focused. Its reporting provides vicarious experience.
6. Some researchers emphasize working from bottom up (e.g., Glaser and Strauss's term "grounded theory," 1967). Indeed, the direction of the issues and foci often emerge during data collection. The picture takes shape as the parts are examined.
7. When done well, its observations and immediate interpretations are validated. Triangulation, the checking of data against multiple sources and methods, is routine. There is a deliberate effort to disconfirm one's own interpretations. The reports assist readers to make their own interpretations, as well as to recognize subjectivity.[4]

QUALITATIVE RESEARCH IN MUSIC EDUCATION

The first decades of research in music education, much as in general education, were characterized by adherence to quantitative models. Little research employed qualitative strategies to illuminate education problems. The late 1960s affected research mores too. National foci on educational equity and back-to-basics curricula swung concern to values, feelings, and minority perspectives. Many recognized that we did not know enough about the educational experience of children "not making it." In general education, qualitative emphasis on understanding the perspective of all participants challenged the idea that the views of those in power are worth more than others. Student perspectives (Jackson, 1968) and the viewing of school as a system of discipline (Dreeben, 1968; Foucault, 1977; Henry, 1966) were widely considered. Concern about student achievement yielded some to concern for what students were actually doing in school. All this stimulated the need for different content, goals, and methods. It opened up educational researchers to qualitative approaches.

Music education, too, followed that route, perhaps delayed by a decade or so. The emphasis in formal music education research on quantitative methodology is reflected in books, reports, journal papers, and dissertations. But researchers and practitioners, teachers and conductors, have always used qualitative observations. To establish pedagogy requires illusive observation of students in order to pinpoint problems and suggest remedies. In an ancient example considered to be the first music pedagogy book, *L'Art de Toucher le Clavicin,* Francois Couperin expressed pedagogical assertions based on observations of student behavior: "It will be necessary to place some additional support under the feet of young people, varying in height as they grow, so that their feet not dangling in the air, may keep the body properly balanced." "With regard to making grimaces, it is possible to break oneself of this habit by placing a mirror on the reading-desk of the Spinet or harpsichord" (p. xx). "It is better and more seemly not to beat time with the head, the body, nor with the feet" (p. xx). The discipline of Couperin's observations and analysis is not known. Should we consider his writings research based?

As Couperin's book illustrates, pedagogical books on performance and conducting are designed to foster learning and remedy problems more than to arrive at causal explanations or understandings of the situation. Use of pictures to express good and bad technique is quite common (Kohut and Grant, 1990). Performance, like some aspects of pedagogy, involves a self-synchronous process of constant listening (either in one's own playing or in ensemble) and comparing it to the score. Through score preparation, the performer not only knows individual details—parts and sections of the score—but also develops a conception of the complete work. The style of performance best suited to any given work; a sound knowledge of music theory, harmonic analysis, and musical form; musicological knowledge to relate the piece to the composer's other works, as well as to other works of the period; all of these shape a performance.

Ethnomusicology is a field in music that draws its intellectual roots and methods from anthropology as well as from musicology. Merriam (1964) and Nettl (1983, 1987) discuss two major approaches in ethnomusicology. The first, a comparative study of musical systems and cultures, is standardized musicology, aiming to record and analyze music in order to produce an accurate structural analysis of the music investigated. Here, the study is primarily based upon a fact-gathering descriptive approach, dealing with such questions as the modes of Persian or Indian music, names of instruments, how they are made, and who owns them.

The second approach, aiming to understand music in the context of human behavior, is an anthropological speciality. Here, the field-worker tries to approximate the anthropologist, for the concern is with much broader questions of the use and function of music, the role and status of musicians, the concepts that lie behind music behavior, and other similar questions (Merriam, 1967; Nettl, 1987). The emphasis is on music but not on music divorced from its total context: The investigator attempts to emerge from the study with a broad and generally complete knowledge of both the culture and the music, as well as the way music fits into and is used within the wider context (Merriam, 1964, p. 42). This second approach is typically a field-oriented naturalistic study. The researcher stays at the site for a considerable amount of time, getting immersed in the culture. The issues, a combination of emic and etic, are progressively focused. The direction of the issues and foci often emerge during and after data collection.[5] With few exceptions (Keil, 1966; Oliver, 1960), ethnomusicological studies typically examine other cultures. Few ethnomusicological studies examine familiar music in familiar settings.

Even though these kinds of knowledge have not, until recently, entered the established domains of music education research, the methods of observation, the interview, the use of archival material, and immersion in the case have long been important tools in music education, and in performance and musicology as well. A pioneering work that drew upon these methods, done within the formal boundaries of music education research, was the Pillsbury Foundation Study (Moorhead and Pond, 1941, 1942, 1944, 1951). Initiated by people outside the field of music education (conductor Leopold Stokowski and composer Donald Pond), the Pillsbury Study was dedicated to the discovery of children's musical development through analysis of free, unhampered musical play. Amazed at the spontaneous outpouring of music in young children, Pond wanted to understand how and why children become musically expressive. Thinking along Deweian lines, he wanted to provide them with opportunities and materials so that they might function in their own ways as musicians. In the study, Pond made a conscious attempt to set aside adult notions about elements of music, processes of learning music, and ways of assessing musical development.

The Pillsbury Study was conducted with 3- to 6-year-old children attending a kindergarten designed specifically for research into musical creativity: an environment full of enticing instruments (e.g., sarong, Chinese and Burmese gongs, Indian drums, and tom-toms) and supportive, musically knowledgeable (but not intrusive) adults. The methods of study involved in-depth observation and analysis. Since the context of sound was of major importance, the observations included such activities as speech and physical movement. All sounds produced were considered musical or "embryonically of musical value." In his reports, Pond provided such examples as when a child calls from the sandbox, "I want a red spoon," in a rhythmic and tonal pattern or a child riding on a tricycle sings over and over to himself in unvarying rhythm, "I ran over a whole basket of cherries." The final report (Moorhead and Pond, 1951), was a set of three short case studies of individual children selected for individual differences and approaches. Data included biographical information such as age, personal, family, and school history.

Some naturalistic studies are taxonomic; others are not. Moorhead and Pond worked toward classification of the musical products. A classification of instrumental music, for example, included flexible and asymmetrical measures, exploring wide intervals, tone colors, and pitch contrast. Another category of sonic physical activity, "insistent and savage," was based on rigid and symmetrical rhythms, indifferent to melody and color variety. Pond distinguished between two types of spontaneous vocal utterances: "song," private rhythmically and melodically complex entities, and "chant," a more public utterance, often spontaneously improvised by groups of children. Social-personal context was seen to be highly relevant; most chants were developed first by one child, continued by that child or undertaken by others to form repartee series. Pond raised issues such as: Are these rhythmic patterns fundamental to the child's musical consciousness? What are the relationships between rhythmic patterns and physical rhythms?

The Moorhead and Pond study was holistic, case oriented, noncomparative. The authors sought more to understand each child than to understand how children differ from each other. The natural setting was stressed, with an emphasis on observables. Moorhead and Pond did not try to intervene but rather to observe, describe, and understand.

The Pillsbury Study set a new direction for investigation of free musical activities and improvisation. For music education research, it provided methodological direction and legitimation of the use of naturalistic methods. In the late 1970s and 1980s, music education saw a spurt of qualitative works, independently done in different locations and universities across the country. Jean Bamberger of Massachusetts Institute of Technology (1977) examined two subjects' perceptions of a melody, noting the strategies used by each to compose a melody and the relationship between perceptions, models, strategies, and the completed melody. A protocol analysis employing an innovative computer-based recording system to study compositional process was included.

Most reported qualitative studies have been dissertations, works of solitary, inexperienced researchers, backed by little financial resource (cf. Gerber, 1975; Freundlich, 1978; Cohen, 1980; Lewers, 1980; L'Roy, 1983; Thiel, 1984; Garrison, 1985; Krueger, 1985; Upitis, 1985; Bresler, 1987; DeLorenzo, 1987; Harwood, 1987). Observing spontaneous musical behavior of children, Douglas Freundlich (1978) of Harvard explored two fifth-grade children's musical thinking, especially focusing on spontaneous solutions to musical problems. Students were to improvise on a simple diatonic xylophone within a traditional musical frame of standard 12-bar blues. The data were collected in the context of a structured "jam session." The research was qualitative not because the situation was loosely structured but because the researcher was refining his interpretation with every observation. Freundlich found that development proceeded down from the chorus-as-a-whole and up from a self-generated two-bar motif. Addressing improvisation's pedagogical value, Freundlich pointed out that the child can generate authentic musical ideas without reference to notation, and that musical concepts furnished by the improvisation procedure are logically organized.

Veronica Cohen (1980) of the University of Illinois also examined the generation of musical ideas in a loosely structured situation. Discussing her methods, Cohen noted the following:

This is not a conventional study in which the researcher set up a plan and then followed it, reporting in what ways it was successful or not. Instead, borrowing on the naturalistic, exploratory and yet scientific tradition exemplified in some of the most important of Piaget's studies, it searched through observations over many years . . . focusing finally on a few of two children's musical productions that held the most promise for revealing the underlying structure and dynamics of children's spontaneous music. (p. 1)

Data collection included a 3-year period of general background observation and immersion in children's free musical play in the kindergarten, followed by a rigorous and detailed study of videotaped data involving two kindergarten children. Cohen discussed the role of intuition and accumulated knowledge of the whole field of music in making the thousands of decisions in data collection in the field. "The researcher becomes the chief instrument who selects, interprets and synthesizes evidence in order to break through to the mind of the child" (p. 2). Engagement in musical dialogues with children was a focus. Descriptors included the role of kindergarten music, teacher special interest, and the *participant-observer* role of the researcher. Cohen reported that she was constantly involved in planning the music curriculum, taught demonstration classes for university students, demonstrated ways of interacting with children at the music center, and discussed and analyzed children's work for classroom teachers, parents, and university students.

Cohen investigated musical gestures, noting how the children organize sounds into "musical ideas." Using videotapes for data collection, Cohen found that such behavior could be nicely placed into three broad categories: exploration, mastery, and generation of musical gestures. She speculated that even at this early age children tended to specialize: some almost always engaged in "mastery" activities (reproduction of known melodies) whereas others "improvised" their own gestures.

Influences of culture and society on the musical behavior of children is a relatively sociology-based area studied by qualitative researchers. In Israel, Devorah Kalekin-Fishman (1981, 1986) investigated the nature of music in kindergartens, examining it from teacher as well as from child perspectives. A kindergarten was chosen as the case because it is here the child encounters society as officially organized by educators and is exposed to conceptual frameworks deliberately arranged to fit at least a dozen years of life in educational organizations. Kalekin-Fishman made intensive observations and conducted semistructured interviews. An analysis of sonal patterns in kindergartens in Germany and Israel showed that with minimal framing (intended pitch and intended rhythm), children produced varieties of typified music making. The framing, however, was not that most commonly employed by kindergarten teachers, who usually have a relatively narrow field of musical knowledge.

Ethnomusicology provides an important model for music education research. At the University of Wisconsin, Madison, Virginia Garrison (1985) examined the transmission process of folk music, a process that is as vital to that tradition as is its product, the music. If folk music is to be included in formal music educational settings, then it is important that those social and musical aspects of the folk music tradition that are essential to that tradition are identified. In order to investigate the transmission process and the effect of changed instructional context on that process, Garrison used ethnomusicological methods of extensive and intensive naturalistic observations of 72 practicing fiddlers and 49 beginning fiddling students in a variety of contexts for a period of 6 years, as well as open-ended interviews and photography.

In a similar vein, Eve Harwood (1987) of the University of Illinois opened her dissertation discussing the difficulty researchers have studying music of a culture different from their own. Whereas at one time it was considered sufficient to analyze musical artifacts in the form of tape recordings and transcriptions, using terms appropriate to traditional western musicology, modern ethnomusicology holds that understanding and describing the cultural context in which music making occurs is a necessary part of understanding the music of a given group. An outsider's analytical tools and observations are not necessarily invalid, but an insider's view of what is significant about the music are thought to illuminate our understanding in a unique way.

In the case of North American children, folklorists and musicians were collecting children's repertoires before 1900, but little scholarship had been directed toward the singers themselves. Harwood's study was based on the assumption that children's music and musical world are distinct from adult counterparts, that what is considered beautiful, attractive, or good to sing and is cherished by children may be different. Not a naturalistic study, Harwood's procedures included semistructured interviews in which the 15 children sang all the songs they could remember, discussed how they had learned each song, and described their singing habits and preferences. A parent of each child answered questions regarding the child's singing habits and preferences and the musical life of the family. Interviews and singing were taped and transcribed, and a fieldwork journal of impressions and visual observations was kept. In conclusion, Harwood once again asserted the need to study children's music as one would that of any outside culture, attempting to appreciate both the insider's and the outsider's view of the material.

In the studies just reviewed, researchers examined relatively uncharted territories in order to understand musical activities in context. The study of innovation is another such uncharted territory. Qualitative methodology not only allows but features the study of contexts. One innovation has been the introduction of instructional computer programming that many music educators claim dramatically affects the music education scene. Case studies are one of many ways to examine accommodation of computers into music classes.

At Stanford, Liora Bresler (1987) studied the integration of computers into a college-level introductory music theory class. The learning environment into which the computer is integrated is far too complex to be condensed to one or even several variables. Complications ranged from implicit and explicit curricula of the music theory class to multiple goals and values of instructors, program designers, and students, all interacting with beliefs, musical aspirations, and perceptions of the innovation. Intensive observations of student work at the computer and unstructured and semistructured interviews with the participants provided the main data, supplemented with questionnaires, computer logs, and collection of materials (e.g., syllabi, tests, and students' composition answer sheets).

Even though initially the class seemed an ideal setting for the use of computers for education (e.g., perfect match between contents of software and curriculum-individualized instruction for a musically heterogeneous population; stable teaching over a number of years), the results fell well short of expectations. Many important issues such as the relevance of music practice to the computer program and the aesthetics of music in the computer program emerged at the site.

Focusing on social and cultural contexts, Saville Kushner (1985) of the University of East Anglia studied an innovative, 3-year course for third- and fourth-year students at the Guildhall School of Music and Drama in London. The course, a response to fundamental misgivings about the education of musicians in conservatoires, arranged student performances and workshops in a range of unconventional community sites. Rather than judging the merits of the training, Kushner was commissioned to collect information that participants would find useful in making such judgments. His report was rich in description of program development over time, noting student and teacher perception and audience response. Through vignettes and vivid pictures, it conveyed conservatory life, its inside rivalries, competitions, participant experiences, implicit and explicit goals, and values. The personal debates about destination, the dreams, the dilemmas—so personal, yet so common to performance-oriented people—captured a reality pertinent to musical lives, innovations, and experiences. The portrayal of student perspectives, including those at the lower social strata, captured personal and cultural meanings of music, confusion over what the role of the professional musician should be, as well as the social context of repertoire.

Case studies are typically confined to one setting. A series of eight case studies portraying ordinary arts instruction in the United States was conducted by the Center for Instructional Research and Curriculum Evaluation (CIRCE) at the University of Illinois under the auspices of the National Arts Education Research Center, funded by the National Endowment for the Arts (see Stake, Bresler, and Mabry, in press). Described in detail were the fundamental differences in program offering for music education specialists and general classroom teachers, not only in curricula and pedagogy, but in impact on scheduling, resources, and use of curricular organizers as well. One etic (original design) issue was the role of community resources and performances. Classroom observations brought out the "hidden curriculum"—art as relief from schoolwork and the regularity with which music was presented without background or interpretation, whether for class participation or as background activity to eating, doing worksheets, or reading. As usual, the emphasis was not on what ought to be, but the study did provide researcher interpretation as to what is needed.

In another federally funded project, the Elementary Subjects Study (funded by the U.S. Department of Education) at Michigan State University, music and the visual arts were studied along with mathematics, science, social studies, and literature. The program focused on conceptual understanding, higher order thinking and problem solving in elementary school teaching through a series of case studies of music and visual arts instruction (May, 1990). Research questions included the following: What content is taught when teaching for conceptual understanding and higher level learning? How do teachers negotiate curricular decisions? How do teachers concentrate their teaching to use their limited resources best? In what ways is good teaching subject matter specific?

Some research in music is done by nonmusicians, where music is but one subject among several others, chosen to highlight larger patterns. Such was a study by Benjamin Bloom (1985), who was interested in the development of talent in a variety of domains—music, math, sculpture, athletics—and the roles of families, teachers, and schools in discovering, developing, and encouraging unusually high levels of competence. The commonalities of music with other domains, as well as its unique properties, were presented by Sosniak (1985).

Music Concepts to Aid Qualitative Study

Extensive use of observation in natural settings with little intervention encourages us to discern the complexity of music education. Taped interviews can capture participant voices, views, and struggles. Qualitative methodology promotes the pursuit of questions like, What music do teachers cherish and participate in outside of school? How are school reform and the accountability movement affecting how teachers perceive the teaching of music? What are children's assumptions about music, about what is beautiful, attractive, or well formed? What musical events are to be found in prekindergarten settings? In school settings? In jam sessions? Are there ways that teachers are using MTV for legitimate music instruction? Qualitative researchers can examine events that reflect latent as well as manifest learnings. They can study interrelationships of school, home, media, and culture as they shape musical skills and attitudes. They do this by studying individual cases, problems, settings.

Capturing reality in its complexity opens up research studies to additional modes of representation: vignettes, photographs, audio-and videotapes, films, and various artifacts of performing and teaching music.

Using tapes to capture musical nuances and qualities in performances as well as intonations of "everyday speech" is useful for musicians, for whom intonation, rhythm, and pitch are specially meaningful.

Having discussed the content and representations that qualitative methodology offers music education research, we now want to draw attention to the symbiotic relation between musicianship and intellectual inquiry—noting that much can be developed along qualitative lines. Musical approach can be an asset in qualitative research in general education. Music educators who turn to research in education can use their musical background to contribute to structural conceptualizations and analysis of school life and teaching.

Teaching and classroom life should sometimes be regarded through aesthetic lenses (cf. Eisner, 1979; Goodman, 1968; Brophy and Good, 1986; Kagan, 1989). Here, it is important to make the distinction between an artwork and a phenomenon analyzed through aesthetic parameters (Dewey, 1958). As Eisner has stated, we can pay attention to the aesthetic qualities of a teaching performance in order to perceive what is later described as its qualitative aspects or its feelingful character. The performance itself may not be artistic; that is, it may not have coherence and unity and might not be particularly inventive. Nevertheless, it still can have aesthetic properties. The opposite of aesthetic is anaesthetic, the thwarting of feeling. Objects, situations, or events that are aesthetic evoke or elicit feeling. Whether the situation of performance is artistic, it can be argued, is another matter (Eisner, private communication, 1990).

Art affords us the unique experience of apprehending the result of one individual's (the artist's) inquiry into the structure of reality and the structure of a medium (Olson, 1978; Arnheim, 1986; Eisner, 1988). Teachers, like artists, create articulated, planned experiences[6] and the portrayal of experience can be disciplined by qualitative methods. Analysis of a lesson, like a work of art in general and a musical work in particular, can benefit by allusion to arts' structural properties: rhythm, line, orchestration, texture, form. Lessons can create drama—introduction, building of tension, and resolution. Formal qualities play a major role in the educational communication, interacting with specific messages and contents to create the impact. These properties help provide standards for teaching, drawing attention to coherence, sequentiality, and comprehension.

Let us examine some musical parameters that we have found helpful for conceptualizing qualitative research, particularly in examining curricula and pedagogies. (1) *Form* relates to the organization of parts and whole, arrangement of repetition and variation, unity and variety. Teaching uses and builds on these. A number of educational models point to the importance of form in teaching: setting up introductory anticipation, development and closure, or the creation of suspense, a dramatic climax and resolution as the summing up of the lesson, of a topic. Every lesson has a form, created by the interplay of new and old material, repetition and variation. A lesson may be conceptualized as a Baroque suite—a series of little, related movements (except for parameters like tonality and orchestration)—or as a classical sonata form, tightly organized, fully developed, and well balanced. (2) *Style*. Just as categorization of musical style[7] is useful for perception and analysis, so is the categorization of teaching style. Parameters of style are qualitative lenses for classroom life, pedagogies, and curricular materials.

Form and style are broad categories, referring to complexes or syndromes. The qualities of melody (or line), tempo and rhythm, orchestration and texture, are more specific. (3) *Tempo* is the pace, quick and slow and all the gradations in between. *Rhythm* refers to relationships of tempi over time as well as to temporal patterns. What are the paces of the lesson? How fast do the ideas flow? How rapidly does the teacher change topic, focus, and assignment? How does this pace raise anticipation, or a sense of development and evaluation? (4) *Orchestration* refers to the character of the interplay among players or participants. What is the character of interplay between teacher and students? How does the teacher get the students to take more initiative? Presentations can be didactic, the teacher assuming the soloist's role, dominating the presentation. Alternatively, the teacher assumes the conductor's role, facilitating student dialogue, yet maintaining control over content and form. Classroom life can take the form of chamber ensembles, a measure of student leadership and autonomy. Orchestration reveals the "colors" of voices in the classroom, for example some extroverted (brass v. string instruments) in higher registers, intense, and interacting. (5) *Melody* refers to the "plot line," its direction ascending, descending, or flat. Is the unit of thought a long one or are there many shorter units? What are the interrelations of the shorter idea units to the whole lesson? Are they complementary, autonomous, or unified? What is the inner form (in terms of anticipation and drama) within each of these plot lines? (6) *Texture* refers to the interrelations of simultaneous lines and their development over time during the lesson. Under the category of texture, the presentation of topics, such as at a board meeting, can be homophonic or contrapuntal, several voices echoing, confronting, ignoring each other.

These music concepts, as well as special concepts of education, are expected content and representation in qualitative music education research. Most important are their contributions to expressivity. Though unobtrusive, the researcher interacts with teaching and learning phenomena, bringing unique experience and scholarship into interpretation. Along with relatively uncontestable descriptions, traces of the researcher's deepest personal understandings are presented. The character and the art form of the researcher are not hidden.

METHODS AND CRITERIA

The primary task of the researcher is interpretation (with interpretations presented eventually not just as findings but as assertions; (Erickson, 1986). The most obvious work of the qualitative researcher is data gathering in the field. The ethic of qualitative research calls for abundant description, sufficient for readers to participate in verification of the researcher's interpretations and to make some of their own (Stake, 1978). Thus, most of the methodological advice in the literature has to do with data gathering. If we were limited to a single recommendation we would name Schatzman and Strauss (1973), *Field Research: Strategies for a Natural Sociology*.

Data Collection

The examples of music education research described earlier identify the main methods for qualitative research: intensive observation in natural settings, examination of documents and other artifacts, and interview. Even when audio- or videotaped, the principal "instrument" is the researcher, a constant arbiter of what is important, of the need for further data, for probing, and for small or large redesign of the study. The design of the study is said to be emergent or progressively focused (Strauss, 1987). The design is based not only on a strong sense of the research questions or issues at hand (Smith, 1978) but on the growing body of interpreted observations in the classroom or wherever.

When assuming the more common nonparticipant role, the researcher observes ordinary activities and habitat, the people, the exercise of authority and responsibility, the expression of intent, the productivity, and especially the milieu. Believing that important understandings are situationally rooted, the researcher carefully describes the contacts, noting not just space and time characteristics, but social, economic, political, historical, and aesthetic contexts. The nonparticipating observer is as invisible and nonintrusive as possible, often even refraining from appearing to record what is going on.

In a participant-observer role the researcher engages in the ordinary activities of the group or program being studied but tries not to redirect those activities. Participation may be marginal, perhaps the role of helpmate with some sharing of interests and problems (Spindler, 1982), or more extensive, such as the teacher as researcher in her own classroom or the researcher as consultant providing inservice training to teachers (Cohen, 1980; Stake and Easley, 1978; Stanley, 1990; Wagner, 1990). The growing interest in action research (teacher as researcher; Carr and Kemmis, 1986) is apparent in recent meetings of the American Education Research Association. Here especially, but even in the more passive roles, as interpreter, the researcher is seen as an interactive force in events.

Document review is an essential component of data collection (Andre, 1983). Needed data on inspiration, obligation, and constraint on personal or group action are often disclosed in formal and informal documents. Many useful documents are fugitive records, stored in places no one can remember, making it necessary for the researcher to look through countless papers to find a useful one. Often the information needed is a marginal notation or not even a document at all, such as an inscription on a trophy or notes on a calendar. Browsing is a common activity for the researcher, with half a mind for the research question but another half just trying to comprehend what sort of place it is.

Interviews are conducted not as surveys of how people feel but primarily to obtain observations that the researcher is unable to make directly, secondly to capture multiple realities or perceptions of any given situation, and, finally, to assist in interpreting what is happening. When standardized information is needed from large numbers of people, the written survey is more efficient, but most qualitative researchers want to probe more deeply than is possible with questionnaires. With a structured interview the researcher assumes questions are comprehensible and consistent in meaning across respondents. Semistructured interviews, with topics or questions predetermined, allow latitude for probing and following the interviewee's sense of what is important. Unfortunately, they are costly to administer and time-consuming in analysis. The degree of structure for individual questions, for the interview as a whole, or for the project as a whole are key decisions to be made and remade (Mishler, 1986).

The qualitative researcher seeks to be unobtrusive, knowing that the more attention is drawn to the study, the more posturing there will be and less ordinary activity available for observation. Even interviewing and testing are interventions, drawing attention to the presence and purpose of the research. The researcher takes advantage of indications of accretion and use, such as graffiti on walls or repair records for tape recorders. Gene Webb and his Northwestern colleagues provided many examples of unobtrusive measures (Webb, Campbell, Schwartz, and Sechrest, 1966), but one of the authors, Don Campbell, later expressed the concern that heavy use of such methods persuade readers that social scientists are covert and deceptive, undermining the credibility of all research. Researchers, often in effect guests at the work space and in the private spaces of others, should be considerate. With its probing orientation, qualitative research easily intrudes into the personal affairs of others. Making the report anonymous is often insufficient to avoid the risk of harming people. Handling data is an ethical as much as a technical matter (Rainwater and Pittman, 1969).

Data Analysis

Techniques vary widely. Both qualitative and quantitative analyses of data are used by the qualitative researcher. Quantitative analysis is used more to work toward generalization across specifics observed in the field. It proceeds largely by coding, classifying, and aggregating observations (Miles and Huberman, 1984). Thus, for example, teaching episodes are increasingly seen to be of perhaps three kinds, and the length of student deliberation in choosing a musical instrument is treated statistically. Uniqueness of each particular situation is given little attention: the typical, aggregate, and generalizable are given more attention. Such an approach is often followed in policy analysis (Yin, 1984).

Qualitative analysis is organized more around the notes and stories the researcher keeps, increasingly focused on a small number of issues or themes. The researcher selects the most revealing instances, identifies vignettes, and composes narratives from day to day, then uses an even smaller selection of them in the final presentation (Goetz and LeCompte, 1984). The choice of what to report is subjective, evolving, emphasizing more what contributes to the understanding of the particulars observed than relating to cases and situations elsewhere, usually giving no more than minor attention to comparisons, not worrying much about typicality or representativeness. Thus, the integrity, complexity, and contextuality of individual cases are probed. Readers fit them in among cases they have known. If theory building is the ultimate intent of the researcher here, qualitative analysis paces it not by years but by decades.

Multiple case studies require a kind of analysis that remains largely unformalized. One tries to preserve the uniqueness of the individual case, yet produce cross-site conclusions. The usual reporting procedure is to present a long or short summary of each case, then chapters on understanding the aggregate (Huberman and Miles, 1984). Panels of interpreters, some of whom may not have observed at any sites, are often useful for enriching and challenging the interpretations—but require more comprehensive site summaries than site-visiting researchers usually provide for themselves. For self-use, panel, or instructional purposes, such summaries provide a synthesis of what the researcher knows about the site, tentative findings, and quality of data supporting them, even indicating what is still left to find out, and perhaps indicating an agenda for the next wave of data collection (Bogdan and Taylor, 1984).

For most qualitative projects, data analysis is an informal and often overwhelming task. There are too many data to keep records of and too few that support prevailing impressions. The researcher works with those seeming most likely to advance understanding, describing them in detail, and frequently restating the issue being pursued. Data analysis is an art form.

Criteria of Quality

The characteristics of quality in quantitative studies are widely agreed upon: representativeness of the sample, reliability and validity of measurement, objectivity in interpretation, and the probabilities of Type I and Type II errors, to name several (Campbell and Stanley, 1966). No such summary of characteristics of quality has been developed for qualitative research. Many of the same concepts are worthy of consideration, but when purposes are different (e.g., a low interest in broad generalization), then the criteria will be different. Whether the alternative purposes are legitimate is a question that researchers continue to debate (Smith and Heshusius, 1986).

The most important criterion for any research is that it is about something important, important to readers as well as to researchers. Researchers are given great respect for recognizing what needs to be studied, and they should not abuse that privilege. Perhaps an overly large share of music education research is the psychological study of musical skills and knowledge; perhaps too little is the study of curriculum change and that of music teaching. Still, the health of any research enterprise depends more on intellectual curiosity, studying what needs to be better understood, rather than on what can be funded or will be pleasing to patrons and readers.

In a response to critics of naturalistic inquiry, Lincoln and Guba (1985, 1988) asked methodologists and philosophers of science for evidence that well-crafted research grounded in qualitative and phenomenological traditions *could* be judged and found (1) systematically congruent with the context, that is, valid; (2) not subject to aberrations in research process or instrumentation, that is, reliable; and (3) not open to charges of bias, prejudice, or political advocacy of the investigators. Lincoln and Guba rejected these more quantitative or positivist criteria on grounds that they were incompatible with the axioms of naturalistic research. They saw the naturalist's criteria to be (1) credibility (rather than internal validity), (2) transferability (rather than external validity or generalizability), (3) dependability (rather than reliability), and (4) confirmability (rather than objectivity). These alternative terms were advocated primarily to make clear the inappropriateness of conventional criteria for qualitative research (House, 1980).

To illustrate these criteria, consider a naturalistic case study of a program for training teachers of introductory band. As does a quantitative researcher, the qualitative researcher unconsciously or deliberately takes into account the experience, sophistication, curiosity, and concerns of the eventual audience and seeks to say mostly what will be credible to them. But unlike the quantitative researcher, the qualitative researcher intends to build upon the uniqueness of personal understanding, offering for each reader a credible account and a vicarious experience for substantiation or modification of existing generalizations.

Transferability refers to the extent to which the research facilitates inferences by readers regarding their own situations and responsibilities. Such are petite generalizations rather than the grand generalizations of the theory builder, relatively context free, and a basis for general policy. Good transfer is based on similarity of situations, intuitively weighted as to what is important and unimportant in the match.

Our campus researcher seeks to describe band director trainees meaningfully to readers, with observations transferable to their situations. Rather than measuring with instrument or frequency count, he observes and portrays the band teacher training experience, clearly describing people, dialogue, settings, expressions of intent and frustration, and so on so as to enable the reader to associate this new vicarious experience with previous experience, recognizing ordinary use of both reasoning and intuition in clarifying views and improving understanding.

Confirmability is a sophisticated way of suggesting accuracy. With qualitative data we seldom have an accurate impression the first time we look; we have to confirm or triangulate[8] (Denzin, 1970), and when we can we have others,

including our readers, confirm the finding. The researcher is not content to note available confirmatory evidence but deliberately seeks new facts that might refute the present facts (Popper, 1969). What are facts? It always happens that several important facts are in some degree interpretations (e.g., a professor's apparent lack of interest in band appearance, particularly synchronous movement—whether or not she confirms it), the meanings differing from observer to observer. The researcher triangulates the observations, working toward some common perception, but expects and reports on certain differences in perception (for example, between male and female faculty members) and goes out of his way to relate certain ways he, with background and value commitment showing, interacted with the scene and arrived at assertions. With different backgrounds, the readers too interpret the account differently. Confirmability is an aim, not an ideal, to be tempered by the indefiniteness of reality and by sticking with questions that matter.

Drawn by his persuasion toward constructed reality, our quantitative researcher finds it of little use to hypothesize some "true account" of the band director training program, an account independent of human observers, an ideal to which actual accounts might be compared. Even those parts of the account most agreed upon are not good grounds for considering "validity"—for many of those easily confirmed facts are of little interest and one way to get confirmation is to omit things, even important things, that people see differently. The account should be dependable among relatively neutral readers, portraying much of what they would have seen, had they been there, and omitting most of what they would have found irrelevant and distracting. The researcher is greatly privileged in what to attend to, but the audience can invalidate, at least for their purposes, the account as off-the-mark and incomplete.

Complete objectivity is unattainable and unsought in this research paradigm (Dilthey, 1900; Barone, 1990). The researcher seeks to diminish subjectivity that interferes with comprehension and to exploit subjectivity for deeper interpretation (Peshkin, 1988). He exposes himself, preferably with grace. Although most readers have little interest in reading the researcher's track record, autobiographical and opinion statements are useful footnotes for deliberately revealing lack of experience, alliances, and value positions. And to carry the handling of subjectivity further, the competent qualitative researcher finds ways of including contrary views and alternative explanations.

The criteria for high-quality inquiry and for high-quality reports are not one and the same. The inquiry process belongs largely to the researcher. Each of the data gathering and analysis methods has its own criteria, sources for which we have footnoted. The criteria for reports (reports being communications requiring both a sender and a receiver) lie in the hands of both the researcher and the user of the research. With quantitative measurement, it is not the test or instrument that has validity, it is each use of the measurements that is valid or invalid (Cronbach, 1971). Similarly with qualitative research, the meanings arrived at by individual readers and the applications to new practice are the ultimate indexes of validity of the reports (Howe and Eisenhart, 1990). A final assertion might be that in the program studied here, band directors are reconsidering their roles in protection and perpetuation of local culture. If readers misinterpret this as indicating the graduates thus are hostile to change, the finding should be considered invalid. The researcher can do much to increase the quality of his work, but it serves no more than to facilitate cautious and insightful use of his accounts.

Strengths and Weaknesses

As summarized by Miles and Huberman (1984), the weakest aspect of qualitative research is its contribution to basic research generalizations and policy study—but such is not its intent. Its purpose is to facilitate understanding of the particular. Still, by charging the researcher with spontaneous responsibility in the field, it lacks good protection against

1. excessive subjectivity in observations,
2. imprecise language in descriptions,
3. vague descriptions of the research design,
4. unwieldy and voluminous reports,
5. implication of generalizability when little is warranted,
6. cost and time overrun, and
7. unethical intrusion into personal lives.

But the strengths of qualitative study are impressive as well. We would summarize those strengths as

1. a holistic, systemic purview, emphasizing inner workings and contexts;
2. a strong, empirical commitment to triangulated description of teaching;
3. an obligation and opportunity to get the most from fieldwork interpretations; and

4. a sense of empathy enhancing the utility of use for applied practice in education.

These features have not characterized the majority of the music education research in our journals. Certainly it would be a mistake were all the issues and developments of music education to be studied naturalistically—but that imbalance is far away.

To close this chapter we would like to quote from Kushner's (1985) case study, his final words:

As can be read throughout this report, the participating students are formidable critics and evaluators—and no one has been spared their scrutiny. MPCS offers a rare occasion in music training for trainees to support each other in a discussion forum and they use it with effect. Guildhall tutors, guest speakers, professional collaborators, prospective employers, those who seek to advise and the principal himself, have all found themselves having to defend statements they have made to MPCS groups in the face of often considerable pressure. There is no evidence on this course, at least, for the often-heard assertion that music students are inarticulate or reticent. This may be both heartening and worrying for the conservatoire facing the prospect of trying to integrate an educational curriculum with a training curriculum. The implications of curriculum integration go beyond finding appropriate slots on a timetable for optional sessions. If there is a vision of new practice enshrined in the Project then it might prove increasingly hard to protect other teaching areas in the School from the consequences of that vision. . . . To date the Project has undoubtedly enjoyed many successes.—but it is still a curriculum 'fledging' enjoying the attention and tolerance needed to nurture it. Its musical products are of a quality which still worry Peter, in educational terms its aims and outcome are still hit-and-miss. There is no certainty that the course will interest conservatoire students other than those (still small) numbers who opt to join and remain on the course. And, of course, MPCS has not had to withstand confrontation with critics one of the few experiences so far denied it.

Notes

1. Vignettes quoted herein are from Stake, Bresler, and Mabry, *Custom and Cherishing,* to be published by the Music Educators National Conference.
2. Guba and Lincoln (1981) have identified gradations of belief in an independent versus a constructed reality. One's belief is linked to belief in how we come to know what we know—but ontology and epistemology are not interdeterminate. Belief in independent reality does not fix one's belief in a simple world, the worlds of Stravinsky's Firebird or seasonal fund drives. Nor does belief in constructionism fix belief in a heterogenous, particularist world. Realists too believe that generalizations are regularly limited by local condition. "Do teachers always prefer authoritarian milieus or only under certain conditions?" Though idealists, relativists, situationalists, contextualists, and other champions of local knowledge often resist broad generalizations and are found to support constructivist ontology, their support for a contextualist epistemology is a correlate, not a derivative, of that ontology.
3. Rorty's perspective on both idealism and positivism moves us toward the role of literature in qualitative methodology. Kant and Hegel, claims Rorty (1989), went only halfway in their repu-

diation of the idea that truth is "out there." They were willing to view the world of empirical science as a made world, to see matter as constructed by mind. But they persisted in seeing mind, spirit, the depths of the human self, as having an intrinsic nature, one that could be known by a kind of nonempirical superscience called philosophy. Thus, only half of truth, the bottom, scientific half, was made. The truth about mind, the providence of philosophy, was still a matter of discovery rather than creation. The idealists confused the idea that nothing has intrinsic nature with the idea that space and time are unreal, that human beings cause the spatiotemporal world to exist. Claiming that truth is not out there, Rorty says that where there are no sentences, there is no truth, that sentences are elements of human languages, and that human languages, as whole vocabularies, are human creations.
4. See naturalistic generalizations, Stake and Trumbull (1982).
5. According to the emic approach, the issues, concepts, and meanings are of the people under study. In the etic approach, researchers apply their own concepts to understand the social behavior of the people being studied (Taylor and Bogdan, 1984). The emic categories of meaning are called first-order

concepts. The etic categories are called second-order concepts, since they are "constructs of the constructs made by actors on the social scene" (Schultz, 1962).

6. The fact that some teachers teach artistically does not necessitate that they articulate it. We find teachers who provide meaningful aesthetic experience in their lessons, yet seem unable to articulate it, just as some musicians create excellent music but find it difficult (and unnecessary) to talk about it. Time and again we are confronted with the difference between "know how" and "know about."

7. Pathos/Dyonsian/Romantic versus Ethos/Apolonian/Classic is a distinction of musical idiom prominent since Plato. Ethos, asso-ciated with restraint and serenity, canon and norm, implies belief in absolute, unalterable values. Pathos, associated with strong feeling, motion, and action implies the personal quest (cf. Sachs, 1946).

8. The term "triangulation" was coined by Webb et al. (1965), an internal index to provide convergent evidence, "the onslaught of a series of imperfect measures." Triangulation is supposed to support a finding by showing that independent measures (checking with different sources, applying different methods, corroborated by different researchers, and examined through different theories) of it agree with it, or at least, don't contradict it.

References

Andre, M. (1983). Use of content analysis in educational evaluation. *Discourse, 4*(1).

Arnheim, R. (1986). *New essays on the psychology of art.* Los Angeles: University of California Press.

Bamberger, J. (1977). Intuitive and formal musical knowing. In Stanley S. Madeja (Ed.), *The arts, cognition, and basic skills.* St. Louis: CEMREL.

Bamberger, J. (1978). In search of a tune. In D. Perkins and B. Leondar (Eds.), *The arts and cognition.* Baltimore: Johns Hopkins.

Barone, T. (1987). Research out of the shadows: A reply to Rist. *Curriculum Inquiry, 17*(4), 453–463.

Barone, T. (1990). *Rethinking the meaning of vigor: Toward a literary tradition of educational inquiry.* Paper presented at the annual meeting of the American Education Research Association, Boston.

Berg, B. L. (1989). *Qualitative research methods for the social sciences.* Boston: Allyn & Bacon.

Bloom, B. (Ed.). (1985). *Developing talent in young people.* New York: Balantine.

Bogdan, R., and Biklen, S. K. (1982). *Qualitative research for education: An introduction to theory and methods.* Boston: Allyn & Bacon.

Bogdan, R., and Taylor, S. (1984). *Introduction to qualitative research methodology.* New York: John Wiley.

Brand, M. (1987). A review of participant observation: Study of a fourth grade music classroom—Cynthia Rhodes Thiel. *Bulletin of the Council for Research in Music Education, 92.*

Bresler, L. (1987). The role of the computer in a music theory class: Integration, barriers and learning. Unpublished doctoral dissertation, Stanford University, Stanford.

Brophy, J., and Good, T. L. (1986). Teacher behavior and student achievement. In M. C. Wittrock (Ed.), *Handbook of research on teaching* (3rd ed.). New York: Macmillan.

Campbell, D. T., and Stanley, J. C. (1966). Closing down the conversation: The end of the quantitative/qualitative debate among educational inquirers. *Educational Researcher, 1*(4), 20–24.

Carr, W., and Kemmis, S. (1986). *Becoming critical: Education, knowledge and action research.* London: Falmer.

Cockshut, A. O. J. (1984). *The art of autobiography.* New Haven: Yale University Press.

Cohen, V. (1980). The emergence of musical gestures in kindergarten children. Unpublished doctoral dissertation, University of Illinois at Urbana-Champaign.

Couperin, F. (1933). *L'Art de toucher le clavecin.* Wiesbaden, Germany: Breitkopf & Hartel. (Originally published in 1717.)

Cronbach, L. J. (1971). Test validation. In R. L. Thorndike (Ed.). *Educational measurement,* 2nd ed. (pp. 443–507). Washington: American Council on Education.

DeLorenzo, L. (1987). An exploratory field of sixth grade students' creative music problem solving processes in the general music class. Unpublished doctoral dissertation, Teachers College, Columbia University, New York.

Denzin, N. K. (1970). *The research act.* New York: Aldine.

Denzin, N. K. (1989). *Interpretative biography.* Beverly Hills: Sage.

Dewey, J. (1958). *Art as experience.* New York: Putnam's.

Dilthey, W. (1900/1976). *Selected writings.* (H. P. Rickman, Ed. and Trans.). Cambridge: Cambridge University Press.

Dilthey, W. (1910). *The construction of the historical world of the human studies. (Der Aufbauder Welt in den Geisteswissenschaften).* Gesammelte Schriften I-VII. Leipzig: B. G. Teubner, 1914–1927.

Dreeben, R. (1968). *On what is learned in school.* Reading: Addison-Wesley.

Eisner, E. (1979). *The educational imagination: On the design and evaluation of school programs.* New York: Macmillan.

Eisner, E. (1988). The primacy of experience and the politics of method. *Educational Researcher, 17*(5), 15–20.

Eisner, E. (1991). *The enlightened eye: Qualitative inquiry and the enactment of educational practice.* New York: Macmillan.

Elbaz, R. (1987). *The changing nature of the self: A critical study of the autobiographical discourse.* Iowa City: University of Iowa Press.

Erickson, F. (1986). Qualitative methods in research on teaching. In Merlin C. Wittrock (Ed.), *Handbook on teaching* (3rd ed.). New York: Macmillan.

Foucault, M. (1977) *Discipline and punish: The birth of the prison.* (Trans. A. Sheridan). New York: Pantheon Books.

Freundlich, D. (1978). The development of musical thinking case-studies in improvisation. Unpublished doctoral dissertation, Harvard University, Cambridge.

Garrison, V. (1985). *Traditional and non-traditional teaching and learning practices in folk music.* Unpublished doctoral dissertation, University of Wisconsin, Madison.

Gerber, L. (1975). An examination of three early childhood programs in relation to early childhood music education. Unpublished doctoral dissertation, University of Illinois at Urbana-Champaign.

Geertz, C. (1973). *The interpretation of cultures.* New York: Basic Books.

Geertz, C. (1988). *Works and lives: The anthropologist as author.* Stanford: Stanford University Press.

Glaser, G. A., and Strauss, A. L. (1967). *The discovery of grounded theory: Strategies for qualitative research.* Chicago: Aldine.

Goetz, J. P., and LeCompte, M. D. (1984). *Ethnography and qualitative design in educational research.* San Francisco: Academic Press.

Goodman, N. (1968). *The languages of art.* Indianapolis: Hackett.

Grumet, M. (1988). *Bitter milk: Women and teaching.* Amherst: University of Massachusetts Press.

Guba, E., and Lincoln, Y. (1981). *Effective evaluation.* San Francisco: Jossey-Bass.

Habermas, J. (1971). *Knowledge and human interests.* (J. J. Shapiro, Trans.). Boston: Beacon Press.

Hamilton, D. (1977). Making sense of curriculum evaluation: Continuities and discontinuities in an educational idea. *Review of Research in Education, 5,* 318–347.

Harwood, E. (1987). The memorized song repertoire of children in grades four and five. Unpublished doctoral dissertation, University of Illinois at Urbana-Champaign.

Hempel, C. (1966). *Philosophy of natural sciences.* London: Prentice Hall.

Henry, J. (1966). *On education.* New York: Random House.

House, E. (1980). *Evaluating with validity.* Beverly Hills: Sage.

Howe, K., and Eisenhart, M. (1990). Standards for qualitative (and quantitative) research: A prolegomenon. *Educational Researcher, 19*(4), pp. 2–9.

Huberman, A. M., and Miles, M. B. (1984). *Innovation up close: How school improvement works.* New York: Plenum.

Jackson, P. (1968). *Life in classrooms.* New York: Holt, Reinhart & Winston.

Jelinek, E. C. (Ed.). (1980). *Women's autobiography: Essays in criticism.* Bloomington: Indiana University Press.

Kagan, D. M. (1989). The heuristic value of regarding classroom instruction as an aesthetic medium. *Educational Researcher, 18*(6), 11–18.

Kalekin-Fishman, D. (1981). Ts'lilim ufikuach: R'chisshath mussag hamusika b'ganei Y'lakim [Sounds and control: The acquisition of the concept of music in the kindergarten.] *Mah'beroth L'mehkar ul'vikoreth [Notebooks of Research and Criticism], 6* 5–16.

Kalekin-Fishman, D. (1986). Music and not-music in kindergartens. *Journal of Research in Music Education, 34*(1), 54–68.

Kant, I. (1969). *Kritik der Urteilskraft* (S. H. Bergman, Trans.). Copyright by The Bialik Institute, Jerusalem.

Keil, C. (1966). *Urban blues.* Chicago: University of Chicago.

Klofas, J. J., and Cutshall, C. R. (1985). The social archeology of a juvenile facility: Unobtrusive methods in the study of institutional culture. *Qualitative Sociology, 8*(4), pp. 368–387.

Kohut, D., and Grant, J. (1990). *Learning to conduct and rehearse.* Englewood Cliffs: Prentice Hall.

Krueger, P. J. (1985). Influences of the hidden curriculum upon the perspectives of music student teachers. Unpublished doctoral dissertation, University of Wisconsin, Madison.

Krueger, P. J. (1987). Ethnographic research methodology in music education. *Journal of Research in Music Education, 35*(2), pp. 69–77.

Kushner, S. (1985). Working dreams: Innovation in a conservatoire. University of East Anglia, United Kingdom.

Kushner, S. (1989). St. Joseph's Hospice: A music performance and communication skills evaluation case study. Unpublished report, University of East Anglia, United Kingdom.

L'Roy, D. (1983). The development of occupational identity in undergraduate music education majors. Unpublished doctoral dissertation, North Texas State University, Denton.

Lewers, J. M. (1980). Rehearsal as the search for expressiveness: Implications for music reading in the high school mixed chorus. Unpublished doctoral dissertation, Teachers College, Columbia University, New York.

Lincoln, Y. S., and Guba, E. G. (1985). *Naturalistic inquiry.* New York: Sage.

Lincoln, Y. S., and Guba, E. G. (1986). But is it rigorous? Trustworthiness and authenticity in naturalistic evaluation. In D. D. William (Ed.), *Naturalistic evaluation: New directions for program evaluation,* No. 30. San Francisco: Jossey-Bass.

Lincoln, Y. S., and Guba, E. G. (1988). *Criteria for assessing naturalistic inquiries as reports.* Paper presented at the annual meeting of the American Education Research Association, New Orleans.

May, W. (1990). Teaching for understanding in the arts. *Quarterly, 1*(1 & 2), 5–16.

Merriam, A. (1964). *The anthropology of music.* Chicago: Northwestern University Press.

Merriam, A. (1967). *Ethnomusicology of the Flathead Indians.* Chicago: Aldine.

Miles, M. B., and Huberman, A. M. (1984). *Qualitative data analysis: A sourcebook of new methods.* Beverly Hills: Sage.

Mishler, E. G. (1986). *Research interviewing.* Cambridge: Harvard University Press.

Moorhead, G., and Pond D. (1941, 1942, 1944, 1951). *Music of young children* (Vols. 1–4). Vancouver: Pillsbury Foundation.

Nash, R. J. (1987). The convergence of anthropology and education. In G. Spindler (Ed.), *Education and cultural process.* Prospect: Waveland.

Nettl, B. (1983). *Twenty-nine issues and concepts.* Urbana: University of Illinois Press.

Nettl, B. (1987). *The radif of Persian music: Studies of structure and cultural context.* Champaign: Elephant & Cat.

Olson, D. (1978). The arts as basic skills: Three cognitive functions of symbols. In S. S. Madeja (Ed.), *The arts, cognition, and basic skills* (pp. 59–81). St. Louis: CEMREL.

Peshkin, A. (1988). In search of subjectivity—One's own. *Educational Researcher, 17*(7), 17–21.

Popper, K. (1959). *The logic of scientific discovery.* New York: Basic Books.

Popper, K. (1969). *Conjectures and refutations.* London: Routledge & Kegan Paul.

Rainwater, L., and Pittman, D. (1969). Ethical problems in studying a politically sensitive and deviant community. In G. J. McCall and J. L. Simmons (Eds.), *Issues in participant observation.* Reading: Addison-Wesley.

Rorty, R. (1982). *Consequences of pragmatism.* Minneapolis: University of Minnesota Press.

Rorty, R. (1989). *Contingency, irony and solidarity.* Cambridge: Cambridge University Press.

Sartre, J.-P. (1981). *The family idiot: Gustave Flaubert* (Vol. 1 1821–1857). Chicago: University of Chicago Press. (Originally published 1971).

Schatzman, L., and Strauss, A. (1973). *Field research: Strategies for a natural sociology.* Englewood Cliffs: Prentice Hall.

Schutz, A. (1962). *Collected Papers, Vol. I: The problem of social reality* (M. Natanson, Ed.). The Hague: Martinus Nijhoff.

Smith, J. K., and Heshusius, L. (1986). Closing down the conversation: The end of the quantitative—qualitative debate among educational inquirers. *Educational Researcher,* 4–12.

Smith, L. M. (1978). An evolving logic of participant observation, educational ethnography and other case studies. In L. Shulman (Ed.), *Review of research in education* (Vol. 6). Chicago: Peacock.

Sosniak, L. A. (1985). Learning to be a concert pianist. In B. Bloom (Ed.), *Developing talent in young people* (pp. 19–67). New York: Ballantine.

Spacks, P. (1976). *Imagining a self: Autobiography and novel in eighteenth-century England*. Cambridge: Harvard University Press.

Spindler, G. (Ed.). (1963). *Education and culture*. New York: Holt, Reinhart, & Winston.

Spindler, G. (1982). *Doing the ethnography of schooling*. New York: Holt, Rinehart & Winston.

Stake, R. E. (1978). The case study method in social inquiry. *Educational Researcher, 7*(2), 5–8.

Stake, R. E., Bresler, L., and Mabry, L. (in press). *Custom and cherishing*. Reston: Music Educators National Conference.

Stake, R. E., Easley, J., Denny, T., Smith, M. L., Peskin, A., Welch, W. W., Walker, R., Serano, R. G., Sanders, J. R., Stufflebeam, D. L., Hill-Burnett, J., Hoke, G., Dawson, B., and Day, J. A. (1978). *Case studies in science education*. Washington: U.S. Government Printing Office.

Stake, R. E., and Trumbull, D. (1982). Naturalistic generalizations. *Review Journal of Philosophy & Social Science, VII*(1, 2).

Stanley, J. (1990). Doing democracy: Cato Park School and the study of education in school settings. Paper presented at the annual meeting of the American Education Research Association, Boston.

Strauss, A. (1987). *Qualitative analysis for social scientists*. Cambridge: Cambridge University Press; Parlett & Hamilton.

Thiel, C. R. (1984). Participant observation: Study of a fourth grade music classroom. Unpublished doctoral dissertation, University of Illinois at Urbana-Champaign.

Upitis, R. (1985). Children's understanding of rhythm: The relationship between development and musical training. Unpublished doctoral dissertation, Harvard University, Cambridge.

Von Gunden, H. (1983). *The music of Pauline Oliveros*. London: Scarecrow.

Von Wright, G. (1971). *Explanation and understanding*. London: Routledge & Kegan Paul.

Wagner, J. (1990). Field research as a full participant in schools and other settings. Paper presented at the annual meeting of the American Education Research Association, Boston.

Webb, E., Campbell, D. T., Schwartz, R. D., and Sechrest, L. (1966). *Unobtrusive measures: Nonreactive research in the social sciences*. Chicago: Rand McNally.

Webb, E., Campbell, D. T., Schwartz, R. D., and Sechrest, L. (1981). *Nonreactive measures in the social sciences*. Boston: Houghton Mifflin.

Weber, M. (1949). *Methodology of the social sciences*. (E. Shils and H. Finch, Trans.). Glencoe: Free Press.

Yin, R. K. (1984). *Case studies in research design: Design and methods*. Beverly Hills: Sage.

Zeller, N. (1987). A rhetoric for naturalistic inquiry. Unpublished doctoral dissertation, Indiana University, Bloomington.

·7·

ON PHILOSOPHICAL METHOD

Estelle R. Jorgensen

INDIANA UNIVERSITY

The doing of philosophy is characterized by certain features or conditions that can be recognized despite differences in individual style, rigor, or orientation. These features are described in terms of how philosophy functions, and I call them "symptoms of the philosophical" because they constitute a profile of aspects that are present to a greater or lesser degree and indicate that philosophy is taking place.[1]

Each of these symptoms will be sketched in turn, with examples cited from the philosophical literatures in aesthetics, education, and music education—literatures from which philosophy of music education properly draws.[2] Some methodological differences between philosophers will then be outlined, followed by remarks on the implications of the analysis for doing philosophy in music education.

SYMPTOMS OF THE PHILOSOPHICAL

Among other things, philosophy clarifies its terms, exposes and evaluates underlying assumptions, relates its parts as a systematized theory that connects with other ideas and systems of thought, and addresses questions that are characteristically philosophical.

Philosophy Clarifies Its Terms The philosopher is vitally concerned with the meaning of words because words are the vehicles for communicating ideas. To select the right words is to clarify meaning and sharpen and refine the ideas being expressed. Although ambiguity, vagueness, and figurative language are common features of discourse, the philosopher works to ensure the greatest possible precision in meaning by clarifying the denotation and significance of words used. Without vigilance, ideas in any system of thought are cluttered and untidy, their meaning unnecessarily vague and ambiguous, making it difficult to compare ideas and systems of thought because one is uncertain of what is being compared.

The philosopher's function is to ensure that the house of ideas is tidy.

Questions such as, What is the nature of music? What is the nature of education? What is the nature of music education? are important to music education because clarifying terms illuminate interrelationships and connections between ideas. For example, if two studies of musical appreciation are compared, unless one has a basis for believing that the expression "musical appreciation" means the same in each case, the comparison does not make sense; the two studies may be about different things.

Clarifying terms also enables one to critique ideas. Such a critique is ineffective unless the meanings of the terms used are as clear as the language permits. Where ambiguities exist (and Scheffler, 1979, reminds us that they play an important part in discourse), the philosopher may simply acknowledge and clarify ambiguities qua ambiguities, and explore the richness they may offer. Having clarified one's terms, one can compare one's ideas with those of another, see points of similarity and difference, weakness and strength, and thereby critique both sets of ideas. Critical dialogue not only illumines one's thinking through sharpening and focusing the meaning attributed to a given term, but it enables careful adjudication of the ideas of others about this term. Through continued criticism, terms used within the field of discourse become more precise in their meaning, understandings become more widely shared, and justifications for positions held are better defended.

To return to our example of musical appreciation, a critique of Scholes's (1935), Wing's (1968), or Crickmore's (1968) concepts of musical appreciation is possible only to the extent that each writer clarifies what musical appreciation means, and that the critic's own concept of music appreciation is clear. Normal usage may constitute a basis on which a term comes to have meaning, as is certainly the case with the notion of musical appreciation. The philosopher, however, is not content to let the matter rest here and asks

91

such questions as: What ambiguities are present in normal usage of the term music appreciation? What do Scholes, Wing, and Crickmore understand by musical appreciation? What weaknesses and strengths characterize their ideas? How do their concepts of musical appreciation stand up to scrutiny in relation to philosophical literature about the nature of musical experience? What specific features ought to characterize musical appreciation? How does such a philosophical view of musical appreciation illumine the common practical usage of the term? What does the philosophical or the common usage concept of musical appreciation imply for instructional practice, for measurement of musical appreciation, and for the identification of factors that might denote it?

Clarifying one's terms enables studies to be devised that utilize these ideas in research and apply them in practice. Not only can the ideas be critiqued, but so too can the research methods that purport to measure or use them, and the applications that ostensibly follow from them. Here, one can move beyond questions of reliability to those of validity, and achieve a penetrating critique of the significance of a particular study or the appropriateness of a given practical application.

For example, tests of musical appreciation such as those developed by Wing (1968) and Crickmore (1968) can be compared with a given concept of musical appreciation, and evaluated not only with respect to the reliability of the measurement scales, but with respect to their validity—that is, whether these tests are in fact measuring musical appreciation or something else. Also, courses that purport to develop musical appreciation can be compared with the concept of musical appreciation, and judgments made as to whether they are accomplishing what they should in terms of the denotation of musical appreciation.

Philosophers often make taxonomies or classifications of the various phenomena they are studying. They do this in order to make distinctions and show similarities and differences not only between different things but within a particular thing. Several examples may be cited. Meyer (1956) distinguishes between various apposed views of the location and character of musical meaning. By way of showing the "morphology" of the musical symbol, Epperson (1967) posits a hierarchy of four orders of musical abstraction in western classical music, the first being the easiest to access and the most particular, the fourth and most abstract being the most difficult to access and most universal. Kivy (1984) develops a taxonomy of musical representations running from the most clearly recognized to the most abstract. And Howard (1982) differentiates various kinds of teacher talk and action involved in communicating to students how to perform music.

Although at first glance some distinctions may seem to be quite fine and of minor significance, upon reflection their importance becomes apparent. For example, Kivy (1980) distinguishes between music as *expressive of* and as *an expression of* emotions, holding that western classical music is expressive of emotion. This distinction is crucial in clarifying various points of view about emotion's specific role in western classical music and other world musics, and evaluating respective philosophical positions. That Kivy makes this distinction and argues the merits of his position enables subsequent philosophical discussion that further illumines the nature of musical meaning.

The rigor of distinction making has been less evident in music education than it should be. For example, his important work in bringing philosophy and advocacy to the attention of the music education community notwithstanding, Reimer (1989) uncritically borrows Meyer's (1956) taxonomy of musical meaning and Langer's (1942, 1953) view of artistic symbolism, thereby failing to take sufficient account of the social context in which individuals are socialized into particular understandings of music. His philosophy, therefore, has restricted application to western school music and does not adequately address artistic aspects of music making, the plethora of world musical traditions, and matters relating to music education conceived of as lifelong experience, ranging from the most elemental to advanced levels of musical instruction. Also, in the absence of further elaboration, Reimer's discussion of the ideas of various philosophers as representative philosophical "schools" tends to caricature their positions rather than clarify differences and similarities between them.[3] Philosophers in music education need to better clarify the meaning of the concepts they employ, and make more penetrating distinctions than they have in the past.

Similarly, descriptive and experimental research in music education could benefit from considerable work in clarifying terms. In much music education research, definitional issues are hastily worked through and concepts borrowed from other fields such as psychology without sufficient consideration as to their meaning. Factor analysis and other statistical techniques are frequently relied upon to clarify the meaning of terms that are then applied within empirical studies. For example, while his efforts in grappling with conceptual and empirical issues are important, in his essay on musical appreciation Crickmore (1968) hurries past a host of philosophical problems implied within the concept of musical appreciation to develop a test to measure something that still remains unclear. If one were now to use Crickmore's musical appreciation test in an empirical study to compare children's musical appreciation in terms of such variables as socioeconomic status, age level, and gender, one would further compound the problem. This is precisely the way in which much descriptive and experimental work in music education is conducted. Statistical analysis cannot substitute for philosophical critique. The function of statistics is to *test* hypotheses, not to *generate* them; that is the work of philosophy. As Goodman (1976, p. 264) reminds us, empirical evidence is a matter of goodness of "fit": fit of the model to the evidence, and the evidence to the model. Without a clearly articulated model to test, a piece of descriptive or experimental research, no matter how cleverly designed, is unscientific and invalid (cf. Gibboney, 1989).

Philosophy Exposes and Evaluates Underlying Assumptions

Assumptions predicate and underlie action. They consist of

beliefs held to be true, taken for granted and acted on. All action is predicated on assumptive sets that may be more or less implicit or explicit. In the process of exposing and evaluating underlying assumptions, the philosopher makes explicit that which otherwise may remain implicit, and clarifies aspects that are prior to and deeper than the actions to which they give rise. As a physician seeks to treat an illness' underlying causes rather than only its symptoms, so the philosopher explicates and exposes the root causes, reasons, and presuppositions of action rather than only its manifestations.

Translating assumptions into practice is difficult. Explicit or implicit assumptions are sometimes highly general and may be transposed into a variety of specific actions, each of which may imply differing and sometimes conflicting specific assumptive sets. In the course of translating theory into practice, one must frequently reconcile desired alternatives with possible or practical alternatives in a particular set of circumstances. This involves bringing together things that are in tension—a process that may not be easy to achieve—so that theory and practice may not have a one-to-one correspondence. Schwab (1971) denotes this complex process whereby one reconciles the variety of potential visions of a particular situation, each of which implies a correspondingly varied assortment of practical implications, as the "arts of eclectic."

In order to expose implicit or unclear underlying assumptions, one utilizes critical and analytical thinking in reasoning from effect to cause. Critical thinking involves the capacity to judge the relative worth of actions and ideas. Analytical thinking entails the ability to take a situation or an idea apart much as a mechanic takes an engine apart. One separates its constituent elements, makes judgments about the significance of those elements, and speculates about the various causes that might have led to a particular thing. This kind of speculative thinking is not undisciplined but is guided by logical and moral rules. Logical rules enable consistency within the analysis itself, whereas moral rules provide consistency of the analysis with the mores of the society or social group. Assumptions lie beneath the surface at various levels like the levels in an archeological dig, and one comes to an understanding of them rationally, intuitively, and imaginatively. Once they have been grasped, though, one can systematically engage in a penetrating critique of each model and deduce those implications that necessarily follow from the analysis. One can then see how they compare, which features are better or worse than others, and how aspects of each may be melded with others.

Evaluating underlying assumptions requires criteria by which these assumptions may be judged. Appeals to precedent, weight of authority, logic, moral claims, realism of expectations, ease of application, and aesthetic appeal are among the criteria by which the worth of assumptions may be adjudicated.

Exposing and evaluating underlying assumptions within music education serve some important purposes. Clarifying that which is implicit or unclear facilitates a more penetrating analysis than would be possible without such clarification. Suppose that a school district plans to adopt a particular

course in musical appreciation for children aged 12 to 15 years. Beyond considerations of the material's age-appropriateness and the measurement of learning gain that may result from taking the course are basic questions about the course's underlying assumptions: What is the author's concept of musical appreciation? On what philosophical grounds is its author's concept defensible? What does the course assume about the ways in which its author believes musical appreciation can be taught and learned? On what grounds can one justify the author's chosen methods? These, among other questions, go beyond an analysis of the course content and its measured effects to look at the factors prior to and behind it, and in so doing reveal the central issues of causation and motivation, offering the tools to answer such questions as, Why is this position being taken? Should it be endorsed?

Explicating assumptions assists in deciding between alternatives. Because education involves selecting alternatives in the worlds of ideas and practice that are ultimately defended philosophically as well as practically, the alternatives must be as clear as possible. For example, one might ask, Is the goal of school music education the development of musical appreciation, composition, or performance? Which is the most desirable alternative? If all are desirable, how are the competing claims of the alternatives to be reconciled? How does one music appreciation curriculum compare with another? The answers to these questions are predicated upon an exposition and evaluation of the underlying assumptions.

Various examples of philosophers exposing and evaluating underlying assumptions may be cited. Dewey (1916, 1938/1963) clarifies the assumptions underlying two approaches to education: a traditional conservative approach rooted in the past; a progressive forward-looking approach utilizing new and different educational methods. Scheffler (1973, pp. 67–81) analyzes the assumptions underlying three philosophical models of teaching based on the ideas of John Locke, St. Augustine, and Immanual Kant. And Alperson (in press) outlines the assumptions underlying three alternative strategies for developing a philosophy of music education and systematically critiques each position.

There has been little analysis of this sort in music education. While some of the suggested approaches to music education have a relatively articulated philosophical basis (e.g., Suzuki, 1969; Kodaly, 1974; Jaques-Dalcroze, 1921/1976), their development has arisen from, and discussions of their merit turn principally on, practical issues rather than the assumptions on which they are based. Such debate as has occurred has seldom benefited from incisive philosophical analysis of underlying assumptions. Teachers have defended their chosen method(s) on the basis of personally held opinions rather than dispassionately reasoned arguments. Many believe that a combination of methods will automatically yield a wider and superior view of music education than just one method, despite the fact that the assumptions on which the methods rest may be contradictory (Jorgensen, 1990).

Were the underlying assumptions of these methods to be systematically explicated, not only would they be better articulated and defended than they are now, but conflicting assumption sets would be exposed and teachers would better understand which methods can or should be combined in given circumstances, and why. Descriptive and experimental researchers would also benefit from such clarification by having access to theories in which methods are carefully described and philosophically grounded.

Philosophy Relates Its Parts as a Systematized Theory That Connects with Other Ideas and Systems of Thought Philosophers seek to construct a body of thought that coheres as a whole yet is structurally organized. Their observations are not isolated phenomena but constitute a systematically analyzed whole. All the parts are present that are needed to form the whole. Every part is necessary and relevant to the whole, and no part is extraneous. Each part is logically consistent with every other part. As such, this body of thought is like a work of art. It is like Langer's (1953) concept of the work of art as a "highly articulated" object, in that its parts seem to fuse to form a whole and yet have a separate existence, so that one understands the whole as well as the constituent parts.

As a systematized theory, the body of thought that the philosopher constructs is intended to have explanatory value. It is purposeful in its clarification of terms and exposition and evaluation of underlying assumptions. Further, it is systematic in its attempt to order that which may otherwise be chaotic. The analogy of the philosopher as the architect of the house, the designer of the ideas that account for a given phenomenon in a meaningful way, suggests that the philosopher articulates the frames of reference within which one sees the world or one's version of it. Through a methodical and careful explication, the philosopher clarifies ideas that may be ambiguous and in disarray, and designs a conceptual framework that is not only ordered but insightful.

Moreover, this system of thought is not isolated but integrated within, or related to, other systems of thought in ways that are clarified by the philosopher. As such, it connects or corresponds to these other systems, be they ideas or phenomena in the empirical world. The evidence of this correspondence may be of varying kinds including logical argument, appeals to authority, precedent, example, or analogy. In the scientific worldview, empirical data constitute the most persuasive evidence. In the philosophical worldview, however, other nonscientific ways of knowing may be equally or more persuasive, and the philosopher admits as evidence that which the scientist may exclude.

Philosophers are inveterate gatherers and citers of examples. Although they differ about the roles examples serve, as we shall see later, philosophers agree that examples are essential to illustrate and test their ideas. Kivy's attempt to clarify the nature of musical expression and representation, to show that musical meaning is found within and without the musical piece, is grounded in examples. In *The Corded Shell* (1980), one encounters Lilian, the St. Bernard dog; and in *Music Alone* (1990), the cast of characters from E. M. Forster's *Howard's End*—Mrs. Munt, Helen, Margaret, and Tibby. These serve not only as exemplars, but as analogies of, or metaphors for, aspects of musical experience. Likewise, Goodman (1976) makes extensive use of examples in

his *Languages of Art.* In distinguishing exemplification as a symbol function, for example, he uses a swatch of cloth, the centaur, Pickwick, Don Quixote, and Pegasus, and metaphors (e.g., "Metaphor, it seems, is a matter of teaching an old word new tricks," p. 69) to make his points. When he speaks of gestures, Goodman cites the example of the orchestra conductor whose gestures "denote sounds to be produced but are not themselves sounds" (p. 61).

Creating a systematized theory that relates to other systems of thought connects the various ways of knowing, be they scientific, artistic, religious, philosophical, or otherwise. Establishing these connections achieves a broader perspective on the world. The scientific way of knowing is only one of a plethora of ways in which we understand ourselves and our world. As we relate these ways of knowing to each other, we come to understand that the realities they address are different, complementary, and intersecting. Restricting one's vision to a particular way of knowing results in a limited view of one's self and the world.

Moreover, such a systematized theory serves to explain why things are as they are, or as they appear to be, in terms of a philosophical worldview. Philosophers' explanations help to illumine the nature of self and the world, one manifestation of the human tendency to reflect on one's place in the world. These philosophical explanations have their own validity, quite apart from questions of how well they interface with other scientific, artistic, or religious explanations: They ultimately are judged in their own terms.

The implications for a philosophy of music education are profound. Not only should it exemplify the characteristics of a systematic theory that relates to other systems of thought (educational, artistic, religious, scientific, or otherwise), but it should ultimately be judged in philosophical, not scientific terms. Science may *enhance* philosophy, but it cannot constitute the *ultimate test* of it. Many philosophical propositions lie outside science's purview and are justified in nonscientific ways. This is not to say that science is unimportant in the study of music education. Quite the contrary. Philosophy draws on science and science on philosophy; each illumines the other. However, one is not judged in terms of the other. Science ultimately judges science; and philosophy, philosophy. Consequently, explanation in music education is understood to be multifaceted rather than monolithic: As nonscientific ways of knowing complement scientific ways of knowing, so music education is properly studied scientifically and nonscientifically. Philosophy thus assumes a central place alongside science in music education research. Such a position requires rethinking the methods of inquiry appropriate to the study of music education and philosophy's place in music education research.

Various examples of philosophers constructing theories that connect with other systems of ideas exist. Schelling (in translation, 1989) proposes a grand schema (to show that the arts, sciences, and social phenomena are emanations of a single absolute) that moves from general principles to specific aspects of the various arts. He follows in the tradition of Plato and Kant, and his ideas relate particularly to those of other German writers such as Schopenhauer (in translation, 1969) and Hegel (in translation, 1975). Langer (1967, 1972, 1982) develops not only a theory of art, but, importantly, a theory of the mind. She constructs an argument within the framework of such ideas as the nature, meaning, and significance of artistic symbols; the virtuality of time and space in artistic apprehension; and the nature of feeling as the basis for artistic cognition. Her work is in the tradition of Kant, Ludwig Wittgenstein, and Ernst Cassirer, and relates especially to the ideas of Dewey (1934/1979) and Meyer (1956), among others. Adorno (1984) elaborates a theory that examines the relevance of aesthetic categories such as form, beauty, truth, content, and objectification, and places the arts within the context of society. His aesthetic theory is apposed to those of Plato, Kant, and Sigmund Freud, among others, and his ideas relate especially to the work of such musicians and philosophers as Busoni (1911/1962) and Bloch (in translation, 1985). Goodman (1976) articulates a theory of symbols in which the arts function as symbol systems or ways of world making. Throughout, he compares his ideas to those of such writers as René Descartes, Jerome Bruner, Emile Jaques-Dalcroze, and Joseph Margolis, and his theory-as-a-whole can be related to the work of various philosophers involved in the study of musical semiotics (see Rantala, Rowell, and Tarasti, 1986; Margolis 1986). Although traditions of documentation vary from one philosopher to another, all place themselves in the context of a philosophical tradition. Even if they specify little about that tradition, an inspection of their ideas and the writers to whom they refer indicates something of the particular traditions from which they draw and to which they contribute.

Relatively few systematic theories of music education have emerged in the twentieth century. Among these, a noteworthy study appears in Small's *Music-Society-Education* (1980). Drawing from two historical paradigms of music and society (the traditional western and "potential" worldviews), Small derives implications for music education and proposes that music education's task is to *reconstruct* culture as well as *transmit* it. His reconceptualist (see Pinar, 1975) view of the music curriculum resonates with work in ethnomusicology, musical anthropology, and sociology, by such writers as Merriam (1964), Blacking (1976), Shepherd, Virden, Vulliamy, and Wishart, (1977), Frith (1978), and Nettl (1985). Following a discussion of the assumptions underlying the potential society that he believes music prophesies, and to which he suggests music educators should aspire, Small develops a model of music education that features an international, inclusive, cooperative, and egalitarian approach to music making within the context of world musics that contrasts with the parochial, exclusive, competitive, and hierarchical approach to music making in the western classical tradition.

Music education would benefit from the development of paradigms that reflect the variety of world musics, the international pervasiveness of music education, its multidisciplinary nature, its relevance to the entire life cycle, under the auspices of the various social institutions that carry it forward. Historically, music educators in search of the boundaries of their field have settled for a definition that is pragmatically rather than philosophically grounded. Music education has been construed mainly as musical instruction in western-style elementary and secondary schools, simply because this is what many music educators do. This limited definition excludes much that properly concerns the interrelationship of music and education.

A more inclusive view suggests that music education is both music in education and education in music, a fusion of two essential elements in a synthesis or integrated whole.[4] The philosopher's challenge is to balance alternative emphases on music and education. An accent on music may devote insufficient attention to the process whereby musical understanding is educed and to music's place in the larger educational enterprise. A focus on education may place inadequate stress on musical knowledge and education's place in the larger musical enterprise. However, a recognition of music education as both education in music and music in education affords a balanced yet broad understanding of the interrelationship of music and education.

Philosophy Addresses Questions That are Characteristically Philosophical As a way of understanding, philosophy addresses questions that differ from those of other ways of knowing, be they artistic, scientific, religious, or otherwise. These questions make up a profile of interests and concerns that are typically philosophical.

Ontological questions have to do with the nature of being and reality. For example, When does music occur? Is it the idea in the composer's head, the notes in the score, the musical performance at a given place and time, or the listener's sensations of sound? What is the nature of the musical experience? What is the nature of the educational experience? For example, Kivy (1990) posits various types of musical experience in the listener to western instrumental classical music, arguing that there is a quantitative rather than a qualitative difference in the experience from the most elemental to advanced levels of training. Sessions (1950/1962) describes three different types of musical experience—those of the composer, performer, and listener. Dewey (1916, 1938/1963) depicts educational experience as potentially educative or miseducative, as the reconciliation of various tensions (doing and undergoing, taking advantage of present desire while also envisioning future possibilities, interfacing person and subject matter, focusing on means and ends, resolving freedom and control, reconciling tradition and change, and balancing the individual's needs with those of the group).

Epistemological questions relate to the nature of knowing and understanding.[5] For example, How does one come to know music? What is the nature of the knowledge implied in understanding music? How is learning educed? Bruner (1963) posits that an understanding of the structure of any subject (whereby one experientially grasps the underlying assumptions, conceptual framework, and methods of inquiry in the subject matter) enables one to gain meaningful knowledge of the material. Like Eisner (1985) and others, Bruner (1979, 1986) holds that the arts provide ways of knowing that contrast with those of the sciences, and consti tute distinct forms of knowledge and perspectives on the world that are uniquely aesthetic or artistic. With Shepherd and others (Shepherd et al., 1977), Bruner (1973, 1986) sees all the symbol systems on which education is based—those of language, music, art, drama, religion, among others—as culturally mediated, and interpreted in corporate or collective as well as individual or personal ways. Although various composers and philosophers agree that music is understood in its own terms in ways that are characteristically musical, there is considerable philosophical disagreement over the precise nature of musical meaning (whether propositional or otherwise), and its location (within or outside the music itself).

Axiological questions regard matters of valuation. For example, Is western classical music "better" than other western genres? Are the arts a necessary part of education or just nice to have (see Broudy, 1979)? Which musical skills are of greatest importance? For example, on musical values, Blacking (1976), Shepherd et al. (1977), Small (1980), Fletcher (1987), Frith (1987), and Swanwick (1988) argue that because the values underlying western classical music do not apply universally to all world musics, music education today must incorporate a variety of musics within the classroom, thereby offering various sets of artistic or aesthetic value systems. Budd (1985) suggests that a new theory of musical valuation is needed. Such a theory would assist teachers in choosing examples for study from a wide array of world musics. The plethora of educational values concerning the arts is illustrated in the contrasting positions of Aristotle (*Works of Aristotle,* 1921), for whom the arts need have no use other than that they enable people to enjoy their lives, and Locke (in a 1913 edition), who is determined that every educational aspect shall have a particular vocational use, thereby marginalizing the arts or excluding them altogether.

Ethical questions refer to the underlying social mores and rules of a given society or social group. For example, When is an elitist system of music education preferable to a universalistic one? How should teachers relate to students? Several examples will illustrate. Peters (1966) grapples with such issues as the concept of education as initiation into a way of life that society's members believe to be worthwhile, the nature of education's ethical foundations and the justifications invoked, and problems of social control. Arguments linking music as one of the arts to "the good" as an educational end go back to antiquity. Plato (*Collected Dialogues of Plato,* 1961) believes that a particular moral quality is associated with any given piece of music. Kant (in translation, 1952) holds that beauty functions as a symbol of the good, and thereby refers to it. Schiller (in translation, 1967) posits that the arts constitute the means whereby the good can be implied before it is understood conceptually, and the way by which the person who has yet to attain full moral development imaginatively or intuitively grasps the idea of the good. Beardsmore (1971) argues that the arts provide an understanding of what the good is. While it is not the artist's intention to moralize, the work of art nevertheless illumines the nature of the good.

Logical questions relate to the rules for reasoning, be they deductive, inductive, analogical, or however conceived. For example, Is this particular justification for music education well taken? Are there logical flaws in this argument? Is this musical curriculum consistent with the theoretical principles it purports to espouse? In their analyses of Kant's aesthetic theory, such writers as Crawford (1974) and McCloskey (1987) expose the logical problems and point to evident strengths they see in Kant's argument. Scheffler (1973) outlines the role of logic in educational decision making, and his analysis of Schwab's curriculum theory constitutes a useful model for examining logical and other aspects of an argument. Budd (1985) exposes some of the logical flaws in arguments about the relationship of music and the emotions by Schopenhauer, Langer, Meyer, and others.

Political questions have to do with issues of governance and social order. For example, How can this theoretical model be applied in practice? How should democratic principles translate into the music classroom? Who should control music education? We see political questions exemplified in the work of Dewey (1916, 1927) and Read (1958), for whom education constitutes the means of preparing citizens for the democracy and the arts the key to its preservation. Notwithstanding its detractions, Dewey holds, democracy illustrates principles of freedom and social control that should be upheld within the classroom. Read argues that the arts are central to the educational process: Only as people are artists will they be fully actualized and productive and cooperative members of society. Discussions of the interface of the arts and politics are also found in the work of such writers as Fischer (1963), Barzun (1974), Taylor (1978), Attali (1985), and Eagleton (1990).

Aesthetic or artistic questions refer to considerations of what is beautiful and how beauty is to be adjudicated. For example, What is a work of art? How does one relate to it? Are there universal aesthetic criteria? What is the nature of artistry? Among the philosophers to explore these sorts of problems, Hanslick (in translation, 1986) examines the nature and basis of beauty in music, Prall (1929, 1936) investigates the nature of aesthetic judgment and analysis, Beardsley (1981) grapples with problems in the philosophy of art criticism, Dahlhaus (1982, 1985) discusses aspects of musical aesthetics as evidenced in the history of western classical music, and the nature of nineteenth-century aesthetic realism, and Ecker and her colleagues (Ecker, 1985) articulate aspects of a feminist aesthetic. Although most philosophers focus on aesthetic apprehension, studies by Howard (1982) and Wolterstorff (1986) are among a comparatively few philosophical studies of the work of musical artists.[6]

These philosophical question sets address a wide range of issues in music education. Their common point of reference is their challenge to the validity of extant ideas and practices: They systematically ask whether these ideas and practices are well grounded. They bypass the peripheral and trivial issues, going to the core of *why* things are as they seem to be and where they seem to be going. As such, they address central questions relating to music education and challenge its very reason for being. That such question sets are already philosophically well established enables philosophers to clarify their terms, expose and evaluate assumptions, and develop systematic bodies of thought that connect with other ideas in respect to a wide range of issues touching on music education.

DIFFERENCES IN APPROACHES

I have sketched symptoms of the philosophical that more or less exemplify the work of philosophy. Philosophers disagree about aspects of how philosophy should be done. To illustrate, I shall briefly outline three interrelated and overlapping sets of contrasting positions—phenomenology/positivism, deduction/induction, and synopsis/analysis—reflecting differences in epistemological stance, perspectives on reasoning, and purposes of doing philosophy, respectively.

Phenomenology and Positivism Reese (1980, p. 428) succinctly describes *phenomenology,* from the Greek *phainomenon* ("appearance") and *logos* ("knowledge of "), as "an approach to philosophy centering on analysis of the phenomena that flood [human] awareness." One of the principal architects of twentieth-century phenomenology is Husserl (in translation, 1931; see Sokolowski, 1988), who regards consciousness as an integral part of reality rather than as "a given," and holds that one cannot describe what one perceives without also describing one's consciousness of what one experiences as one perceives. One therefore intuitively engages in introspection about one's experience of the empirical world with a view to gaining knowledge of self and the world.

Several philosophical studies of music from a phenomenological perspective may be cited, including those by Pike (1970), Schutz (1976), and Smith (1979). Although there are few phenomenologically oriented philosophical studies of music education, a notable example is provided by Bartholomew (in press).

Reese (1980, p. 450) characterizes *positivism* as a related group of philosophies that take an "extremely positive" view of science and scientific method. To the logical positivist (see Hanfling, 1981; Smith, 1986), inference by means of empirical evidence constitutes the predominant means of gathering knowledge, and one bases one's judgments on logic and reason rather than on intuition. The scientific method constitutes the primary means whereby phenomena in the natural world are studied.

The groundwork for educational positivism in the twentieth century was laid by Dewey's (1933) endorsement of the scientific method as the primary source of knowledge and his emphasis on educational experimentation using the scientific method. Subsequently, the ideas of B. F. Skinner and J. Wolpe on operant conditioning and counterconditioning, respectively, building on earlier work by Ivan Pavlov, E. L. Thorndike, and G. B. Watson, among others, gave rise to procedures such as those used in behavior modification, and behavioral models of learning applied in mastery learning and direct instruction, exemplified in teaching/discipline strategies and competency-based music education advocated in Madsen and Madsen (1974) and Madsen and Yarbrough (1980), respectively.

Although phenomenology and positivism are contrasting positions, the lines are less clear in practice: (1) Both make observations and collect empirical data. (2) Philosophers hold positions that have both positivistic and phenomenological elements. For example, while he endorses the importance of reason, Dewey (1916, 1933) also underscores the role of intuition and imagination in the learning process. (3) The excessively narrow interpretation of scientific method that excluded intuitive, emotive, and imaginational aspects of cognition has been challenged by philosophers of science, and the range of acceptable scientific research methods broadened accordingly. (4) Phenomenological research methods such as participant observation and case study approaches have benefited from the insights of positivism in drawing attention to the importance of logic, reason, rigor, and inference in discovering knowledge.

The impact of positivism on music education research in recent decades has downgraded the importance of philosophical research, and detrimentally affected the quality of philosophy of music education teaching and research. The popularity of scientific studies of music and education, the superficiality of philosophical teaching, and the lack of emphasis on philosophical research have resulted in somewhat of a hiatus of serious philosophical research in music education.[7] Fortunately, prominent music education researchers now realize that theory building enhances descriptive, experimental, and historical research; philosophy can make an important contribution to music education research; and both positivistic and phenomenological insights can benefit music education research.

Deduction and Induction Reese (1980, p. 120) describes *deduction* (from the Latin *de,* "from," and *ducere,* "to lead") as reasoning in which the conclusion follows necessarily from the premises, whether from the general to the general, from the general to the particular, or from the particular to the particular. Deduction has its roots in logical rules which establish the conditions under which it can and should proceed. (see Carnap, 1958; Langer, 1967; Simpson, 1988).

For example, in his *Critique of Judgment,* Kant (in translation, 1952) lays out a classic deductive argument that establishes a kind of reason he denotes as "judgment" (rooted in aesthetic and teleological concerns) that links pure and applied reason, and establishes a trilogy of interconnected species of reasoned thought. In Kant's argument, each point follows logically and necessarily from the previous one until the paradigm is complete. Similarly, in *Languages of Art,* Goodman (1976) derives a theory of symbols deductively by establishing the theoretical categories of symbol function, analyzing the specific semantic and syntactic features of various arts, and deducing shared functional qualities that comprise "symptoms of the aesthetic." As with Kant, if any of his assumptions fail to convince, or if his logic is flawed, the argument falls or must be bolstered by other means.

Induction is distinguished from deduction mainly on the

basis of "probable" rather than "necessary inference." As Reese (1980, p. 251) observes, induction and deduction are incorrectly distinguished on the basis of whether the inference moves from "specific facts to general conclusions" (induction) or from "general premises to specific conclusions" (deduction) because such a distinction only compares one sort of induction with one sort of deduction. Indeed, Carnap (1952) posits various species of induction by which a judgment of the probable truth of a particular inference is made. On the basis of evidence, be it example, analogy, predictive quality, or the like, one accepts or rejects a given proposition. Although X does not follow *necessarily* (on the basis of logical rules) from Y, nevertheless, on the basis of certain evidence, one infers that X *probably* follows from Y.

For example, in *Sound and Semblance* (1984), *Sound Sentiment* (1989), and *Music Alone* (1990), Kivy develops an analysis that is pervasively inductive, drawing particularly on example and analogy. He admits that his differences with Goodman include a disagreement over how one should do philosophy. Where Goodman logically derives general propositions, which may then be tested with reference to specific examples, Kivy draws conclusions from various specific examples. Not only do his various characters such as Lilian and Tibby serve as examples, analogies, and metaphors for aspects of musical experience, but Kivy derives his analysis out of an examination of musical examples. Honegger's *Pacific 231* serves, in Kivy's words, as a "paradigm" of "representational" music, and he leans on excerpts from Monteverdi's *Arianna*, Handel's *Messiah*, Beethoven's *Ninth Symphony*, Bach's *Cantata No. 78* ("*Jesu, der du meine Seele*"), Earl Robinson's *The Lonesome Train*, Haydn's *Missa in Tempore Belle*, among others, to derive as well as illustrate ideas regarding aspects of musical expressiveness.

Seldom is the work of one philosopher entirely either deductive or inductive. In practice, philosophers typically combine approaches. For example, in the First Moment of Kant's *Critique of Aesthetic Judgment*, we see the palace, a Rousseau, the Iroquois sachem, and the uninhabited island as Kant elaborates the particular quality of delight that a work of art provides, and a dish of food, Canary wine, among other examples he uses to distinguish between the beautiful and the good. He obviously draws ideas from the examples he considers. Similarly, Kivy lays out his argument in a logical fashion in which deduction forms an integral part. Viewed as a whole, Kivy's analysis is also deductive in the sense that one statement leads to the next that follows necessarily from it, even though each statement is established inductively rather than deductively. One may logically follow the arguments in *Sound Sentiment, Sound and Semblance,* and *Music Alone* from beginning to end as Kivy systematically builds the case for his thesis.

Music educators historically have focused on the inductive development of theories based on empirical evidence, at least to the extent that theory development is of any concern. In so doing, they have followed the predominant research methodologies in education and music. As noted elsewhere (Jorgensen, 1980, 1981), music education would benefit from complementary deductive approaches.

Synopsis and Analysis Synopsis (in the sense in which I am using the term here) involves constructing a comprehensive paradigm that elaborates one's own philosophical perspective while building on the views of other philosophers. One's objective is not so much to critique other points of view (although critique is included) as to utilize them in explicating elements of one's own philosophy for purposes of *verification rather than refutation.* Such synoptic philosophies are often conceived at a high level of generalization; witness Kant's philosophy of reason, Schelling's philosophy of art, Langer's theory of mind, and Dewey's philosophy of experience.

Analysis, as Reese (1980, p. 13) notes, "from the Greek *analytikos,* derived from the verb *analyein,* 'to resolve into its elements,'" involves the breaking down of a thing into its various parts. Analytic philosophers such as Scheffler, Kivy, and Budd approach the ideas of other philosophers critically and use evidence for purposes of *refutation rather than verification.* An important element in their analysis is the clarification of language. Analytic philosophies tend to focus on more specific problems than do synoptic philosophies.

In illustrating the difference between synoptic and analytic approaches to aesthetics, one might cite Goodman (1976) and Collingwood (1938) as examples of a synoptic approach, and Kivy (1989) and Budd (1985) as examples of an analytic approach. What Kivy and Budd attempt to do (and Urmson, 1989, p. 26, suggests that neither Goodman nor Collingwood is primarily concerned with this) is to explicate ideas, often implicit in everyday language, as material to be elucidated rather than as propositions to be critiqued. The former are architects and builders of the house; the latter are its inspectors and appraisers. This is not to say that some analysis does not go on in the midst of synopsis and vice versa. Rather, the focus of philosophical endeavor differs significantly between these approaches.

In music education, philosophical thought has been predominantly synoptic; witness the work of Reimer (1989) and Swanwick (1981, 1988). While there has been relatively little analytic philosophy, useful models include Howard (1982), Alperson (in press) and Elliott (in press).

CODA

Doing philosophy in music education may sometimes be disturbing, uncomfortable, and even painful. To challenge the myths and assumptions that have been held as "received wisdom" is to invite criticism from those for whom a different way of seeing things is provocative and unsettling. We may remember Plato's allegory in which the inhabitants of the cave go so far as to seek to kill the one who brings a different perspective to bear on their situation. So, in music education, to challenge the status quo is to invite hostility or rejection from those with a vested interest in seeing things remain as they are.

Yet despite the potential difficulties of following such a path, the philosopher relentlessly pursues truth, variously understood, however elusive. Whereas Plato finishes his allegory of the cave on a desperate note, a more optimistic story would have concluded with at least some of the cave's inhabitants coming out with their prophet into the sunlight. The critique that philosophy brings and the vision that it offers may be destructive of complacency, yet they appeal to seekers for wisdom and understanding. The disciplined reflection that philosophy demands may fall on some deaf ears, yet it is welcomed by those people who wish to understand what the interrelationship between music and education can and should be. For these persons, philosophy ultimately benefits scholarship and practice in music education.

Notes

1. The term "symptom" is borrowed from Goodman (1976) although here not used narrowly to indicate only the symbolic features of a particular way of understanding.
2. For introductions to the philosophical literatures in music, aesthetics, and education, respectively, see Alperson (1986), Margolis (1987), and Peters (1967). For additional philosophical studies of education see Hirst and Peters (1970), Hirst (1974), Passmore (1980), and Broudy (1988).
3. This is especially true, Bowman (in press) argues, of Reimer's treatment of the contributions of the "formalists" to aesthetic understanding. See Reimer (in press) for a further amplification of his views on aesthetic education.
4. Envisaging music education in this way enables the perspectives of philosophical thought in education as well as music to be brought to bear on music education.
5. Scheffler (1965, p. 1) defines the task of epistemology as "the logical analysis of knowledge."
6. This will doubtless change given the praxialist emphasis in the philosophy of music, evident in the work of Sparshott, among others (see Alperson, 1986).
7. During this time, while various journals such as *The Journal of Aesthetic Education* have published philosophical articles on music and music education, these have been outside the mainstream of music education research.

References

Adorno, T. (1984). *Aesthetic theory* (Trans. C. Lenhardt; Ed. Gretel Adorno and Rolf Tiedemann). London and New York: Routledge and Kegan Paul.

Alperson, P. (Ed.)(1986). *What is music? An introduction to the philosophy of music.* New York: Haven.

Alperson, P. (in press). What should one expect from a philosophy of music education? *Journal of Research in Music Education.*

Attali, J. (1985). *Noise: The political economy of music* (Trans. B. Massumi). Minneapolis: University of Minnesota Press.

Bartholomew, D. (in press). Whole/part relations in music: The application of a distinction. *Journal of Research in Music Education.*

Barzun, J. (1974). *The use and abuse of art.* Princeton and London: Princeton University Press.

Beardsley, M. (1981). *Aesthetics: Problems in the philosophy of criticism* (2nd. ed.). Indianapolis and Cambridge: Hackett.

Beardsmore, R. W. (1971). *Art and morality.* London and Basingstoke: Macmillan.

Blacking, J. (1976). *How musical is man?* London: Faber and Faber.

Bloch, E. (1985). *Essays on the philosophy of music* (Trans. P. Palmer; intro., D. Drew). Cambridge: Cambridge University Press.

Bowman, W. (in press). The values of musical formalism. *Journal of Aesthetic Education*

Broudy, H. S. (1979). Arts education: Necessary or just nice? *Phi Delta Kappan, 60,* 347–350.

Broudy, H. S. (1988). *The uses of schooling.* New York: Routledge, Chapman and Hall.

Bruner, J. (1963). *The process of education.* New York: Vintage Books.

Bruner, J. (1973). *The relevance of education* (Ed. A. Gill). New York: W. W. Norton.

Bruner, J. (1979). *On knowing: Essays for the left hand* (expanded ed.) Cambridge: Harvard University Press.

Bruner, J. (1986). *Actual minds, possible worlds.* Cambridge: Harvard University Press.

Budd, M. (1985). *Music and the emotions: The philosophical theories.* London: Routledge and Kegan Paul.

Busoni, F. (1962). Sketch of a new esthetic of music. In *Three classics in the aesthetic of music.* New York: Dover. (Original work published 1911).

Carnap, R. (1952). *The continuum of inductive methods.* Chicago: University of Chicago Press.

Carnap, R. (1958). *Introduction to symbolic logic and its application* (Trans. W. H. Meyer and J. Wilkinson). New York: Dover.

The collected dialogues of Plato including the letters (1961). (Ed. E. Hamilton and H. Cairns). New York: Pantheon Books.

Collingwood, R. G. (1938). *The principles of art.* Oxford: Oxford University Press.

Crawford, D. W. (1974). *Kant's aesthetic theory.* Madison: University of Wisconsin Press.

Crickmore, L. (1968). An approach to the measurement of musical appreciation (I). *Journal of Research in Music Education, 16,* 239–253.

Dahlhaus, C. (1982). *Esthetics of music* (Trans. W. Austin). Cambridge: Cambridge University Press.

Dahlhaus, C. (1985). *Realism in nineteenth-century music* (Trans. M. Whittall). Cambridge: Cambridge University Press.

Dewey, J. (1916). *Democracy and education: An introduction to the philosophy of education.* New York: Macmillan.

Dewey, J. (1933). *How we think: A restatement of the relation of reflective thinking to the educative process* (rev. ed.). Boston: D. C. Heath.

Dewey, J. (1927). *The public and its problems.* Denver: Alan Swallow.

Dewey, J. (1979). *Art as experience.* New York: G. P. Putnam's Sons. (Original work published 1934)

Dewey, J. (1963). *Experience and education.* New York: Collier Books. (Original work published 1938)

Eagleton, T. (1990). *The ideology of the aesthetic.* Cambridge: Basil Blackwell.

Ecker, G. (Ed.). (1985). *Feminist aesthetics* (Trans. H. Anderson). Boston: Beacon Press.

Eisner, E. W. (Ed.). (1985). *Learning and teaching the ways of knowing.* Chicago: National Society for the Study of Education, 84th Yearbook, pt. 2.

Elliott, D. (in press). Music as knowledge. *Journal of Aesthetic Education.*

Epperson, G. (1967). *The musical symbol: A study of the philosophic theory of music.* Ames: Iowa State University Press.

Fischer, E. (1963). *The necessity of art: A Marxist approach* (Trans. A. Bostock). Harmondsworth: Penguin.

Fletcher, P. (1987). *Music and education.* Oxford: Oxford University Press.

Frith, S. (1978). *The sociology of rock.* London: Constable.

Frith, S. (1978). Towards an aesthetic of popular music. In *Music and society: The politics of composition, performance and reception* (Ed. R. Leppert and S. McClary). Cambridge: Cambridge University Press, 133–149.

Gibboney, R. A. (1989). The unscientific character of educational research, *Phi Delta Kappan, 71,* 225–227.

Goodman, N. (1976). *Languages of art: An approach to a theory of symbols.* Indianapolis: Hackett.

Goodman, N. (1978). *Ways of worldmaking.* Indianapolis: Hackett.

Hanfling, O. (1981). *Essential readings in logical positivism.* Oxford: Basil Blackwell.

Hanslick, E. (1986). *On the musically beautiful* (Trans. G. Payzant). Indianapolis: Hackett.

Hegel, G. W. F. (1975). *Aesthetics* (Trans. A. J. Ellis). Oxford: Clarendon Press.

Hindemith, P. (1952). *A composer's world: Horizons and limitations.* Cambridge: Harvard University Press.

Hirst, P. H. (1974). *Knowledge and the curriculum: A collection of philosophical papers.* London: Routledge and Kegan Paul.

Hirst, P. H., and Peters, R. S. (1970). *The logic of education.* London: Routledge and Kegan Paul.

Howard, V. (1982). *Artistry: The work of artists.* Indianapolis: Hackett.

Husserl, E. (1931). *Ideas: General introduction to pure phenomenology* (Trans. W. R. Boyce Gibson). London: Collier Books.

Jaques-Dalcroze, E. (1976). *Rhythm, music and education* (Trans. H. F. Rubinstein). New York: Arno Press. (Original work published 1921)

Jorgensen, E. R. (1980). On the development of a theory of musical instruction. *Psychology of Music, 8*(2), 25–30.

Jorgensen, E. R. (1981). On a choice-based instructional typology in music. *Journal of Research in Music Education, 29,* 97–102.

Jorgensen, E. R. (1990). Philosophy and the music teacher: Challenging the way we think. *Music Educators Journal, 76*(5), 17–23.

Kant, I. (1952). *The critique of judgement* (Trans., with analytical indexes, J. C. Meredith). Oxford: Oxford University Press.

Kivy, P. (1980). *The corded shell: Reflections on musical expression.* Princeton: Princeton University Press.

Kivy, P. (1984). *Sound and semblance: Refections on musical representation.* Princeton: Princeton University Press.

Kivy, P. (1989). *Sound sentiment: An essay on the musical emotions including the complete text of "The Corded Shell."* Philadelphia: Temple University Press.

Kivy, P. (1990). *Music alone: Philosophical reflections on the purely musical experience.* Ithaca: Cornell University Press.

Kodaly, Z. (1974). *The selected writings of Zoltan Kodaly* (Ed. F. Bonis; Trans. L. Halapy and F. Macnicol). London: Boosey and Hawkes.

Langer, S. K. (1942). *Philosophy in a new key: A study of the symbolism of reason, rite, and art.* Cambridge: Harvard University Press.

Langer, S. K. (1953). *Feeling and form: A theory of art developed from "Philosophy in a New Key."* London: Routledge and Kegan Paul.

Langer, S. K. (1967). *An introduction of symbolic logic* (3rd. rev. ed.). New York: Dover Publications.

Langer, S. K. (1967, 1972, 1982). *Mind: An essay on human feeling* (3 vols.). Baltimore: Johns Hopkins University Press.

Locke, J. (1913). *Some thoughts concerning education.* Cambridge: Cambridge University Press.

Madsen, C. H., and Madsen, C. K. (1974). *Teaching/Discipline: A positive approach for educational development* (2nd. ed). Boston: Allyn and Bacon.

Madsen, C. K., and Yarbrough, C. (1980). *Competency-based music education.* Englewood Cliffs: Prentice-Hall.

Margolis, J. (Ed.). (1987). *Philosophy looks at the arts: Contemporary readings in aesthetics* (3rd ed.). Philadelphia: Temple University Press.

Margolis, J. (Ed.). (1986). On the semiotics of music. In P. Alperson (Ed.), *What is music? An introduction to the philosophy of music.* New York: Haven.

McCloskey, M. A. (1987). *Kant's aesthetic.* Albany: State University of New York Press.

Merriam, A. P. (1964). *The anthropology of music.* Evanston: Northwestern University Press.

Meyer, L. (1956). *Emotion and meaning in music.* Chicago: University of Chicago Press.

Nettl, B. (1985). *The western impact on world music: Change, adaptation, and survival.* New York: Schirmer Books.

Passmore, J. (1980). *The philosophy of teaching.* Cambridge: Harvard University Press.

Peters, R. S. (1966). *Ethics and education.* London: George Allen and Unwin.

Peters, R. S. (Ed.). (1967). *The concept of education.* London: Routledge and Kegan Paul.

Pike, A. (1970). *A phenomenological analysis of musical experience and other essays.* New York: St. John's Press.

Pinar, W. (Ed.). (1975). *Curriculum theorizing: The reconceptualists.* Berkeley: McCutchan.

Prall, D. W. (1929). *Aesthetic judgment.* New York: Thomas Y. Crowell.

Prall, D. W. (1936). *Aesthetic analysis.* New York: Thomas Y. Crowell.

Rantala, V., Rowell, L., and Tarasti, E. (Eds.). (1986). Essays on the philosophy of music. *Acta Philosophica Fennica. 43,* part 1.

Read, H. (1958). *Education through art* (3rd. ed.). London: Faber and Faber.

Reese, W. L. (1980). *Dictionary of philosophy and religion: Eastern and western thought.* Atlantic Highlands: Humanities Press.

Reimer, B. (1989). *A philosophy of music education* (2nd. ed.). Englewood Cliffs: Prentice-Hall, 1989.

Reimer, B. (in press). Essential and non-essential characteristics of aesthetic education. *Journal of Research in Music Education.*

Ross, W. O. (1921). *The works of Aristotle.* London: Oxford University Press.

Scheffler, I. (1965). *Conditions of knowledge: An introduction to epistemology and education.* Chicago: University of Chicago Press.

Scheffler, I. (1973). *Reason and teaching.* Indianapolis: Bobbs-Merrill.

Scheffler, I. (1979). *Beyond the letter: A philosophical inquiry into ambiguity, vagueness and metaphor in language.* London: Routledge and Kegan Paul.

Scheffler, I. (1985). *Of human potential: An essay in the philosophy of education.* Boston: Routledge and Kegan Paul.

Scheffler, I. (1986). *Inquiries: Philosophical studies of language, science, and learning.* Indianapolis: Hackett.

Schelling, F. W. J. (1989). *The philosophy of art* (Ed., Trans., and Intro. D. W. Stott). Minneapolis: University of Minnesota Press.

Schiller, F. (1967). *On the aesthetic education of man in a series of letters* (Ed. and Trans. E. M. Wilkinson and L. A. Willoughby). Oxford: Clarendon Press.

Scholes, P. (1935). *Music, the child and the masterpiece: A comprehensive handbook of aims and methods in all that is usually called 'musical appreciation.'* London: Oxford University Press.

Schopenhauer, A. (1969). *The world as will and representation* (Trans. E. F. J. Payne). New York: Dover.

Schutz, A. (1976). Fragments of a phenomenology of music. *Music and man, 11,* 6–71.

Schwab, J. (1971). The practical: Arts of eclectic. *School Review, 79,* 493–542.

Sessions, R. (1962). *The musical experience of composer, performer, listener.* New York: Atheneum. (Original work published 1950)

Shepherd, J., Virden, P., Vulliamy, G., and Wishart, T. (1977). *Whose music: A sociology of musical languages.* London: Latimer.

Simpson, R. L. (1988). *Essentials of symbolic logic.* London: Routledge.

Small, C. (1980). *Music-society-education* (2nd. ed.) London: John Calder.

Smith, F. J. (1979). *The experiencing of musical sound: Prelude to a phenomenology of music.* New York: Gordon and Breach.

Smith, L. D. (1986). *Behaviorism and logical positivism: A reassessment of the alliance.* Stanford: Stanford University Press.

Sokolowski, R. (Ed.) (1988). *Edmund Husserl and the phenomenological tradition: Essays in phenomenology.* Washington: Catholic University of America Press.

Suzuki, S. (1969). *Nurtured by love: A new approach to education* (Trans. W. Suzuki). New York: Exposition Press.

Swanwick, K. (1981). *A basis for music education.* Windsor: NFER-Nelson.

Swanwick, K. (1988). *Music, mind and education.* London: Routledge.

Taylor, R. L. (1978). *Art, an enemy of the people.* Atlantic Highlands: Humanities Press.

Urmson, J. O. (1989). The methods of aesthetics. In *Analytic aesthetics* (Ed. R. Shusterman). London: Basil Blackwell.

Wing, H. (1968). *Tests of musical ability and appreciation* (2nd. ed.). Cambridge: Cambridge University Press.

Wolterstorff, N. (1986). The work of making a work of music. In P. Alperson (Ed.), *What is music? An introduction to the philosophy of music.* New York: Haven.

·8·

HISTORICAL RESEARCH

George N. Heller
UNIVERSITY OF KANSAS

Bruce D. Wilson
UNIVERSITY OF MARYLAND

Historical research in music education has its roots in American music history. George Hood's *A History of Music in New England,* 1846, was perhaps the first published history of American music. Other early writers on American music, such as Nathaniel Duren Gould (1781–1864), Frederic Louis Ritter (1824–1891), W. S. B. Mathews (1837–1912), and Louis Charles Elson (1848–1920), generally considered music education and its predecessors, psalmody and singing schools, to be important parts of the history of American music.

The most important American music education historian is Edward Bailey Birge (1868–1952). His enduring *History of Public School Music in the United States* remains the single most important volume in the field,[1]* though it has been supplemented in recent times by doctoral dissertations, journal articles, and book-length attempts to replace it.

Allen P. Britton (b. 1914) has followed Birge's pursuit of music education history with pioneering work on early American tune books. Britton has given focus and direction to historical research in music education since 1949. Recent and important work in music education history has been done by James A. Keene, Michael L. Mark, and Carol A. Pemberton. Keene's book *A History of Music Education in the United States* (1982) is a frequently used text in music education history courses. Michael Mark's contributions include his book of readings, his book on contemporary music education, and his most recent collaboration with Charles Gary.[2] Carol Pemberton has authored several studies pertaining to music education history generally and to Lowell Mason in particular.[3]

A recent development of importance to music education historiography is the establishment of the Music Educators National Conference (MENC) Historical Center at the University of Maryland, with Bruce D. Wilson as curator. The Historical Center is included in the facilities of the Special Collections in Music at the University of Maryland, College Park. The University of Maryland and the MENC acted jointly to establish the Historical Center in 1965. Since then it has acquired extensive holdings in music education.

The sesquicentennial celebration of school music in America, in 1988, produced much thought and serious study on music education's past, present, and future. Among the products of that year-long celebration was a series of articles in *Music Educators Journal,* including a special issue edited by Bruce D. Wilson and Charles Gary, and a symposium held at the MENC Historical Center 150 years to the day after the Boston School Committee authorized the hiring of a music teacher.

Present research needs include revision of existing studies, application of new techniques, and cooperation with fields outside music education, especially musicology and educational history. Gaps remain in the present story of people, places, and ideas associated with music teaching and learning. New interpretations of old subjects are needed, especially to discover the roles of ethnic and racial populations and women. Oral history and psychohistory are two relatively new techniques not yet widely used in education historical research.

Cooperation between music educators and American

---

*Editor's Note: In line with practices in historical research, this chapter should have footnotes. At the request of the publisher, the footnotes appear as endnotes.

music historians has been sporadic in the past, but recent breakthroughs have occurred such as the inclusion of music education topics in *The New Grove Dictionary of American Music (*or *AmeriGrove)* and the Sonneck Society's openness to music education history. Cooperation with educational historians has much further to go. Educational historians have shown little interest in music education history, and few music education historians have been actively involved in educational history.

UNDERSTANDING HISTORY

What is historical research in music education, and why is it worth doing? These questions deserve an answer. Jacques Barzun and Henry F. Graff take the position that all research is by definition historical; that is, nothing can be reported that has not already taken place. Research is the careful, systematic, reflective, and objective pursuit of information and understanding, which adds to human knowledge.[4]

History, in the sense used here, has four meanings: (1) the actual past as it happened moment by moment in all of its infinite detail throughout the world; (2) the written account of the past, historians' reconstructions, which are necessarily abstract and incomplete; (3) the memory of the past that exists in the minds of living persons; (4) the discipline or subject matter of history, often called historiography.[5]

Music education is also a broad topic with at least two large categories of meaning: (1) music in public and private schools and (2) music teaching and learning in general. It has a subject matter (rhythm, pitch, quality, form, and context), associated activities (listening, performing, and creating), and pedagogical concerns (goals, objectives, material, equipment, facilities, procedures, and evaluation). There are related matters such as teacher training, research, administration, and supervision.

Why is historical research in music education valued? The reasons advanced to justify historical research in music education may be summarized as follows: (1) to satisfy interest or curiosity, (2) to provide a complete and accurate record of the past, (3) to establish a basis for understanding the present and planning for the future, and (4) to narrate deeds worthy of emulation. Anyone attempting historical research or teaching others about it should have a clear conception of what it is, how it differs from other kinds of research, and why it is important. Failing this, the activity can be aimless or insignificant, or both.[6]

RESEARCHING HISTORY

The main tasks of historical research can be categorized as choosing a topic, building a bibliography, refining the topic, establishing the context, gathering the evidence, and verifying the sources. However, research is only the first stage of a three-stage project, with writing and publishing completing the endeavor. Too many doctoral students fail to allow

ample time for writing, and neglect to seek publication of their work. Since communication is an important goal of writing, this chapter focuses on all three topics, beginning with research.

Choosing a Topic

Something in history itself, encountered either through reading or personal experience, inspires the historical researcher to choose a topic. If one is predisposed to analysis and narrative, an event from the past can command one's attention and study until that event is seen clearly as a topic. Louis Gottschalk defined the four dimensions of a historical topic: biographical (the personalities in history), geographic (the physical setting of history), functional (history as an accounting of the nature of activities), and chronological (meaning the time frame within which history is viewed). The more a researcher focuses on one of these dimensions of human endeavor in history, the easier it is to arrive at a topic that is interesting, original, and manageable as a research project.[7]

Although personal interest alone might sustain a researcher throughout a project, that researcher needs to realize from the outset that, ultimately, others must also find the topic engaging. In shaping a topic, the researcher should imagine the readers and should address their need to know. The researcher can demonstrate that need to know by showing the topic's importance, value, significance, and relevance. The researcher's first task, then, is to determine that knowledge on a particular topic is needed in the field.

An additional requirement, often demanded in academic circles, is that a formal research report be an original contribution to the field, one that adds to the fund of knowledge. A topic is original if it investigates the unexplored or if it is a new study of an old topic. A new interpretation of a previously treated subject can justify its revival. New questions or new evidence can require that old explanations be revised. Although originality does not guarantee interest, it encourages the development of a broad base of historical knowledge, an element needed in music education.

To make a historical topic both manageable and feasible as a project, the researcher expands or contracts its scope to meet the requirements of the intended format. Whether this format be a paper, article, thesis, dissertation, or book, the scope must be narrow enough to allow full documentation and narration, and at the same time broad enough to be of consequence. Time and money are often the limiting factors, and the researcher must anticipate what is required for each. A realistic schedule and budget must take into consideration funding and availability of source materials. The researcher who cannot arrange access to sources must adjust or change topics.

Identifying a topic that satisfies multiple criteria can be a challenge. Attempting to satisfy personal interests and the needs of the discipline, as well as the requirements of originality and manageability, may lead to compromise. Even after adjusting the biographical, geographic, functional, and chronological dimensions of the topic, one may have to move to another topic in order to achieve a satisfactory balance among the three criteria. History, however, is as inexhaustible as time itself; no matter how rapidly historians may write, time continually provides new vantage points from which to examine the past. With imagination and patience the researcher can find a suitable perspective.

Building a Bibliography

Building a bibliography begins with the general references on music education history. General references in the field of music may also be useful because they help outline the history of music as seen by musicologists and music librarians.[8]

Of particular interest to American music historians is Donald W. Krummel's (1987) *Bibliographic Handbook of American Music*. This work is an extension of his article on bibliography in *AmeriGrove*. Krummel's handbook is organized into three main sections: chronological, contextual, and bibliographic, each section containing much of interest to music education historians. The section specifically devoted to music education (pp. 179–186) is rather disappointing for its brevity and spottiness of coverage. Nevertheless, Krummel's work far surpasses its rivals.[9]

Books, articles, proceedings, and yearbooks often contain reports of historical research and even primary sources bearing on music education history. Now somewhat dated but still useful is Ernest E. Harris's 1978 compilation,[10] which indexes generalia, music in education, subject matter areas, uses of music, and multimedia and equipment. Two appendixes list library holdings and music periodicals. Several sources identify the contents of publications of the Music Educators (formerly Supervisors) National Conference.[11]

Doctoral dissertations are listed by University Microfilms Corporation in their publication, *Dissertation Abstracts International*.[12] Listings of master's theses are gathered only sporadically, and then not with great accuracy or anything approaching completeness.[13]

The most comprehensive list of books, periodicals, dissertations, and theses pertaining directly to music education history can be found in a bibliography by George N. Heller, published by the University of Kansas.[14] This bibliography presently runs to 112 pages; it is updated regularly and is to be reissued soon in a more usable topical format.

Computers, compact discs, and other electronic reference tools are making historical research more efficient. Many card catalogs are now available on computer programs for local and remote access. Reference works are stored on compact discs, which lend themselves easily to search. It is difficult to tell where technology will lead and what uses music education historians will have for these and other similar devices, though the potential is vast. Krummel discussed these resources in his *Handbook*.[15]

Refining the Topic

The very act of selecting a topic begins the process of refining it. With the topic defined and delimited as to the bio-

graphical, geographic, functional, and chronological dimensions, the researcher is ready to analyze the issues involved. The result of this analysis is the purpose of the research study. If difficulties arise in stating clearly what is to be undertaken, then it is a good idea for the researcher to rethink the reasons for selecting the topic, questioning again if it adequately meets the criteria of interest, originality, and manageability and if each of the dimensions has been sufficiently explored to make the topic viable.

A researcher embarks on a "diligent and systematic inquiry or investigation into a subject in order to discover or revise facts."[16] At the outset of the quest, the researcher is equipped only with questions. The answers to these questions will be the elements used later in telling a story of who did what, when, and where it happened, and how it happened. To reach these answers, the researcher begins by turning the problem statement itself into a question and continues by asking increasingly precise questions until all known aspects of the subject become avenues of exploration.

The researcher must assume nothing and question everything. One should search for facts and for events known to have happened. Though the search may be motivated by a desire to know why something happened, what caused it, or what effect it had, the search must be for evidence. Questions posed will themselves lead to further questions, and will point the search toward what is ultimately possible to know.

In forming the questions that will guide the research, the researcher finds that the topic and its delimitations become paramount. Questions subsidiary to the main question must pertain to the purpose. All details are in relation to the main topic. With everything open to question, it is possible to be drawn far afield in pursuit of irrelevant answers. Posing additional questions is helpful as long as they do not drag the researcher into tangential pursuits.

The unknown aspects of a topic can create difficulty in anticipating what questions to ask or how much detail is appropriate. One way to resolve this difficulty is to let the known serve as a guide to the unknown, always keeping the purpose in mind. If a particular line of questioning would enhance the purpose, then it is worth pursuing.

Establishing the Context

Establishing the context is important in telling a story. The reader craves to know how the details fit together and how the present story relates to what the reader already knows. Although much of the general reading done by the researcher will not overtly find its way into the work, that reading helps orient the writer to the broader setting. Music education does not occur in isolation; other events going on in the world impinge upon it. Music education has both antecedents and consequences, central and peripheral. General reading makes the historian and the reader more aware of the broader context and how the work at hand fits into it.

World history is a vast topic, and the average music education researcher barely makes a dent in it. Nevertheless, some guidelines exist that help place music education in a world framework. It is impossible, for example, to contemplate music education in sixteenth-century America without consideration of what was happening in Spain, Portugal, France, and England, and without attending to the Reformation and the papacy. Similar concerns touch on music education in America during the seventeenth century. So it goes; each age has its story, and music education relates to each.[17]

American history has been well researched, and many fine summaries exist to help the researcher connect happenings in music education with the larger story of the nation's history and the history of American education. Almanacs provide ready access to chronology. More lengthy surveys, often running to several volumes, are useful not only for the information they provide, but also as models of writing style. As with reading in world history, the goal here is more to learn the scene than to gather facts, names, dates, and places. The researcher and the reader need to know the general context. The particulars will come later.[18]

The premier source of traditional western art music is Donald Jay Grout's monument of musical scholarship.[19] Though it emphasizes music literature and composers, it offers much of value for music education researchers. Another source worth reading for the social and cultural background is the work of Paul Henry Lang.[20] Reading ethnomusicological sources may also prove to be of value, depending on the musical context of the subject under investigation.[21]

American music has a growing body of literature, some of which may be of contextual interest to music education historians. Major works in this field are those of Gilbert Chase, H. Wiley Hitchcock, Charles Hamm, and Daniel Kingman. The *AmeriGrove* dictionary is a major contribution to scholarship in this area. The Sonneck Society's periodical, *American Music,* publishes occasional articles on music education history.[23]

How music education fits into the history of education in general is a fascinating but little-studied problem. Educational historians are generally unaware of music's role in the history of education in western civilization and the New World. Similarly, music educators are equally uninformed about education history and the ways in which music education has paralleled teaching and learning in other subjects. Some collateral reading in this area can contribute to a more complete picture of the topic under consideration.[22]

Other general reading may be inferred from the topic. Geographic topics, sociological questions, or whatever, each demands that the author acquire familiarity with the genre.

Gathering the Evidence

Collecting information on a historical subject takes the researcher to multiple sources. The best evidence comes from primary sources, that is, sources that provide eyewitness testimony of an event or that part of the past under consideration. Historical research requires the use of primary sources.

An account offered by anyone other than an eyewitness is termed a secondary source, a secondhand account to the past. Secondary sources are insufficient evidence to substantiate historical fact. For example, Jere T. Humphreys' article about Patrick S. Gilmore's National Peace Jubilee of 1869[24] is a secondary source, Humphreys not having directly observed the jubilee. Primary sources for that event would be newspaper accounts by covering reporters, the programs, and Gilmore's own reminiscences. An original source—like an original painting versus a copy—is a document as it originated from its author or authors, or lacking that, the earliest available form of the information about the subject under investigation.[25]

Historical sources, or documents, are as varied in their format as there are ways to record words, sounds, pictures, and other information. Printed materials include books, magazines, musical scores, programs, legal documents, pamphlets, reports, and other formats, both published and unpublished. Manuscript materials include letters, memos, diaries, logs, notes, scores, transcripts, financial records, and other writings in hand or typescript, almost by definition unpublished. Since the computer has entered common use, textual documents now include a variety of machine-readable formats.[26]

Aural and visual evidence provides invaluable information in ways that the written word cannot. Photographs, sound recordings, video recordings, and films, along with artifacts such as instruments, clothing, art, and objects of everyday life, can illuminate and enrich the researcher's insights. Preserved sound is especially vital to the music education historian.

Oral history is a special class of historical documentation; it allows the historian to participate in creating the historical document. Oral historians have established guidelines for interviewing individuals about their involvement in matters of historical interest and for preserving the interview as a recording (audio or visual) and a transcript.[27]

How does one judge a document's potential as a source of primary information? The best records are those created contemporaneously with the event. Less reliable are documents created after the event. Of these, confidential or private documents are more reliable than those created for public consumption or larger audiences. Oral histories suffer to the extent that interviewees' memories fail them; but oral histories have the peculiar advantage of preserving accounts that otherwise would be lost.

Other kinds of documents, such as government reports, might gain reliability from being published farther from the date of the original event. Where the intent is to collect or convey opinion, the document will be unreliable as a source of fact. A concert review, for example, is an opinion, not an accurate or objective account of what happened. Documents created for artistic purposes, such as biographical or historical novels or commemorative paintings, may succeed in conveying the essence of historical truth but are not reliable sources of fact. One must study the time and cultural context of a document's origin in order to discover its potential for delivering primary source information.[28]

Regular use of historical documents will soon make it clear to the researcher that single documents are not exclusively primary or secondary sources. A historian looks for the answers to more and more specific questions, a search Gottschalk refers to as the quest for primary particulars. A document may reliably report a particular item of information but may not be reliable as a whole. The more the search for primary particulars succeeds, the more the topic takes definite form, and the better one is able to judge the potential for a document to yield primary information.

Secondary sources are also useful, especially considering that a given document is judged primary or secondary depending on the context of the researcher's inquiry. Gottschalk suggests five reasons to consult secondary sources: (1) to gain an understanding of the times that produced the contemporary evidence; (2) to discover other bibliographic data; (3) to find quotations and citations from contemporary sources; (4) to suggest interpretations of the research problem to be tested, used, improved, or discarded; and (5) to study published examples of how others have reported their historical research. Although the researcher must always be skeptical of secondary sources, such sources do constitute the state of knowledge about the topic, the basis upon which research proceeds.[29]

In the search for pertinent documents, it is frequently necessary to go beyond librarians and archivists to organizations and club officers, school and government officials, institutional and corporate administrators, or private individuals who can arrange access to primary sources. Although bibliographic publications for locating such materials have improved in the past two decades, they are far from adequate. One important reason is that much historical documentation remains outside of archival custody. A proposed research project may itself be the action needed to make a collection of documents available for the first time.

Music education researchers will find the MENC Historical Center at the University of Maryland in College Park of value. The Historical Center documents both the operation of the MENC itself and the history of music education in the United States. The Center was established in 1965, two years after the establishment of the American Bandmasters Association Research Center, a major archival collection devoted to bands, band music, and band conductors. More recently, a number of other archival collections of national and international music organizations have been created, offering heretofore unequalled historical documentation of music education and related topics.[30]

Many state music education organizations have also begun archives or historical collections. These are housed in a variety of locations, most frequently in university libraries. Awareness is growing of the need to preserve historical documents in music education for their use now and in the future, though much remains to be done.[31]

Historical researchers themselves can play an important role in improving access to such historical documents. In their dealings with those who have custody over historical materials, researchers should encourage custodians to place the materials in suitable archival care. Especially in instances where researchers have gained privileged access to documents, they could benefit future researchers by urging the owners to make the materials permanently available through an institution.

Verifying the Sources

Choosing and refining a topic and gathering evidence are distinct phases in a historical research project; the analytic processes of verifying sources of primary information constitute yet another phase. Verifying sources is often called the historical method, mistakenly connoting the whole process of historical research. Strictly speaking, the terms "historical method" and "verification" refer only to the critical analysis of documentary sources that precedes the imaginative construction of a narrative. Two kinds of criticism occur in verification, one for judging the authenticity of documents (external or lower criticism) and another for judging their credibility (internal or higher criticism).

Analyzing a document for its authenticity includes determining such matters as authorship, data, provenance, meaning, original order, variant forms, and forgery. Before using the information in a document, one must question its appearance, examine its survival as an authentic document or as an authentic representation of the author's (or maker's) original version. The following are typical questions about a document's authenticity, many of which can be answered only by searching other sources:

1. Is the handwriting consistent with other identifying marks?
2. Are there autographs or other identifying marks?
3. Does the estimated age of the item match the record?
4. Does any information within the document aid in establishing the missing date?
5. Are there any indications in diaries, newspapers, programs, or other contemporaneous materials that such an item existed?
6. Where was the item originally located?
7. Where is the item now?
8. Are parts of the document or set of documents missing, illegible, or out of order?
9. Can an original order or appearance be discovered?
10. Is this document a variant version or a copy?
11. Does an original or earlier document exist?
12. Does the document have multiple authors?
13. Could this have been written by someone else imitating the purported author's style?
14. Is there any reason to suspect that this item may not be genuine?[32]

Once the document has been established as authentic, its contents must be analyzed for credibility. Even when information in a document is deemed credible, it needs to be corroborated by other independent sources before the account can be assumed to be factual. Identical errors, however, can indicate sources dependent on each other or on a third source that could also be in error. A historian should examine four aspects of an eyewitness account: the reliability of memory, the intention or purpose of writing or speaking, the confidentiality of the account, and the expertness of the writer or speaker. Accordingly, the following questions might be asked to test the credibility of a document or source:

1. Does the document convey hearsay or direct observation of an event?
2. How much time passed between the observation and the creation of the document?
3. Could physical or emotional health factors have affected the accuracy of the observation?
4. Could memory loss have diminished reliability?
5. Was the document created merely to record or report, or was there another purpose or intention?
6. Did the writer or speaker have any known biases that might affect the observation?
7. Does the item have any purpose such as apology, propaganda, promotion, malice, vanity, diplomacy, or good will that might affect its credibility?
8. Is there a reason why the writer or speaker might have ignored certain facts?
9. What was the intended audience for this document?
10. Would the observer have been more or less candid in relation to another audience?
11. Is there any style or mode of address in the document that might obscure the writer's true meaning?
12. Were the writer's training, experience, and knowledge sufficient to support the reliability of the observation?
13. Do other accounts of equally qualified observers agree with this one?[33]

The researcher sets into motion a complex interplay of factors in judging historical evidence, both in searching for it and in using it. One responsibility in gathering evidence is to know when enough has been found and when to stop the search. Then, in making judgments, the researcher must give each piece of evidence its due, no more and no less, omitting personal biases. Confronting the fact that history as it happened can never be known completely, historians must not be afraid to suspend judgment where evidence fails; they must avoid making unsubstantiated assumptions for convenience.

History is a rich resource for the study of music teaching and learning. As each step is taken by the researcher—disciplined inquiry, the gathering of evidence, and verification—the writing of the narrative, which seemed so remote at the outset, will seem both easier and more compelling.

WRITING HISTORY

As important as research is, it constitutes but one-third of the task. Music education historians assume three obligations: telling the truth, telling it in an interesting and memorable way, and making it available to others. It is not suffi-

cient to dig up the facts; nor is it sufficient simply to report them. Facts do not speak for themselves. They must be interpreted, set in context, and assembled into a comprehensible whole that readers can grasp and remember. In short, the story must be told in an intelligible form and with an engrossing style.[34]

Overall Design

When a substantial amount of research has been completed, it is time to decide on a basic plan for the report. Sometimes, as in a thesis proposal, a basic plan is needed even before much of the research is done. Hence the need for preliminary research to settle on a topic, ascertain important secondary sources, locate the primary sources, and build a preliminary bibliography.

Matters of scale are important in putting the overall design together. Short book reviews, journal articles, monographs, and books differ in their dimensions, demands, and approaches. How many parts a given work will have depends on its overall length. How lengthy and detailed each part will be also depends on its overall size.

The first part of any work, whatever its size, is the introduction. The introduction tells the reader what is to follow, helping the reader decide whether or not to examine it further. In the introduction, the writer's task is to establish with the reader a rapport that will continue and develop as the piece progresses. A second task is to present the topic in such a way as to guide the reader toward what follows. The introduction serves as an exposition of the main theme(s) of the work, laying the groundwork for the study.

The longer and more complex the work, the more likely the author is to face the dilemma of chronological versus topical organization. Short pieces typically deal with but one theme or topic and tend to take place over a rather short length of time. In longer works, a multiplicity of themes and extended time frames forces the writer to decide which to present first. Proceeding year by year through the decades can be exceedingly dull. Giving the history of single topics from beginning to end, one after the other, tends to destroy the historicity of the report. It breaks the story up into a series of short stories rather than presenting single topics as parts of a single history.

The best solutions are idiosyncratic, based on themes inherent in the material. General rules are of little use in solving organizational problems. As each study evolves, its author must be thinking of alternative patterns during both the research and the writing stages. What initially seems like a good organization plan may be modified as the writing goes along because the writer finds new points of emphasis and new gradations of meaning.

Planning for illustrations should also be part of the overall design. Illustrations such as charts, maps, photographs, and other figures inform the reader in ways that prose cannot. Again, the size of the whole will govern how many and what kind of illustrations will be chosen, and how and where they will be displayed. The topic itself will also control the selection and placement of illustrations. Because the reader needs a sense of location in time and place as well as a feeling for the artifacts associated with the tale, illustrations that contribute to this feeling must be planned as part of the overall design.

The summary and conclusions in historical research are as vital as a coda is to a piece of music. The ending is as important as the beginning, though for different reasons. The conclusion serves both to bring the long complicated story together in the reader's mind and to leave a distinct impression. To read history is of no value if it is not remembered. The task of the introduction is to stimulate readers to continue; the task of the conclusion is to cause readers to remember what they have read.

In reports of substantial length, end matter is often included, such as tables, lists, and other worthwhile items that would disrupt the narrative. Where the original documents are critical to the story, copies of these may be included. In addition, end matter will usually include a bibliography proportionate to the size of the book.

A preliminary plan of the overall design of the piece must be completed at or near the beginning of the writing. This plan is not carved in stone and often changes as the work progresses, but the plan is necessary to ensure that the finished product has a comprehensible form. No matter how engaging the style, if the form is confusing, the reader will not be able to grasp the story.[35]

Writing Chapters

What is here said about writing chapters also pertains in most cases to articles. Because these writings are approximately the same length, they are subject to many of the same restrictions on form and content.

The average chapter (figuring 250 words per page and 20 pages to the chapter, typewritten and double-spaced) includes about 5,000 words, 33 to 40 paragraphs, a number that can be read comfortably in one sitting. A longer chapter tends to make the eyes glaze over; a shorter one will present an inadequate treatment of most subjects. These figures suggest what most readers find comfortable, and thus are useful guidelines to authors.

After a rough draft is written, the writer may find that some chapters have ballooned uncontrollably, while others are pitifully short. For the overgrown monsters, the best strategy is to look for dividing points, such as a chronological midpoint or a change in subject matter or topic. If a chapter is too short, three options are available. First, a short chapter may be combined with the preceding or the following one to make more comprehensible and convenient units. Second, the shorter chapter may be developed more by going back to the sources and looking for more data, a richer context, or additional arguments to buttress the weaknesses of the chapter. A third possibility, if the sources have already been exhausted, is to expand on the interpretation, to provide a more detailed context for the evidence presented.

Chapters, journal articles, and book reviews are forms with a distinct beginning, middle, and end. Just as an overall design requires attention to these parts, so too does each part. The chapter introduction, unlike the introduction to a journal article, must have transitional materials to connect what precedes and what follows it. For the narrative to flow properly, the chapter introduction must pick up where the previous chapter left off, and the summary and conclusions must point to the chapter ahead. Three to four paragraphs for the introduction and a like amount for the summary and conclusions will be suitable in most cases. Less than that will probably not do the job, while longer introductory and concluding material will begin to take valuable space and attention away from the main body of the chapter.

Three illustrations is an average number for a chapter or a journal article. More than three tends to approach a photo essay—a valid but very different form from the one being discussed here. Fewer or no illustrations will diminish or eliminate a powerful means of helping the reader envision (literally, in many cases) what is being discussed.

Subdivisions within a chapter depend, for the most part, on the unique qualities of the material presented. Some materials are seamless, and the prose naturally flows without interruption from beginning to end. Subheadings in this case tend to distract. Other topics have many natural divisions that can be labeled or that because of their complexity require subheadings for comprehensibility. The use of subdivisions is a matter that only an experienced author or editor can decide.[36]

Paragraphs and Sentences

Whereas the overall design or chapter structure provides shape to a work, it is the paragraphs and sentences that provide the life of the story. These smaller units furnish the architecture with concrete ideas and distinct sentiments; they communicate to the reader what really happened.

Paragraphs are rhetorical units that treat a particular idea in the story. A usual length of 125 to 150 words can, and often should, be altered. However, consistently short paragraphs bespeak weak or undeveloped ideas; they tend to make the flow rather choppy. A single sentence is seldom sufficient for a paragraph. Excessively long paragraphs, on the other hand, are difficult for the reader to grasp because they provide no resting points for the assimilation of ideas. Paragraphs of a page or more cause the reader's attention to stray and ordinarily combine unrelated or poorly related ideas.

Sentences convey the essence of history: people with motives acting in time. Sentences tell who did what with and/or to whom, when, where, why, and how. Stronger sentences answer these questions simply and directly. Weaker sentences, such as passive voice constructions, tend to obscure the subject and make the action difficult to understand. If used too frequently, they can confuse meaning and create a dull, lifeless bureaucratic tone. Sentences unremittingly similar in length and structure create boredom and cause the reader to lose interest.

The good writer accepts the special challenge of keeping readers engaged in the story. Writing history means telling the story in an interesting way. It means conveying to the readers a sense of what happened as conceptualized in the mind of the writer. In short, relating history means communication. Two tasks are implied for the writer of music education history. The first is to impart information as clearly and as succinctly as possible. The second is to create images or sensations that bring that information to life. Both functions of communication are essential if the story is to be read and remembered.

Words and Punctuation

The words one chooses to express ideas and convey images are critical. Words both denote and connote meanings, suggestions, and feelings. Lively, appropriate syntax and an engrossing prose style make the difference between history that is lifeless and history that is lively enough to be remembered. Grammar and rhetoric are part of the author's scholarship; they are critical in bringing to life the story of the past, its relationship to the present, and its implications for the future.[37]

Words denote dictionary meanings important to every author. Distinguishing between the fine graduations between similar words can be vital to communicating exact meaning. The ability to distinguish carefully means more than avoiding malapropisms; it means writing with precision so that the message is sent as intended. This cannot be done well when the author is hurried or under the pressure of a deadline.

Connotation is more elusive but equally important. Connotation is meaning by conveyance, suggestion, implication, hint, allusion, and signification. It is particularly concerned with the transmission of feelings and emotions, with quality and style. The attitude or tone of a report imparts a sense of what happened in the past and how it felt to be part of that scene. Connotation also is a factor in keeping the reader engaged and in making the material memorable.

Dictionaries are not generally of much use here because they are primarily concerned with denotation. Wide reading of literature, both fiction and nonfiction, sensitizes a writer to connotations. Rereading one's own work with a special awareness of the effect of the words also helps to develop the proper tone for a particular report.

Grammar and rhetoric contribute to the accuracy and impact of historical research. Historians who read older texts become aware of changes in usage that have taken place over time. It is not appropriate to write for twenty-first-century audiences using the grammatical and rhetorical styles of the sixteenth or seventeenth century. Textual historical evidence from earlier periods must be assimilated thoroughly so that it can be reported in a contemporary manner. Failure to do this presents an unnecessary barrier for the reader. Direct quotes, when cited to illustrate a point, are expected to be presented in their original form and style, though some modifications are permissible to aid comprehension.

Punctuation styles change as do grammatical and rhetorical usages. It is not now as fashionable as it once was to sprinkle commas throughout a work of prose. Today the function of punctuation is more valued, and its aesthetic role diminished. Punctuation should be deleted if it distracts. That punctuation is best that helps the reader most and is noticed the least.

Documentation

Acknowledging the source of one's work is commonplace in scholarly writing and is normally done through the device of footnotes. Longer works such as books and dissertations also use bibliographies. Each researcher confronts the question of how much or how little documentation is appropriate. The answer depends largely on the audience. Since documentation exists for the information and convenience of the reader, the amount used will vary according to the projected audience.

All direct quotes require documentation. Sources of very close paraphrases (particularly where they might be critical to an argument or where their sources might be of interest to the reader) need to be acknowledged. Beyond that, good judgment is the best guide. Novice writers tend to footnote too much, a tendency that fades with age and experience. A good way to avoid clutter on the page and superscript hazards in the prose is to save all the citations for the end of a paragraph and then use a multiple footnote.

As to form and style, *The Chicago Manual of Style* is the standard in historical research.[38] Although they are largely symbolic in nature, preferences for one style over another bespeak the increasing divisions between those who view research from a perspective of the humanities and those who view it as allied with the natural and social sciences. Here, the convenience of the reader is the important consideration.[39]

The increasingly common tendency toward the use of endnotes is distressing to those concerned with historical research in music education. Few inconveniences in life are more annoying than having to read a book with one finger at the end of the chapter, or worse, at the end of the book, so that references can be consulted as they occur in the text. This arrangement seems to be an acknowledgment that cost savings and convenience for the publisher override concerns for readers.

Titles and Subtitles

The title of a book or article identifies the contents of the piece for the prospective reader. To serve its intended task well, the title should be both accurate and convenient. It should aptly describe what is contained in the work so as not to mislead the prospective reader, but it should also be sufficiently short and interesting to attract readers initially and to be recalled later. This seemingly small task is more difficult than it appears, and it is often not done well.

Titles for whole works or for subsections are often assigned at the close of the project. By then it is clear what the piece is about, so labeling is easier. It is sometimes helpful to assign a working title that is somewhat pedantic, but serviceable to describe the writer's intent. As the project proceeds the writer can jot down titles as they occur, using a process similar to free association. When it comes time to pick a final title, the list of ideas can be surveyed and the best chosen.

Here again, choice of title is guided by accuracy and attractiveness. Historical research strives to be true, but it also strives to be read and remembered. Conscientious and artful labeling of the whole and its constituent parts contributes toward these ends. Titles should therefore be given adequate time and attention and not left until the last moment, then thrown in with the hectic flurry of activity that typically characterizes the conclusion of a project.

PREPARING HISTORY FOR PUBLICATION

Once the research and the writing are completed, the report is two-thirds finished. Facts that have been gathered and assembled into a coherent narrative do not contribute to the accumulation of knowledge unless and until they are put into circulation. History that is thoroughly researched and engagingly written is of little value until it is published. Therefore, the researcher should set aside time for editing, rewriting, revising, proofreading, correcting, and submitting the manuscript for publication.

Editing is a substantial process that entails everything from making small corrections to massive overhauls and redesigns, whatever is necessary to prepare a manuscript for publication. If the researcher, writer, and editor are the same person, it is highly advantageous to allow time between the writing and the editing. If at all possible, an objective person who has not read the manuscript should be enlisted to help with the editing process. A fresh pair of eyes and a new point of view can pick up weaknesses missed by the writer (by then too familiar with the material).

As the manuscript is subjected to subsequent rewriting and revisions, the corrections become smaller and finer, a process somewhat akin to the movement from carpentry, through cabinetmaking, to finishing and polishing a piece of furniture. As the larger problems are solved, it is easier to see the more subtle defects, until at last one is polishing the finished work. Throughout all the steps, the writer should be proofreading, correcting typographical errors so as not to distract readers with unintended slips on the keyboard.

The final stage involves submitting the manuscript to the appropriate outlet for publication. This stage begins when the researcher seeks an appropriate journal or publisher and follows the instructions to authors. Much time and energy are wasted by authors and editors alike when a manuscript is sent to an inappropriate journal or publisher. Submitting the right number of copies, observing style guidelines, and preparing an attractive cover letter are part of this process. If no explicit instructions to authors are available, guidelines or traditions can be inferred from reading back issues of a journal or looking at other books published by a given firm.

Three rules for publishing can be stated. The first rule is self-evident: A piece cannot be sent if it is not written. The second rule is also self-evident: A piece cannot be published if it has not been submitted. The third rule is that once the piece has been written and submitted, anything can happen. No one can predict what an editor or editorial committee will do with a manuscript. Knowing the style and content that a journal or book publisher favors can help in preparing a work for submission, but it does not guarantee results. Once an author has an established reputation, his or her work may be more readily accepted for publication, but until then trial and error is the only way.

STUDYING HISTORY

A survey of the literature of historical research in music education is beyond the purview of this chapter. Numerous examples of outstanding work exist, and a review of even the very best of these would constitute an essay of considerable proportions. A brief but carefully selected bibliography is given at the end of the chapter. The works included there, as well as those scattered through the footnotes of the chapter, offer worthy models for emulation as well as interesting background reading for future studies.

PROPOSING HISTORY

Writing proposals for historical research is a difficult task. The first problem is that many situations require the proposal to be couched in terms suggestive of the scientific model, including hypotheses, literature reviews, designs, statistical treatments of data, statements of summary and conclusions, and suggestions for further study.

A second, related problem is that historians often do not know what they are looking for until they find it. If the object of a search is too well specified, the researcher is almost sure to find it, possibly ignoring more important things and thereby distorting findings. This is a key point that distinguishes history from science; they are two different, though often complementary, ways of investigating and reporting.[40]

Nevertheless, proposals are often necessary. Graduate schools and foundations seldom permit research to proceed without some such document, and so the historian is forced to comply with a system that is unhistorical in nature. In the belief that something useful, however fraught with difficulty, is better than nothing at all, an outline is offered below.

HISTORICAL RESEARCH PROPOSAL FORMAT
1. Title
2. Statement of the problem
3. Statement of the research questions
4. Need for or significance of the study
5. Related literature

6. Sources
  a. Primary
    1. Written: print, manuscript or typescript
    2. Personal interviews
    3. Nonverbal, artifacts
  b. Secondary
7. Criticism of Sources
  a. Authenticity
  b. Credibility
8. Outline of the narrative
9. Preliminary bibliography

SUMMARY AND CONCLUSIONS

The study of history, whether as a reader or researcher, provides a sense of humanity, place, purpose, and time. "The historian can see in the issues of history the issues of today and so be better prepared to attack them with the greatest possible wisdom and so the greatest possible success."[41] The ability to see connections is important if music educators are to become more closely allied with musicologists and theorists (and thus to performers and composers) and with educational historians whose interest in the growth and development of schooling is also important.[42]

The essence of music education can be approached through history, because history is, at least in part, an art. It involves the imagination as well as the intellect, the spirit as well as the mind. History must not only be true; it must also be worthy of remembrance. Social science has its place in the world of scholarship, but it is not the same as history. Historians should not try to imitate or become social scientists. Laws and causes and motives are interesting to the historian, but they are not central. The story of people acting in time is the historian's concern. "History that best serves the profession informs and inspires its readers."[43]

Research, whether historical or scientific, is useful to music educators and to others interested in the field. If the topic is well chosen and appropriate literature is located and carefully surveyed, a worthwhile product can follow. This result depends partially on the writing, editing, and publishing tasks—all of which are essential to ensure that the research joins the literature and so is accessible to readers.[44]

It is a poor endeavor that does not benefit the soul as well as the intellect. With Allen P. Britton, the historical researcher must "side with those who believe that the effort itself is what counts, providing only that it seeks the greatest good for mankind, the most beautiful in music, the most kindness in teaching, the most truth in scholarship. Or something like that."[45] Above all, historical research must be born in a spirit of inquiry. The doing of it as well as the product itself must contribute to the pleasure as well as the enlightenment of the reader and researcher alike.

Notes

1. The first edition of Birge's book was published in 1928 by Oliver Ditson Company of Boston. A reprint edition by Music Educators National Conference was circulated briefly in 1966. The second edition came out in 1937, published by Oliver Ditson Company. It was reprinted in 1966 by the Music Educators National Conference and remains in print to this day.
2. Keene's book, *A History of Music Education in the United States,* is now available in a paperback version (Hanover, NH: University Press of New England, 1988). Three of Mark's contributions are *Source Readings in Music Education History* (New York: Schirmer Books, 1982); *Contemporary Music Education,* 2nd ed. (New York: Schirmer Books, 1986); and Michael L. Mark and Charles L. Gary, *A History of American Music Education* (New York: Schirmer Books, 1992).
3. Most music education historians are familiar with Pemberton's *Lowell Mason: His Life and Work* (Ann Arbor, MI: UMI Research Press, 1985).
4. Barzun and Graff provide numerous examples and sage advice on these and other matters pertaining to research. See their masterful guide, *The Modern Researcher,* 4th ed. (New York: Harcourt Brace Jovanovich, 1985), 1–6.
5. For an extended discussion of these matters, see George N. Heller and Bruce D. Wilson, "Historical Research in Music Education: A Prolegomenon," *Council for Research in Music Education Bulletin* 69 (Winter 1982): 1–20.
6. A good defense of historical research in music education may be found in Roger P. Phelps, *A Guide to Research in Music Education,* 3rd ed. (Metuchen, NJ: The Scarecrow Press, 1986), 152–182.
7. Gottschalk's reference work, *Understanding History: A Primer of Historical Method* (New York: Alfred A. Knopf, 1950), remains a valuable resource for historians of all sorts, especially those concerned with social and cultural topics. See pp. 62–63 for his discussion of the four dimensions in the composition of a historical topic.
8. One of the best general music bibliographies is Vincent H. Duckles and Michael A. Keller, *Music Reference and Research Materials: An Annotated Bibliography,* 4th ed. (New York: Schirmer Books, 1988), though like most others in this genre, it is weak in music education references. See also William S. Brockman, *Music: A Guide to the Reference Literature* (Littleton, CO: Libraries Unlimited, 1987).
9. University of Illinois Press, Urbana, IL, 1987. See also *The New Grove Dictionary of American Music* (1986), s.v. "Bibliographies," by Donald W. Krummel; Donald W. Krummel, Jean Geil, Doris J. Dyen, and Deane L. Root, *Resources of American Music History* (Urbana: University of Illinois Press, 1981). Three other useful tools are David Horn, *The Literature of American Music in Books and Folk Music Collections: A Fully Annotated Bibliography* (Metuchen, NJ: The Scarecrow Press, 1977); David Horn and Richard Jackson, *The Literature of American Music in Books and Folk Music Collections: A Fully Annotated Bibliography, Supplement I* (Metuchen, NJ: The Scarecrow Press, 1988); and Thomas A. Warner, *Periodical Literature on

American Music, 1620–1920: A Classified Bibliography with Annotations (Warren, MI: Harmonie Park Press, 1988).

10. Ernest E. Harris, *Music Education: A Guide to Information Sources* (Detroit, MI: Gale Research Co., 1978).

11. For articles in the *Music Educators Journal* see Arne Jon Arneson, *The Music Educators Journal: Cumulative Index, 1914–1987* (Stevens Point, WI: Index House, 1987). For the *MSNC [MENC] Proceedings,* see Debbie K. Siebert, "Subject and Author Index of the Music Supervisors' National Conference Yearbooks, 1910–1924" (master document, Wichita State University, n.d.) and Marguerite V. Hood, comp., "Index of Yearbooks of the Music Educators National Conference," *MENC Proceedings* (1939–40), pp. 518–552.

12. *Dissertation Abstracts International,* Vols. 1–51. (Ann Arbor, MI: University Microfilms, 1938–1991). The title varies. In vols. 1–11 (1938–51), it was called *Microfilm Abstracts.* With vol. 27 in 1964, the series divided into two sections: A. Humanities and Social Sciences and B. Sciences and Engineering. In 1976, with vol. 37, a third section was added: C. European Abstracts. Music education history dissertations are found in the A. Humanities and Social Sciences section under Education (Music Education) and Music.

13. See Clara Kjerstad, "A Summary of Investigations in Music Education" (master's thesis, Northwestern University, 1932); Jere A. Humphreys, "Bibliography of Theses and Dissertations related to Music Education, 1895–1931," *The Bulletin of Historical Research in Music Education* 10 (January 1989): 1–51; William S. Larsen, ed., *Bibliography of Research Studies in Music Education: 1932–1948,* 2nd ed. (Washington, DC: Music Educators National Conference, 1949); William S. Larsen, "Bibliography of Research in Music Education, 1949–1956," *Journal of Research in Music Education* 5 (Fall 1957): 64–225; Roderick D. Gordon, "Doctoral Dissertations in Music and Music Education, 1957–1963," *Journal of Research in Music Education* 12 (Spring 1964): 7–112; Roderick D. Gordon, "Doctoral Dissertations in Music and Music Education, 1963–1967," *Journal of Research in Music Education* 16 (Summer 1968): 87–216; Roderick D. Gordon, "Doctoral Dissertations in Music and Music Education, 1968–1971," *Journal of Research in Music Education* 20 (Spring 1972): 2–185; Roderick D. Gordon, "Doctoral Dissertations in Music and Music Education, 1972–1977," *Journal of Research in Music Education* 26 (Fall 1968): 128–425; and James R. Heintze, *American Music Studies: A Classified Bibliography of Master's Theses* (Detroit: Information Coordinators, 1984). Heintze's list has some glaring inaccuracies in the music education works and needs to be used with some caution.

14. George N. Heller, *Historical Research in Music Education: A Bibliography* (Lawrence, KS: The Department of Art and Music Education and Music Therapy, 1989).

15. Krummel, *Bibliographic Handbook of American Music,* 189–192.

16. *The Random House Dictionary of the English Language* (1967). For another definition, see Rudolph E. Radocy, "The Research Effort—Why We Care," *Music Educators Journal* 69 (February 1983): 29.

17. A good place to start with this kind of general reading is Bernard Grun's *Timetables of History,* with a foreword by Daniel J. Boorstin (New York: Simon and Schuster, 1979). Based on Werner Stein's 1946 *Kulturfahrplan,* the book has synchronous entries for history and politics; literature and theater; religion, philosophy, and learning, visual arts; music; science, technology, and growth; and daily life.

18. So much literature exists in this field that it is difficult to recommend any one source. By way of example, Arthur M. Schlesinger, Jr.'s excellent almanac, *The Almanac of American History* (Greenwich, CT: Bison Books, 1983) is very useful for events through December, 1982. Almost anything Daniel J. Boorstin has written is worth the time it takes to read. Particularly valuable for surveying American history are his three volumes, *The Americans: The Colonial Experience* (New York: Random House, 1958); *The Americans: The National Experience* (New York: Random House, 1965); and *The Americans: The Democratic Experience* (New York: Random House, 1973). Though a bit out of date, Frank Friedel's *Harvard Guide to American History,* 2 vols. (Cambridge, MA: The Belknap Press of Harvard University, 1974) is still a good reference for this literature.

19. Donald Jay Grout and Claude Palisca, *A History of Western Music,* 4th ed. (W. W. Norton, 1988).

20. Paul Henry Lang's book *Music in Western Civilization* (New York: W. W. Norton, 1941) is a lengthy but eminently readable volume with much social and cultural information.

21. Alan P. Merriam's seminal book *The Anthropology of Music* (Evanston, IL: Northwestern University Press, 1964) contains much that is of value for music education historians, as does Bruno Nettl's *Folk and Traditional Music of Western Continents,* 2nd ed. (Englewood Cliffs: Prentice-Hall, 1973).

22. There are many fine recent educational historians working these days. First among them is the late Lawrence Cremin of Teachers College, Columbia University. Among his many works is an excellent three-volume survey: *American Education: The Colonial Experience, 1607–1783* (New York: Harper & Row, 1970); *American Education: The National Experience, 1783–1876)* (New York: Harper & Row, 1980) and *American Education: The Metropolitan Experience, 1876–1980* (New York: Harper & Row, 1988).

23. The major American music histories in their most recent editions are Gilbert Chase, *America's Music: From the Pilgrims to the Present,* 3rd ed. (Champaign: University of Illinois Press, 1987); H. Wiley Hitchcock, *Music in the United States: A Historical Introduction,* 3rd ed. (Englewood Cliffs: Prentice Hall, 1988); Charles Hamm, *Music in the New World* (New York: W. W. Norton, 1983); and Daniel Kingman, *American Music: A Panorama,* 2nd ed. (New York: Schirmer Books, 1990). For a detailed analysis of the relationship between music education history and American musical scholarship, see George N. Heller, "Music Education History and American Musical Scholarship: Problems and Promises," *The Bulletin of Historical Research in Music Education* 11 (July 1990): 63–75.

24. Jere T. Humphreys, "Strike Up the Band! The Legacy of Patrick S. Gilmore," *Music Educators Journal* 74 (October 1987): 22–26.

25. Primary and secondary sources and original sources are covered in considerable detail in Gottschalk, *Understanding History,* pp. 53–57.

26. The many forms of textual documents, when collected by archival institutions, are generally called "papers" when they represent an individual or family, or "records" when they represent an organization or other corporate entity.

27. A number of manuals offer suggestions to oral historians. Among these are David K. Dunaway and Willa K. Baum, eds., *Oral History: An Interdisciplinary Anthology* (Nashville: American Association for State and Local History, 1984); Raymond L. Gorden, *Interviewing: Strategy, Techniques, and Tactics,* 4th ed. (Chicago: The Dorsey Press, 1987); and Ken Metzler, *Creative Interviewing: The Writer's Guide to Gathering Information by Asking Questions,* 2nd ed. (Englewood Cliffs: Prentice Hall, 1989).

28. Gottschalk, *Understanding History,* 91–117.

29. *Ibid.,* 115–117.
30. As of 1990, the following additional organizations have established archives or research collections: Association of Recorded Sound Collections, American String Teachers Association, College Band Directors National Association, International Association of Music Libraries—U.S. Branch, International Clarinet Society, International Society for Music Education, Music Library Association. Music OCLC Users Group, Mid-West International Band and Orchestra Clinic, National Association of College Wind and Percussion Instructors, and Society of Ethnomusicology. Information about any of these archival collections is available from the Curator, Special Collections in Music, Music Library, 3210 Hornbake, University of Maryland College Park, MD 20742.
31. An incomplete list of states with collections in archival custody would include Colorado, Connecticut, Georgia, Iowa, Illinois, Kansas, Kentucky, Maryland, Minnesota, Missouri, New Jersey, North Carolina, Ohio, and Oregon. For information on any of these collections, contact the state music education association or the MENC Historical Center.
32. See Gottschalk, *Understanding History,* 118–138.
33. *Ibid.,* 90–91.
34. Some excellent guidelines for writing history are offered in Jules R. Benjamin, *A Student's Guide to History,* 4th ed. (New York: St. Martin's Press, 1987), 85–111.
35. Matters of design, as well as many other items of interest to writers of historical essays, are discussed in Anthony Brundage, *Going to the Sources: A Guide to Historical Research and Writing* (Arlington Heights: Harlan Davidson, 1989), 64.
36. A useful handbook for writers is Conal Furay and Michael J. Salevouris, *The Methods and Skills of History: A Practical Guide* (Arlington Heights: Harlan Davidson, 1988). See especially their chapters on "The Written Report," "Writing: Exposition and Narration," and "Historiography," pp. 191–233.

37. Many fine manuals give advice on these matters. One of the best is Jacques Barzun, *Simple and Direct: A Rhetoric for Writers,* rev. ed. (New York: Harper & Row, 1984).
38. *The Chicago Manual of Style,* 13th ed. (Chicago: The University of Chicago Press, 1982). Advice to writers and examples of style usage from the *Chicago Manual* are conveniently presented in Kate L. Turabian, *A Manual for Writers of Term Papers, Theses and Dissertations,* 5th ed., rev. and exp. Bonnie Birtwistle Honigsblum (Chicago: The University of Chicago Press, 1987).
39. Estelle Jorgensen has commented on this problem in a recent article. Unfortunately, she was forced to publish her essentially philosophical article in the scientific style. See Estelle R. Jorgensen, "Towards an Enhanced Community of Scholars in Music Education," *The Quarterly 1* (Spring 1990): 36–42.
40. Jacques Barzun has written very forcefully on this issue. See especially his *Clio and the Doctors: Psycho-History, Quanto-History, and History* (Chicago: University of Chicago Press, 1974).
41. Allen P. Britton, "The Place of Historical Research in Graduate Programs in Music Education," *The Bulletin of Historical Research in Music Education* 5 (July 1984): 56.
42. George N. Heller, "Music Education History and American Musical Scholarship," *The Bulletin of Historical Research in Music Education* 11 (July 1990): 63–75.
43. George N. Heller, "On the Meaning and Value of Historical research in Music Education," *Journal of Research in Music Education* 33 (Spring 1985): 6.
44. See especially Allen P. Britton's reminiscence of his 20-year career as editor of the *Journal of Research in Music Education:* "Founding *JRME:* A Personal View," *Journal of Research in Music Education* 32 (Winter 1984). 233–242. Britton gives a good account of the role of editorial content and style and its effects on the balance between scientific and humanist approaches to research in music education.
45. Ibid., 242.

References

Arneson, A. J. (1987). *The music educators journal: Cumulative index, 1914–1987.* Stevens Point: Index House.

Barzun, J. (1974). *Clio and the doctors: Psycho-history, quanto-history, and history.* Chicago: University of Chicago Press.

Barzun, J. (1984). *Simple and direct: A rhetoric for writers,* rev. ed. New York: Harper & Row.

Barzun, J., and Graff, H. F. (1985). *The modern researcher,* 4th ed. New York: Harcourt Brace Jovanovich.

Benjamin, J. R. (1987). *A student's guide to history,* 4th ed. New York: St. Martin's Press.

Birge, E. B. (1937). *History of public school music in the United States,* 2nd ed. Boston: Oliver Ditson Company. (Reprinted in 1966 by Music Educators National Conference, Washington, DC)

Boorstin, D. J. (1958). *The Americans: The colonial experience.* New York: Random House.

Boorstin, D. J. (1965). *The Americans: The national experience.* New York: Random House.

Boorstin, D. J. (1973). *The Americans: The democratic experience.* New York: Random House.

Britton, A. P. (1984). Founding *JRME:* A personal view. *Journal of Research in Music Education, 32,* 233–242.

Britton, A. P. (1984). The place of historical research in graduate programs in music education. *The Bulletin of Historical Research in Music Education, 5,* 56.

Brockman, W. S. (1987). *Music: A guide to the reference literature.* Littleton: Libraries Unlimited.

Brundage, A. (1989). *Going to the sources: A guide to historical research and writing.* Arlington Heights: Harlan Davidson.

Chase, G. (1987). *America's music: From the pilgrims to the present,* 3rd. ed. Champaign: University of Illinois Press.

Cremin, L. (1970). *American education: The colonial experience, 1607–1783.* New York: Harper & Row.

Cremin, L. (1980). *American education: The national experience, 1783–1876.* New York: Harper & Row.

Cremin, L. (1980). *American education: The metropolitan experience, 1876–1980.* New York: Harper & Row.

Duckles, V. H., and Keller, M. A. (1988). *Music reference and research materials: An annotated bibliography,* 4th ed. New York: Schirmer Books.

Dunaway, D. K., and Baum, W. K. (Ed.). (1984). *Oral history: An inter-disciplinary anthology.* Nashville: American Association for State and Local History.

Friedel, F. (1974). *Harvard guide to American history,* 2 vols. Cambridge: The Belknap Press of Harvard University.

Furay, C., and Salevouris, M. J. (1988). *The methods and skills of history: A practical guide.* Arlington Heights: Harlan Davidson.

Gorden, R. L. (1987). *Interviewing: Strategy, techniques, and tactics,* 4th ed. Chicago: The Dorsey Press.

Gordon, R. D. (1964). Doctoral dissertations in music and music education, 1957–1963. *Journal of Research in Music Education, 12,* 7–112.

Gordon, R. D. (1964). Doctoral dissertations in music and music education, 1963–1967. *Journal of Research in Music Education, 16,* 87–216.

Gordon, R. D. (1964). Doctoral dissertations in music and music education, 1968–1971. *Journal of Research in Music Education, 20,* 2–185.

Gordon, R. D. (1964). Doctoral dissertations in music and music education, 1972–1977. *Journal of Research in Music Education, 26,* 128–425.

Gottschalk, L. (1950). *Understanding history: A primer of historical method.* New York: Alfred A. Knopf.

Grout, D. J., and Palisca, C. (1988). *A history of western music,* 4th ed. New York: W. W. Norton.

Grun, B. (1979). *Timetables of history.* New York: Simon and Schuster.

Hamm, C. (1983). *Music in the New World.* New York: W. W. Norton.

Harris, E. E. (1978). *Music education: A guide to informational sources.* Detroit: Gale Research Co.

Heintze, J. R. (1984). *American music studies: A classified bibliography of master's theses.* Detroit: Informational Coordinators.

Heller, G. N. (1985). On the meaning and value of historical research in music education. *Journal of Research in Music Education, 33,* 6.

Heller, G. N. (1991). *Historical research in music education: A bibliography.* Lawrence: The University of Kansas Department of Art and Music Education and Music Therapy.

Heller, G. N. (July 1990). Music education history and American musical scholarship: Problems and promises. *The Bulletin of Historical Research in Music Education, 11* (July) 63–75.

Heller, G. N., and Wilson, B. D. (1982). Historical research in music education: A prolegomenon. *Council for Research in Music Education Bulletin, 69,* 1–20.

Hitchcock, H. W. (1988). *Music in the United States: A historical introduction,* 3rd ed. Englewood Cliffs: Prentice Hall.

Hood, M. V. (Comp.) Index of yearbooks of the Music Educators National Conference, *MENC proceedings (1939–1940).* Washington: Music Educators National Conference.

Horn, D. (1977). *The literature of American music in books and folk music collections: A fully annotated bibliography.* Metuchen: The Scarecrow Press.

Horn, D., and Jackson, R. (1988). *The literature of American music in books and folk Music Collections: A fully annotated bibliography, Supplement I.* Metuchen: The Scarecrow Press.

Humphreys, J. A. (1989). Bibliography of theses and dissertations related to music education, 1895–1931. *The Bulletin of Historical Research in Music Education, 10,* 1–51.

Keene, J. A. (1982). *A history of music education in the United States.* Hanover: University Press of New England.

Kingman, D. (1990). *American music: A panorama,* 2nd ed. New York: Schirmer Books.

Krummel, D. W. (1986). Bibliographies. In H. Wiley Hitchcock and S. Sadie, (Eds.) *The new Grove dictionary of American music* (pp. 205–213). London: MacMillan Press Limited.

Krummel, D. W. (1987). *Bibliographic handbook of American music.* Urbana: University of Illinois Press.

Krummel, D. W., Geil, J., Dyen, D. J., & Root, D. L. (1981). *Resources of American music history.* Urbana: University of Illinois Press.

Lang, P. H. (1941). *Music in western civilization.* New York: W. W. Norton.

Larsen, W. S. (Ed.) (1949). *Bibliography of research studies in music education: 1932–1948,* 2nd ed. Washington: Music Educators National Conference.

Larsen, W. S. (1957). Bibliography of research in music education, 1949–1956. *Journal of Research in Music Education, 5,* 64–225.

Mark, M. L. (1982). *Source readings in music education history.* New York: Schirmer Books.

Mark, M. L. (1986). *Contemporary music education,* 2nd ed. New York: Schirmer Books.

Mark, M. L., Gary, C. L. (1992). *A history of western music education.* New York: Schirmer Books.

Merriam, A. P. (1964). *The anthropology of music.* Evanston: Northwestern University Press.

Metzler, K. (1989). *Creative interviewing: The writer's guide to gathering information by asking questions,* 2nd ed. Englewood Cliffs: Prentice-Hall.

Nettl, B. (1973). *Folk and traditional music of western continents,* 2nd ed. Englewood: Prentice-Hall.

Pemberton, C. A. (1985). *Lowell Mason: His life and work.* Ann Arbor: UMNI Research Press.

Phelps, R. P. (1986). *A guide to research in music education,* 3rd ed. Metuchen: The Scarecrow Press.

Schlesinger, A. M. Jr. (1983). *The almanac of American history.* Greenwich: Bison Books.

Turabian, K. L. (1987). *A manual for writers of term papers, theses and dissertations,* 5th ed. Chicago: The University of Chicago Press.

Warner, T. A. (1988). *Periodical literature on American music, 1620–1920: A classified bibliography with annotations.* Warren: Harmonie Park Press.

DESCRIPTIVE RESEARCH: TECHNIQUES AND PROCEDURES

Donald E. Casey
NORTHWESTERN UNIVERSITY

Description is fundamental to science. When description is the primary goal of a research project, that project is termed descriptive research. In the simplest terms, descriptive research projects seek to determine "what is," but determinations of needs, trends, and relationships also may be pursued through descriptive research. Along with philosophical, experimental, and historical research, descriptive research is one of the traditional social science research modes. In sheer number of studies completed, the descriptive mode has dominated research endeavors in music education (Yarbrough, 1984, pp. 216–217). The data-gathering techniques of observation, interview, questionnaire, content analysis, and protocol analysis are properly associated with the descriptive research mode. Further, all research studies in which relationship between variables, as they naturally exist, is a focus are properly characterized as descriptive. These may be qualitative in nature, but are more typically quantitative, and include those studies employing any of the full range of correlational statistical treatments (based upon quantitative measures of relationship) from simple correlation, through regressions and canonical correlations, to factor and path analyses. These specific quantitative techniques are discussed in Chapter 11 and so are not discussed here.

Moreover, many research studies not normally characterized as descriptive in mode, especially some experimental and historical studies, also employ descriptive research techniques in data collection and presentation. Experimental studies, which seek to determine cause and effect relationships, often employ descriptive techniques to describe existing conditions before, after, and often during treatment, and to describe the subjects. Historical studies, which seek facts relating to questions about the past and interpretation of these facts, often use data-gathering techniques associated with descriptive research. These techniques are used in the collection of information from living persons who have witnessed or participated in significant historical events, and in content analysis, a descriptive research technique that is applied to the speeches or writings of a person of historical interest.

The topic of descriptive research techniques and procedures in music education, therefore, is quite broad, and cannot be comprehensively covered in any one chapter. Indeed, a strong argument can be made that regardless of paradigm and mode, descriptive research techniques are basic to nearly all inquiry in music education. This chapter's purpose, therefore, is limited to articulating the broad foundations of descriptive research techniques and procedures as they are used in research in education and music education, providing references to studies in which application of these foundational techniques and procedures has been exemplary, and identifying special issues associated with descriptive techniques. Thorough explorations of any of these techniques and procedures can be pursued elsewhere.

Despite some speculation to the contrary, descriptive research should by no means be conceived as any less rigorous, worthwhile, or useful than other research modes. Good research is rigorous, regardless of mode. A research project's value is determined by the problem's importance, the propriety of the design, the researcher's care in following procedures, and the quality of the presentation.

DISCRIMINATIONS BY SCOPE: CENSUS, CASE, AND SURVEY STUDIES

Descriptive research studies that collect data from individuals may be characterized in part by the number of individuals selected for examination and the extent to which they represent a population. In this sense, there are three classifications of studies that collect data from individuals: census, case, and survey studies.

Census Studies

When a researcher seeks to collect information from every member of a population, the study is properly termed a census. Because every member participates, completely accurate representation is possible. The most familiar, expensive, and widely examined census is the U.S. government's decennial population census. With it, the government seeks to collect demographic information from every U.S. resident.

Census studies are rare in education and music education because the populations of interest are typically so difficult and expensive to access (e.g., all American first-graders now learning to read, all beginning orchestra students, all children of single parents, all high school dropouts). Moreover, unless great accuracy is necessary, a much smaller group normally can, with some assurance of good representation, serve the researcher's needs adequately. In short, census studies are rarely appropriate in education or in music education. In a few studies, though, the populations of interest are much more limited and census studies are both feasible and appropriate. Studies collecting information from all Pulitzer Prize–winning composers, doctoral recipients in music education from a particular university, or deans of colleges with membership in the National Association of Schools of Music (NASM) would be properly considered census studies. A recent study of all students participating in the Florida all-state instrumental ensembles is properly categorized as a census study (DeCarbo, Fiese, and Boyle, 1990).

Case Studies

A second classification of descriptive research in which data are collected from individuals is the case study. With it, the researcher selects a single individual, event, or organization to examine. The absolute breadth of the census is sacrificed, but a far greater depth is often obtained. Normally, a single case is selected with the hope that characteristics or relationships found in examination of that single case will allow greater understanding of an entire class. For example, a researcher might study a single dyslexic child learning to read music so that a full understanding of the child's condition might emerge which, in turn, might better enable music teachers to deal more effectively with other dyslexic children.

The most significant disadvantage associated with case studies concerns their generalizability. The researcher may not be able to demonstrate convincingly that the case selected is in fact typical of its class. Additional, more broadly based inquiry may be necessary to make the point and allow readers to accept the original conclusions with confidence.

Case studies tend to generate extremely rich data files, which can be especially useful in examination of complex processes. They are often useful in generating theory or hypotheses, which then can be investigated through other methodologies. An example of a case study within music education is Paul Haack and Rudy Radocy's (1981) study of a chromesthetic individual. Their detailed description of the chromesthetic characteristics of their single subject has helped to illuminate this unusual condition.

Survey Studies

When a researcher examines a portion of the population of interest (more than one and less than all) in the belief that those individuals examined will provide information that is also relatively descriptive of the entire population, that study is properly termed a survey. Surveys are typically less costly and time-consuming than census studies, yet they can still yield valid data sets. Surveys can better represent populations than can case studies, yet still generate rich data sets. Accordingly, surveys are common in music education research.

When information is collected from the subjects only once, the survey is termed *cross-sectional;* when the same type of information is collected from the same subjects at two or more different times, the survey is *longitudinal.* The advantages of cross-sectional surveys are that they can represent the population extremely well and, because data are collected from each subject only once, they can be completed relatively quickly. Price and Yarbrough's (1987) survey of 453 college musicians and nonmusicians designed to assess their opinions of various composers and collect information on their training and record ownership was cross-sectional; a questionnaire was administered to each subject only once, early in the school term.

The advantages associated with longitudinal studies are that the subjects may come to be known in greater depth, the researcher may gain a more accurate assessment of the subjects' stability on the variables of interest, and trends may be identified. One disadvantage to longitudinal surveys is that differential and absolute subject mortality (dropping out of the project) may make later data collections less representative of the population under study.

Alexander Astin and his colleagues have completed a number of large-scale longitudinal survey studies of college students. Several were based on follow-up responses received in later years from an initial sample of 127,000 first-year college students in 1961 (Astin and Panos, 1969). In music education Rainbow's (1981) investigation of the development of rhythmic abilities among preschool-aged children over a 3-year period is exemplary.

SAMPLING IN SURVEY STUDIES

The method employed to identify precisely which individuals to examine in surveys is called "sampling." Obtaining a sample of adequate size and composition to represent the population well is a challenge to survey researchers. Sampling techniques are characterized as either probability or nonprobability according to whether or not every individual member of the population has a chance to be included in the sample. With probability techniques, every individual in the population has some chance, though not necessarily an equal chance, of inclusion in the final sample. With nonprobability techniques, they do not. Accordingly, nonprobability samples offer little assurance that the members of the sample are broadly representative of the population from which they come, and in general, conclusions emerging from studies of nonprobability samples cannot be applied to other settings or groups with as much confidence. Nonprobability techniques include purposive, quota, accidental, and systematic sampling. Probability sampling techniques include simple random, stratified random, and cluster samplings (Williamson, Karp, and Dalphin, 1977).

Nonprobability Sampling Techniques

Nonprobability sampling techniques, while quick and direct, may yield biased samples that do not represent the population well on key variables.

Purposive Sampling In purposive sampling, a nonprobability technique, a researcher simply seeks individuals possessing a particular characteristic of interest, such as perfect pitch or chromesthesia, for study. It is useful when the characteristic is so rare that other sampling techniques might not "capture" enough individuals possessing the characteristic to allow for meaningful analysis. A sociological study of 12 London high schools employed purposive sampling techniques; the researchers selected schools in which they had examined many of the students during an earlier study. The researchers, therefore, had come to know these students rather well, and they used this extra information to enrich the study. In short, they studied those schools in which they already knew the students (Rutter, Maughan, Mortimore, Ouston, and Smith, 1979).

Quota Sampling Quota sampling, another nonprobability technique, occurs when a researcher seeks a sample with sufficient representatives of two or more groups for comparative analysis. It is useful in instances when the researcher wishes to include the full or proportional representation of members from each of two or more groups in the survey sample. Cox (1989) employed quota sampling in his study of the rehearsal structure used by successful high school choral directors; each director identified as successful selected 12 students and two administrators to complete a questionnaire. Duke, Geringer, and Madsen (1988) employed quota sampling in a study of the effect of tempo on perception of pitch, selecting 200 music majors and 200 nonmusic majors as subjects.

Benjamin Bloom (1985) employed quota sampling techniques in his landmark examination of the factors contributing to talent development. He compared 25 young individuals from each of six fields (math, chess, physics, swimming, sculpture, and piano performance) who were identified as qualified for inclusion by virtue of having met some criterion of success. The pianists he studied, for example, had all been finalists in one or more of six major international piano competitions; each of the sculptors had won both a Guggenheim Fellowship and one of the National Endowment for the Arts awards (Bloom, p. 11). Bloom's sampling technique consisted of searching for individuals who met his criteria until his quota of 25 had been secured in each of the six areas. Through examination of the data collected from these 150 talented individuals, Bloom drew conclusions about talent development both within and across the six fields.

Accidental Sampling In accidental sampling, also a nonprobability technique, a researcher collects information from whoever is readily available. It is analogous to "man-on-the-street" reporting, where newscasters interview citizens who just happen to be present. Marketing analysts are fond of this technique, as evidenced by their practice of stationing data collectors inside shopping malls or on street corners to collect responses to carefully structured questions about products, markets, and advertising from shoppers who happen by. Carol A. Prickett's (1987) study of the effect of self-monitoring on the rate of a verbal mannerism among song leaders employed accidental sampling. Its subjects were the 18 students who happened to enroll in one particular junior level music education course one term.

Systematic Sampling The fourth nonprobability sampling technique, systematic sampling, takes place when some regular system for selection is applied to an entire population as, for example, when a researcher selects every tenth name in the phone book of a small town for a telephone interview regarding political preferences there. In a study of a programed instruction technique designed to develop pitch and rhythm error detection skills, Ramsey (1979) employed systematic techniques in developing his instruments and instructional materials. From an initial ordered set of 135 items, he chose every seventh item to form his instrument and every third item of those remaining for a set of programed materials. Those remaining formed an additional longer set, and all combined constituted his final set.

Probability Sampling Techniques

With probability sampling techniques, every member of the population has a chance, though not necessarily an equal chance, of inclusion in the final sample. The advantage of probability sampling over nonprobability sampling is that there is far less chance of a systematic bias in the sample; in other words, the sample is more likely to be representative of the population from which it is drawn.

Simple Random Sample The most basic of the three probability sampling techniques is the simple random sample. From a list of the population's members (the "sampling frame''), the sample is drawn in such a way that each element has an equal chance for inclusion in the sample. Conceptually, this is equivalent to placing all names in a hat, mixing them thoroughly, and drawing names, one at a time, until the sample is fully staffed. More often, a table of computer-generated random numbers is consulted and compared to identification numbers assigned to each element of the sampling frame until the sample is complete. Random samples are useful in assuring good representation of the population. Schmidt (1984), for example, randomly selected 75 subjects from all first-year college music majors at Indiana University in a study of the relationship between certain aspects of cognitive style and language-based perception in a series of aural discrimination tasks. The sample size and random selection procedure gave him confidence that the sample was representative of all first-year college music majors there.

Stratified Random Sample A stratified random sample is a combination of two or more simple random samples. It is used when the researcher wishes to be able to compare two or more subgroups within the larger sample, and so takes steps to ensure their representation. Kratus (1985) employed stratified random sampling techniques in a study of children's original songs. Four students from each of five age levels were randomly selected, in each of four schools; these subjects, then, were stratified by age (five subgroups) and by school attended (four subgroups). Gfeller, Darrow, and Hedden (1990) also employed stratified random sampling in their study of the perceived effectiveness of mainstreaming in Iowa and Kansas schools; 5 percent of the music educators in each state (two subgroups) were randomly selected and surveyed.

Cluster Sampling Cluster sampling is often used when the complete sampling frame would be so large that it would be unwieldy and when close representation remains a real concern. With cluster sampling, the researcher first selects large groups of elements, or clusters, from which the sample will be drawn. From these clusters, the elements of the final sample are identified through simple random, stratified random, or systematic sampling. Coleman (1966) used a complex cluster sampling scheme in a massive study of equality of educational opportunity in America. School clusters were selected on the basis of geographical region of the country, on school size, on racial composition, and on socioeconomic variables and size of the community. From within the clusters, individual students were randomly selected for inclusion in the final sample.

Sample Size

In probability samples, the difference between the characteristics of the sample and those of the population from which it is drawn is known as *sampling error,* and survey researchers work to minimize it. Sampling error is largely a function of sample size, tending to decrease as sample size increases. Deciding on a specific sample size, though, is usually more a matter of judgment than of calculation. Larger samples are more accurate yet usually also more costly to study. In practice, sample size is often determined by the desire to make meaningful comparisons among subgroups of the sample, the researcher including enough in the larger sample to ensure good representation from each important subgroup (Hoinville and Jowell 1977, pp. 57–61). A thorough discussion of considerations relating to sample size can be found in St. Pierre's (1980) article ''Planning Longitudinal Field Studies: Considerations in Determining Sample Size.''

WRITTEN RESPONSES TO QUESTIONS AND STATEMENTS: THE QUESTIONNAIRE

One of the most widely used, and probably most abused, data-gathering techniques in descriptive research is the questionnaire. Questionnaires are printed sets of questions or statements to which the respondents are expected to react in writing. The use of questionnaires is predicated on the assumption that respondents will reply truthfully, at least according to their understanding of the truth. This means the respondents must be both willing and able to provide truthful answers (Berdie, 1974, p. 11). To the extent that this assumption proves false, the data generated through the questionnaire will be invalid.

Undertaking a questionnaire survey is often more difficult than novice researchers might imagine. Borg and Gall (1989, pp. 423–444) prescribe seven major steps that must be completed to carry out a successful questionnaire survey: (1) defining objectives, (2) selecting a sample, (3) writing items, (4) constructing the questionnaire, (5) pretesting the questionnaire, (6) preparing a letter of transmittal, and (7) sending out the questionnaire and follow-ups. Backstrom and Hursh-César (1981) list 16 criteria for determining whether a potential questionnaire item is appropriate. Included among them are concerns for clarity, repleteness, variance, the coding of responses, and item validity. They also recommend a thorough pilot test of every questionnaire to assure that it will function as intended, before primary data collection is begun.

The format of individual questionnaire items may be closed, in which only certain responses are available. Closed-format questions are often of a ''checklist'' type, in which a specific response is checked, circled, or rated (e.g., ''Place the following five items in rank order according to their importance to you.''). Multiple-choice items are in closed format. Open-format items invite respondents to use their own words in response to a question. Questions of attitude may direct the respondents to place a check or an ''X'' at the place along a multipoint scale (e.g., Likert-type scales, semantic differentials) that best reflects their attitude on the issue of interest, or simply to assign a numerical value to the item that would reflect the attitude.

Examples of questionnaire techniques permeate research

in education and music education. Gfeller and colleagues' (1990) study of the perceived effects of mainstreaming in Iowa and Kansas schools employed a carefully developed questionnaire. In constructing it, the researchers reviewed all extant questionnaire items uncovered through a search of the literature on mainstreaming for their suitability, selected some for use in their questionnaire, and carefully constructed additional items in six other areas. The instrument that emerged was submitted to review by a panel of three expert judges, revised according to their comments, submitted to a second panel, and revised again before being used to collect data.

Descriptive researchers often must choose between questionnaire and interview for their data gathering, though some use both to take advantage of the strengths associated with each. Questionnaires possess many advantages, including (1) lower relative cost, (2) ease of contact with respondents, (3) efficient use of researcher time, (4) better control over the effects of any researcher bias, (5) uniform question presentation, and (6) ease of replication. Some significant disadvantages also exist; these may make questionnaires unsuitable for certain kinds of studies. Among the disadvantages are (1) relatively low response rates (which invite criticisms of possible selection bias); (2) limitations associated with written questions and answers, including the inability to decide at the time of questioning to probe deeper after any one response; (3) lack of control over who completes the questionnaire; (4) item dependence (because some respondents may scan the entire instrument before beginning to answer individual items and therefore be affected by their knowledge of the upcoming questions); and (5) sample limitations associated with illiteracy. (Questionnaires are not useful for collecting information from people who are not able to read well.) Researchers can counteract low response rates by repeated follow-up procedures, each of which is likely to improve the total response rate, and/or by sampling the nonrespondents to demonstrate that their responses to key items are not fundamentally different from those of the respondents. Graham Kalton's (1983) *Compensating for Missing Survey Data* provides excellent guidance in data analysis for researchers dealing with low survey response rates and/or high mortality rates in longitudinal projects. A reward for responding, such as money or entry in a raffle, can also increase response rates, but with such material motivation present, some researchers question the validity of the responses that are generated (Berdie, 1974, pp. 17–22).

Analytical techniques for questionnaire data, and for interview data as well, will vary according to the objectives of the research and the format of the questions. Reporting descriptive statistics (measures of frequency, percentage, central tendency, and variance) for closed-format question data is standard practice. Measures of strength of relationship (correlation) may be calculated between items, and statistical difference between subgroups on any item or combination of items may be assessed through analysis of variance (ANOVA) techniques or similar measures. A computer with even a modest statistical package program can handle these analyses easily. Analysis of open-format questions may include frequencies of response "themes," but usually also includes a discursive synthesis of all or most responses.

SPOKEN RESPONSES TO QUESTIONS: THE INTERVIEW

The interview has associated advantages and disadvantages that stem from its interactive condition. The interview's principal advantage is its adaptability. A competent interviewer can guide the course of the interview, as it is developing, in direct support of the research goals; responses can be met with prompts for additional information or with directions to move on to other areas. The result can be more data, greater clarity in the data, and a more complete collection of the specific data desired from the subject. Further, the interview has been shown to be superior to the questionnaire in collecting particularly sensitive information (Jackson and Rothney, 1961).

Unfortunately, the same adaptability that is a strength of the interview technique is also the source of its greatest weakness. Interactions between subject and interviewer are subject to bias from several sources. Borg and Gall (1989, pp. 444–449) specify three potential sources of interview bias: predispositions of the respondent, predispositions of the interviewer, and data collection procedures and conditions. To guard against such possible weaknesses, good researchers (1) train their interviewers carefully, (2) ensure that subjects are exposed to as nearly identical experiences as possible by writing opening and closing statements and all directions beforehand, (3) develop the questions carefully, and (4) pretest the interview guide to expose any problems in the interview plans before beginning primary data collection.

Interviews typically can be described as either structured or unstructured, according to the rigidity of the interview plan. *Structured interviews* ask the respondents to respond to a set series of relatively precise questions (e.g., "How old were you when you began formal music instruction?"). In *unstructured interviews,* the questions are more open-ended (e.g., "What do you remember about your early music study?"). Responses to such questions may range from a few words to several minutes or more of discourse.

In one sense, structured interviews perform the same function as questionnaires. They may be preferred to questionnaires, however, because of the higher response rate, the higher percentage of usable responses, and the greater adaptability associated with interviews, despite the greater expense that frequently accompanies them. A thorough discussion of interview techniques can be found in Douglas's (1985) *Creative Interviewing.*

Bloom's (1985) study of talent development, mentioned earlier, relied exclusively on interviews for primary data collection. Some were conducted in person and were unstructured; others were done on the telephone and were much more structured.

INTERVIEWS AT A DISTANCE: TELEPHONE SURVEYS

One method of survey data collection that can help researchers avoid both the expense of personal interviewing and the relatively low response rates associated with mailed questionnaires is the telephone survey. Surveys by telephone do not provide the interviewer with the same rich contact with the respondent that is available through in-person interviews, but in many cases the potential losses in accuracy are modest and the advantages in quality control over the data collection process, cost efficiency, and speed far outweigh them. The principal disadvantages of telephone interviewing are inherent limitations on the complexity and length of the interview. Simply put, respondents tire much more quickly during telephone interviews than they do during in-person interviews (Lavrakas, 1987, pp. 7–13). Researchers seeking to survey by telephone are well-advised to pursue special instruction in telephone interview techniques (Groves and Kahn, 1979). *Telephone Survey Methods* by Lavrakas (1987) is an excellent resource of telephone survey methodology.

WATCHING "WHAT IS": OBSERVATIONAL RESEARCH

Observational research is a broad classification of several descriptive research types, all characterized by data gathering through observation of the behaviors of others. In some types, specific behaviors are anticipated and recorded as they occur, often by checking an item on a previously constructed observation checklist. Recording in these types of observation studies can be continuous, or it can take place at some small regular interval (e.g., every 5 or 10 seconds), a technique known as behavior sampling. Continuous recording is extremely difficult, as the recorder has to record an event that just happened while concurrently being responsible for recognizing a subsequent event. Videotaping the session, however, allows the recorder to replay the tape and thereby observe the session as many times as necessary to ensure that every pertinent event is ultimately recorded, making continuous recording feasible. Behavior sampling has proved to be more manageable for the observer who chooses not to use videotape. The data that emerge from such observations describe the relative frequency of certain events during the observed period. Comparisons between behaviors and observations may then be easily made. Robert Erbes (1972) employed the behavior sampling and checklist observation form models in developing an instrument suitable for use in observing rehearsals.

Recently, though, researchers in education, and increasingly in music education, have successfully adopted research paradigms originally associated with anthropological and sociological research and applied them to observational research projects. In application, the chief difference is that observers working in the new paradigms seek to observe all that occurs and record all that could be relevant, not just those events that they had anticipated beforehand.

Research in the newer paradigms is often labeled as "ethnographic," and less precisely, as "naturalistic" or "qualitative." The confusion between terms is unfortunate, and the terms may or may not reflect substantial differences in paradigm. Though a comprehensive review of the implications of these alternative paradigms is beyond the scope of this chapter, the interested reader will find it in Guba's (1990) *The Paradigm Dialog*. In simple terms, the *positivist* paradigm has prevailed in science since Descartes and has been virtually the sole model of social science until recently. It supposes that a single reality exists and that it is the function of science to discover it. Researchers operating in this tradition control for bias and error in pursuit of objective "truths" about nature.

The newer *postpositivist* paradigm builds from a "realization" that human bias cannot be completely controlled; postpositivist researchers interpret their work in light of such human "limitations" (Guba, 1990, pp. 17–23). These alternative research types may hold great promise especially for observational research in music education. The techniques associated with them deserve special mention in this handbook, and are discussed at greater length in Chapter 6.

Generally, *qualitative research* is an umbrella term used to describe a wide variety of studies in which the research data are recorded in words as opposed to numbers. Especially within the postpositivist paradigm (which characterizes a great deal of contemporary qualitative research in the field), it is understood that because of idiosyncratic language patterns, the slightly different meanings words may have to different individuals, and because of each researcher's unique set of values and sensitivities, different researchers will describe the same event or phenomenon differently, and then may come to substantially different conclusions. Qualitative research findings are normally viewed, therefore, as at least partly dependent upon the individual collecting and analyzing the data.

Naturalistic research is generally understood to represent one specific type of qualitative research; it is characterized by data gathering that occurs in a "natural" rather than a contrived setting, such as in a laboratory, and under "normal" conditions. Educational researchers long have valued natural settings and normal conditions for their promise in ensuring that subject behaviors and responses are not affected adversely by unfamiliar or artificial conditions. A study of the musical gestures of kindergarten children by Veronica Cohen (1980), based on 3 years of regular observation in a kindergarten, is properly termed a naturalistic study. The study of sixth-graders' creative music problem-solving processes by DeLorenzo (1987) also exemplifies naturalistic techniques applied to music education; it is based on data drawn from field observations of such students functioning within their general music classes. A relatively well-known naturalistic study in music education is Moorhead and Pond's (1941) classic study of children's use of music in school play settings.

More recently, some have used the term "naturalistic research" to describe the entire set of postpositivist research paradigms. Lincoln and Guba (1985, pp. 35–37), for example, assert that postpositivist values are in fact the inverse of those associated with positivism. They propose a shift in terminology that would replace "postpositivist" with "naturalist."

Ethnology is the study of intact cultures; *ethnographic research* is also a type of qualitative inquiry, and a subset of naturalistic inquiry. It is characterized as in-depth investigation and description of an existing culture or aspect or aspects of that culture. Dobbert (1982, p. 4) describes four distinct streams of contemporary ethnographic inquiry: industrial psychology, social psychology, qualitative sociology, and anthropology, and notes that though each employs its own specific terminology and data collection procedures, all are founded on field-based, direct observation methodology. This methodology may reflect simple observation of the cultural scene, or, in pursuit of a fuller understanding of the dynamics of the setting, may involve the researcher as an actual participant in the activities under investigation (Dobbert, 1982, pp. 6–7), a technique known as participant observation. Becker, Geer, Hughes, and Strauss's (1961) sociological case study of first-year medical students at the University of Kansas utilized participant observation. The researchers participated in the role of medical students.

Ethnographic researchers utilize their senses, mediated by their own personal values, to record data in written form. Ethnographers gather data on all human planes: the physical, the emotional, the cognitive, and the ideological. Preparation to do so includes developing a strong self-awareness in terms of personal reactions and learning style so that the full cultural meaning of the events observed may be allowed to emerge. Further, researchers are obliged to report their own theoretical, methodological, and personal preferences and biases to the extent they may impact upon the recording processes and their outcomes (Dobbert, 1982, p. 6).

Still fairly unusual in music education, ethnographic studies are becoming more common. Krueger's (1985) study of student teachers in music and the extent to which their perspectives may shift as a result of that experience and Zimmerman's (1983) study of the musical experiences taking place among two groups of children in one elementary school are examples.

Researchers in education recently have begun to explore a third, "hybrid," paradigm, essentially consisting of a combination of quantitative (positivist) and qualitative (postpositivist) techniques. Some scholars, including Lincoln and Guba (1985) and Smith and Heshusius (1986), consider the two paradigms to be constructed on mutually exclusive philosophical assumptions and therefore incompatible. Others, including Reichardt and Cook (1979) and Howe (1988), have taken a more moderate position, believing that each paradigm is well suited to certain types of questions, and further, that in many cases, a combination of the two is superior to either one alone. In those instances, the qualitative data may illuminate the quantitative and can be validated by it.

Elizabeth Bedsole's (1987) study of the musical abilities of preschool children exemplifies this strategy of combining paradigms. She gave tests on musical tasks, collected questionnaire information from parents and ratings from teachers, and performed analyses of variance on these data; in addition, however, she conducted protocol analyses with several children and compared her conclusions from that exercise with the results of the quantitative analyses.

A second and better-known example of this hybrid paradigm may be found in John Goodlad's (1984) landmark study of American school classrooms. This project was unusually large in scope. Twenty investigators spent a month in the schools of each of 13 communities; 38 schools were involved, and data were collected from 8,624 parents, 1,350 teachers, and 17,163 students. One thousand sixteen complete observations (two or three class periods) were undertaken. Goodlad and his research team pursued the investigation both through the "thick descriptions" of observations that are characteristic of rigorous naturalistic inquiry, and through survey questionnaires and interviews of parents and teachers more characteristic of quantitative inquiry.

The debate regarding the propriety and compatibility of the two general paradigms continues unresolved. Each has a substantial history of scholarly application. There has been an unfortunate tendency to consider quantitative work to be consistent with the "hard" or "real" sciences and to associate qualitative efforts with fuzzy thinking and shoddy research. Both stereotypes are undeserved, but the proper relationship between the two traditions remains a topic of vigorous debate. Both will properly continue as accepted vehicles for the pursuit of understandings in music education, and researchers will no doubt continue to explore designs that combine the two in hopes for an even greater understanding of the phenomena or events under investigation.

A STUDY OF COMMUNICATIONS: CONTENT ANALYSIS

Content analysis is a descriptive research technique that is limited to the study of verbal, symbolic, or other types of communicative data. Content analysts often seek to make inferences from such data to their context, normally the creator or creators of the data (Krippendorff, 1980, pp. 20–21). From these analyses, inferences may be made about the individuals themselves, but the individuals are not the primary focus of the study.

Printed music, which consists of symbolic data, can be appropriate material for content analysis. Indeed, one early and well-known application of content analysis techniques to printed materials took place in eighteenth-century Sweden and concerned the *Songs of Zion,* a controversial publication of hymns. Various church factions counted the religious symbols in these hymns and compared the numbers to those in other publications, drawing inferences about their propriety as songs of worship. The propriety of the procedures employed was vigorously debated among scholars, ultimately contributing to the establishment of a series of methodological conventions now associated with content analysis (Dovring, 1954).

Yarbrough (1984) performed an exemplary content analysis of 30 years of issues of the *Journal of Research in Music Education* and drew conclusions regarding the nature of materials selected for publication therein. Price (1990) executed a content analysis with his examination of the content of orchestral programs performed in a recent 6-year period by the 34 major professional orchestras in the United States, ultimately drawing conclusions regarding musical taste in America.

EXAMINATION OF SPOKEN THOUGHT: PROTOCOL ANALYSIS

Protocol analysis, another type of descriptive research, is closely related to content analysis. In both content and protocol analyses, the researcher examines language or some other symbol system with the hope that a thorough investigation might give insight into the individual(s) who created it. In content analysis, the record examined is extant and the researcher works apart from the individual(s) who created it. In protocol analysis, however, the material under examination is a newly emerging verbalization, and the individual whose verbalization is being examined is present.

With protocol analysis, the researcher hopes to generate information about the subject's cognitive processes by probing the internal states of the subject (Ericsson and Simon, 1984, p. 1). Typically, the goal of protocol analysis is generating or confirming a cognitive processing model. In content analysis, then, the researcher examines a product in hopes of drawing inferences to its context; in protocol analysis, by contrast, the researcher examines a process as it is occurring in pursuit of information about the cognitive processes that are reflected in the emerging verbalization.

In protocol analysis, a subject provides a "running description" of the thought processes he or she is employing or has just employed while undergoing some treatment or engaging in some activity. It is quite literally a "think-aloud" procedure. One advantage that protocol analysis shares with the interview as data-gathering techniques is that both allow the recorder to guide the subjects back to more relevant areas if they start to stray from them, and to probe more deeply with encouragement and/or follow-up questions when key ideas emerge. Richardson (1988) employed protocol analysis successfully in her recent study of the musical thinking of the music critic. In that study, a paradigm of musical thinking was constructed through an examination of the writings of several critics, and this paradigm was tested through a protocol analysis. A "stream of consciousness" narrative of a professional music critic who was listening to an orchestra concert was examined for aspects of similarity to the paradigm. Results of the protocol analysis substantially supported the paradigm.

CONCLUSION

The descriptive process is and no doubt will remain integral to social science, including research activities in education and music education, throughout the foreseeable future. Descriptive researchers in all fields have access to an array of well-established techniques and procedures that can assist them in a wide variety of social science projects. These include study of individuals or groups through census, survey, and case studies and utilizing questionnaires, interviews, and direct observations. Relationships between variables may be examined quantitatively through correlational statistics. Analysis of communicative data is possible through content analysis, and insight into thought processes may be gained through protocol analysis. Each of these techniques is designed to describe, and properly pursued, each continues to be appropriate for certain kinds of rigorous inquiry in all social science fields, including music education.

References

Astin, A. W., and Panos, R. J. (1969). *Educational and vocational development of college students.* Washington: American Council on Education.

Backstrom, C. H., and Hursh-César, G. (1981). *Survey research* (2nd ed.). New York: John Wiley.

Becker, H. S., Geer, B., Hughes, E. C., and Strauss, A. L. (1961). *Boys in white.* Chicago: The University of Chicago Press.

Bedsole, E. A. (1987). A descriptive study of the musical abilities of three- and four-year-old children. Unpublished doctoral dissertation, University of Illinois, Urbana-Champaign.

Berdie, D. R. (1974). *Questionnaires: Design and use.* Metuchen: Scarecrow Press.

Bloom, B. S. (Ed.). (1985). *Developing talent in young people.* New York: Ballantine Books.

Borg, W. R., and Gall, M. D. (1989). *Educational research* (5th ed.). New York: Longman Press.

Cohen, V. W. (1980). The emergence of musical gestures in kindergarten children. Unpublished doctoral dissertation, University of Illinois, Urbana.

Coleman, J. S. (1966). *Equality of educational opportunity.* Washington: United States Department of Health, Education, and Welfare.

Cox, J. (1989). Rehearsal organization structures used by successful high school choral directors. *Journal of Research in Music Education, 37,* 201–218.

DeCarbo, N., Fiese, R. and Boyle, J. D. (1990). A profile of all-state instrumentalists. *Research Perspectives in Music Education, 1,* 32–40.

DeLorenzo, L. C. (1987). An exploratory field study of sixth grade students' creative music problem solving processes in the general music class. Unpublished doctoral dissertation, Columbia University Teachers College, New York City.

Dobbert, M. L. (1982). *Ethnographic research.* New York: Praeger Publications.

Douglas, J. D. (1985). *Creative interviewing.* Beverly Hills: Sage Publications.

Dovring, K. (1954). Quantitative semantics in 18th century Sweden. *Public Opinion Quarterly, 18*(4), 389–394.

Duke, R. A., Geringer, J. M., and Madsen, C. K. (1988). Effect of tempo on pitch perception. *Journal of Research in Music Education, 36,* 108–125.

Erbes, R. L. (1972). The development of an observational system for the analysis of interaction in the rehearsal of musical organizations. Unpublished doctoral dissertation, University of Illinois, Urbana.

Ericsson, K. A., and Simon, H. A. (1984). *Protocol analysis.* Cambridge: MIT Press.

Gfeller, K., Darrow, A. A., and Hedden, S. K. (1990). Perceived effectiveness of mainstreaming Iowa and Kansas schools. *Journal of Research in Music Education, 38,* 90–101.

Goodlad, J. I. (1984). *A place called school.* New York: McGraw-Hill.

Groves, R. M., and Kahn, R. L. (1979). *Surveys by telephone.* New York: Academic Press.

Guba, E. G. (Ed.). (1990). *The paradigm dialog.* Newbury Park: Sage Publications.

Haack, P. A., and Radocy, R. E. (1981). A case study of a chromesthetic. *Journal of Research in Music Education, 29,* 85–90.

Hoinville, G. and Jowell, R. (1977). *Survey research practice.* Aldershot: Gower Publications.

Howe, K. R. (1988). Against the quantitative-qualitative incompatibility thesis or dogmas die hard. *Educational Researcher, 17:* 8, 10–16.

Jackson, R. M., and Rothney, J. W. M. (1961). A comparative study of the mailed questionnaire and the interview in follow-up studies. *Personnel and Guidance Journal, 39,* 569–571.

Kalton. G. (1983). *Compensating for missing data.* Ann Arbor: Survey Research Center of the Institute for Social Research, University of Michigan.

Kratus, J. K. (1985). Rhythm, melody, motive, and phrase characteristics of original songs by children aged five to thirteen. Unpublished doctoral dissertation, Northwestern University, Evanston.

Krippendorff, K. (1980). *Content analysis.* Beverly Hills: Sage Publications.

Krueger, P. J. (1985). Influences of the hidden curriculum upon the perspectives of music student teachers: An ethnography. Unpublished doctoral dissertation, University of Wisconsin at Madison.

Lavrakas, P. J. (1987). *Telephone survey methods.* Newbury Park: Sage Publications.

Lincoln, Y. S., and Guba E. G. (1985). *Naturalistic inquiry.* Beverly Hills: Sage Publications.

Moorhead, G., and Pond, D. (1941). *Music of young children.* Santa Barbara: Pillsbury Foundation for the Advancement of Music.

Price, H. E. (1990). Orchestral programming 1982–1987: An indication of musical taste. *Bulletin of the Council for Research in Music Education, 106,* 23–35.

Price, H. E., and Yarbrough, C. (1987). Expressed opinions of composers, musical training, recording ownership, and their interrelationship. In C. K. Madsen and C. A. Prickett (Eds.), *Applications of research in music behavior.* Tuscaloosa: University of Alabama Press, 232–243.

Prickett, C. A. (1987). The effect of self-monitoring on the rate of a verbal mannerism of song leaders. In C. K. Madsen and C. A. Prickett (Eds.), *Applications of research in music behavior.* Tuscaloosa: University of Alabama Press, 125–134.

Rainbow, E. (1981). A final report on a three-year investigation of the rhythmic abilities of pre-school aged children. *Bulletin of the Council for Research in Music Education, 66–67,* 69–73.

Ramsey, D. S. (1979). Programmed instruction using band literature to teach pitch and rhythm error detection to music education students. *Journal of Research in Music Education, 27,* 149–162.

Reichardt, C. S., and Cook, T. D. (1979). Beyond qualitative versus quantitative methods. In C. S. Reichardt and T. D. Cook (Eds.), *Qualitative and Quantitative Methods in Evaluation Research.* Beverly Hills: Sage Publications, 7–32.

Richardson, C. P. (1988). Musical thinking as exemplified in music criticism. Unpublished doctoral dissertation, University of Illinois, Urbana-Champaign.

Rutter, M., Maughan, B., Mortimore, P., Ouston, J., and Smith, A. (1979). *Fifteen thousand hours: Secondary schools and their effects on children.* Cambridge: Harvard University Press.

St. Pierre, R. G. (1980). Planning longitudinal field studies: Considerations in determining sample size. *Evaluation Review, 4,* 405–415.

Schmidt, C. P. (1984). The relationship among aspects of cognitive style and language-bound/language-optional perception to musicians' performance in aural discrimination. *Journal of Research in Music Education, 32,* 159–168.

Smith, J. K., and Heshusius, L. (1986). Closing down the conversation: The end of the quantitative-qualitative debate among educational researchers. *Educational Researcher, 15,* 4–12.

Williamson, J. B., Karp, D. A., and Dalphin, J. R. (1977). *The research craft.* Boston: Little, Brown and Company.

Yarbrough, C. (1984). A content analysis of the *JRME*, 1953–1983. *Journal of Research in Music Education, 32,* 213–222.

Zimmerman, J. R. (1983). The musical experiences of two groups of children in one elementary school: An ethnographic study. Unpublished doctoral dissertation, Ohio State University, Columbus.

·10·

EXPERIMENTAL RESEARCH METHODOLOGY

John Christian Busch and James W. Sherbon
UNIVERSITY OF NORTH CAROLINA AT GREENSBORO

Objectives

This chapter describes the purpose, logic, and practice of experimental research methodology as conducted in the behavioral and social sciences. Experimental methods are placed within the broad context of disciplined inquiry and are illustrated by contemporary examples from music education literature. We review selected true and quasi-experimental designs for research and the evaluative criteria used to assess their validity.

We had three basic objectives: First, readers should be able to use the chapter as a resource for designing rigorous experiments in music education. Second, the chapter should offer literature for more advanced reading on experimental research methodology, and should be a useful reference in graduate research seminars. Third, the citations to the music education research literature should provide "real" examples that are easily accessible for more detailed analysis and study.

We understand the concept "experimental design" to include the procedures used to select subjects, form treatment groups, impose treatments, control for extraneous influences on research outcomes, collect measurements so that relatively unambiguous causal conclusions can be made, and make the findings applicable to known populations of research subjects. We address many of the issues raised in Campbell and Stanley's (1966) seminal work and in the relevant chapters of such texts as Kerlinger (1973) and Borg and Gall (1989). A somewhat different exposition, also termed "experimental design," focuses primarily on statistical theory and procedure and includes such topics as repeated measures analyses, Latin square designs, and factorial analysis of variance (ANOVA) designs. This focus is exemplified in the excellent work of Hays (1981), Winer (1971), and Edwards

(1972), among others. The present chapter does not focus on statistical theory; however, we do provide a conceptual description of statistical procedures when it is necessary to discuss experimental issues in the broad sense. This chapter is intentionally nonstatistical. Whenever possible, the chapter illustrates each topic with examples from the music education research literature.

Organization of the Chapter

The remainder of this section introduces the concept of disciplined inquiry (Cronbach and Suppes, 1969), of which experimentation is but one tradition. The second section briefly describes the essential characteristics of an experiment by contrasting experimental research with three other quantitative research traditions. The third section leads the reader through various steps in planning and executing an experiment; each step is illustrated with a single experiment (DeCarbo, 1981, 1982) from the music education literature. The fourth section summarizes the relevant philosophical and design requisites necessary to make interpretations that attribute cause. The fifth section introduces several true and quasi-experimental designs and describes several statistical approaches for analyzing quantitative experimental data. The last two sections address ethical principles and methodological issues, such as measurement validity and reliability, statistical power, and practical significance.

Disciplined Inquiry

The scholarly endeavors described in this chapter are a form of the process Cronbach and Suppes (1969) call "disci-

The authors wish to acknowledge the thoughtful comments provided by Richard M. Jaeger, James E. Major, and two unknown reviewers. Their suggestions were very valuable in the completion of the chapter; however, we remain responsible for any sins of omission or commission.

plined inquiry," by means of which scholars attempt to arrive at their understandings of "truth." Experimental research is just one of several approaches to disciplined inquiry. The approaches may be qualitative as well as quantitative, and may be nonscientific as well as scientific.

By definition, inquiry is conducted to answer a question. What sets *disciplined* inquiry apart from other activities intended to answer questions is the disciplined nature of the process. Disciplined approaches are those in which arguments made in answering questions can be examined for their truthfulness and reasonableness. The various areas of study have developed a scholarly tradition of questions that address sources of error that can occur in the inquiry process. The scholar "institutes controls at each step of information collection and reasoning to avoid the sources of error to which these questions refer" (Cronbach and Suppes, 1969, p. 15). In fact, many of the topics discussed in this chapter reflect the questions used by experimental researchers to examine the validity of their truth claims. As a result of these traditional strategies, "the report of a disciplined inquiry has a texture that displays the raw materials entering the argument and the logical processes by which they were compressed and rearranged to make the conclusion credible" (Cronbach and Suppes, 1969, p. 15).

Cronbach and Suppes distinguish between decision-oriented and conclusion-oriented research. *Decision-oriented research* is that which has been initiated by a request from an individual policymaker, a school administrator, or an agency that desires specific information on which to base a decision (e.g., to initiate a new teaching method, to modify a curriculum, to establish new policy). *Conclusion-oriented research* originates with the researcher's own scholarly interest in the issue being investigated. It is intended to contribute to a general understanding of various phenomena. Experimental disciplined inquiry as it is described in this chapter may be decision or conclusion oriented.

WHAT IS AN EXPERIMENT?

In this section we provide a succinct definition of a true experiment and attempt to sharpen that definition by contrasting experimental research with three other quantitative methods of disciplined inquiry: quasi-experiments, causal comparative studies, and correlational studies. An example from the music education literature is used to illustrate each method.

True Experiments

The essential characteristics of a true experiment are control (manipulation) of at least one independent variable, random assignment of subjects to experimental and control groups, control of extraneous variables, and measurement of concomitant variation in at least one dependent variable. If experimenters can rule out the possibility that other variables are responsible, they can conclude that the treatment

variable has caused the effect observed in the dependent variable. True experimental designs are less frequently encountered in the music education literature partially because practical constraints often prohibit random assignment of subjects.

Delzell (1989) conducted a true experiment to evaluate the effectiveness of two training conditions on discrimination skills. The manipulated independent variable, instruction in musical discrimination, had two levels: the experimental group received a tape-recorded discrimination training program using models/discriminator foils and modeling/imitation, while the control group received instruction that did not include these features. The *"Test of Musical Discrimination"* (TMD) (Froseth, 1982), a measure of a dependent variable, was administered prior to initiation of the treatment (as a pretest) and following completion of the treatment (as a posttest).

A pretest-posttest control group true experimental design was used. Although subjects were not randomly sampled, Delzell randomly assigned 43 fifth-grade beginning instrumental music students to an experimental ($n = 21$) or a control group ($n = 22$). The pretest was used as a covariate to adjust for any random preexperimental differences between groups. Delzell examined the covariation of instructional method and discrimination performance and found significant differences ($p < .05$) in composite TMD adjusted posttest means when the groups were compared. To the extent that she could eliminate other plausible explanations, Delzell suggested that differences in instructional method caused differences in music discrimination skills. Therefore, she cautiously concluded that discrimination skills were developed via instruction that could serve effectively in the music classroom. In our opinion, Delzell's study was a "true" experiment because she manipulated the independent variable and she attempted to control for the effects of extraneous variables through random assignment, use of a control (comparison) group, and statistical control.

Quasi-Experimental Research

Quasi-experimental designs may be employed when the researcher cannot constitute groups through random assignment, for example, when preestablished classes in schools are studied. In such designs, intact groups or a single group may be studied; however, the researcher retains control of (i.e., manipulates) a treatment variable. The researcher can strengthen the design by employing various strategies such as repeated measurements or measurement at strategic times.

Kerr (1945) provides an example of a quasi-experiment that utilized an intact, single sample group. Industrial productivity was studied in the presence or absence of music in the working environment. "The Quartz Crystal Experiment," involving 53 subjects employed in a crystal-finishing process, was conducted over a period of approximately 5 months. An equivalent time-samples design was utilized, whereby data were collected throughout a 5-month experiment with repeated random variations of the treatment conditions at different times. External influences in the working environment were thoroughly controlled and periods of music and no music were used during randomly determined times and in random sequence. Three different styles of music were employed. Measurements of productivity under music and no-music conditions were collected on a regular basis throughout the experiment. The results supported the conclusion that exposure to music increased productivity. Campbell and Stanley (1966) state that Kerr's design "seems altogether internally valid. *History,* the major weakness of the time-series [quasi-] experiment, is controlled by presenting X [the treatment] on numerous separate occasions, rendering extremely unlikely any rival explanation based on the coincidence of extraneous events" (p. 44). However, regarding external validity, Campbell and Stanley state that "generalization is obviously possible only to frequently tested populations" (p. 44).

Ex Post Facto Methods: Causal Comparative and Correlational Methods

Causal comparative and correlational research are two examples of ex post facto research. In true or quasi experiments, the researcher manipulates an independent variable, whereas in ex post facto research, the study is conducted after the treatment has occurred. In causal comparative and correlation research (and experiments as well) scholars examine the relationship between independent and dependent variables. In a causal comparative study, the independent variable is categorical, so that two or more groups are compared, while in a correlational study, the independent variable is generally considered to be continuous.

The 1976 outbreak of "Legionnaires' Disease," when many people attending an American Legion convention in Philadelphia became deathly ill, is a classic example of causal comparative medical research. Medical teams, faced with a malady of unknown origin (effect), diligently searched for the cause. In such cases, the testing of possible causes proceeds through trial and error and inspired guesswork.

In a causal comparative music education study, Cox (1989) examined the differences in attitudes toward chorus among students whose directors used three different rehearsal structures: (1) rehearsals beginning with a fast pace, having a slower-paced middle segment, and ending with a fast pace; (2) rehearsals having a fast pace at the beginning and the end, with a slower-paced middle part incorporating a fast-paced "climax"; and (3) rehearsals having a frequently changing pace throughout, with multiple changes in the familiarity and difficulty of the music rehearsed. In this study, the researcher did not manipulate rehearsal structure; he measured it after the fact.

Correlational studies estimate the strength and direction of relationships between variables which are usually measured continuously. Such studies provide the researcher with the ability to predict and estimate using regression procedures. Moore (1990), in a study of 64 high school instru-

mental music students, examined relationships between learning styles and music composition ability. Two learning style inventories and a test of music compositional ability were employed. Moore correlated variables from the composition test with specific learning style constructs, and the results were summarized in a table of correlation coefficients—commonly known as a correlation matrix.

The four categories of research cited above are not an exhaustive classification of all methods used in quantitative research. However, they represent an overview of several very common research techniques found in quantitative music education research.

PLANNING AND CONDUCTING A COMPARATIVE EXPERIMENT IN MUSIC EDUCATION: OVERVIEW AND EXAMPLE

This section describes specific steps in planning and conducting a comparative group experiment in music education. Each of the elements in the process is described briefly, and each is exemplified by a study in the music education literature (DeCarbo, 1981, 1982). DeCarbo sought to evaluate the relative effectiveness of instructional strategies in developing error detection skills among undergraduate conducting students. The two levels of the independent (experimental) variable, different forms of instruction in conducting, were an on-the-podium approach and a programed verbal instruction approach. The research problem was to determine whether there was a causal relationship between instructional approach and skill in error detection, the dependent variable.

An Analysis of Relevant Theory and Empirical Literature

In order that a particular inquiry possess more than immediate significance, the research process is framed within a theoretical perspective. The researcher therefore carefully reviews all relevant theory and previous research reports. The use of a particular theoretical perspective serves an important function in "organizing reality." When one considers the infinite number of research questions that might be posed, the special "worldview" of a theoretical perspective helps the researcher identify phenomena that are "significant" and worthy of study. Unfortunately, commitment to a particular theoretical perspective also may restrict one's perception. Petrie (1973) discusses the interplay between theory and observation. He states that experience (observation) is not neutral and cannot be examined apart from the scientist's theoretical commitments. Petrie states, ". . . two scientists may look at the 'same' thing and, because of different theoretical perspectives, may literally not see the same object. What is relevant for one theory may be totally ignored by another theory and even be logically incapable of being observed" (p. 133).

One theory employed by music education researchers is Piaget's theory of conservation (Piaget, 1969, 1981). Studies by Botvin (1974) on the conservation of melody, Jones (1976) on children's ability to understand and identify meter, Perney (1976) on conservation of metric time, Norton (1979) on auditory and visual conservation, and Nelson (1984) on measuring conservation of rhythm for Suzuki violin students exemplify use of Piaget's theory.

Theory proposes tentative explanations of observable events by using a network of theoretical characteristics or "constructs." This network relates behavioral events to theoretical constructs and attempts to specify relationships among the constructs. The researcher identifies the constructs that are of primary interest and other constructs that must be considered in planning and interpreting the results of a study.

In addition, the experimenter carefully examines empirical literature that relates to the issue of interest. Theory-testing questions that have and have not been posed are identified, and both contradictory and consistent results are noted. Approaches to methodology are also identified. Although DeCarbo (1981, 1982) does not utilize a general theoretical framework in his study, he does provide a statement of practical justification and describes the results of related studies.

Identification of Key Variables and Statement of the Research Problem

Experience suggests that individuals differ with respect to various characteristics. Some people are taller, some are slower, some are more musically proficient, some are male, some are Protestant, some have more extensive musical training, and so on. Sometimes characteristics vary for the same person at different times, as exemplified by the statement, "I am now more knowledgeable about Bach than I was before I completed a seminar on the baroque period." Such characteristics are termed variables. They "are non-uniform characteristics of observational units" (Glass and Hopkins, 1984, p. 5).

Sometimes characteristics do not vary, as exemplified in the following: "All of my graduate students have a bachelor's degree in music education." "This class is composed exclusively of singers." "All of the students in another class teach music at the elementary level." In such situations, the characteristics are constants. All of the previous examples describe the characteristics of individual people; however, the entities also may be aggregate groups of people or individual and collective entities, such as chairs, violins, ensembles, schools, states, countries, and textbook series.

When variability is observed, we may have multiple and contrasting explanations for differences among persons or entities. For example, the following may be used to explain achievement differences: "Students have different genetic heritages." "Some students' backgrounds are advantaged." "Systematic experiences were provided to some of the students that were not available to others." "The measurements of achievement are fallible." How we interpret variation

leads to certain courses of action during inquiry. For example, we might respond to variation caused by errors of measurement by using more reliable instruments or by choosing to study more students. We attempt to rule out sources of variability that we regard as irrelevant by holding those sources constant through physical or statistical methods. We attempt to maximize the effects of sources of variability due to treatment since we have the greatest interest in detecting them. Indeed, a basic principle of experimentation is to optimize variation of the independent variables and to control the remaining variables.

Scientific inquiry, including inquiry that uses experimental approaches, attempts to solve research problems or answer research questions. Kerlinger (1973) defines research problems as interrogative statements that ask whether two or more characteristics (variables) are systematically related. Since the covariation of two characteristics cannot be studied unless there is variation in each characteristic, we study only characteristics that vary naturally or vary as a result of intervention. DeCarbo (1981, 1982), for instance, asked whether there was a systematic relationship between the instructional strategy used (on-the-podium and programed verbal instruction) and success in error detection.

Operational Definition of Independent (Treatment) Variables

The central strategy in an experiment is the manipulation of an independent (treatment) variable and the measurement of a dependent (criterion) variable. The experimenter translates a conceptual definition of the independent variable into specific operations that define the manipulation of the treatment variable. Each "level" of the independent variable is specified, and the researcher determines when the treatment begins and ends.

DeCarbo designed his study to investigate the effects of a single independent variable, instructional method, with two levels: (1) prerecorded programed materials and (2) in-class, on-the-podium instruction. The study did not include a "no-treatment" control group; each level (group) served as a contrast to the other.

Sixteen 30-minute class sessions were devoted to both types of instruction in error detection skills. Students in the programed-materials group used cassette tape facilities, while students in the conducting experience group conducted compositions in class with live performers, under the supervision of the course instructor.

Eight compositions from various style periods were selected and performed by student brass players during on-the-podium instruction. The same compositions were used for the programed-materials instruction but were developed into a programed format and tape-recorded for presentation. Identical "errors" were determined and assigned prior to the lessons for the conducting experience group and prior to taping for the programed-materials group. DeCarbo completed pilot studies to examine the feasibility of using error detection training with "normal" instrumental class instruction, the appropriateness of music selections, the generation of effective error stimuli, and the relationships of the programed materials and conducting experience to the written and conducting tests.

Selection of Measurement Instruments

The researcher next selects instruments for measuring the constructs of interest. Measurements of the dependent (criterion) variable are critical. However, nonmanipulated independent variables may also be measured in order to answer ancillary research questions and to exercise control over other variables. The traditional psychometric criteria of reliability and validity are used to evaluate potential measurement instruments.

In his study, DeCarbo carefully developed separate written and performance (conducting) tests to assess the dependent variable (error detection). In the written test, students listened to a tape produced by professional musicians and marked their responses to four questions regarding the position and kind of each of the errors identified. In the performance (conducting) test, the subjects conducted professional players until perceiving a performance error, at which point they stopped and responded to the same four questions used on the written test. The internal consistency of the written and the performance tests was estimated by using Kuder-Richardson Formula-20 (Crocker and Algina, 1986, p. 139) and yielded coefficients of .83 and .90 respectively. Since the test items were selected from the same error selection list used in instruction, DeCarbo assumed the tests were relevant and appropriate to the instructional treatment.

Identification of the Population and Selection of a Random Sample

Experimenters ask to what population of individuals they wish to generalize their findings. A set of rules is articulated describing who is included in the population and who is not. Then a sample of subjects is selected so that observations made on the sample will be representative of those that would be found for the entire target population. These activities reflect concern for the external validity of the experiment.

One approach to selecting samples is to utilize a "probability" sampling technique such as simple random sampling. We know that there will always be (random) sampling error using probability sampling techniques, but that if the techniques are used properly, the results will be unbiased, or free of systematic errors. Several approaches to probability sampling are available. Unfortunately, many experimenters use samples of "convenience" composed of available intact groups, which may yield results that do not generalize to any population of interest. In such situations, certain types of subjects may be over- or underrepresented. Another issue that must be addressed in planning a study is the number of

subjects who should be sampled. This issue is discussed below.

DeCarbo does not explicitly state a target population for his study. However, he generalizes his results to "undergraduate music students." This generalization is probably too comprehensive since his sample is composed of two accessible undergraduate classes at two universities, an advanced instrumental conducting course and a course on teaching instrumental music. The two classes constitute a sample of convenience and probably limit the external validity of DeCarbo's experiment.

Random Assignment of Subjects to Treatment Groups

The experimenter next assigns the sample of subjects to separate groups that will receive different levels of the treatment (independent) variable. The experimenter wishes to begin the study with equivalent groups so that differences between groups at the conclusion of the study may be attributed to the effect of treatment and not to preexisting differences. Therefore, it is important that subjects with particular backgrounds, skills, aptitudes, expectations, and so forth not be assigned in disproportionate numbers to one or another of the treatment groups. A powerful but simple solution is to assign subjects to groups randomly by numbering each subject and then using a table of random numbers to assign subjects to groups. As a result of this process, any differences between the groups will be chance differences. The experimenter might add the constraint that an equal number of subjects be assigned to the groups. Finally, the randomly formed groups are randomly assigned to levels of the treatment variable. DeCarbo randomly assigned subjects from the two classes to either the conducting ($n = 16$) or the programed-materials group ($n = 17$).

Specifying an Experimental Design to Control Extraneous Variables and to Increase Precision

The research questions guide the preparation of an integrated experimental plan that includes the sampling procedure, the number of treatment groups, a statement of general procedures, the plan for implementing treatments, the frequency and timing of measurements, and the plan for statistical analysis. Table shells (tables without data in their body) are prepared to receive the results of each analysis, and an explicit link is established between each research question and a specific table shell. DeCarbo used a posttest-only control group, true experimental design (Campbell and Stanley, 1966) with random assignment of subjects to two groups, each serving as a control to the other.

The experimenter must attend to systematic and random sources of variation in the design. Some of these issues are addressed in the research plan while others depend on how the study is conducted.

Two sources of systematic variance are a concern. First, the experimenter must monitor the application of the treatment. It must be verified that the operations defined for the different levels of the treatment actually occur as planned. Are the treatment differences between groups maintained throughout the experiment? A second systematic source of variability is irrelevant factors that might mimic treatment "effects" and thus compromise the validity of conclusions. The experimenter monitors the treatment and institutes various physical and statistical measures to control for such effects. An example of a possible extraneous variable in the DeCarbo study was any difference between the scores obtained from the two universities. In order to eliminate the plausibility of that factor, DeCarbo (1) randomly assigned equal members of students from each institution to the two treatment levels and (2) computed *t* tests for independent samples contrasting the written and performance scores of students from the two universities. He reported no significant difference between the two university groups and therefore was able to combine the two groups in subsequent analyses. DeCarbo carefully designed and monitored the treatment as it occurred. In many music education experiments, the length of the treatment period may be inadequate. However, DeCarbo provided sufficient exposure to the independent variable (16 class sessions) so that ample opportunity for the treatment to take effect was ensured.

The influence of random sources of variation is another concern. Random effects within treatment groups may be caused by various factors, including events that occur in the experimental environment (such as physical noise, interruptions, unintended events, and so on) that influence some but not all subjects at various times, as well as factors that influence the reliability of measurements. All of these factors can make statistical analyses less precise. The researcher should take care to use reliable instruments, attempt to reduce the effects of random factors, and use appropriate statistical methods to increase statistical precision. The Kuder-Richardson Formula-20 reliability coefficients for the written and performance measures, which DeCarbo reported, suggested that his analysis was performed with adequate statistical precision.

Collection of Data

Measurements should be recorded carefully and entered into a data file, where they are edited and verified. Various checks should be made to detect recording or copying errors.

Analysis of Data

Appropriate descriptive and inferential procedures are used to summarize the data, test statistical hypotheses, and construct confidence intervals for estimation. Individual measurements should be checked prior to conducting sophisticated statistical analyses by examining simple statistical summaries such as frequency distributions in order to identify any "out-of-bounds" or unusual values. DeCarbo calculated descriptive statistics and computed *t* tests for independent samples comparing the posttest means of the

programed materials group and the conducting experience group for each measure of the dependent variable (written and performance tests). An alpha level of .05 was utilized in all his analyses. He summarized the results in tabular form.

Interpretation of Data

The experimenter should complete each table shell and interpret each statistical result carefully. Each research question should be answered by referring to the relevant part of the analysis. DeCarbo reported no significant difference between the two treatment groups on the written test; however, he found a significant between-group difference ($p < .01$) on the conducting test.

Discussion of Results and Conclusions

The theoretical implications of each result should be thoroughly considered. The experimenter should review the study's strengths and weaknesses and evaluate the trustworthiness of the interpretations of the data. Each conclusion should be evaluated carefully by considering all plausible rival interpretations of the findings. Any unanticipated outcomes should be described, and suggestions for additional research should be made.

DeCarbo stated three purposes for his study, only one of which was a research problem. He successfully achieved the first two purposes: to design two different approaches to teaching error detection skills and to administer the approaches in an experiment. The third purpose, a research question, focused on the differential effectiveness of the two instructional approaches. DeCarbo concluded that on the performance (conducting) test (but not the written test), the on-the-podium conducting instructional method was more beneficial. Although DeCarbo provides a thorough analysis of the implications of his study, since it was not grounded in a theoretical framework, its implications are somewhat limited. In addition, he appears to overgeneralize his results. First, he generalizes to a broader population of subjects than might be warranted. Second, his results suggest that the treatment effects may not be generalized to all measures of the dependent variable.

MAKING INFERENCES ABOUT CAUSALITY

The Attribution of Cause

Music educators (whether as teachers, administrators, or curriculum specialists) frequently ask causal questions. They wonder which teaching method produces the greatest achievement, whether one set of learning conditions is more facilitative than another, and so on. Such questions imply the possibility of going beyond identification of a simple relationship between two or more variables to describe that relationship in a particular way, one in which one variable is considered the cause of a second variable. Philosophers have long debated the validity of inferring cause on the basis of a relationship between variables. Russell (1917/1973), for example, believed that use of the term "cause" was "bound up with misleading associations" (p. 408). Although modern philosophical analysis has pointed out limitations in making causal inferences, a central part of educators' roles dictates that they study and identify interventions that they believe may enhance learning for students.

Some Philosophical Issues It is not our intention to provide an extensive review of philosophical issues related to causality; Cook and Campbell (1979) presented an excellent overview of various philosophical perspectives. However, several preliminary comments may set the issue of inferences based on experimental evidence in its proper philosophical context.

David Hume (1777/1973) suggested that when one event follows the other time after time, the mind associates the two events. He defined cause "to be an object, followed by another, and where all the objects similar to the first are followed by objects similar to the second. Or in other words where, if the first object had not been, the second never had existed" (p. 406). The observer makes the connection between a "cause" and an "effect" when the two events are seen to occur in uniform conjunction. Therefore, Hume equates temporal association with causality. Other writers have addressed the need to identify additional criteria that distinguish causal from noncausal relationships. Mill (1906/1973) stated that "the universality of the law of causation consists in this, that every consequent is connected in this manner with some particular antecedent or set of antecedents" (p. 417); however, he recognized the post hoc fallacy and knew that causes had to be more than events that were invariably followed by other events. For example, is it reasonable to consider night to be the cause of day, simply because night invariably precedes day? Mill defines "the cause of a phenomenon to be the antecedent or the concurrence of antecedents, on which it is invariably and unconditionally consequent" (p. 428). Since day following night is conditional on other events such as the rotation of the earth, night may not be regarded as the "cause" of day. Therefore, causes are events that are linked to subsequent events without conditional statements relating the event to other outside events.

The essence of this discussion is that in order for one to reasonably believe that X causes Y, several conditions must be met. First, there must be covariation between X and Y; that is, they must be systematically related. However, covariation is a necessary but not sufficient condition for causal interpretation. One also must be able to rule out possible effects of other variables. For example, it is not correct to say that X causes Y when in fact X may influence Z, which in turn influences Y. The intervening effect of Z is one of the "conditions" referred to by Mill that can disallow or weaken causal interpretation of relationships. All plausible "conditions" must be identified and eliminated. If the relationship is

to be considered causal, the experimenter also must present evidence to argue for a specific causal direction. This requires evidence to support X as a cause of Y but not the reverse. This is usually accomplished by observing the temporal order of X and Y in the study. That is, if variation in X occurs before the concomitant variation in Y, then Y cannot cause X.

The Validity of Inferences from Experiments

The researcher manipulates an independent variable and then observes the entities being studied to see if there is concomitant variation in a dependent variable. The researcher asks whether the variables covary. If concomitant variation is observed, the researcher must next address the possibility that variables other than the independent variable might be responsible for the covariation. Such variables, sometimes termed "extraneous" variables, threaten the internal validity of the experiment. The effects of these variables must be discounted as reasonable explanations for the observed covariation. To the extent that it is believed that the treatment variable is *the* cause of variation in the dependent variable, the study is said to possess internal validity. Cook and Campbell (1979) state that

> estimating the internal validity of a relationship is a deductive process in which the investigator has to systematically think through how each of the internal validity threats may have influenced the data. Then, the investigator has to examine the data to test which relevant threats can be ruled out. . . . When all of the threats can plausibly be eliminated, it is possible to make confident conclusions about whether a relationship is probably causal. (p. 55)

The experimenter also depends on peer review and criticism for the identification of plausible alternative explanations. Thus, it is important to place one's work before the intellectual community for critical examination and to generate plausible rival hypotheses.

Cook and Campbell have divided validity concerns into four categories: statistical conclusion validity, internal validity (just discussed), the construct validity of causes and effects, and external validity. Threats to each of the four aspects of experimental validity are enumerated in Table 10–1. Since space limitations prevent detailed descriptions of each threat, the reader is referred to Cook and Campbell (1979) for a detailed exposition.

Statistical conclusion validity addresses the possibility that erroneous conclusions based on the statistical analysis may occur. For example, because of weak statistical power, the experimenter may incorrectly conclude that there is no covariation between the independent and dependent variables.

When two variables are observed to covary, the internal validity question asks whether alternative operations also might explain the observed relationship. For example, do an experimental and a control group differ, not because of the treatment, but because of differences in their initial composi-

TABLE 10–1. Four Catergories of Threats to Experimental Validity Described by Cook and Campbell (1979, pp. 37–94)

Statistical Conclusion Validity	Internal Validity	Construct Validity of Cause and Effects	External Validity
Low statistical power	History	Inadequate explication of constructs	Interaction of selection and treatment
Violated statistical assumptions	Maturation	Monooperation bias	Interaction of setting and treatment
Error rate problem	Instrumentation	Monomethod bias	Interaction of history and treatment
Reliability of measures	Statistical regression	Hypothesis guessing	
Reliability of treatment implementation	Selection	Evaluation apprehension	
Random irrelevancies in experimental setting	Mortality	Experimenter expectancies	
Random heterogeneity of respondents	Interactions with selection	Confounding constructs and levels of constructs	
	Ambiguity about direction of causal influence	Interaction of different treatments	
	Diffusion/imitation of treatment	Interaction of testing and treatment	
	Compensatory equalization of treatment	Restricted generalizability across constructs	
	Compensatory rivalry		
	Resentful demoralization		
	Testing		

tion (selection bias)? Construct validity of cause and effects refers to "the approximate validity with which we can make generalizations about higher-order constructs from research operations" (Cook and Campbell, 1979, p. 38). If, for example, a single measure of a construct representing an effect is used, the evidence in support of a construct of cause and effect is potentially limited since that single measure may not adequately define the boundaries of the construct's meaning. External validity refers "to the approximate validity with which conclusions are drawn about the generalizability of a causal relationship to and across populations of persons, settings and times" (Cook and Campbell, 1979, p. 39).

The Experimental Strategy and Sources of Variance

Experimental design deals with the researcher's decisions in planning a study so that valid and efficient interpretations regarding the concomitant variation of treatment (independent) and criterion (dependent) variables may be made. In attempting to answer a research question, the researcher focuses on several sources of variation in the criterion (dependent) variable: random sources of error variance; and two general sources of systematic variance, relevant (treatment) variance and irrelevant (nontreatment) variance.

Error variance in criterion measurements is random. Such errors are equally likely to be positive or negative and are not systematically related to a subject's "true" score. One source of error variance is measurement error (test unreliability). Random errors also result from lack of perfect control over the subjects' experimental environment. The critical task for the researcher in interpreting an experiment's outcome is to evaluate the systematic sources of variance (presumed to be produced by the treatment) against a background of omnipresent error variance. The researcher must determine whether the variance in the criterion measurements is greater than that which would be expected by chance fac-

tors. Excess error variance is potentially problematic because it may obscure the detection of treatment effects. One should attempt, therefore, to minimize such sources of error.

There are two general sources of systematic variation in the criterion. First, there is variation that was created as a function of exposure to the different levels of the experimental treatment. This part of variance is intended, is systematic, is not random, and reflects the effect of the treatment experience, if any. Systematic variability due to treatment is of greatest interest in the experiment. Subjects in treatment and control groups, which did not differ systematically before treatment, may be systematically different following the treatment.

In addition, there are other systematic components of variance that influence criterion variation. These components are not the result of the treatment. They are unwanted and irrelevant sources of variance if they produce an effect that might be misinterpreted as a treatment effect. For example, an independent historical event might occur simultaneously with the manipulation of the treatment and produce systematic effects on criterion variance. Unless this effect is eliminated, the experimenter might erroneously conclude that observed differences in the dependent variable were due to the treatment rather than to the unwanted historical event. This and other threats to internal validity are listed in Table 10–1. An important task for the researcher is to identify potential irrelevant, systematic sources of variation, and to design the study so that these sources can be discounted as implausible alternative explanations of the "treatment" effect.

Kerlinger (1973) discussed a design strategy that he called the "MAXMINCON" principle. This acronym summarizes approaches that a scientist might use in dealing with the three sources of criterion variance just discussed. The "MAX" principle suggests that one should attempt to maximize the treatment source of variation. Kerlinger recommends that the researcher define treatment conditions that are sufficiently different to produce effects that are large enough to detect. Because the researcher must "read" treatment effects against a background of "noise" produced by random sources of error variation, it is important that the treatment effects be large enough to be detectable.

The "MIN" principle recommends that error variance be reduced as much as possible. This is accomplished by selecting well-constructed and reliable measuring instruments, by employing appropriate statistical strategies (such as the analysis of covariance), and by carefully conducting the study, attending to standardization of procedures and monitoring of the experiment.

The "CON" principle states that one should attempt to control for the effects of systematic but irrelevant sources of variation in the criterion measurements. This is accomplished through random assignment of subjects to conditions, through the use of an appropriate experimental design, through a strategy of holding certain variables constant through preassignment matching of subjects who then are assigned randomly to treatment and control groups from matched pairs, and by statistical control. Figure 10–1 illustrates those principles.

Analysis of the Experimental Literature in Music Education

In this section we identify strengths and weaknesses in the recent research literature in music education that are specifically relevant to experimental methodology. In order to accomplish that, we surveyed 27 critiques of experimental studies published in the *Bulletin of the Council for Research in Music Education* (Vols. 99–104) to discover those methodological criticisms that specifically relate to experiments. In this analysis we have not addressed methodological issues that apply equally to other research methods or to other fields. (For a thorough discussion of the role of the critic when reviewing and evaluating dissertation research, the interested reader may wish to consult the works of Gonzo, 1988, Petzold 1988, and Saffle, 1988.)

Reviewers cited the following strengths of the experiments in music education: the use of appropriate experimental designs and correct statistical procedures, the use of nec-

essary treatment controls, and complete description of the treatments.

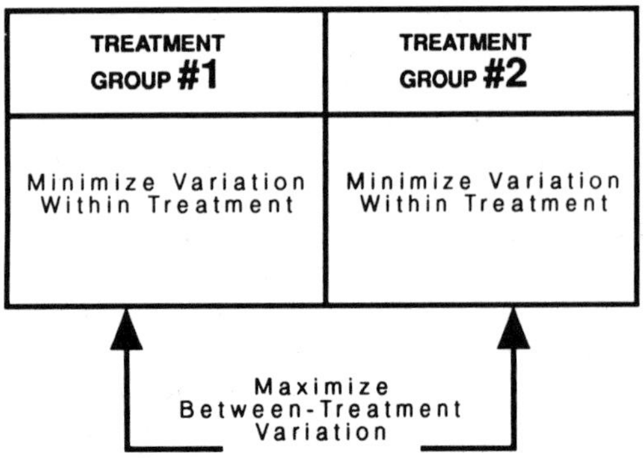

The reviewers cited several negative features: the need for longer treatment periods, failure to establish the reliability and validity of the measuring instruments, lack of attention to the accurate recording of experimental data in the design of the studies, the presence of experimental mortality, and negligence in controlling extraneous factors.

EXPERIMENTAL AND QUASI-EXPERIMENTAL DESIGNS FOR DISCIPLINED INQUIRY IN MUSIC EDUCATION

The classic work on designing experiments for field settings, particularly those in education, is that of Campbell and Stanley (1966). Originally a chapter in the first edition of the *Handbook of Research on Teaching* (Gage, 1963), the treatise has had enormous influence on education and related disciplines and professions. Several authors have extended some of the fundamental concepts presented in Campbell and Stanley's chapter. The most notable extensions include an exposition on external validity (Bracht and Glass, 1968), an extensive analysis of validity issues in quasi-experimental research by Cook and Campbell (1979), and reviews of experimental research appearing in various handbooks, for example, those of Glass (1982) and Porter (1988). In this section we describe three true experimental and three quasi-experimental designs proposed by Campbell and Stanley (1966). Because of space limitations we will not review all of Campbell and Stanley's designs, nor will we provide a complete analysis of strengths and weaknesses of the designs. The reader should consult the sources cited above for additional information.

Notation

Figure 10–2 incorporates the notational system used by Campbell and Stanley (1966) to summarize the designs. The symbols are interpreted in the following way: "R" denotes the use of random assignment of subjects to groups. In designs with two groups, one of those groups is considered to be an experimental group that receives a treatment; and the other, a control group that receives no treatment or an alternative treatment. The symbol "X" designates the application of a treatment. The researcher randomly assigns the treatment levels to the randomly formed groups. "O" indicates that a variable is measured or observed. Measurements of the dependent variable are taken at different time points.

As one reads the figure, the passage of time is represented from left to right. For example, in the first true experimental design, the two randomly assigned groups (experimental and control) are first measured simultaneously (pretests are administered). At a later time, subjects are remeasured (posttests are administered). These pre- and posttests might

FIGURE 10–1. Control of Variance in an Experiment.

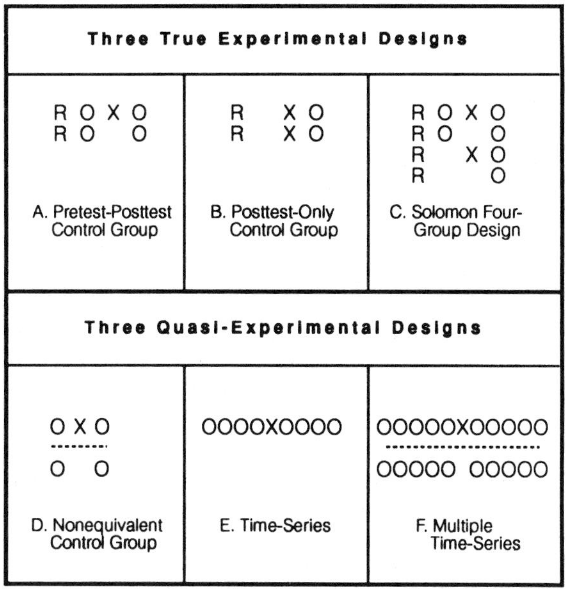

Three True Experimental Designs

R O X O R O O	R X O R X O	R O X O R O O R X O R O
A. Pretest-Posttest Control Group	B. Posttest-Only Control Group	C. Solomon Four- Group Design

Three Quasi-Experimental Designs

O X O ------- O O	OOOOXOOOO	OOOOOXOOOOO ---------------- OOOOO OOOOO
D. Nonequivalent Control Group	E. Time-Series	F. Multiple Time-Series

FIGURE 10–2. Six Selected True Experimental and Quasi-Experimental Designs.

be traditional measuring instruments such as paper and pencil tests or they might be behavioral observations or various types of nonreactive measures (Webb, Campbell, Schwartz, Sechrest, and Grove, 1981).

In two of the quasi-experimental designs shown in Figure 10–2, a broken line separates groups to indicate that the groups are not randomly equivalent; that is, they have not been formed through random assignment of subjects.

Three True Experimental Designs

The first three designs shown in Figure 10–2 are true experimental designs. They are distinguished by the experimenter's ability to manipulate the independent variable and randomly assign subjects to groups. The first of the true experimental designs (A) is a *pretest-posttest control group* true experiment. In this design two (or more) groups are formed through random assignment of subjects and treatments, and the groups are pretested at approximately the same time. Following administration of pretests, an independent variable is manipulated and treatments are administered to the groups. The layouts in Figure 10–2 are somewhat general and permit numerous variations in design. Although it may appear from the figure that just two groups are being compared, two, three, or more levels of one or more treatment variables may be assigned to two, three, or more groups. For example, three different instructional approaches (levels/groups) might be used to teach beginning instrumental students. The designs do not specify the length of the treatment or measurement, nor do they require a single dependent measure. All of those elements are defined appropriately for a particular experiment.

A common misunderstanding is that a pretest-to-posttest comparison alone will test whether the treatment has had an effect; however, that is not the case. The treatment effects are evaluated by contrasting the means of the posttest scores for the experimental and the control groups.

An important feature of design (A) is the presence of pretest scores for each subject, which can be used in several ways. Pretest scores can be used to check on the equivalence of the groups achieved through random assignment. Of greater importance, pretest scores can also be used as statistical covariates to achieve a more precise and efficient analysis of potential treatment effects.

The second of the true experimental designs, is (B) a *posttest-only, control group* true experiment. The difference between this design and the first is the absence of pretest measures. The strategy used to determine whether there is a treatment effect is the same; the experimenter compares posttest scores of the treatment and control groups. Of course, without pretest measures, the equality of groups cannot be examined explicitly, nor can one exercise statistical control. However, with enough cases, it is likely that random assignment has done its job; therefore, examining pretest scores is not essential. In some studies, such as experiments comparing different approaches to teaching beginning instrumentalists, a pretest is inappropriate because none of the subjects has any of the skills assessed by the dependent measure for example, instrumental performance.

The third true experimental design is (C) the Solomon four-group design. Inspection of Figure 10–2 suggests that the Solomon four-group design is a combination of the first two true experimental designs. (The Solomon four-group design is an example of a *factorial* design, i.e., a design that tests the effects of two or more independent variables simultaneously. Pretest condition—presence or absence—is one of the Solomon design's independent variables. Factorial designs are discussed below.) The pool of subjects is randomly assigned to one of four groups. The four groups differ with regard to two characteristics: whether they have received the treatment and whether they have been pretested. The unique feature of this design is that it allows one to test empirically a threat to validity due to pretest sensitization, also termed an interaction of testing and treatment. The potential problem of pretest sensitization is illustrated by a hypothetical study that employed a design with pretesting and in which a treatment effect was found. If one were to replicate the study but use a design without pretests, a treatment effect might not be found. One possible explanation of the finding is that treatment effects may exist only when subjects have been sensitized by pretesting. Of course this limits our understanding of the treatment effect to conditions in which subjects are pretested.

Three Quasi-Experimental Designs

Campbell and Stanley recognize that many research situations in the field do not allow the full experimental control required by true experiments. Although they agree that researchers should always search for settings that maximize the possibility of control, they identify several plausible quasi-experimental designs. Quasi-experimental designs are less demanding with respect to control but are susceptible to more threats to internal validity. Three representative quasi-experimental designs are reviewed in this chapter. These designs, selected because they seem particularly suitable to research in music education, are depicted in Figure 10–2.

The first design is (D) the *nonequivalent control group design*. This design appears similar to true experimental design A, but it differs in one significant feature. In a true experiment, groups are formed by randomly assigning subjects. But in this design, random assignment of subjects to groups is not possible. The broken line separating the two groups in Figure 10–2 emphasizes that the groups are not randomly equivalent. The researcher selects two intact groups that he or she believes are comparable and then randomly assigns treatments to the groups. The design's internal validity depends on the comparability of the intact groups. Campbell and Stanley suggest this design when designs A, B, and C are not feasible.

The second quasi-experimental design is (E) the *time-series design,* in which a single group is studied. The group may have been assembled for other purposes, such as an individual class in a high school. The design's salient feature is the repeated measurement of the group over time. When repeated measurements (such as weekly tests) are a normal part of the group's routine and not likely to be reactive, the design may be plausible. At some randomly determined time, an intervention is introduced, and the researcher attempts to determine whether the treatment might be responsible for any observed changes in the level or trend in the measurements of the dependent variable. That determination is sometimes made with difficulty; for example, when observations gradually increase in magnitude up to the time of the treatment and continue to increase after the treatment.

A variant of the time-series design is (F) the *multiple time-series design*. This design is created by adding one or more intact groups that are selected to be comparable to each other. The design is similar to the nonequivalent control group design (D) except the multiple measurements are taken prior to, and following, administration of the treatment. In general, this design is less vulnerable to threats to its validity than is a simple time-series design (E) because of the addition of a comparison group.

Campbell and Stanley provide detailed summary tables specifying sources of invalidity for the 16 designs covered in their review. However, such information should not be regarded as absolute. Since experiments may have many unique features, the reader is directed to Campbell and Stanley's narrative and to other sources, such as Cook and Campbell (1979). Glass (1982) points out that the validity of experimental findings is not solely dependent on the design used, but must be judged on the collective conditions of a particular experiment. An examination of the tables provided by Campbell and Stanley (1966) does not support unambiguous judgments about the validity of a specific study that employs a particular design. One must examine the features of an individual study to determine whether specific threats to internal and external validity are likely to be present. Glass (1982) points out that even the one-group, pretest-posttest, preexperimental design might be valid under certain circumstances.

The six designs we have presented merit a brief overview of potential threats to experimental validity. Researchers consider internal validity to be a critical factor when designing an experiment. External validity (generalizability), although highly desirable, might be deemed less critical in music education research. All three true experimental designs discussed in this chapter are judged by Campbell and Stanley to control for some threats to internal validity. Of the three quasi-experimental designs discussed, the time-series design (E) provides only weak controls for history (events occurring between measurements), and the nonequivalent control group design (D) is potentially weak in controlling for the interaction of selection and maturation (interaction of selection-maturation confused with the experimental variable). Campbell and Stanley regard the effect of pretesting as a "concern" for all six designs except the posttest-only control group design (B) and the Solomon four-group design (C).

Some Additional Approaches to the Collection and Statistical Analysis of Experimental Data

The designs discussed above may suggest a simple experimental situation in which the researcher focuses attention on a single independent variable with two levels. However, realistic problem solving in experimental research is not well represented by the "idealized" designs of Figure 10–2. In fact, an experimenter has available a substantial number of choices regarding data collection.

This section describes four different data collection strategies: factorial designs, randomized block designs, repeated measures designs, and Latin square designs. In keeping with the approach of this chapter, we will provide a conceptual and nonmathematical overview of the salient features of each design. The interested reader should consult the following excellent statistical sources: Hays (1981), Edwards (1972), Kirk (1968), and Winer (1971) for a more extensive discussion.

In a factorial or multiway design, two or more independent variables are incorporated simultaneously. The experimenter might be interested in testing hypotheses that involve each one. Because there are multiple independent variables, two kinds of information will be available to the experimenter. The first is information about "main effects," which indicates whether there are significant overall differences due to the levels of a given independent variable. Main effects address such questions as, Are there significant differences between the experimental and the control groups? Are there significant differences between woodwind and brass players? The most important characteristic that distinguishes factorial designs from designs with a single independent variable is their ability to yield information about the interaction of two or more of the independent variables. The interaction indicates whether the effects of one independent variable (for example, a treatment variable) are the same at each level

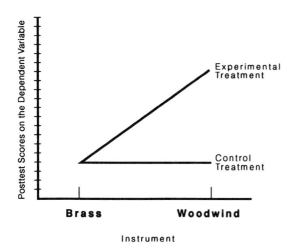

FIGURE 10–3. A Two-Way Interaction Between Treatment and Type of Instrument.

of a second independent variable (for example, woodwind vs. brass players). A graph of a hypothetical interaction is given in Figure 10–3.

In this example, the difference between the experimental group and the control group depends on the type of performer. The treatment does have a differential effect for woodwind players, but does not for brass players. Many different types of interactions are possible in factorial designs.

In completely randomized factorial designs all of the independent variables are "fully crossed." This means that different subjects compose groups formed by all combinations of levels of two (or more) independent variables. In the example shown in Figure 10–3, each woodwind player would be randomly assigned to one of the two levels of treatment and the brass players would be randomly assigned in the same manner.

A study by Asmus (1978) exemplifies a factorial design in the music education literature. Asmus investigated the perception of difference tones among music and nonmusic majors. He randomly selected a sample of 40 subjects from populations of music ($n = 20$) and nonmusic ($n = 20$) majors. He used a 2 (groups) x 7 (frequency settings) factorial design. The first independent variable (groups) had two levels (music and nonmusic major), and the second independent variable (frequency settings) has seven levels (difference tones produced by manipulating the frequencies). The latter variable was a treatment variable.

Measurements of the dependent variable were made to determine the decibel level when a subject first perceived a difference tone and the attenuation level difference between the two tones before the difference tone was no longer perceived. Two separate two-way analyses of variance (ANOVAs) were computed, using the detection levels and the intensity attenuation differences as dependent variables.

A randomized block design is similar to a factorial design in that more than one independent variable is used in the design. However, the second variable is included in the design, not for the purpose of estimating its effects, but to increase

statistical efficiency and to control for its effects. In this strategy, the experimenter first identifies a control variable that is used to form blocks of subjects who are relatively homogeneous with respect to the dependent variable. For this design to be effective, the blocking or control variable must be systematically correlated with the dependent variable. Subjects are classified into different levels of the blocking variable, and subjects from each block are randomly assigned to all treatment and control groups. The randomized block design allows the experimenter to statistically remove the portion of the variability in the criterion measure that is associated with the blocking variable. As a result, the error term is smaller and the analysis is more efficient. The randomized block design is similar to the analysis of covariance in its effects. A critical assumption of the randomized block design is that the blocking variable and the treatment variable do not interact.

An example of a randomized block design is a study by Duke (1985), who investigated intonational patterns of musicians when performing musical intervals. Subjects enrolled in "applied" music were randomly selected from students in junior high school, senior high school, and college. Subjects were assigned to blocks by age/experience level and then randomly assigned to experimental conditions.

In some other designs, subjects are exposed sequentially to *all* of the levels of treatment instead of a single level. Such designs are called repeated measures designs. The order of subjects' exposure to the different treatment levels is usually counterbalanced to control for bias due to sequence effects. With some consideration, it can be seen that a repeated measures design is a special case of the randomized block design. In repeated measures designs the "blocks" consist of subjects matched exactly (with themselves) so that subjects serve as their own control.

If certain restrictions and assumptions are warranted a Latin square design may be chosen. This design is a balanced but incomplete replication of a factorial design. The design requires that the number of levels of each variable and the number of subjects or groups of subjects be the same. An example of a Latin square is shown in Figure 10–4: variables *a* and *b* may be thought of as blocking variables, and variable *c* as a treatment. Note that each treatment level (*c*) occurs just once in each row (variable *a*) and in each column (variable *b*).

Some statistical designs combine several of the features just discussed. For example, in "mixed factorial designs" different subjects may be assigned to the levels of one independent variable, while each level of a second independent variable may be applied to all subjects. This design is a

	b_1	b_2	b_3
a_1	c_1	c_2	c_3
a_2	c_2	c_3	c_1
a_3	c_3	c_1	c_2

FIGURE 10–4. A Latin Square Arrangement.

combination of a repeated measures and a completely randomized design. Other variations are possible.

SOME OTHER IMPORTANT ISSUES

The Importance of Reliable and Valid Measurements

In an experiment, treatment effects are assessed by examining variance in the measurements of the dependent variable. It is essential that those measurements be of sufficient quality that experimental effect can be detected. Two indexes of the quality of a measurement are reliability and validity.

Reliability addresses the issue of consistency of measurement. Less-than-perfect reliability is a function of random (chance) errors that may be due to a variety of factors such as fluctuations in the attention of an examinee, mismarking by an examinee, or sloppy test administration. Such errors contribute to the lack of consistency of response over time, over different forms of the measuring instrument, within the instrument, and so on. The experimenter must attempt to reduce these various sources of random (error) variance. The strategies used to achieve increased reliability are employed during the process of instrument development as well as during data collection. Error variation due to measurement is part of the background "noise" against which treatment effects must be assessed. "Noise" should be minimized as much as possible in order to allow treatment effects to be detected more readily. Because educational and psychological measures are fallible, many sources of inconsistency are unavoidable; however, reducing error variation will increase the statistical power and precision of the analysis of experimental data. Therefore, one should always choose measures that are as reliable as possible.

Validity is the most important consideration when evaluating measurements. Validity refers to the "appropriateness, meaningfulness, and usefulness of the inferences made from test scores" (American Educational Research Association, American Psychological Association, & National Council on Measurement in Education, 1985, p. 9). The kinds of errors associated with measurement validity issues are systematic rather than random. The use of invalid measures in an experiment will lead to incorrect conclusions or inferences concerning the effects of the treatment variable. The experimenter should always consider all evidence that bears on the accuracy of inferences from measurement results, in the context of the particular study.

The assessment of evidence in support of measurement consistency and the accuracy of inferences made from measurements is a complex process. The reader is referred to the *Standards for Educational and Psychological Testing* (American Educational Research Association et al., 1985); annual reviews of educational measurement such as the third edition of *Educational Measurement* (Linn, 1989); specific test reviews in the *Mental Measurement Yearbooks* (Mitchell, 1985); reviews in scholarly journals such as the *Journal of Educational Measurement, Educational and Psychological Measurement, Applied Measurement in Education,* and the *Bulletin of the Council for Research in Music Education.* An excellent resource on classical and modern test theory is Crocker and Algina (1986).

Measuring the Effect of an Experimental Treatment

The hypothesis-testing traditions of the behavioral and social sciences often lead to less-than-complete interpretations of experimental findings. Following a statistically significant outcome, researchers sometimes lose sight of the need to estimate the extent of the treatment effect on the dependent variable. Glass and Hopkins (1984) define the treatment effect size as the difference between the two population means (of the experimental and the control groups) divided by the within-group standard deviation. This index of *effect size* evaluates the size of the difference between the experimental and control group means by taking into account the variability within each group. Therefore, a big difference in means might not be so "big" when subjects *within* a group vary substantially in their scores on the dependent variable. The index is defined in Figure 10–5.

Cohen (1977) interprets treatment effect sizes using the following convention. A small effect size is one that is approximately equal to .2, a medium effect size is approximately equal to .5, and a large effect size is equal to .8. Therefore a "medium" effect is arbitrarily defined as a difference between the experimental group mean and the control group mean that is one-half the within-group standard deviation. Other practical indices of the strength of association of the independent and dependent variables (and therefore of the treatment effect) are the point-biserial correlation coefficient (which can be used as a follow-up to the *t* test) and the eta coefficient (which can be used as an adjunct to the analysis of variance). Cohen (1965) has written a very interesting and readable paper on this topic.

Precision, Statistical Power, and the Size of a Sample

In this section we consider some factors that are important in planning an experiment. These factors are the sample size (n), statistical power, the effect size, and the risk of committing a Type I error (alpha). Each is directly related to the others.

Consideration of statistical power is very important in planning an experiment. Statistical power is the probability of correctly rejecting a false null hypothesis. That is, it is the long-term chance of correctly rejecting the null hypothesis when the treatment has had an effect. In statistical terms, the null hypothesis states that there is no difference between the

$$\text{Effect Size} = \frac{\mu \text{ experimental} - \mu \text{ control}}{\sigma \text{ within}}$$

FIGURE 10–5. Index of Effect Size.

mean scores on the dependent variable in the populations from which the experimental group and the control group have been selected. Therefore, when the treatment has had an effect, the correct decision will be to reject the null hypothesis. Under these conditions, power is the probability of arriving at a correct decision. Cohen (1977) recommends that power, or the probability of making a correct decision, be set at .80 in the absence of specific arguments to the contrary. When power is set at .80, the chance of rejecting an incorrect null hypothesis is 80 out of 100 times if the experiment were to be repeated indefinitely.

Type I error is incorrectly rejecting the null hypothesis. The risk of committing a Type I error (alpha) is set by the experimenter before gathering data. Popular values for alpha are 0.01 (1 percent), 0.05 (5 percent), and 0.10 percent (10 percent).

The effect size (described in the previous section) for a planned experiment can be estimated on the basis of prior experiments with similar populations or may be based on information from a literature review. We know that sample size and statistical power are directly related: With other factors held constant, as the sample size increases, the power of a statistical test increases.

A common scenario in planning an experiment consists of estimating the expected effect size, estimating the desired power and probability of committing a Type I error (alpha), and then calculating the necessary sample size for the study. Tables prepared by Cohen (1977) facilitate such planning and provide systematic and reasonable answers. All things being equal, a good "rule of thumb" for experimenters is that more subjects are better than fewer subjects.

Practical vs. Educational Significance

The term "significance" is generally interpreted to mean something akin to importance or meaningfulness. In the hypothesis-testing tradition, when empirical evidence is evaluated and a decision is made with respect to the null hypothesis, the outcome might be described as statistically significant. Unfortunately, the term "significance" in this sense does not have the same meaning as the more general dictionary definition. In order to better understand the distinction, we will discuss statistical significance in more detail.

Because of sampling error, the experimenter is always confronted with the dilemma of how to interpret differences between mean scores on the dependent variable earned by an experimental group and a control group. Is the observed mean difference due to treatment effects or is it perhaps due to the effects of the sampling process? When experimenters describe an empirical difference between group means as "significant," they assert that the difference probably represents the real effects of the treatment variable on the dependent measure rather than random (sampling) differences.

All that can be concluded after judging a statistic such as t or F as "significant" is that the observed differences are probably not due to chance factors; that is, a real, nonzero difference probably exists in the populations from which the

samples were selected. In our preceding discussion, we indicated that sample size directly influences power: the larger the sample size, the greater the power. Therefore it is almost always possible to detect a small treatment effect if there is a large enough sample. Because a difference is statistically significant does not necessarily mean that it is large enough to be of practical or theoretical significance.

Whether a particular effect size is practically significant is a separate issue from the determination of statistical significance. Determination of practical significance is based on professional and scholarly judgment that is context bound. The scholar must use knowledge and experience to evaluate the practical consequences of using a particular treatment. In one situation, a small effect may be educationally significant but in another it might not.

For example, in music education a large or small treatment effect might influence instructional, budgetary, or administrative decisions. If vocal performance is only slightly stronger when vocal instruction is supplemented with recorder instruction, requiring students to purchase recorders may be justified only if recorders are relatively inexpensive. However, if a small treatment effect size is obtained in an evaluation of several costly basal texts that are being considered for adoption by a state board of education, a larger effect size might be required. Heller and Radocy (1983) have reviewed various meanings of the term "significant."

ETHICAL ISSUES

Although the disciplines, the professions, and various institutions provide standards of appropriate behavior, there is always a constant tension between the researcher's need to know and the experimental subject's need for confidentiality, for freedom from harm, and so forth. The process of measurement, the manipulation of treatment variables, and the interpretation and dissemination of results all have ethical implications that include the protection of subjects from risk of mental and physical harm, and assurance of confidentiality. In this section we discuss broad areas of ethical concern regarding the researcher's responsibility throughout the experimental process.

Treatment of Human Subjects

Music educators must ensure the protection of their research subjects during and after data collection. They must ask whether a study might harm subjects' self-esteem or general psychological or social welfare. Such concerns are particularly relevant when studies utilize powerful treatments or deception. Social psychological experiments that study the conformity of naive subjects to a group majority or to an authority figure—for example, significant studies in music education by Duerksen (1972), Radocy (1975, 1976), and Furman and Duke (1988)—can induce stress and confusion if there is an absence of adequate debriefing and careful follow-up. In studies of this type, inappropriate procedures might affect subjects' self-confidence, level of trust, willingness to participate in future research studies, and attitudes toward music and music research. Risk in music research is not limited to exposure to psychological factors. Consideration must also be given to physical dangers, such as exposure to music at high decibel levels. In all cases, there should be adequate protection from risk factors for all subjects.

Researchers must be concerned with the principle of confidentiality. Personal information provided in trust by individual teachers and students must not be revealed. This issue applies to groups of individuals as well. For example, in studies investigating the effects of teaching strategies on the musical achievement of students, the researcher must take care not to reveal statistical information that places specific schools, programs, or racial or ethnic groups in an unfavorable light unless the groups have been previously informed of the reporting procedures and have agreed to such procedures. Privacy can be invaded when students are observed under false pretenses, as, for example, when a university faculty member visits a school ostensibly to evaluate a student teacher but actually observes the behavior of students in ensembles.

Informed Consent

It is the researcher's responsibility to ensure that informed consent is obtained from subjects. Researchers should provide subjects with sufficient information about the study (the procedures, the nature of involvement, and all costs or reasonably anticipated risks) so that a reasoned and knowledgeable decision can be made by each subject. Other critical elements of informed consent procedures include statements concerning the subject's freedom to withdraw, guarantees of confidentiality, and provisions for poststudy debriefing. In the past, many undergraduate students were required to serve as experimental subjects to obtain course credit; however, current practice requires that they be provided with a reasonable, alternative mode of service. In all situations where the subjects are "captive," such as students, patients, and prisoners, the researcher has a greater obligation to evaluate the ability of the subjects to make informed and free commitments.

Peer Review

In recent years, federal regulations have required institutions to certify that they comply with standards of ethical practice. To accomplish this end, colleges and universities have Institutional Review Boards and Human Subjects Review Committees, which assess potential risks to subjects. Although these safeguards are effective, it is ultimately the individual researchers' obligation when designing an experiment to evaluate carefully all possible factors affecting subjects and to accept responsibility for their subjects' welfare.

In the potential conflict between the researchers' search for knowledge and the subject's interests, there is always a risk that the research process may jeopardize subjects. Furthermore, to the extent that a treatment is "effective," experimental research has greater potential for risk than do other forms of inquiry that are more passive. Nevertheless, ethical issues are not exclusively limited to experimental inquiry methods.

Reporting and Disseminating Research Results

Ethical research practice is undoubtedly the norm; however, the reality of pressures associated with dissertation deadlines and promotion and tenure requirements must be recognized. An example of ethical failure associated with the reporting of research is failure to acknowledge frankly various weaknesses of the study (including design flaws) and unethical practice such as the arbitrary reformulation of Type I error levels in order to gain desired significant results. Tampering with experimental conditions, statistical treatments, and descriptions of findings cannot be tolerated. Integrity must be the principal rule.

Obviously researchers seek an audience for the results of their experimental work, and publication is of considerable concern if the profession is to benefit from research. Guidelines regarding the dissemination of research results are not discussed here. However, the "Code of Ethics" in the *Journal of Research in Music Education* (JRME) is an excellent source on this topic.

SUMMARY

Yarbrough (1984) surveyed the 658 research reports that appeared in the *Journal of Research in Music Education* between 1953 and 1983. Studies that utilized experimental methods comprised about one-third of the published reports, while approximately 40 percent of the articles were classified as descriptive and about 17 percent were historical. The experiment is, therefore, a common but not dominant form of disciplined inquiry in music education as reflected in *JRME*.

As interest and expertise in the conduct of various qualitative methodologies increase, we can expect the research literature to reflect those changes. Certainly, our understanding of the various phenomena we experience in music education will be enriched by utilizing a variety of inquiry approaches, both qualitative and quantitative, to answer different, important research questions.

At the same time, the experimental method has traditionally offered the unique possibility of validly inferring causal relationship. Perhaps one reason that experiments are not used more extensively in music education may be that the requirement for experimental control, such as random assignment to treatment groups, is not easily implemented in educational environments outside the laboratory. For this reason, we suggest that researchers consider the use of various quasi-experimental designs, which typically require less control of the experimental environment. In our opinion, such designs have been vastly underutilized and have great potential utility in music education research.

In summary, we have described the logic and philosophical underpinnings of an inquiry method that attempts to solve research problems regarding possible causal relationships between variables in music education. The traditional methods by which information has been utilized to solve such problems and the questions traditionally posed by scholars to test the validity of truth claims have also been described and evaluated. Music educators have a responsibility to search for and to disseminate reliable knowledge based on inquiry that reflects the richness of the scholarly traditions available to us, including the experimental tradition.

References

American Educational Research Association, American Psychological Association, and National Council on Measurement in Education. (1985). *Standards for Educational and Psychological Testing.* Washington: American Psychological Association.

Asmus, E. P. (1978). Perception and analysis of the difference tone phenomenon as an environmental event. *Journal of Research in Music Education, 26,* 82–89.

Borg, W. R., and Gall, M. D. (1989). *Educational research: An introduction* (5th ed.). New York: Longman.

Botvin, G. J. (1974). Acquiring conservation of melody and cross-modal transfer through successive approximation. *Journal of Research in Music Education, 22,* 226–233.

Bracht, G. H., and Glass, G. V. (1968). The external validity of experiments. *American Educational Research Journal, 5,* 437–474.

Campbell, D. T., and Stanley, J. C. (1966). *Experimental and quasi-experimental designs for research.* Chicago: Rand McNally.

Cohen, J. (1965). Some statistical issues in psychological research. In B. Wolman (Ed.), *Handbook of clinical psychology* (pp. 95–121). New York: McGraw Hill.

Cohen, J. (1977). *Statistical power analysis for the behavioral sciences.* New York: Academic Press.

Cook, T. D., and Campbell, D. T. (1979). *Quasi-experimentation: Design and analysis issues for field settings.* Boston: Houghton Mifflin.

Cox, J. (1989). Rehearsal organizational structures used by successful high school choral directors. *Journal of Research in Music Education, 37,* 201–218.

Crocker, L., and Algina, J. (1986). *Introduction to classical and modern test theory.* New York: Holt, Rinehart, and Winston.

Cronbach, L. J., and Suppes, P. (Eds.). (1969). *Research for tomorrow's schools: Disciplined inquiry for education.* National Academy for Education, Toronto: Macmillan Company.

DeCarbo, N. J. (1981). The effects of conducting experience and programmed materials on error detection scores of college conducting students. Unpublished doctoral dissertation, Kent State University, Kent.

DeCarbo, N. J. (1982). The effects of conducting experience and programmed materials on error detection scores of college conducting students. *Journal of Research in Music Education, 30,* 187–200.

Delzell, J. K. (1989). The effects of musical discrimination training in beginning instrumental music classes. *Journal of Research in Music Education, 37,* 21–31.

Duerksen, G. L. (1972). Some effects of expectation on evaluation of recorded musical performance. *Journal of Research in Music Education, 20,* 268–272.

Duke, R. A. (1985). Wind instrumentalists' intonational performance of selected musical intervals. *Journal of Research in Music Education, 33,* 101–111.

Edwards, A. L. (1972). *Experimental design in psychological research* (4th ed.). New York: Holt, Rinehart, and Winston.

Froseth, J. (1982). *Test of Musical Discrimination.* Unpublished test in J. K. Delzell, *Journal of Research in Music Education, 37* (1989), 21–31.

Furman, C. E., and Duke, R. A. (1988). Effect of majority consensus on preferences for recorded orchestral and popular music. *Journal of Research in Music Education, 36,* 220–231.

Gage, N. L. (Ed.). (1963). *Handbook of research on teaching,* Chicago: Rand McNally.

Glass, G. V. (1982). Experimental validity. In H. Mitzel (Ed.), *Encyclopedia of educational research* (5th ed.). New York: Macmillan, 631–636.

Glass, G. V., and Hopkins, K. D. (1984). *Statistical methods in education and psychology* (2nd ed.). Englewood Cliffs: Prentice Hall.

Gonzo, C. (1988). Bulletin critiques: An analysis. *Bulletin of the Council for Research in Music Education, 97,* 29–58.

Hays, W. (1981). *Statistics* (3rd ed.). New York: CBS College Publishing.

Heller, G. N., and Radocy, R. E. (1983). On the significance of significance: Addressing a basic problem in research. *Bulletin of the Council for Research in Music Education, 73,* 50–58.

Hume, D. (1973). Connectionism and causation. In H. Broudy, R. Ennis, and L. Krimerman (Eds.), *Philosophy of educational research* (pp. 404–407). New York: John Wiley. (Original work published as *An enquiry concerning human understanding* in 1777)

Jones, R. L. (1976). The development of the child's conception of meter in music. *Journal of Research in Music Education, 24,* 142–154.

Kerlinger, F. N. (1973). *Foundations of behavioral research* (2nd ed.). New York: Holt, Reinhart, and Winston.

Kerr, W. A. (1945). Experiments on the effect of music on factory production. *Applied Psychology Monographs,* No. 5, 21–26.

Kirk, R. E. (1968). *Experimental design: Procedures for the behavioral sciences.* Belmont: Brooks/Cole Publishing Co.

Linn, R. (Ed.). (1989). *Educational measurement* (3rd ed.). New York: Collier Macmillan.

Mill, J. S. (1973). Universal causal statements. In H. Broudy, R. Ennis, and L. Krimerman (Eds.), *Philosophy of educational research* (pp. 416–430). New York: John Wiley. (Original work published as *A system of logic* in 1906)

Mitchell, J. V. (1985). *Ninth mental measurements yearbook.* Lincoln: Buros Institute of Mental Measurements.

Moore, B. R. (1990). The relationship between curriculum and learner: Music composition and learning style. *Journal of Research in Music Education, 38,* 24–38.

Nelson, D. J. (1984). The conservation of rhythm in Suzuki violin students: A task validation study. *Journal of Research in Music Education, 32,* 25–34.

Norton, D. (1979). Relationship of music ability and intelligence to auditory and visual conservation of the kindergarten child. *Journal of Research in Music Education, 27,* 3–13.

Perney, J. (1976). Musical tasks related to the development of the conservation of metric time. *Journal of Research in Music Education, 24,* 159–168.

Petrie, H. (1973). Why has learning theory failed to teach us how to learn? In H. Brody, R. Ennis, and L. Krimerman, *Philosophy of educational research* (pp. 131–138). New York: John Wiley.

Petzold, R. G. (1988). Writing a critical review of descriptive or experimental research. *Bulletin of the Council for Research in Music Education, 97,* 19–28.

Piaget, J. (1969). *The child's conception of time.* New York: Basic Books.

Piaget, J. (1981). *The psychology of intelligence.* Totowa: Littlefield, Adams & Company.

Porter, A. (1988). Comparative experimental methods in educational research. In R. M. Jaeger, *Complementary research methods for research in education* (389–442). Washington: American Educational Research Association.

Radocy, R. E. (1975). A naive minority of one and deliberate majority mismatches of tonal stimuli. *Journal of Research in Music Education, 23,* 120–133.

Radocy, R. E. (1976). Effects of authority figure biases on changing judgments of musical events. *Journal of Research in Music Education, 24,* 119–128.

Russell, B. (1973). On the notion of cause, with applications to the free will problem. In H. Broudy, R. Ennis, and L. Krimerman (Eds.), *Philosophy of educational research* (pp. 408–411). New York: John Wiley. (Original work published as *Logic and mysticism* in 1917)

Saffle, M. (1988). Reviewing dissertations in the *Bulletin:* Theory and practice. *Bulletin of the Council for Research in Music Education, 97,* 59–66.

Webb, E. T., Campbell, D. T., Schwartz, R. D., Sechrest, L., and Grove, J. B. (1981). *Nonreactive measures in the social sciences* (2nd ed.). Boston: Houghton Mifflin.

Winer, B. J. (1971). *Statistical principles in experimental design* (2nd ed.). New York: McGraw Hill.

Yarbrough, C. (1984). A content analysis of the Journal of Research in Music Education, 1953–1983. *Journal of Research in Music Education, 32,* 213–222.

·11·

QUANTITATIVE ANALYSIS

Edward P. Asmus
UNIVERSITY OF UTAH

Rudolf E. Radocy
UNIVERSITY OF KANSAS

Research is a systematic process by which investigators gather information, organize it in a meaningful way, and analyze and interpret it. Much information is expressible as quantities or numeric judgments. Researchers may combine and manipulate numbers in a myriad of ways to gain insights and reach conclusions regarding their problems, questions, and hypotheses. After briefly overviewing quantification and measurement, this chapter presents univariate and multivariate statistical techniques for the analysis of research data. The chapter is not a statistical treatise or a critique of the state of the quantitative art in music education research. It is intended to guide the reader in understanding, questioning, and applying basic aspects of quantitative techniques.

Quantification

Quantitative methods greatly enhance the study of musical processes by providing the accuracy and rigor required to produce conclusions upon which the researcher and others can rely (Lehman, 1968). Phelps (1986) points out that researchers who develop their research in a manner that produces quantitative data are in a better initial position to produce research that is significant to the field of music education.

Quantification is the assignment of a number to represent an amount or a perceived degree of something. That is, the association of numbers with behaviors, objects, or events. The units of weight necessary to balance a scale quantify a person's body weight. The height of an enclosed column of mercury quantifies the thermal activity in air. An adjudicator's rating quantifies the apparent quality of a musical performance. Virtually anything is quantifiable, whether in terms of some logical counting unit or some sensory impression. The degree of objectivity varies with the method of quantification. Such variance is a matter of measurement theory in general, and validity in particular.

Quantification has met considerable resistance in music education. The general outlook is that music is so complex and deals with aesthetic elements that are so far beyond tangible matters that it is impossible to quantify musical behaviors, objects, or events. Whybrew (1971, p. 3) has claimed that the precision and objectivity of quantification appear to some as "antithetical" to the aesthetic nature of music. Nevertheless, a significant body of knowledge abut musical phenomena has arisen through the use of quantitative methods. The application of quantitative methods to music has been strongly supported at least since the 1930s. In 1936 Carl Seashore wrote the following:

Musical performance as a form of behavior lends itself surprisingly well to objective study and measurement. However, it requires a rather cataclysmic readjustment in attitude to pass from the traditional introspectional and emotional attitude of the musician to the laboratory attitude of exact measurement and painstaking analysis. (p. 7)

Today, music educators commonly use quantitative methods for such tasks as grading, student evaluation, contest and festival ratings, auditioning students for ensembles, and assigning chairs in an ensemble.

Why Quantitative Research Techniques?

Research is a multifaceted enterprise, and there are many ways to investigate. Numerical expression enhances the precision and specificity of phenomena under investigation. Numbers enable a researcher to describe in specific terms the subject matter under investigation and the results of the investigation. Furthermore, with the aid of statistical techniques, numbers and the resulting quantifications are important tools for framing and answering precise questions.

Quantitative methods have evolved for assigning numeric values to virtually all aspects of music and for the thorough, robust analysis of these values. As Madsen and Madsen (1978, p. 50) have pointed out, "It is the quantification of specific responses and subsequent logical methods of analysis that provide the background for experimental research."

MEASUREMENT: THE SOURCE OF QUANTITIES

The foundation of quantitative methods in research is measurement (Wilks, 1961). Measurement increases the precision and objectivity of observations whose results may be analyzed through statistical methods (Leonhard, 1958). It is the basic means humankind has used for understanding the universe (Finkelstein, 1982). This section discusses measurement because it is the source of quantities, and it imposes certain constraints on the manipulation of the quantities produced.

Definition

S. S. Stevens (1975, pp. 46–47), defined "measurement" as "the assignment of numbers to objects or events according to rule." Payne (1982, p. 1182) stresses that measurement must be more than counting; it must allow "the comparison of something with a unit or standard or quantity of that same thing, in order to represent the magnitude of the variable being measured." Boyle and Radocy (1987, p. 6) simply refer to measurement as quantifying data. Obviously, some observed object or event is expressed numerically. Fortunately for music education research, measurement does not always require using standard counting units, for example, centimeters, hertz, points, lengths of the king's foot. Impressions, judgments, and sensations may be quantified (Radocy, 1986; Stevens, 1975).

Stevens (1959, p.18) described measurement as "the business of pinning numbers on things." Initially, only physical measurements were made by science, which resulted in classical measurement theory being based on additive quantities. Modern measurement theory is predicated on the "correspondence between a set of manifestations of a property and the relations between them and a set of numbers and the relations between them" (Finkelstein, 1982, p. 5).

Good measurement must (1) be operationally defined, (2) be reproducible, and (3) produce valid results. The goal of measurement is to assign numbers in an objective, empirical manner to objects, behaviors, or events for the purpose of their accurate description (Finkelstein, 1982). Care during the measurement process is essential to research, as it forms the foundation for all quantitative methods.

Levels of Measurement

The rules that are applied in the measurement of an object, behavior, or event yield numeric values with specific characteristics. On the basis of these characteristics, a set of numeric values can be placed into different levels of measurement. The levels of measurement, ordered from lowest to highest, are nominal, ordinal, interval, and ratio levels.

At the *nominal level* of measurement the numbers are labels for identifying some classification, as in coding all male subjects as "1" and all female subjects as "2." These numbers provide a means for placing objects or events into particular categories (Moore, 1988). Examples of nominal variables are gender, social security numbers, the numbers on players' football jerseys, and the numbering of individual musicians in a marching band.

The *ordinal level* indicates the position of an item in a set of items ordered from smallest to largest. Ordinal measurement provides no indication of how much more or less one object or event has than another object or event. A common illustration in music is the seating in a band or orchestra, where the principal in a given section presumably plays better than the other section members, but there is no specification of how much better.

The *interval level* of measurement describes the degree to which one unit may differ from another unit on a particular property. Examples of interval variables are scores on music aptitude tests, the number of members in various bands, and scores on music achievement tests.

An interval measure has some arbitrary zero point and a unit interval of constant size. A score of zero on an achievement test and zero degrees on a Fahrenheit or Celsius thermometer exemplify arbitrary zero points: A student who could answer no questions correctly might know something about the subject matter, and the temperature can fall "below zero." Test points and degrees of temperature exemplify measurement units that are presumed to be psychologically or physically equal: It is just as far from a score of 10 to 12 as it is from 55 to 57, and the number of degrees separating Fahrenheit temperatures of 21° and 27° is equal to the number of degrees separating 73° and 79°. It is not legitimate to say that a test score of 50 represents a performance that is "twice as good" as a test score of 25, or that a temperature of 80° is "twice as hot" as a temperature of 40°. Ratio comparisons such as these require a zero point that is a genuine absence of the property in question.

The *ratio level* of measurement describes a unit on the basis of the ratio of the unit's possession of a property in relation to another unit. That is, it describes a unit in terms of its having so many times as much of the property as another unit. Examples of ratio variables are loudness, the proportion of students in a class who passed an examination, and pupil-teacher ratio.

An "absolute" zero is found in ratio measurement. A temperature of 200° on the Kelvin scale is "twice as hot" physically as a temperature of 100°; 0° here is the theoretical absence of heat, a point at which molecular motion ceases. A measure of sound power where no sound results in a power measurement of zero is an example of a ratio scale.

Each succeeding level in the ordered levels of measurement must contain the basic empirical operations of all previous levels (Table 11-1) (Stevens, 1959). Knowing the numbered seat assignment of a member of a hundred-voice choir does not allow the determination of the individual's score on a music achievement test. However, knowing that student's music achievement score will allow the assignment of the student's rank in the class, which may then result in the student's placement into a particular numbered seat. From this, it can be noticed that some data can be expressed at different levels of measurement (Stevens, 1959). For example, the members of a choir may be numbered for identity and ease in keeping records of robe assignments—a nominal level of measurement. This choir may be the first-place choir at a contest where the choirs were ranked—an ordinal level of measurement. The choir may also have received a 99 out of a possible 100 score at the contest—an interval level of measurement. Finally, the choir may also be said to have received a score twice as good as that for their previous performance—a ratio measurement.

There is a relationship between the level of measurement and applicable statistics. In general, the lower the level of measurement, the more limited is the number of available statistical procedures. Asher (1976) has argued that educational researchers should strive for the interval level of measurement because of the variety of analyses available and the ability to test higher-order relationships between variables. However, advances in nonparametric statistics and multivariate analysis have allowed a much greater breadth of analysis than available one decade ago. Indeed, a significant body of relationship in music education has resulted from research that has utilized only nominal and ordinal scales. The complexity inherent in music learning suggests that the researcher should strive for interval measurement because, in comparison with nominal and ordinal data, interval data are more precise and allow use of a wider variety of statistical techniques.

Precision in an Imprecise Enterprise

Music has been said to be a very subjective enterprise. *Subjectivity* implies that there are personal biases and prejudices in operation that may have significant influence on the obtained data. The music researcher should strive for as much objectivity as possible because this will yield data that are the most consistent and sound. The researcher selecting the most appropriate measurement method is involved in evaluating the issues related to reliability and validity.

Reliability In simple terms, reliability is the consistency with which a measuring technique measures. More specifically, as Stanley's (1971) authoritative treatise makes clear, reliability is the portion of variance in the measured property that is attributable to differences in the property itself, rather than to differences in the application of the technique on different occasions, or to other diverse sources of variance due to "error." Reliability affects the precision of measurement as well as the credence that a researcher may give results, so reporting reliability estimates is an important part of presenting the results of quantitative research.

There are several ways to estimate reliability, based on observed consistency across time or within a set of items or observers. Stanley (1971) reviews the "classic" techniques, and Boyle and Radocy (1987) refer to ways appropriate for performance measures. Music education researchers need to be cognizant that reliability is not limited to paper and pencil tests.

Reliability is usually estimated by determining the level of agreement between tests or among observers (Asher, 1976, pp. 93–94). The level of agreement can be determined statistically by the *correlation ratio*. The correlation ratio is a value ranging from −1 to +1 where 0 indicates no relationship, −1 indicates a perfect negative relationship, and +1

TABLE 11-1. Characteristics of Various Levels of Measurement

Scale	Basic Empirical Operations	Example	Measures of Location	Measures of Dispersion	Correlation	Significance Test
Nominal	Determination of equality	Numbering of players—1, 2, 3, . . .	Mode	—	Contingency correlation	Chi-square
Ordinal	Determination of greater or less	Ranking in music competitions	Median	Percentiles	Rank-order correlation	Sign test Run test
Interval	Determination of the equality of intervals of differences	Score on musical aptitude test	Arithmetic mean	Standard deviation	Correlation ratio	t test F test
Ratio	Determination of the equality of ratios	Loudness in sones	Geometric or harmonic mean	Percent variation		

Note: Patterned after S. S. Stevens (1959).

indicates a perfect positive relationship. To calculate a correlation ratio, two matched sets of values are necessary. It is through the type of values the two sets contain that different methods for estimating reliability are derived. *Equivalence* is the agreement between two tests that measure the same attribute. *Internal consistency* is obtained from different subsets of items contained within a measure. Reliability, in its pure sense, is the stability of the measure across time, which may be ascertained by determining the agreement between two different administrations of the same test at some time interval.

Validity Validity refers to the extent to which a measurement technique measures what it is supposed to measure. According to Asher (1976, p. 97), validity is an indication of how effective, truthful, and genuine a measurement is. The validity of a measure may be determined from three primary perspectives: content validity, criterion-related validity, and construct validity.

Content validity is the test's effectiveness in providing a substantive measure of what the test is supposed to measure. *Criterion-related validity* is the level of agreement between a particular test and another indicator known to measure the particular trait of interest. Criterion-related validity may be considered further as *concurrent validity,* when the criterion measure is administered at nearly the same time as the test in question, or *predictive validity,* when the criterion is some future performance, such as eventual classroom or musical achievement. *Construct validity* is the effectiveness of a test to measure specific traits underlying the test (Ebel and Frisbie, 1986). Cronbach (1971, p. 462) indicates that the word "concepts" could be substituted for "constructs," but constructs is more indicative "that the categories are deliberate creations chosen to organize experience into general law-like statements." This has led some to suggest that construct validity is essentially concerned with the scientific variables measured by a test (Asher, 1976).

Music teachers concerned with whether a standardized test truly measures the objectives of their teaching are involved in establishing content validity. A researcher who wishes to determine if a test of auditory acuity is as effective at measuring pitch discrimination as the *Seashore Measures of Musical Talents* (Seashore, Lewis, and Saetveit, 1939/1960) pitch subtest is concerned with criterion-related validity. A researcher who wishes to determine whether a melodic perception test is also measuring rhythm and tonal memory is concerned with construct validity.

Subjectivity Subjectivity is inevitable in measurement and research because people are making judgments regarding what to measure, how to measure, and what the measures mean. Although a multiple-choice achievement test that has high reliability and empirical evidence of validity is more "objective" than a judge assigning ratings at a music festival, there is also subjectivity in writing the test items and in interpreting what the scores mean. The objective-subjective aspect of measurement is a continuum of various degrees: It is not a dichotomy.

Indirect Measurement A measure is conceptually direct when a property is measured in terms in itself. Measuring length in terms of length, as in measuring the length of one side of a room with a carpenter's rule, is an example. In contrast, measuring rhythm perception by judging the precision with which a student claps a pattern after hearing it exemplifies *indirect measurement.* Indirect measures are inevitable in quantifying musical behavior because much behavior is covert and overt behavior often is interpreted as evidence of some knowledge or attitude. Indirect measures abound and include written tests, judgment procedures, and electrical and mechanical measures.

Measurement Types in Music

There are many ways to classify types of measurement applicable to quantitative research in music education. Boyle's (1974) classification of musical test behaviors into performance, reading/writing, listening, and "other cognitive" is useful, as is the Johnson and Hess (1970) grouping of subjects' response behaviors and ways to elicit their responses. Another particularly useful classification scheme for conceptualizing music education research possibilities is the division of measurements into psychomusic tests and mechanized measures.

Psychomusic tests examine some psychomusical construct or psychoacoustical property as it is observed through some indicator created by a subject's conscious efforts, such as a test score or a performance. Psychomusic tests include measures of achievement in general music, musical performance skill, pitch discrimination, musical aptitude, attitude toward music, and sight singing.

Mechanized measurement, which includes electronic measures, employs one or more devices to obtain data from a subject; it does not require that a subject actively complete a form or report, or perform. Examples include monitoring physiological aspects, such as heartbeat and blood pressure, employing stroboscopic devices to monitor a subject's intonation during performance, analyzing a complex tone's frequency components and relative intensities and phases, and studying a room's reverberant properties.

Presumably, mechanized measurement is more reliable and "objective" than most psychomusical measures. A series of stroboscopic readings may be more consistent and easier to "read" than a series of subjective human judgments regarding a performer's intonation. Mechanized measurement avoids inherent problems of error that may be induced in the recording of a subject's response. For instance, a subject may mismark an answer sheet by simply responding to item 5 in the location of item 6. This is avoided by mechanical systems. The greater the error in a measurement, the lower the reliability (Lord and Novick, 1968).

STATISTICAL PRINCIPLES

Strictly speaking, one may quantify without employing statistics, but most quantitative research needs to describe characteristics and draw inferences. Statistical treatments must be appropriate for the research questions and the data. This section reviews basic principles regarding descriptive and inferential statistics, hypothesis testing, and specific properties of statistics.

Descriptive vs. Inferential Statistics

The primary difference between descriptive and inferential statistics is the use to which the statistics will be put. If the purpose is to describe the data, then *descriptive statistics* are used (Borg and Gall, 1979, p. 406). If the purpose is to make inferences about a population of individuals from data gathered from a sample of this population, then *inferential statistics* are used (Best and Kahn, 1989, p. 222). Practically, most research studies begin with descriptive statistics and then, once overall characteristics of the data are known, inferential statistics are applied to determine the characteristics of the population. In some cases, after inferential statistics have been applied, interesting phenomena are noted for particular samples whose data are then treated with descriptive statistics to determine the characteristics of these samples.

The purpose of descriptive statistics is to describe and summarize relatively large amounts of data (Sax, 1979, p. 370), thus reducing the data to a few statistics that simplify interpretation (Borg and Gall, 1979, p. 406). They often describe central tendencies and variability in the data, as well as simply relate how much of what exists. Analysis of the results of a classroom achievement test, a listing of the numbers of students enrolled in particular music classes, grade point averages for all members of a student body, and demographic data exemplify some uses of descriptive statistics.

Inferential statistics are employed to make judgments about some group beyond those subjects who contribute data. A general music class may be considered representative of other general music classes; a set of trumpet mouthpieces may be considered representative of available mouthpieces. On the basis of probabilities and known or surmised properties of the particular sample, a researcher infers characteristics of the larger group. In short, one "draws an inference."

A *statistic* is a numerical characteristic obtained from a sample. A *parameter* is a numerical characteristic obtained from a population. It is the role of inferential statistics to estimate the parameters of a population on the basis of observations derived from a sample (Best and Kahn, 1989, pp. 222–223).

Usually samples are drawn from a population utilizing random sampling techniques. The purpose of random sampling is to produce values for which margins of error can be determined statistically when the sampled values are generalized to a larger population (Borg and Gall, 1979, p. 182). Random sampling provides the most efficient means of providing data that can be generalized to the larger population from which the sample was drawn.

The Elements of Statistics

Populations All members of a particular group of interest comprise the population. Fifth-grade instrumental music students in a city's schools, clarinet reeds available in a music store, learning-disabled students in music classes, string students taught by a Suzuki-based method, or virtually any logical group are populations. Populations may be huge, as in the population of all 6-year-olds, or tiny, as in the population of all students in one school who have absolute pitch. Generalization to a population is implicit in much music education research. In order for researchers to generalize to a specific population, all members of the population need a relatively equal chance to contribute to the data from which the inferences are drawn.

Samples A sample is a subset of a population. A group of voters carefully chosen from "representative" precincts by a polling organization is a sample of a population of voters. The subjects of research in which inferences are to be made are a sample of the population of interest.

Ideally, a sample is obtained in a way that gives each and every member of the population an equal chance of being selected. This is a *random sample.* Selecting subjects on the basis of random number tables, computerized random number generators, tossing fair dice, or drawing numbered slips of paper from a thoroughly mixed set are legitimate applications of randomization. Merely scanning a list of names or looking over a set of objects and in effect saying, "Let's take this one, and that one; we'll eliminate that one . . ." is not a random process. A random sample of sufficient number allows a researcher to generalize results to the population with confidence.

Truly random samples are almost always impossible to obtain. Some reasons include the necessity to work with volunteer subjects, a need to use intact classrooms or ensembles rather than mix subjects across groups, proscriptions caused by informed-consent aspects of using human subjects, and selective loss of subjects. Many samples employed in quantitative research thus are ersatz random samples: samples chosen on the basis of who is available, but deemed to be representative or like the members of some larger population. Researchers must use their training and experience to make an informed decision as to the representativeness of the sample. Many applications of inferential statistics proceed as if the sample were random.

Samples could be obviously nonrandom to a degree where there is no point in claiming that they are representative of a population in any way. Using the first 15 students one meets on campus as somehow representative of the student body clearly is using a nonrandom sample. So is a researcher's employing a group of the general population to answer questions about specific musical phenomena because they are available, without the researcher's having any knowledge of their musical backgrounds.

Sample Size One somewhat controversial issue is sample size. In general, the larger the size of a representative sample, the more stable and representative are the results of the inference. Classical statistical texts (e.g., Li, 1964) clearly show that larger sample sizes enhance the probability of finding a difference between experimental treatments when one "truly" exists in the population. They restrict the range within which some "true" value is likely to fall. Of course, with sufficiently large samples, even population differences that lack any "practical" significance will be statistically significant (Heller and Radocy, 1983).

How large is large enough? Kirk (1982, p. 8) indicates that adequate sample size is a function of experimental effects and the number of treatments, error variance in the population from which the sample comes, and the probability of making a false judgment about the outcome of a statistical test. Since some of these properties are not always known in advance, Kirk also presents procedures for estimating certain sample sizes. Consistent rules of thumb are hard to find. The Bruning and Kintz (1977) statistical "cookbook" recommends 10 to 15 subjects per experimental group. Cohen's (1988) treatise provides various means for estimating minimal sample sizes.

Drawing Inferences

Das and Giri (1986) identify three main characteristics of the inferential process: (1) the inferences are made with observations that are not exact but that are subject to variation making them probabilistic in nature, (2) methods are specified for the appropriate collection of data so that the assumptions for particular statistical methods are satisfied, and (3) techniques for the proper interpretation of the statistical results are devised.

Null Hypotheses Inferences are drawn on the basis of the outcomes of statistical tests. What is tested is a statement of no cause and effect, or no relationship, a *null hypothesis.* The null hypothesis results from a *hypothesis,* a tentative statement of cause and effect or relationship. In turn, the hypothesis is implied by questions that the researcher is trying to answer. Research questions, hypotheses, and null hypotheses are not always stated explicitly in a research report, but are implied by what the researcher investigates and how. Questions are implied in the form of, "What is the effect of _____ on _____?"

Hypotheses lead to deliberate statements of no cause and effect, or no relationship. These null hypotheses are directly testable through techniques of inferential statistics. An example of a null hypothesis statement is, "There is no difference in students' knowledge of excerpts between the beginning of the music appreciation course and the end."

Conceptually, a researcher tests a null hypothesis by judging whether an observed outcome of a statistical test is sufficiently likely to belong to a distribution of events—a distribution that will occur if the null hypothesis is true; that is, there "really" is no difference or relationship in the population. If the observed outcome is not too extreme, in accordance with statistical probabilities, it is deemed to belong to the distribution that exists if the null hypothesis is true. If the observed outcome is too extreme, it is considered to be too unlikely to belong to that distribution—it probably belongs to another and the null hypothesis probably is false. Just

what is "too extreme" is a matter of judgment of just how far from the center of a hypothesized distribution the outcome is.

Statistical Significance The necessary degree of extremity is a matter of statistical significance. Essentially, *statistical significance* is the likelihood that the observed result occurred by chance alone. To say that an outcome is significant at or beyond a certain level is to specify the odds. A researcher claiming statistical significance at the .05 level ($p \le .05$) is saying that the null hypothesis will be rejected 95 times out of 100. Although some researchers have claimed that results are significant at the .10 level ($p \le .10$) or even at the .20 level ($p \le .20$), it is rare that a researcher claims statistical significance unless the .05 level ($p \le .05$) is attained. If the outcome of an experiment may cause a major revision to existing instructional procedures or lead to considerable reallocation of resources, the researcher may require a greater significance level, such as the .01 level or the .001 level.

Statistically significant occurrences are deemed unlikely to have occurred by chance alone, in accordance with a set of statistical probabilities and a researcher's interpretative judgment. Practical significance does not necessarily follow. Large samples, for instance, are prone to produce small but statistically significant differences that have no practical importance. Basically, practical significance comes down to "So what?" (Heller and Radocy, 1983).

Correct Decision vs. Error Although statistical techniques are powerful tools for assessing population characteristics in accordance with sample characteristics, they are not infallible. The correct decision versus error issue may be conceptualized as an interaction of two dimensions. One dimension is reality; that is, whether the null hypothesis is in fact true or false. The other dimension is the researcher's decision to retain or reject the null hypothesis. If the researcher retains a null hypothesis that is in fact true *or* rejects a null hypothesis that is in fact false, that researcher makes a correct decision. If the researcher rejects a null hypothesis that is in fact true, that researcher commits a Type I or alpha error. The researcher who fails to reject a null hypothesis that is in fact false commits a Type II or beta error. Establishing a more stringent criterion for statistical significance, which essentially reduces the number of outcomes that will be deemed too extreme to occur by chance alone, reduces the likelihood of Type I error. Increasing the sample size reduces the likelihood of Type II error.

Parametric vs. Nonparametric Statistics

Parameters are values such as means and variances of some population. *Parametric statistics* are based on distributions of possible outcomes with known parameters. *Nonparametric statistics,* also called "distribution-free" statistics, are based on distributions with unknown parameters. Parametric statistics are applicable to data with at least interval level of measurement while nonparametric statistics are applicable to data with nominal and ordinal levels of measurement (Best, 1981, p. 221). Parametric statistics are more numerous and tend to be more powerful and more frequently used. Nonparametric statistics do not require the same number of assumptions about the underlying population as are required by parametric statistics.

Parametric statistics make a greater number of assumptions about the population parameters. First, the data are at least at the interval level of measurement. Second, the data of the population are normally distributed. Third, the distribution of the data for the various samples is generally the same. To be normally distributed means that the data when graphed create the well-known bell-shaped curve of the normal distribution (Figure 11–1). When the distributions of the various samples are approximately equal, the samples are said to have the characteristic of homogeneity of variance.

Nonparametric statistics require that observations are independent and that measurement is at the nominal or ordinal levels (Madsen and Madsen, 1978, p. 78). Nonparametric tests do not assume that the population is normally distributed, and they do not assume homogeneity of variance in the samples (Rainbow and Froehlich, 1987, p. 230). Siegel and Castellan (1988, p. xv) cite four advantages of using nonparametric statistics: (1) the tests are distribution free in that they do not assume that the data are normally distributed, (2) they can employ ordinal data that are simply ranks, (3) these statistics are simple to calculate, and (4) they are appropriate in the study of small samples.

Puri and Sen (1971, p. 1) point out that researchers seldom know the underlying distribution of a population, and that the use of parametric statistics in situations where the underlying distribution is not normal is highly suspect. However, Borg and Gall (1979, p. 464) recommend the use of parametric statistics when the researcher has interval scores but has neither normally distributed scores nor homogeneity of variance among the samples because (1) the outcome of a parametric technique is affected very little by moderate de-

parture from the technique's theoretical assumptions; (2) nonparametric statistics are generally less powerful; and (3) for many educational research problems, suitable nonparametric tests are not available.

The decision to employ parametric or nonparametric methods depends on the data as well as a researcher's beliefs. Nominal or ordinal data of small sample sizes may be handled more appropriately with nonparametric methods. A researcher who is satisfied that there is no reason to question the propriety of parametric statistics in a particular situation should employ parametric statistics. Assuredly, the researcher should not do both: The researcher either believes that the conditions for parametric statistics are satisfied or does not believe it.

VARIABLES

A *variable,* in the broad sense, is something that does not remain the same under all conditions; that is, it varies. Variables are characterized according to the functions they serve in the research design and in the applicable statistical tests.

Independent Variables

In quantitative research, researchers often compare two or more levels of an *independent variable* on a dependent variable. For example, the effects of two or more instructional approaches could be compared. When investigators are free to decide what will be done and when, they are able to "manipulate" an independent variable. In cases where they must accept previously existing conditions, such as subjects' gender or ethnicity, the independent variable is labeled as an "assigned" variable. The reader should be aware that other labels do exist.

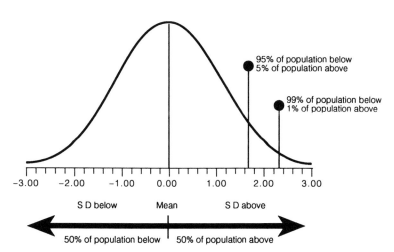

FIGURE 11–1. The Normal Curve with Reference of Population Percentages.

Dependent Variables

Dependent variables presumably "depend" on the effect of independent variables. Changes between pretest and posttest scores exemplify dependent variables. If a researcher is studying the effects of instruction, different forms of instruction constitute an independent variable, and some measure of the result of instruction constitutes a dependent variable. Many quantitative studies contain just one dependent variable, in which case the use of univariate statistics is appropriate. Other studies, especially many contemporary ones, feature simultaneous investigation of the effects of independent variables on more than one dependent variable. In those studies, multivariate statistical techniques are mandatory.

Statistical Conceptualization

In cases where changes in the dependent variable are conceived as resulting from the manipulation of an independent variable, as when attitudes might change as a result of exposure to music across time, or where they are conceived as resulting from a "natural" or assigned independent variable, as when differences in musical taste might be due to gender, there is an underlying *factorial model:* An independent variable clearly is a causal agent or factor that determines what happens to a dependent variable.

In cases where the variables are conceived as a set of relationships—as, for example, where one might relate scores on a measure of musical ability with scores on a test of academic achievement—there is an underlying regression model. Here, depending on the research question, either variable could be "independent" or "dependent." The conception is of related variables, or predictor and criterion variables. For example, Hedden (1982) related a set of predictor variables—attitude toward music, self-concept in music, musical background, academic achievement, and gender—to a criterion variable of musical achievement.

"Other" Variables

Many variables exist that are neither independent nor dependent; most of them are irrelevant. Most research in music education need not be concerned with changing conditions of cosmic ray penetration, eye color, shoe size, hair length, position or rate of the Humboldt current, or subjects' prior exposure to Boolean algebra, for example. However, nuisance or confounding variables could influence a dependent variable. An example would be home musical background in a study of contrasting approaches to teaching instrumental music. Nuisance variables can be controlled by statistical techniques, random selection of subjects, or changing an experimental design and its associated statistical treatment to incorporate a nuisance variable as another independent variable.

Univariate vs. Multivariate Statistics

The distinction between univariate and multivariate statistics varies somewhat from author to author, but the generally distinguishing feature is that *univariate statistics* are used in analyzing the characteristics of one dependent variable (Hair, Anderson, Tatham, and Grablowsky, 1984, p. 5; Harris, 1985, p. 5; Kachigan, 1986, pp. 4–5). *Multivariate statistics,* on the other hand, are used in simultaneously analyzing a number of dependent variables. Multivariate statistics frequently provide a simplification of the data by summarizing the data with relatively few parameters (Chatfield and Collins, 1980, pp. 6–7). Not only do these procedures allow for the testing of hypotheses, but a number are exploratory in nature and can generate hypotheses as well as test hypotheses.

The study of musical processes usually involves multiple variables that could be expected to be affected by some factor. For instance, a 10-week experimental treatment in which fourth-grade students received a particular music-teaching method for 30 minutes each day might be expected to affect both rhythm and pitch skills. With traditional statistical procedures used in music research separate analyses would be performed on each of these skills to determine if the skills had been positively influenced by the treatment. Analyzing each skill separately involves the application of univariate statistics. Unfortunately, the use of separate univariate statistics in such cases increases the possibility of producing a significant result that is actually due to chance (Harris, 1985, pp. 6–7). Thus the research is subject to Type I error. Multivariate statistics provides a means around such problems by providing an overall test to determine first whether the experimental treatment actually produced a significant effect on both skills, and, if so, subanalyses can be performed to determine if the significant effect occurred for each of the skills separately.

Multivariate statistics are an assortment of descriptive and inferential procedures for analyzing the simultaneous effects of phenomena on a number of variables. There exists a multivariate analogue of virtually every univariate procedure. Most research in music will become increasingly involved in the application of multivariate procedures because of the complex nature of music processes. This is most appropriate because multivariate statistics have been claimed to produce more interesting results and to be more scientifically productive (Kachigan, 1986, p. 5). To avoid the use of multivariate statistics will result in research with a greater probability of error and research that does not provide the full range of insights that multivariate statistics provide. Harris (1985, p. 5) has stated that "if researchers were sufficiently narrow-minded or theories and research techniques so well developed or nature so simple as to dictate a single independent variable and a single outcome measure as appropriate in each study, there would be no need for multivariate techniques."

As with univariate statistics, there are both parametric and nonparametric multivariate statistical procedures. For the parametric case, the distribution that forms the foundation for multivariate statistics is the multivariate normal distribution (Muirhead, 1982, p. 1). This distribution is an extension of the normal distribution to more than one variable. As in the univariate case, most sampled measurements tend to be normally distributed.

UNIVARIATE TESTS: ONE INDEPENDENT VARIABLE

Chi-Square Tests

The family of chi-square tests essentially compares an observed classification of frequencies with an expected classification. For example, in a study of elementary students' tempo perceptions, Kuhn and Booth (1988) used chi-square to determine whether the numbers of subjects who classified musical examples as going slower, staying the same, or going faster were significantly different from a chance distribution of the three tempo change classifications.

The assumptions of chi-square include independence of each observation from each other observation, placement of any observation in one and only one cell in the table formed by the classifications of observed and expected, and a sufficiently large sample size (Hays, 1988, p. 772). According to Wike (1971), if the total number of observations exceeds the total number of subjects, some subjects are contributing to more than one observation, and the independence criterion is violated. Sufficient sample size is controversial, but Wike suggests that the total sample size should exceed 20 and the expected frequency in any classification should be at least five. There are various adaptations for smaller numbers and for situations where subjects contribute more than one observation; the Siegel (1956) treatise and Wike's book are good sources of additional information.

t Tests

A widely applicable set of parametric statistical tests is based on a family of statistical distributions called the t distributions. Essentially, the researcher compares an observed t value with a hypothesized t value of zero; if the observed outcome is too far away from zero in accordance with the probabilities of the hypothesized t distribution, the null hypothesis is rejected. In using a t test, one assumes that all samples are drawn randomly from normally distributed populations with equivalent variances. In practice, these assumptions often are violated.

An *"independent"* t test compares two samples that are not matched in any way. The two groups represent two levels of an independent variable, and the t value is computed from the measures of the dependent variable. For example, Darrow, Haack, and Kuribayashi (1987) used independent t tests in comparing preferences for particular musical examples of two groups of subjects who differed in musical experience.

A *"related measures"* t test compares two matched groups. Often, the groups are "matched" because they are

two sets of scores from the same group of people, as in a comparison of pretest and posttest scores. Price and Swanson (1990) used this type of related measures (matched, dependent, paired) t test in comparing their subjects' pretest and posttest scores on cognitive knowledge, attitudes, and preferences.

A less commonly applied t test is a test to compare an observed sample mean with a hypothesized population mean. An investigator might compare a mean score on a standardized musical achievement test administered in his or her school with a hypothesized mean equivalent to a published norm to see if the school's mean was "better" or "worse" than a hypothesized national mean.

A multiplicity of t tests that are testing a series of null hypotheses with data obtained in the same study may be unwise, not only from the standpoint of efficiency but because of increasing the probability of Type I or alpha error. Fortunately, the t test is a special case of a large family of more efficient statistical techniques known as analysis of variance.

Analysis of Variance

The family of t distributions is mathematically related to another family of statistical distributions, the F distributions. Mathematicians can show that $t^2 = F$. Therefore, a t test may be conceived as a special case of analysis of variance, which relies on the F distribution, where there are only two sets of measures to compare. The *analysis of variance* (ANOVA) is much more flexible because it can account for more than two levels of an independent variable and be extended to account for more than one independent variable simultaneously, and, through multivariate techniques, even more than one dependent variable simultaneously.

The assumptions of the analysis of variance are that the samples are obtained randomly from normally distributed populations, with equivalent variances. In practice, the randomization is critical; the other criteria may be "bent" a little (Li, 1964).

Types of ANOVA An ANOVA may be employed to analyze the difference between separate groups and repeated measures of the same group. If a subject can be in one and only one group, the comparison is between separate groups, each of which represents a level of an independent variable. If the same subjects experience different levels of an independent variable, there are *repeated measures* involved. A *mixed design* is one in which any particular subject experiences just one level of one (or more) independent variable(s) while simultaneously experiencing all levels of one (or more) other independent variable(s). For example, in a music preference study, all students in a junior high school can listen to each of five musical styles; the style variable is a repeated measure. If the investigator is interested in differential effects of gender, the gender variable is an independent variable where each subject can be at just one level.

The analysis of variance indicates via one or more F tests whether there is a significant difference between or among the levels of the independent variable. When two or more independent variables are studied simultaneously, F tests also are applied to any possible interaction(s); these are discussed below in the context of factorial designs. The original F tests do not indicate where the significance lies. If there are only two levels, the location of any significant difference is obvious. Otherwise, further testing is necessary.

Post-ANOVA Comparisons Opinions differ regarding multiple comparison tests to follow a significant F value. Kirk (1982) distinguishes between orthogonal and nonorthogonal comparisons and between a priori (planned) comparisons and a posteriori (data snooping) comparisons. Orthogonal comparisons use nonoverlapping information. In general, if there are k levels of the independent variable, there are $k - 1$ orthogonal comparisons. With four groups, for example, the possible comparisons for significant differences between two levels involve the differences between groups 1 and 2, 1 and 3, 1 and 4, 2 and 3, 2 and 4, and 3 and 4. Three pairwise comparisons—the difference between 1 and 2 as compared with the difference between 3 and 4, the difference between 1 and 3 as compared with the difference between 2 and 4, and the difference between 1 and 4 as compared with the difference between 2 and 3—are orthogonal. The other possible comparisons are nonorthogonal; for example, comparing the difference between group 1 and group 2 as compared with the difference between group 1 and group 3 involves group 1 in each difference, so it is nonorthogonal. *Planned comparisons* are hypothesized before the experiment. *A posteriori comparisons* emerge from the data.

In order to reduce the likelihood that some comparisons will be significant by chance alone, various adjustments to the significance level may be necessary, so statisticians have created a family of multiple comparison measures. Kirk describes four situations. When comparisons are limited to planned orthogonal comparisons, a modified form of the t test that incorporates part of the analysis of variance summary (the mean square for error variance) is appropriate. Dunn's test is appropriate for all planned comparisons, whether or not they are orthogonal. For a posteriori comparisons and mixtures of planned and unplanned comparisons, possibilities include Fisher's LSD (least significant difference) test, Tukey's HSD (honestly significant difference) test, Scheffé's test, the Newman-Keuls test, Duncan's new multiple range test, and Dunnett's test. In general, planned orthogonal comparisons are more powerful than the others. Computational procedures differ, and some tests are more versatile regarding the possibility of comparing combinations of levels within an independent variable.

An ANOVA Example The results of an ANOVA are presented in a *source table*. Gfeller, Darrow, and Hedden (1990), in a study of mainstreaming status among music educators, presented a fully documented source table, which appears here as Table 11–2. The grouping variable, or factor, of music education type contained three levels: instrumental, vocal, and general music educator. The dependent variable was the teachers' perception of the instructional support

TABLE 11–2. ANOVA Source Table of Gfeller, Darrow, and Hedden (1990)

Source of Variance	Sum of Squares	df	Mean Squares	F	p
Between groups	186.43	2	93.21	4.84	.010
Within groups	1,327.57	69	19.24		
Total	1,514.00	71			

they were receiving. In the source table, the mean squares are obtained by dividing the sum of squares by the corresponding degrees of freedom. The F value is obtained by dividing the between-groups mean squares with the within-groups mean squares. Note that there was a significant difference at the .01 level between the types of teachers as indicated by p in the table. The post hoc analysis was performed using the Newman Keuls Multiple Range Test (Table 11–3). This analysis indicates that the instrumental music educators have a higher opinion of the instructional support they receive for mainstreaming than do the other music educators.

Analysis of Covariance

A research design may not always control for effects of extraneous or "nuisance" variables. For example, in a study comparing the relative efficacies of two methods of teaching beginning instrumentalists, the two groups might differ significantly in their initial music aptitude, despite randomization. In a study where the researcher must necessarily work with intact groups, the students in one classroom may have some inherent advantage, such as parents who encourage and support private music lessons. Aptitude and parental support variables occasionally may be built into the experimental design as additional independent variables, but when that is not feasible, statistical control may be attained via *analysis of covariance,* where the additional variable functions as a *covariate.* The covariate varies along with the other variables, and its effects are parceled out mathematically; in effect, the researcher is able to indicate the effects of the independent variable with any effects of the covariate under statistical control. Analysis of covariance may be extended to factorial designs, with more than one independent variable and/or covariate, and to multivariate designs, with more than one independent variable, dependent variable, and/or covariate.

TABLE 11–3. Newman Keuls Multiple Range Test of Gfeller, Darrow, and Hedden (1990)

Elementary Music Educators	Vocal Music Educators	Instrumental Music Educators
20.60	22.26	24.81

Note: Rule under values indicates nonsignificance. All other comparisons significant ($p < .01$).

UNIVARIATE TESTS—TWO OR MORE INDEPENDENT VARIABLES

Factorial Design Concepts

The number of independent variables or factors and their associated levels determine which ANOVA model is appropriate. The model extends the partitioning of the total sums of squares beyond the within-treatments and between-treatments sums of squares done by the one-way ANOVA. The *F* value is still the ratio of the sums of squares of interest divided by the sums of squares within treatments now designated as *error* (Edwards, 1968, p. 120).

Figure 11–2 presents three different experiments that all use musical achievement as the dependent variable. In the first experiment, it is desired to determine the effect of three levels of musical aptitude, the single independent variable or factor, on musical achievement. This experimental design would require a *one-way ANOVA*. The second experiment is designed with a two-level factor of gender and a three-level factor of musical aptitude level. This experimental design, because it involves two factors, requires a *two-way ANOVA*. The third experiment extends the second by including a third factor of grade level, which requires a *three-way ANOVA*. ANOVAs with more than one factor may also be referred to by the number of levels of each factor. The second experiment would be referred to as a 2 × 3 ANOVA while the third experiment would be referred to as a 2 × 3 × 3 ANOVA.

The two-way ANOVA required by the second experiment in Figure 11–2 can further partition the between-treatment sums of squares into the *main effects* for each of the factors of gender and musical aptitude as well as for the interaction of these two factors. In this case, the partitioning of the treatment sums of squares yields sums of squares for the gender main effect, the musical aptitude main effect, and the gender × musical aptitude (gender by musical aptitude) *interaction*. An *F* ratio can be produced for each partition by dividing with the appropriate error team. The error term in this case is the within-treatment sums of squares. Thus, tests can be applied to determine if a significant difference exists in musical achievement attributable to gender, musical aptitude, or the interaction between gender and musical aptitude.

A significant interaction in a multiway ANOVA indicates that the effect of the various levels of the factors involved is not uniform. In the case of the second experiment in Figure 11–2, a significant gender × musical aptitude interaction might indicate that girls of high aptitude achieve more than boys of high aptitude while girls of low aptitude achieve less than boys of low aptitude. The opposite also could be true. It would be necessary to plot the means for the cells of the interaction, as in Figure 11–3 (p. 152), to determine the nature of the significant interaction. In this case, our initial supposition is indicated by the graph of the interaction. In general, a plot of significant interaction will reveal prominent nonparallel lines, although the lines may not always intersect.

The concepts presented for the second example can be extended for other multiway ANOVAs. Consider the characteristics of the three-way ANOVA of the third experiment in Figure 11–2. The between-treatments sums of squares can be partitioned into three main effects: gender, musical aptitude, and grade level. In addition, the following combinations of factors produce interactions that can be tested: gender × musical aptitude, gender × grade level, musical aptitude × grade level (two-way interactions), and gender × musical aptitude × grade level (three-way interaction).

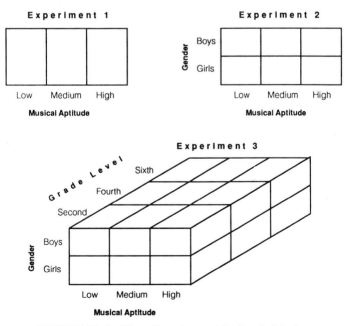

FIGURE 11–2. Three Experimental Designs in Music.

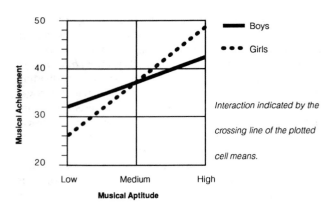

FIGURE 11–3. Hypothetical Interaction Effects for Experiment 2.

Simple Effects

In the example provided by Experiment 2, we may find that there are significant differences due to the main effects of both gender and musical aptitude. For the main effect of gender, there are only two means: one for the boys and one for the girls. Thus, the gender main effect states that the girls and boys performed significantly differently from each other on musical achievement, the dependent variable. For the main effect of musical aptitude, there are three means, one for each of the three musical aptitude levels. A number of methods are available to determine how these means differ through both post hoc and a priori methods. The multiple comparisons that are required to account for the differences among all the means have come to be called *simple effects*.

Simple effects are of two types: planned and unplanned (Kachigan, 1986, p. 306). Comparisons planned prior to data analysis are also known as *a priori comparisons*. Comparisons determined after the completion of an ANOVA where significant differences for the main and interaction effects have been noted are unplanned comparisons also known as *post hoc comparisons*.

A Priori Comparisons   The most accepted method for analyzing simple effects that are preplanned is through the testing of *orthogonal comparisons* (Kachigan, 1986, p. 306). Orthogonal comparisons are established by the assignment of weights to the means so that the sum of all the weights is equal to zero. For instance, in Experiment 2 of Figure 11–2 we might have obtained a significant musical aptitude main effect. This effect has three means. To compare the low aptitude mean $(\overline{x}_l)$ with the medium aptitude mean $(\overline{x}_m)$, we would subtract the second mean from the first mean. This in mathematical formulation would be:

$$\overline{x}_l - \overline{x}_m$$

which is equivalent to

$$(+1)\,\overline{x}_l + (-1)\,\overline{x}_m .$$

Removing the mean symbols leaves the two weights

$$+1 \text{ and } -1,$$

which also sum to zero. Orthogonal contrasts are created in just this manner. They also provide the ability to compare, say, the high musical aptitude mean $(\overline{x}_h)$ against the average of the low and medium level musical aptitude means. This comparison would be mathematically displayed as

$$\overline{x}_h - \frac{\overline{x}_l + \overline{x}_m}{2} = \overline{x}_h - \frac{\overline{x}_l}{2} - \frac{\overline{x}_m}{2} ,$$

which would have the weights of

$$+1 \quad -\frac{1}{2} \quad -\frac{1}{2} ,$$

which also sum to zero.

Two contrasts, to be orthogonal to each other, must have the products of their respective coefficient weights sum to zero. The number of possible orthogonal contrasts is one less than the number of levels in the ANOVA effect of interest. For our musical aptitude effect of Experiment 2, there are three levels, which means that two orthogonal comparisons are possible. It is possible, however, to create a number of different sets of orthogonal comparisons. Table 11–4 presents a number of possibilities for the musical aptitude effect. Note that constants have been used in some of the contrasts to avoid fractions.

The test of the significance of an orthogonal contrast is done by testing whether the sum of the products of each weight times its respective mean is equal to zero. The test requires that the sum (W) of all the Weight (w) × Mean $(\overline{x})$ products is calculated as

$$W = w_1 \overline{x}_1 + w_2 \overline{x}_2 + \cdots + w_k \overline{x}_k .$$

The standard error (s_w) for the sum of all the Weight × Mean products is then calculated as

$$s_w = s \sqrt{\sum \frac{w_i^2}{n_i}} ,$$

where

s = square root of the within-treatment or error mean square,
w_i^2 = squared weight in a contrast, and
n_i = the sample size for a mean in the contrast.

TABLE 11–4. Possible Orthogonal Contrasts
for Musical Aptitude

Contrast	Low Mean	Medium Mean	High Mean
1	2	−1	−1
2	0	1	−1
1	−1	−1	2
2	1	−1	0

The test is distributed as t with the same degrees of freedom as for the within-treatment sums of squares and an alpha twice that selected for the original ANOVA

$$t = \frac{W}{s_w}.$$

An equivalent interval to test this value is

$$W \pm (\alpha/2^t \, df)(s_w)$$

where

$1 - \alpha/2^t$ df = critical value of t for a particular confidence level with the same degrees of freedom as for the within-treatment sum of squares.

The value of using orthogonal contrasts is that both the significance levels of each comparison and the entire set of comparisons are known (Kachigan, 1986, p. 310). If for each of our musical aptitude comparisons we use a significance level of .05, the probability for the entire set is .95 × .95 = .85 that the set is without a Type I error or the probability of one Type I error in the set is .15 (1 − .85). For post hoc, that is unplanned comparisons, the probability in the set of comparisons is not known.

Post Hoc Comparisons Duncan's (1955) multiple range test provides one method for the post hoc determination of which of the differences of the means are significant. Use of post hoc methods assumes that there were no hypothesized differences prior to the implementation of the experiment. The method involves ordering all the means from lowest to highest in a table and calculating the standard error of the mean. A statistical table is then employed to find a multiplier value based on the degrees of freedom for the within-treatment partitioning of the sums of squares. Multipliers are found for two through to the total number of levels. The standard error of the mean and the multipliers are then multiplied. This forms the *shortest significant ranges*. The lowest mean is then subtracted from the highest mean. If this value is larger than the shortest significant range for the spread of levels covered by the lowest to the highest mean, then a significant difference between means has been identified. This process continues comparing the next smallest mean to the highest mean until no difference is noted. A line is drawn under the means from the highest mean to the point where no difference occurs. This entire procedure is then repeated comparing the next highest mean to the smallest values and so on until all significant mean differences have been identified.

Scheffé (1953) proposed another post hoc method for testing any and all comparisons of a set of means. In this procedure a table of all comparisons of interest is created. For the musical aptitude levels of Experiment 2 in Figure 11–2, a table similar to Table 11–5 might result. In the first row of

TABLE 11–5. Scheffé Contrast Vectors for Comparing Means in Experiment 2

Comparison	Means Low	Medium	High	Sum of Squared Weights
Low vs. medium	1	−1	0	2
Low vs. high	1	0	−1	2
Medium vs. high	0	1	−1	2
Low vs. medium + high	2	−1	−1	6
High vs. low + medium	−1	−1	2	6

Table 11–5, the low mean is compared to the medium mean by using the weights 1 and −1 respectively while 0 is assigned to the high-aptitude level as it is not being considered in this contrast. The sum of the squared weights is obtained by squaring each of the weights in the row and adding them together. To test a particular contrast, the difference between the sum of the scores for one compared treatment group is subtracted from the sum of the other and this result is squared. The squared difference between the group sums is then divided by the sum of the squared weights from the table. The resulting value is divided by the error mean square from the analysis of variance producing F. To determine the significance of this F, the number of means minus one is used as the degrees of freedom for the numerator and the within-treatment degrees of freedom is used for the denominator degrees of freedom. With these values, the tabled value for a desired significance level is identified. This value is then multiplied by the number of means minus one to produce F'. To be significant, F must be greater than or equal to F'.

Symbolically, the Scheffé test amounts to:

$$MS_{D_i} = \frac{D_i^2}{n\Sigma w_{\cdot i}^2}$$

$$F = \frac{MS_{D_i}}{s^2}$$

$$F' = (k-1)F_{(k-1),dfw},$$

where

D_i^2 = squared difference of the sum of scores for the contrasted means,
$\Sigma w_{\cdot i}^2$ = sum of the squared weights for the contrast,
n = number of subjects in a treatment level,
k = total number of treatment levels, and
dfw = within-treatment or error mean square degrees of freedom.

Cell Size

The power of an analysis of variance is predicated on the number of subjects that are contained within each of the cells of the experimental design. All things being equal, the greater the number of individuals within a cell, the greater the power. This is related to the assumptions of homogeneity of variance and the measured values being normally distributed. The larger the sample for each cell, the greater the probability that the sampled values for the cell will have these characteristics. The researcher must be cautioned about including too many independent variables within an analysis as the sample size within the cells may become very small. This usually occurs when a researcher decides on a particular analysis of variance after the data are collected rather than before. To avoid such problems, the experiment should be planned carefully in advance to ensure that the number of subjects in each cell will be as equal as possible and as large as feasible. Practically, factorial experiments with fewer than 10 subjects in each cell should be avoided.

Randomized Block Designs

The full factorial designs considered above take the total sample of subjects and randomly assign each subject to one of the treatment level combinations. If one of the treatment, or condition, levels is related to the dependent variable, then a *randomized block design* could be formed. The benefit of the randomized block design is that the error variance—that is, the denominator in the ratio—is reduced, which makes it more likely that a significant ratio will be obtained (Kachigan, 1986, p. 299).

In the randomized block design, blocks are formed of subjects with similar characteristics on a trait. The number of subjects in the block must be equal to the number of treatments, and all subjects in a block must have homogeneous characteristics on the trait related to the dependent variable. Consider an experiment where the dependent variable was

rhythm learning after a 10-week instructional period. Five different treatments were used: (1) Orff method, (2) Kodály method, (3) Education Through Music method, (4) Gordon method, and (5) no-contact control group. The experimenters were interested in the relative effectiveness of these methods in teaching rhythm and, in addition, were interested in determining if a differential effect occurred for various musical aptitude levels. Musical aptitude should be related to rhythm achievement. Therefore, blocks could be formed of high, medium, and low musical aptitude. Because the number of subjects in a block is equal to the number of treatments, there would be five students in each of the three blocks, requiring a total of 15 students. The blocks would be formed by ranking the students according to musical aptitude and placing the first five in the high block, the second five in the medium block, and the last five in the low block. The subjects within each block would be randomly assigned to one of the five treatment conditions.

The statistical treatment of such data is summarized in Table 11–6. The variance in the data is partitioned into total, treatment, blocks, and block × treatment. The block × treatment is used as the error term in the ratios for treatment and block main effects. The fictitious results of this experiment indicate a significant effect for treatment and a significant effect for aptitude. Further analysis for simple effects would be necessary to identify exactly where the differences between means lie.

Repeated Measures Designs

It often occurs that an experiment is designed in which the subjects are measured more than once during the course

TABLE 11–6. A Fictitious Example of a Randomized Block Design

Block Musical Aptitude	Treatment					Block Means
	Orff	Kodály	ETM	Gordon	Control	
Low	22.00	19.00	14.00	26.00	14.00	19.00
Medium	34.00	24.00	19.00	37.00	11.00	25.00
High	39.00	33.00	28.00	42.00	23.00	33.00
Treatment means	31.67	25.33	20.33	35.00	16.00	25.67

Source	SS	df	MS	F	p <
Treatment	735.33	4	183.83	6.66	0.012
Block (musical aptitude)	493.33	2	246.67	8.94	0.002
Treatment × Block	220.67	8	27.58		
Total	1449.33	14			

General Form

Source	SS	df	MS	F
t Treatments	$\Sigma n_j (\bar{x}_{.j} - \bar{x}_{..})^2$	$t - 1$	SS_t / df_t	MS_t / MS_e
b Blocks	$\Sigma n_i (\bar{x}_{.i} - \bar{x}_{..})^2$	$b - 1$	SS_b / df_b	MS_b / MS_e
$t \times b$ Error	$SS_{total} - SS_t - SS_b$	$(t - 1)(b - 1)$	$SS_{t \times b} / df_{t \times b}$	
Total	$\Sigma\Sigma(x_{ij} - \bar{x}_{..})$	$tb - 1$		

$\bar{x}_{..}$ = grand mean		x_{ij} = a cell value	
$\bar{x}_{.j}$ = a treatment mean		n_j = number of cells for a treatment	
$\bar{x}_{.i}$ = a block mean		n_i = number of cells for a block	

of an experiment. This may occur if all the sampled subjects are provided each of the various treatments or when the researcher desires to determine the effects of a treatment a number of times during the experiment. The appropriate analysis of this form of experiment is called repeated measures ANOVA.

Repeated measures ANOVA is a special case of the randomized block design in which each block is a subject. In repeated measures situations, the subject is not randomly assigned to a treatment, but rather is subjected to all treatments. Consider an experiment in which it is desired to know the effects of extraneous sound on an individual's ability to do simple math problems. Four sound conditions exist: (1) silence, (2) sedative music, (3) stimulative music, (4) random pitch durations. In this experiment 10 subjects are tested doing simple math problems during each of the sound conditions.

Data for such an experiment are presented in Table 11–7. Note that the only ratio of interest is the main effect for sound condition. A between-subjects main effect also can be tested using the within-subjects mean square as the denominator in the ratio. Note that the formulas used in deriving the conditions main effect are the same as that used in determining the treatment main effects in the fictitious randomized block design example. To identify exactly where the means differed between the conditions, simple effects would have to be tested.

Other Designs

Analysis of variance provides a very flexible means for analyzing data from virtually all types of experiments and is treated much more extensively in texts by Glass and Hopkins (1984), Hays (1988), Winer (1971), and Winkler and Hays (1975). Full factorial models, randomized blocks, and repeated-measures designs have common applications in music research. Other designs, such as the *nested designs*, where a grouping variable such as type of ensemble, band or chorus, may be nested under school, require different variance partitioning than previously described designs. It is also possible to have various combinations of the types of models presented here, which are known as mixed models. The researcher should consult one of the texts cited for detailed descriptions of how to analyze data from such models.

MULTIVARIATE FACTORIAL DESIGNS

Fundamental Concepts

Frequently a researcher is interested in more than one dependent variable within an experimental design. Referring back to the experiments in Figure 11–2, you may recall these designs all have musical achievement as the one dependent

TABLE 11–7. A Fictitious Example of a Repeated Measures Design

Subject	Sound Condition				Subject Means
	Silence	Sedative	Stimulative	Random	
1	15.00	14.00	8.00	17.00	13.50
2	7.00	9.00	5.00	11.00	8.00
3	12.00	10.00	9.00	15.00	11.50
4	19.00	17.00	10.00	22.00	17.00
5	13.00	14.00	7.00	15.00	12.25
Condition means	13.20	12.80	7.80	16.00	12.45

Source	SS	df	MS	F	p <
Between subjects	170.20	4	42.55	18.11	0.001
Within subjects	202.75	15	13.52		
Sound conditions	174.55	3	58.18	24.76	0.001
Error	28.20	12	2.35		
Total	372.95	19			

General Form

Source	SS	df	MS	F
Between n subjects	$\Sigma n_i\,(\overline{x}_{i.} - \overline{x}_{..})^2$	$n - 1$	SS_b / df_b	MS_b / MS_e
Within subjects	$\Sigma\Sigma(x_{ij} - \overline{x}_{i.})$	$n(t - 1)$	SS_w / df_w	
t Treatments	$\Sigma n_{.j}(\overline{x}_{.f} - \overline{x}_{..})^2$	$t - 1$	SS_t / df_t	MS_t / MS_e
Error	$SS_{total} - SS_t - SS_b$	$(t - 1)(n - 1)$	$SS_{t \times b} / df_{t \times b}$	
Total	$\Sigma\Sigma(x_{ij} - \overline{x}_{..})$	$tn - 1$		

$\overline{x}_{..}$ = grand mean		x_{ij} = a cell value	
$\overline{x}_{.j}$ = a treatment mean		$n_{.j}$ = number of cells for a treatment	
$\overline{x}_{i.}$ = a subject's mean		n_i = number of cells for a subject	

variable. This made univariate ANOVA models the most appropriate for these designs. If the researcher now desired to include two different measures of musical achievement, one being knowledge of musical concepts and the other musical performance skill, the univariate ANOVA would no longer be appropriate. The family of statistical models most appropriate for this new situation would be *multivariate analysis of variance* (MANOVA).

It has been common practice to analyze data from situations such as those just described with two separate univariate ANOVAs. This, however, leads to the great probability of obtaining a significant difference due simply to chance. MANOVA protects from this possibility by first simultaneously testing to determine whether there are any differences across the various dependent variables. MANOVA has the additional benefit of not only providing tests of significance about the dependent variables of interest, but also being able to provide an indication of the pattern of relationships between the dependent variables (Sheth, 1984).

MANOVA

One-way and multiway experimental designs with more than one dependent variable can be analyzed with MANOVA. The overall null hypothesis is tested by reducing the number of measures to a single value by applying a linear combining rule (Harris, 1985, p. 19). The weights of the combining rule are applied in such a way as to produce the largest possible value. It is this value that tests the overall null hypothesis. This set of weights is the discriminant function, which will be discussed in the "Discriminant Analysis" section below.

Overall Test A number of overall tests of MANOVA results exist. Wilks's lambda is the most commonly employed. Harris (1985, p. 169) identifies four reasons for this: (1) historical precedence, (2) it provides a fairly good approximation to the distribution of *F,* (3) it is a more powerful test under certain circumstances, and (4) the discriminant functions on which Wilks's lambda is based are easier to compute than are characteristic roots. In addition, Harris notes that Wilks's lambda has been shown to be more robust against violations of the multivariate normal and homogeneity of variance assumptions of MANOVA than is the greatest characteristic root criterion (p. 170). Many computer programs, such as SPSS^x MANOVA (SPSS, 1988), provide these statistics along with their approximations in the output.

Subanalyses Once a significant overall test has been identified, it is common to then look at the univariate subanalyses of variance in which each dependent variable is analyzed separately. This allows the researcher to identify which of the dependent variables is producing significant differences for the particular effect. Computer programs that compute MANOVA generally provide this output whether the overall test is significant or not. In addition to separate, independent univariate subanalyses, some programs provide step-down subanalyses in which the variance of preceding variables to have been analyzed with ANOVA is removed from the following variables yet to be analyzed. In this manner, the effect of a theoretical ordering of variables on following variables can be determined. For instance, in our Experiment 2 example with the two dependent variables of music knowledge and music skill, it might be desirable to determine if overall differences of the musical aptitude main effect are independent between knowledge and performance. The analysis could be arranged so that the performance subanalysis ANOVA occurred first, with the knowledge subanalysis last. The step-down process would first test the separate, independent ANOVA for performance and remove the performance-related variance from the data prior to testing the final knowledge ANOVA. If the knowledge step-down ANOVA was not significant but the separate performance ANOVA was, it could be concluded that musical aptitude has a profound effect on musical performance achievement. In addition, musical performance achievement is shown to be strongly related to the acquisition of musical knowledge. This is because when the variance of musical aptitude and performance is removed prior to testing musical knowledge, musical knowledge is no longer significant. Of course, this is a hypothetical example, but it does show MANOVA's capacity to provide the researcher with a wealth of information about not only the effects of interest, but the relationships between the dependent variables as well.

MANOVA Example As part of a study on the effectiveness of two forms of instruction on aural and instrumental performance skills, Kendall (1988) reported a MANOVA. The 3 × 2 factorial design included three levels of musical aptitude (above average, average, and below average) and two types of treatment (comprehensive and modeling). The analysis included four dependent variables: Instrumental Eye-to-Hand Coordination Test (IETHCT), Verbal Association Test (VAT), Instrumental Performance Test (IPT), and the Melodic/Rhythmic Sight-Reading Test (MRSRT). An extended source table that includes the multivariate and the univariate ANOVAs for the significant multivariate effect is presented in Table 11–8. As can be seen, there was one significant multivariate main effect for treatment—the type of instruction received. The subanalyses indicate that the effects were attributable to the Verbal Association Test and the Melodic/Rhythmic Sight-Reading Test. Kendall found through inspection of the means that the comprehensive treatment was more effective on these two dependent variables than the modeling treatment.

MANCOVA

As in the univariate case, there is a multivariate analog to the analysis of covariance, the *multivariate analysis of covariance* or MANCOVA. The need for MANCOVA is to provide statistical control for factors that might influence the set of dependent variables of interest. For instance, achievement

TABLE 11–8. MANOVA and Subanalyses from Kendal (1988)

Source	Wilks's Lambda	Hypothesis Mean Square	Error Mean Square	F	p <
Treatment	.425			22.65	.001
IETHCT		314.07	864.74	0.36	NS
VAT		1,433.93	320.32	4.48	.030
IPT		220.11	718.61	0.31	NS
MRSRT		16,869.63	219.40	76.89	1.001
Music aptitude level	.825			1.69	NS
Treatment × Music Aptitude Level	.934			0.58	NS

Note: The degrees of freedom were not completely reported so are not included here.
Abbreviations: IETHCT = Instrumental Eye-to-Hand Coordination Test; VAT = Verbal Association Test; IPT = Instrumental Performance Test; MRSRT = Melodic/Rhythmic Sight-Reading Test.

has been found to be influenced by socioeconomic status. This relationship could be applied to the Experiment 2 of Figure 11–2 where there were two forms of musical achievement measured: knowledge and performance. The influence of socioeconomic status can be removed from the dependent variables prior to testing for main and interaction effects of gender and musical aptitude. This is done by removing the variance that overlaps between the two achievement dependent variables and socioeconomic status, the *covariate*. The result is a clearer picture of the true effects of gender and musical aptitude on the two dependent variables.

MANCOVA can be extended further to include more than one covariate. For instance, a researcher may desire to remove the effect not only of socioeconomic status, but also of home music environment prior to testing the gender and musical aptitude effects. Such procedures allow a great deal of statistical control over the data analysis. However, it is the researcher's responsibility to assure that the initial design is not flawed in some manner that would introduce systematic bias. When the research situation does not allow for early design control of experimental bias, then MANCOVA provides a means for reducing this bias in the data analysis.

Computing Resources

Most major statistical computer packages now provide programs or subroutines for performing complex MANOVA and MANCOVA analyses. Such programs may come under the title of *general linear model*. The choice of computer programs is dependent on the availability of programs to the researcher, the researcher's knowledge of the particular statistical package, the particular procedures that the researcher desires to apply, and the output the program produces. Today's powerful computing environments make the extreme calculating complexity of multivariate statistics no more difficult or time-consuming than simple univariate statistics. The researcher, however, should not choose to use a particular statistical procedure and then design a research study. Rather, the research study should be designed and

then the appropriate statistical procedures should be selected.

CORRELATION

In addition to studying the effects of independent variables on dependent variables and describing populations in various ways, researchers may wish to show relationships among variables or sets of variables. Correlation techniques facilitate quantification of relationships.

In simple terms, a *correlation coefficient,* which may range from -1.00 to $+1.00$, shows the size and direction of a relationship between two sets of scores. The larger the absolute value of the number, the stronger the relationship, whether it be positive or negative. The most common type of correlation, the one most researchers would assume another researcher is talking about without any further qualification, is the Pearson product-moment correlation. The two variables must be measured at at least the interval level, and homoscedasticity is assumed. *Homoscedasticity* essentially means that if all of the scores on one variable are categorized into classes in terms of the other variable, the scores within the classes are normally distributed and the variances of the scores within the various categories are equal. Furthermore, the observations are assumed to be independent, and the underlying relationship is assumed to be linear. In a linear relationship, as one variable changes, the other changes in such a way that a straight line describes the relationship. In a curvilinear relationship, the changes must be described by a curved line or series of line segments that alternate in direction. For a visual depiction of both linear and curvilinear relationships, see the graphing section below.

Two sets of ranks (ordinal measures) may be described by *rank-order correlation,* also known as Spearman's rho. Two sets of dichotomies may be related through *tetrachoric correlation;* one dichotomy and a continuous variable featuring interval measurement may be related through *point-biserial correlation.* Point-biserial correlation is commonly used in psychometrics to express the relationship between answering a particular single item correctly, a dichotomy, and overall test score, the continuous variable.

The relationships between a number of variables can be depicted in a correlation matrix. The correlation matrix is a diagonal matrix in that the values of the lower left portion of the matrix are replicated in the upper right. Hedden (1982), in a study of the predictors of musical achievement for general music students, reported a correlation matrix for one of the participating schools composed of the major variables of the study: Attitude Toward Music Scale (ATMS), Self-Concept in Music Scale (SCIM), Music Background Scale (MB), Iowa Test of Basic Skills (ITBS), students' gender, and Music Achievement Test (MAT). This correlation matrix is reproduced as a complete diagonal matrix in Table 11–9. The lower-left portion of the matrix is not filled in because the correlation for any one variable, say, gender, with another variable, say, MAT, is the same as the correlation for MAT with gender.

EXTENSIONS OF CORRELATION

The concept of the interrelationship among a set of variables has produced a great number of valuable statistical tools. These tools all utilize the variance shared between variables and the variance unique to particular variables to further the understanding of the relationships between the variables and to provide tests of hypotheses about these relationships.

Partial Correlation

It can happen that a researcher wants to know the degree of relationship between variables when the effect of a third variable is removed. In such situations, the researcher is interested in the *partial correlation*. The partial correlation is the correlation between two variables when the common variance of one or more variables is removed. This provides another form of statistical control by removing unwanted variance to provide a clearer view of the relationship between two variables.

The *partial correlation coefficient* can be mathematically defined as

$$r_{12.3} = \frac{r_{12} - r_{13}\,r_{23}}{\sqrt{(1 - r^2_{13})(1 - r^2_{23})}},$$

where

r_{12} = correlation between variables 1 and 2,
r_{13} = correlation between variables 1 and 3, and
r_{23} = correlation between variables 2 and 3.

This partial correlation indicates the relationship between the variables 1 and 2 with the effect of variable 3 removed. Figure 11–4 presents a graphic means of showing this relationship using a Venn diagram. It should be noted that the complete pattern of relationships within the Venn diagram can be determined from such procedures and that these procedures can be extended to indicate the relationship between two variables with the effect of any number of variables removed.

Kendall (1988) provides correlations for three variables related to aural perception and instrumental performance: a measure of student ability to perform on an instrument heard melodic patterns, a measure of student ability to respond in solfege to heard melodic patterns, and a measure of instrumental performance (Table 11–10). A research question could be, "What is the relationship between ability to perform heard melodic patterns and solfege response ability when the variance associated with instrumental performance ability is removed from the relationship?" To answer this question, a partial correlation coefficient would be appropriate. The results of this analysis in Table 11–10 indicate that the partial correlation drops to .59 from the original bivariate correlation of .63 when the variance associated with instrumental performance ability is removed. The difference between the variances (r^2) of the bivariate correlation and the partial correlation indicates that the variance associated with instrumental performance ability in the relationship between the ability to perform heard melodic patterns and the ability to solfege heard melodic patterns is approximately 5 percent.

TABLE 11–9. Full Diagonal Correlation
Matrix from Hedden (1982)

Variable	ATMS	SCIM	MB	ITBS	Gender	MAT
ATMS	1.000	.642	.461	.226	.373	.352
SCIM		1.000	.603	.400	.085	.472
MB			1.000	.535	.159	.450
ITBS				1.000	−.040	.505
Gender					1.000	.034
MAT						1.000

Abbreviations: ATMS = Attitude Toward Music Scale; SCIM = Self-Concept in Music Scale; MB = Music Background Scale; ITBS = Iowa Test of Basic Skills; MAT = Music Achievement Test.

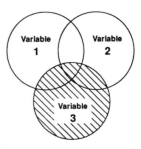

FIGURE 11–4. Partial Correlation between Variables 1 and 2 Controlling for 3.

TABLE 11–10. Example of Partial Correlation Using the Data of Kendal (1988)

	Heard/Played	Heard/Solfege	Instrumental Performance		r	r^2
Heard/Played (P)	1.00			Bivariate$_{(r_{PS})}$	0.63	0.40
Heard/Solfege (S)	0.63	1.00		Partial $_{(r_{IP.S})}$	0.59	0.35
Instrumental Performance (I)	0.40	0.28	1.00	Difference		0.05

Correlation Matrix

Multiple Regression

Multiple regression is the extension of the case of a correlation between two variables to the case where there are a number of variables being related to a single variable. In multiple regression, the set of variables being related to a single variable are known as the *predictor variables*. The single variable to which the independent variables are being related is the *criterion variable.*

Multiple regression extends the bivariate regression

$$y = a + bx,$$

where the value y is predicted by a value of the predictor variable x multiplied by a weight and added to a constant, the *y intercept* in which only one variable x is involved, to

$$y = a + b_1x_1 + b_2x_2 + ... + b_kx_k,$$

where for a number of k variables there are corresponding weights. Thus, a single variable is predicted by a number of other variables.

The results of multiple regression produce a statistic of the degree of relationship between the predictor variables and the criterion variable, the multiple correlation coefficient *(R)*. This statistic ranges from -1 to $+1$ and is interpreted in a manner similar to that used to interpret the simple bivariate correlation. As with the bivariate correlation, when R is squared (R^2), the proportion of variance in the criterion variable accounted for by the predictor variables is revealed. This variance can be tested with an F test. In addition, *beta weights,* the coefficients of the standardized predictor variables, are provided that indicate the relative importance of the predictor variables in predicting the dependent variable. The absolute values of the betas indicate the order of importance of the predictor variables for predicting the criterion. However, these values indicate only the relative importance of the predictor variables and not their absolute contributions to the prediction because their importance depends on other variables included in the analysis. This is because beta weights are related to partial correlation coefficients in that their value is a function not only of the correlation between the criterion variable and the particular predictor variable, but also of the correlations between all of the predictor variables.

The set of independent, or predictor, variables for a particular criterion variable can be analyzed in a number of different ways. The most obvious is to have all predictor variables simultaneously regressed on the criterion variable. Another method is to start with just one predictor variable and the criterion variable, after which another predictor variable is added, and another, until all predictor variables are included. The order of predictor variable entry can be determined on theoretical grounds, or it can be determined statistically. In either case, the amount of variance by which the prediction of the criterion variable is increased (or decreased) with the addition of a predictor variable can be tested. The testing of variance can be used as one basis for selecting which predictor variable should next enter the prediction equation. The variable that is the next largest contributor to the explained variance in the relationship of the predictor variables to the criterion could be selected.

The addition of predictor variables to the regression equation is called *forward stepping. Backward stepping* is also possible where the analysis begins with all predictor variables included in the regression equation and succeeding variables are removed from the equation on the basis of the smallest contribution to the prediction of the criterion variable or on some theoretical basis. A variety of other methods are available, and combinations of these methods are possible. The researcher must select the method that provides the analysis appropriate to the particular research study.

In a study of the factors that contribute to various aspects of work performed in first-year college theory courses, Harrison (1990a) reported a series of multiple regressions using the various aspects of the theory work as the dependent variables. Harrison used a forward-stepping procedure that determined "the best linear combination of statistically significant predictor variables ($p < .05$)" (p. 180). Table 11–11 (p. 160) contains the multiple regression analysis for the written work criterion variable for first-semester college students. In the table, Harrison provides a thorough compilation of the important statistics available for multiple regression. For this variable, the math score on the *Scholastic Aptitude Test* (SAT) is the most important predictor variable, which accounts for 19 percent of the variance (R^2 change), followed in order by high school grade-point average, accounting for an additional 6 percent of the variance, and whether the student was an instrumentalist, accounting for an additional 2 percent of the variance. The total amount of variance in theory written work grade accounted for by these three variables is 27 percent (R^2).

TABLE 11–11. Multiple Regression Predicting First-Semester Written Theory Work Grade from Harrison (1990a)

Variables	r	R	R^2	R^2 Change	F Change	$p <$	B	Beta Weights
SAT math	.43	.43	.19	.19	36.37	.001	.01	.32
HS GPA	.41	.50	.25	.06	12.41	.001	1.92	.26
Instrument	−.15	.52*	.27	.02	5.43	.022	−1.05	−.16

* = .0001 level.

Multiple regression is a very flexible analytical procedure. It can be used not only to identify the degree of relationship between a set of predictor variables and a criterion variable, but also to produce analyses of variance. Researchers who are interested in such uses and a more detailed discussion should consult the text by Kerlinger and Pedhazur (1982) as well as Chapter 15 of this handbook.

Discriminant Analysis

Discriminant analysis is used to study the case where there is a set of continuous independent variables predicting a single discrete grouping variable (Goodstein, 1987). For instance, a researcher may be interested in predicting the beginning band instrument on which students would be the most successful from a set of independent variables such as motivation, preferred sound quality, pitch acuity, parental desire, musical aptitude, physical capabilities, and parental support. This situation would require the use of discriminant analysis.

The particular variables used as independent variables are selected because they are believed to have some relationship with the single categorical dependent variable (Kachigan, 1986, p. 360). This parallels the process that would be used for the selection of the predictor variables for multiple regression. Whereas the calculation of the multiple-regression model centered on the determination of the set of weights for the predictor variables, discriminant analysis involves the determination of the discriminant function. The *discriminant function* is a set of weighted predictor variables for classifying a person or object into one of the groups of the dependent variable. The discriminant function is calculated in such a way as to minimize the classification error. It would hold that the larger the difference between the groups of the dependent variable on the measured independent variables, the fewer classification errors will be made.

The number of discriminant functions necessary to fully characterize the model will be equal to the number of groups in the dependent variable minus one. The process of calculating each of the discriminant functions is based first on determining the discriminant function that will have the greatest success in classifying the persons or objects into one of the dependent groups. Then, the next most successful function is calculated, and so on until all discriminant functions have been calculated. Each discriminant function, then, contains the set of weights that maximally separates persons or objects into one of the dependent variable's groups. Note that the reason for needing only one discriminant function less than the number of groups is that in the two-group case, if we know the person or persons classified into one group, all people left are classified into the other group—the fundamental principle of *degrees of freedom*.

Discriminant functions can be tested for their significance in differentiating the dependent variable groups beyond that expected by chance. The multivariate indicators of this significance are the same as frequently produced by the output of MANOVA: Mahalanobis D^2, Wilks Lambda, and Rao V. This is not surprising since a MANOVA determines the significant differences between groups on continuous variables. Indeed, Tatsuoka and Lohnes (1988, p. 210) have indicated that discriminant analysis is now used more in determining differences between groups than in its original use of classifying persons or objects into groups. This important relationship allows the researcher to gain additional insight into the group relationships of a MANOVA.

An additional method of evaluating the quality of the discriminant functions is to determine their accuracy of classification. The predicted and actual group memberships of a dependent variable can be compared. This process yields the proportion of people or objects correctly classified and the proportion misclassified.

As with multiple regression, the squared standardized discriminant function coefficients or beta weights can be analyzed to determine the relative importance of each independent variable in the classification of the persons or objects into a particular dependent group. The analysis of these weights provides significant insights about the independent variables and the groups of the dependent variable.

May (1985) studied the effects of grade level, gender, and race on first-, second-, and third-graders' musical preferences. As a follow-up to a MANOVA, May presented a table of discriminant analyses for each of these grouping variables. Table 11–12 presents the primary discriminant information for the grade-level effect. As can be seen, only function 1 was significant at $p < .05$ and accounted for 63 percent of the variance in the analysis.

Canonical Correlation

Canonical correlation provides a means of analyzing the relationship between two sets of continuous variables. Usually, one set of variables is considered to be the independent

TABLE 11–12. Discriminant Function Subanalysis for Grade Level from May (1985)

	Function 1	Function 2
Eigenvalue	.101	.060
Percent of variance	62.91	37.09
Canonical correlation	.303	.267
Wilks lambda	.857	.944
Chi-square	86.651	32.397
df	48	23
p	< .0005	< .0902

or predictor variables of the other set of dependent or criterion variables. The process can be conceived as an extension of multiple regression where there are two sets of weighted combinations of variables, one for the predictor variables and one for the criterion variables. The canonical correlation is the correlation between the derived predictor variables and the derived criterion variables. The derived variables are called *canonical variates.* In a manner similar to the calculation of the beta weights of multiple regression, *canonical weights* are derived that maximize the canonical correlation. The number of sets of possible canonical variates is equal to the number of variables in the smaller set of variables minus one.

The squared canonical correlation is the amount of variance shared by the derived canonical variates. The canonical correlation coefficients can be tested for significance. The squared canonical weights show the relative contribution of the individual variables to a derived variable in a manner parallel to the squared standardized regression weights of multiple regression. The amount of variance accounted for by a weighted combination of the original predictor variables in the opposite weighted combination of original criterion variables is not symmetrical. That is, the proportion of variance accounted for in the criterion variables by the predictor variables does not have to be equal. The predictor variables may account for more or less of the variance in the criterion variables than the criterion variables may account for in the predictor variables. This is because we are dealing with the original variables and not the derived canonical variates. The canonical correlation is based on the derived canonical variates, so its square indicates the proportion of variance accounted for by the canonical variates symmetrically. For a detailed example of canonical correlation, see May (1985).

Factor Analysis

Factor analysis is a family of techniques that can be used to study the underlying relationships between a large number of variables. The raw material for factor analysis is the correlation matrix or covariance matrix, which indicates the bivariate interrelationships of a variable set. Three primary techniques are under the factor analysis umbrella: principle components analysis, common factor analysis, and maximum likelihood factor analysis. Principle components analysis creates underlying components that accommodate all the variance within a correlation matrix. Common factor analysis produces underlying factors that are based on the common or shared variance of the variables. Maximum likelihood factor analysis estimates the population parameters from sample statistics and can provide statistical tests of factor models.

Factor analysis can be utilized for a wide variety of research activities, including identifying underlying traits within a data set, developing theory, testing hypotheses, and data set reduction, among others. Having such wide applicability in the research process makes it a very powerful tool.

The various methods for performing factor analysis all attempt to define a smaller set of derived variables extracted from the data submitted for analysis. These derived variables are called factors or components depending on the type of factoring method used. The factors then can be interpreted on the basis of the weights each of the measured variables is assigned on each of the factors. Scores for each subject can be calculated for each factor based on the obtained weights. *Factor scores* then may be used for further statistical analysis.

The steps involved in performing a factor analysis are as follows: (1) determine the substantive reasons for performing a factor analysis, (2) obtain data with sufficient sample size to assure stability of the intercorrelation matrix between all the variables to be factored, (3) select the appropriate factoring method, (4) determine the appropriate number of factors to represent the data, (5) select the appropriate method of factor rotation to derive the weights upon which the interpretations will be based, (6) interpret the derived factors, and (7) compute the factor scores, if desired.

Principal Components Principal components analysis utilizes all the variance associated with the variables without partitioning the variance into constituent parts. The resulting components contain the variance unique to each variable, the variance each variable has in common with the other variables, and variance attributable to error (Asmus, 1989a). The principal components model is most appropriate when the variables being analyzed are believed to be quite different from each other and are considered to have large amounts of unique variance. The principal components model is useful for data reduction purposes in which it is desired to have the reduced set of derived variables account for the greatest amount of variance in the calculated factor scores.

Common Factor Analysis Common factor analysis explains the interrelationships between a set of variables by using only the variance that the variables have in common. Unlike the principal components model, this requires considerably fewer factors than the number of variables (Cureton and D'Agostino, 1983, p. 2). The common factor model partitions the variance associated with a variable into that which is common among the variables, that which is unique to the particular variable, and that which is associated with error. The common factor model is most appropriate when the variables being analyzed are similar to each other, as in a set of items to evaluate musical performance.

Maximum Likelihood Factor Analysis Maximum likelihood factor analysis uses sample statistics to estimate the population parameters of the factoring results. The procedure involves finding the population parameter values that are most likely to have produced the data (Harnett, 1982, p. 333; Lunneborg and Abbot, 1983, p. 222). Gorsuch (1983, p. 127) indicates that as the sample size increases toward that of the population the maximum likelihood estimate will converge to the population parameter, and that across samples the parameter estimates will be the most consistent possible. The maximum likelihood method allows testing hypotheses about the factors extracted through the use of chi-square tests. When the number of factors are tested for, a significant chi-square indicates that there is still significant covariance in the residual matrix (Gorsuch, 1983, p. 129). That is, too few factors have been extracted to this point. Maximum likelihood factor analysis has been developed for use only with large samples. The maximum likelihood model is most appropriate where it is desired to draw conclusions about a population from a large representative sampling of members of that population.

Confirmatory factor analysis extends the maximum likelihood model to allow the testing of a number of hypotheses beyond the number of factors. The most prominent applications have been in testing hypothesized factor structure, in testing the validity of a test or battery of tests, and in causal path analysis (Gorsuch, 1983, pp. 133–140).

Computing a Factor Analysis A factor analysis is based on a correlation matrix. It is imperative that the correlation matrix be as stable as possible, which is to say that the sample size on which the correlation matrix is based should be as large as possible. The subject to variable ratio should never be less than 3:1 and should exceed 5:1 (Asmus, 1989a, p. 4). Sample sizes in excess of 250 tend to produce stable correlation matrices because of the relatively small error term for correlations with samples larger than this value. The measure of sampling adequacy, an indicator available in some computer packages, should never be lower than .5 (Kaiser and Rice, 1974).

Duke and Prickett (1987), as part of a study of applied music instruction, presented a correlation matrix that included the 10 items of a music teaching evaluation form used by 143 observers. This correlation matrix will be factor analyzed to show the steps involved in the factor analytic process. Duke and Prickett's correlation matrix has a subject to variable ratio of 14.3:1 and yields a measure of sampling adequacy of .847. These figures indicate that the correlation matrix had sufficient sample size to warrant factor analysis.

The items of the Duke and Prickett measure were adapted from Moore's (1976) evaluative instrument. All the items were selected to assess important aspects of the domain of music teaching in a private applied music setting. Because of this, it could be expected that there would be considerable variance shared between the items. This suggests that common factor analysis would be the most appropriate factor model for these data. The reason for factoring these data is not only to provide and exemplify the factor analysis process, but to provide some indication of the underlying constructs that are evaluated by the measure. Thus, because of the large common variance expected and because of the exploratory nature of the analysis, common factor analysis will be applied.

One of the most difficult decisions in performing a factor analysis is to determine how many factors best represent the data. Such decisions are usually based on previous research or theory, the eigenvalue-of-one criterion, a scree test in common factor analysis, and interpretation of the resulting factors (Asmus, 1989a, pp. 13–14). In Moore's (1976) original evaluation instrument, the items were divided into three categories: teacher interaction, musicianship, and creativity. In the table overlaying the scree test in Figure 11–5, it can be

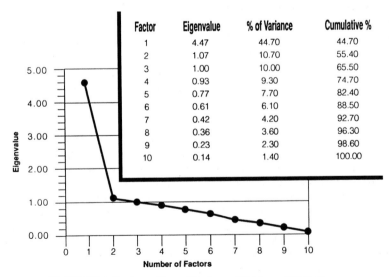

FIGURE 11–5. Scree Test of Duke and Prickett (1987) Data.

seen that three factors are indicated by eigenvalues of one or greater. The scree test of Figure 11–5 does not indicate any significant drop in the plotted line between the eigenvalues after the second eigenvalue so it yields little assistance in determining the number of factors. However, because of Moore's division of items into three categories and the eigenvalue-of-one criterion's indicating three potential factors, the number of factors in the analysis was constrained to three, which accounted for 65.5 percent of the variance in the correlation matrix.

The next decision in the factoring process is to determine the appropriate form of rotation to obtain simple structure. Simple structure maximizes the loading of a variable on one factor while minimizing the variable's loadings on the other factors (Asmus, 1989a, p. 19). Two major forms of rotation are available: orthogonal and oblique. Orthogonal rotation keeps the factors independent of each other and is most appropriate when it is believed that the resulting factors will indeed be independent or when it is desired to have the final factors maximally separated. Oblique rotation allows the factors to be related to each other. In the case of the Duke and Prickett data, the resulting factors logically should be related to each other because the items were selected to evaluate the

single concept of music teaching. Many types of orthogonal and oblique rotations are available. In a practical sense, the researcher is usually limited to those available in the computer statistical package being used. In the present case, SPSS[x] (SPSS, 1988) was the statistical package that provided oblimin oblique rotation for the analysis (Table 11–13). For a capsulated description of the major rotations, see Asmus (1989a).

The *factor pattern matrix* provides the relative weights for the variables on each of the derived factors. Interpretation of the factors is made in light of these weights along with the correlations of the variables with the factor that are presented in the *factor structure matrix*. The absolute values of the pattern weights are usually used to develop the initial conceptualization of a factor. Note that student participation and student attitude have relatively strong weights on the first factor and low weights on the other factors. This factor was labeled "Student Involvement." The second factor had strong weights on items that were interpreted to represent "Teacher Approach With Students." The final factor was interpreted as "Technical Aspects of Instruction."

A few items have relatively strong loadings on more than one factor; that is, the items *cross load*. Overall lesson effec-

TABLE 11–13. Factor Results of Duke and Prickett Data

Variables	Student Involvement	Teacher Approach With Students	Technical Aspects of Instruction
Pattern matrix			
Student participation (StPar)	0.747	−0.169	0.076
Student's attitude (StAtt)	0.588	−0.204	0.042
Quality of instruction (Instr)	0.044	−0.293	−0.001
Overall lesson effectiveness (OvEff)	0.280	−0.469	0.308
Attitude toward students (T-Att)	0.031	−0.849	0.041
Reinforcement effectiveness (Reinf)	−0.041	−1.004	−0.055
Lesson organization (Org)	0.141	0.045	0.931
Teacher's musicianship (Qual)	0.321	−0.087	0.432
Clarity of presentation (Clar)	−0.134	−0.082	0.281
Teacher's creativity (Creat)	0.113	0.008	0.199
Structure matrix			
Student participation (StPar)	0.843	−0.522	0.430
Student's attitude (StAtt)	0.687	−0.472	0.362
Quality of instruction (Instr)	0.165	−0.310	0.184
Overall lesson effectiveness (OvEff)	0.580	−0.764	0.677
Attitude toward students (T-Att)	0.397	−0.886	0.545
Reinforcement effectiveness (Reinf)	0.356	−0.956	0.515
Lesson organization (Org)	0.441	−0.554	0.953
Teacher's musicianship (Qual)	0.505	−0.471	0.592
Clarity of presentation (Clar)	−0.004	−0.189	0.283
Teacher's creativity (Creat)	0.178	−0.154	0.233
Factor Correlation Matrix			
Student involvement	1.000		
Teacher approach with students	−0.414	1.000	
Technical aspects of instruction	0.342	−0.581	1.000

tiveness, for instance, has fairly strong loadings on all factors. Logically a good lesson not only would involve the teacher's approach with students, the factor upon which this item loads most heavily, but also would incorporate significant student involvement and good technical aspects of instruction. Similarly, it is logical that the teacher's musicianship not only would load on the technical aspects of instruction, but also would influence student involvement—a fact long claimed by music teachers.

The factor structure matrix reveals many strong correlations of the items across the factors. This indicates that the derived factors are strongly related. As can be seen in the factor correlation matrix, the factors are indeed related to a considerable degree. Teacher approach, because of its negative weights, is inversely related to student involvement and the technical aspects of instruction. Student involvement, on the other hand, has a fairly substantial relationship with the technical aspects of teaching.

STATISTICAL BASED MODELING

Modeling

The conceptualization of theory generally produces a mental model of the interrelationships between the variables accommodated by the theory (Hanneman, 1988). Visual representations of the model help clarify the theory further. Such models can be evaluated statistically and, through modern computer systems, can be represented and manipulated in graphic form (Asmus, 1989b). The development of theory in music education has been a concern of many in the profession. The statistical methods available for evaluating theoretical models provide powerful tools for the testing and refinement of such theory.

The foundation of statistical based modeling is causation implied in the interrelationships between variables described by a theoretical model. The statistical correlation of variables provides the basis for explaining this causation. Although scientists and philosophers have debated the efficacy of such a position, several authors have clearly articulated the ratio-

nale for using intercorrelations to establish causation (Simon, 1985; Wright, 1921).

Statistical based modeling can be used to both test and develop theory. When theory is being tested, a formal model is established and then the causal links within the model are statistically tested. When theory is being developed, a formal model is evaluated statistically. Then, causal links are added or deleted until a model evolves that has satisfactory statistical and conceptual prowess. Two major types of statistical based modeling are available to researchers: *measured variable modeling* and *latent trait modeling*. In the former, variables that have been measured from a sample are used to form a model. In the latter, the underlying constructs of variables are used as the basis for the model.

Measured Variable Modeling

There are two forms of measured variable modeling: *causal analysis* and *path analysis.* Both are based on multiple regression of real-world data. That is, a variable identified as being caused by other variables in a theoretical model becomes the criterion variable in a multiple regression. The variables that cause the criterion variable are the predictor variables in this regression. The difference between causal and path analyses is that causal analysis uses the unstandardized regression coefficients or beta (b) weights to indicate the contribution of a causal variable to a dependent variable while path analysis uses the standardized regression coefficients or Beta (β) weights to indicate this contribution (Blalock, 1985).

Figure 11–6 presents a path model developed from a correlation matrix of variables extracted from a larger matrix presented by Harrison (1990b) in a study of music theory grade prediction. Harrison calculated the matrix from 121 first-year college music majors. Two types of variables exist within the system. *Exogenous variables,* caused by variables outside the system and linked with the curved line, are represented by total years of experience on musical instruments and whether or not the student had piano experience. *Endogenous variables* are caused by variables inside the system and are linked by the straight lines. The values in the figure

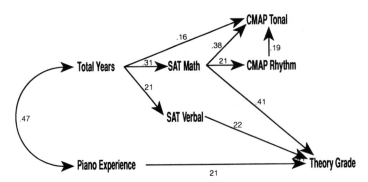

FIGURE 11–6. Path Analysis of Selected Variables from Harrison (1990b). (CMAP = College Musical Aptitude Profile; SAT = Scholastic Aptitude Test.)

are the path coefficients or β weights from the multiple regressions of a variable and its linked causal variables (Table 11–14).

The model was developed by placing the variables in their time ordering. Total years and piano experience would have been primarily determined prior to a student's having taken the SAT in late high school; the SAT would have been taken before the College Musical Aptitude Profile (CMAP; Schleuter, 1978), and the theory grade was assigned after the students had taken the CMAP. As Harrison found, music theory grade has no linkages from the two CMAP variables. Music theory grade is significantly predicted by the two SAT scores and whether or not the student had piano experience. These variables account for 38 percent of the theory grade. The strongest of the linkages is that between SAT math and the theory grade, as indicated by the path coefficient of .41. In the model, two variables play a pivotal role: SAT math and total years of experience. SAT math has substantial linkages with the CMAP variables and the theory grade while total years of experience has strong linkages with the SAT variables and the CMAP tonal variable. Does participation in music influence overall academic achievement? This model may suggest that this is so.

Latent Trait Modeling

Measuring the Unmeasurable Many in the field of music have claimed that a variety of important musical concepts are simply unmeasurable. *Latent trait modeling* provides a means of accounting for these "unmeasurable" concepts in complex systems. As with the measured variable modeling described earlier, latent trait modeling begins with a conceptual model that is depicted graphically. Then, through appropriate specification, the model can be tested using maximum likelihood principles.

A *latent trait* or *latent variable* is estimated from one or more indicators of the hypothetical factor (Cooley, 1978; Jöreskog, 1979). Latent traits are underlying variables that can be conceived as the factors produced by factor analysis. Indeed, latent trait modeling can be considered a blend of multiple regression and factor analysis (Ecob and Cuttance, 1987). The procedure involves the development of structural equations that incorporate latent variables. A general computer program named LISREL (Jöreskog and Sörbom, 1989; SPSS, 1988) provides estimates of the coefficients in these structural equations (Jöreskog, 1982).

There are considerable benefits for the use of latent traits in music education research. Latent traits provide a means for accommodating concepts that are difficult to measure. Many variables in music education research contain considerable measurement error. Latent traits provide a means for compensating for this error (Jöreskog, 1979). Latent trait modeling also provides much greater information about the variables that have been measured, their interrelationships, error, and the theoretical model being investigated.

A Latent Trait Model of Theoretical Understanding The selected subset of Harrison's (1990b) correlation matrix used in demonstrating the concepts of measured variable modeling can be applied in demonstrating latent trait modeling. The model tested is presented in Figure 11–7 (p. 166). The figure follows the conventions that latent traits are indicated by ovals and measured variables are indicated by rectangles. In the model, three latent variables predict the dependent latent variable of theoretical understanding. The three independent latent variables are musical background, scholastic achievement, and musical aptitude. Note that the measured variables' paths do not point toward their associated latent variable. Rather, the opposite is true. This indicates that the latent variables are underlying causes of the observed variables or are intervening variables in a causal chain (Jöreskog, 1982, pp. 83–84). In the present model, the arrows from outside the model pointing toward variables or traits in the

TABLE 11–14. Path Analysis Multiple Regressions of Harrison's (1990b) Data.

Paths to	from	Beta	t	$p <$	R	R^2	df	F	$p <$
Theory Grade									
SAT	Math	0.41	4.80	0.00	0.62	0.38	3,117	23.75	0.01
SAT	Vrbl	0.22	2.68	0.01					
Piano	Exp	0.21	2.82	0.01					
CMAPT	Tonal								
SAT	Math	0.38	4.55	0.00	0.53	0.28	3,117	15.42	0.01
	Rhy	0.19	2.31	0.02					
CMAP									
Totl	Yr	0.16	1.99	0.05					
CMAP	Rhy								
SAT	Math	0.21	2.34	0.02	0.21	0.04	1,119	5.49	0.02
SAT	Math								
Totl	Yr	0.31	3.56	0.00	0.31	0.10	1,119	12.65	0.01
SAT	Vrbl								
Tot	Yr	0.21	2.34	0.02	0.21	0.04	1,119	5.49	0.02

Abbreviations: SAT = Scholastic Aptitude Test; CMAP = College Musical Aptitude Profile.

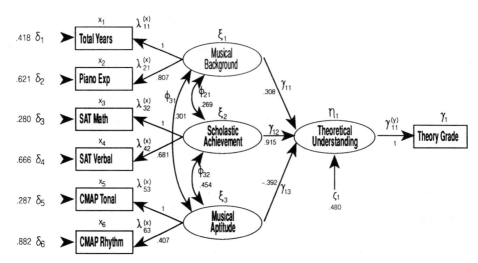

FIGURE 11–7. Latent Trait Model of Theoretical Understanding from Harrison's (1990b) Data.

model indicate measurement error. The various symbology used in latent trait modeling as it is implemented in LISREL is defined in Table 11–15.

The relationship between latent trait modeling and factor analysis is evident in the results of a maximum likelihood factor analysis with oblimin rotation of Harrison's data (Table 11–16). Note that the three factors, which account for 69.9

TABLE 11–15. LISREL Symbol Glossary

Symbol	Character	Description
η	eta	Vector of latent dependent variables
ξ	xi	Vector of latent independent variables
ζ	zetz	Vector of residuals (errors—random disturbances)
β	Beta	Matrix of the direct effects of latent dependent variables on other latent dependent variables
γ	Gamma	Direct effects of latent independent variables on the latent dependent variables
ε	epsilon	Vector of error terms
δ	delta	Vector of error terms
y		Observed dependent variable
x		Observed independent variable
Φ	Phi	Covariance matrix of the latent independent variables
Ψ	Psi	Covariance matrix of the residuals
Θ_ε	Theta$_\varepsilon$	Covariance matrix of the ε error terms
$\Theta_{\varepsilon\delta}$	Theta$_\delta$	Covariance matrix of the δ error terms
$\lambda^{(x)}_{bi}$	lambda$_{bi}$	Path arrow from ξ_i to x_b
$\lambda^{(y)}_{ag}$	lambda$_{ag}$	Path arrow from η_g to y_a
β_{gh}	beta$_{gh}$	Path arrow from η_h to η_g
γ_{gi}	gamma$_{gi}$	Path arrow from ξ_i to η_g
ϕ_{ij}	phi$_{ij}$	Path arrow from ξ_j to ξ_i
Ψ_{gh}	psi$_{gh}$	Path arrow from ζ_h to ζ_g
$\theta^{(\delta)}_{ab}$	theta$^{(\delta)}_{ab}$	Path arrow from δ_b to δ_a
$\theta^{(\varepsilon)}_{cd}$	theta$^{(\varepsilon)}_{cd}$	Path arrow from ε_d to ε_c

percent of the variance, are musical background, musical aptitude, and scholastic achievement. These are the same independent latent traits used in the latent trait model. Theory grade loads with the scholastic achievement variables as would be expected from the previous path analysis of these variables.

The overall goodness of fit for the latent trait model is tested with chi-square. In this case, the fit is quite good ($\chi^2 = 8.91$, $df = 9$, $p < .445$). The model accounts for 52 percent of the variance in the latent trait of theoretical understanding. The model indicates that scholastic achievement has significant impact upon theoretical understanding, musical background has considerably less influence, and musical aptitude is inversely related to theoretical understanding of first-year college music majors. Note that a number of the measured independent variables have error terms that are quite large. The ability of latent trait modeling to compensate for this error is demonstrated as the model does statistically fit the data and accounts for a significant proportion of the variance in theoretical understanding.

MULTIDIMENSIONAL SCALING

Scaling Concepts

Multidimensional scaling refers to a number of methods that provide spatial representations of the relationships between variables on a map (Green, Carmone, and Smith, 1989; Kruskal and Wish, 1978). The map's geometric representation of the data, usually in a Euclidean space of few dimensions, provides a visual means of interpreting the interrelationships of the variables and the variables' dimensionality (Young, 1987). The same mathematical models as employed by factor and discriminant analysis form the basis of multidimensional scaling (Nunnally, 1978). However, multidimen-

TABLE 11–16. Maximum Likelihood Factor Analysis of Harrison's (1990b) Data

Scree Test of Harrison Data

Number of Factors	Eigenvalue	% of Variance	Cumulative %
1	2.70	38.5	38.5
2	1.18	16.9	55.5
3	1.01	14.5	69.9
4	0.72	10.2	80.2
5	0.58	8.2	88.4
6	0.47	6.7	95.0
7	0.35	5.0	100.0

	Pattern Matrix			Structure Matrix		
	Musical Background	Musical Aptitude	Scholastic Achievement	Musical Background	Musical Aptitude	Scholastic Achievement
Piano Experience	1.03	−0.22	−0.09	0.99	0.22	0.19
Total Years	0.41	0.14	0.17	0.50	0.34	0.36
SAT Verbal	−0.10	0.03	0.63	0.24	0.55	0.79
SAT Math	−0.02	0.22	0.69	0.09	0.31	0.62
Theory Grade	0.16	−0.11	0.73	0.34	0.29	0.72
CMAP Tonal	0.02	0.98	−0.09	0.27	0.94	0.39
CMAP Rhythm	0.02	0.28	0.07	0.11	0.31	0.20
Factor Correlation Matrix						
Musical Background	1.00					
Scholastic Achievement	0.28	1.00				
Musical Aptitude	0.29	0.49	1.00			

Abbreviations: CMAP = College Musical Aptitude Profile; SAT = Scholasti c Achievement Test.

sional scaling emphasizes the visual analysis of the variables in a space that reflects the variables' perceived similarities (Miller, 1989, p. 62).

Multidimensional scaling methods employ proximities of variables as input (Kruskal and Wish, 1978). The *proximities* are numbers that represent perceived similarities or differences among the variables. Typically, data are obtained by asking subjects to judge the similarity between two psychological objects. Computational methods are available that allow the use of data reflecting most levels of measurement. However, ordinal data tend to be most commonly employed. Correlations can be considered proximities as they may be conceived as indices of similarity or differences and are appropriate for analysis with multidimensional scaling (Kruskal and Wish, 1978, pp. 10–11).

Miller (1989) cites a number of advantages for multidimensional scaling: It has enormous data reduction power, subjects can easily make the similarity judgments often used for multidimensional scaling, it is easier to visualize and inter-

pret than factor analysis, the dimensions do not require specification prior to the analysis, in more complex stimulus domains it may sort out those attributes that are not important in making the required judgments, data of ordinal and nominal levels can be analyzed, and the data need not be related linearly.

An Application of Multidimensional Scaling

Larson (1977) presented the results of an investigation into undergraduate music majors' aural skills of melodic error detection; melodic dictation; and melodic sight singing in diatonic, chromatic, and atonal pitch categories. As part of his results, Larson presented a matrix of intercorrelations among the various aural tasks. An application of multidimensional scaling can be demonstrated by using Larson's correlations as proximity indices because they do indicate the similarity of the various aural tasks. The purpose

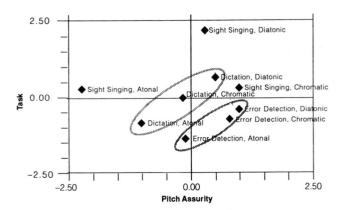

FIGURE 11–8. Multidimensional Scaling Solution of Larson's (1977) Data.

of scaling these data will be (1) to determine the similarities of the nine aural task combinations and (2) to identify the major dimensions characterized by the scaling procedures.

Figure 11–8 presents the variables as points in the two-dimensional Euclidean space of a solution that accounts for 99.1 percent of the variance in the scaled data. The center vertical and horizontal axes represent the two dimensions of the solution. The vertical dimension was interpreted as "task" while the horizontal dimension was interpreted as "pitch assurity." These interpretations were based on the variables' location along the two center axes. The error detection variables cluster along a diagonal plane, as do the dictation variables, and, with the exception of chromatic sight-singing, the sight-singing variables do as well. The tasks appear to be ordered from easy to difficult, with sight singing being the easiest and error detection being the most difficult. Another grouping of the variables can also be made. The atonal variables form a grouping in a diagonal plane opposite to those marked in the figure. The diatonic variables also group well in a similar diagonal plane. With the exception of chromatic sight singing, the chromatic variables form along this diagonal plane. As in the diagonal task planes, the pitch variables appear to be ordered from easy to difficult, with diatonic pitch tasks being the easiest and atonal pitch tasks being the most difficult. The chromatic sight-singing variable defies the overall logic of the map presented here. It could be that sight singing, a production task, interacts differently with pitch structure than the listening tasks of dictation and error detection.

NONPARAMETRIC STATISTICS

Fundamental Concepts

Nonparametric statistical tests have great value in music education as they are based on much less stringent assumptions than parametric statistics described to this point. The primary assumptions of nonparametric statistics are that the observations are independent and that there is underlying continuity to the variable in some cases (Conover, 1980; Gibbons, 1985; Siegel and Castellan, 1988). No assumption is made about the underlying distribution of the population from which the sample was drawn. Nonparametric statistics require only nominal or ordinal data. Parametric statistics, by contrast, require interval or ratio level data, make assumptions about the specific population distribution, and make inferences about population parameters.

Gibbons (1985, p. 29) suggests that nonparametric statistics should be chosen over parametric statistics when the assumptions required by parametric statistics are not satisfied by the data, when the fewest number of assumptions are met by the data, when sample size is small, and when a particular nonparametric test will provide a more adequate test of the null hypothesis. The mathematical simplicity of nonparametric tests adds to their attractiveness in that not only is their calculation simpler, but it is more likely that the user will understand and apply the tests appropriately (Conover, 1980).

Nonparametric Statistical Tests

Selection of the appropriate nonparametric statistical test depends on the particular null hypothesis being tested and the data's level of measurement. There are fewer nonparametric statistical tests than parametric tests. However, statistics are available for most situations involving traditional experimental designs. The nonparametric tests described here focus on tests relating to a single sample, related samples, independent samples, and measures of association. Single-sample tests are for those situations where only one group of subjects has been measured. Related samples are for when two samples have been measured but the samples are related in some way such as the same group being measured twice. Independent samples are two or more measured samples that are not related in any systematic way. Measures of association provide a means for determining the similarity or difference between two measures. For an easy-to-follow description of how to calculate the majority of statistics described here, the reader is directed to the work of Moore in the text by Madsen and Moore (1978) *Experimental Research in Music: Workbook in Design and Statistical Tests*.

One-Sample Tests In the case of research in which the entire set of observations on a variable are to be analyzed, the family of nonparametric one-sample tests may be appropriate.

CHI-SQUARE GOODNESS-OF-FIT TEST. The chi-square goodness-of-fit test determines whether an observed number of cases in each of a number of categories is the same as that expected by some theory. The procedure requires independent observations of a variable with the observations grouped into categories. The statistic assumes that the sample is random and that the variable has at least nominal level of measurement.

Suppose an elementary music teacher had taught a unit on tempo. The instructional goal was to have at least 70 percent

TABLE 11–17. Chi-Square Goodness-of-Fit Test
on Fictitious Data

Category	Observed	Expected	Residual
Faster	78	70.00	8.00
No Change	15	15.00	.00
Slower	7	15.00	−8.00
Total	100		

	Chi-Square	D.F.	Significance
	5.181	2	.075

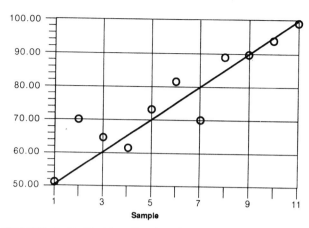

FIGURE 11–9. Fictitious Random Sampling of 11 Scores for a Band History Test.

of the 100 students able to identify a change to faster when it occurred in music. The teacher assumed that 15 percent of the remaining group would not be able to detect any change and that the other 15 percent would indicate that the piece went slower when it indeed went faster. The teacher gave a single-item exam to determine the student's attainment. The data of this fictitious situation are presented in Table 11–17.

Note that in Table 11–17 the chi-square value has degrees of freedom equal to the number of categories minus one. The significance level in our fictitious sample is .075; this is larger than the .05 value of significance traditionally used as the lower bound of significance. Therefore, the statistic indicates no significant difference between the data's observed distribution and the expected distribution. The teacher's assumption that 70 percent of the students would be able to correctly identify an increase of tempo, with 15 percent not being able to detect a tempo change and 15 percent wrongly identifying a decrease in tempo, is supported by the chi-square goodness-of-fit test.

KOLMOGOROV GOODNESS-OF-FIT TEST. Goodness-of-fit tests determine if a random sample of some population matches an expected distribution. That is, goodness-of-fit tests test the null hypothesis that the unknown distribution of the sample is indeed known (Conover, 1980, p. 344). The example cited for the chi-square goodness-of-fit test actually tested the teacher's belief (hypothesis) that 70 percent of the class would be able to correctly identify increases in tempo, 15 percent would be unable to detect any change, and 15 percent would detect a decrease in tempo (a known distribution).

The Kolmogorov goodness-of-fit test provides a means for determining goodness of fit with ordinal data and provides a means for establishing a confidence region for the unknown distribution function. This test has benefits over the chi-square test when sample size is small and appears to be a more powerful test in general. The Kolmogorov test assumes that the data were drawn from a random sample and have some unknown distribution.

Suppose, for example, that a band director gave the 72 band students in the band a test to measure their knowledge of the historical aspects of the music that was being studied. A random sampling of 11 students' scores was taken to determine if the scores were distributed evenly between the minimum score of the class (50) and the maximum score of the

class (100). Figure 11–9 presents the data for the 11 randomly selected students with the hypothesized distribution of the scores plotted as a solid line. Note that distributions that are spread in such a manner are known as uniform distributions. The Kolmogorov goodness-of-fit test for this sample was .494 with an alpha level of .967. Thus, the band director can be statistically certain that the distribution of scores is uniform between the minimum and maximum of this test as based on this sample.

BINOMIAL TEST. The binomial test is used with dichotomous data, that is, data having each individual data point in one of only two categories. For instance, a question is answered either right or wrong, a student listens to the music or does not, or a trumpet student knows the fingerings or does not. Such data are tested with the binomial distribution, which indicates the probability p that the first of two possible events will occur and that the opposite event will occur with probability $q = 1 - p$. The binomial test has great versatility and can be applied in a considerable number of situations (Conover, 1980, p. 96).

The data for the binomial test are the outcomes of a number of trials where the result can be only one thing or another such as right or wrong, good or bad. Each of the trials is assumed to be independent of the others. The outcome of a trial is assumed to have the same probability for each and every trial.

Kuhn and Booth (1988) presented the results of a study on the influence of ornamented or plain melodic activity on tempo perception. In a series of tables they presented binomial comparisons of 95 elementary students' responses to various test items. The items required the students to listen to two musical examples and respond by indicating whether the second example was faster or slower than the first example or whether the tempos were the same (pp. 143–144). To demonstrate the use of binomial comparisons, the data of test item 2 will be used. Students responses for this item, in which there was no change in the second example, were 18 indicating slower, 53 indicating no change, and 24 indicating faster.

Figure 11–10 presents the various possible binomial comparisons for these data where the comparisons were tested for an even distribution of students in each of the two possible categories. That is, the test proportion was .50 or 50:50. Note that both the comparisons made with the correct no-change category are significantly different ($p < .05$) from being the expected proportion of .50. The comparison between the incorrect categories of faster and slower are not significantly different from the expected 50:50 proportion. The fourth pie chart was not contained in the Kuhn and Booth tables, but demonstrates a practical application of this test for music classroom situations. Consider a situation where it was desired that 70 percent of all the elementary students taking a tempo perception test would correctly identify that no change had occurred to the Kuhn and Booth item. After the number of students answering incorrectly either faster or slower were added together, the resulting value could be tested with the number of students answering the item correctly to determine whether the students had attained the 70 percent criterion. As can be seen, the number of correct responses does not achieve the 70 percent criterion level as indicated by the probability value p being less than .05.

Contingency Tables A contingency table is a matrix of frequency data representing two or more categorical variables. Consider the situation where a high school music program wishes to know the makeup of their students by sex (male or female) and primary ensemble participation (band, chorus,

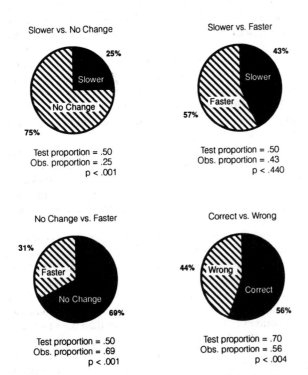

FIGURE 11–10. Binomial Comparisons Using the Data of Kuhn and Booth (1988).

orchestra). The data could be displayed in a matrix such as the following, with sex across the rows of the matrix and ensemble type down the columns of the matrix:

	Band	Chorus	Orchestra
Male	34	30	12
Female	42	67	29

Contingency tables are usually described by their number of rows and number of columns; this is a 2 × 3 contingency table. As can easily be noted, contingency tables display a large amount of information based on nominal data. Additional information could be displayed in such a table, including various percentages based on the number in the rows, the number in the columns, or the total number contained in the table.

CHI-SQUARE TEST FOR INDEPENDENCE. Statistics are also available to determine various characteristics of a contingency table. Chief among these is the chi-square test for independence. The statistic assumes that the sample has been drawn at random and that each observation can be categorized into only one of the cells in the matrix. The hypothesis tested by this statistic is that the two categorical variables that make up the table are independent of each other.

Flowers and Dunne-Sousa (1990) reported a study of 93 preschool "children's abilities to echo short pitch patterns in relation to maintenance of a tonal center in self-chosen and taught songs" (p. 102). Within the report, a 3 × 3 contingency table is presented of students' age by self-chosen song category: modulating, somewhat modulating, and not modulating from the tonal center. Data presented in this table are used to provide an example of the results from a common computer program (CROSSTABS from SPSS^X, 1988) that demonstrates the amount of information that can be obtained from such frequency counts (Table 11–18). The table is an exact copy of the output from the SPSS^x computer program. Note that the area at the top left of the display describes the content of each of the cells. The top-most value in each cell is the frequency for that particular combination of age and self-chosen song. The reader is encouraged to compare the table presented in the excellent article by Flowers and Dunne-Sousa with the computer output presented here. The authors reported the chi-square test for independence for this contingency table, which is contained at the bottom of Table 11–18. Note the significant chi-square value indicating that the two categorical variables are not independent. Rather, age is related to the ability to sing a self-chosen song on the tonal center. This led Flowers and Dunne-Sousa to conclude that "as would be expected, 3-year-olds comprised the largest proportion of modulating singers" (p. 107).

MEASURES OF ASSOCIATION FOR CONTINGENCY TABLES. The smallest form of contingency tables to which the chi-square test of independence can be applied is the 2 × 2 table. When a researcher wishes to establish the degree of association or relationship between the two categorical variables that define the contingency table, the *phi coefficient* is the most ap-

TABLE 11–18. 3 × 3 Contingency Table Using the Data of Flowers and Dunne-Sousa (1990): Age (Preschool Students Age) by SONG (Type of Song Selected)

AGE	Count Row Pct Col Pct Tot Pct	Modulating 1	Somewhat Modulating 2	Not Modulating 3	Row Total
3 years old	3	13 68.4 31.0 14.4	5 26.3 14.7 5.6	1 5.3 7.1 1.1	19 21.1
4 years old	4	10 33.3 23.8 11.1	11 36.7 32.4 12.2	9 30.0 64.3 10.0	30 33.3
5 years old	5	19 46.3 45.2 21.1	18 43.9 52.9 20.0	4 9.8 28.6 4.4	41 45.6
Column Total		42 46.7	34 37.8	14 15.6	90 100.0

Chi-Square	Value	DF	Significance
Pearson	10.35247	4	.03489

propriate. This coefficient is a special case of the Pearson product-moment correlation (Conover, 1980). It is normally calculated from the chi-square value, which will always be positive. Therefore, the phi coefficient is a value that ranges from 0, independence or no association, to +1, dependence or perfect association.

For tables larger than 2 × 2, *Cramer's V* provides an appropriate statistic. It is a slightly modified form of the phi coefficient that accounts for a greater number of rows or columns. Cramer's V, because it is usually calculated from the phi coefficient, will also have a value that ranges from 0, independence, to +1, dependence. Cramer's V obtained from Flowers and Dunne-Sousa's (1990) data is .24.

The contingency coefficient provides another index of association. Its lowest value is 0, but its maximum value varies with the size of the table. The larger the table, the larger the potential maximum value (Gibbons, 1985). It is most appropriate when both nominal variables have the same number of categories. A contingency coefficient of .32 was obtained for the Flowers and Dunne-Sousa (1990) data. Note that there is a discrepancy between the Cramer's V and the contingency coefficient. In the Flowers and Dunne-Sousa case, Cramer's V is the more conservative.

Whereas the measures of association described above are those most commonly employed, a considerable number of other measures of association are available for analysis of contingency tables. These statistics all serve different functions in the analysis of the degree of association between the two categorical variables that comprise the contingency table. For further information, the reader is directed to statistical texts that emphasize contingency table analysis.

Tests For Two Related Samples

SIGN TEST. The sign test compares the differences between pairs of variables by using the sign of the difference between each pair. That is, if the second value of a pair is larger, a plus (+) is assigned; if the second value is smaller, a minus (−) is assigned; and a tie is not counted. The data pairs must have some natural relationship to each other, the data must be at least at the ordinal level of measurement, and the two variables should be mutually independent.

The data from 20 randomly selected high school band students who were measured on their preference for a band piece prior to rehearsing it and then measured again 6 weeks later just prior to the concert performance of this piece will be used to demonstrate the sign test (Asmus, 1987). The sign test will be used to determine whether the students' preference for the band work changed after the 6-week rehearsal period. The results of the analysis are presented in Table 11–19. From the table, we note that 15 students' preference actually declined while five of the students' preference increased. There were no ties. A significant difference ($p < .05$)

TABLE 11–19. Sign Test for Differences in Preference Before and After Rehearsal

Category	Students
− Differences (Preference 2 < Preference 1)	15
+ Differences (Preference 2 > Preference 1)	5
Ties	0
Total	20

2-Tailed $p < .04$

TABLE 11–20. Wilcoxon Matched-Pairs Signed Ranks Test of Price (1988) Data

	Mean Rank	Cases
− Ranks (postcourse < precourse)	13.93	14
+ Ranks (postcourse > precourse)	25.90	29
Ties (postcourse = precourse)		7
Total		50
$Z = -3.3568$	2-Tailed $p < .0008$	

TABLE 11–21. Cochran Q Test of Three Adjudicators' Success Ratings of 16 Marching Bands

	Unsuccessful	Successful
Music adjudicator	10	6
M and M Adjudicator	9	6
Percussion adjudicator	9	7

Number of Bands	Cochran Q	DF	$p <$
16	.4000	2	.8187

Abbreviations: M & M = marching and maneuvering.

between the first and second preference assessments is indicated. In other words, the students' preference for the band work did change significantly in a negative direction.

WILCOXON SIGNED RANKS TEST. The Wilcoxon signed ranks test is used to evaluate matched pairs of data from fairly small samples. The test assumes that the data are of at least the ordinal level of measurement and that the pairs are mutually independent.

Price (1988) used the Wilcoxon signed ranks test to determine if a music appreciation class affects the number of times a traditional composer is mentioned by students when "asked to list and rank their favorite composers" (p. 37). Price provides a thorough listing of these data in his Table 2. The results of the Wilcoxon signed ranks test on Price's data are presented here in Table 11–20.

The Price (1988) data analyzed with the Wilcoxon matched-pairs test produces a significant difference as indicated by the probability of $p < .0008$ for the test statistic Z. That is, there is a significant effect of the music appreciation class on the number of times formal traditional composers are mentioned by students who have completed the course. As the mean ranks in the table indicate, the students are likely to mention more formal, traditional composers after the course than before.

COCHRAN Q TEST. The Cochran Q Test is used to test the effect of a number of treatments when the effect of the treatment forms a dichotomous variable such as "success" or "failure." The data must be independent for each subject, the effects of the treatments are measured in the same manner for each treatment, and the subjects are assumed to have been randomly selected from the population. The Cochran

Q test tests the contention that all the treatments are equally as effective.

Three adjudicators' ratings of 16 marching bands participating in a contest will be used to demonstrate an application of the Cochran Q test. The bands were rated in the categories of music performance, marching and maneuvering, and percussion by an adjudicator assigned to each category. The success ratings were assigned by giving those bands with scores greater than the average in that category a success rating and those bands at or below the average in that category an unsuccessful rating. Table 11–21 presents the results of the Cochran Q test on the successful-unsuccessful data to determine if the judges rated the bands in a similar manner. As the probability figure indicates, there were no significant differences between the ways the judges rated the bands.

FRIEDMAN TEST. The Friedman test is employed in the situation where each subject ranks two or more items on some continuum. The test assumes that each subject's ranking is independent of all the other subjects, that each subject is ranking the same items, and that all subjects rank the items along the same continuum. The Friedman test evaluates the contention that the ranked items are distributed evenly across the continuum on which they were ranked.

LeBlanc, Colman, McCrary, Sherrill, and Malin (1988) presented the results of a study of the effect of tempo variation on the preferences of six age groups for traditional jazz. As part of the study, the authors presented the results of Friedman tests for each age group to determine if tempo affected the preference rating for music. Table 11–22 presents the relevant data taken from the tables and text of the research re-

TABLE 11–22. Means and Friedman Tests of Tempo Effect on Preference From LeBlanc et al. (1988)

Grade Level	Slow	Moderately Slow	Moderately Fast	Fast	Chi-square	df	p <
3	2.99	3.24	3.92	3.99	150.76	3	.01
5	2.47	2.58	3.23	3.50	186.10	3	.01
7	1.91	2.07	2.52	2.64	144.66	3	.01
9,10	2.07	2.40	2.82	2.88	164.38	3	.01
11,12	2.15	2.37	2.83	3.08	213.18	3	.01
College	2.88	3.18	3.51	3.58	91.54	3	.01

Note: The preference ratings had a possible range of 1 to 7.

port. Note that there are significant differences for each of the age groups. An inspection of the means led the authors to conclude that increasingly faster tempos brought increasingly higher preference ratings.

Independent Samples

MEDIAN TEST. The median test is conducted in situations where there are a number of samples measured on the same variable. The test does not require that the number of subjects in each sample be equal. The test does assume that each sample has been drawn at random, that the samples are independent of each other, and that the measurement scale of the variable is at least at the ordinal level. The median test is used to test the contention that all the populations from which the samples were drawn have the same median.

Consider the hypothetical case where a choral music teacher wanted to know if different forms of vocal warm-up would affect vocal performance. The teacher used three different classes: One received no warm-up (control group); another received a warm-up using staccato "ha" on a series of scales, rhythmic patterns, and arpeggios; while the final class received a warm-up on "mah-may-mee-moh-moo" on a comparable series of scales, rhythmic patterns, and arpeggios. After the warm-up, each student was tested as to vocal quality and flexibility using a performance assessment instrument the choral teacher had devised. Because the classes were intact, there was unequal sample size across the classes. The median test was applied to the vocal scores to determine whether the medians were different between the groups. As the results of this analysis indicate (Table 11–23), there was a significant difference between the medians. The table indicates that the control group had more scores below the median than any other group. The distribution of scores above and below the median was evenly split for the "mah-may . . ." warm-up group while the "ha" warm-up group had the majority of scores above the median. It could be concluded that the "ha" warm-up procedure was the most effective in this fictitious example.

MANN-WHITNEY U. The Mann-Whitney U test is used in situations similar to those of the median test, except that it is used when there are only two samples. The test is considered more powerful than the median test because it uses rankings of each sample in its calculation. There is an assumption with this statistic that the samples have been drawn at random from their populations, that the measurement scale of the variable is at least ordinal, and that the two samples are independent of each other. The Mann-Whitney

U tests the contention that the two groups have been drawn from the same population.

Flowers (1988) used the Mann-Whitney U test to determine differences between two groups of elementary education majors on their pretest-posttest differences of rated preference for four symphonic works. One of the two groups received music appreciation lessons on the symphonic works while the other group taught the music to elementary school students. The analysis performed on the posttest gain scores led Flowers to conclude that, "although both groups had increased their preference ratings, there was no significant difference between the groups in amount of gain ($z = -1.45, p = .15$)" (p. 25).

KOLMOGOROV-SMIRNOV TWO-SAMPLE TEST. The Kolmogorov-Smirnov two-sample test is used to test the contention that the scores in two independent samples are distributed in the same manner. The assumptions of this test are that the samples have been drawn at random, that the samples are mutually independent of each other, and that the data are at least at the ordinal level of measurement.

The data from a marching band contest will be used to demonstrate the Kolmogorov-Smirnov two-sample test. In the contest, bands competed in one of two divisions: Class A and Open Class. Class A bands tended to be smaller and not as advanced musically or in their presentation as the Open Class bands. The total scores five adjudicators assigned in the areas of music performance, marching and maneuvering, general effect, percussion, and auxiliary groups are used as data. The Kolmogorov-Smirnov test is applied to determine if the two distributions of total scores were the same for Class A bands as for Open Class bands. The results appear in Table 11–24 and Figure 11–11 (p. 174). A significant difference is detected between the score distributions of the Class A bands and the Open Class bands. As can be seen in Figure 11–11, Open Class bands not only had higher total scores than Class A bands, but the distribution of scores has a different shape.

KRUSKAL-WALLIS ANALYSIS OF VARIANCE. The Kruskal-Wallis ANOVA is used in the situation where there are more than two independent samples. The statistic is based upon a ranking of the entire set of data to test the contention that all of the population distributions represented by the samples are identical. The assumptions are that the samples are drawn from their respective populations at random, that the samples are mutually independent, and

TABLE 11–23. Median Test of Hypothetical Choral Data

	Control Group	Warm-up "ha"	Warm-up "mah-may . . ."
Scores greater than the median	3	11	9
Scores less than the median	15	3	9

Cases	Median	Chi-Square	DF	Significance
50	27.0	12.3303	2	.0021

TABLE 11–24. Kolmogorov-Smirnov 2-Sample Test of Marching Band Contest Scores

Band Level	n
Class A	12
Open Class	4
Total	16

K-S Z	2-Tailed p <
1.732	.005

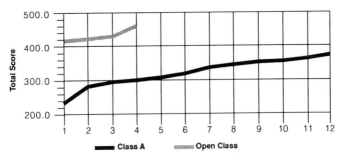

FIGURE 11–11. Distributions of Sorted Marching Band Scores.

that the variable upon which all subjects were assessed is at least at the ordinal level of measurement.

Flowers (1983), in a study of vocabulary and listening instruction on nonmusicians' descriptions of changes in music, used the Kruskal-Wallis ANOVA to test for differences between four experimental groups on pre-post verbal description gain scores. The verbal description scores were obtained by counting the number of references to elements of music made in response to changes heard in a musical excerpt. The four experimental groups included a contact control group, which received no instruction in vocabulary or listening experiences; a vocabulary group, which received instruction in music vocabulary; a listening group, which was provided with music listening experiences; and a vocabulary plus listening group, which received both vocabulary instruction and listening experiences. The Kruskal-Wallis test indicated a significant difference in the mean rankings of the gain scores for each of the four groups ($H = 17.25$, $df = 3$, $p < .001$).

DUNN'S MULTIPLE COMPARISON PROCEDURE. Following a significant Kruskal-Wallis one-way analysis of variance, Dunn's multiple-comparison procedure can be applied to determine the exact location of the mean rank differences. This allows the researcher to determine which of the populations included in the Kruskal-Wallis analysis significantly differ from each other. Flowers (1983), in the study described above, followed the significant Kruskal-Wallis analysis of variance with Dunn's multiple-comparison procedure on the four groups in her study. She found that "vocabulary plus listening produced significantly higher verbal descriptive scores than vocabulary only or contact control conditions, but not significantly different from listening only" (p. 184). Table 11–25 duplicates that provided by Flowers to support her conclusion.

TABLE 11–25. Mean Ranks of Pre-Posttest Differences Described by Flowers (1983)

Contact Control	Vocabulary Only	Listening Only	Vocabulary Plus Listening
46.44	54.37	67.50	81.69

Note: Table is duplicated from Flowers (1983). Underlines represent no differences at the .05 level. Those means not connected are significantly different.

GRAPHIC DATA ANALYSIS METHODS

For most individuals, especially those with little familiarity with statistics, graphic displays of research data provide the most easily grasped methods for understanding the data. The advent of small, yet powerful microcomputers with graphic capabilities has created a wealth of systems for the graphing of research data. Graphic methods can be as simple as a display of the number of people within a certain category through the use of bar graph or pie chart or as complex as the interaction of data through real-time display of data in multidimensional space.

Graphic methods of data analysis are expanding daily. Graphic methods no longer entail only the display of data; graphic interfaces can be used to cause the calculation of various statistics. An example of this was provided in this chapter's section on path analysis. As a whole, graphic methods help the researcher better conceptualize the research and thus allow a better understanding of the variables involved and the nature of the research study than is possible through purely numerical methods. Graphic methods have the additional benefit of utilizing less of the researcher's time in analysis of the data because of the relative ease of interpreting graphic data displays over numeric data displays, though graphic data displays do use a much greater proportion of computer time.

Throughout this chapter various forms of graphic displays have been provided to assist the reader in understanding the various concepts being discussed. This section will present some of the major graphic methods in greater detail. The methods surveyed will only skim the surface of the tremendous number of graphic analysis methods available.

Graphing Frequencies

One-Dimensional Frequency Plots The graphing of frequencies is often needed when the characteristics of a population or phenomenon are required. The graphing of frequencies can be done through the use of bar graphs or pie charts. Figure 11–12 presents a pie chart that displays the proportion of responses teachers made in the final rating of an inservice workshop experience. Note that out of the four possible categories in the rating scale, 84 percent were either

No "poor" ratings were indicated.

FIGURE 11–12. Teacher Ratings About the Quality of an In-service Workshop.

Distribution of Attribution Responses of Austin (1988)

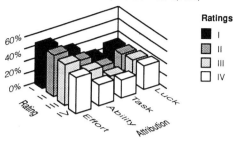

FIGURE 11–13. Proportion of Attributions for Different Division Ratings.

"excellent" or "good." The "fair" portion of the pie chart has been exploded to emphasize the 16 percent of the teachers who may not have had the level of experience that they had actually desired.

Three-Dimensional Frequency Plots An extension of the single-dimension frequency plot is the three-dimensional frequency plot. Consider the data of Austin (1988), where, in a study of elementary band students' music motivation, he provided the number of responses in the attribution categories of "Luck," "Task Difficulty," "Ability," and "Effort" for each of the recipients of four different division ratings: I, II, III, and IV. The frequency data were converted to percentages and are graphically displayed in Figure 11–13. This display is a three-dimensional bar graph where the vertical dimension represents the frequency of response and the other two dimensions represent the various categories involved. It can be seen in the figure that the most-used attribution category by the elementary students for all the division categories was "Effort." The least used was "Task Difficulty". Note, however, that there seems to be a slight increase in the use of Luck attributions with lower performance ratings.

Describing the Distribution of Interval Data

Frequency Polygon The frequency polygon displays data in line graph form with the vertical or *y*-axis representing the frequency with which the particular score occurred. The horizontal or *x*-axis of the frequency polygon is the range of interval scores for the variable under analysis. Figure 11–14 presents a frequency polygon of the scores participants in a

summer music workshop made on a 12-item knowledge test. The figure shows that the most commonly occurring score was 9 and that moving away from this score the frequency of the scores declines. If the sample size approached infinity, we would expect the frequency polygon to resemble the normal curve.

Frequency Histogram The frequency histogram is similar to the frequency polygon, but rather than having the information displayed as a line graph, a bar graph format is used. The *x*-axis remains the range of scores, and the *y*-axis is the frequency of occurrence of the particular scores. Figure 11–15 (p. 176) presents, among other information, the frequency histograms for two different sets of marching band contest scores. The sets of scores are for the same bands at the same contest in two different years. On top of each histogram, the normal curve has been plotted for the data with the same mean and representing the overall distribution of the scores. As can be seen, neither set of scores is distributed normally. Most of the scores tend to be below the mean.

Box Plots Above each frequency histogram in Figure 11–15 is a box plot that also characterizes the distribution of the respective set of marching band scores. The arrows indicate what each of the different points on the box plot represents. If the scores were normally distributed, the median line would be in the center of the box and the box would be centered on the line representing the range of scores from the minimum to the maximum. The small vertical tick mark at the extremes of the range line presents the tenth and nineti-

FIGURE 11–14. Frequency Polygon of Scores on a Summer Music Workshop Knowledge Test.

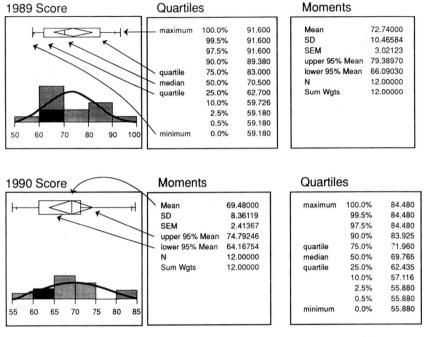

FIGURE 11–15. Frequency Histograms and Box Plots of Marching Bands' Contest Scores for Two Different Years.

eth percentiles respectively. Had the distribution been more normal, the other percentiles in the quantiles table would have been displayed. The diamond characterizes the distribution's mean and the 95 percent confidence intervals for the mean. If the distribution were normal, the median line would appear in the exact center of the diamond.

Figure 11–15 also characterizes the growing trend for graphics analysis programs to provide a wide variety of statistical information. The figure is a slightly modified form of the output from the graphics analysis package JMP (SAS, 1989). The modifications were necessary so that the arrows could be added to define the various points in the box plots.

Plots of Means

Plotting the means for various subgroups on a variable or plotting the means on a number of different variables for a particular sample is a common practice in the analysis and reporting of data. Such plots help determine particular trends inherent in the data or allow the researcher to determine relationships between the groups of variables of interest. In most cases, the vertical y-axis characterizes the value of the mean while the x-axis characterizes the particular subgroups or variables of interest.

One-Dimensional Mean Plots One of the most common forms of mean plots are those created after an analysis of variance that produced a significant interaction. The means for the various groups involved in the interaction are plotted

with the vertical y-axis representing the magnitude of the mean and the horizontal x-axis representing the grouping variable's categories. Kantorski (1986), as part of a study on the effects of accompaniment intervals and register on string instrumentalists' intonation, provided a graph of the significant register by accompaniment interaction that he obtained. Figure 11–16 is a copy of that graph. The crossed lines indicate the interaction. It can be noted that the upper register tends to be further from tempered intonation for all intervals but the unison. For the case of unison intervals, the upper register more closely approximates tempered intonation than the lower register.

LeBlanc et al. (1988, p. 156) presented the results of a study on "the effect of four levels of tempo on the self-reported preferences of six different age-groups for traditional jazz music listening examples." In their report, the authors presented a figure that plotted the preference means across all tempos for each of the age groups. The values reported by the authors were used to replicate this graph in Figure 11–17. The original graph of LeBlanc and colleagues included only the linked squares. As can be seen, the means have a decidedly curvilinear form, with the preference for traditional jazz dropping to its lowest point for the grade 7 group. This version of the graph has utilized the capabilities of the graphing program to overlay a curvilinear trend line and its associated statistics. The fit of the curved line is extremely good with these data. This is verified by the R^2 value, which indicates that 94.5 percent of the variance in the means is accounted for the curved line. This represents an R value of .972, indicating a very substantial fit.

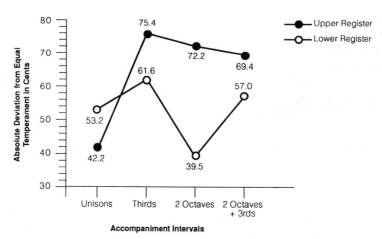

FIGURE 11–16. Plot of Two-Way ANOVA Interaction of Register and Accompaniment Intervals Duplicated from Kantorski (1986).

Two-Dimensional Mean Plots The plots of means in which there are two grouping variables of interest are often best handled by plotting the data in three-dimensional space: one dimension representing the magnitude of the means and the other two dimensions representing the two categories of interest. The data of LeBlanc et al. (1988) described above will be utilized to demonstrate this application. The effect of the grade level and tempo categories are characterized in a single graph in Figure 11–18 (p. 178). The curvilinear relationship between grade level and preference for traditional jazz noted earlier is clearly seen in this three-dimensional plot. The effect, as shown by this plot, is most pronounced for slow pieces, though there appears to be a steeper slope for the lower grades at faster tempos. The figure also indicates a tendency in all age groups for preference to rise as the tempo becomes faster. This effect is lowest for the grade 7 group, which has the overall lowest preference for traditional jazz.

Plotting Relationships

Scattergrams Scattergrams are the plotting of each individual data point by indicating the point's relative magnitude on two variables. One variable's magnitude is characterized by the vertical *y*-axis, and the other variable's magnitude is characterized by the horizontal *x*-axis. The marching band contest data for two consecutive years will be utilized to provide an example of the scattergram. Figure 11–19 (p. 178) displays the location of the juncture of each participating band's 1989 contest score with their 1990 contest score. It can be seen that the scores are distributed in a diagonal form moving from lower left to upper right. This ascending diagonal form is characteristic of variables that have a positive relationship. Variables with a negative relationship distribute the scores in a diagonal from upper left to lower right. No relationship would be indicated by a random spread of the points on the graph.

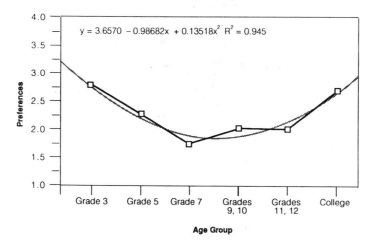

FIGURE 11–17. Plot of Jazz Preference Means from LeBlanc et al. (1988).

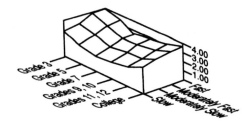

FIGURE 11–18. Three-Dimensional Plot of the Effect of Grade Level and Tempo on Means for Traditional Jazz Obtained by LeBlanc et al. (1988).

Figure 11–19 has the linear trend line plotted on the graph. The tabular information indicates that the two sets of scores have 70 percent of their variance in common. The dotted lines represent the 95 percent confidence intervals for scores predicted with the displayed regression information.

Multidimensional Graphing Multidimensional graphing is possible today in real time. This form of graphing allows items to be plotted as in a scattergram with an additional one or more dimensions added. Usually multidimensional graphing limits the plots to three-dimensional space as this is all that can be easily handled on a computer screen. Each dimension of the space represents another interval or ratio level variable. The interesting aspect of multidimensional graphing is that the data can be "spun" in space so that the relationship between the three variables can be viewed from any possible angle.

Semantic differential data collected from high school students in response to two different musical excerpts provide an excellent example of multidimensional graphing. Semantic scales are bipolar adjectives, such as beautiful-ugly, separated by a seven-point continuum. Subjects respond to an

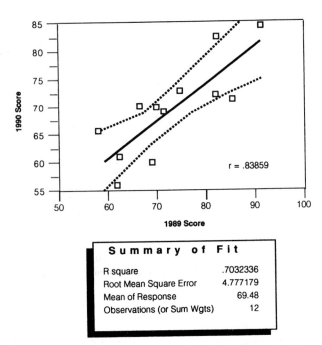

FIGURE 11–19. Plot of the Marching Band Scores for Two Consecutive Years.

object or event by checking the point along the continuum that best reflects their assessment of the object or event on the bipolar adjective scale. Semantic scales typically form three groupings: activity, evaluation, and potency. In the present data, a fourth grouping reflective of preference was added. The pattern weights from a three-dimension, common factor analysis of the data with oblique rotation were plotted using a graphing program with multidimensional capabilities. The plot was rotated in space until the formulation contained in Figure 11–20 was obtained.

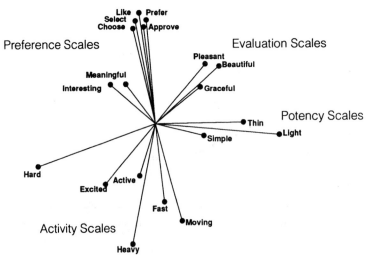

FIGURE 11–20. Three-Dimensional Plot of Four Sets of Semantic Differential Scales.

The display of Figure 11–20 was created by having lines drawn from the central point of the plot to each of the variable points within the graph. This is frequently a useful aid in identifying clusters of variables. The four groups of semantic scales are apparent in Figure 11–20. The figure reveals that the semantic scale hard-soft is across from the potency scales to which it belongs. This is because the scale should have been recorded to soft-hard; this would move it to within the cluster of potency scales. Note also that the interesting and meaningful scales cluster together slightly apart from the evaluation and preference groupings. However, these scales are in the same general region as preference and evaluation. The heavy-light scale is interesting in that it is clearly located within the region of the activity scales, but it is typically found in other studies within the potency scales.

WHEN TO USE WHAT STATISTIC

Selecting the most appropriate statistic to use in a particular situation must be tempered by theoretical and practical considerations. Theoretically, the selection of the statistic should be based on the purpose of the research as specifically described in a research question or null hypothesis. In addition, the characteristics of the data collected will reduce the number of statistical possibilities and aid greatly in the selection of the most appropriate statistic. Practically, researchers will be limited by the computing resources available and their knowledge of statistics. The hope is that the latter limitations have been lessened somewhat by this chapter as lack of knowledge is the weakest excuse for the application of inappropriate statistics.

The initial decision is to use either parametric or nonparametric statistics. Elsewhere in this chapter various facets of this issue have been discussed at length. After the calculation of descriptive statistics and, possibly, the production of frequency histograms and/or box plots, the decision can be made if the sample size is sufficient and the distribution is approximately normal. In general, if these conditions are

met, then parametric statistics should be applied. If not, nonparametric statistics should be applied.

The next decision is to determine the type of statistic that will be applied. This decision is based on the particular research question or null hypothesis that has been established to guide the research process. The choices for parametric statistics are somewhat greater than for nonparametric statistics, as can be seen in Figure 11–21.

The actual statistical procedure that is applied must be determined from both the particular null hypothesis and the type of data collected. For instance, a researcher may wish to predict from five variables, known to be normally distributed, which musical experience a student will have in high school: band, chorus, general music, orchestra. Because there is more than one predictor variable, one of two multivariate relational procedures could be applied: multiple regression or discriminant analysis. Because the dependent variable is a categorical variable that describes the group to which a person belongs, discriminant analysis would be the statistic of choice.

A flow chart describing the various categories of parametric statistics is contained in Figure 11–22 (p. 180), and a flow chart describing the various categories of nonparametric statistics is contained in Figure 11–23 (p. 180). These flow charts do not include all existing statistics, but do cover those that have been discussed in this chapter. These statistics, the authors believe, are those that have found the greatest applicability in music education.

CONCLUSION

This chapter has attempted to describe quantitative methods applicable in music education. It is hoped that, by description and example, the reader has become acquainted with the variety of available quantitative and statistical procedures that can provide significant insight into musical processes. Although they are not the entirety of available quantitative methods, the procedures described here are those

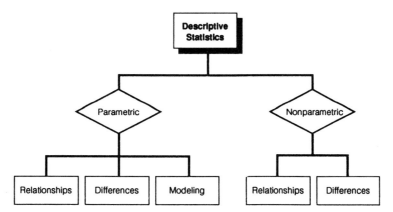

FIGURE 11–21. Flow Chart Leading to Major Type of Statistic To Be Applied.

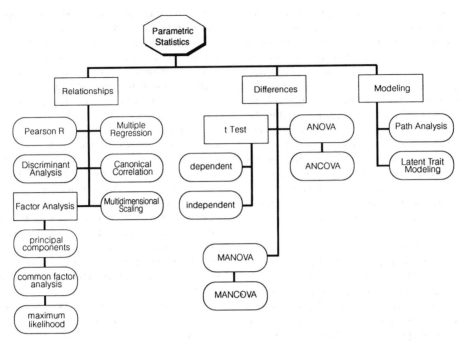

FIGURE 11–22. Flow Chart of Parametric Statistic Categories.

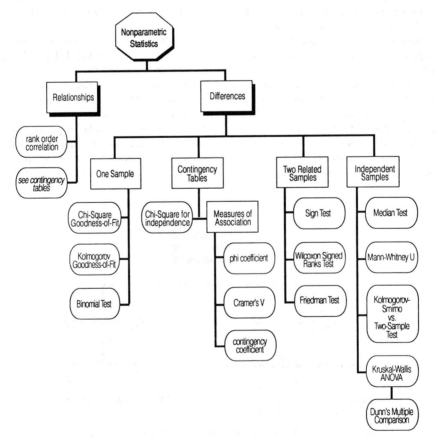

FIGURE 11–23. Flow Chart of Nonparametric Statistic Categories.

frequently applied in music education research, evaluation, and assessment or are those that, in the authors' belief, have significant potential to enhance knowledge about musical processes.

Today the reader need not be discouraged by the mathematical complexity of some of the procedures described here. Rather, if the researcher has selected the appropriate statistic, understands the assumptions that the statistic makes, and can interpret the results produced by the statistical procedure, modern computing power takes care of the mathematical details. This frees researchers from the tedium of the mathematics of the statistic and allows them to spend more time conceptualizing the research and understanding the implications of the results.

References

Asher, J. W. (1976). *Educational research and evaluation methods.* Boston: Little, Brown and Company.

Asmus, E. P. (1987). *The effects of rehearsing a musical work on the aesthetic perceptions of band students: A pilot study.* Paper presented at the Western Divisional Meeting of the Music Educators National Conference, Sacramento, April, 1987.

Asmus, E. P. (1989a). Factor analysis: A look at the technique through the data of Rainbow. *Bulletin of the Council for Research in Music Education, 101,* 1–29.

Asmus, E. P. (1989b). Computer-based modeling of music concepts for testing, evaluating, and refining theory. *Psychomusicology, 8,* 171–182.

Austin, J. R. (1988). The effect of music contest format on self-concept, motivation, achievement, and attitude of elementary band students. *Journal of Research in Music Education, 36,* 95–107.

Best, J. W. (1981). *Research in education* (4th ed.) Englewood Cliffs: Prentice-Hall.

Best, J. W., and Kahn, J. V. (1989). *Research in education* (6th ed.). Englewood Cliffs: Prentice-Hall.

Blalock, H. M. (Ed.) (1985). *Causal models in the social sciences* (2nd ed.). New York: Aldine Publishing.

Borg, W. R., and Gall, M. D. (1979). *Educational research: An introduction.* New York: Longman.

Boyle, J. D. (1974). Overview. In J. D. Boyle (Comp.), *Instructional objectives in music* (pp. 79–82). Vienna: Music Educators National Conference.

Boyle, J. D., and Radocy, R. E. (1987). *Measurement and evaluation of musical experiences.* New York: Schirmer Books.

Bruning, J. L., and Kintz, B. L. (1977). *Computational handbook of statistics* (3rd ed.) Glenview: Scott, Foresman.

Chatfield, C., and Collins, A. J. (1980). *Introduction to multivariate analysis.* London: Chapman and Hall.

Cohen, J. (1988). *Statistical power analysis for the behavioral sciences* (2nd ed.). Hillsdale: Lawrence Erlbaum Associates.

Conover, W. J. (1980). *Practical nonparametric statistics* (2nd ed.). New York: John Wiley.

Cooley, W. W. (October, 1978). Explanatory observational studies. *Educational Researcher, 7*(9), 9–15.

Cronbach, L. J. (1971). Test validation. In R. L. Thorndike (Ed.), *Educational measurement* (pp. 443–507). Washington: American Council on Education.

Cureton, E. E., and D'Agostino, R. B. (1983). *Factor analysis: An applied approach.* Hillsdale: Lawrence Erlbaum Associated.

Darrow, A., Haack, P., and Kuribayashi, F. (1987). Descriptors and preferences for Eastern and Western music by Japanese and American nonmusic majors. *Journal of Research in Music Education, 35,* 237–248.

Das, M. N., and Giri, N. C. (1986). *Design and analysis of experiments* (2nd ed.). New York: John Wiley.

Duke, R. A., and Prickett, C. A. (1987). The effect of differentially focused observation on evaluation of instruction. *Journal of Research in Music Education, 35,* 27–37.

Duncan, D. B. (1955). Multiple range and multiple F tests. *Biometrics, 11,* 1–42.

Ebel, R. L., and Frisbie, D. A. (1986). *Essentials of educational measurement* (4th ed.). Englewood Cliffs: Prentice-Hall.

Ecob, R., and Cuttance, P. (1987). An overview of structural equation modeling. In P. Cuttance, and R. Ecob (Eds.), *Structural modeling by example* (pp. 9–23). Cambridge: Cambridge University Press.

Edwards, A. L. (1968). *Experimental design in psychological research* (3rd ed.). New York: Holt, Rinehart, Winston.

Finkelstein, L. (1982). Theory and philosophy of measurement. In P. H. Sydenham (Ed.), *Handbook of measurement science* (Vol. 1). New York: John Wiley, pp. 1–30.

Flowers, P. J. (1983). The effect of instruction in vocabulary and listening on nonmusicians' descriptions of changes in music. *Journal of Research in Music Education, 31,* 179–189.

Flowers, P. J. (1988). The effects of teaching and learning experiences, tempo, and mode on undergraduates, and children's symphonic music preferences. *Journal of Research in Music Education, 36,* 19–34.

Flowers, P. J., and Dunne-Sousa, D. (1990). Pitch-pattern accuracy, tonality, and vocal range in preschool children's singing. *Journal of Research in Music Education, 38,* 102–114.

Gfeller, K., Darrow, A., and Hedden, S. K. (1990). Perceived effectiveness of mainstreaming in Iowa and Kansas schools. *Journal of Research in Music Education, 38,* 90–101.

Gibbons, J. D. (1985). *Nonparametric methods for quantitative analysis* (2nd ed.). Columbus: American Sciences Press.

Glass, G. V., and Hopkins, K. D. (1984). *Statistical methods in education and psychology.* Englewood Cliffs: Prentice-Hall.

Goodstein, R. E. (1987). An introduction to discriminant analysis. *Journal of Research in Music Education, 35,* 7–11.

Gorsuch, R. L. (1983). *Factor analysis* (2nd ed.). Hillsdale: Lawrence Erlbaum Associates.

Green, P. E., Carmone, Jr., F. J., and Smith, S. M. (1989). *Multidimensional scaling: Concepts and applications.* Boston: Allyn and Bacon.

Hair, J. F., Anderson, R. E., Tatham, R. L., and Grablowsky, B. J. (1984). *Multivariate data analysis with readings.* New York: Macmillan.

Hanneman, R. (1988). *Computer-assisted theory building: modeling dynamic social systems.* Newbury Park: Sage Publications.

Harnett, D. L. (1982). *Statistical methods* (3rd ed.). Reading: Addison-Wesley.

Harris, R. J. (1985). *A primer of multivariate statistics.* Orlando: Academic Press.

Harrison, C. S. (1990a). Relationships between grades in the components of freshman music theory and selected background variables. *Journal of Research in Music Education, 38,* 175–186.

Harrison, C. S. (1990b). Predicting music theory grades: The relative efficiency of academic ability, music experience, and musical aptitude. *Journal of Research in Music Education, 38,* 124–137.

Hays, W. L. (1988). *Statistics* (4th ed.). New York: Holt, Rinehart, and Wiston.

Hedden, S. K. (1982). Prediction of musical achievement in the elementary school. *Journal of Research in Music Education, 30,* 61–68.

Heller, G. N., and Radocy, R. E. (1983). On the significance: Addressing a basic problem in research. *Bulletin of the Council for Research in Music Education, 73,* 50–58.

Johnson, T. J., and Hess, R. J. (1970). *Tests in the arts.* St. Charles: Central Midwestern Regional Educational Laboratory.

Jöreskog, K G. (1979). Structural equation models in the social sciences: Specification, estimation and testing. In K. Jöreskog, and D. Sörbom (Eds.), *Advances in factor analysis and structural equation models* (pp. 105–127). Cambridge: Abt Books.

Jöreskog, K. G. (1982). The LISREL approach to causal model-building in the social sciences. In K. G. Jöreskog and H. Wold (Eds.), *Systems under indirect observation: Causality—structure—prediction* (pp. 81–99). Amsterdam: North-Holland Publishing.

Jöreskog, K. G., and Sörbom, D. (1989), LISREL 7.0 [Computer program]. Mooresville: Scientific Software.

Kachigan, S. K. (1986). *Statistical analysis: An interdisciplinary introduction to univariate and multivariate methods.* New York: Radius.

Kaiser, H. F., and Rice, J. (1974). Little Jiffy, Mark IV. *Educational and Psychological Measurement, 34,* 111–117.

Kantorski, V. J. (1986). String instrument intonation in upper and lower registers: The effects of accompaniment. *Journal of Research in Music Education, 34,* 200–210.

Kendall, M. J. (1988). Two instructional approaches to the development of aural and instrumental performance skills. *Journal of Research in Music Education, 36,* 205–219.

Kerlinger, F. N., and Pedhazur, E. J. (1982). *Multiple regression in behavioral research: Explanation and prediction* (2nd ed.). New York: Holt, Rinehart, and Winston.

Kirk, R. E. (1982). *Experimental design: Procedures for the behavioral sciences* (2nd ed.). Monterey: Brooks/Cole.

Kruskal, J. B., and Wish, M. (1978). *Multidimensional scaling.* Beverly Hills: Sage.

Kuhn, T. L., and Booth, G. D. (1988). The effect of melodic activity, tempo change, and audible beat on tempo perception of elementary school students. *Journal of Research in Music Education, 36,* 140–155.

Larson, R. C. (1977). Relationships between melodic error detection, melodic dictation, and melodic sightsinging. *Journal of Research in Music Education, 25,* 264–271.

LeBlanc, A., Colman, J., McCrary, J., Sherrill, C., and Malin, S. (1988). Tempo preferences of different age music listeners. *Journal of Research in Music Education, 36,* 156–168.

Lehman, P. R. (1968). *Tests and measurements in music.* Englewood Cliffs: Prentice-Hall.

Leonhard, C. (1958). Evaluation in music education. In N. B. Henry (Ed.), *Basic concepts in music education* (The fifty-seventh yearbook of the National Society for the Study of Education). Chicago: University of Chicago Press.

Li, J. C. R. (1964). *Statistical inference I.* Ann Arbor: Edwards Brothers.

Lord F., and Novick, R. L. (1968). *Statistical theories of mental test scores.* Reading: Addison-Wesley.

Lunneborg, C. E., and Abbot, R. D. (1983). *Elementary multivariate analysis for the behavioral sciences.* New York: North-Holland.

Madsen, C. K., and Madsen, C. H. (1978). *Experimental research in music.* Raleigh: Contemporary Publishing.

Madsen, C. K., and Moore, R. S. (1978). *Experimental research in music: Workbook in design and statistical tests.* Raleigh: Contemporary Publishing.

May, W. V. (1985). Musical style preferences and aural discrimination skills of primary grade school children. *Journal of Research in Music Education, 32,* 7–22.

Miller, R. (1989). An introduction to multidimensional scaling for the study of musical perception. *Bulletin of the Council for Research in Music Education, 102,* 60–73.

Moore, D. S. (1988). *Statistics: Concepts and controversies* (2nd ed.). New York: W. H. Freeman.

Moore, R. S. (1976). The effects of videotaped feedback and self-evaluation forms on teaching skills, musicianship and creativity of prospective elementary teachers. *Bulletin of the Council for Research in Music Education, 47,* 1–7.

Muirhead, R. J. (1982). *Aspects of multivariate statistical theory.* New York: John Wiley.

Nunnally, J. C. (1978). *Psychometric theory* (2nd ed.). New York: McGraw-Hill.

Payne, D. A. (1982). Measurement in education. In H. E. Mitzel (Ed.), *Encyclopedia of educational research* (5th ed.; Vol. 3). New York: Free Press.

Phelps, R. P. (1986). *A guide to research in music education* (3rd ed.). Metuchen: Scarecrow Press.

Price, H. E. (1988). The effect of a music appreciation course on students' verbally expressed preferences for composers. *Journal of Research in Music Education, 36,* 35–46.

Price, H. E., and Swanson, P. (1990). Changes in musical attitudes, opinions, and knowledge of music appreciation students. *Journal of Research in Music Education, 38,* 39–48.

Puri, M. L., and Sen, P. K. (1971). Nonparametric methods in multivariate analysis. New York: John Wiley.

Radocy, R. E. (1986). On quantifying the uncountable in musical behavior. *Bulletin of the Council for Research in Music Education, 88,* 22–31.

Rainbow, E. L., and Froehlich, H. C. (1987). Research in music education. New York: Schirmer Books.

SAS Institute. (1989). *JMP: Software for statistical visualization* [Computer program]. Cary: SAS Institute.

Sax, G. (1979). *Foundations of educational research.* Englewood Cliffs: Prentice-Hall.

Scheffé, H. A. (1953). A method for judging all contrasts in the analysis of variance. *Biometrika, 40,* 87–104.

Seashore, C. E. (1936). The objective recording and analysis of musical performance. In C. E. Seashore (Ed.), *Objective analysis of musical performance* (pp. 5–11). Iowa City: The University Press.

Seashore, C. E., Lewis, D., and Saetveit, J. (1960). *Seashore measures of musical talents.* New York: Psychological Corporation. (Original publication in 1939)

Sheth, J. N. (1984). How to get the most out of multivariate methods. In J. F. Hair, R. E. Anderson, R. L. Tatham, and B. J. Grablowsky (Eds.), *Multivariate data analysis with readings* (pp. 19–29). New York: Macmillan.

Siegel, S. (1956). *Nonparametric statistics for the behavioral sciences.* New York: McGraw-Hill.

Siegel, S., and Castellan, N. J. (1988). *Nonparametric statistics for the behavioral sciences* (2nd ed.). New York: McGraw-Hill.

Simon, H. A. (1985). Spurious correlation: A causal interpretation. In H. M. Blalock (Ed.), *Causal models in the social sciences* (2nd ed., pp. 7–21). New York: Aldine Publishing.

SPSS. (1988). *SPSS^x user's guide* (3rd ed.). Chicago: SPSS.

Stanley, J. C. (1971). Reliability. In R. L. Thorndike (Ed.), *Educational measurement* (2nd ed.). Washington: American Council on Education.

Stevens, S. S. (1959). Measurement, psychophysics, and utility. In C. W. Churchman and P. Ratoosh (Eds.), *Measurement definitions and theories* (pp. 18–63). New York: John Wiley.

Stevens, S. S. (1975). *Psychophysics*. New York: John Wiley.

Tatsuoka, M. M., and Lohnes, P. R. (1988). *Multivariate analysis: Techniques for educational and psychological research* (2nd ed.). New York: Macmillan.

Whybrew, W. E. (1971). *Measurement and evaluation in music*. Dubuque: Wm. C. Brown.

Wike, E. L. (1971). *Data analysts*. Chicago: Aldine-Atherton.

Wilks, S. S. (1961). Some aspects of quantification in science. In H. Woolf (Ed.), *Quantification: A history of the measurement in the natural and social sciences (pp. 5–12)*. Indianapolis: Bobbs-Merrill.

Winer, B. J. (1971). *Statistical principles in experimental design* (2nd ed.). New York: McGraw-Hill.

Winkler, R. L., and Hays, W. L. (1975). *Statistics: Probability, inference and decision* (2nd ed.). New York: Holt, Rinehart and Winston.

Wright, S. (1921). Correlation and causation. *Journal of Agricultural Research, 20,* 557–585.

Young, F. W. (1987). *Multidimensional scaling: History, theory, and applications*. Hillsdale: Lawrence Erlbaum Associates.

·12·

REGRESSION-BASED RESEARCH DESIGNS

Randi L'Hommedieu

UNIVERSITY OF OREGON

Kerlinger (1986) writes that "the analysis of variance is not just a statistical method. It is an approach and a way of thinking" (p. 203). And indeed it is. Originally developed for the analysis of agricultural field experiments and quickly appropriated by psychological and educational researchers, this powerful analysis tool has helped shape social science research in the twentieth century. Methodologists have developed a rich literature devoted to the statistical concepts of the analysis of variance (ANOVA), an equally important pedagogical literature for learning and using ANOVA, and, perhaps most important, a systematized set of design principles that support the logic of ANOVA-based experimentation.

But any technique so powerful and robust that it becomes "a way of thinking" also imposes methodological limits on the imagination and aspiration of researchers. The purpose of this chapter is to propose multiple regression analysis, the principle alternative to ANOVA for the analysis of parametric data, as another way of thinking about music education research.

Despite their apparent differences, multiple regression and ANOVA are analogous manifestations of the general linear model. Multiple regression is, in fact, a more general and powerful form of the statistical principles that underpin ANOVA. In a seminal article, Cohen (1968) mused:

If you should say to a mathematical statistician that you have discovered that linear multiple regression analysis and the analysis of variance (and covariance) are identical systems, he would mutter something like, "Of course—general linear model," and you might have trouble maintaining his attention. If you should say this to a typical psychologist, you would be met with incredulity, or worse. Yet it is true, and in its truth lie possibilities for more relevant and therefore more powerful exploitation of research data. (p. 426)

In many respects, music education researchers are in the same situation as the psychological researcher at the time of Cohen's article. Fortunately, however, music education can profit from the pioneering efforts of psychologists, sociologists, economists, and educators who have developed multiple regression techniques in other social science research environments.

But covering this complex topic in a relatively small space presents a dilemma. For the reader who can follow these topics with such shallow explication, the chapter is probably redundant. On the other hand, if these ideas are new and challenging, then the information is too scant to serve a pedagogical purpose. My compromise is to assume a reference function: to outline the main concepts and controversies of contemporary regression analysis and to provide authoritative references for more thorough study. The discussion is intended for readers with a solid background in analysis of variance techniques but with little regression experience beyond bivariate regression and correlation.

This chapter is divided into three parts. The first section outlines the similarities and differences between ANOVA and multiple regression approaches to analysis. The second section introduces some of the basic concepts used in designing and interpreting multiple regression models. The chapter closes with some suggestions for using multiple regression to extend knowledge of music teaching and learning.

COMPARING ANOVA AND MULTIPLE REGRESSION

ANOVA and multiple regression share a common goal: to explain variation from central tendency in one variable (the dependent variable[1]) by recourse to information derived from one or more independent variables. The principal difference between ANOVA and multiple regression analysis involves the level of measurement of the variables in the analysis. When the effects of nominal level independent variables on an interval level dependent variable are of interest, ANOVA has been the traditional analysis technique. When both independent and dependent variables are measured at the interval level, only regression analysis is appropriate.[2] When both nominal and interval level independent variables are analyzed, a hybrid test, the analysis of covariance (ANCOVA), is used.

In all of these multivariate procedures, the analysis strategy is to determine if an alternative estimate of central tendency reduces the amount of variation (measured as the sum of squared deviations). In ANOVA, for instance, nominal level independent variables (e.g., treatment group, sex) are used to separate cases into subcategories, each with a mean and a sum of squared deviations from the mean. If the independent variable has some influence on the dependent variable, then the sum of the sum of squares for each category (*within-groups* sum of squares) will be less than the sum of squares from the grand mean (*total* sum of squares).[3]

Regression analysis takes advantage of the additional information contained in interval level variables to construct a continuously conditional measure of central tendency—the regression line. The regression line graphically represents the magnitude of change in one variable over changes in another; a consistent, dynamic *relationship* between variables, as opposed to a static *difference* between group means. In Figure 12–1, for example, it is clear that there is a strong positive correlation between the dependent variable (first-year college music theory grades) and the independent variable (high school grade-point average [GPA]).[4] Consequently, it is also clear that the angled regression line fits the joint distribution better than the horizontal line representing the average theory grade. The regression line represents an alternative measure of central tendency. If it is a good alternative, the sum of squared deviations from the regression line will be less than the sum of squares from the grand mean.

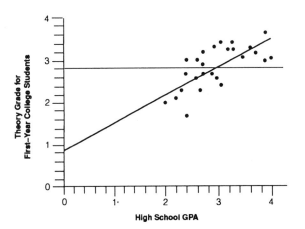

$\bar{Y}$ = 2.793

Sum of squared deviations from $\bar{Y}$ = 7.818

Y' = .832 + .672(X).

Sum of squared deviations from Y' (regression line) = 3.826

FIGURE 12–1. First-Year College Theory Grade by High School GPA.

Fortunately, it is a relatively simple process to determine the best possible line to draw through these data points. The *ordinary least squares* (OLS) line can be arithmetically computed from raw scores.[5] The OLS computations yield two values: (1) an *intercept,* or *constant,* that estimates theory grades (plotted on the Y-axis) when high school GPA equals zero, and (2) a *regression coefficient* that estimates the rise in theory grade for each unit increase of GPA. These two values comprise a linear equation to predict theory grades for first-year students given high school GPA. In this case, the equation is

Theory grade = .832 + .672 (high school GPA).

In a more generalized form, the regression equation is modeled

$$Y' = a + b(X) + E$$

where Y' is the predicted value of the dependent variable (Y), a is some constant value (intercept) of Y when the independent variable (X) equals zero, and b is a functional value that represents the average increase in Y associated with a unit increase in X. This is an expression of what mathematicians call the *general linear model,* which simply states that "an observed value of the dependent variable is equal to a weighted sum of values associated with one or more independent variables" (Hays, 1988, p. 344). Although this model is a perfect predictor of many physical phenomena, for social purposes it is merely a useful conceptual tool and must, because of its limitations, include an error term (E) to account for the unexplained vagaries in behavioral data. Because it is expected that the errors are random and that deviations from the mean error term will sum to zero, the error term is usually dropped from the equation. But the effect of the error is reflected in the sum of the squared deviations from the regression line (*residual* sum of squares). The residual error represents the variation in grades that the regression line fails to explain.

Regardless of the method (regression or ANOVA) used to compute the alternative measure of central tendency, the efficiency and statistical significance of the alternative are determined by the same procedures. The *proportion of explained variation* (called eta^2 in ANOVA and R^2 in regression analysis) is the percentage of error variation that is eliminated by the independent variable. It is computed by first subtracting the alternative estimate of variation (*within-groups* sum of squares in ANOVA or *residual* sum of squares in regression) from the total sum of squares. The difference represents the amount of variation *explained* by the independent variable (*regression* or *between-groups* sum of squares). The explained sum of squares is then divided by the total:

$$\text{Proportion of explained variation} = \frac{\text{Explained sum of squares}}{\text{Total sum of squares}}$$

Equation 1

This value is a good description of the effect of the independent variable.

Determining if this effect is statistically significant is the purpose of the F test. In this test, an estimate of the explained variance is compared to an estimate of the residual variance. If the result reaches the critical value listed in the F table, then the effect is great enough to reject the hypothesis that the difference is due totally to chance.

$$F = \frac{\text{Explained sum of squares/degrees of freedom}}{\text{Residual sum of squares/degrees of freedom}}$$
Equation 2

DESIGNING MULTIPLE REGRESSION STUDIES

The leap from the bivariate to the multivariate regression model is conceptually straightforward, but computationally complex. Whereas the parameters of the bivariate regression model can be computed using simple arithmetic operations, multivariate equations require calculus or matrix algebra (see Hanushek and Jackson, 1977, pp. 24–40, 109–122). Fortunately, computerized statistical packages perform these complex calculations transparently, yielding a banquet of statistics in a fraction of a second. However, the ease with which these statistics are produced belies the complexity of their interpretation. The brief discussion that follows addresses these complexities in only enough depth to illustrate the research design potential of multiple regression analysis. Those interested in a more thorough explanation are referred to Hanushek and Jackson (1977), Berry and Feldman (1985), Hays (1988), Cohen and Cohen (1983), and Pedhazur (1982) for a detailed treatment of these important topics.

Interpreting Multiple Regression Results

Multiple regression equations are of the general form

$$Y' = a + b_1(X_1) + b_2(X_2) + \ldots + b_k(X_k),$$

where Y' is the predicted value of an interval level dependent variable, $X_1 - X_k$ are interval level independent variables, b values are weights or functions assigned to each variable, and a is the intercept or constant value of Y when *all* independent variables equal zero.

Table 12–1a shows part of the output from a multiple regression analysis run by a computerized statistical package. In this example, data on each student's high school GPA and years of private instruction are analyzed to determine a good equation for predicting theory grades for first-year college students.

The results show that, given the available information, the best linear equation is

Theory grade = .885 + .634 (High school GPA)
+ .034 (Years of private instruction).

It is important to note how the results of this analysis differ from the results of two separate bivariate regression analyses. Each regression coefficient in this multivariate model is interpreted as the effect of one variable when all other independent variables in the equation are held constant. In almost all cases, the zero-order regression of one variable on another will yield a different coefficient, but a lower R^2 value.

The beta coefficient displayed in Table 12–1a is a standardized version of the regression coefficient (B). It is calculated by multiplying the unstandardized regression coefficient by the ratio of the standard deviation of X to the standard deviation of Y. Because beta is dimensionless, it allows direct comparisons of the effects of variables measured on different metrics or scales. This feature makes beta weights particularly valuable in some of the more complex interpretations of regression results, such as path analysis and causal modeling (see Loehlin, 1987).

The t value of the regression coefficient is obtained by dividing the regression coefficient by its standard error. The test determines whether the regression coefficient is significantly different than zero.

TABLE 12–1a. Multiple Regression of High School GPA (HSGPA) and Years of Private Study (YEARS) on Theory Grade of First-Year Students (GRADE)

Variables	B	Standard Error	Beta	T	Probability
Dependent Variable = GRADE					
HSGPA	.634	.140	.674	4.528	.0001
YEARS	.034	.056	.091	.612	.5460
Intercept = .885		.383		2.309	.0290

TABLE 12–1b. Analysis of Variance

Source of Variation	Degrees of Freedom	Sum of Squares	Mean Square	F	Probability of F
Regression	2	4.045	2.023	14.474	.0001
Residual	27	3.773	.140		
Total	29	7.818			
Multiple R^2 = .5174					

The multiple R^2 value is a measure of how well the derived model fits the data. It represents the proportion of total variance (Equation 1) that is explained by the new regression line. The statistic is exactly analogous to the bivariate model, except that the line is plotted in k-dimensional space. In the case of one dependent variable and two independent variables, the space is three-dimensional. The F test for the statistical significance of the model is the same as in the bivariate case (Equation 2), but the degrees of freedom are corrected for the number of variables included in the equation (k and $N-k-1$).

Theory Building and Significance Testing in Multiple Regression

Significance testing in multiple regression has three purposes. First, it is used to determine if the equation as a whole is effective; that is, whether the residual error from the line described by the multiple regression equation is significantly less than the total error measured from the mean of the dependent variable. This is accomplished, as in the bivariate case, with an F test comparing the regression sum of squares to the residual sum of squares (Table 12–16).

But this is seldom enough. Rather than simply testing whether the regression model is a better predictor than the mean of the dependent variable, researchers frequently are more interested in comparing the explanatory power of different models or in the unique explanatory power of a single variable in a multiple regression model. Both of these ends are served by the incremental F test.

The Incremental F Test The logic of this test is straightforward. Two regression equations are analyzed and the *difference* in regression sum of squares (Reg SS) between the two models is compared to the residual sum of squares (Res SS). If the difference is statistically significant, the model with the greater proportion of explained variation is a superior predictor.

$$\text{Incremental } F = \frac{\dfrac{\text{RegSS}_2 - \text{RegSS}_1}{(K_2) - (K_1)}}{\dfrac{\text{ResSS}_2}{N_2 - K_2 - 1}}$$

Equation 3

The most frequent use of this procedure is to build efficient, parsimonious regression models from large collections of variables. Variables are entered singularly or in groups into the regression model in order of their theoretical importance, and the incremental change in the regression sum of squares is tested after each iteration. Variables that fail to significantly increase the explanatory power of the model are dropped from the equation. This approach to model building, especially when it is used for theory testing, is called *hierarchical analysis* (see Cohen and Cohen, 1983, p. 120).

An example of the hierarchical method of theory testing would be a test of the null hypothesis of gender equity in college teacher salaries. A simple comparison of male and female instructor salaries would be of no use because many other factors (rank, experience, publications, and grants) affect salaries. To control for these factors statistically and to test for the unique effect of gender, two multivariate models might be analyzed. The first model would include rank (X_1), years of experience (X_2), number of publications (X_3), and number of grants awarded (X_4). The second equation would include sex (X_5) in addition to the four variables from the first model (X_1–X_4). If the change in regression sum of squares associated with the second equation reached significance, a good statistical case could be made for sexual discrimination.

Alternative Methods for Building Regression Models The hierarchical method assumes that all variables have been entered into the equation simultaneously. This analysis procedure is known as *forced entry regression*. With most computerized statistical packages, the hierarchical, forced entry method requires several computer runs and hand calculations to build and test the final model. However, there are methods that accomplish this in one computer run by automatically entering or deleting variables based on post hoc analyses of effect (see Norusis, 1988, pp. 42–53).

There are three alternatives to forced entry regression. In *forward selection multiple regression,* independent variables are added to the equation one at a time in descending order of correlation with the dependent variable. The variable remains in the equation only if the probability of the incremental F value is less than some designated value (usually .05). When the process finally encounters a variable that fails to meet entry criteria, the analysis ends. In *backward elimination multiple regression,* all variables are entered on the first step. Then variables are tested, in reverse order of their partial correlation, to see if they can be removed from the equation on the basis of the statistical significance of the incremental F test. The third and most frequently used type of variable entry is *stepwise selection.* In this method variables are added according to forward selection criteria. However, once the second variable is added to the equation, the model is reexamined after each iteration to see if the previously selected variables should remain in the equation according to backward elimination rules.

In all three of the selection/elimination procedures, the researcher relinquishes control of the theoretical content of the model and gives the computer the final responsibility for the final structure of the regression equation. While these complex permutations may be useful for exploring data or for examining alternative explanations for models that do not reach significance, they violate many of the assumptions underlying the logic of hypothesis testing. The most obvious problem is that computerized model-building procedures use the same data for both generating *and* testing the explanation. Moreover, virtually everything that is done in the three alternative selection procedures can be accomplished in forced-entry regression. Forced-entry, hierarchical analysis requires a few more calculations and a great deal more theoretical rigor, but results in more valid, defensible, and generalizable conclusions.

Accommodating Heterogeneous Variables

Complex field experiments and complicated multivariate designs require statistical procedures that can accommodate heterogeneous variables. Both ANOVA and multiple regression are robust in this regard, but only regression analysis can accommodate heterogeneous variables without loss of statistical power.

Incorporating Continuous Variables in ANOVA Researchers using ANOVA frequently encounter theoretically important independent variables that are measured at the interval or ratio level. This can come about during the design phase, as when a pretest is used to control for initial differences between groups, or post hoc when it may prove interesting to break down results by uncontrolled or unforeseen factors that seem to influence outcomes. In the past, especially before statistical packages for analysis of covariance were widely available, it was customary for researchers to accommodate the analysis of variance by dividing continuous variables (IQ, income, experience) into categories (e.g., high, medium, and low). There are, however, three important reasons to avoid this design strategy.

First, categorization invariably depends on what may be arbitrary cutoff points. How many years equal "high" experience? Shifting the cutoff even slightly can reassign extreme cases and drastically affect the results of the comparison. This is an especially serious problem when categorization criteria are determined after examining the data. It is tempting to select cutoff points that allow more equal distribution to cells or that break the group into cells that correspond to the researcher's expectations.

A second and more technical reason to avoid categorization of interval level data is that it wastes information and decreases statistical power. Because the point of reference for computing the sums of squares is a set of points, rather than a continuous line, the error variation is larger and achieving statistical significance becomes more difficult. In order to reach statistical significance, the increased error sums of squares must be offset by a larger sample or an increased magnitude of effect (Cohen, 1988; Cohen and Cohen, 1983; Kraemer and Thiemann, 1987).

A third and related point concerns the between-groups degrees of freedom in the numerator of the F test. The between-groups mean square ($SS_B/k - 1$) is decreased substantially by increases in the number of categories (k). Note that the numerator in the F test is cut exactly in half by going from a single category to two, by a third by going to three, and so on. On the other hand, the effect on the within-groups mean square ($N - k$) in the denominator of the F test is affected to a much smaller degree. Categorizing a continuous variable into a four-level factor in a 30-subject experiment increases the degrees of freedom in the numerator by 300 percent, while the degrees of freedom in the denominator decrease by only 14 percent. Clearly each increase in the number of categories makes it progressively more difficult to reach a statistically significant F value.

Combining this with the fact that the within-groups sum of squares is generally larger when the variable is categorized, the loss of statistical power can be extreme.[6] When a relationship between variables meets the assumptions for multiple regression analysis, categorization of the independent variable for a factorial ANOVA will always result in a smaller measured effect. This is, of course, especially serious when the F value falls near the cutoff for statistical significance. In such cases, the choice of analysis techniques can mean the difference between a statistically significant result and a "no-difference" study.

Incorporating Categorical Variables in Multiple Regression Whereas categorizing continuous variables in ANOVA entails threats to the construct validity and statistical power of an experiment, incorporating nominal level variables in multiple regression analysis is relatively straightforward and entails no loss of information or statistical power. In fact, as Cohen (1968), Keppel and Zedeck (1989), and others have shown, the analysis of categorical variables with multiple regression yields precisely the same results as ANOVA.

The incorporation of categorical variables is accomplished through special coding procedures. Although there are three distinct types of coding for categorical variables in regression analysis (dummy coding, contrast coding, and effects coding), the most intuitively clear method, and the one on which the other two are based, is *dummy coding.*[7]

Dichotomous variables, such as sex, are the clearest examples of dummy coding. To include sex as a dummy variable in a regression equation, the researcher codes one gender as "1" and the other as "0." To analyze the effect of gender on theory grades, sex can be entered into a regression model as a dummy variable with the coding scheme: 1 = male, 0 = female. The regression equation is

$$\text{Theory grade} = a + b(\text{sex}).$$

Because female is coded "0" (causing the second term of the equation to drop out for women subjects), the intercept, a, represents the average female grade and the regression coefficient, b, estimates the incremental value of being male. The choice of reference "0" category is methodologically irrelevant. If the coding were reversed (1 = female), the regression coefficient would be the same absolute value, but with a different sign.

Note that in the dummy coding system one category of the variable serves as a reference group whose value is represented in the intercept, while the variable term estimates the additive effect of belonging to the alternate group. This becomes clearer when the dummy coding procedure is generalized to variables with more than two categories. Consider, for example, "instrument" as a three-category variable (string, brass, woodwind) to explain theory grades of first-year students. In this case it is possible to do exactly what was done with sex: arbitrarily choose a reference category (string) and construct separate dichotomous variables for the other categories. For this example, the equation would be

$$\text{Theory grade} = a + b_1(\text{brass}) + b_2(\text{woodwind}).$$

TABLE 12-2. Data Table with Theory Grade and Dummy
Codes for Instrument

Subject ID/Instrument	Grade	Brass	Woodwind
01 (cello)	3.30	0	0
02 (trumpet)	2.70	1	0
03 (clarinet)	3.00	0	1
04 (flute)	2.30	0	1
. . .	. . .	. . .	. . .
. . .	. . .	. . .	. . .

If each subject were coded with 1 for belonging to a category and 0 otherwise, the data would look like the sample in Table 12-2.

Analysis of the data would yield an equation for string players [Grade = $a + b_1(0) + b_2(0)$], in which the intercept represented the predicted grade. Predicted grade for the brass players [Grade = $a + b_1(1) + b_2(0)$] and woodwinds [Grade = $a + b_1(0) + b_2(1)$] would be computed in the same way.

In this regression analysis the explained variation and degrees of freedom are exactly the same as in an ANOVA. Therefore, the proportion of explained variance (R^2 or Eta^2) and the F value are precisely the same for both analyses.

There are at least three reasons to favor the regression approach in cases such as this. First of all, the output of the regression analysis provides a substantive measure of the magnitude of effect—the group mean—for each category. Although this information is, of course, available when computing an ANOVA, it is not automatically part of the output. Moreover, despite the availability of descriptive statistics, researchers frequently fail to report the means and standard deviations of statistical tests. This information is important for readers interpreting research, and it is *vital* to reviewers, secondary researchers, and metaanalysts. Note that descriptive statistics are important even when the results do not reach statistical significance (L'Hommedieu, Menges, and Brinko, 1988).

A second reason to favor the regression approach is that it provides the information necessary to test the significance of individual variable categories with the incremental F test. Indeed, the statistical significance of each regression coefficient is usually tested, and the results are reported in the output of most computerized statistical packages. This is seldom the case with ANOVA output.

Finally, the regression model is preferable because it can easily accommodate both interval and categorical variables in a single multivariate equation. This capability makes multiple regression a simple and easily interpretable form of analysis of covariance.

Regression-Based Analysis of Covariance In order to understand the use of multiple regression in the analysis of covariance, it is helpful to consider the traditional, psychological view of ANCOVA, where the covariate is regarded as a way to control systematic error variation in a factorial research design (see, for instance, Blalock, 1979, pp. 527–533). Factorial ANCOVA is used primarily to (1) adjust criterion measures for initial differences between groups due to faulty assignment to treatment or (2) statistically control theoretically irrelevant variables in order to decrease error variation and increase statistical power. From this perspective, the covariate is regarded as an extraneous factor that interferes with the measurement of treatment effect. The covariate is allowed to explain all of the variation it can, and then is discarded as a sort of error "filter."

There is, however, an alternative, more ecological, way to view covariates. The covariate can be understood as simply another influence on the dependent variable; an influence to be measured and explained in a complex, multiple-determined context. This form of explanation is characteristic of regression-based ANCOVA.

In ANOVA-based procedures the covariate is an interval level variable (often a pretest) used to adjust group means statistically. By contrast, the covariate in a regression-based ANCOVA is a categorical dummy variable that is analyzed as an integral part of the explanatory model. The general form of the regression-based ANCOVA model is

$$Y' = a + b_1(X_1) + b_2(X_2) + b_3(X_3) + \ldots + b_k(X_k),$$

where Y' is an interval level dependent variable, a is the intercept value of the dependent variable, X_1–X_k are interval level or dichotomous nominal independent variables, and b_1–b_k are regression coefficients. Note that in an example with one dichotomous covariate (X_1), the equation can be interpreted graphically as two parallel regression lines with different intercepts. This regression model is particularly suited to the quasi-experimental "workhorse" design: a two-group, pretest-posttest study with untreated control group (Cook and Campbell, 1979). A two-dimensional scatterplot of first-year college students' theory grade regressed on sex and high school GPA is shown in Figure 12-2a (p. 190).

A research design including a covariate with more than two levels would be graphed with a scatterplot showing a separate regression line for each category (Figure 12-2b). Models with more than one covariate would yield a scatterplot with as many regression lines as categories in all covariates. The test for the significance of the covariate is whether the difference in intercepts is statistically significant; that is, does the model including the covariate explain significantly more variation than the model without?

Interaction

Researchers who have used ANOVA are familiar with the notion of *interactive* or *conditional* relationships between independent variables in multivariate analyses. In interactive relationships, the effect of one independent variable is conditional on the status of another independent factor, and the effect of the two variables together is different from the sum of the two main effects. Consider again the example in Figure 12-2b. First-year theory grades are clearly influenced by

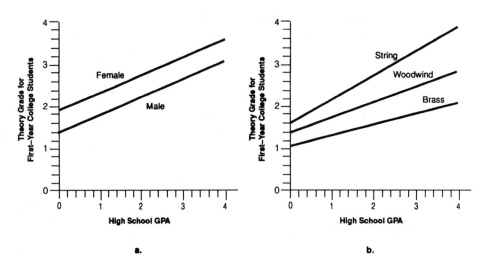

FIGURE 12-2. Plotting Dummy Variables. a. Grade × HS GPA × SEX. b. Grade × HS GPA × Instrument.

high school GPA, but note that the slope for string players is greater than that for woodwinds and brass: There is an interaction between GPA and instrument.

Factorial ANOVA can assess interaction only between nominal level independent variables. Therefore, when interaction with continuous variables has been hypothesized in factorial designs, researchers have been compelled to categorize interval level data. But Cohen and Cohen (1983) caution against this waste of information and loss of statistical power (pp. 308–311) and suggest ways to incorporate interaction terms into multiple regression models.

The explanation of a two-way interaction is sufficient to illustrate the general case. Interaction in a multiple regression equation with two independent variables,

$$Y = a + b_1(X_1) + b_2(X_2),$$

is assessed by adding a computed multiplicative term, $X_3 = X_1 {}^* X_2$. The model then becomes

$$Y = a + b_1(X_1) + b_2(X_2) + b_3(X_3).$$

If the variables are, in fact, interactive, the resulting regression equation will yield different coefficients and a higher R^2 value. The incremental R^2—the proportion of explained variation uniquely associated with the interaction term—indicates the strength of the interaction. The statistical significance of the interaction term is tested with the hierarchical analysis method and the incremental F test. The substantive magnitude and the character of the interaction are determined by the term's regression coefficient. In simple, bilinear interactions, the regression coefficient of the interactive term represents changes in the linear relationship (slope) of one of the independent variables over changes in the other.

Special controversies regarding multicollinearity in multiplicative interaction and the interpretation of interaction co-

efficients remain to be resolved (see Jaccard, Turrisi, and Wan, 1990), but justifiable procedures for computing and interpreting complex interactions in multiple regression analysis are available. Perhaps the best resources for information on interaction in multiple regression are Jaccard and colleagues (1990) for interactions of quantitative variables and complex, nonlinear interaction, and Cohen and Cohen (1983, pp. 301–350) for the explanation of qualitative and qualitative-by-quantitative variable interactions.

Assumptions in Multiple Regression Analysis

As with all statistical techniques, the validity of multiple regression analysis rests in part on specific theoretical and computational assumptions. For expository purposes, these assumptions can be reduced to four important points.[8]

THE DEPENDENT AND INDEPENDENT VARIABLES ARE MEASURED AT THE INTERVAL LEVEL. This basic assumption forms the textbook distinction between multiple regression and other forms of data analysis. However, as the discussion of dummy variables demonstrates, categorical independent variables can easily be incorporated into the model.

Multiple regression can be extended further to the analysis of categorical dependent variables through logit and probit analyses. Like discriminant analysis, logit and probit techniques are used to estimate linear equations that explain categorical events. However, unlike discriminant analyses, logit and probit procedures can be extended to dependent variables with more than two outcomes. Many questions of interest to music education researchers are amenable to these techniques: Do high school music experiences influence students' choice of college major? Do music programs have an effect on at-risk students? What factors are likely to lead to music teacher burnout?

The analysis of logit and probit studies is arcane and difficult (see Hanushek and Jackson, 1977), but these techniques effectively extend the multiple regression model and are becoming more common in the advanced social science literature.

THE RELATIONSHIP BETWEEN THE INDEPENDENT VARIABLES AND THE DEPENDENT VARIABLE IS LINEAR. This is, at first glance, a fairly restrictive assumption. However, regression analysis often gives a good interpretation of data despite deviations from linearity. Moreover, there are data transformation procedures that allow some systematic, nonlinear relationships to be analyzed with multiple regression.

Take the traditional "learning curve," for example, where the initial rapid rate of learning diminishes over time (see Figure 12–3). Clearly, there is a lawful, regular relationship that is theoretically justifiable, but only imperfectly explained by simple linear regression. How, then, can this be reconciled to the linear model? One way is to transform this relationship with a log function. The plotted curve of the relationship can be rendered linear by recoding the independent variable as $\log2(X)$. If the logarithmic model is effective, its R^2 value will be significantly larger than the model based on untransformed data.

Virtually any variable transformation can be used to achieve a better linear fit. Logarithmic, exponential, and polynomial transformations of the explanatory variables are among the more common techniques for adjusting nonlinear relationships. The reciprocal of an independent variable can similarly be used to accommodate curvilinearity. Because the transformations are nonlinear, the problem of linear dependency is avoided, but transformations do present special problems with interpretation (see Berry and Feldman, 1985; Hanushek and Jackson, 1977). The test for the validity of the curvilinear model is the F test for the incremental R^2 compared to the untransformed model.

NO INDEPENDENT VARIABLE IS LINEARLY DEPENDENT ON ANOTHER. Linear dependence, an extreme form of *multicollinearity,* destroys the multiple regression model because it is impossible to determine the unique effect of one independent variable that is perfectly correlated with another. However, some correlation between explanatory variables is almost always present. Though high intercorrelation does not destroy the analysis, it does decrease statistical power by increasing the variance around the regression coefficients. As the correlation between variables increases, so does the amount of information necessary to determine the unique contribution of each variable. This is a particularly important assumption for music education researchers who often use highly correlated standardized tests of academic and musical achievement to construct predictive models (e.g., Harrison, 1990a,b; Hedden, 1982).

Most computer programs provide an error warning and refuse to process linearly dependent variables. Researchers should be careful that in transforming and recoding variables they do not inadvertently construct a variable that contains redundant information. (This is particularly apt to happen when constructing interaction terms.) Less severe intercorrelation is more difficult to detect and control. One indicator of a possible problem is when a multiple regression model has a high multiple-R^2 value, but no single variable proves statistically significant in hierarchical analysis. This is often a sign that the model has been misspecified or inefficiently constructed.

THE VARIATION AROUND THE REGRESSION LINE IS EQUAL FOR EACH OBSERVATION AND THE ERROR TERMS BETWEEN OBSERVATIONS ARE UNCORRELATED. This final assumption is in two parts. They are stated together because violations of both assumptions can be corrected by advanced multiple regression procedures known as *generalized least squares* and *weighted least squares;* (see Hanushek and Jackson, 1977; Wonnacott and Wonnacott, 1990). Although explanation of these arcane techniques is beyond the scope of this chapter, it is possible to describe when the violations that make them necessary are likely to occur.

The first part of the assumption states that for every value of X (or combination of Xs), the distribution of Y around the

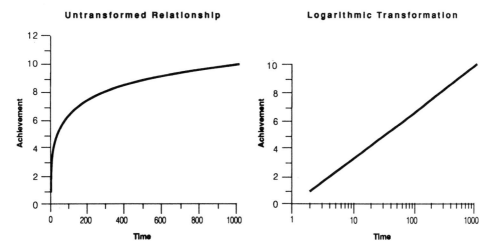

FIGURE 12–3. Learning Curve and Log Transformation.

regression line is equal. When this assumption is violated, the model is said to be *heteroskedastic*. Obviously, the assumption of equal variances (homoskedasticity) is theoretical and all data violate this assumption to some extent. However, when variations around predicted values differ drastically, and especially when the differences seem systematic, heteroskedasticity should be of concern. Heteroskedasticity is most likely to occur when observations are collected from preexisting groups (such as classrooms or schools), so stratified sampling designs are particularly susceptible.

Violations of the second part of this assumption cause *autocorrelation*. Autocorrelation describes regression models in which there is a systematic bias in the error term. When this occurs the error term does not sum to zero and cannot be dropped from the equation. Autocorrelation is often a problem when multiple observations of subjects are analyzed, as in time-series analyses or other longitudinal designs. In such data sets errors are likely to be systematically related to individuals or groups and to bias the error term.

As Hanushek and Jackson (1977) point out, heteroskedasticity and autocorrelation do not affect the unbiasedness of regression coefficients, but these violations do increase the error variance associated with the estimate and make statistical tests of significance unreliable (p. 141). In these cases a better estimate of the model can be calculated with *generalized least squares* or *weighted least squares* procedures. In research designs prone to heteroskedasticity or autocorrelation, the threats can be assessed graphically by plotting the residuals, or statistically through the Durbin-Watson statistic or other estimation procedures.[9]

USING MULTIPLE REGRESSION IN MUSIC EDUCATION RESEARCH

Multiple regression is a powerful and versatile analysis tool, and it is becoming more common in music education research (e.g., Asmus, 1980, 1981; Harrison, 1990a,b; Hedden, 1982; Norton, 1980). Yet methodology in this area has evolved so quickly that recent advances have yet to be completely absorbed by music education researchers. The social science methodological literature suggests some important design and analysis issues that will further enhance the validity and utility of multiple regression designs in music education.

Distinguishing Theory Testing from Data Exploration

One of the most important features of multiple regression analysis is that it is first and foremost a descriptive tool that summarizes the magnitude and strength of multivariate relationships in a given data set. Determining whether these relationships hold for the population from which the data were drawn is a secondary, and more restrictive, consideration. This distinction is important because confusion over these two functions can lead to invalid interpretations of research results.

Because regression accommodates variables at any level of measurement and because assignment to isolated treatments is not strictly necessary in multiple regression studies, almost any information is fair game for analysis. As a result, multiple regression studies frequently contain several demographic variables and archival measures, in addition to measures specially designed for the study. For instance, an analysis may include the subject's sex and income, standardized test scores collected from student records, and a measure of attitude designed by the researcher. This analytical flexibility can tempt the researcher to conduct "kitchen sink" analyses in which every available variable is included.

There are, however, at least two serious problems with this practice. The first is straightforward: Inclusion of a large number of variables increases the chance of a Type I error. With 20 independent variables, for instance, it is likely that one of them would prove statistically significant by chance. The second problem is more easily overlooked: When several variables are indiscriminately entered, highly correlated—even cognate—variables are likely to be included. This intercorrelation will inflate the variance of the regression coefficients and decrease the statistical power of the test.

The problems with indiscriminate modeling are compounded when automatic selection/elimination procedures are employed. These computational options capitalize on sample-specific variation and increase the chances of excluding variables that are theoretically relevant or including variables that are not. This problem is known as *specification error*. Hanushek and Jackson (1977) note that "probably *the most important* element in obtaining reasonable estimates of behavioral models is the statement of the model. The crucial difference between a 'passing' and 'failing' use of regression techniques is the development of the model—the delineation of relevant variables and the relationships among them" (p. 80). A decision of such importance should not be left to an automatic, sample-specific selection procedure.[10]

This is not to say, however, that exploratory data analysis using multiple regression is never justified. Tukey (1977) and Hoaglin, Mosteller, and Tukey (1983) provide clear guidelines and sophisticated methods for exhaustive post hoc data analysis. Indeed, no data should ever be abandoned simply because they fail to support an a priori theory. But for deriving valid and generalizable explanations and predictions of behavior, researchers are obliged to construct a priori models and to analyze all variables simultaneously with the forced-entry method. Refinements of the model should be tested through hierarchical analysis, and confirmation of the derived equation must be tested on new data.

Using the Full Analytical Power of Multiple Regression

Multiple regression analysis is inherently more powerful than ANOVA because it can take advantage of higher levels of measurement in the independent variables. Whereas multiple regression analysis can duplicate the results of most factorial ANOVAs, use of ANOVA with categorized interval level variables results in a severe loss of power. Cohen (1968) notes, for example, that "assuming bivariate normality, when a variable is . . . dichotomized, there is a reduction in R^2_{YX}, the criterion variance it accounts for, and hence in the value of F in the test of its significance, of 36%" (p. 441).

The statistical advantage of multiple regression can be squandered, however, if the multiple regression analysis is not complete. For instance, computerized ANOVA packages compute interaction effects as a default option. Yet, in multiple regression analyses, as Jaccard and colleagues (1990) observe, "interaction effects have received somewhat short shrift in disciplines where such relationships are likely to be the rule rather than the exception" (p. 8). They note that in a sample of 116 published studies in psychology and sociology, only eight analyzed the effects of interaction among independent variables.

Researchers should routinely compute interaction terms. If there is reason to believe that two or more variables have significant main effects, there is every reason to suppose that they may interact. Should the interaction terms fail to show a significant effect, they can be dropped from the model in the interest of theoretical parsimony.

Simple, linear multiple regression analysis can also be less powerful than ANOVA when the relationship between variables is nonlinear. Categorization can capture some of the variation in curvilinear data. (In Figure 12–3, for instance, dichotomizing the independent variable probably would result in significantly different group means.) However, a logarithmic variable transformation might approach linearity and facilitate a more informative and powerful regression analysis.

Researchers should consider correcting for nonlinearity when a theoretical explanation for the transformation can be justifiably proposed. Even when a logical curvilinear form is discovered and thoughtfully explained a posteriori, data transformations may contribute to theoretical advances. But, as with model misspecification, indiscriminate testing of data transformations can lead to spurious or uninterpretable results. Serendipitous a posteriori explanations should be tested against new data.

The validity and power of regression research also can be enhanced by searching for indications of heteroskedasticity and autocorrelation that can make statistical tests of the model unreliable. When one is analyzing designs that are susceptible to these threats or when the form of the data suggests that the threats are operative, GLS and WLS procedures should be applied (perhaps with the help of a consultant) to improve the efficiency of the estimate.

Using the Full Design Potential of Multiple Regression

ANOVA-based factorial analysis remains a powerful tool for exploring the differences between group means, but it is less comprehensive and flexible than multiple regression as a method for analyzing social data. Some methodologists suggest abandoning ANOVA altogether. Pedhazur (1982) concludes that multiple regression is a more comprehensive and general approach to data analysis and should virtually replace ANOVA in social research (p. 328). He notes that multiple regression can be used in all situations in which ANOVA is appropriate and that the statistical results of the two techniques are identical. Furthermore, in situations where (1) any of the independent variables are interval level, (2) cell frequencies are unequal, or (3) trends in the data are to be analyzed, multiple regression is clearly superior to ANOVA.

More temperate authorities suggest limiting its application to classical experimental designs with categorical independent variables. Keppel and Zedeck (1989) suggest that ANOVA is more intuitive and simpler to calculate when the focus of the analysis is the difference between treatment means, while multiple regression is more applicable when the focus is the relationship among variables. Authorities agree, however, that the analysis of nonexperimental and quasi-experimental designs is appropriate only with multiple regression analysis.

So, it seems logical for music education researchers to consider multiple regression analysis when (1) it is not possible to randomly assign subjects to treatment and to maintain group equivalency throughout the course of the study, (2) assignment is likely to result in grossly unequal cells (or when attaining equal cells requires the researcher to underutilize a pool of subjects or to delete cases from the final analysis), (3) a pretest or other covariate is included in the analysis, (4) any of the independent variables are capable of interval level measurement, (5) the relationship between variables is likely to be curvilinear, or (6) complex interactions are of theoretical interest.

Yet even a classical experimental design (random assignment, equal cells, nominal independent variables) does not rule out the use of regression techniques. A truly randomized experiment is exceedingly difficult to implement and maintain in field settings or when the experimental treatment is prolonged. When subject attrition threatens the initial equivalency of treatment groups, the only way to protect the analysis is to use a pretest or other covariate to correct the criterion measures. Cook and Campbell (1979) suggest that in randomized experiments, researchers should always collect data "to test whether attrition from an experiment has been systematically related to treatments" (p. 343). Subject attrition also affects cell frequencies, making analysis more complicated. Although most computer programs include corrections for unequal cell analysis, the calculation and interpretation of results from nonorthogonal designs is more straightforward with multiple regression analysis (Keppel and Zedeck, 1989, p. 555).

Finally, the use of multiple regression to analyze archival data deserves special mention because these sources are so underutilized in music education research. Government agencies and social researchers have established hundreds of social science data sets; large sets of data from individual studies (surveys and polls), and systematic, ongoing data collection projects (e.g., U.S. Census, High School and Beyond, National Education Longitudinal Study). These data sets are based on huge samples and are already coded, cleaned, and stored in a file format that can be read by most statistical packages. A glance at recent issues of the *American Educa-*

tional Research Journal or the *Sociology of Education* shows how far behind music education research is in taking advantage of the important information contained in these huge data sets. Because multiple regression can analyze the relationships between variables without assigning cases to isolated treatments, this technique is particularly applicable for description and theory testing with these archival data sets.

CONCLUSION

Even in such a brief summary some methodological implications are clear. First of all, multiple regression analysis is a powerful, flexible technique that is generally interchangeable with ANOVA in experimental designs and uniquely suited to nonexperimental studies. Second, multiple regression is a clearer and easier method for conducting analyses of covariance. Third, explanations that involve complex interactions or systematic, nonlinear relationships often are more effectively analyzed with multiple regression. Finally, a thorough understanding of multiple regression is a conceptual foundation for understanding more complex analysis tools, such as factor analysis, discriminant analysis, path analysis, structural equation modeling, and latent variable analysis.

Multiple regression is a statistical reflection of the complex, multiple-determined environment in which music is taught and learned. It provides an alternative methodological perspective for researchers and, as one powerful tool among many, can enhance the practice, interpretation, and application of research in music education.

Notes

1. Terminology for variables in regression analysis varies: Independent variables are sometimes called "predictor" or "exogenous" variables, while the dependent variable is often referred to as the "criterion" or "endogenous" variable.
2. Methodologists have not satisfactorily resolved the issue of ordinal level independent variables in multiple regression analysis. Ordinal measures violate the assumptions of continuity and equal intervals of measurement, but statisticians disagree as to the robustness of the F test to violations of this assumption. In practice, researchers often proceed with regression analyses of ordinal data without serious reservation. Stricter methodologists may opt for complicated n-chotomous probit analyses (Hanushek and Jackson, 1977, pp. 210–214) or choose less powerful, but simpler, nonparametric tests. Kerlinger's (1986) advice is to "use parametric statistics . . . routinely, but keep a sharp eye on data for gross departures from normality, homogeneity of variance, and equality of intervals" (p. 268).
3. This process, known as decomposing or partitioning variation, is fully explained in sources such as Blalock (1979, pp. 338–346), Hays (1988, pp. 355–360) and Keppel (1982, pp. 35–42).
4. Using standardized test scores, high school GPA, and other measures to predict (or explain) college achievement is a typical application of regression analysis. The running example in this chapter involves assessing the influence of various high school

measures on achievement in a first-year college music theory course. Several published music education studies address just this issue and can serve as practical illustrations. See, for instance, Asmus (1981) and Harrison (1990a,b).
5. Formulas and computational procedures can be found in most introductory statistics texts (e.g., Blalock, 1979, p. 392).
6. See Cohen and Cohen (1983, pp. 309–311) for a more detailed discussion of the problems associated with categorization of an interval level variable.
7. See Cohen and Cohen (1983, pp. 181–122), Hanushek and Jackson (1977, p. 101–108), Hayes (1988, pp. 671–699), or Keppel and Zedeck (1989, pp. 112–117).
8. For a more complete discussion of these assumptions see Berry and Feldman (1985), Norusis (1988, pp. 24–35), or Pedhazur (1982, pp. 32–39, 101–108), Hayes (1988, pp. 671–699), or Keppel and Zedeck (1989, p. 112–117).
9. Methods for diagnosing and dealing with heteroskedasticity and autocorrelation are discussed in Berry and Feldman (1985), Cohen and Cohen (1983), Hanushek and Jackson (1979), and Wonnacott and Wonnacott (1990).
10. Cohen and Cohen (1983, p. 125) identify some exceptions when automatic selection/elimination procedures may be justifiable, but these conditions are unlikely to occur in music education research.

References

Asmus, E. P., Jr. (1980). Empirical testing of an affective learning paradigm. *Journal of Research in Music Education, 28,* 143–154.

Asmus, E. P., Jr. (1981). Course entry affect and its relationship to course grade in music education and music therapy classes. *Journal of Research in Music Education, 29,* 257–264.

Berry, W. D., and Feldman, S. (1985). *Multiple regression in practice.* Newbury Park: Sage.

Blalock, H. M. (1979). *Social statistics* (2nd ed.). New York: McGraw-Hill.

Cohen, J. (1968). Multiple regression as a general data-analytic system. *Psychological Bulletin, 70,* 426–443.

Cohen, J. (1988). *Statistical power analysis for the behavioral sciences* (2nd ed.). Hillsdale: Lawrence Erlbaum Associates.

Cohen, J., and Cohen, P. (1983). *Applied multiple regression/correlation analysis for the behavioral sciences* (2nd ed.). Hillsdale: Lawrence Erlbaum Associates.

Cook, T. D., and Campbell, D. T. (1979). *Quasi-experimentation: Design & analysis issues for field settings.* Boston: Houghton Mifflin.

Hanushek, E. A., and Jackson, J. E. (1977). *Statistical methods for social scientists.* New York: Academic Press.

Harrison, C. S. (1990a). Predicting music theory grades: The relative efficiency of academic ability, music experience, and musical aptitude. *Journal of Research in Music Education, 38,* 124–137.

Harrison, C. S. (1990b). Relationship between grades in the components of freshman music theory and selected background variables. *Journal of Research in Music Education, 38,* 175–186.

Hays, W. L. (1988). *Statistics* (4th ed.). New York: Holt, Rinehart and Winston.

Hedden, S. K. (1982). Prediction of music achievement in the elementary school. *Journal of Research in Music Education, 30,* 61–68.

Hoaglin, D. C., Mosteller, F., and Tukey, J. W. (1983). *Understanding robust and exploratory data analysis.* New York: John Wiley.

Jaccard, J., Turrisi, R., and Wan, C. K. (1990). *Interaction effects in multiple regression.* Newbury Park: Sage.

Keppel, G. (1982). *Design & analysis: A researcher's handbook* (2nd ed.). Englewood Cliffs: Prentice-Hall.

Keppel, G., and Zedeck, S. (1989). *Data analysis for research designs: Analysis of variance and multiple regression/correlation approaches.* New York: W. H. Freeman.

Kerlinger, F. N. (1986). *Foundations of behavioral research* (3rd ed.). New York: Holt, Rinehart and Winston.

Kraemer, H. C., and Thiemann, S. (1987). *How many subjects? Statistical power analysis in research.* Newbury Park: Sage.

L'Hommedieu, R. L., Menges, R. J., and Brinko, K. T. (1988). Validity issues in meta-analysis: Suggestions for research and practice. *Higher Education Research and Development, 7,* 119–130.

Loehlin, J. C. (1987). *Latent variable models: An introduction to factor, path, and structural analysis.* Hillsdale: Lawrence Erlbaum Associates.

Norton, D. (1980). Interrelationships among music aptitude, IQ, and auditory conservation. *Journal of Research in Music Education, 28,* 207–216.

Norusis, M. J. (1988). *SPSSX advanced statistics guide* (2nd ed.). Chicago: SPSS.

Pedhazur, E. J. (1982). *Multiple regression in behavioral research: Explanation and prediction* (2nd ed.). New York: Holt, Rinehart and Winston.

Tukey, J. W. (1977). *Exploratory data analysis.* Reading: Addison-Wesley.

Wonnacott, R. J., and Wonnacott, T. H. (1990). *Econometrics* (4th ed.). New York: John Wiley.

·13·

CURRICULUM AND ITS STUDY

Lizabeth Bradford Wing
UNIVERSITY OF CINCINNATI

There is no "method" of curriculum discovery, any more than there is a method of exploring the jungle or falling in love. There is just understanding something about jungles, love and school curricula, and the use of a motley collection of skills, disciplines of thought and ideas to make progress in them. There is no "conceptual system" to guide the decision-making. (Barrow, 1984, p. 67)

Discussion about the most appropriate definition of curriculum constitutes a literature in itself (Walker and Schaffarzick, 1974). The various definitions reflect the different ways in which school curriculum is viewed—for example, what subjects should be taught, what students actually experience in school, what is intended to be learned versus what is really learned. Although these different perspectives yield particular insights about schools and learning, each is not, in itself, an adequate conception of curriculum as a field of activity and as a field for study.

As a prelude to their primer on curriculum studies, Taylor and Richards (1985) define curriculum as the "content of education." Curriculum is viewed as the vehicle through which education takes place. Subsumed within this definition are other defining phrases, such as course of study, educational experiences, subjects to be studied, subject matter, and educational activities (p. 3). They note carefully that this definition does not deny the critical importance of considering the interrelatedness of context, teachers, and learners with curriculum; rather, it provides a central point of departure for considering, first, what schools are intentionally about

and, second, how these intents are realized in the lives of schools.

Kliebard (1989) gives Taylor and Richards's general definition the vitality and fluid character that are the essential nature of curriculum by suggesting that the field can most adequately be defined by four central questions: "(a) why certain things should be taught, (b) who should get what knowledge, (c) what rules should govern teaching school subjects, and (d) how the components of curriculum should be interrelated" (p. 5). These questions, which Kliebard poses to clarify the role of values in curriculum (a topic that receives attention later in this chapter), are also useful in delineating the meaning of curriculum as the content of education. The questions suggest educational aims, objectives, materials, scope and sequence, articulation, teaching strategies, learner activities, and outcomes, all of which play a part in curriculum conversations. Inevitably, these conversations are not tidy affairs; the considerations of all that is important—for example, individuals, society, disciplines, and subject matter—are immense. It is critical, however, that these conversations occur, for the curriculum is the concrete ex-

The author is indebted to research assistants Rhonda Levine and Anthony Teehan for help in retrieving literature and conducting some preliminary analysis. Reviewers of the chapter outline and text contributed to content as well as focus: Richard Colwell (Boston University), James Jordan (Westminster Choir School), Rudy Radocy (University of Kansas), Decker Walker (Stanford University), and Ian Westbury (University of Illinois, Champaign). Marti Araujo completed the onerous task of typing and retyping the manuscript. Finally, acknowledgment needs to be made of all the thinkers and writers in the curriculum field on whose work the majority of this chapter is based.

pression of educational values, intents, and experiences and, as such, provides a focus for shared reflection on the educational enterprise.

In the context of these complementary definitions, the study of curriculum is discussed in this chapter. That the thoughts expressed may, at times, be messy is forewarned, for that is the nature of the field. As Walker (1980) notes, "A rich confusion is the right state for curriculum writing" (p. 81).

SETTING THE STAGE

The primary intent of this chapter is to illuminate the field of curriculum study in ways that can be instructive for curriculum work in music education. To do so requires a thoughtful appraisal of past curriculum study efforts. The arena of this inquiry encompasses research and evaluation; techniques and perspectives from both have been employed, and the distinction between the two lines of endeavor is often not clear. (Inquiry related to curriculum has often been most closely related to evaluation, although much of this effort has been called "research.") It seems more appropriate to conceptualize this inquiry as the study of curriculum. The objective of this study is the production of curriculum knowledge. Different approaches to this study yield different kinds of understandings, most of which relate to *these people* at *this time* in *this place* with *these materials*. In addition, some of these understandings seem generalizable in the sense of being principles to guide the thinking, questions, and activities of others.

Difficulty in making sense of curriculum study efforts has been a continual challenge of the field. In an attempt to define curriculum inquiry, Dillon (1985) conducted a content analysis of 171 articles appearing in the 1981 issues of six curriculum journals. On the basis of this examination, he concluded that the study of curriculum includes all kinds of problems, methods, and solutions. Other curriculum scholars have attempted to organize the field with conceptual models (e.g., Goodlad, 1977; Klein, 1983; Kimpston and Rogers, 1986; Ennis, 1986; Chipley, 1989).

Rather than relying on some overall scheme to define curriculum study, discussion in this chapter focuses on the actual patterns of inquiry that may relate to all aspects of the curriculum. Taylor and Richards (1985) delineate these areas as follows:

1. Curriculum development, planning, and design
2. Outcomes or results of the curriculum development process
3. Translation of the intended curriculum into the operational curriculum
4. Operational curriculum
5. "Results" of school curriculum: into the achieved outcomes of curricula experience
6. Relationship between intention and achievement in different parts of the curriculum system—as "evaluation," "congruence," and "appreciation"

7. Relationship between the curriculum system and the wider economic, political, social, and technological systems of society (pp. 165–170)

These dimensions represent a broad view of what constitutes curriculum and what is there to be studied and understood.

From these actual patterns of inquiry and their change over time, there are lessons to be learned. Curriculum efforts in science, aesthetic, arts, and music education have been selected to teach some of these lessons. (The inclusion of curriculum work in areas other than music education is essential as it illustrates the limited way that we have conceived of and studied curriculum; ironically, these other approaches seem to be much more closely aligned with what we teach and deem important than are music education approaches.) In addition, there are general understandings about curriculum and the study thereof that belong to the field today and should inform all curriculum efforts. These are considered to be primary lessons and are discussed at the conclusion of this chapter.

As background to understanding these lessons of curriculum study, perspectives on the curriculum and its study are provided through brief discussions of (1) the history, (2) the relationship between curriculum conversation and teaching practice, (3) conceptions of curriculum as implied by evaluation models and (4) some of the curriculum study frustrations of the last 30 years. Generally overlooked in music education curriculum work, these perspectives can serve to ground and direct our effort toward the production of more useful curriculum knowledge.

Curriculum as a Field of Study

Curriculum has been of interest for as long as thought has been given to teaching. Cremin (1971) suggests that interest in courses of study dates back to the Sophists, if not before. The nature of this interest, until quite recently, was grounded in philosophy.

Attention to curriculum became more collective and systematic as schooling became a public institution. Cremin (1971) marks the work of William Torrey Harris (St. Louis school superintendent in the 1870s) as giving impetus to the systematic curriculum movement, and contends that Harris's course of study represented an analytical paradigm that shaped curriculum making for the next half-century.

There is the learner, self-active and self-willed by virtue of his humanity and thus self-propelled into the educative process; there is the course of study, organized by responsible adults with appropriate concern for priority, sequence, and scope; there are materials of instruction which particularize the course of study; there is the teacher who encourages and mediates the process of instruction; there are the examinations which appraise it; and there is the organizational structure within which it proceeds and within which large numbers of individuals are enabled simultaneously to enjoy its benefits. (p. 210)

Within this paradigm, different curricula took on various central aims such as preparing students to do life activities of adults, capitalizing on the spontaneous activities of the child, or criticizing the social order.

The ways in which attention could be given to curriculum were dramatically altered with the advent of the scientific curriculum movement of the 1920s. Employing Frederick Taylor's concept of scientific management, schools were viewed as "factories," the work of which could be engineered and appraised quantitatively. Curriculum was designed rationally: Desired outcomes (objectives) were identified (initially the source of those outcomes was thought to be adult activities), instructional materials and activities were selected and organized to achieve those outcomes, and the effectiveness of the program was evaluated with respect to the original objectives. Although some twentieth-century curriculum efforts have diverged from this model, it has had remarkable staying power, particularly as interpreted by Ralph Tyler (Reid, 1975). Tanner and Tanner (1980) forward Tyler's model as *the* paradigm that has emerged in the curriculum field.

With the beginnings of the scientific curriculum movement, leading curriculum thinkers (e.g., Tanner, 1982; Cremin, 1971; Kliebard, 1968) mark the appearance of curriculum study as a recognizable field. A landmark work of that time, the *Twenty-Sixth Yearbook of the National Society for the Study of Education* (Rugg, 1927), set the tone for much of the subsequent thinking in curriculum studies when it called for "more scientifically controlled studies of innovation practices" (Tanner, 1982, p. 415).

Tanner (1982) chronicles the growth of the field of curriculum studies through reference to several inaugural events and the production of literature. Two major events in the beginning years were the creation in 1932 of a professional organization specifically devoted to curriculum study (Society for Curriculum Study) and the establishment of curriculum as a field of university study in 1938 (Department of Curriculum and Teaching at Teachers College). Although the literature contains a number of important works from throughout this century ranging from individual contributions (e.g., John Dewey, Franklin Bobbitt, Ralph Tyler) to collective reflections on the field (e.g., *Review of Educational Research,* National Society for the Study of Education yearbooks, National Institutes of Education), it was not until the late 1960s that national/international journals appeared that were dedicated to the study of curriculum. These were *Curriculum Theory Network* (1968), which subsequently became *Curriculum Inquiry* (1976); *Journal of Curriculum Studies* (1969); *Journal of Curriculum Theorizing* (1980); and *Curriculum Perspectives* (1980). In 1985 the *Journal of Curriculum and Supervision* was added to the ongoing and increasingly regular conversations of the field of curriculum studies.

Ralph Tyler (1987), in reviewing the work of the curriculum field during the twentieth century, identifies five important events: (1) the work of Edward Thorndike, (2) John Dewey's monograph on interest in education, (3) the *Twenty-Sixth Yearbook of the National Society for the Study of Education* (Rugg, 1927), (4) the formation of the Society for Curriculum Study, and (5) the curriculum experiments of the 1930s. In a poll of professors of curriculum studies, Shane (1981) found that the writings thought to have most influenced the field since 1906 were *Democracy and Education* by John Dewey (1916) and *Basic Principles of Curriculum and Instruction* by Ralph Tyler (1949).

Curriculum Conversation and Teaching Practice

The territory of conversation within curriculum studies ranges from consideration of broad fundamental questions about the nature of knowledge and the learner to daily and practical questions such as which activities for these students at this time. Responses to these questions have varied over time and, retrospectively, have been said to follow patterns such as the cycle (Schlesinger, 1986) and the pendulum. "Curriculum has been and is a field of shifting emphases, often excesses—from societal needs, to the whole child, to subject disciplines and back around the clock again" (Goodlad et al., 1979, p. 14).

One recurring question is whether instruction should be *teacher centered* or *student centered.* Teacher-centered instruction implies that the teacher provides the student with the information to be learned (textbook, recitation, drill and practice, and memorization figure prominently in this arrangement). As such, conception of the curriculum adheres to the factory or scientific model. Student-centered instruction, by contrast, relates to the agricultural model, where the growth of learners is to be cultivated through approaches such as the discovery method and the use of materials from the everyday world to stimulate motivation. The alternation of these two views of classroom pedagogy figures prominently in curriculum discussion in American education for the last century and a half (Cuban, 1990, p. 4).

To examine the impact of this conversation on classroom practice, Cuban (1984) studied how teachers taught in American classrooms from 1890 to 1980. The periods of most interest were during and after the loudest conversations promoting student-centered instruction (1930s–40s and 1960s–70s). The specific questions guiding his study were:

1. Did teacher-centered instruction persevere in public schools during and after reform movements that had as one of their targets installing student-centered instruction?
2. If the answer is yes, to what extent did it persist and why? If the answer is no, to what extent did instruction change and why? (p. 7)

The concepts of teacher-centered and student-centered instruction were defined by observable measures: teacher talk versus student talk; whole group versus small group and individual instruction; classroom arrangement with rows of desks facing the teacher's desk versus flexible arrangements allowing for small group activities and interest/activity centers; teacher determination versus student involvement or independence in deciding on the use of class time, classroom rules, and movement within the classroom (pp. 3–4). Data sources included photographs, textbooks and tests, student recollections, teacher reports, reports from visitors to the classroom, student writings in school publications, other studies of classroom teacher behaviors, and descriptions of classroom and building architecture (pp. 7–8). The sample included over 1,200 individual classrooms, with an additional 6,000 from other studies incorporated into Cuban's description. The settings included elementary and secondary, rural and urban schools.

One of Cuban's primary findings is that, despite the rather powerful rhetoric and intense level of curriculum activity related to student-centered instruction during the two reform periods of this century, actual teaching practices, in their continued adherence to teacher-centered instruction, remained relatively immune to the conversation; that is, teachers talked most of the time, instruction was mostly whole group, and so on. (Other observation studies, e.g., Stake and Easley, 1978, and Goodlad, 1984, support this conclusion.) The finding is qualified, however, by the observations that some levels of instruction seemed more responsive to change (elementary), some teachers adopted some practices associated with student-centered instruction, and, even in the periods of prevailing emphasis on teacher-centered instruction, there were residues of student-centered practices.

To illustrate the relationship between talk about curriculum and teaching practice, Cuban (1984) used the hurricane as an appropriate metaphor. As hurricanes move across the water, a flurry of activity is generated on the surface. Yet noticeably less movement is apparent a few feet below, and peace reigns on the ocean floor.

[Cuban] compared that hurricane to any newly trumpeted curriculum theory. Professional journals, for example, echo pro and con arguments on a new theory. Letters to editors and sharp rebuttals add to the flurry. Books are written and reputations made. Conferences host both skeptics and advocates. Professors of education teach the new wisdom to their students. Yet most publishers continue producing texts untouched by that theory, and most teachers use methods unmarked by controversy, slogans, journal articles, or convention programs. (p. 2)

Conceptions of Curriculum as Implied by Evaluation Models

Evaluation generally is considered to be the collection and analysis of information in order to make decisions or judgments about the merit of something. The nature of the information collected is a message about what is thought to be important by those concerned with the evaluation; the nature of the analysis is a message about the ways in which the information is important. A brief examination of how school curricula have been evaluated provides another perspective on what has been thought to be important about curriculum, the ways that curriculum has been or can be studied, and the uses to which curriculum knowledge has been put.

Relying heavily on sociological, political, and technological events for definition, Madaus, Stufflebeam, and Serisen (1983) divide the history of program evaluation into six periods. The first period, the Age of Reform (1800–1900), is so named because of "the Industrial Revolution with all of its attendant economic and technological changes" (p. 4). School programs were viewed primarily as enterprises that brought about specific student learnings. Student achievement was measured by test scores. The oral examination was replaced by the essay exam, a European practice of the time. Madaus and colleagues (1983) suggest that the introduction of the essay exam was partially a political move in that the "permanent" nature of written evidence allowed for comparison between schools. Information related to differential achievement outcomes could then play a role in decisions regarding the appointment of principals. (Targets for elimination were those who opposed the abolition of corporal punishment.)

During the last years of this period, Joseph Rice (1893) completed his famous study of spelling. Seeking to provide evidence that extended spelling drills were worthless, Rice compared the test scores of 33,000 students with weekly time spent on spelling instruction in a number of schools. His findings indicated that there were no significant differences in achievement regardless of the time devoted to drills and instruction. The study is one of the first instances of program evaluation employing a comparative experimental design.

During this period the North Central Association of Colleges and Secondary Schools was established. The model of program evaluation used by this and subsequently formed accreditation organizations relies primarily on institutional self study and review by an outside team of professionals according to explicit criteria or standards of the profession.

The period from 1900 to 1930 is labeled the Age of Efficiency and Testing. The influence of scientific management figured heavily in how schools were evaluated. In many large school systems, surveys assessed most of the quantitative dimensions of the educational program: budgets, enrollments, student retention and promotion, student test scores. The standard for these evaluations was efficiency.

The tests used to measure student achievement included locally developed tests in each subject area (which, over time and with annually accumulating scores, could become normative) and standardized tests of specific objectives (created by people like Edward Thorndike), which allowed for between-school comparisons. Test results were used as information about individuals as well as in making decisions and judgments about curricula.

The next 15 years, from 1930 to 1945, is called the Tylerian Age. During these years the seminal influence of Ralph Tyler came to bear on the field of curriculum. Madaus and colleagues (1983) acknowledge him as the father of educational evaluation and credit him with creating the term "educational evaluation." The prototype that Tyler forwarded for evaluating educational programs (known as the "objectives model") is steadfastly linked to behavioral objectives but is not limited to curriculum evaluation as determined by assessment of student achievement alone. His model has application for curriculum development, instructional planning and delivery, assessment of student outcomes, and curriculum revision. As summarized by Hamilton, MacDonald, King, Jenkins, and Parlett (1977), the model consists of a five-step sequence:

1. Secure agreement on the aims of the curriculum.
2. Express these aims as explicit learner behaviors or objectives.
3. Devise and provide experiences that seem likely to enable the learners to behave in the desired way.
4. Assess the congruence of pupil performance and objectives.
5. Vary the "treatment" until behavior matches objectives. (p. 25)

Well known to the general education research community is the Progressive Education Association's (PEA) Eight-Year Study (1932–1940), the classic application of Tyler's model. (The sense of "classic" for many, however, may well be that of Twain's *Pudd'nhead Wilson*—a book that people praise but don't read.) The project grew out of dissatisfaction with viewing the curriculum in terms of Carnegie units and assessing its effectiveness through traditional standardized testing. For the 30 schools involved (ultimately 29), the curriculum work included labored discussions about the aims and purposes of the secondary school. Two major principles guided this discussion and subsequent curriculum development: First, "the general life of the school and methods of teaching should conform to what is now known about the way human beings learn and grow." Second, "the high school in the United States should rediscover its chief reason for existence" (Aiken, 1942, pp. 17–18). Whereas there was consensus that schools should better serve their entire populations rather than catering primarily to the college bound (for five out of six students, high school was the end of formal schooling at this time) and that schools should prepare students for life in a democracy, the realization of these aims in the different schools took a variety of forms. Some schools created curricula incorporating broad-fields courses that were based on subject matter analysis (like a survey course) or the social demands approach reflecting consideration of adult needs. Other schools developed core curricula following the unified studies, cultural epoch, or social demands approaches, or based on adolescent needs. The entire story of the Eight-Year Study is told in a five-volume collection entitled *Adventure in American Education* (Aiken, 1942; Giles, McCutchen, and Zechiel, 1942; Smith, Tyler, and Evaluation Staff, 1942; Chamberlin, Chamberlin, Drought, and Scott, 1942; *Thirty Schools Tell Their Story,* 1942).

What is noteworthy from the standpoint of curriculum evaluation in the Eight-Year Study is that all aspects of the curriculum—from its initial conception to its long-term impact on teachers and students—were considered important for study, a radically new conception. Included in the story are candid accounts of (1) the human challenges in revamping curriculum, (2) the ingredients necessary to bring new curricula into the classroom, (3) the difficulty in creating appropriate learning activities and assessment measures for the new objectives, and (4) the ingenious but labor-intensive ways in which the impact of the new curricula could be assessed through studying the performance of its graduates in college. The information-gathering techniques most often were created for each school, as what was thought to be important was local and interpreted in a much broader and higher-order way than that which could be assessed through traditional standardized testing. Teachers played a large role in creating these techniques and determining their validity, as evaluation was considered integral to instruction. Information was most often used for formative purposes, and the need to look for patterns among scores with some classification of these patterns according to objectives, was found to be essential to adequate interpretation.

Intended to contribute to the evaluation of these curricula but also providing a good example of curriculum research is the college follow-up study. Graduates of study schools were paired with graduates of other schools (1,475 pairs) on a variety of characteristics. College performance was assessed through such indicators as grades, awards, extracurricular activities, interviews with college faculty and students' peers, and students' self-reports. Consideration in analyzing the findings was given to aptitude treatment interaction (ATI) as well as degree of implementation of the new curriculum in each student's high school. Overall conclusion of the follow-up study was "that the thirty schools graduates, as a group, have done a somewhat better job than the comparison group whether success is judged by college standards, by the students' contemporaries, or by the individual students" (Chamberlin et al., 1942, p. 208).

The fourth period in the history of program evaluation, the Age of Innocence (1946–1957), was a time of optimism and growth for education in general, as the country tried to forget the war.

New buildings were erected. New kinds of educational institutions, such as experimental colleges and community colleges, emerged. Small school districts consolidated with others in order to be able to provide the wide range of educational services that were common in the larger school systems, including: mental and physical health services, guidance, food services, music instruction, expanded sports programs, business and technical education, and community education. Enrollments in teacher-education programs ballooned, and, in general, college enrollments increased dramatically. (Madaus et al., 1983, p. 10)

This growth, however, was largely unstudied from the standpoint of curriculum evaluation. Fueled by interest and advances in technology, the period is characterized by marked increase in standardized testing (the Educational Testing Service was established in 1947), the emergence of experimental design as a subject in the professional literature, and large-scale attention to behavioral objectives that included the development of taxonomies. Although the inclusion of behavioral objectives in curriculum discussions reflected the influence of the Tylerian Age, evaluation of curriculum was generally conceived in forms reminiscent of its earliest periods.

The Age of Expansion (1958–1972) was shaped in large measure by the involvement of the federal government in school curriculum activity. Initial involvement took the form of generous financial investment: In 1955, total federal monies devoted to educational enterprises were $1.4 billion; in 1965, $3.6 billion; and in 1968, $8.8 billion (McClure, 1971, p. 61). Between 1963 and 1968, Congress passed 24 legislative acts, more in this time period than it its entire previous history, that focused on all phases of education (p. 51).

Following the investment of federal dollars in the various curriculum efforts allocated through legislation, such as the National Defense Act of 1958 and the Elementary and Secondary Education Act of 1965, came a mandate (through amendment to the latter) to evaluate the effectiveness of the new programs. In response, evaluators drew upon their arsenal of standardized tests, ascertaining congruence of student outcomes with curriculum objectives, professional judgment, and field studies to appraise the new curricula (Madaus et al., 1983, p. 12). The view of program effectiveness based upon the yield of these evaluation approaches, however, was with growing frequency thought to be unsatisfactory. Tests designed for use with students of average ability, for example, were of questionable value for programs concerned with disadvantaged students. Tests of general ability had little utility in assessing the differential effects of planned variation programs such as Head Start and Follow Through. Comparative experiments were similarly inadequate as they failed to be sensitive to the uniqueness of individual programs. The large-scale mathematics and science projects that grew out of complete reconceptualization of the curriculum were attacked at the federal level based on a decline in test scores.

Senator Kennedy is concerned about declining test scores and wonders whether it indicates that "we are moving in the wrong direction." Joanne McAuley asserted that the declining test scores can be "traced directly to the new types of courses" and that this is why there is "such a cry around the country for a return to the basics." (National Institute of Education (NIE), 1976, p. 47)

From dissatisfaction with evaluation results as well as incompatibility between the kinds of information collected through existing approaches to curriculum evaluation and what was thought to be important in new programs emerged the current period of evaluation, the Age of Professionalism (1973 to present).

As in Tanner's (1982) determination of the historical entrance of curriculum as a recognizable field of study, Madaus and colleagues (1983) point to the 1970s and the appearance of professional journals specifically devoted to educational evaluation (*Education Evaluation and Policy Analysis, Studies in Evaluation, CEDR Quarterly, Evaluation Review, New Directions for Program Evaluation, Evaluation and Program Planning, Evaluation News*), the establishment of special organizations given to evaluation concerns (May 12th Group, Division H of AERA, Evaluation Network, Evaluation Research Society), and the creation of educational evaluation programs/centers in universities for marking the dawn of educational evaluation as an identifiable and distinct field (p. 15). Although activities of the maturing field continue to include the testing and research approaches of the past, the current evaluation models go well beyond the limited look at curriculum that is possible through the use of test scores and comparative studies. The flavor and diversity of these models were created by the educational evaluators themselves in order to appreciate the rich complexity of the educational enterprise and the various roles and audiences that evaluation must serve.

A sense of the thinking behind many of these models can be found in an agreement reached among educational evaluation specialists at a 1972 working conference on curriculum evaluation. The core of the agreement included a consensus on the inadequacy of past evaluation efforts that neglected "educational processes including those of the learning milieu" and relied too heavily on "psychometrically measurable changes in student behavior (that to an extent represent the outcomes of the practice, but which are a misleading oversimplification of the complex changes that occur in students)." On the basis of this consensus, a commitment was made to conduct evaluations that were more responsive to actual program events rather than relying only on a preordinate design; recognize the relationship between evaluation design and purpose; employ multiple designs in the evaluation of single programs; make value positions explicit; and consider the political, social, and economic implications of the evaluations (Hamilton et al., 1977, pp. vii–viii).

House (1980) has distilled the repertory of approaches to evaluation into eight basic models. Each model is based on its own perspective of what is important about curriculum, how the curriculum should be studied, and for whom/what this study is important. Table 13–1 (p. 202) is taken from House's analysis (p. 23).

Conceptions of the curriculum implied by these models include such varied perspectives as that the curriculum is (1) a delivery system that is to be economically efficient (systems analysis), (2) a rational, ongoing enterprise that must be informed and guided by the systematic collection and analysis of data (decision making), (3) a human experience that must be represented in ways that communicate the personal and unique (art criticism), and (4) a multifaceted enterprise that is valued and experienced in a variety of ways (case study). Looking at the curriculum through the application of any one of these models (or a combination of them) allows for very specific understandings that are appropriate only for select decisions or judgments about the curriculum. (Colwell [1985] completed a brief analysis of these models with respect to their possible usefulness in the evaluation of music teacher education programs.)

Curriculum Study Frustrations of the Last 30 Years

Much of the hope for improving education, particularly during the 1960s and 1970s, has rested on faith in the impact of curriculum reform. Determining the effectiveness of this impact generally has fallen to two camps: experimental/com-

TABLE 13–1.

Model	How the Curriculum Is Studied	Importance of Study
1. Systems analysis	Program, planning, and budgeting system; linear programing; planned variation; cost-benefit analysis	For: Efficiency To: Economists, managers
2. Behavioral objectives	Behavioral objectives; achievement tests	For: Productivity, accountability To: Managers, psychologists
3. Decision making	Surveys, questionnaires, interviews, natural variation	For: Effectiveness, quality control To: Decision makers, especially administrators
4. Goal free	Bias control, logical analysis, modus operandi	For: Consumer choice, social utility To: Consumers
5. Art criticism	Critical review	For: Improved standards, heightened awareness To: Connoisseurs, consumers
6. Professional review	Review by panel, self study	For: Professional acceptance To: Professionals, public
7. Quasi-legal	Quasi-legal procedures	For: Resolution To: Jury
8. Case study	Case studies, interviews, observations	For: Understanding diversity To: Client, practitioners

parative believers and blind faith believers. Each group has had its share of frustrations.

The large-scale, centrally produced curriculum efforts in mathematics of the 1960s and early 1970s represented a shift in emphasis from drill in arithmetic computation to focus on the mathematical principles underlying computational rules. Among these new programs were the School Mathematics Study Group (SMSG), the University of Illinois Committee on School Mathematics (UICSM), the Ball State Indiana Teachers College Project (Ball State), and the University of Maryland Mathematics Project (UMMaP). (The new school programs of this era came to be known as the alphabet curricula.) The Minnesota National Laboratory conducted a 5-year study of these programs, with volunteer teachers teaching both experimental and control classes (Rosenbloom and Ryan, 1968). A series of achievement tests were administered to assess entering and final levels of achievement, as well as retention. "The results did not show that the experimental programs had a strong influence on increasing (or reducing) student achievement in mathematics as measured by these tests" (Dessart and Frandsen, 1973, p. 1178).

In their review of the Minnesota study and a number of other smaller studies comparing old and new math curricula, Dessart and Frandsen (1973) found little evidence to support the superiority of the new programs, whether they were examined from the standpoint of student achievement or with respect to students' attitudes and interests. They end their review (which is much more extensive than implied here) with a prediction made by Mayor, Henkelman, and Walbesser (1965) "that the decade ending with 1965 was marked by intensive work in curriculum innovation, whereas the following 10-year period would be dominated by research efforts

in the learning and teaching of mathematics" (Dessart and Frandsen, p. 1191).

In an analysis of 26 studies that compared student achievement relative to different curricula in the areas of science, math, social studies, and English, Walker and Schaffarzick (1974) found that "innovative curricula were superior only in their own terms"—that is, that "students using different curricula in the same subject generally exhibited different patterns of test performance, and that these patterns generally reflected differences in content inclusion and emphasis in the curricula" (p. 83). Although most of the studies reviewed suffer from some of the usual threats to external validity (e.g., selection and nonrandom assignment of groups), the authors' thoughtful analysis strongly supports their conclusion that different curricula are perhaps not most appropriately studied by examining general achievement results. Rather, they yield different kinds and levels of outcomes as related to the particularities of each curriculum and should be evaluated accordingly.

Evaluation activities and findings of the Follow Through program, one of the most costly programs supported at the federal level, also provide an account of the frustrations attendant on comparing different programs with common measures. At the same time, however, they illustrate the potential of comparison when appropriate measures are used. Follow Through, which was intended to improve the "life chances" of disadvantaged children through special instruction from kindergarten through grade 3, was initially evaluated by Abt Associates, Inc. "The analysis compared thirteen of the models of early childhood education, using data based on a sample of over twenty thousand students enrolled in Follow Through models for a four year period. The total evaluation of Follow Through cost between $30 and $50 million" (House, Glass, McLean, and Walker, 1978, p. 129).

The primary findings of the Abt evaluation were that each individual program model varied by site and that those models that belonged to the basic skills category were superior to the others. Evaluation of the Abt evaluation, however, revealed serious flaws in the entire study (House et al., 1978). Primarily, the wrong question guided the study. Given the planned and naturally occurring variation across sites, the quest to identify the *one best model* rather than the *specific effectiveness of each model* was inappropriate. Problems with the study accumulated given this false start—the use of common (and available), primarily cognitive assessment measures (one of which may be more of an intelligence test), questionable bases upon which models were categorized, distortion of analysis by confounding sample size and effectiveness, possibly misleading results with the use of ANCOVA, and more. All of these grew out of the effort to conceptualize the evaluation as a comparative experimental project.

In reflecting on other data available from the study of Follow Through during its first 10 years of existence, Hodges (1978) contends that there have been a number of important things learned about and from these programs: (1) the achievement gains of disadvantaged children may be viewed more optimistically if compared with national norms; (2) observations at the various sites indicated that teaching and classrooms changed to reflect the priorities of each program's model; (3) parents of children in Follow Through programs became more interested in the work of the schools and in participating in appropriate ways; (4) program sponsors had documentation that indicated that schools and homes became happier places; (5) a variety of working models were developed for early childhood education; (6) the program represented a new partnership for linking research, theory, and practice; and (7) a new model for teacher training and inservice evolved. Additional information regarding the impact of the Follow Through programs has been obtained through longitudinal studies of program participants (as cited and discussed by Stallings and Stipek, 1986). In general it appears that, in comparison with non–Follow Through students with similar backgrounds, Follow Through participants are more likely to stay in school and graduate, and less likely to be retained in grade or placed in a special education setting.

These additional data about the Follow Through program, collected through onsite and long-term study, are instructive about program impacts in ways well beyond the traditional time-bound comparative study findings; they attend to the people and the places of these programs as well as to indicators of success that perhaps speak more clearly in the grand scheme of education.

Those of the blind faith persuasion, in determining the goodness of curricula, have been satirically portrayed as employing an approach from the "5 C" model (Wolf, 1969). When the Cosmetic Method is used, a program is judged effective if it looks good. The Cardiac Method is based on a heartfelt belief in the program. In the Colloquial Method, goodness is evidenced by group consensus. The degree to which a new program can be implemented without disturbing existing programs is the primary criterion of the Curricular Method. Finally, if program effectiveness relies on agreement about data by two or more clerks, the Computational Method is being employed.

Although Wolf's conceptualization of evaluation models hyperbolizes in making a statement about the superficiality of curriculum evaluation in practice, the lack of rigor in many curriculum evaluations has been a frequently voiced concern. In a major work describing the thinking about and developments in curriculum study for a 30-year period, Taba (1962) laments the inattention given to evaluating curricula and suggests that the problem is not new.

Careful evaluation has not been made of the innovations of the past, nor is it being made today. This failure to assess the effects of innovations against their total outcomes has been perhaps the cause of the fact that in American education curriculum revision proceeds by replacing one scheme with another and one "approach" with another, not necessarily because objective evidence has demonstrated the merits of one or the failures of the other, but merely because the new scheme or approach somehow has gained attention, is in "fashion" for the time being, or is being championed by forceful leaders. (p. 315)

Charged with studying the value to schools of the many federally sponsored curriculum projects of the 1960s and 1970s, the NIE Curriculum Development Task Force (NIE, 1976) interviewed people from over 60 organizations and examined curriculum documents. One conclusion reached by the group was that questions about curriculum were predominantly related to who should do the deciding about school curricula rather than what should be taught. Few concerns were expressed about evaluation.

In their review of music education curriculum projects funded by the government during this same time, Leonhard and Colwell (1977) observe that no systematic evaluation of these projects was undertaken: "They can be appraised as interesting, or musical, or provocative, or some other value-weighted objective, but not in terms of actual results compared with the results of using other materials and methods" (p. 85).

The accumulation of frustrations in the study (or lack thereof) of curriculum has led curriculum scholars to pronounce the field as being "dead" (Huebner, 1976 p. 153), "moribund" (Schwab, 1969, p. 1), or "a discipline in search of its problems" (Westbury and Steimer, 1971, p. 234).

LESSONS FROM THE STUDY OF CURRICULUM

A recurring theme in the curriculum literature is the call to examine and learn from past efforts. In the main, curriculum work has been conducted in an ahistoric context (Goodlad,

1966; Bellack, 1969). Cremin (1971) asserts that neglecting history impoverishes current discussions and makes curriculum reformers victims of the past (p. 216). As mentioned in the preceding section of this chapter, some of the general historical perspectives of the curriculum field that are available and should play a role in current work include the continuing struggle to study curriculum adequately, resulting in increasingly complex and sophisticated conceptions of what curriculum is; the robustness of teaching practices regardless of the pedagogical implications inherent in the espoused curriculum; and the multiple realities of educational programs given voice through different evaluation models.

More particular lessons to be learned from the past may be drawn from an examination of (1) the kinds of questions asked about specific curricula, (2) how these questions were asked (instruments and techniques), (3) the understandings about curriculum that have been gained, and (4) the questions that remain. In what follows are accounts of curriculum work in science, aesthetic, arts, and music education. The size of the projects ranges from large research and development ventures to work conducted by individuals, mostly in completion of their doctoral studies. Although the size of the lessons varies accordingly, there is commonality in their themes, for example, reluctance to conduct thorough curriculum study; the tendency toward and inadequacy of "scientific" study of the curriculum; and the interrelated influences and importance of context, teachers, and learners in curriculum.

Science Education

Two curriculum stereotypes can be used to categorize generally the science education curricula of the past 30 years (White and Tisher, 1986). The first type includes the large, centrally produced programs of the 1950s, 1960s, and early 1970s. These curricula were created primarily by teams of scientists and were intended to prepare students for further study in the sciences. A general assumption underlying these curricula was that science teachers were not capable of intelligent participation in the creation of curriculum. "One of the most pathetic sights on the current educational horizon is the myriad of local school committees, whose members have little or no scientific training, trying to produce a modern science curriculum" (Calandra, 1959, p. 22). The course development process included an initial summer writing conference to prepare instructional materials, field trial of the materials in select schools, a second summer writing conference to revise materials (most often on the basis of debate among project staff rather than feedback from teachers [Welch, 1979]), institutes and workshops to prepare teachers to use the materials, and release of the final version of the curriculum (through commercial publishers) to the schools.

Study of these curriculum packages took a variety of forms. On the local level, the central questions related to planning, development, utility, and student learning.

Is the rationale for the project good? Is it based on sound educational theory?

Are the objectives and purposes clarified enough to serve as a basis for the development of curriculum materials?
Are the materials that are developed teachable?
What is learned by pupils studying the materials?
Do the learners achieve the purposes which the project defined for the learners? (Blackwood, 1965, p. 63)

Early responses to these questions included confirmation of a project's soundness by virtue of its being selected for funding, general group agreement on objectives (although there was some argument over whether objectives could be specified in advance of developing the materials), teachability as a given outcome of trial and revision, and the development of tests to measure student achievement. Few comparisons of the new curricula versus the old curricula were conducted, although sentiment regarding the potential utility of such study was being expressed (Blackwood, p. 64).

By the time that the *Second Handbook of Research on Teaching* (Travers, 1973) appeared, a number of comparative studies had been conducted that sought to determine the differential effects of the various science curricula on student outcomes—for example, knowledge, attitudes, and skills. In general, results indicated that the new curricula were comparable to the old as measured by traditional tests and slightly superior to the old as measured by instruments designed specifically for the new curricula (Shulman and Tamir, 1973).

During the 1976–77 school year, a study funded by the National Science Foundation was undertaken to identify the current status of science education in the schools. The resulting *Case Studies in Science Education* (CSSE; Stake and Easley, 1978) was based on case studies of 11 school systems, site visits to these schools, and a survey administered to a national stratified random sample of about 4,000 school people, parents, and students.

Three of the primary hallmarks of the large-scale curricula that could logically be expected to be in evidence in this study were (1) "variety and flexibility" (multimedia resources for learning), (2) "doing science" (imitating the work of scientists in a lab setting), and (3) "thematic focus" (organizing concepts taken from the disciplines; Welch, 1979). Two of these hallmarks are addressed in the CSSE report summary: (1) the textbook and teacher were the primary source of authority on what was to be learned, and (2) rarely was science taught as inquiry but rather as knowledge forwarded by experts. Although the researchers did observe some remnants of the large-scale curricula, the overall impression was that most instructional settings and teaching practices bore little relationship to the major ideas behind these curricula.

A growing awareness of the complexity of the curriculum enterprise began to emerge from these sorts of studies. No longer did it seem useful to ask simply, What should the curriculum look like? Or, Is curriculum A better than curriculum B? The range of assumptions to be examined and questions to be asked multiplied.

Parallel to this rethinking of what is important about curriculum was the appearance of the second curriculum stereotype (White and Tisher, 1986), whose characteristics are greater teacher involvement in the development and implementation of curricula, development of curricula on the local level, and stronger relationships between science in schools and science in everyday living.

Shulman and Tamir (1973) suggested that study of science curricula would be more informative if it were conceived of as curriculum evaluation and if outcomes were assessed in a multidimensional fashion. They classify studies into five categories:

1. Evaluation of programs through studies of adoption and use
2. Studies of the impact of new programs
3. Comparative evaluation studies
4. Long-term follow-up studies
5. Transaction studies focusing on actual classroom processes rather than exclusively on outcomes (p. 1129)

The types of questions to be asked in any of these studies may include "optimal sequencing, grade level placement, teaching styles, learning styles, change process, and questions relevant to the adoption and use of materials in a wide variety of situations" (Grobman, 1968, p. 5). (For an extensive listing of possible questions related to evaluation of the Biological Sciences Curriculum Study project, see Grobman, 1968, pp. 16–118.)

In their science chapter in the third edition of the *Handbook of Research on Teaching,* White and Tisher (1986) identify a number of new perspectives being brought to the curriculum study enterprise. Impact of the curriculum was being studied with respect to students' perceptions of their classrooms, their listening and classification skills, and teachers' behaviors. The curriculum itself was studied in terms of the validity of its aims and on its actual content. Evaluations had been conducted as an integral part of the development and implementation process. Surveys and observation/interview studies were conducted to determine the degree of implementation of specific curricula and the conditions under which the greatest implementation takes place. A good example of this more comprehensive study of curriculum is provided by investigations of the Australian Science Education Project (ASEP; Fraser, 1978).

Developed over a 5-year period and intended for use in all junior high schools, ASEP was Australia's first national curriculum for any subject area. Key features of the curriculum were organization by independent units providing for teacher choice and variability of sequence, individualization for students, and an emphasis on student activity and inquiry.

Many studies by a number of researchers have been conducted of ASEP in relationship to curriculum development processes, philosophy, materials, learning environment, student outcomes, and dissemination (Fraser, 1978, p. 418). The means used to study each of these dimensions of the curriculum include comparison of the aims of ASEP and the aims for science education expressed in the professional literature, content analysis of the materials to determine major themes, classroom observations, assessment of student per-

ceptions of the learning environment and teacher judgments of the curriculum, case studies, comparisons of student outcomes between ASEP and traditional programs, study of the purchase of materials, and surveys of reported usage and characteristics associated with implementation.

Findings from these studies have been informative in a variety of ways. Content analysis of the materials, for example, revealed some structural weaknesses in thematic presentation. Students learning from revised material performed somewhat better on a test of achievement than did students working with the original material. Study of ASEP and traditional classrooms revealed the ASEP classrooms were, in fact, much more student centered as intended. Students in ASEP programs liked their classes better. Case studies revealed that some teachers had serious misconceptions of what ASEP was all about. There were marked differences in the ASEP experience between schools, classes in the same schools, and students in the same class. Student achievement and attitude/affect were improved by more structured teaching. Teachers who knew more about ASEP and had values similar to those of the program were more likely to use the materials.

Collective findings of these evaluation studies have not yielded immutable knowledge about the curriculum. Rather, they reveal the complexity and the dynamic nature of the curriculum; the critical importance of including teachers, students, and school and social contexts as integral to the actual curriculum; and the need to conduct an evaluation comprehensively and continuously in recognition of what curriculum is and the roles that evaluation can play in efforts to understand and improve.

Aesthetic, Arts, and Music Education

The 1960s and 1970s was also a period of intense activity for curriculum in the arts, which, as with other subject areas, received most of its support from federal sources. Between 1965 and 1971, the Arts and Humanities Program of the U.S. Office of Education funded about 200 projects involving research and development in arts education, at a cost of $10.6 million (Bloom, 1975, p. 4). Other federal programs, such as Titles I and III of the Elementary and Secondary Education Act (ESEA), and private foundations, such as the John D. Rockefeller 3rd Fund and the Kettering Foundation, provided additional resources for the arts education community.

The nature of the curriculum projects undertaken during this time ranged from short-term feasibility studies by individual researchers to large-scale multiyear programs. How curriculum was studied in these different projects depended in large part on the perspectives of the program investigator(s) and the available resources of time, money, and expertise. Evaluation for projects funded under Title III, for example, rested with the project investigator. Initial evaluation reports often included an "imaginative use of attendance figures, narrative descriptions, and letters of appreciation from school faculty members and children to justify the continuation of the projects" (Bloom, 1975, p. 5). Curriculum work of the newly established research and development centers, on the other hand, included basic research; the creation of sophisticated guidelines for curriculum development; and a variety of procedures for the study, revision and testing of curriculum materials. The lessons to be learned from an examination of these projects echo the efforts and understandings of curriculum study in other places and, in many cases, in earlier times.

R & D Center Curriculum Projects in Aesthetic and Music Education

The Aesthetic Education Program (AEP) of the Central Midwestern Regional Educational Laboratory (CEMREL) had as its primary objective the creation of "a resource to help schools develop a generalized course of study for all students using all the arts" (Madeja, 1975, p. 4). Outcome of this study for students was to be "an education of individual sensibilities for varied aesthetic responses, judgments, and actions" (Barkan, Chapman, and Kern, 1970, p. iv).

Conceived in 1967 and conducted until 1976, the program involved two phases. Phase I consisted of the production of guidelines for curriculum development in aesthetic education; Phase II included the development of materials according to these guidelines and the trial, revision, and dissemination of these materials.

Study of the work of Phase I began with consideration of fundamental questions that were at the heart of the entire curriculum: What is an aesthetic experience? What should an aesthetic education accomplish? For whom and to what should this education relate? How and with what should this education be ordered? (Many other issues were addressed, as well, including the primary referents for building a curriculum, i.e., learners, society, and the discipline, and the role of values in the acceptance of the curriculum by schools and teachers.) A National Advisory Committee of the AEP composed of artists, educators, philosophers, educational psychologists, and aestheticians was instrumental in helping program staff arrive at basic understandings for the project. These understandings proceed from the general to the specific in inverted pyramid fashion.

Aesthetic experience is an experience which is *valued* intrinsically.

The general goal for aesthetic education is *to cause the student to increase his capacities to experience qualities in man-made and natural objects and events in his environment.*

Aesthetic education within the context of general education is charged with responsibilities to the *individual,* the *arts,* and the *general environment.*

Ways of responding and *ways of producing* which are consistent with the variety of practices by members of the artistic communities *are authentic sources which can help develop activities for units of instruction.*

Content for units of instruction for aesthetic education should be created out of *combinations of diverse phenomena that can prompt aesthetic encounters and diverse concepts and facts that interpret and document aesthetic qualities.* (Barkan et al., 1970, p. 12)

Within the context of these basic assumptions of the curriculum, a three-stage curriculum development "game" was devised in which formative evaluation played a central role. In the first stage, units were created according to topics contained in an overall plan, four basic rules, technical aids in the form of a thesaurus (student and teacher behaviors and objects of study), curriculum statements, bibliographic sources, checklists to assist in the planning, design and evaluation of the units, and preliminary classroom trials (also known as "messing around") conducted by the unit developers (Bocklage and Meyers, 1975). (The technical aids are presented in Appendices A–D of Barkan et al., 1970.)

In the second stage, Hothouse Trial, the complete set of materials for the unit was implemented in an actual classroom setting by a classroom teacher. Evaluation of this trial was conducted rather systematically through an in-depth interview with the teacher; descriptions of the students, teacher, classroom, and school; and observation/tape recording of the teaching sessions. Focus of the evaluation was on six major concerns:

1. the nature of the student/teacher interaction with the various components of the unit;
2. the design and everyday usability of the materials;
3. the ability of students to demonstrate the behaviors desired by the developer;
4. unanticipated cognitive or affective outcomes;
5. needed revisions and
6. evaluation strategies which may be useful at later stages of the development process. (Blockage and Meyers, 1975, p. 25)

The final stage, Pilot Trials, involved the implementation and study of the materials in three diverse classroom settings. Four questions guided these trials: Can the teacher implement the unit independently? Do students achieve the intended instructional objectives? Do students enjoy the experience? Are the materials durable and in sufficient quantity? Data were collected through questionnaires, interviews, random observations, a few standardized tests, and a variety of student achievement instruments designed specifically for the units.

Beyond the intensive study undertaken during the development of the AEP, there were a number of other investigations conducted relative to the program. Smith and Schumacher (1972), for example, studied through participant observation a statewide extended pilot test of the AEP materials in Pennsylvania. Continued study of the curriculum and its implementation by teachers was accomplished through the establishment of Aesthetic Education Learning Centers (Rosenblatt and Michel-Trapaga, 1975). Bagenstos and Le-Blanc (1975) detail some of the research completed on designing appropriate instruments for assessing student achievement. Smith (1975) conducted a "Piagetian Interview Study" in the attempt to identify a profile of aesthetic development (with the suggestion that the impact of the curriculum could be assessed in relationship to its effects on that profile).

The CEMREL Aesthetic Education Program story is one of a large-scale commitment to the place of aesthetic education within general education, the complex and sophisticated task of translating general ideas and values into instructional specifics, and the enduring questions related to curriculum adoption, survival, and the capacity to know in what ways and by what means the impact of curricula can best be assessed. It is not, however, a story of unqualified success. In addition to there being a lack of adequate resources for dissemination and implementation of the program, some of the basic assumptions underlying the effort were seriously flawed at the practical level—for example, the schools felt no need for a basal curriculum in the arts and did not understand aesthetic education; teachers resisted the shift from teaching the single arts to an approach that included all of the arts; teachers were not comfortable with and had insufficient background to rely on instructional "resources" rather than the textbook (decreasing school finances were also influential in this respect; Madeja, 1986). Lessons learned from the project, on the other hand, spawned four CEMREL-sponsored conferences with subsequent publications devoted to enduring questions of curriculum in the arts (Madeja, 1984). The books are *Arts and Aesthetics: An Agenda for the Future* (Madeja, 1977), *The Arts, Cognition, and Basic Skills* (Madeja, 1978), *The Teaching Process and the Arts and Aesthetics* (Nider and Stallings, 1979), and *Curriculum and Instruction in Arts and Aesthetic Education* (Engel and Hausman, 1981).

The Music Program of the Southwest Regional Laboratory (SWRL) was "designed to provide resources for conducting systematic music instruction in kindergarten through grade six" (Williams, 1976, p. 1). These resources included a sequenced set of behavioral objectives focused on the concepts of rhythm, melody, harmony, form, timbre, and dynamics. Concepts were to be acquired through songs, stories, games, and dances. Intended for use by classroom teachers, the final curriculum package was to be a "ready-made product" that was "state-of-the-art" with respect to "research-based, quality-verified instruction" (Williams, 1975, p. 43). A specific feature of the program that made it usable by classroom teachers was an extensive catalog of audiotapes designed to teach them to perform simple musical tasks, or to be used in actual teaching of children (lesson tapes and song tapes) and to present clearly focused listening lessons that were accompanied by a teacher script (R. Zwissler, personal communication, May 12, 1990).

The SWRL employed a managerial model to develop instructional systems based on research. Initial work included drawing on available research and conducting new research as a basis for each system. Included among SWRL's research efforts in music were a survey of ethnic folksong material as found in elementary music programs (Williams, 1972), the design of an Audio Laboratory System (Williams, 1974) to aid in the conduct of the research, and a series of experiments related to children's perception of melodic patterns (Williams, 1977).

Development and dissemination of the Music Program followed a seven-stage process: *formulation*—objectives were specified and instructional strategies were developed on the basis of the research; *prototype*—strategies were tested to determine sequencing; *component*—units of instruction were tested in a classroom and evaluated with respect to responses to the materials by school personnel and posttest results; *product*—finished products were created on the basis of results of testing; *installation*—training programs were conducted for teachers; *manufacturing* and *marketing*—commercial publishers were to take over the materials and the responsibility for training teachers (Williams, 1975).

For the SWRL Music Program, the final stage did not occur. Copyright clearance for the extensive amount of recorded material (which included performance edition and recording rights) was a formidable challenge and not yet completed at the time (ca. 1982) when funding ceased for this area of the lab's work. A decision was made to leave all as it was at that time. Although some schools purchased the materials from SWRL as a research and development project, the program was not formally completed or disseminated. The Music Program print materials, tapes, student assessment measures (including paper and pencil and some performance measures), and the questionnaire used in field trials are housed in the SWRL archives.

In reflecting on the project, Ruth Zwissler (personal communication, May 12, 1990) indicated that there were important lessons to be learned from SWRL's work. First, it is possible to develop music materials that can be used effectively by classroom teachers. Secondly, student assessment in music—beyond paper and pencil means—is a special challenge (practically and technically) as it is to be conducted by the classroom teacher. Finally, a central idea behind the project—to have classroom teachers play a role in the conduct of the elementary music program—requires a reconceptualization of the role of the elementary music specialists. As with the reorientation required of teachers in the AEP, that call for change was not well received.

The Discipline Based Art Education (DBAE) program, funded by the Getty Center for Education in the Arts (one of seven entities of the J. Paul Getty Trust), has also utilized a research and development approach to curriculum development and implementation. On the basis of a survey of the status of art education in the elementary school and the identification of exemplary art programs, project direction was established to the end that "if art education is to become a meaningful part of the curriculum, its content must be broadened and its requirements made more rigorous" (*Beyond Creating*, 1985, p. v). The DBAE approach promotes the learning of art in four ways: aesthetics, criticism, history, and production.

The development process for DBAE has included summer institutes for staff training; field trials in Los Angeles area schools over a 5-year period; and the establishment of six consortia throughout the nation intended to marshal the resources of schools, colleges, and arts organizations in the design and conduct of school arts education programs in each locale. Central to this development process has been the notion that curricular change is effected through the participation and support of all concerned with the school program, that is, administrators, board members, classroom teachers, arts specialists, and community arts people.

Study of program effectiveness has been integral to project activities.

Just as the Institute [Getty Institute] has evolved, the evaluation has also evolved. Throughout the five years, the question always guiding evaluation activities was: What information is needed in order to make wise decisions? As the nature of the decisions has changed, focusing on more specific problems, the kinds of information collected and how they are analyzed has changed also. (Hoepfner, 1985, p. 15)

On the basis of this evaluation (performed by two independent evaluators, one employing a qualitative approach and the other a quantitative), DBAE has been approved by the National Diffusion Network (NDN) as an "educational program that works" (*Educational Programs,* 1988). Educational effectiveness of the project as it was conducted in the Los Angeles sites was determined according to three "claims." First, DBAE teachers allocated more time to art instruction and displayed more art reproductions in their classrooms. Second, DBAE students performed better than non-DBAE counterparts on tests of achievement related to the curriculum. (An initial finding of similar performance for first-grade students and poorer performance for sixth-grade students was explained by degree of implementation.) Finally, the schools created infrastructures to support DBAE.

Other Curriculum Projects in Music

Descriptions of a few of the smaller curriculum projects undertaken during the curriculum heydays of the 1960s and 1970s illustrate the variety of ways in which curricula were developed and studied. Here again, lessons can be learned from the questions asked (and not asked), from how they were asked, and from the results of those queries.

The Hawaii Music Project was undertaken by the University of Hawaii in an effort to improve K–12 music instruction in the state (Burton, 1975). Philosophical inspiration was drawn from the Yale and Tanglewood meetings and from the publication *Music in General Education* (Ernst and Gary, 1965). The initial activity for the project staff was to create a design statement describing "music as a discipline of knowledge and explain(ing) how a discipline approach could be used to develop a comprehensive program of music education" (Burton, 1990, p. 68). Subsequently, a research and development team consisting of music educators, aestheticians, composers, theorists, performers, and curriculum specialists created a "chronology of skills (behavior statements)" for

each grade level that served as the sequential organizer for comprehensive musicianship development throughout the curriculum: K–12 general music, chorus, band, high school string orchestra, theory and literature, guitar and ukulele. Study of the curriculum materials was conducted through trial, research, and testing in the University of Hawaii's lab school and Hawaii's single statewide public school system.

Implementation of the Hawaii Music Program has relied on inservice workshops for teachers. The method of the inservice at the elementary level "is to have teachers assume the role of students and do all that is expected of students while examining the text material that guides instruction" (Burton, 1990, p. 44). It is estimated that over 75 percent of the island's elementary classroom teachers have voluntarily participated in these workshops, a figure used as evidence of the curriculum's apparent success at that level. Whereas the same general approach to implementation was used with music teachers at the secondary level, the results were not as positive. "The inservice activity was successful," but "it was evident later that little of what had been accomplished found its way to the school programs of the participating teachers" (p. 75). (Can the operation be a success if the patient dies?)

The Icelandic-American Comprehensive Musicianship Framework Project was a cross-cultural effort "to improve musical literacy through unified and sequential curriculum development" (Woods, 1978, p. 23). The idea for the project grew out of the observation by Stefan Edelstein, a visitor from Iceland, that America's music programs represented a vast diversity and that this diversity could result in non-sequential, fragmented learning. Supported by a grant from the Ford Foundation, a group of five music education specialists created a framework for the development of a general music curriculum, preschool through high school. Characteristics of the framework are that it is based on concepts (basic elements of music) that are to be experienced sequentially in spiral fashion and requires that students engage in the behaviors of musicians. Procedural "webs" connecting possible activities and concepts are presented to suggest instructional strategies.

An additional grant by the Ford Foundation in 1977 provided for an actual trial of the common framework by music teachers and college students in Iowa and music teachers in Iceland. The trial included study of curriculum development procedures and the design of curricula for each of the programs or schools involved. During the trial, "teachers from both countries observed and compared the respective programs during specific developmental stages. The cross-cultural setting of the project reinforced the premise that unified concept development can take place if a logical and comprehensive taxonomy of goals, instructional objectives, and concepts is maintained in all facets of the program" (Woods, 1982, pp. 42–43). In addition to finding that the common framework could be employed in different settings using different activities, methods, and materials, the participating teachers reported "that the music literacy of the students at all levels of instruction . . . increased due to the preparation and reinforcement inherent in curriculum planning" (p. 44).

Supported by a grant from the U.S. Office of Education

(USOE), the Manhattanville Music Curriculum Project (MMCP) consisted of two general stages. Convinced of the general lackluster and routine quality of most music programs, Ronald Thomas, project director, set out to identify some exciting and innovative music programs (Thomas, 1967). From a field of 92 programs recommended, he selected 15 for close study. Although these programs were diverse in intent and nature, six common characteristics were identified: (1) each had clearly defined musical objectives; (2) a student was a central referent in consideration of how learning should proceed; (3) skill development and cognitive growth were explicitly addressed; (4) teachers functioned as resources in rather than directors of instruction; (5) teachers respected the students' ability to accept responsibility for learning; and (6) these teachers remained active musically and were individually responsible for the direction of their programs (p. 52).

Based in part on understandings acquired through study of these programs, a 4-year curriculum development project was undertaken to create "an alternative" for music education. Major products of the project were "Synthesis," a comprehensive curriculum for grades 3 through 12; "Interaction," a curriculum for early childhood; and three feasibility studies related to the electronic keyboard, science and music, and instrumental music (Thomas, 1970). Primary characteristics of the curricula include discovery learning, spiral encounters with musical concepts, and personal and creative involvement with music of all varieties.

The process by which these curricula were developed depended heavily on the involvement of music teachers in creating materials, trying them in classrooms, and consulting with one another in the review and redesign of materials and strategies. A series of workshops, implementation in designated experimental and field sites, and annual addition of personnel (expanded to include not only inservice training but initial college preparation as teacher musical qualifications to implement the curriculum became an important issue) provided the forums and impetus for this process. In addition, frequent communications (visits, conferences, group sessions, questionnaires, written reports) among the over 80 musicians and educators involved provided for continuous formative evaluation (Thomas, 1970, p. 11). No assessment instruments were identified that would appropriately measure the important features of the MMCP. Although a preliminary model of assessment was created for the project, no wide-scale testing of the model was conducted (Thomas, 1970, p. 5).

Also supported by a grant from the USOE, Bennett Reimer (1967) developed a 2-year general music curriculum for junior and senior high. During the first year of the project, thorough review of existing philosophies of music education, published curriculum materials, and city and state curriculum guidelines was undertaken. Exemplary programs were also identified and studied for a year. Drawing on understandings about current practices, a particular aesthetic philosophy, and principles and pedagogical approaches from the curriculum field, three assistants under the supervision of the project director created and revised syllabi and

materials through trial in three different communities during the third year of the project. Assessment of students' conceptual understanding and aesthetic perception was integral to the curriculum. The project did not, however, "include a formal analysis of results of the trial teaching as one of its responsibilities" (p. 28). As stated by the project director, "The major implication of this project is that it is indeed possible to carry out at the program level a particular, current, and pervasive aesthetic theory, using educational strategies relevant to that theory" (p.38).

The Rolland string project was yet another USOE-funded curriculum study (Rolland, 1971). The central issue behind the project "was the hypothesis that movement training, designed to free the student from excessive tensions, can be introduced within an organized plan of string instruction, and that such a plan, in the long run, will result in faster learning and better performance in all facets of instruction" (Rolland and Mutschler, 1974, p. 1). Initial phases of the project included developing materials and revising through informal testing. Revised materials underwent an extensive 2-year trial in 22 teaching centers. Final products of the project included 16mm color films, teachers' manuals, wall charts, a curriculum guide, and recordings. Evaluation data available with respect to the project consist largely of testimonials from teachers who have used or examined the materials (Rolland and Mutschler, 1974, pp. 1–3).

Curriculum Conversation in Music Education Research Journals

A search for writings related to curriculum in all issues through 1989 of the *Journal of Research in Music Education* (JRME) and the *Bulletin of the Council for Research in Music Education* (CRME) yielded 88 articles. The majority of these writings (61 percent) appeared in CRME and were related to dissertation studies. Thirty-two percent of the articles for both journals were published from 1969 to 1972. Since that time, only five curriculum-related articles have appeared in JRME; CRME published at least one curriculum study (and as many as four) each of the following years, with the exception of 1979 and the past several years when there have been none.

Casual content analysis of these articles indicates that the kind of attention that has been given to curriculum in music falls into six categories, ranging from talk about curriculum to systematic research of curricula. A listing of these categories, the percentage of articles falling into each category, and a representative example are given in Table 13–2 (p. 210).

Studies falling into categories 5 and 6 (42 total) were further examined to identify those indicators selected to determine curriculum effectiveness. Most frequently (29 studies), indicators were author-constructed pre- and posttests of student achievement. In 20 studies, judgments regarding the goodness of the materials were important. Other effectiveness indicators included student interest/motivation (16), comparison of an experimental group's achievement to that of a control group (14), the use of standardized tests (11),

TABLE 13–2.

Category	%	Example
1. Position statements/Curriculum guidelines	8	"Basic Concepts in Music Education" (Ernst, 1958)
2. Status studies: Survey/analysis	16	"Training of Secondary School Music Teachers in Western Colleges and Universities" (Peterson, 1955)
3. Evaluation of existing curricula	3	"The Piano Major Program at Ithaca College, with Proposals for Future Development" (Nicklett, 1969)
4. Development of curriculum/curricular materials	25	"A Model for a Comprehensive Arts Program with Interdisciplinary Arts Lessons as Unifiers" (Bogusky-Reimer, 1982)
5. Curriculum development and trial	32	"The Design and Evaluation of Study Materials for Integrating Musical Information into the Choral Rehearsal" (Whitlock, 1985)
6. Curriculum development and comparative study	16	"The Effect of Programed Materials on the Vocal Development of Selected Children's Choruses" (Ten Eyck, 1985)

teacher interest/acceptance (8), judgments of the curriculum by external review (3), and assessment of the degree of implementation and teacher understanding of the curriculum (1). (Although it can be generally assumed that most of these studies were based on the work of others through their review of the literature, there appeared to be only one instance in which replication of and improvement upon previous efforts were systematically undertaken by different investigators [Glenn, 1972; Glidden, 1972; Popp, 1972].)

A central mission of the CRME under Colwell's editorship was to improve the quality of dissertation research through published reviews of completed studies. The main points made by reviewers of curriculum studies were classified according to area and to whether the area was cited as a strength or a weakness of the study (Table 13–3).

Content analysis of these writings was undertaken in order to get some sense of the music education research community's attention to and concern with curriculum. There seems to be ample indication that there is dissatisfaction with how most music dissertation curriculum work has been studied (evaluated/researched), that literature reviews are not as thorough and related as should be the case, and that even designing a curriculum for the doctoral project has been thought to be problematic.

Legacies: Perspectives and Tools in Our Current Arsenal for the Study of Curriculum

Despite the similarities between reform movements, the context is never quite the same, the tools of reform are never quite the same, and neither the clients nor their problems are ever quite the same. Beneath the apparent circularity lie linear developments that have transformed both our social problems and our approaches to them. (Kaestle, 1978, p. 136)

Curriculum is an ongoing conversation in which the participants, subject matter, and context are constantly changing. A charge of ahistoricity rings true only to the extent that these conversations are not transformed in some way by experience—that is, that lessons have not been learned.

TABLE 13–3.

Area	Number of Comments	Cited as	
		Strength	Weakness
Study of the curriculum	64	13	51
Design of the curriculum	61	33	28
Review of the literature	41	15	26
Writing	33	15	18
Overall usefulness/generalizability	19	14	5

The disillusionment with curriculum study efforts and results during the large-scale curriculum days of the 1960s and 1970s was followed by a period of curriculum neglect (Ravitch, 1990). Factors other than what happened in schools were thought to be the primary determinants of student achievement. A combination of events, including a decline in test scores, the effective schools research, and a spate of commission reports calling for reform of the educational system, resulted in a renewed interest in curriculum during the 1980s. Response by some to the call for change has been a literal echo from the past. The National Association of State Boards of Education, for example, has urged that schools eliminate the "time-honored" Carnegie unit requirement and, instead, "create a core curriculum made up of six broad areas," institute flexible scheduling, and move toward "performance-based assessments and tests that develop students' creativity and thinking skills" (Rothman, 1988, pp. 1 & 12). These recommendations are being adopted by several states and considered by 15 to 20 others; no mention of the Eight-Year Study appears in the news reports ("Outcome-Based Accreditation," 1990). Other responses indicate an explicit awareness and consideration of past curriculum work.

The projects are aimed, officials of both organizations said, at building a base of support for the proposals among those who will be responsible for implementing them. Previous efforts to change math curricula, such as the New Math of the 1960's, lacked such a base, they maintained. (Rothman, 1990)

What primary lessons should inform current curriculum conversations? There are at least six: the critical importance of good questions to guide curriculum work and study; a thorough understanding and consideration of the complexity of the curriculum enterprise; the role of values; the role and influence of teachers in curriculum; adequate conceptions of assessment; the rich repertory of aids available for the creation and study of curriculum.

On the Questions

Westbury and Steimer (1971) have argued forcefully that curriculum is a discipline in search of its problems. Asking the important questions, sustaining and building on that inquiry, and using the yield of that inquiry to inform understanding and action have not characterized, but should characterize, the activities of the field.

We hold that curriculum is a methodical inquiry exploring the range of ways in which the subject matter elements of teacher, student, subject, and milieu can be seen. A range of ways of viewing these curricular elements serves as a basis for opening a range of choices for deliberative action upon or among these elements, and for making coherent the reasons for choice and action in regard to these elements as they exist in particular real situations. (p. 251)

An attempt was made in the previous section of this chapter to describe curriculum studies with respect to the questions that guided them. This was not possible, in many cases, as either there were no questions or they were unclear. In these many instances, the intent and satisfaction were apparently in just "doing" curriculum.

One reviewer of this chapter indicated that he was not convinced "that there is such a thing as curriculum research, except as it fits into the larger areas of developmental, philosophical, experimental, and even historical research." The particular domain of curriculum research is not in its method(s) but rather in its questions, questions that appreciate the continually shifting coalescence of all of its parts. The degree to which these are the proper questions for curriculum is the degree to which they contribute to useful curriculum knowledge.

The general education research community has been undergoing a fundamental reorientation during the last several decades with respect to defining what knowledge is of most use.

That dream of finding out once and for all how teaching works or how schools ought to be administered no longer animates nearly as many of us as it once did. In its place we have substituted the much more modest goal of trying to figure out what's happening *here and now* or what went on *there and then*. This does not mean that we have given up trying to say things that are true from situation to situation or that we are no longer interested in making generalizations. But the kind of truth in which more and more of us seem interested these days takes a very different form than it once did. As Geertz has pointed out, the change is not so much in our notion of what knowledge as it is in what we want to know. (Jackson, 1990, p. 7)

Methods being employed to address these questions rely heavily on historical, anthropological, ethnographic, philosophical, cognitive science, sociolinguistic, and artistic perspectives.

Doyle (in press) has outlined the general curriculum knowledge that is emerging from this inquiry according to five areas related to curriculum and pedagogy: texts and teachers, content dimensions in conceptions of pedagogy, social context of the curriculum, lesson structures and processes, and classroom structures. The central thesis in his discussion is that curriculum is a series of transformations including the representation of subject matter; the "images" that teachers bring to subject matter, teaching, and classroom life; the representations of subject matter brought or acquired by the learner; and much more. Curriculum knowledge that is useful must account for these transformations.

What kind of curriculum knowledge exists that is specific to music education? It seems as though the bulk of it relates to having good ideas (comprehensive musicianship, sequential organization of concepts to be learned, quality literature, and so on), being able to create curricula based on these ideas, getting teachers to use these programs in varying degrees for a period of time, and seeing some evidence that students learned what was intended from these programs. The profession knows itself largely from the standpoints of stated values and scientifically conducted, quantitative inquiry into some of its curriculum efforts. Not much is known with any certainty about the past or what is really happening in music classrooms today—for example, What and how are teachers teaching? What and how are students learning? What are the primary influences on decisions related to who is taught what and how? What are the long-term outcomes of curricular experience in music? These are questions central to curriculum. That these have not as yet been asked is "an indicator of the developmental stage of our profession" (Colwell, 1985, p. 52).

The beginnings of such inquiry in music education must be local. "A curriculum must be understood in its own terms before being evaluated in other terms" (Westbury, 1970, p. 253). Although this inquiry must continue to remain local, resulting descriptions can become general as the understandings become cumulative to the point of suggesting explanations and patterns. These explanations and patterns would constitute useful curriculum knowledge that could serve as the research basis for continuing to know the music education enterprise and inform the efforts to improve it.

The major challenge, then, that faces the music education research community is the identification and ordering of important questions related to curriculum as an agenda to be acknowledged and pursued collectively and in a variety of ways. Based on the CEMREL curriculum experience, such a task was undertaken for arts and aesthetic education 15 years ago (Madeja, 1977). This would seem to be a very good place to start.

On the Complexity

The curriculum document is only a script. Each performance based on that script is an interpretation brought by the director and actors at different points in time and, perhaps, in different places (Hamilton et al., 1977).

Lee Cronbach's article "Course Improvement Through Evaluation" (1963) often has been cited as one of the earliest statements on the complexity of educational programs and the need to recognize that complexity in how and why programs are studied. Joseph Schwab (1969) has also been influential in directing the field to consider the four commonplaces of education—teacher, student, what is taught, and milieu of teaching-learning—with each being an equally important contributor to the curriculum.

Acknowledgment of what curriculum actually is and how it happens includes new understandings about who should develop curricula and how. Schwab's (1969, 1971, 1973, 1983) arguments for the "practical" and the use of the "arts of the eclectic" undergird much of this thinking. Consequently, some curriculum development is becoming a more collaborative (and necessarily cumbersome) venture among those who are its participants (e.g., McConaghy, 1990; Utterback and Kalin, 1989). This acknowledgment also includes new attempts to understand and portray the meaning of curricula from such perspectives as their sociopolitical messages (Apple, 1988; Giroux, 1988). (For thoughts from this perspective in music education, see Vulliamy and Shep-

herd [1984], phenomenology [Grumet, 1988; Pinar, Reynolds, and Hwu, in press], and artistic criticism/education connoisseurship [Eisner, 1982, 1985].) Although the results of some of these studies are not immediately instructive for doing curriculum, they do shed dramatically new light on our understandings of the curriculum.

Even though curriculum as a fluid, dynamic, and ever-changing phenomenon that is particular to its time, place, and people has continued to receive increasing acknowledgment in the curriculum literature, too little attention is being paid in curriculum study practices. "We researchers have created a language whose primary users seem to be ourselves. We study one thing at a time, oversimplify it for research purposes, and then become wedded to our conception" (Lieberman, 1990, p. 533). What is thought to be the case based on such study often bears little relationship to what is really going on.

Asking the kinds of questions that are appropriate and important, and that reflect the complexity of curricula, is not a simple task, for it is "largely uncharted territory—not unlike the 'new world' of fifteenth-century European maps" (Cornbleth, 1988, p. 91). Walker (1973) has analyzed the rethinking that is necessary in order to conduct meaningful inquiry. Several completed curriculum study projects provide good examples of the magnitude, the method, and the yield of such inquiry (e.g., Cuban's study of nearly a century of teaching practices, the Eight-Year Study, the CEMREL Aesthetic Education Program, Robert Stake and Jack Easley's case studies, and the Australian Science Education Project).

On Values

Values play a large and unbounded role in curriculum. Societal, school, teacher, and learner values all influence what is taught and learned. Where there are differences in value orientation, there is conflict. Curriculum developers, for example, have been accused of being value smugglers. Teachers and learners have been viewed as saboteurs of curriculum intents where discrepancies exist between document and delivery. Wall chart practices are attacked as myopic representations of important school outcomes. Where values are unexamined, there is mindless activity.

Explicitly addressing the question of values is central to good curriculum work (Kliebard, 1989). Choices are made as to what to teach, to whom, in what way, and within what context. "A school and a curriculum are where they are because of judgments from within and from without" (Stake, 1970, p. 181). The goodness of these choices or judgments obviously depends on the quality of the deliberations that lead to their making. Methods for improving these deliberations, the decisions made, and, subsequently, the knowledge of curriculum have been discussed in general by MacDonald and Clark (1973), in the development and study of curriculum by Walker (1970), and in the evaluation of curriculum by Stake (1970) and Schwandt (1989).

On Teachers

The importance of the teacher in the curriculum has been a lesson to be learned over and over again. Degree of implementation and intersite variation are sample indicators of that lesson. Implications from this lesson have been derived for both the design and the study of curriculum.

Connelly and Clandinin (1988) provide perspective on how teachers can create curriculum in considered ways by reflecting on their own experiences in the classroom and on new ideas. The narratives that are a part of this process yield insights into classrooms and teaching that are curriculum knowledge of the "common place." Teacher knowledge in the form of "images" of the classroom, students, and educational processes plays an important contributing role in the curriculum rather than being an obstacle to be overcome (Clandinin, 1986).

In the study of curriculum, Tikunoff and Ward (1979) argue for ecological approaches that attend to the entire "instructional-social system" of classrooms. The primary basis for their argument rests in the substantial literature verifying the critical role of the teacher in bringing about change.

Atkin (1989) identifies and supports the emerging trend of "teacher-as-researcher." The promise of this practice is twofold: a better understanding of educational events at the level of the practitioner, and teachers who are more informed and articulate about what they do. It is in the classroom that the greatest potential for improvement is thought to rest. "Not much progress in education is likely to take place unless teachers become agents in the improvement of their own practice" (p. 204).

On Assessment

Too often the assessment and subsequent evaluation of curriculum have rested in pre- and posttests of student achievement. Although student learning is important and should be included in the study of curricula, the narrowness of testing as an indication of learning and the short-term nature of most projects must be taken into consideration. The inadequacy of this approach for purposes of accountability or instructional decision making is currently receiving formal attention. Expanded conceptions of student learning as implied by assessment programs are being adopted in new statewide plans (Rothman, 1989) and in special subject matter projects such as Arts Propel (Olson, 1988).

Initially, the Program Effectiveness Panel of the NDN limited evidence of effectiveness to "experimentally controlled test score data without regard to the context or the treatment's goals" ("Criteria and Guidelines," 1987, p. 18). Through over 15 years of experience in evaluating projects, the NDN "models" of acceptable evidence have expanded to include changes in student learning skills, improvements in teachers' attitudes and behaviors, improvements in students' attitudes and behaviors, and institutional or schoolwide change. This "suggests a much richer conception of what

constitutes compelling and imaginative evidence suitable for the vast variety of classroom needs and practices" (p. 18).

Determining curriculum "payoff" is only one role of evaluation in the study of curriculum. In most of the systematic curriculum efforts mentioned in this chapter, formative evaluation was as important or more so than summative evaluation in creating and implementing curricula. Although summative statements about curriculum may be more attractive to make (as in nine out of 10 doctors), the work of curriculum is with its people, places, and materials and, therefore, so must be the questions of curriculum study.

On the Repertory of Aids for Curriculum Study

The various segments of the process [curriculum experiences] are as often conflicting as they are complementary, as often random as they are sequential, and as often confusing as they are meaningful. And the very nature of a free and complicated society precludes our ever wholly ordering or rationalizing them—or, I would argue, wanting to. But they can at least be viewed in their full range and complexity whenever we contemplate instruction. (Cremin, 1971, p. 219)

The complexity of the curriculum makes it a challenging phenomenon for study. Systematic study of curriculum is a relatively young field. As awareness of the questions of the field grows, a repertory of approaches and techniques for study continues to develop. As these approaches have been employed, instructive examples of curriculum study are available. Making sense of this arsenal of tools and examples in a way that gives direction to future curriculum study efforts is equally challenging.

Some of the more useful frameworks for organizing and focusing the study of curriculum can be found in general works on educational evaluation (e.g., Bloom, Hastings, and Madaus, 1971; AERA monograph series; Hamilton et al., 1977; House, 1980; Madaus et al., 1983; Taylor and Richards, 1985). Posner (1989) has classified studies considered to be curriculum research with representative examples. Stake (1975) has addressed evaluation of arts education programs with description of his "responsive" approach as well as a bibliography of basic readings and examples of evaluation efforts. Colwell (1985) has reviewed program evaluation in music and made nine recommendations for future study.

Although anthologies of techniques that can be used to study curriculum exist—for example, *Encyclopedia of Educational Evaluation* (Anderson, Ball, Murphy, and Associates, 1975)—the richest sources of means to answer the questions are studies that were thoughtfully conceived to address specific questions for particular situations. Some of those studies are mentioned in this chapter. Others are less accessible as they are inhouse documents whose audience was local. Study of these efforts by curriculum workers, however, is essential, as many lessons are there to be learned. That the "collection of skills, disciplines of thought and ideas" (Barrow, 1984, p. 67) uncovered in these studies can be characterized as motley—"of many colors"—is perhaps appropriate, for that is the kaleidoscopic character of the curriculum.

References

Aiken, W. (1942). *The story of the Eight-Year Study*. New York: Harper and Brothers.

Anderson, S., Ball, S., Murphy, R. et al. (1975). *Encyclopedia of educational evaluation*. San Francisco: Jossey-Bass.

Apple, M. (1988). The culture and commerce of the textbook. In W. Pinar (Ed.), *Contemporary curriculum discourses* (pp. 223–242). Scottsdale: Gorsuch, Scarisbrick.

Atkin, J. M. (1989). Can education research keep up with education reform? *Phi Delta Kappan, 71*(3), 200–205.

Bagenstos, N., and LeBlanc, A. (1975). The role of research in the aesthetic education program. *Bulletin of the Council for Research in Music Education, 43,* 65–85.

Barkan, M., Chapman, L., and Kern, E. (1970). *Guidelines curriculum development for aesthetic education*. St. Louis: CEMREL.

Barrow, R. (1984). *Giving teaching back to teachers*. Brighton, Sussex: Wheatsheaf.

Bellack, A. (1969). History of curriculum thought and practice. *Review of Educational Research, 39,* 283–292.

Beyond creating: The place for art in America's schools. (1985). Los Angeles: J. Paul Getty Trust.

Blackwood, P. (1965). Science. In G. Unruh (Ed.) *New curriculum developments* (pp. 57–67). Washington: Association for Supervision and Curriculum Development.

Bloom, B., Hastings, J., and Madaus, G. (1971). *Handbook on formative and summative evaluation of student learning*. New York: McGraw-Hill.

Bloom, K. (1975). Introduction. In R. Stake (Ed.), *Evaluating the arts in education: A responsive approach* (pp. 3–11). Columbus: Charles E. Merrill.

Bocklage, S., and Meyers, N. (1975). The curriculum development game as played by the aesthetic education program. *Bulletin of the Council for Research in Music Education, 43,* 19–35.

Bogusky-Reimer, J. (1982). A model for a comprehensive arts program with interdisciplinary arts lessons as unifiers (Reviewed by L. Karel). *Bulletin of the Council for Research in Music Education, 69,* 21–25.

Burton, L. (1975). The Hawaii music project. *Educational Perspectives, 14*(2), 24–27.

Burton, L. (1990). Comprehensive musicianship—the Hawaii music curriculum project. *The Quarterly, 1*(3), 67–76.

Calandra, A. (1959). Some observations of the work of the PSSC. *Harvard Education Review, 29*(1), 19–22.

Candinin, D. (1986). *Classroom practice: Teacher images in action*. London: Falmer.

Chamberlin, D., Chamberlin, E., Drought, N., and Scott, W. (1942). *Did they succeed in college? The follow-up study of the graduates of the thirty schools*. New York: Harper and Brothers.

Chipley, D. (1989). Making sense out of curriculum research: Some formative notes and an exploratory model. *Journal of Curriculum and Supervision, 5*(1), 70–80.

Colwell, R. (1985). Program evaluation in music teacher education. *Bulletin of the Council for Research in Music Education, 81,* 18–62.

Connelly, F., and Clandinin, D. (1988). *Teachers as curriculum planners: Narratives of experience*. New York: Teachers College Press.

Cornbleth, C. (1988). Curriculum in and out of context. *Journal of Curriculum and Supervision, 3*(2), 85–96.

Cremin, L. (1971). Curriculum-making in the United States. *Teachers College Record, 1*(2), 207–220.

Criteria and guidelines for the program effectiveness panel. (1987). United States Department of Education.

Cronbach, L. (1963). Course improvement through evaluation. *Teachers College Record, 64*(8), 672–683.

Cuban, L. (1979). Determinants of curriculum change and stability. In J. Schaffarzick and G. Sykes (Eds.), *Value conflicts and curriculum issue* (pp. 139–196). Berkeley: McCutchan.

Cuban, L. (1984). *How teachers taught: Constancy and change in American classrooms 1890–1980*. White Plains: Longman.

Cuban, L. (1990). Reforming again, again and again. *Educational Researcher, 19*(1), 3–13.

Dessart, D., and Frandsen, H. (1973). Research on teaching secondary school mathematics. In R. Travers (Ed.), *Handbook of research on teaching* (pp. 1177–1195). Chicago: Rand McNally.

Dewey, J. (1916). *Democracy and education*. New York: Macmillan.

Dillon, J. (1985). The problems/methods/solutions of curriculum inquiry. *Journal of Curriculum and Supervision, 1*(1), 18–26.

Doyle, W. (1992). Curriculum and pedagogy. In P. Jackson (Ed.), *Handbook of research on curriculum*. New York: Macmillan.

Educational programs that work. (1988). (Supplement: Projects approved since the publication of Edition 14). Longmont: Sopris West Inc.

Eisner, E. (1982). *Cognition and the curriculum: A basis for deciding what to teach*. New York: Longman.

Eisner, E. (1985). *The educational imagination*. New York: Macmillan.

Engel, M., and Hausman, J. (Eds.). (1981). *Curriculum and instruction in arts and aesthetic education*. St. Louis: CEMREL.

Ennis, C. (1986). Conceptual frameworks as a foundation for the study of operational curriculum. *Journal of Curriculum and Supervision, 2*(1), 25–39.

Ernst, K. (1958). Basic concepts in music education. *Journal of Research in Music Education, 6,* 145–148.

Ernst, K., and Gary, C. (1965). *Music in general education*. Washington: Music Educators National Conference.

Fraser, B. (1978). Australian science education project: Overview of evaluation studies. *Science Education, 62*(3), 417–426.

Giles, H., McCutchen, S., and Zechiel, A. (1942). *Exploring the curriculum: The work of the thirty schools from the viewpoint of curriculum consultants*. New York: Harper and Brothers.

Giroux, H. (1988). Liberal arts, teaching, and critical literacy: Toward a definition of school as a form of cultural politics. In W. Pinar (Ed.), *Contemporary curriculum discourses* (pp. 243–263). Scottsdale: Gorsuch, Scarisbrick.

Glenn, N. (1972). A review of recent research in music education. *Bulletin of the Council for Research in Music Education, 27,* 7–16.

Glidden, R. (1972). The development of content and materials for a music literature course in the senior high school. *Bulletin of the Council for Research in Music Education, 27,* 7–16.

Goodlad, J. (1966). *The changing school curriculum*. New York: Fund for the Advancement of Education.

Goodlad, J. (1977). What goes on in our schools? *Educational Researcher, 6*(3), 3–6.

Goodlad, J. (1984). *A place called school*. New York: McGraw-Hill.

Goodlad, J. et al. (1979). *Curriculum inquiry: The study of curriculum practice*. New York: McGraw-Hill.

Grobman, H. (1968). *Evaluation activities of curriculum projects: A starting point*. Chicago: Rand McNally.

Grumet, M. (1988). Bodyreading. In W. Pinar (Ed.), *Contemporary curriculum discourses* (pp. 453–474). Scottsdale: Gorsuch, Scarisbrick.

Hamilton, D., MacDonald, B., King, C., Jenkins, D., and Parlett, M.

(Eds.). (1977). *Beyond the numbers game: A reader in educational evaluation.* Berkeley: McCutchan.

Hodges, W. (1978). The worth of the Follow Through experience. *Harvard Educational Review, 48*(2), 186–192.

Hoepfner, R. (1985). *Evaluation of the 1984 institute: Effects on the growth of students' art achievement.* Tucson: Getty Institute for Educators on the Visual Arts.

House, E. (1980). *Evaluating with validity.* Beverly Hills: Sage.

House, E., Glass, G., McLean, L., and Walker, D. (1978). No simple answer: Critique of the Follow Through evaluation. *Harvard Evaluation Review, 48*(2), 128–160.

Huebner, D. (1976). The moribund curriculum field: Its wake and our work. *Curriculum Inquiry, 6*(2), 153–167.

Jackson, P. (1990). The functions of educational research. *Educational Researcher, 19*(7), 3–9.

Kaestle, C. (1978). Social reform and the urban school: An essay review. In D. Warren (Ed.), *History, education, and public policy* (pp. 127–147). Berkeley: McCutchan.

Kimpston, R., and Rogers, K. (1986). A framework for curriculum research. *Curriculum Inquiry, 16*(4), 463–474.

Klein, M. (1983). The use of a research model to guide curriculum development. *Theory into Practice, 22*(3), 198–202.

Kliebard, H. (1968). The curriculum field in retrospect. In P. Witt (Ed.), *Technology and the curriculum* (pp. 69–84). New York: Teachers College Press.

Kliebard, H. (1989). Problems of definition in curriculum. *Journal of Curriculum and Supervision, 5*(1), 1–5.

Leonhard, C., and Colwell, R. (1977). Research in music education. In S. Madeja (Ed.), *Arts and aesthetics: An agenda for the future* (pp. 81–108). St. Louis: CEMREL.

Lieberman, A. (1990). Navigating the four c's: Building a bridge over troubled waters. *Phi Delta Kappan, 70*(7), 531–533.

MacDonald, J., and Clark, D. (1973). Critical value questions and the analysis of objectives and curricula. In R. Travers (Ed.), *Second handbook of research on teaching* (pp. 405–412). Chicago: Rand McNally.

Madaus, G., Stufflebeam, D., and Serisen, M. (1983). Program evaluation: A historical overview. In G. Madaus, M. Scriven, and D. Stufflebeam (Eds.), *Evaluation models: Viewpoints on educational and human services evaluation* (pp. 3–22). Boston: Kluwer-Nijhoff Publishing.

Madeja, S. (1975). The aesthetics of education: The CEMREL aesthetic education program. *Bulletin of the Council for Research in Music Education, 43*, 1–18.

Madeja, S. (Ed.). (1977). *Arts and aesthetics: An agenda for the future.* St. Louis: CEMREL.

Madeja, S. (Ed.). (1978). *The arts, cognition and basic skills.* St. Louis: CEMREL.

Madeja, S. (1984). Curriculum development in the arts. *Theory Into Practice, 23* (4), 280–287.

Madeja, S. (1986). Reflections on the aesthetic education program. *Journal of Aesthetic Education, 20*(4), 86–91.

Mann, J. (1969). Curriculum criticism. *Teachers College Record, 71*(1), 27–40.

Mayor, J., Henkelman, J., and Walbesser, H., Jr. (1965). An implication for teacher education of recent research in mathematics education. *Journal of Teacher Education, 16*, 483–490.

McClure, R. (1971). The reforms of the fifties and sixties: A historical look at the near past. In R. McClure (Ed.), *The curriculum: Retrospect and prospect: Seventieth yearbook of the National Society for the Study of Education* (pp. 45–75). Chicago: University of Chicago Press.

McConaghy, T. (1990). Curriculum reform in Saskatchewan. *Phi Delta Kappan, 71*(6), 493–496.

National Institute of Education. (1976). *Current issues, problems and concerns in curriculum development.* Washington: Author.

Nicklett, G. (1969). The piano major program at Ithaca College, with proposals for future development (Reviewed by J. Lyke). *Bulletin of the Council for Research in Music Education, 17*, 33–36.

Nider, J., and Stallings, J. (1979). *The teaching process and the arts and aesthetics.* St. Louis: CEMREL.

Olson, L. (1988, November 16). In Pittsburgh: New approaches to testing track arts "footprints." *Education Week,* pp. 1, 22, 23.

Outcome-based accreditation plan advances in Wyoming. (1990, January 31). *Education Week,* p. 14.

Peterson, W. (1955). Training of secondary school music teachers in western colleges and universities. *Journal of Research in Music Education, 3,* 134–135.

Pinar, W., Reynolds, W., and Hwu, W. (In press). *Understanding curriculum: A comprehensive introduction to the study of curriculum.* Scottsdale: Gorsuch, Scarisbrick.

Popp, H. (1972). The implementation and evaluation of developed content and materials for a music literature course in the senior high school (Reviewed by H. Morgan). *Bulletin of the Council for Research in Music Education, 27,* 25–32.

Posner, G. (1989). Making sense of diversity: The current state of curriculum research. *Journal of Curriculum and Supervision, 4*(4), 340–361.

Ravitch, D. (1990, January 10). Education in the 1980's: A concern for quality. *Education Week,* pp. 48, 33.

Reid, W. (1975). The changing curriculum: Theory and practice. In W. Reid and D. Walker (Eds.), *Case studies in curriculum change* (pp. 240–259). London: Routledge and Kegan Paul.

Reimer, B. (1967). *Development and trial in a junior and senior high school of a two-year curriculum in general music* (Report No. OE-6-10-096). Cleveland: Case Western Reserve University. (ERIC Document Reproduction Service No. ED 017 526)

Rice, J. (1893). *The public school system of the United States.* New York: Century.

Rolland, P. (1971). *Development and trial of a two year program of string instruction. Final report* (Report No. BR-5-1181). Urbana: University of Illinois. (ERIC Document Reproduction Service No. ED063323 TE 499832)

Rolland, P., and Mutschler, M. (1974). *The teaching of action in string playing.* Urbana: Illinois String Research Associates.

Rosenblatt, B., and Michel-Trapaga, R. (1975). Through the teacher to the child: Aesthetic education for teachers. *Bulletin of the Council for Research in Music Education, 43,* 36–49.

Rosenbloom, P., and Ryan, J. (1968). *Secondary mathematics evaluation project: Review of results.* St. Paul: Minnesota National Laboratory.

Rothman, R. (1988, November 2). Carnegie 'units' should go, says study by boards: Views curriculum as schools' fatal flaw. *Education Week,* pp. 1, 18–19.

Rothman, R. (1989, November 8). States turn to student performance as new measure of school quality. *Education Week,* pp. 1, 12–13.

Rothman, R. (1990, May 2). Math educators seek to build coalitions to translate reform ideas into practice. *Education Week,* p. 7.

Rugg, H. (Ed.). (1927). *Curriculum-making—past and present: Twenty-sixth yearbook of the National Society for the Study of Education* (Part 1). Bloomington: Public School Publishing Company.

Rugg, H. (Ed.). (1927). *The foundations of curriculum-making: Twenty-sixth yearbook of the National Society for the Study of Education* (Part 2). Bloomington: Public School Publishing Company.

Schlesinger, A. (1986). *The cycles of American history.* Boston: Houghton Mifflin.

Schubert, W. (1982). Curriculum research. In H. Mitzel (Ed.), *Encyclopedia of educational research* (5th ed.; pp. 420–431). New York: Free Press.

Schubert, W. (1986). Curriculum research controversy: A special case of a general problem. *Journal of Curriculum and Supervision, 1*(2), 132–147.

Schwab, J. (1969). The practical: A language for curriculum. *School Review, 78,* 1–23.

Schwab, J. (1971). The practical: Arts of the eclectic. *School Review, 79,* 493–592.

Schwab, J. (1973). The practical: Translation into curriculum. *School Review, 81* 501–522.

Schwab, J. (1983).The practical 4: Something for curriculum professors to do. *Curriculum Inquiry, 13*(3), 238–265.

Schwandt, T. (1989). Recapturing moral discourse in evaluation. *Educational Researcher, 18*(8), 11–16.

Shane, H. (1981). Significant writings that have influenced the curriculum: 1906–1981. *Phi Delta Kappan, 62*(5), 311–314.

Shulman, L., and Tamir, P. (1973). Research on teaching in the natural sciences. In R. Travers (Ed.), *Second handbook of research on teaching* (pp. 1098–1148). Chicago: Rand McNally.

Smith, E., Tyler, R., and Evaluation Staff. (1942). *Appraising and recording student progress: Evaluation, records and reports in the thirty schools.* New York: Harper and Brothers.

Smith, L. (1975). Psychological aspects of aesthetic education: Some initial observations. *Bulletin of the Council for Research in Music Education, 43,* 92–115.

Smith, L., and Schumacher, S. (1972). *Extended pilot trials of the aesthetic education program: A qualitative description, analysis and evaluation.* St. Louis: CEMREL.

Stake, R. (1970). Objectives, priorities and other judgment data. *Review of Educational Research 40*(2), 181–212.

Stake, R. (1975). *Evaluating the arts in education: A responsive approach.* Columbus: Charles E. Merrill.

Stake, R., and Easley, J. (Eds.). (1978). *Case studies in science education.* Urbana: University of Illinois, Center for Instructional Research and Evaluation, and Committee on Culture and Cognition.

Stallings, J., and Stipek, D. (1986). Research on early childhood and elementary school teaching programs. In Wittrock, M. (Ed.), *Handbook of research on teaching* (pp. 727–753). New York: Macmillan.

Taba, H. (1962). *Curriculum development: Theory and practice.* New York: Harcourt, Brace & World.

Tanner, D., and Tanner, L. (1980). *Curriculum development: Theory into practice* (2nd ed.). New York: Macmillan.

Tanner, D. (1982). Curriculum history. In H. Mitzel (Ed.), *Encyclopedia of educational research* (5th ed.; pp. 412–420). New York: Free Press.

Tanner, L. (Ed.). (1988). *Critical issues in curriculum: Eighty-seventh yearbook of the National Society for the Study of Education* (Part 1). Chicago: University of Chicago Press.

Taylor, P., and Richards, C. (1985). *An introduction to curriculum studies* (2nd ed.) Windsor: NFER-Nelson.

Ten Eyck, S. (1985). The effect of programed materials on the vocal development of selected children's choruses. *Journal of Research in Music Education, 33,* 231–246.

Thirty schools tell their story: Each school writes of its participation in the Eight-Year Study. (1942). New York: Harper and Brothers.

Thomas, R. (1967). Innovative music education programs. *Music Educators Journal, 53*(9), 50–52.

Thomas, R. (1970). *Manhattanville music curriculum program. Final report* (Report No. BR-6-1999). Purchase: Manhattanville College. (ERIC Document Reproduction Service No. ED 045865 AA000653)

Tikunoff, W., and Ward, B. (1979). How the teaching process affects change in the school. In G. Knieter and J. Stallings (Eds.), *The teaching process & arts aesthetics* (pp. 100–124). St. Louis: CEMREL.

Travers, R. (Ed.). (1973). *Second handbook of research on teaching.* Chicago: Rand McNally.

Tyler, R. (1949). *Basic principles of curriculum and instruction.* Chicago: University of Chicago Press.

Tyler, R. (1987). The five most significant curriculum events in the twentieth century. *Educational Leadership, 44*(4), 36–38.

Tyler, R. (1988). Progress in dealing with curriculum problems. In L. Tanner (Ed.), *Critical issues in curriculum: Eighty-seventh yearbook of the National Society for the Study of Education* (Part 1; pp. 267–276). Chicago: University of Chicago Press.

Utterback, P., and Kalin, M. (1989). A community-based model of curriculum evaluation. *Educational Leadership, 47*(2), 49–50.

VanSickle, R. (1986). Toward more adequate quantitative instructional research. *Theory and Research in Social Education, 14*(2), 171–184.

Vulliamy, G., and Shepherd, J. (1984). The application of a critical sociology to music education. *British Journal of Music Education, 1*(3), 247–266.

Walker, D. (1970). Toward more effective curriculum development projects in art. *Studies in Art Education, 11*(2), 3–13.

Walker, D. (1973). What curriculum research? *Journal of Curriculum Studies, 5*(1), 58–72.

Walker, D. (1980). A barnstorming tour of writing on curriculum. In A. Foshay (Ed.), *Considered action for curriculum improvement* (pp. 71–81). Washington: Association for Supervision and Curriculum Development.

Walker, D., and Schaffarzick, J. (1974). Comparing curricula. *Review of Educational Research 44*(1), 83–111.

Welch, W. (1979). Twenty years of science curriculum development: A look back. In D. Berliner (Ed.), *Review of research in education* (Vol. 7; pp. 282–306). Washington: American Educational Research Association.

Westbury, I. (1970). Curriculum evaluation. *Review of Educational Research 40*(2), 239–260.

Westbury, I., and Steimer, W. (1971). Curriculum: A discipline in search of its problems. *School Review, 79*(2), 243–267.

White, R., and Tisher, R. (1986). Research on natural sciences. In M. Wittrock, (Ed.), *Handbook of research on teaching* (pp. 874–905). New York: Macmillan.

Whitlock, R. (1985). The design and evaluation of study materials for integrating musical information into the choral rehearsal (Reviewed by C. Hoffer). *Bulletin of the Council for Research in Music Education, 84,* 59–63.

Williams, D. (1972). *SWRL music program: Ethnic song selection and distribution* (Report No. SWRL-TN-3-72-28). Los Alamitos: Southwest Regional Laboratory for Educational Research and Development. (ERIC Document Reproduction Service No. ED 109040 SD008472)

Williams, D. (1974). *The SWRL audio laboratory system (ALS): An integrated configuration for psychomusicology research* (Report No. SWRL-TR-51). Los Alamitos: Southwest Regional Laboratory for Educational Research and Development. (ERIC Document Reproduction Service No. ED 166118 S0011503)

Williams, D. (1975). The research-classroom gap: Has SWRL found an answer? *Music Educators Journal, 61*(5), 41–43.

Williams, D. (1976, March). *An interim report of a programmatic series of music inquiry designed to investigate melodic pattern identification ability in children.* Paper presented at the meeting of the Music Educators National Conference, Atlantic City, NJ.

Williams, D. (1977). *Children's perception of motion in unidirec-*

tional, two-and three-pitch melodic patterns and the related effects of change in timbre, loudness, and duration (Report No. SWRL-ERD-TR-59). Los Alamitos: Southwest Regional Laboratory for Educational Research and Development. (ERIC Document Reproduction Service No. ED 160251 PS010180)

Wolf, R. (1969). A model for curriculum evaluation. *Psychology in the Schools, 6,* 107–108.

Woods, D. (1978). Unified curriculum construction: The Icelandic-American comprehensive musicianship framework project. *Bulletin of the Council for Research in Music Education, 57,* 23–27.

Woods, D. (1982). The American/Icelandic project: A model for curriculum construction in music. *Music Educators Journal, 68*(9), 42–44.

·14·

TOWARD A RATIONAL CRITICAL PROCESS

Carroll Gonzo
UNIVERSITY OF TEXAS

This chapter examines the nature of criticism in general and its application to scholarly works in particular. Criticism of all creative works—artistic, literary, and scholarly—should focus on the "object itself." For the purpose of this chapter, the focus is on scholarly works in music education. The creative works (the objects) include published research, critiques of research, expository articles, critiques of expository articles, book reviews, and rebuttals of research critiques and expository articles.

The chapter's central idea is that the created object has a perceivable inner structure through which meaning is conveyed. The shape and forms through which argumentative patterns move are there for the critic's analysis and assessment, as guided by the rhetorical plan together with the intellectual content. A critic gives meaning beyond that readily apparent in the object. In an effort to develop a blueprint for a rational critical process, the following discussion focuses on the nature and types of criticism, the object created, structural models, the critic, the written critique, and the place of ethics in criticism.

The Nature of Criticism

Everyone makes critical judgments. We make judgments of clothes, movies, people, politics—the list is virtually endless. Some opinions are elegantly stated and carry the force of compelling logic. There are opinions that are emotional, and uninformed opinions that can be irrational and explosive. In short, opinions (forms of criticism) exist in many guises, but there is a significant conceptual distance between an opinion expressed in conjectural rambling and a critical analysis expressed in systematic rational language, the result of reflective thinking. Obviously, to criticize is to say something about something. The critic engages in the act of criticizing and from this a critical analysis emerges.

At this point, the nature of criticism will be addressed; the

critic will be dealt with later. Criticism is an appraisal process that includes the systematic dissection, analysis, and evaluation of another's work. Critics must go beyond describing what a thing is and what it was intended for in order to deal with issues of what its value is and for whom.

The art of criticism enjoys a long history, one that finds its roots in Greek literary criticism. For Aristotle, ideas and values were absolute and unchanging. By logical extension, criticism of art, education, politics, and so on was a matter of conforming to the philosophical constraints of idealism. In *The Politics,* Aristotle advances the assumption that there is an ideal form that serves as the standard by which all forms are judged. Under these conditions, all forms of criticism could conform to existing unequivocal guidelines for judging and evaluating human endeavor.

Over time, and with changing philosophical views of reality, the canons of taste and the methods of applying them to the critical process changed. Contemporary critical theorists such as Raval (1981) point out that "the institution of criticism shows a multiplicity and complexity which is not reducible to the basic premises and certitudes of one or another form of criticism" (p. 253). This view parallels the point made by Esslin (1981), who asserts that "if there are no absolute standards of judgment, similarly there are no absolute standards of critical methodology" (p. 204). He also contends that there is not nor can there be one all-embracing method of criticism simply because there is no objective truth to be uncovered.

The "absolute criterion" becomes an even greater logical impossibility when one considers that the act of criticism not only changes over time but also with respect to genre; for example, criticism of literature, works of art, plays, concerts, recitals, or the writings found in scholarly journals. Esslin suggests that "when thought of as a dialectical process—as discourse, debate, exchange of reactions, impressions, views resulting from widely varying interests and intentions—criticism is clearly a 'collective' endeavor which will at best produce a consensus, sometimes long lasting sometimes short-lived, about individuals, works, problems, techniques and values" (p. 206). The contention that there is no absolute truth or system of judgment creates a sharp dichotomy between the Greek view and contemporary critical theory. However, the "absolute truth or judgment criterion" does not obviate the importance of a *rational critical process*.

Though current critical theorists would have us believe that critical methodology operates in a framework of relativity, it does derive its legitimacy from prevailing tastes, expectations, and conventions that form a standard of judgment in a given time period. The "consensus," as Esslin labels it, while not anchored in immutable laws has at the very least standards acceptable to a collective point of view. Even the thrust of this logic is somewhat blunted by certain obvious limitations. Consensus, like philosophical schools of thought, is subject to continual, albeit gradual, change over time. This inevitable phenomenon does not, however, diminish consensus as a useful starting point for the rational critical process. It is, after all, the basis for much of today's critical activity in spite of certain ambiguities that inhere in this standard of evaluation. Some critics may strive to adhere to perceived consensus standards, while others are controlled by and often limited to their own particular judgmental proclivities—a consequence that can add its own blend of wooliness to the controlling factors of what a critic thinks and writes. If, however, this method produces important creative insights that advance the field, it must be given serious consideration as a standard of criticism.

Inner Criticism

David Hume observed that "no criticism can be instructive which descends not to particulars, and is not full of illustrations" (1875 p. 242). Shumaker (1952) theorized that "the critic's commitment is to reasonable modes of thought. If he communicates his findings in nonrational ways, his writings will not be critical but creative" (p. 76). According to Francis Sparshott, evaluation must be distinguished from enjoying. In judging, the critic must determine how good a thing is, and to call a thing good or bad implies reasons for such a designation.

Considered within the context of these points of view, criticism is a rational procedure, not the expression of prejudice and presupposition. In the criticism of scholarly writings, it can be argued that the nature of the relationship between the critic and the manuscript determines the character of the subsequent analysis and appraisal. What is discovered will depend on where and how the critic decides to look and to comment. In an objective sense, a manuscript has its own essential laws of being. The critic has the option of attending either to the content of the document (inner criticism) or to the critic's musings (outer criticism)—which may be peripheral and/or creative as Shumaker indicates, or some combination of the two. Whatever the format, the critic is confronted with the predicament of deciding what to say and how to say it.

Inner criticism calls for what Matthew Arnold referred to as a free, disinterested play of mind. However, according to Schumaker, no criticism is ever completely inner, since all critics bring prior attitudes and modes of consciousness to their understanding. The best criticism of anything rests on an analysis and appraisal that conforms to recognized standards. After all, according to Sparshott, the merits of criticism are decided not by whether one accepts the critic's verdict, but by the elegance of the logic set forth in making the case: "Like Lawyers, critics are to be esteemed rather for their ability in arguing their cases than for the merits of the cases they argue." Also to the point is Fish's (1981) comment that "the rhetoric of critical argument, as usually conducted in our journals, depends upon the definition between interpretations on the one hand, and the textual and contextual facts that either support or disconfirm them" (p. 204). The limiting factors in inner criticism will depend directly on the critics' knowledge and ability to assess objectively what they have read, and state it in a clear and complete manner in accordance with accepted standards of critical evaluation.

Outer Criticism

Whereas the object (manuscript) and a rational assessment thereof shape inner criticism, the critic is the source of outer criticism. What the critic has to report must be related to the object, even if only minimally. But the critic is, as it were, contextually free to be creative and produce a critique based upon whatever suits his or her fancy in any chosen format. The critique serves as a forum for the critic to expound on personal values, attitudes, and/or a host of topics that are seen as important and relevant. The critic may display reminiscences of the past, or offer a diatribe about the inappropriateness of the author's chosen topic. However, providing a thoughtful explanation of a different question or a different framing of an investigatory method would be valuable and useful. The critic may berate the author's intelligence or cast aspersions on the author's authority and place in the professional community. A single incorrect footnote or typographical error may generate considerable discussion and reprimand, giving the impression that the scholarly worth of the effort has been diminished, while the critic has been elevated through having detected these errors.

Analysis and appraisal of the object are relatively unimportant in outer criticism. Subjectivity dominates, and the critique's only limiting factors are the limits of the critic's outpourings. *In all likelihood, most critiques will contain both inner and outer criticism. Extremes in either direction will probably be of questionable critical value.*

The Object

Literary critics must understand the nature and value of plays, novels, and/or poems, and must adjudicate the merits of these art forms according to the accepted standards that literary critics employ. Critics of the visual and plastic arts also have certain accepted guidelines.

The artistic worth of a musical composition or a musical performance is subject to yet another set of criteria. The constraints that control and direct the playwright, novelist, poet, painter, sculptor, composer, and performer in producing an artistic object are directly related to the artist's imaginative and creative abilities. Even though creative output functions within the framework of stylistic performance practices, the artist is free to bend, break, or disregard the rules and plow new artistic ground. This spontaneous feature offers little or no assistance to the critic in forming analyses and evaluations, thus making the critic's task and findings tenuous.

The discoverable meaning of research practices and products, as well as of other scholarly writing, is not as recondite as that of artistic creations. Whereas scholars and researchers are expected to create new knowledge, they are also expected to achieve this through known and accepted practices. The constituent parts of a research report, for example, are isolable and can be examined for their organic unity within and between parts in terms of appropriate research procedures. Who made it, what it is made of, what led to its production, and what its structural composition is are known. The object is not a mystery that invites inner criticism. There is no disputing that certain research practices change over time, but as the results of new research are published new techniques become available for inspection, application, and evaluation. When this occurs, the critic has the opportunity to assess the merits of these innovative practices. On the other hand, the use of accepted research practices that are technically sound does not in itself obligate the critic to accept the work as a substantive contribution to the field.

The established categories of published research (experimental, historical, descriptive, and philosophical) as well as critiques of research, expository articles, book reviews, and rebuttals are all objects available for critical analysis. Each is discussed in terms of its structural characteristics.

Experimental Research The format of experimental research usually includes a problem statement, hypotheses or questions, sampling techniques, review of the literature, procedures for testing the hypotheses, analyses, interpretation of analyses, and conclusions (see experimental research structural model in Table 14–1, which is a suggested model and should serve only as a point of departure when criticizing experimental research). Although these areas are not mutually exclusive, the manner in which each step is carried out will affect each subsequent step.

A research problem generally arises from an investigator's curiosity and interests. Hypotheses help identify the method of analysis and determine the procedures necessary for data collection and hypothesis testing. The universe or population is defined on the basis of the problem conditions, the hypotheses, or the questions of the investigation. Varied procedures and techniques, both simple and complex, are available; therefore, a critic must determine if the methods used were appropriate to the type of research problem. Evaluation of methodology will, of course, include any statistical procedures in the study. The statistical procedures and the reasoning underlying their application must be appropriate. The hypotheses dictate the analysis design. Finally, the investigator reports the results and conclusions together with recommendations for future research. (For an expanded discussion of the different types of research models, see Gonzo, 1972, "On Writing A Critical Review.")

TABLE 14–1. Experimental Research

A Structural Model

Introductory model
Problem statement
Hypotheses or research questions
Need for the study
Purpose of the study
Limitations of the study
Definition of terms
Underlying assumptions
Review of literature
Delimitation of the population
Selection of an adequate sample
Experimental design
Data collection
Classification of data
Statistical analyses of data
Research decision(s)
Summary and conclusions
Recommendation for future research

Historical Research The function of historical research is to systematically find, evaluate, and synthesize objective evidence relevant to a specific research problem in order to establish facts and draw conclusions about past events. Historical research attempts to explain the past in a framework that emphasizes the social, cultural, economic, and intellectual development of human beings. This type of investigation may place more emphasis on the evaluation of the entire effect of a condition than on specific events and conditions.

In historical research, one expects that the investigator will have (1) defined and delimited a problem, (2) clearly formulated hypotheses or questions, (3) collected primary and secondary source material relevant to the problem, (4) subjected the source material to critical evaluation, (5) adequately synthesized the information contained in the source materials, and (6) through analysis and synthesis rejected or accepted the various hypotheses and made final interpretations and conclusions (see historical research structural model in Table 14–2, a suggested model that should serve only as a point of departure when criticizing historical research.)

Historiographers are expected to bring external and internal criticism to bear on the materials they have selected, thereby providing validity and reliability for their data. (The terms "external criticism" and "internal criticism" as used here refer to a historical research technique and should not be confused with inner and outer criticism.) Reporting of historical information requires that the investigator weigh evidence, pull central ideas and points together, attempt to re-

TABLE 14–2.   Historical Research

A Structural Model

Introductory rationale
Problem statement
Nonhypothesized questions or statistical hypotheses
Need for the study
Limitations of the study
Population
(main source(s) of data)
Data collection
(primary or secondary)
Data authenticity
(external criticism)
Data reliability
(internal criticism)
Data classification
(classifying and/or analyzing techniques)
Interpretation of data
(based on contextual setting)
Summary and conclusions
Proposals for future research

solve inconsistencies apparent in the data, and analyze the data objectively. It can be argued that all types of research should follow these procedures.

Descriptive Research   Descriptive research is devoted to collecting information about prevailing conditions or situations for the purpose of description and interpretation. Descriptive research must meet the same general criteria as other types of research in terms of a research problem, hypotheses or research questions, sampling and data collection techniques, data processing, and evaluation. (See Table 14–3, a suggested descriptive research model that should be used only as a point of departure when criticizing descriptive research.)

Although authorities vary in their categorization of descriptive research, all agree that descriptive research can be

TABLE 14–3.   Descriptive Research

A Structural Model

Introductory rationale
Problem statement
Nonhypothesized questions or statistical hypotheses
Need for the study
Purpose of the study
Limitations of the study
Definition of terms
Review of literature
Population
Sample
Design
Data collection
Data analyses
Research decisions
Summary and conclusions
Recommendations for further research

either qualitative (verbal) or quantitative (mathematical). The following are some examples of descriptive research categories: (1) survey, (2) interrelationship, and (3) developmental. Among the various ways of collecting data in descriptive research are the questionnaire, the opinionnaire, the test, classroom observation, interviews, case studies, ethnography, low-inference coding, and high-inference rating. The type of analysis depends on the questions being asked as well as the nature of the data.

Descriptive research that contains only descriptions and no conclusions has little or no significance, regardless of how extensive the description. How researchers interpret the data will indicate whether or not they understand the data and can convey their meaning to the reader.

Philosophical Research   Philosophical research is unique in the sense that it is based on a priori reasoning. In a priori reasoning, one arrives at a judgment about something without benefit of experiment or examination. Through rational, reflective thinking, the philosophical researcher attempts to arrive at some truth or truths. The objective data are gleaned from past experience and/or accumulated knowledge.

According to Villemain (1953), the philosophical researcher in education has several approaches available. The researcher may decide to "analyze" an educational concept in an effort to render it more meaningful and useful. Or the researcher may wish to "analyze" specific terms currently in vogue so that their meaning might be more accurately served. Finally, the philosophical researcher may decide to "speculate" about objectives and experiences that may be significant in the future. Speculation of this sort requires a priori reasoning that would of necessity include the "analytical" and "critical" procedures in the data collection. In short, the purpose of philosophical research is to provide the theoretical framework for education, while the empiricist's task is to quantify the existing practices in that framework in order to assess their adequacy.

Since the keystone of philosophical research is critical and reflective thinking, one must judge the merits of this type of investigation in terms of the logic and order of the reasoning set forth. The format of the research is scientific in nature because of the method employed, and therefore it should begin with a problem statement. The manner in which the problem is delineated may take one of two forms. Villemain calls these "inquiry" and "argument," and indicates that although they are separate, they are interrelated. The process of inquiry generally follows the procedure used in other types of research: problem statement, hypotheses, procedures for testing them, identification of ideas to be introduced, and collection of data. (See Table 14–4, p. 222, for a suggested philosophical research structural model that should be used only as a point of departure for criticizing philosophical research.) Each step must be logical and in order, and the research must reflect clear rational thinking leading to defensible conclusions.

Expository Writing   It can be argued that research articles, critiques, book reviews, and rebuttals all use the expository

TABLE 14–4. Philosophical Research

A Structural Model
Introductory Rationale
(includes personal theory of author)
Purpose for the study
Problem statement
(may take the form of inquiry and/or argument)
Hypotheses
Procedures for testing hypotheses
(requires critical and reflective thinking)
Framing underlying assumptions
Definition of terms
(follows rules of philosophical reasoning)
Collection of data and relevant theories
Analysis of data
(follows rules of philosophical reasoning)
Conclusions
(evaluation of the evidence)
Recommendation for further philosophical investigation

TABLE 14–5. Expository Article

A Structural Model
Topic
(what the author is writing about)
Thesis
(the main idea)
Exposition
(manner of expression)
Author bias
(viewpoint of the topic)
Mode of expression
(style of writing, e.g., formal, informal)
Rhetorical tone
(cynical, angry, rational, etc.)
Structure
(organizational pattern of ideas)
Explanation
Illustration
Question and answer
Cause and effect
Comparison and contrast
Persuasion
Various combinations of the above
Grammar
Correct rules of grammar
Correct syntax
Correct spelling
Format
Organic flow of ideas
Logical flow of paragraphs
Logical flow between sections

form of writing. Although this may be true, the format of each is controlled by its structural nature together with the writer's style of reasoning. The following discussion is primarily intended for the type of article that does not conform to the above four research categories. In a generic sense, expository writing seeks to explain and clarify an issue. Such writing must interest and stimulate both the author and the reader if it is to be significant. Additionally, it should contribute new information to the field. Exposition presents the what, the how, and the why of matters of human knowledge through interpretation and elucidation. It is certainly the most universal form of composition and serves as the vehicle through which writers make themselves understood.

Dye (1926) states that exposition, unlike forms of writing that are descriptive, narrative, and argumentative, (1) demands a truthful presentation of all the particulars of an object, (2) deals with typical or generalized topics, (3) presents both sides of an issue, and (4) follows no set form. It can utilize the same form followed in descriptive, narrative, or argumentative writing or a combination of these. Consequently, exposition cannot be recognized by any characteristics of external form. It evolves from simple to complex, and its evolution is controlled by the nature of the problem under scrutiny. "Exposition is an intention rather than a hard and fast mold; it is a point of view rather than a form." (See Table 14–5, a suggested expository structural model that should serve only as a point of departure for criticizing expository articles.)

Clearly, expository writing must correctly apply the rules of composition, rhetoric, and grammar. The meaning of each sentence and paragraph should be evident and devoid of obscurity and ambiguity. The logical flow of ideas must move through a coherent arrangement of format and not be disturbed by yawning gaps in the meaning or irrelevant digressions. Although the tone and style of writing vary with each writer, coherence and unity of thought and expression are necessary. In the end, the exposition must cover the concep-

tual ground in a way that clarifies issues for the reader. In the clarifying process, the reader may be led to formulate new questions or doubts about certain issues or beliefs.

Book Reviews The only predictable element in a book review format is a listing of the author or editor's name, the title of the book, the city where the book was published, the publisher, the date of publication, and the number of pages. What follows is usually a discussion of the book's contents, which may include analyses and evaluative statements. Or the discussion may be neutral in character and then be followed by a critique of some sort. The organizational pattern of the review is obviously the reviewer's choice. The scope and bias of the review will be directly related to the reviewer's expertise relative to the topic of the book.

Book reviews in most journals are generally no more than one or two pages in length. Merely recounting the contents of a book in summary fashion is not a book review, even though the term "review" might imply such a procedure. Most reviewers feel qualified to judge a book's merits presumably because they possess expertise about the contents; the "way" in which a book is written and the "depth" and "clarity" of how the subject matter is handled are subject to evaluation and judgment. The reviewer has an object, like a dissertation or expository article, that has been created and that can be subjected to inner criticism. (See Table 14–6 for a

TABLE 14–6. Book Review

A Structural Model

Author or editor
Book title
Place of publication
Publisher
Publication date
Number of pages
Introductory comments
Evaluative comments
Intended audience
Salient features
Uniqueness of ideas
Comparison of book to other books
Value of book to professional community
Organizational merits
Quality of scholarship
Overall assessment
Conclusions

book review structural model.) Moreover, it is useful in a book review to refer for comparison to other books dealing with the same subject. This approach can inform the reader about whether the subject is dealt with adequately.

Frequently the review format parallels the book's format, a tack that can help the reviewer avoid rambling digressions. The reader should expect to find the book's salient features in the review, presented in an orderly fashion. A useful review, to the reader and hopefully to the author, has interpretative information. Explaining the relationship of the book to similar books on the same subject provides readers with a basis for drawing their own conclusions about the book's merits. Is the author breaking new intellectual ground or merely engaging in information juggling? What audience is best served by the book and why? Are there idiosyncrasies in the author's scholarship that make it difficult for the reader to track the book's central ideas and main points? Finally, is the book of major or minor interest to the intellectual community?

Rebuttals Rebuttal is refutation, and to refute is to argue. To argue does not necessarily mean to quarrel (although arguing can certainly take disagreeable forms) but rather to convince someone by dint of reason, to engage in reasoned debate. Rebuttals in professional journals can be reasonable or contentious. Clearly, the tone and logic of rebuttals reflect authors' reactions to the critics who have critiqued their work. Authors frequently take umbrage at what critics say. The sense of anger and offense of authors may make it impossible for them to distinguish between perceived personal affront and a reasonable assessment of the work. If an author takes the former position, the rebuttal may be defensive in nature and may even descend to personal statements directed at the critic, resulting in a quarrelsome challenge rather than a reasoned refutation.

If the format of a rebuttal is to have an identifiable structure, it must be based on the critique structure and/or the

points of disagreement. In both cases, inner criticism is possible. The author now becomes the critic, and through the force of logic must convincingly show how the critic either misinterpreted, misunderstood, or took out of context what the author wrote. If the critique focuses unduly on trivia and fails to address the main substance of an author's work, the rebuttal should expose that inequity. (See Table 14–7, a suggested rebuttal structural model, which should be used only as a point of departure for writing or evaluating a rebuttal.)

In dissertation critiques, expository articles, and book reviews, a critic must choose what to say and in the process decide what not to say. Emotions potentially can play a much greater role in choice making in preparing a rebuttal. It is exceedingly difficult for readers to recognize bias in an author's rebuttal unless they are completely familiar with the original work and the critique. Obviously, the author must set aside personal emotions and hitch the strategy to systematic point-by-point logic, without reference to the critic's persona. Failing this, a rebuttal can be for the reader much like kissing one's cousin—not altogether satisfactory.

The Critic

The reviewing, screening, and judging of a scholarly manuscript begin with a journal editor. Some refereed journals publish the format criteria that authors must meet when submitting a manuscript. If, in the editor's judgment, the manuscript meets the journal's publishing requirements—

TABLE 14–7. Rebuttal

A Structural Model

Introduction
(setting the argumentative tone)
Personal experience
Examples from sources
Historical background
Quotations
Comparison and contrast
Consider the opposition
Issues
(points of contention)
Evidence
(information justifying reasoning and conclusions)
Reasoning
(premises and conclusions)
Refutation
(rhetorical devices)
Example
Description
Narration
Definition
Analysis
Comparison and contrast
Historical background
Conclusions
(summarizing main points)

for example, the professional mission of the journal, timeliness and importance of the article to the profession, clarity and quality of the author's scholarship—the editor can accept or reject the article or can send it to a member or members of an editorial board for their assessment and recommendations. They can recommend to accept as is, accept with specific revisions, reject, or suggest that it be submitted to a different journal more suitable for the topic.

A critique of an unpublished dissertation, a scholarly manuscript, must go through the same screening procedures as an article, a book review, or a rebuttal. When a manuscript is published the reader becomes the final, albeit informal, critic. In all the aforementioned cases—the editor, the editorial board, the critic, and the reader—appraisal occurs in varying degrees; all in their own way are critics. However, the art of formal criticism is practiced by the individual who formally submits for publication a critique, book review, or rebuttal. The work of such serious critics in our profession can be found in such journals as the *Bulletin of the Council for Research in Music Education,* the *Journal of Research in Music Education,* and the *Music Educators Journal,* to mention a few. It is in this arena that critics can be studied to determine more particularly what it is they do.

The Written Critique

Written critiques in scholarly journals usually examine expository articles or books. (For more information about the nature of critiques and writing critiques, see Gonzo, 1988, "Bulletin Critiques: An Analysis.") We may discuss the creation of the critical review in terms of the critic as expert, the critique itself, and the activity of production. Let us start with the premise that the critic is an expert. As was proposed earlier in this chapter, no absolute standards of judgment exist; consensus is a more reasonable basis for appraisal in any given time period. Therefore, this section focuses on the technique of criticism and the critique that it produces.

The method of procedure applied in generating a critique demonstrates knowledge about the subject under review, its structure and its composition. By way of example, let us consider the critical review of research and, in particular, doctoral dissertations. The critic should know rule-governing formulas that serve as a template for judging the research approach, the writing style, and language usage. Moreover, the critic should be able to detect logical dissonances in the investigation, and to explain their cause and effect and provide appropriate solutions.

In the process of dissonance detection, the critic works from the known to the unknown. What is known are the constituent parts of the dissertation, from the standpoint of both format and interplay of ideas. For example, in the chapter on related literature and research the researcher demonstrates the ability to cull sources in such a way that a clear picture emerges concerning present knowledge of the topic under investigation. It serves to point out gaps and omissions, making a case for the proposed research. In short, this chapter provides the underlying information and rationale that lead to the conceptual shaping of the research problem. Once the outcome of the investigation is known, this chapter is revisited (in the summary and conclusion) to state how the new findings square with the research of others. Do the findings confirm or deny their findings? How, and to what extent? The logic between these various elements and the manner in which the author orchestrates them reveal (to the critic) the researcher's thinking, research skill, and scholarly ability.

In examining the problem statement and attendant subproblems, the critic examines whether the subproblems are logical extensions of the problem statement. Does the researcher follow through in solving all aspects of the problem, or get trapped in investigating only the subproblems? Worse, does the study address the wrong problem—one other than the stated problem?

The study's design must be linked to and result from information presented in the chapter on related literature and research, as well as the problem statement and its subproblems. The critic is alert to any link leading to an irrelevant design fostering spurious and therefore unsupportable results, summaries, and conclusions. Additionally, the critic looks for evidence that the laws of logic serve as the intellectual glue binding ideas together. Does the author's scholarship exhibit imaginative and thought-provoking writing in words that demonstrate a substantive command of the English language? In brief, the critic chooses inner criticism and looks to the characteristics of the object to determine the content of the critical review.

Producing a critical review involves more than knowing the structure of a dissertation and whether its constituent parts fit together properly. The critic's disposition and the manner in which the critic enters into the "doing" create the diversity of critical styles found in professional journals. Even if all critics used the general guidelines of inner criticism, varying degrees of divergent thinking and writing would still abound.

"Intention" really determines whether writers (critics) use the knowledge they possess (Flower, 1986). Intention enters the writing process in two places, in "the writer's image of the task itself, and in the form of goals and criteria she brings to bear during her evaluation" (p. 15). Inner criticism requires that critics' image of their task derive directly from the information set forth in the research—the object. In other words, the goals and criteria for critics' judgment should be guided by the structure of the research, filtered through the critics' knowledge, in concert with recognized standards of good research and scholarship.

To attempt to develop rules of or to suggest regulatory boundaries for intention is impossible and, indeed, undesirable. That intentions can take many forms is self-evident. The knowledge that critics choose to apply in their critical doing is also beyond the control of any guidelines. What is arguable is the point of departure. At what juncture does intention shift from inner to outer criticism? When is creative critical activity inner or outer? At the risk of stating the obvious, intention is inner when it deals primarily with appraisal of the object, and outer when it utilizes information wholly unrelated to the object. The critic's creative nature can manifest itself within the constraints of inner criticism, or, it can, as discussed earlier, be contextually free.

In deciding which form of criticism is more desirable, one must ask who is to be served by these critical writings—the critic, the author, the professional community, and/or the public at large? Criticism is certainly beneficial to the critic as a scholarly activity. It is also of value in differing degrees to the author being critiqued, to professionals who read the journals, and to others who simply take an interest in critical activity. So, while many are served by critical appraisals, it would seem that professional colleagues, the author, and the mission of the specific journal are the primary benefactors. The critic and his or her critique are the instrument that accomplishes this end result. Attention then must be given to the object of the criticism, and only minimally, if at all, to the critic's other interests. Thus, a written critique should first present an abstract of the research written by the critic—not the author's abstract, which, with its 250-word limit, does not tell enough. Clearly, the more information concerning the salient features of the research, the greater the reader's opportunity to understand the relationship of the critique to the research.

A critique should, then, be preceded by an abstract and follow the organizational structure of that abstract. The degree to which the critique stems from the abstract must be more than a mere outline. If the critic uses the abstracted research study as the basis for the critique, it then serves as a confining channel by which the content of the critique is kept within bounds. The critique will be characterized by an orderly exposition and a well-defined diagnosis. Where the critic chooses to ignore main features of the research study, selectivity becomes the dominating force, directing both the critic's knowledge and intentions and, ultimately, the organizational shape of the critique.

A critique should focus on the essential features of the research. A sketchy representation of the work or a critique that focuses on trivia fails to serve the author and the research community. Identifying, analyzing, and critiquing the salient features of a research document keep the critic on task. Within the framework of this approach, the clever critic can provides imaginative and creative observations that go beyond the research study while still springing from it.

A critique should not only point out errors, but provide solutions for correction and improvement. To identify certain errors—for example, spelling and typographical errors, grammatical inaccuracies—is to imply the proper correction. Diagnosing flaws in logic in a problem statement and its attendant hypotheses or questions, finding errors in a study's design and procedure, tracing the organic flow of the entire study to determine logical consistency, are all examples in which solutions for corrections are not proffered simply by reporting that problems exist. Conversely, it might be nice to know why its logic or problem statement or organization is

deemed correct, and how its appropriateness contributed to a well-executed investigative endeavor.

A critique should be written according to the rules of good scholarship. Unsupported assertions, unsupported value judgments, formats containing confusing organizational features, paragraphs that have no internal logical flow, successive paragraphs that bear no logical relationship, and convoluted sentences all reflect poor scholarship. Below is a checklist to consider when critiquing someone else's work.

1. Do you have expertise in the area you are evaluating?
2. Have you read the work thoroughly?
3. Have you provided sufficient information about the work for the reader?
4. Does your critique focus primarily on the work?
5. Have you identified the strengths and weaknesses of the work?
6. Have you suggested solutions to diagnosed problems?
7. Have you compared and contrasted the work (where appropriate) to other works on the same subject?
8. Have you been creative and insightful in your assessment of the work?
9. Have you checked your own writing for clarity and correctness?
10. Does your critique help the author and the reader to understand how and where the work succeeds, where it fails, and why?

Ethics and Criticism

James Russell Lowell observed that "nature fits her children with something to do, he who would write and can't write, can surely review" (Henderson, 1986, p. 92). There is an understandable antipathy between authors and reviewers, which perhaps accounts for Lowell's indictment. Critics by nature must be initially skeptical before decrying or applauding the work of others. Writers, and scholars who write, make public their efforts and become fair game for the critics. Critics, however, have an ethical responsibility to take an author's work seriously and recognize that what was accomplished required considerable effort, and should not be summarily dismissed or excoriated.

Samuel Taylor Coleridge wrote that "(Edward) Gibbon's style is detestable; but is not the worst thing about him" (Henderson, 1986, p. 44). A critic of Milton's *Paradise Lost* penned, "His fame is gone out like a candle in a snuff and his memory will always stink" (p. 63). A different Milton critic noted, "I can never read ten lines together without stumbling at some Pedantry that tipped me at once out of Paradise, or even Hell, into the schoolroom, worse than either" (p. 63). Rudyard Kipling received a rejection letter from the *San Francisco Examiner* stating, "I'm sorry, Mr. Kipling, but you just don't know how to use the English language" (p. 56).

The above citings exemplify outer criticism, irresponsible intentions to be hurtful. They tell us nothing of the various works but tell us a great deal about the critics. They are obtrusions of the critics' condemnations. The critic's focus is not so much on the object as it is on the creator. The critical process has been eclipsed by the narrowness and pettiness of the critic's mind.

If the ideational content of anything is to have value for the reader when seen through the critic's eyes, it must be dismantled in a systematic fashion and filtered through thoughtful and objective assessment. A critic who strives to set aside personal prejudices is more likely to render a judgment that is fair, balanced, insightful, and meaningful. A verdict of this nature will be suffused with a larger meaning that will serve the creator, the object, the reader, and the critic. Finally, and certainly a moral imperative, the critic must adjudicate what an author did, not what the critic wished or thought the author should have done. In other words, the critic must identify those aspects of the work that are praiseworthy and those that are with fault and why. For example, the critic may suggest that the problem statement, no matter how cogently stated, is trivial or peripheral or that it was framed in an unproductive way.

SUMMARY

Criticism of scholarly writings should focus primarily on the work itself, the object. The central idea of this chapter is that scholarly writings have perceivable inner structures through which meaning is conveyed. These writings include doctoral dissertations, research articles, rebuttals, and book reviews. The nature of criticism is an appraisal process, which includes the systematic dissection, analysis, evaluation, and valuing of scholarly writings. The criterion for what constitutes acceptable standards for criticism is determined by the prevailing tastes, expectation, and conventional judgmental wisdom in a given time period. Inner criticism directs its attention to the object, while outer criticism focuses on the critic's interests. Most critiques contain both inner and outer criticism. Extremes in either direction are of questionable critical value. The ethics of the art of criticism require that the structure and content of scholarly writing be systematically dismantled in a thoughtful and objective manner, with specific attention given to the object's meaning.

References

Aristotle. (1932). *The politics.* Cambridge: Harvard University Press.

Bell, K. (1990). *Developing arguments: Strategies for reaching audiences.* Belmont: Wadsworth Publishing.

Cavender, N., and Kahane, H. (1989). *Argument and persuasion: Text and readings for writers.* Belmont: Wadsworth Publishing.

Dye, W. (1926). *Expository writing.* Richmond: Johnson Publishing.

Esslin, M. (1981). A search for subjective truth. In P. Hernadi (Ed.), *What is criticism.* Bloomington: Indiana Press.

Fish, S. (1981). Demonstration versus persuasion: Two models of critical activity. In P. Hernadi (Ed.), *What is criticism?* Bloomington: Indiana Press.

Flower, L., Hayes, J. R., Carey, L., Schriver, K. (1986). Detection, diagnosis, and the strategies of revision. *College Composition and Communication, 37* (1).

Gonzo, C. (1972). On writing a critical review. *Bulletin of the Council for Research in Music Education, 28,* 14–22.

Gonzo, C. (1988). Bulletin critiques: An analysis. *Bulletin of the Council for Research in Music Education, 97,* 29–58.

Grinols, A. B. (1988). *Critical thinking: Reading and writing across the curriculum.* Belmont: Wadsworth Publishing.

Henderson, B. (1986). *Rotten reviews.* Stanford: Pushcart Press.

Hume, D. (1875). On simplicity and refinement in writing. In *Essays: Moral, political and literary.* London: Longmans, Green, and Co.

Raval, S. (1981). *Metacriticism.* Athens: University of Georgia Press.

Shumaker, W. (1952). *Elements of critical theory.* Berkeley: University of California Press.

Sparshott, F. (1967). *The concept of criticism.* Oxford: Clarendon Press.

Sparshott, F. (1981). The problem of the problem of criticism. In P. Hernadi (Ed.), *What is criticism.* Bloomington: Indiana Press.

Villemain, F. (1953). *Philosophical research in education.* New York: New York University Press.

·15·

A GUIDE TO INTERPRETING RESEARCH IN MUSIC EDUCATION

Hal Abeles

TEACHERS COLLEGE, COLUMBIA UNIVERSITY

Interpreting research gives meaning to the results of research studies.

RESEARCH AS A SOURCE OF KNOWLEDGE

Research is viewed by many music educators as an esoteric activity that takes place in colleges and universities, and that has little relevance to what real music teachers do. This perspective limits the sources of information music educators have available to make decisions about practice and to assist in understanding the process of music learning. Philosophers usually identify three ways of knowing: tradition, or appeal to authority; personal experience; and systematic study—that is, research. In practice, research results are seldom used in the development of music education's methods and materials. When music teachers make instructional choices—for example, how to teach the concept of meter—they probably refer to what they have done in the past, what some of their more experienced colleagues do, how they themselves were taught, and/or what some notable clinician demonstrated recently. It is less likely that they turn to a research journal for help in the decision. Because research findings can be helpful in decisions about practice in the field as well as in providing a greater understanding of the music-teaching/learning process, it is important for music educators to make use of this resource. The perspective of this chapter is that research is one source of information that music teachers can use in making instructional choices.

Tradition

When the question, "Why do we do this that way?" is answered stereotypically with "Because we always have!," tra-

dition is being used as the justification. Many examples of the use of tradition in decision making in music education exist. Beginning school instrumental instruction in the fifth grade, singing songs about animals with young elementary-age children, and ending a concert with a lively piece such as a march are what we have always done. The problem with decisions based solely on tradition is that the conditions in existence when the tradition started may no longer exist. Children often started both wind and string instruments later than keyboard instruments because of the size of the instruments and the size of children. With string instruments of many different sizes now readily available, the initial reasons for their not starting early with string instruments have disappeared.

Authority

Whether a teacher follows the Orff, Kodály, or Suzuki approach, music teachers as a group depend heavily on authority when making instructional decisions. The process of becoming a performer, of developing musical skills through applied music instruction, is based almost entirely on the notion of authority. This is illustrated in the résumés of performing musicians, where the most highlighted aspect is often the performer-teachers with whom they studied and with whom their teachers studied. A major activity at music education professional association meetings is clinicians' demonstrations of successful techniques. Although sharing materials and procedures is one way music teaching may be improved, most of what a clinician demonstrates has been most successful for that individual clinician, and may or may not work as well for other teachers. The most experienced of our colleagues often have good ideas regarding music teaching, but we must be willing to test their approaches systematically.

Personal Experience

How could music teachers ever be successful without learning from their experiences? The most promising teachers are often those who sense when instruction is going well and when it is not, and modify their teaching accordingly. However, our experiences are limited; they can be a misleading source of knowledge when we assume these experiences represent all the possibilities. Some of the most limiting instruction I have observed occurs when college level music education methods teachers rely solely on their own experience to teach their naive preservice charges. It is disheartening to listen to professors who once were effective school music teachers use reminiscing as their primary mode of instruction. A willingness to compare and contrast systematically the advantages and disadvantages in different music-teaching strategies is what we must nurture, not only in music education method course instructors, but also in their students.

Research

The systematic examination of questions in music education is the most neglected source of knowledge among music teachers. Ideally these systematic investigations are objective. By pursuing the knowledge and trying to be objective regarding questions on teaching, we will be less likely to make wrong decisions or to waste time pursuing unproductive paths. Although research seldom provides complete answers to the practice of music instruction, including research results, with other sources of knowledge for making instructional decisions, could greatly enhance our effectiveness and efficiently.

SCIENCE AS A NETWORK OF KNOWLEDGE

Not all music education research takes place in the music classroom or focuses on issues that have immediate applications to music teaching. Such research may be criticized as irrelevant to practitioners because it focuses on isolated issues too narrow to have much application. In systematic inquiry researchers sometimes must focus on a small, narrow piece of a problem so that they can carefully examine key issues. At other times researchers try to understand basic relationships among variables that appear to be only distantly related to the music classroom. The new knowledge produced by one study must be linked to other knowledge in the field. Rarely does a piece of research stand alone. It is

connected to work done before it, which is usually cited by the author of the study, and to work that will come after. It is necessary to be aware of this context to benefit fully from the knowledge developed. Over time and multiple studies general rules are formulated. These are the prime information sources for music teachers seeking to improve the effectiveness of their programs.

To understand the teaching/learning process in music, we must develop general rules and then determine in what specific music-learning circumstances they apply. Thus, concepts like music achievement, musical talent, aesthetic experience, self-actualization, and musical taste help researchers speculate on principles that may be applied in a variety of music-learning circumstances. The difficulty researchers often encounter in using such terms is a lack of agreement on their precise meaning. To avoid this difficulty researchers try to be quite explicit in defining such terms. This precision in definition is important for understanding the results of a research project. For example, the term "music achievement" may refer to a variety of possible outcomes. For research purposes we must define it more narrowly. For instance, in music performance we might define successful achievement as playing with few wrong notes, rhythmic accuracy, and good tone quality. To interpret and apply a study's outcomes, the reader must know what definition is being used. Researchers often use "operational definitions" to narrow concepts. Operational definitions define concepts in terms of how they are to be measured or observed. Thus, in our example, we could define achievement in music performance operationally as the average rating by a panel of judges on a rating scale of tone quality, or as the number of correct pitches played. We could use both or either one depending on the focus of the investigation, but the use of such definitions allows interpreting a study's results in a way that enables practitioners to apply them. Over time and after numerous studies of "music achievement" that use several operational definitions, it may be possible to arrive at a general rule.

Models

An understanding of a broader context for the particular investigation being reported can make the results more meaningful. Representations of the broader context can be models or conceptual frameworks. They provide both the researcher and the interpreter of research with a means of viewing the specific project and its related research questions and applications. Models suggest relationships and the conditions that can affect these relationships. LeBlanc (1980) proposes a model of factors that influence musical taste. Different levels of the model identify different categories of factors—for example, characteristics of the stimulus and cultural environment—that may influence musical taste. Such models can be used by researchers to plan research and by readers to assist them in understanding the broader context within which a particular study is undertaken (Figure 15–1).

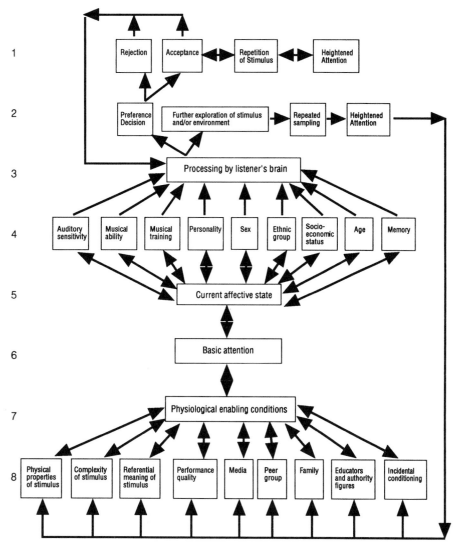

FIGURE 15–1. LeBlanc's Model of Factors That Influence Musical Taste.

Role of Theory

Theories try to explain relationships among several variables. They are generalizations that are applicable in a variety of settings. They aid the music educator in explaining, predicting, and controlling the music-teaching and -learning process. Theories play an important role for both the researcher and the consumer of research. For the researcher they provide guidance in constructing hypotheses. The researcher may use theory to examine under what circumstances the stated relationships are or are not true. The practitioner can use theory to apply the results of a narrow investigation to a wider range of instructional situations. Some theories in science, such as the theory of evolution, appear to be true in a great variety of circumstances. Unfortunately, theories relevant to music learning are not as well tested, but research based on theory can offer the opportu-

nity to apply results beyond the limits of a single investigation, thus providing the general rules by which music teachers can improve the effectiveness of their programs.

Areas in which (1) there has been an ample amount of study to produce theories of music learning, or (2) theory has been proposed that music educators have accepted because of its strong rationale include child development, music listening, and learning. Theorists whose propositions have been tested by music researchers include Jean Piaget, Leonard Meyer, Edwin Gordon, Benjamin Bloom, and Howard Gardner.

Although theory specific to music-learning issues exists in some areas, there are many areas in which there is no such theory. Theories from other areas such as education, psychology, or sociology may provide a base for research in music education. However, many teaching/learning areas in music appear to be sufficiently unique to warrant the development of idiosyncratic theory. The application of science to music teaching and learning is only about four decades old. As our field matures further, it will become increasingly necessary for music educators to develop theory regarding many aspects of the music-teaching and -learning process.

IMPORTANCE OF RELATED RESEARCH TO INTERPRETING RESEARCH

To be most useful, research studies should not be done in isolation but should be well integrated with previous related work, thus providing the opportunity for the development of networks of knowledge. The tradition of research provides for establishing the relationship of the reported study to previous work in the related literature section of a research report. This section is crucial for understanding the study's implications and applying its results. As stated earlier, many research projects focus on narrow issues. To gain insight from such work the reader must understand how this small piece of research fits into a larger context. The researcher is responsible for providing that context. In some disciplines and in a few areas of music education research, the theoretical underpinnings of the research define the area of related literature.

Previous research not only provides a context for interpretation but also guides the planning of the research project. Research closely related to the major research questions or hypotheses of a study may be most helpful in interpreting the results. In the study "Effects of Different Practice Conditions on Advanced Instrumentalists' Performance Accuracy" (Rosenthal, Wilson, Evans, and Greenwalt, 1988), the three key areas identified by the authors as related to the project are modeling, singing, and silent analysis. The literature reviewed in the study includes previous research in these three areas that points to the research questions addressed in the study. The previous research provides an important context, which can lead to understanding how the results of this one study might provide implications for instrumental music instruction generally. In any research study, the related literature may outline a history of work in the area, clarifying the research context within which the present investigation was planned.

Methods

In addition to revealing previous work related to the research questions or hypotheses, a literature review may be helpful in planning and interpreting research, particularly where the research is substantively similar to the current project. This is particularly important if the methods are unique or rarely used in music education investigations. Examining a similar project in a different field may provide powerful insights into possible applications in music education. In a study investigating the relationship between applied music-teaching behavior and selected personality variables, Schmidt (1989) cites several studies that examine the relationship between personality tests and teacher characteristics. Although none of the reviewed studies focused on music teachers, the similarity of the research questions being asked by these investigators provided strong support for the method Schmidt chose to employ in his own investigation.

Subjects

In some studies the particular group of students with which the research is conducted is an important part of the research question. This might apply to studies of specific age groups, for example, the musical behaviors of 3-year-olds, or of other critical characteristics, for example, the sight-reading skill of graduate student piano performance majors. Here again, it may be important for researchers to include studies outside of music that focus on the characteristics of this special group, for example, 3-year-olds, to find context within which the outcomes of the study can be placed. If we do not know what 3-year-olds can do generally, our efforts to apply the results of a study examining their musical behavior will be limited.

Instrumentation

Some research projects in music use quite specific tools during their investigations. The tool might be specific tests (e.g., a particular general reading achievement test) or specific kinds of technology (e.g., certain software packages or a particular electronic keyboard). In such cases it is important for the researcher to report previous studies that have employed the particular materials. Again, the primary purpose is to provide the reader with information that will help in interpreting the results of the investigation. Knowing how equipment or certain tests have been applied in other fields can be valuable in assessing their application to music education questions. In the Schmidt (1989) study cited above, the investigator selected the *Myer-Briggs Type Indicator* (MBTI) to measure the personality of applied music teachers. This selection was well supported by previous studies using the MBTI to investigate the relationship between teachers' personality and teaching behaviors with subjects who were not music teachers.

RESEARCH METHODS FOR MUSIC EDUCATION

As has been stressed throughout this chapter, it is important for the reader to know as much as possible about what questions are being asked and how the answers to those questions are being sought to be able to understand fully the results of research. Most research projects in music education use one of four or five possible strategies. Each of these "research methods" seeks answers to different general questions. Each will be briefly reviewed.

Philosophical Inquiry

Some writers in this area do not classify philosophical inquiry as a research method. Those who do suggest that such work tries to answer either of the following: What should be? or Why do we? Individuals engaged in philosophical inquiry pose questions and solutions and through logic arrive at a proposed solution. Those who reject such work as research do so on the grounds that it does not follow the pattern of the scientific method. Although there is little philosophical inquiry undertaken in music education, there are a few examples in the literature.

Historical Research

Historical research, while more clearly accepted as a research method than philosophical inquiry, is also viewed by some as less scientific than more quantitative methods. Historical research is used to examine hypotheses about the causes, effects, or trends of events that can help us to understand the present and anticipate the future. Although historical research cannot control the events it is examining, it systematically collects evidence, and objectively evaluates the evidence in light of the hypothesis. It tries to answer the question, What was, and why was it that way? so that current practices can be understood better in light of their antecedents. Music education has been a part of the school curriculum in the United States for more than 150 years. Many education practices appear to be cyclical; certain strategies and techniques are adopted and rejected with regularity. Historical researchers attempt to uncover the historical truth, so that we can learn from the past and apply these learnings to today's problems.

Descriptive Research

Descriptive research studies attempt to determine "what is." Descriptive studies constitute a high percentage of the research reported in music education and can provide important information upon which policy and instructional decisions can be made. Descriptive research often focuses on current practice, attitudes, demographic information, relationships among individuals' characteristics (e.g., ethnicity and musical taste), and trends in practice over time. Most researchers recognize several different approaches as descriptive research. Status studies and correlational studies are two frequently used descriptive approaches.

Status Studies Survey research is a common and valuable approach to determine status. Surveys in music education are used to collect information about current instructional practices, characteristics of teachers and students, and description of facilities. Surveys are most often conducted using a portion of the population of interest—that is, a sample—although on occasion all the institutions or individuals of interest might be included in a survey. One of the major factors determining the confidence with which one may view the results of a survey is the portion of the research population that responded to the survey and how representative its characteristics are of the group. Some writers advocate a response rate of at least 70 percent to establish confidence in the results of a survey. Surveys are most often conducted with mailed questionnaires or scheduled interviews, although questionnaires may be distributed in other ways, and interviews, for example, can be conducted over the phone.

Correlational Studies Some writers on research view the correlational study as a subcategory of the descriptive method, while others view it as a distinctly separate method. Correlation studies do describe an existing condition, although they have the specific goal of quantitatively describing the relationship between two or more variables. Often these variables are characteristics of individuals. For example, correlational studies can examine relationships between musical aptitude and intelligence, scores on melodic dictation tests and skill in sight singing, or the number of hours practiced per week and the grade on a final applied jury examination. Often researchers seek relationships between several variables and a central issue such as achievement in music. Although correlation studies can help in making some predictions, correlation does not define causality. If two variables are highly related—for example, interest in learning a musical instrument and success in instrumental music—then knowing one variable, interest, allows us to predict the other variable, success. We may then take action based on this knowledge. Such relationships do not imply cause and effect, but are still useful in prediction.

In addition to status and correlation studies, several other approaches to research are classified as descriptive. These include developmental studies, which describe and compare characteristics of students at different age levels; case studies, which are in-depth descriptions of an individual, group, or institution; and casual-comparative studies, which attempt to determine the causes for existing circumstances. These are explored more extensively in Chapter 9.

Experimental Research

Experimental research is a powerful tool that answers the question, What will be under certain conditions? Experimental research is the only research method that allows the establishing of cause and effect relationships. With this approach the researcher manipulates one aspect of the experimental situation while attempting to control or hold constant all other aspects. Researchers manipulate the aspect they believe will likely cause a change. In experimental studies, this aspect is called either the independent variable, the experimental variable, or the treatment. The effect of this manipulation is assessed by examining changes in some measure, called the dependent variable, the criterion variable, or the posttest. In music education the researchers typically choose as a treatment something that will improve music learning. Treatments might include a newly designed instrumental method book, a computer program for improving melodic dictation skills, or a multicultural curriculum for a music appreciation class. Dependent variables for such studies could be tests that measure, respectively, instrumental performance, melodic dictation skills, or awareness of the music of different cultures. One important issue in reviewing the results of experimental studies is the existence of competing explanations for any change in the dependent variable. If the study's design is appropriate, that fact will provide confidence that the treatment is the best explanation of any effect observed.

Ethnographic Procedures

Recently there has been growing interest among music educators in a research method primarily used by anthropologists and ethnomusicologists. The method is identified by several different labels, including ethnography, qualitative research, naturalistic research, and field research. (Some authors will make finer distinctions among these labels.) The primary goal of ethnographic research is description. It includes intensive data collection in natural settings. In opposition to the researcher using the experimental method, who enters the experimental setting and manipulates variables, the naturalistic researcher attempts to remain unobtrusive. Also, ethnographers commonly collect qualitative instead of quantitative data. Ethnographic studies tend to be exploratory, and whereas related literature based on other research strategies may provide direction for such investigations, ethnographers do not test specific hypotheses, but try to uncover new explanations for phenomena. In music education such methods might be applied to the study of the development of an ensemble, or the implementation of a new teaching method that might be expected to have an impact on students in many ways, not all which can be predicted.

GENERAL GUIDELINES
FOR INTERPRETING INDIVIDUAL STUDIES

The adjusted means for all treatment groups on the item "I feel comfortable singing a solo in front of others" were far lower than the adjusted means on any of the other self-perception items. This finding indicates that elementary education majors feel particularly insecure when singing for others, confirming results reported by Evans. (Phillips and Vispoel, 1990, p. 104)

One of a researcher's obligations is to provide the reader with an interpretation of their research. Researchers should be in the best position to provide the interpretation because they are most familiar with the particular project; they articulated the particular problem, they identified the purpose of the project, they proposed the hypotheses, they provided the model or identified the theory to be tested, they gathered and analyzed the data, and they summarized the previous relevant research. Whereas most parts of the research process are systematic, and relatively objective, the interpretation

section is more subjective because it attempts to relate the project to other projects or to the field. Two competent researchers can examine the same study and arrive at different interpretations.

Purpose of Study

To understand the outcomes, one must understand where the research is heading and what has motivated it. The formulation of the purpose of the study helps provide direction for understanding the results. The purpose identifies the research objective so that the questions the investigator is trying to answer are clear. Statements of purpose are usually short and direct. The following examples illustrate objectives of research studies in music education.

"Specifically, . . . to determine whether vocal knowledge, attitudes, and vocal performance among elementary education majors would improve as a result of an extended time of vocal treatment (ten weeks) with additional emphasis on breath management" (Phillips and Vispoel, 1990, p. 98).

"One purpose of this research was to establish a more consistent means of describing the various stages of child singing-voice development" (Rutkowski, 1990, p. 82).

"This study was designed to test the preferences of subjects for pitch and/or tempo alterations compared to original, unaltered presentations of current popular music excerpts" (Geringer and Madsen, 1987, p. 206).

When the purpose of a study is to "determine whether there is a relationship between variable x and variable y," the reader should expect that certain statements will be included in the study. Statements in results sections might include indices of relationships, such as correlation coefficients, if the study lends itself to quantitative analysis, and the discussion section should comment on the strength of the relationship. In the conclusions of such a study the investigator should be expected to comment about the relationship. For example, in a study by Price and Yarbrough (1987) that examined the relationship between musicians' and nonmusicians' record collections and their expressed opinions of composers, the authors report, "It was found that the frequencies of composer-mention bore significant but moderate correlations to the ownership of corresponding recordings, and the percentage of recordings owned and composers mentioned of a formal tradition were significantly and more strongly related" (p. 241).

Other studies might have as their objectives "to explore a quality or characteristic of a particular group"; the interpretation of the results of such investigation should reflect the exploratory character. The reader of such research should have different expectations because of the type of question being asked. Whereas studies of relationships between variables focus on the variables while acknowledging that subject characteristics may influence the results, studies that focus on the characteristics of groups are much more concerned with how different attributes might interact. Interpretation of the results of such studies might offer several different directions that future research might pursue, rather than a single focused result. A study by Kalekin-Fishman (1986) provides an illustration of an exploratory study. The study, described as a case study by the author, focuses on the music sung in kindergarten classes. The data were collected by observation and tape recordings in 30 kindergarten classes. The results of the research are reported in descriptions and categorizations of the songs recorded. Kalekin-Fishman concludes that teachers constrain what is defined as music in the kindergarten, on the basis of sociocultural criteria.

Studies also may differ in being applied or theoretical. A study by Shehan (1985) is a good example of one that focuses on theoretical concerns. The theory in question is cognitive transfer theory—specifically, Edward L. Thorndike and Robert Woodworth's theory of identical elements. Shehan applies this theory to the area of music preferences, examining whether the preference for taught pieces of nonwestern music transfers to similar pieces not taught. The results show that students did not have similar preferences for taught pieces and for untaught pieces; consequently, the transfer theory as proposed was not supported. A more applied study conducted by Zurcher (1987) examines the effect of three evaluation procedures on the achievement of band students. Zurcher concluded "that daily teacher-issued letter grades are not specific enough to change (rehearsal) behavior" (p. 51). He found that when students recorded their own daily numerical grades, achievement improved. Although most research may have implications for both theory and application, most studies will focus on one or the other; this focus should be apparent in the statement of the purpose. In studies that emphasize a problem's more practical nature the results should be interpreted so as to produce recommendations for what action practitioners should take. Studies that are more theoretical will be directed toward outcomes that will provide directions for future research. Why a study is undertaken is key to understanding what is accomplished.

The Research Hypothesis and Research Questions

Whereas the purpose of a study provides us with a sense of overall direction, the research hypothesis provides the specificity often required by the inquiry. Research hypotheses ideally are based on previous research and theory and inform the reader of what the researcher expects to happen in the study. Not all studies have research hypotheses. Exploratory studies may focus on areas where sufficient information to generate meaningful hypotheses is lacking. In such studies, the material in the problem or introduction section is critically important in providing the reader with the perspective that allows proper interpretation. Dyer (1979) suggests that in many such studies the explanations for the results are supplied after the evidence is collected, rather than before, and that in such studies the researcher's interpretations are

less compelling as they appear to be unexpected. Studies that provide problem- or theory-generated hypotheses prepare the reader so that the author's interpretation logically follows the informed guesses (i.e., hypotheses) provided. Thus readers must be able to critically understand the related research and rationale leading to the hypothesis. Hypotheses can be derived from previous research, theory, or logic. In studies where previous research or theory is inadequate for the development of specific hypotheses, research questions are used. These provide the researcher with guidance without the specificity of hypotheses. Hypotheses provide more confidence in the conclusions. Studies in which researchers specifically predict results are more convincing than those in which a rationale or theory is developed after the data are analyzed.

Most studies in music education use research questions rather than hypotheses. For example:

"Is there a relationship between age and children's responses to analogical tasks using musical concepts?" (Nelson and Barresi, 1989, p. 95).

"What is the attitude of elementary students toward using the computer for music theory drill?" (Willett and Netusil, 1989, p. 221).

"Do music educators perceive specific types of handicapping conditions as more difficult than others to integrate in the mainstream?" (Gfeller, Darrow, and Hedden, 1990, p. 92).

"Do modeling, singing, and silent analysis differ in their effectiveness as aids to practice?" (Rosenthal, et al., 1988, p. 251).

A few studies in music education based on theories or models do use hypotheses. For example:

"The four sensory modes of perceptual modality are proportionally homogeneous across high, moderate, and low groups of students on intuitive musical ability" (Moore, 1990, p. 27).

"The attention subjects would need to devote to the task of reading and playing music in the playing-listening (PL) condition would inhibit their ability to monitor tempo, resulting in slower detection of tempo change than in the listening-only (LO) condition" (Ellis, 1989, p. 289).

Results of Previous Research

As previously mentioned, the related literature section of a research report may serve several functions. It may describe the context in which a research problem exists. It may describe previous studies that have tested the hypothesis being examined and provide clues to strategies for designing the current investigation. Of the various functions of the related literature, the two most important for interpreting results are providing the background for a research problem and examining previous studies that have tested the same or similar hypotheses.

Both areas of literature provide the support for making a hypothesis. Good hypotheses are not wondrous intuitive leaps, but well-thought-out, logical extensions of previous work. The most productive and efficient researchers are those who are well steeped in the literature of their research area. Researchers examine the previous literature and, on the basis of their experience, knowledge, and judgment, determine what is the next most reasonable question to examine. Different researchers may look at the same evidence and come to different conclusions regarding what it shows. An area of research that has several investigators testing related but different hypotheses is more likely to move toward solving problems quickly than one in which there are few researchers examining a narrow group of hypotheses.

This intimacy with the literature surrounding the problem and hypothesis is also important for the consumer of research. Familiarity with this literature enhances the consumer's ability to interpret the results. The results should be presented so that one can determine whether they agree with or contradict previous findings. If the results are contradictory, the researcher should provide an explanation for why the differences might have happened, such as methodological or subject characteristic differences in students. Familiarity with related literature allows the reader to speculate on reasons other than those the investigator proposes for any observed differences and provides the basis on which the consumer may come to different conclusions based on the researcher's evidence.

Theory or Model

For science to be able to contribute to practice it must offer a network of information, not isolated facts. The connecting links between knowledge and science are provided by theory. Theories can provide explanations for events. They may help predict what will happen when a particular intervention is started. They are generalizations, formulated to suggest what is likely to happen, but they may not explain all cases, particularly those that are extreme deviants from the model. Theories are developed through induction, that is, observing events in many instances and a variety of circumstances and developing a statement that appears to explain all the events. Theories are then tested by deduction. A researcher wishing to test a theory develops hypotheses to examine a specific application of the theory. The evidence gathered by testing the hypothesis is then examined to determine how well it supports or refutes the theory. Are there necessary modifications in the theory based upon the research? Comparing the fit of the results of one study with a theory greatly enhances the research consumer's ability to understand a study.

Because of the relative lack of theory in music education,

a researcher is more likely simply to review studies linked to the current investigation and explain their relationship to the current study. It is helpful if researchers also provide a model by which the study being conducted can be viewed in the large context of practice. The LeBlanc (1980) model, presented earlier, is an example of such a model.

RESEARCH DESIGN

Although the specific research method used in a study affects the study's design and interpretation, there are general guidelines for research design issues. These guidelines will be discussed below.

Subjects

The primary question regarding the subjects is, Who are they? What are their characteristics? Are they anything like the subjects that you are interested in? Is there anything about them that might influence or distort the study's results?

Several aspects of subject selection can greatly influence the outcomes of studies. Of these the two that easily generalize across most empirical studies are the sample size and the sample characteristics.

Is the Sample Representative? Research projects are seldom conducted with the entire population in which the researcher is interested. For example, a researcher interested in examining how effective the Curwen hand signs are for developing sight-singing skill among third-grade students will not be able to study all third-grade students in the United States. Thus, the researcher must use a sample of that population. Two questions should be asked regarding the sample. Does the procedure for selecting the sample yield a group that is representative of the target population, and is the sample sufficiently large?

The representative issue is not as clear-cut as it may first appear. One might assume that if the researcher selected only third-grade students from a small city in the middle of the farm belt, the results would not generalize well to an inner city or wealthy suburban population. But, the question the consumer of research must ask is, Are there reasons to believe that the treatment being applied in the study, in this case, hand signs, will interact with the unique characteristics of the sample, in this example, students from a small city in the farm belt? Stated differently, is being from a small city likely to influence how well children learn to sight-sing? This point may be best understood with another illustration. Instead of selecting third-graders from a small farm-belt city, what if the researcher selected third-graders from inner city, suburban, and rural locations, but unintentionally included only communities whose schools had systematic sequential music instruction five days a week beginning in kindergarten? This sample wouldn't be very representative of third-graders across the country regarding music instruction, and it appears that this characteristic would likely interact with the teaching of sight singing.

Although research methods books instruct researchers to use samples randomly selected from the entire population, because of a variety of constraints, research most often is conducted with available samples, for example, "students from 10 third-grade classes from the Lansing (Mich.) School District" or "253 undergraduates from three state-supported universities in the Midwest." If it seems reasonable that the sample available to the researcher (e.g., third-graders from Lansing) is representative of the target population (e.g., third-graders), then the next step is to use an appropriate sampling procedure to choose subjects from those available. There are probably more third-graders in Lansing than it is practical to use in the study, so the researcher will choose a sample of third-graders with which to work, employing a sampling procedure that does not allow the sample to be biased. Using only third-graders enrolled in a special after-school enrichment program may be convenient but is unlikely to be representative of *all* third-graders in Lansing. The most desirable procedure is one in which the students are chosen randomly from the population available, in this case all the third-grade students in Lansing. This procedure ensures that only by chance will the sample selected differ from the population. The generalization of results from this sample of randomly selected third-graders to the population of third-graders in Lansing then can be a statistical matter rather than a logical one. It allows the researcher to use statistics to generalize the results of the study to the larger population.

Further, the generalization of these results to a national population of third-grade students then becomes one of logic rather than statistics. The consumer of research can feel more confident in the results if studies are repeated in different locales (e.g., Stamford, Conn.) and/or with samples with somewhat different characteristics (e.g., third-graders who never have had music instruction in school).

Is the Size of the Sample Adequate? The size of the sample influences confidence in a study's results. A study conducted with only a few subjects often raises questions regarding the uniqueness of those subjects and how the study might apply to a wider range of subjects. Sample size is also affected by the size of the population under study. A study that attempts to generalize to all third-graders has a much larger target population than one that focuses only on third-graders who have taken applied music instruction. Although no specific rules apply in determining adequate sample sizes, there are at least two factors that may help. The ability of statistical procedures to identify small differences in outcomes is influenced by the size of the sample—the larger the sample, the more sensitive statistical procedures are in detecting small differences. (This characteristic of statistics is called power.) If a sample is very large, the results are very likely to be statistically generalizable because the statistical procedures used will be very powerful; and if the sample is very small, the results are not likely to be statistically generalizable because the statistics will not be very powerful.

Certain types of investigations dictate that small or large samples should be used. For example, studies that examine perceptual issues often require an intense focus on a small group or even a single subject. A 1986 study by Cutietta employs a small sample. He examined applications of biofeedback training in music. The subjects for the study were three violinists, two vocalists, a saxophonist, and a percussionist. A parallel control group was formed. The subjects, who were all having some difficulty playing certain musical passages, received four training sessions with biofeedback techniques. The results indicated that all the subjects except the percussionist had less muscle tension during the treatment sessions. Instructors rated the performances of the subjects who had received the biofeedback significantly higher than those of the control group performers. Cutietta concludes that biofeedback can be sucessfully used by musicians to reduce muscle tension and improve their playing.

Instrumentation

Another important aspect of a research project bearing on the interpretation of the results is the way the variables are measured. In research studies the way a variable is measured is really the way in which it is defined for the purposes of that investigation. Thus, if a researcher is examining how musical ability is related to adult attendance at symphony orchestra concerts, the way in which musical ability is measured—for instance with *Musical Aptitude Profile* test scores—is how for the purposes of this study music ability is defined. The effect of defining variables on interpreting a study's results must not be underestimated. With variables such as music ability, the use of different tests is also the use of different theories of music aptitude. Inasmuch as it is necessary to narrow the concept of music aptitude for the purposes of research, there may be disagreement on how that translates back to a broad conception of music ability.

Dyer (1979) presents a two-dimensional scheme for classifying measurement techniques employed in research studies: first, who records the information and, second, the time period in which the information is recorded. This results in three classifications: (1) the subject records information during the study; (2) the researcher records information during the study; or (3) the subject recorded information at some point in the past for purposes unrelated to the present study. The first category includes data collection instruments such as tests, questionnaires, interviews, or even incidental behaviors, such as a trumpeter's rehearsal pencil markings in the score. The second category includes research observations, the use of rating scales, and the measurement of physiological responses such as heart rate. The third category could include school records, original scores, or the choral programs from the 1950 to 1970 seasons.

Each of the measurement categories may have some limitations that limit generalizations of studies using them. A frequent problem for researchers is subjects' awareness that they are being measured. Subjects aware that they are being observed may respond or behave differently than they would in nonresearch circumstances. Such awareness when subjects are taking an achievement test is less important than when they are responding to a questionnaire or interview. With observational approaches used by ethnographic researchers and others, researchers must be particularly sensitive to the influence of the presence of the observer on the behaviors of the students in the class or ensemble. Does the teacher respond differently when someone is sitting in the back of the room recording teacher and student behavior? Are students in a rehearsal able to ignore the presence of a video camera? These are questions that bear on the outcomes of such investigations.

Another factor to be considered in the measurement process is the learning or change in behavior that may occur from participating in an assessment process. Students may acquire skills in test taking or acquire new information as the result of testing. They also may become sensitized to other components of a study as a result of measurement. An example is a study examining whether videotapes illustrating successful uses of multicultural music resources would increase the use of these resources by music teachers exposed to the videotapes. If the inservice music teachers were given an attitude scale on the use of multicultural music resources followed by videotapes illustrating the use of multicultural music resources in elementary school music classes, their reaction to the videotapes might differ from what it would have been without the attitude scale. These reactive effects likely will influence the outcomes of such investigations, so the practitioner may, when applying the experimental treatment (in this case the videotapes), obtain different results from those reported in the research.

Readers should consider whether the recording or scoring of the behavior under investigation changes over time, especially when observers or judges must record or evaluate large amounts of behavior. During auditions, are candidates who perform at 9:00 A.M. viewed with the same "eye" or heard with the same "ear" as those who scheduled right before lunch break, or as those who are scheduled at 4:45 P.M. after the judges have heard more than 20 performances? Researchers must try to control for such influences, and those who examine studies using these kinds of measures must consider how such effects might influence the results.

Data Analysis

The data collected by the researcher can be in several different forms. Data resulting from interviews will likely be verbal statements. Data generated from tests will be in numbers. In some circumstances the data might be music, either notated or aural. Determining what analysis procedures to use will obviously depend on what type of data are generated. In addition, the particular procedures used depend on what problem, research questions, and hypotheses are being investigated. So the question readers of research reports must keep in mind when reading data analysis is, Does the analysis help make a decision regarding the research questions or hypotheses?

The primary function of data analysis is to place the data

in forms that will facilitate a decision regarding the study's results. One established procedure is to summarize the data. Summaries of interview data might consist of what statements interviewees made frequently and what unique statements were made. Questionnaire data often are summarized as the percentage of responses in different categories. Test administration summaries frequently report the group average or mean and how far the scores are spread out around the mean. If the data were music notation, we would expect it to be summarized using analysis techniques—for example, harmonic analysis, or a report of the frequency of appearance of certain melodic intervals. Aural music data might be first converted to notation (not necessarily a straightforward process) and then described in a like manner.

For certain research questions—for example, those determining relationships between variables—very specific data analysis procedures are used. For relational studies, correlation coefficients that show the strength and direction of a relationship are appropriate. For hypothesis-testing studies, one or more tests of statistical inference should be employed. Both of these specialized data analysis procedures will be examined more closely later in this chapter.

Do the Results Support the Research Hypothesis? In a well-designed study the data analysis should lead to a clear decision regarding the research hypothesis. In some studies that use statistical procedures this decision is straightfoward: A statistical test of the hypothesis clearly shows whether the results do or do not support the research hypothesis. In studies that use less clear decision-making strategies, researchers try to weigh the evidence objectively and assist readers in understanding how their decision is supported by the evidence. Often, the data do not lead to overwhelming support for a particular hypothesis. That is, the data may not provide the evidence for a clear decision in which practitioners can place confidence. For instance, in a survey of what beginning method books are used by instrumental music teachers, how does the researcher decide when a difference between two method books is sufficiently important to make a recommendation. If the distribution is 52 percent to 48 percent? If the distribution is 55 percent to 45 percent?; 60 percent to 40 percent? Or how does the historical researcher decide when the evidence is sufficient to show that a composer authored a particular unsigned manuscript? In all data analysis situations it is important that the researcher makes the logic of the decision clear and that the data are presented in such a manner that others may examine them and arrive at their own conclusions.

One way of adding strength to a data-based decision is to compare it with the results of other studies. The researcher is obligated to discuss whether the results agree with other findings and speculate on why they do or do not agree. Agreement with other studies helps researchers develop confidence in their results. Disagreements with other findings may be due to several factors that researchers and research consumers must carefully consider. Was the study sufficiently well designed that the results are not due to "bad data"? Was the population studied sufficiently different to have caused the lack of agreement? If the study is valid and considerable confidence can be placed in conflicting results, then a new relationship might have been uncovered that warrants further study.

Conflicting results highlight an important principal of research: The results of one study do not *prove* a hypothesis. The evidence from one study may support a hypothesis, but proof in science requires more support. This support involves the relationship of the study to previous research and, most importantly, the ability to reproduce the results. If, in fact, a researcher has discovered a truth, a relationship between variables that is stable, repeating the study should produce the same results. Replication is the standard by which researchers gain confidence in their findings. Replications are usually not exact repetitions. For instance, seldom would the same subjects be used. Different subjects in a different location and with somewhat different characteristics further support the results and add to the confidence of generalizing to broader populations and settings. More replications with diverse populations and varied environments allow the researcher to be less tentative in discussing the implications. Although researchers in music education are well aware of the importance of replication, replication studies are seldom undertaken. Consequently, much of what research has added to the knowledge base in music education is based on more tentative findings than are desirable.

Conclusions are statements of what the results say about the problem. They may indicate how well the hypotheses were supported by the results and may make inferences regarding theoretical premises of the investigation. Conclusions are drawn from examining the results of a study in light of the initial problem. If the results are confusing, then additional investigations are necessary before conclusions can be made. If the results are as expected, then the researcher is able to draw conclusions.

When researchers complete investigations and find evidence that supports their hypotheses, an important question for those who wish to apply this tentative new knowledge is, Will it work for me? When the researchers have tested a hypothesis in a particular setting with a particular population, the question of how the results may apply or generalize beyond the study is the determining factor in how useful the research will be to applied music education. If a study has been replicated with different populations, in different environments, and even with different versions of the materials employed, and if each of the replications has yielded similar results, then music teachers can feel confident that the results may work for them. If the results derive from one study of the hypothesis, it is very difficult to determine how broadly they might apply.

The question of generalizability of results is really several different questions, depending on which aspect of a study receives focus. Research procedures—specifically, the selection of a random sample—provides some guidance for generalizing the results to other populations. Strictly speaking, unless a particular subject had the "chance" of being selected through the random selection process, the results cannot be thought to apply to that individual. The reality of conducting

research in music education is that administrative constraints usually limit available research populations to convenient schools, school districts, or small geographical regions. So the researcher can generalize statistically only to the defined available population. To the extent that the available population (e.g., fourth-grade students in the researcher's school district) is similar to students in other school districts, the results may have implications for other settings. This ultimately becomes a rational instead of a statistical decision.

Other issues of generalization are also usually rational decisions instead of decisions designed into the research project. If one study finds that biofeedback techniques result in a decrease in muscle tension and improved performance for pianists, will the results generalize to harpsichordists, or to tubists? Replication studies can confirm such generalizations and ultimately make the finding stronger by confirming its applicability in a variety of situations.

Unhypothesized Results

Researchers and consumers of research must be very cautious in interpreting results that were not hypothesized. These "serendipitous" findings can serve well as the basis for future research designed specifically to test them. Research studies are not "fishing expeditions" in which any "interesting" relationship that is uncovered has the same import as do those the study was designed to examine. For example, in a study designed to examine the effectiveness of an instructional unit on the instruments of the orchestra for fourth-grade students, it may be that while testing students on their ability to aurally identify different instruments the researchers observe that boys seem to exhibit an affinity for certain instruments and girls an affinity for other instruments. Such findings may be documented and reported, but no conclusion should be drawn from them. However, these findings may well serve as the catalyst for additional research.

Research projects are based on carefully developed hypotheses that are logically arrived at from defined problems, experience, theories or models, and previous research. It is this systematic approach that provides confidence in the scientific method of knowledge acquisition. Whereas researchers should report unhypothesized findings and make recommendations regarding their verification through newly designed studies, generalizations based on serendipity are inappropriate.

Practical Significance vs. Statistical Significance

When researchers use inferential statistical procedures, they are able to determine the likelihood that the results obtained in a study would occur again. When results are said to be "statistically significant," that is another way of saying that they are *not likely* due to chance. Such statistically significant relationships would likely occur again and again in replications. Achieving "statistically significant results" is often thought to be so important that researchers discover such relationships, sit back, and do not interpret the importance of the results. Statistical significance might be considered as the first part of a two-step process. The second step involves the question, Do the results have significant implications for practice? Practical significance occurs when the implementation of a research finding results in improvements in practice.

Statistical significance is only a statement regarding the likelihood of recurrence. It is primarily influenced by two factors, size of the sample and size of the effect. The larger the sample, the more likely a result will be significant; and the larger the effect, the more likely a result will be significant. These two factors can work independently; thus a small effect in a study using a large sample can be statistically significant. When this occurs, the practical significance of the results must be considered. If a small difference in test scores is due to a large expenditure of funds, practitioners must question whether the traditionally limited funds available for music education will be well spent to produce such a small improvement. For example, a study might be designed to determine how the intonation of band members might be improved by using "artist model" instruments to replace the "student model" ones currently used. Even if the results of such a study indicated that the band "on average" was five cents more in tune when using the artist model instruments and that this five cents difference was statistically significant, the cost of purchasing artist model instruments for the entire band might well prohibit implementation of such statistically significant findings. It is a curious benefit that because music education research generally is restricted to modest size samples (i.e., 30 to a few hundred students), statistically significant differences are also likely to be practically significant.

INTERPRETING HISTORICAL RESEARCH

Although the recommendations just given are generally applicable to all research methods, each method may have idiosyncratic interpreting issues. These are described below.

Historical research is not conducted to prove a point. Rather it is done to weigh all the evidence available as objectively as possible and determine the truth—that is, what really happened. When interpreting the results of a historical study, the consumer must have confidence in the study's objectivity. Historical researchers spend a considerable amount of their research time determining what evidence should be considered in testing their hypotheses and what evidence should be disgarded. Historical researchers prefer primary rather than secondary sources of information. Primary sources are recorded by eyewitnesses to the event, while secondary sources are those where the reports are at least one step removed from the event's origin. Primary sources can be diaries, music manuscripts, letters, oral interviews, newspaper reports of eyewitnesses, or a range of records and documents. The more primary sources historical researchers have, the better. However, the authenticity and accuracy of the sources are also of concern to historical researchers. Has

a document been developed to project a particularly favorable view of an event that benefits its participants? Do various independent sources present the same or different accounts of an event? These are the types of questions historical researchers must resolve in arriving at conclusions.

The issue of objectivity seems more difficult to resolve in historical research than in other research methods. The historical researcher uses logic instead of statistics to draw conclusions. One danger is the possibility of overlooking or disregarding evidence that contradicts hypotheses. The stereotypical discovery of a previously unknown manuscript in some basement or attic can dramatically alter the view historical researchers have of particular individuals or events. And the possibility of gaining confidence through replication of the historical studies is not available, although several researchers working independently may examine the same evidence. It seems critical for historical researchers to link new studies to previously developed historical research so that the congruity of the results with previous work can add confidence. Of course, there is always the danger of congruent results in false directions. Clearly, historical research requires the sophistication acquired by experience and a strong knowledge base.

Some critics question forming generalizations from the results of historical research. If historical events occur once and the environment in which they occurred can never be exactly duplicated, is it possible to generalize from a historical event? Supporters of historical research point out that most descriptive and experimental research cannot be exactly duplicated either. With historical research, as with generalizing beyond an available population, the closer the circumstances are to the original events the more applicable the results should be.

INTERPRETING DESCRIPTIVE RESEARCH

Status Studies

With descriptive research as with historical research, the major issue of concern in the interpretation of the results is the accuracy of the data. The primary purpose of descriptive research is to report the current state of phenomena, so if the data collection process is flawed, conclusions based upon the data will be misleading.

Certain measurement approaches used in descriptive studies, such as tests and scales to measure attributes like music aptitude or musical taste, include standard procedures for determining the accuracy of measures. Estimates of reliability and validity (see Chapter 16) provide the researcher with information on the type and degree of error that might result from employing such tests and scales. Descriptive researchers can limit the risk of error in their results by using tests and scales that have well-documented reliability and validity. Researchers are particularly at risk in this area when they develop new measures for the research. It is imperative that the reliability and validity of any new measures be clearly established so that the size of the error introduced into the data collection by the measuring instrument can be estimated. Even researchers employing well-documented standardized tests would be wise to check carefully for any sources of error—for example, a change in the recommended procedure for administering the test—that might occur during the study.

With questionnaires, the mainstay of data collection in status studies, the assessment of the quality of information produced is not as direct as with tests and scales. One way to establish the amount of error in questionnaire data is to examine the consistency of responses to similar questions within the questionnaire and to compare the results of a questionnaire with the findings of other studies and/or other measures (such as interviews) used in the same study. This strategy requires the researcher to design into the questionnaire items that serve as consistency checks. Another approach to examining consistency might be to assess whether certain groups of respondents (for instance, college music major undergraduates versus nonmusic major undergraduates) differ in expected ways on certain items on the survey (for instance, the number of "serious music" performances attended). Sometimes it may be possible to obtain an independent measure of some items. Agreement between responses on survey items and other measures provides confidence in survey results. For instance, in a survey of college music departments regarding curriculum issues, responses to questions regarding course offerings might be compared with published college catalogs. Whatever approach is used, some measure of the accuracy of the data collected should be reported in descriptive studies.

Once confidence has been established in the data's accuracy the researcher is responsible for characterizing the results of the study. A survey might hypothetically report that undergraduate music majors attended an average of 12 performances of "serious music" per semester. What does this statement mean? Does the result mean that music majors attend "a lot" "few," or "a satisfactory number" of performances? What additional information is necessary so that we can understand and attach some meaning to the statement? If we knew some comparison information we might be better able to understand the statement. Knowing that there were an average of 25 performances each semester or that non-music majors attended an average of three each semester might provide a context in which to interpret the finding. Determining the average number of performances attended by music majors at other institutions might also provide a context for interpretation. Obviously, it is necessary to obtain some type of comparative data to attach meaning to the results of surveys. The establishment of contrasts or compar-

isons should be an important part of the interpretation of data in status studies.

In addition to being able to generalize from a sample to a target population, those who conduct surveys are often interested in determining trends across time. Measuring related characteristics helps to determine trends across different specific variables and may assist in a broader interpretation of the results. If, in addition to the attendance rate at performances of "serious music," it is also discovered that undergraduate music majors attended more collegiate sporting events and/or student government meetings than nonmusic majors, quite a different interpretation of the "serious music" attendance finding might be made than if music majors exceeded nonmajors in only the one area. More confidence might be placed in the interpretations in our example if data were available for students over a 6- to 10-year period instead of for one specific year in which specific characteristics of the performances might have enhanced or decreased attendance by music majors.

One approach to forming conclusions in status studies is to present a profile of a typical respondent. And it is informative to identify characteristics that show considerable uniqueness. Such approaches must consider relationships between different characteristics in the study. Instead of just reporting average responses or distribution of percent responses to each category, additional insight is often gained by relating the data from two or more questions on a survey. In our illustration, relating the year (e.g., first-year student, sophomore) of the music major respondents and their performance attendance may provide more insight into the data than the results of either question alone. The hypothetical data in Table 15.1 provide an illustration of how this cross-tabulation can be important in interpreting survey results.

Ideally, reports of descriptive research provide enough additional information to make the numbers generated meaningful. Often, surveys can generate so much information that it is difficult to gain an overview. Researchers must remind themselves that the numbers are important only within a meaningful context.

Correlational Studies

With correlational studies as with status studies, confidence in the results depends on the quality of the measures used to collect the data. Reports of the reliability and validity of measures and the results of strategies used to determine the consistency of questionnaire responses should be included in descriptive studies.

Whereas the general issues of sample size and selection should be considered in correlational studies, there is a spe-

TABLE 15.1. Hypothetical Concert Attendance of College Students

	First-Year Students	Sophomores	Juniors	Seniors	Average
Number of performances attended	4	8	16	20	12

cific effect that sampling can have on association studies. If the sample employed represents only a portion of the full range of the variable of interest, then the relationship produced in the study will be inaccurate and misleading. If only students with high music ability are included in a study of the relationship between music aptitude and math aptitude, the resulting correlation between the two aptitudes is unlikely to be the same as if the full range of music ability were represented. The same problem would exist if students with high music ability were excluded from the study. Studies that include only restricted samples are likely to underestimate the relationship between the two variables being investigated. If researchers sample only those students with very high or very low music ability and do not include those in the middle, the estimate of relationship is likely to be overestimated. These consequences underscore the need for samples that are sufficiently large and diverse that the relationships produced will not be distorted. The correlation coefficients produced by studies of relationships provide information on the direction and strength of relationships. Direction can be categorized as either positive or negative. Positive correlation coefficients (e.g., $+0.32$, $+0.80$, $+0.91$) occur when students who receive a high score on one variable tend to receive a high score on the related variable, and students who receive a low score on one variable tend to receive a low score on the related variable. Negative correlation coefficients (e.g., -0.40, -0.72, -0.85) occur when students who receive a low score on one variable tend to receive a high score on the related variable, and vice versa. The scores from two different tests of music aptitude are likely to be positively related while the number of hours students practice is likely to be negatively correlated to the number of mistakes they make at an audition (when hours of practice are high, mistakes should be low).

It is possible to determine the statistical significance of a correlation coefficient. Generally, the stronger the correlation and the larger the sample size, the more likely a coefficient will be statistically significant. A statistically significant correlation is one that probably did not occur by chance. Another investigation likely would yield a similar response.

Generally, of course, more confidence is due coefficients found in studies with 100 subjects than in those with 10.

As stated previously, statistical significance must not be mistaken for practical significance. It is possible for a small coefficient to be statistically significant but have limited practical significance. For interpreting correlational studies, statistical significance is less important than the strength of the relationship. In the interpretation of the strength of the relationship, terms like "strong," "moderate," "substantial," or "negligible" are generally applied. There is little to guide the researcher or the reader in the application of these words to particular ranges of coefficients. One researcher may view a coefficient of 0.72 as strong while another views it as moderate. It is not uncommon for an author in a single study to use the label "moderate" for correlations of .29 and .79.

When correlation coefficients are squared, the resulting number indicates the percentage of variance that is shared by the two variables. Thus even with correlations of .70, less than 50 percent ($.70 \times .70 = .49$) of the variance is common variance. This statistic, r squared, can provide important additional insight into understanding relationships between variables.

Another characteristic of the relationship between two variables is the pattern of the relationship. Identical correlation coefficients can be produced by quite different patterns of relationships. Patterns of relationships, generally represented in scatterplots, are not typically published in journals, so the reader must expect the researcher to have examined the pattern of the relationship and to comment upon it. It may be possible to recognize unusual patterns of relationships by examining basic descriptive information about the variables, such as means and standard deviations if they are reported, but clearly the researcher is in a better situation to comment on asymmetry or the relationship pattern than is the reader. Figure 15–2 illustrates how scatterplots can provide information to assist in understanding a relationship.

It is very tempting to assume causation when a relationship is discovered in a correlational study. Often, the rationale for the investigation and the related literature imply a directionality

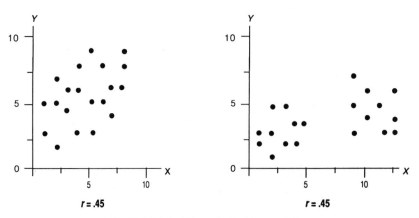

FIGURE 15–2. Hypothetical Scatter Plots.

of a relationship. When medical researchers find that the amount of cholesterol in an individual's blood is related to increased occurrence of heart attacks, clearly causation is implied, although medical researchers cannot do experimental studies with such variables to establish causation. It seems appropriate for researchers to speculate on possible causal relationships, but it should be clear to the reader that the results of a correlational study do not establish causation. Many times strong relationships that are reported may be caused by a combination of several other variables, such as smoking, stress, or obesity in the case of heart disease. Studies that identify a strong positive relationship between participation in instrumental music instruction and general grade point average cannot conclude that if every child were enrolled in instrumental music the educational difficulties of the country would be solved. Many other intervening variables such as aptitude and socioeconomic status may account for such a relationship.

INTERPRETING EXPERIMENTAL RESEARCH

Experimental research methods have as their goal establishing causation. Consequently, when one is assigning meaning to the results of experimental research a major issue that must be resolved is, Are there explanations for the effect observed other than what the researcher has proposed? One way researchers provide answers to this question is by using a well-established procedure, or research design, for conducting their experiment. There are many books written about designing experimental research studies. The major focus of these books is how to control extraneous variables. By controlling the experimental environment, researchers eliminate possible alternative causes. Methods for controlling the experimental environment are in many ways commonsense strategies (they are detailed elsewhere in this volume). If a researcher is comparing two methods of teaching, each group of students exposed to one of the two different methods should have similar experiences for a similar length of time, except for the differences in the method of instruction. Because the area of experimental design is so well developed, most researchers gain some control over the experimental circumstances. Once some confidence has been established in the likelihood that the "cause" produced any observed change, then the issue of generalizability can be raised.

It is unfortunate that control and generalizability in many ways work against each other. If educational researchers press hard to gain as much control as possible over the experimental environment—for instance, to isolate subjects for the period of the experiment—the normal context in which treatment takes place is missing. The resulting artificial environment is not similar to the usual environment in which instruction occurs. Questions regarding generalizations must be raised. Whenever researchers define the circumstances of an experiment, they create conditions that may be different from those under which the results of the research might normally be applied. Students may respond differently if they know they are participating in an experiment. Characteristics of the researcher (e.g., overwhelming enthusiasm) may unintentionally influence the students' behavior. Taking a pretest may sensitize the students to the treatment to which they are being exposed. Fortunately, most researchers compromise this tension between control and generalizability, so that while some control may be sacrificed a gain in the ability to generalize is realized. There is no formula for developing this balance, but it deserves comment by the researcher and consideration by the consumer.

Before generalizing results, most experimental researchers evaluate statistically whether a difference observed in the effect, or dependent variable, is sufficiently large that it is not a chance event. Techniques for accomplishing this task are called inferential statistics, usually accompanied by a statement of probability. In music education studies the typical statement might be that the result is statistically significant at the ".05 level of confidence." This means that there is a small probability, not more than five times out of 100, that the observed result occurred by chance. Consequently, if the experiment was well controlled, the most likely explanation for the effect observed is the "cause," or treatment, focused on by the researcher. Researchers cannot be sure they are right or wrong in this decision, only that they are probably correct. Researchers can design into their experiments the likelihood that they will be able to find statistically significant differences of specific sizes. For instance, researchers may know that they do not wish to purchase an expensive computer-assisted aural dictation laboratory unless it will increase the scores of first-year college music majors by more than 15 points on the standard year-end ear-training examination. With this information researchers can perform a "power analysis" to determine the number of students they will need to include in their study in order to find statistically significant results, at the .05 level of confidence, for a difference of 15 points or more. Most research questions in music education are not framed as practically or specifically as in this illustration. It may be that more should be.

INTERPRETING ETHNOGRAPHIC RESEARCH

Ethnographic researchers take on the challenge of trying to understand processes within their natural context. Rather than controlling the research environment, as the experimental researcher attempts to do, the ethnographic researcher attempts to interfere as little as possible in the events being observed. When readers are interpreting the results of ethnographic studies, Krueger (1987) suggests that they should be concerned with whether the researcher provides enough information so that the study can be replicated, whether the findings are consistent with the data reported, and how the researcher suggests that the results can be generalized. Generalizations are particularly challenging for ethnographers because of the rich uniqueness of the research environment that is the strength of their work.

INTERPRETING AN AREA OF RESEARCH

Role of Research Synthesis

One theme throughout this chapter has been that, in order for research results to be applied to practice in music education, multiple research studies are required. These may be studies related in one or more ways or replication studies. Reports of syntheses of research areas may be most valuable to the practitioner; reports of individual studies may have most value to other researchers who are making efforts to produce new knowledge.

Types of Reviews

Light and Pillemer (1984) suggest that there are three purposes that reviews of research can serve and three particular audiences using research reviews. For policymakers broad generalizations are sought from reviews. Policymakers, such as supervisors of music or department chairs, need to make decisions based on the best information available. They are willing to accept broad generalizations as guidance. Policymakers must make decisions that guide instruction, maintain programs, educate students. Policymakers must take action. For policymakers the ability to supplement political debates with information based on research may be the key to sustaining or strengthening music instructional programs. For policymakers the details from the different studies are unnecessary. Policymakers need more general synopses.

For practitioners, research summaries need to be more specific than for policymakers. Practitioners are charged with implementation, and need reviews that contain sufficient detail so that specific strategies used in a research project are available. If new approaches are to be tried, practitioners need to know enough to use them. Teachers are also interested in feasibility issues, the "will it work here" question. Again, it must be stressed that for the practitioner reviews of research will not provide all the answers. Teachers must rely on their experience and knowledge of the specific setting to make decisions. The point is that research can play a role.

Joel Wapnick's 1976 review of research on music attitude and preference studies illustrates a third function of syntheses. For researchers, syntheses of research provide information on variables that may be important to investigations they are conducting. Reviews may also suggest new directions for research. Questions for which researchers seek answers in reviews are often more specific than those of policymakers or practitioners. Although the average effect provides some direction for the researchers, they wish to know specifics about the population and research settings. Researchers are often most interested in exceptions—that is, circumstances in which the results differed from the general trends—as these may provide direction for future research.

The first question a reviewer must consider is what studies to include in a review. Should every available study be used? Should only works that have been published be included? Should studies that support and contradict both be reviewed? The notion of scientific objectivity seems to suggest that every available study be included, but the reviewer may choose to exclude certain studies that appear to have flaws that have led to incorrect conclusions. When excluding certain studies, reviewers should state the reasons. Other studies may be excluded because they are very difficult to locate.

Studies that represent important issues in an area should be included. Light and Pillemer (1984) suggest that reviewers first identify a few key categories and then divide the available studies into these categories. The next step is to select only a few studies to represent each area, and then analyze in detail a smaller number of selected studies. Another approach might be to include only published studies, as these are often screened by referees and are easier to find. Many authors though (Rosenthal, 1978; Glass, McGaw, and Smith, 1981; Light and Pillemer, 1984) state that including only published documents presents a severe bias. Refereed journals are more likely to publish articles that report statistically significant results, and so researchers hesitate to submit for publication work that results in nonsignificant outcomes. This situation results in a distorted view of effects.

Studies included in reviews often produce results that are in apparent disagreement. One approach to reconciling these differences is by systematically examining how each of the studies may have differed. For a detailed quantitative approach to this topic, readers are referred to G. V. Glass's work on meta-analysis: Glass (1977) and Glass et al. (1981).

Reviews should contain information bearing on the decisions of policymakers, researchers, and practitioners. Reviews of research may provide directions for future research. They may guide researchers away from unproductive directions. If five studies have consistently reported no influence for a particular variable, it is unlikely the sixth study will. Reviews can highlight exceptions to general trends that may warrant further exploration as well as suggest new settings and new populations on which the effect of treatments may be unique.

For policymakers who wish to strengthen the programs they supervise, reviews can provide support for program rationales, and information to suggest what programs will be particularly effective. Reviews can tell policymakers how teachers were prepared, what the critical factors are in a new curriculum, and what type of evidence should be collected to demonstrate the effectiveness of new programs.

For teachers, reviews may stimulate them to try out new strategies. Reviews might serve as a guide for teachers to initiate "action research" projects in their own classroom or ensemble.

FINALE

Interpreting research, attaching meaning to all the numbers that computers can generate, or all the different phrases those interviewed have used, may be the most difficult part of the research process. If research results are going to affect what music educators do, interpreting the results may be the most critical part of the research process. Those who are best prepared to interpret the results of research are those who are most experienced, not only as researchers, but also as policymakers and practitioners. To be well equipped for interpretation, music educators must gain insight from experience and research, as well as tradition and authority. But, as each music educator reads research results, his or her knowledge may provide new insight into the meaning of the results. Involving the community of music educators, policymakers, and practitioners (as well as researchers) in research must be a goal of the profession.

References

Cutietta, R. (1985). An analysis of musical hypotheses created by the 11–16 year old learner. *Bulletin of the Council for Research in Music Education, 84,* 1–13.

Cutietta, R. (1986). Biofeedback training in music: From experimental to clinical applications. *Bulletin of the Council for Research in Music Education, 87,* 35–42.

Dyer, J. R. (1979). *Understanding and evaluating educational research.* Reading: Addison-Wesley.

Ellis, M. C. (1989). The effect of concurrent music reading and performance on the ability to detect tempo change. *Journal of Research in Music Education, 37*(4), 288–297.

Geringer, J. M, and Madsen, C. K. (1987). Pitch and tempo preferences in recorded popular music. In C. K. Madsen, and C. A. Prickett (Eds.), *Applications of research in music behavior* (pp. 204–212). Tuscaloosa: University of Alabama Press.

Gfeller, K., Darrow, A., and Hedden, S. K. (1990). Perceived effectiveness of mainstreaming in Iowa and Kansas schools. *Journal of Research in Music Education, 38*(2), 90–101.

Glass, G. V. (1977). Integrating findings: The meta-analysis of research. *Review of Research in Education,* 5, 351–379.

Glass, G. V., McGaw, B., and Smith, M. L. (1981). *Meta-analysis of social research.* Beverly Hills: Sage.

Kalekin-Fishman, D. (1986). Music and not-music in kindergartens. *Journal of Research in Music Education, 33*(1), 54–68.

Krueger, P. (1987). Ethnographic research in methodology in music education. *Journal of Research in Music Education, 35*(2), 69–77.

Le Blanc, A. (1980). Outline of a proposed model of sources of variation in musical taste. *Council for Research in Music Education, 61,* 29–34.

Light, R. J., and Pillemer, D. B. (1984). *Summing up: The science of reviewing research.* Cambridge: Harvard University Press.

Moore, B. R. (1990). The relationship between curriculum and learner: Music composition and learning style. *Journal of Research in Music Education, 38*(1), 24–38.

Nelson, D. J., and Barresi, A. L. (1989). Children's age-related intellectual strategies for dealing with musical and spatial analogical tasks. *Journal of Research in Music Education, 37*(2), 93–103.

Phillips, K. H., and Vispoel, W. P. (1990). The effects of class voice and breath management instruction in vocal knowledge attitudes and vocal performance among elementary education majors. *The Quarterly, I* (1&2), 96–105.

Price, H. E., and Yarbrough, C. (1987). Expressed opinions of composers, musical training, recording ownership, and their interrelationship. In C. K. Madsen and C. A. Prickett (Eds.), *Applications of research in music behavior,* (pp. 232–243). Tuscaloosa: University of Alabama Press.

Rosenthal, R. (1978). Combining results of independent studies. *Psychological Bulletin, 85,* 185–193.

Rosenthal, R. K., Wilson, M., Evans, M., and Greenwalt, L. (1988). Effects of different practice conditions on advanced instrumentalists' performance accuracy. *Journal of Research in Music Education, 36*(4), 250–257.

Ross, S. L. (1985). The effectiveness of mental practice in improving the performance of college trombonists. *Journal of Research in Music Education, 33*(4), 221–230.

Rutkowski, J. (1990). The measurement and evaluation of children's singing voice development. *The Quarterly, 1*(142), 81–95.

Schmidt, C. P. (1989). Applied music teaching behavior as a function of selected personality variables. *Journal of Research in Music Education, 37*(4), 258–271.

Shehan, P. K. (1985). Transfer of preference from taught to untaught pieces of non-western music genres. *Journal of Research in Music Education, 33*(3), 149–158.

Wapnick, J. (1976). A review of research on attitude and preference. *Bulletin of the Council for Research in Music Education, 48,* 1–20.

Willett, B. E., and Netusil, A. J. (1989). Music computer drill and learning styles at the fourth-grade level. *Journal of Research in Music Education, 37*(3), 219–229.

Zurcher, W. (1987). The effect of three evaluation procedures on the rehearsal achievement of eighth-grade band students. In C. K. Madsen and C. A. Prickett (Eds.), *Applications of research in music behavior* (pp. 51–58). Tuscaloosa: University of Alabama Press.

EVALUATION

·16·

EVALUATION OF MUSIC ABILITY

J. David Boyle
UNIVERSITY OF MIAMI

Information about students' music ability is important to music teachers because it offers objective bases for instructional, curriculum, and program changes that take into account students' individual differences. Despite nearly a century of study by educators and psychologists, however, there is still much controversy regarding definitions, measurement, and implications of music ability. For example, to what extent are music aptitude, ability, and achievement discrete constructs? How do they differ from music talent, music capacity, music intelligence, musicality, music audiation, and music sensitivity?

The lack of consensus about terminology and that which is implied by the respective terms has compounded not only the problems in the measurement and evaluation of students' musical potentials, abilities, and learnings, but also the extent to which music teachers are willing to rely on such information as primary bases for decisions that may have important bearing on individual students' learning opportunities and experiences with music. A premise of this chapter is that a clear understanding of these terms and what they imply is essential to the effective use of such evaluative data in the music education process.

A distinction needs to be made among the terms "*test*," "*measurement*,"and "*evaluation*." For the purposes of this chapter, *test* refers to any systematic procedure for observing a person's behavior relevant to a specific task or series of tasks. A task or series of tasks may be demonstrated completely, partially, or not at all. If one wishes to develop a system for quantifying the extent to which a person can demonstrate the testing tasks, one becomes involved in *measurement*. Most music tests involve quantification through the application of either some scoring system or a rating scale; hence the close relationship and frequent interchangeable use of the terms test and measurement. *Evaluation* is the broadest of the three terms, and it involves making judgments or decisions regarding the level or quality of a music behavior or other endeavor. Evaluation should involve systematic collection, analysis, and interpretation of information relevant to the behavior or other endeavor under consideration (Gronlund and Linn, 1990, p. 5). Although evaluations are usually more accurate when they have a strong basis in test and measurement data, test and measurement data often do not provide complete information regarding the decision to be made. Combining accurate test and measurement data with the enlightened, thoughtful, and professional judgments of experienced music teachers and administrators should facilitate better decision in the evaluation of music ability than judgments without a strong data base.

The first section of the chapter provides a perspective for examining music ability and some related constructs and issues. The constructs examined include music aptitude, music intelligence, music talent, music sensitivity, musicality, and music achievement. Particular issues examined include (1) the relevance of labeling, (2) the role of experience and training, (3) music as an intelligence, (4) the nature of testing tasks, and (5) validity. The second section examines some approaches to assessing various aspects of music ability; specifically, it examines (1) factors to consider in selecting and developing music tests, (2) perceptual and conceptual testing tasks, and (3) approaches to evaluating performance. The chapter concludes with brief mention of some applications of evaluation to research and practice in music education.

PERSPECTIVE AND OVERVIEW OF CENTRAL CONSTRUCTS

Perspective

Efforts to evaluate musical attributes and behaviors of individuals are rooted in western musical and psychological traditions. Early approaches borrowed heavily from general psychological measurement methodologies, especially those used in the measurement of aural sensory discriminations. As traditions developed, a number of constructs were devised to explain individual difference. "A *construct* is a psychological quality that we assume exists in order to explain some aspect of behavior" (Gronlund and Linn, 1990, p. 66). The measurement and evaluation of such constructs as music aptitude, music ability, music talent, music achievement, and musicality became a particular focus of the evolving area of inquiry known as the psychology of music. Assessment of these constructs is of practical significance to music educators.

Carl Seashore's (1919) early efforts to assess music talents provided the model and impetus for much of this work, and as measurement of the various constructs progressed during the first half of the twentieth century, a number of issues related to the theory and methodology for measuring them also evolved. These include long-standing issues relative to (1) the nature/nurture aspects of music aptitude, (2) specific versus global measurements, (3) definitions of terms, (4) the validity of the measures of the various constructs, and (5) the relationships of the various constructs to other experiences and psychological attributes.

More recent developments related to the evaluation of music ability include several theories that are having an impact on contemporary thinking regarding the nature, development, and evaluation of the various constructs. The most prominent of these are Gordon's (1979a, 1987) theory of developmental music aptitude, Gardner's (1983) theory that musical intelligence is one of several loosely related multiple intelligences, and Karma's (1985) view that music aptitude involves perceptual/cognitive structuring of acoustical material.

As it is used by Farnsworth (1969, p. 151) and Shuter-Dyson and Gabriel (1981, pp. 3–7), *music ability* will be used as a generic term referring to that which students demonstrate on any given music testing task, regardless of the nature of the task. Conceivably the tasks may include a wide range of listening, performing, analyzing, and creating behaviors. Farnsworth argues that music ability is the broadest and safest of the various possible terms because it suggests the power to act but makes no inference whether this power is the result of some innate potential, reflects specific learnings, or is predictive of some future potential.

Shuter-Dyson and Gabriel (1981, p. 7) recognize that tests of music aptitude and music achievement are overlapping constructs: "All aptitude tests are to some extent achievement tests, just as all achievement tests necessarily reflect the initial aptitude of the individual." The matter is confounded when one examines the types of items on tests labeled variously as measures of music aptitude, music ability, musicality, music talent, and music achievement. Similar discrimination tasks used on tests often are purported to assess different constructs that are used to differentiate among individuals and groups of individuals who demonstrate different levels of performance on selected musical tasks. "Individuals who perform better on given tasks are considered more 'talented'

or as having higher level 'aptitude' or 'ability' than individuals who perform the tasks less well" (Boyle and Radocy, 1987, p. 4).

Such terms may be meaningful to many music teachers and performers, but the literature suggests that there is not consensus regarding the meanings of these terms (George and Hodges, 1980, p. 401; Shuter-Dyson and Gabriel, 1981, pp. 3–7; Boyle and Radocy, 1987, p. 4). Whether the terms refer to constructs that indeed overlap or whether they are discrete but poorly defined and understood is unclear. The diversity of the ways in which people interact with music seems to compound problems related to defining and understanding the terms.

The various constructs, or "musical attributes" as George and Hodges (1980, pp. 401–403) suggest they be called when considering them as properties of people, are *inferred* from musical behaviors. The musical behaviors from which the respective constructs or attributes are inferred may vary greatly and depend on many factors, including the observers' or test makers' philosophical perspective, theoretical persuasion, musical experience, musical sophistication, and general understanding of the constructs and related issues. The inferential bases that teachers and performers use for labeling someone as "talented," "very musical," or "having great potential" may be quite different from those used in standardized measures of music aptitude, ability, or achievement.

To provide a modicum of order to the labeling problem, Boyle and Radocy (1987, pp. 8–12) take the position that given testing tasks may serve different functions and that the real issue for those concerned with assessment is to establish the appropriate type of validity for the given tasks. Thus, student performance on tasks requiring discrimination between given melodic or rhythmic patterns might be used to demonstrate the learning of specific discrimination skills (achievement function), areas of strength and weakness (diagnostic function), or potential for future success in learning music (aptitude function). The test user, however, must ascertain that the appropriate types of test validity have been established for the various test functions, which in these instances would be content, criterion-related, and predictive, respectively.

Overview of Relevant Constructs

Even with the use of "music ability" as a generic term, the widespread and diverse use of other terms related to the assessment of music ability necessitates an overview of the constructs reflected by the various terms.

Music Ability Music ability refers to what a person is "able" to do musically. The term usually is used in a generic sense with no implications as to its specific source or how it was developed. It is presumed, however, that genetic and maturational potentials, enculturational and environmental influences, and whatever formal instruction one might have had are contributing factors.

Whether music ability is a unitary concept or whether it suggests a range of diverse abilities is an issue that apparently is an outgrowth of philosophical differences underlying early approaches to its assessment. The issue seems to be rooted in the old Carl Seashore/James L. Mursell debate stemming from Mursell's criticisms of the initial Seashore test battery, the *Measures of Musical Talent* (Seashore, 1919). Seashore (1938) maintained that music ability is reflected in several specific but loosely related sensory discrimination tasks, whereas Mursell (1937) argued for an "omnibus" theory, insisting that music ability is an all-pervasive ability. Shuter-Dyson and Gabriel (1981, pp. 51–76) provide an extensive discussion of factor analytic studies related to the issue, but offer no definitive resolution. "With time, it has become evident that musical ability is more than loosely related sensory skills, but the general musical ability factor remains elusive. A person who is musically able can apply diverse skills to particular musical situations. Whether such skills are specific or general is a matter of perspective" (Radocy and Boyle, 1988, p. 298).

Music Aptitude "Music aptitude" is the term used to indicate potential for learning music, particularly for developing musical skills. Many traditional definitions suggest or imply that aptitude is a function of "natural ability or capacity" (Halsey, 1979, p. 47), but more recent accounts (e.g., Boyle and Radocy, 1987, p. 139) recognize it as the "result of genetic endowment and maturation plus whatever musical skills [and sensitivities] may develop without formal music education" (i.e., through the general enculturation process).

Music aptitude may also be defined in terms of those potentials measured by music aptitude tests, but reviews of the content of music aptitude tests (e.g., Lehman, 1968, pp. 37–56; Gordon, 1970, pp. 12–36; George, 1980, pp. 296–315; Boyle, 1982, pp. 14–21; Webster, 1988, pp. 177–182) reveal some differences in the nature of the musical tasks from which music aptitude is predicted. Their reviews reveal that music aptitude tests may include some discrimination tasks relative to pitch, loudness, timbre, and duration of individual pairs of tones; some melodic (also called musical or tonal) memory tasks; and some discrimination tasks related to various aspects of rhythm—tempo, meter, and patterns. Two tests also require preference responses regarding which of two renditions of a musical excerpt is better in terms of its phrasing, rhythm, harmony, balance, or style.

To the extent that such tasks are valid predictors of musi-

cal potential, the tests may be considered adequate. Much of the controversy regarding music testing has evolved from questions about the appropriateness of these tasks for predicting musical potential, especially since research reveals data suggesting that certain nonmusical variables greatly increased the accuracy of prediction (e.g., Rainbow, 1965; Whellams, 1970; Hedden, 1982; Karma, 1983). Rainbow's data reveal that academic achievement, academic intelligence, and socioeconomic background are significant predictors of music ability. Significant music predictors included tonal memory, music achievement, and interest in music. Hedden observed that among several musical and nonmusical variables, academic achievement was the best single predictor of music achievement. Apparently, success, whether musical or academic, is a good predictor of future success in music.

When music aptitude is considered an attribute that people possess in varying degrees, it has strong overtones of being more "mentalistic" than "behavioral," a characteristic that music ability tends to suggest. Perhaps this is because most music aptitude tests primarily involve discrimination tasks, which rely on perception and cognition of differences between pairs of musical stimuli.

Karma (1982, 1983, 1985, 1986) agrees that music aptitude involves perceptual and cognitive processing, but he questions the value of traditional approaches to assessing music aptitude. He maintains that continued reliance on discrimination tasks as measures of music aptitude and the subsequent validation of these tests through correlations with achievement tests is inappropriate and circular (Karma, 1982).

Karma views music aptitude as involving perceptual and conceptual *structuring* of music and has devised information-processing strategies that involve "forming expectations, recognizing, structuring according to strong gestalts, structuring against strong gestalts, changing expectations, timing, and analyzing the internal structures of strong gestalts" (Karma, 1985, p. 11). Essentially, his structuring tasks require the respondent to listen to a short theme that is repeated three times. The themes consist of tones with pitch, duration, or loudness differences, but only one factor is varied within a given item. If the pitch structure (melody) is under consideration, loudness and duration are kept constant. Following a short pause, an "answer" is provided, and the respondent must determine whether the answer is the "same as" or "different from" the recurring pattern. Figure 16–1 shows examples for a pitch and a loudness item.

FIGURE 16–1. Examples of Karma's Themes for Structuring Pitch and Loudness.

Karma contends that these structuring strategies provide a much stronger basis for inferring music aptitude as a psychological construct than do traditional testing tasks. Although Karma's testing tasks for assessing for perceptual and conceptual structuring of music are still evolving, he offers a persuasive argument for considering music aptitude in terms of cognitive structuring.

Another recent development in the literature on music aptitude is the description of developmental music aptitude, a construct advocated by Gordon (1979a, 1984, 1987) to account for fluctuations in children's music aptitude until about the age of 9, after which it becomes stabilized. His apparent recognition of the unstableness of young children's responses on discrimination tasks such as those employed on his music aptitude tests notwithstanding, Gordon holds that "a child's music aptitude will never reach a higher level than that with which he was born" (1984, p. 25). He contends that favorable or unfavorable informal environmental experiences during the developmental years merely allow or do not allow a child to realize in music achievement the level of music aptitude with which he or she was born (1985, p. 25). A seeming paradox, the notion of developmental music aptitude offers an interesting area for research.

Music Intelligence For many years music intelligence was associated with the *Standardised Tests of Musical Intelligence* (Wing, 1939/1961), a test battery that was viewed as the antithesis of Seashore's approach to assessing music ability. The test reflects Wing's belief in a *general* factor of music ability; thus scores from the seven subtests may be combined into a composite or overall measure of music ability. In contrast, Seashore insisted that the subtests on his *Measures of Musical Talents* (Seashore, Lewis, and Saetveit, 1939/1960) provide a profile of six discrete measures. Wing's approach is considered more "musical" than Seashore's in that much of the test involves making judgments regarding which of two renditions of some musical excerpts is better (i.e., more musical). Although Wing (1954) contends that music ability is largely innate, his test, especially the four "appreciation" subtests, requires responses that necessarily reflect sensitivity to western musical practice, thus making "correct" answers much more dependent on experience with music than are answers on the Seashore test. Wing's labeling of his test as a measure of music intelligence instead of aptitude or ability, however, has added to the confusion in terminology.

More recently the term music intelligence has come to be recognized as one of several loosely related multiple intelligences as expounded in Gardner's (1983) theory of multiple intelligences. He established eight criteria for an intelligence, including (1) the potential isolation by brain damage, (2) the existence of idiots savants and prodigies, (3) identifiable core operations such as sensitivity to pitch and rhythm relations, (4) a developmental history that leads to expert performance, (5) an evolutionary history, (6) support from experimental psychological tasks, (7) support from psychometric findings, and (8) the ability to encode the information with which an intelligence deals in a symbol system. Other intelligences identified by Gardner include linguistic, logical-mathematical, spatial, bodily-kinesthetic, and personal intelligences. Although Gardner offers no specific plan for assessing music ability as an intelligence, he questions the relevance of the "specifics" approach and suggests that perhaps a "middle ground" and somewhat eclectic approach might be most useful. "The goal here is to sample musical entities that are large enough to bear nonsuperficial resemblance to genuine musical (as opposed to simple acoustic) entities, yet sufficiently susceptible to analysis to permit systematic experimental manipulations" (p. 107). He goes on to suggest that at a general level people "appear to have 'schemas' or 'frames' for hearing music—expectations about what a well-structured phrase or section of a piece should be—as well as at least a nascent ability to complete a segment in a way that makes musical sense" (p. 108).

Music Capacity "Capacity" is the term traditionally assigned to that portion of a person's ability that is a result of genetic endowment and maturation. Seashore (1938, p. 332) maintained that his test measured inborn or native capacities. Although he made little effort to define the nature of capacity, his writings suggest that he viewed it as an attribute of the mind. Lundin (1967, p. 206) recognized a broader meaning of capacity, arguing that it "is a biological potential serving as a framework within which we develop musical actions." His use of "biological" rather than "inborn" was intended to allow for maturational variables that might have an effect on musical potential to be considered part of capacity.

Capacity is not a useful construct for purposes of evaluation, because satisfactory isolation of genetically determined musical behaviors from environmental influences has yet to be accomplished.

Music Talent Lundin (1967, p. 204), following the lead of Schoen (1940, p. 151), views music talent as a capacity for musical performance. Suggesting that talent is a capacity thus implies that talent is in large part of a result of biological potential. This connotation alone prevents it from being a useful construct for evaluation purposes.

The term "talent" often is used in reference to musical performance, but many would argue that a high level of music performance skill also reflects a high degree of learning. We tend, however, to say that persons are talented if they demonstrate a high level of music performance skill.

Besides this contradiction between definition and usage, the common applications of the term by both musicians and laypersons further complicate its use in evaluation. The criteria by which individuals are designated talented are both diverse and loose. Perhaps evaluators should avoid the term and simply recognize it as an imprecise term that is often applied to individuals whose demonstrated music ability is beyond that of their peers. Nearly everyone has some music ability, but few are recognized as talented. It is doubtful that there will ever be consensus regarding criteria for labeling someone as talented; nevertheless, there appears to be some broad, albeit vague, understanding of what is meant when we say someone is talented.

Music Sensitivity As used by musicians, "music sensitivity" implies something other than the ability to make fine sensory discriminations between the pitch, timbre, or loudness of musical tones. The focus is on *musical* sensitivity rather than sensitivity to small acoustical differences. Sensitivity seems to imply perception of and responsiveness to subtle differences in music, thus reflecting both discriminations and feeling responses. Musical sensitivity may be reflected in both performing and listening to music.

The affective, or feeling, dimension creates problems for some persons concerned with evaluating music ability, but Gordon (1965, p. 5), in making a case for his "Musical Sensitivity" subtest as part of the *Musical Aptitude Profile,* maintains that a musical sensitivity measure "contributes to a more comprehensive appraisal of basic music aptitude, since musical creativity and expression are at least as important to success in music education as the abilities to perceive tonal and rhythmic relationships among notes in a musical phrase." Besides Gordon's *Musical Aptitude Profile,* two other published music tests, the *Wing Standardised Tests of Musical Intelligence* (Wing, 1939/1961) and the *Indiana-Oregon Music Discrimination Test* (Long, 1965), include sensitivity (really a preference for the "better" of two renditions) sections, but correlations between scores on these sections of the three tests are quite low (Gallagher, 1971; Sampsell, 1980; Boyle, 1982). The lack of substantial correlations among the three tests, however, may be because of methodological considerations and/or the familiarity of the examples. Music sensitivity as a construct seems to be generally recognized, but the preference measures designed to assess it have not been well received as isolated measures.

Musicality Also imprecise, "musicality" refers to a state of being "musical"—that is, of being sensitive to the nuances of music. Just as with music sensitivity, the term implies both cognitive and affective dimensions. Lundin (1967, p. 204) suggests that "one may be very musical, having considerable sensitivity toward, feeling for, and appreciation of music, without having any performance ability."

Only one published test, the *Test of Musicality* (Gaston, 1957), purports to measure musicality. Considering the name of the test, one might expect it to include preference tasks to allow respondents to reflect sensitivity, but it does not. Its musical tasks, save one, are discrimination tasks. The one exception asks respondents to indicate the likely direction (higher or lower) of the final tone of a sequence of tones, apparently reflecting the extent to which one has developed certain melodic expectations in tonal music.

Music Achievement Music achievement refers to music accomplishments as a result of experience with music, musical phenomena, or music-related materials. Music achievement reflects what has been learned as a result of such experiences.

The scope of what might be achieved is great and may reflect accomplishments over varying periods of time. Music accomplishments may be quite specific or very general and may include general musical knowledge, knowledge of nota-

tion, aural-visual skills, aural skills, performance skills, and composition.

Music achievement may result from formal learning in schools and other instructional settings, or it may result from less structured, informal settings. Music teachers are most concerned with the kinds of music achievement that result from given instruction.

Because of the diverse yet relatively specific nature of much music instruction, most music achievement is content or task specific; students' music achievements usually reflect their specific learning experiences. The assessment of achievement is important because it provides feedback to learners and teachers regarding the effects of instructional experiences about what has and has not been learned.

Issues Related to Constructs

A number of issues are implicit in the above overview, and several warrant further discussion: (1) the relevance of labeling, (2) the role of experience and training, (3) the implications of Gardner's theory of musical intelligence, (4) the nature of the testing tasks on music ability tests, and (5) the importance of test validity.

Relevance of Labeling We should avoid labeling students on the basis of test results, particularly given the highly inferential nature of the various constructs. Labeling is known to have potentially harmful effects on the interactions between students and teachers (Boyle and Radocy, 1987, pp. 27–28). Music ability testing should be undertaken for educationally valid reasons and should provide information relevant to the individuals being tested and/or the persons responsible for guiding and enhancing the music education of these individuals. Test selection and development should focus on eliciting information relevant to the educational decisions to be made. To the extent that music ability testing provides such information, it is useful.

Experience and Training Most music teachers agree that musical experience and training help develop music ability. Whatever genetic "wiring" individuals have is decided long before they start interacting with music; consequently, music teachers should focus on those factors over which they may have some influence.

With the increasing recognition of the importance of early childhood experiences on musical development—even to the extent that critical periods for music development have been suggested—continued discussion of an individual's inborn aptitude, which can never be known, also seems pointless. What is important, however, is that the nature and quality of music experiences, both informal and formal, appear to have a profound influence on most children's musical development.

Music as an Intelligence Gardner's recognition of music ability as a unique intelligence lends credence to what many music teachers have long believed. The ability to perceive, conceptualize, manipulate through some performance medium, and respond to aural pitch and rhythm patterns appears to involve some cognitions beyond those of traditional academic (linguistic and mathematical) intelligence.

It is surprising, however, that little or no effort appears to have yet been directed toward developing specific measures of Gardner's music intelligence. Whether this is due to apathy, satisfaction with the status quo, or lack of understanding of the construct is not clear.

Nature of Testing Tasks Although formal measures of music ability have been around for more than 70 years, most of the testing tasks on the various measures are still discrimination tasks, usually between pairs of musical stimuli. Over the years the trend has been to make the tasks more musical, even to the extent that several tests include preference sections intended to assess musical sensitivity, but the basic task structures have changed little.

Perhaps it is time for test makers to explore some new approaches. Karma's perceptual and cognitive structuring tasks are quite different from traditional testing tasks and may offer a useful new direction.

Validity of Measures Concerns about the validity of music ability tests have been around since the earliest days of music testing, but the concern is reiterated here to emphasize its importance and to recommend a slight change in emphasis. As Gronlund and Linn (1990, pp. 48–50) note, it is more appropriate to speak of the validity of the interpretation to be made from test results than to speak of the "validity of a test"; a test is valid for some particular use or interpretation. They maintain that validity is a *unitary concept,* for which a test maker provides various kinds of evidence. Depending on the purpose for which the test is to be used, the test maker should provide evidence that is content related, criterion related, or construct related. The important point is that evidence of validity must be appropriate for the purpose of the test.

MUSIC TEST TASK STRUCTURES

In contrast to the previous section in which the terminology and constructs inferred from music tests was considered, in this section the task structures that may be employed in assessing the various aspects of an individual's music ability are examined. The focus is on the music behaviors required in the testing tasks.

The section is in three parts: The first examines factors to consider in selecting and developing measures of music ability, the second reviews approaches that have been used in assessing perceptual and conceptual dimensions of music ability, and the final part reviews approaches to the evaluation of music performance.

The discussion focuses on evaluation of individuals rather than groups, although many of the tasks discussed are administered in group settings. Therefore, procedures for adjudi-

cating ensemble performance are not discussed. Also, there is no discussion of test items for assessing factual information that is ordinarily evaluated through standard paper and pencil objective or essay questions. Readers interested in such information should consult one of the standard references that deal with such items (e.g., Cronbach, 1984; Ebel and Frisbie, 1990; Gronlund and Linn, 1990; Boyle and Radocy, 1987).

Considerations in Selecting and Developing Music Test Tasks

Prior to selecting or developing any measure of music ability, an evaluator must consider a number of factors relevant to the use and design of the instrument. Although these may be obvious to experienced test makers and users, they are sufficiently critical to warrant reiteration here.

Purpose of the Test The primary consideration in selecting or developing any test of music ability is to ensure that it is valid for the function for which it will be used. *Validity* and *reliability* are the two major criteria for selecting any test. Essentially, reliability refers to the consistency with which a test measures, and validity refers to how well a test measures what it claims to measure. A test cannot be valid without being reliable, but a test may be reliable without being valid for the particular purpose for which it is used. (An extended discussion of these concepts is not included because it is assumed that readers are familiar with them. Readers desiring extended discussions of the concepts should consult a standard reference on educational and psychological measurement.) Tests that purport to serve multiple functions should provide validity data for each function. So, the initial step is to define clearly the function for which a test is to be used.

Tests used to make predictions about a student's potential for learning music should provide evidence of how well the test predicts future music learning. Such evidence is criterion related in that scores on the test are correlated with some criterion of future music learning. Music tests used to assess a student's present ability should provide criterion-related evidence of concurrent validity, that is, evidence that scores on the test correlate with some other criterion of present music ability. Tests used for assessing a student's music achievement should provide evidence of content-related validity; these tests should reflect the content of the instructional objectives and learning experiences.

Most published music tests are standardized; they provide data from representative *normative* groups so that teachers may compare their students' performance with the performance of others of similar age or grade level (Lehman, 1968, p. 17). For a test to be standardized also implies that technical evidence of reliability and validity is provided. Since most published tests are developed and refined over a period of years, test manuals usually provide such data. However, the test user should review the technical data and make a judgment regarding the test's validity and overall appropriateness for the purpose for which it is to be used.

Standardized tests are particularly appropriate when one wants to compare the performances of individual students with those of some other students. When objective comparative data are needed as a basis for student selection, a standardized test of music aptitude may be very useful. When the concern is for evaluating music achievement, however, standardized tests may be less useful.

Because achievement tests should be valid measures of the content of the instruction students have been receiving, one must ascertain that the achievement test selected or devised reflects the content of that instruction. Merely selecting one of the published standardized measures of music achievement may be inappropriate for evaluating achievement of specific music skills or knowledge. The far more common practice when assessing music achievement is to use criterion-referenced rather than norm-referenced measures.

Criterion-referenced tests describe student achievement in terms of what a student can do and may be evaluated against a criterion or absolute standard of performance. A student's achievement, therefore, is evaluated in terms of individual performance rather than how well the student does in relation to other students.

Standardized tests have the advantages over teacher-made tests of (1) having been revised several times, thus eliminating weak items, (2) likely being more reliable, (3) having technical superiority, (4) providing norms, and (5) not requiring preparation time. The advantages of teacher-made tests are that they (1) can be adapted to specific needs and objectives, (2) can assess content areas for which there are no suitable standardized tests, (3) are usually less expensive, and (4) allow more leeway for different item types (Lehman, 1968, pp. 28–29).

Teacher-made tests may be analyzed in either a norm-referenced or criterion-referenced manner. When a student's level of achievement is compared to that of other students (e.g., as in grading on a curve), the teacher is evaluating achievement in a norm-referenced sense. However, when each student is evaluated against set criteria (e.g., being able to accomplish a given task), the teacher is evaluating in a criterion-referenced sense. Which approach is "better" depends on the purpose of the evaluation.

Test Takers Testing tasks should be designed to accommodate the general developmental level, academic level, and test-taking experience of the test takers. If the task structure on a test is too complicated, the very complexity of the task structure may prevent a student from demonstrating the given musical skills or knowledge that the test is intended to assess. Reading levels in testing tasks for children should be at or preferably below the reading level for the age or grade of the students being tested. Liberal use of example items with feedback for correct responses should be made to ensure that students understand the given testing tasks.

The musical behaviors required in a testing task also should be designed with test takers' general level of musical experience in mind. Particular care should be taken to ensure that the testing tasks are appropriate to the tests' func-

tion as well as the test takers' general level of experience with the musical behaviors under consideration. For example, interval discrimination and recognition may be examined at several different levels, with different assumptions made each time about the test takers' experience with intervals. Students could merely be asked whether two aurally presented intervals are the same or different, which requires no knowledge of interval names, or they could be asked to name aurally presented intervals, which requires some experience with interval names, or they could be asked to notate the upper note of an aurally presented interval (given the notation for the lower), which requires experience with notating intervals.

Scope and Content Since most teacher-made music tests are intended to evaluate achievement, it is particularly important that they clearly reflect the content of instruction. Critical to this process is having clearly defined instructional objectives that specify the behaviors to be demonstrated, the conditions under which they are to be demonstrated, and the criterion or criteria for acceptable performance. Assuming that instruction is designed to facilitate students' attainment of the objectives, it then becomes a relatively simple matter to design the testing tasks for the respective objectives.

It is especially important that the test reflects an appropriate and balanced sample of behaviors relative to a test's function. In the case of an achievement test, it should reflect the instructional objectives and their relative importance. An achievement test that does not provide such balance is of questionable validity.

Efficiency A test must be designed to elicit the needed information in the most economical way. Ideally, much music testing would involve individually administered performance testing, but this may prove impractical given present-day administrative costs for such testing. Even in group paper and pencil testing, care should be taken to ensure that tests are administered as efficiently as possible.

How much compromise one should make between getting enough samples of behavior to ensure a valid test and considering practical matters is difficult to say. A "perfect" test that is so expensive and time-consuming to administer that it never gets used is inefficient. On the other hand, a test that fails to yield adequate information for its intended function also is inefficient.

Some Principles Some of the considerations examined above have been summarized as "principles" for music test design and for determining music test behaviors. These principles may be useful to persons undertaking the development or selection of music tests.

Principles Underlying Music Test Design

1. Music test content and design must reflect the particular function a test is intended to serve.
2. The scope and specificity of a music test's content must be appropriate and relevant to the test's function.
3. Music test content must reflect consideration for the

general development level, academic level, and test-taking experience of the test takers.

4. The level of cognitive, affective, and psychomotor behaviors required in the test tasks should be appropriate to the test's function and the test takers' general level of experience with the musical behaviors under consideration.
5. A music test must . . . provide a balanced sample of behavior relative to the test's function.
6. A music test must be efficient.
7. A music test must be technically adequate.

Principles for Determining Music Test Behaviors

1. The response behavior(s) required in a testing task should reflect as directly as possible the knowledge, skill, or value being assessed.
2. Whenever possible, evaluation of musical behaviors should involve response to (or production of) aural musical stimuli.
3. The response methodology required on a test should minimize the effects of irrelevant skills and knowledge. (Boyle and Radocy, 1987, pp. 93–98).

Perceptual and Conceptual Tasks

Music perception and conception tasks are intended to assess the extent to which an individual can receive, discern, and/or process music stimuli. The tasks with which test makers have been most concerned may be grouped under three broad headings: (1) aural discrimination, (2) aural recognition, and (3) aural-visual discrimination. Aural discrimination tasks usually require students to discern differences between two or more aurally presented music stimuli, whereas aural recognition tasks place emphasis on identifying various qualities or attributes of an aurally presented music stimulus. Aural-visual discrimination tasks usually are designed to assess students' ability to associate sounds heard with music notation.

Music stimuli for perceptual and conceptual tasks may (1) range from simple to complex, (2) include individual tones and acoustical stimuli; melodic, rhythmic, and harmonic patterns; or musical excerpts or compositions, (3) be either narrowly or broadly focused, (4) be presented either simultaneously or sequentially, and (5) be of varying duration. Variations in a stimulus along any of these continua may radically alter the difficulty of the task. Also, perceptual tasks focus more on discrimination between aural stimuli, while conceptual tasks focus more on analysis, memory, and other cognitive processing of the aural stimuli.

Most tasks on music tests are designed to elicit a "correct" or "best" answer from two or more alternatives, an approach that Webster (1988) notes essentially requires *convergent thinking*, that is, involving consideration of several possibilities and "converging" on the best possible answer. He makes a strong case that the assessment of music ability, particularly music aptitude, should also include *divergent*

thinking tasks, which involve "the generation of many possible solutions to a given task" (Webster, p. 186). He maintains that three important aspects of music creativity—extensiveness, flexibility, and originality—are clearly connected to divergent thinking.

Although Webster's position offers an interesting new perspective toward the assessment of music ability, the profession continues to rely on tasks requiring convergent thinking as basic to assessment of the perceptual and conceptual dimensions of music ability, and the present discussion reflects this focus.

Aural Discrimination Most aural discrimination tasks require the student to detect a difference between two sequentially presented stimuli. As noted above, the stimuli may be individual tones, tonal patterns, or musical compositions or excerpts. The most common stimuli for older music tests have been pairs of individual tones for which the testing task was to discriminate between the tonal attributes of pitch, loudness, timbre, and duration. More recent music testing tasks focus on discrimination between patterns, usually melodic or rhythmic.

Although aural discrimination tasks for tonal attributes generally require a "same" or "different" type of response, which is essentially a one-step process, some discrimination tasks are structured to require additional processing. For example, to determine whether two pitches are merely the "same" or "different" is much easier than determining (1) whether the second tone is "higher" or "lower" than the first tone or (2) if the second pitch is different from the first, the direction it moves (Sergeant and Boyle, 1981). The structure of a discrimination task requiring more than a "same" or "different" response may greatly increase the difficulty.

Aural pattern discrimination tasks in music, particularly tasks requiring discrimination between melodic patterns, have been given various names. Rhythm pattern discrimination tasks usually are called rhythm discrimination tasks, even though their sequential presentation necessarily involves memory. The sections of the rhythm imagery portion of Gordon's well-known *Musical Aptitude Profile* (1965), labeled respectively as "Tempo" and "Meter," each focus on a given dimension of rhythm and simply require a student to indicate whether the dimension of a pattern, albeit in a melodic context, is the "same" or "different."

Most approaches to assessing the ability to discriminate between melodic patterns, however, have been labeled as some type of memory test, usually tonal memory or melodic memory. These approaches are usually one of two broad types. Usually, the type labeled *tonal memory* asks students to indicate which tone in the second rendition of a tonal sequence is changed. The number of tones in a sequence may range from three to 10. Identifying the particular tone that is changed is a more difficult task than simply indicating whether the melodic patterns are the same or different. The Seashore (1939), Wing, (1961), and Bentley (1966) tests employ this approach, although they are labeled respectively as subtests for "memory," "memory for pitch," and "tonal memory." Colwell's (1969–70) *Music Achievement Tests*

(MAT) include a variation of this task. A chord is presented followed by an arpeggiated chord in which one tone may or may not be changed from those in the chord.

The Drake (1957) and Gaston (1957) tasks requiring discriminations between melodic patterns take a different approach: They provide a sequence of tones as a model against which the respondent is asked to compare subsequent (up to six) renditions of the sequence. The subsequent renditions may be the "same" as the model or differ from it in terms of key, notes, or rhythm. Drake's is called a "musical memory" test and Gaston's is called a "tonal memory" test. What makes these tests more "memory" tests than the Seashore, Wing, and Bentley tests is that the respondent must remember the original model while hearing a series of versions that may vary from the model in one of several ways.

Gordon's "tonal imagery" subtest of the MAP appears to be an extension of the melodic discrimination task. His melodic discrimination task provides a model melody followed by either an embellished version of the model melody or a different melody. The task is to determine whether the second melody would be "like" or "different from" the first if the embellishments (added notes) were removed. Gordon extends this task further to a "harmony" test, which is basically the same type of task as for melody; however, the embellished version is in a lower voice played on a cello, while a higher part, played on the violin, accompanies both versions.

Gordon's melodic discrimination task obviously is more complex than the simpler task of discriminating between two melodies, and it appears to have anticipated some recent theories of "hierarchical structuring" in melodic perception (Serafine, 1983). Serafine's data for tasks similar to Gordon's suggest that experienced listeners are able to recognize "basic tonal structures" at levels at which less experienced listeners are not, for example, at "middle ground" levels as well as "foreground" levels.

Aural discrimination tasks appear to be useful to music educators both as predictor tools and as measures of instructional outcomes. Colwell's *Music Achievement Tests* (1969–70), the content of which was based on the instructional objectives of several basal music series, provides discrimination measures for pitch, intervals, meter, and major-minor modes.

Aural Recognition Tasks of this nature are most frequently used as achievement test items. Essentially these tasks ask respondents to identify some attribute or quality of a music stimulus that they have encountered previously. The encounter may have been prior to the time of the testing or it may be part of the testing format. Encounters of the former type may have been during formal instructional sessions; examples of such recognition tasks could be instruction in the identification of intervals or instrument timbres. After instruction in which names or labels are associated with given aurally presented intervals or instrument sounds, students might subsequently be tested to determine whether they can recognize (i.e., label) the respective intervals or instrument timbres.

The other type of recognition task involves presentation of an aural model as part of the test and then asks the test taker to select or identify it, usually from among three or four alternatives, when it is heard again. The focus in both types of recognition tasks is to *remember* and *identify* a previously heard stimulus, whereas the focus of the discrimination tasks is on *differences* between stimuli.

The range of aural recognition tasks in music is virtually limitless; therefore, evaluators need to make every effort to ensure that aural recognition tasks used in student evaluations are relevant and of an appropriate complexity level. Although tests such as Colwell's MAT (1969–70) include a number of recognition subtests, it is more likely that teachers and researchers will need to develop aural recognition tasks specific to their evaluation purposes.

Auditive Structuring Although based primarily on the theory and work of a single researcher, Kai Karma's (1983, 1985), auditive structuring appears to hold a potential for music ability assessment that is perhaps more consistent with contemporary theories of music perception and cognition than are the traditional discrimination and recognition tasks. Based on his theory that defines music aptitude as "the ability to structure acoustical material" (1985, p. 4), Karma's auditive structuring task essentially asks respondents to "detect a small motif in a row of repetitions" (1985, p. 30). The respondent must indicate if a subsequent motif is the "same" or "different" when compared to the three noninterrupted repetitions of a motif. As described earlier, only one tonal dimension is varied in the original motif: pitch, duration of a tone, or loudness of a tone. The number of tones in a sequence may vary, but most are composed of three, four, or five tones; Karma suggests that students can manage sequences of between two and six tones.

Karma presents evidence of the existence of "several cognitive operations involved in structuring sequences of auditive material: forming expectations, recognizing, structuring according to gestalts, changing expectations, timing, and analyzing the internal structures of strong gestalts" (1985, p. 11). Karma argues that the extent to which an individual can use these operations in structuring sound is a reflection of music aptitude. Further, he maintains that the tasks (1) minimize the effect of general (i.e., nonmusical) intelligence, (2) are suitable for use with young children, and (3) correlate highly (.60 to .76) with instrumental teachers' estimates of music aptitude (1983, p. 31.).

Aural-Visual Discrimination Aural-visual discrimination skills involve interaction of hearing and seeing. The most common forms include error detection while following notation and melodic, rhythm, and harmonic dictation. Dictation tasks perhaps go beyond what is implied by the expression aural-visual, since dictation tasks require the added step of holding what is heard in memory and writing it in notation. Because the use of notation implies that some learning is necessary to accomplish aural-visual discrimination tasks, such tasks are most useful for assessing student achievement and diagnosing strengths and weaknesses rather than aptitude.

1. Melody— Up / Down / Same.

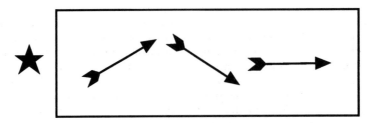

FIGURE 16–2. Response Format "Melody," *Simons Measurements of Music Listening Skills*.

The typical aural-visual discrimination task encountered in published tests includes the notation for a musical example and an accompanying recording of the example that may be the same as the example or differ from it in one or two instances. The respondent must indicate the place (usually by measure) in the notation that differs from the recorded version. Usually such tasks specify the aspect of the notation (rhythm, melody, or chord) in which the discrepancy will occur. A multiple-choice variation of this task is to provide a notated "stem" for an example and several alternatives from which the respondent must select the one that was heard.

Another aural-visual discrimination task that may also use a multiple-choice format provides a line of notation and some alternatives that list the types of possible discrepancies between the notated and heard versions of the example; typically the choices might be "pitch error," "rhythm error," "both," or "no error."

Aural-visual discrimination tasks may be designed for use at a wide range of difficulty and sophistication levels. Tasks asking young children to select or devise iconic notation for examples heard involve associations of visual and aural symbols. A variety of "prenotation" icons have been devised that represent visually certain aspects of musical sounds such as melodic direction, the number of tones in a sound, melodic contour, tempo, or dynamic changes. For example, Simons (1974) asks primary-age students to circle an arrow pointing the direction a melody is going (up/down/same; see Figure 16–2). For comparisons of tonal patterns he presents a picture of two dogs and a cat and a dog. Respondents are to circle the two dogs if the two patterns heard are the same or the dog and cat if the patterns differ (Figure 16–3). Gordon's PMMA (1979a) asks students to circle two smiling faces for pairs of tonal or rhythmic patterns that are the same and a frowning and smiling face if the patterns differ (Figure 16–4). The major concern in devising such tasks is to ensure that the symbols used are appropriate and meaningful for the maturational, educational, and musical experience levels of the children.

At the other end of the sophistication spectrum are the error detection tasks in score-reading studies. Such tasks range from examples with two-, three-, or four-line scores to full scores for which the respondent is to indicate discrepancies between the notated and heard versions. The type and subtlety of errors may vary greatly in these tasks, depending on the experience and sophistication of the listeners and the purposes of the tests. The nearer the task approaches that of a conductor, who must be concerned with detecting errors between all aspects of notation and sound, the more difficult the task. Researchers who have developed error detection tests as part of their research on the development of score-reading skills include Costanza (1971), DeCarbo (1981), Grunow (1980), and Ramsey (1978).

Another type of aural-visual skill, which is perhaps more of a recognition tasks than a discrimination task, involves the recognition of musical themes, compositions, or styles from just the notation. Gordon (1987, pp. 13–15) terms such skill as a type of *audiation,* hearing music silently, that is, when the sound is not present. Essentially involving aural imagery, the tasks require a type of long-term memory through which respondents reflect their ability to imagine aurally how a notated example should sound and then associate it with a given theme, composition, or stylistic or other musical attribute of the example. The difficulty of the task also will vary according to whether the theme, composition, or stylistic or

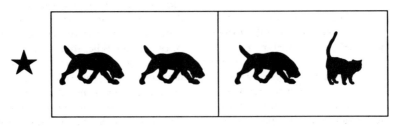

FIGURE 16–3. Response Format, "Form—Tonal Patterns," *Simons Measurements of Music Listening Skills*.

FIGURE 16–4. Response Format, "Tonal Test," Gordon's *Primary Measures of Music Audiation.*

other attributes are to be selected from a list of names or are to be recalled from long-term memory.

Preference/Sensitivity Tasks Three published tests include items that require discrimination between the performance quality of two renditions of given music examples and a stated preference response regarding which version is "better." Although the basic task in each of these tests is the same, they are labeled variously as "appreciation" subtests (*The Standardized Tests of Musical Intelligence,* Wing, 1961), "musical sensitivity" subtests (*Musical Aptitude Profile,* Gordon, 1965), and a "discrimination" test (*Indiana-Oregon Music Discrimination Test,* Long, 1965).

Wing (1968, p. 83) indicated that his subtests, labeled respectively as tests of rhythmic accent, harmony, intensity, and phrasing appreciation, were designed to measure "sensitivity to performance." The "musical sensitivity" portion of Gordon's test includes three subtests: phrasing, balance, and style. The balance subtest essentially requires a discrimination between the appropriateness of the ending phrases of two excerpts and a decision regarding which is better; the style subtest essentially uses tempo as the variable differing in the two renditions of an excerpt. The Indiana-Oregon test also requires a judgment regarding which of two renditions of a musical example is better; in addition, however, the respondent must also indicate (for those examples in which the two renditions are not the "same") whether the change between them was one of rhythm, melody, or harmony, thus making the task somewhat different and more complex than those of the Wing and Gordon tests. Items on the Gordon sensitivity test are unfamiliar melodies, whereas both the Wing and Long tests use familiar melodies.

The "better" version in each item of these tests essentially reflects what "experts" deem to be good performance practices or interpretations within the framework of traditional western art music. Respondents experienced in and knowledgeable about art music or quasi-art music styles should score better on these tests than persons without such experience. In effect, these measures may be assessing achievement.

New Modes of Task Presentation Although the foregoing discussion has focused on the nature of the tasks used in assessing discrimination of, recognition of, and sensitivity to various aspects of music, little has been said about the mode

for presenting the task to the students. The more or less implicit assumption has been that most tasks are administered in group settings, with recorded music stimuli, and requiring a brief letter, number, or check mark to indicate which of two or more alternatives is the appropriate response. The answer sheet may then be scored either by hand or electronically. This has been the most common mode of testing such skills and abilities through the history of music testing.

With the advent and now ready accessibility of computer-aided instruction in music, which requires constant assessment of student achievement, has come a new mode of testing: individualized interactive testing via a computer. Most of the various discrimination tasks may now be generated and presented to a student through headphones and the computer screen. The student usually responds with a simple keyboard response. In most commercially available music software programs, the computer keeps a record of each student's responses. Many programs use the response data to individualize the instructional program via certain "branching" strategies. Essentially, such strategies allow the instructional program to move toward more difficult instructional tasks following a "correct" response or toward less difficult tasks following "incorrect" responses. Such branching serves to make the program more efficient for the individual student.

Similar strategies have been applied to test presentation. Called "adaptive testing," such tests adapt the difficulty level of each succeeding item in accordance with the previous response of the individual. Correct responses are followed by more difficult items, whereas incorrect responses are followed by less difficult ones. Computers make possible immediate scoring and the selection of each subsequent item via complex mathematical calculations in accordance with Item Response Theory. A large pool of items of known difficulty and discrimination level is necessary for adaptive testing to work.

Vispoel (1990) compared the measurement precision, efficiency, and validity of an adaptive test of tonal memory with the Seashore "tonal memory" subtest and three other conventional type tests constructed from items in a 278-item adaptive test pool, which had been developed previously (Vispoel, 1987). His data, based on responses of 468 high school and college students, suggest that the adaptive test provided measurement precision superior to that of the conventional tests while using 34 to 69 percent fewer items. Test reliabilities and validities also exceeded those of the conventional tests.

Besides the testing that is an integral part of many computer-aided instructional programs, several traditional tests have been adapted for individualized presentation via microcomputers: The Seashore "pitch" subtest (McCarthy, 1984), the *Drake Musical Aptitude Tests* (Robinson, 1985), Gordon's *Primary Measures of Musical Audiation* (Forsythe, 1984). Although McCarthy and Robinson both note the advantages of individualization, feedback, and record keeping for the computerized versions, neither provides any evidence of correlations between scores on the computerized tests and the original tests. Forsythe's computerized adaptation of Gordon's PMMA correlated highly with the PMMA (.85 to .88). Split-halves and test-retest reliabilities for Forsythe's adaptation ranged from .80 to .94.

The potential of the computer as a model for testing music perception and cognition is in its infancy, but several articles in the recent special issue of the journal *Psychomusicology* (Vol. 8, Fall 1989) provide perspectives on how microcomputers can be and are being used in research in music perception and cognition. Readers interested in these applications should note in particular the articles by Asmus (1989), Dowling (1989), and Gibson (1989).

Performance Tasks

Cooksey (1982) recognizes music performance as a "complex, multi-dimensional behavior," the evaluation of which has been "plagued by rater subjectivity, the lack of definition of the musical act itself, and the corresponding definitions of component parts of the musical behavior" (p. 209). Performance evaluation is an integral part of any vocal or instrumental lesson or ensemble rehearsal, and for the most part, such evaluations are subjective and reflect either consciously or subconsciously the particular criteria that the individual evaluator considers most important. Although subjectivity will always be an important part of performance evaluation, the precision of performance evaluation may be greatly enhanced with the application of certain procedures that bring more objectivity into the process.

This section examines (1) approaches to objectifying performance evaluation, (2) global approaches to performance evaluation, (3) specific approaches to performance evaluation, (4) the importance of performance-related evaluations, and (5) the role of electronic devices in performance evaluation.

Objectifying Performance Evaluation Performance evaluation necessarily requires an evaluator to make a judgment about a given performance in relation to some standard. The standard may be an ideal, the performance level of others, or some specified criterion for an instructional objective. The most generally accepted procedures for ensuring objectivity or "fairness" in the evaluation process are to establish clear criteria against which the performance will be evaluated and to use some type of rating scale to indicate the extent to which each performer meets the evaluative criteria.

The performance criteria may vary from the *global* approach of traditional auditions, in which a performance is judged in its totality, to the *specifics* approach, in which the evaluator focuses on selected aspects of the performance. Whether to focus on global or specific aspects of a performance depends on the purpose of the evaluation and/or the philosophical perspective of the evaluator. In many cases, evaluators employ some combination of global and specific approaches.

Likert scales are the most commonly used scales for rating people and their behavior along an underlying continuum. A continuum may have a wide or narrow range, but the usual number of points on such a scale is from five to seven; the points might also have verbal designations such as "strongly agree," "agree," "neutral," "disagree," or "strongly disagree." Numbers to circle or blanks to check also are much used formats for Likert scales.

Likert scale responses usually reflect judgments in regard to some statement about a performance or some particular aspect of it. Some typical statements that might be evaluated along such a continuum follow:

	Agree				Disagree
1. This performance is of high musical quality.	___	___	___	___	___
2. The rhythm was performed with precision.	___	___	___	___	___
3. The intonation was accurate.	___	___	___	___	___
4. The phrasing was very "musical."	___	___	___	___	___

Statement 1 reflects a global approach, whereas statements 2, 3, and 4 reflect specific aspects of performance. Ratings from several specific aspects of performance may be *summated* to provide a total performance rating. The Likert scale probably is more appropriate for a specific than a global approach, and one needs to have either a relatively large number of items or judges to establish reliability for Likert scales.

The *semantic differential,* which was developed in an attempt to measure meaning (Osgood, Suci, and Tannenbaum, 1957), has been adapted for rating certain aspects of performance on continua between sets of antonyms. As with Likert scales, the number of points on a continuum between the antonyms may vary, but the procedure is similar. The sets of antonyms or antonym phrases for describing a musical performance might be something like the following:

	1	2	3	4	5	
in tune	___	___	___	___	___	out of tune
good tone quality	___	___	___	___	___	poor tone quality
rhythmic	___	___	___	___	___	arhythmic
musical	___	___	___	___	___	unmusical
sensitive	___	___	___	___	___	insensitive
consistent	___	___	___	___	___	inconsistent

Semantic differential data cannot be summated as can data from Likert scales. Simple "performance profiles" may be sufficient for many evaluative purposes, but sophisticated applications of the semantic differential require a factor analysis to determine the basic underlying *factors,* or *dimensions,* to which the scales are related.

When there is a need to rank several highly similar performances, such as when a number of very fine performers all play the same composition for a concerto composition, application of the *paired-comparisons* technique might allow for greater accuracy of judgment than the traditional auditioning of individual performances. The technique, which is more cumbersome and time-consuming than hearing and rating performances individually, allows systematic comparisons between each pair of performances. All performances are recorded and paired with each other and submitted to several judges who select which of each pair is the better performance. The assumption is that there are ambiguities involved in comparing highly similar performances and that judgments of the differences between each pair will vary in accordance with a normal distribution, centering on the "true" difference. By determining the proportion of times each performance is preferred over each of the others and converting these proportions to z scores in accordance with a normal curve table, one may arrive at mean z scores for the respective performances. For details of the procedure, the reader should consult Boyle and Radocy (1987, pp. 180–183).

When the paired comparisons technique is impractical because of a large number of performances to be compared, the method of *successive intervals* may be useful. In this method, judges categorize rather than rank the performances. Just as for comparative judgments, judges' categorizations are presumed to vary in accordance with the normal distribution. The method involves converting the number of responses in each category, as in the five categories used in rating festival performances, to proportions of judges assigning each performance to a category, converting these to z scores, establishing "true" category boundaries, and determining a mean z value for each performance. Although application of the method is relatively simple, one needs to consult a more detailed description of the procedure to be able to use it. (See Ghiselli, Campbell, and Zedeck, 1981, pp. 404–408, or Boyle and Radocy, 1987, pp. 183–185.) The successive intervals technique offers a viable way for sorting and ranking relatively similar performances.

Radocy (1978, 1982) has employed *magnitude estimation* as a technique for assessing musical performance. Based largely on the work of S. S. Stevens (1975), magnitude estimation was originally used to measure sensations such as loudness, taste, pitch, or brightness. Essentially, the technique involves matching the size, strength, or quality of some stimulus to numbers. The "more" or "better" the size, strength, or quality of the stimulus, the higher the number that is to be assigned to it. Judges are instructed to select any positive number to represent the magnitude of the initial stimulus; subsequent stimuli (i.e., other performances) should be assigned numbers that reflect their magnitudes relative to the original stimulus. Each judge may establish his or her own standard and scale, and the person in charge of the evaluation then establishes a *common modulus,* or standard, and converts each judge's estimates for each performance to reflect a proportionate relationship to the standard. Coeffi-

cient alpha reliabilities of magnitude estimations have been shown to be quite high (Figgs, 1981). The geometric mean is then calculated to provide an average stimulus value for each performance. The procedure is probably more useful for making global evaluations of dissimilar performances than for very similar performances. Also, it requires less listening time for judges than do paired comparisons or successive categories techniques.

The most used formal procedure for evaluating performance is the conventional contest/festival evaluation form. Essentially, the adjudicator must categorize each performance into one of five categories, thus providing a rating from I to V. Typical forms have subheadings such as tone, intonation, technique, balance, interpretation, and overall effect for which judges may rate and make comments about the respective aspects of the performance. Vocal solo forms might include other categories such as diction and breath control. Supposedly the ratings and comments on these subheadings provide the basis for the overall rating into the category I, II, III, IV, or V. Burnsed, Hinkle, and King (1985) report that judges' ratings on the subcategories are significantly related to the final ratings. They also note that there were no significant differences among the judges at each of four band festivals and state that "in most instances, we can be confident that the judges agree on whether our performance was a I, II, III, or IV" (p. 13).

Fiske (1983), however, argues that adjudicator reliability in the application of performance ratings cannot be assumed. He notes that neither high *intra*judge nor high *inter*judge reliabilities are the norm in performance evaluation. Fiske reports that "even highly practiced, experienced adjudicators rarely show a reliability index exceeding .50, that is, 25 percent consistency" (p. 7). Fiske's data suggest that questions concerning the "fairness" of many performance evaluations may be justified. Ideally, inter- and intrajudge reliability coefficients should be above .90.

A final approach to be considered is the use of *anchors* or *models.* To facilitate the setting of a standard for judges, it may be helpful to provide recorded performances of what festival managers (or whoever is in charge of the evaluation) consider "outstanding," "average," and "poor" performances. Such models serve as "anchors" for judges' standards and may be applied to many measurement techniques; their use should lead to more consistent applications of evaluative criteria, hence, yielding more reliable judgments.

Which performance measure to use may ultimately depend on its *usability.* As Colwell (1970, p. 27) notes, "Usability is a common sense consideration of ease in administration and scoring an evaluation device." Factors such as administration and scoring time and cost are the basic concerns when considering usability. However, usability considerations do not negate a test user's responsibility to ensure that the performance measure selected is reliable and valid.

Global Approaches Despite music teachers' ever-present involvement in performance evaluation, the only readily available published performance measures are the *Watkins-Farnum Performance Scale* (WFPS; Watkins and Farnum, 1954) and the *Farnum String Scale* (FSS; Farnum, 1969). The former is for wind instruments and snare drum; the latter, for orchestral string instruments. The WFPS, an outgrowth of a cornet performance measure (Watkins, 1942), has sets of 14 exercises that were adapted (mostly just transposed to appropriate keys and ranges) for treble clef baritone; B flat, alto, and bass clarinet; saxophone and oboe; flute; horn; trombone, bass clef baritone, and bassoon; and tuba. The snare drum measures include only 12 exercises. The FSS includes the 14 exercises adapted for violin, viola, cello, and string bass. Usually administered as sight-reading tests, the scales must be administered individually, and specific criteria and directions are provided in the WFPS for determining errors in pitch, time, change of time, expression, slur, and failure to observe a repeat sign. The FSS substitutes bowing errors for slur errors. The measure is the unit of scoring, and only one error is counted in each measure, no matter how many different types of errors occur. Parallel forms reliability coefficients range from .87 to .94, and correlations between WFPS scores and teachers' rankings of those students' performances range from .67 to .87. Although the test is meant to be scored as it is administered, reliability may be enhanced by having several judges score each performance.

In the 1920s and 1930s, several tests were developed to assess sight-singing skills, but most are no longer available. Over the years, a number of others have been developed as thesis or dissertation projects (e.g., Cooper, 1965; Scofield, 1980), but by and large such tests do not appear to have proved useful enough to music teachers to warrant publication and usage by the profession in the same way that the WFPS has for instrumentalists. Neither has *The Belwin-Mills Singing Achievement Test* (Bowles, 1971), the most recently published sight-singing test. This test has been criticized because of its lack of norms and reliability data (George, 1980, p. 335).

Systematic global approaches to performance evaluation other than traditional auditions or evaluations using contest or festival adjudication forms obviously are lacking. Whether this lack is because the profession does not see a need for such, because the complexity of global measures of performance evaluation makes the development of practical measures infeasible, or because of still other reasons is unclear.

Specific Approaches Perhaps because of the complexities of global evaluation, a number of researchers have undertaken the development of performance evaluation tools to assess varying aspects or facets of performance achievement.

One aspect of performance achievement that has gained the interest of some evaluators is children's vocal development. Long a concern of music teachers, vocal development has until recent years been mostly limited to informal classroom evaluations and classifications of voices into categories or stages of development. Rutkowski (1990) provides a comprehensive review of this literature and notes that many of the classification schemes intermix singing voice and intonation accuracy. She makes a strong case for isolating ratings of voice development from intonation accuracy, and over a period of years she has developed and refined "The Singing Voice Development Measure." The measure, which classifies

children as presingers, speaking-range singers, uncertain singers, initial range singers, or singers, reflects content-related validity and has yielded interrater reliability coefficients of .96 and .97.

The most used specifics approach to performance evaluation is the facet-factorial approach to rating scale development. Abeles (1973) developed 94 statements that might be descriptive of clarinet performance and asked 50 instrumental music teachers to rate some performances of junior high clarinetists on each of the 94 statements. Applying factor analysis to the results of the ratings, Abeles was able to reduce the 94 statements to 30 statements that best reflected six factors of clarinet performance: interpretation, intonation, rhythm continuity, tempo, articulation, and tone. Subsequent evaluations of clarinet performances by 32 instrumental music teachers were used to establish interjudge reliability for the rating scale. Interjudge reliability estimates for the CPRS were consistently high (.90). The CPRS was believed to be both valid and reliable. Essentially, Abeles demonstrated that various facets of a complex behavior (clarinet performance) can be assessed using facet-factorial analysis strategies. Abeles's approach served as a model for two important facet-factorial approaches to developing rating scales for group performance evaluation, one in choral music (Cooksey, 1974) and the other in instrumental music (DCamp, 1980).

The facet-factorial approach to rating scale construction has also been employed in the evaluation of euphonium and tuba performance (Bergee, 1987). An analysis of responses to 112 statements describing euphonium and tuba performance initially yielded five factors, which through subsequent analysis were reduced to four: (1) interpretation/musical effect, (2) tone quality/intonation, (3) technique, and (4) rhythm/tempo. Interjudge reliabilities ranged from .94 to .97; subscale reliabilities ranged from .89 to .99.

Boulton (1974) sought to design a test of flute tone production, intonation, and dexterity. Boulton surveyed 185 instrumental music teachers to validate a list of performance objectives and then devised a performance test to assess tone quality, vibrato, embouchure flexibility, breath capacity, intonation, and tongue and finger dexterity. Test-retest reliability coefficients ranged from .36 to .88, with the lowest coefficient being for intonation. Interjudge reliability coefficients ranged from .61 to .90, and intrajudge coefficients ranged from .78 to .99. Boulton concluded that specific areas of junior and senior high school flutists' performance can be measured with a high degree of reliability.

Kidd (1975) constructed a scale to assess trombone performance skills of elementary and junior high school students. He identified 50 different performance skills necessary to play a select body of grades I and II solo trombone literature and then devised short excerpts focusing on each skill. After piloting, he devised two forms of the test that were administered to 50 grade 6 through 9 trombonists. The performances were recorded and evaluated by three trombone instructors and performers. Interjudge reliabilities were above .90, and the equivalent forms reliability coefficient was .99.

Nelson (1970) developed a short-term objective test designed to assess four aspects of sight-singing: intervals, pitch patterns, rhythm phrases, and melodies. He compared performances on these measures with performance on a dictation test and a long-term sight-singing test (traditional global approach) and concluded that the short-term test was both more efficient and more valid in terms of its higher correlation with the dictation test than the global approach.

Jones (1986) applied the facet-factorial approach to scale construction in the development of rating scales for high school vocal solo performance. Beginning with 168 items, the study resulted in a 32-item rating scale that reflected a five-factor structure of vocal performance: interpretation musical effect, tone, musicianship, technique, suitability/ensemble, and diction. Interjudge reliabilities were acceptable for all but the fourth factor, suitability/ensemble. Criterion-related validity coefficients for subscales, based on correlations with (1) pair-comparison global evaluations and (2) ratings using the "NIMAC Vocal Adjudication Form," range from .72 to .18 for the former and .88 to .35 for the latter.

As part of the Utah State Office of Education's Music Core Curriculum project, Asmus (1990) developed a series of assessment forms through which music teachers might rate, using a five-point scale, the performance achievement of students in relation to the objectives of the curriculum. Music performance objectives were developed for several levels of general music, band, orchestra, and chorus, and pools of assessment items were developed for each level. Items were validated in accordance with teachers' reviews of

(a) whether the item assessed the objective, (b) whether it was appropriate for students of that grade level, (c) whether the task required by the item could be attained by 85 percent of the students if the objective was appropriately taught, and (d) whether the item was understandable by classroom teachers and students at that level. (p. 3)

The assessment forms were designed to (1) accommodate varying numbers of students in a class, (2) clearly indicate the objective being assessed, (3) have clearly labeled indicators of all attributes to be rated, (4) have a response key to anchor and guide the rating process, and (5) allow for numeric ratings that could be totaled to provide an overall index of student attainment of the objective. Essentially, this approach is *objective referenced* in that the teacher rates each student's achievement in relation to the musical performance objective for the given level of the curriculum.

Dressman (1990) sought to develop and validate tests to diagnose selected performance skills of middle/junior high school performers on common wind instruments, which he defined to include flute, clarinet, alto saxophone, trumpet, and trombone. He grouped the competencies to be evaluated under two headings: executive skills and performance skills. The executive skills portion asked music teachers to rate students with respect to embouchure, posture and playing position, hand/finger position and technique, breathing, and tongue movement. The performance skills portion included six types of excerpts for each instrument for which teachers were asked to rate respectively (1) tone quality, (2)

performance of dynamic markings (3) phrasing, (4) articulation, (5) common interpretive notation, and (6) performance of rhythms in common meters. Interjudge reliability coefficients were .90 for the executive skills test and .85 for the performance skills test; intrajudge reliabilities ranged from .91 to .94. In addition to high reliability coefficients and a strong claim for content validity, Dressman's diagnostic tests seem to meet the criterion of "usability" as advocated by Colwell (1970, p. 27).

Performance-Related Evaluation Outcomes of performance classes may involve behaviors other than musical performance per se, and several researchers have undertaken to assess them. This section reviews three such studies.

Mansur (1965) theorized that some skills measurable by a group test that yields objective test scores could, if positively correlated with demonstrated performance achievement, provide an estimate of performance proficiency apart from an audition. In addition to some traditional paper and pencil achievement items, Mansur developed a "Wind Inventory Scale" that presented five original musical phrases to be read silently. Following each phrase, a series of deductive inferences were made about the music, and students were asked to agree or disagree with each inference pertaining to performance of the phrase. Some typical statements follow:

This melody should be played in a rather *marcato* style.
This phrase would require a strict rhythmic accuracy in performance.
A melodic climax is not clearly defined in this phrase.
Stylistic markings indicate a tempo of *andante* or slower.

The test was administered as a screening device to students selected to audition for the Oklahoma all-state band and orchestra. Selection by performing audition was the independent criterion of validity. Although the test reliability was lower than desired (.62), the approach has merit as a way for assessing individual students' performance concepts in a group setting.

Horner (1973) developed a criterion-referenced test of performance-related musical behaviors for upper elementary school instrumentalists. Her test sought to assess student behaviors in relation to a set of objectives that had been developed from a review of instrumental instructional materials and validated through a review by instrumental music teachers. Only behaviors related to objectives agreed upon by 80 percent of the music teachers as appropriate for upper elementary school instrumentalists were included in the test. The test was intended to assess the extent to which students could make discriminations of performances of pitch direction, tonal center, scale and chord patterns, intonation, incorrect performance of notation, timbre, articulations, dynamics, meter, and note and rest values. She concluded that such test data are useful as a diagnostic tool, as a basis for adjusting instructional content to meet individual needs, as a basis for ability grouping, and as one method for providing accountability in the instrumental music program.

Weymuth's (1986) "Cognitive Choral Music Achievement Test" (CCMAT) was designed to assess performance-related objectives in a high school choral setting. He solicited choral directors' views regarding the most important performance-related objectives and devised a four-part test, parts of which required judgments or identification of certain aspects of recorded choral performance: (1) interval identification, (2) rhythmic precision, (3) diction, and (4) vocabulary. The test was essentially objective related in that it assessed student behavior in relation to objectives agreed upon by choral directors. The test's reliability coefficient was .90, and Weymuth maintains that it is a useful tool for assessing performance-related objectives of choral music.

Electronic Devices Electronic measures of the attributes of individual tones are readily accessible commercially, but assessment of real-time musical performance is another matter. Computer analysis of certain aspects of musical performance is possible, but the reality is that few electronic devices have been developed that meet the practical demands of performance evaluation. Some efforts to date show promise, however, and they are reviewed here.

It should be noted briefly that the two most powerful electronic devices for evaluating real-time music performance are the audiotape recorder and the videotape recorder. Recordings provide a record of performance that allows researchers or a music teacher to make repeated listenings to a performance, thus facilitating more careful analysis than might be afforded in a single listening. The videotape recording has the additional advantage of allowing visual reexamination of certain technique aspects of performance. Today both audio and video recording equipment are readily accessible to most music teachers, and they would be remiss not to take advantage of it.

Two noncomputer electronic "teaching machines," the Tap Master and the Pitch Master developed by Temporal Acuity Products, Inc., also have potential for assessment of single-line performance of rhythmic and melodic passages, respectively. Although designed as a tool for teaching rhythm reading, the Tap Master provides a score for the number of notes of a rhythm line tapped correctly on a response button on the machine. The patterns to be evaluated must be preprogramed with a specified tolerance level, but the resultant scores are objective and reliable.

The Pitch Master, which also must be preprogramed for the melodies to be evaluated, provides scores based on the time that a performance is sung or played in tune, that is, within preset tolerance limits. One point is given for every .25 second that the performance is in tune. Although the preparation of the tapes against which to compare students' performances (i.e., the preprograming) requires some planning on both the Tap Master and the Pitch Master, they are useful tools when one has specific performances of rhythmic and melodic patterns to be evaluated objectively.

Bengtsson and Gabrielsson (1977, 1983) have perhaps made the most use of computer analysis of performance to date. Concerned with analysis and synthesis of musical rhythm, they have been able to analyze systematic variations from mechanical regularity in real-time performance of rhythms. They have been able to measure deviations that occur at all levels, that is, for single tones, groups of tones within a beat, at the beat level, the measure level, and so on. Using data from their SYVARD analyses, they have been able to synthesize and demonstrate subtleties of rhythm performance as musicians perform. To date, their computer analyses have been used only for research purposes, and whether such a system can be adapted in a practical way for evaluating instruction remains to be seen.

Perhaps the most interest in electronic analysis of performance has been in computer-based fundamental frequency analysis, also known as pitch extraction. Lorek and Pembrook (1989) note that the technology has been around since the 1960s, but that only recently have advances in microcomputer technology and peripheral devices made such analysis possible on microcomputers; early efforts required mainframe computers. Graves (1980) and Lorek and Pembrook (1989) have each developed systems for evaluating sight-singing. To date such programs appear to be prototypes in which fundamental frequencies of tones in a melody are compared to an equal tempered model. Errors are reported in terms of cents deviation from equal temperament. Obviously, there are many parameters that must be established, and as yet such analyses appear to have been used only for research purposes. Whether refinements of the hardware and software will make them practical and reliable enough for evaluation of sight singing by music teachers has yet to be demonstrated.

APPLICATIONS OF MUSIC ABILITY EVALUATION DATA

The diversity of ways in which music ability is defined, demonstrated, and measured compounds the problems of the application and interpretation of data related to music ability. Such diversity makes it essential for users of music ability data to specify clearly the nature of the test task serving as the basis for evaluation of music ability, especially for those tasks for which there is a high inference level between the test task and the particular construct or dimension of music ability being evaluated. Generally, the inference level is higher for perceptual and conceptual dimensions of music ability than for performance dimensions, although sometimes there appear to be high-level inferences drawn from some music performance tasks that are seemingly rather straightforward and limited in scope. The greater the inference gap between test task and music ability construct, the less likely one is to gain consensus regarding what is being measured.

In a broad sense, music ability evaluation data serve three broad functions: (1) an aptitude or prediction function, which is future oriented, (2) a diagnostic function, which seems to focus on what a student is able to do at the time of testing and which makes no inferences regarding future potential or whether the demonstrated ability is a result of any specific instruction, and (3) an achievement function, which implies that the demonstrated ability is the result of experience, usually some type of formal instruction.

The extent to which music teachers apply and use music ability data to facilitate the educational process in schools varies greatly, perhaps because of (1) diverse philosophies regarding the importance of evaluation in the educational process, (2) varying knowledge and skill in evaluating music ability, and (3) lack of understanding regarding the functions music ability evaluation data may serve in an educational setting. For music ability evaluation data to become an integral part of the instructional process and have an impact on music education in schools, music teachers must develop (1) an understanding of its potential contributions to the educational process, (2) knowledge and skill in applying such data, and (3) a positive predisposition toward increased objectivity in music ability evaluation.

Objective evaluation of music ability is essential to music education research. Much music education research, whether descriptive, developmental, correlational, or experimental, involves measurement of some aspect of music ability either as an independent or dependent variable. To the extent that definitions of music ability are clear and the measurement of it is reliable and valid, music ability is a useful construct for the researcher; however, ill-defined, inaccurately measured, and loosely interpreted music ability data may result in misleading and erroneous research results and conclusions.

References

Abeles, H. F. (1973). Development and validation of a clarinet performance adjudication scale. *Journal of Research in Music Education, 21,* 246–255.

Asmus, E. P. (1989). Computer-based modeling of music concepts for testing, evaluating, and refining theory. *Psychomusicology, 8,* 171–182.

Asmus, E. P. (1990). Development of forms for in-class assessment of musical performance. Paper presented at the Southeastern Music Education Symposium, May 1990, Athens, GA.

Bengtsson, I., and Gabrielsson, A. (1977). Rhythm research in Uppsala. In *Music room acoustics* (pp. 19–56). Stockholm: Royal Swedish Academy of Music.

Bengtsson, I., and Gabrielsson, A. (1983). Analysis and synthesis of musical rhythm. In J. Sundberg (Ed.), *Studies of music performance* (pp. 27–60). Stockholm: Royal Swedish Academy of Music.

Bentley, A. (1966). *Measures of musical abilities.* London: George G. Harrap & Co.

Bergee, M. J. (1987). An application of the facet-factorial approach to scale construction in a rating scale for euphonium and tuba music performance. Unpublished doctoral dissertation, University of Kansas, Lawrence.

Boulton, J. B. (1974). A performance test of flute tone production, intonation and dexterity. Unpublished doctoral dissertation, University of Kansas.

Bowles, R. W. (1971). *The Belwin-Mills singing achievement test.* New York: Belwin-Mills.

Boyle, J. D. (1982). A study of the validity of three published, standardised measures of music preference. *Psychology of Music,* Special Issue, 11–16.

Boyle, J. D., and Radocy, R. E. (1987). *Measurement and evaluation of musical experiences.* New York: Schirmer Books.

Burnsed, V., Hinkle, D., and King, S. (1985). Performance evaluation reliability at select concert festivals. *Journal of Band Research, 21,* 22–29.

Colwell, R. (1969–70). *Music Achievement Tests.* Chicago: Follett Educational Corporation.

Colwell, R. (1970). *The evaluation of music teaching and learning.* Englewood Cliffs: Prentice-Hall.

Cooksey, J. M. (1974). An application of the facet-factorial approach to scale construction in the development of a rating scale for high school choral performance. Unpublished doctoral dissertation, University of Illinois, Urbana.

Cooksey, J. M. (1982). Developing an objective approach to evaluating music performance. In R. Colwell (Ed.), *Symposium in music education* (pp. 197–229). Urbana: University of Illinois.

Cooper, J. J. (1954). The development of a sight-singing achievement test for use with college students. Unpublished doctoral dissertation, University of Colorado, Boulder.

Costanza, A. P. (1971). Programmed instruction in score reading skills. *Journal of Research in Music Education, 19,* 453–459.

Cronbach, E. J. (1970). *Essentials of psychological testing* (4th ed.). New York: Harper & Row.

DCamp, C. B. (1980). An application of the facet-factorial approach to scale construction in the development of a rating scale for high school band performance. Unpublished doctoral dissertation, University of Iowa, Iowa City.

DeCarbo, N. J. (1981). The effects of conducting experience and programed materials on error detection scores of college conducting students. Unpublished doctoral dissertation, Kent State University, Kent.

Dowling, W. J. (1989). Programming small computers to produce experiments in music cognition. *Psychomusicology, 8,* 183–190.

Drake, R. M. (1957). *Drake Musical Aptitude Tests.* Chicago: Science Research Associates.

Dressman, M. B. (1990). The development and validation of a test to evaluate selected wind instrument performance competencies of middle/junior high school instrumentalists. Unpublished doctoral dissertation, University of Miami, Coral Gables.

Ebel, R. L., and Frisbie, D. A. (1990). *Essentials of educational measurement* (5th ed.). Englewood Cliffs: Prentice-Hall.

Farnsworth, P. R. (1969). *The social psychology of music* (2nd ed.). Ames: The Iowa State University Press.

Farnum, S. E. (1969). *Farnum String Scale.* Winona: Hal Leonard.

Figgs, L. D. (1981). Qualitative differences in trumpet tones as perceived by listeners and acoustical analysis. *Psychology of Music, 9*(20), 54–62.

Fiske, H. E. (1983). Judging musical performances: Method or madness. *UPDATE, 1*(3), 7–10.

Forsythe, R. (1984). The development and implementation of a computerized preschool measure of musical audiation. Unpublished doctoral dissertation, Case Western Reserve University, Cleveland.

Gallagher, F. D. (1971). A study of the relationships between the Gordon *Musical Aptitude Profile,* the Colwell *Music Achievement Tests,* and the *Indiana-Oregon Music Discrimination Test.* Unpublished doctoral dissertation, Indiana University, Bloomington.

Gardner, H. (1983). *Frames of mind: The theory of multiple intelligences.* New York: Basic Books.

Gaston, E. T. (1957). *A Test of Musicality* (4th ed.). Lawrence: O'Dell's Instrumental Service.

George, W. E. (1980). Measurement and evaluation of musical behavior. In D. A. Hodges (Ed.), *Handbook of music psychology* (pp. 291–340). Lawrence: National Association for Music Therapy.

George, W. E., and Hodges, D. A. (1980). The nature of musical attributes. In D. A. Hodges (Ed.), *Handbook of music psychology* (pp. 401–407). Lawrence: National Association for Music Therapy.

Ghiselli, E. E., Campbell, J. P., and Zedeck, S. (1981). *Measurement theory for the behavioral sciences.* San Francisco: W. H. Freeman and Co.

Gibson, D. (1989). An effective computer-assisted protocol for music perception experiments. *Psychomusicology, 8,* 191–196.

Gordon, E. (1965). *Musical Aptitude Profile.* Boston: Houghton Mifflin.

Gordon, E. (1970). *The psychology of music teaching.* Englewood Cliffs: Prentice-Hall.

Gordon, E. (1979a). *Primary Measures of Music Audiation.* Chicago: G.I.A. Publications.

Gordon, E. (1979b). Developmental music aptitude as measured by the Primary Measures of Music Audiation. *Psychology of Music, 7*(1), 42–49.

Gordon, E. (1984). *Learning sequences in music.* Chicago: G.I.A. Publications.

Gordon, E. (1987). *The nature, description, measurement, and evaluation of music aptitudes.* Chicago: G.I.A. Publications.

Graves, D. L. (1980). The development of an objective sight singing achievement test employing electronic measurement apparatus. Unpublished doctoral dissertation, University of Georgia, Athens.

Gronlund, N. E., and Linn, R. L. (1990). *Measurement and evaluation in teaching* (6th ed.). New York: Macmillan.

Grunow, R. F. (1980). An investigation of the relative effectiveness of four modes of score preparation on visual-aural discrimination skills development. Unpublished doctoral dissertation, University of Michigan, Ann Arbor.

Halsey, W. D. (Ed.). (1979). *Macmillan contemporary dictionary.* New York: Macmillan.

Hedden, S. K. (1982). Prediction of music achievement in the elementary school. *Journal of Research in Music Education, 30,* 61–68.

Horner, L. K. (1973). A criterion-referenced test in performance-related musical behaviors for instrumentalists in the upper elementary school. Unpublished doctoral dissertation, Pennsylvania State University, University Park.

Jones, H., Jr. (1986). An application of the facet-factorial approach to scale construction in the development of a rating scale for high school vocal solo performance. Unpublished doctoral dissertation, University of Oklahoma, Norman.

Karma, K. (1982). Validating tests of musical aptitude. *Psychology of Music, 10*(1), 33–36.

Karma, K. (1983). Selecting students to music instruction. *Bulletin of the Council for Research in Music Education, 75,* 23–32.

Karma, K. (1985). Components of auditive structuring—Towards a theory of musical aptitude. *Bulletin of the Council for Research in Music Education, 82,* 1-13.

Karma, K. (1986). Item difficulty values in measuring components of musical aptitude. *Bulletin of the Council for Research in Music Education, 89,* 18–31.

Kidd, R. L. (1975). The construction and validation of a scale of trombone performance skills. Unpublished doctoral dissertation, University of Illinois, Urbana.

Lehman, P. R. (1968). *Tests and measurements in music.* Englewood Cliffs: Prentice-Hall.

Long, N. H. (1965). *Indiana-Oregon Music Discrimination Test.* Bloomington: Midwest Music Tests.

Lorek, M. J., and Pembrook, R. G. (1989). Present and future applications of a microcomputer-based frequency analysis system. *Psychomusicology, 8,* 97–110.

Lundin, R. W. (1967). *An objective psychology of music* (2nd ed.). New York: Ronald Press.

Mansur, P. M. (1965). An objective performance-related music achievement test. Unpublished doctoral dissertation, University of Oklahoma, Norman.

McCarthy, J. F. (1984). The pitch test. *Creative computing, 10*(3), 211–212, 216–217.

Mursell, J. L. (1937). *The psychology of music.* New York: W. W. Norton.

Nelson, J. C. (1970). A comparison of two methods of measuring achievement in sight singing. Unpublished doctoral dissertation, University of Iowa, Iowa City.

Osgood, C. E., Suci, G. J., and Tannenbaum, P. H. (1957). *The measurement of meaning.* Urbana: University of Illinois Press.

Radocy, R. E. (1978). The influence of selected variables on the apparent size of successive pitch intervals. *Psychology of Music, 6*(2), 21–29.

Radocy, R. E. (1982). Magnitude estimation of melodic dissimilarity. *Psychology of Music, 10*(1), 28–32.

Radocy, R. E., and Boyle, J. D. (1988). *Psychological foundations of musical behavior* (2nd ed.). Springfield: Charles C Thomas.

Rainbow, E. L. (1965). A pilot study to investigate the constructs of musical aptitude. *Journal of Research in Music Education, 13,* 3–14.

Ramsey, D. (1978). Programed instruction using full-score band literature to teach pitch and rhythm error detection skill to college music education students. Unpublished doctoral dissertation, University of Iowa, Iowa City.

Robinson, R. L. (1985). *Microcomputer adaptation of the Drake Musical Aptitude Tests.* Gainesville: University of Florida.

Rutkowski, J. (1990). The measurement and evaluation of children's singing. *The Quarterly, 1,* 81–95.

Sampsell, S. A. (1980). A study of the comparative validity of three measures of music sensitivity. Unpublished master's thesis, Pennsylvania State University, University Park.

Schoen, M. (1940). *The psychology of music.* New York: Ronald Press.

Scofield, W. R. (1980). The construction and validation of a method for the measurement of the sight-singing abilities of high school and college students. Unpublished doctoral dissertation, Michigan State University, East Lansing.

Seashore, C. E. (1919). *The psychology of musical talent.* New York: Silver Burdett.

Seashore, C. E. (1938). *Psychology of music.* New York: McGraw-Hill.

Seashore, C. E., Lewis, D., and Saetveit, J. G. (1960). *Seashore Measures of Musical Talents.* New York: The Psychological Corporation. (Originally published in 1939.)

Serafine, M. L. (1983). Cognitive processes in music: Discoveries and definitions. *Bulletin of the Council for Research in Music Education, 73,* 1–14.

Sergeant, D., and Boyle, J. D. (1981). The effect of task structure on pitch discrimination. *Psychology of Music, 8*(2), 3–15.

Shuter-Dyson, R., and Gabriel, C. (1981). *The psychology of musical ability* (2nd ed.). London: Methuen.

Simons, G. M. (1974). *Measurements of musical listening skills for young children.* Chicago: Stoetling (printed in 1976).

Stevens, S. S. (1975). *Psychophysics.* New York: Wiley.

Vispoel, W. P. (1987). An adaptive test of musical memory: An application of item response theory to the assessment of musical ability. Unpublished doctoral dissertation, University of Illinois, Urbana.

Vispoel, W. P. (1990). *Computerized adaptive music tests: A new solution to three old problems.* Paper presented at the Music Educators National Conference, Washington, March 1990.

Watkins, J. G. (1942). *Objective measurement of instrumental performance.* New York: Teachers' College Bureau of Publications, Columbia University.

Watkins, J. G., and Farnum, S. E. (1954). *The Watkins-Farnum Performance Scale.* Winona: Hal Leonard.

Webster, P. R. (1988). New perspectives on music aptitude and achievement. *Psychomusicology, 7,* 177–194.

Weymuth, R. W. (1986). The development and evaluation of a cognitive choral music achievement test to evaluate Missouri high school students. Unpublished doctoral dissertation, University of Miami, Coral Gables.

Whellams, F. S. (1970). The relative efficiency of aural-musical and non-musical tests as predictors of achievement in instrumental music. *Bulletin of the Council for Research in Music Education, 21,* 15–21.

Wing, H. D. (1954). Some applications of test results to education in music. *British Journal of Educational Psychology, 24,* 161–170.

Wing, H. D. (1961). *Standardised Tests of Musical Intelligence.* The Mere, England: National Foundation for Educational Research. (Originally published in 1939.)

Wing, H. D. (1968). Tests of musical ability and appreciation. *British Journal of Psychology Monographs,* Supplement, No. 27 (2nd ed.). London: Cambridge University Press.

RESEARCH ON CREATIVE THINKING IN MUSIC: THE ASSESSMENT LITERATURE

Peter R. Webster

NORTHWESTERN UNIVERSITY

BACKGROUND

The systematic study of creative thinking in music and its meaningful assessment are relatively new concerns for researchers. With the exception of a few early descriptive studies, the most useful work has been completed in the last 20 years. This lack of an extensive research tradition for such an important topic has most certainly not been due to lack of interest in the professional as a whole. Many have endorsed the importance of encouraging children to work creatively with music and have written extensive curricular materials (Coleman, 1922; Morgan, 1947; CMP 3, 1966; Thomas, 1970). For over 30 years, approaches to elementary school music education such as those based on the thinking of Carl Orff and Emile Dalcroze have encouraged certain kinds of improvisation and composition. As will be noted below, the reasons for the lack of research tradition have a great deal to do with the enormous problems of definition and assessment validity. It might also be fair to say that, until most recently, researchers in music education have been somewhat conservative in their approaches to assessment research and have chosen to study topics of narrow scope.

Reasons for New Research Interest

Contemporary research interest in the topic of creative thinking ability in children can be explained by factors both inside and outside the profession. It has been clear for some time that traditional measures of music aptitude and achievement are useful only to a point. A broadening of our conception of what constitutes musicality is long overdue (Webster, 1988b). There is also a growing desire to know more about the generative process in music, both in music education circles and in related fields of music psychology, psychomusicology, and music theory (Hargreaves, 1986, pp. 143–178; Sloboda, 1985, pp. 102–150, 1988; Reimer, 1989).

Music researchers have also been influenced by the general psychology literature, particularly the heritage of multiple intelligence theories, such as those of Guilford (1967) and more recently, Gardner (1983). Certain measurement strategies by psychologists such as Torrance (1966) have influenced music researchers who have been interested in a psychometric approach to creative thinking in music.

Recent interest in more varied research techniques, such as ethnographic methodology, extended case studies, and protocol analysis, have given new life to the assessment of creative processes in music. For example, Davidson and Welsh (1988) reported data on working styles and strategies of young adults by systematically observing a music composition task. John-Steiner (1985) has collected the results of self-reports of and interviews with adults known for creative thinking ability. The aim of such work is not to develop a psychometric measure, but rather to observe the cognitive process and report intelligently about it. Such research is in line with the current thinking in cognitive psychology and the interdisciplinary spirit of cognitive science (Gardner, 1985).

There also exists a fresh, new trend in assessment as an educational enterprise aimed at broadening the base of what is considered for evaluation. For example, Wolf (1988) has reported on the use of portfolios, extended student projects, and interviews as means for evaluating student growth in the arts. Such shifts from exclusive reliance on single-grade report systems to more varied mechanisms have affected and will continue to affect the research on creative thinking in music.

Problems That Face the Researcher

There are two fundamental problems that continue to trouble researchers in the field. The first is confusion about creativeness as a concept and what it means in terms of assessment in music teaching and learning. The second, stemming directly from the first, is the more technical problem of achieving valid assessment.

Just what does "creativity" mean? In a study of the term's use in the *Music Educators Journal* from 1914 to 1970, Hounchell (1985) concluded that no clear definition existed and that the term was used largely to encourage acceptance of music education in a general sense. Oehrle (1984), in a study of elementary music textbooks in this country and in England, cited the inconsistency between the relative absence of genuine creative activities and the philosophical endorsement of such activities. This may suggest that the profession confuses generative, divergent music behaviors such as composition, improvisation, and creative listening with convergent skill development (Webster, 1990). This problem is compounded by the selection process for special educational programs for the "gifted" or "talented," which often confuses performance ability in music, high scores on traditional music aptitude tests, and high general intelligence with ability to think creatively in music.

This problem extends to the more systematic literature on assessment. As in general psychology, there is no commonly accepted definition of "creativity," and there is a tendency to use "creative thinking" or "creative ability" for more specificity. Definitions are based on either (1) the creative product as evidence of creative thinking, (2) the mental process during creative activity, (3) cognitive or personality traits of the creator such as flexibility of thought or openness to risk, (4) environmental conditions that encourage creative thinking, or (5) some combination of all four. Fortunately, there are common elements among these definitions both in the music and in the general literatures that help to clarify the problem. These include reference to a problem-solving content, stages in the creative process, convergent and divergent thinking abilities, some aspect of novelty in the product, and a product that makes contextual sense within a domain. However, even with these commonalities, researchers who may be searching for a "clean" problem to study often discard the field as too troublesome.

This complex conceptual base has contributed to problems of valid assessment for both psychometric measurement and more descriptive, content analysis techniques. Problems of definition naturally lead to problems with construct validity. This was a common circumstance in early research efforts when researchers used general creativity measures to assess creative thinking in music—making the questionable assumption that creative ability is generalized across all domains.

The nature of the data must be considered carefully, and special techniques must be used. As Sloboda argues, "It is always easier to collect one's data in the form of responses from a limited and pre-ordained set (for example yes-no decision, same-different decisions) than it is from relatively un-constrained and multidimensional behavior" (1988, p. vii.). This latter kind of assessment is time-consuming, not only for data collection itself but also for the scoring and interpretation of data. Instrumentation is often complicated. Traditional statistical techniques may not always be appropriate or desirable. Because evaluation design is often a one-on-one affair with the notion of group testing being antithetical to the task at hand, large-scale use of these assessment schemes is a major problem.

Finally, each data collection scheme has weaknesses in scorer reliability. Schemes have typically included (1) audio and/or video recording of creative behavior for postanalysis by judges, (2) auditory transcriptions of audiotape performances into conventional or graphic notation for expert analysis, (3) verbal protocol analysis, and (4) classic ethnographic description. Although each approach has decided advantages over traditional paper and pencil tests, problems of scorer bias, numerical coding, and scorer consistency plague such research.

Chapter Focus

Despite these problems—or perhaps because of them—recent systematic study of creative thinking in music offers an interesting literature to review and a challenging field of inquiry for both the new and the seasoned researcher. After a brief review of the important bases in the general literature, the chapter will provide an introduction to many of the important studies in music teaching and learning. Studies that offer special meaning for assessment will be stressed. The chapter will conclude with some thoughts on future directions. Readers interested in a broader review of the literature on creative thinking and music should consult the article by Richardson (1983) and the chapter by Webster (1988a). Richardson outlines the historical perspective by highlighting important writings before 1989 and provides an excellent review of the literature on instruction and its effect on creative ability. Webster provides a general overview of the entire field, including the practical literature. The chapter also contains a literature model that may be helpful for new readers to the field.

BASES IN THE NONMUSIC LITERATURE

A chapter of this sort cannot be complete without some attention to the large and complex literature in psychology on creative thinking and its assessment. Several excellent summaries and anthologies of this writing exist, including those by Bloomberg (1973), Rothenberg and Hausman (1976), Amabile (1983), Davis (1986), and Sternberg (1988). Many of the landmark studies from this general literature are important to note because of their influence on current and future research in music.

It is quite clear that serious interest in creative thinking research began following Guilford's 1950 presidential address to the American Psychological Association (Guilford,

1950). Psychological research flourished for the next two decades, then became more sporadic. Within the last few years, however, fresh perspectives have emerged (Sternberg, 1988, p. viii), especially with the growing interest in cognitive science, social psychology, and mental development. This renewal of research activity parallels that in music education and shares some similar characteristics.

A close study of the content in both the early and the latest general research literature reveals the following categories:

1. *Psychometric research,* which uses both intellectual and personality traits as a basis for the design of measurement tools
2. *Cognitive research,* which centers on identifying mental processes and underlying mental structures
3. *Environment research,* which focuses on the interaction of the creator with the setting in which the creative work occurs

Psychometric research was the dominant characteristic of the early work in psychology. It has also had the most influence on music research. Studies of cognitive process and structure are somewhat newer in the general literature. Work of this sort is just now developing in music education and represents some of the most exciting and challenging research that faces the profession. Finally, research that focuses on the interaction of the creator with the environment is quite new in the general literature. It has not had an effect on music research to date, but has potential to do so as more music researchers speculate on global theories of creative thinking.

Psychometric Research

The psychometric approaches of Guilford (1967), Torrance (1966), and Barron (1969) are all important here. Guilford's Structure of Intellect (SI) model and the resultant factor analytic work are representative of studies of individual difference in creative thinking and their correlation with other mental characteristics. Important are the notions of divergent versus convergent thinking abilities as individuals are asked to perform various tasks. Divergent thinking abilities help individuals generate many possible solutions, while convergent thinking relates to abilities that help the mind focus on the best answer. Divergent thinking concepts include (1) fluency (sheer number of responses), (2) flexibility (different classes of responses), (3) originality (index of novelty of response), and (4) elaboration (extended content of response). These traits are used as the basis for scoring schemes in many standardized measures. Researchers in music have been greatly influenced by these studies, as will be seen.

Studies focused on personality traits of individuals generally known as creative have identified certain common threads (MacKinnon, 1965). Often cited are such traits as confidence, curiosity, humor, risk taking, openness, and in-terest in wide-ranging activities. Tardif and Sternberg (1988, p. 434) list other traits and include personal abilities and styles of thinking common to creative people. This line of inquiry has led to the development of personality inventories that are used to identify creative individuals. There is no evidence that the music assessment literature has been influenced by this approach as yet. Examples of both standardized measures and personality inventories are summarized below.

Published Measures and Inventories The most well-known and researched measure of general creative ability is the *Torrance Tests of Creative Thinking* (Torrance, 1966). For a more extensive treatment of these evaluation tools and others, see Davis (1986), or Amabile (1983). Both verbal and figural content tests are available, and each of these has parallel forms. In the verbal measure, subjects are presented with common objects (e.g., boxes, stuffed animals) and situations (sometimes improbable situations) and asked for the solution to tasks. The tasks are timed and require paper and pencil responses if administered in the normal manner. The responses are measured according to fluency, flexibility, and originality. Elaboration can also be scored. A similar approach is taken with the figural content measure. The link between these measures and those originally designed by Guilford and his associates for the validation of the SI model is quite clear.

Other published measures include the Wallach and Kogan (1965) tests, which take a similar approach to problem solving but are untimed and administered in a gamelike atmosphere. Torrance has also published two other measures—one that uses audio sounds and words as stimuli (Torrance, 1973) and one especially designed for preschool children that uses movement (Torrance, 1981).

Personality and Biographical Inventories Inventories take a descriptive approach by presenting the subjects with statements about themselves and asking for a rating of extent to which the statement seems true. For instance, one item might be worded, "I am very curious," to which the subject must respond "No," "To a small extent," "Average," "More than average," or "Definitely." The profile of responses is then validated against a set of criteria that might include teacher ratings or evidence of real-life creative achievement. These inventories often return subscores for imagination, independence, or confidence, as well as an overall creative index. A good example of this kind of inventory is the *Group Inventory for Finding Talent* (Rimm and Davis, 1980). Other inventories are designed to be used by teachers or parents in rating children.

Cognition Research

Researchers interested in this approach are much less driven by a desire to construct formal measurement instruments. Here, the importance is placed on process and how the mind operates during creative activity. For example, on the basis of the testimony of creative thinkers, Wallas (1926) postulated the existence of four stages during the creative process: (1) *preparation,* when problems are first considered; (2) *incubation,* time away from active consideration of the problem; (3) *illumination,* the moment(s) of insight; and (4) *verification,* the time when solutions are tested and refined. This theory has been confirmed on a number of occasions and in a number of disciplines, although Winner (1982, pp. 39–42) points to the incubation time and its underlying subconscious processes as the most controversial aspect, and Weisberg (1986) argues for caution in overromanticizing illumination. Other stage theories of creative thinking have been offered by scholars, including Abraham Maslow and Ernest Kris. For additional information on stage theories and other theoretical writings on creative thinking, see Baltzer (1990, pp. 18–23).

In a more developmental vein, Gardner believes that the "roots of creativity lie in children's early symbolic products" (Gardner, 1989, p. 114) and in the merger of these with adult understanding of the domain in which the creator operates. Drawing in part on the theory of symbol systems advanced by Goodman (1976), Gardner has devoted his theories and research agenda to a "developmental portrait" of creative mental processes rather than a "trait" view as found in the psychometric literature.

In terms of intelligence theory, Sternberg (1988, pp. 125–147) has argued for a three-facet model of creativity. He cites (1) cognitive skills (drawn from his triadic theory of intelligence) such as the ability to recognize and define problems; (2) intellectual style, which might be "legislative" in nature for creative individuals; and (3) certain personality traits as important in understanding creativity from a cognitive perspective.

Finally, recent interest in creative thinking from an artificial intelligence perspective can be noted in writings by Johnson-Laird (1988) and Shank (1988). The role of memory and memory storage is important in this approach, and computational mechanisms involving elaborate computer models and computer programs are frequently used.

Environment Research

This literature considers the role of culture and cultural expectations. Amabile's work with reward systems, motivation (external and internal), and social interaction is noteworthy (Amabile, 1983). Her conceptual definition of creativity is largely based on the creative product—its novelty and appropriateness. Her approach to assessment uses expert judges to evaluate products, thus relying on a consensus of opinion. (It is interesting to note that music education researchers have used similar techniques to evaluate creative work in music, but have not taken as much care in the training of judges as Amabile's research suggests be taken.) Using data from this approach and from other more psychometric work, she draws conclusions regarding the social aspects of the creative experience.

Others interested in social issues include Feldman (1986)

and Bloom (1985), who investigated child prodigies and their interaction with the environment. Also of primary interest is Csikszentmihalyi (1988) and his system view of creativity, which includes the notions of "person," "domain" (symbol system), and "field" (social organization of the domain).

Readers of music education literature will likely note the relationship between many of these topics and the issues discussed at the third Ann Arbor Symposium (*Documentary Report,* 1983). Assessment research in music has been slow to react to this more general environmental view, although this is likely to change as empirical study increases and as more theory is generated. (One possible exception to this is the work by Simonton on adult composers. One study [Simonton, 1980] investigated thematic fame, a common occurrence in literature about music, and melodic originality, the unusual use of musical material, of 10 classical composers as it might relate to such factors as biological stress and age. Although of interest to music education, this research does not directly deal with the issues of creative thinking in children and its meaningful assessment.)

ASSESSMENT LITERATURE IN MUSIC EDUCATION

Figure 17-1 (p. 270) displays an organizational scheme for the assessment literature on creative thinking in music. This represents a section from the larger category of empirical studies found in the literature on creative thinking in music. Readers interested in a more expanded literature model that includes other empirical study as well as the theoretical and practical literature should see Webster (1988). It should be noted that a number of studies in the empirical category include works that explore relationships between variables, study the effect of creative teaching strategies, describe personality studies, or explore conditions of creative thinking. These studies employ assessment tools but the main focus of the research lies elsewhere. (For example, see Schmidt and Sinor, 1986.) Each study included in this diagram (1) involves the study of individuals from preschool to college age (literature on the systematic study of creative adult musicians is not included), (2) is principally concerned with assessment, and (3) presents empirical evidence. Specialized improvisation literatures, such as those in jazz and ethnomusicology, are not included.

The major categories in the figure have clear parallels with the general literature, and many characteristics of the music studies in each category relate directly to the research summarized above. As with many schemes of this sort, overlap is common and readers should not be surprised to find studies that might be grouped in more than one subdivision. Some studies contain content that might also be placed in theoretical or practical categories as well as the empirical. The placement decision was based on what the major thrust of the work seemed to be.

Within the content analysis category, a distinction is made between studies that have concentrated on assessment of *process* and those that have centered on *product.* Research

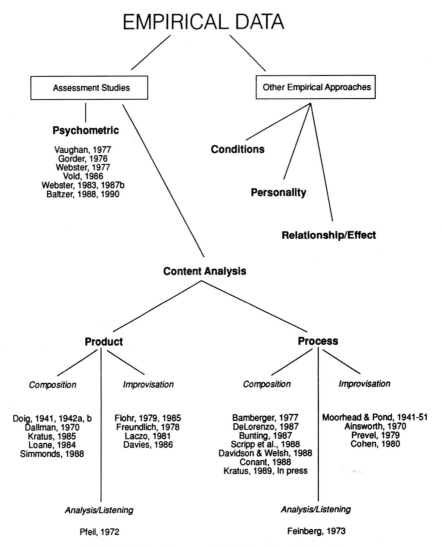

EMPIRICAL DATA

| Assessment Studies | | Other Empirical Approaches |

Psychometric

Vaughan, 1977
Gorder, 1976
Webster, 1977
Vold, 1986
Webster, 1983, 1987b
Baltzer, 1988, 1990

Conditions

Personality

Relationship/Effect

Content Analysis

Product

Process

Composition

Improvisation

Composition

Improvisation

Doig, 1941, 1942a, b
Dallman, 1970
Kratus, 1985
Loane, 1984
Simmonds, 1988

Flohr, 1979, 1985
Freundlich, 1978
Laczo, 1981
Davies, 1986

Bamberger, 1977
DeLorenzo, 1987
Bunting, 1987
Scripp et al., 1988
Davidson & Welsh, 1988
Conant, 1988
Kratus, 1989, In press

Moorhead & Pond, 1941-51
Ainsworth, 1970
Prevel, 1979
Cohen, 1980

Analysis/Listening

Analysis/Listening

Pfeil, 1972

Feinberg, 1973

FIGURE 17–1. Literature Model for Empirical Studies.

strategies for process studies focus on observable behaviors or reported thought processes during the creative act. Assessment techniques employing this kind of research tend to be quite descriptive and include case study and naturalistic studies. The product studies, by contrast, involve work on the end result of the creative act. Findings often center on the nature of musical characteristics as a clue to mental processes.

A final distinction is drawn between studies in the product and process categories that are concerned with composition, improvisation, and analysis/listening. There is some discussion in the literature about the differences between composition and improvisation, especially as one considers the musical products of young children. The distinction made here is quite simple. If subjects are given the opportunity to revise their work in some way before it is considered finished, the product or process is considered more compo-

sitional in nature. If the product or process is not reconsidered for change, it is more improvisatory.

Space restrictions in this chapter will not allow a detailed review of each of these studies. What follows is a description of selected works that are key to understanding the contemporary trends in the field.

Psychometric Studies in Music

Currently there are no published, standardized norm-referenced measures of creative thinking in music. This fact is, in part, a reflection of the measurement problems noted above and the youthfulness of this line of research in traditional music education circles. There is a group of published research studies on measurement development, however, that suggest this will soon change. The works summarized below typically engage subjects in musical tasks and score the process and/or products using a measurement scheme that is related to approaches taken in the general literature. Criterion factors such as musical fluency or musical originality are defined, as are factors of musical relevance or syntax. Multiple judges are often used for more subjective judgments.

Vaughan's Early Work Vaughan (1977) completed the first significant attempts to measure creative thinking in music—a series of four studies from 1969 to 1976 that used a set of six tasks designed for grade school children. These tasks were quite simple in design, asking children to improvise (1) rhythm patterns as a response to a given stimulus, and another set of patterns simultaneously with a given ostinato, (2) melody patterns in a similar manner, and (3) a "piece" showing how the subject feels during a thunderstorm. The final task allowed subjects to use melody bells, tom-tom, and any vocal sounds desired. The scoring scheme used a panel of judges to evaluate factors of musical fluency, rhythmic security, and ideation. Although interjudge reliabilities of .67 to .90 are reported for the various studies using the test, little other validity data is reported for the research.

By contemporary standards, the Vaughan work would be considered incomplete. Its significance, however, is that it represents the first studies to construct *musical* tasks to evaluate creative thinking in music, basing the tasks on established theories in both music and the general literature. Many of the approaches taken to scoring would be repeated in future studies by other researchers.

Research with High School Musicians Gorder (1976) and Webster (1977) completed the first studies of high schoolationships between variables, study the effect of creative teaching strategies, describe personality studies, or explore conditions of creative thinking. These studies employ assessment tools but the main focus of the research lies elsewhere. (For example, see Schmidt and Sinor, 1986.) Each study included in this diagram (1) involves the study of individuals from preschool to college age (literature on the systematic study of creative adult musicians is not included), (2) is principally concernclude this dimension.

Gorder's measure was validated by a panel of musical experts, and construct validity was established in part by factor analysis. Test-retest and split-half reliabilities ranged from .69 to .90. He scored all tests himself; however, a panel of three trained judges scored a sample of the subject records, and interjudge reliability was acceptable. The sample for the main study numbered 81, drawn at random from 542 junior and senior high school band students from eight different schools. Subjects were asked to improvise in four tasks either using their own instruments or by whistling or singing. The tasks themselves were represented as skeletal music notation, and subjects were asked to improvise using the motives, note heads, or contour markings as guides. The approach taken for evaluation used a music content checklist—78 items relating to melody, rhythm, tempo, style, dynamics, timbre, expressive devices, and form. The four tasks were scored for number of phrases (fluency), shifts of content character (flexibility), extent of content beyond the minimum expected (elaboration), unusual content (originality), and musical appeal (quality).

Webster's work also included improvisation: Seventy-seven high school instrumental and choral subjects were asked to perform on melody bells in order to control for performance ability. No notation was used, but subjects were asked to complete tasks of increasing difficulty with the bells. The penultimate task involved a performance of the simple nursery tune "Twinkle" followed by an opportunity to perform the same tune in variation three more times, each time moving further away musically from the original. In the final task, subjects were asked to compose an original tune short enough to play from memory without error but not so short as to be simply a motive or figure. This tune was then to be merged with "Twinkle" in an original composition.

Unlike Gorder, Webster asked the same sample to complete a set of take-home composition and analysis tasks. The composition tasks used a technique similar to Gorder's skeletal improvisation guides, presenting subjects with an outline of a short musical phrase for triangle and some other instrument or voice part. Reference points in the phrase were indicated by note heads, and subjects could use traditional or invented musical notation to complete the phrase. Other tasks used a similar approach, but contained more freedom of choice.

The analysis tasks were probably the most unusual aspect of the study. It is rare to find attention paid to the notion of creative listening/analysis, and this style of assessment is often not explored. The first activity asked subjects to make as many imaginative and original observations as possible about the structure and design of a 14-measure melody extracted from volume 1 of Bartok's *Mikrokosmos*. Although the melody does contain many obvious structural components, there are many that are less obvious relating to tonality, diminution of note values, and melody range. The second and third activities included other musical scores from which a number of observations about musical structure and content could be made. These included a comparison of two duets from the *Mikrokosmos* and a clever twelve-tone composition by Milton Babbit entitled "Play on Notes." The Babbit piece was constructed from two hexachords with a number of permutations, and the text was written as a retrograde that makes sense when read in either direction.

Scoring approaches to each set of tasks were similar to Gorder's, translating notions of fluency, flexibility, originality, and elaboration into musical terms. Scorer reliability ranged from .81 to .93, and interjudge reliability ranged from .70 to .90. A panel of musicians helped establish content validity.

Both the Gorder and the Webster studies are important in the literature because of their success in defining the qualities of creative thinking assessment in music, both theoretically and statistically. Correlations of creative thinking scores in music with traditional music aptitude and general intelligence measures were low and not significant—a tendency that has been shown repeatedly in research on creative thinking in music.

Baltzer's Work with Wang's Measures of Creativity in Sound and Music Psychometric research with younger children has been of recent interest to Baltzer, Wang, and Webster. To date, Baltzer has published two studies that use Wang's *Measures of Creativity in Sound and Music* (MCSM; Baltzer, 1988, 1990). Designed for children ages 3 to 8, this measure is modeled after Torrance's preschool measure (Torrance, 1981) and consists of four activities that provide data on musical fluency and musical imagination. Baltzer describes the measure as follows:

In Activity 1, the child is asked to produce as many different examples of steady beat as possible using two plastic containers and lids as sound sources. The second activity requires the child to imitate, with rhythm instruments, a series of six described events described by the test administrator (thunderstorm with lightning, a giant walking, a horse in motion, popcorn popping, a small river flowing, and someone typing). In Activity 3, the subject is asked to demonstrate as many different ostinatos as possible, given two notes, C and G, on a bass Orff xylophone, and in Activity 4 the subject is asked to move in appropriate ways to six selections of recorded music. (1988, p. 237)

The musical fluency score is determined by adding the number of responses in activities 1 and 3. The musical imagination score is a total of the appropriateness ratings in activity 2 and the quality of movement rating in activity 4. Baltzer (1988) administered the Wang measure to 32 second-grade subjects. Two judges were used to evaluate the tests, with interjudge reliability ranging from .90 to .99. Preliminary data on concurrent validity, expressed in terms of correlations with a music specialist's ratings of creative ability, were moderate to low (.14 to .43). However, such a result must not necessarily be viewed as evidence for poor test validity, since the music specialist's view of students' creative thinking in music is often confused with their convergent achievement skills. This is a classic measurement problem in the literature. Baltzer's most recent use of MCSM was part of an elegant factor analytic investigation of creativity tests in music that involved 90 subjects (Baltzer, 1990). Interjudge reliability results were similar, and factor analysis did help to confirm the construct validity of the fluency and imagination factors.

Wang, herself, has not published data on her work with MCSM as yet. The measure awaits more extensive research and a clearer description of its scoring rationale and theoretical base.

Webster's Measure of Creative Thinking in Music The *Measure of Creative Thinking in Music* (MCTM; Webster, 1987b), designed for children aged 6 to 10, has been used in a number of recent studies. Although it follows many of the traditional approaches outlined above, it does differ in its use of instruments, diversity of tasks, and scoring scheme.

The MCTM uses three sets of instruments: (1) a round "sponge" ball of about 6 inches in diameter that is used to play tone clusters on a piano, (2) a microphone that is suspended in front of the piano and is attached to an amplifier and speaker, and (3) a set of five wooden resonator blocks. There is a brief warm-up period that is not scored and that is designed to familiarize the children with the simple techniques necessary to play the instruments. All tasks are videotaped unobtrusively and scored at a later time. The measure requires about 20 to 25 minutes to administer per child.

There are 10 scored tasks, divided into three parts: exploration, application, and synthesis. The tasks begin very simply and progress to higher levels of difficulty in terms of divergent behavior. The exploration section is designed to help the children become familiar with the instruments used and how they are arranged. The musical parameters of high/low, fast/slow, and loud/soft are explored in this section, as well as throughout the measure. The way the children manipulate these parameters is, in turn, used as one of the bases for scoring. Tasks in this section involve images of rain in a water bucket, magical elevators, and the sounds of trucks.

In the application tasks, children are asked to do more challenging activities that focus on the creation of music with each of the instruments singly. Certain tasks have children enter into a kind of musical question/answer dialogue, with the tester using a mallet and temple blocks, while other activities involve the creation of sound pieces with the round ball and piano or with voice and microphone. Images used include the concept of "frog" music (ball hopping and rolling on the piano) and of a robot singing in the shower (microphone and voice). In the synthesis section, children are encouraged to use multiple instruments in tasks whose settings are less structured. A space story is told in sounds, using line drawings as a visual aid. Finally, children are instructed to create a composition that uses all the instruments and that has a beginning, a middle, and an end.

The scoring of the videotapes involves both objective and subjective techniques. There are four factors used: (1) musical extensiveness—the amount of clock time involved in the creative tasks, (2) musical flexibility—the extent to which the musical parameters of high/low (pitch), fast/slow (tempo), and loud/soft (dynamics) are manipulated, (3) musical originality—the extent to which the response is unusual or unique in musical terms and in the manner of performance, and (4) musical syntax—the extent to which the response is inherently logical and makes musical sense. Musical extensiveness and flexibility are measured objectively by counting the actual seconds of time a child is involved in a task and by observing the manipulation of musical parameters, respectively. For best results, musical originality and syntax are evaluated by a panel of judges; however, one observer is certainly possible. Rating scales based on developed criteria are used for these factors.

Reliability and validity data have been collected in a number of studies (Webster 1983, 1987b; Swanner, 1985; Baltzer, 1990). MCTM has also been used in a study of cognitive style by Schmidt and Sinor (1986). In terms of interjudge reliability for the factors of musical originality and musical syntax, coefficients range from .53 to .78, with an average of .70. Internal reliability, measured in the form of Cronbach Alpha coefficients, ranges from .45 and .80, with an average of .69. Test-retest reliability indicates a range between .56 and .79, with an average of .76.

Content validity was established with a panel composed of music educators, composers, and psychologists. To help establish construct validity, the scoring factors from the first administration of the measure (Webster, 1983) were studied to determine feasibility of factor reduction. Factor analysis showed that each factor significantly contributed to two global factors that represented the theoretical existence of convergent and divergent thinking. Some concurrent validity data exist in the form of significant correlations between music teacher ratings of divergent thinking and scores on the MCTM, although this has not been investigated extensively. All of the studies have shown a lack of correlation between measures of music aptitude and the MCTM, demonstrating that the MCTM is not assessing the same abilities as those shown by musical aptitude tests. Baltzer's work (1990) confirmed much of this information, but did not find factor analysis results that supported the presence of the two global factors of convergent and divergent behavior in the MCTM. As with the Wang measure, more research and revision are needed with the MCTM in order to improve its ease of use, scoring scheme, construct validity, and overall reliability before publication is warranted. The MCTM is made available in unpublished form to any researcher or practitioner who is interested in its use.

Content Analysis

Composition—Product The formal assessment of children's compositions and their musical characteristics has received surprisingly little attention. What work we do have is largely limited to monophonic composition. Advances in computer and sound technology as well as software development may well change this situation dramatically in coming years.

Dorothea Doig's work (1941, 1942a,b) has historical significance for its systematic reporting of experiments in group composition long before any heritage of such research. Working with children between the ages of 6 and 16, she was interested in how children compose music before formal training. In classes arranged by age group, Doig encouraged children to generate melodic phrases individually and then asked the group to vote on those that seemed best—a kind of composition by committee. For the three research reports, the songs were notated by Doig, then analyzed in terms of rhythmic, melodic, and structural characteristics. Tabular data on intervals, nonharmonic tones, phrase structure, key, mode, and range used were presented in each of the three studies, as well as musical examples. She made general conclusions about developmental patterns across ages, but it is difficult to interpret these results given that the music was constructed in groups rather than individually. Doig was also the only judge of the compositions, and it is unclear exactly how she as a teacher might have influenced the final products. Nevertheless, the assessment techniques used are of interest, especially to present-day practitioners who may be interested in experimenting with group composition.

A key research study on children's compositional products was reported by John Kratus (1985). Subjects included 80 children aged 5 to 13 drawn from a sample of volunteers who represented a variety of school settings. Kratus was interested in the developmental nature of children's original compositions, in this case melodies composed on a handheld electronic keyboard. Of special interest were the rhythmic and melodic patterns, rhythmic and melodic motives, and phrase characteristics of music of 5-, 7-, 11-, and 13-year-olds. Kratus engaged subjects individually and used a gamelike format. After a period of experimentation with the small keyboard, he asked each subject to create a "song" that sounded good to him or her. The restrictions were that the melody use only the white keys and that the first pitches be C, D, and E. Kratus reasoned that, although the restrictions did place some constraints on the subjects' creative materials, some framework such as this was needed for initiating the task and for helping to structure meaningful assessment. Such an approach is also consistent with many tasks designed by professional composition teachers and by classroom teachers who work with children. The subjects in this study were given 10 to 12 minutes to complete the melodies. If any finished early, the researcher would encourage continued work, but did not force the subject to go on. At the end of the time period, the melodies were tape-recorded. Subjects were asked to perform the melody once, and then a second time, in order to determine whether the work was really composed or improvised.

Analysis of the data involved measurement of task variables such as the ability to replicate the melodies and melody length, as well as the assessment of 21 music content variables related to the use of rhythm, melody, motive, and phrase. Examples included (1) motivic strength, (2) tonal strength, (3) melodic and rhythmic motion, and (4) phrase repetition and development. The definition of and justification for these variables were supported by a review of important writings in music theory and the psychology of music. A mixture of five-point rating scales (with each point defined separately) and dichotomous scales was used. Two independent judges rated those variables that demanded subjective judgment. Transcriptions of the melodies (pitch levels only) and the audiotapes were given to the judges. Interjudge reliability ranged from .55 to .88. The results demonstrated significant developmental differences on ratings of tempo stability, metric strength, tonal stability and finality, melodic motivic development, and rhythmic motivic repetition.

Such systematic work is important for understanding children's musical thinking and its development over time. Research of this sort helps practitioners understand what to expect in the classroom and provides benchmarks for comparison. This, in turn, adds to our ability to assess musical growth more completely than if one were to use only standardized tests of convergent musical ability.

Before leaving this category, mention should be made of a report in the British literature by Brian Loane (1984). This study, and those by Swanwick and Tillman (1986), Davies (1986), Bunting (1987), and Simmonds (1988) are examples of a long-standing interest of the British music education community in the topic of creative thinking in music and its assessment. Curricula initiatives that encourage creative teaching strategies have inspired practitioners and researchers in Britain to make important contributions to the literature.

Loane's study presented an analysis of music composed by 11- to 14-year-old children with a variety of musical backgrounds. Nine compositions are discussed and an accompanying audiotape—an impressive inclusion by the publishers of the journal—provides original performances of the children's music to supplement the notation in the study. The compositions discussed are of varying lengths and complexities.

Although a detailed analysis according to predefined musical constructs as noted in Kratus's work was not in evidence here, the author did offer many thoughtful comments on the musical structure in relation to the cultural environment of the children. For example, the influence of pop and rock music was noted in the use of musical materials and text choice. Because Loane was also the music teacher of the children, he was able to comment on the use of musical materials in terms of his own teaching strategies. This allowed a level of descriptive analysis that is at once rich with musical detail and revealing of idiosyncratic approaches. Loane's descriptions were also marked by their speculation about the affective state of the music. Because he was in a position to know the children themselves as well as their creative efforts, he was able to observe what he understood to be the embodiment of feeling in their musical gestures. This feature makes the report quite unusual in the literature and, as some might see it, ahead of its time in its attention to both cognition and affect.

Composition—Process Doig, Kratus, Loane, and others have completed studies on the actual product of composition. There also has been recent work on the assessment of process, largely using observational data and interview. Much of this work is oriented toward case study, although some studies have been done with larger groups. A few research efforts in this category, such as the one by DeLorenzo (1987), share important implications for the growing literature in critical thinking in music. The reader is referred to Chapter 43.

Jeanne Bamberger (1977) experimented with a computer-based composition system (long before current technology) as a means for studying decision-making processes in melody writing. Using two untrained college-aged students as subjects, she was interested in how an individual's mental representation of a melody was created and changed during the creative process. The subjects "wrote" melodies by typing characters on the keyboard of a computer, which, in turn, played five "tune blocks" on a small synthesizer next to the subject. No visual cues were used. Each tune block contained no more than six diatonic pitches, had simple quarter and eighth note rhythms, and ventured no larger an interval than a perfect fourth. The task was simply to experiment with the serial order of the tune blocks and arrive at a suitable melody. The blocks could be arranged in any order and used more than once.

Bamberger provided a detailed description (protocol analysis) of all the actions and words of the two subjects as they arrived at their preferred order. An analysis was given of what the actions might mean in terms of mental function. For example, she noted differences in composing strategies, with one student using careful exploration while the other was very impulsive in exploring sound. The way each student used the keyboard also revealed the ability of each to represent internally, or "think in sound." Bamberger was also able to draw several conclusions about the underlying rhythmic structures that were peculiar to each solution by noting the changes made in the use of each tune block.

This use of computer technology as an aid to the assessment of mental processes in composition is remarkable for its time. Recent advances in technology should make this kind of study commonplace in coming years.

In addition to his work on products, Kratus (1989) has also completed work focusing on process. In this study, 60 children were tested using the same hand-held keyboard under similar testing conditions. Kratus recorded not the resultant composition, but the actual 10-minute experimentation that led to the composition. The purpose of this study was to examine how the rehearsal time was used in terms of exploration, repetition, and development of musical materials. Amount of silence used was also of interest. The assessment technique required independent judges to evaluate each 5 seconds of elapsed time in the 10-minute time period in terms of how it was used by the subject. Interjudge reliabilities ranged from .76 to .99. Results indicated distinct differences in the use of musical material with respect to age. This research represents an interesting and meaningful application of assessment techniques used in time management and teaching style research to content analysis in composition. Similar approaches can be imagined with improvisation as well.

In a recent study, Kratus (in press) studied the compositional strategies used by children to compose a melody. Again, 60 children between the ages of 7 and 11 were asked to compose melodies on an electronic keyboard. Two judges listened to tapes of subjects' melodies and rated the "success" of the melodies on a seven-point scale. Success was defined by musical craftsmanship and the ability of the child to replicate the melody. Another set of three judges listened to tapes of the composing periods for the 10 highest and 10 lowest rated songs and completed a content analysis of compositional strategies. This analysis involved the evaluation of each 2-minute interval according to 11 compositional strategies. Strategies included the use of stepping and skipping movement, changes in pitch and rhythm patterns, and repetition of musical ideas. Interjudge reliabilities for all assessment tasks ranged from .77 to .88. Results indicated that children who composed the most successful songs were found to use a variety of exploring, developing, and repeating strategies and also tended to converge on a final solution early in the 10-minute period. Such results are intriguing and hold special promise for a developing theory of creative aptitude in music and for the teaching of compositional process.

Another descriptive study from the British literature is important to include. Robert Bunting (1987) presented a detailed account of three composition projects by two of his fifth-year high school students. The assessment approach here was to present final products together with sketches and fragments that led to the final products. Bunting focused on the musical development of each student while engaged in composition and includes details regarding his interactions with the students and the effect on the compositional process.

For instance, Bunting described the first extended composition assignment of one student who chose to complete a work for bass guitar. The author kept audio records of each sketch and intervened if any phase of the composition process required encouragement. Bunting explained that, at one point, the student's choice of chords was quite limited and not necessarily in context with the key structure. It was unclear if this was because of some desired effect or because the more likely chords were harder to play on the instrument. He described his process of suggesting and teaching the newer chords and notes the results on the final project. It is clear from his descriptions that students made the final choice and that the teacher's suggestions were just that. Again, the journal in which the article appeared published an accompanying tape recording that provided the reader with a clearer picture of the compositions and the creative process that led to them. Bunting concluded his article by asking the following questions that might aid in the assessment of students' creative work:

—what resources of skill and musical experience has the pupil drawn on in composing?
—to what extent has the pupil learned to recognise and avoid mechanical responses, to find the expressive meaning of his materials?
—what exploratory composition processes has the pupil learned to use and with what results?
—to what extent has the pupil learned to articulate his own musical style?
—to what extent can the pupil control the process of individual composition independently of the teacher?
—to what extent can the pupil appraise his own work, development and future needs? (1987, p. 52)

Although Bunting is not a professional researcher in the traditional sense, his work is worth noting. It is also a model of how research can be significantly enhanced by practitioners who are willing to write thoughtfully and carefully about what they observe.

Improvisation—Product Research designed to study improvisation is often difficult to categorize as product or process oriented, and when younger children are subjects, tasks often resemble those in psychometric research. Product studies have used audiotape and independent judges in similar fashion to composition research.

FLOHR. John Flohr has reported two studies on the systematic evaluation of children's improvisations. The first work (Flohr, 1979) involved 4-, 6-, and 8-year-old children in an analysis of improvisations using a two-octave Orff xylophone with a pentatonic scale. Twelve subjects (four children from each age group) met with the researcher for 10 individual 15-minute sessions. The subjects were allowed to (1) freely explore the instrument; (2) participate in guided exploration involving a series of tasks that used melodic and rhythmic echoes, imitation of concrete sounds, given emotions, and musical dialogs; and (3) improvise a melody while the researcher played a simple ostinato on another xylophone. Data analyzed included audio recordings of the sessions, descriptive notes of the researcher, and musical transcriptions of the improvisations. The study was not designed for generalizability and was presented as a series of 12 case studies. The second reported study (Flohr, 1985) was similar in method, but included data on 10 children between the ages of 2 and 5 over a 4-year period. Valuable longitudinal results were reported, leading the author to speculate on developmental stages of improvisational ability.

Results of this work and other studies in this category point to a measurable change in the treatment of musical materials. It seems clear that carefully documented study of improvisations can lead to a better understanding of the musical mind, especially if merged with the more specialized findings in jazz and ethnomusicology. All of the findings are quite tentative and require replication with larger samples.

Improvisation—Process Study of the processes used by children to improvise generally involve careful observation of how materials are manipulated during improvisation and interviews with subjects after the improvisation to determine thought processes involved. There is a strong tendency to endorse naturalistic research techniques in this category, using audio and/or video recordings, field notes, structured and unstructured interview techniques, and other records as sources of assessment.

POND AND THE PILLSBURY FOUNDATION SCHOOL. Perhaps the most well-known series of studies in this category are those associated with the Pillsbury Foundation School in Santa Barbara, California, which operated from 1937 to 1948. These studies are often cited, not so much for their quality of research technique or the richness of their findings, but because they were executed long before the current interest in ethnographic research and in the systematic study of creative thinking in music. The original studies were published from 1941 to 1951 and were reprinted more recently (Moorhead and Pond, 1978). Pond, who was a major force behind the research itself, has reported in retrospect on the studies (Pond, 1981). The school's archives were donated in 1977 to the Music Educators National Conference History Center at the University of Maryland (Wilson, 1981).

In today's terms, the Pillsbury Foundation School would likely be described as a kind of day-care center with a strong music curriculum. According to Wilson's evaluation of records and oral history data (Wilson, 1981, pp. 16–19), its enrollment numbered between 10 and 20 students ranging in age from 1 to 8 years. Some children stayed for only a short time, while others were in residence for a year or two. There was a minimum of structured activity, leaving a great deal of time for free exploration of whatever materials were at hand, including much attention to music.

Pond, a composer by training and disposition, was employed for 8 years (1937–1944) as the school's music director. He began his work with no defined procedures, equipped only with an intense desire to see how children naturally developed musically. His notion was simply to put the children together with a number of unusual oriental musical instruments (bells, xylophones, gongs, drums) and watch what occurred. He intervened only to answer questions or to participate in music making if asked to by the children. Pond reported:

Everything about this research was completely *ad hoc*, completely empirical. It had to be. I had to live, as the saying goes, from hand to mouth. When the researcher knows precisely what he wants to find out (whether, for example, a child can tell the difference between a major and a minor third) he can devise testing procedures. But although I knew there were many things I wanted to learn, I could only learn them from the children, from their spontaneous behaviors; because had I created any kind of artificial situation to inveigle them into telling me something, what they told me would itself had been artificial, and therefore useless. So, carrying on this research was rather like putting together a jigsaw puzzle without knowing what the completed picture was supposed to look like. Such a project takes persistence, acuteness of perception and ability to reason, and, perhaps above all, creative imagination. (1981, pp. 6–7)

Conclusions drawn from this research included (1) observations about timbre and its triggering of curiosity about sound; (2) distinctions between original song and chant, each with its own musical characteristics; (3) and observations about rhythmic complexity and formal properties. By contemporary standards, the reporting of both the methodology and the results seems at times to be unclear and difficult to interpret. The spirit of the research, however, is clear, and the approach to the assessment of creative thinking serves as an important model.

COHEN. One modern study that used Pond's work as a point of departure was reported by Veronica Cohen (1980). Using many of the naturalistic techniques of Pond but with modern videotape technology, Cohen observed a kindergarten setting that featured a "music center" that was open for children to visit during certain times of the day. Cohen spent 3 years observing this activity, both through actual participation with the children and by videotaping behind one-way glass. From this work, Cohen focused attention on two children for more intensive interaction and observation. Her data included observational data as well as personal interviews. She formed conclusions that center around (1) exploration of instruments, musical elements, and relationships between sounds; (2) practice toward the mastery of certain skills, and (3) what Cohen called the production of musical gestures.

Unlike the Pond work, Cohen's provided rich detail about the behavior of the children and did so with an overview as to where the behavior might fit in the mosaic of mental rep-

resentation and process. The assessment approach was clearly enlightened by more than just behavioral reporting. Her many videotape observations of children producing sounds on instruments, for example, suggested that the experience was not just aural but visual, kinesthetic, and tactile as well and that meaningful evaluation of children's work must include this fact. In reporting on the mastery concept, Cohen described fascinating sequences in which children try to match or re-create the musical utterances of their peers—working doggedly at the task with unusual determination until the exact pitches and rhythms are found. One can sense the child's mind struggling with the mental sound image that was retained in memory.

A most important part of Cohen's work was the discussion of musical gesture—a musical idea that may comprise a few notes or a longer musical entity. She attempted to document these gestures and to tie them to evolving mental schemata. In so doing, the researcher brought to the study of musical play in children the very ideas that drive some of the contemporary theories of adult music, including such concepts as surface and deep structure. What is important for this chapter is that she accomplishes this thoughtful assessment of creative thinking by intense observation and interaction with the improvisation process.

Analysis/Learning—Product and Process The concept of "creative" analysis and listening has not been developed in the research literature to any extent, although the practical and theoretical literature often refers to notions of imaginative or divergent listening skills and creative approaches to written analysis (especially in terms of twentieth-century musical languages). Two studies are worthy of close attention, however, and each is a candidate for extension in future research agendas. Each has much to offer assessment.

FEINBERG. The Saul Feinberg study (1973) and a later practical article (1974) argued for an application of creative assessment concepts such as fluency and flexibility of thought to the context of music listening. He presented a theoretical platform for considering music listening in a problem-solving context and included a three-phase model that has close ties with the stages of creative thinking first suggested by Wallas (1926; see above). The concluding section of Feinberg's study demonstrated the application of these ideas to real examples of creative listening. For example, considering the notion of flexibility in music listening, Feinberg writes:

1. After listening to the following composition ["Chester" from Schuman's *New England Triptych*], make up a series of questions that you think relate to what you heard. Remember, the more areas you touch on in your questions, the more flexibly you are thinking.
2. While listening to the following work [the second movement of Hindemith's *Symphonic Metamorphosis of Themes by Weber*], place a check after any of the music qualities listed on your "Aural Flexibility List" . . . whenever they reappear in the music. Each section will be indicated to you. Don't get "stuck" on any one quality.

3. After listening to two different recordings of the same composition [the finale from Bartok's *Concerto for Orchestra*], describe what you think the second conductor did that was different from what the first conductor did. Which version did you find more satisfying? Why? (1974, p. 56)

The "aural flexibilty list" that is mentioned in task 2 above is simply a list of musical qualities such as "change in tempo" or "thick dissonant chords" next to which are several boxes that represent sections of music in serial order. Other example tasks are explained, and accompanying worksheets are included. The implication for assessment is clear for both research and practice.

PFEIL. The other study in this category focused on both the process and the product of creative listening and analysis, but has special meaning for product. Dealing primarily with college-aged students in a "music appreciation" class setting, Clifford Pfeil (1972) held firmly to the belief that traditional courses on this topic attempt to develop listening and analysis skills by the acquisition of a vocabulary of musical elements and events. Students' progress is often tested by their ability to supply a detailed commentary on these events, without much real thinking about them. Pfeil maintained that the fallacy here is the limitation of student experience and expression and the channeling of the listening activity to encourage passivity and discourage questioning and doing. The encouragement of divergent thinking, self-evaluation of one's own ideas, sensitivity to one's environment, and openness to elaboration and discovery should more clearly be the goals.

Pfeil describes several interesting exercises that attempted to involve students in creative thinking on many levels. For example, one improvisation activity that led to creative analytical thinking follows:

Situation: The class members sit in a circle surrounding a tape recorder. Each person decides on one body or voice sound as his property. The piece is performed by the class members making their sounds in rotation once around the circle.
Purpose: To make an interesting collage of sounds. The piece was taped and played back, and the question posed: how can this be made more interesting? The students, who had become acquainted with the principles of deferred judgment suggested many problems and solutions. Problems were listed first, then each problem was considered in turn for solutions. (1972, pp. 91–92.)

Other exercises suggested ways that concepts of notation might be approached. Great use was made of original notation in a number of tasks. Still other experiments involved students with compositional activities surrounding specific musical elements such as timbre and articulation. One large-scale project took the form of a notated composition for orchestra. Simple verbal descriptions were made more accurate and translated to score for actual performance by an ensemble.

Of special interest was the inclusion of a test of creative thinking in sound that employed no traditional notation. The purpose of the measure was to help evaluate the effective-ness of the creative approach to listening and analysis that the author had advocated in class. With the "real world" assessment of the products of meaningful listening/analysis in mind, Pfeil designed the measure using the Guilford factors of intellect for scoring. Task I, for instance, presented a three-stave composition using graphic notation together with the following task description:

Imagine that you have a small band with very limited abilities. . . . Following is a score for your ensemble. The sax player reads left to right across the top space, the trumpet player across the middle space, and the drummer across the bottom space. Each one plays his instrument when a line appears in his space, but is silent when no line appears. As you can see, the piece begins with a saxophone and trumpet playing together, and the drummer silent. Then for a short time, every one is silent. The piece lasts about 25 seconds.
A. Study the score, try to imagine how it sounds, then list as many things about it that you do *not* like as you can.
B. In the blank score below, write a new piece observing the previously mentioned limitations of your band. (1972, pp. 156–157)

These tasks are evaluated for sensitivity to problems (defined as a function of the ability to sense a musical problem in a given notational structure), elaboration, and originality. Another task presented the subject with an electrical wiring diagram and asked the subject to imagine it as a score and to comment on what it might sound like.

Although the measure is based in large part on imagined sound combinations in a composition framework, it attempts to assess the actual result of both divergent and convergent thinking in a music listening/analysis context. It clearly can be applied and adapted to other settings and can be used as a criterion-referenced measure.

FUTURE CONSIDERATIONS

This chapter has summarized important studies in the music education research literature that seem representative of this vital topic. It is relatively young work—tentative, experimental, in need of replication and expansion. It can be said with some confidence that creative thinking in music is a definable and measurable entity that should not be confused with traditional music aptitude, performance achievement, general intelligence, or academic ability. Although there are multiple approaches to these definitions and assessment techniques, few would argue that this is necessarily bad. There is a common core of ideas that unifies this young literature, including (1) focus on mental abilities such as divergent and convergent thinking, thinking "in sound" and mental schemata, (2) personality traits and personal styles of thinking, (3) developmental trends during growth from the young child to the young adult, and (4) stages of thought during the creative act.

What is needed to do to go further, to build on what we have accomplished so far? Certainly the ties to the general literature should be maintained and, in some unexplored areas, expanded. For example, personality and biographical inventories might well be investigated with music criteria, and new research on the environment, including cultural and social influences, should certainly be considered. The work with psychometric materials should be solidified with the publication and distribution of workable measures that can help in research design and in refining measurement and evaluation efforts in the schools. The content analysis work should continue, with special attention to joint research efforts by practicing teachers and professional researchers as they study the actual products and mental processes of our children.

Certainly there is little doubt that the computer, with peripheral sound devices and imaginative software, will need to play an increasing role. Examples of such studies include those by Conant (1988) and by Scripp, Meyaard, and Davidson (1988), which use the computer in a composition setting to study the processes of composition and relate what is observed to the emerging literature on creative thinking. This approach needs to be expanded to include systematic study of improvisation and listening/analysis and needs to be applied to the psychometric literature as an option for test administration.

Finally, *the* most important need that faces researchers interested in this topic is the development of better theory. Working theories of creative thinking give focus to assessment efforts, bring order to the many approaches to defini-

tion and technique and aid in assessment validity. Theoretical work is already in progress that has important implications for assessment. For instance, Swanwick and Tillman (1986) reported a theory of creative musical development based in part on their empirical work with children engaged in musical improvisation and on the writings of other development psychologists. Stages related to age were suggested, together with the belief that there is an internal movement within each stage from personal, egocentric thinking to more social, conventional thinking. Pressing (1988) published a complex theory of improvisation process that is more adult oriented and less developmental. He postulated the existence of "event clusters" that are strung together and that interact with certain cognitive structures. Lastly, Webster (1987a) speculated on creative music process and proposed a conceptual model that includes the interaction of enabling skills and conditions within a framework of divergent and convergent thinking driven by a product intention.

These theories, and others that may follow, are vital if any lasting progress is to be made. Any work in this field, whether it be theoretical, empirical, or practical, presents unusually difficult problems for the researcher and practitioner, yet a quest for solutions to these problems brings us to the very heart of our art form. Quite simply, it will demand the best efforts from the finest, most creative minds in our profession.

References

Ainsworth, J. (1970). Research project in creativity in music education. *Bulletin of the Council for Research in Music Education, 22,* 43–48.

Amabile, T. (1983). *The social psychology of creativity.* New York: Springer-Verlag.

Baltzer, S. (1988). A validation study of a measure of musical creativity. *Journal of Research in Music Education, 36*(4), 232–249.

Baltzer, S. (1990). A factor analytic study of musical creativity in children in the primary grades. Unpublished doctoral dissertation, Indiana University, Bloomington.

Bamberger, J. (1977). In search of a tune. In D. Perkins and B. Leondar, (Eds.), *The arts and cognition.* Baltimore: Johns Hopkins Press.

Barron, F. (1969). *Creative person and creative process.* New York: Holt, Rinehart & Winston.

Bloom, B. (1985). *Developing talent in young people.* New York: Ballantine.

Bloomberg, M. (Ed.). (1973). *Creativity: Theory and research.* New Haven: College & University Press.

Bunting, R. (1987). Composing music: Case studies in the teaching and learning process. *British Journal of Music Education, 4*(1), 25–52.

CMP 3. Experiments in musical creativity. (1966). Washington: Music Educators National Conference.

Csikszentmihalyi, M. (1988). Society, culture, and person: A system view of creativity. In R. Sternberg (Ed.), *The nature of creativity,* (pp. 325–339). New York: Cambridge University Press.

Coleman, S. (1922). *Creative music for children.* New York: Putnam.

Cohen, V. (1980). The emergence of musical gestures in kindergarten children. Unpublished doctoral dissertation, University of Illinois, Urbana.

Conant, B. (1988). A study of cognitive processes of children creating music in a computer learning environment. Unpublished doctoral dissertation, University of Massachusetts, Amherst.

Dallman, R. (1979). A survey of creativity in music through composition in elementary schools of Colorado. Unpublished doctoral dissertation, University of Northern Colorado, Greeley.

Davidson, L., and Welsh, P. (1988). From collections to structure: The developmental path of tonal thinking. In J. Sloboda, (Ed.), *Generative processes in music: The psychology of performance, improvisation and composition* (pp. 260–285). New York: Oxford.

Davis, C. (1986). Say it till a song comes (reflections on songs invented by children 3–13). *British Journal of Research in Music Education, 3*(3), 279–293.

Davis, G. (1986). *Creativity is forever.* Dubuque: Kendall/Hunt.

DeLorenzo, L. (1987). An exploratory field of sixth grade students' creative music problem solving processes in the general music class. Unpublished doctoral dissertation, Teachers College, Columbia University.

DeLorenzo, L. (1989). A field study of sixth-grade students' creative music problem-solving processes. *Journal of Research in Music Education, 37*(3), 188–200.

Documentary report on the Ann Arbor Symposium on the Applications of Psychology to the Teaching and Learning of Music: Session III, Motivation and Creativity. (1983). Reston: Music Educators National Conference.

Doig, D. (1941). Creative music: I. Music composed for a given text. *Journal of Educational Research, 35,* 262–275.

Doig, D. (1942a). Creative music: II. Music composed on a given subject. *Journal of Educational Research, 35,* 344–355.

Doig, D. (1942b). Creative music: III. Music composed to illustrate given music problems. *Journal of Educational Research, 36,* 241–253.

Feinberg, S. (1973). A creative problem-solving approach to the development of perceptive music listening in the secondary school music literature class. Unpublished doctoral dissertation, Temple University, Philadelphia.

Feinberg, S. (1974). Creative problem-solving and the music listening experience. *Music Educators Journal. 61*(1), 53–59.

Feldman, D. (1986). *Nature's gambit: Child prodigies and the development of human potential.* New York: Basic Books.

Flohr, J. (1979). Musical improvisation behavior of young children. Unpublished doctoral dissertation, University of Illinois, Urbana-Champaign.

Flohr, J. (1985). Young children's improvisations: Emerging creative thought. *The Creative Child and Adult Quarterly, 10*(2), 79–85.

Freundlich, D. (1978). The development of musical thinking: Case studies in improvisation. Unpublished doctoral dissertation, Harvard University, Cambridge.

Gardner, H. (1983). *Frames of mind: The theory of multiple intelligences.* New York: Basic Books.

Gardner, H. (1985). *The mind's new science.* New York: Basic Books.

Gardner, H. (1989). *To open minds.* New York: Basic Books.

Goodman, N. (1976). *Languages of art: An approach to a theory of symbols.* Indianapolis: Hackett Publishing.

Gorder, W. (1976). An investigation of divergent production abilities as constructs of musical creativity. Unpublished doctoral dissertation, University of Illinois.

Gorder, W. (1980). Divergent production abilities as constructs of musical creativity. *Journal of Research in Music Education, 28*(1), 34–42.

Guilford, J. (1950). Creativity. *American Psychologist, 5,* 444–454.

Guilford, J. (1967). *The nature of human intelligence.* New York: McGraw-Hill.

Hargreaves, D. (1986). *The developmental psychology of music.* Cambridge: Cambridge University Press.

Hounchell, R. (1985). A study of creativity and music reading as objectives of music education as contained in statements in the "Music Educators Journal" from 1914 to 1970. Unpublished doctoral dissertation, Indiana University, Bloomington.

John-Steiner, V. (1985). *Notebooks of the mind.* New York: Harper & Row.

Johnson-Laird, P. (1988). Freedom and constraint in creativity. In R. Sternberg (Ed.), *The nature of creativity* (pp. 202–219). New York: Cambridge University Press.

Kalmar, M., and Balasko, G. (1987). "Musical mother tongue" and creativity in preschool children's melody improvisations. *Bulletin of the Council for Research in Music Education,* 91, 77–86.

Kratus, J. (1985). Rhythm, melody, motive, and phrase characteristics of original songs by children aged five to thirteen. Unpublished doctoral dissertation, Northwestern University, Evanston.

Kratus, J. (1985). The use of melodic and rhythmic motives in the original songs of children aged 5 to 13. *Contributions to Music Education, 12,* 1–8.

Kratus, J. (1989). A time analysis of the compositional processes used by children ages 7 to 11. *Journal of Research in Music Education, 37*(1), 5–20.

Kratus, J. (In press). Characterization of the compositional strategies used by children to compose a melody. Paper presented at the Thirteenth International Society of Music Education Research Seminar, Stockholm, Sweden (July, 1990).

Laczó, Z. (1981). A psychological investigation of improvisation abil-

ities in the lower and higher classes of elementary school. *Bulletin of the Council for Research in Music Education,* 66–67, 39–45.

Loane, B. (1984). Thinking about children's compositions. *British Journal of Music Education, 1*(3), 205–231.

MacKinnon, D. (1965). Personality and the realization of creative potential. *American Psychologist, 20,* 273–281.

Morgan, H. (Ed.). (1947). *Music Education Source Book,* Washington: Music Educators National Conference.

Moorhead, G., and Pond, D. (1978). *Music for young children.* Santa Barbara: Pillsbury Foundation for the Advancement of Music Education. (Reprinted from the 1941–1951 editions.)

Oehrle, E. (1984). A case for creativity in elementary music education. Unpublished doctoral dissertation, University of Natal (South Africa), Pietermaritzbury-Durban.

Pfeil, C. (1972). Creativity as an instructional mode for introducing music to non-music majors at the college level. Unpublished doctoral dissertation, Michigan State University, East Lansing.

Pond, D. (1981). A composer's study of young children's innate musicality. *Bulletin of the Council for Research in Music Education, 68,* 1–12.

Pressing, J. (1988). Improvisation: Methods and models. In J. Sloboda (Ed.), *Generative processes in music: The psychology of performance, improvisation and composition* (pp. 129–178). New York: Oxford.

Prevel, M. (1979). Emergent patterning in children's musical improvisations. *Canadian Music Educator. 15,* 13–15.

Reimer, B. (1989). *A philosophy of music education* (2nd ed.). Englewood Cliffs: Prentice-Hall.

Richardson, C. (1983). Creativity research in music education: A review. *Bulletin of the Council for Research in Music Education. 74,* 1–21.

Rimm, S., and Davis, G. (1980). Five years of international research with GIFT: An instrument for the identification of creativity. *Journal of Creative Behavior, 14,* 35–46.

Rothenberg, A., and Hausman, C. (1976). *The creativity question.* Durham: Duke University Press.

Schmidt, C., and Sinor, J. (1986). An investigation of the relationships among music audiation, musical creativity, and cognitive style. *Journal of Research in Music Education. 34*(3), 160–172.

Scripp, L., Meyaard, J., and Davidson, L. (1988). Discerning musical development: Using computers to discover what we know. *Journal of Aesthetic Education, 22*(1), pp. 75–88.

Shank, R. (1988). Creativity as a mechanical process. In R. Sternberg (Ed.), *The nature of creativity* (pp. 230–238). New York: Cambridge University Press.

Simmonds, R. (1988). An experiment in the assessment of composition. *British Journal of Music Education, 5*(1), 21–34.

Simonton, R. (1980). Thematic fame and melodic originality in classical music: A multivariate computer-content analysis. *Journal of Personality, 48,* 206–219.

Sloboda, J. (1985). *The musical mind.* New York: Oxford University Press.

Sloboda, J. (Ed). (1988). *Generative processes in music.* New York: Oxford University Press.

Sternberg, R. (Ed.), (1988). *The nature of creativity.* New York: Cambridge University Press.

Swanner, D. (1985). Relationships between musical creativity and selected factors including personality, motivation, musical aptitude and cognitive intelligence as measured in third grade children. Unpublished doctoral dissertation, Case Western Reserve University, Cleveland.

Swanwick, K., and Tillman, J. (1986). The sequence of musical development: A study of children's composition. *British Journal of Music Education, 3*(3), 305–339.

Tardif, T., and Sternberg, R. (1988). What do we know about creativity? In R. Sternberg (Ed.), *The nature of creativity* (pp. 429–440). New York: Cambridge University Press.

Thomas, R. (1970). *Manhattanville Music Curriculum Program: Final report* (Report No. BR6-1999). Purchase: Manhattanville College of the Sacred Heart. (ERIC Document Reproduction Service No. Ed 045 865)

Torrance, E. (1966). *Norms-technical manual: Torrance tests of creative thinking*. Bensenville: Scholastic Testing Service.

Torrance, E. (1973). *Thinking creatively in sound and words*. Bensenville: Scholastic Testing Service.

Torrance, E. (1981). *Thinking creatively in action and movement*. Bensenville: Scholastic Testing Service.

Vaughan, M. (1977). Musical creativity: Its cultivation and measurement. *Bulletin of the Council for Research in Music Education, 50*, 72–77.

Vold, J. (1986). A study of musical problem solving behavior in kindergarten children and a comparison with other aspects of creative behavior. Unpublished doctoral dissertation, University of Alabama, Tuscaloosa.

Wallach, M., and Kogan, N. (1965). *Modes of thinking in young children*. New York: Holt, Rinehart & Winston.

Wallas, G. (1926). *The art of thought*. New York: Harcourt, Brace.

Webster, P. (1977). A factor of intellect approach to creative thinking in music. Unpublished doctoral dissertation, Eastman School of Music, University of Rochester, Rochester.

Webster, P. (1979). Relationship between creative behavior in music and selected variables as measured in high school students. *Journal of Research in Music Education, 27*(4), 227–242.

Webster, P. (1983). An assessment of musical imagination in young children: Technical Report. In P. Tallarico (Ed.), *Contributions to symposium/83: the Bowling Green State University symposium on music teaching & research* (pp. 100–123). Bowling Green: Bowling Green State University.

Webster, P. (1987a). Conceptual bases for creative thinking in music. In J. Peery, I. Peery, and T. Draper (Eds.), *Music and child development* (pp. 158–174). New York: Springer-Verlag.

Webster, P. (1987b). Refinement of a measure of creative thinking in music. In C. Madsen and C. Prickett (Eds.), *Applications of research in music behavior* (pp. 257–271) Tuscaloosa: University of Alabama Press.

Webster, P. (1988a). Creative thinking in music: Approaches to research. In J. Gates (Ed.), *Music education in the United States: Contemporary issues* (pp. 66–81) Tuscaloosa: University of Alabama Press.

Webster, P. (1988b). New perspectives on music aptitude and achievement. *Psychomusicology, 7*(2), 177–194.

Webster, P. (1990). Creativity as creative thinking. *Music Educators Journal, 76*(9), pp. 22–28.

Weisberg, R. (1986). *Creativity, genius and other myths*. New York: Freeman.

Wilson, B. (1981). Implications of the Pillsbury Foundation School of Santa Barbara in perspective. *Bulletin of the Council for Research in Music Education, 68*, 13–25.

Winner, E. (1982). *Invented worlds: The psychology of the arts*. Cambridge: Harvard University Press.

Wolf, D. (1988). Opening up assessment. *Educational Leadership, 45*(4), 24–29.

·18·

CURRICULUM AND PROGRAM EVALUATION

Paul R. Lehman
UNIVERSITY OF MICHIGAN

In 1837 the Boston school board voted to introduce music into the curriculum of the public schools, but the city council failed to appropriate the necessary funds. Lowell Mason agreed to teach at the Hawes School on a trial basis for a year without salary, and at the end of the year the mayor asked the masters of the school for a report on the success of Mason's program. The masters responded:

In reply to your communication, allow us briefly to state that any very positive and splendid results from the introduction of vocal music into the Hawes School cannot yet be reasonably expected, so short has been the time since the first lesson was given and so interrupted have the lessons been. Still, however, enough has, in our estimation, been already accomplished to warrant the belief of the great utility of vocal music as a branch of public instruction. One thing has been made evident, that the musical ear is more common than has been generally supposed. There are but few in the school who make palpable discords when all are singing. Many who at the outset of the experiment believed they had neither ear or voice now sing with confidence and considerable accuracy, and others who could hardly tell one sound from another now sing the scale with ease—sufficiently proving that the musical susceptibility is in a good degree improvable. The alacrity with which the lesson is entered upon and the universal attention with which it is received are among its great recommendations; they show that the children are agreeably employed. . . . We have never known when . . . they were not glad to remain a half-hour or more to pursue the exercise after the regular hours of session. They prefer the play of a hard musical lesson to any out-of-door sports; of course understanding that there are some exceptions. Of the great moral effect of vocal music there can be no question. A song introduced in the middle of the session has been invariabl[y] followed with excellent effect. It is a relief to the wearisomeness of constant study. It excites the listless and calms the turbulent and uneasy. It seems to renerve the mind and prepare all for more vigorous intellectual action.

It is delightful to see how spontaneously a chorus will spring up in any accidental collection of the pupils about the school house, and how soon five will increase to ten and ten to twenty—all tranquil yet intensely happy. How much still, refined enjoyment, accompanied as it is with moderate physical exertion, is to be occasionally preferred to constant, boisterous, over-heating, and sometimes dangerous play. . . . That the music is an attraction is evident from the increased attendance of the pupils on the days of the lessons.

The advantages to be gained from instructing children in vocal music are of little consequence when considered in connection with a school compared with those which are more remote and far less perceptible—such as bear upon their characters, employments, and recreations in after years—upon their condition as social and domestic beings; but with these we have nothing to do.

This brief notice of the results of so important a step in public education is, we are aware, very insufficient—but we hardly know how to go into details; nor indeed have we time to enter upon an elaborate comment. We can only thank you, Sir, for the high privilege which, by your means, we enjoy in having vocal music taught in our seminary. We have been equally delighted with the beautiful simplicity of the system upon which Mr. Mason instructs and with his own personal skill in teaching, and we trust that it will not be for long before vocal music will be every where an essential branch of public instruction.

We are, dear Sir, respectfully
Your obedient servants,
Joseph Harrington, Jr.
John H. Harris
Hawes School, May 25, 1838
(quoted by Birge, 1928, pp. 50–52;
punctuation modernized)

This report represents the first known written evaluation of a music program in an American school. The program itself marks the beginning of formal music education in the public schools of the United States.

The report of Harrington and Harris reflects many of the characteristics of more recent efforts in program evaluation. It was requested near the end of the "experiment." It offered qualitative rather than quantitative results. It was informal. It emphasized judgments and anecdotal evidence. It stressed process but also dealt with outcomes, including ancillary effects. The objectives of the program had not been stated in behavioral terms, but the instruction was obviously considered of intrinsic worth to the evaluators. Apart from quaint language, the report sounds remarkably as though it could have been written during the late 1960s.

BACKGROUND

The term "program evaluation" as used in this chapter refers to the evaluation of curricular and extracurricular offerings sponsored by educational institutions. According to Popham, "systematic educational evaluation consists of a formal assessment of the worth of educational phenomena" (1975, p. 8). Program evaluation provides useful information for decision making. It may help to determine whether a program is achieving its goals, or, perhaps, what goals it is achieving. Evaluation may suggest ways of achieving goals more quickly, more easily, or with a smaller investment of time and funds. It may reveal whether program A is more effective than program B. It may also be used to provide a measure of accountability, to determine whether or not funds are being spent wisely, to locate the source of a perceived problem, to determine whether to continue or terminate a program, to assist in making desired changes, or merely to understand better the status quo.

Program evaluation should be used not simply to validate past instructional efforts but, more important, to shape future policy and directions. The ultimate purpose of program evaluation is to improve instruction. The evaluation of instructional programs should not be confused with the assessment of student learning, though student learning is perhaps the most important single outcome associated with effective programs. Similarly, the evaluation of faculty, textbooks, equipment, and schedules contributes to, but does not constitute, the evaluation of programs.

The history of program evaluation has been summarized by Madaus, Stufflebeam, and Scriven (1983). What is generally recognized as the first formal evaluation of an educational program in America occurred from 1887 to 1898 when Joseph Rice (1897) conducted a comparative study of the value of drill in spelling instruction. In 1949 Tyler established a program evaluation model that endured for almost 20 years when he asserted the following:

The process of evaluation is essentially the process of determining to what extent the education objectives are actually being realized. . . . [Since] the objectives aimed at are to produce certain desirable changes in the behavior patterns of the students, then evaluation is the process for determining the degree to which these changes in behavior are actually taking place. (p. 69)

The era of serious and systematic attention to program evaluation began with the National Defense Education Act, approved in 1958 in response to the Soviet sputnik launched in 1957. This legislation provided funds to improve curricula and instruction in mathematics, science, and foreign languages and, shortly thereafter, to evaluate the programs and projects that it supported. By far the most important impetus to program evaluation came with the massive financial support provided by the Elementary and Secondary Education Act of 1965 (ESEA) and the extensive and specific requirements for evaluation that were mandated by the Congress. Title I, which provided funds for compensatory programs for children from low-income families, required that each school district receiving funds evaluate annually the extent to which these programs had achieved their objectives. Title III, which supplied funds for exemplary programs and services not previously available, also required evaluation. A substantial number of the activities conducted under Title I and Title III included experiences in the arts, but there are no data documenting the role or the effect of music.

As evaluation came to be required in virtually every educational program funded by the federal government, it quickly became apparent that the tools and strategies available to evaluators were often not equal to the task. Everyone recognized that new techniques and new directions were needed, though there was little agreement about the precise details. The concern over program evaluation methodology was especially evident in reading, mathematics, science, and language arts because those were the fields of greatest emphasis, but there were similar difficulties in music.

Program evaluation during the late 1960s relied heavily on hypothesis testing. Evaluators soon discovered, however, that it was often impossible to establish experimental and control groups, and even when it was possible the effects were seldom found to be statistically significant. The major difficulty was a lack of suitable criterion measures. There were very few standardized tests of music achievement, and those that existed were not always valid for the purposes for which tests were needed because they did not measure the skills and knowledge typically sought in compensatory or innovative programs. Further, they were not normed for the populations to which the programs were directed. When new measurement instruments appropriate to the content were developed locally, their reliability and validity were not always investigated adequately.

Aside from the questionable appropriateness of the criterion measures, there were many other reasons why very few studies yielded statistically significant differences. Often the conditions did not satisfy the assumptions of the design. Sometimes the treatment period was too short. In some instances there was excessive turnover in student or faculty personnel. In other instances (1) the evaluation may have occurred too soon, (2) the evaluation may have failed to take into account important outcomes of the program, (3) despite claims to the contrary, the program may never truly have been implemented, (4) important effects may not have been revealed by the hard data collected but might have become apparent if soft data had been sought, or (5) differential effects on diverse student groups may have been masked when data were aggregated (Hill, 1986, pp. 45–53). The programs found to be successful tended to be those in which the objectives were clearly defined and measurable and for which there were satisfactory criterion measures.

Inability to demonstrate convincingly progress toward musical goals, whether primary or ancillary, was a constant source of frustration to music teachers. It was eventually recognized that hypothesis-testing techniques were generally unsuitable for evaluating ESEA programs. The thousands of ESEA programs were independently administered, and they had nothing in common except that they were intended to improve social conditions. The difficulties of evaluating such a diverse array of programs with such nonspecific aims have been described by Weiss and Rein (1983) and by Airasian (1983).

In the political arena, of course, these difficulties were routinely overlooked. The first annual report on ESEA Title I programs suggested that Title I was succeeding even beyond its supporters' highest expectations. No one pointed out initially that the evidence was all anecdotal and was based on an uncritical synthesis of the reports submitted by the 18,000 school districts and 50 states participating (McLaughlin, 1975). These reports were essentially public relations documents intended primarily to ensure continued funding. They tended to be extravagantly favorable. They were often laden with numbers but frequently did not stand up under scrutiny. In discussing the evaluation of government programs, Floden and Weiner suggest the following:

Evaluation may be seen as a ritual whose function is to calm the anxieties of the citizenry and to perpetuate an image of governmental rationality, efficacy, and accountability. The very act of requiring and commissioning evaluations may create the impression that government is seriously committed to the pursuit of publicly espoused goals, such as increasing student achievement or reducing malnutrition. Evaluations lend credence to this image even when the programs are created primarily to appease interest groups (1983, p. 185).

It has traditionally been assumed that insofar as possible evaluation should be divorced from political considerations and used only for educational purposes. In fact, neither the curriculum nor the funding mechanisms of schools can be insulated from the political process, and recently evaluators have recognized the need to cope with this reality. In their 1989 book *Fourth Generation Evaluation,* Guba and Lincoln stated, "We do not treat evaluation as a *scientific* process, because it is our conviction that to approach evaluation scientifically is to miss completely its fundamentally social, political, and value-oriented character" (p. 7).

It is obvious that other factors are often more important than evaluation in determining whether or how widely a particular curriculum is adopted. Systematic evaluation does not appear to have played a decisive role in the acceptance or rejection of any major curriculum in music.

Not only was it found to be extraordinarily difficult to document the results of short-term and innovative curriculum projects, but even the long-term benefits of education proved to be elusive. In their extensive and well-known study *Equality of Education Opportunity* in 1966, Coleman and his colleagues reported that "schools bring little influ-

ence to bear on a child's achievement that is independent of his background and general social context" (p. 325). Some researchers have argued on the basis of these findings that studying the effectiveness of educational programs is pointless because the effect of school variables is minor compared with the effect of family background variables. Others maintain that school effects are nevertheless important and that the influence of the school on student achievement is generally underestimated in the research literature. These conflicting claims are analyzed by Good and Brophy (1986) and by Madaus, Airasian, and Kallaghan (1980).

In recent years the U.S. Department of Education has published an annual *State Education Performance Chart* ("Wall Chart") providing comparative state-by-state data on various measures categorized as student performance, resource inputs, state reforms, and population characteristics. The purpose has been to furnish the public with objective data concerning the effectiveness of the nation's schools. Though extensively criticized on the grounds that it ignored important factors affecting education, the Wall Chart marked a sharp reversal from the view, widely held as recently as a decade earlier, that any direct comparisons between states or school districts were inherently unfair and unwarranted.

Beginning in the mid-1970s, program evaluation emerged as a distinct field of specialization related to, but separate from, research and testing. The literature in the field expanded greatly. Several new journals appeared: *Educational Evaluation and Policy Analysis, Evaluation Review, New Directions for Program Evaluation, Evaluation and Program Planning,* and *Curriculum Inquiry.* Division H of the American Educational Research Association, the American Evaluation Association, and other groups provided opportunities for the exchange of information among program evaluation specialists.

A number of centers were established for the study of evaluation, including program evaluation. These included the Center for the Study of Evaluation at UCLA; the Stanford Evaluation Consortium; the Center for Instructional Research and Curriculum Evaluation at the University of Illinois; the Evaluation Center at Western Michigan University; the Center for the Study of Testing, Evaluation and Educational Policy at Boston College; and the evaluation unit of the Northwest Regional Educational Laboratory (Madaus et al., 1983, p. 15).

MODELS, PARADIGMS, AND APPROACHES

In response to the demands for evaluation of federally funded programs, a variety of new models and paradigms were proposed beginning in the late 1960s. One of the earliest was Stake's (1967) countenance model, in which the evaluator organized possible data in a description matrix containing two columns labeled "intents" and "observations" and a judgment matrix containing columns labeled "standards" and "judgments." Each matrix contained three rows labeled "antecedents," "transactions," and "outcomes." The countenance model was subsequently incorporated in Stake's responsive evaluation model, described below.

Stufflebeam's (1983) CIPP (Context, Input, Process, Product) evaluation model, proposed in 1966, reflected the view that evaluation should focus on the decisions made as new curricula are developed. It was the first widely publicized model to call for evaluation on criteria other than objectives. Context evaluation involves assessment of the needs, problems, and opportunities, as well as of the intended ends. The methods are descriptive and comparative. Input evaluation compares the intended means of achieving the desired ends with the alternative means available. Again the task is largely comparative. Process evaluation monitors the congruence between the actual means and the intended means. Any discrepancies are noted and corrected. Product evaluation compares the actual ends with the intended ends. The emphasis is on the outcomes produced.

In 1967 Scriven drew a distinction between two types of evaluation he labeled formative and summative (pp. 40–43). Formative evaluation, he said, refers to assessing the worth of programs that are still in progress and still capable of being modified. It examines the planning, structure, content, and activities of the program. The emphasis is on making the program better as it proceeds. Summative evaluation refers to assessing the worth of a program that has been completed. It examines the products and the outcomes of the program. The emphasis is on helping users with decisions concerning the adoption or retention of an intact program. The distinction between formative and summative evaluations came to be widely accepted and has proved useful to music teachers as well as to program evaluators.

Observing that unintended effects may be as strong as or stronger than intended effects, Scriven, in 1973, proposed a startling new approach. He suggested that evaluation should disregard the stated objectives of the program entirely and concentrate on identifying the actual effects, which may be either beneficial or detrimental. Scriven's goal-free evaluation requires determining the effects and matching them against existing needs. A program is successful to the extent that it fulfills needs. By emphasizing the side effects of instruction, Scriven showed how evaluation can be helpful when a program does not fulfill its intended goals or when those goals are ill conceived.

The discrepancy evaluation model is based on determining the discrepancy between performance and a standard. The standard must be made explicit, a task requiring clarification of the goals of the program. To collect information about performance, questions are asked about what actually happened. Were the inputs that were supposed to have been available actually available? Did the processes that should have taken place actually take place? Were the anticipated outcomes actually realized? The fewer the discrepancies between the intent and the reality, or between the standard and what actually exists, the more successful the program has been. Examining the nature of the discrepancies can suggest ways to improve the program (Steinmetz, 1983).

As early as 1967, Eisner argued that overreliance on "high-level specification of objectives" is inappropriate for some subject matter and tends to distort the educational process. He distinguished between instructional objectives, which others have referred to as behavioral objectives, and expressive objectives, which he said identify the outcome of an educational activity but do not specify precisely what the student is to do (Eisner, 1969, pp. 14–18). An expressive objective, according to Eisner, identifies the results of "a situation in which children are to work, a problem with which they are to cope, a task in which they are to engage; but it does not specify what . . . they are to learn"(pp. 15–16). Expressive objectives provide an opportunity to explore phenomena, to focus on issues of special interest, and to use a diversity of approaches. In these circumstances neither programs nor individuals can be evaluated by applying a uniform standard to the products generated. What is required instead is reflection on what has been achieved in order to describe its uniqueness and its significance.

Eisner's connoisseurship and criticism model (1979, pp. 190–226; 1983) is derived from his views concerning objectives and is of special interest to music educators. The model is based upon judgments by the trained and experienced observer. The function of the evaluator is similar to that of the art or music critic: to provide a referentially adequate description of the phenomenon. The model has been criticized because different observers may arrive at different conclusions, but it represents a new perspective that has many applications in arts education. "What is the *educational* import or value of what is going on?" (1983, p. 343) Eisner asks. "How do the children participate? What is the quality of what they and the teacher have to say? . . . Is what they are learning worth their time and effort? And just what are they learning?" (p. 344)

Consistent with his earlier criticism of overemphasis on high-level specification of objectives, Eisner stresses two points:

First, the forms of evaluation that are now employed to assess the effectiveness of school programs have profound consequences upon the character of teaching, the content of curriculum, and the kinds of goals that schools seek to attain. Evaluation procedures, more than a reasoned philosophy of education, influence the educational priorities at work within the schools. Second, these evaluation procedures rest upon largely unexamined assumptions that are basically scientific in their epistemology, technological in their application, and have consequences that are often limited and at times inhospitable to the kinds of goals the arts can achieve. (1983, pp. 338–339)

According to Eisner, unless our current approaches to educational evaluation "can be expanded so that they attend to qualities of educational life relevant to the arts, it is not likely that the arts will secure a meaningful place in American schools" (1983, p. 335).

The controversy between quantitative evaluation, or evaluation based on numbers, and qualitative evaluation, or evaluation based on description, is summarized by Cronbach (1982, pp. 22–30) as a conflict between the "scientistic" and the humanistic ideals. The scientistic ideal is based on the true experiment, in which (1) there exist two or more conditions, at least one of which is the result of direct intervention, (2) the individuals or groups are assigned to conditions randomly, and (3) all participants are assessed on the same outcome variables. Internal validity as described by Campbell and Stanley (1963, pp. 5, 23–24) is essential. Humanistic evaluation, at the other extreme, makes no attempt to manipulate or control but seeks merely to assess the events that take place. The program is viewed through the eyes of its users and its developers. The questions asked are those most appropriate to the particular program, not standard questions asked of all programs. The benefits are described rather than quantified. The final report is intended, above all, to be responsive to local needs and interests. Fundamentally, the controversy reflects a disagreement over whether the laboratory or the real world provides the more useful source of information to guide decision making.

Even the strongest advocates of the opposing schools recognize that neither quantitative nor qualitative evaluation is comprehensive and sufficient in itself, and there is increasing evidence that a reconciliation of these views is not only possible but probable (Cronbach, 1982, pp. 26–30; House, 1986, p. 8; Koppelman, 1983). Meanwhile, qualitative techniques can often play a useful role in the assessment of programs in arts education, particularly when quantitative methods are inappropriate. Qualitative evaluation is now widely accepted as legitimate, though it is still considered by some critics to be too subjective, and skirmishing continues between the two camps.

In 1975 Stake outlined what he called a responsive approach to evaluation. His approach was first used to evaluate projects in arts education undertaken by the Arts and Humanities Program of the U.S. Office of Education and the Arts in Education Program of the JDR 3rd Fund. Stake's procedure is more qualitative than quantitative. It is characterized by an emphasis on activities rather than intentions. It responds to the information needs of the persons involved in the program rather than to the information needs of researchers. It incorporates brief narratives, portrayals, displays of products, and the testimony of participants. It is based on observing and reacting. Stake contrasts his approach with preordinate evaluation, which he characterizes as based on formal statements of goals, data-gathering instruments, and experimental designs.

Stake offers responsive evaluation as an alternative to the traditional quantitative procedures. Responsive evaluation sacrifices measurement precision in order to increase the usefulness of the findings. Most important, responsive evaluation is based on the belief that arts education can provide experiences that are of intrinsic value regardless of whether or not any specific behavioral outcomes can be identified. This is a position with strong support among music educators, most of whom would likely agree with Stake (1983b) that measurable outcomes alone do not fully define the value of a program.

Naturalistic, or case history, evaluation is another variety of qualitative evaluation (Guba and Lincoln, 1981, pp. 53–127; 1983). It is based on the field study carried out in a natural setting. It seeks to document how the phenomenon is perceived by those most closely involved in it. Like Stake's responsive evaluation, naturalistic evaluation is concerned with the needs and interests of the user. It employs nontechnical language and is aimed at nontechnical audiences, such as teachers and the public. It attempts to represent as well as possible the feelings, concerns, beliefs, perceptions, and understandings of the participants. In 1989 Guba and Lincoln, who have written extensively on naturalistic evaluation, abandoned the term "naturalistic" in favor of "constructivist" (1989, p. 19). They prefer constructivist because it reflects their view that reality does not exist independently of the observer but consists only of the mental constructs one creates in attempting to make sense out of one's environment.

Wolf's (1983) judicial evaluation method is based on the metaphor of law and is intended to facilitate educational decision making by drawing on the legal concepts of fact-finding, adversarial proceedings, cross-examination, evidentiary rules, and structured argumentation. After the issues are identified, the competing positions are presented at a clarification forum, presided over by a forum moderator, at which evidence is presented and witnesses give testimony and are examined and cross-examined by case presenters. A report is then produced by a clarification panel.

Although the case study method tends to be less highly valued than other methods by some evaluators, it can be helpful, particularly when employed in combination with other methods. Stake (1983a) argues that case studies are useful because a case study that is consistent with readers' experience can give them a basis for generalization. Although a single case cannot represent an entire population, Stake points out that often the need is only for generalizations that apply to that particular case or similar cases and not to an entire population of cases. The case study method provides the basis for many of the program evaluation techniques currently in use.

Nevo (1986, p. 15–16) has proposed 10 questions that any comprehensive evaluation model should address:

1. How is evaluation defined?
2. What are the functions of evaluation?
3. What are the objects of evaluation?
4. What kinds of information should be collected regarding each object?
5. What criteria should be used to judge the merit and worth of an evaluated object?
6. Who should be served by an evaluation?
7. What is the process of doing an evaluation?
8. What methods of enquiry should be used in evaluation?
9. Who should do evaluation?
10. By what standards should evaluation be judged?

Obviously, not all of the models or approaches address directly each of these questions, but the underlying issues should be considered by every administrator or teacher thinking seriously about program evaluation.

PRACTICAL ASPECTS OF PROGRAM EVALUATION

Program evaluation typically begins with a question. For example, is the music curriculum effective? What has been the result of decreasing the number of elementary music specialists in the system? Are there changes that could be made in the program that would reduce the dropout rate in instrumental music? Are the nonperformance music electives recently introduced in the high school effective? What are the strengths and the weaknesses of the program?

There is a large amount of professional literature describing how to become a better music teacher, but very little designed to help teachers evaluate their programs. Much of what does exist is based on the evaluation of short-term programs designed for social or enrichment purposes and funded by the federal government or another external agency. The literature is not well balanced in that it has "tended to focus on public rather than private education, basic and compensatory rather than special or supplemental education, and elementary and secondary versus preschool or higher and continuing education" (Smith, 1983, p. 382). It describes the work of the professional evaluator employed under contract by the district or by a funding agency. The relationship is that of a professional specialist to a client. Some schools seeking evaluation of their programs contract with external agencies to perform the evaluation. Guba and Lincoln (1981, pp. 270–302) and others have discussed the issues that should be addressed in such a contract. Other schools prefer to conduct their evaluations internally. Wick (1987) has offered suggestions for districts performing their own evaluations.

Informal evaluation has gained increased respectability and legitimacy in recent years. Individual teachers evaluate their own instruction continuously and make changes that they believe will increase their effectiveness. The underlying motivation is simply a desire to do a better job. In these circumstances control groups and random assignments typically are not feasible. Familiarity with the principles of program evaluation and with the approaches used by professional program evaluators is helpful in improving the quality of these informal and private decisions. Formal training in evaluation is useful, but in its absence common sense and good judgment can help the teacher greatly in making the evaluation decisions required daily in the classroom.

Hayman and Napier (1975) have offered practical suggestions for a school district seeking to utilize systematic evaluation to bring about improvement. Brinkerhoff, Brethower, Hluchyj, and Nowakowski (1983) have provided materials for the training of teachers and teacher educators to conduct program evaluations. Haller (1974) has suggested ways to estimate the costs of an educational program. Similar efforts in program evaluation are often the focus of what has come to be called action research.

In 1981, as a result of 4 years' work by some 200 individuals, a joint committee appointed by 12 professional organizations concerned with educational evaluation published a comprehensive set of 30 standards to provide guidance in (1) evaluating educational programs, products, and materials, and (2) judging the soundness of such evaluations (Joint Committee on Standards for Educational Evaluation). The standards, which are summarized by Stufflebeam and Madaus (1983), are grouped according to four attributes: utility, feasibility, propriety, and accuracy. In an effort to reform program evaluation, Cronbach and his associates (1980) have offered 95 theses representing suggestions designed to improve practices in the field of program evaluation.

Stake (1985) has summarized three of the major lessons he has learned in almost 30 years of work in program evaluation as follows:

1. For purposes of program evaluation, testing doesn't work. Existing tests simply do not assess what students have learned, and usually neither time nor funds are available to develop suitable tests. Information on student performance is important, but in most evaluation studies there is no justification for treating such data as criteria of program effectiveness.
2. Evaluation concerns are frequently subordinated to political concerns. "What we thought was worth learning was seldom what the clients wanted. They bought our studies mostly because it legitimated them to ask for evaluation" (p. 244).
3. Anything worth knowing should be understood in a practical context. The generalizations valued in the social sciences are of little help in the classroom. There will always be a need for evaluative judgments, though it is not clear that there will always be a need for specialists who call themselves program evaluators.

MUSIC CURRICULA, PROGRAMS, AND PROJECTS

Title IV of ESEA, which amended the Cooperative Research Act of 1954, provided the funds by which almost 200 research and development projects, including more than 60 in music, were supported through the Arts and Humanities Program of the U.S. Office of Education from the mid-1960s through the early 1970s. These included the Manhattanville Project (Thomas, 1970) and the Juilliard Project (Sessions and Dickey, 1967), as well as the work of Reimer (1967), Glenn and Glidden (1966), and Rolland (1971). Projects emphasizing program evaluation included those of Morgan (1966), Lund (1966), Mandle (1967), Spohn (1964), and Thostenson (1966).

The Office of Education also supported work in music curricula and evaluation through the Central Midwestern Regional Educational Laboratory (CEMREL) and several of the other regional educational laboratories as well as through Title I and Title III of ESEA. Some of the curricula developed contained explicit information concerning program evaluation, though others did not. Some of the evaluation procedures described were narrow and superficial, while others proved to be more broadly useful.

Since the mid-1960s American music education has been influenced in important ways by various curriculum movements, many of which originated abroad. Most notable of these are the approaches of Shinichi Suzuki, Zoltán Kodály, and Carl Orff. Despite occasional efforts to evaluate these programs, often in doctoral dissertations, their growth and acceptance has been based not on their success in achieving the aims of music education as determined through systematic evaluation but rather on the results they produce as perceived by music educators and on their popularity with the public.

To many parents and teachers the skills and attitudes developed in the Suzuki program, for example, are obvious. These parents and teachers value the program because they value those skills and attitudes. No further evaluation is needed. Similarly, the school band and other music offerings are valued in proportion to the priority placed on the skills and knowledge they are perceived to develop in young people. Music has held and expanded its position in the curriculum since 1838 almost entirely on the basis of its appeal to students and their parents. In times of curricular or financial stress, music teachers naturally seek data to document the effectiveness of their work. As more sophisticated techniques of program evaluation are developed, it may become possible to provide concrete evidence to buttress the intuitive impressions on which music education has relied heavily for its support.

The Young Audiences Program and the Artists in Education and Arts in Education Programs of the National Endowment for the Arts are examples of enrichment programs that are widely accepted as being of educational value but that have not been subjected to systematic evaluation and for which only anecdotal evidence of effectiveness exists.

Perhaps the most thorough effort thus far to evaluate a well-established music curriculum was the *Silver Burdett Music Competency Tests* of Colwell (1979). Three recorded, criterion-referenced tests were developed for each *Silver Burdett Music* textbook, 1 through 6. The tests were intended to provide information for teachers and students on student achievement. Each test covered the material presented in approximately one-third of the book, and it was expected that three tests would be administered during each school year; for example, in October, February, and May. Most of the items involved aural perception of rhythm, melody, form, tone color, texture, tonality, and dynamics. Colwell (1982, p. 164) suggested that with reasonably effective instruction at least 80 percent of the students could be expected to "master" the content measured. If the students were learning the material presented, the program was presumed to be effective.

The Icelandic-American music education project sought to develop an integrated and comprehensive approach to general music instruction (Edelstein, Choksy, Lehman, Sigurdsson, and Woods, 1980). Its aim was to develop a broad framework to aid individual music teachers in constructing instructional programs suited to the particular needs of their students. Evaluation is an integral part of the program. Student progress may be evaluated in the context of a specific strategy, an activity-content task, an instructional objective, or a goal. Twenty-three evaluative criteria are offered in one appendix and a sample evaluation record in another (Edelstein et al., 1980, pp. 223, 226–227). For each instructional objective, one or more evaluative criteria are identified. The sample evaluation record provides a means of documenting the completion of the various strategies for each objective. As often happens in a program designed to bring about student learning, the line between program evaluation and aggregate student evaluation is blurred.

In some school districts considerable importance is attached to the ratings received in band, orchestra, and choral contests and competitions. School administrators and the public sometimes view these ratings as indications of the quality of the school music program. These inferences are not necessarily valid because the reliability and validity of contest ratings have not been adequately investigated and documented. Further, contests reveal nothing about the balance, comprehensiveness, or quality of the remainder of the K–12 music program. Although contest ratings can be useful as pieces of evidence within a comprehensive program evaluation (Lehman, 1989), music educators should take steps to discourage excessively broad generalizations within their communities concerning the meaning of these results.

CONTEMPORARY MUSIC PROJECT

The Contemporary Music Project (CMP) was funded from 1963 through 1973 by a grant from the Ford Foundation to the Music Educators National Conference. The project sponsored a variety of activities, most of which were evaluated informally, though considerable emphasis was placed on evaluation in the Institutes for Music in Contemporary Education (IMCEs).

From 1966 to 1968, 36 colleges and universities and associated elementary and secondary schools were organized into six regional IMCEs. Courses at all levels followed the comprehensive musicianship model of the CMP, and the student, regardless of level, was expected to function as a practicing musician. The evaluative criteria developed for the IMCEs were intended to be applied to second-year college students.

The evaluation of the local programs was based on an assessment of the students' comprehensive musicianship by means of (1) direct testing and (2) independent student projects designed to demonstrate descriptive competence, performing competence, creative competence, and attitude ("Evaluative Criteria for Music Education," 1968). The direct testing might include, for example, performing a piece at sight and commenting on its structure, its style, and other matters affecting its interpretation. The independent project was intended to allow students to demonstrate their musicianship by completing a musical task over a longer period of time. The local IMCE instructor was responsible for determining the specific questions and tasks and, ultimately, for the evaluation of the students and the program.

PROJECT IMPACT

One of the most thorough and systematic evaluations in the arts during the 1970s was that of Project IMPACT. Project

IMPACT (Interdisciplinary Model Program in the Arts for Children and Teachers) was funded by the U.S. Office of Education from 1970 to 1972 to establish model school programs that were arts centered (Boyle and Lathrop, 1973). The participants were schools in Columbus, OH; Glendale, CA; Eugene, OR; and Philadelphia, PA; and a consortium in southeastern Alabama. The purpose was to make music, art, theater, and dance an integral part of school curriculum. The teachers involved were classroom teachers, arts specialists, and outside consultants.

The principal technique of the evaluation team was to gather data by means of questionnaires. No information is available concerning the reliability or validity of the results, and it is by no means certain that the findings from the questionnaires can be accepted at face value.

The first objective of IMPACT was "to reconstruct the educational program and administrative climate of the school in an effort to achieve parity between the arts and other instructional areas" (p. 43). By the end of the project virtually all teachers at the project sites believed that this had been done.

The second objective was to "develop educational programs of high artistic quality in [visual arts, music, dance, and drama] in each of the participating schools" (p. 43). There was less agreement that this objective had been achieved, though the IMPACT arts programs were generally thought to be of high quality for the level and experience of the students and teachers involved. IMPACT's third objective was to conduct in-service programs for teachers. The responses of the participants, according to the questionnaires, were positive.

The fourth objective was "to develop ways to infuse the arts into all aspects of the school curriculum" (p. 45). A large majority of the teachers at all project sites indicated that the role of the arts in their classrooms had increased as a result of IMPACT, and dramatic shifts were claimed in the extent to which classroom teachers incorporated the arts into their teaching of other subject matter fields. The fifth objective was to bring guest artists to the schools. On the basis of information obtained from teacher questionnaires, the evaluation team drew conclusions concerning the effectiveness of the guest artists and the impact of the instruction on the self-concept of the students and on their attitude toward school.

NATIONAL ASSESSMENT OF EDUCATIONAL PROGRESS

The National Assessment of Educational Progress (NAEP) is an information-gathering project that surveys the skills and knowledge of Americans at ages 9, 13, 17, and 26 to 35 in various subject matter fields, initially including music. Music was assessed in 1971–72 (NAEP, 1974) and again in 1978–79 (NAEP, 1981) using a stratified random sample of approximately 90,000 persons. All items requiring the respondent to sing or play instruments were dropped from the second as-

sessment because of lack of funds. The items were based on a set of objectives developed prior to each assessment.

The results reveal what percentage of Americans at each age level can, for example, sing "America" with and without accompaniment, improvise a rhythmic accompaniment to a melody, sight read a simple musical line, follow a line of printed music, distinguish a trumpet from other instruments, and distinguish the music of Mozart from that of other composers. Data for the nation are reported as well as data by sex, geographic region, race, parental education, and size and type of community. NAEP has provided the most complete and most reliable data available on the musical skills and knowledge of the American public, but it has aroused remarkably little interest on the part of music educators.

Although NAEP is not designed to evaluate programs, it provides methodological models that can be useful in program evaluation. Data have been released only for large geographic regions of the nation, and no state or local results are available, though in some communities music educators have administered the released NAEP items in their own schools in order to compare the skills and knowledge of local students with those of the national sample. Several states have undertaken their own assessments modeled after NAEP, and in those states additional comparisons are possible.

NATIONAL ASSOCIATION OF SCHOOLS OF MUSIC

Accreditation is the process whereby an association or agency recognizes an institution as having met certain qualifications or standards. Accreditation, in a sense, represents criterion-referenced program evaluation. The National Association of Schools of Music (NASM) has been designated by the Council on Postsecondary Accreditation and by the U.S. Department of Education as the agency responsible for the accreditation of music curricula in higher education. Many institutions with teacher education programs are also accredited by the National Council for Accreditation of Teacher Education, and NASM cooperates with the Council in the accreditation of music teacher education programs. NASM also accredits community/junior colleges and non-degree-granting institutions (NASM, 1989).

The process of NASM accreditation involves (1) the preparation of a comprehensive institutional self-study report, (2) a visit by a team of peer music administrators who then prepare a report, and (3) a review by the NASM Commission on Accreditation. The self-study calls for detailed information on a wide variety of topics concerning the operations, programs, and policies of the music unit. Normally an accreditation review is required every 10 years.

NASM (1985) has also published recommendations for the assessment of graduate programs in music for use by institutions that seek to improve their current programs, assess the need for new programs, or implement new programs. Another publication (NASM, 1988) provides recommendations for the assessment of community education programs in music. A parallel publication concerned with undergraduate programs is in preparation.

REGIONAL ACCREDITING ASSOCIATIONS

Elementary and secondary schools are accredited by one of the six regional accrediting associations: Middle States Association of Colleges and Schools, New England Association of Schools and Colleges, Inc., North Central Association of Colleges and Schools, Northwest Association of Schools and Colleges, Southern Association of Colleges and Schools, and Western Association of Schools and Colleges, Inc. The criteria and procedures used in these accreditations have been developed by the National Study of School Evaluation and are set forth in the publication *Evaluative Criteria* (NSSE, 1987, pp. 5–16, 243–262).

The *Evaluative Criteria* is "a profile of the important characteristics of a quality secondary school. It offers a systematic process by which to assess the effectiveness of a school and to stimulate a school and community to establish a planned program of continuous growth so that its school may become progressively better" (NSSE, 1987, p. v). The evaluation process described in the *Evaluative Criteria* consists of three stages: (1) a self-evaluation prepared by a series of subcommittees under the guidance of a steering committee, (2) a visit by a visiting committee to validate the self-study and to suggest changes to improve the educational program, and (3) follow-up activities in which changes are made on the basis of the self-study and the report of the visiting committee.

The *Evaluative Criteria* provides matrices, rating scales, and open-ended items by means of which to assemble information concerning the school, the student body, the community, the school climate, the school's philosophy and goals, and the curriculum. The music section calls for information concerning (1) the major expectations of the program, (2) follow-up activities since the previous evaluation, (3) organization of the school, (4) curricular offerings, (5) components of the instructional program (including faculty, instructional activities, materials and media, student assessment, and program evaluation), (6) facilities and equipment, (7) the learning climate, (8) evaluations, and (9) judgments and recommendations.

STATE DEPARTMENT OF EDUCATION AND LOCAL SCHOOL DISTRICT ACTIVITIES

As a result of the educational reform movement and the demand for accountability, a large majority of the states have adopted an assessment or competency testing program of some sort. Often the results are publicized as measures of the quality of the schools, though most states merely publish test scores.

A number of state departments of education have claimed to be committed to developing or assisting districts to develop plans for the systematic evaluation of educational programs, including music, in the elementary and secondary schools. Information will become available from the state departments of education as their plans develop. States developing plans for program evaluation in music include Minnesota, North Carolina, South Carolina, and West Virginia. Florida currently provides an on-site review by the state music consultant to any district on request. Indiana makes available a self-study evaluative instrument for music programs based on the materials developed by the National Study of School Evaluation and used by the regional accrediting associations.

Many school districts have undertaken to evaluate their programs at the district or building level. These activities can be very helpful when their scope is realistic and when the staff is given adequate time to do the job. One such effort is described by Kimpton (1989). Many states and local districts provide curriculum guides in music. Every curriculum guide should be designed so as to facilitate evaluation of the music program it outlines, and every guide should offer teachers specific information on program evaluation.

MUSIC EDUCATORS NATIONAL CONFERENCE

The Music Educators National Conference (MENC), in cooperation with the Educational Testing Service (ETS), has developed a set of program evaluation materials designed to make possible the comprehensive assessment of the quality of K–12 instructional programs in music at the district level (MENC, In press). Separate assessment instruments have been developed to assess (1) goals and objectives, (2) leadership, (3) staffing, (4) curriculum and scheduling, (5) instructional materials, (6) equipment, (7) facilities, and (8) outcomes.

Additional assessment instruments have been developed for use by elementary school principals, middle or junior high school principals, and high school principals. There are supplementary instruments for the on-site assessment of classroom instruction and large ensemble rehearsals. Finally, assessment instruments have been developed for gathering information from students in general music instruction and elective music instruction.

For goals and objectives, leadership, staffing, curriculum and scheduling, instructional materials, equipment, and facilities, separate assessment instruments have been developed for music administrators and music teachers. For staffing, curriculum and scheduling, instructional materials, equipment, facilities, and outcomes, separate assessment instruments have been developed for elementary school music teachers, middle or junior high school music teachers, and high school music teachers. The assessment instrument for the students in general music instruction is intended for grades 4 through 8. The instrument for students in elective music instruction is for grades 5 through 12 (optional in grade 4).

The instruments are composed of multiple-choice items. The validity of the assessment instruments is based on their derivation from *The School Music Program; Description and Standards* (MENC, 1986), which summarizes the content of the K–12 music program and the standards against which programs should be measured in the collective opinion of the music education profession as determined by MENC. The MENC program evaluation procedures were designed to be (1) sufficiently flexible to be usable in most K–12 public school districts, private school systems, or individual schools throughout the United States, (2) of sufficiently high quality to command the respect of musicians, educators, and the public, and (3) diagnostic in nature and able to provide a basis for improvement rather than merely yield numerical scores.

The assessment instruments are intended to be comprehensive and balanced. They require both facts and opinions. They have been designed so as to give the district the greatest possible flexibility in responding to its own needs and in developing its own assessment profile. Because use of the instruments is strictly voluntary, no national norms will be available. Instead, user profiles will be provided, reporting the aggregate responses to items. Separate profiles will be available for large, mid-sized, and small districts and for urban, suburban, and rural districts. By analyzing these results, according to MENC, a district can identify strengths or weaknesses in its music program that might not otherwise be apparent (Lehman, 1989).

DOCTORAL RESEARCH

A number of doctoral researchers have sought to evaluate the effectiveness of music curricula at a single college or university (Bennett, 1975; Bunch, 1969; Lee, 1981; Meurer, 1975; Prince, 1968; Schumaker, 1978; Simmons, 1979; Thomas, 1981) or a group of colleges or universities (Boyce, 1973; Feil, 1968; Lacy, 1985; Smith, 1969). The usual procedure is to distribute a survey to graduates asking their opinions concerning various aspects of the program. Occasionally information is sought from the graduates' current supervisors or from faculty at the institution under review. The studies frequently offer suggestions for improvement, but no major shortcoming at any institution is known to have been revealed by this method.

Foley (1973) developed an instrument for evaluating high school band programs. Brathwaite (1982) constructed a similar model for evaluating string programs. Bromley (1972) and Daigle (1968) also developed procedures for evaluating music programs. Assessments involving several schools were undertaken by Thurber (1977) and Trotman (1987). Hebert (1984) sought to evaluate the educational usefulness of the television series *From Jumpstreet: A Story of Black Music.*

Other investigators have evaluated courses or curricula they have developed (Biringer, 1974; Fitzpatrick, 1968; Kella, 1984; Nyberg, 1975; Popp, 1969; Segress, 1979; Taylor, 1981). In studies involving both the development and the evaluation of curricula, the amount of attention devoted to evaluation is sometimes minimal.

Mamlin (1974) offered suggestions for revising the *Evaluative Criteria for the Evaluation of Secondary Schools* of the National Study of School Evaluation. Reuer (1987) evaluated the recommended curriculum of the National Association for Music Therapy, while Gilchrist (1986) evaluated an artist-in-residence program.

The usefulness of comparative studies of methodology usually depends on how clearly the treatments are defined and on how appropriate the criterion measures are. Such studies continue to be popular (Hensley, 1982; Olson, 1967; Palmer, 1974; Stephens, 1974; Zemke, 1970).

SUMMARY AND IMPLICATIONS

The following conclusions may be drawn concerning the current state of program evaluation in music:

1. Evaluation should be an integral part of every music program (Boyle, 1989). It is important not only to evaluate what students have learned, but also to evaluate the instructional program itself. Many teachers tend to think of evaluation only in connection with new programs or programs of limited duration, typically supported with external funding, but evaluation is important in established, continuing programs as well. Any program can be improved on, and systematic evaluation can provide the basis for improvement. Evaluation is equally important in small programs and in large ones.

2. Provisions for evaluation should be built into every new program from the earliest planning stages. Evaluation added after the program is under way will be far less satisfactory, though it is preferable to no evaluation at all.

3. The evaluation of music programs is extremely difficult because some of the most important outcomes of music instruction cannot easily be isolated or quantified. Further, music education lacks generally accepted criterion measures, such as widely used standardized tests. There is little agreement among music teachers as to whether the lack of emphasis on standardized testing is an advantage or a disadvantage, but the absence of widely accepted and readily measurable output variables is clearly an impediment to program evaluation.

4. The objectives of an instructional program should be stated explicitly insofar as possible, but the lack of explicit objectives does not preclude evaluation because the field of program evaluation is no longer dominated by objectives-

based models. There is growing recognition of the validity of alternatives, including qualitative, responsive, connoisseurship and criticism, and naturalistic or constructivist evaluation. The alternative approaches offer solutions to some of the problems posed by quantitative models, and they tend to be particularly useful in the arts. Even when applied to subject matter outside the arts, the alternatives tend to promote the values associated with the arts. It is likely that program evaluation will continue to be heavily focused on gathering information to assist in making management decisions, and arts educators should seek to ensure that their concerns and values are reflected in the types of data gathered and in the techniques used in their schools.

5. The evaluation of student achievement is not synonymous with the evaluation of programs, though aggregate data on student achievement provide important information concerning program effectiveness. Other relevant data include (1) the contributions of the program to the long-term general growth and development of the students, (2) the cumulative effects of the program on the artistic, cultural, and intellectual life of the community, and (3) the impact of the program on those less tangible personal and environmental characteristics that affect the quality of life (Edelstein et al., 1980, p. 13). Nevertheless, efforts to improve the evaluation of student achievement may have applications in the field of program evaluation. For example, the work of the Arts Propel Project in portfolio assessment may ultimately provide a methodological model that could be useful in the evaluation of music programs (Wolf, 1988).

6. Evaluation results useful in justifying the music program to school administrators and the public are widely sought but difficult to produce. Music teachers would be delighted if researchers could establish, for example, that children studying music consequently do better in reading and math or become better human beings than children not studying music. Unfortunately, most studies of this type are inconclusive, and those that do claim to show a statistically significant effect usually cannot provide a basis for generalizing to other populations. These studies typically demonstrate correlation but not causation. It is easy to show that students who participate in music do well in other activities, but virtually impossible to show that they do well *because* they participate in music. Since researchers cannot assign students randomly on a long-term basis to study music or not to study it, they cannot isolate the single variable of music participation and measure its effect.

7. Informal evaluation is always useful, even when formal evaluation is not possible. Teachers evaluate their programs continuously. Usually the evaluation is quite informal. Sometimes it is subconscious. Whenever teachers are dissatisfied they will try something different next time. Generalizing on the basis of conclusions reached by informal means is risky but all teachers do it, and a teacher acting on the basis of informal evaluation will probably make the right decision more often than not.

8. Much of the literature that claims to constitute evaluation is of questionable value because the methodology was weak or inappropriate, because there is insufficient evidence of the reliability and validity of the data-gathering instruments used, or because the conclusions are not supported by the evidence.

9. Although there is a rapidly expanding body of literature on program evaluation in the field of education, there is relatively little thus far specifically in music education. This need should be addressed as soon as possible. Efforts should be made to develop a variety of techniques and instruments for program evaluation in music so as to accommodate the great diversity of curricula and activities in which music students are involved.

10. Insofar as possible a comprehensive program evaluation should be based on information from multiple sources and should utilize diverse data-gathering procedures. When results are combined that are derived by various techniques, each of which inevitably has its own methodological strengths and weakness, the composite findings are likely to be more valid than the findings derived by any single technique alone.

11. In many cases effective program evaluation in music education can be facilitated by (1) more focused statements of what the program is intended to achieve, (2) clearer identification of the independent variable(s), (3) creation of an array of reliable and valid instruments for measuring the variable(s), (4) more careful and thorough observation of the results of the program, (5) greater participation and scrutiny by persons independent of the program and the school district, and (6) greater use and acceptance of various alternative techniques so as not to rely exclusively on quantitative methods. However, neither the objectives nor the procedures of the program should be distorted solely to facilitate evaluation.

12. Program evaluation results should themselves be subjected to metaevaluation to examine their technical quality, usefulness, freedom from bias, and other characteristics. Metaevaluation is the practice of evaluating evaluations (Schwandt and Halpern, p. 23). This examination and verification should be conducted by an independent third party in the same manner that a corporation employs an independent accounting firm to audit its books.

Both the strengths and the weaknesses of the report by Harrington and Harris on the music program of Lowell Mason at the Hawes School have become more obvious as a result of the progress made in program evaluation in recent years. Still, it is revealing to compare the philosophical context in which they evaluated the music program with the typical contemporary view, and it is useful to reflect on the program evaluation criteria that they turned to intuitively.

References

Airasian, P. W. (1983). Societal experimentation. In G. F. Madaus, M. S. Scriven, and D. L. Stufflebeam (Eds.), *Evaluation models* (pp. 163–175). Boston: Kluwer-Nijhoff Publishing.

Bennett, R. W. (1975). An evaluation of the effectiveness of the undergraduate music education curriculum at North Texas State University. Unpublished doctoral dissertation, University of North Texas, Denton.

Birge, E. B. (1928). *History of public school music in the United States* (New and augmented ed.). Bryn Mawr: Oliver Ditson Co. (Washington: Music Educators National Conference, 1966)

Biringer, F. A. (1974). The development and evaluation of a systems approach curriculum for a heterogeneous beginning string class. Unpublished doctoral dissertation, University of Miami, Coral Gables.

Boyce, H. W. (1973). A graduate-oriented evaluation of the music education curricula of four state college-university systems in Utah. Unpublished doctoral dissertation, Utah State University, Logan.

Boyle, J. D. (1989). Perspective on evaluation. *Music Educators Journal, 76*(4), 22–25.

Boyle, J. D. and Lathrop, R. L. (1973). The IMPACT Experience: An evaluation. *Music Educators Journal, 59*(5), 42–47.

Brathwaite, A. M. H. (1982). The development of a model for evaluating school music string programs. Unpublished doctoral dissertation, University of Georgia, Athens.

Brinkerhoff, R. O., Brethower, D. M., Hluchyj, T. and Nowakowski, J. R. (1983). *Program evaluation: A practitioner's guide for trainers and educators.* Boston: Kluwer-Nijoff Publishing.

Bromley, A. B. (1972). The development and testing of evaluative checklists for determining the degree of attainment of objectives in music education in the public schools. Unpublished doctoral dissertation, University of Oregon, Eugene.

Bunch, W. F. (1969). An evaluation of the Ph.D. curriculum in music at the University of Iowa from 1931 to 1967 through an analysis of the opinions of its doctoral graduates, Unpublished doctoral dissertation, University of Iowa, Iowa City.

Campbell, D. T., and Stanley, J. C. (1963). *Experimental and quasi-experimental designs for research.* Chicago: Rand McNally.

Coleman, J. S., Campbell, E. Q., Hobson, C. J., McPartland, J., Mood, A., Weinfeld, F. D., and York, R. L. (1966). *Equality of educational opportunity.* Washington: U.S. Department of Health, Education, and Welfare.

Colwell, R. (1979). *Silver Burdett music competency tests.* Morristown: Silver Burdett Company.

Colwell, R. (1982). Evaluation in music education: Perspicacious or peregrine. In Richard Colwell (Ed.), *Symposium in music education.* Urbana-Champaign: University of Illinois.

Cronbach, L. J. (1982). *Designing evaluations of educational and social programs.* San Francisco: Jossey-Bass Publishers.

Cronbach, L. J., Ambron, S. R., Dornbusch, S. M., Hess, R. D., Hornik, R. C., Phillips, D. C., Walker, D. F., Weiner, S. S. (1980). *Toward reform of program evaluation.* San Francisco: Jossey-Bass Publishers.

Daigle, V. E. (1968). Evaluative criteria for programs of music in public secondary schools. Unpublished doctoral dissertation, Louisiana State University, Baton Rouge.

Edelstein, S., Choksy, L., Lehman, P., Sigurdsson, N., and Woods, D. (1980). *Creating curriculum in music.* Menlo Park: Addison-Wesley Publishing Co.

Eisner, E. W. (1967). Educational objectives: Help or hindrance? *The School Review, 75,* 250–266.

Eisner, E. W. (1969). Instructional and expressive objectives: Their formulation and use in curriculum. In *Instructional Objectives* (Vol. 3 of American Educational Research Association Monograph Series on Curriculum Evaluation; pp. 1–31). Chicago: Rand McNally.

Eisner, E. W. (1979). *The educational imagination: On the design and evaluation of school programs.* New York: Macmillan.

Eisner, E. W. (1983). Educational connoisseurship and criticism: Their form and functions in educational evaluation. In G. F. Madaus, M. S. Scriven, and D. L. Stufflebeam (Eds.), *Evaluation Models* (pp. 335–347). Boston: Kluwer-Nijhoff Publishing. [Reprinted from *Journal of Aesthetic Education, 10* (1976), 135–150]

Evaluative Criteria for Music Education: The Airlie House Symposium (1968). *Music Educators Journal, 54*(7), 66–68.

Feil, L. (1968). An analysis and evaluation of the cooperative music program in the Associated Colleges of Central Kansas with recommendations for improvement. Unpublished doctoral dissertation, University of Oklahoma, Norman.

Fitzpatrick, J. B. (1968). The development and evaluation of a curriculum in music listening skills on the seventh grade level. Unpublished doctoral dissertation, University of Iowa, Iowa City.

Floden, R. E., and Weiner, S. S. (1983). Rationality to ritual: The multiple roles of evaluation in government processes. In G. F. Madaus, M. S. Scriven, and D. L. Stufflebeam (Eds.), *Evaluation models* (pp. 177–188). Boston: Kluwer-Nijhoff Publishing. [Reprinted from *Policy Sciences, 9* (1978), 9–18]

Foley, W. J. (1973). The development of an evaluative instrument for high school band programs. Unpublished doctoral dissertation, Indiana University, Bloomington.

Gilchrist, E. R. (1986). Implementation and evaluation of an artist-in-residence classroom teacher in-service program of integrated musical activities. Unpublished doctoral dissertation, Wayne State University, Detroit.

Glenn, N., and Glidden, R. (1966). The development of content and materials for a music literature course in the senior high school. (ERIC Document Reproduction Service No. ED 030 015)

Good, T., and Brophy, J. E. (1986). School effects. In M. C. Wittrock (Ed.), *Handbook of research on teaching* (3rd ed., pp. 570–602). New York: Macmillan.

Guba, E. G., and Lincoln, Y. S. (1981). *Effective evaluation.* San Francisco: Jossey-Bass Publishers.

Guba, E. G., and Lincoln, Y. S. (1983). Epistemological and methodological bases of naturalistic enquiry. In G. F. Madaus, M. S. Scriven, and D. L. Stufflebeam (Eds.), *Evaluation models* (pp. 311–333). Boston: Kluwer-Nijhoff Publishing. [Reprinted from *Educational Communications and Technology Journal, 30,* 4 (1982)]

Guba, E. G., and Lincoln, Y. S. (1989). *Fourth generation evaluation.* Newbury Park: Sage Publications.

Haller, E. J. (1974). Cost analysis for educational program evaluation. In W. J. Popham (Ed.), *Evaluation in education* (pp. 399–450). Berkeley: McCutcheon Publishing.

Hayman, J. L., and Napier, R. N. (1975). *Evaluation in the schools: A human process for renewal.* Monterey: Brooks/Cole Publishing.

Hebert, V. E. (1984). An evaluation of *From Jumpstreet: A Story of Black Music:* Television series' effect on urban senior high school students. Unpublished doctoral dissertation, University of Michigan, Ann Arbor.

Hensley, S. E. (1982). A study of the musical achievement of elementary students taught by the Memphis city curriculum guide and students taught by the traditional approach. Unpublished doctoral dissertation, Louisiana State University, Baton Rouge.

Hill, J. C. (1986). *Curriculum evaluation for school improvement.* Springfield: Charles C Thomas.

House, E. R. (Ed.) (1986). *New directions in educational evaluation.* London: The Falmer Press.

Joint Committee on Standards for Educational Evaluation (1981). *Standards for evaluations of educational programs, projects, and materials.* New York: McGraw-Hill Book Co.

Kella, J. J. (1984). The development and qualitative evaluation of a comprehensive music curriculum for viola, with a historical survey of violin and viola instructional literature from the 16th through 20th centuries, including a review of the teaching concepts of William Lincer. Unpublished doctoral dissertation, New York University, New York.

Kimpton, J. (1989). Toward curricular accountability: A case study in music. *Music Educators Journal, 76*(4), 34–36.

Koppelman, K. L. (1983). The explication model: An anthropological approach to program evaluation. In G. F. Madaus, M. S. Scriven, and D. L. Stufflebeam (Eds.), *Evaluation models* (pp. 349–355). Boston: Kluwer-Nijhoff Publishing. [Reprinted from *Educational Evaluation and Policy Analysis, 1,3* (1979), 59–64]

Lacy, L. C. (1985). A survey and evaluation of music teacher education programs in selected, accredited black private colleges and universities in the United States. Unpublished doctoral dissertation, Ohio State University, Columbus.

Lee, D. (1981). An evaluation of the Louisiana State University School of Music doctoral degree program: A follow-up study of its doctoral graduates. Unpublished doctoral dissertation, Louisiana State University, Baton Rouge.

Lehman, P. (1989). Assessing your program's effectiveness. *Music Educators Journal, 76*(4), 26–29.

Lund, V. E. (1966). *The evaluation of electronic self-instruction on piano keyboard.* (ERIC Document Reproduction Service No. ED 016 391)

Madaus, G. F., Airasian, P. W., and Kallaghan, T. (1980). *School effectiveness: A reassessment of the evidence.* New York: McGraw-Hill Book Co.

Madaus, G. F., Stufflebeam, D. L., and Scriven, M. S. (1983). Program evaluation: An historical overview. In G. F. Madaus, M. S. Scriven, and D. L. Stufflebeam (Eds.), *Evaluation models* (pp. 3–22). Boston: Kluwer-Nijhoff Publishing.

Mamlin, H. R. (1974). A proposed revision of section 4–12 of "Evaluative Criteria," fourth edition, 1969, for use in the evaluation of secondary school music programs. Unpublished doctoral dissertation, Indiana University, Bloomington.

Mandle, W. D. (1967). *A comparative study of programmed and traditional techniques for teaching music reading in the upper elementary schools.* (ERIC Document Reproduction Service No. ED 014 212)

McLaughlin, M. W. (1975). *Evaluation and reform: The Elementary and Secondary Education Act of 1965: Title I.* Cambridge: Ballinger Publishing Co.

Meurer, E. (1974). An evaluation of music teacher education at Indiana State University. Unpublished doctoral dissertation, Indiana University, Bloomington.

Morgan, H. B. (1966). *An evaluation of adequacy of graduate music offerings at California colleges and universities.* (ERIC Document Reproduction Service No. ED 017 066)

Music Educators National Conference. (1986). *The school music program: Description and standards* (2nd ed.). Reston: Music Educators National Conference.

Music Educators National Conference (In press). *Materials for program assessment: K-12 music.* Reston: Music Educators National Conference.

National Assessment of Educational Progress. (1974). *The first music assessment: An overview.* Denver: Educational Commission of the States.

National Assessment of Educational Progress. (1981). *Music 1971–79: Results from the second national music assessment.* Denver: Educational Commission of the States.

National Association of Schools of Music. (1985). *The assessment of graduate programs in music.* Reston: National Association of Schools of Music.

National Association of Schools of Music. (1988). *The assessment of community education programs in music.* Reston: National Association of Schools of Music.

National Association of Schools of Music. (1989). *1989–90 handbook.* Reston: National Association of Schools of Music.

National Study of School Evaluation. (1987). *Evaluation criteria for the evaluation of secondary schools* (6th ed.). Falls Church: National Study of School Evaluation.

Nevo, D. (1986). The conceptualization of educational evaluation: An analytical review of the literature. In E. R. House (Ed.), *New directions in educational evaluation.* London: The Falmer Press.

Nyberg, R. (1975). The development, implementation and evaluation of an introductory course in ethnic music for use in the secondary schools. Unpublished doctoral dissertation, University of Miami, Coral Gables.

Olson, R. G. (1967). A comparison of two pedagogical approaches adapted to the acquisition of melodic sensitivity in sixth-grade children: The Orff method and the traditional method. Unpublished doctoral dissertation, Indiana University, Bloomington.

Palmer, M. H. (1974). The relative effectiveness of the Richards and the Gordon approaches to rhythm reading for fourth-grade children. Unpublished doctoral dissertation. University of Illinois, Urbana.

Popham, W. J. (1975). *Educational evaluation.* Englewood Cliffs, NJ: Prentice-Hall.

Popp, H. A. (1969). The implementation and evaluation of developed content and materials for a music literature course in the senior high school, Unpublished doctoral dissertation, University of Iowa, Iowa City.

Prince, J. N. (1968). An evaluation of graduate music education programs at the University of Illinois. Unpublished doctoral dissertation, University of Illinois, Urbana.

Reimer, B. (1967). *Development and trial in a junior and senior high school of a two-year curriculum in general music.* (ERIC Document Reproduction Service No. ED 017 526)

Reuer, B. L. (1987). An evaluation of the National Association for Music Therapy curriculum from the perspectives of therapists and educators of therapists in view of academic, clinical, and regulatory criteria. Unpublished doctoral dissertation, University of Iowa, Iowa City.

Rice, J. M. (1897). The futility of the spelling grind. *The Forum, 23,* 163–172.

Rolland, P. (1971). *Development and trial of a two-year program of string instruction.* (ERIC Document Reproduction Service No. ED 054 190)

Schwandt, T. A., and Halpern, E. S. (1988). *Linking auditing and metaevaluation.* Newbury Park: Sage Publications.

Scriven, M. S. (1967). The methodology of evaluation. In *Perspectives of curriculum evaluation* (Vol. 1 of American Educational Research Association Monograph Series on Curriculum Evaluation; pp. 39–83). Chicago: Rand McNally.

Scriven, M. S. (1973). Goal free evaluation. In E. R. House (Ed.), *School evaluation: The politics and process.* Berkeley: McCutcheon Publishing.

Segress, T. D. (1979). The development and evaluation of a comprehensive first semester college jazz improvisation course. Unpublished doctoral dissertation, University of North Texas, Denton.

Sessions, R., and Dickey, G. (1967). *The Juilliard Repertory Project, kindergarten through grade 6.* (ERIC Document Reproduction Service No. ED 016 521)

Shumaker, R. B. (1978). An evaluation of the graduate music education programs at East Carolina University. Unpublished doctoral dissertation, University of Illinois, Urbana.

Simmons, J. M. (1979). An evaluation of the music education curriculum at Lamar University through an analysis of the responses of its teaching graduates. Unpublished doctoral dissertation, McNeese State University, Lake Charles.

Smith, G. F. (1969). An evaluation of music appreciation courses in selected institutions of higher learning by measuring change in the sensitivity of the students to form and style in unfamiliar music, Unpublished doctoral dissertation, University of North Texas, Denton.

Smith, N. L. (1983). The progress of educational evaluation. In G. F. Madaus, M. S. Scriven, and D. L. Stufflebeam (Eds.), *Evaluation models* (pp. 381–392). Boston: Kluwer-Nijhoff Publishing. [Reprinted from *Proceedings of the 1980 Minnesota Evaluation Conference on Educational Evaluation: Recent Progress, Future Needs.* Minneapolis: University of Minnesota Press, 1980]

Spohn, C. L. (1964). *An evaluation of two methods using magnetic tape recordings for programed instruction in the elemental materials of music.* (ERIC Document Reproduction Service No. ED 003 611)

Stake, R. E. (1967). The countenance of educational evaluation. *Teachers College Record, 68,* 523–540.

Stake, R. E. (Ed.). (1975). *Evaluating the arts in education: A responsive approach.* Columbus: Charles E. Merrill.

Stake, R. E. (1983a). The case study method in social inquiry. In G. F. Madaus, M. S. Scriven, and D. L. Stufflebeam (Eds.), *Evaluation models* (pp. 279–286). Boston: Kluwer-Nijhoff Publishing. [Reprinted from *Educational Researcher* (February, 1978), 5–8]

Stake, R. E. (1983b). Program evaluation, particularly responsive evaluation. In G. F. Madaus, M. S. Scriven, and D. L. Stufflebeam (Eds.), *Evaluation models* (pp. 287–310). Boston: Kluwer-Nijhoff Publishing.

Stake, R. E. (1985). A personal interpretation. *Educational Evaluation and Policy Analysis, 7,* 243–244.

Steinmetz, A. (1983). The discrepancy evaluation model. In G. F. Madaus, M. S. Scriven, and D. L. Stufflebeam (Eds.), *Evaluation models* (pp. 79–99). Boston: Kluwer-Nijhoff Publishing. [Reprinted from *Measurement in Education, 7,*1 (Winter, 1976), 1–7]

Stephens, R. (1974). A comparative study of two instructional methods in music reading at the grade V and grade VI level. Unpublished doctoral dissertation, University of Oregon, Eugene.

Stufflebeam, D. L. (1983). The CIPP model for program evaluation. In G. F. Madaus, M. S. Scriven, and D. L. Stufflebeam (Eds.), *Evaluation models* (pp. 117–141). Boston: Kluwer-Nijhoff Publishing.

Stufflebeam, D. L., and Madaus, G. F. (1983). The standards for evaluations of educational programs, projects, and materials: A description and summary. In G. F. Madaus, M. S. Scriven, and D. L. Stufflebeam (Eds.), *Evaluation models* (pp. 395–404). Boston: Kluwer-Nijhoff Publishing.

Taylor, F. J. (1981). The development and evaluation of a black music course of study designed for junior high students. Unpublished doctoral dissertation, Temple University, Philadelphia.

Thomas, R. F. (1981). An evaluation of the music education program at Claflin College. Unpublished doctoral dissertation, University of Illinois, Urbana.

Thomas, R. (1970). *Manhattanville Music Curriculum Program.* (ERIC Document Reproduction Service No. ED 045 865)

Thostenson, M. S. (1966). *The study and evaluation of certain programs related to sight-singing and music dictation.* (ERIC Document Reproduction Service No. ED 054 189)

Thurber, D. W. (1977). An evaluation of the music programs in Seventh-Day Adventist academies in the United States. Unpublished doctoral dissertation, University of North Texas, Denton.

Trotman, L. V. (1987). An assessment and evaluation of instrumental music in the school system of the Virgin Islands. Unpublished doctoral dissertation, Ohio State University, Columbus.

Tyler, R. W. (1949). *Basic principles of curriculum and instruction.* Chicago: University of Chicago Press.

Weiss, R. S., and Rein, M. (1983). The evaluation of broad-aim programs: Experimental design, its difficulties, and an alternative. In G. F. Madaus, M. S. Scriven, and D. L. Stufflebeam (Eds.), *Evaluation models* (pp. 143–161). Boston: Kluwer-Nijhoff Publishing. [Reprinted from *Administrative Science Quarterly, 15,*1 (1970), 97–109]

Wick, J. W. (1987). *School-based evaluation.* Boston: Kluwer-Nijhoff Publishing.

Wolf, D. P. (1988). Opening up assessment. *Educational Leadership, 45*(4), 24–29.

Wolf, R. L. (1983). The use of judicial evaluation methods in the formulation of educational policy. In G. F. Madaus, M. S. Scriven, & D. L. Stufflebeam (Eds.), *Evaluation models* (pp. 189–203). Boston: Kluwer-Nijhoff Publishing. [Reprinted from *Educational Evaluation and Policy Analysis, 1, 3*(1979), 19–28]

Zemke, L. (1970). A comparison of the effects of a Kodaly-adapted music instruction sequence and a more typical sequence on auditory musical achievement in fourth grade students. Unpublished doctoral dissertation, University of Southern California, Los Angeles.

·19·

THE MEASUREMENT OF ATTITUDES AND PREFERENCES IN MUSIC EDUCATION

Robert A. Cutietta

KENT STATE UNIVERSITY

ISSUES IN ATTITUDE MEASUREMENT

A frequent assertion of music teachers is that their primary objective is for their students to "love music." Given this interest on the part of the practitioner, it is not surprising to find a parallel interest among researchers. Of the research studies reported in both the *Journal of Research in Music Education* and the *Journal of Music Therapy* during the decade of the 1980s, 27 percent of the research reported had attitude as one of the dependent measures (Flowers and Jellison, 1990). Thus, attitude is one of the most studied dependent measures in the field of music education.

Interest in attitude is understandable given the affective nature of music. However, statements such as "I want my students to love music" often seem to reveal a superficial approach to the issue and nature of attitudes. Furthermore, in music education research attitude measurement has frequently been treated as little more than an afterthought.

It is often unclear what a teacher wishes the student to "love" *about* music. Should the student leave the class with a good attitude toward the music class? (See Broquist, 1961; Crawford, 1972; Hulbert, 1973; Nolin, 1973; Svengalis, 1980; Seidenberg, 1986; VanderArk, Nolin, and Newman, 1980; Taebel and Coker, 1980; Pogonowski, 1985; Chen, Zhang, and Baichuan, 1984.) Toward performing music? (See Spradling, 1985; Hartley, 1991.) Toward listening to a specific style of music? (See May, 1985; LeBlanc, 1986.) Toward marching band? (See Rogers, 1985.) Other attitude studies include feelings concerning handicapped peers in music classes (Jellison, 1985); the attitude of the music student's parents (Brand, 1985); and music teachers' attitudes toward the philosophies of music education (Hanley, 1987). The musical areas in which unique and complex attitudes can be studied seem endless.

Most researchers regard any objective that can be conceptualized or experienced as a valid focus of attitude study. Price (1986), however, believes that one can possess an attitude only toward something that is not physically present. DeCecco (1971) is more extreme, stating that one can hold an attitude only toward another person, never toward a thing or activity. Thus, one could not have an attitude toward "drinking and driving," only toward individuals who drink and drive. Relative to music, DeCecco states that what we feel toward music "is not attitudinal" (DeCecco, 1971, p. 398). A less restrictive definition of attitude will be used in this chapter: Anything that can be conceptualized or experienced will be regarded as an appropriate focus of attitude.

The first step in attitude measurement, then, is to define clearly the focus of the attitude. Although attitudes toward two related concepts or experiences may be similar, the two will also be different in important ways. A clear definition of the object of the attitude is necessary before instruction and accurate measurement can be carried out.

Defining Attitude

Even if one is clear as to the direction and strength of the attitude, there is still the problem of what exactly constitutes an attitude. Attitudes are psychological and perceptual. An attitude is a construct, an abstract concept used to explain and classify the reasons underlying what people say or what they do. Consequently, one cannot directly measure an attitude. Instead, "we can only infer that a person has attitudes by her words and actions" (Henerson, Morris, and Fitz-Gibbon, 1987, p. 12).

The construct of attitude has had more definitions than any other concern in social psychology (Fisher, 1977), and a

295

similar situation holds in the literature of music education. Attitude has been defined in a straightforward manner as "a predisposition to evaluate psychological objects in a favorable or unfavorable manner" (Kuhn, 1980, p. 4), and less specifically as "an implicit, drive producing response considered socially significant in the individual's society" (Doob, 1967, p. 43). Examples between these two extremes can also be found. Either directly or implicitly, the term "music attitude" has also been used to denote a variety of related constructs such as taste, appreciation, preference, interest, and opinion.

The definition of attitude used in this chapter, an adaptation and combination from Henerson and colleagues, (1987, p. 13) and Allport (1967, p. 8), is as follows: An *attitude* is a firmly held mental network of beliefs, feelings, and values that is organized through an individual's experience, and that exerts a directive and dynamic influence on the individual's perception and response to all objects and situations with which it is related. This definition is in the tradition of L. L. Thurstone, who defined attitude as "the sum total of a man's inclinations and feelings, prejudice or bias, preconceived notions, ideas, fears, threats, and convictions about any specific topic" (1928, p. 529). Thus, attitudes are learned networks of complex interactions between facts (as believed), feelings, and values. These networks are, by necessity, highly individualized.

This definition was chosen because it acknowledges the interrelationships inherent in the multifaceted construct of attitude, and thus emphasizes similarities to all cognitive organization (Heider, 1967). By use of this definition, attitude research can be readily assimilated into current cognitive theory, which speaks of concepts in terms of semantic networks, and schema.

Attitudes cannot be directly observed. Instead, the composition of an attitude is inferred from an individual's response to the attitude object or some representation of it. These outward responses that the individual makes are filtered through one of three response modes before they are manifested as observable behavior. This process was conceptualized in the psychological literature by a model proposed by Rosenberg and Hovland (1960).

In their model, attitudes are the result of an individual's experience with stimuli, these latter seen as measurable, independent variables (see Figure 19–1). The individual's attitude is made up of feelings, values, and beliefs interacting with three potential response modes: (1) affect, (2) cognition, and (3) behavior. Rosenberg and Hovland called these three response modes "components" to reflect that all three *collectively* constitute the outward display of attitude; they are collectively referred to as "intervening variables" in Figure 19–1.

For each of the three response components of attitude there are corresponding measurable dependent variables. For example, to measure the affect response component, one can measure nerve responses or verbal statements of affect. For the cognition response component, one can measure perceptual response or verbal statements of belief. Lastly, for the behavior response component, one can measure overt actions or verbal statements indicating behavioral intention (Price, 1986).

The model shows a complex network of possible interactions among and between the attitude construct and the response components. These interactions take place before any attitude can be measured.

There are at least three types of measurement that can be used to infer the attitude of the individual toward a given

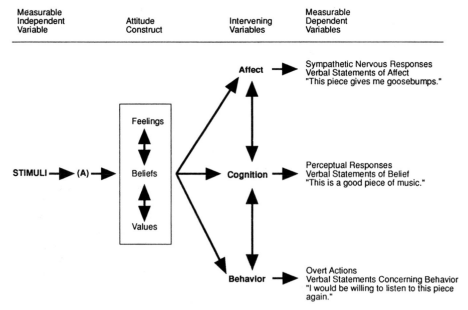

FIGURE 19–1. A Model of Attitude Adapted from Rosenberg and Hovland (1960).

stimulus. These types are action, physiological response, and verbal statements. Only verbal response is common to all three response components of the Rosenberg and Hovland model of attitude.

This three-component model is attractive to researchers for three reasons. First, there is the model's "resemblance to classifications used in other branches of psychology—notably learning theory, where distinctions may be made between conditioned and unconditioned emotions (affect), expectancies (cognition) and operant responses (behavior)" (Eiser, 1987 p. 14). This similarity makes attitude research easy to understand because of the relationship to the objective findings of other studies. This advantage is especially attractive when attitude measurement is just one component among several dependent variables.

The second attraction of the model is the implication that attitudes are learned in response to stimuli that can be systematically provided and objectively measured. Third, the prominence of verbal statements in all three response components of attitude facilitates measurement.

Kuhn (1980) adapted the Rosenberg and Hovland model to attitude toward music. In his adaptation, he specified the role of perception in the attitude formation process. Between the physical stimuli (music) and the attitude construct, he inserted the perceptual process. Perception is denoted as occurring with "A" in Figure 19–1. Perception as part of the process is an important addition; it implies that the actual stimulus (the measurable independent variable in the original model) is dependent on the individual's perception of the stimulus, a perception that may be different among individuals despite the constancy of the stimulus. Thus Kuhn opened the debate of whether the true nature of the stimulus to which the individual is responding can be accurately measured. Unable to resolve this question, Kuhn accepted the three-component model for music.

This model is not without its critics, however. Breckler (1984), for example, has reanalyzed data from experiments conducted during the 1960s and 1970s that explored the interrelationships of the three attitude response components. He sought to determine whether the pattern of intercorrelations was reliable, but following the investigation was unable to say with certainty that it was.

In contrast, Eiser (1987) has argued that one should not expect the intercorrelations among the three response components to be consistent. He believes that since the Rosenberg and Hovland model implies that attitudes are learned over time, each construct should be expected to have its own unique learning history, which may or may not be consistent with the other modes. Measurement of any one construct, then, would reveal a unique interaction among the three specific response components and attitude. Interaction developed (learned) over time in particular situations may or may not parallel the learning history of other constructs.

For example, children are asked their opinion of mice. They state what they have learned through innumerable cartoons and storybooks; namely, that mice are cute, little, gentle, furry animals. Yet, upon seeing one in their bedroom they are terrified and scream for their parents. This reaction demonstrates the conflict *between* cognition, affect, and behavior. The responses would have been learned at different times and in differing contexts.

A difference can also be seen *within* modes, for example, behavior. The same child upon seeing a mouse in a glass cage may speak gently to it and even play with it, whereas when the mouse is out of the cage in the bedroom, the child's response may be to run away.

Similarly, a sixth-grade student may learn through the immediate social environment (i.e., friends), that operatic music is "boring." (Although this is not an attitude, it is used here in the sixth-grade vernacular to denote that common early adolescent attitude with which all teachers are familiar. It is pronounced in a descending fifth pattern with both syllables elongated and accented.) This is abstract cognitive learning in that the actual stimulus of operatic music was probably not present during the learning. Still, when listening to a performance of an opera, the child may feel fear in response to a certain passage of music. The affective mode, therefore, will have a different learned response to the actual stimulus. The same child, involved in the story, becomes curious about what will happen next. Given the choice to stop listening or continue, the child chooses to continue, resulting in a behavioral response. Thus, when the attitude is measured in response to the piece of music, the child could conceivably express fear (affective response), but still express a desire to continue listening (behavioral response). However, when asked about the music, the child might respond that it is "boring" (cognitive response).

So what is the child's attitude toward operatic music in this contrived example? One must conclude that it is the complex network of interconnections between the child's feelings, values, and beliefs (their attitude construct) interacting with the response components of affect, cognition, and behavior.

Such an inherently complex attitude network "may or may not contain inconsistencies" (Abelson, 1967, p. 349). Thus, when measured individually, the modes should not be expected to coincide: the inconsistency of response should be accepted as natural (Eiser, 1987, p. 22). This explanation is given support by the low correlations found between response modes such as verbal statements and behavior in music education research (e.g., Flowers, 1981; Geringer, 1982; Hargreaves, 1988; Kuhn, Sims, and Shehan, 1981).

The reconciling of inconsistencies in the attitude network must be treated with caution (Abelson, 1967). There appears to be a desire on the part of individuals to reduce the differences *once they become aware of their existence.* "There are innumerable inconsistencies in anyone's belief system which may lie dormant and unthought about. Pressure towards . . . balance . . . operates only when . . . 'cognitive work' is applied on the issue" (Abelson, 1967, p. 350).

One method of achieving this balance is through denial. An example of this can be seen by returning to the child who said that operatic music is "boring" but responded differently to an actual piece of music. The child may not realize that this imbalance exists, and if attention is brought to the imbalance, will work to achieve balance through denial of one of the responses. In this case, it is probable that the child will work to change the affective or behavioral responses, since the social pressures on the cognitive response are so strong. Thus, to point out the imbalance to the student may in fact work to change substantively, in a negative manner, the student's response to operatic music.

In the same way, an attitude test that makes students aware of any inconsistencies they may have in their attitude network becomes a reactive measure, which, in turn, leads to a reduction in the internal validity of the experiment in which it is being used (see Best and Kahn, 1989). This reactive effect can influence attitudes so strongly that attitude studies are recommended to use only posttest or Solomon four-group type designs (Adams, 1982).

The reactive nature of attitude tests also has strong implications for test reliability, a topic discussed later in this chapter. Extreme care should be taken when constructing a measure (or planning instruction) to avoid highlighting to the students any differences they may hold.

These issues aside, the three-component view of attitude response provides a model for producing a balanced measurement of the construct of attitude. Measurement should strive to include aspects of all three modes of the model, as Adams (1982) explains:

If a single measure or several measures of the same type are used to measure attitudes, it becomes impossible to distinguish the amount of variance due to the attitude distinguished from that attributable to the characteristic errors inherent in that method. . . . By using a variety of methods, one can make sounder inferences and can have a broader base of support for those inferences than is possible through the use of any single data source. (p. 184)

Unfortunately, this suggestion is not always feasible. The amount of time required to measure cognitive, affective, and behavioral responses separately in subjects would pose a large problem and probably result in much smaller research samples.

A workable compromise is the use of verbal responses that reflect all three response modes of the model. Thus, respondents report what they think they would do or feel in response to the stimuli. However, this technique tends to accentuate the cognitive response mode in that all verbal reports of affect or behavior are filtered through the cognitive response mode.

One way to limit this accentuation is to measure the attitude using the actual stimulus that represents the independent variable rather than a verbal description of the stimulus. Failure to do so results in all responses being filtered through the cognition component (like the child and mice), thus minimizing the effect of affect and behavior. Where the stimulus is present, the subject can report a more direct response. For example, more accurate measurement of attitude toward music or any music education–related construct will result if the response is to the actual music or circumstance.

Thus, verbal response can be used with a certain degree of confidence if the above limitations are understood and steps are taken to reflect all three response modes verbally.

Such steps would begin with the creating of a list of statements which reflect as many interactions between the attitude and the three response components as possible. Once the investigator is satisfied that statements are representative of the ways of manifesting the attitude, the relative weight of each interaction is estimated and items are chosen accordingly. Using this scheme, a survey intended to measure attitude toward "band class" might look something like Figure 19–2. Collectively the statements of the survey deal with feelings, beliefs, and values (the three parts of the construct of attitude) as exemplified through the three intervening response components of affect, cognition, and behavior.

An example may clarify the testing procedure. A part of the construct of attitude towards "band" is the valuing of the band experience. This valuing interacts with the cognitive mode and can be measured through a question such as "Band class is an important part of my life." The valuing is also exemplified through the behavioral mode and can be measured through a question such as "I practice because a good sounding band is important to me." Any attitude has many such combinations inherent in it. The first step in measurement of attitude is to choose the appropriate combinations to measure. This decision will ultimately determine the validity of the measure, an issue to which we now turn.

Reliability and Validity in Measuring Attitudes

Because attitudes are learned over time through one's experiences, they tend to be highly personalized. Disagreement exists as to whether this in fact makes them persistent over time (Summers, 1970; Kuhn, 1980) or fluid and prone to change from day to day as more knowledge is added to the network (Henerson et al., 1987; James and Kuhn, 1988). Be that as it may, in measurement the personalized, fluid quality of attitudes is often negated in favor of a so-called group attitude, which may or may not exist. Although a group attitude seems to exist in emotionally charged and short-lived "mob psychology" situations, more personal attitudes appear to be highly individualized and more long lasting. "The rather large body of literature on attitude clearly indicates that while [a person's attitude] is amenable to change, the alteration of attitude, especially that which is strongly held, requires substantial pressure" (Summers, 1970, p. 2).

The resistance of attitude to change creates an interesting dilemma. As pointed out, one of the pressures that can change an attitude is a reactive measure that makes individuals aware of their own inconsistencies. The prevalence of this phenomenon can be seen in the traditionally low reliabilities resulting from test-retest procedures (Adams, 1982). Therefore, although test-retest is one of the common methods for determining test reliability, it is not recommended for attitude measurement (Adams, 1982, p. 186). Rather, the Kuder-Richardson method is preferred as it measures internal consistency without the need for multiple test administrations (Bohrnstedt, 1970).

Even so, the ambiguities inherent in an attitude tend to be reflected in low reliability scores. "In the case of attitude

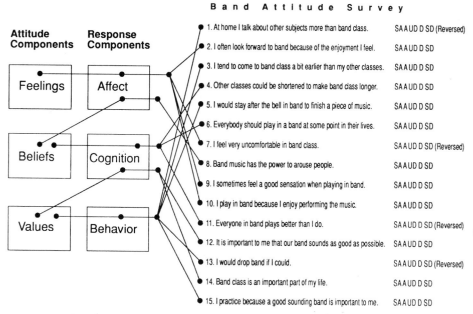

FIGURE 19–2. Construction of an Attitude Scale That Reflects Differing Component Combinations.

measurements, while reliability coefficients of .70 and above are certainly desirable, lower coefficients are sometimes tolerated, although this affects the confidence with which you can make decisions based on measurement results" (Henerson, et al., 1987, p. 154). Bohrnstedt (1970) offers a detailed discussion of reliability in attitude measurement.

The establishment of acceptable validity for an attitude measure is always open to criticism. Because of the abstract nature of the underlying construct of attitude, an unequivocal demonstration that the attitude was accurately measured cannot be achieved.

Still, this ambiguity should not deter the researcher or teacher from attempting to measure the attitude of the groups with which they are working. The validity of a measure is greatly dependent upon accurate indentification and sampling of all possible manifestations of attitude, as described earlier. Careful attention to this step in the measurement procedure can increase an instrument's validity.

Validity should *not* be determined solely by comparing individuals' written responses with their actions or physiological responses. As was discussed, inconsistencies in these responses, rather than displaying that measurements are invalid, instead may highlight the different learning histories of each mode in relation to the stimuli in question. We can expect consistency between the three modes only when the learning histories are similar, a situation that will be the exception in music.

Although numerous methods of validation can be used—such as solicitation of the opinions of "judges," correlation with known measures, factor analysis, or correlation with known groups—we may ultimately be left with having to trust individuals to be honest with their verbal response. In the final analysis, attitudes are so complex that what persons believe their attitude to be might be more valid than direct objective measurement of it, were that possible. Ultimately, individuals' beliefs filter the perception and response to any given stimulus.

Musical Preferences

In the music education research literature "the word 'preference' [is] sometimes used in the manner in which 'attitude' is defined" (Price, 1986, p. 152). This is an error, as attitudes and preferences are fundamentally different.

An attitude is the direct result of prior learnings related to the attitude object. A preference, although influenced by prior experience, does not require prior knowledge of the stimulus. Preference is defined as "an act of choosing, esteeming, or giving advantage to one thing over another" (Price, 1986, p. 154).

For example, most music teachers, lacking previous knowledge of or experience with the music of the Navajo Indians, would not possess a substantive attitude toward the genre. Yet if two pieces of music were played for them, one Navajo and one Blackfoot, teachers could express a preference for one over the other. This is not unlike one's preference for the taste of chocolate ice cream over vanilla ice cream.

Just as one does not need to have any specific knowledge to have a preference, knowledge by itself will not normally change a preference. Knowledge could increase one's appreciation for vanilla ice cream, but one would probably always prefer chocolate. Since preferences are not necessarily based on knowledge, they, unlike attitudes, cannot be taught.

Because preference is defined by an outward act, it is much easier to measure than are attitudes. This does not mean to imply that preferences are not the result of complex influences. Instead, the network of influential variables being measured with a preference test is different from that being measured with an attitude test.

The diversity of influences on preference decisions can be seen in the Model of Musical Preference created by Le-Blanc. LeBlanc proposed his model for musical preference, in detail, in the early 1980s and has subsequently subjected it to empirical tests (e.g., LeBlanc, 1980, 1982, 1986).

LeBlanc attempts to identify all sources that account for musical preference (Figure 19–3). These sources can be arranged in an eight-level hierarchy, which in turn is organized into three broad categories: sources related to the music,

sources related to the listener's cultural environment, and sources related to the personal characteristics of the listener per se.

Those variables that concern both the actual music and the listener's environment are found in level eight of the model; they include the actual properties of the music, referential meaning applied to the music, and the listener's peer group. As the model suggests, the nine variables that constitute level 8 interact in an almost unlimited number of possible combinations and relative weightings.

The next three levels—seven, six, and five—represent filters or gates through which the stimulus must pass before the variables related to the listener can come into play. Basically, levels 7 and 6 suggest that the listener must have the proper physical "equipment" (such as proper hearing) and must be

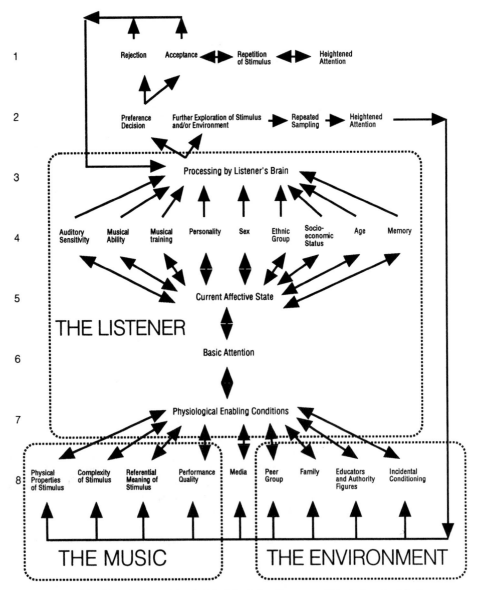

FIGURE 19–3. LeBlanc's Model of the Sources of Variation in Music Preference.

paying attention in order for further processing to continue. Level five, the mood of the listener, is the filter that interacts with all of the variables of level four.

Level four of the model contains the variables that are fairly stable characteristics of the listener, such as gender, auditory sensitivity, musical aptitude, training, personality, and maturation. Like the variables of level eight, the variables of level four interact in almost endless patterns with each other as well as with those of levels three and five.

Level three represents the actual cognitive processing of the music as perceived by the individual. This perception, of course, is the culmination of the influences of all prior levels. As such, the model from levels eight through three can be viewed as a model of musical perception. It is only in levels two and one that the actual personal *decisions* related to musical preference take place. Therefore, levels eight through three, minus the "music" component, could also replace the letter A on Figure 19–1 to create an extremely detailed model of attitudes toward music. LeBlanc (1982) himself supports this assertion.

LeBlanc's Model of Musical Preference provides a wealth of potential independent variables for study relative to the constant dependent variable of music preference. Further, some levels can act, and have acted, as dependent variables—for example, when rewards are given for a student's on-task behavior.

With respect to measurement, the model provides a means for focus and isolation of variables. It also provides some fascinating experimental challenges as attempts are made to measure not only the effects of manipulation of each variable but also the relative weights and interactions of the many sources of variation affecting musical preference.

The measurement techniques used in preference research have quantified the "act of choosing" through both verbal and behavioral means. Verbal preference involves stating a choice in either written or spoken form for one stimulus over another. Behavioral preference, also called operant preference, can be demonstrated through "actions such as concert attendance, recording purchase, choosing to listen to specific music" (Price, 1986, p. 153).

TECHNIQUES OF ATTITUDE MEASUREMENT

This section of the chapter will examine specific techniques for both attitude and preference measurement. Attitude measurement techniques will be described in terms of the outward responses that have been measured to infer attitudes. These techniques fall roughly into the three dependent measures categories described in Figure 19–1: verbal response (both written and spoken), overt action (behavior), and physiological responses. Preference measures will be described separately.

Attitude Measurement Through Verbal Response

Unquestionably the most common type of attitude measurement is that of inferring individuals' attitude from their own words. This type of measurement falls roughly into two categories. In the first, individuals are asked to report their attitude toward an object; this is termed "self-report." In the second, individuals' attitudes are inferred from their writings about an object; this is "content analysis." With the first type of measurement, individuals are aware that their attitude is being measured; with the second they are not.

Before specific self-report techniques are reviewed, two points made above need to be restated. First, regardless of the type of self-report technique chosen, the testing should be conducted in the presence of the actual stimuli. For example, if one is measuring music teachers' attitudes toward rock and roll, the teachers should be asked to respond to actual aural examples of rock music, not just to answer questions *about* rock music. This practice will reduce, thought not eliminate, the biasing effect of filtering all responses through the cognitive response mode that is inherent in any self-report technique.

Second, all self-report measures should include items that reflect all aspects of the attitude as presented in Figure 19–1. Further, relative weightings (Figure 19–2) need to be addressed within the test length limits imposed by administration needs.

Thurstone Method One of the earliest systematic attempts at constructing an attitude scale was that of Thurstone (1928). His technique, although laborious, provides a good example of a technique for item generation. A list of 100 to 150 statements addressing the attitude to be measured is gathered from groups of individuals and by searching appropriate written literature. These statements are selected to cover a wide degree of gradations ranging from one extreme to the other and must be worded so as to be either accepted or rejected. A number of neutral statements are included to assure that the final instrument does not divide itself into two parts and thus measure only two large "groups" of opinions. Typical statements ranging from negative to positive might be the following: "School time is too valuable to be wasted on something as frivolous as music." "It doesn't hurt to have time for music instruction in the school." "Music is central to a proper schooling."

Once gathered, 80 to 100 of the statements are printed, one each, on index cards. A group of 200 to 300 individuals are asked to arrange the statements into 11 piles that are evenly spaced between the two poles of opinion regarding the issue. The piles are numbered from one to 11, and the middle pile (6) is termed "neutral."

The number of the pile into which each individual places the specific statement is noted. The result of this procedure is that each statement will have 200 to 300 individual scores ranging from one to 11. Because of this large number of scores, the responses to many of the questions can be expected to approximate a "normal curve" of distribution. Therefore, after the mean, median, and standard deviation are calculated for each statement, those statements for which scores most closely approximate a normal curve of distribution are chosen as potential items for the final instrument. From this pool of items 20 to 30 statements are selected that span the entire range of the attitude to be measured. These

20 to 30 statements constitute the final version of the measurement instrument. This procedure should ensure that these final questions collectively possess a high degree of validity.

The questionnaire is administered to the group to be measured, participants putting a plus by those statements that they endorse and a minus by those with which they disagree. The attitude of the individual is calculated by averaging the scale value of all the statements that were endorsed.

Although very time-consuming, the Thurstone method holds much value for the music researcher interested in creating valid statements concerning attitudes. The scoring procedure utilizing pluses and minuses, however, has by and large been replaced by the Likert scale, which has been shown to be more reliable.

Likert Method In 1932, Renis Likert proposed a technique of attitude measurement that he claimed was faster, equally or more reliable, and equally or more valid than the Thurstone method. His technique is unquestionably the most common attitude measurement technique used in music education practice and research today.

Like Thurstone, Likert emphasized the importance of statement generation. Unlike Thurstone, he generated statements requiring a "judgement of value" as opposed to a "judgement of fact" (Likert, 1932, p. 22). Consequently, these statements often included words such as "should" and "ought." Most of the statements were drawn from approximately 200 newspapers and magazines, a smaller number coming from books, addresses, and pamphlets. Special emphasis was given to the dogmatic types of statements found in editorials, but the range of statements resembled a normal distribution of the attitude in question.

Once the statements were generated, about half were put into a negative form to disguise the attitude being studied by the researcher. After each proposition, the respondent was provided with the options of (1) strongly approve, (2) approve, (3) undecided, (4) disapprove, (5) strongly disapprove. The "attitude" of the individual is determined by taking a summated score of all the items (being careful to once again reverse the items that were originally reversed).

In attempting to strengthen the reliability of Likert scales, researchers have tried increasing the number of possible responses from five to seven, nine, or even 10. "Increasing the number of response categories beyond five, however, has usually not resulted in increased reliability, for subjects do not use the additional categories to any great extent" (Adams, 1982, p. 186).

Extensive research has examined the claims of increased reliability and validity of Likert's method over Thurstone's. Seiler and Hough (1970) and Flamer (1983) have reviewed this literature. Likert himself reported the same reliability with half the number of items as the Thurstone scale. The findings of others seem to confirm both methods as valid, with the Likert procedure showing better reliability (Seiler and Hough, 1970).

Likert scoring of Thurstone scales has been shown to increase the reliability of those scales. This fact has important implications for music education research in that the Likert method of statement generation does not seem well suited to the issues of music education. Likert created his statements regarding such highly charged issues as war and segregation. In a review of 200 newspapers one could conceivably fail to find a single opinion-based statement regarding music education. For this reason, as well as increased reliability, the combination of Thurstone statement generation procedures with Likert scoring seems appropriate.

Likert intended his scales to be summated. However, this assumes that all statements on the instrument are equally weighted in importance in measuring the attitude. This is a difficult assumption to meet. In practice, therefore, a mean score of all items is often used. In addition to producing a smaller range of scores, this practice creates an interesting analysis dilemma. In the research literature, Likert scales are almost exclusively treated as if they produce parametric data, yet this assumption is open to debate. At issue is whether the points on the scale are truly equidistant.

If the points are not equidistant, the data violate an assumption underlying the use of ANOVAS, *t* tests, and the like. Westerman (1983) found that Likert scales produce parametric data only when certain conditions are met; Hofacker (1984), meanwhile, asserts that points on Likert scales can never be truly equidistant. Still

in assuming interval measurement when only ordinal can be proven, measurement error will occur. [However,] the result of errors generally is the attenuation of relations among variables. That is, one's apparent results will be more attenuated than they are in reality. Thus, it is unlikely that the decision to assume interval measurement when it does not exist will lead to spurious overestimation of results. (Bohrnstedt, 1970, p. 82)

The creation of the equidistant five-point scale was a major contribution of Likert's work. Unfortunately, in much of today's research *any* five-point scale is called a "Likert" scale. In many cases, the words used to describe the five points on the scale are not chosen with the same care as they are in true Likert scales, nor are statements created with the care and attention that either Likert or Thurstone exercised. Consequently, results from these studies must be interpreted with caution.

In music education research, the Likert-type scale is the most common method of attitude measure. Examples would exhaust this chapter (see Kuhn, 1980, for listing). One interesting variation was used in the Attitude Toward Music Scale created by Hedden (1982). Here the items are stated both positively and negatively, one version on each side of the page. The respondent then either agrees with one of the two statements or is "undecided." This method is probably easier for young children to understand than is a traditional Likert scale.

Another variation of the Likert scale involves using cartoon faces to replace the written five-point scale (Peery and Peery, 1986; May, 1985; Brown, 1978; Kuhn 1976). These faces, ranging from smiling to frowning, are useful when assessing the attitudes of young children.

Semantic-Differential The semantic-differential method of attitude measurement is also common in music education research (e.g., Cox 1989; Madsen and Duke 1985; Miller 1980; Ridgeway and Roberts, 1976; Moore 1976). In this method, conceptualized by Osgood, Suci, and Tannenbaum (1957), two bipolar adjectives (such as bad/good, happy/sad, love/hate) are presented to the individual being tested. Spanning each pair of terms are seven points numbered from one to 7. Individuals indicate the number along the continuum they feel best reflects the item being evaluated. Answers to all items are then summed. Thus, if six items are being used in the instrument, the scores might range from six (very negative) to 42 (very positive), with a neutral score of 24. Heise (1970) reports several studies that found high reliability for this measure.

A unique advantage of the semantic-differential technique is one often overlooked in music studies utilizing the technique. Semantic-differential scoring has the potential to measure and report a person's attitude along three dimensions simultaneously, thus allowing for in-depth measuring of subtle differences in attitude. The three dimensions are labeled evaluation, potency, and activity (EPA). Examples of each that could be used with a musical example are nice/awful for evaluation, powerful/powerless for potency, and noisy/quiet for activity. "Using a few pure scales of this sort, one can obtain, with considerable economy, reliable measures of a person's overall response to something" (Heise, 1970, p. 235).

There are two ways to depict the results of this type of measurement. The first is to consider the three scores as coordinates in a three-dimensional graph. The center of this space is complete neutrality toward an object; moves along any of the three axes portray the individual's, or group's, attitude toward the stimulus. Although this method of scoring produces in-depth measurement of an attitude, it is space consuming and scores are not easily compared through traditional statistical analysis.

To overcome these limitations, the three axis points of semantic-differential scales are often combined into what is called a D score. For this procedure the seven scores are arranged $-3, -2, -1, 0, 1, 2, 3$, and subjected to several easy mathematical procedures to produce the combined D score (see Heise, p. 242).

The D score can best be illustrated by an example. The average EPA factor scores for the concepts HOME, OFFICE, and WORK were . . . entered into the formula for D. It was found that the distance between HOME and WORK is about 3.8 units while the distance between OFFICE and WORK is .8 units. Thus, the affective reaction to work is more similar to that for office than to that for HOME. (Heise, 1970, pp. 242–243)

The three factors described above can be altered to accommodate the stimuli toward which attitudes are being measured. For example, Nyberg and Clarke (1982) used evaluation, usefulness, and difficulty to assess students' attitude toward school subjects (including music), while Fujihara and Tagashira (1984) used affective and historical dimensions to rate musical stimuli. Still, Murakami (1984) found high reliability in his measure with slight modifications to the standard EPA structure when measuring response to musical stimuli.

Guttman Scalograms Guttman (1944) proposed an interesting scale that works to categorize individuals according to their attitude toward an object. The individual answers a set of multiple-choice questions regarding the attitude to be measured; the questions are arranged in a hierarchy pattern based on the firmness of the individual's attitude.

The following example could be used for categorizing band directors' attitudes toward their teaching of beginning instrumental music. The directors respond to each of these questions:

1. If you were offered a high school band directing job, what would you do?
   (a) I would take the job.
   (b) I would turn it down if I thought I could get a job that also included beginning instrumental music instruction.
   (c) I would turn it down and look for a job in beginning instrumental music instruction.
2. If you were offered a position in beginning instrumental music instruction, what would you do?
   (a) I would turn it down.
   (b) I would turn it down if I could get a job that also included high school instrumental music instruction.
   (c) I would take the job.
3. If you could not get a high school band directing job, what would you do?
   (a) I would go back to school or look for another job outside of music.
   (b) I would look for a job in beginning instrumental music with some other duties at the high school level.
   (c) I would look for a job in beginning instrumental music.
4. If you could teach anything you want, would it include beginning instrumental music?
   (a) no
   (b) yes

The possible responses are arranged into categories, as shown in Table 19–1 (p. 304).

To interpret this graph, one looks at the common characteristics in each category. For example, category H is made up of those individuals who responded "C,C,C,B" and thus have a strong positive attitude toward beginning instrumental music, whereas individuals in category A (A,A,A,A,) hold a low opinion of beginning instrumental instruction. Individuals in groups B through G hold attitudes that vary between the two extremes.

Admittedly, this type of scale is difficult to construct. Still, it has the advantage of economy: In-depth attitudes can be measured with a minimum of questions. It also indicates categories of beliefs, not just beliefs along a continuous scale, enabling the researcher to look for other characteristics common to each group in order to infer the roots of the attitudes.

No music education studies were located that utilized this

TABLE 19–1. Possible Responses to Questions 1 through 4 with Corresponding Response Categories

Question	Response		
1	Take the job 50%	Turn down if. . . 35%	Turn down 15%
2	Turn down job 40%	Turn down if. . . 30%	Take job 30%
3	Back to school 32%	Look for beginning job with high school 50%	Look for Begin . . . 18%
4	No 50%	Yes 50%	
Categories:	A 40% B 3% C 4% D 3%	E 24% F 3% G 3%	H 20%

technique, although it is common in other fields such as sociology. It is included here as a suggestion for the future.

Double-Digit Analysis James and Kuhn (1988) have developed what they call a "double-digit" technique for measuring attitudes toward music. This scale attempts to address the multidimensionality of attitudes by asking for two sets of responses to each item in a set of statements. For each statement, respondents choose from zero to five for both their "enthusiasm" and their "reservation." These two scores are then combined into delta scores (E − R) and sigma scores (E + R) for analysis.

This method is intended "to cultivate more thoughtful responding in subjects, to move persons beyond mere position taking" (James and Kuhn, 1988, p. 4). James and Kuhn report "surprisingly high" internal reliability but ambiguous test-retest reliability when used with college students. As discussed earlier, this type of ambiguity is to be expected because of the reactive nature of all attitude tests.

Q-Methodology The Q-methodology is similar to the method used by Thurstone to generate statements concerning attitude. Individual statements are printed on index cards, and the subject is asked to sort the cards into piles that span the range of "most like me" or "most like my ideal" to "least like me" or "least like my ideal." This procedure is called a Q-sort. Factor analysis or pretest/posttest correlations are computed to determine the attitude or attitude change of the subject. (See Stephenson, 1953, for a description of the technique and Hanley, 1987, for a music education example.)

Multidimensional Scaling Multidimensional scaling is a two-dimensional technique for measuring the perceived psychological distance between two items. Similar to the three-dimensional semantic-differential, it has been used successfully to "search conceptual structures or to map individual attitude structures" (Adams, 1982, p. 184). An intriguing use of the technique in music can be found in Asada and Ohgushi (1991).

Other Self-Report Measures Other methods of data gathering common to music education attitudinal research include interviews, surveys, polls, and rank orderings. These methods of data collection are familiar to most people in and out of the research field. They collectively possess several strengths and weaknesses. First among the weaknesses is that most tend to be time intensive for both researcher and respondent. This is especially true of the interview, which normally involves not only time to ask questions but also time to allow the respondent to gain confidence in the researcher.

Open-ended surveys also are often time-consuming for the respondent to complete, and for the researcher to tabulate the results; in addition their results are space intensive to report. The advantage of both interviews and open-ended surveys is that they allow for more in-depth responses than do other types of measurement. The time compromise is that these methods are usually used with a much smaller sample than other types of methodologies.

Polls and surveys, common in the popular press, are easily understandable and easy to report. What they lack is the ability to probe beneath the surface of an attitude. A music education example of a poll (with rankings) can be found in Standley (1984).

In the use of self-report methods, unique problems are encountered regarding validity and reliability. Interviews appear to be greatly influenced by the interviewer. For example, when the same questions are asked by different individuals, the respondents often express significantly different attitudes (Fenlason, 1952). Likewise, polls, rankings, and surveys are often used to gather data for a specific situation and as such have a short life of usability. As Best and Kahn (1989) state, "All too rarely do questionnaire designers deal consciously with the degree of validity or reliability of their instrument" (p. 193). Yet, any of these techniques can be constructed and administered with the same attention to reliability and validity as other measures.

Content Analysis Content analysis is an interesting manner of inferring attitudes, one often overlooked in music education research. In content analysis an examination is made of logs, journals, magazines, even advertising for clues to the writer's attitudes toward a given topic. Pemberton (1987) used this methodology to capture changing attitudes in the music education profession by examining written accounts and descriptions of Lowell Mason from 1838 until 1985. Pemberton explains: "Historians are revisionists in that personal and cultural conditioning is automatically reflected in their interpretations. The nature of these views . . . reflects the cultural conditioning and personalities of observers'' (1987, p. 213).

In the same way, Dispenza (1989) examined the pictures used in advertising in the *Music Educators Journal* from 1955 through 1985. He recorded the gender of pictured music teachers according to role (e.g., conducting a band, teaching classroom music) as well as student pictures by instrument played in order to determine changing sex stereotypes over the 30-year span.

Researchers have also examined gender roles by studying the lyrics of popular songs to see changes over time (Cooper, 1985) and within a specific culture (Aho, 1984). This method of studying attitudes holds much promise for many areas of music education.

To ensure the validity of content analysis, primary sources of information must be used. In turn, these sources must meet the standards of internal and external criticism commonly used in historical research methodology. Researcher bias is also a potential threat to both validity and reliability, and care should be taken to ensure objective interpretation of the documents.

Attitude Measurement Through the Observation of Behavior

The measurement of behavior must involve observation of overt actions, a time-consuming and costly process. In 1976, Wapnick observed that the use of this type of measurement was on the increase. The subsequent ready availability of computers and hardware designed specifically for use in measuring behavior suggests that his observation probably is still true.

Cook and Selltiz (1970) recognize three broad classes of measurement of overt actions for the purpose of inferring subject attitudes. The first is one in which subjects are presented "with standardized situations that they are led to believe are unstaged, in which they believe that their behavior will have consequences, and in which the attitudinal object is represented in some way other than by the actual presence of a member of the object-class" (Cook and Selltiz, 1970, p. 30).

For example, a researcher interested in the attitudes of parents toward school music instruction could ask them to sign a petition to increase the instructional materials budget for purchasing printed music for the school's ensembles. The researcher would keep a record of how many parents signed the petition and how many refused, and of qualitative information such as comments that were made while signing. To assess attitude toward music, Pessemier (1960) used a simulated record-purchasing procedure and Sayre (1939) observed the willingness of citizens to pay a tax.

Although this is a time-consuming (and deceptive) technique, one can envision modifications where the public's reaction to purchasing "band candy" or giving donations for a chorus trip to Disney World would be measured in some way, thus providing insightful information for music person-

nel. Examples of similar techniques such as the use of video cameras, one-way mirrors, and other unobtrusive measures can be found in Kuhn (1980).

The second class of behavior measurement of attitude involves role-playing in a staged situation. If the researcher wanted to explore music teachers' attitudes toward allowing disabled students to participate in music ensembles, a scenario such as the following could be arranged: The teachers could be asked to pretend they were the principal of the school, while the researcher pretended to be a parent of a nondisabled student who was upset that the disabled student was preventing his or her child from receiving the best possible musical experience. Stanton and Liwak (1955, reported in Cook and Selltiz, 1970) found that one half-hour session of this type of role-playing was a better predictor of subject behavior than were 12 hours of intensive interviewing by a trained individual.

The third class of behavioral measurement involves choices. This class of behaviors has received the most use in music education research; almost all of it has been used to measure musical preferences, a task to which it seems well suited. In this type of measurement, subjects are asked to make some sort of choice decision about a situation that has highly personal meaning to them. For example, Best and Kahn (1989, p. 207) describe a procedure where students are asked to create a list of the three students from a class whom they would like to invite to their birthday party. Lineburgh (1990) modified this technique to examine "free time" partners in a multiethnic preschool class before and after lessons on world musics.

Another type of behavioral response uses either a dial or a computer input device arranged in five Likert-type categories. As individuals listen to a piece of music, they are free to move the dial or lever to indicate the amount of enjoyment at any given moment. The information is encoded by a computer for analysis, thus making possible the correlational analysis of attitude during a piece of music. It has the drawback of reducing attitude measurement to a one-dimensional construct filtered through the cognitive domain, producing a Likert-type response with the added dimension of recording change over a relatively short period of time.

A somewhat related approach has the respondent manipulate an apparatus to alter some aspect of the music being heard. For example, Killian (1985) asked listeners to adjust the individual volumes of each of the parts in a four-part voice texture until they liked the balance. In this manner she was able to measure attitudes toward choral balance. Other examples of similar techniques can be found in Wapnick (1980), in Geringer (1976), and as early as Farnsworth, Block, and Waterman (1934).

Kuhn (1980) and Boyle and Radocy (1987) list other, less popular, means for measuring attitudes through behavior. The reader is directed to these two sources for more information.

The observation of a person's behavior would seem to provide an accurate measure of the attitude construct; however, individuals often mask their true attitudes for social, professional, political, or other reasons. Frequently, a low correlation exists between an individual's stated attitude and corresponding behavior. Taylor (1984) gives an exhaustive review of the literature related to predicting behavior from stated attitude measurements. Given the difficulties inherent in observation of behavior, it is not surprising that verbal self-report remains the norm in attitude measurement.

Attitude Measurement Through the Measurement of Physiological Responses

Given that the construct of attitude is a subtle and highly personalized phenomenon suffering from a lack of definition and focus, it is not surprising that attempts to measure attitude through physiological response have been infrequently used in recent years. Those attempts that have been made usually seek correlations between attitude-*related* constructs such as mood and physiological responses such as heart rate, blood pressure, skin response, and brain wave patterns.

Reviews of this research can be found in Dainow (1977), Radocy and Boyle (1988), Hodges (1980), and, specifically regarding attitudes, in Kuhn (1980). The results are often contradictory, inconclusive, or worse, both. For example, after reviewing the literature regarding the effect of gender on physiological response to music, Hodges is forced to conclude that "either males and females respond differently or they do not" (1980, p. 395). Radocy and Boyle (1988) question whether these physiological changes are at all related to attitude.

Kuhn seems to have correctly predicted that "research in this area will likely wane" (1980, p. 6). During the decade of the 1980s, little attempt was made to measure attitudes through physiological response. It may be that attitudes, especially those that are not extreme in nature, do not manifest themselves readily through physiological responses. On the other hand, the problem may be in the lack of proper technology or in the failure to identify the proper physiological responses for adequately measuring attitude. Be that as it may, at the present time, no reliable or commonly accepted means are available for measuring attitude through physiological response.

Measurement Techniques for Musical Preference

Preference involves choosing between two or more possibilities; it is patently easier to measure than is attitude. The most common type of preference measure is a pair-comparison method in which individuals are asked to indicate their preference between paired musical examples (e.g., LeBlanc, 1986) or other music-related items such as school activities (MacGregor, 1968).

A multiple-choice comparison is made when individuals are asked to indicate their preference from among several musical examples. Individuals could also be asked to indicate their preferences from a list of statements about music or music education. Kuhn (1980) lists over 50 music education studies that utilize this technique for a variety of dependent variables.

Another technique for assessing preference involves the listening behavior of subjects measured in the amount of time spent listening to a specific piece of music. This technique involves some sort of electronic apparatus that monitors subject choices. Two of these, the Operant Music Listening Recorder and Music Selection Recorder, have different types of music on different channels. The subjects are free to choose, in private, any channel to which they wish to listen. The amount of time spent on each channel is recorded by the device (see Alpert, 1982; Baker, 1980, for examples). Of note is the fact that such behavioral responses have been shown to have very little relationship to verbally expressed preferences (Flowers, 1981; Kuhn et al., 1981).

Comparatively few studies were located that attempted to measure preference through physiological techniques. Recent examples include Peretti and Zweifel (1983), who sought to measure the effects of preferred music styles on anxiety level as measured through physiological skin responses. They found that musical preference had an effect on anxiety but that it affected males and females, as well as music majors and nonmajors, differently. Basically, preferred music lowered anxiety in music majors more than in nonmusic majors, and among females more than males.

Nakamura (1984) attempted to correlate subjects' verbally reported preference, tempo, and "emotional meaning" of music with their galvanic skin response and respiration rates. Significant correlations were found between the two physiological variables and the reported mood (emotional meaning) of the music. Low correlations were found regarding preference.

Since preference is measured as a simple choice between two stimuli, reliability and validity of these measures could be expected to be high where respondents are convinced of their anonymity. Still, the excessively low relationships found between verbally stated preferences and behavioral response seem to argue differently. More research is needed before this question can be answered with confidence.

A major determinant of a preference test's validity would seem to be in the selection and pairing of the musical examples. Care must be taken in the choice and pairing of examples. LeBlanc's (1982) list of "generic styles" of music will be helpful in this selection process.

FUTURE DIRECTIONS IN ATTITUDE MEASUREMENT IN MUSIC EDUCATION

The measurement of attitudes can no longer be regarded as a young discipline. In fact, some support could be given to the notion that the field in general peaked during the World War II era. Indeed, with but few exceptions, the most common means for measuring attitudes were developed and refined during the first half of this century. This by itself does not imply a negative situation. Unfortunately, over the years there seems to have been a somewhat blind acceptance of these techniques and even watered down versions of these techniques.

For example, the early pioneers in attitude measurement fully understood the multifaceted nature of attitudes and intended their tools to be used in a way that would reflect this diversity. In current practice attitudes seem to be measured in whatever manner is easiest and provides the least amount of variability in answers.

In music education research the most common tool for assessing attitudes is unquestionably the Likert-type scale. "Likert-type" is not Likert. Likert emphasized the importance of question creation and distribution along a range of degrees of opinion toward a topic. Often in music education research, any questionnaire that has five points, even if composed of only a handful of questions, is called a Likert scale. This practice is both inaccurate and misleading. Although one may be measuring *something* by asking whether a type of music is "fantastic," "good," "O.K.," or "terrible," such questions fail to capture the inherent depth, diversity, and effervescence of attitudes. The recent work of James and Kuhn (1988) in measuring two degrees of attitude toward music and Murakami (1984) in measuring three levels holds much promise. Much more needs to be done, however, so that a measure that reflects the complexity and depth of attitudes can become as standard in the future as the inadequate "Likert-type" scale is today.

In the creation of an adequate measure, more thought must be given to the many components that make up attitudes toward music. Music education is itself a multifaceted discipline with goals ranging from the perfection of musical skills to the "enjoyment" of music. Researchers can follow the lead of LeBlanc and work to create a useful model for the sources of variability of attitudes toward music. Such a model would help focus the attitude research in music education.

Once a feasible model is created, tests should be developed that are specific to the different areas of music education. For example, we need standardized tests that measure students' attitudes toward playing their instrument, listening to classical music, and the like. For practical reasons, such as ease of administration, scoring, and interpretation, these tests should probably be of the paper and pencil variety.

The opening paragraph of this chapter stated that attitude is one of the most studied dependent variables in the field of music education. It would be more accurate to say that although attitude is frequently measured, it is seldom actually studied. For this to change, three recommendations are given.

First, research into attitude as a construct, worthy of study for its own sake, must be undertaken. This research should identify the makeup of musical attitudes as well as the specific stimuli to which the attitudes are directed. Second, researchers and teachers should work together to produce practical and valid instruments for measuring attitudes, instruments for use by both researchers and teachers in a wide variety of classroom settings. Third, once these instruments are created, they should be a component in most music education research studies and regular musical assessment in the schools.

The reasoning behind these recommendations is simple. Knowledge of whether a new teaching technique produces enhanced learning is of little value if we know nothing of the students' and teachers' attitude toward the procedure. The music education landscape is dotted with supposedly "superior" methodologies that few educators or students like. Likewise, how valuable is it for the teacher to know only the achievement level of students without also knowing something of their attitude? In short, attitude development and measurement need to be treated as a major component of music education (Ernst and Gary, 1965). Acceptance of these recommendations and action toward implementation will go a long way toward focusing the efforts of teachers and researchers in the important area of attitude measurement.

References

Abelson, R. P. (1967). Modes of resolution of belief dilemmas. In M. Fishbein (Ed.) *Readings in attitude theory and measurement* (pp. 349–356). New York: John Wiley.

Adams, G. S. (1982). Attitude measurement. In H. E. Mitzel (Ed.), *Encyclopedia of educational research (5th ed.,* pp. 180–189). New York: The Free Press.

Aho, W. R. (1984). The treatment of women in Trinidad's calypsoes: 1969–1979. *Sex Roles, 10* 141–148.

Allport, G. W. (1967). Attitudes. In M. Fishbein (Ed.), *Readings in attitude theory and measurement* (pp. 1–13). New York: John Wiley.

Alpert, J. (1982). The effects of disc jockey, peer, and music teacher approval of music on music selection and preference. *Journal of Research in Music Education, 30,* 173–186.

Asada, M., and Ohgushi, K. (1991). Perceptual analyses of Ravel's Bolero. *Music Perception, 8,* 241–250.

Baker, D. S. (1980). The effect of appropriate and inappropriate in-class song performance models on performance preferences of third and fourth grade students. *Journal of Research in Music Education, 28,* 3–17.

Best, J. W., and Kahn, J. V. (1989). *Research in education (6th ed.)* Englewood Cliffs: Prentice-Hall.

Bohrnstedt, G. W. (1970). Reliability and validity assessment in attitude measurement. In G. F. Summers (Ed.), *Attitude measurement* (pp. 80–99). Chicago: Rand McNally.

Boyle, J. D., and Radocy, R. E. (1987). *Measurement and evaluation of musical experiences.* New York: Schirmer Books.

Brand, M. (1985). Development and validation of the home musical environment scale for use at the early elementary level. *Psychology of Music, 13*(1), 40–48.

Breckler, S. J. (1984). Empirical validation of affect, behavior and cognition as distinct components of attitude. *Journal of Personality and Social Psychology, 47,* 1191–1205.

Broquist, O. H. (1961). A survey of attitudes of 2594 Wisconsin elementary school pupils toward their learning experience in music. Unpublished doctoral dissertation, University of Wisconsin, Madison.

Brown, A. (1978). Effects of televised instruction on student music selection, music skills, and attitudes. *Journal of Research in Music Education, 26,* 445–455.

Chen, Y., Zhang, D., and Baichuan, Y. (1984). Studies of subject preference in junior high school students. *Information on Psychological Sciences, 6,* 47–49.

Cook, S., and Selltiz, C. (1970). A multiple-indicator approach to attitude measurement. In G. F. Summers (Ed.), *Attitude measurement* (pp. 23–41). Chicago: Rand McNally.

Cooper, V. (1985). Women in popular music: A quantitative analysis of feminine images over time. *Sex Roles, 13,* 499–506.

Cox, J. (1989). Rehearsal organizational structures used by successful Ohio high school choral directors. *Journal of Research in Music Education, 37,* 201–218.

Crawford, J. S. (1972). The relationship of socio-economic status to attitudes toward music and home musical interest in intermediate grade children. Unpublished doctoral dissertation, University of the Pacific, Forest Grove.

Dainow, E. (1977). Physical effects and motor responses to music. *Journal of Research in Music Education, 25,* 211–221.

DeCecco, J. P. (1971). Attitude change in the classroom. In Lee C. Deighton (Ed.), *The encyclopedia of education (Vol 1; pp. 397–402). Macmillan.*

Dispenza, F. (1989). *Gender stereotyping of music teacher roles as reflected in photographs in the "Music Educators Journal" from 1955–1985.* Unpublished paper. Kent State University.

Doob, L. W. (1967). The behavior of attitudes. In M. Fishbein (Ed.), *Readings in attitude theory and measurement* (pp. 42–50). New York: John Wiley.

Eiser, J. R. (1987). *The expression of attitude.* New York: Springer-Verlag.

Ernst, K. D. and Gary, C. L. (1965). *Music in general education.* Washington: Music Educators National Conference Publications.

Farnsworth, P. R., Block, H. A., and Waterman, W. C. (1934). Absolute tempo. *Journal of General Psychology, 10,* 230–233.

Fenlason, A. (1952). *Essentials of interviewing.* New York: Harper and Brothers.

Fisher, R. J. (1977). Toward a more comprehensive measurement of intergroup attitudes: An interview and rating procedure. *Canadian Journal of Behavioral Science, 9,* 283–294.

Flamer, S. (1983). Assessment of multitrait-multimethod matrix validity of Likert scales via confirmatory factor analysis. *Multivariate Behavioral Research, 18*(3), 275–308.

Flowers, P. J. (1981). Relationship between two measures of music preference. *Contributions to Music Education, 8,* 47–54.

Flowers, P. J., and Jellison, J. A. (1990, November). *The measurement of music behavior in music therapy and education.* Paper presented at the annual meeting of the National Association of Music Therapists, Washington, DC.

Fujihara, T., and Tagashira, N. (1984). A multidimensional scaling for classical music perception. *Japanese Journal of Psychology, 55* (2), 75–79.

Geringer, J. M. (1982). Verbal and operant music listening preferences in relationship to age and musical training. *Psychology of Music,* Special Issue: Proceedings of the Ninth International Seminar on Research in Music Education, 47–50.

Geringer, J. M. (1976). Tuning preferences in recorded orchestral music. *Journal of Research in Music Education, 24,* 169–176.

Geringer, J., and Madsen, C. K. (1984). Pitch and tempo discrimination in recorded orchestral music among musicians and nonmusicians. *Journal of Research in Music Education, 32*(3), 195–204.

Guttman, L. (1944). A basis for scaling qualitative data. *American Sociological Review, 9,* 139–150.

Hanley, B. A. (1987). Educators' attitude to philosophies of music education: A Q study. Unpublished doctoral dissertation, University of Minnesota, Minneapolis.

Hargreaves, D. J. (1988). Verbal and behavioral responses to familiar and unfamiliar music. *Current Psychology Research and Reviews, 6,*(4), 323–330.

Hartley, L. (1991). The relationship of student attitude, enrollment, and retention in instrumental music to beginning instructional grade and grade level organization. Unpublished doctoral dissertation, Kent State University, Kent.

Hedden, S. K. (1982). Prediction of music achievement in the elementary school. *Journal of Research in Music Education, 30*(1), 61–68.

Heider, F. (1967). Attitudes and cognitive organization. In M. Fishbein (Ed.), *Readings in attitude theory and measurement* (pp. 39–41), New York: John Wiley.

Heise, D. R. (1970). The semantic differential and attitude research. In G. F. Summers (Ed.), *Attitude measurement.* Chicago: Rand McNally.

Henerson, M. E., Morris, L. L., and Fitz-Gibbon, C. T. (1987). *How to measure attitudes.* Newbury Park: Sage Publications.

Hodges, D. A. (1980). *Handbook of music psychology.* Lawrence: National Association for Music Therapy.

Hofacker, C. F. (1984). Categorical judgment scaling with ordinal assumptions. *Multivaraiate Behavioral Research, 19*(1), 91–106.

Hulbert, H. E. (1972). College freshmen attitudes toward public school music. Unpublished doctoral dissertation, University of West Virginia, Morgantown.

James, P., and Kuhn, T. L. (1988). *Double-digit analysis as a dependent measure of reactions to selected music examples by college students in a music appreciation class.* Paper presented at the Music Educators National Conference, Indianapolis.

Jellison, J. A. (1985). An investigation of the factor structure of a scale for the measurement of children's attitudes toward handicapped peers within regular music environments. *Journal of Research in Music Education, 38,* 167–178.

Killian, J. P. (1985). Operant preferences for vocal balance in four-voice chorales. *Journal of Research in Music Education 33,* 55–67.

Kuhn, T. L. (1976). *Reliability of a technique for assessing musical preference in young children.* Paper presented at the national conference of the Music Educators National Conference: Atlantic City, NJ.

Kuhn, T. L. (1980). Instrumentation for the measurement of music attitudes. *Contributions to Music Education, 8,* 2–38.

Kuhn, T. L., Sims, W. L. and Shehan, P. K. (1981). Relationship between listening time and like-dislike ratings on three music selections. *Journal of Music Therapy, 18,* 181–192.

LeBlanc, A. (1980). Outline of a proposed model of sources of variation in musical taste. *Bulletin of the Council for Research in Music Education, 61,* 29–34.

LeBlanc, A. (1982). An interactive theory of music preference. *Journal of Music Therapy, 19,* 28–45.

LeBlanc, A. (1986). Effects of vocal vibrato and performer sex on children's music preference. *Journal of Research in Music Education, 34,* 222–237.

Likert, R. (1932). A technique for the measurement of attitudes. *Archieves of Psychology, 140,* 12–21.

Lineburgh, N. E. (1990). *The effects of a multicultural music lesson on student interactions in the classroom.* Unpublished paper, Kent State University.

MacGregor, B. (1968). Music activity preference of a selected group of fourth grade children. *Journal of Research in Music Education, 16,* 302–307.

Madsen, C. K., and Duke, R. A. (1985). Observation of approval/disapproval in music: Perceptions versus actual classroom events. *Journal of Research in Music Education, 33,* 205–214.

May, W. V. (1985). Musical Style Preferences and aural discrimination

May, W. V. (1985). Musical style preferences and aural discrimination skills of primary grade school children. *Journal of Research in Music Education, 32,* 7–22.

Miller, R. F. (1980). An analysis of musical perception through multidimensional scaling. Unpublished doctoral disertation, University of Illinois, Urbana.

Moore, R. S. (1976). Effect of differential teaching technique on achievement, attitude, and teaching skills. *Journal of Research in Music Education, 24,* 129–141.

Murakami, Y. (1984). The stratified semantic structure of music: A proposal of a 3-level hierarchical model in semantic differential technique. *Japanese Psychological Research, 26,* 57–67.

Nakamura, H. (1984). Effects of musical emotionality upon GSR and respiration rate: The relationship between verbal reports and physiological responses. *Japanese Journal of Psychology, 55,* 47–50.

Nolin, W. H. (1973). Attitude growth patterns toward elementary school music experiences. *Journal of Research in Music Education, 21,* 123–134.

Nyberg, V. R., and Clarke, C. C. (1982). School subjects attitude scales. *Alberta Journal of Educational Research, 28,* 175–187.

Osgood, C. E., Suci, G. J., & Tannenbaum, P. H. (1957). *The measurement of meaning* Urbana: University of Illinois Press.

Pemberton, C. A. (1987). Revisionist historians: Writers reflected in their writings. *Journal of Research in Music Education, 35,* 213–220.

Peretti, P., and Zweifel, J. (1983). Affect of musical preference on anxiety as determined by physiological skin responses. *Acta-Pschiatrica-Belgica, 83,* 437–442.

Peery, J. C., and Peery, I. W. (1986). Effects of exposure to classical music on the musical preferences of preschool children. *Journal of Research in Music Education, 34,* 24–33.

Pessemier, E. A. (1960). An experimental method for estimating demand. *Journal of Business, 33,* 153–165.

Pogonowski, L. M. (1985). Attitude assessment of upper elementary students in a process-oriented music curriculum. *Journal of Research in Music Education, 33,* 247–258.

Price, H. E. (1986). A proposed glossary for use in affective response literature in music. *Journal of Research in Music Education, 34,* 151–159.

Radocy, R. E. and Boyle, J. D. (1988). *Psychological foundations of Musical Behavior (2nd ed).* Springfield: Charles C Thomas.

Ridgeway, C. L., and Roberts, J. M. (1976). Urban popular music and interaction: A semantic relationship. *Ethnomusicology, 20,* 233–251.

Rogers, G. L. (1985). Attitudes of high school band directors and principals toward marching band contests. *Journal of Research in Music Education, 33,* 259–268.

Rosenberg, M. J., and Hovland, C. I. (1960). Cognitive, affective and behavioral components of attitudes. In M. J. Rosenberg, C. I. Hovland, W. J. Meguire, R. P. Ableson, and J. W. Brehm (Eds.), *Attitude organization and change: An analysis of consistency among attitude components* (pp. 66–84). New Haven: Yale University Press.

Sayre, J. (1939). A comparison of three indices of attitude toward radio advertising. *Journal of Applied Psychology, 23,* 23–33.

Schaub, S. (1983). A scale of basic musical attitudes. *Diagnostica, 29,* 273–280.

Seidenberg, F. (1986). Student preferences and attitudes toward music in school. Unpublished doctoral dissertation, University of Southern California, Los Angeles.

Seiler, L. H., and Hough, R. L. (1970). Empirical comparisons of the Thurstone and Likert techniques. In G. F. Summers (Ed.), *Attitude measurement* (pp. 235–251). Chicago: Rand McNally.

Spradling, R. L. (1985). The effect of timeout from performance on attentiveness and attitude of university band students. *Journal of Research in Music Education, 33,* 123–138.

Standley, J. M. (1984). Productivity and eminence in music research. *Journal of Research in Music Education, 32,* 149–158.

Stanton, H. R., and Litwak, E. (1955). Toward the development of a short form test of interpersonal competence. *American Sociological Review, 20,* 668–674.

Stephenson, W. (1953). *The study of behavior.* Chicago: University of Chicago Press.

Summers, G. F. (1970). Introduction. In G. F. Summers (Ed.), *Attitude measurement* (pp. 1–20). Chicago: Rand McNally.

Svengalis, J. N. (1980). *Music attitude and the preadolescent male.* Paper presented at the Music Educators National Convention, Miami.

Taebel, D. K., and Coker, J. G. (1980). Teacher effectiveness in elementary classroom music: Relationships among competency measures, pupil product measures, and certain attribute variables. *Journal of Research in Music Education, 28,* 250–264.

Taylor, T. R. (1984). Attitude measurement and behaviour prediction: Literature survey. *Council For Scientific and Industrial Research Reports,* January, 150–157.

Thurstone, L. L. (1928). Attitudes can be measured. *American Journal of Sociology, 33,* 529–554.

VanderArk, S. D., Nolin, W. H., Newman, I. (1980). Relationships between musical attitudes, self-esteem, social status, and grade level of elementary children. *Bulletin of the Council for Research in Music Education, 62,* 31–41.

Wapnick, J. (1976). A review of research on attitude and preference. *Bulletin of the Council for Research in Music Education, 48,* 1–20.

Wapnick, J. R. (1980). Pitch, tempo, and timbral preferences in recorded piano music. *Journal of Research in Music Education, 28,* 43–58.

Westerman, R. (1983). Interval scale measurement of attitudes: Some theoretical conditions and empirical testing methods. *British Journal of Mathematical and Statistical Psychology, 36,* 228–239.

·20·

THE EVALUATION OF MUSIC TEACHERS
AND TEACHING

Donald K. Taebel

GEORGIA STATE UNIVERSITY

This handbook is being published at a time when the role of evaluation in schools and in the teaching field is being reshaped in important ways. This reshaping is a result of an increased focus on teachers in the policy environment and of the growing sophistication of basic and applied research in teaching (Darling-Hammond, 1990).

Teacher evaluation is a hazardous and complex undertaking, perhaps because the concepts of teaching and evaluation are multifaceted and complex. What one knows, thinks one knows, and believes about teaching will have a strong bearing on the focus and judgments of an evaluation process. Similarly, one's understandings and beliefs regarding the nature and purposes of evaluation also are central to the process of teacher evaluation. To emphasize the necessity for evaluators to clarify their own views before undertaking the evaluation of music teachers, brief mention is made here of different ways in which teaching and evaluation are viewed.

Scheffler (1973, p. 67) defines teaching as "an activity aimed at the achievement of learning," suggesting that teaching is an intentional activity. Hunter (1988, p. 62) views teaching as the "process of making decisions and implementing decisions, before, during, and after instruction, to increase the probability of learning." Wise, Darling-Hammond, McLaughlin, and Bernstein (1984, pp. 6–9) conceptualize teaching in terms of four models of teaching: teaching as labor, craft, profession, and art, with the respective models reflecting different premises, techniques, and knowledge.

Schulman, in an interview with Brandt (1988), cautions that teaching models and procedures should not be so generic that they ignore the structure of the content areas. Stodolsky (1988) suggests that subject matter seems to shape instructional practice. The many nonteaching expectations of teachers also impact on the teaching process. The extent to which these expectations should be considered in the evaluation of teaching is a matter of perspective.

One's concept of evaluation also has a strong influence on the teacher evaluation process. Evaluation by definition requires judgments, which are usually based on some type of relevant evidence. Evidence may be either objective or subjective, and multiple types of evidence are often available. Ideally, judgments regarding teaching will have a sufficient amount of objective evidence that is relevant to the process.

The relative emphasis one places on formative and summative evaluations, which are recognized as two fundamental purposes of evaluation (Manatt, 1988; Popham, 1988; Stiggins and Duke, 1988), also must be considered. Summative (or job-related) evaluation is the basis for management decisions such as selection, placement, reassignment, tenure, and termination. Formative evaluation is designed to help teachers improve their skills and to provide information or services regarding professional growth needs and opportunities (National Education Association, 1986).

State evaluation systems tend to focus on summative evaluation, although evidence suggests that few teachers lose jobs as a result of summative evaluation. Experts agree that school systems should employ both types of evaluation, but there is consensus that the two approaches should not be commingled (NEA, 1986; Manatt, 1988; Popham, 1988).

A number of generic models of teacher evaluation have been developed in recent years, and each tends to have some unique features. Most notable among these are the models developed by Popham (1988); Medley, Coker, and Soar (1984); Hunter (1979, 1988); McGreal (1983, 1988, 1990); Eisner (1985); and Shulman and associates (Wilson, Shulman, and Richert, 1987). Table 20–1 is an outline comparison of the six models in terms of their purpose (formative or summative—F or S), approach to meeting teacher needs

TABLE 20-1. Developer

Characteristic	Popham	Medley et al.	Hunter	McGreal	Eisner	Shulman
Purpose	S	S or F	S or F	F	F	F
Teacher needs	C	C	C	I	I	I
Source	P	R	T,R	P,R	P	T,P,R
Evidence	ML	SS	SS	ML	SS	ML
Procedure	Fix	Fix	Fix	Flex	Flex	Flex

(common or individualized—C or I), source of content (theory, research, or practice—T, R, or P), evidence base (multiple lines or single source—ML or SS), and procedures (fixed or flexible—Fix or Flex).

During the decade of the 1980s, music teachers, along with the rest of the nation's teachers, began to be evaluated at the state, district, and building levels. Only a handful of research studies that describe and analyze these evaluation systems, however, have been conducted (Wise et al., 1984; McLaughlin and Pfeifer, 1988; Stiggins and Duke, 1988). Furthermore, no research is known other than Taebel's (1990a,b) that examines evaluation practice with respect to music teachers. This chapter examines research studies in music education that provide insight into the evaluation of music teachers. The studies fall into the following categories: (1) specification of music teacher competencies, (2) characteristics of music teachers, and (3) classroom performance of music teachers.

The competency studies detail the expected propositional knowledge, performance skills, and teaching procedures of music teachers. Several studies include desirable teacher dispositions or personality traits. A sizable number of the studies employed observation as a mode of inquiry, and these observational procedures have been reviewed to determine their potential usefulness for evaluative purposes.

RESEARCH ON THE SPECIFICATION OF TEACHER COMPETENCIES

A system of teacher evaluation requires a frame of reference. The frame of reference may be a statement of principles of teaching and learning (McGreal, 1990); it may be a plan for professional development in specific competencies (Sergiovanni, 1987, p. 156); or it may be a set of competencies that describe "best practice" in a particular school system (Medley et al., 1984, p. 65).

Beginning with Baird (1958), 11 researchers have developed lists of successful music teacher competencies. Four of these studies were published (Baird, 1958; Stegall, Blackburn, and Coop, 1978; Taebel, 1979; Fox and Beamish, 1989); reviews of the unpublished studies have been provided by Baker (1981), Parr (1976), and Taylor (1980).

Establishing a Framework for Teacher Evaluation

These studies are important both for their specification of competencies and for the procedures used to produce the lists. Similar procedures may be used to produce guidelines, expectations, or a framework for teacher evaluation: for example, use of expert opinion (teachers, supervisors, professors). The process of dialogue, consensus building, and confirmation by direct observation is essential in constructing a valid evaluation system.

Medley and colleagues (1984, p. 55) state that the most difficult part of designing an evaluation system is to specify the dimensions of teaching in ways that differentiate competent teachers from incompetent ones. McGreal (1990) views the process as having two phases. First, the evaluation system should "include clear criteria established with significant teacher involvement that reflect what the particular school district feels provides a framework for looking at and talking about teaching" (p. 4). The second phase is the selection by the teacher and administrator of particular competencies that the administrator will focus on during a visit to evaluate professional development.

The diversity of tasks among general, choral, and instrumental music teachers makes consensus on evaluative criteria difficult. Raiman (1974), using a Delphi technique, found that ratings of the importance of competencies for music teaching lacked a high degree of consistency when the first questionnaire results were correlated with the second ($r = .65$). Taebel (1979) also found that the music teachers' ratings differed significantly on 45 percent of the music competencies, depending on whether they taught general, choral, or instrumental music. These results indicate that questionnaires by themselves fail to build a consensus; they also suggest that the evaluative criteria must reflect both the common dimensions of music teaching and the more specialized aspects. Parr (1976) and Baker (1981) observed in classrooms before they finalized their list of teaching competencies, providing a reality check, as it were.

Issues in Competency-Based Teacher Evaluation

During the decade of the 1960s, teacher-training institutions and state evaluation systems began to accept the notion that teaching could be defined by a set of competencies. Although specifying the competencies was difficult, it was not the hardest part of the task; it was considerably more difficult to measure competencies and extremely difficult to demonstrate that a teacher who exhibited a competency was necessarily more effective than one who did not. The three major issues of competency-based evaluation turned out to be (1) selection and definition, (2) measurement, and (3) validation of the competencies.

Scope and Specificity of a Competency Medley (1982) defines a competency as any single knowledge, skill, or value that is believed to be relevant to the successful practice of teaching. A similar definition is given by Taylor: "The knowledge, attitude, or behavior that is demonstrated within a given context up to a specified level" (1980, p. 6).

The scope of a competency is an issue illustrated by the varying numbers of competencies included in any list of essential teacher skills. As the number of competencies increased, their scope tended to become more narrow. In 1958, Baird listed 48 competencies; in 1976, Parr listed 511. Eventually, the number of competencies became so unwieldy that researchers and states were forced to broaden the scope and reduce the number of competencies to manageable levels. In his 1987 study, Stafford listed 22, while the state of Alabama considered 15 competencies adequate to evaluate a teacher (Coker and Taebel, 1989).

Related to the problem of scope was the need for stating the minimum level of performance for a given competency. In the early studies the competencies tended to be open; later they were closed, the distinction being that an open competency has an unlimited possibility for improvement whereas a closed competency (e.g., playing a major scale on an instrument from each family) can be specifically defined (Passmore, 1980). If the specified level was not met, the competency was presumed not to be present. Therefore, any competency that was open ended (e.g., sight singing) needed to be reduced to a set of subtasks (e.g., correctly reading simple rhythm patterns). Although the performance level of an open competency may be specified, that level is an arbitrary decision and subject to debate; a closed competency is either present or not.

The definition of teaching as a set of microcompetencies, with the level of performance indicative of the presence or absence of competencies, led some to criticize the movement for emphasizing the trivial and for implying that teaching was only the sum of its parts (Broudy, 1972). For instance, Taba considered teaching "as an organic complex in which each specific behavior . . . acquires a different meaning depending on the nature of the whole complex" (1972, p. 31).

One response to this charge was to cluster specific behaviors under broader teaching activities variously known as teaching functions (Rosenshine and Stevens, 1986; Berliner, 1983), generic competencies (Georgia State Department of Education, 1988), or "keys" (Medley et al., 1984). Baker (1981) grouped competencies as those that might be observable each day and those that required long-term observation. The use of teaching functions of "key" competencies is more manageable for both observers and teachers. When these functions are understood to include a family of related behaviors, it is possible for a teacher to demonstrate those dimensions of the teaching function that are relevant to the context rather than being expected to demonstrate each behavior separately.

Measuring Competencies: Time and Place Whereas propositional knowledge may be evaluated outside the classroom or even prior to employment, procedural knowledge is embodied in classroom interactions. Early in the competency-based teacher education movement it became obvious that some competencies could be measured only by observing a teacher perform in a classroom. Hence, the move from competency-based to performance-based teacher education (Elam, 1971).

Researchers in music education do not discriminate between these two competencies in their lists. For example, among Baker's (1981) competencies are the following:

1. Plays instrument with obvious skill
2. Communicates clearly and concisely
3. Cooperates with fellow teachers and administrators

The first can readily be assessed outside the classroom, the second must be observed during teaching, and the third competency must be measured over time.

The measurement of these competencies is developmental, a view that is delineated by Sergiovanni (1987, p. 157) as having four stages: knowledge of how to do the job, demonstration of this knowledge under actual observation, willingness to sustain the ability continuously, and demonstration of commitment to continuous growth. Sergiovanni considers the first two stages as fairly low level and within the capacity of most teachers. The remaining two stages are those that distinguish the professional from the technician.

The major measurement problem is to control for the effect that the classroom or the school may have on the competencies. Since the context (subject matter, students, equipment, space, schedule) may have a significant effect on a teacher's behavior, one cannot with any certainty assume that a teacher's performance in one situation will be the same as in another (Doyle, 1981; Soar and Soar, 1983).

Teacher Competency/Teacher Effectiveness A competency is believed to be associated with successful teaching; that is, the competency contributes to student learning. Although professional judgment is sometimes the only basis for specifying competencies and establishing minimum performance levels, it is not infallible. Both teachers and principals may err in their assumptions concerning the contribution of certain competencies to student learning (Medley and Coker, 1987). Furthermore, even when research indicates that certain teaching behaviors are possibly linked to student learning, such findings may not be generalized to all teachers in every situation (Brophy, 1988; Perry, 1989). Few music researchers appear to have recognized the error of generalizing competency statements.

Commentary Over the last 15 years school systems have built evaluation systems around specified teaching competencies believed to be generic for all teachers regardless of subject or grade level. These generic competencies were assumed not only to be "right" for all teachers, but also to be major contributors to student learning. In the final analysis, however, the competencies could be considered only minimal expectations and seldom provided guidance or motivation for further professional growth (Duke and Stiggins, 1990). The use of such preestablished competencies as fixed criteria for teacher evaluation may be most appropriate for the beginning teacher or the marginal teacher, but for those who are already effective, a fixed model may be unnecessary or counterproductive. For these teachers, evaluation is more likely to be growth producing when it is flexible and the teacher's self-evaluation is taken into account (Wise et al., 1984; McGreal, 1990). Finally, evaluation of any teacher in terms of demonstrated competencies without consideration of the teacher's purpose, the students, or the situation represents an atrophied conception of teaching.

RESEARCH ON THE CHARACTERISTICS OF MUSIC TEACHERS

Both the competency-based teacher education movement of the 1970s and the process-product research on teaching emerged at the time that behaviorist concepts of teaching and learning predominated; both are also, in some respects, a reaction to earlier, holistic concepts of teaching and learning (Borich, 1986, p. 144). One type of research from this earlier period measured the characteristics of teachers in terms of their personality traits, leadership styles, attitudes, or values (e.g., Barr, 1961; Beecher, 1949; Ryans, 1960).

After reviewing numerous studies of the relationship of teacher personality to effective teaching, Getzels and Jackson (1963) conclude that very little is known for certain about the nature and measurement of teacher personality or about the relationship between teacher personality and effectiveness. Nearly 25 years later, Levis (1987) came to the same conclusion. Evaluation experts have also tended to avoid trait research or personality variables in their evaluation models (Brandt, 1987; Popham and Stanley, 1988).

The popular belief persists, however, that personality traits are important contributors to a teacher's effectiveness, as manifested in official positions of the Music Educators National Conference (MENC) and in school district evaluation instruments. The 1972 MENC report *Teacher Education in Music* listed seven personal qualities and four professional qualities that "may be more a matter of temperament than of education" (p. 7). Fifteen years later, the MENC report (1987) on teacher preparation included numerous references to personal qualities of the music educator. Music teachers also believe personality is important: "The personal qualities of a teacher are many times more important than all of the competencies listed herein as regards success in teaching" (Smith, 1985, p. 87). In many school districts the application process requires some evaluation of traits such as loyalty and cooperation. Gregory Anrig, president of the Educational Testing Service, states that he uses personal qualities as criteria when hiring a new teacher (1987, p. 33). This emphasis on personal qualities is reason enough to examine music education research on the personality traits or leadership styles of music teachers as these relate to student outcomes.

Music Research on Teacher Personality

Research into personality traits of music teachers has almost without exception relied on standardized personality measures to provide scores on various personality traits. Researchers have tried to link global personality traits such as field dependence to criteria of teaching effectiveness such as music festival ratings. Since Barth's 1961 study, researchers have shifted from holistic measures of personality and holistic measures of student outcomes to more specific measures of both. Krueger (1974) and Caimi (1981) provide reviews of early research.

Music researchers appear to assume that a score on a standardized test should, in some way, correspond to a teacher's activities in the classroom; however, in few studies do researchers directly observe teachers in their classrooms. Even those that do (Hepler, 1986; Newman, 1986; Schmidt, 1989) use a standardized measure of their subjects' traits rather than attempt to observe such traits directly. Only Brubaker (1982) compares written measures of a teacher's expectation with classroom performance. Using such standardized measures as their independent variable, the researchers attempted to discover the relationships between a teacher characteristic and one or more student outcomes. On the whole, the results failed to establish such a relationship. Krueger (1974) found that between 12 percent and 17 percent of the variance of the students' gain scores could be explained in terms of the teachers' scores of their motivational characteristics. Bullock (1974), Caimi (1981), Goodstein (1987), Mann (1979), Newman (1986), and Beaver (1973) found practically no relationship between personality measures and student outcomes.

When researchers examined other independent context variables such as school size, ensemble size, budget for the music ensemble, socioeconomic status (SES) of students, and the presence of a teaching assistant, they discovered these variables were strong predictors of "successful" teaching (Mann, 1979; Goodstein, 1987; Beaver, 1973; Caimi, 1981). They concluded that school effects may contribute more to teaching success than any personality trait.

Research into the personality traits of putative successful teachers, as determined by ratings, nominations, or festival ratings, yielded no significant differences between the scores of successful music teachers and randomly selected groups of music teachers (Barth, 1961; Bullock, 1974; Goodstein, 1987).

The work of those researchers who combine a measure of personality with observation deserves further comment. Only Brubaker (1982) tried to observe classroom behaviors that related to her teacher expectation measure; the others used an observation instrument that had no theoretical relation to the personality measure. Newman (1986) found no significant differences between festival ratings and observed classroom behaviors, although there appeared to be a relationship between the management test scores and festival ratings. Hepler (1986) found some relationships between the teacher behaviors exhibited during applied music instruction and the field dependent/independent measures; however, the (few) correlations (of around .50) are as likely to be explained by chance as by a real relationship. Schmidt (1989) grouped teachers into their predominant personality types using the Myers-Briggs Indicator; he compared type of personality with use of behaviors (e.g., approval, disapproval) in applied music lessons. He found significant differences (ANOVA) between the means of observed teaching behaviors and the various personality groups. Brubaker (1982) found that teacher expectations manifested themselves in observable classroom behaviors, especially in the areas of student behavior and musical learning. She concluded that there was some correspondence between what teachers stated as their expectations and their actual behavior. These studies have not been corroborated by other research; thus the findings should be viewed with reservation. Yet, the methodology of direct observation of classroom interactions and the linking of behaviors to specific traits seems to hold more promise than the earlier holistic methodology.

Interpretation of the Findings

The widespread perception that a teacher's personality is a major contributor to student behavior and learning is not supported by these research studies. What explanation may be given for these counterintuitive findings?

First, there is a problem with the construct of personality and its operationalization in the form of a personality inventory. The 13 music education studies cited used 12 different personality measures, suggesting a lack of theoretical coherence. Fiske (1974, p. 1), in commenting on personality theory, states that "neither investigators nor theorists have much consensus on anything," and adds that there is an adherence to global concepts unrestricted by linkages to concrete operations. Rorer and Widiger (1983) in their review of the literature on personality assessment observe that many traits may be associated with a particular behavior.

A second problem is the tendency by researchers to aggregate their data across individuals, which virtually precludes their appropriateness as grounds on which to infer anything about any one individual. The concept of the structure of personality applies to a structure within an individual, not to a population structure; yet it is the latter and not the former that is being estimated in these and other studies (Rorer and Widiger, 1983). Given this perspective, there seems to be little value in reporting the putative characteristics of music teachers as distinct from others, nor does it make much sense to discuss the profile of one sample of "successful" music teachers in contrast to the profile of a random sample, some of whom must also be "successful."

A third problem is the assumption that certain teacher characteristics have some sort of fixed effect on student outcomes regardless of the situational factors. Hersey and Blanchard (1988) concluded that there is no single, all-purpose leadership style, whether autocratic or democratic, direct or indirect, or businesslike or nurturant. The effective leader (or teacher) is one whose style of leadership matches the needs of the group. Therefore, rather than conclude that

teacher characteristics have no effect on students, it may be more productive to consider how teachers may consciously vary certain traits on the basis of their perception of the students' readiness for a task and their psychological/social needs. After more than 30 years of searching for the characteristics of the effective teacher, Barr (1958, p. 696) concluded that "acts are not good or bad, effective or ineffective, appropriate or inappropriate in general but in relation to the needs, purposes, and conditions which give rise to them."

Implications for Teacher Evaluation

Evaluators need to have some understanding of the classroom situation and the musical tasks before they can make sound judgments about the adequacy of a teacher's competencies, personal qualities, or leadership style. Evaluators should avoid imposing a predetermined model on any particular teacher; rather, they need to consider how well the teacher's traits match the learning situation.

Evaluators also must consider that student performance outcomes (e.g., festival ratings) may be partly a function of school/community/home effects. One may attribute marked student achievement to the teacher without negative consequences for the teacher, even though such attribution may be unwarranted; however, care must be taken not to fault the teacher for below-average student achievement when the blame may rest as much with the home, school, and community as with the teacher. Careful consideration of all the variables should be made before judgments are rendered.

RESEARCH ON THE CLASSROOM PERFORMANCE OF MUSIC TEACHERS

Common sense would suggest that a teacher's classroom performance should be the foundation of an evaluation system. Although teaching is the essence of a teacher's work, observation of teaching alone is insufficient for understanding teaching (Green, 1971), failing as it does to provide information about the teacher's expectations or intentions, the teacher's planning, or how materials are selected and matched to students and objectives. Observation provides only a limited perspective on long-range instructional continuity or day-to-day versatility. Although observable, the teacher's involvement in the life of the school, the community, and the profession is unlikely to be evaluated directly. In spite of these limitations, observing life in the classroom is vital to successful evaluation if for no other reason than that it provides the teacher and the evaluator the best starting point for instructional improvement.

Prerequisites for Selection of an Observation System

First, the framework for evaluation must be considered. The concept of the teacher, the system's philosophy of education, and the purposes of evaluation are all factors in the choice of evaluative methods. For example, when the purpose is to identify incompetent teachers, the observational procedures are likely to be highly structured with specified routines and procedures (Wise et al., 1984). However, if the purpose is to improve instruction, the observation procedures are more likely to include pre- and postobservation and to take into account the teacher's objectives, the context, and any information that identifies sources of difficulty and indicates options for change (Wise et al., 1984). Evaluation systems that have multiple purposes—for example, beginning teacher evaluation, marginal teacher evaluation, and professional growth of individual teachers—will require a combination of observational methods.

When the observational procedures are determined, involvement of teachers is important. Natriello and Dornbusch (1980–81) found that teacher satisfaction was strongly related to (1) teachers' ability to affect the criteria for evaluation, (2) their perception that evaluators shared the same evaluative criteria, (3) more frequent samplings of teacher performance, and (4) more frequent communication and feedback. Teachers must agree that observation tools are suited to the purposes of evaluation and match the performance criteria.

Types of Observational Systems

Until recently, teacher evaluations were made by a school principal or supervisor as an annual or semiannual formality. The observer might write a few notes—no special format was required—and make a summary judgment about the teacher's effectiveness or give a few recommendations for improvement (Stodolsky, 1990).

During the 1980s, many states mandated more systematic and more prescriptive observation. Many types of instruments were developed, including category systems, scripting, checklists, and rating scales. A wide range of observation instruments and administrative procedures are referenced and described in Borich and Madden (1977), Evertson and Holley (1981), Medley et al. (1984), Evertson and Green (1986), and Good and Brophy (1987). The historical antecedents of today's classroom observation instruments have been well presented by Medley and Mitzel (1963) and Rosenshine and Furst (1973).

Observation research in music education is not abundant, nor does it have a long history when compared with other types of music education research. Yet, there is a growing body of observational methodology and instrumentation that may be useful in the evaluation of music teaching. Observational systems may be described from three perspectives: type of instrument (open or closed and high or low inference), data-gathering procedures, and content.

Open and Closed Systems In an open system the record is in the form of a script or recording of the events as they occur. No special categories are predetermined nor is any special coding or scoring involved. In taking open records, one

makes an effort to describe fully "all" behavior as it occurs and to avoid interpretation or selection (Stodolsky, 1990). Only a few music researchers have used this approach to observe music teachers (Fiedler, 1982; Zimmerman, 1983; Thiel, 1984; Ingram, 1985; Krueger, 1985; Wohlfeil, 1986; Huff, 1989).

A closed system is one in which specific types of behavior have been identified in advance as codable. Closed systems include category and sign systems, rating scales, and behavior checklists. A category system, such as the *Flanders System of Interaction Analysis* (1967), ordinarily has a small number of categories for coding all actions that fall within the definitions of the categories. One of the earliest observational studies in music education used the Flanders category system, and most observational studies since then also have used category systems (e.g., see Snapp, 1967; Erbes, 1972; Verrastro, 1975; Edwards, 1978). Depending on the system being used, the observer codes the various categories within a time frame of three to 10 seconds.

A sign system usually has more specificity than a category system so that behaviors, such as questioning, may be analyzed in detail. The *Classroom Observation Keyed to Effectiveness Research* (COKER; Taebel and Coker, 1980) is an example of a sign system that has over 100 specific items, including six for questioning. The large number of items requires an expansion of the coding time frame, which in the case of COKER is five minutes. Taebel and Coker (1980) used such a system to observe elementary music teachers. Others in music education have developed sign systems for recording conducting behaviors (Patterson, 1984).

Rating scales have been widely used to make summary judgments about a teacher's performance, but they are rarely used in observational research in music. Kirkwood (1974) rated music teachers on their enthusiasm, clarity, and task focus. Roshong (1978) developed a five-point rating scale for conductors that included rating a conductor's facial expression from mild to intense. Carpenter (1986) used a 26-item rating scale that required the observers to rate such characteristics as leadership style and classroom management skills. Rating scales in music vary in the number of scale points used, from three (Nolin, 1971) to 10 (Wang and Sogin, 1990).

Although rating of teachers as an evaluation technique is ubiquitous, the procedure has its critics, who contend that the categories are too global and ill defined and that the ratings are biased and unreliable, and show weak correlations with student outcomes (Medley et al., 1984; Good and Mulryan, 1990). No rating scales in music education were found that operationally defined the various scale degrees. Consequently, there is no unequivocal basis for distinguishing between a "4" and a "5" or "excellent" and "outstanding."

Low-Inference and High-Inference Variables Another distinction to be made is that between low-inference and high-inference variables. Low-inference variables are behaviorally defined and exemplified; for example, "The teacher smiles." High-inference variables encompass a range of teacher and/or student activity, such as, "The teacher is supportive of student ideas" or "Students are enthusiastic." High-inference variables are likely to be reported narratively or as a rating; furthermore, they are coded less frequently, sometimes only once during an observation period. By contrast, low-inference variables are coded throughout an observation period, with the result that some variables may be coded many times during a lesson.

Researchers who build their instruments around low-inference variables stress the objectivity of the evidence and the quantification of their results; those employing high-inference variables advocate the importance of interpreting the events and placing them in context. While the former makes a clear separation between measurement and evaluation, the latter blends the two. Phillips (1990) points out that all observation is theory laden but adds that low-inference observation, having a higher degree of objectivity, is less susceptible to debate concerning the facts of the case, even when viewed by people of different theoretical orientations. High-inference variables introduce greater subjectivity into an observation; therefore, the data do not stand on their own apart from theoretical persuasions. Even though judgments may vary, the evidence must be there for all to examine.

Multiple Lines of Evidence The complex nature of teaching makes it impossible to evaluate a teacher's performance with a single evaluation instrument (Good and Mulryan, 1990). Peterson (1987, p. 312) contends that no single line of evidence is reliable enough, works for all teachers, addresses all that a teacher does, or is compatible with the varied conceptions of teaching. Travers (1981) states that "if a school can justify evaluating all teachers through identical procedures, then the school is probably devoid of innovations" (p. 22). In the Utah Teacher Evaluation Project, eight lines of evidence were developed from which teachers could select: student report, parent survey, student achievement, teacher tests, peer review, administrator report, documentation of professionalism, and "other" (Peterson, 1987). McGreal (1988) suggests that evaluation be customized by allowing teachers to develop a plan for professional improvement that is monitored by either the principal or another teacher. Good and Brophy (1987) include a variety of observation instruments that are specific to various "problem" areas—for example, management, motivation, expectation, and modeling.

With a few exceptions, music researchers have used only one observation instrument. Carpenter (1986) compared the results of a rating form with those of a low-inference instrument, while Kirkwood (1974) used two instruments, one to record general teaching behaviors and one to record musical activities. Fiedler (1982) used three methods to gather data: systematic observation, interview, and unstructured observation.

Observation and Reporting Procedures

Training When teacher evaluation is not considered a high-stakes activity, training of the school principal as an observer is likely to be minimal. However, when an evaluation system must meet legal standards and has either summative or formative outcomes, the training of competent observers is critical. Training materials and procedures vary considerably, from the provision of a set of category definitions to a complete training package, including a manual of definitions, examples, coding procedures, videotapes of various episodes, and live observation with a trainer. Of course, the amount of training will vary with the complexity of the system, the number of observers, and the resources of the trainer. The Alabama Department of Education required all evaluators to have three days of study and two days of field experience before they were certified (Alabama CIP Project Staff, 1989). Although observational research in music education poses no professional threat to the teachers being observed, the training of the researcher bears directly on the reliability and validity of the data gathered.

Data Gathering: Live vs. Videotape Observation in district and state evaluation involves on-site visits to the classroom where the observational data are gathered as they are observed. In most research studies in music education using observation, the classroom events are videotaped and subsequently coded and analyzed. The advantages and disadvantages of videotaping are listed below:

Advantages	Disadvantages
Repeated viewings are possible	Tendency to microanalyze and lose sense of how students perceive the situation
Useful to sample episodes from the population of classroom events	Limited to the scope of the camera and the perspective of who is shooting the scene
Provides opportunity for future training in developing observation skills	May miss the "real" flavor of the classroom and the development of observation skills more typical of evaluation
Exemplary incidents may be recalled more accurately; transcripts may be prepared	May produce atypical behavior by teacher or student
May be useful in formative evaluation	May intimidate teacher, especially for summative evaluation
	Requires adequate lighting, sound, and space

The videocamera or audio-recorder, and also the microcomputer, are important tools in recording classroom events that may enlighten the teacher as well as the observer (Peterson and Comeaux, 1989; Padilla, 1990). Cassette tape recorders have been used with a computer program to record both the category and the time span of each category (Sommers, 1981). In some studies, several viewings of a videotape were needed to record all categories (Daellenbach, 1970; Patterson, 1984). Such a process is clearly impractical for teacher evaluation. To use a medical analogy, the observation system should work for the general practitioner rather than the microbiologist.

Reporting Results The data reported in music education research are usually given in aggregate form, whereas in teacher evaluation the results that are most meaningful pertain to the individual teacher. Anecdotal accounts that detail significant classroom events, free of interpretive judgments, are recommended (McGreal, 1988). A profile of a teacher's comparative performance with other teachers may also be helpful (Medley et al., 1984). In music research Grechesky (1985) provided a narrative description of each teacher in his sample as did those cited earlier who used the case study method. Case studies describing classroom activities over a lengthy period may uncover variables that may not be in evidence in a single observation.

Observational studies in music education would be more useful for metaanalysis or as baseline data for evaluation of music teachers if the following were observed:

For Descriptive Data

1. Mean scores of categories should be reported as percentages of the total observation period. Although raw scores are sometimes useful, they are difficult to interpret when different time periods are used (e.g., 3 seconds, 10 seconds, 5 minutes). Furthermore, the standard deviation, range, and skewness of each category should be given.
2. Simple correlations are often reported as if the relationships were linear, without mention of a scatterplot analysis. The possibility of a curvilinear relationship should be considered, since low correlations may be explained by that relationship. A high correlation may be obtained from one or two pairs of scores at the upper extreme of the diagonal. Researchers should conduct a follow-up analysis to all important correlations.
3. Researchers should report the reliability of student measures. They should also examine the relationships among the student categories (or items) to determine if there is an underlying factor. Rating scales, in particular, are known to suffer from halo effects that may reduce all categories to a single factor.

For Multivariate Analysis

1. When using multiple regression, discriminant analysis, or path analysis, researchers should be careful in selecting a criterion that is a stable measure of teaching effectiveness. An argument should be made for the validity of the measure, and a reliability coefficient should be given for the criterion.
2. A justification should be given for artificially dichotomizing a sample of teachers in order to do discriminant analysis, especially when cases are lost. Researchers should be aware that other variables, such as school effects, may confound results.
3. Multiple regression analysis should take into account not only active variables but attribute and context variables such as gender, experience, SES, and school size.
4. A multiple regression model (path analysis, discriminant analysis) should include the proper number of predictor variables in relation to the sample size.
5. Multiple regression analysis and discriminant analysis are strengthened if cross-validation is used.

Observer Agreement and Reliability

When decisions are to be made concerning a teacher's classroom performance on the basis of observed scores, it is important that these observed scores are reliable. Although researchers and administrators are likely to understand the concept of reliability when applied to student test scores, there is evidence of some misunderstanding concerning the reliability of observational measures—specifically, the need to separate two statistically related but conceptually different indices: observer agreement coefficients and reliability coefficients (Frick and Semmel, 1978, p. 153). Observer agreement is the degree of consensus between two or more observers during the simultaneous coding of classroom events, which is somewhat analogous to two different readers scoring the same test paper. The reliability of classroom observation scores refers to the stability of a teacher's performance. Observers could agree on the activities of teachers and students on any given occasion, yet these activities may vary greatly on different occasions. Of these two sources of error, the more important contributor to score variance is the instability of teacher/student performance across occasions, not observer disagreement (Medley and Mitzel, 1963). Rowley (1976) demonstrated that frequently coded teacher behaviors are not necessarily associated with high reliability, since a teacher may frequently exhibit a behavior on one occasion but not on another because of different content or topics.

Educational researchers often fail to report the score reliabilities of their observation measures, reporting only observer agreement coefficients (Rowley, 1976; Mitchell, 1979). Similarly, in all but a few studies, music education researchers have reported only observer agreement coefficients, not the reliabilities of measures taken on different occasions. (The exceptions are Froehlich, 1977, 1979; Taebel, 1990a; Baldridge, 1984; and Karpicke, 1987.) Failure to report score reliabilities brings into question the stability of the scores that are reported and makes generalizability of the results somewhat suspect. Furthermore, correlations between teacher behaviors and any student outcome measures are of dubious value when the reliabilities of the measures of teacher behavior are unknown (Frick and Semmel, 1978).

Observer Agreement There are a number of procedures that may be used to calculate observer agreement (Frick and Semmel, 1978; Bartko, 1976; Mitchell, 1979), but most music education researchers restrict themselves to two methods. Researchers who have used instruments based on the Flanders instrument or the Hough-Duncan instrument have used Scott's formula (Scott, 1955; Flanders, 1967). Others who have used a behaviorist model have tended to use the simple percentage of observer agreement formula found in Madsen and Madsen (1981, p. 252). Only a few researchers have used the Pearson correlation coefficient or other intraclass correlation coefficients (Hepler, 1986; Kirkwood, 1974). In all but a few instances the coefficients of observer agreement have been in the .80s to .90s for the various categories included on the instruments, with some categories having coefficients of 1.00.

Frick and Semmel recommend that observer agreement coefficients be determined at three points in a study: before actual data collection, during the study to check observer drift (Evertson and Green, 1986), and after the study.

At the beginning of a study most music researchers compare their scores with those of one or more observers, usually brought in merely to determine observer agreement. Such a procedure is satisfactory only if the researcher is an expert in using the system. Researchers would do well to use an accepted criterion (prescored videotapes, for example) from which they could learn or train others. Researchers who are developing their own instruments should construct a videotape of unambiguous examples of each category by taping a variety of situations and extracting clear examples. An alternative is to prepare such a tape using a simulated situation, perhaps with the researchers themselves giving the instruction (Frick and Semmel, 1978). In music research, Baldridge (1984) provides a good example of this procedure.

Most music researchers use other observers only to determine observer agreement; they seldom have used other observers to gather data independently. Several well-trained observers may gather data on their own, making it possible to increase either the number of teachers to be observed or the number of visits to each teacher. Since most studies have only small samples of teachers (on average about 15) or too few visits, the results would be more valuable if either were increased by using two or more observers independently (Baldridge, 1984; Taebel and Coker, 1980). Erlich and Borich (1979) discount observer error as an important factor in estimating reliability once observers have demonstrated during training that they can code with high levels of agreement.

Reliabilities of the Measures It is misleading to speak of the reliability of a measure, since a number of estimates of reliability are possible, depending on which sources of error variance are included in the calculation of reliability (Nunnally, 1982). Perhaps the most important source of variance is differences in subject (teacher/student) behavior on different occasions (Medley and Mitzel, 1963; Shavelson and Dempsey-Atwood, 1976). Reliability coefficients that take teacher instability into account are known as stability estimates and are calculated using analysis of variance procedures. The use of ANOVA to partition various error components in order to estimate the relative contribution of each source to a reliability coefficient has been recommended by a number of authorities (Ebel, 1951; McGaw, Wardrop, and Bunda, 1972; Medley and Mitzel, 1963).

In music education, stability coefficients of observational measures have been reported by Froehlich (1977, 1979), Taebel and Coker (1980), and Baldridge (1984). These researchers estimated the reliabilities to include variation in subject performance on each of their categories across four to 10 visits. As may be expected, these coefficients were much lower than the typical observer agreement coefficients. Of the 37 observed variables, Froehlich found that 18 to 19 were stable when using $r = .50$ as the criterion of stability. Froehlich also discovered that, when low stability variables were appropriately combined with other variables, the stability coefficients of these composite variables were increased.

Erlich and Borich (1979) and Rowley (1976) investigated relationships between the reliabilities of various categories, the number of observations, and the frequency of occurrence. Erlich and Borich, using the Brophy-Good Teacher-Child Dyadic Interaction System, sought to determine the number of visits required to reach a criterion of .70 for a given category. They concluded that different categories required varying numbers of observational visits, ranging from two to 10, with the average number of observations being five. They recommended that the number of observations should be that required to reach the stability criterion (e.g., .70) for the category needing the most observations. This study, along with those of Froehlich, Baldridge, and Taebel and Coker, provides baseline data on expected reliabilities that can be useful to other researchers in planning their own studies. Borich and Klinzing (1984) provide general guidelines for determining the number of visits and the length of the visits. The criteria for making a decision include (1) the existence of "ground rules" for coding and (2) whether the observed behavior is high or low inference.

Generalizability Studies Cronbach, Glaser, Nanda, and Rajartman (1972) developed a strategy, known as generalizability theory, for examining sources of variation in observational data. When applying the theory, investigators must first identify the universe to which they wish to generalize. "The universe of interest to the decision maker is defined when he tells us what observations would be equally acceptable for his purpose" (Cronbach et al., 1972, p. 15). These might include other observers of equal skill, other teachers from the same group, other times of the day, or other topics. Borich and Klinzing (1984) add other variables, including teacher grade level, teaching method, school, and teacher goals. Only two generalizability studies in music education have been found. Taebel and Medley (1979) considered the variance attributable to three different observers, in two different classes, on four different occasions. Karpicke (1987) defined his universe more narrowly by including only variance between observers and variance due to teaching method.

Generalizability studies provide valuable information about the stability of teaching behaviors and the factors that may contribute to their instability. Generalizability is important in decision studies where stable teaching variables are related to student outcome measures to ascertain the validity of these variables as measures of effective teaching.

Classification of Studies by Observation Instrument

Observational studies can be usefully grouped according to the content embodied in the instrument. The content areas include (1) social-emotional climate emphasis, (2) behavioral modification emphasis, (3) subject matter and music pedagogy, and (4) miscellaneous studies.

Social-Emotional Climate Studies These studies are derived from the work of Withall (1949), Hough (1967), and Flanders (1967). The essential concepts of the Flanders System of Interaction Analysis (FSIA) have been described as follows:

All teacher statements are classified first as either direct or indirect. This classification gives central attention to the amount of freedom the teacher grants to the student. In a given situation, therefore, a teacher has a choice. He can be direct, that is, minimizing freedom of the student to respond, or he can be indirect, maximizing the freedom of the student to respond. (Amidon and Flanders, 1967, p. 121)

The nine music education studies that have used the Flanders observation system, either in its original form or in a modified form, include Snapp (1967), Whitehill (1970), Pagano (1972), Erbes (1972), Hedrick (1976), Hicks (1976), Jessup (1984), Pontious (1982), and Montgomery (1986). One researcher (Verrastro, 1975) used Withall's Social Emotional Climate Index (1949), and two (Nolin, 1971; Reynolds, 1974) used or modified Hough's (1967) Observational System for Analysis of Classroom Interactions (OSACI).

Behaviorally Oriented Studies In the Madsen and Madsen observation system, the most important categories of teacher behavior are approval and disapproval responses. Allowance is also made for errors of approval and disapproval. Student behavior is either on-task or off-task. As Madsen and Madsen (1981) state,

Observations concerning reinforcements focus only on behaviors which follow a student's response. The individual teacher must establish goals and ascertain the most effective strategies of presentation to elicit responses that can be reinforced. . . . Academic instructions pertaining to the academic curriculum are not considered as reinforcement. . . . Questioning, probing, cueing, prompts, illustrations, modeling correct procedures, and so on, seem to be tools of effective teachers, yet these procedures do not necessarily reinforce behavior. (p. 228)

Researchers who have used this approach include Murray (1972); Kuhn (1975); Yarbrough (1975); Forsythe (1975, 1977); Yarbrough, Wapnick, and Kelly (1979); Yarbrough and Price (1981); Moore (1981); Rosenthal (1982); Price (1983); Kostka (1984); Nolteriek (1984); Carpenter (1986); Spradling (1985); Witt (1986); Polachic (1986); Sims (1986); Moore (1987); Madsen and Duke (1985); Madsen, Standley, and Cassidy (1989); and Cox (1990).

Subject-Specific Studies Froehlich (1981) was one of the first music researchers to recognize that "the music teacher's interaction style may vary with the content that is being taught, and it is the content, rather than teaching style which, most of all, determines what students learn" (p. 15). Researchers who have built their instruments around musical activities and content and music-related pedagogy have fo-

cused on musical activities of students (Daellenbach, 1970; Froehlich, 1977, 1979, 1981; Baldridge, 1984; Fiocca, 1989; Gipson, 1978; Wang and Sogin, 1990); conducting activity of the teacher (Ervin, 1975; Lewis, 1977; Thurman, 1977; Patterson, 1984; Roshong, 1978; Berz, 1983; Ellsworth, 1985; Grechesky, 1985; Overturf, 1985; Warner, 1986; Karpicke, 1987); or the teacher/conductor as a user of gesture, demonstration, imagery/metaphorical language, and technical musical language or as one who addresses musical structure, the elements of music, style, theory, or history (Papke, 1972; Thurman, 1977; Caldwell, 1980; Curtis, 1986; Watkins, 1986; Menchaca, 1988).

Miscellaneous Studies Miscellaneous studies include 10 composite studies (Kirkwood, 1974; Edwards, 1978; Wagner and Struhl, 1979; Taebel and Medley, 1979; Taebel and Coker, 1980; Sang, 1982; Scott, 1987; Doane, Davidson, and Hartman, 1990; Taebel, 1990a,b), one single-dimension study (Denicola, 1990), and seven case studies (Fiedler, 1982; Zimmerman, 1983; Thiel, 1984; Ingram, 1985; Krueger, 1985; Wohlfeil, 1986; Huff, 1989).

Summary and Commentary From the perspective of content, the 78 studies cited either use previously constructed observational instruments (48 percent) or use mostly original categories (52 percent). Considering the large number of observation instruments that are available, the derived instruments represent a small fraction of the total (Simon and Boyer, 1974; Borich and Madden, 1977; Evertson and Green, 1986). Twenty-three studies are derived from Madsen and Madsen's work and 13 from socio-emotional climate instruments. Little used is the work of Medley (1977, 1982), Soar and Soar (1983), Good and Brophy (1987), Hunter (1979, 1988), and Stallings (1977), all of whom have made major contributions to observational research. One explanation for this imbalance is that researchers (most of whom were doctoral students) may have had limited access to training in a variety of observation systems, thus being restricted to those instruments that had available training materials or were well-known to their advisers.

As a whole, these studies show little continuity with each other. The authors in the Madsen and Madsen group cite each other but generally do not refer to research outside their group for a descriptive or correlational design. Given the diffuse nature and results of these 78 studies, one is forced to conclude that they have not made a major contribution to the evaluation of music teaching.

Methods Used to Determine Content-Related Validity

More than usability and reliability, the most critical factor in an observation system to be used in evaluating teachers is validity. It is easy to observe whether a teacher is wearing a tie or not, and such a variable can be observed reliably; however, it is improbable that wearing a tie would have anything to do with student learning. The validity of the evaluation system must be established with respect to its content and its relationship to student learning.

The responsibility for establishing such validity falls to both the instrument's developer and its user, that is, the researcher and the evaluator. Before observation, one can consider only content validity, since criterion and construct validity are based primarily on the obtained scores themselves. Content validity is determined by evidence that the observation is a representative sample of the tasks or activities of some defined universe or domain of content (Angoff, 1988; American Psychological Association et al., 1985). Messick (1988) adds that "inferences regarding behaviors require evidence of response or performance consistency and not just judgments of content" (p. 38).

The procedures used to establish content validity include (1) specifying the universe of content (i.e., classroom events) that the measure is intended to represent, (2) making expert judgments concerning the content of the measure and the defined universe, and (3) determining through systematic observation that there is a correspondence between the measure and the defined universe (American Psychological Association et al., 1985, p. 10).

The defined universe of content that reflects one's conception of teaching usually includes teaching activities, content, and student activities. Each of these dimensions may be delineated further as either functions, categories, elements, or variables. For example, teaching activities have been classified as presenting, questioning, managing, and responding (Medley et al., 1984). Musical content may be delineated as musical elements and structure and/or as musical activities— performing, describing, listening, judging, and creating (Music Educators National Conference, 1986). Student activities may be described as academic or nonacademic; as compliant or noncompliant; as cognitive, affective, or psychomotor; or in terms of the musical activities.

Once the universe of interest has been identified, expert opinion may be sought to help define or judge the adequacy of an observation instrument. A problem arises in determining who is an expert. Baker (1981), Baldridge (1984), and Taebel (1979) used practicing teachers as their sources, whereas Hepler (1986) used members of the advisory council of the *Journal of Research in Music Education*. Some studies have used prior research findings (Kostka, 1984; Polachic, 1986) or have borrowed or adapted an existing instrument without further reliance on experts—for example, the behavioral and climate studies.

A second type of evidence is based on preobservation, that is, observation prior to the development or adoption of an instrument. Curtis (1986) spent considerable time in informal observation of six junior high general music teachers. Ervin (1975), Thurman (1977), and Berz (1983) observed videotapes of conductors repeatedly before they determined the categories for their instruments. Both Baker (1981) and Parr (1976) did field observations before they produced the final form of their instruments. Many others, especially researchers studying content-related pedagogy, did pilot studies before their main investigations. Such procedures are essential in the development of a valid evaluation system.

The definition of the universe of classroom events in the majority of music education observational studies is re-stricted. Researchers with a narrow conception of music teaching fail to include music activities or music content; they are following a tradition that has dominated teacher evaluation. The concept of teaching activities as defined by generic principles of classroom management and organization is only a partial picture (Shulman, 1986).

Studies with a behavioral orientation are even more restricted in defining the universe of teaching than those in the socio-emotional climate tradition. Madsen and Madsen concentrate on teacher response to student academic and social behaviors. They omit questioning techniques, presentational skills, content, and specification of student activities other than on-task or off-task. All teacher responses to student behavior are approval, disapproval, or neutral. They see high approval proportionate to disapproval as most conducive to student learning. To be sure, not all music researchers classed as behaviorists have defined the universe of teaching so narrowly. They have, however, retained Madsen and Madsen's global definitions for approval and disapproval, definitions so broad that nearly everything a teacher does falls in one category or the other. For example, under disapproval responses Madsen and Madsen (1981) list the statements "Do your best" and "You're gutless" (p. 246), as well as any stop in a rehearsal. Approval responses include "uh-huh" and "outstanding." The breadth of the categories indicated by these responses makes interpretation of results difficult. When teachers learn that 60 percent of their responses are disapprovals and only 40 percent are approvals, the standard of judgment is not clear enough to provide constructive feedback. Other much more refined classifications for teacher responses are extant. For example, Soar and Soar (1983) classify verbal responses to social behavior as gentle, direct, or harsh; Medley et al. (1984) include the following categories of verbal responses: praises (general), praises (specific), praise (personal), accepts (neutral), gives more information, corrects, waits, interrupts, and criticizes. Good and Brophy (1987) have also classified teacher responses more finely than Madsen and Madsen. These distinctions seem to be important, not only to provide more specific feedback to the teacher but also to ascertain their differential effect, if any, on student behavior and learning.

Fortunately, a number of researchers, especially those in the third and fourth categories above, include subject-related pedagogy, musical materials, and student musical activities. On the other hand, some of these studies fail to include general aspects of teaching, such as management, feedback, structuring, and questioning techniques. It may be that multiple observers using differing instruments designed to capture the various dimensions of teaching are needed for both research and evaluation.

Criterion-Related Validity

A framework for evaluation that includes expectations of a teacher's classroom performance may be based on experience or on generalizations of research findings. The expectations are incorporated into an observation instrument, teachers are observed, and judgments are made. Often, possession of the identified competencies is equated with being an effective teacher, while lack of them requires remediation or dismissal. The relationship between competence and effectiveness often is perceived as one to one; the words are used interchangeably. Medley (1977), however, makes a distinction between competence and effectiveness:

Competence has to do with how a teacher teaches and is measured in terms of the teacher's behavior; how effective a teacher is is measured in terms of pupil learning. In other words, an effective teacher is always competent, but a competent teacher may not always be effective, for a multitude of reasons. (p. 7)

Medley's concern here is the distinction between content-related validity, which relies on professional judgment, and criterion-related validity, where the criterion is pupil learning.

Numerous studies have shown mixed effects of teaching behaviors on student learning (Coker, Medley, and Soar, 1980; Taebel and Coker, 1980; Taebel, 1990b). Furthermore, there is no evidence that research findings are generalizable to other groups of teachers, to students at other grade levels, or to other subject areas (Brophy, 1988; Perry, 1989). At this time the evidence that links particular competencies to predictable student outcomes under all conditions is insufficient; thus evaluation as defined above is a judgment based on incomplete knowledge. The search for valid relationships between teaching and learning must continue. If one accepts the view that the activities of teaching are governed by the subject being taught, it follows that the search should concentrate on the activities of music teachers and students in their classrooms.

In studies investigating the effects of music teachers on student outcomes, a source of some controversy has been the selection of student outcomes. Some studies focused on the relationship between teaching and student attention or on-task behavior; others have investigated how long-term changes in musical achievement are related to selected teacher variables. The attention variable is a learning process variable; long-term achievement is a product variable (Dunkin and Biddle, 1974). Medley (1977), in reviewing studies of teaching effectiveness, eliminated those that did not use long-term pupil gains in achievement as a measure of effectiveness. Gage and Needels's (1989) review of experimental process-product studies included only those that covered most of one school year. Although music teachers appear to agree that effectiveness is measured in terms of pupil achievement over weeks and months (Taebel, 1990a), few studies have used this outcome as a criterion (Kirkwood, 1974; Kuhn, 1975; Taebel and Coker, 1980; Jessup, 1984; Doane et al., 1990).

The Kirkwood, Doane and colleagues, and Taebel and Coker studies are examples of process-product studies in which residualized gain scores on the student measures were correlated with the various measures of teacher performance. Kirkwood used a low-inference, composite observation instrument and a rating scale to derive teachers' scores,

which were then correlated with scores on Colwell's *Music Achievement Tests 1 and 2*. Kirkwood found significant relationships between the rated behaviors of enthusiasm, clarity, and focus and MAT scores. A number of significant relationships, positive and negative, also were found between the low-inference measures and student achievement. The correlation of low-inference measures with high-inference ratings (a form of construct validation) revealed a significant negative relationship between confusion and clarity. Even though Kirkwood visited her teachers six times, she did not determine the stability of her measures.

Doane and colleagues observed teachers in third-grade classes twice, using the state-developed Florida Performance Measurement System and the Music Behavior Observation Form, a researcher-developed instrument. Student achievement was measured using a district music achievement test. Score variance was adjusted by the use of SES, gender, Gordon's PMMA, and other variables. Correlations of residualized gain scores with teacher process variables were all nonsignificant. Doane and colleagues also did not determine the stability of the teachers' scores.

Taebel and Coker (1980) used a composite instrument (COKER) to measure teacher performance, and two criterion measures, MAT 1 and a 10-item attitude measure based on "How I See Myself." Only stable measures of teacher performance were correlated with the residualized gain scores, which had been adjusted for differences in SES and instructional time. Low correlations were obtained.

Kuhn's (1975) study was quasi-experimental and of short duration—six 15-minute lessons. Nevertheless, there were significant gains on MAT 1 and 2 by fifth-grade students. Kuhn's criterion variables were achievement gains, a postexperiment attitude measure of six items, and attention, which was measured simultaneously with teacher approvals and disapprovals. Different ratios of approval and disapproval did not appear to affect attitudes or achievement; however, high approval rates were found to be associated with increased attentiveness.

These studies have been described in some detail, because they are believed to use strong designs to establish the validity of the selected teaching variables as determined by external measures of student learning. Nevertheless, these studies also contain methodological flaws or offer scant evidence of the predictive validity of the teachers' scores.

Other researchers measure student learning either during the observation or at the end of the observation, failing to control for *a priori* status. However, Froehlich's three studies (1977, 1979, 1981) illustrate a methodology that appears to produce dependable relationships between teaching behaviors and student singing and rhythmic activity. Froehlich's cautiousness in correlating only stable teaching behaviors with the student measures is noteworthy, as the criterion validity of a measure is limited by its reliability (Frick and Semmel, 1978). Many studies fail to determine whether the measures of teacher performance are stable. Failure to establish that an obtained measure of a teacher's performance is dependable casts doubts on any inferences based on the correlation coefficient.

Construct-Related Validity

Construct validity is now viewed as the most fundamental and embracing of all types of validity (Angoff, 1988, p. 26). Construct validation is seen as a process, not as a single coefficient; it requires many lines of evidence, not all of them quantitative. Although constructs may be part of a theory, their validation must be behavior relevant and data relevant. Furthermore, all measures that are taken to be behavioral expressions of the construct, including criteria and tests alike, are expected to yield data consistent with the theory of the construct (Angoff, 1988, p. 26). Along with content- and criterion-related validity, other procedures that bear directly on construct validity include factor analysis and convergent and discriminant analysis.

A standard procedure in ascertaining the validity of a construct is to correlate or factor analyze the items that are used to define the construct. This procedure is recommended by Medley and colleagues (1984) in validating a "key," that is, a set of observable behaviors. An example of a key is: "The teacher plans lessons based on student needs and interests." Behaviors that are used to define this construct include student enthusiasm and the teacher's solicitation of student opinion (Taebel and Coker, 1980). In the Alabama teacher evaluation project, 10 competencies were defined by various combinations of observable behaviors. The validation process included item intercorrelations and factor analysis (Alabama CIP Project Staff, 1989). Unlike constructs that are theory based, these examples are empirical interpretations of effective teaching.

A somewhat similar procedure was followed by Kirkwood (1984) when she correlated high-inference ratings with low-inference measures. Her high-inference construct "clarity" correlated positively with a variety of low-inference items, including teacher praise, teacher open-ended questions, creating, and informing. Kirkwood did not report intraclass correlations for these low-inference behaviors; they did not appear to be logically related to each other. Yet another factor may lie behind the low-inference variables. All of Kirkwood's high-inference behaviors were highly correlated with each other ($r > .90$). The notion that these variables are independent constructs may be questioned. Dickson and Wiersma (1980) factor analyzed the competency scores from the Georgia teacher assessment instrument and found that the scores reflected a single factor, which they attributed to the "halo" effect often associated with ratings.

Similar procedures could be used to analyze Flanders's categories of direct and indirect teaching. No investigation by a music researcher has been found that undertakes to determine if each of these categories is, in fact, a unified construct.

Campbell and Fiske (1959) argue that a given measure of a construct should show strong relationships with other measures of the same construct, but weak relationships with measures of other constructs. Their strategy calls for intercorrelations of the scores of two or more different methods of measuring two or more different constructs. Borich, Malitz, and Kugle (1978) employed this validation procedure in a study of five classroom observation systems. The fact that so few dependable findings have emerged from the process-product research is attributed by them to either (1) an inadequate or too simplistic research model implicit in process-product research or (2) psychometric weaknesses within the instruments that obscure any existent underlying relationships. These researchers examined 23 categories found on at least two of the five instruments. Less than half of these "common" categories passed all tests for convergent and discriminant validity. Borich and colleagues (1978) warn researchers that combining results from different observation instruments that appear to have a common construct does not guarantee convergent validity of the construct.

An example of discrepant results in spite of similar-appearing categories is revealed by comparing Taebel's (1990a) report of positive and negative responses by Alabama music teachers with studies by Carpenter (1986) and Kostka (1984), who also examined positive and negative results. In the former study, music teachers gave positive responses 51 percent of the time and negative or corrective responses 28 percent of the time. The latter studies reported that over 50 percent of the responses by music teachers were disapprovals. An interpretation of these conflicting results may be that the researchers used different behaviors to define the construct even though they used the same name.

Positive responses may be viewed without distinction, as Madsen and Madsen (1981) view them. On the other hand, Soar and Soar (1983) point out that positive affect and praise have different effects on learning. Brophy (1983) argues that neither praise nor positive affect is necessarily associated with increased learning. Failure to distinguish between feedback, positive affect, and praise may make interpretation of results imponderable; convergent and discriminant analysis, however, may tease out the relationships, if any, among these variables.

The third method of validating a construct is experimental: Different groups receive different instructional treatments (Messick, 1975). Musical studies of this type include Kuhn's (1975) study, which showed no significant effect of differential ratios of approval and disapproval on student learning, and Yarbrough's (1975) study of the magnitude of conducting behavior on student performance, attitude, and attentiveness, where again no significant treatment effects were found.

In music education the search for valid relationships has been unsuccessful, perhaps because of the use of research designs and/or instruments that are too simplistic or too unreliable. The observation instruments reviewed in this chapter favor relatively low-level teaching and student behaviors. They may be too crude and unsophisticated to capture higher-level teacher-student interactions or make fine-grained distinctions between effective teachers and others. Alternate research methods such as case studies or ethnographic studies may be useful to explain how teachers make decisions as well as what they do. These methods may also be appropriate in evaluation of teachers, particularly those considered "experts." The direction taken by Huff (1989), Ingram (1985), Krueger (1985), Thiel (1984), Wohlfeil (1986), and Zimmerman (1983) may lead to a fuller appreciation of the complexity of teaching and the multitude of variables that interact in the normal classroom. Fiedler's (1982) multi-method approach using a low-inference observation instrument, unstructured observation, and open-ended interview is an example from music research of Shulman's (1988) proposed "union of insufficiencies" as a basis for teacher evaluation.

Future Directions in Observational Research

1. Multiple methods and instruments are needed to record and interpret the richness of classroom events and interactions. Attention should be given to a teacher's thinking—expectations, decisions, and interpretations. A line of research is needed that begins with descriptive studies, is followed by correlational studies, and continues with experimental studies (McGrath, Martin, and Kulka, 1982).

2. Music teaching provides an excellent opportunity for longitudinal studies, since students may have the same music teacher through their elementary or secondary years. Researchers should consider developmental studies in areas such as instrumental music and choral music. Most studies have considered only advanced performing groups; however, habit development is already well advanced in these groups, whereas a teacher's effectiveness may be more readily measured in the formative stages of skill development.

3. Studies of teacher and/or student variability across grades or within grades should be undertaken. Generalizability studies showing class effects or grade effects are needed.

4. Continued work along the lines suggested by Froehlich is encouraged. To what extent is a teacher's behavior guided by teaching objectives or a particular topic? Is there an interaction between generic and content-specific instructional processes?

5. A teacher's use of language, gesture, and signs is a fertile field for study. Consideration should be given to both the form and the content of communication. Few studies have examined the accuracy of given information or its logic (Green, 1971; Needels, 1988; DeNicola, 1990; Osman, 1989). Higher-order thinking of teachers at the analytical and evaluative levels is also in need of further study.

6. Student outcome measures need to be improved, especially performance and attitudinal measures. Attitudes about music, evaluative responses to music, and self-concept are important dimensions that need to be considered.

7. The construct validity of various observational instruments is worth researching, as is the stability of teaching behaviors across time. With so many instruments and so many different categories, there is little chance that a cohesive

body of knowledge will develop unless validated constructs are found between them. Such constructs are unlikely to become known if their constituent behaviors cannot be reliably measured across observations.

8. Research is needed on the purpose, procedures, and outcomes of music teacher evaluation. Such research could take the form of district case studies, impact studies of state-mandated evaluation on music teachers, or professional development practices in music education.

AN AGENDA FOR MUSIC TEACHER EVALUATION

The following are suggested policies for developing an evaluation program for music teachers.

1. A school district should develop a framework for evaluation of its music teachers. All music teachers, music supervisors, and other administrators should have an opportunity to contribute to the development of a framework, even though a "working committee" may actually prepare the documents (McGreal, 1988; Duke, 1990). The framework should include broad goals of musical learning for all students. These goals may be thought of as the outcomes of effective teaching, but they should not be dictated by what can be easily measured. Effectiveness research has been criticized for its tendency to focus only on low-level student outcomes (Passmore, 1980). Goals should be comprehensive and focus on outcomes of learning that are relatively enduring. The framework should include the major components of teaching such as pedagogical and subject matter knowledge; teaching competencies; and contributions to the school, community, and profession. Teaching competencies should be both content specific and generic. Expectations and standards of performance may be specified.

Procedures for evaluation should be described, and the purposes of evaluation must be clearly stated. Evaluators may include the building principal, the music supervisor, a master teacher, or outside consultants. A variety of data-gathering approaches should be available, including structured, low-inference measures and unstructured descriptive tools. Teachers having a record of successful teaching may be given an opportunity to select the evaluation tools that are most appropriate to their professional objectives (Peterson, 1987).

2. The school district should provide for adequate training of the evaluation team. Members of the team should be trained to observe classroom events and make accurate, objective records. Videotape episodes of music teaching, including both positive and negative exemplars, should be used for initial training. Continued training in a live situation should be required (Blackman, 1989; Doane et al., 1990).

Members of the evaluation team should receive training in conferencing with teachers. They should assist a teacher in selecting professional development objectives and in the selection of appropriate evaluation tools. Team members should be aware of the threats to reliability and validity of observation instruments and be sensitive to the context variables that may affect teacher behaviors. Above all, they must learn how to give meaningful feedback to the teacher.

3. The school district should develop a plan for professional development that meets the needs and interest of all teachers, including music teachers, at various stages of professional development. In this chapter evaluation is viewed as a driving force toward professional development rather than as an end in itself. Therefore, provision must be made for professional development activities that are responsive to individual or group interests and needs as identified in the evaluation process. A number of routes should be available such as peer tutoring, mentoring, self-study, special interest groups, and outside consultants (Glickman, 1981; Glatthorn, 1984; Duke, 1990; Joyce, 1990).

4. Finally, the evaluation system itself must be subject to evaluation. The ultimate goal of the system must be to improve learning, which is the result of improved instruction. Evaluation systems that change neither teaching nor learning must be revised. Change in schools and in teaching does not come easily (Cuban, 1984; 1990). The process may be threatening; the outcome may be uncertain. Valid outcomes of evaluation certainly are not easy to produce; the threats that may be associated with teacher evaluation must be weighed in the light of its contribution to professional development, which in turn is guided by a vision of what it means to teach music to students.

References

Alabama CIP Project Staff (1989). *Alabama performance-based career incentive program: A report of the norming study of the spring semester, 1987.* (ERIC Document ED302578).

American Psychological Association, American Educational Research Association, National Council on Measurement in Education (1985). *Standards for educational and psychological testing.* Washington: Author.

Amidon, E., and Flanders, N. (1967). Interaction analysis as a feedback system. In E. J. Amidon and J. B. Hough (Eds.), *Interaction analysis: Theory, research, and application* (pp. 121–140). Reading: Addison-Wesley.

Angoff, W. H. (1988). Validity: An evolving concept. In H. Wainer and H. I. Braun (Eds.), *Test validity* (pp. 19–32). Hillsdale: Lawrence Erlbaum.

Anrig, G. R. (1987). *What is the appropriate role of testing in the teaching profession?* Washington: National Education Association.

Baird, F. J. (1958). Music teaching competencies. *Journal of Research in Music Education, 6,* 25–31.

Baker, P. B. (1981). The development of music teacher checklists for use in evaluating music teacher effectiveness. Unpublished doctoral dissertation, University of Oregon, Eugene.

Baldridge, W. R. (1984). A systematic investigation of listening activities in the elementary general music classroom. *Journal of Research in Music Education, 32,* 79–94.

Barr, A. S. (1958). Problems associated with the measurement and prediction of teacher effectiveness. *Journal of Educational Research, 51,* 691–699.

Barr, A. S. (1961). *Wisconsin studies of the measurement and prediction of teacher effectiveness.* Madison: Dembar.

Barth, G. W. (1961). Some personality and temperament characteristics of selected school music teachers. Unpublished doctoral dissertation, University of Southern California, Los Angeles.

Bartko, J. J. (1976). On various intraclass correlation reliability coefficients. *Psychological Bulletin, 83,* 762–765.

Beaver, M. E. (1973). An investigation of personality and value characteristics of successful high school band directors in North Carolina. Unpublished doctoral dissertation, University of North Carolina, Greensboro.

Beecher, D. E. (1949). *The evaluation of teaching.* Syracuse: Syracuse University.

Berliner, D. (1983). The executive functions of teaching. *Instructor, 93*(2), 28–33.

Berz, W. L. (1983). The development of an observation instrument designed to classify specific nonverbal communication techniques employed by conductors of musical ensembles. Unpublished doctoral dissertation, Michigan State University, East Lansing.

Blackman, M. D. (1989). Development of videotapes illustrating music behaviors within the Texas Appraisal System. Unpublished doctoral dissertation, The University of Texas at Austin.

Borich, G. D. (1986). Paradigms of teacher effectiveness research. *Education and Urban Society, 18*(2), 143–167.

Borich, G. D., and Madden, S. K. (1977). *Evaluating classroom instruction: A sourcebook of instruments,* Reading: Addison-Wesley.

Borich, G. D., Malitz, D., and Kugle, C. L. (1978). Convergent and discriminant validity of five classroom observation systems: Testing a model. *Journal of Educational Psychology, 70*(2), 119–128.

Borich, G. D., and Klinzing, G. (1984). Some assumptions in the observation of classroom process with suggestions for improving low inference measurement. *Journal of Classroom Interaction, 20*(1), 36–44.

Brandt, R. (1987). On teacher evaluation: A conversation with Tom McGreal. *Educational Leadership, 46*(7), 20–24.

Brandt, R. (1988). On assessment of teaching: A conversation with Lee Shulman. *Educational Leadership, 46*(3), 41–45.

Brophy, J. (1988). Research on teacher effects: Uses and abuses. *The Elementary School Journal, 89*(1), 3–22.

Broudy, H. S. (1972). *A critique of performance-based teacher education.* Washington: American Association of Colleges for Teacher Education.

Brubaker, G. L. (1982). Teacher expectation as a factor in the teaching-learning process in junior high school general music classes and in choral ensembles. Unpublished doctoral dissertation, Northwestern University, Evanston.

Bullock, J. A. (1974). An investigation of the personality traits, job satisfaction attitudes, training and experience histories of superior teachers in junior high school instrumental music in New York State. Unpublished doctoral dissertation, University of Miami, Coral Gables.

Caimi, F. J. (1981). Relationships between motivational variables and selected criterion measures of high school band directing success. *Journal of Research in Music Education, 29,* 185–198.

Caldwell, W. M. (1980). A time analysis of selected musical elements and leadership behaviors of successful high school choral conductors. Unpublished doctoral dissertation, Florida State University, Tallahassee.

Campbell, D. T., and Fiske, D. W. (1959) Convergent and discriminant validation by the multitrait-multimethod matrix. *Psychological Bulletin, 56*(2), 81–105.

Carpenter, R. A. (1986). A descriptive analysis of relationships between verbal behaviors of teacher-conductors and ratings of selected junior high and senior high school band rehearsals. Unpublished doctoral dissertation, The Ohio State University, Columbus.

Coker, H., Medley, D. M., and Soar, R. S. (1980). How valid are expert opinions about effective teaching? *Phi Delta Kappan, 62*(2), 131–134, 149.

Coker, H., and Taebel, D. K. (Eds.). (1989). *Alabama career incentive program: Evaluator's manual.* Alabama State Department of Education. (ERIC Document ED298127)

Cox, J. W. (1990). *Choral rehearsal time usage in a high school and a university.* Paper presented at the MENC National Convention, Washington, DC.

Cronbach, L. J., Glaser, G. C., Nanda, H., and Rajartman, N. (1972). *The dependability of behavioral measurements.* New York: John Wiley.

Cuban, L. (1984). *How teachers taught.* New York: Longman.

Cuban, L. (1990). Reforming again, again, and again. *Educational Researcher, 19*(1), 3–13.

Curtis, S. C. (1986). An observational analysis of successful junior high/middle school general music teachers. Unpublished doctoral dissertation, University of Oklahoma, Norman.

Daellenbach, C. C. (1970). Identification and classification of overt musical performance learning behaviors using videotape recording techniques. Unpublished doctoral dissertation, University of Rochester, Rochester.

Darling-Hammond, L. (1990). Teacher evaluation in transition: Emerging roles and evolving trends. In J. Millman and L. Darling-Hammond (Eds.), *The new handbook of teacher evaluation* (pp. 17–32). Newbury Park: Sage Publications.

Dickson, G. E., and Wiersma, W. (1980). *Research and evaluation in teacher education: A concern for competent, effective teachers.* Toledo: The University of Toledo.

DiNicola, D. N. (1990). Historical perspectives on instructional language as applied to an assessment of preservice teachers. *Journal of Research in Music Education, 38,* 39–48.

Doane, C., Davidson, C., and Hartman, J. H. (1990). *A validation of music behaviors based on levels of music achievement in elementary general music students.* Paper presented at the MENC National Convention, Washington, DC.

Doyle, W. (1981). Research on classroom contexts. *Journal of Teacher Education, 32*(6), 3–6.

Duke, D. L. (1990). Setting goals for professional development. *Phi Delta Kappan, 47*(8), 71–75.

Duke, D. L., and Stiggins, R. J. (1990). Beyond minimum competence. In J. Millman and L. Darling-Hammond (Eds.), *The new handbook of teacher evaluation* (pp. 116–133). Newbury Park: Sage Publications.

Dunkin, M. J., and Biddle, B. J. (1974). *The study of teaching.* New York: Holt, Rinehart and Winston.

Ebel, R. L. (1951). Estimation of the reliability of ratings. *Psychometricka, 16*(4), 407–426.

Edwards, B. L. (1978). An investigation of the relationship between selected teacher behaviors and achievement in beginning wind-instrument music classes as measured by the *Watkins-Farnum Performance Scale.* Unpublished doctoral dissertation, University of Connecticut, Storrs.

Eisner, E. W. (1985). *The art of educational evaluation.* Philadelphia: Falmer.

Elam, S. (1971). *Performance-based teacher education.* Washington: American Association of Colleges for Teacher Education.

Ellsworth, E. V. (1985). A descriptive analysis of the characteristics of effective high school orchestra directors including a study of selected rehearsal characteristics. Unpublished doctoral dissertation, University of Wisconsin, Madison.

Erbes, R. L. (1972). The development of an observational system for the analysis of interaction in the rehearsal of musical organizations. Unpublished doctoral dissertation, University of Illinois, Urbana.

Erlich, O., and Borich, G. D. (1979). Occurrence and generalizability of scores on a classroom interaction instrument. *Journal of Educational Measurement, 16*(1), 11–18.

Ervin, C. L. (1975). Systematic observation and evaluation of conductor effectiveness. Unpublished doctoral dissertation, University of West Virginia, Morgantown.

Evertson, C. M. and Holley, F. M. (1981). Classroom observation. In J. Millman (Ed.), *Handbook of teacher evaluation* (pp. 90–109). Beverly Hills: Sage Publications.

Evertson, C. M., and Green, J. L. (1986). Observation as inquiry and method. In M. Wittrock (Ed.), *Third handbook of research on teaching* (pp. 162–213). New York: Macmillan.

Fiedler, S. K. (1982). A methodological study of three observation techniques—an observation schedule, participant observation, and structured observation—in two elementary classrooms. Unpublished doctoral dissertation, Northwestern University, Evanston.

Fiocca, P. D. (1989). A descriptive analysis of the rehearsal behaviors of exemplary junior high and middle school choral directors. *Contributions to Music Education, 16,* 19–33.

Fiske, D. W. (1974). The limits for the conventional science of personality. *Journal of Personality, 42*(1), 1–11.

Flanders, N. A. (1967). The problems of observer training and reliability. In E. J. Amidon and J. B. Hough (Eds.), *Interaction analysis: Theory, research, and application* (pp. 158–166). Reading: Addison-Wesley.

Forsythe, J. L. (1975). The effect of teacher approval, disapproval, and errors on student attentiveness: Music versus classroom teachers. In C. H. Madsen, R. D. Greer, and C. K. Madsen (Eds.), *Research in music behavior* (pp. 49–55). New York: Teachers College Press.

Forsythe, J. L. (1977). Elementary student attending behavior as a function of classroom activities. *Journal of Research in Music Education, 25,* 228–239.

Fox, D., and Beamish, S. R. (1989). A survey of teaching competencies for high school general music. *UPDATE, 8*(1), 33–36.

Frick, T., and Semmel, M. I. (1978). Observer agreement and reliabilities of classroom observation measures. *Review of Educational Research, 48*(1), 157–184.

Froehlich, H. (1977). The relationship of selected variables to the teaching of singing. *Journal of Research in Music Education, 25,* 115–130.

Froehlich, H. (1979). Replication of a study of teaching singing in the elementary classroom. *Journal of Research in Music Education, 27,* 35–45.

Froehlich, H. (1981). The use of systematic classroom observation in research on elementary general music teaching. *Bulletin of the Council for Research in Music Education, 66–67,* 15–19.

Gage, N. L., and Needels, M. C. (1989). Process-product research on teaching: A review of criticisms. *The Elementary School Journal, 89*(3), 253–299.

Georgia State Department of Education. (1988). *Evaluation manual* (Field-test edition). Atlanta: Author.

Getzels, J. W., and Jackson, P. W. (1963). The teacher's personality and characteristics. In N. L. Gage (Ed.), *First handbook of research on teaching* (pp. 506–582). Chicago: Rand McNally.

Gipson, R. C. (1978). An observational analysis of wind instrument private lessons. Unpublished doctoral dissertation, Pennsylvania State University, University Park.

Glatthorn, A. A. (1984). *Differentiated supervision.* Washington: Association for Supervision and Curriculum Development.

Glickman, C. D. (1981). *Developmental supervision.* Washington: Association for Supervision and Curriculum Development.

Good, T. L., and Brophy, J. E. (1987). *Looking in classrooms* (4th ed.). New York: Harper & Row.

Good, T. L., and Mulryan, C. (1990). Teacher ratings: A call for teacher control and self-evaluation. In J. Millman and L. Darling-Hammond (Eds.), *The new handbook of teacher evaluation* (pp. 191–215). Beverly Hills: Sage Publications.

Goodstein, R. E. (1987). An investigation into leadership behaviors and descriptive characteristics of high school band directors in the United States. *Journal of Research in Music Education, 35,* 13–25.

Grechesky, R. N. (1985). An analysis of nonverbal and verbal conducting behaviors and their relationship to expressive musical performance. Unpublished doctoral dissertation, University of Wisconsin, Madison.

Green T. A. (1971). *The activities of teaching.* New York: McGraw-Hill.

Hedrick, G. L. (1976). The development of a verbal analysis system for self-evaluation of pre-service music teachers. Unpublished doctoral dissertation, Florida State University, Tallahassee.

Hepler, L. E. (1986). The measurement of teacher/student interaction in private music lessons and its relation to teacher field dependence/field independence. Unpublished doctoral dissertation, Case Western University, Cleveland.

Hersey, P., and Blanchard, K. H. (1988). *Management of organizational behavior: Utilizing human resources* (5th ed.). Englewood Cliffs: Prentice-Hall.

Hicks, C. E. (1976). The effect of training in interaction analysis on the verbal teaching behaviors and attitudes of prospective school instrumental music education students. Unpublished doctoral dissertation, Michigan State University, East Lansing.

Hough, J. B. (1967). An observation system for the analysis of classroom instruction. In E. J. Amidon and J. B. Hough (Eds.), *Interaction analysis: Theory, research, and application* (pp. 150–157). Reading: Addison-Wesley.

Huff, D. M. (1989). The impact of interactions with students, community, colleagues and the institution of school on the teaching practices of secondary choral music teachers: Two case studies. Unpublished doctoral dissertation, University of Wisconsin, Madison.

Hunter, M. (1979). Diagnostic teaching. *Elementary School Journal, 80*(1), 41–46.

Hunter, M. (1988). Create rather than await your fate in teacher evaluation. In S. Stanley and W. J. Popham (Eds.), *Teacher evaluation: Six prescriptions for success* (pp. 79–108). Washington: Association for Supervision and Curriculum Development.

Ingram, M. H. (1985). A portrait of three elementary music teachers: Their classrooms and self-perceptions. Unpublished doctoral dissertation, University of North Dakota, Grand Forks.

Jessup, L. L. (1984). The comparative effects of indirect and direct music teaching upon the developmental music aptitude and music achievement of early primary grade children. Unpublished doctoral dissertation, Temple University, Philadelphia.

Joyce, B. (Ed.). (1990). *Changing school culture through staff development.* Washington: Association for Supervision and Curriculum Development.

Karpicke, H. A. (1987). Development of an instrument to assess conducting gesture and validation of its use in orchestral performance. Unpublished doctoral dissertation, University of Houston, Houston.

Kirkwood, G. (1974). Teacher behavior and pupil achievement in selected elementary music classrooms. Unpublished doctoral dissertation, University of Texas at Austin.

Kostka, M. J. (1984). An investigation of reinforcements, time use, and student attentiveness in piano lessons. *Journal of Research in Music Education, 32,* 205–214.

Krueger, R. J. (1974). *An investigation of personality and music teaching success.* Unpublished doctoral dissertation, University of Illinois, Urbana.

Krueger, P. J. (1985). Influences of the hidden curriculum upon the perspectives of student teachers: An ethnography. Unpublished doctoral dissertation, University of Wisconsin, Madison.

Kuhn, T. L. (1975). The effect of teacher approval and disapproval on attentiveness, musical achievement, and attitude of fifth-grade children. In C. K. Madsen, R. D. Greer, and C. H. Madsen (Eds.), *Research in music behavior* (pp. 40–48). New York: Teachers College Press.

Levis, D. S. (1987). Teacher's personality. In M. J. Dunkin (Ed.), *The international encyclopedia of teaching and teacher education* (pp. 585–589). New York: Pergamon Press.

Lewis, K. G. (1977). The development and validation of a system for the observation and analysis of choral conductor gestures. Unpublished doctoral dissertation, Texas A & M University, College Station.

Madsen, C. H., and Madsen, C. K. (1981). *Teaching/discipline: A positive approach for educational development* (3rd ed.). Boston: Allyn and Bacon.

Madsen, C. K., and Duke, R. A. (1985). Observation of approval/disapproval in music: Perception vs. actual classroom events. *Journal of Research in Music Education, 33,* 205–214.

Madsen, C. K., Standley, J. M., and Cassidy, J. W. (1989). Demonstration and recognition of high and low contrasts of teacher intensity. *Journal of Research in Music Education, 37,* 85–92.

Manatt, R. P. (1988). Teacher performance evaluation: A total systems approach. In S. Stanley and W. S. Popham (Eds.), *Teacher evaluation: Six prescriptions for success* (pp. 79–108). Washington: Association for Supervision and Curriculum Development.

Mann, P. L. (1979). Personality and success characteristics of high school band directors in Mississippi. Unpublished doctoral dissertation, University of Southern Mississippi, Hattiesburg.

McGaw B., Wardrop, J., and Bunda, M. A. (1972). Classroom observation schemes: Where are the errors? *American Educational Research Journal, 9*(1), 13–27.

McGrath, J. E., Martin, J., and Kulka, R. A. (1982). *Judgment calls in research.* Beverly Hills: Sage Publications.

McGreal, T. L. (1983). *Successful teacher evaluation.* Alexandria: Association for Supervision and Curriculum Development.

McGreal, T. L. (1988). Evaluation for enhancing instruction. In S. Stanley and W. J. Popham (Eds.), *Teacher evaluation: Six prescriptions for success* (pp. 1–29). Washington: Association for Supervision and Curriculum Development.

McGreal, T. L. (1990). *Linking teacher appraisal with staff development.* National Curriculum Study Institute. San Antonio: Association for Supervision and Curriculum Development.

McLaughlin, M. W., and Pfeifer, R. S. (1988). *Teacher evaluation.* New York: Teachers College, Columbia University.

Medley, D. M. (1977). *Teacher competence and teacher effectiveness: A review of process-product research.* Washington: American Association of Colleges for Teacher Education.

Medley, D. M. (1982). *Teacher competency testing and the teacher educator.* Charlottesville: University of Virginia.

Medley D. M., and Mitzel, H. E. (1963). Measuring classroom behavior by systematic observation. In N. L. Gage (Ed.), *First handbook of research on teaching* (pp. 247–328). Chicago: Rand McNally.

Medley, D. M., Coker, H., and Soar, R. S. (1984). *Measurement-based evaluation of teacher performance.* New York: Longman.

Medley, D. M., and Coker, H. (1987). The accuracy of principals' judgments of teacher performance. *Journal of Educational Research, 80*(4), 242–247.

Menchaca, L. A. (1988). A descriptive analysis of secondary instrumental conductor rehearsal problem-solving approaches, addressed musical elements and relationship to student attitude. Unpublished doctoral dissertation, Ohio State University, Columbus.

Messick, S. (1975). The standard problem: Meaning and values in measurement and evaluation. *American Psychologist, 30*(10), 955–966.

Messick, S. (1988). The once and future issues of validity. In H. Wainer and H. I. Braun (Eds.), *Test validity* (pp. 33–46). Hillsdale: Lawrence Erlbaum.

Mitchell, S. K. (1979). Interobserver agreement, reliability, and generalizability of data collected in observational studies. *Psychological Bulletin, 86*(2), 376–390.

Montgomery, C. (1986). A comparative analysis of teacher behavior of jazz and concert ensemble directors. Unpublished doctoral dissertation, University of Oklahoma, Norman.

Moore, R. S. (1981). Comparative use of teaching time by American and British elementary music specialists. *Bulletin of the Council for Research in Music Education, 66–67,* 62–68.

Moore, R. S. (1987). The use of rehearsal time by an experienced choral conductor with a children's choir. *Missouri Journal of Research in Music Education, 5*(5), 39–56.

Murray, K. C. (1972). The effect of teacher approval/disapproval on musical performance, attentiveness, and attitude of high school choruses. Unpublished doctoral dissertation, Florida State University, Tallahassee.

Music Educators National Conference. (1972). *Teacher education in music: Final report.* Washington: Author.

Music Educators National Conference. (1986). *The school music program: Description and standards.* Reston: Author.

Music Educators National Conference. (1987). *Music teacher education: Partnership and progress.* Reston: Author.

National Education Association Board of Directors. (1986). *Unpublished position statement of professional growth and evaluation.* Washington: National Education Association.

Natriello, G., and Dornbusch, S. M. (1980–81). Pitfalls in the evaluation of teachers by principals. *Administrator's Notebook, 29*(6), entire issue.

Needels, M. C. (1988). A new design for process-product research on the quality of discourse in teaching. *American Educational Research Journal, 25*(4), 503–526.

Newman, M. L. (1986). An investigation of selected band programs in the South Carolina public school system. Unpublished doctoral dissertation, University of South Carolina, Columbia.

Nolin, W. H. (1971). Patterns of teacher-student interaction in selected junior high school general music classes. *Journal of Research in Music Education, 19,* 314–325.

Nolteriek, M. A. (1984). A description of teacher and student behavior within single and multiple group teaching structures in elementary and general music education classes. Unpublished doctoral dissertation, University of Minnesota, Minneapolis.

Nunnally, J. C. (1982). Reliability in measurement. In H. E. Mitzel (Ed.), *Encyclopedia of educational research* (Vol. 4; 5th ed., pp. 1589–1601). New York: Macmillan.

Osman, N. E. (1989). The development of the *Communication Skill Evaluation Instrument:* An instrument designed to assess the communication skill of the conductor in the choral rehearsal. Unpublished doctoral dissertation, University of Missouri, Kansas City.

Overturf, M. S. (1985). Implementing concepts of vocal sound: Rehearsal approaches of four conductors of outstanding high school choirs. Unpublished doctoral dissertation, Florida State University, Tallahassee.

Padilla, R. (1990). *Qualitative analysis, computers, and concept modeling.* Paper presented at American Educational Research Association Annual Meeting, Boston.

Pagano, A. L. (1972). A study of the classroom interaction patterns of selected music teachers in first grade and sixth grade general music classes. Unpublished doctoral dissertation, American University, Washington.

Papke, R. E. (1972). An investigation of instrumental music directors' rehearsal behavior utilizing an evaluative instrument with implications for broadening perspectives in secondary school instrumental music curricula. Unpublished doctoral dissertation, Michigan State University, East Lansing.

Parr, J. D. (1976). Essential and desirable music and music teaching competencies for first year band instructors in public schools. Unpublished doctoral dissertation, University of Iowa, Iowa City.

Passmore, J. (1980). *The philosophy of teaching.* Cambridge: Harvard University.

Patterson, R. S. (1984). Conducting gestures used by high school choral directors. Unpublished doctoral dissertation, University of Illinois, Urbana.

Perry, C. (1989). Research finding on teaching: Misuse and appropriate use. *Action in Teacher Education, 11*(3), 12–15.

Peterson, K. D. (1987). Teacher evaluation with multiple and variable lines of evidence. *American Educational Research Journal, 24*(2), 311–317.

Peterson, P. L., and Comeaus, M. A. (1989). Assessing the teacher as a reflective professional: New perspectives on teacher evaluation. In A. E. Woolfolk (Ed.), *Research perspectives on the graduate preparation of teachers* (pp. 132–152). Englewood, Cliffs: Prentice-Hall.

Phillips, D. C. (1990). Subjectivity and objectivity: An objective inquiry. In E. W. Eisner and A. Peshkin (Eds.), *Qualitative inquiry in education* (pp. 19–37). New York: Teachers College, Columbia University.

Polachic, R. W. (1986). Selective descriptors of teacher effectiveness in elementary music education in Medicine Hat, Alberta. Unpublished doctoral dissertation, University of Oregon, Eugene.

Pontious, M. F. (1982). A profile of rehearsal technique and interaction of selected band conductors. Unpublished doctoral dissertation, University of Illinois, Urbana.

Popham, W. J. (1988). Judgment-based teacher evaluation. In W. J. Popham and S. Stanley (Eds.), *Teacher evaluation: Six prescriptions for success* (pp. 56–77). Washington: Association for Supervision and Curriculum Development.

Popham, W. J., and Stanley, S. (1988). *Teacher evaluation: Six prescriptions for success.* Washington: Association for Supervision and Curriculum Development.

Price, H. E. (1983). The effect of conductor academic task presentation, conductor reinforcement, and ensemble practice on performers' musical achievement, attentiveness, and attitude. *Journal of Research in Music Education, 31,* 245–257.

Raiman, M. L. (1974). The identification and hierarchical classification of competencies and objectives of student teaching in music through a partial Delphi survey. Unpublished doctoral dissertation, University of Connecticut, Storrs.

Reynolds, K. (1974). Modifications of the *Observational System of Instructional Analysis* focusing on appraisal behavior of music teachers in small performance classes. Unpublished doctoral dissertation, Ohio State University, Columbus.

Rorer, L. G., and Widiger, T. A. (1983). Personality structure and assessment. *Annual Review of Psychology, 14,* 431–463.

Rosenshine, B., and Furst, N. (1973). The use of direct observation to study teaching. In R. Travers (Ed.), *Second handbook of research on teaching* (pp. 122–183). Chicago: Rand McNally.

Rosenshine, B., and Stevens, R. (1986). Teaching functions. In M. C. Wittrock (Ed.), *Handbook of research on teaching* (3rd ed.; pp. 376–391). New York: Macmillan.

Rosenthal, R. K. (1982). A data-based approach to elementary general music teacher preparation. Unpublished doctoral dissertation, Syracuse University, Syracuse.

Roshong, J. (1978). An exploratory study of nonverbal communication behaviors of instrumental music conductors. Unpublished doctoral dissertation, Ohio State University, Columbus.

Rowley, G. L. (1976). The reliability of observational measures. *American Educational Research Journal, 13*(1), 51–59.

Ryans, D. (1960). *Characteristics of teachers.* Washington: American Council of Education.

Sang, R. C. (1982). Modified path analysis of a skills-based effectiveness model for beginning teachers in instrumental music education. Unpublished doctoral dissertation, University of Michigan, Ann Arbor.

Scheffler, I. (1973). *Reason and teaching.* Indianapolis: Bobbs-Merrill.

Schmidt, C. P. (1989). Applied music teaching behavior as a function of selected personality variables. *Journal of Research in Music Education, 37,* 258–271.

Scott, L. P. (1987). An investigation of attention and perseverance behaviors of preschool children enrolled in Suzuki violin lessons and other preschool activities. Unpublished doctoral dissertation, University of Texas at Austin.

Scott, W. A. (1955). Reliability of content analysis: The case of nominal scale coding. *Public Opinion Quarterly, 19,* 321–325.

Sergiovanni, T. L. (1987). *The principalship.* Newton: Allyn and Bacon.

Shavelson, R., and Dempsey-Atwood, N. (1976). Generalizability of measures of teaching behavior. *Review of Educational Research, 46,* 553–611.

Shulman, L. S. (1986). Those who understand: Knowledge growth in teaching. *Educational Researcher, 15*(2), 4–14.

Shulman, L. S. (1988). A union of insufficiencies: Strategies for teacher assessment in a period of educational reform. *Educational Leadership, 46*(3), 36–41.

Simon, A., and Boyer, E. (Eds.). (1974). *Mirrors for behavior III.* Wyncote: Communication Materials Center.

Sims, W. L. (1986). The effect of high versus low teacher affect and passive versus active student activity during music listening on preschool children's attention, piece preference, time spent listening, and piece recognition. *Journal of Research in Music Education, 34,* 173–191.

Smith, A. B. (1985). An evaluation of music teacher competencies identified by the Florida Music Educators Association. Unpublished doctoral dissertation, Florida State University, Tallahassee.

Snapp, D. (1967). A study of the accumulative musical and verbal behaviors of teachers and students in fifth grade. Unpublished master's thesis, Ohio State University, Columbus.

Soar, R. S., and Soar, R. (1983). Context effects in the teaching-learning process. In D. C. Smith (Ed.), *Essential knowledge for beginning educators* (pp. 65–75). Washington: American Association of Colleges for Teacher Education.

Sommers, P. K. (1981). *The time interval categorical observation recorder.* Cedar Rapids: Grant Wood Area Education Agency.

Spradling, R. L. (1985). The effect of timeout on attentiveness and attitude of university band students. *Journal of Research in Music Education, 33,* 123–137.

Stafford, D. W. (1987). Perceptions of competencies and preparation needed for guiding young singers in elementary school music classes. Unpublished doctoral dissertation, Florida State University, Tallahassee.

Stallings, V. A. (1977). *Learning to look.* Belmont: Wadsworth.

Stegall, J. R., Blackburn, J. E., and Coop, R. H. (1978). Administrators' ratings of competencies for an undergraduate music education curriculum. *Journal of Research in Music Education, 26,* 3–15.

Stiggins, R. J., and Duke, D. (1988). *The case for commitment to teacher growth: Research on teacher evaluation.* Albany: State University of New York.

Stodolsky, S. S. (1988). *The subject matters.* Chicago: University of Chicago Press.

Stodolsky, S. S. (1990). Classroom observation. In J. Millman and L. Darling-Hammond (Eds.), *The new handbook of teacher evaluation* (pp. 175–190). Newbury Park: Sage Publications.

Taba, H. (1972). Teaching strategy and learning. In B. C. Mills and R. A. Mills (Eds.), *Designing instructional strategies for young children* (pp. 28–39). Dubuque: Wm. C. Brown.

Taebel, D. K. (1979). Public school teachers' perceptions of the effect of certain competencies on pupil learning. *Journal of Research in Music Education, 28,* 185–197.

Taebel, D. K. (1990a). An assessment of classroom performance of music teachers. *Journal of Research in Music Education, 38,* 5–23.

Taebel, D. K. (1990b). The validity of general music teaching competencies and specific classroom behaviors as they relate to student musical performance. *Southeastern Journal of Music Education, 1,* 161–174.

Taebel, D. K., and Medley, D. M. (1979). *Generalizability of low inference measures of music teachers across observers, items, and classes.* Paper presented at the annual meeting of the American Educational Research Association, San Francisco.

Taebel, D. K., and Coker, H. (1980). Teaching effectiveness in elementary classroom music. *Journal of Research in Music Education, 28,* 250–264.

Taylor, B. (1980). The relative importance of various competencies needed by choral-general music teachers. Unpublished doctoral dissertation, Indiana University, Bloomington.

Thiel, C. R. (1984). Participant observation study of a fourth grade music classroom. Unpublished doctoral dissertation, University of Illinois, Urbana.

Thurman, V. L. (1977). A frequency and time description of selected rehearsal behaviors used by five choral conductors. Unpublished doctoral dissertation, University of Illinois, Urbana.

Travers, R. M. W. (1981). Criteria for good teaching. In J. Millman (Ed.), *Handbook of teacher evaluation* (pp. 14–21). Beverly Hills: Sage Publications.

Verrastro, R. E. (1975). Verbal behavior analysis as a supervisory technique with student teachers of music. *Journal of Research in Music Education, 23,* 171–185.

Wagner, M. J., and Struhl, E. P. (1979). Comparisons of beginning versus experienced elementary music educators in the use of teaching time. *Journal of Research in Music Education, 27,* 113–125.

Wang, C., and Sogin, D. W. (1990). *A comparative study of self-reported versus observed classroom activities in elementary general music.* Paper presented at the Music Educators National Conference Biennial Convention, Washington, DC.

Warner, D. L. (1986). An investigation of patterns of motivation in rehearsal construction of selected high school choral conductors. Unpublished doctoral dissertation, University of Northern Colorado, Greeley.

Watkins, R. E. (1986). A descriptive study of high school choral conductors' use of modeling, metaphorical language, and musical/technical language related to student attentiveness. Unpublished doctoral dissertation, University of Texas at Austin.

Whitehill, C. D. (1970). The application of Flanders' System of Classroom Interaction Analysis of General Classroom Music Teaching. Unpublished doctoral dissertation, University of West Virginia, Morgantown.

Wilson, S. M., Shulman, L. S., and Richert, A. E. (1987). ''150 different ways'' of knowing: Representations of knowledge in teaching. In J. Calderhead (Ed.), *Exploring teachers' thinking* (pp. 104–123). London: Cassell Educational Limited.

Wise, A. E., Darling-Hammond, L., McLaughlin, M. W., and Bernstein, H. T. (1984). *Teacher evaluation: A study of effective practices.* Santa Monica: The Rand Corporation. (ERIC Document No. ED 246 559)

Withall, J. (1949). The development of a technique for the measurement of socio-emotional climate in classrooms. *Journal of Experimental Education, 92,* 347–361.

Witt, A. C. (1986). Use of class time and student attentiveness in secondary instrumental rehearsals. *Journal of Research in Music Education, 34,* 34–42.

Wohlfiel, M. D. (1986). Effective rural school music teachers: Three profiles. Unpublished doctoral dissertation, University of North Dakota, Grand Forks.

Yarbrough, C. (1975). Effect of magnitude of conductor behavior on students in selected mixed choruses. *Journal of Research in Music Education, 23,* 134–146.

Yarbrough, C., Wapnick, J., and Kelly, R. (1979). Effect of videotape feedback techniques on performance, verbalization, and attitude on beginning conductors. *Journal of Research in Music Education, 27,* 103–112.

Yarbrough, C., and Price, H. E. (1981). Prediction of performer attentiveness based on rehearsal activity and teacher behavior. *Journal of Research in Music Education, 29,* 209–217.

Zimmerman, J. R. (1983). The musical experiences of two groups of children in one elementary school: An ethnographic study. Unpublished doctoral dissertation, Ohio State University, Columbus.

PERCEPTION AND COGNITION

·21·

AURAL PERCEPTION

Lola L. Cuddy and Rena Upitis

QUEEN'S UNIVERSITY AT KINGSTON

Where does "aural perception" belong in the diverse and complex array of musical activities and skills—teaching, singing, playing, improvising, composing, and so forth? In an obvious sense, it has to do with listening to music, but listening to music is itself a complex activity that includes analyzing, contemplating, evaluating, and feeling. Aural perception is part of all musical activity, but is not identical to any one activity. This seemingly simple statement elicits a host of questions for music research: What is the point of isolating aural perception for specialized study? How should we interpret the data collected from experiments that attempt to isolate aural perception? What are the implications for the larger domains of musical understanding, performance, and education?

Music psychology has a long history of concern with these questions, and a great deal of contemporary research has been productive and informative. The answers do not come easily, however, and the issues that arise are controversial. It is impossible, in this chapter, to paint a complete picture of the role of aural perception in musical understanding. What we have decided to discuss, therefore, are selected issues of general concern to the music educator. We attempt to show how research has addressed, or might address, these issues.

The theoretical position underlying our presentation maintains that the aspect of aural perception of greatest importance to the music educator is the ability to hear musical relationships in sounded events. This ability includes a sensitivity to the structure of musical contexts, and a conceptual framework for interpreting the structure. We are concerned, therefore, with obtaining a description of complex mental processes and representations. We want to know how representations of relationships and structures are acquired, what musical experiences they rely on, and how differences might arise both between and within individual listeners.

Under "musical experience" we include both formal intervention and exposure to the idiom of one's musical cul-

ture. The term "intervention" refers to the kinds of interactions that a teacher, coach, or fellow musician has with a student where a concept or skill is introduced, clarified, expanded, or redefined. Interventions can take many forms, from carefully structured lessons for private students or classrooms of students to impromptu interruptions during a rehearsal for an upcoming performance. The term "exposure" refers to something less deliberate—the kinds of encounters one has while listening to music on the beach, attending a concert, dancing at a party, and so forth.

Accompanying our theoretical position is a necessary reliance on scientific method in order to draw inferences about the nature, characteristics, and importance of musical influences on perception. These influences cannot be observed directly in a listener's responses, whether singing, playing, or responding yes/no to a test of pitch discrimination. What we observe in the listener's response is the end result of a complex system that contains many components—including perception, memory, symbolic representation, attention, attitude, and motor control. Thus, the techniques of scientific method are applied in music research to abstract and to isolate the systematic influence of structures and processes under investigation from other possibly influential factors. The goal is to obtain a set of experimental results from which general theoretical principles about music perception and cognition may be derived.

This chapter contains five sections. The first section briefly reviews certain findings from studies of music perception conducted in the tradition of experimental psychology. No attempt at comprehensive summaries of all available research is made. Readers who wish to pursue this topic further are encouraged to consult Deutsch (1982a), Dowling and Harwood (1986), Handel (1989), and Krumhansl (1990). The purpose of the section is to illustrate the kinds of questions asked by psychologists and the conclusions drawn from the results of experimental research.

The next four sections present issues of particular importance for the music educator. The second section is concerned with differences in musical test performance that are found both between and within individuals. The third section is concerned with the problem of inferring aural skills from production skills such as singing. The fourth section is concerned with drawing inferences about perception from observing music-making activities of children. Finally, the fifth section briefly summarizes implications for teaching practice that arise from research findings and directions.

DISCOVERING GENERAL PRINCIPLES: THE USE OF AURAL TESTS TO STUDY MUSIC PERCEPTION

The purpose of aural testing is to discover the influences of musical understanding on the perception of auditorially presented events. In this sense, the term "musical perception" is preferable to the term "aural perception"—to emphasize that the important principles we want to discover are not those of the ear, but more properly the mind.

In order to draw inferences about the complex mental activities that bring about musical perception, researchers employ many of the methods of experimental psychology. Features of these methods, as applied to research on music listening and comprehension, have been reviewed by Krumhansl (1989). They include, first, the careful control of stimulus materials; second, reliance on the law of statistical sampling; third, precise coding of responses so that measures are amenable to numerical analysis; and fourth, focus on the behavior of the "average" musical individual as opposed to the exceptional. An important assumption underlying the application of scientific interference is that the individuals tested are randomly selected from, and thus representative of, a population whose characteristics can be specifically defined. Differences in test scores among and within individuals are attributed to randomness, chance, or unidentified extraneous influences. This assumption is necessary in order to detect systematic effects in the face of inherent variability.

As a first step, data collected with rigorous adherence to scientific procedures are subjected to statistical analyses that produce, among other things, numerical estimates of reliability and replicability. The second step is theoretical interpretation. Here music theory, as well as psychological theory, has provided interpretive constructs (Krumhansl, 1989). Thus, formal quantitative descriptions of different aspects of musical knowledge have been derived. These include descriptions of the hierarchical relations among tones (Krumhansl, 1979; Krumhansl and Kessler, 1982), chords (Krumhansl, Bharucha, and Kessler, 1982), and keys (Krumhansl and Kessler, 1982); of hierarchical relations of pitches in musical sequences (Deutsch and Feroe, 1981) and pitch-time patterns (Jones, 1987); and of hierarchical levels of metrical structure (Palmer and Krumhansl, 1990; Povel and Essens, 1985). Grouping principles, whereby music is segmented into temporal units such as motifs, phrases, and sections, have also been identified (Clarke and Krumhansl, 1990; Deliège, 1987; Deliège and El Ahmadi, 1990; Deutsch,

1982b). The grouping principles formalize traditional Gestalt notions (e.g., proximity and similarity of events) and capture syntactic boundaries in the music, such as cadences. Extensive reviews of research are available (Dowling and Harwood, 1986; Krumhansl, 1990, 1991).

Recent interest has focused on descriptions of the relationships among the components of musical organization. Western tonal music has been described in terms of many different structural dimensions—for example, melody, harmony, rhythm—but it is not clear whether the conceptual distinctions among the dimensions reflect separable mental representations and processes. This is an important question, because it is concerned with how the components of music are connected or linked together to form a rich complex system of relationships. It may also have bearing on listening preferences: If a component is isolable, it may be attended to at the expense of other components.

A growing body of evidence suggests that a number of musical components are (at least to some extent) perceptually separable or isolable. Thus we see, for example, empirical support for the distinction between pitch class and pitch height (Shepard, 1964; Ueda and Ohgushi, 1987); between pitch contour and pitch interval (Dowling, 1978; Dowling and Bartlett, 1981; Dowling and Fujitani, 1971; Edworthy, 1985); between temporal and dynamic structures of rhythm (Gérard and Drake, 1990; Upitis, 1985, 1987a), and between other rhythmic dimensions (Fraisse, 1982; Gabrielsson, 1973; Monahan and Carterette, 1985); and between the organizational principles of harmony and melody (Schmuckler, 1989; Thompson and Cuddy, 1989, in press).

There is also evidence that pitch and temporal structures, as reflected in tonal and rhythmic hierarchies, are perceptually independent. Two recent studies investigated listeners' judgments of the phrase structure of excerpts from a Bach fugue (Palmer and Krumhansl, 1987a) and a Mozart sonata (Palmer and Krumhansl, 1987b). Subjects were asked to make these judgments under conditions in which they were given pitch information only, temporal information only, and both pitch and temporal information (i.e., as notated in the original musical score). In all experiments, judgments for the condition in which both pitch and temporal information were provided were predictable from the linear (additive) combination of the judgments made under pitch-only and temporal-only conditions. Further support for the independence of pitch and temporal organization was obtained by Monahan and Carterette (1985), who identified separable dimensions of pitch and rhythm that contributed to judged similarity of short melodies.

On the other hand, however, other lines of research question this independence (e.g., Deutsch, 1980; Jones, Boltz, and Kidd, 1982). Typically these studies employ auditory patterns in which pitch and temporal structures are either compatible or incompatible. Recall and recognition memory for the patterns are enhanced when the structures are compatible and adversely affected when they are not. Overall, it may be possible to reconcile the findings from these studies with findings from studies that propose independence. According to Krumhansl (1991), "Judgments of higher-order properties . . . would be expected to show joint influences of the tonal and rhythmic components. To say that they are independent (noninteractive) is simply to say that the effects do not require supposing that additional factors emerge when both tonal and rhythmic components are varied. If the two components are varied in a way that is mutually incompatible or inconsistent, then they may well interfere with one other" (p. 298).

There is much yet to be discovered about the relations among the perceptual structures and processes underlying musical understanding. Nevertheless, from the research tradition illustrated in this section, many promising methods for approaching these issues have been developed. Moreover, several general principles that bear on teaching practice may be abstracted. We summarize these principles here, and return to them at the end of the chapter:

1. *Context is important for engaging musical perception.* A historical tradition in auditory research has been to reduce musical materials to their simplest components and to study sensitivity to these components. Krumhansl (1983) argues against this approach, stating, "Quite possibly . . . reducing musical events to elementary components (single tones or isolated intervals) loses significant features in the process. . . . In context, more cognitive processes may interpret the individual tones within the broader framework, substantially altering their perception, diminishing the influence of physical and psychoacoustic properties, and emphasizing certain relationships that are more characteristic of musical structure" (p. 31).

It is not our intention to undervalue the study of auditory sensitivities but, rather, to point out that certain aspects of musical perception may emerge only when tested in musical contexts. For example, Krumhansl (1979, Experiment 1) reported that the perceived relation between two tones preceded by a key-defining context was influenced by their tonal function within the context. The context was either a tonic triad, an ascending scale, or a descending scale, and listeners were asked to rate how well the second tone of the pair followed the first with respect to the musical context. Listeners judged tones that were central to the key as more strongly related than tones outside the key, even if the physical interval between the tones was identical—for example, members of the pair C-G following a C-major context were judged more closely related than members of the pair C♯-G♯. Also, higher ratings were given to pairs in which the second tone was more stable in the key, than to the reverse order pairs. These results, which were highly reliable across listeners, suggest that the context guided listeners to apply musical knowledge in forming their judgments. Here, the knowledge applied was knowledge of tonal function.

2. *Exposure to music, quite apart from formal intervention, plays a role in the acquisition of musical knowledge.* The evidence that formal training leads to elaborated mental representations of musical structure (Dowling and Harwood, 1986; Krumhansl and Shepard, 1979; Palmer and Krumhansl, 1990) is compelling, but not surprising. What is quite striking, however, is the degree to which musically untrained adults show that they too are responsive to both the tonal (e.g., Cuddy, Cohen, and Mewhort, 1981; Cuddy and

Badertscher, 1987) and the rhythmic structures of our culture (e.g., Palmer and Krumhansl, 1990; K. C. Smith, 1989; K. C. Smith and Cuddy, 1989). Although the musically untrained lack the descriptive vocabulary of music theory, it is clear that most are sensitive to regularities in the music they hear, and that they perceive, remember, and interpret musical contexts in terms of knowledge of these regularities. Informal exposure seems adequate to provide the necessary background to make sense of a number of musical tasks. Moreover, the adeptness with which listeners pick up regularities in tonal music implies that they would also be successful at picking up structural regularities in unfamiliar musical idioms; there is now experimental evidence supporting this implication (Castellano, Bharucha, and Krumhansl, 1984; Oram, 1989).

3. *There are many valid ways to evaluate music perception.* Moreover, a variety of experimental measures is highly desirable. As Garner (1974) explained, "We come to know things, usually described as concepts, by carrying out two or more experimental operations that converge on the single concept. . . . A concept that arises as a consequence of converging operations has a reality that is independent of any single experimental observation" (Garner, 1974, p. 187). In music research, a good example is provided by research in perception of tonality. Many experimental procedures have been explored—such as recognition of short melodies varying in tonal structure (e.g., Cuddy, Cohen, and Miller, 1979); ratings of "goodness" or coherence of melodies (e.g., Cuddy et al., 1981); and ratings of goodness-of-fit of each member of the chromatic set to a tonal context (e.g., Krumhansl and Shepard, 1979; Krumhansl and Kessler, 1982). The findings from these studies have converged on a complex description of hierarchical structures and processes. If only one experimental paradigm had been used throughout, there would be the risk that the findings reflected a particular listening strategy (possibly very reliably) but were not conducive to generalizations about tonality perception.

Sometimes, as we shall see in the next section, it is of interest to examine performance on a particular musical task. An important point to remember, however, is that performance may reflect skills specifically engaged by that task, and may not be indicative of overall perceptual ability.

THE PROBLEM OF INDIVIDUAL DIFFERENCES

Up to this point we have discussed methods and theory with respect to general principles of music perception. These methods relied on statistical inference for the making of generalizations. A feature of statistical inference is that differences in test scores obtained under identical testing conditions are attributed to chance—unknown factors whose influence is assumed to be randomly distributed throughout the experiment. The purpose of research design is to provide assurance that the overall results are not likely to be systematically biased in favor of an extraneous influence.

It is not possible totally to eliminate extraneous influences from an experiment. Thus, when considering individual test scores, one cannot conclude that the child scoring below the mean is necessarily poorer in perceptual ability than the child scoring above the mean. Many factors other than perceptual ability may be responsible, or it may even be a matter of luck. This is an important point to keep in mind when one is attempting to interpret a single test score, and, in particular, if one is tempted to use a single test score to predict musical potential.

In everyday practice, however, teachers regularly make inferences about a child's abilities. In some instances, repeated observations may lead to a strong intuition that some children are not representative of a typical collection of individuals. Rather, one child's music-making activities may suggest precocity, while another's may suggest perceptual difficulties. Moreover, in the latter situation, the teacher may suspect that the difficulties are specific to certain musical tasks—for example, a child may have a great deal of difficulty clapping back a rhythm sequence, but be able to identify melodic intervals with ease. The key words here, of course, are "repeated observations": Experienced teachers know enough to consider a child's performance in a number of different settings over time before drawing conclusions about perceptual ability.

In experimental data, "deviant" scores may be evident in several ways. The distribution of scores obtained from an unselected population may not cluster around a representative value (the mode) but may show two or more peak values, suggesting a bimodal or multimodal distribution. Or the distribution of scores may have a long tail, indicating the presence of a set of extreme scores that are not likely to be representative of the population. Both kinds of distributions provide evidence suggesting the presence of separate subgroups.

What do research findings have to say about differences found between and within individuals? Thorough descriptions of the strengths and weaknesses of standardized aptitude tests are available (Shuter-Dyson, 1982; Shuter-Dyson and Gabriel, 1981) and will not be discussed here. What we have chosen to discuss are several research topics of both theoretical and practical relevance. The first topic is concerned with differences between individuals. Two examples are absolute pitch and tone deafness. The second is concerned with differences within individuals. An example is unevenness in musical development: A child may perform adequately in some musical tasks but fail in others. These topics represent continuing challenges to current research and practice.

Differences Between Individuals

Both "absolute pitch" and "tone deafness" are labels that tend to be attached to individuals fairly early in life, and both have been treated as indicative of an individual's musical potential. Moreover, both have been viewed, in traditional musical practice, as reflecting a fixed musical endowment (or lack of it).

Absolute Pitch Ward and Burns (1982) comment that "the ultimate in musical endowment is commonly regarded by musicians to be the possession of 'absolute pitch'" (p. 431). Possessors of absolute pitch reputedly identify or produce isolated musical notes with great facility and without reference to an external standard. This seems to be in striking contrast to the notion that musical perception is evoked by musical contexts, not isolated pitches, which may account for some of the fascination with absolute pitch.

Ward and Burns (1982) trace research interest from the late nineteenth century onward. They summarize four major theories of the genesis of absolute pitch—heredity, learning, unlearning, and imprinting. The first two theories, heredity and learning, occupy extreme poles of the nature-nurture controversy. The first says that absolute pitch is an innate ability that is genetically endowed; the second says that anyone can learn absolute pitch given the appropriate training. The unlearning theory suggests that most people have the potential to acquire absolute pitch, but either do not develop it or "unlearn" it in favor of acquiring good relative pitch. Finally, the imprinting theory suggests that absolute pitch may be learned but only if musical training is begun at an early age.

Of these theories, heredity theory claims that absolute pitch is something that a person "has" or "doesn't have" and that no amount of musical intervention or exposure will alter the situation. There is, in fact, no convincing scientific evidence in support of such a claim.

Rather, research findings suggest that musical experience—both intervention and exposure—plays an important role. The ability to identify pitches can be improved through practice—even adult listeners' ability (Brady, 1970; Cuddy, 1968, 1970, 1971). Superior performance on pitch-naming tasks is almost exclusively associated with musical training and, in fact, is not all that rare among experienced musicians. Sergeant (1969) reported that nearly 70 percent of professional musicians in his survey claimed absolute pitch, and Miyazaki (1988) appears to have obtained at least as high a rate of incidence among music students.

Furthermore, persons claiming absolute pitch tend to report considerable exposure to music in preschool years (Miyazaki, 1988, 1989; Shuter-Dyson and Gabriel, 1981). It is not clear, however, whether it is early exposure per se that guides the development of absolute pitch or whether it is the quality of the exposure. Perhaps the kind of initial musical exposures provided for a 2-year-old contain a critical ingredient that typical initial exposures provided for a 14-year-old do not. But in any case, it again appears that musical experiences are implicated.

Future research may illuminate the specific nature of musical experiences that lead to superior pitch-naming ability. For the present, the more important questions are whether pitch-naming ability itself is a valid reflection of musical perception, whether its development leads to enhanced musical understanding, and thus whether it is worth the trouble to acquire.

Unfortunately, we have very few data to address these questions. Studies of absolute pitch have tended to focus on the note-naming ability of the subjects tested, and have not explored the possible benefits, if any, absolute pitch conveys upon regular music-making activities. Quite possibly, when absolute cues conflict with relative cues, absolute pitch may hinder appreciation and performance. There are many anecdotal stories in this regard—for example, pianists who cannot play accurately on a piano tuned to a standard other than A4 = 440 Hz, music students encountering difficulty learning to play transposing instruments, and so forth. None of these difficulties has been experimentally documented, however.

One experimental study reports a perceptual test that was more difficult for musicians claiming absolute pitch than for musicians not claiming absolute pitch but having equivalent training and experience (Cuddy, 1982). (The accuracy of the claims was verified by a preliminary note-naming test.) The experimental tests involved listening to a correct presentation of a melody and judging whether a subsequent presentation was either correct or mistuned. Melodies were either tonal or nontonal, and were based on either a familiar system of temperament or an unfamiliar one. For most melodies, the absolute pitch claimants were superior to the other listeners in detecting a mistuning. But when the melodies were both nontonal and based on an unfamiliar system of temperament, the absolute pitch claimants were at a distinct disadvantage compared to the other listeners. Perhaps a focus on the categories of the western tonal system rendered the absolute pitch claimants less flexible and less adaptive to the structures of a nonconventional system.

In sum, the evidence suggests that absolute pitch—or a superior ability to identify musical notes—is related to musical experience, quite possibly experiences occurring early in life. It is not at all clear, however, that these experiences are essential to musical growth, or that the ability, once acquired, contributes to musical understanding in a profound way. From an educational viewpoint, it may be more profitable to direct research efforts toward identifying the advantages of a good sense of pitch relationships and structure.

Tone Deafness The term "tone deafness" suggests a pathology of a physiological nature—an inability to hear tones. There is no evidence, however, that the majority of individuals regarded as tone deaf have an auditory pathology. Dictionary entries, such as the entry in Webster's Dictionary (1987), suggest "unable to distinguish differences of pitch in music." (p. 1039) This definition correctly locates the problem as a musical one, but fails to elaborate its complexity. The tone deaf rarely indicate that their inability to hear or to discriminate pitches is the sole, or even the main, source of the problem.

The appellation of tone deafness is in fact quite broad. For example, a survey of 600 university students revealed that those who considered themselves "tone deaf"—about 10 percent of the sample—reported a variety of difficulties of melodic perception and memory, vocal production, and auditory imagery (Mawhinney, 1987). They also reported a low incidence of musical activities in early childhood, and unpleasant memories of the musical education that they did

have. Thus perceptual, productive, environmental, and attitudinal factors were implicated by the respondents; genetic factors may also be important (Shuter-Dyson and Gabriel, 1981). Research evidence, however, for the genesis of tone deafness is even less conclusive than that for the genesis of absolute pitch.

One problem for research investigation of tone deafness is that the label is often applied to individuals who have difficulty with pitch matching, or "carrying a tune." From this evidence alone, it is not possible to conclude that these individuals have difficulties with musical perception; the problem of identifying perceptual difficulties from production errors is discussed in the next section. It is clearly important, however, to identify the source of the difficulty in order to provide appropriate educational experiences to help overcome it.

Very few investigations have been directed toward the question of whether tone deafness involves a perceptual difficulty. An exception is the study of Kalmus and Fry (1980; see also Fry, 1948) that claimed to have isolated a particular perceptual difficulty the authors call dysmelodia, or "tune deafness." One of their experimental tests produced a clear-cut difference in the distributions of scores between subjects considered "musical" and subjects considered "tune deaf" (by themselves and/or others). The test, called the *Distorted Tunes* test, required subjects to listen to 25 excerpts from well-known tunes, and to decide whether the excerpt was correct or whether it contained wrong notes. (Rhythm and tempo were not altered in the incorrect versions of the excerpts.) The "tune deaf" made many more mistakes than the "musical" subjects, and their scores showed a quite different distribution (Kalmus and Fry, 1980, Table 3).

Kalmus and Fry (1980) suggest that difficulty with the *Distorted Tunes* test reflects a failure to have acquired knowledge of the syntactic rules of the western tonal system, or what the authors call the deep structure of melodic aptitude. It would be useful to have converging evidence for this intriguing suggestion. Two further findings provide some indirect support. First, scores on the *Distorted Tunes* test were only weakly correlated with scores on the Seashore test of tonal memory and the Seashore test of pitch discrimination. Thus the problem did not seem to be simply one of pitch discrimination or short-term memory. Second, familiarity with the tunes was not a prerequisite for a good score, so it could be argued that the *Distorted Tunes* test was not merely a test of long-term memory for specific tunes.

As with absolute pitch, as discussed above, both genetic factors (Kalmus and Fry, 1980) and early environment (Kalmus, cited in Shuter-Dyson and Gabriel, 1981) have been implicated in the genesis of tune deafness. It is reasonable to speculate that an impoverished musical upbringing could lead to difficulties with musical syntax. Just as a child acquires natural language syntax from exposure to a linguistic environment, so the syntax of tonality may be acquired through exposure to a musical environment (see Krumhansl and Keil, 1982).

In Mawhinney's (1987) survey, more than half the self-labeled tone deaf attributed the problem to "improper instruction," and over 90 percent thought the problem was correctable. It would seem to be a promising endeavor to investigate the influence of early experiences on, and the tractability of, so-called tone deafness.

Differences within Individuals

We noted above that a teacher may observe unevenness in a child's musical development. Upitis (1990b) reports a case study of a child who appeared, initially, to be "tone deaf" to melody. However, after extensive observations, collected both informally and during music lessons, Upitis concluded that the child paid attention primarily to the rhythmic patterns of a song rather than the pitch patterns, and found the rhythmic patterns easier to learn. Given many chances to hear the music after the rhythm pattern had been learned, the child was able to learn the pitch information as well.

The educational significance of identifying a child's strong and weak points in musical activities cannot be overemphasized. It is unfortunate, therefore, that research on this topic is meager. Promising directions exist, however, one of which arises from the studies investigating relations among perceptual components.

The study by Monahan and Carterette (1985), cited earlier, identified both rhythmic (durational) and pitch dimensions that accounted for the ratings of similarity between brief melodies. Individual differences were also examined, and it was found that whereas most subjects attended to the rhythmic or durational aspects of the melodies in forming their judgments, the judgments of some were most influenced by the pitch aspects. In other words, individual subjects attended to one dimension at the expense of the other. Preference for one aspect over another did not appear to be related to the subject's experience as a solo player or an ensemble player.

In their discussion of the possible functional autonomy of pitch and temporal organization, Peretz and Morais (1989) review studies of dissociations resulting from brain injury. They report a number of clinical findings in which, depending on the nature and location of the damage, melodic processes are spared while rhythmic processes are impaired, or, conversely, rhythmic processes are spared while melodic processes are impaired. These findings suggest some degree of neural independence for rhythmic and melodic processes.

Within a given individual, therefore, certain perceptual components may be privileged over others in the individual's response to music. Various factors may be implicated in the relative status of components—for example, attention, strategy, neural substrates, experience, and development. Moreover, strength or weakness in one component may not be predictive of strength or weakness in another.

INFERRING PERCEPTION FROM PRODUCTION MEASURES

The discussions in the previous sections dealt with tests of listening. In such tests, musical contexts were presented au-

ditorially under carefully controlled conditions, and listeners were asked to form judgments about their content. From these judgments, a description of musical perception was inferred.

In this section and the next, we include musical activities that are part of everyday teaching and learning—singing, playing, and drawing symbolic representations of music. For the classroom teacher, these activities are readily available sources of information about musical development. However, the problems of making inferences about musical perception remain. Theories about production (both in speech and music) do not agree on the extent to which the execution of a motor act or skill reflects the same mental representations and processes as those that underlie perception.

The important point arising from theoretical controversy is that performance cannot be directly identified with perception. Motor production systems leading to performance may share mental resources with systems of perceptual organization, but doubtless engage other resources as well. Performance errors, therefore, may or may not indicate perceptual difficulties. This section will illustrate the point with reference to studies of voice production.

"Why do people sing out of tune?" Sundberg (1987, p. 180) outlines several possibilities, pointing out that formal investigation of these possibilities is far from complete. Singing out of tune may reflect three different types of difficulty. The first type is a perceptual failure. Mistuning may be the result of the singer's having failed to acquire a mental representation of the tonal hierarchy (see first section) that allows one to imagine all the pitches of a piece with reference to the prevailing tonality. This failure results, perhaps, in a poor sense of pitch intervals. The second type is not, however, a perceptual failure. It is the failure of the muscular activities accompanying phonation to produce pitches that have been correctly imagined—the motor commands that produce correct pitch changes have been miscalculated. This is a failure of neural instructions to the production system. The third type is a specific muscular problem; despite correct neural instructions to the correct muscles, some "disturbing additional muscle contraction . . . some irrelevant laryngeal muscle . . . destroys the result" (Sundberg, 1987, p. 180).

Of course, combinations of these types of difficulties are possible, too. A singer may compound perceptual difficulties with poor motor strategies. A single measure of vocal skill is unlikely to reveal the possible underlying causes. A variety of measures is necessary in order to detect consistent patterns that might point to the source(s) of difficulty.

There is a different aspect of the analysis of out-of-tune singing that bears on the question of how musical perception and production are related. Studies with skilled performers have indicated that some tuning deviations may be intentional (Sundberg, 1982; for related developments ascribing performance deviations to musical intent, see, for example, Gabrielsson, 1988; Palmer, 1989; Shaffer and Todd, 1988; Todd, 1985). These deviations are consistent within individuals and appear to reflect an intended style or expression. For example, Hagerman and Sundberg (1980) measured the intervals between tones of various chords as reproduced by a barbershop quartet. They found that intonation deviated from equal temperament in the direction of the intervals of the harmonic spectrum. This was done, presumably, to produce the auditory sensation of vibrato-free (beat-free) chords, a characteristic of barbershop style. Lindgren and Sundberg (cited in Sundberg, 1987) found that large deviations in intonation—normally detectable by listeners—were sometimes acceptable. Instances where deviations were accepted included unstressed metric positions, and passages expressing a tragic mood.

Such studies also raise the issue whether there is such a thing as an ideal (decontextualized) standard for intonation. The most appropriate standard, musically, may vary with style and idiom. According to Francès (1988), "It is difficult . . . to claim that [performance studies] alone disclose the demands of the 'true ear'. . . . [Rather] they demonstrate the adaptation of pitch judgments to those integrative schemes that constitute the foundations of articulation within musical forms" (p. 46). In other words, it is within musical context that accuracy of intonation should be judged and evaluated.

OBSERVATIONS WITH CHILDREN

This section is not intended to describe musical development, which is dealt with elsewhere in this handbook. Rather, our concern here is the extent to which observation of children's musical activities in the classroom might provide information about musical perception. These activities include drawing, notating, clapping, moving to music, and spontaneous singing. Because these activities encompass a broad range of skills—perceptual, cognitive, and motor skills—they are referred to under the broad terms "understanding of rhythm" and "understanding of melody."

A relatively sizable body of literature exists regarding children's understanding of rhythm. Much of our knowledge in this area has been built from observing children's ability to reproduce rhythms and to notate rhythmic sequences using their own invented notations (Bamberger, 1980, 1982; Hildebrandt, 1985; J. E. Smith, 1983; K. C. Smith, 1989; Upitis, 1985, 1987a,b). A good deal of this research has been conducted in classrooms and in other music-making environments. The research tasks for rhythm understanding tend to be similar to tasks that children are expected to perform in school (e.g., clapping back sequences) or in ensemble performance (e.g., keeping time). Also, the stimuli used for these tasks are frequently presented in a "natural" manner—the researcher may clap, sing, or play the sequences, just as a teacher would.

Studies dealing with reproduction of simple rhythmic sequences—that is, where subjects were asked to clap back a sequence they heard—showed that there were two main ways of reproducing a rhythm sequence. Some individuals, usually those with extensive musical training, responded strongly to the metric aspect of rhythm, the underlying or "deep" hierarchical structure of beats. Others responded to figural aspects—the groupings created by surface elements clustered in time. When asked to invent notations to record the events of a rhythmic sequence, both children and adults produced drawings reflecting one of the two structures. The tendency to produce metric notations was again associated with musical training, and figural notations with little or no musical training. Current research has attempted to describe the sequence of development of figural and metric structures contributing to an individual's understanding of rhythm (see Upitis, 1987a,c).

One of the results of this research is that, although a child's notations of rhythm on a particular drawing task may be clearly classified as figural or as metric, the child's performance on other rhythmic tasks often reveals that both figural and metric strategies are available. For example, children who produce accurate figural drawings also respond accurately to perceptual tasks involving detection of metric structure—such as recognizing whether the beats of a metronome are congruent or incongruent with the beats of a melody (Upitis, 1985) or identifying the underlying beat of a rhythmic sequence in the presence of syncopation (K. C. Smith, 1989). Here again is evidence that a single production task does not necessarily provide a direct reflection of perceptual ability. Future research will benefit from continuing to assess performance on a variety of tasks, uncovering the different patterns of responding demonstrated by individual children, establishing the relation between a child's rhythmic performance and rhythmic perceptual abilities, and evaluating the contribution of both to rhythmic understanding.

The understanding of melody has also been studied through observation and description of a variety of musical activities. These include (1) how melody is spontaneously created (Dowling, 1984); (2) how melody is reproduced through singing (Davidson and Colley, 1987; Dowling, 1988); and (3) how melody is notated both to record an original composition (Borstad, 1989; Upitis, 1987b, 1990b) and to record a familiar song of the culture (Davidson and Scripp, 1988; Davidson and Colley, 1987; Davidson, Scripp, and Welsh, 1988; Upitis, 1990a). These observations have resulted in descriptions of an orderly sequence of development (e.g., Dowling, 1984; Davidson and Scripp, 1988; Upitis, 1990a) in which the earliest features mastered are rhythmic-melodic phrase contours, followed by intervals and tonality.

The evidence from listening tests suggests that perceptual structures for tonal music are present very early in life—earlier than might be suspected from observations of skill development. Very young infants abstract the pitch contour of a sequence of tones (Trehub, 1985; Trehub, Bull, and Thorpe, 1984; Trehub, Thorpe, and Morrongiello, 1985, 1987). They are sensitive to the pitch and durational contours that cue phrase endings (Krumhansl and Jusczyk, 1990). In addition, infants are sensitive to musical interval configurations and their invariance under transposition (Cohen, Thorpe, and Trehub, 1987; Trehub, Thorpe, and Trainor, 1990). These early music-processing strategies become further elaborated as demonstrated by studies with preschoolers and first-graders (e.g., Cuddy and Badertscher, 1987; Trehub, Cohen, Thorpe, and Morrongiello, 1986; Trehub, Morrongiello, and Thorpe, 1985). Thus, it appears that children hear and make sense of tonal structures much more complex than those they can record or reproduce. Further research on this notion would have considerable implications for the kinds of music we choose for musical exposure in early school years.

IMPLICATIONS FOR TEACHING PRACTICE

In this section, several implications for music education are summarized. A note of caution: The traditions of research and educational practice have different approaches and methods, and differ in the nature of the evidence on which theories are based. The questions asked by music educators often demand immediate answers that are simply not available from a single research study or even a collection of studies. Nevertheless, while it is important to keep in mind the differing demands and goals of the two traditions, we feel that they can inform each other in profitable ways.

Three points are listed below: first, the value of providing a variety of musical contexts for teaching; second, the desirability of balancing teaching interventions with exposure; and third, the importance of shifting criteria for assessing musical understanding away from decontextualized measures toward measures that emphasize active musical engagement. All three will first be considered in light of teaching practice.

Teaching Practices

Given that there are demonstrated differences in ability, both between and within individuals, an important teaching practice is to use these differences to advantage. Few would argue with the statement that the best way to teach new things is to "teach to the strengths" of the individual, building on prior knowledge and concepts that the child possesses (Dewey, 1902; Papert, 1980). In other words, if a new concept or skill is related to something that is already well understood, it is likely to be learned more readily and more deeply than if presented without reference to something the individual already understands. Teachers are thereby encouraged to use the strengths of the individual to bolster the weaker areas.

The problem then is one of identifying strengths and weaknesses, and attributing each to the correct source. Earlier it was stated that the performance of a song could not be equated with pitch perception, although performance may be influenced by certain perceptual constraints or preferences. It is not a simple matter to identify the source of a singing difficulty, or a difficulty clapping back a rhythm, and clearly more research efforts are needed here. Inaccurate interpretation of a performance difficulty, however, could lead to inappropriate teaching practices, and, quite possibly, a serious underestimation of the musical potential of an individual.

With two general observations in mind—first, that once teachers have identified differences between, or within, individuals they should teach to individuals' strengths, and second, that teachers should carefully consider the possible sources of strengths and weaknesses—we turn to a discussion of the three issues listed above.

1. *Context and relative knowledge.* In this first section, we noted that context was important for engaging musical perception. The ability to judge the tonal relationship between tones may be more valuable than an absolute sense of pitch, and the ability to judge one's intonation relative to the musical context and the intonation of other musicians is arguably more important than being able to identify which pitch is higher or lower than another in an isolated test. Likewise, and on a deeper level, a sense of contour and tonality is more important than an ability to identify and/or reproduce single notes. When the teacher's goal is to enhance skills and sensitivity for the elements of music, pitch perception should be taught within the context of melody, durational concepts within the context of rhythm, and both within the context of music.

2. *Enriching experience.* Research findings suggest that our aural perception of musical structure is dependent to a large degree on exposure to the music of our culture. Young children and musically untrained adults are sensitive to the structures contained in the music to which they are exposed. What is experienced in the day-to-day musical diet affects what can be heard, and perhaps ultimately produced. The structures of aural perception are acquired out of our attempts to make sense of the music around us.

These comments lead to an emphasis on the importance of musical experience, especially musical exposure. Earlier the term "experience" was used to describe two types of situations: interventions and exposure. Indeed, in the learning process, there is a natural tension between these two types of experience; many educators have discussed this tension as it pertains to a variety of subjects (Hawkins, 1974; Whitehead, 1929). In practice, however, there is often more focus on various types of intervention than on exposure.

We suggest that children need be given more opportunity to listen—this includes a variety of music styles both of the children's making, and of other people's making. As we study, through research, the perceptual abilities of children, we can make informed decisions about the kinds of musical exposures from which the children, in turn, can form their own structures with which to hear.

3. *Criteria for assessment.* As we noted above, there are many valid ways to evaluate musical perception. Multiple measures provide evidence that may converge on a particular perceptual strength or weakness. Unfortunately, many criteria for assessment, especially in school settings, are based on a limited number of tests focusing on the isolated components of music. We suggest that children's abilities be assessed in a variety of ways, so that we obtain a full description of their abilities in terms of the structures they build within the musical contexts that surround them.

Musical perception is one important component of all musical activity. We need much more research evidence to uncover how it is reflected in production, performance, and other musical activities. However, the importance of adopting criteria that describe children's active involvement with the music of our culture cannot be overstated. Not only would the use of such criteria encourage teachers to look at the "whole" child in terms of music rather than isolated elements of music, but, in doing so, the musical experiences themselves would change. Thus, interventions and exposures would be likely to become more meaningful, and such meaningful experiences, in turn, might well affect the perceptual structures individuals acquire. As Dowling states, "Differences in prior perceptual experience lead to differences in what is perceived in the present" (1988, p. 126). With richer experiences, leading to more complex perceptual structures, our musical experiences may thereby also be enriched.

References

Bamberger, J. (1980). Cognitive structuring in the apprehension and description of simple rhythms. *Archives de psychologie, 48,* 171–199.

Bamberger, J. (1982). Revisiting children's drawings of simple rhythms: A function of reflection-in-action. In S. Strauss (Ed.), *U-shaped behavioral growth* (pp. 191–226). New York: Academic Press.

Borstad, J. (1989). *But I've been pouring sounds all day.* Paper presented at the annual meeting of the Canadian Society for the Study of Education (CSSE), Quebec City.

Brady, P. T. (1970). Fixed-scale mechanism of absolute pitch. *Journal of the Acoustical Society of America, 48,* 883–887.

Castellano, M. A., Bharucha, J. J., and Krumhansl, C. L. (1984). Tonal hierarchies in the music of North India. *Journal of Experimental Psychology: General, 113,* 394–412.

Clarke, E. F., and Krumhansl, C. L. (1990). Perceiving musical time. *Music Perception, 7,* 213–252.

Cohen, A. J., Thorpe, L. A., and Trehub, S. E. (1987). Infants' perception of musical relations in short transposed tone sequences. *Canadian Journal of Psychology, 41,* 33–47.

Cohen, A. J., Trehub, S. E., Thorpe, L. A., and Morrongiello, B. A. (1989). An approach to the study of melodic perception in infants and young children: Stimulus selection. *Psychomusicology, 8,* 21–30.

Cuddy, L. L. (1968). Practice effects in the absolute judgment of pitch. *Journal of the Acoustical Society of America, 43,* 1069–1076.

Cuddy, L. L. (1970). Training the absolute judgment of pitch. *Perception & Psychophysics, 8,* 265–269.

Cuddy, L. L. (1971). The absolute judgment of musically related pure tones. *Canadian Journal of Psychology, 25,* 42–55.

Cuddy, L. L. (1982). On hearing pattern in melody. *Psychology of Music, 10*(1), 3–10.

Cuddy, L. L., and Badertscher, B. (1987). Recovery of the tonal hierarchy: Some comparison across age and levels of musical experience. *Perception & Psychophysics, 41,* 609–620.

Cuddy, L. L., Cohen, A. J., and Mewhort, D. J. K. (1981). Perception of structure in short melodic sequences. *Journal of Experimental Psychology: Human Perception & Performance, 7,* 869–883.

Cuddy, L. L., Cohen, A. J., and Miller, J. (1979). Melody recognition: The experimental application of musical rules. *Canadian Journal of Psychology, 33,* 148–157.

Davidson, L., and Colley, B. (1987). Children's rhythmic development from age 5 to 7: Performance, notation, and reading of rhythmic patterns. In J. C. Peery, I. W. Peery, and T. W. Draper (Eds.), *Music and child development* (pp. 107–136). New York: Springer-Verlag.

Davidson, L., and Scripp, L. (1988). Young children's musical representations: Windows on music cognition. In J. Sloboda (Ed.), *Generative processes in music: The psychology of performance, improvisation, and composition* (pp. 195–230). New York: Oxford University Press.

Davidson, L., Scripp, L., and Welsh, P. (1988). Happy birthday: Evidence for conflicts of perceptual knowledge and conceptual understanding. *Journal of Aesthetic Education, 22,* 65–74.

Deliège, I. (1987). Grouping conditions in listening to music: An approach to Lerdahl and Jackendoff's grouping preference rules. *Music Perception, 4,* 325–360.

Deliège, I., and El Ahmadi, A. (1990). Mechanisms of cue extraction in musical groupings: A study of perception on Sequenza VI for viola solo by Luciano Berio. *Psychology of Music, 18,* 18–44.

Deutsch, D. (1980). The processing of structured and unstructured tonal sequences. *Perception & Psychophysics, 28,* 381–389.

Deutsch, D. (Ed.). (1982a). *The psychology of music.* New York: Academic.

Deutsch, D. (1982b). Grouping mechanisms in music. In D. Deutsch (Ed.), *The psychology of music* (pp. 99–134). New York: Academic.

Deutsch, D., and Feroe, J. (1981). The internal representation of pitch sequences in tonal music. *Psychological Review, 88,* 503–522.

Dewey, J. (1902). *The child and the curriculum.* Chicago: University of Chicago Press.

Dowling, W. J. (1978). Scale and contour: Two components of memory for melodies. *Psychological Review, 85,* 341–354.

Dowling, W. J. (1984). Development of musical schemata in children's spontaneous singing. In W. R. Crozier and A. J. Chapman (Eds.), *Cognitive processes in the perception of art* (pp. 145–163). Amsterdam: North-Holland.

Dowling, W. J. (1988). Tonal structure and children's early tonal learning of music. In J. Sloboda (Ed.), *Generative processes in music: The psychology of performance, improvisation, and composition* (pp. 113–128) Oxford: Clarendon Press.

Dowling, W. J., and Bartlett, J. C. (1981). The importance of interval information in long-term memory for melodies. *Psychomusicology, 1,* 30–49.

Dowling, W. J., and Harwood, D. (1986). *Music cognition.* New York: Academic Press.

Dowling, W. J., and Fujitani, D. S. (1971). Contour, interval, and pitch recognition in memory for melodies. *Journal of the Acoustical Society of America, 49,* 524–531.

Edworthy, J. (1985). Interval and contour in melody processing. *Music Perception, 2,* 375–388.

Fraisse, P. (1982). Rhythm and tempo. In D. Deutsch (Ed.), *The psychology of music* (pp. 149–181). New York: Academic.

Francès, R. (1988). *The perception of music* (W. J. Dowling, trans.). Hillsdale: Lawrence Erlbaum. (Original work published 1958)

Fry, D. (1948). An experimental study of tone deafness. *Speech, 12,* 4–11.

Gabrielsson, A. (1973). Similarity ratings and dimension analyses of auditory rhythm patterns. I. *Scandinavian Journal of Psychology, 14,* 138–160.

Gabrielsson, A. (1988). Timing in music performance and its relations to music experience. In J. Sloboda (Ed.), *Generative processes in music: The psychology of performance, improvisation, and composition* (pp. 27–51). Oxford: Clarendon Press.

Garner, W. R. (1974). *The processing of information and structure.* New York: Lawrence Erlbaum.

Gérard, C., and Drake, C. (1990). The inability of young children to reproduce intensity differences in musical rhythms. *Perception & Psychophysics, 48,* 91–101.

Hagerman, B., and Sundberg, J. (1980). Fundamental frequency adjustment in barbershop singing. *Journal of Research in Singing, 4,* 3–17.

Handel, S. (1989). *Listening.* Cambridge: MIT Press.

Hawkins, D. (1974). *The informed vision: Essays on learning and human nature.* New York: Agathon Press.

Hildebrandt, C. (1985). A developmental study of children's representations of simple rhythms. Unpublished doctoral dissertation, University of California, Berkeley.

Jones, M. R. (1987). Dynamic pattern structure in music: Recent theory and research. *Perception & Psychophysics, 41,* 621–634.

Jones, M. R., Boltz, M., and Kidd, G. (1982). Controlled attending as a function of melodic and temporal context. *Perception & Psychophysics, 32,* 211–218.

Kalmus, H., and Fry, D. B. (1980). On tune deafness (dysmelodia): Frequency, development, genetics and musical background. *Annals of Human Genetics* (London), *43,* 369–382.

Krumhansl, C. L. (1979). The psychological representation of musical pitch in a tonal context. *Cognitive Psychology, 11,* 346–374.

Krumhansl, C. L. (1983). Perceptual structures for tonal music. *Music Perception, 1,* 28–62.

Krumhansl, C. L. (1989). Issues in theoretical and experimental approaches to research on listening and comprehension. *Contemporary Music Review, 4,* 237–245.

Krumhansl, C. L. (1990). *Cognitive foundations of musical pitch.* New York: Oxford University Press.

Krumhansl, C. L. (1991). Music psychology: Tonal structures in perception and memory. *Annual Review of Psychology, 42,* 277–303.

Krumhansl, C. L., Bharucha, J. J., and Kessler, E. J. (1982). Perceived harmonic structure of chords in three related musical keys. *Journal of Experimental Psychology: Human Perception & Performance, 8,* 24–36.

Krumhansl, C. L., and Jusczyk, P. W. (1990). Infants' perception of phrase structure in music. *Psychological Science, 1,* 70–73.

Krumhansl, C. L., and Keil, F. C. (1982). Acquisition of the hierarchy of tonal functions in music. *Memory and Cognition, 10,* 243–251.

Krumhansl, C. L., and Kessler, E. J. (1982). Tracing the dynamic changes in perceived tonal organization in a spatial representation of musical keys. *Psychological Review, 89,* 334–368.

Krumhansl, C. L., and Shepard, R. N. (1979). Quantification of the hierarchy of tonal functions within a diatonic context. *Journal of Experimental Psychology: Human Perception & Performance, 5,* 579–594.

Mawhinney, T. A. (1987). Tone-deafness and low musical abilities. Unpublished doctoral dissertation, Queen's University, Kingston, Ontario, Canada.

Miyazaki, K. (1988). Musical pitch identification by absolute pitch possessors. *Perception & Psychophysics, 44,* 501–512.

Miyazaki, K. (1989). Absolute pitch identification: Effects of timbre and pitch region. *Music Perception, 7,* 1–14.

Monahan, C. B., and Carterette, E. C. (1985). Pitch and duration as determinants of musical space. *Music Perception, 3,* 1–32.

New Lexicon Webster's Dictionary of the English Language. (1987). New York: Lexicon.

Oram, N. P. (1989). The responsiveness of Western adult listeners to pitch distributional information in diatonic and nondiatonic melodic sequences. Unpublished doctoral dissertation, Queen's University, Kingston, Ontario, Canada.

Palmer, C. (1989). Mapping musical thought to musical performance. *Journal of Experimental Psychology: Human Perception and Performance, 15,* 331–346.

Palmer, C., and Krumhansl, C. L. (1987a). Independent temporal and pitch structures in perception of musical phrases. *Journal of Experimental Psychology: Human Perception & Performance, 13,* 116–126.

Palmer, C., and Krumhansl, C. L. (1987b). Pitch and temporal contributions to musical phrase perception: Effects of harmony, performance timing, and familiarity. *Perception & Psychophysics, 41,* 505–518.

Palmer, C., and Krumhansl, C. L. (1990). Mental representations for musical meter. *Journal of Experimental Psychology: Human Perception & Performance, 16,* 728–741.

Papert, S. (1980). *Mindstorms: Children, computers and powerful ideas.* New York: Basic Books.

Peretz, I., and Morais, J. (1989). Music and modularity. *Contemporary Music Review, 4,* 277–291.

Povel, D.-J., and Essens, P. (1985). Perception of temporal patterns. *Music Perception, 2,* 411–440.

Schmuckler, M. (1989). Expectation in music: Investigations of melodic and harmonic processes. *Music Perception, 7,* 109–150.

Sergeant, D. C. (1969). Experimental investigation of absolute pitch. *Journal of Research in Music Education, 17,* 135–143.

Shaffer, L. H., and Todd, N. P. (1988). The interpretive component in musical performance. In A. Gabrielsson (Ed.), *Action and perception in rhythm and music* (pp. 139–152). Stockholm: Royal Swedish Academy of Music.

Shepard, R. N. (1964). Circularity in judgments of relative pitch. *Journal of the Acoustical Society of America, 36,* 2346–2353.

Shuter-Dyson, R. (1982). Musical ability. In D. Deutsch (Ed.), *The psychology of music* (pp. 391–412). New York: Academic Press.

Shuter-Dyson, R., and Gabriel, C. (1981). *The psychology of musical ability* (2nd ed.). New York: Methuen.

Smith, J. E. (1983). Memory for musical rhythms: The effect of skill. Unpublished doctoral dissertation, Macquarie University, Sydney, Australia.

Smith, K. C. (1989). The representation and reproduction of musical rhythm by children and adults. Unpublished doctoral dissertation, Queen's University, Kingston, Ontario.

Smith, K. C., and Cuddy, L. L. (1989). Effects of metric and harmonic rhythm on the detection of pitch alterations in melodic sequences. *Journal of Experimental Psychology: Human Perception & Performance, 15,* 457–471.

Sundberg, J. (1982). Perception of singing. In D. Deutsch (Ed.), *The psychology of music* (pp. 59–98). New York: Academic Press.

Sundberg, J. (1987). *The science of the singing voice.* Dekalb: Northern Illinois University Press.

Thompson, W. F., and Cuddy, L. L. (1989). Sensitivity to key change in choral sequences: A comparison of single voices and four-voice harmony. *Music Perception, 7,* 151–168.

Thompson, W. F., and Cuddy, L. L. (in press). Perceived key movement in four-voice harmony and single voices. *Music Perception.*

Todd, N. P. (1985). A model of expressive timing in music performance. *Music Perception, 3,* 33–59.

Trehub, S. E. (1985). Auditory pattern perception in infancy. In S. E.

Trehub and B. A. Schneider (Eds.), *Auditory development in infancy* (pp. 183–195). New York: Plenum Press.

Trehub, S. E., Bull, D., and Thorpe, L. A. (1984). Infants' perception of melodies: The role of melodic contour. *Child Development, 55,* 821–830.

Trehub, S. E., Cohen, A. J., Thorpe, L. A., and Morrongiello, B. A. (1986). Development of the perception of musical relations: Semitone and diatonic structure. *Journal of Experimental Psychology: Human Perception & Performance, 12,* 295–301.

Trehub, S. E., Morrongiello, B. A., and Thorpe, L. A. (1985). Children's perception of familiar melodies: The role of intervals, contour, and key. *Psychomusicology, 6,* 39–48.

Trehub, S. E., Thorpe, L. A., and Morrongiello, B. A. (1985). Infants' perception of melodies: Changes in a single tone. *Infant Behavior and Development, 8,* 213–223.

Trehub, S. E., Thorpe, L. A., and Morrongiello, B. A. (1987). Organizational processes in infants' perceptions of auditory patterns. *Child Development, 58,* 741–749.

Trehub, S. E., Thorpe, L. A., and Trainor, L. J. (1990). Infants' perception of good and bad melodies. *Psychomusicology, 9,* 5–19.

Ueda, K., and Ohgushi K. (1987). Perceptual components of pitch: Spatial representation using a multidimensional scaling technique. *Journal of the Acoustical Society of America, 82,* 1193–1200.

Upitis, R. (1985). Children's understanding of rhythm: The relationship between development and musical training. Unpublished doctoral dissertation, Harvard University, Cambridge.

Upitis, R. (1987a). Children's understanding of rhythm: The relationship between development and musical training. *Psychomusicology, 7,* 41–60.

Upitis, R. (1987b). A child's development of musical notation through composition: A case study. *Arts and Learning Research, 5,* 102–119.

Upitis, R. (1987c). Toward a model for rhythm development. In J. C. Peery, I. W. Peery, and T. W. Draper (Eds.), *Music and child development* (pp. 54–79). New York: Springer-Verlag.

Upitis, R. (1990a). Children's notations of familiar and unfamiliar melodies. *Psychomusicology, 9,* 89–106.

Upitis, R. (1990b). *This too is music.* Portsmouth: Heinemann Educational Books.

Ward, W. D., and Burns, E. M. (1982). Absolute pitch. In D. Deutsch (Ed.), *The psychology of music* (431–452). New York: Academic.

Whitehead, A. N. (1929). *The aims of education and other essays.* New York: The Free Press.

·22·

AUDITORY-VISUAL PERCEPTION AND MUSICAL BEHAVIOR

Robert Walker

SIMON FRASER UNIVERSITY

Musical behavior resulting from auditory-visual perception traditionally concerns auditory responses to visual notations. It is important, therefore, to understand the nature of the relationships between notations and musical events, in particular, how notations arose in the first place and what their teleological function in relation to behavior is intended to be. Musical sound came first, and notations were invented later for utilitarian reasons. On the other hand, humans show a proclivity for cross-modal behavior across all the senses, not just auditory and visual, and this inevitably requires attention. In a single chapter it is not possible to mention all the research that might be considered relevant to these broad issues; instead of attempting such a task, I discuss what I consider to be important conceptual problems and in so doing include reference to the work of some researchers merely as examples to illustrate the main arguments. In any case, a chapter such as this should not be simply a catalog of research, but ought to seek to shed some light on the major issues confronting researchers. This is what I have attempted to do.

The chapter comprises two distinct parts. The first part deals with the research problems, particularly those of a teleological nature, associated with investigating auditory-visual behavior in response to orthodox staff notations. The second examines some issues involving both new types of visual notations for music that have arisen in this century and related psychoacoustic perspectives on cross-modal perception. Thus the first part deals with historical notational forms and viewpoints on concomitant cross-modal behavior, whereas the second is concerned with contemporary developments in both music notations and psychoacoustics. Underpinning the whole is the concern that notations for music have never been static in form, intent, or symbolic function. It is this writer's contention that research into auditory-visual

behavior relating to musical notations should be based solidly on an understanding of the variable functions of musical notations across history and particularly on their relationship to musical behavior as a sort of vague adumbration of that behavior. The musical staff notations we now use are the result of editorial decisions taken at a distance of time and location from the originals!

STAFF NOTATIONS

An Introduction to the Research and Problems of Definition

There appears to be general support among researchers and educators in music for the need to develop abilities in some form of integration of information gained from auditory and visual perception. Music, like language, is recorded visually in the form of written symbols that act as mnemonics for the physical actions necessary in the production of musical or spoken sounds. The visual symbols of both speech and music are not in themselves speech or music since the essence of both lies in the interpretations we impose on sound pressure waves. The letters and notations we use in speech and music, respectively, evolved as much as an aid to the memory, in view of the enormous vocabulary used by humans, as they did as a means of recording important words or music for future use.

This functional and historical connection between written symbols and both language and music is an important one, for despite the complexity and flexibility of the written symbol for the physical actions needed to produce the sound, it remains no more than that type of symbol. So when

344

we talk of auditory-visual perception in music, as well as in language, it is essential that the teleological link of sound with the visual symbol is recognized historically as being concerned with the physical actions needed to produce the sound rather than merely with the sound itself. The involvement of auditory perception must, in view of the historical development of such notations, occur with or after the kinesthetic one responsible for producing the sound.

Traditional notational forms in music, from the letter notations of the ancient Chinese and Greek civilizations to modern staff notations, were regarded as the codified versions of important ceremonial acts of producing musical sound on appropriate instruments or with the voice. The information contained in such notations was merely sufficient to remind the performers of the physical actions they needed to make, which they already knew. Such notations did not, and by their very nature could not, represent actions and resultant sounds not already known by performers.

This defines and delineates the nature of auditory-visual perception of such music notations; and such perception is highly dependent on the acquired specialist kinesthetic knowledge and experience of the perceiver. In contrast to such unique historical symbolic forms of notation, some developments in music notations in the twentieth century have produced more perceptually open notational forms with which performers rely less on the recovery of learned acceptable behaviors than on use of the imagination for creating novel, unusual physical behaviors and sounds in response. Indeed, some composers of this century use notations requiring the performer/perceiver to produce auditory events that parallel the two-dimensional deployments of visual shapes in visual space.

The differential teleological issues raised by these various types of music notations cannot be ignored in research into auditory-visual perception in the domain of music. The nature of such perception is likely to be substantively and qualitatively variable according to the teleological properties of notations. One cannot, for example, equate teleologically the staff notations for a Palestrina mass with the graphic notations employed by Earle Brown in an improvisational piece such as "4 Systems." Perception of the former is entirely dependent on previous learning of the special musical behaviors intended—behaviors known only to those who are specially trained and experienced in performing sixteenth-century Roman polyphonic music. In the latter case, perception and performance intentionally relies on more general human behavioral traits in finding cross-modal equivalents across visual and auditory domains.

Much of the research into auditory-visual perception in music education is related to the former teleological province. It has tended to focus on problems in the development of music-reading skills related to previously learned behaviors in the school population, that is, among those who are developing musical skills. Certain assumptions appear to underpin much of the research, assumptions concerning the psychological and musical connections between symbol, physical action, and sound. More specifically, some researchers appear to assume that visual perception of staff notation

somehow involves matching with a mental image of the sound, either in addition to, or rather than with, an image of learned physical movements necessary for setting an appropriate column of air, vocal fold, or string, into vibration. The problems posed by complex interactions between perception of staff notation, images of both learned physical movements and associated sounds, and eventual perceptual feedback involving the actual sound produced are of central concern.

In musical behavior, then, where reading staff notations is concerned, the initial interactions between stimuli (staff notations) and stored images can be characterized psychologically as visual-kinesthetic and kinesthetic-auditory. Following such behaviors, the situation then becomes more complex as auditory perception of the sound produced enters the process. At this stage the difficulty associated with the nature of the stored auditory image becomes apparent. Is this stored auditory image inextricably linked with that of learned physical actions or with some musical ideal associated with the staff notations and toward which performers strive? The point is that it is perfectly possible for someone to look at staff notations and match this perception with a stored image of a musical ideal without any intervening image of physical actions needed to produce sound. Musical directors and scholars do this as part of their professional daily routine. In research into musical behavior among the school population, which is inexperienced and relatively naive musically, it is difficult to imagine that processes involved in perception of musical staff notations mean anything other than matching images of previously learned physical actions with visual notations for those actions. The more sophisticated and experienced the perceiver, the more likelihood there is for the intervention of images of musical auditory ideals.

Instrumentally, then, we can say that music-reading skills, certainly among the masses of the school population, are not concerned solely and simply with auditory-visual integration of information, nor with a simple cross-modal transfer of information between visual and auditory modes of perception. Musical situations requiring an intervening physical response producing musical sound complicate the situation considerably. As we shall see, this complication is of some importance for researchers into music-reading behavior, particularly in view of some apparent teleological similarities between language- and music-reading behaviors. There is physical intervention in both language reading and music reading; both involve a translation into the physical domain of sound pressure waves. Expert readers in both language and music can, in their heads, translate visual symbol into an internal image of sound without physical intervention. The professional musical scholar is as skilled at music reading as is a professional literary scholar at language reading. A main difficulty faced by researchers into music-reading behaviors connected with staff notations is that such music reading is nothing like as ubiquitous a skill as language reading in the general populace. But this is not because of any special difficulty with music reading; it is simply a skill that people do not need to acquire. Historically, language skills were not necessary, and consequently very few people could read language in historical times.

Concerning music reading of staff notations specifically, Radocy and Boyle (1978a, p. 146) explain as follows: "Auditory-visual discrimination involves associating aural stimuli, melodic and harmonic patterns, with their symbolic (notational) representations." They regard this as "receptive" behavior, but make it clear that it is difficult to isolate such behavior from performance behavior, that is, production of sound. Although this does not make the necessary distinction between the learner and the accomplished professional, nor that between the performer and the music scholar or director, it nevertheless indicates an ideal that is attractive to educators. It leaves up in the air the problem of whether or not some sort of auditory-visual perception of notations can occur, musically, without any intervening visual-kinesthetic perception.

Reading music, then, and particularly that involving historical staff notations, is a much more complex process than is found in a straightforward psychological integration or cross-modal transfer of auditory and visual information. Weaver (1943), applying techniques used for investigating language reading in his classic study of ocular movements in music reading, makes the point that "music reading is different from other skills in many ways" (p. 1). I shall argue, among other things, that subsequent research has not identified with any precision how and why music reading is different from other skills such as language reading.

I shall return to this "difference" throughout this chapter. At this stage I want to concentrate on music reading in the school population and the importance of facility in manipulating musical instruments in the process of auditory-visual perception of staff notations. The acquired level of such a facility is of considerable importance. The point here is that levels of fluency in reading music are related to exposure, and those brought up with as much exposure to music reading as to language reading (as in specialist music schools like European residential cathedral schools, for example) probably provide a much more reliable indicator of human facility in this activity. It is suggested that such young people can provide data more comparable to those available on language reading than can the normal school population, which, in terms of music reading attainment, resembles a population more typical of the bulk of medieval Europeans to whom language reading was difficult and almost an unknown art simply because they had no need for it and, therefore, no continual exposure.

Having outlined some of the teleological difficulties and the importance of adequate exposure to regular usage of symbolic forms, I want, now, to look at some samples of research that compares music reading to language reading.

Music Reading and Language Reading

Research from two different perspectives is described here. One is psychological, and covers both mechanistic and cognitive approaches to research; the other shows statistical comparisons of data from tests of music and language reading from within the fields of music and music education. The perspectives are presented below under four subheadings indicating different facets of the issues involved.

The Objective, Mechanistic Approach to Research into Reading Research into language reading has had a major influence on research into music reading. Sight reading (rather than simply playing from a score that might be well-known to the performer) is an obvious choice of study in the latter case. Here, the subjects cannot afford to take their eyes off the score for too long, if at all, and certainly cannot be accused of having memorized passages. In such situations experimental controls can be more effectively applied.

The influence of research into language reading on research into music reading was felt early on, as Sloboda (1985) suggests. He states that language reading is all sight reading (p. 68), and that sight reading in music is, therefore, an obvious focus for research into music reading and for subsequent comparisons with word reading.

This early work referred to utilized various machines for recording subjects' responses. The interest was on the way the eyes move as they focus on the words or musical notations. Basically, in purely mechanistic terms, the eyes move in short, very quick movements from one area of the text being read to another, and then pause in order that the text can be "read." The extent of the movements is a function of the field of vision. Thus, several types of measurement became the focus of early work: the extent of the field of vision, the speed of eye movements between pauses, the length of pauses, and the effects of varying configurations of the visual characters on the operation of reading.

Tinker (1929) used tachistoscopic techniques for measuring and recording eye movements in reading words. He found that a reader can apprehend only a small number of symbols (three to five) at each "reading pause" of the eyes. Similarly, Weaver (1943) reports that in all reading, the eyes move in rapid jerks during which there is no clear vision. The apprehension of material to be read occurs only during the pauses between "jerks" as they scan the material to be read. He suggests that in reading words, pauses constitute about 94 percent of the reading time. Tinker (1929) also comments that in "all reading activity there is a tendency to combine the different elements of a visual impression into higher perceptual units whenever such grouping is possible." (p. 7)

Ortmann (1937) suggests that in music reading the visual field embraces a circular area varying between one-quarter and one-third of an inch in diameter. In such circumstances the size of notations assumes some importance. He goes on to say that, empirically, the chief determinants of the difficulty in note reading not involving actual eye movements (i.e., at the pause between eye movements) are as follows:

1. The number of notes in the field
2. The area covered by the distribution of notes

3. The number of linear dimensions involved (musically speaking)
4. The complexity or symmetry of the note patterns
5. The meaning of the note group from either a harmonic or a melodic standpoint (p.5)

Bean (1938) reports that professional musicians reproduced, at the keyboard, after one visual fixation of the notes, between one and nine notes correctly. The average number of notes accurately reproduced when the music had melodic organization was reported to be 4.72; with polyphonic organization it was 4.9; when chords were used, it was 3.59. On the other hand, nonprofessional musicians reproduced between one and seven notes correctly, and their averages were 2.73 (melodic), 2.15 (polyphonic), and 3.06 (chords). It appears from such data that with an average visual grasp of only three to five notes per reading pause, as Weaver points out, the music reader must achieve a coherent and unified execution of a composition from a visually discrete succession of relatively small groups of notes. An interesting finding reported by Van Nuys and Weaver (1943) in their classic study of eye-hand span among full-time music students playing the piano was that "rhythmic factors constitute the limiting conditions for rate of reading or average reading pause conditions whenever the rhythm is not simple" (p. 50). They go on to suggest that increase in the rate of reading depends on improvement in ability to grasp rhythmic figures. The importance of rhythm reading in music reading is something that appears in much later and very different types of research reported in the literature; it is discussed below in the section on research from within the field of music education. However, one can extend this to include a whole variety of musical elements along with rhythm: harmony, modulations, melody, tessitura, and so on, ad infinitum, and accounting for such things in music reading is, within the traditions of music, regarded as primarily a matter of experience on the part of the perceiver.

Short-term memory also plays a role in this kind of activity. Sloboda (1985) reports that at brief exposures of 100 milliseconds musicians have difficulty recording more than one note correctly from a selection of four. As the exposure time increases both musicians and nonmusicians improve their performance, but when the exposure reaches an optimum 2 seconds, enough time for full grasp of the note patterns, musicians were able to record accurately up to six notes, whereas nonmusicians managed about three. This, as Sloboda points out, indicates the role of musical training and experience. But also this is where the proclivity for perceptual grouping, mentioned by Tinker above, coupled with the effect of higher cognitive processing kicks into the situation. Without some overarching involvement of higher levels of cognitive functioning when recognition tasks are performed enabling the perceiver to categorize from minimum information, it would be impossible to deduce relevant information about a succession of notes or a piece of music from a succession of such small bits of information gained from such quick previews.

But let us look at bit more closely at the supposed connection between word reading and music reading on this mechanistic level. In early work attempting to find the extent of performance of grade school children in reading tasks, Buswell (1920) reports that "for all grades the good readers have a much wider verbal span than poor readers" (p. 2) and that this span is a function of the material read. Fairbanks (1937) also reported that eye-voice spans were a function of both reading ability and the type of material being read.

Weaver (1943) reports that the eye-hand span (for pianists) in music reading corresponds to the eye-voice span for word readers. The term "span" here refers to the extent to which the reader previews the words or musical notes during reading. Typically, it is measured by removing the text and discovering how many words or notes the perceiver can remember from the previewing that occurred before removal. Sloboda (1985) reports that in normal word-reading situations the eye-voice span is between four and six words, and that for "proficient" music readers, the eye-hand span is about seven notes. But whether these two sets of data are equivalent, cognitively, is very difficult to determine. How, for example, does one show that linguistic information from a word is equivalent to musical information from a note? In the purely instrumental terms of an experimental situation involving observations of eye movements, however, it might be said that the numbers of words and musical notes written down are equivalents if they each represent the amount of data obtained from the same span of time taken by the eye in reading movements. Also, there are clear physical differences between responding by manipulating the vocal tract in order to articulate a word, and placing and manipulating the hands to play a piano. This does not, however, mean that one is necessarily easier than the other. It is by no means obvious that it is more difficult to play a piano than to articulate speech for someone without substantial experience and knowledge of either. It may, however, be more physically taxing to play a piano than speak, in which case a more equivalent activity to reading words would be for music scholars to read music without having to respond in the form of a physical performance on musical instruments.

An interesting study by Shaffer (1976) contains reports on the reading behavior of experienced copy typists. The main conclusion was that these experienced typists need to be able to preview at least eight characters ahead in order to maintain a typing speed of 10 characters per second. Unfortunately, as Sloboda points out, no one has yet published experiments with similarly controlled conditions in music reading. But here the business gets messy and complex. Copy typing is not an activity comparable to musical performance, except in purely mechanistic terms of reading visual symbols and making physical movements. Suppose, for example, one persuades a number of highly fluent concert pianists to participate in a similar experiment reading music. An immediate problem arises in measuring the accuracy of their reading. With copy typists, accuracy is a simple matter of comparing the typed words with the original words, but with concert pianists measuring accuracy involves not just accuracy of reproducing notes but musical judgments concerning stylistic and expressive appropriateness. The nearest analogous situation to be found in word reading would be for professional actors to "read" an unseen script of a play or poem, and then similar matters of style and expression would have to figure in any assessment of accuracy.

The task is not impossible, particularly if one applies procedures usually found in concert performances rather than sight reading. For example, there are many international competitions for music performers where such musical judgments are made. Here, the procedure is to get a panel of distinguished and highly experienced performers to reach a consensus about the relative merits of the individual performers entered in the competition and to award prizes after first ranking them in order to merit. Merit, here, means a judgment about the quality of performance in total, including accuracy of notes. It is, however, well-known that some of the most revered performers on the concert stage frequently play inaccurately in terms of simply reproducing the notes written on the musical staff. The great Russian pianist Vladimir Horowitz is a case in point. Almost any recorded performance by this exceptionally gifted pianist will provide evidence of his proclivity to ignore such "mistakes" in the interests of interpretation. His audiences were not at all concerned at this; they, including professional musicians, went to hear his legendary interpretations, including any "wrong notes."

The Cognitive Approach to Investigating Music Reading

The problem for researchers is how to assess such phenomena under the strict experimental conditions usually associated with psychological research into music behavior. In this respect some new directions have emerged in recent years.

Sloboda (1985), in dealing with the problem of accounting for interpretation as it relates in sight reading, reports some interesting developments in recording what he terms the microstructure of sight-reading performance. This includes variations found in such details as minute variations in touch, timing, and intensity. Recent developments in digital recording technology, including the Musical Instrument Digital Interface (MIDI) between microcomputers and synthesizers, make the study of such performance detail relatively easy, but since this technology is so new, researchers have not yet had time to produce studies of a substantive nature.

This general approach, however, was reportedly pioneered by Seashore (1938), but first applied to sight reading by Shaffer (1980). Sloboda suggests that such data might be "particularly important to our understanding of sight reading in situations where there are no explicit instructions in the score to make variations in touch and timing" (p. 7). As for discovering "how principled a performer's expressive playing is," Sloboda suggests this can be done by finding out experimentally from two performances of the same piece by the same performer (p. 7). He cites Shaffer (1981), who argues that "musicians are not better than anyone else at remembering arbitrary analogue information" (p. 7), and if the expressiveness of a performance is replicated in a perfor-

mance task involving relatively unfamiliar music, then the assumption is that it must have musical validity in terms of some overarching strategy for dealing with expressiveness in music-reading situations.

Shaffer (1980) found evidence of such replication in a performance of a Bach fugue from notations where the pianist had not played the work for a number of years. The microstructure of the performance was recorded in the kind of detail referred to above. From such detail Sloboda (1985) indicates how it may be possible to extrapolate some rules for the assignment of "expressive variation." He describes how, using Shaffer's laboratory, he has examined the microstructure of several performances of musical phrases, and how he has found experimental evidence that pianists "are cued rapidly and fairly automatically from a first inspection of the score" into the expressive behaviors he describes in microstructure. Sloboda admits that such preliminary data "leave us a long way from understanding the total process" (p. 7).

What is lacking here is reference to the enormous store of relevant information about such expressive playing in individuals to be found among music teachers with long experience of observing such things. Although it may be true that musicians are no better than anyone else at remembering analogue information, it may also be true that there is something special about the nature of the analogue information contained in music that enables music to be remembered in all its associated detail much more easily than other types of analogue information. We can all remember the words of songs we learned as children far more readily when we go through the melody they are attached to than when we go through the words alone. In a television interview Vladimir Horowitz described how, once he started to play a piece on the piano, all sorts of associated memories returned to his consciousness, including minute details of interpretation associated with the specific piece.

Surprisingly, I know of no studies of such behavior that include input from long experienced music educators, and the more research reports one reads of psychological investigations into musical behavior, the more strident becomes the question: Why ignore the immense body of knowledge about such things that exists among those who are engaged in music performance and music education professionally? For example, for nearly 50 years in England a national organization, the Associated Board of the Royal Schools of Music, has conducted examinations three or four times per year in performance, sight reading, and aural tests on literally millions of children and young people between the ages of about seven and adult. The examinations are graded in difficulty, and such grading of test material is continually refined in the light of successive examiners' experiences of what people at different ages and experience levels can realistically achieve. The music set for examinations at different grade levels as a result of this process is an important source of information concerning expected performance levels, but, additionally, there exist examiner's reports that detail the various aspects of performance, including expression in sight reading and problems of various configurations of harmony, melody, rhythm, and tessitura. Associated Board examinations are conducted across the world as well as in England. Other bodies that perform similar functions include Trinity College in London and the Royal Toronto Conservatory in Canada.

Since the objective of psychological research into music-reading behaviors appears to be to gather information about the perceptual effects of notations for various configurations of musical elements on musical performance of subjects of varying experience and backgrounds, it is difficult to understand why researchers have not started with the enormous body of knowledge on such matters possessed by those who work in the field of music education and examined that before proceeding to laboratory work.

The development of a cognitive approach to investigating musical behavior should herald not merely a change of methodology but also a fresh look at how information is gathered from subjects. The term "cognitive science" began to be used in the early 1970s. Gardner (1985) suggests that it is still a young science and that practically all those working in the field are "still alive and young." He explains that cognitive scientists are concerned with the nature of the human mind, and seek to understand what the mind knows, how it knows it, and how it uses the knowledge. Thus cognitive science is, as Gardner suggests, deeply rooted in the philosophical problems of mind that have exercised the minds of western thinkers for over two thousand years. Essentially, cognitive science is an empirically based effort to answer long-standing epistemological questions about the human mind.

There is at present only a very small body of work in this new field that deals with music, and little that deals specifically with music reading. As Sloboda (1985) states, concerning a cognitive psychology of music, per se, there is a gap that needs to be filled. More importantly, Sloboda suggests that the "psychology of music [has] related rather little to what musicians actually did, and so was failing to tackle questions of central importance" (Preface). He clearly envisages a cognitive psychology of music as subsuming both musical and psychological knowledge in the quest to understand what musicians do.

In addition to the field of music education and testing referred to above, there is also the body of professional musicians from whom equally valuable information can be sought. By this I refer to the full-time professional and orchestral player, as well as those who supply the highest levels of musical experience we all look to for our musical nourishment—top class performers who are revered by their peers. The suggestion is that the full-time professional player is in a different class, behaviorally, from the part-time professional, who may teach as a main source of income and play as a secondary source. The issue here concerns continuous and extensive experience as a performer, not source of income. The professional player has the same kind of exposure to music-reading behavior as literate humans have to language reading. It is from such experience that reliable and musically respectable information can be gained about human behavior in music-reading activities. The last group I refer to are those who are regarded as the finest exponents of musical behavior. In this group, I am, of course, referring to the

likes of Yehudi Menuhin, Paul Tortelier, Luciano Pavarotti, Placido Domingo, Leonard Bernstein, Simon Rattle, and Nigel Kennedy. These people represent the highest levels of human achievement in western music and in any research into music behavior should be the subject of study. In studies of human capabilities in physical sports researchers tend to study the highest achievements of Olympic athletes in order to discover the highest level of physical capabilities of humans. In music research this can be no less important.

Major metropolitan centers like London or New York contain large numbers of highly competent professional musicians, orchestral musicians, and eminent soloists and former soloists who are now teachers—the number is certainly sufficient to conduct experiments in music reading. Outside of these centers there are equally competent performers in the ancient cathedral organ lofts of Europe, or other institutions, such as broadcasting companies, that employ full-time professional musicians of the caliber referred to. Persuading them to participate might be a different matter, of course. However, without experimental data derived from the musical behavior of such people, we have little objective evidence of what the human is capable of in music reading, or of the nature of the differences between such people and musical novices. Do we know, for example, whether Nigel Kennedy, Glenn Gould, or Yehudi Menuhin, as school boys, experienced the same kind of problems in sight reading music to which researchers often refer in research studies using the general population of relatively inexperienced and naive musical subjects? Anecdotally, it is reported that they did not. Without accounting for data from longitudinal studies into the behavior of the musically gifted who subsequently become renowned performers, together with data from the full-time professional performers referred to above, we cannot make any reliable generalizations about the general population of school children. The likelihood is that data from the general population without the levels of experience of the musicians mentioned are likely to be as skewed as data would be from studies of language acquisition among semi-or nonliterate humans in nonliterate societies.

It is the omission of such data in the literature, I believe, that inhibits the further progress of psychological research into musical behavior.

Relationships Between Music Reading and Language Reading Among Children In direct comparisons of children's reading of music and language, a predominant approach favors straight comparisons of performances on music- and language-reading tests. Hutton (1953) produced data yielding little correlation between language-reading scores and those obtained from responses to music-reading tests. In a much larger study, Dalton (1952) found that the better music readers were superior to poor music readers in language reading. Yet although this finding has been replicated in many subsequent studies (see Zinar, 1976), no attempt has been made to prove a connection between the two abilities. Just as music teachers in schools report anecdotally that some children who are poor readers seem to function well in music, so they also report that, generally, children who function well as all-rounders, also function well in school music (Zinar, 1976). Such a generalizable correlation across several subject areas, including mathematical and language skills, was found to exist by Wang (1989) in a study of schoolchildren's performance on various musical tests compared with their performance in several other tests. Wang showed correlations between musical abilities, language and mathematical abilities, and performance on auditory-visual matching tests. In another test, in terms of test measurements of music reading, language reading, and intelligence, positive correlations were shown between language and music-reading abilities, between intelligence and music reading, and between intelligence and language reading (Wheeler and Wheeler, 1952; Cooley, 1961; King, 1954; Maze, 1967).

In view of potential problems over the reliability of such data and the statistical treatment, and the fact that music reading here refers to a rather mechanical process of deciphering visual symbols, it is not at all clear in what ways music-reading abilities, per se, are related to those other abilities, or whether in fact the researchers are testing music-reading abilities at all. What is defined here as music-reading behavior shows little connection with the activity as it occurs in music performance. In Maze's (1967) study the Seashore *Tests of Musical Talents* were used, for example, and in other studies standardized tests of general music-reading abilities were included. Moreover, Zinar reports that in some research the children were not controlled for exposure to music-reading instruction. There also appeared to be great variation among the subjects tested in that some children had had extensive private tuition in music while others had not.

On the more general point of whether or not music-reading instruction can aid development in other areas of instruction, Seides (1967) reports that slow adolescent learners talented in music did display greater achievement in reading, arithmetic, social behavior, and creativity when given formal music lessons. The definitions used were not entirely rigorous or clear, but the general and overall impression was a firm one that music instruction did cause an improvement in general functioning, interest, and attainment. But this is a far cry from linking musical and other behaviors.

Another study by Nicholson (1972) showed similarly that music-reading achievement "can improve abilities in young children who are slow learners" (p. 73), but failed to explain how or why this is so. Monroe (1967) suggests that there are "certain basic principles and practices in music and language reading that involve connections between eye and ear understanding," but whether he refers to purely mechanistic ones such as eye movements or to more cognitive ones is not at all made clear. Pollack (1969) provides some clues to the possible thinking behind such an assertion when she suggests that the "inter-relationships of various sensory approaches is particularly effective for learning (per se) and that music is a valuable aid in this type of presentation" (p. 74); that is, music reading involves several sensory modes—visual, auditory, and kinesthetic. Very little research is published that has followed this up.

All this seems to point to a belief in a general value for children's overall functioning of a multisensory approach to education in general, and in the value of music reading in particular as an aid in this respect. Such views reflect the thinking from an educational movement best described under the umbrella term "whole child" education, a popular term among teachers during the last decade or two. For music education specifically, however, the focus has been on identifying specific elements that facilitate or contribute to children's improved performance in sight reading.

Research into Sight Reading of Staff Notations Within Music Education Not surprisingly, the focus of research into sight reading from within music education is on identifying factors that may facilitate the teaching of sight-reading skills and proficiencies relating to staff notations. Although there may be some overlap with purely psychological research into music reading, and sight reading in particular, there is a substantive difference in that pedagogy is the primary concern of researchers in music education, whereas understanding and describing the mental processes and behaviors of subjects are the main concern of psychologists.

Such studies in music education generally fall into one of two categories:

1. Studies of factors affecting the teaching and learning of music reading and sight reading in general in all of its facets in combination
2. Studies of factors affecting different specific aspects of music reading and sight reading, such as, for example, melody reading, or rhythm reading alone

Generally, there seems to be a conflation of the problems associated with music reading and sight reading in that studies referring to either or both usually present the problems as identical in the learning stages experienced by school children or college and university students. Most, if not all, the research bypasses the possible effects of learned kinesthetic behaviors associated with staff notations and concentrates instead on what may be relatively less intrinsic factors affecting such behavior.

Several researchers conclude that rhythmic control and accuracy constitute the single most important attribute of behavior contributing to overall success in sight reading among schoolchildren. I illustrate this type of research by reference to an interesting study of the effects of select variables on sight-reading behavior. Elliott (1982), in the preamble to the report of his research, suggests that a fundamental question to be resolved concerns the "nature of the sight reading process." By this, and in view of his reported study, one assumes he refers to one or several factors that might accurately predict success in sight reading on a wind instrument. He goes on to explain his seven select variables that might be likely candidates as such factors:

1. Technical proficiency (defined as the ability to perform fluently from memory scale, third, and arpeggio patterns)
2. Sight singing ability
3. Rhythm reading ability

4. Cumulative grade point average on academic work generally
5. Cumulative grade point average in music theory
6. Cumulative music performance jury grade point average
7. Major instrumental grade point average

His subjects were 30 wind instrumentalists from university undergraduate music theory classes. The most promising correlation he found was between rhythm reading ability (No. 3 above), as measured using the procedure developed by Boyle (1968), and sight reading as measured on the *Watkins-Farnum Performance Scale*. This latter test is reported as achieving a reliability coefficient of 0.94 for school children in grades 9 through 12. No evidence was put forward of its reliability beyond this age level or musical experience level. It is particularly interesting at this point to recall the findings of Van Nuys and Weaver (1943) reported above, that reading rhythm was an important factor in eye-hand span in reading music.

Elliott's study is a careful, exemplary one of its type and its strengths and weaknesses are presented and explained meticulously by the author. He is at pains to point out that the results are not generalizable outside wind instrumentalists, and that the selection of the seven variables was made after a careful study of the literature. He mentions the possibility that some of the data suggested that technical proficiency could not be ruled out as a possible main factor. Here, at least, is some indication of awareness of the possibly crucial significance of learned behaviors associated specifically with staff notations. As Elliott points out, much of the research indicating similar findings was also carried out with wind players. In view of the predominance in North American schools of wind performance programs, it is not surprising that the bulk of research into music-reading skills among school children should focus on wind players.

An earlier study (Boyle, 1970) cites the same work of Van Nuys and Weaver (1943) and the finding that increases in the rate of reading music depend on improvement in "ability to grasp rhythmic figures" (p. 307). Thomson (1953) reached essentially the same conclusion, Boyle reports, in his study of violinists and clarinetists in that most errors were in rhythm.

Interjecting a pedagogical note at this point, it is interesting to see that Hoffer (1964) maintains that special rhythm training, through movement, is a "necessary prerequisite to music reading" (P. 308), and several other authors are cited by Boyle in the same vein: Hindemith (1946); Shanet (1956); Dallin (1966); Carlsen (1965). All these maintain that a good feel for rhythm is essential in music reading.

Not surprisingly, then, Boyle's hypothesis was that an approach to music reading that involves bodily movement and rhythm training will aid instrumentalists in reading music, specifically as measured on the *Watkins-Farnum Performance Scale*. In total, all school bands participating in the study spent 30 minutes per week for 14 weeks in rhythm training. The experimental group of bands were asked to incorporate a number of activities into their teaching of rhythm, which involved recognizing the "beat," clapping rhythm patterns while tapping the beat with the foot, and playing rhythm patterns on a single note while marking the beat with the foot.

Boyle reports that high correlation ($r = 0.81$) was observed between ability to read rhythm at sight and ability to read music at sight. Comparison between pretest and posttest scores on rhythm sight reading alone showed that the experimental group made a much greater gain than the control group, and that the control group did not make a statistically significant gain in this respect during the 14 weeks of the experimental program. Both groups made gains on the *Watkins-Farnum Performance Scale* scores in comparisons of pretest and posttest scores, but the experimental group showed significantly higher gains than the control group.

This study seems to provide as much evidence as is necessary to show that, in the specific context of the North American school, rhythm training, particularly that involving bodily movements, significantly improves performance in sight reading generally in such a population. The question remains, however: To what extent is this generalizable? I return to a leitmotif—length of exposure to music reading!

A survey (Walker, 1972) conducted in England among 30 cathedral and collegiate choirs suggested that length and frequency of involvement in actual musical performance in conditions where an audience was present were main predictors of success in music reading, and sight reading in particular as far as vocal performance is concerned. There was considerable agreement among all the respondents (cathedral and collegiate choirmasters) that it takes about two and a half years, for a boy chorister, at the age of 8 or 9 years, to reach the stage of being a "useful" member of the choir in these respects. "Useful," in this context, means capable of reading the large volume of music sung each week at cathedral services well enough to perform satisfactorily on a regular basis. We do not, of course, know what this means in terms of a standardized test of music reading such as the *Watkins-Farnum Performance Scale*, but it can be said that the levels of technical difficulty and musical complexity of melody, harmony, and rhythm of much of the music sung by cathedral choristers daily are much higher than those found in the musical test materials in most, if not all, standardized music-reading tests.

The conclusions derived from the survey were based on the written responses of choirmasters in many of the most prestigious choral establishments in England. There are several points to be borne in mind, however, before any useful comparisons can be made with data from the North American studies cited. The choristers are boys only, and they are selected through competitive open voice trials at the age of 8 years. Those selected attend a boarding school on scholarship as choristers whose main function is to perform at the daily cathedral services. Thus they attend a fee-paying school on a music scholarship—a factor that inevitably applies pressure on them to maintain their function and their performance standards. Their daily musical routines are quite arduous. From the results of the survey mentioned above, they comprise, usually, about two hours of choral practice each day on six days of the week, plus daily performances of three difficult polyphonic choral works from the cathedral repertoire at Evensong (the evening service in the Anglican traditions), plus choral settings of two or three complete psalms each day, possibly a hymn, and in addition to this there is daily music practice on instruments (usually two, including the piano).

In total these choristers receive about 18 to 20 hours each week of musical experience in performance, rehearsal, and practice for something like 30 weeks each year from the age of 8 years to 13 years, at which time many choir schools "graduate" their students to other schools dealing with 13- to 18-year-olds. On a yearly basis this amounts to approximately 500 to 600 hours per year on such musical activities. And if a two and a half year period is necessary in order to reach a good standard, then a total exposure to such musical activities of about 1,250 to 1,500 hours is required. The typical North American school child at the same age would receive about two hours or less each week for about 20 to 25 weeks each year, amounting to a total of about 100 hours over a 2-year period. This activity would predominantly be of the type characterized in many of the studies quoted above as repeated playing of passages in class in order to get the notes right. Very little of it would be in actual performance in front of an audience. We can, therefore, say that the two populations will, qualitatively and quantitatively, have had distinctly different musical experiences.

The cathedral chorister's musical experiences more nearly approximate normal children's experiences with language acquisition in literate societies than their experiences with music reading, and perhaps, in view of this, provide a more reliable indication of human proclivities and capabilities in music reading.

Among the findings from the responses of choirmasters in English cathedrals was a clear unanimity in that none of them used a method or system for teaching melody or rhythm reading to their choristers: All admitted to using only the actual music to be performed and a kind of osmotic approach to this task. As a result the choristers either picked it up or failed to pick it up. However, the failure rate, as signified by withdrawals, is comparatively low in this population.

Concerning training in music-reading skills generally, it can be said empirically that there are significant differences between the North American traditions and those in England, whatever the educational institution. The former are characterized by a reliance on methods and programs of teaching such skills, whereas the latter tend to rely on more general experiential factors to enhance the acquisition of such skills. There is little left at any level in English schools of the traditions of teaching note reading pioneered by Sarah Glover or John Curwen in the nineteenth century. The use of solfege is virtually unknown now in English schools, and Kodály or Orff techniques are difficult to find in their pristine form.

In contrast, in North American schools there is a much more obvious and conscious presence of well-organized, well-constructed methods. Similarly, the North American traditions induce researchers to utilize information gained from standardized tests of music reading rather than experienced music educators' knowledge of children's performances

of actual music, which is the default tradition in England. This latter is more likely to be used in any English monitoring of standards, not solely because of an island mentality that distrusts imported methods and standardization procedures, but because such methods and procedures are not generally known in England. In any case, the proclivity for systematic and pedagogically manufactured approaches to teaching and measuring music reading is the main characteristic found in North American curriculum and testing materials. This is compared with a more improvised, personalized, and osmotic approach to curriculum and assessment materials, often using real music and musicians' opinions, found in the English and European traditions generally.

Some kind of conflation of the two approaches might well produce more musically relevant and interesting results. Unfortunately, I know of no study that has included such subjects as choristers or other students at special music schools in empirical research into music reading among schoolchildren. A comparison of performance on such test batteries as the Watkins-Farnum between normal school children and those in special music schools should at least provide evidence of the scope of such test batteries across a wide range of musical experience. The omission of this type of data in the literature is one that needs rectifying.

In view of the musical differences between English cathedral choristers and typical North American schoolchildren described above, of particular interest is the fact that over three-quarters of the English choirmasters who responded to the survey mentioned above replied that, in their experiences training choristers, not only was length of experience in performing music an important factor in reaching high standards, but so was ability to read rhythms well. A greater number commented that rhythmic problems were more common and difficult to deal with in music reading than were melodic problems. Many admitted that they felt pressure to have their choristers produce the right artistic vocal sound, sometimes to the detriment of rhythmic training. Many suggested that rhythm training was the most desirable addition they would make to their training schedules, if they had time, and that such training needed as much time, at least, as vocal intonation. All admitted that they relied on the music to be performed for materials to be used in daily training.

Such an agreement on the importance of rhythm reading in general music reading for choristers makes for interesting comparisons with the findings of the North American empirical studies of the general school population. It is particularly interesting that such agreement comes from two very different cultural and educational situations.

The importance of considerable time involvement in actual music performance as a factor in the development of good music-reading skills, in particular sight reading of vocal music, is stressed in English traditions. A number of researchers in North America have indicated that some kind of involvement in performance is clearly an aid, or a spur, to improvement in music-reading abilities. Enoch (1978) and Rezits (1972) report that improvement in general sight-reading skills was observed as a result of students' involvement in ensemble playing where they had to account for the performance of others, their own performance was under musical scrutiny as a result, and they had to fit in with the overall musical presentation. Mursell (1956) reports similarly: ''If we want to establish skilled and rapid reading, there is only one way to do it, and that is by extensive reading; i.e. by reading large amounts of music'' (p. 41).

In an interesting and well-organized study of the effect of having to accompany a soloist while sight reading at the piano, Watkins and Hughes (1986) found that piano players who were nonkeyboard majors at a university significantly improved their piano reading scores as a result of accompanying a soloist during sight reading, as compared with similar piano players who did not accompany anyone while playing the same music. Both groups played actual music rather than test batteries, and judgments of their performances were made by three staff members of the university piano faculty—a practice that is increasingly replacing the use of standardized manufactured musical test items and standardized marking schemes, and one that marks a most welcome shift toward gathering data from actual performances of music and the judgments of musicians.

The greater the involvement in performance with other musicians, the more fluent, it appears, music reading becomes. The fact that others are involved must mean that the music reader is obliged to listen, and therefore use auditory modes of behavior as opposed to visual. This would tend to suggest that auditory perception is an important factor in enhancing music-reading skills, but only provided the requisite kinesthetic skills are sufficiently developed to enable ensemble playing to occur.

The inevitable shift toward pedagogical techniques as a focus of enquiry in music education research into music reading is to be expected. And much research of this type in the United States concentrates on the effectiveness of conditions and methodologies that might improve various aspects of the educational process of developing sight-reading and general music-reading abilities. These range from studies of various approaches to teaching rhythm reading (e.g., Palmer, 1976; Colley, 1987; Bebeau, 1982), to various techniques for improving melodic sight reading (e.g., Grutzmacher, 1987; Bobbitt, 1970). To dwell any further on such studies would be to move too far away from the essential research problems of identifying what is meant by auditory-visual perception in music. It is to developments in music notations occurring during this century and to psychoacoustic aspects of auditory-visual perception that I now turn.

MODERN NOTATIONS AND PSYCHOACOUSTICS

Auditory-Visual Perception of Music Notations Beyond the Staff

The history of music notations in modern times shows how, from the seventeenth and eighteenth centuries to the

present, staff notations have become more and more prescriptive. From the skeletal outlines of a seventeenth-century instrumental score showing very little more than a figured bass line, we can see a progression whereby notations showed more and more detail as the choices available to musicians became greater. This reflected a desire of composers and musical directors for greater control over what musicians did in performance. It also reflected a growing awareness of the expressive possibilities of all the parameters of sound available to a musician, not just those of melody, harmony, and rhythm. By the nineteenth century, it was commonplace for composers to specify precisely the instrumentation they required, as well as other information concerning dynamics, phrasing, and performance techniques such as bowing. All these developments signaled a much closer and tighter connection between performance technique and staff notations. It meant that if a performer had not previously acquired the appropriate technique indicated by the staff notations, then this would have to be remedied. The inextricable link between acquired technique and notational function thus became more clearly established.

In the early years of this century new sounds and new performance techniques were increasingly employed by musicians, and notations inevitably followed this trend. One important aspect of this development was to loosen the bond between acquired performance technique and notational representation. Composers began to introduce notations requiring creative leaps of the imagination and a natural proclivity for matching cross-modally information in the visual mode with that in the auditory. For nearly one hundred years now composers have been altering the perceptual basis on which music notations relate to musical actions, and it is, therefore, pertinent to examine the nature of this change and the psychoacoustic issues involved.

Of particular interest from a psychoacoustic perspective is the equality of representational status of all elements of musical sound in many new notations. In particular, pitch is no longer the prime concern and in many cases is subsumed within notations for tone color or timbre—a development that has direct parallels in psychoacoustic research. Several composers show an intuitive grasp of the relationship between pitch and tone color in their notations. Cornelius Cardew in ''The Great Learning'' portrays pitch movements purely in terms of the type of sound employed by using varying thicknesses of graphic shape set above and below a single horizontal line. The pitches are determined more by the nature of the sound source—for example, whistling or singing vowels—than by vertical positioning. The details of pitch are left to the performer, who is required to suit the nature of the sound to the pitches suggested. Psychoacoustically, this relates far more accurately to the nature of human perception of pitch as we shall see below.

John Cage utilizes similar symbols for pitch in such scores as ''Solo for Voice No. 2'' and ''Variations II.'' Here, he employs several transparent sheets upon which he has drawn various graphic shapes to be superimposed at the performer's whim. The performer is expected to display a natural sense of cross-modal information transference in the process of building up the piece by selecting appropriate superimpositions of transparent sheets and their graphic symbols. In "Volumina" by György Ligeti, pitches to be played on the organ are denoted by varying thicknesses and vertical placement of lines. Krzystof Penderecki, in "Dimensionen der Zeit und der Stille," represents pitch movement in whistling sounds by undulating lines set around a single horizontal line, much in the manner of Cardew. Clusters of pitched sounds are portrayed as clusters of graphic shapes set at appropriate points on a staff or arbitrary horizontal reference points in a number of works—for example, in Penderecki's "St. Luke Passion" or Murray Shafer's "Threnody."

Other parameters of sound are shown by means of direct cross-modal links between visual and auditory modalities. Dynamics are shown as varying sizes or thicknesses of shape or line. Examples are as follows: Boguslaw Shäffer's "Azione a due," where different dynamic levels are represented by varying the filling in of a circle, thus involving more parameters of the sound than dynamics; "Four Visions" by Robert Moran, which shows various thicknesses of vertically placed lines to denote various densities of tones; "Circles" by Luciano Berio, which employes frames around a set of graphic shapes where the frames vary in thickness to denote the dynamic levels; "Telemusik" by Karlheinz Stockhausen, where isolated drum sounds are denoted by different sized circles to denote different intensity levels. Duration is shown by horizontal placement, as in Berio's "Circles," Stockhausen's "Momente," or Klaus Hashagan's "Cymbalon," where he also links pitch placement and timbre in the same graphic shape. Timbre is frequently denoted by graphic pattern or shape, and many composers tend to combine several such visual elements intentionally so as to provide clear indication to the performer of the precise sound, or alternatively they provide only vague indications of some parameters in order to leave the performer free for personal interpretation. In the latter case, it becomes not just a matter of personal creativity but also one involving innate cross-modal proclivities for transfer of information from visual to auditory domains.

These developments in new notations raise a number of issues of a psychoacoustic nature, and many such scores appear to reflect or foreshadow findings in modern psychoacoustics. It is to the field of psychoacoustics, therefore, that we must finally turn in order to provide some theoretical explanation of human behavior in interpretations of such notations.

Modern Psychoacoustic Research and the Varying Functions of Music Notations

The subject of sensory integration of information, per se, is felt to be a crucial one in view of the complex evolutionary changes observable in the history of music notations. The varying nature of the relationships between notation and musical action must, it is felt, be accounted for in investigations into auditory-visual perception in music. Research into various psychoacoustic aspects of sensory integration behaviors in humans can inform specific problems associated with intersensory behavior in music.

Information Transfer Across the Senses The phenomenon humans call sound has at least four separable stimulus properties by which an auditory event can be characterized: repetition rate of the pressure wave; its intensity and amplitude envelope; its duration; its frequency components, or spectrum. Similarly, the phenomena that stimulate our peripheral visual receptor systems can be characterized as having varying repetition rates, or frequencies, and varying intensities and durations. We interpret such physical phenomena subjectively in our perceptions of both sight and sound: sound in terms of its pitch (repetition rate), loudness (intensity, or amplitude of the wave form), duration or rhythm, and timbre (its spectral frequency components and other characteristics including its envelope shapes); and sight in terms of hue or color (repetition rates at the red end of the color spectrum are higher than those at the blue end), intensity (amplitude), and shape or length (duration).

Marks (1978) suggests that there are identifiable commonalities across different modes of sensory input. Cross-modal transfer not involving commonalities can and does occur through verbal mediation, but commonalities across the senses can be demonstrated where there is no possibility of such mediation (in preverbal infants, for example). However, the larger problem exists of identifying what precisely facilitates transfer of information, whether common or not, across the sensory modes. It may be due to a recognition of some type of information that is common to the two modes in question. On the other hand, it may be a straight transfer from one mode to another of some information that is not necessarily common to both.

In answer to such speculation, Marks (1978) suggests that "given a direct realist view of perception, a particular property of an object, say its size, is apprehended directly as a property of the object, and is so apprehended regardless of the particular modality through which the property is sensed" (p. 28). As examples, he cites studies showing how sensory magnitude, whatever the sense modality, can be related across the senses. For example, more light intensity can easily be transferred to sound and related with more amplitude or more (i.e., higher) frequency. Magnitude of sensory experience appears to grow with increases in both the duration and size of the stimulus whatever the mode of perception involved. A study by Stevens, Mack, and Stevens (1960) provides data from seven perceptual continua (electric shock to the fingers, lifted weights, pressure on the palm, vibration to the fingertips, white noise, intensity in a 1,000 Hz tone, and white light).

Marks (1978) goes on to describe a number of experiments and modes of expression that show how the different senses, qua senses, that we employ to find out about the world "out there," integrate information across modalities in what might be termed (comparatively speaking) straight stimulus-response situations without a complex intervening physical response being involved. By this I mean that no intervening action is necessary between, say, perception of a visual stimulus and the transfer of the information perceived to the auditory realm. Even if the subject has to make some sort of minimal physical movement in response, such as marking paper with a pencil, this is not to be compared with the complex physical activity necessary in playing a violin or singing an operatic aria from visual notations for such events.

In this way, then, the focus can be on the perceiver's mental integration of two supposedly different *types* of sensory information, which may contain similar content, or content that can easily be translated from one mode into the other. If we do introduce the intervening level of response, whereby the subject is required to display complex physical behaviors in order to externalize a required mental response, then we have to account for the level of technical proficiency in making the appropriate physical movements. And here, skill levels will affect the response, irrespective of any covert mental activity elicited purely from visual-auditory integration processes.

There is evidence that a complex sound containing several frequency components across the spectrum appears to be less "bright," in visual terms, than a pure tone of the same fundamental pitch and overall loudness (Marks, 1978, p. 59). Moreover, Marks found that subjects tended to correlate subjective brightness of tone with increasing loudness and higher frequency, irrespective of common fundamental rates of vibration, behavior he describes as resulting from analogous sensory attributes and qualities. Other studies (Walker, 1987a,b) showed that musically naive subjects (schoolchildren) would often match higher frequencies from pure tones with larger sized two-dimensional visual symbols and smaller such symbols with similar types of lower frequencies. And Bamberger (1982) found that similar subjects would tend to match longer rhythmic durations with larger visual symbols, which they invented in response to their own clapped sounds. Although she does not attribute this to the child's perception that a longer clapped sound is necessarily louder because of the need to make a clap last longer, the evidence from other studies would suggest that this is the most likely explanation.

These and other studies indicate certain proclivities for transfer of analogous information across sensory channels that rely on fairly prosaic properties of the stimulus concerned, such as, for example, perceived size or intensity. In which case, although one is dealing with different types of stimuli in terms of their modality, they appear to have analogous properties (e.g., more of something) when cross-modal transfer occurs. This suggests some kind of correlation between the information in the two types of sense modes involved. It does not refer to a transfer of information across modalities so much as to a recognition of the same or similar properties in different modalities. As Gibson (1969) points out, the term "transfer" may be inappropriate: "Transfer implies a process of mediation, of going from one modality to another through or by means of still something else" (p. 51). Certainly, with more complex types of stimuli, there is evidence that verbal mediation occurs.

There is ample evidence, well documented, that we tend to invent what some term "virtual" reality from some stimuli. This means that we take some stimulus property and invent meaning that is both derived from the property and yet seems remote from it. An example of this "virtual" reality can be seen in pitch perception (Terhardt, 1974, 1979; Ter-

hardt and Seewann, 1982) of both musical sounds and verbal sounds. Terhardt distinguishes between the mental construction of "virtual" pitch concepts from complex sounds found in music and that derived from pure tones that do not occur naturally and are not used in music. In the former case, the perceiver constructs the fundamental pitch from a number of adjacent harmonics. This phenomenon is well reported in the literature (see De Boer, 1976).

To emphasize the subjective nature of our perceptions of such phenomena, we can describe certain frequency spectra in sound as being high pitched by virtue of the distribution of energy across the spectrum. For example, as mentioned above, it is well reported in the literature on speech perception that the subjective "pitch" of a vowel is determined by the frequency of the second formant, or energy peak in the frequency spectrum, in addition to, and quite distinct from, its repetition rate (Delattre, Liberman, Cooper, and Gerstman, 1952). The second formant is usually associated with a concentration of energy in a narrow frequency band around 1.5KHz in sounds produced by the human vocal tract. Newman (1953) reported that some vowels sound brighter or higher pitched than others: (i) as in meet, for example, sounds brighter and subjectively higher than (u) as in moot. The different distributions of spectral energy of such different vowel sounds are achieved because of the way our vocal tract is changed in shape to produce the vowel sound, which in turn moves the positioning of the second formant accordingly (i.e., higher for [i] and lower for [u]). Other studies have shown that "pitch" perceptions do result from varying positions of energy peaks in the spectral envelopes of different musical instruments, or even different tessituras on the same instrument (e.g., Meyer, 1978; Terhardt, 1970, 1979; Terhardt and Grubert, 1987; Ohgushi, 1978).

This prompts a reminder of the work done over the last few decades in pitch perception, particularly that concerning the role of the frequency spectrum in human perception of pitch. Several researchers (Houtsma, 1971; Houtsma and Goldstein, 1972; de Boer, 1976; Terhardt, 1972, 1974, 1979) have demonstrated that pitch can be attributed to complex sounds where little or no energy is contained at the fundamental frequency (the repetition rate itself) and where two or more adjacent harmonics are sounded. Pitch attribution is described by these researchers as being a product of processing information at higher cognitive levels of the cortex. It is, in fact, an invented construct placed upon the information perceived, an invention that is dependent on the background of the perceiver (Terhardt, 1974, 1979; Divenyi, 1979). Instrumentally, this means that music educators cannot rely upon some innate proclivity of humans to match perceived pitch movements with vertically placed visual symbols in the way that they can with different intensities and size of visual symbol or other mode of representation (Marks, 1978). Pitch, as Schoenberg (1911) said, is a "province of timbre" or tone color, not one on its own in music. Thus the interest shown by researchers in perception of vowel sounds and the effects of the placing of the second formant on perceptions of pitch or subjective descriptions such as "brightness" reflects this duality of the notion of pitch and timbre perception in the workings of our peripheral perceptual systems. Pitch, then, is not simply characterized as vertically higher or lower, but rather by sense of the lightness or heaviness that seems to denote pitch sensations subjectively on the basis of perceptions resulting from what might be termed timbre.

In musical sounds we notice the same kind of phenomenon in our perceptions of vocal and instrumental sounds. Some appear to be bright, others dull, and we subjectively interpret these as higher and brighter or duller and lower accordingly, irrespective of their repetition rate. This is also due to the positioning of various formants and the effect of this on our subjective interpretations of such events.

Similarly, in the visual mode we describe some colors or hues as brighter (or higher) by virtue of the effect of higher frequency components in the light waves on our peripheral receptor systems. As already mentioned, light oranges or reds have higher frequency components than blues or blacks, for example. Subjectively, then, we appear to describe visual and auditory information quite readily in similar terms (i.e., brighter or duller, higher or lower) as a result of the perceptual effects of the same physical properties—frequency components.

Marks (1978, p. 77) reports that the sound of a word will elicit particular responses consistently. In citing Kohler (1947) and the responses of his own children, he demonstrates how the pseudowords "maluma" and "takete" will elicit, consistently, a soft rounded visual shape drawn in response to hearing the sound of "maluma," and a jagged, pointed shape for "takete." There is, he maintains, information in vowels and consonants, the phonemes, that suggests such associations across visual and auditory systems: "m" is perceived as a soft consonant, whereas "t" and "k" are hard, and the vowel sounds are correspondingly brighter or duller, as explained above.

In intensity perception, Marks, (1978, p. 120) describes similarities across five sensory modalities (vibration, odor, taste, light, and noise) in intensity discrimination tasks. Interest in quantifying our discriminations of sensory intensity across different modalities can be seen as early as 1860 in the work of Gustav Theodor Fechner. The work of S. S. Stevens is seminal in this field, however, in that he proposed a power law of sensory intensity applicable across all sensory modalities. Stevens' Law states that the subjective strength of intensity of a stimulus is proportional to its physical intensity raised by some power (Marks, 1978, p. 130). Marks reports a number of empirical studies showing that humans readily match visual and auditory intensities. Further, he suggests that poets' use of verbal imagery contains these kinds of cross-modal borrowings that can be quantified. Kipling's "the dawn comes up like thunder" has a greater sensation impact than, say, Browning's "the quiet coloured end of evening" or Poe's "the murmur of gray twilight." Marks quantifies these and other verbal images mathematically, in terms of luminance and sound pressure level.

The proclivity to match sensory input across different modalities appears then to be a direct consequence of stimulus properties and to be innate in humans because of the workings of our peripheral systems. Our ears perform pattern analyses on incoming sound pressure waves in the cochlea, which enable us to receive very complex information from which we make generalizations of the type explained above, and our retinas perform similar tasks on incoming light waves with similar perceptual results. Put this way, it seems a simple matter to relate such similar information across modalities. In fact, a number of researchers demonstrate that infants can perform such tasks as matching information across modes almost from birth. Lewkowicz and Turkewitz (1980), for example, demonstrate the capacity of newborns to modify their visual preferences following exposure to sound. Many other studies show that as infants develop, their ability to match information from one mode to another becomes correspondingly more sophisticated. For example, Bryant, Jones, Claxtion, and Perkins (1972) found that infants were able to match different shapes (e.g., square, rounded, triangular) from tactile to visual modes.

A number of studies were mentioned earlier that dealt specifically with auditory-visual matching of information and that provide some more precise data about the nature of cross-modal behavior from auditory to visual and indicate how this behavior can be viewed as more directly applicable to music and music reading. In two such studies (Walker, 1978, 1981) it was found that both schoolchildren, aged 7 to 18 years, and adults displayed a proclivity for a systematic matching of certain visual shapes with certain sounds. Specifically, it was noted that frequency change was matched with vertically placed visual symbols (visually higher for higher frequencies), different wave forms (with different spectral content) were matched with different visual patterns or shapes, durations were matched with corresponding horizontal lengths, and amplitude with corresponding differences in visual size. This finding was consistent in tasks involving both inventions by the subjects of visual analogies for sounds, and in closed response tasks. Furthermore, a study of responses among congenitally blind subjects (Walker, 1985) yielded essentially the same results in tasks matching sounds with tactile shapes. This finding was replicated in a study using a much larger sample and a much more sophisticated research design involving both closed and open responses from congenitally blind subjects (Welch, 1990). In many ways such findings are consistent with the research from those working in the general field of cross-modal perception, as well as with replication studies (Sadek, 1987), but there are some interesting qualifications to the findings that relate to the business of perception of music notations. The subjects used in these studies were a mixture of the musically experienced and the musically naive, a fact that was later seen to be of some significance.

Further refinement of these findings was derived from data gained from a large sample (838 subjects) from across a variety of musical backgrounds, cultures, and age groups (Walker, 1987b). Here, it was found that musical training was a main factor with subjects choosing a vertical placement for perceived frequency change, and some complex rhythmic durations matched with horizontally placed length, but not for amplitude discriminations matched with visual size, or for waveform discriminations matched with visual pattern or shape. There were exceptions due to the nature of the auditory stimuli presented, but these related to complexity or otherwise, a fact similarly reported in studies of ocular behavior mentioned above. Culture was found to be only a very small factor (with a small amount of variance attributable), as was age.

From these data, and from other studies involving discrimination and subsequent selection tasks (e.g., Siegel and Siegel, 1977; Algom and Marks, 1984; Ward, 1985), it appears that in tasks involving conceptualization of frequency change, exposure to musical training will consistently elicit correspondingly (dependent on the length of training) more systematic responses from subjects than will be found in those with no, or little, such training. The studies cited above (Walker, 1978, 1981, 1987a,b) appear to be somewhat unique in that subjects were required to produce a visual representation of a response to auditory stimulus changes. The other studies cited dealt more in discrimination tasks, per se, than in any form of overt conceptualization of the event that was the object of discrimination.

Applications to Musical Notations Conventional uses of staff notation in music do not provide the type of information that may be characterized as common to both visual and auditory domains, but some categories of contemporary notations do. A louder sound is not conventionally symbolized by a large visual symbol, but in some modern musical scores it would be. Pitch, a crucial attribute of musical sound, is a particularly difficult concept to deal with in both discrete domain terms, that is, auditory and visual. In conventional notation pitch is symbolized by the somewhat arbitrary visual distances of the five-lined musical staff, where, for instance, the minor third looks identical to the major third. In some new graphic notations pitch is shown as a subset of timbre—a most interesting development in view of modern psychoacoustic definitions of pitch sensations mentioned above.

Notwithstanding the arguments made earlier about the nature of music notation, if music notation is either a manifestation of, or is even supposed to facilitate, cross-modal perception, then such mental acts as inventing ''virtual'' pitch obviously cause difficulties since such a perception can be related only indirectly to the actual stimulus properties. That is to say, such properties, as compared with the resulting perception, are qualitatively different from the type of properties of some stimuli reported above that have *analogous* relationships across different perceptual modes. It is possible that the type of symbol used in music notation of any type to denote pitch bears little analogous relationship to the actual pitch sounds symbolized. The manner in which pitch is represented in music notation (i.e., vertically in two-dimensional visual space) does not reflect the known perceptions of stimulus properties found in sounds we usually associate with musical pitch. The same can be said of rhythm notations on the staff: They do not provide cross-modal analogous information about duration. Some contemporary graphic notations are nearer to providing this type of information, however.

Conventional staff notation in music intentionally appears to require some form of verbal mediation in the perceptual process of transferring information derived from such visual symbols across modalities. This concerns transfer both to physical actions (performance) and in the subsequent auditory perception of the performance, as well as in a purely mental response of creating an ideal auditory image of the musical sound suggested by the notations. The same would not be true of certain graphic notations used in this century, and particularly for elements such as dynamics or duration. A certain cross-modal equivalence can be demonstrated between duration and horizontal placing and between dynamics and size of visual symbol.

Modal Properties of Notations Many studies indicate that our natural proclivity for matching auditory with visual information is characterized by two basically different types of information processing: those concerning phenomena that have modal-specific qualities, such as pitch and vertical placing; and those that have amodal properties, such as intensity matched with size.

Modal-specific properties are those that are peculiar and special to a particular modality and are not, therefore, analogous to information in other modalities. Thus any matchings across modalities are artificially contrived, rather than a result of the same type of information being represented in different modes. On the other hand, amodal information is that which involves the same information being presented in different modes. Auditory frequency (pitch) perception and vertical placement of visual symbols are each, clearly, modal-specific types of information, and their connection is a contrived one. Intensity, however, can be perceived across modalities as equivalent information, which Marks (1978) has demonstrated. The former (Walker, 1978a,b) is dependent on learning, and the latter (Marks, 1978; Lewkowicz and Turkewitz, 1980) can be described as more innate and not subject to the learning of specific cultural practices.

Thus it can be said that staff notation, in its relationship with musical sound, is quite clearly modal specific in that each (the sound and notation) is specific in its form to its own particular mode and each reflects no basic equivalents for matching with the other. Pedagogically, this is quite important, for it means that music educators cannot rely on the stimulus properties of musical sound being naturally, or innately, matched with traditional staff notation or vice versa, that is, the staff notation eliciting a cross-modal equivalence in sound. Pitch is not perceived innately as higher or lower, although it appears to be perceived in terms of brightness or dullness innately.

Some recent graphic music notations, on the other hand, require the perceiver to make cross-modal matchings. Loudness is innately perceived to correlate with stimulus size in other modes. Duration, provided it is simple enough in its configuration, appears to be innately linked to horizontal length and placement.

This, I suggest, puts into clearer psychological perspective the nature of the task facing music educators and researchers into music reading and sight reading in relation to the teleological nature of the notations employed. It suggests that music reading skills concerning staff notations are probably in the same category of symbolic function in respect to musical sounds as are words in respect to speech sounds.

The difference lies in the degree of physical involvement required to make a response, in which case there can be psychological and teleological connections established between music reading of staff notations and verbal reading. Both represent cultural conventions of sound production rather than simply innate proclivities for cross-modal representations of similar information. Both concern the cross-modal transfer of modal-specific information from auditory to visual domains. We cannot, therefore, talk of auditory-visual perception in regard to staff notation in music as though there were some innate mental mechanism that readily made cross-modal matchings between music traditional staff notations and musical sounds free of some form of internal mediation between the two modes.

A further complication arises with staff notations that are incomplete and require the perceiver to provide the missing information in the form of improvisations: I refer to baroque figured basses, jazz notations, and other types of improvised tonal music. In such activities perception of notations relies on learned syntactic structures and personal manipulation of these structures in physical acts of performance on various instruments. The intrusion of mediation of stored images of physical action must play a significant role in perception of such notations. In the case of some modern graphic notations, this would not be true. Here, perceivers are dealing in perceptual information that is amodal and, therefore, of an entirely different character to that found in staff notations. A straightforward transfer of stimulus properties across modalities would be essentially a mental phenomenon in terms of information processing.

References

Algom, D., and Marks, L. (1984). Individual differences in loudness processing and loudness scales. *Journal of Experimental Psychology, 113,* 571–593.

Bamberger, J. (1982). Revisiting children's drawings of simple rhythms: A function for reflection-in-action. In S. Strauss (Ed.), *U-shaped behavioral growth* (191–226). New York: Academic Press.

Bean, K. L. (1938). An experimental approach to the reading of music. *Psychological Monographs 50(226),* 80.

Bebeau, M. J. (1982). Effects of traditional and simplified methods of rhythm reading instruction. *Journal of Research in Music Education, 30(2),* 107–119.

Bobbitt, R., (1970). The development of music reading skills. *Journal of Research in Music Education, 18,* 143–156.

Boyle, J. D., (1970). The effects of prescribed rhythmical movements on the ability to read music at sight. *Journal of Research in Music Education, 18,* 307–318.

Bryant, P. E., Jones, P., Claxtion, B., and Perkins, G. M. (1972). Recognition of shapes across modalities by infants. *Nature, 240,* 303–304.

Buswell, G. T. (1920). An experimental study of the eye-voice span in reading. *Supplementary Educational Monograph,* No. 17.

Carlsen, J. C., (1965) *Melodic perception.* New York: McGraw Hill.

Colley, B. (1987). A comparison of syllabic methods of improving rhythm patterns. *Journal of Research in Music Education, 35(4),* 221–236.

Cooley, J. C. (1961). A study of the relation between certain mental and personality traits and ratings of musical abilities. *Journal of Research in Music Education, 9(2),* 108–117.

Dallin, L., (1966). *Introduction to music reading.* Chicago: Scott Foresman.

Dalton, R. S. (1952). A study of the relationship existing between music reading and language reading ability. Unpublished master's thesis, Syracuse University, Syracuse.

De Boer, E. (1976). On the residue and auditory pitch perception. In W. D. Keidel and W. D. Neff (Eds.), *Handbook of sensory physiology* (479–583). Berlin: Springer Verlag.

Delattre, P., Liberman, A. M., Cooper, F. S., and Gerstman, L. J. (1952). An experimental study of the acoustic determinants of vowel color: Observations on one- and two-formant vowels synthesized from spectrographic patterns. *Word 8,* 195–210.

Divenyi, P. L. (1979). Is pitch a learned attribute of sound: Two points in support of Terhardt's theory. *Journal of the Acoustical Society of America 66(4),* 1210–1213.

Elliott, C. A. (1982). The relationship among instrumental sight reading ability and seven selected predictor variables. *Journal of Research in Music Education, 30(1),* 5–14.

Enoch, Y. (1978). *Group piano teaching.* Oxford: Oxford University Press.

Fairbanks, G. (1937). The relation between eye movements and voice in the oral reading of good and poor silent readers. *Psychological Monographs 48,* 78–107.

Fry, D. B. (1976). *The physics of speech.* Cambridge: Cambridge University Press.

Gardner, H. (1985). *The mind's new science.* New York: Basic Books.

Gibson, E. J. (1969). *Principles of perceptual learning and development.* New York: Appleton-Century Crofts.

Gruson, L. M. (1981). *Investigating competence: A study of piano practising.* Paper presented at the 89th annual convention of the American Psychological Association. (Cited in Sloboda, 1985)

Grutzmacher, P. A. (1987). The effect of tonal pattern training on the aural perception, reading recognition, and melodic sight reading achievement of first year instrumental music students. *Journal of Research in Music Education, 35(3),* 171–182.

Hindemith, P. (1946). *Elementary training for musicians.* New York: Associated Music Publishers.

Hoffer, C. R. (1964) *Teaching music in the secondary schools.* Belmont: Wadsworth.

Houtsma, A. J. M. (1971). What determines musical pitch? *Journal of Music Theory, 16(1),* 138–157.

Houtsma, A. J. M., and Goldstein, J. L. (1972). Perception of music intervals: Evidence for a central origin of the pitch of complex tones. *Journal of the Acoustical Society of America, 51,* 520–529.

Hutton, D. (1953). A comparative study of two methods of teaching sight reading in the fourth grade. *Journal of Research in Music Education, 1(2),* 119–126.

King, H. A. (1954). A study of the relationship between music reading and I.Q. scores. *Journal of Research in Music Education, 2(1),* 35–37.

Kohler, W. (1947). *Gestalt psychology.* New York: Liveright.

Lewkowicz, D. J., and Turkewitz, G. (1980). Cross-modal equivalence in early infancy. *Developmental Psychology 20,* 120–127.

Marks, L. E. (1978). *The unity of the senses.* New York: Academic Press.

Maze, N. M. (1967). A study of the correlations between musicality and reading achievement at first grade level in Athens, Georgia. Unpublished doctoral thesis, University of Georgia, Athens.

Meyer, J. (1978). The dependence of pitch on harmonic spectra. *Psychology of Music, 6*(1), 3–13.

Monroe, M. E. (1967). A study of music reading in elementary schools utilizing certain related aspects of language reading. Unpublished doctoral thesis, Columbia University, New York.

Mursell, J. L. (1956) *Music education principles and problems.* New York: Silver Burdett.

Nicholson, D., (1972). Music as an aid to learning. Unpublished doctoral thesis, New York University.

Ohgushi, K. (1978). On the role of spatial and temporal cues in the perception of pitch of complex tones. *Journal of the Acoustical Society of America, 64*(3), 764–770.

O'Regan, K. (1979). Moment to moment control of eye saccades as a function of textual parameters in reading. In P. A. Kolers, M. E. Woolstad, and H. Bouma, (Eds.), *Processing of visible language* (Vol. 1). New York: Plenum Press.

Ortmann, O. (1937). Span of vision in note reading. *Yearbook, Music Educators National Conference,* 88–93.

Palmer, M. (1976). Relative effectiveness of two approaches to rhythm reading for fourth grade students. *Journal of Research In Music Education, 24,* 110–118.

Pollack, C. (1969). *Intersensory reading method.* New York: Book Laboratory.

Radocy, R. E., and Boyle, J. D. (1979). *Psychological foundations of musical behavior.* Springfield: Charles C Thomas.

Rezits, J. (1972). Everyone should try ensemble sight reading. *Clavier,* II(Sept.), 34.

Sadek, A. A. M. (1987). Visualization of musical concepts. *Bulletin of the Council for Research in Music Education Bulletin, 91,* 149–154.

Seashore, C. E. (1938). *The psychology of music.* New York: McGraw Hill.

Schoenberg, A. (1911). *Harmonielehre.* Vienna: Universal Verlag.

Seides, E. (1967). The effect of talent class placement on slow learners in the seventh grade of a New York City junior high school. Unpublished doctoral thesis, New York University.

Shaffer L. H. (1976). Intention and performance. *Psychological Review 83,* 376–393.

Shaffer, L. H., (1980). Analysis of concert pianists. In G. E. Stelmach and J. Requin (Eds.), *Tutorials in motor behavior.* Amsterdam: North Holland.

Shaffer, L. H. (1981). *Creativity in skilled performance.* Paper presented at NATO conference on adaptive control of ill-defined systems. (Cited in Sloboda, 1985).

Shanet, H. (1956). *Learn to read music.* New York: Simon and Schuster.

Siegel, J. A., and Siegel, W. (1977). Categorical perception of tonal intervals. *Perception and Psychophysics, 21,* 399–407.

Sloboda, J. A. (1974). The eye-hand span: An approach to the study of sight reading. *Psychology of Music 2,* 4–10.

Sloboda, J. A. (1985). *The musical mind.* Oxford: Oxford University Press.

Stevens, J. C., Mack, J. D., and Stevens, S. S., (1960). Growth of sensation on seven continua as measured by force of handgrip. *Journal of Experimental Psychology, 59,* 60–67.

Terhardt, E. (1970). Frequency analysis and periodicity detection in the sensations of roughness and periodicity pitch. In R. Plomp and G. F. Smootenberg (Eds.), *Frequency analysis and periodicity detection in hearing* (pp. 258–281). Leiden: Eijhoff.

Terhardt, E. (1972). Zu Tonhohenwahrenmung von Klangen II. Ein Funktionsschema. *Acustica, 26,* 187–199.

Terhardt, E. (1974). Pitch, consonance and harmony. *Journal of the Acoustical Society of America, 55,* 1061–1069.

Terhardt, E. (1979). Calculating virtual pitch. *Hearing Research, 1,* 155–182.

Terhardt, E., and Seewann, M. (1982). Pitch of complex signals according to virtual pitch theory. *Journal of the Acoustical Society of America, 71*(3), 671–678.

Terhardt, E., and Grubert, A. (1987). Factors affecting pitch judgments as a function of spectral composition. *Perception and Psychophysics, 42*(6), 511–514.

Tinker, M. A. (1929). Visual apprehension and perception in reading. *Psychology Bulletin 26,* 223–240.

Thomson, A. G. (1953). An analysis of difficulties in sight reading music for violin and clarinet. Unpublished doctoral thesis, University of Cincinnati, Cincinnati.

Van Nuys, K., and Weaver, H. E. (1943). Memory span and visual pauses in reading rhythms and melodies. *Psychological Monographs, 55,* 33–50.

Walker, R. (1972). A survey of attitudes to musical training among 30 choral directors in cathedral and collegiate choirs of England. Referred to in Walker, R. *Music education: Tradition and innovation* (1984). Springfield: Thomas.

Walker, R. (1978). Perception and music notation. *Psychology of Music, 6,* 21–46.

Walker, R. (1981). The presence of internalized images of musical sounds. *Bulletin of the Council for Research in Music Education, 66–67,* 107–112.

Walker, R. (1985). Mental imagery and musical concepts: Some evidence from the congenitally blind. *Bulletin of the Council for Research in Music Education, 85,* 229–238.

Walker, R. (1987a). Some differences between pitch perception and auditory discrimination by children of different cultural backgrounds. *Bulletin of the Council for Research in Music Educational, 91,* 166–170.

Walker, R. (1987b). The effects of culture, environment, age, and musical training on choices of visual metaphors for sound. *Perception and Psychophysics, 42*(5), 491–502.

Wang, C. C. (1989). Relating musical abilities to visual spatial abilities, mathematics, and languages of fifth grade children. *Canadian Music Educator* (Research Edition), *30*(2), 184–189.

Ward, L. M. (1985). Mixed modality psychophysical scaling. *Perception and Psychophysics, 38,* 512–522.

Watkins, A., and Hughes, M. A. (1986). The effect on an accompanying situation of the improvement of students' sight reading skills. *Psychology of Music, 14,* 97–110.

Weaver, H. E. (1943). A study of visual processes in reading differently constructed musical selections. *Psychological Monographs 55,* 1–30.

Welch, G. (1990). *Visual metaphors for sound: A study of mental imagery, language and pitch perception in the congenitally blind.* Paper presented to the 13th International Research Seminar in Music Education, Stockholm, July, 1990.

Wheeler, L. R., and Wheeler, V. D., (1952). The relationship between music reading and language reading abilities. *Journal of Educational Research, 45*(6), 443–446.

Zinar, R. (1976). Reading language and reading music: Is there a correlation? *Music Educators Journal, 62*(7), 70–74.

·23·

STRUCTURE OF COGNITION AND MUSIC DECISION-MAKING

Harold Fiske

UNIVERSITY OF WESTERN ONTARIO

This chapter is about the structure of music cognition and music decision-making. The construct "music cognition" refers to the mental procedures that take place following prerequisite psychoacoustic processing. Although the potential for carrying out cognitive activity depends on the products of psychoacoustic processing, the cognition construct is generally assumed to refer to procedures and behaviors that are independent of this initial processing. These include any mental behaviors that result in the detection, identification, discrimination, and evaluation of tonal and rhythmic patterns. Three general forms of behavior are involved: (1) the recognition and recall of previously learned tonal-rhythmic patterns; (2) the identification and storage in memory of new patterns; and (3) ongoing comparison of patterns experienced during music listening with appropriately recalled patterns. It might seem that substantial theoretical overlapping occurs between the cognition construct and research in music perception. Ambiguity is avoided, however, by associating cognitive processes with thought processes. These include abstract problem-solving or memory activities such as those involved with identifying tonal-rhythmic patterns, finding functional relationships between musical pattern material, and pattern comparison decision-making that contribute knowledge to or otherwise affect one's understanding and comprehension of the structure of the heard piece.

In short, music cognition is about musical thinking. Musical thinking entails solving problems concerning tonal-rhythmic relationships occurring temporally. Some of these musical decisions are the result of generic (cross-cultural and panstylistic) decision-making activity. Others are the result of learned cultural agreements concerning the manipulation (by composers/performers) of selected tonal-rhythmic material. A theory of the structure of music cognition must explain the contribution and role of each.

The chapter will construct a theoretical framework by reviewing work in three areas: cognition as pattern realization (i.e., pattern formation, recognition, and recall); cognition as pattern processing (e.g., hypothesis testing); and cognition as pattern comparison and decision-making (e.g., decision hierarchies). An attempt will be made to draw the research in the three areas into a unified theory of music cognitive structure.

EARLY THEORIES

Theories about the musical mind originate with the work of philosophers and mathematicians who lived over twenty-five hundred years ago. Pythagoras (ca. 550 B.C.), Plato (ca. 400 B.C.), Aristotle (ca. 300 B.C.), and others introduced hypotheses that in many ways are associated with research today in areas such as psychoacoustics, perception, aesthetics, and music cognition. But most contemporary theories stem from research begun only in the nineteenth century. By then two important developments had occurred: Work in physics and astronomy, begun in the seventeenth century, resulted in the scientific method, an inductive approach to systematic data collection and hypothesis testing; and new discoveries in the structure of nerves and impulse conduction emerged from work in physiology and sensory psychology. These developments led in part to establishing experimental laboratories and early work in experimental psychology such as Fechner's (1860). Some of the first studies conducted were concerned with audition.

In 1863 Hermann von Helmholtz, a German physicist and physiologist, published his text *On the Sensations of Tone*. This book, now a classic in psychophysics, attempted to demonstrate scientifically a unitary connection between measurable features of musical sound objects (such as frequency) and the aural sensations (such as pitch) that result from human auditory processing of such sound objects. It brought together what was then known about the physics of sound wave activity, the physical processing of sound waves by the human ear (psychoacoustics), and auditory perception.

In addition to work in science, Helmholtz was attracted by work in aesthetics, particularly the theories of Friedrich Vischer and Edward Hanslick. Unlike their predecessors, both Vischer and Hanslick restricted musical content and emotional response to perceived musical form or structure and eschewed any claim for content that was not expressly related to tonal-rhythmic relationships. Their influence on Helmholtz is therefore not surprising. Helmholtz concluded that the principles of acoustics and auditory processing totally explained musical practice and experience: scale construction, tonality, tone quality, consonance and dissonance, and chord construction and harmony.

One outcome of this was Helmholtz's resonance or fiber-specific theory of pitch perception. This theory explains musical sensation as the direct and sole result of particular nerve endings on the basilar membrane firing in response to a particular frequency and relaying a signal along particular nerves to specific pitch-associated nerve locations in the brain (something like the key-hammer-string chain of events found in piano construction).

More recent research in both physiology and psychoacoustics has destroyed this particular feature of Helmholtz's work. Such a depiction was found to provide an inadequate account of the process of translating frequency information into a realized pitch sensation. More importantly, however, his theory also failed to take into account mental processing more germane to actual ongoing musical activity such as the realization of tonal and rhythmic patterns, pattern comparison and discrimination activity, or memory and expectation. In short, although Helmholtz provided an important data base for subsequent work in music perception, his theory does not explain musical thinking and decision-making, activity that is today considered by many to be at least equally important in a theory of music to psychoacoustic processing.

Helmholtz was responsible for initiating and shaping several new directions for research in the areas of psychoacoustics, music psychology, and aesthetics. One psychologist so influenced was Carl Seashore, whose work was of particular importance to music education. Seashore too developed a unitary theory of music perception. His reasoning was similar to Helmholtz's: Since an auditory sensation depends on the presence of physical sound waves, then an analysis of the components of sound will explain auditory perception and its outcomes such as music and speech. Seashore (1938) developed an instrument that tracked and graphically notated the progressive frequency and intensity activity of sonic events such as music or speech. The instrument was a rather sensitive one, and resulted in useful analogue performance graphs of, for example, solo musical performances. Seashore used these graphs to study and compare the acoustical components associated with performance attack and vibrato, or those assumed to result in perceived musical expression,

such as subtle changes in intensity. For Seashore, perception held a unitary dependence on the structure of sound waves. The extent of musical understanding and comprehension was determined by the listener's perceptual sensitivity to the performer-shaped sound object: The greater the listener's sensitivity to fine differences in acoustic manipulation, the greater the sensitivity of the listener to the perceived musical product.

Seashore devised a theory that consisted of several sets of psychological capacities. The first set included four capacities, each of which translated a single physical dimension of sound (either frequency, intensity, duration, or wave form) into a perceived psychological correlate (pitch, loudness, time, or timbre). The theory assumed that this set, called "elemental capacities," was inborn, and that threshold and ceiling levels of detection and discrimination sensitivity for each were genetically predetermined. Differences in sensitivity between elemental capacities, or between any particular combination of capacities, were also assumed either for an individual listener or between listeners.

Seashore hypothesized that an individual's profile of elemental capacity sensitivity determined one's potential aptitude for music. Musical ability itself, however, was according to Seashore controlled by a second set of "sensory capacities." These included consonance, volume, rhythm, and tone quality. The activity of each was thought to be more or less the direct outcome of the obviously associated elemental capacity. Unlike the elemental capacities, however, sensory capacities were thought by Seashore to be subject to training and experience to an extent permitted either by the related elemental capacity or by the threshold and ceiling of a particular sensory capacity. For Seashore, musical perceptual and cognitive activity were principally controlled and limited by the listener's own elemental and sensory capacities, which translated the components of the sound object into psychological correlates. (Other sets of capacities that shaped an individual's musical personality type and imagery type were part of Seashore's theory as well, but we will ignore those here.)

Seashore developed a standardized test called *Measures of Musical Talents* (last revision, 1960). The test, designed for grades 4 to 16, consisted of six subtests: pitch, loudness, time, timbre, rhythm, and tonal memory. The primary intent of the test was to measure an individual's elemental capacities plus short-term memory for tonal and rhythmic patterns. The results of the test, reported in percentiles, were intended to serve as one piece of objective information identifying a child's potential for success in music, guiding selection of a musical instrument, and determining suitable musical-educational experiences. Seashore's *Measures* represent an early attempt to tap music cognition activity and to provide information for the development of a theory of musical learning.

NONPSYCHOACOUSTIC REPRESENTATIONS OF PITCH

Shepard (1982) rejects the logic that attributes a unitary relationship to acoustic events and perceived events, or to, for example, physical differences in frequencies and psychological decisions of melodic interval equivalence. Similarly, he rejects attempts of psychophysics to equate scales of relative physical intervallic distance with scales of relative melodic interval distance. The principal reason for this is the demonstrated lack of consistent correspondence between mathematical descriptors of sound objects (such as mel scales, logarithmic scales, frequency ratios, and the emphasis on single or pairs of isolated tones rather than groups of tones) and subjects' perceived equivalence or relative judgments of perceived relationships between sound events. Shepard cites growing evidence that percepts do not vary in any continuous way that corresponds to fixed psychophysical measurement systems. This is particularly so in musical contexts.

In place of psychoacoustic unitary representations, Shepard and other theorists have proposed cognitive models that attempt to represent events as actually perceived by music listeners. The most notable are those of Simon and Sumner (1968), Longuet-Higgins (1976), Deutsch and Feroe (1981), Balzano (1982), Shepard (1982), and Krumhansl (1979, 1990). Although acknowledging the necessity of an acoustic signal for auditory perception, these theorists all claim that a description of the signal is not a sufficient explanation of perception. Each proposes instead a nonpsychoacoustic system, model, or framework that is intended to capture the music listener's cognitive representation of pitch and interpitch relationships. In order to avoid direct reference to either acoustic descriptors or musical descriptors, these models are, in general, highly abstract, often mathematical portrayals of music perception. For example, Shepard's "double helix" (1982) is a multidimensional scale intended to represent the mind's understanding of pitch and intervallic interrelationships in western music. The model incorporates five dimensions, one for pitch height and two each for chroma and the circle of fifths. Deutsch and Feroe (1981) and Simon and Sumner (1968) construct rule sets, expressed mathematically, that describe the representation of tone sequences and musical patterns in memory. Both emphasize and incorporate organized pitch sets, interval classes, chroma, the circle of fifths, octave equivalence, and the use of "operators" that control pattern organization and order. The results of a series of experiments conducted by Krumhansl (1979, 1990) suggest a conical model of pitch stability. The model represents melodic and harmonic interrelationships where the tonic is shown to be the most stable tone followed by other diatonic and nondiatonic tones of decreasing stability. These are specifically portrayed on different hierarchical levels of the model.

Other examples are those of Balzano (1982), who employs group theory, and Longuet-Higgins, who devises a mathematical-notational scheme. Both intend to capture the principles of key, scale, and tonality as comprehended by music listeners.

Although the cognitive models of pitch differ from each other in approach, style, and manner of representation, the theorists find agreement on several points. First, all tend to agree that the understanding and comprehension of musical structure depends upon the brain's genetic predisposition to search for relationships between, and find patterns among,

an array of stimulus events. These patterns are the result of inborn auditory processing rules designed to link auditory events together in certain prescribed ways. The assumption is that, at least for basic sensory experience, these rules operate identically between listeners and result in common auditory percepts.

Second, any cognitive model of musical tone relationships must account for certain phenomena, including the sensation of pitch and pitch height; octave equivalence, pitch class, and chroma (recognizing, for example, that all Cs contain inherent identity that distinguish them from all F♯ s); and a propensity for systematic durational structure (e.g., beat and meter).

Third, agreement is found among these theorists about a distinction between sensory grouping of immediately perceived auditory events and large-scale pattern information stored in long-term memory. The former refers to simple, economical realization of pattern fragment organization and streams of auditory events, usually explained as being under the control of Gestalt principles. The latter refers to the recognition and recall of melodies, sections, whole compositions, and so on. Sensory organization assumes no memory involvement in the formation of certain realized events, and is thought to be genetically controlled and to function panstylistically and cross-culturally. Sensory organization is assumed to be abstract and time independent, and to function by means of heuristics rather than rules of logic (Cross, Howell, and West, 1985). This contrasts with memory systems, both short- and long-term, the musical content of which involves rule-governed organization that is time based, music style specific, and acquired with training and experience. Deutsch (1982) and Dowling and Harwood (1986) report that several factors seem to contribute to immediate sensory organization: rapid presentation of tonal stimuli, extreme differences in pitch range of groups of tones, timbre differences, loudness differences, spatial separation of instruments, rhythmic pattern differences, meter, and different rates of presentation (e.g., polyphonic textures). Each of these has an effect singularly or in combination. Fraisse (1982) reports that rhythmic perception is affected by sensory organization mechanisms as well. These include silence intervals between groups of tones, interduration ratios of tones, consistency of durational organization (meter), accent and stress, and tempo. All of these, again singularly or in combination, contribute to perceived rhythmic organization.

Fourth, cognitive theorists agree that the realization of such organizational principles as tuning, scale, the circle of fifths, and tonality (all usually considered in broad terms so as to apply to both western and nonwestern music) are basic to any models of music perception and cognition (see Watkins and Dyson, 1985).

Critique

Models of pitch representation that portray the features and operating characteristics of pitch percepts are an advance in theory development over unidimensional concepts that directly relate acoustic activity to aural sensation. The principal advantage of these models is the recognition that musical understanding and comprehension are the product of the brain's search for relationships between tonal-rhythmic events and the subsequent identification of melodic, harmonic, and rhythmic patterns.

But a useful model of music cognition must account for other concerns as well. First, it must be shown that the model has psychological reality and validity. The model must be demonstrably related either to one's perceptual experience or to the realized products of perceptual and cognitive activity. Butler (1990), for example, suggests that skilled music listening is mostly intuitive. He suggests that, although pitch interrelationships may have some form of hierarchical order, static models (such as Krumhansl's) are overly complex, implausible, and inappropriate in that they fail to account for more immediately perceived tonal relationships as they occur through time.

Second, in order to satisfy the first concern, the model must generate some hypotheses that are testable. Watkins and Dyson (1985), for example, attempted to do this by first identifying the variables and features of models that have apparent relevance to music cognitive processing. They then synthesized melodic patterns containing likely occurrences of these features for comparison against control patterns consisting of unlikely use of these features (plus an additional "real" melody by Bach). Subjects were then asked to choose from paired comparisons the items they felt were most melodious. In general, the more "likely" manipulations of the features led subjects to select those patterns as being more melodious than patterns containing "unlikely" manipulations. Features found to be relevant included consistent use of scale and key, interval span of less than five semitones, relative differences in redundancy and uncertainty (where, in this case, increased uncertainty led to higher ratings of melodiousness), tuning versus mistuning (where listeners adapted to mistuned contours but not mistuned scales or keys), and contour (which was found to be more important for nontransposed comparisons than for transposed comparisons, and for unfamiliar more than familiar patterns; this agrees with Dowling and Fujitani, 1971).

Third, models of cognition must be generalizable across different musical styles, theory systems, and musical "languages," both interculturally and intraculturally. A weakness of many models is that they are based on the supposed principles of western music while forgetting that these principles may misrepresent the music of other cultures. But a useful theory of music cognition must account for multicultural musical diversity. This must assume at the same time that the auditory and cognitive mechanisms that characterize human brains everywhere are essentially identical in design, function, and structure, although not necessarily identical qualitatively or in their perceptual products. That is, a model must account for a listener's native musical cultural experience while also assuming that there is no logical reason to expect different culture-bound brain types. Some theorists have shown reasonable sensitivity to this concern while others have ignored it.

West and colleagues (1985) offer several other suggestions to model builders. These include concern for listener musical competence, particularly whether what is heard is a musical pattern in total or merely fragmentary structures, listener judgment and behavior, listener understanding of historical context and personal extramusical associations, the need to account for both vertical and horizontal musical structures, and the need to account for immediate percepts and those occurring over an extended amount of time. Shepard (1982) concurs with several of these points as well, and research described below specifically attempts to account for them.

PATTERN REPRESENTATION AND RECOGNITION

Models such as those reviewed above can be seen as either perceptual models (and therefore precognitive) or cognitive processes prerequisite to melodic-rhythmic pattern identity, recognition, and comparison activity. This section is concerned with the features of melodic-rhythmic patterns identified by cognitive mechanisms for the representation of patterns during recognition and recall, processes that require attention and active involvement by the listener. (Some theorists—e.g., Seashore—have referred to pattern representation as musical imagery. For example, see Fiske, 1989.)

Given a pattern P, how is P discriminated from some other pattern K? If heard again, how is P recognized as a replay of P rather than as K or some other pattern N? What features of P represent P in memory and permit one to imagine or recall P? For pattern recognition the problem is compounded by the range of potential distortions of pattern P on subsequent presentations. Pattern P may be transposed, played by different instruments, or played at a different tempo, or it may be embellished or varied by manipulating one of its dimensions (rhythm, for example) while conserving other dimensions (pitch relations, for example). Any one or a combination of these and other distortions makes the recognition task potentially more difficult than a simple P versus P comparison. What information is extracted from a melodic pattern and used by the brain for recognizing the pattern in a wide range of guises?

Several pattern descriptors have been proposed as likely candidates for a theory of music pattern representation. One of these is contour. Dowling (Dowling and Fujitani, 1971; Dowling, 1978) tested the effect of contour on melodic pattern recognition under a number of contextual and experiential conditions. For unfamiliar patterns, discrimination was found to be relatively difficult between patterns based on the same contour but that were structurally different in other ways. Discrimination was easier when comparison patterns were constructed so as to distort the contour of the original model pattern. Not surprisingly, groups of patterns that shared contour were found to be easily distinguished from patterns that did not share that contour. Transpositions of model patterns were relatively difficult to discriminate from interval-distorted, contour-preserving imitations, but it was easier to discriminate either of these from patterns that distorted the model's contour. However, performance improved between transposed tonal patterns and atonal imitations. The above led Dowling to conclude that contour is the most important variable in the representation of unfamiliar patterns.

The situation was complicated by the variable key distance. The more distantly related the key of a pattern imitation was to its model, the more easily it was discriminated. (Dowling relates this result to chroma.) The key distance and contour variables appeared to have an effect on pattern recognition and retention for a time interval of about 30 seconds, after which discrimination of transposed comparisons and tonal imitations improved. That is, discrimination tasks requiring retention of the model pattern for a period greater than 30 seconds resulted in interval information assuming greater importance over those variables found to be initially important. (Dowling presumes that this reflects processes distinguishing short-term memory from long-term memory.)

In the case of familiar patterns, those that distort relative interval distances of a model pattern while preserving its contour were found to be more easily recognized as being related to the model than were patterns that distort both variables. Dowling (1982) points out an apparently important interaction between contour and pitch-interval information. He reports that contour appears to be a useful device for recalling familiar melodies, but that recognition of contour is "critically dependent" on interval information as well (1982, p. 427). So, the contour and interval variable priority for recognition of familiar patterns appears to progress in difficulty as follows: pattern comparisons that preserve both contour and interval; comparisons that preserve contour while maintaining relative interval size; comparisons that preserve contour but that distort interval size; and finally, comparisons that distort both contour and interval size.

Although the evidence provides a reasonable case for the importance of contour in pattern recognition and recall, one might question the validity of the contour variable during actual music listening. Most of the research concerning contour has assumed a post hoc pattern comparison decision. Subjects are usually asked to make their discrimination response following the presentation of a model pattern and one or more comparison patterns. But this task rarely resembles a normal music-listening situation. Instead, music decisions take place more or less continuously while a work is in progress. It is likely that many comparative decisions occur prior to the completion of a presented pattern. It is possible, for example, that a tonal discrepancy may occur in a presented pattern, be identified, and result in a discrimination response prior to the listener's knowing the impact, if any, the discrepancy will have on contour, or prior to the availability of the pattern's contour as a whole. Fiske (1985) tested this possibility in a chronometric analysis study that investigated the effect of several variables, including contour, on decision response time. The task involved the detection of tonal discrepancies between pairs of short melodies. For contour it was found that there was no difference in response time between the detection of tonal discrepancies that caused a change in contour and the detection of those that continued to maintain the contour. A greater number of errors (failures to detect the discrepancy) were found for the contour-main-

taining items than for the contour-distorting items. The difference in error rate supports the findings of Dowling (1978) and Dowling and Fujitani (1971). This was the case despite the fact that the discrepancies occurred (and the response was made) prior to the availability of complete contour information. However, the response time results suggest that for those discrepancies that are detected the contour variable has no effect on processing time. This finding is contrary to Dowling's conclusion concerning the importance of contour, and probably reflects differences between post hoc pattern analysis and ongoing listening activity.

In a study that was essentially identical to Fiske's, Edworthy (1985) compared response times for discrepancy detection in pairs of patterns where the discrepancy either maintained the contour or caused a change in the contour. In several studies she found a statistically significant difference in response times favoring the distorted contour (that is, distorted contours were detected sooner than nondistorted contours). Edworthy concluded that contour is available to listeners under several conditions, including pattern novelty versus familiarity, and transposition versus nontransposition. However, for more lengthy melodies contour information is lost, according to Edworthy, while interval information is more easily retained, particularly for clearly established tonalities. The contradiction in response time results between the Fiske and Edworthy studies may be explained by the way in which the task was explained to the subjects. Edworthy asked her subjects to respond to interval differences between patterns in one task and to compare the contours of pattern pairs in a second task. Edworthy apparently presumed at the outset of the study that contour was a feature of music cognition, and then proceeded to require her subjects to keep track of contour information during the pattern presentations in her second task. Fiske, on the other hand, used contour as a structural variable in the composing of pattern items and merely asked his subjects to respond to any detected tonal or rhythmic discrepancy. Edworthy's study may be an instance of question begging where an influential variable was assumed beforehand and where subjects were asked, and in fact attempted, to employ this variable, although in a manner in which they were not accustomed under more typical listening conditions. Therefore, conclusions concerning processing time in Edworthy's study may be misleading; it may be inappropriate to assume that variables found to be of importance in post hoc situations apply to ongoing listening situations as well.

In ongoing listening tasks (such as Fiske's or Edworthy's), the role of contour in the detection of a tonal discrepancy may revolve around the question of whether the discrepancy maintains or distorts the contour of the comparison pattern up to the point of the actual occurrence of the discrepancy itself. This is different from post hoc studies (such as Dowling's) where the contour of the melody as a whole is in question. If so, perhaps a more realistic view is to consider the contour variable as a series of intervals, each specifying a direction. Dowling and Bartlett (1981) and Bartlett and Dowling (1980) tested this possibility, again for post hoc recognition and recall. Bartlett and Dowling (1980) found that subjects were better able to detect distorted intervals that continued to maintain contour in familiar melodies than in unfamiliar melodies. However, Dowling and Fujitani (1971) found that for immediate recall and comparison of unfamiliar patterns experienced listeners were better at contour recognition than they were at interval recognition. However, the reverse situation was found for inexperienced listeners. So, while the 1980 study perhaps reveals one of the cues that is used by cognition processes for representing melodies in long-term memory across experience levels, the 1971 study suggests that musical experience provides different strategies for learning new melodies. Dowling and Harwood (1986) suggest that inexperienced listeners attempt to learn melodies as a series of intervals while experienced listeners treat the interval patterns as chroma patterns. Perhaps chroma information offers the possibility of a more efficient pattern-learning strategy. However, once learned, interval structure (and therefore the summary contour) seems to be an important cue for both experienced and inexperienced listeners.

Dowling and Harwood further suggest that relative pitch chroma is a more critical factor for long-term storage of melodies than is absolute interval structure. They point to Kallman and Massaro's (1979) study that found a deterioration in pattern recognition when both chroma (essentially, the established tonality) and interval structure were altered, even though contour was maintained, versus the situation where only interval structure was changed. Similar contours and chromas lead to confusing pattern imitations with their original models (Kallman and Massaro, 1979). This is reinforced by the finding that the discrimination ability of both experienced and inexperienced listeners for atonal transpositions versus pattern imitations appears to be more or less equivalent (Dowling and Fujitani, 1971; see also Cuddy, Cohen, and Miller, 1979).

In short, for well-learned patterns, at least for experienced listeners, the cues (in respect to those variables actually tested) employed for representing those patterns in memory appear to have the following priority: chroma patterns, absolute interval structure, and finally contour. Other studies support the importance of these variables. For example, Dowling (1978) found that, for interleaved melodies (well-known when presented individually), pattern identification was assisted when subjects were aware of the contour of target melodies. Contour has also been found to be a critical variable in the discrimination of atonal melodies (Frances, 1958). Krumhansl (1979), Dewar, Cuddy, and Mewhort (1977), and Dowling (1978) all suggest the importance of tonal frameworks, tonal schema, or chroma patterns for establishing a cue set that is useful for recognizing either isolated target pitches or tonal patterns. Pattern discriminations involving relatively unrelated keys have been found to be easier to discriminate than those that are closely related in key (Cuddy et al. 1979). The (intentional) lack of such frameworks in atonal music results in difficulty in learning atonal patterns. At the same time shared tonality frameworks can lead to confusion in attempts to discriminate model patterns from highly related imitations or model patterns from similar transposed patterns.

Croonen and Kop (1989) conducted a series of studies that tested Bartlett and Dowling's conclusion that key distance influences short-term pattern recognition. In addition, on the assumption that different types of melodic contour affect pattern discrimination (either alone or by interacting with other influencing variables), rather than merely the contour variable alone, they also introduced a contour complexity variable. Their results demonstrated that key distance had no influence on pattern discrimination on short-term retention times (up to 30 seconds). They also found that contour complexity had no effect on pattern discrimination. Croonen and Kop's principal conclusion was that tonal clarity is a more critical variable than either key distance or contour. If confirmed in future studies, these results will affect the variable priority list suggested by Dowling.

Croonen and Kop's results conflicted with Edworthy's also. Croonen and Kop found that subjects' retention of a pattern's contour tended to deteriorate after 30 seconds or so. This finding is opposite to that of Edworthy, who found contour to increase in importance in pattern recognition after a period of 30 seconds. The contradiction may again be due to different sets of assumptions underlying the design of Edworthy's and Croonen and Kop's studies concerning the role of the contour variable.

Deutsch and Feroe (1981) demonstrate the influence of both tonal and rhythmic information on pattern representation. They suggest a hierarchy of organizational principles affecting (decreased) pattern recognition: equally spaced, durationally equivalent diatonic tones; equally spaced, durationally equivalent diatonic tones segmented (by inserting rests) in groups of twos, threes, and fours according to a tonal structure; and similarly segmented tone sets in which the groups of twos, threes, and fours conflict with the organized tonal structure.

Critique

The conclusions cognitive researchers have drawn concerning the representation of tonal-rhythmic patterns provide a possible model of melody recognition and recall. One must, however, be aware of potential hazards contained within the typical design of recognition experiments. One hazard, mentioned above, concerns the selection of variables (such as contour) beforehand, testing those variables by explicit manipulation of stimulus materials, and then drawing conclusions about pattern representation on the basis of that preselected variable list. The design is an instance of question begging. That is, the answer to the question concerning what variables are involved in pattern representation is, in such cases, offered by the researcher a priori before the experiment itself is conducted. A second hazard concerns conclusions made implicitly by researchers about the necessity for a variable for music cognitive decision-making. Often a researcher attempts to show that a particular variable holds relative importance against other variables in a priority set. At best, however, we can often rightly conclude that a particular priority has been demonstrated only by the study within the list of variables actually tested. This is merely conditional until it is also shown that the variable is in fact necessary (and possibly also sufficient) for cognitive activity. There may be variables even more important or relevant to the cognitive process that were not among those tested, some that are not immediately apparent from either music notation analyses or introspective reports of music listeners. Fiske (1989, 1990) offers an approach designed to avoid the first hazard. An approach attempted by others for avoiding the second is discussed in the next section.

An understanding of how patterns are encoded and stored in long-term memory is obviously necessary for a theory of music cognition. But such knowledge is insufficient for a complete characterization of cognition since musical comprehension involves processes that go beyond merely recognizing and recalling patterns. Cognitive processes are also required for the purpose of determining the musical function and intention of identified tonal-rhythmic patterns. The next section considers this activity.

PATTERN COMPARISON AND DECISION-MAKING MECHANISMS

Two types of music cognition theories have been discussed so far: (1) psychoacoustic theories that explain musical behavior in respect to the mechanisms involved in auditory perceptual activity, and (2) pattern structure theories, or those that are concerned with musical thinking in respect to the perceptual identification of features or components germane to the recognition and recall of musical patterns. Attention in this section will be directed primarily to a third type: processing-rule theories, or those that assume the presence of languagelike grammatical protocols underlying mental construction of musical patterns. Processing-rule theories tend to deal with generic decision-making activity; that is, they are about mental activity itself rather than the apparent products (e.g., sensations or images) of that activity. They are also the most strongly predictive hypotheses: Strong explanations of generic decision-making activity should subsume the theories of the other two types.

Four points characterize processing-rule theories of music cognition. These points are pretheoretical; that is, they are assumptions held by a theorist or researcher as a foundation to the theory itself. As assumptions they are not usually tested by the research. (Obviously, if the assumptions are found to be wrong, then any theory relying on them would need to be modified or abandoned.) Following is a discussion of the four points.

1. Music cognition is a construction process and not a copy process. That is, musical patterns are the product of cognitive activity and not merely an aural "photocopy" of material contained in sound objects. This assumption (or paradigm) is contrary to notions that musical understanding is simply the product of psychoacoustic mechanisms translating material contained in sound objects. Seashore's theory is an example of copy paradigm; it assumes that the acoustic

object holds or contains all relevant musical order, structure, and content, and that perception of the object is identical for all listeners. Copy paradigm leads to the conclusion that an examination of the sound object will lead to an understanding of what the listener perceives and comprehends musically. Although not strictly construction theorists, Susanne Langer (1942) and Leonard Meyer (1956) helped to crack copy paradigm by introducing perceiver-involved activity including attention and listener-generated expectation. Psycholinguistics assisted too by demonstrating that the similarly perceived /b/ component of words such as "bat," "bit," "bob," and "bet" resulted in a different acoustic description of each. Since some quite different sound objects result in identical percepts, construction paradigm appears to be a more appropriate assumption concerning the perceptual process than is copy paradigm.

The construction paradigm comes in two forms: "soft" construction, which attributes pattern formation to invariant perceptual mechanisms (i.e., the mechanisms always result in the same percept for all listeners) subject in part to the influence of musical experience and concomitant knowledge of style practice and music-culture rule systems; and "hard" construction, which attributes realized percepts and tonal-rhythmic patterns exclusively to a processing system governed by the implicitly known rules of a culturally determined music system. (Proponents of hard construction paradigm may or may not acknowledge a distinction between immediate, invariant sensory organization and flexibility in processing as a result of musical experience and musical knowledge. If the distinction is made, one is apt to refer to the invariant component as sensory perception and the remainder as actual cognitive activity. Soft constructionists tend to see it all as belonging to the same "cognitive" process.) Shepard, Deutsch, Cuddy, Dowling and their associates are perhaps best viewed as soft construction theorists. Examples of hard construction theorists are discussed below.

2. Music cognition is about pattern management and organization; that is, music decision-making involves the detection, identification, and manipulation of patterns, and the ability to recall patterns, discriminate between them, and to realize their function in the larger compositional whole. The emphasis here is on the word "pattern," and although such emphasis is not new to psychological theory (the Gestalt school comes quickly to mind), the idea that music cognitive processes begin with patterns of perceived tonal-rhythmic material rather than discrete, isolated tones is, from the point of view of many contemporary theorists, long overdue.

3. Music cognition consists of two types of components: (a) those that are universal and that operate cross-culturally, and (b) those that are idiom or style specific. Research in music psychology has been long dominated by western musical traditions. Music researchers now realize that emphasis on these traditions is potentially misleading, and that a theory of music must take into account the characteristics of all the world's musics, recognizing at the same time any similarities between them.

4. The ability to listen to music with understanding is the

product of acculturation through shaping inborn mechanisms concerned with auditory pattern construction activity. (There are variations in interpreting how this is accomplished.) The particular impact of this idea is that music listening does not require special training, but that the ability is acquired through active participation and involvement in one's native musical culture. This idea is contrary to notions that musical ability is the result of inheritance, learning to play an instrument, some sort of elemental capacity, or some other special talents or aptitudes.

Space will not be taken here to trace the reasoning or evidence behind these ideas, particularly since others have already done so (see citations in the following paragraph). But it is emphasized that, together, these ideas have shaped the thinking and research behind several recent theories of music cognition. These theories transcend some of the limitations and difficulties of earlier work. A description of four of these theories follows.

The first theory we shall consider is proposed by Jack Heller and Warren Campbell. Their model of music listening emphasizes active, ongoing hypothesis-testing processes. It is based on several premises. The first is that musical structure, like that of language, is founded on an implicitly known set of rules (Heller and Campbell, 1976; Campbell and Heller, 1980a, 1981; see also Campbell and Heller, 1988). These rules define the musical system of a particular culture (e.g., western vs. Javanese), and are concerned with the accepted (grammatical) order of tonal and rhythmic inter- and intrapattern relationships. The rules underlie perceptual and cognitive processes, and guide listener-imposed order and structure on an incoming acoustic signal. These rules are not available to introspection. As in language, these rules are "natural," that is, they have not been established artificially or stated explicitly as have the rules for, say, chess. As for language, such rules may generate an infinite range of tonal-rhythmic patterns within the bounds of a particular rule system.

Second, this implicit set of rules results in tonal-rhythmic orders that are inherently logical within a particular music language system. Heller and Campbell (1976) point out the distinction between designative or referential content of language and the form of linguistic structures devoid of such content (i.e., the propositional content of sentences vs. the form of speech noises that carry that content). For example, the syllogism

All G are H.
All F are G.
Therefore, all F are H.

results, linguistically, in a logical but referentially contentless form. The lines are grammatically acceptable English sentences expressing a demonstrable logical proposition. But they do not specify or designate any particular person, thing, event, or condition. (Noam Chomsky's famous sentence "Colorless, green ideas sleep furiously" also exemplifies the separation of linguistic form and content: Here the individual words are designative and the sentence itself is grammatically acceptable. But, the sentence expresses nothing, at least in an isolated context.) Heller and Campbell suggest that a similar rule set exists for music resulting in formal structures that are musically logical or musically-grammatically correct but nondesignative. That is, the rules result in the realization of tonal-rhythmic patterns appropriate to a particular music language system, but such structures are contentless in a referential sense. These rules are known and understood by the composer, performer, and listener, and underlie the music communication process as a whole.

Third, Campbell and Heller (1980a) suggest that "music (like language) is not of the 'real world' but has its origins as a pattern in the brain of the sender, and is not constituted again until it is evoked as a pattern in the brain of the perceiver" (p. 31). Heller and Campbell's theory reflects a (hard) construction paradigm. They reject the acoustic, notational, and overt behavioral "frames of reference" as equivocal or isomorphic descriptors of actually realized musical patterns and structures. To them the perceptual frame of reference is at least equally important to "objective" consideration of the vibrational frame of reference.

Fourth, Heller and Campbell (1976) suggest that musical behavior is an instance of intelligence characterized by the ability to solve complex, abstract musical problems and to generalize the results to other musical situations. This point emphasizes the view that music cognition is not the result of mechanized and passive perception, nor is it concerned exclusively with matters of history, style, or post hoc analyses of musical form or harmony. Rather, cognition is primarily problem-solving ability that for music includes tonal-rhythmic pattern detection, identification, discrimination, and evaluation, and the active comparison of patterns for the discovery of interpattern relationships. Intellectual activity is viewed here as being at least as demanding for music as it is for other areas more traditionally recognized as demanding "intelligence."

Fifth, music processing has much in common with language processing. Both involve the same sensory network and, at least up to some point, identical auditory-processing mechanisms. This includes both a microlevel and a macrolevel (1976). The microlevel or music interpretive level includes processing changes in stress or timbre that occur within notes or phrases and between notes or phrases, changes that occur within only a very few tenths of a second. These events cannot be symbolized by music notation. Macrolevel processing includes response to motivic, phrase, or section events. These events can be symbolized notationally. The micro- and macrolevels have obvious parallels in language; for example, distinguishing phonemes versus distinguishing verbal phrases. For both music and speech, such processing is assumed to be implicit (see point No. 1). For both, processing involves a search for invariant features between stimuli and the detection of discrepancies between patterns otherwise holding relative invariance.

Points 1 through 5 lead Heller and Campbell to a sixth point: The musical process (composer to performer to listener) requires a successful "social/cultural contract" (1976; this contract is similar to Moles's social-communication matrix, 1958). As with language, the social/cultural contract involves agreement between participants concerning the conventional use of specific tonal-rhythmic events. The agreement is about both the structure of patterns and the interpretation of pitch and durational nuance in respect to expressive intent (point No. 5 again).

Seventh, Heller and Campbell suggest that, again like language, musical ability is dependent upon musically enriched experiences occurring early in a child's life. It is hypothesized that these experiences must take place during a critical period of cognitive development, probably prior to the age of 6 years old (Heller and Campbell, 1981), and that they result in acquiring an appropriate social/cultural contract.

Heller and Campbell use these points to construct a model of the music cognition process. The model (Campbell and Heller, 1981; Heller and Campbell, 1982) demonstrates a parallel between the language communication process and the music communication process. It provides detail of a cognitive-processing stage that they call the "executive." (This model also relies to a great extent on part of Leonard Meyer's [1956] theory.) They propose that the steps occurring in the processing and comparing of musical patterns are:

1. A music-listening context is selected (in respect to composer, style, genre, performer, or listening environment such as concert hall, recording, or football field.
2. Expectations about what will be heard are formulated on the basis of the selected context.
3. Expectations are used to frame questions appropriate to the chosen context in respect to pattern development, overall form of the piece, tempo, expressive nuance, harmonic structure, and so on.
4. These questions are tested against the incoming realized tonal-rhythmic patterns.
5. The answers to the questions are examined and compared against the expectations.
6. Any discrepancies are used to revise the context.

Heller and Campbell's description of the executive has several important features. First, it is an active process rather than a passive copy process, requiring the full attention and participation of the music listener. Second, the depiction of music comprehension is clearly understood as a hypothesis generation/testing process. The hypotheses are an outcome of a musical context as constructed and understood by the individual listener. This context is subject to modification depending on the outcome of the listener's own hypothesis-testing activity. Third, the process accounts for each of the pretheoretical concerns discussed earlier: music cognition as pattern construction and pattern management, universal versus style-specific components, and musical understanding as the product of music acculturation.

Heller and Campbell have tested portions of their model through a series of experiments on "interpretive listening." Again using research in speech perception as a model, Heller and Campbell have investigated the contribution of three segments of the music auditory signal to music perception:

These include the attack portion of a tone, its steady state, and the legato transients between tones. Note that these components concern microlevel within-note activity and between-note activity. The design of their studies (Campbell and Heller, 1979) is quite elegant: A series of tones played by natural instruments serves as a model to be compared with a multiple-choice set consisting of items presented with either the target segment exorcised from the signal (signal minus x) or the segment presented in isolation of the signal (x minus signal). Choice set items (either x alone or signal minus x) are presented either in their natural states, altered instrumentation, or manipulated by synthetically reducing or eliminating other components of the signal such as intensity or selected portions of the harmonic spectrum. Results of subjects presented with the two presentation formats (signal minus x or x minus signal) are interpreted by comparing the pattern of mean differences against a "necessary versus sufficiency" condition; that is, the pattern is shown to converge on one of four possible necessary/sufficient conclusions.

The studies have examined two areas: instrument identification and musical expression. In both cases (Heller and Campbell, 1977; Campbell and Heller, 1978, 1979, 1980b), the scores reflect segment contributions that follow the priority legato transient, attack, and finally steady state. In the identification of six different instruments, Campbell and Heller (1980b) found that scores for legato transients and attack transients were significantly higher statistically than steady state segments for durations greater than 20 milliseconds. (Contrary results, however, were found by Kendall, 1986, who conducted a similar study using musical patterns of somewhat greater length.) Heller and Campbell cite similar research conducted in their laboratory (DeCorso, 1976; Kurau, 1977) demonstrating that information provided by steady state components (e.g., intensity change) fails to result in interpretation discrimination. Instead, legato transients (1978) were again found to result in statistically significantly higher scores than attack or steady state segments in interpretation discriminations. They further hypothesize that additional interpretation information is provided by the upper harmonic spectrum of the signal. They also report evidence for a right-ear (left-brain hemispheric processing) effect for transients versus steady state segments. These results are contrary to some assumptions in psychoacoustics that attribute greater importance to the steady state component in instrument (timbre) identification and for conveying expression (such as fluctuation in dynamics). Heller and Campbell's studies demonstrate that little or no contribution is made by the steady state segment to music perception, even for relatively long presentations of that segment.

Critique

Heller and Campbell's model is an outcome of their six premises. The model concerns cognitive processing that is carried on beyond the mere representation of melodic-rhythmic patterns. However, certain aspects of the model remain untested. It is not clear, for example, what hypotheses are actually tested by the listener or what the substance of the hypotheses might be. Nor is it clear from the model what style or structure describes the hypothesis-testing stage. Are hypotheses tested in succession or are they processed simultaneously? Does processing occur hierarchically or is it singularly directed by the task itself? The theories discussed below offer additional substance to the framework proposed by Heller and Campbell.

Mary Louise Serafine makes a central claim (1988) that music is a form of thought, the product of which is realized tonal-rhythmic organization and comprehension. Serafine bases her theory on the (hard) construction paradigm: Musical understanding is solely the result of cognitive processes; music does not exist as a preformed object external to the perceiver but rather as a "subjective entity springing from mental operations" on the acoustic signal (1988, p. 233). These processes are assumed by Serafine to be universal.

Serafine notes four "facts" about the musical process: (1) universality: all cultures are characterized in part by some form of music, and all people have an understanding of music to some "considerable" degree; (2) diversity: music occurs in a wide variety of styles and types, both within and between cultures; (3) change: any musical type is subject to modification and development over time; and (4) acquisition: musical understanding occurs in large part without formal training.

These "facts" lead Serafine to a set of premises. A few of the more important of these follow. First, Serafine suggests that the working material of composers is something other than individual tones and chords, that tones and chords are not the elements of music but rather are necessary by-products of music analysis. They are merely the result of reflection on music and have "minimal cognitive reality" (1988, p. 7). Instead, only the tonal-rhythmic pattern relationships and organization actually apprehended by listeners have cognitive "reality" or any relevance to music cognition. This idea eliminates from consideration tonal-rhythmic symbols (e.g., descending lines representing death); word spellings (e.g., B.A.C.H.); tonal painting (e.g., thunder); programmatic devices; intellectual manipulation of tonal material that is not actually perceivable (e.g., retrograde inversions, or others that do not result in realized tonal-rhythmic organization).

Second, the same set of mental operations is common to all musical activities (composing, performing, listening) and can be revealed (through experiment) only by how music "is," that is, how music is actually realized by listeners. This point is critical for two reasons. First, it demands that experiments avoid the question-begging fallacy and be designed so that subjects are allowed to respond to what they really hear, rather than prescribing to subjects how they should respond to music or what they are to listen for. Second, it shapes the design of Serafine's own experiments and leads her to the discovery of a cognitive structure.

A third premise is that there are two types of music cognition processes: (1) style specific, or processes that are relevant only to a particular style or type of music (e.g., symphony versus gamelan); and (2) generic, or processes that are universal across all musical types and styles (e.g., pattern clo-

sure). Serafine's theory is specifically concerned with generic processes.

Serafine's research tests the hypothesis that panstylistic music-processing capability is acquired through genetically controlled development of internal cognitive operations. That is, they are acquired without formal musical training but rather by the natural growth and development of cognitive mechanisms concerned with organizing and understanding temporal sonic events. Serafine (1988) reports the results of a series of 15 studies investigating cognitive processes. Included in the studies were subjects 5, 6, 8, 10, and 11 years old and adults. Subjects were pretested for musical training, pitch discrimination abilities, intellectual maturity, and, for younger subjects, cognitive stage. Those having had formal musical training (Suzuki string instruction) were assigned to a separate group; these subjects were not part of the main study. The principal purpose of each study was to determine the extent of success for a particular task and whether this success improved as a function of age. Tasks involved detecting certain tonal-rhythmic relationships in a test item and identifying similar relationships in one or more comparison items. Each subject was tested individually. (This involved some quite imaginative data-gathering techniques, particularly for younger subjects.) The processes tested included the following (which also represents the structure of her resulting theory):

I. Temporal Processes
    A. Processes occurring in succession
        1. Idiomatic construction (e.g., tonality, meter)
        2. Motivic chaining
        3. Pattern detection
        4. Phrasing detection
    B. Processes occurring simultaneously
        1. Timbre synthesis (e.g., recognizing simultaneously employed instruments)
        2. Motivic synthesis (e.g., simultaneous motives)
        3. Textual abstraction (i.e., monophonic vs. polyphonic, etc.)
II. Nontemporal Processes
    A. Tonal closure (in the Gestalt sense)
    B. Transformation
        1. Relative repetition (e.g., matching and discrimination)
        2. Ornamentation (e.g., variation)
        3. Substantive (e.g., conservation)
    C. Abstraction
        1. Motivic abstraction
        2. Rhythmic abstraction
    D. Hierarchic levels (recognizing reductions of tonal-rhythmic patterns)

In general, Serafine found that trends of success supported the principal hypothesis. Children 5 or 6 years old showed the least amount of success on the various tasks and appeared to possess very few of the processes, although there was evidence of a limited degree of success on some of them. Children 8 to 10 years old generally showed rapid growth in their cognitive abilities. And, except for an unexplained dip in success on some of the tasks for 11-year-old children, most subjects older than 10 demonstrated that most of the processes had been acquired.

Some of the tasks were tested using the musically trained Suzuki subjects. These subjects demonstrated an advantage over the untrained subjects for only a few of the tasks. Furthermore, the training needed to be long-term and extensive before showing this advantage. Therefore, age was the principal predictor of success on these tasks, and training seemed neither "necessary nor sufficient for the development of the generic processes" (Serafine, 1988, p. 229).

Critique

Serafine's theory is structured according to three hypothesis levels: Level 1: Music cognition involves a set of processes concerned with panstylistic characteristics of music assumed to be generic. Level 2: Panstylistic processes consist of a specifiable set (shown above). Level 3: Each of the panstylistic processes is acquired through genetically controlled development of internal cognitive operations. Serafine's studies actually directly address the third level only. If we accept the validity of her studies and that the results reflect trends of success, then it seems reasonable to accept the level 3 hypothesis. In doing so we then also have a tentative list of specifiable panstylistic processes (i.e., we find support as well for the level 2 hypothesis). At the same time, however, we must assume that there are other generic processes in operation yet to be discovered, some of which may supersede those already identified.

The studies have little to offer in support of the level 1 hypothesis. There are two reasons for this. First, the hypothesis is the outcome of Serafine's "facts" and premises. If the logic is valid, which it appears to be (however, see Huron, 1990, and Thomson, 1990), then it is reasonable to propose the hypothesis. That is, the hypothesis is first a logical conclusion of a good argument and second a statement that is potentially testable. But, second, the hypothesis will remain untested until the processes specified by level 2 are actually tested cross-culturally. Do the level 2 tasks (rewritten in the style of some other relevant music system) mean anything to nonwestern listeners? Do success trends of nonwesterners reflect those found by Serafine for western subjects? If so, a strong case for level 1 might be made. The answer to these questions, however, remains to date unavailable.

We will next examine the theory of Fred Lerdahl and Ray Jackendoff. Lerdahl and Jackendoff, influenced by Noam Chomsky's contribution to psycholinguistics, have attempted to formulate a generative theory of musical grammar. The term "generative," as used in psycholinguistics, refers to the ability of humans to produce an indefinitely large number of sentences from a finite and specifiable number of sentence-generating rules. Although not all theorists agree, Chomsky suggests that a generative theory of language can account for several aspects of language production: how

speakers (of any culture) are able to continually create and comprehend new sentences; the similarities in function, acquisition, and structure in the world's languages; and the possibility of expressing similar ideas by means of different languages. All of these possibilities are under the control of commonly held speech-generating/receiving mechanisms and cognitive processes. "The intention of a generative theory is to represent what the speaker 'knows' when he knows how to speak a language" (Lerdahl and Jackendoff, 1983, p. 5). It is Lerdahl and Jackendoff's intent to identify a generative grammar for music based on a theory of music cognition similar to Chomsky's theory of language.

Lerdahl and Jackendoff point to five "facts" about music. First, like Serafine, and Heller and Campbell, Lerdahl and Jackendoff assume a (hard) construction paradigm: "A piece of music is a mentally constructed entity" (1983, p. 2). That is, music does not reside in the acoustical signal; rather, the acoustical signal triggers mental (cognitive) operations that impose order on information derived from that signal.

Second, music is a distinctly human activity resulting in a variety of cultural traditions. Since music notation cannot fully capture these traditions, theories of music must account for this variety without resorting to notational analysis.

Third, musical understanding is the product of music acculturation and results in an intuitive listening ability; musical understanding does not depend on formal musical training providing that there is "sufficient exposure" to music. This intuitive ability causes the listener to self-impose "surface structure patterns" on tonal-rhythmic material, the result of a set of perceptual rules acquired from immersion in a particular musical language (see next point). Such rules permit the listener to discriminate between familiar and unfamiliar pieces, and between "grammatical" and "ungrammatical" musical structures. These rules can be discovered by analyzing their use in musical contexts. (This is similar to both Heller and Campbell's implicitly known rule structure, and Serafine's generic rule assumption—although Serafine tries to find the rules through specific listening behavior while Lerdahl and Jackendoff prefer music analyses.) Lerdahl and Jackendoff divide the rules into two types: those that are idiom dependent and those that are universal. (This is also similar to Serafine's point.)

Fourth, organization of musical sounds in any useful way depends on intensive exposure to some particular music language system. Without this exposure no meaningful organization of tonal-rhythmic material will be possible. This idea applies to attempts to comprehend a "foreign" musical language. It also allows for differences in perception between experienced and inexperienced listeners from the same culture.

Fifth, "One hears music as organized patterns" (1983, p. xii), not as a series of discrete pitches. Points 4 and 5 agree with similar assumptions of Serafine and of Heller and Campbell.

Lerdahl and Jackendoff's theory is about universal principles underlying systematic management of patterns by music listeners. The theory is generative in that its intention is to represent what the listener knows when knowing how to listen to music, or to identify the principles known by the listener that permit an internal representation of a piece of music. Lerdahl and Jackendoff's (1983) theory consists of four components and two rules. The four components are the following:

1. Grouping structure, or the "hierarchical segmentation of the piece into motives, phrases, and sections"
2. Metrical structure, or the "regular alternation of strong and weak beats at a number of hierarchical levels"
3. Time-span reduction, or "a hierarchy of 'structural importance' with respect to their position in grouping and metrical structure"
4. Prolongational reduction, or "a hierarchy that expresses harmonic and melodic tension and relaxation, continuity, and progression" (pp. 8–9)

Application of the four components is intended to result in a structural description of a particular piece of music. This may result in ambiguity. Lerdahl and Jackendoff try to solve this dilemma by proposing two "rules" that are supposed to differentiate between different resulting structures. The two types of rules are (1) well-formedness rules, "which specify the possible structural descriptions"; and (2) preference rules, "which designate out of the possible structural descriptions, those that correspond to experienced listeners' hearings of any particular piece" (1983, p. 9).

Lerdahl and Jackendoff have so far derived approximately 50 well-formedness rules and preference rules in respect to the application of each of the four components to particular musical contexts. Generally, the rules emerge progressively beginning with simple rules of rhythmic or tonal organization. The rule set in total constitutes Lerdahl and Jackendoff's generative grammar for music.

A particular feature of Lerdahl and Jackendoff's theory is Schenkerian-like hierarchical layers of adjacent tonal-rhythmic events that emerge from applying the rules to components Nos. 3 and 4 above. This results in a specification of events that are subordinate to other events, layers of events that may be separated somewhat by other surface structure events, but that are found to hold cognitive importance in comprehending larger structures of the piece. (Others—e.g., Deutsch and Serafine—have proposed various hierarchical orders of musical perception or cognitive events as well.)

Critique

The rules of the generative grammar proposed by Lerdahl and Jackendoff are the result of analysis of musical events as practiced by western composers. The rule set appears to rely heavily on the musical experience of the authors and on the implications of music notation. Thus, we cannot be assured by this approach that the "correct" rules will always be discovered. More importantly, there is no reason to assume that the particular identified rules result necessarily in the same rules that drive cognitive mechanisms. It is not surprising that most of the criticism of Lerdahl and Jackendoff's theory

concerns whether or not the particular rules lead to appropriate descriptions of works as actually perceived by listeners, and whether they generalize to all similar musical contexts (i.e., whether the rules have external validity). The opinions to date have been mixed. The theory is, however, logically (internally) valid, and it would be a mistake to condemn the theory on the basis of the particular set of rules that has so far emerged. Since at the very least the rule set provides an array of potentially testable hypotheses, it is more appropriate instead to continue the search for a rule set that does generalize across musical contexts, either until the rules are discovered or until it can be otherwise demonstrated that such a set of rules is impossible.

The final theory we shall consider is the result of research by Fiske. Fiske's theory proposes that music cognition consists in part of a generic decision-making mechanism that is concerned with detecting, identifying, discriminating, and evaluating inter- and intrapattern relationships in tonal-rhythmic material. Briefly, the theory makes the following points: (1) the brain attempts to construct patterns from information provided by auditory sensory stimulation; (2) three types of patterns (only) can be recognized: a given pattern, a variation of the given pattern, and a distinctly different pattern; (3) classification of pattern type is mainly listener determined (according to both processing rules and cultural agreements), and not essentially acoustically determined (or otherwise externally imposed; acoustical structure is seen as a necessary but not sufficient determinant of perceived musical structure); and (4) the brain compares realized patterns in an attempt to discover the function of one pattern with respect to another. The outcome of this process is comprehension by the listener concerning musical relationships between patterns (i.e., pattern repetitions, variations and development of patterns, or the introduction of new tonal-rhythmic pattern material). The remainder of the theory concerns the structure of the cognitive mechanism concerned with making pattern comparisons, and the significance of decisions resulting from this activity for the communication process. (The theory is developed in detail in Fiske, 1990.)

Fiske (1982a,b, 1984, 1985, 1987) conducted a series of studies that sought to determine whether three different musical phrase comparison tasks represent a hierarchy of processing difficulty or whether simultaneous processing of two or more tasks occurs. The three tasks were as follows:

1. Detection of a tonal discrepancy between pairs of tonal patterns, and detection of a rhythmic discrepancy between pairs of rhythmic patterns
2. Detection of a discrepancy, either tonal or rhythmic, between pairs of tonal-rhythmic patterns
3. Identification of the type of discrepancy, either tonal or rhythmic, between pairs of tonal-rhythmic patterns

The tasks consisted of listening to tape-recorded pairs of diatonic musical phrases. Three tape recordings were prepared. One recording consisted of patterns of pitches, all pitches having the same duration. The second recording consisted of rhythmic patterns, all durations played on the same pitch. The third recording consisted of combining the tonal patterns of the first recording with the rhythmic patterns of the second recording, item by item, to form a set of pairs of tonal-rhythmic patterns. All patterns were played at the same tempo. Four seconds of silence separated the given pattern from the comparison pattern. Ten seconds of silence separated one item pair from the next pair. All items were presented on track A of the tape recordings while on track B were recorded brief trigger signals simultaneously occurring with the single discrepancy—tonal or rhythmic—heard in the comparison patterns. The trigger signals were sent to a reaction timer that immediately began to measure processing time in milliseconds. These signals were not heard by the subject. The timer was stopped by the subject's pressing one of two keys indicating an answer to a test item: for example, the answers "same" or "different," or "tonal" or "rhythmic." Reaction times and the subjects' answers were duly noted. A baseline reaction time was also measured for each subject by averaging the responses made to 25 randomly presented beeps. The baseline served as a covariate in a subsequent analysis of covariance statistical design. All 111 subjects were third- and fourth-year university music students, each of whom had completed at least 2 years of ear training. (Chronometric analysis as a tool for investigating microtemporal reaction activity is discussed by Lachman, Lachman, and Butterfield, 1979; Chase, 1978; Taylor, 1976; and Posner 1973.)

In the first study, the combined element patterns were randomly generated and were thus unfamiliar to the subjects. In this study it was found that a greater amount of processing time was required for task 2 than for task 1, and for task 3 than for task 2. This suggests a hierarchy of processing difficulty for these tasks given the type of test item. In a second study, the combined element patterns were familiar to the subjects. In this study task 3 again required a greater amount of processing time than either task 1 and task 2; however, in contrast to the first study, task 1 required a greater amount of processing time than did task 2. Fiske shows that the reason for this reversal probably lies with the nature of the task 1 items: the tonal and rhythmic components of the combined-element patterns of tasks 2 and 3 may have been perceived differently from their isolated presentations in task 1. The familiarity of the items in the second study may have provided a processing advantage for tasks 2 and 3 that was not available for the component-isolated items of task 1. The musical source of the tonal or rhythmic material for task 1 may not have been recognized by the subjects as it was normally for tasks 2 and 3.

Fiske argues that these results suggest a hierarchy of tasks arranged according to required amounts of processing time. The identity of each of the task levels is unknown, but it seems sensible to assume the following: (1) that the tasks extend from an initial "same versus different" comparison task through a range of tasks designed to sort out structural relationships between patterns; (2) that the number of tasks is finite; (3) that the task hierarchy culminates in questions of pattern function; and (4) that musical experience and listening skill determine the extent to which a particular listener can successfully penetrate the hierarchy (that is, different listeners may terminate pattern comparison activity at different levels of the task hierarchy, either voluntarily or involuntarily on the basis of listening ability or personal intent and motivation). Fiske suggests that the outcome of negotiating the hierarchy results in two different decisions regardless of the level of the hierarchy at which the listener terminates pattern comparison activity. The first decision concerns the relationship between the two patterns and is limited to one of three choices: The patterns are identical; the second pattern is a variation or development of, or holds some other sort of structural identity with the first; or the patterns are distinctly different. The second decision concerns the specific relationship between the two patterns with respect to the task defining that particular level of the hierarchy. To place questions of pattern function on the task hierarchy may at first seem surprising. However, pattern function also depends on pattern relationship (relationship having to be sorted out by the listener first), and questions of pattern function appear to be rewritten versions of questions of pattern relationship. For example, the question, what is the function of pattern P at measure N? might be rewritten as, Is pattern P' (a previously identified variation of pattern P) a continuation of pattern development in measure N, or is it the beginning of a new section? The rewritten version now represents a possible upper level of the task hierarchy.

Although the pattern comparison studies suggested a hierarchy of processing stages, it was not clear whether the tasks represented a single processing stage involving levels of increasing processing difficulty or whether, instead, they represented several distinct, but progressively dependent, processing stages. Fiske (1987) examined this question where again reaction time served as the dependent variable while task (two levels—tonal discrepancy detection and discrepancy identification), tonality (two levels—diatonic and chromatic), discrepancy magnitude (two levels—melodic intervals of seconds and sixths), and transposition (two levels—transposed comparison patterns and nontransposed comparison patterns) served as independent variables. Results of this study follow:

1. Levels of task were found to interact with levels of discrepancy magnitude.
2. Levels of tonality were found to interact with levels of transposition.
3. A three-way interaction was found between levels of task, levels of discrepancy magnitude, and levels of tonality.

A further analysis examined the reaction times for the variables discrepancy magnitude, tonality, and transposition, with the two levels of the task variable considered separately. In this analysis it was found that levels of discrepancy magnitude interacted with levels of tonality for the discrepancy detection task, while no interactions occurred for the discrepancy identification task.

Figure 23–1 illustrates the relationship between the four

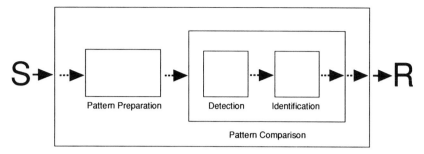

FIGURE 23-1. Decision-Making Dynamics.

variables, including not only the three original interactions but the tonality interaction as well. Two stages are implied. The first stage appears to represent a pattern preparatory stage. That is, rather than there being a single match-mismatch processing stage, an additional preparatory stage was found. At this point it is not clear what the function of this stage is. What may take place is pattern conciliation. Given a pattern K that is to be compared with a previously presented pattern P, the function of this first stage may be to prepare K in such a way that an accurate and efficient comparison with P can be made. This stage may be particularly important for pattern comparisons between P and a transposed version of P.

Since chronometric analysis assigned task to the second processing stage, it seems reasonable to designate pattern comparison activity as the principal function of this stage. At the same time, however, it is clear that pattern structural descriptors define the activity of this stage as well through their interaction with the task variable. All considered, differences in discrepancy magnitude and tonality seem primarily to affect the detection of the discrepancy, while their effect on the identification of the type of discrepancy appears to be additive (i.e., they have no effect on discrepancy identification).

Finally, a study by Fiske (1984) sought to determine whether tonal and rhythmic decisions are made simultaneously or in parallel. Again through chronometric analysis, subjects were tested for the amount of reaction time required for detecting a tonal or rhythmic discrepancy between pairs of tonal-rhythmic patterns. One-half of the group of subjects were provided with advanced cues concerning the discrepancy-producing element; the remaining subjects were not provided with advanced cues. Mean reaction times were compared between the two groups. Fiske also tested for differences between mean reaction times for tonal discrepancies and rhythmic discrepancies, and for differences between the number of subjects demonstrating faster mean reaction time for tonal discrepancy items and the number of subjects demonstrating faster reaction time for rhythmic discrepancy items. No statistically significant difference was found between subjects provided with advanced cues and those not so provided. Response times were faster for rhythmic discrepancy detections than for tonal discrepancies. This difference was statistically significant. A greater number of subjects detected rhythmic dis-

crepancies more quickly than tonal discrepancies. This difference was also statistically significant. Fiske concluded that these results are best represented by a parallel self-terminating model (see Taylor, 1976). This model describes mental activity as the simultaneous processing of different elements such that a response (of some type) may be initiated upon the discovery of a solution to a given task even though processing of any remaining elements is incomplete.

Critique

Measurement of mental behavior is limited to two types of data: an account of the number of correct and/or incorrect responses to a task, and the amount of time required to respond correctly to a task. Music research has given less attention to the second type than to the first. But chronometric analysis offers a powerful tool for analyzing response time of mental activity (see Fiske, 1982a,b). More research is needed that deals with music decision-making, particularly concerning the task hierarchy proposed by Fiske. Is the proposed hierarchy an appropriate construct for representing music-listening decision-making? If so, what are the remaining task levels of the hierarchy? Do some of the tasks interact and result in an acceleration of processing time for higher-level (increasingly complex) listening tasks? Are there additional processing stages beyond the two types identified by Fiske? If so, what influence do they have on pattern comparison and decision-making?

TWO-COMPONENT THEORIES VS. THREE-COMPONENT THEORIES

The theories of Heller and Campbell, Lerdahl and Jackendoff, and Serafine share a "two-component" structural similarity. The research of Fiske introduces an additional component. Following is an explanation of the difference between two-component and three-component music cognition theories. The explanation will tie together the theories and research reviewed above.

Two-component structure characterizes most theories of music cognition. One of the components may be described by a set of processing rules, known to the listener implicitly, which directs the cognitive system to extract certain information from an acoustic signal and to build from that information an internal tonal-rhythmic pattern representation. Its function is pattern detection and pattern identification. The activity described by this component is not available for introspection.

A second component comprises a description of the perceived tonal-rhythmic pattern resulting from exercising the rules of the first component. This description represents the "dynamics of music"; it is the product of introspection and is specified by a set of rules that is unique to the second component. The component's function is pattern recall, recognition, and discrimination. So, we will say that exercising an appropriate set of cognitive rules (component No. 1) leads a listener to experience specific dynamics (or structures) of music (component No. 2).

The attraction of specifying a (component No. 1) rule construct as the essence of cognitive realization of musical order is that we may divide rules into those that are universal, and therefore generic, and those that are style or idiom specific, and therefore culturally determined. By this division the claim is made that concern for musical diversity is satisfied whether we consider such diversity in terms of intercultural style distinctions (e.g., baroque or jazz) or in terms of intracultural music language difference (e.g., symphonies vs. gamelan music). Given, for example, pieces of two different musical styles, two-component theories suggest that we need take only two steps for explaining cognition: (1) attach a different set of style-specific rules to each piece in order to account for style distinctions, and (2) maintain a common set of generic rules in order to account for the fact that human brains of similar genetic structure are involved in both musical types. But there is a problem with this: The temptation is too great to make up generic rules as the need comes along. That is, one might merely assume that the list of generic rules is incomplete, and that when a new discovery is made about what listeners hear, the discovery is satisfied by composing a new rule to account for it. But ad hoc rule invention is poor theorizing. What the theory requires instead is a way to anchor the rules in specific decision-making activity. By doing so one would accept the idea that processing activity itself is generic but that this structure is able to accommodate a range of tonal-rhythmic pattern types, at least within the constraints of known music systems.

The introduction of a third component allows one to represent processing anchors for a generic rule set that we shall call the dynamics of music decision-making. Whereas the dynamics of musical structure (component No. 2) serve as a description of perceived tonal-rhythmic structure (i.e., perceptual products or images), the third component is a description of the activity that leads to realizing those musical structures and interstructural relationships. The result of this description is knowledge—for example, about pattern P and its function with respect to some other pattern K. Given, for example, two patterns heard in a composition, third-component processing leads to one of three decisions: that pattern K is a repeat of pattern P, a variation of P, or the introduction of new tonal-rhythmic material unrelated to P. The decision-making component precedes the question of how P is represented for subsequent recognition and recall and deals first with the problem of how P relates to or is different from K during ongoing music listening activity.

The theories and research reviewed in this chapter can be combined into a single three-component theory of music cognition (see Figure 23–2). A description of the three-component music cognition system assumes the following protocol:

1. The detection and identification of tonal-rhythmic patterns as controlled by style-specific rule-based processing (component No. 1 above). This stage also involves initial (generic) pattern detection as described, for example, by the research of Shepard and others, the laws of Gestalt perceptual processing, and other non-psychoacoustic theories of pitch and rhythmic organization.
2. Comparison of patterns by means of a generic set of decision-making stages; realization of the dynamics of musical structure, pattern function, and interpattern relationships (the third component from above). This stage includes hypothesis-testing activity as described by the dynamics of cognitive processing, or the pattern comparison and decision-making arranged according to a task hierarchy of some finite number of processing levels as suggested by Fiske. It also involves the generic processes of Serafine. The structure of this activity is encapsulated by the executive processing stage proposed by Heller and Campbell.
3. Representation of patterns by a set of encoded features for the purpose of pattern storage, recall, and recognition (component No. 2 above). This entails tonal and rhythmic patterns and their interrelationships that constitute the realized dynamics of music for a particular composition; these dynamics are described (in part at least) by the pattern representation and recognition research of Dowling and his colleagues.

Recall that Heller and Campbell propose a model of the "executive" stage of music cognition. This stage assumes full attention by the music listener and is characterized by active listener-involved hypothesis testing concerning pattern structure and relationships. This activity stems from a listener-assumed context concerning such aspects as expected musical style, performance environment, and interpretative or expressive envelope. All of these context-derived expectations are subject to modification as a result of the listener's own decisions that emerge from hypothesis-testing activity made during the course of a musical event. Hypothesis testing is the focal point of Heller and Campbell's executive component.

The results of Fiske's experiments may be considered as a

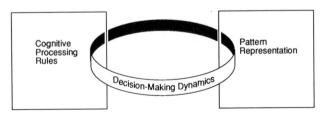

FIGURE 23–2. Three-Component Theory.

description of this hypothesis-testing activity. The style and structure of pattern comparison activity reflected by these experiments, and the decisions that result from this activity, are characterized by the hypothesis-testing stage of the executive model. Therefore, Heller and Campbell's hypothesis stage is best viewed as a description of music cognitive dynamics (step 2 of the above protocol). The products of these decisions—that is, realizations of pattern structure and pattern interrelationships—belong to a separate component, the dynamics of music (step 3 of the above protocol).

The theories of both Lerdahl and Jackendoff and Serafine are likely candidates for further fleshing out Fiske's decision-task hierarchy. Some of the generative grammar rules of Lerdahl and Jackendoff and the process categories proposed by Serafine collapse into questions of discrepancy detection, identity, pattern structure, and tonal-rhythmic function, potentially expanding the task hierarchy into other interdependent comparison decisions. Many of Lerdahl and Jackendoff's rules or Serafine's experiment tasks, for example, can be rewritten as pattern comparison tasks. If tested as such it would not be difficult to show whether these tasks are part of the decision-task hierarchy or whether they are about something else, for example, the dynamics of music rather than the dynamics of music cognition.

The principal advantage of the three-component theory over two-component theories is that the implicit rules assumed by Heller and Campbell and the more specific processes and rules of Serafine or of Lerdahl and Jackendoff take on clarity and flexibility if viewed as being under the control of some form of rule management system such as that identified by Fiske. They find clarity because an experimentally supported rule management system sorts out which rules are useful descriptors of musical pattern realizations and which

are not. They take on flexibility because a rule management system would have to be generic, offering the same structure or control over cognitive processing for any of the world's musics. That is, it would have to fulfill the pretheoretical assumptions identified earlier concerning pattern construction, pattern management and organization, universal versus idiom-specific musical components, and acculturation.

IMPORTANCE TO MUSIC EDUCATION

Skilled listening is the foundation of any musical activity. But such a skill cannot be taken for granted by music education. Neither can we assume the realized products of this skill. Different listeners may come to different conclusions about and understandings of the same piece depending on their musical experience and cultural background. The skill is governed by context (a cultural one) and requires active involvement and musical thinking on the part of the listener. Although it is probably not possible to affect the function, style, or structure of cognitive mechanisms (and thus cognitive processing), it seems likely that we can shape or guide the listening behavior of students to increasingly appropriate, focused, and concentrated musical thinking as controlled by these mechanisms. Such thinking emphasizes the identification of patterns formed by tonal and rhythmic material, and the composer-intended relationships between these patterns within the context of other pattern material presented and manipulated by a composer or performer. In order to nurture the development of listening skills it is helpful for music educators to have some understanding of the form and inherent structure of the music cognitive environment in which such thinking takes place.

References

Balzano, G. J. (1982). The pitch set as a level of description for studying musical pitch perception. In M. Clynes (Ed.), *Music, mind, and brain*. New York: Plenum.

Bartlett, J. C., and Dowling, W. J. (1980). The recognition of transposed melodies: A key-distance effect in developmental perspective. *Journal of Experimental Psychology: Human Perception and Performance, 6,* 501–515.

Butler, D. (1990). A study of event hierarchies in tonal and post-tonal music. *Psychology of Music, 18*(1), 4–17.

Campbell, W., and Heller, J. (1978). The contribution of the legato transient to instrument identification. In E. Asmus (Ed.), *Proceedings of the Research Symposium on the Psychology and Aesthetics of Music* (pp. 30–44). Lawrence: University of Kansas.

Campbell, W., and Heller, J. (1979). Convergence procedures for investigating music listening tasks. *Bulletin of the Council for Research in Music Education, 59,* 18–23.

Campbell, W., and Heller J. (1980a). An orientation for considering models of musical behavior. In D. Hodges (Ed.), *Handbook of music psychology* (pp. 29–36). Lawrence: National Association for Music Therapy.

Campbell, W., and Heller, J. (1980b). Judgments of interpretation in string performance. In W. May (Ed.), *Research Symposium on the Psychology and Aesthetics of Music* (pp. 266–274). Lawrence: University of Kansas.

Campbell, W., and Heller, J. (1981). Psychomusicology and psycholinguistics: Parallel paths or separate ways. *Psychomusicology, 1*(2), 3–14.

Campbell, W., and Heller, J. (1988). Studying the communication process in music. In A. Kemp (Ed.), *Research in music education: A festschrift for Arnold Bentley.* London: International Society for Music Education.

Chase, W. G. (1978). Elementary information processes. In W. K. Estes (Ed.), *Handbook of learning and cognitive processes* (Vol. 5). Hillsdale: Lawrence Erlbaum Associates.

Croonen, W. L. M., and Kop, P. F. M. (1989). Tonality, tonal schema, and contour in delayed recognition of tone sequences. *Music Perception, 7*(1), 49–67.

Cross, I., Howell, P., and West, R. (1985). Structural relationships in the perception of musical pitch. In P. Howell, I. Cross, and R. West (Eds.), *Musical structure and cognition* (pp. 121–142). London: Academic Press.

Cuddy, L., Cohen, A. J., and Miller, J. (1979). Melody recognition: The experimental application of musical rules. *Canadian Journal of Psychology, 33,* 148–157.

DeCorso, T. (1976). The effect of changes in the sound level, frequency, and harmonic structure of clarinet performances on perception of musical interpretation. Unpublished doctoral dissertation, University of Connecticut, Storrs.

Deutsch, D. (1982). The processing of pitch combinations. In D. Deutsch (Ed.), *The psychology of music* (pp. 271–316). New York: Academic Press.

Deutsch, D., and Feroe, J. (1981). The internal representation of pitch sequences in tonal music. *Psychological Review, 88,* 503–522.

Dewar, K. M., Cuddy, L. L. and Mewhort, D. J. K. (1977). Recognition memory for single tones with and without context. *Journal of Experimental Psychology: Human Learning and Memory, 3,* 60–67.

Dowling, W. J. (1978). Scale and contour: Two components of a theory of memory for melodies. *Psychological Review, 85,* 341–354.

Dowling, W. J. (1982). Melodic information processing and its development. In D. Deutsch (Ed.), *The psychology of music perception* (pp. 413–429). New York: Academic Press.

Dowling, W. J., and Bartlett, J. C. (1981). The importance of interval information in long-term memory for melodies. *Psychomusicology, 1,* 30–49.

Dowling, W. J., and Harwood, D. L. (1986). *Music cognition.* Orlando: Academic Press.

Dowling, W. J., and Fujitani, D. S. (1971). Contour, interval, and pitch recognition in memory for melodies. *Journal of the Acoustical Society, 49,* 524–531.

Edworthy, J. (1985). Melodic contour and musical structure. In P. Howell, I. Cross, and R. West (Eds.), *Musical structure and cognition* (pp. 169–188). London: Academic Press.

Fechner, G. T. ([1860], 1966). *Elements of Psychophysics.* Ed. D. H. Howes and E. G. Boring, trans. H. E. Adler. New York: Holt, Rinehart and Winston.

Fiske, H. E. (1982a). Chronometric analysis of selected pattern discrimination tasks in music listening. *Psychology of Music, 10*(1), 37–47.

Fiske, H. E. (1982b). The application of stage reduction theory to music listening. *Psychology of Music,* Special Issue, 31–35.

Fiske, H. E. (1984). Music cognition: Serial process or parallel process. *Bulletin of the Council for Research in Music Education, 80,* 13–26.

Fiske, H. E. (1985). Cognition strategies in music listening. *Bulletin of the Council for Research in Music Education, 85,* 56–64.

Fiske, H. E. (1987). Cognition structure and the perception of music. *Bulletin of the Council for Research in Music Education, 91,* 31–37.

Fiske, H. E. (1989). Musical imagery. *Canadian Music Educator: Research Edition, 30*(1), 5–20.

Fiske, H. E. (1990). *Music and mind.* Lewiston: Edwin Mellen Press.

Fraisse, P. (1982). Rhythm and tempo. In D. Duetsch (Ed.), *The psychology of music* (pp. 149–180). New York: Academic Press.

Frances, R. (1958). *The perception of music.* Paris: J. Vrin.

Heller, J., and Campbell, W. (1976). Models of language and intellect in music research. In A. Motycka (Ed.), *Music education for tomorrow's society* (pp. 40–49). Jamestown: GAMT Music Press.

Heller, J., and Campbell, W. (1977). The relationship between the interpretive element in music and the acoustic microstructure. *Bulletin of the Council for Research in Music Education, 50,* 29–33.

Heller, J., and Campbell, W. (1982). Music communication and cognition. *Bulletin of the Council for Research in Music Education, 72,* 1–15.

Helmholtz, H. (1863/1954). *On the sensations of tone.* Translated from the 4th German edition of 1877 by A. Ellis. New York: Dover Publications. (Originally published in 1863)

Huron, D. (1990). Book review: *Music as cognition: The development of thought in sound,* by Mary Louise Serafine. *Psychology of Music, 18*(1), 99–103.

Kallman, H. J., and Massaro, D. W. (1979). Tone chroma is functional in melody recognition. *Perception and Psychophysics, 26,* 32–36.

Kendall, R. A. (1986). The role of acoustic signal partitions in listener categorization of musical phrases. *Music Perception 4*(2), 185–214.

Krumhansl, C. L. (1979). The psychological representation of musical pitch in a tonal context. *Cognitive Psychology, 11,* 346–374.

Krumhansl, C. L. (1990). *Cognitive foundations of musical pitch.* New York: Oxford University Press.

Kurau, P. (1977). The effect of acoustic modifications on perception of interpretation. Unpublished master's thesis, University of Connecticut, Storrs.

Lachman, R., Lachman, J., and Butterfield, E. (1979). *Cognitive psychology and information processing.* Hillsdale: Lawrence Erlbaum Associates.

Langer, S. (1942). *Philosophy in a new key.* Cambridge: Harvard University Press.

Lerdahl, F., and Jackendoff, R. (1983). *A generative theory of tonal music.* Cambridge: MIT Press.

Longuet-Higgins, H. C. (1976). The perception of melodies. *Nature. 263,* 646–653.

Meyer, L. (1956). *Emotion and meaning in music.* Chicago: The University of Chicago Press.

Moles, A. (1966). *Information theory and esthetic perception* (Trans. J. Cohen). Urbana: University of Illinois Press.

Posner, M. (1973). *Cognition: An introduction.* Glenview: Scott Foresman.

Seashore, C. E. (1938). *Psychology of music.* New York: McGraw-Hill.

Seashore, C. E. (1960). *Measures of musical talents.* New York: The Psychological Corporation.

Serafine, M. L. (1988). *Music as cognition.* New York: Columbia University Press.

Shepard, R. N. (1982). Structural representation of musical pitch. In D. Deutsch (Ed.), *The psychology of music.* New York: Academic Press, 344–390.

Simon, H. A., and Sumner, R. K. (1968). Pattern in music. In B. Kleinmuntz (Ed.), *Formal representation of human judgment.* New York: John Wiley.

Taylor, D. A. (1976). Stage analysis of reaction time. *Psychological Bulletin, 83,* 161–191.

Thomson, W. (1990). On Mary Louise Serafine's *Music and cognition: The development of thought in sound. Bulletin of the Council for Research in Music Education, 103,* 8–28.

Watkins, A. J., and M. C. Dyson. (1985). On the perceptual organization of tone sequences and melodies. In P. Howell, I. Cross, and R. West (Eds.), *Musical structure and cognition.* London: Academic Press, 71–119.

West, R., Howell, P. and Cross. I. (1985). Modeling perceived musical structure. In P. Howell, I. Cross, and R. West (Eds.), *Musical structure and cognition* (pp. 21–52). London: Academic Press.

·24·

DEVELOPMENTAL THEORIES
OF MUSIC LEARNING

David J. Hargreaves
UNIVERSITY OF LEICESTER

Marilyn P. Zimmerman
UNIVERSITY OF ILLINOIS

The potential scope of this chapter is enormous. A survey of developmental theories that might be able to explain empirical research findings on different aspects of music learning and a representative account of those research findings would each in itself be a major undertaking. In this chapter we will of necessity restrict ourselves to those developmental theories that have been specifically developed to explain music learning, and we shall do this by looking at some topical issues in theory building and research.

The current state of theories in developmental psychology as a whole is bewildering and diverse. The relatively clear division into Piagetian, reinforcement, Gestalt, and psychoanalytic theories that might have been made two or three decades ago is no longer adequate to characterize the current plethora of theoretical developments. Alongside derivatives of the earlier approaches, we currently find schema theory, social learning theory, information-processing theory, skill theory, ecological theory, ethological theory, and many more besides. Thomas (1985) and Miller (1989) are two recent textbooks that offer surveys of the field; although both are excellent books in their own ways, they vary quite markedly in their characterizations of the field as a whole.

Both Tunks (1980) and Hargreaves (1986) have carried out broad surveys of the application of different developmental theories to music teaching and learning, and we will not attempt to duplicate those efforts here. What we shall do is to identify three very promising theoretical developments, and to sketch out the general background against which these developments are taking place. They are Swanwick and Tillman's (1986) "spiral" theory of musical develop-

ment; Serafine's (1988) ambitious attempt to identify the generic cognitive processes that underlie musical thinking; and what might be called the "symbol system" approach, which is closely identified with the Harvard Project Zero group (e.g., Gardner, 1973; Davidson and Scripp, 1989). All of these theories are essentially different branches of the cognitive or cognitive-developmental approach, and we focus on them since no comparable developments are taking place within any other area of developmental theory as it applies to music.

In evaluating the relative effectiveness of these three theories, we need to bear certain ground rules in mind. How wide a range of musical phenomena does each theory attempt to explain, and at what level of precision? There are two issues to bear in mind here. First, if we use the term "development" in its widest sense (i.e., simply to refer to overall changes in the patterning of behavior that follow a regular and invariant sequence with age), we need to remember the distinction between changes that are a product of *enculturation* and those that are a product of *training*. The former occur spontaneously in a given culture, without any conscious effort or direction, and the latter are the result of self-conscious, directed efforts. In other words, we need to distinguish between the explanation of music *learning* and music *teaching* when evaluating the claims of different theories.

Second, we need to be clear about the particular modes of musical behavior that are under discussion. Do different theories deal more or less effectively with musical *production* (e.g., composition or improvisation), with *perception* (listening or appreciation), with *performance,* or with *representation* (e.g., in other art forms)? The vast majority of psychological research on musical development has dealt with the second of these, but a comprehensive theory presumably ought to be able to deal with them all. This begs the related question as to whether a given cognitive theory employs explanatory constructs (such as schemes, or processing strategies) that can operate across all of these modalities.

We shall return to these issues in the last section of the chapter. In the next section ("Cognitive Theories of Development: Emerging Issues") we sketch the immediate theoretical background to some current developments: This revolves around a discussion of the ways in which the early but still influential theories of Jean Piaget, Jerome Bruner, and Lev Vygotsky have been modified and adapted to the findings of more recent research. The theories of Keith Swanwick and June Tillman, Mary Louise Serafine, and the symbol system researchers are briefly expounded and evaluated in the next section ("Three Theories of Musical Development"). The penultimate section, "Cognitive Musical Development," contains an overview of the major research findings on musical concept formation; and in the concluding section, "Evaluation and Conclusions," the competing claims of the three theories are evaluated in terms of three critical questions.

COGNITIVE THEORIES OF DEVELOPMENT: EMERGING ISSUES

There can be little doubt that most of the major theoretical developments in developmental psychology in the last decade or two have been part of what might be called the "cognitive approach"; indeed this applies to psychology as a whole. Gardner (1987) speaks of the "cognitive revolution," and has provided a monumentally broad-ranging account of the history of this revolution. One effect of the proliferation of theories is that it has become increasingly difficult to apply the term "cognitive" or "cognitive-developmental" with any degree of precision: Many different approaches are subsumed under this umbrella.

As far as developmental psychology is concerned, one theory in particular has exerted a profound effect on current developments, and a review of its application to the problems of musical development appears in Hargreaves (1986). We might say, broadly speaking, that Piaget's theory has had three direct influences on the developmental psychology of music. The first is the idea that development proceeds according to a series of qualitatively different stages, which occur universally. This idea has had a profound influence on theory and practice in psychology and education, and it has led to specific proposals about artistic development. Swanwick and Tillman's (1986) theory of musical development, for example, while based on a spiral model rather than linear stages, nevertheless makes many assumptions in common with Piaget's theory. We shall return to this issue later. Similarly, Parsons's (1987) theory of aesthetic development

in the visual arts is a specifically Piagetian-style theory, in this case developed along the lines of Kohlberg's cognitive-developmental theory of moral development.

The other two direct influences of Piaget's theory have been in the explanation of symbolic development and in studies of music conservation. Piaget's account of the changes that take place in preschoolers' thinking is based on the development of what he calls the *symbolic function,* which manifests itself in areas such as language, drawings, and make-believe play. Swanwick and Tillman (1986) have drawn directly on this aspect of Piaget's theory, and the symbol system approach also owes a debt to Piaget in this respect.

Third, and most specifically, a considerable body of research has been carried out on what has become known as "music conservation." This field was pioneered by Zimmerman (see, e.g., Pflederer, 1964), and it is based on the application of the Piagetian concept of "conservation"—according to which young children gradually acquire the understanding that two properties of a concrete object can covary to produce an invariant third property—to music. Although there is some debate about the validity of the Piagetian analogy in music, the research evidence is nevertheless generally supportive of the theory, and we shall return to this later in the chapter.

Although Piaget's influence undoubtedly lives on in all of these areas, there are several issues on which subsequent researchers agree that the original theory needs modification and revision. These have been extensively reviewed elsewhere (e.g., Modgil, Modgil, and Brown, 1983), and we will do no more than to outline two major shifts of opinion here. The first is a move away from universal, context-free explanations of developmental change, which are exemplified by the stage model. Various critics have pointed out that the postulation of universal stages simply cannot account for the ways in which environmental objects and experiences actually *mold,* rather than merely reflect, thought (e.g., Bruner, Olver, and Greenfield, 1966). Similarly, several theorists (e.g., Brown and Desforges, 1979) have suggested that the functional coherence of the stages is much less evident than Piaget suggests: that the empirical evidence that stages consist of logically related sets of operations is unconvincing. As a result of both of these shifts of opinion, there is now a distinct move toward theories that are specific to given cultural settings, and to given domains of ability (see, for example, Hargreaves, 1989, for a discussion in the area of artistic development).

Like the theories of Noam Chomsky and Claude Levi-Strauss in linguistics and anthropology respectively, Piaget's theory is primarily structuralist: It is concerned with the explanation of structural regularities in thinking. Beilin (1987), in an extremely broad-ranging review of current trends in cognitive development, points out that many of the recent developments in what is becoming known as "cognitive science" share an emphasis on the identification of regularities in *function* rather than in structure. Information-processing theorists, for example, and those who use other varieties of computational analogy to describe thinking (e.g., Klahr,

1984; Siegler, 1983) are concerned with establishing universals in cognitive function, and this is an area in which different theories are proliferating.

One such growing body of theory has attempted to *combine* developments in functionalist thought with structuralist aspects of Piagetian theory. Some theorists, who have become known as "neo-Piagetians," have attempted to synthesize information-processing concepts with certain aspects of Piagetian theory: Among the most prominent of these are Case (1985) and Fischer (1980). Case's theory, which is a development of Pascual-Leone's (1976) attempt to integrate the two approaches, postulates Piagetian-type stages that are based on different *executive control structures.* These are mental structures that represent the existing cognitive state of the child in relation to particular problem-solving situations. Case proposes four such stages: Thus *sensorimotor control structures* (0–1.5 years) link mental representations to physical movements; *relational control structures* (1.5–5 years) deal with the coordination of relationships among objects and events; *dimensional control structures* (5–11 years) are akin to Piagetian concrete operations in that they concern the manipulation of dimensions in the physical world; and *abstract control structures* (11–18.5 years) allow for abstract or hypothetical operations.

A key feature of this model, which distinguishes it from the Piagetian approach, is that limits in processing capacity constrain the child's logical reasoning ability at any given level: In a sense, processing capacity determines the stage of reasoning, such that each of the stages can be attained to a greater or a lesser degree at any age. The model also implies that stage transitions occur at different ages in different domains, such that the overall character of developmental change is much more complex and diverse than is implied by the concept of universal stages. This insight, which overcomes some of the more intractable theoretical problems associated with the Piagetian stage model, is also incorporated into Fischer's (1980) "skill theory" of development, in which 10 cognitive levels are organized into stagelike tiers. Fischer proposes skills that are domain specific, and that gradually increase in complexity with age; as in Case's theory, it is possible for children to be at different cognitive levels in different domains.

We have spent some time on the ramifications and elaborations of Piaget's theory since the issues raised are at the center of current theoretical developments. Two other early theories should also be mentioned for similar reasons. Bruner (1973) offered an account of the early development of representational systems that is still helpful in contemporary theorizing. He pointed out that early representations, in infancy, are *enactive,* that is, based on motor actions: Action sequences define objects. These are gradually superseded by *iconic* representations, that is, those based on images and direct perceptions; and eventually, *symbolic* representations emerge, that is, in language systems, in which the symbols do not necessarily resemble that which they symbolize. This framework has been adopted by Davidson and Scripp (1989), for example, as a means of describing the early stages of musical thinking; we will return to this later.

The other early theory in which there has been a considerable revival of interest is that of Vygotsky (1978). Vygotsky's approach is very much in tune with recent developments in theories of learning and instruction (see, for example, Wood, 1988), and it challenges the predominant Piagetian view of development as a process of unfolding. "Unfolding" implies that since the child is self-motivated to learn and explore via the process of equilibration, the teacher's role is primarily to provide support for those initiatives that come from the child, that is, to be reactive rather than active. This view is gradually being replaced by one that emphasizes more active training, and Vygotsky's concept of the "zone of proximal development" provides a theoretical rationale. The zone is the discrepancy that exists between the child's performance on a task at any given point in time, and the child's *potential* level of performance given appropriate instruction. The capacity to learn from instruction is much more central to this explanation than in the "unfolding" view. Current studies of teaching and learning in the arts are beginning to move in this direction (see, for example, Hargreaves, Galton, and Robinson, 1989).

In this section we have tried to convey an impression of the changes that are currently taking place in cognitive theories of development so as to provide a background against which to judge the specific theories of musical development that are described next. To summarize, these are (1) a move away from the notion of universal developmental stages that characterize cognition as a whole, and toward greater diversity and domain specificity; (2) an emphasis on the search for universals in function rather than in structure, as exemplified by information-processing and other computational approaches; (3) a growing interest in the development of symbolic representation; and (4) a move away from the view of development as unfolding, and toward one that pays much more specific attention to the active role of the instructor.

THREE THEORIES OF MUSICAL DEVELOPMENT

Swanwick and Tillman's Spiral Model

Swanwick and Tillman's (1986) "spiral" model of musical development emerges from their analysis of some 745 compositions that were collected from 48 British schoolchildren from 3 to 9 years old over a period of several years. June Tillman was herself the class music teacher for many of the children, and she was able to collect the compositions within the framework of regular class music lessons. Ten different types of composition were collected altogether, which varied in complexity from playing rhythm patterns on a pair of maracas and a tambour, through to free improvisations of songs, and instrumental improvisations based on short phrases and sentences.

Swanwick and Tillman's analysis of a sample of their data suggested that there were distinct age-related trends in the nature of the compositions: Three judges' independent ratings of three items from each of seven children, ranging in age from 3 to 9, revealed that the composer's age could be judged fairly accurately. On this basis, Swanwick and Tillman propose a general model of musical development that is based on their detailed characterization of typical compositions at each of several broad age levels (see Figure 24-1). They claim support for this model from their account of Piaget's (1951) theory of play and from Ross's (1984) description of the process of aesthetic development, and draw on the work of Moog (1976a) and Bunting (1977). It also has obvious affinities with Bruner's (1966) spiral curriculum, and with some features of the Manhattanville Music Curriculum Project (Thomas, 1979).

In essence, Swanwick and Tillman's model has three main organizing principles. The first is based on an analogy between musical development and three aspects of children's play, namely, *mastery, imitation,* and *imaginative play.* Swanwick and Tillman suggest these follow a developmental sequence, such that the bottom loop of the spiral is concerned with mastery in that children are primarily dealing with the simple sensory response to and control of sound; the second loop is concerned with imitation, in which children attempt to represent or illustrate aspects of the world

about them by musical means; and the third is based on imaginative play, in which the child makes a creative musical contribution rather than merely imitating what already exists. (On a point of detail, it is not strictly accurate to claim Piaget's support for this proposed developmental sequence. As Swanwick and Tillman point out, Piaget saw imaginative and imitative play as representing different *poles* of behavior—assimilation and accommodation—and both of these are equally likely to occur at any age level. The proposal may nevertheless be applicable to the broad features of real-life musical behavior). Finally, Swanwick and Tillman add a fourth loop to the spiral, which they label "metacognition": This refers to children's increasing awareness of their own musical thinking and experience.

Swanwick and Tillman see their model as one in which the psychological concepts that describe the four levels—which could presumably be applied in other artistic domains—are specifically applied to musical phenomena. They do this by means of their second organizing principle, which is represented by the "boxed" descriptions at the back of each loop of the spiral. These refer to what the authors describe as the musical phenomena that are prominent at each of the levels, namely, *materials, expression, form,* and *value,* respectively.

The four levels, which are now described in two ways, are next subject to a third organizing principle: that there is a developmental shift away from the more individual, personal aspects of musical experience, and toward more schematized forms of "social sharing" on each level. This gives rise to eight distinct "developmental modes," which appear on the spiral, moving from left to right. On the bottom level of mastery, there is a gradual developmental shift from *sensory* to *manipulative* musical behavior: from purely exploratory reactions to sound and its production, toward those that show an increasing control of technique. On the second level of imitation, the move is from *personal expressiveness* to the *vernacular:* The child's initially spontaneous, uncoordinated statements of imitative expression gradually become more attuned to musical conventions such as short melodic and rhythmic sequences, organized into phrases.

On the third level of imaginative play, the move from left to right describes the shift from *speculative* to *idiomatic* composition. The former, which is based on a firm knowledge of vernacular conventions, involves a deliberate attempt to experiment with and to deviate from those conventions; and in the latter, comparable deviations are integrated into a coherent musical style. Finally, within the fourth level of metacognition, Swanwick and Tillman propose a shift from *symbolic* to *systematic* expression. The former involves a strong personal sense of self-awareness, which may be idiosyncratic and highly intense; and the latter incorporates a fullfledged knowledge of one's own awareness of the stylistic principles underlying the chosen musical idiom.

Swanwick and Tillman's model represents a bold and imaginative first attempt to make some sense and coherence out of the rapidly growing body of literature on musical development, and it clearly adopts a broadly cognitive approach. But precisely because this literature is still in its in-

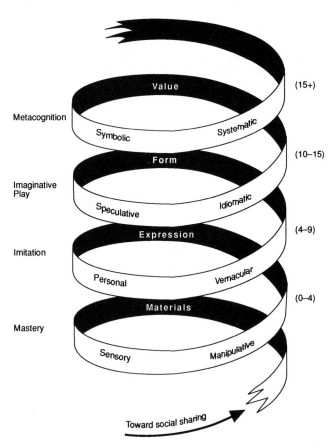

FIGURE 24-1. Swanwick and Tillman's (1986) "Spiral" Model of Musical Development.

fancy, any such model is likely to be overprescriptive. There are two general issues that arise from this dilemma.

The first concerns the relationship between the spiral and stage theories in general. Since the four levels of the spiral are age related, and since the first three are purportedly based on Piagetian theory, each loop is in effect something like a Piagetian stage. The model emerges a spiral rather than as a linear series of stages because the shift from personal to social responding is built into each of the stages. Two problems arise from this. First, as we saw earlier in the chapter, there are a numbers of reasons why universal, Piagetian-type stages have largely been superseded by more context-specific explanations.

The second, related, point concerns the relationship between Swanwick and Tillman's empirical data and their model. The eight developmental modes are primarily characterized by reference to specific examples of children's compositions; there is no specification of the cognitive or affective processes that underlie them as, for example, in the case of Piaget's logical groups and groupings. Although the authors base their proposals on the theoretical work of Piaget (1951), Ross (1984), Bunting (1977), and others, their empirical data collection essentially serves to describe or illustrate the model, rather than to provide a deductive test of it.

Given the importance of the relationship between the empirical data and the fairly elaborate detail of the model, Swanwick and Tillman's description of the analysis and categorization of their data cannot be said to be rigorous. We need to know more about the reliability of the coding scheme: Would independent judges consider a given set of children's compositions to be representative of the same developmental modes? One suspects that the rather high-order, abstract nature of the definitions of these modes might result in low levels of interobserver agreement—but this remains an open question, because no reliability data are presented.

What Swanwick and Tillman *do* present is an analysis of the distribution of the eight developmental modes by age: Broadly speaking, their coding of the compositions does indeed show that the higher-order developmental modes are attained by the older children. But again, this is not to say that the modes themselves are necessarily valid or reliable; further independent tests of the model are clearly necessary. In the meantime, Swanwick and Tillman's model stands as a very useful stimulus for further research and refinement.

Serafine's Theory

Serafine's radical view of "music as cognition" is set out in her book of that title, which was published in 1988, and some of the main strands of her argument were previewed in two previous publications (Serafine, 1983, 1986). In the book she sets out her detailed reconceptualization of the relationship between music and cognition, which has implications for the study of music theory and music history: She describes a new theory that is based on the postulation of a set of core cognitive processes that are present in musical composing, performing, and listening; she describes the development of a series of empirical tasks that are designed to tap the operation of these core processes; and she describes the administration of these tasks to a sample of 168 subjects varying in age from 5 years to adulthood, with a view to establishing a general profile for the acquisition of the core processes.

Serafine begins by making five strong theoretical claims. First, the critical interaction in musical communication is held to be between a person (composer, performer, or listener) and a piece of music; this implies that the communication *among* those persons is not a central issue. Second, music is held to arise from a set of core cognitive processes that are common to composing, performing, and listening, such that there is a direct correspondence between those events that occur "in the head," and those patterns of organization that can be identified "in the music." These processes, thirdly, are of two types, namely *style-specific* and *generic* processes. It is the latter, which are held to occur universally in all musical styles, that are central to Serafine's theory.

Fourthly, Serafine claims that cognition in music is an active, constructive process; and this leads to the question of the extent to which musical properties can be said to preexist in the pieces themselves, or whether they are primarily constructed by the listener. Serafine adopts a fairly strong form of the latter argument, which leads to the fifth claim, that "tones and chords cannot in any meaningful and especially psychological way be considered the elements of music" (p. 7). Rather, she sees these elements as the materials with which the composer works in order to produce sounds that are coded into cognitive units that are then recognized by the listener.

It is easy to see that this view is fundamentally at odds not only with the presumptions of a good deal of music theory, but also with many of the theoretical approaches that have been adopted by psychologists of music, and Serafine spends some time in characterizing these. The views of music as a trait (e.g., in psychometric testing of musical ability); as communication (e.g., in philosophical/aesthetic theories such as that of Meyer, 1967); as behavior (e.g., in behavioristic approaches to music education); as "nature" (as in music theories that postulate immutable "natural" properties of certain intervals or scales); and as sound stimulus (e.g., in psychophysical studies that are primarily concerned with the component parts of music) are all given short shrift on the grounds that they largely miss the point of what is distinctly musical about music. Serafine almost certainly overstates her case in her polemical dismissal of such vast areas of scholarship; but let us concentrate, for now, upon the positive proposals that her viewpoint generates.

Serafine proposes two basic types of general cognitive processes that are supposed to cut across all styles and idioms—temporal processes and nontemporal processes. Temporal processes are those that involve relationships among discrete musical events in time, and nontemporal processes are those that deal with the more general, formal properties of a given piece of music.

There are two distinct types of temporal process, which are based on *succession* and *simultaneity* (cf., in western music, counterpoint and harmony). In successive processes a series or chain of events is conceived in time, and further events are added to it; short chains are gradually built up into longer ones. Serafine proposes four basic types of successive process, namely, *idiomatic construction,* in which the coherence of a sequence of units depends on the organizational rules of a particular musical idiom; *motivic chaining,* in which the addition of one unit to another takes place "retroauditively," that is, with no prior knowledge of the previous units in the chain; *patterning,* in which units are chained repetitively; and *phrasing,* in which the focus is on the way in which boundaries occur between "chunks" of units, that is, on the larger-scale aspects of temporal organization.

In simultaneous temporal processes, the emphasis is on the vertical addition or superimposition of one sound event on another. Examples of this might be the combination of single tones into a chord, the synthesis of timbres, or the simultaneous perception of more than one melody or rhythmic pattern. The criterion for identifying simultaneous processes is whether or not those elements that occur together retain their separate identities, or whether they are perceived as a new, integral whole.

Serafine also proposes four types of nontemporal process that, as we said earlier, are concerned with the overall, formal properties of the musical material. They include *closure* (certain musical patterns imply movement, or a lack of stability, whereas others imply a resolution of that movement—e.g., the intervals of a seventh and an octave respectively); *transformation,* in which two related but nonidentical musical elements might be perceived either as similar or different; *abstraction,* in which some property of a musical event is abstracted from its original context and applied elsewhere; and *hierarchic levels,* which refers to the perception of the formal, "deep" structure of a given piece.

This necessarily brief overview of Serafine's proposed core cognitive processes is essential to the understanding of her account of musical development. She next describes a series of empirical tasks that are designed to operationalize and assess the operation of those processes. As an illustration, let us describe the "motivic chaining" task—which, as we can see from the foregoing, is a successive temporal process.

This task is intended to measure whether subjects understand that motive A, when combined with motive B, will yield phrase AB. In order to do this, Serafine presented the subjects first with motive A, then with motive B, then with a third, longer phrase, and asked them whether the third phrase was made up of the first two. On some trials the "correct" third phrase (AB) was presented, and on other "incorrect" trials either A or B was modified such that the third phrase was either AX or ZB. An example of one of the items appears in Figure 24–2. For the younger subjects, this task was couched in terms of a story involving three elves, represented by small plastic figures; two (A and B) were identical, whilst a third had different clothing, and was placed away from the other two. In the story A and B played some music, and the third elf was asked to play the music of A and B "all together." The experimenter pointed to each figure as the phrases were played, although the music in fact emerged from two adjacent loudspeakers. The subjects were asked whether or not the third elf had accurately played the music of the first two.

This is one example of the 16 such tasks that Serafine carried out with her subjects, who numbered 168 in all, that is, approximately 30 at each age level of 5, 6, 8, 10, and 11 years, and 15 adults. Subjects were also given a pitch discrimination task, a Piagetian number conservation task, and a human figure–drawing task as comparison measures, and there was an additional sample of 34 children 4 to 11 years old who had received intensive violin training under the Suzuki method, who completed three of the tasks. The results were primarily analyzed in terms of developmental trends in the ability to complete the tasks successfully.

In summary, Serafine found that most of the temporal and nontemporal processes had been acquired by the age of 10

FIGURE 24–2.   Serafine's (1988) "Motivic Chaining" Task.

or 11, with the exception of the ability to identify the number of simultaneous parts constituting a complex texture; This was not generally present until adulthood. In contrast, the youngest children in the sample (5- to 6-year-olds) displayed virtually none of the processes, although there were early signs of some emerging abilities. These included the ability to identify phrase boundaries, to recognize (but not identify) differences between textures, and to identify some transformations. The 8-year-olds possessed some but not all of the processes. They performed as well as the 10- and 11-year-olds on the perception of hierarchical levels in simple melodies, on the identification of simultaneous combinations of timbres, and on the discrimination of random melodies. The Suzuki-trained children performed at a comparable level to same-age children unless they had had very intensive, long-term training that was specifically relevant to certain tasks; in these cases, there was evidence of earlier acquisition of some of the generic processes.

Serafine has undoubtedly made an original and important contribution to the study of musical development, although some of her more sweeping claims must be evaluated with caution. Most important for the present chapter are the developmental implications of the research. Serafine's results clearly show that children of different ages, and adults, process music in qualitatively different ways, but as Huron (1990) points out, this raises fundamental difficulties for a theory that starts from the premise that "music" resides in cognitive constructions rather than in the notes themselves. If children and adults construct quite distinctive representations of the same piece, then presumably the essence, or unique identity, of the music must reside in those notes.

Serafine admits that she was surprised by this aspect of the results, since she had originally "considered it likely that children would at least have the same perception of *temporal events* in music as did adults" (pp. 91–92). However, the qualitatively different modes of processing that her results indicate, such as might be predicted by a Piagetian-type model, do not form an integral part of her theory. In this sense, we could say that Serafine's theory claims to deal with developmental processes, but does not put forward a specifically developmental account of age-related changes in music processing.

Serafine's work undoubtedly needs further refinement, as well as replication. Some of her experiments are lacking in rigor with respect to developmental memory controls, control of stimulus material, and subject sampling; and the fundamental distinction between temporal and nontemporal processes is somewhat artificial in that *all* music exists in time, and is therefore strictly speaking temporal. However, there can be no doubt that further work along these lines would be very worthwhile: Serafine has contributed an important new perspective on musical development.

The Symbol System Approach

The "symbol system approach" is probably better thought of as a body of research with a distinct set of theoretical assumptions than as an explicitly stated theory; but an early statement of some of these assumptions can be found in Gardner's (1973) book *The Arts and Human Development.* Hargreaves (1986) has outlined these elsewhere, and so we will do no more than to sketch the essentials here; we shall devote most of our attention to the symbol system research that has been carried out on musical development.

Gardner's theory centers on the acquisition and use of *symbols.* The symbols that are used in different domains, such as in mathematics, language, or music, are organized into different *systems.* These are either *denotational* or *expressive* to different degrees, and they vary in the precision of their correspondence with the real world. Thus numerical notation in mathematics is highly denotational, bearing a very precise relationship with external events, whereas abstract art is wholly expressive, having no clear external reference. Like Piaget before him, Gardner sees the acquisition of these symbol systems as "the major developmental event in the early years of childhood, one decisive for the evolution of the artistic process" (1973, p. 129). However, he diverges from Piaget in his view that artistic developments can be accounted for *within* symbol systems, such that there is no need to postulate general underlying structures such as logical groups and groupings; he also implies that the later concrete and formal operations proposed by Piaget are irrelevant to the arts.

Thus, in his early theoretical statement, Gardner proposed just two broad stages of aesthetic development: a "presymbolic period" in the first year of life, which is largely sensorimotor, and a "period of symbol use" from the ages of 2 to 7 years. More recently, Gardner has developed the idea that there may be certain psychological structures that can be discerned across different symbol systems, and that these may follow a developmental sequence: Wolf and Gardner (1981) suggest that children pass through a series of "waves of symbolisation." They propose, in brief, that "enactive representation" in infancy, that is, infants' ability to organize their actions into symbolic sequences, gives rise to a "mapping wave" of symbolization at around the age of 3 years, in which spatial relationships can be represented in media such as drawing or clay. This is followed by a third wave of "digital mapping" at around the age of 4, which involves an increase in precision—for example, in counting, or in singing pitch intervals—and by the age of 5 or 6 years, children become able to use cultural symbol systems such as musical notation or written language.

The substantial body of research on children's artistic development that has been carried out by the Project Zero group includes some important studies of musical development, including work on composition, song acquisition, and aesthetic appreciation. Davidson and Scripp (1989), for example, have put forward a cognitive-developmental model of music education that is rooted in the symbol system approach, and that draws on the work of Bruner (1973) as well as on Fischer's (1980) model of skill theory. Let us briefly describe one area of research that illustrates this approach: the study of children's graphic representations of music.

In this research, children are typically asked to represent

simple rhythms or tunes on paper in any way that seems appropriate to them (e.g., Bamberger 1982, 1986; Davidson and Scripp, 1988; Upitis, 1987). The early developments of such tasks can be described in terms of Bruner's (1973) representational modes, which we mentioned earlier. Thus, young children typically first use *enactive* means of representation: Their physical actions are mirrored in the drawings, which have been called "action equivalents." Although these actions were physically coordinated with the sounds at the time of drawing, the product itself bears no obvious resemblance to them. This is less true of *iconic* representations, in which icons or images are incorporated: These might include pictures, words, or abstract symbols. Eventually, children begin to invent their own abstract *symbol systems* to represent structural aspects of the music, such as melodic or rhythmic patterns.

Davidson and Scripp (1988) draw on skill theory to describe the subsequent developments in symbolic representation: for example, in the task of writing down a familiar song. An example from their research appears in Figure 24–3: It shows typical notations of the final phrase of "Row, Row, Row Your Boat" by children at the ages of approximately 5, 6, and 7 years. At the first of these age levels, when symbolic representations are just beginning to emerge, children typically record a single dimension of the song, usually its rhythmic pulse. Gradually, they become able to coordinate more than one dimension at a time, for example, the overall pulse as well as the rhythmic structure of the phrase. In skill theory terms, they are simultaneously representing two *relational dimensions* of rhythm. By the age of 7 or so, children can map two relational dimensions of rhythm as well as mapping the contour and pitches of the phrase: They show evidence of representing *relations of systems*.

One interesting aspect of the later development of these representations is the way in which they interact with formally taught staff notation. Bamberger (1982) has made the distinction between *figural* and *metric* representations: The former focus on the broad "chunking" of the stimulus, primarily its overall rhythmic grouping, and the latter on its precise metrical properties. Upitis (1987), like Bamberger, has suggested that formal training in music tends to be associated with the development of the latter type of strategy.

The interaction between development and training is also a key issue in other areas of musical development that have been studied from the symbol system perspective. In singing, for example, children's spontaneous songs inevitably become enmeshed with "standard" songs in the culture, and this must be taken into account in describing their development. Broadly speaking, the research of the Project Zero group (e.g., Davidson, McKernon, and Gardner, 1981; Davidson, 1985a) suggests that there is a gradual progression from the "topological" grasp of songs, in which the emphasis is on its outline properties, toward "digital" understanding, in which features such as pitch, intervals, and key stability are all recognizable, if not fully developed.

Some comparable findings, albeit in a quite different frame of reference, have emerged from studies of composition. Davidson and Welsh (1988) asked beginning and advanced conservatory students to compose a melody based on a rhythmic pattern from a Schubert melody; the melody was to begin in one key, modulate to a second, and return to the original. Analysis of the students' "talk aloud" protocols revealed two distinct modes of tonal thinking, the "enactive" and the "reflective." The beginning students worked enactively, sounding each note at the piano as it was considered; they worked in small units, without any overall awareness of the final shape of the melody that was emerging. The advanced students, on the other hand, worked reflectively in much larger units or "chunks," and were able to conceive these internally before sounding them enactively; they worked out an advance plan, and adapted this to the specific context as they worked through the task.

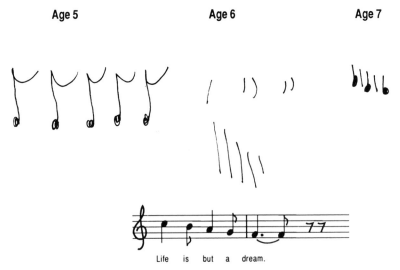

FIGURE 24–3. Children's Notations of the Final Phrase of "Row, Row, Row Your Boat."

As we said at the start of this section, the symbol system approach represents a broad perspective on a large body of research rather than a specifically formulated theory, and as such its distinct claims are more difficult to evaluate than those of the other two theories. However, two general points might be made in summary. The first is that this approach makes a very strong case for viewing developments in music, and indeed in any art form, from a general cognitive perspective. Davidson and Scripp (1989) make this point explicit in the case of music education: "Viewed from a psychological perspective, the symbol system is visible as the co-ordination of motor activities and reflective thinking in notation and performance. The symbol system becomes the transactional medium for physical co-ordination and musical ideas: from the notation to the fingerboard" (p. 84).

Second, this approach is specifically concerned with the process of development, as well as with the interface between development and education. The notion of general "waves of symbolization," while running into some difficulties with the domain-specific orientation of the approach, nevertheless makes some concrete predictions about age-related changes. Our brief review has also shown that the interaction between development (in the broad sense of "enculturation") and musical training is an integral part of the symbol system research, and practitioners must surely welcome this.

COGNITIVE MUSICAL DEVELOPMENT

Concepts and Schemata in Music

The strong interest in concept formation that began during the 1950s persisted into the next decades and is evident today in the emphasis of cognitive developmental psychology on mental structure, representation, and schema. All of these terms have been adopted and readapted from Piagetian theory. When the topic of how one learns is addressed, we are really considering how individuals build mental models of their surrounding worlds (including musical worlds) that will enable them to move, plan, and expand their knowledge and understanding. Various structural concepts form the framework for the musical model in our minds. The child's musical discoveries and improvisations fill in this structural framework. The musical content that fleshes out the framework is important. Conceptual knowledge is rich in relationships and forms a network that embraces and links single concepts into this structural framework.

During an infant's early mental development, perceptions and action patterns furnish both the raw materials and the tools for thinking. As in other areas of perceptual learning, there is increasing differentiation in the infant's responses to sound. Early aural discrimination learnings are to loudness, timbre, and pitch (see Zimmerman, 1982). In musical learning the interdependence of perception and concept is particularly evident. Perceptual learning does not abdicate to conceptual learning at some magical developmental moment.

Each influences the other as together they function in the musical experience. From our various perceptions of music we develop the musical concepts that permit us to make comparisons and discriminations, to organize sounds, to generalize, and, finally, to apply the emerging concepts to new musical situations.

Before we identify the major research findings on musical concept formation, an attempt will be made to link the terms "concept" and "schema" and to indicate their usage by various theorists. The term schema used by contemporary cognitive psychologists is not new; it can be found in Kant's *Critique of Pure Reason* (1781, 1958), where it referred to mental structures. Bartlett (1932) identified the schema as a psychological construct in his book *Remembering: A Study in Experimental and Social Psychology.*

Neisser (1976) uses the term "schemata," which he defines as "cognitive structures that prepare the perceiver to accept certain kinds of information rather than others" (p. 20). He further defines the schema as "that portion of the entire perceptual cycle which is internal to the perceiver, modifiable by experience, and somehow specific to what is being perceived" (p. 54). As the schema accommodates to new perceptions, so also does the individual. Perception is thus selective, and because this is so, individuals determine their own cognition. Schemas are cognitive structures that organize our perceptions and experiences. According to Mandler (1985), "A schema is a category of mental structures that stores and organizes past experiences and guides our subsequent perception and experience" (p. 36).

In Piagetian theory sensorimotor schemata play a major role in the process of adaptation. Mental images, that is, representations of sensorimotor imitations, are accommodated schema, around which new material can be assimilated (Piaget, 1951).

The development of cognitive representations through enactive play leads to preconceptual thought marked by transductive reasoning. Examples of this type of musical thinking are the figural representations and children's explanations identified by Bamberger (1982) and the first symbolic representations (Davidson and Scripp, 1988), which were mentioned earlier in this chapter. In Bamberger's work "coordinating schemas" eventually permit the child to coordinate tune, bells, and earlier figural strategies with a more formal approach to tune representation.

The mental image or concrete example in cognitive representation is a schema of a particular example of the general class of which it is a part. The concept functions at a higher cognitive level and applies to the general class. For example, a child can apply the concept of melody to "Happy Birthday to You" by producing its schematic representation. The schema thus functions at a more concrete level than the concept.

The material for the conceptual structure of music and/or musical schema resides within the elements of music. Concept formation involves labeling, categorizing, and organizing perceptions into meaningful concepts that will provide the key for later study and enjoyment of the complexities of music. Labeling is important since the label helps to clarify the concept. The ability to handle an increasing number of concepts is a fundamental fact of development. A developmental sequence pervades research findings in music concept formation, with concepts developing in the following order: volume, timbre, tempo, duration, pitch, and harmony.

The Development of Musical Concepts

Three federally funded research studies in the United States in the 1960s directed the attention of American music educators to cognitive musical development. Petzold (1966) examined the development of auditory perception in the areas of melodic perception, phrase learning, melodic reproduction with varying harmonies and timbres, and rhythmic ability. His hypothesis that age is a major factor in the development of auditory perception was supported, although with limitations. For most tasks, a plateau in auditory perception was reached by age 8 (third grade), and indications were that the most significant development occurs between ages 6 and 7 (first and second grades).

Andrews and Deihl (1967) designed a battery of musical concept measures to determine elementary school children's responses to the dimensions of pitch, duration, and loudness. The battery consisted of verbal, listening, manipulative, and movement tasks. Results indicated that the concept of loudness was most highly developed, followed by duration and pitch. The authors also concluded that a number of children possessed the concepts but not the vocabulary. Most often confused were the three words "high," "loud," and "fast," and the words "low," "soft," and "slow." Research findings continue to indicate a confusion of these terms (Hair, 1977; 1981; Flowers and Costa-Giomi, 1991).

A series of music conservation studies (Pflederer, 1963, 1964; Zimmerman and Sechrest, 1968) focused attention on children's underlying thought processes as they engaged in musical tasks and activities. These studies were the first to view musical development within the context of a Piagetian cognitive developmental framework. Pflederer (1967) proposed conservation laws in musical development analogous to Piaget's five conservation laws that lead to stability of operational thinking.

Zimmerman and Sechrest (1968) designed musical tasks consisting of tonal and rhythmic patterns and familiar songs with systematic variations of the patterns and songs for each of five experiments in which experimental settings were varied. Children 5, 7, 9, and 13 years old were tested, a total of 697 in all experiments. The findings indicated that (1) performance on the tasks was progressively better from the younger to the older age groups; (2) tonal conservation preceded conservation of rhythm patterns; (3) training to enhance conservation was most marked at the ages of 5 and 7 (according to one experiment); and (4) an ordering of difficulty of the variations emerged, with change of timbre and tempo and the addition of harmony being the easiest to conserve.

The descriptions of the music taken from the protocols were also of interest. These ranged from medium of performance to affective reactions to imagery suggestive of synesthesia. For children sounds have certain images as they try to read a meaning into purely auditory stimuli. For example, in variation of mode:

"The second one got tired" (age 7).
"Half a percent lower" (age 9).
"The sound is getting sorta warped" (age 13).

Since the Zimmerman and Sechrest studies, numerous research studies, articles, and dissertations have had their basis in Piagetian theory. Most of the research has been concerned with conservation and the age at which musical concepts develop. Although the results of these studies are mixed, they seem to indicate that at about age 9 qualitative changes in the child's thinking occur. Two articles (Ramsey, 1978; Serafine, 1980) summarized and critiqued Piagetian research in music, an indication of the interest in and importance of this body of research.

Webster and Zimmerman (1983) extended and replicated an experiment from the Zimmerman and Sechrest (1968) research. Rhythm and tonal conservation tests based on listening were presented to 317 children from second through sixth grades. Results indicated that differences in test scores existed between grade levels, with centers of greatest difference at grade 2, 4, and 6; grades 3 and 5 seemed to be transitory periods. In general, the rhythmic conservation tests were more difficult than those of tonal conservation. Conservation of pentatonic patterns with changing rhythms was more difficult than conservation of major or minor tonal patterns.

Crowther, Durkin, Shire, and Hargreaves (1985) replicated, extended, and modified the Piagetian model developed by Pflederer and Zimmerman. Findings indicated a significant age effect, with the greatest difference occurring between the 5- and 7-year-olds. They also found quite striking accounts at the anecdotal level indicating "that children attend to differences in musical stimuli in ways which take account of characteristics ranging from the cryptic . . . to the quantitative . . . to the figurative" (p. 35).

Rhythmic Development

The study of rhythmic abilities in children includes both perception and performance. Although tasks can be in either category, for a rhythm pattern to be performed, it must first be perceived and/or conceptualized. Rhythm discrimination tasks require perception of whether or not two or more patterns are the same or different. In a definitive study of rhythm, Thackray (1972) found improvements in rhythmic perception but not in performance when comparing 11-year-olds with 8- and 9-year-olds. Examination of general developmental theories reveals that motor development is progressive and age related, an indication that maturation is an important part of the process (see Zimmerman, 1986).

Rainbow and Owen (1979) reported on a 3-year investigation of rhythmic ability of preschool children. Tasks involving speech rhythms were the least difficult to perform. The second easiest tasks were keeping a steady beat with rhythm sticks and clapping a steady beat. Tasks that required large muscle movements were difficult. We shall see later that the words and rhythmic surface of a song are acquired first by young children.

There is some evidence to suggest a developmental sequence in rhythmic concepts from beat to rhythm pattern to meter. Jones (1976) reported that the meter concept seems to develop after age 9.5. Cox (1977) determined a similar developmental pattern. In a meter conservation study, Serafine (1975) concluded that by age 9 there is evidence of a final stage of meter conservation.

Melodic Processing

Melodic processing beginning in infancy is an intriguing research area that has provided new insights into early perceptual awareness and development. The research seems to indicate that the requisite structures for tonal and rhythmic perceptions are available to infants much earlier than our present educational practices indicate. The research evidence also points to the importance of melodic contour as a critical feature of melodies for infants and adults (Dowling and Fujitani, 1971). As Dowling (1988) reminds us, "Contour is one of the most obvious features of a melody to remain invariant across its instances" (pp. 115–116).

Chang and Trehub (1977a,b) determined that infants as young as 5 months can process melodic and rhythmic information. By monitoring changes in the infants' heart rates, they found that the infants discriminated between the transposition of a familiar melody and a new melody, and between two different rhythm patterns.

Trehub, Bull, and Thorpe (1984) examined more precise kinds of melodic transformations recognized by infants of 8 to 11 months. They employed conditioning of head turning to show that the infants were sensitive to changes in immediate repetitions of patterns of six pitches. The changes included key transposition; alteration of intervals within preserved contours; alteration of octaves from which individual notes were drawn with contour preserved; and octave changes within changes of contour. Their findings indicated that "infants treat new melodies or tone sequences as familiar if these sequences have the same melodic contour and frequency range as a previously heard sequence, and as novel if either the contour or range differs" (p. 829). These findings which suggest that infants use a global strategy to process melodic information, add to the evidence that melodic contour is an important feature in melodic perception from early infancy. This global processing strategy parallels that used by adults with atonal or unfamiliar tonal melodies (Dowling and Fujitani, 1971).

Trehub, Morrongiello, and Thorpe (1985) investigated the responses of children and adults to melodies involving contour and interval transformations. Two familiar melodies, "Twinkle, Twinkle Little Star" and "Happy Birthday to You," were subjected to contour and interval variations as established by Zimmerman and Sechrest (1968). Versions of the tunes with interval changes and those with contour changes were rejected by both the children and adults.

Song Acquisition

Moog (1976b) notes that in the development of singing, children begin with the words, then add the rhythm and finally the pitch. Davidson, McKernon, and Gardner (1981) studied spontaneous and learned songs in young children. Four phases in song acquisition were determined: overall topology, rhythmic surface, pitch contour, and key stability. The first three are similar to those identified by Moog.

Davidson (1985b) has proposed a developmental theory of tonal knowledge based on an analysis of the singing of learned and spontaneous songs by preschool children. They first grasped the words, followed by the song's rhythmic shape. This was followed by the contour and finally interval and pitch relationships. The pitches and intervals were not exact since young children lack a sense of tonality, that is, a stable tonal center. By age 6 or 7, children sing familiar and spontaneous songs with increasingly discrete and stable pitch reference (Werner, 1948; McKernon, 1979).

We have noted that contour is important in melodic processing. It is also important in song acquisition. Davidson (1985b) found strong "evidence of the power of contour as an organizing and processing strategy" (p. 31). Contour schemes that refer to specific tonal structures used by preschoolers in their learned and spontaneous songs carry the motion of the melody. They "frame" the interval or unit of melodic organization (the upper and lower boundaries of the melodic unit):

Throughout the development of tonal knowledge, there is a consistent pattern. Once a set of high and low boundaries has been established and integrated into a stable contour scheme, that scheme is used in relation with others to reflect more accurately the tonal material of a given song. (p. 38)

Davidson suggests that a child attempting to match voice modulations while singing is not engaged in pitch matching. Rather the child is "constructing a means of measuring what is initially an undefined and unarticulated vocal space" (p. 34) and becoming oriented to it.

It is interesting to note that in both melodic perception and melodic production, pitch information is stored in contour schemes. Contour schemes guide melodic perception by facilitating the immediate recognition of familiar melodies. And contour schemes guide the early acquisition of song.

Dowling (1982, 1984) has detailed the underlying cognitive processes children use in learning songs. He too found a sequence from an apprehension of the overall melodic contour to a precision in tonality and interval size. This sequence parallels his account of the development of melodic information processing in children.

By the age of 8, children's melodic perception operates

within an increasingly stable tonal system. Now melodic information is stored and processed according to a tonal reference rather than by contour schemes. As mentioned above, this developmental advance also occurs in singing. In both perception and production, children's musical development can be characterized "as progressing rapidly through parallel stages of increasingly systematic knowledge. This development is measured by the emergence of a stable tonal framework. This is in contrast to rote imitation of musical fragments or perception of isolated pitches" (Davidson and Scripp, 1988, p. 199).

Musical Representation

As we saw earlier in the chapter, another dimension in the musical development of children is the ability to represent symbolically what they have heard and sung. According to Krumhansl (1990), "Developing a sufficiently rich and precise representational system is a central problem for any domain" (p. 287).

In a longitudinal study of young children's music notation, Davidson and Scripp (1988) confirmed a sequence in the notation of pitch from units to melodic contour to intervallic boundaries to regulated pitch. This developmental sequence matches the sequences identified in melodic perception and melodic production. Again, a developmental advance or cognitive shift occurs between the ages of 5 and 7.

In their representations of rhythm, the children did not confirm Davidson and Scripp's predicted sequence or Bamberger's (1982) findings. These particular children attempted to represent the underlying pulse before the surface groupings of rhythmic units. (This finding seems to be consistent with earlier rhythmic studies that identified a sequence in rhythmic perception and performance from beat to rhythm pattern to meter.) Although rhythm was the initial focus of the children's representations, pitch emerged as the dominant and stable aspect of their representational development. Davidson and Scripp suggest that pitch is a "prime ingredient" and the most "robust component" of musical cognitive development.

All the research described in this section of the chapter, whether concerned with concept formation; conservation; or melodic and rhythmic perception, production, and/or representation indicates a developmental sequence in the cognitive skills involved. A developmental advance between the ages of 5 and 7 and a stabilizing of concepts around age 9 are also evident. Continued findings that point to definite music developmental advances corresponding to those in other domains place music cognition "more firmly within the framework of general cognitive development than originally thought" (Davidson and Scripp, 1988, p. 227).

EVALUATION AND CONCLUSIONS

In this chapter we have outlined the cognitive-developmental background to the three theories of musical development on which we have focused; we have taken a critical look at each theory; and we have sketched a broad picture of the research findings to which cognitive theories are addressed. In this final section we shall endeavor to draw all the strands together by considering how successfully each theory explains the research findings. We shall do this by asking three critical questions of each.

1. Does each theory deal with musical production, perception, performance, and representation?

In the last section we concluded that there were clear developmental patterns that could be identified in all of these musical modalities: Our analysis of the literature in terms of the notions of musical concepts and schemata implies that there are general cognitive structures that do indeed underlie processes in more than one of the modalities, if not in all. In the area of children's singing, for example, Dowling (1984) has speculated that it may eventually be possible to identify schemata that underlie both musical perception and production. Similarly, an important aspect of Wolf's (1989) proposal that there are three *stances* that people adopt in relation to artworks—the producer, the perceiver, and the reflective enquirer—is that the three stances function together in an integrated way.

Swanwick and Tillman's model is very clearly based on children's compositions, and the developmental spiral model is not specifically designed to explain activities in the other modalities. This is not to say that these authors do not consider the receptive aspects of artistic development to be important, of course, as Swanwick (1990) has recently made clear: He is very concerned that the dimension of aesthetic criticism should be an integral part of developmental theories of the arts. Nevertheless, the spiral model deals primarily with composition, and it does so in a manner that is relatively free from the constraints of conventional pedagogy.

The other two theories are less specific, and are accordingly able to deal more generally with the other modalities. Serafine deals very explicitly with three of the four modalities: Her proposed "core cognitive processes" are designed to underlie musical composing, performing, and listening. They are able to do so because they exist at a relatively high and abstract level; these are translated into actual musical activities in terms of a series of lower-level and specific empirical tasks. Similarly, the symbol system approach deals explicitly with all four modalities by formulating principles at a relatively high level of abstraction. Wolf's notion of artistic stances, mentioned above, is very characteristic of the explanatory constructs of the symbol system approach, and it has a great deal in common with Gardner's (1973) earlier proposal of three interacting systems in development: the making system, the perceiving system, and the feeling system.

2. Does each theory deal specifically with developmental progression?

It is clear from our summary of the research literature in the previous section that there are regular age-related patterns of musical development, and that these occur in all four modalities. Each of the three theories is integrally concerned with changes in children's musical thinking—but does each propose a specific explanation of the course of developmental change?

Of the three, Swanwick and Tillman's model is the most specifically developmental. The four phases of the spiral are explicitly linked to age, and the authors propose that these are grounded in Piagetian theory. Although they stop short of calling these developmental stages in the Piagetian sense, we have argued that they are in fact very similar in their conception.

The other two theories offer explanations that are less specifically developmental. Although Serafine is explicitly interested in age-related changes, and although her data collection is clearly designed to investigate these, her core cognitive processes do not specify developmental mechanisms. Rather, her account of musical development rests on the extent to which the different-aged subjects in her sample did or did not display their possession of the core processes; and this raises some conceptual problems for the theory, as we saw earlier in the chapter.

The symbol system approach falls somewhere in between the two in this respect. On the one hand, Gardner's (1973) earlier theoretical statement was strongly domain specific, and explicitly rejected the need for Piagetian-type stages in the artistic domain. Indeed Gardner proposed just two developmental phases: a "presymbolic period" of sensorimotor development, and a "period of symbol use," which follows. As the later Project Zero research shows, however, developmental regularities clearly can be identified, and these can be rooted in theories of the development of symbols. Wolf and Gardner's (1981) proposed "waves of symbolization" do indeed cut across different art forms, and this represents a partial retreat from full-blown domain specificity.

Perhaps the key question to be posed here is, Are there *stages* in musical development? It is fairly clear by now that the answer to this question is almost certainly no, if "stage" implies the generality and functional coherence of the Piagetian use of the term. But predictable age-related changes *do* exist, and all three of the theories illustrate this in different ways. It is perhaps more realistic to describe musical development in terms of typical modalities of behaviors, maybe designated as *phases,* rather than to speak in terms of monolithic, universal stages; and the neo-Piagetian models, which incorporate concepts from information-processing theory, seem to provide a promising way out of this dilemma.

3. Does each theory deal specifically with music?

The discussion above links this third question with the problem of the validity of developmental stages, since Piagetian stages involve general cognitive structures that influence children's activities across all areas of mental life. None of the three theories under discussion could be thought of as Piagetian in this respect. Although we have argued that the phases of Swanwick and Tillman's spiral are

akin to Piagetian stages, they are clearly not intended to be applicable outside the realm of music. Serafine's model is also very clearly specific to music, and even the symbol system theorists, who are interested in looking for generalities across art forms, would probably pledge their primary allegiance to domain specificity. In other words, all three theories offer specific accounts of development in music.

This specificity may go further in that each theory is essentially based on the analysis of western tonal music. The models of Serafine and the symbol system theorists are probably the most culturally specific in this respect; they rely to a considerable degree on western tonality, harmony, and staff notation, and the symbol system research on representation via notation shows this most clearly. Swanwick and Tillman, on the other hand, are concerned with capturing the essence of children's natural compositions as far as possible away from the influence of musical training. Their approach is less specifically rooted in pedagogical conventions, although their analysis of children's compositions is still carried out by means of tonal notation.

These two orientations are complementary, of course. To refer to a distinction that we made earlier, we might say that musical enculturation needs to be studied alongside musical training, and that the two may well be inseparable in practice. The effects of training and schooling on musical development are an essential part of that development.

This leaves us with something of a paradox in that the basis of the different cognitive approaches is to postulate *general* mechanisms that underlie musical development: The proposal of musical schemes and concepts is intended to work on a more abstract, general level. What will probably emerge is something of a compromise. Specific theories will continue to be developed in each art form: We will need explicit theories of the cognitive bases of musical development, of visual development, of literary development, and so on. But there can be little doubt that there are significant similarities between the cognitive bases of development in each art form. "Waves of symbolization" are one formulation, and the description of broad phases of artistic development is pursued elsewhere by Hargreaves and Galton (in press).

In conclusion, we might say that the similarities between these three theories outweigh the differences between them. They are all cognitive or cognitive-developmental in their orientation, but they operate on different levels of abstraction. Swanwick and Tillman's model is the most specifically developmental, and it deals primarily with composition. Serafine's theory challenges conventional views of the relationship between music and cognition, and it does so by investigating musical processing at a relatively high level of abstraction rather than by considering specific developmental processes. The symbol system approach manages to straddle both of these orientations, but its very flexibility belies its main weakness: It is a synthesis of concepts derived from other theories of symbolism, and from the results of empirical research, rather than an integral theory that proposes explicit mechanisms of development.

In the difficult field of artistic and aesthetic development, we need all the theories we can get. Our overriding impression at the end of this chapter, which has dealt with both theory and empirical research, is the need for a great deal less disjunction between the two. Although the Project Zero team has collected an impressive body of research evidence, this is still a drop in the ocean as compared with the wealth of research on children's mathematical or scientific thinking; and indeed the theories of Serafine and Swanwick and Tillman are based on single samples of data. We urgently need replications of these samples of data; but most important, in conclusion, is the need for research that is theory driven. It is only by testing, developing, and refining theories such as those discussed in this chapter that our understanding of children's music learning will make any real progress.

References

Andrews, F. M. and Deihl, N. C. (1967). *Development of a technique for identifying elementary school children's musical concepts.* Cooperative Research Project 5–0233, The Pennsylvania State University.

Bamberger, J. (1978). Intuitive and formal musical knowing: Parables of cognitive dissonance. In S. S. Madeja (Ed.), *The Arts, cognition and basic skills.* St. Louis: CEMREL.

Bamberger, J. (1982). Revisiting children's drawing of simple rhythms: A function for reflection-in-action. In S. Strauss (Ed.), *U-shaped behavioral growth.* New York: Academic Press.

Bamberger, J. (1986). Cognitive issues in the development of musically gifted children. In R. Sternberg and J. Davidson (Eds.), *Conceptions of giftedness.* Cambridge: Cambridge University Press.

Bartlett, F. C. (1932). *Remembering: A study in experimental and social psychology.* Cambridge: Cambridge University Press.

Beilin, H. (1987). Current trends in cognitive development research: Towards a new synthesis. In B. Inhelder, B. Caprona, and A. Cornu-Wells (Eds.), *Piaget today.* Hove: Lawrence Erlbaum.

Brown, G., and Desforges, C. (1979). *Piaget's theory: A psychological critique.* London: Routledge and Kegan Paul.

Bruner, J. S. (1966). *Toward a theory of instruction.* Cambridge: Harvard University Press.

Bruner, J. S. (1973). The growth of representational processes in childhood. In J. Anlin (Ed.), *Beyond the information given : Studies in the psychology of knowing.* New York: W. W. Norton.

Bruner, J. S., Olver, R. R. and Greenfield, P. M. (Eds.). (1966). *Studies in cognitive growth.* New York: John Wiley.

Bunting, R. (1977). *The common language of music.* Music in the secondary school curriculum working paper 6, Schools Council, York University.

Case, R. (1985). *Intellectual development: Birth to adulthood.* Orlando: Academic Press.

Chang, H., and Trehub, S. E. (1977a). Auditory processing of relational information by young infants. *Journal of Experimental Child Psychology, 24,* 324–333.

Chang, H., and Trehub, S. E. (1977b). Infants' perception of temporal grouping in auditory patterns. *Child Development, 48,* 1666–1670.

Cox, Sr. M. O. (1977). A descriptive analysis of the response to beat, meter and rhythm pattern by children, grades one to six. Unpublished doctoral dissertation, University of Wisconsin, Madison.

Crowther, R., Durkin, K., Shire, B., and Hargreaves, D. (1985). Influences on the development of children's conservation-type responses to music. *Bulletin of the Council for Research in Music Education, 85,* 26–37.

Davidson, L. (1985a). Tonal structures of children's early songs. *Music Perception, 2,* 361–374.

Davidson, L. (1985b). Tonal structure in the songs of preschool children. In J. Boswell (Ed.), *The young child and music: Contemporary principles in child development and music education.* Reston: Music Educators National Conference.

Davidson, L., McKernon, P., and Gardner, H. (1981). The acquisition of song. A developmental approach. In *Documentary report of the Ann Arbor symposium: Applications of psychology to the teaching and learning of music.* Reston: Music Educators National Conference.

Davidson, L., and Scripp, L. (1988). Young children's musical representations. Windows on music cognition. In J. A. Sloboda (Ed.), *Generative processes in music: The psychology of performance, improvisation, and composition.* Oxford: Clarendon Press.

Davidson, L., and Scripp, L. (1989). Education and development in music from a cognitive perspective. In D. J. Hargreaves (Ed.), *Children and the arts.* Milton Keynes: Open University Press.

Davidson, L., and Welsh, P. (1988). From collections to structure: The developmental path of tonal thinking. In J. Sloboda (Ed.), *Generative processes in music: The psychology of performance, improvision and composition.* Oxford: Clarendon Press.

Dowling, W. J. (1982). Melodic information processing and its development. In D. Deutsch (Ed.), *The psychology of music.* New York: Academic Press.

Dowling, W. J. (1984). Development of musical schemata in children's spontaneous singing. In W. R. Crozier and A. J. Chapman (Eds.), *Cognitive processes in the perception of art.* Amsterdam: Elsevier.

Dowling, W. J. (1988). Tonal structure and children's early learning of music. In J. A. Sloboda (Ed.), *Generative processes in music: The psychology of performance, improvisation, and composition.* Oxford: Clarendon Press.

Dowling, W. J., and Fujitani D. S. (1971). Contour, interval and pitch recognition in memory for melodies. *Journal of the Acoustical Society of America, 49,* 524–531.

Fischer, K. W. (1980). A theory of cognitive development: The control and construction of hierarchies of skills. *Psychological Review, 87,* 477–531.

Flowers, P. J., and Costa-Giomi, E. (1991). Verbal and nonverbal identification of pitch change in a familiar song by English and Spanish speaking preschool children. *Bulletin of the Council for Research in Music Education, 107,* 1–12.

Gardner, H. (1973). *The arts and human development.* New York: John Wiley.

Gardner, H. (1987). *The mind's new science: A history of the cognitive revolution.* New York: Basic Books.

Hair, H. I. (1977). Discrimination of tonal direction on verbal and nonverbal tasks by first grade children. *Journal of Research in Music Education, 25,* 197–210.

Hair, H. I. (1981). Verbal identification of music concepts. *Journal of Research in Music Education, 29,* 11–22.

Hargreaves, D. J. (1986). *The developmental psychology of music.* Cambridge: Cambridge University Press.

Hargreaves, D. J. (Ed.). (1989). *Children and the arts.* Milton Keynes: Open University Press.

Hargreaves, D. J., and Galton M. (in press). Aesthetic learning: Psychological theory and educational practice. In B. Reimer and R. A.

Smith (Eds.), *N.S.S.E. Yearbook on the Arts in Education*. Chicago: N.S.S.E.

Hargreaves, D. J., Galton M., and Robinson S. (1989). Developmental psychology and arts education. In D. J. Hargreaves (ed.), *Children and the arts*. Milton Keynes: Open University Press.

Huron, D. (1990). Review of *Music as cognition: The Development of thought in sound*, by M. L. Serafine. New York: Columbia University Press. *Psychology of Music, 18*, 99–103.

Jones, R. L. (1976). The development of the child's conception of meter in music. *Journal of Research in Music Education, 24*, 142–154.

Kant, I. (1958). *Critique of pure reason* (Trans. N. K. Smith). New York: Random House. (Original work published in 1781)

Klahr, D. (1984). Transition processes in quantitative development. In R. J. Sternberg (Ed.), *Mechanisms of cognitive development*. New York: W. H. Freeman.

Krumhansl, C. L. (1990). *Cognitive foundations of musical pitch*. Oxford Psychology Series No. 17. New York: Oxford University Press.

Mandler, G. (1985). *Cognitive psychology: An essay in cognitive science*. Hillsdale: Lawrence Erlbaum.

McKernon, P. (1979). The development of first songs in young children. *New Directions for Child Development, 3*, 43–58.

Meyer, L. B. (1967). *Music, the arts, and ideas*. Chicago: University of Chicago Press.

Miller, P. H. (1989). *Theories of developmental psychology* (2nd ed.). New York: W. H. Freeman.

Modgil, S., Modgil C., and Brown G. (Eds.). (1983). *Jean Piaget: An interdisciplinary critique*. London: Routledge and Kegan Paul.

Moog, H. (1976a). *The musical experience of the pre-school child* (Trans. C. Clarke). London: Schott.

Moog, H. (1976b). The development of musical experience in children of pre-school age. *Psychology of Music, 4*, 38–45.

Neisser, U. (1976). *Cognition and reality*. San Francisco: Freeman Press.

Parsons, M. J. (1987). *How we understand art*. Cambridge: Cambridge University Press.

Pascual-Leone, J. A. (1976). Metasubjective problems of cognitive construction: Forms of knowing and their psychological mechanisms. *Canadian Psychological Review, 17*, 110–125.

Petzold, R. (1966). *Auditory perception of musical sounds by children in the first six grades*. Cooperative Research Project 1051. The University of Wisconsin, Madison.

Pflederer, M. (1963). The responses of children to musical tasks embodying Piaget's principle of conservation. Unpublished doctoral dissertation, University of Illinois, Urbana.

Pflederer, M. (1964). The responses of children to musical tasks embodying Piaget's principle of conservation. *Journal of Research in Music Education, 12*, 251–268.

Pflederer, M. (1967). Conservation laws applied to the development of musical intelligence. *Journal of Research in Music Education, 15*, 215–223.

Piaget, J. (1951). *Play, dreams and imitation in childhood*. London: Routledge and Kegan Paul.

Rainbow, E. L., and Owen D. (1979). A progress report on a three year investigation of the rhythmic ability of pre-school aged children. *Bulletin of the Council for Research in Music Education, 59*, 84–86.

Ramsey, D. S. (1978). Piaget and music: A complementary relationship for music teachers. Pennsylvania Music Educators Association: *Bulletin of Research in Music Education, 9*, 12–21.

Ross, M. (Ed.). (1984). *The aesthetic impulse*. Oxford: Pergamon Press.

Serafine, M. L. (1975). A measure of meter conservation in music based on Piaget's theory. Unpublished doctoral dissertation, University of Florida, Tallahassee.

Serafine, M. L. (1980). Piagetian research in music. *Bulletin of the Council for Research in Music Education, 62*, 1–21.

Serafine, M. L. (1983). Cognition in music. *Cognition, 14*, 119–183.

Serafine, M. L. (1986). Music. In R. F. Dillon and R. J. Sternberg (Eds.), *Cognition and instruction*. New York: Academic Press.

Serafine, M. L. (1988). *Music as cognition: The development of thought in sound*. New York: Columbia University Press.

Siegler, R. S. (1983). Information processing approaches to development. In P. H. Mussen (Ed.), *Handbook of child psychology* (4th ed., Vol I). New York: John Wiley.

Swanwick, K., and Tillman, J. (1986). The sequence of musical development: A study of children's composition. *British Journal of Music Education, 3*, 305–339.

Swanwick, K. (1990). Review of *Children and the arts* (Ed. D. J. Hargreaves). Milton Keynes: Open University Press. *British Journal of Educational Psychology, 60*, 230–231.

Thackray, R. (1972). *Rhythmic abilities in children*. London: Novello.

Thomas, R. (1979). *MMCP Synthesis*. Bellingham: Americole.

Thomas, R. M. (1985). *Comparing theories of child development* (2nd ed.). Belmont: Wadsworth.

Trehub, S. E., Bull, D., and Thorpe, L. A. (1984) Infants' perception of melodies: The role of melodic contour. *Child Development, 55*, 821–830.

Trehub, S. E., Morrongiello B. A., and Thorpe L. A. (1985). Children's perception of familiar melodies: The role of intervals, contour and key. *Psychomusicology, 5*, 39–48.

Tunks, T. W. (1980). Applications of psychological positions on learning and development to musical behavior. In D. Hodges (Ed.), *Handbook of music psychology*. Lawrence: National Association for Music Therapy.

Upitis, R. (1987). Toward a model for rhythm development. In J. C. Peery, I. W. Peery, and T. W. Draper (Eds.), *Music and child development*. New York: Springer-Verlag.

Vygotsky, L. S. (1978). *Mind in society: The development of higher psychological processes*. Cambridge: Harvard University Press.

Webster, P. R., and Zimmerman M. P. (1983). Conservation of rhythmic and tonal patterns of second through sixth grade children. *Bulletin of the Council for Research in Music Education, 73*, 28–49.

Werner, H. (1948). *The comparative psychology of mental development*. New York: International Universities Press.

Wolf, D. P. (1989). Artistic learning as conversation. In D. J. Hargreaves (Ed.), *Children and the arts*. Milton Keynes: Open University Press.

Wolf, D. P., and Gardner H. (1981). On the structure of early symbolisation. In R. Schiefelbush and D. Bricker (Eds.), *Early language intervention*. Baltimore: University Park Press.

Wood, D. (1988). *How children think and learn*. Oxford: Basil Blackwell.

Zimmerman, M. P. (1982). Developmental processes in music learning. In R. Colwell (Ed.), *Symposium in music education: A festschrift for Charles Leonhard*. University of Illinois at Urbana-Champaign.

Zimmerman, M. P. (1986). Musical development in middle childhood: A summary of selected research studies. *Bulletin of the Council for Research in Music Education, 86*, 18–35.

Zimmerman, M. P., and Sechrest, L. (1968). *How children conceptually organize musical sounds*. Cooperative Research Project 5–0256. Northwestern University.

·25·

SURVEYING THE COORDINATES
OF COGNITIVE SKILLS IN MUSIC

Lyle Davidson and Larry Scripp

NEW ENGLAND CONSERVATORY OF MUSIC

A better understanding of the nature of cognitive skills in music is needed. Models from cognitive psychology outside of the domain of music have contributed toward understanding stages of intellectual growth (Piaget, and Inhelder, 1969; Fischer, 1980), the role of social interaction in cognitive development (Vygotsky, 1978), and the difference in how cognitive skills are used by the novice and the expert (Polanyi, 1962). Unfortunately, these models—as yet—carry little meaning for musicians. Psychologists' constructs of cognitive skills lie outside authentic musical practice. Conversely, musicians' descriptions of their practice are difficult for psychologists to interpret.

Psychologists of music have also taken a relatively narrow view of cognitive development. Studies of musical novices based on discrimination tasks of short melodic fragments present a far too limited view on which to base an understanding of music cognition. Interpretability is severely limited by the form of their responses (short answers, filled in blanks), with little or no reference to the symbol systems, performance skills, or critical thinking that musicians normally show in their work.

To attain a comprehensive view of cognitive skills in music, a more inclusive matrix is needed. The matrix should address the coordination of three distinct ways of musical knowing: *musical production* (e.g., compositional and performance skills), *perception* (e.g., discrimination and monitoring skills), and *reflection* (e.g., critical thinking skills and the capacity for reenvisioning work). To ensure musical validity, there is a need to investigate these ways of knowing in two basic conditions: *in performance* and *outside of performance*. By stressing the integration, coordination, and transformation of these ways, this matrix is linked to the "web of understandings" intrinsic to artistic development and practice. Finally, the matrix helps to interpret past research

and formulate future research in musical cognitive skills. Then research can be presented in a more comprehensive scope, rich profiles of developing capacities of young musicians built, and an integrative view of educational practice in music taken.

SITUATING COGNITIVE SKILLS
IN MUSICAL PRACTICE

Anthropology, linguistics, artificial intelligence, philosophy, and psychology have been gathered together under the umbrella "cognitive science" (Gardner, 1985). The impact of taking this broader perspective can be seen in two ways that have bearing on this chapter: (1) the concept of mind has expanded beyond verbal and mathematical knowledge to include several additional "intelligences," including music (Gardner, 1983), and (2) psychological research has extended beyond the laboratory toward a focus on thinking as it occurs in everyday contexts of use (Rogoff and Lave, 1984).

In the first case, the repertoire of skills that have cognitive value has expanded beyond language and numbers. The perceptual coding skills that support performance and other intellectual skills that integrate actions and perceptions become active areas of research. Problem solving, reading, learning strategy, and kinesthetic activities are each considered a cognitive skill worth investigating.

Second, the connection between thinking and the specific context in which thinking occurs becomes a critical factor in research. The context of thought has at least two meanings: the structure of individual domains of thought and the environment or situation within which the thinking occurs.

Increasingly, psychologists consider cognitive skills as intrinsically linked to the disciplines in which they are used (Carey, 1985a,b; Feldman, 1980), and suggest that the study of cognitive skills be conducted within the specific context of a "real world setting" (Newman, Griffin, and Cole, 1989; Rogoff, 1990). These two developments, the expanding concept of mind together with an increasing recognition of the importance of the setting in which the thinking mind works, have a profound effect on the study of cognition and music in general, and on the understanding of cognitive skills in particular.

In this chapter no attempt is made to define the nature of cognitive skills by way of imposing the architecture of current models of cognition outside of music (e.g., Anderson, 1982). Such models of cognitive processing are too distant from the language or the practice of music to be useful for research into cognitive skills in music. Instead, Wohlwill's (1973) suggestion that new efforts most fruitfully begin by offering descriptions of dimensions is followed—in this case, those of cognitive skills in music.

There are various ways to approach such a description. For example, we can borrow from the literature of psychology and nominate sensitivity to *temporal processes* (succession and simultaneity) and *nontemporal processes* (closure, transformation, abstraction, and hierarchical levels) as central measures of cognitive skills in music (Serafine, 1988). Or, we may draw from the intersection of psychology and instruction and nominate *declarative knowledge* (about a musical skill), *procedural knowledge* (of the steps needed to carry out such a skill), and *reflective-knowledge* (of how the skill could be approached differently) as appropriate candidates for categorizing levels of cognitive skills (Perkins 1989a; John Steiner 1985; Dillon and Sternberg, 1986). Another choice of terms can be culled from an educationally based approach to cognitive skills. Inductive and deductive reasoning, comprehension, remembering, study, transfer, problem solving, critical thinking, and creative thinking: these are all skills cited as important for academic performance (Phye, 1986). No doubt, this approach could bear on cognitive skills in music as well.

However, there are several pitfalls to avoid when translating these constructs individually into a paradigm of cognitive skills relevant to musicians. First, descriptions of cognitive skills based on laboratory experiments usually fail to account for the conditions of musical practice. An approach that ignores the context for musical action and thought does not spring out of musical practice and musical knowledge as they are used, says nothing about the use to which knowledge is put, or the role of the situation in which use occurs. Second, these approaches may fail to provide a structure for coordinating observations of cognitive skills into a systematic formulation of cognitive skills. For example, considering cognitive skills in music as temporal, nontemporal, declarative, procedural, and reflective relies on observing these processes and understanding their interrelation to musical practice. Considerable translation must take place before these constructs could have an effect in the workplace and in the arena of education. Finally, the "list approach" to cognitive skills, while useful in some ways, not only fails to differentiate among the contexts of use, but fails to provide a means for establishing the relative importance of individual skills. Although constructing a list of candidate cognitive skills may be useful as a starting place, it is limited by its seemingly arbitrary nature, and its essentially atheoretical stance. For example, problem solving may be a central cognitive skill, but problem solving can cover such a wide expanse of tasks, conditions, and objectives that it is difficult to know what might not be included under problem solving.

In sum, the dimensions for cognitive skills must be directly linked to the domain for reasons of interpretability and use. The dimensions of fundamental processes associated with artistic learning, development, and practice must be identified. This means identifying the nature and relationship of cognitive skills underlying musical production, perception, and reflection—prior to, within, and extending beyond the moment of musical performance.

MUSICAL UNDERSTANDING AS RELATIONAL THINKING

As musicians increasingly produce, perceive, and reflect on their work, new and richer *networks of understandings* are possible. From this view, to act and think like a musician involves an interleaving of cognitive skills that support a broader and deeper understanding of musical processes, works, and affect. David Perkins (1989), a cognitive psychologist who speaks about the unique nature of artistic understandings, comments: "In general one might say that [artistic] understanding is weblike. Understanding involves knowing how different things relate to one another in terms of such relations as symbol-experience, cause-effect, form-function, part-whole, symbol-interpretation, example-generality, and so on" (p. 114).

This view of musical thought as a "web of understanding" is not new. What may be novel for musicians is couching their understanding in terms of developing complex networks of cognitive skills. Consider Arthur Rubinstein's account of an important moment in his early life (Rubinstein, 1973). Although still a child at the time he auditioned for the great violinist, Joachim, he had developed considerable expertise in piano performance skills. Given the high level of skills this young pianist already possessed, what more would Joachim want to know about the precocious child? What recommendations would he make to support and ensure Rubinstein's future musical development?

The master violinist went beyond listening to Rubinstein's performance. He asked Rubinstein to name notes, repeat given notes after they were played, play back notes and melodies that were hummed, harmonize soprano lines, and transpose entire passages from one key to another. Concerned about the future development of the young pianist's ability, Joachim recommended that the child be taken to concerts of good vocal singing and that his sight-reading be improved. Soon the pianist was playing Mozart concertos at sight. Composition and improvisation lessons were taken to ensure that should he have a memory slip, the child could continue playing in the style and the form of the piece.

It is important to note that, as a renowned teacher, Joachim was concerned with far more than the child's performance facility. He was concerned with specific skills that extend beyond the normal lessons: composition, study of form, sight-reading, and the breadth and quality of the child's listening experience. His view of musical ability was obviously broad and one that extended beyond the local and immediate needs of the instrumentalist. He appeared to be concerned with uncovering and developing areas of musical skills, their transfer or reorganization across different contexts (performance, perception, and composition), and their integration into a network of relationships that reflect a coherent understanding of the interdependence of skills. He wanted Rubinstein to have internalized standards of coherence *and* to exhibit creativity in understanding with respect to the standards of contemporary practice within the domain.

Cognitive Skills and Musical Production

Multiple ways of musical thinking arise from the related stances about what music making is. The ability to play an instrument, write a sonata or fugue, or conduct an ensemble—all skills Rubinstein studied—rests on an array of technical skills that support the musical production. Although often thought of as lower-level skills, these must have a place in any description of cognitive skills related to musical practice.

The musician as interpreter, for example, relies on various levels of understanding both in and outside the moment of performance. In rehearsal, this reliance may involve considerable "deconstruction" and "reconstruction" of the score (Schon, 1987). Whether sorting out structural features from ornamental notes in the score, or using metaphor to help shape an interpretation, the performer constructs a sentient version of the composer's world. In addition, the performer's version of the music is continually informed through perception-in-action. As the interpretation unfolds in time, the musician monitors a wide array of musical dimensions at every juncture of the performance. In final production, the performer not only follows the score as a "procedural map," but also provides a distinctive reading of that map in real time—and often in interaction with other performing musicians.

Through interpretive performance, musical expression can be viewed as many versions of a single score, in much the same way that within one world many versions of reality exist, each the product of various systems of interpretation (Goodman, 1976, 1978). The interplay between interpretation and composition—mediated through notation—serves to sharpen the distinction between these two forms of "world making" in music. The score expresses one point of reference—a static set of procedures in fixed relation to one another—while performance brings a dynamic and temporal rendition of this reality into play.

In addition, skilled (interpretive) performance demands constant shifts of attention or awareness among various ways of musical thinking. Often, for example, there are moments in performance when "articulate" awareness of fingering or note decoding is subsidiary to other kinds of awareness, perhaps the feeling of a phrase or thinking about how to portray the rate of a ritardando. Substantial and immediate reorientation of the shifts is possible only if there is an easy exchange between the forms of knowledge.

It is not only simple reflexes that can apparently be controlled without the intervention of awareness. An accomplished pianist can play difficult music beautifully 'with his mind on something else', and need not be aware of the notes on the page, the sounds of his playing or the motions of his hands and fingers. . . . [However,] if he made a mistake, some sort of 'negative feedback' would no doubt shift him to awareness of what he was doing. (Dennett, 1969, p. 123)

Dennett's emphasis on the "thoughtfulness" implicit in kinesthetic activity is welcome. Musicians rehearse constantly and while a musician's rehearsal involves coordinating physical movements, psychologists typically consider such repetitive activity with only accuracy in mind. This limited focus obscures an important characteristic—that thinking infuses the physical acts of performance for a musician from the beginning. Thoughtful and intelligent performance is based on conscious adaptation of instruction, appropriation of gestures, and continual monitoring of actions and goals during practice.

The well regulated clock keeps good time and the well drilled circus seal performs its tricks flawlessly yet we do not call them 'intelligent'. . . . To be intelligent is not merely to satisfy criteria, but to apply them to regulate one's actions and not merely to be wellregulated. A person's performance is described as careful or skillful, if in his operations he is ready to detect and correct lapses, to repeat and improve upon successes, to profit from the examples of others and so forth. He applies criteria in performing critically, that is, in trying to get thing right. (Ryle, 1949, pp. 28–29)

In addition, a formulation of cognitive skills that does not take into account the perceptual acuity musical experts demonstrate in various musical contexts cannot begin to capture the scope or standards of the skills required of professionals working in the domain. Cognitive skills in music include sensitivity to the nature of the materials and the ability to make fine discriminations among them. Master musicians exhibit remarkable abilities to discriminate among pitches, durations, and aspects of nuance, including timbres, voices, harmonic progressions, and formal structures. For example, the range of musical situations in which discrimination of pitch occurs is important. Some skills are relatively simple, such as identifying a second tone as the same or different from the first one. Consideration of the issue of pitch discrimination as a cognitive skill becomes extremely complex when the conditions for discrimination approach the situation in which conductors work.

In sum, dimensions of cognitive skill must be linked to all levels of musical production, whether playing a tune, improvising, or composing a piece. For example, tuning to a note sounding on an instrument is relatively simple when compared to playing a melody with an intonation that supports the tonal relationships implicit in the key. In both cases matching a model and monitoring the result is important, but in the second case a wider range of responses or solutions may be considered. When the task is even more complex, as when one is composing or improvising a melody, the balance between novel and conventional "moves" is far less defined and resolved. Moving along this path of instances of musical production takes one from relatively rule-based activities toward the more novel choices reflecting realms of aesthetic awareness.

Reflecting Transformations During Musical Development

Although Rubinstein's account is a valuable window on the scope of cognitive skills in production and perception, the account of the conceptual transformations that accompanied his development is missed. With training, most musicians learn to reflect on the dynamic and relational aspects of their musical skills. As musical thinking rapidly becomes more relational, the need for reflective skills becomes increasingly critical for supporting reconceptualized productions. Reflections written during intensive musical training provide one way of opening windows into this process (Davidson, Scripp, and Fletcher, 1991; Scripp, in press). In this example, the student uses reflective thinking skills to approach the question of modulation in acappella singing in his journal. Commenting on the increasing role of internal aural references over time in relation to musical performance, he muses:

The temporality of the space is [also] complicated. Past, present and future must be almost simultaneously present. The tonic, whether sounding or not, must always be there. If its literal, external sound has passed, the mind keeps it in the space always in play. With modulation, the future must also be actively engaged. While changing keys, a new—future/past—memory tone arises. In very effective ways, then, what is in the mind is brought into consonance with what lies outside it. Imagined time and real time flow together, imagined sound and real sound are the same, the world within and that without are brought together. (Robinson, 1989, p. 8)

Finally, if artistic knowing involves constructing complex webs of understanding, one also needs to approach the quandary of knowing *when* full and complete musical understanding is reached. Taking a developmental stance, Perkins offers a narrative that serves to illuminate the provisional stages for acquiring full musical understanding:

If understanding is a matter of knowing and playing out a web of relations about something, then when do you understand it all? What is it to 'fully understand'? Plainly this is an endless quest. What is it to understand the sun? As a child, I learn the word that stands for the presence in the sky. I learn some effects of the sun—warm days, cold nights. Later, I learn some physics of the sun, the earth rotates around it, it's a big continuously exploding hydrogen bomb. I also learn of metaphoric and symbolic uses, 'Juliet is the sun' teaches me

by example about the sun as a well of resonant associations. Van Gogh's sunflowers bind joy to sun to flower to wilting and death. Thus the web grows. When we say we understand the sun or anything else, the most we could mean is that we understand some things about it adequately for certain purposes. (Perkins, 1989, p. 116)

Similarly, there may be no limits in building relational knowledge in music. For a first-year conservatory student, reflection on musical concepts that emerge from a sight-singing course reveals a growing web of understanding. Reading skills serve as a context for building a fully functioning coordination of musical knowledge. Again, our music learner, in his journal, ponders the relation of music notation to music making:

For better or worse, musical notation was the only means we had of acceding to the past prior to the invention of the phonograph (of course, things aren't this simple, as musical notation also allows access to a future—the performance of a piece as yet unheard). At any rate one must learn how to cope with musical notation. It would seem from this perspective that the purpose of solfege is precisely to teach individuals how to go behind or through visual symbols to aural and kinesthetic realms. All that is solid melts into air. Nothing is as it seems in musical notation. What is static black on white, dots more or less opaque aligned on rigid grids accompanied or surrounded by various hieroglyphs through solfege, is transformed into movement, rhythm, tone, music. (Robinson, 1990, n.p.)

Going beyond the reflective writings and anecdotes supporting Perkins's metaphor of the web of understanding we need to more precisely specify and survey the coordinates of the cognitive skills musicians develop. The following matrix represents an attempt to identify, situate and relate the dimensions of cognitive skills. This, in turn, will enable us to explore and interpret the intersection of dimensions crucial to the discussion of cognitive skills in music.

A MATRIX OF COGNITIVE SKILLS IN MUSIC

The cognitive skills matrix provides an important tool for a more comprehensive and integrative understanding of how musicians think (Figure 25–1). If multiple ways of knowing exist for the master practitioner, we must see these as essential components of music cognition rather than as a list of highly trained yet fundamentally isolated actions. Directing and redirecting focus across various representations of cognitive skills allows us to see many levels of processing involved in the array of skills supporting artistry. Based on the framework, artistic thinking is richly relational and, at the highest levels of development, integrated throughout its various guises in musical production, perception, and reflection.

The matrix is based on three categorically different *ways of knowing* that musicians exhibit in their work—during and beyond musical performance. Each captures a necessary and distinctly different set of cognitive skills. *Production* is the

Cognitive Skills Matrix
Ways of Knowing

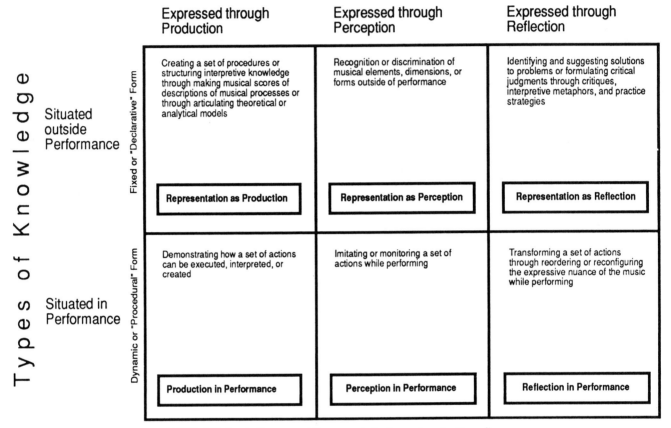

FIGURE 25–1. A Conceptual Framework for Surveying the Coordinates of Cognitive Skills in Music.

initial component. It encompasses a wide range of musical thinking, for example, as expressed in composition or interpretive performance. Without production there is no music. *Perception,* the second component, reflects the need for making discriminations and informed judgments. Perceptive thinking supports the translation and shaping of sounds physically present in live performance and silently heard from the musical score. Without perception music making is insensitive to its sensorial elements. Finally, *reflection* acknowledges the essential role of reenvisioning, reconceptualizing, and reworking a musical composition or an interpretative performance. Reflective thinking supports a wide range of musical transformations. Without reflective thinking, music making is limited to a narrow range of interpreting and understanding the processes behind artistic production.

A particularly crucial feature of the framework is the *cross-referencing of the three ways of knowing with two conditions of knowledge.* Exploring the difference between musical knowledge situated during performance and outside of

performance allows the distinction between two very different manifestations of musical production, perception, and reflection.

With *knowledge-in-performance,* for example, we see examples of how musical understanding is embedded in the action itself. Dynamic in nature, this type of knowledge is linked to a particular course of action that occurs in the context of performance. The musician knows the music as it unfolds in time. This knowledge takes three distinct forms: *action-procedural* (expressed in the action itself), *perception-in-action* (the result of monitoring the expression and notation during performance), and *reflection-in-performance* (as the performance is influenced by new events in the performance).

In the second case, *knowledge-beyond-performance* (outside of performance time) is the focus. Musical knowledge in this form occurs in more static or "declarative" representations such as musical notation and written or spoken statements. From the *production* point of view, composing musical scores involves creating the ideal set of procedures that the performing artist is obliged to interpret in performance. From a more *perceptual* view, musicians "declare" their knowledge of music through recognition or discrimination of musical elements such as pitch, rhythm, or form. Critical thinking outside of performance is essentially *reflective*. In this framework, new practice strategies or ideas for reinterpretation suggest evidence of *reflective understanding* of music independent from the performance.

These categories of cognitive skills that are necessary for describing the work of mature practicing musicians are each independent measures of cognitive skill development. Consequently, master musicians may exhibit strong indications of musical thinking on all these fronts, while less developed musicians may not. The disconnectedness of musical cognitive skills in immature, untrained, or relatively inexperienced musicians, therefore, should not be surprising given the current framework. For example, the abilities to perform from memory, imitate another's phrasing, and transform the style of playing in reaction to a conductor are not only independent forms of cognition-in-action, but may also be independent of any knowledge of this action outside of performance. The ability to create a score does not necessarily carry with it the skills needed to construct a cogent interpretation of the score in performance. Similarly, successful recognition of notes on a paper and pencil test may not predict, by itself, the ability to sight-read or compose music.

Children and adult beginners show similar origins and development of cognitive skills. The foundation from which we work is the issue: the various ways of knowing, the nature of our representations, and what we understand about what we see, hear, or do. To know more about the linkage of productions, perceptions, and reflections, we need to explore the source of musical actions and thoughts, and to follow their development as they interact with training. The predominant theoretical model of cognitive development is based on the work of Piaget.

THE COGNITIVE SKILL MATRIX FROM A PIAGETIAN POINT OF VIEW

For Piaget, thought emerges from actions. Placing the origins of thought in action has implications for the relationships among of production, perception, and reflections about what we do, and for the role played by perception and memory in our performance experience. What does Piaget say about the relationship of these ways of knowing? Ways of knowing, perception, and our memory play different roles in what we know. Furthermore, these roles can reflect different levels of development.

In one study, Piaget considered the asymmetrical relationship between actions, imitations, and descriptions, or in the language of cognitive skills (Sincoff and Sternberg, 1989), two types of procedural knowledge (actions and imitations) and declarative knowledge (the description). Children of dif-

ferent ages were asked to crawl on the floor, show how they did it using a small doll, and finally tell someone else how to do it. Although all children were able to crawl, only the oldest were able to both imitate crawling with the doll and describe how they did it (Piaget, 1976). The ability to use action knowledge (procedural knowledge) to correct or monitor other forms of knowing, including declarative knowledge and what is seen, does not develop all at once, but as separate "ways" in the stream of development. The three forms are strikingly independent.

Looking at the relationship of schema and physical actions, Piaget found an asymmetrical relation between a mental image, our understanding, and its physical accomplishment—again, action and image are independent for a surprisingly long time (Piaget, 1963). Piaget found that whereas children failed to draw sticks accurately while looking at them, they drew more accurate renditions *from memory* (not from physical experience) 6 months later. Their drawing appears to be based on what they understand, not what they see. Again, this points to the influence of understanding as the basis on which comparisons are made.

These studies also suggest that reorganization and integration more likely result from changes in mental representation than from increased ability to make faithful copies of objects—indeed, one could argue it is difficult to make copies at all without a sufficiently articulated internal representation in memory. It is striking that the ability to use what is seen and the ability to use what is known (represented in memory) are, at first, so independent. A most important factor in development is that memory becomes increasingly integrated with respect to these representations.

These studies carry important implications for musicians and the study of cognitive skills in music. First, this work challenges the idea that knowledge is "of a piece"—that is, that we can innocently infer what is known overall from the evidence obtained from one 'chunk' or type of behavior. Learning and knowing something in one way or representation does not automatically enable us to predict with certainty what it will look like through the window of another modality. The Project Zero longitudinal studies of childrens' singing, invented notations, and reflections in interviews show that similar results can be obtained in the domain of music (Davidson and Scripp, 1988d). Furthermore, evidence gathered from work with older subjects suggests that this finding holds for them as well, regardless of training (Davidson, Scripp, and Welsh, 1988). Second, Piaget's research shows that memory is not a passive faculty, a slate to be enscribed, but a continuously active process of construction. Similar studies in music reveal that memory actually shapes experience and that the outcomes reflect changes in understanding (Sloboda and Parker, 1985; Davidson and Torff, 1991). This suggests, then, that it is necessary to continually revisit what was learned in the past in order to maintain contact with what we know today.

The cognitive skills that support musical production and perception and the interpretative act are embodied in the explicit and tacit knowledge of the expert. This knowledge extends beyond the expert's individual skills. The standards of this knowledge encompass those of the culture, as well as the values expressed by experts. Because of the comprehensiveness of the expert's perspective and skills, it is necessary to base research and investigation squarely in the center of experts' practice as well as musical practice as it is defined by the culture through its educational and professional organizations. In this way, one can be assured that the findings are informed by the values and standards on which the best musical practice rests.

EXPLORING THE ORIGINS OF COGNITIVE SKILLS IN MUSIC

Whether observing a master class in vocal repertoire or a young child singing, we can look for common strands of cognitive skill development. On the one hand, we expect master musicians to excite us with their performances, demonstrate impressive perceptive skills when listening, or reflect with experienced ease about their work with others. Master musicians easily discuss issues of music and expressive interpretation of their own work and the work of others, using musical references, concepts, and metaphors (Blum, 1986). But those abilities do not spring up in full form without a period of apprenticeship. What at first passes for a perfectly stable performance by a student often disintegrates under cross examination. On the other hand, masterful performances are so compact and seamless that it is difficult to observe the subskills or components supporting a fluent production. By looking at the performances of children and the less musically developed, we can see some of the fissures that betray the presence of less integrated components of musical skills and knowing. But, if we assume that a full array of discrimination and reflective thinking skills are to some degree always present in mature artistic production, then this configuration of cognitive skills should also appear to some degree at relatively early levels of music making.

The song reproduced in Figure 25–2, performed by a typical 6-year-old student, provides a reference point for how an entire network of cognitive skills begins to surface in early childhood. Her production suggests a flattering story about a first-grader's musical competence in performance. What does this say about her cognitive skills development? On further probing, other stories might emerge based on measures of her perceptual or reflective understanding of the music. For example, when Janet is asked to make a notation about the song, she invents the notation shown in Figure 25–3. Reminiscent of Piaget's seriation task, she is able to represent melodic contour through her patterning of the notes of the song. However, during the course of her work more is learned about her perceptive and reflective knowledge of the song through dialogue:

Researcher: How do you know the song "Row, Row, Row Your Boat"?

Janet: We always sang this song to quiet my sister.

Researcher: So you know the song. Can you write down the song so that another kid who doesn't know how the song goes can read it?

Janet: Uh-huh. (sings to herself and makes slash marks on the paper at the same time)

Researcher: Can I hear you sing it from here (pointing to phrase 2)?

Janet: (sings the phrase "Row, row, row your boat" accurately)

Researcher: Can I hear it from here (pointing to phrases 4 and 5)?

Janet: (sings with confidence until she loses the tune and in the middle of phrase 5 stops and says) I can't do it. It's hard to sing from a different part.

Researcher: How about singing from here (pointing to the first phrase)?

Janet: Okay. (sings the introductory phrase accurately recovering the sense of the melody)

Researcher: Tell me, why do you use different shapes in your notation?

La La La La   La   Row, Row,   Row Your Boat   Gently Down The   Stream

Merrily Merrily   Merrily Merrily   Life Is But A Dream.

FIGURE 25–2. A Transcription of Janet's Song, "Row, Row, Row Your Boat."

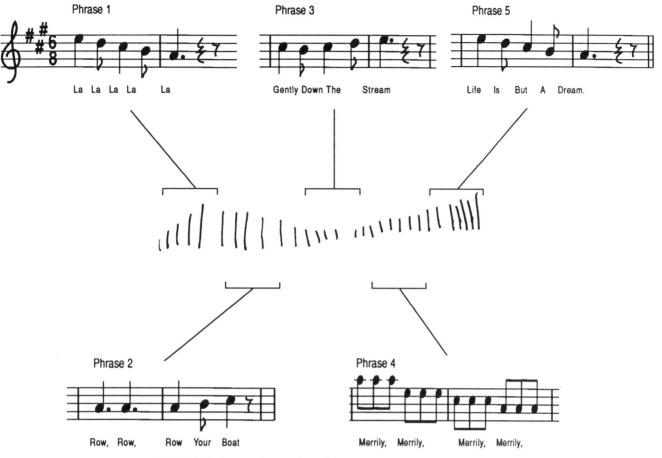

FIGURE 25–3. Janet's Notation of Song "Row, Row, Row Your Boat."

Janet: Because it started up higher (pointing to the small marks) and went lower and lower and lower (pointing to the gradually enlarged marks).

Researcher: How about trying again? Can I hear you sing the last part (pointing to phrase 5)?

Janet: No. I can't. It's hard to do without going from the beginning on. (She hums phrases 2 and 3 quietly, and sings loudly as she begins the fifth phrase. She sings it accurately, except she uses the syllable "la" instead of the canonical text.)

Researcher: Can I hear this part again (pointing to phrase 1)?

Janet: (She sings it and then announces) They're twins!

Researcher: What do you mean?

Janet: Those two are the same (pointing to the first and last phrases)

Researcher: Did you write them the same?

Janet: Nope.

Researcher: Why not?

Janet: At first, I didn't notice they were the same

Summarizing Janet's in-performance skills, she has a grasp of the elements required to render an acceptable version of the song. Her performance accurately represents the phrase structure of the song, the rhythms of the phrases, and the pitches within each phrase of the song (which she is also able to coordinate as she moves from one phrase to another). Furthermore, she can sing the melody of the song without the words and, with the help of her notations, can sing phrases of the song in various orders.

With the support provided by the structure of this experiment (Davidson and Scripp, 1988d), Janet is able to produce another version of the song as a depiction (not a performance) of how her voice goes when she sings the song. The notation she constructs is itself a production. In this representation of her musical knowledge, she invents a way to depict what she understands the song to be (or for the more cautious, which features of the song she considers important to show using pencil and paper). Put another way, what Janet considers to be focal in her understanding is revealed by what she includes and excludes in her notation. She discriminates among the high and low notes of the melody and invents ways of showing those perceptions. She also decides it is important to indicate the presence of phrases through her notation by leaving more space between the phrases than within the phrases.

Her ability to reflect on her knowledge of the song in its various forms is equally impressive, especially the relation between her performance and her notation. She can sing the phrases when they are pointed out in her notation. She is able to talk about the high and low pitches of the song. When asked about her notation, Janet is able to describe her system of notation, making explicit reference to the dimensions of the song, the way the long and short marks on the page reflect the pitches of the song.

Identifying specific structural relationships is more problematic for Janet. In the interview, she appears unaware of the melodic repetition that occurs in the introductory and the last phrases. As her comments show, she is apparently unable to simultaneously "hear" what she has done in performance and "read" what she has notated. Evidently, this relationship was not a focal object of attention during song singing and the making of notation. Only after being asked to decode phrases out of order is she able to "rediscover" the structural features of the melody (since one could argue she had already presented the relationship when she produced her notation). Only after given sufficiently guided opportunity to reconsider those two phrases from a new point of view is she able to extend the frontier of her knowing, to suddenly grasp the similarity of phrase relationship and capture that relationship in a succinct and revealing metaphor. "They're twins!" she exclaims.

What she knows about the song is, at last, in focus. We can now tell a far richer story about what Janet knows. Focusing our inquiry on her production, perception, and reflective thinking skills, we not only gain a fuller view of what she knows and a deeper understanding of the relation of different modes of representation, but we help her create and understand new relationships in the song she has sung many times. As shown in Figure 25–4, *production* involves various modes of representation (singing and inventing notations); *perception* provides a vehicle for feedback and the beginnings of reflection necessary to monitor the production: and the *reflective moment* provides opportunities for relating performance and perception and discovering new relationships. Through activity, discrimination, and thoughtful ob-

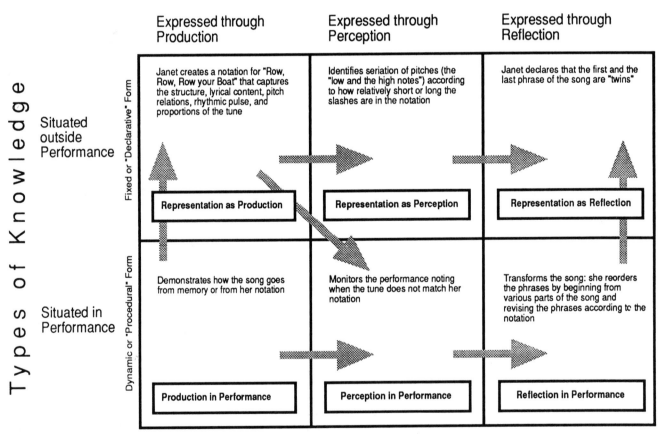

FIGURE 25–4. Profile of Cognitive Skills Janet Displays While Inventing a Notation for "Row, Row, Row Your Boat."

servation, multiple perspectives of the same event or object are generated, differentiated from one another, and during reconsideration, integrated into a new and more comprehensive understanding.

The cognitive skills framework provides a way to trace the flow of cognitive skills from one way or type of knowing to another in early childhood. Similarly, the framework becomes a useful tool for threading together various levels of cognitive skills that support musicians' work at various intermediary levels of development, and beyond, to support music making in later stages of musical training. We can see this by observing how master musicians employ these skills to teach, practice, and rehearse.

COGNITIVE SKILLS AND EDUCATION

How a musical novice develops musical skills and moves toward mastery is the business of education. But are music educators sufficiently focused on cognitive skill development? From the perspective of the framework, education in music implies a direct concern for development and the integration of six kinds of skills. A lack of comprehensive cognitive skill development raises the spectre of music educators graduating performers who can neither perceive, critique, nor revise their performances, or who may not be able to coordinate their skills sufficiently if their skills *do* exist, even in isolation. Although we assume that skills develop simultaneously with musical training, research suggests, unfortunately, that in most cases they do not.

For example, students talented and trained enough to begin conservatory training may be extremely adept at one kind of cognitive skill yet lacking in many of the others. Researchers report that when entering students in a major music school are asked to sing, write out, and discuss their notation of "Happy Birthday," radically unbalanced profiles of cognitive skills emerge (Davidson, Scripp, and Welsh, 1988, 1989). Clark, whose notation appears in Figure 25–5, is typical.

Unlike Janet's invented notation, Clark's notation uses standard notation. The familiar staff, clef, notes, and rhythmic symbols are there. A closer view, however, reveals some disturbing deficiencies. For example, he indicates the meter is in common time (4/4). The song should be in triple meter. The appropriate contour of the melody is indicated, but the exact distance between notes is not always correct. The third phrase has wrong notes—the leaps in the melody are notated as steps. The last phrase is not in the right key! Along with about 80 percent of the many students who took part in this study over a 5-year period, this student failed to accurately

notate this well-known song (Davidson, Scripp, and Welsh, 1988, 1989).

When asked to sing the song from his notation, Clark apparently disregards his notation and sings the canonical version without perceiving the difference between his notation and his sung performance. Indeed, he even points to his notation as he sings, as if proving the identity—yet still without noticing the difference. (Later, however, when his melody is played back to him on the piano, he is shocked, and at first doubts that his notation is being correctly played.) When pushed to describe the relation of the first and last notes of the song, he quickly explains that the song begins and ends on the same note. Essentially he does not link the different ways of knowing, using one to explain another. For Clark, performance, notation, and analytical questions about the music are all completely separate considerations.

Although Clark's vocal rendition of the song is accurate, his notation, music reading and comments are neither commensurate nor linked with his performance knowledge. His comments are puzzling. He states that songs begin and end in the same key, generalizing from a principle without realizing its inappropriateness and the lack of correspondence to this case. Although students like Clark have superior performance skills, their ability to show their knowledge of music in any other form is seriously impaired. Disconnected from one another, various ways of making representations showing his knowledge of the song only reveal a general lack of integrative knowledge about the song (Figure 25–6).

Comparing Clark's and Janet's work suggests that relatively simple musical tasks—writing down a very familiar tune—require a complete array of cognitive skills. For both of them, it appears that performance skills, if not guided by perception or representation through notation or reflective comments, convey only a portion of what they know. Differences between coordinations of these skills also suggest that Janet and Clark fall into distinctly different cognitive skill profiles. Although both show a knowledge of music via a competent performance of a song, they clearly differ in other forms of representation. Janet, for example, invents a notation while singing the song. As Piaget suggests, Janet's knowledge of the song stems from her kinesthetic actions, and her notation functions as a window into her understanding of the song (Davidson and Scripp, 1988d). Concepts about the song emerge from her actions. Clark, on the other hand, quickly abandons performance and perceptual knowledge in favor of concepts about songs in general (Davidson, Scripp, and Welsh, 1988, 1989). The assumption that simple tunes begin and end with the tonic guides his representation of the song. Conceptual knowledge, disconnected from his perceptual knowledge-in-action, guides his action (Figure 25–7). As Piaget might have it, a concrete operational level of

FIGURE 25–5. Clark's Notation of the Song, "Happy Birthday to You."

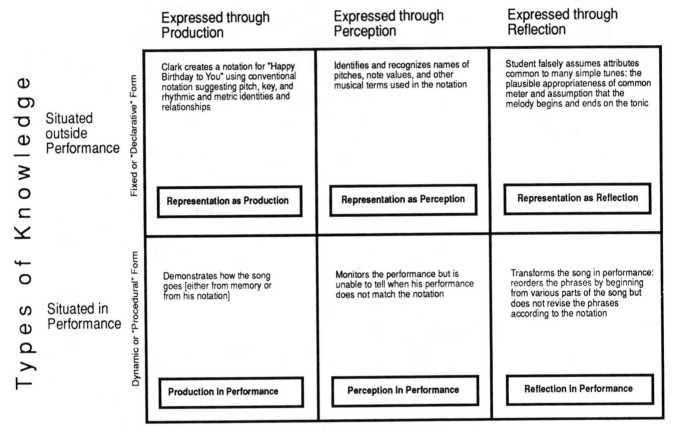

Ways of Knowing

Expressed through Production

Expressed through Perception

Expressed through Reflection

Types of Knowledge

Situated outside Performance

Fixed or "Declarative" Form

Clark creates a notation for "Happy Birthday to You" using conventional notation suggesting pitch, key, and rhythmic and metric identities and relationships

Representation as Production

Identifies and recognizes names of pitches, note values, and other musical terms used in the notation

Representation as Perception

Student falsely assumes attributes common to many simple tunes: the plausible appropriateness of common meter and assumption that the melody begins and ends on the tonic

Representation as Reflection

Situated in Performance

Dynamic or "Procedural" Form

Demonstrates how the song goes [either from memory or from his notation]

Production in Performance

Monitors the performance but is unable to tell when his performance does not match the notation

Perception in Performance

Transforms the song in performance: reorders the phrases by beginning from various parts of the song but does not revise the phrases according to the notation

Reflection in Performance

FIGURE 25–6. Profile of Cognitive Skills Clark Displays in the "Happy Birthday" Experiment.

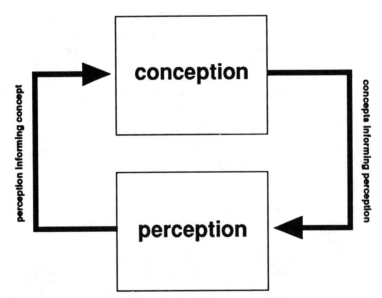

FIGURE 25–7. The Difference between Janet's and Clark's Orientation to Notation of Simple Songs.

understanding of conservation signals a phase in cognitive development where logical necessity may overrule conflicting sensorial evidence (Piaget and Inhelder, 1969).

This narrow interpretation of cognition implies that one type of knowledge governs or determines the limits of another, separate kind of knowledge. A broader interpretation is needed to explain what happens as Janet and Clark proceed with their notations. As opposed to Piaget, Neisser (1976) suggests their knowledge can be seen as more *mutually regulated* by "separate" ways of knowing the music. Janet's knowledge of music is embedded in her performance of the song, but some of her specific insights into particular dimensions of the song appear to come from another form of production—the notation. She produces her marks enactively—following the rhythm of the song—and uses her powers of discrimination to test her notation against "how the song should go." Her increasingly astute comments about differences in pitch appear to come from engaging in this "perceptual cycle." This continuous reexamination of musical knowledge from different points of view describes a wider net of awareness than is suggested by focusing only on the performance (Figure 25–8).

In addition, when different forms of knowledge are at odds, conflict between actions and concepts may stimulate further reconciliation. In Janet's case, she may make use of this cyclical process to decide to revise the notation in favor of the performance. In Clark's case, this process is begun when he is finally faced with the possibility of his notation not matching his performance and consideration of the tune's constituting an exception to his implicit concept of how a simple song is most often structured (in common time with the tonic at the beginning and the end). Although performance skill is an essential entry point, there appear to be several distinct and essential forms of knowledge necessary for a comprehensive view of musical knowl-

edge. From this view it is the reconciliation and mutual regulation of these forms of knowledge that form the hallmark of cognitive skills in musical development.

In other words, developing musical knowledge requires multiple views. The criteria for what constitutes a rich example of musical knowing emerges from the various stances and truths. Looking at a 6-year-old's singing, notating, pointing, and talking are required for a meaningful assessment of her music cognitive skills. The resulting profile suggests a network of relational knowledge essential to artistic thinking. Musical thinking during and beyond the performance is no better exemplified than in her exploration of the relationship between the tune, her performance, and her invented notational system. This interaction stimulated exciting discoveries about musical structure with a tune she knew "all my life."

To appreciate the "standards of coherence" of relational thinking in music we need only recall the misunderstandings exhibited by the entering conservatory student. In Perkins's terms, this student makes mistakes in coordinating the perceptual with the notational (Perkins, 1988). From the perspective of the framework, reflective knowing separate from the performance may support a view about the expected features in a simple tune, while it is necessary to use perception or reflection during performance to sort out a more contextually resonant set of supporting relationships. Relational knowledge is substantially facilitated by knowing where to look for a consensus. Significantly, when musical novices (adults with little or no formal musical training) or music students are asked to sing the last phrase of "Happy Birthday" and begin the tune immediately afterwards, they discover that the last note and the first note cannot be the same. This phenomenon suggests that musical understanding relies on the *linking* of a number of independent cognitive skills rather than the development of musical skills in isolation.

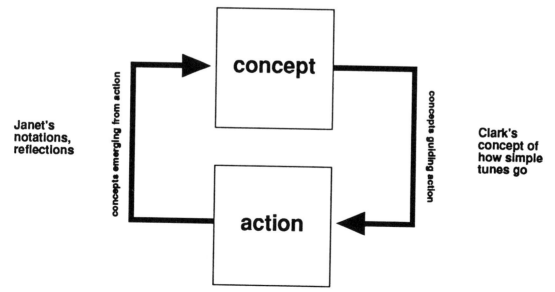

FIGURE 25–8. Perceptual Cycle Where Perception and Action are in Constant Interaction and Mutually Regulated.

COGNITIVE SKILLS AS TOOLS OF MASTERY

Another way to view cognitive skills in action is to see what tools musicians use to guide, organize, and support the thought processes inherent in musical performance. Looking across diverse musical cultures, musicians apply cognitive skills as tools for more efficient conception, discrimination, and refinement of skills as they approach the problem of mastering repertoire.

What are examples of "cognitive tools" for musicians in lessons, rehearsals, or master classes? *Modeling* and *metaphor* are two approaches to musical performance that feature very different, yet equally essential interplays of cognitive skills (Davidson, 1989; Davidson and Scripp, 1990). In both cases reflective thinking during and beyond the performance is used to enhance perceptual and performance skills.

In the case of *modeling*, the focus is directed to the teacher's performance (production-in-action). Through the process of imitating the model (perception-in-action), students work toward transforming musical understanding from their own point of view. Although information is experienced principally through wholesale imitation, the explicit and tacit exchange of information between the master musician and the apprentice is at the heart of this process. "The apprentice unconsciously picks up the rules of the art, including those which are not explicitly known to the master himself. These hidden rules can be assimilated only by a person who surrenders himself to that extent uncritically to the imitation of another" (Polanyi, 1962, p. 53).

Polanyi's analysis of skills suggests that in both playing an instrument and reflecting about performance, we explore the meaning and scope of both words and tools through imitative use. In doing so, we make them a part of ourselves. This construction is social in nature. It does not occur in isolation. The context is important; it becomes a "heuristic field" in which discoveries are possible. Imitation goes far beyond rote matching of physical gestures and techniques. In the music lesson imitation functions as a tool for building perceptive and reflective thinking into musical practice.

Throughout the dialogue of a Yang Ch'in (similar to a hammered dulcimer) lesson, for example, learning begins with the student's ability to imitate new ways of performing:

The student plays through a piece in its entirety. The remainder of the lesson is then devoted to issues which the student brings up in [relation to] that first performance. The structure of the dialogue is clear. Throughout the lesson, the teacher would show what he wanted by playing the passage in question. He would then ask the student to show what she understood from his instruction by playing the same passage back to him. (Davidson, 1989, p. 89)

Here the student grasps new ideas through listening and watching the master play. The dialogue is carried out through modeling: presenting an initial aural or perhaps physical image that can be grasped only through imitation. The student has to select relevant dimensions from her teacher's performance of the piece. In doing so, she reveals her understanding of the structural and expressive aspects, as

well as her understanding of the degree to which the notation must be supplemented by nuance. For example, the teacher demonstrates the physical technique on the instrument (in the language of the domain), drawing attention explicitly to specific issues. Whereas the beginner can match only a portion of the master's grace by following the general dynamic shape of his physical motions, the more advanced student is able to take in additional features of the performance, taking in more of the shape, nuance, and purpose of the demonstration. Thus, what the student takes from the modeling can function as an index of her level of development.

Modeling becomes increasingly the basis for reflection as the student revises her work on the basis of her understanding of the model presented. Selecting the most important features of the demonstration, the student is challenged to invent ways to control, exaggerate, and expand on external or internalized actions in order to grasp the model. Understood in this way, modeling functions as a tool for comparing versions of the work, creating new versions, and evolving a repertoire of concepts that then may be applied across diverse contexts.

Thinking of the interplay of the teacher, student, and curriculum in this light underscores the special relationship within which cognitive skills develop in music lessons, performance studios, and classes. The teacher and the student are constantly engaged in a social exchange in which each acts, interprets, questions, and grows. The teacher acts from explicit knowledge of the field as well as with considerable tacit knowledge. The student invents, adapts, and actively assimilates or appropriates new information by making some activity the focus of attention. In this context, the tacit components of the teaching are assimilated from within the focal task. A student's unconscious imitation of a revered teacher's mannerisms illustrates both the power and the range of the tacit component of learning (Figure 25–9).

Throughout the exchange, the teacher and student influence one another in ways not suggested by the concept of the student's mind as an empty vessel. The instruction, modeling, criticism, and feedback are based on a close, interactive working process that lies at the core of the educational transaction. This is the context in which tools of inquiry are formed, explored, and adapted. Rejecting the superordinate or exclusive role of any single kind or condition of cognitive skill, musicians avail themselves of purposeful integrative use of tools such as physical imitation to support and develop richer levels of explicit and tacit musical understanding through the coordination of a larger set of cognitive skills.

Modeling as Guide to Interpretation

Modeling demonstrates how musicians work and think, but it can also provide occasions for generative work of the highest order. Imitation may prove to be a tool for skills in ways the student may not grasp at first. Citing his experience with Pablo Casals, Bernard Greenhouse reports painstakingly replicating Casals's idiosyncratic fingerings and bowings for a Bach suite. Only after performing the piece pre-

Ways of Knowing

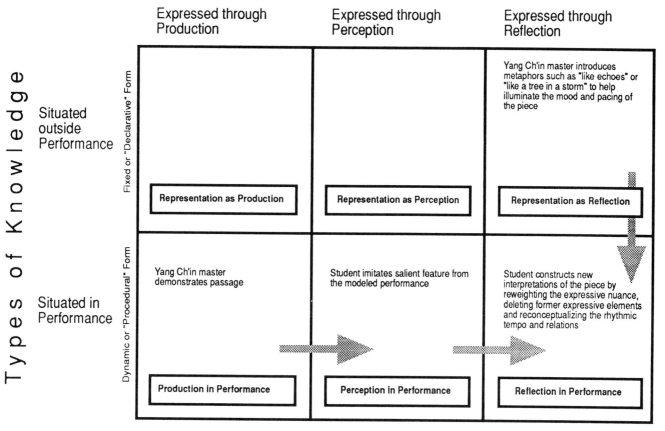

FIGURE 25–9. Profile of Cognitive Skills Demonstration by the Use of Metaphor and Modeling in a Yang Ch'in Lesson.

cisely in the manner of Casals did he realize that Casals intended the model to function as a point of departure for Greenhouse's own personal interpretive "improvisation."

He was extremely meticulous about my following all the details of his performance. And after several weeks of working on that one suite of Bach's, finally, the two of us could sit down and perform and play all the same fingerings and bowings and all of the phrasings alike. . . . And at that point, when I had been able to accomplish this . . . he played through the piece and changed every bowing and every fingering and every phrasing and all the emphasis within the phrase. I sat there, absolutely with my mouth open, listening to a performance which was heavenly, absolutely beautiful. And when he finished he turned to me with a broad grin on his face, and he said, 'Now you've learned how to improvise in Bach. From now on you study Bach this way.' (Delbanco, 1985, pp. 50–51)

Greenhouse's encounter with Casals produces a particular pattern of cognitive skills in interaction. Beginning with Casals's initial performance demonstrations, Greenhouse imitates (perception-in-reaction). What makes this interaction successful is Greenhouse's ability to imitate reflectively, that is, to select the salient aspects of the demonstration. Casals, we assume, repeats the demonstration as necessary while

continuing to articulate a particular interpretive version of the score. It is easy to imagine Casals making additional use of declarative statements outside of or interjected during performance focusing on how this is to be achieved. Casals later uses a new version of the piece to force Greenhouse to reflect on the purpose of the initial demonstrations. Finally, after a metaphoric statement, "You've learned to improvise in Bach," Greenhouse is asked to invent a new interpretation of his own (Figure 25–10).

Metaphor as Guide to Interpretation

While the teacher often uses modeling to focus and control one central aspect of learning music—the physical control of the instrument—various forms of *metaphors* are used to focus and control the affective qualities that enhance the expression of the music. Here, a new set of cognitive skills is called into play in important ways that support reflective discourse: Some comments may correct and address specific issues, others act as a catalyst to spark new insights or stimulate further exploration, still others serve to spur greater effort. Metaphors in particular function as cognitive tools for

Ways of Knowing

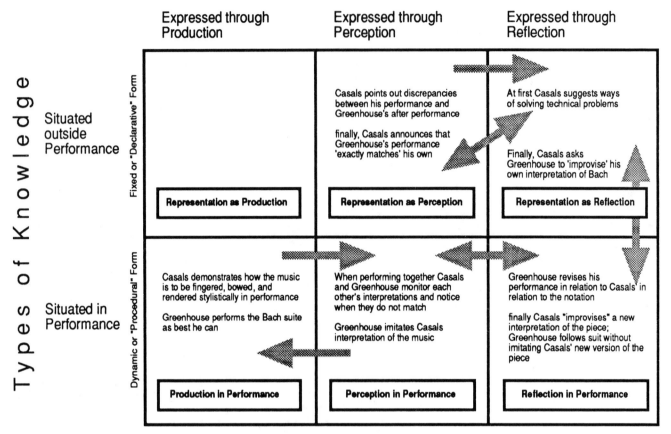

FIGURE 25–10. Profile of Cognitive Skills at Work in Greenhouse's Encounter with Casals's Teaching.

imaginative and purposeful recourse to ideas concerning expressive nuance or interpretive revision.

Revisiting the Yang Ch'in lesson described earlier, we find many examples of metaphor that support reflective thinking skills. Take, for example, the use of the metaphor of echoes as a way of approaching the issue of dynamic contrasts in performance (Davidson, 1989). The teacher in one case mentions "echoes" while demonstrating dynamic contrasts in the music. For him, the atmosphere of echoes evokes the setting for the piece, defines the character of the music, and as a whole provides the context for ensuing sections of the piece. However, the metaphor does not function unilaterally. Carrying through with a metaphor means selecting a "thinking frame" that is dynamic in its relation to the whole as well as the parts (Perkins, 1987). If, for example, the teacher is not satisfied with the student's grasp of the broad metaphor in relation to a particular section of the piece, more specification may be necessary. By describing a scene, "This is the quiet of the early morning," the metaphor is particular to the opening, yet may still work with the broader context of the piece.

Also, metaphors need to be pitted against alternative metaphors for clarification. Here the presentation of declarative

knowledge is the focus. Asking the student to provide a quality of "feeling inside" asks for a provocatively reflective stance. Rather than more static qualities of restraint or calm, the phrase "feeling inside" evokes a quality of gesture and timbre that supports a particular set of otherwise elusive expressive nuances.

The use of metaphors is as likely to be used in a master piano class of Western classical music as in the Yang Ch'in lesson. Commenting on a performance of a student during a master class, the teacher (a world class pianist) sorts through a series of metaphors to describe an interpretive approach to the piece:

My main criticism, it is, . . . I find it a little too gentle . . . too gentle, believe it or not, for this piece (Schubert op 15, 'The Wanderer'). . . . You are making it a little too unified. The same between loud and soft. It can be, you know, this piece, a sort of expression of despair. (Schon, 1987, pp. 183–184)

Centering on the affective state of despair, the master pianist launches into a set of descriptions and demonstrations conveying a regulating device for maintaining an integrated interpretation: "It's not terribly beautiful what I did, not terribly beautiful, but I don't think it has to be. You make it sort of triumphant (plays a little, 'triumphantly') it isn't triumphant. It's desperate, you know" (Schon 1987, p. 186).

Working within various polarities of performance characteristics, the master teacher introduces a higher level of differentiation—triumph versus despair, for example—through metaphor. Metaphor must be regulated by other, more technical concerns. This regulation can be further demonstrated by imitation or perhaps parody. It need not be "beautiful" in sound, but it must be "balanced" in its phrasing. Direction as to how this can be achieved technically is appropriate.

Deciphering the score, controlling the physical means of expression, and constructing an interpretation all point to an impressive combination of skills that may be integrated with considerable insight and practice. The value of observing the master class situation is that we see more explicitly the level of discourse required for musicians to learn from each other. The cognitive underpinnings are clearer in the rapid exchange and shifts of focus necessary for making use of musical concepts. Schon, an astute observer of professional practitioners at work, summarizes his impressions of the master class in these terms:

Thus, in his treatment of these first two phrases of the piece—some six measures in all—Franz (a pseudonym for a world-class pianist) has executed four shifts of attention. He begins with the feelingful quality of desperation and then turns to phrasing, metric order, the all-important pause, and finally balance of sound. In each instance, his improvised response to Amnon's playing goes beyond the manifest content of Schubert's score to its further meanings. Through qualitative description, technical instruction, and demonstration, he shows Amnon how to make more of what is there. (Schon, 1987, p. 190)

Thus, the interpretive act is informed by continual use of demonstration and metaphor in lessons, master classes, and rehearsal. Differentiating among various features of a modeled activity involves highly reflective and analytical acts, while the process of responding to those features requires a highly creative act. In this sense the metaphor functions very differently from the model. Metaphors depend on the musician's personal experience with words and images. Metaphors grow from an inquiry into musical meaning in performance not always emanating from technical concerns, motor skills, or standard theoretical terms. The master teacher uses references to narrative imagery, description of musical qualities, and gestures to "describe and make operational" a clearly defined and well-established image of Schubert's piece (Schon, 1987). Although the model is initially approached through imitation, the metaphor creates an affective state within which the performer can return to the model for further insight.

Cognitive Skills as Tools for Achieving New Levels of Understanding

It is important to consider cognitive skills, and this matrix, from the vantage point of the tools psychologists, musicians, and educators use to express their thoughts. Although the concept of tools and the role they play in thought are relatively unexplored, certain seminal works about tools and the formation of mind are available (Polanyi, 1962; Vygotsky, 1978; Winnicott, 1971; and Hodgkin, 1985). It is appropriate to consider the relationship of tools to thinking.

Tools function as extensions of thought and skills. They are based on principles abstracted from other complex systems (e.g., a probe from the finger, a camera from the eye, a string instrument from the voice) and take their meaning from the skill within which they function. This is a subtle process. For example, when one is learning an instrument, there is a developmental path that reflects the user's shift of attention. During the first phase of work, the focus is on acquiring and mastering the techniques required to play the instrument. Later, as technique becomes automatic, the focus shifts from technique to expression of musical thought. At the same time, there is a corresponding inverse shift in subsidiary awareness. At first, expression is subsidiary to the focal attention on the instrument; later the instrument is subsidiary to the focal expression of musical thought (Polanyi, 1962). At this level, instruments are used to express our personal experience and interpretation. Thus, our awareness of instruments, tools for musical thinking and expression, shifts as they become extensions of our body and integrated into our thought (as interpretative frameworks for and expressions of our intentions).

We establish a unique bond to a tool, whether it is an instrument or a concept (like the matrix of cognitive skills). We make it an extension of ourselves and establish a relationship to it that Polanyi refers to as "dwelling in" a tool. As we come to know it through use, a tool, by degrees, constrains our efforts and goals, enables us to probe our knowledge, and propels our understanding beyond our starting point. Our tools play a special role in problem solving and exploration that makes possible new achievements of understanding (Brown, Collins, and Duguid, 1990; Polanyi, 1962).

The transformation and use of our musical and psychological tools, instruments and concepts alike, can be seen as a dialogue among three phases of object use. Once a natural object becomes a personal tool for expression in a cultural context, we treat it differently, reflecting out intention. During one phase, it is a *toy*, where it can be used to explore new expressive forms. For example, playing with a concept or a sound without constraints can lead to novel constructions that can lead into unforeseen directions. The same object or concept as a *tool* serves an explicit or specific intention that lies beyond itself and its identity. And as a musical tool, it changes its position in our consciousness. The piano as a tool for musical expression is transparent because it serves as a vehicle for, not as the object of, musical expression. The piano is subsidiary to our focal intention of expression. Finally, as a *symbol* we can use the same object or concept to explore multiple levels of meaning. For instance, the instrument piano can be used as a symbol for nineteenth-century music (Winnicott, 1971).

Applying these ideas to the matrix of cognitive skills, musical creativity requires a progressively deeper and broader mastery of all six levels of cognitive skills as tools. In music learning, instruments begin as "things for use" and then become "things for meaning." The beginning of imaginative and intuitive dreaming, of original vision and interpretation, implies a creative cycle where tools play an ever increasing role. The phenomenology of tools traverses a wide range. It includes the selection of an object from nature, a chip of stone that becomes a plaything, a tool, a gadget, a trinket. The child or explorer picks up a natural object, uses it intentionally, and enters a world of culture. And the transformation works in both directions. Sometimes there is the playing, sometimes the sharpening of tools (Hodgkin, 1985).

Tool use may begin with picking up a natural object as a toy, and, as it is used intentionally, the toy becomes a tool as play turns into purposeful skill. Finally tools become, if levels of skill increase, extensions of the user. This extension implies an exploration of what is known in which the knower plays and extends beyond the perimeter of knowledge by considering ambiguities and possible solutions (Bruner, 1968; Papert, 1980; Polanyi, 1962; Winnicott, 1971).

The importance of a model of cognitive skills as tools lies in our thinking about creativity, while maintaining the values of the metaphors generated by the creative personality. With this view of tools as cognitive skills, play and discipline, critical and creative thinking, are complementary aspects of learning. The use of modeling and metaphor meets these criteria. It is of particular importance to the cognitive skill framework that, although much of teaching may be spent modeling and imitating, the process of understanding the true intentions of the teacher rests in the reflective thinking skills of the student or colleague. The transformation, elaboration, or abstraction of the model or metaphor must occur in the process of revision in performance. Reflecting new levels of understanding, musicians reorder and redirect their vision of music through this fundamental activity.

The concept of tools as the mind's instrument is crucial when considering cognitive skills, and especially when considering the issue of creativity and invention. Because tools impose limitations, and yet are open-ended toward new meanings and frontiers, it is important to acknowledge the role they play in our thinking and our concepts.

PROFILING THE COURSE OF COGNITIVE SKILL DEVELOPMENT

What is the path of cognitive skill development from the first instrumental lesson to the master class? Given that models and metaphors can all be used at all levels of instruction, what distinguishes novice from expert development? Rather than looking for deficiencies in cognitive skills, we can look for levels of awareness as indicative of development: For the beginner, the focus may be entirely on the fingers. For the expert, this focus may be peripheral to the more reflective and perceptive concerns for the music. Consider what happens when various cognitive skills are uncoordinated.

For example, consider the actual performance given by a beginning guitar student who is called on to perform a piece in front of his peers at a primary school assembly. He knows the music "by heart" and gets through the piece without the slightest hesitation. Finishing, he receives applause and beams. Clearly, he is pleased with his performance. However, the performance was perplexing to the audience. Although the piece was listed in the program as "Down in the Valley," those who knew the tune heard little resemblance to the version they knew. Apparently, in his haste or confusion, the student tuned his guitar to the wrong pitches before concentrating on the performance.

Several factors suggest what may be the overriding difference between the beginner and the experienced musician. However, the most obvious feature, the accuracy of the rendition of the tune, may be the least important. In terms of the framework, it is the lack of coordination among and integration of cognitive skills that is most disturbing. For the young student, this may occur because of an overriding focus on one kind of cognitive skill at the expense of all others.

Shifts of Awareness in Expert Performance

Perhaps the beginner and expert differ most in what focus is brought into play in musical performance. In this example, the beginning instrumentalist focuses primarily on a set of physical movements, and, in some cases, these actions may be uninformed by an aural image of how the music should sound. For the expert this situation is inconceivable. Although technical concerns are ever present, the musical interpretation is of paramount interest. What is most salient for the master may not be a primary interest to the beginner. Thus as artistry develops, cognitive skills reflect changing levels of focal or subsidiary awareness of aural, sensory motor, and musical dimensions. We see technical considerations disappearing from primary focus as they are mastered, with this focal-to-subsidiary shift signaling cognitive development in music (Polanyi, 1962).

For Glenn Gould, fingering had ceased to be the primary focal awareness in musical performance. It was the spontaneous interaction with the musical score and the conception of the performance in relation to the score that governed choice of fingering: "For me, a fingering is something which springs spontaneously to mind when one looks at a score, and is altered, if at all, when a shift of emphasis alters the way of looking at the score" (Dubal, 1984, p. 180). What ceases to be an articulate awareness of technique, that is, a predisposed set of fingerings, becomes tacit knowledge of what fingerings can be appropriate for producing the music. This, in turn, is subject to change as awareness of the score is altered during the course of the performance. Thus, for the mature performer, mastery of technique is deliberately subjugated to the concerns of interpretation. Perhaps through earlier routinization of technique, the expert performer finally can afford to focus entirely on other musical issues. In rehearsal, this focus can be altered to attend to issues that need to become focal, if only temporarily, in order to solve problems of technique or phrasing, or to develop new avenues of interpretation. What is most striking about Gould is his view of physical coordination skills as peripheral when compared to the more focal mental image of performance. For him it was not unusual to *not practice at all,* a full 48 hours before recording sessions:

Interviewer: Don't [you] find that the fingers simply refuse to cooperate at first, that it takes a certain number of days just to reestablish coordination?

Gould: On the contrary, when I do go back I probably play better than at any other time, purely in a physical sense, because the image, the mental image, which governs what one does is normally at that point at its strongest and is most precise because of the fact that it has not been exposed to the keyboard, and it has not, therefore, been distracted from the purity of its conception, of one's ideal relationship to the keyboard. (Dubal, 1984, p. 183)

Spanning the range from the beginning instrumentalist to the master performer suggests that the diversity in levels of awareness is enormous. In addition, the increasingly internalized musical conception suggests a level of cognitive skill that allows the performer to flexibly focus and reflect on aspects of structure and form that are at the heart of musical comprehension. As a conductor, Daniel Barenboim, for example, learns to perform and interpret a work by first memorizing the music away from the instrument. For Barenboim, both as a pianist and as a conductor, this focus on learning the music before physically producing the sound is the "first step in the process of 'de-composing' the music at hand, that is, to recreate the process whereby the composer himself created it" (Hart, 1979, p. 32).

For other master musicians, the primary focus of skills appears to shift developmentally from one set of representations to another. Beginning with the fingers and the ear, a necessary and successful way to begin musical skill development, one becomes focused in one's musical growth on the information in the score and the active internal imaging of the music. Eric Leinsdorf, the conductor and teacher, insists that musical growth for prospective conductors involves deepening cognitive skills independent of imitating through listening, that is, perception outside of the act of performance. In his book *The Composer's Advocate,* he states:

My overall purpose in these chapters has been to wean professional musicians from learning their music through the ear [through recordings] and guide them toward an independent and more reliable method of learning through the eye and the mind . . . to undertake a personal search for the deeper truths in great music. (Leinsdorf, 1981, p. 209)

The poles between the beginning performer and the master interpreter can be seen by the increasingly subsidiary awareness that musicians have the physical coordination necessary for performance. This change of focus suggests an underlying development of cognitive skills necessary for the study and performance of music in the broader and deeper sense of the master musician. The instrumentalist may begin with fingering or rote learning of folk songs as the focal point of performance, but it is the development of a richer array of underlying cognitive skills that marks the mature performer.

INDICES OF DEVELOPMENT IN PRODUCTION, PERCEPTION, AND REFLECTION

Drawing on practical experience and elaborated in educational contexts, this framework serves as a tool for tracing the development of cognitive skills in music. Three ideas surface most clearly. First, each of the types of cognitive skill contains *qualitatively different levels of skill.* Different levels of cognitive skill, whether framed as levels of complexity or levels of application, exist within all of the three ways of knowing music in or outside of performance. Second, it is the *integration and coordination of cognitive skills* that most clearly signal musical development. In this case, indicators of development appear to relate areas of attention and increasingly flexible levels of awareness when coordinating cognitive skills. Third, shifts of awareness among and transformations within underlying cognitive skills can be used to differentiate the master from the novice. In this case, the shift from focal to subsidiary awareness of technical concerns allows the expert to engage in the interpretative act.

Beginning with Janet, not only was there evidence for initial coordination of cognitive skills but also there were compelling examples of the form these fledgling skills may take. Janet's example of cognitive skills, however, is further amplified by corroborating research in individual areas of children's cognitive skill development. Outside of performance, for example, untrained children are able to produce increasingly detailed notations to show properties of rhythm (Bamberger, 1986) and pitch (Davidson and Scripp, 1988b), more often declare stable *perception* of pitch or rhythmic patterns (Zimmerman and Sechrest, 1968), and construct increasingly reflective questions and critiques of ensemble performance (Davidson and Scripp, 1990; Kennell, 1989). Similarly researchers also report development in performance skills (Davidson and Scripp, 1988b), perception skills related to music reading performance (Wolf, 1976), and reflective thinking in interpretive performance (Gabrielsson, 1988; Sloboda, 1985). Taken together, these skills suggest a broad and comprehensive network of cognitive skills. When one looks across the matrix of cells within the framework, this research offers considerable descriptive evidence for how these cognitive skills emerge (Figure 25–11).

For example, as young children control more musical dimensions in their singing, their notations begin to focus on a wider array of events. However, musical development needs be measured by more than the accrual of dimensions. Looking more carefully at notational and performance productions, researchers also see evidence for increasingly rela-

Ways of Knowing

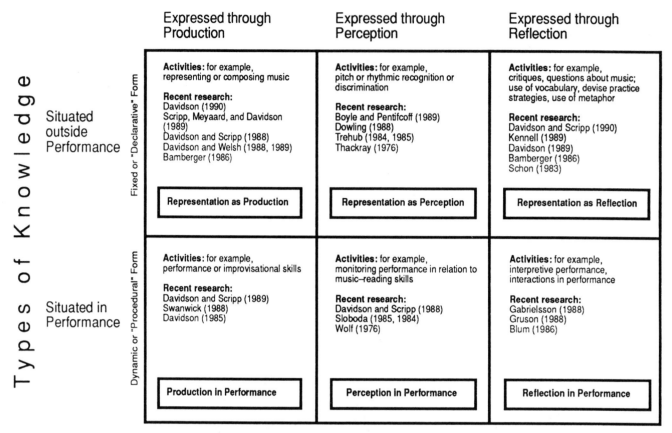

FIGURE 25–11. Relevant Research in Music Cognition in Relation to the Cognitive Skills Matrix.

tional, systematic, and integrative thinking in action. As Fischer (1980) suggests, evidence for cognitive skill development rests as much with level of complexity of dimensions in performance as with the process of arriving at the result.

Accordingly, research suggests that children who represent musical performance as a note to note process are very different from those who take a more systematic or relational approach by relating the performance to scalar frameworks (Bamberger 1986). Research also suggests development continues in composition (Scripp, Meyaard, and Davidson, 1988; Davidson and Welsh, 1988) or in improvisation (Swanwick and Tillman, 1986) in terms of increasingly rich dimensions, systematic reference to musical practice, and the construction of personal methods. In perception tasks, researchers report young children first recognize short melodies only at pitch, later transpositionally, and finally in terms of broad schema (Chang and Trehub, 1977; Dowling, 1982). Perception in music-reading conditions offers a path from simple sequential decoding of the musical novice toward more inferential and structurally aware readings of the more expert performer (Sloboda, 1984). Finally, in reflection outside of performance, there is evidence young musicians become

more sophisticated listeners and critics of music (Davidson and Scripp, 1990; Scripp, In press). As they progress, young ensemble musicians, for instance, offer more specific and perspicuous critiques of ensemble performance and are eventually able to offer and implement increasingly sophisticated practice strategies related to their critiques (Wolf and Pistone, In press; Swinton, 1989; Gruson, 1988).

The framework supports not only a comprehensive view of musical cognitive skill development but also a broader view of musical development through the coordination and integration of separate yet essentially webbed constellation of independent cognitive skills. More than simply distributing research in musical development, this framework provides essential links for connecting the understanding of musical development to continuing musical practice.

Thinking of production, perception, and reflective practice as differentiated by categorically different levels of development forces musicians to view musical practice in terms of a rich cognitive map. Unfolding along separate dimensions of skills, we see a picture of emerging mindfulness in music that grows more sophisticated with time, training, experience, and eventually the desire to draw the various strands of musical thinking together. Comparing the nature of cognitive skills in the novice and the expert allows the researcher, educator, and practitioner to explore the landscape.

CONCLUSION

Wanting to learn about elephants, the king sent his wise men to examine the beast. Each one being blind, and each examining a different part of the animal, they brought back dramatically different descriptions. The king became more confused. Like the blind men's description of the elephant, the term "cognitive skills" means different things, depending on which part of the "animal" is being examined. For the psychologist it refers to the thought processes that take place between the ears of the animal, the musician is concerned with the flow of the animal's performance, and the educator worries about how to train and educate the young. As long as each constituency speaks only to its own group, there is no conflict of definition. However, we need an integrated perspective if we are going to advance beyond local knowledge.

Cognitive skills are best *not* divided among various individual domains: psychology, music, and education. Nor should they be isolated as belonging to mind, body, private or social settings, idiosyncratic and cultural contexts, but rather encompass the situations in which cognitive skills appear in everyday practice (Scribner and Cole, 1973; Lave, 1988). Cognition, intelligence, and mind are not matters of the head alone, nor is music a matter of kinesthetic performance untouched by discrimination and reflection. A comprehensive approach to cognitive skills in music reveals the relation and integration of production, perception, and reflection supporting musical artistry.

Consequently, cognitive skills must be defined by considering the points of view of the psychologist, the musician, and the educator—one providing a systematic interpretation of individual observations, another providing the tacit knowledge that comes from practice and informal observations, while the third helps establish the setting that links the first two. The examples illustrate the differences between cognitive skills under various levels of development and in the context of the networks of understanding necessary for attaining artistic and educational objectives (Davidson and Scripp, 1989).

A cognitive skills model should integrate psychological models of cognition and musically situated knowledge. One way this integration might be achieved is by introducing a framework that coordinates aspects of various cognitive skills in relation to musical practice. Musicians employ any number of such "thinking frames" or tools to guide, organize, and support musical processes. The framework of cognitive skills requires consideration of various frames of reference in order to construct and support meaning when engaging in musical values and learning. This has several implications for education: First it expands the scope of learning in music by positioning knowledge both in and outside of musical performance, that is, within mainstream musical values; second, it elaborates the scope of those types of knowledge by situating them in activities that require production, perception, and reflection; third, it places emphasis on musical practice as the source of models; and fourth, it shifts the focus of development to the integration, coordination, and transformation of a range of cognitive skills.

Of course, if psychologists, musicians, and educators don't talk to one another, the inquirer is left with a bewildering impression of what the term cognitive skills or musical thinking might mean. With the cognitive skills matrix, we are no longer able to take musicians' performances alone as de facto knowledge of music, nor will a historical or analytical view of music in isolation serve as an example of comprehensive musical thinking. Psychological tests of discrimination are not necessarily good predictors of broader aspects of musical perception. In order to consider the question of cognitive skills seriously, we need to identify individual skills, take their coordinates and attempt to construct a perspective that integrates their diversity. Listening to psychologists, we search for concepts about knowledge, its development, and its relation to music. We look to musicians to identify significant musical problems, establish musical values, and better understand the tools of music making. We rely on the experience of the teacher and the variety of educational settings as well as the everyday instances of professional practice for our investigation of cognitive skills. In this way, a framework for exploring and relating relationships between the worlds of musical practice and systematic research can be constructed and used for the betterment of both.

References

Alexander, F. M. (1932). *The use of the self: Its conscious direction in relation to diagnostic, functioning and the control of reaction.* New York: E. P. Dutton.

Anderson, J. R. (1982). Acquisition of cognitive skill. *Psychological Review, 89,* 369–406.

Apfelstadt, H. (1989). Musical thinking in the choral rehearsal. In E. Boardman (Ed.), *Dimensions of musical thinking.* Reston: Music Educators National Conference.

Bamberger, J. (1986). Cognitive issues in the development of musi-

cally gifted children. In R. Sternberg and J. Davidson (Eds.), *Conceptions of giftedness.* Cambridge: Cambridge University Press.

Baron, J. B., and Sternberg, R. J. (1987). *Teaching thinking skills: Theory and practice.* New York: W. H. Freeman.

Blum, D. (1986). *The Guarneri Quartet.* New York: W. W. Norton.

Brown, A. L. (1990, April). *Distributed expertise in the classroom.* Paper read at AERA, Boston.

Brown, J. S., Collins, A., and Duguid, P. (1990). Situated cognition and the culture of learning. *Educational Researcher,* 32–42.

Bruner, J. (1968). *Toward a theory of instruction.* Cambridge: Harvard University Press.

Bruner, J. (1973). The growth of representational processes in childhood. In J. Anglin (Ed.), *Beyond the information given: Studies in the psychology of knowing.* New York: W. W. Norton.

Bruner, J., and Hudson, L. (1966). *Contrary imaginations.* London: Methuen.

Carey, S. (1985a). Are children fundamentally different kinds of thinkers and learners than adults? In S. F. Chipman, J. W. Segal, and R. Glaser (Eds), *Thinking and learning skills: Research and open questions* (Vol. 2). Hillsdale: Lawrence Erlbaum.

Carey, S. (1985b). *Conceptual change in childhood.* Cambridge: MIT Press.

Chang, H. and Trehub, S. (1977). Auditory processing of relational information by young infants. *Journal of Experimental Child Psychology, 24,* 324–331.

Davidson, L. (1989). Observing a Yang-ch'in lesson: Learning by modeling and metaphor in China. *Journal of Aesthetic Education, 23,* 1, 85–99.

Davidson, L. (1990, May). Tools and environments for musical creativity. *Music Educators Journal,* May, 47–51.

Davidson, L., and Scripp, L. (1988a). A developmental view of sight-singing: The internalization of tonal and temporal space. *Journal of Music Theory Pedagogy, 2,* (1), 10–23.

Davidson, L., and Scripp. L. (1988b). Sight-singing ability: A quantitative and qualitative point of view. *Journal of Music Theory Pedagogy, 2,* (1), 51–68.

Davidson, L., and Scripp, L. (1988c). Sightsinging at New England Conservatory of Music. *Journal of Music Theory Pedagogy, 2,* (1), 3–9.

Davidson, L., and Scripp, L. (1988d). Young children's musical representations: Windows on music cognition. In J. Sloboda (Ed.), *Generative processes in music.* Oxford: Oxford University Press.

Davidson, L., Scripp, L., and Welsh, P. (1988e) "Happy Birthday": Evidence for conflicts of perceptual knowledge and conceptual understanding. *Journal of Aesthetic Education, 22,* 1, 65–74. Also in Gardner, H. and Perkins, D. (Eds.), 1989, *Art, mind, and education: Research from Project Zero.* Urbana: University of Illinois Press.

Davidson, L., and Scripp, L. (1989). Education and development in music from a cognitive perspective. In D. J. Hargreaves (Ed.), *Children and the arts: The psychology of creative development.* Leicester: Open University Press.

Davidson, L., and Scripp, L. (1990). Tracing reflective thinking in the performance ensemble. *The Quarterly, 1,* (1&2).

Davidson, L., and Torff, B. (1991). *Singing, listening, and critiquing: Adults' knowledge of children's songs.* Harvard Project Zero, Graduate School of Education, Cambridge.

Davidson, L., and Welsh, P. (1988). From collections to structure: The developmental path of tonal thinking. In J. Sloboda (Ed.), *Generative Processes in Music* (pp. 260–285). Oxford: Oxford University Press.

Davidson, L., Ross-Broadus, L., Charlton, J., Scripp, L, and Waanders, J. (1991). *Recent advances in the state of assessment: arts propel in Pittsburgh.* Special Research Interest Group in Measurement and Evaluation, MENC, 11.

Davidson, L., Scripp, L., and Fletcher, A. (1991). *Writing as scaffolding for learning in solfege class.* Boston: New England Conservatory of Music.

Delbanco, N. (1985). *The Beaux Arts Trio: A portrait.* New York: Willian Morris & Co., Inc.

Dennett, D.C. (1969). *Content and consciousness* London: Routledge & Kegan Paul.

Dillon, R. F., and Sternberg, R. J. (1986). *Cognition and instruction.* San Diego: Academic Press.

Dowling, W. J., (1982). Melodic information processing and its development. In D. Deutsch, (Ed.), *The psychology of music.* New York: Academic Press.

Dubal, D. (1984). *Reflections from the keyboard: The world of the concert pianist.* New York: Summit Books.

Feldman, D. H. (1980). *Beyond universals in cognitive development.* Norwood.: Ablex.

Fischer, K. (1980). A theory of cognitive development: The control and construction of hierarchies of skills. *Psychological Review, 87* (6), 477–531.

Gabrielsson, A. (1988). Timing in music performance and its relations to music experience. In J. Sloboda (Ed.), *Generative processes in music: The psychology of performance improvisation, and composition* (pp. 27–51) Oxford: Clarendon Press.

Gardner, H. (1983). *Frames of mind.* New York: Basic Books.

Gardner, H. (1985). *The mind's new science: A history of the cognitive revolution.* New York: Basic Books.

Goodman, N. (1976). *Languages of art: An approach to a theory of symbols.* Indianapolis: Hackett Publishing Company.

Goodman, N. (1978). *Ways of worldmaking.* Indianapolis: Hackett Publishing Company.

Gordon, E. (1965). *Musical aptitude profile.* Boston: Houghton Mifflin Co.

Gruson, L. (1988). Rehearsal skill and musical competence: Does practice make perfect? In J. Sloboda (Ed.), *Generative processes in music: The psychology of performance, improvisation, and composition.* London: Oxford Science Publications.

Hart, P. (1979). *Conductors: A new generation.* New York: Scribner.

Hodgkin, R. A. (1985). *Playing and exploring: Education through the discovery of order.* London: Methuen.

Howard, V. A. (1982). *Artistry: The work of artists.* Indianapolis: Hackett Publishing Company.

John-Steiner, V. (1985) *Notebooks of the mind: Explorations of thinking.* Harper & Row: New York.

Kennell, R. (1989). Musical thinking in the instrumental rehearsal. In E. Boardman (Ed.), *Dimensions of musical thinking.* Reston: Music Educators National Conference.

Lave, J. (1988). *Cognition in practice: Mind, mathematics and culture in everyday life.* Cambridge: Cambridge University Press.

Leinsdorf, E. (1981). *The composer's advocate.* New Haven: Yale University Press.

Marzano, R., Brandt, R., Hughes, C., Jones, B., Presseisen, B., Rankin, S., and Suhor, C. (1988). *Dimensions of thinking: A framework for curriculum and instruction.* Alexandria: The Association for Supervision and Curriculum Development.

Neisser, U. (1976). *Cognition and reality: Principles and implications of cognitive psychology.* San Francisco: W. H. Freeman.

Newman, D., Griffin, P., and Cole, M. (1989). *The construction zone: Working for cognitive change in school.* Cambridge: Cambridge University Press.

Ortmann, O. (1925). *The physiological mechanics of piano technique.* New York: E. P. Dutton.

Papert, S. (1980). *Mindstorms: Children, computers and powerful ideas.* Brighton: Harvester.

Perkins, D. (1986). *Knowledge as design.* Hillsdale: Lawrence Erlbaum Associates.

Perkins, D. (1987). Thinking frames: An integrative perspective on teaching cognitive skills. In J. Baron, and R. Sternberg (Eds.), *Teaching thinking skills: Theory and practice.* New York: W. H. Freeman and Company. 41–61.

Perkins, D. (1989). Art as understanding. In H. Gardner and D. Perkins (Eds.), *Art, mind, and education: Research from Project Zero* (pp. 111–131). Urbana: University of Illinois Press.

Perkins, D. (1989a). *Mindware: The new science of learnable intelligence*. Paper presented & published by the Fourth National Conference on Thinking. San Juan, Puerto Rico.

Pflederer, M., and Sechrest, L. (1968). Conservation-type responses of children to musical stimuli. *Bulletin of the Council for Research in Music Education 13*, 19–36.

Phye, G. D. (1986). Practice and skilled classroom performance. In Phye G. D. and Andre, T. (Eds.), *Cognitive classroom learning: Understanding, thinking, and problem solving* (pp. 141–168). New York: Academic Press.

Phye, G. D., and Andre, T. (1988). *Cognitive classroom learning*. Orlando: Academic Press.

Piaget, J. (1963). Mental images. In H. Gruber and J. Voneche (Eds.), *The essential Piaget*. New York: Basic Books.

Piaget, J. (1966). Memory and the structure of image-memories. In H. Gruber and J. Voneche (Eds.), *The Essential Piaget*. New York: Basic Books.

Piaget, J. (1976). Walking on all fours. *The grasp of consciousness*. Cambridge: Harvard University Press.

Piaget, J., and Inhelder, B. (1969). *The psychology of the child*. New York: Basic Books.

Polanyi, M. (1962). *Personal knowledge*. Chicago: University of Chicago Press.

Reahm, D. E. (1986). Developing critical thinking through rehearsal techniques. *Music Educators Journal, 74* (1), 29–31.

Robinson, P. (1989). The geography of solfege: An interim report. Unpublished manuscript, New England Conservatory.

Robinson, P. (1990). Solfege class journals from the New England Conservatory. Unpublished manuscript.

Rogoff, B. (1990). *Apprenticeship in thinking: Cognitive development in social context*. New York: Oxford University Press.

Rogoff, B. and Lave, J. (1984). *Everyday cognition: Its development in social context*. Cambridge: Harvard University Press.

Rubinstein, A. (1973). *My young years*. New York: Alfred Knopf.

Ryle, G. (1949). *The concept of mind*. London: Hutchinson House.

Schon, D. A. (1983). *The reflective practitioner: How professionals think in action*. New York: Basic Books.

Schon, D. A. (1987). *Educating the reflective practitioner: Toward a new design for teaching and learning in the professions*. San Francisco: Jossey-Bass.

Scribner, S., and Cole, M. (1973). *The psychology of literacy*. Cambridge: Harvard University Press.

Scripp, L. (in press). Transforming teaching through portfolios: A case study of the high school performance ensemble. *The Quarterly*.

Scripp, L., and Davidson, L. (1988). Framing the dimensions of sight-singing: Teaching towards musical development. *Journal of Music Theory Pedagogy, 2*(1), 24–50.

Scripp, L., Meyaard, J., and Davidson, L. (1988). Discerning musical development. *Journal of Aesthetic Education, 22*, 1, 75–88. Also in Gardner, H. and Perkins, D. (Eds.), (1989). *Art, mind, and education: Research from Project Zero*. Urbana: University of Illinois Press.

Seashore, C., Lewis, D., and Saetveit, J. (1960). *The Seashore Measures of Musical Talents*. New York: The Psychological Corporation.

Serafine, M. L. (1988). *Music as cognition: The development of thought in sound*. New York: Columbia University Press.

Shaffer, L. H. (1981). Performance of Chopin, Bach and Bartok: Studies in motor programming. *Cognitive Psychology, 13*, 326–376.

Siegel, J., and Siegel, W. (1977). Categorical perception of tonal intervals: Musicians can't tell sharp from flat. *Perception and Psychophysics, 21*, 399–407.

Sincoff, J. B., and Sternberg, R. J. (1989). The development of cognitive skills: An examination of recent theories. In A. M. Colley and J. R. Beech (Eds.), *Acquisition and performance of cognitive skills*. Chichester: John Wiley.

Sloboda, J. (1984). Experimental studies of music reading: A review. *Music Perception, 2,*2.

Sloboda, J. (1985). *The musical mind: The cognitive psychology of music*. Oxford: Oxford University Press.

Sloboda, J., and Parker, D. H. H. (1985). Immediate recall of melodies. In P. Howell, I. Cross, and R. West (Eds.), *Musical structure and cognition*. London: Academic Press.

Swanwick, K., and Tillman, J. (1986). The sequence of musical development: A study of children's composition. *British Journal of Music Education, 3*(3), 305–339.

Swinton, S. (1989). Assessment of production, perception, and reflection in beginning music. *Portfolio: The Newsletter of Arts Propel*. Princeton: Educational Testing Service.

Trehub, S. E., Morrongiello, B. A., and Thorpe, L. A. (1985). Children's perception of familiar melodies: The role of intervals, contour and key. *Psychomusicology, 5*, 39–48.

Upitis, R. (1985). Children's understanding of rhythm: The relationship between development and musical training. Unpublished doctoral dissertation, Harvard University, Cambridge.

Upitis, R. (1987). Toward a model for rhythm development. In Peery, J. C., Peery, I. W., and Draper, I. W. (Eds.), *Music and child development*, New York: Springer Verlag.

Vygotsky, L. (1978). *Mind in society*. Cambridge: Harvard University Press.

Vygotsky, L. (1986). *Thought and language*. Cambridge: MIT Press.

Werner, H. (1948). *Comparative psychology of mental development*. New York: International Universities Press.

Winnicott, D. W. (1971). *Playing and reality*. London: Travistock.

Wohlwill, J. F. (1973). *The study of behavioral development*. New York: Academic Press.

Wolf, D., and Pistone, N. (in press). *Taking full measures: Rethinking assessment through the arts*. Princeton: College Board.

Wolf, T. (1976). A cognitive model of musical sight-reading. *Journal of Psychological Research, 5*, 143–171.

Zimmerman, M. P., and Sechrest, L. (1968). *How children conceptually organize musical sounds*. Cooperative Research Project 5-0256. Northwestern University, Chicago.

We gratefully acknowledge support from the following foundations: the Spencer Foundation, The Carnegie Corporation, the Markle Foundation, and the Rockefeller Foundation. We wish to thank Howard Gardner, Keith Swanwick, and Richard Colwell for their valuable comments and suggestions. Finally, we wish to thank our Project Zero colleagues, David Perkins, Dennie Wolf, Joe Walters, Joan Meyaard, Donna Plasket, and Bruce Torff, for their contributions and suggestions relating to our musical research.

·26·

AFFECTIVE RESPONSE

Robert F. Miller

UNIVERSITY OF CONNECTICUT

The terms "affect" and "affective response" are not consistently used in the literature. A varied list of constructs has been subsumed under affect, including emotion, aesthetic response, mood or character response, interests, values, appreciations, preferences, attitudes, and taste (Radocy and Boyle, 1988). Abeles (1980) adds to this list the topics of anxiety and arousal. Some of the uses of the term affect reflect physiological properties; some, judgment processes; some, direct and apparently unmediated responses; others imply large schemata, plans, motivations, and other features of cognition.

In the absence of an agreed-upon classification system for musical affective responses, this discussion uses an arbitrary scheme. Affective responses are divided into "preferences," "appraisals," and "subjective responses." This classification system is less finely divided than it might be, but another taxonomy would be tedious, and probably no better. In any case, the three-part division should be treated only as a rhetorical organizer.

Two points of view prejudice this discussion of affect. The first is that all forms of music are potential stimuli for affective response, whether the music is heard, remembered, performed, or translated by the mind from a musical score, as long as there is established some relationship between the music user ("the perceiver") and the music itself ("the object"). This relationship can vary in closeness. It might be completely detached and apparently objective. The relationship might include a nonmusical organizer, such as language, to mediate between perceiver and object. The relationship might be intimate, like that of a performer or composer concentrating on the music being created. The transaction between the perceiver and the object can produce a passive, detached result, or one completely integrated and subjective, involving the perceiver totally.

The second point of view is that affective response involves meaning. In instances of affective response the perceivers use part or all of their mental system (cognitive, affective, and/or psychomotor) to search out and attach meaning to the musical object. The search can be spontaneous (and sometimes highly idiosyncratic) or the result of an experimental or pedagogical situation in which responses are circumscribed by the questions asked. The search for meaning can be unconscious, conscious, or both.

In the first division of affect the result of the meaning search is to make decisions about approaching, liking, or continuing interest in musical objects. This category is called *preferences,* with no special meaning implied.

The second division is *appraisals.* It includes all types of indices about the music, usually arrived at through introspection: assignment of a place within a value system, rank orderings along some musical/technical dimension, purely associative and rhetorical responses, and cognitive judgments that are "about" emotional qualities, but involve no emotional response. Responses in this division usually result from the imposition of an extramusical mediation structure or classification scheme on the musical judgment task. In many of the studies addressing this category, subjects may be asked to respond to music using a verbal scheme that might or might not be used in a natural, nonlaboratory musical situation (O'Briant and Wilbanks, 1978; Crozier, 1974; Hevner, 1936).

The last division, least understood but intuitively the most important, can be labeled *subjective involvements.* Such responses are fascinating to musicians, but often deliberately excluded from discussion in music education. For example, within this division are studies that examine emotion in terms of the relationships between physiological response and cognition.

PREFERENCES

The preferences division of affective response includes those responses that reflect a value hierarchy of any sort. Research

414

in this division includes both studies in which subjects use various scales and rating schemes to respond about musical preferences and also those that use other indicators of liking, usually behavioral indices that measure presumed interest, such as listening time or choice of musical material in a free listening situation. In this discussion, preferences will include studies of musical taste.

The literature on musical preferences is broad and diverse. Aside from pseudotheories concerning the relationships between familiarity or complexity and preference, the literature suffers from a general lack of direction and from theoretical shallowness. Many of the studies have clearly stated hypotheses, but often the research is not clearly related to other studies or to a preexisting theory. In that way, they seem like pieces without a puzzle into which they might be fitted. There are, however, some common themes that join these studies into loose categories, and certain of them will be addressed here. Extensive reviews of the literature are reported elsewhere in this volume and in Abeles (1980) and Radocy and Boyle (1988).

Preference and Its Relationship to Various Factors
One extensive group of studies investigates various personality characteristics and their relationships to preference. For instance, Cattell and Anderson (1953) devised a test that measures personality variables through the rating of 100 musical examples. The relationship of music to other personality variables has been examined by Butler (1968; unconventionality and radicalism), Keston and Pinto (1955; introversion/extroversion), Mikol (1988), and Zagona and Kelly (1966; dogmatism), Fisher and Fisher (1951; clinical anxiety), and Inglefield (1968; conformity).

Of particular interest to music educators are studies relating preference for particular musical styles with age and peer group membership. The behaviorists who use music as a reinforcer often examine this variable, music with higher preference ratings having greater utility as a reinforcer. Greer, Dorrow, and Hanser (1973); Greer, Dorrow, and Randall (1973); and Greer, Dorrow, Wachaus, and White (1973) are examples. Johnstone and Katz (1957) and Inglefield (1974) examined the effect of peer relationships on musical preference.

Radocy and Boyle agree with Abeles that the effects on musical preference of gender, socioeconomic status, musical achievement, musical aptitude, race, and other potential influences have been neither documented well enough nor replicated to establish any reliable relationships. Some studies investigating effects of training on musical preferences demonstrate a weak but positive effect. For instance, Duerksen (1968) concluded that the degree to which students recognize tonal relationships in complex music is only weakly related to preference strength. Some multidimensional scaling studies indicate that musical preference dimensions are more salient for musically naive subjects than for musically sophisticated ones (Hare, 1975). Hargreaves (1986) concludes that specific training may affect preferences in a positive way, but that, again, "it is difficult to make generalisations about the results of these studies because of the wide variation in their aims and methods, and in the types of training investigated" (p. 102).

A number of variables that are characteristics of the music itself, rather than of the listener, *do* seem to have a relationship to preference, and these variables are of potential importance in establishing a theory of musical affective response. Information rate, complexity, and repetition are all explored more closely below.

Inverted-U Theories and Information Rate
In the 1970s D. E. Berlyne (1970) and his associates from the University of Toronto began a series of publications in what they described as a "new" or at least "re-newed" field of study, experimental aesthetics. Within both the visual arts and music, Berlyne examined the relationships between what he identified as "collative variables" of visual and acoustic stimuli (sound sequences rather than actual musical examples) and certain affective responses (Berlyne, 1971). The collative variables (e.g. complexity, novelty, redundancy, and orderliness) were related to the information rate in the sound sequence, and were treated as independent variables in relation to aesthetic/affective dependent variables such as liking, interest, subjective familiarity, and subjective complexity.

This line of empirical work, continued later by Hargreaves and his associates (Hargreaves, 1986; Sluckin, Hargreaves, and Colman, 1982, 1983) has important antecedents in Abraham Moles's application of information theory to music and his notion that music is a stochastic system dependent for its aesthetic effect on the rate at which the information is perceived by the listener. Information, in this context, is defined as novelty (Moles, 1968). There are, Moles contends, both minimum and maximum information rates beyond which a given listener may no longer be interested in a piece or sound sequence. Leonard B. Meyer made a similar connection with information rate as an important variable in arousal state and musical meaning (Meyer, 1957).

The result of all of this is what Walker calls a hedgehog theory, so named because it is so widely applicable to a large number of different settings and variables (Walker, 1980). (The hedgehog, to mix a metaphor or two, is a "one trick pony." No matter what the situation, fear, anger, or whatever, a hedgehog simply rolls up into a ball.)

Walker's theory states that one generalized function, an "inverted-U," or quadratic function (Figure 26–1) accounts for the relationship between almost any of the above-mentioned independent variables and any of the dependent ones. That is, generalized preference (or interest or pleasure) increases with stimulus complexity up to a point for each listener. When complexity (i.e., the amount of information per unit time) is increased beyond that point, interest, pleasure, or preference declines. For each perceiver the function will be different in its position along the abscissa, but the shape of the function will remain roughly the same. More experienced, better trained, or more acculturated listeners will have the curve shifted in a positive direction. They prefer, to a point, more complex music.

Complexity in this model is seen as presenting novelty through time. Its opposite is redundancy. The extension to

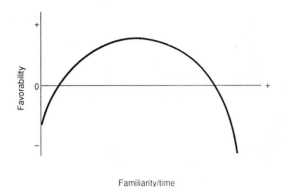

FIGURE 26–1. The Inverted-U Curve.

familiarity and unfamiliarity of particular musical examples is direct. So it makes sense that the American social scientist Harry Triandis would say that after a number of years of listening to music in New Delhi he not only began to get a sense of "how it goes," but even found that he "enjoyed it once it got there." Through repetition the Indian musical system went from complete novelty, with every musical event unanticipated, to a more optimum level of perceived complexity (personal communication).

There is considerable experimental evidence for the inverted-U function. Vitz (1966), Heyduk (1975), Crozier (1974), and Davies (1978) all provide confirmation. Davies takes great pains to make a potentially very important point for educators. The information rate (or complexity or novelty) contained in a musical work is not the result of the notes the composer puts there, but rather of the perceptions of the listener (Davies, 1978, p. 93):

A person, who as the result of his past musical experience is able to predict to a large extent what is going to happen will find a piece of music less complex than does his neighbor who cannot predict so well. Furthermore, since musical experience is something which is a continuous process for most people, pieces which an individual finds highly complex at first may become less complex with the passage of time and the acquisition of new musical experiences. . . . Preferred levels of complexity [can undergo] a steady rise [with the passage of time.]

A conflicting theory to the inverted-U, presented by Zajonc (1968), is called the "mere exposure theory." It states that "mere exposure of the individual to a stimulus is sufficient condition for the enhancement of his attitude toward it" (p. 1). Zajonc's theory, however, may result from stopping short, not allowing enough exposure for the eventual decline in the slope of the curve. His results may represent only the first half of the inverted U.

APPRAISALS

Musical appraisals include two broad groups of studies: first, those using direct associative meanings and meanings derived from conventions; second, those relying on the use of measurement scales and methods that involve either verbal or nonverbal responses. What characterizes the second group is reliance on mediation—processes that "intercede" between the musical object and the responder. In most but not all studies the data under analysis are verbal reports and are at least partially the result of introspections.

Fundamentally, the task for the listener in every appraisal is some kind of sense making. The senses pass to the mind a stream of incoming music information that must be sorted out and integrated into the listener's mental structure. Many cognitive processes may be activated at one time: memory, categorization, both top-down and bottom-up strategies, representation, and more—all addressing the problem of sense making. Some of the meaning that results from this processing comes from the musical object, but the mind contributes as well. In a discussion of verbal report techniques, the process has been described as follows:

A foundation [of this model] is the constructionist premise that meaning exists only in the mind and results from the mind's ability to impose order on the data coming from the senses. . . . The data received through the senses are actually sparse and impoverished compared to the mind's responses, which are [more] complete and rich. The mind combines sensory data, thought, memory, and construction strategies of various kinds to 'build up' meanings of an object or event. (Miller, 1990, p. 64)

Many of those meanings will share certain features with feelingful responses. Some meanings may actually engender feeling, but many will be purely cognitive registrations that share only the cognitive features of other feeling-laden experiences. In contrast with the "cold emotions" discussed elsewhere in this chapter, these can be called "hot cognitions." They are important examples of sense making.

Associations and Rhetorical Devices

Some (trivial) examples of associations are the meanings attached to a bugle call, pride on hearing a patriotic tune, or nostalgia on hearing an old school song. The association process is the same one by which a stop sign or a logo carries meaning: The meaning of one object is substituted in a straightforward way for the meaning of another object that has been associated with it. For example, the meanings associated with repeated car horn blasts (busyness, activity, anxiety, and so forth) are more or less directly attached to the same sounds used in a musical way in *An American in Paris*. The listener does not have to "interpret" these sounds. They carry direct meaning. Susanne Langer (1957) called these "signs" and the process by which they have meaning, "signification."

More abstract examples of appraisals would include purely conventional musical meanings, such as fanfares and fanfarelike expressions, and the musical/rhetorical devices used by composers in the early seventeenth century and in the baroque period. Explained in music theory by references to classical Greek rhetorical devices, such conventions as an *aposiopesis* (an unexpected silence) or an *antitheton* (a sudden melodic contrast to express the idea of conflict) were employed regularly by composers with the clear expectation that they would be understood. Although listeners no longer respond to them fully—nor to the slightly later baroque "doctrine of affections," nor the North German *Empfindsamkeit*—these were highly developed systems that carried assigned meanings from composer to listener. There is no direct experimental corroboration of their effectiveness with listeners untrained in the conventions.

Nonverbal Response Methods

Because music is a nonverbal medium, nonverbal methods seem to be intuitively the most "true" to musical settings. They are, however, difficult to conceive, execute, analyze, and interpret, and thus are not frequently used. Enough studies have demonstrated their utility, however, to encourage further use.

Jeanne Bamberger (1977) has used computers and synthesizers to study ways in which cognitive sense-making problems are solved. Her system uses musical fragments, "tune blocks," to present experimental problems. For example, subjects may be presented with a set of tune blocks and asked to reorder the blocks so as to form tunes they know. At other times, the subjects are presented with blocks that can be combined in many ways, some musically "sensible" and some not. The subjects' exploratory manipulations of the blocks are studied as they attempt to create a "sensible" tune. Using this nonverbal system, Bamberger has examined such questions as: What musical features form cognitively important units? How do musical embedded figures work? What distinguishes one music unit (a "block") from another for various ages and experience levels of subjects? What features signal the beginning, middle, and end of musical phrases? Bamberger and Brody (1984) have studied other nonverbal representation schemes for sense making. There are, they claim, multiple representations of musical events, different among different individuals at various stages of their musical development, that should be subject to empirical examination. Other nonverbal methods include the examination of musical similarities. In these studies musical examples are compared by subjects who rate their similarity on whatever features they deem perceptually important at the time. Through various scaling techniques, usually multidimensional scaling algorithms (MDS), the data are reduced to a graphic or spatial representation of relatively few dimensions. Shepard (1972) says that the result is that the investigator can "get ahold of whatever pattern or structure may otherwise [lie] hidden in the data" (p. 1).

Although MDS techniques have most often been used to study musical elements such as timbre (Grey, 1978; Gordon and Grey, 1978), or pitch (Shepard, 1982a,b), they have been used for more global affective assessments as well. Wedin (1972) examined what he called "emotional qualities." Several studies have contrasted the affective response structures of musicians and nonmusicians (Howard and Silverman, 1976; Hare, 1975; Miller, 1979). A finding for these studies is that for both nonmusicians and musicians, an important dimension of the perceptual space is a "dynamism" dimension related somehow to qualities of activity and arousal discussed later in this chapter.

Verbal Appraisal Methods

People talk about music easily and naturally. Perhaps because of this, verbal reports of internal states are often encountered. The remarkable thing about verbal reports of musical stimuli, especially those concerning mood and affect, is that they are consistent from person to person, and reliable across time for a given person.

Those consistencies were noted by Schoen and Gatewood (1927), who studied the verbal responses of over 20,000 subjects to recorded examples of both vocal and instrumental music. Despite differences in age and musical experience, verbal characterizations of the mood of musical examples were strikingly similar.

The differences that do exist in verbal reports of musical mood are related to the character of the stimuli. Pieces characterized by negative terms like "despair," "agony," or "grief" are more reliably characterized than more positive moods like joy or a loving feeling (Hampton, 1945).

Adjective Studies The landmark use of verbal reports is the Hevner adjective studies (Hevner, 1935, 1936). Initially, subjects listened to five musical pieces of widely differing character and checked adjectives appropriate to each piece from a list of 66 adjectives with emotional connotations. The adjectives were grouped into eight clusters, arranged in a circle. The groupings were Hevner's own, accomplished intuitively (Figure 26–2). The study found listener agreement on broad characterizations of each piece.

Later investigations by Hevner included the effects of various alterations on the mood category responses of listeners. Melodic direction had little effect ascending or descending. Minor and major modes elicited consistent responses: minor treatments interpreted in cluster 2 (sad, pathetic, and doleful) and major treatments of the same musical material interpreted in cluster 6, (bright, happy, and joyous). Other musical features eliciting consistency of response included "firm" versus "flowing" rhythm, and "simple" versus "complex" harmony. Hevner's studies, and confirmations by Farnsworth (1954) and Scherer and Oshinsky (1977; using other types of stimuli) indicate that certain musical features are systematically related to listeners' verbal reports of general character states.

Semantic Differential Studies Other verbal report methods have utilized factor analysis of adjective ratings of musical examples. The most productive of these have employed semantic differential (SD) technique, as described by Osgood, Suci, and Tannenbaum (1957). (A recent theoretical review of SD technique applied to musical study is provided by Miller, 1990.) SD technique calls for subjects to rate a num-

FIGURE 26-2.   The Hevner Adjective Circle.

ber of stimuli on a number of five- or seven-point bipolar adjective scales. The data are then collapsed along (usually) the subject dimension and subjected to factor analysis. The factors emerging from the use of a wide variety of adjectives in numerous languages applied over many classes of stimuli have proved to be remarkably consistent. The factors are most often labeled Evaluation, Potency, and Activity (often abbreviated simply E,P,A). The E,P,A structure has been so consistent and stable that Osgood has considered it to be a universal of affective meaning.

The factors that have emerged from musical studies are consistent. One factor is usually an evaluative factor (often related to liking), and one is a combination of activity and potency usually described as "dynamism."

Semantic differential technique has been fecund. The following abbreviated list demonstrates the diversity of research settings in which it has been invoked. It has been used to examine the effects of complexity on musical meaning by Crozier (1974), Hare (1975), and Bragg and Crozier (1974). Accurso (1967) used SD to examine the affective differences between serious and popular music for naive and sophisticated listeners. Keil and Keil (1966) used it cross-culturally. SD technique was used by O'Briant and Wilbanks (1978) to determine the effects of previously existing mood states on the meaning of a piece for the listener.

Several important criticisms of the semantic differential deserve mention. First, like all verbal report methods, it engages subjects in a behavior that may not happen outside the experimental setting. Second, the use of a short list of adjectives or an even shorter list of factors does violence to the richness of the musical experience. The technique is by definition reductionist. Third, it shares with all factor analytic schemes the problem that the answers are completely determined by the experimenter's choice of scales and stimuli. Fourth, the technique requires a good deal of skill to apply. Fifth, and most important of all, the real applicability of SD technique is bounded by its theoretical basis, Osgood's neobehaviorist theory of "Representational Mediation." Most researchers ignore the theory, using the technique because it is handy and reliable. This is, of course, dangerous. Although it seems to "work" every time, phenomenology by itself is not sufficient for solving psychological problems.

SUBJECTIVE INVOLVEMENTS

The point of departure for this final discussion is intended to be Hegelian, at least in spirit. It will rely for its proof on the dictum that anything that is true is rational and anything that is rational is true. That notion, which bestows upon constructs and models a special usefulness, has allowed psychology to move away from its reliance on behaviorism. The behaviorist idea that if one cannot directly observe it in action, it isn't worthy of consideration satisfies only the most naive view of scientific principles while doing violence to some of the most interesting qualities of humans. Behaviorism reduces the importance of several qualities that distinguish humans, such as thought, intention, and mind. The idea that a thing might be true solely on the basis of its rationality has permitted psychologists to better use a convention often found in other scientific disciplines, "the useful fiction." These entities, like quarks in physics, are true because they rationally must be, even if one cannot actually observe them. It may be that the idea of affect itself is a useful fiction. Familiar instances of such fictions are "ideas," "memories," "predispositions or sets," and indeed the useful fiction of the mind itself. So, behaviors aside, emotions like fear, anger, love, rage, and the rest exist, and there are fine shadings and gradations of emotion that may not always be made evident from overt behavior.

Physiological Responses to Music

The view that music concerns communication has been central to the psychology of music, especially in the last 50 years or so. What is communicated or represented is often described in terms of emotions or feelings. This emphasis on emotions or feelings is not hard to understand. Many who have been drawn to music have been motivated by the emotional "kick" that music provides to both performer and listener.

The term "kick" is used here advisedly. Feelings are intimately concerned with bodily functions. In distinguishing between feelings and inclinations, Gilbert Ryle (1949, pp. 83–84) says:

By 'feelings' I refer to the sorts of things which people often describe as thrills, twinges, pangs, throbs, wrenches, itches, prickings, chills, loads, glows, qualms, hankerings, curdlings, sinkings, tensions, gnawings and shocks. Ordinarily, when people report the occurrence of a feeling, they do so in a phrase like 'a throb of compassion,' 'a shock of surprise,' or 'a thrill of anticipation.'

It is an important linguistic fact that these names for specific feelings, such as 'itch,' 'qualm,' and 'pang,' are also used for specific body sensations.

While listening to certain pieces under certain conditions, almost everyone has at one time or another been aware of somatic or bodily changes that seem to have concomitant events in the musical stream. Musical events seem to have correlates literally in one's guts. Often one experiences a feeling "in the pit of the stomach," a nondifferentiated visceral response that is intuitively significant.

Other more specific bodily responses to musical stimuli have been noted for years and have been studied extensively. Lundin (1967), Farnsworth (1969), and Radocy and Boyle (1988) have provided good summaries of these studies. Exemplars of work of this type are the studies done by the psychologists G. and H. Harrer of Salzburg (G. Harrer and H. Harrer, 1977). A useful fiction in physiology has provided us with something called the autonomic nervous system (ANS). Ordinarily, the ANS is charged with the responsibility for maintaining stasis in the organism. It is charged with responding to the environment to readjust the organism's energy use. If one is cold, for instance, it is one's autonomic nervous system that closes down blood vessels to keep one from losing heat. If one is running, it is the autonomic system that calls for an increase in respiration and heart rate to compensate for the lack of blood oxygen sensed by the hypothalamus. Those changes are readily measurable, and scientists are drawn to measurable things. They ascribe almost magical powers to anything measurable, so ANS responses are measured often and for a wide variety of purposes.

The Harrers noticed what almost all musicians have noticed. Sometimes a person's heart speeds up not because of running, not in response to a need for more oxygen, but to accompany some perceived emotion. This can happen when listening to music. In spite of a lack of any real theory, the Harrers minutely described changes in the activation of the autonomic nervous system by noting changes in blood pressure, respiration, psychogalvanic reflex, and other autonomic functions.

Somatic responses are situational. The Harrers have described distinct and predicted changes in respiration and psycholgalvanic response by persons listening to music with emotional involvement ("into it," as the idiom would suggest) and contrasted these responses with those of the same persons listening to the same pieces while being asked to analyze critically what is being heard. The analytical task did block the physical responses.

In a famous case study, the Harrers examined the pulse rates of Herbert von Karajan while he conducted the *Leonora Overture No. 3*. The highest rates were not achieved during the most vigorous physical activity, but rather were reserved for those portions of the music that the conductor singled out in later conversations as being the most emotionally touching. At times in this condition his pulse rate was twice his resting pulse. When a tape of the performance was later played for him, and further measurements were made, there was "evidence of considerable qualitative parallelism between both tracings" (Harrer and Harrer, 1977, p. 204).

To allow for better understanding of these performance-induced pulse rates, von Karajan allowed his pulse rates to be recorded while he piloted his jet aircraft through a series of tricky maneuvers known as "touch and goes," where a landing approach is followed by a sudden and steep ascent. In each case, these maneuvers were preceded by a rapid increase in heart rate. But neither the magnitude of the increase nor the eventual upper limit of the heart rate was as high during the flying as during the more emotion-laden parts of the musical performance, a time when he attained heart rates as high as 150 beats per minute.

Through other experimental manipulations the Harrers have determined that these physiological responses and many others (like muscle strength, ankle jerk response, and general muscle tone) are affected by a number of factors that seem to mediate the eventual somatic reaction. Many of the factors seem to be correlative to physical characteristics of the subject, such as age, general health, sex, and physical fitness. Others seem to be related to a subject's general emotional reactivity and momentary mind set. None of the factors described by the Harrers seems to be directly cognitive, or subject to learning effects or prior training.

The laboratory confirmation that somatic changes are somehow "in sync" with musical activities is not really satisfying, however. It is once again phenomenology without psychology. It fails to present any particular theory from which a prediction might be made. These studies are unfortunately typical of much of recent psychology. Emotional behaviors—observable, measurable—were acceptable for study. Emotional experiences—mental events—were not.

Emotional Responses to Music

The past twenty-some years of American psychology notwithstanding, emotions have always fascinated psychologists, and the fascination is almost a perverse one. As civilization progresses, it seems, it wants to view itself as increasingly intelligent, ever more rational, exhibiting action that is ever more controlled and circumscribed. The rational, intelligent progress of humans seems demonstrable prima facie, except for those evil emotions that muck things up. We seem, despite our rationality, no closer than we ever were to doing away with war and anger, dominance and lust. Clinical psychology itself grew up in part around Freud's attempt to understand how emotions cause abnormalities in otherwise intelligent people. Emotions are relentless. Emotions are intuitively significant. Emotions are undeniable. Emotions are undeniably central to humanness.

Mandler's Explanations of Emotion

The most recent complete and understandable explanations of the psychology of emotion have been presented by George Mandler (1979, 1988). Much of the discussion on general theories of emotion that follows is based on his writings. Mandler points out that there are two major traditions in the study of emotion; each focuses on a different human mechanism. One asserts the primacy of central nervous system (CNS) processes in the emotional experience (Mandler, 1984). He labels this a "mentalist" view of emotion, a position that holds that emotional experience is a process only of the mind. The second view, the "organic tradition," asserts the primacy of the peripheral nervous system, particularly the autonomic nervous system. The first holds that emotional experiences are mentally caused; the other, that they are organically caused.

The mentalist view holds that during emotional experience, organic events are the products of psychic events. The organic view says that physiological events occur first, and that it is these events that are brought to consciousness by the mind and experienced as emotions. The organic tradition has the richest history.

The Organic Tradition The organic tradition begins where much of psychology begins, in the work of William James. In an 1884 article he wrote, "My thesis is . . . that the bodily changes follow directly the *perception* of the exciting fact, and that our feeling of the same changes as they occur IS the emotion" (James, 1884, p. 189). A person might see a bear, and decide quite rationally to leave without any emotional response at all, while another might perceive the bear and be driven to bodily action—flight for instance. That flight would kick off the experience of emotion. To James, we do not cry because we are sad, we cry and it is that physical act that we experience as sadness.

At a distance of over a hundred years it seems impossible that James did not consider the need for some chain of cognitive process between the initial perception of the bear and the gut wrenching that triggers the actual experience of fear. James insisted that particular perceptions cause bodily changes directly, without any interpretation, without any awareness of the external events on the part of the perceiver.

This theory, modified by Lange (1887) and now known as the James-Lange theory, was a dominant one for many years. It was attacked by some of the greatest of the early psychologists, like Wilhelm Wundt in the 1890s, but it still remained popular. The most telling criticisms came from Walter Cannon (1927). He attacked it to support his own theory, a theory that has never had many adherents. The criticisms, however, set the tone for 50 years' examination of the James-Lange theory.

Cannon's criticisms focused on visceral response, the "feeling in the pit of one's stomach" that seems present in all emotional experience. Whereas Cannon made many points, there are two that are important. First, he reasoned that if James and Lange were correct, if he surgically separated the brain from the sympathetic nervous system (or severed the spine in an accident so there could be no feedback from the gut to the brain), persons would be unable to experience emotion. Observation showed him, though, that even sympathectomized people experience emotions. This weakened the James-Lange theory. (There is recent evidence, however, that persons thus afflicted do have a difficult time acquiring emotional responses to new experiences.)

Second, if the James-Lange theory were correct, and if our experience of emotion depended on our perception of gut feelings, then there should be distinctly discernible differences in the gut feelings for fear, lust, and anxiety. There did not seem to be. All the gut feelings seemed the same, so how could the brain distinguish among the emotions? This question further weakened the theory of James and Lange.

These points, and the other less obvious ones made by Cannon, encouraged an extensive research tradition into the psychophysiology of emotion, research and experimentation that is important to understanding the musical emotional response.

Cold Emotions—the "As if" Experience In the 1920s G. Marañon (1924) found that when he injected a large number of people with the extract of the adrenal glands called "adrenaline," about a third of them described some sort of emotional state. The rest did not report any emotional state, but merely perceived a physiological state of arousal. Those who reported an emotional state did not say that they were angry, or sad, or happy. Rather they said that they felt "as if" they were angry or sad. That response was not a total emotional response. The classic "as if" response has been called a "cold" emotion. If Marañon, however, discussed a recent emotional event, say, the death of a family member, with one of the patients so treated, the patient then actually *became* sad, and had a full emotional response. There are thus three outcomes to the experiment: simple arousal; a "cold" or "as if" emotion; and a full emotional experience if cognitive support is available (Mandler, 1984).

In the 1960s Stanley Schachter and his colleague J. Singer refined Marañon's experiments (1962). They told their subjects that they would receive a vitamin injection; some were then given a placebo and others were given a shot of adrenaline. Both the placebo and the adrenaline receivers were then told one of three stories. Group 1 was told to expect a set of effects from the shot, and the proper effects of adrenaline were then described. (Anger or euphoria are the ordinary effects.) Group 2 was given no information about what would happen, and group 3 was given misinformation about what would happen.

They later were placed in a room with another person they believed to be an experimental subject but who actually was a stooge of the experimenters. Depending on whether the subject reacted with anger or euphoria to the adrenaline, the stooge either tried to engage them in play, or exhibited angry behaviors, becoming more and more insulting, asking insulting questions and then angrily leaving the room. The behavior of the subjects was observed surreptitiously.

Subjects who had received a placebo had no predictable responses. A state of no visceral arousal was associated with emotionally neutral behavior. Those who felt what they expected to feel (the informed group) reported very low levels of emotional response (self-report) and displayed low levels of emotional behavior. Those who were misinformed about the effects of the adrenaline, those who had the greatest need for an explanation of why they felt the opposite of how they expected to feel, reported the greatest levels of emotional feelings. These subjects joined in the emotional behaviors to a greater extent and reported a more intense feeling.

Several important conclusions can be drawn from this experiment and from the many attempts at replicating it. First, an internal, organic, or visceral arousal state alone is not enough to be experienced as emotion. Second, cognitive information alone may not be enough to produce emotional experience. Third, identical visceral arousal can be interpreted as completely different emotional states depending on the cognitive information available at the time. The last conclusion is the most important. The depth and intensity of emotional experience are increased when an unexpected result is encountered, that is, when the cognitive information available in the environment is at odds with what one has been led to believe will happen. If what is expected to happen does happen, one feels less emotion than if something unexpected happens (Mandler, 1984).

During the last 25 years Singer and Schachter's work has been extended, and further investigations of the involvement of visceral response in emotional experience have been made (Reisenzein, 1983). Mandler (1984) decided that there is no evidence for specific visceral precedence for specific emotional reactions. There is in a variety of emotional states, including anger, fear, and euphoria, an adrenaline release. Consistent with the data from the von Karajan studies, Frankenhaeuser (1975) has demonstrated that the greatest adrenaline release is in euphoric situations. ANS arousal is undifferentiated.

Mandler (1984) concludes that

the perception of autonomic or visceral activity is in fact an extremely powerful variable in manipulating emotional response. . . . The important modern insight is that what is subjectively registered by the experiencing individual influences emotional experience. In that sense, James and Lange have been partially vindicated. . . . (p. 17)

The Mentalist Tradition

The mentalist tradition has a distinguished history. Traces of it can be found in Plato. This view holds that emotion is a purely mental event; the physiological components of the experience are consequences of the emotional state, not precursors of it.

A popular version of the mentalist view holds that there are a number of fundamental, innate processes that might be ascribed to neural patterns resulting from common evolutionary history. These fundamental patterns are limited in number, and each gives rise to a fundamental emotion. There are other, more complex emotions, but they are seen as combinatory results of the fundamental ones. These theories, like the ones postulated by Tompkins, by Izard, and by Plutchik, seem to state that there are about 10 such fundamental emotions (differing only in specifics; Mandler, 1984). These emotions are always present in the mind and are activated by external events, or internal events such as memory or image. Although the specific emotions vary from list to list, Izard's list is instructive: fear, anger, joy, disgust, interest, surprise, contempt, shame, sadness, and guilt.

The fundamental emotion theories pose several major problems. Mandler (1984) has pointed out two. First, all of the theories require a great deal of cognitive processing before the registration of emotion; and the processing would seem to be complex, including current and prior knowledge, expectation, and plans. This is true of even the "fundamental" emotions, but for the secondary ones the processes are even more complex. To Mandler they are too complex to support the supposition that these emotions are fundamental, primary states.

Mandler's second criticism is more obtuse. It is similar to the criticism of factor analytic studies of mental processes. Just because a response is regular, there is no reason to conclude it is fundamental to the organism. These regularities may be only the result of common regularities in action in the world, which induce regularities in cognition, especially in perception action sequences.

Conflict Theories

Quite apart from the fundamental emotion theorists, another line of thought within the mentalist tradition groups together the various "conflict" theories of emotion. The most famous of these was Freud's psychoanalytic theory, which viewed all emotional response as the result of long-standing frustration in the history of each individual. Those frustrations were for Freud so soundly rooted in the Judeo/Christian ethic and the environment of Calvinism that they are impossible to apply to a general pancultural understanding of the mind. Thus Freud's idea is interesting, but not particularly useful in the present case.

More important are the general conflict theories, like the theory of Frederic Paulhan (1930). Paulhan noted that whenever any affective experience happens it is always in the presence of the same condition: the arrest of tendencies. Paulhan believed that no two emotions were alike, and did not provide an atomistic list of "fundamentals." Rather, he believed the particular emotion experienced was a function of whatever specific tendencies were established and the particular conditions under which they were arrested. John Dewey (1895) advanced a similar theory, which reemphasized that an interruption of orderly progression is resisted by humans, and that resistance results in actual tensions and internal conflict. Thus conflict forms the emotional experience.

Hebb's (1949) theory was also a conflict theory, but with an important twist. Hebb said that one can learn the regularities that are interrupted to cause emotional reaction. He formed his model after watching monkeys react to the presence of a severed monkey head. The monkeys became terrified, but the intensity of that terror was a function of their experience. The older they were, and the more they "expected" to see only whole monkeys, the greater their terror. His theory requires an acquired, rather than innate, sense of orderliness to the world.

One conflict theory of particular importance in music is a part of the music theory literature of the 1950s. That theory is described in Leonard B. Meyer's *Emotion and Meaning in Music*. Meyer (1956) contends that an emotion is "aroused when a tendency to respond is arrested or inhibited" (p. 19). Meyer contends that the feeling so engendered is undifferentiated. (Note the similarity to the organic theorists.) The emotional experience, on the other hand, is differentiated "because it involves awareness and cognition of a stimulus situation which itself is necessarily differentiated" (p. 19).

Meyer's theory is that emotion or affect arises when a musical tendency is established and then arrested, or delayed, or modified. At this point purely cognitive processes take over to "explain" why the established plan turns out differently than thought.

As an example of how emotional experiences are differentiated from essentially undifferentiated emotions, Meyer (1956) cites the sensation of falling through the air. If we are in a dark place and simply find ourselves falling without explanation, we are likely to have an unpleasant emotional experience. We have no cognitive model to fit to the visceral response. If, however, we are in an amusement park, in, say, a parachute drop ride, the same visceral activation will give rise to an emotional experience of pleasure or even fun.

Meyer's explanations have some deficiencies. Chief among them are two: First, he postulates no real mechanism for sorting out affect or emotion after the arousal takes place. That is, his explanations of the eventual differentiation of the undifferentiated arousal states are unsatisfying. Second, there is not a good explanation of why pleasant emotions are aroused. Most interruptions would seem to cause surprise, at least, or frustrations, and annoyances.

Mandler's theory as summarized by Dowling and Harwood (1986) informs about the first criticism:

Human cognition operates by means of perceptual-motor schemata through which (largely unconscious) expectancies are generated for upcoming events and by which future behaviors are planned. The interruption of an ongoing schema or plan brings about biological arousal [our good old visceral activation]—a signal that something has gone wrong. This reaction in turn triggers a search for a cognitive interpretation of what happened—a search for meaning. The arousal and interpretation join together in producing an emotional experience of a particular quality. (p. 214)

Musical Schemata One learns how music goes. One learns in general terms (e.g., the whole western music system) and in more specific terms (e.g., a particular style) and in more particular terms (e.g., a particular composer) and even in the most specific terms (e.g., a particular piece as it unfolds for the first time). These instances of "the way music goes" are reduced to patterns, or directions, or models that are called

schemata. Individuals have expectations in the form of these "maps" or models. When a particular piece is encountered, as many schemata are activated as are known, and when they are exhausted, the individual begins to build a newer and more specific one. It is the violation of a schema or several schemata that causes the activation of visceral response (or even responses that are not so conscious as "that feeling in the pit of one's stomach"). The archetypical schemata that organize it all are by some theories based on patterning of motor events. Some manifestations of interruptions may be so slight as to escape conscious notice, but they are there.

In listening to a particular piece, one follows the schemata, projecting them forward in time to provide expectancies. Most of this, these plans, the projections, is unconscious. When an interruption occurs and arousal takes place, cognitive activity is triggered that searches for an interpretation of the novel event.

Dowling and Harwood (1986) liken this to walking down a forest path. There is a general schema for all paths, and more specific schemata as well. We "expect" what will happen. We will often encounter small trees down in our way, and we will be blocked. But the path doesn't simply end; we search around the interruption and find our way forward again. "The happiest outcome occurs when in the course of the detour we come upon an especially beautiful flower that we would have missed on the main path. Meyer argues persuasively that especially meaningful moments in music arise from the violation of specific expectations followed by creative and felicitous resolutions of the disruptions" (p. 219).

This experience may be unconscious most of the time. Why is there agreement on the emotional content of a piece, at least at the conscious level? Why does it make sense to say that a particular piece is angry or sad, or that it makes us feel "as if" angry? Because when those cognitive processes cast around for meaning after those interruptions, they often activate other schemata that are not schemata of musical experience, but rather of ordinary experience. That is to say, there are enough similarities between a schema representing a fist fight and the schema representing parts of the *Rite of Spring* so that the conclusion is easily reached. Parts of *Rite of Spring* may sound angry, or sensual, or lustful.

The second criticism of Meyer—that while Meyer does a good job of explaining anger or surprise, he fails to account for delight or joy—is more difficult, until one makes the connection with the literature concerning the "inverted-U" hedgehog theory. Information theory is, of course, another example of a conflict theory. By the inverted-U theory, there is an optimum level of information, and thus of arousal. That optimum arousal, more or less continuously refreshed by the stream of musical information, may itself be experienced as pleasure.

The potential effects of experience and education are plain in this context. The better the grounding in the musical tradition, the more solidly a perceiver can have expectations. Meyer asserts that music is a stochastic process—an unfolding that produces certain elements according to certain probabilities. Further, music is a special kind of stochastic known as a Markoff chain. As such, the probabilities of any event depend on the events that went before. Musical memory, often cited as a part of musical ability, plays a part in musical response. There is a certain level of tacit understanding of those probabilities inherent in any member of a culture. The resolution of a dominant chord in a perfect cadence is expected by everyone. In fact, so many of the expectations are picked up simply by living and developing in the culture that children are to an extent functioning listeners to ordinary music at a very early age.

The establishment of more complex expectations, and the affective responses that accompany them, require more specialized experience than that afforded by growing up in the popular culture. The cognitive processing of art music is quite complex. A full set of expectations requires the activation of many schemata that are developed only through experiences like those gained in specialized study. Music education of all sorts, performing, creating, listening, analyzing, and the rest, helps to establish the schemata that form the expectations that are the roots of affective response.

References

Abeles, H. (1980). Responses to music. In D. Hodges (Ed.), *Handbook of music psychology* (pp. 105–140). Lawrence: National Association of Music Therapy.

Accurso, R. (1967). The development and application of a semantic differential for sounds. Unpublished master's thesis, University of Illinois, Urbana.

Bamberger, J. (1977). In search of a tune. In D. Perkins and B. Leondar (Eds.), *Arts and cognition,* (pp. 284–319). Baltimore: Johns Hopkins University Press.

Bamberger, J., and Brody, M. (1984). Perceptual problem solving in music: Some proposals for future research. *Psychomusicology, IV*(1&2), 33–57.

Berlyne, D. (1970). Novelty, complexity and hedonic value. *Perception and Psychophysics, 8,* 279–286.

Berlyne, D. (1971). *Aesthetics and psychobiology,* New York: Appleton-Century-Crofts.

Bragg, B., and Crozier, J. (1974). The development with age of exploratory sound sequences varying in uncertainty level. In D. E. Berlyne (Ed.), *Studies in the new experimental aesthetics.* New York: John Wiley.

Butler, J. (1968). The effect of personality variables, dogmatism, and repression-sensitization, upon response to music. Unpublished doctoral dissertation, University of Georgia, Athens.

Cannon, W. (1927). The James-Lange theory of emotions: A critical examination and an alternative theory. *American Journal of Psychology, 39,* 106–124.

Cattell, R., and Anderson, J. (1953). The measurement of personality and behavior disorders by the IPAT Music Preference Test. *Journal of Applied Psychology, 37,* 446–454.

Crozier, J. (1974). Verbal and exploratory responses to sound sequences varying in uncertainty level. In D. E. Berlyne (Ed.), *The new experimental aesthetics* (pp. 27–90). New York: John Wiley.

Davies, J. (1978). *The psychology of music,* Stanford: Stanford University Press.

Dewey, J. (1895). The theory of emotion. *Psychological Review,* 553–569.

Dowling, W., and Harwood, D. (1986). *Music cognition.* Orlando: Academic Press.

Duerksen, D. (1968). A study of the relationship between the perception of musical processes and the enjoyment of music. *Bulletin of the Council for Research in Music Education, 12,* 1–8.

Farnsworth, P. (1954). A study of the Hevner adjective list. *Journal of Aesthetics and Art Criticism, 13,* 97–103.

Fisher, S., and Fisher, R. (1951). The effects of personal insecurity on reactions to unfamiliar music. *The Journal of Social Psychology, 34,* 265–273.

Frankenhaeuser, M. (1975). Experimental approaches to the study of catecholamines and emotion. In L. Levi (Ed.), *Emotions, their parameters and measurement.* New York: Raven Press.

Gordon, J., and Grey, J. (1978). Perception of spectral modifications of orchestral instrument tones. *Computer Music Journal, 2,* 24–31.

Greer, R., Dorrow, L., and Hanser, S. (1973). Music discrimination training and the music selection behaviour of nursery and primary level children. *Bulletin of the Council for Research in Music Education, 35,* 30–43.

Greer, R., Dorrow, L., and Randall, A. (1973). Music listening preferences of elementary school children. *Journal of Research in Music Education, 21,* 284–291.

Greer, R., Dorrow, L., Wachaus, G., and White, E. (1973). Adult approval and students' music selection behavior. *Journal of Research in Music Education, 21,* 345–354.

Grey, J. (1978). Multidimensional perceptual scaling of musical instrument timbres. *Journal of the Acoustical Society of America, 63,* 1270–1277.

Hampton, P. (1945). The emotional element in music. *Journal of General Psychology, 33,* 237–250. Cited in Lundin, R. (1985). *An Objective Psychology of Music.* New York: Ronald Press.

Hare, F. (1975). The identification of dimensions underlying verbal and exploratory responses to music through multidimensional scaling. Unpublished doctoral dissertation, University of Toronto, Toronto.

Hargreaves, D. (1986). *The developmental psychology of music.* Cambridge: Cambridge University Press.

Harrer, G., and Harrer, H. (1977). Music, emotion, and autonomic function. In M. Critchley and R. Henson (Eds.), *Music and the brain* (pp. 202–216). Springfield: Charles C Thomas.

Hebb, D. (1949). *The organization of behavior.* New York: John Wiley.

Hevner, K. (1935). Expression in music: A discussion of experimental studies and theories. *Psychological Review, 42,* 186–204.

Hevner, K. (1936). Experimental studies of the elements of expression in music. *American Journal of Psychology, XLVIII,* 245–268.

Heyduk, R. (1975). Rated preference for musical composition as it relates to complexity and exposure frequency. *Perception and Psychophysics, 17*(1), 84–91.

Howard, J., and Silverman, E. (1976). A multidimensional scaling analysis of 16 complex sounds. *Perception and Psychophysics, 19*(2), 193–200.

Inglefield, H. (1968). The relationship of selected personality variables to conformity behavior reflected in the musical preferences of adolescents when exposed to peer group influences. Unpublished doctoral dissertation, Ohio State University, Columbus.

Inglefield, H. (1974). Conformity behavior reflected in the musical preferences of adolescents. Unpublished paper presented at the in-service meeting of the Music Educators National Conference, Anaheim, CA. Cited in Radocy, R., and Boyle, J. (1988). *Psychological foundations of musical behavior.* Springfield: Charles C Thomas.

James, W. (1884). What is an emotion? *Mind, 9,* 188–205. Cited in Mandler, G. (1984). *Mind and body.* New York: Norton.

Johnstone, J., and Katz, E. (1957). Youth and popular music: A study of the sociology of taste. *American Journal of Sociology, 62,* 563–568.

Keil, C., and Keil, A. (1966). Musical meaning: A preliminary report. *Ethnomusicology, 10*(2), 153–173.

Keston, M., and Pinto, I. (1955). Possible factors influencing musical preference. *Journal of Experimental Psychology, 70,* 101–113.

Lange, C. (1887). *Über Gemuthsbewegungen.* Leipzig: Theodor Thomas. Cited in Mandler, G. (1975). *Mind and emotion.* New York: John Wiley.

Langer, S. (1957). *Philosophy in a new key,* Cambridge, Harvard University Press.

Lundin, R. (1967). *An objective psychology of music* (2nd ed.). New York: Ronald Press.

Mandler, G. (1979). Emotion. In E. Hearst (Ed.), *The first century of experimental psychology.* Hillsdale: Lawrence Erlbaum Associates.

Mandler, G. (1984). *Mind and body.* New York: Norton.

Mandler, G. (1988). Emotion. In the *Oxford companion to the mind.* London: Oxford University Press.

Marañon, G. (1924). Contribution à l'étude de l'action émotive de l'adrenaline. *Revue Française d'Endocrinologie, 2.* Cited in Mandler, G. (1984). *Mind and body.* New York: Norton.

Meyer, L. (1956). *Emotion and meaning in music.* Chicago: University of Chicago Press.

Meyer, L. (1957). Meaning in music and information theory. *Journal of Aesthetics and Arts Criticism, XV,* 412–424.

Mikol, B. (1960). The enjoyment of musical systems. In M. Rokeach (Ed.), *The open and closed mind.* Cited in Radocy, R. and Boyle, J. (1988). *Psychological foundations of musical behavior* (2nd ed.). Springfield: Charles C Thomas.

Miller, R. (1979). An analysis of musical perception by multidimensional scaling. Unpublished doctoral dissertation, University of Illinois, Urbana.

Miller, R. (1990). The semantic differential in the study of musical perception: A theoretical overview. *The Quarterly, I*(1&2), 63–73.

Moles, A. (1968). *Théorie de l'information et perception esthétique.* Paris: Flammerion.

O'Briant, M., and Wilbanks, W. (1978). The effect of context on the perception of music. *Bulletin of the Psychonomic Society, 12*(6), 441–443.

Osgood, C., Suci, G., and Tannenbaum, P. (1957). *The measurement of meaning.* Urbana: University of Illinois Press.

Paulhan, F. (1930). *The laws of feeling* (Trans. C. K. Ogden). New York: Harcourt, Brace and Co. Cited in Meyer, L. B. (1956). *Emotion and meaning in music.* Chicago: University of Chicago Press.

Radocy, R., and Boyle, J. (1988). *Psychological foundations of musical behavior* (2nd ed.), Springfield: Charles C Thomas.

Reisenzein, R. (1983). The Schachter theory of emotion: Two decades later. *Psychological Bulletin, 94*(2), 239–264.

Ryle, G. (1949). *The concept of mind,* London: Hutchinson.

Schacter, S., and Singer, J. (1962). Cognitive, social and psychological determinants of emotional state. *Psychological Review, 69,* 379–399.

Scherer, K., and Oshinsky, J. (1977). Cue utilization in emotion attribution from auditory state. *Motivation and Emotion, 1,* 331–346.

Schoen, M., and Gatewood, E. (1927). The mood effects of music. In M. Schoen (Ed.), *The effects of music.* New York: Harcourt, Brace, and World.

Shepard, R. (1972). Introduction to Volume One. In R. Shepard, K. Romney, and S. Nerlove (Eds.), *Multidimensional scaling, Vol. I: Theory.* New York: Academic Press.

Shepard, R. (1982a). Structural representations of pitch. In D. Deutch (Ed.), *Psychology of music.* New York: Academic Press, 275–287.

Shepard, R. (1982b). Geometrical approximations to the structure of musical pitch. *Psychological Review, 89,* 305–333.

Sluckin, W., Hargreaves, D., and Colman, A. (1982). Some experimental studies of familiarity and liking. *Bulletin of the British Psychological Society, 35,* 189–194.

Sluckin, W., Hargreaves, D., and Colman, A. (1983). Novelty and human aesthetic preferences. In J. Archer and L. Birke (Eds.), *Exploration in animals and humans.* London: Van Nostrand Reinhold.

Vitz, P. (1966). Affect as a function of stimulus variation. *Journal of Experimental Psychology, 71,* 74–79.

Walker, E. (1980). *Psychological complexity and preference: A hedgehog theory of behavior.* Monterey: Brooks-Cole.

Wedin, L. (1972). A multidimensional study of perceptual/emotional qualities in music. *Scandinavian Journal of Psychology, 13,* 228–240.

Zagona, S., and Kelly, M. (1966). The resistance of the closed mind to novel and complex audiovisual experience. *Journal of Social Psychology, 70,* 123–131.

Zajonc, R. (1968). Attitudinal effects of mere exposure. *Journal of Personality and Social Psychology, 9, Monograph Supplement 2,* Cited in Hargreaves, D. (1986). *The developmental psychology of music.* Cambridge: Cambridge University Press.

·27·

MOTIVATION

Nancy G. Thomas

UNIVERSITY OF MICHIGAN

> I must admit that when I started the flute in the fifth grade, I picked it
> because it was the lightest to carry. But as I progressed in the flute choir,
> to flute lessons, to all-state, and finally to music camp, I realized I'd made
> a good decision. Right now I'm fourth chair in the high school symphony
> band, and I'm an up-and-coming clarinet player in the wind ensemble.
> But I didn't start out this way. When I was in elementary school I was
> pretty bad. But I was just starting out. We all know you have to start
> somewhere.
>
> Eleventh-grade witness

This testimony comes from a student speaking against a school board's proposal to eliminate fifth-grade instrumental music in its district schools. Her plea reveals both a determination to make music and a recognition that the current level of her instrumental "mastery" rests on having begun young and persisted over time.

What do we know about this course of events? What do we understand about how students take up an instrument or somehow come to take singing seriously, possibly before they understand much at all about what making music entails? Then—and this is more critical—what makes them give themselves over to the protracted effort needed to progress? How do they move from the initial stage of "romance" toward a stage of greater "precision" (Whitehead, 1929)? The research that would address these questions is under way and is the focus of this chapter.

Motivation to learn music may be similar to that governing learning in other academic subjects. As with other school learning, the pursuit of music training is multiply determined. Accomplishment in music, as in other fields, rests on a network of skills, strategies, and techniques, and discipline is key (Covington, 1983). Also as in other subjects, teachers face the full gamut of student sentiment, from indifference to enthusiasm to unreasoned anxiety. If similar cognitive skills thus serve the arts, the humanities, and the sciences (Gard-

ner, 1977; Root-Bernstein, 1984), the motivation to acquire those skills should generalize across fields. But is there more to learning music? A case is made here that although these parallels pertain, there is more to the story: The nature of music learning and music's unique function in students' lives point to important additional challenges to understanding the motivation to learn music, and ultimately to understanding how music affects intellectual, social, and emotional development. The following discussion first reviews research evidence on what we know about music's place in young students' lives. Then follow reflections on the special challenges music learning offers to the study of motivation and some proposed directions for future investigation.

EMPIRICAL RESEARCH IN REVIEW

The degree to which music learning is thought to resemble other learning in school appears to have shaped the direction taken thus far by the research of student motivation in music. Theorizing and investigations to date have either lifted directly or adapted to their purpose constructs from the more general literature on achievement motivation. Although research on the music pursuits of school-age children lacks its equivalent of the early classic studies of the "need for achievement" (McClelland, 1961), the work picks up where psychoanalytic theory leaves off, with personality and motivational studies of self constructs, attitudes, and the wish for success and fear of failure (Atkinson and Raynor, 1974). Research on motivation in music has focused on investigations of (1) the relationship between attitudes about music and self-esteem, (2) the self-concept of ability, and (3) attributions to success and failure. All three avenues of research take their inspiration from the classic work on achievement motivation.

Early Studies of Attitudes and Self-Esteem

Initial studies (Nolin, 1973; Nolin and Vander Ark, 1979; Vander Ark, Nolin, and Newman, 1980) sought to trace developing attitudes about music and their relationship to self-esteem over the middle grades (third through ninth) in schools differing in socioeconomic status (SES). As with the research on attitudes about school in general (Eccles, Midgley, and Adler, 1984), students' attitudes toward music were found to become increasingly negative with age, but with girls' attitudes being more positive than those of boys. Higher self-esteem was associated with the study of music and generally with higher SES.

In addition to problems in sampling and design, these early studies are unsatisfying on other counts. First, the measures of "attitudes," consisting of the *Musical Attitude Quotient* (MAQ) and the *Musical Attitude Inventory* (MAI), were limited to students' "liking" of various music activities. Absent are any consideration of student interest beyond enjoyment and measures of task value or difficulty, variables that are known to be important components of motivation (Parsons, 1983; Nicholls, 1984). Further, despite the proffering of various causal hypotheses, these studies are essentially descriptive. It is posited, for instance, that music experience in school fosters positive attitudes and self-esteem (Nolin and Vander Ark, 1979), and the authors interpret the results as supporting this hypothesis. But this is an unwarranted conclusion. Since a correlation does not tell us the direction of effect, the causal relationship could as well be in the opposite direction, with the students with higher self-esteem and more positive attitudes being more likely to elect music.

Other findings in these studies seem contradictory or at least difficult to interpret. For instance, students were found to prefer singing over instrumental music, but in one study performing was preferred, especially where it involved playing instruments (Nolin, 1973). Similarly, reading music was glaringly the most unpopular activity, except in connection with playing instruments. These apparent interactions between preferences and activities need further explanation.

The effect of SES was mixed and the authors' conclusions unconvincing. In one study (Nolin, 1973) lower SES students had more positive attitudes toward music, but in another study (Vander Ark et al., 1980) students in a middle SES school had more positive attitudes than students in either a lower or higher SES school. Although this U-shaped relationship was seen to be important, no theoretical interpretation was offered. In discussing the finding in a third study that student self-esteem varied with SES, Nolin and Vander Ark (1979) pointed out that students in the high SES school had a particularly outstanding music program and teacher. The obvious possibility that students may simply like music better and experience an enhancement of self-esteem when the program is good and the subject well taught, regardless of SES factors, was not discussed.

Finally, these early studies did not address the fundamental question of what students were *learning* in music. Research in other areas of education has found a consistent link between measures of achievement and motivational disposition (Byrne, 1984). The following studies explored whether such a relationship also holds for music.

Self-Concept and Academic Achievement

Subsequent research has continued to reflect the influence of the classic literature on motivation through studies of the relationship of academic achievement and measures of self-concept of ability in music to achievement in general music. Citing four previous studies that had found general achievement scores to be a consistent predictor of achievement in instrumental performance, one investigator (Hedden, 1982) devised a study to test the comparative effects on achievement in general music of five predictors: (1) academic achievement, (2) attitudes toward music, (3) self-concept in music, (4) music background (extensive experience with music outside school), and (5) gender. Participants in the study were the fifth- and sixth-grade students ($N = 144$) in two schools in two towns.

Regression analyses revealed that in the first school, academic achievement and self-concept in music were significant predictors of achievement in general music classes, accounting jointly for 34 percent of the variance; in the second school, the combined effect of academic achievement and attitudes toward music accounted for 61 percent of the variance in music achievement. Self-concept and attitudes were found to be highly correlated, however, which led the authors to conclude that the best single predictor of achievement in general music was not music self-concept or attitudes but overall academic achievement: The best all-around students also do well in music. What may be masked in these results is an assessment of music's place in the lives of the less good students over and beyond its strictly academic value, a consideration to be taken up later.

A recent study (Stewart, 1991) used survey data from a nationally representative sample ($N = 9195$) to explore high school students' participation in music. Preliminary analyses of data from the "High School and Beyond" survey, the second of three federally-funded studies of the National Education Longitudinal Studies program, found no difference between music and nonmusic students in global self-concept, as measured by a scale made up of four questions about self-worth and general ability. Students who took music, however, had significantly higher achievement scores than nonmusic students. The correlation between overall academic achievement and global self-concept, although significant, was modest, .13, and did not differ for music and nonmusic students. Although one could wish for a more discriminating conception of self-concept, the study is nevertheless valuable in that it takes a broad stroke in examining the effects of music participation in a large sample, and subsequent causal modeling analyses may serve to clarify the interrelationships among variables.

Attributions to Success and Failure

Other recent work (Asmus, 1985, 1986, 1989) adapting attribution theory (Weiner, 1984) brings a third body of empirical evidence to bear on our understanding of motivation in music. The hypothesis was that differences in *motivation* might account for variability in music achievement that was not accounted for by differences in general academic achievement. Differences in motivation were explored by assessing the attributions students make, that is, the reasons they give, to explain why a person does well or poorly in music. The underlying assumption of this approach is that students' motivation to commit themselves to a task is determined in large part by whether they expect to be successful at it, and that these expectancies for success are in turn influenced by their sense of how much they can control the outcome; success may be seen to rest, for instance, on their own effort or on the possession of some requisite ability. The first two studies considered here (Asmus, 1985, 1986) drew on Weiner's earlier two-dimensional model (1974). Four attributions consisting of two to internal causes (i.e., ability and effort) and two to external causes (i.e., task difficulty and luck), combined with a stable/nonstable dimension, were employed to assess a person's views of what explains success, or failure, at a task and how this bodes for prospects of future success.

A preliminary study of sixth-graders in three schools generally replicated other attributional research findings (Asmus, 1985). In responses typical of the age group, the students attributed both success and failure to a combination of ability and effort. The results, however, varied with school, an interesting finding that would recur in subsequent investigation.

A more rigorous study assessed the attribution patterns of 589 fourth- to twelfth-graders in music in eight schools (Asmus, 1986). The assessment was open-ended, with students being asked to give five reasons why other students do well or do not do well in music. The focus was on students' attributions for others, not for themselves, a measure likely to elicit trait rather than situational perceptions (Weiner, 1984). Results largely paralleled findings from the existing attribution literature. As with the earlier study of sixth-graders, the internal attributions of ability and effort were overall the most cited determinants of success or failure. Additional patterns were detected, however—possibly stemming from the increased sample size and age range. Success was attributed to stable internal and external causes, namely, ability and

task difficulty, while failure was attributed to the unstable causes, namely, effort and luck. Unexpectedly, girls made more attributions to ability than boys, which contrasts with other attribution studies that have shown boys to be more likely than girls to cite ability as responsible for success and failure (Parsons, Meece, Adler, and Kaczala, 1982). The author speculated that the greater emphasis on ability may be the result of emphasis on competition in music in our schools and the general societal view that superior inborn talent is responsible for achievement in music. No interpretation of the sex difference finding was proposed.

As would be expected from other research results (Nicholls and Miller, 1984), the data also revealed a gradual shift with increasing age from an internal, unstable attribution to effort to an internal, stable attribution to ability, such that by early adolescence students cited ability as the major reason for doing well in music. This finding was taken as evidence that students should begin music early while they still view effort as the legitimate route to mastery, a conviction echoing Nicholls (1984; also Nicholls and Miller, 1984), who has demonstrated that the shift to ability attributions to the exclusion of effort tends to be maladaptive to continuing persistence.

Finally, the results differed once more "by school" in this study, yet no specific school level patterns could be identified. The differences were interpreted, rather, as a *teacher* effect calling for more intensive exploration. In a follow-up study, the 5,000 attributions supplied by the participants of the 1986 study were reduced to 125 statements (Asmus, 1989). These statements were then rated in turn by 540 high school students to derive five "factors" accounting for success or failure in music: effort, musical ability, musical background, classroom environment, and affect for music. This set of attributions thus introduced new variables that diverge from the Weiner model.

Initial analyses showed that, of the five categories, high school students still emphasized effort and ability and that highly motivated students make more attributions to effort while less motivated students emphasize ability. The author explored the relationship of these five categories to three outcomes: students' commitment to music study, their liking of music, and "motivation magnitude," which included personal commitment, interest in school music, and interest in music compared with other subjects. Specific attention was given to determining if patterns varied by teacher. Ninth- to twelfth-graders (N = 498) in five high schools representing different geographical areas and both rural and urban settings provided responses on the independent measure of the five categories and the dependent measures of commitment, liking, and motivation magnitude.

In reporting results the author chose to highlight, more than the motivational patterns themselves, the finding that the relationship between independent and dependent variables differed by teacher for all the categories *except* musical background—the only category among the five not under school teacher control. This was taken as evidence that the teacher in the school music-learning process has special importance. But the assertion also serves to raise one's curiosity about the actual teacher differences in this study. What were these teachers like? What was their training? How, indeed, *did* they teach music? It seems crucial that the relationship between students' achievement and teachers' practices be explored.

The report concluded that teachers should have superior musical skill and knowledge and strong "motivational" skills, the latter to involve encouraging an attribution pattern that ties achievement more to effort than ability. Teachers should motivate students "not only for short-term musical development but also for long-term musical involvement" (Asmus, 1989, p. 20). Empirical investigation to substantiate this set of claims would take us a long way toward a better understanding of what teachers already do or might learn to do to foster students' continuing motivation in music.

CHALLENGING THE RESEARCH STATUS QUO

Studies of music learning and motivation have proceeded to this point under the aegis of the older, established literature on academic achievement motivation. And this fledgling body of research has been fruitful in drawing the comparison between students' music learning and learning in other areas. The evidence that positive attitudes toward music decline over age, that self constructs are related to achievement, and that attributions to ability gradually overtake those to effort as children get older all corroborate that the motivation to learn and do music operates very much like that observed in other academic areas. A few hints that all is not completely harmonious have been addressed, however. Perhaps most provocative is the work of Asmus with its five-category inventory that includes both "background in music" and "affect for music" as departures from the standard models. Also intriguing are the indications that differences between schools, music programs, or teachers may be potent determinants of student persistence and enjoyment.

Where should the research on motivation and music turn next? What considerations might help shape research design and choice of measures? First, learning music has special characteristics that lend it a unique status among school subjects at-large—characteristics that have implications, singly and in counterpoint, for how the conduct of research could proceed (Covington, 1983). In addition, a burgeoning literature of more recent thinking and evidence on academic motivation and achievement in general offers a wealth of new theory and tools for formulating studies of music motivation. Indeed some research directives already seem to be pushing for new approaches, and the discussion that follows is indebted to the presentations of the 1983 Ann Arbor Symposium III on the Application of Psychology to Music Teaching and Learning and the 1987 Denver Conference on the Biology of Music Making: Music and Child Development.

A new wave of thinking about students' motivation to learn and achieve is moving away from viewing motivation as relatively fixed and "traitlike," to emphasizing its fluidity and interconnectedness to situations-over-time. The cognitive and emotional *meanings* attached to learning are crucial to understanding what accounts for why a student turns one way or the other. The full menu offers a rich and complex array of constructs: perceived competence (Harter, 1982), self-worth (Covington, 1984), illusory incompetence (Phillips, 1987), the motives to get ahead and get by (Hartman, 1987), learned helplessness (Diener and Dweck, 1978), a third-generation theory of attributions (Weiner, 1984), attributions to task-inherent strategies (Clifford, 1984), personal investment (Maehr, 1983, 1984), the differentiation of ability (Nicholls, 1984; Nicholls and Miller, 1984), and the expectation of success and a codification of task value (Eccles, 1983).

Hardly one of this grand set of constructs would not be applicable to the study of music and motivation. An exhaustive discussion would be prohibitive here, so what follows is a selection of what might prove most useful: (1) some reflections on how music differs from most other school learning, and (2) how these distinctions, coupled with recent developments in theory, might lead us to ask different research questions or modify our study of motivation in music.

Music's Unique Role in the School Curriculum

To begin contrasting music learning to that of other subject areas, we first need only imagine the unlikely possibility that our young woman of the opening testimony would go before her school board to attest to the importance of fifth-grade reading or fifth-grade mathematics. It's an improbable image in the case of reading or math, but not so for music, which too often is thought a "frill," a subject outside the core curriculum. That this troubling state of affairs is the rule, that music is "definitely a side thing" as one young person raised in America's public schools puts it, is the topic for another day. Suffice it to say that music is not required in school in the same way reading, writing, and arithmetic are required. Students in most schools know they can pass from grade to grade without "passing" music; they can graduate from high school and go on about their life course without ever attaining a modicum of musical proficiency. As "functionally illiterate" in music, many students reach adulthood lacking the capacity, as either listener or performer, to "take meaning" from music (Heath, 1982) or to apply the skills of "audiation" (Gordon, 1990).

That music is a live performance art sets it apart from most other kinds of school learning. Several important implications for studying students' music involvement follow from this characteristic. First, a student's accomplishment is most crucially revealed in the *doing,* in present and prescribed time, not in problem solutions, written assignments, or passed examinations. This is not to say that learning to listen is unimportant or that music training does not have attached to it an extensive body of knowledge that is testable in the conventional sense, but "making music" is the essential activity. "Music is available for use and exists only in performance" (Blacking, 1990, p. 71). Ultimate literacy, even for the good listener, is best grounded in the experience of making music oneself.

That music is a performance art means also that the social context is an especially powerful factor underlying the learning process and the defining of student goals. Cooperative efforts among students, the student-teacher relationship, and very often the parent-child collaboration take on a special salience beyond that present in most other areas of learning. The making of music in ensembles, for instance, that typifies much school music can serve explicitly to enhance interest and requires a kind of student "teamwork," not unlike that in sports, but uncharacteristic of most other classroom learning. The music teacher not only has to cover the basic skills but also must be the mentor who enculturates students to a whole world of aesthetic meaning, historical perspective, and multicultural tradition. It is not that the exceptional, self-taught musician does not exist, but the essence of music, for the accomplished performer and literate listener alike, *cannot* be learned from a book or a computer program. In the case of high-achieving musicians (Bloom, 1985), the teacher's central role has been well documented: "Most excellent performers start really young, practice a lot, and *have rigorous mentors*" (Treffinger, 1983, p. 58). Parental mentorship also comes into play, with the most extreme example, the mother-prodigy phenomenon, being a topic unto itself. It would seem that a child's initiation and appreciation are best fostered in the presence of a knowledgeable and responsive adult who provides individual attention, even within the group setting.

Few, if any, other pursuits in school require from the student the extremes of combined private and public effort that characterize the learning of music. Whoever has experienced the demanding and often lonely and isolating routine of private practice knows that the multiplication tables or the identity of the adverb is more readily mastered. Yet at the other end comes the special exhilaration of a school program, sung or played in consort with one's peers for friends and family. To emphasize the contrast, we don't usually publicly celebrate the child's mastery of the 12s table or growing command of reading comprehension or written communication with anything approaching the same social intensity as that that accompanies the making of music.

It also follows that what constitutes "success" may be different in music learning than in other school subjects. Mastery in music is both highly elusive and protracted. Conquering the shaping of a phrase one day, or even at one moment, does not mean it will be there the next moment, let alone tomorrow. Learning to play or sing in tune, watching the metronome hand inch upwards notch by notch, wondering if a twinge of vibrato will ever come to sweeten the sound—these can consume an entire childhood and more. Since students who would attain even a modest competence in music must commit themselves before they realize what will be required, they should be able to appreciate small signs of growth, and they must be willing to take risks and accept disappointment (Sosniak, 1990). If "success value," as we will see shortly, is an important construct of the theorizing on motivation, then it matters that "success" in music might be defined more reservedly than in other subjects.

Finally, music's ethological significance may also afford it special status among school subjects and have implications for our understanding of how it is learned and to what end. The kinship of music acquisition, if only analogously, to language acquisition (Blacking, 1990; Hargreaves, 1986; Jackendoff and Lerdahl, 1980) speaks to its very basic role in human activity. Cohesive societies have certainly in the past and may yet in the future carry on admirably without formal mathematics or even written language—but *without music?* Might one contend even that societal cohesion and communal music making go hand in hand (Thomas, 1980; see also Feintuch, 1983)? We do not rally around a geometry proof or even a great poem in the same way that we take strength from a hymn or even a school "fight" song—from "Take Me Out to the Ball Game," much less "We Shall Overcome." "The real power of music lies in the fact that it can be 'true' to the life of feeling in a way that words cannot: Its significant forms have an *ambivalence* of content which words cannot" (Langer, 1960, p. 243). Strangely, the capacity of music to uplift and transcend, which would seem to be its most striking characteristic, is all but ignored in the literature on motivation. Is it because the "life of feeling" is too difficult, if not impossible, to measure? In that internalized sound imagery of rhythm and song runs deep in our collective soul, the extent to which this is so ought not be ignored in our attempts to understand more fully music's place in a child's development.

Self-Concept Revisited

When these distinguishing features of music learning are taken as a point of departure, revisions in our view of the self-concept as it applies to music may be in order. The global self-concept of the "High School and Beyond" study (Stewart, in progress) or even the more specific self-concept of music ability employed in the Hedden (1982) or Asmus studies (1989) may not do justice to the self-meanings attached to musical activity in school. It may not be enough to ask, "Are you a person of worth?" or, even more specifically, "How good are you at music?" because the student's motivation to do music may be governed by more than perceived self-worth or ability.

Demonstrating a relationship between a general or academic self-concept and music motivation or achievement may therefore prove difficult. A "hierarchical" conception (Shavelson, Hubner, and Stanton, 1976) that relates, instead, different aspects of the person's sense of self to specific activities or fields of study may be more useful (Marsh and Holmes, 1990; Thomas, 1986). And the self-concept construct might well profit from a still further revision that expands the hierarchical model to incorporate a broader conception of music's place in school life.

The operationalizing of such an expansion presents a challenge to anyone wanting to represent a more comprehensive music self-concept: Yes, music is in part academic, but it is also nonacademic and subsumes social, physical, and affective elements, with "music self-concept" crossing the existing theoretical boundaries (Figure 27–1). As more stud-

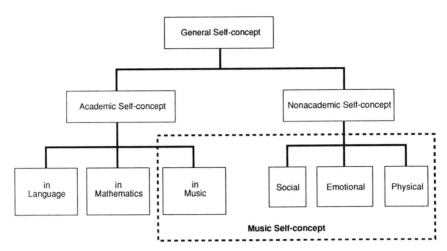

FIGURE 27–1.   Music Self-Concept: A Revised Hierarchical Model.

ies break out of the standard conceptual mold, the affective element may, for instance, take on a more central position. The emergence of "affect for music" (Asmus, 1989) as a factor to be reckoned with may signal such a shift. In two studies that investigated students' explanations of why they elected music in high school, "love of music" (Frakes, 1984), "pride in the group," and "enjoyment of performance" (Koutz, 1987) overshadowed all other considerations of ability or accumulated skill.

Intrinsic and Extrinsic Motivation

Task vs. Ego Involvement Because the external pressure in school to study music is much less than it is in other areas, the degree to which motivation is intrinsic rather than extrinsic may be especially crucial to persistence in music (Covington, 1983; Nicholls, 1983). Students may pursue mathematics as "a way to get ahead," but music has rarely been thought a route to fame and fortune. Thus the motive "to do one's best" or "just enjoy," as opposed to "being better than" the next person, may be not only desirable but essential to maintaining students' continuing motivation in music. These contrasting motives are termed: *task involvement,* which refers "to states where our concern is to develop or demonstrate (primarily to oneself) high ability in the less differentiated sense"; and *ego involvement,* which refers "to states where our concern is with developing or demonstrating (to self or others) high rather than low ability" (Nicholls, 1984, p. 43).

Unfortunately many schools typically promote ego involvement rather than task involvement—that is, extrinsic rather than intrinsic motivation (Nicholls, 1983, 1984). As the salience of students' "rank in the hierarchy" increases over the grades, this may be exactly, and ironically, the wrong emphasis if motivation is to be sustained. As students become more certain that ability means capacity, a "maturity" attained at about age 11 and consolidated by early adolescence (Nicholls, 1984), they come in turn to view ability as something innate and unchangeable; with the result that, if

they are not doing well, they may judge further striving as not worth their best effort. "When we are ego-involved and believe our capacity is low, we will avoid moderate normative-difficulty levels or 'realistic' challenges and will perform our worst if obliged to work on such tasks" (Nicholls, 1984, p. 49). At the extreme, students may completely abandon further effort. "Hopelessness and resignation are elicited, given an attribution for a negative outcome to stable factors [i.e., ability]. That is, if the future is expected to remain as bad as the past, then hopelessness is elicited" (Weiner, 1984, p. 30).

New research might well investigate the relationship of classroom practices to students' task and ego involvement in music to clarify the comparative importance of intrinsic and extrinsic motivation as predictors of persistence in music. Evidence suggests that adult musicians, who have obviously persisted, may experience more satisfaction in their profession than many other professionals for the very reason that motivation is inherently more intrinsic (see McKeachie, 1981). Interview material from a study of 25 professional string quartets (Murnighan, 1981) speaks to the lure of the elusiveness of success and the intrinsic attraction of music's complexities:

One thing that might contribute to the continued liveliness of string quartet players is their seeming inability to produce exactly the sound they want. Most [of the quartet members] I asked mentioned that there were only rare times when they were able to produce exactly the sound they wanted, and that these times were particularly brief. . . . I don't think anyone was able to say that they had even played an entire movement *exactly* right. The occasional successes gave them hope and something to shoot for. To have established an almost unattainable ideal and to be able to say that, however briefly and occasionally, the goal is reached, helps explain even further the commitment of string quartet musicians. (pp. 1–2)

Competition and Performance Anxiety Competitiveness in music is ubiquitous. The opportunity for public comparison in music takes many forms—from everyday playing or singing before one's peers to actual competitions, from auditions to "Bloody Friday," a famed and long-standing practice of the Interlochen National Music Camp in Michigan, whereby students "challenge" one another to determine section seating in orchestra or band. However widespread such practices are, though, a paucity of empirical studies leaves us knowing almost nothing about their actual effects on student motivation. As one participant of the Denver conference queried, "Competitions—are they anti-educational and destructive, or are they predictive of or essential to a successful career?" (Brandfonbrenner, 1990, p. 308).

Anyone who has experienced the stress of competing must sometimes question the wisdom, let alone efficacy, of the competition mystique: adrenalin gone berserk, the heart in the throat, a narrowed awareness reducing what was secure in the practice room to less than one's best—memory lapse, muddle at the keyboard, or the dreaded fluttering of the bow across the strings—it is not a pretty picture. Yet it has been proposed (Peery, Nyboer, and Peery, 1987) that while competitions may have some negative influence, most of the effect is positive. In this view, winners and non-winners alike benefit from preparing for a competition, and alerting students that winners may not necessarily be "the best" and that judges' views are not always consistent and accurate will cushion the blow of possible losses. A recent informal poll of students' reactions to a concerto competition at a summer music festival found a variety of face-saving responses (called "protective" by Pruett, 1990): "You have to take it all with a grain of salt." "I look on it as a 'moral obligation,' not a lot of fun." "There's always politics involved."

It may be that for many students, competition poses no problem. Indeed, for some the excitement of the contest may even improve performance, and for the student who can't wait to get out on stage, opportunities to compete or perform can be greatly enhancing. "If . . . we believe we have high capacity, ego-involving situations will present relatively little threat to our sense of competence. We will expect to succeed and, thereby, to demonstrate high ability at moderate normative-difficulty levels" (Nicholls, 1984, p. 49). We can wonder still about students with low perceived ability, and even the highest achievers are known to feel the pinch of performance anxiety—from the seasoned, world-renowned performer who is haunted by "chronic nerves," to the violin prodigy, at age 9, well before she should be viewing ability as capacity, observed to wipe her small hands on her concert dress as she launches into the Tchaikovsky Concerto.

The ego involvement resulting from classroom practices that emphasize public comparisons among students may well serve to incite achievement and provide many students with important creative outlets. And competitive structures may simply provide students with a model of the meritocratic system they will enter as adults (Nicholls, 1984; Peery et al., 1987). But the competitive classroom structure also inevitably creates an inequality of motivation (Ames, 1984; Nicholls, 1984): Since there must be both "winners" and "losers," students' achievements are negatively interdependent. One person's triumph requires another's relative loss. The evidence is that winning is less enhancing than losing is damaging, with "losing in competitive settings creating a

condition for self-criticism even in the high-self-concept child" (Ames, 1984, p. 186). Under competitive conditions, students focus on their ability differences and give unrealistically high and low estimates of their ability, with winners' estimates being overly self-aggrandizing and losers' estimates overly self-deriding (Ames, 1984; Nicholls, 1983). If competitive structures pose little problem to the "elite" (Maehr, 1983; Nicholls, 1984) or to students with perceived high ability, we still need to ask what effect such practices have on the very young, the shy, the talented but insecure, the ordinary, the less aggressive, or otherwise "noncompetitive" student. These are empirical questions, worthy of study.

NEW DIRECTIONS FOR RESEARCH

Assuming that making music involves more than winning and losing and that it does have other meanings, what different questions should we be asking to capture a broader perspective? Researchers might begin by acknowledging that a student's motivational disposition toward music is not static but a constantly shifting interaction of the person with the environment and situation (Raynor, 1983); and the design of research should incorporate more explicitly the social and developmental context in which students are making choices relevant to music. Students face a broad array of possible pursuits in school, and while the offering may be quite prescribed in the early grades, alternatives expand as they get older, such that by high school, many students, whether they realize it or not, are making choices that can indelibly affect their future options. How do students go about calculating where to expend their "time, talent, and energy" (Maehr, 1984)? And more specifically for our purposes, how does the pursuit of music weigh into such a formula? Two current theoretical approaches, which overlap conceptually but differ in detail, suggest new directions. One is a model of interlocking motivational constructs that has guided extensive research in mathematics learning (Eccles, 1983), and the other is a model of "personal investment" (Maehr, 1983, 1984).

Current Models of Motivation

A Model of Motivation in Mathematics Learning Eccles's (1983) model of motivation in mathematics learning focuses on students' subjective *reasoning* about the choice to pursue or avoid a given activity. Two interrelated factors, "expectations of success" and "subjective task value," predict student choice and persistence; each factor subsumes a set of variables, some of which are already familiar and have been studied as separate predictors:

1. A student's *expectation of success* is determined by
   (a) self-concept of ability
   (b) attributions for success and failure
   (c) stereotypes of ability (akin to Nicholls' ability differentiation)

2. *Subjective task value,* not touched on directly in the discussion thus far, refers to the student's sense of the task's relevance or its value.

    (a) Task importance is defined by its attainment value—the potential of the accomplished task to enhance one's sense of competence; intrinsic value—its attraction as a source of enjoyment for its own sake; and utility value—its usefulness as a means to other ends.

    (b) Sex role stereotypes held by the student may also affect choices, a consideration perhaps more important in the study of mathematics than of music.

    (c) Cost of participation—what the pursuit of one activity may take away from another—is, in a sense, the reciprocal of the enhancement of self.

    (d) Previous and anticipated affective experience adds a crucial emotional ingredient that is often implied but operationally ignored in much of motivational theory.

Personal Investment Maehr's (1984) personal investment model offers an alternative cognitive approach that sets student choice within the larger social and educational context. As in the model above, students choose to invest their efforts on the basis of the *meanings* they attach to the pursuit of one activity or another, and these meanings are determined by a set of contextual antecedents:

1. *Meaning* is seen as made up of three interrelated cognitive constructs—
    (a) beliefs about self
    (b) goals related to ego, social solidarity, and extrinsic rewards
    (c) action possibilities, i.e., the perceived available behavioral alternatives
2. *Contextual antecedents* influence the meanings students attach to various activities—
    (a) personal experience
    (b) teaching-learning situation
    (c) information
    (d) sociocultural context

Goals and Expectations of Success in Music

Both of these models of motivation highlight the importance of student perceptions of anticipated outcome—of goals and expectations of success. At present we know next to nothing about what students consider to be the important goals of studying music or even what they think of as "success" in music. Granted, we might find consensus that winning a competition or receiving a superior rating at "state contest" constitutes success, but students may differ in how they define success day to day. Because the learning of music is so protracted and one may never truly "arrive," students might be expected to view success as more ephemeral in music than in arithmetic or social studies. But do they? It has been suggested that a pervasive desire in our culture for "immediate success" clouds what students can learn from "less-

than-successful experiences" (Sosniak, 1990, p. 288–289). Does a serious music student appreciate this subtlety? And what about the average student or the student with low perceived ability? These are empirical questions ready-made for investigation. One piece of indirect evidence comes in a recent study in which students were found to view attributions to faulty strategy (e.g., poor practice habits) as a more constructive response to failure in music than either ability or effort attributions. Attributions to strategy were seen to avoid the negative effect so often associated with failure and to point to expectations of improved future performance (Vispoel and Austin, 1990).

Not knowing what students themselves consider the purpose of music study to be, we know only a little more about what teachers believe it is. What we do know, however, could stimulate a potentially valuable study of student perceptions. A compilation of music educators' views of music's role in early childhood education, taken from 108 textbooks spanning the years 1887 to 1982, provides an impressive list of teachers' purposes shown in Figure 27–2 (Draper and Gayle, 1987, p. 197).

The authors proceed to point out that *Child Development Abstracts* between 1927 and 1983 include few empirical studies demonstrating that such purposes are actually served. Some exceptions appearing in the late 1970s and early 1980s dealt with music study's relationship to concept formation and Piagetian conservation. Examination of the *Abstracts* since 1983 reveals a comparable dearth of studies of music's role in development and schooling, save those reviewed here. Despite the lack of research evidence relating music teaching to its stated goals, the list is nevertheless provocative. Presuming that teachers' goals help determine students' goals, an investigation of students' and teachers'

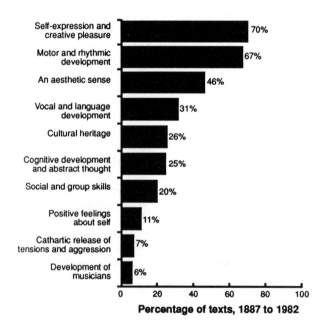

FIGURE 27–2. The Purposes of Music Education.

perceptions of these purposes would seem to offer a gold mine of research possibilities.

Toward a Developmental and Social Perspective

I started playing an instrument, like many other people, in the fifth grade, and I think if I hadn't done that, if I'd had to wait until I went to junior high, I wouldn't have started that instrument—that when I got to junior high I was too worried about other things, meeting new people and things like that. And band was the only thing I was involved in, right from the start, and it really helped me get involved and meet new people . . . it gave me a head start.

Junior high witness

If the frequency of mention of goals in textbooks is taken as a measure of their importance, a kind of hierarchy of teachers' purposes emerges. It appears that providing self-expression and creative pleasure is most important and the development of musicians least important. But let us keep in mind that these are early childhood education goals. If we take a developmental perspective, we might well ask how such goals shift in priority over time or even disappear as others move in to take their place. One such purpose of teaching or learning music, for instance, not mentioned for the very young child, is how participation in music may serve to ease a student through difficult developmental transitions. That the junior high witness quoted above can say that being in band gave him a "head start," that being in band helped him "get involved and meet new people," poignantly attests to the social function served by music participation.

Sustaining Students through Transitions The well-documented deterioration of students' attitudes and self-esteem over the course of schooling, which we have seen mirrored in studies of attitudes about music, can be exacerbated at points of transition. Entering junior high school and the transition into high school are such junctures. The particular low point associated with transition to junior high has been shown (Eccles et al., 1984) to be related to an unfortunate mismatch between the student's developmental stage, with its early-adolescent vulnerabilities, and an environment that is suddenly less hospitable and increasingly competitive compared to the relative security of the elementary years. A study discussed early in this chapter (Nolin and Vander Ark, 1979) investigated sixth-, and seventh-, ninth-graders' attitudes about music, thus touching on this sensitive period, but the report failed to provide a description of school type or structure that would allow assessment of transition in these students' lives. The three-way interaction of Grade × Sex × School, however, with boys' attitudes about music in one school actually improving from grades 6 to 7, raises the possibility that music participation may have facilitated a more positive transition for these particular students in one particular school. One wonders if music participation in some subset of schools with strong and well-supported music programs might not serve as an antidote to the sagging self-concept and attitudes typical of junior high and high school students.

About the Unit of Analysis The leitmotif of school differences that has sounded repeatedly throughout this chapter bears special comment. To characterize students' motivation to pursue music requires a two-part strategy—a strategy that traces the developmental process within the individual student over time *and* describes the contexts within which optimal development can occur. Longitudinal and cross-sectional designs that track students' development and compare students of different ages serve the first tack. But that is only part of the story, since research has already shown that development can vary across settings with different "teacher-learning situations" (referring to the Maehr personal investment model, 1984). Analysis of data at the classroom (or teacher) and school levels will be needed to fill out the picture of how different contexts affect student outcomes.

Science educators have used the "pipeline" analogy (U.S. Congress, 1988) to alert the public that students who fail to master requisite skills and knowledge over the course of schooling gradually lose options. The vast majority of high school graduates have a science and mathematics background so meager that they could not go in these fields even if they wanted to: They are out of the pipeline. The same metaphor can be applied to music learning, and one wonders—about science and music—whether "age-related changes in the concept of ability and in teaching practices appear designed to ensure attainment of minimum levels of competence in most of the population before ego-involvement is given full rein" (Nicholls, 1984, p. 65). Even if schools are not under pressure to produce musicians at the same rate as engineers, would we not like to think that an educated populace should be "musically literate," that a schooled citizenry should be equipped to "take meaning" from both music and science? The contrary seems rather to be the case, with too many students also outside the music pipeline long before they leave school.

The research on motivation and music would make a fine contribution to the field of education if it could identify the teacher and school practices that promote the task involvement and resultant equality of motivation that is thought to be requisite to the "optimal development of intellectual potential" (Nicholls, 1984, p. 64). Given such a state of equality of motivation distributed across students of varying musical abilities, we could then trust to the seductive powers of music itself to move and inspire students, with "affect for music" (Asmus, 1989) or "love of music" (Frakes, 1984) serving to keep them engaged within, not outside, the pipeline.

Research has demonstrated that deteriorating attitudes and self-concept are not inevitable (Eccles et al., 1984). Some schools that downplay competitive structures and build student-teacher trust manage to sustain students' good will. Could music have a main theme to play in helping set a more cooperative tone? One music educator whose classes over 25 years have produced both musicians and literate listeners, when asked what she holds to be her main purpose in teaching music states, "I see the school running more smoothly because of the music program. In making music, the kids work together . . . they have a sense of belonging to a community, of feeling good, that they can't get in any other way"

(B. Moore, personal communication, 1990). This potential role of music programs, assessed at both the individual and the school levels, needs investigation.

Toward an Ecological Perspective

To round out our understanding of what may be involved in students' motivation to pursue music, researchers will need to assess not only individual student development and what constitutes optimal contexts within schools, but also finally the world beyond schools. To comprehend varying levels of personal investment, a broader, ecological perspective will be necessary.

The following statement from a dedicated musician would be difficult to evaluate, for example, without a broader conception of the motivation to make music: "If someone said I could never play again, it would be disastrous. The parting would be very strong. I'm not sure I could ever go to a concert again. It's all of my life. It would mean giving up the greatest love of my life" (Creager, 1990 p. F2). It would seem unlikely that this level of commitment to music would be traced to schooling factors alone; more probably it is attributable to some combination of schooling and extrascholastic influences. In fact, this young concertmaster explained that her mother is a violinist, that she began attending conservatory at a very young age, and that her childhood was totally devoted to music. "There are sacrifices to be made. I was strongly encouraged by my parents" (Creager, 1990, p. F2).

Such an artist may well be an outlier in the context of the present discussion, which has focused more on everyday schooling and has avoided the distinctions between "elite" and "amateur," or "performer" and "fan" (Eccles, 1983; Maehr, 1983). But the exogenous factors outside the immediate setting (Bronfenbrenner, 1979)—parental beliefs and practices (Stevenson and Lee, 1990), and the sociocultural context (Maehr, 1984)—may ultimately account for important variability in students' initial willingness to sing, dance, or pick up an instrument, let alone their desire to persist.

It is parents who provide for children's private instruction, which doubtlessly contributes to proficiency. The demonstrated independence of Asmus's (1989) "background in music" from other school-related categories predicting achievement attests to the separate contribution made by children's out-of-school experience in music. Music lessons may be viewed as a variable connoting a whole set of parental attitudes about children's education, but out-of-school instruction cannot be the end-all to widespread music literacy. One participant of the Denver Conference, in fact, offered a counterobservation: that we spend too much time "worrying about prizes, and not enough time developing people's ability to interpret and appreciate. That's why a very large segment of American society stops making music the day the lessons stop" (Wilson and Roehmann, 1990, p. 416). How do home and school complement one another in contributing to children's continuing motivation in music? The question calls for investigation of this connection.

Finally, families exist within a sociocultural context, already posited earlier as a critical determinant of children's personal investments (Maehr, 1983). In the choice to pursue music, a child's "action possibilities" are constrained both practically and psychologically. What of the child, for instance, whose family cannot afford lessons, or the child whose range of perceived alternatives for self includes one mode of music making, but excludes another? "What of those citizens . . . who find themselves in an environment that has denied them full representation in the artistic tradition, that for the most part has inhibited their creative expression?" (Lewis, 1977, p. 397). Schools must reach for optimal creative opportunities for all, and research can contribute vitally to this effort by exploring how sociocultural factors influence student perceptions of choice.

CODA: RESEARCH AND PUBLIC POLICY

Research on motivation in music is clearly in a preliminary stage of development, but to draw on the opening quotation: "We all know you have to start somewhere." The prospects are exciting, and not the least of the challenges to the research community is funding. To compare the arts with science, the National Science Foundation (NSF) funding for science education alone is greater than the total funding of its parallel agency, the National Endowment of the Arts (NEA)—approximately $170 million. And while the NSF clamors for a $6 million appropriation for *research* in science education, the NEA has no comparable funding stream to support the type of research in music education projected here. All the research reviewed in this chapter, for instance, was either subsidized by the authors themselves or supported by local funds. One can surmise only that this negative contrast arises because we are in a time of scarce resources and because science is considered more important. The NEA itself acknowledges the dilemma, that "the arts are in triple jeopardy: they are not viewed as serious; knowledge itself is not viewed as a prime educational objective; and those who determine school curricula do not agree on what arts education is" (NEA, 1988, p. 7). But "our own civility can be questioned because we regard music as a minor subject" (Sidlin, 1990).

How do we go about raising music's standing in the public consciousness? Research itself can be a worthy lobbyist, and the Congress has explicitly called for more rigorous data collection (NEA, 1990). A good descriptive statistic can be very persuasive when the member of Congress asks: "What's this about music illiteracy? Just how many people are we talking about?" Some scholars have expressed concern that the research on motivation in music is still only descriptive (Colwell, 1990), but let us keep in mind that the barest facts are yet to be established. Can researchers say how many students move to sound, how many can "carry a tune," read notes, or distinguish one instrument from another? Can they tell us what school practices serve to promote students' musical competence, their "pride in the group," or their sheer enjoyment?

Public commitment to research must be encouraged. To

understand how children come to make music a part of their lives that will carry into adulthood, we need both the bare facts and an explication of the processes involved, many of which have been commented on in this chapter. There remain thus important data to gather, relationships to understand, and accumulating wisdom to put into practice.

References

Ames, C. (1984). Competitive, cooperative, and individualistic goal structures: A cognitive-motivational analysis. In C. Ames and R. Ames (Eds.), *Research on motivation in education* (Vol. 1). San Diego: Academic Press.

Asmus, E. P. (1985). Sixth graders' achievement motivation: Their views of success and failure in music. *Bulletin of the Council for Research in Music Education, 85,* 1–13.

Asmus, E. P. (1986). Student beliefs about the causes of success and failure in music: A study of achievement motivation. *Journal of Research in Music Education, 34,* 262–278.

Asmus, E. P. (1989). The effect of music teachers on students' motivation to achieve in music. *Canadian Journal of Research in Music Education, 30,* 14–21.

Atkinson, J. W., and Raynor, J. O. (Eds.). (1974). *Motivation and achievement.* New York: John Wiley.

Blacking, J. (1990). Music in children's cognitive and affective development. In F. R. Wilson and F. L. Roehmann (Eds.), *Music and child development: The biology of music making.* Proceedings of the 1987 Denver Conference. St. Louis: MMB Music.

Bloom, B. S. (Ed.). (1985). *Developing talent in young people.* New York: Ballantine Books.

Brandfonbrenner, A. G. (1990). A former prodigy looks back: Commentary on a filmed interview with Yo-Yo Ma. In F. R. Wilson and F. L. Roehmann (Eds.), *Music and child development: The biology of music making.* Proceedings of the 1987 Denver Conference. St. Louis: MMB Music.

Bronfenbrenner, U. (1979). *The ecology of human development.* Cambridge: Harvard University Press.

Byrne, B. M. (1984). The general/academic self-concept nomological network: A review of construct validation research. *Review of Educational Research, 54,* 427–456.

Clifford, M. M. (1984). Thoughts on a theory of constructive failure. *Educational Psychologist, 19,* 108–120.

Colwell, R. (1990). Comments. In F. R. Wilson and F. L. Roehmann (Eds.), *Music and child development: The biology of music making.* Proceedings of the 1987 Denver Conference. St. Louis: MMB Music.

Covington, M. V. (1983). Musical chairs: Who drops out of music instruction and why? In *Ann Arbor Symposium III on the Application of Psychology to Music Teaching and Learning: Motivation and Creativity.* Reston: Music Educators National Conference.

Covington, M. V. (1984). The motive for self-worth. In C. Ames and R. Ames (Eds.), *Research on motivation in education* (Vol. 1). San Diego: Academic Press.

Creager, (1990). World on a string. *Detroit Free Press,* January 12, F1–2.

Diener, C. I., and Dweck, C. S. (1978). An analysis of learned helplessness: Continuous changes in performance, strategy, and achievement cognitions following failure. *Journal of Personality and Social Psychology, 36,* 451–462.

Draper, T. W., and Gayle, C. (1987). An analysis of historical reasons for teaching music to young children: Is it the same old song? In J. C. Peery, I. W. Peery, and T. W. Draper (Eds.), *Music and child development.* New York: Springer-Verlag.

Eccles, J. S. (1983). Children's motivation to study music. In *Ann Arbor Symposium III on the Application of Psychology to Music Teaching and Learning: Motivation and Creativity.* Reston: Music Educators National Conference.

Eccles, J. S., and Midgley, C. (1989). Stage-environment fit: Developmentally appropriate classrooms for young adolescents. In C. Ames and R. Ames (Eds.), *Research on motivation in education* (Vol. 3). San Diego: Academic Press.

Eccles, J., Midgley, C., and Adler, T. F. (1984). Grade-related changes in the school environment: Effects on achievement motivation. In M. L. Maehr (Ed.), *Advances in motivation and achievement* (Vol. 3). Greenwich: Jai Press.

Feintuch, B. (1983). Examining musical motivation: Why does Sammie play the fiddle? *Western Folklore, 42,* 208–215.

Frakes, L. (1984). Differences in music achievement, academic achievement, and attitude among participants, dropouts, and nonparticipants in secondary school music. Unpublished doctoral dissertation, University of Iowa, Iowa City.

Gardner, H. (1977). Sifting the special from the shared: Notes toward an agenda for research in arts education. In S. S. Madeja (Ed.), *Arts and aesthetics: An agenda for the future.* St. Louis: CEMREL.

Gordon, E. (1990). Comments. In F. R. Wilson and F. L. Roehmann (Eds.), *Music and child development: The biology of music making.* Proceedings of the 1987 Denver Conference. St. Louis: MMB Music.

Hargreaves, D. J. (1986). *The developmental psychology of music.* Cambridge: Cambridge University Press.

Harter, S. (1982). The perceived competence scale for children. *Child Development, 53,* 87–97.

Hartman, A. (1987). The role of students' goals and perceptions of instrumental value in the development of achievement motivation at junior high school. Unpublished doctoral dissertation, University of Illinois, Urbana.

Heath, S. B. (1982). What no bedtime story means: Narrative skills at home and school. *Language in Society, 11,* 49–76.

Hedden, S. K. (1982). Predictions of music achievement in the elementary school. *Journal of Research in Music Education, 30,* 61–68.

Jackendoff, R., and Lerdahl, F. (1980). *A deep parallel between music and language.* Bloomington: Indiana University Linguistics Club.

Koutz, T. A. (1987). An analysis of attitudinal differences toward music performance classes in secondary school by nonparticipants. Unpublished doctoral dissertation, University of Missouri-Columbia.

Langer, S. (1941). *Philosophy in a new key.* Cambridge: Harvard University Press.

Lewis, S. (1977). Art and aesthetics, a minority report. In S. S. Madeja (Ed.), *Arts and aesthetics: An agenda for the future.* St. Louis: CEMREL.

Maehr, M. L. (1983). The development of continuing interest in music. In *Ann Arbor Symposium III on the Application of Psychology to Music Teaching and Learning: Motivation and Creativity.* Reston: Music Educators National Conference.

Maehr, M. L. (1984). Meaning and motivation: Toward a theory of personal investment. In C. Ames and R. Ames (Eds.), *Research on motivation in education* (Vol. 1). San Diego: Academic Press.

Marsh, H. W., and Holmes, I. W. (1990). Multidimensional self-concepts: Construct validation of responses by children. *American Educational Research Journal, 27,* 89–117.

McClelland, D. C. (1961). *The achieving society.* New York: Free Press.

McKeachie, W. J. (1981). National symposium on the application of psychology to the teaching and learning of music. *American Psychologist, 36,* 408–410.

Murnighan, J. K. (1981). Preliminary report on interviews of professional string quartets in Britain. Unpublished document.

National Endowment for the Arts. (1988). *Toward civilization: Overview from a report on arts education.* Washington: U.S. Government Printing Office: 1988-213-993.

National Endowment for the Arts. (1990). *Arts in America.* Washington: Author.

Nicholls, J. G. (1983). Task involvement in music. In *Ann Arbor Symposium III on the Application of Psychology to Music Teaching and Learning: Motivation and Creativity.* Reston: Music Educators National Conference.

Nicholls, J. G. (1984). Conceptions of ability and achievement motivation. In C. Ames and R. Ames (Eds.), *Research on motivation in education* (Vol. 1). San Diego: Academic Press.

Nicholls, J. G., and Miller, A. T. (1984). Development and its discontents: The differentiation of the concept of ability. In M. L. Maehr (Ed.), *Advances in motivation and achievement* (Vol. 3). Greenwich: Jai Press.

Nolin, W. H. (1973). Attitudinal growth patterns toward elementary school music experience. *Journal of Research in Music Education, 21,* 123–134.

Nolin, W. H., and Vander Ark, S. D. (1979). A pilot study of patterns of attitudes toward school music experiences, self-esteem, and socioeconomic status in elementary and junior high students. *Contributions to Music Education, 5,* 31–46.

Parsons, J. E. (1983). Expectancies, values and academic behaviors. In J. T. Spence (Ed.), *Achievement and achievement motives: Psychological and sociological approaches.* San Francisco: W. H. Freeman.

Parsons, J. E., Meece, J. L., Adler, T. F., and Kaczala, C. (1982). Sex differences in attributions and learned helplessness. *Sex Roles, 8,* 421–432.

Peery, I. W., Nyboer, D., and Peery, J. C. (1987). The virtue and vice of musical performance competitions for children. In J. C. Peery, I. W. Peery, and T. W. Draper (Eds.), *Music and child development.* New York: Springer-Verlag.

Phillips, D. A. (1987). Socialization of perceived academic competence among highly competent children. *Child Development, 58,* 1308–1320.

Pruett, K. D. (1990). Coping with life on a pedestal. In F. R. Wilson and F. L. Roehmann (Eds.), *Music and child development: The biology of music making.* Proceedings of the 1987 Denver Conference. St. Louis: MMB Music.

Raynor, J. O. (1983). Step-path theory and the motivation for achievement. In *Ann Arbor Symposium III on the Application of Psychology to Music Teaching and Learning: Motivation and Creativity.* Reston: Music Educators National Conference.

Root-Bernstein, R. S. (1984). Creative process as a unifying theme of human cultures. *Daedalus, 113,* 197–219.

Shavelson, R. J., Hubner, J. J., and Stanton, G. C. (1976). Validation of construct interpretations. *Review of Educational Research, 46,* 407–441.

Sidlin, M. (1990). Comments. *Robert Sherman conversations: Music education in America.* Aspen Music Festival.

Sosniak, L. (1990). From tyro to virtuoso: A long-term commitment to learning. In F. R. Wilson and F. L. Roehmann (Eds.), *Music and child development: The biology of music making.* Proceedings of the 1987 Denver Conference. St. Louis: MMB Music.

Stevenson, H. W., and Lee, S. (1990). Contexts of achievement. *Monographs of the Society for Research in Child Development, 55,* (1–2).

Stewart, C. (1991). Who takes music? Social and school factors related to high school music course enrollment. Unpublished Doctoral dissertation, University of Michigan, Ann Arbor.

Thomas, N. G. (1980). Music as an analogue in the study of language acquisition. Unpublished manuscript.

Thomas, N. G. (1986). The effects of parental attitudes and classroom climate on children's self-concept of mathematics ability. Unpublished doctoral dissertation, University of Illinois, Urbana.

Treffinger, D. J. (1983). Fostering creativity and problem-solving. In *Ann Arbor Symposium III on the Application of Psychology to Music Teaching and Learning: Motivation and Creativity.* Reston: Music Educators National Conference.

U.S. Congress, Office of Technology Assessment (1988). *Educating scientists and engineers: Grade school to grad school.* OTA-SET-377. Washington: U.S. Government Printing Office.

Vander Ark, S. D., Nolin, W. H., and Newman, I. (1980). Relationships between musical attitudes, self-esteem, social status, and grade level of elementary children. *Bulletin of the Council for Research in Music Education, 62,* 31–41.

Vispoel, W. P., and Austin, J. R. (1990). *Constructive responses to failure in music: The role of goal structure and outcome attribution feedback.* Paper presented at the annual meeting of the American Educational Research Association, Boston.

Weiner, B. (1974). *Achievement motivation.* Morristown: General Learning Press.

Weiner, B. (1984). Principles for a theory of student motivation and their application within an attributional framework. In C. Ames and R. Ames (Eds.), *Research on motivation in education* (Vol. 1). San Diego: Academic Press.

Whitehead, A. N. (1929). *The aims of education.* New York: Macmillan.

Wilson, F. R., and Roehmann, F. L. (Eds.) (1990). *Music and child development: The biology of music making.* Proceedings of the 1987 Denver Conference. St. Louis: MMB Music.

·28·

THE TRANSFER OF MUSIC LEARNING

Thomas W. Tunks

SOUTHERN METHODIST UNIVERSITY

In his highly influential book *The Process of Education,* Jerome Bruner (1960) states, "The first object of any act of learning . . . is that it should serve us in the future. Learning should not only take us somewhere; it should allow us later to go further more easily"(p. 17). This is Bruner's elegant way of underscoring the central role of transfer in all learning. Our entire educational system, in fact, is based on the premise that what is learned in school will apply in other settings, and that what is learned earlier will have some effect on later learning or performance. For over one hundred years, transfer of learning (or transfer of training) has been the object of systematic investigation by psychologists and educators.

That transfer of learning is of paramount importance to the enterprise of music teaching and learning seems axiomatic. As Edwards (1988) puts it, "Thoughtful performance teachers would admit that transfer (i.e., arranging experiences to influence subsequent performance) pretty well summarizes their whole mission in life" (p. 123). Yet perhaps because transfer is accepted as ubiquitous, its nature has not received widespread attention in the music education research literature. An overview of music instruction literature in general reveals numerous tacit, sometimes erroneous assumptions teachers and other musicians seem to make about transfer. Chief among them are the following:

Transfer is automatic—that it happens by itself, without particular attention.

Transfer is not limited to specific skills, but also extends to general abilities, even across learning domains.

Transfer is positive—that learning necessarily facilitates, rather than inhibits, later learning or performance.

Transfer is always forward—that learning new things does not retroactively facilitate or inhibit performance of things previously learned.

These and other assumptions about transfer are addressed in this chapter, as examined in the research literature of edu-

cation, psychology, music education, military training, and artificial intelligence. Although transfer of learning has not received much attention in the music education research literature, careful inspection reveals more research on transfer than may be immediately apparent because many studies that address issues related to transfer are "hidden" under other titles and topic areas. For example, application of skills or habits gained in rehearsal to a performance situation must involve transfer; practicing etudes in order to be better at playing the patterns encountered in "real" music assumes transfer; and investigating whether music study causes students to have more success in academic pursuits is really investigating transfer effects.

Given the discussion thus far, it becomes clear that transfer of learning can potentially include the effect of doing anything on doing anything else, so long as they are not simultaneous. For this chapter, transfer is defined as the effect of learning skills, knowledges, or attitudes on the later learning of other skills, knowledges, or attitudes. It also includes the application of learned skills, knowledges, or attitudes in novel settings. The first part of this definition (effect of learning on later learning) implies a causal relationship. Accordingly, investigations of this aspect of transfer included for review are those appropriate to address cause and effect relationships. Unfortunately, many studies, especially in music, that profess to address transfer of learning turn out either to be simple correlational studies or to lack the control needed to make valid conclusions about cause.

TRANSFER THEORIES IN HISTORIC PERSPECTIVE—A BRIEF OVERVIEW

Because learning and transfer are inextricably bound, theories of learning and transfer necessarily go together. Various explanations of learning have corresponding explanations of transfer. A widely accepted nineteenth-century learning theory, faculty development, held that various mental faculties such as analysis, judgment, and memory could be strengthened through exercise, just as could various physical capacities. The corresponding formal discipline theory of transfer was that transfer automatically resulted from strengthening the various faculties through certain studies, such as Latin and Greek (general training of the mind), logic and mathematics (reasoning), and rote learning (memory) (Bruner, 1960; O'Connor, 1971). When in 1890 William James and his students determined that practicing poem memorization did not shorten the time needed to memorize poems, "the theory that exercising the faculty of memory improved future memorization had not stood up to the first direct test" (O'Connor, 1971, p. 97).

In contrast to the view of transfer as automatic and ubiquitous in human learning, Thorndike proposed an "identical elements" theory (Thorndike and Woodworth, 1901; Thorndike, 1903) based on the premise that transfer occurs only if tasks share identical elements, or common features. Although not unchallenged, "identical elements" remained the prominent theory of transfer for most of this century. It served as the basis for later elaboration and extension, and is still presented in textbooks today. The issue of what, exactly, constitutes "identical" elements was the subject of considerable debate (Ellis, 1965), and has been revisited consistently through the years, most recently by Singley and Anderson (1989), who state that, in relation to Anderson's ACT* (pronounced act-star) theory, "single productions are the units of cognitive skill, the elements that Thorndike was searching for" (p. 31). An environmental theory (in that it rests on observable similarities or differences in stimulus or response characteristics), "identical elements" came under criticism from other learning theorists, primarily because of its mechanistic, stimulus-response nature, which was in opposition to the older idea of transfer as incorporating flexibility and adaptation. An opposing view of transfer was posed by Judd (1908), who demonstrated that transfer in situations where the task is based on a "guiding principle" is facilitated by the learner being made aware of the principle. In a dart-throwing experiment in which the target was under water, boys who had learned the principle of light refraction transferred the task to different water depths more readily than boys who had not learned about refraction. This fundamental distinction between the importance of factors external to the learner (identical elements, for example) and factors internal to the learner (knowledge of guiding principles, for example) has continued as the subject of investigation and debate to the present, particularly as evidenced by literature on "learning to learn" (Brown and Kane, 1988) and "thinking skills curricula" (Adams, 1989). It also constitutes, of course, the major difference between the behavioral (environmental) theories that dominated the first half of the century and the more recent cognitive theories of learning and transfer.

Cognitive Theories of Transfer

Although cognitive theories of learning and transfer are not new (it can be argued that they grew directly out of the Gestalt theories of the 1930s and earlier "mentalist" views), cognitive psychology has grown rapidly in prominence since the early 1960s.

Ausubel (1963) included in his theory of meaningful verbal learning the concept of "advanced organizers," which may be thought of as tools for transfer. The theory is based on the idea that for new material to be incorporated into a learner's existing cognitive structure, it must have some point of relationship to what the learner already knows (be meaningful). Advance organizers are presented to the learner prior to presentation of new material for the purpose of providing a conceptual bridge between new material and the existing cognitive structure. Defined by Ausubel (1963, p.29) as being at a higher level of abstraction than the new material, advance organizers allow for learning to proceed in a "top-down" way, from a general conceptual framework into which specifics presented later can be fit. This is a major difference between Ausubel's theory and more recent cognitive theories, which view learning as taking place in a "bottom-up" fashion, moving from subordinate to basic to superordinate concepts (Rosch, 1973; Royer, 1979). The more recent (bottom-up) theories seem to have gotten more empirical support (Royer and Cable, 1975, 1976). Barnes and Clawson (1975), on the basis of a review of 32 studies of the effects of advance organizers, concluded "that advance organizers, as presently constructed, generally do not facilitate learning" (p. 651). They went on to stipulate, however, that most studies to that time had concerned only short-term effects and to recommend that longer-term effects of advance organizers be studied.

The information-processing approach, which is generally considered to be at the root of modern cognitive psychology, concerns the flow of information—how we acquire, transmit, store, retrieve, and transform it. Beginning in the 1950s, this approach has developed rapidly, leading to schema theory and computer-based artificial intelligence study. Information-processing theory holds strong implications for how transfer takes place. The basic premises are that memory is a highly structured and interconnected system, comprehension has resulted from relating new information to existing knowledge, and recall is performed by entering memory at a particular point (node) and searching outward to connecting nodes (spreading activation) until the target is found (or the search stops). Transfer is dependent on the learner's encountering the relevant prior information (Royer, 1979; Shuell, 1986). This is compatible with the identical elements theory, in that what constitutes relevant prior information depends partly on shared stimulus features with the new information. The emphasis, however, is on the search process rather than the stimulus features.

From information processing emerged schema theory. The main distinguishing characteristic of this theory (or really, a broad set of theories) is the view of the way memory is structured. Schemata are seen as complex, interrelated, hierarchically organized structures the elements of which are other schemata, facts, concepts, procedures, variables, or slots (placeholders) (Anderson, 1984). Memory is generally thought of as consisting of two main categories—declarative and procedural (Singley and Anderson, 1989; Shuell, 1986).

Procedural memory may take the form of intellectual procedures (harmonic analysis, for example) or motor schemata (Schmidt, 1975, 1982; LaBerge, 1981). Transfer is dependent on the activation of appropriate schemata, which in turn can activate subschemata or other related schemata.

Applications of schema theory to music learning are currently in progress, as exemplified by the work of Jones (1982, et seq.) and Bharucha (1987). Jones, in studying music processing by listeners, has postulated a theory of "ideal prototypes," or durable conceptual models formed through past experience. Prototypes, in conjunction with incoming music information, are the basis for "expectancy schemata," which serve as templates for comparison with musical input. This is directly related to transfer in music listening. If, for example, a listener has established an ideal prototype of music from a particular style period, or even of a specific composer, processing of later musical input, novel or not, would be facilitated by activation of appropriate expectancy schemata. Comparison of incoming sounds with expectancies would account for listeners' ability to classify music they have not previously heard as being composed by Palestrina rather than Monteverdi, or Shostakovich rather than Hindemith. Bharucha (1987) has been studying computer simulation models of spreading activation of schemata and the effects of "priming" listeners with tonal contexts on their musical processing.

The most recent descendants of schema theory are termed "production systems" (Singley and Anderson, 1989), and use computer programs to model human cognition. Most prominent among these is Anderson's (1983) ACT* theory. The theory incorporates two kinds of long-term memory—production memory and declarative memory. In this respect, the theory is similar to earlier cognitive theories, in that productions constitute procedural memory and declarative structures are used to encode facts (Singley and Anderson, 1989, p. 30). The major point of difference with earlier theories lies in the nature of productions and the relationship between productions and declarative structures. Productions take the form of "condition-action" rules:

IF	a specified condition exists,
THEN	do a specified action.

In skill acquisition, initial representations of skills are declarative, and interpreted by general-purpose analogy mechanisms, but quickly are transformed (by a process of "knowledge compilation") into domain-specific productions. Applying ACT* to the transfer of computer programing skill and text-editing skill, treating productions as identical elements, yielded successful results. This led to the "identical productions" theory of transfer, with productions considered the elements for which Thorndike had searched. Interestingly, because productions differ from Thorndike's elements in that they are "mentalistic abstractions containing variables and goal structures" (Singley and Anderson, 1989, p. 229), Singley and Anderson suggest that "it might be possible to revive the doctrine of formal discipline in our framework by finding a production system cast at a high enough level of abstraction so that it applies profitably to a wide range of problems" (p. 229). This has the potential of bringing transfer theory full circle (better, full spiral) across the course of about a century. More detailed reviews of transfer theories are presented by Ellis (1965), Cormier and Hagman (1987), and Singley and Anderson (1989).

DIMENSIONS OF TRANSFER

Certain types or aspects of transfer addressed throughout the research literature are associated with more than one transfer theory. These I refer to as dimensions of transfer. All have been used to classify or otherwise clarify transfer phenomena.

General and Specific Transfer

Sometimes referred to as specific and nonspecific transfer, this dimension is central to the differences between identical elements and the earlier formal discipline theories. Whereas the earlier approach assumed wide-ranging transfer, not restricted to similar tasks, the notion of transfer as dependent on identical elements shared by the original and transfer task redefined transfer as necessarily specific to closely related tasks, and in effect discounted the possibility of general transfer. The general-specific dimension is in ways synonymous with, or inclusive of, other transfer dimensions to be discussed separately, such as cross-domain transfer, near and far transfer, and vertical and lateral transfer.

Conclusions vary as to whether general transfer is a feasible outcome of instruction. Lipman's Philosophy for Children program has produced significant gains in reading comprehension and logical thinking (Lipman, 1985). Royer and Cable (1975, 1976) have shown nonspecific transfer effects, but within the domain of prose materials. Harlow (1949), Postman (1969), and Brown and Kane (1988) have all demonstrated general transfer effects in "learning to learn" settings. Brown and Kane concluded, "Preschool children can form a *mind set* to look for analogous solutions to problems that differ in surface features but share deeper relational commonalities. The learning to learn effect is rapid and dramatic" (p. 516). In the Brown and Kane studies, the tasks were similar, in that they were based on the same solution principle, but the children were not told that the similarity existed, and surface similarity was minimized. This prompts the question of whether this really constituted general transfer. How general is general? Royer (1979) states that specific transfer involves clear similarity between stimulus elements in original and transfer tasks that is detected by the learner (p. 54). With respect to what constitutes similarity, Goodman (1978, as reported in Salomon and Perkins, 1989) pointed out a circularity of definition, in that "what transfers to what may itself be part of our tacit standards for similarity" (p. 115). Research on the effect of music study on extramusical achievement, reviewed later in this chapter, has produced mixed results.

On the negative side, results of motor transfer studies mainly argue against the presence of a general motor ability, and in favor of extreme specificity of tasks (Schmidt and

Young, 1987). In addition, Singley and Anderson (1989) review numerous studies failing to show general transfer effects, and conclude, "A long line of research (starting with the work of Thorndike and James) casts a gloomy pall on the prospect of general transfer" (p. 230).

Vertical and Lateral Transfer

Gagné (1965) used the terms "lateral" and "vertical" to represent types of transfer similar to those other theorists called "general" and "specific" transfer. Lateral transfer generalizes to a broad set of situations at roughly the same level of complexity. In contrast, vertical transfer occurs if a capability to be learned is acquired more rapidly when it has been preceded by previous subordinate learning. Gagné cites research evidence for vertical transfer, but not for lateral.

Near and Far Transfer

Gick and Holyoak (1987) have defined a continuum of transfer task similarity ranging from repetitious tasks (termed self-transfer), through highly similar tasks (near transfer), to very different tasks (far transfer). They add that not only task similarity but time between performance of tasks can be the basis for nearness of transfer. Ferrara, Brown, and Campione (1986) studied transfer distance effects in relation to both age and IQ of elementary school children learning letter series completion tasks. Data were gathered on initial learning of tasks, maintenance, near transfer, far transfer, and very far transfer. Results indicated marked interactions between age and transfer distance, and between IQ and transfer distance. The higher IQ group displayed more efficiency on initial learning, and the difference between IQ groups widened as transfer distance increased. Essentially the same effect was found for age, in comparing fifth-graders to third-graders. These results indicate that those children who learn more efficiently also transfer more efficiently, increasingly so as transfer distance increases. Also, because all children were brought to the same criterion level in initial learning, these results demonstrate that bringing learners to equivalent mastery of problem-solving rules or procedures does not ensure their equivalency on later application. Mayer (1975) studied near and far transfer in relation to "meaningful" and "rote" learning of binomial probability. Instruction was characterized either by emphasis on algorithms and correct answers (rote), or by presentation of basic ideas and their relation to the computational procedures (meaningful). Mayer found that rote instruction resulted in good near transfer, but poor far transfer performance, while the "meaningful" instruction resulted in poor near transfer, but good far transfer performance. The near-far transfer dimension seems essentially the same as the general-specific transfer dimension.

Cross-Domain Transfer

Research on transfer across domains of learning is virtually ignored in the transfer literature. Studies that are relevant to this discussion all fall within the realm of music education research, and are reviewed later in the chapter. As with general transfer, there is little evidence to suggest that significant transfer occurs across domains. Shuell (1988) concluded that little if any cross-domain transfer can be expected. He cites no research in support of this conclusion, which is not surprising, given the fact that cognitive psychology, as a discipline, has not pursued affective issues.

Positive and Negative Transfer

That learning can not only facilitate later learning or performance but also inhibit or interfere has been recognized since the earliest transfer research. The so-called Bruce-Wylie laws (Bruce, 1933; Wylie, 1919; reported in Gick and Holyoak, 1987), pertaining to the relationships among task similarity and transfer magnitude and direction, state that (1) the amount of transfer depends on the degree of similarity between the two situations, and (2) the direction of transfer (positive or negative) depends on the similarity of the two responses. Thus, the greater the perceived similarity between tasks, the more likely that use of the previously learned response will be made. However, given perceived task similarity, the less similarity there is between correct responses for the two tasks, the less likely that the previously learned response will be appropriate. These basic principles have reappeared, in different language and with some extension, through the years and form the basis for the most recent explanations of negative transfer. *Einstellung* (Luchins, 1942), which is German for "set" (the unthinking repetition of the same response for repeated tasks), represents the same effect—negative transfer as inappropriate repetition of a learned strategy resulting from seeming similarity of tasks. Osgood (1949) extended the relationship to include not only transfer, but also "retroaction"—the effect of new learning inserted between initial learning of a task and its later repetition. Either retroactive facilitation or retroactive inhibition could occur, depending on stimulus or response similarity. Retroaction varies directly with transfer. That is, where transfer is negative, retroaction is also negative, and vice versa. Most recently, Singley and Anderson (1989) have restated what amounts to the same relationship, but in terms of productions, or condition-action rules. In this relationship, conditions function as stimuli and actions as responses. Negative transfer results from condition-action rule overgeneralization, where the transfer action elicited is inappropriate because the transfer condition does not match the previously learned condition, even though it was a perceived match. This situation is corrected by making the condition statement more specific. The opposite situation, condition-action rule undergeneralization, results in no transfer attempt because the potential transfer condition is not perceived as a match with the previously learned condition. This situation is corrected by making the condition statement less specific. Recently, an important distinction has been made between "surface" similarity and "structural" similarity of tasks (Holyoak, 1985; Gick and Holyoak, 1987). Structural components of a learning situation are those that are "causally or functionally related in outcomes or goal attainment" (Gick and Holyoak, p. 16). Surface components are more superficial than functional. Perceived similarity between tasks, resulting from shared surface or structural elements, increases the likelihood of transfer attempts. However, it is the amount of structural similarity (apparent or not) between tasks that determines whether attempted transfer will be positive or negative. If tasks are perceived as similar on the basis of surface components but in fact are different structurally, transfer is negative. If, by contrast, tasks are not perceived as similar, even though structural similarity may be present, transfer will not occur. In rhythm reading, for example, two excerpts might contain identical patterns of a dotted quarter note followed by three eighths. This constitutes surface similarity. If they are in the same meter, structural similarity is present as well. If, however, one passage is in 3/4 time and the other in 6/8, they are structurally different, and to transfer interpretation of one to the other would create a mistake in accent. If, on the other hand, two rhythmic passages should sound identical, but one is written in 4/2 time and the other in 4/8 time (surface dissimilarity, but structural similarity), transfer of performance from one to the other would be unlikely unless the learner were already aware of the rules governing these meters.

High-Road and Low-Road Transfer

Salomon and Perkins (1989) have proposed what they term a tentative theory of the internal mechanisms of transfer. They identify two classes of transfer, dealing with different mechanisms and different types of information. "Low-road" transfer is characterized by involuntary transfer of skills that are highly practiced, even to automaticity. "Low-road transfer is the trend when a performance is unintentional, implicit, based on modeling and driven by reinforcement. This is typical of . . . socialization, acculturation, and experience-based cognitive development, resulting in the acquisition of habitual behavior patterns, . . . cognitive strategies and styles, expectations" (p. 122). Low-road transfer does not include reflective activity. "High-road" transfer, in contrast, depends on "mindful abstraction" of rules, patterns, prototypes, categories, and so on. Salomon and Perkins refer to the "decontextualization" of information and rerepresentation in a new, more general form. True comprehension of the relationship between information in context and the abstraction (as opposed to being learned as a formula) is seen as important for high-road transfer. The issue of transfer as a conscious effort, then, seems to be the chief difference between the high and low roads. High-road transfer can be either "forward reaching" or "backward reaching." During training or instruction, conscious attention to possible future applications of the material being learned constitutes a forward-reaching transfer effort. When one is confronted with a novel situation and searches through memory for a previously learned rule or principle extracted from an analogous situation, this constitutes a backward-reaching transfer attempt. Salomon and Perkins present a strong case for the high- and low-road concepts of transfer, and demon-

strate that some earlier inconsistencies in transfer research results can be explained as differences between high- and low-road transfer effects. In a music setting, low-road transfer might well involve the highly repetitive, modeled psychomotor skills or music-listening strategies that do not lend themselves well to mindful abstraction, intellectualization, or even discussion. High-road transfer might involve more "abstractable" skills, such as music reading, stylistic interpretation, and formal analysis.

Consideration of high-road transfer raises the issue of metacognition and its role in transfer. Sometimes referred to as "knowing about knowing," metacognition involves both thinking about what we know or do not know and thinking about how to use what we know. High-road transfer involves conscious transfer effort, and is in line with findings (Newell, 1980; O'Sullivan and Pressley, 1984) that awareness of transfer task requirements enhances transfer, particularly with novice learners. Because research in metacognition is a relatively recent pursuit, the current body of information is not large. Garner and Alexander (1989) provide a useful review of findings in metacognition.

RESEARCH ON MUSIC AND TRANSFER

Numerous studies of the relationship between music and other skill areas appear in the literature. Many of these, however, are either simple correlational research or descriptive comparisons of music participants with nonparticipants on some achievement or aptitude variable. Neither of these research types, valuable as they may be for certain purposes, addresses the question of whether music learning causes people to perform differently in other areas. A major concern in participation studies is that nonrequired participation is always self-selected, and thus can never be isolated as the only cause for a difference in anything else (Holland and Andre, 1987). However, to create an artificial situation wherein participation that would normally be voluntary is required changes the nature of the independent variable, thus threatening ecological validity.

Still other studies, for whatever reason, are simply inconclusive or offer conclusions not supported by the data gathered. Such research is not reviewed here.

Music to Nonmusic Abilities

Results are mixed concerning transfer of music learning to other skills. Modified Suzuki and Kódaly instruction showed positive transfer to body percept (Bain, 1978), and Kódaly instruction had a positive effect on temporal/spatial abilities, but only for boys (Hurwitz, Wolff, Bortnick, and Kokas, 1975). Both of these studies, however, indicated no transfer of music instruction to verbal abilities. Positive effects of music instruction on verbal abilities have been shown, but with special populations of disadvantaged children (Aten, Smith, and Tunks, 1984) and neurologically impaired children (Pirtle and Seaton, 1973). Both of these studies used music-learning activities aimed specifically at verbal gain. Another study of a special population (Seides, 1967) demonstrated positive effects of an arts-intensive talent class on academic achievement and creative thinking of "slow learners" (IQ from 70 to 90). Using successive approximation techniques to train for conservation of melody across tempi, Botvin (1974) showed that melody conservation transferred to conservation of number, weight, and mass, but not liquid volume. Two studies (Lauder, 1976; Sharman, 1981) showed no transfer from music activities to reading skill, even though the music instruction was coupled with reading instruction. Kodaly-based instruction (Hurwitz et al., 1975), on the other hand, had a facilitative effect on reading achievement.

Wolff (1978), following an excellent review of research to that time on nonmusical outcomes of music education, concluded that "there may be measurable effects of music education on the development of cognitive skills and understanding." (p. 19) She goes on to state, however, that "the conclusions drawn generally remain unconvincing. This is due largely to obvious inadequacies in the experimental designs." (p. 21) Wolff's concerns still hold. Some of the research cited in her review was included here, but most was not. What the collective results of research reviewed here seem to support is that effects of music instruction can transfer to other areas of study, but only when the instruction is aimed specifically at transfer and is highly structured toward that aim.

Music to Music Skills

Study of transfer within the realm of music has addressed a variety of music skills, such as performance, memorization, critical listening, analysis, and affective response. Research considered here was all aimed at the effect of music learning on a different type of music learning or application.

Transfer and Performance

The way a music-reading task is practiced has been shown to have a transfer effect to later reading of the same music. More specifically, mental practice, although not significantly different from no practice when pitch, rhythm, and articulation are considered together (Ross, 1985), or in facilitating note accuracy alone, is superior to aural models, physical practice, singing, and no practice, in facilitating rhythmic accuracy (Rosenthal, Wilson, Evans, and Greenwalt, 1988). Mental practice is superior to both singing and no practice in facilitating accuracy in phrasing and dynamics, and tempo (Rosenthal et al., 1988). These results are only partially consistent with other mental practice results in motor learning (Twining, 1949) and physical education (Weinberg, 1982), which indicate that mental practice is almost as efficient as physical practice. This may be because those studies dealt with much less complex tasks than playing through a music etude. Aural models have shown superiority to physical practice in facilitating rhythmic accuracy (Rosenthal et al., 1988; Rosenthal, 1984) and note, dynamic, and tempo accuracy (Rosenthal, 1984). These results were all obtained with

advanced (at least college level) instrumentalists. With beginning students, aural models seem to have no effect on performance achievement (Hodges, 1975). Practice that follows a predetermined structured approach has been shown to be more facilitative of accurate performance than free practice (Barry, 1990). Amount of practice time does not alone determine performance success (Wagner, 1975). With respect to an isolated musical task (vocal imitation of a pitch interval), Harvey, Garwood, and Palencia (1987) found that training on a variety of intervals resulted in less transfer to the task of imitating a single interval than did training on a different single interval. This superiority of constant practice over variable practice in promoting transfer is opposite to most research results concerning variable practice (Schmidt and Young, 1987). The inconsistency might be explained by the fact that the variable practice intervals were extremely varied (from two to 16 semitones) and randomly distributed. Such extreme variability in practice has not been as successful as low-to-high ordering of variability (Nitsch, 1977). Another possible explanation is that other practice variability studies dealt with high-road transfer effects, whereas interval imitation can be argued to fit a low-road transfer model (Salomon and Perkins, 1989).

Practice method affects not only music reading, but also music memorization. Guided analysis of music before playing has a facilitative effect on its memorization by pianists (Rubin-Rabson, 1941) and wind instrumentalists (Ross, 1964). Memorization of a song and a second transfer song was facilitated by memorization training stressing whole (versus part) practice, analysis, attending to intermediate memory goals, and self-testing (Williamson, 1964). For pianists, practicing with hands together (Rubin-Rabson, 1939); distributing practice sessions across time rather than using fewer, but longer sessions (Rubin-Rabson, 1940); and mental rehearsal (Rubin-Rabson, 1941) all seem to facilitate memorization.

Other training factors have been studied with relation to music-reading skill. MacKnight (1975) found that training with tonal patterns, as opposed to focusing on one note at a time, is superior in facilitating sight-reading ability. With respect to music notation, Peitersen (1954) found that training with notation spaced according to note duration had no superiority over training with nonspaced notation in facilitating reading of printed music.

Training in aural discrimination has not been shown to have a transfer effect to music performance skill, either at the junior college level (Kinser, 1975) or with beginners (Delzell, 1989). These results are consistent with Marciniak's (1974) finding of no significant relationship between high school students' music perception skills and band performance.

A different question is whether, once a performance skill is mastered, application is affected by the context in which the application is made. Duke and Pierce (1990) found that melodic context (difficulty of surrounding measures) did not affect pitch and rhythm accuracy of performance, but did affect tempo accuracy. In addition, performing the transfer task at a faster tempo than that at which the skill was learned negatively affected pitch accuracy, but performing at a slower tempo than that at which it was learned negatively affected tempo accuracy. The best tempo for the transfer task was the tempo at which the task was learned. This result is consistent with findings in motor transfer research (Schmidt and Young, 1987) and context interference research (Shea and Morgan, 1979; Shea and Zimny, 1983).

Listening and Analytic Skills

Transfer of music-listening skills has been studied with respect to melodic recognition, style discrimination, and music structure. Repeated listening to music examples results in thematic extraction by musicians, and transfer to new examples has been shown (Pollard-Gott, 1983). For untrained listeners, however, repeated listening facilitates discrimination of harmony and other structural elements, but discrimination does not necessarily transfer to music of different styles (Bartlett, 1973). In training for discrimination among musical styles, a mixture of positive and negative training examples promotes better performance on transfer examples than does use of all positive training examples (Haack, 1972). This is consistent with most research findings dealing with variability of examples (Gick and Holyoak, 1987). In melodic dictation, amount of unstructured practice does not account for facilitation of dictation with novel tasks (Langsford, 1959). This is consistent with results indicating that amount of practice does not affect transfer of performance skill (Wagner, 1975). Highly structured successive approximations in attaining melodic conservation do result in young children's transfer of conservation to novel melodies (Botvin, 1974). Music discrimination and vocabulary are achieved more effectively by addressing them directly in instruction than by relying on transfer from rehearsal experiences that are not aimed at these objectives (Gebhardt, 1973; Nierman, 1985), but a variety of music experience does seem to be more effective than concentration of time on a single type of music activity (Pembrook and Taylor, 1986). Hedden (1981) concluded that, in general, music-listening skills achieved in classroom settings may not transfer to listening situations outside the classroom. DeTurk (1988) provides a good review of research relating experience in performing groups and gain in listening and analytic skills.

Transfer and Affect

Even though music educators and others often assume that learning about music will increase musical enjoyment or preference, the small amount of research addressing causal relationships between music study and affect are in support of the idea that not much cross-domain transfer can be expected (Shuell, 1988). Bartlett (1973) found that an increase in structural discrimination ability did not transfer to increased preference for classical music. Shehan (1985) noted a significant increase in preference for nonwestern music that had been studied, but the preference did not transfer to matched pieces of music that had not been studied. Taking the opposite approach, Asmus (1980) studied the effect of

prior affective set on cognitive task performance in a music acoustics class. Using a path analytic method, he determined that although entering affect seemed to have an effect on early task performance, as the course progressed affect had little effect on cognitive gain. Taken together, these results point out, again, that desired gain in any area of learning is more likely to occur if addressed directly by instruction or if instruction is structured specifically to achieve transfer.

Cross-Sensory Perception and Response

A phenomenon closely related to cross-domain transfer is what I will call cross-sensory perception and response. It involves relating information entering through one sense mode to analogous information in another mode (aural to visual, for example) or to responding in one mode to a task presented in another mode (verbally describing music phenomena, for example). These effects do not fall within the definition used here for transfer of learning because they do not involve the effect of learning one task on the later learning or performance of another task. They are closely enough related, however, to be included in the discussion. As with cross-domain transfer, there is little reason to expect that cross-sensory response occurs as naturally as response within the same sense mode. Young children are not able to describe adequately with words various musical phenomena that they can demonstrate or imitate by playing. This has been shown for duration and rhythm (Van Zee, 1976) and tonal direction (Hair, 1977). Also, Olson (1976) found that first-grade children had more success at matching two aurally presented melodic contours than matching visual (line) contours with aurally presented contours. This is related to a problem identified in Piagetian conservation research (Tunks, 1980). Often such research relies on children's verbalizations of what they perceive, or verbal reasons for their responses, in determining their understanding of physical or musical concepts. With older learners, however, multisensory input has been applied with some success in instructional situations. Learners displayed better theme recall when aural presentation was accompanied by music notation, even if they had no music-reading training (Smith, 1953). Intonation was better with a combination of visual and aural feedback, both for college vocalists and instrumentalists matching a recorded model (Heller, 1969), and for college-age beginning guitarists performing tuning tasks (Codding, 1985). Heller suggested further study to determine whether the superior intonation performance with visual feedback would transfer to more usual music situations in which there is only aural feedback. Codding, in effect, did just that. She determined that although guitarists tuned with more accuracy using visual feedback in training sessions, the effect did not transfer to a posttest without the visual feedback.

Transfer and Music Teacher Training

Simulation training, which relies directly on transfer from a simulated situation to "real" applications, has been used in military and industrial training for over 50 years (Baudhuin, 1987). In music teacher training, simulation is quite common, but rarely studied. Two notable exceptions appear in the literature. In the teaching of behavior management techniques, videotapes of simulated behavior problems were no more effective than presentation of the same content in a lecture-discussion format with school observation, based on the results of a written test of attitudes and behavior management skills. However, the simulation training transferred more effectively to a classroom teaching situation (Brand, 1977). DeCarbo (1982) compared the effectiveness of error detection training in a conducting situation with programed instruction in error detection. He found that, although the two training groups did not score differently on a written error detection test, the conducting experience group scored higher on a conducting-based error detection test. This suggests that the conducting training transferred to the written application, but the programed instruction did not transfer as well to the conducting application.

SUMMARY

Results of research on transfer of music learning are not entirely consistent. However, they provide enough information, when coupled with transfer research results from other areas of study, to allow some general statements about transfer:

- Transfer from music to other skills can be achieved, but results from music activity specifically designed for that transfer.
- Low-road transfer is more likely to occur automatically than high-road transfer.
- Application of learned skills (especially motor) is highly sensitive to context.
- Varied teaching examples promote more transfer than single examples, especially for high-road transfer.
- Ordering of examples (near to far) promotes more transfer than random ordering.
- For high-road transfer, informing learners of structural rules or guiding principles (including how a specific skill fits within a broader context) promotes more transfer than leaving them uninformed.
- Transfer depends on perceived similarity between tasks, either surface or structural.
- For transfer to be positive, task similarity must be structural.
- Retroaction, either facilitative or inhibitive, seems to vary directly with transfer.
- Mental practice is beneficial for high-road transfer, more for rhythm and interpretive elements than for note accuracy.
- Distributed practice promotes more transfer than massed practice.

- Amount of practice does not alone account for transfer.
- Structured practice facilitates more transfer than unstructured practice.
- Aural models are beneficial for attaining performance accuracy of advanced students.
- Transfer depends on the extent and efficiency of initial learning.

Both Edwards (1988) and Shuell (1988) have taken many of the above generalizations into account, and provide excellent practical suggestions regarding music teaching for transfer.

SUGGESTED APPROACHES FOR STUDYING TRANSFER OF MUSIC LEARNING

Clearly, much remains to be studied concerning transfer of music learning (or transfer of other learning to music learning, which seems not to have been addressed at all). Questions of importance to music instruction are practically limitless. I suggest three research models for such study. In all three models, measurement of transfer can vary, depending on the nature of the learning involved. In past transfer study, measures of efficiency (trials to criterion, time to criterion, time to completion) and measures of accuracy (score within a fixed time or number of trials, score without time or trial limits) have all been used effectively. Boldovici (1987) reviews various ways of calculating amount of transfer, ranging from simple raw score comparison between treatment group and control group to more sophisticated calculations of percentage of transfer. I suggest direct raw score comparison for music education transfer research because it yields a straightforward, directly interpretable result. For relative comparisons between different sorts of transfer tasks, percent of transfer may be important, but should still be reported with accompanying raw score results, to avoid the quagmire of false, confusing, or counterintuitive metrics.

Model I—Training Effectiveness

Most transfer research completed thus far falls within this general model, which is essentially an experimental design. It assumes random assignment of subjects to treatment and comparison groups, or at least matching groups on multiple variables. The basic design involves a training task (A) and a transfer task (B):

$$
\begin{array}{cc}
A & B \\
- & B
\end{array}
$$

Direct comparison of the groups on B shows the amount of transfer from A to B. If an efficiency measure is used for both A and B (trials or time to criterion or completion), it may be desirable to add the trials on A to the trials on B for the treatment group and compare the sum to trials on B for the control group. If A + B (treatment) is no less than B (control), no efficiency of training time has been gained. A similar comparison can be made with variation of the basic design:

$$
\begin{array}{cc}
A & B \\
B & B
\end{array}
$$

Another variation useful in studying relative order effects of A and B, each as a possible facilitator of the other, is:

$$
\begin{array}{cc}
A & B \\
B & A
\end{array}
$$

This design coupled with relative (percent of transfer) measures could be useful in determining which of two tasks is subordinate to the other. Still another variant of the basic design was suggested by Osgood (1949) for studying retroaction:

$$
\begin{array}{ccc}
A & B & A \\
A & - & A
\end{array}
$$

With any of these designs a pretest or other covariate measure could be used to help reduce noise in the data.

Model II—Context of Application

This model is for determining whether, after a task has been learned (to some predetermined criterion), its performance is affected by the performance context. This is the model used by Duke and Pierce (1990). The model is descriptive, and involves a task (A) and a variable number of application settings (1,2,3 . . . n):

Train to criterion	Compare applications		
A	A_1	A_2	A_3

The order of application would vary among individual subjects, and analysis would be for repeated measures.

Model III: Training × Context of Application Interaction

This combines models I and II to determine not only whether different training or practice methods (A,B,C) have different facilitative effects on the performance of a task (T), but also whether performance, once learned, is affected by application setting (1,2,3 . . . n) and if training and application setting interact:

Train to criterion using method	Compare applications		
A	T_{A1}	T_{A2}	T_{A3}
B	T_{B1}	T_{B2}	T_{B3}
C	T_{C1}	T_{C2}	T_{C3}

Data, if appropriate, would be analyzed using a split-plot (repeated measures) analysis, with method as the between-groups variable and application setting as the repeated factor. The order of application would vary among individual subjects. A variation of this model would be used to determine whether transfer from a training task (A) to a transfer task (B) was affected by learning context of B:

A	B_1	B_2	B_3
—	B_1	B_2	B_3

Again, if data were appropriate, a split-plot analysis would be used, with presence or absence of the training task (A) as the between-groups variable and application setting as the repeated factor. Application order would vary by subject.

References

Adams, M. J. (1989). Thinking skills curricula: Their promise and progress. *Educational Psychologist, 24*(1), 25–77.

Anderson, R. C. (1984). Some reflections on the acquisition of knowledge. *Educational Researcher, 13*(9), 5–10.

Asmus, E. P. (1980). Empirical testing of an affective learning paradigm. *Journal of Research in Music Education, 28*(3), 143–154.

Aten, J., Smith, G., and Tunks, T. (1984). *Music in a remedial oral language program: Final evaluation of cycle I.* Paper presented at the Texas Music Educators Association conference, San Antonio.

Ausubel, D. P. (1963). *The psychology of meaningful verbal learning.* New York: Grune and Stratton.

Bain, B. (1978). The cognitive flexibility claim in the bilingual and music education research traditions. *Journal of Research in Music Education, 26*(2), 76–81.

Barnes, B., and Clawson, E. (1975). Do advance organizers facilitate learning? Recommendations for further research based on an analysis of 32 studies. *Review of Educational Research, 45*(4), 637–659.

Barry, N. H. (1990). *The effects of different practice techniques upon technical accuracy and musicality in student instrumental music performance.* Paper presented at the Music Educators National Conference national convention, Washington.

Bartlett, D. L. (1973). Effect of repeated listenings on structural discrimination and affective response. *Journal of Research in Music Education, 21*(4), 302–317.

Baudhuin, E. S. (1987). The design of industrial and flight simulators. In S. M. Cormier and J. D. Hagman (Eds.), *Transfer of learning.* New York: Academic Press.

Bharucha, J. J. (1987). Music cognition and perceptual facilitation: A connectionist framework. *Music Perception, 5*(1), 1–30.

Boldovici, J. A. (1987). Measuring transfer in military settings. In S. M. Cormier and J. D. Hagman (Eds.), *Transfer of learning.* New York: Academic Press.

Botvin, G. J. (1974). Acquiring conservation of melody and cross-modal transfer through successive approximation. *Journal of Research in Music Education, 22*(3), 226–233.

Brand, M. (1977). Effectiveness of simulation techniques in teaching behavior management. *Journal of Research in Music Education, 25*(2), 131–138.

Brown, A. L., and Kane, M. J. (1988). Preschool children can learn to transfer: Learning to learn and learning from example. *Cognitive Psychology, 20,* 493–523.

Bruce, R. W. (1933). Conditions of transfer of training. *Journal of Experimental Psychology, 15,* 343–361.

Bruner, J. (1960). *The Process of Education.* Cambridge: Harvard University Press.

Codding, P. A. (1985). The effect of differential feedback on beginning guitar students' intonational performance in tuning strings. Unpublished doctoral dissertation, Florida State University, Tallahassee.

Cormier, S. M. and Hagman, J. D. (1987). *Transfer of learning.* New York: Academic Press.

Decarbo, N. J. (1982). The effects of conducting experience and programed materials on error detection scores of college conducting students. *Journal of Research in Music Education, 30*(3), 187–200.

Delzell, J. (1989). The effects of musical discrimination training in beginning instrumental music classes. *Journal of Research in Music Education, 37*(1), 21–31.

DeTurk, M. S. (1988). The relationship between experience in performing music class and critical thinking in music. Unpublished doctoral dissertation, University of Wisconsin, Madison.

Duke, R. A., and Pierce, M. A. (1990). *Effects of tempo and context on transfer of performance skills.* Paper presented at the Music Educators National Conference national convention, Washington.

Edwards, R. H. (1988). Transfer and performance instruction. In C. Fowler (Ed.), *The Crane Symposium: Toward an understanding of the teaching and learning of music performance.* New York: Potsdam College of the State University of New York.

Ellis, H. C. (1965). *The transfer of learning.* New York: Macmillan.

Ferrara, R. A. , Brown, A. L., and Campione, J. C. (1986). Children's learning and transfer of inductive reasoning rules: Studies of proximal development. *Child Development, 57,* 1087–1099.

Gagné, R. M. (1965). *The conditions of learning.* New York: Holt, Rinehart, and Winston.

Garner, R., and Alexander, P. A. (1989). Metacognition: Answered and unanswered questions. *Educational Psychologist, 24*(2), 143–158.

Gebhardt, L. R. (1973). The development and evaluation of an integrated plan of study providing for increased musical perception and skills by students in the junior high school band. Unpublished doctoral dissertation, Indiana University, Bloomington.

Gick, M. L., and Holyoak, K. J. (1987). The cognitive basis for knowledge transfer. In S. M. Cormier and J. D. Hagman (Eds.), *Transfer of learning* (pp. 239–260). New York: Academic Press.

Goodman, N. (1978). *Ways of worldmaking.* Indianapolis: Hackett.

Haack, P. (1972). Use of positive and negative examples in teaching the concept of musical style. *Journal of Research in Music Education, 20*(4), 456–461.

Hair, H. I. (1977). Discrimination of tonal direction on verbal and non-verbal tasks by first grade children. *Journal of Research in Music Education, 25,* 197–210.

Harlow, H. F. (1949). The formation of learning sets. *Psychological Review, 56,* 51–65.

Harvey, N., Garwood, J., and Palencia, M. (1987). Vocal matching of pitch intervals: Learning and transfer effects. *Psychology of Music, 15*(1), 90–106.

Hedden, S. K. (1981). Music listening responses of groups differing in listening achievement. *Psychomusicology, 1*(2), 52–58.

Heller, J. J. (1969). Electronic graphs of musical performance: A pilot study in perception and learning. *Journal of Research in Music Education, 17*(2), 202–216.

Hodges, D. (1975). The effects of recorded aural models on the performance achievement of students in beginning band classes. *Journal of Band Research, 12,* 30–34.

Holland, A., and Andre, T. (1987). Participation in extracurricular activities in secondary school: What is known, what needs to be known? *Review of Educational Research, 57*(4), 437–466.

Holyoak, K. J. (1985). The pragmatics of analogical transfer. In G. H. Bower (Ed.), *The psychology of learning and motivation (Vol. 19).* New York: Academic Press.

Hurwitz, I. Wolff, P., Bortnick, B., and Kokas, K. (1975). Nonmusical effects of the Kodaly Music Curriculum in primary grade children. *Journal of Learning Disabilities, 8*(3), 167–174.

Jones, M. R. (1982). Music as a stimulus for psychological motion: II. An expectancy model. *Psychomusicology, 2*(1), 1–13.

Judd, C. H. (1908). The relation of special training and general intelligence. *Educational Review, 36,* 28–42.

Kinser, T. (1975). An investigation of the effects of guided listening upon instrumental music performances of junior college students. Unpublished doctoral dissertation, North Texas State University, Denton.

LaBerge, D. (1981). Perceptual and motor schema in the performance of music. *Documentary report of the Ann Arbor Symposium.* Reston: Music Educators National Conference.

Langsford, H. M. (1959). An experimental study of the effect of practice upon improvement in melodic dictation. Unpublished doctoral dissertation, Michigan State University, East Lansing.

Lauder, D. C. (1976). An experimental study of the effect of music activities upon reading achievement of first grade students. Unpublished doctoral dissertation, University of South Carolina, Columbia.

Lipman, M. (1985). Thinking skills fostered by philosophy for children. In J. W. Segal, S. F. Chipman, and R. Glaser (Eds.), *Thinking and learning skills, Vol. I: Relating instruction to research.* Hillsdale: Lawrence Erlbaum Associates.

Luchins, A. (1942). Mechanization in problem solving. *Psychological Monographs, 54* (No. 248).

MacKnight, C. B. (1975). Music reading ability of beginning wind instrumentalists after melodic instruction. *Journal of Research in Music Education, 23*(1), 23–34.

Marciniak, F. M. (1974). Investigation of the relationships between music perception and music performance. *Journal of Research in Music Education, 22*(1), 35–44.

Mayer, R. E. (1975). Different problem-solving competencies established in learning computer programming with and without meaningful models. *Journal of Educational Psychology, 67,* 725–734.

Newell, A. (1980). One final word. In D. T. Tuma and F. Reif (Eds.), *Problem solving and education.* Hillsdale: Lawrence Erlbaum Associates.

Nierman, G. E. (1985). The differences in descriptive abilities of band, choral, and orchestral students. *Psychology of Music, 13*(2), 124–132.

Nitsch, K. E. (1977). Structuring decontextualized forms of knowledge. Unpublished doctoral dissertation, Vanderbilt University, Nashville.

O'Connor, K. (1971). *Learning: An introduction.* Glenview: Scott, Foresman and Co.

Olson, G. B. (1976). Task difficulty in inter-and intrasensory transfer of melodic contour perception by first-grade children. Unpublished doctoral dissertation, University of Iowa, Iowa City.

Osgood, C. E. (1949). The similarity paradox in human learning: A resolution. *Psychological Review, 56,* 132–143.

O'Sullivan, J. T., and Pressley, M. (1984). Completeness of instruction and strategy transfer. *Journal of Experimental Child Psychology, 38,* 275–288.

Peitersen, D. N. (1954). An experimental evaluation of the transfer effects of rhythm training in spaced notation on subsequent reading of commercially printed music. Unpublished doctoral dissertation, University of Minnesota, Minneapolis.

Pembrook, R. G., and Taylor J. A. (1986). Relationships between scores on a melodic discrimination test and the background variables of prospective music students. *Bulletin of the Council for Research in Music Education, 88,.* 1–21.

Pirtle, M., and Seaton, K. P. (1973). Use of music training to actuate conceptual growth in neurologically handicapped children. *Journal of Research in Music Education, 21*(4), 292–301.

Pollard-Gott, L. (1983). Emergence of thematic concepts in repeated listening to music. *Cognitive Psychology, 15*(1), 66–94.

Postman, L. (1969). Experimental analysis of learning to learn. In G. H. Bower and J. T. Spence (Eds.), *The psychology of learning and motivation* (Vol. 3). New York: Academic Press.

Rosch, E. H. (1973). Natural categories. *Cognitive Psychology, 4*(3), 328–350.

Rosenthal R. (1984). The relative effects of guided model, model only, guide only, and practice only treatments on the accuracy of advanced instrumentalists' musical performance. *Journal of Research in Music Education, 32*(4), 265–273.

Rosenthal R., Wilson, M., Evans, M., and Greenwalt, L. (1988). Effects of different practice conditions on advanced instrumentalists' performance accuracy. *Journal of Research in Music Education, 36*(4), 250–257.

Ross, E. (1964). Improving facility in music memorization. *Journal of Research in Music Education, 12*(4), 269–278.

Ross S. L. (1985). The effectiveness of mental practice in improving the performance of college trombonists. *Journal of Research in Music Education, 33*(4), 221–230.

Royer, J. M. (1979). Theories of the transfer of learning. *Educational Psychologist, 14,* 53–69.

Royer, J. M., and Cable, G. W. (1975). Facilitated learning in connected discourse. *Journal of Educational Psychology, 67,* 116–123.

Royer, J. M., and Cable, G. W. (1976). Illustrations, analogies, and facilitative transfer in prose learning. *Journal of Educational Psychology, 68,* 205–209.

Rubin-Rabson, G. (1939). Studies in the psychology of memorizing piano music: I. A comparison of unilateral and coordinated approaches. *Journal of Educational Psychology, 30,* 321–345.

Rubin-Rabson, G. (1940). Studies in the psychology of memorizing piano music: II. A comparison of massed and distributed practice. *Journal of Educational Psychology, 31, 270–284.*

Rubin-Rabson, G. (1941). Studies in the psychology of memorizing piano music: VI. A comparison of two forms of mental rehearsal and keyboard overlearning. *Journal of Educational Psychology, 32,* 593–602.

Salomon, G., and Perkins, D. N. (1989). Rocky roads to transfer: Rethinking mechanisms of a neglected phenomenon. *Educational Psychologist, 24*(2), 113–142.

Schmidt, R. A. (1975). A schema theory of discrete motor skill learning. *Psychological Review, 82,* 225–260.

Schmidt, R. A. (1982). *Motor control and learning: A behavioral emphasis.* Champaign: Human Kinetics Publishers.

Schmidt, R. A., and Young, D. E. (1987). Transfer of movement control in motor skill learning. In S. M. Cormier and J. D. Hagman (Eds.), *Transfer of learning* (pp. 47–79). New York: Academic Press.

Seides, E. (1967). The effect of talent class placement on slow learners in the seventh grade of a New York City junior high school. Unpublished doctoral dissertation, New York University, New York.

Sharman, E. (1981). The impact of music on the learning of young children. *Bulletin of the Council for Research in Music Education, 66,* 80–85.

Shea J. B., and Morgan, R. L. (1979). Contextual interference effects on the acquisition, retention, and transfer of a motor skill. *Journal of Experimental Psychology: Human Learning and Memory, 5,* 179–187.

Shea J. B., and Zimny, S. T. (1983). Context effects in memory and learning movement information. In R. A. Magill (Ed.), *Memory and control of action.* Amsterdam: North Holland.

Shehan, P. K. (1985). Transfer of preference from taught to untaught pieces of non-Western music genres. *Journal of Research in Music Education, 33*(3), 149–158.

Shuell, T. J. (1986). Cognitive conceptions of learning. *Review of Educational Research, 56*(4), 411–436.

Shuell, T. J. (1988). The role of transfer in the teaching and learning of music: A cognitive perspective. In C. Fowler (Ed.), *The Crane Symposium: Toward an understanding of the teaching and learning of music performance.* New York: Potsdam College of the State University of New York.

Singley, M. K., and Anderson, J. R. (1989). *The transfer of cognitive skill.* Cambridge: Harvard University Press.

Smith, E. H. (1953). The value of notated examples in learning to recognize musical themes aurally. *Journal of Research in Music Education, 1*(2), 97–104.

Thorndike, E. L. (1903). *Educational psychology.* New York: Lemcke and Buechner.

Thorndike, E. L., and Woodworth, R. S. (1901). The influence of improvement in one mental function upon the efficiency of other functions. *Psychological Review, 8,* 247–261.

Tunks, T. W. (1980). Applications of psychological positions on learning and development to musical behavior. In D. Hodges (Ed.), *Handbook of music psychology.* Lawrence: National Association for Music Therapy.

Twining, W. E. (1949). Mental practice and physical practice in learning a motor skill. *Researchers Quarterly, 20,* 432–435.

Van Zee, N. (1976). Responses of kindergarten children to musical stimuli and terminology. *Journal of Research in Music Education, 24*(1), 14–21.

Wagner, M. J. (1975). The effect of a practice report on practice time and musical performance. In C. K. Madsen, R. D. Greer, and C. H. Madsen (Eds.), *Research in music behavior: Modifying music behavior in the classroom.* New York: Teachers College Press.

Weinberg, R. S. (1982). The relationship between mental preparation strategies and motor performance: A review and critique. *Quest, 33*(2), 195–213.

Williamson, S. C. (1964). The effect of special instruction on speed, transfer, and retention in memorizing songs. Unpublished doctoral dissertation, University of Kansas, Lawrence.

Wolff, K. (1978). The nonmusical outcomes of music education: A review of the literature. *Bulletin of the Council for Research in Music Education, 55,* 1–27.

Wylie, H. H. (1919). An experimental study of transfer of response in the white rat. *Behavioral Monographs, 3*(16).

TEACHING AND
LEARNING STRATEGIES

·29·

THE ACQUISITION OF
MUSIC LISTENING SKILLS

Paul Haack

UNIVERSITY OF MINNESOTA

RATIONALE AND PARAMETERS

The Significance of Music Listening

Listening is the fundamental music skill. Some aestheticians argue or imply that until sounds are heard and perceived as music, there is no music. Clearly this is the practical truth as concerns music listening: Music exists for hearing and listening. Such listening is a skill in and of itself, as well as a vital part of all other musical skills. Yet music listening is among the last and least studied aspects of music. Aspects of musicology have long received scholarly attention under rubrics such as music history, theory, and ethnomusicology. Performance skills have received a considerable amount of more or less scientific attention under rubrics such as developmental methodology, performance practice, and interpretation.

Only in recent decades has the acquisition of listening skills received notable attention from researchers and pedagogues—probably fostered by developments in sound reproduction technology and spurred on by the general music movement. The significant body of research that has developed over recent years in this fundamental area will be sampled and examined according to the following general format:

1. An examination of research reviews dealing with the acquisition of music listening skills
2. Research dealing with developmental aspects of music-listening skill acquisition
3. Research on teaching to enhance music-listening skill acquisition and development
4. Conclusions and observations relating to the state of the field and further research needs

Parameters

The area of music listening skills is so fundamental that virtually any study could be seen as related to it. This fact along with practical limits of space dictates the setting of priorities. Thus a fairly close interpretation of the topic of this chapter has been made to arrive at the following areas of focus:

1. Emphasis is given to findings from developmental and methodological studies rather than unidimensional or status quo studies, for example, comparisons and evaluations of methods designed to enhance listening skills and studies focusing on skill changes over time as contrasted with singular assessments of skills at a given point in time.
2. Emphasis is given to research dealing with actual *music* stimuli, with contextual music listening, in contrast to more "clinical" studies of the perception of sounds not necessarily in musical context and covered elsewhere in this book, for example, studies dealing with intact rhythmic, melodic, and/or harmonic selections or excerpts in contrast to pure tone pitch discrimination research.
3. Emphasis is given to listening *skills* in contrast to values, attitudes, and preferences—some aspects of which are considered elsewhere in this book—except where such aspects may be affected methodologically, for example, research dealing with the development of stylistic recognition or changing style values in contrast to a status quo survey of stylistic preference.
4. Finally, emphasis is given to research of the 1980s, because of necessary space limits and because several comprehensive summaries of prior research are already available. Pertinent aspects of these earlier summaries

451

will be included to provide the basis for the current review, but generally references to specific studies will be to those of the decade of the 1980s. This emphasis will not rule out inclusion of several examples of earlier landmark or "classic" contributions.

REVIEWS DEALING WITH MUSIC LISTENING SKILLS ACQUISITION

Earlier reviews tend to be of a more general or comprehensive nature. They focus on the studies of the 1960s and 1970s, a time rich in research on various aspects of music listening. More recent reviews tend to be less extensive and more focused on limited aspects of the topic. Both formats can be beneficial in providing insights into research trends if not detailed findings in an area of study.

Earlier Reviews

In Hodges's (1980) *Handbook of Music Psychology,* the chapter by Haack, "The Behavior of Music Listeners," provides the most extensive review of research literature to date. The review is organized into four broad areas: physiological aspects (including physiological responses, synesthesia, verbalization, and music in the physical environment); psychological aspects (including types of listeners, affective/mood responses, taste and preference responses); sociological aspects (including teacher, peer, and disc jockey influences; socioeconomic factors; and music in the social environment); and developmental/educational aspects. Whereas all relate to the acquisition of music listening skills at least peripherally, the last section provides the most direct information concerning the priorities of the current review.

This section begins with an overview of research in the developmental aspect of music listening skills as stimulated by the work of Jean Piaget. Pflederer was the prime contributor in the investigation of Piaget's theories, particularly those relating to conservation as applied to music education. Among other findings she verified the ability of 8-year-olds to conserve meter and tonal and rhythmic patterns, and the inability of 5-year-olds to do likewise (1964). Subsequent researchers found that melodic permutations tended to be consistent with Piaget's developmental stages theory, and that children identified as "field independent" accomplished musical conservation tasks more easily than those categorized as "field dependent."

In a pioneering series of longitudinal/developmental studies, Petzold (1963, 1966, 1969) studied the musical sound perception responses of hundreds of elementary school children over a 6-year time span. His findings revealed certain gender differences, and early improvements from grade to grade, with a marked leveling off of response accuracy to his tonal-rhythmic tasks from grade 3 on. Petzold's work remains a classic and oft-cited example of longitudinal research in music education. In a subsequent and substantial cross-sectional study, Hufstader (1977) found evidence for a music listening learning sequence wherein, according to his criteria, timbres were satisfactorily perceived by first-graders, rhythm by fifth-graders, and melodic pitch pattern at some point between fifth and seventh grades, with the harmony criterion only partially satisfied by the seventh-graders.

Development of recognition skills for varied or altered themes received considerable attention in the 1960s and 1970s. Such skills generally improved with age and experience, with findings ranging from a general lack of structural perception prior to age 8, to the point of no difference between high school and college nonmusic majors at the other end of the spectrum. These skills can, however, be notably improved with training in high school and beyond. The role of memory in this regard has received some attention as well.

Though peripheral to the acquisition of listening skills per se, preference studies have shown student preferences tending toward the popular styles from the early to middle grades onward, with the preferences, particularly for forms of rock music, growing stronger as grade levels increase. Training was generally found to have a broadening effect, but not so as to replace the preference for popular music.

Used in bridging the developmental to educational emphases in Haack's (1980) review, Mark's (1978) synopsis of National Assessment of Educational Progress testing results remains informative as a basis for comparisons with more recent data relating to listening skills and preferences according to age/grade variables. The 1960s and 1970s were rich in the research and development of various types of materials and means of teaching for the acquisition of listening skills. Related testing centered on assessment of ways to direct listening via instructions and visual aids, as well as methods employing activities and approaches ranging from the deductive to the inductive. In a landmark project Reimer (1967) developed an extensive set of curricular materials that focused on listening skills and served as a basis for additional experimental research in this area.

Training in conservation skills was found to be effective, as were most of the other reported approaches and materials. This portion of Haack's (1980) review concludes with an extensive summary of programed learning research, much of which was found to be effective as well. Although presumably less than successful results were found at times, the reported research demonstrates that the acquisition of listening skills can be readily enhanced through a variety of educational processes.

In another 1980 research review, Serafine concentrated on Piagetian research in music. She summarized those aspects of Piagetian theory that she considered particularly susceptible to music research and application, and followed this with a comprehensive and detailed review of the existing research literature in music. The reviews were punctuated with frank and insightful commentary sections. She concluded the following:

1. Some progress has been made toward the beginnings of a theoretical framework for Piagetian research in music.
2. Tasks (both individual and group administered) for mea-

suring certain constructs have been developed, but not validated.

3. Although performance on most Piagetian music tasks has been found to improve with age, well-defined stages of development have not been identified.

4. There is scant information on the effects of other variables (e.g., environment, experience, memory, aural perception) on task performance.

5. In various studies the effects of training on task performance have ranged from negligible to positive.

6. A positive relationship has been found in some studies between music conservation tasks and Piaget's conservation tasks. (p. 19)

Her general conclusion was that (in 1980) there was an absence of conclusive research to demonstrate that Piagetian theory can extend comfortably to the field of music education. Thus any but the most general claims in terms of implications and applications were probably premature.

Two additional earlier reviews by Hedden (1980, 1981) are notable with regard to the acquisition of music listening skills. In the 1980 review Hedden included 28 references from the 1960s and 1970s and organized them into three categories. In reviewing studies that deal with "notated themes or visual representations," his first category, he concludes that using such devices in the development of music recognition skills does not appear to be superior to instruction without them at the elementary school level. However, definite advantages seem to accrue when they are used at the junior high school level.

Hedden's second category, "guided listening," included studies that demonstrated that seventh-graders can be taught to track formal properties of symphonic movements, but that attitude shifts do not necessarily accompany the skill development. Guided listening via some form of programed instruction received considerable attention in Hedden's review; however, he found it difficult to generalize or summarize findings because of the uniqueness of each study. Most programs dealt with development of repertoire, music memory, or analytical skills. Virtually all facilitated learning, and in those studies where control groups were employed, approximately half showed superior results for the experimental group. The effect of such materials on attitudes, where formally assessed, appeared to be positive.

Hedden's third, or "other methods and techniques," category included two specific listening skills studies comparing certain aspects of Kodály and Orff methodology to "traditional" approaches. Kodály won and Orff tied. Two other studies demonstrated the superiority of using both positive and negative exemplars over only positive exemplars in listening for stylistic recognition, and the benefits of employing visual arts exemplars in the same area of skills development. Hedden's final two studies indicated that both compositional activities and attendance at a live concert that included instructional commentary were viable means of enhancing various listening skills.

Hedden's 1981 review focused in part on music listening skills, with the 33 studies cited all completed in the 1960s

and 1970s. A degree of consensus emerged in at least a couple of areas. With respect to sequential listening skills development, there was agreement that awareness of differences in loudness is followed by ability to discriminate differences in timbre. Melodic or rhythmic discriminations are apparent next, followed by sensitivity to harmony. Another consistent finding was that students from culturally limited or economically deprived backgrounds performed more poorly on tests of listening skills.

More Recent Reviews

Hedden's 1988 review concentrated on music listening in the sixth through ninth grades, drawing on 10 studies completed in the 1980s. Implications were summarized as follow: When music perception and auditory discrimination are goals of instruction, it is helpful to focus student attention directly on the musical elements; students appear to be most comfortable with and capable of discussing the elemental/formal properties of music; students want to hear more about a specific piece of music the more they like it; acceptance of and liking for unfamiliar nonwestern music can be elevated through focused teaching; and, again, visual representations of musical forms and content can be helpful in aural instruction. In virtually each case, the findings and implications are congruent with and reinforce the findings of prior research.

Lewis (1989b) draws implications for the acquisition of listening skills among other aspects of music teaching and learning from her excellent review focusing on movement-based instruction research. With the notable exception of rock concerts, the general view of music listening is one of physical passivity. Lewis begins by citing expert opinion, not research, that presents a different view. From John Dewey to Emile Jaques-Dalcroze and Carl Orff, action is regarded as a key to auditory acuity and musical perception and response. Music educators tend to endorse and apply the latter viewpoint, at least at the preschool and elementary school levels. However, research findings do not uniformly support such opinions and practices. In fact, Lewis found movement studies relating to listening skills per se to be quite evenly divided between significant and nonsignificant effects. In various other studies, both positive and nonpositive effects were noted for rhythm discrimination ability, meter discrimination, and dynamic/volume and pitch discriminations.

Lewis observed that, generally, longer treatment periods tended to result in more notable skill acquisition, and that effects of movement-based instruction over relatively short periods of time may not be noticeable. She also suggested an alternative hypothesis that motivation may be more decisive than instructional mode, and may even present limitations to skill acquisition regardless of instructional method. Her conclusions pertaining to listening include the caveat that patient, well-sequenced experiences, and time in terms of years are needed to gain maximal effect from movement activities. In addition, students will benefit differentially from such experiences, which seem more essential and helpful for field-dependent children, for children in whom physical response tends to heighten aesthetic response, and for handicapped children.

Also with regard to handicapped children, Darrow (1989) surveyed 36 studies relating to music and the hearing impaired, and provided an excellent example of a focused review. Her implications for music educators include the following listening-related suggestions: Hearing-impaired children can benefit from participation in music though they may require louder stimuli than students with normal hearing and more time to attain instructional goals; hearing-impaired children do have preferences concerning types of sound sources and listening conditions, including intensity; they are more responsive to rhythmic than tonal aspects of music, and their rhythmic performance accuracy is better in the moderate tempo range; instruments that provide sustained tones may provide more useful feedback than percussive instruments; like normal hearing children, hearing-impaired children can improve in the realm of ear training and can develop a more sensitive ear over time; the supplemental use of tactile stimuli and vibrotactile devices can be very helpful in the instruction of hearing-impaired children; and finally, they, like most other children, could benefit from enhanced musical vocabulary.

A final example of a helpful review in the area of music-listening skill acquisition is provided by Allman (1990). The focus is on brain function, with recent research results drawn from the work of some leading researchers in the field. Diana Deutsch (University of California at San Diego) is cited for findings that suggest that musical perception is influenced by the sounds people employ in speaking; that is, speech sounds affect and assist the brain in categorizing tones with reference to a scale established deep within the mind. Furthermore, such perceptions and categorizations appear to vary with the mother tongue. Deutsch also studied the physical and biological factors that allow persons to concentrate on music in an environment of many different sounds via a kind of directional sorting. She believes that the sorting itself may be based on the brain's assumption that the ear that hears the highest (and thus weakest) tones is most proximate to the musical sound source. Allman also mentions Deutsch's work with musical illusions such as those resulting from the rapid alteration of high and low notes and the simultaneous presentation of differing complex sound patterns to each ear.

Allman's review article lends further support to Leonard Meyer's theories relating to expectation and affect. According to findings by psychologists Sandra Trehub (University of Toronto) and Michael Lynch (University of Miami), the neurobiological bases for Meyer's theories are already in the process of development in children only 1 year old. Jamshed Bharucha (Dartmouth College), working with a computer model of brain cells in a so-called neural network, found that without explicit instructions, the model network, upon continuing exposure to music, organized itself in a way that reflected the organization of the music itself. Bharucha's work has provided further support for Meyer's emphasis on musical expectations via insights into the brain's tendency to organize by patterns, and to compare specific incoming musi-

cal patterns with stored patterns of music in general (expectations). Extensions of such modeling and theorizing may lead to possible explanations for the development and sustenance of music preferences based on even more sophisticated neural networking and pattern comparisons. Finally, Richard Voss (IBM: Thomas J. Watson Research Center) is cited for his development of mathematical models that demonstrate strong theoretical similarities between the tonal-rhythmic organization and ebb and flow of music and many other natural phenomena. The speculation here is that in music listening, the appreciation that results has its roots in nature itself. The unanswered question, and in this review the unasked question, is, Does awareness of such relationships and congruity enhance music-listening skill and appreciation? Nevertheless, Allman's article may be regarded as an insightful, thought-provoking overview of the state of the art as concerns listening and brain function.

In closing this section on research reviews, one additional effort should be noted, and that is Lewis's (1989a) overview of the literature on measurement of children's music-listening skills. Her review does not deal with research findings regarding listening, and thus it will not be detailed here, other than to note its value to anyone contemplating research into children's music listening skills.

DEVELOPMENTAL ASPECTS OF MUSIC LISTENING SKILLS

As demonstrated in the preceding reviews, developmental and educational aspects of music learning overlap. Indeed, it is a prime purpose of education to enhance social and maturational development, so these aspects cannot be totally isolated as discrete categories of research. Nevertheless, this section will attempt to review studies having more of a developmental focus, while the ensuing section will deal with studies having more of an educational nature—in the formal teaching and methodological sense. As per stated priorities and limitations, the sampling of studies that follows is drawn largely from music education research of the 1980s.

Perception and Cognition of Music Elements and Their Interactions

A major emphasis in listening skills research in recent years has been study of the development of aesthetic sensitivity. Aesthetic sensitivity has been defined generally and operationally in research and practice as the ability to perceive and deal cognitively with musical elements and their relationships. Pitch is an element that has received and continues to receive much attention from music researchers.

Walker (1987) designed an imaginative study to learn if musically untrained subjects conceptualize pitch/frequency changes in the same manner as subjects who had music as a part of their regular school curriculum. Through their choices of visual responses to discrete tonal and glide-tone stimuli, Walker found that the trained students were much more likely than the untrained students to select drawn responses representing movement along a vertical axis. He felt that learning the concept of pitch seemed to involve the identification of movement as up or down on a vertical tone ladder. Thus he concluded that the musically trained subjects were able to employ the concept of pitch while the untrained subjects seemed to be at a more arbitrary level of conceptualization in this ability. The differential response practices of the trained and nontrained groups are clearly demonstrated in Walker's study, though his "ladder" premise relating to the concept of pitch may warrant further discussion and research—for instance, is up always a higher frequency in this concept area? What of cellists and accordionists who learn to go down to go up, or pianists who use lateral rather than ladder movements? Or is the concept totally dominated by visual experience with the staff? Then what of "ear-players'" pitch concepts? The role of personal experience and learning style may be influential and worthy of additional research in this aspect of concept development.

Two pitch (and pulse/tempo) studies of the mid-1980s are particularly notable because of their employment of large samples. Mills (1985) analyzed the responses of 1,715 children in the age range 6 through 16 on a pitch test patterned after Arnold Bentley's and a pulse test after Raleigh Drake's. The results of the two tests demonstrate that the measured abilities are age related, with the most notable increases taking place up to ages 10 or 11, and continuing beyond more slowly. The norms of some earlier tests have suggested similar phenomena, so the more interesting and novel findings here are that the nature of these perceptions may change with age; that is, rising pitch sequences were heard more accurately than falling pitch sequences by children up to approximately age 10. The reverse was true thereafter. With regard to marking time passage, counting was notably too slow through age 10, and notably too fast from age 14 on. In addition to implications for optimal developmental/educational ages, these findings suggest possible error tendencies that when known by teachers can be more effectively anticipated and nullified.

The second large sample study involved 200 musicians and 200 nonmusicians listening to paired (repeated) orchestral excerpts (Geringer and Madsen, 1984). One of most pairs was altered in terms of pitch and/or tempo. The college student subjects exhibited greater difficulty in dealing with pitch increase than pitch decrease discriminations. This statistically significant finding is consistent with previous findings, but the finding that tempo increase excerpts were identified correctly more often than tempo decrease excerpts was not in keeping with most previous findings. The data revealed no significant differences in correct responses of musicians and nonmusicians in these abilities.

Kuhn and Booth (1988) found that their fifth-grade subjects, though instructed in beat awareness and tempo perception, nevertheless were more influenced in their tempo judgments by degree of melodic activity than by actual tempo changes between 90, 102, and 118 beats per minute. The report is somewhat unique in that it encompasses two studies, the second resulting from a good self-critique of the first. An excellent capsulization of recent tempo research is included, as is also the case in the Geringer and Madsen study.

In related studies on beat and meter perception, Boyle (1987) found that his college music major subjects had little difficulty discriminating between musical excerpts according to traditional definitions of duple and triple. Of greater interest may be the finding that at faster tempi—for example, MM = 200—responses suggested a possible feeling for a superimposed beat. Duke's (1989) study relates here and is of sufficient importance to be mentioned even though it was not carried on in a musical context. Subjects were asked to tap their perceived beat or pulse in response to sets of periodic beep tones of differing tempi. Tempo rates greater than 120 tones per minute tended to be responded to as subdivisions of a slower perceived pulse, and rates slower than 60 tended to be responded to in terms of subdivisions of the basic rate. Thus perception/responses of these music major subjects were generally confined to the pulse range of 60 to 120 tones per minute.

Clearly more research is needed in these areas, particularly with a broader range of subjects in terms of age and musical experience. In addition, the profession would do itself a service to come to agreement, however arbitrary, on the meanings of apparently related and at times interchangeably used terms such as beat, pulse, takt, meter, and tempo.

As with tempo, some rhythm research involved the possible effects of melodic context. Boisen (1981) found that single-pitch rhythm patterns and rhythm patterns in the context of melodic patterns that exhibited like qualities of completeness both yielded more accurate responses than did nonmatched patterns. He suggested that rhythm-reading instruction might be enhanced by using a contextual approach involving feeling for musical style rather than a measure-based arithmetic approach, and called for additional research in this direction. Sink (1983) studied how varying melodic contours might affect rhythm perception, and also how dissimilar some rhythm alterations might be perceived to be. As a result it was hypothesized that there may be a relationship between rhythm alterations and degree of perceived dissimilarity. Moreover, melodic contexts were found to alter perception of rhythm dissimilarity. A finding that presenting rhythm in melodic context may result in reduced attention to the essential rhythmic aspect of the music holds implications for selection of teaching materials. When instructional goals focus on rhythm awareness and rhythm concepts, complexity of the melodic context as well as that of the rhythm patterns should be considered. Sink's report offers an excellent review of related literature based on an impressive list of references.

Piaget's theories, particularly those relating to conservation, continued to foster research activities in the 1980s, though not at the pace of preceding decades. Webster and Zimmerman (1983) gathered listening test data from 317 second- through sixth-grade children and concluded the ability to conserve tonal and rhythm patterns is essentially a linear growth process through this age range. Tonal conservation was easier than rhythm conservation, and graphic as well as traditional notation was a notable aid in each task area. The interaction between grade and test order for rhythm conservation again suggests the need to approach rhythm tasks and concepts for younger children with careful attention to materials selection. Crowther, Durkin, Shire, and Hargreaves (1985) investigated "conservation-type" responses and found a significant age effect akin to the linear development noted by Webster and Zimmerman. They reported as surprising the fact that type of music had little effect on responses of the test takers.

The theories of Edwin Gordon continue to attract researchers. Taggart (1990) developed the "Test of the Stages of Tonal Audiation," which was used along with the tonal test of the *Intermediate Measures of Music Audiation*, in an effort to study Gordon's six stages of tonal audiation. The testing of second- and fourth-grade subjects suggested that the overall hierarchy of the stages is valid, though stages two and three may be reversed for the younger group. Tonal music aptitude appeared to be related to general ability to audiate and to all stages of tonal audiation except the last for the fourth-grade subjects. Similar relationships were not evident for the second-grade subjects, indicating the value of further research in this area.

It seems appropriate to conclude with another reference to the foundational work of Petzold (1963, 1966, 1969) particularly as it relates to the findings above. His developmental studies with children in the first six grades provides solid evidence concerning the significance of the age factor in the development of auditory perception. Subsequent studies have done much to illuminate the intricacies of the age factor, its varying developmental plateaus, and possible gender effects. Clearly, investigation of the developmental aspects of music perception and cognition vis-à-vis listening ability has provided much guidance for music education practice and continues to warrant our best research efforts.

Listener Responses to Music

Developmental aspects of listener responses to music have been approached from a variety of viewpoints, such as the perceptual/aesthetic responses reviewed above, mood responses, personality-related responses, verbal responses, movement responses, and familiarity. Mood, in terms of "happy," "sad," "angry," and "frightened," was ascribed to musical examples by college students in a study by Dolgin and Adelson (1990). When children aged 4, 7, and 9 were provided the same stimuli, all age levels were able to recognize the emotional qualities to a fairly consistent degree, and the ability was found to improve through, and presumably beyond, the age levels employed. In a large sample cross-cultural study, 487 college students in Japan and America were tested for mood and emotion responses to eastern and western musics. There was no greater consistency by one group or the other in selecting verbal descriptors for the music of its own culture, but as a whole, the subjects were more in

agreement on descriptors for western than for eastern examples (Darrow, Haack, and Kuribayashi, 1987).

Lewis and Schmidt (1990) employed Hedden's "Music Listening Response Scale" to study different personality types as identified by the *Meyers-Briggs Type Indicator*. The Response Scale is a self-assessment instrument that provides information on listening styles along various dimensions such as active-passive and formal-associative listening. The Response Scale data revealed statistically significant mean differences among various Meyers-Briggs personality-type subgroups.

Radocy (1990) studied verbal responses to music and arrived at a classification scheme that has implications for the development and enhancement of students' musical vocabularies. The musical (tone properties) category was favored by the fourth-grade subjects, while the "liking" category was used more by the seventh-grade subjects. High school subjects tended to make more balanced comments, including the third major category of "extra-musical." Flowers and Giomi (1990) had their English- and Spanish-speaking preschool subjects respond by clapping or using words to indicate a range change in the music they were hearing. Although many of the younger children failed to respond via clapping, nearly all employed verbal indicators of perceived change. An inference one might draw from these studies is that verbalization is an important tool in musical awareness, and may need more attention to be more useful as children mature.

Like verbal responses to music, movement responses have received increasing attention over the past decade. Metz (1989) investigated preschool children's responses in a free-choice participation format. Analysis of her qualitative data resulted in the definition of several theoretical core categories underlying movements to music: *conditions* that influence movement responses; *interactions* between students and teachers; and *outcomes* in terms of music and non-music-related responses. Her theoretical work may provide a useful basis for further research, just as her bibliography provides a good sampling of prior studies. This line of research should extend well beyond the preschool level in an effort to understand why and how responses appear to become more restricted with increasing age levels and for differing types of music—seemingly to the point of very little movement response to almost any kind of music.

Finally, an imaginatively designed and executed study serves to demonstrate the rapidity with which environmental/developmental influences can result in perceptive and discriminating responses with music. Excerpts of Mozart minuets, altered by the insertion of brief pauses at phrase points in some and at nonphrase points in others, were played for 4.5- and 6-month-old infants. Lights above a speaker would draw the infant's attention, at which time an excerpt with either natural or unnatural breaks would begin and continue until the infant looked away. The time of looking favored the naturally broken excerpts by a substantial margin. Krumhansl and Jusczyk (1990) concluded that protracted musical experience may not be necessary in order to perceive, discriminate, and respond favorably to common phrase structure in music.

Imagery and Memory

Listening skills relating to music imagery and memory have received substantial attention in recent years. In a series of reports, Walker (1981, 1983, 1985) considered visual imagery responses to musical stimuli. His 1981 experiments involved a subject age range of 7 to 15 years and revealed that all age groups scored significantly beyond chance in relating auditory and visual stimuli. Significant linear relationships were revealed as concerns age and intelligence, with ability growth appearing to level off after age 13.

Walker's 1983 report is based on a brief but perceptive review of literature relating to visual imagery and melodic perception. One of his prime concerns is that melodic perception and experience involve much more than isolated pitch/duration discriminations, yet much of the available research focuses on the latter. Because there seems to be much more interest in music education and research in the ability to reproduce written sound than in the intuitive use of sound, relatively little is known about auditory imagery. Walker points out that melodies in different musical contexts will be perceived differently and that even inexperienced listeners will have different mental images for them. Thus he argues that teaching young children about melody by using short isolated pitch segments and then progressing to larger, more complete representations is not appropriate for music education, regardless of how well it may apply to some other curricular areas. He concludes that young children need and can deal with music wherein the melody is in its complete context, and melody should even initially be approached holistically.

In his 1985 study Walker had congenitally blind subjects respond to musical sounds by selecting what they felt to be appropriate tactile shapes, while sighted subjects responded with visual shapes. He found no difference in the tactile and visual externalizations for subjects' internal sound images and concluded that neural sound stimulation induces the same internal imagery even without visual experience. However, he also recognized that both groups had the same cultural and language background, and that this circumstance requires further study for possible linking factors and an explanation for response similarity between groups.

Abel-Struth (1981) studied various aspects of musical audiation in 5- to 7-year-old children and found them able to listen sensitively and to evaluate music in images and terms as "marchlike" and "signallike" (highest preference); "dancelike," "songlike," and "animal sounds" (moderate liking); with "flowing sound" far behind. In a study that bridges imagery and memory, Moore and Staum (1987) employed a computer game that produced color and sound stimuli to study auditory short-term memory skills of English and American children, also in the 5 to 7 age range. They found 5-year-olds could deal effectively with three- or four-tone patterns (accompanied by color imagery), while 7-year-olds

were mastering five-tone/symbol patterns. Follow-up studies indicated that this memory ability continued to improve with age beyond childhood. English children tended to score better with increased age than their American counterparts, and there were no significant differences between boys and girls in either group. The researchers concluded that both the auditory tonal stimuli and the visual color imagery contributed to the demonstrated abilities, though further research would be required to determine the precise extent for each. All of this begs the question of chromesthesia, a phenomenon not yet receiving much attention in arts education even though it is more common than generally acknowledged. The persistent presence of colorful visual imagery when hearing music has implications for music education in terms of individual perceptual differences that may significantly influence learning style and possibly even cause learning problems, for example, the reported tendency to dissect melodies into individual tones (and colors) rather than hearing tonal-rhythmic flow and relationships (Haack and Radocy, 1981).

Williams (1982) also employed visual imagery in his memory studies, which he reviews in this article along with studies by several others concerned with memory processing. He identifies gaps in research to date of his publication and raises questions for study such as: Is recognition of melodies essentially a contour-based (and visual imagery–based) task while recall is a pitch-based task? Do different strategies govern recall for novel as contrasted with familiar patterns? And, how can memory research be approached in more holistic, musical ways?

Davies (1981) also examined several memory studies and concluded the following: Melody is a psychological not a physical event; melody is based on a sequence of intervals, not durations, but a sequence of intervals is not necessarily a melody; and transpositions of tunes are remembered and recognized more effectively than transpositions of isolated intervals. Davies emphasized conclusions suggesting that explanations for complex phenomena such as music memory may be beyond the range of current neurophysiology, and that work on music memory may benefit more from serious inquiry into what people do than from premature attempts to learn how they do it.

Cutietta (1984), testing a large national sample of 11- to 16-year-old subjects, found a marked advance in tonal memory ability at or immediately after age 14. He recommended that training in that skill might be more effectively and efficiently done if delayed until students move from what he found to be an apparent learning plateau prior to that age.

Short-term music memory research has demonstrated the enhancing effect of tonal-rhythmic context on memory for both pitch and rhythm sequences. Rhythm appears to be more than merely a grouping mechanism for pitch, and having students practice pitch or rhythm sequences in isolation of one another may not be advantageous to learning and remembering at all, particularly in the early stages of instruction (Fiske, 1982; Schellenberg, 1985). These findings seem resonant with the above-mentioned findings of Walker, Williams, and Davies.

Madsen and Staum (1983) found that the ability to remember melodies was apparently highly developed in their 400 non–music major college student subjects. Recall of melodies in duple meter appeared to be affected less by the interference of very similar melodies than recall of those in triple meter and those having modal changes. This article is also noteworthy for having an excellent literature review, most of which will not be rereviewed herein. However, a recent interference/memory study by Beckett and Byrnes (1990) revealed that absolute pitch subjects had significantly less difficulty remembering and labeling music intervals in various interference situations than did their relative pitch counterparts.

Experience does seem to make a difference in the task of learning a popular-type tonal melody by listening, according to a study by Oura and Hatano (1988). Their musically experienced fourth-grade subjects listened and learned more effectively than their nonexperienced college student subjects. The difference was not maintained, however, when the task focused on a nontonal Japanese folk song. The researchers speculated that the tonal melodic memory discrepancy may have been due to learned strategies specific to tonal music.

Tempo has been found to be a significant factor in melodic memory and error detection. Maximum effectiveness appears to reside in the 100 to 240 MM range, below and above which performance seems to diminish significantly (Tunks, Bowers, and Eagle, 1990). And in one of the few memory studies to focus on rhythm, Love (1989) found that perception of rhythms and memory for rhythm patterns appear to be affected more by pattern length in terms of the number of sound events than by pattern length in terms of time duration.

Summary

A thoughtful and stimulating article by Cuddy (1982) remains relevant to all aspects of this section on developmental aspects of music-listening skills. The article is titled "From Tone to Melody to Music: Some Directions for a Theory of Musical Cognition." Research in pitch scaling, identification, and memory is considered, to the conclusion that musical context is of major importance, a conclusion also reached by several of the aforementioned researchers. Cuddy also contemplates research in pitch perception, memory, and musical cognition, and emphasizes the psychological reality of tonal systems and their role in providing cognitive structures for music listening. She posits a major question: How do other dimensions interact with and influence the apprehension of a melodic line? As is clear from the preponderance of melodically oriented research found in the search for this review, much research information is needed in other elemental areas, and in their contextual interactions within more holistic approaches. This latter aspect, the need for research that explores listening phenomena in a more holistic, contextual manner, is emphasized by many researchers, and particularly by those concerned with more direct applications of findings to teaching/learning processes.

TEACHING FOR THE ACQUISITION OF MUSIC-LISTENING SKILLS

Whereas many of the preceding research reports concerned with social and maturational effects on music listening skill acquisition provided implications for music education, the ensuing reports deal with studies designed specifically to provide information directly concerned with music teaching and learning. Thus we proceed to a sampling of research, again drawn largely from the 1980s, that focuses on instructional processes, including strategies and approaches to enhance the acquisition of music listening skills.

Perception and Cognition of Musical Elements and Their Interactions

Teaching to enhance perception and cognition of music can take many forms, as demonstrated by the following studies dealing with subjects ranging from preschool children to college students. Ramsey's (1983) study of the effect of instrumental experience on preschool children's melodic perception demonstrated no advantage for the experimental approach. Although more exposure to the experimental treatment might provide different results, some secondary findings may be of more immediate interest: Among the 3- to 5-year-old subjects, perception of melodic rhythm appeared to precede perception of melodic intervals. Improvement in perception of melodic contour was evident as well, though this seemed to progress at a more gradual pace. The ability to retain a tonal center when vocally reproducing a melody appeared neither well developed nor improving with age in the 3- to 5-year-old subjects of the study.

First- and third-grade children were the subjects for Lewis's (1986) study of the effects on listening skills of incorporating a strong movement component into the normal general music curriculum. In tests in the areas of melodic direction, meter, rhythm, dynamics, and tempo, the experimental approach bested the traditional in dynamics, melodic direction (third grade only), and the composite score (third grade only). Other differences were not significant. This again brings to light an area of considerable discrepancy between strong practical beliefs and weak research support.

Shehan's (1986) sixth-grade subjects who had instruction before or before and after a live concert demonstrated significantly greater pre- to posttest gains in musical element and style perceptions when compared with subjects who attended the concert only. Apparently the additional one or two classes spent in preparation or preparation and follow-up on the concert experience enhanced the learning outcomes substantially, though attitudinal/preference effects were mixed. Shehan concluded that lack of specific preparation for concert experiences means a loss in the learning potential of those experiences. Her findings support the similar conclusions in Hedden's earlier mentioned 1980 review (p. 8).

On a slightly different tack, Baldridge (1984) systematically observed 18 elementary general music teachers in an effort to learn the extent to which the teachers initiated music-listening activities, as well as what activities and materials were employed. Major findings revealed that the teacher-subjects tended to regard music listening as a separate activity rather than one underlying and permeating all music instruction and activity. In this sense listening received very little emphasis in the observed classrooms, particularly compared to singing and performance in general. Furthermore, verbal instruction in listening tended to dominate actual listening. If "assumed" listening including performance activities is added in, the proportions seem more balanced; however, if listening tends to be regarded as an isolated activity, the benefits of assumed listening may be difficult to realize and claim.

College student musicians (music majors) and nonmusicians (less than 3 years of music instruction) were studied by Madsen and Geringer (1990) in an effort to learn if instructional experience resulted in different music-listening foci. Clear and statistically significant differences were found. Musicians attended most to melody, then to rhythm and dynamics almost equally, then to timbre, and lastly to "everything." Nonmusicians focused mostly on dynamics, then melody, timbre, everything, and rhythm in a fairly steady decreasing order. The very low proportion of time spent attending to rhythm by the nonmusician subjects seemed particularly interesting.

Listener Responses to Music

Teaching to enhance listener responses to music has created research interests and needs that go beyond the perceptual and cognitive aspects discussed above to include mood responses, movement responses, verbal responses, and liking/preference responses. Kucenski's (1977) study is mentioned in this sampling because of its innovative and imaginative approach to teaching and evaluating 60 3-month-old infant subjects. Three subgroups underwent conditions of 6 months', 3 months', and no instruction. Instruction groups were exposed to six songs through a series of four differing modes of presentation. Infant response inventories and developmental indicators revealed statistically significant gains for the treatment groups over the control group in terms of infants' responsiveness to music and general developmental effects.

The listening behaviors of 3- through 5-year-old children were videotaped and analyzed according to differing instructional conditions by Sims (1986). Active listening behaviors resulted in similar or higher attention to the music than passive activities. Also, high teacher affect was associated with higher levels of attending behavior, though not with preferences, listening time, or piece recognition.

The school music experience of college undergraduates studied by Burnsed and Fiocca (1990) did not relate notably to their listening perceptions of complexity, interestingness, or pleasingness, though instrumental experience did relate positively to familiarity with the standard concert literature

employed in the study. They found an inverted-U relationship between pleasingness and complexity, which appears consistent with the optimal complexity model discussed extensively by Radocy and Boyle (1988). This model of aesthetic preference theorizes that the relationship of complexity and affective value is best described by an inverted U-shaped curve. Hargreaves's (1986) text provides an excellent review of the literature on this topic and indicates that the results of studies divide approximately in half in terms of support for the inverted-U hypothesis.

A considerable amount of recent research in music listening has focused on verbal aspects of instruction, that is, on the words and vocabularies used by teachers and by students in the instructional process. O'Brien (1990) tested theories espoused by Regelski (1981) and Tait and Haack (1984) concerning the need for varied vocabulary development in music education. Her well-designed study involved two groups of seventh-grade general music students, one of which was instructed in and encouraged to use analytical language, while the other used analytical and figurative language including similes, analogies, and metaphors. Data from both her attitudinal and conceptual understanding measures revealed that the latter group consistently scored higher than the former. Similarly, Bula (1987) reported that instructional techniques for 13- to 15-year-old students that involved descriptive, figurative, and emotional vocabularies appeared to have significant positive attitude effects. A notable exception occurred when students expressed strong attitudes on initial hearings. At this point it appears distinctly advantageous to include substantial experience with figurative/affective language in music instruction, at least for the age levels represented in the studies to date.

Nierman (1985) tested hundreds of high school musicians in an effort to assess their ability to describe changes in music they were hearing with musical terms as opposed to with common vernacular descriptions. He found that these subjects lacked a broad and representative music vocabulary to describe many aspects of music, particularly terms to deal with loudness and textural and stylistic aspects. In the same vein Flowers (1983) studied nonmusicians' ability to describe musical changes and found that learning to use a technical vocabulary while hearing music leads to increased use of such terminology when describing musical events. However, this employment of technical vocabulary seemed to have no real effect on the sheer number of changes described in the music.

Zalonowski (1986) assigned subjects to listening instruction groups that variously emphasized paying attention, free-form mental imagery, story program, abstract verbal program, and analytical program. Subject responses were evaluated in terms of attention, enjoyment, understanding, and memory with musical stimuli including programmatic and absolute music examples. The imagery instruction resulted in the greatest enjoyment of both types of music; the story program led to the greatest understanding of the programmatic piece; while the abstract and concrete analytical programs did not improve any aspect of absolute music appreciation. The analytic instructions did seem to benefit left-hemisphere-oriented subjects more, while imagery better served the right-hemisphere subjects. Cognitive style interacted with instructional programs, further suggesting that, while descriptive techniques seemed to be of most benefit in the aggregate, no single type of instruction can serve all students equally well.

In conclusion, a notable aspect of this portion of the review is the amount of recent work done with verbal aspects of music-listening skill instruction and acquisition. By virtue of their training, music teachers are usually well versed in the technical/analytic vocabularies of music, and apparently instruction in this area can also be advantageous to students' musical development. But probably the greatest need in the verbal area at this time is the development and evaluation of student vocabularies in the figurative/experiential realm. Certainly the limited mood terms commonly employed in music discussions—happy, lively, sad—need expansion to include expressions of more subtle shades of feeling, as stated or implied in several references mentioned above.

Although words about musical experiences can never be the experiences themselves, nor can they ever be an adequate substitute for the essentially nonverbal art of music, the combining of musical experience with verbal information about it remains the most likely and most potent means of imparting music education. A continuing research emphasis in this area could be of substantial value to the profession and the students it serves.

Imagery and Memory

Imagery and memory have received only marginal attention in research dealing with instructional methods and materials for the development of listening skills, though they are recognized as vital factors in listening for the aesthetic qualities of more complex forms of western music. Remembering a theme well enough to recognize its related permutations and developments is important to intrinsic listening, and visual or verbal imagery is at times employed to assist the memory in terms of melodic contours and rhythmic patterns.

These factors have received some attention in several of the studies cited previously; for example, in the preceding section O'Brien (1990) and Bula (1987) deal with verbal imagery and Zalonowski (1986) employs free-form mental imagery. In exploring the potential of visual imagery, Haack (1982) found that his musically experienced high-school-age subjects were able to identify visual arts styles more effectively than musical styles. This helped to explain earlier findings (1970) wherein his subjects who studied the style concepts of classical and romantic with the help of visual arts examples made significantly better categorizations of musical examples than those who spent all of their time listening to and studying musical examples. Barry (1983) provided additional explanation for these findings in a study that analyzed formal/expressive characteristics of music and painting in terms of classical-romantic polarities. Her resulting charts are good subjects for experimental research and evaluation,

and her bibliography provides a remarkably extensive base for such efforts.

Both visual imagery and memory were involved in Hair's (1982) study of first- through fourth-grade children's ability to remember and discriminate melodic directional patterns. Her computerized instruction/testing package indicated that the aural/aural-matching tasks yielded more success than the aural/visual mode at these age levels. This finding was consistent with the earlier findings of Olson (1981). Hair regarded her results as affirming the Pestalozzian adage "sounds before signs," and suggested the best teaching sequence would appear to be aural/aural matching, then aural with moving visual stimuli, and finally aural with stationary visual stimuli.

Pembrook (1987) studied the use of singing as a reinforcer of short-term memory for melodic stimuli. The data yielded by his college-age subjects led him to conclude that singing is not an advantageous means of reinforcing melodic memory unless the singing is done with a high degree of accuracy, one beyond the ability of most of his subjects. This sampling of recent work again demonstrates an emphasis on the melodic element in music. It may also be noted that though there is not an abundance of research, that which is available suggests the efficacy of using various kinds of imagery in the development of listening skills.

New Dimensions

One of the foremost challenges in furthering the investigation of music-listening skills is the need to develop new and increasingly sophisticated means of measurement. Because measurement of music skills is the topic of another portion of this text, only brief mention will be given here to several examples of innovative work relating specifically to listening skills.

Herberger (1983) examined ways to explore mental and emotional processes in music listening, while Olson (1984) studied ways to measure musical awareness as well as related mental imagery. Ladànyi (1990) sought means of evaluating listening skills in terms of preferences for more and less appropriate interpretations of music. Use of the Continuous Response Digital Interface by Madsen and Geringer (1990) to get a continuously ongoing record of subjects' nonverbal responses to music provides an example of specially designed technology for the music-listening measurement process, a direction that several researchers are taking in this new era of high-tech development.

A truly different aspect of music listening was explored by Shehan (1987). Her sixth-grade students received an hour lesson during each of 5 weeks during which time they studied southeast Asian music in its cultural context. Her testing indicated a notable growth in learning about and liking for the music. She also tested for changes in attitudes relative to ethnocentricity and prejudice. Though trends were indicated, there were no statistically significant findings in this respect. It was speculated that attitude is a relatively stable construct that may require longer periods of development than normal information acquisition. Shehan's study is considered significant because, while it deals with aesthetic aspects of listening, it goes beyond that function in new and timely directions to examine social aspects, in this case ethnocentricity and prejudice. These directions receive further consideration and comment in the closing sections of this chapter.

SUMMARY

Although research in teaching for the acquisition of music listening skills during the 1980s does not seem to have kept pace quantitatively with that of the late 1960s and early 1970s, quality work continues to be done. That work, however, continues to focus heavily on the melodic aspect of music, leaving information gaps in aspects such as harmony, rhythm, timbre, texture, direction, and location—aspects being increasingly emphasized in contemporary music. Interest in the verbal aspects of teaching for listening skills, including verbal imagery, is increasing, and this appears to be a promising area for further research. Advanced technology is now being employed for measurement purposes in some music listening research, and a recent report indicated that cutting edge technology is coming into the general music classroom as well (Moore, 1989).

A final observation is that the age span of subjects in listening research is increasing, particularly in the direction of younger children. The sampling of cited studies involves infants to adults, preschool children through college students. However, there still appears to be a notable lack of research relating to the junior and senior high school years. It is natural that most research in listening skill acquisition should involve subjects associated with general music curricula that have substantial listening content, but this raises several questions. Is music listening skill enhancement not regarded as a goal in the performance curricula that dominate secondary education? Has the mid-1980s resurgence of interest in secondary school general music yet to bear fruit in terms of related research activity? And finally, how do we rationalize an apparent lack of interest in an age/developmental span during which possibly the most influential and intense listening interactions with music take place?

CONCLUDING COMMENTARY

Comments about listening research characteristics made in the intermittent summaries will not be rehearsed here other than to note that they related primarily to matters such as

1. the primacy of pitch and melody in music listening research and the need for more comprehensive and contextual research that deals with other elements and the interactions of elements;

2. the continuing importance of tonality as a structural agent for listening, and the need for different strategies for listening to nontonal musics;
3. the importance of verbal imagery and the value of verbal skills in teaching and learning about music listening;
4. the age/grade levels that tend to be favored and slighted in music listening research; and
5. the inroads of technology.

In general, the quality of music listening research is high, though the quantity appears to have diminished in some areas, most notably in the development and evaluation of teaching methods and materials, and particularly at the secondary school level. In the late 1960s and early 1970s, the "golden days of junior high general music," listening skills received much emphasis. When this brief era waned, research on teaching for listening skills seemed to wane as well. There have been recent signs of a resurgence of interest in secondary school general music and related arts, at least in part as a result of state mandates for arts education, initiatives of the Getty Trust, and several seminal conferences, but there is as yet no notable effect on music education research activity and focus.

Past Conclusions Revisited

In comparing today's music listening skills acquisition research scene with that of Haack's pre-1980s review in the *Handbook of Music Psychology*, several of the earlier concluding comments appear to remain particularly pertinent:

1. Research findings often are not readily or obviously applicable to practice. High-level practitioners in music education and music therapy could lend great assistance to the profession by adopting more of a researcher's role in helping to extend and evaluate research findings on listening theories, methods, and materials in their classrooms and clinics.
2. Large-scale studies and longitudinal designs are still the exception while reliance on small or special group samples remains. Such circumstances limit generalizability and applicability, particularly in as broad and complex an area as music listening skills acquisition, and they limit understanding the metamorphosis of such skill acquisition and development. Again, a closer alliance of researchers and high-level practitioners could do much to improve this situation.
3. Cross-cultural research remains virtually untapped as a source of information on the development of various kinds of listening skills, for example, memory, imagery, and association. The fruits of anthropological approaches may be helpful not only for a better understanding of our own behaviors and values, but even more directly because our classrooms are increasingly populated by persons with strong cultural roots in other countries, or in various subcultures of our own country;

for example, how and why some recent immigrants from Southeast Asia may regard, listen to, and respond to various musics very differently from the majority population is crucial but largely unavailable information for teachers working with such children.

4. There remains a timely need for applied research into the three C's of cognitive style, creativity, and critical thinking vis-à-vis music-listening behaviors. In particular, little is known about the development of skills that foster truly imaginative, thoughtful, and feelingful listening.

5. Several sociofunctional concerns were cited as well in the earlier review. Because their importance, or awareness of it, has grown so enormously over the intervening decade, they will be discussed in more detail in the ensuing sections in terms of priority needs and expanding research horizons.

Additional Research Needs and Priorities

As a result of the foregoing sampling and review of the literature, it appears that additional aspects of music listening skills acquisition that need to be informed by research include the following.

The role, and particularly the educational enhancement, of music memory skills remain vital listening research topics. Cady's (1981) speculations from the Ann Arbor Symposium, while controversial in terms of brain function, remain relevant and provide excellent questions for research efforts.

Recent developments in discipline-based art education, including Broudy's aesthetic-scanning techniques for the development of responsiveness to the expressive qualities of the arts, appear to call for immediate attention for music education researchers.

The relationship of guided-imagery experiences to the acquisition of music-listening skills has surfaced as a pedagogical and a research question recently, possibly in part as a result of the use of guided-imagery techniques in some music therapy settings. The effects of such experiences in the music classroom, in contrast to more traditional methods employing program music, also may warrant study as we enter the "new age." In this respect as well as many others, the growing interactions between music education researchers and music therapy researchers (many of whom are also certified music educators) bodes well for the profession at large, particularly in light of their significantly overlapping interests, objectives, and clientele.

There seems to be reason to question and research further the notion that simply knowing more about elemental/formal music properties per se promotes acceptance and liking of music, and to continue to investigate the hypotheses that enhancement of feelingful interactions, development of functional awareness, and teacher enthusiasm may be more important factors in this respect. For example, were the hypothesis concerning teacher enthusiasm to be supported, particularly with younger subjects, broadening children's acceptance of a variety of styles and types including ethnic and

contemporary musics might be more effectively accomplished at an earlier and more open and impressionable age.

Expanding Music-Listening Research Horizons

In admittedly broad terms, it may be noted that much listening skills research has focused primarily on perception and cognition relating to formal/elemental properties of the *object,* the music. Some recent attention has been accorded the thoughtful, feelingful nature of the *subject,* the listener. And most recently, researchers have begun to explore some essential *interactions* between listener and music, for example, awareness of feelingful effects and their relationships to musical structures, reflecting the growing need to study seriously the entire, holistic context of music listening behavior. These emphases have not developed in isolation from expanding philosophical/aesthetic viewpoints, that is, objectivists focusing on the formal/expressive properties of the music, subjectivists focusing on the responses and values of the listener, and contextually/functionally oriented aestheticians concerned with matters of enlightened interaction between listeners and their music.

If feeling is influenced by form, and the quality of the interaction affects function and value, the need for broadened, holistic exploration becomes clear. And although the more subjective and complex feelingful and functional aspects of music listening may be more difficult to research, reality dictates that they be recognized as vital to our times and studied accordingly. New technological tools as well as information from fields such as communications studies, psychology, sociology, anthropology, physiology, and neurology will be increasingly helpful in this endeavor.

In an age where music increasingly permeates the environment, an age of drugs, youth depression, and teen suicide, problems at times closely linked to music, researchers cannot ignore the feelingful and functional, positive and negative, aspects of music listening. Student knowledge of the personal and social influences and functions of music may provide the base for skills in choosing and using music wisely, not only in terms of its aesthetic and nonverbal communication functions, but also in its functions as an enhancer of verbal communications, as an environment modifier, stress buffer, emotion and mood controller, physical activator, and so on.

There is a serious and growing need for music research to study and inform some of the prime contemporary social issues that center on music listening. As some citizens call for arts labeling and censorship, others are concerned with development of understandings and skills that allow for discrimination and judgment, abilities of an informed citizenry that neutralize the need for the kind of censorship that runs contrary to the principles of a free society. An effectively free, capitalist society demands a public equipped for socially conscious self-determination via an understanding of the influences and functions of music in society. Researching and developing curricular units and materials that enable teachers to prepare such listeners are activities essential to responsive schooling. Shehan's (1987) study dealing with ethnocentricity and prejudice is one excellent example of research that is abreast of and directed toward the societal needs of the times.

At a time when music education again seems less than secure in its curricular standing, it becomes even more important that we rationalize and publicize its values not narrowly, on the basis of aesthetic function alone, but on as broad a functional/useful needs base as research can legitimately support. Speaking to this point, a study currently in progress (Haack, in preparation) has revealed that over 90 percent of the persons surveyed more often linked the word "aesthetic" to terms like "nicety" and "frill" than to words like "vital" and "necessary." Yet members of the same community responded overwhelmingly (in an unscientific radio survey) in favor of record "labeling and categorization" as a means for parents to guide their children's listening. They believe, even if they do not understand clearly how or why, that music has the power to be used negatively as well as positively in their children's lives. Such concerns should not be dealt with on the basis of well-publicized, unscientific data. So the basic question becomes, How can young listeners be helped to become more aware of and knowledgeable about music's many functions and influences, and more free to choose and use it wisely to program their own world of sound, to meet their own humane needs? A research base in this broadened area of functionality may support a rationale that clarifies not only the nicety but the necessity of music education in the basic core of our educational curriculum.

Obviously, people are becoming more aware that music is being used not just for aesthetic and entertainment purposes, but increasingly to influence behavior for commercial and political gain. There are questions of personal freedom in Muzak-like environments where people may unwittingly experience "stimulus-progression" effects or other musical manipulations. There are concerns about music that disrupts personal privacy and the environment and causes children to suffer hearing loss. There are concerns about music associated with words and deeds of drugs, obscenity, sexism, and violence. Music education needs to come to terms with these aspects of music listening, needs to provide students the skills and knowledge to function in their contemporary sonic environment, and needs to have a research base to do so effectively. To ignore such issues seems as insensible and self-defeating as it would be for health educators and researchers to ignore current concerns about physical well-being, mental illness, and sexually transmitted diseases.

The fact that there is a significant body of youth music that is considered socially detrimental by a significant segment of society raises researchable questions such as, do youth generally develop the ability to enjoy their music while tuning out the message and effects of any antisocial lyrics? Or, does the naturally positive valence of the music attach to and make for acceptance of the message, regardless how repugnant? The great preponderance of television violence studies, and there now have been hundreds, indicates that the violence does influence viewer behaviors and attitudes, at least in the short term. Does MTV have similar effects? Does audio only music have similar effects?

To date most of the research touching on these areas has come from the medical, psychological, sociological, and communication communities, and has been reported without direct implications for curricular applications to music educators. A prime case in point is an analysis of 140 research reports and other sources titled "Popular Music in Early Adolescence." The report was prepared by Christenson and Roberts (1989) for the Carnegie Council on Adolescent Development. The insights it provides into young people's music behaviors and responses are fascinating and indicate again the need for listening skills relating to understanding and managing music's affects, effects, and functions in daily life. A recent article by Brown and Hendee (1989) in the *Journal of the American Medical Association* is based on a similar review of the youth music listening literature. The physician authors recommend that doctors be aware of the role of music in the lives of their young patients, and that they use musical behaviors and preferences as valid clues to the emotional and mental health of these youth. The authors stress the need for much additional research, begging the question by whom. Clearly the music education and music therapy professions have the expertise and the major responsibility in this respect.

In closing, it seems appropriate to recall that listening is the first communication skill humans develop, and it is the foundation of all other communication skills, including music. Just as we cannot learn to speak well without learning to listen well, we cannot fully enjoy or make music well without learning to listen well. Music is essentially an aural art and we cannot use or appreciate it effectively without well-developed listening skills—skills relating to perception, cognition, memory, understanding, discrimination, uses and functions, judgment, and valuing. The fact that music increasingly permeates and at times even seems to dominate our environment and our society, points with growing importance to not just the nicety, but the *necessity* of music listening education—and the concomitant need to expand the research base that supports this essential aspect of contemporary music education.

References

Allman, W. F. (1990). The musical brain. *U.S. News and World Report,* June 11, 56–62.

Abel-Struth, S. (1981). Frankfurt studies on musical audiation of five to seven year old children. *Bulletin of the Council for Research in Music Education.* 66–67, 1–7.

Baldridge, W. R. (1984). A systematic investigation of listening activities in the elementary general music classroom. *Journal of Research in Music Education, 32,* 79–94.

Barry, M. M. (1983). An analysis of classic and romantic style in painting and music as a possible approach to aesthetic awareness. Unpublished doctoral dissertation, Columbia University, New York.

Beckett, C., and Byrnes, S. (1990). Effects of aural interference on pitch labelling and memory tasks. Unpublished research paper, McGill University. (Presented at MENC, Washington)

Boisen, R. (1981). The effect of melodic context on students' aural perception of rhythm. *Journal of Research in Music Education, 29,* 165–172.

Boyle, J. D. (1987). An exploratory investigation of meter perception. *Bulletin of the Council for Research in Music Education, 91,* 10–14.

Brown, E., and Hendee, W. (1989). Adolescents and their music: Insights into the health of adolescents. *Journal of the American Medical Association, 262*(12), 1659–1663.

Bula, K. (1987). The participation of the verbal factor in perception of musical compositions. *Bulletin of the Council for Research in Music Education, 91,* 15–18.

Burnsed, V., and Fiocca, V. H. (1990). The relationship between school music instruction and the perceived complexity, pleasingness, and familiarity of selected concert literature. Unpublished research paper, Virginia Polytechnic Institute and State University. (Presented at MENC, Washington)

Cady, H. (1981). Children's processing and remembering of music: Some speculations. *Documentary report of the Ann Arbor Symposium: Applications of psychology to the teaching and learning of music* (pp. 81–87). Reston: Music Educators National Conference.

Christenson, P. G., and Roberts, D. F. (1989). *Popular music in early adolescence* (manuscript). Carnegie Council on Adolescent Development.

Crowther, R., Durkin, K., Shire, B., and Hargreaves, D. (1985). Influences on the development of children's conservation-type responses to music. *Bulletin of the Council for Research in Music Education, 85,* 26–37.

Cuddy, L. (1982). From tone to melody to music: Some directions for a theory of musical cognition. *Bulletin of the Council for Research in Music Education, 71,* 15–29.

Cutietta, R. (1984). The musical hypothesis-testing ability of the adolescent learner. *Bulletin of the Council for Research in Music Education, 80,* 27–50.

Darrow, A. A., Haack, P. A., and Kuribayashi, F. (1987). Descriptors and preferences for Eastern and Western music by Japanese and American nonmusic majors. *Journal of Research in Music Education, 35,* 237–248.

Darrow, A. A. (1989). Music and the hearing impaired: A review of the research with implications for music educators. *Update, 7,* 10–12.

Davies, J. B. (1981). Memory for melodies and tonal sequences: A brief note. *Bulletin of the Council for Research in Music Education, 66–67,* 9–14.

Dolgin, K. G., and Adelson, E. H. (1990). Changes in the ability to interpret affect in sung and instrumentally-presented melodies. *Psychology of Music, 18,* 87–98.

Duke, R. A. (1989). Musicians' perception of beat in monotonic stimuli. *Journal of Research in Music Education, 37,* 61–71.

Fiske, H. E. (1982). Chronometric analysis of selected pattern discrimination tasks in music listening. *Psychology of Music, 10,* 37–47.

Flowers, P. J. (1983). The effect of instruction in vocabulary and listening on nonmusicians' descriptions of changes in music. *Journal of Research in Music Education, 31,* 179–190.

Flowers, P. J., and Giomi, E. C. (1990). Verbal and nonverbal identification of pitch changes in a familiar song by English and Spanish speaking preschool children. Unpublished research paper, Ohio State University, Columbus. (Presented at MENC, Washington)

Geringer, J. M., and Madsen, C. K. (1984). Pitch and tempo discrimination in recorded orchestral music among musicians and nonmusicians. *Journal of Research in Music Education, 32,* 195–204.

Haack, P. A. (1970). A study involving the visual arts in the development of musical concepts. *Journal of Research in Music Education, 18,* 392–398.

Haack, P. A. (1980). The behavior of music listeners. In D. A. Hodges (Ed.), *Handbook of music psychology.* Dubuque: Kendall/Hunt.

Haack, P. A. (1982). A study of high school music participants' stylistic preferences and identification abilities in music and the visual arts. *Journal of Research in Music Education, 30,* 213–220.

Haack, P. A. (in preparation). A verbal matrix study of the word "aesthetic." University of Minnesota.

Haack, P. A., and Radocy, R. E. (1981). A case study of a chromesthetic. *Journal of Research in Music Education, 29,* 85–90.

Hair, H. I. (1982). Microcomputer tests of aural and visual directional patterns. *Psychology of Music, 10,* 26–31.

Hargreaves, D. J. (1986). *The developmental psychology of music.* Cambridge: Cambridge University Press.

Hedden, S. K. (1980). Development of music listening skills. *Bulletin of the Council for Research in Music Education, 64,* 12–22.

Hedden, S. K. (1981). Music listening skills and music listening preferences. *Bulletin of the Council for Research in Music Education, 65,* 16–26.

Hedden, S. K. (1988). Music listening in grades six through nine. *Update, 7,* 17–18.

Herberger, R. (1983). Presenting a method of analyzing mental and emotional processes in secondary school students while they are listening to music. *Bulletin of the Council for Research in Music Education, 75,* 41–48.

Hodges, D. A. (Ed.). (1980). *Handbook of music psychology.* Dubuque: Kendall/Hunt.

Hufstader, R. A. (1977). An investigation of learning sequence of music listening skills. *Journal of Research in Music Education, 25,* 184–196.

Krumhansl, C. L., and Jusczyk, P. W. (1990). Infants' perception of phrase structure in music. *Psychological Science, 1,* 70–73.

Kucenski, D. (1977). Implementation and empirical testing of a sequential musical sensory learning program on the infant learner. Unpublished doctoral dissertation, Northwestern University, Evanston.

Kuhn, T., and Booth, G. (1988). The effect of melodic activity, tempo change and audible beat on tempo perception of elementary school students. *Journal of Research in Music Education, 36,* 140–155.

Ladányi, H. (1990). Test of evaluative listening skills in regard to musical interpretations. Unpublished research paper. (Presented at MENC, Washington)

Lewis, B. E. (1986). The effect of movement-based instruction on the aural perception skills of first and third-graders. Unpublished doctoral dissertation, Indiana University, Bloomington.

Lewis, B. E. (1989a). The measurement of children's listening skill: An overview of the literature. *Contributions to Music Education, 16,* 50–66.

Lewis, B. E. (1989b). The research literature in movement-based instruction with children: Implications for music teaching and learning. *Update, 7,* 13–17.

Lewis, B. E., and Schmidt, C. P. (1990). Listener's response to music as a function of personality type. Unpublished research paper, University of North Dakota. (Presented at MENC, Washington)

Love, D. B. (1988). The relationship of tempo, pattern length, and grade level on the recognition of rhythm patterns. Unpublished doctoral dissertation, Virginia Polytechnic Institute & State University, Blacksburg.

Madsen, C. K., and Staum, M. (1983). Discrimination and interference in the recall of melodic stimuli. *Journal of Research in Music Education, 31,* 15–32.

Madsen, C. K., and Geringer, J. M. (1990). Differential patterns of music listening: Focus of attention of musicians versus nonmusicians. *Bulletin of the Council for Research in Music Education, 105,* 45–57.

Mark, M. (1978). *Contemporary music education.* New York: Schirmer Books.

Metz, E. (1989). Movement as a musical response among preschool children. *Journal of Research in Music Education, 37,* 48–60.

Mills, J. I. (1985). Some developmental aspects of aural perception. *Bulletin of the Council for Research in Music Education, 85,* 140–145.

Moore, B. R. (1989). *Music in education research summary.* Grand Rapids: Yamaha Corporation of America.

Moore, R. S., and Staum, M. (1987). Effect of age and nationality on auditory/visual sequential memory of English and American children. *Bulletin of the Council for Research in Music Education, 91,* 126–131.

Nierman, G. (1985). The role of vernacular in assessing students' perceptive/descriptive capabilities of music components. *Bulletin of the Council for Research in Music Education, 85,* 156–165.

O'Brien, W. (1990). The effects of figurative language in music listening instruction. Unpublished research paper, Montgomery. (Presented at MENC, Washington)

Olson, G. B. (1981). Perception of melodic contour through intrasensory matching and intersensory transfer by elementary students. *Journal of Educational Research, 74,* 358–362.

Olson, I. (1984). Measurement of musical awareness. *Bulletin of the Council for Research in Music Education, 77,* 31–42.

Oura, Y., and Hatano, G. (1988). Memory of melodies among subjects differing in age and experience in music. *Psychology of Music, 16,* 91–109.

Pembrook, R. G. (1987). The effect of vocalization on melodic memory conservation. *Journal of Research in Music Education, 35,* 155–169.

Petzold, R. G. (1963). The development of auditory perception of musical sounds by children in the first six grades. *Journal of Research in Music Education, 11,* 21–43.

Petzold, R. G. (1966). *Auditory perception of musical sounds by children in the first six grades.* Final Report, Cooperative Research Project Number 1051, U.S. Office of Education.

Petzold, R. G. (1969). Auditory perception by children. *Journal of Research in Music Education, 17,* 82–87.

Pflederer, M. (1964). The response of children to musical tasks embodying Piaget's principles of conservation. *Journal of Research in Music Education, 12,* 251–268.

Radocy, R. E. (1990). Toward measuring aesthetic sensitivity: Classifying students' initial verbal reactions to music. Unpublished research paper, University of Kansas, Lawrence. (Presented at MENC, Washington)

Radocy, R. E., and Boyle, J. D. (1988). *Psychological foundations of musical behavior.* Springfield: Charles C Thomas.

Ramsey, J. H. (1983). The effects of age, singing ability, and instrumental experience on preschool children's melodic perception. *Journal of Research in Music Education, 31,* 133–145.

Regelski, T. A. (1981). *Teaching general music: Action learning for middle and secondary schools.* New York: Schirmer Books.

Reimer, B. (1967). *Development and trial in a junior and senior high school of a two-year curriculum in general music.* Final Report to the U.S. Office of Education Bureau of Research.

Schellenberg, S. (1985). The effect of tonal-rhythmic context on short-term memory of rhythmic and melodic sequences. *Bulletin of the Council for Research in Music Education, 85,* 207–217.

Serafine, M. L. (1980). Piagetian research in music. *Bulletin of the Council for Research in Music Education, 62,* 1–21.

Shehan, P. K. (1986). Music instruction for the live performance. *Bulletin of the Council for Research in Music Education, 88,* 51–57.

Shehan, P. K. (1987). Stretching the potential of music: Can it help reduce prejudices? *Update, 5,* 17–20.

Sims, W. L. (1986). The effect of high versus low teacher affect and passive versus active student activity during music listening on pre-school children's attention, piece preference, time spent listening, and piece recognition. *Journal of Research in Music Education, 34,* 173–191.

Sink, P. E. (1983). Effects of rhythmic and melodic alterations on rhythmic perception. *Journal of Research in Music Education, 31,* 101–113.

Taggart, C. C. (1990). An investigation of the hierarchical nature of the stages of tonal audiation. Unpublished doctoral dissertation, Temple University, Philadelphia.

Tait, M., and Haack, P. (1984). *Principles and processes of music education.* New York: Teachers College Press.

Tunks, T. W., Bowers, D. R., and Eagle, C. T. (1990). The effect of stimulus tempo on memory for short melodies. Unpublished research paper, Southern Methodist University. (Presented at MENC, Washington)

Walker, R. (1981). The presence of internalized images of musical sounds and their relevance to music education. *Bulletin of the Council for Research in Music Education, 66-67,* 107–111.

Walker, R. (1983). Children's perceptions of horses and melodies. *Bulletin of the Council for Research in Music Education, 76,* 30–41.

Walker, R. (1985). Mental imagery and musical concepts: Some evidence from the congenitally blind. *Bulletin of the Council for Research in Music Education, 85,* 229–237.

Walker, R. (1987). Some differences between pitch perception and basic auditory discrimination in children of different cultural and musical backgrounds. *Bulletin of the Council for Research in Music Education, 91,* 166–170.

Webster, P. R., and Zimmerman, M. P. (1983). Conservation of rhythmic and tonal patterns of second through sixth grade children. *Bulletin of the Council for Research in Music Education, 73,* 28–49.

Williams, D. B. (1982). Auditory cognition. A study of the similarities in memory processing for music tones and spoken words. *Bulletin of the Council for Research in Music Education, 71,* 30–44.

Zalonowski, A. H. (1986). The effects of listening instructions and cognitive style on music appreciation. *Journal of Research in Music Education, 33,* 43–53.

·30·

THE ACQUISITION
OF MUSIC READING SKILLS

Donald A. Hodges
UNIVERSITY OF TEXAS AT SAN ANTONIO

Music reading is the process of converting special visual symbols—music notation—into sounds. These sounds may be conceived internally, or they may be produced externally through voices or musical instruments. This process may seem rather simple, but there are a number of more complex issues to be explored. It is the purpose of this section to review and synthesize the research on music reading. The work is organized into the following sections: basic research, applied research, and commentary.

BASIC RESEARCH ON MUSIC READING

One of the most common areas of basic research in music reading has been eye movement. The sensation most of us experience in reading is one of fluid eye movement scanning a line of printed music. However, the actual mechanics of reading involve a rapid series of stops (fixations) and starts as the eye focuses on pertinent information and then sweeps (saccade) to the next focal point. Information is brought into the visual system at a fixation, when the eye is not moving and is focusing on a circular area about one inch in diameter. Fixations can last from less than 100 milliseconds to 500 milliseconds, or half a second (Goolsby, 1989).

Several studies have been conducted on the saccadic, or eye movement, patterns during music reading. Evidence suggests that an individual's level of musical experience significantly influences eye movement. Experienced music readers read ahead of the point of performance in units or chunks. This "previewing" allows the eye to fixate on structurally important features, such as chords or melodic fragments, and to skip over less important details, that may be filled in.

It appears that saccadic movements alter to suit the music (Van Nuys and Weaver, 1943; Weaver, 1943). When one is

sight playing piano music of a homophonic nature, the saccadic movements tend to consist of a vertical sweep down from treble to bass, then over to the next chord for another vertical sweep downward, and so on. Contrapuntal music elicits a horizontal sweep along an upper line for a unit, followed by a return for a parallel horizontal sweep along a lower line. It has also been found that better keyboard readers economize on eye movements, keeping their eyes focused on the music, while poorer readers engage in many needless shifts from the music to the hands (Fuszek, 1990).

Researchers are beginning to learn more about the units of information that are perceived during fixations. Sloboda (1976b) found that musicians were superior to nonmusicians in the recognition of briefly exposed pitch notation patterns of more than three notes if the exposure was longer than 150 milliseconds. At exposure times of less than 100 milliseconds, musicians were no better than nonmusicians at identifying specific pitches, but they were superior at retaining the contour of notational patterns (Sloboda, 1978). For isolated pitches, musical experience would not necessarily be advantageous, since the task would be more related to visual-spatial acuity. However, for longer patterns, musical experience would provide an advantage, since individual notes can be grouped into meaningful patterns (e.g., an arpeggio or a scalelike passage). These results suggest that a time interval shorter than 150 milliseconds is too brief for the eye, musically experienced or not, to obtain information. However, Goolsby (1989), using sophisticated equipment that determined eye positions 1,000 times per second, discovered that skilled music readers use fixations of less than 100 milliseconds. (Perhaps the difference in results is due to the fact that Sloboda's subjects viewed patterns flashed on a screen, then transcribed what they saw to paper, while Goolsby's subjects were monitored during the act of vocalizing melodies.)

466

How long are the units of previewed information? Sloboda (1974, 1977) asked instrumentalists to read a single line of music. At some point in the process, the music was removed, and the musicians continued to play as long as possible from memory. Poorer readers could produce only another three or four correct notes, while better readers could produce up to seven additional notes. The actual number of notes was somewhat conditioned by how many notes were left in a phrase unit. (It is interesting to note that this number corresponds to the magic number 7± 2 that Miller (1956) established as the average memory buffer for bits of information.) When the same task was given to keyboard players (Sloboda, 1977), it was found that structural markings (important chords or melodic fragments) increased eye-hand span and tended to extend the memory unit to a phrase boundary.

There is an interesting phenomenon, similar to "proofreader's error" in language reading, that corroborates the evidence that experienced musicians read in units. When reading a book, one reads in context and thus may skip over simple typographical errors. The mind infers the meaning of the sentence by taking in the key words, and the eyes skip over less important details. Pianists were asked to sight-read a piece of music that contained carefully implanted notational errors (Sloboda, 1976a). All subjects "corrected" some of the mistakes; that is, they played notes that would normally have been written rather than the errors that were implanted. On a second performance of the piece, the number of proofreader's errors actually increased slightly as the subjects made even more "corrections"; this indicates that more familiarity with the music allowed for greater reliance on units rather than specific details. Also, notational errors were less likely to be detected in the middle of phrases, indicating that subjects made more inferences about middles of phrases than about beginnings or endings. These inferences were based on structural elements of the music.

Taking a different approach, a number of researchers have been interested in discovering what relationships might exist between music-reading skills and other related variables. Boyle (1970) obtained a correlation coefficient of .81 and Elliot (1982) a coefficient of .90 between total sight-reading scores and sight-reading rhythm patterns.

A number of researchers have obtained correlations for other related variables that are positive but too low to be of predictive value. These include music reading correlated with standardized tests (Cooley, 1961; Erlings, 1977), tests of tonal memory and error detection (Kanable, 1969), sight-reading skills and leadership status (Luce, 1965), socioeconomic and musical backgrounds (Daniels, 1986), and IQ and reading achievement (Hutton, 1953; King, 1954; Luce, 1965).

A summary of basic research on music reading indicates that eye movements are influenced by the nature of the music being read. Experienced music readers scan up to seven notes ahead of performance and are guided by structural elements in the music. They also tend to group notes in units that are viewed within the context of a musical style. Good keyboard readers exhibit an economy of eye shifts between the music and their hands. Studies of relationship between music reading and rhythm reading have provided the only correlation coefficients high enough to be of predictive value.

APPLIED RESEARCH ON MUSIC READING

Teaching Music Reading

A moderate body of literature may be grouped under the rubric of teaching music reading. Unfortunately, these studies are so scattered as to render overall conclusions exceedingly difficult. In 40 selected studies there are no replications and few that use similar strategies. Even where several studies can be grouped together, there is rarely enough consensus to lead to a broader conclusion.

Bebeau (1982), Colley (1987), Palmer (1976), and Shehan (1987) concluded that the use of syllables, or related mnemonic devices, is an effective pedagogical approach for teaching music-reading skills. However, there is a decided lack of continuity among the approaches used and in the results obtained. It is not clear, for example, whether one particular approach has a distinct advantage, or whether the use of nearly any kind of syllabic or mnemonic device is sufficient.

The results of three studies indicate that tonal pattern instruction is an effective technique for improving melodic sight-reading (Grutzmacher, 1987; MacKnight, 1975; Richardson, 1972).

Results were mixed in a group of studies that centered around the use of tape-recorded aural models. Anderson (1981) and Hodges (1975) found them to be ineffective, but Barnes (1964), Heim (1976), Kanable (1969), Owen (1973), and Puopolo (1971) found that taped examples led to improvement in music reading.

Christ (1966), DiFronzo (1969), and Hammer (1963) all found the tachistoscope to be an effective means of teaching music-reading skills, while Stokes (1965) did not. From the dates of these studies it would appear that the tachistoscope is no longer popular equipment. In a study using computers, Willett and Netusil (1989) found that a drill program was effective in improving note placement skills but not in note naming.

Several researchers tested the effects of different notational systems, with varying results. The notational changes made by Bukspan (1979), notation based on a binary system, and Kyme (1960), shape notes, led to improvement in music reading. Notational schemes used by Byo (1988) and Gregory (1972) had no observed effect on music-reading test scores.

The use of body movements in music reading was effective in two experiments with instrumentalists (Boyle, 1970; Skornicka, 1972) but not in another (Salzburg and Wang, 1989). Neither Autry (1975) nor Klemish (1970) found hand signs and/or body movements to be helpful in sight singing.

Class piano students who sang piano materials did not improve music-reading skills (Hargiss, 1962), but similar students did have better rhythmic accuracy when they practiced accompaniments with tape recordings of soloists (Watkins and Hughes, 1986). Emphasizing vertical aspects of the score did not help class piano students to become better music readers (Lowder, 1973).

Creative activities, such as composing, performing, and listening, led to improvements in music-reading scores (Bradley, 1974; Hutton, 1953). Experiencing music-reading activities prior to formal explanations produced higher music-reading scores (Hewson, 1966). Placing song texts higher and lower in conjunction with higher and lower melodic pitches was found to facilitate music reading (Franklin, 1977).

From this brief review of the basic research on music reading, it is apparent that the bulk of these studies are technique or strategy driven rather than based on any underlying theory of music reading. With the mixed results obtained and the lack of replications, it is difficult to draw any major conclusions about teaching music reading that are derived from research.

Error Detection in Score Reading

One of the areas that has received a certain amount of attention from researchers is the detection of errors in a musical performance while reading a score. Because younger musicians rarely have the opportunity to be involved in score reading, the subjects of these studies are primarily college students or music teachers. The research in error detection can be organized into two subcategories: the improvement of error detection skills and the relationship of error detection skills to other variables.

In view of the importance of score reading and error detection to ensemble conductors, a central question is, What techniques might be effective in improving error detection? Several researchers (Behmer, 1988; Costanza, 1971; Ramsey, 1979; Sidnell, 1971) demonstrated that programed instruction, using written musical scores and aural examples, was an effective technique for improving error detection skills. Deal (1985) found that a computerized version of Ramsey's programed instructional materials was equally as effective as the original, but not more so. DeCarbo (1982) found that programed instructional materials were equal to podium-based conducting experiences on a written error detection test, but not on an actual conducting test that included error detection. Forsythe and Woods (1983) found error detection scores were lower when the subjects were actually conducting than when they were only listening. These last two studies suggest that the use of programed instructional materials needs to be integrated into conducting experiences.

In terms of the correlational literature in error detection, several researchers started with the premise that various aspects of studies in music theory would be related to error detection. Ear-training grades and dictation and sight-singing scores were highly related to error detection scores; for example, Larson (1977) obtained a correlation coefficient of .80

between error detection and dictation on tonal examples, and Ottman (l965) obtained a coefficient of .73 between melodic sight singing and error detection. Also, students with 2 years of theory did better on an error detection test than students with only 1 year (Hansen, 1961), and "A" students did better than students with lower grades in music theory classes (Gonzo, 1971). Conversely, Brand and Burnsed (1981) found almost no relationship between error detection skills and music theory grades ($r = -.19$) or sight singing and ear training grades ($r = .07$).

Music performance and teaching experiences have provided additional variables for study. Keyboard study was related positively to the ability to hear vertical aspects (chords) of the score (Pagan, 1973), and pianists performed better than instrumentalists on a test of error detection (Hansen, 1961). However, a lack of relationship was found between error detection skills and number of instruments played, ensemble experience, and years of private instruction (Brand and Burnsed, 1981). Also, mixed results were obtained when teachers were compared with students (Gonzo, 1971). Essentially, there were no differences between choral teachers and undergraduate students in their ability to detect pitch errors while reading a choral score. However, choral directors with 6 to 10 years of experience did better than college seniors but not juniors. DeCarbo (1984) found that teachers with 11 years or more of teaching experience scored higher on an error detection test than did teachers who had less experience. He also found that a subject's principal instrument made no difference in error detection scores.

Briefly, then, it appears that error detection skills might be improved through the use of programed instructional materials. These results have prompted the publication of at least two commercially available sets of programed instructional materials, one choral (Grunow and Fargo, 1985) and one instrumental (Froseth and Grunow, 1979). However, such programs should be integrated into podium-based conducting experiences. Students who have good keyboard and music theory skills are more likely to perform better on error detection tests than other students, but the relationship between these skills and music reading is not yet clearly defined.

COMMENTARY ON MUSIC-READING RESEARCH

When one considers the research base in music reading, there is perhaps a natural tendency to make some comparisons with research in language reading. Aside from the fundamental differences in the two different reading skills, there are at least three other major differences. One difference is in the amount of research. According to Singer (1983), more than 12,000 studies in language reading were conducted between 1879 and 1972. There were perhaps fewer than 250 such studies on music reading. Of those studies done on music reading, few can be grouped together to provide a core of research leading toward a solid grasp of a particular issue.

The second major difference concerns the role of theory in reading research. The first major theory in language reading was proposed in 1953, and a significant amount of research has been conducted to test this theory along with the others that have since been proposed (Gentile, Kanil, and Blanchard, 1983). In music there is no theory devoted specifically to an explication of music reading; thus, the bulk of the research appears to be devoid of a theoretical underpinning. Music Learning Theory, proposed by Gordon (1984), includes music reading, but does not represent a comprehensive theory of music reading per se. Explicit theories of music reading, theories that would organize knowledge and research about music reading into a system of assumptions, principles, and procedures, do not exist. Such theories would be useful in predicting and explaining the phenomenon of music reading. Implicit theories, theories that one might construct on the basis of observations of what teachers do, abound. Unfortunately, these are of lesser value in providing the solid ground that is necessary to guide research.

The third major difference has to do with the fact that as a profession, music educators have never decided whether music reading is necessary or not. Certainly in traditional music performance experiences, music reading is deemed integral and necessary. But in general music, the issue of "rote versus note" is more than a historical curiosity since there is still disagreement over whether all children should engage in music-reading activities as a basic part of music education.

It is within this context that research on music reading must be viewed: There is much less research than is desirable, much of it is not guided by an overarching theory, and the music education profession has not made a clear statement regarding the role of music reading in general music. On the latter point, it would seem to be important for the profession to have a formal definition of music literacy that would include a clear position statement on the value of music reading in general music education.

Future research efforts might be guided toward two complementary goals: (1) basic research geared toward understanding the process of music reading, and (2) applied research designed to determine the most effective means of training proficient music readers. An important step toward reaching these goals would be a comprehensive theory of music reading.

Several previously unrelated factors that emerge from the diffuse data base might be considered as a basis for the construction of a music-reading theory. One important factor might well be the basic research that indicates that good music readers read ahead in meaningful units and that structural units (e.g., phrases) are important signposts. This could be bolstered by the applied research in tonal pattern instruction. However, since rhythmic sight reading is a strong predictor variable, the focus should be broadened to include rhythm pattern instruction. Gordon's taxonomy of tonal and rhythm patterns might be important in this regard (Gordon, 1976).

Researchers should take advantage of the latest in technological developments. Sophisticated equipment, such as the Stanford Research Institute Dual Purkinje-Image Eyetracker used by Goolsby (1989), can provide enormous research potential. Other improvements might include the presentation of music notation on a computer screen, measurement of responses by Musical Instrument Digital Interface (MIDI) equipment, and the conversion of programs to run on more accessible personal computers. Keeping abreast of developments in language reading research is particularly important for persons interested in doing basic research in music reading.

Similarly, technological advances can be utilized by applied researchers. Early research using the tachistoscope could easily be replicated and extended on modern computers. Since this research yielded primarily positive results and it appears to support the previously identified direction of tonal and rhythm patterns, it is a line of experimentation that should be pursued. One can imagine, for example, a beginning band student sitting at a computer and controlling the presentation of briefly presented tonal and rhythm patterns (perhaps by means of a foot pedal). The student would play the pattern—one of a series of carefully graded exercises—receive immediate feedback on the performance, and hear a correct performance in response. Such a program could be adapted to group format by means of large-screen projection.

Research on music reading has provided some insights into what is a very complicated process. However, there is much to be learned. With creative theory construction and a focusing of research efforts on several key issues, exciting progress could be made. Critically important to the success of these efforts, at least in terms of sustaining an emphasis over a period of time, will be a strong philosophical stance on the part of the music education profession about the value of music reading in general music.

References

Anderson, J. N. (1981). Effects of tape-recorded aural models on sight-reading and performance skills. *Journal of Research in Music Education, 29,* 23–30.

Autry, M. R. (1975). A study of the effects of hand signs in the development of sight singing skills. Unpublished doctoral dissertation, University of Texas, Austin.

Barnes, R. A. (1964). Programed instruction in music fundamentals for future elementary teachers. *Journal of Research in Music Education, 12,* 187–198.

Bebeau, M. J. (1982). Effects of traditional and simplified methods of rhythm-reading instruction. *Journal of Research in Music Education. 30,* 107–119.

Behmer, C. F. (1988). The effect of a learning program on the ability of undergraduate music students to detect errors in performance.

(Rev. by R. C. Sang). *Bulletin of the Council for Research in Music Education, 97,* 81–84.

Boyle, J. D. (1970). The effect of prescribed rhythmical movements on the ability to read music at sight. *Journal of Research in Music Education, 18,* 307–318.

Bradley, I. L. (1974). Developments of aural and visual perception through creative processes. *Journal of Research in Music Education, 22,* 234–240.

Brand, M., and Burnsed, V. (1981). Music abilities and experiences as predictors of error-detection skill. *Journal of Research in Music Education, 29,* 91–96.

Bukspan, Y. (1979). Introduction of musical literacy to children by means of a binary system of music notation: An experimental study. *Bulletin of the Council for Research in Music Education, 59,* 13–17.

Byo, J. (1988). The effects of barlines in music notation on rhythm reading performance. *Contributions to Music Education, 15,* 7–14.

Christ, W. B. (1966). The reading of rhythmic notation approached experimentally according to techniques and principles of word reading (Rev. by John W. Shepard). *Bulletin of the Council for Research in Music Education, 7,* 78–82.

Colley, B. (1987). A comparison of syllabic methods for improving rhythm literacy. *Journal of Research in Music Education, 35,* 221–235.

Cooley, J. C. (1961). A study of the relation between certain mental and personality traits and ratings of musical abilities. *Journal of Research in Music Education, 9,* 108–117.

Costanza, A. P. (1971). Programed instruction in score reading skills. *Journal of Research in Music Education, 19,* 453–459.

Cutietta, R. (1979). The effects of including systemized sight-singing drill in the middle school choral rehearsal. *Contributions to Music Education, 7,* 12–20.

Daniels, R. D. (1986). Relationships among selected factors and the sight-reading ability of high school mixed choirs. *Journal of Research in Music Education, 34,* 279–289.

Deal, J. J. (1985). Computer-assisted instruction in pitch and rhythm error detection. *Journal of Research in Music Education, 33,* 159–167.

DeCarbo, N. J. (1982). The effects of conducting experience and programmed materials on error-detection scores of college conducting students. *Journal of Research in Music Education, 30,* 187–200.

DeCarbo, N. J. (1984). The effect of years of teaching experience and major performance instrument on error detection scores of instrumental music teachers. *Contributions to Music Education, 11,* 28–32.

DiFronzo, R. F. (1969). A comparison of tachistoscopic and conventional methods in teaching grade three music sight-playing on a melody wind instrument (Rev. by Warren F. Prince). *Bulletin of the Council for Research in Music Education, 16,* 50–54.

Elliot, C. A. (1982). The relationships among instrumental sight-reading ability and seven selected predictor variables. *Journal of Research in Music Education, 30,* 5–14.

Erlings, B. (1977). A pilot investigation of relationships between elementary keyboard sight-reading achievement by music majors in college and selected musical profile tests. *Bulletin of the Council for Research in Music Education, 50,* 14–17.

Forsythe, J. L. and Woods, J. R. (1983). The effects of conducting on the error detection ability of undergraduate and graduate instrumental conductors. *Contributions to Music Education, 10,* 27–31.

Franklin, E. (1977). An experimental study of text notation. *Bulletin of the Council for Research in Music Education, 50,* 18–20.

Froseth, J. O., and Grunow, R. F. (1979). *MLR instrumental score reading program.* Chicago: G.I.A. Publications.

Fuszek, R. M. (1990). Sight-reading sight-playing at the keyboard. Unpublished paper, California State University, Fullerton.

Gentile, L. M., Kanil, M. L., and Blanchard, J. S. (Eds.). (1983). *Reading research revisited.* Columbus: Charles E. Merrill.

Gonzo, C. L. (1971). An analysis of factors related to choral teachers' ability to detect pitch errors while reading the score. *Journal of Research in Music Education, 19,* 259–271.

Goolsby, T. (1989). Computer applications to eye movement research in music reading. *Psychomusicology, 8,* 111–126.

Gordon, E. E. (1976). *Tonal and rhythm patterns: An objective analysis.* Albany: State University of New York Press.

Gordon E. E. (1984). *Learning sequences in music: Skill, content, and patterns.* Chicago: G.I.A. Publications.

Gregory, T. B. (1972). The effects of rhythmic notation variables on sight-reading errors. *Journal of Research in Music Education, 20,* 462–468.

Grunow, R. F., and Fargo, M. H. (1985). *The choral score reading program.* Chicago: G.I.A. Publications.

Grutzmacher, P. A. (1987). The effects of tonal pattern training on the aural perception, reading recognition, and melodic sight-reading achievement of first-year instrumental music students. *Journal of Research in Music Education, 35,* 171–181.

Hammer, H. (1963). An experimental study of the use of the tachistoscope in the teaching of melodic sight singing. *Journal of Research in Music Education, 11,* 44–54.

Hansen, L. A. (1961). A study of score reading ability of musicians. *Journal of Research in Music Education, 9,* 147–156.

Hargiss, G. (1962). The acquisition of sight singing ability in piano classes for students preparing to be elementary teachers. *Journal of Research in Music Education, 10,* 69–75.

Heim, A. J. (1976). An experimental study comparing self-instruction with classroom teaching of elementary rhythm reading in music. *Bulletin of the Council of Research in Music Education, 46,* 52–56.

Hewson, A. T. (1966). Music reading in the classroom. *Journal of Research in Music Education, 14,* 289–302.

Hodges, D. A. (1975). The effects of recorded aural models on the performance achievement of students in beginning band classes. *Journal of Band Research, 12,* 30–34.

Hutton, D. (1953). A comparative study of two methods of teaching sight singing in the fourth grade. *Journal of Research in Music Education, 1,* 119–126.

Kanable, B. (1969). An experimental study comparing programed instruction with classroom teaching of sightsinging. *Journal of Research in Music Education, 17,* 217–226.

King, H. A. (1954). A study of the relationship of music reading and I.Q. scores. *Journal of Research in Music Education, 2,* 35–37.

Klemish, J. J. (1970). A comparative study of two methods of teaching music reading to first-grade children. *Journal of Research in Music Education, 18,* 355–364.

Kyme, G. H. (1960). An experiment in teaching children to read music with shape notes. *Journal of Research in Music Education, 8,* 3–8.

Larson, R. C. (1977). Relationship between melodic error detection, melodic dictation, and melodic sightsinging. *Journal of Research in Music Education, 25,* 264–271.

Lowder, J. E. (1973). Evaluation of a sight-reading test administered to freshmen piano classes. *Journal of Research in Music Education, 21,* 68–73.

Luce, J. R. (1965). Sight-reading and ear-playing abilities as related to instrumental music students. *Journal of Research in Music Education, 13,* 101–109.

MacKnight, C. B. (1975). Music reading ability of beginning wind instrumentalists after melodic instruction. *Journal of Research in Music Education, 23,* 23–34.

Miller, G. A. (1956). The magic number seven, plus or minus two. Some limits on our capacity for processing information. *Psychological Review, 53,* 81–97.

Ottman, R. (1965). A statistical investigation of the influence of selected factors on the skills of sight singing (Rev. by Merrell L. Sherburn). *Bulletin of the Council for Research in Music Education, 5,* 42–48.

Owen, N. L. (1973). Teaching music fundamentals to the seventh grade via programed materials. *Journal of Research in Music Education, 21,* 55–60.

Pagan, K. A. (1973). An experiment in the measurement of certain aspects of score reading ability (Rev. by Carroll Gonzo). *Bulletin of the Council for Research in Music Education, 31,* 29–35.

Palmer, M. (1976). Relative effectiveness of two approaches to rhythm reading for fourth-grade students. *Journal of Research in Music Education, 24,* 110–118.

Puopolo, V. (1971). The development and experimental application of self-instructional practice materials for beginning instrumentalists. *Journal of Research in Music Education, 19,* 342–349.

Ramsey, D. S. (1979). Programmed instruction using band literature to teach pitch and rhythm error detection to music education students. *Journal of Research in Music Education, 27,* 149–162.

Richardson, H. V. (1972). An experimental study utilizing two procedures for teaching music reading to children in second grade (Rev. by Janice J. Klemish). *Bulletin of the Council for Research in Music Education, 30,* 47–50.

Salzburg, R. S., and Wang, C. C. (1989). A comparison of prompts to aid rhythmic sight-reading of string students. *Psychology of Music, 17,* 123–131.

Shehan, P. K. (1987). Effects of rote versus note presentations on rhythm learning and retention. *Journal of Research in Music Education, 35,* 117–126.

Sidnell, R. G. (1971). Self-instructional drill materials for student conductors. *Journal of Research in Music Education, 19,* 85–91.

Singer, H. (1983). A critique of Jack Holmes's study: The substrate-factor theory of reading and its history and conceptual relationship to interaction theory. In L. M. Gentile, M. L. Kanil, J. S. Blanchard (Eds.), *Reading research revisited.* Columbus: Charles E. Merrill.

Skornicka, J. E. (1972). The function of time and rhythm in instrumental music reading (Rev. by Alan H. Drake). *Bulletin of the Council for Research in Music Education, 27,* 44–46.

Sloboda, J. A. (1974). The eye-hand span: An approach to the study of sight-reading. *Psychology of Music, 2,* 4–10.

Sloboda, J. A. (1976a). The effect of item position on the likelihood of identification by inference in prose reading and music reading. *Canadian Journal of Psychology, 30,* 228–237.

Sloboda, J. A. (1976b). Visual perception of musical notation: Registering pitch symbols in memory. *Quarterly Journal of Experimental Psychology, 28,* 1–16.

Sloboda, J. A. (1977). Phrase units as determinants of visual processing in music reading. *British Journal of Psychology, 68,* 117–124.

Sloboda, J. A. (1978). Perception of contour in music reading. *Perception, 7,* 323–331.

Sloboda, J. A. (1985). *The musical mind: The cognitive psychology of music.* Oxford: Clarendon Press.

Stokes, C. F. (1965). An experimental study of tachistoscope training in reading music (Rev. by William F. Wakeland). *Bulletin of the Council for Research in Music Education, 5,* 60–64.

Van Nuys, K., and Weaver, H. E. (1943). Memory span and visual pauses in reading rhythms and melodies. *Psychological Monographs, 55,* 33–50.

Watkins, A., and Hughes, M. A. (1986). The effect of an accompanying situation on the improvement of students' sight-reading skills. *Psychology of Music, 14,* 97–110.

Weaver, H. E. (1943). A study of visual processes in reading differently constructed musical selections. *Psychological Monographs, 55,* 1–30.

Willett, B. E., and Netusil, A. J. (1989). Music computer drill and learning styles at the fourth-grade level. *Journal of Research in Music Education, 37,* 219–229.

THE ROLE OF MENTAL PRESETS
IN SKILL ACQUISITION

Roger R. Rideout
UNIVERSITY OF OKLAHOMA

Mental presets are models of (musical) knowledge, skill, and values formed from one's prior experience and learning. These presets are deeply imbedded in memory and can be invoked, as needed, to provide models of exemplary musical behaviors that focus attention and guide musical learning. Research in mental presets has centered on defining preset components and how presets affect attention, practice, and performance. Authors have deduced strategies for minimizing the external and internal interference that adversely affects musical performance, devised techniques for improving concentration, and proffered schemas for understanding how attention functions. Music educators, in turn, have applied this research in various settings in order to examine how presets make music skill learning more efficient and effective.

In an effort to summarize this research, this section contains an overview of two opposing theories that suggest how presets focus attention, followed by a discussion of mental imagery research applied to music learning, and suggestions about developing and using presets.

MENTAL PRESETS AND ATTENTION

William James (1890) defined attention as "the taking possession by the mind, in clear and vivid form, of one out of what seem several simultaneously possible objects or trains of thought. Focalization, concentration of consciousness are of its essence. It implies withdrawal from some things in order to deal effectively with others'' (pp. 403–404). James saw attention as exclusory, functioning as a means of denying certain objects or events access to consciousness.

A century after James formulated his definition, the pro-

cess of attention still eludes psychologists, although many theories have been suggested. Nideffer (1976) argues that attention is relative, falling, at any moment, at points along two continua. The first ranges from broad to narrow and sets the field in which attention operates. The second determines the degree to which individuals select the information they need for a given task by attending internally to thoughts or feelings or externally to things going on around them. Attention's intersect point on these continua establishes the criteria for selecting stimuli from sensory cues. Attention scans all of the possible sources received through the senses at any one time via the limitations of the first continuum and selects a given object or event according to the criteria of the second continuum. Musicianly attention, for example, may fall anywhere along these continua, depending on the task. A conductor may need a broad external focus in order to monitor progress of the ensemble players, while the concertizing pianist might need a narrow internal focus to control the keyboard demands during performance. Because practice and performance problems can change at any moment, one's position along the continua changes in response, altering both the fields and the sources of attention.

While attention focuses on the requirements of the moment, the procedures controlling the selection of a given object are constructed from one's prior experience and learning, which exist in memory as mental presets. These presets establish the criteria for analyzing the task at hand by consciously and unconsciously providing models for action. Such presets contain aural, visual, and kinesthetic models of good musical behavior that have been developed over years of study, instruction, listening, and performing. In any task, they serve as preexisting guides for focusing attention and improving concentration.

How presets focus attention has been the subject of much

experimentation. During the 1950s and 1960s, physiologists and psychologists devised many theories of mental operations based on empirical investigations into response time, muscle movement, and auditory and visual perception. One outgrowth of their work was the single-channel theory of mental operations, which posits that the brain processes only one event at a time. The speed at which this is done is in milliseconds, and the event may be very simple, such as a muscle jerk in response to a loud sound, or very complex, such as visually perceiving music notation while performing. Welford (1967) suggests that when the brain perceives an event or stimulus, it is sent along a single channel to another processing center, which then determines the movements necessary to operate on it and forwards the proper commands to the appropriate muscle groups. Although other events may be perceived at time intervals that seem simultaneous, in reality the brain selects only one event for passage, reserving other stimuli until that portion of the brain transmitting the event is free to select another.

How the brain selects a specific stimulus from a myriad of concurrent options was studied by Kalsbeek and Sykes (1967), who concluded that one function of attention is to control the entrance to this single channel by recognizing, selecting, and admitting familiar and appropriate stimuli. A stimulus that attention deems familiar may contain much more information than one deemed unfamiliar. For example, a portion of a difficult contrapuntal keyboard passage might be admitted into processing in toto because all of the information needed to perform the passage is known from practice. The many discrete muscle movements required by this complex stimulus can be lumped together for processing by the second center because the entire excerpt is seen by attention as a familiar stimulus.

Channel theories, such as that espoused by Kalsbeek and Sykes, often contain a view of attention in which some portion of mental operations is believed to control actions. A "second self" exists within the brain that governs other mental activity. This view has been criticized in recent years by authors who insist attention is an emergent phenomenon made up of layers of consciousness rather than a linear single-channel or single-event processing procedure. Searle (1984) believes the channel theory claim for a governing function to be a fallacious dualism based on outmoded research. As such it must be replaced by a more biologically accurate view of consciousness and attention in which such mental operations are unitary. This alternate view is represented, in part, by Reubart's (1985) adaptation of Arthur Koestler's serialistic and hierarchical model. Koestler (1975) suggests attention increases from automatic response instilled at near autonomic levels to a set of governing perceptions that filter out unessential or conflicting information. Muscle movements, note reading, technical aspects of performance, style, and so on are stored at lower levels of consciousness over years of practice and study. When a specific task arises, upper level processors are invoked that read the present mental models—and relevant environmental cues—in order to select the right mental and physical responses. In this view, attention is but one aspect of an overall mental consciousness capable of filtering through sensory stimuli and selecting relevant events. Preexisting models, or mental mindsets, serve as referees for this selection and instruct appropriate muscle groups to operate.

An advantage of this theory can be shown by the familiar example of practicing and performing while thinking of something else. Everyone has driven to work only to arrive and not remember a single event of the trip, or has had attention drawn away from a musical passage only to return and find measures were played correctly during the lapse. Such experiences seem to demand that attention has a layering or sorting function capable of locating and acting on vital information relevant to a task, and yet interact with other stimuli unrelated to the task. Consider the keyboard example above. A single-channel theory based on single-event processing procedures is inadequate to explain how the multiple muscle movements required in keyboard playing can be processed sequentially while attention is drawn away to an unrelated task. The many distinct aural, visual, and kinesthetic responses needed to execute the movements would seem to require a theory that explains how consciousness is capable of attending to many competing sensory cues while processing the appropriate muscle commands from stored memory.

Whether one subscribes to the single-channel theory or other theories about mental processing, the implication remains that mental presets, as functions of memory and consciousness, provide multifaceted, integrated contexts that allow the brain to process large amounts of information. Regardless of which theory may eventually be shown to explain attention best, mental presets appear to provide a shepherding function by setting up composite models that concentrate mental-processing procedures on specific information in the preset itself, thereby shutting out all competing sources of attention and generating the appropriate responses to musical problems.

MENTAL PRESETS AND MUSIC IMAGING

These arguments suggest that all people, musicians especially, can improve learning by concentrating attention on a preset that the brain can process and translate into appropriate behavior. Although these presets are composites of an individual's musical learning and experience, one component of their construction seems to be vivid, dynamic aural and kinesthetic models of proper behaviors that are invoked, as needed, to govern the selection of objects for attention. As an example, Dale Clevenger, solo horn for the Chicago Symphony, is quoted as insisting, "I never practice. I always perform," meaning he plays every musical passage in light of preexisting aural/kinesthetic models of the perfect performance, models that are stored in memory (Trusheim, 1987). Clevenger's attention is focused on these models as he interprets every note of an exercise. These mental presets contain the musical information necessary to perform stylistically and the technical information needed to realize a musical passage through physical action. Yet the preset is so ingrained that information about specific muscle actions is not identified or attended to consciously, but subsumed within the model. The brain dissects the composite model into the appropriate muscle responses as needed by the specific task.

Seashore (1938) calls this phenomenon "imaging" in music. "Imagery is analogous to the development of thinking [and] consists largely in forming the habit of noting relationships which become fixed in memory so that when a situation is anticipated or recalled, the image presents it in accurate and vivid detail" (pp. 170–171). Although Seashore centers his discussion on auditory imaging as an indication of musical ability, he recognizes the necessity for and the existence of mental presets containing other kinesthetic and musical information necessary to complete any musical task.

In refining Seashore's ideas, Gordon (1987) has coined the verb "to audiate" to define the dynamic act of mentally hearing sounds either stored in memory or heard only recently in performance. He insists the term accurately indicates musicianly mental activity because it delimits a purely aural sensation, free of any pictoral reference. Although the concept is an integral part of Gordon's definition of musical aptitude and ability and skill at noting pitch relations, he recognizes the interaction of prior learning and active mental recall as a vital component of musical performance.

Throughout this century music education studies of mental imagery have confirmed its importance as part of the preset models that guide practice and performance. Agnew (1922) studied the letters and autobiographies of noted composers to determine if and how they used mental imagery. Similar efforts by Khatena (1984), Chapman (1985), and Bradle (1983) illustrate that composers and conductors as varied as Tchaikovsky, Brahms, Wagner, Copland, Cowell, and Bernstein attest to the importance of auditory imagery in their musical creativity. Betts (1909) examined the use of auditory imagery by undergraduate theory students. In a series of experiments, he assessed the use of imagery, the occurrence of imagery in music reading, and the presence of imagery in music listening. In all three instances a majority of his 19 students used imagery to aid their learning and increase their musical enjoyment. In an extension of this work, Bergan (1965) measured musical imagery and pitch discrimination skills. He concluded there are statistically significant differences between genders in discrimination skills and the capacity to form images. In a later study, Bergan (1967) administered a questionnaire with selected items relating to musical imagery and correlated the items to pitch judgment measures. He found strong positive correlations between imagery and pitch judgment. Serafine (1981) interviewed students aged 2 to 5 to measure the imagery they used to identify certain musical timbres. Basing her work on theories by Jean Piaget and Barbel Inhelder, she concluded that the results supported Piaget's claim that developmental stages account for some of the child's ability to form and use auditory images.

Research indicates that while images may vary in kind and strength depending on the need a person has for them, they are important for developing affective reactions to music and as an accompaniment to learning music skills. Also, these dis-

tinct aural, visual, and kinesthetic images are present in the thinking of musicians *prior to the act of performing or practicing* and are, themselves, the objects of attention.

Additional research has centered on mental rehearsal techniques and the influence of mental presets on improving physical performance. A host of research studies in physiology, psychology, and physical education indicate significant improvement can occur in the development of skills through mental practice, the act of mentally rehearsing or practicing model behaviors without accompanying physical movement (Richardson, 1969). Andre and Means (1986) compared the effects of slow-motion imagery and mental practice in reducing mistakes in execution. Beasley and Heikkinen (1983) applied physical and mental practice techniques to the development of laboratory psychomotor skills of first-year college chemistry students. Prather (1973) used mental practice to review flight training skills. Yamamoto and Inomata (1982) examined its use in the development of backstroke swimming skills. Wichman and Lizotte (1983) measured improvement in dart throwing. All found increased refinement of motor skills through the use of mental practice prior to and in conjunction with physical practice.

In music education specifically, Rubin-Rabson (1941) worked with nine piano students on music memorization, interspersing two methods of mental practice between physical trials and analytical prestudy. She concluded that there were limitations on the ability of mental practice to increase performance skills, but that such work "allows further analysis and reorganization of points of confusion and presents a 're-seeing' of the small musical figures against the general background" (p. 601). Her work, in turn, was based on an earlier experiment by Kovacs (1916) in which students were required to concentrate on a musical score with their eyes closed and to hear the notes mentally until the material was memorized. When compared to memorizing by repetition, the results favored the mental image procedure.

Ross (1985) randomly assigned 30 university student trombonists to five different practice conditions and individually measured their success at performing an etude. After a pretest in which everyone sight-read the etude, the first five students practiced the music by playing it three times with 30-second rest periods between each attempt. The second five were instructed to mentally practice the etude without any accompanying physical movement. The third group combined both techniques by physically practicing the second of the three trials. The fourth group was allowed to move the slide while mentally practicing three times. The last group did not practice, but merely read a short article on sight-reading techniques. As a posttest, the students were measured on their skill at performing the etude a fifth time. The students who combined mental and physical practice techniques improved most on the posttest.

In a variation of Ross's approach, Coffman (1987) alternated three types of mental and physical practice in an effort to improve piano performance skills of 80 undergraduate music majors who were not piano majors. Those students who alternated mental practice with physical practice improved significantly over those students in the control group, but were not significantly better than those who utilized only physical practice. Since the subjects were not pianists, one would expect their unformed or sketchy mental presets to contribute minimally to improving pianistic skill. Yet Coffman's study implies that, even at this early stage of development, the addition of mental practice may aid skill development.

Trusheim (1987) interviewed 27 professional brass players to determine their use of imagery in practice and performance. Twenty-five of them

reported that they could easily form an aural image of their sound, or an ideal sound in their mind. The majority of these players have also managed to incorporate the manipulation of the image into important aspects of their approach to performance. In so doing, these players have given recognition to the mental side of performance and identified it—by their actual performance practices—as the guiding function behind musical artistry. (p. 330)

Trusheim concluded, "All musicians could easily spend some of their practice time using mental rehearsal to refine their mental concept and to solve technical or mechanical difficulties in their playing. Research has shown mental rehearsal to be an effective and efficient supplement to actual practice in many areas involving skilled physical activity" (p. 345).

After a series of experiments on visual discrimination, Finke (1986) gives some insight into how such discrimination works. He concludes that mental imaging may "enhance the perception of an object by causing selective priming of appropriate neural mechanisms in the visual system. In other words, forming a mental image of an object might initiate certain neural events that are equivalent to those occurring at the moment the object is seen, thereby facilitating the perceptual process" (p. 92). Similarly, an aural or kinesthetic mental image may serve to review and reinforce a sequence of muscle movements by setting up the initial mental commands in a manner similar to actual performance. In support, Schmidt (1982) writes, "A common belief about this activity is that performers are actually running off a motor program with the 'gain' turned down, obtaining additional practice that will help when time to perform overtly comes along" (p. 520). Kohut (1985) affirms this in claiming that "mental practice involves training the unconscious brain to efficiently process and organize information (goals specified by the conscious brain) and transform it into specific nerve signals to the muscles. In this context, mental practice is directed toward development of neuromuscular coordination" (p. 127).

DEVELOPING MENTAL PRESETS

Music educators are challenged to develop means for formulating proper mental presets and instructing students in their use. Yet, few authors have suggested techniques for doing this. Although psychological theory and research confirm the importance of mental presets and mental practice in

controlling attention, improving concentration, and increasing performance, few guidelines are available by which the learner can "practice" developing and using presets in skill learning. One possible approach has been suggested by Timothy Gallwey (1974), who identified discrete levels of negative psychological conditioning that tennis players must supervene in order to achieve their fullest potential. These levels were defined in an effort to clarify aspects of mental activity that a student needed to remove or overcome in developing proper performance behavior. These steps are familiar to musicians because they apply directly to the practice and performance behaviors of music students.

Step 1: Criticize or Judge Past Behavior
The student relies on past behavior to judge and critically assess the present task, which serves to divide the student's concentration between performing and criticizing, thus increasing the potential for error. As more errors occur, criticism increases, concentration is divided further, and a negative cycle of action and criticism is set in motion.
Step 2: Tell Yourself to Change, Instructing with Word Commands Repeatedly
Upon realizing the proper action (either missed or anticipated), the student then instructs the performing self to make the correct action, thereby creating a third "observer" who constantly monitors action. This observer further divides concentration by coming between the mental sequence of thought and action.
Step 3: Try Hard, Make Yourself Do It Right
Self-doubt and frustration destroy concentration, tighten muscles, and control the performer's actions, thereby preventing the ease and fluidity necessary to complete the task.
Step 4: Critical Judgment about Results Leading to Repetition of Process
"When one has tried hard to perform an action 'right,' it is difficult not to become either frustrated at a failure or excited by success. Both these emotions are distracting to one's concentration and prevent full experiencing of what happens. Negative judgment of the results of one's efforts tends to make one *try* even harder; positive evaluation tends to make one *try* to force oneself into the same pattern on the next shot. Both positive and negative thinking inhibit spontaneity" (p. 82).

Achieving a proper learning style that eliminates these habits then becomes one practical goal of music instruction. Barry Green (1986) adapted Gallwey's ideas specifically for musicians and suggests four steps to improving attention through focusing on existing mental presets.

Awareness

In this first step, the student removes the judgmental self from the act of learning and focuses instead on the object to be learned. Green suggests four modes of awareness. First, is *being present by paying attention to sight,* which means attending to the present moment by focusing on the notes on the score, hand position, the musical instrument, etc. The second, *being present by paying attention to sound,* requires that one use listening in the same manner as viewing to assure complete attention to the required aural elements. These two steps help the learner "to silence the critical voice inside, . . . draw . . . attention more fully into the music and . . . relax" (p. 40). *Being present by paying attention to feelings* is defined as attending to one's own emotional reactions while playing the music. *Being present by paying attention to what you know* asks the student to use all prior knowledge of the music (style, articulation, composer's intent) to shade the performance with appreciation and understanding.

Will

Will is the ability to define the object to be learned and to focus all desire toward it, including ordering one's daily actions and decisions to serve this clearly defined goal. Will controls one's commitment to achieve the desired visual, aural, and kinesthetic skills, and to acquire the mental knowledge necessary to learn a particular passage of music or to perform it in a certain style. Will is the one aspect of the critical self that is allowed to remain because it infuses the performing self with desire and commitment but does not interfere with the efforts to focus concentration.

Trust

After will and awareness have provided the necessary skills and experiences, trust allows the student to believe the desired musical ends can be achieved. The doubts and fears accompanying learning and performing cause one to question whether the task can be accomplished, revealing a basic insecurity or mistrust of one's capabilities. Conscious reflection on the level of skill and experience appropriate to the task is necessary to build trust. For example, a trumpet player facing a rapid chromatic passage must trust the performing self to know and to execute the necessary fingerings and articulations. The student must be convinced to trust the performing self by the long hours of practice and years of experience preceding this performance.

Letting Go

This fourth aspect is, in the practical sense, something all musicians understand, that is, giving oneself over completely to the act of listening, performing, or composing, etc., being fully immersed in the act, ignoring the self as actor. This advanced stage is possible only after the other three stages are ingrained in the student/performer.

Underlying these learning procedures is the familiar assumption that the mind is divided, with one part critically analyzing and evaluating all action in light of previous behavior

and a second part trying to act intuitively, spontaneously, and in near-autonomic control of the mental presets of stored musical knowledge and skill that memory can make available to it at any moment. The second self constantly struggles with the first to free its actions from inhibitions and criticism. Although this view may not meet the standards of some models of mental activity, clearly successful learning/performance requires conscious development of attentive behavior.

Gallwey, Green, and others insist such efforts must be undertaken obliquely, by focusing attention not on the effort or the act of learning/performing, but on the mental preset that sets the standards for the action at hand. Normally for musicians this is the preexisting mental image of the music notation, the musical line, the feel of the instrument, or any entity that can guide direct expression in behavior *at that moment.* Full attention is demanded by the immediate task, and identity with the moment must be so complete that no other stimulus can interfere and confound the action. In controlling attention in this way, the object of attention, the mental preset, aids in eliminating conflicting external and internal sources that might come between the mental image of the music and the physical act of performing.

In commenting on the difference between expert and inexpert performers, Sloboda (1985) illumines this process:

Inexpert performance is typically controlled by superficial characteristics of the musical 'foreground'. . . . The inexpert performer cannot exercise higher-level control because his resources are fully committed to managing the solution of these immediate local problems . . . What allows expert performers to make feedback adjustments so effectively is that they are not dependent on consciously monitored feedback at all times and levels. . . . Thus a performer can choose how and when to monitor his performance knowing which aspects can be safely left to learned programming procedures. (p. 101)

While research and common experience affirm the importance of mental presets in controlling attention, a student learner still needs guidelines for constructing them. In his review of mental practice research, the psychologist Singer (1968) suggests three guides for formulating and implementing correct presets.

1. Mental practice is effective only to the degree that the student is familiar with the physical requirements of the task. Mental practice can be effective only if the mental preset contains all of the behaviors necessary to achieve the desired end. Without the experience and prior training that allow a thorough understanding of the skills needed to perform a particular passage, mental practice will contain gaps that will impede the desired progress.
2. Alternating physical practice with mental practice appears to be as good or better than physical practice alone. Alternating practice styles appears to add a critical dimension of reflective self-evaluation that improves model behaviors more quickly than with physical trials alone.

3. Mental practice allows students to concentrate on a task in their own time and at their own rate. For many this is superior to more structured practice. Taking the time to mentally rehearse a passage seems to help the student think through the problems of performance more methodically, thereby aiding concentration and attention. Doing this in the relative ease and comfort of practice reinforces the preset model behaviors, contributing to more rapid and efficient learning.

In summary, mental practice appears to be a valid technique for improving performance skills. This claim is based on research that examines the role of mental presets in providing aural, visual, and kinesthetic imagery of model musical behaviors. When a student has the experience and training to understand the subtle and complex behaviors attendant on a particular task, mental practice allows the systematic reexamination of those behaviors and reinforces their later presence in actual performance.

MENTAL PRESETS, MUSICAL IMPROVISATION, AND MUSICAL ANXIETY

Determining precisely how mental presets improve skill development and musical performance is hampered by lack of access to a subject's mental processes during the act of performing, composing, or listening. Measurements are limited to after-the-fact examinations. Yet observing and analyzing musical improvisation and musical anxiety can illustrate indirectly how preexisting models might serve as guides for immediate solutions to performance problems. For example, while improvising, the player's attention is centered on creating the best musical realization allowed by the constraints of form, harmonic style, tempo, meter, and so on. Preexisting models, learned through years of listening and practice, guide selection. Also, the performer attends to the musical idea being generated by the preset information stored in musical memory, not the fingerings or vocal techniques needed to realize the idea, thus illustrating the extent to which motor skill learning is subsumed within aural imaging.

In reviewing improvisational methods and models, Pressing (1988) illuminates the value of presets in his observation that

by the time advanced or expert stages have been reached, the performer has become highly attuned to subtle perceptual information and has available a vast array of finely timed and tuneable motor programmes. This results in the qualities of efficiency, fluency, flexibility, and expressiveness. All motor organization functions can be handled automatically (without conscious attention) and the performer attends almost exclusively to a higher level of emergent expressive control parameters. (p. 139)

Reducing the anxiety associated with musical performance is another area in which presets seem to serve attention. Borrowing from the earlier Gallwey/Green discussion,

anxiety can be defined as the process and product of a critical and evaluative self disassembling focused concentration by manifesting itself in physiological and psychological conditions that preclude confident, controlled performance. Anxiety is expressed by nervousness, self-doubt, fear, tense muscles, and inability to concentrate, and a host of other physiological and psychological conditions. Efforts to minimize or contain anxiety have centered either on altering specific physiological aspects of playing such as posture and breathing, or on redirecting attention through training, meditation, and so on. Alexander (Barlow, 1973), Havas (1973), and others have developed techniques for correcting a performer's physical problems, while Ristad (1982) has suggested ways of attending to issues other than the specific manifested anxiety. As Reubart's (1985) examination of these techniques reveals, they serve the end of directing attention and controlling it so intensely that distractions and sensory cues that might interfere with performance are ignored or handled at a sufficiently minimal level of consciousness that normal performance operations are not disturbed. Such observations imply that presets can assist in screening and blocking environmentally, physiologically, and psychologically induced distractions.

Research studies in musical anxiety have centered on solving specific instrument- or voice-related problems (Faulkner, 1980; Leglar, 1978; Waite, 1977). Whereas such studies generally skirt the specific topic of presets, they describe the kinds and levels of musical knowledge and skill necessary to develop confidence and free attention for musical issues. Their discussions clearly embrace the realization that attending to potential musical errors, breathing, embouchure, or technique dooms the performer because attention is drawn away from the musical idea that mental presets serve. Without defining presets as such, these studies support the contention that presets are the mental tools for channeling attention away from manifestations of anxiety and for assuring the musical goal or model remains foremost in consciousness.

OBSERVATIONS

Most of the music research cited in this short summary was undertaken outside of a larger theory of mental operations that might provide the contextual framework for understanding behavior. Serafine's effort to examine the responses of young children in the light of Piaget's developmental stages is one of the few examples of research in preset development that proceeds from an existing theoretical framework. Her research was based on a model of how children learn; it served the dual purposes of testing the model and examining the pedagogical problem as well.

After studying the research, one remains uncertain about the mental processes involved in developing and employing mental presets and how these processes work. Here, the tentative and popular answers by Gallwey and Green, or the scholarly theories of Searle and Koestler, lack the research studies in music learning to confirm or refute them. This is because the adjuvable relationships that exist between mind and body, mental activity and muscle response, are still too complex and ill defined for a clear synergetic model of mental activity in music skill acquisition to be set forth. Music educators must still rely on the conclusions of individual and isolated studies to indicate a pedagogical direction, and await the underlying principles or theories of mental actions that provide the solid foundation for method and practice.

Finally, most music educators spend their time trying to develop the initial skills that form presets. They teach posture, breath support, articulation, musical style, and the many other cognitive, affective, and psychomotor skills that

are the grist of specific presets. Young children and adolescents, by the fact of their age, lack the experience and passage of time necessary for these different knowledges to settle into memory, combine in their various possibilities, and be integrated into the model presets described above. In order for research in mental activity and the development of presets to be meaningful, studies will have to account for the differences and limitations that are imposed by the maturation of the learner. Although such problems may only confound efforts to devise a comprehensive model, the improvement of musical learning and the efficient and effective acquisition of musical skills will occur only when a model arises that can be practically applied to teaching students of all ages.

References

Agnew, M. (1922). A comparison of the auditory images of musicians, psychologists, and children. *Psychological Monographs, 31,* 268–278.

Andre, J. C., and Means, J. R. (1986). Rate of imagery in mental practice: An experimental investigation. *Journal of Sport Psychology, 8,* 124–128.

Barlow, W. (1973). *The Alexander technique.* New York: Warner Books.

Beasley, W. F., and Heikkinen, H. W. (1983). Mental practice as a technique to improve laboratory skill development. *Journal of Chemical Education, 60*(6), 488–489.

Betts, G. H. (1909). *The distribution and functions of mental imagery.* New York: Teachers College, Columbia University.

Bergan, J. R. (1965). Pitch perception, imagery, and regression in the service of the ego. *Journal of Research in Music Education, 13*(1), 15–32.

Bergan, J. R. (1967). The relationships among pitch identification, imagery for musical sounds, and musical memory. *Journal of Research in Music Education, 15*(2), 99–109.

Bradle, S. (1983). Itzhak Perlman. *The Instrumentalist, 37*(6), 14–18.

Chapman, R. (1985). Vincent Cichowicz, The man behind the trumpet. *The Instrumentalist, 40*(1), 35–42.

Clynes, M. (1977). *Sentics: The touch of emotions.* Garden City: Doubleday.

Coffman, D. D. (1987). The effects of mental practice, physical practice, and aural knowledge of results on improving piano performance. Unpublished doctoral dissertation, University of Kansas, Lawrence.

Faulkner, M. (1980). The science of creative intelligence—transcendental meditation: A correlative study with the art of violin playing. Unpublished doctoral dissertation, University of Cincinnati, Cincinnati.

Finke, R. A. (1986). Mental imagery and the visual system. *Scientific American, 254*(3), 88–95.

Gallwey, W. T. (1974). *The inner game of tennis.* New York: Random House.

Gordon, E. E. (1987). *The nature, description, measurement, and evaluation of music aptitudes.* Chicago: G.I.A. Publishers.

Green, B. (1986). *The inner game of music.* Garden City: Anchor Press.

Haider, M. (1967). Vigilance, attention, expectation and cortical evoked potentials. In A. F. Sanders (Ed.), *Attention and performance* (pp. 246–352). Amsterdam: North-Holland Publishing Co.

Havas, K. (1973). *Stage fright: Its causes and cures with special reference to violin playing.* London: Bosworth Publishers.

James, W. (1980). *Principles of psychology.* New York: Henry Holt.

Kalsbeek, J. W. H., and Sykes, R. N. (1967). Objective measurement of mental load. In A. F. Sanders (Ed.), *Attention and performance* (pp. 253–261). Amsterdam: North-Holland Publishing Co.

Khatena, J. (1984). *Imagery and creative imagination.* Buffalo: Bearly Limited.

Koestler, A. (1975). *The ghost in the machine.* London: Pan Books.

Kohut, D. (1985) *Musical performance: Learning theory and pedagogy.* Englewood Cliffs: Prentice Hall.

Kovacs, S. (1916). Untersuchungen uber das musikalische gedachtnis. *Zeitschrift fur angewandte Psychologie und charakterkunde, 11,* 113–135.

Leglar, M. A. (1978). Measurement of indicators of anxiety levels under varying conditions of musical performance. Unpublished doctoral dissertation, Indiana University, Bloomington.

Nideffer, R. M. (1976). *The inner athlete: Mind plus muscle for winning.* New York: Crowell.

Prather, D. C. (1973). Prompted mental practice as a flight simulator. *Journal of Applied Psychology, 57*(3), 353–355.

Pressing, J. (1988). Improvisation: Methods and models. In J. A. Sloboda (Ed.), *Generative processes of music: The psychology of performance, improvisation and composition* (pp. 129–178). Oxford: Clarendon Press.

Reubart, D. (1985). *Anxiety and musical performance: On playing the piano from memory.* New York: Da Capo Press.

Richardson, A. (1969). *Mental imagery.* New York: Springer.

Ristad, E. (1982). *A soprano on her head.* Moab: Real People Press.

Ross, S. L. (1985). The effectiveness of mental practice in improving the performance of college trombonists. Unpublished doctoral dissertation, Northwestern University, Evanston.

Rubin-Rabson, G. (1941). Studies in the psychology of memorizing piano music. VI: A comparison of two forms of mental rehearsal and keyboard overlearning. *Journal of Educational Psychology, 32*(8), 593–602.

Schmidt, R. A. (1982). *Motor control and learning: A behavioral emphasis.* Champaign: Human Kinetics Publishers.

Searle, J. R. (1984). *Mind, brains, and science.* Cambridge: Harvard University Press.

Seashore, C. E. (1938). *Psychology of music.* New York: McGraw-Hill.

Serafine, M. L. (1981). Musical timbre imagery in young children. *The Journal of Genetic Psychology, 139,* 97–108.

Singer, R. M. (1968). *Motor learning and human performance.* New York: Macmillan.

Sloboda, J. A. (1985). *The musical mind—the cognitive psychology of music.* Oxford: Clarendon Press.

Trusheim, W. H. (1987). Mental imagery and music performance: An inquiry into imagery use by eminent orchestral brass players in the United States. Unpublished doctoral dissertation, State University of New Jersey, Rutgers.

Waite, J. R. (1977). Reducing music performance anxiety: A review of the literature and a self-help manual. Unpublished doctoral dissertation, University of Oregon, Eugene.

Welford, A. T. (1967) Single-channel operation in the brain. In A. F. Sanders, (Ed.), *Attention and performance* (pp. 5–22). Amsterdam: North-Holland Publishing Co.

Weinberg, R. S. (1981). The relationship between mental preparation strategies and motor performance: A review and critique. *Quest, 33*(2), 195–213.

Wichman, H., and Lizotte, P. (1983). Effects of mental practice and locus of control on performance of dart throwing. *Perceptual and Motor Skills, 56,* 807–812.

Yamamoto, K., and Inomata, K. (1982). Effect of mental rehearsal with part and whole demonstration models of acquisition of backstroke swimming skills. *Perceptual and Motor Skills, 54,* 1067–1070.

·32·

TECHNOLOGY

William Higgins
MESSIAH COLLEGE

The term "technology" is derived from two Greek words: *techne,* meaning "art," and *logos,* meaning "discourse"— "the art of discourse." The derivation of the word and the essence of its application in teaching and learning have to do with *communication.* Technology has become a vital part of education because it increases our ability to communicate with the learner, and thus our effectiveness as teachers. This chapter reviews the research literature on the use of technology in music instruction beginning with programed instruction, audio recording, and the introduction of teaching machines. Studies in the use of television, computers, scientific equipment, and current technologies are described. As a direction for future research, a paradigm is delineated.

It is accurate to state from the outset that research in the use of technology in music instruction has been limited. However, development of technologies to adapt them to music instruction has been extensive, both in the academic community and in the music industry. Among the possible reasons for the lack of research is the fact that rapid changes in technologies have not allowed the limited number of researchers in the profession to gain a solid foothold. Also of importance is the fact that academic developers are interested in the cutting edge of technology and elect to continue developing newer technologies instead of investigating the effects of the "in place" technologies. Bales (1986) states that in order to use technology in music research the investigator must be proficient in musical acoustics, electrical engineering, computer science, mathematics, and teaching.

This discussion is limited to technology used in research that is directly related to music teaching and learning. Several technological developments are presented that are not research based but that are important to understanding the background of the technology, the directions that have been taken within the music education community, and the research potential that exists. Research involving music composition and analysis, music performance, and musicology is not included. Comprehensive references to research in these areas as well as several of those addressed in this discussion may be found in the bibliographies of Boody (1975), Davis (1988), and Kostka (1974). Hewlett and Selfridge-Field (1989) provide an annual directory of musicology research. Descriptions of computer and video software developed for instructional purposes have been omitted but may be found in Bartle (1987), Boody (1990), Gilkes (1986), Hofstetter (1988), Rudolph (1984), and Waters (1989). Alphonce (1988) provides a view of computer applications to research in music theory. Directions for designing, developing, and programing computer-based instruction (CBI) in music can be found in Dowling (1989), Hofstetter (1985), Williams and Bowers (1986), and Wittlich, Schaffer, and Babb (1986).

PROGRAMED INSTRUCTION

Credit for the initial use of programed and mediated instruction in formal education is best attributed to B. F. Skinner. Not only did Skinner bring into the classroom the results of experimental research on learning principles but he introduced the concept that well-planned and sequenced instruction by teachers can be supported by technological mediation (Skinner, 1968). The principles of Skinnerian theory (Skinner, 1954) form the basis for much of the mediated instruction today regardless of the learning theory on which it is based.

In 1965 the Music Educators National Conference (MENC) held a conference on the uses of educational media in the teaching of music that included discussions on (1) film and television, (2) audio devices, (3) teaching machines, (4) programed instruction, (5) electronic devices, and (6) printed materials. Recommendations were given for the improvement and expansion of the uses of the media for more effective teaching of music (Maltzman, 1965). Rogers and Almond (1970) published an extensive bibliography of studies and articles on programed instruction up to 1967 containing reports of studies in music theory, psychology of music, and instrumental methods, many of which utilize technology. Carlsen and Williams (1978) compiled an annotated bibliography of music research on programed instruction covering the two decades from 1952 to 1972. The work contains a taxonomy of 17 topics and subtopics that categorize the research. Sections on equipment requirements and presentation format identify 34 studies that utilize technology including the tape recorder, videotape, slide or overhead projector, and phonograph. Nine of these studies used some form of teaching machine for displaying or recording data.

Teaching Machines

To achieve a combined aural and visual presentation, several researchers utilized various "auto-tutor" devices in conjunction with audiotape. Woelflin (1961) studied the transfer of clarinet fingerings, names of instrument parts, and ranges using a teaching machine connected to a slide projector containing 150 slides that were available for random access and pictorial branching. Maltzman (1964) tested the effects of reinforcement on the aural/visual discrimination of tone matching. Mears (1965) investigated the effects of aural, visual, and descriptive presentations along with reinforcement on the learning of rhythms. Rasmussen (1966) integrated slides, audiotape, and a teaching machine to teach ear training and recognition and identification of specific musical events to improve listening skills. Sanders (1966) utilized programed instructional techniques to teach recognition and identification of musical styles in orchestra music. Jeffries (1967) looked at the effects of the order of presentation and type of reinforcement in melodic dictation. Ihrke (1971) modified a teaching machine by connecting it to an electronic organ and stereo tape recorder to make a rhythm-trainer that required the student to play along with music that was matched to an inaudible track of the tape providing immediate feedback concerning whether a note was played early, in time, or late. The device was effective in developing rhythmic steadiness and a favorable attitude to the task. Greenburg and Huddelston (1971) used a Videosonic teaching machine, 35 mm slides, and synchronized tape to teach aural discrimination of tone colors in instrumental music to elementary children. Although this form of programed instruction was found to be effective, the high cost of equipment and difficulty in locating suitable materials were seen as problems for future solution.

Audio Recording

A logical extension of printed programed instruction in music was instruction through the use of audio recording. Williams and Hoskin (1974) developed an audio laboratory system for generating recorded audiotapes for research in psychomusicology that controlled the basic vibrational properties of recorded tones. Bodenstein (1975) explored the teaching of selected musical concepts in a college music

survey course utilizing a taped guided-listening technique. Salvi (1981), investigating conceptual/nonconceptual and verbal/nonverbal combinations of instructional strategies using programed instruction with workbooks and cassette tapes to teach musical style recognition in Gregorian chant, found that the conceptual/verbal model was best for self-instructional materials in musical style recognition. Bridges (1982) designed programed instructional materials to teach the concepts of musical form to undergraduate elementary education majors. A 13-lesson instructional audiotape lesson was presented to two experimental groups individually and in a whole-class setting. Control groups were instructed individually or in class settings by a teacher. With the use of immediate and delayed posttests, the teacher-presented whole-class format was more effective in developing discrimination skills.

Several studies focused on melodic dictation. Carlsen (1962) explored branching and linear presentation of recorded melodic dictation examples. Spohn (1962) investigated the use of the language laboratory for ear training as compared with traditional presentation. Spohn (1963), Tarratus and Spohn (1967), and Unsworth (1970) continued the research on the effects of audiotaped instruction in melodic dictation. Spohn and Poland (1964) combined melodic and rhythmic dictation as an extension of the earlier work. Simpson (1970) and Puopolo (1971) applied audio programed instruction to instrumental music. Simpson used exercises in ear training to teach tone production and sight-reading, while Puopolo used a self-instructional tape to improve recognition of musical styles and performance techniques for beginning instrumentalists. Wilson (1970) used a programed tape to present music fundamentals, while Sidnell (1971) prepared self-instructional tapes in score reading to improve undergraduate conducting techniques in detection and identification of pitch and rhythm errors in instrumental performance. Through the use of the tapes and workbook, students improved in these skills. Fiorillo (1973) explored the efficacy of channel-alternated tape recordings with related visual materials in the development of aural discrimination.

Slides, Filmstrips, and Motion Pictures

Collins and Diamond (1967), using 8 mm silent film loops, taught music majors to identify clarinet fingering, embouchure, and hand position errors. The film loops worked best for nonclarinet majors and were equally effective for experienced and nonexperienced instrumentalists. Zalampas (1973) produced a 35 mm slide and cassette tape modified autotutorial presentation of music fundamentals and skills for prospective elementary classroom teachers. Dvorak (1973) utilized sound filmstrips in the instruction of instrument repair. Hlynka (1980) provided a critical review of the behavioral research on film music. He discussed the dichotomy between background music for entertainment and for educational purposes and the nonverbal communication function of film music, concluding that affective learning is influenced by music while cognitive learning is not. March (1980) prepared an animated film to aid students in perceiving the differences in musical texture. The film demonstrated monophonic, polyphonic, homophonic, and mixed textures by synchronizing a visual presentation of the text of the music with the actual sound. Results indicated that students who viewed the film achieved higher posttest scores than students who only listened and followed "call charts." Sebald (1981) conducted a formative evaluation of automated slide/cassette/workbook instructional packages to teach music education majors oboe reed making, single-reed factual knowledge, and information about single-reed mouthpieces. Data indicated that this was a successful technique in teaching content and fostered a positive attitude toward learning supplemental woodwind information.

TELEVISION

The history of the use of televised music instruction is a macrocosm of the use of a technology in instruction. Educational television had a slow beginning in the years following 1948 characterized by great interest but held back by high costs. This was followed by a period of rapid growth, with high hopes, great developmental activity, and modest research. Finally, there was a sharp decline in general educational use as the availability of the technology and associated instructional materials failed to meet the promises of the 1950s and 1960s.

Television was the first technology that came with the promise of being a panacea, propelling it into the developmental stage so rapidly that research to discover how to use it and what the effects would be was never conducted. Carpenter (1973) reports that during the first decade "televised music instruction differed little from face-to-face instruction in either learning sequence or content and that the second decade did not see much change in that program format or approach. Many telelessons appeared to the viewer as if a television camera simply had been transported to the back of a classroom" (pp. 38, 50, 83).

During the period from 1950 to 1960, financial and administrative support from foundations, government, and regional cooperatives was available for development and dissemination of materials. Much was written about the use of television in music instruction, and many local, regional, and national programs and series were produced, but little research was conducted. Individual telelessons and series were informally evaluated usually for production purposes since the primary impetus was to extend the traditional classroom to more students to offer (1) more uniform teaching, (2) enrichment, and (3) supplemental instruction.

Music and Television

The potential of television in music education is delineated by Carpenter (1966). Berg (1962) developed a series of telecasts sponsored by the Regents Educational Television Project. Allen (1966) summarized the state of instructional television in music education at that time. Davis (1968) investigated the National Educational Television (NET) status to see if it was fulfilling its artistic potential while Dasher (1968) was concerned with the music programing of NET. Henney (1968) evaluated the *Bell Telephone Hour* series and its impact. Carpenter (1969) described the use of instructional television in music education in general, while Glenn (1972) examined the potential use of television for early childhood music education. Giles (1981) prepared a 30-program telecourse for adult beginners in applied piano with an accompanying textbook and student guide. Testing of the sequence was conducted via closed circuit in a piano lab and broadcast on public television. Motivated adult students were able to complete the first semester of piano study at least as successfully with televised instruction as with more conventional instruction in class or private study.

Video Recording

At the outset of the development of video recording, Skapski (1969) prepared synchronized videotapes of musical scores as instructional aids to the identification of specific musical concepts. Repeated melodic and rhythmic figures, canon, and free imitation were experienced in this setting with graphs and notation displayed with the music. No specific conclusions were drawn. In a later study, Skapski (1971) compared programed instruction by audiotape and videotape. Miller (1973) used videotape simulation to teach embouchure formation problems to instrumental music education majors. Gonzo and Forsythe (1976) prepared videotapes as teaching aids for music education classes to teach rehearsal techniques and principles at the junior high, senior high, and college levels. Three approaches were utilized: (1) introduction, viewing, and discussion, (b) view independently, and (c) view and test. All treatments were found to reinforce subject matter and to maintain interest in the topic. Williams (1978) used a videotape in the solution of selected problems in oboe playing. Albin (1979) constructed videotaped instructional units for percussion instruction. Robbins (1979) developed and evaluated a series of videotape lessons to supplement a college course in advanced music theory. Stuart (1979) combined videotape, recordings, and slides with textural materials and class discussion to increase teacher trainees' error detection skills in orchestral rehearsal techniques. The aural-visual training was found to be somewhat more effective than traditional classroom approaches. Jordan (1980) evaluated the effectiveness of videotape instruction as a supplement to classroom instruction in the conducting of fermatas and cues. Students had printed materials or printed materials and videotape instruction for a 5-week treatment period. Those with visual reinforcement performed better than those without. Practice alone was considered by the students to be the least effective of the approaches between in-class instruction and videotape. Saker (1982) found that videotape training of simulated band rehearsal behavior management problems produced in student teachers a perceived ability to handle the situation, but that in actual practice they were not observed to be better than those without the training. Dibble (1983) prepared four 5-to-8 minute videotaped segments to teach pitch discrimination (same/different) through the use of Bandura's imitation and modeling strategies using puppets. With the use of *Primary Measures of Music Audiation* (PMMA), preschool children were assigned to two groups: those with good and those with poor tonal skills. The treatment produced gains in all subjects. Correlation of musical home environment and achievement was also significant. Berg (1984) presented a historical synopsis of music video. Furman (1984) studied the effects of four feedback conditions on the development of competency to lead group singing using the guitar. It was found that a checklist alone was as effective as a videotape alone, videotape and checklist, or teacher feedback. Michelson (1984) developed a series of videotaped models of conducting behaviors and techniques that generate and sustain maximum mental and physical effort by singers in a rehearsal. University choral students were given instruction in identifying these behaviors and techniques in a rehearsal. Two modes of instruction were used: lecture only and videotape of the models. Posttraining evaluations by subjects revealed that the videotape-trained students were better at identifying the conducting behaviors than the lecture-trained group, particularly in the more subtle and difficult-to-identify behaviors. Miller (1973) examined embouchure instruction by videotape in a pilot study using simulation as a technique to determine the ability of instrumental music majors to analyze woodwind embouchure problems.

COMPUTERS IN MUSIC EDUCATION

The use of computers in music education parallels the introduction of the use of computers in general education, with music educators playing an active role in computer-based instruction since the late 1950s. Two works chronicle the early uses of computers in music instruction and should not be overlooked by the researcher: a complete bibliography of computer uses in music up to 1974 (Kostka, 1974) and a survey of noncompositional computer uses in music up to 1972 (Boody, 1975). Throughout this discussion, computer-based instruction (CBI) will be synonymous with computer-assisted instruction (CAI), computer-mediated instruction (CMI), and computer-aided music instruction (CAMI).

By the late 1960s, research in music CBI was being conducted on the IBM 1500 system at Stanford University (Allvin, 1967; Kuhn and Allvin, 1967) and Pennsylvania State University (Deihl and Radocy, 1969a). At the same time, the University of Illinois was developing the Programed Logic for Automatic Teaching Operations (PLATO) system on a Control Data computer.

Britton (1968), reporting on the Tanglewood Symposium, *inaccurately* assessed the involvement of music research at that time by stating, "The explosion of knowledge, which applies much more to the exact sciences than to the social

sciences and humanities, may account in part for our comparative lack of involvement in the swiftly moving tides of technological change and development" (p. 123).

Deihl and Partchey (1973), Killiam (1981), Kuhn and Allvin (1967), Lincoln (1969), Lincoln (1974), and Spohn (1969) all provided essays on the early use of computers in music research. Allvin (1971), Deihl and Radocy (1969a), Ihrke (1972), Knuth (1971), and Peters and Eddins (1978) delineated the early prognosis of the use of computers in music education, and Hullfish (1969) described the possibilities of computer use in music theory. However, as early as 1970, Allvin was questioning the validity of using computer learning laboratories.

National Consortium for Computer-Based Instruction

In 1975, Hofstetter and others formed the National Consortium for Computer-Based Music Instruction (NCCBMI) as an affiliate of the Association for the Development of Computer-Based Instructional Systems (ADCIS). This organization is now known as the Association for Technology in Music Instruction (ATMI), which better illustrates the broad concerns of technology in music teaching and learning. ATMI annually publishes one of the most complete lists of technology for music instruction (Boody, 1990).

Microcomputer Development

Throughout the early 1970s, research was centered around universities with mainframe computers, even though the third generation of computers (microcomputers) was becoming increasingly available. By 1975 the development of the microprocessor had reduced the price and size of computers by 80 to 90 percent; and by 1977 the Commodore Pet, Radio Shack TRS-80, and Apple II microcomputers were available. The language developments, especially in BASIC, made programing accessible. Peters (1979) discussed the transfer of courseware from mainframe computers (PLATO) to microcomputers and the hardware and software problems associated with this transition. Williams and Shrader (1980) described the microcomputer-based music education laboratory implemented at the Illinois State University that was started in 1976 utilizing the Kim-1 microcomputer connected to an Arp 2600 synthesizer. In 1977 Chamberlin (1980, 1985) of Micro Technology Unlimited designed a digital to analog converter board (DAC) that used software-based sound generation utilizing Fourier computation of waveform tables. By 1979 Williams and Shrader (1980) developed Apple II software and a music card based on the Chamberlin DAC. This provided the basis of what became the Micro Music Software library now published by Temporal Acuity Products. In 1980 Prevel described the construction of a low-cost computer-assisted ear-training system developed for aural skills training at the University of Laval, Quebec. This article is noteworthy for the unusual choices made in equipment selection and program compromises for the sake of budgetary constraints.

Research Studies

Descriptive Studies Descriptive studies examining the state of the art in music instruction have been conducted by several researchers. Ihrke (1972) visited 30 departments of music and found that there was very little computer use and very few signs of interest. Deihl and Partchey (1973) reported the status of research with educational technology in music education, and Jones (1975), who surveyed 434 colleges and universities concerning CBI in music education, indicated that little research was being conducted, that there were few quality course materials available, and that there was no formal mechanism for sharing efforts in CBI. Taylor and Parrish (1978) conducted a national survey on the uses of and attitudes toward programed instruction and computers in public school and college music education, finding that there was, at that time, substantial use of programed instruction but minimal computer utilization in instruction. Arenson (1978) surveyed hardware at 28 NCCBMI member schools, finding that 26 were using mainframe computers, 20 had minicomputer systems, and 5 had microcomputers. Only 14 of the schools had audio devices at that time. Rumery (1986) surveyed postsecondary schools, reporting that a significant number of institutions had or were planning music computer facilities for music research, instruction, and administration. Grijalava (1986) found that 31 percent of independent elementary and secondary music teachers in California were using computers for administrative purposes and 26 percent for CBI. Bresler (1987) studied the role of the computer in introductory music theory instruction using qualitative evaluation to determine the impact of integration, the barriers to its use, and its effect on learners. The computer was found to have substantial impact on the learning of some students, primarily those who (1) had the ability to self-diagnose learning difficulties, (2) were analytical thinkers, (3) had systematic work habits, and (4) had long concentration spans. Bresler found that even when an educational innovation offers significant advantages, its adoption and use may create problems for teachers and students that make the innovation less successful than it might otherwise have been. Krout (1988) surveyed the extent to which microcomputers were being used in music therapy, finding that computer use in college music therapy programs was minimal. Results indicated that, in the research situation, integration was hindered by instructor apathy and adherence to tradition and authority. The poor quality of software and hardware was identified by students as a barrier to learning. Schmidt (1989) studied computer use in undergraduate curricula, reporting that 60 percent incorporate courses in the use of technology for prospective teachers.

Music Fundamentals and Ear Training Computer-based instruction in the areas of music fundamentals, elements, and ear training constitutes the bulk of the available software in music education. Although much of this material was developed in an academic setting, only a small portion has been evaluated using research techniques. Kuhn and Allvin (1967) developed the first instructional programs in music at Stanford University. The IBM 1620 mainframe was equipped with a typewriter terminal and pitch discrimination device for the presentation of sight-singing exercises and criterion tests. Placek (1972) developed random access audio for drill and practice in rhythmic perception on the PLATO system. Herrold (1973) described the Stanford CBI ear-training program including a survey of student's attitudes to CBI as well as a description of the hardware and software. Utilizing the PLATO system, Eddins (1978) described a random access audio system he developed for use in music lessons.

Thostenson (1978) collected data on the aural interval identification of music major subjects with an analysis to determine the types of difficulties students had with this task. Findings indicated that confusion patterns existed and that individual intervals were important to performance. Humphries (1978) studied the effects of CBI time on achievement in interval identification. Lamb and Bates (1978) developed a complete ear-training system that branched according to the progress of the student's performance. After 3 years of development, Hofstetter (1978, 1979, 1981) developed the GUIDO system of ear training on PLATO. This research-based complete curriculum of interactive ear training in intervals, melodies, chords, harmonies, and rhythms was made available in a commercial personal computer edition. Vaughn (1978) and Lamb (1979) compared CBI and traditional teacher/learner situations in basic musicianship. Ottman et al. (1980) describe the development of an ear-training CBI system at North Texas State University based on a concept-centered instructional philosophy. The program correlated, supported, and reinforced students' classroom experiences in theory. The MElodic DIctation Computerized Instruction (MEDICI) system was developed on the PLATO system at Florida State University. MEDICI contained an interactive music editor for writing dictation on the screen and into the computer where it was then analyzed (Newcomb, Weage, and Spencer, 1980). Garton (1981) pitted media versus media in a Solomon four-group time-series design comparing the effectiveness of CBI and tape-recorded assistance in ear-training instruction. Both procedures provided significant gain scores ($p < .01$), and reactions to CBI were positive. Wilson (1981) described the development of CBI programs for teaching music fundamentals to undergraduate elementary education music methods classes. The fundamentals included rhythm, pitch notation, key signatures, scales, intervals, chords, and terminology. No results of the effectiveness of the programs were provided. Kuyper (1981) developed the Music Instruction System in Theory—Iowa (MISTI), which presented modules in written music theory and fundamentals interrelating various approaches to instruction including drill and practice, tutorial, and programed instruction. The system contained a forerunner of expert systems with an algorithm to represent the entire system of tonal theory providing a theoretical basis for a system that solves problems itself and presents a model of the learning process.

Watanabe (1981) developed a computer-assisted drill program to aid in the aural identification of instruments. A PLATO program presented computer-controlled random access audio drill and practice in instrument identification. Following a one-month treatment period, no significant difference was noted in identification ability between control and experimental groups. Shannon (1982) compared CBI instructional drill in interval recognition to traditional instruction with first-year college students. He found that CBI was not as effective as the traditional approach in aural-visual interval recognition and that human interaction may be the reason for the effectiveness of a traditional approach. Deal (1983) replicated and compared previous audiotape research in pitch and rhythm error detection to computer-based instruction in these skills. Interactive computer examples of four-voice reductions of band literature were used to present and identify errors. Results indicated significant gains for audiotape and CBI groups but no significant difference between groups. Findings also suggested that repeated hearings may not be beneficial in developing error detection skill. Robinson (1984) developed a CBI program to increase tonal memory in elementary through high school students. The software provided no significant gains in 16 half-hour treatments as measured by the appropriate portions of four standard measures (those of Seashore, Drake, Wing, and Gaston). Dangelo (1985) investigated the effects of short-term CBI in music fundamentals on intermediate elementary level students with no previous music fundamentals instruction. Results did not differ from students taught in a classroom situation. Jacobsen (1986) compared instruction in music notation and rhythm as applied to instruction in classes for elementary education majors. Nine 50-minute CBI treatment periods produced results that indicated that note types and counting were best taught by traditional methods, while the learning of note names, key signatures, and rhythm was not significantly different from that with conventional instruction. Glass (1986) explored the effects of a microcomputer-assisted tuning program on junior high school computer students' pitch discrimination and pitch-matching abilities. Eighth-grade computer students practiced on a CBI tuning program for 25 minutes per day for 10 days. Subjects showed no gain on pre-posttest measures of the pitch section of the *Seashore Measures of Musical Talents,* but showed increases in achievement on two built-in computer rating systems. Whiston (1986) used two commercial microcomputer music programs as supplemental instructional material to teach first-graders aural perception skills of up/down/same. CBI consisted of 20 minutes per week for 8 weeks. When compared to traditional instructional techniques, all methods were equally successful. Pembrook (1986) surveyed students' attitudes toward computer-based melodic dictation programs, providing suggestions for designing future CBI in this area. Using a nonrandomized, intact class, control group, pretest-posttest design, Hesser (1988) evaluated the results of three methods of instruction in music-reading skills at the reinforcement stage. Third-grade students received six teacher-taught lessons addressing the music-reading skills of staff, pitch, and duration identification. Three methods of reinforcement provided the independent variables, including (1) untimed CBI in which students worked at their own selected period and length of time, (2) CBI class laboratory for 30 minutes per week, or (3) control group, which received teacher-presented group reinforcement. CBI in a structured setting is more effective than individual presentation at this level.

Music Theory Cooper (1975) compared the efficacy of CBI with traditional teacher-taught and self-taught methods of teaching beginning music theory. With the development of the Gooch Synthetic Woodwind computer-controlled, digital music output device on the PLATO system (Gooch, 1978) and the update of PLATO IV's dumb terminals to 8080 based microcomputer systems, programs in ear training, composition, and theory were developed on the PLATO system. Several studies have evaluated methods or strategies of CBI presentation in music theory. Canelos, Murphy, Blombach, and Heck (1980) evaluated three instructional strategies for learning intervals. Wittlich (1980) described the developments in computer-based music theory instruction and research at Indiana University. Arenson (1982) conducted an early study employing a program to teach fundamental music theory skills to non–music majors. The control group received homework assignments, while the experimental group received competency-based instruction via the PLATO system. Conclusions support the use of competency-based techniques, which may or may not be attributable to the CBI delivery. Newcomb (1983) developed LASSO, a computer-based tutorial in sixteenth-century counterpoint. The program simulated the role of the teacher in a one-to-one learning situation. Through the use of a 104 rule base, help sequences, and computer-generated "remarks," the computer guided the student through seven categories of exercises. Results of the program's effectiveness were not included. Bowman (1984) investigated precollege theory remediation using selected equivalent ability groups, one group of which received traditional classroom remedial instruction while the treatment group received a multimedia learning sequence including a programed text, rhythm tapes, and CBI. Although both methods were found to be effective, the multimedia approach was deemed to be more efficient. Dalby (1989) researched a Harmonic Intonation Training Program on the PLATO system to develop judgment on harmonic intonation utilizing intervals, triads, and four-part harmonic context presented in equal temperament and just intonation. Treatment included listening, judging, and tuning intonation errors. Substantial intonation discrimination gains were produced by all ability levels. There was no difference in abilities to judge sharp and flat mistunings. It was also noted that harmonic intonation discrimination skill is not highly correlated with harmonic analysis skill.

Instrumental Music Deihl and Radocy (1969b) designed a program in instrumental music that taught musicianship to intermediate level wind instrumentalists emphasizing ear training in articulation, phrasing, and rhythm. Kent (1970) developed and tested an elementary keyboard instruction system, finding that it was both educationally and economically feasible. Peters (1974) explored the feasibility of CBI using the computer to judge the pitch and rhythm accuracy of trumpet performance. He also developed a course in percussion pedagogy presenting interactive instruction via PLATO to teach the cognitive aspects of percussion playing and teaching (Peters, 1978b). Sanders (1980) studied the effects of a traditional approach and CBI for visual diagnostic skills training of instrumental music education students. Identical materials were presented in class lecture and by mediation. Although no differences were found between the posttest scores of control and experimental groups, examination of the practice characteristics of the two groups revealed that the computer-based method was a more efficient method of delivery. Higgins (1981) investigated the feasibility of teaching applied clarinet to music education majors entirely through CBI. Subjects who had not previously played the clarinet progressed through the equivalent of a first lesson book utilizing individualized CBI only. CBI was successful for the self-motivated, self-critical learner but less successful for those who needed feedback on performance achievement, which the computer did not provide. Eisele (1985) developed a computer-assisted instructional program designed to improve pitch discrimination of junior high violin and viola students. The program was a fingering and pitch-matching tutorial and drill program. Research subjects achieved significantly higher posttest scores ($p < .05$) on the pitch section of the *Music Achievement Test* (MAT) and a researcher-designed performance test. Results suggest that pitch perception can be improved through CBI. Kent (1970) and Weeks (1987) utilized commercial software as a supplement to lessons to compare traditional instruction in trumpet fingerings with CBI. Ten minutes of each 30-minute lesson was spent at the computer. No difference in performance results were noted, but subjects using CBI scored significantly higher ($p < .001$) in cognitive skills on a written fingering test. Banks (1990) correlated 24 independent, commercially available computer programs with the activities presented in the "Alfred Basic Piano Library." The results provided charts and information on how to integrate computer lessons into instruction utilizing this particular piano method. Colman (1990) created a computerized diagnostic test to measure music theory achievement of incoming first-year college students and to see if the test had predictive value. The 90-item instrument was implemented in HyperCard on the Macintosh.

Conducting Platte (1981) reported the effects of microcomputer program developed to increase melodic sight-reading ability of college choral ensemble members. Schwaegler (1984) developed a computer-based music conducting trainer that tested four modes of practice feedback on steadiness of beat and pattern shape. Results indicated that conducting steadiness and pattern shape were best when feedback was concurrent with or following a performance. It was noted that supplemental information feedback should be removed as soon as possible in order to develop intrinsic feedback.

Creativity Composition in the classroom was investigated by Kozerski (1988). He found that the effects of interactive participation with computers in compositional activities offered a better paradigm than present music education software, which is primarily built around a drill and practice format that is neither stimulating nor necessary. Nelson (1988) used the compositional and orchestrational capabilities of the computer to extend a general music curriculum built on the Music Learning Theory model to include experience with timbre variation as well as to reinforce melodic and rhythmic content. A curriculum was developed and tested. It was concluded that the computer and synthesizer were an efficient adjunct to the general music curriculum. Conant (1988) found that utilizing computer notational software to have fifth- and sixth-grade students write their own melodies, harmonize them, and develop a rhythmic accompaniment facilitated learning music fundamentals, creative revisions, aural recognition, recognition of texture, melody, contour, and abstraction. Students were also highly motivated to continue. Upitis (1989) described the application of computer software to creative compositional activities with children, emphasizing the creation of notational systems and the use of traditional notational software. Specific composition software and its application in the research of creativity are outlined by Webster (1989). Computer compositional programs are listed, with suggestions for their use in investigating music intelligence, imagery, cognitive style and affect, mental representation, meaning, and stages of development.

Computer-Based Testing Radocy (1971) developed a computerized criterion-referenced test in musical nonperformance behaviors. Herrold (1977) outlines the development of a computer-managed test in music fundamentals for college level theory. Two portions of separate standardized musical aptitude tests have been prepared for computer presentation. Peters (1978a) found that computerized versions of the *Music Achievement Test* (MAT) were effective because of immediate feedback and individual pacing. Testing was greatly enhanced by computer mediation. The question of the most appropriate mode of item presentation was left unresolved. Forsythe (1984) adapted Gordon's *Primary Measures of Music Audiation* (PMMA) for use with preschoolers. The length was shortened, and the response mode was changed to, "Which one is not like the others?" The *Preschool Measures of Musical Audiation* (PSMMA) indicated that age and intelligence were related to music audiation. Means on the PSMMA were compared to scores of a similar population of 6- to 8-year-olds on the PMMA and found to have a strong positive correlation. A partial stabilization of musical aptitude was found to occur around age 5, with the strongest stabilization at about age 10. McCarthy (1984) wrote a computer version of the pitch test from Seashore's *Measures of Musical Talents* that provides results as a difference limen in addition to the standard percent score. Robinson (1988b) created a computer version of the *Drake Musical Aptitude Test* in which the computer administers, scores, and records the data. The advantages gained from converting these tests to computer mediation include convenience and reliability of administration and ease and accuracy of scoring.

Computer-Based Research Modeling Abeles (1969) developed a computer-based research experiment simulator that permits students to conduct simulated research without all the problems associated with data collection. The computer program provides background information and an introduction to simulated research. Students select appropriate independent and dependent variables, and formulate hypotheses. The computer designs an experiment to test the hypotheses. Students use the Stastical Package for the Social Sciences (SPSS) to analyze data and design follow-up studies. Asmus (1989) has written two computer-based research modeling systems in Hypertext on the Macintosh. The computer graphic path analysis permits the researcher to manipulate and link predefined variables shown graphically on the screen. The program then computes multiple regression analysis of the linked results. Paths can be deleted or added and new regressions calculated. A second model statistically allows for the contributions of latent variables that are not directly measurable. This software provides a method for testing, evaluating, and refining theory and for conducting mock experiments in a flexible environment.

Expert System Blombach (1983) designed a semiintelligent computer-assisted music ear-training system. Schaffer (1988) explored the possibilities of using PROLOG to write an intelligent theory tutorial based on the principles of expert system technology. Music theory lends itself readily to artificial intelligence because it has a comprehensive rule-based knowledge structure. The results of this work are being prepared commercially as a program called Harmony Coach.

Utilizing heuristically guided discovery, a concept based on learning by rehearsal, Ashley (1989) has developed an expert system program called BigEars to teach analytic listening skills. Students make a visual thematic graph describing the hierarchical structure and identify relationships. The system guides the student on the basis of a plan that most closely resembles that which the student seems to be following. A trace of the student's actions can be saved and replayed for analysis. The rules for decision making can be delineated, and most problems can be solved using these structural rules.

OTHER TECHNOLOGY APPLIED TO MUSIC RESEARCH

Scientific and medical technology has been used in music research in effective ways. As with all technology, the primary deterrents to extensive research are the lack of availability of specialized equipment and the lack of research training.

TAP Shrader (1970) developed a special audiotape teaching machine (TAP) and instructional tapes to evaluate and provide feedback on rhythm performance accuracy based on principles of programed learning. Swope (1977) investigated the capabilities of the TAP system to improve rhythm sight-reading ability. Students who used the TAP program for 9 hours scored significantly higher ($p < .001$) on rhythmic sight-reading posttests. Parker (1979) investigated the effectiveness of the TAP system in developing sight-singing proficiency as compared to traditional instruction. First- and second-year music majors utilized the TAP Master for 15 minutes a day for 6 weeks. Sight-singing achievement tests were used for statistical analysis. Conclusions indicated that the system was an effective tool, but the role of rhythmic study in sight-singing achievement has not been established.

Oscilliscope Fernandes (1980) utilized the oscilloscope to produce visual models of the waveform of "good" cornet/trumpet tone that subjects attempted to copy in practice sessions. Junior high subjects with judged poor tone quality practiced for 12 to 15 minutes twice a week using an oscilloscope to which a transparent waveform of a good tone on specified notes was attached. Subjects attempted to match their waveform to that of the overlay. From posttest results, the oscilloscope was not effective as a device for improving tone quality under the conditions of the study.

Electroencephalogram Wagner (1975) suggested that the electroencephalogram (EEG) and other biofeedback is a way to study music attention focus, but very little research has been conducted using this technology. Wagner suggested that the EEG provides information on music attention that might lead to a better understanding of how perception and music processing take place.

Phonoelectrocardiogram A three-channel phonoelectrocardiogram was used by Buchanan (1988) to monitor 3-, 4-, and 5-year-old children's ability to tap to their heart rate and to beats 15 percent faster and slower than their heart rate. Highest synchronization occurred at heart rate, with faster and slower rates following. The device proved to be effective in monitoring and collecting data for use with music synchronization studies, although the variance in the data was high.

Continuous Response Digital Interface Two models of a Continuous Response Digital Interface (CRDI) have been developed at the Center for Music Research at Florida State University (Gregory, 1989). These devices connect to a microcomputer to record three types of behavior: switch manipulation, intensity levels, and tracking of switch manipulation across time. Both models use analog potentiometer input, which is translated into digital information by the computer. Model one consists of a horizontal slider while model two is a rotary dial. By dividing the areas of the slider or the dial into discrete sections, one can record various responses on a continuous basis. The advantages of CRDI for inputting research data are its simplicity of use, adaptability to research projects, and capability to gather continuous data. Robinson (1988a) had 120 diverse evaluators rate choral performance tapes by using the CRDI and a written response on adjudication forms. No results of the effectiveness of the CRDI were reported.

EMERGING TECHNOLOGIES IN MUSIC RESEARCH

Digital Sound Synthesis

Between 1978 and 1980, several companies began producing computer digital to analog converter (DAC) boards that permitted the reproduction of music of acceptable quality for music instruction and research. Micro Technology Unlimited, Alf, Micro Music, and several other companies produced computer DAC boards for sound reproduction, none of which were software compatible with the others. Passport Designs and Syntauri produced digital synthesizers utilizing the Mountain Computer DAC connected to an Apple II computer. With the exception of the Micro Music Software Library now available from Temporal Acuity Products, these companies produced only a limited amount of software for performance, composition, notation, and instruction. Several research studies were based on this equipment, although by the time they were completed the systems were no longer being manufactured (Jigour, 1981; Turrietta and Turrietta, 1983; Nelson, 1988).

Musical Instrument Digital Interface

By 1980 analog synthesizers were being replaced with polyphonic digital synthesizers containing onboard microprocessors for controlling the interactions between modules within the synthesizers. In 1981 David Smith of Sequential Circuits proposed the Universal Synthesizer Interface (USI), which was to be a hardware design and communications protocol for the transmission of data to and from synthesizers and computers. To reflect the broader scope of the final standard, the name was changed to the Musical Instrument Digital Interface (MIDI).

Because MIDI clearly defines and makes available the digital representation of most of the parameters of musical performance, it provides a vehicle for the collection of information for research. Higgins (1989) described MIDI parameters and how they might be used for research purposes and provided a resource guide of available hardware and software to aid in using MIDI in music research.

Research utilizing MIDI is just beginning. Todd, Boltz, and Jones (1989) have designed a MIDILAB Music Research System for the automatic recording of response and reaction data and for the presentation of research stimuli. The input device consists of a panel of 10 push buttons that record three types of responses: (1) panel push buttons, (2) MIDI keyboard, and (3) computer keyboard. A commercial version is available for researchers. Lee (1989) studied pianist touch control utilizing a MIDI keyboard to record temporal and dynamic parameters of left-hand leap patterns. Through the removal of audio and/or visual feedback, note accuracy, dynamics, tempo, and articulation were studied. Results indicated that visual sensitivity can be strengthened by the removal of auditory feedback and vice versa. Sebald (1990) reported a project in progress using MIDI in the general music classroom to teach theoretical musical understanding, creativity, performance skills, and motivation. If current interest in MIDI is any indicator, this will become a prime vehicle for research in the near future.

Pitch Extraction

Pitch extraction on mainframe computers was reported in the first published research in music CBI by Kuhn and Allvin (1967), who evaluated vocal pitch deviation in terms of percent deviation from equal-tempered tuning. Singing was performed to a metronomic beat and rhythm was not evaluated. Peters (1974) evaluated the pitch and rhythm accuracy of trumpet players utilizing a pitch and rhythm extractor on the PLATO system. The program, permitting only a 2 percent tolerance in pitch discrepancy, was found to be too confining in a musical context. The Computer-Based Music Reading project initiated by Peters at the University of Illinois on the PLATO system used a pitch extractor to communicate digital analysis of the accuracy of singing or playing a musical instrument. This project was extended by research at Laval University, Florida State University, and the University of Delaware (Peters, 1990b). Most research on pitch accuracy has been evaluated in real time by judges with statistical procedures used to factor for error of measurement. Performance research would be strengthened if it were possible to compare data on the perception of pitch and deviation with the actual parameters of the pitch as it occurred. Goodwin, Lord, and Wang (1989) identified the problems of onset, timbre, fluctuation, vocal vibrato, noise, and input inaccuracies as parameters that complicate the task of extracting the fundamental pitch from analog input. Graves (1980) found the instability of the fundamental vocal pitch to be a major problem in tracking accuracy. Although tuning devices that extract both the pitch and pitch deviation in real time have been in use since the late 1950s, these did not collect and store data on the event for later analysis or comparison. Several computer-based pitch extractors have been developed for the purpose of evaluating and teaching sight-singing accuracy. Pygraphics' Amadeus displayed real-time fluctuation in pitch much like the sweep hands of the hand-held tuner. Temporal Acuity Product's stand-alone Pitch Master matches the input pitch with a standard on tape for the purpose of identifying and reinforcing singing accuracy.

Several proprietary hardware systems have been developed for pitch extraction. Early studies by Graves (1980) and Kolb (1984) used the Gentle Electric Model 101 Pitch and Envelope Follower to identify fundamental pitch through pitch to voltage transformation. Graves used the information to create a 40-item sight-singing achievement test based on the Berkowitz (1976) *A New Approach to Sight-Singing*. Informal comparisons between teacher ratings and computer scores indicated that the system was both reliable and valid. Kolb's software provided feedback to students on the accuracy of pitches and notated examples of the student's singing on the computer screen for comparison with the original music. Dworak (1985) has developed a pitch detector algorithm that attempts to simulate the workings of the human ear. The Apple II software has been used successfully in sight-singing instruction. Goodwin et al. (1989) have developed an extractor board for the Apple II computer that reportedly overcomes the problems of other pitch extractors in extracting and following singing in real time. Lorek and Pembrook (1989), utilizing the Roland VP-70 Voice Processor, MIDI synthesizer, and Atari microcomputer at the Center for Music Research of Florida State University, developed a sight-singing evaluation system. Pitch discrepancies of up to 50 cents were acceptable, and rhythm accuracy using computer clock ticks within a plus/minus 15 percent range were considered accurate. Feedback was provided at the end of each exercise including pitch and rhythm errors, starting and ending pitch, and starting and ending tempo. Electronic Courseware Systems has produced a computer-based pitch extractor to be used in a national Computer-Based Music Skills Assessment Project currently being conducted by Peters (1990a). TeAchnology has also developed hardware and software for the instruction of sight singing using the Apple II computer and a specially designed pitch extractor board (Warren, 1989). With the exception of Lorek and Pembrook (1989), attempts to utilize pitch-to-MIDI converters such as the IVL Pitchrider 4000, the Fairlight Instruments Voicetracker, and the Roland VP-70 Voice Processor have met with little success.

Interactive Multimedia

"Interactive multimedia" is a broad term coined by Ambron and Hooper (1988) describing the integration of many technologies into a single flexible unit. This might be analogous to the concept of the humanities or related arts synthesizing the facets of several art forms to produce a richer and more complex discipline. Ambron and Hooper (1990) have edited a collection of applied research in developing multimedia tools in education that should be of interest to music researchers working in this area.

Interactive Media Technologies has developed the IMTX 8000 desktop multimedia integration system that can control CD-ROM, tape recorders, MIDI devices, video cameras, videocassette recorders (VCRs), and laser discs working in conjunction with a microcomputer. The "black box" has a proprietary central processing unit (CPU) for control of up to 10 devices simultaneously and can be daisy chained for additional interaction. The Yamaha Corporation, in collaboration with music educators, has developed a technology-assisted music curriculum, Music in Education, which consists of hardware and courseware including MIDI keyboards, interactive audio/video, computer-based instruction, and curriculum materials.

Hypertext and Hypermedia. "Hypertext" is a term coined in the early 1960s to mean nonsequential writing. In the late 1970s the term "hypermedia" was used to describe an integrated information delivery system into an aural/visual/textual communication system. Today, "hypermedia" usually refers to a software application that links data of many different types in many different ways so that the user is free to peruse the linked information in any sequence. Information can be in the form of words, numbers, pictures, interactive video, audio, or control of electronic devices. Hypermedia is unique in that it is a tool to arrange information of all kinds so that it can be accessed in ways intuitive to the task or learner. This should be of great interest to the researcher who can precisely control the sequence of learning, provide several avenues of learning, or permit subjects to control the learning environment, sequence, and structure. There are two principal divisions of hypermedia: the information delivery system and the authoring environment. The information delivery module permits the presentation of linked lists of data prepared by the author/programer. The authoring module is a simple icon-oriented environment for preparing the presentation of data. Sophisticated authoring is easily learned and can be extended by integrating programing language commands to handle specialized tasks. Examples of hypermedia are HyperCard from Apple Computer for the Macintosh, ToolBook from Asymetrix for MS-DOS computers, and HyperStudio from Roger Wagner for the Apple IIgs. Franklin (1988) provided examples of hypermedia applications for music and explained how it can be used in association retrieval, manipulation, and storage of music, video, text, graphics, and audio. Williams (1989a) has prepared research materials and tools utilizing HyperCard in psychomusicology as well as HyperCard stacks to assist in the writing of hypermedia for research and instruction in music. Adams (1989) used Hypercard and interactive audio stored on hard disk to teach tempo markings, dynamics, articulations, ornamentation/special effects, and form to high school wind instrumentalists. The program integrated professionally recorded audio examples that students heard and were instructed to imitate. The computer-based interactive multimedia approach was found to be effective for instruction in interpretive aspects of wind instrument notation. This is an example of updating previous research (Deihl and Zeigler, 1972) to new technology.

CD-ROM and Interactive Audio. Compact Disc Read Only Memory (CD-ROM) has supplanted the vinyl recording as the medium of choice for audio storage and playback. Data stored on CD-ROM is in digital form like the data used by computers. CD-ROM drives can be connected to a computer and an audio system to be used as an interactive audio instructional delivery system. The computer application program and music data may be on the CD or the music can be on the CD and the computer program on traditional magnetic media. The Voyager company has developed a HyperCard stack called AudioStack, which utilizes the necessary XCMDs and XFCNs for complete control of computer/CD interaction to within a 1/75 second accuracy. Voyager publishes HyperCard control stacks for *The Rite of Spring* and the Beethoven *Ninth Symphony*. Utilizing this system, Aitken and Adams have developed interactive ear-training stacks using standard music repertoire, which the students notate within the interactive environment. Williams (1989b) has also developed a HyperCard stack for controlling CD interaction and utilized it in melodic recognition research. New developments in compact disc technology include compact disc interactive (CD-I), compact disc with graphics (CD + G), compact disc and full motion video (CD-V), and compact disc with MIDI (CD + MIDI). Unfortunately, CD-V, CD-I and CD + G are based on entirely different engineering specifications, and each requires a different type of CD player. Warner New Media has taken advantage of a specification for CD audio disks that provides for 5 percent of the storage capacity to be reserved for subcode. They use this space for graphics and MIDI data to produce a series of discs called Audio Notes utilizing HyperCard to control CD-I, CD + G, and CD + MIDI providing an interactive interface for the study of music. At the present time, *The Magic Flute, The Rite of Spring,* Beethoven's *String Quartet No. 14, Symphony Fantastique,* and *A German Requiem* are available.

Laser Disc and Interactive Video. Video disc technology has been a parallel development of CD audio technology. The advantage of video disc technology is that it provides all of the advantages of interactive CD with the addition of full motion video, all of which is controllable at the frame level. As with CD, computer control of courseware presentations can be written with traditional programing languages or hypertext. The University of Delaware's Video Disc Music Series (Hofstetter, 1986) offers controlled video instruction including the capability to select performance style, score analysis, form analysis, still pictures, random access of any aspect, types of display modes, and single frame motion. Four discs covering 12 performances are available.

In order to prepare video disc performances for instructional use, all the information on the disc must be cataloged. Peterson (1989) has started a series of indexes of video discs that include information for random access of performance data as well as charts and essays about the composition. There are presently two operas in the series, *La Boheme* and *The Magic Flute.* Video discs for music instruction are also available from Image Entertainment, Pioneer Laserdisc, Teaching Technologies, and Encyclopedia Britannica Educational Corporation. Emerging Technologies (1989) provides a comprehensive list of educational video discs in music. The ORAT Review Shell that Williams (1989a) designed at Illinois State University provides the educator with a content-free environment to easily design interactive computer-based reviews using both video laser disc and CD audio.

Rees (1986) developed a self-instructional video disc on the PLATO system for teaching string vibrato techniques. Miller (1987) investigated the feasibility of using interactive video disc to teach oboe reed making. Developmental time as well as costs are considered reasonable for the project. Formative evaluation indicated that this approach was as successful in teaching these skills as traditional teacher instruction. Atwater (1990) developed a laser disc interactive instructional program to present various problems in trombone performance to be analyzed visually and aurally by music education students.

SUMMARY

Although activity in the use and development of technology in music instruction has kept pace with that in other disciplines, experimental research on the effects of technology on music learning has been limited. The present body of research is attempting to apply new technology to traditional environments and concerns. Programed instruction research provided an impetus for technology research that was not continued in the following four decades. The computer era has fostered considerable developmental research, much of which has centered around hardware not generally available to the profession. Instructional application of the latest technologies to music education is being conducted primarily by isolated individuals who have as a primary goal the utilization of the technology in CBI and not the research of the effects of that development.

CONCLUSIONS

Some of the problems of the present body of research in technology are due to (1) the lack of a good research design, (2) an inadequate treatment time, (3) the lack of researcher expertise, (4) the quality of the treatment, and (5) the lack of designs that protect validity in favor of comparative studies that are used to factor out the effects of treatment interaction.

Action, descriptive, and developmental research designs have been utilized because of (1) the rapid change in the development of new technologies, (2) the delay of acceptance or implementation of the technology into the instructional process, (3) the narrow view of the instructional environment (in school, in class), (4) a focus on the didactic aspects of music to the exclusion of the heuristic, (5) reluctance to extend the research base by applying new technology to solve problems identified by earlier research, and (6) the lack of qualified people to develop the technology.

Major changes in technological tools occur in decreasing time intervals, and the apparent inability of the educational system to incorporate them compounds the research problem. Because of these rapid changes, many researchers today are opting to participate in the development of new technologies, experimenting with the possibilities of these devices, rather than conducting research on the effects of pedagogical applications. Compounding the problem is that much of the research is being conducted by doctoral students who lack experience with the technology and who, because of financial restrictions, are sometimes conducting research on previous generations of technology. Few experimental designs have been employed to determine the cause and effect of the technology or to discover the attributes of the technology that have potential for instruction. No research in music has been conducted on the correlation of technology attributes with learner traits. Research in the use of technology in music instruction needs to be conducted within the framework of a specific pedagogical taxonomy with the intent of discovering what attributes of the technology produce what specific results for what type of learner. The need is to combine research in the areas of the psychology of music and learning theory with the yet to be defined knowledge of the instructional attributes of technology.

We have no clear answer about which music-learning tasks are intrinsic to specific types of technology mediation (Guilliford, 1973); and we do not know what type of learners respond to mediated learning. For example, Hawkins (1985) concluded that sex differences in computer use emerge in relation to the functions computers serve. Matching the learning task to the goals of individual students removes the differentiated interest seen between boys and girls. It is the application of the technology, not the technology itself, that influences interest and consequently success with the technology.

PARADIGM FOR FUTURE RESEARCH

Why Is Technology Research Important?

Salomon (1984) states that "the development of television was left to the entertainment industry." Extensive research must be implemented within the music education community. Researchers have the opportunity to set the future direction of music education, which will become more highly technology intensive than has yet been imagined. This is possible because, as Salomon continues, "the computer, being the brainchild of a number of academic disciplines, is not only their product but also their tool of development, attracting the best minds around" (p. 8).

A Direction for Technology Research in Music Education

Unlike academic research in the fields of science, medicine, and psychology, educational research has not found a way to legitimize applied research and thus has had difficulty in accepting action research, which develops approaches to utilizing technology in education, as opposed to experimental research on the effects of mediated instruction. The concern with legitimizing music education research within the research community has resulted in the selection of research hypotheses that are acceptable to the research community but inappropriate to the solution of the problem. Many of the studies in music education technology have been based on quality ideas but were presented with unsuitable hypotheses. Technology research in music instruction, like that in general education, has been overly concerned with evaluative comparison (Hall, 1977; Salomon and Clark, 1977). In attempting to conduct quality empirical research, we have been concerned with the generalizability of results based on Gaussian criteria. We have concentrated on studies with dependent variables intended to answer the question, Does it

teach better than traditional instruction? assuming that the technology itself is what effects learning rather than the manner in which the technology is utilized, or the individual interaction of the media and the learner, or that some specific attributes of the technology effect learning. Salomon and Gardner (1986) stated that "when everything else is indeed held constant, save the medium, not much of an effect can be observed." (p. 14). For this reason, a great percentage of technology research in music learning has shown no significant results.

There are many feasibility/developmental studies in technology applications to music instruction, and most of these studies were structured to observe only specific research variables, failing to report important findings related to (1) the specific features of the technology that influenced learning, (2) the design elements of the materials and the pedagogical basis for their choice, and (3) the types of learners that respond to various aspects of mediated instruction. Research has generally ignored these elements, attempting to define the parametric elements of technology instruction. It is intrinsic to mediated instruction that the effect will not be equal for all learners. Research designed to evaluate comparative judgments based on normative results is missing the essence of the value of mediated instruction, individualization, and is predestined to produce superficial results even when statistically significant.

Designing Technology Research

We have not laid a proper foundation of exploratory, open-ended, holistic observations of the effects of technology instruction in music before entering into analytic experimental research (Gibbs, 1979). Instead of identifying the essential variables of technology-based instruction and the types of learning and learners affected by those variables, much research has assumed that there is no interaction between the technology's attributes and the learning styles of the students and that the learning environment of mediated instruction and traditional classroom instruction plays a relatively insignificant role in learning outcomes.

A unique feature of technology instruction is the effect of the manner in which each individual learner approaches the media and the choices made in the interaction. While researchers plan for equal control and experimental groups, they forget the fact that learner ability, prior knowledge, and motivation are crucial in determining how the subject will interact with the technology (Salomon and Gardner, 1986).

Because technology-based instruction has become multifaceted, with an endless variety of instructional paths, the manner in which individual learners perceive the task, move through the presentation, and execute problem solving has as much impact on the outcome as the definable parameters of media, materials, and sequence. "This issue proves to be of particular relevance to the study of computer activities in which the learner is assumed to exercise significant control over the material" (Salomon and Gardner, 1986, p. 16).

Researchers make parametric assumptions that equal environments and treatments produce consistent learning results for a given population. However, with technology research, where there are a multitude of interactive choices, the individual characteristics of the learner have an effect on the instructional environment to such a degree as to be a dependent variable.

It becomes apparent then that questions such as (1) Does it teach? (2) Does it teach better than. . . ? (3) Which is the best approach? are pedantic questions about enigmatic pedagogical conditions. Therefore, researchers should be concerned not with uniform or normative effects but with discovering the correlations between technology attributes and individual learning styles. Research questions should ask how much and what type of learning takes place in a given mediated instructional situation for what type of learner. It is important to be aware that mediated instruction, because of the diversity of choices of the learner, may produce divergent results from the same application. Research designs must be flexible enough to identify all learning that occurs, measuring the effects of the technology that affects learning and to what degree and what type of learning takes place in what style of learner. "Instead of incorporating technology into the curriculum, we need to reconstruct the curriculum for design-oriented learning to accommodate the new technology" (Balzano, 1987, p. 91).

The Imperative of Time

It is important that formative, open-ended observational research be conducted as soon as possible to codify properly the complex issues that will become the dependent variables for summative, analytic, experimental research after relationships have been identified. Time becomes an increasingly important factor as technology invades everyday life. Because technology is so quickly assimilated into society, it soon becomes difficult to find control groups not already biased by interactions with the technology.

References

Abeles, H. F. (1969). *Using an EXPER SIM (experimental simulation) model in teaching graduate research courses in music education.* Bloomington: Indiana University (ERIC Document Reproduction Service No. ED 175 463)

Adams, S. (1989). The development of a computer-based interactive multimedia program for teaching interpretive aspects of wind instrument notation. Unpublished doctoral dissertation, University of Southern California, Los Angeles.

Albin, W. R. (1979). The development of videotaped instructional units for teaching selected aspects of mallet-played, Latin American, and accessory percussion instruments. Unpublished doctoral dissertation, Indiana University, Bloomington.

Allen, C. (1966). *Instructional television in music education.* Bloomington: National Center for School and College Television.

Allvin, R. L. (1967). The development of a computer-assisted music instruction system to teach sight-singing and ear-training. Unpublished doctoral dissertation, Stanford University, Stanford.

Allvin. R. L. (1970). Do colleges and universities need an automated music learning center? *Bulletin of the Council for Research in Music Education, 21*(2), 32–46.

Allvin, R. L. (1971). Computer-assisted music instruction: A look at the potential. *Journal of Research in Music Education, 19*(2), 131–143.

Alphonce, B. (1988). Computer applications in music research: A retrospective. *Computers in Music Research, 1*(Fall), 1–74.

Ambron, S., and Hooper, K. (1988). *Interactive multimedia.* Redmond: Microsoft Press.

Ambron, S. and Hooper, K. (Ed.). (1990). *Learning with interactive multimedia: Developing and using multimedia tools in education.* Redmond: Microsoft Press.

Arenson, M. A. (1978). An examination of computer-based educational hardware at twenty-eight NCCBMI member schools. *Journal of Computer-Based Instruction, 5*(3), 38–40.

Arenson, M. A. (1982). The effect of a competency-based computer program on the learning of fundamental skills in a theory course for non-majors. *Journal of Computer-Based Instruction, 9*(3), 55–58.

Ashley, R. D. (1989). A computer system for learning analytic listening. In D. Butler (Ed.), *Proceedings of the international computer music conference.* San Francisco: Computer Music Association.

Asmus, E. P. (1989). Computer-based modeling of music concepts for testing, evaluating, and refining theory. *Psychomusicology, 8*(2), 171–182.

Atwater, D. (1990). The development of computer-based videodisc courseware for teaching visual diagnostic skills of selected problems in trombone performance. Unpublished doctoral dissertation, University of Illinois, Urbana.

Bales, W. K. (1986). Computer-based instruction and music technology in education. *Journal of Computer-Based Instruction, 13*(1), 2–5.

Balzano, G. J. (1987). Reconstructing the curriculum for design: Music, mathematics, and psychology. *Machine Mediated Learning, 2*(1–2), 83–109.

Banks, D. W. (1990). The Correlation of selected precollege music computer programs with the 'Alfred Basic Piano Library'. Unpublished doctoral dissertation, University of Oklahoma, Norman.

Bartle, B. K. (1987). *Computer software in music and music education: A guide.* Metuchen: Scarecrow Press.

Berg, C. M. (1984). *Visualizing music: The archaeology of music video.* Paper presented at the annual meeting of the Speech Communication Association, Chicago.

Berg, R. C. (1962). The teaching of music on a series of telecasts sponsored by the regents educational television project. Unpublished doctoral dissertation, Columbia University, New York.

Berkowitz, S., Fontrier, G., and Kraft, L. (1976). *A new approach to sight singing.* (rev. ed.). New York: Norton.

Blombach, A. K. (1983). OSU's GAMUT: Semi-intelligent computer-assisted music ear training. *Proceedings of the sixth international conference on computers and the humanities,* (pp. 14–15). Rockville: Computer Science Press.

Bodenstein, N. M. (1975). The teaching of selected musical concepts in the college music survey course utilizing the taped guided listening technique. Unpublished doctoral dissertation, Boston University, Boston.

Boody, C. G. (1975). Non-compositional applications of the computer to music: An evaluative study of the materials published in America through June 1972. Unpublished doctoral dissertation, University of Minnesota, Minneapolis.

Boody, C. G. (Ed.). (1990). *Technology directory 1990–1991*. Columbus: Association for Technology in Music Instruction.

Bowman, J. A. (1984). An investigation of two methods of preparation for college level music theory: Precollegiate remediation, CAI. Unpublished doctoral dissertation, University of Rochester, Rochester.

Bresler, L. (1987). The role of the computer in a music theory classroom: Integration, barriers, and learning. Unpublished doctoral dissertation, Stanford University, Stanford.

Bridges, N. (1982). The development of aural perception of selected percepts of musical form utilizing programed instruction. Unpublished doctoral dissertation, Boston University, Boston.

Britton, A. P. (1968). Committee on the impact and potentials of technology. In R. A. Choate (Ed.), *Documentary report of the Tanglewood Symposium,* Washington: Music Educators National Conference.

Buchanan, J. C. (1988). An exploratory study of preschool children's synchronization of a selected rhythmic activity with music set at their heart rates. Unpublished doctoral dissertation, University of South Florida, Tampa.

Canelos, J. J., Murphy, B. A., Blombach, A. K., and Heck, W. C. (1980). Evaluation of three types of instructional strategy for learner acquisition of intervals. *Journal of Research in Music Education, 28*(4), 243–249.

Carlsen, J. C. (1962). An investigation of programed learning in melodic dictation by means of a teaching machine using a branching technique. Unpublished doctoral dissertation, Northwestern University, Evanston.

Carlsen, J. C., and Williams, D. B. (1978). *A computer annotated bibliography: Music research in programed instruction 1952–1972.* Reston: Music Educators National Conference.

Carpenter, T. H. (1966). An analysis of past, present, and potential uses of instructional television in the teaching of music. Unpublished doctoral dissertation, Boston University, Boston.

Carpenter, T. H. (1969). *The utilization of instructional television in music education.* Bethesda: U.S. Department of Health Education and Welfare, Office of Education. (ERIC Document Reproduction Services No. ED 032 788)

Carpenter, T. H. (1973). *Televised music instruction.* Washington: Music Educators National Conference.

Chamberlin, H. (1980, April). Advanced real-time music synthesis techniques. *Byte, pp. 70–196.*

Chamberlin, H. (1985). *Musical applications of microprocessors* (2nd ed.). Hasbrouck Heights: Hayden.

Collins, T. C., and Diamond, R. M. (1967). The use of 8mm loop films to teach the identification of clarinet fingering, embouchure, and hand position errors. *Journal of Research in Music Education, 15*(3), 224–228.

Colman, J. P. (1990). The development and validation of a computerized diagnostic test for the prediction of success in the first year music theory sequence by incoming freshman at Michigan State University. Unpublished doctoral dissertation, Michigan State University, East Lansing.

Conant, B. H. (1988). A study of cognitive processes of children creating music in a computer learning environment. Unpublished doctoral dissertation, University of Massachusetts, Amherst.

Cooper, R. M. (1975). The efficacy of computer-assisted instruction compared with traditional teacher-taught and self-taught methods of teaching beginning music theory. Unpublished doctoral dissertation, University of North Carolina, Greensboro.

Dalby, B. F. (1989). A computer-based training program for the development of harmonic intonation discrimination skill. Unpublished doctoral dissertation, University of Illinois, Urbana.

Dangelo, E. M. (1985). The use of computer based instruction in the teaching of music fundamentals. Unpublished doctoral dissertation, University of Pittsburgh, Pittsburgh.

Dasher, R. T. (1968). The musical programming of national educational television. Unpublished doctoral dissertation, University of Michigan, Ann Arbor.

Davis, C. W. (Ed.). (1968). *National educational television: Fulfilling the artistic potential.* Washington: Music Educators National Conference.

Davis, D. S. (1988). *Computer applications in music: A bibliography.* Madison: A-R Editions.

Deal, J. J. (1983). Computer-assisted programmed instruction to teach pitch and rhythm error-detection skill to college music education students. Unpublished doctoral dissertation, University of Iowa, Iowa City.

Deihl, N. C., and Partchey, K. C. (1973). Status of research: Educational technology in music education. *Bulletin of the Council for Research in Music Education, 35*(4), 18–29.

Deihl, N. C., and Radocy, R. E. (1969a). Computer-assisted instruction: Potential for instrumental music education. *Bulletin of the Council for Research in Music Education, 15*(Winter), 1–7.

Deihl, N. C., and Rodocy, R. E. (1969b). *Development and evaluation of computer-assisted instruction in instrumental music* (USOE Project No. 7-0760). University Park: Pennsylvania State University. (ERIC Document Reproduction Service No. ED 035 314)

Deihl, N. C., and Zeigler, R. H. (1972). *Evaluation of computer-assisted instruction in instrumental musicianship* (Report No. OEG-3-72-0011). Washington: National Center for Educational Research and Development. (ERIC Document Reproduction Service No. ED 067 897)

Dowling, W. J. (1989). Programing small computers to produce experiments in music cognition. *Psychomusicology, 8*(2), 183–190.

Dibble, C. A. (1983). Videotape pitch discrimination instruction of five-year-old children from different home musical environments. Unpublished doctoral dissertation, Boston University, Boston.

Dvorak, D. D. (1973). The use of filmstrip-sound materials instrument repair instructions. Unpublished doctoral dissertation, Arizona State University, Tempe.

Dworak, P. (1985). A real-time pitch detector for instructional and research applications. In G. C. Turk (Ed.), *Proceedings of the research symposium on the psychology and acoustics of music* (pp. 84–93). Lawrence: University of Kansas.

Eddins, J. M. (1978). Random access audio in computer-assisted music instruction. *Journal of Computer-Based Instruction, 5*(1–2), 22–29.

Eisele, M. J. (1985). Development and validation of a computer-assisted instructional lesson for teaching intonation discrimination skills to violin and viola students. Unpublished doctoral dissertation, Indiana University, Bloomington.

Fernandes, G. M. (1980). The oscilloscope as an aid in changing tone quality in the performance of junior high school cornet and trumpet students. Unpublished doctoral dissertation, University of Iowa, Iowa City.

Fiorillo, R. J. (1973). The efficacy of channel-alternated tape recordings with related visual materials in the development of aural discrimination. Unpublished doctoral dissertation, University of Maryland, College Park.

Forsythe, R. (1984). The development and implementation of a computerized preschool measure of music audiation (aptitude, ability, testing). Unpublished doctoral dissertation, Case Western Reserve University, Cleveland.

Franklin, C. (1988). The hypermedia library. *Database, 11*(3), 43–48.

Furman, C. E. (1984). Behavior checklist and videotapes versus standard instructor feedback in the development of a music teaching competency. Unpublished doctoral dissertation, Florida State University, Tallahassee.

Garton, J. C. (1981). The efficacy of computer-based and tape-recorded assistance in second-semester freshman ear-training instruction. Unpublished doctoral dissertation, Louisiana State University and Agricultural and Mechanical College, Baton Rouge.

Gibbs, J. (1979). The meaning of ecologically oriented inquiry in contemporary psychology. *American Psychologist, 2,* 127–140.

Giles, A. L. (1981). Teaching beginning piano to adults by television. Unpublished doctoral dissertation, Columbia University, New York.

Gilkes, L. W. (1986).*Commodore 64 & 128 music software guide.* Drexel Hill: Unsinn Publications.

Glass, J. S. (1986). The effects of a microcomputer-assisted tuning program on junior high school students' pitch discrimination and pitch-matching abilities. Unpublished doctoral dissertation, University of Miami, Coral Gables.

Glenn, K. J. (1972). The potential use of television for early childhood music education. Unpublished doctoral dissertation, University of Michigan, Ann Arbor.

Gonzo, C., and Forsythe, J. (1976). Developing and using videotapes to teach rehearsal techniques and principles.*Journal of Research in Music Education, 24*(1), 32–41.

Gooch, S. (1978). *PLATO music system.* Paper presented at the annual meeting of the Association for the Development of Computer-Based Instructional Systems, Dallas, TX.

Goodwin, A., Lord, C., and Wang, C. (1989). *Techniques for extracting voice pitch information with personal computers.* Paper presented at the Music Educators National Conference special conference on music and technology, Nashville.

Graves, D. L. (1980). The development of an objective sight-singing achievement test employing electronic measurement apparatus. Unpublished doctoral dissertation, University of Georgia, Athens.

Greenburg, M., and Huddelston, D. R. (1971). A program for developing aural discrimination of instrumental tone colors using a videosonic teaching machine.*Journal of Research in Music Education, 19*(1), 51–61.

Gregory, D. (1989). Using computers to measure continuous music responses. *Psychomusicology, 8*(2), 127–134.

Grijalava, F. J. (1986). Factors influencing computer use by music educators in California independent elementary and secondary schools. Unpublished doctoral dissertation, University of San Francisco, San Francisco.

Gulliford, N. L. (1973). Current research on the relative effectiveness of selected media characteristics. Pittsburgh: Westinghouse Electric Corporation. (ERIC Document Reproduction Service No. ED 098 968)

Hall, K. A. (1977). A research model for applying computer technology to the interactive instructional process. *Journal of Computer-Based Instruction, 3*(3), 68–75.

Hawkins, J. (1985). Computers and girls: Rethinking the issues. *Sex Roles, 13*(3–4), 165–180.

Henney, T. H. (1968). The Bell Telephone Hour: Who needs it? In R. A. Choate (Ed.), *Documentary report of the Tanglewood symposium* (pp. 87–88). Washington: Music Educators National Conference.

Herrold, R. M. (1973). Computer-assisted instruction: A study of student performance in a CAI ear-training program. Unpublished doctoral dissertation, Stanford University, Stanford.

Herrold, R. M. (1977). The development and trial of a computer managed test of music fundamentals. *Oregon Council for Research in Teacher Education* (p. 21). (ERIC Document Reproduction Service No. ED 171 312)

Hesser, L. A. (1988). Effectiveness of computer-assisted instruction in developing music reading skills at the elementary level. Unpublished doctoral dissertation, State University of New York, Albany.

Hewlett, W. B., and Selfridge-Field, E. (1989). *Computing in musicology: A directory of research.* Menlo Park: Center for Computer Assisted Research in the Humanities.

Higgins, W. R. (1981). The feasibility of teaching beginning applied clarinet with the microcomputer. Unpublished doctoral dissertation, Pennsylvania State University, University Park.

Higgins, W. R. (1989). Resource guide for using MIDI in psychomusicology research. *Psychomusicology, 8*(2), 197–205.

Hlynka, D. (1980). *Film music: Implications for instructional films and television.* Paper presented at the annual conference of the Australian Society for Educational Technology, Melbourne, Australia.

Hofstetter, F. T. (1978). Computer-based recognition of perceptual patterns in harmonic dictation exercises. *Journal of Research in Music Education, 26*(2), 111–119.

Hofstetter, F. T. (1979). Evaluation of a competency-based approach to teaching aural interval identification. *Journal of Research in Music Education, 27*(4), 201–213.

Hofstetter, F. T. (1981). Applications of the GUIDO system to aural skills research, 1975–1980. *College Music Symposium, 21*(Fall), 46–53.

Hofstetter, F. T. (1985). *Making music on micros: An approach to computer programming.* Westminster: Random House.

Hofstetter, F. T. (1986). *Videodisc music series.* Newark: University of Delaware.

Hofstetter, F. T. (1988). *Computer literacy for musicians.* Englewood-Cliffs: Prentice-Hall.

Hullfish, W. R. (1969). A comparison of response-sensitive and response-insensitive decision rules presenting learning materials in music theory by computer-assisted instruction. Unpublished doctoral dissertation, State University of New York, Buffalo.

Humphries, J. A. (1978). The effects of computer assisted aural drill time on achievement in musical interval identification. Unpublished doctoral dissertation, Arizona State University, Tempe.

Ihrke, W. R. (1971). Automated music training: Final report on phase one.*Journal of Research in Music Education, 19*(4), 474–480.

Ihrke, W. R. (1972). *A study of the present state of electronic music training including computer-assisted instruction: A bibliography.* Storrs: University of Connecticut (ERIC Document Reproduction Service No. ED 063 806)

Jacobsen, J. R. (1986). Effectiveness of a computer-assisted instruction program in music fundamentals applied to instruction for elementary education majors. Unpublished doctoral dissertation, University of Northern Colorado, Greeley.

Jeffries, T. B. (1967). The effects of order of presentation and knowledge of results on the aural recognition of melodic intervals. Unpublished doctoral dissertation, University of California, Los Angeles.

Jigour, R. J. (1981). *The Alphasyntauri instrument and software programmable digital synthesizer system.* Paper presented at the symposium on small computers in the arts, Philadelphia.

Jones, M. J. (1975). Computer-assisted instruction in music: A survey with attendant recommendations. Unpublished doctoral dissertation, Northwestern University, Evanston.

Jordan, G. L. (1980). Videotape supplementary instruction in beginning conducting. Unpublished doctoral dissertation, University of Illinois, Urbana.

Kent, W. P. (1970). *Feasibility of computer-assisted elementary keyboard music instruction.* Falls Church: System Development Corporation. (ERIC Document Reproduction Service No. ED 038 039)

Killiam, B. (1981). Research applications in music CAI. *Bulletin of the College Music Society,* (Fall), 37–44.

Knuth, A. M. (1971). Integration of the systems approach and electronic technology in learning and teaching music. *Bulletin of the Council for Research in Music Education, 25*(Summer), 34–46.

Kolb, R. M. (1984). A real-time microcomputer-assisted system for translating aural monophonic tones into music notation as an aid in sight-singing. Unpublished doctoral dissertation, Louisiana State University and Agricultural and Mechanical College, Baton Rouge.

Kostka, S. M. (Ed.). (1974). *A bibliography of computer applications in music.* Hackensack: Joseph Boonin.

Kozerski, R. A. (1988). Computer microworlds for music composition and education. Unpublished doctoral dissertation, University of California, San Diego.

Krout, R. E. (1988). Microcomputer applications in music theory. Unpublished doctoral dissertation, Columbia University, New York.

Kuhn, W. E., and Allvin, R. L. (1967). Computer-assisted teaching: A new approach to research in music. *Journal of Research in Music Education, 15*(4), 305–315.

Kuyper, J. Q. (1981). MISTI: A computer-assisted instruction system in music theory and fundamentals. Unpublished doctoral dissertation, University of Iowa, Iowa City.

Lamb, M. R. (1979). The computer as a musicianship teaching aid. Unpublished doctoral dissertation, University of Canterbury, New Zealand.

Lamb, M. R., and Bates, R. H. T. (1978). Computerized aural training: An interactive system designed to help both teachers and students. *Journal of Computer-Based Instruction, 5*(1–2), 30–37.

Lee, S. H. (1989). Using the personal computer to analyze piano performance. *Psychomusicology, 8*(2), 143–149.

Lincoln, H. B. (1969). The computer and music research: Prospects and problems. *Bulletin of the Council for Research in Music Education, 18*(Fall),

Lincoln, H. B. (1974). Use of the computer in music research: A short report on accomplishments, limitations, and future needs. *Computers and the Humanities, 8*(5–6), 285–289.

Lorek, M. J., and Pembrook, R. G. (1989). Present and future applications of a microcomputer-based frequency analysis system. *Psychomusicology, 8*(2), 97–109.

Maltzman, E. (1964). An investigation of key-tone matching with children and adults. Unpublished doctoral dissertation, Boston University, Boston.

Maltzman, E. (1965). *Proceedings of the national conference on the uses of educational media in the teaching of music,* (Washington: Music Educators National Conference. (ERIC Document Reproduction Service No. ED 003 168)

March, H. C. (1980). The development and evaluation of an animated film to improve listening skills of junior high school general music students. Unpublished doctoral dissertation, University of Michigan, Ann Arbor.

McCarthy, J. (1984, March). The pitch test. *Creative computing,* pp. 211–217.

Mears, W. G. (1965). Tri-sensory reinforcement of a rhythmic learning program. Unpublished doctoral dissertation, Florida State University, Tallahassee.

Michelson, S. K. (1984). The use of videotaped models to teach rehearsal techniques. Unpublished doctoral dissertation, Arizona State University, Tempe.

Miller, A. W. (1987). Feasibility of instruction in instrumental music education with an interactive videodisc adapted from existing media. Unpublished doctoral dissertation, University of Illinois, Urbana.

Miller, V. K. (1973). Simulation: Embouchure instruction by videotape. A pilot study using simulation as a technique to determine the ability of instrumental music majors to analyze woodwind embouchure problems. Unpublished doctoral dissertation, University of Oregon, Eugene.

Nelson, B. J. P. (1988). The development of a middle school general music curriculum: A synthesis of computer-assisted instruction and music learning theory. Unpublished doctoral dissertation, University of Rochester, Rochester.

Newcomb, S. R. (1983). LASSO: A Computer-based tutorial in sixteenth-century counterpoint. Unpublished doctoral dissertation, Florida State University, Tallahassee.

Newcomb, S. R., Weage, B. K., and Spencer, P. (1980). *The MEDICI tutorial in melodic dictation.* Tallahassee: Florida State University. (ERIC Document Reproduction Service No. ED 196 426)

Ottman, R. W., Killam, R. N., Adams, R. M., Bales, W. K., Bertsche, S. V., Gay, L. C., Marshall, D. B., Peak, D. A., and Ray, D. (1980). Development of a concept centered ear-training CAI system. *Journal of Computer-Based Instruction, 6*(3), 79–86.

Parker, R. C. (1979). The effectiveness of the TAP system in instruction in sight-singing: An experimental study. Unpublished doctoral dissertation, University of Miami, Coral Gables.

Pembrook, R. G. (1986). Some implications of students' attitudes toward a computer-based melodic dictation program. *Journal of Research in Music Education, 34*(2), 121–133.

Peters, G. D. (1974). Feasibility of computer-assisted instruction for instrumental music education. Unpublished doctoral dissertation, University of Illinois, Urbana.

Peters, G. D. (1978a). *Computer-assisted instruction applications to standardized music achievement testing.* Paper presented at the annual meeting of the Association for the Development of Computer-Based Instructional Systems, Dallas.

Peters, G. D. (1978b). Percussion instruction methods by computer. *The Instrumentalist, 32*(6), 41–43.

Peters, G. D. (1979). *Courseware development for microcomputer-based instruction in music.* Paper presented at the Association for the Development of Computer-Based Instructional Systems, San Diego.

Peters, G. D. (1990a). *Computer-based music skills assessment project.* Washington: National Endowment for the Arts and the United States Department of Education.

Peters, G. D. (1990b). *Illinois technology-based music instruction project.* Urbana-Champaign: University of Illinois, School of Music.

Peters, G. D., and Eddins, J. M. (1978). Applications of computers to music pedagogy, analysis, and research: A selected bibliography. *Journal of Computer-Based Instruction, 5*(1&2), 41–44.

Peterson, L. W. (1989). *Videodisc index series.* Newark: University of Delaware.

Placek, R. W. (1972). Design and trial of a computer-assisted lesson in rhythm. Unpublished doctoral dissertation, University of Illinois, Urbana.

Platte, J. D. (1981). The effects of a microcomputer-assisted instructional program on the ability of college choral ensemble members to sing melodic configurations at sight. Unpublished doctoral dissertation, Ball State University, Muncie.

Prevel, M. (1980). Low-cost computer-assisted ear-training. *Journal of Computer-Based Instruction, 6*(3), 77–78.

Puopolo, V. (1971). The development and experimental application of self-instructional practice materials for beginning instrumentalists. *Journal of Research in Music Education, 19*(3), 342–349.

Radocy, R. E. (1971). Development of a computerized criterion-referenced test for certain nonperformance musical behaviors requisite to teaching music. Unpublished doctoral dissertation, Pennsylvania State University, University Park.

Rasmussen, W. I. (1966). An experiment in developing basic listening skills through programed instruction. Unpublished doctoral dissertation, University of Southern California, Los Angeles.

Rees, F. J. (1986). A PLATO-based videodisc self-instructional program for directing the development of string vibrato technique. *Journal of Educational Technology Systems, 14*(4), 283–296.

Robbins, D. E. (1979). The development and evaluation of a series of video-tape lessons to supplement a college course in advanced music theory. Unpublished doctoral dissertation, North Texas State University, Denton.

Robinson, C. R. (1988a). Differentiated modes of choral performance evaluation using traditional procedures and a continuous response digital interface device. Unpublished doctoral dissertation, Florida State University, Tallahassee.

Robinson, R. L. (1984). The development and evaluation of microcomputer-assisted instruction for the improvement of tonal memory. Unpublished doctoral dissertation, University of Miami, Coral Gables.

Robinson, R. L. (1988b). *Drake musical aptitude test* [Computer program]. Bellevue: Temporal Acuity Products.

Rogers, K., and Almond, F. (1970). A bibliography of materials on programed instruction in music. *Journal of Research in Music Education, 18*(2), 178–183.

Rudolph, T. E. (1984). *Music and the Apple II.* Drexel Hill: Unsinn Publications.

Rumery, K. R. (1986). Computer applications in music education. *Technological Horizons in Education, 14*(2), 97–99.

Saker, J. R. (1982). An evaluation of a videotaped simulation training program on the perceived ability of band student teachers to deal with behavior-management problems encountered during student teaching. Unpublished doctoral dissertation, University of Iowa, Iowa City.

Salomon, G. (1984). Computers in education: Setting a research agenda. *Educational Technology, 24*(10), 7–11.

Salomon G., and Clark, R. E. (1977). Reexamining the methodology of research on media and technology in education. *Review of Educational Research, 47*(1), 99–120.

Salomon, G., and Gardner, H. (1986). The computer as educator: Lessons from television research. *Educational Researcher, 15*(1), 13–19.

Salvi, D. A. (1981). A comparison of instructional strategies in programmed materials in musical style recognition. Unpublished doctoral dissertation, Columbia University, New York.

Sanders, L. E. (1966). An introduction to style in orchestra music: A self-tutoring program. Unpublished doctoral dissertation, Indiana University, Bloomington.

Sanders, W. H. (1980). The effect of computer-based instructional materials in a program for visual diagnostic skills training of instrumental music education students. Unpublished doctoral dissertation, University of Illinois, Urbana.

Schaffer, J. W. (1988). Developing an intelligent music tutorial: An investigation of expert systems and their potential for microcomputer-based instruction in music theory. Unpublished doctoral dissertation, Indiana University, Bloomington.

Schmidt, C. P. (1989). An investigation of undergraduate music education curriculum content. *Bulletin of the Council for Research in Music Education, 99,* 42–56.

Schwaegler, D. G. (1984). A computer-based trainer for music conducting: The effects of four feedback modes. Unpublished doctoral dissertation, University of Iowa, Iowa City.

Sebald, D. C. (1981). The development and formative evaluation of multi-media learning packages in supplementary woodwind techniques for use in teacher training. Unpublished doctoral dissertation, Michigan State University, East Lansing.

Sebald, D. C. (1990). *A public school creative music project using computers and MIDI technology.* [Research in Progress]

Shannon, D. W. (1982). Aural visual interval recognition in music instruction: A comparison of a computer-assisted approach and a traditional in-class approach. Unpublished doctoral dissertation, University of Southern California, Los Angeles.

Shrader, D. L. (1970). An aural approach to rhythmic sight-reading based upon principles of programed learning, utilizing a stereotape machine. Unpublished doctoral dissertation, University of Oregon, Eugene.

Sidnell, R. (1971). Self-instructional drill materials for student conductors. *Journal of Research in Music Education, 19*(1), 85–91.

Simpson, E. (1970). Investigating the effectiveness of programed listening in secondary instrumental music instruction. *Bulletin of the Council for Research in Music Education, 19*(4), 16–19.

Skapski, G. J. (1969). *Feasibility of producing synchronized videotapes as instructional aids to the study of music* (Report No. OEG-1-7-070052-4272). Washington: Office of Education (DHEW) Bureau of Research. (ERIC Document Reproduction Service no. ED 030 313)

Skapski, G. J. (1971). Electronic video recording as a new resource in music education. *Journal of Research in Music Education, 19*(4), 408–421.

Skinner, B. F. (1954). The science of learning and the art of teaching. *Harvard Educational Review, 24,* 86–97.

Skinner, B. F. (1968). *The technology of teaching.* New York: Appleton-Century-Crofts.

Spohn, C. E. (1969). Individualizing instruction through new media research. *Journal of Research in Music Education, 17*(1), 94–99.

Spohn, C. L. (1962). Music instruction in the language laboratory: Theory into practice. *Journal of Research in Music Education, 11*(2), 25–29.

Spohn, C. L. (1963). Programing the basic materials of music for self-instructional development of aural skills. *Journal of Research in Music Education, 11*(3), 91–98.

Spohn, C. L., and Poland, W. (1964). *An evaluation of two methods using magnetic tape recordings for programed instruction in the elements of music.* Columbus: Ohio State University. (ERIC Document Reproduction Service No. ED 003 611)

Stuart, M. (1979). The use of videotape recordings to increase teacher trainees' error-detection skills. *Journal of Research in Music Education, 27*(1), 14–19.

Swope, R. L. (1977). Improvement of rhythm sight reading ability through use of the TAP system. *Pennsylvania Music Educators Association Bulletin of Research in Music Education, 8*(1), 23–26.

Tarratus, E., and Spohn, C. L. (1967). Cooperative research in programed learning: Taped interval discrimination drills. *Journal of Research in Music Education, 15*(3), 210–214.

Taylor, J. A., and Parrish, J. W. (1978). A national survey on the use of and attitudes toward programed instruction and computers in public school and college music education. *Journal of Computer-Based Instruction, 5*(1–2), 11–21.

The 1989–1990 videodisc compendium. (1989) St. Paul: Emerging Technologies.

Thostenson, M. S. (1978). Project in aural interval identification, Phase one. *Proceedings of the annual meeting of the Association for the Development of Computer-Based Instructional Systems,* Dallas: (ERIC Document Reproduction Service No. ED 160 087)

Todd, R. E., Boltz, M., and Jones, M. R. (1989). The MIDILAB music research system. *Psychomusicology, 8*(2), 83–96.

Turrietta, A. A., and Turrietta, C. R. (1983). Computer music applications in education: The Soundchaser computer music system. *Proceedings of the twenty-first annual convention proceedings. Frontiers in Educational Computing* (pp. 346–349). Portland.

Unsworth, A. E. (1970). A comparison of programed and teacher oriented instruction in teaching diatonic modes. Unpublished doctoral dissertation, Arizona State University, Tempe.

Upitis, R. (1989). The craft of composition: Helping children create music with computer tools. *Psychomusicology, 8*(2), 151–162.

Vaughn, A. C. (1978). *A study of the contrast between computer assisted instruction and the traditional teacher/learner method of instruction in basic musicianship.* Unpublished doctoral dissertation, Oregon State University, Corvallis.

Wagner, M. J. (1975). Brainwaves and biofeedback: A brief history, implications for music research. *Journal of Music Therapy, 12*(2), 46–58.

Warren, J. (1989). *Micro^Notes music theory. St. Louis: TeAchnology.*

Watanabe, N. T. (1981). Computer-assisted music instruction utilizing compatible audio hardware in computer-assisted aural drill. Unpublished doctoral dissertation, University of Illinois, Urbana.

Waters, W. J. (1989). *Music and the personal computer: An annotated bibliography.* New York: Greenwood Press.

Webster, P. (1989). Composition software and issues surrounding its use in research settings with children. *Psychomusicology, 8*(2), 163–169.

Weeks, D. G. (1987). The effectiveness of using computer-assisted instruction with beginning trumpet students. Unpublished doctoral dissertation, Boston University, Boston

Whiston, S. K. (1986). The development of melodic concepts in elementary school age children using computer-assisted instruction as a supplemental tool. Unpublished doctoral dissertation, Ohio State University, Columbus.

Williams, D. B. (1989a). The office of research in arts technology. *Wheels of the mind, 5*(1), 35–42.

Williams, D. B. (1989b). *Toney* [Computer program]. Normal: Office Research in Arts Technology, Illinois State University, Normal.

Williams, D. B., and Bowers, D. R. (1986). *Designing computer-based instruction for music and the arts.* Bellevue: Temporal Acuity Press.

Williams, D. B., and Hoskin, R. K. (1974). *The SWRL audio laboratory system (ALS): An integrated configuration for psychomusicology research.* Los Alamitos: (ERIC Document Reproduction Service No. ED 166 118)

Williams, D. B., and Shrader, D. L. (1980). *The development of a microcomputer-based music instruction lab.* Paper presented at the NCCBMI/ADCIS National Conference, Arlington, VA.

Williams, E. C. (1978). The use of videotape in the solution of selected problems in oboe playing: A field study. Unpublished doctoral dissertation, University of Illinois, Urbana.

Wilson, G. (1970). The development and evaluation of a self-instructional audio-tutorial system for use in teaching basic musical concepts and skills to college students. Unpublished doctoral dissertation, University of Southern California, Los Angeles.

Wilson, M. L. P. (1981). The development of CAI programs for teaching music fundamentals to undergraduate elementary education music methods classes. Unpublished doctoral dissertation, Louisiana State University and Agricultural and Mechanical College, Baton Rouge.

Wittlich, G. E. (1980). Development in computer based music instruction and research at Indiana University. *Journal of Computer-Based Instruction, 6*(3), 62–71.

Wittlich, G. E., Schaffer, J. W., and Babb, L. R. (1986). *Microcomputers and music.* Englewood-Cliffs: Prentice-Hall.

Woelflin, L. E. (1961). An experimental study on the teaching of clarinet fingerings with teaching machines. Unpublished doctoral dissertation, Southern Illinois University, Carbondale.

Zalampas, M. S. (1973). Techniques for the planning, production and use of 35mm slides and cassette tapes in a modified autotutorial method as applied to teaching selected music fundamentals and skills to prospective elementary classroom teachers. Unpublished doctoral dissertation, University of Kentucky, Lexington.

·33·

METHODOLOGIES IN MUSIC EDUCATION

Peter Costanza

OHIO STATE UNIVERSITY

Timothy Russell

NAPLES PHILHARMONIC CENTER FOR THE ARTS

In music education, ways of doing things have variously been called techniques, methods, curricula, and methodologies. The assumption that they all have the same meaning is erroneous. Yet even though these terms are employed with regularity by professionals, they are not clearly defined. The following definitions, as applied to teaching and learning, define the terms as they will be used in this chapter:

Technique: a teaching activity or strategy that is used to achieve an objective

Method: "a procedure or process for obtaining an objective, as a systematic plan followed in presenting material for instruction" *(Webster's Seventh New Collegiate Dictionary,* 1963, p. 533)

Curriculum: a plan or course of study that describes what is to be taught and in what order and that may or may not include information regarding how it is to be taught

Methodology: a body of techniques, methods, and curricula that is based on a philosophical system and a foundation of research

The activities, materials, and procedures used to teach music may be based on (1) suggestions in a set of music books (perhaps the most common of occurrences), (2) an original approach to teaching music (a less common occurrence), or (3) what is known about the art and science of music, the nature of the learner, the learning environment, and the effectiveness of the experiences (the rarest of occurrences).

Music education uses the activities of singing, playing, moving to, listening to, and creating music. These activities may employ techniques that could evolve into a method, which may achieve the status of a curriculum, and, with the appropriate philosophical base and foundation of research, may ultimately result in a methodology. Thus, these terms may be considered hierarchical. They may also be considered cyclical in that new techniques, methods, and curricula may come from the research in a methodology.

Although music educators have techniques, methods, and curricula that are effective for them, they are constantly in search of the perfect methodology. Workshops abound in the latest technique and/or method of teaching music. The pitfall is when music educators incorporate into their teaching a new technique or method without ever considering "why" it is done or to be done. The ultimate danger is, as Bennett (1986) concludes, that technique or method becomes authority.

In the field of music, as with most educational disciplines, curricula and methodologies are often related and interdependent. In the broadest terms, they can be divided into those in which teacher-learner contact is a prerequisite (e.g., classroom instruction; applied music lessons) and those in which teacher-learner contact is optional (e.g., programed/computer-assisted instruction).

There is an extensive tradition of teaching techniques and methods that have been transmitted historically from one generation of teachers to the next, not always codified into an actual methodology. In the field of teacher training, there is speculation as to whether such strategies are systematically taught at the university level, or merely "caught," as young teachers often end up teaching just as they were taught. New teachers often fail to explore the best possible teaching techniques, methods, curricula, and methodologies.

This chapter is restricted to an exploration of selected research applications in the following areas: general music education (including Dalcroze, Orff, Kodály, Gordon, and general music series textbooks), choral music education, instrumental music education (including instrumental methods books, string music education, and Suzuki), and trends in music education methodologies (modeling and imitation, individualized instruction, the discovery method, and comprehensive musicianship).

GENERAL MUSIC EDUCATION

The majority of the studies in general music education have compared the effects of one technique or method with those of another in the teaching and learning of music or compared a defined technique or method with a "traditional" method. This latter treatment (the "traditional method") is not well defined and typically uses materials that have been employed by a particular individual, within a particular course, or within a particular music series.

There have been few studies that have attempted to establish the effectiveness of a well-defined methodology (e.g., Dalcroze, Orff, Kodály). These studies tend to examine one aspect or several aspects of the methodology and rarely deal with the methodology in its entirety. Studies that have attempted to compare the effectiveness of two methodologies are rare indeed.

The methodologies in general music education that are present in the classroom today can be traced to a number of individuals whose philosophy of music in the education of children incorporated the nature of music, the learner, and a particular approach to instruction. Among these individuals were Johann Pestalozzi, who contributed to the ideas of sequence, repetition, and rote; Lowell Mason, who advocated the Pestalozzian principles and their importance in the education of the child; and John Dewey, who advocated the discovery method for the solving of problems. Methodologies in use in the general musical education of children incorporate many of the principles of Pestalozzi, Mason, and Dewey, but have evolved into specific applications as advocated by such individuals as Emile Jaques-Dalcroze, Carl Orff, and Zoltan Kodály.

Emile Jaques-Dalcroze Dalcroze had Pestalozzian influences in his musical training, and his methodology reflects these influences. It began as an attempt to improve hearing in a sight-singing class by incorporating movement and evolved into the use of body movement to develop rhythmic concepts associated with pulse, meter, and rhythm (Landis and Carder, 1972).

Several comparisons of Dalcroze and traditional approaches have been examined. Crumpler (1983) examined the melodic musical growth of children in the first grade by a comparison of the Dalcroze methodology and musical activities as found in the music books of Silver Burdett Publishers (1974). Four groups of first-grade children were exposed to

an experimental treatment: Two control groups taught using the Silver Burdett series and two experimental groups using the Silver Burdett series and Dalcroze eurythmics. A dependent measure of the ability to identify the direction of groups of two and five tones was administered as a pre- and posttest. Crumpler found no significance in the change in achievement scores of the control group, but she did find a significant increase in achievement in the Dalcroze/Silver Burdett series students (p < .0001).

The rhythmic movement and improvisation achievement of kindergarten students was examined by Joseph (1983). Contrasting the effects of three types of musical instruction (informal instruction, Dalcroze with improvisation activities, and Dalcroze excluding improvisation activities), Joseph measured randomly selected subjects from each group on their ability to recognize and respond to familiar rhythm patterns and on their ability to use rhythm patterns while performing on a set of bells. Joseph concluded that the Dalcroze methodology should be considered for inclusion in early childhood education.

Carl Orff The methodology developed by Carl Orff implements the activities of singing, saying, dancing, and playing (Shamrock, 1986). These behaviors are considered central to the methodology because Orff Schulwerk teachers believe they are a natural part of the behavior of children. Active music making begins with rhythm and is based on speech patterns. The techniques used are exploration, imitation, improvisation, and creation. Children must have experiences in exploration and imitation before any improvisation and creation take place.

Olson (1964) compared the effects on melodic sensitivity of Orff techniques and various techniques commonly used in elementary music classrooms. Groups matched on IQ, musicality, melodic memory, attitude, experiences, and socioeconomic status were provided instruction in both approaches. Although the difference in gain scores between groups was not significant, both groups did improve significantly.

A comparison of musical achievement and attitude of students taking part in Orff-inspired instruction and those in a traditional approach is reported by Siemens (1967, 1969). Her posttest-only design compared students who had participated in the Orff approach for at least 1 year (some as long as 3 years) and students who had received "traditional" music instruction in general music. Students who participated in the Orff program scored significantly higher in interest and attitude and reported greater enjoyment of part singing and rhythm activities. Munsen (1986) used an Orff approach to examine the ability of students to improvise melodically and rhythmically. She concluded that students' abilities to improvise peaked at about grade 3 and that their attitudes became increasingly negative from grades 1 through 5.

Zoltan Kodály Zoltan Kodály developed a methodology primarily to teach choral musicianship to the children of

Hungary (Landis and Carder, 1972). Using the folk music of his own country, Kodály devised a methodology that stresses the teaching of music-reading and -writing skills and includes walking, running, and marching movements to accompany the singing activities.

Studies that have compared the Kodály methodology and other approaches include those by McDaniel (1974) and Palmer (1974). McDaniel (1974) compared the Kodály methodology, as presented in the *Threshold to Music* materials (Richards, 1966), and musical activities represented in the *Making Music Your Own* music books (Landeck et al., 1968). Results showed no significant differences between the groups in posttest or mean change scores, although the non-Kodály group did have higher mean improvement scores.

Palmer (1974) investigated the effects on rhythm reading of Kodály (as presented in the *Threshold to Music* books), a learning sequence by Gordon (1971; as presented in *The Psychology of Music Teaching),* and a version of a traditional approach that did not include instruction in rhythm reading. Students in two schools were randomly assigned to either the Kodály or the Gordon approach, and students in a third school received the traditional instruction, minus rhythm-reading activities. Palmer, using the *Musical Aptitude Profile* as a dependent measure, reported no significant difference between the Kodály and Gordon approaches, although a significant difference was found between the Kodály and Gordon approach groups and the traditional approach group. The mean improvement of the group taught using the Gordon approach was slightly higher than that of the group taught by the Kodály approach. Darazs (1966) utilized the Kodály method with high school students and found that music reading increased for students in a select group.

Gordon Learning Theory One of the recent developments in the teaching and learning of music is the learning theory of Edwin E. Gordon (1989a). This theory explains how persons gain knowledge, comprehension, or mastery when they study music. Gordon (1989b) writes:

"Music learning theory includes three categories of music learning sequence. They are 1) skill learning sequence, 2) tonal content learning sequence, which includes tonal pattern learning sequence, and 3) rhythm content learning sequence, which includes rhythm pattern learning sequence" (p. 88).

These music-learning sequences are divided into two general types: discrimination and inference. When the music-learning sequences are incorporated into their teaching, students learn not only what to learn but how to learn.

Gordon (1986, 1987) has incorporated the music-learning theory and sequences into a curriculum for both general music education and instrumental music education. Shuler (1986) investigated the effects of Gordon's music-learning sequence on music achievement, with the intent of improving music pedagogy. He found that no conclusions could be drawn regarding the effects of learning sequence activities

on music performance achievement but that some teachers may be more effective when they incorporate learning sequence activities into their instructional procedures. Stockton (1983) investigated the use of rhythm-learning sequence activities with older (nonmusic major college) students. His experimental group received a rote performance method derived from the Gordon rhythm-learning sequence, and the control group received a lecture-demonstration approach incorporating notational skills without performance. Stockton concluded that the rhythm-learning sequence was superior to the reading and listening approach presented in the lecture-demonstration. In the previously cited study, Palmer (1974) found no significant difference between groups (cf. p. 7).

The Music Learning Theory, as presented in the *Jump Right In* series for general music and instrumental music, is a curriculum that incorporates techniques and methods of sequencing. A foundation of research to verify the effectiveness of this curriculum has yet to be established.

General Music Series Textbooks Whereas music books have been used in the teaching of music to elementary and secondary school children in the United States for many years, several series of music textbooks published since 1970 differ from their predecessors. Particular note should be made of the general music series textbooks published by the Silver Burdett Publishers and by Holt, Rinehart, and Winston.

Reimer (1989) calls the series of textbooks entitled *Silver Burdett Music* (Crook et al., 1978) "my own attempt to build a comprehensive curriculum for general music classes in grades 1-8" (p. 151). The philosophy upon which the series is based is that, as Reimer writes, "music education is valuable because the art of music is valuable" (p. 148). The series is unique in that competency tests were developed to accompany the curricular materials (Colwell, 1979). Boyle and Radocy (1987) describe the tests as "very comprehensive, especially regarding perception of melody, rhythm, timbre, texture, form, tonality, and dynamics" (p. 168).

The *Silver Burdett Music* series is a curriculum in that there is a plan of study that describes what is to be taught and includes methods and techniques for achieving the objectives. It approaches a methodology in that it is a body of techniques and methods, and a curriculum that is based on a philosophical system. All that remains is for a foundation of research to verify the effectiveness of the curriculum.

The general music series textbooks *Holt Music* are based on the Generative Theory of Music Learning (Boardman, 1988a, 1988b). The basic assumptions of this theory are that (1) the basic unit is a system, of which the whole is greater than the parts, (2) symbols and symbol systems not only serve to represent our view of reality, but mold that view, and (3) the purpose of knowledge is generative—to make possible the expansion of not just one's personal grasp of existing information but the total body of possible knowledge (p. 5). This theory (philosophical system), based on the writings of Jerome Bruner, Howard Gardner, Susanne Langer, Charles Morris, and Nelson Goodman, has been incorporated into the techniques and methods as presented in the music series *Holt Music*. Until a foundation of research that verifies the effectiveness of the Holt series has been established, the *Holt Music* general music series textbooks can be called a curriculum, but not yet a methodology.

Summary

Findings from these studies in general music education are variable, at best. The studies that have compared various techniques or methods with each other or with a "traditional method" have found no differences between experimental and control groups, but have reported increases (some significant, some not) in gain scores for the experimental groups. The methodologies of Orff, Kodály, and Dalcroze have been shown to be effective in increasing musical learning. The effectiveness of one methodology over any other has not been demonstrated as controlled comparisons of methodologies have not yet appeared in the literature. The theories and philosophies of Gordon, Reimer, and Boardman, as presented in their music books, are best designated as curricula that approach methodology. They lack the foundation of research that is essential to a methodology.

In the studies reported, it appears that those techniques, methods, curricula, and methodologies that are most effective and bring about increased learning are those that the teacher knows best. The teacher's knowledge of what is to be taught and confidence about how it is being taught enhance the musical learning of students.

CHORAL MUSIC EDUCATION

An examination of the research in choral music education does little to shed light on the techniques, methods, curricula, or methodologies employed. Topics in the journal literature discuss choral compositions, analyses of compositions, stylistic characteristics, choral composers, and various aspects of literature, including its appropriateness and difficulty. The research that is reported tends to examine techniques to improve choral singing (including the teaching of music reading), aspects of the choral rehearsal, and techniques that the choral conductor uses to improve choral singing (including those that assist the choral conductor in detecting performance discrepancies).

If there is any area of choral music education that will produce intense debate, it is whether students should learn the music by sight-reading or through rote learning. Sight-reading may remain one of the weakest components in choral programs. Choral music education has followed the patterns of rote teaching established in the teaching of songs. Weyland (1955) and Hales (1961) have reported that rote learning is the predominant approach in the teaching of choral music. Daniels (1986) notes that the occasional use of rote procedures to teach music improved the ability to sight-read music. Shehan (1987) showed that a combination of rote and

note presentations provided the best performance and retention of rhythm patterns among younger students.

It is surprising that sight singing or sight-reading remains one of the weakest components in the teaching of choral music in that it is one of the few areas in choral music education that has specific methods. These include movable *do,* fixed *do,* numbers and letter names, shape notes, and hand signals. Each of these will be discussed briefly, with the relevant research.

Movable *do* is the most common method used in the teaching of sight singing in the United States. With its roots in the system of Guido d'Arrezo (ca 955–1050), its primary advantage is in its tonal relationships. There are several variations on the movable *do* method, including the English or Lancashire method (advocated by John Curwen [1816–1880]), which disregarded *do* and *re* and used letter names instead of syllables (Zinar, 1983). Rainbow (1979) notes that this was a supplemental device meant to lead to notation on the staff, not replace it. Among those who have been advocates of the movable *do* method include Johann Pestalozzi, Carl Orff, Zoltan Kodály, and Fred Waring. Bonham (1977) has suggested that movable *do* is unsuitable to atonal music. Winnick (1987) disagrees and is a strong advocate of the method.

Fixed *do,* also known as the conservatory French fixed *doh,* or stationary *do,* has its roots in the European conservatories. Its advantages are that it is not affected by modulations and letter names and keys are not used. The traditional fixed *do* method does not distinguish between natural and chromatic pitches, so that the pitches C and C♯ are both called *do.* One variation of fixed *do* does include chromatic names for the flats and sharps. Advocates of fixed *do* include Emile Jaques-Dalcroze, Robert Shaw, and Robert Page.

Other techniques for the teaching of sight singing include the intervallic method, in which students are presented with the different intervals as found in popular melodies, and practice and drill is provided until the intervals are learned. Shape notes, a distinctively American method in use in the southern United States, substitutes shapes for notes and has been shown to be an effective approach to sight singing (Kyme, 1960). The use of hand signals, as advocated by Kodály, is another popular method to teach sight singing, although this is a predominantly diatonic method.

Summary

Hylton (1983) concluded from his survey of the research in choral methods that the scope of the research was narrow and fragmented. Stockton (1983) found that there are no universally accepted methods of choral teaching. The adaptations are diverse and reflect the skills and interests of the teachers. Corbin (1982) reported that the research in choral rehearsal techniques was extremely limited and was primarily based on subjective opinions, and that no one technique was better than any other. Unfortunately, little has changed since Gonzo (1973) reported that the structure of the choral curriculum has not changed in 60 years.

INSTRUMENTAL MUSIC EDUCATION

There exist in the field of music education a plethora of method books. With the exception of those traditions passed on from one generation of teachers to another, the oldest systematic materials in music education were singing books and instrumental instruction books, such as *The Modern Musick-Master,* or *The Universal Musician,* published in 1791. Many of these are curricula; others constitute genuine methodologies (e.g., Suzuki).

This section presents selected research applications related to instrumental methods books; string music education; the Suzuki methodology; developments in the areas of modeling and imitation; individualized instruction (including programed instruction and computer-assisted instruction); the discovery method; and comprehensive musicianship.

Instrumental Methods Books From the time of England's "Maidstone Movement" to the present, there has been an interest in teaching instrumental music to large numbers of students. Countless methods and method books have been developed to teach piano, as well as stringed, wind, and percussion instruments, to individuals and groups. Even though this source of teacher/student material is the largest in music education, there is, unfortunately, very little research regarding its validity or effectiveness.

Texter (1975) offered a comparative analysis of selected instrumental music books written between 1910 and 1972. She concludes that, with few exceptions, pedagogical approaches consistent with current knowledge of the music teaching-learning process are not present in contemporary instrumental method books used in music education.

Sampson (1968) investigated deficiencies in beginning band method books. He concluded that, in many respects, a majority of beginning band method books do not measure up to the aims and expectations of instrumental teachers and that little systematic study of band method books is occurring.

Kress (1981) compared *The Individualized Instructor* (Froseth 1976), which applied Piaget's theory of conservation to the conservation of music concepts, to the *First Division Band Method* (Weber, 1968), which was found to encourage conservation only indirectly. The researcher found no significant difference between the conservation of musical concepts when compared to the students' musical achievement and musical performance.

String Music Education Nelson (1983) reviewed the research findings in the teaching of strings and string performance. He notes that "string teaching and performance are among the least researched areas of music education" (p. 39). His overview of this subfield of instrumental music education includes two sections: "Suzuki Studies" and "Techniques of String Instruction."

Gillespie (1991) presents results from the research regarding techniques and methods of strings instruction that string teachers should consider. Among his implications are the following:

1. Teacher modeling with student imitation, accompanied by a minimum of verbal description, may be the best mode of instruction for very young students.
2. Starting violin students in third position rather than first position does not significantly increase students' intonational accuracy or rhythmic skills.
3. Developing students' intonational accuracy with or without finger placement markers is directly related to the overall string competence of the teacher.
4. Teachers must be careful to diagnose and train their students to correct motions in string playing that may impair intonational accuracy.
5. Delaying note-reading training does not impair the technical progress of beginning students' performance development and may help to facilitate it.
6. Suzuki pedagogy and materials may be successfully adapted for beginning heterogeneous class string teaching.

This list includes results from those research studies that could be considered to deal with techniques and methods of string music teaching. Research in curricula has not been reported in the literature, and where curricula do exist (e.g., Rolland), their effectiveness has not been established. However, in string music education, there is a methodology that meets all of the guidelines of the definition. That methodology is the one set forth by Shinichi Suzuki.

The Suzuki Methodology The Suzuki methodology is based on an interplay of the following groups of pedagogical tenets: the child's exposure to music at an early age; listening, imitation, tonalization, and modeling; sound before signs and rote learning; sequential materials; review, repetition, and mastery learning; and parental involvement (Suzuki, 1969). In specifically considering Suzuki's principles in a research context, one must distinguish between those that are curricular and those that are methodological. The Suzuki books alone are a curriculum. Teachers who merely utilize the sequentially presented repertoire pieces and do not make use of the remaining principles clearly cannot be considered to be using the Suzuki methodology.

Nelson notes that Project Super (1966–1968) evaluated the feasibility and potential effectiveness of Suzuki instruction administered by North American teachers (Wensel, 1970). An evaluation of the project revealed that (1) the Suzuki methodology could be adapted to the social and educational systems of the United States, (2) string teachers could manage the Suzuki approach with minimal training under Dr. Suzuki, and (3) the approach could be used in a variety of school systems and communities of different socioeconomic levels (Nelson, 1983, pp. 40–41).

Several projects have been undertaken to study the Suzuki methodology as well as the adaptation of Suzuki to other areas of instrumental music education. Sperti (1970) and Blaine (1976) conducted studies that applied the Suzuki principles to wind instrumental music classes. Sperti (1970) adapted three concepts of the Suzuki methodology (use of rote teaching, parental involvement in the child's home study, and implementation of a comprehensive listening program) to clarinet instruction and compared their effectiveness to that of widely accepted practices in teaching the clarinet. Achievement of the subjects in the Suzuki group was significantly superior to that of the control group in all categories of performance.

Blaine (1976) adapted the Suzuki-Kendall methodology to the teaching of trumpets and trombones, comparing it to what he called a traditional methodology. Results of the data analysis indicated that the Suzuki group achieved higher performance scores on the Whybrew *Performance Evaluation Scale* (subjective elements of musicality such as breath and control of tone and the subdivisions of technique, articulation, fingering dexterity), whereas the control group performed higher on the *Watkins-Farnum Scale* (sight-reading ability).

Although the Suzuki methodology was designed as an individual approach, Brunson (1969) investigated its application in a fourth-grade heterogeneous string class. The investigator judged the program a success on the basis of acceptable student performance, no dropouts, and positive student feedback.

Adaptations of the Suzuki methodology to the teaching of piano and other instruments have been proposed, although reports of these adaptations have not yet appeared in the research literature. Clearly, the teaching of instrumental music as presented by Shinichi Suzuki can be called a methodology. It has a philosophical base that is clearly articulated, and research studies that demonstrate its effectiveness.

TRENDS IN MUSIC EDUCATION METHODOLOGIES

As the profession of music education has expanded since the decade of the 1960s, research activities and productivity have also expanded. Much of this research has explored the techniques, methods, curricula, and methodologies in music teaching and learning. Some of this research has explored applications of techniques and methods of instruction from other areas of research associated with music education, including education and psychology. Among the research results that hold promise for application and/or adaptation to music education are those relating to the areas of modeling and imitation, individualized instruction, and the discovery method. These, as well as comprehensive musicianship, a methodology that has existed for some time in music teaching and learning, will be discussed and relevant research presented.

Modeling and Imitation Research studies have investigated the use of modeling and/or imitation in instrumental music education. One study examined students in two groups that were taught using the same approach, with the exception that one of the groups listened to recorded models of the music being studied. As reported by Duerkson (1972), a panel of experts judged the performance of the group that had been prepared with the aid of recorded models superior in expression, accuracy, intonation, and balance to the group prepared without the aid of recorded models. Sang (1987) examined the relationship between instrumental students' performance behavior and teachers' modeling skills, and concluded that a teacher's ability to model and the frequency of demonstrations in rehearsals have an effect on student performance level. Delzell (1989) found that the incorporation of models/discriminator foils and modeling/imitation in the classroom is effective in developing the rhythmic and melodic musical discrimination skills of beginning instrumentalists.

Research in the use of recorded models in instrumentalists' home practice has produced a variety of findings. Zurcher (1972) found that beginning brass players who used cassette-recorded models and instructions had fewer pitch and rhythm errors and developed pitch-matching skills better than those who followed traditional practice methods. Yet in contrast to these results, Anderson (1981) found that there was no significant difference in regard to pitch reading, rhythm reading, tempo accuracy, and intonational accuracy between sixth-grade clarinetists who had used tape-recorded aural models and those who had not.

Modeling and its effects on advanced wind players' musical performances have been examined in two more recent studies. Rosenthal (1984) studied the effects of four modeling conditions—guided model (verbal and aural), model only (aural), guide only (verbal explanations), and practice only—on the musical performance of advanced instrumentalists. Subjects in the "model only" group scored significantly higher than all other groups. Second in effectiveness was the guided model group, with the subjects scoring significantly higher than subjects in the guide only and practice only groups. A similar study by Rosenthal, Wilson, Evans, and Greenwalt (1988) examined five practice conditions (modeling, singing, silent analysis, free practice, and control-practice of an unrelated musical composition) and their relationship to the performance accuracy of advanced instrumentalists. Modeling and practice were most effective, while singing and silent analysis were generally no more effective than sight-reading.

Individualized Instruction Individualized instruction may take the form of programed instruction (PI) or computer-based instruction (CBI)/computer-assisted instruction (CAI). Programed instruction may be used to replace a particular area of teacher instruction or to supplement conventional teacher and classroom instruction. Results from these studies show no significant differences between groups and that individualized instruction is an effective technique.

Shaw (1971) tested the effects of programed learning on the development of musical psychomotor skills (snare drum technique) and reported that the method developed for his study did not efficiently teach the elements of snare drum technique. Higgins (1981) investigated the feasibility of teaching beginning applied clarinet with a microcomputer.

The attitudes of the students were positive toward the program, but the lack of feedback was viewed as a drawback.

Woelflin (1961) investigated the use of a teaching machine program to teach clarinet fingerings. There were three groups in the experiment: the control group, which received all of the instruction from the teacher, and two experimental groups, which used the teaching machine. Both experimental groups had a clarinet to hold and finger while using the teaching machine, but only one group had a mouthpiece to play. All three groups received classroom instruction about embouchure and breath support. Results indicated that the three groups made equal gains in knowledge of fingerings. In a similar study, Drushler (1972) compared the use of classroom instruction and programed instruction in the teaching of fingerings and pitch notation to beginning instrumentalists. The data showed that the scores for students in the programed instruction group exceeded those of the classroom instruction group, but the differences were not significant. Puopolo (1971) found that students who used self-instructional materials, printed lesson material, and cassette tape recordings of the required lesson materials for the week scored significantly higher on the *Watkins-Farnum Performance* Scale than did students who practiced the same material for the same amount of time without using the tape-recorded materials.

Individualized instruction within an instrumental music classroom has been investigated by McCarthy (1974, 1980). In both studies a heterogeneous band class approach was compared to an individualized instructional program in which students practiced exercises on their own. The instructor provided only individual help or permission to proceed to new material. Results from the 1974 study indicated that students at the extreme ends of intelligence, musical aptitude, and personal adjustment (those with high or low levels) received the greater benefit, in terms of performance achievement, from the individualized instruction program. Findings from the 1980 study indicated that individualized instruction resulted in higher performance test scores for students with above-average academic reading skills.

Research indicates that it is logical and practical for the instrumental music educator to use technology to further the teaching and learning of music. If used properly, "instructional technology seems to lead to more effective instruction in instrumental music" (Duerkson, 1972, p. 21). Abeles, Hoffer, and Klotman (1984) write:

> The question of the ability of PI and CBI to provide effective instruction seems to have been answered. Literally hundreds of studies comparing PI and CBI materials with "traditional approaches" have been conducted. . . . They indicate, in general, that automated instructional materials are equally as effective as teacher-presented instruction. (p. 224)

The Discovery Method The discovery method actively involves students in the learning process. A teacher utilizing the discovery method does not provide all the answers and directions for the student, but guides the student through leading questions and clues to discover the correct answers.

D'Aurelio (1973), investigating the effects of a teacher-dominated strategy and a teacher-guided strategy (discovery method) on the abilities of beginning instrumental music students to detect and correct pitch and rhythm errors, found no significant differences between the two strategies. However, the teacher-guided group obtained higher scores on pitch and rhythm error detection than the teacher-dominated group.

Groeling (1977) investigated the effects of the discovery approach on beginning instrumentalists. An experimental group explored sounds, beginning with nonmusical sound sources and later writing short sound compositions, explored the sounds of real instruments by family groupings, and then chose one instrument on which to specialize. Groeling found that while the experimental and control groups were equal in playing skill and musical comprehension, students in the experimental group maintained a high level of enthusiasm during the duration of the experiment (one academic year), whereas students in the control group lost interest in the lessons after 3 months, and all the students in the experimental group completed the course of instruction, while 30 percent of the control group dropped out.

Reimer (1989) writes, "Artistic decisions are those which are made to carry forward the process of exploring and discovering the expressive potentials of some materials" (p. 64). Students who have the opportunity to make artistic decisions develop a deeper sense of musical understanding and aesthetic awareness. A philosophical basis has been established for discovery learning as a methodology. All that remains is a foundation of research to verify its effectiveness.

Comprehensive Musicianship Comprehensive musicianship methodology differs from the strictly performance-oriented approach in that music concepts such as melody, harmony, style, rhythm, form, texture, and the historical context of music are studied in addition to the development of performance skills. Parker (1974) compared two methods of band instruction at the middle school level. Students in the comprehensive program received full band instruction 50 percent of the time and related musical activities (listening sessions, class electronic piano lessons, music theory lessons, fundamentals of popular music classes, and music and related area) the remaining 50 percent of the time. Students in the performance-oriented program received full band instruction 75 percent of the time, with the remaining 25 percent spent in small/large performance ensembles. Results indicated that the performance-oriented group did not perform significantly better or evaluate their experience significantly differently than students in the comprehensive program.

Comprehensive musicianship concepts were studied by Garofalo and Whaley (1979). Two groups studied the same compositions, but one group followed traditional rehearsal procedures, while the other followed a comprehensive music program developed by Garofalo. Students taught with this methodology acquired conceptual knowledge, aural skills, and performance proficiency to a significantly greater degree than students taught with the traditional approach. Whitener (1983) also compared a comprehensive music methodology to the traditional performance-oriented approach. Findings indicated that members of both groups performed equally well and, in the areas of interval, major-minor mode, and auditory-visual discrimination skills, those students who were taught through the comprehensive music methodology scored significantly higher than those students who were taught through the traditional performance-oriented approach.

Findings from these studies would support the inclusion of the comprehensive musicianship methodology in the music curriculum. Music educators tend to believe that because of the time necessary for a methodology such as this, the development of their students' performance skills would be hindered. Results from the aforementioned studies would refute this belief. One of the main goals of a music education program is to develop musical literacy. Comprehensive musicianship appears to be one way of achieving that goal.

Conclusions

There are many factors inherent in the success of any music education program. Some of these include the techniques, methods, curricula, and methodologies employed by the teacher; the students' backgrounds, previous musical experiences, and motivations; and the instructional setting. This chapter has presented selected research findings and applications of the techniques, methods, curricula, and methodologies in selected areas of music education teaching and learning.

There has been a good deal of research regarding the techniques, methods, and curricula used in the field of music education; however, because of the absence of a philosophical basis and a foundation of research for many of these techniques, methods, and curricula, there have not been many exemplary studies dealing with music education methodologies. Following are conclusions that are based on results of those research studies:

1. Findings from those research studies in general music education are variable, at best. Few differences have been reported in those studies that have compared various techniques or methods with each other or with a "traditional method." The effectiveness of one methodology over any other has not been demonstrated as controlled comparisons of methodologies have not yet appeared in the literature. The methodologies of Orff, Kodály, and Dalcroze have been shown to be effective in increasing musical learning. The theories and philosophies of Gordon (in his learning theory), Reimer (in the *Silver Burdett Music* series), and Boardman (in the *Holt Music* series), because they lack the conclusive research findings essential to demonstrate their effectiveness, are best designated as curricula that approach methodology.
2. Research studies in choral music education have focused on selected aspects of techniques to improve choral singing (including the teaching of music reading), aspects of the choral rehearsal, and techniques that the choral conductor uses to improve choral singing (including those that assist the choral conductor in detecting performance discrepancies). The research that has been reported is so narrow in scope as to render unchanged the choral curriculum. A philosophical base and a foundation of research for methodologies in choral music education do not exist at the present time.
3. Research in instrumental music education has shown that there are very few conclusive findings regarding the validity or effectiveness of instrumental methods books, the largest source of teacher/student material in music education. The research in string music education has been limited to selected aspects of string teaching techniques and methods. The teaching of instrumental music as presented by Shinichi Suzuki, because it has a philosophical base that is clearly articulated, and research studies that demonstrate its effectiveness, can be called a methodology.
4. Comprehensive musicianship can also be considered a methodology and clearly should be incorporated into music education teaching and learning. Modeling and imitation, individualized instruction, and the discovery method hold high promise as methodologies. A foundation of research should bring that promise to realization.
5. Although much has been learned in recent years about the teaching/learning process, it would appear that, in the research literature in music education regarding methodologies, no new conclusions have been reached as profound as the one highlighted in the famed *First Grade Reading Studies*. Stauffer (1967) writes that, while these studies were conducted in different localities across the country, were directed by individuals with varying training, and explored many different approaches to the teaching of reading, "in almost every instance the experimental populations made significantly greater gains than the control populations" (p. v). Those techniques, methods, curricula, and methodologies that are most effective and bring about increased learning are those that the teacher knows best. Seemingly, in music education the teacher's knowledge of what is to be taught, and confidence about how it is to be taught, enhance the musical learning of students.

As researchers in music education formulate and shape their questions, hypotheses, and designs, it is hoped that they will find ways to investigate the effectiveness of the techniques, methods, curricula, and methodologies in music education; that they will examine the relationships and interactions between and among the techniques, methods, curricula, and methodologies and the numerous teacher, learner, and setting variables; and that their investigations will address the perspectives of those teaching, as well as those being taught, in relationship to both achievement and attitude. Most importantly, study of these variables should be conducted in a longitudinal manner. The ongoing challenge is still the identification and utilization of effective research-based methodologies.

References

Abeles, H., Hoffer, C., and Klotman, R. (1984). *Foundations of music education*. New York: Schirmer Books.

Anderson, J. (1981). Effects of tape-recorded aural models on sight-reading and performance skills. *Journal of Research in Music Education, 29*(1), 23–30.

Bennett, P. (1986). When "method" becomes authority. *Music Educators' Journal, 72*(9), 38–40.

Blaine, R. (1986). Adaptation of the Suzuki-Kendall method to the teaching of a heterogeneous brass-wind instrumental class of trumpets and trombones. Unpublished doctoral dissertation, Catholic University of America, Washington.

Boardman, E. (1988a). The generative theory of musical learning, Part 1. *General Music Today, 2*(1), 4–5, 26–30.

Boardman, E. (1988b). The generative theory of musical learning, Part 2. *General Music Today, 2*(2), 3–6, 28–32.

Bonham, G. (1977). Australian music education-traditions of the enlightenment. *The Australian Journal of Music Education, 20,* 17–21.

Boyle, D., and Radocy, R. (1987). *Measurement and evaluation of musical experiences*. New York: Schirmer Books.

Bridges, D. (1982). Fixed and movable *doh* in historical perspective. *The Australian Journal of Music Education, 30,* 11–15.

Brunson, T. R. (1969). An adaptation of the Suzuki-Kendall violin method for heterogeneous stringed instrument classes. Unpublished doctoral dissertation, University of Arizona, Tempe.

Colwell, R. (1979). *Music competency tests*. Morristown: Silver Burdett.

Corbin, L. (1982). Vocal pedagogy in the choral rehearsal: The influence of selected concepts on choral tone quality, student understanding of the singing process and student attitudes toward choir participation. Unpublished doctoral dissertation, Ohio State University, Columbus.

Crook, E., Reimer, B., and Walker, D. (1978). *Silver Burdett Music*. Morristown: Silver Burdett Company.

Crumpler, S. E. (1983). The effect of Dalcroze eurythmics on the melodic growth of first grade students. Unpublished doctoral dissertation, University of Kansas, Lawrence.

D'Aurelio, G. C. (1973). An investigation of the effects of two teaching strategies on the development of skills in detecting and correcting pitch and rhythm errors by beginning instrumental music students. Unpublished doctoral dissertation, University of Wisconsin, Madison.

Daniels, R. D. (1986). Relationships among selected factors and the sight reading ability of high school mixed choirs. *Journal of Research in Music Education, 34*(4), 279–289.

Darazs, A. (1966). The Kodály method for choral training. *American Choral Review, 8*(3), 8–12.

Delzell, J. (1989). The effects of musical discrimination training in beginning instrumental music classes. *Journal of Research in Music Education, 37*(1), 21–31.

Dickey, M. R. (1982). A comparison of the effects of verbal instruction and nonverbal teacher-student modeling on instructional effectiveness in instrumental music ensembles. Unpublished doctoral dissertation, University of Michigan, Ann Arbor.

Drushler, P. (1972). A study comparing programmed instruction with conventional teaching of instrumental fingerings and music pitch notation for beginning students of clarinet, flute, and trumpet in a flexible scheduled curriculum. Unpublished doctoral dissertation, State University of New York, Buffalo.

Duerksen, G. (1972). *From research to the classroom no. 3: Teaching instrumental music*. Washington: Music Educators National Conference.

Froseth, J. (1976). *The individualized instructor*. Chicago: GIA Publications.

Garofalo, R. J. and Whaley, G. (1979). Comparison of the unit study and traditional approaches to teaching music through school band performance. *Journal of Research in Music Education, 27*(3), 137–142.

Gillespie, R. (1991). Research in string pedagogy for developing the playing skills of students in string classes. *Dialogue in Instrumental Music Education, 15*(1), 1–9.

Gordon, E. (1971). *The psychology of music teaching*. Englewood Cliffs: Prentice-Hall.

Gordon, E. (1986). *Jump Right In; The music curriculum*. Chicago: GIA Publications.

Gordon, E. (1987). *Jump Right In; The instrumental curriculum*. Chicago: GIA Publications.

Gordon, E. (1989a). *Learning sequences in music: Skills, content and patterns. A music learning theory*. Chicago: GIA Publications.

Gordon, E. (1989b). Music learning theory. *Proceedings of the Suncoast Music Education forum on creativity*. Tampa: University of South Florida.

Gonzo, C. (1973). Research in choral music education. *Bulletin of the Council for Research in Music Education, 35*(2), 1–9.

Green, D. R. (1973). An investigation of the effects of two modes of notating and structuring the rhythmic content of a beginning instrumental method book on the rhythmic reading ability of beginning instrumental students. Unpublished doctoral dissertation, University of Wisconsin, Madison.

Groeling, C. (1977). A comparison of two methods of teaching instrumental music to fourth grade beginners. *Bulletin of the Council for Research in Music Education, 51,* 41–44.

Hales, B. (1961). A study of music reading programs in high school choruses in the Rocky Mountain States. Unpublished doctoral dissertation, University of Oregon, Eugene.

Higgins, W. R. (1981). The feasibility of teaching beginning applied clarinet with the microcomputer. Unpublished doctoral dissertation, Pennsylvania State University, University Park.

Hylton, J. (1983). A survey of choral music education research: 1972–1981. *Bulletin of the Council for Research in Music Education, 76,* 1–29.

Jones, M. S. (1979). An investigation of the difficulty levels of selected tonal patterns as perceived aurally and performed vocally by high school students. Unpublished doctoral dissertation, University of Michigan, Ann Arbor.

Joseph, A. (1983). A Dalcroze eurhythmics approach to music learning in kindergarten through rhythmic movement, ear training, and improvisation. Unpublished doctoral dissertation, Carnegie-Mellon University, Pittsburgh.

Kress, H. (1981). An investigation of the effect upon musical achievement and musical performance of beginning band students exposed to method books reflecting Piaget's theory of conservation. Unpublished doctoral dissertation, University of Colorado, Boulder.

Kyme, G. (1960). An experiment in teaching children to read music with shape notes. *Journal of Research in Music Education, 8*(1), 3–9.

Lander, R. (1980). *The talent education school of Shinichi Suzuki: An analysis.* Hicksville: Exposition Press.

Landeck, B., Crook, E., and Youngberg, H. (1968). *Making music your own.* Morristown: Silver Burdett Company.

Landis, B., & Carder, P. (1972). *The eclectic curriculum in American music education: Contributions of Dalcroze, Kodály, and Orff.* Reston: Music Educators National Conference.

McCarthy, J. (1974). The effect of individualized instruction on the performance achievement of beginning instrumentalists. *Bulletin of the Council for Research in Music Education, 38,* 1–16.

McCarthy, J. (1980). Individualized instruction, student achievement, and dropout in an urban elementary instrumental music program. *Journal of Research in Music Education, 28*(1), 59–69.

McDaniel, M. (1974). A comparison of *Music Achievement Test* scores of fourth-grade students taught by two different methods - Kodály (Threshold to Music) and traditional (Making Music Your Own). Unpublished doctoral dissertation, Louisiana State University, Baton Rouge.

Major, J. (1982). The effect of subdivision activity on rhythmic performance skills in high school mixed choirs. *Journal of Research in Music Education, 30*(1), 31–47.

Meske, E., Pautz, M., Andress, B., and Willman, F. (1988). *Holt Music.* New York: Holt, Rinehart and Winston.

Mount, T. (1982). Pitch and rhythm error identification and its relevance in the use of choral sectional rehearsals. Unpublished doctoral dissertation, University of Southern California, Los Angeles.

Munsen, S. C. (1986). A description and analysis of an Orff-Schulwerk program of music education (improvisation). Unpublished doctoral dissertation, University of Illinois, Urbana.

Nelson, D. (1983). String teaching and performance: A review of research findings. *Bulletin of the Council of Research in Music Education, 74,* 39–46.

Olson, R. G. (1964). A comparison of two pedagogical approaches adapted to the acquisition of melodic sensitivity in sixth grade children: The Orff method and the traditional approach. Unpublished doctoral dissertation, Indiana University, Bloomington.

Palmer, M. H. (1974). The relative effectiveness of the Richards and Gordon approaches to rhythm reading for fourth grade children. Unpublished doctoral dissertation, University of Illinois, Urbana.

Parker, R. (1974). Comparative study of two methods of band instruction at the middle school level. Unpublished doctoral dissertation, Ohio State University, Columbus.

Puopolo, V. (1971). The development and experimental application of self-instructional practice materials for beginning instrumentalists. Unpublished doctoral dissertation, Michigan State University, East Lansing.

Rainbow, B. (1979). Curwen, Kodály and the future. *The Australian Journal of Music Education, 25,* 33–35.

Reimer, B. (1989). *A philosophy of music education (2nd ed.).* Englewood Cliffs: Prentice Hall.

Richards, M. (1966). *Threshold to music.* Palo Alto: Fearon Publishers.

Rosenthal, R. K. (1984). Relative effects of guided model, model only, guide only, and practice only treatments on the accuracy of advanced instrumentalists' musical performance. *Journal of Research in Music Education, 32*(4), 265–273.

Rosenthal, R. K., Wilson, M., Evans, M., and Greenwalt, L. (1988).

Effects of different practice conditions on advanced instrumentalists' performance accuracy. *Journal of Research in Music Education, 36*(4), 250–257.

Sampson, U. (1968). An identification of deficiencies in past and current method books for beginning heterogeneous wind-percussion class instrumental music instruction. Unpublished doctoral dissertation, University of Michigan, Ann Arbor.

Sang, R. (1987). A study of the relationship between instrumental music teachers' modeling skills and pupil performance behaviors. *Bulletin of the Council for Research in Music Education, 91,* 155–159.

Shamrock, M. (1986) Orff Schulwerk: An integrated foundation. *Music Educators Journal, 72*(6), 51–55.

Shaw, A. (1971). The development and evaluation of a programmed learning approach in teaching the elements of snare drum technique. Unpublished doctoral dissertation, Indiana University, Bloomington.

Shehan, P. (1987). Effects of rote versus note presentations on rhythm learning and retention. *Journal of Research in Music Education, 35*(2), 31–47.

Shuler, S. (1986). The effects of Gordon's learning sequence activities on music achievement. Unpublished doctoral dissertation, Eastman School of Music of the University of Rochester, Rochester.

Siemens, M. T. (1969). A comparison of Orff and traditional instructional methods in music. *Journal of Research in Music Education, 17*(3), 272–285.

Siemens, M. T. (1967). Current status, practices, and procedures of two instructional methods of music education of Jefferson County elementary schools. Unpublished doctoral dissertation, University of Toledo, Toledo.

Small, A. R. (1983). The effect of male and female vocal modeling on pitch matching accuracy of first grade children. *Journal of Research in Music Education, 31*(3), 227–233.

Sperti, J. (1970). Adaptation of certain aspects of the Suzuki method to the teaching of the clarinet: An experimental investigation testing the comparative effectiveness of two different pedagogical methodologies. Unpublished doctoral dissertation, New York University, New York.

Spillane, K. (1987). Breath support directives used by singing teachers: A delphi study. Unpublished doctoral dissertation, Columbia University, New York.

Stauffer, R. G. (1967). *The first grade reading studies: Findings of individual investigations.* Newark: International Reading Association.

Stegall, J. R. (1978). Shape notes and choral singing. *The Choral Journal, 24*(2), 5–10.

Sterling, P. (1985). The effects of accompanying harmonic content on vocal pitch accuracy of a melody. *Psychology of Music, 13*(2), 72–80.

Stockton, J. (1983). An experimental study of two approaches to the development of aural meter discrimination among students in a college introductory class. Unpublished doctoral dissertation, Temple University, Philadelphia.

Suzuki, S. (1969). *Nurtured by love.* Jericho: Exposition Press.

Texter, M. E. (1975). A historical analytical investigation of the beginning band method book. Unpublished doctoral dissertation, Ohio State University, Columbus.

Weber, F. (1968). *First division band method.* Rockville Center: Belwin, Incorporated.

Webster's Seventh New Collegiate Dictionary. Springfield: G. & C. Merriam and Company, 1963.

Wensel, V. (1970). *Project Super 1966-1968.* Eastman School of Music.

Weyland, R. (1955). The effects of a workshop on certain fourth-grade teachers' skills in teaching music reading. Unpublished doctoral dissertation, University of California, Berkeley.

Whitener, W. T. (1983). Comparison of two approaches to teaching beginning band. *Journal of Research in Music Education, 31*(1), 5–13.

Winnick, W. (1987) Hybrid methods in sight-singing. *The Choral Journal, 28*(1), 24–30.

Woelflin, L. (1961). An experimental study on the teaching of clarinet fingerings with teaching machines. Unpublished doctoral dissertation, Southern Illinois University, Carbondale.

Zinar, R. (1983). John Curwen: Teaching the tonic sol-fa method 1816-1880. *Music Educators' Journal, 70*(9), 46–47.

Zurcher, Z. (1972). The effect of model-supportive practice on beginning brass instrumentalists. Unpublished doctoral dissertation, Columbia University, New York.

THE STUDY OF BIOMECHANICAL AND PHYSIOLOGICAL PROCESSES IN RELATION TO MUSICAL PERFORMANCE

Frank R. Wilson
UNIVERSITY OF CALIFORNIA, SAN FRANCISCO

Franz L. Roehmann
UNIVERSITY OF COLORADO, DENVER

There is probably no aspect of musical behavior that does not invite questions concerning its physical origins or correlates. Brain mechanisms responsible for the perception of musical sound have been the subject of both speculation and inquiry for centuries, and since the time of Hermann Helmholtz have offered serious investigative challenge to both psychologists and physiologists. Not only do auditory and acoustic sciences attract an avid following of musicians, these sciences have benefited considerably from the contributions of these musicians (e.g., Pierre Boulez and Milton Babbitt, to cite two prominent contemporary examples).

Given the demonstrated compatibility and productivity of this interdisciplinary experience, it is curious that biomechanical and physiological studies of movement have attracted neither the attention nor the participation of musicians in any systematic or serious way. Indeed, when one considers the imposing accumulation of pedagogical writing on the subject of musical technique (and the example of a thriving partnership between athletic coaches, sports psychologists, and physiologists), the comparative inactivity of this branch of music research is noteworthy.

This is not to suggest that the issue has been ignored. In the context of his review of the psychological and musical foundations of motor learning, Sidnell (1981) asks a series of questions that a decade later continue to serve as a point of departure for music researchers interested in questions related to motor control in musical tasks. Hedden's (1988) review of the literature demonstrates that researchers have

The senior author's research was carried out while he was Guest Professor, Department of Neurology, University of Düsseldorf, under a grant from the Sonderforschungsbereich 200; MIDI-equipped pianos and a C1 computer were supplied by Yamaha Europa, GmbH, and Yamaha Music Corporation, USA. Sequence programming was done with the kind assistance of Mr. Hiro Kato, Director of InfoSoft Systems Lab, Yamaha Corporation, Hamamatsu, Japan, and Mr. Stefan Huschenbeck, Computer Engineer at the Neurologic Rehabilitation Center, Düsseldorf. Biomechanical evaluations were obtained through the generous assistance of Mr. D. Drescher and Mrs. E. Santo at the Institut für Musikphysiologie at the Hochschule für Musik und Theater in Hannover, Germany. A number of individuals contributed to the development of ideas expressed in this chapter during its early planning and writing, among whom I wish particularly to thank Hans-Joachim Freund, Professor and Chairman, Department of Neurology, University of Düsseldorf; Professor Christoph Wagner, Director of the Institut für Musikphysiologie in Hannover; Dr. Volker Hömberg, Director of the Neurologic Rehabilitation Center, Düsseldorf; Professor George Moore, University of Southern California; Professor Johannes Noth, Director of the Department of Neurology, Alfried Krupp Krankenhaus, Essen, Germany; Dorothy Taubman and Patrick O'Brien, both of Brooklyn, New York; and Professor C. David Marsden, The National Hospital, Queen Square, London.

been interested in this subject from a variety of perspectives: the power of proprioceptive feedback (e.g., Salzberg, 1980; Ward and Burns, 1978); transferability of motor learning (e.g., Brick, 1984); aspects of neurophysiology (e.g., Dennis, 1984); and motor control models (e.g., Welch, 1985).

What is of concern is the predominant emphasis on psychological questions (the "psycho" in psychomotor) and the apparent lack of interest in replication of studies of potential importance. Psychological issues of complex movement, such as the effect of feedback in refining motor skills, the usefulness of mental practice in learning a motor skill, and the importance of developmental readiness specific to a motor task, have, as Hedden's discussion points out, received a fair amount of attention, while other questions of fundamental importance, like those asked by Sidnell, remain largely unexamined:

1. What motor skills are important to musical growth?
2. What about the timing sequence and consideration of motor responses—how are they accomplished? What physiological mechanisms are at work? How do we make so-called automatic patterns from irregular sets?
3. How does motor memory function?

That these questions, which focus more on neurological and physiological issues (the "motor" in psychomotor), have not been examined systematically as part of a music research agenda is understandable in light of their multidisciplinary nature and their demand for specialized laboratory space, equipment, and research protocols. Even so, speaking for himself and Sidnell, Hedden summarizes the status of psychomotor research related to music by observing, "In 1978, Sidnell and the present author found it astounding that the profession had so little *confirmed* knowledge about an area that is such a basic part of all music education programs; in 1986 the astonishment remains" (p. 28, emphasis added).

There must be many explanations for this largely unexploited potential; whatever they may be, two suffice to explain the impasse. First, the scientific study of locomotion, limb, and oculomotor control encompasses such a wide range of questions and investigative techniques that no central disciplinary focus can be said to exist. In other words, there is no such thing as a "field" of movement science; instead, there is an ad hoc and shifting affiliation of psychologists, biomechanical engineers, mathematicians, anthropologists, prosthesis and robot builders, cockpit designers, sports and dance trainers, neurologists and neurophysiologists, physical therapists, Feldenkrais and Alexander practitioners, and sundry stationary human workstation ergonomists. Consequently, were music educators interested in a serious working relationship with movement scientists, the realization (and the achievements) of such a collaboration would depend almost entirely on chance.

Symptomatic of the mosaic character of work carried out under the "movement science" rubric is a lack of agreement concerning the name by which an integrated discipline ought to be known. At one of the few American universities where such a department enjoys an autonomous existence,

there is a continuing search for a better way to formally designate themselves and their endeavors. At present the departmental title is Kinesiology, but inquiries from potential students indicate that outsiders are unsure of the nature of their work, and sometimes (for example) suppose this to be a place where chiropractors are trained.

Second, science (as applied to music instruction) attracts only a limited following among music educators. Otto Ortmann, a notable early exception to the rule, published two major works during his career, leaving a substantial body of research whose importance seems undiminished decades later. Although his published work demands more than a modest familiarity with biological science, it never loses its immediate connections with pedagogy. In his discussion of the skeletal system and joint movement, for example, his conclusions and advice are the following:

1. Any key on the piano can be reached effectively in a multitude of ways.
2. The position in which a key is played is determined by the position and manner of playing the preceding and succeeding keys.
3. The best manner of making a movement to a certain point on the keyboard varies with the individual, and among other things, is determined by skeletal structure.
4. The physiologically best movement is the one permitting motion near the middle range of the joints involved. (Ortmann, 1929, 1981, p. 33)

Despite the great care taken by Ortmann to make his work applicable to the teaching of music, his contemporaries and their successors were, and remain, largely unaware that performance research might have anything to offer them in their work, and in some cases overtly hostile toward a pedagogy based on mechanistic principles and practices.

Kochevitsky (1967), in a very interesting brief monograph, attempted to revive the scientific approach to music teaching. He performed a particularly valuable service by extensively reviewing non-English publications and bringing to light a number of lesser-known but highly worthwhile research efforts undertaken by other music teachers. For example, he discusses the work of Oscar Raif (1901/1967), who had established convincingly that technical training at the keyboard produces results not by increasing speed of finger movement, but by reducing delays *between* movements. Such observations are reinforced by contemporary studies of timing mechanisms in control of skilled movement, to which we shall turn later in this chapter.

Although lack of interest and skepticism toward a scientific approach to pedagogy are understandable among music educators, they are hard to reconcile with actual pedagogical practice, which takes the structure and delivery of music teaching very seriously. The discrepancy suggests nothing so much as a failure of consensus among teachers concerning basic procedures of training in music performance. Thus, for example, teachers may assert that technical study has only one purpose: to give the student mastery of the full range of sound-producing possibilities latent in the instrument—in other words, technical study should promote refinement of touch and hearing, and should be defined solely in terms of artistic imagination and realization.

Alternatively, technical training may be seen as a kind of gymnastics course designed to develop arms, hands, lips, breathing, and so forth, so that the musician will be prepared to meet the purely *physical* demands of music performance. The fully developed musician, according to this line of thought, should be prepared to play any piece of music, no matter what the location or number of notes to be played might be, or what instrument the music was written or transcribed for.

If it is doubted that these really are contrasting aims, a recent dialogue between pianists Fernando Laires and Dorothy Taubman is instructive. The discussion concerned the value, and the problems, associated with the well-known *Exercises for Independence of the Fingers* published by Isidor Philipp (1898, 1926), with whom Laires had studied.

Laires: You must realize that this is part of the romantic tradition of sound. When Philipp talks about full, round, even tone, he's talking about romantic sound. And if we're talking about romantic sound, we are also talking about romantic procedures of handling things. I also can hold the note with the pedal.

Wilson: If I understand Mr. Laires correctly, the intent of Philipp in retaining the hand in a certain position was to produce a particular effect in the sound, and he expected experienced pianists to understand what he intended them to do.

Laires: That is correct; these are not for beginners.

Taubman: I must tell you something. The pianists who come to me are all concert artists with careers that are virtually finished. It was only by going through the whole history of what they had been doing that I found how often exercises of this sort were dangerous. I know Philipp believed this was the way to produce a beautiful tone, but for me it amounts to total incoordination, and there has to be a healthier way to achieve beautiful tone. (Wilson, 1988)

Opinions about technical training comprise what might best be considered part of the respected folklore of music pedagogy, representing the shared experience of countless thoughtful and caring teachers, and many lifetimes of working, observing, reflecting on and refining the teaching of music. One should not make the mistake of ignoring or even mistrusting folklore simply because it is unsupported by scientific research; in most cases when teaching succeeds, it must do so because its underlying assumptions about the learning process are not misguided.

The teacher's job, of course, is not to defend or explain pedagogical practice but to produce musicians. Still, the need for objectivity should not be in doubt. Technical exercises, for example, are an invariant staple of performance curricula in music, despite the fact that their role has never been systematically investigated. Books of technical exercises do not normally contain descriptions of validation studies to which they have been subjected, detailed rules for their implementation, or advice about limitations or risks of which the student should be aware. Is it not possible to determine how much time can usefully be expended on technical training, and what the elements and timing of that training should be? Without an improvement in the liaison between teachers and movement scientists, the answer is probably no.

Efficiency and effectiveness in technical training—the shorter and smoother path to virtuosity—is not the only issue. The contemporary environment of competitiveness surrounding the musical career sometimes leads to the adoption of excessive or irrational training programs whose pursuit may be worse than fruitless; when undertaken blindly, or in pursuit of ill-considered commitments or frantic schedules, instrumental practice can have disastrous consequences.

The senior author conducts a medical practice in California that includes a concert artist who, after winning an important competition, received a teaching appointment on the performance faculty at a major university. After taking up his new position, he found himself obliged to teach technical exercises that he had never done himself. As a matter of conscience he began to practice the exercises his students were obliged to study, but found that most of his young piano students could play everything faster than he could. Horrified, he began to work intensively at these exercises; within a very short time he had developed severe pain in one of his hands, and was forced to abandon the instrument for an extended period. Stories of this kind abound in medical clinics where musicians are evaluated for performance-related pain.

BIOMECHANICS IN MUSIC: BEGINNING AGAIN

From the scientist's perspective, the folklore of music pedagogy is perhaps best seen as a rich source of ideas and questions about the structure and control of skilled movement. It was his experience as a teacher that led Ortmann to seek ways to demonstrate the details of movement of the pianist's hand at the keyboard, and to use the objective study of hand and key behavior to inform and advance pedagogical practice.

Folklore also figured as an impetus for an extremely important ongoing German investigation of the role biomechanics might play in the development of musical skill. One often hears claims that a particular individual has "perfect pianists's hands," yet it was not until the early 1970s that a serious attempt was made to examine anatomic structure quantitatively and to correlate findings with individuals' training and performing experiences in music. It was at that time that Christoph Wagner, then a physician, conductor, and pianist working at the Max Planck Institut für Arbeitsphysiologie in Dortmund (now the Institut für Systemphysiologie) established a laboratory for the study of individual biomechanical and anthropomorphic differences among musicians.

Having studied a variety of industrial and occupational hand and arm problems in Dortmund, Wagner moved to the Hochschule für Musik und Theater in Hannover, a leading conservatory in West Germany, where he expanded his research focus to include investigation of biomechanical sources of performance-related pain and injury. His Institut für Musikphysiologie in Hannover is the only establishment of its kind in the world, and the studies carried out there have begun to attract increasing attention in other European countries and in the United States. In a series of English language publications, Wagner (1974, 1977, 1988a, b) has provided details of the static and dynamic characteristics of movement in the upper extremities of musicians whose ages range from 16 to 72 years, and who play virtually all instruments in common use.

Fixed anatomic measures obtained in the Hannover laboratory include the following:

- Hand size, including length measured from wrist to the tip of the longest finger
- Hand width, measured from the base of the index to the base of the small finger
- Wrist width, measured at the widest point of the wrist

Dynamic measures are divided into two groups:

- Maximum interdigit spans and maximum flexion, extension, or rotational movements achieved at selected joints by maximum voluntary effort
- Maximum interdigit spans and maximum flexion, extension, or rotational movements produced by passive movement of the same joints using standard forces

Measurement of excursions are made after mechanical isolation of the joint being measured. Joint ranges surveyed include the following:

- Elbow rotation (pronation and supination) by active movement and passively at low, medium, and high torque
- Wrist movement (radial and ulnar abduction) by active movement
- Knuckle joint movement (extension) passively at low and high force
- Thumb flexion (the metacarpophalangeal joint) by active movement

These measures yield precise and reproducible descriptions of several innate properties of the hand and arm of the musician, and permit consideration of both isolated and composite characteristics of upper limb movement in relation to instrumental playing.

By 1990 nearly 1,000 individuals (plus 300 young children both with and without musical training) had been examined by Wagner, and a number of conclusions had emerged. First, (as expected) musicians come in an extraordinary range of sizes and shapes, and neither size nor shape alone has any predictive value as to success or failure in music. Second, once hand and arm have reached adult size (and in the absence of disease, injury, or surgical intervention), none of these measures appears to be significantly altered as a function of age or training.

Because he was interested in learning whether there might be any correlation between the biomechanical properties of the upper extremity and complaints of pain or technical difficulty, Wagner designed a graphic plot of the measurements obtained in his subjects, called the *hand profile* (Figure 34–1), and has used this form to help identify characteristics that might be sources of trouble for the musician.

The profile is divided into three sections for both left and right sides. The top section describes *static* measures; the middle, *active* ranges of motion; and the bottom, *passive* ranges of motion. Raw scores are converted to rank, or decile scores, so the diagram depicts each measure in relation to normal values for other musicians. The profile associates increased functional advantage with higher rank scores—the farther to the right of the diagram, the greater the likelihood that a specific characteristic is an advantage. This is because (all other things being equal) a small, immobile hand tends to present greater limitations to the musician than a large, flexible hand. As a practical matter, however, it would be naive to interpret the test in such a simplistic way. In particular, it is clear that

- mobility measurements at a single joint do not predict values for other joints in the same limb;
- individual structural elements never function in isolation, and functional groupings may be ultimately far more significant than their components in contributing to success or failure in performance on a particular instrument; and
- the relationship between size/flexiblity and functional advantage is neither linear nor certain; what is a biomechanical advantage (or disadvantage) in playing one type of instrument may not prove to be so in playing another type, and high rank values in size and flexibility may occasionally confer *increased* risk of disturbed movement.

Although limitations of space do not permit a full discussion of the implications of Wagner's work, a number of important conclusions have emerged, among which are the following:

- There is a strong correlation between complaints of pain in the arms and reduced pronation-supination values, *particularly among string players with low rank supination scores in the left arm.*
- Extremely low rank scores at multiple (and sometimes single) joints are often associated with complaints of difficulty achieving and maintaining control of high-speed finger movements.

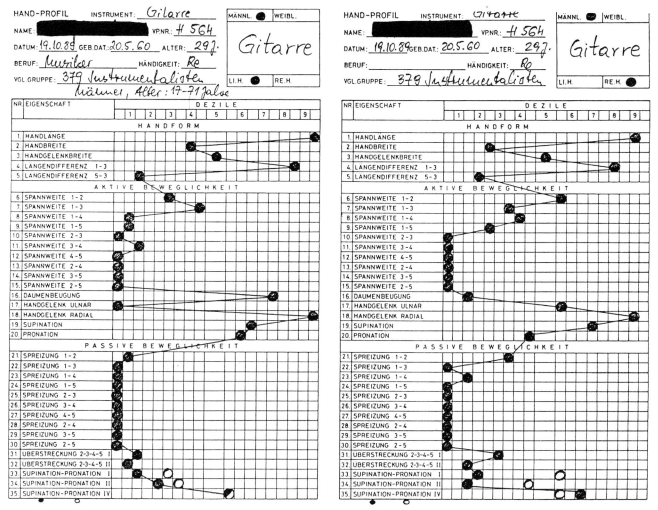

FIGURE 34–1. The subject is a 26-year-old conservatory graduate with a performance degree in classical guitar. Following graduation, he discontinued study and performance of classical literature and spent 1 year as a "street musician," followed by another year of virtually no contact with the instrument. He then resumed serious work under extreme pressure, after setting the goal of recording a guitar trio within several months. While preparing for the recording and practicing a thumb tremolo he began to experience pain at the metacarpal-phalangeal (MP) joint of the right thumb. Despite increase in the pain, he intensified his practicing until he found that any thumb stroke produced forced flexion of his index finger. He rapidly lost the ability to separate control of thumb and index finger movements, and, 4 years later, no longer plays.

The hand profile (see text for explanation) shows several features of interest:

• Right hand is extremely long (line 1).
• All active and passive finger spans excluding the thumb and the left 3–4 active span are at or below the .5 decile range (lines 10–15 and 25–30).
• While thumb-index span is *above average* in the right thumb (line 6), the MP joint flexion angle (line 16) is at the 1.5 decile level, compared to the 7.5 decile level on the left (i.e., there is marked limitation in one of the two joints involved in the tremolo move that was being practiced).

It is clear that this work has considerable implications for music pedagogy, and deserves the attention of anyone concerned with the physical basis of musical technique.

A complementary presentation of functional anatomy in relation to musical performance has been published by Raoul Tubiana (1988) and his associates (Tubiana and Chamagne, 1988; Tubiana, Chamagne, and Brockman, 1989). Tubiana, a hand surgeon and director of the Institut Français de la Main, Paris, has published a discussion of functional anatomy in relation to specific instruments, and emphasizes the special problems in movement faced by guitarists (Tubiana et al., 1989). The benefit to musicians of a detailed understanding of anatomy has been stressed by other hand surgeons who see these individuals as patients (Nolan and Eaton, 1989; Watson and Kalus, 1987).

Less obvious than the purely orthopedic issues is the apparent tendency of the developing nervous system to establish preset patterns of functional control related to type of hand use. It is clear, as Ortmann pointed out, that any instrumentalist has an enormous range of possible ways to support and manipulate keys, valves, strings, bows, fingerboards, and sticks in order to produce and control instrumental sound. Conceivably, some of those choices could lead to suboptimal movement in some situations, or poorly coordinated muscular control of finger and hand movement during certain musical passages on certain instruments, for neurological as well as for orthopedic reasons.

An illuminating introduction to this issue has been published by Elliott and Connolly (1984), who classify hand movements by pattern of synergistic use. In calling attention to the differences between movements whose purpose is to manipulate objects within the hand (*intrinsic* movements) and movements in which the hand displaces a held object toward or away from the body (*extrinsic* movements), they lay a useful theoretical foundation for consideration of the importance specific postures and combined muscle use might play in instrumental study and performance.

If the motor system were biased toward the selection of muscles arranged in functional "presets" as described by Elliott and Connolly, the hand could prove not only resistant to training but susceptible to overt malfunction in the face of inappropriate muscle selection under special conditions. Thus, when faced with particularly demanding motor tasks (or phylogenetically novel limb use, such as playing the piano), and perhaps especially when movement must be extremely rapid and accurate at the same time, the performer may be extremely limited in options available for configuring movement in ways that will satisfy sequence, timing, and force criteria demanded by the task. To complicate the situation further, those options would almost certainly be unique for each musician as well as for individual tasks rehearsed to a level of stable performance.

On the other hand, there is good evidence that there are general rules that might apply for many situations. Taubman (1988), for example, has implicated reliance on deep flexors of the fingers in the etiology of hand problems among pianists, and a similar warning for guitarists has been sounded by Patrick O'Brien (Hays, 1987). Despite the considerable differences in the instruments they teach, both Taubman and O'Brien also regard active thumb opposition (pulling the thumb into the center of the palm, toward the small finger) as highly undesirable because of the tendency of such movement to cause synergistic flexion in other fingers. Both also pay particular attention to the development of movements involving abduction, or stretching, of the fingers.

It must be emphasized, however, that *direct* observation of muscle activity in performing musicians has never been achieved, and that all statements about muscle interactions and the underlying neurological control mechanisms are pure speculation. Documentation remains a major research challenge and, in view of the inherent anatomic, physiological, and technological complexities, an exceedingly distant prospect.

Another dimension to the movement configuration problem is added by psychologists concerned with higher-order control of complex movement. Wade (1990) has reviewed this problem from the perspective of musical performance, pointing out that serious questions now exist concerning the mechanisms whereby the nervous system is able to store, recall, and use detailed information about previous movement in highly skilled performance.

The contemporary view of motor control, he says, suggests that the central nervous system is functionally organized around cognitive, biomechanical, and environmental circumstances, and, as a way of overcoming the handicap of limited memory capacity, configures itself into "coordinative structures." These are seen as task-oriented control assemblies within the nervous system that must learn to "make adjustments to the external forces, e.g., the mechanical features of the movement related to the instrument to be played; the feedback about muscle length and tension; the inertia of a moving finger or a moving arm. In addition, even postural states are accounted for by the establishment of a coordinative structure" (Wade, 1990 p. 176). For more extended discussions of behavioral psychology and neurophysiology germane to the development of musical skill, the reader is referred to Holding (1981), Smyth and Wing (1984), Phillips (1985), Wilson (1986), and Jennerod (1988).

STUDIES OF MUSCLE AND BRAIN ACTIVITY

The physiological control of limb movement occupies a central position in contemporary neurological and neurophysiological research. Studies of physiological control of rapid limb movements among mammals show that the nervous system has a remarkable capacity to regulate precise timing of contraction and relaxation of muscles working reciprocally in rapid sequential movements (Brooks, 1979a, b; DeLong and Strick, 1974) and imply that the slightest interference in control of such movements could substantially degrade the timing and accuracy of such movements (Freund, 1983, pp. 422–425; Thach, 1987, p. 218).

With the recent emergence of specialty clinics for performing artists, standard techniques for the study of muscle, nerve, and brain activity have been applied to musicians. These include electrical measurements of muscle contraction (electromyography) and measurement of the speed of impulse conduction in both motor and sensory nerves (nerve conduction testing). More elaborate measurements permit the estimation of conduction rates within the brain and spinal cord (Noth, Podoll, and Friedemann, 1985) and, to some extent, localization of specific regions of the brain active during motor planning and execution, or in response to sensory stimulation (Fox, Raichle, and Thach, 1985; Gevins et al., 1987). Musicians, for good reason, have already attracted the attention of contemporary neuroscientists, and will increasingly be the subject of study by positron emission tomography, high-resolution somatosensory evoked potential recordings, and other elaborate (and expensive!) brain-imaging techniques.

Although the conduct and interpretation of such tests requires extensive training and experience in clinical neurology or neurophysiology, there is no real impediment to the musical researcher's acquiring some degree of familiarity with such tests and an understanding of how they might contribute to the clarification of physiological processes involved in skill acquisition or loss.

A number of clinical studies of muscle, nerve, and brain activity in musicians have been recently published. Lederman (1986) has described several forms of nerve entrapment seen in musicians, and in his most recent study (1989) reported finding peripheral nerve disorders in 29 percent of 226 instrumentalists seen at the Medical Center for Performing Artists at the Cleveland Clinic Foundation. Although improvements in some patients came about through alterations in technique, no attempt was made to correlate specific problems or their correction with specific pedagogical interventions.

On the long list of physical disorders to which musicians are prey, occupational cramp (or *focal dystonia,* as it is currently designated by most neurologists) is easily the most mysterious and fascinating. Thought to be primarily the result of emotional disturbance until the early 1980s, cramp has recently assumed heightened theoretical importance because of the discovery by Sheehy and Marsden (1982) of characteristic patterns of abnormal muscular activity in musicians and other skilled hand users disabled by this condition. They, and others who have studied this problem, have repeatedly demonstrated that simultaneous cocontraction of agonist-antagonist muscles is the physiological sine qua non of this disorder (Rothwell, Day, Obeso, Beradelli, and Marsden, 1988; Panizza, Hallett and Nilsson, 1989).

What is not clear is *why* occupational cramp develops, or what to do about it. If it is simply a neurological disorder (akin to Parkinson's disease, for example), cramp will never represent a research problem in music education. If, by contrast, it can be associated with particular aspects of either the learning process, or performance, the problem would assume equal (and major) theoretical significance for both motor physiology and music pedagogy.

The most recent studies of musicians with occupational cramp have called attention to the frequent association between onset of symptoms and specific work circumstances or triggers. Lederman (1988) reported 21 patients, of whom 14 were in this category. "These included excessive practicing or playing in 5, a change in technique or instrument in 4, trauma in 3, and unusual emotional distress in 2. There was evidence of nerve entrapment in three patients" (p. 46). Newmark and Hochberg (1987) evaluated 59 musicians with cramp, with similar suggestions of predisposing events in over half the cases. "In 37 of the 59 musicians we elicited histories of either trauma, inflammation, or increased demands upon the hand preceding the onset of symptoms, sometimes by years" (p. 293). It was their conclusion that most cases could be explained on the basis of peripheral causes (which is to say that the disorder did not appear to be precipitated by an underlying neurological disorder or disease).

Despite the apparent connections between occupational cramp and what is referred to as the *overuse syndrome* (Fry, 1986), there is a major impediment to conceptualizing cramp as simply the far end of a spectrum of soft tissue or peripheral nerve trauma induced by overindulgence in instrumental practice. That impediment (and the reason for continued interest in central nervous system involvement in this disorder) is that the symptoms simply do not go away with rest. In fact, except in extremely unusual instances, the symptoms do not go away at all, no matter what is done medically, surgically, or by way of all but extremely protracted, heroic retraining attempts.

In a recent review of research on writer's cramp, Sheehy, Rothwell, and Marsden (1988) call attention to the recurrent theme of task *complexity* in individuals who develop occupational cramps.

However, it is striking how often focal manual dystonia strikes first at an individual's most skilled motor accomplishment. Perhaps this is not surprising. The exquisite motor mechanisms developed to enable humans to play musical instruments, professional sports, and even to write must be vulnerable. (p. 472)

A similar view opinion is held by the author (Wilson, 1988, 1989):

Success at a high level of musical skill must be utterly dependent on the capacity of the control system to maintain agonist and antagonist (muscular) activity in strict reciprocal balance. Any contrary condition, whether it be motor or sensory malfunction (central or peripheral) or simply the springing of a trap unwittingly laid by the rehearsal of movements incompatible with the agonist/antagonist paradigm ("faulty technique") could put the system (meaning hand and arm) out of commission. The final misery in this situation—its normal tendency toward irreversibility—may simply reflect the paradoxical consequence of the distraught musician practicing in an abnormal condition, thereby effectively locking in an end-stage, chaotic ballistic program (possibly at the spinal level) that can only degrade further each time the movement is attempted again. (1989, p. 150)

The suggestion, in other words, is that occupational cramps (or focal dystonia) in musicians do not ordinarily develop in the absence of movement rehearsal, and that they must therefore in such cases represent an aberrant form of motor learning.

In order to explore further the interrelationship between physical, training, and physiological factors in musician's cramp, a collaborative study was initiated in West Germany in 1989. Although analysis of the data obtained in the study is incomplete, one preliminary finding (entirely unexpected) was that biomechanical factors appear to have been of considerable importance in this group of musicians (Wilson, Wagner, Hömberg, and Noth, 1991):

In addition to extended performance, clinical and electrophysiologic examination, 21 subjects (including 15 with occupational cramp) underwent a quantitative biomechanical assessment. . . . All 15 fully tested musicians with occupational cramp demonstrated individual, functionally critical biomechanical conditions which correlated either with earlier training problems or with the phenomenology of the subsequent motor disorder (usually with both). . . . These findings strongly implicate both biomechanical preconditions and learning protocols in the etiology of occupational cramp among musicians.

Although this finding adds weight to the argument that the disorder arises out of the interplay of multiple elements integrated during the learning of complex motor skills, it still does not explain the *persistence* of the control problem. Jancovic and Shale (1989) theorize that a region of the frontal cortex known as the supplementary motor area (SMA) is involved:

This part of the motor cortex is critical for proper execution of sequential and simultaneous movements, such as those required for playing musical instruments. . . . The task specific dystonias, such as those seen in musicians, possibly result from an abnormal sensory feedback to the SMA. The impairment of sensory input may explain the paresthesias and discomfort experienced by some patients, even without objective evidence of sensory deficit. (p. 143)

There are, in fact, quite compelling reasons to regard sensory learning as another of those multiple elements whose contribution must be accounted for in both the acquisition and the loss of skilled movement. Michael Merzenich and his colleagues in San Francisco have demonstrated in monkeys that cortical sensory representation of the upper extremity is dynamic in its properties, and exquisitely responsive to stimuli reaching the cortex during movement taking place under conditions of "high cognitive drive"—for example, instrumental practice (Jenkins, Merzenich, Ochs, Allard, and Guic-Robles, 1990). Whether these findings can be extended to studies of human manual performance remains to be seen.

What seems most clear is that musician's cramp represents a specific (though polymorphic), persistent, and so far unexplained breakdown of skilled performance, probably in association with multiple risk factors, and that the explanation will emerge from a patient and thorough consideration of biomechanics, pedagogy, instrument design, neurophysiology, psychiatry, and economics. Musician's cramp ap-

pears, in other words, to be an appropriate topic for research by music educators.

TIME, TRILLS, AND MIDI

Through the use of newer technologies (e.g., Musical Instrument Digital Interface [MIDI], infrared light-emitting diodes [LEDs], and high-speed photography, traditional instruments modified to accept sensors and computers), researchers are examining ever more subtle aspects of musical performance. Using LEDs, high-speed cameras, and a computer, Winold and Thelen (1989) are studying the performance of graduate level university cello students by examining the strategies used to coordinate bow movements and to vary them according to tempo and expressive intent. McArthur (1989), using analogous imaging technologies, has recorded the hand, wrist, forearm, elbow, and upper arm movements of two expert pianists. The data allow the researcher to observe the biomechanics of the performances in great detail, with analysis intended to yield both an objective basis for the improvement of pedagogy and insight into factors that may lead to performance-related injury.

Sang-Hie Lee (1989), using an electronic piano and MIDI-computer interface, has explored left-hand piano technique under three conditions: with auditory and visual feedback, audio feedback only (blindfolded with earphones), and visual feedback only (no earphones). Under these conditions she has measured such variables as the velocity of key descent, the time elapsed from the beginning of one key strike to the beginning of the next key strike, the time a key was depressed, and the time from the release of a key to the next key strike. She seeks to model the idea of pianistic "touch" as an expressive component of performance.

With few exceptions (e.g., Moore, Hary, and Naill, 1988; Lashley, 1951), researchers studying the biomechanics of motor control remain far removed from the performing arts. The problem is that although the principles that govern the acquisition, refinement, and conservation of motor control are a central concern, the study of such problems in the laboratory requires controls that can rarely be exercised in real-life behavior. Consequently, a developed description of the behavior of the neuromuscular system of performing musicians is presently regarded as unattainable by experienced members of the motor research community.

Psychologists and neurophysiologists are increasingly interested in the nature of biological time, but musicians are the real authorities on this subject. Tempo, pulse, beat, meter, rhythm, polyrhythm, rubato, and syncopation represent just a small fraction of the rich vocabulary by which musicians seek to denote and convey the temporal character of their thought and work.

The musician represents an ideal subject for the study of timing operations of the central nervous system. Ernst Pöppel (1989), who hopes to establish the origins and role of psychophysical time constants shaping human perception, puts the issue this way:

If tempo is so fundamental to music, then we must ask ourselves how we find the right tempo and how we maintain it once it has been found. How can we throw light on this problem from the standpoint of brain research and experimental psychology? (p. 83)

One way of throwing light on the problem has been adopted by David Epstein, a pianist, conductor, and music educator interested in the temporal basis of musical performance (Epstein, 1985). He proposed earlier (Epstein, 1979) that in classical music the tempo relations between movements can be described by ratios of simple integers: 1:1, 1:2, 2:3, and 3:4. Interested in learning whether these observations could be extended to other musical forms, he examined examples of improvised music (including "musical" speech and music-dance events) in recordings obtained in a variety of nonwestern cultures. By a technique for locating attack points on a reel-to-reel tape and then measuring intervals between them, he was able to show that musically salient selections of these performances also resolve into ratios of simple integers.

Epstein's conclusion was that the ubiquity of this aspect of musical performance implies biological origins; that is, it is somehow related to the operation of an internal clocking mechanism. His *musical* conclusion is that aesthetics are constrained by biological factors; in this case, that effectiveness of musical communication demands observance by performers of the proportionality rule described in the study.

An unexpected dividend in the Epstein study derives from his discussion of the elusive musical terms tempo, rhythm, beat, and pulse. He defines *tempo* as "large scale time durations," in contrast to *rhythm,* "which involves durations on a smaller scale." *Beat* is the duration of the basic time unit of a measure (the denominator of the time signature), and is fixed by the composer's metronome settings. Thus, where the time signature is 2/4, and MM = 60, there are 60 beats per minute and each quarter note occupies one beat lasting one second.

Without formally defining the term *pulse,* Epstein nevertheless appears to intend it to refer to a sensation that the musician will experience, or seek, while listening to music or analyzing a score, hence to reflect a judgment concerning the temporal structure (specifically, the beat) of the music. Used this way, "pulse" seems to denote an internal sensation contingent upon a perceptual event (specifically, the analysis of temporal relationships between sequential auditory events having a unitary source) and is therefore analogous to the term "pitch," an observer judgment about the audible spectral frequency of a single musical event.

What might explain the origin of pulse? According to Epstein, "most tempos lie within or only slightly beyond the MM 60–120 range. Tempos much slower than 60, say below 54, often require musicians to subdivide in order to find a beat to control the music in practical terms. . . . " (p. 42). Epstein's fascinating study appears to raise any number of questions suitable for further musical-biological investigation. Could it be that pulse, restricted to a musical context, is a subjective sensation of synchrony with musical events having a stable recurrence rate lying between 60 and 120 per minute? Could it mark the recruitment of the motor system by an auditory scanner that paces, and has locked onto, the most salient time interval that can be extracted from a coherent, extended auditory signal? Does such a conceptualization help to explain audiation of pulse in the absence of real-time sound stimulation? Finally, does it point to, and help explain, a biological basis for the temporal stability found in the many examples of musical performance he examined?

Of the many intriguing questions arising in the middle ground between physiological and musical constructs of time, perhaps the most interesting concerns the resolution of aesthetic, physiological, and astronomical rules affecting the execution and perception of music. Writing in the landmark Critchley and Henson volume *Music and the Brain; Studies in the Neurology of Music,* William Gooddy (1977) put the situation in these words:

Personal time is a biological matter within each of us, dependent on all that we are, in ancestry and genetic make-up, in age and state of health, mood and present surroundings, alert or weary, . . . or in getting a few bars of music right as we practice them. . . . It is in complete contrast with government time, which is a standardized, specially non-human technological arrangement for the convenience of society in order to obviate the disorder which would result if public life were dependent upon the vagaries of innumerable personal times. (p. 138)

How, for example, did Glenn Gould and Leopold Stokowski settle on a particular tempo for their 1966 performance of Beethoven's *Emperor Concerto* with the American Symphony Orchestra? At a rehearsal, this dialogue is recorded by Gould (1984):

"What is your tempo?" the Maestro inquired, as I settled into the instrument.

"My tempo is your tempo," I responded in a bad imitation of Rudy Vallee. "I hope, however, that, whatever the tempo, we can make this piece into a symphony with piano obbligato; I really don't think it ought to be a virtuoso vehicle." After a preamble in which I outlined my views on this matter, Stokowski asked again, rather warily this time: "May I hear your tempo?" I explained that I had, in fact, two tempos at the ready and demonstrated with a few sentences from the opening movement's tutti and from the beginning of the finale. . . . To my delight, the Maestro expressed his preference for the slow set. . . . " (pp 269–270)

Just what are the implications of this negotiation? Pöppel's question disguises a veritable cornucopia of large-scale puzzles. How free is the pianist to adjust the rate at which he distributes an incalculably complex set of motor commands to his own musculature? How does the maestro adjudicate the disparities between his and the artist's intentions and capabilities, and align those with the vastly larger set of possibilities that exist among the musicians of the orchestra? How quickly and in what ways can any of these people react to mistakes, fatigue, problems with their instruments, acoustical illusions, or distortions in the hall? Yet these two gentlemen smile, banter, and decide it all in an instant, knowing they can do precisely what they have agreed to do.

One of the reasons this supreme self-confidence is so well placed is that such individuals have had long experience with the smooth and reliable operation of their own auditory and neuromuscular systems, including their temporal acuteness and consistency. Perhaps with the advent of increasingly precise tools for measuring and analyzing such performances, and with greater experience applying these tools to the study of high musical development, it will become possible to assist young artists more effectively as they work toward higher levels of achievement.

The relationship of the human auditory and motor systems to music perception and music performance, as implied by both Epstein's work and the Gould-Stokowski dialogue, represents one of the most challenging of all areas of inquiry for music researchers. Freund and Hefter (1990) have provided an exciting example of the prospects for the discovery of coherence in fundamental neurophysiological and musical phenomena, having demonstrated the influence of motor system oscillators in control of rapid serial and repetitive movements.

Most of our natural motor acts are not single, but instead consist of sequences of alternating movements. This certainly does apply for most musical performances. Serial movements can be conceived as a sequence of single movements or as a group of continuous sinusoids. Such serial movements can be subjected to spectral analysis, so that any regularity, or the major frequency components, of single contractions making up the serial movements will be revealed. A spectral analysis is shown [Figure 34-2] indicating the preferred frequencies of fast finger taps plotted along the abcissa and amplitude along the ordinate. The consistent performance of one subject is characterized by a sharp peak indicating that this is a preferentially sinusoidal movement performed at a rather stable frequency. In contrast, the spectral analysis of a second subject, whose performance was intentionally irregular, shows a shallow profile with a wide scatter over many frequencies. (p. 182)

Pointing to Epstein's work, Freund and Hefter comment:

He advances a theory that proportional tempo represents a universal principle in music, which infers the existence of a biological mechanism underlying such temporally invariant behavior. An intrinsic cerebral oscillator that generates tremor and attracts alternating move-

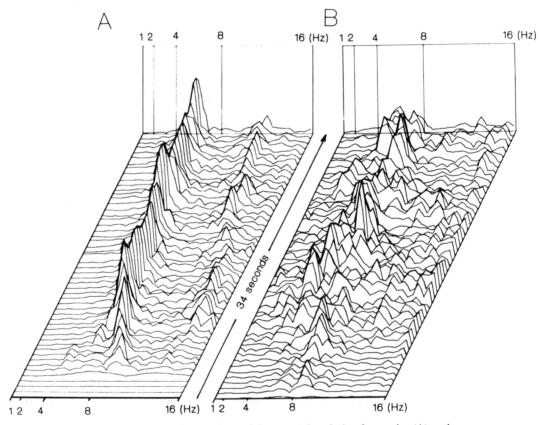

FIGURE 34–2. Comparison of the spectral analysis of a regular (A) and an irregular (B) series of most rapid voluntary alternating index finger movement of two untrained normal subjects. Compared to (A), where a single dominant peak with its harmonics is seen, the record in (B) shows both considerable variation of the dominant frequency and many nonharmonic peaks. Consecutive power spectra are shown from bottom to top. (Adapted with permission from Freund and Hefter, 1990.)

ments towards a preferred frequency would be (such) a mechanism. (p. 186)

Another example deserving close attention also concerns timing accuracy on a very small scale: the control of trills. George Moore, a neurophysiologist and cellist, has recently devised an elegant technique for examination of the interface between muscular and musical activity. Using a specially equipped cello and a MIDI grand piano, he and his colleagues at the University of Southern California have produced a highly detailed picture of the interaction of physical, musical, and physiological events in instrumental playing (Moore et al., 1988; Moore, 1991). (See Figure 34–3.)

The impact energy in the finger is derived, in part, from contraction of the flexor muscles; in addition, during the extensor phase of the trill, energy is stored in the elastic tissues of the finger and in the flexor muscles themselves, to be released when the extensors cease their contraction. Thus, the impact velocity of the finger, and hence the energy imparted to the key, are dependent on both the flexor and extensor phases of the movement.

It is notable in this example how well matched the notes are in duration, velocity, and cycle length. According to the MIDI data, the note durations for D and E (averaged over a 3-second period containing 36 notes) were 64 milliseconds, the off-durations were 104 milliseconds, and the cycle durations were 167 milliseconds.

Since the upper limit in the trill rate seems to be about 12 to 14 notes/second, or 6 to 7 notes/second per finger, there is only a limited time available in each cycle for immediate control to operate. That time would include sensory feedback, potentially available from proprioceptive, touch, and auditory modalities, and the time required to integrate that information into appropriate modifications in motor command signals.

The physiologist, in other words, discovers interactions in the hand and arm as complex and as smoothly orchestrated as is the orchestra itself. And he is able to do this because the electronic instrument of the performer doubles as the investigative instrument of the scientist.

Can musical instruments actually become part of the advanced technology for the study of human performance? The prospects for such adaptation are, in fact, extremely good. Studies using electronic keyboards—and synthesizers in other configurations—together with MIDI technology and sequencing software are already making their way into the scientific literature. Caroline Palmer has demonstrated the utility and versatility of digital recordings as a source of both computer graphics and statistical evaluations that can assess strategies used by the musician for refining musical interpretation (Palmer, 1989a). The potential for making explicit the basis for achieving artistic intent seems considerable (Palmer, 1989b).

It has also been shown that this technology has potential for the study of changes in performance produced by physical problems, and, theoretically at least, for improving strategies for diagnosis and treatment of neuromuscular problems related to performance (Salmon and Newmark, 1989). The study of occupational cramp (Wilson et al., 1991) discussed

earlier included data collected from a MIDI grand piano and development of software for statistical analysis and display of digital piano files. As shown in Figure 34–4, and as discussed by Moore, MIDI-generated data appear not only suitable for importation into a scientific environment but sufficiently sensitive and reliable to support detailed study of musical performance.

TRAINING AND EDUCATION

Looking to the future of research in music education, Duerksen (1988) offers some realistic advice about how researchers in music will need to be trained and educated. He encourages the provision of more research experiences throughout the entire music education system and particularly emphasizes the need for Ph.D. candidates to have more opportunities to practice *doing* research prior to beginning a dissertation. In addition to his recommendations, Ph.D. programs in music might also include a series of "short courses" that give candidates practical interactive experiences with researchers from other disciplines; for example, a systematic study of experimental designs, research protocols, and parametric strategies used by investigators from the biological and medical sciences would seem to be particularly useful.

A highly interactive research environment is not merely a future prospect; it is a present and expanding reality where the demand for researchers capable of working across traditional disciplines will inevitably increase. Witness the rise of university programs, centers, and institutes built on the multidisciplinary paradigm. In music, in addition to the Cluster on Music Cognition and Development at Eastman and the University of Rochester Medical School, examples include: Health Program for Performing Artists at the University of California at San Francisco Medical School; and the Center for Music Research at Florida State University. These and other units either operating or in the planning stages represent a determined effort to understand how humans acquire and maintain performance skills, what internal and external forces may intrude on these skills, and how performance health can be maintained throughout life.

Few, if any, universities graduating music Ph.D.'s have the capacity to provide comprehensive training in the study of complex motor behaviors. The reasons for this are twofold. First, as pointed out earlier, issues of motor control fall into several domains: neurological, physiological, psychological, behavioral, developmental, and biomechanical; second, it is simply impossible for any single graduate campus to commit resources to more than a portion (usually small) of the motor skill research agenda. It may therefore be time to think seriously about the feasibility of multiinstitutional consortia. In the absence of a single or cohesive discipline from which to address the questions, the development of consortial arrangements among institutions with mutually supportive capabilities and shared concerns may be a realistic means for getting on with the matter.

Most Ed.D. and D.M.A. candidates will never engage in

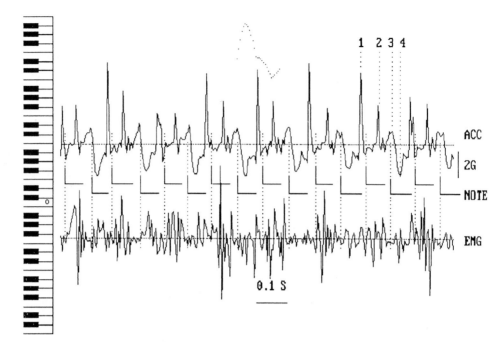

FIGURE 34–3. This figure associates finger acceleration, key movement (timing and velocity of keystrikes), and EMG activity (electrical potentials produced by muscle contraction). The subject is a highly trained pianist without a history of impaired performance.

Top line (ACC): Deflections above the baseline signify either increase in finger velocity as it lifts off the key or decrease in velocity (braking) as the finger moves downward; deflections below the baseline signify either increasing velocity of the finger as it moves downward or decreasing velocity (braking) as it moves upward.

Four important acceleration peaks for the finger playing the upper trill note are identified:

1. Maximal deceleration, associated with initial finger contact with the key
2. Second rapid deceleration, associated with key striking key bed
3. Maximal acceleration of the finger as it lifts off the key
4. Maximal downward acceleration of the finger as it moves toward the key for a second strike

Middle Line (NOTE): As indicated on the keyboard graphic, the notes of the trill are E and D. The length of the line (called "gatetime") is a measure of the duration of the key press. The vertical segment is a measure of the speed of hammer movement.

Bottom Line (EMG): Muscle activation potentials measured by electrodes placed over the belly of the extensor digitorum communis, the muscle that lifts the trill finger. Note that bursts of activity begin just after finger contact with the key and peak just prior to or at the point of key contact with the key bed. Note, also, that the muscle has become electrically silent (i.e., has ceased active contraction) *prior to* the attainment of maximum finger velocity. (Adapted with permission from Moore, 1991.)

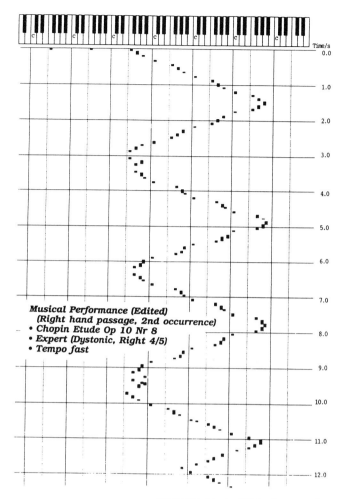

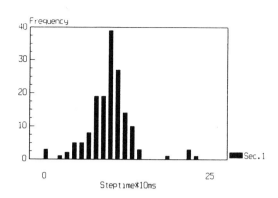

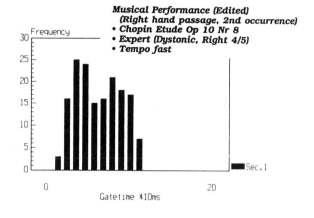

FIGURE 34–4. With the use of a sequence editing program, a performance of the Chopin Etude Op. 10, No. 8, been edited to remove all left-hand key strikes. The upper histogram shows the distribution of intervals between onset of successive notes in the sequence ("steptime"); the lower histogram shows the distribution of duration of all key strikes in this performance ("gatetime"). Ninety-eight key strikes are recorded in the first 10 seconds.

experimental research; they will teach and perform and teach others to teach and perform. Because they are in a unique position to observe student performers at all levels of ability and all stages of life, they can make an enormous contribution to clinical research. Were they, as a part of their education, trained to keep records of what they observed in class piano situations, private and group lessons, master classes, and the wide variety of performance venues they share with student and professional musicians, the profession would have available to it an invaluable base of longitudinal data. Its value would be so much the greater if the observations were made using predefined protocols. Although not every teacher-performer would be inclined to take on such an arduous task, and fewer still might commit themselves to it for the long haul, some would—and the effort would make a difference.

CONCLUSION

For music education, the study of movement in musical performance will be undertaken in pursuit of questions germane to pedagogy itself. However, the same investigations may prove a powerful way to advance the goals of movement science, where attention will increasingly be drawn toward the study of humans who are not only exploiting but *defining* the behavioral limits of the human motor system.

An additional goal of music research should be to connect

human biomechanics with instrumental design. The experience of performing arts medicine clinics suggests strongly that instrumental configuration may occasionally contribute to injuries in musicians. Examples include rigid-surface drum pads; rigid supports for drum sets used by marching bands and by drum and bugle corps; fixed ("one size fits all") configurations of keys on musical instruments; and of course, the utter lack of rules ("mix and match") governing the design of acoustic and electrical fretted instruments. Instrumental ergonomics is an untapped mine for the music researcher.

Another reason to study musical physiology and biomechanics derives from both the longevity of the musical career and some of the special working conditions encountered throughout the career of the musician—for example, travel exposes both musicians and instruments to sudden changes in climate and altitude, and imposes the further mundane but burdensome obligation to transport (usually in a rush and without help) bulky and heavy instruments. These and other such logistic considerations have long-reaching implications not only for the health of musicians, but for their prospects for performing as they wish to, and sustaining their artistic vitality. Keeping the career musician at work, productive, and content, is neither an obscure nor a trivial challenge.

Without the slightest intent to suggest priorities or to circumscribe the domain of the researcher, the following is offered as a rough guide to topics that seem appropriate to future biomechanical and physiological research in music education. The list is certain to grow with time.

- Collection of normative data on performance, including changes expected as a consequence of age and training

- Expanding biomechanical research to assist in injury prevention; developing ergonomics for the same reason
- Evaluation of technology; the role of sound and video recordings; MIDI technology, synthesizers, and music software; special recordings, such as high-speed computerized video, accelerometers, neurophysiologic, and brain-imaging techniques
- Study of physiological parameters of motor learning; recording of timing, force, and trajectory of movement; recording of muscular activity in instrumental playing, especially in relation to the process of skill refinement, and in relation to the musician-instrument "fit"
- Study of the relationship between automatic and variable aspects of automatized movement (coping with sticking keys and valves, for example)
- Study of muscular fatigue
- Study of technical exercises and their influence of measurable behavior
- Study of cognitive strategies in motor learning—visualization, handedness differences, memory; the role of stress in learning
- Linking studies of auditory and visual performance to research on motor skills in music
- The use of *all the above* in research on music therapy in learning-impaired or injured and ill individuals; in addition, design and evaluation of adaptive instruments for special learning situations
- The role of "adjunctive" procedures in the learning process and in health maintenance—posture, rest, diet, sensorimotor training (e.g., Feldenkrais therapy, Alexander technique)

References

Brick, J. S. (1984). An exploratory study of the effects of self-instructional programme utilizing the Pitch Master on pitch discrimination and pitch accuracy in performance of young trombonists. *Psychology of Music, 12,* 119–125.

Brooks, V. (1979a). Control of intended limb movements by the lateral and intermediate cerebellum. In H. Asanuma and V. Wilson (Eds.), *Integration in the nervous system.* Tokyo: Igaku-Shoin.

Brooks, V. (1979b). Motor programs revisited. In R. Tablott and D. Humphrey (Eds.), *Posture and movement: Perspectives for integrating sensory and motor research on the mammalian nervous system* (pp. 13–49). New York: Raven Press.

DeLong, M., Strick, P. (1974). Relation of basal ganglia, cerebellum and motor cortex to ramp and ballistic limb movements. *Brain Research, 71,* 327–35.

Dennis, A. (1984). The effect of three methods of supporting the double bass on muscle tension. *Journal of Research in Music Education, 32,* 95–103.

Duerksen, G. L. (1988). Research and music education: Needs for the next decade. *Bulletin of the Council of Research in Music Education, 90,* 60–64.

Elliott, J. M., and Connolly, K. J. (1984). A classification of manipulative hand movements. *Developmental and Child Neurology, 26,* 283–296.

Epstein, D. (1979). *Beyond Orpheus.* Cambridge: MIT Press.

Epstein, D. (1985). Tempo relations: A cross-cultural study. *Music Theory Spectrum* (The Journal of the Society for Music Theory), 7 [Rhythm and Time in Music], pp. 34–71.

Fox, P., Raichle, M., and Thach, W. T. (1985). Functional mapping of the human cerebellum with positron emission tomography. *Proceedings of the National Academy of Sciences, USA, 82,* 7462–7466.

Freund, H. -J. (1983). Motor unit and muscle activity in voluntary motor control. *Physiological Reviews, 63*(2), 387–436.

Freund, H. -J., and Hefter, H. (1990). Timing mechanisms in skilled hand movements. In F. Wilson and F. Roehmann (Eds.), *Music and child development: Proceedings of the 1987 Denver conference* (pp. 179–190). St. Louis: MMB Music.

Fry, H. (1986). Overuse syndrome in musicians—100 years ago: An historical review. *Medical Journal of Australia, 146,* 620–625.

Gevins, A., Morgan, N., Bressler, S., Cutillo, B., White, R., Illes, J., Greer, D., Doyle, J., and Zeitlin, G. (1987). Human neuroelectric patterns predict performance accuracy. *Science, 235,* 580–585.

Gooddy, W. (1977). The timing and time of musicians. In M. Critchley and R. A. Henson (Eds.), *Music and the brain: Studies in the neurology of music* (pp. 131–155). London: Wm. Heinemann Medical Books.

Gould, G. (1984). Stokowski in six scenes. In T. Page (Ed.), *The Glenn Gould Reader* (pp. 258–282). New York: Alfred A. Knopf. [First published in *Piano Quarterly*, Winter 1977–78 through Summer 1978]

Hays, B. (1987). "Painless" hand problems of string pluckers. *Medical Problems of Performing Artists, 2*(1), 39–40.

Hedden, S. K. (1988). Recent research pertaining to psychomotor skills in music. *Bulletin of the Council of Research in Music Education, 90,* 25–29.

Holding, D. (Ed.). (1981). *Human skills: Studies in human performance.* New York: John Wiley.

Jancovic, J., and Shale, H., (1989). Dystonia in musicians. *Seminars in Neurology, 9*(2), 131–135.

Jenkins, W., Merzenich, M., Ochs, M., Allard, T., and Guic-Robles, E. (1990). Functional reorganization of primary somatosensory cortex in adult owl monkeys after behaviorally controlled tactile stimulation. *Journal of Neurophysiology, 63*(1), 82–104.

Jennerod, M. (1988). *The neural and behavioral organization of goal-directed movements* (Oxford psychology series no. 15). Oxford: Oxford University (Clarendon) Press.

Kochevitsky, G. (1967). *The art of piano playing: A scientific approach.* Princeton: Summy-Birchard.

Lashley, K. S. (1951). The problem of serial order in behavior. In L. A. Jeffress (Ed.), *Cerebral mechanisms in behavior: The Hixon Symposium.* New York: John Wiley.

Lederman, R. (1986). Nerve entrapment syndromes in musicians. *Medical Problems of Performing Artists, 1*(2), 45–48.

Lederman, R. (1988). Occupational cramp in instrumental musicians. *Medical Problems of Performing Artists, 3*(2), 45–51.

Lederman, R. (1989). Peripheral nerve disorders in instrumentalists. *Annals of Neurology, 26,* 646–650.

Lee, S. (1989). Using the personal computer to analyze piano performance. *Psychomusicology, 8*(2), 143–149.

McArthur, V. H. (1989). The use of computers to analyze performance motions of musicians. *Psychomusicology, 8*(2), 135–141.

Moore, G. P. (1987). The study of skilled performance in musicians. In F. Roehmann and F. Wilson (Eds.), *The biology of music making: Proceedings of the 1984 Denver conference* (p. 77). St. Louis: MMB Music.

Moore, G. P. (1991). Piano trills. *Music Perception.*

Moore, G. P., Hary, D., and Naill, R. (1988). Trills: Some initial observations. *Psychomusicology, 7,* 153–162.

Newmark J., and Hochberg, F. (1987). Isolated painless manual incoordination in musicians. *Journal of Neurology, Neurosurgery, and Psychiatry, 50,* 291–295.

Nolan, W., and Eaton, R. (1989). Thumb problems of professional musicians. *Medical Problems of Performing Artists, 4*(1), 20–24.

Noth, J., Podoll, K., and Friedemann, H. -H. (1985). Long-loop reflexes in small hand muscles studied in normal subjects and in patients with Huntington's disease. *Brain, 108,* 65–80.

Ortmann, O. (1981). *The physiological mechanics of piano technique.* New York: DaCapo Press. (Originally published in 1929)

Palmer, C. (1989a). Computer graphics in music performance research. *Behavior Research Methods, Instruments & Computers, 21*(2), 265–270.

Palmer, C. (1989b). Mapping musical thought to musical performance. *Journal of Experimental Psychology: Human Perception and Performance, 15*(12), 331–346.

Panizza, M, Hallett, M., and Nilsson, J. (1989) Reciprocal inhibition in patients with hand cramps. *Neurology, 39,* 85–89.

Philipp, I. (1926). *Exercises for independence of the fingers.* New York: G. Schirmer. (Originally published in 1898)

Phillips, C. G. (1985). *Movements of the hand.* Liverpool: Liverpool University Press.

Pöppel E. (1989). Measurement of music and the cerebral clock: A new theory. *Leonardo, 22*(1), 83–89.

Raif, O. (1967). Finger preparation in piano playing. In G. Kochevitsky (Ed.), *The art of piano playing: A scientific approach* (pp. 12–13). Princeton: Summy-Birchard. (Originally published in 1901)

Roehmann, F. L., and Pierson, S. (1986). Music and medicine: A marginal interdisciplinary history. *Bulletin of the Council of Research in Music Education,* No. 88, 58ff.

Rothwell, J., Day, B., Obeso, J., Beradelli, A., and Marsden, C. D. (1988). Reciprocal inhibition between muscles of the human forearm in normal subjects and in patients with idiopathic torsion dystonia. In S. Fahn, C. D. Marsden, D. B. Calne (Eds.), *Dystonia 2: Advances in neurology, Vol. 50* (pp. 133–140). New York: Raven Press.

Salmon, P., and Newmark, J. (1989). Clinical applications of MIDI technology. *Medical Problems of Performing Artists, 4*(1), 25–31.

Salzberg, R. S. (1980). The effects of visual stimulus and instruction on intonation accuracy of string instrumentalists. *Psychology of Music, 8,* 42–49.

Sheehy, M. P., and Marsden, C. D. (1982). Writer's cramp—a focal dystonia. *Brain, 105,* 461–481.

Sheehy, M. P., Rothwell, J. C., and Marsden, C. D. (1988). Writer's cramp. In S. Fahn, C. D. Marsden, D. B. Calne (Eds.), *Dystonia 2: Advances in neurology, Vol. 50* (pp. 457–473). New York: Raven Press.

Sidnell, R. G. (1981). Motor learning in music education. In R. G. Taylor (Ed.), *Documentary report of the Ann Arbor Symposium* (pp. 28–35). Reston: MENC.

Smyth, M., and Wing, A. (Eds.), (1984). *The psychology of human movement.* New York: Academic Press.

Taubman, D. (1988). A teacher's perspective on musicians' injuries. In F. Roehmann and F. Wilson (Eds.), *The biology of music making: Proceedings of the 1984 Denver conference* (pp. 144–153). St. Louis: MMB Music.

Thach, W. T. (1987). Cerebellar inputs to motor cortex. In G. Bock, M. O'Conner, and J. Marsh (Eds.), *Motor areas of the cerebral cortex: Ciba Foundation Symposium 132.* New York: John Wiley.

Tubiana, R. (1988). Movement of the fingers. *Medical Problems of Performing Artists, 3*(4), 123–128.

Tubiana, R., and Chamagne, P. (1988). Functional anatomy of the hand. *Medical Problems of Performing Artists, 3*(3), 83–87.

Tubiana, R. Chamagne, P., and Brockman, R. (1989). Fundamental positions for instrumental musicians. *Medical Problems of Performing Artists, 4*(2), 73–76.

Wade, M. (1990). Motor skills and the making of music. In F. Wilson and F. Roehmann (Eds.), *Music and child development: Proceedings of the 1987 Denver conference* (pp. 157–178). St. Louis: MMB Music.

Wagner, C. (1974). Determination of finger flexibility. *European Journal of Applied Physiology, 32,* 259–278.

Wagner, C. (1977). Determination of the rotary flexibility of the elbow joint. *European Journal of Applied Physiology, 37,* 47–59.

Wagner, C. (1988a). The pianist's hand: Anthropometry and biomechanics. *Ergonomics, 31,* 97–131.

Wagner, C. (1988b). Success and failure in musical performance: Biomechanics of the hand. In F. Roehmann and F. Wilson (Eds.), *The biology of music making: Proceedings of the 1984 Denver conference* (pp. 154–179). St. Louis: MMB Music.

Watson, H., and Kalus, R. (1987). Achieving independent finger flexion—the guitarist's advantage. *Medical Problems of Performing Artists, 2*(2), 58–60.

Ward, W. D., and Burns, E. M. (1978). Singing without auditory feedback. *Journal of Research in Singing, 1,* 24–44.

Welch, G. F. (1985). A schema theory of how children learn to sing in tune. *Psychology of Music. 13,* 3–18.

Wilson, F. (1986). *Tone deaf and all thumbs? An introduction to music making for late bloomers and non-prodigies.* New York: Viking-Penguin.

Wilson, F. (1987). Fernando Laires and Dorothy Taubman discuss the exercises of Isidor Philipp. *Piano Quarterly, 138,* 36–39.

Wilson, F. (1988). Teaching hands, treating hands. *Piano Quarterly, 141,* 34–41.

Wilson, F. (1989). Acquisition and loss of skilled movement in musicians. *Seminars in Neurology, 9*(2), 146–151.

Wilson, F., Wagner, C., Hömberg, V., and Noth, J. (1991) Interaction of biomechanical and training factors in musicians with occupational cramp/focal dystonia. *Neurology, 41 3, Supplement 1,* 292–292.

Winold, H., and Thelen, E. (1989). Study in perceptual, cognitive, and motor aspects of highly skilled cellist [Abstract]. *Psychomusicology, 7*(2), 163–164.

·35·

TEACHING STRATEGIES AND STYLES

Malcolm J. Tait

EAST CAROLINA UNIVERSITY

Teaching strategies and styles have to do with the "how" of music teaching. They represent actions and interactions that take place in classrooms and studios after curriculum goals and procedures have been established. Teaching strategies involve vocabulary choice and usage, various forms of modeling, and management and implementation procedures. A combination of several strategies may be referred to as a teaching style; for example, an applied music teacher's style might involve a combination of certain kinds of modeling and certain kinds of questions based on a carefully chosen vocabulary. The same teacher working in another situation may choose another combination of strategies, which would produce a somewhat different teaching style. Moreover, just as several teaching strategies may define a teaching style, it is also true to say that several teaching styles may contribute to the teaching profile of a particular teacher.

Successful music teachers develop many strategies and styles in order to address the varied needs of their students. Accordingly, there is no one best style for teaching music, but rather a repertoire of strategies and a range of teaching styles.

An examination of the literature indicates that in the past, character traits were often considered to play an important role in determining the effectiveness of music teaching. Many basic music education texts provided long lists of desirable personality characteristics, such as tolerance, cooperativeness, dedication, and emotional stability. But lists of desirable combinations of character traits are not limited to music teaching. In a careful examination of 10 independent studies, Cruickshank (1990) notes a large number of items occurring across different subject areas and at different student age levels. The research suggests that

teachers are effective when they are enthusiastic, stimulating, encouraging, warm, task-oriented, and businesslike, tolerant, polite, tactful, trusting, flexible, adaptable and democratic. Also, they hold high expectations for pupils, do not seek personal recognition, care less about being liked, are able to overcome pupil stereotypes, are

less time-conscious, feel responsible for people learning, are able to express feelings and have good listening skills. (p. 82)

Several studies of effectiveness in music teaching reveal support for traits similar to those identified in Cruickshank's review. Baker (1982) asked over one hundred music educators and administrators to identify the competencies essential for effective music teaching. Among the most frequently identified characteristics were a sense of humor, qualities of enthusiasm and caring, and a sense of fairness. Fox and Beamish (1989) undertook a teaching competency study with one hundred high school general music teachers in New York State who identified four major "personal characteristics" they considered important for teaching. Flexibility was rated highest on a five-point scale (4.62), followed by creativity (4.58), sense of humor (4.57), and knowledge of student interests (4.44).

Just as it is helpful to identify character traits that can have a positive effect on teaching, the reverse may also be true: It is helpful to identify character traits that can contribute to ineffective music teaching and may ultimately lead to teacher burnout.

Rosenman and Friedman (1983) report that teaching burnout is most likely to be associated with such characteristics as aggressiveness, hostility, ambitiousness, competitiveness, tenseness, impatience, inability to relax away from work, suppressed hostility, orientation toward achievement, and denial of failure. Teachers with these characteristics feel pressured, are often engaged in multiple activities, are overly conscious of time in relation to output, are greatly influenced by criticisms, and are in need of constant social approval. Further, Hamann (1986) indicates that public school music educators have significantly higher burnout levels than do public school general classroom teachers. According to Hamann, factors that contribute to this state of affairs include insufficient funds and materials, students who are emotionally or physically abused, lack of parental or administrative support, chemical abuse, students dropping out, and widely varying interest and skill levels among the students.

Although it appears that character traits can influence music-teaching effectiveness, many additional variables need to be considered. In addition, the identification of character traits is essentially subjective, and research suggests that independent observers often disagree on whether or not a teacher has a particular character trait. Brand (1990) claims that

personalities of master teachers vary. Some are charismatic, some have great personal warmth, while others are more staid, their classroom and rehearsal styles differ too. Some are gentle and congenial, others rule more firmly. Most are master teachers as a result of some combination of skill, local customs, tastes, personal magnetism, and political savvy. (p. 23)

Schmidt (1989) notes that though a substantial amount of evidence exists implicating personality characteristics in classroom music teaching, far less evidence exists concerning relationships between personality variables and specific music teacher strategies (p. 259). Schmidt set out to explore the relationships among applied music-teaching behaviors and personality variables measured by the *Myers-Briggs Personality Type Indicator*. Subjects consisted of 43 college level applied music instructors in several different performing areas. The observed teacher behaviors in order of frequency were (1) teacher talk, (2) student performance, (3) teacher model, (4) approvals, (5) questions, and (6) disapprovals. When Schmidt analyzed relationships between the observed teacher behaviors and the Myers-Briggs measure he found that (1) extroverted and introverted subgroups did not differ significantly on the variables of disapprovals, talk, teacher model, and teacher questions but that (2) significant differences existed between these two subgroups and the rates of reinforcement and approvals. "Relatively extroverted subjects had a significantly higher rate of reinforcement and approvals than those subjects who were relatively introverted" (p. 264). Additionally, Schmidt found that "relatively intuitive, applied teachers tended to provide significantly more approvals and models/performances, had a higher rate of reinforcement, and conducted lessons at a faster pace than relatively sensing subjects." Schmidt concluded that "relationships between personality variables and other dimensions of applied teaching behavior such as nonverbal approvals and disapprovals, use of verbal imagery, and appropriate and inappropriate uses of approvals and disapprovals, should be the focus of future research" (p. 269).

The foregoing research illustrates the need for detailed descriptive research that focuses on specific teaching strategies to offer the profession a clearer understanding of the many variables involved in effective music teaching. Whereas research into personality traits and their effects on music teaching is likely to continue, other avenues of more specific teaching strategies hold greater potential for understanding music teaching.

Over a decade ago there was a strong call for experimental investigation that would test correlational findings in process/product studies to provide a positive influence within the arts education profession and in arts teacher programs in particular (Koehler, 1979 p. 57). In spite of increased awareness of the need for this basic research, the profession does not presently have a comprehensive body of research on which to build models for music-teaching effectiveness.

Most texts used in music teacher preparation include sections on methods of music teaching. However, the methodologies are derived not from research but from theories based in educational psychology. These offer general guidelines but lack specific strategies for classroom implementation. There is a dearth of empirical research that can shape effective music teaching, but increasing ethnographic research is beginning to disclose some of the subtle and complex events that take place in music classrooms. The purpose of this chapter is to review recent research that clarifies those procedures contributing to effective music teaching.

VERBAL STRATEGIES

Even though music teachers use language extensively in teaching, the research does not indicate predictable patterns of vocabulary usage for different ages or subject areas. Some studies have analyzed the frequency of teacher statements and questions, and the effects of verbal reinforcement, but the vocabularies used at particular ages and for particular purposes remain unclear.

Basically, the vocabulary options are threefold: first, a *professional* vocabulary derived from the music itself, which may be technical, conceptual, or aesthetic. Words such as vibrato, articulation, and legato are technical; words such as tone, rhythm, and crescendo are conceptual; words such as blend, balance, and intensity are aesthetic.

A second vocabulary can be termed *experiential* in that it helps integrate musical knowledge with personal experience of that knowledge. The three dimensions of an experiential vocabulary are imagery, with words that have colorful, pastoral, or religious connotations; metaphor, with words that evoke qualities of feeling or movement, such as dry, violent, or nervous; and analogy with living processes, with words such as cohesion, expectation, and stability.

A third vocabulary has to do with the *process* of music teaching and includes words such as analyze, imagine, describe, explore, express, and demonstrate. These words express processes that combine overt and covert musical behaviors. Such processes have not been the subject of rigorous scrutiny or research, but they do provide options for teacher directives and student behaviors, and may therefore be expected to occur in educational contexts. The three vocabularies derive from a theory of verbal and nonverbal strategies discussed by Tait at the Ann Arbor Symposium (1981).

Many studies claim that more than 50 percent of studio lesson and ensemble rehearsal time is spent in teacher verbal behavior (Carpenter, 1988; Kostka, 1984; Yarbrough and Price, 1981, 1989). However, Baxter and Stauffer (1988) rate the proportion of verbal usage as less than 50 percent of the total instructional time (Caldwell, 1980—35 percent; Thurman, 1977—40 percent; Papke, 1972—20 percent to 42 percent; Gipson, 1978—33 percent; Kostka, 1984—42 percent).

In spite of this variance in the reported data, at least one-third of music instructional time clearly involves a verbal component. Perhaps more significant is that the verbal component appears to be one directional: It is initiated by the teacher and continues to flow from teacher to students.

Hepler (1986) found that 40 percent of teacher-student interactions consisted of statements by the teacher, while only 3.52 percent of the interactions were teacher questions.

The ratio of teacher statements to teacher questions was 11.36 to 1.00. The ratio of teacher statements to student statements was 16.06 to 1.00 and the ratio of teacher questions to student questions was 6.07 to 1.00. Combined statements and questions show that the teachers dominated lessons by a ratio of 14.8 to 1.00. (p. 166)

In view of such dominance, one might expect the research to reveal a positive correlation between teacher verbal usage and increased teaching effectiveness. In fact, the opposite appears to be the case. According to Price (1989), ample research indicates that increased teacher talk can lead to decreased student attentiveness of all age levels (Forsythe, 1977; Kostka, 1984; Madsen and Alley, 1979; Moore, 1987; Price, 1989; Sims, 1986; Spralding, 1985; Witt, 1986; Yarbrough and Price, 1981). Price notes that "experienced music teachers use less teacher verbalization time than inexperienced ones" (p. 43). But we do not know the reasons for this phenomenon. If increased teacher talk lowers student attentiveness, a number of factors may be involved, including choice of vocabulary, ratio of student/teacher questions and statements, timing and pacing of the verbalization, as well as quality of the articulation.

With rich vocabularies available, one might expect varied, colorful, and imaginative language usage in classrooms, but this apparently is not the case. In their verbal statements in a lesson or rehearsal, teachers employ a largely professional vocabulary that focuses on technical and conceptual areas more than aesthetic or experiential areas.

Carpenter (1988), in a study of 14 teachers conducting 56 junior and senior high school band rehearsals, found that teachers made very little use of verbal imagery. The main vocabulary usage focused on technical directions (approximately 80 percent of the time). Similarly, Hepler (1986) found that college teachers in general studies courses in music placed greater emphasis on conceptual and technical statements than on expressive or aesthetic areas.

By contrast, Funk's (1982) study of three university choral directors found verbal imagery to be a prominent feature of choral rehearsals. Funk found verbal imagery to be an especially effective force when student vocal skills are lacking. He also claims that verbal imagery provides a means for establishing a relationship between the music, life experiences, and the students involved in making the music.

Similarly Elliott (1983) claims that "the use of metaphoric language [as distinct from professional language] is particularly recommended in the beginning stages of jazz instruction" (p. 323). Elliot's comment is particularly interesting

when compared with Hair's (1981) findings that children are able to perceive differences and changes in music stimuli long before they are able to label these changes appropriately, leading her to conclude that perhaps sound descriptive terms such as banging, choppy, or fast would be more appropriate than the traditional vocabulary. Hair's comment that "researchers should continue exploring how much and when associative training is needed before conceptual labels for aural-stimuli become meaningful" (p. 20) might well be directed to teachers.

Adding further weight to this need for experiential vocabulary to precede a professional vocabulary, Flowers (1983) found in a study based on 124 undergraduate nonmusic majors that increased study and familiarity with conceptual/technical vocabularies had little, if any, effect on recognition of musical changes in a subsequent musical task.

Putting labels on sound phenomena may be helpful in assessing accumulated knowledge, but it does not indicate the depth, intensity, or value of a musical experience. Elementary school music texts often include lists of words considered appropriate for different grade levels, words drawn primarily from a professional vocabulary. The foregoing evidence suggests that word recognition will not necessarily increase recognition of musical events for which the words stand. In order for the words to become personally useful, students need to describe and express their perception and experience of musical events in their own words, words drawn initially from an experiential vocabulary. Thus, use of questioning skills and problem-solving strategies needs to increase so that musical events can lead to shared experience and growth.

Music teachers use language to reward effort, to praise, or to disapprove of student behaviors. Although research indicates that specific approval encourages student attention and positive attitudes, music teachers are found to be more frequently disapproving than approving (McCoy, 1985; Price, 1989). According to Carpenter (1988), "Teachers are inclined to be specific when giving disapproval and more likely to be general when giving approving feedback" (p. 37). According to Yarbrough and Price (1989), band directors may be disapproving as much as 80 percent of the time, and although some of that disapproval may be registered nonverbally, the majority involves verbal behavior. Whereas praise tends to be general most of the time, Salzburg and Salzburg (1981) found that specific praise that reinforced desired response leads to improved motor skills among elementary string players.

Kostka (1984) investigated teacher reinforcements, lesson time use, and student attentiveness in private piano lessons. Subjects were divided into elementary, secondary, and adult age groups. She found that teacher approvals and disapprovals were nearly equal, with more reinforcements given for performance than for social behavior. Students were on-task for the majority of the observed periods; lesson time was primarily divided between student performance (56 percent) and teacher talk (42 percent).

Nichols (1983) made an interesting distinction between praise and encouragement: He claimed praise focuses on personality and ego involvement while encouragement focuses on the particular task at hand. McCoy's (1985) statement that "neither elaborate praise nor strong criticism has any positive correlations with achievement" (p. 12) might be borne in mind here.

Summary

Research into verbal strategies in music teaching reveals an imprecise picture. Though music teachers talk for significant periods of time, the talk does not appear to relate positively to student learning. In addition, teacher vocabularies generally do not represent the broad scope of the musical experience. Language is employed for awarding praise or reinforcement and is nonspecific and general. Verbal strategies appear to be too generalized and teacher initiated for depth of interaction and communication. The challenge is to use words that enliven and enrich the musical experience. Imaginative and detailed research is needed to move the profession forward in more appropriate and effective directions.

NONVERBAL STRATEGIES

In a general sense nonverbal communication can serve many functions. For example, in addition to conveying warmth and affection, approval or disapproval, nonverbal communication can regulate the pace of verbal exchanges; it can reveal emotional states, values, and attitudes; and most importantly, it can influence the behavior and performance of others.

Music teaching makes considerable use of nonverbal communication as it occurs in three major areas: first, musical modeling in which teacher performance provides a total image of what is desired either vocally or instrumentally; second, aural modeling in which a teacher employs phonetic vocalization including humming and syllables in order to convey particular meanings or points of emphasis within the music; and third, physical modeling including facial expressions, physical gestures, and more formal conducting. It should be noted that physical and aural modeling frequently accompany and reinforce one another.

The relationships between nonverbal strategies and music-teaching effectiveness have not been the subject of extensive research. Music teachers seem to employ various kinds of modeling both intuitively and spontaneously and as reinforcement for verbal strategies. Therefore, although it is possible to distinguish between three kinds of nonverbal strategies, the research tends to group them together under the general rubric of modeling. Several recent developments suggest the profession would benefit from a closer examination of the values of various forms of modeling and nonverbal strategies in music teaching. These include the educational theories of Bandura (1986) and subsequent research by Sang (1987) and others.

Bandura's learning theories bear on music teaching be-

cause he has drawn attention to the importance of observed behaviors in the role of imitation in the learning process. He distinguishes between observed behaviors that are learned and those that are actually displayed. According to Bandura's theory of social cognition, children learn not simply through imitation per se but through complex cognitive processing of the observed behaviors. Children are natural imitators regardless of the quality of the model; therefore, in a sophisticated art form such as music, modeling can greatly affect the quality of the learning.

Sang (1987) undertook a study of the relationships between instrumental music teacher's modeling skills and pupil performance behaviors. Sang's findings—that teacher talk represented 40 percent of class time, whereas modeling time represented only 26 percent—support data on verbal strategies presented earlier in this chapter. Of more relevance here is Sang's claim that modeling is more efficient than verbalizing about performance behaviors by a margin of nearly three to one. On the basis of these results Sang argues that "teachers who have stronger modeling skills and apply these skills in teaching are more likely to produce students who perform better than teachers who do not" (p. 158).

Studies by Anderson (1981), Vereen (1968), and Thurman (1977) produced evidence that further supports modeling as effective for music skill development. Rosenthal (1984) studied 44 college music education students to determine the relative effectiveness of musical and verbal models alone and in combination and found that direct musical modeling without additional verbal explanation was the most effective means for improving performance. Even more dramatically, in a study of college-age advanced instrumentalists, Rosenthal, Wilson, Evans, and Greenwalt (1988) determined that listening to a musical model without opportunity to practice was nearly as effective as practicing with the instrument. Such a finding would be unlikely with students who are not technically advanced.

Although research supports modeling as an effective means for improving musical performance, Pontious (1982) and Kostka (1984) found that teachers in ensemble settings use modeling less than 10 percent of the instructional time. One wonders if this is because teachers believe modeling is inappropriate or because they feel inadequate for the task. The choice not to model stems from a different pedagogical viewpoint. The pianist Andre Watts (1989) shares some reservations about modeling when he says,

I try to avoid playing for students. There are some who may not be up to par technically so I'll probably play a bit more for them. But I don't play for those who have a lot of technical equipment, because they are also very good at imitating. Once they've copied the sound, they just repeat it and it doesn't mean anything. (p. 13)

A similar attitude is noted by Nichols (1983) in an account of Isaac Stern teaching while on a visit to China.

I particularly recall his treatment of a girl whose playing was stilted. He asked her to hum the piece. She was embarrassed but eventually hummed it more lyrically than she had played it. Stern beamed and told her to play it that way. She did so to Stern's visible delight. She appeared to not only learn from this encouraging treatment but to enjoy the music more. (p. 3)

Clearly Stern chose not to model for this student but rather to help her define her own sense of musicality by developing an aural model for her own benefit. The student's humming provided an opportunity to clarify and intensify the musical image.

It is important to note that while Stern did not provide a model, he did call forth a model from the student. One might make a comparison with a verbal strategy in which the teacher asks a question rather than making a statement, thus forcing the student to seek an answer from within.

Although it is apparent that musical skill development can be enhanced by teacher modeling, some concern exists as to whether the resulting skills are superficial and impersonal or whether they do in fact enhance students' musical expressive abilities. The apparent dilemma here is whether in facilitating performance through teacher modeling we may bypass expressive and creative maturational processes; musical performance may "improve," but students' musical growth may be inhibited. Yet the dilemma may be more apparent than real: Both skill and creativity are intrinsic to musical growth, and both can be nourished with appropriate teaching strategies.

Gardner (1973) sees imitation based on teacher modeling as a legitimate stage in aesthetic development, but he argues that carried to extremes it can limit a child's creativity. Gardner recommends a developmental perspective in which

first the child should be allowed to explore the medium as fully and completely as possible; next, through careful guidance and posing problems he should have the opportunity to build up sufficient skills to capture the qualities and create the effects he desires; finally, having a sense of his own abilities and goals, he should be exposed to the great works of his medium and be encouraged to study and imitate them so that he can see how effects have been achieved by others working in the same craft. (p. 286)

Further discussion of Gardner's theories are found later in this chapter.

The word "imitation" needs clarification in terms of Bandura's and Gardner's use of it as well as the loose connotation it has in teaching. Whereas imitation is essentially a function of students and modeling a function of teachers, these distinctions are not always clear. For example, sometimes a teacher may choose to imitate a student in order to highlight a student's particular problem. Sometimes a student may model another student or a style of performance derived from a source other than the teacher. Just as verbal communication should be more than a single teacher-to-student act, so imitation and other forms of nonverbal communication can go far beyond one-directional teaching.

Aural modeling is one nonverbal strategy that can enhance both skill and creative development. "This method has become a direct and economical means of communicating nonverbally and noninstrumentally because no highly

technical skill is required; simply a desire or willingness to share and a vivid repertoire of sound syllables to draw on" (Tait and Haack, p. 86, 1984).

Aural modeling has always been a natural and intrinsic part of jazz, where body language reinforces felt accents, syncopations, phrase beginnings and endings, climaxes, cadence points, dramatic gestures, and dynamic growth and decay. Scat syllables, a form of phonetic vocalization, provide the jazz educator with opportunities to share "insights about time—feel patterns, jazz phrasing and articulation, dramatic events, sound qualities and overall style features" (Elliott, p. 334, 1983).

Professional musicians, and particularly conductors, make considerable use of aural modeling in their rehearsal procedures. We do not know the extent to which this strategy is employed in the school classroom or rehearsal situations, but it is a form of modeling and nonverbal communication that can be quite precise, and is therefore a valuable music teaching strategy.

In addition to musical modeling and aural modeling, there is physical modeling, in which gestures and facial expressions anticipate, clarify, and coordinate the musical events. Clearly dance and conducting are forms of physical modeling that require a wide range of qualitative movement and feeling.

Yarbrough (1975) studied the magnitude or intensity of conductor's nonverbal gestures, including such things as facial expressions, gesture, and vocal inflexion and found that students were more attentive during high-magnitude conditions but that no significant improvement in the actual musical performance resulted. A study by Yarborough and Price (1981) showed that eye contact has a strong relationship to on-task behavior; the least teacher eye contact produced more off-task behavior. More recently, Madsen, Standley, and Cassidy (1989) concluded that intensity may be an important attribute of effective music teaching. Although intensity includes several nonverbal behaviors such as eye contact, body movements, postures, and gestures, behaviors similar to those in Yarbrough's magnitude concept, the authors claim that "teacher intensity is an attribute that can be learned and demonstrated by preservice music teachers and that almost everyone can recognize it with very high reliability" (p. 92).

Researchers need to determine the short- and long-term effects of nonverbal teaching strategies in the music classroom and studio. In some instances modeling appears helpful in clarifying musical images in creative and essentially artistic ways. In other instances it can evoke imitation behaviors, thus reducing student initiative. And while the short-term gains may seem impressive, growth in individual musicianship and problem solving may be inhibited.

The research indicates that music lessons are frequently dominated by teacher verbal and nonverbal strategies. Students do not interact verbally, and for the most part their nonverbal behaviors are limited to actual performance. This situation is unlikely to change so long as music education places greater emphasis on teacher-directed musical products than on student-centered processes.

STRATEGY SELECTION AND SEQUENCING

Strategy selection and sequencing may be considered at various levels of complexity. In classrooms and studios, selection and sequencing often take place from moment to moment based on specific goals and student progress. In the larger arena the process of strategy selection and sequencing involves profound philosophical and psychological considerations. This section will begin with a review of studies focusing on strategy selection within lessons, then move toward larger and more far-reaching considerations.

Model development for effective classroom teaching took a major step forward in the 1970s and 1980s with the work of Madeline Hunter (1986). In her Instructional Theory Into Practice (ITIP) model, teachers learn to design lessons using very specific components in a five-step sequence, beginning with activities aimed at getting students involved in the lesson. The second step develops very clear and observable objectives; the third step breaks up the instruction into conceptual blocks or segments; the fourth step provides opportunities for checking student understanding and for guided practice; and the fifth step leads to final checks and independent practice. Hunter's ITIP model has been particularly effective in the areas of reading and mathematics, in terms of both teacher effectiveness and student achievement. Although derived from the academic classroom, Hunter's ITIP model has important implications for music classrooms and studios; for example, Hunter supports the use of modeling to introduce new concepts, and her emphasis on more precise verbal and nonverbal strategies is certainly appropriate for music.

Price (1989), building on the data from earlier studies, argues for a three-step sequence in music-teaching and rehearsal situations, as follows: The first step involves the teacher's presenting the task, either verbally or nonverbally. The second step involves students interacting with the task and/or the teacher, again either verbally or nonverbally. The third step in the cycle requires the teacher to give feedback, also verbal and nonverbal: The feedback must be task oriented and as specific as possible. Price claims the three-step sequence "will likely result in more efficient use of class/rehearsal time in which students pay better attention, perform better and are more positive about the teacher and the music" (p. 44).

Favorable aspects of this approach include clarification of student expectations, greater interaction between teacher and learners, and feedback that supports and reinforces desired responses. Within each step there are opportunities for additional research with regard to vocabulary usage, the role of questioning, and the employment of nonverbal strategies. Research is also needed to determine whether the three-step sequence is more appropriate to traditional performance training than it is to a more creativity-centered, open-ended philosophy focusing on the exploration of music.

In a study of 29 elementary music classes over the period of 1 year, Taebel and Coker (1980) attempted to establish correlations between effective music teaching and student achievement. Their findings were somewhat disappointing. Although the data demonstrated that the teacher was the most important factor in pupil learning, the data did not reveal which variables contributed most significantly to improved student performance. Some evidence suggested that more effective teaching takes place when the lesson objectives are related to student interests and needs, and also when students initiate verbal interaction with the teacher.

There have been many process/product studies similar to those conducted by Taebel and Coker but exploring subjects other than music. Cruickshank (1990) summarized 10 such studies and concluded that

effective teachers demonstrate clarity, provide variety, establish and maintain momentum, make effective use of small groups, encourage more pupil participation, monitor and attend to pupils and structure teaching and learning. Also, they take advantage of unexpected events (teachable moments), monitor seat work, use both open-ended and lower-order questions, involve pupils in peer teaching, use programmed materials and manipulation, use large group instruction, avoid complexity by providing information in small chunks, use less busy work and use fewer traditional materials. Additionally they show pupils the importance of what is to be learned, demonstrate the thinking processes necessary for learning, anticipate and correct pupil misconceptions and are reflective about what they are doing with respect to teaching and learning. (p. 83)

Many of the detailed strategies outlined by Cruickshank clearly call for depth interactions between teachers and students that involve both verbal and nonverbal communication. The data suggest images of learning environments that are structured yet flexible, resourceful, and innovative. One would hope that many of the above qualities would be observed in music classrooms throughout the country, but no data exist to substantiate (or contradict) that hope.

Indications from the few process/product studies in music-teaching effectiveness may enable us to make certain assumptions about the bases for strategy selection. Perhaps the main bases are beliefs about the nature of music and beliefs about the teacher's own learning experiences, which together result in beliefs about what will work best for the teacher's own students.

If teachers believe that art is as Bronowski (1978) says, "an unfinished statement" (p. 126), then many open-ended and creative strategies are likely to be encouraged in music classrooms and studios. According to Thomas (1970), teachers who favor an open-ended approach are

likely to be as unintrusive as possible and resist the impulse to inflict their expertise on students. They must be guides, creators of problems, resource people, stimulators of creative thinking and astute musicians capable of responding to complex musical ideas while remaining sensitive to the creative insight of students. It is not their prerogative to impose judgments but rather cultivate them. Their function is to stimulate not dominate, to encourage not to control, to question far more than to answer. Discovery may be guided but never dictated. (p. 23)

If, on the other hand, music is considered to be an art form with strong traditions and canonic standards, then individual investment and interpretation are likely to be replaced by carefully sequenced skill development and an emphasis on authentic replication. The role of the teacher in this instance is that of providing a very clear model, probably a musical model that the student will be expected to copy as faithfully as possible. The teacher will establish a tight regimen of expectations both within the lessons and during practice sessions so there will be few opportunities for dialogue, exploration, or shared experience.

If teachers view their role as limited to instruction, then they become transmitters of information and developers of skill. Consequently, teaching strategies will be relatively limited and inflexible. They may produce rapid learning in selected areas, but learnings that are narrow and short-lived. On the other hand, teachers who view their role as learning facilitators will plan environments that challenge individual growth. Teaching strategies will be many and varied. Students as a result may learn as much about themselves as about the subject or skill they are involved with. Progress may be slower than in the above example but may also be sustained for longer periods.

It would seem that elements of both philosophical viewpoints are desirable and not mutually exclusive, appropriately receiving different emphases at different times. If philosophical considerations about the nature of music provide one basis for strategy selection, psychology may provide another.

The field of cognitive psychology has generated learning theories, which in turn have produced new teaching strategies. According to Rabinowitz (1988), ''Knowledge about the how, where and why of strategy use [is] important if students are to take control of their cognitive processing'' (p. 234). He argues that students need to be provided with metacognitive knowledge concerning the value of a particular strategy and its appropriate contexts. In applying this theory to music teaching, one would go beyond a single strategy and employ whatever verbal or nonverbal strategies heighten the student's self-awareness of newly acquired skills and concepts. If students' self-awareness is nourished, it is argued, they are more likely to retain the new knowledge and be able to apply it in new situations.

Increased emphasis on cognitive processing encourages learnings that foster relationships and interconnectedness. Joyce and Weil (1986) state that there are several ''points of entry'' to increased understanding, including scholarly knowledge derived from academic disciplines, personal knowledge derived from internal experience or realization, and social interaction that draws on group dynamics. These general models break down into several subgroups or families of models. Joyce and Weil claim that ''teaching is the creation of learning environments and different environments are directed toward or nurture different kinds of learning'' (p. 418). For example, in music situations a strategy that utilizes an experiential vocabulary is likely to assist in the development of personal knowledge. ''Metaphoric activity thus depends and draws from the students' knowledge helping them connect ideas from familiar content to those from new content, or view familiar content from a new perspective'' (p. 166). In a music rehearsal situation the environment

model might be one that draws on the social situation to help develop diagnostic skills and remediation. The choral director who encourages interaction is then building cooperative problem-solving skills. In supporting the concept that models and families of models are not mutually exclusive, Joyce and Weil add credence to the argument that effective music teaching derives from many strategies and many styles. Resourceful teachers adapt their strategies to the needs of learners, so that where one strategy is not effective an alternative strategy or a composite model is employed. Music teaching that is dominated by a single strategy such as musical modeling may hamper a learner's self-awareness as well as opportunities for creative self-investment.

A third area of influence in selecting music-teaching strategies has to do with the kinds of knowledge that need to be developed. Since types of knowledge differ, so do the ways of knowing or learning. Schuell (1988, p. 150) suggests seven types of knowledge in music education: propositional knowledge (the organized body of verbal knowledge); procedural knowledge (intellectual skills such as analysis); psychomotor knowledge (performing skills); images (aesthetic implications of notation); aural knowledge (ability to think in sound); attitudes (knowledge of how to practice); and emotions (visceral involvement).

If there are indeed seven types of musical knowledge, then it is important to determine whether certain teaching strategies fit more naturally with certain bodies of knowledge. For example, it seems likely that propositional knowledge would fit with verbal strategies based on a professional vocabulary. Psychomotor knowledge would fit with modeling strategies but also with experiential and behavioral vocabularies if metacognition were considered to be important. It would seem that aural knowledge might include verbal strategies within a social context so that perception and problem solving could be shared experiences. Similarly, procedural knowledge might best be developed through the use of verbal strategies in social settings so that dialogue and discussion could assist problem solving. Image knowledge and attitude knowledge probably receive less attention in the classroom than do some other forms of knowledge, and, according to Schuell, this could be detrimental for learners because ''the learner passes through a series of stages involving different types of learning. If the teacher ignores the various stages and focuses only on the terminal performance, then learning could be haphazard and inefficient'' (p. 151).

Schuell's thesis offers implications as to why students drop out of music education, for if certain types of knowledge are omitted from their learning process, they will feel frustrated with their progress. Similarly, a poor fit between the knowledge to be gained and the strategies employed to gain that knowledge will result in frustration for the student.

Piagetian psychologists support the concept of appropriate learnings for certain ages based on developmental profiles. In the context of this chapter, the question of appropriate teaching strategies for appropriate ages assumes considerable importance. One might argue that this is the most important consideration in determining the sequence of teaching strategies.

Gardner (1990) believes that within the American school system students up to the age of about 7 should have ample opportunity to explore materials and media on their own, building structures and deriving meanings as they discover their own cognitive processes. Between the ages of 7 and 14, the focus should be on the development of literacies and skills within an apprenticeship environment that encourages imaginative applications. Gardner proposes a third 7-year phase after age 14 when the two earlier phases should come together to focus on more extended projects that are both personally and socially significant.

Gardner's theory recognizes the importance of both creativity and skill development within a developmental framework. It also implies a comprehensive range of teaching strategies based on a broad interpretation of music and recognition of individual potential.

The references in this section suggest that many variables influence the selection and sequencing of teaching strategies. The music-teaching profession needs to address the question of teaching strategies on several levels. More detailed and longitudinal studies are needed to explore relationships between categories of musical knowledge and strategies for teaching that knowledge. More studies are needed to determine how teaching strategies are affected by a teacher's perception of music. The profession needs to explore the implications of open-ended teaching strategies vis-à-vis more traditional approaches and their appropriateness for particular ages. These topics have far-reaching implications for the nature of music and how it can best be taught.

SUMMARY

The general model for teaching music has often been derived from the conservatory master teacher where the focus is on the musical score and the teacher analyzes the performance, identifies problems, and suggests remedies. In some situations the learning process is one of strict imitation of the master teacher, but in others there is room for flexibility so that dialogue can develop and students are encouraged to share their opinions. However, the general model remains essentially teacher centered, with minimal opportunities for students to become aware of their own roles in the music-learning process. Knowledge and skill are usually teacher based and teacher developed. This model appears to be reasonably successful with musically motivated students and where large amounts of practice time are dedicated to achieving or refining desired responses. But given the appar-

ent need for instant gratification in so many sectors of contemporary society, the model is not suited to the vast majority of students.

Education fails if it does not help students understand their experiences. By the same token, music education fails if it does not help them understand their musical experiences. A musical experience must have significance for a participant if it is to be educationally worthwhile. Clearly this is a primary goal for music education regardless of the social or cultural context. Therefore the focus must be on teaching strategies that will enhance the significance of a musical experience for each participant.

Students who drop out of music generally do so because musical experiences are not significant for them. In other words, experiences have not been internalized or personalized. A personal experience will most likely be a significant experience. It appears that music education has not challenged sufficient numbers of students to define musical problems and explore musical options and solutions. Diagnosis and remediation have more often than not been the teacher's activity, and as a result music education has gradually become divorced from its own vital roots—namely, the creative and imaginative lives of children.

Society is going to need many more creative people in the next decade, and knowledge of the creative process is going to help fulfill that need. Needed are people who will think imaginatively, divergently, and intuitively as well as logically, deductively, and analytically; people who will involve their feelings as well as their thinking and who will share those feelings in constructive ways, including musical events of their own making.

The studies in the chapter suggest that music-teaching strategies can encourage greater amounts of student input into the educational enterprise. Since increased teacher talk leads to lower student attention, there is at least some justification for increasing student talk. Expanded vocabularies tied to developmentally appropriate verbal and nonverbal strategies can enliven the environment and encourage students to invest themselves more fully in the learning process. By the same token, teaching strategies need to become more specific in terms of tasks and feedback.

The profession would benefit greatly from a range of teaching models that could demonstrate relationships between desired student outcomes and potential strategies for achieving those outcomes. Collaborative research between classroom teachers and university teachers should be encouraged as being one of the most appropriate means for achieving this goal.

References

Anderson, J. N. (1981). Effects of tape-recorded aural models on sight reading and performance skills. *Journal of Research in Music Education, 29,* 23–30.

Baker, P. J. (1982). The development of a music teacher checklist for use by administrators, music supervisors and teachers in evaluat-

ing music teaching. Unpublished doctoral dissertation, University of Oregon, Eugene.

Bandura, A. (1986). *Social foundations of thought and action: A social cognitive theory.* Englewood Cliffs: Prentice Hall.

Baxter, S. G., and Stauffer, S. L. (1988). Music teaching: A review of common practice. In C. Fowler (Ed.), *The Crane Symposium: Toward an understanding of the teaching and learning of music performance*. Potsdam: College of the State University of New York.

Brand, M. (1990). Master music teachers: What makes them great? *Music Educators Journal, 77*(2), 22–25.

Bronowski, J. (1978). *The visionary eye*. Cambridge: M.I.T. Press.

Caldwell, W. M. (1980). A time analysis of selected musical elements and leadership behaviors of successful high school choral conductors. Unpublished doctoral dissertation, Florida State University, Tallahassee.

Carpenter, R. A. (1988). A descriptive analysis of relationships between verbal behaviors of teacher-conductors and ratings of selected junior and senior high school band rehearsals. *Update, 7,* 37–40.

Cruickshank, D. (1990). *Research that informs teachers and teacher educators*. Bloomington: Phi Delta Kappa Educational Foundation.

Elliott, D. J. (1983). Descriptive philosophical and practical bases for jazz education: A Canadian perspective. Unpublished doctoral dissertation, Case Western Reserve University, Cleveland.

Flowers, P. J. (1983). The effect of instruction in vocabulary and listening on nonmusicians' descriptions of changes in music. *Journal of Research in Music Education, 31,* 179–189.

Forsythe, J. L. (1977). Elementary student attending behavior as a function of classroom activity. *Journal of Research in Music Education, 25,* 228–239.

Fox, D., and Beamish, S. R. (1989). A survey of teaching competencies for high school general music. *Update, 8,* 33–36.

Funk, G. (1982). Verbal imagery: Illuminator of the expressive content in choral music. Unpublished doctoral dissertation, Arizona State University, Tempe.

Gardner, H. (1973). *The arts and human development*. New York: John Wiley.

Gardner, H. (1990). *To open minds*. New York: Basic Books.

Gipson, R. C. (1978). An observational analysis of wind instrument private lessons. Unpublished doctoral dissertation, Pennsylvania State University, University Park.

Hair, H. I. (1981). Verbal identification of music concepts. *Journal of Research in Music Education, 29,* 11–21.

Hamann, D. L. (1986). Burnout and the public school orchestra director. *Update, 4,* 11–14.

Hepler, L. E. (1986). The measurement of teacher/student interaction in private music lessons and its relation to teacher field dependence/field independence. Unpublished doctoral dissertation, Case Western Reserve University, Cleveland.

Hunter, M. (1986). *Mastery teaching*. University of California, Los Angeles, El Segundo: TIP Publications.

Joyce, B., and Weil, M. (1986). *Models of teaching* (3rd ed.). Englewood Cliffs: Prentice-Hall.

Koehler, V. (1979). Research on teaching: Implications for research on the teaching of the arts. *The teaching process and arts and aesthetics*. St. Louis: CEMREL.

Kostka, M. J. (1984). An investigation of reinforcements, time use and student attentiveness in piano lessons. *Journal of Research in Music Education, 32,* 113–122.

Madsen, C. K., and Alley, J. (1979). The effect of reinforcement on attentiveness: A comparison of behaviorally trained music therapists and other professionals with implications for competency-based academic preparation. *Journal of Music Therapy, 16,* 70–82.

Madsen, C. K., Standley, J. M., and Cassidy, J. W. (1989). Demonstration and recognition of high and low contrasts in teacher intensity. *Journal of Research in Music Education, 37,* 85–92.

McCoy, C. W. (1985). The ensemble director as effective teacher: A review of selected research. *Update, 3,* 9–12.

Moore, R. S. (1987). Effect of age, sex and activity on children's attentiveness in elementary school music classes. In C. K. Madsen and C. A. Prickett (Eds.), *Applications of Research in Music Behavior* (pp. 26–31). Tuscaloosa: University of Alabama Press.

Nicholls, J. G. (1983). Task involvement in music. *Documentary report of the Ann Arbor symposium on the applications of psychology to the teaching and learning of music. Session III: Motivation and creativity*. Reston: Music Educators National Conference.

Papke, R. E. (1972). An investigation of the instrumental music director's rehearsal behavior utilizing an evaluative instrument with implications for broadening perspectives in secondary school instrumental curricula. Unpublished doctoral dissertation, University of Minnesota, Minneapolis.

Pontious, M. F. (1982). A profile of rehearsal technique and interaction of selected band conductors. Unpublished doctoral dissertation, University of Illinois, Urbana.

Price, H. E. (1989). An effective way to teach and rehearse: Research supports using sequential patterns. *Update, 8,* 42–46.

Rabinowitz, M. (1988). On teaching cognitive strategies: The influence of accessibility of conceptual knowledge. *Contemporary Educational Psychology, 13,* 229–234.

Rosenthal, R. K. (1984). The relative effects of guided model, model only, guide only, and practice only treatments on the accuracy of advanced instrumentalists' musical performance. *Journal of Research in Music Education, 32,* 265–273.

Rosenthal, R. K., Wilson, M., Evans, M., and Greenwalt, L. (1988). Effects of different practice conditions on advanced instrumentalists performance accuracy. *Journal of Research in Music Education, 36,* 250–257.

Salzburg, R. A., and Salzburg, C. L. (1981). Praise and corrective feedback in the remediation of incorrect left-hand positions of elementary string players. *Journal of Research in Music Education, 29,* 125–133.

Sang, R. C. (1987). A study of the relationship between instrumental music teachers' modeling skills and pupil performance behaviors. *Bulletin of the Council for Research in Music Education, 91,* 155–159.

Schmidt, C. P. (1989). Applied music teaching behavior as a function of selected personality variables. *Journal of Research in Music Education, 37,* 258–271.

Schuell, T. J. (1988). The role of transfer in the learning and teaching of music: A cognitive perspective. In C. Fowler (Ed.), *The Crane Symposium: Toward an understanding of the teaching and learning of musical performance*. Potsdam: College of the State University of New York.

Sims, W. L. (1986). The effect of high versus low teacher affect and passive versus active student activity during music listening on preschool children's attention, piece preference, time spent listening, and piece recognition. *Journal of Research in Music Education, 34,* 173–191.

Spralding, R. L. (1985). The effect of time out from performance on attentiveness and attitude of university band students. *Journal of Research in Music Education, 33,* 123–127.

Taebel, D. K., and Coker, J. G. (1980). Teaching effectiveness in elementary classroom music: Relationships among competency measures, pupil product measures, certain attribute variables. *Journal of Research in Music Education, 28,* 250–264.

Tait, M. J. (1981). Motivation and affect. *Documentary report of the Ann Arbor Symposium: Applications of psychology to teaching and learning music*. Reston: Music Educators National Conference.

Tait, M. J., and Haack, P. (1984). *Principles and processes of music education: New perspectives.* New York: Teachers College Press, Columbia University.

Thomas, R. B. (1970). *MMCP synthesis.* Bardonia: Media Materials.

Thurman, V. L. (1977). A frequency and time description of selected rehearsal behaviors used by five choral conductors. Unpublished doctoral dissertation, University of Illinois, Urbana.

Vereen, W. N. (1968). A study of rehearsal techniques for symphonic band. Unpublished doctoral dissertation, University of Missouri, Kansas City.

Watts, A. (1989). Andre Watts on teachers and teaching. In E. Mach (Ed.), *American Music Teacher.* April–May.

Witt, A. C. (1986). Use of class time and student attentiveness in secondary instrumental music rehearsals. *Journal of Research in Music Education, 34,* 34–42.

Yarbrough, C. (1975). Effects of magnitude of conductor behavior on students in selected mixed choruses. *Journal of Research in Music Education, 23,* 134–146.

Yarbrough, C. and Price, H. E. (1981). Prediction of performer attentiveness based on rehearsal activity and teacher behavior. *Journal of Research in Music Education, 29,* 209–217.

Yarbrough, C. and Price, H. E. (1989). Sequential patterns of instruction in music. *Journal of Research in Music Education, 37,* 179–187.

·36·

SEQUENCING FOR EFFICIENT LEARNING

Darrel L. Walters

TEMPLE UNIVERSITY

Arthur Pryor, internationally acclaimed trombonist with the Sousa band, allegedly attributed his musicianship to having come from a little town in Missouri where there were "no teachers to get in my way." More recently, neurologist and amateur musician Frank Wilson, commenting about the impatience of music students, observed that "beginners tend to resent the learning process, as though it were some sort of obstacle in their way" (Wilson, 1986, p. 191). The last thing a teacher wants to do is obstruct learning, and the best way to avoid that is to present students with well-sequenced learning experiences. Good teachers think about more than what to teach and how to teach; they think about when and when not to teach particular lessons.

The most damaging characteristic of inefficient teaching/learning is that it compounds itself. Introducing Barry Green's *The Inner Game of Music,* Timothy Gallwey, author of *The Inner Game of Tennis,* made an important observation about young players: "I found that much of the self-interference in the practice of sports originated in the way they [the children] were taught" (Green, 1986, p. vii). In simplest terms, if the teacher of sports (or music) works cross-grain to Mother Nature, the student practices and performs cross-grain to Mother Nature long after the teacher has departed.

Some of Barry Green's "naturalist" statements in *The Inner Game of Music* align with fundamental tenets of learning theories and research findings. He reflects on hearing bassist Gary Karr perform: "What I learned from that concert was worth ten years of lessons" (p. 132). How important is modeling to the early stages of a music-learning sequence? Investigating the influence of several factors on the tonal memory of young children, Mitchell (1985, p. 47) found the one statistically significant factor to be the "presence of older musical siblings" who served as constant in-house models. Green elaborated further on the value of the Karr model, saying that he could "translate" what he saw and heard into his own playing. Reflecting on what he learned in

the process of that translation, he added, "Maybe there are 'information' subjects where verbal instruction works best, but music is something the body is going to have to perform and it's best learned by the body that's going to do the performing" (p. 132). Emile Jaques-Dalcroze is smiling; he knew a century ago that musical performance improved when preceded by body performance.

Teachers necessarily sequence material, usually on the basis of intuition and experience, and they judge how well published materials are sequenced. Do "fundamental" materials that contain exercises in note naming (e.g., spell "cabbage" and "baggage" on the staff) take student and teacher to the starting point of music learning as the name implies? Are music "methods" truly methodical? Music teachers need to decide what is fundamental and what constitutes a method, they need to base curricula on that knowledge, and then they need to take charge of the learning process. The purpose of this chapter is to add to the intuition and experience of teachers a measure of insight from theorists and scientists about how sequencing of teaching in general and sequencing of music teaching in particular may facilitate efficient learning.

Public and parochial school music teachers need to be especially confident of their product because they often need to assert themselves when opposed by persons who conceive of school music as entertainment and competition with a little note spelling thrown in. "If we won't tell the people what we are trying to accomplish," wrote Arthur Foshay, "they will tell us . . . and their efforts are full of mistakes" (1980, p. 93). Although music teachers (like music students) gain expertise principally by doing, their doing spawns more vivid, more comprehensive, and more accurate learning if combined with reading and thinking. This chapter, indeed this entire handbook, is intended to add measurably to the reading and thinking material available to music teachers.

CONCEPTS OF READINESS
AND SEQUENCING

In *Musical Growth and Development,* McDonald and Simons (1989) assert that "effective instruction is as much dependent upon the teacher's possession of scientific knowledge of children's musical development as upon skills and imagination" (p. 23); they follow with information not about the work of music-learning theorists but about the work of the general learning theorists Jean Piaget, Jerome Bruner, and Maria Montessori. Fowler writes, "It is sometimes assumed that there exists in research a corpus of knowledge that identifies correct procedures for teachers of music to follow. The authors have found this not to be the case" (1988, p. 60). Even more boldly, McDonald and Simons write that "no fully developed theory of music learning has yet been developed" (p. 23), a statement with which some music psychologist may disagree. Those glum statements notwithstanding, there does exist valuable information about the sequencing of learning, much of which is applicable to the teaching of music.

Teaching sequences are built on the concept of readiness. Exactly what is readiness? Early in this century Edward Thorndike, a pioneer in learning theory, described readiness in terms of "satisfying" conditions and "annoying" conditions. He stated that one who is ready for an activity and is given that activity experiences satisfaction, and one who is not ready and is given the activity experiences annoyance. Satisfaction, therefore, is a sign of readiness, and annoyance a sign of what Thorndike calls "unreadiness" (1930, pp. 125–133). (Interestingly, Thorndike points out a third possibility, that being the creation of annoyance by withholding the activity from one who is ready.) Decades later, Skinner and Gagne described readiness in more specific terms that imply a responsibility of the educator to create readiness rather than to simply observe and react to it. Skinner (1953), thinking within the framework of operant conditioning, described readiness as the "behavioral repertoire" brought to the learning situation (p. 156), and Gagne (1985), thinking in terms of his theorized conditions of learning, wrote about the need to have "previously learned capabilities . . . readily accessible" (p. 268).

Both Skinner and Gagne insisted that readiness as an element of the learning process should be separated from the issues of growth readiness and the readiness to internalize logical forms. Piaget, on the other hand, spoke of readiness in terms of acquiring prerequisite cognitive structures (Wadsworth, 1971, p. 121), and in terms of acknowledging and wanting to resolve conflicting statements (Bell-Gredler, 1986, p. 222).

The preceding two paragraphs, read with specific subject matter and students in mind, will probably generate a few sketchy thoughts about efficient music-learning sequences. More detailed information about learning sequences brings to light at least three specific issues: maturational readiness versus experiential readiness, the sequencing of individual sessions versus large-picture sequencing, and subjective sequencing versus objective sequencing.

Maturational Readiness vs. Experiential Readiness On the subject of maturational readiness, Jensen (1969) states:

It is a well-established fact that at any given age it is much easier to teach some things than others; some skills seem to be acquired almost spontaneously *after* a certain age and it is practically impossible to teach a child to perform certain skills *before* a certain age. (p. 135)

Montessori (1936) observed that maturation and individual preference together create "sensitive periods" during which a child exhibits optimal readiness for specific learning. Maturational readiness is important to all teachers from the start, which is why the Educational Testing Service has developed tools by which a child's readiness for school is assessed. (*Let's Look at Children* and *CIRCUS* are widely used ETS assessment tools for potential kindergarten students [Hsia, 1975]. For a five-part series about pushing preschool children to achieve prior to maturational readiness, begin with Shirley J. O'Brien, 1988.) Readers interested in knowing more about maturational readiness will want to study the work of Jean Piaget.

The teacher's control over maturational readiness is slight. In contrast, teachers methodically provide students with a large portion of their experiential readiness. The premise behind experiential readiness is that new learning "becomes incorporated into a learner's cognitive structure by becoming subsumed by something previously learned" (Gubrud and Novak, 1973, p. 179). Gordon uses the term "musical age," which is parallel to the term "mental age," to describe the level of a student's experiential readiness for music learning. He asserts that "musical age [as opposed to chronological age] . . . is the determining factor" in considering a child's readiness for a specific element of music instruction (1979, p. 55). The focus of this chapter is on experiential readiness. When a music teacher thinks of designing a learning sequence, all other environmental considerations—the teacher's own learning experiences, which activities seem attractive to children, what materials are on hand, what might be cute for the next performance—should be secondary to consideration for the student's experiential readiness.

Individual-Session Sequencing vs. Large-Picture Sequencing Another important question is whether teaching is being sequenced for today, this week, this year, or multiple years. Reigeluth (1983) refers to "micro-strategy variables" for organizing presentations of a single idea and "macro-strategy variables" for organizing the presentation of multiple ideas (p. 19). If microsequencing and macrosequencing refer to lesson plans and curricula, we might think of a super-macrosequence in reference to a learning hierarchy such as Gagne's (1965, pp. 33–57) or Gordon's (1988, p. 37). Recommendations for microsequencing, which are plentiful, usually resemble those presented by Blaine (1986, p. 248), paraphrased here in five stages: (1) review the prerequisite skill(s), (2) pretrain difficult aspects of the new skill, (3) teach the new skill, (4) provide experience in using the new skill, and (5) maintain the new skill through review. Perhaps because the larger picture is more difficult to see, recommendations for macrosequencing, and more so for super-macrosequencing, are less plentiful. Briggs (1977) observed that "most of the research on sequencing of instruction has dealt with sequencing at a smaller 'size of chunk'" (p. 111). Of course that is only natural, because research directed at a "large chunk" is usually poor research. Large-chunk insight into sequencing is dependent on persons who are persistent enough and prolific enough in their research to put many small chunks together into one insightful large chunk.

Subjective Sequencing vs. Objective Sequencing Biases work against our differentiating easily between subjective sequencing and objective sequencing. Subjective sequencing in everyday life might be brushing your teeth before showering or putting silverware away ahead of dishes, and in music education it might be introducing quarter notes, half notes, and whole notes before eighth notes or teaching a pre-notational system of icons before teaching music notation. In each case sequence is a matter of habit, preference, or attitude rather than a matter of objectively determined advantage. Objective sequencing in everyday life might be putting pants on ahead of boots or spreading seed and fertilizer before watering the lawn, and in music education it might be having children hear, sing, and move to music before presenting them with formal instruction or teaching them to discriminate aurally among elements of music before expecting them to understand and appreciate a variety of music. In each case sequence affects efficiency of learning and outcome in a fundamental and universal way. To be responsible about the learning sequences that they apply, teachers need to learn what is objectively efficacious and then teach accordingly.

TWO CONSIDERATIONS BEARING ON SEQUENCE

Two pieces of business need to be taken care of prior to examining learning theories. One is to differentiate between two very different yet interdependent kinds of learning, those being the assimilation of content and the acquisition of skill. The other is to present some thoughts about the controversial issue of whether learning should be initiated by studying the whole or by studying its parts.

Content and Skill Learning involves two fundamental elements: content and skill. Content consists of characteristics of the material being learned. In the case of music learning, examples of content are minor tonality, triple meter, and tonic function. Skill is the action that the learner applies to the material being learned. In the case of music learning, examples of skill are the association of rhythm syllables with rhythm patterns, the interpretation of symbols found in

music notation, and the production of a characteristic clarinet tone.

Of course, content in music cannot be studied without applying some specific level of skill, nor can skill be exercised in relation to music except as it is applied to specific content. The two are as interdependent as a lock and key, neither able to function meaningfully without the other.

Memory functions are critical to learning both content and skill because meaningful learning implies remembering. Sylvester (1985) writes about recent memory research in terms of two primary memory mechanisms, which he labels "declarative memory" and "procedural memory." Inferences drawn from Sylvester's work might lend insight to relationships between content and skill, and ultimately to the issue of learning sequence. Characteristics of the two categories of memory as presented or implied by Sylvester are shown in condensed form in Table 36–1.

What insight can be gleaned from this information? It is apparent that content learning is the province of declarative memory and skill learning is the province of procedural memory. Content-related information is learned quickly and accumulated to a saturation point, specifics are lumped into general categories because of limited memory space, and one by one many specifics slip out of the memory as easily as they were put in. In contrast, skills are acquired over time, they reside as autonomous processes in what Sylvester refers to as the "automatic pilot" of the brain, actually the cerebellum (p. 71), they guide routine motor activity and thinking activity year after year, and they remain until they are removed by an explicit force such as the aging process or a stroke.

Applying this information to classroom practice, one would expect short-term learning to predominate when the teacher emphasizes content (tomorrow you will each recite the "Preamble to the Constitution"), and one would expect long-term learning to predominate when the teacher emphasizes skill ("If you were to start a new country, what would you consider to be the most pressing issues?"). Educational reformers have heavily criticized schools for emphasizing the former (Holt, 1964, 1967, 1983; Silberman, 1970; Illich,

TABLE 36–1. A Comparison of Memory Mechanisms

Declarative Memory	Procedural Memory
Explicit facts and symbols are processed	Motor and problem-solving skills are processed
Visualization and mapping are effective tools for learning	Sequencing is an effective tool for learning
Pieces of learning tend to become lumped into categories over time	Pieces of learning tend to retain autonomy over time
Learning is quick and easy	Learning is time-consuming and difficult
Forgetting is easy	Forgetting is difficult

1970). Happily, the newest craze dominating thought in schools of education is the teaching of thinking. (*Educational Leadership, 45*(7), April 1988, is devoted entirely to articles about the teaching of thinking.)

Content learning occurs predominantly through mapping and visualizing (in the case of music learning, audiating), and skill learning occurs predominantly through sequencing. To an extent, content learning also depends on sequence, and skill learning on visualization, mapping, and audiation, because the characteristics shown in Table 36–1 are only dominant, not exclusive. Content learning and skill learning overlap continuously: Neither stands on its own.

Two major premises of the preceding few paragraphs are that (1) the role of content and the role of skill need to be considered separately but implemented jointly in the construction of music-learning sequences, and (2) sequence is more critical to skill learning than to content learning. Because music learning is realized in performance, and because performance is dependent on demonstrable skill, efficient music learning is more dependent on appropriate sequential teaching than is efficient academic learning. That is especially true considering the imbalance between academic skill and music skill that kindergarten children bring to school from the home. Parents are much more likely to have taught their children the skills of thinking, speaking, and calculating simple problems than they are to have taught them the skills of audiating music, singing in tune, and moving in a consistent tempo.

It is difficult to read about procedural memory, skill development, and sequential learning without thinking back to Barry Green's experience with Gary Karr's bass playing. Sylvester (1985), writing about declarative and procedural memory, states: "Researchers recommend that people who are learning a skill frequently observe experts performing it, practice it often . . . and integrate mastered prerequisite skills into the mastery of the more advanced skill" (p. 72). Sylvester continues with what amounts to a paraphrase of one of Green's statements: "It's difficult to recall a skill except through its execution. It's also difficult to explain or discuss a skill" (p. 71). Marzano and Arredondo, writing about how to teach thinking skills, also say that "concepts should be first introduced to students at an experiential level" (1986, p. 22). By virtue of the dominant role of skill in music learning, it becomes clear that the front end of a music-learning sequence should be an active music experience.

Whole-Part/Part-Whole The educationist's version of the chicken-or-the-egg question is the whole-or-the-part question. More than two centuries ago Comenius offered nine teaching principles, the sixth of which was, "Nature, in its formative process, begins with the universal and ends with the particular" (Wiman, 1969, p. 12). As often as that wisdom has been questioned since, evidence remains strong that teachers should begin learning sequences with the whole rather than with the part (Ausubel, 1968; p. 148; Abou-Rass, 1972; Houser, 1974; Condello, 1975; Mayer, 1979, p. 372; Robinson and Crawford, 1978, p. 9).

Houser (1974), studying the effect of instructional se-

quences on math learning, found that learning of the whole transferred so powerfully to learning of the parts that many students were able to teach new parts to themselves through generalization. Condello (1975) hypothesized that the learning of general materials at a low technical level would facilitate the learning of specific materials at a higher technical level, and conversely that the learning of specific materials would facilitate the learning of general materials so long as the technical levels of the two were equivalent. He found evidence that the general-to-specific hypothesis was true, but labeled the status of the specific-to-general hypothesis "unclear." A skill-learning experiment involving dental procedures (Abou-Rass, 1972) produced evidence of decreased learning time when learning progressed from the simple (whole) to the complex (parts). Robinson and Crawford (1978, p. 9) recommend whole-to-part learning sequences in the teaching of typing skills. Ausubel (1968), whose research has led him to the use of a kind of induced readiness that he calls "advance organizers," states that the organizers "are introduced in advance of the learning material itself and are also presented at a higher level of abstraction, generality, and inclusiveness" (p. 148). Mayer (1979) reinforces the approach further in stating a theory that has been supported by a body of research: "Subjects given a general model or general experience in thinking about examples will have a meaningful learning set for encoding the subsequent new specifics and hence will be able to assimilate the material to a broader set of past experiences" (p. 372).

Although Sylvester (1985) minimized the importance of sequence to content learning in general, he believed that when pieces of content are presented to learners apart from the whole, content sequence becomes critical. Wedman (1981) writes: "The more the content sequence distorts the relationships between the content topics, the more the content structure, indeed, the content itself, is changed" (p. 13). Even with careful sequencing, the presentation of parts to learners ignorant of the whole can lead to inefficient learning. Tulvig (1966) and Bower and Lesgold (1969) each concluded that learning part of a list of items impeded subsequent learning of the whole list. It appeared that if learners were presented with material that was obviously part of an unavailable whole, the tendency was for them to create a whole based on the parts known to them—a whole that they may later need to unlearn.

THE LEARNING HIERARCHY: GENERAL EDUCATION

A learning hierarchy is an arrangement of the components of learning into a series of stages that progress from the simple to the complex, each successive stage subsuming all stages that have preceded it. The hierarchies on which general educationists most frequently base curricular decisions are those of Jean Piaget, Jerome Bruner, and Robert Gagne. Of the two types of readiness, maturational readiness and experiential readiness, Piaget's hierarchy is maturationally based and the others are experientially based. Of course the reader knows that this small space cannot begin to represent the prolific work of these researchers. There is room only to point out some relationships among their work and some implications for the teaching of music, leaving readers to seek other sources if they wish to understand their work in any substantial way.

Piaget is known for having conducted exhaustive clinical investigations of the thought process of children of all ages. A skeletal view of his developmental hierarchy, constructed from information contained in *An Outline of Piaget's Developmental Psychology* (Beard, 1969) and *Piaget's Theory of Cognitive Development* (Wadsworth, 1971) is shown in Table 36-2.

Achievements during the sensorimotor period are extremely important, as they underlie all further cognitive advances, but the practical value of that information to a teacher of older children is minimal. Study of the other periods may help a teacher to sequence learning material by understanding the immediate developmental circumstances of students and by predicting the emergence of future developmental capabilities.

Jerome Bruner has stated plainly that "the sequence in which a learner encounters materials within a domain of knowledge affects the difficulty he will have in achieving mastery" (1966, p. 49). Bruner believes that proper learning sequence nearly renders content irrelevant—that is, almost anyone of almost any age can learn almost anything given the power of an appropriate learning sequence. The three stages of Bruner's learning hierarchy, taken from *Ways Children Learn* (Lall and Lall, 1983, pp. 9–13) are shown in Table 36-3. Bruner (1965) emphasizes the importance of (1) orientation to the whole, which he labels "structure," (2) readiness, (3) intuitive and analytical thinking, and (4) motivation.

Robert Gagne refers to the learning hierarchy that he has constructed as types of learning, each of which may occur if specific conditions of learning are present. Gagne's types of learning, paraphrased from *Conditions of Learning* (1965) are shown in Table 36-4. (Gagne's types of learning are less clearly delineated in his 1985 text [see References].)

TABLE 36-2. Piaget's Hierarchy of Children's Intellectual Development

Sensorimotor Period—birth to about 18 months
  Reflex exercises
  Primary circular reactions
  Secondary circular reactions
  Coordination of secondary schemas
  Tertiary circular reactions
  Invention of new means through mental combinations

Preoperational Period—about 18 months to about 7 yr
  Preconceptual state—to about 4.5 yr
  Intuitive stage—to about 7 yr

Concrete Operations—about 7 to 11–12 yr

Formal Operations Period—about 12 to 15 yr

TABLE 36-3. Bruner's Three-Stage Model of the Process of Knowledge Acquisition

Enactive Stage

This is a time of action. Learning is acquired principally through manipulation, and the child's attention span is short.

Iconic Stage

This is a time of imagery. Learning involves the building of mental pictures, with previous experiences supplying the raw material. Images facilitate the child's understanding of concepts.

Symbolic Stage

This is a time of weighing options. Problems can be solved by choosing from among multiple approaches. Concepts can be conveyed to others through verbalization.

MUSIC LEARNING AND SEQUENCE: A PRELUDE TO THE MUSIC LEARNING HIERARCHY

Several questions might be asked in anticipation of creating a music-learning hierarchy. First, how do children learn music? There could be no more legitimate stimulus for creating a learning hierarchy than insight into how children, by nature, learn. Second, can some insight into visual learning be generalized to aural learning? If so, extra mileage can be taken from existing research. And last, can some of our insight into language learning provide insight into the important issue of how to teach children to read music?

TABLE 36-4. Gagne's Hierarchy of Types of Learning

1. *Signal Learning:* simply react to a stimulus, as with Pavlov's dog

2. *Stimulus Response Learning:* respond to a solitary stimulus, but purposely rather than as a simple reaction (signal learning); synonym: trial and error

3. *Chaining:* respond to multiple stimuli in a sequence that accomplishes a more complex task than encountered in stimulus response learning

4. *Verbal Association:* associate words with objects by building verbal chains

5. *Multiple Discrimination:* establish numbers of different chains, group them by similarities into "collections," and learn to make different responses to different members of the same collection

6. *Concept Learning:* respond to collections as a whole in such a way as to extend thought beyond present members of each collection

7. *Principle Learning:* acquire knowledge by chaining concepts into an infinite variety of relationships

8. *Problem Solving:* use knowledge of principles to generate new principles that carry with them the insight needed to solve problems

Natural Learning Scientists have known for decades that the fetus responds to sound (Murphy and Smyth, 1962, p. 972), and recent research by Eimas (1985) demonstrates that infants not only hear acutely but discriminate extraordinarily well among minute changes in sound (pp. 46–52). Apparently nature cannot be blamed for the predominance of visual learning over aural learning.

Victorino Tejera has found "doing" to be particularly important to learning in the arts: "In the sphere of art what is wanted is not a theoretical knowledge of art but some sort of intimacy with the subject matter which, while it may not always lead to original production, will properly lead to the enjoyment and understanding of art" (1965, p. 7). "Intimacy with the subject matter" relative to music learning would entail aural rather than visual experiences. Perhaps regressive music learning is attributable primarily to a dirth of well-chosen and well-sequenced aural experiences (p. 127).

Extensive interview studies with children ages 3 to 8 have shown that to children "learning means to become more able by experience." Fewer than 10 percent of the 8-year-old subjects of Pramling's study (1983, p. 128) thought of learning in terms of "to understand." Pramling elaborates:

Very young children can sing songs and tell nursery rhymes but they think they have learnt them just by hearing them, and perhaps they have. But what these children are not able to do is to decide consciously to learn a new song or nursery rhyme. . . . A small group of six and seven-year-olds and 40 percent of eight-year-olds have a conception of using their thinking for learning (p. 132).

Natural learning for young children appears to require a great amount of freedom, in which they are not bothered by formal instruction and by encounters with uninterpretable parts of the whole.

The Visual/Aural Connection Medical research has demonstrated functional independence between visual and auditory processes by testing patients with dominant temporal lobe lesions (Jensen, 1969, p. 139). Still, high correlation between the two (Jensen, 1969, p. 140) as major systems for sensory intake gives reason to believe that learning processes that engage one might engage the other in similar ways. Some educators believe that to be the case, judging by the partial list of readiness skills categorized by "visual channel" and "auditory channel," shown in Table 36–5 (Denver Public Schools, 1982, pp. 11–13). Aural/visual parallels have been explicitly drawn.

Randhawa (1976) lists four assumptions underlying visual learning, all of which may well apply to aural learning. Aural terms are inserted into Randhawa's statements in brackets to encourage the reader to think in terms of both senses.

1. Visual [aural] learning encompasses all changes in behavior arising from visual [aural] stimulation.
2. Visual [aural] learning is dependent upon maturation level and prior experiences.
3. Visual [aural] learning develops in an invariant sequence of stages, each stage subsuming the abilities acquired at

TABLE 36–5. Partial List of Readiness Skills for Special Education, Denver Public Schools

Visual Channel	Auditory Channel
Attends visual stimuli	Attends auditory stimuli
Matches concrete objects	Discriminates sounds
Separates same from different objects	Locates sources of sound
Matches objects to pictures	Associates sound with given stimuli
Separates same from different pictures of objects	Sequences auditory stimuli
Sorts objects into groups by colors	Discriminates environmental sounds as same or different

earlier stages. Early stages are critical, because repertoire is needed for subsequent instruction.

4. Visual [aural] learning will most likely result from active participation of the learner, i.e., conscious processing of incoming information and relation of that information to what was learned previously. (pp. 1–2)

Randhawa's assumptions coincide with most of the theories and research findings cited previously. If taken to be valid for aural learning, they amount to a mandate for the construction of a music-learning sequence.

Reading Language/Reading Music Sticht and James (1984, p. 293) relate the concepts of Donald P. Brown, a blind educator, about skill in processing spoken language. Brown reasoned that processing written language for comprehension is more than just looking, and therefore is given a unique term, "reading." Similarly, he reasoned that processing spoken language for comprehension is more than just listening, and therefore requires a unique term. The term that he coined was "auding" (Brown, 1954). Despite the utility that the word enjoys as a result of its specificity, most reading researchers continue to use "listening" where "auding" would enable them to say more.

Great numbers of researchers have found that competence in reading and writing language is heavily dependent on competence in speaking the language (Loban, 1963, p. 88; Hillerich, 1977, p. 41) and on listening (auding) skills (Duker, 1969). A concentration of studies is available in the *Handbook of Reading Research* (Pearson, 1984). Downing (1969) found reading ability dependent on concepts of "letter," "word," and "sentence," and Stanovich (1980) found both oral language development and beginning reading acquisition to rely heavily on the use of context, especially for those of least ability. Piagetian scholars add the acquisition of thinking skills to the long list of prerequisites for the teaching of reading (Waller, 1977).

Hahn (1985) taught music reading to children in grades 4 to 6 by use of strategies used by fluent readers of written language (p. 119). Students who learned to sing specific patterns in a melodic context learned to read those familiar patterns, as well as unfamiliar patterns that were related to them, more effectively than did a group of students whose starting point was to learn notation in isolation from sound.

Kluth (1986) conducted research similar to Hahn's, except that her experimental instruction consisted of sequential rhythm patterns. Differences in rhythm-reading scores between the higher-scoring experimental group and the lower-scoring control group were statistically significant.

Language vocabularies are listening, speaking, reading, and writing. The basic unit of language is the word, and words combined into phrases or sentences create context. The ability to read and give meaning to sentences is clearly dependent on one's having acquired a listening and speaking vocabulary, and having become familiar with contexts within which that vocabulary might reside. Having done so, one can read sentences containing unfamiliar words, providing that those sentences contain enough familiar words to provide a context.

Parallel music vocabularies might be thought of as listening, singing (and moving), reading, and writing. The basic unit of a music vocabulary analogous to a word would have to be a sound pattern, which could consist of tonal variants, rhythmic variants, or both tonal and rhythmic variants. Those patterns can be combined into phrases to create context. The ability to read and give meaning to phrases of music would then be dependent on one's having acquired a listening and singing (and moving) vocabulary, and having become familiar with contexts within which the patterns reside. Having done so, one could read phrases containing unfamiliar patterns, providing that those phrases contained enough familiar patterns to provide a context. Some of the prerequisites to music reading cited by Heffernan (1968) in his rather extensive treatise on teaching music reading conform to just such a parallelism between the teaching of language reading and the teaching of music reading.

THE LEARNING HIERARCHY: MUSIC EDUCATION

Music educators of this century whose approaches have won acclaim have all had strong convictions about the most fundamental aspect of learning sequence—the starting point. At the turn of the century Emile Jaques-Dalcroze claimed that his work in Geneva demonstrated the importance of beginning music instruction with movement and singing, namely, because the acquisition of kinesthetic and aural sensibilities represents the foundation for all music learning. He subsequently built a teaching approach based on solfège, eurhythmics (his term), and improvisation (1921, 1980).

In the 1920s Carl Orff (1978) collaborated with a movement expert, Dorothee Gunther, and "drew up a plan for an 'Elemental Music Practice' that would only be suitable in a movement school" (p. 12). Like Dalcroze, Orff saw the ideal beginning of music learning to be movement: "It is difficult to teach rhythm. One can only release it" (p. 15). His quest ultimately led him to conclude that improvisation was the natural starting point.

In the 1930s, composer Zoltan Kodály took great interest in the process by which children learn music. He concluded that the starting point needed to include aural/vocal training by use of solfège, rhythm training by use of active (as opposed to passive) rhythms, and the use of only the finest literature (Choksy, 1988).

In the 1930s Shinichi Suzuki developed his "Mother Tongue" approach to the teaching of violin. The starting point for language learning, he reasoned, was for the child to hear it spoken and repeat it many, many times with the guidance of parents. For him, music learning properly began at the same point and in the same way as language learning (Suzuki, 1969).

The point of this litany is that the most prominent music educators of this century have identified a common starting point for the intelligent sequencing of music learning, and that starting point matches the "inner game" philosophy; the whole-before-part theory; the evidence of researchers from numerous fields including reading, general education, and music education; and the work of prominent learning theorists. One grand amalgamating statement might be that music learning begins with active, holistic experiences that combine the seeing and hearing of models with doing and experimenting, and that doing, experimenting, verbalizing, and comparing oneself with models leads to the acquisition of skills in performing and discriminating, and finally to skills in conceptualizing musical sound and relating it to printed symbols.

Like Brown (1954), who found a lack of specificity relative to the description of language processing and responded by coining the term "auding," Gordon (1988) found a lack of specificity relative to the description of music processing and responded by coining the term "audiation." The term might be thought of as a counterpart to "visualization," which describes the act of "seeing" (thinking about) visual sensations in the absence of those sensations. That is, "audiation" describes the act of "hearing" (thinking about) aural sensations, specifically musical sensations, in their absence.

Gordon developed a skill-learning hierarchy specific to music. Divided into two subhierarchies, discrimination learning and inference learning, Gordon's hierarchy bears resemblance to Piaget's (sensorimotor and preoperational periods preceding concrete and formal operations) and to Gagne's (response, verbal association, and discrimination preceding concept and principle learning).* Gordon's hierar-

---

*(Readers interested in research relating Piaget's work to the teaching of music might want to consult Pflederer [1967], Zimmerman and Sechrest [1970], Botvin [1974], Foley [1975], and Warrener [1985]. And for additional comparisons of the Gagne and Gordon hierarchies, see Grunow [1991].)

chy also shows the influence of prominent music educators who preceded him with advice about delaying theoretical learning until after the student has had sufficient experience with rhythmic movement and singing. Gordon's skill-learning hierarchy is shown in Table 36–6, along with a brief interpretation of each level.

Gordon (1990) has identified early stages of music learning as music babble, which he describes in relation to a concept he labels "preaudiation." Procedurally, preaudiation learning belongs to the aural/oral level of the hierarchy, but Gordon differentiates between the informal learning that occurs during preaudiational stages and the formal learning that the hierarchy is meant to explain and guide.

Gordon (1988) has constructed music content learning hierarchies as well, but the greater importance of sequential learning to functions of procedural memory as compared with functions of declarative memory causes the skill-learning hierarchy to be of foremost importance. Still, there are three important points relative to Gordon's concept of music content learning. First, he attaches importance to teaching two opposing classifications of content in proximity within a given dimension—for example, major tonality in proximity to minor tonality. The rationale is that learning what something is not is part of learning what it is. Second, he developed taxonomies of tonal patterns and rhythm patterns that are meant to guide content learning from easy to difficult (pp. 92–110, 156–166). Difficulty level is based on audiational

difficulty, which coincides to an extent but not completely with performance difficulty (pp. 184–186). Third, he believes that the dimensions of music must be taught separately as a regular part of instruction. That is, tonal instruction and rhythm instruction should occur in isolation from one another.

It is important to note that Gordon's theory is not a method, but rather provides guidelines by which methods of instruction can be constructed. In the process of amalgamating approaches to music learning, some music educators have identified relationships between Gordon's concept of sequence and sequencing aspects of other prominent approaches. Dalcroze lamented the reliance of piano teachers and students on tactile associations prior to their having developed aural associations, and he responded with a hearing-moving-singing sequence that appears to have influenced Gordon's skill-learning hierarchy at its most elementary level (Shehan-Campbell, 1989, p. 307). Cernohorsky (1989), in comparing learning sequence in the Orff and Gordon approaches, found the only firm commonality to be that "aural experiences precede visual experiences" (p. 272), although she made a tenuous link between Orff's process of experience-imitate-explore-create and Gordon's skill-learning sequence (p. 275). Feierabend (1989) has compared the Kodály learning sequence of preparation, presentation, and practice with the discrimination portion of Gordon's skill-learning sequence (p. 295). The attendant implication that inference learning within the Kodály curriculum is not formally structured is not alarming; discrimination learning is a matter of teacher-teaching-student, whereas inference learning is a matter of student-teaching-self with guidance from the teacher.

TABLE 36–6. Gordon's Skill-Learning Hierarchy Briefly Interpreted

Discrimination Learning: A Subhierarchy Featuring Rote Learning	
Aural/oral	—hearing/moving, chanting, singing
Verbal association	—associating words, tonal syllables, and rhythm syllables with sound
Partial synthesis	—recognizing characteristics of wholes (series of patterns rather than isolated patterns) that are heard
Symbolic association (reading, writing)	—associating syllables and sounds with music notation
Composite synthesis reading, writing	—recognizing characteristics of wholes (series of patterns rather than isolated patterns) that are seen in notation and translated to sound in audiation

Inference Learning: A Subhierarchy Featuring Conceptual Learning	
Generalization (aural/oral, verbal, symbolic)	—identifying the unfamiliar on the basis of similarities to and differences from the familiar
Creativity/improvisation (aural/oral, symbolic)	—using skill and content learned at lower levels of learning to improvise and create music
Theoretical understanding (aural/oral, verbal, symbolic)	—learning the mechanics of music notation

MUSIC EDUCATION AND THE WHOLE / PART CONTROVERSY

Gordon's hierarchical approach to music learning, embodied in lessons that he refers to as learning sequence activities, appears to promote a part approach to learning in contrast to the whole approach that most researchers and theorists agree is most effective. Gagne's hierarchy, which is closely related to Gordon's, gives the same impression. Gagne, in fact, has been more of an adherent to part learning than any other general learning theorist of recent times. If the greater picture of music learning is examined, meaning a lifetime of sequenced music learning, what will the relative roles of whole learning and part learning be?

A whole-part-whole sequence of learning may allow music educators and their students to enjoy the advantages of both whole-part learning sequences and part-whole learning sequences. Students might be given a general view of the whole, something that Bruner would refer to as a sense of structure, in preparation for their being able to study the parts within the proper context. The study of the parts might then be followed by another experience with the whole, one that would be more enlightened as a result of the specific

TABLE 36–7. A Whole-Part-Whole Learning Process
Resulting from the Coordination of Learning Sequence
Activities and Classroom Activities

I	II	III
(Introduction)	(Application)	(Reinforcement)
Classroom activities	Learning sequence activities	Classroom activities
Overview of the whole	Specific study of the parts	Greater understanding of the whole

learning of the parts. Some learning theorists refer to the whole-part-whole learning model as "introduction, application, and reinforcement." A logical line of thought, given the information contained in this chapter, might be that music educators should follow a whole-part-whole sequencing model similar to the one shown in Table 36–7, taken from a publication that assumes part study to consist of the learning sequence activities prescribed by Gordon (Walters, 1988). In practice, teachers could create unique parts of an infinite variety to complement whatever the whole is that they are trying to teach.

APPLICATION ACROSS THE MUSIC CURRICULUM

To make the most of information contained in this chapter, individual teachers will need to generalize the principles of readiness and sequencing that it contains to their specific teaching assignments. A high school ensemble conductor, for example, might draw these conclusions:

1. Hearing aural models is an important readiness for subsequent learning. I'll build a collection of recorded solo performances, convert one practice room to a listening room, and arrange for at least one annual trip to a good concert.
2. Singing and moving may be legitimate readinesses for instrumental performance even at the secondary level. I'll incorporate a few minutes of such exercises into my rehearsal warm-ups.
3. A whole-part-whole design for a rehearsal may make learning more efficient. When I rehearse a piece or section, I will
   (a) play the whole
   (b) make comments and take questions about the whole
   (c) rehearse parts, and relate them to what is known about the whole
   (d) play the whole again
   (e) make evaluative comments about the progress

The reverse approach may also be valuable. Rather than build sequences by the light of insights gained here, music

teachers might compare the order in which they teach content or skills with any number of theories or models. If an adjustment seems worth trying, either in a short-term sequence or a long-term sequence, the teacher can experiment with some expectation of being engaged in more than simple trial and error.

VOICES FROM THE PAST

The concepts of readiness and sequence as facilitators of learning are hardly new. Ausubel's (1968) statement that "the acquisition of knowledge is a process in which every new capability builds on a foundation established by previously learned capabilities" (p. 159) might have been made in 1868, 1768, or 1668. In the seventeenth century John Amos Comenius wrote that information learned will tend to be retained and understood if "a thorough grounding precedes instruction" and if "all that comes later be based on what has gone before" (Keatinge, 1896/1967, p. 143). In the eighteenth century Pestalozzi admonished that "the child must be brought to a high degree of knowledge, both of things seen and words, before it is reasonable to teach him to spell and read" (Hayward, 1979, p. 50). In the nineteenth century Lowell Mason built music curriculum guidelines for the Boston schools (Mason, 1838) on the foundation of seven Pestalozzian principles of music-learning sequence. (Those Pestalozzian principles had been introduced to Boston by William C. Woodbridge in 1830 in a paper that he delivered to the American Institute of Instruction [Monroe, 1969, p. 145.]) In brief form, the first five of those principles follow:

1. Teach sound before sign.
2. Lead the student to observe by hearing and imitating instead of explaining.
3. Teach but one thing at a time—rhythm, melody, and expression—before the child is called to attend to all at once.
4. Require mastery of one step before progressing to the next.
5. Give principles and theory after practice.

The Glover/Curwen approaches of the mid-nineteenth century were built on a similar foundation (Curwen, 1843/1985; Bennett 1984).

Reading of the Pestalozzian approach and observing its lineage through the nineteenth and twentieth centuries causes one to realize that the music education establishment is not so much in need of information about how to sequence learning as it is in need of resolve to make good use of centuries-old information, information that has been amply enriched over the years. Following Pestalozzi's two-hundred-year-old lead, teachers and educational researchers may decide that the most exciting prospects for future research lie in discovering relationships among principles of learning for diverse disciplines. Which fundamentals are shared between visual learning processes and aural learning processes and which are unique? To what extent do language reading and music reading share eye-to-ear-to-mind processes? By virtue of its reliance on procedural memory and skill acquisition, and consequently on effective learning sequences, music as a discipline within education may have the potential to lend more insight than it borrows. By practicing what is known about efficient music learning sequence, and by recording and analyzing results, music educators may bring edification not only to music education, but to education as a whole.

References

Abou-Rass, M. (1972). Effects of method of sequencing and amount of training on the acquisition and performance of psychomotor skills in preclinical endodontics. Unpublished doctoral dissertation, University of Pittsburgh, Pittsburgh.

Ausubel, D. P. (1968). *Educational psychology: A cognitive view.* New York: Holt, Rinehart, and Winston.

Beard, R. M. (1969). *An outline of Piaget's developmental psychology for students and teachers.* London: Routledge & Kegan Paul.

Bell-Gredler, M. E. (1986). *Learning and instruction.* New York: Macmillan.

Bennett, P. D. (1984, Spring). Sarah Glover: A forgotten pioneer in music education. *Journal of Research in Music Education, 32*(1), 49–64.

Blaine, D. (1986). *Memory and instruction.* Englewood Cliffs: Educational Technology.

Botvin, G. J. (1974). Acquiring conservation of melody and cross-modal transfer through successive approximation. *Journal of Research in Music Education, 22*(3), 226–233.

Bower, G. H., and Lesgold, A. M. (1969). Organization as a determinant of part-to-whole transfer in free recall. *Journal of Verbal Learning and Verbal Behavior, 8,* 501–506.

Briggs, L. E. (Ed.). (1977). *Instructional design: Principles and applications.* Englewood Cliffs: Educational Technology.

Brown, D. P. (1954). Auding as the primary language ability. Unpublished doctoral dissertation, Stanford University, Stanford.

Bruner, J. (1965). *Process of education.* Cambridge: Harvard University Press.

Bruner, J. (1966). *Toward a theory of instruction.* Cambridge: Belknap Press of Harvard University.

Cernohorsky, N. (1989). Integrating music learning theory into an Orff program. In D. L. Walters and C. C. Taggart (Eds.), *Readings in music learning theory.* Chicago: G.I.A.

Choksy, L. (1988). *The Kodály method* (2d ed.). Englewood Cliffs: Prentice Hall.

Condello, R. A. (1975). Effects of sequencing on meaningful learning. Unpublished doctoral dissertation, Hofstra University, Hempstead.

Curwen, J. S. (1985). *Singing for schools and congregations.* Kilkenny, Ireland: Boethius. (Originally published in 1843)

Denver Public Schools, Department of Special Education. J. M. O'Hara, Executive Director. (1982). *Special education instructional skills guide for IPCD and SIEBD.*

Downing, J. (1969). How children think about reading. *The Reading Teacher, 23,* 217–230.

Duker, S. (1969). Listening. In R.L. Ebel (Ed.), *Encyclopedia of educational research.* New York: Macmillan.

Eimas, P. D. (1985). The perception of speech in early infancy. *Scientific American, 252*(1), 46–52.

Feierabend, J. (1989). Integrating music learning theory into the Kodály curriculum. In D. L. Walters and C. Crump Taggart (Eds.), *Readings in music learning theory.* Chicago: G.I.A.

Foley, E. A. (1975). Effects of training in conservation of tonal and rhythmic patterns on second-grade children. *Journal of Research in Music Education, 23*(4), 240–248.

Foshay, A. W. (1980). Curriculum talk. In *Yearbook of the Association for Supervision and Curriculum Development.* Alexandria: ASCD.

Fowler, C. (Ed.). (1988). *The Crane Symposium: Toward an understanding of the teaching and learning of music performance.* Potsdam: Potsdam College of the State University of New York.

Gagne, R. M. (1965). *The conditions of learning.* New York: Holt, Rinehart, and Winston.

Gagne, R. M. (1985). *The conditions of learning and theory of instruction.* New York: Holt, Rinehart, and Winston.

Gordon, E. E. (1979). [Manual] *Primary Measures of Music Audiation.* Chicago: G.I.A.

Gordon, E. E. (1988). *Learning sequences in music: Skill, content, and patterns.* Chicago: G.I.A.

Gordon, E. E. (1990). *A music learning theory for newborn and young children.* Chicago: G.I.A.

Green, B. and Gallwey, W. T. (1986). *The inner game of music.* New York: Anchor Press/Doubleday.

Grunow, R. F. (1991). The evolution of rhythm syllables. *The Quarterly* Vol. 2 (1&2): 97–105. Greeley: University of Northern Colorado.

Gubrud, A. R., and Novak, J. D. (1973). Learning achievement and the efficiency of learning the concept of vector addition at three different grade levels. *Science Education, 57*(2), 179–191.

Hahn, L. B. (1985). Correlations between reading music and reading language with implications for music instruction. Unpublished doctoral dissertation, University of Arizona, Tucson.

Hayward, F. H. (1979). *The educational ideas of Pestalozzi and Froebel.* Westport: Greenwood.

Heffernan, C. W. (1968). *Teaching children to read music.* New York: Appleton-Century-Crofts.

Hillerich, R. L. (1977). *Reading fundamentals for preschool and primary children.* Columbus: Charles E. Merrill.

Holt, J. (1964). *How children fail.* New York: Pitman.

Holt, J. (1983). *How children learn* (rev. ed.). New York: Delacorte Press/Seymour Lawrence. (Originally published 1967)

Houser, L. L. (1974). Toward a theory of sequencing: Study (2,3)-1: An exploration of the effects of three instructional sequences on achievement of selected instructional objectives in conversion of units in the metric system of measure. Unpublished doctoral dissertation, Pennsylvania State University, University Park.

Hsia, J. (1975). *Assessing young children.* Paper presented at the statewide meeting on early childhood education, May 3, Minneapolis. (ED 110469)

Illich, I. (1970). *Deschooling society.* New York: Harper and Row.

Jaques-Dalcroze, E. (1980). *Rhythm, music, and education.* London: The Dalcroze Society. (Originally published in 1921)

Jensen, A. (1969). Hierarchical theories of mental ability. In B. Dockrell (Ed.), *On intelligence.* London: Methuen.

Keatinge, M. W. (1967). *The great didactic of John Amos Comenius.* New York: Russell and Russell. (Originally published 1896)

Kluth, B. (1986). A procedure to teach rhythm reading: Development, implementation, and effectiveness in urban junior high school music classes. Unpublished doctoral dissertation, Kent State University, Kent.

Lall, G. R., and Lall, B. M. (1983). *Ways children learn: What do experts say?* Springfield: Charles C Thomas.

Loban, W. D. (1963). *The language of elementary school children.* Urbana: National Council of Teachers of English.

Marzano, R. J., and Arredondo, D. E. (1986, May). Restructuring schools through the teaching of thinking skills. *Educational Leadership, 43,* 20–26.

Mason, L. (1838). *Manual of the Boston Academy of Music for instruction in the elements of vocal music, on the system of Pestalozzi.* Boston: J. H. Wilkins and R. B. Carter.

Mayer, R. E. (1979). Twenty years of research on advance organizers: Assimilation theory is still the best predictor of results. *Instructional Science, 8*(2) 133–167.

McDonald, D. T., and Simons, G. M. (1989). *Musical growth and development: Birth through six.* New York: Schirmer.

Mitchell, D. H. (1985). The influences of preschool musical experiences on the development of tonal memory. Unpublished doctoral dissertation, University of Southern California, Los Angeles.

Monroe, W. S. (1969). *History of the Pestalozzian movement in the United States.* New York: Arno Press and the New York Times.

Montessori, M. (1936). *The secret of childhood.* London: Longmans, Green and Co.

Murphy, K., and Smyth, C. (1962, May). Response of foetus to auditory stimulation. *The Lancet,* 972–973.

O'Brien, S. J. (1988, Fall). For parents particularly: Early learning guidelines. *Childhood Education, 65,* 33–34.

Orff, C. (1978). *The Schulwerk.* New York: Schott Music.

Pearson, P. D. (Ed.). *Handbook of reading research.* New York: Longman.

Pflederer, M. (1967). Conservation laws applied to the development of musical intelligence. *Journal of Research in Music Education, 15*(3) 215–223.

Phye, G. D., and Andre, T. (1986). *Cognitive classroom learning.* New York: Academic Press.

Pramling, I. (1983). *The child's conception of learning.* Göteborg, Sweden: Kompendiet, Lindome.

Reigeluth, C. M. (Ed.). (1983). *Instructional-design theories and models: An overview of their current status.* Hillsdale: Lawrence Erlbaum Associates.

Randhawa, B., Back, K. T., and Myers, P. J. (1976). *Visual learning.* Paper developed at the Lake Okoboji Educational Media Leadership Conference, August 26, Miami Beach. (ED 143319)

Robinson, J. W., and Crawford, T. J. (1978). Fundamental considerations in sequencing and teaching basic typing applications. *Balance Sheet, 60*(1), 4–7.

Shehan-Campbell, P. (1989). Dalcroze reconstructed: An application of music learning theory to the principles of Jaques-Dalcroze. In D. L. Walters and C. C. Taggart (Eds.), *Readings in music learning theory,* Chicago: G.I.A.

Silberman, C. E. (1970). *Crisis in the classroom.* New York: Random House.

Skinner, B. F. (1953). *Science and human behavior.* New York: Macmillan.

Stanovich, K. (1980). Toward an interactive-compensatory model of individual differences in the development of reading fluency. *Reading Research Quarterly, 16*(1), 32–71.

Sticht, T. G., and James, J. H. (1984). Listening and reading. In P. D. Pearson (Ed.), *Handbook of reading research.* New York: Longman.

Suzuki, S. (1969). *Nurtured by love.* New York: Exposition Press.

Sylvester, R. (1985, April). Research on memory: Major discoveries, major educational challenges. *Educational Leadership, 42,* 69–75.

Tejera, V. (1965). *Art and human intelligence.* New York: Appleton-Century-Crofts.

Thorndike, E. (1930). *Educational psychology: Vol. I. The original nature of man.* New York: Columbia University.

Tulvig, E. (1966). Subjective organization and the effects of repetition in multitrial free recall learning. *Journal of Verbal Learning and Verbal Behavior, 5,* 193–197.

Van De Riet, V., Van De Riet, H. and Sprigle, H. (1968–69). The effectiveness of a new sequential learning program with culturally disadvantaged preschool children. *Journal of School Psychology, 7*(3), 5–15.

Wadsworth, B. J. (1971). *Piaget's theory of cognitive development.* New York: David McKay.

Waller, T. G. (1977). *Think first, read later.* Newark: International Reading Association.

Walters, D. L. (1988). *Jump Right In: Coordinating classroom activities and learning sequence activities.* Chicago: G.I.A.

Walters, D. L. (1989). Skill learning sequence. In D. L. Walters and C. C. Taggart (Eds.), *Readings in music learning theory.* Chicago: G.I.A.

Walters, D. L., and Taggart, C. C. (1989). *Readings in music learning theory.* Chicago: G.I.A.

Warrener, J. J. (1985). Applying learning theory to musical development: Piaget and beyond. *Music Educators Journal, 75*(3) 22–27.

Wedman, J. F. Jr. (1981). The relationships among task complexity, content sequence, and instructional effectiveness in procedural learning. Unpublished doctoral dissertation, University of Oklahoma, Norman.

Wilson, F. (1986). *Tone deaf and all thumbs.* New York: Vintage Books.

Wiman, R. V. (1969). A historical view of communications in the classroom. In R. V. Wiman and W. C. Meierhenry (Eds.), *Educational media: Theory into practice.* Columbus: Charles E. Merrill.

Zimmerman, M. P. and Sechrest, L. (1970). Brief focused instruction and musical concepts. *Journal of Research in Music Education, 18*(1), 25–36.

37

CRITICAL THINKING AND MUSIC EDUCATION

Carol P. Richardson

NORTHWESTERN UNIVERSITY

Nancy L. Whitaker

UNIVERSITY OF NORTH CAROLINA

The concept of "critical thinking" functions in educational research in a fashion similar to "creative thinking": Investigation of the literature becomes a process of making sense of the concept as viewed through the lenses of a variety of researchers. The process of making sense of the term is concurrent with development of implications for music education. This review of research on critical thinking is organized into three areas of consideration found in extant research: (1) How is critical thinking defined? (2) What is the relationship of critical thinking to subject or content area? and (3) How can critical thinking be evaluated? Two bodies of literature are considered: research on critical thinking in education and research on musical thinking in music education.

CRITICAL THINKING IN EDUCATION

Examination of the literature on critical thinking includes philosophical analyses of the concept of critical thinking; description of self-contained instructional materials; suggestions for implementation of critical thinking techniques in social studies, mathematics, and other subject areas; reviews of critical thinking tests; and research on implementation of critical thinking techniques. The term "critical thinking" supports a variety of definitions, and appears to be used synonymously, on occasion, with such terms as "reflective thinking," "informal logic," "problem solving," and "higher-order thinking."

The process of making sense of critical thinking requires

following a series of research directions; tracing development of ideas from one theorist to another; and comparing definitions, descriptions, and conditions under which critical thinking may take place. The tracing of ideas is confounded by the presence of approaches to the instruction of critical thinking that lack explicit theoretical support, approaches that act as prescriptive overlays that can be superimposed on any content area to create critical thinking. These approaches in the form of curricular packages are omitted from this review of literature as they lack any identifiable concern with a theoretical basis for instruction.

Four philosophers provide ideas that are illustrative of the literature in education on critical thinking: John Dewey, John McPeck, Robert Ennis, and Richard Paul. Dewey serves a dual function: His conception of reflective thinking serves as a historical source for contemporary views of critical thinking even as it is being revisited by researchers concerned with the teaching of thinking (Farra, 1988; Kitchener, 1983; Rosen, 1987; Tanner, 1988; VanSickle, 1985).

The first section of the chapter presents the views of each philosopher with regard to the questions of definition, relation of critical thinking to subject matter, and evaluation of critical thinking. Examination of critical thinking in education would not be complete without consideration of extant research. The process of selecting research studies required severe delimitation, for the studies of critical thinking are numerous. The studies can be organized into four large groupings: (1) consideration of theories of critical thinking; (2) assessment of the implementation of instructional interventions; (3) correlation studies that investigate the relationship between critical thinking and a given variable; and (4) research in which the author sought either to evaluate baseline critical thinking ability or to evaluate or create assessment instruments. The studies selected for consideration in this analysis of critical thinking were from the first group.

Defining Critical Thinking

In *How We Think* (1933), Dewey defines reflective thinking as uniquely different from other modes of thought. Specifically, for Dewey, "active, persistent, and careful consideration of any belief or supposed form of knowledge in the light of the grounds that support it and the further conclusions to which it tends constitutes reflective thought" (p. 9). He provides four kinds of thinking that all individuals use that are not reflective. The first is the transient, continuous undercurrent of thinking, without perceptible purpose or order, which surfaces occasionally to the level of consciousness. Dewey describes this as daydreaming—disconnected mental impressions that leave little lasting impression. A second type of thinking appears as imaginative elaboration: "In this sense, a thought or idea is a mental picture of something not actually present, and thinking is the succession of such pictures" (p. 5). Inventive elaboration such as that found in storytelling is an example of this type of thinking. Storytelling has an element of connectedness yet is not based wholly on direct experience. The third type is thought transformed into unconsidered belief, subsisting at the level of prejudice: "From obscure sources and by unnoticed channels they insinuate themselves into the mind and become unconsciously a part of our mental furniture" (p. 7). Dewey later describes a fourth type of thinking resembling reflective thinking in all but one respect. As part of reflective thought, it is necessary for an experience or idea to suggest other ideas to serve as evidence for belief in the first. The suggestions must be considered before action or belief is established.

This near-reflective type of thinking results in action on suggestion without consideration (p. 16). This fourth type of thinking resembles reflective thinking in all but the critical aspect. The critical aspect of thinking precludes adoption of action or belief on reaching a conclusion; the action is suspended while an evaluation of the grounds of the initial solution takes place.

The act of consideration and reflection frees the individual from actions done on impulse in response to a perceived impediment or difficulty. Dewey views the unreflective state as being unnatural, in the sense that humans have certain natural tendencies that can be cultivated: curiosity, spontaneous suggestion, and a basic sense of orderliness of thinking (pp. 36–49). In a stronger sense, Dewey equates unreflectiveness with subjection: "To cultivate unhindered, unreflective external activity is to foster enslavement, for it leaves the person at the mercy of appetite, sense, and circumstance" (p. 88).

The concept of "funding" is linked inextricably with the individual nature of reflective thinking. According to Dewey, a given difficulty or problem appears unique to the individual experiencing it directly, and that individual's past experiences direct the process of making sense of the perplexity. The process of making sense of an experience engages intellectual, emotional, and imaginative capacities in a web of funded information. The act of reflection, then, involves a fund of experience leading a person to have and interpret an experience in a particular way, purposeful thought directed from assessment of the experience to funded knowledge, and suspension of action or belief until possible directions of action have been formulated. Whereas the characteristics of reflective thinking can be generalized into phases, the individual experiences cannot be discounted: "Thinking is specific, in that different things suggest their own appropriate meanings, tell their own unique stories, and do this in very different ways with different persons" (p. 46). The examination of any thinking must take into account the continuum represented by the natural resources of curiosity, suggestion, and orderliness of thought.

The establishment of individual meaning is the result of two general stages of the process: (1) a state of indecision, which challenges the individual to think further, and (2) an investigative phase, "an act of searching, hunting, inquiring to find material that will resolve the doubt, settle and dispose of the difficulty" (p. 12). The initial difficulty serves as a guide, directing the flow of thought within channels dependent on the thinker's prior experience, not necessarily linear, yet always moving toward the eventual resolution of the difficulty: "The nature of the problem fixes the end of thought, and the end controls the process of thinking" (p. 15). The sequence of thoughts appears as one of continuous reference to the situation itself and to a store of past experiences with similar situations. This investigative process of searching through a mass of information presented in a given situation, selecting the salient aspects of the present problem and useful past experiences, is one of weighing, judging, and evaluating at each step. The problem accesses for the thinker a rich store of possible suggestions from funded experience, which are brought forth and examined in the light of the problem. This analytical process is accompanied by a willingness to suspend judgment until all the demands of the situation have been satisfied by emergent suggestions, to delay synthesis until response to all facets of the perceived problem occurs. The process of moving from a directly experienced situation to a conclusive one is characterized not only by judgment, but by the use of controlled inference that tests each inference by thought, in imagination, by action, or by both means (p. 96).

John McPeck, in *Critical Thinking and Education* (1981), performs a conceptual analysis of critical thinking. He distinguishes critical thinking from other types of thinking, such as creative thinking and imaginative thinking. McPeck defines critical thinking as "the propensity and skill to engage in an activity with reflective skepticism" (1981, p. 9). "Skepticism" is the process of suspension of belief, of consideration of alternative solutions. McPeck describes the adjective "reflective" as a quality of thinking that is a "level of deliberation that at least appears to be capable of offering a plausible alternative" (1981, p. 9). Critical thinking is involved in "any activity requiring deliberation" (1981, p. 153).

For McPeck, critical thinking is differentiated from logic by the fact that the critical thinker is not merely looking for the truth of statements or detecting fallacies (1984, pp. 30–31). The exclusive employment of argument analysis through the use of informal logic (e.g., seeking fallacies, identifying assumptions) necessitates conscious disregard for the complexity of everyday problems. McPeck suggests that argument analysis is only part, not the whole, of critical thinking. Employment of this "assumption hunting," as he phrases it, relates to the nature of the problems encountered: "We are not analyzing arguments as much as evaluating data, information, and putative facts" (1984, p. 36).

His definition requires a subject or content area, as described in the sentence "I teach critical thinking about X." McPeck contends that if one drops the emphasis on "X", the meaning of the statement becomes similar to "I teach creativity" or "I teach imagination," thus relegating critical thinking to a set of general skills (1981, p. 4). For McPeck, critical thinking is a combination of disposition and skill, used to address problems within a particular discipline. The skills component of critical thinking entails the application of methods, strategies, and techniques within the context of a discipline.

McPeck describes critical thinking as involving both the cognitive and the affective domains. The affective domain is engaged as part of the creation of a disposition to think critically, to voluntarily adopt an attitude of reflective skepticism when confronted with a problem. The critical thinker must have some knowledge of the discipline to be able to recognize a problem or challenge to that knowledge, and to be able to apply the skills used in questioning and evaluating the problem, aspects of the situation, and possible courses of action. The focus on the use of critical thinking is on the process involved in achieving a particular decision or answer, rather than the answer itself (1981, p. 44).

Robert Ennis's most recent definition of critical thinking is, as stated previously, "reasonable reflective thinking that is focused on deciding what to believe or do" (1987b, p. 10). The first component of this definition is rationality, the employment of some form of reasoning. The form of reasoning employed becomes clearer when his taxonomy is examined: Ennis is referring to the employment of reasoning abilities (1987b, pp. 12–15). The second component of the definition is implied by the use of the term "reflective." This is problematic, as Ennis does not clarify the usage of this term. Does he mean reflective in the sense of Deweyan reflective thinking? The remaining components of the definition ("deciding what to believe or do") imply that the solutions include decisions made about the truth of a proposition or the applicability of a course of action. The use of terminology as apparently interchangeable (higher-order thinking, reflective thinking, and critical thinking) is made increasingly unclear by the inclusion of "informal logic" as something connected with critical thinking in a limited fashion (1987b, p. 11). As a result, the reader is left with the impression that critical thinking includes reflective thinking, creative thinking, and

higher-order thinking, and is roughly equivalent to informal logic in some instructional settings.

The definition of critical thinking is accompanied by a taxonomy proposed as a possible curriculum for a college level course in critical thinking. The taxonomy is in two parts: dispositions and abilities. The same dispositions and abilities could, Ennis states, be infused into the total curriculum at the elementary, secondary, or college level through incorporation of a spiral curriculum (1987b, p. 15). The taxonomy fails to make clear whether all of the abilities are involved when a problem occurs that necessitates critical thinking. Must the thinker move sequentially through *all* of the listed abilities, using *all* of the dispositions, to think critically? The "conception" of critical thinking represented by the taxonomy is evidently distinct from the definition of critical thinking: The conception functions simultaneously as an elaboration of the definition and as a curriculum. Therefore, if one uses all of the abilities and dispositions to address a problem, is one accomplishing curricular goals? If so, Ennis's conception of critical thinking is not on a continuum: Either one employs the abilities and dispositions or one does not.

Richard Paul is associated with philosophers writing on critical thinking through his writings on "dialogical thinking," which he also refers to as dialectical reasoning. Paul's theory of critical thinking is divided into critical thinking in a weak sense and critical thinking in a strong sense. The weak sense consists of a set of thinking skills that can be applied to multiple subject areas (similar to Ennis's general approach to critical thinking). The strong sense includes technical reason in the form of basic thinking skills, and emancipatory reason in the form of dialogical thinking. The fundamental difference between the two forms of reason is the presence in the latter of self-awareness and criticism of one's own thinking processes: "skills that generate not only fundamental insight into but also some command of one's own cognitive and affective processes" (Rudinow and Paul, 1987, p. 152). Critical thinking in the strong sense, in contrast to what Paul refers to as "vocational" thinking skills, becomes an intrinsic part of the thinker through the thinker's analysis of his or her "cognitive and affective processes" (1987, p. 152).

Dialogical thinking (critical thinking in the strong sense) is similar to the construction of a legal case, involving consideration of alternatives and investigation of consequent and logical strength of assertions (Paul, 1984a, p. 12). The logical strength of a frame of reference or case can be tested in two ways: (1) by listening to a proponent of the case, then listening to the competing view, or (2) by framing both sides of the argument in imagination while suspending judgment. Paul describes this use of imagination as an indicator that dialogical thinking is creative as well as rational (1987, p. 128). Thinking is not driven by procedures but is governed by principles, "rational and comprehensive" thinking similar to that used in the law (1984a, p. 14).

Paul characterizes the monological, rationally naive thinker as egocentric. This thinker is bound by the unconsidered acceptance of assumptions and beliefs from teachers, parents, friends, and other cultural sources. Ego- and ethnocentric thinkers are irrational by definition, as their thinking omits any rational examination of the reasonability of their beliefs. If one thinks monologically, one "may have an overwhelming inner sense of the correctness of one's views and still be wrong" (1987, p. 131). Rational thinkers have gained control of logic structures through employment of their own reasoning, have moved beyond the egocentrism of unconsidered ideas. Paul cites C. Wright Mills on the three types of believers to illustrate the distinction between types of thinking. The first type of believer is called "vulgar," one who functions by egocentric identification with the beliefs of others. A second type, labeled "sophisticated," intellectually examines and espouses one and only one point of view. The "critical" believer considers personal point of view as "something to be developed continually and refined by a fuller and richer consideration of the available evidence and reasoning through exposure to the best thinking in alternative points of view" (1987, p. 138). Clearly, Paul's dialogical thinker is Mills's critical believer.

The Relationship of Critical Thinking to Content Area

The question of whether critical thinking is either content specific or applicable to any discipline is one that needs to be considered by music education researchers. If one considers musical thinking to be different from other types of thinking, then does critical thinking in music differ from critical thinking in other subject areas?

Dewey's view of reflective thinking is not subject specific: Reflective thinking may occur in response to any problem. Reflective thinking occurs when a challenge or question to the funded experience of the thinker creates a state of doubt or perplexity. As funded experience is individually unique within a given discipline, the reflective thinking process must satisfy the demands of the problem as perceived by the individual. The combination of the individual's perception of the problem and funded experience determines the extent of reflective thinking. Thus, reflective thinking may be characterized as individually specific rather than subject specific. Reflective thinking can occur in musical settings, in response to a disparity or challenge to the funded experience of the individual. A musical problem set by the teacher may not be recognized by all students as a problem to be considered reflectively—some students may consider the problem unreflectively.

McPeck's view is that critical thinking is framed within the subject-specific epistemology of a given field. He defines epistemology as "the analysis of good reasons for belief" (1981, p. 24). Understanding a subject-dependent proposition entails understanding the unique meaning of the proposition as couched in the language of that field, not merely debating the adequacy of the logical relationship. Epistemology is involved in the critical thinking process as part of the suspension of decision. For McPeck, the suspension of decision or judgment is the hallmark of a critical thinker, for the thinker's particular knowledge of field, represented by the

thinker's reasons for belief, functions as the lodestone that organizes the problem and generates possible solutions.

Teaching critical thinking involves concurrent teaching for knowledge of field. The student develops a disposition to use those skills in other fields, given adequate knowledge of those fields. McPeck refers to this approach as the "knowledge and information" approach. The knowledge selected is presented to the student in such a way as to be considered fallible, not rigidly sacred. Rather than teaching a set of general, apparently easily transferable critical thinking skills, McPeck advocates considering a transfer of knowledge of fields. He poses the question: What knowledge and information will have the most transfer? (1984, p. 40) His answer is to (1) identify knowledge that is the most rich/powerful, and (2) seek to cultivate an attitude toward that knowledge. A liberal education fulfills the requirements for a source of potentially transferable knowledge. The attitude toward the knowledge gleaned from a liberal education is one of skepticism, perhaps insight into the temporary nature of the truth and permanence of knowledge. This attitude is the antithesis of unreflective, passive acceptance of field-related truths: It represents a disposition to think critically.

McPeck's view of critical thinking is based on an assumption readily applicable to music education. The assumption is that music, like any other discipline, is a unique discipline with an intrinsically different epistemology, language, and structure. There are no generally applicable principles, no use of tests for validity through informal logic.

As with his definition of critical thinking, Ennis has modified his views on subject specificity and critical thinking (1985, 1987a, b, 1989). Ennis rejects the argument (espoused by McPeck) that if critical thinking is thinking about something it must necessarily be tied to some subject matter rather than taught separately. His refutation hinges on terminology: the definitional difference between "subject" and "discipline." Ennis states that "subject" has two meanings: (1) a specific meaning, such as psychology or mathematics, and (2) a more general sense, as a "topic." He advocates consideration of general principles that bridge subjects, such as "conflict of interest," "straw person fallacy," and "denial of the consequent" (1987a, pp. 43, 45).

A recent article continues the discussion of subject specificity through an analysis of the types of specificity and implications for instruction (Ennis, 1989). Ennis moves through several levels of analysis to delineate distinct modes of instruction. The first level of analysis involves clarification of four modes of instruction: general, infused, immersed, and combination. The general approach to teaching critical thinking is in the form of a separate course, in which "non-school" problems are examined using skills of formal or informal logic. In the second mode of instruction, the infused mode, some critical thinking skills are taught within the context of a subject matter area, and these skills are made explicit to the students. The immersion approach differs from the infusion approach only in that critical thinking skills are implicit rather than explicit. Ennis describes the fourth approach as a combination of teaching some abstract skills and utilization within subject matter area (1989, pp. 4–5). Teachers of critical thinking base their choice of instructional modality on acceptance/rejection of three principles of "domain specificity." The three principles are (1) critical thinking involves some background knowledge of a discipline; (2) transfer is dependent on some practice in the disciplines used; and (3) general critical thinking instruction is ineffective (1989, p. 5). The theorist who accepts all three principles unilaterally will advocate the infusion instructional approach. A theorist accepting only the first two would most likely use a combination approach to teaching critical thinking (p. 6). In addition to the domain specificity viewpoint, Ennis analyzes two others: epistemological subject specificity and conceptual subject specificity. McPeck is cited as an advocate of epistemological subject specificity, and also of the immersion approach to critical thinking instruction.

Ennis proposes the combination approach to instruction of critical thinking, including a "separate thread or course aimed at teaching general principles of critical thinking" as well as instruction in critical thinking that is subject matter specific (1989, p. 5).

Can Ennis's view of critical thinking be applied to musical problems? This question can best be answered through references to his taxonomy of dispositions and abilities (1987b, pp. 12–15). If the assumption is made that the critical thinker uses all of the dispositions and abilities, then musical problems might not be considered using this description of critical thinking. Does the musical thinker analyze arguments when thinking about a musical problem? Does the musician use induction and deduction, and make value judgments? Finally, are musical problems generally considered using a group of abilities that Ennis considers critical: interaction with others in the form of "discussion, debates, and written pieces" as criteria for being "sensible" (1987b, p. 23)? The problematic areas are the abilities involved in the use of argument analysis through informal logic and the necessity of interaction with others. An example of this lack of conceptual "fit" is a problem of musical interpretation being considered by a performer or conductor—should the musician use forms of logic, discuss the problem with a colleague, to derive a satisfactory conclusion? Similarly, a problem may result when a composer is seeking a particular musical effect. Ennis has made certain assumptions about critical thinking that may not be defensibly utilized when approaching musical problems.

Paul makes a fundamental connection between types of thinking and different disciplines. He describes two distinctly different types of disciplines: monological or technical and multi- or dialogical. Monological or technical disciplines include mathematics, physics, and chemistry; the dialogical disciplines are history, psychology, sociology, anthropology, economics, and philosophy. This distinction is based on the different reasoning or logical systems involved in each discipline. Paul posits that technical disciplines have in common certain logic systems that lead the thinker through a procedure directly to an answer. Technical domains are atomistic, involving monological thinking. As an example of thinking that occurs in technical disciplines, Paul cites Dewey's scientific method (1984a, p. 11). Dialogical disciplines involve more than one logical system and thinking that may involve multiple, possibly conflicting, viewpoints or frames of reference.

Can one teach for dialogical thinking in music? Paul has bypassed consideration of this question through his omission of music, visual art, dance, drama, and literature from the list of disciplines he categorized as fundamentally either monological or dialogical. Can his view of critical thinking adapt itself as a framework to superimpose upon musical thinking about musical problems? Several questions must be asked. First, is music a technical or dialogical discipline? If music is a technical discipline, then it follows that critical/dialogical thinking cannot, if one accepts Paul's assumption, take place. One concern in adapting dialogical thinking instruction to the music setting is whether there are any musical problems that suggest alternative viewpoints. A second consideration is whether such problems are typically considered using verbal discussion, or are thought through without interaction with others. A similar obstacle occurred in considering Ennis's prerequisite of interaction with others for critical thinking. However, Paul has inserted the caveat that dialogical thinking may occur in the imagination, with the thinker generating the case for both sides of the argument. This caveat facilitates the potential adaptation of the process to musical problems, as many musical problems are not, and perhaps cannot be, thought through using discussion with others. Problems representing diverse viewpoints would include, for example, problems of musical interpretation, or perhaps choice of appropriate teaching method. Certainly, many musical problems have a so-called technical aspect, an either-or element: Either a fingering works or it doesn't, or an instrument is out of tune or it is in tune. However, if one accepts that the apparently technical discipline of music may have dialogical problems occurring in real life within that discipline, then Paul's generalizable concept of dialogical thinking is in question.

The Evaluation of Critical Thinking

Three of the philosophers (Dewey, McPeck, and Paul) suggest that the process, rather than the product, of thinking must be evaluated. Ennis, as evidenced by both multiple-choice and essay test formats, considers both the product and the process to be areas of possible evaluation.

Two widely used tests of critical thinking are the *Watson-Glaser Critical Thinking Appraisal* (Watson and Glaser, 1980) and the *Cornell Tests of Critical Thinking* (Ennis and Millman, 1985). Glaser and Ennis have developed definitions of critical thinking that are described as a set of subskills. The definitions of critical thinking focus on a conception of critical thinking as argument analysis. This focus is easily discernible from the subtests. The Cornell tests contain seven subtests, including evaluation of deductive and inductive reasoning, identification of assumptions, detection of fallacies, reliability of observations, generalizations, and hypotheses. The Watson-Glaser test contains subtests that purport to assess ability to evaluate inferences, recognition of assumptions, deduction, evaluation of generalizations, and evaluation of the logical strength of arguments. The skills and dispositions are presented as lists of attributes or, as in the Cornell test, "dimensional categories."

Is music education an appropriate area for the use of tests to evaluate critical thinking? The answer to this question depends on which definition and description of critical thinking the music educator accepts. Several questions may aid in making such a choice: (1) Can critical thinking skills and subskills be discriminated from other skills? (2) Is evaluation focused on the process or the product of critical thinking? (3) Are critical thinking skills generalizable? (4) Do differences in background knowledge affect the results of an evaluation of critical thinking? (5) When can evaluation of critical thinking take place? The question of the discrimination of critical thinking skills from other skills is vital. Can critical thinking skills be discriminated from reading comprehension, writing ability, or general intelligence? If such discrimination is not possible, then perhaps tests of basic skills may be scored differently to reveal critical thinking ability, or items added to assess such ability. Morante and Ulesky argue that, given a definition of critical thinking as argument analysis, strong positive correlations exist between selected standardized tests (*Cornell Critical Thinking Test* [Ennis and Millman, 1985], *New Jersey Test of Reasoning Skills* [Shipman, 1983]) and all sections of the *New Jersey College Basic Skills Placement Test* (1984, p. 74). Such correlations may be due to the inclusion of questions that did not sufficiently discriminate between critical thinking skills and questions drawing on the student's academic achievement.

In an article focused on issues in the assessment of critical thinking, Norris (1988) discusses the differences involved in the evaluation of critical thinking as process or product. But can process be separated from product for the purposes of assessment? Can we, as Norris suggests, judge process quality by the "propensity of the processes to yield good products" (p. 135)? He lists several alternative forms of evaluation: essay tests, observation, and one-on-one oral testing. In designing his own tests of critical thinking, Norris utilized verbal protocols for test questions within the context of stories. The students were asked to think aloud while solving the questions, and the test adjusted until "good and poor thinking were associated, by and large, with keyed and unkeyed answers" (1985, p. 42). It may be worth noting that one essay test is available for the assessment of critical thinking: the *Ennis-Weir Critical Thinking Essay Test* (1985).

Carpenter and Doig (1988) suggest that observation may provide an alternative means of evaluation. Carpenter and Doig take the idea of an essay test one step further. They suggest that the student respond in essay format, then "attach to the completed essays brief explanations of the thinking process involved in their writing"—asking students to turn their thinking inward in an attempt to utilize metacognition. In addition to a strong reliance on writing skills, this approach assumes that students will be able, without benefit of instruction, to recall and describe their thought processes (1988, p. 37).

Suggestions for research into the possibility of assessment of critical thinking in music are based on consideration of the questions involved in a theoretical basis for instruction: definition of critical thinking, discrimination of critical thinking skills from other skills, generalization of critical thinking skills, background knowledge, and use of application of assessment instruments. Another consideration of particular interest is the question of process and product: Are they really a dichotomy, or can there be truly some evaluation of process that does not lead to an expected conclusion? Can the thinking process about a music problem be critical where the product of that thinking is not under concern? Do students use critical thinking about music problems, even in the absence of explicit instruction in critical thinking? The area of assessment of critical thinking is one that appears to generate as many questions as it satisfies, creating many implications for future research.

Research in Critical Thinking in Education

Research on critical thinking includes a vast number of studies, including philosophical research, curricular research, explorations of the correlation of critical thinking to another variable, and investigations of the validity of assessment instruments. As stated at the beginning of this chapter, space constraints have restricted the focus to studies focused on the theoretical bases for critical thinking.

Carroll (1981) performs an extensive review of existing literature about critical thinking in social studies education. Social studies education has produced the majority of articles and studies about critical thinking because of the connection between critical thinking and teaching for a goal of responsible citizenship. Carroll describes the need for the study as a "critical thinking gap" between the theories of social studies education that include critical thinking as essential and the actual practice of teaching critical thinking. Carroll hypothesizes that this gap is due to "conceptual confusion": lack of a common definition or description of the process of critical thinking. The review of literature is directed by the hypothesis of definitional vagueness and by a search for reasons for the "critical thinking gap." His conclusions suggest that (1) a gap exists between theory and practice; (2) the gap is due to conceptual imprecision; and (3) attitudes held by faculty and students about the nature of critical thinking appear to be responsible for the continuation of the problem.

The theme of semantic confusion is also the focus of Norton's (1980) examination of the relationship between critical thinking and selected theories of cognitive development. He justifies his combination of critical thinking theories with theories of cognitive development on the grounds that cognitive development is essential for any curriculum development. Norton proposes four groupings of theorists representing critical thinking: critical thinking as problem solving, Gestalt act, information processing, and judgment. Rather than focusing on the differences, Norton synthesizes common features of all the approaches into a list of 10 conclusions about critical thinking. Predictably, there is no one theory that satisfies all the theorists.

The next step of the procedure, following the review of critical thinking literature, involved examination of the 10 common features of critical thinking through the lens of eight cognitive development theories. When developmental theories are superimposed, a limited number of common features result, based on the fit of the theorist to the 10 general features of critical thinking (pp. 113–115). Norton concludes that critical thinking is both general and context specific. It is general in the sense that logic, values, and judgment are incorporated, and specific elements in each context will influence process.

Maiorana (1984) uses content analysis to examine the works of John Dewey for common elements with which to build a model for instruction in business education. However, following the derivation of common features of Dewey's descriptions of thinking, he introduces another model for representation of the thinking process rather than using Dewey's description. This rather vague model (p. 35) looks like this:

INPUT	**PROCESS**	**RESULT**
subject matter	critical thinking	learning
	teaching	

The content analysis, in the form of theme lists, is based on the categories of subject matter, critical thinking, teaching, and learning. Following the content analysis, Maiorana selects, without any explicit justification, certain ideas that he considers the primary considerations within each category. In the final chapter, he creates a sample plan for instruction in productivity.

Can these studies be used as exemplars for further philosophical examination of the concept of critical thinking? There are certain limitations common to this area of research. First, there are disappointingly few examples of research into the theoretical foundations of critical thinking. These studies are dated prior to 1984, when the national interest in critical thinking moved once more to the forefront of educational journals. When compared to the problems of clarification found in the literature since 1984, there are similarities: Conceptual confusion still exists in the literature; the process of thinking critically is not as apt to be evaluated as the product of critical thinking; and there is equivocation of Dewey's description of reflective thinking with critical thinking.

RESEARCH ON THINKING IN MUSIC EDUCATION

For the music education researcher venturing into the area of critical thinking research, the issues of definition, content, and evaluation must be dealt with. Two questions, which parallel those of the first section, organize this section:

(1) How can one best define critical thinking as it occurs in the musical encounter? (2) How has critical thinking been evaluated by music educators?

Defining Critical Thinking in Music

Among the various definitions proposed for critical thinking, problem solving, or decision making, which one best describes the student's encounter with music? Is it Dewey's definition of reflective thinking, the "active, persistent, and careful consideration," or McPeck's "propensity and skill to engage in an activity with reflective skepticism"? Can Ennis's definition—"reasonable reflective thinking that is focused on deciding what to believe or do"—be applied to musical experiences for which no belief or action is the result? The music education researcher need not engage in a complete conceptual analysis to make a decision about definition, but choosing the conceptual basis that most clearly fits the aspect of musical thinking under consideration is an important first step in research design, and one that seems to have been neglected in this rather unexplored area of music education research. Suppose the researcher chose, as many do, to equate critical thinking in music with musical problem solving. Is this a valid equation? Does an encounter with music have any of the problem-solving characteristics as cited in the previous section? Does every encounter with music present every student with a problem to be solved? If so, does the nature of the problem change depending on whether this is the student's first or fifth encounter with a particular piece of music? Do students formulate their own problems to make sense of the musical stimulus, or is musical problem formulating something done by music educators and given to students to solve?

Focus on another definition, such as musical decision making, would require a different set of questions. What are the musical decisions to be made by the student? To report whether the first phrase is the same as or different from the second requires one kind of musical decision; for the violin section to agree on the most expressive way to shape a difficult phrase requires a different kind of decision-making process. And in what ways is musical decision making different from or similar to critical thinking as defined by any of the previously cited theorists?

One way to clarify the notion of critical thinking in music is to consider the various roles undertaken by the student in a variety of encounters with music. For example, in one instance the student merely listens to the teacher perform a difficult passage, while in another instance the student is asked to perform the passage after the teacher models the correct fingering. Does critical thinking occur in both instances? If that same student is asked to evaluate her own performance of the modeled passage, does she use the same critical thinking processes as those used in the imitation exercise? Suppose this same student is asked to listen to a phrase and create her own appropriate ending. Will critical thinking be involved, and if so, are different critical thinking processes used to arrive at the product?

One way to clarify musical problem solving is to look at the variety of tasks that music teachers typically set. These generally require the student to apply previously acquired cognitive knowledge in a new situation, such as conducting a passage, improvising a musical answer, or adding appropriate sound accompaniment to a story. Suppose the choral director asks a chorus member to conduct the final section of the piece being rehearsed. Is this a musical problem? From the student's perspective, it may be a tremendous physical problem (How can I get my arms to show the different dynamic levels while keeping the beat pattern going?), a social problem (Will my peers do as I ask?), or an academic problem (If I can't do this correctly, I'll blow my A in this course). The general music student given the musical problem of improvising a musical answer on a xylophone may encounter a musical memory problem (How many beats have I played already?) as well as a coordination problem (Do I start with my left or right hand? Will I forget to alternate hands?) The group of children faced with the musical problem of adding an appropriate sound accompaniment to a story may be faced with an equipment problem (We don't have enough cymbals in this room to make the crash loud enough), an image problem (No one ever takes my suggestions seriously), or even a teacher appeasement problem (Which sounds will Miss Jones like the best?). Although every teacher-assigned task constitutes some type of problem to the student, the researcher needs to clearly distinguish musical problems from nonmusical ones and determine how the problem-solving process differs in each instance. Perhaps the most important feature of setting problem-solving tasks is the Deweyan notion of presenting the problem solvers with situations that require them to sense, identify, and define many layers of the problem for themselves, and work these through to completion. A second question is, To what degree did the problem-solving process differ in arriving at the solution of each?

Another distinction that needs to be considered by the researcher is the difference between problem solving, as defined by the critical thinking theorists, and creative problem solving (terms that are often used interchangeably in the research literature). If the researcher wanted to look at the value or correctness of the proposed musical solution or the process through which the solution was generated, a search of critical thinking literature might be in order. If, however, the focus were on the various ways the musical materials were manipulated, the researcher would more appropriately consult the creative thinking literature outlined by Peter Webster in Chapter 17. Whereas the problem-solving process defined by the critical thinking theorists focuses on procedure and evaluation of ideas or solutions to a problem, the creative problem-solving literature conveys the fluency, originality, and adaptability of the subject's thinking by presenting the solution to the problem.

Summary

There are many distinctions that can be made among the definitions of critical thinking and the terminology related to it in the research literature. Because this is a rather young area of research for music educators, no single conception of critical thinking has emerged as the best definition for critical thinking in music.

Evaluating Critical Thinking in Music: The Research

To date there are four different types of music education research that have examined the student's critical thinking in and about music: (1) descriptive studies that focus on musical problem solving; (2) correlation studies that focus on musical problem solving; (3) correlation studies of the relationship between musical and nonmusical variables and measures of critical thinking; and (4) verbal protocol analyses of musical thinking based on a Deweyan definition of reflective thinking.

Descriptive Studies of Musical Problem Solving

Although each of the studies included in this section focuses on musical problem solving, each stems from a distinctly different theoretical base. Taken together, the results of these studies serve to expand, rather than clarify, thinking about thinking in music.

DeLorenzo (1987) used naturalistic observation techniques to study sixth-grade students' problem-solving behavior while engaged in three different types of creative group composition activities: sound composition, event- or story-based composition, and composition based on a stated musical concept (p. 82). The researcher visited four school sites and observed students at work on 16 different group composition assignments. A variety of data was gathered, including videotapes, student and music teacher interviews, field notes, transcriptions of students' musical responses, and information about both the student and the school setting.

Although DeLorenzo emphasized the creative aspect of problem solving by focusing on the musical product, she clearly approached musical problem solving as a process with the same thought components as described by Ennis, Sternberg, and Dewey—such as judgment, decision making, analysis, synthesis, evaluation, and enquiry (p. 4). Her focus was the process by which students come to make musical decisions, and her findings are both informative and useful. DeLorenzo observed two types of problem-solving behavior: highly involved and uninvolved. Those students who were highly involved in the problem explored and organized sound for its expressive qualities, while the uninvolved rarely based their musical decisions on musical concerns. The degree of personal involvement in the problem-solving task appeared to DeLorenzo to be related to two main factors: the student's perception of the problem structure, and how closely the problem structure relates to that individual student's personal definition of what music is (p. 157). Two additional factors affecting student involvement emerged. The fewer choices students believed were available to them in solving the problems, the lower was their level of involvement; and unless the musical problem was within the student's existing understanding of music, only superficial musical investigation resulted (p. 158).

One important finding in this study is consistent with the Deweyan model of reflective thinking. The way in which students cognitively represented the problem structure to themselves influenced their perception of choices within the musical problem more than did the given, teacher-provided choices within the assignment. In other words, the ways in which students represent the problem to themselves have a greater influence on which choices they make in solving the problem than do the choices provided by the teacher. This crucial step of making the problem one's own, knowing first that there is a problem and recognizing that it is something outside of one's own head that can be looked at and turned over, is referred to in the critical thinking literature as sensing the problem. Unless the student senses the problem *as a problem,* and not just as an activity that will take the next 40 minutes, there is no problem solving. There may be acquiescence, outward appearance of on-task behavior, and even experimentation with sound. But these are mere teacher-pleasing behaviors, not problem-solving behaviors. This single result makes DeLorenzo's study a landmark, for it provides the beginnings of a well-formulated definition of musical problem solving.

Whereas DeLorenzo looked at the process of musical problem solving in group composition assignments, Barrett (1990) examined the musical problem-solving process involved in transforming a familiar melody into a resonator bell performance. Barrett considered three variables involved in the solution of the musical problem: melodic schemata, forms of representation, and cognitive strategies. After a warm-up task, 20 randomly sampled fourth-graders with no previous private music lessons were asked first to sing "Are You Sleeping?" and then determine how to play it on a set of resonator bells. The researcher videotaped the entire procedure and asked those subjects who completed the task a set of follow-up questions about the contour of the melody, interval relationships, and their strategies for solving the problem. Data included transcribed musical solutions and verbal reports given during the song solutions task, answers to follow-up questions, and stimulated recall of thought processes made by the subjects while watching the videotape.

Barrett found that, of 20 subjects, only one was unable to reproduce either the pitches or the contour of the melody, leading her to conclude that children possess contour and interval schemata for known songs (p. 187). Barrett identified three cognitive strategies used by the subjects: temporal order strategies, comparison strategies, and inferring strategies. The temporal order strategies included starting over from the beginning and adding the next phrase, starting over from the beginning and playing the whole song, solving the next adjacent phrase, and solving the next pitch. The comparison strategies included a systematic interval search and interpolating the correct pitch between known pitches. Inferring strategies included holding musically plausible, though not correct, answers as solutions. Barrett also identified three types of musical problem solvers among her 20 subjects: aural solvers, nonsolvers, and visual solvers (p.

186). The aural solvers easily solved the problem using aural forms of representation, song-specific schemata, whole-song-ordering strategies, systematic interval searches, and interpolations. The nonsolvers had no song-specific schemata, were able to use iconic forms of representation to a limited extent, and showed few identifiable cognitive strategies. The visual solvers were greatly helped by the use of iconic representations of the melody, and used ordering, comparing, and inferring strategies.

Barrett's study is unique in that the focus is on the solution of the musical problem as well as the process by which it was solved. Although the music education researcher can learn much from analyzing the metamorphosis of earlier attempts into the performance of the completed melody, Barrett uncovered an even richer source of data through her subject's verbal reflections on the solution process, and this methodology holds promise as a research tool in the field.

Correlation Studies of Musical Problem Solving

Cutietta (1982) examined another component of problem solving in the music listener: hypothesis testing. He developed a listening task in which subjects heard eight musical examples and were asked to hypothesize what each pair of pieces had in common. Subjects were given 3 seconds to write their hypotheses, and these results were analyzed to identify hypothesis-testing techniques and to identify which of two scanning strategies was used: successive (subject tested one hypothesis at a time) or simultaneous (subject tested more than one hypothesis at a time).

The theoretical basis for Cutietta's research was derived from *A Study of Thinking,* written by Bruner, Goodnow, and Austin in 1956. These researchers define a hypothesis as an assertion that a particular attribute identifies the concept; once learners create a hypothesis, they then test it against the musical stimulus perceived. For Bruner and colleagues, this testing is problem solving, and it is the means through which concepts are shaped and refined (Bruner et al., p. 104). This is not a definition of critical thinking per se but rather a conception of the thinking that is requisite to learning. This study is included here as another example of just how widely varied the music education researcher's conception of "problem solving" and "thinking" has been.

Cutietta found that the percentage of subjects using hypothesis testing increased progressively between ages 11 and 15, with a slight drop between ages 15 and 16. He also found that while the percentage of subjects who used hypothesis testing rose gradually, 11- to 13-year-olds used successive scanning, while 15- to 16-years-olds used simultaneous scanning. Cutietta concluded that while the musical knowledge of the 11- to 16-years-olds did not increase noticeably, the ability to manipulate hypotheses seemed to expand, perhaps as a result of the development of formal operational thought during this period.

Several issues important to an understanding of musical problem solving/critical thinking arise from this study. What is the link between musical concept formation and problem solving? Can we equate the hypothesis testing undergone in the process of concept formation with musical problem solving? If so, to what degree can the teacher guide the student to formulate correct hypotheses, ones that lead to correct definitions or conceptions of the concept, rather than the proportionately large number of incorrect hypotheses Cutietta found? How effective would be the teaching of strategies of successive scanning before the age of 14?

The second study in this section is Morgan's 1984 correlation study of musical problem solving by high school instrumentalists, which investigated the relationship between musical and nonmusical variables to the performance of musical problem-solving tasks. Morgan inspected several factors that may influence the instrumentalist's musical problem-solving ability, including musical background, cognitive style and creativity, age and maturation, and task type by using data from several types of instruments, including *Watkins-Farnum Performance Scale,* and Colwell's *MAT2.* He then developed his own criterion measure, the *Musical Problems Test* (MPT) which consisted of three tasks: learning an unfamiliar piece, transposing, and creating an ending. Morgan administered all of the measures to 94 high school instrumentalists, 43 in grade 9, 51 in grade 11. He found that performance on the three subtests of the MPT was more strongly related to musical variables than to psychological variables, and that the eleventh-grade students scored higher on all three subtests than did the ninth-graders.

Although the results of this study may not be particularly surprising, the study is unusual in that the author proposes a definition of musical problem-solving ability as musical independence and initiative, based on an in-depth synthesis of several definitions of problem solving, including those by Ausubel, Gagne, Davis, Dewey, Hilgard, and Bruner (p. 8). Since musical independence and initiative are such dearly held goals of music teaching, the link that Morgan proposes between musical problem solving and musical independence is an important one, especially for researchers trying to tease out the meaning of critical thinking/musical problem solving as practiced in the music classroom.

Correlation Studies: Verbal Measures of Critical Thinking

The following studies focus on the correlation between various musical and nonmusical variables and scores on verbal measures of critical thinking.

DeTurk (1988) examined the relationship between number of years of experience in performance and critical thinking skills about music. High school juniors (n = 279) listened twice to two musical selections and wrote essays about the pieces during their English class period. DeTurk instructed the students to describe, compare, contrast, and make evaluative statements about the quality of the two pieces, and to ''utilize the most sophisticated musical concepts and vocabulary'' (p. 61). Students had a total of 20 minutes to complete both essays. A structure of learning outcomes (SOLO) taxonomy was used to categorize the level of musical understanding exhibited in each essay. DeTurk found that students with 6 or more years of performance experience wrote essays that

exhibited the highest levels of critical thinking, according to the taxonomy. He also found that the student's most recent English grade strongly correlated with the SOLO taxonomy rating.

Anyone wishing to replicate this particular study should carefully consider two things. First, great care needs to be taken in choosing a definition for the unknown variable, critical thinking in music. Second, the means for measuring the unknown variable needs to allow the researcher to get as close to the thinking process as possible. Perhaps some form of nonwritten response, either verbal or computerized, would be a more fruitful means for evaluating critical thinking in music.

Another correlation study was undertaken by Small (1990). In the first part of the two-part study, 114 students enrolled in a school of music were given the *Watson-Glaser test of critical thinking.* Results were compared with *Scholastic Aptitude Test* (SAT) scores and cumulative grade point averages (GPAs), and evaluated by types of major: vocal versus instrumental, performance versus music education, and undergraduate classification. Results indicated that seniors did the best, with no significant difference between vocal/instrumental and music education/performance. No significant relationship was found between critical thinking scores and GPA, but a weak (.378) positive relationship was found between critical thinking score and SAT score.

In the second phase, the researcher gave an experimental group (n = 8) in her undergraduate elementary music methods class written exercises in the content area and evaluated their writing for the following critical thinking skills: recognition of assumptions, inference, and evaluation of arguments. Small found no differences between the experimental and the control group's critical thinking results, and the experimental group showed only slightly higher mean gain scores.

The results of Small's studies are consistent with findings in critical thinking research in other fields: namely, that verbal measures such as SAT scores often correlate positively with critical thinking test scores because they are so verbally oriented. Small's second-phase results, even with a small *n,* are consistent with critical thinking results that show that instruction in critical thinking skills in isolation from a content area doesn't affect the student's critical thinking scores.

Although they both focused on verbal products of critical thinking in the broad field of music education, the two researchers included in this section relied on written measures of critical thinking for insight into thinking *about* music and music education. In the next section, the researchers look at the process, instead of the product, through another methodology: verbal protocol analysis.

Verbal Protocol Analyses

Two studies based on a definition of musical thinking as the reflective thinking defined by Dewey (1933) were undertaken by the authors of this chapter. Richardson (1988) and Whitaker (1989) formulated paradigms for the ways in which adult musical experts (performer, conductor, arranger, and listener/critic) think reflectively in the musical encounter.

Using what Richardson termed a "philosophical, speculative approach" (p. 28), both Richardson and Whitaker relied heavily on verbal protocol analysis as a source of data.

Richardson focused on the thinking of the music critic engaged in a musical experience by looking at three distinct types of data. First, works of several metacritics were surveyed and synthesized into a paradigm of the thought processes involved in the formulation of music criticism. Next, 30 randomly selected pieces of written music criticism by six different critics were examined to determine if they supported the paradigm. Further support for the paradigm was sought in a recorded and transcribed stream-of-consciousness verbal narrative produced by one music critic as he listened to a live orchestral concert. The similarities and differences between the written and verbal examples of the critic's thinking were noted, and Richardson proposed that the process of arriving at a musical judgment is a series of distinct functions: expectation, comparison, prediction, and evaluation. These functions are nonlinear and occur continually while the critic is engaged in the music (p. 134).

Whereas Richardson focused on the music critic's thinking, Whitaker (1989) investigated the extent to which the performer, arranger, and conductor use Dewey's conception of reflective thinking when making decisions about musical problems (p. 462). Whitaker relied heavily on two sources of data to verify the Deweyan paradigm of musical thinking. First, writings of pianists, arrangers, and conductors were surveyed, and problem statements were extracted and categorized as evidence of Dewey's phases of reflective thinking. Comparisons were then made between the thinking of pianists, arrangers, and conductors. Whitaker's second source of data was a series of stream-of-consciousness verbal protocols produced by two pianists, two arrangers, and two instrumental conductors while engaged in a variety of tasks, such as selecting a piece of music, studying the score, and rehearsing. Whitaker found evidence that the thinking of the subjects was individual, as Dewey claims, and that reflective thinking was present in five of the six subjects (p. 466). Reflective thinking did not seem to be tied to any particular type of funded knowledge or problem, but appeared in a variety of forms, in response to the experience each individual brought to the data-gathering settings

Although the results of these two studies have yet to be taken to the level of practical, classroom applications, they do offer promising directions for future researchers looking for a theoretical base for thinking in music. Pursuing the Deweyan definition of reflective thinking seemed to be particularly useful: feeling, imagination, and the thinkers' con-

stant dipping into their fund of previous musical experience. The affective component included in Dewey's definition is especially important, since it figures in affective knowing, while the critical thinking theorists include only the cognitive, factual representations of knowledge to be counted in support of a viewpoint or decision. Although Dewey may not be the answer to the current lack of a theoretical base, he does provide one conception that seems compatible with both the cognitive and the affective aspects of music education.

Implications for Further Research

Because the area of critical thinking research in music education is relatively young, much important work has yet to be undertaken. First, and most importantly, there is a need to explore the musical implementation of a single theoretical base. There is a need for philosophical studies in which meanings are clarified, conceptions refined, and clear connections made between critical thinking and musical thinking. A definition of critical thinking in music that is able to encompass adequately the whole of the student's experience with music—including the cognitive as well as the affective components of musical thinking—needs to be forged. In an enlightening article entitled "Critical Thinking and the Perception of Aesthetic Form," Dressel (1988) argues eloquently that our affective response to works of art is central, not peripheral, to our thinking about the works. She states:

Our understanding of learning cannot be complete until we recognize the symbiotic relationship between the cognitive and affective means of knowing. In our attempts to understand and explain higher-level thinking processes, we have talked about thinking as if it could be emotion-free, about affective response as if it were the antithesis of critical thought. And in so doing we have created a false and dangerous dichotomy between cognition and affect. Thoughts are not emotion-free, emotions are not devoid of thought. (p. 568)

We no longer need to operate as if the traditionally held Western dichotomy between feeling and thinking were true. Whatever definitions come to be used for musical thinking must include both kinds of knowing—cognitive and affective. Once we become more adept at theory building and have some of our own theoretical studies in place, we can proceed to develop the pilot curricula that enable students to become better thinkers in music, and develop instruments to quantify musical thinking in ways that are not wholly dependent on the student's verbal ability.

References

Barrett, J. (1990). Melodic schemata, forms of representation, and cognitive strategies used by fourth graders in the recall and reproduction of familiar songs. Unpublished doctoral dissertation, University of Wisconsin, Madison.

Bruner, J. S., Goodnow, J., and Austin, G. A. (1956). A study of thinking. New York: John Wiley.

Carpenter, C. B., and Doig, J. C. (1988). Assessing critical thinking across the curriculum. New Directions for Teaching and Learning, 34, 33–46, San Francisco, Jossey-Bass.

Carroll, R. J. (1981). An examination of conceptual problems in teaching critical thinking in social studies education. Unpublished doctoral dissertation, University of North Carolina, Chapel Hill.

Cutietta, R. (1982). The analysis of listening strategies and musical focus of the 11–16-year-old learner. Unpublished doctoral dissertation, Pennsylvania State University, University Park.

DeLorenzo, L. C. (1987). An exploratory field study of sixth grade students' creative musical problem solving processes in the general music class. Unpublished doctoral dissertation, Columbia University, New York.

deTurk, M. S. (1988). The relationship between experience in performing music class and critical thinking about music. Unpublished doctoral dissertation, University of Wisconsin, Madison.

Dewey, J. (1933). *How we think*. Lexington: D.C. Heath.

Dressel, J. H. (1988). Critical thinking and the perception of aesthetic form. *Language Arts, 65*(6), 567–572.

Ennis, R. H. (1962). A concept of critical thinking. *Harvard Educational Review, 32*, 81–111.

Ennis, R. H. (1985). A logical basis for measuring critical thinking skills. *Educational Leadership, 43*(2), pp. 44–48.

Ennis, R. H. (1987a). Critical thinking and the curriculum. In M. Heiman, and J. Slomianko (Eds.), *Thinking skills instruction: Concepts and techniques* (pp. 40–48). Washington: National Educational Association.

Ennis, R. H. (1987b). A taxonomy of critical thinking dispositions and abilities. In J. B. Baron and R. J. Sternberg, (Eds.), *Teaching thinking skills: Theory and practice* (pp. 9–26). New York: Freeman.

Ennis, R. H. (1989). Critical thinking and subject specificity: Clarification and needed research. *Educational Researcher, 48*(3), pp. 4–10.

Ennis, R. H., and Millman, J. (1985). *Cornell Critical Thinking Test, levels X and Z*. Pacific Grove: Midwest Publications.

Ennis, R. H., and Weir, E. (1985). *The Ennis-Weir Critical Thinking Essay Test*. Pacific Grove: Midwest Publications.

Farra, H. (1988). The reflective thought process: John Dewey revisited. *Journal of Creative Behavior, 22*(1), 1–9.

Kitchener, K. S. (1983). Educational goals and reflective thinking. *Educational Forum. 63*(1), 75–93.

Maiorana, V. P. (1984). A model of teaching business management based on John Dewey's concept of critical thinking. Unpublished doctoral dissertation, New York University, New York.

McMillan, J. H. (1987). Enhancing college students' critical thinking: A review of studies. *Research in Higher Education, 26*(1), 3–29.

McPeck, J. E. (1981). *Critical thinking and education*. New York: St. Martin's Press.

McPeck, J. E. (1984). Stalking beasts but swatting flies: The teaching of critical thinking. *Canadian Journal of Education, 9*(1), 28–44.

McPeck, J. E. (1985). Paul's critique of critical thinking and education. *Informal Logic, 7*(1), 45–54.

Morante, E. A., and Ulesky, A. (1984). Assessment of reasoning abilities. *Educational Leadership, 42*(1), 71–74.

Morgan, S. G. (1984). Dimensions of musical problem solving by high school instrumentalists: An exploratory investigation. Unpublished doctoral dissertation, University of Wisconsin, Madison.

Norris, S. P. (1985). Synthesis of research on critical thinking. *Educational Leadership, 42*(8), 40–45.

Norris, S. P. (1988). Research needed on critical thinking. *Canadian Journal of Education, 13*(1), 125–137.

Norton, J. R. (1980). An analysis of the relationship of critical thinking to specified theories of cognitive structures. Unpublished doctoral dissertation, University of Southern California, Los Angeles.

Paul, R. W. (1984a). Critical thinking: Fundamental to education for a free society. *Educational Leadership, 42*(1), 4–14.

Paul, R. W. (1984b). The Socratic spirit: An answer to Louis Goldman. *Educational Leadership, 42*(1), 63–64.

Paul, R. W. (1985a). Bloom's taxonomy and critical thinking instruction. *Educational Leadership, 42*(8), 36–39.

Paul, R. W. (1985b). Critical thinking research: A response to Stephen Norris. *Educational Leadership, 42*(8), 46.

Paul, R. W. (1985c). McPeck's mistakes. *Informal Logic, 7*(1), 35–43.

Paul, R. W. (1987). Dialogical thinking: Critical thought essential to the acquisition of rational knowledge and passions. In J. B. Baron and R. J. Sternberg, (Eds.), *Teaching thinking skills: Theory and practice* (pp. 127–148). New York: Freeman.

Richardson, C. P. (1988). Musical thinking as exemplified in music criticism. Unpublished doctoral dissertation, University of Illinois, Urbana.

Rosen, J. G. (1987). Problem-solving and reflective thinking: John Dewey, Linda Flower, Richard Young. *Journal of Teaching Writing, 6*(1), 69–78.

Rudinow, J., and Paul, R. W. (1987). A strategy for developing dialectical thinking skills. In M. Heiman, and J. Slomianko, (Eds.), *Thinking skills instruction: Concepts and techniques* (pp. 92–98). Washington: National Educational Association.

Shipman, V. (1983). *New Jersey Test of Reasoning Skills*. Montclair: IAPC, Test Division, Montclair State College.

Small, A. R. (1990). An investigation of critical thinking skills among college music majors. Unpublished manuscript, Stetson University, DeLand.

Tanner, L. N. (1988). The path not taken: Dewey's model of inquiry. *Curriculum Inquiry, 18,* 471–479.

VanSickle, R. (1985). Research implications of a theoretical analysis of John Dewey's "How We Think." *Theory and Research in Social Education, 8*(3), 1–20.

Watson, G., and Glaser, E. M. (1980, 2 forms). *The Watson-Glaser Critical Thinking Appraisal*. Cleveland: The Psychological Corporation.

Whitaker, N. L. (1989). Reflective thinking as exemplified in musical decision making. Unpublished doctoral dissertation, University of Illinois at Urbana.

THE TEACHING OF SPECIFIC MUSICAL SKILLS AND KNOWLEDGE IN DIFFERENT INSTRUCTIONAL SETTINGS

38

ISSUES AND CHARACTERISTICS COMMON TO RESEARCH ON TEACHING IN INSTRUCTIONAL SETTINGS

Hildegard C. Froehlich

UNIVERSITY OF NORTH TEXAS

NOTE. This chapter is an introduction to chapters 39–43. The purpose of the introduction is to point out that despite the seemingly different instructional settings described and the specific musical skills and knowledge researched, likenesses and commonalities of concerns do exist and can be observed. These transcend each particular teaching and research environment and may therefore be viewed as the bond that makes the five chapters a unit.

In section F, the status of knowledge gained through research on formal teaching processes in different instructional settings is described. There are chapters on the teaching of vocal music, instrumental music, keyboard music, elementary general music, and general music at the middle school/junior high school level. This variety of settings suggests a diversity of goals and objectives that—particularly those for school music instruction—have been discussed in depth elsewhere, most recently by McDonald (1990) and Elliott and Rao (1990). Here, a brief overview may suffice.

Both at the elementary and the secondary levels of instruction, general music focuses on strategies that foster in the learner a conceptual understanding of music through skills of musical discrimination. Through both in-depth and exploratory experiences in the areas of music history and theory, composition, and improvisation, the learner is to integrate the acquired skills and knowledge with those gained in purely academic subject matter areas. Performance skills are being developed to the degree that either discriminatory and conceptual skills need honing or transfer to other knowledge areas demands it.

Particularly at the elementary school level where general music is usually compulsory, the goal is to equip a person to make educated choices about music in the future. At the middle school or junior high school level, general music may be either elective or compulsory, depending on the laws of the state or the decisions of the local school boards. In all cases general music focuses more on the integration of knowledge and discovery learning than on the attainment of testable musical skills and knowledge.

Most commonly, music instruction at the high school level emphasizes performance through elective participation in choir, band, or orchestra. Such instruction stresses the development of instrumental or vocal skills and is often quite competitive. It includes basic knowledge about musical styles so that two interrelated goals can be reached: (1) The student becomes a functional member of a large music ensemble within the school, and (2) the student has the foundation from which to develop into an active, self-sufficient, and lifelong performer.

Private music study, both in vocal and instrumental studios, has traditionally emphasized a one-on-one teaching approach between pedagogue and student. The pedagogue can thus strive for individualized objectives that are dependent on and commensurate with the learner's abilities and motivations. Nonetheless, a dichotomy between the development of specific performance skills and the teaching of conceptual skills exists here as it does in school music instruction. In fact, independent vocal and instrumental teachers, piano pedagogues included, debate perhaps more often and stringently than school music teachers, which of the two goals to teach.

In this section, all five authors address the impact of technological advances on the teaching of music under various instructional conditions; both measurement of learning and improvement in instruction are often closely associated with advances in music technology and educational technology. Considering the history of school music instruction, one may surmise that curricular changes have frequently occurred as the result of technological advances. From the introduction of the phonograph and radio to the use of films and videos; from teaching machines to programed instruction, computer-assisted instructional packages, and the synthesizer; from the electronic keyboard to personal computers for each student, technological innovations have had and continue to have ramifications for the role the teacher plays in the music instructional process. Before this assertion can become fact, however, we need systematic studies on this topic for elementary and secondary general music, performance groups in the schools, and private studio teaching.

The purpose of this section is to provide the reader with a comprehensive overview of research in instructional settings and with references for important issues germane to each area of instruction. Questions common to all research on instructional settings are the focus of this particular chapter, outlining some of the concerns that arise as the result of defining the purpose of music teaching, its methods and approaches toward the sequencing of instruction, and methods of researching their effectiveness.

THE PURPOSE OF MUSIC TEACHING

Music is a discipline with a rich history of performance and scholarship. From that history emanates a body of knowledge whose mastery is as important as the mastery of any instrument. Because teaching toward the acquisition of technical skills cannot or should not do without the teaching of conceptual knowledge, we must find a middle ground where both purposes can meet. If I want my students to advance as performers, the very repertoire I select carries with it the need for the students to deal with conceptual issues of music. On the other hand, if I am in charge of general musical learning, I cannot make the musical concepts concrete unless I first provide my students with an adequate amount of performance skills. We must therefore recognize the uniqueness of each performance medium and, at the same time, acknowledge that all efforts at improving instrumental and vocal skills must lead to an understanding of *music* as a special form of knowledge.

Music instruction becomes concrete in the relationship between the activities of the teacher to facilitate learning and the behaviors by which the students show that learning has taken place. As its title suggests, this section addresses primarily the aspect of teaching since other parts in the book are devoted to the issue of learning. But, the distinction is less clear in practice than in print since a teacher judges how to proceed in the instructional process by observing students' learning behavior. A certain degree of overlap between issues of learning and teaching is therefore inevitable.

All responsible teaching emphasizes the intentional se-

quencing of activities that lead to preestablished learning results. Here, the two key elements are "intentional sequencing of activities" and "preestablished learning results." Although other sections in the *Handbook* address both topics, a brief discussion of the act of sequencing will follow here.

The Nature of Sequencing

We define sequencing as an orderly and continuous progression of teaching activities from point A to point B. The progression is intentional and may go from the simple to the complex, from the familiar to the unfamiliar, from the easy to the difficult, or from the known to the unknown. There is, however, disagreement among music textbook authors, music education researchers, and teachers about what may be simple, familiar, easy, or known to the learner in music. Thus, "sequencing" does not suggest that music educators follow an agreed-upon order of teaching activities. It merely acknowledges a music teacher's effort to move from one point to another in an orderly, continuous way.

As the views of what constitutes an orderly, continuous progression of learning activities differ widely between teachers and researchers, teachers depend either on their own experiences or on music textbooks to determine where to begin their teaching sequence. Researchers spend their lifetime of work on that question and have documented specific musical knowledge and skills that may serve as a beginning point of musical learning. Although not stated in those terms, the research questions reflecting those efforts have addressed the acquisition of skills in instrumental performance, skills in the symbolization of musical sounds as well as their aural discrimination, and skills of reading/singing at sight. These questions have been studied for learners of different ages and musical backgrounds, in relationship to specific teaching methodologies, and in the context of varying theoretical frameworks. Thus, even questions about musical perception, conservation theory, learning theories in application to music, and comparisons of methodologies have contributed to the question of defining point A in a teaching sequence. The chapters in this section describe some of those research efforts in depth, documenting the state of our knowledge in that regard.

Defining Learning Outcomes

Whenever we seek to define point B in a teaching sequence, it is inevitable that we address the relationship of goal setting and educational policy (Colwell, 1990). The latter being a political as much as an educational issue, music educators have shied away from tackling it in a systematic way. Or, perhaps, they merely have not considered it to be under their purview.

When describing what we know about the teaching of music, we must look to the purpose for which we teach: Where do instructional sequences lead us? What do we want our students to know? What should the learning outcomes be? Who determines them? Where are we taking our students? To what degree are curricular decisions based on consensus among experts? Does this consensus emanate from knowledge about and agreement on the developmental levels of the learners? Or, is the consensus a result of preferences for specific teaching content on the part of the teacher?

Efforts at answering these and related questions fall as often into the realm of philosophical research as they do into the realm of empirical inquiry. Both venues are likely to result in further questions: What has been the relationship between objectives that address the attainment of musical performance skills and those that address knowledge? Can we say with a degree of certainty that all students enrolled in secondary school music programs will gain comparable musical skills and knowledge? Will those skills transcend the playing of an instrument and impact a person's musical understanding and ability to conceptualize musical sound and compositional structures? Could such understanding be termed musical literacy? Finally, is the research that speaks to these issues conclusive enough that curricular decisions can and should be based on the evidence provided?

Surprisingly little research exists on what teachers believe the purpose of music teaching to be. Similarly, rarely have there been studies about the expectations of teachers as to what their students may or may not be able to do. The isolated dissertations on these issues will continue to have a low impact until supported by additional research.

There are hardly any investigations on what students themselves consider important to learn. Rather, one must surmise this from research about preferences among adolescents (e.g., Anderson, 1961; Asmus, 1986; Boyle, Hosterman, and Ramsey, 1981; Broquist, 1961; Deihl, Schneider, and Petress, 1983; Haack, 1972; Hylton, 1981; Pearsall, 1980; Sturgess, 1986; Wapnick, 1976). Because attitudes change over time, this type of study requires constant updating and replication before the findings can aid music educators in setting instructional goals.

Comparisons of teacher and student viewpoints toward specific and desirable learning outcomes are still isolated (e.g., Murphy and Brown, 1986; Stone, 1983) but should be encouraged in future research efforts. Such information could guide music educators in the forecasting of how students are likely to react toward certain instructional assignments and class activities. The planning of teaching activities would benefit from such knowledge.

The "Learning of Musical Concepts" and "Conceptual Learning in Music"

The chapters in this section reflect the principle that regardless of the instructional setting and performance medium, all of music teaching should occur for one overriding purpose: to instill in our students the ability to conceptualize music as a craft, an art, a body of knowledge, and a medium of self-expression and creativity. Such a comprehensive goal implies distinguishing between (1) the learning of musical concepts and (2) conceptual learning in and through music.

The *learning of musical concepts* would entail the teaching of the knowledge and skills needed to identify organized sound according to its elements. Conceptual knowledge in this sense would mean (1) knowing the musical elements by labeling them; (2) understanding the form of a composition by naming its parts; and (3) articulating the relationship between the musical elements and those parts. As I pointed out earlier, this type of knowledge is particularly stressed in general school music.

Some researchers have attempted to show how performance teachers at the secondary level might stress the acquisition of conceptual knowledge as well (see, for example, Burris, 1989; Flom, 1971; Whitener, 1981; Whitlock, 1982). Such efforts have often taken place under the label of comprehensive musicianship. The researchers listed above sought ways in which the teacher might strike a balance between the acquisition of knowledge about music and the advancement of performance skills.

Less research exists on the second approach, *conceptual learning in and through music,* that is, the application of performance skills and content knowledge to new musical situations. The result of such conceptual learning might be creativity and aesthetic sensitivity (e.g., Baudo, 1983; Reimer, 1990; Webster, 1979, 1990), critical decision making about music, and skills of musical transfer (e.g., Shehan, 1985). In education, these aspects of musical thought are often referred to as "higher-level thinking skills." They are assumed to be applicable to all areas of knowledge acquisition (Baron and Sternberg, 1987; Cormier and Hagman, 1987) and are learned by adapting problem-solving techniques from one subject matter to tasks in another subject area.

Thus far, music educators have relied heavily on research conducted outside the field of music for information concerning principles of higher-level thinking skills in music. For example, Boardman's *Dimensions of Musical Thinking* (1989) contains references to many different educational theorists and learning psychologists as evidence that music study does, indeed, contribute to all levels of thinking.

The methodological and logistic difficulties embedded in transfer research are immense. Therefore, only relatively few researchers have even begun to explore systematically aspects of problem solving in music. Most notably among them are Cutietta (1984, 1985); deTurk (1988); Greer and Ludquist (1976); Howard (1971); Morgan (1985); Schmidt (1984, 1985); and Serafine (1988). Also, our interest in investigating skills in musical thinking and processing should give us reason to pay renewed attention to research on a learner's listening strategies (Cutietta, 1983; Fiske, 1984; Hedden, 1981; Hufstader, 1977; LeBlanc, Colman, McCrary, Sherrill, and Malin, 1988; Turk, 1985; and Zumbrunn, 1968).

The most crucial aspect of transfer learning—that is, the actual application of musical skills and knowledge to the solution of nonmusical problems—has not been explored. It seems safe to say, therefore, that integration of knowledge in an interdisciplinary sense has not been the focus of researchers either in music education or in general education. Furthermore, there is still a relative paucity of research on the issue of how students use knowledge gained in music class beyond the performance of their instrument. We need research on the question of what students may gain from their involvement in music activities in and outside of school. Do band students acquire the same knowledge as students enrolled in choir? What concepts about music, the history of music, and musical style do they take with them after graduation? To what degree does the chosen instrument determine the person's knowledge about music as a discipline, about music as a form of human expression, about the place and value of music in society? What does private music study contribute in that regard and how do its effects differ from those of school music instruction?

Assessing Teaching Success

Once the profession has defined and agreed on specific educational goals and objectives, a second, related set of questions arises: Who judges the appropriateness and the success of the teaching activities? What evaluation procedures are being employed in that regard? Do the evaluations occur on a continuing basis and is the revision of the curriculum an integral part of the teaching methodology? Do we consider different learners' needs and motivations as well as cultural and experiential differences? Any or all of these questions contribute to defining point B in the instructional sequence to the same degree as does the decision toward what goals to teach.

Very little research on assessing teaching success is available for either vocal or instrumental studio instruction. In contrast, research that evaluates teaching success in school music abounds. Two reasons may be given. First, individualized instruction allows an immediacy of feedback impossible to obtain in a group instructional setting. Secondly, the school music teacher is subject to accountability measures, whereas private music teachers can rely on the trust of their clientele for continuing their work.

The definitions for teaching success underlying extant studies on teacher evaluation vary from researcher to researcher. They have ranged from learning gains on the part of each student to performance quality of the ensemble, from motivation and enthusiasm for music to "liking" the teacher, and from positive ratings by the teachers' immediate superiors to the teachers' own perceptions about their students' learning gains. Approaches toward measuring teaching success are discussed in detail elsewhere in the *Handbook*. We should recognize that both the testing of knowledge and skills and systematic observations of learner behaviors exist primarily for school instruction, not for studio teaching.

COMMON PROBLEMS IN RESEARCH IN INSTRUCTIONAL SETTINGS

Research in instructional settings brings with it a variety of methodological and philosophical concerns that determine the usefulness of findings for practical application. First of all, there is the need to distinguish between description and experiment. Second, most research in classroom or studio settings relies on volunteers whose availability limits sampling procedures. This means the reported findings may not be generalizable to a larger population. Finally, in no other area of inquiry within music education than in research on instruction is there such a need to understand the difference between thinking as an educator and as a scientist/scholar. There is a conceptual difference between the questions asked by a researcher and those asked by a teacher.

Description vs. Experiment

Researchers who conduct investigations in music instructional settings must keep classroom or studio procedures intact if they want to study the nature of teaching and learning. This means they cannot easily interfere with either the objectives toward which a teacher aspires, or the sequence of activities established in a particular setting. Furthermore, the replacement of one teacher with another or one group of students with another for the purpose of experimentation can have lasting effects on the people under investigation. For this reason, most studies reported in this section rely on the description of behaviors rather than on experimenting with them.

The behaviors are cataloged as they occur in the observed environments. Regardless of whether such environments represent experimental or control groups, the observed behaviors themselves are not actually being manipulated. This is why in research on music instruction, experiments can be, at best, quasiexperimental (Broudy, Ennis, and Krimerman, 1973; Rainbow and Froehlich, 1987; Campbell and Stanley, 1967). This makes the determination of cause and effect relationships between specific variables difficult; behavior is hard to predict, and it takes many replications of research to test specific instructional theories.

Even if we were to conduct true experimental research in instructional settings where we could test for causal differences in learning gains, we would have to contend with some ethical concerns. We are referring not to major breaching of trust, to deceit or physical harm (Smith, 1973), but to the fact that the slightest reason to believe that one method of instruction might be inferior to another should stop us from exposing subjects to the inferior one—even in the name of improving learning on a long-term basis. In fact, one might make the case that experimental designs in instructional research may be harmful to learning and, thus, undesirable in music education.

Sampling

A second dilemma the researcher faces when conducting research in instructional settings is that of sampling. Much of the research reported in this chapter relies on the voluntary participation of teachers (and their students). Usually, a researcher obtains just enough volunteers to include all of them in the population. To draw a randomized sample from such a population is in most cases counterproductive. Therefore, the researchers often report their results for the total population. This means they cannot generalize from the observed behavior to that of other teachers. To resolve this problem, many more replication studies than are currently the norm in our field are needed (Easley, 1973).

Because of the voluntary nature of subject participation in the investigations described, comparing research results across age and learning levels becomes difficult. Such comparisons are needed, however, to generalize findings for programs across one state and across the United States.

Currently, reporting and comparing the results from different studies is the function of the related literature section of a research report or dissertation. Often such comparisons remain unreported in published articles because of space limitations. We need to expand our research agenda in music education by juxtaposing and systematically studying data from different studies through metaanalyses. The comparisons would be made by the application of the same research question to all available raw data; the comparison itself would be the focus of the study.

In addition to metaanalyses, we need replications of investigations whose data corroborate previous findings. We also need to be reminded of one of the most basic insights into probability research: We cannot verify theories, we can only falsify them (Popper, 1959, 1973). Thus, we need more research in music education that refutes the relative merit of one accepted methodology and instructional technique over another.

Acknowledging the Difference Between Questions Asked in Research and in Teaching

Because of methodological concerns about research in instructional settings, the application of research findings to actual teaching situations is a complicated process. As researchers, we must identify the causes for problems before we can resolve them. That in itself takes a long time. Thus, in most cases and for reasons discussed above, we cannot easily dictate prescriptive measures for how to act differently in the future. How to act, however, is what would interest us the most in our role as teachers.

From a teacher's point of view, our concerns might be practical ones: how to motivate our students from day to day and over the years that they are with us; how to deal efficiently with any given restrictions in the routine of doing our job; and how to maintain a productive and smoothly running rehearsal, lesson, or class in spite of any disturbances that inevitably occur. Our questions would address how to resolve specific problems we view as disruptions in our daily activities.

For us as researchers, those questions trigger several investigations about which we could get excited. The results, however, are not likely to provide complete answers to the dilemmas we as teachers would wish to resolve. The results certainly do not trigger teacher excitement.

Although the agenda we have as instructors may differ from the agenda we have as researchers, a relationship exists between the questions we ask as researchers and the meaning our answers may have for everyday teaching practice. Whereas the findings of one study will never be able to answer the broad-based concerns of the teacher, the findings can contribute to the total body of knowledge within which the concerns may be embedded. Likewise, while the results of an investigation should not cause us to change our teaching behavior lock, stock, and barrel, they could increase our sensitivity for observing ourselves and our instructional behavior.

To sum up: We have in music education a wide variety of approaches toward thinking about teaching purposes as well as toward the employment of specific instructional methods and techniques. We also have a variety of belief systems as to what may be acceptable or unacceptable research behavior and methodologies. Such varieties of purpose, methodology, and techniques do not deserve criticism per se. Any review of research literature, however, is affected by the theoretical and methodological choices a researcher makes about them. Thus, the clarity and uniformity of this section depend on (1) the clarity and uniformity of conceptual framework behind the research agenda of our profession; (2) the degree of agreement among the profession on the relative importance of specific teaching goals and learning objectives; and (3) the degree of consensus among the research community about what is considered acceptable and unacceptable research.

As Colwell (1990) has suggested, music educators have very little agreement on what it is they are looking for. Therefore, research on instruction in different settings suffers from a piecemeal approach toward solving the myriads of problems both teachers and researchers have identified. Beyond that, music educators lack an agreed-upon research agenda in which they address policy issues relevant to the practice of and research on teaching. As Pankratz (1989) has identified for all of arts education, we might begin to explore the following issues:

1. The role of research on music instruction in teaching practice now and in the future
2. The relationship of basic to applied research on music instructional questions
3. The relationship of learning theory in music to music-teaching practice, and the impact of learning theory on teaching
4. The relationship between music educators as (a) a professional decision-making body, (b) public servants, and (c) self-employed entrepreneurs
5. The relationship between public school music teachers, studio teachers, and researchers
6. The feasibility of a research agenda as the basis of action for all music educators

Once we have begun to understand the above issues, we might engender more specific questions concerning how we act as music teachers in the general music classroom, rehearsal hall, and private studio. The reader is encouraged to keep this in mind when contemplating the findings reported in this section.

References

Anderson, K. E. (Ed.). (1961). *Research on the academically talented student.* Washington: National Education Association.

Asmus, E. (1986). Student beliefs about the causes of success and failure in music: A study of achievement motivation. *Journal of Research in Music Education, 34*(4), 262–278.

Baron, J. B., and Sternberg, R. J. (Eds.) (1987). *Teaching thinking skills. Theory and practice.* New York: W.H. Freeman.

Baudo, J. M. (1982). The effectiveness of jazz education on the enhancement of the characteristic traits associated with creativity in music: Implications for curriculum planning. Unpublished doctoral dissertation, State University of New York, Buffalo.

Boardman, E. (Ed.). (1989). *Dimensions of musical thinking.* Reston: Music Educators National Conference.

Boyle, J., Hosterman, G., and Ramsey, D. (1981). Factors influencing music preferences of young people. *Journal of Research in Music Education, 29*(1), 47–55.

Broquist, O. (1961). A survey of the attitudes of 2,594 Wisconsin elementary school pupils toward their learning experiences in music. Unpublished doctoral dissertation, University of Wisconsin, Madison.

Broudy, H. S., Ennis, R. H., and Krimerman, L. I. (Eds.). (1973). *Philosophy of educational research.* New York: John Wiley.

Burris, D. L. (1988). A systematic and integrated approach to teaching comprehensive musicianship and voice in high school performance oriented choirs. Unpublished doctoral dissertation, Southern Illinois University, Carbondale.

Campbell, D. T., and Stanley, J. C. (1967). *Experimental and quasiexperimental designs for research.* Chicago: Rand McNally.

Colwell, R. (1990). The posture of music education research. *Design for Arts in Education, 91*(5), 42–52.

Cormier, S. M., and Hagman, J. D. (Eds.). (1987). *Transfer of learning: Contemporary research and applications.* San Diego: Academic Press.

Cutietta, R. (1982). The analysis of listening strategies and musical focus of the 11- to 16-year-old learner. Unpublished doctoral dissertation, Pennsylvania State University, University Park.

Cutietta, R. (1984). The musical hypothesis-testing ability of the adolescent learner. *Bulletin of the Council for Research in Music Education, 80,* 27–50.

Cutietta, R. (1985). An analysis of musical hypotheses created by the 11-16 year-old learner. *Bulletin of the Council for Research in Music Education, 84,* 1–13.

Deihl, E., Schneider, M., and Petress, K. (1983). Dimensions of music preference: A factor analysis study. *Popular Music and Society, 9,* 41–50.

deTurk, M. (1988). The relationship between experience in performing music class and critical thinking about music. Unpublished doctoral dissertation, University of Wisconsin, Madison.

Easley, J. A., Jr. (1973). The natural sciences and educational research: A comparison. In H. S. Broudy, R. H. Ennis, and L. I. Krimerman (Eds.) *Philosophy of educational research* (pp. 53–64). New York: John Wiley.

Elliott, D. J., and Rao, D. (1990). Musical performance and music education. *Design for Arts in Education, 91,* (5), 23–34.

Fiske, H. E. (1984). Cognition strategies in music listening. 10th ISME Research Seminar. *Bulletin of the Council for Research in Music Education, 85,* 56–64.

Flom, J. H. (1971). An investigation of growth in musical facts and concepts, in musical discrimination, and in vocal performance proficiency as a result of senior high school vocal music experiences. *Journal of Research in Music Education, 19*(4), 433–442.

Greer, R., and Ludquist, A. (1976). The discrimination of musical form through "conceptual" and "non-conceptual" successive approximation strategies. *Council for Research in Music Education, 47,* 8–15.

Haack, P. (1972). A study of high school music participants' stylistic preferences and identification abilities in music and the visual arts. *Bulletin of the Council for Research in Music Education, 30,* 213–220.

Hedden S. (1981). Music listening skills and music listening preferences. *Bulletin of the Council for Research in Music Education, 65,* 16–26.

Howard, C. (1969). An experimental study in developing and evaluating musical understandings in a high school choir. Unpublished doctoral dissertation, Boston University School for the Arts, Boston.

Hufstader, R. (1977). An investigation of a learning sequence of music listening skills. *Journal of Research in Music Education, 25*(3), 184–196.

Hylton, J. B. (1981). Dimensionality in high school student participants' perceptions of the meaning of choral singing experience. *Journal of Research in Music Education, 29*(4), 287–303.

LeBlanc, A., Colman, J., McCrary, J., Sherrill, C., and Malin, S. (1988). Tempo preferences of different age music listeners. *Journal of Research in Music Education, 36*(3), 156–168.

McDonald, D. (1990). General music in education. *Design for Arts in Education, 91*(5), 15–22.

Morgan, S. G. (1984). Dimensions of musical problem solving by high school instrumentalists: An exploratory investigation. Unpublished doctoral dissertation, University of Wisconsin, Madison.

Murphy, M., and Brown, T. (1986). A comparison of preferences for instructional objectives between teachers and students. *Journal of Research in Music Education, 34*(2), 134–139.

Pankratz, D. B. (1989). Policies, agendas, and arts education research. *Design for Arts in Education, 90*(5), 2–13.

Pearsall, G. K. (1980). A curriculum for ninth grade general music: Meeting student needs through areas of designated interest (Vol. I, II). Unpublished doctoral dissertation, Carnegie-Mellon University, Pittsburgh.

Popper, K. R. (1959). *The logic of scientific discovery.* New York: Basic Books.

Popper, K., Sir (1973). Corroboration, or how a theory stands up to tests. In H. S. Broudy, R. H. Ennis, and L. I. Krimerman (Eds.), *Philosophy of educational research* (pp. 280–306). New York: John Wiley.

Rainbow, E. L., and Froehlich, H. C. (1987). *Research in music education: An introduction to systematic inquiry.* New York: Schirmer Books.

Reimer, B. (1990). A comprehensive arts curriculum model. *Design for Arts in Education, 90*(6), 2–16.

Rosenshine, B., and Furst, N. (1973). The use of direct observation to study teaching. In R. M. W. Travers (Ed.), *Second handbook of research on teaching* (pp. 122–183). Chicago: Rand McNally.

Schmidt, C. P. (1985). The relationship among aspects of cognitive style and language-bound/language-optional perception to musicians' performance in aural discrimination tasks. *Journal of Research in Music Education, 32*(3), 159–168.

Schmidt, C. P. (1983). The relationship among aspects of cognitive style and language-bound/language optional perception to musicians' performance in selected aural discrimination tasks. Unpublished doctoral dissertation, Indiana University, Bloomington.

Serafine, M. (1988). *Music as cognition: The development of thought in sound.* New York: Columbia Press.

Shehan, P. K. (1985). Transfer of preference from taught to untaught pieces of nonwestern music genres. *Journal of Research in Music Education, 33*(3), 149–158.

Smith, M. B. (1973). Conflicting values affecting behavioral research with children. In H. S. Broudy, R. H. Ennis, and L. I. Krimerman (Eds.), *Philosophy of educational research* (pp. 140–150). New York: John Wiley.

Stone, M. (1983). Some antecedents of music appreciation. *Psychology of Music, 11*(Spring), 26–31.

Sturgess, P. A. (1986). An exploration of the character, expressive qualities and attitudes towards arts activities of exceptional adolescent students. The Ontario Institute for Studies in Education. Ontario Department of Education, Toronto.

Turk, G. C. (1984). Development of the music listening strategy tempo: Computer assisted instruction in music listening. Unpublished doctoral dissertation, University of Kansas, Lawrence.

Wapnick J. (1976). A review of research on attitude and preference. *Bulletin of the Council for Research in Music Education, 48,* 1–20.

Webster, P. (1979). Relationship between creative behavior in music and selected variables as measured in high school students. *Journal of Research in Music Education, 27*(4), 227–242.

Webster, P. (1990). Creative thinking, technology, and music education. *Design for Arts in Education, 91*(5), 35–41.

Whitener, W. T. (1980). An experimental study of a comprehensive approach to beginning instruction in instrumental music. Unpublished doctoral dissertation, Indiana University, Bloomington.

Whitlock, R. H. S. (1981). The design and evaluation of study materials for integrating musical information into the choral rehearsal. Unpublished doctoral dissertation, North Texas State University, Denton.

Zumbrunn, K. L. F. (1968). *Effects of a listening program in contemporary music upon the appreciation by junior high school students of representative literature of other periods.* Final report. Washington: Office of Education (DHEW), Bureau of Research.

·39·

RESEARCH ON THE TEACHING
OF SINGING

Kenneth H. Phillips
UNIVERSITY OF IOWA

Singing is a psychomotor skill. It involves both the physiological process of motor coordination and the psychological processes of pitch perception and memory. This chapter presents research in these areas as it affects the teaching of singing for school-age children (K–12). Included are clinical voice studies that are applicable to the classroom setting, as little research has been conducted using children as subjects in the motor coordination area. Research directly involving children and adolescents is, however, the focus of this article, which concludes with a summary of the adolescent and changing-voice literature. The goal of all voice instruction is confident and beautiful singing, and those studies that are included here were chosen for their contribution to making this goal a reality among school-age children.

The Science and Art of Singing

Numerous books have been written on the teaching of singing. Although many of these are commendable, most of what has been written is not based on scientific investigation. This is because the pedagogy of singing is divided between schools that can be broadly interpreted as being science and art. Even those noted authors who have written from a scientific base (Appelman, 1967; Klein and Schjeide, 1972; Stanley, 1929/1958; Vennard, 1967) have reported their findings in terms of the practitioner, and not the researcher. This combination of art and science, while noteworthy for its attempt to base method on scientific inquiry, has resulted in teaching approaches that are sometimes contradictory.

The study of singing will never be free from subjectivity. Singing is an art, and will remain so. Nevertheless, there is a growing belief among vocal pedagogues and researchers that

the schism between art and science can be bridged, and that a standardized system of vocal teaching is possible. Large (1980), in publishing one of the first college-level texts on voice research, *Contributions of Voice Research in Singing,* was a leader in calling attention to the need for a vocal pedagogy that is based on knowledge gained from rigorous, scientific study. Miller (1986) likewise has written one of the first texts for the teaching of singing that includes references to contemporary vocal research literature. Bunch (1982) and Sundberg (1987) have contributed valuable reviews and summaries of research on the science of the singing voice.

Teaching Children to Sing

Music teachers have long agreed that children can and should learn to sing. It is the process that remains open to question; and whether or not it is appropriate to "teach" children to sing also is an issue. According to one medical opinion (Brodnitz, 1983), the formal training of the child's voice should be delayed until the vocal folds have completely adjusted to the physical changes related to puberty. Other medical experts (Sataloff and Spiegel, 1989) note that "it is possible and proper to train young voices to sing" (p. 36). They caution against vocal abuse, and recommend an approach based on "gradual development of vocal musculature and control" (p. 36). Mayer and Sacher (1964) state that it is really a matter of endurance; one should not expect youthful voices to endure long periods of vocal practice. Ross (1948) concludes:

There is no doubt that the actual singing of songs should be the artistic side of singing. However, when a singer is unable to meet the demands that the literature for his particular voice calls for, then he

568

must call on science for the development of a physical skill that will meet those demands. (p.3)

PHYSIOLOGICAL PARAMETERS

Respiration and Posture

Most vocal authorities recognize proper breathing as the basis for good singing technique. Dawson (1902), an early twentieth-century expert on children's voices, states that "disordered muscular conditions" are among the greatest causes for poor singing, and that "children who come to school unable to sing breathe defectively, i.e., in the upper part of the lungs and do not at all in the lower part" (p. 21).

Breathing technique for singing has been an area of active research interest among vocal scientists. Much has been learned concerning functional anatomy, lung volume, air flow, subglottic pressure, and the relationship of the breathing musculature to phonation. Although these are important areas of research, the "theoretical" nature of the findings is beyond the scope of this chapter. The reader interested in this type of research should refer to the article by Sundberg and Leanderson (1986), which presents research findings and references for the physiological characteristics of phonatory breathing.

The process of breathing, as taught by a wide range of vocal teachers, appears generally to be consistent in emphasizing "deep breathing," via diaphragmatic contraction, as the inhalation phase for singing (Phillips, 1983). The actual management of the breath, however, has been a source of disagreement among teachers of singing and vocal scientists. The focus of this disagreement is the approach to breath management for "support" of vocal production. Three general approaches to breath support are known: The first states that for proper support and control the singer should "bear down" or "push out" in the abdominal area upon exhalation. The second technique is just the opposite; singers are taught to "draw in" vigorously the abdominal muscles for needed support. The third teaches that a high and expanded rib cage should be maintained for singing, while the gentle pressure of the contracting abdominal muscles "supports" an energized air column for phonation.

Miller and Bianco (1985) investigated the three known approaches to breath management. Trained singers were asked to sustain single pitches while using, in succession, each of the three techniques. The movement (relaxation speed/control) of the diaphragm of each subject was monitored through fluoroscopic (X-ray) pictures. The results of the study showed that for the "bear down" and "draw in" approaches, the diaphragm relaxed and ascended very quickly. For the "expanded ribcage and gentle abdominal contraction" technique, the diaphragm was found to have its slowest rate of relaxation/ascent control. On the basis of these results, the authors reported the "expanded ribcage and gentle abdominal contraction" approach to be the most efficient technique of breath management. This finding confirms the technique advocated by many voice teachers. Continued research on respiration is necessary for establishing techniques that will help students to develop the correct mode of breathing for singing.

Vocal authorities agree that correct posture is a basic element in the development of proper breathing for singing (Phillips, 1983). Emphasis is on a balanced and erect torso, free of tension. Research in this area of singing is almost nonexistent, although the Alexander technique is one approach gaining an international reputation among musicians for freeing the physical body of performance-related tension (Duarte, 1981). Emphasis is on the identification and correction of postural positions that inhibit freedom and flexibility of performance. Lewis (1984) reports the results of a survey of professional teachers of singing. Among her findings she notes that those teachers who had Alexander instruction "recognized counterproductive tensions in more different parts of the body than those in the non-Alexander group . . . [and] the more extensive a teacher's Alexander experience, the more likely it is that that teacher believes vocal training focuses to a significant extent on changing counterproductive habits" (p. 16). Although such statements support the view that posture development is a basic necessity for singing technique, there is a need for research in this area on the measured benefits for singing. Studies using the Alexander technique and other postural approaches should aid in understanding the relationship of posture and singing.

A study by Brody (1948) is among the earliest investigations known to have examined the effects of breath management instruction with children. The purpose of the study was to improve the singing of subjects in grades 4 through 12, by means of better motor or muscular control. Although the design of the study is weak, the study is significant for showing that research on physiological parameters as related to singing is possible with children and adolescents. Brody measured subjects' breathing patterns with the use of pneumograph instrument (expandable bands placed around the torso), and found that shallow breathers increased their depth and capacity for breathing through greater diaphragmatic contraction as reflected in a greater measure of abdominal expansion. She noted the improved quality of the subjects' singing voices, concluding the latter to be the result of the improved breathing process.

A long-range study of the child's singing voice was begun in Russia in the 1940s and reported by Gembizakaja (1962). Of importance in this study is the finding that the lungs of first-grade children are not fully developed, and therefore not capable of extensive deep breathing. The study reports that the ability to breathe deeply develops in the child during the second grade (on the average), accompanied by a broadening vocal range and greater accuracy of intonation.

Phillips (1983) investigated the effectiveness of group breath control training on physical and vocal singing measures among subjects in grades 2, 3, and 4. Pre- and posttraining data for each subject on four dependent measures (vocal range, vocal intensity, tonal duration, and pitch accuracy) were analyzed for the effects of the treatment (reflected in measures of abdominal and thoracic movement and vital capacity) between groups and among grade levels. Results of the study showed that breath control training significantly differentiated between groups, but not among grade levels. The subjects in the experimental group responded to training in such a way as to reflect a change in breathing from "shallow" to "deep" breathing, with improvements in vocal range, intensity, and pitch accuracy.

Phillips (1983) used the same instrumentation (pneumograph) for the recording of breathing patterns as did Brody (1948). Such a recording device was a precursor to more sophisticated equipment used to measure breathing in a study by Phillips and Vispoel (1990). In the latter study, breathing patterns were measured using a Respitrace™ instrument, which consists of gauzelike bands placed around the subject's torso to measure displacement during breathing. The use of sophisticated measuring devices for the study of singing provides for the researcher highly reliable means of data collection. Advancements in technology have made such devices possible, and those interested in the investigation of singing should be aware of the possibilities that now exist with scientific instrumentation.

Gackle (1987) studied the effects of breath management instruction and other vocal techniques on tone production of adolescent females. Although Gackle collected no data on specific breathing patterns, she found that the experimental group, as the result of the treatment, improved in their ability to sustain a pitch, and had greater pitch security (less deviation from pitch center). Gackle's research (1987) is significant in that it is the only study known to have investigated the effects of vocal technique and breath management instruction with adolescent females. Although Gackle did not find significant results for improved tone quality (possibly because of the short period of treatment), such a study is worthy of replication. Of note, also, is Gackle's use of the Kay Elemetrics Visi-Pitch, an instrument for analyzing pitch accuracy. Such equipment provides reliable data and should be considered by researchers for pitch accuracy investigations.

A study by Aaron (1990) also used the Visi-Pitch in analyzing the pitch accuracy of inaccurate singers in grades 4, 5, and 6. Although Aaron did not measure breathing patterns, he did employ a treatment with the experimental group that emphasized posture and breathing exercises. After a semester of instruction, Aaron (1990) found that subjects in the experimental group showed significant improvement over those in the control group on measures of pitch accuracy (especially among highly inaccurate boys) and vocal range. This study adds further evidence to findings of earlier studies (Brody, 1948; Gould, 1968; Joyner, 1969; Romaine, 1961; Roberts and Davies, 1975) that inaccurate singers can be helped to sing with greater pitch accuracy through a program that emphasizes proper posture, breathing, and the coordination of vocal production with the respiration process.

Phonation and Resonant Tone Production

Gould (1968) conducted an extensive study on children's singing, and found that attention to the speaking voice is a vital "link" in the development of the singing voice. Poor speech habits often result in poor singing habits, and Brodnitz (1983) reports numerous cases of vocal nodules among children as a result of improper use of the voice. Nilson and Schneiderman (1983) report that in a program emphasizing prevention of vocal abuse (shouting, speaking too low, and so on) among 6- to 8-year-olds, results pre- to posttest show that students do benefit from such a program with improved speech habits. More research is needed to help teachers better understand the importance of phonation as it relates to speaking and singing. The use of speech devices for "finding" the upper singing register (e.g., imitating the voice of Mickey Mouse) are widely used, but empirical study has not resulted in a knowledge base that can help teachers know what techniques are most beneficial.

A beautiful voice is one that is rich in resonance. Such a voice can be characterized as having uniformity of vowel production, depth, fullness of tone, and projection or "ring." Whereas such terms are highly subjective, these qualities are recognized by vocal authorities (Alderson, 1979; Appelman, 1967; Klein and Schjeide, 1972; Miller, 1986; Vennard, 1967) as being characteristic of the resonant voice. Opinions as to what qualifies as a beautiful voice vary among persons and from culture to culture, and must be considered and/or controlled for in studies of vocal resonance.

Modern technology has made it possible to analyze vocal resonance with scientific instrumentation. Appelman (1967) invented the Vowelometer, which plots the optimum resonance for vowels as fixed points on a TV monitor. When a vowel is sung into a microphone, a luminescent dot of light appears on the screen. The closer the dot of light appears to the fixed position of the vowel, the greater the optimum resonance. This instrument is costly, and relies on subjective opinion as to what constitutes the optimum resonance for each voice model programed into the computer. As mentioned earlier, a balance of science and art is difficult in a field of study that relies heavily on cultural and personal preferences.

The Real-Time Vowel Spectrum Analyzer is another instrument that can be used for studying the complexity of waveforms. Using such equipment, Sundberg and Nordstrom (1983) have demonstrated how raised or lowered laryngeal positions can affect the vowel formant frequencies (overtone regions), resulting in a brighter (raised larynx) or darker (lowered larynx) vocal quality. In an earlier study, Sundberg (1977) reports the presence of an extra "singer's formant" in the voices of trained singers, resulting in the carrying power necessary to sing over orchestral accompaniment. Advances in modern technology have made such discoveries possible, but research in these areas is limited because few people have access to and knowledge of such instrumentation.

Vocal vibrato is heard as a slight undulation of pitch at between 5 and 6 cycles per second. The pioneering studies by Carl Seashore (1931) at the University of Iowa validate the overwhelming presence of vibrato in the voices of trained singers. Although voice scientists have established a number of theories as to the source of vocal vibrato (McLane, 1985), good breath management and a relaxed throat seem to be essential to its emergence (Appelman, 1967). Vibrato is considered, at least in western cultures, a phenomenon of the beautiful singing voice. Opinions differ as to the presence of a vibrato in the child's voice, and research is needed to study objectively this parameter of vocal production.

Most vocal authorities teach that the soft palate should be arched for maximizing pharyngeal space and resonance. However, Scotto di Carlo and Autesserre (1987) have shown in their research with trained singers that the velopharyngeal port (opening into the nasopharynx) is not actually closed for singing, but rather that the "arching" of the soft palate, to which singers commonly refer, is a transversal tension of the velum, resulting in the "feeling" of a raised soft palate. The authors recommend that the soft palate be lowered for singing in order that the entire pharynx remain open. However, Troup and colleagues (1989) take exception to this earlier finding, and note that "velum closure in singing depends on many factors: the instructor, the language, the singer and the style of singing" (p. 35). The authors report case studies of singers studied by xeroradiographic analysis, and note the wide range of results as to velum closure at differing pitch levels. Even with the use of sophisticated equipment, two sets of researchers have produced conflicting results. This should remind the reader that research, in general, must be read with a certain amount of circumspection—especially in an area that is as clearly subjective and personal as the singing voice.

Vocal Registration

The parameter of vocal registration is one that is very important, especially when considering appropriate vocal ranges for young singers. In fact, most studies that have investigated children's singing ranges have not taken into account the influence of vocal registration on range, and the results of such studies must be viewed with caution.

One study in which the interaction of vocal register and range has been taken into consideration is that by Brown (1988), who investigated the effects of self-selected pitch and prescribed pitch with a model on the vocal range of children in grades 1, 3, and 5. In the first assessment, subjects were asked to sing a familiar song at a pitch level of their own choosing. Range was then measured, ascending and descending, from the final pitch of the song. In the second assessment, the investigator provided a vocal model in the head register, and guided subjects with vocal activities (speech to song) that helped them to locate their "upper" voices. The subjects then repeated the familiar song, beginning on the pitch B above middle C. Range was measured as before, beginning this time on the pitch G above middle C, the last note of the song. Results of the analysis of the data for vocal range demonstrated a significantly wider range for singing in the higher vocal register. As a group, subjects, when permitted to choose their own singing level, chose a lower range and register for singing. When exposed to a higher vocal register, subjects were able to make the transition quickly to this "new" voice, resulting in a wider vocal range. Had the subjects not been instructed in the use of the

"head" register, the results of the vocal range assessment would have been quite different, that is, lower. Brown (1988) did not limit her assessment to one register, and therefore produced results more reflective of the "true" vocal range of her subjects. Further research as to vocal range should make provision for the registration factor as it affects optimum singing range.

The presence of registers in children's singing voices has long been recognized by authorities on the child's voice. Appelman (1967) notes that "in the human voice, registration is a physiological and acoustical fact. Years of research . . . have contributed evidence of its existence and have verified that all voices have three registers that may be utilized in singing" (p. 86). There is little research in the area of vocal registration as it affects singing, especially among children and adolescents. Brown's study (1988) is important for its contribution to this area, and replication and further research are needed to bring greater understanding to this area of vocal development.

Diction and Expression

Another important area of instruction in singing is that of diction. Voice teachers stress the proper pronunciation of language, and most spend time "shaping" vowels and drilling on consonant articulation. Fisher (1986) has identified two approaches to diction, which he has studied for the effects that such approaches have on word intelligibility and beauty of vocal sound. The first approach is known as "sung-speech diction," and the second he calls "rhythmic diction."

"Sung-speech" proponents suggest that spoken language is discerned in "patterns" or acoustical blends of vowels and consonants. Therefore, the practice of connecting syllable to syllable and word to word is advocated. This style of diction was made popular by Fred Waring over a generation ago, and continues to be used today.

"Rhythmic diction" for singing has appeared in recent years as a counterapproach to "sung-speech." Proponents of this system base their technique on the underlying rhythmic nature of the music, separating every sound in every syllable within a metered rhythmic structure.

Fisher (1986) investigated listener preference to taped examples of 10 paired choral excerpts sung by the same choir using "sung-speech" and "rhythmic" approaches. Adult subjects ($n = 102$) were asked to identify which of the excerpts they liked the most. Fisher found an overall preference rating of 69 percent for the "rhythmic diction" approach. He concludes that "phonological studies, psychoacoustical research, and listener preferences appear to support the 'rhythmic diction' approach over that of the 'sung-speech' approach" (Fisher, 1986, p. 18). The area of diction is of great importance to teachers of singing and choral ensembles, and more of this type of research is needed.

Good singing is more than a well-supported, resonant tone. Good singing is expressive; it conveys the meaning and life of the text. Parameters such as phrasing, dynamics, tempo, agility, and affect are all elements of expressive singing about which little is known from a research base.

A study by McCoy (1986) is one example of research that investigated the expressive elements of singing. McCoy sought to determine if movement (phrasing/conducting gestures, stepping the pulse, or the like) as a choral rehearsal technique would improve the vocal performance and attitude of high school choral ensemble members. Although posttest ratings of the singing of two select high school choirs (experimental and control) did not demonstrate overall significant performance differences between groups, the experimental group did score significantly higher than the control group on subscales of tempo and balance/blend. A significant difference in favor of the experimental group also was found for student attitude.

Whereas much of the ability to "interpret" music is the responsibility of the teacher/conductor, there are a number of expressive elements that can be studied, and McCoy's research (1986) is one such attempt. A problem with such research is that it relies heavily on the subjective judgment of human raters, who often have their own ideas about what constitutes a good performance. Uniform instruction and established qualifications of judges are necessary if rating measures are to be reliable. The development and use of precise rating instruments also is important in order to control for the subjective bias of the judges. As long as these concerns are taken into account the study of expressive singing can and should be investigated.

PSYCHOLOGICAL PARAMETERS

Confident singing relies on the psychological parameters of pitch perception-discrimination and tonal memory. Poor pitch perception may have psychological and physical origins. Fortunately, most students do not have a physical hearing problem. The psychological problems of poor pitch perception-discrimination and tonal memory may be due to a number of factors. Among those in which research has been conducted are inattention to pitch, motivation, and mode of teaching.

Pitch Discrimination

Inattention or lack of "focus" is especially problematic among younger children. This lack of attention to pitch may be simply a result of where the child is seated within the classroom, or it may be a result of inadequate feedback. Without aural knowledge, either in the form of verbal feedback or self-discrimination, the child may not be able to recognize pitch differences.

Welch (1985) states that "children who sing out-of-tune can become pitch accurate if the learning condition contains both qualitative information about the pitch error and sufficient practice for this information to be applied" (p. 246). He encourages feedback in both auditory and kinesthetic modes.

A study by Welch, Howard, and Rush (1989) further explores the relationship of visual feedback to pitch accuracy in singing. The authors used a microcomputer-based system to provide real-time visual feedback of vocal pitch production with a class of 7-year-old subjects ($n = 32$), which was divided into three matched groups based on pretest singing accuracy. During the treatment period of seven weekly sessions, the first two groups used an author-designed software program, SINGAD. Group 1 had singing lessons in pairs or threes with one of the authors, while group 2, similarly in pairs or threes, used the software without any adult help. The control group undertook group singing activities of a traditional nature, and received verbal feedback as to pitch accuracy.

The results of the study by Welch and colleagues (1989) found that on a posttest of pitch accuracy, there was a significant difference between experimental group 1 and the control group, but no significant difference between experimental group 2 and the control group, nor between the two experimental groups. A further reassessment of group 1 after 6 months revealed that the improvement was generally sustained. The authors note that all groups showed improvement over the treatment period, but conclude that a microcomputer-based system may promote individual development in singing, in that "verbal feedback on its own appears to be less powerful in promoting learning than real-time, meaningful visual feedback" (p. 156).

This study by Welch and colleagues (1989) should be of major interest to music teachers as to one application of microcomputers in the music classroom. The computer provides the opportunity for students who are inaccurate singers to receive remedial help and feedback on an individual basis. The results of the study show that the program is effective with and without teacher assistance. However, the findings must be interpreted with caution for at least two reasons. First, students were required to match single pitches only; there is no evidence to suggest that matching single pitches results in general singing accuracy of song phrases. Second, it is possible for students to learn to match pitch to a visual image using improper vocal technique, that is, straining at the laryngeal level. Although the use of microcomputers in the music class has obvious advantages, care must be taken to monitor for both psychological and motor responses in the psychomotor process.

Children who develop only an "aural" means of discrimination may hear or perceive pitch correctly but be unable to reproduce it accurately. A number of investigators have found that students who sing inaccurately may not necessarily have poor pitch discrimination (Aaron, 1990; Anderson, 1939; Brody, 1948; Fieldhouse, 1937; Pollock, 1950; Porter, 1977; Roberts and Davies, 1975). Likewise, children who relate to singing only as a kinesthetic experience, without auditory feedback, may not link the kinesthetic production of pitch to its psychological parameter. Goetze (1986) found that primary children are more likely to sing in tune individually than in a group. A similar finding is reported by Smale (1988). Perhaps an aural "masking" effect takes place in group singing that interferes with aural perception. Thus, young children who do not hear their own voices are forced to sing only by kinesthetic association, which by itself is not sufficient to produce accurate singing results. Goetze notes that by the third grade, pitch accuracy no longer seems to be affected by group singing; older children who sing inaccurately will do so in either situation—individually or in a group.

Pitch perception also may be affected by motivation. Students who don't like to sing and who do not willingly participate may be observed to drone along without interest. American boys, especially, seem to think that singing is less a masculine activity than a female one (Castelli, 1986), and withdraw early from active participation. Teachers must work to overcome this "macho" attitude, using male role models, whenever possible, to note the contributions of male singing to musical culture. The relationship of attitude to singing is an important area in which little research has been conducted.

How much teaching and learning mode affects pitch perception is a question that has begun to interest researchers in music education (Apfelstadt, 1986a,b; Persellin, 1988). There are three general learning modalities—visual, auditory, and kinesthetic—and individuals learn best in one of these modes (primary modality). A visual learner will respond better to books, visual aids, and other written forms than an auditory learner, who prefers aural stimuli, or a kinesthetic learner, who learns best through touching or manipulating.

A study by Persellin (1988) indicates that the teaching modality preference of teachers does influence their teaching direction; that is, those who are visual learners teach with an emphasis toward visual instruction. Many students, however, are not good visual learners, and respond better to an auditory or a kinesthetic approach. Persellin notes that in learning a song, visual activities may include learning to read musical notation and using word sheets, while auditory learning may use modeling and echo singing. The kinesthetic component may involve movement and adding actions to songs. For students whose primary mode of learning is not auditory, pitch perception may be aided by both visual and kinesthetic activities (Apfelstadt, 1986a,b; Persellin, 1988; Welch, 1985). This is an important area for continued research.

A final parameter that affects pitch perception is vocal modeling. A number of studies have shown that children are more likely to perceive pitch accurately if what they hear is an accurate model of what they are to produce. Both Petzold (1966) and Clegg (1966) found that children match pitch more accurately when it is presented in the child's singing range. The male voice singing an octave below seems especially troublesome for children who are inexperienced singers (Kramer, 1986).

Voice quality, as part of the vocal model, also affects accuracy of pitch perception-production. The female vocal model is superior for this purpose (Clegg, 1966; Petzold, 1966; Sims, Moore, and Kuhn, 1982; Small and McCachern, 1983), and Green (1987) found the child's voice to be an excellent model for vocal matching in grades 1 through 6. Kramer (1986), Montgomery (1988), and Wolf (1984) all report that children find pitch level at a higher rate of accuracy when the male teacher sings in the "falsetto" voice, as op-

posed to the fuller, natural male quality. It would seem that males who work with children's singing need to develop the ability to sing an octave higher than normal, so as not to confuse pitch perception, especially among younger, inexperienced children.

Tonal Memory

Tonal memory is another psychological parameter that may interfere with confident singing. Research indicates that tonal memory seems to be affected by age and the amount of material to be remembered. Memory span generally increases with age, and Cady (1981) notes that "children's songs are short, and their listening experiences are also. At least, our pedagogical folklore implies an agreement that the timespan of remembered works increases with age" (p. 84). Long (1977) reports that tonal memory decreases as the length of patterns increases, and that both perception and melodic contour appear to affect tonal memory (p. 281). Studies by Bentley (1968), Joyner (1969), Petzold (1966), and Zwissler (1972) all indicate that inaccurate singers may be deficient in tonal memory. The parameter of tonal memory should be included as a variable in research on singing accuracy.

THE ADOLESCENT CHANGING VOICE

A number of descriptive studies in the 1950s (Beall, 1958; Ekstrom, 1959; Joseph 1959; Swanson, 1959) provided an overview of the male changing voice and the problems associated with teaching young adolescent males to sing. Whereas these studies, in some cases, did little more than to summarize the confusion existing about how best to handle voices during puberty, they should have served as an impetus for greater research in this area. This has not been the case. Numerous articles and books have been written on the topic of the boy's changing voice, but little real experimental research has been conducted to verify techniques advocated by different teachers.

One point on which American authors on the topic of voice change agree is that students in the pubescent years should continue to sing. Contrary to the English tradition of having boys sing in their "upper" voices throughout the voice change until the voices "break," teachers in the American system have favored the gradual lowering of boys' singing ranges in relation to the newly emerging lower compass of the voice. Nevertheless, different American schools of thought have emerged as to the best way of handling the changing voice among adolescent boys.

Two "schools" that have been prominent in teaching about the male changing voice are represented by Cooksey (1977) and Swanson (1977). Both of these men have collected and charted the vocal ranges, tessituras, and maturational stages of hundreds of boys in the process of voice change, only to report conflicting results. Cooksey has found that the voices of boys change according to a rather slow, predictable schedule, that at least three stages of voice change can be noted, and that tenor or bass voices, in the "true" sense, are not frequent at the junior high or middle school level. Swanson, by contrast, has found that many boys go through the voice change quickly, that the voice change can be quite erratic, and that "true" tenors and basses are quite abundant in the early adolescent years. How can two researchers collect so much data and arrive at such different results?

The conflicting nature of the findings of Cooksey and Swanson may be due to a topic discussed earlier—vocal registers. When researchers are measuring the vocal ranges of adolescents, it is as important as it is with elementary-age children that they consider the effects of register changes on range. Wolverton (1986) found that both tessitura and register factors were stronger predictors of appropriate voice classification among adolescent singers than vocal range when high school choral directors were asked to determine the relative importance of selected vocal characteristics. As stated previously, studies of vocal ranges that ignore the register factor need to be read with caution. If the adolescent male has not been exposed to singing in his newly developing "chest" voice, his range will be limited to that which he can sing with his previous child's voice, or a mixed registration of "head" and "chest" voice, which also can limit the extent of vocal production at either end of the vocal range continuum.

The effect of register on range among adolescent males has been identified by Mayer and Sacher (1964) in the following illustration:

In a summer camp where Dr. Mayer recently conducted the junior high school chorus, there was one twelve year old boy singing soprano and five boys singing alto on the advice of their teachers. The five altos, when first tested, were capable of reaching about "a" below middle "c," but, when they were introduced to the use of the lower register in their voices, three of them were immediately capable of singing "d" below middle "c." One sang to "e flat" and the other maintained a bottom pitch of "a." . . . The following morning, during the demonstration, the boy soprano performed as expected, but the five "altos" all sang with ease to "d" below middle "c." These voices did not develop over night, but, by finding the use of the lower register, which was already a reality when the boys first came to the camp, they were able to sing about a fifth lower in a day's time. (p. 11)

This illustration by Mayer and Sacher clearly demonstrates how vocal registration can confound the accurate charting of vocal ranges. Once the boys were able to experience singing kinesthetically in a lower register (i.e., with shorter, thickened vocal folds), their ranges extended lower.

Swanson (1977) gives evidence in his writing of having taught the boys under his supervision to find and sing in their lower "chest" registers. Thus, his findings as to vocal ranges reflect lower extremes than do those of Cooksey. Swanson also advocates that adolescent boys continue to vocalize in their "old" upper registers, so as to successfully "bridge the gap" between the two vocal registers. This would result in higher vocal ranges than those found by Cooksey, who

warns against boys' continuing to use the upper vocal register of childhood. The hypothesis that vocal registers directly affect the quantification of vocal ranges among adolescents is one worthy of investigation, and should be considered by those interested in vocal research on the topic of the changing voice.

While some research has been conducted on the problem of the changing voice among males, almost none has been conducted on the vocal problems of adolescent female subjects. The study by Gackle (1987), discussed earlier, is one such example. Clearly, a research emphasis is needed in the profession that investigates the voice change problems of both males and females.

SUMMARY

Research on singing (voice production) and research on the teaching of singing are two separate areas of investigation, but not mutually exclusive ones. Far more research exists in the area of voice production, and much is known from this about how the voice operates. Since vocal production is basically the same from childhood through adulthood, the knowledge gained in the voice science area needs to be more actively disseminated among those who teach singing at the elementary and secondary school levels. At the same time, more research into the physiological parameters of child and adolescent voices would help to draw distinctions between adult and student vocal phenomena, such as the presence or absence of vocal vibrato. However, voice science research often requires an in-depth knowledge of vocal physiology and sophisticated instrumentation for data-gathering purposes. Persons seeking to do such research must have more than a basic knowledge of voice science in order to pursue such study adequately.

Research on the teaching of singing is more common in the music education profession, and has produced a considerable amount of knowledge. Numerous techniques involving breathing, speech devices, pitch perception, modeling, resonance enhancement, register production, diction, movement, and so on have been investigated, and a valuable contribution has been made to understanding the means by which singing may be taught at the elementary and secondary school levels. However, many of the areas discussed in this chapter are represented by only one or two studies, which means that the results have to be interpreted with caution. One area in which a considerable amount of research has been conducted is that of vocal modeling, and the results from this research form a more substantial base for teaching practice.

The numerous areas of research covered under the physiological and psychological parameters presented in this chapter represent a wealth of possibilities for future research in vocal music education. Many of the techniques commonly used for the teaching of singing (e.g., imitating sirens to discover the "head" voice) have never been investigated as to their real benefits. Perhaps some techniques are more productive than others or work better for some age groups than others. Investigating the appropriateness and results of various techniques for confident and accurate singing among children is an important area of study in music education, one that should continue to interest researchers, for much remains to be learned.

References

Aaron, J. C. (1990). The effects of vocal coordination instruction on the pitch accuracy, vocal range, pitch discrimination, and tonal memory of inaccurate singers. Unpublished doctoral dissertation, University of Iowa, Iowa City.

Alderson, R. (1979). *Complete handbook of voice training.* West Nyack: Parker Publishing Co.

Anderson, T. (1939). Variations in the normal range of children's voices, variations in the range of tone audition, variations in pitch discrimination. Unpublished doctoral dissertation, University of Edinburgh, Edinburgh.

Apfelstadt, H. (1986a). Melodic perception instruction—what is its effect upon pitch discrimination and vocal accuracy among kindergarten children? *Update, The Applications of Research in Music Education, 4*(2), 6–8.

Apfelstadt, H. (1986b). Learning modality: A potential clue in the search for vocal accuracy. *Update, The Applications of Research in Music Education, 4*(3), 4–6.

Appelman, R. D. (1967). *The science of vocal pedagogy: Theory and application.* Bloomington: Indiana University Press.

Beall, L. M. (1958). Elementary and junior high school voice training. Unpublished doctoral dissertation, American University, Washington.

Bentley, A. (1968). *Monotones: A comparison with "normal singers" in terms of incidence and musical abilities.* Music Education Research Papers, No. 1. London: Novello.

Brodnitz, F. S. (1983). On change of the voice. *Journal of the National Association of Teachers of Singing, 40*(2), 24–26.

Brody, V. A. (1947). An experimental study of the emergence of the process involved in the production of sound. Unpublished doctoral dissertation, University of Michigan, Ann Arbor.

Brown, C. J. (1988). The effect of two assessment procedures on the range of children's singing voices. Unpublished master's thesis, Indiana University, Bloomington.

Bunch, M. (1982). *Dynamics of the singing voice.* Vienna: Springer-Verlag.

Cady, H. (1981). Children's processing and remembering of music: Some speculations. *Documentary report of the Ann Arbor symposium on the applications of psychology to the teaching and learning of music* (pp. 81–87). Reston: Music Educators National Conference.

Castelli, P. A. (1986). Attitudes of vocal music educators and public school secondary students on selected factors which influence decline in male enrollment occurring between elementary and secondary public school vocal music programs. Unpublished doctoral dissertation, The University of Maryland, College Park.

Clegg, B. (1966). A comparative study of primary grade children's ability to match tones. Unpublished master's thesis, Brigham Young University, Salt Lake City.

Cooksey, J. M. (1977). The development of a contemporary, eclectic theory for the training and cultivation of the junior high school male changing voice—Part III. *The Choral Journal, 18*(4), 5–15.

Dawson, J. J. (1902). *The voice of the boy.* New York: E. L. Kellog.

Duarte, F. (1981). The principles of the Alexander technique applied to singing: The significance of the "preparatory set." *Journal of Research in Singing, 5*(1), 3–21.

Ekstrom, R. C. (1959). Comparison of the male voice before, during, and after mutation. Unpublished doctoral dissertation, University of Southern California, Los Angeles.

Fieldhouse, A. E. (1937). A study of backwardness in singing among school children. Unpublished doctoral dissertation, London Institute of Education, London.

Fisher, R. E. (1986). Choral diction with a phonological foundation. *The Choral Journal, 27*(5), 13–18.

Gackle, M. L. (1987). The effect of selected vocal techniques for breath management, resonation, and vowel unification on tone production in the junior high school female voice. Unpublished doctoral dissertation, University of Miami, Coral Gables.

Gembizakaja, E. (1962). Systematic development of the child's singing voice in Russia. *International Music Educator, 5,* 146–148.

Goetze, M. (1985). Factors affecting accuracy in children's singing. Unpublished doctoral dissertation, University of Colorado, Boulder.

Gould, A. O. (1968). *Developing specialized programs for singing in the elementary school* (Final Report). Washington: Research in Education. (ERIC Reproduction Service No. ED 025530 24 TE 499967)

Green, G. A. (1987). The effect of vocal modeling on pitch-matching accuracy of children in grades one through six. Unpublished doctoral dissertation, Louisiana State University and Agricultural and Mechanical College, Baton Rouge.

Joseph, W. A. (1959). The relationship between vocal growth in the human adolescent, and the total growth process. Unpublished doctoral dissertation, Boston University Graduate School, Boston.

Joyner, D. R. (1969). The monotone problem. *Journal of Research in Music Education, 17,* 114–125.

Klein, J. J., and Schjeide, O. A. (1972). *Singing technique: How to avoid vocal trouble.* Anaheim: National Music Publishers.

Kramer, S. J. (1985). The effects of two different music programs on third and fourth grade children's ability to match pitches vocally. Unpublished doctoral dissertation, Rutgers University, Rutgers.

Large, J. (1980). *Contributions of voice research in singing.* Houston: College-Hill Press.

Lewis, P. (1984). The Alexander influence: A comparative study. *Journal of Research in Singing, 7*(2), 6–20.

Long, P. A. (1977). Relationships between pitch memory in short melodies and selected factors. *Journal of Research in Music Education, 25*(4), 272–282.

Mayer, F. D., and Sacher, J. (1964). The changing voice (II). *American Choral Review, 6*(3), 9–11.

McCoy, C. W. (1986). The effects of movement as a rehearsal technique on performance and attitude of high school choral ensemble members. Unpublished doctoral dissertation, University of Iowa, Iowa City.

McLane, M. (1985). Artistic vibrato and tremolo: A survey of the literature, Part I. *Journal of Research in Singing, 8*(2), 21–43.

Miller, R., and Bianco, E. (1985). Diaphragmatic action in three approaches to breath management in singing. *Transcripts of the fourteenth symposium: Care of the professional voice, Vol. II—Pedagogy* (pp. 357–360). New York: The Voice Foundation.

Miller, R. (1986). *The structure of singing: System and art in vocal technique.* New York: Schirmer Books.

Montgomery, T. (1988). A study of the associations between two means of vocal modeling by a male music teacher and third grade students' vocal accuracy in singing pitch patterns. Unpublished doctoral dissertation, University of North Carolina, Greensboro.

Nilson, H., and Schneiderman, C. R. (1983). Classroom program for the prevention of vocal abuse and hoarseness in elementary school children. *Language, Speech, and Hearing Services in Schools, 14*(2), 121–127.

Persellin, D. C. (1988). The influences of perceived modality preferences on teaching methods used by elementary music educators. *Update, The Applications of Research in Music Education, 7*(1), 11–15.

Petzold, R. (1966). *Auditory perception of musical sounds by children in the first six grades.* Cooperative Research Project No. 1051, Madison: University of Wisconsin.

Phillips, K. H. (1983). The effects of group breath control training on selected vocal measures related to the singing ability of elementary students in grades two, three, and four. Unpublished doctoral dissertation, Kent State University, Kent.

Phillips, K. H., and Vispoel, W. P. (1990). The effects of class voice and breath-management instruction on vocal knowledge, attitudes, and vocal performance among elementary education majors. *The Quarterly, 1*(1&2), 96–105.

Pollock, T. (1950). Singing disability in school children. Unpublished master's thesis, University of Durham, Durham.

Porter, S. Y. (1977). The effect of multiple discrimination training on pitch-matching behaviors of uncertain singers. *Journal of Research in Music Education, 25*(1), 68–82.

Roberts, E., and Davies, A. (1975). The response of "monotones" to a programme of remedial training. *Journal of Research in Music Education, 23,* 227–239.

Romaine, W. B. (1961). Developing singers from nonsingers. Unpublished doctoral dissertation, Teachers College, Columbia University, New York.

Ross, W. E. (1948). *Sing high, sing low.* Bloomington: Indiana University Press.

Sataloff, R. T., and Spiegel, J. R. (1989). The young voice. *Journal of the National Association of Teachers of Singing, 45*(3), 35–37.

Scotto di Carlo, N., and Autesserre, D. (1987). Movements of the velum in singing. *Journal of Research in Singing and Applied Vocal Pedagogy, 11*(1), 3–13.

Seashore, C. (1931). The natural history of the vibrato. *Proceedings of The National Academy of Sciences, 17,* 623.

Sims, W. L., Moore, R. S., and Kuhn, T. L. (1982). Effects of female and male vocal stimuli, tonal pattern length and age on vocal pitch-matching abilities of young children from England and the United States. *Psychology of Music,* Special Issue: Proceedings of the IX International Seminar on Research in Music Education, 104–108.

Smale, M. J. (1987). An investigation of pitch accuracy of four- and five- year old singers. Unpublished doctoral dissertation, University of Minnesota, Minneapolis.

Small, A., and McCachern, F. L. (1983). The effect of male and female vocal modeling on pitch-matching accuracy of first-grade children. *Journal of Research in Music Education, 31*(3), 227–233.

Stanley, D. (1958). *The science of voice.* New York: Carl Fischer. (Originally published in 1929)

Sundberg, J. (1977). The acoustics of the singing voice. *Scientific American.* H. W. Freeman, 82–91.

Sundberg, J. (1987). *The science of the singing voice.* Dekalb: Northern Illinois University Press.

Sundberg, J., and Leanderson, R. (1986). Phonatory breathing—physiology behind voice pedagogy: A tutorial. *Journal of Research in Singing and Applied Physiology, 10*(1), 3–21.

Sundberg, J., and Nordstrom, P. E. (1983). Raised and lowered larynx: The effect of vowel formant frequencies. *Journal of Research in Singing, 6*(2), 7–15.

Swanson, F. J. (1959). Voice mutation in the adolescent male: An experiment in guiding the voice development of adolescent boys in general music class. Unpublished doctoral dissertation, University of Wisconsin, Madison.

Swanson, F. J. (1977). *The male voice ages eight to eighteen.* Cedar Rapids: Ingram Press.

Troup, G. J., Welch, G., Volo, M., Tronconi, A., Ferrero, F., and Farnetani, E. (1989). On velum opening in singing. *Journal of Research in Singing and Applied Vocal Pedagogy, 13*(1), 35–39.

Vennard, W. (1967). *Singing—the mechanism and the technique.* New York: Carl Fischer.

Welch, G. F. (1985). Variability of practice and knowledge of results as factors in learning to sing in tune. *Bulletin of the Council for Research in Music Education, 85,* 238–247.

Welch, G. F., Howard, D. M., and Rush, C. (1989). Real-time visual feedback in the development of vocal pitch accuracy in singing. *Psychology of Music, 17,* 146–157.

Wolf, J. H. (1984). An investigation of natural male voice and falsetto male voice on fourth grade children's ability to find pitch level. *Missouri Journal of Research in Music Education, 5*(2), 98–99.

Wolverton, V. (1985). Classifying adolescent singing voices. Unpublished doctoral dissertation, The University of Iowa, Iowa City.

Zwissler, R. N. (1971). An investigation of the pitch discrimination skills of first-grade children identified as accurate singers and those identified as inaccurate singers. Unpublished doctoral dissertation, University of California, Los Angeles.

·40·

RESEARCH ON THE TEACHING
OF INSTRUMENTAL MUSIC

Richard Weerts

NORTHEAST MISSOURI STATE UNIVERSITY

Research consists of findings based on scientifically controlled studies. Practitioners in music education, much like medical practitioners, need to be aware of research findings and how such findings might apply to their work. The purpose here is to report on various kinds of research completed in the area of teaching instrumental music. The areas selected for inclusion in this chapter are some of the most crucial in the field today. The studies included were selected on the basis of their significance and relevance to the specific topics appearing in this chapter. It is hoped that this material will whet the appetite of readers to the point where they will look into research studies on their own on a regular and continuing basis.

The material in this chapter was adapted from the sources cited in the text and listed in the references. In several cases, paraphrasing was not done because of the possibility of distorting a researcher's message, thus misleading the reader and doing a disservice to the researcher. The specific topics included are:

Dropouts from Instrumental Music
Improving Beginning Instruction in Instrumental Music
Effectiveness of Wind Chamber Music Ensemble
    Experience vs. Large Ensemble Experience
Research in Teaching Strings
The Effect of Vocalization on the Development of
    Instrumental Performance Skills
Improving Sight Reading in Instrumental Music
    Fluoroscopic Studies
Teaching Instrumental Music to the Handicapped
Class Size: Private vs. Group Instruction

DROPOUTS FROM INSTRUMENTAL MUSIC

The retention of students in instrumental music continues to be a major concern among instrumental music teachers. Kruth (1964) dealt with student dropouts from instrumental music in the secondary schools of Oakland, CA. He found that 46.4 percent of the students who started instrumental music in Oakland dropped out before graduation. Some of the reasons cited were lack of time because of required courses, scheduling problems, vocational conflicts, counseling, and outside activities. Ineffective teacher-student-parent relationships also appeared to be a general problem regarding dropouts, as was the articulation between junior and senior high school instrumental programs (Kruth, 1964, pp. 170–171). Anthony (1974) studied the school districts of Des Moines, Davenport, and Cedar Rapids, IA. He found that the students' perception of the band directors' attitude was of significant importance (Anthony, 1974, pp. 23, 79.) This research tends to support that of Mercer (1970), who found that success depends on the kind of person the band director is and the director's personal commitment to and involvement in band activities (Mercer, 1970, p. 79). In a study conducted in Lincoln, NE., Rawlins (1979) found the reasons for students dropping out of the instrumental music program to be rather typical. They included scheduling, conflict with the instrumental teacher, and students' feelings about themselves. Poor articulation of the instrumental program in general was also cited as being a problem, as was a lack of opportunities to perform after graduation (Rawlins, 1979). Martignetti (1965) noted that each of the three groups included in his study (teachers, students, parents) presented different reasons as the major cause of students dropping out of the elementary instrumental music program. While the teachers suggested that lack of support at home caused a loss of interest, the parents indicated that time required for practice was the important reason. The students listed the difficulty of mastering the instruments as the chief reason for dropping out of the program. Martignetti concluded that the problem of dropout from the elementary instrumental music program must be dealt with in its entirety; that is, it needs to include all those involved—the teacher, the students, and the parents (Martignetti, 1965, p. 183). Solly (1986) found that 55 percent of the students involved in her study dropped out because of loss of interest. It was noted that 73 percent of the withdrawal group and 70 percent of the comparison group were never contacted by instructors from higher educational levels to encourage them to continue their studies of (and participation in) instrumental music on those levels. Twelve percent of the students withdrew from the program after 6 or more years of participation. Her study also revealed that transportation to before-school rehearsals was a serious problem for junior high school (grades seven and eight) students and parents (Solly, 1986).

Two studies that deal extensively with the problems of recruitment and retention are *The Gemeinhardt Report* (Brown, 1982) and *The Gemeinhardt Report II* (Brown, 1985). Better communication among parents, teachers, and students as well as more instrument rental awareness and more program awareness (appreciation) is recommended for maximizing recruitment and retention efforts. Minimizing scheduling conflicts, presenting a better perception of the program, and decreasing the student's fear of failure are suggested as being viable ways for retaining instrumental music students (Brown, 1985, p. 27; Brown, 1982, pp. 6–9). In another report, the Research Committee of the American School Band Directors Association (Gerheart et al., 1984) indicated that the use of awards, contests, challenges, and testing all helped to retain students. In order to achieve maximum retention and minimize dropout, this report recommends that the elementary instrumental program begin in the fifth grade and meet five times a week during the school day for 40 minutes per period. Two programs per year were recommended for such groups (Gerheart et al., 1984, pp. 11–12).

BEGINNING INSTRUCTION IN INSTRUMENTAL MUSIC

Puopolo (1970) investigated the feasibility of structured, programed practice with tape-recorded materials and its effect on the performance achievement of beginning elementary cornet and trumpet students. Specific objectives were with the effect of programed practice upon performance achievement and the relationships of music achievement, social status, and IQ with both programed practice and performance achievement. He found that beginning instrumental-

ists demonstrated a substantial increase in efficiency when they practiced with the lesson material structured on the taped self-instructional format used in his research. When programed practice was included, students of above-average music achievement exhibited no significant difference in performance achievement from students of below-average music achievement. Although there was a positive relationship between IQ and performance achievement, almost no relationship existed when the programed practice was used (Puopolo, 1970, pp. 65, 71–72).

Alexander and Dorrow (1983) developed a study that compared the pretest and posttest music performance of beginning band students in tutor and student pairs with students in regular band class instruction. The effect of tutor approval and disapproval techniques was also observed. Their research concluded that tutoring is beneficial whether the tutor used approval (positive reinforcement) or disapproval (error corrections). Although the specific reasons why the tutor and student relationship is beneficial were not clear, this study suggests that significant benefits come to those being tutored, particularly when the tutor uses approval techniques. This research indicated that tutoring benefits are derived from any or all of the following: (1) opportunity to respond, (2) provision of a model at each stage of the learning process, and (3) individualization of tasks and consequences (Alexander and Dorrow 1983, pp. 33, 46).

A study completed by McCarthy (1980) involved fifth- and sixth-grade students in an urban school system. Both individual instruction in instrumental music classrooms and student subject variables were examined for their influence on an audiovisual music-reading test, a performance sight-reading test, and dropout rate from the music program. McCarthy concluded that no relationship existed between students' ethnic or racial background and their music achievement. Also of interest was that differences in teachers had virtually no effect on differences in students' *Music Achievement Test* (MAT) scores, *Watkins-Farnum Performance Scale* test scores, or dropout rate. Individualized instruction did have a significant interactive effect on the performance sight-reading measure, and scores on the Watkins-Farnum test were significantly higher for individually taught students with above-average scores on a reading achievement test than for similar students in ensemble classes (McCarthy, 1980, pp. 59–68).

The purpose of Milak's study (1980) was to compare two instructional methods for trumpet and trombone students in the fourth- and fifth-grade levels at two schools. The methods were one semester in length and were organized according to the types of learning set forth by Robert Gagne. The experimental group was introduced to pitch notation beginning with a one-line staff and progressing to a five-line staff, as well as rhythmic notation beginning with beat signs and groupings and progressing to traditional rhythmic notation. Supervised practice was advocated with this group. The control group was introduced to pitch and rhythmic notation through traditional techniques found in two well-known beginning band methods. Unsupervised practice was advocated with the control group. Colwell's *Elementary Music*

Achievement Test was administered before and after the treatments, and a performance test was administered after the treatments. The results of the analysis indicated a significant difference between the achievement and performance levels of the students, with the classes in the experimental group scoring significantly higher than the classes in the group that used traditional methods of beginning instrumental instruction (Milak, 1980, Abstract).

WIND CHAMBER MUSIC ENSEMBLE EXPERIENCE VS. LARGE ENSEMBLE EXPERIENCE

Olson (1975) found that, in general, students who participated in chamber music ensembles showed gains in cognitive music achievement over those who participated only in large ensembles. Gains were also noted in music performance achievement. Students who participated in chamber music ensembles demonstrated a more desirable attitude toward music, but test results indicated that the attitude alteration was not statistically significant. Tests employed in this investigation included the Colwell *Music Achievement Tests,* the *Oregon Test for Attitude Toward Music,* and the *Watkins-Farnum Performance Scale* (Olson, 1975, pp. 71–74).

Zorn (1969) conducted a similar study that included ninth-grade students. He found that although the experimental (chamber) groups indicated greater gains in performance abilities than the control groups, these gains were not statistically significant. The chamber music ensemble groups demonstrated no significant difference in their learning of cognitive information as compared with the control groups. The experimental (chamber) groups did, however, achieve significantly greater results in terms of developing positive attitude than the control sectional rehearsal groups. Zorn employed a series of six tests to gather data for his study. He designed three of the tests himself: the *Music Attitude Inventory,* the *Individual Recorded Performance,* and the *Music Information Inventory.* The three standardized tests used in his research were the *Music Aptitude Profile* (Part II: Musical Sensitivity), the *California Test of Mental Maturity* and the *Differential Aptitude Test* (Zorn, 1969, pp. 99–104).

RESEARCH IN TEACHING STRINGS

The Suzuki method brought about a major change in the attitude toward and philosophy toward the study of the violin. This approach considers the whole personality of the child, thus fostering a greater respect for the students, which also encourages them to perform their best—not always in an atmosphere of competitiveness. Today this method of string teaching is widespread in the United States. In a pilot study, Wensel (1970) found that the Suzuki philosophy could be adapted to the social and educational systems of the United States. Although this system of string pedagogy was

originally developed as an individual approach to string teaching, Brunson (1969) found that he was able to achieve success as he used the Suzuki system in a fourth-grade heterogeneous string class. In addition, Keraus (1973) compared the violin performance skills of 20 Suzuki students taught privately with those of 16 elementary Suzuki violin students taught in a class setting. After a 42-week period of instruction, there was no apparent difference in the performances of the two groups as judged by three experienced Suzuki teachers (Nelson, 1983, p. 41). Questions raised by Nelson (1983) include the following: "What is the most effective way to mainstream the Suzuki student into the ensemble experience?" "How and when can technical learnings on a string instrument be balanced with conceptual learnings?" and "What effect does the physical and mental maturation of children have on their technical and conceptual learning abilities?" (Nelson, 1983, p. 45). These kinds of questions will need to be addressed by researchers.

Rolland, Mutschler, Colwell, Miller, and Johnson (1971) conducted a study that included the development of a series of films that focused on movement education and rhythm training in string playing, with emphasis on the violin. The central issue of the project was the hypothesis that movement training, designed to free the student from excessive tensions, can be introduced within an organized plan of string instruction, and that such a plan, in the long run, will result in faster learning and better playing in all facets of instruction. The materials were used and tested in a 2-year trial involving 22 teaching centers in Illinois and additional out-of-state testing centers (Rolland et al., 1971, p. vii). Smith (1989) offers an extensive compilation of research findings that have been developed in recent years that have implications for public school string class instruction. She divided the data into the following four topic areas: the development of basic kinesthetic skills, the development of accurate intonation, the teaching of music reading, and the development of basic musicianship. The studies included in Smith's article focus primarily on group instruction and offer specific suggestions that can be used within the public school string class setting (Smith, 1989, p. 47). Romeo (1986) has designed a comprehensive curriculum for young violinists, using both group and private instructional settings to teach music history, music theory, aural skills, ensemble playing through chamber music, and violin technique. Her curriculum stresses two major areas: detailed structure and individual creativity (Romeo, 1986, p. 176).

VOCALIZATION AND THE DEVELOPMENT OF INSTRUMENTAL PERFORMANCE SKILLS

McGarry (1967) conducted a study to determine the extent to which vocalization of music contributes toward the development of several music performance skills in the area of instrumental music. These skills included tempo fluctuation, technical accuracy, duration, rests, slurs, observation of expression marks, holds, and repeats. As a result of his research, McGarry concluded that vocalization is, in fact, significantly effective with below-average students who did not take private lessons. Beyond this, vocalization had a leveling influence that narrowed the achievement range within the performing groups. McGarry also found that vocalization affected gains made by brass and woodwind sections to essentially the same extent (McGarry, 1967, pp. 1–2, 46–47).

Smith's (1984) study dealt with the effects of vocalization on the intonation of college level wind performers. He used 94 subjects who were wind instrumentalists in the Florida State University Bands. His results indicated no significant difference in the intonational deviation between female and male students included in the study. On the other hand, significant differences were noted between woodwind players and brass players (Smith, 1984).

Davis (1981) conducted a study that dealt with the effects of structured singing activities and self-evaluation practice on elementary band students' performance, melodic tonal imagery, self-evaluation, and attitude. He concluded that although no experimental condition provided an effective technique for developing melodic tonal imagery, self-evaluation practice and the combination of singing and self-evaluation practice provided a significant approach for the development of instrumental performance skills, attitude, and self-evaluation. It was noted that the results did differ for the first- and second-year students. This study indicated that the traditional approach employed during the second year of instruction provided a significantly effective approach for the development of both instrumental performance skills and attitude (Davis, 1981).

IMPROVING SIGHT-READING IN INSTRUMENTAL MUSIC

Streckfuss (1984) designed a study to test the effectiveness of his sight-reading pacer machine for improving the sight-reading ability of college instrumentalists. Sixty college instrumentalists served as subjects in his study. Experimental and control groups read the same sight-reading exercises during a 6-week period, but the experimental group read them with the aid of Streckfuss's sight-reading pacer machine. Forms A and B of the *Watkins-Farnum Performance Scale* served as pretest and posttest measures of sight-reading ability. The conclusions of this research showed that the sight-reading ability of students involved in this study was improved as measured by the *Watkins-Farnum Performance Scale*. Sight-reading ability appears to be correlated with years of private study and does not appear to be related to pitch and rhythm error detection ability as measured by the *Musical Achievement Test 2, Part 3*. Finally, there appeared to be no statistically significant relationship between sight-reading ability and years of large ensemble experience (Streckfuss, 1984, pp. 42, 65–68). The specific problem of Grutzmacher's (1987) research was to compare two courses of study—one emphasizing tonal concept development by using tonal patterns as content with harmonization and vo-

calization as teaching techniques; the other utilizing a single-note identification approach. This approach consisted of a set of musical symbols and a range of pitches taught from notation. It also emphasized technical skill development. The subjects were 48 fifth- and sixth-grade students who were studying wind instruments in three elementary schools in the same school system. It was found that the sight-reading skills of these students were noticeably improved by the instruction that used tonal pattern content presented through the use of harmonization and vocalization activities (Grutzmacher, 1987, pp. 173–179). Rosenthal (1984) utilized four experimental conditions in order to examine the effect of aural and verbal models on musicians' ability to accurately perform a musical selection. Included were (1) a guided model, a combined verbal and aural example of a relatively complex musical selection, (2) the model only, and aural example only, (3) the guide only, a verbal explanation only, and (4) practice only. The selection, Etude No. 22 by Kopprasch, was chosen to be modeled because it fulfilled the criteria of being relatively obscure, within the range of all woodwind and brass instruments (once transcribed), and complex enough to be challenging for graduate students in music education. Subjects for this study were 44 graduate and upper level undergraduate students majoring in either a woodwind or a brass instrument. They were enrolled in the B.M.Ed. or M.M.Ed. program at the VanderCook College of Music, Chicago, during the summer of 1982. Each subject was randomly assigned to one of the four treatments.

Results of this study demonstrated that different modeling conditions can affect subjects' performance. It was noted that the guided model did not appear to enhance the subjects' ability to perform the etude accurately despite the fact that the guide was designed to help subjects focus their attention on the most critical and complex aspects of the etude. It was thought that the guide may have helped the subjects to describe the selection verbally. This research also demonstrated that verbal instruction alone may be no more effective than independent practice in helping subjects to perform accurately. The implications for music teachers who elect to use modeling in their private instruction and in their ensemble rehearsals include the following: Direct modeling, without any added verbiage, may be most effective in helping a student perform accurately. If the teacher chooses to provide a verbal explanation, it may be most effective if it is done in conjunction with a direct model. Verbal explanation isolated from a direct example does not appear to have any immediate benefits for performance accuracy (Rosenthal, 1984, pp. 267–272).

The purpose of Ciepluch's study (1988) was to investigate the correlations between sight-reading achievement in instrumental performance, as determined by the *Watkins-Farnum Performance Scale*, with each of the following factors: (1) field-dependence/field-independence; (2) sensory mode preference(s): (a) visual, (b) written work, (c) listening, (d) activity; (3) musical aptitude; (4) grade point average; (5) math achievement; and (6) reading achievement. An analysis of the data indicated a significant relationship between sight-reading achievement in instrumental music performance and (1) field-dependence/field-independence; (2) musical aptitude; (3) written word sensory mode preference; (4) grade point average; (5) math achievement; and (6) reading achievement. This study did not find any significant differences between sight-reading achievement in instrumental performance and the sensory mode preferences of listening and activity (Ciepluch, 1988).

FLUOROSCOPIC STUDIES

Fluoroscopic and x-ray techniques continue to be used by researchers to identify what the performers are actually doing during performance as opposed to what they say they are doing. Merriman and Meidt (1968) set out to investigate what takes place in the oral cavity of horn and trumpet players during actual musical performance. Theirs was a pilot study that concluded that although cinefluorography is a valuable investigative technique, the diverseness of tongue and throat movements among subjects emphasizes the point that successful playing of a wind instrument is an extremely complicated process that has numerous variables. For example, the tongue position of four performers included in this study remained essentially constant during the playing of ascending passages, but six of the players moved their tongues upward and forward while playing such passages (Merriman and Meidt, 1968, pp. 31–38.). Subjects used in the Amstutz (1971) study employed similar consistent tongue positions; that is, the tongue was arched for the higher tones. Amstutz also found that tongue positions were not exactly the same for slurred tones as for detached tones (Amstutz, 1971, p. 35).

Wheeler (1973) operated under the assumption that his intraoral images (tongue techniques) could be substantially different from those of other clarinetists. His research, however, indicated that intraoral techniques had to be very nearly identical for all clarinetists. Wheeler indicated that the most significant finding of his research is that although specific tongue positions or shapes are essential for stabilizing tones in the several registers of each instrument (and even for adjusting intonation on the clarinet or saxophone), a specific shape cannot be altered to improve tone *quality* for any given tone, assuming that tone has been reasonably stabilized. His research dealt with both single- and double-reed instruments (Wheeler, 1973, pp. 3–4).

Frohrip (1972) investigated the physiological adjustments in teeth opening, pharyngeal opening, and over/underbite of the upper and lower jaw of trombone players using the videofluorographic technique. He found that no differences appeared to exist in the physiological adjustments made in the over- and underbite as well as in the teeth openings of the trombone players in his study. He also found that the speed of tongue release is an important factor in achieving legato or marcato articulation (Frohrip, 1972). Carr (1978) conducted a videofluorographic study of throat and tongue positions on the saxophone, bassoon, clarinet, oboe, and flute. He found that the major differences between instrument groups were in the area of throat positioning. Except with the bassoon group, the throat apertures opened as the playing range was extended into the upper registers. The throat apertures of the bassoon group, however, closed as the bassoonists played in the upper registers. Carr also discovered that the tongue was found to be in a higher position during the double-tonguing process. All performers were videofluorographed by radiologists as they performed on their instruments (Carr, 1978).

TEACHING INSTRUMENTAL MUSIC TO THE HANDICAPPED

In a study dealing with handicapped children and youth, Probst (1985) found that the mentally retarded demonstrated much progress in their social behavior as a result of instrumental study. The physically handicapped showed improvement in their social behavior and their capability to learn and to perform. The so-called slow learners demonstrated the greatest achievements in their social behavior. Of the three groups of handicapped students, the slow learners profited the most from instrumental lessons. In all groups, the students from the "lower class" displayed the most progress both in mental ability and in the field of physical movement. This group also showed the greatest interest in participating in the instrumental music lessons. The students involved in this research were allowed to select the particular musical instrument they wished to learn. The teachers were trained over a period of 2 years; at the end of this period they were required to successfully complete an examination prior to being qualified as instrumental teachers for handicapped children. The setting for this study was the Federal Republic of Germany (Probst, 1985, pp. 169, 173–174).

CLASS SIZE

The purpose of Jackson's (1980) research was to determine the effect of class size on individual achievement in beginning piano classes. She concluded that there were no statistically significant differences in individual achievement in piano classes of two, four, six, eight, or (by related comparison) 12 beginners at the ages of 4.9 years, 10 years, 15 years, or 19 years. Jackson indicated, however, that these data would not necessarily be valid for piano classes of other sizes or other levels. She points to the need for further research, using a number of group sizes and students at various levels of advancement in order to produce conclusive results (Jackson, 1980, pp. 162–166).

In a somewhat similar study, Seipp (1976) found that class instruction is more appropriate for lower-ability first-year college music majors while private instruction is more beneficial for higher-ability students. Sight-reading improvement was found to be significantly greater among the class students than those receiving private study. However, students in class instruction were much less satisfied with their type of instruction than were the students involved in private instruction. Both groups tended to doubt that applied class instruction could be as effective as applied private instruction. Seipp concluded that, for practical purposes, the differences between class and private instruction were slight and of no practical significance for the types of attitudes and learnings included in his study (Seipp, 1976, pp. 156–160).

Waa (1965) conducted a study designed to evaluate the effect of class and private methods of instruction on musical achievement and musical aptitude of instrumental beginners at the elementary level. One school in the study had beginning band twice a week for 40-minute periods, three schools had band twice a week for 20-minute periods, and two schools had no beginning band program at all. The difference in scores on the *Watkins-Farnum Performance Scale* reflected the difference of the band/no-band variable. Although private instruction appeared to be superior to class instruction concerning performance skills, Waa indicated that another study would need to be developed in which the band/no-band variable would be eliminated (Waa, 1965, pp. 100–109).

LOOKING TOWARD THE FUTURE

Additional research needs to be done in several areas. For example, a nationally normed and standardized test instrument needs to be developed to assess effectively the instruction of instrumental music. At present only generic test instruments are in use throughout the United States; thus we have, in most cases, the same evaluative instrument being used to assess the teaching of instrumental music and the teaching of calculus.

Numerous journal articles continue to appear that address the evaluation of individual instrumental performance as well as the evaluation of ensemble performance. Much more research is needed in both areas in order to develop assessment instruments to accomplish such evaluations objectively.

Although significant progress has been made over the past 25 years in the construction of musical instruments, more research will need to be done in order to improve such areas as intonation, tone quality, and the general construction of the instruments. For example, can musical instruments of the future be manufactured from different material to good advantage? Will the clarinet of the future be made of metal rather than of wood, much as the modern flute has evolved?

The rapid growth of technology should be of great assistance both in helping people to teach more effectively and also in aiding the researcher. Research is needed in the area of using twentieth-century musical materials such as mixed meters, nonmetric material, atonality, and improvisation. Certainly, many method books now in studio use are well over a hundred years old and do not address the technical and musical problems of today.

Finally, it is safe to say that the research efforts of most doctoral candidates end with the completion of the dissertation. Those who have demonstrated genuine skill in conducting viable research should be encouraged to continue such activities by their institutions, whether these are universities, colleges, or public school systems. Time and research stipends or grants need to be made available to such people so they might continue their research efforts. More endowed chairs for researchers are needed on the college and university levels. Once research has been completed, the results should be made available, in concise and readable language, to practitioners in the field. This is now being accomplished through such publications as the *Journal of Research in Music Education* and *Update: Applications of Research in Music Education* (both MENC publications), the *Bulletin of the Council for Research in Music Education* (available from the School of Music, University of Illinois), and *The Quarterly* (available from the School of Music, University of Northern Colorado).

References

Alexander, L. and Dorrow, L. G. (1983). Peer tutoring effects on the music performance of tutors and tutees in beginning band classes. *Journal of Research in Music Education, 31,* 33.

Amstutz, A. K. (1971). A videofluorographic study of the teeth aperture, instrumental pivot and tongue arch and their influence on trumpet performance. *NACWPI Journal, 20,* 34.

Anthony, J. (1974). Student perception of factors related to discontinuance from Iowa Public High School band programs in districts of 10,000 or more students. Unpublished doctoral dissertation, University of Iowa, Iowa City.

Brown, J. D. (1982). *The Gemeinhardt report.* Elkhart: The Gemeinhardt Company.

Brown, J. D. (1985). *The Gemeinhardt report II.* Elkhart: The Gemeinhardt Company.

Brunson, T. R. (1969). An adaption of the Suzuki-Kendall violin method for heterogeneous stringed instrument classes. Unpublished doctoral dissertation, University of Arizona, Tempe.

Carr, W. E., Jr. (1978). A videofluorographic investigation of tongue and throat positions in playing flute, oboe, clarinet, bassoon, and saxophone. Unpublished doctoral dissertation, University of Southern California, Los Angeles.

Ciepluch, G. M. (1988). Sightreading achievement in instrumental music performance, learning gifts and academic achievement: A correlation study. Unpublished doctoral dissertation, University of Wisconsin, Madison.

Davis, L. M. (1981). The effects of structured singing activities and self-evaluation practice on elementary band students' instrumental music performance, melodic tonal imagery, self-evaluation and attitude. Unpublished doctoral dissertation, Ohio State University, Columbus.

Frohrip, K. R. (1972). A videofluorographic analysis of certain physiological factors involved in performance of selected exercises for trombone. Unpublished doctoral dissertation, University of Minnesota, Minneapolis.

Gerheart, D. E., Anderson, D. L., Burdick, J., Chandler, T., Criss, L., Foster, W. J., Hanna, D. L., McMath, C. F., Moore, J. F., Phillips, P. A., Priest, J. R., Rauso, J., Sloanaker, J., Snider, S., and Williams, R. L. (1984) *Recruitment techniques and the beginning band.* American School Band Directors Association Research Committee report. 32nd annual convention of the American School Band Directors Association, Akron.

Grutzmacher, P. A. (1987). The effect of tonal pattern training on the aural perception, reading recognition, and melodic sight-reading achievement of first-year instrumental music students. *Journal of Research in Music Education, 35*(3), 171.

Heim, N. M. (1984). *Clarinet literature in outline.* Hyattsville: Norcat Music Press.

Jackson, A. (1980). The effect of group size on individual achievement in beginning piano classes. *Journal of Research in Music Education, 28*(3), 162.

Keraus, R. K. (1973). An achievement study of private and class Suzuki violin instruction. Unpublished doctoral dissertation, University of Rochester, Rochester.

Kruth, E. C. (1964). Student drop-out in instrumental music in the secondary schools of Oakland, California. Unpublished doctoral dissertation, Stanford University, Stanford.

McCarthy, J. F. (1980). Individualized instruction, student achievement, and dropout in an urban elementary instrumental music program. *Journal of Research in Music Education, 28*(1), 59.

McGarry, R. J. (1967). A teaching experiment to measure the extent to which vocalization contributes to the development of selected instrumental music performance skills. A comparison of the effectiveness of two teaching techniques on instrumental music performance utilizing the Watkins-Farnum Performance Scale. Unpublished doctoral dissertation, New York University, New York.

Martignetti, A. J. (1965). Causes of elementary instrumental music dropouts. *Journal of Research in Music Education, 13*(3), 177.

Mercer, R. J. (1970). *The band director's brain bank.* Northfield: The Instrumentalist Co.

Merriman, L. C., and Meidt, J. A. (1968). A cinefluorographic investigation of brass performance. *Journal of Research in Music Education, 16*(1), 31.

Milak, J. J. (1980). A comparison of two approaches of teaching brass instruments to elementary school children. Unpublished doctoral dissertation, Washington University, St. Louis.

Nelson D. J. (1983). String teaching and performance: A review of research findings. *Bulletin of the Council for Research in Music Education, 74,* 39.

Olson, E. E. (1975). A comparison of the effectiveness of wind chamber music ensemble experience with large wind ensemble experience. Unpublished doctoral dissertation, University of Southern California, Los Angeles.

Probst, W. (1985). Instrumental lessons with handicapped children and youths. *Bulletin of the Council for Research in Music Education, 85,* 166.

Puopolo, V. (1970). The development and experimental application of self-instructional practice materials for beginning instrumental-

ists. Unpublished doctoral dissertation, Michigan State University, East Lansing.

Rainbow, E. (1973). Instrumental music: Recent research and consideration for future investigations. *Bulletin of the Council for Research in Music Education, 33,* 8.

Rawlins, L. D. (1979). A study of the reasons for students dropping out of the instrumental music program of the Lincoln, Nebraska, Public Schools. Unpublished doctoral dissertation, University of Nebraska, Lincoln.

Rolland, P., Mutschler, M., Colwell, R., Miller, D. L., and Johnson, A. (1971). *Development and trial of a two year program of string education.* Final Report. U.S. Department of Health, Education, and Welfare; Office of Education; Bureau of Research, Project Number 5-1182.

Romeo, K. W. (1986). A five year comprehensive curriculum for young violinists. Unpublished doctoral dissertation, Ohio State University, Columbus.

Rosenthal, R. K. (1984). The relative effects of guided model, model only, guide only, and practice only treatments on the accuracy of advanced instrumentalists' musical performance. *Journal of Research in Music Education, 32*(4), 265.

Seipp, N. F. (1976). A comparison of class and private music instruction. Unpublished doctoral dissertation, West Virginia University, Morgantown.

Smith C. M. (1989). Research-based string class instruction. *Update: Applications of Research in Music Education, 8,* 47.

Smith, E. R. (1984). The effects of vocalization on the intonation of college wind performers. Unpublished doctoral dissertation, Florida State University, Tallahassee.

Solly, B. (1986). A study of attrition from the instrumental music program in moving between grade levels in Cherry Hill, New Jersey. Unpublished doctoral dissertation, Temple University, Philadelphia.

Streckfuss, R. J. (1984). The effect of a sight reading pacer machine upon the sight reading ability of college wind instrumentalists. Unpublished doctoral dissertation, Catholic University of America, Washington.

Waa, L. R. (1965). An experimental study of class and private methods of instruction in instrumental music. Unpublished doctoral dissertation, University of Illinois, Urbana.

Wensel, V. F. (1970). Project Super 1966–1968. Unpublished paper, Eastman School of Music, University of Rochester, Rochester.

Wheeler, R. L. (1973). Tongue registration and articulation for single and double reed instruments. *National Association of College Wind and Percussion Instructors Journal, 22*(1), 3.

Wheeler, R. L. (1977). Pedagogic concepts for reed instrument performance, based on cineradiographic research of the oral cavity. *National Association of College Wind and Percussion Instructors Journal, 25*(3), 3.

Zorn, J. D. (1969). The effectiveness of chamber music ensemble experience for members of a ninth grade band in learning certain aspects of music and musical performance. Unpublished doctoral dissertation, Indiana University, Bloomington.

·41·

RESEARCH ON THE TEACHING
OF KEYBOARD MUSIC

Marienne Uszler
UNIVERSITY OF SOUTHERN CALIFORNIA

An examination of keyboard teaching in the twentieth century might be approached in several ways, each having equal merit. No single focus is completely representative. The focus of this chapter will be documented research related to keyboard (primarily piano) teaching, together with commentary on what that research implies about trends, investigations, and issues. This is a limited approach, admittedly, but one that seems reasonable. It will enable readers to examine cited references and reach their own conclusions; be alerted to unfamiliar research; consider undertaking studies that fill research gaps; trace movements of particular interest; discover materials appropriate for building a personal or institutional library; and see their own place in the scheme of things with greater clarity.

In the twentieth century, what has remained the same about keyboard teaching is just as important as what has changed. Thus this chapter examines the private lesson and the master teacher—areas in which the scope of research has remained relatively constant—before discussing matters relating to technical instruction, and awareness techniques, areas in which research seems to be leading in new, albeit evolutionary, directions. Concert or recital performance as the primary goal of piano teaching has been recognized in the twentieth century. However, alterations of this goal are reflected in new teaching materials, use of divergent instructional formats (studio, classroom, small group, and laboratory), and the preparation of teachers able to integrate multipurpose instruction and to function in different educational settings. Research related to these matters is abundant; attention to it constitutes the bulk of this chapter. Inspection of the current scene suggests that electronic technology, new student populations, and education of the keyboard teacher are the focus of recent research.

It must be recognized that the keyboard teacher looking toward the twenty-first century is quite different from the piano teacher for whom *The Etude* was written at the turn of the last century.

TUTORIAL INSTRUCTION

The music lesson, particularly the piano lesson, is one of the most enduring forms of tutorial teaching. The relationship between teacher and student carries on the master-apprentice tradition. The master is the model who demonstrates, directs, comments, and inspires. The apprentice is the disciple who watches, listens, imitates, and seeks approval. Although the authoritarian position assumed by the master is open to question and criticism, notably by those who advocate learner-oriented teaching and by proponents of adult education, the presence of a master model is a powerful, universal motivating force. Research affirms this repeatedly, although "model" may be designated by different titles and function in varied situations. The stimulation of following a model over nearly an entire lifetime is observable, for example, in certain biographical studies (Groves, 1981). The influence of the "master teacher" is often referred to, and the search for pedagogical secrets of significant model teachers forms a continuing thread in research literature (Gordon, 1965; Machnek, 1966; Holland, 1973; Pucciani, 1979; Fang, 1978; Kern, 1984; Roberson, 1985).

Teaching by modeling is at the heart of the conservatory tradition, and while the conservatory as an institution has not been heavily documented, such studies are numerous enough to warrant attention (Skyrm, 1962; Robinson, 1969; Phillips, 1979; Kogan, 1987; Kingsbury, 1988). The motivating power of the model is a recurrent theme in learning theory and psychological literature, where at times it is referred to as mentorship and wherein negative aspects (such as the "apprentice complex" and "the limitations of the ego ideal") are also discussed (Bandura, 1969; Maslow, 1970; Gagné, 1977; Colarusso and Nemiroff, 1981; Babikian, 1982; Bloom, 1985; Kennell, 1989).

TECHNICAL INSTRUCTION

Another abiding concern of research is the matter of technique. A universally accepted definition of technique remains elusive, yet each performer and teacher discusses technique as if technical terminology was commonly understood, or as if the importance of certain experiences (such as relaxation) was unassailable. The abundance of technical manuals and documents is daunting. A bibliography pertaining to technique alone would be a formidable undertaking. All that is attempted here is to note several aspects of technique singled out for attention within the twentieth century either by particular groups (schools of technique) or at rather clearly defined times (trends).

Investigations of technique are as varied as they are numerous. Studies may offer detailed instructions on the teaching of particular techniques (Mathews, 1901; Brée, 1902; Matthay, 1903; Breithaupt, 1909; Whiteside, 1961; Sándor, 1981; Banowetz, 1985; Brodsky, 1986), or may examine complexities relating to technique in a more global context (Roeder, 1941; Boardman, 1954; Gerig, 1974; Taylor, 1981; Bardas, 1982; Dumm, 1988). Written documents about technique are often pedantic and verbose. The complex material in "scientific" works (Ortmann, 1929/1962; Schultz, 1936; Kochevitsky, 1976; Gát, 1974) cited in courses or bibliographies on technique is perforce digested slowly. The practical influence of such works may become perceptible only much later.

In some ways, however, research related to the teaching of technique is exploring unfamiliar territory or is reexamining older issues from new perspectives. In the last few decades there has been a decided interest in viewing technique as a psychophysical totality, as more than concern merely with fingers, hands, arms, and muscles. Emphasis has shifted to developing greater understanding of the interconnections between body and brain (Wilson, 1986). Earlier performers and teachers were certainly cognizant of the important role played by imagination and audiation (internally hearing beforehand the sound one wishes to make) in the development of technical facility, and it is astonishing how new research often appears to verify the usefulness of time-honored practice techniques. But the relationship between "inner" and "outer" aspects of playing was often expressed in relatively ambiguous language. Anton Rubinstein cautioned students to "begin the piece mentally" (Hofmann, 1920, p. 58) before touching the keys. Rosina Lhevinne exhorted students to "imagine the sound you wish to produce, and then . . . produce it" (Sargeant, 1963, p. 52).

The detailed anatomical studies of Ortmann and Schultz were largely reactionary works, determined to explain the physiological realities behind notions such as tone quality and methodology on the basis of weight and relaxation principles. Ortmann's research, for example, was dismissed by many in great part "because of his insistence upon accounting for muscular tension and fixation in joints at a time when focus was directed toward relaxation and freedom of movement" (Uszler et al., 1991, p. 337). Although neither Ortmann nor Schultz attracted ardent followers, as did Matthay and Whiteside, for example, some later writers reflect similar opinions and beliefs (Gát, 1974; Newman, 1984).

Ortmann himself realized that his research was preliminary to further exploration in realms involving psychophysical study. Other works following Ortmann's, though not necessarily in direct response to his research, also discussed technique in psychophysical terms (Bonpensiere, 1952; Kochevitsky, 1976; Bardas, 1982; McArthur, 1987) or at least in relation to interaction of larger playing units (e.g., torso, whole arms) with mental concepts (Whiteside, 1961). Bonpensiere's idea of "ideo-kinetics," though abstractly expressed and incompletely understood, has proved provocative, particularly to those with interest in correlations between perceptual imaging and motor response. Kochevitsky's study, done in association with a neurophysiologist, drew attention to the role of the central nervous system, likening the cerebral cortex to an intricate switchboard, transmitting orders for motor activity by means of electrochemical processes involving nerve fibers. For Whiteside, the direction of the entire playing organism is "driven by inner aural images and basic rhythmic impulse" (Uszler et al., 1991, p. 345). Although her approach to playing is criticized for what appears to some as undue attention to large—at the expense of smaller—playing units, Whiteside's ideas continue to influence teaching philosophies (Camp, 1981).

AWARENESS TECHNIQUES

Some writers and teachers, with the pendulum perhaps swinging heavily toward the "psycho" side of the psychophysical issue, dwelt on what has come to be known as awareness techniques. The popularity of the *inner game* approach to the teaching of sports movements (Gallwey, 1974) gave rise to discussion and writing dealing with musical performance movements in inner game terms (Green and Gallwey, 1986), or was reflected in humanistic explorations of these movements, mostly with a view to counteracting physical problems and inhibitions caused by inappropriate use of the body (Bernstein, 1981; Ristad, 1982; Kohut, 1985). Other research undertaken not in relation to inner game theories but as the result of interest in physical/inhibition difficulties of performers in general (Alexander, 1969; Feldenkrais, 1972) is also currently flourishing.

The technique associated with F. Matthias Alexander is not new. It arose in the 1890s as a result of Alexander's self-diagnosis of a recurring laryngitis problem. Improvement in body posture and general body mechanics is the result of dealing with an integrating mechanism, termed by Alexander the "primary control." Alexander training activates both unconscious learning (the teacher's hands "trigger the student's primary control" [Rosenthal, 1989]) and conscious learning (the student becomes aware of habits and what is necessary to redirect these). Regarded by its practitioners as an educational discipline, the movement has teachers and students rather than clinicians and patients. For Moshe Feldenkrais awareness of movement is a means of coming in touch with, and raising, self-image. Although components of the waking state also include sensation, feeling, and thought, Feldenkrais focuses on the continual interconnections between the making of movement and the nervous system. Since all muscular activity is movement, breathing is as significant an expression of one's physical state and self-image as sitting or standing. Feldenkrais exercises heighten awareness of the body functioning from within as much as from without. Achieving physical equilibrium is linked to an *understanding* of how one moves; carrying out an action with *awareness* is what distinguishes human, from animal, movement. Interest in techniques such as those associated with Alexander and Feldenkrais has burgeoned in recent decades, partly as an outgrowth of generally sharpened awareness of mind/body interaction among performers in many fields (sports as well as arts), partly also in reaction to the "curative" powers attributed to these techniques by musicians with physical problems and emotional blocking.

THE PIANO: INSTRUMENT ON WHICH TO TEACH FUNCTIONAL SKILLS

Much private piano instruction focuses on preparing the learner to play pieces. Nonetheless, more than other teachers, the keyboard teacher feels responsible for ensuring that the student can read, count, harmonize, transpose, memorize, improvise, and know theoretical principles—all this in addition to preparing for recital performance. Seldom is an early vocal, string, wind, or brass instructor faulted for not enabling a student to be an independent consumer of music in general. When has a voice teacher been criticized for not having taught key signatures? Or a string teacher reproached for not having taught tonic and dominant? Or a flute teacher discredited for not having explained intervals? "Someone else" in the instruction chain of command is held accountable; this is quite often the keyboard teacher. The nature of the instrument itself, of course, makes it an ideal teaching tool, and the keyboard teacher, by inference, is held answerable for the imparting of comprehensive knowledge, responsibility the keyboard teacher has acquired gradually but willingly.

A reasonable balance between exercises/etudes and repertoire was not characteristic of nineteenth-century keyboard tutors. Many were little more than technical manuals, and what literature was included tended toward the etude genre. Moreover, adequate grading of technical and repertoire materials did not exist in American tutors until the very end of

the nineteenth century (Mathews, 1892–94). Early graded materials were created in response to an audience that regarded music study as a pastime. The great majority of piano students were decidedly amateurs—as were most of their teachers. Although repertoire in these early graded books was more substantial than salon music, the market for such material was the "parlors" of America, not conservatory studios. Soon keyboard educators, the usual authors of keyboard materials, began to accommodate student needs in other ways.

The most significant change in keyboard tutors in the early twentieth century was the inclusion of materials for the purpose of developing reading and rhythmic skills along with materials for recital performance. Since pianos as furniture "status symbols" were found in many homes, it was advantageous that students be offered keyboard instruction that was both practical and "general." Two concomitant phenomena resulted. One of these was a change of goal, from emphasis on teaching *piano* to emphasis on teaching *music at the piano.* The other was to recognize class piano instruction as the most effective way to impart this wider instruction. These two phenomena will be examined in turn, even though cause and effect relationships between them are not direct.

Development of the Twentieth-Century Keyboard Method

Primary attention was focused on the process of teaching reading. The approach to rudiments of pitch reading used by the majority of tutors (Blake, 1916; Diller and Quaile, 1918; Williams, 1925; Thompson, 1936) has since come to be known as the *middle-C approach.* Middle C was the focal note from which all others were to be located, and the presentation of notes was presented in small increments, based on the five-finger position emanating from the thumb side of each hand. This reading approach underpins the majority of twentieth-century American keyboard methods and, with some adaptation, is still the stock-in-trade of most keyboard teachers.

Other reading approaches, however, also originated in the earlier years of the twentieth century (Giddings and Gilman, 1919; Miessner, 1924; Schelling, McConathy, Haake, and Haake, 1928). One approach was based on moving from the known to the unknown. Singing was the "known;" playing familiar songs on the keyboard was the "unknown." The keyboard reading process began, therefore, in keys comfortable for the child voice, via rote teaching of keyboard five-finger patterns in multiple keys (notably G, F, and A major) and the playing of "songs" in those keys. The student came to understand that a song, once learned, could be played in many keys by relocating finger patterns wherever desired. Thus the *multi-key reading approach* incorporated emphasis on transposition (Burrows and Ahearn, 1941, 1945; Pace, 1961). This practical skill—being able to play in many keys— used the piano as an instrument on which one could "play along" rather than as one designed primarily for solo performance. Understanding harmonic function was a corollary of this approach since songs were harmonized, almost from the outset, by basic chord progressions. "Chording" was also a practical piano skill and enhanced the value of the keyboard as a functional tool.

Another approach to the reading process centered on the perception of intervals; hand shapes and fingerings were learned that facilitated placement of intervals on the keyboard. This approach initially used a variant of staff notation without reference to an exact clef (Faelton and Faelton, 1904). By the 1950s the *intervallic approach* had evolved, which advocated extensive off-staff reading experiences prior to reading from partial (one- through four-line) staves (Clark, 1955). "Grand staff reading [thus evolved] as a development of all preceding reading activities" (Uszler et al., 1991, p. 106). This approach cultivated remembrance of a few focal note placements called "landmarks" (often treble clef G, bass clef F), from which further reading, by intervallic distance, was possible. Proponents of this approach maintain that although certain hand shapes correlate with certain intervals (even for very advanced readers), the hands at the beginning of study are not fixed in specific keyboard locations nor "locked into" five-finger positions (with the RH thumb, LH fifth finger as the bottom pitch of each position). The reading range is thereby quickly broadened since new "landmarks" may be positioned at will.

Most methods written in the 1980s use an eclectic mix of all three approaches, acknowledging that each has advantages and disadvantages (Uszler et al., 1991, pp. 107–108). The above classification of piano methods is somewhat simplistic, since many other factors contribute to a method's efficacy. It is nonetheless true that many teachers base their opinions about an entire method largely on the reading approach it uses.

The approach to reading is only one illustration of how keyboard methods have changed in the twentieth century. The expansion of the idea that keyboard instruction should facilitate generalized musicianship grew from simple harmonizing experiences to integrated approaches where concepts (scale formation, key signature, form) were interwoven with activities that enabled students to experience them before defining them. For example, students played "in keys" (all accidentals written out) before key signature was introduced as a way to simplify the notational process. Understanding of "scale" evolved from the playing of overlapping tetrachords (or simple single-note crossings) and moved only gradually to single-hand scale playing with regularly alternating groups of three and four fingers.

The incorporation of creative activities also contributed to greater comprehension, activities planned so that the student owned each concept and skill before reaching out to the next. Reinforcement pieces were included in core texts, quite unlike John Thompson's promise of "Something New Every Lesson" (1936, Table of Contents). Encouragement to create came in many forms; opportunities were given to vary, to accompany, to develop, to improvise, and to generate original ideas. Some inclusion of pop and jazz idioms (albeit highly simplified) was presented in such a way that both students and teachers would be drawn into experimenting with, and developing, new avenues of expression. Some strategies from group situations—for example, improvising over an ostinato or supplying "answers" to "questions"— also proved useful in any keyboard lesson.

The type of keyboard text in general use at the beginning of the twentieth century—a graded mix of exercises, etudes, and repertoire—ultimately emerges at the end of the century as a method that integrates the playing of etudes and repertoire with rhythmic activities, a technical regimen, sight reading, harmonization, transposition, broad musical comprehension, and creativity/improvisation. A program of such scope cannot be contained in a single set of graded volumes. Current keyboard methods generally offer an assortment of interrelated books—a "library"—with the implicit understanding that the teacher will mix and match books within a series (or books from different series) according to a personal teaching philosophy or the needs and desires of individual students.

The number of available libraries (methods) is now impressive. The plethora of divergent materials with their complex educational goals is in fact a unique feature of American keyboard methods. Curricula prepared as official courses of study in other countries (especially those under English influence) do not provide such comprehensive programing, nor the wide choice of methods. It should be noted, however, that some American keyboard teachers use none of the teaching libraries, preferring to teach keyboard performance much as it has always been taught by selection of materials from standard sources—for example, the *Anna Magdalena Bach Notebook*—combining these with perhaps a more strict technical regimen.

The amount of material available for survey in a keyboard pedagogy course can be overwhelming, and one of the primary goals of such a course is to supply the novice with tools for sorting through and evaluating this extensive body of materials (Uszler et al., 1982–1985; Bastien, 1988; Uszler et al., 1991). Despite the profusion and diversity of piano methods, and the attention paid to them in pedagogy classes and elsewhere, there is no scientific research into the relative effectiveness of these methods. Here, indeed, is an area to which those engaged in pedagogical research must turn their attention.

Group Teaching

The trend in the United States throughout the twentieth century toward group keyboard instruction is well-known. This does not mean that group teaching is the preferred instructional environment of most keyboard teachers (far from it), nor that group teaching itself can be circumscribed in a generally accepted definition.

To some, group teaching implies that the group dynamic itself is an important component of the instruction; thus instruction using multiple electronic keyboards, with each student on headphones communicating directly with the teacher, would not be considered true group instruction. To others, the presence of more than one student reacting to the directions of a single teacher, by whatever means, constitutes a group experience.

Most teachers would agree that a keyboard laboratory is not essential to group teaching, yet most teachers who work with group situations use a laboratory setup. Teachers who deal with smaller groups (two to four students) in a studio equipped with only one or two acoustic instruments use group time for specific tasks: presentation of concepts, ensemble experiences, creative and improvisatory activities, directives related to learning of new repertoire. Additional individual or partner lessons focus on technique, refinement of performance skills, repertoire development, and solving individual problems. It is possible to regard a master class, especially one in which the master teacher relates to those in the audience, as a type of group teaching. In short, exactly what constitutes "group" teaching is more a matter of perspective than of common agreement.

Group teaching, although not common, was practiced in the nineteenth century. Reference to such is found in individual tutors (Logier, 1816; Burrowes, 1818) or in accounts of study with master teachers (Boissier, 1927; Holland, 1973; Fay, 1978). But group teaching was given a strong emphasis by early twentieth-century American educators who advocated keyboard instruction in the classroom. As noted earlier, these educators regarded the keyboard as a music teaching tool; curriculum content focused on practical rather than performance skills.

Educators seeking to provide music instruction for the general population found that appropriate teaching materials were wanting. These educators wrote new books and methods (Giddings and Gilman, 1919; Miessner, 1924; Schelling et al., 1928; Curtis, 1933; Burrows and Ahearn, 1941, 1945). In so doing they not only provided for the specific needs of classroom keyboard teaching, but also called into question numerous time-tested strategies—such as teaching rhythm and reading primarily by means of memorization and repetition. Thus arose a further difficulty. Although helpful materials (some even with teacher manuals) became available, teachers were not prepared to use them. Classroom teachers, skilled in teaching groups, were not skilled in music making. Although most classroom teachers could sing and some were even amateur pianists, they lacked the confidence and the background required to teach harmonization and transposition or to guide creative activities. Keyboard teachers, on the other hand, informed in musical matters, had no group teaching experience. To organize a general presentation of conceptual information for a divergent group of learners was outside their training. Teaching techniques linking singing and movement to keyboard playing were equally foreign to professional studio and "parlor" instructors. Seeking the solution to this problem constitutes the history of group keyboard teaching throughout the remainder of this century.

In the first half of the century, especially the 1920s and 1930s, a major effort was directed toward establishing successful group piano in the elementary school (Beer, 1952; Monsour, 1960; Miller, 1962; Richards, 1962; McDermid, 1967). Pioneers in this endeavor—Thaddeus Giddings, Hazel Kinscella, Otto Miessner, Helen Curtis, Charles and Gail Haake, Polly Gibbs, Ada Richter, Raymond Burrows, Ella Mason Ahearn, Fay Templeton Frisch—were themselves classroom music teachers. Through demonstrations and lectures to professional music organizations, they "spread the word" and offered good examples. Giddings, Kinscella, Curtis, and Miessner were active throughout the 1920s; the Haakes, Gibbs, Richter, Burrows, Ahearn, and Frisch followed in succeeding decades. In 1949 the Music Educators National Conference (MENC) published a national survey, *Piano Instruction in the Schools,* prepared by the Piano Instruction Committee, which Burrows chaired (Wagner, 1968).

Although the initial intent of these educators was to prepare music teachers for the school classroom, many of them came to see the importance of training piano teachers to function in other group situations. Burrows and Ahearn in particular helped develop group instruction for adults both in the college setting and in the workplace. Richter and Frisch were creating materials for group instruction of preschool children.

The emergence of the electronic piano laboratory in the late 1950s (Page, 1968; Goltz, 1975; Rhea, 1972) increased group keyboard offerings at the college level. Many colleges purchased these labs in order to use their features (such as headphones and linkage to the teacher console) for a generalized instructional format as well as for individualization within the group framework. In many cases class piano was viewed as an adjunct to theory instruction; the curricular emphasis was almost entirely on the teaching of functional skills. Once again, appropriate instructors for these classes were in short supply. Often members of the existing keyboard faculty, trained in performance instruction, were pressed into service. In many cases such individuals became skilled in group techniques through self-instruction; they also attended intensive training programs offered, frequently in summer sessions, by those continuing the work of the pioneers.

Content for these courses gradually expanded to include repertoire and technical instruction as well as improvisatory and ensemble experiences. Although keyboard classes usually originated as courses for music students whose major was other than piano, classes were also instituted for the non–music major. In small institutions, especially in 2-year junior and community colleges, music majors and non-majors were (and still are) forced to coexist in the same classroom. Research reflects study of activities specific to certain locales/schools (Rast, 1964; Lyke, 1968; Holsclaw, 1969; Hunter, 1973; Exline, 1977; Osadchuk, 1984), to certain majors (Albers, 1973; Brown, 1983; Johnson, 1987; McDonald, 1989), and to the acquisition of certain skills (Lowder, 1971; Beehler, 1978; Micheletti, 1980; Bogard, 1983; Fincher, 1983; Bozone, 1986). What seems to have proved valid, or at least practical, in American class piano programs at the tertiary level is now finding its way elsewhere (Sabry, 1965; Kou, 1985; Lee, 1986).

As a consequence of the success of these classes, and also of the acumen of the instructors involved, colleges began to offer class piano teacher training, as an individual course or as an emphasis or major. In the early years a pedagogy major, usually at the master's level, concentrated on college-level group teaching. Although this is no longer the case, it does illustrate the influence that group teaching philosophy and practice have had on the development of the keyboard pedagogy major (Lancaster, 1978; Uszler and Larimer, 1986).

THE CURRENT SCENE

The 1970s and 1980s witnessed a tremendous growth in keyboard pedagogy. Among the developments are establishment of keyboard pedagogy majors at both undergraduate and graduate levels (Uszler and Larimer, 1984, 1986); the inauguration of the National Conference on Piano Pedagogy; the expansion of technology via digital keyboards, computers, and Musical Instrument Digital Interface (MIDI) capabilities; the importance of the independent studio teacher in the face of dwindling keyboard music in the school system; awareness of the adult student as a unique entity, and the effect an aging population will have on all educational and recreational resources; great interest by independent music teachers in preschool instruction, arising from the prevalence of Orff, Suzuki, Kodály, and Yamaha instructional programs; and the growing image of undertaking independent music instruction as a business, as well as an artistic or educational, endeavor.

The Keyboard Pedagogy Major

The keyboard teacher currently finds it possible and/or desirable to function in a number of categories: as an independent teacher of adults, children, and preschool children in both studio and group situations; as a group piano teacher at the college level, teaching nonmusic majors and/or music majors; as a group piano teacher in a public school program; as a studio teacher at the college level; as a teacher of college-level functional harmony classes; as a teacher of keyboard literature; and as a teacher of keyboard pedagogy. Each of these situations requires special pedagogical mastery. Moreover, in each of these areas there is an abundance of print material from which to select instructional texts and music; surveying the literature itself demands considerable time and effort. Many skills that the instructor is expected to teach in these situations (e.g., harmonization, improvisation, sight reading) are skills not often developed within the performance-oriented studio. Thus, unless the keyboard major is provided with such instruction in other classes, these skills are learned either on the firing line or not at all. Although no one would contend that a primary purpose of courses designed to fulfill a major in pedagogy is the teaching of functional skills to the pedagogy major, it must be admitted that a discussion of teaching such skills to others cannot proceed unless the skill has become comfortable to the would-be teacher.

Appreciation of the learning characteristics of varied age groups is also a major part of the effective teacher's equipment. The amount of educational psychology required for the incipient teacher to understand the needs of preschool, elementary, secondary, tertiary, and other adult students gives an implication of the scope of what must be covered in yet other pedagogy courses. A large amount of time must also be spent on a scrutiny of instructional materials and how they may be used. In schools where pedagogy instruction is confined to one or a few classes, surveys of this sort often constitute the bulk of the class activity.

Pedagogy teachers, however, see intern teaching as the focal point of a pedagogy major—the internship to include observation, guided student teaching, and frequent observation by a master teacher, with feedback (Baker, 1982; Collins, 1982, 1984; Goss, 1982; Uszler and Larimer, 1984, 1986; Mann, 1986; Pearce, 1986). Since most keyboard teachers will need to work in varied situations in their professional careers, realistic intern teaching experiences should include both individual and group instruction. The National Conference on Piano Pedagogy provides guidelines for establishing and organizing the pedagogy major (Uszler and Larimer, 1984, 1986), and has been effective in influencing the National Association of Schools of Music in the formation of its own handbook policy regarding pedagogy competencies.

New Technology

The keyboard teacher, like everyone in the educational sector, has been inundated by information about electronic technology. Not yet clear is how to evaluate the educational implications of this technology beyond seeing the new tools as the ultimate drillmasters, record keepers, and providers of "enhanced" backgrounds. Since much new technology is keyboard driven, those with a vested interest in keyboard performance must play a vital role in the exploration of this equipment and what it offers to the keyboardist and the musician. When speaking of electronic equipment in this context, it is necessary to distinguish between new instruments per se (such as electronic/digital keyboards, synthesizers) and other hardware (such as computers, drum machines, sequencers) that influence instruction and performance, often through a keyboard MIDI interface.

New instruments are generators of new sounds. The most effective use of these instruments is (or at least should be) creative, discovering ways in which each new instrument can speak its own voice. Where their principal use is remedial (e.g., to drill, correct, or report) or ancillary (e.g., to embellish, vary, or manipulate familiar sounds), their most valuable contribution is being overlooked. Most keyboard players and teachers are still busy exploring the remedial/ancillary properties of the new keyboards (Young, 1990). Although this use is important and may eventually be the key to finding the "new voice," *musical* judgment and evaluation must ultimately carry the day. Few are addressing this issue at present.

Efforts are being made by individuals (Anderton, 1986; Hofstetter, 1987; Carden, 1988), by professional organizations (Association for Technology in Music Instruction [ATMI]; Music Teachers National Association [MTNA], MENC), and by periodicals and other print/video publications to inform teachers of what is available, how to choose among products, and how to use this equipment.

Computer-assisted instruction (CAI) is another valuable adjunct to the educational scheme (Banks, 1990). Most CAI music programs treat the subject (whether notation, rhythm, or ear training, for example) in fairly rudimentary fashion. This is helpful since a great percentage of keyboard students work at elementary, or near elementary, levels. Authors of keyboard methods are now designing computer software to accompany the print material; computer software and videotapes are being reviewed on a frequent, if irregular, basis in keyboard periodicals. Video programs may soon assume the task of direct teaching of keyboard performance, although how evaluation will occur in this type of instruction is not clear.

There are now keyboard teachers in all categories: those who embrace with enthusiasm all that new technology offers and immerse themselves in this heady world; those who explore and experiment, sifting and weighing pros and cons as best they can; those who try the waters, dabbing here and there to see if they can remain afloat in the techno-world; those who ignore issues raised by technology and its panoply of products; and those who worry that western art music is under siege and avoid any vestige of "techno-taint." Thus has it always been. When the fortepiano was a new instrument, most keyboardists continued for nearly a quarter century to play it like a harpsichord.

New Student Populations

Two sectors of the potential student population represent new areas of interest for keyboard teachers: the preschool student and the adult student. These two groups are growing in number and are good candidates for enrichment programs such as music instruction. They have thus attracted the attention of teachers who might otherwise not have sought either of these student types as studio prospects. College music instructors are also looking with interest at the same groups. As the music student population diminishes and administrators urge out-reach programing, the development of piano classes for adults of all ages and backgrounds represents a new and challenging opportunity. College pedagogy teachers have reason to develop interest in the preschool population as well, seeing there an area to which their pedagogy students must be introduced. Thus, from either necessity or educational devotion, keyboard teachers in general are now more eager to develop instructional programs for these divergent student groups.

Attention to Adults Keyboard texts designed for the adult have been around for a long time (Uszler et al., 1991, pp. 150–153). The more recent ones have learned to target specific audiences and provide attractive features such as graphic sophistication, practice cassettes, and clever verbal analogies and summaries. But because "adult" can describe so many different types of student—each with separate interests, needs, and capabilities—it is often not so simple to find the workable match between student and text.

Preschool Instruction Interest in teaching the preschool child has been stimulated by phenomena within music education, within general education, and within society. By the 1970s Suzuki instruction (Maris, 1984; Landers, 1984) seemed to be proving that preschoolers had enough small muscle control to succeed at serious instrumental music making. At the same time Yamaha schools (Lancaster, 1984–85) were taking a different approach, offering musical training in a more global context and stressing creativity and exploration rather than developing instrumental technique. In the 1980s authors of keyboard methods were seriously into the business of creating preschool materials, and the writing of preprimers and musical coloring books continues to flourish.

The independent instrumental teacher became aware that preschool classes could fill the vacant places in the teaching schedule when other students were in school. Keyboard teachers, in particular, began preschool classes—some on a modest basis, others joining forces with a local care or educational program. Once again this required on-the-spot learning, as most pedagogy programs did not, and still do not, spend time on training relating to preschool instruction. Those that do are usually institutions whose adjunct or preparatory faculty include Suzuki or Yamaha teachers.

There is a single issue underlying all decisions relating to preschool instruction. Should music teaching involving preschool children be instrument specific, teaching the child how to play a piano or violin, or should it offer a general exposure to musical experiences of many kinds on varied instruments such as pianos, organs, mallet, and percussion instruments? (Aronoff, 1969, 1988; Bridges, 1984; Elkind, 1987; Scott, 1987, 1989). That issue, for most keyboard teachers, remains currently unresolved. In-service or degree-related pedagogical education within the next decade may not satisfactorily unravel that particular knot, but it will surely need to examine the territory.

KEYBOARD TEACHERS: A HYBRID WORLD

The reason this chapter has addressed so many, and such varied, issues may be partly explained by considering the hybrid world of keyboard teachers. They are essentially performance teachers, engrossed in matters relating to technique, literature, performance practice, and instrumental technological development. They are, however, responsive to the learning process and the application of educational psychology to piano performance. Many are attracted to pedagogical research, either delving into what others have produced or contributing to ongoing research themselves.

Formerly the pianist found nothing in the professional curriculum speaking to education. This was the situation in which Raymond Burrows found himself a half century ago. His solution was to pursue performance at Juilliard and education at Teachers College, Columbia. In the decades that followed, pianists sharing Burrows' dual interests were often counseled into the field of music education, particularly at graduate degree levels. This was an often unsatisfactory solution, as the music education focus was on preparing the classroom and school ensemble instructor, and piano teachers wished to investigate educational theories with reference to the studio and keyboard class.

The advent of the pedagogy major has succeeded in allowing for this fusion of interests (Kowalchyk, 1989). Enthusiasm for this major grows steadily. Some pianists, looking realistically at the world into which they will emerge after graduation, see it as the only rational curriculum. Admittedly, a pedagogy curriculum is not yet as standardized as that for a performance major; courses and experiences con-

stituting that major still differ from institution to institution. Nonetheless, attention to the learning process is addressed from the perspective of performance, the best illustration being the internship teaching, teaching that occurs in the studio (at various advancement levels, depending on the institution) and in settings involving keyboard study in small and/or large groups.

The inclusion of a chapter on keyboard teaching in a music education handbook underscores the issue of focus addressed at the chapter's opening. A report on keyboard teaching might have examined only keyboard education in the classroom. Yet that would have been an inadequate description of what has evolved in the area of twentieth-century keyboard education, and would not have presented the interconnections in the hybrid discipline discussed above. The keyboard teacher approaching the twenty-first century is coming closer to a sought-after ideal—one in which the performer and the educator are equally alive, equally committed, and equally informed.

References

Albers, C. H., Jr. (1973). An analysis and evaluation of the class piano course for non-music majors. Unpublished doctoral dissertation, Northwestern University, Evanston.

Alexander, F. M. (1969). In E. Maisel (Ed.), *The resurrection of the body*. New York: University Books.

Anderton, C. (1986). *MIDI for musicians*. New York: Amsco Publications.

Aronoff, F. W. (1969). *Music and young children*. New York: Holt, Rinehart & Winston.

Aronoff, F. W. (1988). Reaching the young child through music: Howard Gardner's theory of multiple intelligences as model. *International Journal of Music Education, 12,* 18–22.

Babikian, H. M. (1982). The psychoanalytic treatment of the performing artist: Superego aspects. *Journal of the American Academy of Psychoanalysis, 13*(1), 148.

Baker, M. J. (1982). When piano pedagogy is an 'option': A solution to the practice-teaching dilemma. *Proceedings of the National Conference on Piano Pedagogy,* 53–56.

Bandura, A. (1969). *Principles of behavior modification*. New York: Holt, Rinehart and Winston.

Banks, D. W. (1990). The correlation of selected pre-college music computer programs with the Alfred Basic Piano Library. Unpublished doctoral dissertation, University of Oklahoma, Norman.

Banowetz, J. (1985). *The pianist's guide to pedaling*. Bloomington: Indiana University Press.

Bardas, W. (1982). *On the psychology of piano technique*. Brooklyn: Beechwood Press.

Bastien, J. W. (1988). *How to teach piano successfully* (3rd ed.). San Diego: Neil A. Kjos.

Beehler, S. R. (1978). A plan of instruction for teaching music majors basic open score reading at the keyboard in class programs. Unpublished doctoral dissertation, University of Arizona, Tucson.

Beer, A. S. (1952). Class piano as an adjunct to the classroom music program. Unpublished masters thesis, Northwestern University, Evanston.

Bernstein, S. (1981). *With your own two hands*. New York: Schirmer Books.

Blake, D. (1916). *Melody book*. Cincinnati: Willis.

Bloom, B. (Ed.). (1985). *Developing talent in young people*. New York: Ballantine.

Boardman, R. (1954). A history of theories of teaching piano technique. Unpublished doctoral dissertation, New York University, New York.

Bogard, D. M. (1983). An exploratory study of first year music theory, ear training/sight singing, and piano class: An interrelated approach. Unpublished doctoral dissertation, University of Colorado, Boulder.

Boissier, A. (1927). *Liszt pédagogue: Lecons de piano données par Liszt a Mademoiselle Valérie Boissier a Paris en 1832*. Paris: Honoré Champion.

Bonpensiere, L. (1952). *New pathways to piano technique: A study of the relations between mind and body with special reference to piano playing*. New York: Philosophical Library.

Bozone, J. M. (1986). The use of sight singing as a prestudy aid for the improvement of the sight-reading skill of second semester class piano students. Unpublished doctoral dissertation, University of Oklahoma, Norman.

Brée, M. (1969). *The groundwork of the Leschetizky method*. St. Clair Shores: Scholarly Books. (Originally published 1902)

Breithaupt, R. (1909). *Natural piano-technic* (Trans. J. Bernhoff). Leipzig: C. F. Kahnt Nachfolger.

Bridges, D. (1984). Eclecticism in early music education. *Music Education [International Society for Music Education], 3,* 35–37.

Brodsky, E. (1986). Piano tone colors: Its scientific foundations and their implication for the performer. Unpublished doctoral dissertation, Stanford University, Stanford.

Brown, B. A. (1983). The organization and analysis of selected repertoire for the teaching of comprehensive musicianship to non-piano majors through group piano instruction. Unpublished doctoral dissertation, Teachers College, Columbia, New York.

Brown, M. C., and Sommer, B. K. (1969). *Movement education: Its evolution and a modern approach*. Reading: Addison-Wesley.

Burrowes, J. F. (1818). *The piano-forte primer or new musical catechism*. London: Original publisher unknown.

Burrows, R., and Ahearn, E. M. (1941). *The young explorer at the piano.* Cincinnati: Willis Music.

Burrows, R., and Ahearn, E. M. (1945). *Young America at the piano.* Cincinnati: Willis Music.

Camp, M. W. (1981). *Developing piano performance.* Chapel Hill: Hinshaw.

Carden, J. (1988). *A piano teacher's guide to electronic keyboards.* Milwaukee: Hal Leonard Publishing.

Clark, F. (1955). *Time to begin.* Secaucus: Summy-Birchard.

Colarusso, C., and Nemiroff, R. (1981). *Adult development.* New York: Plenum Press.

Collins, A. (1982). How can successful teaching experience be included in piano pedagogy programs? *Proceedings of the National Conference on Piano Pedagogy, 15–21.*

Collins, A. (1984). Report of the committee on practice teaching. *Proceedings of the National Conference on Piano Pedagogy, 39–42.*

Curtis, H. (1933). *Curtis class piano course: Teacher's manual.* Chicago: Roosa.

Diller, A., and Quaile, E. (1918). *First solo book.* New York: G. Schirmer.

Dumm, R. (1988). *Pumping ivory.* Katonah: Ekay Music.

Elkind, D. (1987). *Miseducation, preschoolers at risk.* New York: Alfred A. Knopf.

Exline, J. M. (1977). Development and implementation of a program in functional piano skills designed for undergraduate music and non-music majors at the State University College at Oswego, New York. Unpublished doctoral dissertation, University of Rochester, Rochester.

Faelton, C., and Faelton, R. (1904). *The Faelton system of fundamental piano instruction.* Boston: Arthur P. Schmidt.

Fang, S. (1978). Clara Schumann as teacher. Unpublished doctoral dissertation, University of Illinois, Urbana.

Fay, A. (1978). *Music study in Germany.* New York: Da Capo Press.

Feldenkrais, M. (1972). *Awareness through movement.* New York: Harper & Row.

Fincher, B. J. (1983). The effects of playing the melody by rote during the prestudy procedure upon sight-reading skills development of beginning class piano students. Unpublished doctoral dissertation, University of Oklahoma, Norman.

Gagné, R. (1977). *The conditions of learning* (3d Ed.). New York: Holt, Rinehart and Winston.

Gallwey, W. T. (1974). *The inner game of tennis.* New York: Random House.

Gát, J. (1974). *The techniques of piano playing.* New York: Boosey & Hawkes.

Gerig, R. (1974). *Famous pianists and their technique.* Washington and New York: Robert B. Luce.

Giddings, T. P., and Gilman, W. (1919). *Public school class method for the piano.* Boston: Oliver Ditson.

Goltz, J. D. (1975). A survey of class piano laboratories. Unpublished doctoral dissertation, Florida State University, Tallahassee.

Gordon, S. L. (1965). Cecile Staub Genhart: Her biography and her concepts of piano playing. Unpublished doctoral dissertation, Eastman School of Music, University of Rochester, Rochester.

Goss, L., (1982). Should there be a standardized curriculum for practice teaching? *Proceedings of the National Conference on Piano Pedagogy, 25–28.*

Green, B., and Gallwey, W. T. (1986). *The inner game of music.* Garden City: Anchor Press/Doubleday.

Groves, R. W. (1981). The life and works of W. S. B. Mathews 1837–1912. Unpublished doctoral dissertation, University of Iowa, Iowa City.

Hofmann, J. (1920). *Piano playing with questions answered by Josef Hofmann.* Philadelphia: Theodore Presser.

Hofstetter, F. T. (1987). *Computer literacy for musicians.* Englewood Cliffs: Prentice-Hall.

Holland, J. (1973). Chopin's teaching and his students. Unpublished doctoral dissertation, University of North Carolina, Chapel Hill.

Holsclaw, J. L. (1969). An analysis of instructional techniques relative to class piano in selected institutions of higher education in California. Unpublished master's thesis, California State University, Fullerton.

Hunter, R. J., Jr. (1973). The teaching of ten functional piano skills to undergraduate music education majors at selected west coast four-year colleges and universities. Unpublished doctoral dissertation, University of the Pacific, Stockton.

Johnson, G. W. (1987). Group piano instructional priorities for music majors in higher education settings in the United States. Unpublished doctoral dissertation, Brigham Young University, Salt Lake City.

Kennell, R. (1989). Three teacher scaffolding strategies in college applied music instruction. Unpublished doctoral dissertation, University of Wisconsin, Madison.

Kern, R. F. (1984). Frances Clark: The teacher and her contributions to piano pedagogy. Unpublished doctoral dissertation, University of Northern Colorado, Greeley.

Kingsbury, H. (1988). *Music, talent, and performance.* Philadelphia: Temple University Press.

Kochevitsky, G. (1976). *The art of piano playing: A scientific approach.* Princeton: Birch Tree.

Kogan, J. (1987). *Nothing but the best.* New York: Random House.

Kohut, D. (1985). *Musical performance: Learning theory and pedagogy.* Englewood Cliffs: Prentice-Hall.

Kou, M. (1985). Secondary piano instruction in the colleges and universities of the Republic of China with recommendations for incorporating American group piano instructional methods in the curriculum. Unpublished doctoral dissertation, University of Oklahoma, Norman.

Kowalchyk, G. (1989). A descriptive profile of piano pedagogy instructors at American colleges and universities. Unpublished doctoral dissertation, Teachers College, Columbia, New York.

Lancaster, E. L. (1978). The development and evaluation of a hypothetical model program for the education of the college and university group piano instructor. Unpublished doctoral dissertation, Northwestern University, Evanston.

Lancaster, E. L. (1984–85). The Yamaha music education system. *The Piano Quarterly, 128,* 19–29.

Landers, R. (1984). *The talent education development of Shinichi Suzuki: An analysis* (3d Ed.). Athens: Ability Development.

Lee, Y. (1986). A survey and study of the piano teaching materials for use in promoting comprehensive musicianship to college non-piano majors in Korea. Unpublished doctoral dissertation, Teachers College, Columbia, New York.

Logier, J. (1816). *A companion to the royal patent chiroplast, or hand director.* London: I. Green.

Lowder, J. E. (1971). An experimental study of teaching reading concepts and keyboard fingering patterns to freshman college piano classes. Unpublished doctoral dissertation, Indiana University, Bloomington.

Lyke, J. B. (1968). An investigation of class piano programs in the six state universities of Illinois and recommendations for their improvement. Unpublished doctoral dissertation, University of Northern Colorado, Greeley.

Machnek, E. J. (1966). The pedagogy of Franz Liszt. Unpublished doctoral dissertation, Northwestern University, Evanston.

Mann, J. (1986). Optimizing observation and evaluation of student teachers: A high-tech approach, *Proceedings of the National Conference on Piano Pedagogy, 55–57.*

Maris, B., (1984). The Suzuki method . . . and piano school. *The Piano Quarterly, 127,* 32–47.

Maslow, A. (1970). *Motivation and personality.* New York: Harper & Row.

Mathews, W. (1892–94). *Standard graded course of studies* (10 vols.). Philadelphia: Theodore Presser.

Mathews, W. (1901). *Teacher's manual of Mason's pianoforte technics.* Chicago: Music Magazine Publishing Co.

Matthay, T. (1903). *The act of touch in all its diversity.* London: Bosworth & Co.

McArthur, V. (1987). An application of instructional task analysis and biomechanical motion analysis to elementary cognitive and psychomotor piano learning and performance. Unpublished doctoral dissertation, Florida State University, Tallahassee.

McDermid, C. M. (1967). Thaddeus P. Giddings: A biography. Unpublished doctoral dissertation, University of Michigan, Ann Arbor.

McDonald, S. R. (1989). A survey of the curricular content of functional keyboard skills classes designed for undergraduate piano majors. Unpublished doctoral dissertation, University of Oklahoma, Norman.

Micheletti, L. H. (1980). An assessment of the vertical method and the ensemble approach to teaching sight reading to secondary class piano students. Unpublished doctoral dissertation, University of Miami, Coral Gables.

Miessner, O. (1924). *The melody way to play the piano.* Chicago: Miessner Institute of Music.

Miller, S. D. (1962). W. Otto Miessner and his contributions to music in American schools. Unpublished doctoral dissertation, University of Michigan, Ann Arbor.

Monsour, S. A. (1960). The establishment and early development of beginning piano classes in the public school. Unpublished doctoral dissertation, University of Michigan, Ann Arbor.

Newman, W. S. (1984). *The pianist's problems.* New York: Da Capo Press.

Ortmann, O. (1962). *The physiological mechanics of piano technique.* New York: E. P. Dutton and Co. (Originally published in 1929).

Osadchuk, E. G. (1984). Class piano instruction in junior colleges accredited by the North Central Association of Colleges and Schools. Unpublished doctoral dissertation, University of Oklahoma, Norman.

Pace, R. (1961). *Music for piano.* Milwaukee: Lee Roberts (Distributed by Hal Leonard).

Page, C. L. (1968). Keyboard experience and electronics. Unpublished doctoral dissertation, University of Michigan, Ann Arbor.

Pearce, E. (1986). Report of the committee on practice teaching, *Proceedings of the National Conference on Piano Pedagogy,* 12–19.

Phillips, L. M. (1979). The Leipzig Conservatory: 1843–1881. Unpublished doctoral dissertation, Indiana University, Bloomington.

Pucciani, D. (1979). Olga Samaroff (1882–1948). American musician and educator. Unpublished doctoral dissertation, New York University, New York.

Rast, L. R. (1964). A survey and evaluation of piano requirements for students enrolled in programs of teacher-training in elementary education at selected colleges and universities in the state of Illinois. Unpublished doctoral dissertation, Northwestern University, Evanston.

Rhea, T. L. (1972). The evolution of electronic musical instruments in the United States. Unpublished doctoral dissertation, Peabody Conservatory. Baltimore.

Richards, W. H. (1962). Trends of piano class instruction, 1815–1962. Unpublished doctoral dissertation, University of Missouri, Columbia.

Ristad, E. (1982). *A soprano on her head.* Boulder: Myklas.

Roberson, S. (1985). Lili Kraus: The person, the performer, and the teacher. Unpublished doctoral dissertation, University of Oklahoma, Norman.

Robinson, R. E. (1969). A history of the Peabody Conservatory of Music. Unpublished doctoral dissertation, Indiana University, Bloomington.

Roeder, C. (1941). *Liberation and deliberation in piano technique.* New York: Schroeder & Gunther.

Rosenthal, E. (1989, October/November). The Alexander Technique: What it is and how it works. *American Music Teacher, 39*(2).

Sabry, H. (1965). The adaptation of class piano methods as used in the United States of American for use in the Egyptian educational system. Unpublished doctoral dissertation, Indiana University, Bloomington.

Sándor, G. (1981). *On playing piano.* New York: Schirmer Books.

Sargeant, W. (1963, June). The leaves of a tree. *The New Yorker, 38*(47), 52.

Schelling, E., McConathy, O., Haake, C. J., and Haake, G. (1928). *Oxford piano course.* New York: Oxford University Press.

Schelling, E., McConathy, O., Haake, C. J., and Haake, G. (1929). *Oxford piano course: Teacher's first manual.* New York: Oxford University Press.

Schultz, A. (1936). *The riddle of the pianist's finger and its relationship to a touch-scheme.* New York: Carl Fischer.

Scott, C. (1987). Introduction to the ISME Seminar: Reaching the young child through music. *International Music Education, 14,* 11–20.

Scott, C. (1989). How children grow—musically. *Music Educators Journal,* 28–31.

Skyrm, R. D. (1962). Oberlin Conservatory: A century of musical growth and influence. Unpublished doctoral dissertation, University of Southern California, Los Angeles.

Taylor, K. (1981). *Principles of piano technique and interpretation.* London: Novello.

Thompson, J. (1936). *Teaching little fingers to play.* Cincinnati: Willis Music.

Uszler, M., Bognar, A., Camp, M., Johnson, D., Lancaster, E. L., Larimer, F., Lyke, J., Maris, B., Miller, M. (1982–85). A survey of American beginning keyboard methods [reviews of ten different methods]. *The Piano Quarterly,* 120–128.

Uszler, M., Gordon, S., Mach, E. (1991). *The well-tempered keyboard teacher.* New York: Schirmer Books.

Uszler, M., and Larimer, F. (1984, 1986). *The piano pedagogy major in the college curriculum. Part I: The undergraduate piano pedagogy major; Part II: The graduate piano pedagogy major.* Princeton: National Conference on Piano Pedagogy.

Wagner, E. (1968). Raymond Burrows and his contributions to music education. Unpublished doctoral dissertation, University of Southern California, Los Angeles.

Whiteside, A. (1961). *Indispensables of piano playing* (2nd ed.). New York: Scribner.

Williams, J. (1925). *Very first piano book.* Boston: Boston Music Co.

Wilson, F. R. (1986). *Tone deaf and all thumbs?* New York: Viking Penguin.

Young, B. G. (1990). The use of keyboard and computer technology in selected independent piano studios. Unpublished doctoral dissertation, University of Oklahoma, Norman.

RESEARCH ON THE TEACHING
OF ELEMENTARY GENERAL MUSIC

Betty W. Atterbury

UNIVERSITY OF SOUTHERN MAINE

Music education for children in grades 1 through 6 has been influenced by many diverse factors throughout our nation's history. The singing schools of the colonists, the Pestalozzian schools concept imported from Europe, and the advocacy efforts of Lowell Mason with the Boston School Committee shaped the beginning of elementary school music. In the years following Mason's historic breakthrough, public school music teaching spread throughout the country; eventually methods that promoted more active learner involvement and curricula emphasizing all facets of music replaced the earlier emphasis on reading and singing and on rote teaching techniques. Three important influences on teaching and learning in elementary general music are discussed here: conceptual curricula organization, developmental child psychology and instructional activities. These are the selection markers for the exemplary research discussed in this chapter.

First, the influence of a seminal text, *The Study of Music in the Elementary School—A Conceptual Approach* (Gary, 1967), is recognized by members of the profession as profound. The compilers of this text proposed (1) that music curricula should be based on the structure of music and (2) that musical concepts (see also Leonhard and House, 1959; Woodruff, 1970) could be taught to children in an intellectually honest manner. These theses had an important influence on the writers of subsequent series textbooks, and these texts often serve as a substitute for independent curriculum development by elementary music teachers. The first portion of this chapter will offer a description of exemplary research on how children learn musical concepts. It will be obvious that some musical concepts have enjoyed greater attention in the research literature than others.

Second, the influence of child psychology on music teaching and learning is noteworthy. The structure of elementary music curricula can be easily traced to Jerome Bru-

ner. In addition, the theories of Jean Piaget and other developmentalists have contributed to the emphasis on concrete experiences and the activity approach in elementary music, as well as to a differentiation of teaching approaches at successive grade levels. Research into the possibility that developmental levels exist in music-learning ability will be covered in the second section of this chapter.

The third major influence in elementary music instruction is the impact of several individuals in relation to classroom experiences (singing, moving, listening, playing). In the decades following the 1960s there has been an inclusion of experiences for children based on the approaches of Carl Orff, Zoltan Kodály, Emile Jaques-Dalcroze, and most recently Edwin Gordon. While many teachers rely exclusively on one of these approaches, many others use a combination of these methods, incorporating the strengths of each (Carder, 1990). The final section describes selected research into some of these activities and approaches.

MUSICAL CONCEPTS

Multiple Concepts

Only one report of research with elementary children focuses on more than one musical concept. In one of the federally supported research projects of the 1960s, Andrews and Diehl (1967) investigated conceptual understanding of pitch, duration, and loudness of fourth-graders. They developed three types of evaluation: written (including both a verbal and a listening measure), manipulative (playing), and overt (movement). The written tests were administered to 429 fourth-graders in 12 different school districts, and the individual measures were administered to a random selection of 214 of these subjects. The researchers' primary focus was the development of tests, but their findings indicated that children in fourth grade could indeed demonstrate an understanding of these three musical concepts.

Rhythm

Rhythm Reading Several researchers have investigated the efficacy of an approach to teaching rhythm reading that includes a simultaneous speech cue. Palmer (1974) compared the approaches of Gordon (1971) and Richards (1964) in a 5 month experiment with fourth-graders. The number of subjects (n = 136), the amount of time (5 months—three times a week), and the use of a standardized pre- and posttest (*Music Achievement Test,* Colwell, 1970) in addition to a pretest of music aptitude (*Music Aptitude Profile,* Gordon, 1965) used as a covariance measure, are notable strengths of the study. Palmer found that, although there was no difference between the Gordon and Richards approaches, there was a significant difference in rhythm-reading achievement between the two experimental groups and the control group. One concern is that the researcher did not also teach the control classes.

Colley (1987) compared the effect of three methods of rhythm reading: those of Kodály and Gordon and an experimenter-designed word method. Strengths of the study include the use of the three contrasting spoken cues with the same rhythm patterns, number of subjects (*n* = 160), and experimenter instruction for eight experimental and control classes of second-and third-graders. However, the experiment included only nine 35-minute weekly lessons. The researcher's finding that the spoken rhythm reading of the two classes that learned the word approach was superior may be related to the ability of second-and third-grade children to remember words more easily than meaningless syllables.

The importance of carefully selecting the age of one's subjects for such short-term research is supported by the findings of Shehan (1987), who tested the short-term retention of rhythmic patterns. The researcher presented rhythms visually and aurally with and without a mnemonic cue to second-and sixth-graders. The younger students in the study required more than twice the time of older subjects to master the eight-beat rhythm patterns.

Effect of Tempo A substantive body of research has been conducted to determine the effect of tempi on listening to music. A series of studies by LeBlanc and others (LeBlanc, 1981; LeBlanc and Cote 1983; LeBlanc and McCrary, 1983) offer conclusions that fifth- and sixth-graders prefer music with a fast tempo. In one project (LeBlanc and McCrary, 1983) the listening examples were from one style, jazz, and one performing medium, instrumental. A listening test that contained examples representing four different tempi was administered to 163 students in fifth and sixth grades. The results indicate that with each increase in tempo there was a similar (and close to linear) increase in preference. The instructional implication offered by LeBlanc is that when teachers introduce a new genre of music to students in these grades, the initial examples should be with a fast tempo.

Tempo preference in younger children has also been explored. Sims (1987) employed a pictographic response to indicate "like," "no preference," or "dislike" with children from nursery school age through grade 4. Preference for fast tempi (in the piano music of Mozart and Beethoven) was apparent by fourth grade, and the third-graders seemed to be in a transitional stage in their preference (see also Baker, 1977; Flowers, 1988).

Rhythmic Understanding and Symbolic Representation
Bamberger (1982) suggests that once human beings have internalized the music notional system, they experience a "wipe out phenomenon." They are no longer able to think about rhythm in isolation, in the way young children do. In an attempt to probe these cognitive differences, she has researched the ways children represent rhythms. Subjects were asked to first reproduce a rhythm and then notate the sounds so they and others could later reproduce the sound from the drawing. Bamberger suggests that children's representations of rhythm occur in categories she describes as (1) figural, an attempt to translate the experience of movement or action into shapes, and (2) metric, a representation of time duration (see Figure 42–1).

Bamberger's conclusions are based on data from two studies. One was a pilot study with 25 children 8 to 9 years old, and the second included 186 children aged 4 to 12. Al-

Musical Notation

Figural Representation

Metric Representation

FIGURE 42–1. Contrasting Representations of Rhythm, Bamberger (1982)

though her research design does not control for the confounding variables of music education, intelligence, memory, or musical aptitude, she offers an approach to determining children's rhythmic understanding that contrasts with the perception and performance focus of previous rhythm research. Subsequent researchers have explored this hypothesis, and their work is summarized below under "Developmental Levels."

Pitch

There is scant research in the teaching and learning of pitch reading. In one germane report (Klemish, 1968), the researcher taught first-grade children to read pitch either from graphic representation or from conventional music staff and note heads. Strengths of the study include time and investigator involvement. The research design contains two matters of concern. First, differences between the pretest scores of the two groups were not treated statistically in the comparison with posttest scores. Second, there was a relatively short transition time from graphic to traditional notation (2 weeks) for the second group, and the posttest used traditional notation. This amount of time could have been inadequate for young children to assimilate traditional notation and may account for the researcher's finding that the differences in pitch reading tended to favor the first method (traditional notation). Of particular interest is the finding that following this period of instruction, first-grade children could actually sight sing familiar and new pitch patterns such as found in Figure 42–2.

The tradition of research on the teaching of register, direction, contour, timbre, form, dynamics, and harmony is limited in music education. Each of these topics represents a rich area for investigation by future researchers.

DEVELOPMENTAL LEVELS

The research summarized in this section is based on cognitive, stage-developmental theory in the field of psychology and an assumption that children develop musically in a parallel manner through elementary school years. However, the studies summarized here must be considered with caution.

FIGURE 42–2. Examples of Pitch Patterns from Klemish (1968)

All findings of improvement in various musical tasks by age are confounded by uncontrollable variables in educational research, including the influence of home environment, private and school music instruction, and the development of memory and attention with age.

One of the most important studies was conducted by Petzold (1966), who investigated the auditory perception of musical sounds by children in grades 1 to 6. He tested an impressive number of subjects ($n = 509$) annually during a 5-year period, using a test of 45 tonal patterns. Aural perception was measured through a sung response. The performance of all subjects improved at a fairly uniform rate, although at least a 2-year interval was necessary to produce significant differences between grade levels.

In addition, Petzold investigated the perception of timbre, harmonic accompaniment, and rhythmic production in single-year studies. The timbre and harmony tests were constructed with the same 45 pitch patterns. In the timbre study the contrasting sounds were piano, flute, violin, and voice. The data analysis for 500 children in all six grades indicated significant increases at 2-year intervals. In the harmony study the three accompaniments were (1) single chord, (2) three-chord progression, and (3) different chord for each tone. There was a noticeable improvement between grades 1 and 2, and then 2-year intervals were again evident in the 360 subjects. The rhythm test contained 30 examples in three meters (2/4, 3/4, 6/8, and children responded to the melodic rhythm by tapping or singing. In this test, the researcher did not report a developmental progression but rather a finding that the ability to respond rhythmically was attained by second grade.

The study is recommended to readers as a significant contribution to the research literature in elementary music. Each of the tests used was piloted several times, and the report contains a rich array of descriptive data concerning construction as well as results.

The fact that auditory musical perception was judged primarily by sung responses is of some concern, however. The variable of accurate use of the singing voice was not addressed by the researcher. Therefore, the developmental changes documented in this study may be confounded by the factor of vocal control.

A study that directly relates music education research to developmental psychology was reported by Zimmerman and Sechrest (1968). Their tasks were designed to measure musical conservation; they attempted to translate Piaget's conservation experiments with volume and weight into an equivalent set of auditory tasks. Zimmerman and Sechrest administered five different experiments to a large number of subjects ($n = 679$) and reported progressively better responses throughout successive grades. Readers should note that the conservation response demanded by these musical tasks was highly dependent on memory. A critique of this and subsequent Piagetian-labeled research can be found in Serafine (1980).

The findings of the above major studies suggest that developmental levels exist; later researchers continue to test this hypothesis. Although a number of studies do support the development hypothesis, there is no replication of tasks or approaches in the literature, making it impossible to compare and generalize findings.

Three researchers have reported linear improvement in tasks that require children to listen and respond, in various ways, to musical changes. Taebel (1972) tested 260 children in kindergarten, first grade, and second grade for their ability to discriminate successive positive and negative examples of change in dynamics, tempo, register, and duration. Hufstader (1977) constructed a listening test that included alterations of timbre, rhythm, pitch, or harmony in the same musical excerpts. This test was administered to 596 children in the first, third, fifth, and seventh grades. In 1984 O'Hearn individually tested 108 children in grades 1, 3, and 5 to determine their ability to discriminate changes of timbre, dynamics, pitch, and duration. Each of these studies offers support for a developmental music-listening ability.

Other research exists that supports a developmental view. Two massive studies by Thackray (1972, 1973) in England—one of rhythmic ability, and the other of harmonic perception—indicate linear improvement in both these areas of musicality from age 8 to 15 (see also Serafine, 1975).

Two researchers have extended the rhythmic representation work of Bamberger. Hildebrandt (1985) individually tested children in kindergarten, grade 2, and grade 5 with tasks that required children to represent rhythm patterns in four different media: with drawings, numbers, circles of two sizes, and a mechanical toy. She reported significant differences between kindergartners' and second-graders' representations for all four simple rhythms. However, differences between second- and fifth-graders' representations were evident for only two rhythms on one task. Upitis (1985) focused on a more complex view of rhythm, including pulse, rhythm pattern, and meter, and reported that children's accuracy in representing and reading rhythms increased with age (7–12).

Findings of developmental differences are also reported by Serafine (1988) in her study of children aged 5, 6, 8, 10, and 11, and adults. Serafine's work is posited on the thesis that music cognition is the activity of thinking in or with sound; that is, how we think about music is what matters as opposed to the perception of specific musical concepts such as pitch, duration, and rhythm. Serafine suggests that the most important characteristic of music is that it moves through time, and therefore an individual's ability to cognitively organize successive and simultaneous musical events is the basis for all musical activity. To probe this hypothesis, she designed 16 tasks that she administered individually to approximately 15 subjects at each age. Instructions were worded appropriately for the age level. Her findings indicate that 10- and 11-year-olds could succeed on the tasks she presented, while 8-year-olds performed as well as these older subjects on only three tasks. The youngest children, while possessing almost none of the processes necessary to complete the tasks, did show signs of emerging understanding. An unexpected decline at age 11 led Serafine to hypothesize that decrements in some types of musical cognition may be necessary for gains to occur in others. This thesis and experimental approach seem worthy of replication and expansion.

The area of children's singing voice development is one in which a substantial body of research exists and fairly definite conclusions can be reached (see also Davidson, McKernon, and Gardner, 1981, for a discussion of the acquisition of song). Two studies from the 1930s (Hattwick, 1933; Jersild and Bienstock, 1934) contain findings of the existence of an expansion of singing range by successive ages. Hattwick tested 95 children from preschool through second grade to determine the average range of the songs that individual subjects selected to sing. Jersild and Bienstock tested over four hundred children to determine the musical pitches they could sing. Two longitudinal studies of vocal range development (Wilson, 1970; Wassum, 1979) also include descriptions of a linear improvement in vocal range.

These generalized findings of developmental levels in singing do not imply the absence of individual differences in rate of development. Indeed, in Wilson's study there were three sets of twins among the subjects for whom the variables of home experience and music instruction were automatically controlled; differences in the rate of vocal development were found in each pair of twins.

An important aspect of all evaluation, whether for research or instructional purposes, is the mode of response. Studies in which young children are asked to respond to musical change with accurate musical terms must be critically evaluated—indeed, two of the reports described above (Andrews and Diehl, 1967; Zimmerman and Sechrest, 1968) contain cautions regarding the extent of their subjects' musical vocabulary. An excellent discussion of this topic is provided by Hair (1987).

INSTRUCTIONAL ACTIVITIES

Music classes often appear quite different from other types of elementary instruction because children are continuously involved in group music producing through singing, listening, moving, and playing classroom instruments. A research topic noted by Forsythe (1977) is whether such active involvement actually results in greater musical learning.

Singing

Several facets of instruction in singing have been probed by researchers, including harmonic accompaniment, the effect of text, breath control instruction, intervention, and contrasting vocal models. Findings regarding the effect of harmonic accompaniment on children's singing are rare but worthy of consideration. Petzold's subjects (Petzold, 1966) were evaluated on their ability to sing 10 melodic patterns with three different harmonic accompaniments (a single chord, a simple three-chord progression, or a different chord for each tone of the pattern). He reported significant differences irrespective of harmonic accompaniment between the scores of the first-graders and all other subjects (grades 2–6). As with so many studies in this field, it is not clear if these findings are the result of instruction or maturation.

Sterling (1984) reported differences in the singing of familiar melodies by subjects in grades 1, 3, 5, and 7 with no harmonic accompaniment and traditional tonal accompaniment. Stauffer (1985) taught first-, second-, and third-graders and included melodic echo training with and without harmonic accompaniment. The researcher reported that the first- and second-grade groups that received the no-harmony treatments scored higher than the groups that were taught the melodic echoes accompanied by harmonic background.

The effect of text has been investigated by two researchers. Goetze (1985) tested the ability of children ($n = 165$) to sing a researcher-taught unison song in groups of three and individually, using text and the syllable "loo." The youngest subjects sang more accurately without text, but this finding may be attributable to memory differences between kindergartners and children in grades 1 and 3. Levinowitz (1987) explored Goetze's finding in a year-long instructional setting with three kindergarten and three first-grade classes. At each level instruction varied as follows: (1) songs taught primarily with words, (2) songs taught primarily without words, (3) songs taught only with words. She reported no significant effects for type of treatment. A second finding of Goetze, that her 165 subjects sang more accurately individually than with others, is intriguing.

Pedagogical aspects can also influence singing development. Phillips (1983) included breath control exercises in 18 weeks of instruction for second-, third-, and fourth-graders and reported significant changes in vocal range and pitch accuracy at the end of the experiment. Welch (1985) indicated that intervention, in the form of knowledge of results, had a significant effect on children's singing. Green (1987) evaluated the responses of 282 children in grades 1 to 6, to a child, female adult, and male adult singing model and reported more correct responses to the child and female voices than to the male voice. Studies by Montgomery (1988) and Small and McCachern (1983) also contain suggestions that there may be a negative effect when a male vocal model is used in teaching young children.

Listening

Three studies, although they are not methodological in nature, seem to have important implications for method and materials as well as future research. O'Hearn (1984) reported that subjects in grades 1, 3, and 5 recognized changes in familiar music ("Twinkle, Twinkle, Little Star") significantly more than changes in unfamiliar music. The approach taken in this study is particularly recommended for consideration in future work since the children were not required to remember and compare musical examples. Rather, they responded to change by pressing a buzzer in real time during the listening process.

A learning sequence for musical elements has been suggested by Hufstader (1977) based on the results of his listening test, administered to almost 600 children in grades 1, 3, 5, and 7. Ordering of the musical concepts of timbre, rhythm, melodic pitch pattern, and harmony was based on the results

of a task where subjects compared two selections as being the same or not the same. For first-graders, only the category of timbre produced scores higher than chance. These findings must be considered with caution because of the written test format.

Also germane to this topic is a report by Hair (1982), who investigated different combinations of modalities as well as single-modality approaches to discriminating musical direction. The task contained sets of two, three, or four synthesized tones, followed by a similar or contrasting stationary or moving visual representation, or another set of aural stimuli. The 102 subjects in grades 1 through 4 all scored higher on the task with no visual representation. Although the research task is not completely analogous to classroom instruction in listening to music, the results are worthy of consideration because of the inclusion of visual illustrations of listening selections (e.g., listening maps, icons) in music textbooks for children and because Hair reports that the most difficult task for her subjects was associating tonal direction with stationary visual images.

Moving

Both the Dalcroze and the Orff methods stress the importance of physical response to music. In a research study with three groups of children (physically handicapped with normal intelligence, low intelligence, and nonhandicapped), Moog (1979) reported that the physically handicapped children had limitations in their rhythmic perception nearly to the extent of those with low intelligence. Lack of movement experience was a factor contributing to poorer rhythmic perception, a finding worthy of consideration by researchers and practitioners.

Cheek (1979) taught two groups of fourth-graders the same music, but included movement (systematic psychomotor experiences including creative movement, body rhythms, and hand gestures) in only one group. Her findings support the notion that instructional strategies that include movement are valuable, especially when done on a consistent basis. Of a similar nature is Moore's report (1984) of improvement in rhythmic aptitude by second- and third-graders after instruction that incorporated movement and rhythm exercises based on the Orff and Weikart (1982) approaches.

Organized Approaches

Considering the vast popularity that three specific approaches—Orff-Schulwerk, Kodály, and Dalcroze—enjoy with many general music teachers, supporting evidence of the validity of these methods should be readily available. However, there is a dearth of substantial research exploring any one of these approaches. Some findings that tend to support the effectiveness of the Kodály approach are found in Zemke (1973), and Dalcroze is studied in Crumpler (1982) and Joseph (1982). However, the results of this and similar work are inconclusive at best. The claims of superiority of each approach still await objective substantiation.

One other approach in general music that has numerous supporters is the sequential teaching of pitch and rhythmic patterns advocated by Gordon (1984). Gordon's influence is apparent in a spate of research reports using either his sequence of patterns or his *Primary Measures of Music Audiation* (1979). Jarjisian (1981) investigated the effects of pitch pattern instruction using diatonic, pentatonic, or a combination of both patterns with first-graders. She found that children who received instruction with the combination of patterns performed rote songs significantly better than those in the other two groups. This finding suggests to Jarjisian that the use of solely pentatonic (Orff-Schulwerk and Kodály) or solely diatonic (Gordon) materials provides less adequate foundation for the development of rote singing ability than the use of both. Her study did not include a control group. However, a study by Feierabend (1984) did include a control group, and his findings are of interest. After 7 weeks of daily instruction (5 minutes) in singing major tonic and dominant patterns on a neutral syllable, the control group of first-graders who had no pitch pattern training had greater gains between a pretest and a posttest. Considering the brief amount of instructional time for music in most schools, the efficacy of drilling on repeated tonal and rhythmic patterns should be carefully considered.

CONCLUSION

The research studies described above contain valid conclusions that should be considered in the development of future teaching materials as well as by classroom practitioners. Elementary children are indeed able to understand musical concepts, and the findings of Andrews and Diehl (1967) support this statement. The finding of Palmer (1974) that children read rhythms better with a verbal cue as well as the findings of LeBlanc and others (1981, 1983) that older children prefer faster tempi should be considered most carefully by practitioners. The differences between the younger and older subjects on the musical tasks of O'Hearn (1984) and Serafine (1988) clearly suggest that from kindergarten through sixth grade the ways in which children hear and learn music change. And the findings of a successively wider

singing range in children by Jersild and Bienstock (1934) and others suggest the careful consideration of much of the song material presently available for children.

Implications for directions for future research have been noted throughout this chapter. There is a need for researchers to compare and evaluate instruction in elementary general music, including ways of teaching individual musical concepts, singing and listening skills, strategies that incorporate multiple modalities, and the efficacy of the major approaches, such as those based on the thinking of Orff, Kodály, Dalcroze. Also awaiting exploration is the development of effective methods of evaluation for general music and the question of whether the "activity" approach is the best type of musical education for youngsters. The hypotheses of Serafine that music cognition is not the same as music perception, and of Bamberger that children's rhythmic understanding is apparent through symbolic representation, are also worthy of serious consideration by music education researchers.

Readers will note the lack of many longitudinal research reports in this summary. Because so much of music education research is the result of doctoral dissertations, it is recommended that cluster research be done by future doctoral students, each researcher focusing on one aspect of an area in which the doctoral adviser is expert. In this way it might indeed be possible for shorter-term research to contain applicability to daily music education practice.

Finally, an important way for the profession to accumulate valid research results about contrasting teaching practices will be through serious attempts to incorporate into the research community those professionals who daily interact with children. Approaches to the research enterprise that encourage active practitioners to engage in qualitative and quantitative research—perhaps as members of a select team—will yield far more relevant and meaningful findings than is currently the case.

The focus of this chapter has been to describe exemplary research in selected aspects of elementary general music. It does not represent, in any way, an inclusive summary of extant research in elementary general music. Readers are directed to other chapters of this *Handbook* for information on additional topics pertinent to elementary music instruction including creative and critical thinking, exceptional learners, music reading, music preference, philosophy, methodology, and curriculum.

References

Andrews, F. M., and Deihl, N. C. (1967). *Development of a technique for identifying elementary school children's music concepts.* Cooperative Research Project No. 5-0233. University Park: The Pennsylvania State University.

Baker, D. S. (1977). The effect of appropriate and inappropriate in-class performance models on performance preference of third and fourth grade students. Unpublished doctoral dissertation, University of Maryland, College Park.

Bamberger, J. (1982). Revisiting children's drawings of simple rhythms: A function for reflection-in-action. In S. Strauss (Ed.), *U-shaped behavioral growth* (pp. 191–226). New York: Academic Press.

Carder, P. (Ed.). (1990). *The eclectic curriculum in American music education.* Reston: Music Educators National Conference.

Cheek, Y. (1979). The effects of psychomotor experiences on the perception of selected musical elements and the formation of self-concept in fourth grade. Unpublished doctoral dissertation, University of Michigan, Ann Arbor.

Colley, B. (1987). A comparison of syllabic methods for improving rhythm literacy. *Journal of Research in Music Education, 35,* 221–225.

Colwell, R. (1970). *Music Achievement Tests.* Chicago: Follett Educational Corporation.

Crumpler, S. E. (1982). The effect of Dalcroze eurhythmics on the melodic musical growth of first grade students. Unpublished doctoral dissertation, Louisiana State University and Agricultural and Mechanical College, Baton Rouge.

Davidson, L., McKernon, P., and Gardner, H. E. (1981). The acquisition of song: A developmental approach. *Documentary report of the Ann Arbor symposium* (pp. 301–314). Reston: Music Educators National Conference.

Feierabend, J. M. (1984). The effects of specific tonal pattern training on singing and aural discrimination abilities of first grade children. Unpublished doctoral dissertation, Temple University, Philadelphia.

Flowers, P. J. (1988). The effects of teaching and learning experiences, tempo, and mode and undergraduates and children's symphonic music preferences. *Journal of Research in Music Education, 36,* 19–34.

Forsythe, J. L. (1977). Elementary student attending behavior as a function of classroom activities. *Journal of Research in Music Education, 25,* 228–239.

Gary, C. (Ed.). (1967). *The study of MUSIC in the elementary school: A conceptual approach.* Washington: Music Educators National Conference.

Goetze, M. (1985). Factors affecting accuracy in children's singing. Unpublished doctoral dissertation, University of Colorado, Boulder.

Gordon, E. E. (1965). *Musical Aptitude Profile.* Chicago: G.I.A. Publications.

Gordon, E. E. (1979). *Primary Measures of Music Audiation.* Chicago: G.I.A. Publications.

Gordon, E. E. (1971). *The psychology of music teaching.* Englewood Cliffs: Prentice-Hall.

Gordon, E. E. (1984). *Learning sequences in music: Skill, content, and patterns.* Chicago: G.I.A. Publications.

Green, G. (1987). The effect of vocal modeling on pitch-matching accuracy of children in grades one through six. Unpublished doctoral dissertation, Louisiana State University and Agricultural and Mechanical College, Baton Rouge.

Hair, H. (1982). Microcomputer tests of aural and visual direction patterns. *Psychology of Music, 10,* 26–31.

Hair, H. (1987). Children's responses to music stimuli: Verbal/nonverbal, aural/visual modes. In C. Madsen, and C. Prickett (Eds.), *Applications of research in music behavior* (pp. 59–70). Tuscaloosa: The University of Alabama Press.

Hattwick, M. (1933). The role of pitch level and pitch range in the singing of preschool, first grade and second grade children. *Child Development, 4,* 281–191.

Hildebrandt, C. (1985). A developmental study of children's representations of simple rhythms. Unpublished doctoral dissertation, University of California, Berkeley.

Hufstader, R. A. (1977). An investigation of a learning sequence of music listening skills. *Journal of Research in Music Education, 25,* 184–196.

Jarjisian, C. (1981). The effects of pentatonic and/or diatonic pattern instruction on the rote singing achievement of young children. Unpublished doctoral dissertation, Temple University, Philadelphia.

Jersild, A. T., and Bienstock, S. F. (1934). A study of the development of children's ability to sing. *The Journal of Educational Psychology, 25,* 481–503.

Joseph, A. S. (1982). A Dalcroze eurhythmics approach to music learning in kindergarten through rhythm movement, ear-training and improvisation. Unpublished doctoral dissertation, Carnegie-Mellon University, Pittsburgh.

Klemish, J. (1968). A comparative study of two methods of teaching music reading to first grade children by developing a vocabulary of tonal patterns. Unpublished doctoral dissertation, University of Wisconsin, Madison.

LeBlanc, A. (1981). Effects of style, tempo, and performing medium on children's music preference. *Journal of Research in Music Education, 29,* 143–156.

LeBlanc, A., and Cote, R. (1983). Effects of tempo and performing medium on children's music preference. *Journal of Research in Music Education, 31,* 57–66.

LeBlanc, A., and McCrary, (1983). Effect of tempo on children's music preference. *Journal of Research in Music Education, 31,* 283–294.

Leonhard, C., and House, R. W. (1959). *Foundations and principles of music education.* New York: McGraw-Hill.

Levinowitz, L. M. (1987). An experimental study of the comparative effects of singing songs with words and without words on children in kindergarten and first grade. Unpublished doctoral dissertation, Temple University, Philadelphia.

Montgomery, T. D. (1988). A study of the associations between two means of vocal modeling by a male music teacher and third-grade students' vocal accuracy in singing pitch patterns. Unpublished doctoral dissertation, University of North Carolina, Greensboro.

Moog, H. (1979). On the perception of rhythmic forms by physically handicapped children and those of low intelligence in comparison with non-handicapped children. *Bulletin of the Council for Research in Music Education, 59,* 73–78.

Moore, J. L. S. (1984). Rhythm and movement: An objective analysis of their association with music aptitude. Unpublished doctoral dissertation, University of North Carolina, Greensboro.

O'Hearn, R. (1984). An investigation of the response to change in music events by children in grades one, three and five. Unpublished doctoral dissertation, University of Wisconsin, Madison.

Palmer, M. (1974). The relative effectiveness of the Richards and Gordon approaches to rhythmic reading for fourth grade students. Unpublished doctoral dissertation, University of Illinois, Urbana.

Petzold, R. (1966). *Auditory perception of musical sounds by children in the first six grades.* Washington: U.S. Department of Health, Education and Welfare, Cooperative Research Project No. 1051.

Phillips, K. H. (1983). The effects of group breath control training on selected vocal measures related to the singing ability of elementary students in grades two, three and four. Unpublished doctoral dissertation, Kent State University, Kent.

Richards, M. H. (1964). *Threshold to music.* Belmont: Fearon Publishers.

Serafine, M. L. (1975). A measure of meter conservation in music, based on Piaget's theory. Unpublished doctoral dissertation, University of Florida, Gainsville.

Serafine, M. L. (1980). Piagetian research in music. *Journal of Research in Music Education, 62,* 1–21.

Serafine, M. L. (1988). *Music as cognition: The development of thought in sound.* New York: Columbia University Press.

Shehan, P. K. (1987). Effects of rote versus note presentations on rhythm learning and retention. *Journal of Research in Music Education, 35,* 117–126.

Sims, W. L. (1987). Effects of tempo on music preference of preschool through fourth-grade children. C. Madsen and C. Prickett

(Eds.), *Applications of research in music behavior*, (pp. 15–25). Tuscaloosa: The University of Alabama Press.

Small, A. R., and McCachern, F. L. (1983). The effect of male and female vocal modeling on pitch-matching accuracy of first-grade children. *Journal of Research in Music Education, 31*, 227–234.

Stauffer, S. L. (1985). An investigation of the effects of melodic and harmonic context on the development of singing ability in primary grade children. Unpublished doctoral dissertation, University of Michigan, Ann Arbor.

Sterling, P. A. (1984). A developmental study of the effects of accompanying harmonic context on children's vocal pitch accuracy of familiar melodies. Unpublished doctoral dissertation, University of Miami, Coral Gables.

Taebel, D. K. (1972). The effect of various instructional modes on children's performance of music concept tasks. Unpublished doctoral dissertation, University of Southern California, Los Angeles.

Thackray, R. (1972). *Rhythmic abilities in children.* London: Novello.

Thackray, R. (1973). Tests of harmonic perception. *Psychology of Music, 1,* 49–57.

Upitis, R. B. (1985). Children's understanding of rhythm: The relationship between development and musical training. Unpublished doctoral dissertation, Harvard University, Cambridge.

Wassum, S. (1979). Elementary school children's vocal range. *Journal of Research in Music Education, 27,* 214–226.

Weikart, P. (1982). *Teaching movement and dance.* Ypsilanti: High Scope Press.

Welch, G. (1985). Variability of practice and knowledge of results as factors in learning to sing in tune. *Bulletin of the Council for Research in Music Education, 85,* 238–247.

Wilson D. S. (1970). A study of the child voice from six to twelve. Unpublished doctoral dissertation, University of Oregon, Eugene.

Woodruff, A. D. (1970). How music concepts are developed. *Music Educators Journal 56,* 51–54.

Zemke, S. L. (1973). The Kodály method and a comparison of the effects of a Kodály-adapted music instruction sequence and a more typical sequence, on auditory musical achievement in fourth grade students. Unpublished doctoral dissertation, University of Southern California, Los Angeles.

Zimmerman, M. P., and Sechrest, L. (1968). *How children conceptually organize musical sounds.* Evanston: Northwestern University. (Department of H.E.W. Office of Education Report No. 6-10-285).

·43·

RESEARCH ON TEACHING JUNIOR HIGH AND MIDDLE SCHOOL GENERAL MUSIC

Patricia E. Sink

UNIVERSITY OF NORTH CAROLINA AT GREENSBORO

Junior high and middle schools provide students, between 11 and 15 years of age, access to the world's rich and varied heritage of information of which music is a part. Melton (1990) maintains that junior high or middle school education is the most important level of education, during which time lifelong values are formed. This belief may inspire intense debate; yet research supports that adolescent music preferences, for example, are recapitulated during the senior years of life (e.g., Gibbons, 1977). Music behaviors, stabilized and changed during adolescence, strongly influence desires and directions for continued music learning and participation as a consumer, composer, and performer.

Frequently, junior high or middle school music instruction is divided between two instructional tracks (Music Educators National Conference, 1986). One track focuses on music as an avocation and encourages classroom experiences in music; the other track emphasizes music as a vocation and is dominated by performance education. The vast majority of adolescent students choose to study music avocationally and are tracked into general music education. Even though the profession urges that general music instruction is an essential part of a child's 12 years of formal education, the sixth-, seventh-, or eighth-grade general music course is often the last formally required music study for the majority of adolescent students (85 percent to 88 percent; Reimer, 1989). These facts highlight the critical importance of effective general music teaching and learning.

General music is a "core" course of study for adolescent students; it is a "nonperforming" music course providing a broad scope of learning experiences to foster development of music literacy and individual music preferences and attitudes. Ultimately, general music study is designed to help students acquire knowledge, skills, and values necessary to

continue music learning and participation as composers, performers, and consumers.

Assimilating research findings relevant to junior high and middle school music teaching and learning is imperative for providing the highest quality and most motivating music instruction possible. In this chapter the past three decades of research on adolescent general music education is analyzed. The purpose of this chapter is to identify and discuss replicated research findings concerning junior high and middle school general music education, and offer recommendations and identify unanswered questions for music teachers and researchers. The chapter is divided into four major sections: "General Music Instruction," "Music Literacy," "Music Preferences and Attitudes," and "Implications for Adolescent General Music Education." Within the first three sections, replicated research findings are highlighted and supportive studies are discussed. Before the first major section is presented, processes the author used to select and review the research are discussed briefly.

Grade Level Organization

Various plans are used in the United States to cluster 12 grades into three different schools or instructional units, including the 6-3-3, 5-3-4, 5-4-3, and 4-4-4 grade-clustering plans (Teske, 1990). The labels "junior high school" and "middle school" usually are used to identify the middle unit of instruction in each plan. One may assume that there are major effects of each grade-clustering plan on adolescent general music teaching and learning, including influences on scheduling and course content. Minimal research, however, exists investigating effects of grade level organization on general music education. Providing a detailed account and description of the impact of this unresolved organizational problem is not within the scope of this chapter, but should be in the minds of teachers and researchers in the coming years.

An examination of the different plans for clustering grades in schools reveals that the middle level of instruction could include students in grades 5 through 9. Regelski (1981) maintains that middle school usually begins and ends with sixth and eighth grades, and junior high school usually begins and ends with seventh and ninth grades. Among the sampled research on general music education, 200 studies involved students between 11 and 15 years of age. Eighty-nine studies (45 percent) *specifically* focused on general music students, teachers, or curricula within a junior high or middle school setting. The remaining studies, 111 or 55 percent, focused on general music teaching and learning involving students between 6 and 18 years of age. Three primary research emphases have recurred throughout the past 30 years; these are 67 studies on general music instruction (33.5 percent), 69 studies on music literacy (34.5 percent), and 64 studies on music preferences and attitudes (32 percent).

Sources of Information

The primary sources of research for this chapter have been music education dissertations and research published in the *Bulletin of the Council for Research in Music Education* and the *Journal of Research on Music Education*. The author has analyzed several characteristics of the reviewed research: (1) research methods, (2) music behaviors examined, (3) subject and/or manipulated variables examined, (4) data collection procedures, (5) statistical treatments of data, (6) decade of the research study, (7) magnitude of emphasis on adolescent students, and (8) findings deduced. To remain within the limitations of a chapter, the author chose to report a general overview of the research summarizing replicated and generalizable findings. Replicated research findings from the primary sources are identified numerically and highlighted, and supporting research studies are discussed.

GENERAL MUSIC INSTRUCTION

This section includes a discussion of replicated research findings in two general areas: (1) evaluating music teacher effectiveness, and (2) using music as a reinforcer for learning in other subject areas. In many of these studies, research methods did not permit generalization of findings beyond the specific samples. Of the studies reviewed, only six general music instruction research studies used empirical methods to analyze teacher effectiveness evaluation procedures (e.g., Taebel, 1990) or to describe characteristics of successful general music teachers (e.g., Curtis, 1986). Five research studies used experimental methods to investigate (1) effects of music instruction or contingent music listening on academic achievement or self-esteem (e.g., Michel and Farrell, 1973),

and (2) effects of listening to different music styles on adolescent students' personality traits (e.g., Fromm, 1981). Only 24 of the 67 general music instruction research studies were conducted in junior high or middle school settings. Four replicated research findings were identified that have implications for junior high and middle school general music education.

1. *Generic evaluations of teacher effectiveness may not be appropriate for measuring music teacher effectiveness.* Taebel (1990) conducted an extensive analysis of 10 broad teaching competencies and numerous subcompetencies to compare music teachers' and nonmusic teachers' performances as measured by a widely used generic teacher effectiveness assessment tool based on a model defined by Hunter (1983). Taebel found that music teachers scored below average on seven of the 10 broad competencies. As a whole, music teachers scored higher than other teachers in using materials and equipment and in eliciting student responses, and lower than other teachers in using various types of questions. Questions were defined as verbal questions. Nonverbal questions, used by many music teachers, were not recognized by the generic assessment tool.

The highest rated competencies for middle school music teachers were using materials and equipment, and monitoring student behaviors, whereas the lowest rated competency was presenting organized instruction. Music teachers generally felt positive about the generic measure of teacher effectiveness, yet they questioned its validity for music teaching. Among 26 music-teaching behaviors analyzed in an earlier study, Taebel and Coker (1980) found that using advance organizers, positive teacher/student interactions, and high time on task produced increases in students' music achievement. A teacher's use of varied teaching methods and student inclass discussions produced favorable attitudes toward music study. Taebel (1990) questioned the value of using the Hunter (1983) model to evaluate music teacher effectiveness.

2. *High teaching intensity and a teacher's knowledge of subject matter interact to positively affect student attention; yet, these factors may not positively affect long-term learning.* Madsen, Standley, and Cassidy (1989) investigated high and low contrasts in teaching intensity as defined by teacher affect and enthusiasm. They found that effective music teaching was defined by a teacher's knowledge of the subject matter, enthusiasm, and sense of timing; and that teaching intensity involves a combination of attributes associated with enthusiasm and timing. Teachers who were perceived as highly intense were enthusiastic and managed class time appropriately.

In a later report, Madsen (1990) identified two basic elements of general music teaching effectiveness: (1) extensive knowledge of subject matter, and (2) effective delivery and sequencing of subject matter. Madsen associated effective subject matter delivery and high teaching enthusiasm with high teaching intensity. Highly intense teaching increased student attention, yet high teaching enthusiasm made little impact on long-term learning.

3. *Two factors that contribute to successful junior high general music teaching are pacing and lecturing.* Curtis

(1986) analyzed behaviors of successful junior high school general music teachers. He developed an assessment tool with two broad categories of behaviors that were labeled "nonverbal" and "verbal." Ten music teachers were identified as successful. Observers noted the amount of time each teacher used eight nonverbal and 11 verbal behaviors across 100 videotape-recorded general music lessons. Successful teachers maintained eye contact with students much of their lesson times (89.76 percent), used their hands frequently (35.74 percent), and moved around the room throughout their lessons (21.82 percent). Two factors were associated with successful general music teaching: *pacing* (eye contact, hand gestures, and positive pacing) and *lecturing* (moving, closed questions, and lecture).

Yarbrough (1975), in a study of choral music teachers, found that students were more responsive to a high magnitude of pacing, eye contact, and closeness. High magnitudes of modulated voice intensities, gesturing, and facial expressions contributed to high student responsiveness, but these qualities failed to contribute to higher choral performance evaluations. As Madsen (1990) explained, a high magnitude of student attention is essential to conveying information; however, such attention does not seem related to long-term music learning.

4. *Music reinforces learning in other subject areas of an educational curriculum.* Three studies were found that experimentally documented the reinforcing value of music with 11- to 15-year-old students. Additionally, numerous accounts were found of music's reinforcing value with young children and young adults in school and therapeutic settings. Madsen and Forsythe (1973) investigated the effects of contingent (earned) music listening on correct responses of sixth-grade students in a middle school. Students were assigned to one of four groups, including three contingent reward groups (i.e., dance plus music listening, music listening only, and math games) and one contact control group. Popular music listening and dance plus popular music listening contingencies evoked significantly higher correct math responses than math games ($p < .05$), but effects of the two music contingencies on correct math responses were not significantly different ($p > .05$). The researchers concluded that popular music listening alone has strong reinforcement value for sixth-grade students' math achievements.

Michel and Farrell (1973) examined music's reinforcing value for increasing self-esteem and socially acceptable behaviors of 10- to 14-year-old boys with behavioral disorders and from culturally disadvantaged homes. An experimental group of students received ukulele instruction; a control group of students received no music instruction. The ukulele group's mean scores on a self-esteem inventory and behavioral rating form significantly increased. Fromm (1981) examined personality traits of adolescent students when exposed to no music, rock music, and classical music. Students were defined as highly compliant or highly noncompliant. Noncompliant students valued independence more while hearing classical music than while hearing no music or hearing rock, and thereby expressed less peer group conformity.

MUSIC LITERACY

During the past 30 years of general music research, numerous music behaviors related to music literacy have been investigated. Researchers have analyzed adolescent students' knowledge of tonal and rhythmic characteristics; skills in reading music symbols, performing with a music instrument or the human singing voice; and music listening and creating. Sixty-nine general music research studies were identified that described adolescent music literacy.

The majority of music literacy research focused on characteristics of music listening behaviors and effects of instructional strategies on aural and aural-visual discrimination skills. Some researchers examined performing and composing skills by describing creative music behaviors and by examining relationships between music listening and performing skills or music reading and performing skills.

During the 1960s, most music literacy research investigated effects of teaching strategies on music listening and/or reading skills. Additionally, descriptions of music cognition and perception evolved from Piaget and Bruner human development theories. A major concern during the late 1960s and throughout the 1970s was the effects of socioeconomic conditions and cultural advantages or disadvantages on adolescent music teaching and learning (e.g., Hill, 1968; Gordon, 1970). Researchers attempted to define the impact of equal educational opportunities on culturally advantaged and disadvantaged students' music achievement as measured by music listening, reading, and instrumental performance skills. Other research interests during the 1970s included (1) music listening sequences associated with rhythmic and tonal characteristics of music (conceptual development), (2) relationships between music performance and perception skills, (3) effects of allied or interdisciplinary arts programs on music listening skills, (4) effects of instructional materials that use popular or youth music on music literacy, and (5) effects of programed music instruction on music literacy. Emphasis on developing music reading skills diminished somewhat during the 1970s, except to the extent that iconic or visual symbols enhanced music-listening skill development.

Generally, research on adolescent students' music literacy decreased somewhat during the 1980s and migrated from analyses of music conservation skills to music problem solving and abstract thinking. During the last few years of the 1980s, position papers reflected a growing concern for junior high and middle school general music education (e.g., Gerber, 1989; 1990), and for music creativity and creative thinking skills (e.g., Webster, 1990).

1. *Music notation enhances junior high and middle school students' aural discrimination skills.* Peterson (1965) investigated effects of music notation on music listening skills developed in elementary and junior high school general music classes. Unlike elementary students, junior high school students made a marked improvement in their ability to recognize variations of melodic themes when they used

music notation. Nelson (1973) also found that music notation of melodic themes enhanced seventh-grade students' abilities to track unfolding music forms. However, improved form-tracking abilities did not improve students' abilities to recognize (label) music forms.

Smith (1973) confirmed Nelson's findings and showed that seventh-grade students could be taught to track an unfolding music form (e.g., minuet). He maintained that form-tracking abilities related to abilities to use music notation and to discriminate aurally presented changes in music elements as a form progressed through time. Hartshorn (1958) provided support for Smith's hypothesis. He explained that form discrimination does not mean determining if the form is a sonata-allegro or theme and variation, but rather recognizing an exact repetition, a variation that is the same melodically with the rhythm changed, or a variation that is the same rhythmically with a different melody.

2. *Programed music instruction is no more or less effective than traditional general music instruction in developing sixth- and seventh-grade students' music listening skills.* Harrison (1974) investigated effects of programed and traditional general music instruction on adolescent students' abilities to aurally discriminate major and minor modes. She provided an experimental group with supplementary programed audiotape recordings in addition to traditional general music instruction. A control group received general music instruction with no supplementary programed materials. Both groups' aural discriminations of mode variations increased, and no noticeable difference between the groups was observed as a result of programed instructional materials. In an earlier study, Kohn (1971) also examined programed music instruction. He investigated the effects of the timing of supplementary programed instruction on students' knowledge of music fundamentals. One group received supplementary materials upon completion of a music fundamentals unit; another group (experimental) received supplementary materials intermittently throughout the unit. He found no statistically significant difference between groups (p > .05); both groups increased their abilities to define music terms and read music symbols.

3. *Use of positive and negative exemplars of music styles facilitates adolescent students' aural discrimination of stylistic concepts of music.* Haack (1972) investigated the effects of positive and negative exemplars of romantic music styles on junior high school students' recognition of romantic music excerpts. He defined positive exemplars as romantic music styles and negative exemplars as nonromantic styles of music. Students who received instruction using both positive and negative exemplars improved their test scores on romantic music recognition 75 percent more than students receiving only positive exemplars. Haack suggested that music teachers should progress from the known to the unknown, first accentuating differences and then similarities in instructional examples of music concepts. Cutietta (1984) also found that adolescent students were able to use positive and negative exemplars to discover specific music concepts functioning across different styles of music.

4. *Visual arts and music instructional materials can be used cooperatively to enhance adolescent students' listening skills.* Haack (1970) examined effects of an allied arts course using both music and visual arts instructional materials on junior high school students' recognition of romantic and classical styles. A control group received only music exemplars of romantic and classical music styles, and an experimental group received both music and visual arts exemplars of the styles. Control and experimental groups improved pretest scores by 33 percent and 51 percent respectively. His findings replicated results from research on allied arts instruction with college-age students (Wehner, 1966). Although numerous interdisciplinary curricula using music have been developed during the past 30 years for adolescent students (e.g., Schneider, 1986), few empirical studies have tested the effectiveness of such curricula.

5. *Tempo, melodic pattern activity, and intervallic relationship organize adolescent students' performances and aural perceptions of melodic-rhythmic patterns in music.* Kuhn and Gates (1975) investigated first- through twelfth-grade students' abilities to clap notated rhythmic excerpts while trying to maintain an established tempo at 90 beats per minute. Students clapped three phrases containing 12 beats of half-note, quarter-note, and eighth-note durations. Of the three phases of beats, quarter note durations were performed at a faster tempo than half-note and eighth-note durations. Across all notated phrases, each student's clapping tempo gradually increased from the beginning to the end of phrases. Petzold's (1969) research also confirmed that elementary children (including sixth-grade students) were more adept at performing fast tempi than slow tempi.

Most research on tempo perception supported that tempo increases were more difficult to perceive than tempo decreases. Mills (1985) analyzed elementary and junior high school students' perceptions of ascending and descending pitches, and tempo increases and decreases. She found that adolescent students attended more to descending pitches and decreasing tempi than to ascending pitches and increasing tempi.

Recent research demonstrated that adolescent students' perceptions of tempo were affected not only by the speed of recurring pulses (tempo), but also by melodic activities within the music patterns being perceived. Kuhn and Booth (1988) examined effects of melodic activity (ornamented and plain melodies) and beat dominance (intensity of metrical beats) on third- and sixth-grade students' perceptions of fast and slow tempi. Melodic activity was the most influential variable affecting students' tempo perceptions; ornamented melodies were perceived as faster than plain melodies. Beat dominance and age did not noticeably affect students' tempo perceptions. Boisen (1981) confirmed this finding, showing that seventh- and ninth-grade students' perceptions of the completeness and incompleteness of rhythmic phrases were influenced by the melodic context of the rhythmic phrases.

Tillotson (1972) investigated fifth and seventh grade students' aural-visual discrimination skills and pitchmatching acuity while perceiving and singing intervals in melodic contexts and in isolation. Students most accurately perceived intervals in isolation, and most accurately performed intervals in melodic contexts. Small intervals (minor and major seconds and thirds) were performed and perceived most accurately. Even though a clear link between music perception and performance skills was not defined by the reviewed research, tempo, melodic activity, and intervallic relationships seem to organize both skills.

6. *Adolescent students can use critical thinking skills and hypothesis testing to learn about music concepts.* Cutietta (1984; 1985) completed two studies to determine if adolescent students used critical thinking skills to solve music problems. In the 1984 study, the researcher investigated students' abilities to make decisions about, judge and select common music elements interacting in music excerpts presented aurally, and thereby to create and test music hypotheses. Students used hypothesis-testing strategies to study three music concepts: polyphony, melodic variation, and rhythmic repetition. Cutietta described scanning strategies students used to test hypotheses. Successive scanning was described as testing one hypothesis until it was refuted, and then forming and testing another hypothesis until it was refuted. Simultaneous scanning was described as testing more than one music hypothesis simultaneously. Use of hypothesis testing increased with age. Students used successive scanning to test hypotheses prior to 14 years of age and used simultaneous scanning after 14 years of age. Accurate identification of music concepts occurred most frequently when students used simultaneous scanning strategies. Cutietta (1985) also analyzed characteristics of adolescent students' music hypotheses. He found that the majority of students (69 percent) wrote hypotheses about music elements focusing on music instrument sounds, tempo, and beat. Hypotheses were written also about music style focusing on opera, rock, and church music.

Cutietta maintained that analysis of music hypotheses should provide music educators insight into how adolescent students create cognitive networks and organize music information. Tunks (1981) emphasized the importance of identifying those elements people use to organize music information so that it means something. The uniformity of the content of adolescent students' hypotheses in the Cutietta studies reflected the music characteristics students used as music information organizers and also felt most comfortable discussing verbally. Other researchers also showed that adolescent students used tempo and melodic information to organize their perceptions of melodic-rhythmic patterns in music (Kuhn & Booth, 1988; Mills, 1985).

7. *If early adolescent students perceive a music composition task as relevant and their capacities permit completion of the task, a balanced progression of exploration, repetition, development, and silence is used while composing music.* Kratus (1985) investigated developmental differences among children while composing original songs. Sixth grade students explored sounds, repeated preferred sounds, developed melodic phrases, and used silent time to think about ideas. Sixth-grade students distributed their time equally across exploration, repetition, development and silence;

they also left time at the end of the process to practice original songs. As compared to younger students, early adolescent students were more product oriented.

DeLorenzo (1989) also examined sixth-grade students' music composition skills and their uses of problem solving processes while composing. The process students used while composing depended on students' perceptions of their capacities to complete the compositional task and of the relevance of the task. Students who were motivated to complete the compositional task used exploration, development and repetition while composing. Students who were not motivated to complete the task were easily distracted, used excessive repetition of music ideas, and showed minimal emotional responses.

MUSIC PREFERENCE AND ATTITUDE

During the last three decades, 64 investigations have provided foundations for understanding adolescent students' music preferences and attitudes. Some researchers analyzed characteristics of adolescent preferences as related to attributes of music information (e.g., tonal and rhythmic characteristics of generic music styles) and attributes of students (e.g., socioeconomic conditions, gender, and age). Many preference studies considered instructional methodology as a secondary issue. Other studies evaluated the effects of instruction and teaching strategies on attitudes toward music learning experiences or on preferences for a variety of music styles.

During the 1960s and 1970s, the majority of researchers described students' attitudes toward general music learning experiences or analyzed effects of instruction on music preferences. Major studies of the 1980s described sociocultural reasons for adolescent music preferences, adolescent students' motivations to continue music study, and relationships among music attitude and achievement variables.

1. *Repeated hearings of a composition exert a positive influence on junior and middle school students' preferences. The optimum number of repetitions facilitating increased preferences depends in part on music complexity.* Evans (1965) presented junior high school students with repeated hearings of eight compositions throughout a one-semester general music course. The compositions represented a wide variety of styles and included both instrumental and vocal performance. Evans found that students' preferences increased across all music styles (e.g., art music styles, American folk music, and jazz). He concluded that repeated hearings seemed to increase students' preferences for the music presented.

Getz (1966) extended Evans's study. Five compositions, embedded in a series of 40 compositions for string orchestra, were presented 11 times to adolescent students during a one-semester period. An increase in students' expressed liking for the repeated music occurred between the first hearing and the sixth through eighth hearings. Getz recommended that to maximize adolescent music preferences, six to eight hearings of a composition should be planned throughout one semester of study. Finnäs (1989), by contrast, found that repeated listening to complex art music increases music preferences, but that repeated listening to simple and uncomplicated music decreases preferences.

In an effort to determine optimum music complexity levels across age levels, Hargreaves and Castell (1987) compared preference ratings for familiar and unfamiliar melodies by students across widely spaced ages (including 10 to 14 years of age). Adolescent preference ratings for familiar melodies, upon one hearing, decreased with age. Their preference ratings for all melodies were the lowest among students participating in the study. The reviewed research showed that adolescent students expressed low preferences for unfamiliar and, sometimes, familiar music; however, repeated hearing may be used to the point at which student preferences peak, or are sustained and then diminish. In the Hargreaves and Castell research, this preference point interacted with music complexity and students' familiarity with the music presented. Pribram (1963) explained that human beings, regardless of age, need just the right portion of novelty (unfamiliar) and redundancy (familiar) when interacting positively and creatively with the environment. Walker (1981) maintained that this balance is represented at a point on a psychological complexity scale that is most preferred by an individual. The optimum number of repetitions and amount of music complexity that increase preferences for music was not established by the reviewed research.

2. *Junior high and middle school students react positively to music that has a fast tempo, a variety of loudness levels, dominant beats, and conjunct, diatonic melodic repetitions. Conversely, adolescent students react negatively to music that has slow to moderate tempi, disjunct and tonally vague melodies, dissonance, and melodies in minor modes.* Getz (1966) found that adolescent students liked music using fast tempi, diverse loudness levels, driving rhythms, and melodic repetition. Students reacted negatively to loud classical music, "jumpy" melodies, dissonance, and minor modes. Prince (1972) confirmed these findings and also found that adolescent students liked clear-cut music structures and disliked disjunct, tonally vague melodies, and a vocal performance medium.

Between 1979 and 1988, LeBlanc participated in a series of studies of music characteristics affecting early adolescent students' music preferences. LeBlanc and other researchers (1979, 1981) found that early adolescent students prefer fast tempi and instrumental performance media across popular, jazz, art, band, and country music styles. LeBlanc and Mc-Crary (1983) compared effects of four tempo levels on fifth- and sixth-grade students' preferences for traditional jazz music performed and recorded between 1925 and 1940. Statistically significant increases in preferences occurred at each faster tempo level ($p < .01$).

3. *Adolescent students prefer music styles that are popular and regarded as their own, yet "nonpopular" music style preferences can be enhanced when presented with preferred music elements (e.g., fast tempo and instrumental music performance medium).* Greer, Dorrow, and Randall

(1974) investigated music preferences of elementary children (including sixth-grade students). The researchers found that children liked music that they perceived as their own. After grade three, rock music preferences increased with age, and the pivotal point for increased popular music preference seemed to occur between third and fourth grades.

LeBlanc (1979) examined the function of popular music preferences amidst other allegedly "nonpreferred" music styles. He found that easy-listening popular music was most preferred by early adolescent students, with its competitors being rock, ragtime, Dixieland, band marches, and country western/bluegrass. Four factors were identified and used to cluster music styles as related to students' verbal descriptions of the music they heard. *Establishment Music* included instrumental and choral classical and modern swing music styles, with the descriptors "serious adult" and "not fun" music associated with this preference factor. *Novel Timbres* contained avant garde and electronic popular music styles and students' descriptions of electronic sounds. *Rhythmic Dynamism* included band marches, ragtime, Dixieland, and easy-listening music styles, with "happy," "upbeat," and "fast tempo" commonly used to describe music associated with this factor. The fourth factor was labeled *People's Music* and included folk, country western/bluegrass, Dixieland, black gospel, and rock music styles. Students frequently characterized the music as "nonestablishment" and "music of the people."

Another investigation focused on effects of tempo, music style, and performance medium on early adolescent preferences (LeBlanc, 1981). The rank order of students' preferences, from most to least preferred, was popular, country, band, new jazz, old jazz, and art music. Students preferred an instrumental performance medium and a fast tempo. LeBlanc recommended that to motivate students to listen to art or jazz music styles, teachers should present both in the following combination of tempo and performance medium attributes: fast-instrumental, slow-instrumental, fast-vocal, and slow-vocal.

4. *Music preferences can be modified by peers and mass media personalities. The reinforcing strength of peer and media approval depends on a student's personality, gender, music training, and age.* Ingelfield (1968) attempted to bias preference responses of ninth-grade students by providing bogus preference information allegedly acquired from two peer groups including social leaders and rebel leaders. Results from a personality test were used to identify students for the study. Results indicated that (1) highly dependent students conformed to those music preferences allegedly supplied by their group leaders, (2) jazz music preferences were most susceptible to bogus peer influence, (3) classical music preferences were well established as negative and were immune to change regardless of peer influence and student personality traits, and (4) bogus social leader preferences produced greater conformity than bogus preferences of rebel leaders.

Boyle, Hosterman, and Ramsey (1981) analyzed the importance of music and sociocultural variables in junior high school students' self-reported reasons for popular music preferences. Music characteristics such as melody, rhythm, instrument sounds, and harmony were the most influential in students' popular music preferences. Sociocultural reasons generally were less important than music reasons for preferences. Some students, depending on age, gender, and music training, were influenced by sociocultural reasons, such as hearing music on the radio, peer influence, and "danceability" of the music. Seventh- grade students considered media, peer, and social reasons as more important than did ninth-grade students. Additionally, females rated lyrics, melody, and music sentiment as important; males rated instrument sounds and peer influence as important. An inverse relationship was found between years of music training and importance of peer influence; also, musically trained students considered hearing the music on the radio and being able to dance to it as unimportant. Statistically significant positive correlations occurred between amount of preference for popular music and ratings of music's "danceability" and lyrics ($p < .01$). In an earlier study, Kelly (1961) also confirmed that musically trained students seemed relatively free from peer group influences and were able to form their own preferences. The reinforcing strength of peer approval, however, depended on age. Eighth-grade students preferred popular music styles more than classical or semiclassical music styles regardless of music training. Killian (1990) investigated junior high school students' preferences for popular music performers and solo performances as a function of race and gender. Students expressed which solo performance they preferred among the 21 different solo performances in the audio-video recording of "We Are the World." Students also indicated which performer they would prefer to emulate if given the opportunity to sing one of the solos in the song. Students tended to choose same-race and same-gender performances and performers to model. The tendency was stronger for males than for females. Killian explained that choices possibly resulted from uncontrolled variables including preference for perceived success and popularity of preferred performers. Boyle, Hosterman and Ramsey (1981) explained that music characteristics seemed more important than sociocultural factors affecting adolescent music preferences. In the Killian study, student preferences also were possibly affected by the music characteristics of the solos (e.g., melody or rhythm of solo passages).

Substantial research confirmed that adolescent music preferences are affected by peer and media approval. A recent study did not confirm this finding for privately expressed music preferences. Finnäs (1989) found that adolescent music preferences were higher for classical and folk music when expressed privately than when expressed publicly. Adolescent students' typical conformity to assumed popular music preferences existed in the presence of peers regardless of perceived peer-leadership qualities. Finnäs explained that adolescent students misunderstand peer approved music which varies when expressed privately and publicly.

5. *During general music classes, junior high and middle school students like playing music instruments and participating in rhythmic experiences (playing and moving). They dislike unaccompanied singing, music listening, and music reading. Expressed attitudes toward music instructional experiences may vary as a function of socioeconomic status (SES) and gender.* Broquist (1961), in a foundational study of elementary students' attitudes toward general music activities (including sixth-grade students), found that general music classes appealed more to females than to males; both female and male attitudes toward general music became more negative with advancing grade levels. Playing instruments received the most favorable responses from all students. Music reading using syllables, numbers, or letter names received the least favorable responses from all students. Unaccompanied singing and singing alone were disliked by all students, particularly sixth grade students.

Nolin (1973) also analyzed elementary students' attitudes toward general music (including sixth-grade students); his research confirmed Broquist's findings. Nolin suggested that creative experiences elicited neutral attitudinal responses because minimal class time was given to creativity. Playing instruments elicited the most positive responses from sixth-grade students. They also liked music reading and listening if paired with audio-video instructional media or with playing music instruments.

Subsequent research supported the Nolin and Broquist research findings with elementary children; however, these findings were extended to show effects of socioeconomic status (SES) and gender on attitudes toward general music. Bowman (1990) and Pogonowski (1985) found that fifth- and sixth-grade students' attitudes toward general music interacted with SES and gender. Females exhibited the most positive attitudes; however, low-SES female and high-SES male attitudes were the least positive attitudes expressed by all students. There was a decline in positive attitudes toward general music study between fifth and sixth grades.

6. *Junior high and middle school students' motivations to continue music study depend on students' perceptions of their music abilities.* In 1980 Hoffer assessed enrollment trends in secondary music courses. He explained that only two courses (junior high general music and glee club) showed a decrease in the number of students enrolled. Between 1964 and 1976, there was a 46.2 percent decrease in junior high school general music enrollment. In a recent discussion of enrollment trends in music, the enrollment scenario was even more disconcerting than in the Hoffer (1980) report. As documented by the National Center for Educational Statistics, Reimer (1989) said that less than 2 percent of all high school students in the United States are enrolled in any nonperformance music course; and of those students, a large percentage also is involved in music performing ensembles. Performance motivates junior high or middle school students to continue studying music.

Frakes (1984) conducted an ex post facto study of factors contributing to students continuing or discontinuing music study. She analyzed students' scores on Colwell's *Music Achievement Tests* and on the *Iowa Test of Basic Skills,* and analyzed reasons students expressed for continuing or discontinuing music study. Students who continued music study had high music and academic achievement scores (above average), tended to like teachers, and studied music privately. Students who discontinued music study perceived themselves as less musically able than other students, and received minimal family encouragement to study music. Frakes also maintained that junior high or middle school music instruction was a strong predictor of continuation of music study.

Lillemyr (1983) found that fourth-grade students with high levels of interest in school music study believed they were musically capable, were motivated toward success, had positive perceptions of their abilities, and avoided situations conducive to failure. Asmus (1986) completed research on music achievement motivations and pertinent to understanding adolescent students' motivations to continue music study. He examined effects of gender, grade and school on reasons students cited for success and failure in music. Asmus indicated that achievement with a music task is mediated by an individual's beliefs about causes of success and failure. Eighty percent of the reasons students cited for success in music were attributed to students' perceptions of their music abilities. Junior high school students, however, attributed successes in music to both level of music abilities and required efforts to succeed. Failures were often attributed to luck. In a discussion of music student dropouts, Covington (1983) explained that as age increases students believing that music abilities are stable and affected by effort probably will dropout of music study. The Asmus and Frakes findings cooperatively provided evidence that students discontinue general music study because of low self-concept about their music abilities. Frakes recommended that adolescent music students be encouraged to feel musically able, particularly male adolescent students. She also suggested that effective and motivating adolescent general music education were essential to encourage continued music study.

7. *Increased aural and aural-visual music discrimination skills are only slightly related to music preferences.* Standifer (1970) investigated the relationship between students' music preferences and proficiencies in perceiving music elements. Students' abilities to aurally discriminate repetitions and variations of music elements were increased by instruction; however, positive attitudes toward music did not increase. Zumbrunn (1972) and Prince (1974) found minimal positive effects of guided-listening instruction on junior high school students' attitudes toward art music. Nelson (1973) also found that increases in music listening skills did not positively affect students' attitudes toward music.

In a psychoacoustical study of music behaviors, Burns (1980) found only a slight relationship between junior high school students' perceptions of and preferences for tonal information in avant garde music. She concluded that preferences were not altered by perceived tonality; perceptions of tonality were influenced by acculturation to or experience with tonality. A possible confounding variable was use of nonpreferred music styles.

8. *Positive attitudes toward music decrease between elementary and junior high school; however, certain teaching strategies maintain positive attitudes toward music and increase music achievements.* Nolin (1971) analyzed teacher and student verbal and nonverbal behaviors in junior high

school general music classes. Nolin concluded that music teachers judged to be most effective and liked tended to avoid static behavioral patterns that resulted from remaining in a single area for an extended time. Teacher demonstrations also seemed to be effective in eliciting music learning and positive student attitudes.

Taebel and Coker (1980) examined relationships among music achievement, music attitudes, and teaching competencies in 29 schools, including grades 3 through 7. Socioeconomic conditions, grade, time spent in general music class, and private music study were not strongly related to music attitudes and achievements. Attitudes across all grades remained relatively positive; however, there was a significant decrease of positive attitudes with each advancing grade level ($p < .01$). Gains in positive attitudes were associated with teachers using a variety of teaching methods and student-initiated verbal interactions.

IMPLICATIONS FOR ADOLESCENT GENERAL MUSIC EDUCATION

Generalizable research findings specifically focusing on teaching and music's reinforcing value in junior high and middle schools is limited, and numerous questions remain unanswered. Are generic teacher evaluation programs (e.g., Hunter, 1983) appropriate for evaluating music teacher effectiveness? What are the effects of a teacher's subject matter knowledge, instructional pacing, and enthusiasm on student attention, acquisition of music literacy, and student and teacher on-task behaviors? The reviewed research includes several descriptions of using music to enhance learning in other subject areas. The validity of these descriptions has not been tested empirically, and further research is needed.

In the area of general music curricula in junior high and middle school settings, researchers have devoted much effort to answering questions pertaining to the current status of music education curricula. What factors contribute to discrepancies between desired outcomes in music education and actual music achievements and attitudes acquired and expressed by many adolescent students?

Unresolved problems of grade level distribution in a junior high school or middle school perplex many music educators. The lack of standardized grade level organization affects scheduling, curriculum content, and emphasis on general music study. Should general music be offered as an exploratory, 9- week to 18-week course or as a course requiring a complete academic year of indepth study? Educational administrators stress achievement in all subject areas, yet exploratory courses in music and the other arts are provided (Gerber, 1990). Teske (1990) emphasizes that labeling junior high or middle school general music as "exploratory" may diminish the value of such study for adolescent students. One may assume that the negative characterizations of exploratory music courses are supported by an extensive, well-established body of research. To the contrary, there is minimal empirical research analyzing effects of exploratory music courses on students' development of music literacy and music values.

Knowing about music's rhythmic and tonal characteristics and being able to read, create, perform, and listen to these characteristics in a music form are essential to being a musically literate person. An important function of adolescent general music education is to reinforce and enhance each student's music literacy. Research is needed to clarify the effects of instructional strategies and musical materials on adolescent music literacy. Research in this area has focused primarily on music listening and music reading behaviors, but several questions remain unanswered.

How do music teachers help students acquire meaning from an aurally presented music form? What teaching strategies will help focus students' attention on those qualities that clarify or illuminate a specific concept being studied? Some researchers suggest that knowledge of characteristics that attract students' attentions will aid in a teacher's choice of teaching strategies. Researchers have identified music characteristics that attract adolescent students' attention, such as characteristics of recurring beats (i.e., beat intensity and tempo) and melodic activity (i.e., intervallic relationships and melodic contour). Additional research is needed to test effects of teaching strategies on adolescent students' organization of music information.

Recent editions of music textbooks have employed critical thinking skills and have increased emphasis on music creativity (Culp, Eisman, and Hoffman, 1988; Meske, Andress, Pautz, and Willman, 1988). A growing body of research evidence describes adolescent students' music creativity and critical thinking skills. Such research indicates that adolescent students can use hypothesis-testing strategies and positive and negative exemplars to solve music problems. Early adolescent students use exploration, repetition, development, and silence while composing music. The generalizability of these descriptions is questionable. Continued research, however, should strengthen the external validity of the findings.

Ability to evaluate music experiences and to make decisions is based on a person's music preferences and attitudes. Naturally, music educators hope that preferences and attitudes are expanded by school music experiences. To expand music students' preferences, LeBlanc (1981) maintains that an effective presentation sequence for nonpreferred music styles is fast-instrumental, slow-instrumental, fast-vocal, and slow-vocal. This recommendation has not been verified empirically and requires additional research. Music educators assume that guided music listening lessons enhance music listening skills and music preferences; research does not support this assumption. Several questions remain unanswered regarding the use of guided music-listening instruction. Is a student's reception of music listening experiences enhanced by using repeated listening and student-preferred music elements? How do complexity levels of music compositions inhibit or enhance positive effects of repeated listening and student-preferred music elements? Additional research is needed to analyze effects of students' perceptions and motivations on continued general music study throughout junior and senior high school.

Among the 200 studies reviewed, there were many "one-shot" studies. The body of research on adolescent general music education includes many unrelated bits of research information acquired via diverse procedures and designs. Throughout this chapter, replicated research findings have been identified and discussed. The research reviewed in this chapter is inadequate to explain and predict adolescent music behaviors in teaching and learning settings with precision and accuracy. In some areas, music researchers are beginning to provide rather precise and accurate explanations. The majority of adolescent general music research, however, is in need of replication to generalize and apply research findings. In an essay on medical research, Thomas (1979) cautions physicians against accepting cures and causes evolving from *immediate* applications of findings without necessary replications and careful control of research efforts. The music education profession likewise must use caution concerning magical cures and causes or "tricks that click." In this chapter, replicated findings are not provided as "tricks that click;" they have evolved from replicated research efforts, and continuously are being refined. Continued research on the fascinating and sometimes puzzling music behaviors of junior high and middle school students should provide precise and systematic descriptions of music behaviors functioning in many facets of an adolescent student's life.

References

Asmus, E. P. (1986). Student beliefs about the causes of success and failure in music: A study of achievement motivation. *Journal of Research in Music Education, 34,* 262–278.

Boisen, R. (1981). The effects of melodic context on students' aural perception of rhythm. *Journal of Research in Music Education, 29,* 165–172.

Bowman, R. (1990, March). *A descriptive study of elementary students' attitudes toward school music activities.* A paper presented at the Music Educators National Conference, Washington, D.C.

Boyle, J. D., Hosterman, G. L., and Ramsey, D. S. (1981). Factors influencing pop music preferences of young people. *Journal of Research in Music Education, 29,* 47–56.

Broquist, O. H. (1961). A survey of the attitudes of 2594 Wisconsin elementary school pupils toward their learning experience in music. Unpublished doctoral dissertation, University of Wisconsin, Madison.

Burns, M. M. T. (1980). Aural perception of tonality in avant garde music and its relationship to preference. Unpublished doctoral dissertation, Florida State University, Tallahassee.

Covington, M. V. (1983). Musical chairs: Who drops out of music instruction and why? in *Third Ann Arbor Symposium Session III: Motivation and creativity.* Reston: MENC.

Culp, C. E., Eisman, L., and Hoffman, M. E. (1988). *World of music.* Morristown: Silver Burdett-Ginn.

Curtis, S. C. (1986). An observational analysis of successful junior high/middle school general music teachers. Unpublished doctoral dissertation, University of Oklahoma, Norman.

Cutietta, R. (1984). The musical hypothesis-testing ability of the adolescent learner. *Bulletin of the Council for Research in Music Education, 80,* 27–50.

Cutietta, R. (1985). An analysis of musical hypotheses created by the 11–16 year old learner. *Bulletin of the Council for Research in Music Education, 84,* 1–13.

DeLorenzo, L. C. (1989). A field study of sixth-grade students' creative problem-solving processes. *Journal of Research in Music Education, 37,* 188–200.

Evans, J. G. (1965). The effect of especially designed music listening experiences on junior high school students' attitudes toward music. Unpublished doctoral dissertation, Indiana University, Bloomington.

Finnäs, L. (1989). How can musical preferences be modified? A research review. *Bulletin of the Council for Research in Music Education, 102,* 1–59.

Frakes, L. (1984). Differences in music achievement, academic achievement, and attitude among participants, dropouts, and nonparticipants in secondary school music. Unpublished doctoral dissertation, University of Iowa, Iowa City.

Fromm, M. (1981). The effects of music upon the values of compliant and non compliant adolescents. Unpublished doctoral dissertation, University of Colorado, Boulder.

Gerber, T. A. (1989). *The quality quotient for young adolescents' exemplary general music teachers in the middle grades.* Paper presented at the Symposium on Research in General Music, Tucson.

Gerber, T. A. (1990, March). *Addressing problems of music instruction in the middle school.* Panel presentation at the Music Educators National Conference, Washington, DC.

Getz, R. P. (1966). Effects of repetition on listening responses. *Journal of Research in Music Education, 14,* 178–192.

Gibbons, A. C. (1977). Popular music preferences of older people. *Journal of Research in Music Therapy, 14,* 180–189.

Gordon, E. (1970). First-year results of a five-year longitudinal study of the musical achievement of culturally disadvantaged students. *Journal of Research in Music Education, 18,* 195–213.

Greer, D., Dorrow, L. G., and Randall, A. (1974). Music listening preferences of elementary school children. *Journal of Research in Music Education, 22,* 284–291.

Haack, P. A. (1970). A study involving the visual arts in the development of musical concepts. *Journal of Research in Music Education, 18,* 392–398.

Haack, P. A. (1972). Use of positive and negative examples in teaching the concept of musical style. *Journal of Research in Music Education, 20,* 456–461.

Hargreaves, D. J., and Castell, K. C. (1987). Development of liking for familiar and unfamiliar melodies. *Bulletin of the Council for Research in Music Education, 91,* 6569.

Harrison, L. N. (1974). The development and evaluation of supplementary programed materials for teaching meter and major-minor discrimination to elementary school children. Unpublished doctoral dissertation, Columbia University, New York.

Hartshorn, W. C. (1958). The role of listening. In N. Henry (Ed.), *Basic concepts in music education.* Chicago: National Society for the Study of Education.

Hill, J. D. (1968). A study of the musical achievement of culturally deprived children and culturally advantaged children at the elementary school level. Unpublished doctoral dissertation, University of Kansas, Lawrence.

Hunter, M. (1983). *Master teaching: Improved instruction.* El Sequendo: TIP.

Ingelfield, H. G. (1968). The relationship of selected personality variables to conformity behavior reflected in the musical preferences of adolescents when exposed to peer group leader influences. Unpublished doctoral dissertation, Ohio State University, Columbus.

Kelly, D. T. (1961). A study of the musical preferences of a select group of adolescents. *Journal of Research in Music Education, 9,* 118–125.

Killian, J. N. (1990). Effect of model characteristics on musical preferences of junior high students. *Journal of Research in Music Education, 38,* 115–124.

Kohn, H. D. (1971). Effect of timing of supplementary materials on programed learning in music. *Journal of Research in Music Education, 19,* 481–487.

Kratus, J. (1985). A time analysis of the compositional processes used by children ages 7 to 11. *Journal of Research in Music Education, 37,* 5–20.

Kuhn, T. L., and Booth, G. (1988). The effect of melodic activity, tempo change, and audible beat on tempo perception of elementary school students. *Journal of Research in Music Education, 36* 140–155.

Kuhn, T. L., and Gates, E. E. (1975). Effect of notational values, age, and example length on tempo performance accuracy. *Journal of Research in Music Education, 23,* 203–210.

LeBlanc, A. (1979). Generic style music preferences of fifth-grade students. *Journal of Research in Music Education, 27,* 255–271.

LeBlanc, A. (1981). Effects of style, tempo, and performing medium on children's music preference. *Journal of Research in Music Education, 29,* 143–156.

LeBlanc, A., and McCrary, J. (1983). Effect of tempo on children's music preference. *Journal of Research in Music Education. 31,* 283–294.

Lillemyr, O. F. (1983). *Achievement motivation as a factor in self-perceptions.* A paper presented at the Annual Meeting of the American Educational Research Association, Montreal.

Madsen, C. K., (1990). Teacher intensity in relationship to music education. *Bulletin of the Council for Research in Music Education, 104,* 38–46.

Madsen, C. K., and Forsythe, J. L. (1973). Effect of contingent music listening on increases of mathematical responses. *Journal of Research in Music Education, 21,* 176–181.

Madsen, C. K., Standley, J. M., and Cassidy, J. W. (1989). Demonstration and recognition of high and low contrasts in teacher intensity. *Journal of Research in Music Education, 37,* 85–92.

Melton, G. M. (1990, March). *Addressing problems of music instruction in the middle school.* Panel presentation at the Music Educators National Conference, Washington.

Meske, E. B., Andress, B., Pautz, M. P., and Willman, F. (1988). *Holt music.* New York: Holt, Rinehart and Winston.

Michel, D. E., and Farrell, D. M. (1973). Music and self-esteem: Disadvantaged problem boys in an all-black elementary school. *Journal of Research in Music Education, 21,* 80–84.

Mills, J. I. (1985). Some developmental aspects of aural perception. *Bulletin of the Council for Research in Music Education, 85,* 140–145.

Music Educators National Conference Committee on Standards. (1986). *The school music program: Description and standards* (2nd ed.). Reston: Music Educators National Conference.

Nelson, G. O. (1973). A chronometric approach to the study of form in seventh-grade general music series. Unpublished doctoral dissertation, University of Minnesota, Minneapolis.

Nolin, H. W. (1971). Patterns of teacher-student interaction in selected junior high school general music classes. *Journal of Research in Music Education, 19,* 314–325.

Nolin, H. W. (1973). Attitudinal growth patterns toward elementary school music experiences. *Journal of Research in Music Education, 21,* 123–134.

Peterson, A. V. (1965). A study of developmental listening factors in children's ability to understand melody. Unpublished doctoral dissertation, University of Rochester, Rochester.

Petzold, R. G. (1969). Auditory perception by children. *Journal of Research in Music Education, 17,* 82–87.

Pogonowski, L. M. (1985). Attitude assessment of upper elementary students in a process-oriented music curriculum. *Journal of Research in Music Education, 33,* 247–258.

Pribram, K. H. (1963). The new neurology: Memory, novelty, thought, and choice. In G. H. Glaser (ed.), *EEG and behavior.* New York: Basic Books.

Prince, W. F. (1972). Some aspects of liking responses of junior high school students for art music. *Contributions to Music Education, 1,* 25–35.

Prince, W. F. (1974). Effects of guided listening on musical enjoyment of junior high school students. *Journal of Research in Music Education, 22,* 45–51.

Regelski, T. A. (1981). *Teaching general music.* New York: Schirmer.

Reimer, B. (1989). *A philosophy of music education,* (2nd ed.). Englewood Cliffs: Prentice Hall.

Schneider, J. R. (1986, October). Our world in miniature: Bringing more international education into today's classrooms. *Councilor, 46,* 13–17.

Standifer, J. A. (1970). Effects on aesthetic sensitivity of developing perception of musical expressiveness. *Journal of Research in Music Education, 18,* 112–125.

Smith, A. (1973). Feasibility of tracking musical form as a cognitive listening objective. *Journal of Research in Music Education, 21,* 200–213.

Taebel, D. K. (1990). An assessment of the classroom performance of music teachers. *Journal of Research in Music Education, 38,* 5–23.

Taebel, D. K., and Coker, J. G. (1980). Teaching effectiveness in elementary classroom music: Relationships among competency measures, pupil product measures, and certain attribute variables. *Journal of Research in Music Education, 28,* 250–265.

Tatarunis, A. M. (1976). The effect of two teaching methods utilizing popular music on the ability of seventh-garde students to perceive aurally and identify musical concepts. Unpublished doctoral dissertation, Boston University, Boston.

Teske, P. W. (1990, March). *Addressing problems of music instruction in the middle school.* Panel presentation at the Music Educators National Conference, Washington.

Thomas, L. (1979). *The medusa and the snail.* New York: Viking.

Tillotson, J. R. (1972). A study of learning characteristics as identified in the music reading process. Unpublished doctoral dissertation, Northwestern University, Evanston.

Tunks, T. A. (1982, February). *Perceptual research: Definitions of areas which contribute to theories of music instruction.* Panel presentation at the music educators national conference, San Antonio.

Walker, E. L. (1981). Hedgehog theory and music education. In *Documentary report of the Ann Arbor Symposium: Applications of Psychology to the teaching and learning of music.* Reston: Music Educators National Conference.

Webster, P. R. (1990). Creative thinking in music: Introduction. *Music Educators Journal, 76,*(9), 21.

Wehner, W. L. (1966). The relation between six paintings by Paul Klee and selected musical compositions. *Journal of Research in Music Education, 15,* 220–224.

Yarbrough, C. (1975). The effect of magnitude of conductor behavior on performance, attentiveness, and attitude of students in selected mixed choruses. *Journal of Research in Music Education, 23,* 134–146.

Zumbrunn, K. (1972). A guided listening program in twentieth-century music for junior high students. *Journal of Research in Music Education, 20,* 370–378.

SCHOOLS/CURRICULUM

RESEARCH REGARDING STUDENTS WITH DISABILITIES

Kate Gfeller
UNIVERSITY OF IOWA

According to the U.S. Office of Education (Bureau of Education for the Handicapped, October 1989), over four million persons under the age of 22 receive special education services. While federal guidelines regarding educational practices for students with disabilities indicate specific terminology for particular categories (e.g., emotionally disturbed, speech-impaired), one finds considerable variety in terminology within research publications, regulations, and from one educational setting to the next. For example, some school systems use the term "mentally handicapped" while others use the term, "developmentally disabled" to describe persons with mental retardation. Some federal regulations use the term, "handicapped" while others use the term, "disabilities." There is and will continue to be debate among educators, medical personnel, and advocates concerning the appropriateness of labels that categorize persons with special medical and developmental conditions.

These children deviate significantly from others in one or more of the following areas: mental, physical, behavioral, social, or emotional development. It is well documented that disabilities can affect educational progress in subjects such as language arts or mathematics. Do these same disabilities have a significant impact on learning music? Do children with specific disabilities have musical potential similar to that of their nondisabled peers? What level of achievement can the music educator anticipate? Are there particular instructional practices in music education that are more effective for disabled children?

These questions have been addressed in varying degrees through systematic inquiry. This chapter is a review of selected research on (1) the musical aptitude and achievement of children with disabilities and (2) the effectiveness of specific instructional practices for such children. Although considerable research exists concerning therapeutic applications

of music for children with disabilities, that literature is beyond the scope of this chapter.

MUSICAL CHARACTERISTICS OF STUDENTS WITH DISABILITIES

Music educators have long based instructional decisions on known principles of child development and learning theories—principles and theories that reflect typical patterns of maturation. This knowledge assists the teacher in establishing realistic educational objectives, and in the selection of appropriate instructional methods. The patterns of children with disabilities, however, do differ from typical developmental patterns in one or more functional areas: Their mental, physical, or social/emotional development may or may not reflect that of age group peers. Without a clear understanding of musical aptitude or achievement, the educators can err in one of two ways: (1) underestimation of the abilities of the child, resulting in educational experiences that are demeaning or that fail to foster potential, or (2) unrealistically high expectations that end in frustration and failure. This section focuses on research concerning the musical characteristics of persons with specific types of disabilities.

Children with Mental Retardation

Of all classifications of disabilities none has been studied as extensively in regard to musical behaviors as has mental retardation (Kalenius, 1977). To some extent, this research interest may reflect the belief that individuals with particular types of retardation have unusual musical sensitivity. According to Stratford and Ching (1983), reference to musical ability among persons with Down syndrome (one particular etiology of mental retardation) appeared in the literature as early as 1876. Descriptions such as "love of music," "marked sense of rhythm," and "idea of time as well as tune" have been associated with this group of the mentally retarded (Stratford and Ching, 1983, p. 23).

Another possible explanation for this large body of research has to do with subject availability. Children with mental retardation comprise a sizeable percentage of those students served in special education (Graham and Beer, 1980; U.S. Office of Education, Bureau of Education for the Handicapped, October 1989). In addition, prior to the integration of disabled students into school communities in 1978, children with mental retardation were often educated in large residential institutions (Graham and Beer, 1980). Within those settings, researchers had easy access to subjects with mental handicaps.

The musical characteristics of children with mental retardation have been investigated through a variety of means: Some researchers have utilized published standardized tests of aptitude or achievement, while others have devised measures to assess specific musical skills. Extant studies vary in many important factors, including subject characteristics, test constructs, and procedures; however, the majority of these research efforts can be classified under the categories of general musical aptitude, musical achievement, or specific skill attainment.

Musical Aptitude Children with mental retardation fall below their chronological peers in many cognitive and physical tasks. Should the music educator also expect significant differences in musical aptitude? Several researchers have examined musical aptitude of children with mental retardation using standardized measures.

In research using the *Musical Aptitude Profile* (MAP) (Gordon, 1965) with mentally retarded children, both Bixler (1968) and Ianacone (1977) adapted the test protocol in order to reduce negative effects of poor attention span, distractability, and difficulty with complex instructions. For example, following unsuccessful trials with the original format of the MAP, Bixler administered portions (Rhythm, Melody, and Expression Tests) of the full test protocol. In addition, he used an adaptive answer sheet with color coding (coefficients for split-half and test-retest reliability of the composite test were .91 and .72, respectively).

In order to determine the relationship between musical aptitude as measured on the MAP and other mental and musical tasks, Bixler calculated correlation between scores on the MAP, age, measures of academic achievement, and intelligence, and ranked ability in an instrumental music program. Bixler found low correlations between chronological age and subtests of the MAP (coefficients ranged from .08 to .27); moderate to low correlations (.55 to .04) were reported for the MAP and academic or intelligence tests. According to Bixler, these results implied that musical aptitude as measured by the MAP was relatively independent of intellectual and academic achievement. In contrast, a stronger relationship was demonstrated (correlations ranging from .69 to .70)

between performance on the MAP and success in music instruction (observer rankings for musical ability of 17 children enrolled in an instrumental music program).

Ianacone (1977) compared the traditional test protocol of the MAP with an audio and an audiovisual format (split-half reliability on the modified subtests ranging from .87 to .88). In addition to determining whether test format had a significant effect on aptitude measurement, he also wished to determine whether a relationship existed between musical aptitude and intelligence. Three groups of subjects were compared: nondisabled children (mean age of 120 months), educable mentally retarded (EMR) children matched for chronological age (mean age of 122 months), and EMR children with mental age comparable to that of the nondisabled children (mean chronological age of 202 months). Educable mentally retarded children matched for chronological age (122 months) scored significantly lower than nondisabled children and EMR children who were matched for mental age. However, EMR children did show significantly improved test performance on the adapted as opposed to the traditional test format. Granted, alterations in a standardized protocol limit comparison to published norms because it can be questioned whether the Ianacone version tested the same things as the original MAP. Nevertheless, there are real benefits in using an adapted test protocol that reduces effects of administrative factors, and that is more representative of the child's musical aptitude.

Other researchers have used alternative measures of aptitude to determine the musical potential of students with mental retardation. McLeish and Higgs (1982) compared results on two standardized tests, each with different constructs regarding musical aptitude: The *Seashore Measures of Musical Talents* (Seashore, Lewis, and Saetveit, 1960), which views musical abilities as a set of loosely related basic sensory discrimination skills, and the Bentley *Measures of Musical Ability* (1966), a test that combines psychoacoustic with "musical" tasks.

Despite the difference in testing philosophy among the Seashore test, the Bentley test, and the MAP, research using all of these measures indicated that the musical aptitude of mentally retarded children is more similar to that of nondisabled children of comparable mental age than to those of the same chronological age. However, in using Seashore's and Bentley's tests, McLeish and Higgs (1982) found that musical aptitude of children with mental retardation may not be adequately represented by one composite score of aptitude. Rather, various subskills appeared to be differentially influenced by subnormal mental capacity. For example, test items reliant on memory or reasoning were more troublesome than those requiring simple discrimination.

What follows are implications of these findings for the music teacher: The student's mental age is a better predictor of aptitude than is chronological age, and should be considered when selecting developmentally appropriate curricular goals and activities. Furthermore, the teacher should expect to find uneven performance among various musical activities, depending on the cognitive requirement associated with each task.

Musical Achievement In comparison with aptitude studies, less research has been conducted on musical achievement of students who are mentally retarded. In 1981 Sona Nocera compared the musical achievement of mainstreamed (integrated into a regular music class) educable mentally retarded children with that of nondisabled children. Subjects from grades 2 and 5 (intact classrooms) from eight different elementary schools were tested using the *Silver Burdett Music Competency Test* (SBMCT; Colwell, 1979). Possible instructional differences across the classes were not addressed in the research design; however, according to Nocera, an examination of the curriculum for the eight classes revealed similar instructional objectives, all related to concepts tested in the SBMCT. Nocera indicated that suitability of the test instrument (in its original format) for mildly retarded students was determined through pilot testing (details concerning pilot procedures were not provided). No reliability data were reported for this administration of the SBMCT.

Nocera reported that EMR children showed overall achievement significantly below that of their nondisabled peers (.01). However, no significant differences existed on particular subtests (meter, texture, and intervals in second grade; meter, form, and melody in fifth grade), and both EMR and nondisabled children showed similar order for difficulty of subtests. EMR children (both grade levels) performed significantly lower than nondisabled students on items requiring interpretation of nonverbal symbols (.01).

In the following year, another study (Ellis, 1982) compared music achievement of EMR children, average children, and gifted children, using the *Music Achievement Test* (1 and 2) (Colwell, 1969). Ellis found no significant differences between EMR and average children except for the pitch discrimination subtest (.01). However, when gifted children were compared with average and EMR children, significant differences were found in each subtest and composite score of both MAT1 and MAT2 (.0001). Ellis concluded that children with mild (educable) retardation could be effectively mainstreamed with nondisabled children in music class. However, he recommended provision of different lessons and objectives for gifted and talented children.

These test results should be interpreted with caution. First, Ellis provided little detail concerning the appropriateness of this test for EMR children. Second, reliability coefficients were not reported. Third, information regarding subjects' music education experiences prior to testing was not provided. Therefore, it is not possible to determine whether differences in educational experiences contributed to test results.

Basing conclusions regarding musical achievement on such a limited research base is unwise. However, there are certain trends that can be inferred from these two studies: Achievement, like aptitude, appears to vary among specific skill areas. Furthermore, success in testing is influenced by the differential requirements of the test items themselves. For example, Nocera reported significant differences between nondisabled and EMR children for several skill areas. In contrast, Ellis found that only pitch discrimination was significantly lower for EMR children than for average children.

These different outcomes may be a function of methodological factors such as differences in test content or administration (e.g., the SBMCT vs. the MAT).

Test appropriateness itself is an important concern in research regarding both aptitude and achievement. Given the unique learning and behavioral characteristics of children with mental handicaps (e.g., poor short-term memory, attention deficits, difficulty with abstract concepts), the researcher must use care in selecting or administering most published tests of musical achievement and aptitude. Standardized instructions and the response mode found in some test protocols may be too difficult or confusing for some students with disabilities. Adaptations in administration may be necessary in order to obtain data that are truly representative of the subjects' potential or ability (Lidz, 1981, pp. 112–113).

One direction for future research is the norming of preexisting achievement and aptitude tests adapted for exceptional learners. Another option is the construction of new measures designed specifically for children with disabilities. One example of inquiry directed toward testing of disabled children was conducted by Kaplan (1977). In this study, Kaplan developed a criterion-referenced test, the *Test of Rhythmic Responsiveness,* to assess EMR children's ability to respond to beat, tempo change, metric accent, durational pattern, and ostinatos. Responses were elicited by a stimulus pattern (woodblock sound) superimposed on tape-recorded musical examples. The children listened to the tape over earphones, and then tapped the rhythmic pattern on the Tap Master, which automatically tabulated each correct response.

The rationale for test content and procedures was established in a careful review of literature. The procedure section provided a detailed account of the steps taken to determine the content and refine the protocol used in the test. All of these measures were assessed through a pilot study to ensure that the directions, length of testing, and items were realistic for administration. Kaplan provided test-retest data of a small sample prior to the actual study.

In order to study developmental effects in rhythmic abilities, Kaplan chose subjects to represent three different age groups (6, 7, and 8 years of age). The EMR children matched for mental ages 6, 7, and 8 were compared to a nondisabled sample. In order to ensure good matches, both nondisabled and EMR children were tested using a standardized measure of mental age, the *Peabody Picture Vocabulary Test* (PPVT). In addition, the author screened subjects for sensory impairments that can confound test outcome. Kaplan attempted to control for possible maturational changes by testing within a 2-week period. Test-retest coefficients were determined for the final test form; coefficients ranged from .434 to .992 for the 10 subtests.

Kaplan reported that beat maintenance and tempo change were more highly developed than other rhythmic abilities for both nondisabled and EMR children. Echo tapping was the only skill in which nondisabled children showed significantly greater degree of success (.01) than did EMR children matched for mental age. While both nondisabled and EMR children responded more accurately to a synchronization task in moderate and fast tempos than in slow tempos, the 8-year-old EMR children also showed greater accuracy in moderate than faster tempos. This finding suggests that the music educator may assist children in rhythmic accuracy by presenting rhythmic patterns for subsequent production at a moderate rather than a slow or fast tempo.

There are several limitations to Kaplan's test as a "standardized" measure of rhythmic ability, including a relatively weak test-retest coefficient of .434 for one of the 10 sections. A total sample size of 72 is also relatively small for norming a test for two different populations covering three ages. In addition, the overall number of test items sampled a limited number of skills. However, because short attention span is a problem for many children who are mentally retarded, a longer test may have produced diminishing returns. Despite these concerns, the careful steps taken by this author provide a helpful example for other researchers interested in test construction. More important, Kaplan's test is a rare example of a test battery developed specifically for disabled children. Further efforts in this vein would be welcome additions to the field. The development of reliable and valid achievement tests could subsequently facilitate research on musical ability in relation to such factors as severity of disability, classroom placement (i.e., the regular music classroom vs. a special classroom), early childhood instruction, and a variety of instructional practices (e.g., Orff, Kodály, multisensory instruction).

Specific Skill Attainment In addition to using standardized measures of aptitude and achievement, researchers have designed special tests to study specific musical skills. The majority of these researcher-designed tests have examined rhythmic discrimination or production.

RHYTHMIC SKILLS. Studies regarding the rhythmic skills of children with mental retardation have examined accuracy on differing tasks (e.g., steady beat vs. rhythm patterns) with differing treatment variables. Several studies have looked at factors associated with mental retardation as they interact with the complexity of a rhythmic task. Kenneth Bruscia (1981) investigated rhythmic production in view of one particular behavioral characteristic frequently associated with persons with mental retardation: namely, the failure to observe elements of stimuli that are task relevant while inhibiting those that are irrelevant.

Bruscia hypothesized that recall and subsequent production of rhythm patterns by people with mental retardation may be impacted by poor attentional control, and that deficits in selective attention may differ depending on the level of intelligence (mild vs. moderate retardation). In order to test these hypotheses, subjects from the two groups (mild and moderate levels of retardation) listened to taped rhythm patterns (each item contained four short rhythmic motifs) and were then asked to tap the patterns on a drum. Some of the patterns were accompanied by irrelevant, distracting musical stimuli. Subject responses were collected on tape and then rated by observers for accuracy, motif by motif. One point was awarded for each of the four motives correctly produced in each item.

Bruscia found that presentation of irrelevant, competing stimuli resulted in significant decrement (.01) in short-term recall of rhythm patterns for both mildly and moderately retarded subjects. In other words, selective attention appeared to be a problem for both groups. However, the overall rhythmic performance of mildly retarded subjects was significantly more accurate (.01) than that of moderately retarded subjects independent of stimuli complexity. These data suggest that music educators, when introducing rhythmic patterns, should reduce potential distractors until the basic rhythmic task is mastered. In addition, some rhythmic tasks may be appropriate for a child with mild retardation but prove too difficult for a child with greater mental limitations.

Bruscia presented his problem and methodology clearly and thoroughly. Bruscia's care in subject selection was illustrated by the fact that he screened 600 individuals in order to attain a sample of 46 that met specific and predetermined criteria for participation. These criteria included (1) an IQ score between 40 and 60 on the *Wechsler Adult Intelligence Scale* or the *Wechsler Intelligence Scale for Children (Revised),* (2) no known sensorimotor impairment, (3) no behavioral problem that would interfere with task performance, (4) ability to pass a screening test of motor and rhythmic skills, (5) willingness to participate, and (6) parental consent. He thoroughly described the test stimuli and scoring system, thus facilitating replication. Test stimuli were selected and prepared in order to reduce possible impact of subject fatigue, attention deficits, and order effects. One limitation of Bruscia's study, however, was the relatively subjective analysis of beat accuracy determined through observer ratings and assignment of points. The determination of beat accuracy through observer ratings of "correct" or "incorrect" cannot fully address the continuum of small to gross temporal differences that can occur in rhythmic production.

In the past decade, testing of rhythmic ability has been further objectified through advances in technology. Stratford and Ching (1983) utilized a computer to record subjects' production of rhythmic patterns varying in complexity. Rather than comparing subjects by level of retardation, as did Bruscia (1981), these researchers investigated whether the etiology of mental retardation would have a significant effect on rhythmic precision. Using the PPVT, they compared three contrasting test groups matched for mental age: nondisabled children, children with retardation resulting from Down syndrome, and children with mental retardation of an etiology other than Down syndrome (no specific etiologies were provided for the third group, but could potentially include causes as different as birth trauma and genetic anomalies). Criteria for subject selection were (1) ability to understand and follow verbal instruction, (2) motor skills required to tap a metal plate, and (3) no behavioral disturbances that might interfere with the testing procedure.

In this study, extensive pilot testing was conducted in order to develop instrumentation both precise and usable with disabled children. Subjects listened to three different rhythms of increasing complexity and were asked to tap them simultaneously with the stimuli. After a practice session, responses were collected using a computer that quantified temporal deviations between the rhythmic model and the children's responses. Stratford and Ching found no significant difference in rhythmic abilities of nondisabled children and children with Down syndrome who were matched for mental age. In contrast, subjects with mental retardation resulting from other etiological bases performed significantly poorer (.05) than either the nondisabled or Down syndrome group. This relative similarity of rhythmic precision between subjects with Down syndrome and nondisabled subjects may contribute to perceptions stated in prior studies concerning the musicality of children with Down syndrome.

Precise instrumentation is only one strength apparent in their study. Stratford and Ching were unusually thorough in their critical review of past studies and the rationale for their own investigation. They challenged past claims concerning extraordinary musical abilities of children with Down syndrome, cautioning the reader that many of these statements were based on opinion or questionable research methodology. For example, the authors cited one study in which mentally retarded children were assessed with a test of the kind "given to candidates for examination for the Royal College of Music" (p. 24)!

From an educational standpoint, this study suggests that students identified under a generic classification such as mental retardation may demonstrate different rhythmic abilities for a variety of reasons, including the specific type of mental retardation. Differences from one etiology to another are particularly noticeable when the cause of retardation has a significant negative impact on motor functioning (e.g., spastic cerebral palsy).

Some researchers have examined rhythmic accuracy in relation to the mode of rhythmic presentation. Freeman (1986), like Stratford and Ching (1983), suggested that rhythmic response of persons with Down syndrome may be unique as a result of neurophysiological characteristics specific to that disability (including proportionately different distribution of brain mass). She cited several studies about cerebral characteristics of persons with Down syndrome that implied that visual-motor response may be more accurate than auditory-motor response. Therefore, the type of cue used to elicit a rhythmic response (e.g., visual cue paired with auditory information vs. auditory information only) might influence rhythmic accuracy. Rather than emphasizing the effects of attentional deficits or irrelevant stimuli as did Bruscia (1981), Freeman emphasized the sensory modality through which the task was presented.

Like Stratford and Ching (1983), Freeman (1986) selected a precise and objective measure of rhythmic production. A computer was used both to generate the musical stimuli for beat reference and to collect the response. Subjects were asked to tap a steady beat on a button-press in response to recorded music with a dominant pulse. The mean beat interval and beat deviation were recorded in milliseconds by computer.

In comparing rhythmic production of subjects with Down syndrome to that of a nondisabled reference group, Freeman reported significantly greater rhythmic consistency for the nondisabled children. Information about the reference group, such as mental or chronological age and details of musical training, was not provided. Therefore, comparisons of mental age, IQ, or chronological age for these groups are not possible.

From a music education standpoint, the primary findings of Freeman's study were as follows: In comparison with nondisabled children who tended to anticipate beats, children with Down syndrome tended toward a delayed beat response to a rhythmic musical selection. The provision of exaggerated conducting (visual cue), however, assisted in beat accuracy for those with Down syndrome. These findings suggest that success in rhythm activities (at least for children with Down syndrome) might be improved through instructional methodology, such as the use of visual cues, or visually clear conducting styles.

The benefits of visual cues in rhythmic activities were further supported in a study by Grant and LeCroy (1986), in which the researchers compared accuracy of rhythmic duplication (played on a hand drum) of five different rhythm patterns under the following conditions: tactile presentation, auditory presentation, auditory-visual presentation, and auditory-visual-tactile presentation. The authors did not indicate the etiology of retardation but described subjects as mildly retarded and having no sensory impairments. The data indicated a significant main effect for sensory conditions (.0001). Subjects of all ages scored higher with the auditory-visual mode. The tactile-only mode of presentation resulted in the lowest rhythmic accuracy—an unexpected finding considering how often educators tap on a student's knee in an attempt to aid rhythmic consistency. This research suggests that such a seemingly appropriate instructional strategy may be counterproductive with some mentally retarded students.

MELODIC SKILLS. In comparison with research on rhythmic abilities, little testing has been done specifically for melodic discrimination. In 1975, Arlette Zenatti compared the discrimination and recall abilities of 480 nondisabled and 396 mentally retarded children on a "same-different" task for three- or four-note melodic patterns. In addition to comparing the melodic discrimination of nondisabled and mentally retarded children of the same chronological and mental age, Zenatti investigated whether tonal versus atonal melodic structure would have a significant impact on discrimination accuracy.

Zenatti reported that the melodic discrimination of mentally retarded children was inferior to that of nondisabled children of the same chronological age, but approximated that of nondisabled children of the same mental age. The author also concluded that tonal acculturation (meaning more accurate discernment of melodic changes in tonal than in atonal melodic series) in subjects with mental retardation was a function of perceptual acuity and mental age, and that tonal acculturation emerged at approximately 8 to 9 years mental age.

This particular study had an unusually large sample size ($N = 876$) compared with many extant studies of musical characteristics of children with disabilities. Replication is hindered, however, by a sketchy description of testing procedures and subject selection criteria.

In conclusion, extant research regarding the musical skills of children who are mentally retarded focuses predominately on rhythmic tasks. Many questions relative to other skill areas remain unanswered. For example, what level of motor precision can be expected in activities using large-muscle control (e.g., movement activities)? How accurately do children with retardation replicate melodic contour during singing activities?

Research regarding musical characteristics should take into account the range of motor deficits and behavioral characteristics as well as the continuum of intellectual ability found among children with mental retardation. Some children with mental retardation may have concomitant orthopedic or sensory disabilities. For example, according to Rigrodski, Prunty, and Glovsky (1961), as many as 60 percent of Down syndrome residents in institutions have hearing loss. Factors such as physical impairments or behavioral problems interact with subnormal mental functioning, resulting in a unique profile of musical ability, and should be addressed in the design and interpretation of research.

Children with Hearing Impairments

Because hearing is the sense that is most typically associated with musical involvement, it is reasonable to assume that a significant hearing loss precludes musical enjoyment or achievement. Through the research efforts of music educators, music therapists, audiologists, and psychologists, it is known that people with hearing impairments do have the capacity to perceive and appreciate differential aspects of music.

The extent to which a hearing-impaired person can perceive and enjoy various aspects of music will vary, however, depending on a number of factors such as severity of hearing loss (mild to profound) and onset (congenital or acquired well after language development), the type of assistance hearing device (e.g., hearing aids, FM units) used by the individual, and experimental conditions (e.g., pure tone vs. complex waveforms, acoustic environment during testing, intensity and frequency of sound stimuli). These variables complicate the design and interpretation of research on the musical abilities of the hearing impaired. Furthermore, since hearing impairment is a low-incidence population, obtaining an adequate sample size is problematic. Despite these methodological challenges, a growing body of research is available concerning rhythmic and pitch or melodic perception of the hearing impaired (Darrow, 1979, 1984, 1987; Darrow and Goll, 1989; Ford, 1988; Kracke, 1975; Korduba, 1975; Rileigh and Odom, 1972; Sterritt, Camp, and Lippman, 1966).

Rhythmic Skills To date, the greatest focus of research interest has been rhythmic perception. Audiologists and psychologists have used a variety of temporally based discrimination and production tasks in order to determine the impact of auditory deprivation on temporal estimation and sequencing. Some researchers maintain that hearing is the sense through which awareness of time is best developed, and that early auditory deprivation results in deviant or delayed development in rhythmic perception (Rileigh and Odom, 1972; Sterritt et al., 1966). Therefore, even if intensity levels of the test stimuli are accessible to the listener, perception of the sound signal may differ from that of persons with normal hearing. These findings have implications for music educators whose concern is musical potential. To what extent does a hearing impairment affect musical aptitude and skill development?

Some data suggest that hearing-impaired children perform as effectively on rhythmic tasks as children with normal hearing while other studies show poorer accuracy. Why this inconsistency? Variability in the test stimuli and response mode may account for some differences in research outcomes. For example, some studies require reproduction of a rhythmic pattern or steady beat (Korduba, 1975; Darrow, 1979, 1984, 1987). Other studies measure discrimination of complex rhythm patterns or rhythmic change (e.g., eighth note to sixteenth note) (Darrow, 1987; Darrow and Goll, 1989). Still other researchers have used visual or tactile modes of presentation in addition to or in contrast to auditory stimuli (Darrow, 1979; Darrow & Goll, 1989; Korduba, 1975).

Subject characteristics (e.g., age, severity of hearing loss) can also influence outcome (Darrow, 1984, 1987). A study by Darrow (1984) illustrates how variability in task as well as subject characteristics can influence test outcome. In this study, Darrow used the *Test of Rhythmic Responsiveness* (Kaplan, 1977) as the measure for rhythmic abilities. This test has six different tasks: beat identification, tempo change, accent in meter discrimination, melodic rhythm duplication, rhythm pattern duplication, and rhythm pattern maintenance. Instructions were signed for hearing-impaired subjects at the language level of the child. Subjects listened to the rhythmic stimuli over earphones. Those subjects with hearing impairments heard the stimuli at a sound level of 35 dB greater than the intensity at which the subject could perceive speech sounds (SRT). Rhythmic responses were collected on a Tap Master, with one point recorded for each pattern tapped correctly. No points were awarded for partially correct responses.

In addition to assessing different types of rhythmic skills, Darrow analyzed the data with respect to four age levels and five categories of hearing status (normal hearing to profound hearing loss). The onset of loss was not reported. Darrow reported significant differences (.05) due to hearing status and for various subtests. Hearing-impaired and normally hearing subjects showed similar accuracy on beat maintenance, tempo changes, and metric accent. Normally hearing subjects, however, performed significantly more accurately (.05) on duplication of melodic rhythms and rhythm patterns. Subjects with profound hearing losses performed significantly more poorly (.05) than hearing-impaired subjects with mild or moderate losses. These findings demonstrate that rhythmic abilities may vary, depending on the nature of the task itself and the hearing status of the subject.

It is clear from this study using multiple measures that one indicator of rhythmic ability provides an incomplete picture of the capabilities of students with hearing impairments. For example, some research suggests that rhythmic information is more easily accessed than melodic information (Darrow, 1987). This may account for poorer performance among hearing-impaired subjects on such tasks as melodic rhythm. Furthermore, the varied abilities of the same subject from task to task underscore the importance of thoughtfully sequenced avenues of inquiry. Too often, research efforts with disabled subjects consist of individual and unrelated studies, each using dependent measures and response tasks with little regard for prior research.

Frequency Based Perception In comparison with rhythmic studies, little investigation has been conducted on the melodic or pitch perception of the hearing impaired (Darrow, 1987; Ford, 1988). Testing with the *Primary Measures of Music Audiation* (PMMA) (Gordon, 1979) indicated that hearing-impaired children are significantly less accurate than children with normal hearing (.05) in melodic discrimination. Furthermore, mean scores on the Tonal subtest were lower than mean scores on the Rhythm subtest (Darrow, 1978). Ford's (1988) test of pitch perception suggests factors that might have contributed to the errors on the melodic subtest of the PMMA.

Ford investigated effects of school music experience, age, academic level, and gender on pitch discrimination (same-different task) at 250 and 500 Hz. Hearing-impaired subjects listened to paired pitches of either no change or changes ranging from a minor second to greater than an augmented fourth. Stimuli were presented over stereo earphones at the most comfortable level of loudness (MCL), which for these subjects ranged from 90 to 110 dB.

Over 50 percent of subjects were able to discriminate a change of a minor third with 75 percent accuracy at both 250 and 500 Hz. Intervals smaller than a minor third proved difficult for hearing-impaired subjects, the same small frequency changes found in many items of the PMMA Tonal subtest. Ford found no differences for pitch discrimination due to age or music training, but discrimination proved more accurate at 250 Hz than at 500 Hz (.05). The researcher concluded that hearing-impaired children may benefit from listening activities (1) that are in an optimal pitch range (around B below middle C to an interval of a twelfth above middle C) and (2) that start with gross pitch differentiation, gradually reducing the size of the interval change.

One of the notable strengths of Ford's study is the reporting of subject characteristics: IQ, age (6–9; 11–12), type of loss (sensorineural loss only), onset of loss (all subjects were congenitally or prelingually deafened), musical background (home environment), music education (schools for the deaf with and without a music curriculum), and status regarding multiple disabilities (subjects with multiple disabilities were excluded). All too often, researchers have been less thorough in reporting subject characteristics such as onset of hearing loss and extent of musical training and experience. Even the etiology of hearing loss may be of interest in some circum-

stances. For example, deaf subjects whose hearing loss was due to meningitis may manifest neurological complications that influence perception and motor precision. Although obtaining a large, homogeneous sample for all factors is not realistic, thorough reporting of characteristics is an important step in interpretation and generalization of research findings.

In any research with hearing-impaired subjects, clear communication between the subject and tester is a critical factor in test reliability. If the subject uses manual communication, instructions should be given in the specific system (e.g., American Sign Language, manually coded English, cued speech) used by the subject in everyday interactions. In addition, since many hearing-impaired children lag behind normally hearing peers in language development (e.g., knowledge of vocabulary, correct use of syntax), instructions should be clear and reflect the language level of the individual subject (Darrow and Gfeller, 1988). For example, Darrow's (1984) use of sign language at the subject's level of language difficulty increases confidence that the subject understood the task at hand. Even if appropriate communication is used, the tester should provide enough sample trials to ensure that the subject understands the task requirements. Visual aids and demonstration can facilitate understanding.

Children with Visual Impairments

Whereas the musical potential of hearing impaired is often underestimated, it is too often assumed that persons with visual impairments have unusual musical abilities (Pitman, 1965). As early as 1918, Seashore and Ling challenged the notion that the blind have an inherently superior auditory sense. The "compensation hypothesis," which states that the other senses of the blind become "quicker," has been abandoned in favor of the theory that the blind probably use their intact sensory channels to fuller capacity (Stankov and Spilsbury, 1978).

A series of studies investigating auditory perception of the blind as it relates to musical ability supports the notion that the sighted and blind are, for the most part, similar in musical aptitude (Drake, 1939; Heim, 1963; Kwalwasser, 1955; Madsen and Darrow, 1989; Sakurabayashi, Satyo, and Uehara, 1956; Seashore and Ling, 1918; Stankov and Spilsbury, 1978). However, persons with visual impairments may excel in particular subtests of a larger battery of auditory perception (e.g., tonal memory; Stankov and Spilsbury, 1978).

According to Stankov and Spilsbury (1978), many studies have failed to consider the onset or the severity of visual impairment. These are factors that should be controlled or addressed as an independent variable in future research. Despite limitations in past research, there is relative agreement that the blind are not unusually talented in music or auditory acuity. This conclusion leads the researcher in music education away from inquiry concerning extraordinary talent, and toward the determination of instructional techniques that will allow the visually impaired student to function successfully alongside nondisabled peers.

Children with Learning Disabilities

Children with specific learning disabilities constitute a substantial group of those disabled students served within the educational mainstream. Yet this group is meagerly represented within research on the musical characteristics of disabled students. This dearth of research may be due in part to the methodological difficulties in subject selection.

By definition, this category is made up of students who have learning problems but whose difficulties cannot be attributed to other disabilities such as mental retardation, sensory impairments, or emotional disturbance. In a sense, it is definition by exclusion, covering a population with widely divergent types of academic difficulties (e.g., math, reading, spelling) that vary considerably in severity. Furthermore, there is a variety of etiologies associated with learning disabilities, including minimal brain dysfunction, perceptual disorders, and aphasia, to name just a few. Many of these etiologies are difficult to assess and identify, so the cause for many learning disabilities may be unreported, unknown, or misdiagnosed. Even leaders in the field of learning disabilities disagree concerning what actually constitutes this condition (Mercer, 1987). It is not surprising, therefore, that those researchers who have attempted to study music perception of students with learning disabilities have failed to control for or report all possible subject differences.

Complete reporting of subject selection criteria and types of specific disabilities is absent in Gilbert's (1983) study of motor music skills. Only age and years of academic discrepancy are provided. Nevertheless, Gilbert's study also had notable strengths. The author reported impressive test-retest (.91–.94), interjudge (.98–.94), and internal consistency (.78–.89) coefficients for her self-devised assessment tool. Furthermore, details about test development were reported in a previous publication (Gilbert, 1979).

Gilbert's findings are of practical interest to the music educator. In comparing musical motor skills of nondisabled and learning-disabled children, nondisabled children showed greater performance on the composite test score (.001). Given the heterogeneous nature of the learning-disabled population, it could be expected that the standard deviation for learning-disabled children would be greater than that for nondisabled children. In addition, significantly more erratic motor development over age among learning-disabled children compared with nondisabled peers (.02) is consistent with theories of immature or idiosyncratic neurological development reported in the special education literature (Gfeller, 1982).

Betty Atterbury (1983) also investigated motor and rhythmic capabilities of learning-disabled children in comparison with nondisabled children. A self-constructed assessment of rhythm perception and rhythm performance was conducted using three modes of presentation: tapped, melodic, and tapped and spoken (ta, titi, etc.). In addition, a modified form of the PMMA (Rhythm subtest) was administered (paper and pencil responses were eliminated in favor of a pointing response). Atterbury piloted the protocol of her author-constructed test to determine its suitability for the population.

Although she did not provide in-depth documentation concerning how observers were trained for rating the rhythmic production test, she achieved an interrater reliability of .96.

Atterbury selected learning-disabled subjects by type of disability, including only subjects with problems in reading. This criterion alone cannot ensure homogeneity of etiology or specific learning characteristics, but it is an effort to control subject variables. Further, Atterbury limited the age of subjects to 7 and 8 years, which helped to control for possible developmental effects. She also matched learning-disabled and nondisabled subjects for socioeconomic status as well as gender.

Like Gilbert, Atterbury found significant differences (.01) in favor of nondisabled children for reproduction of a rhythmic task. In addition, nondisabled children showed significantly greater accuracy on the PMMA (.01). The author concluded that while learning-disabled children with reading difficulty perceived simple rhythmic patterns similarly to nondisabled listeners, they had greater difficulty with more complex rhythm patterns, and performed more poorly on rhythmic reproduction tasks. However, mode of presentation appeared to have an impact on rhythmic performance, since subjects performed with significantly greater accuracy under the condition of tapped and spoken rhythmic syllables (e.g., "ta-titi") than with tapped or melodic presentations alone. These findings suggest that learning-disabled children with reading difficulties may not only struggle in classroom activities requiring reading (e.g., lyrics to songs, or instructions in texts), but also have difficulty with production of difficult rhythm patterns. However, the instructor may reduce learning difficulty through the use of spoken as well as tapped presentation modes when introducing new rhythmic tasks.

There exists a scant body of research concerning the musical aptitude and achievement of learning-disabled children. Perhaps researchers have been discouraged by subject selection factors or difficulty obtaining reliable data. This is one of many populations in which the researcher should consider alternatives to more traditional testing procedures and research designs. For example, additional response time or simplification of test instructions can make a difference in test performance. The specific disability reported by the special education staff (e.g. problems with reading, difficulty understanding spoken language) should be accommodated in the test protocol. Given the intersubject variability, research with this population may lend itself to single-subject designs in which the subject also serves as control across treatment conditions. Although complete homogeneity in a large sample is unrealistic, interpretation of the study can be supported by controlling for those variables most relevant to the primary research question, and through detailed documentation of subject characteristics.

Persons with Other Disabilities

The previous sections include only a portion of those disabilities listed under federal guidelines for special education.

Other classifications include emotionally disturbed, speech-impaired, other–health-impaired, orthopedically impaired, and multihandicapped. Although several of these categories make up a sizeable proportion of those children served in special education and music classrooms, these populations are minimally represented within research on musical characteristics.

Children with Emotional Disturbances The category of emotionally disturbed children includes those with such widely divergent problems as aggressive behavior, social withdrawal, and psychoses. When a single classification encompasses such diverse subgroups, criteria for subject selection should be thoughtfully determined and clearly articulated.

At present, little data exist concerning musical characteristics of emotionally disturbed children. One study (Giacobbe and Graham, 1978) regarding musical response has addressed the heterogeneity of this classification by including only children with aggressive behaviors. Participants were screened using several clinical measures (PPVT and Behavior Problem Checklist, hearing acuity, and school records of behavioral problems). All subjects were American Caucasian males between the ages of nine and 11 years. Nondisabled and emotionally disturbed children with aggressive behaviors were compared on responses to 51 different taped musical stimuli. Responses included three evaluative dimensions (like/dislike, happy/sad, and good/bad) and a summed response, resulting in a total of 204 variables.

In general, responses were more similar than different across the two groups: Significant differences (.05 and .01) were reported for only six of the 204 variables. Both groups tended to respond in the same manner to selected musical stimuli, though the emotionally disturbed subjects demonstrated greater variability than nondisabled children.

Investigation of one subcategory of emotional disturbance in comparison with a control group is one way to approach such a heterogeneous population. Contrasting different types of disturbance (e.g., depression versus psychotic disorders) is another appropriate comparison. Whatever the comparison, screening procedures for subject selection should be clear and thoroughly reported. Furthermore, in studies related to perception, affective response, or motor precision, any use of medication should be indicated since drugs can influence cognitive processes or alter mood and affect.

Children with Autism Although autism is not a separate classification within federal guidelines for special education, it is a unique condition. Considered a pervasive developmental disorder, autism manifests itself through an unusual interactive style and bizarre behaviors (*Diagnostic and Statistical Manual of Mental Disorders-III-R,* APA, 1987). Several researchers have observed, and then studied empirically, musical interest in this population. Measures such as duration of time committed to musical stimuli (Thaut, 1980), interviews of parents (DeMyer, 1974), and vocal imitation (Applebaum, Engel, Koegel, and Imhoff, 1979) have been

used to investigate the question of musical interest or ability. Studies by Thaut (1980) and DeMyer (1974) support the notion of preference for music over other types of environmental stimuli. Furthermore, Applebaum and colleagues (1979) found that vocal imitation of three children with autism was equal to or better than that of three nondisabled children on 62 percent of trials. However, Applebaum and colleagues pointed out that imitation is a very limited skill, and that the social and interactive skills required for full musical involvement are sadly lacking in children with autism. In short, musical aptitude and achievement are only two factors in classroom participation. Accompanying behavioral characteristics (e.g., unusual interactive style, compliance problems) are as important in classroom success.

Children with Speech Impairments Speech-impairment is a heterogeneous category that includes a wide range of problems, including delayed speech, aphasia, dysfluency (stuttering), articulation problems, and voice disorders. Etiology can be attributed to mental retardation, brain injuries, physical trauma, hearing losses, or functional causes (e.g., understimulation, emotional conflicts).

Given the range of presenting symptoms and etiological bases along with the dearth of systematic inquiry, it is difficult to identify trends of musical abilities. One obvious area of inquiry regarding music education is vocal production in activities such as singing. Research by Sato (1960), for instance, indicated that the vocal range of cerebral palsied children is lower and more narrow than that of nondisabled children. Furthermore, extended vocal training (e.g., 3 years) using traditional vocal exercises did not benefit vocal range. This study illustrates that certain physical conditions may not respond to remediation strategies. Rather, compensatory activities may be more realistic. In addition to problems with vocal production, a few studies (Eisenson, Kastein, and Schneiderman, 1958; Bergendal and Talo, 1969) suggest that persons with various speech impairments may have poorer perceptual abilities (as measured by the *Seashore Measures of Musical Talents,* Seashore et al., 1960) on tasks related to pitch or melodic discrimination.

As can be seen, a small body of research exists regarding the musical characteristics of children with emotional disturbance, autism, and speech impairments. As researchers do contribute to these areas of inquiry, it is important to address the heterogeneity of these populations through meticulous criteria for sample selection and careful reporting of subject characteristics. For those subjects with motor or communication deficits, adaptation in test instructions or response mode is critical. In the cases of small samples, single-subject designs and nonparametric analyses along with qualitative research would be of value.

In conclusion, the practitioner might argue that studies of musical aptitude, achievement, and specific skills do not directly address instructional methodology. An understanding of the musical potential and abilities of such children, however, assists the music educator in setting realistic educational objectives and selecting appropriate instructional methods.

MUSIC EDUCATION PRACTICES
WITH DISABLED STUDENTS

A perusal of literature on music education practices for disabled students reveals many methodological articles recommending particular instructional practices, or advocating music for the disabled. Collections of musical repertoire and activities, application of traditional instructional approaches and philosophies (e.g., Orff, Kodály, Dalcroze), and recommendations for adaptive instruments or nontraditional notation have been utilized by countless music educators.

In contrast to the wealth of methodological resources, actual research in which educational practices are objectively evaluated through accepted methods of structured inquiry is scarce (Hopkins, 1976; Kalenius, 1977). The relative dearth of research investigating educational practices in the classroom setting is unfortunate but not particularly surprising, since the design and implementation of such research tends to be labor intensive and potentially expensive, and poses many methodological challenges. For example, measurable gains resulting from educational interventions usually occur over time for all students, but the time required for change may be even longer when testing students who have specific learning disabilities or subaverage intelligence. Even with extended instructional time, possible gains may be difficult to measure since many of the existing tests in music education are designed for and normed on nondisabled students, and may be inappropriate for children with cognitive, behavioral, communicative, or motor deficits. In addition, it is often difficult to obtain adequate sample sizes. To the extent possible, students with disabilities are now educated in home communities within each state. Therefore, intact groups of students who fit selection criteria may not be available in one school or area.

The Buckley Amendment and the National Research Act of 1984 have also influenced research practice (Borg and Gall, 1979). These regulations, which protect the privacy and safety of participants, require informed consent and parental permission. The ethical value of these regulations is clear. Nevertheless, these regulations contribute to the challenge of subject acquisition. Although it is true that parental approval is a necessary component of research with all children, students with disabilities may be medically fragile and have often endured extensive diagnostic assessment, and so parents may be especially hesitant to permit yet another test.

Despite these barriers, researchers have endeavored to study various components of music education for disabled students. These studies include evaluation of mainstreaming, teacher preparation, and specific instructional practices for students with specialized educational needs.

Mainstreaming

Perhaps no single event has had such a profound effect on the education of children with disabilities as the passage and implementation of Public Law (PL) 94-142, the Education for All Handicapped Children Act of 1975. This particular bill mandated that students with all types of disabilities be educated in the least restrictive environment, with educational placement closest to normal as possible while still providing adequate instructional support. In many instances, this means that students with disabilities are placed in classrooms with nondisabled peers. This practice of integrating the disabled with nondisabled learners, often called mainstreaming, has been the focus of numerous research efforts. To date, the bulk of inquiry has been descriptive studies regarding the present status of mainstreaming.

Descriptive Studies The questionnaire has been a common tool for gathering descriptive information about mainstreaming and music education. Studies by Damer (1979), Brown (1981), Gilbert and Asmus (1981), Gavin (1983), Stein (1983), Atterbury (1986), and Gfeller, Darrow, and Hedden (1990) have examined the following factors: placement procedures, administrative support for mainstreaming, teacher attitude toward mainstreaming, and teacher knowledge and preparation for working with disabled students. Sampling has been as limited as a citywide group of instructors (Brown, 1981; Gavin, 1983) or as inclusive as a nationwide sampling of music educators (Gilbert and Asmus, 1981).

Results from these questionnaires indicate that placement of children with disabilities in the regular music class is a common practice. A national survey of music educators (Gilbert and Asmus, 1981) indicated that as many as 63 percent of music educators have had professional involvement with disabled children. With regard to specialty area and grade level, mainstreaming occurs more frequently in general music and in elementary schools than in performance ensembles or high schools (Gfeller et al., 1990). Data indicate that music educators are seldom involved in placement decisions, and that administrative support (e.g., provision of teacher aides in the music classroom, extra preparation time, special teaching materials, or inservice) is limited (Atterbury, 1986; Gfeller et al., 1990; Gilbert and Asmus, 1981).

Teachers' attitudes toward mainstreaming might be described as ambivalent. In one study (Gfeller et al., 1990), 52 percent of music educators reported that the needs of children with disabilities were being met in the regular music class, but 50 percent of educators indicated that children with disabilities were better served in special classes. Furthermore, 61 percent of the respondents indicated that the presence of disabled children in the music class hampered the progress of nondisabled children. Specific concerns stated in another study (Gilbert and Asmus, 1981) included too large a number of disabled children in one classroom and difficulty adjusting for individual differences. Children with emotional disorders were reported as those most difficult to accommodate in the regular music classroom (Gfeller et al., 1990).

Perhaps the ambivalence toward mainstreaming is related to lack of preparation for working with students who have disabilities. In 1981 Gilbert and Asmus reported that 80 percent of respondents expressed a need for information regarding music programs for students with disabilities. In research conducted almost a decade later (Gfeller et al., 1990), only one-third of educators stated that they receive any in-service education, and that is only on direct request. Thirty-eight percent of respondents indicated that they had never attended any workshops or college courses directly related to the education of students with disabilities.

The care with which questionnaires regarding mainstreaming have been prepared and analyzed varies greatly. Documentation of reliability or efforts to establish validity is present in only a few studies (Damer, 1979; Gilbert and Asmus, 1981; Gfeller et al., 1990). Other investigations give little or no detail concerning questionnaire development. Despite the variance in methodological care found in extant research, there is nevertheless remarkable agreement across these studies concerning the present state of mainstreaming. These research findings, spanning more than 10 years, point up some consistent trends regarding the continued need for teacher preparation and administrative support (Damer, 1979; Gfeller et al., 1990; Gilbert and Asmus, 1981).

One of the limitations of a questionnaire in assessing teacher attitude toward children with disabilities is the fact that many instructors have had limited experience with different types of disabilities. Opinions expressed in a questionnaire may reflect an isolated experience with a particular child and disability. In order to investigate attitudes of music education students toward a variety of disabilities, Stuart and Gilbert (1977) used stimulus tapes of disabled children engaged in musical activities. The tape included examples of conditions ranging from mild to severe. These prospective teachers indicated that they were less comfortable, less confident, and more hesitant to work with children as the severity of physical or behavioral problems demonstrated on the tapes increased. These findings suggest that music educators could benefit from preservice training on the educational needs of children with severe disabilities.

The aforementioned methods assessed teacher perceptions concerning mainstreaming. Descriptive research concerning the present status of mainstreaming can also evaluate the participation of students actually integrated in regular music classrooms. For example, in 1986, Keith Thompson evaluated the efficacy of mainstreaming by measuring participation of "mildly handicapped" students and their nondisabled peers. Thompson (1986) used an observation scale to determine on-task behavior and extent of successful participation for 14 mildly disabled and 14 nondisabled students in mainstreamed general music. Contrary to what some educators might expect, no significant differences were noted between the two student groups for off-task behaviors. However, Thompson also found that nondisabled students were significantly (.05) more "successful" than disabled students. The study did not specify criteria for determination of successful participation.

In addition to evaluating student participation, Thompson quantified time spent in specific activities. He found the most frequent activities (in percentage of time spent) to be teacher talk (49 percent), singing (31 percent), listening (10 percent), and playing instruments (08 percent). Moving to music and activities involving writing occurred infrequently (1 percent each). Thompson concluded that the high percentage of teacher talk and infrequent use of multisensory activities may have hampered successful participation by students with disabilities.

Clear interpretation of Thompson's study is difficult since a generic description such as "mildly handicapped" can cover a diverse group of disabilities. Thompson noted that specific data were not available as a result of school policy. Some schools do indeed have a restrictive interpretation of regulations concerning confidentiality of student records. Obtaining access to files that indicate the specific disability, mental age, and other informative subject variables can be troublesome, or even impossible.

Obtaining permission for access to relevant subject characteristics in school records prior to testing is ideal. In circumstances where such information is withheld, the researcher should consider alternative methods for defining the population tested. For example, some researchers (Bixler, 1968; Kaplan, 1977; Gfeller, 1982) have administered their own screening measures (e.g., PPVT, *Slosson Intelligence Test*) as a part of the research methodology. Direct observation of target behaviors relevant to the research questions could be obtained prior to testing, and subsequently reported as part of subject selection criteria.

Descriptive studies give some indication about the effectiveness of mainstreaming. From the aforementioned studies, it is clear that some aspects of mainstreaming practices can be improved: (1) teacher preparation for working with disabled students, (Atterbury, 1986; Gfeller et al., 1990; Gilbert and Asmus, 1981); (2) disabled childrens' success in the mainstream music classroom (Thompson, 1986); and (3) teacher acceptance of mainstreaming practices (Gfeller et al., 1990). These findings provide a good point of departure for research intended to improve educational practice. One example of research designed to investigate the efficacy of different instructional approaches in regard to mainstreaming focused on student involvement and attitude as positive outcomes.

Student Involvement and Attitude Jellison, Brooks, and Huck (1984) investigated the effect of different instructional approaches on two variables: extent of peer involvement between disabled and nondisabled students, and peer acceptance of severely disabled students in a mainstreamed setting. In this study, integration consisted of the placement of five or six severely disabled students in four regular music classrooms (grades 3–6). Disabled students were screened to ensure a minimal level of eye contact, ability to communicate with peers, and compliant behavior.

These researchers used both systematic observation of student interaction and two measures of self-report, the *Acceptance Within Music Scale* (AMS) and an *Acceptance Scale,* (AS) (Meyer, 1981), to determine attitude of nondisabled students toward peers with disabilities. The AMS was developed by Jellison as a situation-specific tool to parallel a more general measure (AS) with demonstrated validity and reliability. (Subsequent factor analysis by Jellison [1985] indicated that the AMS has similar dimensions to those suggested by Meyer [1981] in the AS.)

Using these measures, Jellison and colleagues studied the effects of three different teaching conditions on frequency and quality of interaction between disabled and nondisabled students and peer acceptance. The three conditions were as follows: (1) large group activities, (2) small group activities, and (3) small group activities with contingencies for completion of an assigned group task. The contingency reward consisted of the opportunity to listen to rock music known to be of interest to classroom members. In this multiple baseline design, each classroom was exposed to each experimental condition but at staggered intervals over a period of 13 weeks. Through visual inspection of data illustrated in graphic form, the investigators were able to determine whether changes in interaction occurred sequentially as the treatment was introduced for each subsequent group.

The researchers reported that the percentage of heterogeneous (disabled and nondisabled) social interaction was highest under the teaching conditions of small groups with contingencies offered for cooperative behavior. The lowest percentage of interactions occurred in the more traditional large group activities. Three of the four classrooms showed significantly higher acceptance of disabled classmates (.05) from pre- to posttest. Jellison and colleagues concluded that meaningful integration of disabled students does not occur as a result of proximity alone. Small groups, clear teacher expectations, and opportunities for cooperative activities were important factors in successful integration.

These researchers studied a sizeable sample ($N = 126$; 100 nondisabled and 26 disabled students) and used multiple measures (two measures of attitude and extent of integrated interaction) to determine treatment effectiveness, thus providing a more thorough view of the various aspects of integration than would be possible with a single, global measure. Confidence in the observation date was established through a reliability coefficient of .93.

The research design had particular advantages in an educational setting. The multiple baseline permitted each classroom to serve as its own control. This has ethical advantages over research designs using control groups, since potentially advantageous interventions are not withheld from any subjects. This type of design, however, does not control for the different lengths of time groups spend under contrasting treatment conditions.

The instructional approach of small groups and contingencies is only one of many variables that potentially affect the success of mainstreaming practice. Additional factors such as placement policies, sensitivity training for nondisabled students, administrative support, and the selection of instructional objectives are just a few of the areas of inquiry needed regarding integration of disabled children in the regular music classroom. One factor that influences student success in music, whether in the mainstream or self-contained classroom, is the extent to which the music educator is prepared to serve the student with special needs.

Teacher Preparation

According to responses by educators garnered in questionnaires (Gfeller, et al., 1990; Gilbert and Asmus, 1981), music teachers believe they need additional information on music programming for students with disabilities. Studies by Sheridan (1979), Kearns (1986), Smith (1987), Lehr (1977),

and Dickinson (1976) have presented a variety of instructional options designed to prepare music teachers to work with disabled students.

Both Sheridan (1979) and Kearns (1986) addressed the provision of inservice at the state level. Sheridan's (1979) detailed account of a statewide inservice program provided an example of possible components of instructional units and the process of program implementation. Objective evaluation of outcomes, such as teacher satisfaction with the inservice or resulting instructional outcomes by participants, was not included in the study. Kearns (1986) conducted a post hoc evaluation of an existing arts inservice program in the state of Pennsylvania. Her description of the inservice program itself was quite sketchy. Therefore, it is impossible to attribute positive attitude to any particular component of the inservice. But the data do reflect strong consensus among the 254 respondents that inservice was helpful: Ninety-four percent indicated that inservice was valuable, and another 89 percent reported a positive effect on teaching practice.

In addition to state-level inservice workshops, collegiate classroom instruction has been the focus of research inquiry (Lehr, 1977; Smith, 1987). Smith (1987) examined whether music education majors who had participated in a 5-day unit on the exceptional child would demonstrate greater ability than would a control group (music education majors with no concentrated instruction on this topic) in generating adaptive teaching strategies in a mainstream context. In order that their instructional effectiveness could be evaluated, subjects were required to apply their knowledge of educational practices by generating instructional adaptations in response to videotaped teaching segments with four different types of disabled students (visual impairment, hearing impairment, mental retardation, and emotional impairment). Testing took place three weeks after instruction of the experimental group.

Smith found that students receiving classroom instruction on students with disabilities performed significantly better (.01) than a control group on the total number of adaptive strategies generated. When analyzed by specific disabilities, the experimental group generated a significantly greater number of strategies for the categories of emotional and visual impairments (.05). Both groups produced the smallest number of adaptations for working with emotionally disturbed children. This is consistent with findings by Gfeller and colleagues (1990) that teachers find students with emotional disturbances the most difficult group to mainstream. Categorical analysis of adaptations (e.g., use of auditory cues, visual cues, classroom management) indicated that the experimental group more frequently devised adaptations consistent with instructional material on education of the exceptional child than did the control group, suggesting that the students were able to transfer the instructional information to a related task.

Although a larger sample size ($N = 23$) and greater effort to control for possible initial group differences would have strengthened the study, the dependent variable nevertheless seems a very appropriate one. The ability to adapt instruction reflects a "real-life" teaching skill critical to successful mainstreaming.

Lehr's (1977) research concerning a preparatory class offered at Dartington College of Arts (United Kingdom) offers an interesting contrast to the study by Smith (1987), both in research methodology and in content of the course investigated. Rather than evaluating the educational experience through behavioral outcomes as did Smith, Lehr chose primarily qualitative methods of inquiry. Evaluation was composed of in-depth description of course content, including relative strengths and weaknesses.

The instructional focus of the class studied by Lehr was substantially different from that proposed by Smith (1987). Lehr noted the emphasis on musical development of the classroom teacher, and the lesser emphasis on what was termed "special education" information, such as characteristics of learners with disabilities and instructional adaptations. The class described by Lehr also included direct, but loosely structured exposure to several special music programs within the United Kingdom, a contrast with the outlined learning objectives facilitated within Smith's classroom. Research comparing differing approaches to inservice (such as the two contrasting models evaluated by Smith and Lehr) and subsequent outcomes warrants additional investigation.

The aforementioned studies on teacher preparation have focused on the music specialist, with evaluative emphasis placed on the teacher as learner. Dickinson's (1976) study explored the feasibility of classroom teachers (as opposed to music specialists) leading music activities for students with mild mental retardation. This study also evaluated the end result of teacher preparation, that is, student participation and musical growth.

Dickinson's study required exceptional commitment of time and resources: This field study represented more than one year of sustained effort, including initial training of classroom teachers, pretesting of student abilities, implementation of weekly music activities, daily observation of teacher and student behaviors, and posttesting for student ability at the end of one academic year. The implementation and assessment of the program required wholesale cooperation on the part of administrators and teachers in the two schools involved (one treatment, one control).

Dickinson provided an extensive rationale for the content of the musical program implemented in the schools, and included numerous examples of instructional materials and approaches. She also specified sampling procedures for the treatment group (a school program receiving the special music program) and a control group (a school with only incidental music experiences), as well as evaluative components of the project. She selected both quantitative and qualitative measures to evaluate student progress and teacher effectiveness, providing a rationale for each measure. Dickinson discussed, at length, measurement of musical aptitude, achievement, and ability as she built a case for using Bentley's (1966) *Measures of Musical Ability* to assess learning outcomes. Not all would agree that the use of the Bentley test was appropriate in this circumstance. Nevertheless, her description of the adaptive *Measures of Musical Ability* was clear and complete, thus facilitating replication. More detailed description of other questionnaires, observation forms, and statistical analyses used in the study would have been desirable.

Dickinson determined through pre- and posttest mea-

sures of specific musical skills and the modified Bentley *Measures of Musical Abilities* that those children involved in the special music program showed significantly superior (confidence level not indicated) performance to that of children receiving only incidental musical experiences. In short, classroom teachers trained in the provision of specially designed music activities were effective in enhancing the musical skills of children described as educationally subnormal (IQ ranging from 50 to 90 on the *Wechsler Intelligence Scale for Children*).

Because Dickinson's music program was designed for disabled students placed in self-contained educational institutions, some of the program recommendations may not generalize to the integrated instructional settings in the American educational system. Furthermore, the program's emphasis on teaching basic musical skills to the classroom teacher is not relevant for preparing the music specialist to work with disabled students. But Dickinson's study does provide an example of ongoing professional inservice, and illustrates possible measures for determining instructional outcomes. Furthermore, Dickinson's findings suggest that students with mild mental retardation can show measurable gains in musical ability as a result of ongoing and developmentally appropriate music activities.

The topic of preservice and inservice effectiveness will continue to be an important topic as teachers provide music education for students with unique learning characteristics. Given the variability of music programs, placement policies and procedures, and administrative structure from school to school, this small group of studies only begins to cover the range of factors that influence teacher preparation.

Instructional Practices

All students benefit from appropriate, quality instruction, but for many disabled students such instruction is the difference between success and abject failure. Therefore, it is of real concern that so few research studies investigate specific instructional practices (Kalenius, 1977). Many of the existing resources concerning the disabled learner are collections of musical activities, lists of how to's, or opinion articles advocating the use of existing approaches or such methods as Orff, Kodály, or Dalcroze. Actual systematic evaluation of instructional practices in which clear research questions are hypothesized and tested is all too rare.

As a group, existing studies consist primarily of singular studies on widely ranging topics such as curricular development, instrumental instruction, vocal ensemble participation, and notational and rhythmic training (Beal, 1980; Buker, 1966; Hughes, Robbins, Smith, and Kinkade, 1987; Rosene, 1976; Strockbine, 1982). The group best represented in this small body of research is probably students with mental retardation.

Students with Mental Retardation

GENERAL MUSIC CURRICULA.   Concern about the appropriate curricular content for students with mental disabilities has long been of interest to music educators. Several studies have addressed curricular content relative to the self-contained music classroom. Beal (1980) and Strockbine (1982) utilized contrasting research approaches in their studies on curricula for disabled students. Beal (1980) developed and evaluated a music curriculum for a self-contained class of trainable (moderate) mentally retarded adolescents. The curriculum included sequenced instructional objectives in the areas of rhythm, melody, harmony, form, tone color, expression, singing, and playing instruments.

In order to assess the effectiveness of the curriculum, Beal compared gains on a self-devised skills assessment (pretest-posttest) for two experimental groups involved in her model curriculum and one control group (intact classrooms—no random assignments). Following four weeks of instruction (three times weekly for 30-minute sessions), significant gains on curricular objectives (.001) were achieved by both experimental groups compared with the control group.

Beal provided little information about subject characteristics, specific observational criteria used during assessment, and validity of the curriculum or test items. Test reliability was not discussed. This masters thesis, however, did include extensive detail concerning the curriculum tested, including activities, instructional methods, and sample assessment sheets. Her curricular materials could be readily replicated, and represent basic skill areas commonly found in general music. Of particular merit in Beal's model curriculum was the attention to behavioral management. As those educators who have served mentally retarded students can attest, slow rate of learning is one of many educational hurdles. Inappropriate social behaviors, short attention span, and distractibility are not uncommon, and can interfere with the most efficacious educational objectives and methods. In short, this study provides an example of research that is directly related to actual instructional concerns and practices.

Frank Strockbine Jr. (1982) approached curricular development in a manner quite different from Beal (1980). Rather than evaluating appropriateness through behavioral measures, Strockbine supported his suggested curriculum through the logical application of Piaget's developmental theories of perception, imitation, and mental imagery. Strockbine first outlined and analyzed Piagetian theory of child development in the sensorimotor and preoperational stages of child development, relating cognitive stages to particular musical tasks. The author also reviewed Piagetian-based research concerning the development of children with mental retardation, using these examples as rationale for modifications in the learning environment. His study is an example of qualitative research regarding curriculum for mentally retarded students. A follow-up study, using quantitative methods that evaluate educational gains and student involvement in a field setting, would be a logical extension of this study.

In 1966, Guy Buker conducted an experimental program of rhythm reading for educable mentally retarded children aged 9 to 13. He wished to determine whether reading rhythmic notation was a reasonable addition to the music education curriculum of EMR students. In this study, EMR children were assigned to either traditional music classes or a program

of rhythmic reading based on methods by Mary Helen Richards (1964). Children receiving structured rhythmic reading instruction (7 weeks of special rhythmic instruction) showed significant (.001) gains (pre- to posttest) in rhythmic reading over a control group. Buker also found that higher IQ was shown to be positively correlated with gain scores. It appears that when higher functioning mentally retarded students are provided with appropriate instructional methods they may experience success in this traditional musical skill.

Buker tested an impressive sample size ($N = 78$), and specified many important subject characteristics (i.e., chronological age, mental age, IQ, socioeconomic status, laterality, and home musical environment) of his population. He included a control group as part of his research design, and reported reliability coefficients for his self-constructed test ($r = .82$), and for interrate reliability ($r = .98$). Furthermore, he justified his choice of instructional methodology by reviewing characteristics of mentally retarded learners and theories about normal and delayed or unusual learning behaviors.

CHORAL AND INSTRUMENTAL INSTRUCTION. Although descriptive research indicates that disabled students are less frequently enrolled in performance ensembles (Gfeller et al., 1990; Gilbert and Asmus, 1981), experimental research regarding instructional practices suggests that these limitations need not exist. Hughes and colleagues (1987) studied the effects of a nine-month choral music program on the singing ability of adolescents with trainable mental retardation. This choral program included planned reinforcement (e.g., verbal praise, singing solos, wearing uniforms, parental support, certificates, positive role models) and multisensory activities (e.g., use of pictures and graphs, physical gestures, modeling breathing) for teaching vocal skills along with traditional choral teaching techniques (e.g., standard elementary school music texts and traditional choral techniques and repertoire).

Performances of 40 students attending choral rehearsal three times weekly were compared to those of 18 subjects in a no-contact control group. Gains over the nine-month period were measured (pre- and posttest) using the Singing Ability Evaluation Scale that assessed articulation, pitch, and melodic contour. Whereas the control group showed no significant gains in posttesting, the experimental group showed significant improvement (.05) in articulation, contour, and pitch accuracy. These outcomes suggest that music educators can expect more than "enjoyment" and "socialization" from disabled students involved in a properly designed choral program. These researchers were successful in obtaining a reasonable sample size, using a control group, and attaining impressive interrater reliability ($r = .97$) within a "real-life" educational setting.

Paul Rosene, in his dissertation (1976), investigated the efficacy of instrumental music study for students with mental retardation. Thirteen EMR children (IQs ranging from 50 to 80; chronological age from 9.11 to 12.0) participated in an 18-week program of instrumental music instruction that included stages of recruitment, individual lessons, group instruction, and public performances. According to Rosene, the behaviors demonstrated by these disabled children were not unlike those of nondisabled children. Eight of the 13 students enrolled in the instrumental program subsequently met minimum requirements (tone quality, facility, rhythmic accuracy, note reading) to be accepted into a school band. However, Rosene noted that immature or disruptive behaviors (a tendency to be overly enthusiastic) had to be controlled in order to attain successful integration.

Rosene used several quantitative measures to reflect change resulting from instruction. Significant gains (.001) were made from pre- to posttests on both the *Musical Aptitude Profile* (Gordon, 1965) and the *Music Achievement Test* (Colwell, 1969, 1970). Of the two tests, however, the MAT proved to be a better predictor for instrumental skill achievement.

Although these data are interesting, perhaps the primary educational contribution of Rosene's study is found in the in-depth qualitative information presented in case studies for each of the 13 subjects. On the basis of the successes and problems experienced by these children, Rosene recommended several adaptations to traditional instrumental pedagogy when teaching students with mental retardation: initial 1:1 instruction, emphasis on rote learning, use of iconic notation, and direct instruction of instrument care. Furthermore, behavior management and gradual introduction to the group ensemble were recommended.

Students with Visual Impairments To date, only a few studies relate directly to instructional methodology for the students with visual impairments. This small body of research may reflect the fact that visual impairment is a low-incident disability; therefore, few teachers have extensive experience with blind students.

Anita Jackson's (1975) study examined the efficacy of group keyboard instruction for beginners (six high school students enrolled in a residential school for the blind). Given data from aptitude studies, it is not unusual that these students showed no auditory or tactile superiority to the typical sighted student of this age. In addition, the visually impaired students showed cognitive acquisition of musical concepts similar to that expected of nondisabled high school students.

However, there were important differences that have implications for music educators. Blind students required approximately three times longer than sighted learners to acquire the necessary psychomotor responses (spatial orientation at the keyboard). This suggests the need for extended practice time. In addition, formation of visual imagery was problematic. Jackson also noted that music instructors would find a dearth of appropriate materials for the older blind learner.

Bruscia and Levinson's (1982) study, ''Predictive Factors in Optacon Music-Reading,'' examined variables such as figure complexity and time of instruction in efficacy of Braille music reading. A negligible relationship was found between the amount of training and reading speed. What is most intriguing, perhaps, is that figure complexity was negatively correlated with speed of reading. Because of the unique coding characteristics of the optacon, and ''searching'' process, the types of reading tasks that are relatively simple for sighted

readers (e.g., single line melodies) were not for the visually impaired. Rather, clusters of notes (i.e., chords) were easier to read in a short time. Bruscia and Levinson concluded that some alterations in repertoire and exercises may be necessary for the student using Braille musical notation. These data suggest that music educators working with a visually impaired student should familiarize themselves with the basic coding idiosyncrasies of Braille notation before planning an appropriate sequence for notationally based activities.

Students with Hearing Impairments To date, research concerning instructional methodology for hearing-impaired students is descriptive in nature, and focuses primarily on educational practices in residential schools for the deaf. Historical studies (Darrow and Heller, 1985; Edwards, 1974) demonstrate a long tradition of music for the deaf student, but the rationale for music has often included therapeutic outcomes in addition to aesthetic growth. Information gleaned from surveys of residential and day programs for the deaf (Ford, 1987; Shroyer and Ford, 1986) gives some insight into teacher preparation, program size, and organizational features of music programs.

Little research is available, however, concerning efficacy of actual instructional methodology. Some teaching strategies can be implied from audiological and perceptual characteristics of deaf students (e.g., better rhythmic than melodic perception, better hearing acuity in lower frequencies). For example, Robbins and Robbins's (1980) instructional manual on music for the hearing impaired based many of the instructional suggestions on data obtained regarding the acoustic properties of various musical instruments and audiological characteristics of students with hearing impairments. Similarly, Sposato's (1982) study regarding curriculum planning for students with hearing impairments emphasized the implication of residual hearing (usable hearing) in designing appropriate music education programs. Additional research is needed regarding the efficacy of particular instructional practices in the mainstream as well as in self-contained programs.

As can be seen, these instructionally based studies are few in number and widely divergent in focus. Of particular concern is the limited extent to which these studies reflect approaches and methodology advocated in educational resource books. For example, Orff activities, Kodály hand signals and time names, and Dalcroze eurythmics are often recommended in activity collections and music series textbooks designed for exceptional learners. Yet studies on these methods and approaches are conspicuously absent in the research. Buker's dissertation (1966) testing methods by Mary Helen Richards is unique in its study of an existing instructional method.

The minds of music educators and pages of music textbooks are filled with instructional theories and methods that may be more or less effective for various segments of the disabled population. Because these remain unsubstantiated through objective evaluation, classroom teachers continue to rely all too heavily on trial and error when serving students with disabilities.

How can researchers focus their study when so much remains unknown? One strategy is to examine studies of aptitude, achievement, and specific skill attainment, seeking implications for classroom instruction. For example, studies by Freeman (1986) and Grant and LeCroy (1986) regarding rhythmic production of students with mental retardation indicated that visual cues may enhance rhythmic accuracy. This finding might be applied in research regarding instructional methodology for music activities requiring rhythmic synchrony (e.g., movement activities, playing rhythm instruments). Ford's (1988) study of pitch perception in deaf students calls for subsequent research identifying vocal selections most readily perceived and reproduced in the classroom, based on range and intervallic structure. The research questions emerging from existing studies offer endless opportunities for inquiry, and include the advantage of establishing trends in research, a much needed change from the present pattern of singular unrelated studies.

SUMMARY

From extant research, educators have gained some insights regarding the musical potential and achievement of students with disabilities. In addition, various instructional practices have undergone the scrutiny of systematic inquiry. The depth and breadth of knowledge vary greatly depending on the particular category of disability and musical task. For example, the largest proportion of research regarding musical aptitude and achievement has focused on children with mental retardation. In contrast, little is known about the potential and abilities of children with other types of disabilities. From a review of the aptitude and achievement research of students with disabilities, one thing is clear: Musical potential and ability vary greatly from one disability to another, but also within each category of exceptionality, depending on the severity of the condition as well as the particular musical task.

In comparison with the wealth of methodological resources on music education for students with disabilities, there exists a relatively small body of research investigating the efficacy of instructional practices with this population. The primary areas of focus have been mainstreaming effectiveness, teacher preparation, and evaluation of specific instructional practices. Additional research is needed, particularly on the effectiveness of educational methods and approaches advocated in instructional texts.

Whatever the focus of research, the heterogeneous nature of the population of exceptional learners makes test appropriateness, subject selection criteria, and design issues particularly problematic. Future efforts are needed in the area of testing and measurement (achievement and aptitude) in order to determine adequately the native aptitude of disabled students, as well as to assess the relative merits of instructional practices. Meticulous selection and reporting of subject characteristics will assist in interpretation and generalization of research findings. These efforts, in addition to judicious selection of design, will assist the researcher in the critical evaluation of educational practices for students with disabilities.

References

American Psychiatric Association. (1980). *Diagnostic and statistical manual for mental disorders* (3rd ed.). Washington: Author.

Applebaum, E., Engel, A. L., Koegel, R. L., and Imhoff, B. (1979). Measuring musical abilities of autistic children. *Journal of Autism and Developmental Disorders, 9*(3), 279–285.

Atterbury, B. W. (1983). A comparison of rhythm pattern perception and performance in normal and learning-disabled readers, age seven and eight. *Journal of Research in Music Education, 31*(4), 259–270.

Atterbury, B. W. (1986). A survey of present mainstreaming practices in the southern United States. *Journal of Music Therapy, 23*(4), 202–207.

Beal, M. R. (1980). Music curriculum guidelines for moderately retarded adolescents. Unpublished master's thesis, University of Kansas, Lawrence.

Bentley, A. (1966). *Measures of musical abilities.* London: George A. Harrap.

Bergendal, B., and Talo, S. (1969). The response of children with reduced phoneme systems to the Seashore Measures of Musical Talents. *Folio Phoniatrica, 21,* 20–38.

Bureau of Education for the Handicapped (1989, October). Table: Number of Children Served Under Chapter 1 of ESEA (SOP) and EHA-B by age group. U.S. Department of Education. Washington, D.C.

Bixler, J. (1968). Musical aptitude in the educable mentally retarded child. *Journal of Music Therapy, 5*(2), 41–43.

Borg, W. R., and Gall, M. D. (1979). *Educational research.* New York: Longman.

Brown, M. C. (1981). Problems in mainstreaming programs in the Los Angeles Unified School District as perceived by junior high school music teachers. Unpublished doctoral dissertation, University of Southern California, Los Angeles.

Bruscia, K. E. (1981). Auditory short-term memory and attentional control of mentally retarded persons. *American Journal of Mental Deficiency, 85*(4), 435–437.

Bruscia, K. E., and Levinson, S. (1982). Predictive factors in optacon music-reading. *Journal of Visual Impairment and Blindness,* October, 76(8), 309–312.

Buker, G. (1966). A study of the ability of the educable mentally retarded to learn basic music rhythm reading through the use of a specified structured classroom procedure. Unpublished doctoral dissertation, University of Oregon, Eugene.

Colwell, R. (1969). *Music Achievement Tests 1 and 2.* Chicago: Follett Educational Corporation.

Colwell, R. (1970). *Music Achievement Tests 3 and 4.* Chicago: Follett Educational Corporation.

Colwell, R. (1979). *Silver Burdett Music Competency Tests.* Morristown: Silver Burdett.

Damer, L. K. (1979). A study of attitudes of selected public school music teachers toward the integration of handicapped students into music classes. Unpublished doctoral dissertation, University of North Carolina, Greensboro.

Darrow, A. A. (1979). The beat reproduction of subjects with normal and impaired hearing: An empirical comparison. *Journal of Music Therapy, 16*(2), 91–98.

Darrow, A. A. (1984). A comparison of rhythmic responsiveness in normal and hearing-impaired children and an investigation of the relationship of rhythmic responsiveness to the suprasegmental aspects of speech perception. *Journal of Music Therapy, 21*(2), 48–66.

Darrow, A. A. (1987). An investigative study: The effect of hearing impairment on musical aptitude. *Journal of Music Therapy, 24*(2), 88–96.

Darrow, A. A., and Gfeller, K. E. (1988). Music therapy with hearing impaired children. In C. Furman (Ed.), *Effectiveness of music therapy procedures: Documentation of research and clinical practice* (pp. 137–175). Washington: National Association for Music Therapy.

Darrow, A. A., and Goll, H. (1989). The effect of vibrotactile stimuli via the SOMATRON on the identification of rhythmic concepts by hearing-impaired children. *Journal of Music Therapy, 26*(3), 115–124.

Darrow, A. A., Heller, G. N. (1985). Early advocates of music education for the hearing impaired: William Wolcott Turner and David Ely Bartlett. *Journal of Research in Music Education, 33*(4), 269–279.

DeMyer, M. K. (1974). *Parents and children in autism.* Washington: V.H. Winston.

Dickinson, P. (1976). *Music with educationally subnormal children: A guide for the classroom teacher.* Atlantic Highlands: Humanities Press.

Drake, R. M. (1939). Factorial analysis of music tests by the Spearman tetrad difference technique. *Journal of Musicology, 1,* 6–10.

Edwards, E. M. (1974). *Music education for the deaf.* South Waterford: Merriam-Eddy Co.

Eisenson, J., Kastein, S., and Schneiderman, N. (1958). An investigation into the ability of voice defectives to discriminate among differences in pitch and loudness. *Journal of Speech and Hearing Disorders, 23*(5), 577–582.

Ellis, D. (1982). Differences in music achievement among gifted and talented, average, and educable mentally handicapped fifth- and sixth-grade students. Unpublished doctoral dissertation, University of North Carolina, Greensboro.

Ford, T. A. (1987). Survey of music teachers in residential and day programs for hearing-impaired students. *Journal of the International Association of Music for the Handicapped, 3*(1), 16–25.

Ford, T. A. (1988). The effect of musical experience and age on the ability of deaf children to discriminate pitch. *Journal of Music Therapy, 25*(1), 2–16.

Freeman, I. A. (1986). Rhythmic beat perception in a Down's syndrome population: A computerized measure of beat accuracy and beat interval response. Unpublished doctoral dissertation, The University of North Carolina, Greensboro.

Gavin, A. R. (1983). Music educators' practices and attitudes toward mainstreaming. Unpublished doctoral dissertation, Washington University, St. Louis.

Gfeller, K. E. (1982). The use of melodic-rhythmic mnemonics with learning disabled and normal students as an aid to retention. Unpublished doctoral dissertation, Michigan State University, East Lansing.

Gfeller, K. E., Darrow, A. A., and Hedden, S. K. (1990). On the ten-year anniversary of P.L. 94-142: The perceived status of mainstreaming among music educators in the states of Iowa and Kansas. *Journal of Research in Music Education, 38*(2), 90–101.

Giacobbe, G. A., and Graham, R. M. (1978). The responses of aggressive emotionally disturbed and normal boys to selected musical stimuli. *Journal of Music Therapy, 15*(3), 118–135.

Gilbert, J. P. (1979). Assessment of motoric music skill development in young children: Test construction and evaluation procedures. *Psychology of Music, 7*(2), 3–12.

Gilbert, J. P. (1983). A comparison of the motor music skills of non-handicapped and learning disabled children. *Journal of Research in Music Education, 31*(2), 147–155.

Gilbert, J. P., and Asmus, E. P. (1981). Mainstreaming: Music educators' participation and professional needs. *Journal of Research in Music Education, 29*(1), 283–289.

Gordon, E. E. (1965). *Musical Aptitude Profile.* Boston: Houghton Mifflin.

Gordon, E. E. (1979). *Primary Measures of Music Audiation.* Chicago: G.I.A. Publications.

Graham, R., and Beer, A. (1980). *Teaching music to the exceptional child.* Englewood Cliffs: Prentice-Hall.

Grant, R., and LeCroy, S. (1986). Effects of sensory mode input on performance of rhythmic perception tasks by mentally retarded subjects. *Journal of Music Therapy, 23*(1), 2–9.

Heim, K. E. (1963). Musical aptitude of seven high school students in residential schools for the blind as measured by the Wing *Standardized Test of Musical Intelligence.* Unpublished master's thesis, University of Kansas, Lawrence.

Hopkins, C. D. (1976). *Educational research: A structure for inquiry.* Columbus: Charles E. Merrill.

Hughes, J. E., Robbins, B. J., Smith, D. S., and Kinkade, C. F. (1987). The effects of participation in a public school choral music curriculum on singing ability in trainable mentally handicapped adolescents. *Music Education for the Handicapped Bulletin, 2*(4), 19–35.

Ianacone, R. N. (1977). The measurement of music aptitude for the mentally retarded. Unpublished doctoral dissertation, University of Florida, Gainesville.

Jackson, A. L. (1975). An exploratory study using a group piano approach in an original comprehensive course for the older blind beginner. Unpublished doctoral dissertation, Northwestern University, Evanston.

Jellison, J. A. (1985). An investigation of the factor structure of a scale for the measurement of children's attitudes toward handicapped peers within regular music environments. *Journal of Research in Music Education, 33*(3), 167–177.

Jellison, J. A., Brooks, B. H., and Huck, A. M. (1984). Structuring small groups and music reinforcement to facilitate positive interactions and acceptance of severely handicapped students in regular music classrooms. *Journal of Research in Music Education, 32*(4), 243–264.

Kalenius, W. G., Jr. (1977). *What is the state of research pertaining to arts and handicapped?* Washington: The National Committee, Arts for the Handicapped.

Kaplan, P. R. (1977). A criterion-referenced comparison of rhythmic responsiveness in normal and educable mentally retarded children. Unpublished doctoral dissertation, University of Michigan, Ann Arbor.

Kearns, L. H. (1986). Outcomes of inservice programs on the arts in special education: The arts in special education project of Pennsylvania. Unpublished doctoral dissertation, Pennsylvania State University, University Park.

Korduba, O. M. (1975). Duplicated rhythm patterns between deaf and normal hearing children. *Journal of Music Therapy, 12*(3), 136–146.

Kracke, I. (1975). Perception of rhythmic sequences by receptive aphasic and deaf children. *British Journal of Disorders of Communication, 10,* 43–51.

Kwalwasser, J. (1955). *Exploring the musical mind.* New York. Colman Ross.

Lehr, J. K. (1977). An investigation of music in the education of mentally and physically handicapped children in the United Kingdom, with particular reference to the course, Music for Slow Learners, at Dartington College of Arts. Unpublished doctoral dissertation, Ohio State University, Columbus.

Lidz, C. S. (1981). *Improving assessment of schoolchildren.* San Francisco: Jossey-Bass.

Madsen, C. K., and Darrow, A. A. (1989). The relationship between music aptitude and sound conceptualization of the visually impaired. *Journal of Music Therapy, 26*(2), 71–78.

McLeish, J., and Higgs, G. (1982). Musical ability and mental subnormality: An experimental investigation. *British Journal of Educational Psychology, 52,* 370–373.

Mercer, C. D. (1987). *Students with learning disabilities* (3rd ed.). Columbus: Charles E. Merrill.

Meyer, L. H. (1981). *The acceptance scale: Upper elementary level.* (Available from L. H. Meyer, Division of Special Education and Rehabilitation, Syracuse University, Syracuse, NY 13244)

Nocera, S. D. (1981). A descriptive analysis of the attainment of selective musical learnings by normal children and by educable mentally retarded children mainstreamed in music classes at the second and fifth grade level. Unpublished doctoral dissertation, University of Wisconsin, Madison.

Pitman, D. J. (1965). The musical ability of blind children. *American Foundation for Blind Research Bulletin, 11,* 63–79.

Richards, M. H. (1964). *Thresholds to music.* Palo Alto: Fearon Publishers.

Rigrodski, S., Prunty, F., and Glovsky, G. (1961). A study of the incidence, types, and associated etiologies of hearing loss in an institutionalized mentally retarded population. *Training School Bulletin, 58,* 30–44.

Rileigh, K. K., and Odom, P. B. (1972). Perception of rhythms by subjects with normal and deficient hearing. *Developmental Psychology 7,* 54–61.

Robbins, C., and Robbins, C. (1980). *Music for the hearing impaired.* St. Louis: Magnamusic-Baton.

Rosene, P. E. (1976). A field study of wind instrument training for educable mentally handicapped children. Unpublished doctoral dissertation, University of Illinois, Urbana.

Sakurabayashi, H. Y., Satyo, Y., and Uehara, E. (1956). Auditory discrimination of the blind. *Japanese Journal of Psychology of the Blind, 1,* 3–10.

Sato, C. (1960). Survey on vocal pitch range of cerebral palsied children. *Cerebral Palsy Review, 21*(5), 4–5, 8–9.

Seashore, C. E., Lewis, D., and Saetveit, J. G. (1960). *Seashore Measures of Musical Talents.* New York: The Psychological Corporation.

Seashore, C. E., and Ling, T. (1918). The comparative sensitiveness of blind and seeing persons. *Psychological Monographs, 25,* 148–158.

Sheridan, W. F. (1979). Public law 94-142 and the development of the Oregon plan for mainstreaming in music. Unpublished doctoral dissertation, University of Oregon, Eugene.

Shroyer, E. H., and Ford, T. A. (1986). Survey of music instruction and activities in residential and day schools for hearing-impaired students. *MEH Bulletin, 2*(1), 28–45.

Smith, D. S. (1987). The effect of instruction on ability to adapt teaching situations for exceptional students. *MEH Bulletin, 2*(4), 3–18.

Sposato, M. (1982). Implications of maximal exploitation of residual hearing on curriculum planning in music education for hearing impaired children. Unpublished doctoral dissertation, State University of New York, Buffalo.

Stankov, L., and Spilsbury, G. (1978). The measurement of auditory abilities of sighted, partially sighted, and blind children. *Applied Psychological Measurement, 2,* 491–503.

Stein, A. R. (1983). The efficacy of the curriculum of special area teachers for serving the needs of handicapped students and its implications for curriculum planning. Unpublished doctoral dissertation, State University of New York, Buffalo.

Sterritt, G. M., Camp, B. W., and Lippman, B. S. (1966). Effects of early auditory deprivation upon auditory and visual information processing. *Perceptual and Motor Skills, 23,* 123–130.

Stratford, B., and Ching, E. Y. (1983). Rhythm and time in the perception of Down's Syndrome children. *Journal of Mental Deficiency Research, 27,* 23–38.

Strockbine, F. (1982). An approach to teaching music to mentally retarded children based on Piagetian constructs. Unpublished doctoral dissertation, Temple University, Philadelphia.

Stuart, M., and Gilbert, J. P. (1977). Mainstreaming: Needs assessment through a videotape visual scale. *Journal of Research in Music Education, 25*(4), 283–289.

Thaut, M. H. (1980). Music therapy as a treatment tool for autistic children. Unpublished master's thesis, Michigan State University, East Lansing.

Thompson, K. P. (1986). The general music class as experienced by mainstreamed handicapped students. *MEH Bulletin, 1*(3), 16–23.

Zenatti, A. (1975). Melodic memory tests: A comparison of normal children and mental defectives. *Journal of Research in Music Education, 23*(1), 41–52.

·45·

RESEARCH ON MUSIC IN EARLY CHILDHOOD

Carol Scott-Kassner

SEATTLE PACIFIC UNIVERSITY

Though the idea of utilizing music in a planned way with pre-school children has been promoted for nearly four hundred years, preschool music education did not begin in the United States until the mid-1800s (McDonald and Simons, 1989). By the early 1900s, reflecting the work of Frederick Froebel, music became a standard part of the kindergarten curriculum, and children's songs an important educational tool (Alvarez, 1981). The presence of young children in school settings also provided a ready source of subjects for study. Limited study of children's musical progress began in the United States with the child study movement of the late 1800s (Humphreys, 1985). This research was generally conducted by psychologists and (nonmusician) child study experts. The Iowa studies in the 1930s (Seashore, 1939; Stoddard, 1932; Williams, 1933) are important early attempts to measure the musical discriminations and physical responses to music of children under 5. This early research, generally clinical in orientation, measured discrete responses. An exception to this pattern, the Pillsbury Studies (1937–1958) represent the first long-term observational study of preschool children's spontaneous creative musical behavior in America (Moorhead and Pond, reprinted 1978). A shift away from clinical toward developmentally oriented research occurred in the mid-1950s when both child psychologists and music educators began to focus on questions of "perceptual and cognitive development and the accompanying issues of the transformation and structure of systems, the developmental stages and transitions, and the mechanisms of developmental change" (Zimmerman, 1985, p. 66).

Subsequent research emphasis on music with the young child appears to have gone through cycles. Simons (1978, 1986) reported 99 studies from 1960 to 1975, a downturn of interest through the 1970s, and renewed interest beginning

again in 1981, which was attributed by Simons to the stimulus of the Ann Arbor Symposium on the *Applications of Psychology to the Teaching and Learning of Music,* held in 1978–79.

The 1984 Music in Early Childhood Conference in Provo, UT, brought together music educators and early childhood educators to explore the place of music in early child development.

Scott (1988), in an overview of research with young children, identified eight questions that seem to undergird most of the completed research.

1. What can young children do musically, if anything?
2. How does what young children do change over time and how is that related to general development?
3. What is the relationship between what young children do musically and other factors such as heredity, environment, parenting, intelligence, social class, and race?
4. How does instruction affect what young children can do in music?
5. What is the nature of the development of musical intelligence and how can it be tested?
6. How is the development of musical intelligence related to theories of general development?
7. What factors influence the development of musical intelligence?
8. What is the nature of musical valuing in the young child and how does that develop? (pp. 74–75)

Because much of that research was basic developmental research, scattered in terms of theory, usually not replicated, and often based on short-term instruction, the implications for practice remain tentative.

GOALS FOR CHAPTER

This chapter reviews research with the very young, looks at issues in early childhood music as well as existing theories of development, summarizes the key music research on children through the age of 8, and reviews research on various educational methods. Suggestions for future research are included throughout the chapter. The years from birth through age 8 were selected because they are officially designated as the years of early childhood by the National Association for the Education of Young Children (NAEYC).

CONDUCTING RESEARCH WITH THE VERY YOUNG

A range of methodologies and techniques is available for examining musical growth in the young child. This section highlights studies using a number of those methodologies and techniques, and discusses their advantages and limitations.

Qualitative Research

Though often viewed with suspicion by traditional, trained researchers, qualitative research has increasingly gained a place in educational settings (Borg and Gall, 1989). Often support for this methodology questions the validity of the more traditional means of conducting research, particularly in regard to the uniqueness of each setting and of the persons being studied. Qualitative research, carefully performed in the home or school setting, can provide a wealth of data about musical development and musical behavior specific to settings and individuals, which can become the genesis of theories to be tested by other empirical means.

Ethnographic Research The Pillsbury Foundation Studies performed from 1937 to 1948 (reprinted in Moorhead and Pond, 1978) represent an early example of the application of ethnographic techniques of an indepth analytical cultural description to the music setting. Children from the ages of 1.5 to 8.5 years were placed in a musically rich environment, and their actions, both individual and group, were recorded by a trained musician. Daily anecdotal notes were kept, and the musical artifacts the children produced were "phonographically" recorded. Data on the evolution of chant, personal songs, movement to music, musical notation, and free instrumental exploration were reported and summarized.

Zimmerman (1985) lists the following insights gained from these studies: "(a) For young children, music is primarily the discovery of sound; (b) music time with children should include their purposive action or involvement; (c) in planning music time, it is necessary to consider social, environmental, and procedural conditions; and (d) spontaneous music making should be carefully observed" (p. 73).

Shelley (1981) conducted observations in a similar setting, recording free musical behavior twice weekly for 10 weeks using a Music Study Observation Form and a cassette recorder. Shelley's discussion of the challenges of doing on-the-spot coding of complex musical behaviors over a long period is informative.

Naturalistic Research Naturalistic study attempts to develop theory gained from data gained through observation rather than imposing theory in an a priori manner. Miller (1986) applied these techniques in a number of preschools working with 3- to 5-year-old children. Baseline data on the children were established using observations of musical behavior as well as teacher interviews and parent surveys. A musical behavior observation matrix was developed based on the emergent behaviors of the children and the data analyzed for age, sex, and race. The results were discussed in terms of existing research and theory in music education. Miller suggests that research combining both qualitative and quantitative methods may help to give a more complete picture of musical development.

Metz (1989) took the naturalistic research process one step further in her study of movement as musical response in preschool children. With concern that previous studies in rhythmic movement used adult standards and failed to involve teacher interaction, Metz examined the movements of 2-, 3-, and 4-year-olds in three preschools. A baseline description of the students and the setting was established during the first three weeks, and during the next five weeks the researcher acted as observer and teacher. To establish reliability, classes were videotaped, and those records plus parent and staff surveys and interviews were examined by three people. Observed aspects of behavior were organized into theoretical categories. From this, Metz developed a model for viewing the relationships of the categories and put forth seven propositions for teaching arising from the conditions of her study.

Case Study The case study, which allows for in-depth study of a single subject or group, has been used to a limited extent with young children in music. Problems of generalizability are inherent in this type of research but can be mitigated to a degree by using multiple case studies. Kelley and Sutton-Smith (1987) used that approach in their study of the musical responses of three firstborn females. One was a child of professional musicians, another of musically oriented parents, and the third of nonmusically oriented parents. Each was observed weekly beginning at birth and extending for a two-year period. Observations lasted from 15 minutes to half a day. The observer recorded spontaneous music productions, contingencies for those productions if any, the presence of instruments, and family reports of musical activities and history of family music making. Each case was analyzed in terms of family musicality, child's responses, song, song form, substructures such as beat and tonality, and the role of performance. Results were discussed in terms of existing theory, including that on nature/nurture questions.

Papousek and Papousek (1981), both trained psychologists, documented the psychobiological evolution of their child musically. They recorded her behavior audiovisually and analyzed responses with a spectrograph and computerized digital analysis. Their theoretical discussion is wide-ranging, covering a number of fields including psychology, biology, and music.

Quantitative Research

Quantitative designs have been more frequently used than qualitative in examining musical growth in young children. The attempts of researchers to generate knowledge claims through theory development and controlled examination of musical behavior have led to an increasingly large body of information regarding music and the young child.

Experimental Research The experimental or quasi-experimental study has been used by numerous researchers; the preponderance of studies with these designs is with children ages 3 to 8. It is particularly difficult to assess the very young child because of the limits of language development. Though young children understand more than they can express, it is difficult for the researcher to discern accurately the young child's level of understanding of a task or to ask for verbal explanations of phenomena.

In addition, situational variables often result in a Type I error—overestimation of a child's ability—or a Type II error or underestimation (Flavell, 1985). Some of these testing problems include:

1. The amount of cognitive or physical load on the child—is the task too simple or too difficult?
2. The naturalness of the task—is it like real life or is it so contrived and abstract that generalization is impossible?
3. The metacognitive demands—is the child being forced to develop problem-solving strategies to think about his or her thinking that are beyond the child's abilities developmentally?
4. Human involvement—does the presence of a person result in bias because of nonverbal cues or distractors?
5. Memory load—are the task demands on remembering too much for the child developmentally?
6. Language development—is it the case that the child really understands but is committing errors because of lack of consensual vocabulary or because of a tendency to overextend a concept and apply it to too many instances? Or, is the child responding correctly on the basis of contextual cues without really understanding?
7. Perceptual complexity and bias—is the child committing an error because there is too much to pay attention to or because some dimension of the stimulus is so dominant that it creates a bias?
8. The naturalness of the environment—is the child performing a certain way because of being in a laboratory, removed from familiar surroundings and familiar people?

These concerns, added to the normal concerns for internal and external validity, make the challenges almost overwhelming (see Donaldson, 1978; Flavell, 1985; Kail, 1984).

In spite of these challenges a number of researchers have succeeded in developing means for testing musical discrimination, perception, preference, and conception in infants and young children.

INFANT RESPONSE. A cogent summary of research regarding infant response to auditory stimuli can be found in Standley and Madsen (1990, Table 1). Typical measures have included: (1) physiological measures such as change of heart rate, eye blink, or weight gain; (2) operant measures such as conditioned head turn, changes in sucking patterns, or discriminative toy play; and (3) observation measures of vocalization, behavioral state, and bodily activity.

Bridger (1961) recorded startle responses in a habituation study as a measure of discrimination of pitch change in neonates. Summers (1984) and Trehub (1987) utilized a conditioned head-turning response to novel stimuli as a measure of discrimination of pitch patterns in infants. Standley and Madsen (1990) measured infant preference for various auditory stimuli via a mercury switch attached to a foot of each subject. These and numerous other studies with infants suggest that the infant is a seeker of novel stimuli and perceiver of a range of differences in auditorily presented materials.

SUNG RESPONSE. A number of researchers have utilized the sung response as evidence of cognitive growth in infants and young children. This response is assumed to test capacities of discrimination, awareness of tonality, and perceptual shifts in pitch processing. The work of Papousek and Papousek (1981), Davidson (1985), Dowling and Harwood (1986), Kessen, Levine, and Wendrich (1979), Moog (1976), Sergeant and Roche (1973), and Davidson, McKernon, and Gardner (1981) all speaks to theories of the relation between vocal production and thought in young children. Results of this research are discussed in detail in a later section.

NOTATED RESPONSE. Several researchers have utilized children's symbolic notations to measure perception of and memory for rhythm and melody (Bamberger, 1982; Upitis, 1987; Hildebrandt, 1987; Davidson and Colley, 1987). The findings are that younger children, aged 4 and 5, use iconic notation (pictures describing the activity) to represent rhythms, then move into figural drawings (depictions of the rhythmic figures) about the age of 6, followed by metric representation in older children (Upitis, 1987). Upitis found that musical training of at least one year made a difference in the ability to read both figural and metrical forms. Kindergartners were generally unable to represent rhythms in any type of one-to-one correspondence, while second-graders were able to show one-to-one correspondence plus groupings of durations (Hildebrant, 1987). Davidson and Colley (1987) studied a group of children from the ages of 5 to 7 and found that text influenced performance and perception of rhythm in the 5- and 6-year-olds but that 7-year-olds were able to separate text from the musical setting.

Davidson and Scripp (1986) examined the development of children aged 5 to 7 years in representing melodic information through drawing. The stages are pictures and symbols in the 5-year-olds, language and melodic contours in the

6-year-olds, and language and symbols representing melodic features at 7 years of age. Children from 6 to 9 used icons and words to represent a familiar melody but resorted to discrete marks and melody lines with an unfamiliar melody (Upitis, 1990).

NONVERBAL, MANIPULATIVE RESPONSES. Various studies have been conducted to determine whether children 3 to 6 years of age are able to nonverbally demonstrate musical understandings. Scott (1977) developed a series of small boxes that activated recorded pitch stimuli when they were lifted. Children aged 3 to 5 were asked to group boxes into categories representing pitch concepts of high/low, melodic contour, and interval size. Stimuli were presented on two different timbres, a sine wave and a xylophone, to determine whether timbre would affect the perceptual salience of the patterns.

Hair (1977) tested first-grader's ability to show perception of pitch motion via a written response, via performance on bells, and verbally. Hair noted that children were more accurate in showing understanding using the nonverbal response modes. Spontaneous gestural responses were used by 66 percent of the children. Webster and Schlentrich (1982) utilized verbal, gestural, and bell performance response modes for 4- and 5-year-olds to indicate pitch direction. For children who had not fully attained the concept of pitch direction, the performance mode was the most successful. For those who had, mode was not a factor. Girls at age 5 verbalized more successfully than boys, and boys at age 5 tended to prefer the gestural response. In a study by Van Zee (1976), kindergartners were more successful demonstrating pitch and rhythm responses on a keyboard than verbalizing about them. Spontaneous gestures and sung responses were often used by children to demonstrate perception. This emergence of physical responses appears to lend credence to theories of the existence of verbal/tactile substructures that may help children mediate their musical experiences.

White, Dale, and Carlsen (1990) used an oddity task format to identify the discrimination and categorization of pitch direction by children from 3.5 to 5 years of age. In an oddity task, children are asked to group together two out of three stimuli. Children responded by touching visual images on a touch screen, which in turn activated the auditory stimuli of various three-note pitch sequences. In spite of the fact that the touch screen allowed repeated listenings to stimuli, children had difficulty with the categorization task. Perhaps children in these age categories must physically or vocally replicate the musical stimuli to get at the substructure.

Sims (1990) theorizes that children go through a sequence in their capacity to identify and label contrasting aspects of conceptual stimuli in music. Sims suggests that, for a given music element, preschool children (3 to 6 years) are able to demonstrate contrasts, first, through sung imitation, labeling characteristics in their own performances, second and recorded music, third, and applying the characteristic to their own performance last. She is currently testing whether single discrimination tasks (e.g., smooth/choppy) are easier than double discrimination tasks (e.g., smooth/choppy and fast/slow). Sims has tested these ideas using movement as the response mode to various types of music. Sims (1984) used a combination of videotape, time sampling, and observer grid sheets as means for objectifying the coding of children's creative movement responses to music.

VERBAL RESPONSE. The question of children's confusion over the use of consensual music labels, particularly in the area of pitch change, continues to arise in the literature. Young (1982) and McMahon (1982) found that 4-year-olds verbally substituted loud and soft for high and low, and performed loud for fast and quiet for slow. They both conclude that loudness is perceptually dominant over pitch in 4-year-olds. Hair (1981, 1987) discovered older children in grades K–6 had difficulty labeling pitch changes correctly yet found no problems with fast/slow and loud/soft. Pictures of high and low objects in space were difficult for these children to associate with pitch change.

Flowers and Costa-Giomi (1990) theorized that the problem in understanding might be due to the confusion about the spatial connotations of high and low, the spatial analogies often used by teachers. They tested 4- and 5-year-old children in America and Argentina to determine the effect that language and age had on response to two-octave pitch changes in a familiar song. The words for high/low in Spanish, *agudo/grave,* are not spatial in connotation nor are they confused with loud/soft in meaning. Children were taught in their own language to use the terminology in response to music. English-speaking children were more accurate in responding to pitch differences when asked to identify changes by clapping. Spanish-speaking children were more accurate when asked to verbalize the pitch changes. Spanish-speaking children were also more reflective in their responses, taking more time to think before verbalizing.

COMPUTER-BASED RESPONSES. The computer appears to hold potential for teaching and testing children beginning at the age of 3. Williams and Fox (1983) and Monsour and Knox (1985) have developed computer games that train and test preschool children's discrimination and perception of a range of musical stimuli. These programs or similar ones could become powerful means for measuring musical growth. Touch-screen technology (White et al., 1990) also represents an efficient and direct means for generating stimuli as well as recording and analyzing data.

Descriptive Research The most direct and commonly used methodology with children under 5 has been the observational or descriptive study. As researchers have attempted to document normal musical growth in children, observation over time has been the logical method of study. These observations are typically of singing, moving, creating, or playing in response to musical stimuli or environments.

Simons (1964) observed 12 pairs of same-sex twins and matched singletons between the ages of 9 months and 31 months. The observations occurred every month for four months in the home environment, and each observation lasted for 40 minutes with periods of musical stimuli followed by periods of silence. Responses to various musical stimuli were tape-recorded and coded by two trained observers using predetermined criteria. Data reporting frequency of responses were reported and discussed. Alford (1971) continued to study these same subjects over periods of two months each at intervals of one and two years later, thereby adding to the data on the effects of maturation. Statistical comparisons of differences in responses between the two groups studied were made.

Moog (1976) made over 8,000 individual tests of 500 children and analyzed observations of 1,000 parents in an observational study. In terms of sheer magnitude of data, this study is one of the most extensive. Children from 6 months to 5.5 years were observed. Moog's procedures involved going into the homes of the children and playing recorded songs, words with rhythms, pure rhythms, tonal and atonal instrumental music, cacophonies, and environmental sounds, and recording the children's responses to those stimuli. Summaries of percentages of responses in the various categories occur throughout the discussion. The 1976 report of his study does not discuss methods used to record the responses or other controls for objectivity. Because of the extent of the study, it is often cited as a key reference in the musical growth of infants and preschoolers.

Two descriptive studies of infant vocalization demonstrate the usefulness of current technology in recording observations. Wendrich (1981), in a study of pitch matching, observed 23 infants three times between 3 and 6 months of age. Lacking technological aid, Wendrich determined accuracy via aural analysis and the help of a colleague with absolute pitch. Fox (1990) observed 12 infants at monthly intervals from 3 to 9 months of age. Recordings of vocalizations were made with high-quality tape and equipment, and vocal segments were analyzed using analog to digital conversion and computer graphics display procedures. Though concerns exist regarding the possible intrusiveness of video and audio recording, such recording can help to enhance the objectivity of the researcher.

Goetze (1985) in examining factors affecting vocal accuracy in kindergarten, first-, and third-grade children, attained more objective control over her analysis of pitch accuracy through the use of the Visi-Pitch. This electronic instrument gives a visual display in graphic form as well as a numerical value in hertz. Goetze was able to determine the frequency for each pitch unit of the singing tasks.

Correlational/Causal-Comparative Research The correlational and causal-comparative methods have also been utilized by music researchers in studying the young child. Studies using these techniques have focused on discovering relationships between factors such as the following:

1. Home environment and musical response (Brand, 1986; Moore, 1973)
2. Aptitude, perception, and/or intelligence and various aspects of the musical response (Geringer, 1983; Schleuter and Schleuter, 1989)
3. Different training or testing conditions and musical responses (Gilbert, 1979; Ramsey, 1983; Walters, 1986)

4. Differences due to age and to gender (Schleuter and Schleuter, 1985)
5. Differences due to cognitive style (Schmidt and Sinor, 1986)

With the advent of the *Primary Measures of Musical Audiation* (PMMA) as a vehicle for testing young children's musical aptitude, many researchers have utilized that device as one variable in correlational studies. As a result, there are emerging data to suggest the degree of relation between scores on the two subtests of the PMMA and vocal, motor, and creative responses to music.

Needed Research

Zimmerman (1981), in a presentation at the Ann Arbor Symposium, called for more longitudinal studies to document the development of aspects of musicality in children. However, given the realities of the mobility of society and the changing school boundaries, she suggests the use of (1) cross-sectional studies, covering wide geographical areas, (2) convergence, in which a series of shorter-term longitudinal studies with overlapping age range is implemented, (3) the clinical approach, case studies with or without depth analysis, and (4) scalogram analysis, using an ordinal scale, in which a series of tasks of increasing difficulty is ordered and children are ranked on their performance of a task. An added suggestion is for cross-cultural research to determine which aspects of musicality are global and which are unique to particular cultures or reflect a high degree of cultural influence.

Zimmerman further suggests a series of proposals for a sequential program of research in child development put forth by Wohlwill (1973). They are to (1) define a set of scales along which consistent developmental changes can be observed and mapped, (2) collect facts to provide a descriptive study of the changes, (3) correlate the developmental changes in music with other behaviors developing simultaneously, (4) study the variables that affect developmental changes, and (5) study individual differences in development.

Systematic implementation of any or all of these suggestions by researchers plus an increased dialogue between psychologists, psychomusicologists, music educators, and early childhood experts conducting research with the young child would add a richness and depth to our understanding.

THEORIES OF CHILD DEVELOPMENT IN MUSIC

Several factors have contributed to the emergence of comprehensive theories of musical development. The entry of developmental and cognitive psychologists into the study of children's musical growth has stimulated research activity linked to existing theories. Summaries of the work of these individuals and that of music psychologists interested in musical growth can be found in a range of resources (Deutsch, 1982; Dowling and Harwood, 1986; Hargreaves, 1986; Peery,

Peery, and Draper, 1987; Serafine, 1988; Shuter-Dyson and Gabriel, 1981; Sloboda, 1985). Though the following theories emerge primarily from outside of music education, they have implications for both research and practice.

Jean Piaget

Jean Piaget's biologically based theory of cognitive growth was brought to music education in the 1960s by Marilyn Pflederer Zimmerman. Zimmerman (1982) outlines Piaget's stage theory and theorizes that musical intelligence might develop along similar lines. Zimmerman (Pflederer, 1964) and Zimmerman and Sechrest (1968) developed a variety of tasks to test conservation of tonal and rhythmic patterns in the face of deformation by changes in tone color, tempo, harmony, rhythm, contour, or interval. Children aged 5 to 13 were tested. A difference was found between the 5- and the 8-year-olds in their capacity to recognize some aspect of the stimuli as the same as well as different, suggesting a shift in the thinking process in music. It was labeled a conservationlike response.

This research stimulated additional studies in music conservation. Foley (1975) found second-grade children able to benefit from short training procedures focused on creating melodic and rhythmic pattern awareness in producing conservation responses of melody in the face of rhythmic change and rhythm in the face of melodic change. Hargreaves, Castell, and Crowther (1986) tested 6- and 8-year-olds from England and the United States on their ability to conserve familiar and unfamiliar melodies with rhythmic transformation and transposition. They found that there were more conservation-type responses to familiar melodies than unfamiliar and that 8-year-olds performed significantly better than 6-year-olds. There were no cultural differences as the familiar songs used were common to both cultures. Nelson (1984) used Suzuki violin students, aged 4 to 8 years, to help validate a Piagetian-based rhythmic conservation task. Results suggest that rhythmic conservation as tested by his measure is more a function of age than training.

Other studies applying conservation theory to music learning have been conducted by Ashbaugh (1983), Jones (1976), and Norton (1979, 1980). Summaries of much of that research and discussions of it by Serafine (1980) and Hargreaves (1986) raise valid concerns about the nature of the tasks and whether it is ever possible to measure conservation in music because of the temporal nature of music. Hargreaves (1986) also raises questions about the effect of melodic memory and processing on conservation-type responses in music and suggests a dialogue between researchers pursuing these different theoretical paths.

Howard Gardner

Gardner and his colleagues at Project Zero at Harvard have been conducting extensive research since the late 1960s on artistic growth. Although Gardner acknowledges the power of Piagetian theory as a developmental theory, he critiques some of that theory in terms of its limited definition of thought and lack of examination of the quality of thought. His 1973 publication, *The Arts and Human Development*, outlines basic premises regarding the uniqueness of learning in and thinking about the arts. He hypothesizes that artistic thinking combines affect and cognition (or feelings and thought) and that artistic behaviors consist of systems of making, perceiving, and feeling. His early research focused on the use of symbols by children and the meaning of artistic symbols for them (Gardner, 1982). Research regarding children's notation of rhythms and melodies was stimulated by Gardner's theories.

A key area of interest of the Project Zero researchers has been to examine children's artistic development in artistic production, artistic valuing, and aesthetic responding. Wolf and Gardner (1980) propose three levels of artistic development. In stage one, the time from birth to 18 to 24 months, they see the child as director/communicator gaining practical knowledge from acting on the world. During this time the child learns to communicate, to trust others, and to gain an awareness that the world consists of stable objects about which one can communicate. The role of the educator is to be responsive to the child's needs and communications. In stage two, from 18 to 24 months to 5 to 7 years, the child is a symbol user. During this time the child's artistic work is in the creation and "reading" of artistic symbols gained by discovery through play. The challenge for education is to respect children's spontaneity, originality, and individuality while they move from their own idiosyncratic forms of representation to those dictated by society. It is a time to cherish and nurture the child's individual expression. In stage three, from 5 to 7 years to 11 to 13 years, the youth is a craftsperson, one who stands back from his or her work and perceives it in a more objective sense, often in terms of societal standards. The child in this stage is more subject to peer influences and is moving from childhood to young adulthood. The challenge of education is to help the child combine artistic craftsmanship and criticism with self-expression without being paralyzed by feelings of inadequacy.

Music Aptitude

Musical aptitude has been defined as the capacity to learn music and to think musically. An ongoing question in music has been the degree to which musical aptitude (versus being responsive to training or environmental factors) is fixed. The nature/nurture question was raised by Revesz (1953), based on research by V. Haecker and Th. Ziehen in the 1920s. Revesz states that the musicality of musically talented children is revealed at an early age, for 50 percent of children between the ages of 2 and 6. For the remaining 50 percent musicality is usually demonstrated before puberty.

Bentley (1966) based his studies of musical aptitude on his observations of rhythmic and vocal responses in infants and preschoolers but did not systematically test children under the age of 7. Gordon (1979) proposed a theory of developmental music aptitude based on widespread measures of children's responses to his *Primary Measures of Music Audiation,* standardized for ages 5 through 8, and his *Intermediate Measures of Music Audiation* (IMMA), standardized for ages 6 through 9. Both instruments measure perception of tonal patterns devoid of rhythm and rhythmic patterns devoid of melody. On the basis of a factor analytic study of these various batteries, Gordon (1986) claims that developmental music aptitude and stabilized music aptitude have little in common. He also believes that music preference measures are a part of stabilized music aptitude, which he feels occurs at the age of 9. Gordon summarizes his beliefs regarding the nature/nurture issue as follows:

Neither side of the nature/nurture controversy is correct. Music aptitude is a product of both nature and nurture. A child born with a high degree of music aptitude who does not receive appropriate early informal environmental influences, will lose his potential. Conversely, a young child can profit from early exposure to music. The interaction between capacity and environment continues from birth, or possibly prenatally, until about age nine. The effect of environment on a child's music aptitude decreases substantially with age. (1986, pp. 18–19)

The existence of the PMMA and the notion of the role of training in developmental musical aptitude have led to research designed to identify aspects of or influences upon aptitude in young children. Norton (1979, 1980) determined the degree to which auditory conservation, visual-tactile conservation, intelligence, and music aptitude are related in children of 6 years of age. She found a high relation between IQ, music aptitude, and auditory conservation, though only 22 percent of the 1980 subjects were auditory conservers. Flohr (1981) found that 12 weeks of music instruction in 5-year-old children positively affected their scores on the PMMA.

Musical Creativity

Models of creative thinking (Webster, 1988) and creative development (Tillman, 1989) in music have recently emerged, and each shows promise as a basis for the exploration of developmental musical thought and behavior in children.

Webster (1988) asserts that "musically divergent" production skills are not significantly related to traditional measures of musical aptitude and play an independent role in musical intelligence. Webster suggests that the development of musical aptitudes is susceptible to environment during early childhood and possibly into adulthood. He defines those aptitudes as skills of tonal and rhythmic imagery as measured by Gordon, musical syntax (sensitivity to musical whole), musical extensiveness, flexibility, and originality. These aptitudes, in combination with conceptual understandings, craftsmanship, and aesthetic sensitivity, comprise the enabling skills Webster believes are necessary for the creative process to occur. Those skills develop with age and are, to some degree, dependent on the presence of enabling conditions. Those conditions are motivation, subconscious imagery, personality, and environment. The influence of various environments on creativity in music is an especially potent area for research.

Tillman (1989), in collaboration with Keith Swanwick, has proposed a model of musical development in creativity. Her main study involved analyzing compositions of children from ages 3 to 11. Tillman postulates a spiral development. She calls the first level mastery, and suggests the the child from birth to age 4 is mainly concerned with materials, first sensing the range of sounds various instruments can make. Around the age of 4, children move to a manipulative mode where they try to control the sounds for effect or demonstrate the joy of mastering a skill. From 4 to 9, the imitation stages, the child creates more expressive sounds, first in a personal mode where spontaneous use of dynamic expression and heightened pitch and activity level are common. By the age of 9, the child composes in a vernacular mode, using musical conventions and musical cliche.

Though both of these models have been developed through practical experience, they remain highly theoretical.

REVIEW OF THE LITERATURE

Questions asked by most early childhood researchers fall within three large categories: production, cognition, and affect. The categories are interactive, not discrete. Emphasis is on research completed during the last 20 years. The results of prior research can be found in Simons (1978, 1986), McDonald and Simons (1989), and Shuter-Dyson and Gabriel (1981).

Production

Research in musical production has been based on one of three responses: the rhythmic, the vocal or sung, or the creative. The research has attempted to describe these responses; develop means of measuring them; or, in some instances, determine factors affecting the development of those responses.

Motor Learning and Rhythmic Development Sidnell (1981), in his address on motor learning to the Ann Arbor Symposium, stated that although music educators have assumed that motor learning is a means to the end of rhythmic achievement, little inquiry into that assumption exists. A review of studies subsequent to 1981 indicates that that connection has yet to be made, at least with young children. Research findings describe age-related motor responses to musical stimuli without examining the connection between motor training and rhythmic achievement.

Moog's (1976) description of the development of the movement response charts the following course. From infancy to 1.6 years, the child develops from showing pleasure in sounds to swaying, bouncing, and conducting. At 1.6 years Moog noticed a decrease in movement, more focused listening, and an increase in the variety of movements as the child walks, spins, claps, taps, and moves in larger space. By the age of 3, the number of coordinated movements increases, and by the age of 4, though there are fewer total movements, the movements become more complex and dancelike. The ages of 4 to 6 show a decline in spontaneous movements and an increase in clapping, though this clapping is usually not accurate and with the beat.

Rainbow (1981) in the United States, and Frega (1979) in Argentina conducted parallel studies with 3- to 5-year-old children to determine whether they could learn certain rhythmic tasks and to discern any age-related differences. The Rainbow study lasted three years, and the Frega, eight months. In both instances, children were taught by music educators who included rhythmic activities as one of many activities. Music classes occurred two to three times per week. No control groups were tested. Children were observed (videotaped) on a variety of tasks, including beat maintenance and rhythm echoing to recorded piano music—all at a tempo approximating MM = 104. Children were asked to respond through clapping hands, slapping knees, marching, clapping hands while marching, tapping with rhythm sticks, and vocalizing patterns. Three-year-olds were most successful when vocalizing their responses, followed by clapping after vocalizing, clapping a steady beat, and tapping a steady beat with rhythm sticks. Echo clapping, marching, and marching and clapping in time to music were more difficult. Four-year-olds were relatively better on all tasks, the pattern of difficulty of the tasks remaining the same. Frega experimented in varying the tempo and found the slower tempo to be the most difficult.

Gilbert (1979) developed and tested a measure of motoric music skill development (MMST) in young children. Her measures involved testing 808 children from 3 through 6 on various motor tasks typically used in music-learning situations. These tasks included tests of motor pattern coordination, eye-hand coordination, speed of movement, range of movement, and compound factors. Significant age-related improvements were found on all subtests, and girls outscored boys on tests of motor pattern coordination, eye-hand coordination, and compound factors. A subsequent two-year longitudinal test (1981) of a random sample of children from each 6-month age level of the original study confirmed the validity of the cross-sectional testing and indicated that initial performances may be used to predict later performance. Because this sample of children now ranged from 4 to 7, a test was conducted to determine whether any one age period differed in absolute gain scores. In every subtest the gain of the 4-year-olds was greater than that of the 7-year-olds. Gilbert suggests that these results substantiate claims of motor theorists that most fundamental motor patterns emerge before the age of 5 and are merely stabilized beyond that age.

Schleuter and Schleuter (1985) conducted a study to determine the relationship of grade level and sex differences in rhythmic responses of clapping, chanting, and stepping with children from kindergarten to grade 3. A Rhythm Response Test (RRT) was developed that required children to respond to 12 tape-recorded items (six duple and six triple) over four tempo beats. Chanting was easiest for kindergartners, and

chanting and clapping for grades 1 and 2 students, while clapping was easiest for grade 3 students. All responses improved with age. Stepping was the most difficult for all children. Girls in grades 1 to 3 consistently scored higher than boys. A later study (1989) tested these variables in light of the effect of school music training. Two schools were chosen, one that received general music instruction twice weekly and another that offered no formal music instruction. Results were similar to those of the first study. Girls benefited more from instruction than boys. Chanting was most influenced by music training, although all three responses were influenced by training.

Two studies (Vaughan, 1981; Walters, 1986) examined children's personal tempi. Vaughan studied children from 41 to 190 months of age (3.6 to 16 years) in Canada, Argentina, Colombia, Denmark, and England. Children were asked to walk comfortably at their own speed for a distance of 30 meters while a tester tapped the pulse near the microphone of a cassette recorder. Across culture, the tempo curve started generally high in the very young, at a mean metronome marking of 118.6 in kindergarten, dropping gradually to MM = 104.5 for grade 3, then rising gradually back to MM = 118.6 at grade 7. Older children preferred slower walking tempos. Leg length may have been a factor in tempo choice. Walters, in testing children from kindergarten through grade 3, found the mean tempo at kindergarten to be MM = 114.6, and in grade 3, MM = 99.5. He also found that on tests of synchronization with recorded music, children of all ages had more difficulty the greater the divergence from their personal tempo.

Vocal Response The vocal response has been studied more frequently than any other response in young children. Michel (1973), Moog (1976), Davidson and colleagues (1981), Davidson (1985), and Papousek and Papousek (1981) have all helped to document and outline the course of vocal growth in infants and/or young children. The very young infant seems to engage in a variety of vocalizations. About the age of 3 to 4 months, experimentation with sounds begins, pitch matching can occur, and musical babbling—experimentation with pitch—goes on. Pitch contours are usually descending, the pitch range can be remarkably wide, and glissandi are used. From 1 to 2 years, discrete bits of songs with words and rhythms are produced. Pitch may or may not be accurate. From 2 to 3 years, songs assume their characteristic melodic shape, and words and rhythms are increasingly accurate. From 3 to 4 years, children become fairly accurate in mastering songs. Their average range is from c to c'. From 4 to 5 years, singing becomes quite accurate but tonality is not always stable across phrases, and spontaneous singing is less frequent. By the age of 5 to 6, a sense of key stability and scale emerges and the child can sing expressively. Davidson and colleagues (1981) outlined phases of song acquisition in 5-year-olds, noting that the first stage focuses on either the words or the most distinctive phrases with some attention to pulse and overall pace. The second stage is attention to rhythmic surface, demonstrated by playing patterns on a drum, but the child still does not attend to tonality across phrases. The third stage is attention to pitch contour, which becomes more accurate, but interval accuracy and maintenance of tonality are still a problem. In the fourth stage, key stability, separation of pulse from rhythm, and expressive qualities emerge. Precise intervals throughout the song are not present.

Ries (1987) performed cross-sectional research with 48 children of ages 7, 11, 19, and 30 months, and Fox (1990) studied 12 children from the ages of 3 to 9 months. Ries found the overall range to be A3 to G5 with the most common contour to be descending intervals. Fox found actual frequencies ranging from 195 Hz to 1036 Hz and mean frequencies for all subjects from 313 Hz to 599 Hz. No differences due to gender were discovered. Eighty-two percent of the contours were descending.

Kessen and colleagues (1979) studied pitch matching in 23 infants between 3 and 6 months of age. Pitches of D4, F4, and A4 were sung by the mothers. Infants responded by vocalizing the given pitch. A follow-up study (Wendrich, 1981) of nine of those children at the age of 3.5 showed that seven of the nine had lost their propensity for pitch matching. Additional data were collected from nine 3.5-year-old children of musically active families, and they could match pitch accurately. This finding adds support to the importance of home music environment.

The loss of pitch matching capacity in some children and the presence of modulating tonality led Flowers and Dunne-Sousa (1990) to examine sung responses in 3-, 4-, and 5-year-olds. Children were tested individually on their ability to sing a song of their choice, sing a taught song, and echo-sing 20 different pitch patterns varying from one to four notes, performed at two different tempi, and covering, across all patterns, a range from A3 to D4. The largest percentage of children at all three ages were still modulating singers. Children who were modulating tonality had greater difficulty in matching pitches and contours than those who were somewhat modulating or not modulating. Vocal range was reduced in children in both the chosen and the taught songs but expanded when matching short patterns. Ability to match contour increased with age. Exact replication of pitches in patterns was difficult. Low correlations between echoing pitch patterns and maintaining a tonality indicated those are separate skills in young children. Roberts and Davies (1975) tried for eight weeks to improve the singing accuracy of monotone singers, 6 to 8 years of age. The remedial group improved significantly in their vocal range and single note and interval production, but there was no improvement in the ability to accurately sing a song.

Assuming the age of 6 was a key time for vocal problems in boys, Buckton (1983) inspected the vocal accuracy of 6-year-olds in New Zealand. A random sample of 1,089 children from 49 schools was tested in groups of 10, singing songs their teacher believed they could sing best. Each child was recorded via individually worn microphones. Results were analyzed by gender and ethnic background. The children of Polynesian heritage, whether from Maori or Pacific Island, sang more accurately than children of European descent. Girls sang more accurately than boys, although the gender difference was negligible in Polynesian children and more marked in European children. Later testing showed little to no relationship between children's singing accuracy and their ability to demonstrate pitch concepts of high and low on bells.

Buckton's description of the importance of singing in Polynesian cultures and the clear finding of the superiority of singing in those children strengthens the argument for the strong effect of home/cultural environment in the development of the singing response.

The relationship between aspects of melodic perception, pitch discrimination, and vocal accuracy has been examined by several persons. Geringer (1983) examined the relationship between pitch discrimination using a same/different response and vocal pitch matching of a simple three-measure song in preschoolers and in fourth-graders. Fourth-graders were more successful on pitch matching than were the preschoolers. However, there appeared to be no relationship between success in pitch matching and success in pitch discrimination, with the exception of a moderate correlation in high-ability fourth-graders.

Ramsey (1983) used sung responses of 3- to 5-year-olds to measure their perception of absolute pitch, melodic rhythm, melodic contour, tonal center, and melodic interval. Children were allowed to sing a song of their choice and three task songs that had always been taught in the same key. Very few children paid attention to the absolute pitch value of the task songs in singing them on their own. Overall, descending contours were easier to sing, and accuracy in contours increased with age. The tonal center typically changed three or more times during a song. Intervals of unison, major second, and minor third were the easiest to sing, and the ascending minor seventh was the most difficult. Apfelstadt (1984) tested the effect of instruction in melodic perception on pitch discrimination and singing accuracy of kindergarten children. One group received vocal instruction that utilized movement, iconic notation, and step-bells to highlight melodic movement. A second group received vocal instruction highlighting imitation as a technique. Group three received traditional, nonconceptual music instruction using rote songs with no emphasis on melodic perception. There was no correlation between pitch discrimination and vocal accuracy. Both forms of melodic perception instruction seemed to help improve performance of pitch patterns but not of rote songs. Each of these studies leaves open the question of the relationship between discrimination or perception and singing accuracy in young children.

Other studies of vocal accuracy include the following. Goetze (1985) and Goetze and Horii (1989) compared unison with group singing, and the effects of use of text with the effects of neutral syllables on singing accuracy of kindergarten, first-, and third-graders. The findings of gender differences (girls superior to boys) and improvement with age mirror other studies. They also found greater accuracy for singing alone than in a group and that, especially for kindergartners and first-graders, using a neutral syllable such as "loo" enhances accuracy. Levinowitz (1989) conducted a five-month study to determine the effect of singing a song with words versus singing a song with neutral syllables on the tonal and rhythmic accuracy of 4- and 5-year-old children. During the last month, criterion songs having similar melodic/harmonic qualities were taught, one using words and one using neutral syllables. No difference was found in rhythmic accuracy, but tonal accuracy was better on the song with words. Differences in the results of these two studies in terms of the effect of neutral syllables may be due to differences in age, sample, or experimental design.

Dunne-Sousa (1990) examined 3- to 5-year-olds to determine whether speech rhythm, melody, or movement was most useful to them in identifying a song, and which was most useful in helping children to learn a song. Results suggest that movement followed by melody produced on "loo" was the most effective in cuing a learned song for children. Chanting the melodic rhythm on "ta" was the least effective. No significant relationship was found between style of song presentation and learning of the song.

A final question regarding vocal accuracy in young children centers on the effect of male and female vocal modeling on pitch accuracy. The results are mixed. Small and McCachern (1983) found a negligible difference in favor of female vocal modeling, while Sims, Moore, and Kuhn (1982) found a significant positive effect in favor of female voices. This is an issue that may need to be explored further as more and more men move into early childhood music instruction.

Creative Response On one level, it could be said that everything the very young child does musically is creative in that it is unique, exploratory in nature, and a means of discovering what the child can do musically. Certainly theories of artistic or creative development (see Wolf and Gardner, 1980; Webster, 1988; Tillman, 1989) view these early years as times of spontaneous expression, exploration, and emerging mastery or control.

Studies examining creative development in the young are limited and generally focus on the child from 5 years on. Flohr (1984) studied 2- to 5-year olds' exploratory improvisations on xylophones. He found that 2-year-olds are mostly driven by motor energy; by age 3 children begin to create pattern through repetition of ideas, particularly rhythmic repetition characterized by even rhythms and sometimes a feeling of triple meter; by the age of 5, steady beat emerges as a forming device and both melodic and rhythmic repetition occur structurally.

Kratus (1985, 1989) observed that melodies of 5-year-olds tend to have a wide pitch range with no tonal context but some use of repeated melodic patterns. Rhythmic organization tended not to be present. By the age of 7, attention to tonal center at the ends of melodic patterns was common, but tempo and meter remained uncertain. Stepwise motion was often used. Very few 7-year-olds could repeat a melody they had just composed, indicating that these children are still in an improvisatory stage.

Kalmar and Balasko (1987) examined sung improvisations on a given text by 6-year-old children from two different schools in Hungary. All children had been in nursery school for 2.5 years. Children were divided into three groups, all of which received the typical Hungarian music program for nursery schools, utilizing Hungarian folk songs, chants, and simple rhythm patterns. The control group received only that instruction. The experimental group received additional

30-minute classes twice a week for three years, featuring special playful singing-music activities taught by Katalin Forrai. The third group received the basic instruction but was taught by a teacher of high musicianship who used highly creative musical activities with the children. Torrance measures were used to evaluate the quality of the 169 improvisational responses. The third group excelled in virtually every respect, having the highest numbers of improvisations (fluency); and the highest originality in use of tonal resources, unique phrasing, atypical rhythm forms, and other interesting elements such as sequences. The experimental group gave the second most advanced performance but adhered more strictly to taught materials such as use of the full pentatonic scale and typical but complex song forms. The performance of the control group was the least interesting.

Schmidt and Sinor (1986) studied the relationship of music audiation (measured by the PMMA), musical creativity (measured by the *Webster Measure of Creative Thinking in Music* [MCTM]), and cognitive style (reflective/impulsive) in second-grade children. Children with a reflective style tended to score significantly higher on the tonal test of the PMMA than those with an impulsive style. These differences did not exist for the rhythm test. No relationship was found between cognitive style and measures of divergent thinking in music as evidenced by the children's compositions. Reflectivity/impulsivity appeared to be more related to convergent thinking. No gender differences appeared on the MCTM except that boys produced more divergent responses.

Future Research in Musical Productive Behaviors The following questions (Scott, 1990) may help to guide ongoing research in music production in young children. Some have begun to be studied; many have implications for cross-cultural or cross-sectional study.

1. How does one explain the amount of individual variation in musical capacity and sensitivity between different children at a very early age? Are some children born with a musical "predisposition"?
2. Are there universal patterns of musical development in singing, moving, listening, creating? If not, how does culture, including language, seem to affect those behaviors?
3. What production skills can be developed? What variability can be found across cultures? What can be learned from that variability?

Cognition

Several researchers, either through their own study or through summarizing the work of others, have proposed general sequences in the development of music cognition. Dowling (1982) links children's perception of melodic features to their song production, suggesting movement from perception of gross features such as melodic contour to more precise features of tonality and interval. McDonald and Simons (1989) propose a sequence of conceptual development moving from timbre to dynamics, rhythm, melody, form, texture, and harmony. Zimmerman (1984) suggests that the developmental sequence of concepts is volume, timbre, tempo, duration, pitch, and harmony. Most of the existing research from which these orders have been extracted is atomistic, considering single attributes rather than the multiple variants that typify musical events.

Pitch In the area of pitch, Bridger (1961) found that infants up to 5 days old could discriminate fairly fine differences in frequency. Chang and Trehub (1977) conditioned 5-month-old infants to ignore a six-tone melodic pattern through habituation. They then switched to either a transposition of the standard pattern or a scrambled order. Infants showed a differential response to the scrambled pattern but seemed to treat tonal shape as being the same, indicating that 5-month-old infants are aware of extracting information in tonal patterns.

Summers (1984) used a visually reinforced head-turn technique to determine whether 6-month-old infants could be trained to discriminate (1) a melody from its transposition, (2) a melody from a variant, and (3) two melodies of contrasting contour using the same pitch set. Infants were successful on the first two tasks but had difficulty with the latter. Summers found that some infants could learn to conserve short melodies regardless of changes due to transposition. Trehub, Thorpe, and Trainor (1990) found that infants aged 7 to 10 months were successful at discriminating a semitone change in a well-structured western melody based on an underlying major or minor triad but not in a poorly structured western melody or nonwestern melody. The researchers suggest that patterns based on major or minor triads may be more readily encoded by infant listeners than non-triadic patterns.

Scott (1977) examined children from 3 to 5 years of age on their ability to group pitch stimuli based on register, contour, and interval size. A fairly high percentage of 4-year-olds had attained the concept of register; a smaller percentage demonstrated acquisition of the other two concepts. Timbre was not a factor. White and colleagues (1990) tested children from 3.5 to 5 years on their ability to group three-note unidirectional pitch patterns on the basis of direction, first note, and pitch set. In a same/different test, younger children tended to group on the basis of absolute value (pitch set), and the 5-year-olds on the relational (directional) features. The categorization task produced no age-related results.

Jordan-DeCarbo (1989) studied the effect of three different modes of brief perceptual pretraining on 3- to 5-year-olds' pitch discrimination of common three-note patterns. The first training mode consisted of same/different verbal responses to patterns, the second used vocal imitation of the patterns, and the third involved only listening. Three- and 4-year-olds responded similarly to each other, and 5-year-olds were significantly better at discrimination.

In a replication of this study, teachers of these children sang simple directions for classroom activities using the four pitch patterns across 10 days prior to testing. Again, there were age-related effects, but this time each older age group scored better than the previous one. Webster and

Schlentrich (1982) found that active response improved preschool children's ability to discriminate differences in pitch patterns, with performance (playing patterns on bells) being more effective than a gestural response or a verbal response. Buckton (1982) found 5- to 7-year-olds able to identify high/low with isolated sounds. The terms "getting higher" and "getting lower" were easily used to describe pitch events.

Litke and Olsen (1979) found 4- to 5-year-olds much faster and more accurate than older subjects in tuning frequencies in octave relationship to a variable reference stimulus. They theorize that children of this age may be particularly susceptible to the acquisition of relative pitch perception.

Timbre In the area of tone color or timbre, Michel (1973) found that infants of 2 to 3 months can distinguish between two different timbres as evidenced through an eye-blinking response in a conditioning paradigm. Loucks (1974) found that 5-year-olds discriminated instrument timbre better than 4-year-olds. Fullard (1967) trained preschool children to identify various orchestral instruments and categories of instruments. Wooderson and Small (1981) found second-graders more able to associate the sound of an instrument with its visual representation than first-graders.

Training Several researchers have examined the effects of training and/or testing on the ability of kindergarten, first- and second-graders to recognize various musical concepts. Buckton (1982) tested children from 5 to 7 on a variety of perceptual and conceptual tasks, some verbal and some performance based. The children successfully identified high/low, loud/soft, fast/slow, and long/short. Concepts of loudness seemed easier than those of pitch.

Piper and Shoemaker (1973) discovered that prior to their formal training, kindergarten children already could distinguish between same and different phrases, identify gross features of melodic contour, distinguish between accompanied and unaccompanied music, and distinguish between loud and soft and fast and slow. They also found kindergarten children able to benefit from instruction across a wide range of concept tasks. Taebel (1974) examined the effects of four modes of test instruction (discovery, verbal cue, verbal response, motor response) on the ability of kindergarten, first-, and second-grade children to identify louder, faster, higher, or shorter in a given melody. Age had the greatest effect, with concepts of loudness manifested by all ages, tempo by first- and second-graders, pitch by first-graders, and duration by first and second. Mode of instruction had a minimal effect on most concepts. Kindergartners and first-graders were similar in verbal responses, but first-graders were more able to demonstrate their understandings. Second-graders were as accurate as first-graders but more able to explain their choices verbally.

Future Research in Perception and Cognition The following questions (Scott, 1990) call for careful quantitative study and cooperation between music education researchers, psychomusicologists, and cognitive psychologists interested in musical growth. Though suggested by previous research, most remain to be addressed.

1. Are there clear stages in the development of musical thought in the young child? Are these mainly a function of maturation, or do these vary from culture to culture and from individual to individual?
2. What is "normal" musical thought and "normal" musical behavior during the preschool years? Does this vary across cultures?
3. What can be learned about normal musical thinking by studying the musically gifted?
4. What is the relationship between production and perception? Are there vocal or kinesthetic/tactile substructures that affect aural perception? If so, how and when do they develop? Are they subject to instruction?
5. What is the effect of active "musicing" on the musical/cognitive as well as the general intellectual development of the very young child? How is this related to the period of rapid growth of language?
6. When does perceptual expectancy begin to influence musical decision making in preschoolers?
7. What are the links between musical constructive behavior (composing) and musical analytical behavior (listening) and the development of musical thought?
8. Is the development of musical thought related to general cognitive development?
9. What are the links between accuracy of production of the singing or the motor response to music and musical intelligence and sensitivity?

Affect

Discussions concerning affective response to music have been confounded by attempts to differentiate the aesthetic response from the affective, and by questions about what role preference plays in either one. Affect is usually defined as the emotional aspect of responding, which may or may not lead to valuing. Preference is the selection of certain stimuli over others and may or may not imply valuing.

Standley and Madsen (1990) studied sound preference in infants from age 2 to 8 months. They recorded a simple story read by the mother, read by a female graduate student, and sung by a male and female. The infants were videotaped, and their auditory, vocal, and motoric responses and eye movements were analyzed. Seconds of listening time and number of preference changes per interval were recorded. The mother's voice was most highly preferred, followed by music and the other female voice. The older infants preferred the mother's voice almost equally to that of the other female. All babies seemed to listen more intently to the music than the other stimuli.

Peery and Peery (1986) studied preschool children (mean age: 4 years, 7 months) to determine the effects of positive social experience on musical preference. Children were pre- and posttested on preference for a range of musical works using a semi-Likert scale with five different qualities of facial expression. The experimental group received 10 months of weekly 45-minute classes using classical music in a variety of activities and positive reinforcement responses. Results of the pretest suggested that, at age 4.5 years, children liked all kinds of music. The posttest showed that whereas the experimental group retained their enjoyment of all kinds of music, the control group children (now 5 or older) had begun to show preferences for popular music. This result may show the increasing influence of media over children.

May (1985) measured musical preferences of children from 6 to 8 years old via a pictographic response form using faces with various expressions from like to dislike. Aural skills and factors of age, race, gender were also analyzed. Generally 6-year-olds were open to a wider variety of music than the older children. All children preferred popular styles, and that preference became more established with age. Females tended to prefer lower dynamism in music than males. The only differences were preferences associated with a particular race, such as music by black singers or with texts about Afro-American culture. Correlations between aural skills and preference were not definitive.

The aesthetic is generally considered a combination of the affective and the cognitive. It is also thought to be affected by both age and experience. McMahon (1987) tested 3- to 5-year-olds in their ability to make and justify aesthetic choices with visual, tactile, and auditory musical stimuli. She found that children could more easily verbalize their responses to objects in the tactile and visual realm than the auditory. Nelson (1985) attempted to apply Parson's theory of aesthetic growth in the area of music with 3- to 17-year-olds. Seven standard questions in response to musical stimuli allowed them to demonstrate preference and respond emotionally, empathically, and qualitatively. A high correlation was found between quality of aesthetic response and age; children under 6 had the most difficult time responding. The trend in responding was from egocentric standards in the young children to more external standards in the older.

Future Research in Affective Responding Some questions of potential interest to researchers in the area of musical valuing are as follows.

1. At what age does a child start making choices between types of music? At what age do distinct preferences begin to emerge?
2. When does the child start making a clear commitment to certain pieces or types of music? How does that response develop? How is it influenced by environment? By instruction?
3. How do early approach tendencies toward music affect later musical behaviors?
4. What are the stages of growth in aesthetic responding to music? How are those impacted by environment including schooling? (Scott, 1990)

Models and Methods of Instruction

Peery and Peery (in Peery, Peery, & Draper 1987) suggest that music should be included in the childhood curriculum because of its inherent merit; that it is desirable that children be exposed to, trained in, and enculturated with music. Further, musical skills have attendant benefits in terms of personal and social competence. Certainly, research into the validity of these assumptions would contribute to a broad theory of musical learning that would be helpful, not only in planning and implementing instruction but in building the case for music. Researchers such as Michel (1973) and Heller and Campbell (1981) have asserted that the years from birth through age 6 may be the most crucial for musical development. In spite of these assertions, the development and testing of comprehensive models of music instruction with the young have been minimally explored.

Katz (1987), in a book devoted to issues of early schooling, raises the concern that in the absence of a body of relevant studies, the tendency is to use broad developmental data and to attempt to make valid and reliable inferences from them. She states, "It is a general principle that any field characterized by a weak data base has a vacuum which is filled by ideologies" (p. 151).

This problem is especially critical in the field of early childhood music education, where a coherent body of general developmental data in music is lacking. As a result, music educators have intuitively advocated early childhood music programs based on play theory, cognitive/conceptual programs, methods inherent in early childhood approaches such as that of Montessori, and programs from other cultures such as those of Orff, Kodály, Dalcroze, and Suzuki. Arguments for and against these various approaches abound. Most such arguments remain at the speculative level, given the limited research examining short- or long-term effects of a structured program on musical development, musical attitudes, musical creativity, or other factors such as personal and social competence as suggested by Peery and Peery (1987). Further, very few studies report either formative or summative evaluations of early childhood music programs.

Philosophical Models Some researchers have attempted to use a strong philosophical/theoretical base in proposing the form early childhood music programs might take. Hawn (1975) researched Piaget's play theory as a basis for a complete music program in the preschool years. Romanek (1980) adapted the Cantometrics classification system (the study of song style as a measure of culture) as a means of developing a world music curriculum for early childhood. Andress (1986) proposed that a variety of developmental theories in play, language, and cognition be utilized as a basis for constructing early childhood music programs.

Specific Curricula Other researchers have examined music principles and materials in two categories: (1)music-based curricula such as Kodály and Suzuki, and (2) general curricula such as Montessori.

MONTESSORI. Miller (1981) describes both the historical and the current practice in Montessorian music. Rubin (1983) summarizes previously unpublished works resulting from the collaboration of Montessori and Maccheroni, a musician who worked with Montessori over a long period of time. Fitzmaurice (1971) developed and refined an experimental music program based on Montessori principles.

KODÁLY. Effects of the Kodály preschool curriculum have been tested in Hungary, including a descriptive study by Forrai (1970) of her musical observations of children from 1 to 3 years of age; a study by Kalmar (1989) of the effect of music training on the development of qualitative concepts in kindergarten children; a study by Kalmar (1982) of the effects of the Kodály program on nursery school children; and another study (reported earlier) by Kalmar and Balasko (1987) on children's creativity as a function of a training program. Kalmar, a psychologist, studied growth of various kinds of thinking stimulated within the context of the music setting. The 1989 study reports that children who had been in a special music group for 2.5 years (in which antonym pairs were used as descriptive language to describe musical events, e.g., loud/soft, fast/slow) improved their correct use of such descriptors far beyond that of a control group matched for gender, intelligence, and age.

Two studies—Jarjisian (1983) and Sinor (1984)—have examined assumptions underlying aspects of the Kodály system. Jarjisian was curious to determine whether use of materials based on pentatonic scales would have a positive effect on vocal performance of first-graders. She studied three training groups for four months: one pentatonic only, one diatonic only, and one mixed diatonic and pentatonic. First-graders who learned both diatonic and pentatonic patterns were more successful in singing than either of the other groups.

Sinor (1984) studied the capacity of 96 children ranging in age from 36 to 71 months to reproduce common tonal patterns. Age was the most significant variable. Sinor discusses her results in terms of assumptions of the Kodály system that (1) half steps are easier to sing than whole steps (this was not supported), (2) that large intervals are more difficult to sing than smaller ones (there was limited support for this), (3) that the descending minor third is the easiest interval to sing (it was the second easiest), (4) that descending patterns are easier to sing than ascending (divided evidence), and (5) that successive leaps are difficult to sing (successive leaps in the same direction are not, v-shaped leaps seem to be).

SUZUKI. In spite of the widespread enthusiasm over Suzuki instruction, the question of whether instruction at the age of 2 or 3 is of long-term emotional or musical benefit to the child remains unanswered. It is clear that young children can be taught to play at advanced levels by rote. Price (1979) developed and tested a short-term program to train 4- and 5-year-olds to play Suzuki violin in a day-care setting. After a period of from 12 to 23 weeks of training, music achievement was rated outstanding and parent and teacher support very strong. Long-term research would help to answer questions posed at the beginning of this paragraph.

Evaluation of Models As more instructional programs in music are developed for the very young child, both formative and summative evaluations of their ineffectiveness will be needed.

Greenberg (1974) reports on the development and evaluation of a music curriculum for preschool and Headstart children designed to develop cognitive and affective responses to music and also to help teachers with limited musical backgrounds teach sequentially. Five experimental and two control groups were pretested on their music achievement, teacher training in use of the curriculum was accomplished, and the program implemented. Children were posttested six months later. Observers ranked teacher effectiveness, and teachers ranked program effectiveness. Rhythmic development was the only aspect significantly affected by the training. Teachers rated the affective component as high. They felt cognitive and aesthetic growth was possible and important.

Piper and Shoemaker (1973) performed a formative evaluation of a kindergarten music program based on concept mastery and performance skill. Using a pretest/posttest design, they tested children across a wide range of common concepts and skills. They found the program successfully taught new things but not all it purported to teach. The information gathered was used to modify the program.

Future Research in Music Instruction The following questions (Scott, 1990) are presented to stimulate thinking about needed research in music instruction with the very young. It is hoped that researchers will work cooperatively with educators to answer these and other questions.

1. At what age do children begin to benefit most from structured music instruction versus learning that is more the result of enculturation?
2. What ways of engaging music contribute most significantly to musical development? Sound play, live music, recorded music?
3. What instructional models seem to work best at what ages? What role should language play? Experimentation with sound? Parent involvement? Cognitive reasoning? Movement? Should models be developed that are unique to music or should they be adapted from other early childhood models?
4. What media (computers, synthesizers, instruments, recordings) should be used at different ages? How does this relate to the ability to handle use of the media? How does this relate to the ability to learn from the media?
5. What are the long-range effects of short-term instruction as well as of long-term instruction on children's valuing of music, perception of music, understanding of music, and/or performance of music? What are the long-term effects of early instruction in music on other factors such as intelligence, personal competence, social competence?
6. What are effective methodologies for training parents to be agents for their children's musical growth?
7. What are effective models for training preschool teachers to use music in a significant fashion? Is the preschool teacher a better agent for music instruction than the music specialist?
8. Does early musical stimulation, including prenatal stimulation, result in long-term significant musical development in children, including musical sensitivity and memory?

In developing programs in music for the very young, one must consider the concerns raised by Katz (1987) and Elkind (1988) about the dangers of starting children too early on certain kinds of tasks, with certain kinds of pressures, and with homogeneous programs. Data in the general development and educational literature are ample to guide people in developing programs that clearly reflect the needs as well as the readiness of the very young.

Closing Remarks

This is an exciting time to explore theories related to musical development and music instruction in the very young child. Organizational interest in issues regarding music and the very young is building. The International Society for Music Education (ISME) approved the establishment of an Early Childhood Commission in 1980. The Music Educators National Conference (MENC) has included standards for early childhood music settings in its recent, (1986) description and standards publication. An MENC-appointed early childhood task force has issued a call for more publications of research and practice in early childhood music education. The Early Childhood Special Research Interest Group (SRIG) of MENC, established in 1978, continues to provide a forum for persons interested this area.

It is hoped that the current interest in music and the very young will continue and that researchers will be stimulated to conduct studies that will help establish a clear foundation of understanding on which to base ideas of musical development and practice.

References

Alford, D. L. (1971). Emergence and development of music responses in preschool twins and singletons: A comparative study. *Journal of Research in Music Education, 19,* 222–227.

Alvarez, B. J. (1981). Preschool music education and research on the musical development of preschool children: 1900 to 1980. Unpublished doctoral dissertation, University of Michigan, Ann Arbor. Review by C. Scott in *Bulletin of the Council for Research in Music Education, 87,* 1986, 57–60.

Andress, B. (1986). Toward an integrated developmental theory for early childhood music education. *Bulletin of the Council for Research in Music Education, 86,* 10–17.

Apfelstadt, H. (1984). Effects of melodic perception instruction on pitch discrimination and vocal accuracy of kindergarten children. *Journal of Research in Music Education, 32*(1), 15–24.

Ashbaugh, T. J. (1983). The effects of training in conservation of duple and triple meter in music with second-grade children. *Bulletin of the Council for Research in Music Education, 73,* 67–72.

Bamberger, J. (1982). Revisiting children's drawings of simple rhythms: A function for reflection-in-action. In S. Straus (Ed.), *U-Shaped behavioral growth.* New York: Academic Press.

Bentley, A. (1966). *Musical ability in children.* New York: October House.

Borg, W. R., and Gall, M. D. (1989). *Educational research* (5th ed.). New York: Longman.

Boswell, J. (Ed.). (1985). *The young child and music: Contemporary principles in child development and music education.* Reston: Music Educators National Conference.

Brand, M. (1986). Relationship between home musical environment and selected musical attributes of second-grade children. *Journal of Research in Music Education, 34*(2), 111–120.

Bridger, W. H. (1961). Sensory habituation and discrimination in the human neonate. *American Journal of Psychiatry, 117,* 991–996.

Buckton, R. (1982). An investigation into the development of musical concepts in young children. *Psychology of Music,* Special issue: ISME IXth Research Seminar, pp. 17–21.

Buckton, R. (1983). *Sing a song of six-year-olds.* Wellington, New Zealand: New Zealand Council for Educational Research.

Chang, H. W., and Trehub, S. E. (1977). Auditory processing of relational information by young infants. *Journal of Experimental Child Psychology, 24,* 324–335.

Davidson, L. (1985). Preschool children's tonal knowledge: Antecedents of scale. In J. Boswell (Ed.), *The young child and music* (pp. 25–40). Reston: Music Educators National Conference.

Davidson, L., and Colley, B. (1987). Children's rhythmic development from age 5 to 7: Performance, notation, and reading of rhythmic patterns. In J. C. Peery, I. W. Peery, and T. W. Draper, *Music and child development* (pp. 107–136). New York: Springer-Verlag.

Davidson, L., McKernon, P., and Gardner, H. (1981). The acquisition of song: A developmental approach. In *Documentary report of the Ann Arbor Symposium: National Symposium on the Application of Psychology to the Teaching and Learning of Music.* Reston: Music Educators National Conference.

Davidson, L., and Scripp, L. (1986). Young children's musical representation: Windows on music cognition. In J. Sloboda (Ed.), *Generative processes in music* (pp. 195–230). New York: Oxford University Press.

Deutsch, D. (Ed.). (1982). *The psychology of music.* New York: Academic Press.

Donaldson, M. (1978). *Children's minds.* New York: W. W. Norton.

Dowling, W. J. (1982). Melodic information processing and its development. In D. Deutsch (Ed.), *The psychology of music.* New York: Academic Press.

Dowling, W. J., and Harwood, D. L. (1986). *Music cognition.* Orlando: Academic Press.

Dunne-Sousa, D. (1990). *The effect of speech rhythm, melody, and movement on song identification and performance of preschool children.* Paper presented at the biennial meeting of the Music Educators National Conference, Washington.

Elkind, D. (1988). Educating the very young: A call for clear thinking. *NEA Today, 6*(6), 65–70.

Fitzmaurice, T. J. (1971). An experimental music program based on

Montessorian principles. Unpublished doctoral dissertation, Boston University, Boston.

Flavell, J. H. (1985). *Cognitive development.* Englewood Cliffs: Prentice-Hall.

Flohr, J. W. (1981). Short-term music instruction and young children's developmental music aptitude. *Journal of Research in Music Education, 29*(3), 219–224.

Flohr, J. W. (1984). *Young children's improvisations.* Paper presented at the bienniel meeting of the Music Educators National Conference, Chicago.

Flowers, P. J., and Costa-Giomi, E. (1990). *Verbal and nonverbal identification of pitch changes in a familiar song by English and Spanish speaking preschool children.* Paper presented at the biennial meeting of the Music Educators National Conference, Washington.

Flowers, P. J., and Dunne-Sousa, D. (1990). Pitch-pattern accuracy, tonality, and vocal range in preschool children's singing. *Journal of Research in Music Education, 38*(2), 102–114.

Foley, E. (1975). Effects of training in conservation of tonal and rhythmic patterns on second-grade children. *Journal of Research in Music Education, 23*(4), 240–248.

Forrai, K. (1970). *Musical observations among children of one to three years of age.* Kecskemét, Hungary: Kodály Seminar. [monograph]

Fox, D. B. (1990). An analysis of the pitch characteristics of infant vocalizations. *Psychomusicology, 9*(1), 21–30.

Frega, A. L. (1979). Rhythmic tasks with 3-, 4-, and 5-year-old children: A study made in the Argentine Republic. *Bulletin of the Council for Research in Music Education, 59,* 32–34.

Fullard, W. G., Jr. (1967). Operant training of aural musical discriminations with preschool children. *Journal of Research in Music Education, 15*(3), 201–209.

Gardner, H. (1973). *The arts and human development.* New York: John Wiley.

Gardner, H. (1982). *Art, mind & brain: A cognitive approach to creativity.* New York: Basic Books.

Gardner, H. (1983). *Frames of mind: The theory of multiple intelligences.* New York: Basic Books.

Geringer, J. M. (1983). The relationship of pitch-matching and pitch-discrimination abilities of preschool and fourth-grade students. *Journal of Research in Music Education, 31*(2), 93–100.

Gilbert, J. P. (1979). Assessment of motoric music skill development in young children: Test construction and evaluation procedures. *Psychology of Music, 9*(1), 3–12.

Gilbert, J. P. (1981). Motoric music skill development in young children: A longitudinal investigation. *Psychology of Music, 7*(2), 21–25.

Goetze, M. (1985). Factors affecting accuracy in children's singing. Unpublished docotral dissertation, University of Colorado, Boulder. Review by K. Phillips in *Bulletin of the Council for Research in Music Education, 102,* 1989, 82–85.

Goetze, M., and Horii, Y. (1989). A comparison of the pitch accuracy of group and individual singing in young children. *Bulletin of the Council for Research in Music Education, 99,* 57–73.

Gordon, E. (1979). Developmental music aptitude as measured by the *Primary Measures of Music Audiation. Psychology of Music,* 7(1), 42–49.

Gordon, E. (1986). A factor analysis of the *Musical Aptitude Profile,* the *Primary Measures of Music Audiation,* and the *Intermediate Measures* of *Music Audiation. Bulletin of the Council for Research in Music Education, 87,* 17–25.

Greenberg, M. (1974). The development and evaluation of a preschool music curriculum for preschool and Headstart children. *Psychology of Music, 2*(1), 34–38.

Hair, H. I. (1977). Discrimination of tonal direction on verbal and nonverbal tasks by first grade children. *Journal of Research in Music Education, 25*(3), 197–210.

Hair, H. I. (1981). Verbal identification of music concepts. *Journal of Research in Music Education, 29,* 11–21.

Hair, H. I. (1987). Descriptive vocabulary and visual choices: Children's responses to conceptual changes in music. *Bulletin of the Council for Research in Music Education, 91,* 59–64.

Hargreaves, D. J. (1986). *The developmental psychology of music.* Cambridge: Cambridge University Press.

Hargreaves, D. J., Castell, K., and Crowther, R. (1986). The effects of stimulus familiarity on conservation-type responses to tone sequences: A cross-cultural study. *Journal of Research in Music Education, 34*(2), 88–100.

Hawn, C. (1975). Implications and adaptations of Piaget's theory of play for the preschool music curriculum. Unpublished doctoral dissertation, Southern Baptist Theological Seminary, Louisville. Reviewed by M. Greenberg in *Bulletin of the Council for Research in Music Education, 56,* 1978, 21–24.

Heller, J., and Campbell, W. (1981). A theoretical model of music perception and talent. *Bulletin of the Council for Research in Music Education, 66-67,* 20–24.

Hildebrandt, C. (1987). Structural development research in music: Conservation and representation. In J. C. Peery, I. W. Peery, and T. W. Draper (Eds.), *Music and child development* (pp. 80–95). New York: Springer-Verlag.

Humphreys, J. T. (1985). The child-study movement and public school music education. *Journal of Research in Music Education, 33*(2), 79–86.

Jarjisian, C. S. (1983). Pitch pattern instruction and the singing achievement of young children. *Psychology of Music, 11*(1), 19–25.

Jones, R. L. (1976). The development of the child's conception of meter in music. *Journal of Research in Music Education, 24*(3), 142–154.

Jordan-DeCarbo, J. (1989). The effect of pretraining conditions and age on pitch discrimination ability of preschool children. *Journal of Research in Music Education, 37*(2), 132–145.

Kagan, S., and Zigler, E. (Eds.). (1987). *Early schooling: The national debate.* New Haven: Yale University Press.

Kail, R. (1984). *The development of memory in children.* New York: W. H. Freeman.

Kalmar, M. (1982). The effects of music education based on Kodály's directives in nursery school children from a psychologist's point of view. *Psychology of music* [Special issue: ISME IXth Research Seminar].

Kalmar, M. (1989). The effects of music education on the acquisition of some attribute-concepts in preschool children [special supplement, XIIth International Research Seminar in Music Education]. *Canadian Music Educator, 30*(2), 51–59.

Kalmar, M., and Balasko, G. (1987). "Musical mother tongue" and creativity in preschool children's melody improvisations. *Bulletin of the Council for Research in Music Education, 91,* 77–83.

Katz, L. C. (1987). Early education: What should young children be doing? In S. Kagan and E. Zigler (Eds.), *Early schooling: The national debate.* New Haven: Yale University Press.

Kelley, L., and Sutton-Smith, B. (1987). A study of infant musical productivity. In J. C. Peery, I. W. Peery, and T. W. Draper, (Eds.) *Music and child development* (pp. 35–53). New York: Springer-Verlag.

Kessen, W., Levine, J., and Wendrich, K. A. (1979). The imitation of pitch in infants. *Infant Behavior and Development, 2,* 93–99.

Kratus, J. (1985). Rhythm, melody, motive, and phrase characteristics of children's original compositions. Unpublished doctoral dissertation, Case Western Reserve University, Cleveland.

Kratus, J. (1989). A time analysis of the compositional processes used by children ages 7 to 11. *Journal of Research in Music Education, 37,* 5–20.

Levinowitz, L. M. (1989). An investigation of preschool children's comparative capability to sing songs with and without words. *Bulletin of the Council for Research in Music Education, 100,* 14–19.

Litke, E., and Olsen, C. C. (1979). Acquiring relative pitch perception as a function of age. *Journal of Research in Music Education, 27*(4), 243–254.

Loucks, D. G. (1974). The development of an instrument to measure instrumental timbre concepts of four-year-old and five-year-old children: A feasibility study. Unpublished doctoral dissertation, Ohio State University, Columbus.

May, W. V. (1985). Musical style preferences and aural discrimination of primary grade school children. *Journal of Research in Music Education Bulletin, 33*(1), 7–22.

McDonald, D. T., and Simons, G. M. (1989). *Musical growth and development: Birth through six.* New York: Schirmer Books.

McMahon, O. (1982). A comparison of language development and verbalization in response to auditory stimuli in pre-school age children. *Psychology of Music* [Special issue: ISME IXth Research Seminar], pp. 82–85.

McMahon, O. (1985). Young children's perceptions of the dimensions of sound. *Bulletin of the Council for Research in Music Education, 85,* 131–139.

McMahon, O. (1987). An exploration of aesthetic awareness in preschool age children. *Bulletin of the Council for Research in Music Education, 91,* 97–102.

Metz, E. (1989). Movement as a musical response among preschool children. *Journal of Research in Music Education, 37*(1), 48–60.

Michel, P. (1973). The optimum development of musical ability in the first years of life. *Psychology of Music, 1,* 14–20.

Miller, J. K. (1981). The Montessori music curriculum for children up to six years of age. Unpublished doctoral dissertation, Case Western Reserve University, Cleveland.

Miller, L. B. (1986). A description of children's musical behaviors: Naturalistic. *Bulletin of the Council for Research in Music Education, 87,* 1–16.

Moog, H. (1976). *The musical experience of the pre-school child.* London: B. Schott. (Original work published in German in 1968)

Monsour, S., and Knox, C. (1985). *Magic musical balloon game* [Computer program]. Bellevue: Temporal Acuity Products.

Moore, D. L. (1973). A study of pitch and rhythm responses of five-year-old children in relation to their early musical experiences. Unpublished doctoral dissertation, Florida State University, Tallahassee.

Moorhead, G., and Pond, D. (1978). *Music of young children.* Santa Barbara: Pillsbury Foundation for the Advancement of Music Education.

MENC Committee on Standards. (1986). *The school music program: Description and standards* (2nd ed.). Reston: MENC.

Nelson, D. J. (1984). The conservation of rhythm in Suzuki violin students: A task validation study. *Journal of Research in Music Education, 32*(1), 25–34.

Nelson, D. J. (1985). Trends in the aesthetic responses of children to the musical experience. *Journal of Research in Music Education, 33*(3), 193–203.

Norton, D. (1979). Relationships of music ability and intelligence to auditory and visual conservation of the kindergarten child. *Journal of Research in Music Education, 27*(1), 3–13.

Norton, D. (1980). Interrelationship among music aptitude, IQ, and auditory conservation. *Journal of Research in Music Education, 28*(4), 207–217.

Papousek, M., and Papousek, H. (1981). Musical elements in the infants vocalization: Their significance for communication, cognition and creativity. In L. P. Lipsitt (Ed.), *Advances in infancy research* (Vol. 1, pp. 163–224). Norwood: Ablex Publishing.

Peery, J. C., and Peery, I. W. (1986). Effects of exposure to classical music on the musical preferences of preschool children. *Journal of Research in Music Education, 33*(1), 24–33.

Peery, J. C., Peery, I. W., and Draper, T. W. (1987). *Music and child development.* New York: Springer-Verlag.

Pflederer, M. (1964). The responses of children to musical tasks embodying Piaget's principle of conservation. *Journal of Research in Music Education, 12,* 251–268.

Piper, R. M., and Shoemaker, D. M. (1973). Formative evaluation of a kindergarten music program based on behavioral objectives. *Journal of Research in Music Education, 21*(2), 145–152.

Price, C. V. G. (1979). A model for the implementation of a Suzuki violin program for the day-care center environment: An evaluation of its effectiveness and impact. Unpublished doctoral dissertation, University of Michigan, Ann Arbor.

Rainbow, E. (1981). A final report on a three-year investigation of rhythmic abilities of preschool aged children. *Bulletin of the Council for Research in Music Education, 66-67,* 69–73.

Ramsey, J. H. (1983). The effects of age, singing ability, and instrumental experiences on preschool children's melodic perception. *Journal of Research in Music Education, 31*(2), 133–145.

Ries, N. L. (1987). An analysis of the characteristics of infant-child singing expressions: Replication report. *The Canadian Journal of Research in Music Education, 29,*(1), 5–20.

Revesz, G. (1953). *Introduction to the psychology of music.* London: Longmans Green.

Roberts, E. and Davies, A.D.M. (1975). Poor pitch singing: Response of monotone singers to a program of remedial training. *Journal of Research in Music Education, 23* (4), 227–239.

Romanek, M. L. (1980). *Cantometrics and world music for the early childhood music curriculum.* Paper presented at XIV International Society of Music Education World Conference in Warsaw.

Rubin, J. S. (1983). Montessorian music method: Unpublished works. *Journal of Research in Music Education, 31*(3), 215–226.

Schleuter, S. L., and Schleuter, L. J. (1985). The relationship of grade level and sex differences to certain rhythmic responses of primary grade children. *Journal of Research in Music Education, 33*(1), 23–30.

Schleuter, S. L., and Schleuter, L. J. (1989). The relationship of rhythm response tasks and PMMA scores with music training, grade level, and sex among K-3 students. *Bulletin of the Council for Research in Music Education, 100,* 1–13.

Schmidt, C. P., and Sinor, E. (1986). An investigation of the relationships among music audiation, musical creativity, and cognitive style. *Journal of Research in Music Education, 34*(3), 160–172.

Scott, C. R. (1977). Pitch concept formation in preschool children. Unpublished doctoral dissertation, University of Washington, Seattle.

Scott, C. R. (1988). Getting there from here: The examination of musical growth in young children. In A. Kemp (Ed.), *Research in music education: A festschrift for Arnold Bentley* (pp. 74–80). London: International Society for Music Education Edition No. 2.

Scott, C. R. (1990, August). *Closing the gap between research and practice.* Paper presented at XIX International Society of Music Education World Conference in Helsinki.

Seashore, C. E. (1939). *Music before five.* (Child welfare pamphlets, no. 72). Iowa City: University of Iowa.

Sergeant, D., and Roche, S. (1973). Perceptual shifts in the auditory information processing of young children. *Psychology of Music, 1*(2), 39–48.

Serafine, M. L. (1983). Cognitive processes in music: Discovering vs. definitions. *Bulletin of the Council for Research in Music Education, 73,* 1–14.

Serafine, M. L. (1988). *Music as cognition. The development of thought in sound.* New York: Columbia University Press.

Serafine, M. L. (1980). Piagetian research in music. *Bulletin of the Council for Research in Music Education, 62,* 1–21.

Shelley, S. (1981). Investigating the musical capabilities of young children. *Bulletin of the Council for Research in Music Education, 68,* 26–34.

Shuter-Dyson, R., and Gabriel, C. (1981). *The psychology of musical ability.* London: Methuen.

Sidnell, R. (1981). Motor learning in music education. In *Documentary report of the Ann Arbor Symposium: National Symposium on the Applications of Psychology to the Teaching and Learning of Music.* Reston: Music Educators National Conference.

Simons, G. (1964). Comparisons of incipient music responses among very young twins and singletons. *Journal of Research in Music Education, 12*(3), 212–226.

Simons, G. (1978). *Early childhood musical development: A bibliography of research abstracts, 1960–1975.* Reston: Music Educators National Conference.

Simons, G. (1986). Early childhood musical development: A survey of selected research. *Bulletin of the Council for Research in Music Education, 86,* 36–52.

Sims, W. L. (1984). *Young children's creative movement to music: Categories of movement, rhythmic characteristics, and reactions to changes.* Paper presented at the biennial meeting of the Music Educators National Conference, Chicago.

Sims, W. L. (1988). Movement responses of preschool children, primary grade children, and preservice classroom teachers to characteristics of musical phrases. *Psychology of Music, 16*(2), 110–127.

Sims, W. L. (1990). Characteristics of young children's music concept discrimination. *Psychomusicology, 9*(1), 79–88.

Sims, W. L., Moore, R. S., and Kuhn, T. L. (1982). Effects of female and male vocal stimuli, tonal pattern length, and age on vocal pitch-matching abilities of young children from England and the United States. *Psychology of Music* [Special issue], 104–108.

Sinor, E. (1984). The singing of selected tonal patterns by preschool children. Unpublished doctoral dissertation, Indiana University, Bloomington. Reviewed by L. Damer in *Bulletin of the Council for Research in Music Education, 103,* 1990, 64–67.

Sloboda, J. A. (1985). *The musical mind.* Oxford: Clarendon Press.

Small, A. R., and McCachern, F. L. (1983). The effect of male and female vocal modeling on pitch-matching accuracy of first-grade children. *Journal of Research in Music Education, 31*(3), 227–234.

Standley, J. M., and Madsen, C. K. (1990). Comparison of infant preferences and responses to auditory stimuli: Music, mother, and other female voice. *Journal of Music Therapy, 26*(4).

Stoddard, G. D. (Ed.). (1932). *The measurement of musical development* (University of Iowa Studies in Child Welfare, 7(1)). Iowa City: University of Iowa.

Summers, E. K. (1984). Categorization and conservation of melody in infants. Unpublished doctoral dissertation, University of Washington, Seattle. Reviewed by M. Greenberg. (1987). *Bulletin of the Council for Research in Music Education, 94,* 69–72.

Taebel, D. K. (1974). The effect of various instructional modes on children's performance of music concept tasks. *Journal of Research in Music Education, 22*(3), 170–183.

Tillman, J. (1989). Towards a model of development of children's musical creativity [Special supplement, XIIth International Research Seminar in Music Education]. *Canadian Music Educator, 30*(2), 169–174.

Trehub, S. E. (1987). Infant's perception of musical patterns. *Perception and Psychophysics, 41*(6), 635–641.

Trehub, S. E., Thorpe, L. A., and Trainor, L. J. (1990). Infant's perception of good and bad melodies. *Psychomusicology, 9*(1), 5–19.

Upitis, R. (1987). Toward a model for rhythmic development. In J. C. Peery, I. W. Peery, and T. W. Draper, *Music and child development* (pp. 54–79). New York: Springer-Verlag.

Upitis, R. (1990). Children's invented notations of familiar and unfamiliar melodies. *Psychomusicology, 9*(1), 89–106.

Van Zee, N. (1976). Response of kindergarten children to musical stimuli and terminology. *Journal of Research in Music Education, 24*(1), 14–21.

Vaughan, M. M. (1981). Intercultural studies in children's natural singing pitch and walking tempo. *Bulletin of the Council for Research in Music Education, 66-67*, 96–101.

Walters, D. L. (1983). The relationship between personal tempo in primary-aged children and their ability to synchronize movement with music. Reviewed by M. Vaughan (1986) in *Bulletin of the Council for Research in Music Education, 88*, 85–89.

Wassum, S. (1980). Elementary school children's concept of tonality. *Journal of Research in Music Education, 28*(1), 18–33.

Webster, P. R. (1988, April). *A model for creative thinking in music with implications for music education.* Paper presented at the biennial meeting of the Music Educators National Conference, Indianapolis.

Webster, P. R., and Schlentrich, K. (1982). Discrimination of pitch direction by preschool children with verbal and nonverbal tasks. *Journal of Research in Music Education, 30*(3), 151–162.

Wendrich, K. A. (1981). Pitch imitation in infancy and early childhood: Observations and implications. Unpublished doctoral dissertation, University of Connecticut, Storrs.

White, D. J., Dale, P. S., and Carlsen, J. C. (1990). Discrimination and categorization of pitch direction by young children. *Psychomusicology, 9*(1), 39–58.

Williams, D. B., and Fox, D. B. (1983). *Toney listens to music* [Computer program]. Bellevue: Temporal Acuity Products.

Williams, H. M. (1933). *Musical guidance of young children* (Child welfare pamphlets, no. 29). Iowa City: University of Iowa.

Wohlwill, J. F. (1973). *The study of behavioral development.* New York: Academic Press.

Wolf, D., and Gardner, H. (1980). Beyond playing or polishing: A developmental view of artistry. In J. Hausman (Ed.), *Arts and the schools* (pp. 47–77). New York: McGraw-Hill.

Wooderson, D. C., and Small, A. R. (1981). Instrument association skills: Children in first and second grade. *Journal of Research in Music Education, 29*(1), 39–46.

Young, L. (1982). An investigation of young children's music concept development using nonverbal and manipulative techniques. Unpublished doctoral dissertation, Ohio State University, Columbus.

Zimmerman, M. P. (1981). Child development and music education. In *Documentary report of the Ann Arbor Symposium: National Symposium on the Applications of Psychology to the Teaching and Learning of Music.* Reston: Music Educators National Conference.

Zimmerman, M. P. (1982). Developmental processes in music learning. In R. Colwell (Ed.), *Symposium in music education.* Urbana: University of Illinois Press.

Zimmerman, M. P. (1984). The relevance of Piagetian theory for music education. *International Journal of Music Education, 3*, 31–34.

Zimmerman, M. P. (1985). State of the art in early childhood music and research. In J. Boswell (Ed.), *The young child and music* (pp. 65–78). Reston: Music Educators National Conference.

Zimmerman, M. P., and Sechrest, L. (1968). *How children conceptually organize musical sounds* (Cooperative research project No. 5-0256). Evanston: Northwestern University.

·46·

RESEARCH ON MUSIC ENSEMBLES

Jere T. Humphreys
ARIZONA STATE UNIVERSITY

William V. May
UNIVERSITY OF NORTH TEXAS

David J. Nelson
UNIVERSITY OF IOWA

Since the early years of the twentieth century, elementary, secondary, and postsecondary performing music ensembles have enjoyed increasing popularity in American schools. Throughout most of this century, bands, choirs, and orchestras have been the mainstay of the music curriculum, serving as the primary means of formal music education for tens of thousands of students spanning several generations. Even today, these ensembles constitute all, or nearly all, of the music curriculum in many secondary schools, and they play a key role in college-level music programs as well. Despite their popularity and importance to music curricula, meaningful research on bands, choirs, and orchestras has been difficult to formulate, especially research related to the teaching-learning process.

The difficulties experienced by researchers who attempt to study music ensembles should not reflect negatively on either the ensemble experience or the research process. The music ensemble is a unique educational phenomenon, the success of which has been attributed to its wide-ranging appeal as well as to the directness and simplicity of its objectives (Leonhard, 1980). For some teachers and researchers, however, the objectives of music ensembles are neither simple nor direct. Given the ensemble's preeminent role within the music curriculum, some music educators believe that ensembles should provide students with opportunities not only to participate in music making but also to experience the aesthetic satisfaction of an art form. The failure of the music education profession and society at large to agree on more specific objectives for music ensembles has blurred the

research process. Nevertheless, the legitimate quest for improved instruction via ensembles continues to be of interest to the music education research community.

Toward that end, selected research on school and college instrumental and choral ensembles is reviewed in this chapter. Unlike earlier reviews of research related to instrumental and choral ensembles (Benner, 1972; Gonzo, 1973; Hylton, 1983; Nelson, 1983; Rainbow, 1973; Ramsey, 1978), this chapter consists of an overview of research on issues associated with the ensemble setting. Specifically, the chapter focuses on research that addresses the following factors: (1) predictors related to student participation and achievement in the ensemble; (2) results of teaching-learning strategies, related ensemble activities, and program types; (3) effects of ensemble participation; and (4) instrument choice, attitudes, and conductor characteristics. Implications for researchers and teachers, based on the overview, are also included.

PREDICTORS OF STUDENT PARTICIPATION AND ACHIEVEMENT

Student Participation

The ability to predict which students will choose to participate in school music ensembles is of vital importance to a music education program. Though activities associated with the recruitment, as well as retention, of ensemble participants typically occupy a large portion of directors' time and attention, there is little research on the characteristics of students who do or do not participate in school music ensembles. Because among extant studies the topic usually was incidental to the main purposes, and because the studies usually do not include inferential methodology, a common body of knowledge about participation versus nonparticipation has not been identified.

In a study of elementary school students, Bailey (1975) reported statistically significant higher intelligence quotient test scores (IQ), subtest scores on the *SRA Achievement Series* (SRA), and scores on the Colwell *Music Achievement Tests* (MAT), parts 1 and 2, among sixth-grade band and orchestra participants than among nonparticipants. When the years-of-piano-study variable (1 year or more) was held constant, there were no statistically significant differences between participants and nonparticipants on IQ, SRA, or MAT. This suggests that piano study may be more closely related to IQ, SRA, and MAT scores than ensemble participation.

In a study of high school band participation (Koutz, 1987), students cited interest in music and enjoyment of the social aspects of the program as reasons for participation. As might be expected, nonparticipants reported conflicts with other interests and activities as the primary reason for not choosing band. Kourajian (1982) and Castelli (1986) explored factors leading to nonparticipation of male high school students in choir programs. Family influence, peer pressure, gender stereotypes, adolescent voice change, and future occupational choice were identified as related issues, although cause and effect relationships between those factors and participation were not clearly established. In a more comprehensive study of high school music participation, Frakes (1984) noted that both choral and instrumental music participants scored significantly higher than nonparticipants on the MAT, part 2, and the *Iowa Tests of Basic Skills* (ITBS), both of which had been taken by the students in the sixth grade.

In studies of college band participation, Mountford (1977), McClarty (1968), and Milton (1982) found that band students decided while still in high school whether to participate in a college band. The main predictors for those who did participate were enjoyment of the college band's musical and social activities, enjoyment of playing the instrument, and a favorable image of the particular college band (McClarty, 1968). In another study (Clothier, 1967), amount of practice time in high school, participation in solo and ensemble competitions in high school, students' assessment of their own playing ability, ownership of an instrument, and the influence of parents and the high school band director were significant predictors of college band participation. In a study by Milton (1982), significant predictors of band participation in small colleges were found to include frequency of playing instruments other than in college band, college academic major, ability to obtain an instrument from the band, sex, encouragement by a college professor to join band, instrument played, and parental encouragement. Nonsignificant predictors of college band participation found in the various studies, some of which conflict with the significant predictors cited above, were self-assessment of playing ability, influence of friends and high school band director, private lessons, high school solo and ensemble ratings, musical background of parents, grade in which instrumental study was begun, ownership of an instrument, enjoyment of high school band, the perceived value of the high school band experience (Milton), private lessons in high school, size of high school (Clothier), and students' assessment of the quality of the high school band (Clothier; Milton). Other factors influencing college band nonparticipation were lack of interest (Mountford, McClarty), nonmusical demands and conflicts (McClarty), and apprehension over the college band's musical standards or audition process (McClarty).

Student Retention

Trustworthy studies of retention and dropout rates in music programs are more numerous than studies of participation versus nonparticipation. Klinedinst (1989) reported that socioeconomic factors, self-concept in music, overall scholastic ability, and reading and mathematics achievement predicted an extraordinarily high 74 percent of the variance in retention of elementary instrumental students. These same variables predicted student dropout rate less well. Similarly, McCarthy (1980) noted that socioeconomic status (SES), sex, and academic reading achievement did not predict rate of dropout from an elementary instrumental program. Young (1971) reported that fifth-grade dropouts from an instrumental music program scored significantly lower on Gordon's *Musical Aptitude Profile* (MAP) than those who continued. The largest difference occurred on the MAP rhythm subtest, perhaps because, according to Young, most method books for young bands emphasize rhythm. IQ was not significantly different between dropouts and continuers in Young's study.

Bailey (1975) found that sixth-grade dropouts in instrumental music scored significantly lower on the MAT than continuers, and Mawbey (1973) reported that British instrumental primary and secondary students with low music aptitude scores on the Bentley *Measures of Musical Abilities* dropped out at significantly higher rates than students with high scores. Similarly, Frakes (1984) observed that instrumental dropouts scored lower than continuers on the MAT, part 2, and on the ITBS. On the other hand, McCarthy (1980) found that students' dropping out was not predicted by MAT scores. In general, these findings suggest that elementary students who perform well on music tests tend to remain in music ensembles—not an unexpected conclusion.

Studies of high school attrition are less common. Anthony (1974) gathered data on perceptions of high school seniors who had dropped out of band programs and those who remained. Continuers held significantly more positive attitudes toward public band performance, the music performed in band, memorizing music for performance, their own musical ability, the band director's attitude, and the band program as a whole. Dropouts cited significantly more problems with the scheduling of rehearsals. Anthony found no significant differences between continuers' and dropouts' perceptions of their parents' actual attendance at public band performances. The researcher concluded that "a negative reaction to a single factor apparently does not lead to dropout, but negative reactions to several factors apparently do" (p. 79).

Anthony's conclusions about student dropouts from bands largely were corroborated for choral students by Perez and Ramsey (1990). Their study of middle school males revealed that a desire to continue improving musical skills, confidence in their own musical ability, and social involvement were the primary motives for continuing. Negative previous experiences in choir, the director's personality, and negative social factors were the main reasons for dropping out.

Student Achievement

In his review of research completed prior to 1950, Manor (1950) concluded that low achievers in instrumental music differed significantly on IQ scores from middle and high achievers. Subsequently, IQ has been shown to predict individual achievement in instrumental music by Bailey (1975), Cramer (1958), Culbert (1974), Hufstader (1974), McCarthy (1974), and Strachan (1964). Composite scores on Gordon's MAP predicted achievement in instrumental music in studies by Baer (1987), Delzell (1989), Gordon (1967), McCarthy (1974), Schleuter (1978), and Young (1976).

Additional variables that have been shown to predict success in instrumental music include subtests of various standardized music aptitude and achievement tests (Bailey, 1975; Cramer, 1958; Gordon, 1986; Hufstader, 1974; Kovacs, 1985; Young, 1976), personality development (Cramer, 1958; Kaplan, 1961), and psychomotor skills (Cramer, 1958; Hufstader, 1974; Kovacs, 1985). Some of the strongest correlations were identified by Gordon (1986), who found that MAP scores and a test of instrument timbre preference predicted success after two years of beginning instrumental music. Cutietta and Foustalieraki's (1990) review of recent research seems to confirm Gordon's findings about the predictive power of the instrument timbre preference variable. Young (1971) found that, for dependent variable measures not involving musical notation, the MAP was the best predictor of performance achievement for fifth-grade band and orchestra students. For sight-reading achievement, a test of academic achievement (the ITBS) was the strongest predictor.

Factors found not to correlate significantly with achievement in instrumental music include previous piano experience (Young, 1976), general motor development (Baer, 1987), various physical measurements (Lamp and Keys, 1935), lateral dominance (Schleuter, 1978), sex (Hill, 1987; McCarthy, 1980; Schleuter, 1978; Young, 1976), race or ethnicity (Hill, 1987; McCarthy, 1980), SES (Hill, 1987; McCarthy, 1980), and overall physical growth (Cramer, 1958). Researchers have obtained mixed results when correlating various measures of academic achievement and achievement in music (Hill, 1987; McCarthy, 1974).

Generally, research has failed to reveal significant predictors of jazz improvisation ability among school-age instrumentalists (Bash and Kuzmich, 1985). Researchers have reported low correlations between improvisation and MAP scores (Bash, 1983) and between improvisation and IQ (Young, 1971). Research findings are contradictory with regard to correlations between sight-reading and improvisation ability (Bash, 1983; Burnsed, 1978).

Summary

Clearly, more studies are needed that focus on differences between students who choose to participate in elective school music ensembles and those who do not. Bailey's findings that IQ, SRA, and MAT scores differentiate between participants and nonparticipants is meaningful, but factors that attract students to ensemble programs have not yet been identified through systematic research. Conversely, research on college ensemble participation has tended to rely on student perceptions of their own attitudes and background experiences. Demographic data that might confirm those findings are not available.

Research has identified several factors that seem to predict which students will remain in a musical organization. SES, self-concept in music, music aptitude, social attitudes, and various measures of scholastic ability have been identified as sources of variation in statistically significant differences between continuers and dropouts. Little is known about the effects of different types of instruction, teacher-related variables, and the interactions of these and other factors on dropout and retention.

Successful participation in school music ensembles is more difficult to define than the dichotomous, concrete variables of participation/nonparticipation and continuation/dropping out. Nevertheless, research regarding predictors of student success in music ensembles has attained some fairly consistent results. IQ scores, MAP scores, MAT scores, *Seashore Measures of Musical Talents* subtest scores, instrument timbre preferences, personality development, and certain psychomotor skills each seem to predict success to a moderate degree.

RESULTS OF TEACHING-LEARNING STRATEGIES, ACTIVITIES, AND PROGRAM TYPES

The short-term effects of different teaching-learning strategies, program types, and activities have been studied by a relatively large number of researchers. These research endeavors have focused on the effects of modeling, competition, jazz improvisation training, and various other teaching, rehearsing, and conducting strategies. The effects of different class-rehearsal structures and teaching strategies on perceptual and conceptualization skills have been of particular interest.

Modeling

Modeling, or the use of recorded or live musical performance in the instructional setting, has been an area of some research interest. Hodges (1975) found that the use of recorded models in beginning band classes did not result in significant improvement of performance. Dickey (1988), however, reported that regular modeling by a teacher improved imitative and kinesthetic responses. Delzell (1989) found that musical discrimination skills were significantly improved through modeling, while performance skills were not. Kendall (1988) found that a teacher-modeling approach which incorporated music-reading activities resulted in significantly better solfège and sight-reading skills than a modeling approach with no music reading.

Direct comparisons have not been made between teacher modeling and recorded modeling. The research does suggest that an approach incorporating both teacher modeling and music reading might improve certain aural and kinesthetic skills among young band students, although probably not traditional performance skills. It would appear also that to be effective modeling should "be used in more than a cursory manner" (Hodges, 1975, p. 34); however, other research has shown that only a small percentage of ensemble rehearsal time typically is devoted to modeling and verbal imagery (Carpenter, 1988; Edwards, 1978; Pontious, 1982). Future research should investigate the optimum percentage of rehearsal time that should be devoted to modeling, the effects of different modeling procedures, and the effects of particular modeling strategies on different types of students.

Competitions

Historically, musical competitions have been an integral part of the American school music scene. Given the extraordinary amount of effort and attention currently devoted to competition in music education, research on the phenomenon is relatively rare and unusually contradictory.

LaRue (1986) found that students in programs that did not emphasize competitions "consistently rated outcomes pertaining to broad musical growth higher" (p. 97) than students from highly competitive programs. To the contrary, Head (1983) reported no significant differences in attitudes toward musical activities between students whose band directors emphasized competitions and those who did not. A third researcher (Maddox, 1973) reported a significant positive correlation between recent high school graduates' plans to support classical music and the contest ratings of the bands in which they had participated.

Mixed results also have been noted in correlational studies of the effects of competition on student achievement. Temple (1973) reported that scores on the MAT were significantly higher for high school students in bands that competed than in bands that did not compete. Similarly, West (1985) found that students in high school bands that competed successfully scored significantly higher on an unpublished musicianship test than students in less successful bands and that individual students who competed successfully in solo and ensemble contests also scored significantly higher on the musicianship test. He found no interactions between band and solo/ensemble success and musicianship. Conversely, Jarrell (1971) found that the number of weeks devoted to band concert contest preparation was inversely related to high school students' scores on an unpublished test of ability to evaluate musical performance. Finally, Temple (1973) found no significant differences in sight-reading ability, as measured by the *Watkins-Farnum Performance Scale* (WFPS), between high school band students from competitive and noncompetitive bands.

In the only experimental studies found on the effects of music competition, Austin (1988) reported no significant difference in achievement motivation between elementary band students who participated in a solo contest for ratings and those who received comments only. In a subsequent study (1990), he found no significant differences on the rhythm subtest of the MAT, performance ratings at a contest, or achievement motivation between elementary band students who participated in competitive solo and ensemble festivals and those who participated in noncompetitive festivals. Austin's study did produce some evidence, however, that students with low self-esteem in music performance performed better under the noncompetitive conditions.

There seems to be fairly consistent evidence that the more a band competes, the more favorably competitive activities are viewed by members of the organization (Burnsed and Sochinski, 1983). Research also suggests that most of the benefits of marching band competition, as perceived by students, directors, parents, and administrators, are extramusical (Burnsed and Sochinski, 1983; Rogers, 1985).

Improvisation

Research indicates that jazz improvisation can be taught. However, mixed results have been found in studies of the effects of jazz improvisation training on other aspects of musical achievement. In studies designed to test methods of teaching jazz improvisation to high school students, Bash (1983) and Damron (1973) found significant differences between control and treatment groups on investigator-designed improvisation tests. Bash noted that the aural perceptive task of singing improvised solos was particularly effective for teaching jazz improvisation. Wilson (1970) reported that high school wind instrumentalists who practiced improvisation scored significantly higher on the WFPS and the *Aliferis Music Achievement Test, College Entrance Level* than control subjects. Burnsed (1978), on the other hand, found no significant difference in WFPS scores between intermediate band students who participated in 20 minutes of daily improvisation training and those who did not. In a study by Briscuso (1972), high, medium, and low levels of MAP scores by high school jazz band students did not interact significantly with an improvisation training program, which suggests that improvisational ability may be dependent on different abilities than those measured by the MAP.

Dependent variables used in the studies by Bash, Damron, and Briscuso—that is, test instruments developed specifically to measure improvisation—would seem to be more appropriate research tools than traditional sight-reading measures such as the WFPS.

Class Structure

Despite the central role of traditional bands, orchestras, and choirs in the secondary and postsecondary music curriculum, nontraditional organizational structures for musical ensembles have also received some attention in the research literature. Olson (1975) found significant gain score differences on the WFPS between secondary students who participated in band and chamber music and those who participated in band only. No significant gain score differences were noted on the three sections of the MAT. Sorensen (1971) reported significant differences in sight-reading, intonation, MAT subtest scores, and attitude toward the school music program in favor of an experimental group of junior high school band students that received small ensemble experience as opposed to a control group that received extra technical instruction. He found no significant differences in attitude toward music in general between the two groups. Carmody (1988) found significant differences in attitude toward music and ability to play in tune in favor of junior high school string students who participated in chamber music and large ensemble over those who participated in large ensemble only. Zorn (1969) reported that ninth-grade band students who performed chamber music one time per week outside of class had a significantly more positive change in attitude toward band than students who participated in section rehearsals. However, he found no significant differences between the groups on individual performance or conceptual understanding. Sherburn (1984) found that high school band students who performed daily in a large ensemble and took part in various other musical activities during the school day demonstrated significantly more improvement in music knowledge than students who participated in two daily large ensemble rehearsals. There were no significant differences in attitude toward music between the two groups. In a study of group achievement (McLarty, 1963), high school bands that received superior contest ratings were shown to provide significantly more solo and small ensemble experiences for students than lower-rated bands. Although the results of this line of research are not entirely consistent, the literature does seem to suggest that sight-reading ability and attitudes toward school music may be enhanced by chamber music and other small group performance experiences.

Private lessons and other forms of individualized instruction have also received some attention in the research literature. In studies by Froseth (1971) and McCarthy (1974), individualized instruction within classroom settings resulted in significantly higher levels of performance among beginning instrumentalists than did traditional group instruction. Individualized instruction seemed to be more effective for high-IQ students and students with low levels of personal adjust-

ment. It should be noted that in a later study McCarthy (1980) obtained no significant differences in sight-reading achievement between individualized and group instruction among fifth- and sixth-grade instrumentalists. However, a significant interaction occurred between the treatment and an academic test of reading achievement. In short, the more capable students fared better with individualized instruction. In a study that compared private lesson instruction with traditional class instruction in instrumental music, Shugert (1969) found that private instruction resulted in significantly higher levels of performance than did group instruction. Given the importance of group dynamics in the class setting, not to mention fiscal and instructional time limitations, it seems that more research on the possible benefits of individualized instruction is warranted.

Rehearsal Structure and Teaching Strategies

In his study of rehearsal structure, Pascoe (1973) recommended that faster-paced, more familiar activities be placed at the beginning and end of the rehearsal, while slower-paced, less familiar, more difficult activities be placed in the middle portion. He also suggested that a climactic moment of high intensity take place approximately two-thirds through the rehearsal period. Other researchers have determined that the structure of rehearsals affects student behavior and attitudes (Cox, 1986, 1989; Menchaca, 1988; Murray, 1975; Price, 1983; Thurman, 1977). Specifically, rehearsals in which there is a balance of varied musical activities and intensity levels seem to improve student attention to tasks and to the teacher (Spradling, 1985; Witt, 1986; Yarbrough and Price, 1981). The variation of intensity levels seems to be strongly related to positive responses on the part of students.

In recent years, there has been increased interest in the effective use of instructional time. Studies by Montgomery (1986), Pontious (1982), Spradling (1985), Witt (1986), and Yarbrough and Price (1989) have addressed the issue in relation to the instrumental rehearsal setting. The research shows that approximately 42 percent of rehearsal time for both concert and jazz bands is devoted to verbal communication. The percentage of time devoted to performance, including large group, section, and individual, ranges from about 43 percent to 57 percent, with the vast majority of performance time devoted to full ensemble performance.

Similar observations were recorded by Caldwell (1980) in the high school choral setting. Generally, 65 percent of a choral conductor's rehearsal time was spent rehearsing one or more voice parts in isolation, while 35 percent of the time was spent using verbal descriptions to teach elements and skills such as diction, phrasing, tone color, and style. Subjects for the study, each identified as "successful" choral directors, spent about 50 percent of the rehearsal time with choir members singing all voice parts together as written.

Off-task behavior in one study of junior and senior high school bands and orchestras ranged from 3.4 percent during performance time to 17.8 percent during nonperformance time (Witt, 1986). In an experimental study (Spradling,

1985), the off-task behavior rate for students in a college band was 8.86 percent during instructional periods and 4.19 percent during performance periods. There were no significant differences in off-task rates between instructional periods of 15, 30, and 45 seconds, leading the researcher to conclude that a 45-second nonperformance period is well within the attention span of college students.

Some researchers have gone further in their analysis of teaching-rehearsal strategies. Yarbrough and Price (1989) identified a three-part teaching cycle that they believed represents good teaching in the ensemble setting. The cycle consists of (1) presentation of task, (2) student response, and (3) reinforcement. They found that band directors spent only 18.39 percent of their instructional time within such a framework and 81.61 percent outside the framework. Choral directors were "somewhat better" in this regard. Yarbrough and Price also noted that comparatively little rehearsal time was spent on reinforcement. Among band directors, reinforcement consisted of 6.93 percent of total time in disapprovals and only 1.62 percent in approvals, while choral directors were, again, "somewhat better." Similarly, Carpenter (1988) and Erbes (1972) found that ensemble directors, elementary through high school, tended to be disapproving rather than approving in their responses to student performance.

In a controlled study of teacher behavior, Price (1983) found that conductor reinforcement of student performance consisting of 80 percent approvals and 20 percent disapprovals resulted in significantly greater gains on performance measures and significantly higher student attitude ratings toward a college band than did a strategy employing no feedback on student performance. Similarly, Edwards (1978) and Alexander and Dorow (1983) reported significant correlations between positive reinforcement and beginning band students' performance achievement.

Conducting Strategies

Research on the effects of specific conducting strategies is virtually nonexistent. Reasons for this scarcity may be partially explained by a study in which instrumental students were asked to identify specific videotaped conducting gestures (Sousa, 1988). Results indicated that precollege students were unable to identify or respond to a wide variety of gestures.

Familiarization with conducting gestures should be a result of the ensemble experience. However, if inconsistent or otherwise inappropriate conducting strategies are employed, students may become oblivious to most gestures. Casual observation reveals that some teachers, even in elementary ensemble settings, conduct with gestures more appropriately reserved for professional ensembles. Clearly, research that measures actual student responses to conducting gestures of all types is warranted. This notion is underscored by Yarbrough (1975), who determined that drastic variations in a choral conductor's vocal inflections, facial expressions, rehearsal pace, eye contact, and general excitement level all affected students' attitudes toward the conductor, although they made no difference in performance quality.

Perceptual Skills and Conceptualization

In many cases, the ensemble experience is a student's only musical activity. In essence, the band, orchestra, or choir often serves as the only forum for a broad musical experience that should include the development of perceptual skills and conceptual understanding, coupled with enhanced technical development. Fortunately, there is a growing body of research that addresses this crucial issue. Although some of the studies suffer from poor design and analysis, they offer some support for devoting a portion of the rehearsal to nonperformance learning activities. It seems clear that nonperformance learning activities do not necessarily diminish, and may actually improve, performance skills.

Elliott (1974) found that beginning band students who vocalized on a syllable scored significantly higher on measures of pitch discrimination and tonal memory than those who did not. Vocalization also appears to have improved the ability to relate musical sounds to notation. In a similar study, Jarvis (1981) found that syllabic verbalization resulted in improved scores on a test of notation recognition given to junior high school band students. The technique did not improve performance achievement. Several other studies, some involving high school and college students, have shown similar results with the use of vocalization and/or verbalization (Grutzmacher, 1987; Harris, 1977; Smith, 1984). Unfortunately, research suggests that many high school and college band directors choose to employ little vocalization in their rehearsals (Burton, 1988).

Boyle (1970) found that junior high school band students who tapped beats with their feet and clapped rhythms with their hands showed significantly more improvement on rhythmic sight-reading and overall sight-reading than students who did not tap or clap. He also concluded that "the ability to sight read music is dependent in large part upon the ability to read rhythms" (p. 14). Similarly, Elliott (1982) reported that of seven variables, the ability to read rhythms was the strongest predictor of sight-reading ability among college instrumental music majors.

Grutzmacher (1987) and MacKnight (1975) found that the aural-visual discrimination and sight-reading skills of elementary band students who were taught tonal patterns improved significantly more than the skills of students taught by traditional note-by-note methods. MacKnight observed that, among other factors, singing, chanting, and listening helped students with low music aptitude improve their sight-reading skills. She also noted that the same activities helped students with high music aptitude improve in aural-visual discrimination.

Harris (1977) implemented an intonation training program for junior and senior high school band students. The instructional program, which included some vocalization, taught instrumental intonation tendencies and beat elimination. The treatment group improved significantly more than the control group on an individual test of intonation skills. Private study appears to have contributed to intonation gain scores also.

Whitener (1983) compared a comprehensive musicianship approach and a more traditional performance-oriented approach with two groupings of junior high school beginning bands. Results indicated no significant performance differences between the two groups. However, the group exposed to the comprehensive approach scored significantly higher on subsections of the MAT that measured interval discrimination, meter discrimination, major-minor mode discrimination, and auditory-visual discrimination. In a study by Parker (1974), there were no significant differences in performance or attitude toward band between middle school bands taught by comprehensive musicianship and those taught by traditional approaches.

In a similar study, Culbert (1974) investigated the effects of an experimental program designed to improve students' skills in describing music. The program included classroom discussions, writing, listening, and performing. The experimental group, randomly selected from a high school band, attended three regular full band rehearsals and one experimental class each week. The control group attended the same three full band rehearsals, plus an additional weekly rehearsal. The researcher found significant differences in favor of the experimental group on sections of the MAT that measured tonal memory and auditory-visual discrimination and recognition of melody, pitch, instruments, style, chords, and cadences.

Hedberg (1975) compared the effects of a similar nonperformance instructional program to those of a more traditional performance-dominated choral program. The nonperformance curriculum produced significantly better performance skills when students were confronted with unfamiliar music. Discrimination skills, performance skills with familiar works, and attitudes toward participation remained unaffected by the two different instructional strategies.

Finally, both Bangstad (1975) and Hill (1979) sought to increase choral music students' awareness of form and style in the rehearsal setting. Although neither researcher effectively evaluated the results of the programs, both provided detailed descriptions of teaching strategies that might be of value in future research endeavors.

Summary

Some of the research literature on the effects of various teaching-rehearsal strategies, related ensemble activities, and program types tends to exhibit certain procedural weaknesses, including lack of randomization, failure to control confounding variables, poor sampling procedures, and weak measurement tools. Nevertheless, certain findings can be posited with a reasonable degree of confidence: (1) improvisation skills, which are important to general musical development, can be taught to instrumental students; (2) chamber music experiences can improve sight-reading skills and enhance students' attitudes toward school music; (3) individ-

ualized instruction can improve the performance of young instrumentalists, especially those with high IQ, high reading achievement, and low levels of personal adjustment; (4) teacher modeling can improve certain aspects of students' musicianship; (5) syllabic vocalization and verbalization can improve pitch discrimination, tonal memory, and the ability to relate music to notation; (6) training in tonal patterns can enhance aural-visual discrimination and sight-reading skills among elementary instrumental students; (7) rhythm-reading skills appear to be strongly related to sight-reading skills, and both skills can be improved through kinesthetic movement; (8) instrumental intonation skills can be taught to secondary students through systematic instruction; (9) performance skills are not diminished and certain musicianship skills may be improved when a portion of the ensemble rehearsal is devoted to nonperformance learning activities; (10) there appears to be no difference in music achievement as a result of either competitive or noncompetitive instrumental contests at the elementary level; (11) high levels of positive reinforcement in the rehearsal setting result in higher levels of student performance; and (12) young students cannot identify many typical conducting gestures.

EFFECTS OF ENSEMBLE PARTICIPATION

Given the current emphasis on educational accountability, the music education community often finds it necessary to outline the numerous reasons for providing ensemble experiences in the secondary and postsecondary curriculum. Although it is clear to musicians and others that music enriches people's lives through experiences unique to the art form, it is incumbent upon the research community to provide research-based rationales for the inclusion of music in the schools. A review of research on the possible effects of participation in school and college musical ensembles reveals an extremely broad and unfocused body of literature. Areas of concentration can be categorized into the possible relationships between the ensemble experience and the following variables: adult activities, musical preferences and attitudes, personality, musical and nonmusical achievement, musical perception and discrimination, and creativity.

Ensemble Participation and Adult Activities

There is a lack of research on the effects of the school ensemble experience on musical activity in later life. Generally speaking, extant studies tend to be ex post facto in design. Carefully controlled longitudinal studies are nonexistent.

Goodrich (1965) found a positive relationship between music participation in high school and in adult life, but he noted that most former high school musicians did not continue musical activities other than purchasing recordings, watching musicals on television, and listening to music. Peterman (1954) found that six years after high school graduation, there was little difference in the level or type of musical activities between adults who had been labeled as high and those who had been labeled as low participants in secondary music activities. Falkner (1957) reported that ownership of an instrument while in high school, as opposed to renting one, correlated positively with later interest and participation in music. He also noted that participation in two or more high school musical groups and personal selection of an instrument, as opposed to teacher selection, were important factors. Fuller (1973) found that 73.7 percent of the members of nine adult community bands had been first-chair players in their respective high school instrumental ensembles. He also noted, as did Patterson (1985), that players in adult bands considered their high school years to have been the most influential period in their musical development.

Farrell (1972) explored the perceived meaning derived by adult recreational singers from their participation in choral ensembles. Through factor analyses, she identified eight underlying dimensions that defined meanings: integrative, spiritualistic, incidental, communicative, music purist, social status, psychological, and collective. Though research efforts have not included attempts to connect early ensemble experience to meanings held by adults, Hylton (1981) explored many of these same dimensions using high school chorus members as subjects. He found factors similar to those identified by Farrell, which he labeled achievement, spiritualistic, musical-artistic, communicative, psychological, and integrative. Both these studies revealed the large variety of feelingful response and associated meaning resulting from individuals' participation in choral ensembles.

Ensemble Participation, Musical Preference, and Attitudes

In general, research suggests that individuals who participate in high school ensembles hold more positive attitudes toward music, both while in school and later as adults, than those who do not participate in such activities. The studies also suggest that school ensemble experiences do not influence an individual's preference for different types of music. Unfortunately, the ex post facto design of the studies makes it impossible to point to causal relationships among the numerous variables.

In a study of preferences for art music, popular music, and folk music, Rubin (1952) found little difference between seventh-, ninth-, and twelfth-graders with little experience in music and those with a great deal of experience. Despite considerable variance in the musical experiences among the students studied, the overall correlation between private lessons/ensemble participation and regular radio listening was extremely low. Contemporary results might differ from those found in 1952, given the wide access to radios by young people today.

Stewart (1961) observed no significant differences in preferences for different types of music between high school students who participated in music and those who did not. Preferences of band, choir, and orchestra participants were also not significantly different. Fulbright (1964) found no significant relationship between precollege music ensemble participation and private lessons or between participation

and preference for selected types of orchestral compositions. Rubin-Rabson (1940) found no relationship between the number of semesters of music taken before and during college and preference for classical and romantic music. However, she did report a significant positive relationship between school music training and an affinity for modern art music. Long (1971) reported significant positive correlations between expressed preference for "concert-type" music and experiences in choral and instrumental ensembles among students in elementary through college levels. Interestingly, he found a larger correlation between preference for concert music and piano experiences. Frakes (1984) noted that former secondary school music participants held significantly more positive attitudes toward music than nonparticipants or music dropouts, and Erneston (1961) observed that the previous experiences in school and community music ensembles among first-year college students related significantly to attitudes toward music in general. Previous experiences were not related to preference for different types of music in the study by Erneston. Little (1979) and Noble (1977) found that favorable attitudes toward music among high school seniors and adults, respectively, were related to their experience in school instrumental and vocal ensembles. Colwell (1961) found no significant differences between fifth-grade vocal and instrumental students' attitudes toward music.

Ensemble Participation and Personality Characteristics

The ex post facto design of studies of ensemble participation and personality characteristics precludes an attribution of causal relationships among any of the variables. In other words, students who elected to join school music ensembles may have already possessed a certain personality characteristic, such as high self-esteem, prior to joining an ensemble, or they may have developed it with or without the musical experience. In any case, the research literature indicates that high school music students are significantly more self-confident, self-controlling and intellectualizing and possess higher self-esteem than nonmusic students (Kaplan, 1961; Koutz, 1987; Nolin and Vander Ark, 1977). Additionally, self-evaluation of musicality seems to correlate with ensemble experiences (Long, 1971).

Ensemble Participation, Musical Achievement, and Nonmusical Achievement

The effects of ensemble participation on both musical and nonmusical achievement is of considerable interest to teachers in general. It is to be expected that students in a school ensemble would show some degree of achievement in musical performance. It is less clear, however, whether ensemble participation affects musical achievement other than performance achievement. Quite simply, there is little research on the subject.

Johnson (1979) did find that twelfth-grade students with three or more years experience in school music ensembles scored significantly higher on a test of classical and popular music knowledge than twelfth-graders with less (or no) school music ensemble experience. Luce (1965) reported that school band and orchestra experiences significantly predicted sight-reading and ear-playing abilities among high school students. In contrast, other researchers (Brand and Burnsed, 1981; Daniels, 1986; Dean, 1937; Emig, 1978; Ernst, 1957; Tucker, 1969) have concluded that prior musical experiences at precollege and college levels, including private lessons, did not predict sight-singing skills or grades in college theory and ear-training classes.

Researchers have also found that choral and instrumental experiences have similar effects on musical learning. Generally speaking, no significant differences have been found in the achievement of instrumental and choral students in improvisation skills, composition skills, musical analysis skills (Webster, 1977), knowledge of notation, overall musical cognition, or general musicality (Tuley, 1967). An exception was noted by Daniels (1986), who found that sight-reading skills were less closely related to choral experiences than to other factors, such as home piano study and instrumental ensemble experiences.

The effects of ensemble experiences on general academic achievement are not entirely clear. Indeed, one may wonder why the effects of musical study need to be equated with other subject areas. Regardless of the motivations involved, the perceived need to justify music participation in the schools through the identification of extramusical benefits of musical study has led to several studies.

In studies on the effects on academic achievement of excusing elementary students from regular classes to participate in instrumental music, there were no significant differences between music and nonmusic students in reading, mathematics, or overall academic achievement (Friedman, 1959; Groff, 1963; Kvet, 1985; Robitaille and O'Neal, 1981). Further, when music and nonmusic students were equated on the basis of IQ, sex, ranking of the classroom teacher, and other factors, significant differences in academic achievement were not found.

Other related studies have been conducted. In one such study, Gordon (1979) reported that fourth-grade inner-city students who were given instrumental music instruction contingent upon their reading achievement in the classroom showed significant improvement over students given the same instruction on a noncontingent basis. Anello (1972) found that students with school band and orchestra experience made significantly higher grades in high school mathematics, English, and social science than did nonperforming students, although the differences were not significant when the effects of IQ were held constant. Similarly, Whitener (1974) found no significant differences in overall grade point average between first-year college students with four or more semesters of high school art or music and those with less (or no) high school art or music experience.

Ensemble Participation, Musical Perception, and Discrimination

As one would expect, students with ensemble experience generally display higher levels of musical perception and dis-

crimination skills than students who lack such experience. Stewart (1961), Erneston (1961), McCarthy (1969), Horner (1973), Hoffren (1962), Zimmerman (1971), and Duerksen (1968) have all studied the phenomenon by administering various musical tests.

Stewart, for example, found significant differences in favor of high school music students over nonmusic students on both the *Kwalwasser-Ruch Test of Musical Accomplishment* and the *Knuth Achievement Tests in Music.* Similarly, Erneston reported significant differences in music discrimination based on high school music experiences among first-year college students on the revised edition of the *Wing Standardized Tests of Musical Intelligence,* and McCarthy found significant differences on his test of musical perception in favor of high school band and orchestra students over noninstrumental students.

Horner reported significant differences in musical discrimination between instrumentalists and noninstrumentalists in grades 4 through 6, and Hoffren found significant differences in favor of junior and senior high school band students over nonband students on a test of phrasing expression. Similarly, Zimmerman found significant differences between high school performers and nonperformers on a test designed to measure the ability to describe verbally musical stimuli perceived aurally. By contrast, Duerksen found no significant difference in the ability of secondary school music and nonmusic students to discriminate between repeated and altered musical themes.

Some researchers have studied the musical perception and discrimination abilities of students with ensemble experience, but without comparing them to other students. Marciniak (1974), for example, found a significant relationship between the number of years of high school band membership and general musical perception. Similarly, Long (1971) reported significant correlations between both instrumental and choral experiences at the elementary school through college levels and general music discrimination as measured by the *Indiana-Oregon Music Discrimination Test.*

Various individuals have investigated specific rather than general perception or discrimination abilities of students with ensemble experience. For instance, Heritage (1986) found that the ability of junior-level college music majors to hear musical intervals was related to their high school choral experiences and that their rhythmic discrimination ability correlated with their high school band experiences. Iltis (1970) observed significant relationships between ensemble experiences and students' ability to detect errors in intonation, tone quality, interpretation, ensemble, and technique. Boisen (1979) found that seventh-, ninth-, and eleventh-grade students' experiences in band, orchestra, or chorus were significantly related to their ability to perceive complete rhythmic patterns.

Not all studies have revealed significant relationships or differences. Rubin (1952) found low correlations between membership in band, orchestra, or chorus and scores on his test of music discrimination, while Deihl (1963) found a significant relationship between performance experience and listening achievement, but no significant relationship between performance experience and musical concept development. Haack (1969) observed no significant difference on a test designed to measure perception of thematic relationships in high school students with high and low levels of band experience. Similarly, Madsen, Duke, and Geringer (1984) found little difference in tempo and pitch variation discrimination ability between high school and college band students, which suggests that the additional ensemble experiences may not have contributed to the development of that skill.

A few studies have compared perception and discrimination abilities of students with various kinds of ensemble experiences. Nierman (1982) asked secondary school ensemble participants to describe verbally their perceptions of various musical components presented in recorded excerpts. He found that ensemble experience was positively related to students' abilities to perceive musical events within a larger musical context. Students who participated in orchestra were significantly better than band and chorus students at the musical perception and description tasks. This finding was similar to that of May and Elliott (1980), who reported no significant differences on Gaston's *A Test of Musicality* between fourth-grade students in band, choir, orchestra, and more than one ensemble. However, they did find significant differences between the various groups of ensemble participants at the ninth-grade level, where orchestra students exhibited the greatest skill gains, followed closely by band students. Choral students' scores were significantly lower than both orchestra and band students' scores. Similarly, Colwell (1961) found significant differences between instrumental and choral students at various grade levels. Specifically, at the levels of sixth, seventh, eighth, and ninth through twelfth grades, instrumental students scored higher than choral students on the Knuth *Achievement Tests in Music*. McCarthy (1969) also found that high school band and orchestra students scored significantly higher than choral students on a test of musical perception. The scores of the band and orchestra students were not significantly different from each other. Zimmerman (1971) administered a test designed to measure students' abilities to describe music verbally. He found that high school orchestra students were significantly better than band students and that band students were significantly better than choral students. While standardizing their musical achievement test of auditory-visual discrimination in 1950, Stecklin and Aliferis (1957) established a relationship between instrumental study and scores on the test. They noted that string students attained the highest total scores, followed by students who had studied piano, woodwinds, brass, voice, and percussion. Sisler (1975), on the other hand, found no significant differences between seventh-grade instrumental, choral, and general music students on a test of music perception. It should be noted that the effects of music aptitude, as measured by the MAP, and the effects of IQ were held constant in Sisler's study. Finally, Duerksen (1968) found that band students scored lower than any other group of students who participated in one or more ensembles on a test designed to measure the recognition of alterations in musical themes. Despite some contradictory findings and the absence of clear cause and effect relationships, it does appear that there may be different skill development effects related to the type of ensemble participation.

Attempts have been made to discover relationships between the ensemble experience, as structured within the contest and competition setting, and musical perception and discrimination. West (1985) found that individuals' success in solo and ensemble competition, together with their bands' performance ratings, predicted scores on an unpublished test of musicianship. Findings by Marciniak (1974), however, suggest that band contest ratings alone do not predict music perception. Jarrell (1971), in his administration of Iltis's error detection test to high school band students in 31 schools, found positive correlations between test scores and participation in summer band programs, the difficulty of repertoire performed in the schools, teachers' objective grading procedures, time spent by bands on sight-reading, and the presence of an assistant director in the band programs. He found negative relationships between test scores and the number of annual marching performances and the number of weeks devoted to concert contest preparation.

Creativity, although difficult to specify, is generally regarded as a positive outcome of the instructional process. A growing body of research in this area may ultimately have important implications for the future structure of the school ensemble experience. Creative interactions with music may help to mold individual aesthetic experiences, compositional skills, interpretive abilities, aesthetic judgment and sophistication, and critical thinking skills.

Gorder (1976) found that musical creativity among secondary band students may not be related to musical training, while Shelton (1986) reported that music-performing experiences, regardless of their length or type, did not predict the type of verbal responses to music given by black college students. On the other hand, De Turk (1988) found a significant, but low, correlation between ensemble experiences and the level of critical thinking about music among high school students. Furthermore, he noted that at least six years of experience was required before significant differences in critical thinking skills occurred. Similarly, Cowles (1963) found that six or more years of school orchestra experience seemed to be related to students' aesthetic judgment in music. For unknown reasons, he found significant differences among orchestra, band, and choral students, with the orchestra students displaying the highest levels of aesthetic judgment. Simpson (1969) did find, however, that high school band and choral students improved significantly more in the areas of elaboration and flexibility than did nonmusic students placed in a control group for research purposes.

INSTRUMENT CHOICE, ATTITUDES, AND CONDUCTOR CHARACTERISTICS

Issues that pertain to students' choice of instrument are extremely important. One issue of obvious concern to the profession is the gender stereotyping that often occurs in the selection process. In a general review of the literature, Delzell and Leppla (1990) found that the flute, cello, violin, and clarinet were associated with femininity, while the saxophone, percussion instruments, and the trumpet had masculine connotations. Such stereotyping seemed to occur at the college level also, where the rankings of music majors differed little from those of nonmajors. Although the magnitude of this problem appears to have lessened in recent years, the concern for its effects remains. Research has identified additional factors in instrument choice. Delzell and Leppla suggest that the most often cited reason for instrument choice among elementary students was preference for a particular sound. There also appears to be a relationship between personality characteristics and instrument type among high school and college students (Hyden, 1979; Sherman, 1983).

In general, society's support for the ensemble experience seems to be strong. Researchers who have attempted to discover the nature of this positive attitude have arrived at some interesting conclusions. Whitelegg (1986) and Franklin (1979) found general agreement on the importance of various band activities among school administrators, band students, parents, directors, and community members.

Students have tended to identify music-related reasons for band participation. Broquist (1961) and Fox (1986) noted that students at the elementary and high school levels, respectively, believe that the opportunity to play an instrument and perform are the most beneficial aspects of participation. Mills (1988) found that among 71 benefits attributed to band participation, high school students rated the need to be more responsive to music as the chief reason for choosing the experience. Parents of band students, by contrast, have tended to identify nonmusical factors as most important. In one survey, sense of accomplishment, responsibility, teamwork, discipline, and self-esteem were among the factors considered to be most important, while appreciation of music as an art form ranked eleventh (Brown, 1981).

Still others have focused on the perceived benefits of competition. Head (1983) found no significant attitudinal differences toward band among high school band students whose directors emphasized (1) basic music skills, (2) marching, (3) competition, or (4) an equal attention to marching and concert performance. LaRue (1986), however, found that students from high school band programs that did not emphasize competitions "consistently rated outcomes pertaining to broad musical growth higher than did students from major contest emphasis programs" (p. 97). Despite these conflicting findings, researchers have generally found that band directors, band students, parents, and school administrators believe that marching band and the competitive experience are beneficial to students (Burnsed and Sochinski, 1983; Jorgensen, 1974; LaRue, 1986; Rogers, 1985).

In a study of attitudes toward musically intrinsic and extrinsic outcomes of band participation, LaRue (1986) found that high school students and their parents tended to agree with items most highly valued by band directors. The intrinsic outcomes included skills related to technique, expressive playing, tone quality, a desire to improve, and intonation.

The outcomes least valued included the ability or desire to make valid judgments about the quality of the music, promote music to friends, perform in small ensembles, play popular tunes or hymns by ear, and improvise on a 12-bar blues progression. Extrinsic outcomes most highly rated by band directors included pride in the quality of work, self-discipline, sense of responsibility, sense of personal pride, and group cooperation. It is interesting to note that the National Assessment of Educational Progress (1974) concluded that adults who continued to play musical instruments rated improvisation as one of the two most important musical skills. It appears that directors, and perhaps students and parents as well, value most highly the skills that contribute to high-quality ensemble performance. They seem less concerned with attitudes, values, and skills that could "enhance the students' musical lives after high school" (LaRue, 1986, p. 71).

There has been research focusing on the perceptions of ensemble directors about the adequacy of their musical training and the competencies that are needed to do their jobs. It seems clear, given the current body of research, that more studies are needed that relate specific teaching competencies to educational outcomes (Taebel, 1980). Such studies are lacking at present.

Other research studies have attempted to identify academic predictors of teaching success (see Chapter 48). Benner (1963), for example, found significant correlations between success ratings of ensemble directors, as judged by their school administrators, and the directors' previous student teaching grades, professional education grades, and music education methods class grades. Undergraduate grade point averages, major instrument grade point averages, conducting grades, keyboard grades, theory grades, and music history grades did not correlate significantly with the success ratings. In a similar study, Borkowski (1967) found no significant relationships between the quality of band directors' undergraduate work—including overall grades, student teaching grades, music history grades, music theory grades, and major instrument grades—and their students' knowledge of music, their students' individual performance, or the overall performance of the band.

A few studies have been completed under the assumption that competent ensemble directors need advanced skills in error detection and detailed knowledge of instrumental idioms. DeCarbo (1984, 1986) found that senior high school directors and directors with more than 10 years' teaching experience scored significantly higher in this area than did junior high school directors and directors with fewer than 10 years of experience. McAdams (1988) found significant differences in the knowledge of tuba pedagogy between brass-playing and nonbrass-playing band directors, while Wallace (1979) found that some band directors could not distinguish between cornet and trumpet timbres within an ensemble context. In one of the few studies that relates director competency and success in the field, Woods (1979) found a significant relationship between band directors' scores on a visual error detection test of instrumental performance skills and ratings of the directors' beginning students' performance abilities.

IMPLICATIONS FOR RESEARCHERS AND TEACHERS

Music in elementary, secondary, and postsecondary schools has maintained its broad appeal to students over the years. In fact, the presence of instrumental and choral ensembles has never been stronger. Why, then, is there a need for more research on the topic? As contemporary society evolves and the driving forces behind the educational establishment change, it becomes incumbent upon the profession to articulate clearly the benefits of a musical experience. For example, music educators and researchers have some insights into the types of individuals who participate in elective school music programs, but it is less clear why certain individuals are attracted to these programs while others are not. It is not enough for the profession to lobby for higher levels of participation or to seek entrance and exit standards that include a fine arts or music component. The need for music and the desire for music as a curricular necessity must have a logical research base.

It is not altogether clear why certain individuals remain in an ensemble program while others drop out. Extramusical factors obviously come into play. Research suggests that self-concepts, social attitudes, and even certain scholastic abilities of students may play a part in the decision-making process. It is less clear whether various types of instruction or different teacher-related issues have any effect on continued participation.

At first glance, teachers might conclude that successful students are those who play or sing well, enjoy their ensemble experience, display some level of musical achievement, and choose to continue specific musical activities later in life. However, other factors need to be considered. For example, what are the lasting effects of the ensemble experience, even an experience that may last for a relatively short period of time? Is the experience of playing an instrument in a band or orchestra, or singing in a choral ensemble, however brief, enough to produce a lasting effect? At this time, answers to such questions are speculative at best.

As was noted earlier, research on the effects of various teaching-rehearsal strategies, related ensemble activities, and program types has been difficult to formulate, and much of it to date has tended to suffer from procedural difficulties. However, certain recommendations for both teachers and researchers can be made from the extant body of literature.

There needs to be a concerted effort by both the research and the teaching communities regarding curricular issues. For example, many teachers believe that improvisation skills should be taught, and the research literature suggests that they can be taught. It is not clear, however, exactly how to incorporate the basic skills underlying improvisational performance into the curriculum. It would seem also that an exploration of alternative forms of literature and ensemble settings could help in the instructional process. Students who participate in school-based ensembles may need improvisational skills if they choose to participate in music during their adulthood. Chamber music experiences have been shown to enhance students' sight-reading skills and attitudes toward the ensemble experience. Once again, it is not clear how best to incorporate such experiences into the curriculum. Private music instruction for the general student body, as an integral part of the ensemble experience, is often found in only the most affluent schools and colleges. Indeed, the elementary, secondary, and postsecondary ensemble experience rarely includes private lessons. How then to best utilize instructional time generally reserved for large-group rehearsals and to offer private or small-group lessons has not been explored thoroughly. If the ensemble experience is to address issues of individual musical growth, methods and procedures that allow for individualized attention need to be examined. Given the present state of the ensemble curriculum, it seems that individuals who cannot afford private lessons outside of school may not be able to achieve their full musical potential.

Research indicates that teacher modeling can improve certain aspects of student musicianship. Perhaps the modeling role is one of motivation as much as demonstration. In any case, it seems that the performing ensemble teacher could have the greatest impact on student perceptions of musical integrity. It is a challenge to talk about musical performance, but it may be much more effective to demonstrate it.

In general, research indicates that instructional time spent on movement, vocalization, and verbalization can enhance students' abilities in pitch discrimination, tonal memory, music reading, sight-reading, rhythmic skills, and intonation. Such activities do not always fit into the traditional model of the ensemble rehearsal, yet they remain essential to musical growth and understanding. It would also seem that ensemble students could benefit from some exposure to "academic-based" music studies.

Researchers and teachers need to evaluate several other aspects of ensemble-related activities. As noted earlier, student achievement does not seem to be related to competition. Although the competitive atmosphere of contemporary music education programs does reap benefits in the areas of student motivation, program prominence, and perhaps public support, it is important for those in the profession to study carefully any possible ill effects of the competitive experience. Further, positive reinforcement is as essential in music as in other areas of education. In fact, research indicates that a positive rehearsal setting, a relaxed music-making atmosphere, and a sense of cooperative spirit lead to higher-quality public performances. Finally, there are indications that young students are unable to identify typical conducting gestures. Perhaps the need for refined conducting needs to be communicated to the ensemble. In other words, students need some sense of the art of conducting before they can respond to it.

There is a need for longitudinal research that tracks students through their ensemble experiences into adulthood. If one of the chief goals of music education programs is the development of lifelong attitudes and understandings in music, and if the ensemble experience is to be the major catalyst for the development of such attitudes and understandings, then it behooves the research community to come to a greater understanding of the long-term effects of various musical experiences within the ensemble. Longitudinal research can help provide an understanding of the underlying societal forces that cause students to choose certain forms of musical participation, the motivational factors that keep them active in music, and the reasons why certain individuals ultimately grow in their support and appreciation of the art of music.

In general, extant research is plagued with most of the nagging problems and inadequacies that characterize most research in music education. Random subject selection and assignment to experimental conditions typically is impossible. Usually, the researcher is limited to intact ensembles for purposes of study, which severely limits the control of confounding variables and the manipulation of experimental variables. Action or naturalistic research designs might be helpful in solving this dilemma, yet few such studies are conducted and even fewer are published in the literature.

Current research endeavors also tend to suffer from insufficient sample size, the inability to confirm cause and effect relationships, weak measurement instruments, and the overuse of ex post facto–type research designs with many complex validation problems. These weaknesses, which exist in some form in the vast majority of ensemble-related studies, produce false contradictions in findings, render most data untrustworthy, and make clear conclusions difficult to support. Additionally, perhaps the most limiting factor in this area is the widespread lack of participation in, understanding of, or appreciation for the research process among those most intimately associated with music ensembles—the ensemble directors.

Although solutions to these problems are not simple, at present the most expedient solution to methodological limitations might be replication of extant studies. This is not to suggest that constant attention to the improvement of research strategies in this area should be abandoned, only that the most important issues in the current, limited body of knowledge should be recognized systematically and the studies replicated. More replication could result in greater insights in spite of the perhaps inherent design weaknesses in the research on music ensembles. At the same time, more sophisticated research designs and evaluation procedures must be developed if research is to provide some much needed higher-quality direction to school music ensembles.

Considered as a whole, the studies reviewed in this chapter suggest that bands have received far more attention from researchers than choirs. Orchestras have been studied least of all, except in cases in which strings were grouped with winds and percussion for research purposes. There are dangers inherent in generalizing research findings across performance media, but at this point the temptation to do so is strong because of the quantitative disparity in research among media. This disparity underscores the need for future research in orchestral and choral settings.

The attitudinal limitations among potential benefactors of research are far more difficult to rectify. Research efforts to date have tended to produce more suspicion and skepticism among some individuals than answers to questions. As a result, researchers must strive not only to continue building a body of knowledge but to present that knowledge convincingly to those for whom findings might have the greatest value.

Those uninvolved directly in the research process should also examine certain of their own attitudes and recognize that research is a confirmatory rather than an exploratory process. Discoveries and findings with immediate and far-reaching application are rare. To the contrary, researchers most often seek to confirm systematically that which they believe to be correct theoretically. This requires lengthy, often tedious work, the scope of which is limited and which must be replicated before trustworthy conclusions can be reached. Once complete, the results infrequently are revolutionary in effect. Findings, however, may provide guidance for more efficient use of instructional and rehearsal time, more productive musical and pedagogical processes, more incisive understandings of teaching-learning phenomena, and a host of other valuable issues. For this reason, the research needs discussed throughout this chapter deserve the attention of ensemble directors and the music education research community. The music ensemble occupies a central position in the school music curriculum, constitutes the only formal music education for many students, and demands a large share of the time and attention of music educators. In sum, a cogent, thoroughly confirmed body of knowledge is much needed in this important area.

References

Alexander, L., and Dorow, L. (1983). Peer tutoring effects on the music performance of tutors and tutees in beginning band classes. *Journal of Research in Music Education, 31,* 33–47.

Anello, J. A. (1972). A comparison of academic achievement between instrumental music students and non-music students in the El Dorado and Valencia high schools of the Placentia Unified School District, 1971–72. Unpublished doctoral dissertation, Brigham Young University, Provo.

Anthony, J. (1974). Student perceptions of factors related to discontinuance from Iowa public high school band programs in districts of 10,000 or more students. Unpublished doctoral dissertation, University of Iowa, Iowa City.

Austin, J. R. (1988). The effect of music contest format on self-concept, motivation, achievement, and attitude of elementary band students. *Journal of Research in Music Education, 36,* 95–107.

Austin, J. R. (1990). *Competitive and noncompetitive goal structures: An analysis of motivation and achievement outcomes among elementary band students.* Paper presented at the biennial meeting of the Music Educators National Conference, Washington.

Baer, D. E. (1987). Motor skill proficiency: Its relationship to instrumental music performance achievement and music aptitude. Unpublished doctoral dissertation, University of Michigan, Ann Arbor.

Bailey, J. Z. (1975). The relationships between the Colwell *Music Achievement Tests* I and II, the *SRA Achievement Series,* intelligence quotient, and success in instrumental music in the sixth grade of the public schools of Prince William County, Virginia. Unpublished doctoral dissertation, University of Illinois, Urbana.

Bangstad, G. (1975). Developing a choral rehearsal program designed to increase perception of form and style in choral music. Unpublished doctoral dissertation, Arizona State University, Tempe.

Bash, L. (1983). The effectiveness of three instructional methods on the acquisition of jazz improvisation skills. Unpublished doctoral dissertation, State University of New York, Buffalo.

Bash, L., and Kuzmich, J. (1985). A survey of jazz education research: Recommendations for future researchers. *Bulletin of the Council for Research in Music Education, 82,* 14–25.

Benner, C. H. (1963). The relationship of pre-service measures to ratings of music teachings success. Unpublished doctoral dissertation, Ohio State University, Columbus.

Benner, C. H. (1972). *Teaching performing groups.* Washington: Music Educators National Conference.

Boisen, R. L., Jr. (1979). The effects of selected factors on the aural perception of rhythmic material by seventh, ninth, and eleventh grade students. Unpublished doctoral dissertation, University of Wisconsin, Madison.

Borkowski, F. T. (1967). The relationship of quality of work in undergraduate music curricula to effectiveness of instrumental music teaching in the public schools. Unpublished doctoral dissertation, West Virginia University, Morgantown.

Boyle, J. D. (1970). The effect of a program for teaching sight reading in junior high school training bands. *Journal of Band Research, 7,* 7–15.

Brand, M., and Burnsed, V. (1981). Music abilities and experiences as predictors of error-detection skill. *Journal of Research in Music Education, 29,* 91–96.

Briscuso, J. J. (1972). A study of ability in spontaneous and prepared jazz improvisation among students who possess different levels of musical aptitude. Unpublished doctoral dissertation, University of Iowa, Iowa City.

Broquist, O. H. (1961). A survey of the attitudes of 2,592 Wisconsin elementary school pupils toward their learning experiences in music. Unpublished doctoral dissertation, University of Wisconsin, Madison.

Brown, J. D. (1981). *The Gemeinhardt report.* Elkhardt: Gemeinhardt Company.

Burnsed, C. V. (1978). The development and evaluation of an introductory jazz improvisation sequence for intermediate band students. Unpublished doctoral dissertation, University of Miami, Coral Gables.

Burnsed, V., and Sochinski, J. (1983). Research on competitions. *Music Educators Journal, 70,* 25–27.

Burton, J. B. (1988). A study to determine the extent to which vocalization is used as an instructional technique in selected public school, public junior college, and state university band rehearsals. *Journal of Band Research, 23,* 30–39.

Caldwell, W. (1980). A time analysis of selected musical elements and leadership behaviors of successful high school choral conductors. Unpublished doctoral dissertation, Florida State University, Tallahassee.

Carmody, W. J. (1988). The effects of chamber music experience on intonation and attitudes among junior high school string players. Unpublished doctoral dissertation, University of Southern California, Los Angeles.

Carpenter, R. A. (1988). A descriptive analysis of relationships between verbal behaviors of teacher-conductors and ratings of selected junior and senior high school band rehearsals. *UPDATE: Applications of Research in Music Education, 7,* 37–40.

Castelli, P. A. (1986). Attitudes of vocal music educators and public

secondary school students on selected factors which influence a decline in male enrollment occurring between elementary and secondary public school vocal music programs. Unpublished doctoral dissertation, University of Maryland, College Park.

Clothier, R. I. (1967). Factors influencing freshmen with high school band experience to elect or not to elect band membership at five liberal arts colleges in Iowa. Unpublished doctoral dissertation, Colorado State College, Fort Collins.

Colwell, R. J. (1961). An investigation of achievement in music in the public schools of Sioux Falls, South Dakota. Unpublished doctoral dissertation. University of Illinois, Urbana.

Cowles, C. V. (1963). Aesthetic judgment of high school music students. Unpublished doctoral dissertation, University of Southern California, Los Angeles.

Cox, J. (1986). Choral rehearsal time usage in a high school and a university: A comparative analysis. *Contributions to Music Education, 13,* 7–23.

Cox, J. (1989). Rehearsal organizational structures used by successful high school choral directors. *Journal of Research in Music Education, 37,* 201–218.

Cramer, W. F. (1958). The relation of maturation and other factors to achievement in beginning instrumental music performance at the fourth through eighth grade levels. Unpublished doctoral dissertation, Florida State University, Tallahassee.

Culbert, M. E. (1974). The effects of using a portion of the rehearsal time for developing skills in describing music on the performance level and musical achievement of high school band students. Unpublished doctoral dissertation, Temple University, Philadelphia.

Cutietta, R. A., and Foustalieraki, M. (1990). Preferences for select band and non-band instrument timbres among students in the United States and Greece. *Bulletin of the Council for Research in Music Education, 105,* 72–80.

Damron, B. L., Jr. (1973). The development and evaluation of a self-instructional sequence in jazz improvisation. Unpublished doctoral dissertation, Florida State University, Tallahassee.

Daniels, R. (1986). Relationships among selected factors and the sight-reading ability of high school choirs. *Journal of Research in Music Education, 34,* 279–289.

Dean, C. D. (1937). Predicting sight-singing ability in teacher-education. *Journal of Educational Psychology, 28,* 601–608.

DeCarbo, N. (1984). The effect of years of teaching experience and major performance instrument on error detection scores of instrumental music teachers. *Contributions to Music Education, 11,* 29–32.

DeCarbo, N. (1986). The effects of teaching level and teaching experience on common performance errors of instrumental music teachers. *Journal of Band Research, 22,* 20–28.

Deihl, N. C. (1963). Certain relationships among concept development, listening achievement, musicality, and the quantification of musical performance experience. Unpublished doctoral dissertation, Pennsylvania State University, University Park.

Delzell, J. K. (1989). The effects of musical discrimination training in beginning instrumental music class. *Journal of Research in Music Education, 37,* 21–31.

Delzell, J., and Leppla, D. (1990). *Gender association of musical instruments and preferences of fourth-grade students for select instruments.* Paper presented at the biennial meeting of the Music Educators National Conference, Washington, DC.

De Turk, M. S. (1988). The relationship between experience in performing music class and critical thinking about music. Unpublished doctoral dissertation, University of Wisconsin, Madison.

Dickey, M. R. (1988). A comparison of the effects of verbal instruction and nonverbal teacher-student modeling on instructional effectiveness in instrumental music ensembles. Unpublished doctoral dissertation, University of Michigan, Ann Arbor.

Duerksen, G. L. (1968). Recognition of repeated and altered thematic materials in two selected communities. *Journal of Research in Music Education, 16,* 3–30.

Edwards, B. L. (1978). An investigation of the relationship between selected teacher behaviors and achievement in beginning wind-instrumental music classes as measured by the *Watkins-Farnum Performance Scale.* Unpublished doctoral dissertation, University of Connecticut, Storrs.

Elliott, C. A. (1974). Effect of vocalization on the sense of pitch of beginning band class students. *Journal of Research in Music Education, 22,* 120–128.

Elliott, C. A. (1982). The relationships among instrumental sight-reading ability and seven selected predictor variables. *Journal of Research in Music Education, 30,* 5–14.

Emig, S. J. (1978). The relationships of selected musical, academic, and personal factors to performance in the freshman and sophomore music theory and ear training sequences at the Ohio State University. Unpublished doctoral dissertation, Ohio State University, Columbus.

Erbes, R. L. (1972). The development of an observational system for the analysis of interaction in the rehearsal of musical organizations. Unpublished doctoral dissertation, University of Illinois, Urbana.

Erneston, N. (1961). A study to determine the effect of musical experience and mental ability on the formulation of musical taste. Unpublished doctoral dissertation, Florida State University, Tallahassee,

Ernst, K. D. (1957). A study of certain practices in music education in school systems of cities over 150,000 population. *Journal of Research in Music Education, 5,* 23–30.

Falkner, K. W. (1957). The influence of music education and private study on adult interest in music in two selected communities. Unpublished doctoral dissertation, University of Iowa, Iowa City.

Farrell, P. (1972). The meaning of the recreation experience in music as it is defined by urban adults who determined typal singer profiles through Q-technique. Unpublished doctoral dissertation, Pennsylvania State University, University Park.

Fox, E. J. (1986). An investigation of the public high school band programs of a large city in Southeast Louisiana, including attitudes of senior band students. Unpublished doctoral dissertation, Louisiana State University, Baton Rouge.

Frakes, L. (1984). Differences in music achievement, academic achievement, and attitude among participants, dropouts, and nonparticipants in secondary school music. Unpublished doctoral dissertation, University of Iowa, Iowa City.

Franklin, J. O. (1979). Attitudes of school administrators, band directors, and band students toward selected activities of the public school band program. Unpublished doctoral dissertation, Northwestern State University of Louisiana, Natchitoches.

Friedman, B. (1959). An evaluation of the achievement in reading and arithmetic of pupils in elementary school instrumental classes. Unpublished doctoral dissertation, New York University, New York.

Froseth, J. O. (1971). Individualizing instruction in the beginning instrumental music class. *Journal of Band Research, 8,* 11–23.

Fullbright, E. G. (1964). An investigation of relationships between cultural background and attitudes toward classical orchestral music among college undergraduates. Unpublished doctoral dissertation, Indiana University, Bloomington.

Fuller, J. E. (1973). Colorado adult amateur bands and the implications for music educators. Unpublished doctoral dissertation, University of Northern Colorado, Greeley.

Gonzo, C. (1973). Research in choral music. *Bulletin of the Council for Research in Music Education, 33,* 21–33.

Goodrich, D. E. (1965). The musical activities of graduates of the Hastings public schools. Unpublished doctoral dissertation, University of Nebraska Teachers College, Lincoln.

Gorder, W. D. (1976). An investigation of divergent production abilities as constructs of musical creativity. Unpublished doctoral dissertation, University of Illinois, Urbana.

Gordon, E. E. (1986). Final results of a two-year longitudinal predictive validity study of the *Instrumental Timbre Preference Test and the Musical Aptitude Profile. Bulletin of the Council for Research in Music Education, 89,* 8–17.

Gordon, E. E. (1967). *A three-year longitudinal predictive validity study of the Musical Aptitude Profile: Studies in the psychology of music* (Vol. 5). Iowa City: University of Iowa.

Gordon, M. (1979). Instrumental music instruction as a contingency for increased reading behavior. *Journal of Research in Music Education, 27,* 87–102.

Groff, F. H. (1963). Effect on academic achievement of excusing elementary school pupils from classes to study instrumental music. Unpublished doctoral dissertation, University of Connecticut, Storrs.

Grutzmacher, P. A. (1987). The effect of tonal pattern training on the aural perception, reading recognition, and melodic sight-reading achievement of first-year instrumental music students. *Journal of Research in Music Education, 35,* 171–181.

Haack, P. A. (1969). A study in the development of music listening skills of secondary school students. *Journal of Research in Music Education, 17,* 193–201.

Harris, T. J. (1977). An investigation of the effectiveness of an intonation training program upon junior and senior high school wind instrumentalists. Unpublished doctoral dissertation, University of Illinois, Urbana.

Head, J., Jr. (1983). Attitudes toward musical activities among North Carolina high school band students with directors using varying teaching emphases. Unpublished doctoral dissertation, University of North Carolina, Greensboro.

Hedberg, F. (1975). An experimental investigation of two choral rehearsal methods: Their effect on musical attitude, music discrimination, music achievement, and music performance. Unpublished doctoral dissertation, University of Northern Colorado, Greeley.

Heritage, R. A. (1986). A study of the effect of selected environmental and instructional factors on the aural skill achievement of college music majors. Unpublished doctoral dissertation, University of Southern Mississippi, Hattiesburg.

Hill, J. (1979). An instructional program for high school vocal music performance classes based upon recent theories of aesthetic perception and response. Unpublished doctoral dissertation, Ball State University, Muncie.

Hill, W. L., Jr. (1987). A comparison of factors related to participation and achievement in instrumental music at the middle school level in the Denver Public Schools. Unpublished doctoral dissertation, University of Colorado, Boulder.

Hodges, D. A. (1975). The effects of recorded aural models on the performance achievement of students in beginning band classes. *Journal of Band Research, 12,* 30–34.

Hoffren, J. A. (1962). The construction and validation of a test of expressive phrasing in music. Unpublished doctoral dissertation, University of Illinois, Urbana.

Horner, L. K. G. (1973). A criterion-referenced test in performance-related musical behaviors for instrumentalists in the upper elementary school program. Unpublished doctoral dissertation, Pennsylvania State University, University Park.

Hufstader, R. A. (1974). Predicting success in beginning instrumental music through use of selected tests. *Journal of Research in Music Education, 22*, 52–57.

Hyden, J. M., Jr. (1979). Musical style and instrument preferences as correlates of personality variables. Unpublished doctoral dissertation, Texas Agricultural and Mechanical University, College Station.

Hylton, J. (1981). Dimensionality in high school student participants' perceptions of the meaning of choral singing experience. *Journal of Research in Music Education, 29*, 287–303.

Hylton, J. (1983). A survey of choral education research: 1972–1981. *Bulletin of the Council for Research in Music Education, 76*, 1–25.

Iltis, J. L. (1970). The construction and validation of a test to measure the ability of high school students to evaluate musical performance. Unpublished doctoral dissertation, Indiana University, Bloomington.

Jarrell, J. A. (1971). An analysis of achievement, procedures, and activities of selected high school band programs in Oklahoma. Unpublished doctoral dissertation, University of Oklahoma, Norman.

Jarvis, W. C. (1981). The effectiveness of verbalization upon the recognition and performance of instrumental music notation. Unpublished doctoral dissertation, Rutgers University, New Brunswick.

Johnson, K. L. (1979). The relationship between the components of musicality and ethical values among high school students. Unpublished doctoral dissertation, Boston College, Boston.

Jorgensen, J. C. (1974). A study of motivations for band participation as perceived by band section leaders, band instructors, and principals in selected North Central Association high schools. Unpublished doctoral dissertation, University of Nebraska, Lincoln.

Kaplan, L. (1961). The relationship between certain personality characteristics and achievement in instrumental music. Unpublished doctoral dissertation, New York University, New York.

Kendall, M. J. (1988). Two instructional approaches to the development of aural and instrumental performance skills. *Journal of Research in Music Education, 36*, 205–219.

Klinedinst, R. E. (1989). The ability of selected factors to predict performance achievement and retention of fifth-grade instrumental music students. Unpublished doctoral dissertation, Kent State University, Kent.

Kourajian, B. J. (1982). Non-participation of freshman and senior boys in high school choirs. *Missouri Journal of Music Education, 5*, 108–117.

Koutz, T. A. (1987). An analysis of attitudinal differences toward music performance classes in secondary schools by non-participants, current, and former participants. Unpublished doctoral dissertation, University of Missouri, Columbia.

Kovacs, B. E. (1985). An exploratory study of the relationships of flute, clarinet, and trumpet playing achievement, psychomotor ability, and selected physical characteristics of fifth and sixth graders. Unpublished doctoral dissertation, University of Maryland, College Park.

Kvet, E. J. (1985). Excusing elementary school students from regular classroom activities for the study of instrumental music: The effect on sixth-grade reading, language, and mathematics achievement. *Journal of Research in Music Education, 32*, 45–54.

Lamp, C. J., and Keys, N. (1935). Can aptitude for specific musical instruments be predicted? *Journal of Educational Psychology, 26*, 587–596.

LaRue, P. J. (1986). A study to determine the degree of consensus regarding outcomes of band participation and the competitive elements in band programs among band directors, band members

and members of parent booster groups. Unpublished doctoral dissertation, University of Illinois, Urbana.

Leonhard, C. (1980). Toward a contemporary program of music education. *Bulletin of the Council for Research in Music Education, 63*, 1–10.

Little, J. P. (1979). Differences in attitudes toward music between twelfth grade music and non-music students. Unpublished doctoral dissertation, University of Kentucky, Lexington.

Long, N. H. (1971). Establishment of standards for the *Indiana-Oregon Music Discrimination Test* based on a cross-section of elementary and secondary students with an analysis of elements of environment, intelligence, and musical experience and training in relation to music discrimination. *Bulletin of the Council for Research in Music Education, 25*, 26–35.

Luce, J. R. (1965). Sight-reading and ear-playing abilities as related to instrumental music students. *Journal of Research in Music Education, 13*, 101–109.

MacKnight, C. B. (1975). Music reading ability of beginning wind instrumentalists after melodic instruction. *Journal of Research in Music Education, 23*, 23–34.

Maddox, R. L. (1973). The construction and validation of an instrument to measure relevance perception in band students. Unpublished doctoral dissertation, New York University, New York.

Madsen, C. K., Duke, R. A., and Geringer, J. M. (1984). Pitch and tempo discrimination in recorded band music among wind and percussion musicians. *Journal of Band Research, 20*, 20–29.

Manor, H. C. (1950). A study in prognosis: The guidance value of selected measures of musical aptitude, intelligence, persistence, and achievement in tonette and adaption classes for prospective instrumental students. *Journal of Educational Psychology, 41*, 31–50.

Marciniak, F. M. (1974). Investigation of the relationships between music perception and music performance. *Journal of Research in Music Education, 22*, 35–44.

Mawbey, W. E. (1973). Wastage from instrumental classes in schools. *Psychology of Music, 1*, 33–43.

May, W. V., and Elliott, C. A. (1980). Relationships among ensemble participation, private instruction, and aural skill development. *Journal of Research in Music Education, 28*, 155–161.

McAdams, C. A. (1988). Investigation of instrumental music teachers' knowledge of the tuba. Unpublished doctoral dissertation, University of Illinois, Urbana.

McCarthy, J. F. (1974). The effect of individualized instruction on the performance achievement of beginning instrumentalists. *Bulletin of the Council for Research in Music Education, 38*, 1–16.

McCarthy, J. F. (1980). Individualized instruction, student achievement, and dropout in an urban elementary instrumental music program. *Journal of Research in Music Education, 28*, 59–69.

McCarthy, K. J. (1969). Effects of participation in school music performance organizations on the ability to perceive aesthetic elements in recorded music. Unpublished doctoral dissertation, Case Western Reserve University, Cleveland.

McClarty, J. L. (1968). An investigation to determine the reasons former high school band members elect to participate or not to participate in band upon entering the University of Montana. Unpublished doctoral dissertation, University of Montana, Missoula.

McLarty, C. L. (1963). Characteristics related to the festival performance of Mississippi high school bands. Unpublished doctoral dissertation, University of Mississippi, Oxford.

Menchaca, L. A. (1988). A descriptive analysis of secondary instrumental conductor rehearsal problem-solving approaches, addressed musical elements and relationship to student attitude. Unpublished doctoral dissertation, Ohio State University, Columbus.

Mills, D. L. (1988). The meaning of the high school band experience and its relationship to band activities. Unpublished doctoral dissertation, University of Miami, Coral Gables.

Milton, G. K. (1982). The effects of selected factors on the choice of freshmen instrumentalists in small colleges to participate or not to participate in the college concert band. Unpublished doctoral dissertation, Ohio State University, Columbus.

Montgomery, M. F., Jr. (1986). A comparative analysis of teacher behavior of jazz and concert ensemble directors in selected Oklahoma high schools. Unpublished doctoral dissertation, University of Oklahoma, Norman.

Mountford, R. D. (1977). Significant predictors of college band participation by college freshmen with high school band experience. Unpublished doctoral dissertation, Ohio State University, Columbus.

Murray, K. C. (1975). The effect of teacher approval/disapproval on musical performance, attentiveness, and attitude of high school choruses. In C. K. Madsen, R. D. Greer, and C. H. Madsen (Eds.), *Research in music behavior: Modifying music behavior in the classroom* (pp. 165–181). New York: Teachers College Press.

National Assessment of Educational Progress. (1974). *The first national assessment of musical performance.* Washington: Education Commission of the States.

Nelson, D. J. (1983). String teaching and performance: A review of research findings. *Bulletin of the Council for Research in Music Education, 74,* 39–46.

Nierman, G. E. (1982). The differences in descriptive abilities of band, choral, and orchestral students. *Psychology of Music, 13,* 124–132.

Noble, R. F. (1977). A multivariate analysis of factors in attitudinal levels of Wyoming adults toward music. *Journal of Research in Music Education, 25,* 59–67.

Nolin, W. H., and Vander Ark, S. D. (1977). A pilot study of patterns of attitudes toward school music experiences, self-esteem and socio-economic status in elementary and junior high students. *Contributions to Music Education, 5,* 31–46.

Olson, E. E. (1975). A comparison of the effectiveness of wind chamber music ensemble experience with large wind ensemble experience. Unpublished doctoral dissertation, University of Southern California, Los Angeles.

Parker, R. A. (1974). Comparative study of two methods of band instruction at the middle school level. Unpublished doctoral dissertation, Ohio State University, Columbus.

Pascoe, C. B. (1973). Golden proportion in musical design. Unpublished doctoral dissertation, University of Cincinnati, Cincinnati.

Patterson, F. C. (1985). Motivational factors contributing to participation in community bands of the Montachusett region of North Central Massachusetts. Unpublished doctoral dissertation, University of Connecticut, Storrs.

Perez, J., and Ramsey, D. S. (1990). *An investigation of variables related to the decision of selected sixth-grade male students to participate in seventh-grade choir.* Paper presented at the Southern Division Convention of the Music Educators National Conference, Winston-Salem, NC.

Peterman, W. J. (1954). An investigation of influences contributing to the post-school musical activities of adults in the city of Milwaukee, Wisconsin. Unpublished doctoral dissertation, Northwestern University, Evanston.

Pontious, M. F. (1982). A profile of rehearsal techniques and interaction of selected band conductors. Unpublished doctoral dissertation, University of Illinois, Urbana.

Price, H. E. (1983). The effect of conductor academic task presentation, conductor reinforcement, and ensemble practice on performers' musical achievement, attentiveness, and attitude. *Journal of Research in Music Education, 31,* 245–257.

Rainbow, E. (1973). Instrumental music: Recent research and considerations for future investigations. *Bulletin of the Council for Research in Music Education, 33,* 8–20.

Ramsey, D. S. (1978). A review of research related to the teaching of the beginning band. *Journal of Band Research, 13,* 15–24.

Robitaille, J. P., and O'Neal, S. (1981). Why instrumental music in elementary schools? *Phi Delta Kappan, 63,* 213.

Rogers, G. L. (1985). Attitudes of high school band directors and principals toward marching band contests. *Journal of Research in Music Education, 33,* 259–267.

Rubin, L. (1952). The effects of musical experience on musical discriminations and musical preferences. Unpublished doctoral dissertation, University of California, Berkeley.

Rubin-Rabson, G. (1940). The influence of age, intelligence, and training in reactions to classic and modern music. *Journal of General Psychology, 22,* 413–429.

Schleuter, S. (1978). Effects of certain lateral dominance traits, music aptitude, and sex differences with instrumental music achievement. *Journal of Research in Music Education, 26,* 22–31.

Shelton, R. O. (1986). The relationship between formal and informal music education and patterns of black college students' verbal response to musical excerpts from diverse stylistic traditions. Unpublished doctoral dissertation, University of Alabama, Tuscaloosa.

Sherburn, E. F. (1984). Student achievement and attitude in high school instrumental music education: A comparison of the effects of a lab approach and a more traditional approach. Unpublished doctoral dissertation, University of Southern California, Los Angeles.

Sherman, R. C. (1983). The relationship between personality traits of selected Michigan high school band members and their selection of an instrument. Unpublished doctoral dissertation, University of North Carolina, Greensboro.

Shugert, J. M. (1969). An experimental investigation of heterogeneous class and private methods of instruction with beginning instrumental music students. Unpublished doctoral dissertation, University of Illinois, Urbana.

Simpson, D. J. (1969). The effect of selected musical studies on growth in general creative potential. Unpublished doctoral dissertation, University of Southern California, Los Angeles.

Sisler, H. (1975). Relative effects of traditional general music and performance experience on the ability to perceive selected musical events. Unpublished doctoral dissertation, Case Western Reserve University, Cleveland.

Smith, E. R. (1984). The effects of vocalization on the intonation of college wind performers. Unpublished doctoral dissertation, Florida State University, Tallahassee.

Sorensen, J. M. (1971). The effects of small ensemble experience on achievement and attitude of selected junior high school instrumental music students. Unpublished doctoral dissertation, University of Illinois, Urbana.

Sousa, G. D. (1988). Musical conducting emblems: An investigation of the use of specific conducting gestures by instrumental conductors and their interpretation by instrumental performers. Unpublished doctoral dissertation, Ohio State University, Columbus.

Spradling, R. L. (1985). The effect of timeout from performance on attentiveness and attitude of university band students. *Journal of Research in Music Education, 32,* 123–127.

Stecklin, J. E., and Aliferis, J. (1957). The relationship of instruments to music achievement test scores. *Journal of Research in Music Education, 5,* 3–15.

Stewart, J. W. (1961). Influence of public school music education as revealed by a comparison of forty selected high school music and nonmusic students. Unpublished doctoral dissertation, Florida State University, Tallahassee.

Strachan, E. D. (1964). The designation of the appropriate grade level for beginning instrumental study. Unpublished doctoral dissertation, Colorado State College, Fort Collins.

Taebel, D. K. (1980). Public school music teachers' perceptions of the effect of certain competencies on pupil learning. *Journal of Research in Music Education, 28,* 185–197.

Temple, C. P. (1973). A study of the effectiveness of competition festivals in the music education process. Unpublished doctoral dissertation, Ohio State University, Columbus.

Thurman, V. L. (1977). A frequency and time description of selected rehearsal behaviors used by five choral conductors. Unpublished doctoral dissertation, University of Illinois, Urbana.

Tucker, D. W. (1969). Factors related to musical reading ability of senior high school students participating in choral groups. Unpublished doctoral dissertation, University of California, Berkeley.

Tuley, R. J. (1967). A study of musical achievement of elementary and junior high school pupils at Malcolm Price Laboratory School of the State of Iowa. Unpublished doctoral dissertation, University of Illinois, Urbana.

Wallace, S. C. (1979). A study of high school band directors' ability to discriminate between and identify modern cornet and trumpet timbres. Unpublished doctoral dissertation, Pennsylvania State University, University Park.

Webster, P. R. (1977). A factor of intellect approach to creative thinking in music. Unpublished doctoral dissertation, University of Rochester, Rochester.

West, J. T. (1985). The effect of performance success on the musical achievement of high school band students in four Florida counties. Unpublished doctoral dissertation, Florida State University, Tallahassee.

Whitelegg, C. P. (1986). An investigation of conflicts in the perceptions of band directors, school administrators, and selected members of the community about their respective band programs. Unpublished doctoral dissertation, North Texas State University, Denton.

Whitener, S. (1974). Patterns of high school studies and college achievement. Unpublished doctoral dissertation, Rutgers University, New Brunswick.

Whitener, W. T. (1983). Comparison of two approaches to teaching beginning band. *Journal of Research in Music Education, 31,* 5–13.

Wilson, J. H. (1970). The effects of group improvisation on the musical growth of selected high school instrumentalists. Unpublished doctoral dissertation, New York University, New York.

Witt, A. C. (1986). Use of class time and student attentiveness in secondary instrumental music rehearsals. *Journal of Research in Music Education. 34,* 34–42.

Woods, J. R. (1979). A study designed to develop an aural-visual test for measuring instrumental teachers' abilities to diagnose common wind instrument performance problems. Unpublished doctoral dissertation, University of Michigan, Ann Arbor.

Yarbrough, C. (1975). Effect of magnitude of conductor behavior on students in selected mixed choruses. *Journal of Research in Music Education, 23,* 134–146.

Yarbrough, C., and Price, H. E. (1981). Prediction of performer attentiveness based on rehearsal activity and teacher behavior. *Journal of Research in Music Education, 29,* 209–217.

Yarbrough, C., and Price, H. E. (1989). Sequential patterns of instruction in music. *Journal of Research in Music Education, 37,* 179–187.

Young, W. T. (1971). The role of musical aptitude, intelligence, and achievement in predicting the musical attainment of elementary instrumental music students. *Journal of Research in Music Education, 19,* 385–398.

Young, W. T. (1976). A longitudinal comparison of four music achievement and music aptitude tests. *Journal of Research in Music Education, 24,* 97–109.

Zimmerman, W. W. (1971). Verbal description of aural musical stimuli. *Journal of Research in Music Education, 19,* 422–432.

Zorn, J. D. (1969). The effectiveness of chamber music ensemble experience for members of a ninth grade band in learning certain aspects of music and musical performance. Unpublished doctoral dissertation, Indiana University, Bloomington.

STUDENT OUTCOMES OF TEACHING SYSTEMS FOR GENERAL MUSIC, GRADES K–8

Steven K. Hedden

UNIVERSITY OF ARIZONA

David G. Woods

UNIVERSITY OF OKLAHOMA

The teaching systems used in general music classes in grades K–8 reflect a variety of philosophies and styles of teaching music. There are "methods," which provide a great deal of structure for both musical content and teaching strategy, as well as "approaches," which emphasize exploration and experimentation. For example, Kodály specialists generally refer to the Kodály system as a method because it involves a sequential and developmental course of study. Orff specialists generally refer to the Orff system as the Orff approach because it emphasizes exploration and experimentation. Of course, sometimes the textbook is the system.

The purpose of this chapter is not to differentiate between "method" and "approach," but rather to provide a brief overview of each of several "systems" of teaching general music in grades K–8, and, for each system, the experimental research on student outcomes as reported by American and Canadian researchers. Sometimes the research results are interspersed throughout the overview, and sometimes the materials appear in a self-contained section. Generally the research on a given system exhibits a number of deficiencies as noted in the closing portion of the chapter, which identifies several recommendations about needed research on "teaching systems."

The first four systems of teaching music addressed in this chapter have their roots in Europe. The order in which they are discussed reflects the amount of extant research bearing on the system: (1) the Kodály system; (2) the Orff Schulwerk; (3) Dalcroze eurhythmics; and (4) Laban movement.

A similar ordering strategy is used for the remaining four systems, which have their roots in the United States: (5) Gordon music learning theory; (6) the Manhattanville Music Curriculum Project; (7) the comprehensive musicianship system of the Contemporary Music Project (CMP); and (8) the basal music textbooks, used as adopted text materials for general music classrooms throughout the United States.

TEACHING SYSTEMS FOR GENERAL MUSIC CLASSROOMS

Kodály System

Designed and implemented in Hungary by Zoltán Kodály (1882–1967), the Kodály system is a sequential and developmental course of musical study that has universal musical literacy as its goal, for Kodály asserted that each person can become musically literate. He also believed that (1) singing is the most important foundation of music education; (2) singing experiences should begin at a very young age; (3) the curriculum should use the indigenous songs of a child's own culture as the source of early music learning because of their inherent simplicity of musical style and language; and (4) only music of the highest quality (folk and composed) should be utilized as pedagogical resources and musical materials. The sequence of the Kodály system is presumably based on developmental characteristics of children rather than subject/logic considerations; learning experiences in music are arranged in a pedagogical order from sound to sight and from the concrete to the abstract.

One of the tenets of his system is that children can achieve better intonation at a quicker rate without the complication of diatonic patterns; thus, the pentatonic folk songs of Hungary are best suited for the musical experiences of Hungarian preschool- and kindergarten-age children. The results from Sinor's (1984) investigation of the singing of selected tonal patterns by American preschool children did not support this belief; on the basis of the responses of her 96 subjects, she concluded that the minor second was not consistently more difficult to sing than the major second. Casting additional doubt on the assertion are the results of a study by Jarjisian (1983), in which American first-graders worked on pentatonic and/or diatonic pitch patterns and songs over a four-month instructional period. Those students who learned both pentatonic and diatonic materials demonstrated significantly ($p < .05$) greater skill in singing pentatonic and diatonic songs than did students who worked on only pentatonic or diatonic patterns; she recommended the use of both pentatonic and diatonic patterns and songs with young children.

Kodály stressed that musical development should begin with pentatonism and rapidly progress to diatonic and chromatic musical structures. Today the students and advocates of Kodály's system believe in a sequence of melodic development beginning with the minor third (*sol–mi*) and then progressing to the *la* above. The value of starting with the descending minor third has experimental support in the results from Sinor's research (1984); when she asked preschool students to echo-sing a variety of tonal patterns, the minor third was contained in a majority of the easiest items.

Kodály borrowed hand signs developed in England by John Spencer Curwen (1816–1880) to provide a symbolic association for the solmization system used to teach melodic reading skills. The assumptions underlying the use of the hand signs include the following: Hand signs present a visualization of the high-low relationship among the notes being sung and thus help reinforce intervallic feeling; and hand signs help students develop cognitive knowledge regarding notation so that they become able to read music by translating it into body motions and actions.

Many teachers who embrace the Kodály system assert that students improve their sight singing as they become more skilled in utilizing hand signals. Unfortunately, the experimental evidence provided in two recent dissertations has not demonstrated that the use of the Curwen hand signals provides any additional advantage to students. For example, Martin (1987) found a nonsignificant difference ($p > .05$) in students' scores on a researcher-constructed test of sight singing between first-grade students who were taught solfège and hand signals during a semester and those who were taught only solfège. Similar results were obtained by Jones (1981) in her six-week investigation of music learning by

seven-year-olds. That is, there was not a significant difference ($p > .05$) in pitch discrimination between students who received the experimental treatment (spatial reinforcement that included movement and Curwen hand signals) and those who received control treatments (no spatial reinforcement).

Another of the tenets of the system is that the teacher should employ designated syllables to represent expressions of duration. Research by Palmer (1976) investigated the use of rhythm syllables to teach rhythm reading to fourth-graders over a six-month period. The experimental treatments were presented during three 20-minute periods each week; one was based on Mary Helen Richards's adaptation of the Kodály system, while the other was predicated on the ideas of Edwin Gordon. Employing the *Musical Aptitude Profile* (Gordon, 1965) and a rhythm-reading achievement measure as covariates, Palmer observed a significant difference ($p < .01$) on the achievement measure (written and performance components). The aggregated treatment groups had higher scores than the control group that received no special instruction in rhythm reading. A multivariate analysis of covariance indicated that there was not a significant difference ($p > .20$) between the scores of the two treatment groups.

A mixed picture emerges from the research studies in which researchers have compared the effect of the Kodály system on student outcomes with that of a "traditional" approach. For intermediate grades, Zemke (1973) prepared 35 lessons for use by fourth-graders over one semester of instruction; she labeled the experimental treatment she provided as a Kodály-adapted sequence. Another music specialist taught a control treatment, "more traditionally oriented," while a classroom teacher instructed a third group. In a comparison of pretreatment and posttreatment mean scores there were significant differences ($p < .01$) for the experimental group ($n = 25$) on four of the eight comparisons of *Music Achievement Test* scores (Colwell, 1969)—for Pitch Discrimination (Test 1), Auditory-Visual Discrimination (Test 2), and the total scores for Test 1 and Test 2. There were two such gains for the control group taught by the music specialist ($n = 32$)—Pitch Discrimination and total score for Test 1—as well as a significant ($p < .05$) decline for Major-Minor Mode Discrimination (Test 2). The only significant change ($p < .01$) for the control group taught by the nonspecialist ($n = 38$) was a decline on Major-Minor Mode Discrimination. The researcher stated that the results were equivocal, and noted that the treatment variable was confounded with the teacher variable. That is, the lesson plans and objectives were unique to each of the three teachers.

McDaniel (1974) also tested the effects of a Kodály-based approach on student outcomes when he taught several classes of fourth-grade students in 18 lessons over the course of one semester. Richards's *Threshold to Music: The First Three Years* (Richards, 1964) served as the basis of the experimental treatment, and the teacher's edition of *Making Music Your Own* (Landeck, Crook, Youngberg, and Luening, 1968) was the source for the "traditional" approach. Analysis of covariance with pretreatment scores on Tests 1–3 of the *Music Achievement Test* (Colwell, 1969) as the covariate indicated that there was not a significant difference ($p > .05$) between the two treatments.

The results obtained by Hudgens (1987) with primary students are also equivocal regarding the effect of the Kodály system on student outcomes. Subjects for the eight-week experiment were first-graders from five classes in four elementary schools ($N = 121$). Hudgens identified four treatments for the students: Kodály; traditional; eclectic, with a Kodály emphasis; and eclectic, with an Orff Schulwerk emphasis. The testing devices were the *Primary Measures of Music Audiation* (PMMA; Gordon, 1979) and investigator-designed performance tests of the ability to match pitches and to echo rhythms. Each measure was administered twice, and pretreatment scores were used in an analysis of covariance. The differences among adjusted posttreatment mean scores were statistically significant ($p < .05$) for the two investigator-designed measures in favor of the Kodály group, and the PMMA rhythm score, where those taught by the eclectic approaches had lower scores; however, the treatment variable was confounded with the teacher effect.

Orff Schulwerk

Carl Orff (1895–1983) founded his approach to musical learning on the premise that music, movement, and speech are inseparable, and he called the unity of these three components "elemental music." (As used in the Orff Schulwerk, "elemental" refers both to the early music of humankind and to the music of young children.) He developed his ideas and theories in Germany, and in 1924 collaborated with the dancer Dorothea Günther to establish the Günther Schule to train physical education teachers in movement. His goal was to develop and to stimulate artistic creativity in the adult students by using improvisation of movement and music by the students as a major focus of the program. (Improvisation of music was accomplished through a variety of sound sources, including xylophones and metallophones, glockenspiels, recorders, and various pitched and unpitched percussion instruments.)

The extensive development and implementation of Orff's ideas regarding improvisation and the use of instrumental ensembles were interrupted by World War II, during which the Günther Schule and the instruments constructed for the educational experiences at the Schule were destroyed. After the war, Orff decided that his approach might produce better results with young children than with adults.

With the collaboration of Gunild Keetman, Orff began to implement his approach in the infant schools and kindergartens in Germany. Known as the Orff Schulwerk, the elemental approach has a pedagogical structure that stresses improvisation through speech, movement, playing, and singing. Children begin with repetition and imitation, then gradually proceed to improvisatory activities. The songs included in *Music for Children*—Orff's five-volume compilation of rhymes, songs, and instrumental arrangements—provide improvisatory models for the children and the teachers to follow in conjunction with several improvisational devices, for example, melodic and rhythmic ostinato patterns.

The studies that have considered overall differences in effectiveness between a Schulwerk approach and a "traditional" approach generally have indicated that there is no difference between the two; in one investigation described below, the significant difference in test scores was in favor of the "traditional" approach. Unfortunately, these investigations have not provided a clear test of the underlying assumption of the Schulwerk—that improvisation of sound and movement will help young children develop the concepts of form, texture, timbre, dynamics, melody, harmony, and rhythm, as well as their creativity. The criterion measures in these studies typically are of limited scope, or the subjects are "older children" (from the upper elementary grades).

For example, Olson (1964) used scores on an author-designed test of melodic sensitivity—with a focus on aural/aural and aural/visual discrimination—to compare two approaches that he designated Orff method and traditional method. The test scores of the two groups of sixth-grade subjects ($N = 52$) at the end of the 18 lessons indicated that the two treatments were equally effective ($p > .05$). In her post hoc study of 458 fifth-graders, Siemens (1969) concluded that there was a significant difference ($p < .05$) in scores on the Knuth *Achievement Tests in Music* (Knuth, 1936) in favor of students in three schools who had received "traditional" instruction when compared with those in two "similar" schools who had received at least one full year of "Orff method" instruction. In a study of 10 weeks' duration, Moore's (1984) results were more positive regarding the value of a Schulwerk approach in that she obtained a significant difference ($p < .01$) in rhythm aptitude (PMMA rhythm score) in favor of the experimental group of primary students; however, this group did not receive a "pure" Schulwerk approach, and, more importantly, the teacher effect could not be separated from that for treatment.

Dalcroze Eurhythmics

Dalcroze eurhythmics is an approach to music education developed and implemented by the Swiss musician and educator Emile Jaques-Dalcroze (1865–1950). The goals of the Dalcroze approach to music education, which was based on the idea that the source of musical rhythm is the natural locomotor rhythm of the human body, include helping students to become aware of and to develop the expressive possibilities of their own bodies. The three basic components of the approach are rhythmic movements, solfège, and piano improvisation.

In a typical eurhythmics class, children move freely in bare feet to music that is improvised at the piano by the teacher. Believing that immediate physical response is essential to the comprehension of the musical idea, Dalcroze emphasized that rhythmic movement is an important means through which musical understanding can be gained.

Solfège activities are always a part of the Dalcroze class; students sing intervals, sing songs with syllables, and improvise vocally. Dalcroze asserted that the fixed *do* solmization system should be used in order to develop students' sense of musical pitch, awareness of tonal relationships, and tonal memory.

With the Dalcroze method, a teacher must be able to improvise freely at the piano in order to create a different movement feeling for every exercise used during a class. Also, the teacher should be able to play piano accompaniments spontaneously to specific movements improvised by the children. Finally, improvisation with the voice and with other melodic percussion instruments is encouraged in the Dalcroze method.

Apparently, only one study has provided empirical data regarding the use in K–8 settings of the Dalcroze approach to music education (Crumpler, 1982). The intent of this experiment was to determine whether first-grade students who worked on Dalcroze eurhythmics for six weeks in combination with their regular musical materials would attain higher scores on an investigator-designed criterion measure of pitch discrimination than students who worked only on their usual materials. Unfortunately, intact groups were utilized, and the statistical design made it impossible to determine whether the observed pre- and posttest gain for the experimental group should have been attributed to statistical regression.

Laban Movement

A fourth European whose ideas on music education have found adherents in this country is Rudolf von Laban (1879–1958), who developed an approach to learning that focuses on the language of movement. In Laban movement, the body sways or moves in space, and movement activities are developed that emphasize locomotion and the basic body elements. Locomotor movements include stretching, bending, twisting, circling, lifting, collapsing, swinging, swaying, and shaking. When the body moves from one place to another within the conceptual experience of space, as defined by Laban, locomotor steps are used. These steps include walk, run, leap, jump, hop, skip, gallop, and slide.

A sequential structure is used for the movement experiences. The initial focus is on the child's own body and self-space, and activities often focus on body-part identification, body control, and creative body shaping. Later in the sequence, experiences and activities designed to connect the child with other children within the classroom space are used. Children are taught to be aware of spatial relationships and the conservation of energy through space. The teacher then expects to use these awarenesses to help students develop greater sensitivity to music.

Advocates of the Laban approach to movement education assert that students taught by means of the approach become more controlled in their musical performances. Apparently, no research studies have been conducted that would evaluate this rather global assertion.

Gordon Music Learning Theory

The music learning system developed by Edwin E. Gordon (1927–) in the United States is built on the premise that in order to understand music one must be aware both interpretively and descriptively of its basic aural elements. Furthermore, to achieve this awareness, one must develop a sense of tonality and a sense of meter. Also, Gordon suggests that both the sense of tonality and the sense of meter are de-veloped through a skill-learning sequence and a content-learning sequence.

The learning sequence for skills is based on Gordon's belief that music learning has two aspects that are not mutually exclusive: discrimination and inference. Based on perception, discrimination includes five hierarchical levels; emphasizing conceptualization, inference learning includes three levels.

The content-learning sequence of the system is based on the premise that the learning of tonal patterns and rhythm patterns will lead to the learning of music form, style, timbre, and dynamics, as well as other aspects of music. Accordingly, Gordon has developed a complex sequence of tonal patterns to be used developmentally with skill-learning sequence. In addition to tonal syntax, Gordon has defined a rhythmic syntax, again based on sequential patterns. Tonal content learning and rhythmic content learning are not to be combined in Gordon's system for music education; they are to be used separately by the teacher.

Gordon's system has been subjected to experimental scrutiny in several dissertations that have investigated various aspects of music learning theory. For example, the evidence provided by three dissertations completed under Gordon's direction in the early 1980s indicates that the benefits of the approach may not become apparent until the upper primary grades.

In the first of these dissertations, Holahan (1983) administered the *Primary Measures of Music Audiation* (Gordon, 1979) as a pre- and posttest to four intact groups of kindergartners. Students in three of the groups worked on tonal patterns that the teacher performed and labeled, while the teacher for the fourth group neither performed nor labeled tonal patterns. The improvement in Tonal total scores over the eight weeks between pretest and posttest was significant ($p < .05$) for all groups, but there were no significant differences ($p > .05$) attributable to the treatment variable.

Feierabend (1984) also obtained a "no difference" result ($p > .05$) among four treatment groups of first-graders; in his experiment, each treatment was provided for five minutes each day over a seven-week period. Three of the groups received training in echoing various tonal patterns, but he discovered that the adjusted posttest scores of the group that had no special training did not differ significantly on the measures of singing skill and of aural discrimination ability from those of the three treatment groups.

In the third of the dissertations to obtain a "no difference" result, DiBlassio (1984) investigated music learning among first-graders over a period of 12 weeks. Four types of tonal pattern instruction and four types of rhythm pattern instruction were provided to separate groups during the 12 weeks. The differences in posttreatment mean scores on the *Primary Measures of Music Audiation* (Gordon, 1979) were nonsignificant ($p > .05$).

The remaining studies used third-graders as subjects. McDonald (1987) taught one group of randomly assigned third-graders ($n = 13$) soprano recorder through an approach that followed Gordon's suggestions regarding sequence. In the 48 lessons, taught over 12 weeks, each song was taught by rote, then melodic and rhythmic patterns of a song were rehearsed separately using a verbal association system with singing and chanting, and then the notation eventually was introduced. In teaching the other third-graders ($n = 14$) McDonald stressed individual fingerings, pitches, and rhythm symbols, which were presented in isolation before being assembled in order to play songs from notation. Significant differences ($p < .05$) were observed in favor of the experimental group, not surprisingly, on the rhythm score of the *Primary Measures of Music Audiation* (Gordon, 1979), as well as the investigator-designed recorder performance scale. It is unclear from the dissertation whether McDonald was equally skilled and enthusiastic when presenting the two treatments.

In the other study of third-graders, Shuler (1987) administered two treatments to 126 third-grade students—three classes using a "traditional" approach and three classes in which the initial quarter of each instructional period was devoted to Gordon's music learning sequence activities (LSA)—over one school year. Design difficulties and low test reliability prevented him from discerning any effect of the LSA on performance achievement or on a modified version of the *Music Achievement Test* (Colwell, 1969).

Manhattanville Music Curriculum Project

Named for the Manhattanville College of the Sacred Heart in Purchase, NY, where it originated, the Manhattanville Music Curriculum Project (MMCP) began in 1965 with funding provided by a grant from the U.S. Office of Education. A major objective of the project under the direction of Ronald B. Thomas was to develop a music curriculum for a sequential music learning program for the primary grades through high school. The resulting publication—*Synthesis,* a comprehensive music curriculum for grades 3 through 12—embraced a spiral curriculum concept, and included a sequential series of problem-solving situations for the students to encounter in the roles of composer, conductor, performer, listener, and critic. The emphasis of the curriculum was on inherent concepts that pertain to all music rather than idiomatic ones that apply only to some music; this reflected the authors' belief that using such a focus would discourage students from making specific value judgments that apply only to some music.

Experimental evidence pertaining to student outcomes from the MMCP system in grades K–8 is virtually nonexistent. Gibbs (1972) conducted an ex post facto study on static groups of fifth- and eighth-graders—taught according to an MMCP approach or taught according to what he called "conventional" means. He utilized measures of music aptitude and intelligence in a multiple regression equation and determined that there were nonsignificant differences ($p > .05$) on the two criteria—*Music Achievement Test* 2 (Colwell, 1969) and an attitude scale. Attitudes also were explored in a study by Pogonowski (1983). She worked with more than 400 students in grades 4 through 6 whose music instruction had been based on a process-oriented music curriculum (in turn, based on the MMCP model). With attitude as the variable of interest, she discovered a significant three-way interaction ($p < .05$) among grade level, gender, and socioeconomic status, but did not choose to explore this further by conducting a multiple regression analysis.

Comprehensive Musicianship

The underpinnings of comprehensive musicianship (CM) teaching emerge from the activities of the Contemporary Music Project for Creativity in Music Education (CMP), funded by a grant from the Ford Foundation. Four basic premises guided the program, experiments, and seminars of the CMP during its existence from 1963 to 1973: (1) the course of study for education in music should be based on all types and kinds of music; (2) music students will benefit from close association and contact with practicing musicians and composers; (3) music education should utilize to the greatest extent the creative capacities of the learner; (4) education in music from the preschool through the university should develop broad-based musicianship through listening, performing and creating music.

The comprehensive musicianship framework of teaching music at any level of instruction stresses that a focus on common elements—melody, harmony, rhythm, for example—is effective in helping students gain an awareness and understanding of the structural characteristics of music of any culture, tradition, or style. Also, advocates of a comprehensive musicianship approach to music teaching believe that students best develop personal musical competencies through a balance of experience among three musicianly functions—analysis, composition, and performance.

Research on the student outcomes of a comprehensive musicianship approach in grades K–8 is scanty. Apparently, the only "A vs. B" study is one by Madhosingh (1984), in which students received voice and ukulele instruction through either a "traditional" approach or one based on comprehensive musicianship; her experiment concluded that the CM system was significantly more effective ($p < .05$) in helping sixth- and seventh-graders acquire skill in pitch recognition as measured by an author-designed test. In his evaluation of a curriculum that emphasized comprehensive musicianship, Woods (1973) examined changes in scores over the course of a school year on several teacher-constructed measures of creating, performing, and listening. The results of this analysis suggested that an approach based on CM principles was effective at the preschool through high school levels, although the author emphasized that there was no control group in the investigation.

Basal Music Textbooks

There are four major music series currently available to school systems. They include *Music and You* from Macmillan/McGraw-Hill (Staton and Staton, 1988); *Jump Right In!* from G. I. A. Publications (Gordon & Woods, 1986); *Holt Music,* from Holt, Rinehart and Winston (Meske, Andress, Pautz, and Willman, 1988); and Silver Burdett & Ginn's *The World of Music* (Beethoven, Davidson, and Nadon-Gabrion, 1988).

The four music series generally include activities and experiences using the Orff Schulwerk, the Kodály method, Dalcroze eurythmics, Laban movement, comprehensive musicianship, Manhattanville Music Curriculum Project activities, and other approaches and methodologies. Also, they incorporate experiences for children that focus on performance, analysis, and creation, and they focus on the integration of the related arts. Each basal series is sequenced by the difficulty of the musical element being explored and by the categories of the musical materials.

Given the prevalence of the basal series in music classrooms across this country (most music classrooms contain at least one series), there is an appalling lack of research attention to the instructional efficacy of these materials. What is known at present is that (1) generally there are no differences in achievement ($p > .05$) over a semester, as measured by the *Music Achievement Test*, Tests 1–3 (Colwell, 1969), when some fourth- and fifth-grade students are taught with materials and approaches contained in *Exploring Music* (Boardman and Landis, 1966) and other students are taught with materials and approaches contained in the Memphis (TN) curriculum guide (Hensley, 1981); and (2) seventh-grade students who work for five weeks on materials from a concept-centered text attain a higher score on measures of listening skills than students who work on materials that emphasize singing skills almost exclusively (Smith, 1984).

As noted at the outset of this chapter, sometimes the textbook is the "system." Unfortunately, controlled research on the current basal texts apparently does not exist.

SUMMARY AND RECOMMENDATIONS

The picture that emerges from considering the research on student outcomes of teaching systems for general music, grades K–8, is a bleak one. There is very little research on the topic; the few studies that appear in this chapter result from using almost 40 search terms in an exhaustive search of all the pertinent data bases, and virtually all the "identified studies" are included.

For all the "systems" considered in this chapter—Kodály, Orff, Dalcroze, Laban, Gordon, Manhattanville Music Curriculum Project, comprehensive musicianship, and basal texts—there apparently exists no empirical evidence that any of them is effective as a system. There are a few studies that have detected a difference in "A vs. B" comparisons, but these investigations generally suffer from one of the problems identified in the two paragraphs that follow.

The measurement tools employed in several of the studies are ones that consider only a small aspect—a facet—of the system. As a result, the investigations generally do not examine or test the objectives of the method/approach. Instead,

they tend to focus on lower-level skills such as pitch discrimination and do not address the kinds of outcomes identified in the section on subject matter achievements for grades 1–3, 4–6, 6–8, and 7–9 in *The School Music Program: Description and Standards* (Music Educators National Conference, 1986).

Another problem of the studies that have detected an "A vs. B" difference is the experimental design. Sometimes the control groups in these investigations were not comparable to the treatment group(s) for a number of reasons: (1) the lesson plans, materials, and objectives were unique to the treatment and control groups; (2) groups were not assigned randomly, and regression could not be dismissed as the source of the observed differences; or (3) an ex post facto design was used, which prevented the researcher from unequivocally identifying a causal variable.

Detecting a difference was further complicated by the short treatment period employed in several of the studies. The treatment period for five of the studies included in this chapter extended over not more than 10 weeks. The last complication to be mentioned is the lack of multidimensionality in several of the extant studies. It was quite common to find that the researcher made the "A vs. B" comparison on the basis of only one test score; multivariate analyses of variance or covariance were uncommon.

An agenda for research on student outcomes of teaching systems for general music, grades K–8, follows quite logically from the items mentioned in the several preceding paragraphs. For example, the criterion measures that future researchers should assemble are ones that deal with the higher-level outcomes implied by the objectives, goals, or philosophical approach of each system. As a starting point, the outcomes listed under "Subject Matter Achievements" in *The School Music Program: Description and Standards* (Music Educators National Conference, 1986) could serve as a guide in the construction of these instruments. Perusing these subject matter achievements also will encourage future researchers to use multidimensional evaluations that simultaneously consider several instructional outcomes.

Also, those who wish to conduct research on student outcomes attributable to various teaching systems should plan experiments of at least one semester's duration (preferably one school year). It seems unreasonable to expect "A vs. B" differences to emerge if the total instructional time is only five or six hours over five to 10 weeks. Of course, researchers in these studies will want to use control groups that are directly comparable to the treatment group(s), with the expectation being that all groups would be addressing similar objectives and would be utilizing similar student materials, exercises, and songs, and that treatments will not be nested within teachers.

References

Beethoven, J., Davidson, J., and Nadon-Gabrion, C. (1988). *The world of music*. Morristown: Silver Burdett & Ginn.

Boardman, E., and Landis, B. (1966). *Exploring music*. New York: Holt, Rinehart and Winston.

Colwell, R. (1969). *Music achievement test.* Chicago: Follett Educational Corporation.

Crumpler, S. E. (1982). The effect of Dalcroze eurythmics on the melodic musical growth of first-grade students. Unpublished doctoral dissertation, Louisiana State University and Agricultural and Mechanical College, Baton Rouge.

DiBlassio, R. V. (1984). An experimental study of the development of tonal and rhythmic capabilities of first-grade children. Unpublished doctoral dissertation, Temple University, Philadelphia.

Feierabend, J. M. (1984). The effects of specific tonal pattern training on singing and aural discrimination abilities of first-grade children. Unpublished doctoral dissertation, Temple University, Philadelphia.

Gibbs, R. A. (1972). Effects of the Manhattanville Music Curriculum Program on the musical achievement and attitude of Jefferson County, Colorado, public school students. Unpublished doctoral dissertation, University of Colorado, Boulder.

Gordon, E. E. (1965). *Musical aptitude profile.* Chicago: Riverside Publishing.

Gordon, E. E. (1979). *Primary measures of music audiation.* Chicago: G. I. A. Publications.

Gordon, E. E., and Woods, D. G. (1986). *Jump right in!* Chicago: G. I. A. Publications.

Hensley, S. E. (1981) A study of the musical achievement of elementary students taught by the Memphis City curriculum guide and students taught by the traditional approach. Unpublished doctoral dissertation, Louisiana State University and Agricultural and Mechanical College, Baton Rouge.

Holahan, J. M. (1983). The effects of four conditions of "same" and "different" instruction on the developmental music aptitudes of kindergarten children receiving tonal pattern training. Unpublished doctoral dissertation, Temple University, Philadelphia.

Hudgens, C. K. (1987). A study of the Kodály approach to music teaching and an investigation of four approaches to the teaching of selected skills in first-grade music classes. Unpublished doctoral dissertation, North Texas State University, Denton.

Jarjisian, C. S. (1983). Pitch pattern instruction and the singing achievement of young children. *Psychology of Music, 11,* 19–25.

Jones, B. A. (1981). A comparative study of spatial reinforcement as a means for improving the pitch discrimination of seven year olds. Unpublished doctoral dissertation, University of Mississippi, Oxford.

Knuth, W. E. (1936). *Achievement tests in music.* Philadelphia: Educational Test Bureau.

Landeck, B., Crook, E., Youngberg, H. C., and Luening, O. (1968). *Making music your own.* Morristown: Silver Burdett Company.

Madhosingh, D. F. (1984). An approach to developing comprehensive musicianship in the intermediate grades using the voice and the ukulele. Unpublished doctoral dissertation, University of British Columbia, Vancouver.

Martin, B. A. (1987). The effect of hand signs, verbal tonal syllables, and letter representations of tonal syllables on the verbal and symbolic acquisition of tonal skills by first-grade students. Unpublished doctoral dissertation, University of Oklahoma, Norman.

McDaniel, M. A. (1974). A comparison of 'music achievement' test scores of fourth-grade students taught by two different methods—Kodály ("Threshold To Music") and traditional ("Making Music Your Own"). Unpublished doctoral dissertation, Louisiana State University and Agricultural and Mechanical College, Baton Rouge.

McDonald, J. C. (1987). The application of Edwin Gordon's empirical model of learning sequence to teaching the recorder. Unpublished doctoral dissertation, University of Arizona, Tucson.

Meske, E. B., Andress, B., Pautz, M. P., and Willman, F. (1988). *Holt music.* New York: Holt, Rinehart and Winston.

Moore, J. L. S. (1984). Rhythm and movement: An objective analysis of their association with music aptitude. Unpublished doctoral dissertation, University of North Carolina, Greensboro.

Music Educators National Conference. (1986). *The school music program: Description and standards.* Reston: Author.

Olson, R. G. (1964). A comparison of two pedagogical approaches adapted to the acquisition of melodic sensitivity in sixth-grade children: The Orff method and the traditional method. Unpublished doctoral dissertation, Indiana University, Bloomington.

Palmer, M. (1976). Relative effectiveness of two approaches to rhythm reading for fourth-grade students. *Journal of Research in Music Education, 24,* 110–118.

Pogonowski, L. M. (1983). Attitudinal assessment of upper elementary students in a process-oriented music curriculum. Unpublished doctoral dissertation, Temple University, Philadelphia.

Richards, M. H. (1964). *Threshold to music: The first three years.* Palo Alto: Fearon Publishers.

Shuler, S. C. (1987). The effects of Gordon's learning sequence activities on musical achievement. Unpublished doctoral dissertation, University of Rochester Eastman School of Music, Rochester.

Siemens, M. T. (1969). A comparison of Orff and traditional instructional methods in music. *Journal of Research in Music Education, 17,* 272–285.

Sinor, E. (1984). The singing of selected tonal patterns by preschool children. Unpublished doctoral dissertation, Indiana University, Bloomington.

Smith, C. M. (1984). Effects of two music series texts on seventh grade students' musical perception and musical sensitivity. *Bulletin of the Council for Research in Music Education, 77,* 43–51.

Staton, B., and Staton, M. (1988). *Music and you.* New York: Macmillan.

Woods, D. G. (1973). The development and evaluation of an independent school music curriculum stressing comprehensive musicianship at each level, preschool through senior high school. Unpublished doctoral dissertation, Northwestern University, Evanston.

Zemke, L. (1973). The Kodály method and a comparison of the effects of a Kodály-adapted music instruction sequence and a more typical sequence on auditory musical achievement in fourth-grade students. Unpublished doctoral dissertation, University of Southern California, Los Angeles.

·48·

MUSIC TEACHER EDUCATION

Ralph E. Verrastro and Mary Leglar
UNIVERSITY OF GEORGIA

Since the time of Lowell Mason (1792–1872), American music educators have searched for more effective ways to train teachers. Not until well into the twentieth century, however, could these efforts be described as research, and only recently has validating teacher education practices and programs through research become a major professional concern. Critics contend that, as a whole, research in music teacher education is unfocused, methodologically uncertain, and not clearly conceptualized, and that the individual studies fail to form a cohesive body of knowledge. Although these concerns are justified to an extent, valuable information can be gleaned from the diverse efforts to explore and reflect on the complex art of training an effective music teacher.

RESEARCH CATEGORIES

The topics most frequently investigated suggest several organizational categories that reflect traditional divisions in music teacher education: undergraduate music teacher education, music education for elementary classroom teachers, and inservice education. Not surprisingly, the majority of investigations have focused on various aspects of undergraduate music teacher education.

Undergraduate Music Teacher Education Many studies of undergraduate education have explored the relationships between various characteristics of the candidates and their success in completing the program and gaining entrance to the profession. Studies in this category attempt to predict or *presage* professional effectiveness on the basis of personal qualities, academic standing, aptitude, or intellectual and musical competencies.

Researchers also have demonstrated interest in the *process* of training music teachers, examining in some detail the effectiveness of certain strategies and curricular patterns. Studies of the teacher-training process are concerned with such topics as competency development, instructional techniques, early field experiences, and student teaching.

Assessment of the outcomes, or *product,* of the music teacher education process is the third major area of interest. Comprehensive program evaluation is complex and demands considerable theoretical sophistication. In music teacher education, program evaluation is not well developed, consisting largely of isolated site-specific studies. Yet even this limited focus on curricular and program outcomes represents an important step toward establishing a more cohesive body of information.

Music Education for Elementary Classroom Teachers The musical training of the classroom teacher is of universal concern to music educators and has received considerable research attention. Although studies in this area have much in common with research on preparing music teachers, the unique practical and theoretical problems of educating the nonspecialist require separate treatment in this chapter.

Inservice Education Inservice education, including graduate education, inservice conferences, and workshops, has received less attention from the research community than the other categories. Several recent studies have proposed models to assist universities in meeting the needs of inservice teachers (Stencel, 1988; Warren, 1989). A few others have been concerned with designing and evaluating inservice courses (e.g., Parkes, 1988; Warnick, 1979). Although these studies offer some insights, they do not provide a sufficient basis for drawing general conclusions and therefore will not be discussed further.

History and Philosophy Two of the classic modes of inquiry, historical and philosophical, are so seriously underrepresented in music teacher education that lengthy consideration is not warranted. It should be noted, however, that although a comprehensive history of music teacher education has yet to be written, a number of contributing steps have been taken—for example, Claudson (1969), Koch (1975), James (1968), Navarro (1989), and Platt (1973). Likewise, a few scholars have demonstrated an interest in philosophical inquiry. Representative of the occasional efforts to develop the philosophical and theoretical basis of music teacher training are Dorman (1973), Drew (1974), Glennon (1979), Parker (1982), and Rosenthal (1982). Although Reimer's (1989) influential work on the philosophy of music education is applicable, it is not directed specifically toward teacher training.

The research, then, has been concentrated in two areas: the undergraduate education of the music teacher, under the general themes of presage, process, and product; and the training of elementary classroom teachers. This pattern is reflected in the organization of the present chapter. The intent is to review the literature selectively, providing sufficient information about methodology, approaches, and research problems to give a fairly comprehensive outline of the research as it has evolved and to suggest patterns that future research may logically follow. Although technical merit was a primary consideration for citing studies, some were included because the results contributed uniquely to the body of knowledge or because they best illustrated a particular mode or method of inquiry. Conversely, since a number of informative studies were available on certain topics, it was occasionally necessary to make rather arbitrary choices.

A brief historical introduction is offered as a prologue to the chapter, with the intention of providing a context for evaluating existing research and a point of reference in setting an agenda for future scholarship.

THE HISTORICAL CONTEXT

In its earliest form, music teacher training was simply music training. The qualifications of the typical New England singing school master in the late eighteenth century consisted of successful completion of a singing school course. The singing school conventions that began in 1829 represent the first signs of progress in music teacher training, which was furthered in 1833 with the opening of the Boston Academy under the aegis of Lowell Mason. One of the academy's stated purposes was to provide instruction in the teaching of music (Birge, 1937), and in 1834 it sponsored a convention featuring lectures on teaching methods (Keene, 1982). With the conventions, significant progress was made in music teacher education even before the introduction of music into the public schools of Boston in 1838.

After music found a place in the school curriculum, music teacher training gradually became more closely allied with teacher education. The first public normal school, an institution established specifically for the preparation of teachers, opened in Lexington, MA, in 1839. For many years thereafter, however, special training was not generally required for teachers, and many had little formal preparation for their work. Normal schools were opened throughout the country in the years after the Civil War and proved to be an important

factor in the improvement of teacher education. However, the supply of normal school graduates never met the demand, especially in rural areas, and teachers were still certified on the basis of an examination, without higher education (Colwell, 1985). The normal school curriculum included instruction in the rudiments of music for the classroom teacher, but not until the 1880s did the normal schools offer courses for music specialists (Keene, 1982).

In the first quarter of the twentieth century, the curriculum of the normal schools was gradually expanded to four years, and the training of music teachers and supervisors also became a four-year program. At about the same time, there was a movement toward music teacher training at existing four-year colleges and universities. In some conservatories, such as Oberlin, music degrees had been in place since the mid-nineteenth century, and departments of music were established at several colleges, beginning with Harvard, during the 1870s. During the 1920s it became increasingly common for school music supervisors to hold a bachelor's degree (Birge, 1937). An indication of the growing importance of the colleges in music teacher training is the 1921 report of the Educational Council of the Music Supervisors National Conference, which recommended a four-year curriculum for music specialists (Keene, 1982). Not until the 1960s, however, did the baccalaureate degree become a requirement for music teacher certification in every state (Boardman, 1990).

The National Association of Schools of Music (NASM), founded in 1924, also issued recommendations on curricula for music teacher training. The purpose of the NASM was "securing a better understanding among institutions of higher education engaged in work in music; . . . establishing a more uniform method of granting credit; and . . . setting minimum standards for the granting of degrees and other credentials" (NASM, 1989, p. 5). In setting uniform minimum standards for accreditation in all areas of music, the NASM encouraged examination of the teacher education curriculum and attempted to ensure that teachers graduating from accredited institutions would have adequate training in both music and pedagogy.

The acceptance of music teacher education on the campuses of colleges and universities in the 1920s was crucial to the development of research. Studies dealing directly or indirectly with music teacher education began to appear soon afterward. For example, in 1927 Kwalwasser assessed the musical knowledge of schoolchildren and blamed the preparation of teachers for the students' shortcomings. McEachern (1937) conducted a thorough study of music teacher training programs, teacher educators, and teachers, finding a variability that is still characteristic today, in spite of the standardizing influence of the NASM.

Doctoral dissertations in music teacher training became more common after World War II. Several of these mostly descriptive studies, because of their comprehensive nature and substantive content, are still worthy of imitation. Doctoral dissertations continue to account for the vast majority of research in music teacher education, and a large proportion of published articles in the field are based on dissertations.

The founding of the *Journal of Research in Music Educa-*

tion in 1953 provided a much-needed outlet for the publication of research in music education, including teacher training. The very first issue included an article on developing the musical competencies of elementary classroom teachers (Fleming, 1953). Linton (1954) also wrote a JRME article on music for elementary teachers, but it cannot be classified as a research study. W. J. Peterson (1955, 1956) was interested in the training of secondary music teachers, and Clarke (1958) published the results of a descriptive survey of supervisors of student teachers.

Since the 1950s research in music teacher education has grown along with research in music education as a whole. Increased financial support for educational research benefited research in teacher training during the 1960s. The number of studies increased sharply in the 1970s, partly because of the growth of graduate education. The advent of competency-based teacher education (CBTE) prompted the influential *Teacher Education in Music: Final Report* (1972) by the Music Educators National Conference (MENC), plus a flurry of research studies, the chief purpose of which was to identify the characteristics and abilities of an effective teacher. Another interest of the 1970s was the prediction of success in music teaching, often by means of various personality tests.

Concurrently with the focus on CBTE in the mid-1970s and the cry for reform in the 1980s, researchers have expended effort in investigating the kinds of instructional practices that actually do contribute to the making of a good teacher. Studies have been conducted involving simulation, microteaching, self-assessment, interpersonal communication and interaction with students, and behavior modification. Interest has also been shown in alternate paradigms for research design and methodology.

A direction for future research is suggested in the 1987 MENC report *Music Teacher Education: Partnership and Process,* which emphasizes that the making of a teacher is a lifelong endeavor to which many people in partnership contribute. The report calls for "a new focus on the manner in which prospective teachers are prepared to teach music in the next decade and beyond. The task likely will require teachers who have been stimulated to be inquisitive, self-critical, questioning, and eager to solve instructional problems on a daily basis" (MENC, 1987, p. 13). The MENC report further recommends that the teacher-training program emphasize educational technology, individualized instruction, and education for special learners. That such crucial issues remain inadequately explored is due partly to the tendency toward isolation and overlap that is characteristic of an immature research field. The patterns that become apparent from studies building on other studies, replication without unnecessary duplication, are not yet discernible.

UNDERGRADUATE EDUCATION: PREDICTING THE SUCCESS OF THE CANDIDATE

The reform literature of the 1980s, which sharply criticized the quality of the nation's teachers, called attention to the need for more careful selection of candidates for the teaching profession. Traditionally, teacher education programs have not been selective in admission or retention practices. Colleges of education surveyed in the Research About Teacher Education (RATE) project, sponsored by the American Association of Colleges of Teacher Education (AACTE), reported that only about 20 percent of applicants are rejected (Galluzzo and Arends, 1989). Of this 20 percent, most reapply to the same program or to a less selective institution and are eventually admitted. Further, it is very unusual for preservice teachers to fail out of the program after admission, or for inservice teachers to have certification revoked (Pugach, 1984).

According to Galluzzo and Arends (1989), the most common criterion for admission to colleges of education is grade point average (GPA); many institutions also require letters of recommendation (Howey and Strom, 1987). Recently, many states have attempted to control the quality of candidates for certification. More than half of all states require some form of basic skills test for admission to candidacy. The *Preprofessional Skills Test* (PPST), developed by the Educational Testing Service to assess the reading, writing, and mathematics skills of students seeking admission to teacher education programs, is currently required in several states. Although use of the PPST seems to be spreading, the disproportionately high rate of failure among minority candidates has caused great concern (e.g., Smith, Miller, and Joy, 1988). The effect of such tests on music teacher education is not yet known.

Aside from state-mandated admissions standards, most programs admit and retain students principally on the basis of academic and/or musical skills–oriented criteria. Of 105 NASM member institutions surveyed by Shellahamer (1984), 73 percent employed initial selection criteria, most frequently an audition on principal instrument or voice, music placement exams, and/or an entry interview with faculty. Retention criteria were used in 90.5 percent of the responding institutions; most frequently employed were overall GPA, piano proficiency, jury on principal instrument or voice, and GPA in all music courses.

In spite of the number of institutions that employ various means of selection, there is little research on the subject; only 12.4 percent of the schools in Shellahamer's (1984) sample had attempted to validate selection practices. The body of research available for consultation can be divided into two categories: studies concerned with the prediction of academic success and studies that investigate the larger issue of teaching effectiveness.

Predicting Academic Success

The general consensus is that, in addition to high school GPA and scores from standardized tests such as the *Scholastic Aptitude Test* (SAT), more comprehensive measures should be employed to predict academic success in undergraduate programs (Howey and Strom, 1987). Although traditional measures such as GPA and SAT scores have more consistent support in the literature, personality traits, motivation, and socioeconomic status have also been considered as possible criteria for predicting academic success at the undergraduate level. "Academic success," in the context of prediction research, is usually either equated with program completion or measured by undergraduate GPA.

George (1969), LeBlanc (1971), and Melton (1973) used completion of a degree program as the criterion for academic success. LeBlanc investigated the feasibility of using the scholastic and personal information provided on the American College Testing Program (ACT) score report to predict completion of a music degree. Employing a geographically diverse and random sample, LeBlanc found statistically significant correlations between program completion and both high school GPA and ACT scores, but only 13 of 103 nonacademic items included on ACT reports were significantly correlated with graduation. George investigated the effectiveness of a variety of variables—for example, high school GPA, overall college GPA, scores on standardized ability and achievement tests, and GPA in various music and nonmusic courses—in predicting completion of a four-year music degree program. On the basis of multiple regression analyses, he identified a significant battery of predictors, of which the most important were high school achievement and achievement in music theory and ear training. Melton tested a number of variables in two general categories: (1) standardized tests of aptitude, achievement, and interest; and (2) course grades and GPA. In contrast to George, he found no variable that distinguished dropouts from music students who graduated.

Ernest (1970) and R. D. Walker (1977) employed GPA as a measure of success. Walker found support for relating ACT scores and selected background, demographic, and motivational measures to undergraduate achievement as measured by applied instructor ratings and GPA. The traits that correlated most highly were ACT scores, parents' education, race, and the Sweetheart-Spouse Sentiment from the *Motivation Analysis Test.* Ernest reported that undergraduate success, as measured by cumulative GPA and GPA in music, correlated significantly (at the .01 level) with high school rank and with scores on the *Triggs Reading Survey* and the *Minnesota Scholastic Aptitude Test.* High school rank constituted the best single predictor. In contrast to Walker, Ernest found that the correlation between ACT scores and college GPA was not statistically significant.

The weight of the evidence suggests that high school grades and standardized test scores provide the best indication of academic performance in teacher-training programs. This seems to be the case for both types of success measures. However, research results are often contradictory, and a great deal of work remains to be done before success or failure in a music education degree program can be predicted with any degree of confidence.

Predicting Effectiveness in Teaching

The problem that most directly concerns music teacher educators is not the prediction of success in college course work but the prediction of success in teaching. There is considerable evidence that undergraduate academic achievement does not necessarily predict success in actual teaching situations (Howey and Strom, 1987; G. S. Smith, 1975). A variety of nonacademic characteristics have been suggested as related to teaching success, notably self-concept, empathy, interest in people, flexibility, and creativity (Griffin, 1986). Regardless of the predictor variables chosen for investigation, there are two arenas in which the criterion variables have been measured: student teaching and inservice teaching.

Predicting Effectiveness in Student Teaching Anderson (1965) and Wink (1970) found evidence that certain personality traits may predict student-teaching performance. Anderson studied the predictive effectiveness of a battery of standardized personality, creativity, and talent tests. He concluded that the *Guilford-Zimmerman Temperament Survey,* the *Kwalwasser Music Talent Test,* and the *Symbol Reproduction Test* of the *Project Potential Creativity Test* had possible value in measuring the potential of student teachers of music. Wink found a positive relationship between students' concept of their own teaching ability and the grade received in student teaching. Wink reported high negative correlations between anxiety and adjustment.

Duda (1961) assembled a set of personality characteristics that might contribute to success in student teaching of music. Although Duda found that certain psychological factors showed statistically significant correlations with ratings of student teachers' effectiveness, the strongest single predictor was overall undergraduate GPA. Turrentine (1962) confirmed and refined Duda's findings about the relationship of GPA to final grade in student teaching of music. He established that the best single predictor of success was GPA in teacher-training courses. The two best predictor variables were GPA in teacher-training courses and high school class rank. Scores on the *Ohio State University Psychological Test,* the SAT, and the *Otis Quick-Scoring Mental Ability Test* failed to correlate strongly with student-teaching performance.

Faculty ratings in various forms appear to have considerable support as a predictor of student-teaching success. Chadwick (1972) and Chadwick, Michael, and Hanshumaker (1972) reported that, of 32 variables tested, the best predictors were recommendations of the student teacher's college instructors, GPA in groupings of music courses, and overall GPA. Schmidt and Hicken (1986) concurred, reporting moderate but statistically significant correlations between (1) success in student teaching as measured by a Likert scale rating completed by the cooperating teacher and (2) music GPA and personality attributes as assessed by music education faculty, among other variables. The composite measure of personality attributes proved to be the best single predictor variable. The findings of these studies support those of Turrentine (1962) concerning the lack of statistically significant correlation between standardized ability and/or psychological tests and teaching effectiveness.

Predicting Effectiveness in Inservice Teaching The assumption underlying studies of student teachers is that candidates who function well in the student-teaching environment are likely to function well as inservice teachers. Several researchers have studied possible correlations between undergraduate student-teaching performance and the effectiveness of inservice teachers. Others have focused on the identification of characteristics common to successful inservice teachers for the ultimate purpose of identifying these traits in teacher-training candidates.

Benner (1963) reported positive correlations significant at the .01 level between success as measured by ratings of principals and supervisors and student-teaching grade, music education GPA, and professional education GPA. Like Chadwick (1972) and Schmidt and Hicken (1986), Benner found that the most accurate predictor of classroom effectiveness is the judgment of music education faculty.

When measures of pupil achievement are included in the criteria for success, the results are entirely different. Borkowski (1967) postulated that if teacher education programs are preparing effective teachers, the quality of undergraduate work should be positively related to effectiveness in the classroom. Borkowski used a comprehensive set of success measures, including various measures of pupils' performance and several evaluations of classroom teaching. He found no statistically significant correlations between teacher effectiveness as measured by comprehensive criteria and quality of undergraduate work.

A classic example of a study based on comprehensive criteria for teacher effectiveness is provided by R. J. Krueger (1976), who investigated the relationship between music teacher effectiveness and selected personality and motivational variables. Krueger measured two distinct facets of success: (1) pupil achievement as measured by gain scores on the *Music Achievement Tests* and (2) the opinions of pupils, principals, supervisors, peers, and the teachers themselves. He reported that "personality and motivation are related to music teaching success in fairly powerful ways" (p. 23). Krueger also found statistically significant differences in personality and motivational characteristics between teachers who were successful in terms of pupil achievement and those who were successful in terms of opinion ratings. He commented that "no study to date has found a significantly stable relationship between objective measures of teaching success in terms of gain scores . . . and subjective measures of success such as ratings or observational instruments" (p. 24).

Consideration of the results obtained by Borkowski and Krueger suggests an important conclusion for prediction research: that the construction of a comprehensive profile of the effective music teacher must include pupil gain as well as what is commonly accepted to be effective teacher behavior. The further development of prediction research will be seriously hampered until research on teacher effectiveness establishes a more valid and reliable profile to serve as a standard for measuring the potential of preservice teachers.

UNDERGRADUATE EDUCATION: REFINING THE INSTRUCTIONAL PROCESS

During the first half of the twentieth century, such organizations as NCATE and NASM succeeded in establishing widely accepted guidelines for the training of teachers. Through specification of the courses to be included in the curriculum, these standards ensure that prospective teachers are exposed to a basic core of knowledge. By the early 1960s, however, critics of the educational system began to object that the possession of theoretical knowledge gained in college course work did not guarantee that graduates could actually put that knowledge into practice. Reformers began to call for the development of specific performance criteria, to be stated in terms of behavioral objectives.

The continuing effort to unite theory and practice in teacher training culminated in the early 1970s with the competency-based teacher education movement. The CBTE movement, developed in response to demands for teacher accountability and philosophically rooted in the behavioral objectives movement, sought to combine the practical emphasis of the normal school and the theoretical orientation of the university. Although interest in CBTE peaked in the 1970s, the movement left its mark in the form of an almost universal concern with the importance of competency-based objectives, a legacy of technological innovations in classroom instruction, and an increased emphasis on field experiences.

Research interest in the past two decades has also attempted to combine the theoretical and the practical. This is apparent in the framing of research questions relating to all components of the undergraduate curriculum: goals and objectives, classroom instruction, and field-based instruction.

Goals and Objectives

CBTE programs by definition have a list of observable behaviors that students are expected to demonstrate, an individualized approach to guiding students in acquiring the competencies, and a field-based setting. Of the many research problems suggested by CBTE, perhaps the most interest was shown in delineating the personal and professional characteristics, or competencies, of a good teacher. Although few music teacher education programs ever fully implemented CBTE principles, the emphasis on observable competencies has had widespread and persistent influence in developing program goals and objectives.

Studies before the CBTE movement identified teaching competencies, but usually in the context of a follow-up evaluation survey in which respondents rated the importance of each competency and/or the success of the undergraduate program in teaching it. As early as 1953, J. L. Fleming conducted a program evaluation study in which he identified 116 competencies for the elementary teacher, but not until the advent of CBTE were studies conducted for the sole purpose of developing lists of competencies that might serve as program objectives.

Design of Competency Studies Several methods have been used to identify teaching competencies. Most frequently, an exhaustive list is compiled based on the literature, the opinions of experts, or a combination of sources. Validity is established by submitting the list to a review panel that rates each competency on a value scale. The competencies are then ranked on the basis of the panel's ratings, and lower-ranked competencies are deleted to produce a list of manageable length.

An important decision to be made in designing a competency study, and an important factor to be considered in evaluating the resulting list, is the makeup of the review panel. In general, evaluation panels can be classified as either "expert" or "representative." Meske (1982) suggested that the decision whether to employ experts (e.g., teacher educators or teachers identified as superior) or a cross-section of music educators may influence the results of the study. The choice between representative and expert panels is often determined by the purpose of the study. The relationship between purpose and choice of panel may best be illustrated by a brief synopsis of two studies: Stegall (1975), which used expert opinion, and Taebel (1980), which used a representative panel.

On the basis of information gleaned from a survey of a national sample, Stegall (1975) compiled a list of competencies that would have NASM support and could serve as program objectives for the undergraduate curriculum in music education. The heads of 400 NASM schools were asked to rank, according to importance, an initial list of 99 competencies derived from the opinions of experts. On the basis of a 58 percent return, a final rank order list of 83 competencies was compiled using the categories of basic musicianship, applied music, and music education methods (see also Stegall, Blackburn, and Coop, 1978).

Taebel (1980) attempted to determine the teacher competencies that music teachers considered most important in contributing to the achievement of their students. Using the representative opinion approach, he developed a preliminary list of competencies based on informal interviews with music teachers and consultants from five schools in one metropolitan area. To these competencies, Taebel added the highest- and lowest-rated competencies from a "generic" list previously evaluated for inclusion on the Georgia *Teacher Performance Assessment Instruments*. The resulting list was then evaluated by a panel composed of teachers, supervisors, and university faculty members to determine which competencies should be included in the survey questionnaire. In the final stage of the study, 201 public school music teachers in all areas and at all levels rated the competencies, which were then ranked on the basis of the mean rating. Taebel's list included both generic and musical competencies.

Numerous other studies, utilizing variations of the basic procedure described above, were conducted throughout the 1970s and early 1980s for the purpose of identifying competencies. Some, such as those of Medley (1974), Parr (1976), and Taylor (1980), were limited to compiling lists of competencies suitable to specific areas such as band, choral, or general music. Reeves (1980) took a different approach, asking four groups of respondents—principals, music supervisors, college music educators, and beginning teachers—to rate a list of 60 competencies compiled from lists published by MENC, NASM, the National Association of State Directors of Teacher Education and Certification, and the Virginia State Department of Education. He found that the competencies expected by all four groups were basically compatible.

Beazley (1981) addressed the problem of test construction to satisfy the needs of competency-based programs by developing and validating a test to measure selected singing, conducting, keyboard, and diagnostic rehearsal skills. The test was based on competencies identified in professional literature, doctoral dissertations on music teacher training and assessment, and course outlines and examinations used in undergraduate courses. Beazley's work documents the probability that valid and reliable instruments can be devised to measure objectives of CBTE programs.

Limitations of Competency Studies Although much work remains to be done in competency research, fewer studies have appeared in recent years, partly because of conceptual and methodological weaknesses in current research approaches. First, many of the lists produced so far have been of unmanageable length, with competencies numbering in the hundreds. Second, the validity of competency statements compiled solely on the basis of opinion, whether expert or representative, has been called into question. Mountford (1976), attempting to address the concern, cited 29 research findings, gleaned from a survey of over 200 studies completed between 1964 and 1974, that supported or related to the competency statements found in *Teacher Education in Music: Final Report* (MENC, 1972). Finding little or no evidence to support many of the statements included in the MENC report, he concluded that until research empirically establishes those characteristics that identify successful teaching, the criteria for the measurement of the success or failure of CBTE programs cannot be considered valid or reliable.

Mountford's work highlights an important problem for music teacher training. Descriptive research has established the competencies that music educators consider crucial, and it is possible to measure whether teacher education programs are successful in developing these competencies. Yet it is not clear that assembling lists of competencies based largely on opinion accomplishes anything more than simply reinforcing the status quo in music education. Additional research is needed to establish whether the competencies identified in descriptive studies actually do contribute to the learning of music in the classroom. The importance of research in this area is underlined by the growing emphasis on teacher accountability and state-mandated precertification competency testing. Further progress in music teacher education awaits a concerted effort to establish a coherent set of musical and nonmusical competencies that are validated by research.

Classroom Instruction

In music teacher education, classroom instruction takes a variety of forms: major applied courses, secondary applied, conducting, music theory and history, professional education, and music methods. Of these, the only sequence that is the exclusive responsibility of music education faculty in most institutions is music methods. Courses commonly taught by applied faculty or in the college of education are beyond the scope of this chapter, and research in these areas will be discussed only insofar as it is applicable to the methods classroom.

Many of the research areas that attracted great interest among scholars in colleges of education during the 1980s are only now beginning to draw the attention of music teacher educators. These include such important issues as reflective teaching and teaching for transfer. Instead, research in music teacher education has concentrated on specific practical approaches to helping students acquire teaching competencies. These techniques, inspired by the practical focus of CBTE and made possible by technological advances (Freiberg and Waxman, 1990), include programed instruction, videotape and videodisc, observational systems, microteaching, and techniques for behavioral self-assessment and modification.

Programed Instruction Since the early 1960s, programed instruction techniques in teacher training have become increasingly elaborate, advancing in format from simple booklet to interactive videodisc. Programed instruction using computer-based technology is now usually termed "computer-assisted instruction" (CAI), but the concept—a format that enables students to learn independently and at their own pace while receiving appropriate feedback—has not changed.

Programed instruction in various guises has been used for many years in classes that require extensive drill, such as music theory. In two carefully conceived pioneer studies, Sidnell (1967, 1971) extended the principles of programed instruction in error detection to teacher training. Sidnell's materials were designed to assist prospective teachers in transferring aural skills acquired in college theory classes to music they were likely to conduct in the school setting— namely, full-score band literature. He found that students who used programed drills achieved higher mean gain scores than those who used nonprogramed materials. The effectiveness of programed learning has since been supported by Ambrose (1989), Costanza (1971), Lemke (1979), Ramsey (1978), Stuart (1979), and Wyatt (1974).

Videotape and Videodisc The potential of technology to bring the school classroom into the methods classroom is underscored in a study by Brand (1977), who investigated using videotapes of simulated critical incidents in teaching behavior management skills. Subjects who did not view the videotapes scored as well as experimental subjects on paper and pencil tests of behavior management skills. However, when subjects were placed in actual classroom situations, the experimental subjects were more effective in dealing with behavioral problems. Michelson (1984) observed that videotaped models were particularly beneficial when the concepts and techniques being taught were subtle and thus more difficult to understand and identify.

In another application of technology to music teacher training, Gonzo and Forsythe (1976) developed an extensive set of videotapes to help prospective music teachers under-

stand the relationship among teacher, learner, and subject matter. They found that subjects exposed to the video material developed better observation skills and a higher level of interest. In a feasibility study applying advanced technology, Miller (1987) concluded that instruction via interactive videodisc was as effective as traditional classroom instruction in teaching students to make oboe reeds.

The theory that videotapes are an effective way to provide feedback is supported by Jordan (1980), who provided data on the effectiveness of videotape feedback in teaching conducting skills. Nelson (1980) compared the effects of systematic self-observation of videotaped music lessons, unguided videotape self-observation, instructor verbal feedback without videotape observation, and absence of feedback on selected skills and attitudes of prospective music teachers. Although all groups who received feedback scored significantly higher than the control group, no differences were found among the experimental groups. According to Nelson, the important element is feedback, regardless of the form it takes.

The common element in all feedback systems may be that they encourage student self-assessment. Furman (1984) evaluated the effects of four feedback conditions on the development of a single competency: the ability to lead group singing with guitar accompaniment. The feedback methods employed were behavior checklist only, videotape only, videotape and checklist, and standard instructor feedback. Findings indicated that the use of the checklist alone was as effective as its use with videotape feedback.

Observational Systems The checklist developed by Furman is a form of observational system, which, as described by Dorman (1978), "consists of a set of categories which can be used to describe what occurs in a classroom" (p. 35). The majority of observational systems can be applied to any subject area. In music, most of the research on developing and using observational instruments was conducted in the 1970s (e.g., Erbes, 1972; Hedrick, 1976; Hicks, 1976; Reynolds, 1974; Verrastro, 1975; Whitehill, 1970). Observational systems aid preservice teachers in analyzing and evaluating their own performance and that of others.

Microteaching Microteaching, in which students give a short, focused demonstration of a specified teaching technique, may also contribute to preservice teachers' preparation for the classroom experience. Petty (1987) found an organized series of lectures, modeling, and microteaching to be an effective means of improving pacing in the choral rehearsal, and Reifsteck (1980) reported that microteaching was as effective as field experiences in improving the music-teaching skills of elementary classroom teachers.

Behavioral Self-Assessment and Behavior Modification Clusters of related studies that examine a single problem in several aspects are rare. Among the few efforts to conduct ongoing research on a specific problem is the work of Yarbrough and associates on the effectiveness of behavioral self-assessment in the teacher-training program. Over a period of years, Yarbrough studied various aspects of using student self-assessment in teaching rehearsal and conducting skills (e.g., Yarbrough, 1978; Yarbrough, Wapnick, and Kelly, 1979; Yarbrough, 1987). Summarizing the results of her research in this area, Yarbrough concluded that "students can efficiently change their conducting and/or rehearsal behavior by studying operational definitions, participating in practical conducting experiences, observing themselves via videotape, taking data through systematic observation, and writing self-evaluative critiques" (1987, p. 184). Portions of Yarbrough's work have been replicated by Alley (1980), Price (1985), and Rosenthal (1985).

Behavior modification, an area of research well developed by Madsen, was studied in the context of teacher education by Madsen and Duke (1987), who investigated the effect of training in behavioral techniques on the ability to modify preservice teacher behavior. Subjects who received training in behavioral techniques showed gains in the ability to recommend the appropriate teacher responses to specific classroom situations.

Areas for Further Research All of the techniques discussed above helped lay the groundwork for the use of more sophisticated technology in teacher training. For example, techniques developed for programed instruction in the 1970s were transferred directly to CAI in the 1980s, and experience gained with videotaping in the 1980s can be expected to contribute to the development of interactive videodisc programs in the 1990s. Interactive videodisc applications in particular have the potential to increase the effectiveness and efficiency of instruction in music methods and are a promising field for new research.

Although investigations of new techniques and applications of new technology have indicated that some innovations are effective in improving instruction in methods courses, it has been questioned whether the effects of these techniques persist beyond the methods classroom. Using a pretest-posttest control group design, Walters (1972) examined the effect of videotapes of simulated teaching situations on the attitudes of instrumental majors. On the posttest the experimental group showed a significant increase in positive attitudes toward pupils and toward teaching music. However, a second posttest, administered 30 days later, revealed no significant differences between experimental and control groups. Walters's findings make clear the need for longitudinal studies, which are rare in music teacher education research.

Studies are also needed in areas other than practical techniques. Research in general education has delineated several areas of importance for music teacher education, and the advent of performance-based teacher certification has highlighted several competencies, ranging from lesson planning to teaching for transfer, that are currently problem areas for beginning music teachers. Research in technology and techniques has proved valuable but is not sufficient to effect lasting improvements in music methods instruction. Furthermore, field experience research suggests that influences beyond the university setting, such as the cooperating teacher and the school context, may interfere with the ability of the preservice teacher to transfer what was learned in the methods class to the actual teaching situation.

Field-Based Instruction

In spite of the importance attached to the practicum, the research base supporting field experience as an essential part of teacher training is insubstantial and contradictory (e.g., Applegate, 1986, 1987; Griffin, 1986; Guyton and McIntyre, 1990; Waxman and Walberg, 1986; Zeichner, 1986, 1987). As Rosenshine and Furst commented in 1973, "The research on teaching in natural settings to date has tended to be chaotic, unorganized and self-serving. . . . There seems to be no simple route through the chaos which has developed" (p. 122).

Although numerous studies have dealt directly or indirectly with the practicum in music teacher preparation, in the final analysis very little has been firmly established (Boardman, 1990). This is the case even for student teaching, which is a virtually universal feature of teacher training curricula and has attracted a great deal of research attention.

Field Experience Programs: The Status Quo Beginning in the 1950s, several dissertations included descriptive statistics concerning field experiences in the music education program (Clarke, 1954; Gelvin, 1956; Janszen, 1962; Ricks, 1974). Coy (1976), in an in-depth survey of 12 selected institutions, reported considerable diversity among the respondents. Student-teaching terms ranged from seven to 18 weeks for full-time programs, and credit from six to 17 semester hours. The number of early field experiences varied from two to 90. Student teachers in one responding institution were observed by the college supervisor only once; in another, the typical student teacher was observed 24 times. Panhorst (1971) found similar variations. The 375 institutions responding to Panhorst's questionnaire required from 20 to 540 clock hours in student teaching, with a mean of 212 and a median of 200.

In 1989 Schmidt confirmed the earlier findings of wide variability among programs. The 111 teacher-training institutions responding to his survey (62 percent return rate) reported from 0 to 300 hours of required prestudent-teaching field experiences. The distribution was highly skewed, with a mean of 66.1 and a standard deviation of 73.20. The percentage of total curricular hours allotted to student teaching was more consistent, with a mean of 6.92 and a standard deviation of 3.7.

A consequence of this variation among programs is that the results of a study using subjects drawn from the student population at one institution may not be generalizable to other institutions. Because most research studies in music field experiences are based on site-specific samples, few broad-based conclusions can be drawn about field experiences in music teacher training. However, from a survey of the literature it is possible to glean a modicum of useful information and pinpoint promising areas for research.

The Effects of Field Experiences Both inservice (Corbett, 1977; Griffin, 1986) and preservice teachers (Applegate, 1986) consider field experiences one of the most valuable parts of the teacher-training curriculum. Numerous studies, usually based on opinion surveys, recommend the strengthening of the field experience component of the music education curriculum.

Yet there is no solid body of research that demonstrates conclusively the value of preservice classroom experience. According to Waxman and Walberg (1986), who summarize the findings of the research in teacher education, various studies have shown that field experiences increase interest in a teaching career, improve teaching behavior and performance, increase professional orientation and promote professional socialization, reduce racial prejudice and increase acceptance of disadvantaged children, increase the use of indirect methods of teaching, and encourage a preference for a democratic teaching style. Other studies have found that field experiences foster the development of merely utilitarian teaching perspectives, increased authoritarianism, and rigidity; they also encourage preservice teachers to become more controlling, restrictive, custodial, and impersonal, and less pupil centered, accepting, and humanistic (Becher and Ade, 1982; Tabachnick, 1980).

A brief glance at such contradictory results leads to the conclusion that one of the central components of music teacher training rests on an insubstantial theoretical and empirical base. The field experience concept simply evolved, unquestioned and unexamined, from the early apprenticeship model of teacher training (Guyton and McIntyre, 1990). As Boardman has observed, "No studies exist in the field of music education that verify that this apprenticeship model results in better prepared teachers" (1990, p. 730).

Examination of the few empirical studies on the effects of field experience in music teacher training confirms Boardman's assessment. Epley (1971), investigating the effects of early field experiences on students' attitudes toward teaching, reported results that varied depending on the instrument used to measure attitude. Comparing an experimental group that received teaching experience with a control group of students receiving no field experience, Epley found a significant difference in favor of the experimental group in pre- and posttest scores on the *Miller Attitude Scale Toward Teaching* and the *Cady Survey of Musical Career Preferences,* but no significant difference on the *Minnesota Teacher Attitude Inventory* (MTAI). Although the results were not uniform, Epley concluded that field experience had a positive effect on attitudes. However, Aurand (1964) found no significant differences in knowledge, as measured by *National Teacher Examination* scores, or attitude, as measured by the MTAI, between students whose field experiences included teaching and those who were restricted to observation.

Similar results are found in studies of field experiences in the music training of classroom teachers. Reifsteck (1980) investigated the effects of field and peer teaching experiences on the music-teaching competencies of preservice elementary classroom teachers, as measured by judges' ratings of teaching ability. Both groups showed gains, but there were no statistically significant differences between the groups. Reifsteck's results confirm Morten's (1975) findings that elementary education majors enrolled in field-based and campus-based music methods courses made gains during the course but that there were no significant differences between the groups.

Although it has not been shown that field experiences improve teaching ability, they may serve other important ends. According to Applegate (1987), one of the purposes of field experience is to encourage the student to develop career commitment and a sense of occupational identity. There is evidence that music education students often fail to develop a strong sense of identity with the teaching profession before graduation. Froehlich and L'Roy (1985) investigated occupational identity using a questionnaire and interviews with undergraduate music education majors. In all three instructional areas studied (band, chorus, orchestra), the students ranked occupational labels in the following order: performing musician, music educator, musician. The students also indicated that they placed more importance on the opinions of applied instructors and fellow students than on those of music education faculty. This performance orientation seemed to increase from the first year of college to the senior year. The researchers described the students' self-concepts as educators and their commitment to the profession as "weak" (p. 72). However, students with teaching experience reported a stronger perception of themselves as music educators and a stronger commitment to staying in the profession (L'Roy, 1983).

The Field Experience Triad Much of the research on field experiences centers on the "triad": the university supervisor, the cooperating teacher, and the student teacher or field experience student. Studies in education point to the cooperating teacher as the most influential member of the triad, at least from the student teacher's point of view (McIntyre, 1984; Watts, 1987; Yee, 1969; Zeichner, 1987). Zimpher (1987) argued that the cooperating teacher is indeed the dominant member of the triad, although the university supervisor tends to be more tolerant, secure, and independent.

Numerous studies in teacher education have called attention to the lack of training for cooperating teachers and the lack of communication between school and university regarding the roles and expectations of triad members (Griffin, 1986; Waxman and Walberg, 1986). These studies predictably recommend more training and better communication, but the results of empirical studies on the training of cooperating teachers are inconclusive, suggesting that it effects changes in attitude only (Griffin, 1986).

Research on the role of the cooperating teacher in music teacher training is sparse. Brand, in a 1982 study of 47 music student teachers and their cooperating teachers, administered inventories of behavior management skills and beliefs near the beginning and at the end of student teaching. No statistically significant difference was found between the pre- and posttest scores. He also administered the inventories to the cooperating teachers and reported that the student teachers' scores did not differ from the scores of the cooperating teachers on either the pretest or the posttest. Brand concluded that student teaching did not affect the classroom management beliefs and skills of the student teachers in the sample and that the classroom management beliefs and skills of the student teachers were similar to those of the cooperating teachers, both near the beginning and at the end of the student-teaching term. Gray (1962) compared the teaching concepts of student teachers with those of selected "effective" teachers. He found that the teaching concepts of the student teachers changed during the student-teaching period, becoming more like those of effective teachers.

The role of the university supervisor in the student-teaching experience has been explored in several dissertations, most of which are based on questionnaire data. Snyder (1961), D. E. Walker (1972), and Wortman (1965) called attention to weaknesses in supervision of field experiences and to lack of communication between the university and the cooperating school. More recently, D'Arca (1985) identified a trend toward a higher, more consistent level of qualifications for university supervisors.

Qualitative Studies of the Triad

Perhaps because of the difficulty of designing and implementing controlled quantitative studies on field experiences, a few researchers in the 1980s turned to ethnography, a methodology adapted ultimately from anthropology. The ethnographer differs from the experimental researcher in that he or she "obtains very detailed and elaborate descriptions of activities in a particular setting. . . . Ethnographic research makes few claims regarding representativeness, concentrating instead on explaining social processes in great detail" (Slavin, 1984, p. 16).

Ethnographic studies in music teacher education center on the student member of the triad. One of the first to employ the methodology was Bennett (1982), who studied shifts of perceptions among early field experience students. Bennett's work provides a good model for collecting and analyzing data in the field. Schleuter (1988) conducted a sophisticated study of changes in the curricular thinking of student teachers in elementary general music. Schleuter made a case for emphasizing the development of teacher thinking as well as classroom performance.

In 1985 P. J. Krueger completed an in-depth ethnographic study of two choral/general music student teachers. Krueger reported that the role perspectives of the two subjects were highly influenced by the practices of the cooperating teacher and the organizational structure of the school, that they perceived existing situations and methods as "given and unalterable," and that "student teaching experiences significantly modified student teacher perspectives and actions toward increased acceptance of existing school structures and practices" (Krueger, 1987, p. 70).

If, as Krueger's research suggests, the student-teaching experience decreases the likelihood that the student teacher will develop a reflective attitude toward the teaching situation, an important question arises: What can be done to ensure that field experiences produce positive results?

The Role of the University

The strongest possibility for improving field experiences and minimizing the reactionary effects of the experience is to strengthen or expand the role of the college or university. As Zimpher (1987) implied, the university has the potential to be a liberalizing influence, encouraging in the field experience student a more reflective and evaluative attitude toward the status quo. Considerable research in music education has focused on the effects of supervisory techniques and college-based programs on the development of given skills and/or attitudes. For the sake of clarity, these techniques may be divided into two categories: those that are or can be implemented before the field experience term and those that are implemented during the field experience, as part of the supervisory process.

Preparation for the Field Experience

The first phase of field experience programs is usually observation, which is often unsupervised and for which no special training is thought necessary. Duke and Prickett (1987), however, documented the need for careful preparation for field observations. On the basis of a thorough review of the literature, they noted several problems with observation. Observers tend to form opinions at the very beginning of the observation period, and these opinions affect and perhaps distort perceptions of subsequent events. Observers do not use all available information but instead are selective. Unexpected events may seem unduly important or meaningful, and there is evidence that the observer's own goals and values may influence what is noticed and recalled.

To examine the extent to which the observer's perspective affects observation and evaluation, Duke and Prickett videotaped a violin lesson from three different visual perspectives: teacher centered, student centered, and combined. The researchers found that teacher attitude was rated lowest by subjects viewing the teacher-centered tape and that student attitude was rated lowest by those evaluating the student-centered tape; subjects viewing the tape focused equally on teacher and student rated both teacher and student attitude higher. Moreover, subjects directed specifically to observe teacher behavior showed a higher mean disapproval estimation.

Duke and Prickett's study has interesting implications for music teacher education. As the researchers note, field experience students focus their observations on the teacher's behavior and thus may perceive the classroom climate as less positive and more disapproving than it actually is. They may later model this perceived negative teacher behavior. When the observer's attention is directed toward the teacher, whose attention is focused on the student, he or she may form a distorted picture of the classroom situation. While noting that the use of music majors rather than nonmajors as experimental subjects might produce different results, the researchers conclude that "the many hours presently devoted to observation in teacher education curricula may be of great benefit; however, it seems imperative that the time spent be carefully structured so that observers 'see' what is actually taking place" (p. 37).

Supervisory Techniques Evidence that the supervisory process can have a measurable effect on the verbal behavior patterns of music student teachers was provided by Verrastro (1975). The 39 subjects were observed with the use of the Withall (1951) procedure for verbal statement classification, which identifies verbal behavior as learner oriented or teacher oriented. Supervisory conference sessions were held with all subjects; experimental group conferences emphasized a cause and effect analysis of verbal behavior. The experimental group demonstrated more variability in verbal behavior patterns and more learner-oriented verbal behavior. Experimental subjects also tended to be more objective in the self-assessment of teaching effectiveness. The study concluded that verbal behavior analysis provided a constructive focus for the supervisory process, was an effective means for providing feedback on teaching performance, and was helpful in fostering objective self-assessment.

Merrell (1973) developed a self-instructional packet designed to improve the questioning techniques of student teachers in music. The packet, consisting of a programed text and an aural tape, took about four hours to complete and involved no follow-up instruction. Merrell compared an experimental group that completed the packet with a control group that did not, and reported that the experimental group used more examining behaviors. Merrell's research implies that fairly simple procedures may be effective for achieving specific improvements in teaching techniques.

Colnot (1977) reported that audio-cuing can increase the rates of teacher approval responses and the ratios of approval responses to disapproval responses while maintaining a low rate of approval error. Data indicated that the attitude of all groups worsened during student teaching, but positive attitude increases were observed most consistently in the group receiving audiocuing.

The effects of directive versus nondirective counseling techniques on selected personality variables were examined by Rossman (1977). Rossman employed the introversion-extraversion scale of the *Myers-Briggs Type Indicator* to divide his sample of 12 music student teachers into two groups, each containing an equal number of introverts and extraverts. In regular conference sessions during the student teaching term, nondirective counseling techniques were used with one group and directive techniques with the other. According to the extraversion-introversion scale of the Myers-Briggs, the nondirective group became more extraverted. Rossman concluded that nondirective counseling techniques can be highly effective in increasing extraversion among student teachers of music.

Taking an innovative approach to supervision, Saker (1982) videotaped simulated incidents based on 12 critical behavior management problems. The experimental group viewed and discussed the videotape; the control group listened to and discussed a narrative account of the incidents. Saker found that the experimental subjects were more confident of their ability to deal with behavior problems. However, cooperating teachers' evaluations showed no difference in the ability of the two groups to deal with actual classroom behavior incidents.

Implications of Field Experience Research The literature suggests, directly and indirectly, that the crucial problem in field experiences is lack of involvement on the part of university faculty, both before and during the experience. Field experiences, from observation to student teaching, not only may fail to contribute to the goals of the teacher training program, but may actually negate those goals. Research shows that university faculty involvement is essential in every phase—from the selection of the cooperating teacher through the counseling of the student teacher to the final evaluation—to ensure that the field experience does not reflect Thomas Regelski's scenario: "Welcome to the real world. Forget everything you were taught in college methods classes, and I'll teach you how to teach" (Fowler, 1988, p. 192).

EVALUATING PROGRAM OUTCOMES

Sophisticated research in program evaluation is a key to improving teacher education. Although most institutions, to meet NCATE and/or NASM standards, do conduct periodic evaluations of their music teacher education programs, these evaluations are seldom if ever sufficiently broad in scope and rigorous in methodology to effect fundamental improvements in the education of music teachers. In teacher training as a whole, program evaluation is a complex, slowly evolving field, handicapped by a lack of sophistication in theory and methodology and by a poorly developed network for scholarly communication (Galluzzo and Craig, 1990).

Approaches to Program Evaluation

Evaluation of Education Programs Teacher-training institutions have historically relied heavily on product-oriented goal attainment approaches for program evaluation. The most common means of collecting data have been follow-up studies of graduates. Before 1970 these were most often in the form of a single mailed questionnaire seeking graduates' perceptions of the quality of the teacher preparation program or, in rare instances, the opinion of the graduates' employers regarding their teaching success.

After 1970, even though other, more comprehensive approaches to evaluation had been introduced, the objectives-based follow-up study of graduates continued to be favored and, in fact, became more popular. In a survey of 444 institutions that trained teachers in various fields, Adams and Craig (1983) reported that 326 were conducting follow-up studies. Slightly over half of these sent questionnaires to first-year graduates, although only nine to 10 percent reported visiting first-year teachers for the purpose of classroom observations and interviews. The continued popularity of the follow-up study is at least partially attributable to the influence of NCATE. Both the 1970 and 1982 NCATE standards called for follow-up studies of graduates, and the 1987 revised standards continue to define success in teacher education in terms of how well graduates demonstrate program objectives.

Some researchers (e.g., De Voss and Hawk, 1983; Nelli and Nutter, 1984; Zimpher and Loadman, 1986) contend that evaluation methods should be more comprehensive and that data-gathering methods should be expanded to include methodology from the social sciences as well as the natural and behavioral sciences. According to this view, field methods such as ethnography are better suited to program evaluation in teacher education than are methods relying on quantitative data such as questionnaire results.

Methodology is dependent on purpose, and failure to define clearly the purpose and intended audience of the evaluation is a major weakness in program evaluation research. Education research has adapted several comprehensive program evaluation models from other disciplines (see Galluzzo and Craig, 1990), practically all of which are preferable to the summative follow-up study. Many of these models are formative rather than summative, and several are quite comprehensive, including program inputs and processes as well as products. The broader the purpose of the study, the more comprehensive is the model required.

Evaluation of Music Education Programs In music education, as in general education, the vast majority of program evaluation studies have been summative, based on follow-up questionnaires. These site-specific surveys of graduates have provided the subject matter for numerous dissertations and constitute much of the literature available to music educators on program evaluation. According to Colwell (1985), who provides the only extensive published discussion of the theory and practice of program research in music teacher training, just five studies—the latest conducted in 1958—dealt with a sufficiently large population to be of general value. McEachern (1937) visited approximately 20 institutions, surveyed 32 music teacher educators and 370 school music teachers, and studied the catalogs of 150 institutions. She was the first to document the immense variability among programs on a national level. Barrett (1950) collected data from the registrars of 160 universities, teachers' colleges, and liberal arts colleges and used it to identify course work common to all institutions. He found that, although average course requirements were similar among types of institutions, considerable variation existed among individual programs. Peterson (1954) surveyed a national sample of 374 outstanding music teachers regarding the value of their undergraduate training; he determined that while teachers tended to blame local situations for their difficulties, teacher education programs did not address the realities of public school teaching. Ehlert (1950), in a survey of 233 school superintendents, found that personality and lack of teaching ability, not lack of musical ability, were the factors that most often caused teachers to fail. English's 1958 study of 452 vocal music teachers from 44 states found that teachers were most concerned about their preparation in administrative, teaching, and social areas, and that problems dealing with musical knowledge were minimal.

More recently, Schmidt (1989) surveyed the music department chairpersons of 111 randomly selected teacher-training institutions in the United States. The survey sought to determine which topics are generally included somewhere in the aggregate of music education courses, the amount of time devoted to each, the extent to which they are covered, and the extent to which demographic variables influence their inclusion. Results indicated great variability regarding the topics included and the amount of time allotted to each. Substantial variability was also found between institutions in the number of hours given to the curricular components: The share for music courses and general education ranged from 17 to 55 percent and 15 to 57 percent respectively. Over 80 percent of the respondents indicated that all students studied the following topics: lesson planning, evaluation/grading, music education philosophy, curriculum construction, child development in music, classroom management, and creative music activities.

Program Evaluation Results in Music Teacher Education

The numerous studies that have attempted to analyze and evaluate individual teacher education programs are generally site specific and too narrow in scope to allow general conclusions to be drawn. The results of such studies are therefore often dismissed. Although the studies considered separately are not particularly informative, a synthesis of the results of 55 selected program evaluations conducted between 1955 and 1985 provides some broad conclusions regarding the teacher-training curriculum and its effectiveness. As Cady noted, however, such a synthesis provides "tentative conclusions rather than facts or concepts . . . beyond questioning" (1964, p. 7).

Even though the 55 studies yielded a total of 47 different findings, a substantial majority, at least 80 percent, mentioned the lack of practicality in teacher training. Approximately 50 percent reflected this concern in statements regarding student teaching or prestudent-teaching field experiences. Among the most frequent recommendations were the following: (1) More time should be spent in applying theory to practice; field experiences and possibly student teaching should occur earlier in the curricular sequence. (2) Supervision of student teaching should be improved; the student should receive more feedback from both the college supervisor and the cooperating teacher, and there should be more coordination among members of the triad. (3) During the field experiences, more time should be spent in teaching and less time in observing.

Methods classes were indicted for being impractical in 30 percent of the studies. As Peterson noted, "The most frequent comment . . . was the demand for a functional curriculum which presents materials that are easily adapted to high school classes and practical in application rather than traditional and theoretical in nature" (1955, p. 133). Findings reported most frequently indicated that (1) classes should be taught as if addressing real rather than ideal situations; more specific details and "tricks of the trade" should be emphasized; (2) classes should teach more organizational and administrative skills, especially for prospective high school teachers; and (3) classes should introduce a wider variety of materials and repertoire.

Twenty-nine percent of the studies targeted preparation to teach elementary and secondary general music. The needs mentioned most often were that there should be (1) more time devoted to elementary general music methods; (2) more preparation for teaching general music in the upper grades, and especially at the secondary level; (3) more training in Orff, Kodály, and other up-to-date approaches; (4) more exposure to contemporary and ethnic music and ways to teach it. Conducting and secondary methods (both instrumental and vocal) also received criticism in about 30 percent of the studies. Major concerns were the need for (1) more emphasis on rehearsal techniques in conducting classes, (2) more guided experience in applying conducting skills and rehearsal techniques, as in laboratory or early field experiences, and (3) more and better instruction in secondary methods classes, with the emphasis on pedagogy rather than on playing or singing.

Other needs reflected at a lower level of frequency (between 15 and 20 percent) were (1) more practical keyboard knowledge, (2) more emphasis on teaching the creative aspects of music, (3) adequate preparation in all phases of school music (band/choral, elementary/secondary) to meet certification requirements, and (4) stage and marching band techniques. There was also some evidence that graduates consider applied music and music theory the strongest areas of preparation in teacher training and that professional education classes were regarded as weak and useless.

Research Needs in Program Evaluation

Findings based on teacher opinions are of limited usefulness, because the results of follow-up studies are affected by factors not within the control of the program—for example, the graduates' aptitude, motivation, current teaching situation, and years of experience (Colwell, 1985). Perhaps this is why there is so little indication that programs are changed as a result of evaluation. As Galluzzo suggested, "One could draw the conclusion that the faculty nods in agreement when the evaluation data are presented but continues to offer the same program that apparently had been failing" (1986, p. 233).

The alternative—formative program evaluation based on a comprehensive model—is expensive, time-consuming, and conceptually complex. It requires considerable faculty involvement at each step, but this ensures that faculty have an investment in the evaluation process and in the implementation of the recommendations. More important, such a comprehensive evaluation process provides a broad understanding of each component of the program and of the ecology of the program as a whole.

INSTRUCTION FOR CLASSROOM TEACHERS

The music education of the elementary classroom teacher is a stepchild of sorts, living on the fringes of both music and education. Elementary classroom teachers have historically played a crucial role in the musical education of children, and the musical training of these teachers has been the focus of considerable research interest. Yet basic questions remain unanswered.

Although most universities include one or more music courses as part of the required elementary education curriculum (Brown, 1988; Sarvis, 1969), research has not advanced sufficiently to provide a sound basis for determining the goals and content of these courses. As always, lack of clarity in theory has produced confusion in practice. Brown (1988), surveying all NASM member institutions in six Great Lakes states, found that among the responding institutions (80, or 76.1 percent), a great variety of methods and approaches was used. Brown's data point not only to a confusion of methods but also to variations in goals: Some institutions offered courses in methodology, fundamentals, or a combination of the two; some offered piano study; and in some the required course was music appreciation. Atsalis (1987) found wide diversity in the content of music curricula for elementary education majors within a single state. This lack of agreement is likely to continue until research has established a basis for evaluating aims, objectives, and methods for the music training of elementary teachers.

Research questions in music education for the classroom teacher can be grouped into two broad categories: (1) What factors contribute to a classroom teacher's willingness and ability to teach music? and (2) What approaches, methods, and materials are most effective in preparing elementary education majors to teach music? Many studies have been conducted in both areas, and, although the results as a whole are inconclusive, a selected number of these are presented as representative efforts to address important issues.

Attitudes Toward Teaching Music

Studies investigating factors influencing the teaching of music in the elementary classroom have consistently found that one of the most important is precollege music background. Logan (1966) surveyed 358 Florida State University alumni who held a degree in elementary education and had taught at the elementary level for at least one year. He found that those who had sufficient music preparation to enable them to exempt the required fundamentals course considered themselves better prepared to teach music than did those who did not exempt the course. They used their skills more often in the classroom and were more enthusiastic about teaching music.

Gelineau (1960) surveyed 204 classroom teachers in two New England states, achieving a return rate of 100 percent by visiting school sites to distribute the questionnaire. She reported that those who enjoyed teaching music had a greater proportion of musical experiences from elementary school through college and a higher proportion of vocal activities than those who disliked it. They also exhibited the following characteristics: They had more music-teaching experiences during student teaching; the largest percentage had been teaching for over 25 years; and the majority had done most of their teaching at the primary level. Other influences were related to the school situation. None of these factors seems to be related to the music courses the respondents took as elementary education majors.

More recently, A. B. Smith (1985) reported that only one-fifth of the K–6 classroom teachers in six counties on the Eastern Shore of Maryland were teaching music. Significant relationships were found between music teaching and the following factors: the college attended and the degree received; musical background; whether music was taught during student teaching; county and grade level, presence of a music supervisor, teaching of music early in the career, and number of years in the profession; teachers' perceptions about their college preparation in music and their own music teaching; and whether they were involved in teaching mostly because of school district guidelines or as a matter of personal choice.

Goodman (1985) found that classroom teachers in Ohio rated their music-teaching competencies and their undergraduate music courses as "somewhat effective." The factor exerting the greatest influence on their perceptions was experience in private music lessons—again indicating that, although classroom teachers are not dissatisfied with their undergraduate preparation in music, factors unrelated to the required music courses are most influential in determining attitudes toward teaching music. Goodman recommended that undergraduate music courses for elementary education majors be reexamined to ensure that students acquire the needed competencies for teaching music.

On the theory that willingness to teach music is related to confidence and attitude, M. L. Smith (1969) studied the effects of student teaching on confidence level and attitudes toward the teaching of music. Comparing the results of pretest and posttest scores, Smith found a slight increase in the percentage who favored having a music specialist teach in their classrooms (a 6 percent increase, to 92.4 percent), and that 40.9 percent expressed a slight increase in their estimates of the amount of time per day they would spend teaching music (from 17 minutes, 38 seconds, to 18 minutes, 15 seconds). They expressed positive changes in confidence about teaching and in confidence about teaching music.

Tunks (1973) developed an attitude scale for measuring attitudes of preservice elementary teachers toward the value of music in the elementary classroom. Tunks's carefully researched and validated instrument is an important contribution to the field (see Greenberg, 1976), which can be consulted by researchers attempting to measure attitudes among elementary education majors. That it so far has not been utilized in other studies points to a characteristic weakness of scholarship in music teacher training: failure to build on previous research.

In summary, the preponderance of evidence suggests that elementary teachers who have experience in making music are most likely to include music in the daily classroom routine. The factor that seems to contribute most to a teacher's willingness to teach music is precollege musical background, especially private lessons. Unfortunately, this factor is beyond the control of teacher educators, who must attempt to find effective and time-efficient methods for instilling musical competence and confidence in all preservice elementary teachers, including those who have had no musical experience at all.

Preparation for Teaching Music

Considerable attention has been devoted to the content of music courses for elementary education majors without producing concrete results, and several of the more important studies deal with approaches that are now outdated. However, given the close relationships between programed instruction and computer-assisted instruction, and between videotaped observations and interactive videodisc technology, a brief glance at research on earlier techniques may prove fruitful.

Several studies in the 1960s and 1970s investigated the effectiveness of programed instruction, for example, but the conclusions were often contradictory. Barnes (1964) found that elementary education majors using a programed text to supplement classroom instruction in music fundamentals were superior to the control group on both posttest and retention test. Liberles (1975) reported differences in favor of programed listening instruction. Cribb (1965) compared three forms of individual out-of-class assignments: conventional study assignments, use of a programed textbook, and use of a "teaching machine program." In contrast to Barnes and Liberles, Cribb found no significant differences among the groups in pretest, posttest, or retention test scores on a test of knowledge of music fundamentals.

A small group of studies deals with the effects of videotape feedback or observations on various aspects of classroom teacher training in music. No significant differences were found between control and experimental groups in musicianship and creativity (Moore, 1976), confidence (Simpkins, 1980), attitudes (Tunks, 1973), or music skills and achievement (Kelly, 1984).

Recently, research on the uses of technology in music teacher education has focused on computer-assisted instruction. Jacobsen's 1986 study of CAI and music fundamentals produced mixed results, with significant differences favoring the experimental groups on two subtests and no significant differences on three. Given the wide availability of computers on college campuses, further work on the effects of CAI on all aspects of music teacher education will presumably be forthcoming.

In summary, no conclusive evidence has yet been presented that programed or technology-based approaches are particularly effective in increasing confidence or developing skills. Other methods that have not been shown to affect various outcomes of music courses for elementary education students include intensity training (Cassidy, 1988), ability grouping (McGlothlin, 1970; Tunks, 1973), and combined comprehensive courses versus separate courses in fundamentals, methods, and/or music history (Duffy, 1973; Hudson, 1973).

Directions for Future Research

A stepping stone for future research may be found in Kinder's 1987 descriptive study of 400 randomly selected elementary education graduates of one university. Of the 93 percent who returned the survey, over 50 percent of those who were teaching music in the classroom reported using the following seven activities: singing, listening to recordings, correlating music with other subjects, playing rhythm instruments, preparing music programs, motor movements such as singing games and dancing, and teaching concepts of beat/rhythm and loud/soft. Ninety percent of the respondents rated the following skills as very important or important: ability to use game or action songs to teach music concepts, ability to organize musical activities around holidays, ability to use rhythm and melody instruments as accompaniments, and ability to sing. The same percentage also considered it important to have the opportunity to observe music being taught by a specialist in an elementary classroom. A logical follow-up study would investigate the extent to which the college curriculum provides for these skills and activities.

One of the few established facts about the classroom teacher and music is that teachers who had experience with music before and during college are more likely to teach music in their classrooms. Further research is needed to establish what can be done in the college music methods course for the large proportion of preservice elementary teachers who have never been involved in music.

More important, there is no evidence that music instruction for classroom teachers has changed substantially in the recent past, although the circumstances in which they teach and the materials they use have changed drastically. Funding for elementary music specialists in many states increases or decreases as the economy expands or contracts, and the classroom teacher's role in music education changes accordingly. The availability of general music series texts with accompanying recordings may have lessened the demands placed on the elementary teacher's musical skills, but the extent to which these texts are used in the classroom is unknown. All these factors should be considered in setting the objectives of the music sequence for elementary education majors. Continuing research is needed to ensure that the objectives of the methods classes are congruent with the duties required of the classroom teacher.

DISCUSSION

Research in music teacher education has opened many doors, but a vast terra incognita remains to be explored. Few definitive answers have been found to the basic questions of the profession. In a mature research field, scholars expand and build upon the work of others. Problems are identified, conceptualized, and explored in the light of what is already known about the topic. The failure of music teacher education research to reach useful, far-reaching conclusions is due in great measure to the lack of cohesive groups of studies.

This situation can be attributed to the relative newness of the field, and there are indications that it is changing. In recent years, there has been increasing interest in organizing symposia for the purpose of synthesizing knowledge pertaining to the teaching of music and the preparation of music teachers, for example, the Crane Symposium (Fowler, 1988). Groups of studies on related topics are beginning to appear; examples include Yarbrough's research on self-assessment techniques and Madsen's research on behavior modification. Further, an examination of topics covered in recent dissertations and dissertations in progress reveals renewed interest in several fields that were initially investigated in the 1970s, for example, programed instruction and verbal interactions, personality characteristics, and relationships between the student teacher and the cooperating teacher.

This does not suggest that research can afford to confine itself to fields in which the ground has already been broken. The failure of investigators to show more than faint interest in inservice education, for example, is inexplicable. As the RATE research shows, the average teacher age and length of service have risen steadily in the past decade, and beginning teachers form a shrinking sector of the profession. Continued neglect of research in inservice teacher education has become impossible to justify.

Music teaching and the elementary classroom teacher is an area that demands much more attention than it has heretofore received. The time is ripe for entirely new questions about the function of the classroom teacher in music education. Competent studies have been published on various discrete aspects, such as factors that influence elementary teachers to include music instruction in the classroom. Many equally important issues remain to be investigated: for example, how much of the responsibility for teaching music rests with the classroom teacher in American schools, what the relationship is between the classroom teacher and the music specialist, and how successful classroom teachers are in teaching music.

Further, the education of teachers of music teachers has received very little attention. The RATE project has gathered demographic information about teacher educators, and various studies have focused on issues of status. It must be said, however, that even in general education the body of research is not advanced, and in music education it is practically nonexistent.

Equally remarkable is the neglect of philosophical and historical research, both of which are vital to a deeper understanding of the field. The lack of a comprehensive, interpretive history of music teacher training has hindered progress, although teacher training is included in the standard histories of music education. With some notable exceptions, historians have been content to chronicle facts and trends in teacher training rather than explore the relationship between teacher education and the demands of the societal context. The lack of interest in historical/philosophical inquiry among music teacher educators is perhaps reflected in the inability of music teachers to articulate a coherent and persuasive rationale for music education.

Not surprisingly, many of the strengths and weaknesses of

the research in music teacher training are paralleled in general education. The Macmillan *Handbook of Research in Teacher Education* (Houston, 1990), which contains Boardman's excellent chapter on music teacher education, is a valuable resource for scholars in music education. The American Educational Research Association (AERA) has sponsored the publication of a series of handbooks on research in teaching. The second (Travers, 1973) contains a chapter on teacher education by Peck and Tucker, which is worthy of examination even though much of the information is outdated. Several other chapters in the 1973 AERA *Handbook* provide valuable guidance on matters of methodology. The third *Handbook* also has a chapter on teacher education (Lanier and Little, 1986). These volumes are useful not only in suggesting promising areas for research but also in providing an overview of methodological issues.

The research methods used in music teacher education have been adopted, virtually without critical analysis, from education, which in turn borrowed from the natural and behavioral sciences. Research in music teacher training has traditionally relied on a limited group of research designs, most commonly the questionnaire survey and quasi-experimental designs using experimental and control groups. Even within this framework, the execution of research methods leaves much to be desired. In the many descriptive studies based on questionnaire results, the most common weaknesses are a low return rate and failure to validate the instrument. The typical quasi-experimental study relies on a "convenience" sample consisting of students in a single college. In view of the ample evidence that music education programs differ widely, the vast majority of such studies are not generalizable.

Even in the minority of studies that utilize a true experimental design, the length and complexity of the experimental treatment, particularly in areas such as student teaching, often make it difficult to be certain that the treatment is the sole cause of the observed effects. Instrumentation is also a threat to internal validity in many studies, particularly those requiring observation by judges, raters, or coders. Many researchers have attempted to minimize instrumentation threats. Still, differences among observers, or among observations made by the same rater in different circumstances, must be considered a potential threat to validity.

It is possible to compensate for design and methodological flaws in a variety of ways. Perhaps the most important, and least used, tool for doing so is replication. Replication of a study using a restricted sample increases generalizability and may help to compensate for unidentified variables in the treatment, or at least to identify these unknown variables. At present, replication is effectively discouraged by the poor preparation of abstracts and by lack of encouragement from the scholarly community. Dissertation abstracts should be carefully constructed to provide sufficient information on which to base preliminary decisions about whether a given study is worthy of or suitable for replication. The development of outlets for the publication of the results of replication studies would constitute a major step forward for music education research.

It is likely that music teacher education research will broaden its modes of inquiry to include concepts and methodologies from other fields. Ethnography, a qualitative methodology borrowed from the social sciences via education, shows promise in helping researchers place the results of quantitative studies in the context of the school classroom. The chief value of the methodology probably lies in its ability to identify hitherto unknown factors that may affect the results of empirical studies. More broadly, descriptive ethnographic studies may provide a framework within which to evaluate other types of research.

This is not to suggest that descriptive methodologies, however innovative, can entirely replace experimental designs. Although descriptive studies are useful, they provide information about what *is*, not what *ought* to be. Well-designed experimental research is required to either validate or impeach current practices, very few of which are now substantiated on the basis of research. This is a glaring paradox for a profession that engages in guiding the research of others and whose practitioners very often lament the fact that in-service teachers are reluctant to put research results into practice in the classroom. One may perhaps be forgiven for wondering why we are not practicing what we preach.

Ultimately, progress is dependent on an expanded concept of research and its place in music teacher training. Individual research efforts will continue to provide useful information, but, as Reimer (1985) has suggested, broadening the knowledge base on many vital issues will require cooperation among faculty researchers at different institutions. The establishment of a clearinghouse for research in teacher training would make a lasting contribution to the profession. An effort is needed to establish research priorities in order to build a coherent body of knowledge about the questions deemed most vital. Finally, and most fundamentally, progress requires a commitment among music teacher educators to the firm grounding of practice in theory, an insistence on understanding not only what we are doing, but why we are doing it and how we might do it better.

References

Adams, R. D., and Craig, J. R. (1983). A status report of teacher education program evaluation. *Journal of Teacher Education, 34*(2), 33–36.

Alley, J. M. (1980). The effect of self-analysis of videotapes on selected competencies of music therapy majors. *Journal of Music Therapy, 17*, 113–132.

Ambrose, S. C. (1989). The development and trial of programmed materials for teaching selected clarinet performance skills in college woodwind techniques courses. Unpublished doctoral dissertation, University of Cincinnati, Cincinnati.

Anderson, J. M. (1965). The use of musical talent, personality and vocational interest factors in predicting success for student music teachers. Unpublished doctoral dissertation, University of Southern California, Los Angeles.

Applegate, J. H. (1986). Undergraduate students' perceptions of field experiences: Toward a framework for study. In J. D. Raths and L. G. Katz (Eds.), *Advances in teacher education* (Vol. 2, pp. 21–37). Norwood: Ablex.

Applegate, J. H. (1987). Early field experiences: Three viewpoints. In M. Haberman and J. M. Backus (Eds.), *Advances in teacher education* (Vol. 3, pp. 75–93).

Atsalis, L. A. (1987). A comparison of curricula requirements in music for students majoring in elementary education at selected colleges and universities in southwestern Ohio. Unpublished doctoral dissertation, Ohio State University, Columbus.

Aurand, W. O. (1964). An experimental study of college music methods class laboratory school participation experience. Unpublished doctoral dissertation, University of Illinois, Urbana.

Barnes, R. A. (1964). Programed instruction in music fundamentals for future elementary teachers. *Journal of Research in Music Education, 12*(3), 187–198.

Barrett, J. H. (1950). The education of the music teacher. Unpublished doctoral dissertation, University of Northern Colorado, Greeley.

Beazley, H. V. (1981). Development and validation of a music education competency test. *Journal of Research in Music Education, 29*(1), 5–10.

Becher, R. M., and Ade, W. E. (1982). The relationship of field placement characteristics and students' potential field performance abilities to clinical experience performance ratings. *Journal of Teacher Education, 33*(2), 24–30.

Benner, C. H. (1963). The relationship of pre-service measures to ratings of music teaching success. Unpublished doctoral dissertation, Ohio State University, Columbus.

Bennett, B. L. (1982). Differential effects of initial early field experience on the concerns of preservice music teachers. Unpublished doctoral dissertation, University of Texas, Austin.

Birge, E. B. (1937). *History of public school music in the United States.* Bryn Mawr: Oliver Ditson.

Boardman, E. (1990). Music teacher education. In W. R. Houston (Ed.), *Handbook of research on teacher education* (pp. 730–745), New York: Macmillan.

Borkowski, F. (1967). The relationship of quality of work in undergraduate music curricula to effectiveness of instrumental music teaching in the public schools. Unpublished doctoral dissertation, West Virginia University, Morgantown.

Brand, M. (1977). Effectiveness of simulation techniques in teaching behavior management. *Journal of Research in Music Education, 25*(2), 131–138.

Brand, M. (1982). Effects of student teaching on the classroom management beliefs and skills of music student teachers. *Journal of Research in Music Education, 30*(4), 255–265.

Brown, R. L. (1988). A descriptive study of college level music courses for elementary education majors at NASM institutions in the western Great Lakes region of the United States. Unpublished doctoral dissertation, Michigan State University, East Lansing.

Cady, H. L. (1964). The synthesis of music education research. *Bulletin of the Council for Research in Music Education, 3,* 12–15.

Cassidy, J. W. (1988). The effect of training in intensity on accuracy of instruction and effectiveness of delivery among preservice elementary education majors in a music setting. Unpublished doctoral dissertation, Florida State University, Tallahassee.

Chadwick, C. A. S. (1972). The prediction of success in student-teaching in music at the University of Southern California. Unpublished doctoral dissertation, University of Southern California, Los Angeles.

Chadwick, C. S., Michael, W. G., and Hanshumaker, J. (1972). Correlates of success in practice teaching in music at the University of Southern California. *Educational and Psychological Measurement, 32,* 1073–1078.

Clarke, S. M. (1954). A study of practices in student-teaching in selected universities with recommendations for the improvement of the full-time student-teaching program in music at the Ohio State University. Unpublished doctoral dissertation, Ohio State University, Columbus

Clarke, S. M. (1958). Opinions and practices of supervisors of student teachers in selected music schools. *Journal of Research in Music Education, 6*(1), 62–67.

Claudson, W. D. (1969). The philosophy of Julia E. Crane and the origin of music teacher training. *Journal of Research in Music Education, 17*(4), 399–407.

Colnot, C. L. (1977). An exploratory study of different modes of presenting behavioral principles and their effect upon the cognitive understandings, attitudes and teaching skills of instrumental music student-teachers. Unpublished doctoral dissertation, Northwestern University, Evanston.

Colwell, R. J. (1985). Program evaluation in music teacher education. *Bulletin of the Council for Research in Music Education, 81,* 18–62.

Corbett, D. L. (1977). An analysis of the opinions of recent music education graduates from Kansas teacher training institutions regarding the adequacy of their preparation to teach music. Unpublished doctoral dissertation, University of Kansas, Lawrence

Costanza, P. (1971). Programed instruction in score reading skills. *Journal of Research in Music Education, 19*(4), 453–459.

Coy, K. F. (1976). A study of the student-teaching programs in music of selected institutions of higher education. Unpublished doctoral dissertation, University of Maryland, College Park.

Cribb, G. R. (1965). The comparative effectiveness of conventional and programed instructional procedures in teaching fundamentals of music. Unpublished doctoral dissertation, University of North Texas, Denton.

D'Arca, L. A. (1985). A comparative study of the qualifications, training, and function of supervisors of student teachers in music at selected midwestern colleges and universities. Unpublished doctoral dissertation, University of Missouri, Columbia.

De Voss, G., and Hawk, D. (1983). Follow-up models in teacher education. *Educational Evaluation and Policy Analysis, 5*(2), 163–171.

Dorman, P. E. (1973). Relationship between teaching incidents and Taba's theoretical construct. *Journal of Research in Music Education, 21*(2), 182–186.

Dorman, P. E. (1978). A review of research on observational systems in the analysis of music teaching. *Bulletin of the Council for Research in Music Education, 57,* 35–45.

Drew, E. J. (1974). An application of the Manhattanville Music Curriculum Program to the preparation in music of elementary school classroom teachers. Unpublished doctoral dissertation, Boston University School for the Arts, Boston.

Duda, W. B. (1961). The prediction of three major dimensions of teacher behavior for student-teachers in music education. Unpublished doctoral dissertation, University of Illinois, Urbana.

Duffy, M. E. W. (1973). An investigation of two teaching methods for rudimental and historical music study by elementary education majors in Southern Connecticut State College. Unpublished doctoral dissertation, University of Michigan, Ann Arbor.

Duke, R. A., and Prickett, C. A. (1987). The effect of differentially focused observation on evaluation of instruction. *Journal of Research in Music Education, 35*(1), 27–37.

Ehlert, J. K. (1950). The selection and education of public school music teachers. Unpublished doctoral dissertation, University of Colorado, Boulder.

Eisenberg, T. E., and Rudner, L. M. (1988). State testing of teachers: A summary. *Journal of Teacher Education, 39*(4), 21–22.

English, W. S. (1958). Learning experiences that prepare school music teachers for selected activities. Unpublished doctoral dissertation, George Peabody College for Teachers of Vanderbilt University, Nashville.

Epley, W. C. (1971). Modifying attitudes toward school music teaching through sophomore level experience in elementary or secondary schools. Unpublished doctoral dissertation, Arizona State University, Tempe.

Erbes, R. L. (1972). The development of an observational system for the analysis of interaction in the rehearsal of musical organizations. Unpublished doctoral dissertation, University of Illinois, Urbana.

Ernest, D. J. (1970). The prediction of academic success of college music majors. *Journal of Research in Music Education, 18*(3), 272–276.

Fleming, J. L. (1953). The determination of musical experiences designed to develop the musical competencies required of elementary school teachers in Maryland. *Journal of Research in Music Education, 1*(1), 59–67.

Fowler, C. (Ed.). (1988). *The Crane Symposium: Toward an understanding of the teaching and learning of music performance.* Potsdam: Potsdam College of the State University of New York.

Freiberg, H. J., and Waxman, H. C. (1990). Changing teacher education. In W. R. Houston (Ed.), *Handbook of research on teacher education* (pp. 617–635). New York: Macmillan.

Froehlich, H., and L'Roy, D. (1985). An investigation of occupancy identity in undergraduate music education majors. *Bulletin of the Council for Research in Music Education, 85*, 65–75.

Furman, C. E. (1984). Behavior checklists and videotapes versus standard instructor feedback in the development of a music teaching competency. Unpublished doctoral dissertation, Florida State University, Tallahassee.

Galluzzo, G. R. (1986). Teacher education program evaluation: Organizing or agonizing? In J. D. Raths and L. G. Katz (Eds.), *Advances in teacher education* (Vol. 2, pp. 221–237). Norwood: Ablex.

Galluzzo, G. R., and Arends, R. I. (1989). The RATE Project: A profile of teacher education institutions. *Journal of Teacher Education, 40*(4), 56–58.

Galluzzo, G. R., and Craig, J. R. (1990). Evaluation of preservice teacher education programs. In W. R. Houston (Ed.), *Handbook of research on teacher education* (pp. 599–616). New York: Macmillan.

Gelineau, R. P. B. (1960). Factors influencing attitudinal variation among classroom teachers in the teaching of music. Unpublished doctoral dissertation, University of Connecticut, Storrs.

Gelvin, M. P. (1956). A comparative analysis of the preparation and practices in student teaching in music. Unpublished doctoral dissertation, Northwestern University, Evanston.

George, W. E. (1969). Significant predictors for college achievement in specified areas of music education and identification of potential graduates. Unpublished doctoral dissertation, University of Kansas, Lawrence.

Glennon, M. C. (1979). Carl Rogers' theory of facilitation as a basis for the preparation of student teachers in music education. Unpublished doctoral dissertation, Temple University, Philadelphia.

Gonzo, C., and Forsythe, J. (1976). Developing and using videotapes to teach rehearsal techniques and principles. *Journal of Research in Music Education, 24*(1), 32–41.

Goodman, J. L. (1985). Perceived music and music-teaching competencies of classroom teachers in the state of Ohio. Unpublished doctoral dissertation, Ohio State University, Columbus.

Gray, T. L. (1962). An investigation of the changes in teaching concepts of student teachers of music. Unpublished doctoral dissertation, State University of Iowa, Iowa City.

Greenberg, M. (1976). [Review of Attitudes of elementary classroom teachers toward elementary general music: The effects of certain aspects of preservice training]. *Bulletin of the Council for Research in Music Education, 47*, 51–60.

Griffin, G. A. (1986). Issues in student teaching: A review. In J. D. Raths and L. G. Katz (Eds.), *Advances in teacher education* (Vol. 2, pp. 239–273). Norwood: Ablex.

Guyton, E., and McIntyre, D. J. (1990). Student teaching and school experiences. In W. R. Houston (Ed.), *Handbook of research on teacher education* (pp. 514–534). New York: Macmillan.

Hedrick, G. L. (1976). The development of a verbal analysis system for self-evaluation of preservice music teachers. Unpublished doctoral dissertation, Florida State University, Tallahassee.

Hicks, C. E. (1976). The effect of training in interaction analysis on the verbal teaching behaviors and attitudes of prospective school instrumental music education students studying conducting. Unpublished doctoral dissertation, Michigan State University, East Lansing.

Houston, W. R. (Ed.). (1990). *Handbook of research on teacher training.* New York: Macmillan.

Howey, K. R., and Strom, S. M. (1987). Teacher selection reconsidered. In M. Haberman and J. M. Backus (Eds.), *Advances in teacher education* (Vol. 3; pp. 1–34). Norwood: Ablex.

Hudson, L. H. (1973). A study of the effectiveness of teaching music fundamentals and methods to prospective elementary school classroom teachers using two different approaches within a course. Unpublished doctoral dissertation, Indiana University, Bloomington.

Jacobsen, J. R. (1986). Computer-assisted instruction program in music fundamentals applied to instruction for elementary education majors. Unpublished doctoral dissertation, University of Northern Colorado, Greeley.

James, R. L. (1968). A survey of teacher-training programs in music from the early musical convention to the introduction of four-year degree curricula. Unpublished doctoral dissertation, University of Maryland, College Park.

Janszen, R. H. (1962). The organization and administration of off-campus student teaching in music at selected institutions. Unpublished doctoral dissertation, Columbia University, New York.

Jordan, G. L. (1980). Supplementary instruction in beginning conducting. Unpublished doctoral dissertation, University of Illinois, Urbana.

Keene, J. A. (1982). *A history of music education in the United States.* Hanover: University Press of New England.

Kelly, M. M. (1984). The differential effects of modeling and discrimination training on selected music teaching skills, confidence level, and achievement among elementary education majors. Unpublished doctoral dissertation, Ohio State University, Columbus.

Kinder, G. A. (1987). A survey of the musical activities of classroom teachers with implication for undergraduate music courses for elementary education majors. Unpublished doctoral dissertation, Indiana University, Bloomington.

Koch, M. H. (1975). Music teacher training in the public normal schools of Wisconsin: A history focused on the school at Milwaukee. Unpublished doctoral dissertation, Northwestern University, Evanston.

Krueger, P. J. (1985). Influences of the hidden curriculum upon the perspectives of music student teachers: An ethnography. Unpublished doctoral dissertation, University of Wisconsin, Madison.

Krueger, P. J. (1987). Ethnographic research methodology in music education. *Journal of Research in Music Education, 35*(2), 69–77.

Krueger, R. J. (1976). An investigation of personality and music teaching success. *Council for Research in Music Education, 47,* 16–25.

Kwalwasser, J. (1927). *Tests and measurements in music.* Boston: Birchard.

L'Roy, D. (1983). The development of occupational identity in undergraduate music education majors. Unpublished doctoral dissertation, University of North Texas, Denton.

Lanier, J. E., and Little, J. W. (1986). Research on teacher education. In M. C. Wittrock (Ed.), *Handbook of research on teaching* (3rd ed., pp. 527–569). New York: Macmillan.

LeBlanc, J. R., Jr. (1971). The ACT test battery as a predictor of completion of a baccalaureate degree of music education. Unpublished doctoral dissertation, University of Southern Mississippi, Hattiesburg.

Lemke, W. R. (1979). A comparison of the effectiveness of a programed instructional technique and a technique using advance organizers and study questions as ancillary learning activities for brass techniques classes at the college level. Unpublished doctoral dissertation, University of Iowa, Iowa City.

Liberles, J. (1975). Developing selected musical concepts for the preservice elementary school classroom teacher utilizing programed instruction. Unpublished doctoral dissertation, Boston University School for the Arts, Boston.

Linton, S. S. (1954). Music for the preservice classroom teacher. *Journal of Research in Music Education, 2*(1), 3–10.

Logan, J. C. (1966). An analysis of in-service teacher evaluations of teacher preparatory courses in elementary school music at Florida State University. Unpublished doctoral dissertation, Florida State University, Tallahassee.

Madsen, C. K., and Duke, R. A. (1987). The effect of teacher training on the ability to recognize need for giving approval for appropriate student behavior. *Bulletin of the Council for Research in Music Education, 91,* 103–109.

McEachern, E. (1937). A survey and evaluation of the education of school music teachers in the United States. In *Contributions to education* (p. 166). New York: Columbia University, Teachers College, Bureau of Publications.

McGlothlin, D. (1970). An investigation of the efficacy of ability grouping prospective teachers enrolled in elementary music methods and materials courses. Unpublished doctoral dissertation, University of Iowa, Iowa City.

McIntyre, D. (1984). A response to the critics of field experience supervision. *Journal of Teacher Education, 35*(3), 42–45.

Medley, G. W. (1974). An identification and comparison of competencies for the pre-service education of secondary vocal music teachers in Texas. Unpublished doctoral dissertation, Texas Tech University, Lubbock.

Melton, E. E., Jr. (1973). A study of differences among various groups of Michigan State University music students. Unpublished doctoral dissertation, Michigan State University, East Lansing.

Merrell, R. C. (1973). The development and evaluation of a self-instructional packet to change the questioning techniques of music student-teachers. Unpublished doctoral dissertation, Pennsylvania State University, University Park.

Meske, E. B. (1982). Educating the music teacher: Participation in a

metamorphosis. In R. Colwell (Ed.), *Symposium in music education: A festschrift for Charles Leonhard* (pp. 249–265). Urbana-Champaign: University of Illinois.

Michelson, S. K. (1984). The use of videotaped models to teach rehearsal techniques. Unpublished doctoral dissertation, Arizona State University, Tempe.

Miller, A. W. (1987). Feasibility of instruction in instrumental music education with an interactive videodisc adapted from existing media. Unpublished doctoral dissertation, University of Illinois, Urbana.

Moore, R. S. (1976). The effects of videotaped feedback and self-evaluation forms on teaching skills, musicianship and creativity of prospective elementary teachers. *Bulletin of the Council for Research in Music Education, 47,* 1–7.

Morten, H. E. (1975). A suggested field-based teacher education program: Construction of modules for music education, their implementation and evaluation. Unpublished doctoral dissertation, University of South Dakota, Vermillion.

Mountford, R. D. (1976). Competency-based teacher education: The controversy and a synthesis of related research in music from 1964 to 1974. *Council for Research in Music Education, 46,* 1–12.

Music Educators National Conference (MENC). (1972). *Teacher education in music: Final report.* Washington: Author.

Music Educators National Conference (MENC). (1987). *Music teacher education: Partnership and process.* Reston: Author.

National Associations of Schools of Music (NASM). (1989). *1989–1990 Handbook.* Reston: Author.

Navarro, M. L. (1989). The relationship between culture, society, and music teacher education in 1938 and 1988. Unpublished doctoral dissertation, Kent State University, Kent.

Nelli, E., and Nutter, N. (1984). *A model for evaluating teacher education programs.* Washington: American Association of Colleges for Teacher Education.

Nelson, J. K. (1980). A comparison of differential feedback procedures on music teaching skills of prospective elementary and special education teachers. Unpublished doctoral dissertation, University of Texas, Austin.

Panhorst, D. L. (1971). Current practices in the evaluation of student teachers in music. *Journal of Research in Music Education, 19*(2), 204–207.

Parker, C. A. (1982). A model with four training components for pre-internship teacher education in music. Unpublished doctoral dissertation, University of Washington, Seattle.

Parkes, M. B. (1988). The development and implementation of an in-service course in comprehensive musicianship for elementary band directors: Measurement of teacher attitude shift, student attitudes and student achievement. Unpublished doctoral dissertation, University of Rochester, Eastman School of Music, Rochester.

Parr, J. D. (1976). Essential and desirable music and music-teaching competencies for first-year band instructors in the public schools. Unpublished doctoral dissertation, University of Iowa, Iowa City.

Peck, R. F., and Tucker, J. A. (1973). Research on teacher education. In R. M. W. Travers (Ed.), *Second handbook on research in teaching.* Chicago: Rand McNally.

Peterson, W. J. (1954). Training of secondary school music teachers in the undergraduate programs of colleges and universities of seventeen western states. Unpublished doctoral dissertation, University of Oregon, Eugene.

Peterson, W. J. (1955). Training of secondary school music teachers in western colleges and universities. *Journal of Research in Music Education, 3*(2), 131–135.

Peterson, W. J. (1956). The place of the performance area in training high school music teachers. *Journal of Research in Music Education, 4*(1), 52–56.

Petty, R. A. (1987). Evaluation of procedures to develop selected choral rehearsal skills with undergraduate choral methods students. Unpublished doctoral dissertation, Ohio State University, Columbus.

Platt, M. C. (1973). The history and development of the American Institute of Normal Methods, 1914–1950. *Contributions to Music Education, 2,* 31–39.

Price, H. E. (1985). A competency-based course in basic conducting techniques: A replication. *Journal of Band Research, 21,* 61–69.

Pugach, M. C. (1984). The role of selective admissions policies in the teacher education process. In L. G. Katz and J. D. Raths (Eds.), *Advances in teacher education* (Vol. 1, pp. 145–169). Norwood: Ablex.

Ramsey, D. S. (1978). Programed instruction using full-score band literature to teach pitch and rhythm error detection skill to college music education students. Unpublished doctoral dissertation, University of Iowa, Iowa City.

Reeves, J. M. (1980). Expected competencies for beginning music teachers by music supervisors, principals, college music educators and beginning music teachers: A comparative study. Unpublished doctoral dissertation, Catholic University of America, Washington.

Reifsteck, C. S. (1980). A comparison of field and peer teaching experiences on the development of music teaching competencies of pre-service elementary classroom teachers. Unpublished doctoral dissertation, Pennsylvania State University, University Park.

Reimer, B. (1985). Toward a more scientific approach to music education research. *Bulletin of the Council for Research in Music Education, 83,* 1–21.

Reimer, B. (1989). *A philosophy of music education* (2nd ed.). Englewood Cliffs: Prentice-Hall.

Reynolds, K. (1974). Modification of the observational system for instructional analysis focusing on appraisal behaviors of music teachers in small performance classes. Unpublished doctoral dissertation, Ohio State University, Columbus.

Ricks, B. S. (1974). Innovations in undergraduate music education curricula from 1968 through 1973 in colleges and universities which are members of the National Association of Schools of Music. Unpublished doctoral dissertation, University of Mississippi, Oxford.

Rosenshine, B., and Furst, N. (1973). The use of direct observation to study teaching. In R. M. W. Travers (Ed.), *Second handbook of research on teaching* (pp. 122–183). Chicago: Rand McNally.

Rosenthal, R. K. (1982). Elementary general music teacher preparation. Unpublished doctoral dissertation, Syracuse University, Syracuse.

Rosenthal, R. K. (1985). Improving teacher effectiveness through self-assessment: A case study. *Update, 3,* 17–21.

Rossman, R. L. (1977). A study of directive and non-directive counseling techniques with music student-teachers and their relationship to selected personality factors. Unpublished doctoral dissertation, Ohio State University, Columbus.

Saker, J. R. (1982). An evaluation of a videotaped simulation training program on the perceived ability of band student teachers to deal with behavior-management problems encountered during student teaching. Unpublished doctoral dissertation, University of Iowa, Iowa City.

Sarvis, G. L. (1969). An investigation of the nature and conditions of music education courses in teacher training programs in selected universities in the United States. Unpublished doctoral dissertation, University of Oregon, Eugene.

Schleuter, L. J. (1988). An analysis of elementary general music stu-dent teachers' preactive and postactive thinking about curriculum. Unpublished doctoral dissertation, Kent State University, Kent.

Schmidt, C. P. (1989). An investigation of undergraduate music education curriculum content. *Bulletin of the Council for Research in Music Education, 99,* 42–56.

Schmidt, C. P., and Hicken, L. (1986). An investigation of selected variables as predictors of achievement in music student teaching. *Contributions to Music Education, 13,* 39–47.

Shellahamer, B. R. (1984). Selection and retention criteria in undergraduate music teacher education programs: Survey, analysis, and implications. Unpublished doctoral dissertation, Ohio State University, Columbus.

Sidnell, R. G. (1967). The development of self instructional drill materials to facilitate the growth of score reading skills of student conductors. *Bulletin of the Council for Research in Music Education, 10,* 1–6.

Sidnell, R. G. (1971). Self-instructional drill materials for student conductors. *Journal of Research in Music Education, 19*(1), 85–91.

Simpkins, R. (1980). The effect of videotape feedback on the confidence of prospective elementary classroom teachers. Unpublished doctoral dissertation, Ohio State University, Columbus.

Slavin, R. E. (1984). *Research methods in education: A practical guide.* Englewood Cliffs: Prentice-Hall.

Smith, A. B. (1985). An evaluation of music teacher competencies identified by the Florida Music Educators Association and teacher assessment of undergraduate preparation to demonstrate those competencies. Unpublished doctoral dissertation, Florida State University, Tallahassee.

Smith, G. P., Miller, M. C., and Joy, J. (1988). A case study of the impact of performance-based testing on supply of minority teachers. *Journal of Teacher Education, 39*(4), 45–57.

Smith, G. S. (1975). The construction and validation of the Smith-Ryan Proficiency Teachers Examination grades K–12. *Bulletin of the Council for Research in Music Education, 44,* 1–17.

Smith, M. L. (1969). A study of elementary student-teacher confidence in and attitudes toward music and changes that occur in a student-teaching experience. Unpublished doctoral dissertation, Michigan State University, East Lansing.

Snyder, J. F. (1961). Techniques and practices for effective supervision of student-teachers in music. Unpublished doctoral dissertation, University of Nebraska, Lincoln.

Stegall, J. R. (1975). A list of competencies for an undergraduate curriculum in music education. Unpublished doctoral dissertation, University of North Carolina, Chapel Hill.

Stegall, J. R., Blackburn, J. E., and Coop, R. H. (1978). Administrators' ratings of competencies for an undergraduate music education curriculum. *Journal of Research in Music Education, 26*(1), 3–15.

Stencel, P. L. (1988). The value and feasibility of offering field-based courses as components of a master's degree program in music education for in-service teachers: The development of two models. Unpublished doctoral dissertation, University of Rochester, Eastman School of Music, Rochester.

Stuart, M. (1979). The use of videotape recordings to increase teacher trainees' error detection skills. *Journal of Research in Music Education, 27*(1), 14–19.

Tabachnick, B. R. (1980). Intern-teacher roles: Illusion, disillusion, and reality. *Journal of Education, 162,* 122–137.

Taebel, D. K. (1980). Public school music teachers' perceptions of the effect of certain competencies on pupil learning. *Journal of Research in Music Education, 28*(3), 185–197.

Taylor, B. P. (1980). The relative importance of various competencies needed by choral-general music teachers in elementary and secondary schools as rated by college supervisors, music supervisors and choral-general music teachers. Unpublished doctoral dissertation, Indiana University, Bloomington.

Travers, R. M. W. (Ed.). (1973). *Second handbook of research on teaching.* Chicago: Rand McNally.

Tunks, T. W. (1973). Attitudes of elementary classroom teachers toward elementary general music: The effects of certain aspects of preservice training. Unpublished doctoral dissertation, Michigan State University, East Lansing.

Turrentine, E. M. (1962). Predicting success in practice teaching in music. Unpublished doctoral dissertation, University of Iowa, Iowa City.

Verrastro, R. E. (1975). Verbal behavior analysis as a supervisory technique with student teachers of music. *Journal of Research in Music Education, 23*(3), 171–118.

Walker, D. E. (1972). College supervision of student-teachers in instrumental music. Unpublished doctoral dissertation, University of Northern Colorado, Greeley.

Walker, R. D. (1977). An investigation of the relationship of selected background and motivational variables to achievement in the music curriculum of undergraduate music education majors at Mississippi State University. Unpublished doctoral dissertation, Mississippi State University, State College.

Walters, D. H. (1972). The development of simulated critical teaching situations for use in instrumental music teacher education. Unpublished doctoral dissertation, Michigan State University, East Lansing.

Warnick, E. M. (1979). An inservice music teaching performance-based laboratory for classroom teachers: A feasibility study. Unpublished doctoral dissertation, Carnegie-Mellon University, Pittsburgh.

Warren, M. D. L. (1989). The development of models for inservice music teacher education based on selected school-university collaborations. Unpublished doctoral dissertation, Columbia University Teachers College, New York.

Watts, D. (1987). Student teaching. In M. Haberman and J. M. Backus (Eds.), *Advances in teacher education* (Vol. 3, pp. 151–167). Norwood: Ablex.

Waxman, H. C., and Walberg, H. J. (1986). Effects of early field experiences. In J. D. Raths and L. G. Katz (Eds.), *Advances in teacher education* (Vol. 2, pp. 165–184). Norwood: Ablex.

Whitehill, C. D. (1970). The application of Flanders' system of classroom interaction analysis to general classroom music teaching.

Unpublished doctoral dissertation, University of West Virginia, Morgantown.

Wink, R. L. (1970). The relationship of self-concept and selected personality variables to achievement in music student teaching. *Journal of Research in Music Education, 18*(3), 234–241.

Withall, J. (1951). The development of a climate index. *Journal of Educational Research, 30,* 93–99.

Wortman, H. R. (1965). A critical analysis of the student teaching program in music in selected midwestern liberal arts colleges with specific application to the program at Sioux Falls College, Sioux Falls, South Dakota. Unpublished doctoral dissertation, University of Northern Colorado, Greeley.

Wyatt, L. (1974). The development and testing of auto-tutorial instructional materials for choral conducting students. Unpublished doctoral dissertation, Florida State University, Tallahassee.

Yarbrough, C. (1978). Competency-based conducting: An exploratory study. In *Proceedings of the Symposium on Current Issues in Music Education* (Vol. 11, pp. 89–99). Columbus: Ohio State University.

Yarbrough, C. (1987). The relationship of behavioral self-assessment to the achievement of basic conducting skills. *Journal of Research in Music Education, 35*(3), 183–189.

Yarbrough, C., Wapnick, J., and Kelly, R. (1979). Effect of videotape feedback techniques on performance, verbalization, and attitude of beginning conductors. *Journal of Research in Music Education, 27*(2), 103–112.

Yee, A. H. (1969). Do cooperating teachers influence the attitudes of student teachers? *Journal of Teacher Education, 20,* 327–332.

Zeichner, K. M. (1986). Individual and institutional influences on the development of teacher perspectives. In J. D. Raths and L. G. Katz (Eds.), *Advances in teacher education* (Vol. 2, pp. 135–163). Norwood: Ablex.

Zeichner, K. M. (1987). The ecology of field experience: Toward an understanding of the role of field experiences in teacher development. In M. Haberman and J. M. Backus (Eds.), *Advances in teacher education* (Vol. 3, pp. 94–117). Norwood: Ablex.

Zimpher, N. L. (1987). Current trends in research on university supervision of student teaching. In M. Haberman and J. M. Backus (Eds.), *Advances in teacher education* (Vol. 3, pp. 118–150). Norwood: Ablex.

Zimpher, N. L., and Loadman, W. E. (1986). *A documentation and assessment system for student and program development.* Washington: American Association of Colleges for Teacher Education.

GENERAL MUSIC CURRICULUM

Maria Runfola

STATE UNIVERSITY OF NEW YORK AT BUFFALO

Joanne Rutkowski

PENNSYLVANIA STATE UNIVERSITY

Traditionally, the focus of the general music program has been singing, playing instruments, listening to music, moving to music, and creating music, the so-called fivefold program. Bergethon and Boardman (1970) added reading to this list. Boardman (1989) said that "creating, listening, and performing are musical behaviors upon which activities basic to most music education curriculums are developed" (p. 11). This activities-centered approach has provided varied and enriched music experiences for children and has been viewed as an efficient way to accomplish the ultimate goal of music education: appreciation of music, including a desire for continued participation in music.

Nonetheless, many of the recipients of this instruction have been "turned off" to music class (Steinel, 1984), even though music is viewed as important to their lives (Leming, 1987; Munsen, 1986). In this chapter, extant research on the general music curriculum as well as relevant areas is reviewed in an attempt to clarify issues that underlie the design of effective general music curricula.

Definition of Terms

The use of terms relevant to curriculum is not consistent in the literature; a discussion of several of these terms follows.

Curriculum Webster's dictionary defines "curriculum" as "the whole body of courses offered by an educational institution" (Gove, 1976, p. 557). This general definition is appropriate to represent the totality of individual courses that constitute the general music curriculum. MacDonald stated

that curriculum development should be a process of creating the best possible range of alternatives for students (1971, p. 122). Several music educators provide descriptions of curriculum. In the Manhattanville Music Curriculum Project (MMCP), for example, "curriculum" was defined as having "four constituents which must be taken into account: music, the student, the process for learning, and the educational environment; . . . Decisions on each component seriously affect the nature and objectives of the total learning program" (Thomas, 1970, p. 15). Gordon (1988) wrote that "the most important part of a music curriculum is appropriate method and when it is supported by appropriate techniques and materials, the result is ideal music education" (p. 31). Labuta (1982) concluded that "Curriculum is frequently defined in terms of experience. It consists of all of the planned and incidental experiences the child has under the direction of the school" (p. 112). In this chapter, "curriculum" refers to "an organized set of formal educational and/or training intentions" (Pratt, 1980, p. 4). "Curriculum planning" refers to the process by which that organized set of intentions is developed.

General Music The term "general music," widely used by music educators, usually refers to music instruction that takes place in a K-8 classroom setting. The outcome of this instruction is typically not performance for an audience. More recently, a concern regarding music offerings for the general student population at the senior high school level has prompted the expansion of this definition to include these students as well. The authors concur with this definition but also support Collins (1987) who has suggested that a new term be used since the word "general" implies nonspecific instruction.

Eclectic Curriculum Since the first publication of *The Eclectic Curriculum in American Music Education* (Landis and Carder, 1972), "eclectic" has been a buzzword for the potpourri of music activities available for use in the general music curriculum. More specifically, the term "eclectic" has been used to mean a combination of the approaches of Carl Orff, Zoltán Kodály, and Emile Jaques-Dalcroze. These three approaches "are vast—in philosophy, in teaching style, in material—in every important aspect save one: each is a legitimate and honest path to genuine musicianship" (Choksy, Abramson, Gillespie, and Woods, 1986, p. 342).

"Eclectic" means "selecting what appears to be best or true in various and diverse doctrines or methods . . . composed of elements drawn from various sources" (Gove, 1976, pp. 719–720). Some music educators, however, extract only activities and techniques from the approaches, so that "eclectic" has become the rationale for an activities-dominated curriculum. In an eclectic curriculum the techniques and activities should be sorted to match the objectives that they best support. The activities approach focuses on only the experience; the eclectic approach uses an activity as a means to accomplish a specific learning outcome.

Goals, Objectives, Techniques and Activities An objective is "something toward which effort is directed: an aim or end of action" (Gove, 1976, p. 1556). The term "goal" is similarly defined by Webster (Gove, 1976, p. 972). Educators generally use goal to mean broad, general purposes that are reached through accomplishing objectives. A technique, on the other hand, is "a teaching aid which is employed to achieve one or more . . . objectives" (Gordon, 1988, p. 28). Some music educators prefer to use activities rather than techniques. Labuta (1982) stated that "learning activities are not preplanned, but planned cooperatively by the teacher and pupils" (p. 114).

Eisner (1985a) offered two types of objectives, expressive and behavioral: A behavioral objective defines specific outcomes of instruction while an expressive objective deals with an experience from which each participant will probably draw different conclusions. When this is applied to music learning, it may be said that music appreciation objectives are expressive whereas objectives that systematically lead to music understanding are behavioral. Moreover, Eisner maintained that the outcomes of expressive objectives are not measurable and that they usually deal with higher levels of learning. Eisner concluded that most teachers tend to teach toward expressive objectives. Once objectives have been specified, techniques can be identified to assist in accomplishing them, but without specific objectives, the techniques, games, and activities cannot have predictable learning outcomes.

Evaluation and Research Scholars typically recognize the distinction between evaluation and research but are generally more interested in evaluation as an integral part of research. Isaac and Michael (1981) stated that evaluation and research are two distinct types of disciplined inquiry, having differing characteristics. "Research is oriented toward the development of theories and its most familiar paradigm is the experimental method, in which hypotheses are logically derived from theory and put to a test under controlled conditions" (p. 2). The emphasis on evaluation, on the other hand, "is not on theory building but on product delivery or mission accomplishment" (p. 2). The authors will maintain this distinction between evaluation and research.

Two final terms need clarification. In this chapter, "method" refers to the systematic delivery of instruction; "approach" refers to the suboptimization that may occur within, or displace, a method.

Major Influences on the General Music Curriculum

General music curricula have been affected by a great number and variety of influences, several of which are presented here. Extant research dealing with each category is reviewed.

Basic Series Textbooks Music series of the type used widely in America have been published since the 1870s (Jones, 1954), but research regarding them has been scarce. The main studies provide a historic overview of the changes that have occurred within specific time periods. For example, Diaz (1980) analyzed the elementary school music series published in the United States between 1926 and 1976. She found that the focus of objectives broadened over the 50 years from those associated only with music reading to those dealing with music understanding, performance skills, and aesthetic responsiveness. Diaz also noted a change from topical organization based on extramusical considerations to one based on music growth, and a great increase in the number and frequency of series published during that 50-year period.

Growman (1985) looked at the basic series over an 80-year period, from 1900 to 1980, and analyzed their treatment of the concepts of music and the five activities—singing, playing instruments, moving, listening, and creating. She concluded, as did Diaz, that the focus moved from singing and music reading to a more multicentered approach, but the emphasis, as well as her own analysis, centered on activities. Growman recommended that objectives of the music program from level to level be clearly articulated in the series texts.

Harris (1985) examined series texts to derive information about how a general music curriculum has been articulated over time. She used a curricular model when analyzing elementary music series published by the Silver-Burdett Company from 1885 to 1975. She compared the various series on (1) philosophy, (2) objectives, (3) methods and materials, (4) experiences provided for the students, and (5) evaluation of students. A comparison was also made of articles published by authors of the series with statements made by them in the teachers' manuals.

Harris found, as did the other researchers, that a narrow content dealing with sight-reading expanded to a more complex music program over the 90 years. Objectives were consistent with the pedagogical outlook of the period. The scope of materials greatly increased over the years and experiences reflected the "fivefold program." Harris found that few statements regarding evaluation were included, and that those were inconsistent.

The limited research conducted on basic series texts seems to indicate that the focus of most series has been on activities and generally has not provided means of student evaluation. In addition, researchers and other professionals in music education have had a decreasing influence over what is actually included in the series in spite of the fact that many teachers use these series as their sole curriculum guides.

Textbooks for Teacher Training Obviously, textbooks used in college level general music methods courses, especially if they provide the course of study for the class, can greatly influence the type of instruction provided. Research concerning the influence of college texts does not appear to have been conducted. Wunderlich (1980) developed a field-based design for an undergraduate course in elementary music methods. Her study indicated the need for cogent curriculum design: documentation of objectives, course content, procedures, and evaluation. She recommended careful attention to specification of subject matter, teaching procedures, and evaluation in college methods courses. These authors recommend an analysis of methods textbooks as well.

Current Trends and Doctrines Current trends and doctrines have had a major influence on the general music curriculum. The approaches of Kodály, Orff, Dalcroze, and more recently Boardman and Gordon have received some research attention (Beatty, 1989; Burtenshaw, 1983; Byrd, 1989; Harding, 1988; Hudgens, 1987; Munsen, 1986; Shuler, 1987). In general, most studies have investigated the efficacy of specific techniques advocated by the approaches. The results have been inconclusive. However, that these approaches are influential on general music-teaching practices is apparent from articles in the *Music Educators Journal* (MEJ; see, for example, the February 1986 issue.) Among the books published on these approaches are those by Carder (1990), Choksy (1988), Gordon (1988), Kaplan (1985), Walters and Taggart (1989), and Warner (1991). The basic series have shown a growing influence of specific doctrines, but research indicates that teaching techniques and activities continue to be emphasized rather than specific objectives based on a cogent psychology of music learning.

Teacher Experience and Preference Although teacher experience and preference undoubtedly have an effect on general music curricula, the extent of such influence has not received much study. In fact, the knowledge base regarding teachers and student teachers is limited. Krueger (1985) and Schleuter (1988) investigated factors relating to the general music curriculum in student teaching. Schleuter, who studied general music student teachers' thinking about curriculum, found that they felt they received inadequate curriculum information from their cooperating teachers prior to

planning lessons. Perhaps the teachers cannot articulate a curriculum to the student teachers because they do not have one.

Teacher effectiveness (Froelich, 1977, 1979; Polachic, 1986; Wohlfeil, 1986), teachers' perceptions of their pre-professional training (Taebel, 1980), and teachers' experience and emphasis in teaching assignments (Thompson, 1986) have also been investigated. Collins (1987) proposed the implementation of a "specialization in music teacher training to include an emphasis in general music for prospective teachers at both public school and college levels" (p. 6). It seems reasonable to assume that teachers' attitudes toward general music affect the quality of instruction. Teachers' curricular perceptions have not been studied.

State and Local School System Curriculum Guides These guides constitute perhaps one of the strongest influences on application of curriculum in the classroom. Numerous guides are available from state and local departments of education, and some have been included in Boyle (1974). Research regarding these guides has generally focused on the status of music in state and/or local programs (Barndt, 1979; Carter, 1986; Caylor, 1973; DeLaine, 1986; Jothen, 1989; Rasor, 1988; Walker, 1988). It appears that neither these curricula nor their implementation has been evaluated.

Information Disseminated by Professional Organizations A wealth of information is made available to teachers through professional journals such as MEJ, *General Music Today* (GMT), and *Update,* and books published by MENC. Except for *Update, Instructional Strategies* (Merrion, 1989) was the first attempt to provide research-based information about general music curricula to teachers. However, as Madsen stated in his foreword (Merrion, 1989), "There appears to be no consensus as to what our music education curriculum or instructional strategies should be. In this context, perhaps the primary function of this document should be to ask better questions concerning curricular substance in addition to finding effective strategies" (p. ii). The *School Music Program: Descriptions and Standards* (George, Hoffer, Lehman, and Taylor, 1986) attempted curricular recommendations; however, the authors noted that the order in which the desired outcomes are listed here does not imply any ranking according to importance or sequence of instruction (p. 16).

Tradition Both society's beliefs about music education and teachers' traditional practices strongly influence what happens in today's classrooms, yet these issues have received almost no attention by the research community. De-Ory (1989) described the role of music in society, particularly regarding music and young children. MacDonald (1971) expressed the opinion that schooling has become a process of encountering what society thinks one *ought* to learn, not what there *is* to learn. He concluded that "there is no *objectively discoverable* curriculum to be found 'out there'" (p. 121). Britton implied that the content included in the general music curriculum was affected more by social values—specifically "politeness"—than the need to provide materials for a rigorous program in music education (1966, p. 18). None of these ideas has been subjected to research.

Technological Advances Beginning with the formation, in 1911, of an education department by the Victor Talking Machine Company, advances in technology have influenced general music curricula (Miller, 1991). Recordings that were included with series texts "influenced many teachers across the nation to develop music listening programs within the general music class" (p. 1). Since that date, students have had increasing access to music via technology and media. The influence of technology on students' musical skills has received some research attention (Alpert, 1982; Boyle, Hosterman, and Ramsey, 1981; Christenson and Roberts, 1989; Frith, 1981; Killian, 1990; Sessions, 1987; Thompson, in press). Developments in computer and electronic technologies have enabled more students to create and perform music. These technological developments certainly affect the general music curricula and their effectiveness. Moore advocated "constant awareness and revision of current practice to realize technology's potential as a learning and teaching resource" (1989, p. 116).

Preparing for the Twenty-First Century

As the last decade of the twentieth century unfolds, technological innovations have the potential to revolutionize the general music curriculum and provide unimaginable opportunities for improvement of instruction. The boundaries of knowledge continue to expand; what better time for a discipline to review past performance, assess current capacities, and select goals for its future? Who is better suited or more duty bound to orchestrate that future than the musician-educators who comprise the profession? Armed with a vision of successful general music outcomes in the new century, music educators must break the cycle of focus on technique and/or activity driven general music classes and implement general music curricula based on legitimate models for curriculum development. Research should provide some models.

EXTANT MODELS FOR CURRICULA

Models for curriculum in general and music curricula in particular are presented below. Though differences do exist among these models, their similarities will be emphasized.

Eisner

Elliot Eisner (1985b) presented the following dimensions of curriculum planning, stating that "the sequence of these dimensions is, to a large degree, arbitrary" (p. 136): goals and their priorities, content of the curriculum, types of learning opportunities, organization of learning opportunities, organization of content areas, mode of presentation and mode of

response, and types of evaluation procedures. His discussion of goals and their priorities (how objectives should be formulated) included the distinction between aims, goals, and objectives, with aims being the most general and objectives the most specific. Selection of content is an important curriculum consideration usually not specified by goals. Regarding learning opportunities, Eisner stated, "educationally appropriate means must be created to enable students to interact with problems or situations that will yield an understanding of these concepts and generalizations" (p. 140).

Eisner offered two images of curricular sequences for organizing learning opportunities. The first, a "staircase model," refers to "independent steps that lead to a platform from which one exits" (p. 143). Working toward completion of a college degree is perhaps a good example. The second, a "spiderweb model," is one where "the curriculum designer provides the teacher with a set of heuristic projects, materials, and activities whose use will lead to diverse outcomes among the group of students" (p. 144). Eisner did not support one model over the other, but rather recommended application of each when appropriate. Of concern to Eisner were the "modalities through which students encounter and express what they learn" (p. 149) and evaluation, "a process that pervades curriculum decision making" (p. 152).

Taba

Hilda Taba presented a logical order for curriculum design (Parker and Rubin, 1966). Her seven steps are "diagnosis of needs, formulation of objectives, selection of content, organization of content, selection of learning experiences, organization of learning experiences, and determination of what to evaluate and of the ways and means of doing it" (Taba, 1962, p. 12).

Diagnosis determines what the curriculum should be for a particular population and is an important first step. The formulation of objectives determines "what content is important and how it should be organized" (p. 12).

The next steps, selection and organization of content, involve issues such as the validity and significance of the curriculum as well as "the making of proper distinctions between the various levels of content, and decisions about the level of development at which to introduce it . . . [and] consideration of continuities and sequences in learning and of variations in the capacity to learn" (p. 12).

Taba considered the next steps, selection and organization of learning experiences, to be vitally important. "To the extent that learning activities are used to implement some objectives, the planning and learning experiences become a part of a major strategy of curriculum building instead of being relegated to incidental decisions made by the teacher at the moment of teaching" (p. 13).

The final step asks the following questions: "How should the quality of learning be evaluated . . . ? How does one make sure that there is consistency between the aims and objectives and what is actually achieved by students? Does the curriculum organization provide experiences which offer optimum opportunities for all varieties of learners to attain independent goals?'' (p. 13).

Reimer

Bennett Reimer's (1989) model of the total curriculum, based on an initial conceptualization suggested by John Goodlad, included seven interacting phases. The values phase must be the starting point for all curriculum development: "Why and for what purpose should we educate?" (p. 153). The conceptualized phase (what?) is when the philosophy is "actuated through psychology, child development, research, the history of education, the nature of the subject(s), the structure of schools, etc." (p. 152). The systematized phase (when?) deals with the nature of the subject area and human development. The interpreted, operational, and experienced phases (how?) refer to professionals' understanding of the previous phases and their choice for implementation, the interaction of students and teachers, and what students bring to the process and undergo as a result of the previous phases. The expectational phase, which is applied to the other six phases, accounts for the influences and expectations of "students, teachers, administrators, school boards, parents, citizens, politicians" (p. 165).

Gordon

Edwin Gordon (1984) proposed an outline for a course of study. His categories were purpose, current class achievement, comprehensive objectives (music, executive, literary), sequential objectives (method, techniques, materials), individual differences (aptitude, achievement), and measurement and evaluation (p. 206). Gordon asserted that "although the purpose does not provide specific direction . . . if a teacher does not know why he is teaching music, teaching will be haphazard" (p. 206). "Sequential objectives are the core of a course of study," according to Gordon, and "appropriate method and sequential objectives become one when they are based on learning sequence" (pp. 209–210). Music aptitude must be evaluated to diagnose individual differences, and then "students' achievement of sequential objectives in learning sequence activities may be measured and evaluated" (p. 211).

Other Models

Other scholars have developed models for curriculum planning. MacDonald (1971) presented linear and circular models: "Circularity is intended to indicate a process whereby all relevant participants take part in curriculum development in a much more dynamic fashion" (p. 128). The four constituents of music curriculum as presented by the authors of MMCP are "music, the student, the process for learning, and the educational environment" (Thomas, 1970, p. 15). Gammage (1980) presented a triangle, the three points of which ("what, when, and how") interact with each other.

Edelstein, Choksy, Lehman, Sigurdsson, and Woods (1980) discussed three levels of planning: establishment of broad concepts and long-range goals, synthesis of musical elements, and development of suitable instructional procedures. Principles, aims, objectives, and experiences are the planning levels included by Tait and Haack (1984). Coates (1983) investigated a behavioral model for curriculum design based on the writings of B. F. Skinner. Sidnell (1973) presented a model with goal identification based on sociological, philosophical, and experimental research as the first step, development and implementation as the second step, and evaluation the final step. Labuta (1982) proposed six different modes of curriculum organization derived from current public school practice. These include "1) rational systems and objectives, 2) concepts, 3) materials, 4) music, 5) activities, and 6) methods" (p. 123). He did not suggest that these categories exist in pure form, but that one seems to dominate the curricular organization of a school.

Although the models presented all have their own identity, a pattern does emerge (see Table 49–1). That pattern includes the questions why, what, who, when and where, and how. Evaluation plays an important role at all stages. The premise of this chapter is to look at similarities rather than stress differences. The persons whose models were presented may not agree that the models are similar; however, disagreement would most likely involve the relative emphasis placed on each component rather than its inclusion or exclusion. The next section of this chapter reviews research that provides insight regarding the component parts of a curriculum.

DISCUSSION OF COMPONENT PARTS OF A CURRICULUM

Why?/Philosophy

All of the models stress the importance of a philosophical base for curriculum planning. Music educators use the term "philosophy" rather loosely to reflect a set of values, a widely shared point of view, or a rationale for the inclusion of a music program within the total school curriculum. However, philosophy and rationale are not synonyms: Philosophy is the ideology on which a rationale is built. Jorgensen (1990) emphasized that philosophy undergirds the music curriculum, and Reimer (1989) stated that we need "a philosophy of sufficient importance to provide a strong foundation for the curriculum built upon it" (p. 153). Our philosophical stance is fairly consistent, at least insofar as there is agreement that musical education is important for the total development of every child. Nonetheless, major differences exist regarding how our common philosophical stance is realized through goals, objectives, and techniques. Leonhard and House (1972) pointed out that every teacher's way of teaching is an expression of that teacher's philosophy, whether or not the philosophy has been expressed or critically reviewed (p. 85). To date, "philosophy" and its effect on general music curricula have not been empirically studied.

TABLE 49–1. Components of Curriculum Models.

	Why?	What?	Who?	When? Where?	How?	Evaluation
Eisner	Goals and priorities	Content		Types of learning opportunities	Organization of learning and content Modes of presentation	Evaluation procedures
Taba		Forming objectives Selecting content	Diagnose needs		Select and organize learning experiences	What and how to evaluate
Reimer	Values	Conceptualized phase		Systematized phase	Interpreted operational experienced phases	
Gordon	Purpose	Comprehensive objectives	Current class achievement Individual differences		Sequential objectives	Measurement and evaluation

What?/Content and Objectives

Selection of what should be taught and articulation of this content through objectives are basic to curriculum development. Primarily because of the differences that exist regarding implementation of philosophy, agreement regarding the content that should be included in the general music curriculum is difficult. Whereas Boardman stated that "our content has become fairly well defined" (1989, p. 2), Edelstein and colleagues (1980) had previously expressed concern regarding the specificity of content recommendations: "If the suggestions offered are too vague, teachers are left without expected guidance; if too specific, teachers may feel bound by prescribed ideas and fail to make adaptations or adjustments which would increase the benefit of the activities for their students" (p. 1). Gordon claimed that "many so-called curriculums in music education are nothing more than a compilation of techniques and the gathering of materials. Techniques and materials are used haphazardly in those programs because they are not associated with the logical order of objectives" (1988, p. 28). Kimpton (1989) believed that curriculum must be organized around specific music objectives, not music experiences given a certain group of students. Interestingly the authors of the MMCP described music education as "a series of exercises and experiences devised to assist the student to gain skills and knowledge and become involved in the art of music" (Thomas, 1970, p.1).

That is not to say that techniques and activities are not important. Learning by doing has been found to be highly effec-

tive (Ferrara, 1986; Shehan, 1985, 1986; Webster, 1990), whereas learning about music in a cognitive, theoretical manner has not been effective: "Being knowledgeable about music is not knowing music" (Webster, 1990, p. 37). However, techniques and activities must contribute to the accomplishment of a music objective. A study (Baloche, 1985) to explore "the design and implementation of an elementary school music curriculum whose materials and activities are aimed specifically at the facilitation of growth in creativity and cooperation" (p. 1549) illustrates the trap that one can fall into when objectives are not related directly to musical goals. Creativity and cooperation may be noble aims of a curriculum, but they are not the primary aims of a music curriculum.

Who?/Nature of the Student

Appropriate objectives cannot be specified without knowledge of the nature of the students, specifically knowledge of how students learn music. The psychology of music learning has been investigated by some, but knowledge about this area is sketchy. The Ann Arbor Symposium (MENC, 1981, 1983), an attempt to link current knowledge in psychology with music education, appears to have had little real impact.

Several researchers have investigated the relevance of Piaget's theory of developmental stages, particularly conservation, to music education (Hargreaves et al., 1986; Warrener, 1985; Webster and Zimmerman, 1983; Zimmerman and Sechrest, 1970), but conclusions drawn from these studies have mainly raised questions about the relevance of Piaget's theory as applied to music education.

Willmann (1983) investigated similarities between the Kodály approach and Bruner's instructional theory and concluded that the Kodály approach "is based in principles of [Bruner's] general instructional theory" (p. 822). An instructional design for music based on Asahel Woodruff's cybernetic model was created by Gjerdingen (1982). She concluded that the lessons were effective, but did not include objectives for the lessons. Learning styles of students have also been investigated (Moore, 1986; Nelson and Barresi, 1989), and results indicate relationships between learning styles and children's musical responses and abilities. Some research has also been conducted on cerebral hemispheres and their role in music. Gates and Bradshaw (1977) reported not one hemisphere dominant for music but rather an interaction between the two. Recent contributions by Gardner (1983) and Gordon (1988) cannot be ignored. Gardner has proposed a separate intelligence for music, and Gordon has provided a learning theory for "how we learn when we learn music" (1988, p. 19). One notion consistent with current learning theory in music is that aural discrimination should precede cognitive understanding (Zimmerman, 1986). As early as 1835, Lowell Mason had adopted this viewpoint from Pestalozzian educators.

Other student characteristics are relevant to planning the general music curriculum. Heller (1990), in a review of recent research on student characteristics, affirmed that age and grade level, music aptitude, music achievement, interest, and handicapping conditions all affect music learning. Teachers should also consider the musical capabilities of students, because this information would inform the specification of objectives and the selection of content. Auditory memory has been investigated by Moore and Staum (1987) and Walker (1987); they generally concluded that tonal memory improves with age and that all children can hear differences in pitch but not all can attribute that change to pitch. In related studies, Dittemore (1968) and DeYarman (1972) found that children who sang in a variety of modes actually sang more accurately in major and minor than those students who sang only in major and minor.

This research is a sample of what has been undertaken regarding the nature of music students. The psychology of learning applied to music learning perhaps needs to be utilized by the profession and to receive more attention by the research community. More knowledge about how music is learned is necessary if appropriate curricula are to be established.

When? and Where?/Context

When and where instruction takes place should also be of concern in developing curricula. According to MacDonald (1971), curriculum developers have failed "to respond to the total context of our curriculum needs and problems" (p. 121). The nature of the community and its accompanying social forces, the needs of the students within that community, and the political and social nature of the school institution, as well as seemingly mundane issues such as teaching space, materials and equipment availability, and scheduling, are all valid considerations when planning curricula. Research on how these matters affect music learning is almost nonexistent. Hale [Runfola] (1977) found that kindergarten children who attend music class twice a week achieve significantly more than those children who attend music class only once a week. Rutkowski (1990) also concluded that frequency, rather than total amount of instruction, may significantly affect students' music achievement. The School Music Program: Descriptions and Standards (George et al., 1986), a document that makes recommendations for "When? and Where?," stated that in a basic program "each child, K–6, receives music instruction in school at least three times weekly" (p. 24) and that for grades 6–8/ 7–9 "nonperformance classes meet for a minimum of 90 class periods each year" (p. 33). These issues need to be addressed empirically to provide a knowledge base for curriculum development.

How?/Techniques, Activities and Materials

Certainly, how content is presented to students and how the techniques and materials are used for attaining objectives are of importance. Content may be presented as a whole (many concepts presented simultaneously), or in parts (content presented independently). Comprehensive musicianship (Burton and Thompson, 1982a,b, 1983a,b) is an example of a whole approach, whereas MMCP (Thomas, 1970), which presents elements interdependently, and Jump Right In: The Music Curriculum (Gordon and Woods, 1986), which presents rhythm and tonal concept development separately, are examples of a more ontogenetic approach.

The use of whole versus elements in content presentation has received little research attention. Individual techniques, activities, and materials, however, have been well studied, most importantly by Clifford Madsen and those whom he has influenced. These studies have been covered in other chapters, and only a few representative areas will be mentioned here. The activities of the fivefold general music program are well represented in the research: singing and melodic/tonal activities (Forsythe and Kelley, 1989; Goetze et al., 1990; Gould, 1966; Hale [Runfola], 1977; Kavanaugh, 1982; Oura, 1987; Stafford, 1987); moving and rhythmic activities (Callen, 1985; Colley, 1987; Kluth, 1986; Kuhn and Booth, 1988; Ludowise, 1985; Schleuter and Schleuter, 1985; Searle, 1985; Shehan, 1987; Wang, 1984); listening (Baldridge, 1984; Bartlett, 1973; Brinson, 1986; Goolsby, 1984; Haack, 1966; Kirschenmann, 1970; Shehan, 1975); creating (DeLorenzo, 1987, 1989; Pogonowski, 1985); and playing instruments (Charboneau, 1980; Nebb, 1988; Wig and Boyle, 1982). Cliatt (1975) established criteria for selecting music activities.

The use of media and computer technology has been well researched (Deal, 1985; King, 1988; Mee, 1988; Prevel, 1982; Turk, 1984; Whiston, 1986; Willett and Netusil, 1989). The selection and evaluation of materials have also been investigated (Bledsoe, 1984; Curry, 1982; Diaz, 1980; Rhoden, 1969; Roberts, 1982; Rutkowski, 1986). Although music educators are to be commended for the vast amount of research on techniques and materials, well-integrated behavioral objectives must be available to guide the use of these techniques.

Finally, student attitudes and preferences should not be ignored when selecting techniques, activities, and materials. Students' identification of their music activity preferences makes planning and implementing general music programs more efficient and enjoyable. Research has shown, generally, that achievement is enhanced when students are encouraged to assist in choosing class activities (Combs, 1962, 1979; Mc-Cully, 1979; Purkey, 1970, 1978). In addition, Maslow (cited in Combs, 1962) stated that, "in the normal development of the normal child, it is now known that most of the time, if he is given a really free choice, he will choose what is good for his growth" (p. 39). Some representative studies dealing with attitudes and preferences of general music students include Bowman (1988), Finnäs (1989), Gernet (1940), Hargreaves (1984), Hargreaves and Castell (1987), LeBlanc and Cote (1983), LeBlanc and McCrary (1983); May (1985), Pearsall (1980), Prince (1974); Pogonowski (1983, 1985); Seidenberg (1986), and Thompson (in press).

Evaluation

Evaluation of student achievement of objectives is an essential step in curriculum development. Therefore, identifying appropriate and valid measurement instruments is necessary. "Planning new curricula and revising the old necessitate a look at objectives and the ways in which achievement of these objectives can be measured" (Colwell, 1974, p. 127). Boyle and Radocy (1987) advocated that evaluation "is an essential and critical aspect of the music curriculum" (p. 285). Since techniques and objectives have often been confused, evaluation of the success of instruction has frequently been confined to questions such as whether or not students remained on-task or appeared to be enjoying themselves. A thorough presentation of program evaluation is included in *Measurement and Evaluation of Musical Experiences* (Boyle and Radocy, 1987). A few curricula have been designed, implemented, and evaluated (Fitzpatrick, 1968; Kimpton, 1989; McCaskill, 1989; Nelson, 1988; Paraskevopoulos, 1989; Quay, 1987; Reimer, 1967; Scarborough, 1979). Unfortunately, many of these evaluated curricula were designed for a particular research project and have not been implemented on a larger scale. Conversely, the curricula that are most often implemented, those of state and local education agencies, have not been evaluated in any formal sense. Kuehmann (1987) followed curriculum design principles when developing a theoretical model for a general music curriculum for fundamentalist Christian elementary schools; however, the model does not appear to have been evaluated.

TO PROVE OR TO IMPROVE?

Much research that pertains to the general music curriculum is quasi-experimental. Although numerous studies of this type have been, and continue to be, conducted, researchers appear to be 'doing their own thing' in an effort to justify personal pedagogical choices. A more concerted, coordinated effort is needed as well as "large-scale, long term research, which is notable, in music education, by its almost complete absence" (Reimer, 1985; p. 17).

The focus of current and past research is generally "to prove"; is research, then, enough when dealing with curricular issues? Perhaps evaluation, with its purpose "to improve," is a more reasonable and appropriate method of disciplined inquiry as a tool for shaping the general music curriculum. Evaluation studies take much time, effort, and money.

Usually, less energy is required to get knowledge than is required to develop and perfect the means by which to use it. Furthermore, because knowledge is cumulative one can draw upon a store of existing knowledge gained from experience and research spanning centuries of intellectual effort. On the other hand, the actual development requires a contemporary design, the selection and/or production of materials, the cooperation and education of those who are to employ the new program, continuing evaluation of its effectiveness, and making improvements as needed. Both research and development are important . . . but their relative costs are different. (Tyler, 1975, pp. 168–169)

CONCLUSIONS

The large amount of research that has been conducted in music education illustrates the complexity of the discipline. Part of that complexity is caused by music's dependency on more than one learning domain in sequencing learning in the classroom. Recalcitrant problems are encountered when teaching such a discipline (Colwell, 1987). Accordingly, a great deal of sophistication is needed in order to design, implement, and evaluate effective curricula. This fact poses a dilemma to the profession: Should there be a national curriculum guide for general music developed by curriculum specialists and music education scholars that teachers could adapt to local needs, or should the general music curriculum be developed independently at the local level by teachers? In either case, are teachers being prepared to cope with and select from the diversity of information that is available to them? Is the inability to cope with information overload the reason why so many teachers latch onto an activities and/or techniques driven program? The students "who attend American schools are entitled to encounter [general music] educational programs that result from the application of the most sophisticated tools that we have available" and "to create such programs will probably require not less sophistication and insight into the processes of learning, but more sophistication'' (Eisner, 1971, p. 164).

In order to accomplish this lofty goal, the scholars within the profession must begin to work together, emphasizing their similarities rather than their differences. The lack of research objectives that stimulate creative thinking may have contributed to this isolation.

Whatever the outcome of future research efforts, it remains in the province of each teacher to apply or not to apply research-based knowledge in instruction. The teacher faces many nonresearch-related pressures from students, administrators, colleagues, family members, and citizens in the community; research-based instruction may meet with initial difficulties in its implementation. Eisner (1971) is right: American students deserve the best we can offer. Success requires that teachers have not only knowledge but also the courage to use it.

References

Alpert, J. (1982). The effect of disc jockey, peer, and music teacher approval of music on music selection and preference. *Journal of Research in Music Education, 30*(3), 173–186.

Baldridge, W. R. (1984). A systematic investigation of listening activities in the elementary general music classroom. *Journal of Research in Music Education, 32*(2), 79–93.

Baloche, L. (1985). Facilitating creativity and group-cooperative skills in the elementary music classroom: A model, a curriculum, and a study (poetry, imagery). Unpublished doctoral dissertation, Temple University, Philadelphia.

Barndt, J. G. (1979). A survey and study of current practices and problems in music education in accredited and nonaccredited public and nonpublic secondary schools in Pennsylvania. Unpublished master's thesis, Temple University, Philadelphia.

Bartlett, D. L. (1973). Effect of repeated listenings on structural discrimination and affective response. *Journal of Research in Musical Education, 21*(4), 302–317.

Beatty, R. J. (1989). A comparative study of a Kodály-based developmental music program and a traditional public school music program at the kindergarten level. Unpublished master's thesis, Queen's University, Kingston.

Bledsoe, J. C. (1984). Efficacy of popular music in learning music concepts in seventh grade music classes. *Psychological Reports, 54*(2), 381–382.

Boardman, E. (Ed.). (1989). *Dimensions of musical thinking.* Reston: Music Educators National Conference.

Bowman, B. A. (1988). A cross sectional descriptive study of intermediate elementary students' attitudes toward school music activities. Unpublished doctoral dissertation, University of Kansas, Lawrence.

Boyle, J. D., (ed.) (1974). *Instructional objectives in music.* Vienna: Music Educators National Conference, National Commission of Instruction.

Boyle, J. D., Hosterman, G. L., and Ramsey, D. S. (1981). Factors influencing pop music preferences of young people. *Journal of Research in Music Education, 29*(1), 47–56.

Boyle, J. D., and Radocy, R. E. (1987). *Measurement and evaluation of musical experiences.* New York: Schirmer Books.

Brinson, B. A. (1986). Individualized listening modules for the high school student in general music. Unpublished doctoral dissertation, Florida State University, Tallahassee.

Britton, A. (1966). Music education: An American specialty. In B. C. Kowall (Ed.), *Perspectives in music education: Sourcebook III,* (pp. 15–28). Washington: Music Educators National Conference.

Burtenshaw, L. J. (1983). The construction and validation of a criterion-referenced test to measure the musical outcomes of the upper elementary school pupils instructed in the Kodály method in the U.S.A. (United States). Unpublished doctoral dissertation, University of Colorado, Boulder.

Burton, L. H., and Thompson, W. (Eds.). (1982a). *Music: Comprehensive musicianship program. Teacher text. Grade 6.* Hawaii University, Honolulu: Curriculum Research & Development Group.

Burton, L. H., and Thompson, W. (Eds.). (1982b). *Music: Comprehensive musicianship program. Grade 6.* Hawaii University, Honolulu: Curriculum Research & Development Group.

Burton, L. H., and Thompson, W. (Eds.). (1983a). *Music: Comprehensive musicianship program. Teacher Text. Grade 5.* Hawaii University, Honolulu: Curriculum Research & Group.

Burton, L. H., and Thompson, W. (Eds.). (1983b). *Music: Comprehensive musicianship program. Grade 5.* Hawaii University, Honolulu: Curriculum Research & Development Group.

Byrd, M. E. (1989). A comparative analysis of Edwin Gordon's approach to sequential musical learning and learning sequences found in three elementary general music series (music learning). Unpublished doctoral dissertation, University of Illinois, Urbana.

Callen, D. M. (1985). Moving to music—for better appreciation. *Journal of Aesthetic Education, 19*(3), 37–50.

Carder, P. (Ed.). (1990). *The eclectic curriculum in American music education* (rev. ed.). Reston: Music Educators National Conference.

Carter, K. G. (1986). The status of vocal/general music programs in Oklahoma elementary schools. Unpublished doctoral dissertation, University of Oklahoma, Norman.

Caylor, F. B. (1973). Contemporary practices and problems in music education in the elementary public schools of the United States: A survey and study. Unpublished doctoral dissertation, Walden University, Minneapolis.

Charboneau, M. L. (1980). The effect of bell playing instruction and music listening on kindergarten students' preferences and attitudes. Unpublished doctoral dissertation, Syracuse University, Syracuse.

Choksy, L. (1988). *The Kodály method: Comprehensive music education from infant to adult* (2nd ed.). Englewood Cliffs: Prentice-Hall.

Choksy, L., Abramson, R. M., Gillespie, A. E., and Woods, D. (1986). *Teaching music in the twentieth century.* Englewood Cliffs: Prentice-Hall.

Christenson, P. G., and Roberts, D. F. (1989). *Popular music in early adolescence.* Carnegie Council on Adolescent Development.

Cliatt, M. J. P. (1975). Criteria for the selection of music activities for young children. Unpublished doctoral dissertation, University of Mississippi, Oxford.

Coates, P. S. (1983). Music education: A behavioral model for curriculum design. Unpublished doctoral dissertation, Georgia State University, Atlanta.

Colley, B. (1987). A comparison of syllabic methods for improving rhythm literacy. *Journal of Research in Music Education, 35*(4), 221-235.

Collins, I. (1987). General music: A call for reform. *General Music Today, 1*(1), 3-6.

Colwell, R. (1987). Test item difficulty and perception. *Bulletin of the Council for Research in Music Education, 91*, 19-22.

Colwell, R. J. (1974). Musical achievement: Difficulties and directions in evaluation. In J. P. Boyle (Ed.) *Instructional objectives in music* (pp. 127-135). Vienna: Music Educators National Conference.

Combs, A. W. (1962). *Perceiving, behaving, becoming: A new focus for education.* Washington: Association for Supervision and Curriculum Development.

Combs, A. W. (1979). *Myths in education: Beliefs that hinder progress and their alternatives.* Boston: Allyn & Bacon.

Curry, B. A. B. (1982). An evaluation of African and Afro-American music in selected elementary music textbook series and recommendations for supplemental song materials. Unpublished doctoral dissertation, University of Houston, Houston.

Deal, J. J. (1985). Computer-assisted instruction in pitch and rhythm error detection. *Journal of Research in Music Education, 33*(3), 159-166.

DeLaine, T. H. (1986). The status of music education in the public schools of Maryland, 1983-84 (program, curriculum, elementary, high school, arts). Unpublished doctoral dissertation, Catholic University of America, Washington.

DeLorenzo, L. C. (1987). An exploratory field study of sixth grade students' creative music problem solving processes in the general music class. Unpublished doctoral dissertation, Columbia University Teachers College, New York.

DeLorenzo, L. C. (1989). Field study of sixth-grade students' creative music problem-solving processes. *Journal of Research in Music Education, 37*(3), 188-200.

De-Ory, E. Z. (1989). Young children and music making. *Early Child Development and Care, 44*, 73-85.

DeYarman, R. M. (1972). An experimental analysis of the development of rhythmic and tonal capabilities of kindergarten and first grade children. In E. E. Gordon (Ed.), *Experimental research in the psychology of music* (Vol., pp. 1-44). Iowa City: University of Iowa Press.

Diaz, M. C. (1980). An analysis of the elementary school music series published in the United States from 1926 to 1976. Unpublished doctoral dissertation, University of Illinois, Urbana.

Dittemore, E. E. (1968). An investigation of some musical capabilities of elementary school students. Unpublished doctoral dissertation, University of Iowa, Iowa City.

Documentary report of the Ann Arbor Symposium: Applications of Psychology to the Teaching and Learning of Music. (1981). Reston: Music Educators National Conference.

Documentary report of the Ann Arbor Symposium session III: Applications of Psychology to the Teaching and Learning of Music. (1983). Reston: Music Educators National Conference.

Edelstein, S., Choksy, L., Lehman, P., Sigurdsson, N., and Woods, D. (1980). *Creating curriculum in music.* Reading: Addison-Wesley Publishing Company.

Eisner, E. W. (1971). Persistent dilemmas in curriculum decision-making. In E. Eisner (Ed.), *Confronting curriculum reform.* Boston: Little, Brown and Company.

Eisner, E. W. (1985a). *The art of educational evaluation: A personal view.* London: The Falmer Press.

Eisner, E. W. (1985b). *The educational imagination: On the design and evaluation of school programs* (2nd ed.). New York: Macmillan Publishing Company.

Ferrara, L. (1986). Music in general studies: A look at content and method. *College Music Symposium, 26*, 122-129.

Finnäs, L. (1989). How can musical preferences be modified? A research review. *Bulletin of the Council for Research in Music Education, 102*, 1-58.

Fitzpatrick, J. B. (1968). The development and evaluation of a curriculum in music listening skills on the seventh grade level. Unpublished doctoral dissertation, University of Iowa, Iowa City.

Forsythe, J. L., and Kelley, M. M. (1989). Effects of visual-spatial added cues on fourth-graders' melodic discrimination. *Journal of Research in Music Education, 37*(4), 272-277.

Frith, S. (1981). *Sound effects: Youth, leisure, and the politics of rock 'n' roll.* New York: Pantheon Books.

Froehlich, H. C. (1977). An investigation of the relationships of selected observational variables to the teaching of singing. Unpublished doctoral dissertation, University of Texas, Austin.

Froehlich, H. C. (1979). Replication of a study on teaching singing in the elementary general music classroom. *Journal of Research in Music Education, 1*(3), 3-6.

Gammage, P. (1980). School curricula—A social-psychological view. In L. G. Katz (Ed.), *Current topics in early childhood education* (Vol. III). Norwood: Ablex Publishing Corporation.

Gardner, H. (1983). *Frames of mind: The theory of multiple intelligences.* New York: Basic Books.

Gates, A., and Bradshaw, J. L. (1977). The role of the cerebral hemispheres in music. *Brain and Language, 4*(3), 403-431.

George, W. E., Hoffer, C. R., Lehman, P. R., and Taylor, R. G., (Eds.) (1986). *The school music program: Description and standards* (2nd ed.). Reston: Music Educators National Conference.

Gernet, S. K. (1940). *Musical discrimination at various age and grade levels.* College Place: The College Press.

Gjerdingen, K. M. (1982). An instructional design for the music classroom based on Asahel Woodruff's cybernetic model. Unpublished doctoral dissertation, Arizona State University, Tempe.

Goetze, M., Cooper, N., and Brown, C. J. (1990). Recent research on singing in the general music classroom. *Bulletin of the Council for Research in Music Education, 104*, 16-37.

Goolsby, T. W. (1984). Music education as aesthetic education: Concepts and skills for the appreciation of music. *Journal of Aesthetic Education, 18*(4), 15-44.

Gordon, E. E. (1984). *Learning sequences in music: Skill, content, and patterns.* Chicago: G. I. A. Publications.

Gordon, E. E. (1988). *Learning sequences in music: Skill, content, and patterns.* Chicago: G. I. A. Publications.

Gordon, E. E., and Woods, O. (1986). *Jump right in: The music curriculum.* Chicago: G. I. A. Publications.

Gould, A. O. (1966). *Developing specialized programs for singing in the elementary school: Interim report* (Report No. CRP-3047 (2541). Macomb: Western Illinois University. (ERIC Document Reproduction Service No. ED 010 527)

Gove, P. B. (Ed.). (1976). *Webster's third new international dictionary, unabridged.* Springfield: G. & C. Merriam.

Growman, F. (1985). The emergence of the concept of general music as reflected in basal textbooks: 1900—1980. Unpublished doctoral dissertation, Catholic University of America, Washington.

Haack, P. A. (1966). A study of two approaches to the development of music listening skills within the context of the music appreciation class for secondary school students. Unpublished doctoral dissertation, University of Wisconsin, Madison.

Hale, M. [Runfola] (1977). An experimental study of the comparative effectiveness of harmonic and melodic accompaniment in singing as it relates to the development of a sense of tonality. *Bulletin of the Council for Music Education, 53,* 23–30.

Harding, M. H. (1988). Improving music skills of elementary students with notation-reading and sight-singing. Unpublished doctoral dissertation, Nova University, Ft. Lauderdale.

Hargreaves, D. J. (1984). The effects of repetition of liking for music. *Journal of Research in Music Education, 32*(1), 35–47.

Hargreaves, D. J., Castell, K. C., and Crowther, R. D. (1986). The effects of stimulus familiarity on conservation-type responses to tone sequences: A cross cultural study. *Journal of Research in Music Education, 34*(2), 88–100.

Hargreaves, D. J., and Castell, K. C. (1987). Development of liking for familiar and unfamiliar melodies. *Bulletin of the Council for Research in Music Education, 91,* 65–69.

Harris, J. N. (1985). The instructional philosophies reflected in the elementary music series published by Silver Burdett Company. Unpublished doctoral dissertation, University of Illinois, Urbana.

Heller, G. N. (1990). Research on student characteristics: Important considerations in planning music instruction. *Update, 8,* 6–10.

Hudgens, C. K. K. (1987). A study of the Kodály approach to music teaching and an investigation of four approaches to the teaching of selected skills in first grade music classes. Unpublished doctoral dissertation, University of North Texas, Denton.

Isaac, S., and Michael, W. B. (1981). *Handbook in research and evaluation.* San Diego: Edits Publishers.

Jones, W. R. (1954). An analysis of public school music textbooks before 1900. Unpublished doctoral dissertation, University of Pittsburgh, Pittsburgh.

Jorgensen, E. R. (1990). Philosophy and the music teacher: Challenging the way we think. *Music Educators Journal, 76*(5), 17–23.

Jothen, M. (1989). Steps to a successful curriculum. *Music Educators Journal, 75*(7), 40–43.

Kaplan, B., (Ed.). (1985). *Concept: A bibliography for music education. Kodály: A dynamic tradition I.* Whitewater: Organization of American Kodály Educators.

Kavanaugh, J. M. (1982). The development of vocal concepts in children: The methodologies recommended in designated elementary music series. Unpublished doctoral dissertation, University of North Texas, Denton.

Killian, J. N. (1990). Effect of model characteristics on musical preferences of junior high students. *Journal of Research in Music Education, 38*(2), 115–123.

Kimpton, J. (1989). Toward curricular accountability: A case study in music. *Music Educators Journal, 76*(4), 34–36.

King, R. V. (1988). The effects of computer-assisted music instruction on achievement of seventh-grade students. Unpublished doctoral dissertation, University of Illinois, Urbana.

Kirschenmann, W. P. (1970). The teaching of music listening skills to elementary school children. Unpublished doctoral dissertation, University of Northern Colorado, Greeley.

Kluth, B. L. (1986). A procedure to teach rhythm reading: Development, implementation, and effectiveness in urban junior high school general music classes. Unpublished doctoral dissertation, Kent State University, Kent.

Krueger, P. J. (1985). Influences of the hidden curriculum upon the perspectives of music student teachers: An ethnography. Unpublished doctoral dissertation, University of Wisconsin, Madison.

Kuehmann, K. M. (1987). A theoretical model for curriculum development in general music for fundamentalist Christian elementary schools. Unpublished doctoral dissertation, Arizona State University, Tempe.

Kuhn, T. L., and Booth, G. D. (1988). The effect of melodic activity, tempo change, and audible beat on tempo perception of elemen-

tary school students. *Journal of Research in Music Education, 36*(3), 140–155.

Labuta, J. A. (1982). Curriculum development for music education. In R. Colwell (Ed.), *Symposium in music education: A festschrift for Charles Leonhard.* Urbana-Champaign: University of Illinois.

Landis, B., and Carder, P. (1972). *The eclectic curriculum in American music education: Contributions of Dalcroze, Kodály, and Orff.* Washington: Music Educators National Conference.

LeBlanc, A., and Cote, R. (1983). Effects of tempo and performing medium on children's music preference. *Journal of Research in Music Education, 31*(1), 57–66.

LeBlanc, A., and McCrary, J. (1983). Effect of tempo on children's music preference. *Journal of Research in Music Education 31*(4), 283–294.

Leming, J. (1987). Rock music and the socialization of moral values in early adolescence. *Youth and Society, 18*(4), 363–383.

Leonhard, C., and House, R. (1972). *Foundations and principles of music education* (2nd ed.). New York: McGraw Hill.

Ludowise, K. D. (1985). Movement to music: Ten activities that foster creativity. *Childhood Education, 62*(1), 40–43.

McCaskill, M. E. (1989). A comparative study of general music education curricula in elementary schools of the United States of America and the Russian Soviet Federation Socialist Republic. Unpublished doctoral dissertation, University of Kentucky, Lexington.

McCully, T. M. (1979). Curriculum planning: Teacher concerns in affective learning. Unpublished doctoral dissertation, SUNY, Buffalo.

MacDonald, J. B. (1971). Responsible curriculum development. In E. Eisner (Ed.), *Confronting curriculum reform.* Boston: Little, Brown and Company.

May, W. V. (1985). Musical style preferences and aural discrimination skills of primary grade school children. *Journal of Research in Music Education, 33*(1), 7–22.

Mee, R. A. (1988). The integration and evaluation of 'Musicland' in a music listening course and acoustics course for tenth grade students (CAI). Unpublished doctoral dissertation, University of Rochester, Eastman School of Music, Rochester.

Merrion, M., (Ed.). (1989). *What works: Instructional strategies for music education.* Reston: Music Educators National Conference.

Miller, S. D. (1991). 'The Music Hour' (1927–1941) and its pioneer listening-appreciation program. *The Bulletin of Historical Research in Music Education, 12*(1), 1–12.

Moore, B. R. (1986). Music composition and learning style: The relationship between curriculum and learner. Unpublished doctoral dissertation, University of Wisconsin, Madison.

Moore, B. (1989). Musical thinking and technology. In E. Boardman (Ed.), *Dimensions of musical thinking.* Reston: Music Educators National Conference.

Moore, R. S., and Staum, M. (1987). Effect of age and nationality on auditory/visual sequential memory of English and American children. *Bulletin of the Council for Research in Music Education, 91,* 126–131.

Munsen, S. C. (1986). A description and analysis of an Orff-Schulwerk program of music education (improvisation). Unpublished doctoral dissertation, University of Illinois, Urbana.

Nebb, G. D. (1988). Improving sixth graders' basic music skills and developing compositional skills through the use of the ukulele. Unpublished doctoral dissertation, Nova University, Ft. Lauderdale.

Nelson, B. J. P. (1988). The development of a middle school general music curriculum: A synthesis of computer-assisted instruction and music learning theory (CAI). Unpublished doctoral dissertation, University of Rochester, Eastman School of Music, Rochester.

Nelson, D. J., and Barresi, A. L. (1989). Children's age-related intellectual strategies for dealing with musical and spatial analogical tasks. *Journal of Research in Music Education, 37*(2), 93–103.

Oura, Y. (1987). *What kind of knowledge facilitates memory of melodies?* Presented at the 9th biennial meeting of the International Society for the Study of Behavioral Development. Tokyo, Japan.

Paraskevopoulos, A. A. (1989). Metaphor and knowledge: Exploring the cognitive aspects of music through the development of a workbook for the study of notation in junior high school. Unpublished doctoral dissertation, Columbia University Teachers College, New York.

Parker, J. C., and Rubin, L. J. (1966). *Process as content: Curriculum design and the application of knowledge.* Chicago: Rand McNally & Company.

Pearsall, G. K. (1980). A curriculum for ninth grade general music: Meeting student needs through areas of designated interest (Vol. I, II). Unpublished doctoral dissertation, Carnegie-Mellon University, Pittsburgh.

Pogonowski, L. M. (1983). Attitudinal assessment of upper elementary students in a process-oriented music curriculum. Unpublished doctoral dissertation, Temple University, Philadelphia.

Pogonowski, L. M. (1985). Attitude assessment of upper elementary students in a process-oriented music curriculum. *Journal of Research in Music Education, 33*(4), 247–257.

Polachic, R. W. (1986). Selective descriptors of teacher effectiveness in elementary music education in Medicine Hat, Alberta. Unpublished doctoral dissertation, University of Oregon, Eugene.

Pratt, D. (1980). *Curriculum design and development.* New York: Harcourt Brace Jovanovich.

Prevel, M. (1982). The development of open drills in the context of computer-based ear training. *Journal of Computer Based Instruction, 9*(2), 74–77.

Prince, W. F. (1974). Effects of guided listening on musical enjoyment of junior high school students. *Journal of Research in Music Education, 22*(1), 45–51.

Purkey, W. W. (1970). *Self-concept and school achievement.* Englewood Cliffs: Prentice-Hall.

Purkey, W. W. (1978). *Inviting school success: A self-concept approach to teaching and learning.* Belmont: Wadsworth Publishing.

Quay, J. S. (1987). The differential effects associated with two music curricula on eighth grade students. Unpublished doctoral dissertation, University of Cincinnati, Cincinnati.

Rasor, S. H. (1988). A study and analysis of general music education, K–8, in the public schools of Ohio, 1987. Unpublished doctoral dissertation, University of Cincinnati, Cincinnati.

Reimer, B. (1967). *Development and trial in a junior and senior high school of a two-year curriculum in general music.* Cleveland: Case Western Reserve University.

Reimer, B. (1985). Towards a more scientific approach to music education. *Bulletin of the Council for Research in Music Education, 83,* 1–21.

Reimer, B. (1989). *A philosophy of music education* (2nd ed.). Englewood Cliffs: Prentice Hall.

Rhoden, J. O. (1969). A history of music written for preschool children. Unpublished doctoral dissertation, Florida State University, Tallahassee.

Roberts, M. B. (1982). A comparison of elementary general music educator practices and rationale for the inclusion of musical variety in aesthetic education toward broadening musical taste. Unpublished doctoral dissertation, Washington University, St. Louis.

Rutkowski, J. (1986). The effect of restricted song range on kindergarten children's use of singing voice and developmental music aptitude. Unpublished doctoral dissertation, State University of New York, Buffalo.

Rutkowski, J. (1990). *The comparative effectiveness of individual and group singing activities on kindergarten children's use of singing voice and developmental music aptitude.* Presented at the national meeting of the Music Educators National Conference. Washington, DC.

Scarborough, I. G. (1979). General music in the secondary school: A curricular framework for program development. Unpublished doctoral dissertation, George Peabody College for Teachers of Vanderbilt University, Nashville.

Schleuter, L. J. (1988). An analysis of elementary general music student teachers' preactive and postactive thinking about curriculum. Unpublished doctoral dissertation, Kent State University, Kent.

Schleuter, S. L., and Schleuter, L. J. (1985). The relationship of grade level and sex differences to certain rhythmic responses of primary grade children. *Journal of Research in Music Education, 33*(1), 23–29.

Searle, J. W. (1985). An investigation of movement to music and rhythmic pattern reading flash-slide training in fifth- and sixth-grade music classes. Unpublished doctoral dissertation, University of Michigan, Ann Arbor.

Seidenberg, F. P. D. (1986). Students' preferences and attitudes toward music in school. Unpublished doctoral dissertation, University of Southern California, Los Angeles.

Sessions, G. L. (1987). Adolescent identity formation, regressions, and music videos. Unpublished doctoral dissertation, California School of Professional Psychology, Berkeley/Alameda.

Shehan, P. (1975). The effects of two methods of teaching basic music concepts utilizing twentieth-century music. Unpublished doctoral dissertation, Washington University, St. Louis.

Shehan, P. (1985). To educate is to activate. *Music Educators Journal, 71*(8), 41–43.

Shehan, P. K. (1986). Major approaches to music education: An account of method. *Music Educators Journal, 72*(6), 26–31.

Shehan, P. K. (1987). Effects of rote versus note presentations on rhythm learning and retention. *Journal of Research in Music Education, 35*(2), 117–162.

Shuler, S. C. (1987). The effects of Gordon's learning sequence activities on music achievement. Unpublished doctoral dissertation, University of Rochester, Eastman School of Music, Rochester.

Sidnell, R. (1973). *Building instructional programs in music education.* Englewood Cliffs: Prentice-Hall.

Stafford, D. W. (1987). Perceptions of competencies and preparation needed for guiding young singers in elementary school music classes. Unpublished doctoral dissertation, Florida State University, Tallahassee.

Steinel, D. V. (Ed.). (1984). *Music and music education: Data and information.* Reston: Music Educators National Conference.

Taba, H. (1962). *Curriculum development theory and practice.* New York: Harcourt, Brace and World, Inc.

Taebel, D. K. (1980). Public school music teachers' perceptions of the effect of certain competencies on pupil learning. *Journal of Research in Music Education, 28*(3), 185–197.

Tait, M., and Haack, P. (1984). *Principles and processes of music education: New perspectives.* New York: Teachers College Press.

Thomas, R. (1970). *MMCP synthesis.* Bardonia: Media Materials.

Thompson, K. P. (1986). Status of music in Pennsylvania schools. *Pennsylvania Music Educators Association Bulletin of Research, 17,* 1–24.

Thompson, K. P. (in press). Media, music, and adolescents. In R. Lerner (Ed.), *Early adolescence: Perspectives on research, policy, and intervention.* Hillsdale: Lawrence Erlbaum Associates.

Turk, G. C. (1984). Development of the music listening strategy—

tempo: Computer assisted instruction in music listening. Unpublished doctoral dissertation, University of Kansas, Lawrence.

Tyler, R. W. (1975). The school of the future: Needed research and development. In L. Rubin (Ed.), *The future of education: Perspectives on tomorrow's schooling.* Boston: Allyn & Bacon.

Walker, B. C. (1988). The status of elementary school general music programs in selected elementary schools in the Charlotte-Mecklenburg County school system in North Carolina. Unpublished doctoral dissertation, University of North Carolina, Greensboro.

Walker, R. (1987). Some differences between pitch perception and basic auditory discrimination in children of different cultural and musical backgrounds. *Bulletin of the Council for Research in Music Education, 91,* 166–170.

Walters, S. L., and Taggart, C. C., (Eds.). (1989). *Readings in music learning theory.* Chicago: G.I.A. Publications.

Wang, C. C. (1984). Effects of some aspects of rhythm on tempo perception. *Journal of Research in Music Education, 32*(3), 169–176.

Warner, B. (1991). *Orff-Schulwerk: Applications for the classroom.* Englewood Cliffs: Prentice-Hall.

Warrener, J. J. (1985). Applying learning theory to musical development: Piaget and beyond. *Music Educators Journal, 72*(3), 22–27.

Webster, P. R. (1990). Creative thinking, technology, and music education. *Design for Arts in Education, 91*(5), 35–41.

Webster, P. R., and Zimmerman, M. P. (1983). Conservation of rhythmic and tonal patterns of second through sixth grade children. *Bulletin of the Council for Research in Music Education, 73,* 28–49.

Whiston, S. K. (1986). The development of melodic concepts in elementary school age children using computer-assisted instruction as a supplemental tool. Unpublished doctoral dissertation, Ohio State University, Columbus.

Wig, J. A., Jr., and Boyle, J. D. (1982). The effect of keyboard learning experiences on middle school general music students' music achievement and attitudes. *Journal of Research in Music Education, 30*(3), 163–172.

Willett, B. E., and Netusil, A. J. (1989). Music computer drill and learning styles at the fourth-grade level. *Journal of Research in Music Education, 37*(3), 219–229.

Willmann, M. M. (1983). An investigation of conceptual congruencies between the Kodály method and Jerome Bruner's instructional theory. Unpublished doctoral dissertation, University of Texas, Austin.

Wohlfeil, M. D. (1986). Effective rural school music teachers: Three profiles. Unpublished doctoral dissertation, University of North Dakota, Grand Forks.

Wunderlich, J. C. (1980). A field-based design for an undergraduate course in elementary school general music methods. Unpublished doctoral dissertation, Carnegie-Mellon University, Pittsburgh.

Zimmerman, M. P., and Sechrest, L. (1970). Brief focused instruction and musical concepts. *Journal of Research in Music Education, 18*(1), 25–36.

Zimmerman, M. P. (1986). Music development in middle childhood: A summary of selected research studies. *Bulletin of the Council for Research in Music Education, 86,* 18–35.

SOCIAL AND INSTITUTIONAL CONTEXTS

·50·

SOCIOLOGY AND MUSIC EDUCATION

Charles R. Hoffer
UNIVERSITY OF FLORIDA

The process of teaching and learning music can be examined from a variety of viewpoints. One of them is in terms of the social context in which music takes place, the sociological view. This orientation is not one of analyzing organized sounds or studying how people perceive those sounds. Instead, it treats music as a form of human behavior that is subject to the same influences as other forms of behavior ranging from selecting clothes to preparing food to engaging in conversation.

One tenet of the sociological view is that almost everything human beings do is learned, and not the result of genetic disposition. Regardless of whether the learning takes place in school or from informal encounters, people learn to be human in terms of their particular culture. Therefore, the ways in which people use music and the kinds of music they sing and play are a result of learning.

Because music is learned, it is manifested in a wide variety of ways for a wide variety of purposes. The chant of the ox driver in India to soothe his team is created for very different reasons than the operatic aria in Europe, which is designed to move the audience emotionally. Because the two examples were created for such different purposes, it is not surprising that they are musically very different. Different functions significantly affect how each type of music sounds, what people do with those sounds, and how they are taught and learned. For this reason, examining music from the sociological viewpoint can contribute much to understanding how music is used and learned in a particular social context.

FUNCTIONS AND USES OF MUSIC

There are probably as many uses of music as there are people who use it. Merriam (1964, pp. 209–227) lists 10 functions:

1. Emotional expression: the venting of emotions and the expression of feelings.

2. Aesthetic enjoyment: the use of music for deep emotional and intellectual enjoyment.

3. Entertainment: the use of music as amusement and diversion.

4. Communication: the conveying of emotions that are understood within a particular society.

5. Symbolic representation: The expression of symbols exists in the texts of songs and in the cultural meaning of the musical sounds.

6. Physical response: the use of music for dancing and other physical activity.

7. Enforcement of conformity to social norms: the use of music to provide instructions or warnings.

8. Validation of social institutions and religious rituals: the use of music in religious services and state occasions.

9. Contribution to the continuity and stability of culture: Merriam states that "music is in a sense a summation activity for the expression of values, a means whereby the heart of the psychology of a culture is exposed" (1964, p. 225).

10. Contribution to the integration of society: The use of music brings people together, as when the school fight song is performed at an athletic contest.

Kaplan (1990, p. 28) lists eight "social" functions of music: as a form of knowledge, collective possession, personal experience, therapy, a moral and symbolic force, an incidental commodity, a symbolic indicator of change, and a link with the past and future. Honigsheim identifies several functions: ceremonial, entertainment, accompaniment for work, use in the home, concerts, and oratorios (1989, pp. 60–65). Gaston (1968) lists the need for aesthetic experience, the enhancement of religion, communication, emotional expression, rhythmic response, gratification, and the potency of music in the group situation. Clearly there is some overlap of Gaston's list of functions with those of Kaplan, Merriam, and Honigsheim, which is what one would expect.

713

Other classifications and functions can also be named. An important function in contemporary America is as a "sonic background" for nonmusical activities ranging from studying to jogging to shopping in a store. In other instances music is used as a social accoutrement or trapping, in the same manner as is designer clothing or certain makes of automobiles.

The amount of research dealing with the various uses of music is small, if one limits the search to only the *uses* of music. Sociological research on the functions of music in contemporary western civilization consists largely of ethnographic studies of music in particular situations. A classic descriptive study in the use of popular music is Horton's analysis of the lyrics in popular songs (Horton, 1957). Bridges and Denisoff (1986) conducted a subsequent study analyzing the changes in such lyrics that had taken place over a 29-year period.

The limited amount of research in this area may result from the obviousness of the fact that music has different functions. Who hasn't observed the playing of the fight song of the home team during the final minutes of a close college basketball game or heard music used to enhance the dramatic impact of a scene in a film? What is obvious may be so self-evident that it is neglected in the education of students. Do students understand the difference between singing their school song and singing a motet in the school choir? Do they understand the different reasons for singing these two pieces of music and the effect such differences will have on the way they sing them?

Casual observation leads one to conclude that most people in contemporary America never think about the various functions of music and how these uses affect their experiences with a particular type of music. The need for such skill was articulated in 1965 in Ernst and Gary's *Music in General Education,* which lists discrimination as one of the 11 outcomes for students by the conclusion of the twelfth grade.

XI. He will discriminate with respect to music. *The generally educated person has good taste.* He has learned to make sensitive choices based upon musical knowledge and skill in listening. He evaluates performances and exercises mature judgments in this area. He is not naive with respect to the functional use of music for commercial purposes nor to the commercial pressures which will be exerted to obtain what money he can spend for music. (p. 8)

There is a clear need for study and research on this topic.

CULTURAL FACTORS

Everyone grows up in a particular cultural setting with all the attendant beliefs, social practices, and viewpoints. People are not born with ideas about economics, religion and ethics, politics, and the arts; such things are learned. The process of learning one's culture is termed *enculturation,* or sometimes, *socialization.* Without such a process, there would be chaos.

The type and form of individuals' convictions depend on the particular culture or subculture into which they are born. A child growing up in India in a Hindu family will practice vegetarianism; eat with the first two fingers and thumb of the right hand; accept a marriage partner arranged for by the parents; speak Hindi or another of the 14 major language groups of the country; often sit on his or her haunches; believe in reincarnation; think that things change but do not improve; and assume that Indian art, music, and dance are the right and appropriate expressions of those art forms.

The cultural pattern is not a simple phenomenon. Each culture is composed of elements, some of which are in conflict with one another. This is exemplified in the elements of "high culture" and "mass culture." As described by Bantock (1968), high culture is "legitimized" by the dominant cultural group, while mass or popular culture is manufactured for the mass market. Mass culture is marked by a separation between those who create it and those who consume it. This process of creating the popular culture, sometimes referred to as the "massification hypothesis" (Fox and Wince, 1975), is seen by some critics as revealing a lack of integrity in the quest for the lowest common denominator.

Vulliamy (1977) outlines the application of the massification hypothesis to music:

(a) High culture ('serious' music) is not subject to commercial pressures; commercial gain must inevitably lead to inartistic works.
(b) High culture ('serious' music) results from the unique creative potential of the artist.
(c) Mass culture ('popular' music) is produced solely for a mass market. Its commercial nature therefore leads to standardisation of the product. This in turn denies the possibility of creativity to the artist.
(d) Mass culture ('popular' music) is a homogeneous category whilst high culture ('serious' music) is subdivided into many different types with strict boundaries.
(e) Mass culture ('popular' music) inhibits the growth of high culture ('serious' music) mainly due to the former's sheer quantity in the mass media.
(f) Mass culture ('popular' music) is imposed from above and the audience (teenagers) are therefore exploited. (p. 191–192)

This massification hypothesis has by no means met with full acceptance. Fox and Wince (1975) studied the musical preferences of sociology students according to nine styles of music, from which the researchers identified five factors or "taste cultures." These were analyzed with the researchers controlling for seven demographic factors including sex, age, and religious preference. The results did not support the mass culture idea. Instead, they indicate a diverse pattern. Robinson and Hirsch (1969) provide further evidence of the diversity of taste. Hirsch (1971) concludes, "The stratified teenage audience . . . is an aggregate of individuals who form distinct popular music subcultures" (p. 379).

Regardless of the culture or subculture into which people are socialized, they tend to think of it as right, true, and good, as the best way of life. This universal tendency is called *ethnocentrism.* It was coined in the early part of this century by Sumner, who defined it as "that view of things in which one's own group is the center of everything and all others are scaled and rated with reference to it" (1906, p. 13). There is a logical basis for ethnocentrism: People understand their own culture and know how to function in it, so *for them* it is superior. Ethnocentrism not only applies at the individual level; it also applies to groups within society. Caplow and McGee (1958) found in a study of 55 sets of six organizations each—colleges, insurance companies, churches, fraternities, among others—that members overestimated the prestige of their own organization eight times as often as they underestimated it (p. 105).

This sociological view of life, including the arts, means that beauty is indeed "in the eye of the beholder." It is ascribed by people to art and music only to the extent that the objects exhibit properties that are familiar and understood in the particular culture. The wide differences among the types of music found around the world support the idea of the importance of the cultural basis of art and music.

This view of the arts is at odds with the idea that objective or intrinsic qualities within works of art hold the secret to their quality, which is generally the approach in aesthetics and music appreciation courses. Instead of looking for such qualities in artworks, the sociological approach calls for examining the social and psychological processes that have encouraged artists and musicians to create certain kinds of works and their shared convictions about the nature of art works (Mueller, 1958, p. 100). The challenge, according to the sociological view, should be to search for norms and beliefs that exist in the minds of people in a particular culture. For example, a climactic moment in a symphony by Brahms is climactic only to persons familiar with western art music. They are the ones who have been taught that certain sound patterns are climactic; people from central Africa or China would probably not react to the sounds in that way.

Although social scientists may describe the characteristics of a culture, there is no clear, objective way to evaluate cultural phenomena as a whole. Even among expert music critics writing within a cultural tradition with which they are thoroughly familiar, there are sometimes quite varying opinions about the merits of a work or a performance of it. The reason why such differences are possible, and even probable, is the fact that *qualities* cannot accurately be transformed into *quantities*. The weight, height, and other objective measurements can be recorded for a beautiful woman, and such data can be compared with those of other women. However, the qualities of beauty cannot be compared in this way. In addition, whether the woman would be more beautiful were she somewhat taller or shorter, heavier or lighter is a qualitative judgment that is largely the result of one's cultural bias. Even within the same culture these judgments can vary over the centuries. The "beauties" in Rubens's seventeenth-century paintings look to most twentieth-century Americans like candidates for a football team, not models of feminine loveliness. The norms for the arts are subject to similar cultural variation.

Studies by Mueller and Hevner (1942) and Mueller (1951) also indicate variation in the preferences for symphonic music over the years. These changes are not rapid, as they are in the case of popular music, but shifts do occur in the

popularity of Tchaikovsky, Bach, and Brahms as indicated by performances by major symphony orchestras.

Because cultural standards do not exist, according to the sociological viewpoint, one culture's music cannot be said to be superior to that of another culture. Standards for music and the arts are culturally relative and nonrational in the sense that one cannot logically argue that one is better than another. Different cultures and different types of music exist; they are what they are.

Furthermore, although art objects can be seen to progress from one to another in terms of historical order, the later objects do not necessarily represent "progress" in the sense of being better. While it is possible to develop a strong case that modern automobiles are superior to the models of the 1920s in terms of comfort, performance, and reliability, it is not possible to make a case that the music of Bartok and Stravinsky is superior to that of Bach and Telemann. The two ages of music are *different*, but one is not superior to the other according to any objective criteria. For this reason, musicians do not discard any music as being of little value simply because it is old, a fact that every college level music major learns when taking music history courses. The reason for this is the fact that each work of music stands as an end or object by itself. Its value does not depend on what music was created previously or will be created in the future.

Does the sociological viewpoint imply that all works of music are of equal value? Strictly speaking, the answer seems to be yes. However, aestheticians have suggested that some distinctions can be made in terms of the relative sophistication of artworks. In music it can be demonstrated that one work is more sophisticated than another. Meyer, in *Emotion and Meaning in Music* (1956) and *Music, the Arts, and Ideas* (1967), has developed an interesting and somewhat objective means of examining works in terms of sophistication or "maturity," to cite a term Meyer uses (1967, p. 33). The differences exist in the delay of gratification and the degree to which the music follows expected patterns. According to Meyer, the less sophisticated work follows its anticipated musical path with few or no diversions or delays. It is, therefore, less interesting and of less cultural value. According to such analysis, then, Bach's *Magnificat* is of more cultural value than the latest hit tune.

Some research on predictability in music has been conducted by Berlyne and his associates. In some of his experiments, the subjects rated melodic phrases created according to a mathematical formula of differing degrees of complexity/uncertainty. The university student subjects rated each melody according to its uncertainty and how beautiful they thought it was. The very simple melodies were not considered beautiful, but the rating for beauty increased as complexity/uncertainty increased. However, an optimum point was reached. Beyond that point, further complexity/uncertainty resulted in a reduction in the rating for beauty (J. B. Crozier in Berlyne, 1974, pp. 38–46). Berlyne's research also shows some differences between music majors and non-music majors in terms of willingness to accept uncertainty. The effects of training in music appear to discourage favorable ratings for melodies that do not fit the expected mould.

Further research in this area was conducted by Sluckin, Hargreaves, and Colman (1982, 1983). While confirming Berlyne's basic conclusions, they gave greater emphasis to the degree of familiarity of a melody. Such an analysis accounts better for the many musical works, highly regarded today, that initially received chilly receptions. However, the available research data suggest that pleasantness and familiarity interact to affect the listeners' opinions.

The potential for research in the area of cultural values and expectations appears to lie in the "experimental aesthetics" of Berlyne and in ethnographic studies that explore the development of values about music and the arts. Such matters are generally complex. Although they are usually difficult to test experimentally, they certainly need to be subjected to careful, objective analysis. To date, probably because the topic lies between music and sociology, few such studies have been undertaken by either sociologists or researchers in music.

The formation of culture and its characteristics and standards is an important topic in a nation like the United States with its many subcultures, to say nothing of the increasing importance of worldwide cultural contacts, a point that is discussed specifically in another section of this book. The plea here is not to abandon research studies that confirm the differences in cultures and subcultures, but to go deeper into the development of and reasons for these differences.

SOCIAL STRATIFICATION

The concept of stratification, or classification by layers or levels, has been used by sociologists in their research on social structure. In much of that research, the stratification dimension has been operationalized as *social class* or *socioeconomic status* (SES). Social classes in American society seem to be broad groupings of people that vary in terms of social rank, prestige, and life-style. Such groupings are rather diffuse compared with those in some European societies, where stratification is highly articulated. In the United States as in other urban-industrial societies, individuals initially inherit the social rank of their parents, but they often can move from one level to another; they are socially mobile.

Social inequality exists in every society. As Roach states, "Sociologists generally concur that social stratification in some form and degree is a feature of all societies" (Roach, Cross, and Grusslin, 1969, p. 11). Even in societies that claim to be "classless," people are not treated equally or accorded equal esteem, as is evident in communistic societies, where the leaders and upper-level party members are given better housing, more material goods, and extra privileges. It is not clear why social stratification exists. The origin of stratification seems to be a consequence of the establishment of a system of social roles. Someone inevitably comes to exercise leadership in an organization, while others are required to do more menial tasks. Some roles call for highly specialized knowledge or skill, while other jobs can be done by almost anyone who is physically able.

The classic studies of stratification in America were done by Warner (1960) in the 1940s through the 1960s. Since that time over a thousand studies on the topic have been reported by sociologists. In the past decade, however, interest in the topic has waned, probably because it has been studied so thoroughly and perhaps because it has become a less popular idea during a time when egalitarian ideas are being actively promoted.

In his study of Yankee City (Newburyport, MA), Warner found three broad classes with two subdivisions each: upper upper, lower upper, upper middle, lower middle, upper lower, and lower lower. He assigned persons to these classifications according to a rating scheme that considered occupation, income, education, and place of residence. Of these factors, occupation and education were the most important. Strong intercorrelations existed among these factors. Other researchers have found consistent positive correlations between occupation, educational level, and place of residence.

Various polls have been conducted over the years on the prestige or socioeconomic status of various occupations. Although some changes have occurred over time, in general, the professions have ranked higher than "white-collar" jobs such as insurance agent or salesperson. In turn, white-collar occupations have ranked well ahead of "blue-collar" jobs such as plumber, mechanic, and farm laborer. Furthermore, stratification exists among the subgroups within an occupational group. Medical doctors with specializations have more prestige than general practitioners, medical doctors rank higher than dentists, registered or specialized nurses rank higher than nurses who do more practical work, and so on.

The concept of SES is rich in subtlety and nuance. As with all findings in sociology, these phenomena are not uniform or absolute; rather, they represent trends. It is known, for example, that upper and lower SES persons differ on matters as diverse as churches attended (lower-strata persons are more likely to belong to more fundamentalist groups while the upper strata are more likely to belong to more liberal churches), civic activity (lower-strata persons are much less likely to join civic organizations or vote in elections), gum and tobacco chewing (much more common in the lower strata), marriage and family practices (upper-level couples tend to marry later and have fewer children but maintain an influence on them longer), style of speech (the "he don't" grammatical error is found often in the lower strata, and the variety and pronunciation of words is quite different), amount and type of television viewed and books read, and preferences in sports (upper-strata persons support tennis and soccer while lower-strata persons are more likely to follow boxing and automobile races).

There are also significant differences in music preferences among the different SES levels. The consumers of art music, both in terms of concert attendance and listening to recorded music, are overwhelmingly persons with college degrees, that is, people who are in the upper strata. In 1978 DiMaggio, Useem, and Brown synthesized the available research on arts audiences. They reported that 83.4 percent of the audience for classical music had at least attended college, with 63 percent having graduated (DiMaggio et al.,

1978, pp. 20, 22). Further analysis of the data reveals this fact even more impressively. Although they constituted only 25.5 percent of the total employed population, persons in professional and managerial positions made up 70.8 percent of the concert audience. Furthermore, although they made up only 4.1 percent of the total employed population, school and college teachers made up 22.1 percent of the audience, a better than 5:1 ratio, much larger than would have been expected. Only artists, performers, and writers exceeded that ratio. Baumol and Bowen offer further evidence of the importance of SES in determining attendance at concerts. They found that only two or three percent of the arts audience consisted of blue-collar workers, who were at the time 60 percent of the working population (1966, p. 96). In contrast, men who had done graduate work were five percent of the population but 55 percent of arts audiences.

Sociological phenomena are complex, and this fact is certainly true of the causes for the differences in interest in the fine arts and concert music among the various social classes. Economic factors probably account for only a minor portion of the differences. Some blue-collar workers (plumbers, truck drivers, and others) earn as much money as schoolteachers, and almost all workers generally have the money to buy the things they really value.

Some of the differences in arts consumption appear to be the result of the view among the lower social strata that the fine arts are not important or appropriate. A knowledge and consumption of the arts have not been traditionally part of the blue-collar life-style or self-image. In fact, the opposite is often true: Some people in lower SES levels speak almost boastfully about how little they know about the arts.

Another reason for the differences in interest in the arts and music among those at various SES levels is the amount of cultural reinforcement provided by the social group. Persons in the lower strata know of the existence of concert music, but they are not sufficiently familiar with such music to find attending a concert meaningful. Some years ago Schuessler (1948) pointed out that social class operates to channel music experiences in a way that tends to form favorable attitudes toward certain kinds of music. He states, "Likewise, familiarity affects musical taste, and socio-economic position may cause an individual to be regularly exposed to some kinds of music and remain virtually isolated from other kinds" (pp. 330–335). Children grow up hearing the music their families and friends hear and talk about.

A self-reinforcing cycle of music preferences operates in almost everyone's experience. A person tends to listen to the type of music he or she likes, which strengthens further that preference for that kind of music. For most young people the school is their main potential avenue to becoming educated in types of music that they do not encounter routinely in their social environment. If the children of blue-collar workers, for example, are going to learn about Mozart or English ballads, in all probability it will happen in school.

Other factors are also involved in the relationship between social class and music preferences and activities in the arts. One of these can be termed the "comfort factor." People enjoy things that are familiar to them, both in music and in other aspects of their lives. Not only do they enjoy listening to their favorite (and more familiar) type of music, they also feel better about doing so in circumstances with which they are familiar. Some research indicates that persons in the lower social strata do not feel comfortable at symphony concerts in elegant concert halls surrounded by upper-strata persons. Even if they might enjoy the music played in such circumstances, they do not feel confident in knowing what to say, what to wear, and how to act in such a situation; they tend to feel that they do not "belong." And the opposite is probably true: Avid upper-class concertgoers would not feel they belonged at a performance of country music.

Some years ago the Danish State Radio conducted an experiment in which it played on a particular program the same music during two successive weeks. It was a selection of ear-appealing and not-too-difficult classical music (Geigor, 1950, pp. 453–460). The first week the program was introduced as "popular recorded music." The identical program was repeated a week later, only this time it was introduced as "classical music." The size of the listening audience was cut in half, a phenomenon Geigor termed "reverse snobism." Apparently the highbrow trappings and image of concert music are an impediment to concert music for many people, at least in Denmark.

Another factor that may account for some of the differences in musical interests among persons at various social levels is what sociologists term the *deferred gratification pattern* (Schneider and Lysgaard, 1953). This pattern is the willingness to postpone immediate satisfaction in order to gain a more important objective. Delaying the purchase of a new automobile until after one has completed college is an example of deferred gratification. The willingness to defer gratification is characteristic of the middle and upper social strata, while persons in the lower strata generally are not willing to do this. One feature of art music is its inhibition of expected tendencies, in which instead of moving promptly as expected, it does so with delays and detours, all of which make it more interesting to experienced listeners. They find the permutations of Bach and Brahms stimulating and enjoyable; to them, music that lacks complexity and imagination is boring.

All this invites speculation concerning a possible association between socioeconomic status, the deferred gratification pattern, and enjoyment of concert music. To a person who is not inclined to defer gratification, waiting out a development section in sonata form can be irritating or cause the mind to wander. On the other hand, if one senses that the music is leading somewhere in an imaginative way, then listening to such music is a rewarding experience.

The connection between socioeconomic status and music consumption is in need of further investigation. The limited amount of extant research does have some interesting and useful implications for music teachers. For example, casual observation indicates a strong association between the percentage of high school graduates attending college and successful string programs. However, conclusive evidence is not available on this issue. Another suggested strategy that merits more research is the presentation of art music in ways without the usual trappings of the concert hall. Various means of implementing such strategies also call for study.

AGE-LEVEL STRATIFICATION

Another dimension of stratification, in addition to social class, is that of age. The fact that teenagers differ from their seniors (anyone over the age of 30?) is apparent in their style of dress, hair, speech, and taste in music and television shows. Advertisers have clearly identified "markets" for several age-level groupings within American society, and they design advertising campaigns based on those classifications.

The differences within the American population that are due to age appear to be increasing, for a number of reasons. One is increasing life expectancy. The percentage of persons who live into their eighties grows each year.

A second reason is the rapid rate of social change. One can easily think of assumptions about life that were accepted in the early 1900s but no longer prevail. "A woman's place is in the home" is one such assumption, as is the idea that the United States can effectively isolate itself from the rest of the world and its conflicts and problems. The rate of change is exemplified by the fact that it was only 66 years from the first flight of the Wright brothers in 1903 to the time Neil Armstrong walked on the moon in 1969. Change has increased the cultural gap between the oldest and the youngest members of American society.

A third reason for the increasing differences among age groups is the sheer size of America's population. At the time of the Civil War it was 31,500,000, and it had increased to 80,000,000 by the turn of the century. Today it has grown to over 250,000,000.

A fourth reason is the economic power wielded by the large number of persons in each age group, including teenagers and even children. Young people today are able to buy recordings, clothes, movie tickets, and other items to an extent that was out of the question only a generation or two ago. Today there is a "youth market" and a "yuppie market" and a "senior citizen market" that are all commercially important.

A fifth reason, which is partly a consequence of the factors previously mentioned, is the increased separation existing among different age groups. At one time grandparents, parents, and children all lived close together on a farm or in a small town. Today they may be separated by hundreds or thousands of miles, or the grandparents may live in a retirement community or similar restricted situation. Even when families are living together, it is unusual for them to all be present for the evening meal because of school or work activities. And seldom do families have extended contact with each other, except perhaps for the once-a-year vacation.

For all these reasons, as well as some social psychological ones that will be mentioned later, it should not be surprising that the type of music various age groups prefer differs. Again, businesses are well aware of this fact. Some radio stations design their product for the teenage market, while others are "upscale" and play music for persons who are 40 and older.

Age level differences were clearly evident in the 1972 National Assessment of Educational Progress on musical knowledge, skills, and preferences of four age-level groups: 9-year-olds, 13-year-olds, 17-year-olds, and adults between the ages of 26 and 35. The data are presented in Table 50–1. The responses were to the questions "What kind of music do you *most* like to listen to?" and "What type of music do you *least* like to listen to?"

Striking differences are revealed among the various age groups with respect to their preferences for "instrumental art" and "rock." (The categories were designated by the researchers.) Instrumental art music is preferred by a very small portion (between 3 and 5 percent) of the younger age groups; among adults it is noticeably more popular (12 percent). Rock is preferred by 32 percent of the 9-year-olds, and that preference nearly doubles for the two teenage groups (57 and 62 percent, respectively). But among adults, the preference for rock slips back to 14 percent, scarcely more than that for instrumental art music! The pattern of liking for

TABLE 50–1. Most Enjoyed Type of Music by Age Level

	Age Level			
	9	13	17	Adult
Instrumental art (e.g., classical, symphonic)	3%	4%	5%	12%
Vocal art (e.g., opera)	1	0	0	1
Jazz	4	5	4	6
Folk	4	2	4	5
Rock	32	57	62	14
Country-western	8	7	5	29
Soul	1	3	5	0
Popular ballads (e.g., barbershop, male vocalists, romantic)	2	2	2	8
Blues	1	1	2	2
Background music	0	0	0	3
Other popular	3	5	4	8
Other types (e.g., unclassifiable responses)	17	7	6	11

Least Enjoyed Type of Music by Age Level

	Age Level			
	9	13	17	Adult
Instrumental art (e.g., classical, symphonic)	4%	9%	14%	9%
Vocal art (e.g., opera)	5	16	15	24
Jazz	2	4	4	7
Folk	2	3	2	1
Rock	8	7	11	25
Country-western	6	12	18	10
Soul	1	1	2	1
Popular ballads (e.g., barbershop, male vocalists, romantic)	4	3	1	0
Blues	1	1	2	1
Other popular	3	5	2	3
Other types (e.g., unclassifiable responses)	18	7	4	1

Source: National Assessment of Educational Progress. *A perspective on the first music assessment,* Report no. 03-MU-02. Denver, 1974.

country music is interesting: The younger age groups express little preference for it, while the adults like it (29 percent) more than any other type.

The data on music liked least also show some interesting contrasts among different age groups. Some types of music seem to accumulate more "negatives" as young people mature from age 9 to their late teens, namely, instrumental and vocal art music, rock, and country. The gap between the teenage listeners and the adults spans the most dramatic shifts in taste. Among adults the dislike for vocal art music and rock rises dramatically, while that for instrumental art music and country music declines quite noticeably.

At the time of the first National Assessment of Educational Progress in the area of music (1972), rock was the youth music of the day. The preferences of the 26- to 35-year-olds were much more varied than was the case by 1981. Unfortunately, financial constraints prevented the second National Assessment, which at the time of this writing is the most recent one in music, from including adults (who had to be contacted individually instead of at school).

In general, the data from the National Assessment are consonant with previous research cited by Farnsworth (1969, pp. 124–125). His summary of several studies concludes that music taste grows more like adult tastes as a young person matures.

The differences among various age groups present music educators with some real challenges. For one, they need to devise ways of breaking down what Rieger (1973) refers to as "the phoniness-stuffiness-jeweled-dowager syndrome," which represents the inaccurate perception that art music is for older people, is something out of date, and has about it an air of stuffiness and false morality. Rieger suggests establishing a "beachhead" by letting students "discover the parallels between the music they know and the music they don't know" (p. 31). His suggestion reaffirms what music educators have long known but often seem to forget: Begin where the students are. When teachers have their students draw parallels between art music and popular music, they are achieving another desirable educational outcome: They are diverting attention from thinking about music as being "ours" and "theirs" to the nature of the musical sounds, which is one of the goals of music education.

Although there is some research that documents age-level differences in musical interests among the various groups within the American population, there is little on how such differences can or should affect the teaching of music. Some writings on the topic are based on empirical experiences. However, most teachers deal with age-level differences by intuition and unsystematic observations. In summary, it is another area that is ripe for research investigation.

SOCIAL PSYCHOLOGICAL FACTORS

A field that is partly sociological and partly psychological involves the study of the effect of the group on the behavior of individuals: social psychology. Several topics associated with social psychology merit inclusion in this chapter: conformity, expectations and roles, and self-image.

Conformity

Casual observation confirms the idea that people learn from and are influenced by what the group does and thinks. However, until the work of Asch in the early 1950s, this phenomenon had not been systematically studied. He conducted a classic series of experiments that consisted of showing subjects two cards like the ones shown in Figure 50–1. The subjects were asked to select the line on the right-hand card that was closest in length to the line that stands alone on the left-hand card. Several sets of cards with similar sets of lines were used. The responses of the subjects were made verbally and observed by the other subjects in the small group.

All subjects responded correctly to the first several sets of cards. However, after these initial trials, some of the subjects (who had been coached to give incorrect responses) began to give wrong answers. After the first four subjects gave incorrect responses, the fifth and uncoached participant faced the choice of either conforming with the rest of the group and answering incorrectly or standing alone in giving the correct response. The results were impressive: Over the course of many experiments subjects went against their own perceptions about 35 percent of the time (Asch, 1952).

Similar experiments have been conducted in listening to music. Ingelfield had ninth-grade students indicate music preferences by pushing buttons on a small box. The equipment purported to show also the preferences of the other subjects, but in fact did not. False responses were fed into the system to test the influence of the "preferences" of their peers on the subjects. Individuals who scored high on measures of other-directedness, need for social approval, and dependency showed greater amounts of conformity behavior. The results indicated that the pressure to conform significantly affected the subjects' responses (Inglefield, 1968, pp. 175–176). Radocy (1975) replicated the Asch design in a study that showed college music majors changed their reported perceptions of pitch (30 percent changed) and loud-

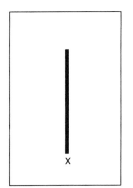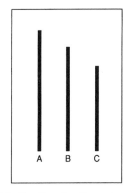

FIGURE 50–1.   Cards for Asch's Conformity Experiments.
© Solomon E. Asch. Used by permission.

ness (50 percent changed) because of the influence of false peer responses.

In a later experiment Radocy (1976) played paired excerpts from what were actually the same recordings, but provided bogus information about the performers. The alleged information about composers and imaginary prior listeners' opinions significantly influenced the subjects' judgments.

If conformity behavior is strong among college students and adults, it appears to be unassailable among adolescents. Virtually any observation of youngsters between the ages of 11 and 17 reveals the effect of conformity pressure almost to the point of uniformity in terms of dress, use of slang, and preferences in music. This phenomenon can be seen in Table 50–1 with the high reported preference for rock music by the 13- and 17-year-old students, which is in contrast to the much lower percentage for 9-year-olds and adults.

Although a number of studies have been conducted on teenage musical preferences, including many by Blaukopf and others associated with the International Institute for Music, Dance, and Audio-Visual Media (IMDT) in Vienna, such descriptive research tends to become dated within a few years. Of greater value are studies concerning how music teachers, both in school and in the private studio, can use the strong need for conformity among teenagers to motivate them to learn music. Is the matter as simple as letting the students perform some popular music? Or are the circumstances in which music is learned more important? If so, what situations and what methods are best for taking advantage of the need for conformity and peer approval among students, especially adolescents?

Expectations and Roles

People do what is expected of them to a surprising degree. From infancy they learn, subtly and sometimes not so subtly, certain behaviors and roles. For example, people learn that they are to shake hands when being introduced to strangers, to drive on the right-hand side of the road, and not to sob or laugh aloud when listening to music. They also learn such diverse roles as being a college professor, student, and parent.

One interesting manifestation of the role system involves "gender typing" in music. Abeles and Porter (1978) sampled the opinions of adults about which instrument they would like their sons and daughters to play. The clarinet, flute, and violin were preferred for the daughters, while drums, trombone, and trumpet received the nod for the sons. In a second study discussed in the same report Abeles and Porter attempted to determine the age at which gender/instrument associations first appear in children. Youngsters from kindergarten through grade 5 were shown pictures of instruments and asked their preferences, No strong preferences became evident until about grade 3, after which time the preferences were well established, with boys selecting "masculine" instruments and the girls preferring "feminine" instruments.

For many years various tests of musical ability and achievement have rather consistently shown girls scoring somewhat higher than boys. The National Music Assessment, for example, revealed that girls consistently were higher in both musical ability and interest (1974 and 1981). A major research question here is: To what degree are such results due to socialization? There has been a long tradition in America that males are supposed to be interested in sports and things like that, not in the arts. This view seems to be receding to some degree, but it is an issue that merits much more study.

It is interesting to compare the importance attached to music in American society with that in countries such as Hungary or Korea. In Hungary the ability to sing has become strongly associated with Hungarian nationalism, which has provided young people in this rather small nation—often in its history occupied by foreign powers—with strong motivation to do well in music. The beneficial results can be heard in the high quality of singing in Hungarian schools. Korea is another country in which the "message" to children is that they should do well in music—and they do. Visiting educators from America often comment on the fact that they never encounter a Korean child who can't sing. Probably there are some such children in Korea, but apparently they learn how to cover their musical inadequacies. In any case, the expectation of musical competency provides a strong impetus for young people in these two countries to succeed in music.

Ascertaining people's views about the importance of music in their lives is no easy task. Such feelings are subtle and complex, but they have a major impact on how well people learn music and what use they make of it. Even more difficult, but equally important, is the matter of how such views of music are formed. If American males think that music is not really for them, then how can such views be changed? Are there actions that arts councils or music teachers can take that will in the long run alter such thinking? These are matters of much importance to the future of music education and the cultural health of American society.

Self-Image

The classic work in self-image was done by Cooley in the early years of this century (1902, pp. 102–103). He coined the phrase "looking-glass self" to describe the process of developing a sense of one's self with the aid of the reactions of others. According to Cooley, there are three dimensions of this process: (1) one's perception of how one appears to others; (2) one's perceptions of their judgments about him or her; and (3) one's reactions to those perceptions. The idea of the looking-glass self can be illustrated with a musical example: (1) You may think (for whatever reason) of yourself as a good singer, but (2) no one ever asks you to sing, and when you do it is greeted with glazed, bored looks. (3) This situation is not a pleasant one for you, and you begin to adjust your views about your singing ability.

Probably the most crucial element in the three-part looking-glass self is the perception of the opinions of others. Do one's perceptions of other's opinions agree with their actual judgments? Calvin and Holtzman (1953) found that individuals vary significantly in the accuracy of their perceptions about what others think. Well-adjusted persons do this quite well; less well-adjusted persons have problems with it.

Mead (1934, part 3, pp. 140–141) added an important element to Cooley's analysis of the looking-glass self: the "significant other." Mead thus took account of the fact that it is the persons closest to us and/or those whom we consider important who have the most influence in shaping our self-image. As the circle of interaction widens, the individual begins to perceive the consensus of the broader community; that is, the "generalized other." Mead emphasized the importance of indiviudals' capacity to project themselves into the position of other people, to see things as others see them, to "take the role of the other." In this sense, the self is inherently a *social* product, and people's views of themselves are profoundly affected by their involvement in social interaction and social groups.

One's musical interests and abilities are a part of one's self-image. It is a part of a complex view of what one is or wants to be. However this view is formed, it is crucial in guiding one's actions in almost every area of life, including music. Examples would include the person who wants to be "seen" at a certain concert, the person who disdains a certain kind of music, thinking it "tacky" because of its association with undesirable people, and the young man who plays the trumpet in the community band after graduating from high school because of the sense that it is something he does better than most people and part of his identity is associated with the trumpet.

Many people use music as an accoutrement or trapping to a particular self-image or socioeconomic level. For example, the man who wears a necktie to work and the woman who puts on hose both have a self-image that is likely to see a knowledge of art music as something important, because art music is likely to be thought of as necessary to being considered "educated" or "cultured." Those who are motivated by prestige drives may also be careful to use correct English, wear clothes with the "right" labels, and drive certain kinds of automobiles.

The discussion of self-image sometimes raises concerns in people's minds about the exploitation of music for purposes of elitism or snobbery. Unfortunately, music has been so used sometimes over the centuries, but it does not need to be that way. In order to make a living, Mozart, for example, had to compose for the "beautiful" people of his day, but his music can speak to everyone, not just the rich and famous. Snobbery's aim is to set oneself above or apart from others; it is an attitude of "I am better than most other people." What music educators should attempt to instill in their students is a self-image of honesty and self-respect and a motivation to be well-informed. The message to the students should be, "Don't be ignorant about music; don't miss out on something that can really make your life richer," instead of implying, "Knowing music makes you better than others."

As is true of most aspects of sociology and music education, the relationship of music and self-image has received only limited attention by researchers. It is a complex topic rich with overtones. However, it also carries many important ramifications for the impact of music instruction. Like an iceberg, of which only about an eighth is visible, the impact of social factors runs deep in the music teaching and learning process.

TECHNOLOGICAL FACTORS

It is hardly news that technology has had an enormous impact on life in the twentieth century. The changes over the centuries have been as dramatic as that from quill pens to word processors and that from the unaccompanied singing of ballads to the synthesized sounds emanating from electronic keyboards. These changes have affected the way people think about music, how they use it, and how they learn it.

First, with respect to how people think about music: At one time hearing some music was a special event. Someone had to play or sing it, and capable performers above the level of campfire song and lullaby were not readily or easily available. Today there is music everywhere—in supermarkets, on car radios and small tape players with headphones, and even in doctors' offices and operating rooms. Instead of being something special, music is now commonplace almost to the point of being trivial. Even concert music has been affected. A hundred years ago a person would probably never had had the opportunity to listen to a symphony orchestra, and the odds were even smaller that the person would hear Beethoven's *Fifth Symphony*, for example. Composers realized this and indicated that the exposition sections in their symphonies and concertos were to be repeated. Because of tapes and recordings, one can listen to orchestras and Beethoven's *Fifth Symphony* as often as one desires, so that what was formerly rare is now ordinary. For this reason, conductors today usually ignore the repeat signs at the ends of the exposition sections.

Perhaps the most significant change in the way people think about music is the fact that its pervasiveness causes people *not* to think about it. Human beings simply cannot give concentrated attention to all the music they hear each day, any more than they can give careful attention to each commercial message they see on television or hear on the radio or see in newspapers and magazines. In addition, often the conditions under which the music is heard (while jogging, shopping, reading) do not encourage careful, contemplative listening. Therefore, people, especially young people, learn to ignore much of what they hear. In fact, the word "listen" does not mean anywhere near the same thing to most people that it does to musicians. The high school or college male who has the "bazooka" speakers in his car booming away may say that he is "listening," when in fact what he is doing is reveling in the sound vibrations without giving them any conscious attention.

The music created to be simply "absorbed" almost has to be of a different character from most of the music composed for contemplative listening in a concert hall. Music to be absorbed cannot be subtle or complicated, and it cannot require more than a minimum of thought and attention. People who hear mostly popular music tend to develop a set of habits in listening to it that are inimical to listening to art music. They are accustomed to music that is loud, simple, and short. Even the normal timbre of instruments has been altered by distortion intentionally introduced during the recording process or through electronic manipulation.

The impact of technology and the easy availability of music are a rich lode for research study in perception and the teaching of listening skills. Can students be taught to listen to different kinds of music with different mental viewpoints, one for absorbing sounds and one for attentive listening? How successfully can those students who are accustomed to short, simple works blasted at them at very loud dynamic levels be taught to value the subtleties of art music? If so, by what means? What effect has MTV and its visual images had on the listening habits of teenagers?

Another fertile area for research is the use of technology in the teaching of music. One aspect of this question that has received quite a bit of research attention is the teaching of basic skills and knowledge with the aid of computer programs. As of this writing, over 60 such programs are commercially available, and more are coming out each year. Most of these programs have been subjected to some evaluation prior to being marketed. Writings by Hair (1985), McGreer (1984), and Robinson (1987) synthesizing research on computers in music education have described their educational efficacy. Instruction in listening skill can also be aided by tapes and various computer programs.

The ease with which music can be made on some electronic instruments raises some problems for music educators in motivating students to learn to sing or play traditional instruments. The students may wonder why they should devote so much time and effort to learning to make music on a conventional piano or clarinet when music can be made so easily and quickly on an electronic instrument. Why should they learn to make music when it is so readily available in recorded versions performed far better than they may ever learn to perform it? Clearly, here is another issue that merits study.

To some music educators, technology is a curse; to others, it is a blessing. The electronic means of making and reproducing music can be either, depending on how well music educators understand it and its effects on their students. For this reason, it is an important area for additional research.

References

Abeles, H. F., and Porter, S. Y. (1978). The sex-stereotyping of music instruments. *Journal of Research in Music Education, 22*(2).

Asch, S. E. (1952). *Social psychology.* Englewood Cliffs: Prentice-Hall.

Bantock, G. H. (1968). *Culture, industrialisation and education.* London: Routledge & Kegan Paul.

Baumol, W., and Bowen, W. (1966). *The performing arts: The economic dilemma.* Cambridge: The M.I.T. Press.

Berlyne, D. E. (1974). *Studies in the new experimental aesthetics.* Washington: Hemisphere Publishing.

Bridges, J., and Denisoff, R. S., (1986). Changing courtship patterns in the popular song: Horton and Carey revisited. *Popular Music and Society, 10*(3), 29–45.

Calvin, A. D., and Holtzman, W. H. (1953). Adjustment to the discrepancy between self-concept and the inferred self. *Journal of Consulting Psychiatry, 17.*

Caplow, T., and McGee, R. J. (1958). *The academic marketplace.* New York: Basic Books.

Cooley, C. H. (1902). *The nature of human nature.* New York: Charles Scribner's Sons.

DiMaggio, P., Useem, M., and Brown, P. (1978, November). *Audience studies of the performing arts and museums: A critical review.* Washington: The National Endowment for the Arts (research report 9).

Ernst, K., and Gary, C. (1965). *Music in general education.* Reston: Music Educators National Conference.

Farnsworth, P. R. (1969). *The social psychology of music* (2nd ed.). Ames: Iowa State Press.

Fox, W. S. and Wince, M. H. (1975). Music taste cultures and taste publics, *Youth and Society, 7,* 198–224.

Gaston, E. T. (1968). Factors contributing to responses in music. In E. T. Gaston (Ed.), *Music therapy.* Lawrence: The Allen Press.

Geigor, T. (1950). A radio test of musical taste. *Public Opinion Quarterly, 14,* 453–460.

Hair, H. I. (1985). Teaching music with the computer: Guidelines for teachers. *Update: The Applications of Research in Music Education, 3*(2), 9–12.

Hirsch, P. (1969). *The structure of the popular music industry.* Ann Arbor: Survey Research Center, University of Michigan.

Honigsheim, P. (1989). *Sociology and music* (2nd ed.). (K. P. Etzkorn, Ed.). New Brunswick: Transaction Publishers.

Horton, D. (1957). The dialogue of courtship in popular songs. *American Journal of Sociology, 62,* 561–578.

Inglefield, H. G. (1968). The relationship of selected personality variables to conformity behavior in the musical preferences of adolescents when exposed to peer group leader influences. Unpublished doctoral dissertation, Ohio State University, Columbus.

Kaplan, M. (1990). *The arts: A social perspective.* Rutherford: Fairleigh Dickinson University Press.

McGreer, D. M. (1984). The research literature in computer-assisted instruction. *Update: The Applications of Research in Music Education, 3*(1), 12–15.

Mead, G. H. (1934). *Mind, self and society.* Chicago: University of Chicago Press.

Merriam, A. (1964). *The anthropology of music.* Evanston, Northwestern University Press.

Meyer, L. B. (1956). *Emotion and meaning in music.* Chicago: University of Chicago Press.

Meyer, L. B. (1967). *Music, the arts, and ideas.* Chicago: University of Chicago Press.

Mueller, J. H. (1951). *The American symphony orchestra: A social history of musical taste.* Bloomington: Indiana University Press.

Mueller, J. H. (1958). Music and education: A sociological approach. In N. Henry (Ed.), *Basic concepts in music education.* Chicago: National Society for the Study of Education.

Mueller, J. H., and Hevner, K. (1942). *Trends in musical taste.* Indiana University Publication, Humanities Series, No. 8.

Music 1971–79: Results from the second national music assess-

ment. (1981). Denver: National Assessment of Educational Progress (report 10-MU-01).

A perspective on the first music assessment. (1974). Denver: National Assessment of Educational Progress (report 03-MU-02).

Radocy, R. (1975). A naive minority of one and deliberate majority mismatches of tonal stimuli. *Journal of Research in Music Education, 23*(2), 120–133.

Radocy, R. (1976). Effects of authority figures biases on changing judgments of musical events. *Journal of Research in Music Education, 24*(3), 119–128.

Rieger, J. (1973). Overcoming the phoniness-stuffiness-jeweled dowager syndrome with young people. *Music Educators Journal, 59*(9).

Roach, J. L., Cross, L., and Grusslin, O. R., (1969). *Social stratification in the United States.* Englewood Cliffs: Prentice-Hall.

Robinson, J. P., and Hirsch, P. M. (1969). *Teenage response to rock and roll protest songs.* Paper presented to annual meeting of the American Sociological Association, San Francisco.

Robinson, R. L. (1987). Uses of computers in music education: Past, present and future. *Update: The Applications of Research to Music Education, 5*(2), 12–16.

Schneider, L., and Lysgaard, S. (1953). The deferred gratification pattern. *American Sociological Review, 18.*

Schuessler, K. F. (1948). Social backgrounds and musical taste. *American Sociological Review, 13,* 330–335.

Sluckin, W., Hargreaves, D. J., and Colman, A. M. (1982). Some experimental studies of familiarity and liking. *Bulletin of the British Psychological Society, 35,* 189–194.

Sluckin, W., Hargreaves, D. J., and Colman, A. M. (1983). Novelty and human aesthetic preferences. In J. Archer and L. Birke (Eds.), *Exploration in animals and humans.* London: Van Nostrand Reinhold.

Sumner, W. (1906). *Folkways* (3rd ed.). Boston: Ginn and Co.

Vulliamy, G. (1977). Music and the mass culture debate. In J. Shepherd, P. Virden, G. Vulliamy, and T. Wishart (Eds.), *Whose music? A sociology of musical languages,* London: Latimer.

Warner, W. L. (1960). *Social class in America.* New York: Harper and Brothers.

·51·

PROFESSIONAL ORGANIZATIONS AND INFLUENCES

Samuel Hope
NATIONAL ASSOCIATION OF SCHOOLS OF MUSIC

Music is complex, and the world of music an interlocking system of complexities. Thus, the study of music itself as well as the context in which music functions presents sets of issues and problems to challenge the most learned and gifted minds. Much intellectual activity is concerned with creation and performance. Important work is under way regarding psychological and scientific aspects of musical phenomena; other studies consider history, musical cultures, and education. Intellectual effort is also involved in providing financial, administrative, and technical support for music and music-related activities and businesses. Each of these activities proceeds essentially according to the artistic, analytical, or management nature of the task, following regnant norms for pursuit of goals and objectives. These norms change as times and values change, producing new, or at least different, interrelationships. In this way, America's musical organizations and their members are influenced by a wide variety of factors, both internal and external to the music community.

Identifying, placing, and evaluating various elements of the composite puzzle is a daunting task, partially because the relative importance of each element varies given the musical subject under consideration and the location in which the subject is being addressed, and partially because values and ideas, not facts and figures, are the elemental building blocks of the work. A significant degree of comfort with uncertainty and willingness to engage in a speculative enterprise is needed. Of course, methods based in science and history are important. Statistical analyses and studies of who did what, when, and to what effect are extremely useful. However, there is no known science that explains human valuing, primarily because values differ about the same idea or object. The ambiguities and lack of replicability are too inexact for science. Further, no historical event or set of understandings can be extrapolated exactly to explain current conditions.

The world of organizations and influences represents a set of conditions in constant flux. The intellectual target is constantly moving, and answers have varying lengths of usefulness.

The speculative nature of work with interrelationships of organizations and influences presents specific practical challenges. Professional and economic rewards for music education researchers now seem tied to production of work immediately or readily verifiable by others. Speculative intellectual activity, on the other hand, carries the conditions inherent in the nature of speculation. Without willingness to take risks, significant rewards cannot be expected. Exploration is more important than exactitude. Another problem is that professional speculation about organizations and influences in music proceeds in a much larger world of speculation and action. This world is a marketplace of ideas full of interacting and conflicting agendas concerned with economic, political, social, and intellectual interests. Academe occupies some but not all stalls in this marketplace, even though academics often are prominent influences on the mood or direction of the market. The marketplace of ideas influences decisions that affect the operation of society—policy-making in other words. In this chapter, a few basic issues in this speculative world of policy-making that has so much ultimate influence on the progress of music and music teaching are explored. Our goal is to discover as many questions needing attention as possible, and to propose a few basic formats for structuring inquiry about them.

Although the text of this paper is original and through-composed, the thoughts presented are derived from years of study and experience. Many organizing principles are the result of work with the Futures Committee of the National Association of Schools of Music that met in 1987–89. Many issues were distilled from work on papers for *Design for Arts in Education* magazine and the *Journal of Aesthetic Education.* Many insights came from connecting the ideas of various authors whose works are presented in the References.

ORGANIZATIONS

The professional music and music-teaching communities in the United States are represented by hundreds of organizations. Operating at local, regional, and national levels, these organizations undertake a wide variety of responsibilities. A survey of these entities would reveal a broad spectrum for almost every parameter: history, objectives, financial resources, and scope of service. Various matrices could be developed to categorize organizations and their attributes. But it is important to remember that we are seeking not the one correct matrix or pattern, but rather ways of working with the elements before us that provide valuable and usable insight. Therefore, to proceed, it is necessary to choose one particular pattern at a time and use it to best advantage, knowing that it is not the only pattern and that each pattern chosen can be combined with others in infinite variation.

By studying perceived historical objectives, it is possible to divide organizations concerned with music and music teaching into three groups. The first group involves organizations whose primary purpose is to support professional work in the creation and presentation of music. The second group involves organizations founded to further the teaching of music. A third group involves organizations whose primary concern is supporting music and music teaching. It is hard to find organizations that are pure examples of any one of these categories. The American Symphony Orchestra League, for example, has its most fundamental historic objectives in the presentation of symphonic music, but the League also has objectives in education and in support. At any given point, the League's activities would exhibit a certain profile with respect to each of these three basic functions.

Our tripartite division of functions—creation/presentation, education, support—can be overlaid with another kind of division: whether fundamental objectives are grounded in history, the present, or the future. For example, organizations devoted to historical scholarship concern themselves with the creation and performance function, the teaching function, and the support function, while organizations in the speculative world of policy analysis and formulation deal with these three functions from a very different perspective.

Another way of dividing the field is to consider that some organizations have objectives to provide professional exchange and services for their members, while others are more concerned with influencing change in society as a whole. Again, it is hard to find an organization that is a pure example of either of these activities. But it is obvious that some organizations active in the fields of music and music teaching are far more involved in interprofessional discourse than in arts advocacy.

These three sets of descriptors—creation/presentation, education, support; past, present, future; interprofessional discourse, public advocacy—produce a stunning complexity. Making weighted profiles for various organizations with just these descriptors provides comparisons that will go some way to explain the natural attractions and polarizations among various groups in the music community. Bringing more descriptors to the analytical process may be useful in refining the picture. Such refinements may include judgments about the relative effectiveness of organizations. Note, however, that effectiveness is not unidimensional. An organization can be extremely effective in one arena and completely ineffective in another. This may be by design or by default. Organizations should not be expected to be effective in areas where they have no particular objectives. In fact, basic effectiveness is often based on the extent to which the organization has balanced its objectives, resources, and program in a logically consistent and mutually reinforcing way.

From a research perspective, organizations can be studied as utilizing various operating techniques. Organization theory provides numerous frameworks for pursuit of the relevant questions. But the researchers engaged in either historic, current, or futures issues confront not just questions of technique, but also questions regarding content and purpose. Organizational research can produce reams of data. The data may reveal previously unknown patterns. But data are of minimal value until compared against a specific research objective that is centered in values and content, a difficult concept to work with, particularly at a time when value is so often described in quantitative rather than qualitative terms. For example, if the effectiveness of an organization is to be determined primarily in terms of the growth or decline of membership, a particular set of values and operational premises comes into play. Different objectives highlight different sets of values and operational premises. And, as already noted, these values and premises are perpetually in a state of flux and thus harder to capture in the present than in the past or the future where the urgencies of immediate time have less effect.

The orientation of an organization toward music is another fundamental analytical consideration. The complexity of musical endeavor makes this a challenging inquiry, not a matter of assigning organizations to definite categories but rather of discovering the weight of various elements in the mix of what the organization most values in the range of musical activity. For example, what profile does an organization exhibit with respect to doing music versus doing something with or about music, for example, study, promotion, economic advancement? There is no right or wrong answer with respect to these profiles; they become meaningful only when compared against content expressed in subject matter, objectives, and the like. It is illogical to expect that an organization of performers would hold the same objectives regarding historical musicology as would an organization of musicological scholars. In the best of circumstances, the variety of organizational objectives creates conditions for the optimum exchange of expertise.

A variation is provided by analyzing an organization's perspective on the purposes of music. For example, how does the organization's profile relate to music-as-center versus music-as-means? Music-as-center indicates music's being created, taught, and received on its own terms. Music-as-means indicates that music is present primarily in service of other goals—social, political, economic, philosophical. Evaluation of an organization's place on the spectrum between pure music-as-center and pure music-as-means is particularly valuable in studying the evolution of organizational policies and activities.

In summary, fundamental research into organizations is based on discerning master ideas and fundamental objectives that are driving decision making. Most of the operational activities of any organization evolve essentially from the values created by interrelationships of these ideas and objectives. How do these objectives and master ideas come to be? Perhaps more important than their current manifestation is how they will evolve: the impact of this evolution on the organization itself, on its relationship with other organizations, and on the nature of its contribution to the development of the field.

INFLUENCES

If the world of organizational behavior is complex, the world of influences on organizations is even more so. Even contemplative individuals with significant intrapersonal intelligence have difficulty tracing the impact of influences on their own lives. This difficulty, compounded by the fact that organizations are made up of individuals with various levels of skill in analyzing influences, demonstrates the maze faced by any researcher. Psychology, sociology, and marketing are three disciplines significantly concerned with influences. Research in these disciplines can be connected to problems concerned with music and music teaching. However, the nature of these connections depends on the extent to which they are made on scientific, historic, artistic, pedagogical, or other grounds. For example, scientific studies of the psychology of hearing have relationships to scientific studies about musical perception. A more tenuous relationship surely exists between scientific studies in the psychology of hearing and historical studies of the way music is valued.

The researcher has many ways to approach the issue of influences. Influences can be considered as historic, current, or projected. They can be tied to ideas, personalities, and organizations. They can be considered in terms of basic elements and/or conditions, change factors, and change mechanisms. They can be considered in terms of basic strategic orientations. And then there is the movement of all of these analyses in time and over time. As moments pass, conditions change. The extent to which these changes produce real differences in the influences under consideration is one of the most challenging intellectual puzzles. In order to approach such puzzles, a discussion of 10 influences with significant impact on music study and the field of music education follows, starting with ideas/values. Obviously, there are far more influences than those presented in this text. Choices were made to produce a particular pattern of coverage, not to indicate exclusivity or to promote a certain set of priorities for researchers.

Ideas/Values

Traditions, the economic environment, and education are primary forces creating ideas and values. In considering these forces, the researcher confronts a world of conventional wisdom and professional activity, but relatively little comparative analysis of individual ideas and values about music and music study. Where do such ideas come from? Can they be generalized and assigned on the basis of other groups of ideas and values individuals possess? Is there a way that education in music can be structured to intervene significantly in the development of ideas and values? Thoughtful and successful speculation on these and similar questions is important because ideas and values tend to govern all else: By definition, only one set of ideas/values can hold first priority as the basis for individual or organizational action at a given time. When operational decisions must be made, values and ideas have overriding influence. With respect to music study, such decisions touch everything from curriculum content to budget support to whether music education programs will exist at all.

Information and Knowledge

Drawing fine distinctions between information and knowledge could occupy the lifetimes of many philosophers. For current purposes, it seems important to make such a distinction because present mass media conditions include constant inundation of every individual by a gushing stream of information. The stream's volume and intensity is an influence in and of itself in addition to the content of the information it carries. For example, is it possible that the current popularity of single-interest political action organizations is partially derived from reactions to the constant flood of information? Rather than producing a holistic view, the flood produces high anxiety, frustration, and confusion. In response, many individuals find psychological refuge by taking one issue and focusing on it to the exclusion of all else. Faction, not cooperation, is the overall result.

Knowledge implies the result of consciously processing information in a way that involves intellectual use of ideas and values. In another sense, knowledge is what resides in memory irrespective of the flood of information we experience. In yet another sense, knowledge implies information and understandings that we have apprehended, that are truly and centrally our own property, that we are able to work with in creative and evolutionary ways. One's native language is the best example. At any given moment, it is hard to *un*know what one knows.

Leaders and members of organizations are also subject to volumes of information, and they also apprehend various bodies of knowledge. What roles do ideas and values play in this process? Obviously, the answer is different for every organization. In searching for answers, it is helpful to consider the extent to which an organization is consciously or unconsciously making choices about what to abstract from the flood of information as the basis for developing its program.

Economic Conditions

The quest for favorable economic conditions for music and music teaching is one of the most powerful factors in determining how the field evolves. Ideas, values, information, and knowledge are all significantly influenced by economic interests. General values about music held by most Americans are insufficient to allow comfort about the continuity of any musical enterprises beyond those associated with entertainment or popular culture; and even in that arena, technological advances now generate economic uneasiness. The search for continuity of support has produced many harsh realities for the music and music-teaching communities. For example, competition for scarce resources has influenced perceptions about the practicality of broad-scale collaboration and cooperation: The quarter-to-quarter orientation of American business seems so ingrained in the American psyche that the idea of long-term investment allied with strategic planning has little real power. To those on the outside, the music community often seems excessively fragmented. Given its precarious economic position, more integrated cooperation might be expected.

To the researcher, economic patterns and the relative security of financial support for various elements of the musical enterprise reveal much about the underlying basis for many policy decisions. The music-as-center/music-as-means distinction is an important analytical tool. Often, the most effective way to provide financial means to do music is to use music primarily as means for other ends. Thus, gaining the means to do music often results in reinforcing the idea that music has little meaning in and of itself. Continuous reinforcement of this idea produces values about music that prevent it from being broadly considered as a basic in education. The potential impact on economic designs affecting music and music study is obvious. The status of this idea is of continuing strategic concern with respect to tax-based funding for music education programs in the public schools.

The further one pursues such analysis, the more interrelationships tend to reveal themselves: for example, between (1) ideas/values/information/knowledge about music and (2) ideas/values/information/knowledge about economic conditions either locally, regionally, or nationally. Since economic conditions play such an important role in the advancement of music and music teaching, expanding knowledge and understanding of these interrelationships is a critical research priority.

Public Relations

The connection between public relations and economic well-being is generally perceived to be so strong that the two are hard to separate. Yet, it is useful to make the division for analytical purposes. Even though a good image is considered of vital importance by most individuals and organizations, knowledge of and competence in public relations technique vary widely. Further, to the extent that public relations can be purchased, there is great disparity among organizations and groups: Image power in arts policy is often a function of wealth rather than accomplishment in arts or policy terms. Exploring this relationship is an important priority for researchers directly concerned with policy formulation.

Public relations, marketing, and advertising are interrelated fields of study, each with a literature and contending sets of methodologies and practices. Conditions are far from static in these fields. Value changes, technological advances, and subject matter shifts cause evolutions and, at times, rapid extrapolations or demarches.

For the researcher, a first premise might be that public relations will always exist as a primary factor among various influences. The major line of inquiry becomes not the presence or necessity of public relations, or even analyses of public relations technique, but rather (1) the place public relations holds in the objectives profile of an individual or organization, (2) how ideas about public relations relate to ideas about music and/or music study, (3) how values are reflected in the content of public relations activities, and so forth. Another line of inquiry pursues the extent to which individual and organizational public relations are consistent with ideas indigenous to the nature of the work being done, or to relationships between the specific work being done and the general work necessary to support the musical enterprise in a comprehensive sense.

Technology and Technique

Technology and technique are central to music and music teaching. Technology enables much and promises more in terms of machinery and processes that facilitate musical activities. Technique—the application of the philosophy of technology in nonmachine contexts—is a two-edged sword of portentous dimensions. Without technique, one can do little. But overemphasis on technique is almost as problematic. For example, overemphasis can diminish both the will and the means for individual application of knowledge and skills in discrete circumstances. Technique out of control can become means for manipulation and power acquisition rather than means for facilitating individual effort toward substantive results.

Fortunately, there is a small but significant literature exploring the wider impact of technology and technique on contemporary affairs. At its best, this literature analyzes and cautions about misuse without taking the untenable position that technology and technique should be either removed from the scene or frozen at their present state of development. The music education profession and its research component need to be involved with such ideas on a continuing basis.

Interchanges of ideas, values, information, and knowledge about technology and technique constitute a major influence on what individuals and organizations do. Both economic conditions and public relations are deeply affected by what is thought and known about technology and technique. Further, technology and technique are such central mechanisms in contemporary life that information is easily translated into values without first being filtered through a set of ideas or considered against principles or bodies of knowledge. Images and image making through technical means have thus replaced discourse in many decision-making arenas. Technology and technique are commonly thought to be capable of overriding historic and physical conditions. General faith in public relations technique, management technique, teaching technique, polling technique, and so on seldom waivers, even though specific technical procedures within these larger categories come and go in response to various influences. This general faith is so pervasive that it is hard to imagine understanding the contemporary world and the interplay of organizations and individuals concerned with music and music teaching without a thorough understanding of technology, technique, and the technological mentality, both as influences in and of themselves and as means for delivering other influences.

Demographics

The demographic issue has recently emerged from relative obscurity and exploded on the policy analysis scene. All sorts of connections are currently being made between demographic statistics and projected conditions. But demographics remain an important influence irrespective of public notice. Researchers in music and music education have significant challenges in pursuing this influence. Consider the extent to which there is an immediate linear correlation between demographic statistics and evolving individual or organizational values. Groups used as demarcators in any specific demographic projection evolve as time passes. A specific community expected to grow or diminish in numbers over a 10-year period may or may not have an identical set of values at the end of the 10-year period. Correlating the extent to which demographics may change values in a given period is perhaps the most salient problem in bringing demographics research into a useful relationship with policies for music and music teaching.

Philosophical Climate

The philosophical climate is an aggregation of the political, religious, intellectual, and cultural climates, each of which is multifaceted. Here the researcher has a rich set of conditions. A first step might be determining what aspect of the philosophical climate has which influences on the subject of specific research. This step is not easy because connections between philosophical climates and ideas/values are regularly drawn in superficial terms. News media, party politics, and all manner of public relations efforts usually try to distill complicated issues into their most simple, potent, and effective formulations for swaying public opinion. Fortunately, there is much to be discovered in exploring such issues in greater depth. For one thing, elements of the philosophical climate do much to fashion and refashion ideas and values. The notion of refashioning values is of extreme importance to the music and music-teaching communities because, as previously noted, ideas and values about music and music study are often insufficiently favorable to provide economic and other kinds of support needed by the field. Philosophical positions developed and articulated with force create influences to be reckoned with in every arena where decisions are made about music and music education. The capability to interrelate analysis of and creation of the philosophical climate is a critical skill that must be present with sufficient force if the field is to be effectively proactive on its own behalf. The most knowledgeable and sophisticated research efforts are needed as a basis for this work.

Governance Patterns and Change Mechanisms

Governance patterns are the subject of much study, particularly as they occur in government and business. These patterns are interesting in and of themselves, and they have many applications to the organization and management of all aspects of the musical enterprise. Numerous research paths for relating governance to music are clearly charted. Researchers need only produce studies having the same objectives as those about other enterprises.

The more difficult and less understood territory involves connections between governance patterns and change mechanisms. The mix is even more challenging if one adds other influences; patterns then begin to appear for comprehensive studies of interrelationships among all three areas. A few pertinent change mechanisms include funding patterns, reward systems, legislation/regulation, standards-setting mechanisms, policy analysis/development mechanisms, consultant/advisory systems, industry- or field-wide decisions, technological applications, advertising, research reports, content presented by the electronic media, content of formal education, and path-breaking conceptual work. All of these mechanisms regularly influence music and music education. Each also has connections to the evolution of economic conditions and to the availability of technical means. Each influences and is influenced by ideas, values, information, and knowledge. Each impacts the information, knowledge, and values base for governance patterns and policy decisions. All these connections and their relationships to the progress of music and music education constitute a rich field for research. Their specific relationships to the operations of professional organizations are a subset of such a field.

The Presence, Will, and Commitment of Visionaries

Visionary work has the potential to produce immediate influence. There is an equal potential for truly visionary work to be ignored, or even opposed, at least for a time. Work can also be considered visionary at one point, wrongheaded at another. The notion of vision with respect to music and music education deserves intense scrutiny. The most understood sort of vision is that of composers and performers whose visionary work illuminates the musical universe in pure musical terms. This is easy to compare to visionary work in scientific, humanistic, or other artistic disciplines. Vision, however, is also associated with politics and particularly with political personalities.

Public relations technique is heavily engaged in churning out images of vision along with images of competence, integrity, accountability, and compassion. Research interest in visionaries, or even visionary enterprises, can be promotional or otherwise protective. Nonpartisan analysis, on the other hand, reveals the presence or absence of logical inconsistencies, old ideas in new guises, trendiness, images masking lack of substance, and so on. Vigorous analysis of self-announced visionary proposals emanating from all sorts of entities is essential. The absence of such analysis limits possibilities for informed debate. The result is often a substitution of public relations nonstrums for content. Music, and particularly music education, can be profoundly affected.

In order to analyze historic, present, or prospective influences of real or self-anointed visionary ideas, the researcher must be able to draw upon various disciplines. This ability is particularly important because different visions have different impacts: What may be perceived as a benefit by one sector of music or music education may be seen as negative by another. As noted previously, visions tied to certain music-as-means agendas have significant potential to harm public ideas and values about music and music study, particularly if supported by extensive, sustained public relations operations. Analysis of this kind is well-known in politics. A primary role of political analysts is to evaluate the consequences of proposals based on content rather than on source, or on the presence of will and commitment, and particularly on the presence of money. Any field that does not have and utilize extensive capabilities in this regard is severely disadvantaged in the current marketplace of ideas.

Wild Cards

The term "wild card" is used to designate phenomena that appear without warning. A mercantile example is extreme weather conditions that cause rises or falls in the prices of commodities. Wild cards portend significant changes in one or more of the elements of influence that, in turn, can precipitate new sets of conditions for the pursuit of music and music study. Thus, diagnosis and evaluation of potential wild cards is an important research activity. Consider the battle of ideas taking place under the rubric of education reform. Some ideas, if rapidly and pervasively implemented, would have a devastating impact on current music education programs. In fact, back-to-basics directions in education reform produced just such a result in some localities. But education reform also contains ideas of tremendous benefit for the furtherance of music education.

The responsibility of the researcher is to analyze ideas and make forecasts about wild cards inherent in them that will assist those who are in positions to influence decision mak-

ing. Not every wild card and its ramifications can be predicted, but this does not stop significant forecasting and contingency planning in many other fields. The music and music education communities need to know, for example, how they might deal with a massive recession, or with the impact of new levels of competition with an expanded and united Europe, or with the potential development of home-centered life-styles made possible by technological advances, life-styles that can maximize passive use of music even to the extent of minimizing incentives for individuals to attend live performances. These and many other contingency questions deserve continuing consideration.

SAMPLE RESEARCH ISSUES

Multiple combinations of the issues raised concerning organizations and influences provide a virtually endless array of research topics. There are countless permutations as influences develop, intermingle, and collide both within and among music and music education organizations, and within the entire nonmusic context. Despite this complexity and the ebb and flow of change, there are various perennial issues of critical concern to music education. Positions on these issues are not static, but most often they do not change quickly. An interesting question is the extent to which evolutions occur primarily as individuals move in and out of the system (a generational shift) or because individuals within the system change their basic point of view (an internal values shift). Studying such shifts, their interrelationships, their evolution, and their multiple connections to organizations and influences demands a philosophical and artistic approach to intellectual work. Analysis of these matters is not fundamentally scientific, although scientific methodologies may be part of the information-gathering process. The orientations and techniques most involved are those of strategic analysis: evaluations of evolving collections and movements of force, projections about potential developments, preparation for proactive leadership, if possible, and carefully developed contingencies to be used if necessary. At its most sophisticated levels, the work combines scientific, historical, and artistic means for dealing with ideas and information. It is not, however, a search for truth in scientific or historical terms, but rather an attempt to understand and manage an evolving state of affairs.

In order to demonstrate how research about organizations and influences can be interwoven with several perennial issues, four areas have been chosen for a brief analysis. These four are illustrative rather than exhaustive, both in their presence and in their presentation. They are closely interrelated. They touch on basic values and challenges for the future of music education. They represent truly strategic questions that are always being answered in some fashion. The issue here is whether at any specific time answers result from an aggregation of random events, or whether policy intellectuals in music education have provided the kind of analysis and debate that sharpens the awareness of individual decision makers with influence on the work of the field.

Music Education and Music as an Art Form

The values held by music teachers and their organizations about the art of music and the relationship of their work to the furtherance of this art provide tremendous influences on all factors involved in comprehensive considerations of relationships between music education and its context. Everyone recognizes that music has many purposes. Its major purpose in contemporary American society is clearly entertainment. For most individuals, this means that music is something to hear rather than something to do. Most listening is passive in musical terms, although it may be active in other terms—the social or political import of lyrics, for example. Music also has psychological functions. It produces joy and richness on many levels. In its folk manifestations, it binds cultures together and provides cultural identifications, even for those outside a specific culture. Music seems so indigenous to human existence that it springs up naturally in every society. Just as individuals build shelter for various purposes, communicate with words, make pictorial representations, and establish codes of conduct, so they also make music. But history shows that these and other goals of human activity can be pursued on a variety of levels. A structure can be a simple pioneer hut or it can be the Chartres Cathedral, words can be a concert notice or a Shakespearean play, visual representation can be a teacher's blackboard illustration or a painting by Rembrandt, social organization can be the unspoken behavior codes of a family or the American Constitution. Just so, music can be a folk melody or a symphony, a popular melody or a jazz improvisation, a simple hymn or a Palestrina motet. Although the examples given here are all from western culture, the same types of examples can be rendered for many other cultures. The difference between the two examples in each pair comes from the fact that the second in each pair represents conscious objectives to bring the highest level of intellectual technique to expressive communication. Reaching for and achieving this fusion of intellect and emotion is one of the greatest cultural legacies. The existence of this legacy and the promise it holds provide the fundamental rationale for formal study of any of the arts. By definition, vernacular culture does not need formal education to be transmitted from generation to generation.

This basic idea demarcates a certain perspective. It suggests that the primary reason for music education is to develop knowledge and skills that provide capabilities for and orientation to work and works that exemplify the fusion of intellectual technique and expressive intent. This is not to be pejorative about vernacular music. It is simply to state that vernacular music and art music represent different objectives in the use of musical materials. Both are useful, both are to be respected on a variety of levels, but one is based on formal education and pursuit of the world through conscious application of intellectual means while the other is not. This idea presents only one of the many possible frames of reference for analysis, but keeping the idea in mind for the moment, it is clear that the values held by the music education community about this idea have a powerful impact on the agendas and aspirations of organizations. These values also have a tre-

mendous impact on the extent to which cultural influences are broadly considered things that the field has a mission to create, or whether they are things expected to create the field. A related question is the choice of arena or arenas the field makes with respect to taking leadership. To what extent does the music education community at any one time exhibit aspirations for leadership in artistic development? What position does artistic development have on lists of organizational priorities? Considerations of this issue lead to a critical matter: the impact of values about the music/art relationship on the long-term health of the field.

Certain ideas held by individuals, organizations, and societies are so strong that they transcend influences. (Influences primarily change means of working with the idea as time passes. They hardly alter the basic idea.) One such idea is that every student should study mathematics as a serious educational discipline. It is not necessary to produce fundamental arguments for the cause of mathematics. Questions are about how, how long, and how much, not whether. There are many reasons why mathematics is considered inherently valuable, but one reason is that common understanding of the connection between mathematics and the achievements that benefit everyone. Mathematics is considered the basis for our scientific and technological culture, our economic well-being, our security. Contrast this situation with the position of music. Instead of being considered inherently valuable, music is regularly considered ornamental. As a result, proponents of music education constantly redefine and repackage the rationale for music study on the basis of current perceptions about what will sell. Music education—and much of art in general—is thus constantly defined in trendy terms. There is no transcendent presence as a basic. This set of conditions leads to a most interesting and strategic research question: the extent to which music's position in education is related to the position of the music education community about the extent to which its work is centered in the furtherance of music as an art form. For, to the extent that such aspirations for music-art connections are not present, to that same extent there is no continuing visibility for ideas that connect basic study of music to high accomplishment in cultural terms. There is no parity of aspiration with the other basics, at least in terms of serious contributions to intellectual life.

This set of conditions is rich with possibilities in research and strategic analysis. If some subjects in the curriculum are understood for their connection to the basic work of economic and cultural formation, while others are not so understood, the result is obvious in terms of public values. Questions of interest are (1) how is music education valued? and (2) what options does the music education community have to deal with the answers? Further analyses can be made about which sectors of influence can bring either evolutionary or rapid change, and under what conditions.

Many other questions are related to the extent to which the driving force of music education is an artistic agenda. Two of the most interesting are (1) the extent to which aspirations for teaching music are centered on forming culture or reflecting culture and (2) the extent to which music teaching is involved in the advancement of intellectual capabilities in both musical and nonmusical terms. Another set of questions involves the problem of mixtures and balances given the nature of aspirations for teaching music as an art form. Many influences bear on this question in specific circumstances. For example, ideas and concepts considered inherently valuable by students, parents, other teachers, administrators, education policy intellectuals, and arts advocates regularly produce varying but tremendous arrays of force against music programs with an artistic agenda. These conditions present both short-term and long-term realities that often alter the best, most well-intentioned plans of music teachers. A critical strategic question is the extent to which these conditions create a downward spiral of public values. If all energies are spent on constant redefinition and repackaging of the rationale for music study in response to trends, to counterproductive ideas, or to both, too little is left to execute long-term campaigns that would cause music to be regarded as inherently valuable as an educational basic. For example, what is the long-term effect of constantly changing public rationales for music instead of a perennial agenda focused on vital issues such as individual competence and general cultural formation? To the extent that the music education community presents an ever-changing public position about its basic purposes, is the public being taught that music has no fundamental purpose beyond entertainment, no basic connection to the life of the mind that transcends the parade of temporary influences and their interrelationships?

Social Responsibility

Issues of social responsibility are intricately related to values about the role of music education in the advancement of music as an art form. Consider the difference between holding (1) that the most socially responsible course for music education is providing individuals with the knowledge and skills to work with music on their own terms as their capabilities and philosophies evolve and (2) that immediate social action is the first objective and that music study is primarily useful only to the extent that it promotes the best definitions of social responsibility extant at the time of study. Position (1) might be defined as a music-as-center position while position (2) might be defined as a music-as-means position. Since definitions of social responsibility are constantly changing, the music-as-means position is consistent with operations that redefine and repackage rationales for music study in response to changing conditions.

Effective strategic analysis is not based on taking either/or positions in matters of this kind, but rather on looking at the current presence and projected impacts of various mixtures and balances—any real world music-teaching activity has both music-as-center and music-as-means rationales, agendas, and results. Weight in favor of music-as-center approaches, however, produces a far different curriculum and set of expectations than does a music-as-means agenda. At the K–12 level the first will focus on basic knowledges and skills, while the second will emphasize experiences with

ideas, events, and knowledge, all filtered to achieve the primary agenda for which music has become a means. The primary agenda sets the content rather than the discipline itself.

Decisions about the nature of social responsibility in music education have influence far beyond specific ramifications for curricular content. Analysis of these matters is made more interesting by the ubiquity and intensity of public relations battles devoted to defining and redefining social responsibility. The presence of mass communication capabilities keeps the arsenals of combatants brimming. Much effort is centered on attempts to convince the public that direct linear extrapolations of current conditions and traditions will produce the future. While sophisticated analysts know that exhortations based on such premises are seriously flawed, the public gets whipsawed by set after set of trendy projections calculated to manufacture urgencies. The analytical challenge is to distinguish among fads, trends, and real long-term change.

Since grist for public relations mills can develop or be developed from any influence or set of influences, the strategic analyst has a significant task. Sophisticated persons realize that underlying questions about social responsibility are based on such distinctions as the balance at a given time between emphasis on individual versus group responsibility, or citizen versus state responsibility, or private sector versus public sector responsibility. A wise analyst also knows that popular culture definitions of social responsibility, though fickle, can be powerful driving forces on decisions taken for the short term. These standard operating conditions present an extremely challenging set of strategic problems. One of these is the impact of rapidly changing popular culture definitions of social responsibility on music study focused on music-as-center values with its concomitant reliance on long-term, incremental development. There are also intriguing questions about the relationship of rapidly changing popular values about social responsibility and the more transcendent and permanent agenda of enterprises devoted to crafting and presenting works of high art in any of the world's great cultural traditions. These two latter problems provide excellent examples of the distinction between measuring value and productivity in terms of efficiency and measuring them in terms of sustained ability. Different mixtures and balances regarding efficiency and sustained ability have different impacts on definitions of social responsibility. These definitions have profound impact on the context in which music is taught and learned.

The Impact of Technology and Technique

Technology (mechanical devices) and *technique* (use of technological methods in essentially nonmechanical or nonmachine contexts) are constants of contemporary existence. Technical advances have been so great in so many fields that technological values have inordinate influence. Most usual approaches to technology and technique focus on either creation, advancement, explanation, or application of technical means. Centered on quests for immediate efficiency and mathematical replicability, these represent important intellectual activities that rightly command significant resources. However, such activities in and of themselves are not always intrinsically strategic. The usual focus is on what technology and technique can do rather than on what should be done. Strategic analysis, on the other hand, considers such questions as the interrelationship of what is feasible and what is best, the working relationships of means and ends, and the philosophical impact of means on ends. Such questions have significant import for music education. Consider two issues: First, the art of music itself requires the acquisition of technique. Technique and content are interwoven in basic music-centered activities such as composition, improvisation, performance, and analysis. Second, technique, in the form of teaching methodology, has driven much of the intellectual effort for music education since its early beginnings in the United States. Critics of music education often suggest that teaching methods have become far more important than content, that the pursuit of methodology has obscured or even obviated an artistic or cultural formation agenda. For the analyst, such charges invite exploration of relationships among technological, artistic, and social values in the world of music education.

One of the most interesting and pertinent technological/artistic/social connections is the relationship of faith in technique to responsibilities for individual craftsmanship. Consider three questions. If techniques can be discovered that will guarantee success under any conditions, why should an individual acquire professional competence in a discipline sufficient to make personal decisions and craft individualized approaches to instruction? If teachers are only technicians monitoring the delivery of prepackaged methods, can they be truly regarded by themselves or others as practicing professionals? How are aspirations for the development of individual intellect encouraged in an educational environment driven primarily by faith in technique? It is easy to see that these questions have strategic and tactical connections with issues raised in previous sections on art and social responsibility.

Another powerful connection involves technique and values concerning work and time. Conquering both work and time is a primary objective of technology and technique. However, this objective obscures a basic fact: In certain areas, the presence of technology and technique does not change the fundamental nature of the task, including the time and effort needed to accomplish it. Acquiring an education is one such area, especially if education is defined as (1) acquiring a holistic and interreferential education that enables and facilitates deep thought and wise action rather than (2) the acquisition of facts to be tested by multiple-choice examinations and then essentially forgotten. The distinction between efficiency and sustained ability becomes particularly poignant here. Consider one powerful connection. The technological environment with its constant promise of diminishing both work and time on task has significant impact for a field such as music where patient, incremental acquisition of knowledge and skills is so central to basic competence.

All these issues demonstrate why strategic attention to technology and technique is important for the professional research community in music education. The internal impact of technical values is significant in everything from curriculum building to teacher preparation. However, these internal issues pale in comparison to the impact of technology and technique on the context in which music education functions.

In the previous section, we indicated the power of media to promote constant redefinitions of social responsibility. Public relations, management, political, social, and psychological techniques used to advocate continuous redefinitions are utilized everywhere values formation and policy development occur throughout and across the interlocking set of systems that make up American society. As noted previously, many of these techniques regularly focus on replacing reasoned discourse with image making. This, in turn, has significant impact on abilities to make long-term plans and work steadily toward their achievement. The penchant of a technologically driven value system for newness also contributes to these conditions.

Techniques to change public values are regularly used to develop images of power—who is powerful and who is powerless. Techniques to create substitutions of meaning are also well developed. In language, for example, "elitism" has become widely used as a pejorative to indicate snobbish condescension rather than pursuit and achievement of excellence. At another level, substitution of meanings produces conditions whereby expertise in one field (law, social and political positioning, business) is equated with expertise in another (arts and arts education policy, for example). Images of power and expertise created by such substitutions have an impact on the context for music education, and particularly on patterns of influence derived from what and who is covered by the mass media.

Issues of technology and technique provide another platform from which to view the music-as-center versus music-as-means distinction. For example, when music education programs must be justified by contest winning to the extent that all aspirations are cast aside except those that demonstrate the acquisition of technique sufficient to present a highly polished performance of a small number of works, ensemble development technique has become the means for providing content for public relations technique that will justify the music program in terms of prevailing values. With all of the benefits that may come from such conditions, the driving idea considered inherently valuable is winning competitions rather than advancing musical competence. The strategic analyst might interpret this in light of the fact that competition is not confined to music. Competition is adisciplinary. If competition is considered inherently valuable but music study is not, to what extent does this leave music education vulnerable to the vagaries of public opinion? What are the futures of these linkages given the expansion of competition from athletic teams and musical organizations to test scores in disciplines broadly considered inherently valuable?

The music-as-center/music-as-means distinction is also useful in reviewing the values supporting music in many schools and educational systems. The connections between these values, technological development, and proposals to change the status of music instruction deserve constant attention. This is particularly important as computer technology advances. Strategic analysts would consider this development not only in terms of technical capabilities, but also the meaning of these capabilities for the maintenance of important distinctions between ideas and information, linear and nonlinear thought, scientific innovation and artistic creativity, communication and understanding, art and entertainment, and so on. The results could then be reviewed against older pairs of contrasting ideas that are also influenced by technical capabilities and values: images/substance, notoriety/achievement, experience/study, coverage/depth. Such a review would provide the basis for comprehensive forecasting about impacts of the computer advance on values and ideas supporting various types of music education. Other technological advances deserve the same research treatment.

Promotion and Policy Development

The music education community is responsible for promotion and policy development on its own behalf. In both these arenas, all of the issues previously discussed have significant influence on results.

One of the first analytical issues is exploring various distinctions between promotion and policy development. A promotional posture at a given moment may or may not be obviously consistent with a long-term policy development plan. Promotional technique can produce feints as well as direct movement toward objectives. Both promotion and policy development can be adversely impacted by an overreliance on technology and technique. The use of technical means prepared for other subjects and contexts can be devastating when misapplied to music and music education. Direct appropriation of technical means can also result in unintended effects—redefinition and repackaging of music education in terms that enhance nonmusical objectives at the expense of musical ones.

Often, promotion and policy development are considered exclusively in terms of the acquisition, maintenance, or enhancement of a funding base. Whereas funding is an important objective of promotional and policy development efforts, there are many other significant dimensions. Distinctions between short-term funding decisions and a long-term base of values supporting perpetual funding need careful consideration as promotional plans and operational policies are developed. Distinctions between efficiency and sustained ability are useful once again.

The relationship between values and content is a critical element in analyses that support promotion and policy development. This consideration brings us full circle as it connects back to attitudes and positions about music as an art form, social responsibility, and technological means. The content of promotional campaigns and policy initiatives teaches the public as much about the music education profession's values for music as anything that is said and done in classrooms and rehearsal halls. Promotional activities and policy initiatives thus join teaching as primary means of advancing the cause of music education. The research agenda is huge, complex, and perennially urgent.

CONCLUSION

This chapter has presented a long yet incomplete list of areas of inquiry concerning professional organizations and influences. Understanding where the field has been, where it might go, or where it might be led clearly involves understanding complex interplays of ideas, agendas, and aspirations. Organizations are crucibles in which all of these elements are mixed. Although organizations are interesting on many levels, their impact on the advancement of the discipline primarily resides in the extent to which they help the field answer strategic questions both individually and collectively, both for specific local circumstances and for the nation as a whole. There are many lessons to be learned from historical, current, and projective studies of organizations and influences and the impact of their interrelationships on values and content.

To date, the interdisciplinary research challenge represented by these issues and relationships is relatively unmet by researchers centered in music and music study. This current condition needs remediation because failure to be effective in such research as the basis for initiative condemns music and music teaching to the status of reactor rather than proponent in the marketplace of ideas. Changing this present condition is contingent not only on individuals' taking action but also on action being taken in enough locations by enough individuals to create a significant presence for music-centered policy studies in the firmament of the music enterprise. Such initiatives should not be based on hopes for unanimity or on expectations for breakthroughs in technique that will solve all problems before they arise, but rather on faith in the exploratory spirit of policy analysis combined with recognition that the crucible of reasoned debate is, for all its faults, far better than the mailed fist of orthodoxy or the random walk produced by the multiple interactions of various myopic sensibilities. The questions posed and implied by the text above are research questions first and last, yet as previously noted they are only partially scientific and historical. Expanding the music education research base beyond science and history has every prospect of connecting scientific and historical findings back into the daily operations of the musical enterprise. Strategic analysis of influences and organizations and policy development based on such analysis provides the optimum way to make this important and long-awaited connection.

References

Attali, J. (1985). *Noise: The political economy of music.* Minneapolis: The University of Minnesota Press.

Barzun, J. (1989). *The culture we deserve.* Middletown: Wesleyan University Press.

Berke, J. H. (1988). *The tyranny of malice.* New York: Summit Books.

Best, H. M. (1988, September/October). Arts education: Culture, the media, and the church. *Design for Arts in Education, 90*(1).

Brantlinger, P. (1988). *Bread and circuses: Theories of mass culture as social decay.* Ithaca: Cornell University Press.

Bruckner, P. (1986). *Tears of the white man.* New York: The Free Press.

Campbell, J. (1989). *The improbable machine: What the upheavals in artificial intelligence research reveal about how the mind really works.* New York: Simon & Schuster.

Chapman, L. H. (1982). *Instant art, instant culture: The unspoken policy for American schools.* New York: Teachers College, Columbia University.

Drucker, P. F. (1989). *The new realities.* New York: Harper & Row.

Ellul, J. (1965). *Propaganda.* New York: Alfred A. Knopf.

Ellul, J. (1985). *The humiliation of the word.* Grand Rapids: Eerdmans Publishing Company.

Ellul, J. (1964). *The technological society.* New York: Alfred A. Knopf.

Garreau, J. (1981). *The nine nations of North America.* Boston: Houghton-Mifflin.

Gilder, G. (1989). *Microcosm: The quantum revolution in economics and technology.* New York: Simon & Schuster.

Ginsberg, B. (1986). *The captive public: How mass opinion promotes state power.* New York: Basic Books.

Gitlin, T. (Ed.). *Watching television.* New York: Pantheon Books.

Glidden R. (1990). Finding the balance. *Design for Arts in Education 91*(5).

Hamrin, R. (1988). *America's new economy: The basic guide.* New York: Franklin Watts.

Hodgkinson, H. L. (1985). *All one system.* Washington: Institute for Educational Leadership.

Hofstadter, R. (1963). *Anti-intellectualism in American life.* New York: Vintage Books.

Hope, S. (1987). Overview of strategic issues in arts education. *Journal of Aesthetic Education, 21*(4).

Hope, S. (1987). Media and arts education policy. *Design for Arts in Education, 88*(6).

Hope, S. (1988). Searching for common ground. *Design for Arts in Education, 89*(5).

Hope, S. (1989). From past to future. In Symposium: Civilization and arts education. *Journal of Aesthetic Education, 23*(23). Urbana: The University of Illinois Press.

Hope, S. (1989). National conditions and policy imperatives. *Design for Arts in Education, 91*(1).

Hope, S. (1990). Technique and arts education, *Design for Arts in Education* Vol. 91, (1).

Kramer, H. (1989). Studying the arts and humanities: What is to be done. *The New Criterion.*

Lasch, C. (1978). *The culture of narcissism.* New York: W. W. Norton.

Lipman, S. (1986). Art and patronage today. *The New Criterion, 4,*(9).

Lipman, S. (1988). The NEA: Looking back, looking ahead. *The New Criterion, 7*(1).

Lipman, S. (1989). Redefining culture in democracy. *The New Criterion, 8*(4).

Lipman, S. (1990). Backward and downward with the arts. *Commentary, 89*(5).

Manoff, R. K. and Schudson, M. (Eds). (1986). *Reading the news.* New York: Pantheon Books.

Mendell, J. S. (1985). *Nonextrapolative methods in business forecasting.* Westport: Quorum Books.

Mumford, L. (1956). *The dehumanization of art.* New York: Doubleday.

Mumford, L. (1963). *Technics and civilization.* New York: Harcourt, Brace, and World.

Music Educators National Conference. (1986). *K-12 arts education in the United States: Present context, future needs.* Reston: MENC.

National Association of Schools of Music. (1989–91). *Executive summaries, futureswork,* September 1989–March 1992. [Summaries cover demographics, values and traditions, professional education, economics, K-12 education, technology, the values context, research, administrative leadership, and an overview.] Reston: Author.

National Association of Schools of Music. (1990). *Sourcebook for futures planning.* Reston: Author.

Ortega y Gasset, J. (1961). *The modern theme.* New York: Harper & Row.

Oxford Analytica. (1986). *America in perspective.* Boston: Houghton-Mifflin.

Postman, N. (1988). *Conscientious objections.* New York: Alfred A. Knopf.

Rifkin, J. (1989). *Time wars.* New York: Touchstone Books, Simon & Schuster.

Rozak, T. (1986). *The cult of information.* New York: Pantheon Books.

Smith, R. A. (1986). The question of elitism. *Excellence in art education: Ideas and initiatives.* Reston: National Art Education Association.

Von Laue, T. H. (1987). *The world revolution of westernization.* New York: Oxford University Press.

Zuboff, S. (1988). *In the age of the smart machine: The future of work and power.* New York: Basic Books.

·52·

MULTICULTURAL MUSIC EDUCATION
IN A PLURALISTIC SOCIETY

Joyce Jordan
UNIVERSITY OF MIAMI

American educators have initiated many programs in recent years in an effort to deal with such issues as billingual/bicultural education, racial awareness, and multicultural education. American schools, by design, are places in which young people are provided opportunities to attain knowledge and skill. Not by design they also have become centers for social change and the preservation of values. When ideals are postulated or differences arise, the aftershocks or disagreements almost always manifest themselves in the schools. Schools either covertly or overtly are pressured to meet the challenges, counteract injustices, or attempt to balance the forces between extremism and mediocrity. One such movement receiving attention from nearly all strata of society today is multiculturalism.

Music education has been a part of this movement. This chapter will focus on a broad range of research studies related to multicultural music education—studies that reflect historical, philosophical, and practical issues that impact on music education in elementary and secondary schools as well as on teacher-training programs. Long before social movements forced these issues, interest in musics of various world cultures could be found in music instruction. Anderson (1974) traces this interest back to the early years of the progressive education movement.

HISTORICAL BACKGROUND

In 1916, Satis Coleman, a piano teacher at the Lincoln School of Teachers College, Columbia University, developed classes in creative music. She believed that music study should begin with the sounds of instruments. Children were encouraged to collect or construct a variety of percussion,

wind, and string instruments and compose and perform their music. Among the instruments mentioned were panpipes, ocarinas, Swiss bells, Chinese gongs, aerophones, and chordophones. Coleman's (1927) *Creative Music in the Home* contained, among other information, instructions for making instruments from India, Polynesia, Africa, and China. In 1924, this growing interest in nonwestern musics was reflected in a songbook series for public schools called *The Music Hour* (McConathy, 1927–1941).

This interest of American educators in the music of other cultures may have been fostered by two international conferences held by the Music Supervisors National Conference (MSNC) in Lausanne, Switzerland, the first in 1929 and the second in 1931. In the decade of the 1930s, textbooks published by C. C. Birchard and Company, Ginn and Company, and Silver Burdett and Company continued to include songs and pictures relating to various dimensions of cultural life in foreign countries. In 1937 a three-year investigation of young children's capacity for musical expression and creativity in a natural setting was begun. Instruments mostly of eastern origin were utilized in the project. The project, supported by the Pillsbury Foundation, resulted in a publication by Moorhead and Pond (1941).

In 1939, attention focused on hemispheric unity among peoples of North and South America. A music division of the Pan-American Union, the Music Educators National Conference (MENC), and other organizations initiated intercultural exchanges among musicians and educators in the United States and Latin American countries. Encouraged by individuals such as James Mursell, teachers began to familiarize themselves with the music found in both Americas.

In 1948, the United Nations Educational, Scientific, and Cultural Organization (UNESCO) laid the groundwork for the establishment of the International Music Council, which became operational in 1949. In the 1960s, attention was directed to the study of foreign musics, and colleges and universities began to offer courses in ethnomusicology. Foreign musics were discussed at conferences on music education at Yale University in 1963 and at Tanglewood in 1967, both promoting musics of all periods, styles, forms, and cultures in curricular development. As a result of this renewed emphasis on music of other cultures by professionals in music education and the blossoming field of ethnomusicology, textbook publishers employed consultants on musics from foreign countries and increased the use of authentic versions of both vocal and instrumental music examples. In addition, several research studies resulted in which elementary or secondary students were introduced to the music of various cultures—May and Hood (1962), Larson and Anderson (1966), May (1967), and Anderson (1970).

Moore (1977) discusses three events reflective of upheavals in the social structure that gave impetus to multicultural awareness: the Civil Rights Movement of the mid-1950s and early 1960s, the Civil Rights Act of 1964, and the college student activism that led to the student activism in education during the mid to late 1960s and early 1970s. "The concerns of minority students for the inclusion of studies that reflected their culture (Black, Chicano, and Native American studies) and accurately represented their ancestors as well as themselves filtered downward to the elementary and secondary levels to become the ground for multicultural education in its beginning stages of implementation throughout the United States" (Moore, 1977, p. 71).

The humanistic philosophy so prevalent during this period influenced education by advocating the development of the individual's total potential, including the intellectual, physical, and affective domains. The hope was that generating positive images of minorities within the classroom setting would carry over into larger societal interaction. Federal legislation provided the needed funding, and wide-scale reforms began.

The impact of humanistic education had a strong effect on music education. Music instruction, performance driven or not, was advocated for all children. Educators felt strongly that exposure to various world cultures was a viable vehicle for instilling pride in the broadening tapestry of ethnic America.

The impetus for a truly multicultural curriculum came in 1972 with the enactment of Public Law 92-318, Title IX, established by the 92nd Congress of the United States (Montague, 1988). The law promotes multicultural education in that it recognizes

the heterogeneous composition of the Nation and the fact that in a multiethnic society a greater understanding of the contributions of one's own heritage and those of one's fellow citizens can contribute to a more harmonious, patriotic, and committed populace, and in recognition of the principle that all persons in the educational institutions of the Nation should have an opportunity to learn about the . . . nature of their own cultural heritage, and to study the contributions of the cultural heritages of other ethnic groups of the nation [Sec. 901]. (quoted in Montague, 1988, p. 3)

This pronouncement prompted many states to enact specific legislation to implement multicultural education. A survey taken in 1973 by the National Project of Ethnic America indicated that 33 of the 40 states responding had published materials related to multicultural mandates; 26 had formal policy statements; 13 had specific laws on the books; and four had passed bilingual laws.

Montague (1988) updated the status of legislative activity in the 1980s with responses from all 50 states plus the District of Columbia. Her study reported "twenty-one states with legislation affecting multicultural/bicultural education, five states with related legislation affecting multicultural education, nine states with policies affecting multicultural education, and twelve states plus The District of Columbia with a law affecting bilingual education" (p. 176). Among those 21 states with legislation, both instructional materials and teacher certification were addressed. The 14 states with either related legislation or policies affecting multicultural education have publications that encourage multicultural education, publications of resource materials, or programs operating at local levels.

Montague found that although laws do tend to foster compliance on some level, her data do not support a law's being the main reason for multicultural music education programs in higher education. In addition, many laws are addressed to elementary and secondary education rather than higher education. In only five instances do the laws address teacher certification, which indirectly impacts higher education and, according to the results of her study, was one of the reasons for involvement by universities. The second and most frequent reason was the individual faculty member's own training or personal background. Professors and administrators promoting multiculturalism had received training in college classes or workshops, had some close experience with another culture, or were themselves of an ethnic background.

SEARCH FOR A PHILOSOPHICAL BASE

Two common misconceptions regarding multiethnic diversity and musical expression, are (1) that music is a universal language, and (2) that America is a cultural melting pot. Concerning the first, despite a general acceptance of the existence of a multiplicity of musical languages, until recent years, and continuing to the present in our music institutions and schools, many professionals have tended to perpetuate the validity of only one musical tradition—western art music. As our scholarship has broadened, we now know that music can also create divisions among peoples. Often, this is true because a people's music is inseparable from the people themselves and accepting or rejecting a culture's music is, in fact, acceptance or rejection of the individuals within that culture. Elliott (1989) believes that the profession's preoccupation with the aesthetic aspects of nonwestern music has led educators to overlook the fact that music in any culture is first and foremost a human practice. The aesthetic perspective, by definition, tends to exclude nonformal considerations such as the technical and social aspects that impact profoundly on the processes of music making and music listening within the culture. In music education practice, music is often separated from its context of use and production so the listener can experience it in some "pure" form.

The second notion, that America is a cultural melting pot, which glorified the eradication of ethnic differences, never truly materialized. Music is not necessarily a harmonious thread to unite peoples. But because it is a major means of distinguishing, identifying, and expressing differences across cultures, it is a window to the minds that created it (Elliott, 1989).

This brings us to an alternative view, that of cultural pluralism. John Dewey, an avid proponent of pluralism, viewed public education as a system plagued by numerous dualisms, many of which we recognize as the philosophical targets of the last 50 years: academic versus artistic study, process versus product, specialized music versus comprehensive musicianship, music for the talented versus music for every child, fine arts versus practical arts, cognitive versus affective domain. Steinecker (1976, p. 13) quotes from Dewey's writings: "Men still want the crutch of dogma, of beliefs fixed by authority, to relieve them of the trouble of thinking and the responsibility of directing their activity by a thought."

Much of this conflict stems from an increasingly pluralistic society. Leonard Meyer postulates:

Our sense of crisis stems largely from the pluralism of our society; but this unease is related to the expectation that society should, in fact, be linear and nonpluralistic. Pluralism does not produce conflict unless the expectation is for unity. Once one recognizes pluralism as the dominant fact of our society, the ability to live with and understand and appreciate the divergent ideologies is not necessarily a source of unease. (quoted in Steinecker, 1976, p. 7)

The advancement of cultural pluralism allows many different groups to maintain their cultural heritage or to assimilate other cultural traits, as they will. Such is the basis of a democracy. Differences among groups become a national resource and the emerging common culture a mosaic of subsidiary cultures.

Palmer (1975) considered the philosophical and practical problems of including the world's musics in public school curricula. His investigation sought to probe the question of why music and music education were on a plane of such global dimensions, and to explore the problems relative to broadening the pedagogical base to a world perspective.

In his search for a philosophical base, Palmer enumerated four categories of philosophical ideation:

1. The "global village" concept, introduced by Marshall McLuhan, recognized the impact on music in each culture of technology in travel and communications media. The notion of western cultural superiority began to diminish as scholars and musicians began to realize that other music cultures were valid and artistic expressions of human needs and aspirations not unlike those of the west. Intercultural study was a natural consequence of this realization.

2. The western ideal of aesthetic value as a closed system warranted fresh inquiries since many music cultures in the world value functional, ritualistic, or religious ends either in place of, or in addition to, aesthetic values. The search for musical significance began to be intertwined with an emerging sociological view of music.

3. As indigenous music became endangered in the last two hundred years through western colonialism, missionary ventures, and more recently, urbanization and scientific technology, acculturation dominated where change was rapid. Many music traditions, whether covertly or overtly, were in danger of extinction. Countermovements advocated principally by musicians, scholars, and educators emerged. Two important organizations fostering global exchanges were The International Society for Music Education and the International Institute for Comparative Music Studies and Documentation. In addition, the rise of social turmoil in the United States in the 1960s focused increased attention on ethnic minorities. Intercultural education was viewed as a viable means of promoting cultural identity and fostering racial and ethnic equality. If through education the values of music in various world traditions could be viewed objectively, this experience might advance a deeper understanding of one's own culture.

4. Academic scholarship and increased ethnomusicological fieldwork resulted in the awareness that while the end products of various music systems were different, the process of music making retained more similarities than differences. Universals emerged, not on the grounds of music as a "universal language," but on psychophysiological grounds of aesthetic response. "Music in this circumstance is accepted for its own intrinsic values and as a unique human endeavor to be beheld and contemplated for its own sake" (Palmer, 1975, p. 122).

Palmer offers implications for a pedagogical framework for music education. Without adequate preparation to understand the structural nature of various world musics and their value systems, inaccurate pictures of the culture itself can result. Moreover, the power of music to evoke peace and understanding between peoples often exists only within a specific cultural setting; therefore, music taught under such a guise is a highly questionable means-ends philosophical conception of music education. To utilize music to achieve cultural identity is perhaps too narrow a basis for inclusion of such musics in the curriculum. However, given the cultural pluralism of today's schools, the music educator must recognize that many different musics are worthy of inclusion in music education programs, with the major goal being a truly world perspective rather than a vantage point from which to establish any one musical tradition as "superior." If students can be brought to the realization that all traditions of music reflect in some way a full range of human emotions, then the potential for a beneficial exploration of various musical systems has some validity.

MULTICULTURAL MUSIC EDUCATION—PRACTICAL PROBLEMS

Given the premise that a pluralistic view of music is philosophically sound, certain practical problems emerge in the implementation of a world music curriculum. Palmer (1975) summarizes problem areas as they relate to the learner, the teacher, and the educational institution.

The primary problems related to the learner involve musical capacity; in essence, a musicianship that allows an individual to practice one or more musical systems as either a performer or a listener is questionable. The music education profession is based on the premise that all children have a right to music education. The assumption that all students, regardless of talent, have the capacity to achieve a functional level of proficiency within their own culture's musical system remains a dichotomy. The commercial world invests large amounts of capital on the premise that the listener is somehow affected by the musical medium. Reports from both the Yale Seminar and the Tanglewood Symposium reaffirm that all possess sufficient musicality to warrant music instruction. However, the music education profession continues to be performance oriented, with selectivity based primarily on perceived "talent." School music requirements are by no means consistent and universal. What then is the implication for a world music curriculum within the context of mass public education?

Another issue involves the question of multimusicality. Can one's capacity to interpret an indigenous musical system be expanded to include other musical systems? The results of some early studies tend to affirm that "restraints on the musicality of peoples are culture bound rather than intrinsic limitations of the human intellect and musical capacity" (Palmer, 1975, p. 142).

In 1962, May and Hood (1962) experimented with teaching Javanese songs to a first- and a fifth-grade class of elementary-age children. While the older children demonstrated more delay than the younger group in grasping the nonequal-tempered system, with practice, both groups were able to grasp the scalar subtleties of *pelog* and *slendro* Javanese tuning systems. May (in Palmer, 1975) reported similar findings in working with Australian children using music of the Australian aboriginal peoples, and in a later replication with American children (in Palmer, 1975) obtained similar findings. No recent studies were found that sought to address the issues of multimusicality or capacity of young children to function within cultures other than their own.

The second problem related to the learner involves the emotional-attitudinal mind-set of the student, necessary not only for the motivation to master a foreign musical system but also to foster responsiveness at beginning levels of understanding. Although no research exists specific to the issue of foreign musics, research results reported by Rokeach (1960) tend to reinforce the proposition that conceptual and perceptual processes have strong correlations. The willingness of a subject to be open or closed to new ideas may be related to personality development in early childhood. Es-

tablishing an openness to various world cultures may need to occur with the very young. Although the work by Rokeach was based on experiments with serial music and has little significance to the question under discussion here, it does open up an aspect of potential research pertinent for educators, especially with early childhood issues surfacing in so many areas.

Lomax (1968) discussed several factors within the cultural fabric that act to inhibit one from transcending one's own cultural base. The Indian Council for Cultural Relations, convening in Delhi, India, in 1964, was particularly significant in light of problems of cultural transcendency. Peter Crossley-Holland, a participant of the conference, enumerated three specific problems encountered in listening to music of another culture:

1. There is a natural tendency to judge music by one's own criteria, which frequently are not appropriate for the music being perceived.
2. There is a lack of background information on aesthetic factors, logic, and convention, which assist in focusing attention in the proper way.
3. The presence of nonmusical factors—such as mind wandering, expectations of a work prior to hearing it, assumption of superiority or inferiority—all cause distraction from focusing on the sound of the music (in Palmer, 1975, p. 151).

Thus, while students in elementary and secondary schools may be capable of engaging in musical activities within their own culture and even expanding to additional musical systems, personal and cultural factors may create obstacles to this end. The notion that the younger the child, the fewer conditioned barriers there are is not validated by research but certainly holds a glimmer of hope for those who espouse enrichment through exposure to cultures other than our own.

Problems related to the teacher are, in many ways, similar to those encountered by students. Issues involved in a music education program that incorporates world musics are (1) teacher preparation, (2) authenticity of performers, (3) methods and materials, (4) feasibility and practicality, (5) selection of specific musical traditions, and (6) other miscellaneous considerations. Many of these issues discussed by Palmer (1975) were revisited in discussions held at the Wesleyan Symposium in 1984. In a summary report entitled *Becoming Human Through Music* (1985), symposium participants reiterated the importance of viewing the music of nonwestern cultures within their own social structures and realizing that in most cultures music is interrelated with dance, drama, ritual, and visual elements. Many questioned whether music teachers confronting a folk song found in a book isolated from its cultural context would have the background to do this. Music teachers expressed openly their skepticism respecting adequate training, performance skills, and cultural competence.

Montague (1988) investigated teacher training in multicultural music education in selected universities and colleges. Her review of literature is notable and covers a broad range of issues. She reports that a number of multicultural teacher-training conferences in the 1970s were prompted by passage of Title IV of the 1964 Civil Rights Act. Publications from these conferences indicated that preservice education in the area of multicultural training was far from ideal. A comprehensive project, reported in four volumes, was undertaken in 1980 by the Commission on Multicultural Education of the American Association of Colleges for Teacher Education. Volume one discussed implementation of multicultural education, preservice and inservice teacher-training programs, models for training activities, and the importance of interpersonal skills training for personal cultural orientation necessary to affect educational practice. Volume two was a collection of case studies that provided alternative strategies for implementing programs in various settings. Volume three was an annotated bibliography of resources and reference materials for use in preservice, inservice, and graduate classes. Volume four presented guidelines for planning and evaluating programs based on National Council for Accreditation of Teacher Education (NCATE) standards. Other publications devoted to the training of educators were produced by Webb (1979), Moody (1979), and Moody and Vergon (1979). Two additional sources devoting large portions of their publications to teacher preparation are *Multicultural Education and Ethnic Studies in the United States: An Annotated Bibliography of Selected ERIC Documents* (1976), by Gollnick, and Baker (1983), *Planning and Organizing for Multicultural Instruction.* Finally, a dissertation by Johnson (1980) explores preservice teacher perceptions of a lecture series provided by the School of Education at the University of Michigan. These references deal with multicultural education and not multicultural music education, but they do provide an important base for teacher preparation since many issues of teacher training are in some ways unaffected by specific content areas and many of the ideas related to methodology lend themselves to the area of music.

Reports related specifically to music and multicultural issues began to appear in the late 1970s and 1980s. Duncan (1977), in a survey of junior high school general music teachers, recommended that teachers be given training to develop in-depth cultural, sociological, and psychological understanding of the disadvantaged student. A similar recommendation resulted from a study by Jones (1985) in an investigation with teachers in rural settings.

One of the first dissertations specifically on the preparation of music teachers was conducted in North Carolina public schools and dealt with performance practices of black gospel music. The study yielded some interesting results. The 1980 study by Gilchrist, as summarized by Montague (1988), reported that (1) public school students were perceived by teachers to be enthusiastic about the study and performance of black gospel music, (2) black gospel music was perceived by teachers to be less significant than other music forms, (3) teachers did not feel adequately prepared to teach black gospel music, (4) teachers did not receive training in preservice programs to teach black gospel music, and

(5) teachers were generally unable to recognize distinctions between traditional and more contemporary forms of black gospel music.

Another dissertation related to preservice training is by Stephens (1984). The study examined the effect of a course that integrated Afro-American music into a musical setting. Seventy-eight undergraduates received training in the form of lectures, films, listening activities, readings, and discussion. Results showed some effect on the degree of preference for Afro-American music, a strong effect on the degree of acceptance of this music, and mixed effects on the subjects by race.

Additional dissertations that stress the need for adequate teacher training but are primarily concerned with either the development or the analysis of resource materials are by Anderson (1970), Moore (1977), Horton (1979), and Britt (1980).

The most relevant information regarding preservice undergraduate training for teachers is a study by Montague (1988) identifying courses and/or course content related to multicultural music education in select universities and colleges. Information was obtained through a questionnaire with a follow-up interview requested. Of 31 professors contacted, interviews were obtained with 22 music educators and eight ethnomusicologists. Information from these interviews provided descriptions for 40 courses. The investigation gathered data from eight universities in the West, 11 in the Midwest, four in the South, two in the East, and two in the islands. Courses mandated for undergraduate music education programs rather than elective offerings were given priority since the former were considered to have the most long-lasting effect on multicultural goals within the profession.

Of the 40 courses described, five were special multicultural music education courses required for undergraduate music education students and taught by a music educator; 20 were music education methods courses with a multicultural component, required for music education students and taught by a music educator; seven courses were elective for undergraduate or graduate music education students and taught by a music educator; and eight were world music or ethnomusicology courses required or elective for undergraduate or graduate music education students. Because the investigation concerned required preservice courses within music education departments, courses in the first and second categories were sought after more diligently than those in categories three and four, which accounts somewhat for the lower numbers in the latter; in reality, many more courses could have been cited in categories three and four.

While category one courses focused primarily on nonwestern musics and presumably involved more in-depth study, many more courses were found in category two. Montague speculates that it is easier to incorporate a unit into an existing course than to introduce an additional course within already overcrowded curricula. Although the incorporation of multicultural materials into a methods course is far from ideal, it does provide some information to students and can serve to increase awareness of the need for further study at a later time. Courses in categories three and four were in no way minimized by Montague. Elective courses were considered to be an immediate way to move toward required courses, and courses in category four were viewed as the most desirable situation where two departments, music education and ethnomusicology, work together to prepare students. Many of the music educators interviewed believed that multicultural education could not be accomplished without first being addressed in higher education at the preservice level of instruction. The ethnomusicologists agreed, but in general saw competence as the most essential need, stating that without the proper experience with varied musics, essential listening and/or performance skills, and knowledge of musical terms in contexts beyond western traditions, students would be reluctant to introduce music of other cultures in public school settings. In addition, ethnomusicologists felt that collaboration between departments must be initiated before advancement in multicultural education could be fully realized on a scale broad enough to make a difference.

CURRICULUM DEVELOPMENT

The largest number of studies relating to multicultural music education fall into the category of curricular issues or development of resource materials for general use for either a particular age group or a specific population.

Palmer (1975), in determining realistic projections for the incorporation of world musics into the elementary and secondary music curricula, discussed three areas of concern—materials, methodology, and students. He viewed the availability of specific materials as essential for implementation. Three proposals were outlined to address what he felt were major problem areas.

The first proposal addresses the problem of great diversity of pitch phenomena of various music systems. He suggested the development of an electronic instrument capable of producing various scale structures and tunings not possible for the equal-tempered piano or other classroom instruments. Palmer envisioned the project to be carried out by a team of individuals qualified in electronics design and implementation, musical theory, and acoustics; scholars in various world music traditions; and a knowledgeable music educator to validate the pedagogy. Today's technology has produced such an instrument, but its widespread use in conjunction with the study of world musics in schools has not occurred.

The second proposal called for source books about various world music traditions designed especially for use in elementary schools. Most essential are textbooks including authentic examples of world music as a normal part of music instruction, supplementary books that concentrate on specific cultures or genres within a culture, and storybooks related to various aspects of nonwestern cultural traditions. The increase in availability of such sources, many of which include accompanying tapes to ensure more authentic aural examples, is indeed notable. An increasing number of children's books with themes related to other cultures are available in public libraries and catalogs.

The third proposal suggested the establishment of an extensive data bank cross-referenced for various kinds of information and materials for music specialists. The data bank should be designed for easy retrieval, utilize a system for ongoing expansion, indicate level of difficulty or age appropriateness, and be inexpensive. The need for such a system still exists.

With regard to methodology, two approaches have dominated curricular formats in the studies reviewed. One approach organizes instruction around universal musical concepts, and the other emphasizes performance. To give the reader some perspective on the nature of curricular studies, several are briefly reviewed here. However, they are not organized around these two basic approaches, although both are reflected in the studies discussed. Rather, the studies are grouped according to higher education curricula, K–12 curricula, and curricula developed as a result of urban issues, and there are a few studies focusing on curricula in an international context.

Higher Education Curricula

Studies targeted for adult or undergraduate multicultural experience are sparse. Butcher (1970) developed materials for a course in African music as part of a project at Howard University. Schmid (1971) developed a curriculum for use in undergraduate music education, providing a syllabus for the course and a select bibliography, discography, and film list. The first three chapters discuss, respectively, the rationale for the study, the need for it, and projections of educational models pertaining to tribal, Oriental, and folk music of nonwestern cultures. The remaining chapters address orientation for the study, the music of tribal cultures. the music of Oriental cultures, European folk music, and folk music in the Americas.

Levine and Standifer (1981) produced *From Jumpstreet: Television and the Humanities,* a series of 13 half-hour television programs for preservice and inservice training that focus primarily on the black musical heritage from its African beginnings to its influences in modern American music. Another publication designed particularly for teacher training was a manual by Rodriguez and Sherman (1983) in which the music of three culture groups is explored—black Americans, American Indians, and Hispanic Americans. Detailed background on the uses of music in each culture and general information on musical performance are included along with specific classroom activities.

Three other studies present a somewhat different emphasis. Gartin (1981) assessed the intercultural perspectives provided in music appreciation textbooks used in the five-college consortium of western Massachusetts. Mumford (1984) developed an instrument to measure the attitudes of prospective music educators toward black popular music and its use in the classroom. He concluded that direct contact with ethnic and popular music was superior to lectures and readings in effecting positive attitudinal change. Stephens (1984) used the Mumford Afro-American Popular Music Attitude

Scale to measure possible effects of the integration of Afro-American popular music into the undergraduate curriculum. Treatment consisted of lectures, films, listening, readings, and discussion. The results indicated that the degree to which a subject preferred Afro-American popular music was slightly affected, and that the degree of acceptance of this music was strongly affected.

Elementary and Secondary Music Curricula

A number of studies were found that specifically sought to synthesize and organize various musics for use in schools across a wide spectrum of ages. Heidsiek (1966) undertook to collect authentic music of the Luiseño Indians of Southern California and relate it to a program of music education for schools in the area. Fifteen songs found in thè Southwest Museum, Los Angeles, were transferred to tape, transcribed into standard notation, and organized into eight study units of Luiseño music for use by teachers. Each unit is a body of information and music related to a ceremony or other social activity. Each unit consists of background information, related mythology, dance directions, and descriptions of instruments, implements, and costumes.

Freebern's study (1969) was designed as a guide and resource for incorporating the cultures of India, China, Japan, and Oceania into the classroom. Information on each culture includes historical and geographical data; references to the art, architecture, drama, and literature; and a list of resource materials such as recordings and films to augment the musical study of these cultures.

Anderson (1970) explored the teaching of two nonwestern musics—Javanese and Indian—in American elementary schools. Included were basic historical backgrounds for each of the cultures; descriptions of various types of vocal and instrumental forms; and activities designed for use with children, such as singing, the playing of instruments, listening to prepared tape recordings, and viewing slides and films.

A similar study for junior high school general music classes was conducted by Okimoto (1974). Using the structural and taxonomic base of the Hawaii Music Program as a framework in which basic musical concepts were introduced and reinforced, Okimoto selected additional music of the three largest immigrant cultures in Hawaii—the Chinese, Japanese, and Filipino cultures. The use of nonwestern music was not treated as the sole basis of study or even as a separate unit, but rather as one aspect of the wide range of material available expressing the universal existence of basic musical concepts.

Behnke (1975) collected musical material and cultural and bicultural resources for the study of Mexican and Mexican-American music, including the history and style characteristics of Mexican Indian music, folk music, art music of both the Spanish colonial period and the twentieth century, and Chicano rock music. Music and materials were organized into units with emphasis on the cultural-social setting, the elements of musical structure, and style characteristics.

Gamble (1978) designed a curriculum that emphasized the principles of the spiral curricular model using the music of Java and Bali as content. Concepts of pitch, rhythm, form, dynamics, and timbre were identified and reinforced at four different levels of increasing complexity, from kindergarten to eighth grade. Musical behaviors were described for each level for each concept and constructed in such a way that students must achieve the objectives for one level before proceeding to the next level. Suggested activities were included to accomplish the desired objectives. Students were expected to perform, create, listen, move, notate, interpret, and evaluate each of the levels. The curriculum employed the music and cultural traditions of Java and Bali as an example of how to incorporate a specific type of ethnic music in a conceptually based approach. Lists of source materials, covering recordings, songs, gamelan compositions, and films, were included.

Harpole (1980) gathered data about Hispanic vocal and instrumental music of the southwestern United States in order to design curricular units for use at the middle school level (grades 6 through 9). The term "Hispanic" referred specifically to all types of music in the Southwest that evidence the Spanish language and cultural background. Two major types of Hispanic music were chosen for unit development—the mariachi ensemble and its accompanying song type, the *son,* and the *corrido* ballad form. One set (of two units) represented Mariachi music; the second set (also two units) was devoted to the *corrido.* Each set includes an introduction to the topic utilizing a cassette tape containing both narration and musical examples, supportive materials including teaching instructions and suggestions, transcripts of the tape in both English and Spanish, maps, and vocabulary sheets. Each introductory unit is designed to be used by classroom teachers with minimal music background as well as music specialists. The second unit involves the student directly in musical activities incorporating singing and playing of instruments and composition.

Shehan (1981) sought to determine the effectiveness of two different methods of introducing gamelan music of Indonesia to groups of sixth-grade students. The heuristic method emphasized the performance of gamelan compositions by the students singing and playing instruments. The didactic method was more traditional in format, in that students discussed musical style and culture of Indonesia as presented by the teacher through lectures, films, slides, and so on. Results suggested that involving students actively with the vocal and instrumental performance of gamelan music not only improved cognitive skills but increased preference for the music under study.

Even though the Anderson, Harpole, and Shehan studies suggested that actively involving students in making music as opposed to learning about music of other cultures resulted in positive responses from students, it is not an argument that necessarily validates the teaching of world musics. The value of active involvement is well established irrespective of the content under study. Inferior performances of music by students with little skill or the performance of Indonesian scales on diatonic instruments points out the limitations of school settings. On the other hand, there is nothing to indicate that these limitations cause irreparable harm. Students as well as teachers enjoy and can benefit from the variety of "new" musics.

The Gamble and Okimoto studies focused on the use of ethnic musics as an alternative to more traditional musics in educational settings in the learning of musical concepts. Credence for multicultural music is enhanced by any approach that can verify that students are accomplishing basic musical goals.

Although these studies indicate that students can benefit from the study of ethnic musics, curricular oriented studies simply do not provide the research base to satisfy the enormous philosophical and practical issues mentioned earlier.

Multicultural Studies Related to Urban Issues

Many dissertations and funded studies that relate to multicultural music education curricula are reflective of the 1972 mandate by the government's passage of Public Law 92-318 discussed above under "Historical Background." Many of the studies in the mid to late 1970s take on a decided "urban" character, attempting to identify problems, introduce an innovative curriculum within the cultural context of the school's urban ethnicity background, and investigate attitude changes as a result of multicultural initiatives.

Reyes-Schramm (1975) investigated *The Role of Music in the Interaction of Black Americans and Hispanos in New York City's East Harlem*. The data base for the investigation was the music performed by live musicians, whether they were formally structured, informally structured, or contextually structured groups. A study by Lampkins (1976) investigated the history of the Lakeside School of Music and its role in fostering understanding and the teaching of Afro-American music. A similar study by Whitworth (1977) exposed students in predominantly black inner-city Chicago high schools to music units based on cultural and historical contributions of blacks. Results showed improvement in both achievement and attendance for students exposed to the experimental curriculum.

The purpose of a study by Diaz-Cruz (1979) was to investigate and describe the music programs and their relationship to the bilingual-bicultural programs of a Chicago high school and elementary feeder schools. An ethnographic study by Merrill-Mirsky (1988) investigated the musical play of children from four major ethnic groups in Los Angeles elementary schoolyards—Euro-American, Afro-American, Latino, and Southeast Asian. A total of 342 variants of 117 items was collected over a period of five years, including hand clapping and ring games, jump rope chants, and cheers. The repertoire represents games that have been passed from generation to generation through oral tradition, as well as games of recent creation, recycled within local communities and transmitted from area to area.

An underlying assumption of these curricular studies seems to be that focusing on a minority's indigenous culture can mitigate the inequities that are responsible for the problems of that minority in the home, community, and school. There is an inherent danger in advocating an ethnocentric curriculum to replace established curricula in an effort to raise the self-esteem and academic achievement of children from ethnic or minority backgrounds. To imply that the only way to reach self-determination is through one's own heritage (history, art, music, and so forth) intimates that self-identity is preserved by divorcing oneself from a common culture, that is, the American culture. Such extremism is notably different from the cultural pluralism that recognizes diversity as an organizing principle of American society, acknowledges the racism and discrimination of the past and present, and advocates the notion that our common culture is defined by immigrants, native Americans, and Africans and their descendants; and that American music, art, literature, language, food, customs, all reflect the commingling of diverse cultures. Such an extremist approach would seem to be closing the minds of children, isolating them from any hope of an enriched cultural life, and narrowing the path that lies ahead of them.

International Studies

Multicultural issues in music education have been studied by researchers from other countries. Nakazawa (1988) investigated the lack of interest shown by Japanese youth toward their own traditional music. Nakazawa (1) investigated music education in Japan and found that a conscious effort was made to subordinate Japanese traditional musics to western classical music; (2) surveyed the attitudes of Japanese parents living in the United States and found that they feared the loss of Japanese identity in their children; and (3) compared the music preferences of youth in Japan with those of youth in the states and found that children exposed to the most intercultural interaction showed increased interest in both ethnic musics and traditional Japanese music. Similarly, in an effort to involve Korean schools in the preservation of Korean traditional music by making it the core of the school music curriculum, Lee (1988) conducted a study that compared the use of Korean-based materials and western-based materials in two senior high schools in Seoul. Not surprisingly, Lee found that instruction in traditional Korean music idioms contributed significantly to the development of students' perception of Korean music.

Ekwueme (1988), recognizing the lack of indigenous music in Nigerian primary schools, developed a curriculum utilizing folk music and materials through which students were sensitized to musical elements, improvisation strategies, local musical materials, and the expressive aspects of their own indigenous music. The study provided a basis for teacher training and a curriculum consistent with Nigerian cultural values.

These studies indicate that even within cultures other than American culture, there is evidence that students do not relate to their own traditional musics. Elliott (1989) suggests that to achieve the goals we have set for multicultural authenticity we must decipher objectively the various curricular models that have emerged over the past several decades. He introduces the work of Richard Pratte, entitled *Pluralism in Education* (1979), which details six different curriculum models; Elliott adapts these for the study of music.

The first model focuses on the major musical styles of western art music. Because it is concerned with development of "taste," the goal is to break down students' affiliations with popular and/or subculture musics, especially the affiliations of minority students. The second curricular model, while it includes some ethnic and subculture musics (e.g., gospel, rock, Mexican, African, baroque) sees them only as inspiration for new music composed in accepted styles and forms; in this way, values of minorities are accepted as a source for their potential contribution to a stronger, hybrid society. The third curricular model views cultural heritage as an impediment to progress, proposing that only "now" music has the power to draw all to a national identify. Value is placed on everything that is contemporary, with musical values pivoting on political and economic whim. Self-expression is validated through such musics as fusion, punk, commercial, electronic, and aleatoric. The *explicit* goal shared by these three curricular models supports the inculcation of majority values; the *implicit* goal promotes the unification of a culture (melting pot theory) and the elimination of cultural diversity.

In contrast to these three models, the last three curricula share a common concern for the preservation of cultural diversity. In the fourth model the core repertoire is selected from within the largest minority group of a local community. Although this model seems "multicultural" because it permits alternative musics, it actually serves to insulate the population from the broad scope of world musics' enrichment.

The fifth model distinguishes itself from the fourth (1) by incorporating musics on the basis of regional and/or national boundaries of culture, ethnicity, religion, function, or race; (2) by organizing the curriculum itself conceptually by the musical elements, processes, roles, and behaviors accepted by majority value; and (3) by introducing musics in much the same way as they are learned and taught in their original cultures. While Elliott views this model as the one that comes closest to achieving the criteria for multicultural music education, he believes it has two basic weaknesses. First, it is biased at the outset by the "aesthetic" perspective inherent in the notion of teaching within a conceptual framework, a perspective that judges all musics within a standard set by the ideal the "aesthetic" represents. Second, it tends to be limited to the styles available in the contemporary musical life of the host culture, with only those styles being selected that have some relativity to the students in that setting.

The sixth model discussed by Elliott, and the one that he feels has the most potential for multicultural music education practice, is called dynamic multiculturalism. The model preserves the integrity of past musical traditions yet is open to unfamiliar values, procedures, and behaviors necessary to understand the music of a variety of cultures. This approach allows students to develop ideas about music without the didactic preservation of unconscious prejudice, be it academic or social.

The combination of the widest possible range of world musics and a world view of musical concepts separates the dynamic curriculum model from all the rest. Thus, in addition to developing students' abilities to discriminate and appreciate the differences and similarities among musical cultures, a dynamic curriculum has the potential to achieve two fundamental 'expressive objectives' or ways of being musical: 'bimusicality' at least, and 'multimusicality' at most. (Elliott, 1989, p. 18)

Miscellaneous Resource Guides

A number of published materials are available for use with varying age groups and settings. Two issues of the *Music Educators Journal* (October 1972; May 1983) were devoted to the topic of world musics and multicultural music education. Standifer and Reeder (1972) published the *Source Book of African and Afro-American Materials for Music Educators,* which combined the concepts of comprehensive musicianship and multicultural music education. A more recent MENC publication by Anderson and Campbell (1989) provides detailed information on utilizing the musics of various nonwestern cultures in elementary and secondary general music. In both of these collections the focus for multicultural insistence lies within the musical elements, and direct contact with the music is suggested as the catalyst for openness toward the music itself.

In 1983, the Seattle School District published a series of booklets under the title *Selected Multicultural Instructional Materials.* The booklets list and describe major U.S. holidays and events and American ethnic minority and majority individuals and their achievements, including those of the Chinese, Korean, Vietnamese, Hawaiian, Mexican, Japanese, and American Indian ethnic groups. Although most of the booklets do not focus on music specifically, they offer guidance in all subject areas in achieving the stated goals and objectives.

One curriculum guide that specifically includes music was developed by the Los Angeles Unified School District. Entitled *Incorporating Multicultural Education into the Curriculum* (1981), it focuses on the aspects of cultural similarities and differences and is designed to develop acceptance of individual and group heritage. There are nine sections, each related to a specific culture. Each section contains activities pertaining to interdisciplinary goals and to specific goals and objectives in art, reading, health, physical education, music, language arts, and social sciences for grades 4–8. Cultural groups include blacks, European Americans, Hispanics, American Indians and Eskimos, and Asian Americans and Pacific Islanders.

Ethnomusicological Studies

Another group of studies related to multicultural music education is primarily ethnomusicological. These studies provide more in-depth information about specific cultures, which can serve as resource material for teaching purposes. Many such dissertations can be found in the references to this chapter. Only continued collaboration between the ethnomusicologist and the music educator can assist in the realization of the goal of multicultural authenticity.

SOME ISSUES FOR THE FUTURE

The research discussed illustrates a movement that was labeled as "multicultural" and that has emerged slowly and, to a great extent, as a reaction to other more dynamic expressions of ethnomusicological or sociological happenings. Despite the recognition by the Yale Seminar, the Tanglewood Symposium, school textbooks, and MENC and ISME publications, the inclusion on nonwestern musics in elementary and secondary curricula is far from global.

If philosophy has provided at least a glimmer of a theoretical pathway, there still remain a number of practical problems. Both preservice and inservice training for teachers have been inadequate. A host of related problems is identified by Schwadron (1984): "the availability of native instruments, informants and performers; issues of authenticity and compromise; tuning and scalar differences; national and political attitudes; place in the shrinking K–12 curriculum; teacher preparation; and, not the least, the musical maturity of children" (p. 94).

Research has provided much information regarding the background of various music cultures and curricular sources. Materials alone will not solve the problems of teacher competency. It is doubtful that even traditional programs are meeting the goals set by the profession given the present constraints in time, facilities, staff, and administrative support. Justification for additional multicultural goals must be found in rationales that go beyond availability of content materials.

Research has yet to answer the questions regarding the effects of cross-cultural exposure on musical perception, the developmental readiness of various ages for the study of world musics, the effectiveness of various approaches, and the question of bimusical and multimusical capacity. With this notion of bimusicality and multimusicality, we return full circle to ideas discussed earlier by Palmer (1975). The reality of bimusicality and/or multimusicality needs to be revisited in the 1990s by researchers sensitive to both sides of the issues, who are familiar with the performance and discrimination abilities of students throughout the age spectrum.

A more immediate need is that of addressing the fundamental issues relevant to both philosophy and practice. Schwadron continues:

Put simply, we are not agreed on matters of values or directions of study. In the U.S. there still is some confusion between liberal outcomes and socio-ethnic goals which identify more readily with such movements as affirmative action, equality of opportunity, and other concerns for minority rights. The idealistic hope is that by searching out value systems in music cultures throughout the world, music education will assume an inclusively valuable humanistic role—one that is alert to cultural differences and commonalities while nurturing

aesthetic self-realization from a rich field of musical potential. (Schwadron, 1984, p. 94)

This focus on "value" is not inconsistent with writings from the dawn of the multicultural movement. Dolce (1973) discussed several ideas plaguing the multicultural movement in the early 1970s. The Board of Directors of the American Association of Colleges for Teacher Education issued statements as early as 1972 that differed significantly from "model American archetype" and the ideal of assimilation represented by the "melting pot theory." Dolce marveled then, that for such a revolutionary idea, there was little hostility evidenced toward proponents of multiculturalism. He believed that the word itself carried a number of interpretations that actually masked conflicts among value systems. In addition, for many the changes implied were either of such superficiality that change was inevitable or so radical that it could never be accomplished.

Three types of multicultural advocates emerged throughout the 1970s, each with their own value statement. The first perceived the movement as a utilitarian vehicle for achieving larger ends, that is, to increase the leverage and power of minority ethnic groups. The second saw the movement as an opportunity for something new, a spark for innovative approaches and novel content. The third envisioned multiculturalism as near the top of a hierarchical scale of values; hence, compliance implied a willingness to reevaluate one's most basic ideas and behaviors.

Dolce (1973) outlined several characteristics of multicultural education, which still seem viable today:

1. Multiculturalism is a reflection of a value system which emphasizes acceptance of behavior differences deriving from differing cultural systems and an active support of the right of such differences to exist. . . . Advocates often wrongly assume that all share basic cultural values.
2. The concept of multiculturalism transcends matters of race. A one-to-one correlation between race and culture is simply not supported by the evidence.
3. Multiculturalism is not simply a new methodology which can be grafted onto an educational program. The concept of multiculturalism in education is based upon a different view of society than that which appears to exist. . . . A single course on multicultural education in such a setting is an attempt to capture the appearance without the substance.
4. A multicultural state of affairs is not one which is devoid of tensions. All differing cultures are not complementary. The interaction of such cultures will tend to create new tensions and possibly increase existing tensions.
5. Based upon mutual respect among different cultures, multiculturalism is not a euphemism for disadvantaged. Cultures are neither inherently superior nor inferior to each other. (pp. 282–283)

In 1979, the Commission on Multicultural Education of the American Association of Colleges for Teacher Education issued a statement that acknowledged that cultural diversity should be preserved and extended, not just tolerated. The statement defines multicultural education as (1) sets of courses or skills involved in coping successfully with a culturally diverse society; and (2) a general approach to education that seeks to organize schooling around both the fact and the value of cultural pluralism (Rodriguez, 1979).

Is it possible that in an age where even the global market of fashion has sensed the urgency of multicultural awareness, we in education will follow rather than lead in issues that shape the future? Rodriguez (1979) cautioned the profession a decade ago. "Only a well-conceived, sensitive, thorough, and continuous program of multicultural education can create the broadly based ethnic literacy necessary for the future of our nation" (p. 14).

References

Akpabot, S. E. (1974). Functional music of the Ibibio people of Nigeria. Unpublished doctoral dissertation, University of Pennsylvania, Philadelphia.

Al Faruqi, L. I. (1974). The nature of the musical art of Islamic culture: A theoretical and empirical study of Arabian music. Unpublished doctoral dissertation, Syracuse University, Syracuse.

Anderson, W. M., Jr. (1970). A theoretical and practical inquiry into the teaching of music from Java and India in American elementary schools. Unpublished doctoral dissertation, University of Michigan, Ann Arbor.

Anderson, W. M. Jr. (1974, Autumn). World music in American education. *Contributions to Music Education.* 23–42.

Anderson, W. M., Jr., and Campbell, P. S. (1989). *Multicultural perspectives in music education.* Reston: Music Educators National Conference.

Multicultural, nonsexist teaching strategies reference (K–6). (1980). Cedar Falls: Area Education Agency 7. (ERIC Document Reproduction Service No. ED 241967)

Bahree, P. (1986). *Asia in the European classroom: The CDCC's teachers bursaries scheme.* Council for Cultural Cooperation, Strasbourg.

Baker, G. (1983). *Planning and organizing for multicultural instruction.* Reading: Addison-Wesley Publishing Company.

Becker, J. M. O. (1972). Traditional music in modern Java. Unpublished doctoral dissertation, University of Michigan, Ann Arbor.

Becoming human through music. (1985). *The Wesleyan Symposium on the Perspectives of Social Anthropology in the Teaching and Learning of Music.* Reston: Music Educators National Conference.

Behnke, M. K. (1975). Resources and suggested organizational procedures for courses in Mexican and Mexican-American music. Unpublished doctoral dissertation, University of Colorado, Boulder.

Benary, B. L. (1973). Within the Karnatic tradition. Unpublished doctoral dissertation, Wesleyan University, Middletown.

Berliner, P. F. (1974). The soul of Mbira: An ethnography of the Mbira among the Shona people of Rhodesia. Unpublished doctoral dissertation, Wesleyan University, Middletown.

Blum, R. S. (1972). Musics in contact: The cultivation of oral repertoires in Meshed, Iran. Unpublished doctoral dissertation, University of Illinois, Urbana.

Bragg, D. A. (1971). The teaching of music concepts in the elementary schools of Puerto Rico. Unpublished doctoral dissertation, Florida State University, Tallahassee.

Britt, M. R. (1980). The assimilation of Afro-American music Idioms into the music education curriculum. Unpublished doctoral dissertation, Stanford University, Stanford.

Buckner, R. T. (1980). A history of music education in the black community of Kansas City, Kansas, 1905–1954. *Journal of Research in Music Education, 30,* 91–106.

Burman-Hall, L. C. (1974). Southern American folk fiddling: Context and style. Unpublished doctoral dissertation, Princeton University, Princeton.

Butcher, V. (1970) *Development of materials for a one-year course in African music for the general undergraduate student.* (Research project No. 6-1179, Final Report). Washington: U.S. Department of Health, Education, and Welfare, Bureau of Research.

Carriuolo, R. E. (1974). Materials for the study of Italian folk music. Unpublished doctoral dissertation, Wesleyan University, Middletown.

Chen, L. (1983). Development of a Chinese music listening program. Unpublished doctoral dissertation, Columbia University Teachers College, New York.

Chi, C. Y. (1975). The influence of Chinese music on Korean music. Unpublished doctoral dissertation, University of Northern Colorado, Greeley.

Cho, G. J. (1975) Some non-Chinese elements in the ancient Japanese music: An analytical-comparative study. Unpublished doctoral dissertation, Northwestern University, Evanston.

Coleman, S. N. (1927). *Creative music in the home.* New York: The John Day Company.

Diaz Cruz, H. (1979). A descriptive study of the music programs in Roberto Clemente High School and selected feeder schools as they relate to bilingual-bicultural education. Unpublished doctoral dissertation, University of Illinois, Urbana.

Dolce, C. J. (1973). Multicultural education—some issues. *Journal of Teacher Education, 24,* 282–285.

Duncan, R. A. (1977, March). *Teacher perceived problems in general music in inner city junior high schools with implications for teacher education.* Research report presented to the North Carolina and Southwestern Division Conference, Music Educators National Conference, Kansas City.

Ekwueme, L. U. (1988). Nigerian indigenous music as a basis for developing creative music instruction for Nigerian primary schools and suggestive guidelines for implementation. Unpublished doctoral dissertation, Columbia University Teachers College, New York.

Elliott, D. J. (1989). Key concepts in multicultural music education. *International Journal of Music Education, 13,* 11–18.

Ferguson, D. L. (1988). A study of Cantonese opera: Musical source materials, historical development, contemporary social organization and adaptive strategies. Unpublished doctoral dissertation, University of Washington, Seattle.

Franklin, J. C. (1976). Relationship between teacher viewpoints towards a culturally oriented music program and black pupils' achievement and viewpoints towards the program. Unpublished doctoral dissertation, Purdue University, West Lafayette.

Freebern, C. L. (1969). The music of India, China, and Oceania: A source book for teachers. Unpublished doctoral dissertation, University of Arizona, Tucson.

Frissell, S. (1985). A historical study of the implications of black music and its relationship to the selected aspects of social, cultural, and educational experiences of black Americans: 1955–1980. Unpublished doctoral dissertation, Loyala University, Chicago.

Gamble, S. (1978). A spiral curriculum utilizing the music of Java and Bali as a model for teaching ethnic music from kindergarten through grade eight. Unpublished doctoral dissertation, Pennsylvania State University, University Park.

Gartin, B. A. H. (1981). Intercultural perspectives in music appreciation: A survey of five college textbooks. Unpublished doctoral dissertation, University of Massachusetts, Amherst.

Gilchrist, C. H. (1980). An assessment of the preparation of North Carolina public school music teachers in performance practices of black gospel music: Implications for curriculum revisions in higher education. Unpublished doctoral dissertation, University of North Carolina, Greensboro.

Giles, M. M. (1977). A synthesis of American Indian music as derived from culture: Examination of style, performance practices, and aesthetic for music education. Unpublished doctoral dissertation, University of Oklahoma, Norman.

Gollnick, D. (1976). *Multicultural education and ethnic studies in the United States: An analysis and annotated bibliography of selected ERIC documents.* Washington: Ethnic Heritage Center for Teacher Education of the American Association of Colleges for Teacher Education.

Hallman, C. L., Capaz, A., and Capaz, D. (1983). *Value orientations of Vietnamese culture.* Office of Bilingual Education and Minority Languages Affairs, Washington: (ERIC Document Reproduction Service No. ED 269533)

Harpole, P. W. (1980). Curricular applications of Hispanic music in the southwestern United States. Unpublished doctoral dissertation, University of California, Los Angeles.

Harrell, M. L. (1974). The music of the gamelan degung of West Java. Unpublished doctoral dissertation, University of California, Los Angeles.

Hartenberger, J. R. (1974). Mrdangam manual: A guidebook of South Indian rhythm for Western musicians. I. Rhythmic theory. II. Analysis of Mrdangam lessons. III. Mrdangam lessons in Mrdangam notation. Unpublished doctoral dissertation, Wesleyan University, Middletown.

Haughton, H. S. (1984). Social and cultural reproduction in the (music) curriculum guideline process in Ontario education: Ethnic minorities and cultural exclusion. Unpublished doctoral dissertation, University of Toronto, Toronto.

Heidsiek, R. G. (1966). Music of the Luiseño Indians of Southern California—a study of music in Indian culture with relation to a program in music education. Unpublished doctoral dissertation, University of California, Los Angeles.

Hendon, W. S. (Ed.). (1980). *The arts and urban development: Critical comment and discussion.* (Monograph Series in Public and International Affairs No. 12), University of Akron: Center for Urban Studies.

Heth, C. A. W. (1975). The stomp dance music of the Oklahoma Cherokee: A study of contemporary practice with special reference to the Illinois district council ground (Vols. I & II). Unpublished doctoral dissertation, University of California, Los Angeles.

Hicks, C. E., Standifer, J. A., and Warrick L. C., (Eds.). (1983). *Methods and perspectives in urban music education.* Lanham: University Press of America.

Horton, C. D. (1979). Indigenous music of Sierra Leone: An analysis or resources and educational implication. Unpublished doctoral dissertation, University of California, Los Angeles.

Hughes, S. E. (1987). A compilation of Afro-American and Puerto Rican music materials for use in the New York City public schools. Unpublished doctoral dissertation, Columbia University Teachers College, New York.

Incorporating multicultural education into the curriculum. Grades four through eight. (1981). (Publication No. GC-89-1981). Los Angeles: Los Angeles Unified School District, Office of Instruction. (ERIC Document Reproduction Service No. ED 231 905)

Isaku, P. M. (1973). An introduction to Japanese folk music. Unpublished doctoral dissertation, Wesleyan University, Middletown.

Johnson, J. T. Jr. (1988). Enculturation in a formal setting: A study of programs and prospects in Afro-American music education. Unpublished doctoral dissertation, University of Pittsburgh, Pittsburgh.

Johnson, M. L. R. (1980). An exploration of preservice teacher perception on the effectiveness of multicultural lecture series. Unpublished doctoral dissertation, University of Michigan, Ann Arbor.

Jones, B. J. (1985). Preservice programs for teaching in a rural environment: Survey and recommendations. Summary of results and recommendations. Ann Arbor. (ERIC Document Reproduction Service No. ED 26 1826)

Jones, L. J. (1977). The Isawiya of Tunisia and their music. Unpublished doctoral dissertation, University of Washington, Seattle.

Keene, J. A. (1982). *A history of music education in the United States.* Hanover: University Press of New England.

Klein, G. and King, E. W. (1984). *Resources for teaching about antiracism and multiethnic education: Recent outstanding materials from Britain selected especially for American teachers.* Washington: National Institute of Education. (ERIC Document Reproduction Service No. ED 260 160)

Knight, R. C. (1973). Mandinka Jaliya: Professional music of the Gambia (Vols. I & II). Unpublished doctoral dissertation, University of California, Los Angeles.

Lampkins, E. H. (1976). The understanding and teaching of Afro-American music. Unpublished doctoral dissertation, University of Pittsburgh, Pittsburgh.

Larson, P., and Anderson, W. (1966, December). Sources for teaching nonwestern music. *The School Music News, 30,* 27–31.

Lau, C. A. (1971). An inquiry into the traditional music of Tahiti and its pedagogy. Unpublished doctoral dissertation, University of Oregon, Eugene.

Lee, H. (1988). The development and trial of resource materials focusing on traditional Korean music idioms for a senior high school general music course in Korea. Unpublished doctoral dissertation, University of Michigan, Ann Arbor.

Levine, T., and Standifer, J. (1981). *From jumpstreet: Television and the humanities. A workshop on multicultural education in secondary schools.* Washington: WETA-TV. (ERIC Document Reproduction Service No. ED 220 388)

Lomax, A. (1968). *Folk song style and culture.* Washington: American Association for the Advancement of Science.

Lundin, J., and Smith, T. (Eds.). (1982). *Visual and performing arts framework for California public schools: Kindergarten through grade twelve.* Sacramento: California State Department of Education. (ERIC Document Reproduction Service No. ED 231 708)

May, E. (1967, December). An experiment with Australian aboriginal music. *Music Educators Journal, 54,* 47–50.

May, E., and Hood, M. (1962, April–May). Javanese music for American children. *Music Educators Journal, 48,* 38–41.

Mbabi-Katana, S. (1972). Proposed music curriculum for first eight years of schooling in Uganda. Unpublished doctoral dissertation, Northwestern University, Evanston.

McConathy, O. (Ed.). (1927–1941). *The music hour.* New York: Silver Burdett and Company.

McKeller, D. A. (1987). Sociomusicology: The next horizon for music education. *International Society for Music Education Yearbook,* Vol. II, 173–179.

Menez, H. Q. (1986–87). Aoyu and the skyworld: The Philippine folk epic and multicultural education. *Amerasia Journal, 13*(1), 35–49.

Merrill-Mirsky, C. (1988). Eeny, meeny pepsadeeny: Ethnicity and gender in children's musical play. Unpublished doctoral dissertation, University of California, Los Angeles.

Montague, M. J. (1988). An investigation of teacher training in multicultural music education in selected universities and colleges. Unpublished doctoral dissertation, University of Michigan.

Moody, C. D. (Ed.). (1979). *Cross cultural communication in the schools.* Ann Arbor: Program for Educational Opportunity, University of Michigan.

Moody, C. D., and Vergon, C. B. (Eds.). (1979). *Approaches for achieving a multicultural curriculum.* Ann Arbor: Program for Educational Opportunity, University of Michigan.

Moore, M. C. (1977). Multicultural music education: An analysis of Afro-American and native American folk songs in selected elementary music textbooks of the periods 1928–1955 and 1965–1975. Unpublished doctoral dissertation, University of Michigan, Ann Arbor.

Moorhead, G. E., and Pond, D. (1941). *Music of young children.* Santa Barbara: Pillsbury Foundation Studies.

Mumford, J. E. (1984). The effect on the attitudes of music education majors of direct experiences with Afro-American popular music ensembles—A case study. Unpublished doctoral dissertation, Indiana University, Bloomington.

Nakazawa, N. (1988). School music, environment, and music preferences: A comparison of Japanese students living in Japan and Japanese students living in the United States. Unpublished doctoral dissertation, Columbia University Teachers College, New York.

Nelson, E. J. (1981). Black American folk song: An analytical study with implications for music education. Unpublished doctoral dissertation, Stanford University, Stanford.

Nyberg, J. L. (1974). An examination of vessel flutes from prehistoric cultures of Ecuador. Unpublished doctoral dissertation, University of Minnesota, Minneapolis.

Okimoto, R. I. (1974). Folk music of the dominant immigrant cultures of Hawaii as resource for junior high school general music. Unpublished doctoral dissertation, George Peabody College for Teachers, Nashville.

Olsen, D. A. (1973). Music and shamanism of the Winikina-Warao Indians: Songs for curing and other theurgy (Vols. I & II). Unpublished doctoral dissertation, University of California, Los Angeles.

Ornstein, R. S. (1971). Gamelan Gong Kebjar—the development of a Balinese musical tradition. Unpublished doctoral dissertation, University of California, Los Angeles.

Palmer, A. J. (1975). World musics in elementary and secondary music education: A critical analysis. Unpublished doctoral dissertation, University of California, Los Angeles.

Pinkston, A. A. (1975). Lined hymns, spirituals, and the associated lifestyle of rural black people in the United States. Unpublished doctoral dissertation, University of Miami, Coral Gables.

Portland Public Schools. (1986–87). *A statistical portrait of the multicultural/multiethnic student population in Portland Public Schools.* Portland: Management Information Services.

Pratte, R. (1979). *Pluralism in education: Conflict, clarity and commitment.* Springfield: Charles C Thomas.

Reid, J. L. (1977). The Komagaku repertory of Japanese gagaku (court music): A study of contemporary performance practice. Unpublished doctoral dissertation, University of California, Los Angeles.

Reyes-Schramm, A. The role of music in the interaction of black Americans and Hispanos in New York City's East Harlem. Unpublished doctoral dissertation, Columbia University, New York.

Riddle, R. W. (1976). Chinatown's music: A history and ethnography of music and music-drama in San Francisco's Chinese community. Unpublished doctoral dissertation, University of Illinois, Urbana.

Ringer, A. L. (1971). Kodály and education: A musicological note. *College Music Symposium, 11,* 60–65.

Rodriguez, Fred. (1979). *Accreditation and teacher education: a multicultural perspective.* (ERIC Document Reproduction Service No. ED 177 253)

Rodriguez, F., and Sherman, A. (1983). *Cultural pluralism and the arts. A multicultural perspective for teacher trainers in art and music.* Lawrence: Kansas University, School of Education. (ERIC Document Reproduction Service No. ED 232795)

Rokeach, M. (1960). *The open and closed mind.* New York: Basic Books.

Rosenfelt, D. S. (Ed.). (1982). *Cross-cultural perspectives in the curriculum: Resources for change.* California State University, Long Beach: Office of the Chancellor.

Schmid, W. R. (1971). Introduction to tribal, oriental, and folk music: A rationale for undergraduate music education curricula. Unpublished doctoral dissertation, University of Rochester, Eastman School of Music, Rochester.

Schwadron, A. A. (1984). World musics in education. *International Society for Music Education, 11,* 92–98.

Selected multicultural instructional materials. (1983). Seattle School District 1, Washington, Office of the State Superintendent of Public Instruction, Olympia. (ERIC Document Reproduction Service No. ED 240 217)

Shamrock, M. E. (1988). Applications and adaptations of Orff-Schulwerk in Japan, Taiwan and Thailand. Unpublished doctoral dissertation, University of California, Los Angeles.

Shehan, P. K. (1981). The effect of didactic and heuristic instruction on the preference, achievement, and attentiveness of sixth grade students for Indonesian gamelan music. Unpublished doctoral dissertation, Kent State University, Kent.

Shumway, L. V. (1974). Kibigaku: An analysis of a modern Japanese ritual dance. Unpublished doctoral dissertation, University of Washington, Seattle.

Simon, R. L. (1975). Bhakti ritual music in South India: A study of the Bhajana in its cultural matrix. Unpublished doctoral dissertation, University of California, Los Angeles.

Small, C. (1977). *Music, society, education: A radical examination of the prophetic function of music in Western, Eastern and African cultures with its impact on society and its use in education.* London: J. Calder.

Smith, E. P. (1976). Assessments of the cultural elements by generic areas of teaching competence in multi-cultural settings and their socio-demographic correlates. Unpublished doctoral dissertation, University of Houston, Houston.

Standifer, J. A. (1990). Comprehensive musicianship: A multicultural perspective—looking back to the future. *The Quarterly, 1*(3), 10–19.

Standifer, J. A., and Reeder, B. (1972) *Source book of African and Afro-American materials for music educators.* Reston: Music Educators National Conference.

Starks, G. L., Jr. (1973). Black music in the Sea Islands of South Carolina: Its cultural context-continuity and change. Unpublished doctoral dissertation, Wesleyan University, Middletown.

Steinecker, J. L. (1976). *John Dewey's empirical pluralism: Implications for music education.* Unpublished doctoral dissertation, Temple University, Philadelphia.

Stephens, R. W. (1984). The effects of a course of study on Afro-American popular music in the undergraduate curriculum. Unpublished doctoral dissertation, Indiana University, Bloomington.

Swadener, E. B. (1986, April 16–20). *Implementation of education that is multicultural in early childhood settings: A case study of two day care programs.* Paper presented at the 67th annual meeting of the American Educational Research Association, San Francisco.

Tellstrom, T. (1976). *Music in American education: Past and present.* New York: Holt, Rinehart, and Winston.

Tewara, L. G. (1974). Folk music of India: Uttar Pradesh. Unpublished doctoral dissertation, Wesleyan University, Middletown.

Washington Office of the State Superintendent of Public Instruction. (1983). *Guidelines for multicultural Education.* Olympia: Office of Equity Education.

Washington Office of the State Superintendent of Public Instruction. (1983). *Selected multicultural instructional materials.* Olympia: Seattle School District.

Webb, L. (1979). *Implementing multicultural curriculum: A handbook.* Ann Arbor: Program for Educational Opportunity, University of Michigan.

Whitworth, L. E. (1977). Determination of attitude change toward high school general music resulting from instruction in curricular units incorporating cultural and historical contributions of blacks. Unpublished doctoral dissertation, Northern Illinois University, DeKalb.

Wisconsin State Department of Public Instruction. (1979). *Asian and Pacific American education: Directions for the 1980s.* Madison: Bureau for Food and Nutrition Services.

·53·

TRENDS AND ISSUES IN POLICY-MAKING FOR ARTS EDUCATION

Ralph A. Smith

UNIVERSITY OF ILLINOIS AT URBANA-CHAMPAIGN

In recording observations about trends and issues in policy-making for arts education, I am conscious of the pitfalls of selectivity and personal vantage point. What stands out in my perception of attempts to influence policy may seem less important from another's standpoint. Even if agreement could be obtained about what is an obvious trend—the increasing support of arts education by public and private agencies—the significance of this trend can be variously interpreted. If my disposition is to be critical, it is because I am influenced by a tradition of British and American cultural criticism that has as one of its principal objectives what F. R. Leavis, the British literary critic, once called the repulsing of the confident destructive follies of reformers of all stripes, not least educational reformers, who often come to the policy task with ideological agendas to advance. Leavis further believed that it is the obligation of the university in its function as a center of civilization to undertake the work of criticism. I too believe that those privileged to hold university posts have special responsibilities. High on my list of obligations is a continuing effort to exert some control over the quality of thinking that characterizes policy deliberations about art and arts education.

What follows consists of observations I've made about policy-making over the past several years. The principal concern is to indicate a number of mistakes policymakers typically make. Any assessment of policy-making, however, should be preceded by a statement of assumptions about the nature, meaning, and value of art. Mere recommendations intended to encourage support for the arts in general or simply to increase levels of funding may be called policies, but they lack substantive teeth.

By ''art'' here is understood a humanly made artifact or performance that has the capacity to induce a high level of aesthetic experience, a kind of experience that is noteworthy for both its constitutive and its revelatory values. That is, the aesthetic experience of art can both shape the human personality in positive ways and provide humanistic insight. The purpose of arts education, it follows, is to develop in young people the capacity to experience works of art for the sake of such values. Arts education should further be general education for the nonspecialist and a requirement for all students. This stipulation stems from the assumption that all persons in a democratic society should have opportunities to develop basic human capacities, one of these being the ability to experience works of art. All other purposes and objectives of arts education—social, psychological, political, and so forth—are secondary. This image of arts education does not deny the importance of creative and performing activities in the aesthetic education of the young, but it does put them in the service of developing aesthetic awareness. An accent on response to art is consistent with the way the large majority of people encounter art in our society. Persons visit museums and galleries, attend musical performances, go to the theater and movies, and watch television.

TRENDS

One of the most obvious trends since the 1960s has been the involvement of a considerable number of public and private agencies in supporting arts education. Or perhaps one should speak of a dialectic of involvement and disengagement, for there have been both advances into and retreat from arts education on the part of various public and private groups, though the line between such papers is not a sharp one. For example, a common tactic, say of a private foundation, is to secure endorsements for its ideas and activities from other private and public agencies and from professional arts education organizations in order to help justify its intervention in the field. Such partnerships may or may not be in the best interests of art and arts education. In the 1970s, for example, a new policy-making complex in arts education seemed more concerned to use art as a means to solve social problems than to teach what is unique about art itself.[1] The ideas, rhetoric, and strategy of this complex can be conveniently examined in *Coming to Our Senses: The Significance of the Arts for American Education,* to which I now turn.[2]

Although undertaken with good intentions by the philanthropists and agencies who instigated it, the Rockefeller report, as it came to be called, exemplifies much that has been wrong and questionable in efforts to influence policy-making for arts education. Three aspects of the report will be discussed here: its multiplicity of aims, its ideas about organizing teaching and learning, and its recommendations for policy.

Coming to Our Senses is a product of the now defunct Arts, Education, and Americans Panel that was organized under the auspices of the American Council for the Arts in Education. The report took two years to complete, was reported to have cost $300,000, and was supported by such organizations as the Ford Foundation, the JDR 3rd Fund, the National Endowment for the Arts, the Rockefeller Brothers Fund, the Rockefeller Foundation, and the Office of Education—15 organizations and foundations in all. It is a distillation of several kinds of information: the testimony of numerous witnesses invited to participate in regional meetings conducted by a 25-member panel, the standard literature on the report's topics, and several commissioned research studies. After chapters devoted to its purposes; historical background; elementary, secondary, and higher education; and so forth, the report concludes with 15 recommendations. The report contains nearly a hundred reproductions, illustrations, and diagrams, and reveals a preference for action photographs. Attention to the visual design of this report is appropriate inasmuch as its central complaint about arts education concerns an alleged overvaluation of verbal learning. Ostensibly, the report was intended to improve arts education in the schools, but in actuality it questions whether the schools can be as effective as, say, cultural organizations in the community.

To judge by the aims it sets for arts education, the report understands the teaching of art as a means of learning and accomplishing a rather large number of things. True, the report does refer in a general way to art as a kind of knowing, but it manages to present only half an epistemology of art. It emphasizes, for example, not the cognitive status of the art object but a psychological conception of making or performing. While half an epistemology vitiates the report's aesthetic theory, a loosely differentiated cluster of aims—everything from worldly awareness to the improvement of basic skills—vitiates its educational theory. Having no firm idea of art's distinctive functions, the report's authors opt for a plethora of outcomes that are limited only by their ability to think up additional ones. Any approach to arts education, however, that is not grounded solidly in aesthetic theory and that attempts to achieve too much is not likely to achieve any one thing very well.

How is arts education to foster aesthetic knowing? After some unnecessary and foolish remarks about pedagogy, the report concludes that this can be done by a curricular strategy that stresses learning in, about, and through the arts—the first because it has unique educational value, the second because it sensitizes one to the environment, and the third because it stimulates the desire to learn. It is clear, however, that the report favors learning through art. This preference is evident in a not always hidden agenda, an agenda that takes the reform of the whole curriculum and school milieu as its goal. The aim is nothing less than to humanize the purportedly gray fortresses of schooling with the potent instrument of art. The model of reform is borrowed from the British concept of the integrated day popularized by Charles Silberman's *Crisis in the Classroom* (1970).[3] The report thus endorses the notions of open education, the nongraded school, and team teaching, especially at the elementary level, where the report concentrates its attention, notions that place an inordinate emphasis on children's interests, altered configurations of classroom space, flexible scheduling, and interdisciplinary teaching. But most of all, in its preference for integration the report manifests an almost pathological fear of specialization. It abhors subjects, divisions, and compartments. Yet, it is only reasonable to suppose that before art can be used instrumentally to achieve nonaesthetic outcomes, or as a catalyst of educational reform, it is first necessary to know what aesthetic learning means in the context of understanding art itself.

Commitments to nongraded schooling, open classrooms, and interdisciplinary teaching, however, do not necessarily demand the dismantling of school subjects. One can redesign classroom space and experiment with sequence and learner placement and still teach subjects with more or less clearly defined boundaries. And although paying serious attention to the interests of the young is certainly laudable, it is not incompatible with taking into account their needs as well, needs that require students to study things that may not be of immediate interest to them. As for the efficacy of interdisciplinary teaching, it depends on how it is done. What the report advocates gives one pause:

The visit of a master dancer and drummer from Ghana inspired one sixth-grade class to focus on the arts of Africa for two weeks, during which time they created African art of their own. After discussing the influence of African art on the early cubists, they became especially intrigued with Picasso's work and eagerly attempted to make art objects in his style.

As a result of working with the plywood and paint used for these projects, their inventive minds conceived the idea of reproducing a World War I airplane. As construction of the airplane progressed, they asked the drama teacher to help them write a play about the Red Baron, a character made familiar to them by the Peanuts cartoon. They not only wrote the play but presented an effective production to the rest of the school. It can be assumed these vivid learning experiences were not only satisfying but will be long remembered.

In other words, one exciting thing can lead to another. And here is what can be accomplished when artists, in this instance performing artists, are invited into schools as part of an artists-in-schools program.

As we continued to explore movement, the students began to see its importance in the curriculum. We developed our social studies unit around Career Education and the roles people play at their job and with their families. We improved our handwriting by tracing letters with our bodies. We worked on geometric shapes in math and studied athletes (during the Olympics) by doing various sports movements in a controlled sequence. Each day the (dance) specialist continued to say, "you can do better," and "don't scatter your mind."[4]

It comes as no surprise to read "that the students in the project had made gains in reading and mathematics and were displaying superior problem-solving ability. In addition, the school climate seemed more positive and parents had become more supportive of the schools."[5] But of what was learned about the art of dance nothing is said. The question, of course, is not whether it is worthwhile to enliven the atmosphere of classrooms and schools, but rather where it all leads. What does it connect with or how does it fit into a larger pattern of learning? Surely the value of the arts and aesthetic learning does not lie in such free association. But if art is principally used as a motivating device and not treated as a distinctive subject, then, of course, almost anything goes.

The above descriptions are of elementary school activities. The report's discussion of secondary schooling can be simply ignored as it reveals little more than a misty-eyed countercultural attitude toward youth and the arts. Invoking the Woodstock festival, the writers say that "Woodstock was a phenomenon that demonstrates youth's full support for the arts and the power of the arts as a unifying force." But it was, of course, nothing of the sort. Once again, however, we encounter an uncritical faith in the catalytic and integrative functions of art. Today, all this sounds merely quaint, although there are still those who would like to bring it all back.[6]

Even though the rhetoric has changed and there is now more serious discussion about teaching art as a subject in its own right, the policy of inviting artists and performing arts groups into schools is still with us. The retention of this policy is principally due to the education policy of the National Endowment for the Arts, with which an artists-in-schools program is associated. But questions can also be raised about this policy.[7]

As originally conceived, the Artists-in-Schools program (AIS) of the Arts Endowment and of other agencies and groups that endorsed it was a confused and contradictory affair. Obviously intending to give employment to artists, agency officials equivocated on basic purposes; they were not sure whether the Endowment was or was not in the education business. What is more, when the Endowment did speak with an educational voice it attempted to justify the use of artists in schools on highly dubious grounds. It seemed to believe that by importing a relatively small number of artists into a limited number of schools for varying periods of residence it could actually bring about fundamental educational change and reform. Thought was also given to the possibility that artists could gradually replace certified teachers of art. Among other things this would have meant

diverting millions of education dollars from the support of existing school programs and the strengthening of teacher education to the employment of artists. But it was not pedagogical arguments so much as fascination with artists and performers that made the AIS program popular. Artists and performers, it may be argued, should receive their fair share of governmental support, but it is doubtful that they should be made schoolmasters.

The report further compared the creativity of adolescents favorably with that of artists and uncritically endorsed alternative education. Ultimately, however, alternative education proved to be little more than suggestions by educational reformers of the 1960s and 1970s to relieve the young of routine, study, and hard work. Freewheeling alternative education is now under a cloud and is regarded as a peculiar moment in modern educational history when adults affected fond tolerance toward practically every divagation of youth.[8] Looking back at this period is not pleasant, but it is the countercultural ethos of the 1960s that informed the conceptions of learning and arts education in *Coming to Our Senses*.

As far as the report's policy recommendations are concerned, they are largely restricted to business at the top of the stairs: that is, special advisers in the cabinet, the then HEW (Department of Health, Education, and Welfare), and the White House; the creation of new federal agencies for research and publication; a national citizens' council; state-level appointments; and numerous networks to hold everything together. This is action on a grand scale. But policy thinking also consists of small-scale textural considerations that involve the decisions of local school boards, curriculum committees, and classroom teachers. Such kinds of activity are not inherently dramatic and do not lend themselves to the machinery of public relations and advocacy. *Coming to Our Senses,* however, from its inception to all the hoopla and hype that attended its publication, was nothing if not an exercise in modern public relations. The problem with public relations and advocacy is that the whole truth can seldom be told because efforts are directed toward securing approval for ideas. In fact, not a little distortion and outright fabrication tend to occur.

Coming to Our Senses deserves the space given to it here because it is not just another instance of cultural and educational advocacy. It is a document that says much about the cultural attitudes and values of American society. The report is, in fact, a typical product of what Jacques Barzun has called the Art Epoch, an epoch that attributes to art almost unbelievable curative and redemptive powers.[9] Yet it is highly unlikely that art and arts education can perform the multiple functions the report assigns to them or that art can be a potent force for educational reform. Exclaiming approvingly over every artist's and young child's expressive gesture is not the way to acquaint young minds with the complex nature of art. Because art is indeed a formidable power, there is a need for a serious analysis of the relationships among art, society, and education, but *Coming to Our Senses* is not that analysis. Not only that. The report debases educational discourse when it ignores a standard and traditional literature on a given topic. One example of this is its use of the slogan "The arts in general education," or AGE, as the approach came to be known.[10]

Bypassing the standard associations of the term "general education," the report exploits only one meaning, that of general education as nonspecialized education. That meaning, moreover, is used to criticize practically any kind of specialization. Distinctions, compartments, and separations in general are denounced in favor of integration. Over and over we read that the arts should be used to integrate and animate interdisciplinary studies. Yet the report's interpretation of "interdisciplinary" is as empty as its definition of "general education." It amounts to little more than the use of artistic activities to make things exciting. Such activities can consist of everything from singing campaign songs and making posters for a social studies lesson to the use of dancers to illustrate geometric shapes and angles in math classes. The use of "interdisciplinary" to describe what resourceful teachers have always done to make their subjects interesting and appealing is simply an instance of trading on an honorific concept to confer significance and prestige on ordinary activities, an example, that is, of the inflation of pedagogical language. But in truth such misuse of terms invites ridicule. Consider, for example, the remarks of one advocate of AGE who wrote that "these [arts in general education] approaches can be the catalyst that brings about a restructuring of all education and that moves us closer to the goal of humanizing education that so many educators desire for the schools."[11] It is difficult to believe today that such views could be expressed about the nature and role of art and that so many in the arts education professions found them unobjectionable.

The major mistake of this period of thinking about arts education derived from its underlying assumption about the nature and function of art. The arts were construed as a palliative for whatever ailed society and the schools. They were nothing less than potent patent medicine to be administered without any fear of side effects. The arts could raise the "energy levels" not only of teachers and students but also of school principals, janitors, and members of the community. The arts could stimulate learning and creativity generally; help develop the basic skills of reading, writing, and computing; lower the dropout rate; and on and on and on.

The effects of art, however, are not always benign or redemptive. This awareness explains Plato's recommendation to censor certain kinds of art and makes the question of obscenity and pornography a relevant one today. But perhaps even more important than this underlying assumption about art's redeeming powers is the implicit belief that art has no inherent value or energies of its own, only instrumental value. Conceiving art as a kind of social lever or lubricant, AGE in effect redefined it as a social service. Though AGE advocates would recoil at the charge, the attitude is anti-art. To be sure, one risks the charge of elitism in acknowledging that an artwork is a privileged object that demands contemplation and appreciation for its distinctive values and that it is to be understood as something special and set apart. But the egalitarian outlook of AGE was not willing to incur such condemnation. AGE's thinking about art, then, was as anemic as

its thinking about the nature of general education and interdisciplinary studies. Anemic yet not inconsequential, for when the arts are so insufficiently valued for themselves that they can scarcely be identified with the great moments and monuments of their history, arts education is in danger of becoming disoriented. And when the arts are channeled into the mainstream and made part and parcel of everything, arts education is in danger of becoming intolerably diffuse. And, to get down to cases, when teachers are encouraged to think that they can discharge their obligations to arts education by letting dancers imitate shapes in a mathematics class or students make posters for a history lesson, arts education is in danger of becoming perilously diluted.

In short, what is distressing about the reform movement in question is that it showed so little interest in the arts themselves. Its commitment is not primarily to aesthetic learning but to school reform. One has only to run down the index of *Coming to Our Senses,* the magnum opus of the mentality under discussion, to detect where the real interest lies. Every educational reform of the preceding two decades is accorded space: open education, nongraded schooling, team teaching, special education, racial integration, alternative education, free schools, schools-without-walls, voucher systems, competency-based learning, career education, and basic education. The value of these reforms is, of course, to be assessed independently. The point here is that an excessively instrumental conception of art's functions is inimical to art. It is even inimical to the idea of a professional art education association.

SOME MISTAKES OF POLICY THINKING

The desire to be socially helpful and the failure to be reflective about the nature of art are responsible for a number of errors made by policy thinking over the past three decades. These mistakes are the sentimentalizing, the politicizing, the bureaucratizing, and the fashionabilizing of cultural and educational matters.[12] The sentimentalizing of policy thinking is an expression of the philanthropic attitude in cultural and educational contexts. When the arts and arts education are placed in the service of extraaesthetic political objectives, policy reflects a misconstrued instrumentalism. The bureaucratizing of policy consists of substituting inflated procedure for substantive accomplishment, while the fashionabilizing of culture confers credibility on policies by associating them with the celebrities of the worlds of business, government, and entertainment.

THE SENTIMENTALIZING OF POLICY

In claiming that the sentimentalizing of policy in cultural and educational activities is an expression of the philanthropic disposition, implied is a disposition to take attitudes toward cultural and educational affairs attitudes that are more appropriate to the church, settlement house, and psychiatric clinic.[13] The consequence is that good will, sincerity, and compassion obscure the true character and complexity of art and underestimate the need for disciplined intelligence to create and appreciate it.

Instances of the sentimentalizing of culture and arts education are everywhere apparent. We recognize it not only in romantic child-centered conceptions of art education in which clues to curriculum design are taken less from the demands of society, subjects, and learning than from the interests of young students, but also in the doctrine of relevance associated with the pedagogical prescriptions of alternative education popular in the 1960s and 1970s; in the beliefs of multicultural educators today who expound an unqualified cultural relativism; and in populist rhetoric that constantly invokes art of, by, and for the people. When applied to cultural matters, the philanthropic disposition is harmful because it results in the restraint of judgment and the dilution of standards, failure to concentrate resources and energies, and preference for a flaccid tolerance over critical decisiveness. It is antiintellectual because it fails to discharge the obligations of intellect. Compassion is not being criticized here, only the disproportionate emphasis it receives. Marva Collins's school for minority children in the inner city of Chicago, on the other hand, conveys something of the balance that teachers should keep in mind. Caring and helping in her school mean showing concern not only for the disadvantages suffered by urban youngsters but also for their intellectual development.

THE POLITICIZING OF POLICY

Sentimentalism pervades the politicizing of policy insofar as policymakers endorse what is essentially a social-welfare concept of cultural policy in which cultural services are assimilated to social services and expected to achieve similar results: improving the psychological condition of clients. Keeping potentially disruptive social conflict at bay may be an additional objective. For example, in his discussion of the policies of the Arts Endowment in the 1970s, Ronald Berman tells the story of how "art," a distinctive accomplishment with a history of achievement and standards of excellence, was transformed into "the arts," by which he meant the institutionalized expenditure of funds provided for the purpose of solving social problems. The arts were in effect cultural aid to prisons, hospitals, urban ghettos, rural regions, community centers, and other agencies of public welfare. Such aid, it was believed, was justified on the grounds that the arts could, among other things, sublimate violence, provide an alternative to drug addiction, discourage crime, create jobs, animate the elderly, and encourage craftsmanship.

The effect of such beliefs, says Berman, is that justification for the support of art had little to do with its distinctive values and still less with scholarship, criticism, and training. Moreover, since money for solving social problems is not typically given to individuals, social and cultural organizations became the principal beneficiaries of cultural support.

One might venture the opinion that cultural policy has in fact inspired more creativity in fund-raising than in the making and performing of art. Perhaps Berman had something like this in mind when, writing in 1979, he said that "in the fourteen years since the inception of this agency [the Arts Endowment] and after the expenditure of the better part of a billion dollars, *we are hard put to name a single work of art worth recollecting that it has made possible.* Nor can we associate its support with a productive idea affecting the understanding of art either by artists or their audience."[14] This encompassing judgment included the Endowment's Artists-in-Schools program, its premier educational venture.

But then, it might be asked, isn't it the case that anything at all done in behalf of the arts is worthwhile? Is there really any occasion for alarm? The reason for expressing concern is the damage done by misconceptions about the nature of art and about the way social problems can be solved. When art undergoes redefinition as a social service, as something intended either to relax, soothe, cure, or entertain, when it becomes essentially the institutionalized expenditure of funds, then it can no longer be what the works of genius have persuaded us that it is; it is no longer the expression of a unique vision and the embodiment of distinctive values. If one accepts the redefinition of art just described, one conclusion is unavoidable; it is, says Berman, that "art has no particular value in itself."[15] This is, I think, the major problem with the politicizing of arts education; it corrupts the concept of art. The politicizing of the arts and arts education is therefore a matter of grave concern. One cannot have it both ways: art cannot be an object the understanding of which requires long training, cultivated skills, and special sensibility, and at the same time be a social lubricant. We do well in this connection to mention something said by Iris Murdoch, the British philosopher and novelist. She thinks that while art is far and away the most educational thing we have, it has as such no formal social role to play, and it serves us well when artists simply create the very best and most beautiful art of which they are capable.[16] In brief, the politicizing of art and arts education, the framing of policy in social service terms, and the use of art as a social palliative further obscure the fact that art is a human activity with a history of distinguished accomplishment, standards of excellence, and a capacity to provide worthwhile experiences merely in being looked at, listened to, or read.

THE BUREAUCRATIZING OF POLICY

The mistakes do not end with the sentimentalizing and politicizing of policy; we must also contend with the bureaucratizing of policy, about which I will be mercifully brief. The bureaucratizing of policy substitutes elaborate procedures for substantive accomplishment, or at least guarantees the almost eternal delay of the latter. Endless studies, position papers, reviews, meetings, conferences, panels, commissions, and recommendations for more of the same are characteristic activities of bureaucratization. The net effect is a waste of resources and human energy. This realization was not lost on one reviewer of *Coming to Our Senses* who observed of its 17 pages of recommendations that one experienced administrative assistant working a long weekend for $100 a day with pencils could have thought all of them up and written them down. The welter of recommendations, moreover, were said to have been enough to make a New Dealer blanch.[17]

THE FASHIONABILIZING OF POLICY

By the fashionabilizing of policy, I have in mind an observation made by art critic Harold Rosenberg: When the avant-garde ran out of ideas, it fashionabilized itself in order to remain in the public eye.[18] I understand "fashionabilizing" as the tendency to transform art and arts education into show business and to associate them with the celebrities of politics, business, and entertainment. The dangers of this tendency are obvious. Culture itself comes to be associated with show biz. And this is, in fact, one of the capital city's concepts of culture that Charles Frankel discovered while serving as Assistant Secretary of State for Cultural and Educational Affairs during the Johnson administration. The others were culture as the dead hand of the past, culture as people-to-people relations, and culture as cultural lag.[19] Fashionabilizing has another meaning—keeping up. State art education guides, for example, often reveal a futile effort to keep abreast of trends and issues. It doesn't matter if the recommendations crowding their pages are ill-considered or contradictory. The important thing is to be perennially modern, or postmodern as the case may be. And this is understandable, for often there are no criteria for assessing the value of new ideas other than the criterion of newness.

These remarks are not intended to take easy advantage of persons whose principal responsibility may be the implementation of policy and not reflection about its substance. It is the task of responsible criticism, however, to try to understand these tendencies and to point out their consequences. With this function of criticism in mind I have alluded to some mistakes of policy thinking. The way to correct these mistakes is obvious: It would consist of *de*sentimentalizing, *de*-politicizing, *de*bureaucratizing, and *de*glamorizing policy thinking and behavior. We can begin to do this if we keep in mind certain basic questions.

SOME POLICY QUESTIONS

The first question: Is a purported policy actually a policy; that is, is it clear about what should be done and toward what end?[20] This question presupposes that a policy in any significant sense of the term is something carefully thought out and adopted only after considerable deliberation. Such deliberations have a special flavor because they issue in decisions regarding what to do. Policy, therefore, is always addressed to actions. More precisely, policies are designed to determine,

organize, regulate, or systematize activities in order to bring about a state of affairs that manifests a policy's purpose. Under this description policy-making might appear to be an eminently pragmatic enterprise, relying mainly on know-how and empirical knowledge of what will work in accomplishing a policy's objectives. But this impression is somewhat deceptive; theory is also necessary in framing defensible policies. Aesthetic theory is needed to articulate the principal conceptual baggage of instruction in arts education, and educational theory is required to develop the contexts within which to locate specific pedagogical activities. This is to say there is a two-step process involved in justifying policy: first, the generals goals of arts education must be formulated; and second, the ways in which pedagogical activities are related to these goals must be indicated. But for the moment we may simply ask of any policy for arts education, from whatever source it emanates, whether it is clear about the state of affairs it is intended to bring about.

A second question: Is the view of education underlying a purportedly educational policy compatible with the very idea of a policy? The aspects of policy isolated here involve the compatibility of a given conception of education with a definition of policy that emphasizes activities directed toward previsioned educational goals. That is to say, a policy implies a formal institutional setting within which policies can be enacted and assessed. This may seem obvious except as one considers policy recommendations that are inimical to formal institutional arrangements, and hence to policy. Hands off! is not really a policy.

A third question: Is the policy a truly educational policy or does it subserve noneducational objectives? Many policies enacted for schooling have a purpose that is only marginal or conditional to formal learning. Policies are enacted for the security and well-being of pupils while in school and, increasingly, for their safe conduct to and from school. Technical training is also generally conceded to be not distinctively educational in nature. Schooling becomes essentially educational only as students come to understand and appreciate the point of engaging in worthwhile activities. This means that a policy of arts education could not be justified if it did not go beyond the learning of skills. Textbook authors and advocates of education often simply assume that what they propose is educational in character, but it is clear that they do not always make the relevant distinctions. Earlier on, for example, officials of the Arts Endowment were quite confused and ambivalent about the uses of artists in the schools. Despite stated pedagogical aims, their real interest was in giving financial aid and employment to artists. In short, it was an example of a purported educational policy that, in fact, subserved noneducational purposes.

A fourth question: Does the policy emphasize the distinctive purposes of a domain of instruction or does it promote other instructional and educational purposes? This question is similar to the last one with the difference that it asks not whether a policy subserves a noneducational purpose but whether it serves an extraaesthetic objective that may be an educational one. There can be legitimate differences of opinion regarding whether the curriculum should be organized around subjects or areas of study. But if it is advisable to speak in terms of subjects, especially at the secondary level, the question, again, is whether art education should try to achieve its own domain objectives or be instrumental to extradomain outcomes. That aesthetic education as an area of study should pursue its own peculiar aims does not sound like an unreasonable recommendation. Yet it has not persuaded policymakers, who generally ignore it. Consider, for example, the following remarks by a once influential establishment figure, who also happened to be an administrator at a prominent university:

Our great need today is to do with the arts in the nation's schools what was done with technology and science when America woke up to the news that a Sputnik was circling the skies. That is, to employ, through children, teachers, administrators and artists, for the full benefit of the country, one of the great areas of human experience, fulfillment, and promise—the arts—to offer the arts, not as an alternative or substitute to education in traditional subjects, but as an ideal context, a context for a euphoric kind of synthesis, in which better, richer, more profoundly humanizing education can take place.[21]

How works by Rembrandt, Jane Austen, and Igor Stravinsky can constitute "an ideal context" that will produce "a euphoric kind of synthesis" may seem difficult to imagine, but as a sample of policy rhetoric the remarks are typical of the panacea mentality that dominated thinking in the government, foundations, and like-minded university and school people for a period of time.

That educational policy can be diverted from its proper course rather easily by a variety of external interests and pressures—prevailing federal winds, funding patterns, philanthropic caprice—is, of course, not news. However, that this should happen with art and art education policies, that they should be justified primarily on extraaesthetic grounds, is particularly deplorable since in important respects the arts are cherishable in their own right and not merely as a means.

On to a fifth question: Is a policy an effective policy? Effectiveness is a deceptive notion. It refers not only to the actual attainment of a state of affairs that marks a policy's purpose but also to the probable or likely effectiveness of a given proposal. We may thus say about a proposal that even though the state of affairs that marks its purpose has not yet been attained, we at least have good reason for believing that the course of action intended to bring it about is an appropriate or sensible one. There is another point to be made about effectiveness. A policy is not necessarily justified because it does in fact bring about an intended state of affairs. Both the state of affairs and the methods that helped to bring it to pass can be questioned. Neither does the popularity of a policy necessarily justify it. Policy purposes, states of affairs, and methods must be worthwhile and capable of being defended with good reasons. And so when we hear that a given policy or procedure works, we should inquire into the significance of such a statement for any number of things might work.

This leads to the sixth and last question: Have alternatives to a policy been duly considered? All I will say here is that if this question were asked more insistently there would be far

more thoughtfulness about policy matters. The sad fact is that all too often people simply don't bother to think about alternatives.

TOWARD A NEW POLICY FOR ARTS EDUCATION

One example of thoughtful reflection on an alternative to a social-service conception of art and arts education is the recent writings of Samuel Lipman, a music critic and publisher. Lipman, a former member of the National Council of the Arts, not only advocates the strengthening of the link between the arts and education; he also unequivocally assigns a role of educational leadership to the Arts Endowment.

According to Lipman, the foremost governmental agency with responsibility for cultural policy would discharge its obligations to the greatest benefit of society and culture if it accepted and took seriously the task of educating the public about the arts. As educator, the agency should concern itself primarily "with communicating to our citizens the particular kind of knowledge about ourselves, our world, and most especially the civilized heritage that art enshrines."[22] Such a commitment to teaching implies that the Arts Endowment would not only emphasize the substance and content of its programs over such considerations as the size of audiences reached or the amounts of money generated; it would also encourage the presentation of less popular and contemporary art as an extension of the well-known repertoire and do so by stressing not the revolutionary character of new art but its evolution from the past. Toward these ends, the Endowment should enlist the cooperation of the educational establishment and make wiser use than it has of teachers and artists. The agency's mission, in other words, is too important to be left to a congeries of cultural administrators.

Lipman's suggestion of a predominantly educational role for the Arts Endowment implies a major reordering of priorities and a new agenda. We may also read his recommendations as an expression of despair that the agency hasn't realized its earlier promise and that government support for the arts has reaped but meager results or results of the wrong kind. Lipman's assessment is supported by the judgment of Ronald Berman, whose criticism of the Endowment was mentioned earlier.

Both Lipman and Berman point out that the current state of affairs in cultural policy is the consequence of both unavoidable trends and deliberate policy decisions. The agency could hardly have gone untouched by the trend toward centralization of decision making and the bureaucratization of modern institutions. This bureaucratization has produced a new class of cultural officials increasingly preoccupied with political considerations and administrative procedure. Cultural officials were nonetheless free to choose the policies that they thought would best serve culture. Yet the record of the past two decades demonstrates they have increasingly elected to provide cultural services in the form of unspecified "arts experiences" that are "delivered" by cultural organizations which in turn believe it to be their function to secure government grants for making available the experiences in question. Thus it happened that the National Endowment for the Arts, the agency founded as the champion and protector of the arts, came to be looked on, and appealed to, mainly as a dispenser of funds to cultural organizations. But whenever public monies are available for disbursement, numerous groups surface to demand their share. As a result a good deal of the agency's energy must be spent trying to satisfy competing interests.

Contributing to the politicizing of cultural policy-making is what was previously referred to as a social-welfare mentality. Recall that Berman said that it was during the 1970s in particular that cultural services were justified by in effect assimilating them to social services and expecting them to meliorate social problems. The arts became one more weapon in the government's arsenal to fight poverty, crime, alienation, and racial segregation. Yet a social-welfare conception of culture tends to obscure the realization that art is worthwhile for its distinctive values, that its creation requires genuine talent and creativity, and that it has left a legacy of admirable achievement worthy of preservation. In short, a social service concept of aesthetic learning inhibits a concern for quality and standards.

Other factors mentioned by Lipman that have influenced culture and cultural policy today are the use of the arts to help restore the legitimacy of modern governments; the importance the arts have assumed in a secular age as a source of spiritual values; the devastating blow dealt to the life of culture, art, and learning during the 1960s; and the neglect evident in justifications of support for the arts of the distinction between public benefits and private pleasures. Problems and disappointments notwithstanding, Lipman thinks there is considerable good will toward the arts in society and that a public well educated about the nature of high culture and the government's proper role in supporting it would welcome a truly educational Arts Endowment.

Deferring momentarily an estimate of the Endowment's chances of functioning effectively as educator, there are two reasons for an educator's feeling encouraged by Lipman's essay. The first is his avowal of the importance of education to the life of the arts and culture. The second is his essentially humanistic conception of the arts. When art is understood not only as a source of enjoyable experience but also as the communicator of values and knowledge, it is easily accommodated to the purposes of humanistic education in the best sense of the term.

Lipman's belief that the Endowment's most important educational function should be that of federal leadership is perhaps overly optimistic. But if we hope to engender in the young and in the society an appreciation of excellence in art, then an Endowment that unwaveringly espouses the importance of high artistic standards would perform an invaluable service to arts educators and the public alike. Yet much would have to change for this to happen. The Endowment would have to pay more attention to what it stands for—that is, for excellence and thoughtful, defensible statements of its aims and purposes—than to the size of its budget and staff and to questionable self-promotion.

The outlines of such a statement may be found in the Endowment's most recent report on arts education, *Toward Civilization,* a report that stands in polar contrast to *Coming to Our Senses* in its conceptions of art, arts education, and the role of the Endowment. Although it reflects the kinds of political compromises and the sort of writing characteristic of government publications in general, its outlook and tone suggest what is needed to reshape policy for arts education. The report, moreover, bears the unmistakable stamp of Lipman's thinking. In other words, if *Coming to Our Senses* was a product of the countercultural sentiments of the 1960s, *Toward Civilization* is the traditional culture's response to the 1960s obsessions and excesses. One immediately senses this in the report's statement of the purpose of arts education: "Arts education should provide all students with a sense of the arts in civilization, of creativity in the artistic process, of the vocabularies of artistic communication, and of the critical elements necessary to make informed choices about the products of the arts."[23]

In the chapter on arts education, the report's writers recall some of the Endowment's past educational efforts and draw attention to current changes in policy. In 1980, for example, the agency's Artists-in-Schools program was renamed the Artists-in-Education program, and in 1986 it was further renamed the Arts-in-Education program. The change in language signaled the agency's unequivocal commitment to art education, in particular its commitment to making the arts a basic and sequential component of the school curriculum from kindergarten through high school. Support for artist residencies is still retained, but residencies are now clearly intended to help achieve educational objectives. Of particular interest is a category called Arts in Schools Basic Education Grants (AISBEG), whose purpose is to encourage state and local agencies to work with schools to design arts education programs, K–12. The report describes several of the initial efforts of this funding category. A Special Grants Category also places emphasis on a range of educational projects, including centers for research and learning. Disciplines Programs in the areas of media arts, folk arts, materials, design, interarts, opera/musical theater, and literature also support educational programs in the schools. The Challenge Program does likewise, one of its new ventures being in the area of art appreciation. Most significantly, particularly in light of its earlier waffling on the subject, the report admits that the Endowment had all along been more concerned to help artists and cultural institutions than to address problems of curriculum design in the schools. This latter concern is said to have grown out of an increasing awareness that the arts were not figuring importantly in the lives of American people. Yet criticisms of the Endowment's policies obviously have had their effect. The Endowment's funding of arts education, however, still remains a relatively small portion of its budget and is less than the percentage spent on education by the National Endowment for the Humanities and the National Science Foundation.

Looking forward, the report envisages long-term involvement in arts education. It realizes, for example, that 10 years may be required to assess the effectiveness of the Endowment's current initiatives. The report therefore recommends "that the current direction of the Arts in Education Program be continued and strengthened over the next decade, and that in preparation for the Endowment's reauthorization in the mid-90s a second arts education report to congress be prepared."[24] Toward this end the report makes a number of recommendations that encompass arguments for teaching art, various kinds of collaboration, developmental activities, and review and research efforts. Appendixes describe the educational activities of the Humanities Endowment, the National Science Foundation, and the Department of Education, the latter's involvement in arts education consisting principally of support of the Kennedy Center's educational activities for example, its efforts in behalf of special education and the Alliance for Arts Education.

TOWARD THE FUTURE

Some of the considerations that figure in the following speculations about the future of policy-making for arts education derive from recent changes in the rhetoric and substance of writings about arts education: for example the increasing emphasis being placed on art as a substantive subject of schooling, which stands in contrast to a social service concept of art's function; the continuing critique of cultural and educational policies; the location of the teaching of the arts within the humanities; and, more worrisome, the emergence of multiculturalism as a political movement. At the time of this writing this last consideration is perhaps the most serious challenge to policy-making for arts education, not least because of the decision certain groups have made that in order to advance their own cultural interests it is necessary to denigrate the cultural heritage of western civilization.

It is not overstating matters to say that during the 1980s more and more policymakers and art educators came to realize that the proper object of study for arts education is art itself, and that art should be taught for the characteristic effects it is capable of inducing and not as a means for solving or meliorating a host of social problems. This redirection of thought is the result of at least three major developments. Foremost was the change from a Democratic to a Republican administration during the 1980s that eventually resulted in the more conservative attitude taken toward art and arts education in *Toward Civilization*. This change at this center of policy-making was largely the result of the efforts of conservative cultural critics. I use "conservative" in the best sense of the term, the sense in which we are all, or should be, conservative. That is, "conservatism" implies a commitment to the preservation of standards, traditions, institutions, and civility in place of the penchant for change and novelty that plays havoc with enduring and lasting values. The difference

is precisely the one between the mentality of *Coming to Our Senses* and that of *Toward Civilization*. Having said all this, however, I do not necessarily imply that the curriculum recommendations of *Toward Civilization* will be thoroughly and enthusiastically implemented. Indeed, as this is being written there are some indications that efforts are under way to get around them, and that Endowment officials are returning to earlier ways of thinking.

If conservative cultural criticism played a major role in altering attitudes, so did the criticism by a number of writers within the arts education professions, notably Elliott W. Eisner, Laura Chapman, and Samuel Hope.[25] Characteristically, the observations of these writers were first ignored, then ridiculed, and finally taken seriously as their cogency became clearly apparent. The writings of educational critics were also largely responsible for the directions taken by the major arts-educational event of the 1980s, the advocacy of the Getty Center for Education in the Arts of discipline-based art education (DBAE).[26] This approach to arts education repudiated (at least implicitly) the arts-educational orientation of the 1960s, and it sought to accommodate the best art-educational thinking of the 1970s. The idea of discipline-based art education assumes that art should be taught as a basic subject (i.e., a subject apart from others) in a program of general education and be grounded in the concepts and methods of four interrelated disciplines—artistic creation, art history, art criticism, and aesthetics (philosophy of art). As such, the approach has much to recommend it. Although it has concentrated its efforts on the visual arts, other groups have been listening in, and the Getty Center has supported some modest efforts in music education. True the Center has not managed to escape all of the policy mistakes discussed earlier. It is, for example, prone to the pitfalls of proceduralism and public relations. But it has in large part abjured the politicizing of art and arts education and has opted for a substantive rather than a social-service concept of the field. It has further foresworn the rhetoric of innovation and made conspicuous efforts to acknowledge the origins of its ideas in the literature of art education. In other words, it has tried to avoid some past policy errors. But it is also receptive to criticism of its policies and actually encourages it through the sponsorship of issue seminars. In all these respects, the Getty Center provides something of a model for the intervention of a private agency in educational matters. Critiques of the Center notwithstanding, it has the endorsement of most of the major figures in the field of art education, several of whom are directors of its regional curriculum centers. In 1983 I wrote that if we have learned anything from the policy-making of the 1960s and 1970s, it is the foolishness of relying on career civil service personnel and philanthropists for ideas about arts education. That same year the Getty Center was established, and it has since been attempting to establish itself as a counterexample to past reform efforts.

There is, however, one implication of recent developments that has not yet been systematically entertained. This consequence follows from the increasing acceptance by arts educators of the study of art as a field with a history of accomplishment, peculiar excellences, and critical issues and puzzles. Now to think of the teaching of the arts not only in terms of creative and performing activities but also in terms of historical and critical studies is in effect to locate the arts within the humanities and to conceive of the teaching of art as a humanity. The policy ramifications of this stance could profoundly affect the way we think about arts education. A humanities-based arts education could also affect how and when we prepare teachers of the arts and how we design curriculums and assess learning. The fact that the Humanities Endowment spends a greater percentage of its budget on education than the Arts Endowment does further suggests that the federal leadership for arts education might well originate with this agency and not with the Arts Endowment, and that the implementation of the recommendations of *Toward Civilization* should be the concern of the NEH, not the NEA.

From all this it would also seem to follow that teachers of art, especially at the secondary level, should be prepared as humanities teachers in departments of the humanities in colleges of liberal arts and sciences. Readers can envision further consequences of the ripple effects of such a change. To raise these possibilities is, once more, simply to take what seems to be the next logical step in current thinking about arts education. Were these suggestions to be taken seriously, ample resources could be found for reconceptualizing the field of arts education. Albert William Levi has written insightfully about a redefinition of the humanities that is congruent with the objectives of arts education.[27] And Leonard Meyer, in a wide-ranging essay, has probed the relations of the sciences, the arts, and the humanities in an illuminating way.[28] It may also well be that a humanities conception of

arts education is indirectly relevant to meliorating some of the problems besetting American society and education, not least the problem of the low level of cultural literacy in the society, the loss of historical memory that such illiteracy implies, and the ubiquitous assault on reason and judgment.[29] A humanities conception of arts education that locates the teaching of the arts within a common cultural heritage may also be a response to the challenge of multiculturalism, whose advocates are increasingly composed of a coalition of interests that deplores the influence of western civilization on the grounds that its values are inherently racist, sexist, and elitist. Critics of this way of thinking express concern that instead of promoting a healthy and mutually respectful cultural pluralism, the current criticism of "Eurocentrism" will encourage a divisive cultural particularism.[30] Though it may be an overstatement, cultural particularism is said to be sweeping the country, especially in large urban school systems. Cultural particularism, however, is a prescription for multiple enclaves, not a unified society. The policy question is whether cultural diversity can be celebrated without denying the existence of a common political and cultural heritage. If the advocates of an enclave prevail, then any talk of a humanities conception of art education will be beside the point, for the humanities traditionally have placed a high value on social integration, effective communication, and mutual sympathy, all rooted in a continuous historical tradition whose classics and masterworks enshrine these values. If cultural particularism comes to pass, then the critical intelligence that rescued thinking about art and arts education from its sentimentalism and antiintellectualism will have new issues to address.

Notes

1. Ralph A. Smith, "The New Policy-making Complex in Aesthetic Education," *Curriculum Theory Network* 4, nos. 2 and 3 (1974): 159–168.
2. *Coming to Our Senses: The Significance of the Arts for American Education* (New York: McGraw-Hill, 1977).
3. Charles Silberman, *Crisis in the Classroom* (New York: Random House, 1970).
4. *Coming to Our Senses,* pp. 81–82.
5. Ibid., p. 121.
6. See, for example, Charles Fowler, *Can We Rescue the Arts for America's Children: Coming to Our Senses—Ten Years Later* (New York: American Council for the Arts, 1988). It is symptomatic of the current atmosphere that this follow-up report has been almost totally ignored by professional arts educators.
7. My observations about AIS programs are contained in "An Analysis and Criticism of the Artists-in-Schools program of the National Endowment for the Arts," *Art Education* 50, no. 5 (September 1977): 12–19.
8. For a judicious assessment of alternative arts education, see Barbara Leondar, "The Arts in Alternative Schools: Some Observations," *Journal of Aesthetic Education* 5, no. 1 (January 1971): 75–91.
9. This is one of the themes in Jacques Barzun's, *The Use and Abuse of Art* (Princeton: Princeton University Press, 1974).
10. See my observations in "Critical Reflections of the AGE Idea," *Musical Educators Journal* 64, no. 5 (January 1978): 88–97; and "The Arts in General Education Ideology," *Art Education* 36, no. 4 (July 1983): 34–38.
11. Gene Wenner, "Arts in the Mainstream of Education," *Music Educators Journal,* 62, no. 8 (April 1976): 34–35. See, for example, Jacques Barzun, "Art and Educational Inflation," *Journal of Aesthetic Education* 12, no. 4 (October 1978): 9–20.
12. I have discussed these mistakes and tendencies in "Policy and Art Education. A Review of Some Fallacies," *High School Journal* 63, no. 8 (May 1980): 353–361, and "Reshaping Policy for Arts Education," *Controversies in Art and Culture* 1, no. 1 (1987): 31–44.
13. See Jacques Barzun, *The House of Intellect* (New York: Harper & Brothers, 1959), pp. 21–24.
14. Ronald Berman, "Art vs. the Arts," in his *Culture and Politics* (New York: University Press of America, 1984), p. 133.
15. Ibid., p. 144.
16. Iris Murdoch, *The Fire and the Sun: Why Plato Banished the Artists* (New York: Oxford University Press, 1977), p. 86.
17. Roger Rosenblatt, *The New Republic,* 2 July 1977. Rosenblatt further says that all the logistics "bespeaks not an idea but a method for promulgating an idea, a style which finds the method before it understands the problem, and then proceeds

with all good intentions to solve the method instead of the problem" (p. 42).

18. Harold Rosenberg, "Avant-Garde," in *Quality: Its Image in the Arts* (New York: Atheneum, 1969).

19. Charles Frankel, *High on Foggy Bottom: An Outsider's Inside View of the Government* (New York: Harper & Row, 1969), pp. 101–106.

20. I have discussed these questions in a number of places, for example, "Formulating a Defensible Policy for Arts Education," *Theory Into Practice* 23, no. 4 (Autumn 1984): 273–279; and "Some Policy Questions," *Journal of Aesthetic Education,* 12, no. 3 (July 1978): 5–11.

21. From testimony given before a House Committee on Select Education in the fall of 1975.

22. See, for example, Samuel Lipman, "Cultural Policy: Whither America, Whither Government?" *The New Criterion* 3, no. 3 (November 1984): 7–15. In a subsequent essay, "The NEA: Looking Back, Looking Ahead" (*The New Criterion* 7, no. 1 [September 1988]), Lipman says of the Rockefeller report *Coming to Our Senses* that it is a "monument to the destruction of the idea of serious general arts education" (p. 9). This was also my assessment in "The Naked Piano Player: Or, What the Rockefeller Report *Coming To Our Senses* Really Is," *Journal of Aesthetic Education* 12, no. 1 (January 1978): 45–61. For my response to Lipman, see "Policy for Arts Education: Whither the Schools, Whither the Public and Private Sectors?" *Design for Arts in Education* 89, no. 4 (March/April 1988): 2–11. The "piano player" referred to is not Mr. Rockefeller, but a photograph of a naked youth seated at a piano, which I took to be representative of the report's sentimentalism.

23. *Toward Civilization: A Report in Arts Education* (Washington: National Endowment for the Arts, 1988), p. 35.

24. Ibid., p. 171.

25. See, for example, Elliott W. Eisner, "Is the Artist in the School Program Effective?" *Art Education,* 27, no. 2 (February 1974):

19–24; Laura Chapman, *Instant Art, Instant Culture* (New York: Teachers college, Columbia University, 1982); and Samuel Hope, "An Overview of Strategic Issues in American Arts Education," *Journal of Aesthetic Education* 21, no. 4 (Winter 1987): 25–40. See also the briefing papers on policy prepared by members of the various professional art and arts education associations. Available from the Music Educators National Conference office in Reston.

26. For discussions of the antecedents, character, and disciplines of DBAE, see R. A. Smith, ed., *Discipline-based Art Education, Origins, Meaning, and Development* (Urbana: University of Illinois Press, 1987). The volume consists of the contents of the Summer 1987 issue of the *Journal of Aesthetic Education.*

27. See, for example, Albert William Levi, *The Humanities Today* (Bloomington: Indiana University Press, 1970); and A. W. Levi and R. A. Smith, *Art Education: A Critical Necessity* (Urbana: University of Illinois Press, 1991), which presents a humanities interpretation of discipline-based art education. I have also spelled out a humanities interpretation in my *The Sense of Art: A Study in Aesthetic Education* (New York: Routledge, 1989).

28. Leonard B. Meyer, "Concerning the Sciences, The Arts—AND the Humanities." *Critical Inquiry* 1, no. 1 (September 1974): 163–217. Cf. my "Teaching Music as One of the Humanities," *Journal of Aesthetic Education* 25, no. 3 (Fall 1991): 115–128.

29. For a description of the state of cultural literacy in American society, see E. D. Hirsch, Jr., *Cultural Literacy: What Every American Needs to Know* (New York: Vintage Books, 1988). Cf. R. A. Smith, ed., *Cultural Literacy and Arts Education* (Urbana: University of Illinois Press, 1991), a product of the National Arts Education Research Center at the University of Illinois of Urbana-Champaign.

30. See Diane Ravitch, "Multiculturalism: E Pluribus Plures," *The American Scholar* (Summer 1990): 337–354, and her further comments in the same journal, 60, no. 2 (Spring 1991): 272–276.

THE NATURE OF POLICY
AND MUSIC EDUCATION

Anthony L. Barresi and Gerald Olson

UNIVERSITY OF WISCONSIN

Policy decisions affect nearly every aspect of our lives. Whether overtly or covertly, they regulate and influence our daily actions. They also guide most decisions affecting the music education profession at national, state, and local (community and school) levels. In order to comprehend the philosophical and practical ramifications of such policy initiatives, music educators need to develop a realistic understanding of how society values music and music education. Music educators need to recognize the formulators of policy in society, government, and educational institutions in order to assess their motives. Through an understanding of the bases upon which policymakers act and function, music educators will be better able both to develop strategies for influencing the direction of policies and to initiate the formulation of policy at various levels.

Finally, by developing sophistication in policy understanding and analysis, music educators can learn to anticipate the "hidden" or "resultant" effects that may occur as a consequence of the policy process. The ability to perceive such covert effects results from a thorough understanding of the nature of policy formulation and its implementation.

Because it would be impossible in this short chapter to acquire all of the understandings and analytical skills necessary to achieve the goals stated above, we will address broad issues surrounding the development of policy. Further, we will provide a framework in which language, process, and policy types are discussed as possible paradigms for future music education research. Finally, we will identify selected policy research efforts that may shed light on various aspects of the policy development process.

THE NATURE OF POLICY

An examination of the research reveals very little systematic study directed specifically to the development and implementation of effects on music education of policy decisions. In addressing the nature of policy, we offer in the following section a definition of policy, stages of the policy-making process, and specific policy types.

Definition of Policy

Mayer and Greenwood (1980) state that policy has three characteristics: (1) it involves an intended course of action; (2) it occurs at the highest or most inclusive level of decision making relative to the action to be taken; and (3) it incorporates consideration of complex implications anticipated from the proposed action (p. 4). Some definitions of policy add qualifying components of self-interest and relationship to values that also appear to be valid. Such qualifiers, however, are quite general in meaning, and their relationship to specific policy is sometimes elusive.

Policy may be formally stated, developed, and implemented or it may occur informally in the absence of stated policy. Formal and informal policies influence the process of education at levels ranging from broad principle to specific, program-based regulations. Although informal policy may have several characteristics in common with formal policy, it is usually less clearly defined in its formulation and implementation. While it is probable that such informal and unstated policy initiatives have profound influences on various aspects of the profession, this chapter focuses on articulated policies and those effects that may result as consequences of the implementation of stated policies.

Policy can be divided into two classifications—explicit policy, which is formally stated and clearly defined, and implicit policy, which occurs "where the absence of specific policy, in effect, constitutes a policy or where the behavior of decision makers or administrators alters the stated goals or implementation strategies of policy" (Pankratz, 1989). Clearly, Pankratz accepts a broad definition of policy that extends to implications arising from implementation and/or alteration of an explicit policy and the adoption of consistent action (policylike initiative) in the absence of a specific policy initiative.

Mayer and Greenwood (1980) outline the formulation process for explicit policy in nine stages. The process begins with the determination of goals in which the philosophical framework and values of the formulator are considered. Next, a needs assessment is made and specific objectives are derived. After a design of alternative courses of action and an estimation of the consequences of alternate courses is completed, a selection of course(s) of action is made and implementation begun. After the implementation phases of the process, evaluation of policy compliance is made and "feedback" data are considered by the formulators (p. 9).

On the basis of this model, the authors have devised a descriptive four-stage policy process model that can serve for policy analysis in music education. The first stage, *formulation,* deals with the development of policy. An examination of the philosophical underpinnings and values that support the eventual goals and objectives will reveal much about the formulator's motivations and intentions. Stage two, *implementation,* requires the researcher to study methods of enacting the policy as well as possible sanctions that may result from noncompliance. Stage three, *response of constituents,* roughly coincides with the evaluation step of Mayer and Greenwood. Since, to a great degree, the response of constituents is a determinant of the success or failure of a policy initiative, this stage is essential in any analytical process. Finally, an analysis of the application of *possible sanctions* and the type of sanction applied helps the researcher to assess the policy effects on the constituents. Further, it allows one to identify covert policies that may arise as a result of the explicit policy under scrutiny. The roles of policy participants clearly relate to each of these process stages. Formulators of policy devise, implement, and sanction for noncompliance while constituents accept or ignore policy and when applicable, accept sanctions.

Explicit Policy Types

Mayer and Greenwood (p. 14) maintain that the effectiveness and feasibility of an explicit policy is related to the effects of the policy on its constituency. Compliance, therefore, is a major determinant of policy success or failure, and the relative power of the policymaker is related directly to the ability to require compliance. Three types of explicit policy, based upon the formulator's ability to require compliance, have been identified as aides for analysis of music education policy.

Formulators of *imposed policy* require constituents to comply with policy under penalty of sanction, either economic or professional. Although this type of policy is the most effectively implemented, it is often negatively imposed on constituents who comply out of fear of sanctions. Organizations, agencies, or institutions granting funds, salaries, or other types of economic support make effective use of this policy type because their control of financial resources provides them with powerful sanctioning mechanisms. Further, some formulators possess professional sanctioning powers that allow them to disassociate themselves from constituents who are in noncompliance.

A less stringent mechanism for requiring compliance is evident in the *endorsed policy* type. Compliance with this type of policy is often motivated by a desire to receive some benefit from the policy-making body. Constituents voluntarily apply for organizational approval that may or may not be granted depending on the qualifications or actions of applicants. The power to bestow approval resides with the policymaker as the constituents must meet the requirements specified within the policy statement in order to gain the beneficial rights and privileges.

Advocated policy is characterized by completely voluntary compliance to its dictates. Because some organizations have no sanctioning powers they employ this policy type, which relies on acceptance by constituents of the "suggestions" made by the policymakers. Obviously, for such policy to be successful—for majority compliance—constituents must be in philosophical and/or practical agreement with the policy in order to actively support its tenets. Frequently, formulators of advocated policy do not see themselves as policymakers but rather as leaders in educational thought and action who look to and rely on their constituency for the implementation of ideas. The authors, who take a broad view of policy formulation and implementation, regard such initiatives as policy in that they are developed through a policylike process and call for *consistent action* from constituents.

Implicit Policy Types

The concept of implicit policy furnishes the basis for more subtle policy types—policylike initiatives that are less specific in explication yet clear in consequence. The first, *adjusted policy,* refers to a new policy resulting from alteration of an explicit policy by its formulators. Such alteration, often covert, may occur in stated goals or in implementation strategies that result in an adjusted policy that is active but unstated.

Constituent action is responsible for the second implicit

policy type. What shall be called *resultant effects* is a policylike initiative that occurs as a covert consequence of the imposition of an explicit policy causing constituents to take action in response. Because no "stated" policy exists, the authors hesitate to refer to such initiatives as policy. Yet, to be sure, such initiatives do in fact act as policy in that they guide the consistent action of constituents in policylike ways.

Informal Policy Initiatives

Although this chapter offers insights into a relatively structured process wherein policy is made *for* the public by powerful agencies such as state departments of education or the courts, the steps to policy decisions are influenced *by* many special interest groups who move in and out of the policy arena through opinions, statements, and actions. A few examples are identified below to illustrate the variety of special interests that help to shape policy development through such informal initiatives.

The business community and their commercial interests have influenced policy regarding school curricula for many years. In general, community business leaders often lobby for secondary school courses that teach specific skills that produce useful prospective employees. To that end, donated expertise, programs, and money often are made available to educational institutions. Further, corporations such as Apple Computer, Inc. make equipment and materials available to schools, thus reshaping approaches to learning in a dramatic fashion. Music publishers, book publishers, and musical equipment companies traditionally have supported (and sometimes have led) new directions in music curricula and in the manner in which that instruction is delivered.

Finally, organizations or individuals who critique the "state of education" or who have a specific philosophical goal for the outcomes of education participate actively in informal policy initiatives. As examples of this kind of influence one need only recall the writings and speeches of Robert M. Hutchins, James Conant, and John Goodlad; the work of the Carnegie Task Force on Teaching as a Profession, and the Holmes Group in the past decade; or the current initiatives on behalf of the arts by the J. Paul Getty Center for Education in the Arts.

EXPLICIT AND IMPLICIT POLICIES

In order to describe more clearly the explicit imposed, endorsed, and advocated policy types, specific examples of each will be discussed in the following section. In each case, formulators will be identified, formulation and implementation processes described, and possible implicit effects (adjusted or resultant) of a policy's implementation presented.

Imposed Policy Examples

In order to impose policy, a formulator must have the power of sanction—the ability to require constituents to ad-

here to the policy under the threat of some sort of punitive action, either legal, financial, professional, or social. In reference to education, most of the imposed policy initiatives have come from government agencies that dispense funds, licensing, accreditation and/or certification.

Federal Government Policy Since the 1950s, federal government agencies have become increasingly active in the development of policy affecting arts education. With the establishment of the National Defense Education Act of 1958 and the designation of music as a critical subject of national concern, the United States Department of Education (USDOE) signaled its interest in music education. Further, its financial support of the 1963 Yale Symposium lent it official credence and, some would argue, raised the conclusions and recommendations of that meeting to the level of implicit policy. Policies associated with the improvement of the quality of education and the equalization of educational opportunities for all children led to the enactment of the Elementary and Secondary Education Act of 1965, which empowered the USDOE to award federal funds for a number of purposes: the establishment or improvement of arts education programs in schools; the purchase of learning materials and equipment; the establishment of regional laboratories for the development of curriculum and instructional materials; the support of research activities in universities and development centers; and, finally, the strengthening of state departments of education.

Enabling legislation for the National Endowment for the Arts (NEA) in 1966 was liberally laced with education rhetoric due to the sociocultural imperatives of the late 1960s. This federal agency adopted three broad goals: the achievement of availability of the arts; the development of cultural resources; and the advancement of cultural heritage. In order to accomplish such policy initiatives, the NEA developed a number of educational programs that sought to promote arts awareness and understanding in schools and communities through artistic presentations. One such program, established with cooperative funding and development with the USDOE was the Artists-in-Schools (AIS) program, which placed artists in schools to teach and demonstrate their art. Nancy Hanks, chair of the Endowment, claimed in 1975 that AIS, the agency's most active educational program, was intended to "open up new avenues of awareness," excite the development of new talent, and give "many students a new appreciation of life and of themselves, a new sense of identity and purpose" (Hanks, 1975, p. 45).

Despite the stated intentions for this program, NEA and its state agencies came under criticism from various quarters. Arts educators such as Ralph Smith (1977) and Elliot Eisner (1974) questioned whether residency programs were just work programs for artists or, given their general objectives, were capable of being evaluated. Others feared that such programs were "deschooling" the arts by replacing traditionally conceived school-based programs with educationally ephemeral residencies. The Artists-in-Schools program, later renamed the Artists-in-Education program, was the ground on which traditional philosophical positions of artists and educators were played out. Representing the arts establishment, artists often hold the conviction that experiencing the art is sufficient for the development of artistic valuing and commitment in students. Arts educators, on the other hand, have been traditionally committed to more balanced discipline-based/experiential programs in which learning is achieved through a variety of approaches.

Because artist residency programs are supported by substantial government funds, their design, content, and operation are influenced by federal and state arts agencies. Further, program policies are imposed under the possible sanction of removal of government funds for noncompliance. Barresi (1983; Taylor and Barresi, 1984) and Udell (1990) examined the historical development of AIS programs and identified points of conflict arising between artists and arts educators. Mok (1983) described a number of residency programs, paying particular attention to the statement and implementation of goals. Further research into the influences of imposed policies on participants—artists, arts educators, and students—is called for if some of the questions raised are to be addressed in precise, systematic ways.

In the mid-1980s, spurred by the congressional requirements for more educational emphasis attached to the agency's appropriations, the Endowment and state arts councils instituted a project called Arts in School Basic Education Grant (AISBEG). In order to receive federal monies, constituents—state departments of education, state arts councils, universities, artists, school systems, arts advocacy groups and cultural institutions—were required by program policy to develop cooperative school-based programs in which these groups would have direct input into curricular design and program content (Barresi, 1988; Carol R. H. Ford Associates, 1987). Hope (1985) and Hutchens (1989) saw this kind of incursion by the "arts establishment" into curricular content as antithetical to the tenets of traditional music education. Further, Hope raised policy questions related to curricular content and the effects of strategic control and funding in partnership situations. As such partnership efforts proliferate, these questions should furnish a needed framework for research into such resultant effects.

State Departments of Education State departments of education are among the most powerful policymakers as they have a legislative mandate to oversee and regulate the operation of public education and teacher preparation, and the policy that they devise can be imposed under the threat of financial or professional sanction. One policy area that has been most influential on programs in music education relates to high school graduation requirements. A survey of state department of education arts supervisors revealed their concern over changes in graduation requirements that have deleterious effects on arts programs (Council of Chief State School Officers, 1985, p. 25). The "back to basics" philosophy has caused many state educational agencies to impose policy requiring more instruction in math and science areas, and, in a number of states, courses in language and computer science are highly recommended. Periodic evaluation of school programs ensures compliance with these policies under threat of withdrawal of state financial aid.

As a consequence of such policy imperatives, a number of resultant effects have already been noted. In order that students meet the necessary graduation requirements with dispatch, school officials frequently advise them to "front load" their high school schedules with required courses. This practice leads to "course cramming" wherein scheduling flexibility is reduced and the ability to register for music courses consecutively throughout the high school experience is curtailed significantly. Further, the importance given to "required" curricular offerings by state departments of education has the effect of reducing the importance of music offerings in the eyes of school administrators, students, and community members. Much more research into the effects of mandated changes in graduation requirements upon the scheduling of music programs is needed before solutions to this escalating problem can be addressed. Additionally, policies relating to arts requirements for high school graduation, where such mandates exist, should be examined concerning motivations for such requirements, number of courses required, and recommended course content.

Matters of teacher certification and licensing also fall within the jurisdiction of state departments of education. For years, such agencies, through the vehicle of imposed policy, have mandated that teachers must be certified in their specific subject areas in order to teach in state-supported schools. Under the belief that certain preparatory courses and educational experiences were necessary before a teacher would be capable of providing effective instruction in a specified area of knowledge, state education agencies have worked with teacher preparation institutions to provide programs that would culminate in certification and licensing. Periodically, these programs are evaluated by the state agency to determine if compliance has been achieved. Failure to comply could result in the nonlicensing of graduating teachers which, in effect, renders them unemployable.

In recent years, however, an adjusted policy has become evident. While maintaining the principle of traditional certification programs, many state agencies are altering their certification and licensing policies. Erbes (1990) reported that teacher shortages in some curricular areas have encouraged departments of education in 48 states to develop alternative licensing procedures that bypass traditional preparation regulations. This adjusted policy, in effect, sets up a contrary policy that contradicts previously held beliefs—that certain prescribed experiences and course content are necessary for the preparation of quality teachers. Research into such adjusted policies can provide valuable information on the motivations for such alteration and the degree of alteration. Perhaps investigations of this kind may provide the profession with data useful for the development of appropriate coping strategies

The Courts No more powerful policy arena exists than the courts, as they are often involved in education decisions because of failures in some other part of the political or social system (Spring, 1988). Legal judgments are clear examples of explicit imposed policy, and in recent years a number of decisions have altered traditional practice in music education.

Richmond (1990) identifies many school-related legal cases in his research on equal opportunity for aesthetic development in the schools. Recent separation of church and state rulings regarding public school settings have brought into question the performance of religious art music in school curricula. Clearly, these actions have forced school boards and music teachers to reassess the role of music in the school and the type of music literature appropriate for study and performance.

The effects of court-ordered busing to achieve racial desegregation (an imposed explicit policy) in the Milwaukee city school district provides one example of unintended deleterious results on the instrumental music programs of the district. While court-mandated busing allowed students to attend the schools of their choice within the city, the district initiated a flexible transfer program to specialty schools as their own policy initiative (Murphy and Pawasarat, 1986). The latter had implicit resultant effects on elective instrumental music programs. As the "community" support of students, families, and business leaders became dissipated by transfers away from neighborhood elementary, middle, and secondary schools, and through the loss of students to private schools, the number of students in bands and orchestras declined over the years. Certainly, studies into policies emanating from court decisions merit the attention of researchers as such investigations may furnish educators with a clearer understanding of the ramifications of such decisions (Hawley, 1990).

Endorsed Policy Examples

The explicit endorsed policy model has a sanctioning mechanism that is less stringent than that of the imposed model. Compliance with endorsed policies is often motivated by a desire of the constituent to receive some official approval from the policy implementor. For example, accreditation, certification, or credentialing by some organization or agency may be given or withheld depending on constituent compliance. Those seeking official acceptance by the organization or agency are motivated to comply voluntarily with the dictates of the policy in order to receive official "approval," even though such approval may not be required for continued existence or operation.

National Association of Schools of Music The accreditation policy of the National Association of Schools of Music (NASM) is among the best examples of endorsed policy. This organization is composed of music divisions from postsecondary educational institutions that have applied for and received the endorsement of member schools. Further, NASM offers one of the clearest examples of a self-regulating accrediting organization that promotes high standards in the preparation of music educators.

In order to achieve membership, applying institutions must meet certain qualifications or standards and satisfy concerns of educational quality and institutional probity (NASM, *Handbook* 1989–90). NASM offers a number of goals for ac-

creditation that give testimony to the organization's professional intentions and operation. In short, the association aims to set and maintain standards for schools of music; encourage the continued development and improvement of member institutions; provide assurances that members clearly conceive and effectively deliver quality programs in music; encourage members to develop effective programs within their unique institutional setting; and act as an advocate for member institutions against encroachments that might jeopardize their educational effectiveness or academic freedom (p. 26).

All institutions filing successful initial applications are granted a 5-year period of accreditation. After the first 5-year period, it is NASM's explicit policy to reexamine each member institution on a 10-year cycle to determine if the institution is in compliance with the association's code of ethics and standards. If an institution is found to be in noncompliance, it is placed on probation until it files a probationary response to the examining commission, which either accepts it or revokes membership (pp. 35–36).

NASM has explicit policy related to music education programs of member institutions. It recommends program proportions in the areas of music studies (at least 50 percent), general studies (30–35 percent), and professional education studies (15–20 percent), and it describes the recommended procedures for the development and preparation of music educators and the essential competencies and desirable personal qualities of those teachers (pp. 65–69).

NASM's accreditation policy and program recommendations have had a number of resultant effects that appear to be most beneficial to music education. The periodic reevaluation requires music schools and departments to maintain quality in their education programs and facilities. Further, members are encouraged to examine issues that relate to their institutional offerings and programs. For example, NASM published an Executive Summary, NASM Futureswork, November 1990, entitled "K-12 Issues and Influences," which discusses factors of arts education in American schools and concludes with general suggestions for members as to curricular or advocacy actions that they can take in support of school-based arts education.

There is some conjecture in the profession that the program standardization recommended by NASM has worked contrary to the association's "encouragement of diversity" goal. These critics assert that opportunities that were once available in teacher preparation programs unique to universities, teachers colleges, or liberal arts colleges have been reduced significantly as a result of standardization resulting from NASM accreditation policies. This assertion is, at this time, a moot point but one that could merit study by policy researchers.

A most awkward resultant effect regarding NASM policy is occurring in some states. Significant changes in music education programs initiated and mandated by state departments of education are bringing to the fore questions of compliance with some of the NASM standards. For example, a number of states are now investigating the certification and licensing of teachers with significantly fewer credits in content music courses. By utilizing the power of explicit imposed policy, these state agencies could cause a dilemma for NASM member institutions that are most anxious to remain in compliance with the association's endorsed mandates. Researchers might wish to watch for potential conflicts of this kind and to study how NASM and departments of education, either separately or cooperatively, address such dichotomous situations.

Professional Credentialing Organizations Endorsed policy has been used effectively by professional organizations that focus on classroom pedagogy. Under the belief that the methodology they espouse will educate all children in the most efficient, effective, and musical manner, these groups have structured themselves to help teachers achieve these ends. For example, organizations dedicated to Kodály, Orff, and Dalcroze methods for teaching music have endorsed policies for credentialing teachers who wish to learn the method and receive official certification in the pedagogy.

A certification brochure issued by the Organization of American Kodály Educators (OAKE) explains the group's philosophy and generally states that those teacher education programs wishing to receive OAKE certification must offer preparatory experiences in choral ensembles, solfeggio, conducting, and folk song analysis at three proficiency levels (OAKE, 1990). Similar credentialing policies that exist for the Orff and Dalcroze organizations are endorsed in type as they require voluntary compliance with certification requirements before official recognition is given. Methodology groups, less formal in organization and structure, employ policylike approaches in their recommendations that teachers wishing to learn the method attend workshops and clinics on its application.

Policy research into the effects of special credentialing organizations on classroom instruction, teacher preparation, instructional materials, and teacher effectiveness appears essential in this day of proliferating methods and instructional materials. Additionally, an in-depth investigation into the reasons for proliferation of method and its effect on professional direction seems imperative.

Advocated Policy Example

Advocated policy is unique among explicit policy types in that no form of traditional sanctioning power rests with the formulators. Thus, policy formulators must look to other modes of operation in order to gain voluntary compliance by constituents. Nonetheless, advocated policy can be a pervasive and effective phenomenon in music education.

Music Educators National Conference As a large, self-interested professional organization, the Music Educators National Conference (MENC) has a rich tradition of establishing advocated policy, though its leadership may not have viewed MENC as a policy-making agency. If one holds a very limited definition of policy—the "imposed" type only—then this view is understandable. Clearly, MENC does not possess the power to sanction its members for noncompliance with certain philosophical stances. A close examination of the history of MENC and the themes it has championed, however, leads one to understand that it does advocate specific policy. Its policy initiatives address philosophical positions such as viable rationales for music in our nation's schools, or descriptions and standards for effective school music programs. Certain policylike positions carry a consistent and long-term commitment, such as "music for every child, and every child for music," though that mission is still unfulfilled. MENC has initiated advocated policies of a very broad nature and has sought voluntary compliance from its constituency. To the degree that compliance has been gained, it has resulted from "trickle-down" implementation made possible by the structure, practices, and publications of the organization.

One example of advocated policy was the commitment made by MENC leadership in the late 1960s and early 1970s to teaching ethnic music as a way of addressing cultural diversity. The formulation stage for this policy initiative developed over some time and can be seen as a response to the changing sociocultural environment in the United States during that period. The MENC-Boston University Tanglewood Symposium addressed such issues in broad terms through papers, speeches, and discussions by artists, sociologists, educators, and the many participants in attendance. In 1969 the Goals and Objectives Project of MENC was established to respond to the recommendations from the Tanglewood Symposium. Eight priority objectives were identified by the MENC National Executive Board from the original 35 objectives. High on the list of priorities was MENC's decision to "lead in efforts to develop programs of music instruction challenging to all students, whatever their socio-cultural condition, and directed toward the needs of citizens in a pluralistic society" (Mark, 1986, p. 58). One aspect of this objective was focused on the desire to expose schoolchildren to a variety of ethnic musics so that cultural awareness and respect would be fostered.

Implementation of advocated policy by MENC has been carried out through a variety of avenues that complement each other and reinforce the theme of a policy initiative. Three avenues are identified here to illustrate the process of implementation through the "trickle-down" approach: (1) the formal structure of MENC—national, regional, and state officers and committees, (2) conventions and special workshops at the national, regional, and state levels, and (3) the publications of MENC, especially the *Music Educators Journal* and the special publications (books and pamphlets) promoted through the MENC "Professional Resources Catalog."

Within a 3-year period following the Goals and Objectives Project, the sociocultural theme and attendant issues (multicultural awareness, ethnic musics, demographic changes, and urban education) had been addressed through each of the avenues discussed above. National, regional, and state leadership hosted conferences and workshops wherein this mission was addressed. For example, the 22nd biennial meeting of MENC in Chicago in March 1970 carried the theme "Interpreting Tradition, Understanding Change."

One of the featured topics involved continuing work on the GO Project by committee No. 18, Musics of Nonwestern Cultures. Further, that conference presented 10 sessions related to ethnic musics in an effort to promote awareness and to assist constituents with material selection and pedagogical advice.

In addition, the *Music Educators Journal* published special issues on related matters within the same period of time—January 1970, "Facing the Music in Urban Education," and October 1972, "Music in World Cultures." Both of these issues of the *Music Educators Journal* also were published as pamphlets by MENC and offered to its constituents over the next few years. Lacking the ability to make imposed policy, MENC has developed and utilized consistent procedures for seeking philosophical and/or pedagogical agreement in advocated policy from its extremely varied clientele. Its well-designed network enabled process to support the goal. It succeeded in making the profession aware of the philosophical reasons for advocating change, and it provided like-minded constituents with the tools to seek compliance.

The resultant effects of this positive initiative have been substantial. MENC identified and appointed multicultural chairpersons to highlight their objective. Music educators who acted as editors and writers of book series for classroom music instruction altered the contents of their books in subsequent revisions. Teacher preparation institutions included ethnic musics and multicultural issues in university curricula. Finally, elementary and secondary school students began studying and performing music literature representing a variety of cultural heritages. There seems little doubt that this example of advocated policy has influenced the direction of the profession over the past 20 years.

POLICY INVESTIGATION AND DISCUSSION

In addition to the work of authors and researchers already cited, there have been a number of investigative efforts of policy as it relates to the arts and arts education. Although some of these reports might not meet specific or rigorous definitions of research, their descriptive, philosophical, and/or directive value to future researchers of policy seems important. Further, this brief review of policy writings is not meant to be exhaustive but rather a compilation of those works that appear to be representative of insightful and provocative thinking and research in arts education policy. Finally, the pieces cited in this section will be divided into those related to public policy and the arts and those that discuss various aspects of policy relating to arts education.

Public Policy and the Arts

"Public arts policy" is a term that is heard often these days and yet is one that defies specific definition. The term implies action based on the desires and attitudes of the public, when, in fact, those who make public policy transfer, shape, and recast those attitudes into policy that may or may not reflect broad public consensus. In 1984, Taylor and Barresi published a book on the historical development of the National Endowment for the Arts during the Roger Smith and Nancy Hanks years (1966–1976). In it, historical federal commitment to the arts was discussed—public interest in and support for the arts as reflected in government support were identified as an expression of public policy. Although some may view this approach to determining public arts policy as too limited (those who highlight the role of arts advocates and others in lobbying for public policy), it is nevertheless a way of evaluating public attitudes as expressed through the legislative actions of elected officials (Taylor and Barresi, 1984).

Art, Ideology and Politics, edited by Balfe and Wyszomirski (1983), is composed mostly of papers presented at the 10th Annual Conference on Social Theory and the Arts by social scientists who are, as the editors state, "aesthetically *engagé.*" This collection of empirical papers addresses the apparent paradox in arts for political as well as aesthetic purposes and discusses various relationships of arts world issues with the social and political concerns of a wider society (Balfe and Wyszomirski, 1983, pp. vii–x). It should be noted that the fourth segment of this volume, entitled "Aesthetic Ideologies and Public Policy," focuses entirely on government actions relating to the arts.

In their book, editors David Pankratz and Valerie Morris have solicited chapters from some of the leading arts policy analysts in the nation. Entitled *The Future of the Arts: Public Policy and Arts Research,* the book has major segments that include: "Visions of Public Arts Policy"; "Policy Research on the Arts"; "Social Trends and Research on Public Participation in the Arts"; "Emerging Aesthetic Ideologies and Cultural Choice"; and "Arts Policy, Research, and the Future" (Pankratz and Morris, 1990). It seems clear that the focus of this book stresses the major role played by the government in planning arts policy for the public. And, much of this public policy is accomplished through the National Endowment for the Arts.

Hope (1989a) addresses public policy imperatives as they are related to arts education. Through his discussion of a variety of speculations centered on four powerful sources of ideas—the arts-as-center/arts-as-means dichotomy, our European heritage, the arts/humanities relationship, and the economic context in which arts programs must operate—Hope leads the reader to recognize the possible implications and effects of such ideas on arts education. Further, he makes the case for a carefully considered, art-as-center curriculum as a means of combating the art-as-means (entertainment) climate presently affecting arts educators and their efforts. He calls for strong, assertive professional leadership to chart strategies for the retention of arts education initiatives by arts educators.

Arts Education Policies

With the publication of *Toward Civilization* in 1988, the National Endowment for the Arts, at the urging of Congress, began to promulgate arts educational policies that it hoped would characterize the agency as a champion for arts education. This report noted what were perceived to be the weaknesses of arts education in American schools and cited basic reasons for arts education: to provide the young of America a sense of their civilization and those that have contributed to it; to foster creativity, especially in relation to problem solving and reasoning; to teach the skills of effective communication, both verbal and nonverbal, in various of the graphic and performing arts; to provide a basis for critical thinking about the arts so that consumers of the arts will be able to make discriminating, well-informed choices in artistic matters (NEA, 1988). Frank Hodsoll (1989), chair of the Endowment, listed five areas where recommendations thought to be especially important were made in the report—curriculum, testing and evaluation, teacher preparation, research, and leadership. Hodsoll further articulated what later became policy in the AISBEG program, that partnerships of state education and arts agencies should work cooperatively with regional and local education and arts agencies, professional organizations, artists, and arts institutions to provide leadership and support for improving arts education. In describing the Endowment's role in this process, the NEA chair stated that control of American schools belongs to states and local communities and that the agency's efforts are directed toward encouraging and funding collaborations between "state arts agencies and state educational authorities with the view to including the arts as basic and required parts of the state and local curriculum guides" (p. 14). Sponsoring research through research centers supported by the Department of Education and the NEA was cited as an additional facet of policy action on the national level. Finally, Hodsoll stated that the Endowment is trying to reach local decision makers such as school board members, state education officers, and others through the dissemination of the *Toward Civilization* report in hopes that it will enlighten them to the necessity for action on behalf of arts education (Hodsoll, 1989).

Investigations of the early stages of the NEA's Arts in School Basic Education Grants program identified collaborative efforts, special preparation of teachers and artists, and more effective assessment efforts as policies requiring compliance before initial funding would be awarded to state arts agencies (Barresi, 1988; Jensen, 1991). Concurrently, other arts educators/policy analysts were examining these same NEA policies in an effort to project the possible effects of such federally sponsored efforts.

A report of a symposium on civilization and arts education summarized in the *Journal of Aesthetic Education* presented the reactions of three arts educator/policy analysts to *Toward Civilization*. In the brief preface, Ralph Smith recalled his early opposition to Endowment education programs and observed that while there had been changes in rhetoric and attitude about arts education, the agency's restructuring of educational goals and programs was modest (Smith, 1989).

Samuel Hope recounted earlier Endowment policies and attitudes toward arts education (especially during the Nancy

Hanks years as chair) and observed that *Toward Civilization* is a document that clarifies the choices available for arts education and states that "arts education is at a decision point with two basic paths as oppositions" (Hope, 1989b, pp. 85–91). The first is the path of advocacy and experiential arts encounters—"hedonistic wallowing in the pleasures of the senses" that leads to artistic crisis and cultural dissolution. The second path involves the provision of "basic knowledge and skill in the various arts" that will enable a lifelong intellectual and emotional interaction with the arts. Hope points out that the primary failure of federal arts education policy is not the absence of committees but rather a failure to support the idea of serious, committed teaching. Moreover, *"Toward Civilization* points philosophically towards teaching, but operationally the text seeks solutions by requesting leadership from the whole educational establishment, much of which has no expertise in, and often little empathy for, the real work of arts education" (p. 89).

Hope concludes that Endowment-recommended policy coalitions, where everyone interested in arts education is equally represented, leave those who know the most about arts education—the arts teachers, arts education intellectuals, and artists—in the minority, a formulation for future policy development not likely to produce quick orientation to the civilization agenda (p. 90).

Symposium participant Kevin Mulcahy noted that the Endowment's claim to sponsorship of arts education matters, much like those of the National Endowment for the Humanities (NEH) and the National Science Foundation (NSF), is not backed with concrete action. The Humanities Foundation spent 12.8 percent of its budget on humanities education, while the Science Foundation spent over five percent, and the NEA, 3.3 percent (Mulcahy, 1989, pp. 93–94). Further, he maintained that the Endowment's focus on curricular development is lacking in specifics and vague about the role of the NEA in arts education. Mulcahy concludes that "the NEA should commit itself to a policy of cultural democracy that would seek to broaden public appreciation of, and participation in, the arts." Specifically, he recommends that the agency should reorganize its administrative structure and funding priorities to recognize the centrality of arts education.

James Hutchens (1989) maintained that the inadequacies in arts education highlighted in *Toward Civilization,* were situated in the society as well.

I believe that the most serious problem facing arts education is a value system antithetical to serious study of the arts in education. Greater literacy in the arts will become a goal of the curriculum only when concerned citizens demand study of the arts in education. This demand will arise when leadership in education, the arts, the private sector, and government emerge to promote it. The NEA should influence the course of the development of arts education through the next decade by helping to create this concerned citizenry. (p. 98)

Hutchens warns that the arts education establishment should attend to how the Endowment goes about the task of supporting arts education. It would be unfortunate if the NEA used national concern for arts education mainly as a way to strengthen its present educational programs and challenge grant programs. Educational policies of the Endowment should be more clearly specified, and increased funding should be provided. Hutchens concludes by reminding readers that "policy-oriented efforts focus attention on issues and maintain intellectual and political pressure to keep the idea of arts education alive; . . . that the sectors of arts education need not be united on every issue in order to work together effectively;" . . . and that we must "acquire a holistic sense of the issues, for this is the informed perspective from which policy actively ought to emerge" (p. 101).

The question of partnerships in the cause of arts education is the subject of a book edited by Jonathan Katz. Designed to encourage cooperative efforts at local, state, and national levels, this book is divided into three parts: "Opportunities for Cooperative Efforts" by C. Fowler; "Working Effectively with Public Schools" by T. Baker; and "How to Get the Most Out of State and Local Arts Agencies" by R. Lynch, A. Jennings, and J. Katz (Katz, 1988). Policy analysts seeking to understand collaborative structures and operations would find this work a useful point of departure.

Curricular Policy

There appears to be agreement among arts educators that school-based curricula can be improved, that opportunities for education in the arts must be available to all students, and that such curricula should be regarded as an intrinsic part of the educative process. In fact, these goals, common among the writers already cited, appear to be regarded by them as desirable policy imperatives. In the following segment, writings about the development of curricula that flow from such goals are discussed, and curricular ideas as expressed by three leaders in the field of arts education and policy analysis are presented.

In a 1988 document prepared for the Getty Center for the Arts in Education, Elliot Eisner presented rationale, philosophical bases, and implementation suggestions for a curriculum policy that is discipline based (Eisner, 1988). Concerned with cultural and artistic literacy, Eisner stated that the arts, when well taught, can provide opportunities for the use of imagination and the creation of multiple solutions to problems. Ultimately, such interactions can lead to the "most exquisite of human intellectual abilities—judgment." In a discussion of the status of the arts in schools, Eisner identifies two beliefs that have, in effect, served as policy imperatives in schools. The first of these, fostered by some arts educators and teachers, maintains that the arts should be used mainly to develop creative abilities and that overly structured programs stifle creativity. The second belief, which has led to consistent action on the part of some administrators, teachers, and artists, is that the ability to create requires talent that only a few people possess. When such views become pervasive, they create a self-fulfilling prophecy and meaningful programs and adequate instructional time in the arts are not provided. Eisner maintains that such views have

had a chilling effect on arts education and have blocked access to the arts by a majority of children.

In a very lucid and carefully conceived description, Eisner identifies the four major activities of discipline-based arts education: "One can create art, perceive and respond to its qualities, understand its place in history and culture, and make reasoned judgments about art and understand the grounds upon which those judgments rest." These activities clearly demonstrate the educational aims of this approach to arts education, and as Eisner states, "aims are important as a kind of educational policy statement—they tell the world what is valued for a school or classroom" (pp. 14–17).

In order for this curriculum to be successful, teachers with expertise in artistic creation, aesthetics, history, and critical thinking must be available to motivate the students and guide instruction. The use of artists and cultural institutions in such a curricular setting is also discussed. Like Barresi (1983), Eisner sees artists acting in a supportive role, as valuable resources. Cultural institutions also should be used to enrich what the school provides. But Eisner cautions that "Suggesting the creation of permeable boundaries between the school and the cultural human resources in the community is not to say that the major source of instruction be provided by visiting artists or craftsmen. These human resources are supplementary, not primary" (p. 30).

Eisner is suggesting policy for arts educators when he states that discipline-based arts education must be based upon an in-place curriculum, dedicated teachers, adequate instructional time, and serious administrative support.

Ralph A. Smith, a leading arts educator and writer on policy issues, published a book entitled *Excellence in Arts Education* in 1986 that offered a specific proposal for an "excellence" arts curriculum for grades 7–12 that is common as well as general (p. 42). Smith characterized this program as general in that it was intended for all students and common in that all students would learn basic concepts, content, and skills. Unlike other curricula that focused on performance and creation with select students, this program would in large part stress the study of masterpieces. Recognizing that such a plan could be condemned as elitist, Smith advocated this humanities approach in the belief that all students should have the opportunity for exposure to classic works of art and that they, in fact, have the right to such experiences.

In a 1988 article appearing in the *Design for Arts in Education* Smith further discussed an excellence curriculum in the context of policy. On one policy level he discusses the roles of the various players who may influence the curriculum, and on a second level he eloquently describes the rationale, general content, and organization of an exemplary curriculum.

Citing Samuel Lipman (1984), who thinks that the National Arts Endowment would best benefit society if it would assume the task of educating the public about the arts, Smith stated that the agency's most important educational function should be to set an example that "unwaveringly espouses the importance of high culture." To do this, however, the Endowment must "learn to think educationally and not confuse patronage, revenue sharing, and show business with teaching and learning" (p. 7). Smith later comments that the Humanities Endowment might be a more appropriate agency to advance his conception of a humanities-based arts curriculum. He views museums and other cultural institutions as adjuncts to the school programs, not as substitutes. As for advocate groups from the private sector, Smith senses a new spirit.

The new breed of private sector representative emphasizes that art should be taught as a demanding subject in a curriculum of general education that aims at cultivating educated commerce with art. It is realized that to achieve this objective substantive content from art history, art criticism, and the philosophy of art must be incorporated into both teacher preparation and arts education programs. (p. 8)

In short, Smith sees the possibility for an enlightened private sector whose role in the arts education process will be to facilitate and support arts educators and scholars.

In support of his excellence curriculum for secondary education, Smith makes an effective argument for placing it within a humanities framework. Using instructional approaches that incorporate the study of the historical framework of art, the techniques of analysis, the process of creation, and the experiencing of significant artworks, he asserts that students should value the arts and integrate them into their lives. While some of these positions are still open to debate, researchers into curricular policy and design should examine Smith's ideas seriously as they speak to many of the controversial issues and policies related to arts education. Finally, one should note that Smith's conception of a humanistic curriculum for arts education is a contemporary expression of one of the curricular policy streams (the humanistic curriculum) that have waxed and waned at various times throughout the twentieth century (Kliebard, 1986).

Believing that it is time for the arts education profession to develop a program that will promote aesthetic literacy for all children and extended opportunities for some who have special artistic interests and abilities, Bennett Reimer (1989) proposed a comprehensive arts curriculum model that could be applied to curriculum development in any arts education specialty area. Unlike most previous curricula that focused primarily on skill development and creation, instruction in Reimer's model would be directed toward the improvement of each student's quality of aesthetic experiences through interaction with artworks; toward the creation of works of art as a way of illuminating the perceptions of other creations and understanding the creative process; toward the development of conceptual understandings as an essential means for heightening aesthetic understanding, and toward the development of abilities to apply standards of judgment so that students might exercise control over artistic choice. Like Smith and Eisner, Reimer suggests a curricular model that includes a variety of approaches to learning, but he maintains that his strikes a balance of general and creative experiences.

In addition to suggesting a policy for a comprehensive curriculum, Reimer advocates the building of curriculum by arts educators and artists with the support of private advocacy organizations. He suggests that advocate assistance is needed in the effort to change schools, and that this requires both persuasion and action. "Persuasion," he writes, "is a matter of education." We need to focus our advocacy toward clear, understandable, convincing policies that enlighten influential school constituencies about the value of the arts and the need for an arts curriculum as an essential component of schooling. This effort will be directly related to the parallel curriculum effort, the latter providing ammunition for the former" (p. 16). Clearly, Reimer's curricular and advocacy suggestions present several implications for future arts education policy research.

Other Policy Studies

While considerable policy investigation has been related to public policy and arts or curriculum development and implementation, a number of efforts in other policy areas of arts education are in evidence. In October 1990, the University of Wisconsin-Madison, the Committee on Institutional Cooperation (CIC), the Wisconsin Music Educators Conference, and the North Central Division of MENC sponsored the "Robert Petzold Research Symposium on Policy Issues in Music Education." Researchers from the Big Ten universities were invited to present papers on policy issues that addressed special areas of interest. Paul Haack (University of Minnesota) presented a paper on advocacy for music education and policy development, Robert Erbes (Michigan State University) on influences of educational reform on policy in teacher education, and James Standifer (University of Michigan) on policy development in multicultural arts education. Arts education policies for students with disabilities was the topic of Kate Gfeller's (University of Iowa) paper; Jean Sinor (University of Indiana) presented on policy development in arts education for early childhood programs; and Carol Richardson and Peter Webster (Northwestern University) prepared a paper on educational policies influencing children's thinking in music. A paper on gender equity and policy in music education was given by Julia Koza (University of Wisconsin); approaches to evaluation of policy issues was the topic of the paper presented by Peter Costanza (Ohio State University); and finally, Mary Hoffman (University of Illinois) delivered a paper in which she questioned whether MENC has been or will ever be a policy-wielding organization. The symposium proceedings (Olson, Barresi, and Nelson 1991) provide a resource and several models for research into special topics in music education.

The notion that policy decisions made somewhere in the education establishment can exert influences that are unknown to teachers—the hidden curriculum phenomenon so well explicated by Apple (1979)—has sparked several investigations by music educators. Krueger (1985) examined the influences of the hidden curriculum (factors of schooling procedures and cooperating teacher influence) on the perspectives of music student teachers. Huff (1989) took a broader perspective in examining the hidden curriculum effects of interactions with students, community, colleagues, and institutions of schooling on the teaching practice of two secondary choral music educators. Both of these studies address aspects of arts education that are influenced by policy imperatives, both explicit and implicit. Further, they employ research paradigms and pose questions that might prove useful to future policy researchers.

The influence of the hidden agenda on gender issues in music education has interested a number of researchers in music education. A 1978 study by Abeles and Porter investigated sex stereotyping of students regarding factors that influenced their selection of an instrument. Study results revealed that there was a significant interaction between student gender and the method of presentation for the instrument. A study by Griswold and Chroback (1981) examined the sex-role associations of music instruments and occupations by gender and major. Study results revealed that sex-role associations to instruments did exist. Koza (1991) examined policies of music textbook companies as regards sex equity in illustrations. Using iconographic analysis techniques on her data, Koza revealed that overt sex bias did exist. In fact, while explicit policy militating against sex bias exists, it appears that an implicit adjusted policy reinforcing traditional sex biases was in operation.

Perhaps some of the most powerful examples of policy dynamics are acted out on the local school level. Imposed, endorsed, and advocated policies formulated by school boards, administrators, and teachers' unions (and policies from federal and state officials that filter through these local bodies) all affect the development and operation of music education programs. Although a number of studies (e.g., Radocy, 1988; Anderson, 1986; Brown, 1987) have examined some issues that are tangential to policy, there is a need for policy studies that are focused specifically on this arena and that must be accomplished if the profession is ever to understand the effects of the local political process on school-based music instruction.

The studies and discussions presented above represent exemplary efforts of arts educators and researchers in coming to grips with policy issues. Whereas this section was not intended to be an exhaustive review of the literature, the selected examples contain bibliographic information that will lead researchers to influential sources not cited in this chapter.

THE NEED FOR POLICY RESEARCH

While much of the research reported here examined policy issues related to arts education in general, few studies addressed issues related directly to music education. In fact, the specific examples of the various forms of explicit and implicit policy require in-depth investigation in order for further influences on professional direction and day-to-day operations in music education to be determined.

Toward a Proactive Stance

Because teachers have never had a strong voice in the policy-making and implementation process, they have found themselves in a reactive relationship to policy dictates emanating from a variety of sources within and outside of the school. In this regard, Rose (1990) reported a sense of powerlessness and accompanying frustration felt by many of the teachers she interviewed. Zeichner and Tabachnick (1984) argued that a knowledge of the factors that influence one's behavior as a professional will allow teachers to engage in a strategic redefinition of the situation. They will be able to alter operational parameters, thereby increasing their ability to move from a traditionally reactive stance to a proactive one.

Hope (1989a) notes that arts educators need to become active on the national level if they are ever to gain control of the direction of their profession in the struggle with "image powerful" agencies, organizations, and institutions. Hoffa (1988) asserted that for arts educators

the task is, therefore, more than tactical. It calls for strategic planning that is comparable to a military or an electoral campaign with short-term and long-term goals, the collection and assessment of data, a marshalling and allocation of resources, contingency planning, phased operations, and so forth. . . . Fabricating some kind of agenda for collective action is, therefore, one of the sterner challenges that faces arts education. (p. 7)

Like Hoffa, Hope recognized that, to move forward, arts educators must "create a posture toward the future that avoids superficial approaches, that takes high aspirations for art and teaching and uses them as the basis for policy analysis and vigorous action" (p. 15). Both individuals recognize that a lack of policy action by educators and their professional organizations has placed them in a reactive mode and that the path to proactivity lies in the direction of political consciousness and awareness.

Research and Proactivity

Pankratz (1989) states that arts education as a field has yet to develop a capacity for policy research. Such research, he asserts, can make educators more aware of policies related to curriculum and evaluation as well as additional factors such as leadership, funding, alternative delivery systems, and change strategies. Further he asserts that policy research can assess the potential impact of demographic, economic, sociological, political, ideological, and aesthetic trends in order that policy options can be developed that are within the decision-making control of leaders within the many sectors of arts education.

Research into policy issues may benefit the music education profession in a number of ways. It may assist in determining appropriate rationales for public support of music; it may provide a history of policy efforts that affect music education, identify policymakers and their motivations (both overt and covert), and furnish information relating to leadership styles of policymakers. Further, it may identify potential champions for arts education and determine their usefulness in future policy endeavors. Finally, such research may identify vital information that could lead to efficient and effective development, implementation, and compliance procedures for use by music educators and their professional organizations.

Hope (1989a) poses a question that gets to the heart of necessity for policy research. "What common vision does the arts community have to counterpose against economic and political vision?" His contention is that common vision as expressed through policy will allow arts education to vie for its rightful place in an American society that often views the arts "as a frill," as "having little value but importance as a means to accomplish other ends," or other "art-as-means" agendas (p. 21). Music education as a major partner in arts education must achieve proactive stances in its professional organiza-

tions, in its teacher education programs, and through its advocates in government and in arts-inclined organizations. But translation into policy can come about only when music educators understand the sociocultural forces that affect policy-making; when they can identify the policymakers that affect the profession; when they can pinpoint those persons and organizations in the profession that can effectively develop and implement policy; and when they fully understand the process of formulating, implementing, and evaluating policy that can advance the goals and aspirations on which the profession agrees.

References

Abeles, H. and Porter, S. Y. (1978). The sex-stereotyping of musical instruments. *Journal of Research in Music Education, 26*(2), 65–75.

Anderson, J. E. (1986). A comparison of music teachers' perceptions of individual efficacy in school districts without district music coordinators. Unpublished doctoral dissertation, Columbia University Teachers College, New York.

Apple, M. (1979). *Ideology and curriculum.* London and Boston: Routledge and Kegan Paul.

Apple, M. (1986). *Teachers and texts.* London and Boston: Routledge and Kegan Paul.

Balfe, J. H., and Wyszomirski, M. J. (Eds.). (1983). *Art, ideology and politics.* New York: Praeger.

Barresi, A. L. (1983). The Artists-in-Schools program: A precedent or a fad? In P. T. Tallarico (Ed.), *Bowling Green State University Symposium on Music Teaching and Research, 2,* 68–99.

Barresi, A. L. (1988). The Arts-in-Education program: State arts agencies in assistance to school arts programs. *Design for Arts in Education, 89*(6), 18–23.

Brown, P. A. (1987). An investigation of problems which cause stress among music teachers in Tennessee. Unpublished doctoral dissertation, University of Tennessee, Knoxville.

Carol, R. H. and Ford Associates. (1987). *Summary analysis: Arts-in-Education information exchange questionnaire.* Report compiled for and distributed to Arts-in-Education coordinators. Obtained from the Wisconsin Arts Board.

Council of Chief School Officers. (1985). *Arts, education and the states: A survey of state education policies.* Washington: Author.

Eisner, E. (1974). Is the Artists-in-Schools program effective? *Arts Education, 27*(2), 20.

Eisner, E. (1988). *The role of discipline-based art education in American schools.* Los Angeles: The Getty Center for Education.

Erbes, R. (1990). Influences of education reform on policy in teacher education. In G. Olson, A. Barresi, and D. Nelson (Eds.), *Proceedings of the Robert Petzold Research Symposium on Policy Issues in Music Education.* Madison: School of Music, University of Wisconsin.

Fowler, C. (1989). Why the arts in education: Saving our cultural future. *NASSP Bulletin, 73*(519), 90–95.

Griswold, P. A., and Chroback, D. A. (1981). Sex-role associations of music instruments and occupations by gender and major. *Journal of Research in Music Education, 29*(1), 57–62.

Hanks, N. (1975). *Statement of Nancy Hanks, chairman, National Endowment for the Arts, before the joint hearings of the Special Subcommittee of the Arts and Humanities of the Committee on Labor and the Public Welfare of the United States Senate and the*

Select Subcommittee on Education of the Committee on Education and Labor of the United States house of Representatives on S. 1800, S. 1809, and H. R. 9657, H.R. 7490. November 12, 1975, Washington: U.S. Government Printing Office.

Hawley, W. D. (1990). Systematic analysis, public policy-making and teacher education. In W. R. Houston (Ed.), *Handbook of research on teacher education.* New York: Macmillan Publishing Company.

Hodsoll, F. (1989). Toward civilization: Next responsibilities. *Design for Arts in Education, 90*(3), 10–15.

Hoffa, H. (1988). Arts education and politics: The odd coupling. *Design for Arts in Education, 89*(6), 2–12.

Hope, S. (1985). *Policy questions in music education.* Reston: Music Educators National Conference.

Hope, S. (1989a). National conditions and policy imperatives. *Design for Arts in Education, 90*(7), 15–35.

Hope, S. (1989b). Symposium: Civilization and arts education: From past to future. *Journal of Aesthetic Education, 23*(2), 85–91.

Huff, D. M. (1989). The impact of interactions with students, community, colleagues, and the institution of schooling on the teaching practice of secondary choral educators: Two case studies. Unpublished doctoral dissertation, University of Wisconsin, Madison.

Hutchens, J. (1989). Symposium: Civilization and arts education. Some cautionary observations. *Journal of Aesthetic Education, 23*(2), 96–101.

Jensen, J. L. (1991). An analysis of federal arts education policy and its implementation at the state level: A modified Delphi study of collaborations as ends and means of the policy process in arts education. Unpublished doctoral dissertation, University of Texas, Austin.

Katz, J. (Ed.). (1988). *Arts and education handbook: A guide to productive collaborations.* Washington: National Assembly of State Arts Agencies.

Kliebard, H. M. (1986). *The struggle for the American curriculum 1893–1958.* London and Boston: Routledge and Kegan Paul.

Koza, J. E (1991). Sex equity and policy in music education: A change of vision, a change of values. In G. Olson, A. Barresi, and D. Nelson (Eds.), *Proceedings of the Robert Petzold Research Symposium on Policy Issues in Music Education.* Madison: School of Music, University of Wisconsin.

Krueger, P. (1985). Influences of the hidden pedagogy upon the perspectives of music students: An ethnography. Unpublished doctoral dissertation, University of Wisconsin, Madison.

Lipman, S. (1984). Cultural policy: Whither America, whither government? *The New Criterion, 3,* 14.

Mark, M. (1986). *Contemporary music education.* New York: Schirmer Books.

Mayer, R. R., and Greenwood, E. (1980). *The design of social policy research.* Englewood Cliffs: Prentice Hall.

McLaughlin, J. (Ed.). (1987). *A guide to national and state arts education services.* New York: ACA Books.

MENC. (1970). *Interpreting traditional, understanding change.* Program for the twenty-second biennial meeting of the MENC, Chicago, March 6–10, 1970.

MENC. (1970, January). Facing the music in urban education [Special issue]. *Music Educators Journal.*

MENC. (1972, October). Music in world culture [Special issue]. *Music Educators Journal.*

Mills, E. A., and Thomson, D. R. (1986). *A national survey of art(s) education, 1984–85: A national report on the state of the arts in the states.* Reston: National Art Education Association.

Mok, J. L. (1983). Artists-in-Education program of the National Endowment for the Arts using educational criticism and congruence. Unpublished doctoral dissertation, New York University, New York.

Mulcahy, K. (1989). Symposium: Civilization and arts education. Civilization through arts education. *Journal of Aesthetic Education, 23*(2), 92–96.

Murphy, B., and Pawasarat, J. (1986). Why it failed: School desegregation 10 years later. *Milwaukee Magazine, 11*(9), 34–50.

NASM. (1989–90). *Handbook 1989–90.* Reston: National Association of Schools of Music.

NASM Futureswork. (1990, November). *Executive summary: K–12 issues and influences.* Brochure for members, National Association of Schools of Music.

National Endowment for the Arts. (1988). *Toward civilization: A report on arts education.* Washington: U.S. Government Printing Office.

Olson, G. B., Barresi, A. L. and Nelson, D., (Eds.), (1991). *Proceedings of the Robert Petzold Symposium on Policy Issues in Music Education.* Madison: School of Music, University of Wisconsin.

Organization of American Kodály Educators (1990). *What is a Kodály certification program?* Brochure of the Organization of American Kodály Educators.

Pankratz, D. (1989). Policies, agendas, and arts education research, *Design for Arts in Education, 90*(5), 2–13.

Pankratz, D., and Mulcahy, K. (Eds.). (1989). *The challenge to reform arts education: What role can research play?* New York: ACA Books.

Pankratz, D., and Morris, V. (1990). Arts policy research for the 1990's and beyond. In D. Pankratz and V. Morris (Eds.), *The future of the arts: Public policy and arts research.* New York: Praeger.

Radocy, R. (1988). Through superintendents' eyes: Attitudes towards the arts in Kansas schools. *Research Paper Abstracts,* MENC National Convention, Indianapolis, April 20–23.

Rebell, M. A., and Block, A. R. (1982). *Educational policy making and the courts: An empirical study of judicial activism.* Chicago: University of Chicago Press.

Reimer, B. (1989). A comprehensive arts curriculum model. *Design for Arts in Education, 90*(6), 3–16.

Richmond, J. W. (1990). Equal opportunity for aesthetic development: The arts, the schools, and the law. Unpublished doctoral dissertation, Northwestern University, Evanston.

Rose, A. M. (1990). Music education in culture: A critical analysis of reproduction, production, and hegemony. Unpublished doctoral dissertation, University of Wisconsin, Madison.

Smith, R. A. (1986). *Excellence in art education: Ideas and initiatives.* Reston: National Arts Education Association.

Smith, R. A. (1977). A policy analysis and criticism of the Artists-in-Schools program of the National Endowment for the Arts. *Arts Education, 30*(5), 17–18.

Smith, R. A. (1988). Policy for the arts: Whither the schools, whither the public and private sectors? *Design for Arts in Education, 89*(4), 2–11.

Smith, R. A. (1989). Symposium: Civilization and arts education [Preface]. *Journal of Aesthetic Education, 23*(2), 83–84.

Sorenson, G. P. (Ed.). (1988). *Critical issues in education law: The role of the federal judiciary in shaping public education.* Topeka: National Organization on Legal Problems of Education.

Spring, J. (1988). *Conflict of interests: The politics of American education.* White Plains: Longman.

Taylor, F., and Barresi, A. L. (1984). *The arts at a new frontier: The National Endowment for the Arts.* New York: Plenum.

Udell, S. (1990). A historical/descriptive study of the Wisconsin Arts Board and its involvement in arts education. Unpublished doctoral dissertation, University of Wisconsin, Madison.

Zeichner, K., and Tabachnick, R. (1984). *Social strategies and instructional control in the socialization of beginning teachers.* Madison: Wisconsin Center for Educational Research.

·55·

RESEARCH METHODS IN INTERNATIONAL AND COMPARATIVE MUSIC EDUCATION

Anthony Kemp
UNIVERSITY OF READING

Laurence Lepherd
UNIVERSITY OF SOUTH QUEENSLAND

Greater facility of communication, particularly through advances in technology and travel, has provided music educators with considerable opportunity for broadening their perspectives on music education. The result has been a heightened awareness of the various ways education is carried out in other countries and cultures, together with increased knowledge of the problems and attempted solutions by colleagues.

In this chapter the essential features of international and comparative music education over approximately the last three decades are described. Also described are the developments in the field of general comparative education, and suggestions are made about the ways in which advances in this field might be applied to music education.

It is concluded that although there have been achievements in international and comparative music education, greater emphasis needs to be placed on the development of comparative theories, conceptual frameworks, and methods specifically appropriate to music education and music-cultural transmission to enable more rigorous, reliable, valid, and beneficial comparisons to take place.

BACKGROUND TO RESEARCH

The modern era of research in international and comparative music education commenced in 1953 with a conference in Brussels organized by the United Nations Educational, Scientific, and Cultural Organization (UNESCO) in association with the International Music Council. The conference, titled "The Role and Place of Music in the Education of Youth and Adults," was attended by delegates from 29 member states of UNESCO.

The aim of this conference was to study in their entirety problems connected with nonspecialized music education, the purpose of which is not to form professional musicians, but to develop the appreciation, taste and critical judgement of the listener from his earliest youth, so as to train him and enable him to appreciate the beauty and wealth of musical masterpieces. (UNESCO, 1955, p. 9)

The proceedings from the conference were published in 1955 and drew attention to the further aims of the conference, indicating the scope of papers presented and discussions held. The conference "set out to define" methods used in schools, teaching adults and training teachers. It placed particular emphasis on the international exchange of information, people, and materials; the activities of government institutions; and the "role of music education as a means to international understanding." At the conference, "representatives of all branches of musical activity, educators, composers, music teachers, students and performers met together . . . to exchange ideas and attempt to compare the experience gained in their particular fields" (p. 12). Discussions held resulted in a series of recommendations that advocated "specific solutions" for most of the problems common in a number of countries.

The Brussels Conference was a most important event because it formally brought together a group of people involved in music education in a variety of international, national, and musical circumstances. The papers presented constituted the first attempt at a structured analysis of research in international music education. The report of its proceedings included such broad topics as the philosophy of music education; the role of music in international understanding; the overviewing of music education in the occidental world, Europe, and the American continent; and new trends in music education. Chapter headings included "Music Education in the Curriculum," "Music Education in Society," "Methods and Aids in Music Education," "Teacher Training," and "The Contribution of the Professional to Music Education."

One of the principal outcomes of the Brussels Conference was the establishment of the International Society for Music Education (ISME). This organization has continued to function since that time and has been the principal body accepting responsibility for continuing the work of the Brussels Conference. This has been carried out through its conferences and seminar activities as well as the publication of journals and yearbooks.

Initially, ISME established a journal—the *International Music Educator*—which was issued at first three times and later twice each year from 1960–1971. The journal included material written in English, French, and German simultaneously and aimed to "publish views, exchange information and mutual criticism" (International Society for Music Education, 1960, p. 5). It also included reports on activities within particular countries from national organizations affiliated with ISME. This journal was discontinued in 1971 and replaced in 1973 by an annual yearbook and other "occasional" publications. The yearbook, which has been published in most years since then, is devoted to the publication of papers presented either at biennial conferences or at seminars organized by the ISME commissions. The yearbooks are usually centered on a particular theme, with perspectives from a wide variety of countries. Some themes have been the education of professional musicians, national culture: an inspiration for music education, tradition and change in music education, music for a small planet, new perspectives in music: new tasks for music education, a world view of music education.

In 1983 ISME reintroduced a journal—now called the *International Journal of Music Education* (IJME)—which is published twice yearly. Although it is now published for general distribution only in the English language (a Hungarian edition is also published independently), its concept has been expanded to include a greater number of articles and reviews of books relating to music education pedagogy or music for children, as well as reports from affiliated national organizations, matters related to the functioning of the society, and details of the activities of its seven commissions.

One of the most important functions of ISME in the development of international and comparative music education is through the work of its commissions, each of which has a specific focus:

Community Music
Early Childhood

Mass Media Policy
Music Therapy and Special Education
Research
Schools and Teacher Training
The Education of the Professional Musician

The commissions promote the exchange of ideas relating to each of these topics and often arrange for the publication of commission seminar papers independently.

Through its activities ISME has been the prime organization responsible for a coordinated approach to providing international perspectives for music education. It has focused on broad issues, and because of its disparate membership (spanning some 60 countries), it has been able to identify salient aspects of music education as far as both global matters and individual national matters are concerned.

Another conference, not dissimilar to that at Brussels, was the Fourteenth Symposium of the Colston Research Society held at the University of Bristol in 1962. The symposium was designed to examine the current state of music education in England and Wales, but it also included papers from colleagues in other parts of the world, essentially Europe and America. The implication was that the consideration of these international presentations would provide English and Welsh music educators with the opportunity to see their own music in broader perspectives.

While ISME has undertaken a specifically international role, other organizations and publications have attempted occasional international perspectives even though their briefs have had more national orientation. National organizations such as the Canadian Music Educators Association, the Australian Society for Music Education and societies for music education in Hungary and Sweden, to name a few, have all published material of wider than national interest. Between 1970 and 1983 the *Australian Journal of Music Education* assumed the role of providing international perspectives while the international journal was in abeyance. The *British Journal of Music Education* (established in 1984) regularly includes articles of international interest, while the *Music Educators Journal*, the magazine of the American Music Educators National Conference, occasionally does so. The implied purpose of these publications is to provide some international perspective for national music educators.

Other research studies have emanated as the result of varying motivations. One study that attempted to juxtapose provisions for music education in a variety of countries was undertaken by the Schools' Music Association in Britain. The association wrote to many embassies and other organizations seeking information on national provisions for music education and received 48 responses ranging from one paragraph to 1,000-word articles. The information was published in 1964 (Schools' Music Association, 1964). The purpose of collating and publishing this material was stated in the following terms:

Advances in music education in the last thirty years have been revolutionary and standards today are far higher than those attained in schools during the early part of this century. It becomes increasingly important that countries should keep each other fully informed of what each is doing in this field, as progress can thereby be accelerated when all interested persons are aware of what is being done in countries other than their own. (p. 5)

No detailed guidelines for the collection of data were evident, and the information published was so diverse that the book's value in accelerating progress must have been questionable.

National studies that are either entirely devoted to an analysis of the complete provisions for music education or a preliminary to other studies are evident in separate forms outside of journal publications. These include Choksy (1974)—Hungary; Taylor (1979)—England; Lepherd (1988)—The People's Republic of China; Comte (1988)—Australia; and Gates (1988)—the United States. The framework for each description varied considerably, and the rationale for adopting a particular framework was not always stated.

Most studies that have appeared since the Brussels Conference and that have documented international meetings and endeavors appear to have two common themes. First, there is a belief in the value of music in a diversity of forms as a vital element in human, aesthetic, and artistic development and as an integral part of life if it is not life itself. Second, there should be a commitment to education in and through music as a means whereby that development can be implemented. As far as the first theme is concerned, one of the most significant trends over the last 40 years has been the increasing recognition of the diversity of world music to the extent that the term "musics" is frequently used. It is noteworthy that the findings of the original Brussels conference included only sparse reference to music of nonwestern origins but that over recent years there has been an increasing recognition of the traditional indigenous musics of many societies that were previously regarded as virtually monocultural.

For a time when emphasis was placed on western music in most music education, music was termed "the universal language." This phrase is now regarded as inappropriate. The wide variety of musical styles and genres in all cultures has been increasingly recognized in international and comparative music education as contributing to wider aesthetic experience and involves "musical languages" that need to be learned to facilitate wider communication and understanding.

NATURE OF INTERNATIONAL AND COMPARATIVE STUDIES

The results of research reported in the various sources listed above can be categorized into three main areas:

1. Studies that amount to philosophical statements relating to education and that are designed to be global in their concept
2. Studies that relate to formal, systemic provisions for music education that can be either an overview or a thematic study of provisions in full or in part, and that can be in the form of single national studies or of comparative studies involving two or more nations
3. Studies that relate to nonsystemic cultural transmission and that can be either monocultural studies or cross-cultural comparative studies where the cultural basis is of ethnic origin

Some comparative studies have attempted to bridge the gap between nonsystemic and systemic education (see Figure 55–1).

Global Statements

In an endeavor to draw together the disparate elements of music internationally, many editions of journals, other publications, and conference reports include statements that are designed to stimulate international thinking on what might be regarded as areas of common concern. The unifying feature of many of these papers is the philosophy of music education.

A frequently used approach is to identify problems that are common in a variety of circumstances, refer to these circumstances, and make generalizations about the problems. Hoggart (1976), for example, draws attention to a challenge that he perceived to exist in the latter part of the twentieth century. This challenge involved determining what to do in the face of greatly increased attention to and funding in the arts. He refers to the United States and the Soviet Union as examples of countries that "provide massively" for the arts (p. 3) and also mentions the United Kingdom in this vein. His thesis is that the place of the arts in society needs to be questioned. He perceives a universal problem—if immense amounts of funding are being expended, we should be sure that they are appropriately placed. Therefore, society needs to know what disciplines constitute the arts and what benefit they are to society.

Elliott (1984) epitomizes much of the discussion on universal issues that has taken place during the last decade when he advocates that thinking about the philosophy of music education has been too closely related to western concepts of music and aesthetics. According to Elliott, "We are unlikely to develop a full explanation of the role of music and musical experience in modern society, or bases for multi-cultural music education, from the current principles of aesthetic education" (p. 3). He postulates that western aesthetics, musicology, and descriptive ethnomusicology focus on music that is severely limited in its more technical and academic aspects—its notation, practices, and technology—and that these cannot be applied to "the music of all times and all places" (p. 3). Elliott proceeds to discuss aspects of the internalization of music, a concept that, he believes, is more common to music of all cultures and should therefore be a focal point in all music education.

To deny a place in music education to the musical metaphors, forms and behaviors of other cultures is to deny students access to sources

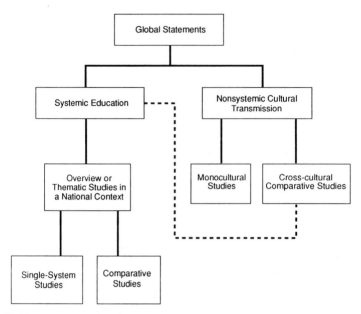

FIGURE 55-1.   Classification of Existing International and Comparative Studies

particularly qualified for and successful at integrating the prototypical experiences of human mental life. (p. 7)

Similar arguments for the recognition of "musics" rather than "music" have been expressed in global terms by Nketia (1978), Schwadron (1984), and Gieseler (1986). Gieseler, however, makes some penetrating observations on the reasons for musics being included in music education. He warns against the concept of leveling musical expression to one kind of "world music," and advocates a strengthening of indigenous musics around the world so that the "concealed musical energies of a region should be freed" (p. 6).

Many arguments have been raised advocating the greater recognition in music education of what is loosely termed (synonymously) folk, indigenous, national, or traditional music. A nation's own national music has generally been regarded as being a fundamental part of its music education. Many countries, however, include national music of other countries in their own music programs. This is probably a manifestation of the global trends indicated above. Advocates of this position have included Vikar (1983), De Azevedo (1983), and Jayatilaka (1984). ISME regarded the concept with such importance that a theme for its fourteenth international conferences was "National Culture: An Inspiration in Music Education"; SME subsequently published 12 of the papers presented there (Taylor, 1981).

Another global theme that has emerged over the last two decades has been the result of the increased recognition of pluralist cultures based on ethnic origins—frequently referred to as multiculturalism. Western countries have tended to believe that immigrants from other countries and cultures should be assimilated by the dominant host culture. In real-

ity, this has not happened. What occurred was originally termed a "melting pot" but more latterly recognized as a "mosaic" of cultures. The fusion was really confusion until there was a recognition that the imported cultures assisted in developing more colorful and diverse societies and musical expressions.

With this realization came the need for music educators to recognize the pluralist concept in music education. The concept has been addressed by various music educators including Dobbs (1982), Lewin (1984), Standifer (1986a), Walker (1986), and Swanwick (1988). Kemp (1989) expresses it in this way:

Trends towards a multi-cultural music curriculum will, without doubt, bring a greater and a more detailed understanding of the different musics of the world: but it will do more than this. . . . Multicultural awareness will allow us to recognize and respect essential differences between musics of the world and to be sensitive to calls to maintain cultural purity; it will also help us clarify those underlying principles which bind us together. Music is a worldwide manifestation of our human condition and reflects human needs to engage in communication of a very special kind. (p. 37)

Systemic Education

The major source of international studies has been related to national systems of education. The underlying assumption for this is that in the contemporary world all countries are committed to education for the development of their societies in economic, scientific, and cultural ways. As nations have geographical, administrative, and political boundaries and each government has a system of education within which music is a part, it is logical that music educators frequently view their profession within this framework. The two major forms of study associated with systemic education relate to the whole or part of system overview, or themes or components within a system.

National, Single-System Studies The main purpose of using a national system as a basis for study has been to describe the provisions for music education within the system. In the more detailed single-system studies, a number of different methods used in analysis have been evident.

Choksy (1974) approaches an analysis of music education in Hungary from a pedagogical position. Her purpose in discussing music education in Hungary is to indicate the way in which the Kodály method has been used in that national system, and thus to demonstrate its potential use in other contexts. She begins her description of music education with a brief statement on the current musical context in Hungary and the influence that Kodály's method has had on it, and goes on to describe the Kodály method in detail. She then discusses the structure of public education in Hungary and the place of music in that structure, dealing briefly with elementary and secondary schools, and finishes with a description of colleges and conservatories. Because of the appropriateness of the Kodály method to the elementary school, and its possible application to American music education, the description of the music curriculum in Hungary is restricted to grades 1 to 8. This overview has its limitations, probably because of its intent to focus on the application of the Kodály method in America. However, it hints at comparative study because it involves a prediction based on the assumption that because the Kodály method is good in one context it can therefore be applied successfully in another.

The scope of the eight year music program in Hungary includes a formidable amount of teaching material when thought of in terms of the typical American school situation of music once or twice per week. However, the sequence of the Kodály method is a valid one, and it is possible to accomplish much through it in the six years of American elementary school. (p. 49)

Taylor (1979) uses a model for analysis that has a historical framework. In keeping with the title of her monograph *Music Now*, Taylor outlines the historical antecedents of music in England, commencing briefly with music ideas from Ancient Greece and the role of the Church in the Middle Ages, through to a more detailed account of mass music education in the nineteenth century and the first half of the twentieth century.

Taylor draws attention to international developments in music education in her description of post–World War II initiatives, particularly her reference to the 1953 Brussels Conference. She makes a specific reference to the influence of one paper at the conference, "The Orff-Bergese Method" (Kraus and Twittenhoff, 1955; Taylor, 1979, p. 14), on the development of British music education.

Within the historical framework, Taylor covers progressively the influence on music education of such factors as the media and developments in mass communication; the ap-

pointment of advisers and inspectors; and the development of instrumental schemes, music centers, and youth orchestras. Having arrived at the 1970s, Taylor turns to the curriculum as the focal point for the analysis. She discusses issues such as curriculum values and goals, objectives, cognitive behaviors, affective behaviors, psychomotor behaviors, and instructional objectives. She then outlines the major influences on the curriculum and draws particular attention to psychological influences. She refers then to the "creativity" element of the 1960s and the three major music educators Carl Orff, Zoltan Kodály, and Shinichi Suzuki.

Taylor next turns her attention to the monitoring of achievement and describes in some detail the examination systems in England. She then deals with advanced music education in colleges of education, university departments of music, colleges of music (conservatories), polytechnics, and adult education. In essence, this section of her work has been concerned with the structure and content of the music curriculum at various levels.

Taylor then goes on to describe the influences that have been exerted on the educational system. She mentions some of the organizations that have been involved in supporting and influencing developments; of these she numbers more than 100. She also refers to government reports and curriculum development influences, patronage and sponsorship, and the rise of the leisure industry. Finally, Taylor concludes with a reference to the changing face of education. She identifies emerging trends in music education and identifies a number of current issues.

In summary, Taylor's approach is to describe English music education in a historical context with specific relevance to psychology and with emphasis on curricular aims, objectives and assessment, influences on musical development and issues.

Lepherd (1988), in a study of music education in the People's Republic of China, used a conceptual framework for the description of a national system of music education adapted from the work of Holmes (1981) and Bereday (1966, 1967).

There are six categories that can be used in a model for the analysis of a national system of music education. Because it is recognized that music education should have purpose, the first aspect of education that it is logical to address is *aims*. Aims are usually expressed at different levels of education starting with such policy documents as a national constitution and continuing in more specific terms through provincial legislation, local curricula, influential music educators, and professional associations. Aims can be found in three subclassifications. *Child-centered* aims are those in which the child is the focus of education. *Society-centered* aims are those in which education is seen as the means through which society develops. *Subject-centered* aims relate to the way in which the continued development of the subject is considered to be of paramount importance. In reality, the aims of music education can rarely be categorized absolutely in these terms. All three aims are expressed in various documents, and the comparative interest is in the degree of emphasis placed on each.

The second category for analysis is *administration*. It is suggested that after aims are expressed and promoted nationally they need to be implemented. Governments develop administrative systems that assist in this implementation. Administrative systems usually encompass three levels—national, provincial, and local. Description of a system involves identifying the relationship between these levels, particularly observing the various responsibilities associated with each.

In order to implement any educational program there is a need for *finance*. Comparative interest lies in the way in which finance is provided, who provides it, and how it is expended. This generally includes government provision at the system level and can include commercial, philanthropic, and parental provision. An important issue in financial considerations is accountability, and related to this is system evaluation.

The next level of interest is associated with the *structure and organization* of music education. This involves an analysis of the educational continuum from early childhood through to tertiary institutions and adult education. Of particular interest is the way in which provision is made for music at each level, how transition from one level to another is facilitated, and how progression is assessed.

The fifth category concerns *curricula*. Once the aims have been determined, provision made for administration, sources of finance determined, and the structure established, the curricula for all levels (from preschool to higher education) need to be developed. Curriculum design includes the formation of specific objectives for music education and the content and learning strategies for each level of instruction. There are three theories under which curricula generally fall. These are *essentialism*, the question of what subjects are essential for general education; *encyclopedism*, the assertion that all knowledge should be found in a curriculum, and *pragmatism*, the consideration of what is important to face the problems of living. The presence of music for all children aged 6 to 12 years, for example, suggests essentialism. The nature of curriculum content would determine if the curriculum was encyclopedic (if all aspects of music were in the curriculum) or pragmatic (if there was an emphasis on the teaching of social skills or developing specific societal aims). Of further interest is curriculum development—how it is carried out and by whom.

The final category is that of *teacher education*. Curricula need implementation. How teachers are educated and trained to implement curricula both before and during employment is of comparative interest. Before employment the issue of length, type, and balance of courses and the methods of assessment are important. During employment, types of teacher and teacher status, and promotion and professional development opportunities are important considerations.

This model for analysis has been developed with the view to standardizing the method of presentation of national systems. Standardization facilitates comparison because the variables can be identified.

George Bereday (1966, 1967), however, some years previously, developed a comparative method that can be used in conjunction with the above model, and with further extension enables even more rigorous comparison. National systems can be compared in four stages. It is important to *describe* and *interpret* a system first. These two processes can be undertaken simultaneously and can be carried out using the categories outlined above. Once this process has been completed, the third stage of *juxtaposition* and preliminary comparison can be carried out. In this process data can be placed side by side to determine comparability. The fourth stage involves *comparison proper*; that is, after the comparable data have been determined, detailed comparison can take place.

One of Bereday's principles is that the data to be described are interpreted in the light of the variety of factors that influence the education process, which can include sociological, economic, historical, and geographical considerations. It is appropriate to review these factors before examining the provisions for music education by including an overview of the context for music education in a report that addresses the nature of contemporary society of a particular country and its history, geography, and economy.

In music education there is also a need to examine the musical context of the society. This includes the nature of the music (a nation's traditional music as well as other forms) and also the current national climate for music (the extent to which national or local organizations of a variety of kinds influence directly the provisions for music education). Within this framework it is possible to establish a link between the educational context, the musical context, and the direct provisions. Music education does not exist in a vacuum. A national system is the way it is because of the factors that have influenced its development. Often the factors differ from one country to another, and it is important to recognize this in the description and interpretation, and, above all, the comparison.

Lepherd (1988) used this conceptual framework in his study of music education in China. He described and analysed current provisions in each of Holmes' six categories and demonstrated the way that history and traditions have influenced current practices.

Comte (1988) edited a special edition of the *Australian Journal of Music Education* as a contribution to Australia's bicentennial celebration of European settlement and coinciding with the eighteenth ISME conference held in Canberra. The format for this publication was based on a structural analysis within a historical framework that made reference to current context. After a statement concerning the formation and development of the Australian Society for Music Education, the historical framework and current context components were provided by two initial papers that referred to the relationship between aboriginal music and Australian music education, and the current cultural context, and a concluding paper that traced the important developments in Australian music education over the last 50 years. In between were papers addressing aspects of music education such as music therapy; private studio music teaching; early childhood, primary, secondary, and tertiary music education; and teacher training.

Gates (1988) edited a major contemporary analysis of music education in the United States based on a series of symposia at the University of Alabama. The resultant publication was reviewed by Rainbow (1990).

A comprehensive statement of current challenges confronting American music education and suggested ways of resolving them emphatically deserves the notice of teachers elsewhere. Provided, that is, readers in other lands do not expect to find in it a ready-made panacea for their own ills. (p. 75)

National System Thematic Studies Although there have not been many comprehensive national system overviews of music education, there have been a considerable number of smaller papers published in various journals, some of which present a brief overview but most of which focus on a particular theme.

One collection of papers was published in the *British Journal of Music Education.* Paynter (1987), as coeditor, arranged for a special edition of the journal to address music education in Nordic countries. The seven papers presented were eclectic in nature, drawing attention to a variety of issues having, as a whole, a regional rather than a national concept, although individual papers were certainly nationally oriented. The edition included:

"The Development and Structure of the Icelandic Community Schools"
"Music Education in Teacher Training in Denmark"
"Danish Music Education—A Crafts Museum?"
"It Takes Time to be Creative—More Time?" (a paper addressing some issues relating to the Danish Grammar School)

Paynter's rationale for the use of such an edition is interesting.

Yet although it may be true to say that, over the last twenty years or so, music educators in the Nordic countries have drawn quite a lot of inspiration from beyond their own borders (Finland and Sweden tending to look towards Hungary, Norway, Iceland and Denmark perhaps turning to Britain and the United States), it would be a serious error to imagine that they have no significant ideas of their own! Indeed, an enormous amount has been achieved in these countries from which the rest of us can usefully learn. (p. 251)

In this way Paynter draws attention to two aspects of comparative music education. First, the acknowledgment that borrowing of ideas has already occurred, and second, that one of the aims is to transfer ideas from one environment to another. The problem with this kind of statement is that although music educators acknowledge that it is possible (and probably desirable) to learn by observing what takes place in other environments, the question of the most appropriate ways to achieve this transfer is largely ignored.

In this editorial introduction Paynter draws attention to a very significant problem of comparative study, and that is language facility. He acknowledges that colleagues in Nordic countries may read what is written in English but that the reverse does not happen so frequently. At least in the English-speaking world, comparative studies are often one-way, a reason for there being few references in this chapter to comparative studies that take place in non-English-speaking countries.

Terry (1985), in his description of music education in France, commences with a statement of the organizational structure of music education, particularly since the reforms of 1975. He draws attention to the dualism of provision for music education that sees the Ministry of Culture as having responsibility for the large variety of conservatories existing in France, and the system of education as being provided for all students by the minister of education. Methodologically he places this in the area of introduction and of contextual influence. Having drawn attention to this in the "structural" introduction, Terry then uses the structure outline to indicate the curriculum provisions in each level. Included in the primary music section on curriculum are statements on the training of teachers. Terry concludes his overview with a summary of some of the main problems evident in French music education and poses some questions that relate to British music education. As far as methodology is concerned, Terry states that "an effort has been made to restrict value judgements to those made by French teachers themselves" (p. 227). The problem of value judgments in comparative music education will be addressed later.

The *Music Educators Journal* has occasionally included articles on national systems of music education. One edition carried two such articles, Abdoo (1984) on music education in Japan, and Kaplan (1984), in Israel. A subsequent edition published a paper on aspects of Chinese music education (Standifer, 1986b).

Abdoo commences with a historical introduction drawing attention to the nonsystemic nature of centuries of Japanese music education through the imitating of gagaku music from one generation to the next. In 1879 the Tokyo National University of Fine Arts and Music commenced a formal education program. The modern system of music education was instituted in 1945 and was based on the U.S. model. Abdoo then gives a thumbnail anecdotal sketch of the current curriculum of elementary school, the high school, and college. He progresses to a specific description of school performances, which would no doubt be of considerable interest to the American clientele of the journal. He gives a broad description of teaching techniques, paragraphs on funding sources—and again, some oblique comparison with the United States.

A distinctly different approach is taken by Kaplan (1984) in her essay on music education in Israel. Her approach commences with a reference to the music opportunities offered in the Kibbutz, and she makes the observation that this music education available outside of the formal system is of a very high standard. Music teachers in the Kibbutz are paid by the Ministry of Education and Culture, as are music teachers in the public school system. Kaplan then follows an approach that simultaneously describes music in schools and Kibbutzim, referring to resources available and teachers and performing groups. Reference is also made occasionally to higher education and entrance requirements. Finally, the problems of music education are discussed. The overall linking theme of this overview is what Kaplan describes as "the elusive dream of music literacy for all" (p. 60). Kaplan's paper is an oblique comparison of nonsystemic education with systemic education.

The *International Journal of Music Education,* since its appearance in 1983, has included at least one article in most editions covering some aspects of one country's music education. In the second issue, for example, there are three articles relating to Asian countries. Jayatilaka (1984) focuses on indigenous music as a basis for music education in Malaysia. He commences with a sociogeographic picture of Malaysian society indicating pluralism, and then proceeds to outline the need for a recognition of the development of indigenous music but not necessarily in the formal system. Jayatilaka believes it is the basis of "music education" (he does not specify formal or informal). He advocates this because

extramural factors which are not always considered by the 'outsider', have a way of binding themselves tenaciously to the musical tones and rhythms of organized sound patterns. These may include the community's psychophysical attributes and capacities—musical, social, moral, spiritual or otherwise—which may be inextricably bound with each other and essential for making music. . . . It is only when educators are prepared to study the creative musical processes of the indigenous people that they will be able gainfully to transmit to others what it is one ought to be listening for in the ethnic music of these peoples. (p. 45)

One difficulty with the proposal is that the writer does not suggest how this might be achieved in the formal or the informal context. Given the position taken, it would appear to be difficult to transmit these societal nuances in a formal system.

Kasilag (1984) adopts a similar position regarding the importance of folk music. She draws attention to the historical influences on the multicultural aspects of society and the way in which Filipino music is being developed.

Leong (1984), in a description of music education in Singapore, has taken a structural approach. After a brief introductory note on the sociocultural background, he indicates the basic provision of primary school music education and then describes the nonelective music, extracurricular activities, and elective music programs in secondary schools leading to provision for teacher training. He outlines some of the influences on children's development, including concerts, music tuition, youth orchestras, festivals, competitions, and music camp. Leong's approach is descriptive without being critical. There is no indication of problems or discussion of aims or content. Critical analysis of relevant issues is an important component of any educational study.

In a subsequent edition of IJME Merkuriyev (1984) contributes a paper that also adopts a structural approach to an overview of music education, in this instance, in the U.S.S.R. After a historical introduction, he moves to a description of class music and extracurricular activities in the general education school and outlines the influence on this music by

some organizations available in Russian society. He then moves to special music education in schools, music colleges, and conservatoires, with an outline of the influence of the U.S.S.R. Composer's Union on this level of music.

Describing aspects of music education in the Soviet Union, Bartle (1986) also offers a structural approach with a detailed analysis of music in general education with the inclusion of music available in the special music schools. He then goes into considerable detail on the training of professional musicians and music teachers and describes curriculum purpose, content, and outcomes in three different kinds of institution. Bartle's focus is on the training of professional musicians and the purpose of the introduction at the lower levels of education is to provide a context into which the professional training is set.

Two other small studies are by Guardabasso (1989) and Achilleoudis (1989). Under the respective headings of "Music Education in Italy: What is Going On?" and "Music in Secondary Education in Cyprus," the authors focus on particular aspects of music education. Guardabasso, for example, indicates some of the problems currently evident in Italy. Achilleoudis, on the other hand, follows a curriculum approach that outlines aims, classroom content, timetable, resources, and musical activities. The various activities associated with secondary school music are then listed. Again, although there is description, there is little analysis.

Studies in a National Context—Comparative Studies One of the first genuinely comparative studies in the modern era was carried out by Cykler (1960). Cykler's goals for the study were quite clear.

Obviously the goals of music education at elementary and secondary levels vary between countries. Moreover the school systems of Europe in general are difficult to compare with those of the United States of America. However, a comparison of the education of classroom teachers and special music teachers in a few selected countries may help to point out strengths as well as weaknesses in the various systems. . . .

This study in no way purports to be an exhaustive one in comparative education. Areas of significant comparison are dealt with in the hope that further and deeper probing may bring to light practices, strengths, weaknesses, and contemplated reforms that might be mutually helpful. (p. 31)

Without enunciating a rationale for the methodology he uses, Cykler systematically examines four aspects of teacher education in Austria, Germany, and the United States. These aspects are the preprofessional musical training for teachers responsible for music education in elementary and secondary schools, the professional musical training of elementary and then secondary school music teachers, and the certification of teachers.

The description of preprofessional training is a statement providing the context for the other three aspects. Cykler compares progressively. Having drawn attention to the similarities and differences in the structural contexts in the three countries, he proceeds to describe the provisions for each country in the other three aspects, making comparative observations within the text of the descriptions. The observed model that Cykler uses is structural and thematic. The background description is structurally based, while the principal theme is that of teacher education within the elementary and secondary school structure.

Two comparative studies by Bartle (1988, 1990) reveal different methods of comparison. The first is based on the comparison of two models of music tuition in two different countries: the Private Teacher Model in Australia and the Music School Model in the U.S.S.R. He describes each of the models first separately (including some background), and then places the salient features alongside one another, teasing out perceived advantages of each model. In the second study Bartle describes the professional training of musicians in six occupational categories in six countries. As an introduction he provides a historical background to the study and then delineates the commonalities (of commission and omission) in the training between the countries.

One of the major international comparative studies currently being undertaken is being carried out by Bartle in conjunction with ISME and the Callaway International Music Education Resource Centre based at the University of Western Australia. Because of the scope of this study, its purpose, methodology, and outcomes have been fully described (Bartle, 1984). The project aims to classify and record music degree and diploma courses in as many countries as possible in order to facilitate the employment of graduates of institutions in countries other than the one in which they graduated, or to facilitate the transference of students from one institution to another in the event of migration.

It is an attempt to devise means whereby accurate, detailed and up-to-date information may be available on courses for degrees and diplomas anywhere in the world, and in such a form as to be immediately comprehensible to those who need it. (p. 127)

Bartle recognizes the need to standardize the categorization of the courses through a description of length, content, assessment details, and the compulsory or optional nature of subjects. The model further divides information into six main types of subjects. He draws attention to the immense amount of data that could be collected and the value of using a computer data base for the storage of the information and the necessity to update the information every three years to maintain currency. In the development of the data base he carried out a pilot study using information obtained from Australian institutions. This study is a good example of the recognition of the need for purpose in comparison, standardization for comparability, a data collection method based on a pilot study, and a recognition of the long-term implications of the study which addresses a logistical music education problem—the transference of musicians from one situation to another.

Three editions of the *International Journal of Music Education* (Lepherd 1985a,b, 1986) carried comparative studies based on themes involving a problem. The themes selected were Music Education in a Multicultural Society, the

Education of Exceptionally Musical Children, and Bicultural Music Education. In each case contributions were invited from music educators in different countries. They were provided with a set of guidelines designed to facilitate comparability. Lepherd, as the section editor, introduced each section with a broad statement of the problems as they appeared in a variety of contexts, and the writers provided information about their own national system. A comparative comment, drawing attention to features emerging from the papers, was given by the section editor at the end. The overall aim of these sections was to provide a standardized conceptual framework within which it was possible to enable comparison. The framework in each case commenced with a background statement to the theme followed by a discussion of the implied problem and posed solutions within the writer's own environment.

A similar thematic study was published in another edition of IJME (Dobbs and Kemp, 1987) where the theme was adult music education, and the five papers addressed various issues related to the topics from an overall perspective in two cases and from the perspective of three countries in the other three papers. Comparison was implied rather than explicit.

Nonsystemic Cultural Transmission

Nonsystemic cultural transmission refers to the music education that takes place outside a national system of music education. In this case children (and adults) learn music through the socialization process that takes place within their environment. Some of this transmission takes place formally—community teachers transmitting their music consciously because of the desire to ensure cultural continuity. Other transmission occurs informally because the recipient happens to be in a cultural environment that facilitates the educational process in music. Although this transmission takes place in almost every society, the emphasis in this chapter will be on the transmission of a culture's traditional music in the situation where there is little provision for it in the national system. The cultures referred to will have an "ethnic" basis. Documentation of this situation in the forums referred to in the foregoing is mostly related to Asian and African countries, although it is also prevalent in countries with significant indigenous minority populations such as the Indians of North America, the aborigines of Australia, and the Maoris in New Zealand. Many of the studies are monocultural in nature in that they refer to the way in which the transmission takes place within one cultural group. Some studies have been cross-cultural in that they compare the processes of music education in two or more groups and others in that they compare transmission between a "nonsystem" and a system.

Monocultural Studies Okafor (1988, 1989) outlines some of the issues appropriate to music and music education in Nigeria. The basis of music education is oral tradition, and he draws attention to the fact that to Africans "music remains a veritable way of life, and no occasion, whether sad or joyful, is without its attendant musical expression. . . . Music . . . is a social fact—a cultural expression'' (1988, p. 10). Okafor indicates that the most formal method of transmission in Nigeria is the apprenticeship tradition. He cites an example of a group of scouts who invite a teaching team of appropriate dance and music instructors to their activities who will be billeted by the group and who will carry out instruction for a week or more before returning to their homes.

Okafor, however, draws attention to a significant amount of informal music education that takes place when, for example, people have attended a festival in another region and have discovered new dances and music. He states that these people will return home and practice informally, whether unconsciously or deliberately. He also draws attention to the fact that cultural assimilation, where one stronger cultural group may unconsciously absorb another, takes place through this procedure.

Booth (1987) draws attention to a similar means of transmission in the music of India. He suggests that the traditional transmission of music in India is oral—that students learn by ''hearing, watching, and then imitating their teacher, in just the same way young children learn to speak a language'' (p. 7). He points out that notation plays a virtually nonexistent role in this form of learning. He also suggests that much learning is incidental or casual and that the method is highly contextual and ''takes place in a familial, or family-like, environment, with multiple, positive, socio-musical models'' (p. 7).

He extols this method of learning because he sees that it focuses on music as communication. He ''compares'' this with western traditions by suggesting that lessons might be learned from this oral tradition when so much western music is notationally and literacy based.

Touma (1976) and Ohazaki (1976) draw attention to a considerable problem existing in some societies that have a long history of traditional music. This relates to their taking on an educational system that has a European origin and the tendency to take with it a penchant for European music to the detriment of the country's traditional music. Touma suggests that one reason for this, for example, in the case of Arabian music, is that it is orally oriented and therefore lacks a printed, visual base. Ohazaki points to a historical reason in Japan associated with the nation's desire to curb extreme nationalism after World War II and the embracing of the American educational model.

It is interesting to note that although these studies are monocultural, in that they refer to cultural transmission in one cultural group, there is a tendency to relate the study to systemic provisions—a recognition of the increased importance of educational systems and a desire to retain the oral, often informal tradition in the more formal, systemic environment.

Cross-Cultural Comparative Studies There is a very fine line between the monocultural studies referred to above and specific comparative cross-cultural studies. The tendency of monocultural writers to make oblique cross-cultural comparisons has already been mentioned.

Most writers referred to below acknowledge the essential differences between cultural transmission in traditional environments and formal education in systems. This observation relates to some more than others. Lewin (1984) notes the integration of the arts with life in traditional societies and recognizes that because of mass migrations there has been considerable integration of cultures in formal systems. She also recognizes that more study needs to be done; however, she does not suggest how. Borris (1981) presents a similar argument. In recognizing the value of a diverse cultural experience in music education, he suggests that one of the most appropriate ways to study different cultures is through ''live confrontation'' (p. 73). Again, even though he implies that this can be achieved in formal education, how it can be done is not delineated.

Without going in to specific detail on comparative teaching methods, Burton (1986) attempts to provide a preliminary conceptual framework by drawing attention to the commonalities of music across all cultures with the object of defining a ''basic structure for designing programs of music education that would accurately reflect music as a discipline of knowledge'' (p. 111). Burton's thesis is that it would be more possible to develop a comprehensive program of music education incorporating world musics if the common elements of such musics were identified. The five commonalities he identifies are (1) musical concepts, (2) musical processes, (3) musical media, (4) musical functions, and (5) performance considerations (p. 115). This preliminary approach to comparative study follows the process referred to earlier, that of standardizing the variables so that comparison can take place. The implication of Burton's paper is that after the variables of music evident in a variety of cultures have been standardized, appropriate techniques can be determined to assist in cross-cultural transfer.

New (1983) and Darko, Darko, and Roach (1983) refer to problems experienced in Africa and Nigeria, respectively, of resolving the tension between cultural transmission in the traditional sense and formal music education in the national system. In a very real way this is a cross-cultural problem because it draws attention to the traditional indigenous culture and the imported western educational system model. New's topic, ''Progressive Western Methods and Traditional African Methods of Teaching Music—A Comparison,'' is immediately controversial and loaded with value judgments. The immediate implication of such a title is that because the methods are western they are progressive, but New's content allays such fears. For example, New writes, ''Many of the innovations in the West seem to be a laborious rediscovery of what the African has done for centuries'' (p. 25).

After drawing attention to the inherent nonmusical concepts of African music referred to by other authors above, New concludes that the introduction of the western educational system is having a ''devastating effect on African culture. Few Africans seem to have any idea of the price that is being paid in social dislocation, cultural erosion and even economic catastrophe, all in the name of progress'' (p. 29).

New points out that traditional African music is a powerful cohesive force. The tendency to separate music into a variety of components in the western education system is incongruous with the African tradition. New recognizes the value of western education system models but asserts that it will require vision and flexibility for African music to be integrated successfully into the classroom.

Darko and colleagues, after drawing attention to the nature of traditional Ghanaian music, explain the way in which it has been integrated into the western system and taught alongside western-oriented music. They allude to the influence of the Church on early formal development of the education system but conclude that they have no fears for the continuity of traditional Ghanaian music. They do not address the issue of the different concepts of traditional music and systemic education that are seen to be a considerable problem by other writers.

Trimillos (1983, 1984, 1988) has carried out in-depth comparative studies addressing these issues. In a major report to the East-West Centre in Honolulu, he compared the methods of cultural transmission of ancient Hawaii, India, the Southern Philippines, and Japan. Methodologically, he discusses the concept of formalized transmission of culture first before describing the method of transmission used in each of the examples he cites. He defines this transmission as including "any process in which a mutually acknowledged transactional relationship has been established between teacher and learner" (1983, p. 2). Trimillos recognizes that this transmission takes place in societies of diverse cultural or ethnic backgrounds. In traditional cultures he acknowledges that there is far more sociological meaning than is normally associated with western culture. He concludes that in traditional cultures process is just as important as performance (or, the product). He specifies the problem of cross-cultural transmission in the traditional versus systemic concept.

For those designing new approaches for teaching traditional arts, a reliance upon product-oriented transmission structures (such as conservatories, leaving examinations, etc.) should be reevaluated. Using such strategies to teach traditions with a significant process orientation weakens both the conceptual frame and the rationale of the tradition. Further, it often adversely affects the product. (p. 9)

Although Trimillos (1984) does not make specific reference to music education, he does advocate the necessity for the music educator to be aware of common issues in cross-cultural music. He maintains that all music no matter what its culture should recognize the presence of truth, beauty, politics, and applause, with the fundamental recognition that there will be a commensurate human reward.

Trimillos addresses the issue of cross-cultural transmission in detail (1988) by quoting specific examples of learning in four different contexts. He refers to the Hawaiian halau, the German Musikhochschule, the Lowland Philippine maystro, and the Japanese ryu-ha. Each he regards as a system, but in the context of this chapter each could be redefined as a method. Only one of them, the German method, has relation to a national education system. For the purposes of de-

scription and comparison, he observes that each method can be subjected to five categories of protocol:

1. Musical aspects emphasized
2. Statuses in the learning context
3. Development of performance technique
4. Areas for creativity and individual expression
5. Ritual and ceremonial and social rites of passage

Trimillos then proceeds to compare each of the methods. The interesting aspect of this paper is that it provides a methodology for comparison across cultures and across the national system/nonsystemic boundary. Although this distinction has been made for the purposes of analysis in this chapter, for the reasons previously stated the distinction is not really arbitrary because so much of international education is systemic. By presenting a methodology that transcends the barriers and that embraces the inherent qualities of the music itself, Trimillos has provided a stimulus to what is an important problem in international music education. This relates to the need to recognize, in a world increasingly aware of a diversity of cultures, the necessity to cross-fertilize diverse musical qualities.

COMPARATIVE EDUCATION AS A FIELD OF STUDY

From the above studies in international and comparative music education, it can be inferred that there is a need for a consolidation and further development of theories, conceptual frameworks, and methods in comparison. The need for rigorous and systematic comparative studies is of concern not only in music education. This need has been recognized for many decades within the field of international and comparative education generally. If international and comparative music education is going to achieve greater integrity it would do well to take greater notice of developments in the "parent" field.

It is evident that colleagues in comparative education have already experienced the kind of difficulties that are now being encountered in international and comparative music education.

Many authors have described a history of the development of comparative education. Jones (1971) suggests that the prehistory of the study goes back at least to Herodotus and Xenophon, when, for example, the Greek Xenophon described in some detail the military training methods of the Persians. Jones records that Marc-Antoine Jullien is claimed to be the father of comparative education in the more modern sense. Jullien, who published a work in 1817, was described by Bereday (1966, p. 7) as "the first scientifically minded comparative educator" because he attempted to systematize approaches to comparison.

Between 1817 and 1960 many educators postulated various methodological positions in relation to comparison.

Isaac Kandel (b. 1881), for example, attributed the development of a nation's education system to historical causes. Sir Michael Sadler (early twentieth century) recognized the need to study schools in their social context and was thus an advocate of a sociological approach to comparison. Nicholas Hans, writing in the 1940s and 1950s, followed Kandel's tradition and moved toward a consideration of national character as an additional determinant of national systems, a position further developed by Mallinson (1975).

Comparativists began to realize the need for a theoretical base for international studies, and the debate on appropriate methodologies commenced in 1961, a date that is regarded as the watershed for comparative education (Halls, 1990).

The 1960s saw the development of a new thrust in comparative education through the work of UNESCO and also through the formation of professional associations dedicated to the furtherance of the field of study. The establishment of comparative education societies and the resultant publications saw the commencement of significant debates on all aspects of comparative education. The common recognition was that there were obvious advantages in comparative study. Observing how education was carried out in another place had intellectual as well as pragmatic value. There was also the recognition that education was not just a description of what was taking place but involved a recognition and assessment of problems. Educators saw in comparative study a means of seeing what problems existed in other countries, finding that they were also apparent in their own, and looking for solutions from the other source. They then realized that the environment differed from one country to another and that the solution to a problem in one country might not be the same solution in another possessing a completely different environment. They then became determined to carry out more rigorous studies and establish methods that would facilitate comparison.

From about 1960 to 1970 there sprung up many educators who endeavored to find an approach to comparison that would overcome the problems of cross-cultural borrowing. Some turned to the principles of science to establish that rigor. Holmes (1965), for example, centered his study on an approach that recognized that in education there are problems that need to be recognized, selected, and analyzed. The policies relevant to the problem need to be articulated, followed by an identification of the factors influencing those policies. The final element involves prediction and verification, what Holmes regards as "essential ingredients in planned reform" (p. 44). The duty of the comparative educationist, states Holmes,

is to ensure that the difficulties of comparing educational systems and ideas are not overlooked. His task is to compare only what is comparable by making sure that educational terms, contextual variables, and criteria of success are stated unambiguously and in a manner which makes them meaningful across the cultural boundaries of comparison. (p. 47)

It was in an endeavor to provide the systematic framework for comparison that Holmes developed the taxonomies

for description of a national system used by Lepherd (1988). Bereday (1964 and 1967) also attempted to systematize comparison using the four stages outlined earlier in this chapter and using area study as the basis for analysis.

King (1968), also searching for a scientific approach to comparative education, suggests five elements in a conceptual framework, followed by comparative steps. The first element is a recognition of social change, which is inevitable in society, and the second is that comparative education's role is to assist in decision making by supplying educational insights. The third element involves a commitment to education and educational reform that is realized using academic comparative studies for practical purposes. The fourth element is the recognition of a pragmatic approach to study using hypotheses, and the fifth element is the belief that there is a difference between study in the physical sciences and the social sciences. He argues this because he believes that the environment of the physical sciences can be more controlled than that in the social sciences. He asserts, though, that this does not make the results less reliable, just more difficult to obtain.

King's methods involve the collection of data as the first stage of comparison, followed by analysis. In this way meaningful patterns can be discovered. Comparative analysis can then be made where sets of data from different countries can be placed side by side. In order to determine comparability, it is necessary to distinguish patterns of significance in particular cultures so that the cultural context for different societies can be recognized. Once this is completed, conclusions can be reached and predictions made on the results of possible reforms. King, however, warns against long-term predictions on the basis that society can change so rapidly that the circumstances under which the reform was mooted will alter within a short time, making the reforms obsolete.

Noah and Eckstein (1969) are fully committed to a belief in the value of scientific method in the study of comparative education. They believe in the strength of its explanatory power, the necessity to formulate and to test hypotheses, and the use of techniques of quantification and research control. They draw attention to the weaknesses in a nonscientific approach to comparative study—specifically, the susceptibility to bias and lack of accepted criteria. They see in the scientific method an ability to self-correct and minimize the possibility of observer bias. The method is open to scrutiny by anyone at each step of the investigation and also at its conclusion.

In practice, this method commences with a clearly articulated hypothesis. In the testing of this hypothesis, the researcher will quantify the data, rendering them more neutral and allowing them to be handled with greater objectivity. In the physical sciences researchers attempt to carry out experiments by maintaining control over certain dependent variables. Experimenting in the social sciences is more difficult, but Noah and Eckstein maintain that control in investigation is still possible. They finally suggest that the formulation of hypotheses in the true scientific fashion must be rooted in theory, or an interrelated set of hypotheses. They are, however, conscious of possible pitfalls in the use of the scientific method: "The gloss of science may lend a temporary fake respectability to thoroughly bad or trivial findings but investigators who blindly apply advanced statistical techniques to poorly formulated concepts and imperfect data are inviting disaster" (pp. 110–111).

Another area of international comparison that has achieved particular prominence in recent years has been educational achievement. The International Association for the Evaluation of Educational Achievement (IEA) has been active since 1961 and has carried out comparative studies that have embraced such subjects as science, reading, comprehension, literature, English as a foreign language, French as a foreign language, and civic education. Each study involved a number of nations with widely divergent cultures. Altogether, 35 countries have participated in the research projects already carried out, and another 15 have expressed interest in future projects. The achievement of the research can be summarized in a conclusion reached in the pilot project that prefaced the first series of studies. It was stated that "cross-national comparisons of educational performance can be made and can give comparable results" (cited in Purves, 1987, p. 12). It has been claimed that the organization of the projects has resulted in "one of the most influential research efforts in the history of educational research" (Husen, 1987, p. 29).

The studies have involved the development of comparative models that vary from project to project but that have as a purpose the measurement of achievement, mostly in the school situation, and the identification of the determinants of achievements. Measuring instruments are developed to enable the collection and analysis of statistical and comparable data. Through the use of these instruments, it is possible to compare the achievements of different countries and postulate the reasons for higher achievements in some countries rather than others. Policymakers can then evaluate the information and consider the possibilities of implementing desirable determinants of high achievement in their own situation or eliminating the determinants of low achievement. Context has an important role in the development of such models.

Apart from the IEA studies, comparative education appeared to go into the doldrums from 1970 to the mid-1980s. This may have been due to the debate over which was the most appropriate research method to adopt. Another reason for the apparent decline and the recognized depression was the belief that education generally was not providing the answers to society's problems, resulting in major cuts in educational spending.

Two more recent publications have attempted to review the current status of the field. Altbach and Kelly (1986) have suggested that at last there has been a realization that no single method can be used to carry out comparison.

Scholars in comparative education have recently adopted a range of methodologies and approaches to develop innovative ways of dealing with complex research issues and in analyzing educational data creatively in a cross-cultural frame. The new approaches reflect eclectic and creative ways of dealing with a broad spectrum of issues. (p. 1)

The focus of studies during this time has shifted from national studies to subject studies within national systems and to studies independent of national systems. Up to 1977 the focus was on schooling within the nation-state, but scholars have argued that often influences on national system education come from outside a nation, and therefore the notion of the discreteness of a nation is not valid in analyzing education. It is also argued that often variances between regions of a nation are sometimes more marked than variances between nations. Although Altbach and Kelly make this assertion regarding nation-states, there is no doubt that such units are still being used as a basis for description. Postlethwaite (1988), for example, edited an encyclopedia that describes and analyzes national systems in some 120 countries. It can be argued that while such studies may not offer a complete approach to analysis and comparison, they will provide an important contextual perspective and an introduction for many thematic studies.

The most recent comparative challenges have related to such issues as women in research, ways of examining the relationship between institutions and society concerning educational planning, quality and inequality, and the promotion of talent.

Halls (1990) edited a publication that overviews the development of comparative education since 1961. Writers in this volume have come to conclusions similar to those of Altbach and Kelly, particularly in relation to the shift of emphasis from the nation-state unit to thematic studies.

One of the debates referred to by Halls concerns whether comparative education is in fact a field of study or has acquired the status of a discipline. Many maintain that if it were a discipline it would have developed sets of accepted theories within which comparisons could be undertaken. The lack of acceptance of many theories militates against a consensus that discipline status has been reached.

THE FUTURE OF INTERNATIONAL AND COMPARATIVE MUSIC EDUCATION

Summary of Music Studies Reviewed

Most of the studies reviewed here involve either overviews or thematic studies relating to single nation-states. This provides a national basis. An international perspective is gained through their appearance in what are designed to be international forums. They aim to describe what is perceived to be the researcher's observation of the actual situation. These studies have a systemic foundation in that they refer to music education within "official" national education.

Other studies are monocultural or cross-cultural, and many of these refer to music education outside a formal system. Some try to straddle the "barrier" between systemic and nonsystemic education.

Very few music educators formally engage in either systemic comparison or cross-cultural comparison. It can always be argued that music educators looking at the way music education is carried out in other places are informally carrying out comparison because they are viewing the other situation from the perspective of their own context and using their own value judgments. This situation, however, is not satisfactory in the area of public music educational development because the informal comparisons and the value judgments are not open to scrutiny and verification. Comparison in the academic sense of the word must involve at least two phenomena. For comparison to take place music educators need to learn from generalist colleagues that conceptual frameworks should be developed alongside the methods to be used. The current problem in international music education is that very little attention is paid to the development of theory and comparative methods. A consequence of this is that there may be no conscious recognition of differences in context or allowances made for cultural bias and personal value judgments. One of the difficulties that comparative researchers face is trying to be objective in judgments. This is particularly taxing for a researcher coming from outside a cultural group and attempting to understand the musical nuances that are endemic to that group. Well-developed theories and methods could substantially contribute to overcoming this kind of problem.

The discipline bases for the studies referred to have varied considerably. Some have been historical, arguing that music education is as it is because of the way it has developed. Other studies have at least recognized historical influences. Some studies have been sociocultural or sociological in that they have emphasized the socialization process that has taken place in music education. Some have reflected anthropological tendencies. Other studies have been based on psychology, a very prominent characteristic during the last decade particularly in its close links with pedagogy. This is very evident, for example, in the methods of Kodály, Orff and others who have related their methods to aspects of developmental psychology.

Some studies have used structure as their conceptual framework and have related this to curriculum development. Although this is not a discipline, it provides a starting point for analysis. However, structures differ considerably from one system to another, and comparison needs elements of commonality. In fact, validly identifying similarities and differences is another prime difficulty in comparative music education.

One or two studies with considerable potential for development draw on the discipline of music itself, examining inherent concepts, qualities, and characteristics and observing the ways in which these are transmitted in a variety of circumstances.

It might be noted that there are very few papers making use of the discipline of economics in comparative studies. Wood (1986) draws attention to the relationship between music education and Canada's economy, but similar studies are few. There appears to be a particular need for more music educators with an economic background to assist in determining the most cost-efficient approaches to music education in times of almost universal economic restraint.

The lack of theoretical development in the field of international and comparative music education over the last three decades has already been noted. If this situation continues, there is a danger that international music education will be in its current position in another three decades. Developing theories, frameworks, and methods that will facilitate cross-cultural borrowing, a principal purpose of comparative music education, should enable a greater reliability in such borrowing. A structured approach to comparison and prediction should have economic benefits through being more efficient, as well as achieving another principal goal of providing better music education.

CONCLUSION

International and comparative music education has made important progress in two areas since 1955. In the first instance, increased awareness has resulted in a wider number of forums for the promulgation of the benefits of international music education. The publishing of many papers and the discussions at conferences and seminars of issues affecting this topic have resulted in a greater awareness of international problems. Ernst (1966) realized the importance of comparative music education when he recognized that "the teaching of music involves common problems which transcend national boundaries" (p. 459). In the second instance, increased exposure has resulted in a significant thrust in the direction of cross-cultural music education. In the attempt to overcome the problems of music education, a welcome side effect has been the greater awareness of the music of other cultures per se.

Cykler (1961) was one of the first to summarize succinctly the aspirations of comparative music education and to advocate the need for a systematic approach.

The term, comparative music education, implies that its subject matter deals with the various aspects of music education as these are pursued in various countries and cultures all over the world.

Such studies must include private as well as institutional or public instruction in all phases—instrumental—vocal—theoretical—aesthetic—and creative.

It should be the function of a study of comparative music education to gather systematically information concerning not only the practices and methodology used in all phases of music education but to investigate the bases, historical, pedagogical, psychological, social, and aesthetic, for any and all such practices. Only in this way can a true understanding of various practices be assessed and determined. Only in this way can a true value be placed on any and all practices pursued in various places. Only in this way can one establish whether a practice which seems to work so well in one situation can actually serve as well under other and different conditions (p. 140)

Although these words were penned in 1961, they are still eminently applicable. They epitomize the aspirations of comparative music education study. Continued development may in time lead to the establishment of comparative music education as a discipline in its own right.

References

Abdoo, F. B. (1984). Music education in Japan. *Music Educators Journal, 70*(6), 52–56.

Achilleoudis, C. N. (1989). Music in secondary education in Cyprus. *International Journal of Music Education, 13,* 37–41.

Altbach, P. G., and Kelly, J. P. (Eds.). (1986). *New approaches to comparative education.* Chicago: University of Chicago Press.

Bartle, G. (1984). The ISME Degree and Diploma Co-ordination Project—A move towards international standing. In J. Dobbs (Ed.), *International Music Education: ISME Yearbook Vol XI,* 126–130.

Bartle, G. (1986). Music education in the Soviet Union. *International Journal of Music Education, 8,* pp. 33–37.

Bartle, G. (1988). The grass on the other side of the fence . . . Two contrasting models for the organization of music education for the beginner performer. In J. Dobbs (Ed.), *International Music Education: ISME Yearbook Vol XV,* 196–202.

Bartle, G. (1990). How 1,250,000,000 people train their performing musicians: A microscopic view of the training of pianists, opera singers, orchestral musicians, conductors, organists and sound recording technicians in six countries. *International Journal of Music Education, 15,* 31–36.

Bereday, G. Z. F. (1964). *Comparative method in education.* New York: Holt, Rinehart and Winston.

Bereday, G. Z. F. (1967). Reflections in comparative methodology in education 1964–1966. *Comparative Education Review, 3*(1), 169–187.

Booth, G. D. (1987). The north Indian oral tradition: Lessons for music education. *International Journal of Music Education, 9,* 7–9.

Borris, S. (1981). National idioms and universal elements: Their relation to music and music education. In D. Taylor (Ed.), *International Music Education: ISME Yearbook VIII,* 67–73.

Burton, L. H. (1986). Commonalities in the musics of diverse cultures. In J. Dobbs (Ed.), *International Music Education: ISME Yearbook XIII,* 111–118.

Choksy, L. (1974). *The Kodály method.* Englewood Cliffs: Prentice Hall.

Comte, M. (Ed.). (1988). Music in Australian education. *Australian Journal of Music Education, 1.*

Cykler, E. (1960). Some salient areas of comparison in the training of music teachers in Austria, Germany, and the United States of America. In *International Music Educator, 2,* 31–35.

Cykler, E. (1961). Comparative music education. *International Music Educator, 4,* 140–142.

Darko, S. F., Darko, M. C., and Roach, D. W. (1983). Ghana music education: A merging of cultures. *International Journal of Music Education, 2,* 11–16.

De Azevedo, L. H. C. (1983). Aural education and traditional music. *International Journal of Music Education, 1,* 32–34.

Dobbs, J. (1982). Music as multi-cultural education. In J. Dobbs (Ed.), *International Music Education: ISME Yearbook Vol IX,* 142–147.

Dobbs, J., and Kemp, A. E. (Eds.). (1987). Adult music education. *International Journal of Music Education, 9,* 23–36.

Elliott, D. J. (1984). The role of music and musical experience in modern society: Toward a global philosophy of music education. *International Journal of Music Education, 4,* 3–8.

Ernst, K. D. (1966). An international scope for music education. *International Music Educator, 14,* 457–460.

Gates, T. (Ed.). (1988). *Music education in the U.S.: Contemporary issues.* Tuscaloosa: Alabama University Press.

Gieseler, W. (1986). New perspectives and new tasks. *International Journal of Music Education, 8,* 3–6, 12.

Guardabasso, G. (1989), Music education in Italy: What is going on? *International Journal of Music Education, 13,* 35–36.

Halls, D. W. (Ed.). (1990). *Comparative education: Trends and issues.,* London: Jessica Kingsley Publishers and UNESCO.

Hoggart, R. (1976), The arts and education in the late 20th century: Challenge and response. In F. Callaway (Ed.), *Challenges in music education* (pp. 3–8). Department of Music, University of Western Australia, Perth .

Holmes, B. (1965). *Problems in education: A comparative approach.* London: Routledge and Kegan Paul.

Holmes, B., (1981). *Comparative education: Some considerations of method.* London: George Allen & Unwin.

Husen, T. (1987). Policy impact of IEA research. *Comparative Education Review, 31*(1), 29–46.

International Society for Music Education. (1960). *International Music Educator, 1.*

Jayatilaka, B. (1984). Indigenous music: A basis for music education in Malaysia. *International Journal of Music Education, 3,* 43–45.

Jones, P. E. (1971). *Comparative education: Purpose and method.* Brisbane: University of Queensland Press.

Kaplan, B. (1984). Music education in Israel. *Music Educators Journal, 70*(6) 57–60.

Kasilag, L. R. (1984), Forging a Philippine identity in music. *International Journal of Music Education, 3,* 45–47.

Kemp, A. E., (1989). Current developments in music curriculum thinking in the United Kingdom. *Studier au den Pedagogiska Vaven, 8,* 34–37.

King, E. J. (1968), *Comparative studies and educational decision.* London: Methuen.

Kraus, E., and Twittenhoff, W. (1955). The Orff-Bergese method. *Music in Education* (pp. 241–244). Paris: UNESCO.

Leong, S. (1984). The present state of music education in Singapore. *International Journal of Music Education, 3,* 48–50.

Lepherd, L. (Ed.). (1985a). Music education in a multi-cultural society. *International Journal of Music Education, 5,* 47–59.

Lepherd, L. (Ed.). (1985b). The education of exceptionally musical children. *International Journal of Music Education, 6,* 39–58.

Lepherd, L. (Ed.). (1986). Bi-cultural music education. *International Journal of Music Education, 7,* 23–39.

Lepherd, L. (Ed.). (1988). *Music education in international perspective: The People's Republic of China.* Darling Heights: Music International. Queensland

Lewin, O. (1984). Inter-cultural music education within a nation. J. Dobbs (Ed.), *International Music Education: ISME Yearbook Vol XI* (pp. 51–54).

Mallinson, V. (1975). *An introduction to the study of comparative education.* London: Heinemann.

Merkuriyev, P. (1984). Music education in the USSR. *International Journal of Music Education, 4,* 41–45.

New, L. H. (1983). Progressive western methods and traditional African methods of teaching music: A comparison. *International Journal of Music Education, 1,* 25–31.

Nketia, J. H. (1978). New perspectives in music education. In E. Kraus (Ed.), *International Music Education: ISME Yearbook Volume V* (pp. 104–111).

Noah, H. J., and Eckstein, M. A. (1969). *Toward a science of comparative education.* Toronto: Macmillan.

Ohazaki, T. (1976). The place of traditional music in the cultivation of music in Japan. In F. Callaway, (Ed.), *Challenges in music edu-*

cation (pp. 374–376). Department of Music, University of Western Australia, Perth.

Okafor, R. C. (1988). Focus on music education in Nigeria. *International Journal of Music Education, 12,* 9–17.

Okafor, R. C. (1989). Popular music education in Nigeria. *International Journal of Music Education, 14,* 3–13.

Paynter, J. (Ed.). (1987). Music education in Nordic countries. *British Journal of Music Education, 4*(3) 251–252.

Postlethwaite, T. N. (1988). *The encyclopedia of comparative education and national systems of education.* Oxford: Pergamon Press.

Purves, A. C. (1987). The evolution of the IEA: A memoir. *Comparative Education Review, 31*(1) 10–28.

Rainbow, B. (1990). Review of "Music education in the U.S.: Contemporary issues." *British Journal of Music Education, 7*(1), 75.

Schools' Music Association. (1964). *Music in schools: A world survey.* London: Schoolmaster Publishing Co.

Schwadron, A. A. (1984). World musics in education, *International Journal of Music Education, 4,* 9–12.

Standifer, J. (1986a), China's multi-cultural population: Insights from minority nationalities and their music. *International Journal of Music Education, 8,* 17–24.

Standifer, J. (1986b), Everyday music in a Chinese province. *Music Educators Journal, 73*(3) 32–34, 39–40.

Swanwick, K. (1988). Music education in a pluralist society. *International Journal of Music Education, 12,* 3–8.

Taylor, D. (1979). *Music now.* Bristol: The Open University Press.

Taylor, D. (Ed.). (1981). *International Music Education: ISME Yearbook Vol. VIII.* 11–79.

Terry, R. (1985). Music Education in France. *British Journal of Music Education, 2*(3), 227–251.

Touma, H. (1976). Music education in Arabian society: Its implementation, efficacy, handicaps and dangers. In F. Callaway (Ed.), *Challenges in Music Education* (pp. 370–373). Department of Music, University of Western Australia, Perth.

Trimillos, R. D. (1983). The formalized transmission of culture: Selectivity in traditional teaching/learning systems in four high skill music traditions. *Report* (pp. 1–9). Honolulu: East-West Culture Learning Institute.

Trimillos, R. D. (1984). Truth, beauty, politics, and applause: Cross-cultural dimensions in music and the performing arts. In J. Dobbs (Ed.), *International Music Education: ISME Yearbook Vol XI* (pp. 15–24).

Trimillos, R. D. (1988). Halau, Hochschule, Maystro, and Ryu cultural approaches to music learning and teaching. In J. Dobbs (Ed.), *International Music Education: ISME Yearbook XV* (pp. 10–23).

UNESCO. (1955). *Music in education.* Paris: Author.

Vikar, L. (1983). Folk music research and music education. In J. Dobbs (Ed.), *International Music Education: ISME Yearbook Vol X* (pp. 31–35).

Walker, R. (1986). Music and multi-culturalism. *International Journal of Music Education, 8,* 43–50, 52.

Wood, G. (1986). Music education in the Canadian economy. *International Journal of Music Education, 8,* 53–59, 70.

ABOUT THE CONTRIBUTORS

Hal Abeles is director of the Division of Instruction, and professor of music and education at Teachers College, Columbia University. His research interests include measurement and evaluation of musical behaviors, sex-stereotyping of musical instruments, and musical preference behavior. He is the editor of the *Music Researchers Exchange* and a coauthor of *Foundations of Music Education.* Dr. Abeles earned his bachelor's and master's degrees at the University of Connecticut, and his Ph.D. at the University of Maryland

Edward P. Asmus is associate professor in the Department of Music at the University of Utah, where he serves as director of graduate studies and of music education. His research has centered on affective response to music, music motivation, nonmusical outcomes of music instruction, quantitative methodology, and evaluation of music programs. He has produced many articles, books, presentations, tests, measures, and computer programs. Dr. Asmus earned his B.M.E. at Ohio State University and his M.M.E. and Ph.D. at the University of Kansas.

Betty W. Atterbury is associate professor of music and coordinator of music education at the University of Southern Maine. Her research centers on elementary general music teaching, including the development of the child singing voice, and learning and teaching problems resulting from mainstreaming. She is the author of *Mainstreaming Exceptional Learners in Music,* as well as numerous journal articles. Currently Dr. Atterbury chairs the editorial committee of the *Music Educators Journal* and is president of the Maine Music Educators Association.

Anthony L. Barresi is professor of music and education at the University of Wisconsin at Madison, where he directs undergraduate and graduate programs in choral music education. His research deals with public arts policy and music education issues. He is the author of *The Arts at a New Frontier: The National Endowment for the Arts.* Barresi is a member of the MERC Executive Council and a former chair of the Social Sciences SRIG.

J. David Boyle is professor and chair of the Department of Music Education and Music Therapy, School of Music, University of Miami. His primary research interest is program evaluation. He compiled and edited the MENC publication *Instructional Objectives in Music,* and coauthored *Measurement and Evaluation of Musical Experiences* and *Psychological Foundations of Musical Behavior.* Dr. Boyle has served on the evaluation teams for the Arts IMPACT Project and the Contemporary Music Project. He received his Ph.D. in music education from the University of Kansas.

Liora Bresler is an assistant professor in the Department of Curriculum and Instruction at the University of Illinois at Urbana-Champaign. She is a pianist, a musicologist, and a former director of music at the Tel-Aviv Museum in her native Israel. Her primary research interests are aesthetic education and qualititative research methodology. Dr. Bresler was involved in the J. Paul Getty Arts Education study (1982–1984). She is coauthor of *Customs and Cherishing,* the result of case studies conducted at the National Arts Education Research Center from 1987 to 1990.

John Christian Busch is associate professor of educational research and evaluation at the University of North Carolina at Greensboro. His major research interests lie in standard-setting methods for licensure and certification examinations, and in the application of operations research to the solution of practical measurement problems. Dr. Busch has master's and bachelor's degrees in psychology and English; he received his Ph.D. in educational psychology from the University of Tennessee. He was a 1990 Coolidge Colloquium Fellow.

Henry L. Cady is professor emeritus at the University of Delaware. His main research interest is the social aspects of music in the schools. Dr. Cady received his doctorate from the University of Kansas and taught for many years at Ohio State University. His analysis of research studies (with Erwin Schneider) which was completed under an office of education grant remains the seminal synthesis of music education research. Widely published, he aided in the reform of MENC's music education research council.

Donald E. Casey is associate professor and coordinator of undergraduate studies in music education at Northwestern University. He is active in Northwestern's Center for the Study of Education and the Musical Experience, and a contributor to the group's forthcoming publication, *Toward a Description of the Musical Experience.* Dr. Casey's research interests include the effect of teacher behaviors on students, experiential variance among student musicians, talent development in outstanding composers, and the development of support materials for bibliographic resources in music education.

Peter Constanza is professor of music and director of graduate studies in the School of Music at Ohio State University. Among his numerous current professional activities is his service on the National Advisory Board for the Yahama Corporation-funded *Project 2000,* designed to implement the recommendations of the MENC report *Music Teacher Education: Partnership and Process.* Dr. Costanza earned his bachelor's degree from West Chester University and his master's and doctoral degrees from Pennsylvania State University.

Lola L. Cuddy is professor of psychology at Queen's University, Ontario, Canada, where she directs the acoustical laboratory. Her research interests are music perception and cognition, especially absolute pitch, perception of melody, harmony, and rhythm, and the perception of novel musical structures. She is currently collaborating with Queen's composers on a study of temporal organization in music. Dr. Cuddy earned her Ph.D. in psychology at the University of Toronto and her associate of music degree at the University of Manitoba.

Robert A. Cutietta is associate professor and coordinator of music education at Kent State University. His wide research interests include sight-singing methodologies, noise-induced hearing loss, biofeedback techniques, and musical preferences in different cultures. His recent efforts have centered on how the brain organizes music through the use of verbal and nonverbal strategies. Doctor Cutietta has published many articles and is the coauthor of two books on the teaching of music.

Lyle Davidson is chair of the Undergraduate Theory Department and a member of the composition faculty at the New England Conservatory of Music. He was a senior research associate with the Arts Propel group of the Harvard Project Zero. Dr. Davidson is the author and coauthor of many articles on musical cognition in child development, composition, and pedagogy.

Roger H. Edwards is director of research and assessment for the Rockwood School District in suburban St. Louis, Missouri. He spent eleven years as an instrumental music teacher. His research interests lie in the design and validation of psychometric instruments, and in the cross-pollination of musical and nonmusical research. He was a contributor to the Crane Symposium and serves on the Learning Theory Committee of the National Conference

on Piano Pedagogy. Dr. Edwards earned his Ph.D. at the University of Illinois.

Harold Fiske is professor of music at the University of Western Ontario, where he teaches courses in the psychology of music and music education. He has published many articles on these topics and is the author of *Music and Mind.* He is completing a second book, that analyzes major twentieth-century theories of music. Dr. Fiske is the current chair of the Research Commission of the International Society for Music Education. He received his B.M. and M.M from Boston University and his Ph.D. from the University of Connecticut.

Hildegard C. Froehlich is professor of music at the College of Music, University of North Texas, in Denton. Her research and teaching areas include the sociology of music, comparative music education, and music teacher education and training. She is the author of a book on research methods in classroom observation (published in German) and the coauthor of *Research in Music Education: An Introduction to Systematic Inquiry.* She is active in many national and international organizations. Dr. Froehlich earned her Ph.D. in music education at the University of Texas at Austin.

Kate Gfeller is associate professor at the University of Iowa, where she directs the music therapy program and teaches music in special education. Her research emphases include music for the hearing-impaired and mainstreaming practices in music education. Dr. Gfeller is coauthor of *An Introduction to the Theory and Practice of Music Therapy* and a contributor to *Musical Growth and Development: Birth Through Six* and several music research journals.

Carroll Gonzo is professor of music at the University of Texas at Austin, where he teaches courses in the history and philosophy of music education, tests and measurements, current trends and issues in music education, and choral music education. He has over forty publications to his credit. Dr. Gonzo received his Ph.D. from the University of Wisconsin at Madison.

Paul Haack heads the Music Education/Therapy Division of the School of Music, University of Minnesota. His teaching and research interests include instrumental, general music, and related arts methods, and the psychology, sociology, and aesthetics of music. He is the coauthor of *Principles and Processes of Music Education,* several book chapters, and over eighty journal articles. Currently he chairs the Yamaha National Music Education Research Project. Dr. Haack earned his Ph.D. at the University of Wisconsin.

David J. Hargreaves is senior lecturer in psychology at the University of Leicester, England, where his current teaching and research interests are in developmental psychology, psychology of music, and arts education. His numerous publications include *The Developmental Psychology of Music, Children and the Arts,* and (as coauthor) *Devel-*

opmental Psychology and You. He also serves as editor of *Psychology of Music.* Dr. Hargreaves is codirector of the DELTA (Development of Learning and Teaching in the Arts) project, and of the Leicester Music Research Group.

Steven K. Hedden is professor and coordinator of music education at the University of Arizona. His areas of research interest include the psychology of music, behavioral research in music, foundations of music education, and curriculum development in music. Dr. Hedden's articles have appeared in a variety of music education research journals, and he currently serves on the editorial boards of the *JRME,* the *CRME Bulletin,* and *The Quarterly.*

George N. Heller is on the faculty in music education and music theory at the University of Kansas. His special interests include secondary general music methods, ethnic music, and the history of music education and music therapy. Dr. Heller is the author of *Ensemble Music for Wind and Percussion Instruments,* the editor of *The Bulletin of Historical Research in Music Education,* and was the music education area advisor for the *The New Grove Dictionary of American Music.* Dr. Heller received his bachelor's, master's, and doctoral degrees from the University of Michigan.

William Higgins is professor of music at Messiah College in Grantham, Pennsylvania, where he teaches music education and computer science. His primary research interest is computer applications in music education. He is the author of a computer-based instruction course in applied clarinet, three computer programs in music education, a textbook on computer programing, and numerous journal articles. Dr. Higgins earned his B.M.E at Lebanon Valley College, his M.M. at Boston University, and his Ed.D. in music education at Pennsylvania State University.

Donald Hodges is coordinator of music education at the University of Texas at San Antonio. In addition to his teaching responsibilities, he conducts the chamber and symphony orchestras at UTSA. Dr. Hodges' special research interests include the neurophysiological aspects of musical behavior. He is contributing editor of the *Handbook of Music Psychology* and the author of several articles. He has served on the editorial committees of *Update* and *Music Educators' Journal.*

Charles R. Hoffer is professor of music and coordinator of music education at the University of Florida at Gainesville. His research has focused on curriculum development and sociological factors of music education. He has written numerous articles and books on music and music education, including *Teaching Music in the Secondary Schools* and (as coauthor) *Foundations of Music Education.* Hoffer is the current vice president of the Music Educators National Conference.

Samuel Hope is executive director of the National Association of Schools of Music and an executive editor of the magazine *Design for Arts in Education.* His primary re-

search interests are policy analysis and developments for the arts and education, and he has published widely on the arts, education, and accreditation. Hope holds degrees in composition from the Eastman School of Music and Yale University; he studied composition with Nadia Boulanger. His works have been performed by major American orchestras, chamber groups, and choral organizations.

Jere T. Humphries is professor and chair of the Division of Music Education/Therapy at Arizona State University at Tempe. His major research and teaching interests lie in instrumental music methods and the history of music education. He is the author of many publications, serves on the editorial boards of four scholarly journals, and is a member of the Executive Committee of the MENC Music Education Council. Dr. Humphries holds degrees from the University of Mississippi, Florida State University, and the University of Michigan.

Joyce Jordan is associate professor of music education at the University of Miami, where she is involved primarily in the teacher-training program and as supervisor for all general music internships. Dr. Jordan has published on the capabilities of preschool children, and she continues to research many aspects of musical learning in young children. Currently she coordinates and teaches Kindermusik, a music program for three- to five-year olds.

Estelle R. Jorgensen is professor of music at Indiana University at Bloomington, where she teaches philosophical, historical, and curricular foundations of music education. She has published widely in these areas in various scholarly and professional journals.

Anthony Kemp is head of the Department of Arts and Humanities in Education at the University of Reading, England. He is also director of the Music Education Research and Information Centre, which he established at the university in 1978. His teaching and research interests lie in the psychology of musicianship, music learning, and music curriculum development, as well as international music education. He is coeditor of the *International Journal of Music Education,* the associate editor of *Psychology of Music,* and on the editorial board of the *British Journal of Music Education.*

Mary Leglar is associate professor of music and coordinator of undergraduate music education at the University of Georgia. Her research in teacher education has centered on early field experiences and applications of technology to teacher education. She is the editor of the *Georgia Music News* and current chair of the MENC Council of State Editors. Dr. Leglar received her Ph.D. in music education from Indiana University.

Paul R. Lehman is professor of music and senior associate dean in the School of Music at the University of Michigan. He has taught widely at the secondary and college levels and also served as music specialist with the United States Department of Education in Washington, D.C. Dr. Lehman is the author of several books and over one hundred articles and reviews concerned with curriculum, teacher education, and measurement and evaluation.

Laurence Lepherd is associate professor and associate dean at the University of South Queensland, Australia, where he is responsible for the coordination of research and the academic program in the School of Arts. He has contributed to a variety of scholarly music education journals. Mr. Lepherd earned his B.A. and M.E. at the University of New England in Australia, with specializations in education and comparative education. He also studied in London, the United States, and China.

Randi L'Hommedieu is assistant professor of music at the University of Oregon, where he teaches foundation and research courses for music education majors as well as music appreciation courses for nonmajors. His research has focused on teacher effectiveness, faculty development, and research methodology. He has published articles in *Higher Education Research and Development* and the *Journal of Educational Psychology*.

Michael L. Mark is professor of music and dean of the Graduate School at Towson State University. His primary research interest is historical music education studies. He is coauthor of *A History of American Music Education* and author of *Contemporary Music Education* and *Source Readings in Music Education*, as well as numerous articles in various professional journals.

William V. May is chair of the Division of Music Education in the College of Music of the University of North Texas, Denton. His teaching specialties are choral music education, tests and measurement, and educational psychology. He serves on the editorial boards of *JRME* and *Update*. Dr. May holds degrees from Baylor University, the University of North Texas, and the University of Kansas.

Robert F. Miller is associate professor of music and coordinator of the music education program at the University of Connecticut in Storrs. A former instrumental music teacher and high school band director, Dr. Miller also served as director of the Aesthetic Education Program at CEMREL, Inc., a National Institute of Education regional laboratory. He is active as a conductor, clinician, and adjudicator. Dr. Miller earned his undergraduate degree at the College of William and Mary, his master's degree at East Carolina University, and his Ph.D. at the University of Illinois.

David J. Nelson is director of the School of Music at the University of Iowa and former director of the School of Music of the University of Wisconsin, Madison. Professor Nelson has done extensive research in the psychology of music and has published extensively. He was formerly editor of the journal *Dialogue in Instrumental and Music Education*.

Gerald Olson is professor of music and education at the University of Wisconsin at Madison, where he guides the undergraduate through doctoral programs in instrumental

music education. Dr. Olson is the founder and editor of *Dialogue in Instrumental Music Education* and serves on the Executive Board of the Wisconsin Music Educators Association. He chaired the MENC task force report, *Music Teacher Education: Partnership and Process.*

Kenneth H. Phillips is associate professor of music education at the University of Iowa, where he has been twice honored for excellence in teaching. His area of specialization is vocal technique for young singers. He is the author of *Teaching Kids to Sing* and many articles, and he has presented numerous workshops on the child and adolescent voice. He served as guest editor for the *Music Educators Journal* issue (December 1988) on choral music instruction. Dr. Phillips earned his Ph.D. in music education at Kent State University.

Rudolf E. Radocy is professor in the Department of Art and Music Education and Music Therapy at the University of Kansas, where he teaches courses in such topics as music psychology, musical acoustics, and the sociology of music. He has conducted research on music perception, musical preference, and evaluation. He is the coauthor of *Psychological Foundations of Musical Behavior* and *Measurement and Evaluation of Musical Experiences*. Dr. Radocy serves as editor of *JRME*, on the editorial boards of the *Journal of Music Therapy* and *Psychology of Music,* and as an evaluation consultant for arts evaluation.

Bennett Reimer holds the John W. Beattie Endowed Chair in Music at Northwestern University, where he is director of the Center for the Study of Education and the Musical Experience. His research has focused on the philosophy of music education, curriculum theory, and the place of music in arts education. Reimer's many publications include *A Philosophy of Music Education, Developing the Experience of Music,* and the *Silver Burdett Music* series of textbooks for grades 1–8. Dr. Reimer also coedited the 1992 NSSE yearbook, *The Arts, Education, and Aesthetic Knowing.*

Carol P. Richardson is assistant professor of music education at Northwestern University, where she teaches undergraduate and graduate methods courses in general music, high school nonperformance classes, and a doctoral research class. Her research has produced articles on creativity testing, educational reform, gifted and talented music education, and career issues for women in music education. Currently, she is focusing on musical thinking in children. Dr. Richardson serves on the editorial board of the *Music Educators Journal.*

Roger R. Rideout is associate professor of music education and coordinator of graduate programs in the School of Music of the University of Oklahoma. He teaches in the areas of instrumental music methods, learning theory, and research techniques. He has published in major music education journals on a variety of topics relating to music curricula. His master's degree was in musicology at the

Hartt School of Music and his doctorate in music education from the University of Illinois.

Franz L. Roehmann is chair of the Department of Music at the University of Colorado at Denver. He also serves as president of the Biology of Music Making, Inc., a non-profit educational corporation. His research interests are in music and medicine.

Maria Runfola is on the faculty of music at the University of Buffalo, where she also serves as associate dean of the Graduate School. She has authored materials for music teaching and learning, consulted in the creation of school music curricula throughout the country, guest-conducted regional elementary and junior high school choruses across the nation, and been active in the New York State School Music Association as a clinician, adjudicator, and research chair. Dr. Runfola was educated at Nazareth College of Rochester, the Eastman School of Music, and the State University of New York at Buffalo.

Timothy Russell is music director of the Naples Philharmonic and the Pro Musica Orchestra of Columbus, Ohio. He also serves as director of music education for the Naples Philharmonic Center for the Arts. Dr. Russell has held teaching and conducting positions at Ohio State University, the University of Rochester, and the Eastman School of Music. His research interests include conducting, leadership styles, and string pedagogy.

Joanne Rutkoswki is on the faculty of music education at Pennsylvania State University. Her primary research interest is the child's singing voice, and techniques and materials for helping the problem singer in a classroom setting. The results of her research have been presented in a variety of professional journals and at many conferences and symposia. She is a contributor to the book, *Early Adolescence: Perspectives on Research, Policy, and Intervention.* Dr. Rutkowski received her B.M. from Miami University, Ohio, and her M.F.A. and Ph.D. from the State University of New York at Buffalo.

Carol Scott-Kassner is a professor and the chair of Department of Music at Seattle Pacific University. Her research centers on the development of musical thought in children from three to five years of age. She has published many articles on this topic. She is also the author of the elementary series of the TAP rhythm training program and coauthor of the *World of Music.* Dr. Kassner was co-founder and first chair of the ISME Early Childhood Commission; she has chaired the Music Education Research Council of the Society for Research in Music Education.

Larry Scripp is on the faculty at the New England Conservatory of Music in education and undergraduate theory. His research has centered on young children's artistic development in musical performance, perception, musical representation, and the development of computer-supported curricula. Dr. Scripp is currently researching reflective thinking in the arts, in conjunction with the Arts

Propel portfolio assessment project. He plans to publish further material in musical development and to develop college textbooks based on his research.

James W. Sherbon is professor of music education and director of graduate studies in music in the School of Music of the University of North Carolina at Greensboro. His primary research focus has been in areas associated with hearing acuity and musical achievement. He has published articles in and served on the editorial boards of a number of music education research journals. He has been active in the MENC and recently served as the chair of higher education for the North Carolina Music Educators' Association. Dr. Sherbon received his Ph.D. in music education from the University of Kansas.

Patricia E. Sink is associate professor of music in the School of Music at the University of North Carolina at Greensboro, with primary responsibilities in the graduate music program. She has published articles on music listening behaviors, general music instruction, music and exceptional learners, and electronic media in music education. Dr. Sink received her Ph.D. in music education and music therapy at the University of Kansas. She is also a Registed Music Therapist with the National Association for Music Therapy.

Ralph A. Smith is professor of cultural and educational policy in the Department of Educational Policy Studies at the University of Illinois at Urbana-Champaign. He is the author and coauthor of several books on arts education, aesthetics, and policy analysis, including, most recently, *Excellence in Art Education, The Sense of Art: A Study in Aesthetic Education,* and *Art Education: A Critical Necessity.* He is also the coeditor of *Public Policy and the Aesthetic Interest* and the NSSE yearbook *The Arts, Education, and Aesthetic Knowing.*

Robert E. Stake is professor of education and director of the Center for Instructional Research and Curriculum Evaluation (CIRCE) at the University of Illinois. His specialty is the evaluation of educational programs. He is the author of *Quieting Reform* and *Evaluating the Arts in Education,* and the coauthor of *Case Studies in Science Education.* He has been active in the American Education Research Association and participated in the formation of the two groups which merged into the American Evaluation Association. Dr. Stake earned his Ph.D. in psychology at Princeton University.

Eleanor V. Stubley is chair of the Music Education Area in the Faculty of Music, McGill University, Montreal Canada where she teaches graduate and undergraduate courses in brass, conducting, curriculum, and aesthetics. She is a graduate of the University of Toronto and completed her Ph.D. at the University of Illinois at Urbana-Champaign. Her research focuses on philosophical issues pertaining to the nature and value of music and musical performances and she has published extensively on Canadian music for student performers.

Donald K. Taebel is associate professor of music at Georgia State University where he serves as director of graduate studies in music and teaches courses in research, assessment, and instrumental music education methods. He has presented papers on teacher evaluation and teaching effects at state and national professional conferences, and served as a consultant on teacher evaluation in school systems in several states. He is also the former codirector of the Alabama Career Incentive Project.

Malcolm J. Tait is dean of the School of Music at East Carolina University. His primary research interests include the philosophy of music education, curriculum development, and teaching styles and their impact on musical learning. He is the author of several books, including *Music Education in New Zealand, Comprehensive Musicianship Through Choral Performance,* and (as coauthor) *Principles and Processes of Music Education: New Perspectives.* Dr. Tait was educated in New Zealand and earned his Ed.D. at Columbia University. He has made many public appearances as a choral conductor, pianist, and accompanist.

Nancy G. Thomas is a developmental psychologist and musician who serves as associate director of the Michigan Program in Child Development and Social Policy at the University of Michigan. She also holds appointments as a lecturer and research investigator at the University of Michigan. Dr. Thomas edits the *Social Policy Report,* the publication of the Society for Research in Child Development. She regularly participates and performs as a violist at the Aspen Music Festival and performs with the Ann Arbor Symphony.

Thomas W. Tunks is head of the Music Education Department in the Meadows School of the Arts at Southern Methodist University. He has published numerous articles and book chapters on music learning and music perception, and he has served on the editorial boards of several music education journals and as associate editor of *Psychomusicology.* He is research chair of the Texas Music Educators Association. Dr. Tunks has taught in the Michigan public schools and at the Conservatario del Tolima in Columbia, South America. He earned his Ph.D. in music at Michigan State University.

Rena Upitis is a member of the Faculty of Education at Queen's University, Ontario, Canada, and teaches at the J.G. Simcoe School in Kingston, Ontario. Her primary research interests are in children's musical development, especially in the areas of composition and notation. She is the author of *This Too Is Music* and *The Development of Notation,* as well as articles in *Psychomusicology* and other journals. Dr. Upitis has degrees in music, mathematics, law, education, and human development from the University of Toronto, Queen's University, and Harvard University.

Marienne Uszler is professor of keyboard studies in the School of Music of the University of Southern California. Her area of specialization is American keyboard method. She is coauthor of *The Piano Pedagogy Major in the College Curriculum* and *The Well-Tempered Keyboard Teacher,* contributing editor of *The Piano Quarterly,* and review editor for *American Music Teacher.* Dr. Uszler chairs the Committee on Historical Research for the National Conference on Piano Pedagogy.

Ralph Verrastro is professor of music and director of the School of Music of the University of Georgia. His teaching and research interests are in the areas of curriculum, teacher effectiveness, and music in higher education. He has published articles in general interest periodicals and research journals in music education. He is a contributor to *Symphony Orchestras of the United States.* Dr. Verrastro was associated with the Contemporary Music Project and the Manhattanville Music Curriculum Project while on the faculty at East Carolina University.

Robert Walker is professor of music education at Simon Fraser University, British Columbia, Canada. His research has focused on auditory and visual perception and the acoustics of the voice. He is the author of several articles and books, including *Musical Beliefs: Psychoacoustic, Mythic, and Educational Perspectives.* He is the editor of the *Canadian Journal of Research in Music Education* and coeditor of the *Canadian Journal of Music Education.* Dr. Walker received his B.M. and Ph.D. from London University, England, and his performer's diploma from the Royal College of Music in London.

Darrel L. Walters is assistant professor of music education at Temple University, where he teaches graduate and undergraduate courses and advises master's and doctoral students in music education research. He is active in the Pennsylvania Music Educators Association and represents the state at the Society for Music Teacher Education. Dr. Walters earned his B.A. and M.A. in music education at the University of Michigan School of Music and his Ph.D. in supervision and administration at the University of Michigan School of Education.

Peter R. Webster is associate professor of music education at Northwestern University, where he teaches courses in research and measurement, the psychology of musical behavior, creative thinking in music, and music technology. He has publications on music perception, preference, technology, and creative thinking. Dr. Webster holds a bachelor's degree in music from the University of Southern Maine, and master's and doctoral degrees from the Eastman School of Music.

Richard Weerts is professor of music at Northeast Missouri State University, in Kirksville. He teaches graduate courses in research and directs theses. Dr. Weerts is the author of several books and a number of articles on music and music education. He is editor of the National Association of College Wind and Percussion Instructors *Journal,* a frequent reviewer of doctoral dissertations for the *CRME Bulletin,* and a member of the national board of editors of *The Quarterly.*

Nancy L. Whitaker is clinical assistant professor of music education at the University of North Carolina at Chapel Hill, where her areas of specialization include general music education, instrumental music education, and music education research. Dr. Whitaker's research and publications have focused on the musical thinking process involved in instrumental performance, conducting, arranging, and musical composition.

Bruce D. Wilson is curator of Special Collections in Music at the University of Maryland at College Park. He administers the archives of numerous national and international music organizations and is active in the interpretation of archival collections through exhibitions, publications, and public programs. Dr. Wilson is a frequent guest speaker on music education history, American music, historical research methods, and archival issues. He is coauthor of an article on historical research in music education and coeditor of *Music in American Schools, 1838–1988: A Symposium.*

Frank R. Wilson is associate clinical professor of neurology at the University of California School of Medicine and director of research and education for the Health Program for Performing Artists. He is the author of *Tone Deaf and All Thumbs? An Invitation to Music Making for Late Bloomers and Non-Prodigies.* He is on the board of directors of the Performing Arts Medicine Association and on the advisory board of the International Arts Medicine Association. Dr. Wilson graduated from Columbia College in New York and received his M.D. from the University of California School of Medicine.

Lizabeth Bradford Wing is head of the Division of Music Education and associate professor at the College-Conservatory of Music, University of Cincinnati. Her areas of special interest include teacher education, secondary general music, and evaluation. Dr. Wing was educated at Luther College, the University of Cincinnati, and the University of Illinois.

David G. Woods is dean of Fine Arts at the University of Oklahoma. His area of specialization is in early childhood music education. He is the author and coauthor of numerous articles and books, including *Jump Right In!,* a comprehensive music series for grades K–8, *Teaching Music in the Twentieth Century,* and *Creating Curriculum in Music;* he has presented workshops throughout the United States, Europe, and Australia. He holds a B.M. from Washington University in Topeka, and the M.M. and Ph.D. from Northwestern University.

Marilyn P. Zimmerman is professor of music at the University of Illinois at Urbana-Champaign. She has taught at every level from kindergarten through graduate music education. Her research has focused on the application of Piaget's theory of cognitive development to musical development. She has published widely in the areas of early musical development and early childhood music education. Currently, Dr. Zimmerman is the editor of the *CRME Bulletin.*

NAME INDEX

SUBJECT INDEX

A priori comparisons, in statistics, 152
Ability, and motivation in music learning, 427
Absolute pitch
  theories about, 336
  and music perception, 336–337
Academic achievement, and music achievement, 426–427
Acceptance Scale (AS), 625
Acceptance Within Music Scale (AMS), 625
Accidental sampling, 117
Accreditation, regional associations for, 289
Accuracy, in music reading, 347–348
Achievement, of students in music ensembles, 653. *See also* Academic achievement; Musical achievement; Nonmusical achievement
Achievement Test in Music (Knuth), 659, 671
Acoustics, and empiricism, 5
ACT* (act-star) theory of learning transfer, 438
Activities
  in curriculum, defined, 698
  studies of, in general music curriculum, 703
Adjective studies in music appraisal, 417
Adjusted policy
  defined, 761
  in teacher certification and licensing, 763
Advance organizers theory of learning transfer, 438
Advocated policy
  defined, 761
  by MENC, 765–766
AEP. *See* Aesthetic Education Program
AERA. *See* American Educational Research Association
Aesthetic Education Program (AEP), of the Central Midwestern Regional Educational Laboratory (CEMREL), 56, 206–207
Aesthetic questions in music education research, 96
Aesthetic sensitivity, development of, 454
Affect, and learning transfer in music, 443
Affective response
  categories of, 414
  nonverbal methods of study in, 417
  research on, 414–423
  verbal methods of study in, 417–418

of young children to music, 644
Africa, music education in, 782–783
Afro-American music, 739, 740
AGE. *See* Arts in general education approach
AHP. *See* Arts and Humanities Program
Age-level stratification, and music behavior, 718–719
Alexander technique, 585–586
  in singing, 569
Aliferis Music Achievement Test, 654
Alternative education, and arts education, 751
American Association of Colleges for Teacher Education, 739, 744
American Bandmasters Association Research Center, 106
American College Testing Program (ACT), 679
American Council for the Arts in Education, 750
American Educational Research Association (AERA), 49
  Handbooks, 691
American Indian music
  experimental use of, in schools, 741
  teacher training in, 740
American Music (Sonneck Society), 105
American music, scholarship on, 105
American Symphony Orchestra League, 725
AmeriGrove. See New Grove Dictionary of American Music
Analysis, as philosophical approach, 98
Analysis of covariance, 150
  regression-based, 189
Analysis of variance (ANOVA), 149–155
  incorporating continuous variables in, 188
  and regression analysis, 184–186, 192–194
Analytical thinking in exposing assumptions, 93
ANOVA. *See* Analysis of variance
Anxiety. *See* Performance anxiety
Appraisal, as category of affective response, 415–418
Arabian music, 782
Arranging, reflective thinking in, 556
Art
  defined, 749

erroneous assumptions about, 752
  as a kind of knowing, 750
  social-welfare concept of, 753, 756
Art Epoch (Barzun), 751
Art, Ideology and Politics (Balfe and Wyszomirski), 766
Art music, versus vernacular music, 730
Artist residency programs, 763
Artistry (Howard), 14
Artists-in-Education program (of NEA), 751, 756, 762–763
Artists-in-schools programs, 751, 763
Arts and Human Development, The (Gardner), 383, 638
Arts and Humanities Program (AHP), 55–56
Arts education
  curricular policy studies in, 768–769
  curriculum studies in, 205–208
Arts education policy, 749–770
  by the courts, 763–764
  effect of local politics on, 770
  by federal government, 762–763
  future of, 757–758
  mistakes of thinking in, 752–754
  recommendations for, 755–757
  research in, 766–768
  by state education departments, 763
  trends in, 749–752
Arts, Education, and Americans Panel (of American Council for the Arts in Education), 750
Arts in general education approach (AGE), 752
Arts-in-Education program (of NEA), 756, 757
Arts in Schools Basic Education Grant (ASBEG) program (NEA), 756, 763, 767
Arts of eclectic (Schwab), 93
ASBEG. *See* Arts in Schools Basic Education Grant
ASEP. *See* Australian Science Education Project
Assessment of creative thinking in music
  of analysis and listening skills, 276–277
  British literature on, 273–274
  content analyses in, 273–277
  psychometric studies of, 270–273
Assessment of curriculum, 213. *See also* Program evaluation

816